Word Study Series

AMG's
ANNOTATED STRONG'S DICTIONARIES

JAMES STRONG, LL.D., S.T.D.
EDITORS: WARREN BAKER, D.R.E. AND SPIROS ZODHIATES, Th.D.

AMG's Annotated Strong's Dictionaries
By James Strong
Edited by Warren Baker and Spiros Zodhiates
Copyright © 2009 by AMG Publishers
Published by AMG Publishers
6815 Shallowford Road
Chattanooga, TN 37421

ISBN 13: 978-089957-710-4
ISBN 10: 0-89957-710-5

Excerpts taken from the following:

The Complete Word Study Dictionary: Old Testament
by Warren Baker and Eugene Carpenter
©2003 by AMG Publishers. All Rights Reserved.

The Complete Word Study Dictionary: New Testament
by Spiros Zodhiates
©1992 by AMG International. All Rights Reserved.

First Printing—November 2009

Printed in the United States of America
13 12 11 10 09 –Di– 8 7 6 5 4 3 2 1

AMG's Annotated Strong's Hebrew Dictionary Of the Old Testament

Additional materials in this dictionary were taken from
The Complete Word Study Dictionary: Old Testament
by Warren Baker and Eugene Carpenter.

Transliteration of Hebrew Consonants

Hebrew Consonant	Name	Trans–literation	Phonetic Sound	Example
א	Aleph	ʾ	Silent	Similar to h in honor
בּ	Beth	*b*	b	as in boy
ב	Veth	*b*	v	as in vat
גּ	Gimel	*g*	g	as in get
ג	Gimel	*g*	g	as in get
דּ	Daleth	*d*	d	as in do
ד	Daleth	*d*	d	as in do
ה	Hē	*h*	h	as in hat
ו	Waw	*v*	w	as in wait
ז	Zayin	*z*	z	as in zip
ח	Cheth	*ch*	ch	Similar to ch in the German *ach*
ט	Teth	*ṭ*	t	as in time
י	Yodh	*y*	y	as in you
כּ	Kaph	*k*	k	as in kit
כ	Chaph	*k*	ch	Similar to ch in the German *ach*
ל	Lamed	*l*	l	as in lit
מ	Mem	*m*	m	as in move
נ	Nun	*n*	n	as in not
ס	Samekh	*s*	s	as in see
ע	Ayin	ʿ	Silent	Similar to h in honor
פּ	Pē	*p*	p	as in put
פ	Phē	*ph*	f	as in phone
צ	Tsadde	*ts*	ts	as in wits
ק	Qoph	*q*	q	as in Qatar
ר	Resh	*r*	r	as in run
שׂ	Sin	*ś*	s	as in see
שׁ	Shin	*sh*	sh	as in ship
תּ	Taw	*t*	t	as in time
ת	Thaw	*th*	th	as in this

Transliteration of Hebrew Vowels

Hebrew Vowel	Name	Position	Trans-literation	Sound
ְ	Shewa (Silent)	מְ	*Not transliterated or pronounced*	
ְ	Shewa (Vocal)	מְ	*e*	u as in but
ַ	Pathah	מַ	*a*	a as in lad
ֲ	Hateph Pathah	מֲ	*ă*	a as in lad
ָ	Qamets	מָ	*â*	a as in car
ֳ	Hateph Qamets	מֳ	*ŏ*	a as in car
ֵי	Sere Yodh	מֵי	*êy*	ey as in prey
ֵ	Sere	מֵ	*ê*	ey as in prey
ֶ	Seghol	מֶ	*e*	e as in set
ֱ	Hateph Seghol	מֱ	*ĕ*	e as in set
ִי	Hiriq Yodh	מִי	*îy*	i as in machine
ִ	Hiriq	מִ	*i*	i as in pin
ָ	Qamets Qatan	מָ	*o*	o as in hop
ֹ	Holem	מֹ	*ô*	o as in go
וֹ	Holem	מוֹ	*ôw*	o as in go
ֻ	Qubbuts	מֻ	*u*	u as in put
וּ	Shureq	מוּ	*û*	u as in tune

Special Symbols

:— (*colon and one-em dash*) are used within each entry to mark the end of the discussion of syntax and meaning of the word under consideration, and to mark the beginning of the list of word(s) used to render it in translation.

() (*parentheses*) denote, in the translation renderings only, a word or syllable given in connection with the principal word it follows.

+ (*addition symbol*) denotes a rendering in translation of one or more Hebrew words in connection with the one under consideration.

× (*multiplication symbol*) denotes a rendering within translation that results from an idiom peculiar to the Hebrew.

א (Aleph)

1. אָב, **'âb,** *awb*; a primitive word; *father* in a literal and immediate, or figurative and remote application:—chief, (fore-) father ([-less]), × patrimony, principal. Comparative names in "Abi-".

A masculine noun meaning father, head of a household, ancestor, patron of a class, benevolence, respect, honour. This word is primarily used to mean either a human or spiritual father. There are numerous references to a father as a begetter or head of a household (Ge 24:40; Jos 14:1). When referring to an ancestor, this word can be collective; Naboth would not give up the inheritance of his fathers (1Ki 21:3). One of the most important meanings is God as Father (Isa 63:16). It can also mean originator of a profession or class; Jabal was called the father of nomadic farmers (Ge 4:20). A father is also one who bestows respect or honour (Jgs 17:10).

2. אָב, **'ab** (Chaldee), *ab*; corresponding to 1:—father.

An Aramaic masculine noun meaning father or ancestor. The primary meaning is a male biological parent (Da 5:11, 13). In the plural, its meaning is ancestors or forefathers (Ezr 4:15). See the Hebrew cognate *'âb* (1).

3. אֵב, **'êb,** *abe*; from the same as 24; a *green plant*:—greenness, fruit.

4. אֵב, **'êb** (Chaldee), *abe*; corresponding to 3:—fruit.

5. אֲבַגְתָא, **'Ăbagthâ',** *ab-ag-thaw´*; of foreign origin; *Abagtha*, a eunuch of Xerxes:—Abagtha.

6. אָבַד, **'âbad,** *aw-bad´*; a primitive root; probably to *wander* away, i.e. *lose* oneself; by implication to *perish* (causative *destroy*):—break, destroy (-uction), + not escape, fail, lose, (cause to, make) perish, spend, × and surely, take, be undone, × utterly, be void of, have no way to flee.

A verb meaning to perish, to be lost, to wander, or, in a causative sense, to destroy, to reduce to some degree of disorder. It is used to signify God's destruction of evil, both threatened (Le 26:38) and realized (Nu 17:12[27]); Israel's destruction of the Canaanites and their altars (Nu 33:52; Dt 12:2, 3); the perishing of natural life (Ps 49:10[11]; 102:26[27]; Ecc 7:15); the perishing of abstract qualities such as wisdom and hope (Isa 29:14; La 3:18); and an item or animal being lost (Dt 22:3; Ecc 3:6).

7. אֲבַד, **'âbad** (Chaldee), *ab-ad´*; corresponding to 6:—destroy, perish.

An Aramaic verb meaning to perish, to be destroyed, or, in a causative sense, to destroy. This term is closely connected to death. It is used for the passing away of false gods (Jer 10:11); the execution of the Babylonian wise men (Da 2:12, 18, 24); the bodily destruction of Daniel's apocalyptic "beast" (Da 7:11). See the Hebrew cognate *'âbad* (6).

8. אֹבֵד, **'ôbêd,** *o-bade´*; active participle of 6; (concrete) *wretched* or (abstract) *destruction*:—perish.

An abstract noun meaning destruction. The word is used this way only in Nu 24:20, 24 where Balaam prophesies the destruction of three nations or areas, one of which is Eber. If Eber refers to the Hebrews, then the destruction is not to be understood as absolute. Other occurrences of this form, although spelled identically, are used differently and are included under *'âbad* (6).

9. אֲבֵדָה, **'ăbêdâh,** *ab-ay-daw´*; from 6; (concrete) something *lost*; (abstract) *destruction*, i.e. Hades:—lost. Compare 10.

A feminine noun meaning a lost object or possession. The term is employed only in a legal context in the Hebrew Bible (Ex 22:8; Le 6:4[5:23]; Dt 22:3). To keep a lost item in one's possession and lie about it to the rightful owner

1

is listed among sins, such as deception concerning a deposit or pledge and robbery and fraud (Le 6:3[5:22]).

10. אֲבֵדָה, **'ăbaddôh,** *ab-ad-do´*; the same as 9, miswritten for 11; a *perishing:*—destruction.

A noun referring to the place of the dead, indistinguishable in meaning from *'ăbaddôwn* (11). This form occurs only in Pr 27:20 where, along with Sheol, it identifies death as a place that can always hold more just as the eyes of humans always want more. This word originally may have been *'ăbêdâh* (9) or *'ăbaddôwn* (11) but was changed in the transmission of the ancient manuscript.

11. אֲבַדּוֹן, **'ăbaddôwn,** *ab-ad-done´*; intensive from 6; (abstract) a *perishing;* (concrete) Hades:—destruction.

A feminine noun meaning destruction (that is, death). It may also mean a place of destruction. It is used extensively in wisdom literature and connotes the abode of the dead. It commonly forms a word pair with *shě'âl* (7594) (Job 26:6; Pr 15:11; 27:20) but is also linked with death (Job 28:22) and the grave (Ps 88:11[12]). See the Hebrew verb *'âbad* (6).

12. אַבְדָן, **'abdân,** *ab-dawn´*; from 6; a *perishing:*—destruction.

A noun, probably masculine, meaning destruction. It occurs only in Est 9:5 where the Jews striking their enemies with the sword results in slaughter and destruction. A similar form, *'obdân* (13), also meaning destruction, occurs in Est 8:6 in a similar context: the desire of the Jews' enemies to bring destruction on them. These two forms may be identical.

13. אֹבְדָן, **'obdân,** *ob-dawn´*; from 6; a *perishing:*—destruction.

A masculine noun meaning destruction. This term conveys the slaughter of the Jews (Est 8:6; 9:5). See the Hebrew verb *'âbad* (6).

14. אָבָה, **'âbâh,** *aw-baw´*; a primitive root; to *breathe* after, i.e. (figurative) to *be acquiescent:*—consent, rest content, will, be willing.

A verb meaning to be willing, to consent, to be acquiescent, to yield, to desire. Its primary meaning is to be positively inclined to respond to some authority or petition. The word is used to signify willingness or desire (Ge 24:5, 8; Jgs 19:25; 2Ch 21:7; Isa 30:15); agreement in prin-

ciple (Jgs 11:17; 1Ki 20:8); consent to authority (Job 39:9; Isa 1:19); yielding, as to sin (Dt 13:8[9]; Pr 1:10); and, by extension, to be content (Pr 6:35; Ecc 7:8).

15. אָבֶה, **'âbeh,** *aw-beh´*; from 14; *longing:*—desire.

16. אֵבֶה, **'êbeh,** *ay-beh´*; from 14 (in the sense of *bending* toward); the *papyrus:*—swift.

17. אֲבוֹי, **'ăbôwy,** *ab-o´ee*; from 14 (in the sense of *desiring*); *want:*—sorrow.

18. אֵבוּס, **'êbûws,** *ay-booce´*; from 75; a *manger* or *stall:*—crib.

19. אִבְחָה, **'ibchâh,** *ib-khaw´*; from an unused root (apparently meaning to *turn*); *brandishing* of a sword:—point.

20. אֲבַטִּיחַ, **'ăbaṭṭîyach,** *ab-at-tee´-akh*; of uncertain derivation; a *melon* (only plural):—melon.

21. אֲבִי, **'Ăbîy,** *ab-ee´*; from 1; *fatherly; Abi,* Hezekiah's mother:—Abi.

22. אֲבִיאֵל, **'Ăbîy'êl,** *ab-ee-ale´*; from 1 and 410; *father* (i.e. *possessor*) *of God; Abiel,* the name of two Israelites:—Abiel.

23. אֲבִיאָסָף, **'Ăbîy'âsâph,** *ab-ee-aw-sawf´*; from 1 and 622; *father of gathering* (i.e. *gatherer*); *Abiasaph,* an Israelite:—Abiasaph.

24. אָבִיב, **'Âbîyb,** *aw-beeb´*; from an unused root (meaning to *be tender*); *green,* i.e. a young *ear* of grain; hence the name of the month *Abib* or Nisan:—Abib, ear, green ears of corn.

25. אֲבִי גִבְעוֹן, **'Ăbîy Gib'ôwn,** *ab-ee´ ghib-one´*; from 1 and 1391; *father* (i.e. *founder*) *of Gibon; Abi-Gibon,* perhaps an Israelite:—father of Gibeon.

26. אֲבִיגַיִל, **'Ăbîygayil,** *ab-ee-gah´yil*; or shorter אֲבִיגַל, **'Ăbîygal,** *ab-ee-gal´*; from 1 and 1524; *father* (i.e. *source*) *of joy; Abigail* or *Abigal,* the name of two Israelitesses:—Abigal.

27. אֲבִידָן, **'Ăbîydân,** *ab-ee-dawn´*; from 1 and 1777; *father of judgment* (i.e. *judge*); *Abidan,* an Israelite:—Abidan.

28. אֲבִידָע, **'Ăbîydâ‘,** *ab-ee-daw´*; from 1 and 3045; *father of knowledge* (i.e. *knowing*); *Abida,* a son of Abraham by Keturah:—Abida, Abidah.

29. אֲבִיָּה, **'Ăbîyyâh,** *ab-ee-yaw´*; or prolonged אֲבִיָּהוּ, **'Ăbîy-yâhûw,** *ab-ee-yaw´-hoo*; from 1 and 3050; *father* (i.e. *worshipper*) *of Jah*; *Abijah,* the name of several Israelite men and two Israelitesses:—Abiah, Abijah.

30. אֲבִיהוּא, **'Ăbîyhûw',** *ab-ee-hoo´*; from 1 and 1931; *father* (i.e. *worshipper*) *of Him* (i.e. *God*); *Abihu*, a son of Aaron:—Abihu.

31. אֲבִיהוּד, **'Ăbîyhûwd,** *ab-ee-hood´*; from 1 and 1935; *father* (i.e. *possessor*) *of renown*; *Abihud*, the name of two Israelites:—Abihud.

32. אֲבִיחַיִל, **'Ăbîyhayil,** *ab-ee-hah´-yil*; or (more correctly) אֲבִיחַיִל, **'Ăbîychayil,** *ab-ee-khah´-yil*; from 1 and 2428; *father* (i.e. *possessor*) *of might*; *Abihail* or *Abichail*, the name of three Israelites and two Israelitesses:—Abihail.

33. אֲבִי הָעֶזְרִי, **'Ăbîy hâ'Ezrîy,** *ab-ee´-haw-ez-ree´*; from 44 with the article inserted; *father of the Ezrite*; an *Abiezrite* or descendant of Abiezer:—Abiezrite.

34. אֶבְיוֹן, **'ebyôwn,** *eb-yone´*; from 14, in the sense of *want* (especially in feeling); *destitute*:—beggar, needy, poor (man).

35. אֲבִיּוֹנָה, **'ăbîyyôwnâh,** *ab-ee-yo-naw´*; from 14; *provocative* of *desire*; the *caper* berry (from its *stimulative* taste):—desire.

36. אֲבִיטוּב, **'Ăbîyţûwb,** *ab-ee-toob´*; from 1 and 2898; *father of goodness* (i.e. *good*); *Abitub*, an Israelite:—Abitub.

37. אֲבִיטַל, **'Ăbîyţal,** *ab-ee-tal´*; from 1 and 2919; *father of dew* (i.e. *fresh*); *Abital*, a wife of King David:—Abital.

38. אֲבִיָּם, **'Ăbîyyâm,** *ab-ee-yawm´*; from 1 and 3220; *father of* (the) *sea* (i.e. *seaman*); *Abijam* (or *Abijah*), a king of Judah:—Abijam.

39. אֲבִימָאֵל, **'Ăbîymâ'êl,** *ab-ee-maw-ale´*; from 1 and an elsewhere unused (probably foreign) word; *father of Mael* (apparently some Arab tribe); *Abi-mael*, a son of Joktan:—Abimael.

40. אֲבִימֶלֶךְ, **'Ăbîymelek,** *ab-ee-mel´-ek*; from 1 and 4428; *father of* (the) *king*; *Abimelek*, the name of two Philistine kings and of two Israelites:—Abimelech.

41. אֲבִינָדָב, **'Ăbîynâdâb,** *ab-ee-naw-dawb´*; from 1 and 5068; *father of generosity* (i.e. *lib-eral*); *Abinadab*, the name of four Israelites:—Abinadab.

42. אֲבִינֹעַם, **'Ăbîynô'am,** *ab-ee-no´-am*; from 1 and 5278; *father of pleasantness* (i.e. *gracious*); *Abinoam*, an Israelite:—Abinoam.

43. אֶבְיָסָף, **'Ebyâsâph,** *eb-yaw-sawf´*; contracted from 23; *Ebjasaph*, an Israelite:—Ebiasaph.

44. אֲבִיעֶזֶר, **'Ăbîy'ezer,** *ab-ee-ay´-zer*; from 1 and 5829; *father of help* (i.e. *helpful*); *Abiezer*, the name of two Israelites:—Abiezer.

45. אֲבִי-עַלְבוֹן, **'Ăbîy-'albôwn,** *ab-ee al-bone´*; from 1 and an unused root of uncertain derivation; probably *father of strength* (i.e. *valiant*); *Abialbon*, an Israelite:—Abialbon.

46. אָבִיר, **'âbîyr,** *aw-beer´*; from 82; *mighty* (spoken of God):—mighty (one).

47. אַבִּיר, **'abbîyr,** *ab-beer´*; for 46:—angel, bull, chiefest, mighty (one), stout [-hearted], strong (one), valiant.

An adjective meaning mighty or strong. Used frequently as a noun, the word applies to God as the Mighty One (Ps 132:2, 5; Isa 1:24). It also designates angels (Ps 78:25); men (Ps 76:5); bulls (Ps 22:12[13]); and horses (Jer 8:16). When used to describe a person or a person's heart, it normally refers to a strength independent of or opposed to God (Job 34:20; Ps 76:5[6]; Isa 46:12). It is used once to mean chief of the shepherds (1Sa 21:7[8]).

48. אֲבִירָם, **'Ăbîyrâm,** *ab-ee-rawm´*; from 1 and 7311; *father of height* (i.e. *lofty*); *Abiram*, the name of two Israelites:—Abiram.

49. אֲבִישַׁג, **'Ăbîyshag,** *ab-ee-shag´*; from 1 and 7686; *father of error* (i.e. *blundering*); *Abishag*, a concubine of David:—Abishag.

50. אֲבִישׁוּעַ, **'Ăbîyshûwa',** *ab-ee-shoo´-ah*; from 1 and 7771; *father of plenty* (i.e. *prosperous*); *Abishua*, the name of two Israelites:—Abishua.

51. אֲבִישׁוּר, **'Ăbîyshûwr,** *ab-ee-shoor´*; from 1 and 7791; *father of* (the) *wall* (i.e. perhaps *mason*); *Abishur*, an Israelite:—Abishur.

52. אֲבִישַׁי, **'Ăbîyshay,** *ab-ee-shah´ee*; or (shorter) אַבְשַׁי, **'Abshay,** *ab-shah´ee*; from 1 and 7862; *father of a gift* (i.e. probably *generous*); *Abishai*, an Israelite:—Abishai.

53. אֲבִישָׁלוֹם, **'Ăbîyshâlôwm,** *ab-ee-shaw-lome´*; or (shortened) אַבְשָׁלוֹם, **'Abshâlôwm,** *ab-shaw-lome´*; from 1 and 7965; *father of peace* (i.e. *friendly*); *Abshalom*, a son of David; also (the fuller form) a later Israelite:—Abishalom, Absalom.

54. אֶבְיָתָר, **'Ebyâthâr,** *eb-yaw-thawr´*; contracted from 1 and 3498; *father of abundance* (i.e. *liberal*); *Ebjathar*, an Israelite:—Abiathar.

55. אָבַךְ, **'âbak,** *aw-bak´*; a primitive root; probably to *coil* upward:—mount up.

56. אָבַל, **'âbal,** *aw-bal´*; a primitive root; to *bewail*:—lament, mourn.

57. אָבֵל, **'âbêl,** *aw-bale´*; from 56; *lamenting*:—mourn (-er, -ing).

58. אָבֵל, **'âbêl,** *aw-bale´*; from an unused root (meaning to *be grassy*); a *meadow*:—plain. Compare also the proper names beginning with Abel-.

59. אָבֵל, **'Âbêl,** *aw-bale´*; from 58; a *meadow*; *Abel*, the name of two places in Palestine:—Abel.

60. אֵבֶל, **'êbel,** *ay´-bel*; from 56; *lamentation*:—mourning.

61. אֲבָל, **'ăbâl,** *ab-awl´*; apparently from 56 through the idea of *negation; nay,* i.e. *truly* or *yet*:—but, indeed, nevertheless, verily.

62. אָבֵל בֵּית־מֲעֲכָה, **'Âbêl Bêyth Mă'akâh,** *aw-bale´ bayth ma-a-kaw´*; from 58 and 1004 and 4601; *meadow of Beth-Maakah; Abel of Beth-maakah*, a place in Palestine:—Abel-beth-maachah, Abel of Beth-maachah.

63. אָבֵל הַשִּׁטִּים, **'Âbêl hash-Shiṭṭîym,** *aw-bale´ hash-shit-teem´*; from 58 and the plural of 7848, with the article inserted; *meadow of the acacias; Abel hash-Shittim*, a place in Palestine:—Abel-shittim.

64. אָבֵל כְּרָמִים, **'Âbêl Kᵉrâmîym,** *aw-bale´ ker-aw-meem´*; from 58 and the plural of 3754; *meadow of vineyards; Abel-Keramim*, a place in Palestine:—plain of the vineyards.

65. אָבֵל מְחוֹלָה, **'Âbêl Mᵉchôwlâh,** *aw-bale´ mekh-o-law´*; from 58 and 4246; *meadow of dancing; Abel-Mecholah*, a place in Palestine:—Abel-meholah.

66. אָבֵל מַיִם, **'Abêl Mayim,** *aw-bale´ mah´-yim*; from 58 and 4325; *meadow of water; Abel-Majim*, a place in Palestine:—Abel-maim.

67. אָבֵל מִצְרַיִם, **'Âbêl Mitsrayim,** *aw-bale´ mits-rah´-yim*; from 58 and 4714; *meadow of Egypt; Abel-Mitsrajim*, a place in Palestine:—Abel-mizraim.

68. אֶבֶן, **'eben,** *eh´-ben*; from the root of 1129 through the meaning to *build; a stone*:— + carbuncle, + mason, + plummet, [chalk-, hail-, head-, sling-] stone (-ny), (divers) weight (-s).

69. אֶבֶן, **'eben** (Chaldee), *eh´-ben*; corresponding to 68:—stone.

70. אֹבֶן, **'ôben,** *o´-ben*; from the same as 68; *a pair of stones* (only dual); a potter's *wheel* or a midwife's *stool* (consisting alike of two horizontal disks with a support between):—wheel, stool.

71. אֲבָנָה, **'Ăbânâh,** *ab-aw-naw´*; perhaps feminine of 68; *stony; Abanah*, a river near Damascus:—Abana. Compare 549.

72. אֶבֶן הָעֵזֶר, **'Eben hâ'êzer,** *eh´-ben haw-e´-zer*; from 68 and 5828 with the article inserted; *stone of the help; Eben-ha-Ezer*, a place in Palestine:—Ebenezer.

73. אַבְנֵט, **'abnêṭ,** *ab-nate´*; of uncertain derivation; a *belt*:—girdle.

74. אַבְנֵר, **'Abnêr,** *ab-nare´*; or (fully) אֲבִינֵר, **'Ăbîynêr,** *ab-ee-nare´*; from 1 and 5216; *father of light* (i.e. *enlightening*); *Abner*, an Israelite:—Abner.

75. אָבַס, **'âbas,** *aw-bas´*; a primitive root; to *fodder*:—fatted, stalled.

76. אֲבַעְבֻּעָה, **'ăba'bu'âh,** *ab-ah-boo-aw´*; (by reduplication) from an unused root (meaning to *belch* forth); an inflammatory *pustule* (as *eruption*):—blains.

77. אֶבֶץ, **'Ebets,** *eh´-bets*; from an unused root probably meaning to *gleam; conspicuous; Ebets*, a place in Palestine:—Abez.

78. אִבְצָן, **'Ibtsân,** *ib-tsawn´*; from the same as 76; *splendid; Ibtsan*, an Israelite:—Ibzan.

79. אָבַק, **'âbaq,** *aw-bak´*; a primitive root; probably to *float* away (as vapor), but used only as denominative from 80; to *bedust*, i.e. *grapple:*—wrestle.

80. אָבָק, **'âbâq,** *aw-bawk´*; from root of 79; light *particles* (as *volatile*):—(small) dust, powder.

A masculine noun meaning dust, especially extremely fine, powdery particles in contrast to the coarser dust or *'âphâr* (6083). It is used to signify the dust easily driven by the wind (Isa 5:24) and dust raised by the hooves of galloping horses (Eze 26:10). As a metaphor, it signifies the notion of utter insignificance (Isa 29:5); conditions of drought (Dt 28:24); and clouds as the dust of God's feet (Na 1:3).

81. אֲבָקָה, **'ăbâqâh,** *ab-aw-kaw´*; feminine of 80:—powder.

82. אָבַר, **'âbar,** *aw-bar´*; a primitive root; to *soar:*—fly.

83. אֵבֶר, **'êber,** *ay-ber´*; from 82; a *pinion:*—[long-] wing (-ed).

84. אֶבְרָה, **'ebrâh,** *eb-raw´*; feminine of 83:—feather, wing.

85. אַבְרָהָם, **'Abrâhâm,** *ab-raw-hawm´*; contracted from 1 and an unused root (probably meaning to *be populous*); *father of a multitude; Abraham*, the later name of Abram:—Abraham.

86. אַבְרֵךְ, **'abrêk,** *ab-rake´*; probably an Egyptian word meaning *kneel:*—bow the knee.

87. אַבְרָם, **'Abrâm,** *ab-rawm´*; contracted from 48; *high father; Abram*, the original name of Abraham:—Abram.

88. אֹבֹת, **'ôbôth,** *o-both´*; plural of 178; *waterskins; Oboth*, a place in the Desert:—Oboth.

89. אָגֵא, **'Âgê',** *aw-gay´*; of uncertain derivation [compare 90]; *Agè*, an Israelite:—Agee.

90. אֲגַג, **'Agag,** *ag-ag´*; or אֲגָג, **'Agâg,** *ag-awg´*; of uncertain derivation [compare 89]; *flame; Agag*, a title of Amalekitish kings:—Agag.

91. אֲגָגִי, **'Agâgîy,** *ag-aw-ghee´*; patrial or patronymic from 90; an *Agagite* or descendant (subject) of Agag:—Agagite.

92. אֲגֻדָּה, **'ăguddâh,** *ag-ood-daw´*; feminine passive participle of an unused root (meaning to *bind*); a *band, bundle, knot,* or *arch:*—bunch, burden, troop.

93. אֱגוֹז, **'ĕgôwz,** *eg-oze´*; probably of Persian origin; a *nut:*—nut.

94. אָגוּר, **'Âgûwr,** *aw-goor´*; passive participle of 103; *gathered* (i.e. *received* among the sages); *Agur*, a fanciful name for Solomon:—Agur.

95. אֲגוֹרָה, **'ăgôwrâh,** *ag-o-raw´*; from the same as 94; probably something *gathered*, i.e. perhaps a *grain* or *berry*; used only of a small (silver) *coin:*—piece [of] silver.

96. אֶגֶל, **'egel,** *eh´-ghel*; from an unused root (meaning to *flow* down or together as drops); a *reservoir:*—drop.

97. אֶגְלַיִם, **'Eglayim,** *eg-lah´-yim*; dual of 96; a *double pond; Eglajim*, a place in Moab:—Eglaim.

98. אֲגַם, **'ăgam,** *ag-am´*; from an unused root (meaning to *collect* as water); a *marsh*; hence a *rush* (as growing in swamps); hence a *stockade* of reeds:—pond, pool, standing [water].

99. אָגֵם, **'âgêm,** *aw-game´*; probably from the same as 98 (in the sense of *stagnant* water); (figurative) *sad:*—pond.

100. אַגְמוֹן, **'agmôwn,** *ag-mone´*; from the same as 98; a marshy *pool* [others from a different root, a *kettle*]; by implication a *rush* (as growing there); (collective) a *rope* of rushes:—bulrush, caldron, hook, rush.

101. אַגָּן, **'aggân,** *ag-gawn´*; probably from 5059; a *bowl* (as *pounded* out hollow):—basin, cup, goblet.

102. אֲגַף, **'ăgâph,** *ag-af´*; probably from 5062 (through the idea of *impending*); a *cover* or *heap*; i.e. (only plural) *wings* of an army, or *crowds* of troops:—bands.

103. אָגַר, **'âgar,** *aw-gar´*; a primitive root; to *harvest:*—gather.

104. אִגְּרָא, **'iggᵉrâ'** (Chaldee), *ig-ger-aw´*; of Persian origin; an *epistle* (as carried by a state courier or postman):—letter.

105. אֲגַרְטָל, **'ăgartâl,** *ag-ar-tawl´*; of uncertain derivation; a *basin:*—charger.

106. אֶגְרֹף, **'egrôph,** *eg-rofe´*; from 1640 (in the sense of *grasping*); the *clenched* hand:—fist.

107. אִגֶּרֶת, **'iggereth,** *ig-eh´-reth;* feminine of 104; an *epistle:*—letter.

108. אֵד, **'êd,** *ade;* from the same as 181 (in the sense of *enveloping*); a *fog:*—mist, vapor.

109. אָדַב, **'âdab,** *aw-dab´;* a primitive root; to *languish:*—grieve.

110. אַדְבְּאֵל, **'Adbeʼêl,** *ad-beh-ale´;* probably from 109 (in the sense of *chastisement*) and 410; *disciplined of God; Adbeël,* a son of Ishmael:—Adbeel.

111. אֲדַד, **'Ădad,** *ad-ad´;* probably an orthographical variation for 2301; *Adad* (or Hadad), an Edomite:—Hadad.

112. אִדּוֹ, **'Iddôw,** *id-do;* of uncertain derivation; *Iddo,* an Israelite:—Iddo.

113. אָדוֹן, **'âdôwn,** *aw-done´;* or (shortened) אָדֹן, **'âdôn,** *aw-done´;* from an unused root (meaning to *rule*); *sovereign,* i.e. *controller* (human or divine):—lord, master, owner. Compare also names beginning with "Adoni-".

A masculine noun meaning lord or master. The most frequent usage is of a human lord, but it is also used of divinity. Generally, it carries the nuances of authority rather than ownership. When used of humans, it refers to authority over slaves (Ge 24:9; Jgs 19:11); people (1Ki 22:17); a wife (Ge 18:12; Am 4:1); or a household (Ge 45:8; Ps 105:21). When used of divinity, it frequently occurs with *yĕhôwâh* (3068), signifying His sovereignty (Ex 34:23; Jos 3:13; Isa 1:24). See the Hebrew noun *'ădônây* (136).

114. אַדּוֹן, **'Addôwn,** *ad-done´;* probably intensive for 113; *powerful; Addon,* apparently an Israelite:—Addon.

115. אֲדוֹרַיִם, **'Ădôwrayim,** *ad-o-rah´-yim;* dual from 142 (in the sense of *eminence*); *double mound; Adorajim,* a place in Palestine:—Adoraim.

116. אֱדַיִן, **'ĕdayin** (Chaldee), *ed-ah´-yin;* of uncertain derivation; *then* (of time):—now, that time, then.

117. אַדִּיר, **'addîyr,** *ad-deer´;* from 142; *wide* or (general) *large;* (figurative) *powerful:*—excellent, famous, gallant, glorious, goodly, lordly, mighty (-ier, one), noble, principal, worthy.

An adjective meaning excellent, majestic, lofty, or great. When describing physical objects, it often denotes strength of the waters of the sea (Ex 15:10; Ps 93:4); the precious value of a bowl (Jgs 5:25); or both the strength and beauty of trees (Eze 17:23; Zec 11:2). When describing humans, it refers to those who lead, either as rulers or royalty (Jer 14:3; 25:34–36; 30:21; Na 3:18). When describing God, this word describes His majestic power (1Sa 4:8; Ps 8:1[2], 9[10]; Isa 10:34) that is greater than the breakers of the sea (Ps 93:4).

118. אֲדַלְיָא, **'Ădalyâʼ,** *ad-al-yaw´;* of Persian derivation; *Adalja,* a son of Haman:—Adalia.

119. אָדַם, **'âdam,** *aw-dam´;* to *show blood* (in the face), i.e. *flush* or turn rosy:—be (dyed, made) red (ruddy).

A verb meaning to be red, ruddy, dyed red. It is used to describe people: Esau (Ge 25:25); David (1Sa 16:12; 17:42); and princes (La 4:7). As for things, it describes ram skins that were dyed red (Ex 25:5; 26:14; 35:7) and red wine (Pr 23:31). Metaphorically, this word describes sin as "red like crimson" (Isa 1:18).

120. אָדָם, **'âdâm,** *aw-dawm´;* from 119; *ruddy,* i.e. a *human being* (an individual or the species, mankind, etc.):— × another, + hypocrite, + common sort, × low, man (mean, of low degree), person.

A masculine noun meaning a male, any human being, or generically the human race. The word is used to signify a man, as opposed to a woman (Ge 2:18; Ecc 7:28); a human (Nu 23:19; Pr 17:18; Isa 17:7); the human race in general (Ge 1:27; Nu 8:17; Ps 144:3; Isa 2:17); and the representative embodiment of humanity, as the appellation "son of man" indicates (Eze 2:1, 3). The first man used this word as a proper noun, "Adam" (Ge 2:20).

121. אָדָם, **'Âdâm,** *aw-dawm´;* the same as 120; *Adam,* the name of the first man, also of a place in Palestine:—Adam.

122. אָדֹם, **'âdôm,** *aw-dome´;* from 119; *rosy:*—red, ruddy.

A masculine adjective meaning red, ruddy, the colour of blood (red to reddish brown). The meaning of the word is best demonstrated in 2Ki 3:22, where the Moabites saw the sunrise reflecting off the water which the Lord had miraculously provided. The Moabites thought the water was "as red as blood." This word is also used to describe the colour of lentil stew (Ge 25:30); the health or attractiveness of a man (SS 5:10); the colour of garments (Isa 63:2); the colour of animals, like a red heifer (Nu 19:2) or chestnut or bay–coloured horses (Zec 1:8; 6:2).

123. אֱדֹם, **'Ĕdôm,** *ed-ome´*; or (fully) אֱדוֹם, **'Ĕdôwm,** *ed-ome´*; from 122 *red* [see Ge 25:25]; Edom, the elder twin-brother of Jacob; hence the region (Idumæa) occupied by him:— Edom, Edomites, Idumea.

124. אֹדֶם, **'ôdem,** *o´-dem*; from 119; *redness,* i.e. the *ruby, garnet,* or some other red gem:— sardius.

125. אֲדַמְדָּם, **'ădamdâm,** *ad-am-dawm´*; reduplicated from 119; *reddish:*—(somewhat) reddish.

An adjective meaning reddish. This word is used only six times in the OT. It signifies the reddish appearance of leprosy on the skin (Le 13:19, 24, 42, 43); the mark of leprosy on a garment (Le 13:49); or the mark of leprosy within a house (Le 14:37). It is related to the verb *'âdam* (119), meaning to be red, and the adjective *'âdôm,* meaning red (122).

126. אַדְמָה, **'Admâh,** *ad-maw´*; contraction for 127; *earthy; Admah,* a place near the Dead Sea:—Admah.

127. אֲדָמָה, **'ădâmâh,** *ad-aw-maw´*; from 119; *soil* (from its general *redness*):—country, earth, ground, husband [-man] (-ry), land.

A feminine noun meaning dirt, ground, earth, clay. In the narrow sense of the word, it signifies the earth or clay God used to form man (Ge 2:7); dirt put on the head during mourning (2Sa 1:2; Ne 9:1); the ground itself (Ex 3:5); cultivated land (Ge 4:2; Zec 13:5). In a broader sense, it means the inhabited earth (Isa 24:21; Am 3:2). The first man, Adam, both came from the ground and was assigned the task of tending the ground (see Ge 2:7, 15).

128. אֲדָמָה, **'Ădâmâh,** *ad-aw-maw´*; the same as 127; *Adamah,* a place in Palestine:—Adamah.

129. אַדְמִי, **'Ădâmîy,** *ad-aw-mee´*; from 127; *earthy; Adami,* a place in Palestine:—Adami.

130. אֲדֹמִי, **'Ĕdômîy,** *ed-o-mee´*; or (fully) אֱדוֹמִי, **'Ĕdôwmîy,** *ed-o-mee´*; patronymically from 123; an *Edomite,* or descendant from (or inhabitant of) Edom:—Edomite. See 726.

131. אֲדֻמִּים, **'Ădummîym,** *ad-oom-meem´*; plural of 121; *red* spots; *Adummim,* a pass in Palestine:—Adummim.

132. אַדְמֹנִי, **'admônîy,** *ad-mo-nee´*; or (fully) אַדְמוֹנִי, **'admôwnîy,** *ad-mo-nee´*; from 119; *reddish* (of the hair or the complexion):—red, ruddy.

An adjective meaning red, ruddy. Esau is the prime example of someone who was red (Ge 25:25). The Edomites, or "red ones," descended from Esau. David is the other notable figure whose complexion was characterized as good-looking, bright-eyed, and ruddy (1Sa 16:12).

133. אַדְמָתָא, **'Admâthâ',** *ad-maw-thaw´*; probably of Persian derivation; *Admatha,* a Persian nobleman:—Admatha.

134. אֶדֶן, **'eden,** *eh´-den*; from the same as 113 (in the sense of *strength*); a *basis* (of a building, a column, etc.):—foundation, socket.

135. אַדָּן, **'Addân,** *ad-dawn´*; intensive from the same as 134; *firm; Addan,* an Israelite:—Addan.

136. אֲדֹנָי, **'Ădônây,** *ad-o-noy´*; an emphatic form of 113; the *Lord* (used as a proper name of God only):—(my) Lord.

A masculine noun used exclusively of God. An emphatic form of the word *'âdôwn* (113), this word means literally "my Lord" (Ge 18:3). It is often used in place of the divine name YHWH (3068), which was held by later Jewish belief to be too holy to utter. This designation points to the supreme authority or power of God (Ps 2:4; Isa 6:1). The word was often combined with the divine name to reinforce the notion of God's matchlessness (e.g., Eze 20:3; Am 7:6).

137. אֲדֹנִי־בֶזֶק, **'Ădônîy-Bezeq,** *ad-o´-nee-beh´-zek*; from 113 and 966; *lord of Bezek; Adoni-Bezek,* a Canaanitish king:—Adoni-bezek.

138. אֲדֹנִיָּה, **'Ădônîyyâh,** *ad-o-nee-yaw´*; original (prolonged) אֲדֹנִיָּהוּ, **'Ădônîyyâhûw,** *ad-o-nee-yaw´-hoo*; from 113 and 3050; *lord* (i.e. worshipper) of Jah; *Adonijah,* the name of three Israelites:—Adonijah.

139. אֲדֹנִי־צֶדֶק, **’Ădônîy-Tsedeq,** *ad-o´-nee-tseh´-dek*; from 113 and 6664; *lord of justice; Adoni-Tsedek,* a Canaanitish king:—Adonizedec.

140. אֲדֹנִיקָם, **’Ădônîyqâm,** *ad-o-nee-kawm´*; from 113 and 6965; *lord of rising* (i.e. *high*); *Adonikam,* the name of one or two Israelites:—Adonikam.

141. אֲדֹנִירָם, **’Ădônîyrâm,** *ad-o-nee-rawm´*; from 113 and 7311; *lord of height; Adoniram,* an Israelite:—Adoniram.

142. אָדַר, **’âdar,** *aw-dar*; a primitive root; to *expand,* i.e. *be great* or (figurative) *magnificent:*—(become) glorious, honourable.

A verb meaning to magnify, glorify, or, in the passive sense, to be magnified. Whereas the Hebrew noun *kâbôwd* (3519) pictures glory in terms of weight, this word pictures it in terms of size. The Hebrew word is used only three times in the OT: to celebrate God's power and holiness after the deliverance of Israel from Egypt (Ex 15:6, 11); and to describe the Law given on Sinai as great and glorious (Isa 42:21).

143. אֲדָר, **’Ădâr,** *ad-awr´*; probably of foreign derivation; perhaps meaning *fire; Adar,* the 12th Hebrew month:—Adar.

144. אֲדָר, **’Ădâr** (Chaldee), *ad-awr´*; corresponding to 143:—Adar.

145. אֶדֶר, **’eder,** *eh´-der*; from 142; *amplitude,* i.e. (concrete) a *mantle;* also (figurative) *splendor:*—goodly, robe.

146. אַדָּר, **’Addâr,** *ad-dawr´*; intensive from 142; *ample; Addar,* a place in Palestine; also an Israelite:—Addar.

147. אִדָּר, **’iddar** (Chaldee), *id-dar´*; intensive from a root corresponding to 142; *ample,* i.e. a threshing-*floor:*—threshingfloor.

148. אֲדַרְגָּזֵר, **’ădargâzêr** (Chaldee), *ad-ar´-gaw-zare´*; from the same as 147, and 1505; a *chief diviner,* or *astrologer:*—judge.

An Aramaic masculine noun meaning counselor. It is found only in the book of Daniel. When Nebuchadnezzar erected his statue for all to bow down to, he sent a decree to all the important people (i.e. satraps, administrators, counselors) to come for the dedication ceremony (Da 3:2, 3).

149. אַדְרַזְדָּא, **’adrazdâ’** (Chaldee), *ad-raz-daw´*; probably of Persian origin; *quickly* or *carefully:*—diligently.

150. אֲדַרְכֹּן, **’ădarkôn,** *ad-ar-kone´*; of Persian origin; a *daric* or Persian coin:—dram.

A noun meaning monetary value and weight. This word is used only in 1Ch 29:7, where David collected money for the first temple, and in Ezr 8:27, where it tells the weight of gold basins for use in the second temple. The word may refer to the Greek *drachma,* which weighed 4.3 grams, or to the Persian *daric,* which weighed about twice as much.

151. אֲדֹרָם, **’Ădôrâm,** *ad-o-rawm´*; contraction for 141; *Adoram* (or Adoniram), an Israelite:—Adoram.

152. אַדְרַמֶּלֶךְ, **’Adrammelek,** *ad-ram-meh´-lek*; from 142 and 4428; *splendor of* (the) *king; Adrammelek,* the name of an Assyrian idol, also of a son of Sennacherib:—Adrammelech.

153. אֶדְרָע, **’edrâ‘** (Chaldee), *ed-raw´*; an orthographical variation for 1872; an *arm,* i.e. (figurative) *power:*—force.

154. אֶדְרֶעִי, **’edre‘îy,** *ed-reh´-ee*; from the equivalent of 153; *mighty; Edrei,* the name of two places in Palestine:—Edrei.

155. אַדֶּרֶת, **’addereth,** *ad-deh´-reth*; feminine of 117; something *ample* (as a *large* vine, a *wide* dress); also the same as 145:—garment, glory, goodly, mantle, robe.

156. אָדַשׁ, **’âdash,** *aw-dash´*; a primitive root; to *tread* out (grain):—thresh.

157. אָהַב, **’âhab,** *aw-hab´*; or אָהֵב, **’âhêb,** *aw-habe´*; a primitive root; to *have affection* for (sexually or otherwise):—(be-) love (-d, -ly, -r), like, friend.

A verb meaning to love. The semantic range of the verb includes loving or liking objects and things such as bribes (Isa 1:23); wisdom (Pr 4:6); wine (Pr 21:17); peace, truth (Zec 8:19); or tasty food (Ge 27:4, 9, 14). The word also conveys love for other people (Ge 29:32; Ru 4:15; 1Ki 11:1); love for God (Ex 20:6; Ps 116:1); and also God's love of people (Dt 4:37; 1Ki 10:9; Hos 3:1).

158. אַהַב, **’ahab,** *ah´-hab´*; from 157; *affection* (in a good or a bad sense):—love (-r).

A masculine noun meaning love or lover. Both occurrences of this noun are in the plural. In Pr 5:19, it refers to marital love, while in Hos 8:9, the word refers to Israel's trust in foreign alliances rather than in God. The foreign nations are Israel's hired lovers.

159. אֹהַב, **'ôhab,** *o´-hab*; from 156; meaning the same as 158:—love.

A masculine noun meaning loved one. It occurs twice in the Hebrew Bible, both times in the plural (Pr 7:18; Hos 9:10). Both occurrences are associated with illicit sexual relations.

160. אַהֲבָה, **'ahăbâh,** *ă-hab-aw´*; feminine of 158 and meaning the same:—love.

A feminine noun meaning love. The word often signifies a powerful, intimate love between a man and a woman (Ge 29:20; SS 2:4, 5, 7); love between friends (2Sa 1:26); God's love for His people (Isa 63:9; Hos 3:1). Frequently, it is associated with forming a covenant, which enjoins loyalty (Dt 7:8). When used in an abstract way, the word designates a desirable personal quality, which connotes affection and faithfulness (Pr 15:17; 17:9).

161. אֹהַד, **'Ôhad,** *o´-had*; from an unused root meaning to *be united; unity*; Ohad, an Israelite:—Ohad.

162. אֲהָהּ, **'ăhâh,** *ă-haw´*; apparently a primitive word expressing *pain* exclamatorily; Oh!:—ah, alas.

163. אַהֲוָא, **'Ahăvâ',** *ă-hav-aw´*; probably of foreign origin; Ahava, a river of Babylonia:—Ahava.

164. אֵהוּד, **'Êhûwd,** *ay-hood´*; from the same as 161; *united*; Ehud, the name of two or three Israelites:—Ehud.

165. אֱהִי, **'ĕhîy,** *e-hee´*; apparently an orthographical variation for 346 *where*:—I will be (Hos 13:10, 14) [*which is often the rendering of the same Hebrew form from* 1961].

166. אָהַל, **'âhal,** *aw-hal´*; a primitive root; to *be clear*:—shine.

167. אָהַל, **'âhal,** *aw-hal´*; a denominative from 168; to *tent*:—pitch (remove) a tent.

168. אֹהֶל, **'ôhel,** *o´-hel*; from 166; a *tent* (as clearly conspicuous from a distance):—covering, (dwelling) (place), home, tabernacle, tent.

A masculine noun meaning tent. It is used literally as a habitation of nomadic peoples and patriarchs (Ge 9:21; 25:27). It can be used figuratively for a dwelling (Ps 91:10; 132:3); or a people group (Ge 9:27; Jer 35:7; 49:29). As a generic collective, it describes cattle (Ge 4:20) or wickedness (Job 15:34; Ps 84:10[11]). The word is also employed in reference to the tabernacle, the "tent" (Nu 12:5, 10; Eze 41:1).

169. אֹהֶל, **'Ôhel,** *o´-hel*; the same as 168; *Ohel*, an Israelite:—Ohel.

170. אָהֳלָה, **'Ohŏlâh,** *ŏ-hol-aw´*; in form a feminine of 168, but in fact for אָהֳלָהּ, **'Ohŏlâh,** *ŏ-hol-aw´*; from 168; *her tent* (i.e. idolatrous *sanctuary*); Oholah, a symbolical name for Samaria:—Aholah.

171. אָהֳלִיאָב, **'Ohŏlîy'âb,** *ŏ´-hol-e-awb´*; from 168 and 1; *tent of* (his) *father*; Oholiab, an Israelite:—Aholiab.

172. אָהֳלִיבָה, **'Ohŏlîybâh,** *ŏ´-hol-ee-baw´*; (similarly with 170) for אָהֳלִיבָה, **'Ohŏlîybâh,** *ŏ´-hol-e-baw´*; from 168; *my tent (is) in her*; Oholibah, a symbolical name for Judah:—Aholibah.

173. אָהֳלִיבָמָה, **'Ohŏlîybâmâh,** *ŏ´-hol-e-baw-maw´*; from 168 and 1116; *tent of* (the) *height*; Oholibamah, a wife of Esau:—Aholibamah.

174. אֲהָלִים, **'ăhâlîym,** *â-haw-leem´*; or (feminine) אֲהָלוֹת, **'ăhâlôwth,** *ă-haw-loth´*; of foreign origin; *aloe* wood (i.e. sticks):—(tree of lign-) aloes.

175. אַהֲרוֹן, **'Ahărôwn,** *ă-har-one´*; of uncertain derivation; Aharon, the brother of Moses:—Aaron.

176. אוֹ, **'ôw,** *o*; presumed to be the "constructive" or genitival form of אַו, **'av,** *av*, shortened for 185 *desire* (and so probably in Pr 31:4); hence (by way of alternative) *or*, also *if*:—also, and, either, if, at the least, × nor, or, otherwise, then, whether.

177. אוּאֵל, **'Ûw'êl,** *oo-ale´*; from 176 and 410; *wish of God*; Uel, an Israelite:—Uel.

178. אוֹב, **'ôwb,** *obe*; from the same as 1 (apparently through the idea of *prattling* a father's name); probably a *mumble*, i.e. a water-*skin* (from its hollow sound); hence a *necromancer* (ventriloquist, as from a jar):—bottle, familiar spirit.

A masculine noun meaning a conjured spirit, a medium or necromancer; or a leather bottle. The primary use of the word is connected to the occult practice of necromancy or consulting the dead. It is used to signify a conjurer who professes to call up the dead by means of magic, especially to give revelation about future uncertainties (1Sa 28:7; Isa 8:19); a man or woman who has a familiar spirit (Le 20:27; 1Ch 10:13; Isa 29:4); the conjured spirit itself, particularly when speaking through the medium (1Sa 28:8; 2 Kgs 21:6; 2Ch 33:6). The Israelites were strictly forbidden from engaging in such practices or consulting mediums (Le 19:31; Dt 18:10–12). Interestingly, the word is used once to signify a leather bottle that may burst under pressure (Job 32:19). There is no convincing evidence that this particular reference has any occult connotations. Rather, the connection between the two divergent meanings of this Hebrew word is probably that a medium was seen as a "container" for a conjured spirit.

179. אוֹבִיל, **'Ôwbîyl**, *o-beel´*; probably from 56; *mournful*; *Obil*, an Ishmaelite:—Obil.

180. אוּבָל, **'ûwbâl**, *oo-bawl´*; or (shortened) אֻבָל, **'ubâl**, *oo-bawl´*; from 2986 (in the sense of 2988); a *stream*:—river.

181. אוּד, **'ûwd**, *ood*; from an unused root meaning to *rake* together; a *poker* (for *turning* or *gathering* embers):—(fire-) brand.

182. אוֹדוֹת, **'ôwdôwth**, *o-dōth´*; or (shortened) אֹדוֹת, **'ôdôwth**, *o-dōth´* (only thus in the plural); from the same as 181; *turnings* (i.e. *occasions*); (adverbial) on *account* of:—(be-) cause, concerning, sake.

183. אָוָה, **'âvâh**, *aw-vaw´*; a primitive root; to *wish* for:—covet, (greatly) desire, be desirous, long, lust (after).

A verb meaning to desire, to be inclined. This word is used to signify coveting, as in the tenth commandment (Dt 5:21[18]; but *châmad* [2530] is used in Ex 20:17). The word may also signify acceptable desires for objects such as food or beauty (Ps 45:11[12]; Mic 7:1); as well as for righteousness and God (Isa 26:9; Mic

7:1). Both God and humans can be the subject of this word (Ps 132:13, 14).

184. אָוָה, **'âvâh**, *aw-vaw´*; a primitive root; to *extend* or *mark* out:—point out.

185. אַוָּה, **'avvâh**, *av-vaw´*; from 183; *longing*:—desire, lust after, pleasure.

186. אוּזַי, **'Ûwzay**, *oo-zah´ee*; perhaps by permutation for 5813, *strong*; *Uzai*, an Israelite:—Uzai.

187. אוּזָל, **'Ûwzâl**, *oo-zâwl´*; of uncertain derivation; *Uzal*, a son of Joktan:—Uzal.

188. אוֹי, **'ôwy**, *ō´-ee*; probably from 183 (in the sense of *crying* out after); *lamentation*; also interjectional Oh!:—alas, woe.

189. אֱוִי, **'Ĕvîy**, *ev-ee´*; probably from 183; *desirous*; *Evi*, a Midianitish chief:—Evi.

190. אוֹיָה, **'ôwyâh**, *o-yaw´*; feminine of 188:—woe.

191. אֱוִיל, **'ĕvîyl**, *ev-eel´*; from an unused root (meaning to be *perverse*); (figurative) *silly*:—fool (-ish) (man).

192. אֱוִיל מְרֹדַךְ, **'Ĕvîyl M͏ͤrôdak**, *ev-eel´ mer-o-dak´*; of Chaldee derivation and probably meaning *soldier of Merodak*; *Evil-Merodak*, a Babylonian king:—Evil-merodach.

193. אוּל, **'ûwl**, *ool*; from an unused root meaning to *twist*, i.e. (by implication) *be strong*; the *body* (as being *rolled* together); also *powerful*:—mighty, strength.

194. אוּלַי, **'ûwlay**, *oo-lah´ee*; or (shortened) אֻלַי, **'ulay**, *oo-lah´ee*; from 176; *if not*; hence *perhaps*:—if so be, may be, peradventure, unless.

195. אוּלַי, **'Ûwlay**, *oo-lah´ee*; of Persian derivation; the *Ulai* (or Eulæus), a river of Persia:—Ulai.

196. אֱוִלִי, **'ĕvilîy**, *ev-ee-lee´*; from 191; *silly, foolish*; hence (moral) *impious*:—foolish.

197. אוּלָם, **'ûwlâm**, *oo-lawm´*; or (shortened) אֻלָם, **'ulâm**, *oo-lawm´*; from 481 (in the sense of *tying*); a *vestibule* (as *bound* to the building):—porch.

198. אוּלָם, **'Ûwlâm**, *oo-lawm´*; apparently from 481 (in the sense of *dumbness*); *solitary*; *Ulam*, the name of two Israelites:—Ulam.

199. אוּלָם, **'ûwlâm,** *oo-lawm'*; apparently a variation of 194; *however* or *on the contrary*:—as for, but, howbeit, in very deed, surely, truly, wherefore.

200. אֻלֶּת, **'ivveleth,** *iv-veh'-leth*; from the same as 191; *silliness*:—folly, foolishly (-ness).

201. אוֹמָר, **'Ôwmâr,** *o-mawr'*; from 559; *talkative; Omar,* a grandson of Esau:—Omar.

202. אוֹן, **'ôwn,** *ōne*; probably from the same as 205 (in the sense of *effort,* but successful); *ability, power,* (figurative) *wealth*:—force, goods, might, strength, substance.

203. אוֹן, **'Ôwn,** *ōne*; the same as 202; *On,* an Israelite:—On.

204. אוֹן, **'Ôwn,** *ōne*; or (shortened) אֹן, **'Ôn,** *ōne*; of Egyptian derivation; *On,* a city of Egypt:—On.

205. אָוֶן, **'âven,** *aw'-ven*; from an unused root perhaps meaning properly to *pant* (hence to *exert* oneself, usually in vain; to *come to naught*); strictly *nothingness*; also *trouble, vanity, wickedness*; specifically an *idol*:—affliction, evil, false, idol, iniquity, mischief, mourners (-ing), naught, sorrow, unjust, unrighteous, vain, vanity, wicked (-ness). Compare 369.

A masculine noun meaning nothingness, trouble, sorrow, evil, or mischief. The primary meaning is that of emptiness and vanity. It is used to signify empty or futile pursuits (Pr 22:8; Isa 41:29); nothingness, in the sense of utter destruction (Am 5:5); an empty word, implying falsehood or deceit (Ps 10:7; Pr 17:4; Zec 10:2); wickedness or one who commits iniquity (Nu 23:21; Job 22:15; Ps 14:4[5]; 36:4; 101:8; Isa 58:9; Mic 2:1); evil or calamity (Job 5:6; Pr 12:21; Jer 4:15); and great sorrow (Dt 26:14; Ps 90:10; Hos 9:4). In a metaphorical sense, the word is used once to signify an idol, strongly conveying the futility of worshiping an idol, which is, in fact, "nothing" (Isa 66:3).

206. אָוֶן, **'Âven,** *aw'-ven*; the same as 205; *idolatry; Aven,* the contemptuous synonym of three places, one in Coele-Syria, one in Egypt (On), and one in Palestine (Bethel):—Aven. See also 204, 1007.

207. אוֹנוֹ, **'Ôwnôw,** *o-no'*; or (shortened) אֹנוֹ, **'Ônôw,** *o-no'*; prolonged from 202; *strong; Ono,* a place in Palestine:—Ono.

208. אוֹנָם, **'Ôwnâm,** *o-nawm'*; a variation of 209; *strong; Onam,* the name of an Edomite and of an Israelite:—Onam.

209. אוֹנָן, **'Ôwnân,** *o-nawn'*; a variation of 207; *strong; Onan,* a son of Judah:—Onan.

210. אוּפָז, **'Ûwphâz,** *oo-fawz'*; perhaps a corruption of 211; *Uphaz,* a famous gold region:—Uphaz.

211. אוֹפִיר, **'Ôwphîyr,** *o-feer'*; or (shortened) אֹפִיר, **'Ôphîyr,** *o-feer'*; and אוֹפִר, **'Ôwphir,** *o-feer'*; of uncertain derivation; *Ophir,* the name of a son of Joktan, and of a gold region in the East:—Ophir.

212. אוֹפָן, **'ôwphân,** *o-fawn'*; or (shortened) אֹפָן, **'ôphân,** *o-fawn'*; from an unused root meaning to *revolve*; a *wheel*:—wheel.

A masculine noun meaning wheel (although it is feminine in one usage). God caused the chariot wheels of the Egyptians to come off while they were chasing the Israelites through the Red Sea (Ex 14:25). This word is also used to describe the movable stands in Solomon's Temple (1Ki 7:30, 32, 33); the wheels of threshing carts (Pr 20:26; Isa 28:27); and the wheels of Ezekiel's chariot that supported the four living creatures (Eze 1:15, 16, 19–21).

213. אוּץ, **'ûwts,** *oots*; a primitive root; to *press*; (by implication) to *be close, hurry, withdraw*:—(make) haste (-n, -y), labour, be narrow.

214. אוֹצָר, **'ôwtsâr,** *o-tsaw'*; from 686; a *depository*:—armoury, cellar, garner, store (-house), treasure (-house) (-y).

215. אוֹר, **'ôwr,** *ore*; a primitive root; *to be* (causative *make*) *luminous* (literal and metaphorical):— × break of day, glorious, kindle, (be, en-, give, show) light (-en, -ened), set on fire, shine.

216. אוֹר, **'ôwr,** *ore*; from 215; *illumination* or (concrete) *luminary* (in every sense, including *lightning, happiness,* etc.):—bright, clear, + day, light (-ning), morning, sun.

A masculine noun meaning light. In a literal sense, it is used primarily to refer to light from heavenly bodies (Jer 31:35; Eze 32:7) but also for light itself (Ge 1:3; Ecc 12:2). The pillar of fire was a light for the wandering Israelites (Ex 13:21). One day God, who is clothed with light (a manifestation of His splendor), will replace the light of the heavens with His own light (Ps 104:2; Isa 60:19, 20; cf. Rev 21:23; 22:5). Light is always used as a positive symbol, such as for good fortune (Job 30:26); victory (Mic 7:8, 9); justice and righteousness (Isa 59:9); guidance (Ps 119:105); and a bearer of deliverance (Isa 49:6). Expressions involving light include the light of one's face, meaning someone's favour (Ps 44:3[4]); to see light, meaning to live (Ps 49:19[20]); and to walk in the light, meaning to live by God's known standards (Isa 2:5).

217. אוּר, *'ûwr, oor*; from 215; *flame*, hence (in the plural) the *East* (as being the region of light):—fire, light. See also 224.

A noun meaning fire. It refers to the fire of God's judgment (Isa 31:9) and God's destruction of the wicked (Eze 5:2). In Isa 44:16 and 47:14, the noun is used to speak of a form of idol worship.

218. אוּר, *'Ûwr, oor*; the same as 217; *Ur*, a place in Chaldea; also an Israelite:—Ur.

219. אוֹרָה, *'ôwrâh, o-raw'*; feminine of 216; *luminousness*, i.e. (figurative) *prosperity*; also a plant (as being *bright*):—herb, light.

A feminine noun meaning light, brightness, splendor, herbs. The primary stress of the word is on the life-giving properties. It is used to signify light (Ps 139:12); joyous well-being (Est 8:16); vibrant green herbs (2Ki 4:39). The word also conveys the quality of living (Isa 26:19).

220. אֻוְרָה, *'ăvêrâh, av-ay-raw'*; by transposition for 723; a *stall*:—cote.

221. אוּרִי, *'Ûwrîy, oo-ree'*; from 217; *fiery; Uri*, the name of three Israelites:—Uri.

222. אוּרִיאֵל, *'Ûwrîy'êl, oo-ree-ale'*; from 217 and 410; *flame of God; Uriel*, the name of two Israelites:—Uriel.

223. אוּרִיָּה, *'Ûwrîyyâh, oo-ree-yaw'*; or (prolonged) אוּרִיָּהוּ, *'Ûwrîyyâhûw, oo-ree-yaw'-hoo*; from 217 and 3050; *flame of Jah; Urijah*, the name of one Hittite and five Israelites:—Uriah, Urijah.

224. אוּרִים, *'Ûwrîym, oo-reem'*; plural of 217; *lights; Urim*, the oracular brilliancy of the figures in the high priest's breastplate:—Urim.

A masculine plural noun, which occurs seven times in the OT, usually with "the Thummim." Our knowledge of the Urim and Thummim is limited. They were kept in the breastplate which the high priest wore over his heart (Ex 28:30; Le 8:8) and were given to the Levites as part of Moses' blessing (Dt 33:8). Some believe they were flat objects which were cast to determine the will of God, one providing a negative answer and the other a positive, much like casting lots. However, that is somewhat conjectural. Joshua received God's revelation by Eleazer's use of the Urim (Nu 27:21). God didn't answer Saul when he consulted the Lord with the use of the Urim (1Sa 28:6). The Urim and Thummim were also used to approve priestly qualifications (Ezr 2:63; Ne 7:65).

225. אוּת, *'ûwth, ooth*; a primitive root; probably to *come*, i.e. (implication) to *assent*:—consent.

226. אוֹת, *'ôwth, ōth*; probably from 225 (in the sense of *appearing*); a *signal* (literal or figurative), as a *flag, beacon, monument, omen, prodigy, evidence*, etc.:—mark, miracle, (en-) sign, token.

A masculine noun meaning sign, signal, mark, miracle. This word is used most often to describe awe-inspiring events: God's work to bring the Hebrew people out of Egypt (Ex 4:8, 9; Nu 14:22; Dt 7:19; Ps 78:43; Jer 32:20, 21); miracles verifying God's message (1Sa 2:34; 10:7, 9; Isa 7:11, 14). Moreover, this word may also denote signs from false prophets (Dt 13:1[2], 2[3]; Isa 44:25); circumstances demonstrating God's control (Dt 28:46; Ps 86:17). Associate meanings of the word denote physical emblems (Nu 2:2); a promise to remember (Ge 17:11; Dt 6:8; Jos 2:12; 4:6); an event to occur in the future (Isa 20:3; Eze 4:3).

227. אָז, *'âz, awz*; a demonstrative adverb; *at that time* or *place*; also as a conjunction, *therefore*:—beginning, for, from, hitherto, now, of old, once, since, then, at which time, yet.

An adverb meaning then, at that time, or since. This word may introduce something that used to be so (Ge 12:6); what happened next in a narrative (Ex 15:1); or what will happen in the future (Isa 35:5, 6). On occasion, it is also used as a preposition, such as in Ru 2:7: "Even from the morning" (KJV).

228. אֲזָא, **'ăzâ'** (Chaldee), *az-aw´*; or אֲזָה, **'ăzâh**, *az-aw´*; (Chaldee); to *kindle*; (by implication) to *heat*:—heat, hot.

229. אֶזְבַּי, **'Ezbay**, *ez-bah´ee*; probably from 231; *hyssop-like*; *Ezbai*, an Israelite:—Ezbai.

230. אֲזַד, **'ăzâd** (Chaldee), *az-awd´*; of uncertain derivation; *firm*:—be gone.

231. אֵזוֹב, **'êzôwb**, *ay-zobe´*; probably of foreign derivation; *hyssop*:—hyssop.

232. אֵזוֹר, **'êzôwr**, *ay-zore´*; from 246; some-thing *girt*; a *belt*, also a *band*:—girdle.

233. אֲזַי, **'ăzay**, *az-ah´ee*; probably from 227; *at that time*:—then.

234. אַזְכָּרָה, **'azkârâh**, *az-kaw-raw´*; from 2142; a *reminder*; specifically *remembrance-offering*:—memorial.

235. אָזַל, **'âzal**, *aw-zal´*; a primitive root; to *go away*, hence to *disappear*:—fail, gad about, go to and fro [*but in Eze 27:19 the word is rendered by many* "from Uzal," *by others* "yarn"], be gone (spent).

236. אֲזַל, **'ăzal** (Chaldee), *az-al´*; the same as 235; to *depart*:—go (up).

237. אֶזֶל, **'ezel**, *eh´-zel*; from 235; *departure*; *Ezel*, a memorial stone in Palestine:—Ezel.

238. אָזַן, **'âzan**, *aw-zan´*; a primitive root; prob-ably to *expand*; but used only as a denominative from 241; to *broaden out the ear* (with the hand), i.e. (by implication) to *listen*:—give (perceive by the) ear, hear (-ken). See 239.

A verb meaning to give an ear, to lend an ear, to listen, to hear. This word is almost always found in poetic texts of the OT and is often found in songs. The SS of Moses begins with an exhortation for the heavens to lend its ear (Dt 32:1); Jeremiah asked for the people of Israel to listen to his prophecy (Jer 13:15). God's people commonly asked the Lord to listen to their prayers and petitions; this significant use is found many times throughout the Book of Psalms (Ps 5:1[2]; 77:1[2]; 80:1[2]).

239. אָזַן, **'âzan**, *aw-zan´*; a primitive root [rather identical with 238 through the idea of *scales* as if two ears]; to *weigh*, i.e. (figurative) *ponder*:—give good heed.

240. אָזֵן, **'âzên**, *aw-zane´*; from 238; a *spade* or *paddle* (as having a *broad* end):—weapon.

241. אֹזֶן, **'ôzen**, *o´-zen*; from 238; *broadness*, i.e. (concrete) the *ear* (from its form in man):—+ advertise, audience, + displease, ear, hearing, + show.

A masculine noun meaning ear. The word is often used metaphorically as an instrument of obedience (Pr 25:12) and intellect (Job 12:11; 13:1; Pr 18:15; Ecc 1:8). In Jer 6:10, the disobe-dient or inattentive are said to have uncircum-cised ears. The Hebrew idiom for revealing something or making one aware is to open the ears (Ru 4:4; 1Sa 20:2, 12, 13; Isa 35:5).

242. אֹזֶן שֶׁאֱרָה, **'Uzzên She'ĕrâh**, *ooz-zane´ sheh-er-aw´*; from 238 and 7609; *plat of Sheerah* (i.e. settled by him); *Uzzen-Sheërah*, a place in Pales-tine:—Uzzen-sherah.

243. אַזְנוֹת תָּבוֹר, **'Aznôwth Tâbôwr**, *az-nōth´ taw-bore´*; from 238 and 8396; *flats* (i.e. *tops*) *of Tabor* (i.e. situated on it); *Aznoth-Tabor*, a place in Palestine:—Aznoth-tabor.

244. אָזְנִי, **'Oznîy**, *oz-nee´*; from 241; *having (quick) ears*; *Ozni*, an Israelite; also an *Oznite* (collective), his descendants:—Ozni, Oznites.

245. אֲזַנְיָה, **'Ăzanyâh**, *az-an-yaw´*; from 238 and 3050; *heard by Jah*; *Azanjah*, an Israelite:—Aza-niah.

246. אֲזִקִּים, **'ăziqqîym**, *az-ik-keem´*; a variation for 2131; *manacles*:—chains.

247. אָזַר, **'âzar**, *aw-zar´*; a primitive root; to *belt*:—bind (compass) about, gird (up, with).

248. אֶזְרוֹעַ, **'ezrôwa'**, *ez-ro´-ă*; a variation for 2220; the *arm*:—arm.

249. אֶזְרָח, **'ezrâch**, *ez-rawkh´*; from 2224 (in the sense of *springing up*); a spontaneous *growth*, i.e. *native* (tree or persons):—bay tree, (home-) born (in the land), of the (one's own) country (nation).

250. אֶזְרָחִי, **'Ezrâchîy**, *ez-raw-khee´*; patronymic from 2246; an *Ezrachite* or descendant of Zer-ach:—Ezrahite.

251. אָח, **'âch,** *awkh*; a primitive word; a *brother* (used in the widest sense of literal relationship and metaphorical affinity or resemblance [like 1]):— another, brother (-ly), kindred, like, other. Compare also the proper names beginning with "Ah-" or "Ahi-".

A masculine noun meaning brother. The word is used not only of those with common parents but also of those with common ancestors. Thus, the descendants of Israel are brothers (Le 19:17; 25:46), as are two nations with common ancestors (Am 1:11, Ob 1:10, 12). It further describes a close friend outside the immediate physical family (2Sa 1:26).

252. אָח, **'ach,** *akh*; corresponding to 251:— brother.

An Aramaic masculine noun meaning brother. It occurs only in Ezr 7:18 and is the equivalent of the Hebrew word *'âch* (251).

253. אָח, **'âch,** *awkh*; a variation for 162; *Oh!* (expressive of grief or surprise):—ah, alas.

254. אָח, **'âch,** *awkh*; of uncertain derivation; a fire-*pot* or chafing-dish:—hearth.

255. אֹחַ, **'ôach,** *o'-akh*; probably from 253; a *howler* or lonesome wild animal:—doleful creature.

256. אַחְאָב, **'Ach'âb,** *akh-awb'*; once (by contraction) אֶחָב, **'Echâb,** *ekh-awb'*; (Jer 29:22), from 251 and 1; *brother* [i.e. *friend*] *of* (his) *father; Achab,* the name of a king of Israel and of a prophet at Babylon:—Ahab.

257. אַחְבָּן, **'Achbân,** *akh-bawn'*; from 251 and 995; *brother* (i.e. *possessor*) *of understanding; Achban,* an Israelite:—Ahban.

258. אָחַד, **'âchad,** *aw-khad'*; perhaps a primitive root; to *unify,* i.e. (figurative) *collect* (one's thoughts):—go one way or other.

259. אֶחָד, **'echâd,** *ekh-awd'*; a numeral from 258; probably *united,* i.e. *one;* or (as an ordinal) *first:*—a, alike, alone, altogether, and, any (-thing), apiece, a certain, [dai-] ly, each (one), + eleven, every, few, first, + highway, a man, once, one, only, other, some, together.

260. אָחוּ, **'âchûw,** *aw'-khoo*; of uncertain (perhaps Egyptian) derivation; a *bulrush* or any marshy grass (particularly that along the Nile):—flag, meadow.

261. אֵחוּד, **'Êchûwd,** *ay-khood'*; from 258; *united; Ehud,* the name of three Israelites:— Ehud.

262. אַחֲוָה, **'achvâh,** *akh-vaw'*; from 2331 (in the sense of 2324); an *utterance:*—declaration.

263. אַחֲוָה, **'achăvâh** (Chaldee), *akh-av-aw';* corresponding to 262; *solution* (of riddles):— showing.

264. אַחֲוָה, **'achăvâh,** *akh-av-aw';* from 251; *fraternity:*—brotherhood.

A noun meaning brotherhood. It is used only in Zec 11:14 where it signifies the unity between Judah and Israel whose common ancestor is Jacob. The brotherhood is symbolically broken by Zechariah's breaking his staff.

265. אֲחוֹחַ, **'Ăchôwach,** *akh-o'-akh*; by reduplication from 251; *brotherly; Achoach,* an Israelite:—Ahoah.

266. אֲחוֹחִי, **'Ăchôwchîy,** *akh-o-khee';* patronymically from 264; an *Achochite* or descendant of Achoach:—Ahohite.

267. אֲחוּמַי, **'Ăchûwmay,** *akh-oo-mah'ee*; perhaps from 251 and 4325; *brother* (i.e. *neighbour*) *of water; Achumai,* an Israelite:—Ahumai.

268. אָחוֹר, **'âchôwr,** *aw-khore';* or (shortened) אָחֹר, **'âchôr,** *aw-khore';* from 299; the *hinder* part; hence (adverbial) *behind, backward;* also (as facing north) the *West:*—after (-ward), back (part, -side, -ward), hereafter, (be-) hind (-er part), time to come, without.

269. אָחוֹת, **'âchôwth,** *aw-khōth';* irregular feminine of 251; a *sister* (used very widely [like 250], literal and figurative):—(an-) other, sister, together.

A feminine noun meaning sister. Besides a biological sister, it also refers to more intimate female relatives. SS of Solomon uses the word to refer to a bride (SS 4:9, 10, 12; 5:1, 2). In Nu 25:18, it is used as a generic term for female relatives. Poetically, it sometimes refers to a geographical location (Jer 3:7, 8, 10; Eze 16:45, 52). For inanimate objects, it can often be translated as the English word *another* (Ex 26:3, 5, 6, 17; Eze 1:9; 3:13).

270. אָחַז, **'âchaz,** *aw-khaz';* a primitive root; to *seize* (often with the accessory idea of holding in possession):— + be affrighted, bar, (catch, lay, take) hold (back), come upon, fasten, handle, portion, (get, have or take) possess (-ion).

271. אָחָז, **'Âchâz,** *aw-khawz´*; from 270; *possessor; Achaz,* the name of a Jewish king and of an Israelite:—Ahaz.

272. אֲחֻזָּה, **'ăchuzzâh,** *akh-ooz-zaw´*; feminine passive participle from 270; something *seized,* i.e. a *possession* (especially of land):—possession.

A feminine noun meaning possession, literally meaning something seized. The word usually refers to the possession of land, especially of the Promised Land (Ge 48:4; Dt 32:49). Because the Promised Land is "an everlasting possession" (Ge 17:8), this word often refers to land that is to pass down within families, never being permanently taken away (Le 25; Nu 27:4, 7, Eze 46:16–18). The Levites had God, instead of land, as their "possession" (Eze 44:28).

273. אַחְזַי, **'Achzay,** *akh-zah´ee*; from 270; *seizer; Achzai,* an Israelite:—Ahasai.

274. אֲחַזְיָה, **'Ăchazyâh,** *akh-az-yaw´*; or (prolonged) אֲחַזְיָהוּ, **'Ăchazyâhûw,** *akh-az-yaw´-hoo*; from 270 and 3050; *Jah has seized; Achazjah,* the name of a Jewish and an Israelite king:—Ahaziah.

275. אֲחֻזָּם, **'Ăchuzzâm,** *akh-ooz-zawm´*; from 270; *seizure; Achuzzam,* an Israelite:—Ahuzam.

276. אֲחֻזַּת, **'Ăchuzzath,** *akh-ooz-zath´*; a variation of 272; *possession; Achuzzath,* a Philistine:—Ahuzzath.

277. אֲחִי, **'Ăchîy,** *akh-ee´*; from 251; *brotherly; Achi,* the name of two Israelites:—Ahi.

278. אֵחִי, **'Êchîy,** *ay-khee´*; probably the same as 277; *Echi,* an Israelite:—Ehi.

279. אֲחִיאָם, **'Ăchîy'âm,** *akh-ee-awm´*; from 251 and 517; *brother of the mother* (i.e. *uncle*); *Achiam,* an Israelite:—Ahiam.

280. אֲחִידָה, **'ăchîydâh** (Chaldee), *akh-ee-daw´*; corresponding to 2420, an *enigma:*—hard sentence.

281. אֲחִיָה, **'Ăchîyâh,** *akh-ee-yaw´*; or (prolonged) אֲחִיָהוּ, **'Ăchîyâhûw,** *akh-ee-yaw´-hoo*; from 251 and 3050; *brother* (i.e. *worshipper*) *of Jah; Achijah,* the name of nine Israelites:—Ahiah, Ahijah.

282. אֲחִיהוּד, **'Ăchîyhûwd,** *akh-ee-hood´*; from 251 and 1935; *brother* (i.e. *possessor*) *of renown; Achihud,* an Israelite:—Ahihud.

283. אַחְיוֹ, **'Achyôw,** *akh-yo´*; prolonged from 251; *brotherly; Achio,* the name of three Israelites:—Ahio.

284. אֲחִיחֻד, **'Ăchîychud,** *akh-ee-khood´*; from 251 and 2330; *brother of a riddle* (i.e. *mysterious*); *Achichud,* an Israelite:—Ahihud.

285. אֲחִיטוּב, **'Ăchîyṭûwb,** *akh-ee-toob´*; from 251 and 2898; *brother of goodness; Achitub,* the name of several priests:—Ahitub.

286. אֲחִילוּד, **'Ăchîylûwd,** *akh-ee-lood´*; from 251 and 3205; *brother of one born; Achilud,* an Israelite:—Ahilud.

287. אֲחִימוֹת, **'Ăchîymôwth,** *akh-ee-mōth´*; from 251 and 4191; *brother of death; Achimoth,* an Israelite:—Ahimoth.

288. אֲחִימֶלֶךְ, **'Ăchîymelek,** *akh-ee-meh´-lek*; from 251 and 4428; *brother of* (the) *king; Achimelek,* the name of an Israelite and of a Hittite:—Ahimelech.

289. אֲחִימַן, **'Ăchîyman,** *akh-ee-man´*; or אֲחִימָן, **'Ăchîymân,** *akh-ee-mawn´*; from 251 and 4480; *brother of a portion* (i.e. *gift*); *Achiman,* the name of an Anakite and of an Israelite:—Ahiman.

290. אֲחִימַעַץ, **'Ăchîyma'ats,** *akh-ee-mah´-ats*; from 251 and the equivalent of 4619; *brother of anger; Achimaats,* the name of three Israelites:—Ahimaaz.

291. אַחְיָן, **'Achyân,** *akh-yawn´*; from 251; *brotherly; Achjan,* an Israelite:—Ahian.

292. אֲחִינָדָב, **'Ăchîynâdâb,** *akh-ee-naw-dawb´*; from 251 and 5068; *brother of liberality; Achinadab,* an Israelite:—Ahinadab.

293. אֲחִינֹעַם, **'Ăchîynô'am,** *akh-ee-no´-am*; from 251 and 5278; *brother of pleasantness; Achinoam,* the name of two Israelitesses:—Ahinoam.

294. אֲחִיסָמָךְ, **'Ăchîysâmâk,** *akh-ee-saw-mawk´*; from 251 and 5564; *brother of support; Achisamak,* an Israelite:—Ahisamach.

295. אֲחִיעֶזֶר, **'Ăchîy'ezer,** *akh-ee-eh´-zer*; from 251 and 5828; *brother of help; Achiezer,* the name of two Israelites:—Ahiezer.

296. אֲחִיקָם, **'Ăchîyqâm,** *akh-ee-kawm´*; from 251 and 6965; *brother of rising* (i.e. *high*); *Achikam,* an Israelite:—Ahikam.

297. אֲחִירָם, **'Ăchîyrâm,** *akh-ee-rawm´*; from 251 and 7311; *brother of height* (i.e. *high*); *Achiram,* an Israelite:—Ahiram.

298. אֲחִירָמִי, **'Ăchîyrâmîy,** *akh-ee-raw-mee´*; patronymically from 297; an *Achiramite* or descendants (collective) of Achiram:—Ahiramites.

299. אֲחִירַע, **'Ăchîyra',** *akh-ee-rah´*; from 251 and 7451; *brother of wrong; Achira,* an Israelite:—Ahira.

300. אֲחִישַׁחַר, **'Ăchîyshachar,** *akh-ee-shakh´-ar*; from 251 and 7837; *brother of* (the) *dawn; Achishachar,* an Israelite:—Ahishar.

301. אֲחִישָׁר, **'Ăchîyshâr,** *akh-ee-shawr´*; from 251 and 7891; *brother of* (the) *singer; Achishar,* an Israelite:—Ahishar.

302. אֲחִיתֹפֶל, **'Ăchîythôphel,** *akh-ee-tho´-fel*; from 251 and 8602; *brother of folly; Achithophel,* an Israelite:—Ahithophel.

303. אַחְלָב, **'Achlâb,** *akh-lawb´*; from the same root as 2459; *fatness* (i.e. *fertile*); *Achlab,* a place in Palestine:—Ahlab.

304. אַחְלַי, **'Achlay,** *akh-lah´ee*; the same as 305; *wishful; Achlai,* the name of an Israelitess and of an Israelite:—Ahlai.

305. אַחֲלַי, **'achălay,** *ak-al-ah´ee*; or אַחֲלֵי, **'achălêy,** *akh-al-ay´*; probably from 253 and a variation of 3863; *would that!:*—O that, would God.

306. אַחְלָמָה, **'achlâmâh,** *akh-law´-maw*; perhaps from 2492 (and thus *dream-stone*); a gem, probably the *amethyst:*—amethyst.

307. אַחְמְתָא, **'Achmᵉthâ',** *akh-me-thaw´*; of Persian derivation; *Achmetha* (i.e. *Ecbatana*), the summer capital of Persia:—Achmetha.

308. אֲחַסְבַּי, **'Ăchasbay,** *akh-as-bah´ee*; of uncertain derivation; *Achasbai,* an Israelite:—Ahasbai.

309. אָחַר, **'âchar,** *aw-khar´*; a primitive root; to *loiter* (i.e. *be behind*); by implication to *procrastinate:*—continue, defer, delay, hinder, be late (slack), stay (there), tarry (longer).

310. אַחַר, **'achar,** *akh-ar´*; from 309; probably the *hind* part; generally used as an adverb or conjunction, *after* (in various senses):—after (that, -ward), again, at, away from, back (from, -side), behind, beside, by, follow (after, -ing), forasmuch, from, hereafter, hinder end, + out (over) live, + persecute, posterity, pursuing, remnant, seeing, since, thence [-forth], when, with.

311. אַחַר, **'achar** (Chaldee), *akh-ar´*; corresponding to 310; *after:*—[here-] after.

312. אַחֵר, **'achêr,** *akh-air´*; from 309; probably *hinder;* generically *next, other,* etc.:—(an-) other (man), following, next, strange.

313. אַחֵר, **'Achêr,** *akh-air´*; the same as 312; *Acher,* an Israelite:—Aher.

314. אַחֲרוֹן, **'achăryôwn,** *akh-ar-one´*; or (shortened) אַחֲרֹן, **'achărôn,** *akh-ar-one´*; from 309; *hinder;* generically *late* or *last;* specifically (as facing the east) *western:*—after (-ward), to come, following, hind (-er, -ermost, -most), last, latter, rereward, ut(ter)most.

315. אַחְרַח, **'Achrach,** *akh-rakh*; from 310 and 251; *after* (his) *brother; Achrach,* an Israelite:—Aharah.

316. אַחְרְחֵל, **'Ăcharchêl,** *akh-ar-kale´*; from 310 and 2426; *behind* (the) *intrenchment* (i.e. *safe*); *Acharchel,* an Israelite:—Aharhel.

317. אָחֳרִי, **'ochŏrîy** (Chaldee), *okh-or-ee´*; from 311; *other:*—(an-) other.

318. אָחֳרֵין, **'ochŏrêyn** (Chaldee), *okh-or-ane´*; or (shortened) אָחֳרֵן, **'ochŏrên,** *okh-or-ane´*; (Chaldee); from 317; *last:*—at last.

319. אַחֲרִית, **'achărîyth,** *akh-ar-eeth´*; from 310; the *last* or *end,* hence the *future;* also *posterity:*—(last, latter) end (time), hinder (utter) -most, length, posterity, remnant, residue, reward.

A feminine noun meaning the end, last time, latter time (Ge 49:1; Nu 23:10; 24:14, 20; Dt 4:30; 8:16; 11:12; 31:29; 32:20, 29; Job 8:7; 42:12; Ps 37:37, 38; 73:17; 109:13; 139:9; Pr 5:4, 11; 14:12, 13; 16:25; 19:20; 20:21; 23:18, 32; 24:14, 20; 25:8; 29:21; Ecc 7:8; 10:13; Isa 2:2; 41:22; 46:10; 47:7; Jer 5:31; 12:4; 17:11; 23:20; 29:11; 30:24; 31:17; 48:47; 49:39; 50:12; La 1:9; Eze 23:25; 38:8, 16; Da 8:19, 23; 10:14; 11:4; 12:8; Hos 3:5; Am 4:2; 8:10; 9:1; Mic 4:1).

320. אַחֲרִית, **'achăriyth** (Chaldee), akh-ar-eeth´; from 311; the same as 319; later:—latter.

321. אָחֳרָן, **'ochŏrân** (Chaldee), okh-or-awn´; from 311; the same as 317; other:—(an-) other.

322. אֲחֹרַנִּית, **'ăchôrannîyth**, akh-o-ran-neeth´; prolonged from 268; backwards:—back (-ward, again).

323. אֲחַשְׁדַּרְפַּן, **'ăchashdarpan**, akh-ash-dar-pan´; of Persian derivation; a satrap or governor of a main province (of Persia):—lieutenant.

324. אֲחַשְׁדַּרְפַּן, **'ăchashdarpan** (Chaldee), akh-ash-dar-pan´; corresponding to 323:—prince.

A Chaldean noun meaning satrap. Satraps were officials who governed large provinces in Persia as representatives of the Persian sovereign. Pechâh (6346) denotes a smaller office within a satrapy. Daniel was one of three rulers over the satraps and became an object of their evil schemes (Da 6:1–4[2–5], 6[7], 7[8]; the word also occurs in Da 3:2, 3, 27). All occurrences of this Chaldean word are in the book of Daniel, but the Hebrew equivalent (323) is spelled the same and occurs in Ezra and Esther.

325. אֲחַשְׁוֵרוֹשׁ, **'Ăchashvêrôwsh**, akh-ash-vay-rōsh´; or (shorter) אַחַשְׁרֹשׁ, **'Ăchashrôsh**, akh-ash-rōsh´ (Est 10:1); of Persian origin; Achashverosh (i.e. Ahasuerus or Artaxerxes, but in this case Xerxes), the title (rather than name) of a Persian king:—Ahasuerus.

326. אֲחַשְׁתָּרִי, **'ăchashtârîy**, akh-ash-taw-ree´; probably of Persian derivation; an achastarite (i.e. courier); the designation (rather than name) of an Israelite:—Haakashtari [including the article].

327. אֲחַשְׁתְּרָן, **'ăchashtᵉrân**, akh-ash-te-rawn´; of Persian origin; a mule:—camel.

328. אַט, **'aṭ**, at; from an unused root perhaps meaning to move softly; (as a noun) a necromancer (from their soft incantations), (as an adverb) gently:—charmer, gently, secret, softly.

An adverb meaning gently, with gentleness. It occurs five times (Ge 33:14; 2Sa 18:5; 1Ki 21:27; Job 15:11; Isa 8:6).

329. אָטָד, **'âṭâd**, aw-tawd´; from an unused root probably meaning to pierce or make fast; a

thorn-tree (especially the buckthorn):—Atad, bramble, thorn.

330. אֵטוּן, **'êṭûwn**, ay-toon´; from an unused root (probably meaning to bind); probably twisted (yarn), i.e. tapestry:—fine linen.

331. אָטַם, **'âṭam**, aw-tam´; a primitive root; to close (the lips or ears); by analogy to contract (a window by bevelled jambs):—narrow, shut, stop.

332. אָטַר, **'âṭar**, aw-tar´; a primitive root; to close up:—shut.

333. אָטֵר, **'Âṭêr**, aw-tare´; from 332; maimed; Ater, the name of three Israelites:—Ater.

334. אִטֵּר, **'iṭṭêr**, it-tare´; from 332; shut up, i.e. impeded (as to the use of the right hand):—+ left-handed.

335. אֵי, **'êy**, ay; perhaps from 370; where hence how:—how, what, whence, where, whether, which (way).

336. אִי, **'îy**, ee; probably identical with 335(through the idea of a query); not:—island (Job 22:30).

337. אִי, **'îy**, ee; shortened from 188; alas!:—woe.

338. אִי, **'îy**, ee; probably identical with 337 (through the idea of a doleful sound); a howler (used only in the plural), i.e. any solitary wild creature:—wild beast of the islands.

339. אִי, **'îy**, ee; from 183; probably a habitable spot (as desirable); dry land, a coast, an island:—country, isle, island.

340. אָיַב, **'âyab**, aw-yab´; a primitive root; to hate (as one of an opposite tribe or party); hence to be hostile:—be an enemy.

341. אֹיֵב, **'ôyêb**, o-yabe´; or (fully) אוֹיֵב, **'ôwyêb**, o-yabe´; active participle of 340; hating; an adversary:—enemy, foe.

342. אֵיבָה, **'êybâh**, ay-baw´; from 340; hostility:—enmity, hatred.

A feminine noun meaning hostility, animosity, or ill will. It is used to signify acrimony, as between the woman and the serpent (Ge 3:15); malice that leads to violent acts against another (Nu 35:21); and the lingering hatred between mortal enemies (Eze 25:15; 35:5).

343. אֵיד, *'êyd, ade*; from the same as 181 (in the sense of *bending* down); *oppression*; by implication *misfortune, ruin*:—calamity, destruction.

A masculine noun meaning calamity or disaster. The word refers to a time of trouble when a person is in special need of help (Pr 27:10); a calamity so severe that men and women should not rejoice or take selfish advantage of those whom the disaster renders helpless before God (Job 31:23; Pr 17:5; Ob 1:13). The calamity may result from a deliberate violation of principles (Pr 1:26) or a more explicit judgment of God (Jer 18:17). It may even befall a righteous person (2Sa 22:19; Ps 18:18[19]).

344. אַיָּה, *'ayyâh, ah-yaw'*; perhaps from 337; the *screamer*, i.e. a *hawk*:—kite, vulture.

345. אַיָּה, *'Ayyâh, ah-yaw'*; the same as 344; *Ajah*, the name of two Israelites:—Aiah, Ajah.

346. אַיֵּה, *'ayyêh, ah-yay'*; prolonged from 335; *where*:—where.

347. אִיּוֹב, *'Îyyôwb, ee-yobe'*; from 340; *hated* (i.e. *persecuted*); *Ijob*, the patriarch famous for his patience:—Job.

348. אִיזֶבֶל, *'Îyzebel, ee-zeh'-bel*; from 336 and 2083; *chaste*; *Izebel*, the wife of king Ahab:—Jezebel.

349. אֵיךְ, *'êyk, ake*; also אֵיכָה, *'êykâh, ay-kaw'*; and אֵיכָכָה, *'êykâkâh, ay-kaw'-kah*; prolonged from 335; *how* or *how!*; also *where*:—how, what.

350. אִי־כָבוֹד, *'Îy-kâbôwd, ee-kaw-bode'*; from 336 and 3519; (there is) *no glory*, i.e. *inglorious*; *Ikabod*, a son of Phineas:—Ichabod.

351. אֵיכֹה, *'êykôh, ay-ko*; probably a variation for 349, but not as an interrogative; *where*:—where.

352. אַיִל, *'ayil, ah'-yil*; from the same as 193; probably *strength*; hence anything *strong*; specifically a *chief* (politically); also a *ram* (from his strength); a *pilaster* (as a strong support); an *oak* or other strong tree:—mighty (man), lintel, oak, post, ram, tree.

353. אֱיָל, *'ĕyâl, eh-yawl'*; a variation of 352; *strength*:—strength.

354. אַיָּל, *'ayyâl, ah-yawl'*; an intensive form of 352 (in the sense of *ram*); a *stag* or male deer:—hart.

355. אַיָּלָה, *'ayyâlâh, ah-yaw-law'*; feminine of 354; a *doe* or female deer:—hind.

356. אֵילוֹן, *'Êylôwn, ay-lone'*; or (shortened) אֵלוֹן, *'Êlôwn, ay-lone'*; or אֵילֹן, *'Êylôn, ay-lone'*; from 352; *oak-grove*; *Elon*, the name of a place in Palestine, and also of one Hittite, two Israelites:—Elon.

357. אַיָּלוֹן, *'Ayyâlôwn, ah-yaw-lone'*; from 354; *deer-field*; *Ajalon*, the name of five places in Palestine:—Aijalon, Ajalon.

358. אֵילוֹן בֵּית חָנָן, *'Êylôwn Bêyth Chânân, ay-lone' bayth-khaw-nawn'*; from 356, 1004, and 2603; *oak-grove of* (the) *house of favour*; *Elon of Beth-chanan*, a place in Palestine:—Elon-beth-hanan.

359. אֵילוֹת, *'Êylôwth, ay-lōth'*; or אֵילַת, *'Êylath, ay-lath'*; from 352; *trees* or a *grove* (i.e. palms); *Eloth* or *Elath*, a place on the Red Sea:—Elath, Eloth.

360. אֱיָלוּת, *'ĕyâlûwth, eh-yaw-looth'*; feminine of 353; *power*; by implication *protection*:—strength.

361. אֵילָם, *'êylâm, ay-lawm'*; or (shortened) אֵלָם, *'êlâm, ay-lawm'*; or (feminine) אֵלַמָּה, *'êlammâh, ay-lam-maw'*; probably from 352; a *pillar-space* (or colonnade), i.e. a *pale* (or portico):—arch.

362. אֵילִם, *'Êylim, ay-leem'*; plural of 352; *palm-trees*; *Elim*, a place in the Desert:—Elim.

363. אִילָן, *'îylân* (Chaldee), *ee-lawn'*; corresponding to 356; a *tree*:—tree.

364. אֵיל פָּארָן, *'Êyl Pâ'rân, ale paw-rawn'*; from 352 and 6290; *oak of Paran*; *El-Paran*, a portion of the district of Paran:—El-paran.

365. אַיֶּלֶת, *'ayyeleth, ay-yeh'-leth*; the same as 355; a *doe*:—hind, Aijeleth.

366. אָיֹם, *'âyôm, aw-yome'*; from an unused root (meaning to *frighten*); *frightful*:—terrible.

367. אֵימָה, *'êymâh, ay-maw'*; or (shortened) אֵמָה, *'êmâh, ay-maw'*; from the same as 366; *fright*; (concrete) an *idol* (as a bugbear):—dread, fear, horror, idol, terrible, terror.

A feminine noun meaning fear, terror, dread, or horror. The basic meaning is that of fear. It is used to signify the dread of the darkness that fell on Abraham (Ge 15:12); a fear of hostile opponents (Jos 2:9; Ezr 3:3); the terror of the Lord's judgment (Ex 15:16; 23:27; Job 9:34); dread of the wrath of an earthly king (Pr 20:2); something fierce or fearsome (Job 39:20). In a metaphorical sense, it refers once to pagan idols (Jer 50:38).

368. אֵימִים, **'Êymîym**, *ay-meem´*; plural of 367; *terrors; Emim*, an early Canaanitish (or Moabitish) tribe:—Emims.

369. אַיִן, **'ayin**, *ay´-yin*; as if from a primitive root meaning to *be nothing* or *not exist*; a *nonentity*; generally used as a negative particle:—else, except, fail, [father-] less, be gone, in [-curable], neither, never, no (where), none, nor (any, thing), not, nothing, to nought, past, un [-searchable], well-nigh, without. Compare 370.

370. אַיִן, **'ayin**, *ah-yin´*; probably identical with 369 in the sense of *query* (compare 336); *where* (only in connection with prepositional prefix, *whence*):—whence, where.

371. אִין, **'îyn**, *een*; apparently a shortened form of 369; but (like 370) interrogative; is it *not*:—not.

372. אִיעֶזֶר, **'Îy'ezer**, *ee-eh´-zer*; from 336 and 5828; *helpless; Iezer*, an Israelite:—Jeezer.

373. אִיעֶזְרִי, **'Îy'ezrîy**, *ee-ez-ree´*; patronymically from 372; an *Iezrite* or descendant of Iezer:—Jezerite.

374. אֵיפָה, **'êyphâh**, *ay-faw´*; or (shortened) אֵפָה, **'êphâh**, *ay-faw´*; of Egyptian derivation; an *ephah* or measure for grain; hence a *measure* in general:—ephah, (divers) measure (-s).

375. אֵיפֹה, **'êyphôh**, *ay-fo´*; from 335 and 6311; *what place*; also (of time) *when*; or (of means) *how*:—what manner, where.

376. אִישׁ, **'îysh**, *eesh*; contraction for 582 [or perhaps rather from an unused root meaning to *be extant*]; a *man* as an individual or a male person; often used as an adjunct to a more definite term (and in such cases frequently not expressed in translation):—also, another, any (man), a certain, + champion, consent, each, every (one), fellow, [foot-, husband-] man, (good-, great, mighty) man, he, high (degree), him (that is), husband, man [-kind], + none,

one, people, person, + steward, what (man) soever, whoso (-ever), worthy. Compare 802.

A masculine noun meaning a man or an individual. It is also used to mean male or husband. This word does not indicate humankind but the male gender in particular. Its feminine counterpart is a woman or wife. In Hos 2:16[18], this word describes God's special relationship to Israel. He will be their protective husband, not their master. Curiously, the word is also used of animals (Ge 7:2), referring to a male and his mate.

377. אִישׁ, **'îysh**, *eesh*; denominative from 376; to *be a man*, i.e. act in a manly way:—show (one) self a man.

378. אִישׁ־בֹּשֶׁת, **'Îysh-Bôsheth**, *eesh-bo´-sheth*; from 376 and 1322; *man of shame; Ish-Bosheth*, a son of King Saul:—Ish-bosheth.

379. אִישׁהוֹד, **'Îyshhôwd**, *eesh-hode´*; from 376 and 1935; *man of renown; Ishod*, an Israelite:—Ishod.

380. אִישׁוֹן, **'îyshôwn**, *ee-shone´*; diminutive from 376; the *little man* of the eye; the *pupil* or *ball*; hence the *middle* (of night):—apple [of the eye], black, obscure.

381. אִישׁ־חַיִל, **'Îysh-Chayil**, *eesh-khah´-yil*; from 376 and 2428 *man of might*; by defective transcription (2Sa 23:20) אִישׁ־חַי, **'îysh-Chay**, *eesh-khah´ee*; as if from 376 and 2416; *living man; Ish-chail* (or *Ish-chai*), an Israelite:—a valiant man.

382. אִישׁ־טוֹב, **'Îysh-Ṭôwb**, *eesh-tobe´*; from 376 and 2897; *man of Tob; Ish-Tob*, a place in Palestine:—Ish-tob.

383. אִיתַי, **'îythay** (Chaldee), *ee-thah´ee*; corresponding to 3426; (properly) *entity*; used only as a particle of affirmation, there *is*:—art thou, can, do ye, have, it be, there is (are), × we will not.

384. אִיתִיאֵל, **'Îythîy'êl**, *eeth-ee-ale´*; perhaps from 837 and 410; *God has arrived; Ithiel*, the name of an Israelite, also of a symbolical person:—Ithiel.

385. אִיתָמָר, **'Îythâmâr**, *eeth-aw-mawr´*; from 339 and 8558; *coast of* the *palm-tree; Ithamar*, a son of Aaron:—Ithamar.

386. אֵיתָן, **'êythân,** *ay-thawn´*; or (shortened) אֵתָן **'êthân,** *ay-thawn´*; from an unused root (meaning to *continue*); *permanence*; hence (concrete) *permanent*; specifically a *chieftain*:— hard, mighty, rough, strength, strong.

387. אֵיתָן, **Êythân,** *ay-thawn´*; the same as 386; *permanent; Ethan,* the name of four Israelites:— Ethan.

388. אֵתָנִים, **'Êythânîym,** *ay-thaw-neem´*; plural of 386; always with the article; the *permanent* brooks; *Ethanim,* the name of a month:— Ethanim.

389. אַךְ, **'ak,** *ak*; akin to 403; a particle of affirmation, *surely*; hence (by limitation) *only*:— also, in any wise, at least, but, certainly, even, howbeit, nevertheless, notwithstanding, only, save, surely, of a surety, truly, verily, + wherefore, yet (but).

390. אַכַּד, **'Akkad,** *ak-kad´*; from an unused root probably meaning to *strengthen*; a *fortress*; *Accad,* a place in Babylon:—Accad.

391. אַכְזָב, **'akzâb,** *ak-zawb´*; from 3576; *falsehood*; by implication *treachery*:—liar, lie.

392. אַכְזִיב, **'Akzîyb,** *ak-zeeb´*; from 391; *deceitful* (in the sense of a winter torrent which *fails* in summer); *Akzib,* the name of two places in Palestine:—Achzib.

393. אַכְזָר, **'akzâr,** *ak-zawr´*; from an unused root (apparently meaning to *act harshly*); *violent*; by implication *deadly*; also (in a good sense) *brave*:—cruel, fierce.

394. אַכְזָרִי, **'akzârîy,** *ak-zaw-ree´*; from 393; *terrible*:—cruel (one).

395. אַכְזְרִיּוּת, **'akzᵉrîyyûwth,** *ak-ze-ree-ooth´*; from 394; *fierceness*:—cruel.

396. אֲכִילָה, **'ăkîylâh,** *ak-ee-law´*; feminine from 398; something *eatable,* i.e. *food*:—meat.

397. אָכִישׁ, **'Âkîysh,** *aw-keesh´*; of uncertain derivation; *Akish,* a Philistine king:—Achish.

398. אָכַל, **'âkal,** *aw-kal´*; a primitive root; to *eat* (literal or figurative):— × at all, burn up, consume, devour (-er, up), dine, eat (-er, up), feed (with), food, × freely, × in … wise (-deed, plenty), (lay) meat, × quite.

399. אֲכַל, **'ăkal** (Chaldee), *ak-al´*; corresponding to 398:— + accuse, devour, eat.

400. אֹכֶל, **'ôkel,** *o´-kel*; from 398; *food*:—eating, food, meal [-time], meat, prey, victuals.

401. אֻכָל, **'Ukâl,** *oo-kawl´*; or אֻכָּל, **'Ukkâl,** *ook-kawl´*; apparently from 398; *devoured; Ucal,* a fancy name:—Ucal.

402. אָכְלָה, **'ôklâh,** *ok-law´*; feminine of 401; *food*:—consume, devour, eat, food, meat.

403. אָכֵן, **'âkên,** *aw-kane´*; from 3559 [compare 3651]; *firmly*; (figurative) *surely*; also (adversely) *but*:—but, certainly, nevertheless, surely, truly, verily.

404. אָכַף, **'âkaph,** *aw-kaf´*; a primitive root; apparently meaning to *curve* (as with a burden); to *urge*:—crave.

405. אֶכֶף, **'ekeph,** *eh´-kef*; from 404; a *load*; by implication a *stroke* (others *dignity*):—hand.

406. אִכָּר, **'ikkâr,** *ik-kawr´*; from an unused root meaning to *dig*; a *farmer*:—husbandman, ploughman.

407. אַכְשָׁף, **'Akshâph,** *ak-shawf´*; from 3784; *fascination; Acshaph,* a place in Palestine:— Achshaph.

408. אַל, **'al,** *al*; a negative particle [akin to 3808; *not* (the qualified negation, used as a deprecative); once (Job 24:25) as a noun, *nothing*:— nay, neither, + never, no, nor, not, nothing [worth], rather than.

409. אַל, **'al** (Chaldee), *al*; corresponding to 408:—not.

410. אֵל, **'êl,** *ale*; shortened from 352; *strength*; as adjective *mighty*; especially the *Almighty* (but used also of any *deity*):—God (god), × goodly, × great, idol, might (-y one), power, strong. Compare names in "-el."

A masculine noun meaning God, god, mighty one, hero. This is one of the most ancient terms for God, god, or deity. It appears most often in Genesis, Job, Psalms, and Isaiah and not at all in some books. The root meaning of the word mighty can be seen in Job 41:25[17] and Mic 2:1. This word is used occasionally of other gods (Ex 34:14; Dt 3:24; Ps 44:20[21]; Mal 2:11) but is most often used to mean the one true God (Ps 5:4[5]; Isa 40:18). It expresses various ideas of deity according to its context. The most common may be noted briefly: the holy God as contrasted to humans (Hos 11:9); the High God El (Ge 14:18; 16:13; Eze 28:2); the Lord (Yahweh) as a title of Israel according to the Lord's own claim (Ge 33:20; Isa 40:18); God or god in general (Ex 34:14; Dt 32:21; Mic 7:8); the God of Israel, the Lord (Nu 23:8; Ps 118:27); God (Job 5:8).

This word is used with various descriptive adjectives or attributes: *'êl* is God of gods (Ps 50:1); God of Bethel (Ge 35:7); a forgiving God (Ps 99:8). He is the holy God (Isa 5:16). Especially significant are the assertions declaring that *'êl* is with us, Immanuel (Isa 7:14); and He is the God of our salvation (Isa 12:2); a gracious God (Ne 9:31); a jealous God (Ex 20:5; 34:14). The closeness of this God is expressed in the hand of God (Job 27:11).

In the human realm, the word also designates men of power or high rank (Eze 31:11); mighty men (Job 41:25[17]); or mighty warriors (Eze 32:21). The word is used to designate superior and mighty things in nature, such as mighty or high mountains (Ps 36:6[7]), lofty, high cedars, or stars (Ps 80:10[11]; Isa 14:13).

In conjunction with other descriptive words, it occurs as *'êl shaday*, "God Almighty" (7706) (Ge 17:1; 28:3; Ex 6:3) or *'êl 'elyôwn*, "God Most High" (5945) (Ge 14:18, 19; Ps 78:35). Used with hand (*yâd*) in some settings, the word conveys power, strength (Ge 31:29; Dt 28:32; Pr 3:27), or ability.

411. אֵל, **'êl,** *ale*; a demonstrative particle (but only in a plural sense) *these* or *those*:—these, those. Compare 428.

412. אֵל, **'êl** (Chaldee), *ale*; corresponding to 411:—these.

413. אֵל, **'êl,** *ale*; (but used only in the shortened construction form אֶל, **'el,** *el*; a primitive particle, properly denoting motion *toward*, but occasionally used of a quiescent position, i.e. *near*, *with* or *among*; often in general, *to*:—about, according to, after, against, among, as for, at, because (-fore, -side), both … and, by, concerning, for, from, × hath, in (-to), near, (out) of, over, through, to (-ward), under, unto, upon, whether, with (-in).

414. אֵלָא, **'Êlâ,** *ay-law´*; a variation of 424; *oak; Ela,* an Israelite:—Elah.

415. אֵל אֱלֹהֵי יִשְׂרָאֵל, **'Êl 'ĕlôhêy Yiśrâ'êl,** *ale el-o-hay´ yis-raw-ale´*; from 410 and 430 and 3478; the *mighty God of Jisrael; El-Elohi-Jisrael,* the title given to a consecrated spot by Jacob:—El-elohe-israel.

416. אֵל בֵּית־אֵל, **'Êl Bêyth-'Êl,** *ale bayth-ale´*; from 410 and 1008; the *God of Bethel; El-Bethel,* the title given to a consecrated spot by Jacob:—El-beth-el.

417. אֶלְגָּבִישׁ, **'elgâbîysh,** *el-gaw-beesh´*; from 410 and 1378; *hail* (as if a *great pearl*):—great hail [-stones].

418. אַלְגּוּמִּים, **'algûwmmîym,** *al-goom-meem´*; by transposition for 484; sticks of *algum* wood:—algum [trees].

419. אֶלְדָּד, **'Eldâd,** *el-dâd´*; from 410 and 1730; *God has loved; Eldad,* an Israelite:—Eldad.

420. אֶלְדָּעָה, **'Eldâ'âh,** *el-daw-aw´*; from 410 and 3045; *God of knowledge; Eldaah,* a son of Midian:—Eldaah.

421. אָלָה, **'âlâh,** *aw-law´*; a primitive root [rather identical with 422 through the idea of *invocation*]; to *bewail*:—lament.

422. אָלָה, **'âlâh,** *aw-law´*; a primitive root; proper to *adjure,* i.e. (usually in a bad sense) *imprecate*:—adjure, curse, swear.

A verb meaning to curse, to put under oath. It is used in many cases of persons bringing curses on themselves if they are guilty of doing wrong (Jgs 17:2). Similarly, *'âlâh* is used to prove someone's guilt or innocence. The person is guilty if the curse occurs but is innocent if the curse does not occur (1Ki 8:31; 2Ch 6:22). In 1Sa 14:24, the word is used to put someone under an oath. In Hosea, the word refers to a curse placed on a person who makes a covenant or treaty and does not keep his word (Hos 10:4).

423. אָלָה, **'âlâh,** *aw-law´*; from 422; an *imprecation*:—curse, cursing, execration, oath, swearing.

A feminine noun meaning an oath, a sworn covenant, or a curse. The word signifies an oath to testify truthfully (Le 5:1; 1Ki 8:31); a sworn covenant, bearing a curse if violated (Dt 29:19; Ne 10:29[30]); a curse from God for covenant violations (Dt 29:20; 2Ch 34:24; Da 9:11); God's judgment on sin (Dt 30:7; Isa 24:6; Zec 5:3); and that which is accursed because of unfaithfulness, such as an adulterous wife or the erring tribe of Judah (Nu 5:27; Jer 29:18; 42:18; 44:12).

424. אֵלָה, **'êlâh,** *ay-law´*; feminine of 352; an *oak* or other strong tree:—elm, oak, teil tree.

425. אֵלָה, **'Êlâh,** *ay-law´*; the same as 424; *Elah,* the name of an Edomite, of four Israelites, and also of a place in Palestine:—Elah.

426. אֱלָהּ, **'ĕlâh** (Chaldee), *el-aw´*; corresponding to 433; *God:*—God, god.

An Aramaic masculine noun meaning deity, divinity. This word can be used in a general sense to indicate a god (Da 3:15) or gods (Da 2:11; 3:12, 18, 25). In a specific sense, it signifies the God of Israel, namely, Yahweh (Ezr 5:1, 2, 8; 6:14; 7:15; Da 2:20, 28; 3:17).

427. אֲלָה, **'allâh,** *al-law´*; a variation of 424:—oak.

428. אֵלֶּה, **'êlleh,** *ale´-leh*; prolonged from 411; *these* or *those:*—an- (the) other; one sort, so, some, such, them, these (same), they, this, those, thus, which, who (-m).

429. אֵלֶּה, **'êlleh** (Chaldee), *ale´-leh*; corresponding to 428:—these.

430. אֱלֹהִים, **'ĕlôhîym,** *el-o-heem´*; plural of 433; *gods* in the ordinary sense; but specifically used (in the plural thus, especially with the article) of the supreme *God*; occasionally applied by way of deference to *magistrates*; and sometimes as a superlative:—angels, × exceeding, God (gods) (-dess, -ly), × (very) great, judges, × mighty.

A masculine plural noun meaning God, gods, judges, angels. Occurring more than 2,600 times in the OT, this word commonly designates the one true God (Ge 1:1) and is often paired with God's unique name *yĕhôwâh* (3068) (Ge 2:4; Ps 100:3). When the word is used as the generic designation of God, it conveys in Scripture that God is the Creator (Ge 5:1); the King (Ps 47:7[8]); the Judge (Ps 50:6); the Lord (Ps 86:12); and the Saviour (Hos 13:4). His character is compassionate (Dt 4:31); gracious (Ps 116:5); and faithful to His covenant (Dt 7:9). In fewer instances, this word refers to foreign gods, such as Dagon

(1Sa 5:7) or Baal (1Ki 18:24). It also might refer to judges (Ex 22:8[7], 9[8]) or angels as gods (Ps 97:7). Although the form of this word is plural, it is frequently used as if it were singular—that is, with a singular verb (Ge 1:1–31; Ex 2:24). The plural form of this word may be regarded (1) as intensive to indicate God's fullness of power; (2) as majestic to indicate God's kingly rule; or (3) as an allusion to the Trinity (Ge 1:26). The singular form of this word *'ĕlôwah* (433) occurs only in poetry (Ps 50:22; Isa 44:8). The shortened form of the word is *'êl* (410).

431. אֲלוּ, **'ălûw** (Chaldee), *al-oo´*; probably prolonged from 412; *lo!:*—behold.

432. אִלּוּ, **'illûw,** *il-loo´*; probably from 408; *nay,* i.e. (softened) *if:*—but if, yea though.

433. אֱלוֹהַּ, **'ĕlôwah,** *el-o´-ah*; rarely (shortened) אֱלֹהַּ, **'ĕlôah,** *el-o´-ah*; probably prolonged (emphatic) from 410; a *deity* or the *Deity:*—God, god. See 430.

A masculine noun meaning god or God. It is thought by some to be the singular of the noun *'ĕlôhiym* (430). This word is used of *yĕhôwâh* (3068) (Ps 18:31 [32]) and, with a negative, to describe what is not God (Dt 32:17). Most occurrences of this word are in the book of Job, where the speakers may not be Israelites and thus use other generic names for God (Job 3:4), of which this is one. It is used once in the name, "God of Jacob" (Ps 114:7) and once in the phrase, "God of forgiveness" (Ne 9:17).

434. אֱלוּל, **'ĕlûwl,** *el-ool´*; for 457; good for *nothing:*—thing of nought.

435. אֱלוּל, **'Ĕlûwl,** *el-ool´*; probably of foreign derivation; *Elul,* the sixth Jewish month:—Elul.

436. אֵלוֹן, **'êlôwn,** *ay-lone´*; prolonged from 352; an *oak* or other strong tree:—plain. See also 356.

437. אַלּוֹן, **'allôwn,** *al-lone´*; a variation of 436:—oak.

438. אַלּוֹן, **'Allôwn,** *al-lone´*; the same as 437; *Allon,* an Israelite, also a place in Palestine:—Allon.

439. אַלּוֹן בָּכוּת, **'Allôwn Bâkûwth,** *al-lone´ baw-kooth´*; from 437 and a variation of 1068;

oak of weeping; Allon-Bakuth, a monumental tree:—Allon-bachuth.

440. אֵלוֹנִי, **'Êlôwnîy,** *ay-lo-nee´*; or rather (shortened) אֵלֹנִי, **'Êlônîy,** *ay-lo-nee´*; patronymic from 438; an *Elonite* or descendants (collective) of Elon:—Elonites.

441. אַלּוּף, **'allûwph,** *al-loof´*; or (shortened) אַלֻּף, **'alluph,** *al-loof´*; from 502; *familiar;* a *friend,* also *gentle;* hence a *bullock* (as being tame; applied, although masculine, to a *cow*); and so a *chieftain* (as notable like neat cattle):—captain, duke, (chief) friend, governor, guide, ox.

An adjective meaning docile or a masculine noun meaning tame, friend, intimate, chief, captain. Even though the adjectival usage is rare, it is found in the well-known description, "Like a docile lamb to the slaughter" (Jer 11:19). In the nominal form, this word connotes the closest of companions; such companions can be separated by a whisperer (Pr 16:28). In another aspect, this term was used to describe a leader of a nation or group. Esau's descendants were listed as chiefs of Edom (Ge 36:15).

442. אָלוּשׁ, **'Âlûwsh,** *aw-loosh´*; of uncertain derivation; *Alush,* a place in the Desert:—Alush.

443. אֶלְזָבָד, **'Elzâbâd,** *el-zaw-bawd´*; from 410 and 2064; *God has bestowed; Elzabad,* the name of two Israelites:—Elzabad.

444. אָלַח, **'âlach,** *aw-lakh´*; a primitive root; to *muddle,* i.e. (figurative and intransitive) to *turn* (moral) *corrupt:*—become filthy.

445. אֶלְחָנָן, **'Elchânân,** *el-khaw-nawn´*; from 410 and 2603; *God (is) gracious; Elchanan,* an Israelite:—Elkanan.

446. אֱלִיאָב, **'Êlîy'âb,** *el-ee-awb´*; from 410 and 1; *God of* (his) *father; Eliab,* the name of six Israelites:—Eliab.

447. אֱלִיאֵל, **'Êlîy'êl,** *el-ee-ale´*; from 410 repeated; *God of* (his) *God; Eliel,* the name of nine Israelites:—Eliel.

448. אֱלִיאָתָה, **'Êlîy'âthâh,** *el-ee-aw-thaw´*; or (contracted) אֱלִיָתָה, **'Êlîyyâthâh,** *el-ee-yaw-thaw´*; from 410 and 225; *God of* (his) *consent; Eliathah,* an Israelite:—Eliathah.

449. אֱלִידָד, **'Êlîydâd,** *el-ee-dawd´*; from the same as 419; *God of* (his) *love; Elidad,* an Israelite:—Elidad.

450. אֶלְיָדָע, **'Elyâdâ',** *el-yaw-daw´*; from 410 and 3045; *God (is) knowing; Eljada,* the name of two Israelites and of an Aramaean leader:—Eliada.

451. אַלְיָה, **'alyâh,** *al-yaw´*; from 422 (in the original sense of *strength*); the *stout* part, i.e. the fat *tail* of the Oriental sheep:—rump.

452. אֵלִיָּה, **'Êlîyyâh,** *ay-lee-yaw´*; or prolonged אֵלִיָּהוּ, **'Êlîyyâhûw,** *ay-lee-yaw´-hoo;* from 410 and 3050; *God of Jehovah; Elijah,* the name of the famous prophet and of two other Israelites:—Elijah, Eliah.

453. אֱלִיהוּ, **'Êlîyhûw,** *el-ee-hoo´*; or (fully) אֱלִיהוּא, **'Êlîyhûw',** *el-ee-hoo´*; from 410 and 1931; *God of him; Elihu,* the name of one of Job's friends, and of three Israelites:—Elihu.

454. אֶלְיְהוֹעֵינַי, **'Ely°hôw'êynay,** *el-ye-ho-ay-nah´ee;* or (shortened) אֶלְיוֹעֵינַי, **'Elyôw'êynay,** *el-yo-ay-nah´ee;* from 413 and 3068 and 5869; *toward Jehovah* (are) *my eyes; Elijehoenai* or *Eljoenai,* the name of seven Israelites:—Elihoenai, Elionai.

455. אֶלְיַחְבָּא, **'Elyachbâ',** *el-yakh-baw´*; from 410 and 2244; *God will hide; Eljachba,* an Israelite:—Eliahbah.

456. אֱלִיחֹרֶף, **'Êlîychôreph,** *el-ee-kho´-ref;* from 410 and 2779; *God of autumn; Elichoreph,* an Israelite:—Elihoreph.

457. אֱלִיל, **'ĕlîyl,** *el-eel´*; apparently from 408; *good for nothing,* by analogy *vain* or *vanity;* specifically an *idol:*—idol, no value, thing of nought.

A masculine noun meaning worthlessness. The term is frequently used to describe false gods and idols (Le 19:4; Ps 96:5; Isa 2:8; Hab 2:18). Sometimes, this noun is used in a prepositional phrase, such as in Zec 11:17, where the Hebrew literally says "shepherd of worthlessness," and in Job 13:4, "physicians of worthlessness." In those verses, *'ĕliyl* functions as an adjective.

458. אֱלִימֶלֶך, **'Êlîymelek,** *el-ee-meh´-lek;* from 410 and 4428; *God of* (the) *king; Elimelek,* an Israelite:—Elimelech.

459. אַלֵּין, **'illêyn** (Chaldee), *il-lane´*; or shorter אַלֵּן, **'illên**, *il-lane´*; prolonged from 412; *these*:— the, these.

460. אֶלְיָסָף, **'Elyâsâph,** *el-yaw-sawf´*; from 410 and 3254; *God* (is) *gatherer; Eljasaph,* the name of two Israelites:—Eliasaph.

461. אֱלִיעֶזֶר, **'Ĕlîy'ezer,** *el-ee-eh´-zer*; from 410 and 5828; *God of help; Eliezer,* the name of a Damascene and of ten Israelites:—Eliezer.

462. אֱלִיעֵינַי, **'Ĕlîy'êynay,** *el-ee-ay-nah´ee*; probably contraction for 454; *Elienai,* an Israelite:— Elienai.

463. אֱלִיעָם, **'Ĕlîy'âm,** *el-ee-awm´*; from 410 and 5971; *God of* (the) *people; Eliam,* an Israelite:— Eliam.

464. אֱלִיפַז, **'Ĕlîyphaz,** *el-ee-faz´*; from 410 and 6337; *God of gold; Eliphaz,* the name of one of Job's friends, and of a son of Esau:—Eliphaz.

465. אֱלִיפָל, **'Ĕlîyphâl,** *el-ee-fawl´*; from 410 and 6419; *God of judgment; Eliphal,* an Israelite:— Eliphal.

466. אֱלִיפְלֵהוּ, **'Ĕlîyph^elêhûw,** *el-ee-fe-lay´-hoo*; from 410 and 6395; *God of his distinction; Eliphelehu,* an Israelite:—Elipheleh.

467. אֱלִיפֶלֶט, **'Ĕlîyphelet,** *el-ee-feh´-let*; or (shortened) אֶלְפֶּלֶט, **'Elpelet,** *el-peh´-let*; from 410 and 6405; *God of deliverance; Eliphelet* or *Elpelet,* the name of six Israelites:—Eliphalet, Eliphelet, Elpalet.

468. אֱלִיצוּר, **'Ĕlîytsûwr,** *el-ee-tsoor´*; from 410 and 6697; *God of* (the) *rock; Elitsur,* an Israelite:—Elizur.

469. אֱלִיצָפָן, **'Ĕlîytsâphân,** *el-ee-tsaw-fawn´*; or (shortened) אֶלְצָפָן, **'Eltsâphân,** *el-tsaw-fawn´*; from 410 and 6845; *God of treasure; Elitsaphan* or *Eltsa-phan,* an Israelite:—Elizaphan, Elza-phan.

470. אֱלִיקָא, **'Ĕlîyqâ',** *el-ee-kaw´*; from 410 and 6958; *God of rejection; Elika,* an Israelite:— Elika.

471. אֶלְיָקִים, **'Elyâqîym,** *el-yaw-keem´*; from 410 and 6965; *God of raising; Eljakim,* the name of four Israelites:—Eliakim.

472. אֱלִישֶׁבַע, **'Ĕlîysheba',** *el-ee-sheh´-bah*; from 410 and 7651 (in the sense of 7650); *God of*

(the) *oath; Elisheba,* the wife of Aaron:— Elisheba.

473. אֱלִישָׁה, **'Ĕlîyshâh,** *el-ee-shaw´*; probably of foreign derivation; *Elishah,* a son of Javan:— Elishah.

474. אֱלִישׁוּעַ, **'Ĕlîyshûwa',** *el-ee-shoo´-ah*; from 410 and 7769; *God of supplication* (or *of riches*); *Elishua,* a son of King David:—Elishua.

475. אֶלְיָשִׁיב, **'Elyâshîyb,** *el-yaw-sheeb´*; from 410 and 7725; *God will restore; Eljashib,* the name of six Israelites:—Eliashib.

476. אֱלִישָׁמָע, **'Ĕlîyshâmâ',** *el-ee-shaw-maw´*; from 410 and 8085; *God of hearing; Elishama,* the name of seven Israelites:—Elishama.

477. אֱלִישָׁע, **'Ĕlîyshâ',** *el-ee-shaw´*; contraction for 474; *Elisha,* the famous prophet:—Elisha.

478. אֱלִישָׁפָט, **'Ĕlîyshâphât,** *el-ee-shaw-fawt´*; from 410 and 8199; *God of judgment; Elishaphat,* an Israelite:—Elishaphat.

479. אִלֵּךְ, **'illêk** (Chaldee), *il-lake´*; prolonged from 412; *these*:—these, those.

480. אַלְלַי, **'allay,** *al-lah´ee*; by reduplication from 421; *alas!*:—woe.

481. אָלַם, **'âlam,** *aw-lam´*; a primitive root; to *tie* fast; hence (of the mouth) to be *tongue-tied*:—bind, be dumb, put to silence.

482. אֵלֶם, **'êlem,** *ay´-lem*; from 481; *silence* (i.e. mute justice):—congregation. Compare 3128.

483. אִלֵּם, **'illêm,** *il-lame´*; from 481; *speechless*:—dumb (man).

484. אַלְמֻגִּים, **'almuggiym,** *al-moog-gheem´*; probably of foreign derivation (used thus only in the plural); *almug* (i.e. probably sandalwood) sticks:— almug trees. Compare 418.

485. אֲלֻמָּה, **'ălummâh,** *al-oom-maw´*; or (masculine) אָלֻם, **'âlum,** *aw-loom´*; passive participle of 481; something *bound*; a *sheaf*:—sheaf.

486. אַלְמוֹדָד, **'Almôwdâd,** *al-mo-dawd´*; probably of foreign derivation; *Almodad,* a son of Joktan:—Almodad.

487. אַלַּמֶּלֶךְ, **'Allammelek,** *al-lam-meh´-lek*; from 427 and 4428; *oak of* (the) *king; Allammelek,* a place in Palestine:—Alam-melech.

488. אַלְמָן, **'almân,** *al-mawn´*; prolonged from 481 in the sense of *bereavement; discarded* (as a divorced person):—forsaken.

An adjective meaning forsaken or widowed. It occurs only in Jer 51:5, assuring Israel and Judah that, even in exile, they have not been forsaken by their God. Although this Hebrew word is similar to the Hebrew word for widow, the context of this verse does not support the idea that Israel is pictured as the wife of the Lord.

489. אַלְמֹן, **'almôn,** *al-mone´*; from 481 as in 488; *bereavement:*—widowhood.

490. אַלְמָנָה, **'almânâh,** *al-maw-naw´*; feminine of 488; a *widow*; also a *desolate* place:—desolate house (palace), widow.

A feminine noun meaning widow. The word occurs many times in the Law and the Prophets, where the well-being and care of the widow are the subject (Dt 14:29; Isa 1:17; Jer 7:6; Zec 7:10). Israel's concern for the widow was founded in the Lord's own concern (Ps 68:5[6]; 146:9; Pr 15:25; Jer 49:11). Figuratively, the term occurs twice in reference to a devastated city: Jerusalem (La 1:1) and Babylon (Isa 47:8).

491. אַלְמָנוּת, **'almânûwth,** *al-maw-nooth´*; feminine of 488; (concrete) a *widow*; (abstract) *widowhood:*—widow, widowhood.

492. אַלְמֹנִי, **'almônîy,** *al-mo-nee´*; from 489 in the sense of *concealment; some one* (i.e. *so and so*, without giving the name of the person or place):—one, and such.

493. אֶלְנַעַם, **'Elna'am,** *el-nah´-am;* from 410 and 5276; *God* (is his) *delight; Elnaam,* an Israelite:—Elnaam.

494. אֶלְנָתָן, **'Elnâthân,** *el-naw-thawn´*; from 410 and 5414; *God* (is the) *giver; Elnathan,* the name of four Israelites:—Elnathan.

495. אֶלָּסָר, **'Ellâsâr,** *el-law-sawr´*; probably of foreign derivation *Ellasar,* an early country of Asia:—Ellasar.

496. אֶלְעָד, **'El'âd,** *el-awd´*; from 410 and 5749; *God has testified; Elad,* an Israelite:—Elead.

497. אֶלְעָדָה, **'El'âdâh,** *el-aw-daw´*; from 410 and 5710; *God has decked; Eladah,* an Israelite:—Eladah.

498. אֶלְעוּזַי, **'El'ûwzay,** *el-oo-zah´ee*; from 410 and 5756 (in the sense of 5797); *God* (is) *defensive; Eluzai,* an Israelite:—Eluzai.

499. אֶלְעָזָר, **'El'âzâr,** *el-aw-zawr´*; from 410 and 5826; *God* (is) *helper; Elazar,* the name of seven Israelites:—Eleazar.

500. אֶלְעָלֵא, **'El'âlê',** *el-aw-lay´*; or (more properly) אֶלְעָלֵה, **'El'âlêh,** *el-aw-lay´*; from 410 and 5927; *God* (is) *going up; Elale* or *Elaleh,* a place east of the Jordan:—Elealeh.

501. אֶלְעָשָׂה, **'El'âśâh,** *el-aw-saw´*; from 410 and 6213; *God has made; Elasah,* the name of four Israelites:—Elasah, Eleasah.

502. אָלַף, **'âlaph,** *aw-lof´*; a primitive root, to *associate* with; hence to *learn* (and causative to *teach*):—learn, teach, utter.

A verb meaning to learn or, in a causative sense, to teach. The meaning apparently derives from a noun meaning association, familiarity, which leads to learning. This root idea appears in Pr 22:25 where association with an angry man causes one to learn his ways. Other usages mean to teach without obvious reference to learning by association (Job 15:5; 33:33; 35:11).

503. אָלַף, **'âlaph,** *aw-laf´*; denominative from 505; causative to *make a thousandfold:*—bring forth thousands.

A masculine verb meaning thousand. It presents the idea of bringing forth thousands or making a thousandfold. It comes from the noun *'eleph* (505) and is found only once in the OT. The psalmist asked God for his granaries to be filled and his sheep to bring forth thousands (Ps 144:13).

504. אֶלֶף, **'eleph,** *eh´-lef;* from 502; a *family*; also (from the sense of *yoking* or *taming*) an *ox* or *cow:*—family, kine, oxen.

505. אֶלֶף, **'eleph,** *eh´-lef;* properly the same as 504; hence (an ox's head being the first letter of the alphabet, and this eventually used as a numeral) a *thousand:*—thousand.

A masculine noun meaning a thousand or clan. The word was commonly used for people, weights (including money), measures, and livestock (Jgs 8:26). Though the word is usually literal, sometimes it is used poetically to suggest a large number (Ge 24:60; Job 9:3). In a few cases, it carries the sense of an extended family or clan (Jgs 6:15).

506. אֱלַף, **'ălaph** (Chaldee), *al-af´*; or אֶלֶף, **'eleph**, *eh´-lef*; (Chaldee); corresponding to 505:—thousand.

An Aramaic masculine noun meaning one thousand. This word is found only in the book of Daniel. For example, Belshazzar held a magnificent feast and invited the lords of the land, whose total number was one thousand (Da 5:1). Daniel had a dream of people ministering to the Ancient of Days; Daniel called these people the thousand thousands (Da 7:10).

507. אֶלֶף, **'Eleph**, *eh´-lef*; the same as 505; *Eleph*, a place in Palestine:—Eleph.

508. אֶלְפַּעַל, **'Elpa'al**, *el-pah´-al*; from 410 and 6466; *God* (is) *act*; *Elpaal*, an Israelite:—Elpaal.

509. אָלַץ, **'âlats**, *aw-lats´*; a primitive root; to *press*:—urge.

510. אַלְקוּם, **'alqûwm**, *al-koom´*; probably from 408 and 6965; a *non-rising* (i.e. *resistlessness*):—no rising up.

511. אֶלְקָנָה, **'Elqânâh**, *el-kaw-naw´*; from 410 and 7069; *God has obtained*; *Elkanah*, the name of seven Israelites:—Elkanah.

512. אֶלְקֹשִׁי, **'Elqôshîy**, *el-ko-shee´*; patrial from a name of uncertain derivation; an *Elkoshite* or native of Elkosh:—Elkoshite.

513. אֶלְתּוֹלַד, **'Eltôwlad**, *el-to-lad´*; probably from 410 and a masculine form of 8435 [compare 8434]; *God* (is) *generator*; *Eltolad*, a place in Palestine:—Eltolad.

514. אֶלְתְּקֵא, **'Elt°qê'**, *el-te-kay´*; or (more proper) אֶלְתְּקֵה, **'Elt°-qêh**, *el-te-kay´*; of uncertain derivation; *Eltekeh* or *Elteke*, a place in Palestine:—Eltekeh.

515. אֶלְתְּקֹן, **'Elt°qôn**, *el-te-kone´*; from 410 and 8626; *God* (is) *straight*, *Eltekon*, a place in Palestine:—Eltekon.

516. אַל תַּשְׁחֵת, **'Al tashchêth**, *al tash-kayth´*; from 408 and 7843; *Thou must not destroy*; probably the opening words of a popular song:—Al-taschith.

517. אֵם, **'êm**, *ame*; a primitive word; a *mother* (as the *bond* of the family); in a wide sense

(both literal and figurative) [like 1]:—dam, mother, × parting.

A feminine noun meaning mother, a woman with children (Ex 20:12; Ps 35:14). The word may also signify a female ancestor, animals, or humans in general (Ge 3:20; 1Ki 15:13). A nation or city is sometimes viewed as the mother of its people. So in that sense, this word is sometimes used to refer to a nation (Isa 50:1; Hos 2:2[4], 5[7]).

518. אִם, **'im**, *eem*; a primitive particle; used very widely as demonstrative, *lo!*; interrogative, *whether*; or conditional, *if, although*; also *Oh that!, when*; hence as a negative, *not*:—(and, can-, doubtless, if, that) (not), + but, either, + except, + more (-over, if, than), neither, nevertheless, nor, oh that, or, + save (only, -ing), seeing, since, sith, + surely (no more, none, not), though, + of a truth, + unless, + verily, when, whereas, whether, while, + yet.

519. אָמָה, **'âmâh**, *aw-maw´*; apparently a primitive word; a *maid-servant* or female slave:—(hand-) bondmaid (-woman), maid (-servant).

520. אַמָּה, **'ammâh**, *am-maw´*; prolonged from 517; properly a *mother* (i.e. *unit*) of measure, or the *fore-arm* (below the elbow), i.e. a *cubit*; also a door-*base* (as a *bond* of the entrance):—cubit, + hundred [*by exchange for* 3967], measure, post.

521. אַמָּה, **'ammâh** (Chaldee), *am-maw´*; corresponding to 520:—cubit.

522. אַמָּה, **'Ammâh**, *am-maw´*; the same as 520; *Ammah*, a hill in Palestine:—Ammah.

523. אֻמָּה, **'ummâh**, *oom-maw´*; from the same as 517; a *collection*, i.e. community of persons:—nation, people.

A feminine noun meaning tribe, people. This word occurs three times in the Hebrew Bible (Ge 25:16; Nu 25:15; Ps 117:1) and is always plural. It is synonymous with *gôwy* (1471).

524. אֻמָּה, **'ummâh** (Chaldee), *oom-maw´*; corresponding to 523:—nation.

An Aramaic feminine noun meaning nation. This word corresponds to the Hebrew word *'êm* (517) meaning mother, and when carried into the Aramaic, this word shifts to mean mother in a collective sense (i.e. nation). Often a nation is found in the expression "peoples, nations, and languages" (Da 3:4, 7; 4:1[3:31]; 5:19; 6:25[26]; 7:14; cf. Ezr 4:10). For example, after Shadrach, Meshach, and Abednego came through the fiery furnace, Nebuchadnezzar issued a decree to every people, language, and nation concerning the God of the Hebrews (Da 3:29).

525. אָמוֹן, **'âmôwn,** *aw-mone´*; from 539, probably in the sense of *training; skilled*, i.e. an architect [like 542]:—one brought up.

A masculine noun meaning architect or craftsman. The word is used in Pr 8:30 as the personification of wisdom. Wisdom is portrayed as a craftsman at God's side, involved in designing the creation.

526. אָמוֹן, **'Âmôwn,** *aw-mone´*; the same as 525; *Amon*, the name of three Israelites:—Amon.

527. אָמוֹן, **'âmôwn,** *aw-mone´*; a variation for 1995; a *throng* of people:—multitude.

A masculine noun of uncertain derivation, meaning either a skilled craftsman or a throng of people. It is used only twice in the OT. In Pr 8:30, the sense is that of a master architect or artisan (525). The other appearance in Jer 52:15 seems to designate a general multitude of people.

528. אָמוֹן, **'Âmôwn,** *aw-mone´*; of Egyptian derivation; *Amon* (i.e. Ammon or Amn), a deity of Egypt (used only as an adjunct of 4996):—multitude, populous.

A masculine noun meaning artisan or master craftsman. The legs of the beloved are said to be the work of an artisan (SS 7:1[2]). This word is also a proper name of an Egyptian god (Jer 46:25; Na 3:8). The Egyptian god was the local deity of Thebes but came to be the supreme god in Egypt.

529. אָמוּן, **'êmûwn,** *ay-moon´*; from 539; *established*, i.e. (figurative) *trusty*; also (abstract) *trustworthiness*:—faith (-ful), truth.

A masculine noun meaning trustworthiness, faithfulness, or dependability. It is used to signify the rare and beneficial quality of trustworthiness in an individual (Pr 13:17; 14:5; 20:6); the character of a righteous nation (Isa 26:2); and in a negative sense, a fundamental lack of dependability or faithfulness (Dt 32:20).

530. אֱמוּנָה, **'ĕmûwnâh,** *em-oo-naw´*; or (shortened) אֱמֻנָה, **'ĕmunâh,** *em-oo-naw´*; feminine of 529; (literal) *firmness*; (figurative) *security*; (moral) *fidelity*:—faith (-ful, -ly, -ness, [man]), set office, stability, steady, truly, truth, verily.

A noun meaning truth, faithfulness. It is used to describe God's character and His actions in Dt 32:4. The psalmists often use this word in their praise of the Lord and His faithfulness (Ps 33:4; 100:5; 119:90). When people are faithful, good comes their way (2Ch 19:9; Pr 12:22; 28:20). The word *'ĕmûnâh* is also used with righteousness to describe the character (Pr 12:17; Isa 59:4; Jer 5:1).

531. אָמוֹץ, **'Âmôwts,** *aw-mohts´*; from 553; *strong*; *Amots*, an Israelite:—Amoz.

532. אָמִי, **'Âmîy,** *aw-mee´*; an abbreviation for 526; *Ami*, an Israelite:—Ami.

533. אַמִּיץ, **'ammîyts,** *am-meets´*; or (shortened) אַמִּץ, **'ammits,** *am-meets´*; from 553; *strong* or (abstract) *strength*:—courageous, mighty, strong (one).

534. אָמִיר, **'âmîyr,** *aw-meer´*; apparently from 559 (in the sense of *self-exaltation*); a *summit* (of a tree or mountain):—bough, branch.

535. אָמַל, **'âmal,** *aw-mal´*; a primitive root; to *droop*; by implication to *be sick*, to *mourn*:—languish, be weak, wax feeble.

536. אֻמְלַל, **'umlal,** *oom-lal´*; from 535; *sick*:—weak.

537. אֲמֵלָל, **'ămêlâl,** *am-ay-lawl´*; from 535; *languid*:—feeble.

538. אָמָם, **'Âmâm,** *am-awm´*; from 517; *gathering* spot; *Amam*, a place in Palestine:—Amam.

539. אָמַן, **'âman,** *aw-man´*; a primitive root; properly to *build up* or *support*; to *foster* as a parent or nurse; (figurative) to *render* (or *be*) *firm* or *faithful*, to *trust* or believe, to be *permanent* or *quiet*; moral to *be true* or certain; once (Isa 30:21; by interchange for 541) to *go to the right hand*:—hence assurance, believe, bring up, establish, + fail, be faithful (of long continuance, steadfast, sure, surely, trusty, verified), nurse, (-ing father), (put), trust, turn to the right.

A verb meaning to be firm, to build up, to support, to nurture, or to establish. The primary meaning is that of providing stability and confidence, like a baby would find in the arms of a parent. It is used to signify support of a pillar (2Ki 18:16); nurture and nourishment (Nu 11:12; Ru 4:16; thus, a nurse, 2Sa 4:4); cradling in one's arms (Isa 60:4); a house firmly founded (1Sa 2:35; 25:28); a secure nail that finds a solid place to grip (Isa 22:23); a lasting permanence (Ps 89:28[29]; with negative particle, Jer 15:18). Metaphorically, the word conveys the notion of faithfulness and trustworthiness, such that one could fully depend on (Dt 7:9; Job 12:20; Ps 19:7[8]; Isa 55:3; Mic 7:5). Therefore, the word can also signify certitude or assurance (Dt 28:66; Job 24:22; Hos 5:9) and belief, in the sense of receiving something as true and sure (Ge 15:6; Ex 4:5; 2Ch 20:20; Ps 78:22; Isa 53:1; Jnh 3:5).

540. אֲמַן, **'ăman** (Chaldee), *am-an´*; corresponding to 539:—believe, faithful, sure.

An Aramaic verb meaning to trust in, to put one's faith in someone or something. This verb occurs only three times in the Hebrew Bible. In Da 6:23(24), it states that Daniel trusted in his God. In the other occurrences, the verb is in the form of a passive participle and functions as an adjective meaning trustworthy or faithful: the interpretation of the king's dream is trustworthy (Da 2:45); and Daniel is described as a faithful man without negligence or corruption (Da 6:4[5]).

541. אָמַן, **'âman**, *aw-man´*; denominative from 3225; to take the *right hand* road:—turn to the right. See 539.

A verb meaning to go to the right or to use the right hand. This word is identical to *yâman* (3231) and is related to the noun *yĕmâniy* (3233), meaning right hand. In the OT, this word is always used with its opposite, *śâma'l*, meaning to go to the left or to use the left hand. Lot could choose which direction he wanted to go (Ge 13:9). God would guide Israel where they needed to go (Isa 30:21). God commanded Ezekiel to go the way God directed him (Eze 21:16[21]).

542. אָמָן, **'ommân**, *ow-mawn´*; from 539 (in the sense of *training*); an *expert*:—cunning workman.

543. אָמֵן, **'âmên**, *aw-mane´*; from 539; *sure*; (abstract) *faithfulness*; adverb *truly*:—Amen, so be it, truth.

An adverb meaning verily or truly. The word is used more often as the declaration may it be so. It comes from a root meaning to confirm; to support; to be faithful. The major idea behind this word is constancy and reliability. It is used as a declaration to acknowledge affirmation of a statement (1Ki 1:36); acceptance of a curse (Ne 5:13); affirmation of a prophecy (Jer 28:6). It is also used in response to worship and praise (1Ch 16:36; Ne 8:6). The English word *amen* comes from this word and means, "I agree; may it be so."

544. אֹמֶן, **'ômen**, *oh-men´*; from 539; *verity*:—truth.

545. אָמְנָה, **'omnâh**, *om-naw´*; feminine of 544 (in the specific sense of *training*); *tutelage*:—brought up.

546. אָמְנָה, **'omnâh**, *om-naw´*; feminine of 544 (in its usual sense); adverbial *surely*:—indeed.

An adverb meaning verily, truly, indeed. Abraham used this word to express that he was being truthful when he said Sarah was his sister (Ge 20:12)—although, in fact, he was lying. When Achan took loot from Jericho, he admitted his sin by saying he had indeed sinned against God (Jos 7:20).

547. אֹמְנָה, **'ômᵉnâh**, *o-me-naw´*; feminine active participle of 544 (in the original sense of *supporting*); a *column*:—pillar.

548. אֲמָנָה, **'ămânâh**, *am-aw-naw´*; feminine of 543; something *fixed*, i.e. a *covenant*, an *allowance*:—certain portion, sure.

A feminine noun meaning agreement, faith, support. It occurs in Ne 9:38[10:1] and 11:23. In Ne 9:38, it is the object of the verb *kârath* (3772), which is also used in the idiom "to make (lit., cut) a covenant," suggesting a possible semantic overlap.

549. אֲמָנָה, **'Ămânâh**, *am-aw-naw´*; the same as 548; *Amanah*, a mountain near Damascus:—Amana.

550. אַמְנוֹן, **'Amnôwn**, *am-nohn´*; or אֲמִינוֹן, **'Ămîy-nôwn**, *am-ee-nohn´*; from 539; *faithful*; *Amnon* (or *Aminon*), a son of David:—Amnon.

551. אָמְנָם, **'omnâm,** *om-nawm´*; adverbial from 544; *verily*:—indeed, no doubt, surely, (it is, of a) true (-ly, -th).

An adverb meaning admittedly, truly, or surely. The word is used to acknowledge that something is true but not the whole truth. Hezekiah admitted that Assyria destroyed other nations and their gods but claimed that it was because they were false gods (2Ki 19:17; Isa 37:18). Job admitted the truth of his friends' sayings but claimed that they did not see the whole truth (Job 9:2; 12:2, 19:4, 5). Eliphaz used the word to deny negative statements about God and himself (Job 34:12; 36:4).

552. אֻמְנָם, **'umnâm,** *oom-nawm´*; an orthographic variation of 551:—in (very) deed; of a surety.

An interrogative particle meaning verily, truly, indeed. It always occurs in questions. An example is Ge 18:13, where Sarah doubted that she would have a child, "Shall I of a surety bear a child . . . ?"

553. אָמַץ, **'âmats,** *aw-mats´*; a primitive root; to *be alert*, physically (on foot) or mentally (in courage):—confirm, be courageous (of good courage, steadfastly minded, strong, stronger), establish, fortify, harden, increase, prevail, strengthen (self), make strong (obstinate, speed).

554. אָמֹץ, **'âmôts,** *aw-mohts´*; probably from 553; of a *strong* colour, i.e. *red* (others *fleet*):—bay.

555. אֹמֶץ, **'ômets,** *o´-mets*; from 553; *strength*:—stronger.

556. אַמְצָה, **'amtsâh,** *am-tsaw´*; from 553; *force*:—strength.

557. אַמְצִי, **'Amtsîy,** *am-tsee´*; from 553; *strong; Amtsi,* an Israelite:—Amzi.

558. אֲמַצְיָה, **'Ămatsyâh,** *am-ats-yaw´*; or אֲמַצְיָהוּ, **'Ămatsyâhûw,** *am-ats-yaw´-hoo*; from 553 and 3050; *strength of Jah; Amatsjah,* the name of four Israelites:—Amaziah.

559. אָמַר, **'âmar,** *aw-mar´*; a primitive root; to *say* (used with great latitude):—answer, appoint, avouch, bid, boast self, call, certify, challenge, charge, + (at the, give) command (-ment), commune, consider, declare, demand,

× desire, determine, × expressly, × indeed, × intend, name, × plainly, promise, publish, report, require, say, speak (against, of), × still, × suppose, talk, tell, term, × that is, × think, use [speech], utter, × verily, × yet.

A verb meaning to say. It is translated in various ways depending on the context. It is almost always followed by a quotation. In addition to vocal speech, the word refers to thought as internal speech (2Sa 13:32; Est 6:6). Further, it also refers to what is being communicated by a person's actions along with his words (Ex 2:14; 2Ch 28:13).

560. אֲמַר, **'ămar** (Chaldee), *am-ar´*; corresponding to 559:—command, declare, say, speak, tell.

An Aramaic verb meaning to say, to tell, to command. This root carries the same semantic range as its Hebrew cognate, *'âmar* (559) (Ezr 5:3, 15; Da 2:4; 3:24–26; 4:7–9[4–6]; 7:23).

561. אֵמֶר, **'êmer,** *ay´-mer*; from 559; something *said*:—answer, × appointed unto him, saying, speech, word.

A masculine noun meaning word, speech, saying. The primary meaning is something said. The word is used like *dâbâr* (1697); however, it occurs (with the exception of Joshua 24:27) only in poetry, usually in the plural, often in the phrase "the words of my mouth" (Dt 32:1; Ps 19:14[15]). Words are seen as taking from their context qualities such as truth (Pr 22:21); beauty (Ge 49:21); deception (Isa 32:7); knowledge (Pr 23:12). This word may refer to God's words (Job 6:10; Ps 138:4) as well as people's words.

562. אֹמֶר, **'ômer,** *o´-mer*; the same as 561:—promise, speech, thing, word.

A masculine noun meaning utterance, speech, word. It is used only in poetry in parallel constructions with *dâbâr* (1697), meaning word (Ps 19:3[4]; Pr 2:16; 4:10, 20); *millîm* (4405), meaning words (Job 32:12, 14; 33:3; 34:37); *mitswâh* (4687), meaning commandment (Job 23:12; Pr 2:1; 7:1).

563. אִמַּר, **'immar** (Chaldee), *im-mar´*; perhaps from 560 (in the sense of *bringing forth*); a *lamb*:—lamb.

564. אִמֵּר, **'Immêr,** *im-mare'*; from 559; *talkative; Immer,* the name of five Israelites:—Immer.

565. אִמְרָה, **'imrâh,** *im-raw'*; or אֶמְרָה, **'emrâh,** *em-raw'*; feminine of 561, and meaning the same:—commandment, speech, word.

A feminine noun meaning word. This rare poetic term occurs more in Ps 119 than everywhere else combined. It is used in parallel with teaching, covenant, commandment, and voice (Dt 32:2; 33:9; Ps 119:172; Isa 28:23). This noun most often designates God's Word, which is the psalmist's guide for life and his basis for requesting God's kindness, graciousness, and deliverance (Ps 119:11, 41, 58, 76, 116, 133, 154, 170). The keeping of God's Word is a frequent topic in Scripture (Dt 33:9; Ps 119:67, 158; cf. Isa 5:24). God's Word is pure, sweeter than honey, and has been magnified with His name (Ps 119:103; 138:2; Pr 30:5).

566. אִמְרִי, **'Imrîy,** *im-ree'*; from 564; *wordy; Imry,* the name of two Israelites:—Imri.

567. אֱמֹרִי, **'Ĕmôrîy,** *em-o-ree'*; probably a patronymic from an unused name derived from 559 in the sense of *publicity,* i.e. prominence; thus a *mountaineer;* an *Emorite,* one of the Canaanitish tribes:—Amorite.

568. אֲמַרְיָה, **'Ămaryâh,** *am-ar-yaw'*; or (prolonged) אֲמַרְיָהוּ, **'Ămaryâhûw,** *am-ar-yaw'-hoo*; from 559 and 3050; *Jah has said* (i.e. promised); *Amarjah,* the name of nine Israelites:—Amariah.

569. אַמְרָפֶל, **'Amrâphel,** *am-raw-fel'*; of uncertain (perhaps foreign) derivation; *Amraphel,* a king of Shinar:—Amraphel.

570. אֶמֶשׁ, **'emesh,** *eh'-mesh*; time *past,* i.e. *yesterday* or *last night*:—former time, yesterday (-night).

571. אֶמֶת, **'emeth,** *eh'-meth*; contraction from 539; *stability;* (figurative) *certainty, truth, trustworthiness*:—assured (-ly), establishment, faithful, right, sure, true (-ly, -th), verity.

A feminine noun meaning truth, faithfulness. It is frequently connected with lovingkindness (Pr 3:3; Hos 4:1) and occasionally with other terms such as peace (2Ki 20:19); righteousness (Isa 48:1); and justice (Ps 111:7). To walk in truth is to conduct oneself according to God's holy standards (1Ki 2:4; 3:6; Ps 86:11; Isa 38:3). Truth was the barometer for measuring both one's word (1Ki 22:16; Da 11:2) and actions (Ge 24:49; Jos 2:14). Accordingly, God's words (Ps 119:160; Da 10:21) and actions (Ne 9:33) are characterized by this Hebrew term also. Indeed, God is the only God of truth (Ex 34:6; 2Ch 15:3; Ps 31:5[6]).

572. אַמְתַּחַת, **'amtachath,** *am-takh'-ath*; from 4969; properly something *expansive,* i.e. a *bag*:—sack.

573. אֲמִתַּי, **'Ămittay,** *am-it-tah'ee*; from 571; *veracious; Amittai,* an Israelite:—Amittai.

574. אֵמְתָּנִי, **'êmtânîy** (Chaldee), *em-taw-nee'*; from a root corresponding to that of 4975; *well-loined* (i.e. burly) or *mighty*:—terrible.

575. אָן, **'ân,** *awn*; or אָנָה, **'ânâh,** *aw'-naw*; contraction from 370; *where;* hence *whither, when;* also *hither* and *thither*:— + any (no) whither, how, where, whither (-soever).

576. אֲנָא, **'ănâ',** *an-aw'*; (Chaldee); or אֲנָה, **'ănâh,** *an-aw'*; (Chaldee); corresponding to 589; *I*:—I, as for me.

577. אָנָּא, **'ânnâ',** *awn'-naw*; or אָנָּה, **'ânnâh,** *awn'-naw*; apparently contraction from 160 and 4994; *oh now!*:—I (me) beseech (pray) thee, O.

An interjection of entreaty meaning I beg you, ah now, alas, or oh. The primary use of the word is to intensify the urgency of request or the gravity of a given situation. It is used to signify the pressing desire for forgiveness (Ge 50:17); the great weight of sin (Ex 32:31); earnestness in prayer of petition (2Ki 20:3; Ne 1:5, Jnh 1:14).

578. אָנָה, **'ânâh,** *aw-naw'*; a primitive root; to *groan*:—lament, mourn.

579. אָנָה, **'ânâh,** *aw-naw'*; a primitive root [perhaps rather identical with 578 through the idea of *contraction* in anguish]; to *approach;* hence to *meet* in various senses:—befall, deliver, happen, seek a quarrel.

580. אֲנוּ, **'ănûw,** *an-oo'*; contraction for 587; *we*:—we.

581. אִנּוּן, **'innûwn,** *in-noon'*; (Chaldee); or (feminine) אִנִּין, **'innîyn,** *in-neen'*; (Chaldee);

corresponding to 1992; *they:*— × are, them, these.

582. אֱנוֹשׁ, **'ĕnôwsh,** *en-oshe´*; from 605; properly a *mortal* (and thus differing from the more dignified 120); hence a *man* in general (singly or collectively):—another, × [blood-] thirsty, certain, chap [-man], divers, fellow, × in the flower of their age, husband, (certain, mortal) man, people, person, servant, some (× of them), + stranger, those, + their trade. It is often unexpressed in the English Version, especially when used in apposition with another word. Compare 376.

A masculine noun meaning man. In the singular, this word occurs in poetry and prayers (2Ch 14:11[10]). This word may derive from *'ânash* (605), meaning to be weak or sick. In comparison to *'îsh* (376), which also means man, *'ĕnôwsh* often occurs in passages emphasizing man's frailty (Job 7:17; Ps 8:4[5]; 90:3). However, the plural of *'ĕnôwsh* serves as the plural of *'îsh* and occurs throughout the OT.

583. אֱנוֹשׁ, **'Ĕnôwsh,** *en-ohsh´*; the same as 582; *Enosh*, a son of Seth:—Enos.

584. אָנַח, **'ânach,** *aw-nakh´*; a primitive root; to *sigh*:—groan, mourn, sigh.

585. אֲנָחָה, **'ănâchâh,** *an-aw-khaw´*; from 584; *sighing*:—groaning, mourn, sigh.

586. אֲנַחְנָא, **'ănachnâ',** *an-akh´-naw*; (Chaldee); or אֲנַחְנָה, **'ănachnâh,** *an-akh-naw´*; (Chaldee); corresponding to 587; *we:*—we.

587. אֲנַחְנוּ, **'ănachnûw,** *an-akh´-noo*; apparently from 595; *we:*—ourselves, us, we.

588. אֲנָחֲרָת, **'Ănâchărâth,** *an-aw-kha-rawth´*; probably from the same root as 5170; a *gorge* or narrow pass; *Anacharath*, a place in Palestine:—Anaharath.

589. אֲנִי, **'ănîy,** *an-ee´*; contraction from 595; *I:*—I, (as for) me, mine, myself, we, × which, × who.

590. אֳנִי, **'onîy,** *on-ee´*; probably from 579 (in the sense of *conveyance*); a *ship* or (collective) a *fleet:*—galley, navy (of ships).

591. אֳנִיָּה, **'onîyyâh,** *on-ee-yaw´*; feminine of 590; a *ship:*—ship (-men).

592. אֲנִיָּה, **'ănîyyâh,** *an-ee-yaw´*; from 578; *groaning:*—lamentation, sorrow.

593. אֲנִיעָם, **'Ănîy'âm,** *an-ee-awm´*; from 578 and 5971; *groaning* of (the) *people; Aniam,* an Israelite:—Aniam.

594. אֲנָךְ, **'ănâk,** *an-awk´*; probably from an unused root meaning to be narrow; according to most a plumb-*line*, and to others a *hook:*—plumb-line.

595. אָנֹכִי, **'ânôkîy,** *aw-no-kee´*; (sometimes *aw-no´-kee*); a primitive pronoun; *I:*—I, me, × which.

596. אָנַן, **'ânan,** *aw-nan´*; a primitive root; to *mourn,* i.e. *complain:*—complain.

597. אָנַס, **'ânas,** *aw-nas´*; to *insist:*—compel.

598. אֲנַס, **'ănas** (Chaldee), *an-as´*; corresponding to 597; (figurative) to *distress:*—trouble.

599. אָנַף, **'ânaph,** *aw-naf´*; a primitive root; to *breathe* hard, i.e. *be enraged:*—be angry (displeased).

A verb meaning to be angry, enraged, or to breathe through the nose. The word derives its meaning from the heavy breathing and snorting typical of anger. It is used solely in reference to God's anger or severe displeasure with His people: Moses (Dt 1:37; 4:21); Aaron (Dt 9:20); Solomon (1Ki 11:9); and Israel (Dt 9:8; 1Ki 8:46; 2Ki 17:18; Ps 60:1[3]; 79:5) all provoked this divine anger. In Ps 2:12, this word is used in reference to the Messiah.

600. אֲנַף, **'ănaph** (Chaldee), *an-af´*; corresponding to 639 (only in the plural as a singular); the *face:*—face, visage.

601. אֲנָפָה, **'ănâphâh,** *an-aw-faw´*; from 599; an unclean bird, perhaps the *parrot* (from its *irascibility*):—heron.

602. אָנַק, **'ânaq,** *aw-nak´*; a primitive root; to *shriek:*—cry, groan.

603. אֲנָקָה, **'ănâqâh,** *an-aw-kaw´*; from 602; *shrieking:*—crying out, groaning, sighing.

604. אֲנָקָה, **'ănâqâh,** *an-aw-kaw´*; the same as 603; some kind of lizard, probably the *gecko* (from its *wail*):—ferret.

605. אָנַשׁ, **'ânash,** *aw-nash´*; a primitive root; to *be frail, feeble,* or (figurative) *melancholy*:—desperate (-ly wicked), incurable, sick, woeful.

606. אֱנָשׁ, **'ĕnâsh,** *en-awsh´*; (Chaldee); or אֲנַשׁ, **'ĕnash,** *en-ash´*; (Chaldee); corresponding to 582; a *man*:—man, + whosoever.

An Aramaic masculine noun meaning man or mankind. This word is often used to differentiate man from deity. It can also be synonymous with human beings. The most frequent usage occurs in the book of Daniel. It is used in a general, collective sense to mean everyone (Ezr 6:11; Da 3:10); and in the phrase "son of man" to mean a human being (Da 7:13). See the related Hebrew noun *'ĕnôwsh* (582).

607. אַנְתָּה, **'antâh,** *an-taw´*; (Chaldee); corresponding to 859; *thou*:—as for thee, thou.

608. אַנְתּוּן, **'antûwn,** *an-toon´*; (Chaldee); plural of 607; *ye*:—ye.

609. אָסָא, **'Âsâ',** *aw-saw´*; of uncertain derivation; *Asa,* the name of a king and of a Levite:—Asa.

610. אָסוּךְ, **'âsûwk,** *aw-sook´*; from 5480; *anointed,* i.e. an oil *flask*:—pot.

611. אָסוֹן, **'âsôwn,** *aw-sone´*; of uncertain derivation; *hurt*:—mischief.

A masculine noun meaning mischief, evil, harm, hurt, or damage. It signifies potential danger during a journey (Ge 42:4, 38), bodily harm or personal loss (Ex 21:22, 23).

612. אָסוּר, **'êsûwr,** *ay-soor´*; from 631; a *bond* (especially *manacles* of a prisoner):—band, + prison.

613. אֱסוּר, **'êsûwr** (Chaldee), *es-oor´*; corresponding to 612:—band, imprisonment.

614. אָסִיף, **'âsîyph,** *aw-seef´*; or אָסִף, **'âsiph,** *aw-seef´*; from 622; *gathered,* i.e. (abstract) a *gathering* in of crops:—ingathering.

615. אָסִיר, **'âsîyr,** *aw-sere´*; from 631; *bound,* i.e. a *captive*:—(those which are) bound, prisoner.

616. אַסִּיר, **'assîyr,** *as-sere´*; for 615:—prisoner.

617. אַסִּיר, **'Assîyr,** *as-sere´*; the same as 616; *prisoner; Assir,* the name of two Israelites:—Assir.

618. אָסָם, **'âsâm,** *aw-sawm´*; from an unused root meaning to *heap* together; a *storehouse* (only in the plur.):—barn, storehouse.

619. אָסְנָה, **'Asnâh,** *as-naw´*; of uncertain derivation; *Asnah,* one of the Nethinim:—Asnah.

620. אָסְנַפַּר, **'Ôsnappar,** *os-nap-par´*; of foreign derivation; *Osnappar,* an Assyrian king:—Asnapper.

621. אָסְנַת, **'Âs°nath,** *aw-se-nath´*; of Egyptian derivation.; *Asenath,* the wife of Joseph:—Asenath.

622. אָסַף, **'âsaph,** *aw-saf´*; a primitive root; to *gather* for any purpose; hence to *receive, take away,* i.e. remove (destroy, leave behind, put up, restore, etc.):—assemble, bring, consume, destroy, fetch, gather (in, together, up again), × generally, get (him), lose, put all together, receive, recover [another from leprosy], (be) rereward, × surely, take (away, into, up), × utterly, withdraw.

A verb meaning to gather, to take away, to harvest. The meaning of the word varies depending on the context. The word can mean to gather people for different purposes (Ge 29:22; 42:17; Ex 3:16; 4:29). It is used of a nation collecting armies for fighting (Nu 21:23; Jgs 11:20; 1Sa 17:1; 2Sa 10:17); and the Lord taking away Rachel's disgrace of childlessness (Ge 30:23). Oftentimes it refers to gathering or harvesting food or gathering other objects, such as animals (Jer 12:9); quail (Nu 11:32); eggs (Isa 10:14); money (2Ki 22:4; 2Ch 24:11). The word also refers to death or burial, literally meaning to be gathered to one's people (Ge 25:8, 17; 35:29; 49:29, 33); to be gathered to one's fathers (Jgs 2:10); or to be gathered to one's grave (2Ki 22:20; 2Ch 34:28).

623. אָסָף, **'Âsâph,** *aw-sawf´*; from 622; *collector; Asaph,* the name of three Israelites, and of the family of the first:—Asaph.

624. אָסֹף, **'âsôph,** *aw-sof´*; passive participle of 622; *collected* (only in the plural), i.e. a *collection* (of offerings):—threshold, Asuppim.

A masculine noun meaning a collection, treasury, or storehouse. The primary meaning of the root is that which is gathered. It is used three times in the OT to signify the storehouses near the gates of a temple (1Ch 26:15, 17; Ne 12:25).

625. אֹסֶף, **'ôseph,** o´-sef; from 622; a *collection* (of fruits):—gathering.

A masculine noun meaning a collection, ingathering, harvest. The Hebrew word especially refers to a harvest of summer fruit, as is depicted in Mic 7:1, "Gather the summer fruits" (NKJV). The prophet Isaiah is the other biblical author to use this term. In Isa 32:10, he states that the complacent people will be troubled and insecure because "the gathering will not come," but, then in Isa 33:4, the prophet uses the same word to refer to the Lord's spoil being collected like "the gathering of the caterpillar."

626. אֲסֵפָה, **'ăsêphâh,** as-ay-faw´; from 622; a *collection* of people (only adverbial):— × together.

A feminine noun meaning a gathering or a collection. This word is related to 'âsaph (622), which means to gather or collect. This particular word occurs only in Isa 24:22, "And they will be gathered together, as prisoners are gathered in the pit" (NKJV).

627. אֲסֻפָּה, **'ăsuppâh,** as-up-paw´; feminine of 624; a *collection* of (learned) men (only in the plural):—assembly.

A feminine noun meaning council or assembly. It comes from a root meaning to gather. Although there are many usages of the different forms of the root, this particular word is used only once in the Hebrew Bible, and the usage is plural instead of singular. It is used with the word for master and can be translated as "the gathering of masters"; "the council of scholars"; or "the collected sayings of scholars" (Ecc 12:11).

628. אֲסַפְסֻף, **'ăsaphsuph,** as-af-soof´; by reduplication from 624; *gathered up together,* i.e. a promiscuous *assemblage* (of people):—mixt multitude.

A masculine noun meaning a gathering or mixed multitude. This word is related to 'âsaph (622), which means to gather or collect. It occurs only in Nu 11:4, "And the mixed multitude that was among them fell a lusting" (KJV).

629. אָסְפַּרְנָא, **'osparnâ'** (Chaldee), os-par-naw´; of Persian derivation; *diligently:*—fast, forthwith, speed (-ily).

630. אַסְפָּתָא, **'Aspâthâ',** as-paw-thaw´; of Persian derivation; *Aspatha,* a son of Haman:—Aspatha.

631. אָסַר, **'âsar,** aw-sar´; a primitive root; to *yoke* or *hitch;* by analogy to *fasten* in any sense, to *join* battle:—bind, fast, gird, harness, hold, keep, make ready, order, prepare, prison (-er), put in bonds, set in array, tie.

632. אֱסָר, **'êsâr,** es-awr´; or אִסָּר, **'issâr,** is-sawr´; from 631; an *obligation* or *vow* (of abstinence):—binding, bond.

633. אֱסָר, **'êsâr** (Chaldee), es-awr´; corresponding to 632 in a legal sense; an *interdict:*—decree.

634. אֵסַר־חַדּוֹן, **'Êsar-Chaddôwn,** ay-sar´ chaddohn´; of foreign derivation; *Esar-chaddon,* an Assyrian king:—Esar-haddon.

635. אֶסְתֵּר, **'Estêr,** es-tare´; of Persian derivation; *Ester,* the Jewish heroine:—Esther.

636. אָע, **'â'** (Chaldee), aw; corresponding to 6086; a *tree* or *wood:*—timber, wood.

637. אַף, **'aph,** af; a primitive particle; meaning *accession* (used as an adverb or conjunction); *also* or *yea;* adversatively *though:*—also, + although, and (furthermore, yet), but, even, + how much less (more, rather than), moreover, with, yea.

638. אַף, **'aph** (Chaldee), af; corresponding to 637:—also.

639. אַף, **'aph,** af; from 599; properly the *nose* or *nostril;* hence the *face,* and occasionally a *person;* also (from the rapid breathing in passion) *ire:*—anger (-gry), + before, countenance, face, + forbearing, forehead, + [long-] suffering, nose, nostril, snout, × worthy, wrath.

A masculine noun meaning nose, nostril, and anger. These meanings are used together in an interesting wordplay in Pr 30:33. This word may, by extension, refer to the whole face, particularly in the expression, to bow one's face to the ground (Ge 3:19; 19:1; 1Sa 24:8[9]). To have length of nose is to be slow to wrath; to have shortness of nose is to be quick tempered (Pr 14:17, 29; Jer 15:14, 15). This Hebrew term is often intensified by being paired with another word for anger or by associating it with various words for burning (Nu 22:27; Dt 9:19; Jer 4:8;

7:20). Human anger is almost always viewed negatively with only a few possible exceptions (Ex 32:19; 1Sa 11:6; Pr 27:4). The anger of the Lord is a frequent topic in the OT. The OT describes how God is reluctant to exercise His anger and how fierce His anger is (Ex 4:14; 34:6; Ps 30:5[6]; 78:38; Jer 51:45).

640. אָפַד, **'âphad,** *aw-fad´*; a primitive root [rather a denominative from 646]; to *gird* on (the ephod):—bind, gird.

641. אֵפֹד, **'Êphôd,** *ay-fode´*; the same as 646 shorter; *Ephod*, an Israelite:—Ephod.

642. אֲפֻדָּה, **'ăphuddâh,** *af-ood-daw´*; feminine of 646; a *girding* on (of the ephod); hence generally a *plating* (of metal):—ephod, ornament.

643. אַפֶּדֶן, **'appeden,** *ap-peh´-den*; apparently of foreign derivation; a *pavilion* or palace-tent:—palace.

644. אָפָה, **'âphâh,** *aw-faw´*; a primitive root; to *cook*, especially to *bake*:—bake, (-r, [-meats]).

645. אֵפוֹ, **'êphôw,** *ay-fo´*; or אֵפוֹא, **'êphôw',** *ay-fo´*; from 6311; strictly a demonstrative participle, *here*; but used of time, *now* or *then*:—here, now, where.

646. אֵפוֹד, **'êphôwd,** *ay-fode´*; rarely אֵפֹד, **'êphôd,** *ay-fode´*; probably of foreign derivation; a *girdle*; specifically the *ephod* or high priest's shoulder-piece; also generally an *image*:—ephod.

647. אֲפִיחַ, **'Ăphîyach,** *af-ee´-akh*; perhaps from 6315; *breeze*; *Aphiach*, an Israelite:—Aphiah.

648. אָפִיל, **'âphîyl,** *aw-feel´*; from the same as 651 (in the sense of *weakness*); *unripe*:—not grown up.

649. אַפַּיִם, **'Appayim,** *ap-pah´-yim*; dual of 639; *two nostrils*; *Appajim*, an Israelite:—Appaim.

650. אָפִיק, **'âphîyq,** *aw-feek´*; from 622; (properly) *containing*, i.e. a *tube*; also a *bed* or *valley* of a stream; also a *strong* thing or a *hero*:—brook, channel, mighty, river, + scale, stream, strong piece.

651. אָפֵל, **'âphêl,** *aw-fale´*; from an unused root meaning to *set* as the sun; *dusky*:—very dark.

An adjective meaning dark or gloomy. This word is related to *'ôphel* (652), which means darkness or gloom. The only time this word occurs in the OT is in Am 5:20, "Shall not the day of the Lord be darkness, and not light? even very dark, and no brightness in it?" (KJV).

652. אֹפֶל, **'ôphel,** *o´-fel*; from the same as 651; *dusk*:—darkness, obscurity, privily.

A masculine noun, used only in poetry to denote darkness, gloom, especially a thick darkness. Although the term can be used in reference to physical darkness (Job 28:3; Ps 91:6), it is more often used in a figurative sense to designate things like obscurity (Job 3:6); death (Job 10:22); evil (Job 23:17; 30:26; Ps 11:2). In Isa 29:18, the term has both a literal and a figurative meaning in reference to the blind.

653. אֲפֵלָה, **'ăphêlâh,** *af-ay-law´*; feminine of 651; *duskiness*, (figurative) *misfortune*; (concrete) *concealment*:—dark, darkness, gloominess, × thick.

A feminine noun meaning darkness or gloominess. It signifies physical darkness: the plague of darkness (Ex 10:22); the naïve walking in darkness (Pr 7:9); the darkness which causes people to stumble and grope (Pr 4:19; Dt 28:29). Metaphorically, it is used to describe the calamity and misfortune that comes to the wicked (Isa 8:22; Jer 23:12) or the darkness of the day of the Lord (Joel 2:2; Zep 1:15).

654. אֶפְלָל, **'Ephlâl,** *ef-lawl´*; from 6419; *judge*; *Ephlal*, an Israelite:—Ephlal.

655. אֹפֶן, **'ôphen,** *o´-fen*; from an unused root meaning to *revolve*; a *turn*, i.e. a *season*:—+ fitly.

656. אָפֵס, **'âphês,** *aw-face´*; a primitive root; to *disappear*, i.e. *cease*:—be clean gone (at an end, brought to nought), fail.

657. אֶפֶס, **'ephes,** *eh´-fes*; from 656; *cessation*, i.e. an *end* (especially of the earth); often used adverbially *no further*; also (like 6466) the *ankle* (in the dual), as being the extremity of the leg or foot:—ankle, but (only), end, howbeit, less than nothing, nevertheless (where), no, none (beside), not (any, -withstanding), thing of nought, save (-ing), there, uttermost part, want, without (cause).

658. אֶפֶס דַּמִּים, **'Ephes Dammîym,** *eh´-fes dam-meem´*; from 657 and the plural of 1818;

boundary of blood drops; *Ephes-Dammim*, a place in Palestine:—Ephes-dammim.

659. אֶפַע, **'epha',** *eh´-fah*; from an unused root probably meaning to *breathe*; (properly) a *breath*, i.e. *nothing:*—of nought.

660. אֶפְעֶה, **'eph'eh,** *ef-eh´*; from 659 (in the sense of *hissing*); an *asp* or other venomous serpent:—viper.

661. אָפַף, **'âphaph,** *aw-faf´*; a primitive root; to *surround:*—compass.

662. אָפַק, **'âphaq,** *aw-fak´*; a primitive root; to *contain*, i.e. (reflexive) *abstain:*—force (oneself), restrain.

663. אֲפֵק, **'Âphêq,** *af-ake´*; or אֲפִיק, **'Âphîyq,** *af-eek´*; from 662 (in the sense of *strength*); *fortress; Aphek* (or *Aphik*), the name of three places in Palestine:—Aphek, Aphik.

664. אֲפֵקָה, **'Âphêqâh,** *af-ay-kaw´*; feminine of 663; *fortress; Aphekah*, a place in Palestine:—Aphekah.

665. אֵפֶר, **'êpher,** *ay´-fer*; from an unused root meaning to *bestrew*; *ashes:*—ashes.

666. אֲפֵר, **'ăphêr,** *af-ayr´*; from the same as 665 (in the sense of *covering*); a *turban:*—ashes.

667. אֶפְרֹחַ, **'ephrôach,** *ef-ro´-akh*; from 6524 (in the sense of *bursting* the shell); the *brood* of a bird:—young (one).

668. אַפִּרְיוֹן, **'appiryôwn,** *ap-pir-yone´*; probably of Egyptian derivation; a *palanquin:*—chariot.

669. אֶפְרַיִם, **'Ephrayim,** *ef-rah´-yim*; dual of a masculine form of 672; *double fruit; Ephrajim*, a son of Joseph; also the tribe descended from him, and its territory:—Ephraim, Ephraimites.

670. אֲפָרְסָי, **'Âphâr'say** (Chaldee), *af-aw-re-sah´*; of foreign origin (only in the plural); an *Apharesite* or inhabitant of an unknown region of Assyria:—Apharsite.

671. אֲפַרְסְכָי, **'Âphars'kay** (Chaldee), *af-ar-sek-ah´ee*; or אֲפַרְסַתְכָי, **'Âpharsathkay,** *af-ar-sath-kah´ee*; (Chaldee); of foreign origin (only in the plural); an *Apharsekite* or *Apharsathkite*, an unknown Assyrian tribe:—Apharsachites, Apharsath-chites.

672. אֶפְרָת, **'Ephrâth,** *ef-rawth´*; or אֶפְרָתָה, **'Ephrâ-thâh,** *ef-raw´-thaw*; from 6509 *fruitfulness; Ephrath*, another name for Bethlehem; once (Ps 132:6) perhaps for *Ephraim*; also of an Israelite woman:—Ephrath, Ephratah.

673. אֶפְרָתִי, **'Ephrâthîy,** *ef-rawth-ee´*; patrial from 672; an *Ephrathite* or an *Ephraimite*:—Ephraimite, Ephrathite.

674. אַפְּתֹם, **'app'thôm** (Chaldee), *ap-pe-thome´*; of Persian origin; *revenue*; others *at the last:*—revenue.

675. אֶצְבּוֹן, **'Etsbôwn,** *ets-bone´*; or אֶצְבֹּן, **'Etsbôn,** *ets-bone´*; of uncertain derivation; *Etsbon*, the name of two Israelites:—Ezbon.

676. אֶצְבַּע, **'etsba',** *ets-bah´*; from the same as 6648 (in the sense of *grasping*); some thing to *seize* with, i.e. a *finger*; by anal. a *toe:*—finger, toe.

677. אֶצְבַּע, **'etsba'** (Chaldee), *ets-bah´*; corresponding to 676:—finger, toe.

678. אָצִיל, **'âtsîyl,** *aw-tseel´*; from 680(in its secondary sense of *separation*); an *extremity* (Isa 41:9), also a *noble:*—chief man, noble.

A masculine noun designating side, corner, chief. This term can indicate the sides or borders of the earth, thereby referring to its extremities or remotest countries (Isa 41:9); or it can be used figuratively to mean nobles (Ex 24:11).

679. אַצִּיל, **'atstsîyl,** *ats-tseel´*; from 680(in its primary sense of *uniting*); a *joint* of the hand (i.e. *knuckle*); also (according to some) a *party-wall* (Eze 41:8):—[arm] hole, great.

680. אָצַל, **'âtsal,** *aw-tsal´*; a primitive root; (properly) to *join*; used only as a denominative from 681; to *separate*; hence to *select, refuse, contract:*—keep, reserve, straiten, take.

681. אֵצֶל, **'êtsel,** *ay´-tsel*; from 680 (in the sense of *joining*); a *side*; (as a preposition) *near:*—at, (hard) by, (from) (beside), near (unto), toward, with. See also 1018.

682. אָצֵל, **'Âtsêl,** *aw-tsale´*; from 680; *noble; Atsel*, the name of an Israelite, and of a place in Palestine:—Azal, Azel.

683. אֲצַלְיָהוּ, **'Ătsalyâhûw,** *ats-al-yaw´-hoo;* from 680 and 3050 prolonged; *Jah has reserved; Atsaljah,* an Israelite:—Azaliah.

684. אֹצֶם, **'Ôtsem,** *o´-tsem;* from an unused root probably meaning to *be strong; strength* (i.e. *strong*); *Otsem,* the name of two Israelites:—Ozem.

685. אֶצְעָדָה, **'ets'âdâh,** *ets-aw-daw´;* a variation from 6807; properly a *step-chain;* by analolgy a *bracelet:*—bracelet, chain.

686. אָצַר, **'âtsar,** *aw-tsar´;* a primitive root; to *store* up:—(lay up in) store, (make) treasure (-r).

687. אֵצֶר, **'Êtser,** *ay´-tser;* from 686; *treasure; Etser,* an Idumæan:—Ezer.

688. אֶקְדָּח, **'eqdâch,** *ek-dawkh´;* from 6916; *burning,* i.e. a *carbuncle* or other fiery gem:—carbuncle.

689. אַקּוֹ, **'aqqôw,** *ak-ko´;* probably from 602; *slender,* i.e. the *ibex:*—wild goat.

690. אֲרָא, **'Ărâ',** *ar-aw´;* probably for 738; *lion; Ara,* an Israelite:—Ara.

691. אֲרִאֵל, **'er'êl,** *er-ale´;* probably for 739; a *hero* (collective):—valiant one.

692. אַרְאֵלִי, **'Ar'êlîy,** *ar-ay-lee´;* from 691; *heroic; Areli* (or an *Arelite,* collective), an Israelite and his descendants:—Areli, Arelites.

693. אָרַב, **'ârab,** *aw-rab´;* a primitive root; to *lurk:*—(lie in) ambush (-ment), lay (lie in) wait.

694. אֲרָב, **'Ărâb,** *ar-awb´;* from 693; *ambush; Arab,* a place in Palestine:—Arab.

695. אֶרֶב, **'ereb,** *eh´-reb;* from 693; *ambuscade:*—den, lie in wait.

696. אֹרֶב, **'ôreb,** *o´-reb;* the same as 695:—wait.

697. אַרְבֶּה, **'arbeh,** *ar-beh´;* from 7235; a *locust* (from its rapid *increase*):—grasshopper, locust.

698. אָרְבֶה, **'orbâh,** *or-baw´;* feminine of 696 (only in the plural); *ambuscades:*—spoils.

699. אֲרֻבָּה, **'ărubbâh,** *ar-oob-baw´;* feminine participle passive of 693 (as if for *lurking*); a *lattice;* (by implication) a *window, dove-cot* (because of the pigeonholes), *chimney* (with its apertures for smoke), *sluice* (with openings for water):—chimney, window.

700. אֲרֻבּוֹת, **'Ărubbôwth,** *ar-oob-both;* plural of 699; *Arubboth,* a place in Palestine:—Aruboth.

701. אַרְבִּי, **'Arbîy,** *ar-bee´;* patrial from 694; an *Arbite* or native of Arab:—Arbite.

702. אַרְבַּע, **'arba',** *ar-bah´;* masculine אַרְבָּעָה, **'ar-bâ'âh,** *ar-baw-aw´;* from 7251; *four:*—four.

703. אַרְבַּע, **'arba'** (Chaldee), *ar-bah´;* corresponding to 702:—four.

704. אַרְבַּע, **'Arba',** *ar-bah´;* the same as 702; *Arba,* one of the Anakim:—Arba.

705. אַרְבָּעִים, **'arbâ'îym,** *ar-baw-eem´;* multiple of 702; *forty:*—forty.

706. אַרְבַּעְתַּיִם, **'arba'tayim,** *ar-bah-tah´-yim;* dual of 702; *fourfold:*—fourfold.

707. אָרַג, **'ârag,** *aw-rag´;* a primitive root; to *plait* or *weave:*—weaver (-r).

708. אֶרֶג, **'ereg,** *eh´-reg;* from 707; a *weaving;* a *braid;* also a *shuttle:*—beam, weaver's shuttle.

709. אַרְגֹּב, **'Argôb,** *ar-gobe´;* from the same as 7263; *stony; Argob,* a district of Palestine:—Argob.

710. אַרְגְּוָן, **'arg^evân,** *arg-ev-awn´;* a variation for 713; *purple:*—purple.

711. אַרְגְּוָן, **'arg^evân** (Chaldee), *arg-ev-awn´;* corresponding to 710:—purple.

712. אַרְגָּז, **'argâz,** *ar-gawz´;* perhaps from 7264 (in the sense of being *suspended*); a *box* (as a pannier):—coffer.

713. אַרְגָּמָן, **'argâmân,** *ar-gaw-mawn´;* of foreign origin; *purple* (the colour or the dyed stuff):—purple.

714. אַרְדְּ, **'Ard,** *ard;* from an unused root probably meaning to *wander; fugitive; Ard,* the name of two Israelites:—Ard.

715. אַרְדּוֹן, **'Ardôwn,** *ar-dohn´;* from the same as 714; *roaming; Ardon,* an Israelite:—Ardon.

716. אַרְדִּי, **'Ardîy,** *ar-dee´;* patronymic from 714; an *Ardite* (collectively) or descendants of Ard:—Ardites.

717. אָרָה, **'ârâh,** *aw-raw´*; a primitive root; to *pluck*:—gather, pluck.

718. אֲרוּ, **'ărûw** (Chaldee), *ar-oo´*; probably akin to 431; *lo!*:—behold, lo.

719. אַרְוַד, **'Arvad,** *ar-vad´*; probably from 7300; a refuge for the *roving; Arvad,* an island city of Palestine:—Arvad.

720. אֲרוֹד, **'Ărôwd,** *ar-ode´*; an orthographical variation of 719; *fugitive; Arod,* an Israelite:—Arod.

721. אַרְוָדִי, **'Arvâdîy,** *ar-vaw-dee´*; patrial from 719; an *Arvadite* or citizen of Arvad:—Arvadite.

722. אֲרוֹדִי, **'Ărôwdîy,** *ar-o-dee´*; patronymic from 721; an *Arodite* or descendant of Arod:—Arodi, Arodites.

723. אֻרְוָה, **'urvâh,** *oor-vaw´*; or, אֲרָיָה, **'ărâyâh,** *ar-aw-yah´*; from 717 (in the sense of *feeding*); a *herding-place* for an animal:—stall.

724. אֲרוּכָה, **'ărûwkâh,** *ar-oo-kaw´*; or אֲרֻכָה, **'ăru-kâh,** *ar-oo-kaw´*; feminine passive participle of 748 (in the sense of *restoring* to soundness); *wholeness* (literal or figurative):—health, made up, perfected.

A feminine noun meaning the healing of a wound, restoration, repair. The intuitive meaning is healing caused by the fleshly covering of a physical wound. It signifies the restoration of Israel, both the need for it (Jer 8:22) and the reality of it (Isa 58:8); and also the rebuilding of Jerusalem's walls that had been torn down (Jer 33:6).

725. אֲרוּמָה, **'Ărûwmâh,** *ar-oo-maw´*; a variation of 7316; *height; Arumah,* a place in Palestine:—Arumah.

726. אֲרוֹמִי, **'Ărôwmîy,** *ar-o-mee´*; a clerical error for 130; an *Edomite* (as in the margin):—Syrian.

727. אָרוֹן, **'ârôwn,** *aw-rone´*; or אָרֹן, **'ârôn,** *aw-rone´*; from 717 (in the sense of *gathering*); a *box*:—ark, chest, coffin.

A common noun meaning a box, chest, or ark. It is treated as masculine in some passages and as feminine in others. This word refers to the chest for collecting money offerings (2Ki 12:9[10], 10[11]); or the sarcophagus in which the mummy of Joseph was placed (Ge 50:26). In a sacred or cultic context, the term identifies the Ark of the Covenant (Nu 10:33), which at one time contained the tablets of the law (Dt 10:5); a copy of the Law which Moses had written (Dt 31:26); a pot of manna (Ex 16:33, 34); Aaron's rod (Nu 17:10). This word is often used with another word to denote the Ark of the Covenant: "the ark of the LORD your God" (Jos 4:5); "the ark of God" (1Sa 3:3); "the ark of the God of Israel" (1Sa 5:7); "the holy ark" (2Ch 35:3).

728. אֲרַוְנָה, **'Ăravnâh,** *ar-av-naw´*; or (by transposition) אוֹרְנָה, **'Ôwrnâh,** *ore-naw´*; or אֲנִיָּה, **'Aniy-yâh,** *ar-nee-yaw´*; all by orthographical variation for 771; *Aravnah* (or *Arnijah* or *Ornah*), a Jebusite:—Araunah.

729. אָרַז, **'âraz,** *aw-raz´*; a primitive root; to be *firm*; used only in the passive participle as a denominative from 730; of *cedar*:—made of cedar.

730. אֶרֶז, **'erez,** *eh´-rez*; from 729; a *cedar* tree (from the tenacity of its roots):—cedar (tree).

731. אַרְזָה, **'arzâh,** *ar-zaw´*; feminine of 730; *cedar* wainscoting:—cedar work.

732. אָרַח, **'ârach,** *aw-rakh´*; a primitive root; to *travel*:—go, wayfaring (man).

733. אָרַח, **'Ârach,** *aw-rakh´*; from 732; *way-faring; Arach,* the name of three Israelites:—Arah.

734. אֹרַח, **'ôrach,** *o´-rakh*; from 732; a well trodden *road* (literal or figurative); also a *caravan*:—manner, path, race, rank, traveller, troop, [by-, high-] way.

A masculine noun meaning path, way, byway, or highway. It describes the literal path one walks on (Jgs 5:6); the path or rank one walks in (Joel 2:7). Figuratively, this word describes the path of an individual or course of life (Job 6:18); the characteristics of a lifestyle, good or evil (Ps 16:11); righteousness or judgment (Pr 2:13). It is further used to mean traveler or wayfarer (Job 31:32). In the plural, it means caravans or troops (Job 6:19).

735. אֳרַח, **'ărach** (Chaldee), *a´-rakh*; corresponding to 734; a *road*:—way.

736. אֹרְחָה, **'ôrᵉchâh,** *o-rekh-aw´*; feminine active participle of 732; a *caravan*:—(travelling) company.

737. אֲרֻחָה, **’ăruchâh,** *ar-oo-khaw´*; feminine passive participle of 732 (in the sense of *appointing*); a *ration* of food:—allowance, diet, dinner, victuals.

738. אֲרִי, **’ărîy,** *ar-ee´*; or (prolonged) אַרְיֵה, **’aryêh,** *ar-yay´*; from 717 (in the sense of *violence*); a *lion*:—(young) lion, + pierce [*from the margin*].

739. אֲרִיאֵל, **’ărîy’êl,** *ar-ee-ale´*; or אֲרִאֵל, **’ări’êl,** *ar-ee-ale´*; from 738 and 410; *lion of God*, i.e. *heroic*:—lionlike men.

740. אֲרִיאֵל, **’Ărîy’êl,** *ar-ee-ale´*; the same as 739; *Ariel*, a symbolical name for Jerusalem, also the name of an Israelite:—Ariel.

741. אֲרִאֵיל, **’ări’êyl,** *ar-ee-ale´*; either by transposition for 739 or, more probably, an orthographical variation for 2025; the *altar* of the Temple:—altar.

742. אֲרִידַי, **’Ărîyday,** *ar-ee-dah´-ee*; of Persian origin; *Aridai*, a son of Haman:—Aridai.

743. אֲרִידָתָא, **’Ărîydâthâ’,** *ar-ee-daw-thaw´*; of Persian origin; *Aridatha*, a son of Haman:—Aridatha.

744. אַרְיֵה, **’aryêh** (Chaldee), *ar-yay´*; corresponding to 738:—lion.

745. אַרְיֵה, **’Aryêh,** *ar-yay´*; the same as 738; *lion*; *Arjeh*, an Israelite:—Arieh.

746. אַרְיוֹךְ, **’Aryôwk,** *ar-yoke´*; of foreign origin; *Arjok*, the name of two Babylonians:—Arioch.

747. אֲרִיסַי, **’Ărîysay,** *ar-ee-sah´-ee*; of Persian origin; *Arisai*, a son of Haman:—Arisai.

748. אָרַךְ, **’ârak,** *aw-rak´*; a primitive root; to *be* (causative *make*) *long* (literal or figurative):—defer, draw out, lengthen, (be, become, make, pro-) long, + (out-, over-) live, tarry (long).

A verb meaning to be long, prolong, draw out, or postpone. In most instances, it refers to the element of time. Most commonly, it bears the causative sense: to prolong one's days (Dt 5:16); to show continuance (Ex 20:12); tarry or stay long (Nu 9:19); to survive after (Jos 24:31); to postpone or defer anger (Isa 48:9); to draw out (1Ki 8:8). Used literally, it describes the growth of branches (Eze 31:5); and as a command, to lengthen one's cords (Isa 54:2).

749. אֲרַךְ, **’ărak** (Chaldee), *ar-ak´*; properly corresponding to 748, but used only in the sense of *reaching* to a given point; to *suit*:—be meet.

750. אָרֵךְ, **’ârêk,** *aw-rake´*; from 748; *long*:—long [-suffering, -winged], patient, slow [to anger].

An adjective meaning long, drawn out, or slow. This word primarily describes feelings pertaining to a person: either being slow of temper or patient. In wisdom literature, the person who is patient and does not anger quickly is extolled as a person of understanding (Pr 14:29; Ecc 7:8). When used to describe God, the Hebrew word means slow to anger and is immediately contrasted with God's great love, faithfulness, and power, demonstrating His true nature and His longsuffering (Ex 34:6). Also, this Hebrew word is used of an eagle's long pinions or feathers (Eze 17:3).

751. אֶרֶךְ, **’Erek,** *eh´-rek*; from 748; *length*; *Erek*, a place in Babylon:—Erech.

752. אָרֹךְ, **’ârôk,** *aw-roke´*; from 748; *long*:—long.

An adjective meaning long. It occurs only in the feminine singular tense and is used to modify exile (Jer 29:28); war (2Sa 3:1); and God's wisdom (Job 11:9). See the verb *’ârak* (748).

753. אֹרֶךְ, **’ôrek,** *o´-rek*; from 748; *length*:—+ for ever, length, long.

A masculine noun meaning length, long. It is primarily used in describing physical measurements, for example, Noah's ark (Ge 6:15) and the land (Ge 13:17). It is also used for the qualities of patience (forbearance) in Pr 25:15 and limitless presence (forever) in Ps 23:6. In perhaps its most significant theological usage, it speaks of long life or "length of your days" (NASB), a desirable state of existence embodied in the Lord (Dt 30:20), given to those who walk in obedience (Ps 91:16; Pr 3:2) and wisdom (Pr 3:16). This kind of existence begins in the eternity of God and is granted to those He has chosen.

754. אַרְכָא, **’arkâ’** (Chaldee), *ar-kaw´*; or אַרְכָה, **’arkâh,** *ar-kaw´*; (Chaldee); from 749; *length*:—lengthening, prolonged.

An Aramaic feminine noun meaning lengthening, prolonging. It is used temporally (Da 4:27[24]; 7:12).

755. אַרְכֻבָה, **'arkubâh** (Chaldee), *ar-koo-baw´*; from an unused root corresponding to 7392 (in the sense of *bending* the knee); the *knee*:—knee.

756. אַרְכְּוָי, **'Ark^evay** (Chaldee), *ar-kev-ah´ee*; patrial from 751; an *Arkevite* (collective) or native of Erek:—Archevite.

757. אַרְכִּי, **'Arkîy,** *ar-kee´*; patrial from another place (in Palestine) of similar name with 751; an *Arkite* or native of Erek:—Archi, Archite.

758. אֲרָם, **'Ărâm,** *arawm´*; from the same as 759; the *highland; Aram* or Syria, and its inhabitants; also the name of a son of Shem, a grandson of Nahor, and of an Israelite:—Aram, Mesopotamia, Syria, Syrians.

759. אַרְמוֹן, **'armôwn,** *ar-mone´*; from an unused root (meaning to *be elevated*); a *citadel* (from its *height*):—castle, palace. Compare 2038.

A masculine noun meaning fortress, citadel. Amos frequently equated God's judgment with the destruction of a fortress (Am 3:11). The word is used in parallel construction with strength (Am 3:11); siege tower (Isa 23:13); rampart (Ps 122:7; citadel, NIV; palace, NASB, NKJV, KJV); fortification (La 2:5; palace, NASB, NKJV, KJV, NIV).

760. אֲרַם צוֹבָה, **'Ăram Tsôwbâh,** *ar-am´ tso-baw´*; from 758 and 6678; *Aram of Tsoba* (or Coele-Syria):—Aram-zobah.

761. אֲרַמִּי, **'Ărammîy,** *ar-am-mee´*; patrial from 758; an *Aramite* or Aramæan:—Syrian, Aramitess.

762. אֲרָמִית, **'Ărâmîyth,** *ar-aw-meeth´*; feminine of 761; (only adverbial) *in Aramæan*:—in the Syrian language (tongue), in Syriack.

763. אֲרַם נַהֲרַיִם, **'Ăram Nahărayim,** *ar-am´ nah-har-ah´-yim*; from 758 and the dual of 5104; *Aram of* (the) *two rivers* (Euphrates and Tigris) or Mesopotamia:—Aham-naharaim, Mesopotamia.

764. אַרְמֹנִי, **'Armônîy,** *ar-mo-nee´*; from 759; *palatial; Armoni*, an Israelite:—Armoni.

765. אֲרָן, **'Ărân,** *ar-awn´*; from 7442; *stridulous; Aran*, an Edomite:—Aran.

766. אֹרֶן, **'ôren,** *o´-ren*; from the same as 765 (in the sense of *strength*); the *ash* tree (from its toughness):—ash.

767. אֹרֶן, **'Ôren,** *o´-ren*; the same as 766; *Oren,* an Israelite:—Oren.

768. אַרְנֶבֶת, **'arnebeth,** *ar-neh´-beth*; of uncertain derivation; the *hare*:—hare.

769. אַרְנוֹן, **'Arnôwn,** *ar-nohn´*; or אַרְנֹן, **'Arnôn,** *ar-nohn´*; from 7442; a *brauling* stream; the *Arnon*, a river east of the Jordan; also its territory:—Arnon.

770. אַרְנָן, **'Arnân,** *ar-nawn´*; probably from the same as 769; *noisy; Arnan*, an Israelite:—Arnan.

771. אָרְנָן, **'Ornân,** *or-nawn´*; probably from 766; *strong; Ornan*, a Jebusite:—Ornan. See 728.

772. אֲרַע, **'ăra',** *ar-ah´*; corresponding to 776; the *earth*; by implication (figurative) *low*:—earth, interior.

An Aramaic, feminine noun meaning earth. Functioning as an adverb, it also carries the idea of downward, below, or toward the earth. This concept appears in Jer 10:11 in conjunction with the phrase "under the heavens" to say that the gods who did not make heaven and earth will perish. It is also used to mean the realm where humans live (Da 2:35). The word also occurs twice in Da 2:39; in the first instance, it means inferior or less than, and in the second occurrence, it means earth. See the equivalent Hebrew noun *'eres* (776).

773. אֲרָעִי, **'ar'îy** (Chaldee), *arh-ee´*; feminine of 772; the *bottom*:—bottom.

774. אַרְפָּד, **'Arpâd,** *ar-pawd´*; from 7502; *spread out; Arpad*, a place in Syria:—Arpad, Arphad.

775. אַרְפַּכְשַׁד, **'Arpakshad,** *ar-pak-shad´*; probably of foreign origin; *Arpakshad*, a son of Noah; also the region settled by him:—Arphaxad.

776. אֶרֶץ, **'erets,** *eh´-rets*; from an unused root probably meaning to *be firm*; the *earth* (at large, or partitively a *land*):— × common, country, earth, field, ground, land, × nations, way, + wilderness, world.

A noun meaning the earth, land. It is used almost 2,500 times in the OT. It refers to the whole earth under God's dominion (Ge 1:1;

14:19; Ex 9:29; Ps 102:25[26]; Pr 8:31; Mic 4:13). Since the earth was God's possession, He promised to give the land of Canaan to Abraham's descendants (Ge 12:7; 15:7). The Promised Land was very important to Abraham's descendants and to the nation of Israel that possessed the land (Jos 1:2, 4). Israel's identity was tied to the land because it signified the fulfillment of God's promise to Abraham. If the Israelites were disobedient, however, they would be cursed by losing the land (Le 26:32–34, 36, 38, 39; Dt 28:63, 64; Jer 7:7).

777. אַרְצָא, **'artsâ'**, ar-tsaw´; from 776; *earthiness; Artsa*, an Israelite:—Arza.

778. אֲרַק, **'ăraq** (Chaldee), ar-ak´; by transmutation for 772; the *earth*:—earth.

An Aramaic, feminine noun meaning earth. Related to the Hebrew word *'eres* (776), it corresponds to the term planet. This Aramaic word occurs only once in the Hebrew Bible in Jer 10:11. The English word *earth* occurs twice in this verse, but it does not translate the same Aramaic word. The first is the Aramaic word being defined here; the second is the Aramaic noun *'ăra'* (772). Both of these words mean world.

779. אָרַר, **'ârar,** aw-rar´; a primitive root; to *execrate*:— × bitterly curse.

A verb generally denoting to inflict with a curse. There are at least five other Hebrew verbs with the same general meaning. This verb, in a more specific sense, means to bind (with a spell); to hem in with obstacles; to render powerless to resist. It is sometimes used as an antonym of *bârak* (1288). In Ge 3, God renders curses on the serpent, the woman, and the man for their sins in the Garden of Eden. To the serpent, God says, "Cursed are you more than all cattle, and more than every beast of the field" (Ge 3:14 NASB), meaning that the serpent would be the lowest of all animals. Then to the man, God says, "Cursed is the ground because of you," meaning that he would have difficulties in producing food from the soil. In Nu 22:6, King Balak of Moab asks Balaam to curse the Israelites. His desire is for the Israelites to be immobilized or rendered impotent so he can defeat them, his superior enemy.

780. אֲרָרַט, **'Ărâraṭ,** ar-aw-rat´; of foreign origin; *Ararat* (or rather Armenia):—Ararat, Armenia.

781. אָרַשׂ, **'âraś,** aw-ras´; a primitive root; to *engage* for matrimony:—betroth, espouse.

782. אֲרֶשֶׁת, **'ăresheth,** ar-eh´-sheth; from 781 (in the sense of *desiring* to possess); a *longing* for:—request.

783. אַרְתַּחְשַׁשְׁתָּא, **'Artachshashtâ',** ar-takh-shash-taw´; or אַרְתַּחְשַׁשְׁתְּא, **'Artachshasht',** ar-takh-shasht´; or by permutation אַרְתַּחְשַׁסְתְּא **'Artachshast',** ar-takh-shast´; of foreign origin; *Artachshasta* (or Artaxerxes), a title (rather than name) of several Persian kings:—Artaxerxes.

784. אֵשׁ, **'êsh,** aysh; a primitive word; *fire* (literal or figurative):—burning, fiery, fire, flaming, hot.

785. אֶשָּׁא, **'eshshâ'** (Chaldee), esh-shaw´; corresponding to 784:—flame.

786. אֵשׁ, **'ish,** eesh; identical (in origin and formation) with 784; *entity*; used only adverbially, there *is* or *are*:—are there, none can. Compare 3426.

787. אֹשׁ, **'ôsh** (Chaldee), ohsh; corresponding (by transposition and abbreviation) to 803; a *foundation*:—foundation.

788. אַשְׁבֵּל, **'Ashbêl,** ash-bale´; probably from the same as 7640; *flowing; Ashbel*, an Israelite:—Ashbel.

789. אַשְׁבֵּלִי, **'Ashbêlîy,** ash-bay-lee´; patronymic from 788; an *Ashbelite* (collective) or descendants of Ashbel:—Ashbelites.

790. אֶשְׁבָּן, **'Eshbân,** esh-bawn´; probably from the same as 7644; *vigorous; Eshban*, an Idumæan:—Eshban.

791. אַשְׁבֵּעַ, **'Ashbêa',** ash-bay´-ah; from 7650; *adjurer; Asbeä*, an Israelite:—Ashbea.

792. אֶשְׁבַּעַל, **'Eshba'al,** esh-bah´-al; from 376 and 1168; *man of Baal; Eshbaal* (or Ishbosheth), a son of King Saul:—Eshbaal.

793. אָשֵׁד, **'âshêd,** awsh´-shade; from an unused root meaning to *pour*; an *outpouring*:—stream.

794. אֲשֵׁדָה, **'ăshêdâh,** ash-ay-daw´; feminine of 793; a *ravine*:—springs.

795. אַשְׁדּוֹד, **'Ashdôwd,** *ash-dode´*; from 7703; *ravager; Ashdod,* a place in Palestine:—Ashdod.

796. אַשְׁדּוֹדִי, **'Ashdôwdîy,** *ash-do-dee´*; patrial from 795; an *Ashdodite* (often collective) or inhabitant of Ashdod:—Ashdodites, of Ashdod.

797. אַשְׁדּוֹדִית, **'Ashdôwdîyth,** *ash-do-deeth´*; feminine of 796; (only adverbial) *in the language of Ashdod:*—in the speech of Ashdod.

798. אַשְׁדּוֹת הַפִּסְגָּה, **'Ashdôwth hap-Pis-gâh,** *ash-doth´ hap-pis-gaw´*; from the plural of 794 and 6449 with the article interposed; *ravines of the Pisgah; Ashdoth-Pisgah,* a place east of the Jordan:—Ashdoth-pisgah.

799. אֶשְׁדָּת, **'eshdâth,** *aysh-dawth´*; from 784 and 1881; a *fire-law:*—fiery law.

800. אֶשָּׁה, **'eshshâh,** *esh-shaw´*; feminine of 784; *fire:*—fire.

801. אִשֶּׁה, **'ishsheh,** *ish-sheh´*; the same as 800, but used in a liturgical sense; properly a *burnt-offering*; but occasionally of any *sacrifice:*—(offering, sacrifice), (made) by fire.

A feminine noun meaning offering made by fire, fire offering. Its usage is highly religious and theological in a ritual context. The word describes how the various offerings were presented to the Lord; that is, they were offerings made by means of fire. This practice gave rise to referring to all the offerings the priests presented as fire offerings; hence, some consider this term a general term that applied to all the sacrifices of the Israelites (Dt 18:1; 1Sa 2:28). The fire was actually not offered. Instead, it was the means by which the various offerings were presented to God. The fire caused the offering to go up in smoke, a fact indicated by the causative form of the Hebrew verb, and that created a pleasant aroma to the Lord. The fire also purified what was offered. In this sense, the offerings could be called fire offerings or offerings made by fire. The other words for sacrifice in the OT are specific and describe a certain sacrifice, although *qorbân* (7133) is used in a general sense a few times. The word *'ishsheh* is slightly more specific.

The Levites were put in charge of all the offerings by fire to the Lord (Jos 13:14). Both animal sacrifices and nonanimal sacrifices were presented to the Lord by fire (Le 1:9; 2:10), as well as such items as the sacred bread and frankincense placed in the Holy Place (Le 24:7). These offerings by fire cover at least the burnt offering (Le 1:3–17; 6:8–13); the grain offering (Le 2:1–16; 6:14–23; 7:9, 10); the fellowship or peace offering (Le 3:9; 7:11–21, 28–34); the sin offering (Le 4:1–35; 5:1–13; 6:24–30); the guilt offering (Le 5:14–19; 7:1–10). All of these offerings were the Lord's (Nu 28:2), but the phrase "to the Lord" is explicitly stated most of the time (Ex 29:18; Le 2:11; Nu 28:13). As noted above, the offering by fire produced a pleasing or soothing aroma to the Lord as it ascended (cf. Le 1:9; Nu 15:13, 14; 29:13, 36), a phrase indicating that the Lord had accepted the sacrifice.

802. אִשָּׁה, **'ishshâh,** *ish-shaw´*; feminine of 376 or 582; irregular plural נָשִׁים, **nâshîym,** *naw-sheem´*; a *woman* (used in the same wide sense as 582):—[adulter]ess, each, every, female, × many, + none, one, + together, wife, woman. Often unexpressed in English.

A feminine noun meaning woman, wife, or female. The origin of this word has been recorded in Ge 2:23, where Adam said, "She shall be called Woman (*'ishshâh* [802]), because she was taken out of Man (*'iysh* [376]) (NASB)." While this word predominantly means woman or wife, it is further used in various ways: those able to bear children (Ge 18:11); a widow (Ru 4:5; 1Sa 27:3); an adulteress (Pr 6:26; 7:5); female children (Nu 31:18); or female animals (Ge 7:2).

803. אֲשִׁיָּה, **'ăshyâh,** *ash-yah´*; feminine passive participle from an unused root meaning to *found; foundation:*—foundation.

804. אַשּׁוּר, **'Ashshûwr,** *ash-shoor´*; or אַשֻּׁר, **'Ashshur,** *ash-shoor´*; apparently from 833 (in the sense of *successful*); *Ashshur,* the second son of Shem; also his descendants and the country occupied by them (i.e. Assyria), its region and its empire:—Asshur, Assur, Assyria, Assyrians. See 838.

805. אֲשׁוּרִי, **'Ăshûwrîy,** *ash-oo-ree´*; or אַשּׁוּרִי, **'Ash-shûwrîy,** *ash-shoo-ree´*; from a patrial word of the same form as 804; an *Ashurite* (collective) or inhabitant of Ashur, a district in Palestine:—Asshurim, Ashurites.

806. אַשְׁחוּר, **'Ashchûwr,** *ash-khoor´*; probably from 7835; *black; Ashchur,* an Israelite:—Ashur.

807. אֲשִׁימָא, **'Ăshîymâ'**, *ash-ee-maw'*; of foreign origin; *Ashima*, a deity of Hamath:—Ashima.

808. אָשִׁישׁ, **'âshîysh**, *aw-sheesh'*; from the same as 784 (in the sense of *pressing* down firmly; compare 803); a (ruined) *foundation*:—foundation.

809. אֲשִׁישָׁה, **'ăshîyshâh**, *ash-ee-shaw'*; feminine of 808; something closely *pressed* together, i.e. a *cake* of raisins or other comfits:—flagon.

810. אֶשֶׁךְ, **'eshek**, *eh'-shek*; from an unused root (probably meaning to *bunch* together); a *testicle* (as a *lump*):—stone.

811. אֶשְׁכּוֹל, **'eshkôwl**, *esh-kole'*; or אֶשְׁכֹּל, **'eshkôl**, *esh-kole'*; probably prolonged from 810; a *bunch of grapes* or other fruit:—cluster (of grapes).

812. אֶשְׁכֹּל, **'Eshkôl**, *esh-kole'*; the same as 811; *Eshcol*, the name of an Amorite, also of a valley in Palestine:—Eshcol.

813. אַשְׁכְּנַז, **'Ashkᵉnaz**, *ash-ken-az'*; of foreign origin; *Ashkenaz*, a Japhethite, also his descendants:—Ashkenaz.

814. אֶשְׁכָּר, **'eshkâr**, *esh-cawr'*; for 7939; a *gratuity*:—gift, present.

815. אֵשֶׁל, **'êshel**, *ay'-shel*; from a root of uncertain signification; a *tamarisk* tree; by extension a *grove* of any kind:—grove, tree.

A masculine noun meaning tamarisk tree. This tree has small leaves and survives well in the dry, hot climate of Israel. The word appears only three times in the OT: when Abraham planted a tamarisk tree near the well in Beersheba (Ge 21:33); the place where Saul and his men gathered (1Sa 22:6); and where Saul's bones were buried at Jabesh (1Sa 31:13).

816. אָשַׁם, **'âsham**, *aw-sham'*; or אָשֵׁם, **'âshêm**, *aw-shame'*; a primitive root; to *be guilty*; by implication to *be punished* or *perish*:— × certainly, be (-come, made) desolate, destroy, × greatly, be (-come, found, hold) guilty, offend (acknowledge offence), trespass.

A verb meaning to be guilty or to do wrong. This word is most often used to describe the product of sin—that is, guilt before God. It may be used of individuals (Le 5:2–5; Nu 5:6, 7); congregations (Le 4:13); or nations (Eze 25:12; Hos 13:16[14:1]). Because of the close connec-tion between guilt and sin, this word may be used as a synonym for sin (Hos 4:15; 13:1), while often the idea of punishment for a wrong done is implied (Hos 10:2; Zec 11:5). See the related nouns, *'âshâm* (817), meaning guilt, and *'ashmâh* (819), meaning guiltiness.

817. אָשָׁם, **'âsham**, *aw-shawm'*; from 816; *guilt*; by implication a *fault*; also a *sin-offering*:—guiltiness, (offering for) sin, trespass (offering).

A masculine noun used to express the concept of guilt or offence. It can connote the deeds which bring about guilt (Ps 68:21[22]). It can also express the condition of being guilty, that is, the results of the actions as shown in Ge 26:10 (NIV), "You would have brought guilt upon us." This word can also refer to the restitution that the guilty party was to make to the victim in the case of property damage (Nu 5:7). The biblical writer also uses this term to designate the guilt offering, the offering which is presented to the Lord in order to absolve the person guilty of an offence against God or man, which can be estimated and compensated (Le 5:6).

818. אָשֵׁם, **'âshêm**, *aw-shame'*; from 816; *guilty*; hence *presenting a sin-offering*:—one which is faulty, guilty.

An adjective meaning guilty. This word comes from the verb *'âsham* (816), meaning to be guilty and is related to the nouns *'âshâm* (817), meaning guilt, and *'ashmâh* (819), referring to guiltiness. Thus, the adjective describes one who is in a guilty state. It describes Joseph's brothers, who declared, "Truly we are guilty concerning our brother" (Ge 42:21, NASB); David in not bringing back Absalom (2Sa 14:13); and priests who had married foreign wives (Ezr 10:19).

819. אַשְׁמָה, **'ashmâh**, *ash-maw'*; feminine of 817; *guiltiness*, a *fault*, the *presentation of a sin-offering*:—offend, sin, (cause of) trespass (-ing, offering).

A feminine noun suggesting the concept of sin or guilt. It is similar in meaning to *'âshawm* (817). It can represent wrong actions (2Ch 24:18); the status of guilt which comes on a person by virtue of his or her wrong actions (Ezr 10:10); the guilt offering itself (Le 6:5[5:24]).

820. אַשְׁמָן, **'ashmân,** *ash-mawn´*; probably from 8081; a *fat* field:—desolate place.

821. אַשְׁמֻרָה, **'ashmurâh,** *ash-moo-raw´*; or אַשְׁמוּרָה, **'ashmûwrâh,** *ash-moo-raw´*; or אַשְׁמֹרֶת, **'ashmô-reth,** *ash-mo´-reth*; (feminine) from 8104; a night *watch*:—watch.

822. אֶשְׁנָב, **'eshnâb,** *esh-nawb´*; apparently from an unused root (probably meaning to *leave interstices*); a latticed *window*:—casement, lattice.

823. אַשְׁנָה, **'Ashnâh,** *ash-naw´*; probably a variation for 3466; *Ashnah*, the name of two places in Palestine:—Ashnah.

824. אֶשְׁעָן, **'Esh'ân,** *esh-awn´*; from 8172; *support*; *Eshan*, a place in Palestine:—Eshean.

825. אַשָּׁף, **'ashshâph,** *ash-shawf´*; from an unused root (probably meaning to *lisp*, i.e. *practise enchantment*); a *conjurer*:—astrologer.

A masculine noun meaning enchanters, conjurers of spirits, necromancers, or astrologers. Found only in the plural, this word is borrowed from the Aramaic language. It is found only in the book of Daniel in relation to wise men or diviners (Da 2:2; 5:11).

826. אַשָּׁף, **'ashshâph** (Chaldee), *ash-shawf´*; corresponding to 825:—astrologer.

An Aramaic masculine noun which denotes a conjurer, enchanters, magicians. It is closely related to the Hebrew word *'ashshâph* (825). This designation, in both the Aramaic and the Hebrew forms, appears only in the book of Daniel. Since no etymology is apparent, its meaning must be determined by its context. The word always occurs in a list with one to three or four other words, whose meanings clearly refer to people with occult knowledge in the practice of divination (Da 2:10, 27; 4:7[4]; 5:7, 11, 15).

827. אַשְׁפָּה, **'ashpâh,** *ash-paw´*; perhaps (feminine) from the same as 825 (in the sense of *covering*); a *quiver* or arrow case:—quiver.

828. אַשְׁפְּנַז, **'Ashp'naz,** *ash-pen-az´*; of foreign origin; *Ashpenaz*, a Babylonian eunuch:—Ashpenaz.

829. אֶשְׁפָּר, **'eshpâr,** *esh-pawr´*; of uncertain derivation; a measured *portion*:—good piece (of flesh).

830. אַשְׁפֹּת, **'ashpôth,** *ash-pohth´*; or אַשְׁפּוֹת, **'ashpôwth,** *ash-pohth´*; or (contracted) שְׁפֹת, **shephôth,** *shef-ohth´*; plural of a noun of the same form as 827, from 8192 (in the sense of *scraping*); a heap of *rubbish* or *filth*:—dung (hill).

831. אַשְׁקְלוֹן, **'Ashq'lôwn,** *ash-kel-one´*; probably from 8254 in the sense of *weighing*-place (i.e. *mart*); *Ashkelon*, a place in Palestine:—Ashkelon, Askalon.

832. אֶשְׁקְלוֹנִי, **'Eshq'lôwnîy,** *esh-kel-o-nee´*; patrial from 831; an *Ashkelonite* (collective) or inhabitant of Ashkelon:—Eshkalonites.

833. אָשַׁר, **'âshar,** *aw-shar´*; or אָשֵׁר, **'âshêr,** *aw-share´*; a primitive root; to *be straight* (used in the widest sense, especially to *be level, right, happy*); (figurative) to *go forward, be honest, prosper*:—(call, be) bless (-ed, happy), go, guide, lead, relieve.

A verb meaning to go straight, to go on, to advance forward, to be called blessed, or to be made happy. Of blessing or happiness, this verb is primarily used causatively: to call one blessed (Ps 72:17); to pronounce happiness (Ge 30:13); to be made happy or blessed (Pr 3:18). Used figuratively, it means to follow a straight path in understanding (Pr 9:6) or in one's heart (Pr 23:19). When it is used intensively, it means going straight or advancing (Pr 4:14).

834. אֲשֶׁר, **'ăsher,** *ash-er´*; a primitive relative pronoun (of every gender and number); *who, which, what, that*; also (as adverb and conjunction) *when, where, how, because, in order that*, etc.:— × after, × alike, as (soon as), because, × every, for, + forasmuch, + from whence, + how (-soever), × if, (so) that ([thing] which, wherein), × though, + until, + whatsoever, when, where (+ -as, -in, -of, -on, -soever, -with), which, whilst, + whither (-soever), who (-m, -soever, -se). As it is indeclinable, it is often accompanied by the personal pronoun expletively, used to show the connection.

835. אֶשֶׁר, **'esher,** *eh´-sher*; from 833; *happiness*; only in masculine plural construction as interjection, how *happy!*:—blessed, happy.

A masculine noun meaning a person's state of bliss. This Hebrew word is always used to refer to people and is never used of God. It is almost exclusively poetic and usually exclamatory, "O the bliss of . . ." In Proverbs, this blissfulness is frequently connected with wisdom (Pr 3:13; 8:32, 34). This term is also used to describe a person or nation who enjoys a relationship with God (Dt 33:29; Job 5:17; Ps 33:12; 146:5). In some contexts, the word does not seem to have any religious significance (1Ki 10:8; Pr 14:21; Ecc 10:17), and at least in one context, it has no religious significance (Ps 137:8, 9).

836. אָשֵׁר, **'Âshêr**, *aw-share´*; from 833; *happy*; *Asher*, a son of Jacob, and the tribe descended from him, with its territory; also a place in Palestine:—Asher.

837. אֹשֶׁר, **'ôsher**, *o´-sher*; from 833; *happiness*:—happy.

A masculine noun meaning happiness. The Hebrew word is found once in the Bible describing a feeling of joy (Ge 30:13).

838. אָשֻׁר, **'âshur**, *aw-shoor´*; or אַשֻּׁר, **'ashshur**, *ash-shoor´*; from 833 in the sense of *going*; a *step*:—going, step.

839. אֲשֻׁר, **'ăshur**, *ash-oor´*; contraction for 8391; the *cedar* tree or some other light elastic wood:—Ashurite.

840. אֲשַׂרְאֵל, **'Ăsar'êl**, *as-ar-ale´*; by orthographical variation from 833 and 410; *right of God*; *Asarel*, an Israelite:—Asareel.

841. אֲשַׂרְאֵלָה, **'Ăsar'êlâh**, *as-ar-ale´-aw*; from the same as 840; *right toward God*; *Asarelah*, an Israelite:—Asarelah. Compare 3480.

842. אֲשֵׁרָה, **'ăshêrâh**, *ash-ay-raw´*; or אֲשֵׁירָה, **'ăshêy-râh**, *ash-ay-raw´*; from 833; *happy*; *Asherah* (or Astarte) a Phoenician goddess; also an *image* of the same:—grove. Compare 6253.

A feminine noun which signifies the Canaanite fertility goddess believed to be the consort of Baal. Because of this association, the worship of Baal and Asherah was often linked together (Jgs 3:7; 1Ki 18:19; 2Ki 23:4). The noun is most often used for a carved wooden image of the goddess instead of a proper name (Jgs 6:26; 1Ki 14:15). This image was frequently associated with high places and fresh (i.e. green) trees—the latter contributing to the misleading translations of the Septuagint and Vulgate that the word denoted "groves" (Dt 12:3;

1Ki 14:23; Jer 17:2). The Israelites were commanded by God to cut down and burn the images (Ex 34:13; Dt 12:3), and occasionally the Israelites took steps to eliminate them (1Ki 15:13; 2Ki 23:4, 6, 7). Nevertheless, throughout much of Israel's preexilic history, false worship was a problem, even to the extent that Asherah's image was erected in God's temple itself (2Ki 21:7; Isa 27:9).

843. אָשֵׁרִי, **'Âshêrîy**, *aw-shay-ree´*; patronymic from 836; an *Asherite* (collective) or descendants of Asher:—Asherites.

844. אַשְׂרִיאֵל, **'Aśrîy'êl**, *as-ree-ale´*; an orthographical variation for 840; *Asriel*, the name of two Israelites:—Ashriel, Asriel.

845. אַשְׂרִאֵלִי, **'Aśrî'êlîy**, *as-ree-ale-ee´*; patronymic from 844; an *Asrielite* (collective) or descendants of Asriel:—Asrielites.

846. אֻשַּׁרְנָא, **'ushsharnâ'** (Chaldee), *oosh-ar-naw´*; from a root corresponding to 833; a *wall* (from its uprightness):—wall.

847. אֶשְׁתָּאֹל, **'Eshtâ'ôl**, *esh-taw-ole´*; or אֶשְׁתָּאוֹל, **'Eshtâ'ôwl**, *esh-taw-ole´*; probably from 7592; *intreaty*; *Eshtaol*, a place in Palestine:—Eshtaol.

848. אֶשְׁתָּאֻלִי, **'Eshtâ'ulîy**, *esh-taw-oo-lee´*; patrial from 847; an *Eshtaolite* (collectively) or inhabitant of Eshtaol:—Eshtaulites.

849. אֶשְׁתַּדּוּר, **'eshtaddûwr** (Chaldee), *esh-tad-dure´*; from 7712 (in a bad sense); *rebellion*:—sedition.

850. אֶשְׁתּוֹן, **'Eshtôwn**, *esh-tone´*; probably from the same as 7764; *restful*; *Eshton*, an Israelite:—Eshton.

851. אֶשְׁתְּמֹעַ, **'Esht^emôa'**, *esh-tem-o´-ah*; or אֶשְׁתְּמוֹעַ, **'Eshtemôwa'**, *esh-tem-o´-ah*; or אֶשְׁתְּמֹה, **'Eshtemôh**, *esh-tem-o´*; from 8085 (in the sense of *obedience*); *Eshtemoa* or *Eshtemoh*, a place in Palestine:—Eshtemoa, Eshtemoh.

852. אָת, **'âth** (Chaldee), *awth*; corresponding to 226; a *portent*:—sign.

853. אֵת, **'êth**, *ayth*; apparently contracted from 226 in the demonstrative sense of *entity*; properly *self* (but generally used to point out more definitely the object of a verb or preposition, *even* or *namely*):—[as such unrepresented in English.]

854. אֵת, **'êth,** *ayth*; probably from 579; properly *nearness* (used only as a preposition or adverb), *near*; hence generally *with, by, at, among*, etc.:— against, among, before, by, for, from, in (-to), (out) of, with. Often with another preposition prefixed.

855. אֵת, **'êth,** *ayth*; of uncertain derivation; a *hoe* or other digging implement:—coulter, plowshare.

856. אֶתְבַּעַל, **'Ethba'al,** *eth-bah´-al*; from 854 and 1168; *with Baal*; Ethbaal, a Phoenician king:—Ethbaal.

857. אָתָה, **'âthâh,** *aw-thaw´*; or אָתָא, **'âthâ',** *aw-thaw´*; a primitive root [collaterally to 225 contraction]; to *arrive*:—(be-, things to) come (upon), bring.

858. אֲתָה, **'ăthâh,** *ah-thaw´*; (Chaldee); or אֲתָא, **'ăthâ',** *ah-thaw´*; corresponding to 857:—(be-) come, bring.

859. אַתָּה, **'attâh,** *at-taw´*; or (shortened) אַתָּ, **'attâ,** *at-taw´*; or אַת, **'ath,** *ath*; feminine (irregular) sometimes אַתִּי, **'attîy,** *at-tee´*; plural masculine אַתֶּם, **'attem,** *at-tem´*; feminine אַתֶּן, **'atten,** *at-ten´*; or אַתֵּנָה, **'attênâh,** *at-tay´-naw*; or אַתֵּנָּה, **'attênnâh,** *at-tane´-naw*; a primitive pronoun of the secondary person; *thou* and *thee*, or (plural) *ye* and *you*:—thee, thou, ye, you.

860. אָתוֹן, **'âthôwn,** *aw-thone´*; probably from the same as 386 (in the sense of *patience*); a female *ass* (from its docility):—(she) ass.

861. אַתּוּן, **'attûwn** (Chaldee), *at-toon´*; probably from the corresponding to 784; probably a *fire-place*, i.e. *furnace*:—furnace.

862. אַתּוּק, **'attûwq,** *at-tooke´*; or אַתִּיק, **'attîyq,** *at-teek´*; from 5423 in the sense of *decreasing*; a *ledge* or offset in a building:—gallery.

863. אִתַּי, **'Ittay,** *it-tah´ee*; or אִיתַי, **'îythay,** *ee-thah´ee*; from 854; *near*; *Ittai* or *Ithai*, the name of a Gittite and of an Israelite:—Ithai, Ittai.

864. אֵתָם, **'Êthâm,** *ay-thawm´*; of Egyptian derivation; *Etham*, a place in the Desert:—Etham.

865. אֶתְמוֹל, **'ethmôwl,** *eth-mole´*; or אִתְמוֹל, **'ithmôwl,** *ith-mole´*; or אֶתְמוּל, **'ethmûwl,** *eth-mool´*; probably from 853 or 854 and 4136; *heretofore*; (definite) *yesterday*:— + before (that) time, + heretofore, of late (old), + times past, yester[day].

866. אֶתְנָה, **'ethnâh,** *eth-naw´*; from 8566; a *present* (as the price of harlotry):—reward.

867. אֶתְנִי, **'Ethnîy,** *eth-nee´*; perhaps from 866; *munificence*; Ethni, an Israelite:—Ethni.

868. אֶתְנַן, **'ethnan,** *eth-nan´*; the same as 866; a *gift* (as the price of harlotry or idolatry):—hire, reward.

869. אֶתְנַן, **'Ethnan,** *eth-nan´*; the same as 868 in the sense of 867; *Ethnan*, an Israelite:—Ethnan.

870. אֲתַר, **'ăthar** (Chaldee), *ath-ar´*; from a root corresponding to that of 871; a *place*; (adverb) *after*:—after, place.

871. אֲתָרִים, **'Ăthârîym,** *ath-aw-reem´*; plural from an unused root (probably meaning to *step*); *places*; Atharim, a place near Palestine:—spies.

ב (Beth)

872. בִּאָה, **bi'âh**, *bi-aw´*; from 935; an *entrance* to a building:—entry.

873. בְּאִישׁ, **bî'ysh**, *beesh´*; (Chaldee); from 888; *wicked*:—bad.

874. בָּאַר, **bâ'ar**, *baw-ar´*; a primitive root; to *dig*; by analogy to *engrave*; (figurative) to *explain*:—declare, (make) plain (-ly).

875. בְּאֵר, **be'êr**, *bĕ-ayr´*; from 874; a *pit*; especially a *well*:—pit, well.

876. בְּאֵר, **Be'êr**, *bĕ-ayr´*; the same as 875; *Beër*, a place in the Desert, also one in Palestine:—Beer.

877. בֹּאר, **bô'r**, *bore*; from 874; a *cistern*:—cistern.

878. בְּאֵרָא, **Be'êrâ'**, *bĕ-ay-raw´*; from 875; a *well*; *Beëra*, an Israelite:—Beera.

879. בְּאֵר אֵלִים, **Be'êr 'Êlîym**, *bĕ-ayr´ ay-leem´*; from 875 and the plural of 410; *well of heroes*; *Beër-Elim*, a place in the Desert:—Beer-elim.

880. בְּאֵרָה, **Be'êrâh**, *bĕ-ay-raw´*; the same as 878; *Beërah*, an Israelite:—Beerah.

881. בְּאֵרוֹת, **Be'êrôwth**, *bĕ-ay-rohth´*; feminine plural of 875; *wells*; *Beëroth*, a place in Palestine:—Beeroth.

882. בְּאֵרִי, **Be'êrîy**, *bĕ-ay-ree´*; from 875; *fountained*; *Beëri*, the name of a Hittite and of an Israelite:—Beeri.

883. בְּאֵר לַחַי רֹאִי, **Be'êr la-Chay Rô'îy**, *bĕ-ayr´ lakh-ah´ee ro-ee´*; from 875 and 2416 (with prefix) and 7203; *well of a living* (One) *my Seer*; *Beër-Lachai-Roï*, a place in the Desert:—Beer-lahai-roi.

884. בְּאֵר שֶׁבַע, **Be'êr Sheba‘**, *bĕ-ayr´ sheh´-bah*; from 875 and 7651 (in the sense of 7650); *well of an oath*; *Beër-Sheba*, a place in Palestine:—Beer-shebah.

885. בְּאֵרֹת בְּנֵי־יַעֲקָן, **Be'êrôth Benêy-Ya‘ăqan**, *bĕ-ay-roth´ bĕ-nay´ yah-a-can´*; from the feminine plural of 875, and the plural contraction of 1121, and 3292; *wells of* (the) *sons of Jaakan*; *Beeroth-Bene-Jaakan*, a place in the Desert:—Beeroth of the children of Jaakan.

886. בְּאֵרֹתִי, **Be'êrôthîy**, *bĕ-ay-ro-thee´*; patrial from 881; a *Beërothite* or inhabitant of Beëroth:—Beer-othite.

887. בָּאַשׁ, **bâ'ash**, *baw-ash´*; a primitive root; to *smell* bad; (figurative) to *be offensive* morally:—(make to) be abhorred (had in abomination, loathsome, odious), (cause a, make to) stink (-ing savour), × utterly.

A verb meaning to stink, to be offensive, to be repulsive. It denotes a bad physical smell, like the reeking odor of blood in the Nile River (Ex 7:21) or the odor of spoiled manna (Ex 16:20). In a figurative sense, it speaks of a person who becomes strongly revolting to another, a metaphorical "stench in the nostrils." Jacob worried that his sons' retributive murder of the Shechemites caused him to stink before the people of the land (Ge 34:30). The Israelites fretted that Moses' preaching caused them to be offensive to Pharaoh (Ex 5:21), thus risking their lives. The verb also negatively expresses the actions of the wicked (Pr 13:5); folly (Ecc 10:1); and the stinking of wounds resulting from God's reproof of sin (Ps 38:5[6]).

888. בְּאֵשׁ, **be'êsh**, *bĕ-aysh´*; (Chaldee); corresponding to 887:—displease.

889. בְּאֹשׁ, **be'ôsh**, *bĕ-oshe´*; from 877; a *stench*:—stink.

890. בָּאְשָׁה, **bo'shâh**, *bosh-aw´*; feminine of 889; *stink-weed* or any other noxious or useless plant:—cockle.

891. בְּאֻשִׁים, **be'ushîym**, *bĕ-oo-sheem´*; plural of 889; *poison-berries*:—wild grapes.

892. בָּבָה, **bâbâh,** *baw-baw´*; feminine active participle of an unused root meaning to *hollow* out; something *hollowed* (as a *gate*), i.e. the *pupil* of the eye:—apple [of the eye].

893. בֵּבַי, **Bêbay,** *bay-bah´ee*; probably of foreign origin; *Bebai*, an Israelite:—Bebai.

894. בָּבֶל, **Bâbel,** *baw-bel´*; from 1101; *confusion; Babel* (i.e. Babylon), including Babylonia and the Babylonian empire:—Babel, Babylon.

895. בְּבֵל, **Bâbel,** *baw-bel´*; (Chaldee); corresponding to 894:—Babylon.

896. בַּבְלִי, **Bablîy,** *bab-lee´*; (Chaldee); patrial from 895; a *Babylonian:*—Babylonia.

897. בַּג, **bag,** *bag*; a Persian word; *food:*—spoil [*from the margin for* 957].

898. בָּגַד, **bâgad,** *baw-gad´*; a primitive root; to *cover* (with a garment); (figurative) to *act covertly*; (by implication) to *pillage:*—deal deceitfully (treacherously, unfaithfully), offend, transgress (-or), (depart), treacherous (dealer, -ly, man), unfaithful (-ly, man), × very.

A verb meaning to deal treacherously with, to be traitorous, to act unfaithfully, to betray. The verb connotes unfaithfulness in relationships like marriage (Ex 21:8; Jer 3:20; Mal 2:14); Israel's covenant with the Lord (Ps 78:57; 119:158); friendships (Job 6:15; Jer 3:20; Mal 2:10); leadership (Jgs 9:23).

899. בֶּגֶד, **beged,** *behg´-ed*; from 898; a *covering*, i.e. clothing; also *treachery* or *pillage:*—apparel, cloth (-es, -ing), garment, lap, rag, raiment, robe, × very [treacherously], vesture, wardrobe.

900. בֹּגְדוֹת, **bôgᵉdôwth,** *bohg-ed-ōhth´*; feminine plural active participle of 898; *treacheries:*—treacherous.

901. בָּגוֹד, **bâgôwd,** *baw-gode´*; from 898; *treacherous:*—treacherous.

902. בִּגְוַי, **Bigvay,** *big-vah´ee*; probably of foreign origin; *Bigvai*, an Israelite:—Bigvai.

903. בִּגְתָא, **Bigthâ’,** *big-thaw´*; of Persian derivation; *Bigtha*, a eunuch of Xerxes:—Bigtha.

904. בִּגְתָן, **Bigthân,** *big-thawn´*; or בִּגְתָנָא, **Bigthânâ’,** *big-thaw´-naw*; of similar derivation to 903; *Big-than* or *Bigthana*, a eunuch of Xerxes:—Bigthan, Bigthana.

905. בַּד, **bad,** *bad*; from 909; (properly) *separation*; (by implication) a *part* of the body, *branch* of a tree, *bar* for carrying; (figurative) *chief* of a city; especially (with prepositional prefix) as adverb, *apart, only, besides:*—alone, apart, bar, besides, branch, by self, of each alike, except, only, part, staff, strength.

906. בַּד, **bad,** *bad*; perhaps from 909 (in the sense of *divided* fibres); flaxen *thread* or yarn; hence a *linen* garment:—linen.

907. בַּד, **bad,** *bad*; from 908; a *brag* or *lie*; also a *liar:*—liar, lie.

908. בָּדָא, **bâdâ’,** *baw-daw´*; a primitive root; (figurative) to *invent:*—devise, feign.

909. בָּדַד, **bâdad,** *baw-dad´*; a primitive root; to *divide*, i.e. (reflexive) *be solitary:*—alone.

910. בָּדָד, **bâdâd,** *baw-dawd´*; from 909; *separate*; adverb *separately:*—alone, desolate, only, solitary.

911. בְּדַד, **Bᵉdad,** *bed-ad´*; from 909; *separation*; *Bedad*, an Edomite:—Bedad.

912. בְּדְיָה, **Bêdᵉyâh,** *bay-dĕ-yaw´*; probably shortened for 5662; *servant of Jehovah; Bedejah*, an Israelite:—Bedeiah.

913. בְּדִיל, **bᵉdîyl,** *bed-eel´*; from 914; *alloy* (because *removed* by smelting); (by analogy) *tin:*— + plummet, tin.

914. בָּדַל, **bâdal,** *baw-dal´*; a primitive root; to *divide* (in variation senses literal or figurative, *separate, distinguish, differ, select*, etc.):—(make, put) difference, divide (asunder), (make) separate (self, -ation), sever (out), × utterly.

A verb meaning to separate, to divide, to detach. This word is used most often of the various words that indicate these ideas. It is used both literally and figuratively in two different stems. The first stem is reflexive or passive in its function, and the second is causative. The reflexive sense of the word is used to express Israel's separation of themselves from intermarriage and the abominations and pollution of the nations around them (Ezr 6:21; 10:11) in order to dedicate themselves to the Lord and His Law (Ne 10:28[29]). Its passive usage indicates those being set apart for something (1Ch 23:13) or, in a negative sense, being excluded from something (e.g., from the community of Israel [Ezr 10:8]).

The verb is used most often in its active causative meanings that are the active counterparts to its passive reflexive meanings. Perhaps the most famous example of this is found in the creation story as God produces a separation between light and darkness (Ge 1:4). Just as significant is the distinction He makes between His people Israel and the peoples and nations surrounding them (Le 20:24). The fact that Moses set aside the Levites to administer and to carry out their holy duties is described by this word (Nu 8:14), as is the exclusion of a person from the Israelite community (Dt 29:21[20]). In the religious and ritualistic sphere, this word indicates a sharp division between the holy and unholy (profane) and the clean and unclean (Le 20:25). It also describes priests dividing sacrificial animals into pieces (Le 1:17).

The use of this word by the writer indicates that God desires to make discriminations between this people and the nations, among groups within His own people and within His larger creation, both animate and inanimate. These differences are important to God and are to be observed carefully, especially by His chosen nation.

915. בְּדָל, **bâdâl,** *baw-dawl´*; from 914; a *part*:— piece.

916. בְּדֹלַח, **bᵉdôlach,** *bed-o´-lakh*; probably from 914; something in *pieces*, i.e. *bdellium*, a (fragrant) gum (perhaps *amber*); others a *pearl*:—bdellium.

917. בְּדָן, **Bᵉdân,** *bed-awn´*; probably shortened for 5658; *servile*; *Bedan*, the name of two Israelites:—Bedan.

918. בָּדַק, **bâdaq,** *baw-dak´*; a primitive root; to *gap* open; used only as a denominative from 919; to *mend* a breach:—repair.

919. בֶּדֶק, **bedeq,** *beh´-dek*; from 918; a *gap* or *leak* (in a building or a ship):—breach, + calker.

920. בִּדְקַר, **Bidqar,** *bid-car´*; probably from 1856 with prepositional prefix; *by stabbing*, i.e. *assassin*; *Bidkar*, an Israelite:—Bidkar.

921. בְּדַר, **bᵉdar,** *bed-ar´*; (Chaldee); corresponding by transposition to 6504; to *scatter*:— scatter.

922. בֹּהוּ, **bôhûw,** *bo´-hoo*; from an unused root (meaning to be empty); a *vacuity*, i.e. (superficially) an undistinguishable *ruin*:—emptiness, void.

923. בַּהַט, **bahat,** *bah´-hat*; from an unused root (probably meaning to *glisten*); white *marble* or perhaps *alabaster*:—red [marble].

924. בְּהִילוּ, **bᵉhîylûw,** *bĕ-hee-loo´*; (Chaldee); from 927; a *hurry*; only adverbial *hastily*:—in haste.

925. בָּהִיר, **bâhîyr,** *baw-here´*; from an unused root (meaning to be bright); *shining*:—bright.

926. בָּהַל, **bâhal,** *baw-hal´*; a primitive root; to *tremble* inwardly (or *palpitate*), i.e. (figurative) be (causative *make*) (suddenly) *alarmed* or *agitated*; by implication to *hasten* anxiously:—be (make) affrighted (afraid, amazed, dismayed, rash), (be, get, make) haste (-n, -y, -ily), (give) speedy (-ily), thrust out, trouble, vex.

A verb meaning to be dismayed or terrified. It is sometimes used when a sudden threat conveys great fear (Ex 15:15; 1Sa 28:21). This word can also mean hasten or to be in a hurry (2Ch 26:20; Ecc 8:3).

927. בְּהַל, **bᵉhal,** *bĕ-hal´*; (Chaldee); corresponding to 926; to *terrify, hasten*:—in haste, trouble.

An Aramaic verb meaning to be in a hurry; to be troubled, to be disturbed. It occurs only in the book of Daniel, where it is used of someone in a hurry (Da 2:25; 3:24; 6:19[20]) or someone who is terrified, frightened, or troubled (Da 4:5[2], 19[16]; 5:6, 9; 7:15, 28). In each of these cases, the people are terrified because of a dream or a vision from God.

928. בְּהָלָה, **behâlâh,** *beh-haw-law´*; from 926; *panic, destruction*:—terror, trouble.

A feminine noun meaning dismay, sudden terror, or fright. One of the curses for not obeying the commands of the Lord is sudden terror (Le 26:16). When God makes the new heaven and earth, children will not be doomed to this terror (Isa 65:23). But the people in Jerusalem will be the object of such terror for not remaining faithful to God (Jer 15:8).

929. בְּהֵמָה, **bᵉhêmâh,** *bĕ-hay-maw´*; from an unused root (probably meaning to be *mute*); properly a *dumb* beast; especially any large quadruped or *animal* (often collective):—beast, cattle.

930. בְּהֵמוֹת, **bᵉhêmôwth,** *bĕ-hay-mōhth´*; in form a plural of 929, but really a singular of Egyptian derivation; a *water-ox,* i.e. the *hippopotamus* or Nile-horse:—Behemoth.

931. בֹּהֶן, **bôhen,** *bo´-hen*; from an unused root apparently meaning to *be thick;* the *thumb* of the hand or *great toe* of the foot:—thumb, great toe.

932. בֹּהַן, **Bôhan,** *bo´-han*; an orthographical variation of 931; *thumb; Bohan,* an Israelite:—Bohan.

933. בֹּהַק, **bôhaq,** *bo´-hak*; from an unused root meaning to *be pale;* white *scurf:*—freckled spot.

934. בַּהֶרֶת, **bahereth,** *ba-heh´-reth*; feminine active participle of the same as 925; a *whitish* spot on the skin:—bright spot.

935. בּוֹא, **bôw',** *bo*; a primitive root; to *go* or *come* (in a wide variety of applications):—abide, apply, attain, × be, befall, + besiege, bring (forth, in, into, to pass), call, carry, × certainly, (cause, let, thing for) to come (against, in, out, upon, to pass), depart, × doubtless again, + eat, + employ, (cause to) enter (in, into, -tering, -trance, -try), be fallen, fetch, + follow, get, give, go (down, in, to war), grant, + have, × indeed, [in-]vade, lead, lift [up], mention, pull in, put, resort, run (down), send, set, × (well) stricken [in age], × surely, take (in), way.

936. בּוּז, **bûwz,** *booz*; a primitive root; to *disrespect:*—contemn, despise, × utterly.

937. בּוּז, **bûwz,** *booz*; from 936; *disrespect:*—contempt (-uously), despised, shamed.

938. בּוּז, **Bûwz,** *booz*; the same as 937; *Buz,* the name of a son of Nahor, and of an Israelite:—Buz.

939. בּוּזָה, **bûwzâh,** *boo-zaw´*; feminine passive participle of 936; something *scorned;* an object of *contempt:*—despised.

940. בּוּזִי, **Bûwzîy,** *boo-zee´*; patronymic from 938; a *Buzite* or descendant of Buz:—Buzite.

941. בּוּזִי, **Bûwzîy,** *boo-zee´*; the same as 940, *Buzi,* an Israelite:—Buzi.

942. בַּוַּי, **Bavvay,** *bav-vah´ee*; probably of Persian origin; *Bavvai,* an Israelite:—Bavai.

943. בּוּךְ, **bûwk,** *book*; a primitive root; to *involve* (literal or figurative):—be entangled (perplexed).

944. בּוּל, **bûwl,** *bool*; for 2981; *produce* (of the earth, etc.):—food, stock.

945. בּוּל, **Bûwl,** *bool*; the same as 944 (in the sense of *rain*); *Bul,* the eighth Hebrew month:—Bul.

946. בּוּנָה, **Bûwnâh,** *boo-naw´*; from 995; *discretion; Bunah,* an Israelite:—Bunah.

947. בּוּס, **bûws,** *boos*; a primitive root; to *trample* (literal or figurative):—loath, tread (down, under [foot]), be polluted.

A verb that signifies to tread down, to trample underfoot. This term generally has a negative connotation, implying a destructive action (Zec 10:5). God is often the subject of this verb, when He states that He will trample His enemies (Ps 60:12[14]); Isa 14:25; 63:6). It can also be used with people as the subject but with the understanding that they are only God's instruments (Ps 44:5[6]). This expression can also have a figurative meaning: to reject (Pr 27:7) and to desecrate (Isa 63:18).

948. בּוּץ, **bûwts,** *boots*; from an unused root (of the same form) meaning to *bleach,* i.e. (intransitive) *be white;* probably *cotton* (of some sort):—fine (white) linen.

949. בּוֹצֵץ, **Bôwtsêts,** *bo-tsates´*; from the same as 948; *shining; Botsets,* a rock near Michmash:—Bozez.

950. בּוּקָה, **bûwqâh,** *boo-kaw´*; feminine passive participle of an unused root (meaning to *be hollow*); *emptiness* (as adjective):—empty.

951. בּוֹקֵר, **bôwqêr,** *bo-kare´*; properly active participle from 1239 as denominative from 1241; a *cattletender:*—herdman.

952. בּוּר, **bûwr,** *boor*; a primitive root; to *bore,* i.e. (figurative) *examine:*—declare.

953. בּוֹר, **bôwr,** *bore*; from 952 (in the sense of 877); a pit *hole* (especially one used as a *cistern* or *prison*):—cistern, dungeon, fountain, pit, well.

A masculine noun meaning pit, cistern, well. The term can refer to rock-hewn reservoirs or man-made wells. When empty, such cisterns served as perfect prisons (i.e. Joseph [Ge 37:20, 22, 24, 28, 29] and Jeremiah [Jer 38:6, 7, 9–11, 13]). The semantic range extends to prisons in general. Joseph refers to Pharaoh's dungeon as *bôwr* (Ge 40:15). Figuratively, it carries positive and negative connotations. Positively, it can signify a man's wife (Pr 5:15), and Sarah is the cistern of Israel (Isa 51:1). Negatively, it represents death (Pr 28:17); Sheol (Ps 30:3[4]); exile (Zec 9:11).

954. בּוֹשׁ, **bôsh**, *bosh*; a primitive root; (properly) to *pale*, i.e. by implication to *be ashamed*; also (by implication) to *be disappointed*, or *delayed*:—(be, make, bring to, cause, put to, with, a-) shame (-d), be (put to) confounded (-fusion), become dry, delay, be long.

A verb meaning to be ashamed, to act shamefully, or to put to shame. It is both an external and a subjective experience, ranging from disgrace (Hos 10:6) to guilt (Ezr 9:6). In Ge 2:25, shame is related to the sexual nature of humans. Moreover, to act shamefully is equivalent to acting unwisely (Pr 10:5; 14:35). To be ashamed is to experience distress, as farmers with no harvest (Jer 14:4; Joel 1:11), but the blessing of God means that one will never be put to shame (Ps 25:20; Joel 2:26, 27).

955. בּוּשָׁה, **bûwshâh**, *boo-shaw'*; feminine participle passive of 954; *shame*:—shame.

A feminine noun meaning shame. Although this word is used only four times in the OT, its meaning is clear from an understanding of the verb *bôwsh* (954) meaning to be ashamed, to act shamefully, or to put to shame. This word refers to the shame that came on David during his distress (Ps 89:45[46]), as well as the shame associated with the destruction of an enemy (Mic 7:10); of Edom (Ob 1:10); and of the people in the land of Israel (Eze 7:18).

956. בּיּת, **bîyth**, *beeth*; (Chaldee); apparently denominative from 1005; to *lodge* over night:—pass the night.

957. בַּז, **baz**, *baz*; from 962; *plunder*:—booty, prey, spoil (-ed).

958. בָּזָא, **bâzâ'**, *baw-zaw'*; a primitive root; probably to *cleave*:—spoil.

959. בָּזָה, **bâzâh**, *baw-zaw'*; a primitive root; to *disesteem*:—despise, disdain, contemn (-ptible), + think to scorn, vile person.

960. בָּזֹה, **bâzôh**, *baw-zo'*; from 959; *scorned*:—despise.

961. בִּזָּה, **bizzâh**, *biz-zaw'*; feminine of 957; *booty*:—prey, spoil.

962. בָּזַז, **bâzaz**, *baw-zaz'*; a primitive root; to *plunder*:—catch, gather, (take) for a prey, rob (-ber), spoil, take (away, spoil), × utterly.

963. בִּזָּיוֹן, **bizzâyôwn**, *biz-zaw-yone'*; from 959:—*disesteem*:—contempt.

964. בִּזְיוֹתְיָה, **bizyôwthᵉyâh**, *biz-yo-thĕ-yaw'*; from 959 and 3050; *contempts of Jah*; *Bizjothjah*, a place in Palestine:—Bizjothjah.

965. בָּזָק, **bâzâq**, *baw-zawk'*; from an unused root meaning to *lighten*; a *flash* of lightning:—flash of lightning.

966. בֶּזֶק, **Bezeq**, *beh'-zek*; from 965; *lightning*; *Bezek*, a place in Palestine:—Bezek.

967. בָּזַר, **bâzar**, *baw-zar'*; a primitive root; to *disperse*:—scatter.

968. בִּזְתָא, **Bizzᵉthâ'**, *biz-ze-thaw'*; of Persian origin; *Biztha*, a eunuch of Xerxes:—Biztha.

969. בָּחוֹן, **bâchôwn**, *baw-khone'*; from 974; an *assayer* of metals:—tower.

970. בָּחוּר, **bâchûwr**, *baw-khoor'*; or בָּחֻר, **bâchur**, *baw-khoor'*; participle passive of 977; (properly) *selected*, i.e. a *youth* (often collective):—(choice) young (man), chosen, × hole.

971. בָּחִין, **bachîyn**, *bakh-een'*; another form of 975; a *watch-tower* of besiegers:—tower.

972. בָּחִיר, **bâchîyr**, *baw-kheer'*; from 977; *select*:—choose, chosen one, elect.

973. בָּחַל, **bâchal**, *baw-khal'*; a primitive root; to *loathe*:—abhor, get hastily [*from the margin for 926*].

A verb meaning to abhor or to obtain by greed. This word has two different, unrelated meanings. The first meaning is to abhor and comes from a Syriac word meaning to be nauseated by or to experience disgust with. It is used only in Zec 11:8 to refer to the flock who abhorred the shepherd. The second meaning, to obtain by greed, comes from an Arabic word with a similar meaning. This word only appears in Pr 20:21. However, a textual problem exists, and some people read the verse with the Hebrew word *bâhal* (926), meaning to be in haste.

974. בָּחַן, **bâchan,** *baw-khan´*; a primitive root; to *test* (especially metals); (general and figurative) to *investigate:*—examine, prove, tempt, try (trial).

A verb meaning to examine, to try, to prove. This verb can refer to any type of test. Joseph tested his brothers (Ge 42:15, 16); while Job and Elihu indicated that the ear tests words as the palate tastes food (Job 12:11; 34:3), thereby indicating that the hearer should be able to vindicate his or her assertions. However, it generally refers to God's testing of humanity. The psalmist acknowledges this fact (Ps 11:4, 5) and even requests it (Ps 139:23). The biblical writers sometimes compare God's testing to the refining of precious metals, like gold and silver (Job 23:10; Zec 13:9). There are also a few passages in which people test God, but these clearly state that this is not normal (Ps 95:9; Mal 3:10, 15).

975. בַּחַן, **bachan,** *bakh´-an*; from 974 (in the sense of keeping a *look-out*); a watch-*tower:*—tower.

976. בֹּחַן, **bôchan,** *bo´-khan*; from 974; *trial:*—tried.

A masculine noun meaning testing. This word is derived from the verb *bâhan* (974), meaning to examine, try, or prove. The idea is that the testing verifies or authenticates. In Eze 21:13[18], the strength of the sword is verified in its testing. In Isa 28:16, the stone is verified in that it has been tested and proved.

977. בָּחַר, **bâchar,** *baw-khar´*; a primitive root; properly to *try*, i.e. (by implication) *select:*—acceptable, appoint, choose (choice), excellent, join, be rather, require.

A verb whose meaning is to take a keen look at, to prove, to choose. It denotes a choice, which is based on a thorough examination of the situation and not an arbitrary whim. Although this word rarely means to prove, it does communicate that sense in Isa 48:10, where it describes the way God tested Israel in order to make a careful choice: "I have tested

you in the furnace of affliction." In most contexts, the word suggests the concept to choose or to select. It can designate human choice (Ge 13:11; Dt 30:19; Jos 24:15; Jgs 10:14) or divine choice (Dt 7:7; 1Sa 2:28; Ne 9:7; Ps 135:4); however, in either case, it generally has theological overtones. This word can also have the connotations to desire, to like, or to delight in. A good example is Isa 1:29, where the word is in synonymous parallelism with *châmad* (2530), meaning to desire or take pleasure in.

978. בְּחֲרוּמִי, **Bachărûwmîy,** *bakh-ar-oo-mee´*; patrial from 980 (by transposition); a *Bacharumite* or inhabitant of Bachurim:—Baharumite.

979. בְּחֻרוֹת, **bᵉchurôwth,** *bekh-oo-rothe´*; or בְּחוּרוֹת, **bechûw-rôwth,** *bekh-oo-roth´*; feminine plural of 970; also (masculine plural) רִים, בֶּח, **bechurîym,** *bekh-oo-reem´*; *youth* (collective and abstract):—young men, youth.

980. בְּחֻרִים, **Bachurîym,** *bakh-oo-reem´*; or רִים, בֶּחוּ, **Bachûw-rîym,** *bakh-oo-reem´*; masculine plural of 970; *young men; Bachurim,* a place in Palestine:—Bahurim.

981. בָּטָא, **bâṭâ´,** *baw-taw´*; or בָּטָה, **bâṭâh,** *baw-taw´*; a primitive root; to *babble*; hence to *vociferate* angrily:—pronounce, speak (unadvisedly).

A verb meaning to speak rashly or thoughtlessly, to babble. It connotes a foolish utterance with an oath spoken thoughtlessly or flippantly (Le 5:4).

982. בָּטַח, **bâṭach,** *baw-takh´*; a primitive root; (properly) to *hie* for refuge [but not so *precipitately* as 2620]; (figurative) to *trust*, be *confident* or *sure:*—be bold (confident, secure, sure), careless (one, woman), put confidence, (make to) hope, (put, make to) trust.

A verb indicating to trust, to be confident. It expresses the feeling of safety and security that is felt when one can rely on someone or something else. It is used to show trust in God (2Ki 18:5; Ps 4:5[6]; Jer 49:11); in other people (Jgs 9:26; 20:36; Isa 36:5, 6, 9); or in things (Ps 44:6[7]; Jer 7:4; Hab 2:18). In addition, this expression can also relate to the state of being confident, secure, without fear (Jgs 18:7, 10, 27; Job 11:18; Pr 28:1).

983. בֶּטַח, **betach,** *beh´-takh*; from 982; (properly) a place of *refuge*; (abstract) *safety*, both the fact (*security*) and the feeling (*trust*); often (adverb with or without preposition) *safely*:— assurance, boldly, (without) care (-less), confidence, hope, safe (-ly, -ty), secure, surely.

A masculine noun or adjective meaning security. As a noun, it primarily means security or calm assurance (Ge 34:25; Isa 32:17). As an adjective, it means assurance or confidence. It is primarily a positive term: to dwell in safety because of God's protection (Le 25:18); to lie down safely or in security (Hos 2:18[20]); to walk securely or assuredly (Pr 10:9). In other instances, it is a negative term meaning to be too self-assured or careless (Eze 30:9; 39:6).

984. בֶּטַח, **Betach,** *beh´-takh*; the same as 983; *Betach*, a place in Syria:—Betah.

985. בִּטְחָה, **bitchâh,** *bit-khaw´*; feminine of 984; *trust*:—confidence.

A feminine noun meaning trust, confidence. It is used only in Isa 30:15 where this trust was to characterize the people of God. Used as such, it explicates a key theme of Isaiah's theology: true belief in God should be exhibited by implicit trust (confidence) in Him (cf. Isa 26:3, 4). The people of God, even in their sinful failure, should glorify Him by quiet trust instead of reliance on self-stratagems and other powers (cf. Isa 7:4). This confident trust would bring divine strength and salvation. The failure to trust could only provoke judgment (cf. Isa 31:1). Such trust or confidence as indicative of belief is echoed throughout the OT, particularly in the Psalms.

986. בִּטָּחוֹן, **bittâchôwn,** *bit-taw-khone´*; from 982; *trust*:—confidence, hope.

A masculine noun meaning trust or hope. It is used to signify Hezekiah's trust in God when Jerusalem was under siege (2Ki 18:19); or the hope that living people possess (Ecc 9:4).

987. בַּטֻּחוֹת, **battuchôwth,** *bat-too-khōth´*; feminine plural from 982; *security*:—secure.

A feminine plural noun meaning security, safety. Its only occurrence is Job 12:6.

988. בָּטֵל, **bâtal,** *baw-tal´*; a primitive root; to *desist* from labour:—cease.

989. בְּטֵל, **bᵉtêl,** *bet-ale´*; (Chaldee); corresponding to 988; to *stop*:—(cause, make to), cease, hinder.

990. בֶּטֶן, **beten,** *beh´-ten*; from an unused root probably meaning to be hollow; the *belly*, especially the *womb*; also the *bosom* or *body* of anything:—belly, body, + as they be born, + within, womb.

A feminine noun meaning belly, womb, inner body, rounded projection. With perhaps the general meaning of inside, *beten* often refers to the physical belly. It also frequently refers to the womb, where it is at times significantly linked with God's sovereign care, comfort, and the calling of His elect (Ps 22:9[10]; 139:13; Isa 44:2; 49:1; Jer 1:5). Defined as womb, the Hebrew word is sometimes used with the word *rechem*, also meaning womb (7358). First Kings 7:20 uses the word to refer to a rounded projection of a temple pillar. In a figurative sense, *beten* means the inner being of a person. Ancient wisdom literature pictured the belly, or inmost part, as the place where thoughts were treasured and the spiritual being expressed itself and was satisfied (Job 32:18; Pr 20:27).

991. בֶּטֶן, **Beten,** *beh´-ten*; the same as 990; *Beten*, a place in Palestine:—Beten.

992. בָּטְנָה, **botnâh,** *bot´-nah*; from 990; (only in plural) a *pistachio* nut (from its form):—nut.

993. בְּטֹנִים, **Betônîym,** *bet-o-neem´*; probably plural from 992; *hollows; Betonim*, a place in Palestine:—Betonim.

994. בִּי, **bîy,** *bee*; perhaps from 1158 (in the sense of *asking*); (properly) a *request*; used only adverbially (always with "my Lord"); *Oh that!*; *with leave,* or *if it please*:—alas, O, oh.

995. בִּין, **bîyn,** *bene*; a primitive root; to *separate* mentally (or *distinguish*), i.e. (general) *understand*:—attend, consider, be cunning, diligently, direct, discern, eloquent, feel, inform, instruct, have intelligence, know, look well to, mark, perceive, be prudent, regard, (can) skill (-ful), teach, think, (cause, make to, get, give, have) understand (-ing), view, (deal) wise (-ly, man).

A verb meaning to discern, to perceive, to observe, to pay attention to, to be intelligent, to be discreet, to understand; in the causative sense, to give understanding, to teach; in the reflexive sense, to consider diligently. People can perceive by means of their senses: eyes (Pr 7:7); ears (Pr 29:19); touch (Ps 58:9[10]); taste (Job 6:30). But actual discerning is not assured. Those who hear do not always understand (Da 12:8). In the final analysis, only God gives and conceals understanding (Isa 29:14).

996. בֵּין, **bayin,** *ba-yin´*; (sometimes in the plural masculine or feminine); (properly) the constructive contraction form of an otherwise unused noun from 995; a *distinction*; but used only as a preposition, *between* (repeated before each noun, often with other particles); also as a conjunction, *either … or:*—among, asunder, at, between (-twixt … and), + from (the widest), × in, out of, whether (it be … or), within.

997. בֵּין, **bêyn,** *bane*; (Chaldee); corresponding to 996:—among, between.

998. בִּינָה, **bîynâh,** *bee-naw´*; from 995; *understanding*:—knowledge, meaning, × perfectly, understanding, wisdom.

A feminine noun meaning understanding, comprehension, discernment, righteous action. The word is found mainly in wisdom literature, the Psalms, in several of the major prophets, and 1 and 2 Chronicles. In nearly all the literary contexts in the Bible where it occurs with these basic meanings, it carries strong moral and religious connotations. In Job 28:28, the act of turning away from evil was said to be understanding and was based on a prior proper discernment of what was evil. A lack of this kind of understanding was morally culpable and resulted in sin and even drove away God's compassion for persons who did not have it (Isa 27:11). Happily, understanding as a moral or religious entity can be acquired (Pr 4:5, 7) and even increased (Isa 29:24) by seeking after it diligently. The understanding that God desires has a cognitive dimension, therefore, as further illustrated when the author of Proverbs spoke of words of "understanding" (Pr 1:2). The understanding and discernment that is the object of all knowing is the knowledge of the Holy One (Pr 9:10). Understanding is to mark God's people. It is not surprising, therefore, to learn that by means of understanding, God made all His created order (cf. Ps 136:5).

God has graciously endowed human beings with the ability of understanding and compre-hension, but this faculty is not infallible, and, therefore, we are to ask God for guidance at all times (Pr 3:5). Our own ability of understanding should, however, function to give us discernment, for instance, in showing a proper attitude toward seeking the riches of this world (Pr 23:4). Our understanding is also the ability that enables us to understand languages (Isa 33:19), literature, visions, and dreams (Da 1:20). It is the ability that decodes the symbols of communication for us. The writer of Proverbs personifies understanding along with wisdom in the famous wisdom chapter of Proverbs (Pr 2:3; 8:14).

999. בִּינָה, **bîynâh,** *bee-naw´*; (Chaldee); corresponding to 998:—knowledge.

An Aramaic feminine noun meaning understanding. The Hebrew root for this word means to distinguish, to separate, to perceive. Therefore, this word carries the idea of discernment, as one separates the truth from lies (Da 2:21).

1000. בֵּיצָה, **bêytsâh,** *bay-tsaw´*; from the same as 948; an *egg* (from its whiteness):—egg.

1001. בִּירָה, **bîyrâh,** *bee-rah´*; (Chaldee); corresponding to 1002; a *palace*:—palace.

1002. בִּירָה, **bîyrâh,** *bee-raw´*; of foreign origin; a *castle* or *palace*:—palace.

1003. בִּירָנִיּוֹת, **bîyrânîyyoth,** *bee-raw-nee-yoth´*; from 1002; a *fortress*:—castle.

1004. בַּיִת, **bayith,** *bah´-yith*; probably from 1129 abbreviation; a *house* (in the greatest variation of applications, especially *family*, etc.):—court, daughter, door, + dungeon, family, + forth of, × great as would contain, hangings, home[born], [winter] house (-hold), inside (-ward), palace, place, + prison, + steward, + tablet, temple, web, + within (-out).

A noun meaning house, dwelling, family, temple, palace. It is used basically to denote a building in which a family lives (Dt 20:5) but can also refer to the family or household itself (Ge 15:2; Jos 7:14; 24:15). It often is used of a clan such as "house of Aaron" (Ps 115:10, 12; 118:3). Sometimes it means palace or dynasty when employed in the Hebrew phrase "house of the king" (Ge 12:15; 1Ki 4:6; Jer 39:8). When the OT speaks of the house of the Lord, it obviously refers to the Temple or tabernacle (Ex

23:19; Da 1:2). The word is also found in place names: Bethel, meaning "house of God" (Ge 12:8); Beth-shemesh, meaning "house of the sun" (Jos 15:10); and Bethlehem, meaning "house of bread" (Ge 35:19).

1005. בַּיִת, **bayith,** *bah-yith*; (Chaldee); corresponding to 1004:—house.

1006. בַּיִת, **Bayith,** *bah´-yith*; the same as 1004; *Bajith*, a place in Palestine:—Bajith.

1007. בֵּית אָוֶן, **Bêyth 'Âven,** *bayth aw´-ven*; from 1004 and 205; *house of vanity; Beth-Aven*, a place in Palestine:—Beth-aven.

1008. בֵּית־אֵל, **Bêyth-'Êl,** *bayth-ale´*; from 1004 and 410; *house of God; Beth-El*, a place in Palestine:—Beth-el.

1009. בֵּית אַרְבֵּאל, **Bêyth 'Arbê'l,** *bayth ar-bale´*; from 1004 and 695 and 410; *house of God's ambush; Beth-Arbel*, a place in Palestine:—Beth-Arbel.

1010. בֵּית בַּעַל מְעוֹן, **Bêyth Ba'al Me'ôwn,** *bayth bah´-al me-own´*; from 1004 and 1168 and 4583; *house of Baal* of (the) *habitation of* [apparently by transposition]; or (shorter) מְעוֹן בֵּית, **Bêyth Me'ôwn,** *bayth me-own´*; *house of habitation of* (Baal); *Beth-Baal-Meön*, a place in Palestine:—Beth-baal-meon. Compare 1136 and 1194.

1011. בֵּית בִּרְאִי, **Bêyth Bir'îy,** *bayth bir-ee´*; from 1004 and 1254; *house of a creative* one; *Beth-Biri*, a place in Palestine:—Beth-birei.

1012. בֵּית בָּרָה, **Bêyth Bârâh,** *bayth baw-raw´*; probably from 1004 and 5679; *house of* (the) *ford; Beth-Barah*, a place in Palestine:—Beth-barah.

1013. בֵּית־גָּדֵר, **Bêyth-Gâdêr,** *bayth-gaw-dare´*; from 1004 and 1447; *house of* (the) *wall; Beth-Gader*, a place in Palestine:—Beth-gader.

1014. בֵּית גָּמוּל, **Bêyth Gâmûwl,** *bayth gaw-mool´*; from 1004 and the passive participle of 1576; *house of* (the) *weaned; Beth-Gamul*, a place East of the Jordan:—Beth-gamul.

1015. בֵּית דִּבְלָתָיִם, **Bêyth Diblâthayim,** *bayth dib-law-thah´-yim*; from 1004 and the dual of 1690; *house of* (the) *two figcakes; Beth-Diblath-ajim*, a place East of the Jordan:—Beth-diblathaim.

1016. בֵּית־דָּגוֹן, **Bêyth-Dâgôwn,** *bayth-daw-gohn´*; from 1004 and 1712; *house of Dagon; Beth-Dagon*, the name of two places in Palestine:—Beth-dagon.

1017. בֵּית הָאֱלִי, **Bêyth hâ-'Êlîy,** *bayth haw-el-ee´*; patrial from 1008 with the article interposed; a *Beth-elite*, or inhabitant of Bethel:—Bethelite.

1018. בֵּית הָאָצֵל, **Bêyth hâ'êtsel,** *bayth haw-ay´-tsel*; from 1004 and 681 with the article interposed; *house of the side; Beth-ha-Etsel*, a place in Palestine:—Beth-ezel.

1019. בֵּית הַגִּלְגָּל, **Bêyth hag-Gilgâl,** *bayth hag-gil-gawl´*; from 1004 and 1537 with the article interposed; *house of the Gilgal* (or *rolling*); *Beth-hag-Gilgal*, a place in Palestine:—Beth-gilgal.

1020. בֵּית הַיְשִׁימוֹת, **Bêyth ha-Ye shîymôwth,** *bayth hah-yesh-ee-mōth´*; from 1004 and the plural of 3451 with the article interposed; *house of the deserts; Beth-ha-Jeshimoth*, a town East of the Jordan:—Beth-jeshimoth.

1021. בֵּית הַכֶּרֶם, **Bêyth hak-Kerem,** *bayth hak-keh´-rem*; from 1004 and 3754 with the article interposed; *house of the vineyard; Beth-hak-Kerem*, a place in Palestine:—Beth-haccerem.

1022. בֵּית הַלַּחְמִי, **Bêyth hal-Lachmîy,** *bayth hal-lakh-mee´*; patrial from 1035 with the article inserted; a *Beth-lechemite*, or native of Bethlehem:— Bethlehemite.

1023. בֵּית הַמֶּרְחָק, **Bêyth ham-Merchâq,** *bayth ham-mer-khawk´*; from 1004 and 4801 with the article interposed; *house of the breadth; Beth-ham-Merchak*, a place in Palestine:—place that was far off.

1024. בֵּית הַמַּרְכָבוֹת, **Bêyth ham-Markâbôwth,** *bayth ham-mar-kaw-both´*; or (shortened form) בֵּית מַרְכָבוֹת, **Bêyth Mar-kâbôwth,** *mar-kaw-both´*; from 1004 and the plural of 4818 (with or without the article interposed); *place of* (the) *chariots; Beth-ham-Markaboth* or *Beth-Markaboth*, a place in Palestine:—Beth-marcaboth.

1025. בֵּית הָעֵמֶק, **Bêyth hâ'Êmeq,** *bayth haw-Ay´-mek*; from 1004 and 6010 with the article interposed; *house of the valley; Beth-ha-Emek*, a place in Palestine:—Beth-emek.

1026. בֵּית הָעֲרָבָה, **Bêyth hâ-'Ărâbâh,** *bayth haw-ar-aw-baw´;* from 1004 and 6160 with the article interposed; *house of the Desert; Beth-ha-Arabah,* a place in Palestine:—Beth-arabah.

1027. בֵּית הָרָם, **Bêyth hâ-Râm,** *bayth hawrawm´;* from 1004 and 7311 with the article interposed; *house of the height; Beth-ha-Ram,* a place East of the Jordan:—Beth-aram.

1028. בֵּית הָרָן, **Bêyth hâ-Rân,** *bayth haw-rawn´;* probably for 1027; *Beth-ha-Ran,* a place East of the Jordan:—Beth-haran.

1029. בֵּית הַשִּׁטָּה, **Bêyth hash-Shiṭṭâh,** *bayth hash-shit-taw´;* from 1004 and 7848 with the article interposed; *house of the acacia; Beth-hash-Shittah,* a place in Palestine:—Beth-shittah.

1030. בֵּית הַשִּׁמְשִׁי, **Bêyth hash-Shimshîy,** *bayth hash-shim-shee´;* patrial from 1053 with the article inserted; a *Beth-shimshite,* or inhabitant of Bethshe-mesh:—Bethshemite.

1031. בֵּית חָגְלָה, **Bêyth Choglâh,** *bayth choglaw´;* from 1004 and the same as 2295; *house of a partridge; Beth-Choglah,* a place in Palestine:—Beth-hoglah.

1032. בֵּית חוֹרוֹן, **Bêyth Chôwrôwn,** *bayth khorone´;* from 1004 and 2356; *house of hollowness; Beth-Choron,* the name of two adjoining places in Palestine:—Beth-horon.

1033. בֵּית כָּר, **Bêyth Kâr,** *bayth kawr;* from 1004 and 3733; *house of pasture; Beth-Car,* a place in Palestine:—Beth-car.

1034. בֵּית לְבָאוֹת, **Bêyth Lᵉbâ'ôwth,** *bayth leb-aw-ōth´;* from 1004 and the plural of 3833; *house of lionesses; Beth-Lebaoth,* a place in Palestine:—Beth-lebaoth. Compare 3822.

1035. בֵּית לֶחֶם, **Bêyth Lechem,** *bayth leh´-khem;* from 1004 and 3899; *house of bread; Beth-Lechem,* a place in Palestine:—Beth-lehem.

1036. בֵּית לְעַפְרָה, **Bêyth lᵉ'Aphrâh,** *bayth lĕ-af-raw´;* from 1004 and the feminine of 6083 (with preposition interposed); *house to* (i.e. *of*) *dust; Beth-le-Aphrah,* a place in Palestine:—house of Aphrah.

1037. בֵּית מִלּוֹא, **Bêyth Millôw',** *bayth mil-lo;* or בֵּית מִלֹּא, **Bêyth Millô',** *bayth mil-lo´;* from 1004 and 4407; *house of* (the) *rampart; Beth-Millo,* the name of two citadels:—house of Millo.

1038. בֵּית מַעֲכָה, **Bêyth Ma'ăkâh,** *bayth mah-ak-aw´;* from 1004 and 4601; *house of Maakah; Beth-Maakah,* a place in Palestine:—Beth-maachah.

1039. בֵּית נִמְרָה, **Bêyth Nimrâh,** *bayth nimraw´;* from 1004 and the feminine of 5246; *house of* (the) *leopard; Beth-Nimrah,* a place East of the Jordan:—Beth-nimrah. Compare 5247.

1040. בֵּית עֵדֶן, **Bêyth 'Êden,** *bayth ay´-den;* from 1004 and 5730; *house of pleasure; Beth-Eden,* a place in Syria:—Beth-eden.

1041. בֵּית עַזְמָוֶת, **Bêyth 'Azmâveth,** *bayth az-maw´-veth;* from 1004 and 5820; *house of Azmaveth,* a place in Palestine:—Beth-azmaveth. Compare 5820.

1042. בֵּית עֲנוֹת, **Bêyth 'Ănôwth,** *bayth an-ōth´;* from 1004 and a plural from 6030; *house of replies; Beth-Anoth,* a place in Palestine:—Beth-anoth.

1043. בֵּית עֲנָת, **Bêyth 'Ănâth,** *bayth an-awth´;* an orthographical variation for 1042; *Beth-Anath,* a place in Palestine:—Beth-anath.

1044. בֵּית עֵקֶד, **Bêyth 'Êqed,** *bayth ay´-ked;* from 1004 and a derivative of 6123; *house of* (the) *binding* (for sheep-shearing); *Beth-Eked,* a place in Palestine:—shearing house.

1045. בֵּית עֶשְׁתָּרוֹת, **Bêyth 'Ashtârôwth,** *bayth ash-taw-rōth´;* from 1004 and 6252; *house of Ashtoreths; Beth-Ashtaroth,* a place in Palestine:—house of Ashtaroth. Compare 1203, 6252.

1046. בֵּית פֶּלֶט, **Bêyth Peleṭ,** *bayth peh´-let;* from 1004 and 6412; *house of escape; Beth-Palet,* a place in Palestine:—Beth-palet.

1047. בֵּית פְּעוֹר, **Bêyth Pᵉ'ôwr,** *bayth pĕ-ore´;* from 1004 and 6465; *house of Peor; Beth-Peor,* a place East of the Jordan:—Beth-peor.

1048. בֵּית פַּצֵּץ, **Bêyth Patstsêts,** *bayth pats-tsates´;* from 1004 and a derivative from 6327; *house of dispersion; Beth-Patstsets,* a place in Palestine:—Beth-pazzez.

1049. בֵּית צוּר, **Bêyth Tsûwr,** *bayth tsoor´*; from 1004 and 6697; *house of* (the) *rock; Beth-Tsur,* a place in Palestine:—Beth-zur.

1050. בֵּית רְחוֹב, **Bêyth Rᵉchôwb,** *bayth rĕkhobe´*; from 1004 and 7339; *house of* (the) *street; Beth-Rechob,* a place in Palestine:—Bethrehob.

1051. בֵּית רָפָא, **Bêyth Râphâ’,** *bayth raw-faw´*; from 1004 and 7497; *house of* (the) *giant; Beth-Rapha,* an Israelite:—Beth-rapha.

1052. בֵּית שְׁאָן, **Bêyth Shᵉ’ân,** *bayth shĕ-awn´*; or also בֵּית שָׁן, **Bêyth Shân,** *bayth shawn´*; from 1004 and 7599; *house of ease; Beth-Shean* or *Beth-Shan,* a place in Palestine:—Beth-shean, Beth-Shan.

1053. בֵּית שֶׁמֶשׁ, **Bêyth Shemesh,** *bayth sheh´-mesh*; from 1004 and 8121; *house of* (the) *sun; Beth-Shemesh,* a place in Palestine:—Bethshemesh.

1054. בֵּית תַּפּוּחַ, **Bayth Tappûwach,** *bayth tappoo´-akh*; from 1004 and 8598; *house of* (the) *apple; Beth-Tappuach,* a place in Palestine:—Beth-tappuah.

1055. בִּיתָן, **bîythân,** *bee-thawn´*; probably from 1004; a *palace* (i.e. *large house*):—palace.

1056. בְּכָא, **Bâkâ’,** *baw-kaw´*; from 1058; *weeping; Baca,* a valley in Palestine:—Baca.

1057. בָּכָא, **bâkâ’,** *baw-kaw´*; the same as 1056; the *weeping* tree (some gum-distilling tree, perhaps the *balsam*):—mulberry tree.

1058. בָּכָה, **bâkâh,** *baw-kaw´*; a primitive root; to *weep*; (generally) to *bemoan*:— × at all, bewail, complain, make lamentation, × more, mourn, × sore, × with tears, weep.

1059. בֶּכֶה, **bekeh,** *beh´-keh*; from 1058; a *weeping*:— × sore.

1060. בְּכוֹר, **bᵉkôwr,** *bek-ore´*; from 1069; *first-born*; hence *chief*:—eldest (son), firstborn (-ling).

1061. בִּכּוּרִים, **bikkûwrîym,** *bik-koo-reem´*; from 1069; the *first-fruits* of the crop:—first fruit (-ripe [figurative]), hasty fruit.

1062. בְּכוֹרָה, **bᵉkôwrâh,** *bek-o-raw´*; or (shortened) בְּכֹרָה, **bᵉkôrâh,** *bek-o-raw´*; feminine of 1060; the *firstling* of man or beast; abstract *primogeniture*:—birthright, firstborn (-ling).

1063. בִּכּוּרָה, **bikkûwrâh,** *bik-koo-raw´*; feminine of 1061; (figurative) the *early*:—firstripe (fruit).

1064. בְּכוֹרַת, **Bᵉkôwrath,** *bek-o-rath´*; feminine of 1062; *primogeniture; Bekorath,* an Israelite:—Bechorath.

1065. בְּכִי, **bᵉkîy,** *bek-ee´*; from 1058; a *weeping*; by analogy, a *dripping*:—overflowing, × sore, (continual) weeping, wept.

1066. בֹּכִים, **Bôkîym,** *bo-keem´*; plural active participle of 1058; (with the article) the *weepers; Bokim,* a place in Palestine:—Bochim.

1067. בְּכִירָה, **bᵉkîyrâh,** *bek-ee-raw´*; feminine from 1069; the *eldest* daughter:—firstborn.

1068. בְּכִית, **bᵉkîyth,** *bek-eeth´*; from 1058; a *weeping*:—mourning.

1069. בָּכַר, **bâkar,** *baw-kar´*; a primitive root; (properly) to *burst the womb,* i.e. (causative) *bear* or *make early fruit* (of woman or tree); also (as denominative from 1061) to *give the birthright*:—make firstborn, be firstling, bring forth first child (new fruit).

1070. בֶּכֶר, **bêker,** *bee´-ker*; from 1069 (in the sense of *youth*); a young *camel*:—dromedary.

1071. בֶּכֶר, **Beker,** *beh´-ker*; the same as 1070; *Beker,* the name of two Israelites:—Becher.

1072. בִּכְרָה, **bikrâh,** *bik-raw´*; feminine of 1070; a young *she-camel*:—dromedary. בִּכְרָה, **bᵉkôrâh.** See 1062.

1073. בַּכֻּרָה, **bakkurâh,** *bak-koo-raw´*; by orthographical variation for 1063; a *first-ripe* fig:—first-ripe.

1074. בֹּכְרוּ, **Bôkᵉrûw,** *bo-ker-oo´*; from 1069; *first-born; Bokeru,* an Israelite:—Bocheru.

1075. בִּכְרִי, **Bikrîy,** *bik-ree´*; from 1069; *youthful; Bikri,* an Israelite:—Bichri.

1076. בַּכְרִי, **Bakrîy,** *bak-ree´*; patronymic from 1071; a *Bakrite* (collective) or descendants of Beker:—Bachrites.

1077. בַּל, **bal,** *bal*; from 1086; (properly) a *failure*; (by implication) *nothing*; usually (adverbial) not at all; also *lest*:—lest, neither, no, none (that …), not (any), nothing.

1078. בֵּל, **Bêl,** *bale*; by contraction for 1168; *Bel,* the Baal of the Babylonians:—Bel.

1079. בַּל, **bâl,** *bawl*; (Chaldee); from 1080; (properly) *anxiety,* i.e. (by implication) the *heart* (as its seat):—heart.

An Aramaic noun which means heart, mind. There is only one occurrence of this word in Scripture (Da 6:14[15], NKJV), where King Darius "set his heart on Daniel." The phrase expresses the concern the king had for Daniel.

1080. בְּלָא, **bᵉlâ',** *bel-aw'*; (Chaldee); corresponding to 1086 (but used only in a mental sense); to *afflict*:—wear out.

1081. בַּלְאֲדָן, **Bal'ădân,** *bal-ad-awn'*; from 1078 and 113 (contracted); *Bel* (is his) *lord; Baladan,* the name of a Babylonian prince:—Baladan.

1082. בָּלַג, **bâlag,** *baw-lag'*; a primitive root; to *break off* or *loose* (in a favourable or unfavourable sense), i.e. *desist* (from grief) or *invade* (with destruction):—comfort, (recover) strength (-en).

1083. בִּלְגָּה, **Bilgâh,** *bil-gaw'*; from 1082; *desistance; Bilgah,* the name of two Israelites:—Bilgah.

1084. בִּלְגַּי, **Bilgay,** *bil-gah'ee*; from 1082; *desistant; Bilgai,* an Israelite:—Bilgai.

1085. בִּלְדַּד, **Bildad,** *bil-dad'*; of uncertain derivation; *Bildad,* one of Job's friends:—Bildad.

1086. בָּלָה, **bâlâh,** *baw-law'*; a primitive root; to *fail*; (by implication) to *wear out, decay* (causative *consume, spend*):—consume, enjoy long, become (make, wax) old, spend, waste.

1087. בָּלֶה, **bâleh,** *baw-leh'*; from 1086; *worn out*:—old.

1088. בָּלָה, **Bâlâh,** *baw-law'*; feminine of 1087; *failure; Balah,* a place in Palestine:—Balah.

1089. בָּלַהּ, **bâlah,** *baw-lah*; a primitive root [rather by transposition for 926]; to *palpitate*; hence (causative) to *terrify*:—trouble.

1090. בִּלְהָה, **Bilhâh,** *bil-haw'*; from 1089; *timid; Bilhah,* the name of one of Jacob's concubines; also of a place in Palestine:—Bilhah.

1091. בַּלָּהָה, **ballâhâh,** *bal-law-haw'*; from 1089; *alarm;* hence *destruction*:—terror, trouble.

1092. בִּלְהָן, **Bilhân,** *bil-hawn'*; from 1089; *timid; Bilhan,* the name of an Edomite and of an Israelite:—Bilhan.

1093. בְּלוֹ, **bᵉlôw,** *bel-o'*; (Chaldee); from a root corresponding to 1086; *excise* (on articles consumed):—tribute.

1094. בְּלוֹא, **bᵉlôw',** *bel-o'*; or (fully) בְּלוֹי, **bᵉlôwy,** *bel-o'ee*; from 1086; (only in plural construct) *rags*:—old.

1095. בֵּלְטְשַׁאצַּר, **Bêltᵉsha'tstsar,** *bale-tesh-ats-tsar'*; of foreign derivation; *Beltshatstsar,* the Babylonian name of Daniel:—Belteshazzar.

1096. בֵּלְטְשַׁאצַּר, **Bêltᵉsha'tstsar,** *bale-tesh-ats-tsar'*; (Chaldee); corresponding to 1095:—Belteshazzar.

1097. בְּלִי, **bᵉlîy,** *bel-ee'*; from 1086; (properly) *failure,* i.e. *nothing* or *destruction;* usually (with preposition) *without, not yet, because not, as long as,* etc.:—corruption, ig[norantly], for lack of, where no … is, so that no, none, not, un[awares], without.

1098. בְּלִיל, **bᵉlîyl,** *bel-eel'*; from 1101; *mixed,* i.e. (specific) *feed* (for cattle):—corn, fodder, provender.

1099. בְּלִימָה, **bᵉlîymâh,** *bel-ee-mah'*; from 1097 and 4100; (as indefinite) *nothing whatever*:—nothing.

1100. בְּלִיַּעַל, **bᵉlîyya'al,** *bel-e-yah'-al*; from 1097 and 3276; *without profit, worthlessness;* (by extension) *destruction, wickedness* (often in connection with 376, 802, 1121, etc.):—Belial, evil, naughty, ungodly (men), wicked.

A masculine noun of unknown origin meaning worthlessness. Often a strong moral component in the context suggests the state of being good for nothing and therefore expresses the concept of wickedness (Job 34:18; Pr 6:12; Na 1:11). It is always used in reference to persons with only two exceptions, once for a disease and once for a nonspecific thing (Ps 41:8[9]; 101:3). The term is applied to the hard-hearted (Dt 15:9; 1Sa 30:22); perjurers (1Ki 21:13; Pr 19:28); and those promoting rebellion against a king's authority (2Sa 20:1; 2Ch 13:7) or God's authority (Dt 13:13[14]). This word was not treated as a proper name by the Septuagint translators of the OT, but it does appear in its Greek form as a name for the devil in the Dead Sea scrolls and in the NT (cf. 2Co 6:15).

1101. בָּלַל, **bâlal,** *baw-lal´*; a primitive root; to *overflow* (specifically with oil); (by implication) to *mix*; also (denominative from 1098) to *fodder*:—anoint, confound, × fade, mingle, mix (self), give provender, temper.

A verb meaning to mix, to mingle, to tangle, to confuse, to bewilder, to perplex, to anoint. The word is often used in a technical sense to signify the mixing of oil with the fine flour used to bake cakes without yeast that were then presented as grain offerings (Le 2:4; 14:21). Similarly, oil was mixed with fine wheat flour to bake wafers without yeast in a sacrificial setting (Ex 29:2). Sometimes oil was simply mingled with fine flour itself as part of a drink offering (Ex 29:40). While these food items readily combined with positive results, the verb can also indicate confusion, bewilderment, or perplexity. The language of the whole earth was confused by the Lord at the tower of Babel so that people could not understand each other (Ge 11:9).

Since the verb could mean to moisten or to dampen when used in the technical sacrificial examples noted above, it is a reasonable extension of that usage to the anointing of a person with oil. This usage is found (Ps 92:10[11]) where the psalmist rejoiced that he was anointed with fine oils.

The verb is used one time also to indicate the feeding of donkeys, (i.e. providing fodder for the animal to eat [Jgs 19:21]), but in this case, the verb is probably from a different original root.

1102. בָּלַם, **bâlam,** *baw-lam´*; a primitive root; to *muzzle*:—be held in.

1103. בָּלַס, **bâlas,** *baw-las´*; a primitive root; to *pinch* sycamore figs (a process necessary to ripen them):—gatherer.

1104. בָּלַע, **bâla',** *baw-lah´*; a primitive root; to *make away with* (specifically by *swallowing*); generally to *destroy*:—cover, destroy, devour, eat up, be at end, spend up, swallow down (up).

A verb meaning to swallow or engulf. The literal meaning of this word is to swallow, as a person swallows a fig (Isa 28:4) or as the great fish swallowed Jonah (Jnh 1:17[2:1]). It further describes how the earth consumed Pharaoh's army (Ex 15:12) and the rebellious Israelites (Nu 16:32); and a consuming destruction that comes on people (2Sa 17:16; Job 2:3; Ps 21:9[10]); cities (2Sa 20:19); or nations (La 2:5).

1105. בֶּלַע, **bela',** *beh´-lah*; from 1104; a *gulp*; (figurative) *destruction*:—devouring, that which he hath swallowed up.

A masculine noun meaning what is swallowed or devoured. This is derived from the verb *bâla'* (1104), meaning to swallow or engulf. It is used only twice in the OT: In Ps 52:4[6], it speaks of "devouring words." In Jer 51:44, the word is used of the things the god Bel has swallowed. In both cases, the word connotes a destructive action.

1106. בֶּלַע, **Bela',** *beh´-lah*; the same as 1105; *Bela*, the name of a place, also an Edomite and of two Israelites:—Bela.

1107. בִּלְעֲדֵי, **bil'ădêy,** *bil-ad-ay´*; or בַּלְעֲדֵי, **bal'ă-dêy,** *bal-ad-ay´*; constructed plural from 1077 and 5703; *not till*, i.e. (as preposition or adverb) *except, without, besides*:—beside, not (in), save, without.

1108. בַּלְעִי, **Bal'îy,** *bel-ee´*; patronymic from 1106; a *Belaite* (collective) or descendants of Bela:—Belaites.

1109. בִּלְעָם, **Bil'âm,** *bil-awm´*; probably from 1077 and 5971; *not (of the) people,* i.e. *foreigner; Bilam,* a Mesopotamian prophet; also a place in Palestine:—Balaam, Bileam.

1110. בָּלַק, **bâlaq,** *baw-lak´*; a primitive root; to *annihilate*:—(make) waste.

1111. בָּלָק, **Bâlâq,** *baw-lawk´*; from 1110; *waster; Balak,* a Moabitish king:—Balak.

1112. בֵּלְשַׁאצַּר, **Bêlsha'tstsar,** *bale-shats-tsar´*; or בֵּלְאשַׁצַּר, **Bêl'shatsar,** *bale-shats-tsar´*; of foreign origin (compare 1095); *Belshatstsar,* a Babylonian king:—Belshazzar.

1113. בֵּלְשַׁאצַּר, **Bêlsha'tstsar,** *bale-shats-tsar´*; (Chaldee); corresponding to 1112:—Belshazzar.

1114. בִּלְשָׁן, **Bilshân,** *bil-shawn´*; of uncertain derivation; *Bilshan,* an Israelite:—Bilshan.

1115. בִּלְתִּי, **biltîy,** *bil-tee´*; constructed female of 1086 (equivalent to 1097); (properly) a *failure of,* i.e. (used only as a negative particle, usually with prepositional prefix) *not, except, without, unless, besides, because not, until,* etc.:— because un[satiable], beside, but, + continual, except, from, lest, neither, no more, none, not, nothing, save, that no, without.

1116. בָּמָה, **bâmâh,** *baw-maw´*; from an unused root (meaning to *be high*); an *elevation:*— height, high place, wave.

A feminine noun meaning high place. This word may refer to a physical high place, like a mountain (Ps 18:33[34]; Hab 3:19); or a place of worship. Although Samuel conducted sacrifices in these locations (1Sa 9:13), they were predominantly places of idol worship, which God hates (Ps 78:58). These high places became symbolic of the idolatry of the Israelites (2Ki 12:3[4]; 14:4; 15:4; Jer 19:5).

1117. בָּמָה, **Bâmâh,** *baw-maw´*; the same as 1116; *Bamah,* a place in Palestine:—Bamah. See also 1120.

1118. בִּמְהָל, **Bimhâl,** *bim-hawl´*; probably from 4107 with prepositional prefix; *with pruning; Bimhal,* an Israelite:—Bimhal.

1119. בְּמוֹ, **beʹmôw,** *bem-o´*; prolonged for prepositional prefix; *in, with, by,* etc.:—for, in, into, through.

1120. בָּמוֹת, **Bâmôwth,** *baw-môth´*; plural of 1116; *heights;* or (fully) בָּמוֹת בַּעַל, **Bâmôwth Baʻal,** *baw-môth´ bah´-al;* from the same and 1168; *heights of Baal; Bamoth* or *Bamoth-Baal,* a place East of the Jordan:—Bamoth, Bamoth-baal.

1121. בֵּן, **bên,** *bane*; from 1129; a *son* (as a *builder* of the family name), in the widest sense (of literal and figurative relationship, including *grandson, subject, nation, quality* or *condition,* etc., [like 1, 251, etc.]):— + afflicted, age, [Ahoh-] [Ammon-] [Hachmon-] [Lev-]ite, [anoint-]ed one, appointed to, (+) arrow, [Assyr-] [Babylon-] [Egypt-] [Grec-]ian, one born, bough, branch, breed, + (young) bullock, + (young) calf, × came up in, child, colt, × common, × corn, daughter, × of first, + firstborn, foal, + very

fruitful, + postage, × in, + kid, + lamb, (+) man, meet, + mighty, + nephew, old, (+) people, + rebel, + robber, × servant born, × soldier, son, + spark, + steward, + stranger, × surely, them of, + tumultuous one, + valiant[-est], whelp, worthy, young (one), youth.

A noun meaning son that occurs almost five thousand times in the OT. Although the most basic meaning and general translation is son, the direct male offspring of human parents (Ge 4:25; 27:32; Isa 49:15), it is more generally a relational term because of its variety of applications. This word can express an adopted child (Ex 2:10); children in general, male and female (Ge 3:16; 21:7; Ex 21:5); descendants, such as grandsons (Jos 22:24, 25, 27; 2Ki 10:30); relative age (Ge 5:32; 17:12; Pr 7:7; SS 2:3); the male offspring of animals (Le 22:28; Dt 22:6, 7; 1Sa 6:7, 10); a member of a guild, order, or class (1Ki 20:35; 1Ch 9:30; Ezr 4:1); a person with a certain quality or characteristic (1Sa 14:52; 2Sa 3:34; 2Ki 14:14). It may also have a gentilic sense and designate a person from a certain place (Ge 17:12; Ps 149:2; Eze 23:15, 17).

1122. בֵּן, **Bên,** *bane*; the same as 1121; *Ben,* an Israelite:—Ben.

1123. בֵּן, **bên,** *bane*; (Chaldee); corresponding to 1121:—child, son, young.

A masculine noun meaning son. This is the Aramaic equivalent of the Hebrew word *bên* (1121), meaning son. Thus, it is only used in the Aramaic sections of the OT (Ezr 4:8—6:18; 7:12–26; Da 2:4—7:28; Jer 10:11). Although it may refer to the offspring of animals (Ezr 6:9), it is used mostly of the sons of particular groups of people: of Israel (Ezr 6:16); of captives (Da 2:25; 5:13; 6:13[14]); of kings (Ezr 6:10; 7:23); of those who accused Daniel (Da 6:24[25]); of people in general (Da 2:38; 5:21).

1124. בְּנָא, **beʹnâ’,** *ben-aw´*; (Chaldee); or בְּנָה, **beʹnâh,** *ben-aw´*; (Chaldee); corresponding to 1129; to *build:*—build, make.

1125. בֶּן־אֲבִינָדָב, **Ben-’Ăbîynâdâb,** *ben-ab-ee´-naw-dawb´*; from 1121 and 40; (the) *son of Abinadab; Ben-Abinadab,* an Israelite:—the son of Abinadab.

1126. בֶּן־אוֹנִי, **Ben-’Ôwnîy,** *ben-o-nee´*; from 1121 and 205; *son of my sorrow; Ben-Oni,* the original name of Benjamin:—Ben-oni.

1127. בֶּן־גֶּבֶר, **Ben-Geber,** *ben-gheh´-ber*; from 1121 and 1397; *son of* (the) *hero; Ben-Geber,* an Israelite:—the son of Geber.

1128. בֶּן־דֶּקֶר, **Ben-Deqer,** *ben-deh´-ker*; from 1121 and a derivative of 1856; *son of piercing* (or *of a lance*); *Ben-Deker,* an Israelite:—the son of Dekar.

1129. בָּנָה, **bânâh,** *baw-naw´*; a primitive root; to *build* (literal and figurative):—(begin to) build (-er), obtain children, make, repair, set (up), × surely.

1130. בֶּן־הֲדַד, **Ben-Hădad,** *ben-had-ad´*; from 1121 and 1908; *son of Hadad; Ben-Hadad,* the name of several Syrian kings:—Ben-hadad.

1131. בִּנּוּי, **Binnûwy,** *bin-noo´ee*; from 1129; *built* up; *Binnui,* an Israelite:—Binnui.

1132. בֶּן־זוֹחֵת, **Ben-Zôwchêth,** *ben-zo-khayth´*; from 1121 and 2105; *son of Zocheth; Ben-Zocheth,* an Israelite:—Ben-zoketh.

1133. בֶּן־חוּר, **Ben-Chûwr,** *ben-khoor´*; from 1121 and 2354; *son of Chur; Ben-Chur,* an Israelite:—the son of Hur.

1134. בֶּן־חַיִל, **Ben-Chayil,** *ben-khah´-yil*; from 1121 and 2428; *son of might; Ben-Chail,* an Israelite:—Ben-hail.

1135. בֶּן־חָנָן, **Ben-Chânân,** *ben-khaw-nawn´*; from 1121 and 2605; *son of Chanan; Ben-Chanan,* an Israelite:—Ben-hanan.

1136. בֶּן־חֶסֶד, **Ben-Chesed,** *ben-kheh´-sed*; from 1121 and 2617; *son of kindness; Ben-Chesed,* an Israelite:—the son of Hesed.

1137. בָּנִי, **Bânîy,** *baw-nee´*; from 1129; *built; Bani,* the name of five Israelites:—Bani.

1138. בֻּנִּי, **Bunnîy,** *boon-nee´*; or (fuller) בּוּנִי, **Bûwnîy,** *boo-nee´*; from 1129; *built; Bunni* or *Buni,* an Israelite:—Bunni.

1139. בְּנֵי־בְרַק, **Beney-Beraq,** *ben-ay´-ber-ak´*; from the plural construct of 1121 and 1300; *sons of lightning, Bene-berak,* a place in Palestine:—Bene-barak.

1140. בִּנְיָה, **binyâh,** *bin-yaw´*; feminine from 1129; a *structure:*—building.

1141. בְּנָיָה, **Benâyâh,** *ben-aw-yaw´*; or (prolonged) בְּנָיָהוּ, **Benâyâhûw,** *ben-aw-yaw´-hoo*; from 1129 and 3050; *Jah has built; Benajah,* the name of twelve Israelites:—Benaiah.

1142. בְּנֵי יַעֲקָן, **Beney Ya'ăqân,** *ben-ay´ yah-ak-awn´*; from the plural of 1121 and 3292; *sons of Yaakan; Bene-Jaakan,* a place in the Desert:—Bene-jaakan.

1143. בֵּנַיִם, **bênayim,** *bay-nah´-yim*; dual of 996; a *double interval,* i.e. the space between two armies:— + champion.

1144. בִּנְיָמִין, **Binyâmîyn,** *bin-yaw-mene´*; from 1121 and 3225; *son of* (the) *right hand; Binjamin,* youngest son of Jacob; also the tribe descended from him, and its territory:—Benjamin.

1145. בֶּן־יְמִינִי, **Ben-yemîynîy,** *ben-yem-ee-nee´*; sometimes (with the article inserted) בֶּן־הַיְמִינִי, **Ben-hayyemînîy,** *ben-hah-yem-ee-nee´*; with 376 inserted (1Sa 9:1) בֶּן־אִישׁ יְמִינִי, **Ben-'îysh Yemîynîy,** *ben-eesh´ yem-ee-nee´*; *son of a man of Jemini;* or shortened (1Sa 9:4; Est 2:5) יְמִינִי אִישׁ **'Îysh Yemîynîy,** *eesh yem-ee-nee´*; *a man of Jemini;* or (1Sa 20:1) simply יְמִינִי **Yemîynîy,** *yem-ee-nee´*; *a Jeminite;* (plural בְּנֵי יְמִינִי **Benay Yemîynîy,** *ben-ay´ yem-ee-nee´*;) patronymic from 1144; a *Benjaminite,* or descendant of Benjamin:—Benjamite, of Benjamin.

1146. בִּנְיָן, **binyân,** *bin-yawn´*; from 1129; an *edifice:*—building.

1147. בִּנְיָן, **binyân,** *bin-yawn´*; (Chaldee); corresponding to 1146:—building.

1148. בְּנִינוּ, **Benîynûw,** *ben-ee-noo´*; probably from 1121 with pronoun suffix; *our son; Beninu,* an Israelite:—Beninu.

1149. בְּנַס, **benas,** *ben-as´*; (Chaldee); of uncertain affinity: to *be enraged:*—be angry.

An Aramaic verb denoting to be angry. This verb is used often in the Aramaic translations but only once in the Hebrew Bible (Da 2:12), where Daniel states that Nebuchadnezzar was angry because his diviners could not reveal to him his dream and its interpretation. It is followed by the phrase *qĕtsaph* (7108) *śaggî'* (7690), meaning he was very angry.

1150. בִּנְעָא, **Bin'â**, *bin-aw´*; or בִּנְעָה **Bin'âh,** *bin-aw´*; of uncertain derivation; *Bina* or *Binah,* an Israelite:—Binea, Bineah.

1151. בֶּן־עַמִּי, **Ben-'Ammîy,** *ben-am-mee´*; from 1121 and 5971 with pronoun suffix; *son of my people; Ben-Ammi,* a son of Lot:—Ben-ammi.

1152. בְּסוֹדְיָה, **Bᵉsôwdᵉyâh,** *bes-o-deh-yaw´*; from 5475 and 3050 with prepositional prefix; *in* (the) *counsel of Jehovah; Besodejah,* an Israelite:—Besodeiah.

1153. בֵּסַי, **Bêsay,** *bays-ah´-ee*; from 947; *domineering; Besai,* one of the Nethinim:—Besai.

1154. בֶּסֶר, **beser,** *beh´-ser*; from an unused root meaning to *be sour;* an *immature* grape:—unripe grape.

1155. בֹּסֶר, **bôser,** *bo´-ser*; from the same as 1154:—sour grape.

1156. בְּעָא, **bᵉâ**', *beh-aw´*; (Chaldee); or בְּעָה, **bᵉâh,** *beh-aw´*; (Chaldee); corresponding to 1158; to *seek* or *ask:*—ask, desire, make [petition], pray, request, seek.

A verb meaning to ask, seek, or request. An Aramaic word found only in Daniel, it connotes the idea to ask, request, or petition (Da 2:18). It also conveys the idea of praying to God or seeking out a person (Da 2:13); asking a person for something (Da 6:7[8]); making other inquiries (Da 7:16); or seeking out a fault (Da 6:4[5]).

1157. בְּעַד, **ba'ad,** *ba-ad´*; from 5704 with prepositional prefix; *in up to* or *over against;* generally *at, beside, among, behind, for,* etc.:—about, at, by (means of), for, over, through, up (-on), within.

1158. בָּעָה, **bâ'âh,** *baw-aw*; a primitive root; to *gush* over, i.e. to *swell;* (figurative) to *desire* earnestly; (by implication) to *ask:*—cause, inquire, seek up, swell out.

A verb which means to cause to swell or boil up; to seek, to ask, to request. This verb describes a swelling of water (Isa 64:2[1]); or a rising of desire or interest (Isa 21:12). In the latter interpretation, the verb is also used in the passive form, to be searched (out), with the implication of being ransacked or plundered. This meaning is evident by the context and by the synonymous parallelism in the following verse, "But how Esau will be ransacked, his hidden treasures pillaged!" (Ob 1:6 NIV).

1159. בָּעוּ, **bâ'ûw,** *baw-oo´*; (Chaldee); from 1156; a *request:*—petition.

A feminine noun meaning petition. An Aramaic term related to *be'â'* (1156), meaning to ask, seek, or request, this word occurs only twice in Scripture, both times in Daniel. It conveys the idea of petition (Da 6:7[8], 13[14]).

1160. בְּעוֹר, **Bᵉ'ôwr,** *beh-ore´*; from 1197 (in the sense of *burning*); a *lamp; Beör,* the name of the father of an Edomitish king; also of that of Balaam:—Beor.

1161. בְּעוּתִים, **bi'ûwthîym,** *be-oo-theme´*; masculine plural from 1204; *alarms:*—terrors.

1162. בֹּעַז, **Bô'az,** *bo´-az*; from an unused root of uncertain meaning; *Boaz,* the ancestor of David; also the name of a pillar in front of the temple:—Boaz.

1163. בָּעַט, **bâ'at,** *baw-at´*; a primitive root; to *trample* down, i.e. (figurative) *despise:*—kick.

1164. בְּעִי, **bᵉ'îy,** *beh-ee´*; from 1158; a *prayer:*—grave.

A masculine noun meaning ruin (heap), against a ruin, entreaty; figuratively, a grave. In its only use in Job 30:24, it is probably best interpreted as an occurrence of the preposition *bᵉ* ("for" or "against") and *'iy* (5856, "ruin"), and should be translated as "against a ruin." However, some have interpreted this word as a derivative of *bâ'âh* (1158) and translated it as "entreaty" or "prayer," or in a derived meaning, "grave." Either translation would fit the context, for both communicate that the outstretched hand of God is present in the midst of destruction. This destroying hand has either brought a person (in this case, Job) to utter ruin or is the very thing against which there is no entreaty or prayer. Job is speaking from the shattered depths of utter personal ruin, where he perceives the hand of God as against him.

1165. בְּעִיר, **bᵉ'îyr,** *beh-ere´*; from 1197 (in the sense of *eating*); cattle:—beast, cattle.

1166. בָּעַל, **bâ'al,** *baw-al´*; a primitive root; to *be master;* hence (as denominative from 1167) to *marry:*—have dominion (over), be husband, marry (-ried, × wife).

A verb meaning to marry, have dominion, or to rule over. In relation to marriage, it refers to marrying a woman (Dt 24:1); or a woman to be married (Pr 30:23). Figuratively, it is used in connection with God's marriage to Israel (Jer

3:14), as well as Judah and Israel's marriage to the daughter of a foreign god (Mal 2:11). Other times, this verb means to have dominion over land (1Ch 4:22) or people (Isa 26:13). Used as a participle, it means to be married to (Ge 20:3).

1167. בַּעַל, **ba'al,** *bah´-al*; from 1166; a *master*; hence a *husband*, or (figurative) *owner* (often used with another noun in modifications of this latter sense):— + archer, + babbler, + bird, captain, chief man, + confederate, + have to do, + dreamer, those to whom it is due, + furious, those that are given to it, great, + hairy, he that hath it, have, + horseman, husband, lord, man, + married, master, person, + sworn, they of.

A masculine singular noun meaning lord, husband, owner, the title of a Canaanite deity (Baal). It can also denote rulers and leaders (Isa 16:8). Commonly, it refers to legally owning something such as an ox or bull (Ex 21:28); house (Ex 22:8[7]); or land (Job 31:38). The word can also describe possessing a quality, attribute, or characteristic like anger (Pr 22:24); wrath (Pr 29:22); hair (2Ki 1:8); appetite (Pr 23:2); wisdom (Ecc 7:12). When Joseph is called a dreamer, he is literally a possessor of dreams (Ge 37:19). Further, the word can connote husband as used of Abraham (Ge 20:3) and elsewhere (Ex 21:3; Dt 22:22). It often refers to the Canaanite deity, generally known as Baal in the OT and other local manifestations (Nu 25:3). Worship of this deity seems to have been common in the Northern Kingdom which is attested in the preponderance of the Baal theophoric element in many proper nouns. The Lord may also have been referred to with this generic term for "lord." But in light of the worship of Baal in the north, Hosea longed for a time when this usage would cease (Hos 2:16[18]).

1168. בַּעַל, **Ba'al,** *bah´-al*; the same as 1167; *Baal*, a Phoenician deity:—Baal, [*plural*] Baalim.

1169. בְּעֵל, **be'êl,** *beh-ale´*; (Chaldee); corresponding to 1167:— + chancellor.

A masculine Aramaic noun meaning lord, master, overlord, owner. It is used in Ezr 4:8, 9, and 17 as an official title for Rehum, a Persian provincial officer, the "chancellor." It corresponds to the Hebrew word *ba'al* (1167), which

also means lord or owner but is used with broader variations in meaning ranging from man, ruler, owner, and husband to the description of false gods.

1170. בַּעַל בְּרִית, **Ba'al Be'rîyth,** *bah´-al bereeth´*; from 1168 and 1285; *Baal of* (the) *covenant; Baal-Berith,* a special deity of the Shechemites:—Baal-berith.

1171. בַּעַל גָּד, **Ba'al Gâd,** *bah´-al gawd*; from 1168 and 1409; *Baal of Fortune; Baal-Gad,* a place in Syria:—Baal-gad.

1172. בַּעֲלָה, **ba'ălâh,** *bah-al-aw´*; feminine of 1167; a *mistress:*—that hath, mistress.

A feminine singular noun meaning lady, owner, or possessor. It is the feminine form of *bâ'al* (1167). The word occurs three times in the Bible, and twice it refers to possessing occult abilities: possessor of ghosts (1Sa 28:7); and spells (Na 3:4).

1173. בַּעֲלָה, **Ba'ălâh,** *bah-al-aw´*; the same as 1172; *Baalah,* the name of three places in Palestine:—Baalah.

1174. בַּעַל הָמוֹן, **Ba'al Hâmôwn,** *bah´-al hawmone´*; from 1167 and 1995; *possessor of a multitude; Baal-Hamon,* a place in Palestine:—Baal-hamon.

1175. בְּעָלוֹת, **Be'âlôwth,** *beh-aw-lōth´*; plural of 1172; *mistresses; Beäloth,* a place in Palestine:—Bealoth, in Aloth [*by mistake for a plural from 5927 with prepositional prefix*].

1176. בַּעַל זְבוּב, **Ba'al Ze'bûwb,** *bah´-al zeb-oob´*; from 1168 and 2070; *Baal of* (the) *Fly; Baal-Zebub,* a special deity of the Ekronites:—Baal-zebub.

1177. בַּעַל חָנָן, **Ba'al Chânân,** *bah´-al khawnawn´*; from 1167 and 2603; *possessor of grace; Baal-Chanan,* the name of an Edomite, also of an Israelite:—Baal-hanan.

1178. בַּעַל חָצוֹר, **Ba'al Châtsôwr,** *bah´-al khawtsore´*; from 1167 and a modification of 2691; *possessor of a village; Baal-Chatsor,* a place in Palestine:— Baal-hazor.

1179. בַּעַל חֶרְמוֹן, **Ba'al Chermôwn,** *bah´-al kher-mone´*; from 1167 and 2768; *possessor of Hermon; Baal-Chermon,* a place in Palestine:—Baal-hermon.

1180. בַּעֲלִי, **Ba'ălîy,** *bah-al-ee´*; from 1167 with pronoun suffix; *my master; Baali,* a symbolical name for Jehovah:—Baali.

1181. בַּעֲלֵי בָּמוֹת, **Ba'ălêy Bâmôwth,** *bah-al-ay´ baw-mōth;* from the plural of 1168 and the plural of 1116; *Baals of* (the) *heights; Baale-Bamoth,* a place East of the Jordan:—lords of the high places.

1182. בְּעֶלְיָדָע, **Be'elyâdâ',** *beh-el-yaw-daw´;* from 1168 and 3045; *Baal has known; Beëljada,* an Israelite:—Beeliada.

1183. בְּעַלְיָה, **Be'alyâh,** *beh-al-yaw´;* from 1167 and 3050; *Jah* (is) *master; Bealjah,* an Israelite:—Bealiah.

1184. בַּעֲלֵי יְהוּדָה, **Ba'ălêy Yehûwdâh,** *bah-al-ay´ yeh-hoo-daw´;* from the plural of 1167 and 3063; *masters of Judah; Baale-Jehudah,* a place in Palestine:—Baale of Judah.

1185. בַּעֲלִיס, **Ba'ălîys,** *bah-al-ece´;* probably from a derivative of 5965 with prepositional prefix; *in exultation; Baalis,* an Ammonitish king:—Baalis.

1186. בַּעַל מְעוֹן, **Ba'al Me'ôwn,** *bah´-al meh-one´;* from 1168 and 4583; *Baal of* (the) *habitation* (of) [compare 1010]; *Baal-Meön,* a place East of the Jordan:—Baal-meon.

1187. בַּעַל פְּעוֹר, **Ba'al Pe'ôwr,** *bah´-al peh-ore´;* from 1168 and 6465; *Baal of Peor; Baal-Peör,* a Moabitish deity:—Baal-peor.

1188. בַּעַל פְּרָצִים, **Ba'al Perâtsîym,** *bah´-al per-aw-tseem´;* from 1167 and the plural of 6556; *possessor of breaches; Baal-Peratsim,* a place in Palestine:—Baal-perazim.

1189. בַּעַל צְפוֹן, **Ba'al Tsephôwn,** *bah´-al tsef-one´;* from 1168 and 6828 (in the sense of *cold*) [according to others an Egyptian form of *Typhon,* the destroyer]; *Baal of winter; Baal-Tsephon,* a place in Egypt:—Baal-zephon.

1190. בַּעַל שָׁלִשָׁה, **Ba'al Shâlishâh,** *bah´-al shaw-lee-shaw´;* from 1168 and 8031; *Baal of Shalishah, Baal-Shalishah,* a place in Palestine:—Baal-shalisha.

1191. בַּעֲלָת, **Ba'ălâth,** *bah-al-awth´;* a modification of 1172; *mistressship; Baalath,* a place in Palestine:—Baalath.

1192. בַּעֲלַת בְּאֵר, **Ba'ălath Be'êr,** *bah-al-ath´ beh-ayr´;* from 1172 and 875; *mistress of a well; Baalath-Beër,* a place in Palestine:—Baalath-beer.

1193. בַּעַל תָּמָר, **Ba'al Tâmâr,** *bah´-al taw-mawr´;* from 1167 and 8558; *possessor of* (the) *palm-tree; Baal-Tamar,* a place in Palestine:—Baal-tamar.

1194. בְּעֹן, **Be'ôn,** *beh-ohn´;* probably a contraction of 1010; *Beön,* a place East of the Jordan:—Beon.

1195. בַּעֲנָא, **Ba'ănâ',** *bah-an-aw´;* the same as 1196; *Baana,* the name of four Israelites:—Baana, Baanah.

1196. בַּעֲנָה, **Ba'ănâh,** *bah-an-aw´;* from a derivative of 6031 with prepositional prefix; *in affliction; Baanah,* the name of four Israelites:—Baanah.

1197. בָּעַר, **bâ'ar,** *baw-ar´;* a primitive root; to *kindle,* i.e. *consume* (by fire or by eating); also (as denominative from 1198) to *be* (-*come*) *brutish:*—be brutish, bring (put, take) away, burn, (cause to) eat (up), feed, heat, kindle, set ([on fire]), waste.

1198. בַּעַר, **ba'ar,** *bah´-ar;* from 1197; (properly) *food* (as *consumed*); i.e. (by extension) of cattle *brutishness;* (concrete) *stupid:*—brutish (person), foolish.

1199. בָּעֲרָא, **Bâ'ărâ',** *bah-ar-aw´;* from 1198; *brutish; Baara,* an Israelite woman:—Baara.

1200. בְּעֵרָה, **be'êrâh,** *bĕ-ay-raw´;* from 1197; a *burning:*—fire.

A feminine singular noun meaning burning. Its only occurrence is in Ex 22:6[5] where it connotes burning offerings.

1201. בַּעְשָׁא, **Ba'shâ',** *bah-shaw´;* from an unused root meaning to *stink; offensiveness; Basha,* a king of Israel:—Baasha.

1202. בַּעֲשֵׂיָה, **Ba'ăsêyâh,** *bah-as-ay-yaw´;* from 6213 and 3050 with prepositional prefix; *in* (the) *work of Jah; Baasejah,* an Israelite:—Baaseiah.

1203. בְּעֶשְׁתְּרָה, **Be'eshterâh,** *beh-esh-ter-aw´;* from 6251 (as singular of 6252) with prepositional prefix; *with Ashtoreth; Beështerah,* a place East of the Jordan:—Beeshterah.

1204. בָּעַת, **bâ‘ath,** *baw-ath´*; a primitive root; to *fear*:—affright, be (make) afraid, terrify, trouble.

A verb meaning to fear, to be or to make afraid, to startle. The basic ideas of this word can be summarized as an individual's realization that he or she is less powerful than someone or something else and can be overcome. An evil spirit tormented Saul (1Sa 16:14, 15), but God is also accused of making people afraid (Job 7:14; 9:34). It is used of humans, as when Haman was terrified (Est 7:6). This word can also mean to fall upon or to overwhelm (Job 3:5; Ps 18:4[5]).

1205. בְּעָתָה, **be‘âthâh,** *beh-aw-thaw´*; from 1204; *fear*:—trouble.

1206. בֹּץ, **bôts,** *botse*; probably the same as 948; *mud* (as *whitish* clay):—mire.

1207. בִּצָּה, **bitstsâh,** *bits-tsaw´*; intensive from 1206; a *swamp*:—fen, mire (-ry place).

1208. בָּצוּר, **bâtsûwr,** *baw-tsoor´*; from 1219; *inaccessible*, i.e. *lofty*:—vintage [*by confusion with* 1210].

1209. בֵּצַי, **Bêtsay,** *bay-tsah´ee*; perhaps the same as 1153; *Betsai*, the name of two Israelites:—Bezai.

1210. בָּצִיר, **bâtsîyr,** *baw-tseer´*; from 1219; *clipped*, i.e. the *grape crop*:—vintage.

1211. בְּצָל, **bâtsâl,** *baw´-tsawl*; from an unused root apparently meaning to *peel*; an *onion*:—onion.

1212. בְּצַלְאֵל, **Betsal'êl,** *bets-al-ale´*; probably from 6738 and 410 with prepositional prefix; *in* (the) *shadow* (i.e. protection) *of God; Betsalel*; the name of two Israelites:—Bezaleel.

1213. בַּצְלוּת, **Batslûwth,** *bats-looth´*; or בַּצְלִית, **Batslîyth,** *bats-leeth´*; from the same as 1211; a *peeling; Batsluth* or *Batslith*; an Israelite:—Bazlith, Bazluth.

1214. בָּצַע, **bâtsa‘,** *baw-tsah´*; a primitive root to *break* off, i.e. (usually) *plunder*; (figurative) to *finish*, or (intrans.) *stop*:—(be) covet (-ous), cut (off), finish, fulfill, gain (greedily), get, be given to [covetousness], greedy, perform, be wounded.

A verb meaning to cut off, to gain by violence. Figuratively, it bears the sense of being destroyed or judged (Job 27:8; Isa 38:12; Jer 51:13). In some cases, it is used to express the dispensing of the Lord's judgment (Isa 10:12; La 2:17). The word also describes taking from someone out of greed (Pr 1:19; Jer 8:10; Eze 22:12).

1215. בֶּצַע, **betsa‘,** *beh´-tsah*; from 1214; *plunder*; (by extension) *gain* (usually unjust):—covetousness, (dishonest) gain, lucre, profit.

1216. בָּצֵק, **bâtsêq,** *baw-tsake´*; a primitive root; perhaps to *swell* up, i.e. *blister*:—swell.

1217. בָּצֵק, **bâtsêq,** *baw-tsake´*; from 1216; *dough* (as *swelling* by fermentation):—dough, flour.

1218. בָּצְקַת, **Botsqath,** *bots-cath´*; from 1216; a *swell* of ground; *Botscath*, a place in Palestine:—Bozcath, Boskath.

1219. בָּצַר, **bâtsar,** *baw-tsar´*; a primitive root; to *clip* off; specifically (as denominative from 1210) to *gather* grapes; also to *be isolated* (i.e. *inaccessible* by height or fortification):—cut off, (de-) fenced, fortify, (grape) gather (-er), mighty things, restrain, strong, wall (up), withhold.

1220. בֶּצֶר, **betser,** *beh´-tser*; from 1219; strictly a *clipping*, i.e. *gold* (as *dug* out):—gold defence.

1221. בֶּצֶר, **Betser,** *beh´-tser*; the same as 1220; an *inaccessible* spot; *Betser*, a place in Palestine; also an Israelite:—Bezer.

1222. בְּצַר, **betsar,** *bets-ar´*; another form for 1220; *gold*:—gold.

1223. בָּצְרָה, **botsrâh,** *bots-raw´*; feminine from 1219; an *enclosure*, i.e. *sheep-fold*:—Bozrah.

1224. בָּצְרָה, **Botsrâh,** *bots-raw´*; the same as 1223; *Botsrah*, a place in Edom:—Bozrah.

1225. בִּצָּרוֹן, **bitstsârôwn,** *bits-tsaw-rone´*; masculine intensive from 1219; a *fortress*:—stronghold.

1226. בַּצֹּרֶת, **batstsôreth,** *bats-tso´-reth*; feminine intensive from 1219; *restraint* (of rain), i.e. *drought*:—dearth, drought.

1227. בַּקְבּוּק, **Baqbûwq,** *bak-book´*; the same as 1228; *Bakbuk*, one of the *Nethinim*:—Bakbuk.

1228. בַּקְבֻּק, **baqbuq,** *bak-book´*; from 1238; a *bottle* (from the gurgling in *emptying*):—bottle, cruse.

1229. בַּקְבֻּקְיָה, **Baqbuqyâh,** *bak-book-yaw´*; from 1228 and 3050; *emptying* (i.e. *wasting) of Jah; Bakbukjah,* an Israelite:—Bakbukiah.

1230. בַּקְבַּקַּר, **Baqbaqqar,** *bak-bak-kar´*; reduplicated from 1239; *searcher; Bakbakkar,* an Israelite:—Bakbakkar.

1231. בֻּקִּי, **Buqqîy,** *book-kee´*; from 1238; *wasteful; Bukki,* the name of two Israelites:—Bukki.

1232. בֻּקִּיָּה, **Buqqîyyâh,** *book-kee-yaw´*; from 1238 and 3050; *wasting of Jah; Bukkijah,* an Israelite:—Bukkiah.

1233. בָּקִיעַ, **bâqîya‘,** *bawk-ee´-ah*; from 1234; a *fissure:*—breach, cleft.

1234. בָּקַע, **bâqa‘,** *baw-kah´*; a primitive root; to *cleave;* (generally) to *rend, break, rip* or *open:*—make a breach, break forth (into, out, in pieces, through, up), be ready to burst, cleave (asunder), cut out, divide, hatch, rend (asunder), rip up, tear, win.

1235. בֶּקַע, **beqa‘,** *beh´-kah*; from 1234; a *section* (half) of a shekel, i.e. a *beka* (a weight and a coin):—bekah, half a shekel.

1236. בִּקְעָא, **biq‘â’,** *bik-aw´*; (Chaldee); corresponding to 1237:—plain.

1237. בִּקְעָה, **biq‘âh,** *bik-aw´*; from 1234; (properly) a *split,* i.e. a wide level *valley* between mountains:—plain, valley.

1238. בָּקַק, **bâqaq,** *baw-kah´*; a primitive root; to *pour* out, i.e. to *empty,* (figurative) to *depopulate;* (by analogy) to *spread* out (as a fruitful vine):—(make) empty (out), fail, × utterly, make void.

1239. בָּקַר, **bâqar,** *baw-kar´*; a primitive root; (properly) to *plough,* or (generally) *break* forth, i.e. (figurative) to *inspect, admire, care for, consider:*—(make) inquire (-ry), (make) search, seek out.

1240. בְּקַר, **beqar,** *bek-ar´*; (Chaldee); corresponding to 1239:—inquire, make search.

1241. בָּקָר, **bâqâr,** *baw-kawr´*; from 1239; a *beeve* or *animal* of the ox kind of either gender (as used for *ploughing*); (collectively) a *herd:*—

beeve, bull (+ -ock), + calf, + cow, great [cattle], + heifer, herd, kine, ox.

1242. בֹּקֶר, **bôqer,** *bo´-ker*; from 1239; (properly) *dawn* (as the *break* of day); (generally) *morning:*—(+) day, early, morning, morrow.

1243. בַּקָּרָה, **baqqârâh,** *bak-kaw-raw´*; intensive from 1239; a *looking after:*—seek out.

1244. בִּקֹּרֶת, **biqqôreth,** *bik-ko´-reth*; from 1239; (properly) *examination,* i.e. (by implication) *punishment:*—scourged.

1245. בָּקַשׁ, **bâqash,** *baw-kash´*; a primitive root; to *search* out (by any method, specifically in worship or prayer); (by implication) to *strive after:*—ask, beg, beseech, desire, enquire, get, make inquisition, procure, (make) request, require, seek (for).

1246. בַּקָּשָׁה, **baqqâshâh,** *bak-kaw-shaw´*; from 1245; a *petition:*—request.

1247. בַּר, **bar,** *bar;* (Chaldee); corresponding to 1121; a *son, grandson,* etc.:— × old, son.

1248. בַּר, **bar,** *bar;* borrowed (as a title) from 1247; the *heir* (apparent to the throne):—son.

1249. בַּר, **bar,** *bar;* from 1305 (in its various senses); *beloved;* also *pure, empty:*—choice, clean, clear, pure.

An adjective meaning pure, clean, radiant. This term is extremely rare and occurs only in the poetic books. The word typically means purity or cleanness of heart (Ps 24:4; 73:1; cf. Job 11:4). This term also describes a clean feeding trough (Pr 14:4). Radiance is ascribed to both the commandments of the Lord and the Shulamite (Ps 19:8[9]; SS 6:10). The only other occurrence of this word also applies to the Shulamite and seems to indicate a select status, but this status is probably based on her purity (SS 6:9).

1250. בָּר, **bâr,** *bawr;* or בַּר, **bar,** *bar;* from 1305 (in the sense of *winnowing*); *grain* of any kind (even while standing in the field); (by extension) the open *country:*—corn, wheat.

1251. בַּר, **bar,** *bar;* (Chaldee); corresponding to 1250; a *field:*—field.

1252. בֹּר, **bôr,** *bore;* from 1305; *purity:*—cleanness, pureness.

A masculine noun indicating cleanness, purity. The connotation is a cleanness or pureness in the spiritual sense rather than the physical. Note the synonymous parallelism between this Hebrew word and *tsedeq* (6664), which means righteousness as the basis for divine reward or recompense (2Sa 22:21, 25; Ps 18:20[21], 24[25]). It occurs only once by itself (2Sa 22:25). It usually occurs with *yâd* (3027), meaning hand (2Sa 22:21; Ps 18:20[21], 24[25]), or *kaph* (3709), meaning palm (Job 9:30; 22:30).

1253. בֹּר, **bôr**, *bore*; the same as 1252; vegetable *lye* (from its *cleansing*); used as a *soap* for washing, or a *flux* for metals:— × never so, purely.

1254. בָּרָא, **bârâ'**, *baw-raw'*; a primitive root; (absolute) to *create*; (qualified) to *cut down* (a wood), *select, feed* (as formative processes):— choose, create (creator), cut down, dispatch, do, make (fat).

A verb meaning to create. Only God is the subject of this verb. It is used for His creating: heaven and earth (Ge 1:1); humanity (Ge 1:27); the heavenly host (Isa 40:26); the ends of the earth (40:28); north and south (Ps 89:12[13]); righteousness; salvation (Isa 45:8); evil (Isa 45:7). David asked God to "create" in him a clean heart (Ps 51:10[12]). Isaiah promised that God will create a new heaven and earth (Isa 65:17).

There are other roots that are spelled the same, but have different meanings. These include: to make fat (1Sa 2:29); to clear timber (Jos 17:15, 18; Eze 23:47); and to choose (Eze 21:19[24], KJV).

1255. בְּרֹאדַךְ בַּלְאֲדָן, **Berô'dak Bal'ădân**, *ber-o-dak' bal-ad-awn'*; a variation of 4757; *Berodak-Baladan*, a Babylonian king:—Berodach-baladan.

1256. בְּרָאיָה, **Berâ'yâh**, *ber-aw-yaw'*; from 1254 and 3050; *Jah has created*; *Berajah*, an Israelite:—Beraiah.

1257. בַּרְבֻּר, **barbur**, *bar-boor'*; by reduplication from 1250; a *fowl* (as fattened on *grain*):—fowl.

1258. בָּרַד, **bârad**, *baw-rad*; a primitive root, to *hail*:—hail.

1259. בָּרָד, **bârâd**, *baw-rawd'*; from 1258; *hail*:—hail ([stones]).

1260. בֶּרֶד, **Bered**, *beh'-red*; from 1258; *hail*; *Bered*, the name of a place south of Palestine, also of an Israelite:—Bered.

1261. בָּרֹד, **bârôd**, *baw-rode'*; from 1258; *spotted* (as if with *hail*):—grisled.

1262. בָּרָה, **bârâh**, *baw-raw'*; a primitive root; to *select*; also (as denominative from 1250) to *feed*; also (as equivalent to 1305) to *render clear* (Ecc 3:18):—choose, (cause to) eat, manifest, (give) meat.

1263. בָּרוּךְ, **Bârûwk**, *baw-rook'*; passive participle from 1288; *blessed*; *Baruk*, the name of three Israelites:—Baruch.

1264. בְּרֹמִים, **berômîym**, *ber-om-eem'*; probably of foreign origin; *damask* (stuff of variegated thread):—rich apparel.

1265. בְּרוֹשׁ, **berôwsh**, *ber-ōsh'*; of uncertain derivation; a *cypress* (?) tree; hence a *lance* or a *musical* instrument (as made of that wood):— fir (tree).

1266. בְּרוֹת, **berôwth**, *ber-ōth'*; a variation of 1265; the *cypress* (or some elastic tree):—fir.

1267. בָּרוּת, **bârûwth**, *baw-rooth'*; from 1262; *food*:—meat.

1268. בֵּרוֹתָה, **Bêrôwthâh**, *bay-ro-thaw'*; or בֵּרֹתַי, **Bêrôthay**, *bay-ro-thah'ee*; probably from 1266; *cypress* or *cypresslike*; *Berothah* or *Berothai*, a place north of Palestine:—Berothah, Berothai.

1269. בִּרְזוֹת, **Birzâvith**, *beer-zaw-vith'*; probably feminine plural from an unused root (apparently meaning to *pierce*); *holes*; *Birzoth*, an Israelite:—Birzavith [*from the margin*].

1270. בַּרְזֶל, **barzel**, *bar-zel'*; perhaps from the root of 1269; *iron* (as *cutting*); (by extension) an iron *implement*:—(ax) head, iron.

1271. בַּרְזִלַּי, **Barzillay**, *bar-zil-lah'ee*; from 1270; *iron* hearted; *Barzillai*, the name of three Israelites:—Barzillai.

1272. בָּרַח, **bârach**, *baw-rakh'*; a primitive root; to *bolt*, i.e. (figurative) to *flee* suddenly:—chase (away), drive away, fain, flee (away), put to flight, make haste, reach, run away, shoot.

1273. בְּרַחְמִי, **Barchumîy,** *bar-khoo-mee´*; by transposition for 978; a *Barchumite*, or native of *Bachu-rim*:—Barhumite.

1274. בְּרִי, **b^erîy,** *ber-ee´*; from 1262; *fat*:—fat.

1275. בְּרִי, **Bêrîy,** *bay-ree´*; probably by contraction from 882; *Beri*, an Israelite:—Beri.

1276. בְּרִי, **Bêrîy,** *bay-ree´*; of uncertain derivation; (only in the plural and with the article) the *Berites*, a place in Palestine:—Berites.

1277. בָּרִיא, **bârîy**, *baw-ree´*; from 1254 (in the sense of 1262); *fatted* or *plump*:—fat ([fleshed], -ter), fed, firm, plenteous, rank.

1278. בְּרִיאָה, **b^erîy'âh,** *ber-ee-aw´*; feminine from 1254; a *creation*, i.e. a *novelty*:—new thing.

1279. בִּרְיָה, **biryâh,** *beer-yaw´*; feminine from 1262; *food*:—meat.

1280. בְּרִיחַ, **b^erîyach,** *ber-ee´-akh*; from 1272; a *bolt*:—bar, fugitive.

1281. בָּרִיחַ, **bârîyach,** *baw-ree´-akh*; or (shortened) בָּרִחַ, **bâriach,** *baw-ree´-akh*; from 1272; a *fugitive*, i.e. the *serpent* (as *fleeing*), and the constellation by that name:—crooked, noble, piercing.

1282. בָּרִיחַ, **Bârîyach,** *baw-ree´-akh*; the same as 1281; *Bariach*, an Israelite:—Bariah.

1283. בְּרִיעָה, **B^erîy'âh,** *ber-ee´-aw*; apparently from the feminine of 7451 with prepositional prefix; *in trouble; Beriah*, the name of four Israelites:—Beriah.

1284. בְּרִיעִי, **B^erîy'îy,** *ber-ee-ee´*; patronymic from 1283; a *Beriite* (collective) or descendants of Beriah:—Beerites.

1285. בְּרִית, **b^erîyth,** *ber-eeth´*; from 1262 (in the sense of *cutting* [like 1254]); a *compact* (because made by passing between *pieces* of flesh):—confederacy, [con-]feder[-ate], covenant, league.

A feminine noun meaning covenant, treaty, alliance, agreement. The word is used many times in the OT. Its basic uses are outlined here. It describes covenants, or agreements between and among human beings: between Abraham and the Amorites, Abraham and the Philistines, Jacob and Laban, etc. (Ge 14:13; 21:27, 32; 31:44). The nations were said to have made a covenant against Israel (Ps 83:5[6]). It is used figuratively to depict a covenant with death (Isa 28:15, 18) or with the stones of the field (Job 5:23).

It denotes an alliance, ordinance, or agreement between persons. References to covenants between people included Abraham's military treaty with the Ammorites (Ge 14:13); Jonathan and David's pledge of friendship (1Sa 18:3); David's covenant with Abner (2Sa 3:12); the covenant of marriage (Pr 2:17). The word *bĕriyth* is often preceded by the verb *karath* to express the technical idea of "cutting a covenant."

This word is used to describe God's making a covenant with humankind. It may be an alliance of friendship (Ps 25:14). The covenants made between God and humans defined the basis of God's character in the OT. They showed the strength of His divine promise from Adam all the way through to the exile and restoration. It is employed many times: God's covenant with Noah (Ge 9:11–13, 15–17; Isa 54:10) in the form of a promise; with Abraham, Isaac, and Jacob (Ge 15:18; 17:2, 4, 7, 9–11, 13, 14, 19, 21; Ex 2:24; Le 26:42) to increase their descendants, giving them Canaan and making them a blessing to the nations; with all Israel and Moses at Sinai (Ex 19:5; 24:7, 8; 34:10; Dt 29:1 [28:69]) with the stipulations of the Ten Commandments, including the guiding cases in the Book of the Covenant. The words of this covenant (*dibrêy habbĕriyth*) were kept in the ark in the Holy of Holies (Ex 34:28; 40:20). A covenant with Phinehas established an everlasting priesthood in Israel (Nu 25:12, 13). It is used to refer to the covenant established with David and his house (Ps 89:3[4], 28[29]; Jer 33:21), an eternal covenant establishing David and his descendants as the inheritors of an everlasting kingdom. Jeremiah refers to a new covenant (Jer 31:31) that God will establish in the future. The concept is personified in a person, a Servant who becomes the covenant of the people (Isa 42:6; 49:8).

In addition to the verb *kârath* mentioned above, the verb *qûm* is employed with *bĕriyth* meaning to establish a covenant (Ge 6:18; 9:9; Ex 6:4) or to confirm a covenant (Le 26:9; Dt 8:18). The word is used with *nâthan*, to give, meaning to give or make a covenant (Ge 17:2; Nu 25:12). Five other verbs are used in this way less often (Dt 29:12[11]; 2Sa 23:5; 2Ch 15:12; Ps 50:16; 111:9; Eze 16:8). A covenant could be transgressed or violated (Dt 17:2; Jgs 2:20); but the Lord never broke His covenants; He always remembered a covenant (Ge 9:15, 16; Ex 2:24; 6:5; Le 26:42).

1286. בְּרִית, **Bᵉrîyth,** *ber-eeth´*; the same as 1285; *Berith*, a Shechemitish deity:—Berith.

1287. בֹּרִית, **bôrîyth,** *bo-reeth´*; feminine of 1253; vegetable *alkali*:—soap.

1288. בָּרַךְ, **bârak,** *baw-rak´*; a primitive root; to *kneel*; (by implication) to *bless* God (as an act of adoration), and (vice-versa) man (as a benefit); also (by euphemism) to *curse* (God or the king, as treason):— × abundantly, × altogether, × at all, blaspheme, bless, congratulate, curse, × greatly, × indeed, kneel (down), praise, salute, × still, thank.

A verb meaning to bless, kneel, salute, or greet. The verb derives from the noun knee and perhaps suggests the bending of the knee in blessing. Its derived meaning is to bless someone or something. The verb is used when blessing God (Ge 9:26) or people (Nu 24:9). God used this verb when He blessed Abraham in the Abrahamic covenant (Ge 12:3). The word is used intensively when God blesses people or people bless each other (Jos 17:14). When the word is used reflexively, it describes a person blessing or congratulating himself (Dt 29:19 [20]). Other meanings are to bend the knee (2Ch 6:13); and to greet someone with a salutation or friendliness (1Sa 25:14).

1289. בְּרַךְ, **bᵉrak,** *ber-ak´*; (Chaldee); corresponding to 1288:—bless, kneel.

1290. בֶּרֶךְ, **berek,** *beh´-rek*; from 1288; a *knee*:—knee.

1291. בְּרֵךְ, **bᵉrêk,** *beh´-rake*; (Chaldee); corresponding to 1290:—knee.

1292. בַּרַכְאֵל, **Barak'êl,** *baw-rak-ale´*; from 1288 and 410, *God has blessed; Barakel*, the father of one of Job's friends:—Barachel.

1293. בְּרָכָה, **Bᵉrâkâh,** *ber-aw-kaw´*; from 1288; *benediction*; (by implication) *prosperity*:—blessing, liberal, pool, present.

A feminine noun meaning blessing. The general idea of this word is one of good favour bestowed on another. This may be expressed in the giving of a tangible gift (Ge 33:11; 1Sa 25:27) or in the pronouncing of a verbal bless-

ing (Ge 27:36; 49:28). Most often, however, this word speaks of God's favour on the righteous (Ge 12:2; Mal 3:10). It is related to the common verb *bârak* (1288), meaning to bless and is often used to contrast God's blessing and His curse.

1294. בְּרָכָה, **Bᵉrâkâh,** *ber-aw-kaw´*; the same as 1293; *Berakah*, the name of an Israelite, and also of a valley in Palestine:—Berachah.

1295. בְּרֵכָה, **bᵉrêkâh,** *ber-ay-kaw´*; from 1288; a *reservoir* (at which camels *kneel* as a resting place):—(fish-) pool.

1296. בֶּרֶכְיָה, **Berekyâh,** *beh-rek-yaw´*; or בֶּרֶכְיָהוּ, **Berekyâhûw,** *beh-rek-yaw´-hoo*; from 1290 and 3050; *knee* (i.e. *blessing*) of *Jah; Berekjah*, the name of six Israelites:—Berachiah, Berechiah.

1297. בְּרַם, **bᵉram,** *ber-am´*; (Chaldee); perhaps from 7313 with prepositional prefix; (properly) *highly*, i.e. *surely*; but used adversatively, *however*:—but, nevertheless, yet.

1298. בֶּרַע, **Beraʿ,** *beh´-rah*; of uncertain derivation; *Bera*, a Sodomitish king:—Bera.

1299. בָּרַק, **bâraq,** *baw-rak´*; a primitive root; to *lighten* (lightning):—cast forth.

1300. בָּרָק, **bârâq,** *baw-rawk´*; from 1299; *lightning*; (by analogy) a *gleam*; (concrete) a *flashing* sword:—bright, glitter (-ing, sword), lightning.

1301. בָּרָק, **Bârâq,** *baw-rawk´*; the same as 1300; *Barak*, an Israelite:—Barak.

1302. בַּרְקוֹס, **Barqôws,** *bar-kose´*; of uncertain derivation; *Barkos*, one of the Nethinim:—Barkos.

1303. בַּרְקָן, **barqôn,** *bar-kon´*; from 1300; a *thorn* (perhaps as burning *brightly*):—brier.

1304. בָּרֶקֶת, **bâreqeth,** *baw-reh´-keth*; from 1300; a gem (as *flashing*), perhaps the *emerald*:—carbuncle.

1305. בָּרַר, **bârar,** *baw-rar´*; a primitive root; to *clarify* (i.e. *brighten*), *examine, select*:—make bright, choice, chosen, cleanse (be clean), clearly, polished, (shew self) pure (-ify), purge (out).

A verb signifying to purify, select. God declares that He will purge the rebels from Israel (Eze 20:38) and that He will give the people purified lips (Zep 3:9). The term can also mean to polish or make shine like polished arrows (Isa 49:2; Jer 51:11). Primarily used in the books of Chronicles, it points out that which was choice or select: men (1Ch 7:40); gatekeepers (1Ch 9:22); musicians (1Ch 16:41); sheep (Ne 5:18). It can also carry the connotation of testing or proving (Ecc 3:18).

1306. בִּרְשַׁע, **Birshaʿ,** *beer-shah´;* probably from 7562 with prepositional prefix; *with wickedness; Birsha,* a king of Gomorrah:—Birsha.

1307. בֵּרֹתִי, **Bêrôthîy,** *bay-ro-thee´;* patrial from 1268; a *Berothite,* or inhabitant of Berothai:—Berothite.

1308. בְּשׂוֹר, **Beʿsôwr,** *bes-ore´;* from 1319; *cheerful; Besor,* a stream of Palestine:—Besor.

1309. בְּשׂוֹרָה, **beʿsôwrâh,** *bes-o-raw´;* or (shortened) בְּשֹׂרָה, **beʿsôrâh,** *bes-o-raw´;* feminine from 1319; *glad tidings;* (by implication) *reward for good news:*—reward for tidings.

1310. בָּשַׁל, **bâshal,** *baw-shal´;* a primitive root; (properly) to *boil* up; hence to *be done* in cooking; (figurative) to *ripen:*—bake, boil, bring forth, roast, seethe, sod (be sodden).

1311. בָּשֵׁל, **bâshêl,** *baw-shale´;* from 1310; *boiled:*— × at all, sodden.

1312. בִּשְׁלָם, **Bishlâm,** *bish-lawm´;* of foreign derivation; *Bishlam,* a Persian:—Bishlam.

1313. בָּשָׂם, **bâsâm,** *baw-sawm´;* from an unused root meaning to *be fragrant;* [compare 5561] the *balsam* plant:—spice.

1314. בֶּשֶׂם, **beśem,** *beh´-sem;* or בֹּשֶׂם, **bôśem,** *bo´-sem;* from the same as 1313; *fragrance;* (by implication) *spicery;* also the *balsam* plant:—smell, spice, sweet (odour).

1315. בָּשְׂמַת, **Bâśemath,** *baw-se-math´;* feminine of 1314 (the second form); *fragrance; Bosmath,* the name of a wife of Esau, and of a daughter of Solomon:—Bashemath, Basmath.

1316. בָּשָׁן, **Bâshân,** *baw-shawn´;* of uncertain derivation; *Bashan* (often with the article), a region East of the Jordan:—Bashan.

1317. בָּשְׁנָה, **boshnâh,** *bosh-naw´;* feminine from 954; *shamefulness:*—shame.

1318. בָּשַׁס, **bâshas,** *baw-shas´;* a primitive root; to *trample* down:—tread.

1319. בָּשַׂר, **bâśar,** *baw-sar´;* a primitive root; (properly) to *be fresh,* i.e. *full, rosy;* (figurative) *cheerful;* to *announce* (glad news):—messenger, preach, publish, shew forth, (bear, bring, carry, preach, good, tell good) tidings.

A verb meaning to bring news or to bear tidings. The general idea of this word is that of a messenger announcing a message, which may either be bad news (1Sa 4:17, the death of Eli's sons) or good news (Jer 20:15, the birth of Jeremiah). It is often used within the military setting: a messenger coming from battle lines to report the news (2Sa 18:19, 20, 26) or victory (1Sa 31:9; 2Sa 1:20). When used of God's message, this word conveys the victorious salvation which God provides to His people (Ps 96:2; Isa 40:9; 52:7; 61:1).

1320. בָּשָׂר, **bâśâr,** *baw-sawr´;* from 1319; *flesh* (from its *freshness*); (by extension) *body, person;* also (by euphemism) the *pudenda* of a man:—body, [fat, lean] flesh [-ed], kin, [man-] kind, + nakedness, self, skin.

A masculine noun whose basic meaning is flesh. The basic meaning is frequently observed in the OT, especially in the literature concerning sacrificial practices (Le 7:17) and skin diseases (Le 13). It also is used of the animal body (Ge 41:2–4, 18, 19); the human body (Isa 10:18); the penis (Ge 17:11, 13, 14, 23–25); blood relations (Ge 2:23, 24; 29:14); and human frailty (Ge 6:3; Job 10:4). This word is further used in the phrase *kôl* (3605) *bâśâr,* meaning all flesh, to indicate all living beings (Ge 6:17, 19; 7:21); animals (Ge 7:15, 16; 8:17); humanity (Ge 6:12, 13).

1321. בְּשַׂר, **beśar,** *bes-ar´;* (Chaldee); corresponding to 1320:—flesh.

A masculine noun meaning flesh. It is an Aramaic word found only in the book of Daniel. When used figuratively, it signifies all flesh or humankind (Da 2:11) and all creatures (Da 4:12[9]). It is also used in relation to the devouring of flesh in a literal sense (Da 7:5).

1322. בֹּשֶׁת, **bôsheth,** *bo´-sheth;* from 954; *shame* (the feeling and the condition, as well as its cause); (by implication, specifically) an *idol:*—

ashamed, confusion, + greatly, (put to) shame (-ful thing).

1323. בַּת, **bath,** *bath*; from 1129 (as feminine of 1121); a *daughter* (used in the same wide sense as other terms of relationship, literal and figurative):—apple [of the eye], branch, company, daughter, × first, × old, + owl, town, village.

1324. בַּת, **bath,** *bath*; probably from the same as 1327; a *bath* or Hebrew measure (as a means of *division*) of liquids:—bath.

1325. בַּת, **bath,** *bath*; (Chaldee); corresponding to 1324:—bath.

1326. בָּתָה, **bâthâh,** *baw-thaw´*; probably an orthographical variation for 1327; *desolation*:—waste.

1327. בַּתָּה, **battâh,** *bat-taw´*; feminine from an unused root (meaning to *break* in pieces); *desolation*:—desolate.

1328. בְּתוּאֵל, **B**e**thûw'êl,** *beth-oo-ale´*; apparently from the same as 1326 and 410; *destroyed of God; Bethuel,* the name of a nephew of Abraham, and of a place in Palestine:—Bethuel. Compare 1329.

1329. בְּתוּל, **B**e**thûwl,** *beth-ool´*; for 1328; *Bethul* (i.e. *Bethuel*), a place in Palestine:—Bethuel.

1330. בְּתוּלָה, **b**e**thûwlâh,** *beth-oo-law´*; feminine passive participle of an unused root meaning to *separate*; a *virgin* (from her *privacy*); sometimes (by continuation) a *bride*; also (figurative) a *city* or *state*:—maid, virgin.

A feminine noun meaning virgin. Some scholars prefer to translate the term loosely as maiden or young woman. Yet in Ge 24:16, Rebekah is described as a beautiful woman and a bĕthûlâh. The text states that no man had known Rebekah—that is, had sexual relations with her. Also, Jgs 21:12 states that there were "four hundred young bĕthûlâh, that had known no man by lying with any male." In these verses, this Hebrew word certainly connotes virginity. But in Joel 1:8, the Lord describes the bĕthûlâh mourning for the husband of her youth. In this case, the word means young woman. Moreover, the word also refers

to cities or countries that are personified as females (Isa 37:22; 47:1; Jer 18:13; 31:4, 21; Am 5:2). For further occurrences of this Hebrew word, see Dt 22:23, 28; Jgs 19:24; 2Sa 13:2, 18; 1Ki 1:2; Est 2:2; Zec 9:17.

1331. בְּתוּלִים, **b**e**thûwlîym,** *beth-oo-leem´*; masculine plural of the same as 1330; (collective and abstract) *virginity*; (by implication and concretely) the *tokens* of it:— × maid, virginity.

A feminine noun meaning virginity, virgin, or maiden. It is primarily used to describe the sexual purity or chastity of a young woman. Variations on this theme show it is used in contrast to a defiled or impure woman (Dt 22:14); to signify the virginal state of a woman to be married (Le 21:13); or to signify the virginal state of young women in general (Jgs 11:37).

1332. בִּתְיָה, **Bithyâh,** *bith-yaw´*; from 1323 and 3050; *daughter* (i.e. worshipper) *of Jah; Bithjah,* an Egyptian woman:—Bithiah.

1333. בָּתַק, **bâthaq,** *baw-thak´*; a primitive root; to *cut* in pieces:—thrust through.

1334. בָּתַר, **bâthar,** *baw-thar´*; a primitive root, to *chop* up:—divide.

1335. בֶּתֶר, **bether,** *beh´-ther*; from 1334; a *section*:—part, piece.

1336. בֶּתֶר, **Bether,** *beh´-ther*; the same as 1335; *Bether,* a (craggy) place in Palestine:—Bether.

1337. בַּת רַבִּים, **Bath Rabbîym,** *bath rab-beem´*; from 1323 and a masculine plural from 7227; the *daughter* (i.e. *city*) *of Rabbah*:—Bath-rabbim.

1338. בִּתְרוֹן, **Bithrôwn,** *bith-rone´*; from 1334; (with the article) the *craggy* spot; *Bithron,* a place East of the Jordan:—Bithron.

1339. בַּת־שֶׁבַע, **Bath-Sheba**‘, *bath-sheh´-bah*; from 1323 and 7651 (in the sense of 7650); *daughter of an oath; Bath-Sheba,* the mother of Solomon:—Bath-sheba.

1340. בַּת־שׁוּעַ, **Bath-Shûwa**‘, *bath-shoo´-ah*; from 1323 and 7771; *daughter of wealth; Bathshuä,* the same as 1339:—Bath-shua.

ג (Gimel)

1341. גֵּא, gê', *gay'*; for 1343; *haughty:*—proud.

1342. גָּאָה, gâ'âh, *gaw-aw'*; a primitive root; to *mount* up; hence in general to *rise*, (figurative) be *majestic:*—gloriously, grow up, increase, be risen, triumph.

A verb meaning to rise, to grow up, to exalt, to lift up. It is used physically of a stream in Eze 47:5, "The waters were risen"; and of plants in Job 8:11, "Can the rush grow up without mire?" In a figurative sense, it speaks of a lifting up or exaltation (specifically of God). The verb emphatically describes God's matchless power in Miriam's song (Ex 15:1, 21). This is the key usage of *gâ'âh:* The Lord only is highly exalted. The horse and rider He easily casts into the sea; He alone legitimately lifts up the head, as Job admits in Job 10:16. None can stand before Him. Some Hebrew words derived from this one express an important negative theme—that of lifting up of one's self in wrongful pride against the rightful place of God: *gê'eh* (1343); *ga'ăwâh* (1346); and *gâ'ôwn* (1347).

1343. גֵּאֶה, gê'eh, *gay-eh'*; from 1342; *lofty;* (figurative) *arrogant:*—proud.

1344. גֵּאָה, gê'âh, *gay-aw'*; feminine from 1342; *arrogance:*—pride.

1345. גְּאוּאֵל, Ge'ûw'êl, *geh-oo-ale'*; from 1342 and 410; *majesty of God; Geüel*, an Israelite:—Geuel.

1346. גַּאֲוָה, ga'ăvâh, *gah-av-aw'*; from 1342; *arrogance* or *majesty;* (by implication and concretely) *ornament:*—excellency, haughtiness, highness, pride, proudly, swelling.

1347. גָּאוֹן, gâ'ôwn, *gaw-ohn'*; from 1342; the same as 1346:—arrogancy, excellency (-lent), majesty, pomp, pride, proud, swelling.

1348. גֵּאוּת, gê'ûwth, *gay-ooth'*; from 1342; the same as 1346:—excellent things, lifting up, majesty, pride, proudly, raging.

1349. גַּאֲיוֹן, ga'ăyôwn, *gah-ăh-yone'*; from 1342; *haughty:*—proud.

1350. גָּאַל, gâ'al, *gaw-al'*; a primitive root, to *redeem* (according to the Oriental law of kinship), i.e. to *be the next of kin* (and as such to *buy back* a relative's property, *marry* his widow, etc.):— × in any wise, × at all, avenger, deliver, (do, perform the part of near, next) kinsfolk (-man), purchase, ransom, redeem (-er), revenger.

A verb meaning to redeem or act as a kinsman-redeemer. The word means to act as a redeemer for a deceased kinsman (Ru 3:13); to redeem or buy back from bondage (Le 25:48); to redeem or buy back a kinsman's possessions (Le 25:26); to avenge a kinsman's murder (Nu 35:19); to redeem an object through a payment (Le 27:13). Theologically, this word is used to convey God's redemption of individuals from spiritual death and His redemption of the nation of Israel from Egyptian bondage and also from exile (see Ex 6:6).

1351. גָּאַל, gâ'al, *gaw-al'*; a primitive root, [rather identical with 1350, through the idea of *freeing*, i.e. *repudiating*]; to *soil* or (figurative) *desecrate:*—defile, pollute, stain.

1352. גֹּאַל, gô'al, *go'-al*; from 1351; *profanation:*—defile.

1353. גְּאֻלָּה, ge'ullâh, *geh-ool-law'*; feminine passive participle of 1350; *redemption* (including the right and the object); by implication *relationship:*—kindred, redeem, redemption, right.

A feminine singular noun meaning redemption. The term is typically used in legal texts denoting who can redeem (Le 25:24, 31, 32, 48); what they can redeem (Le 25:26); when (Le 25:26, 51, 52); and for how much (Le 25:26, 51, 52). Redemption was a means by which property remained in families or clans. The best picture of this custom in the Bible is Ru 4:6, 7.

1354. גַּב, **gab,** *gab;* from an unused root meaning to *hollow* or *curve;* the *back* (as *rounded* [compare 1460 and 1479]; by analogy the *top* or *rim,* a *boss,* a *vault, arch* of eye, *bulwarks,* etc.:—back, body, boss, eminent (higher) place, [eye] brows, nave, ring.

1355. גַּב, **gab,** *gab;* (Chaldee); corresponding to 1354:—back.

1356. גֵּב, **gêb,** *gabe;* from 1461; a *log* (as *cut* out); also *well* or *cistern* (as *dug*):—beam, ditch, pit.

1357. גֵּב, **gêb,** *gabe;* probably from 1461 [compare 1462]; a *locust* (from its *cutting*):—locust.

1358. גֹּב, **gôb,** *gobe;* (Chaldee); from a root corresponding to 1461; a *pit* (for wild animals) (as *cut* out):—den.

1359. גֹּב, **Gôb,** *gobe;* or (fully) גּוֹב, **Gôwb,** *gobe';* from 1461; *pit; Gob,* a place in Palestine:—Gob.

1360. גֶּבֶא, **gebe',** *geh'-beh;* from an unused root meaning probably to *collect;* a *reservoir;* by analogy a *marsh:*—marsh, pit.

1361. גָּבַהּ, **gâbah,** *gaw-bah';* a primitive root; to *soar,* i.e. *be lofty;* (figurative) to *be haughty:*—exalt, be haughty, be (make) high (-er), lift up, mount up, be proud, raise up great height, upward.

1362. גָּבֹהַּ, **gâbôah,** *gaw-bo-ah';* from 1361; *lofty* (literal or figurative):—high, proud.

1363. גֹּבַהּ, **gôbah,** *go'-bah;* from 1361; *elation, grandeur, arrogance:*—excellency, haughty, height, high, loftiness, pride.

1364. גָּבֹהַּ, **gâbôah,** *gaw-bo'-ah;* or (fully) גְּבוֹהַּ, **gâbôwah,** *gaw-bo'-ah;* from 1361; *elevated* (or *elated*), *powerful, arrogant:*—haughty, height, high (-er), lofty, proud, × exceeding proudly.

1365. גַּבְהוּת, **gabhûwth,** *gab-hooth';* from 1361; *pride:*—loftiness, lofty.

1366. גְּבוּל, **gᵉbûwl,** *geb-ool';* or (shortened) גְּבֻל, **gebul,** *geb-ool';* from 1379; (properly) a *cord* (as *twisted*), i.e. (by implication) a *boundary;* (by extension) the *territory* inclosed:—border, bound, coast, × great, landmark, limit, quarter, space.

1367. גְּבוּלָה, **gᵉbûwlâh,** *geb-oo-law';* or (shortened) גְּבֻלָה, **gebulâh,** *geb-oo-law';* feminine of 1366; a *boundary, region:*—border, bound, coast, landmark, place.

1368. גִּבּוֹר, **gibbôwr,** *gib-bore';* or (shortened) גִּבֹּר, **gibbôr,** *gib-bore';* intensive from the same as 1397; *powerful;* (by implication) *warrior, tyrant:*—champion, chief, × excel, giant, man, mighty (man, one), strong (man), valiant man.

1369. גְּבוּרָה, **gᵉbûrâh,** *geb-oo-raw';* feminine passive participle from the same as 1368; *force* (literal or figurative); (by implication) *valor, victory:*—force, mastery, might, mighty (act, power), power, strength.

1370. גְּבוּרָה, **gᵉbûwrâh,** *geb-oo-raw';* (Chaldee); corresponding to 1369; *power:*—might.

1371. גִּבֵּחַ, **gibbêach,** *gib-bay'-akh;* from an unused root meaning to *be high* (in the forehead); *bald* in the forehead:—forehead bald.

1372. גַּבַּחַת, **gabbachath,** *gab-bakh'-ath;* from the same as 1371; *baldness* in the forehead; (by analogy) a *bare spot* on the right side of cloth:—bald forehead, × without.

1373. גַּבַּי, **Gabbay,** *gab-bah'ee;* from the same as 1354; *collective; Gabbai,* an Israelite:—Gabbai.

1374. גֵּבִים, **Gêbîym,** *gay-beem';* plural of 1356; *cisterns; Gebim,* a place in Palestine:—Gebim.

1375. גָּבִיעַ, **gâbîya',** *gawb-ee'-ah;* from an unused root (meaning to *be convex*); a *goblet;* (by analogy) the *calyx* of a flower:—house, cup, pot.

1376. גְּבִיר, **gᵉbîyr,** *geb-eer';* from 1396; a *master:*—lord.

1377. גְּבִירָה, **gᵉbîyrâh,** *geb-ee-raw';* feminine of 1376; a *mistress:*—queen.

1378. גָּבִישׁ, **gâbîysh,** *gaw-beesh';* from an unused root (probably meaning to *freeze*); *crystal* (from its resemblance to *ice*):—pearl.

1379. גָּבַל, **gâbal,** *gaw-bal';* a primitive root; (properly) to *twist* as a rope; only (as a denominative from 1366) to *bound* (as by a line):—be border, set (bounds about).

1380. גְּבַל, **Gᵉbal,** *geb-al';* from 1379 (in the sense of a *chain* of hills); a *mountain; Gebal,* a place in Phoenicia:—Gebal.

1381. גְּבָל, **Gᵉbâl,** *geb-awl´*; the same as 1380; *Gebal,* a region in Idumæa:—Gebal.

1382. גִּבְלִי, **Giblîy,** *gib-lee´*; patrial from 1380; a *Gebalite,* or inhabitant of Gebal:—Giblites, stone-squarer.

1383. גַּבְלֻת, **gabluth,** *gab-looth´*; from 1379; a twisted *chain* or *lace*:—end.

1384. גִּבֵּן, **gibbên,** *gib-bane´*; from an unused root meaning to be *arched* or *contracted; hunchbacked*:—crookbackt.

1385. גְּבִנָה, **gᵉbinâh,** *geb-ee-naw´*; feminine from the same as 1384; *curdled* milk:—cheese.

1386. גַּבְנֹן, **gabnôn,** *gab-nohn´*; from the same as 1384; a *hump* or *peak* of hills:—high.

1387. גֶּבַע, **Gebaʻ,** *geh´-bah*; from the same as 1375; a *hillock; Geba,* a place in Palestine:—Gaba, Geba, Gibeah.

1388. גִּבְעָא, **Gibʻâʾ,** *gib-aw´*; by permutation for 1389; a *hill; Giba,* a place in Palestine:—Gibeah.

1389. גִּבְעָה, **gibʻâh,** *gib-aw´*; feminine from the same as 1387; a *hillock*:—hill, little hill.

1390. גִּבְעָה, **Gibʻâh,** *gib-aw´*; the same as 1389; *Gibah;* the name of three places in Palestine:—Gibeah, the hill.

1391. גִּבְעוֹן, **Gibʻôwn,** *gib-ohn´*; from the same as 1387; *hilly; Gibon,* a place in Palestine:—Gibeon.

1392. גִּבְעֹל, **gibʻôl,** *gib-ole´*; prolonged from 1375; the *calyx* of a flower:—bolled.

1393. גִּבְעֹנִי, **Gibʻônîy,** *gib-o-nee´*; patrial from 1391; a *Gibonite,* or inhabitant of Gibon:—Gibeonite.

1394. גִּבְעַת, **Gibʻath,** *gib-ath´*; from the same as 1375; *hilliness; Gibath*:—Gibeath.

1395. גִּבְעָתִי, **Gibʻâthîy,** *gib-aw-thee´*; patrial from 1390; a *Gibathite,* or inhabitant of Gibath:—Gibeathite.

1396. גָּבַר, **gâbar,** *gaw-bar´*; a primitive root; to *be strong;* (by implication) to *prevail, act insolently*:—exceed, confirm, be great, be mighty, prevail, put to more [strength], strengthen, be stronger, be valiant.

1397. גֶּבֶר, **geber,** *geh´-ber;* from 1396; (properly) a *valiant* man or *warrior;* (generally) a *person* simply:—every one, man, × mighty.

A masculine noun meaning man, mighty (virile) man, warrior. It is used of man but often contains more than just a reference to gender by referring to the nature of a man, usually with overtones of spiritual strength or masculinity, based on the verb *gâbar* (1396), meaning to be mighty. The word is used to contrast men with women and children (Ex 10:11) and to denote warrior ability (Jer 41:16). The fifteen occurrences of the word in Job are significant, presenting a vast contrast between the essence of man (even a good one) and God (Job 4:17; 22:2). This contrast only adds more force to the passage in Zec 13:7 where God calls Himself *geber.* This passage points to the coming of Jesus—the One who as God would take on sinful human nature. He is the Man (the Shepherd of the sheep).

1398. גֶּבֶר, **Geber,** *geh´-ber;* the same as 1397; *Geber,* the name of two Israelites:—Geber.

1399. גֶּבֶר, **gᵉbar,** *geb-ar´*; from 1396; the same as 1397; a *person*:—man.

A masculine noun meaning man. This is the construct of the Hebrew word *geber* (1397) and has the same meaning. It is found in the Psalms to describe a male who is upright before the Lord. He is described as a blameless man, literally, a man of no shame (Ps 18:25[26]).

1400. גְּבַר, **gᵉbar,** *geb-ar´*; (Chaldee); corresponding to 1399:—certain, man.

An Aramaic masculine singular noun meaning man. It occurs ten times. See the word *geber* (1397).

1401. גִּבָּר, **gibbâr,** *gib-bawr´*; (Chaldee); intensive of 1400; *valiant,* or *warrior*:—mighty.

An Aramaic masculine noun meaning mighty one, warrior, hero. This word is used only once in the Bible, where it is attached to another word meaning strength. It translates as "mighty one" or "strongest soldier" (Da 3:20).

1402. גִּבָּר, **Gibbâr,** *gib-bawr´*; intensive of 1399; *Gibbar,* an Israelite:—Gibbar.

1403. גַּבְרִיאֵל, **Gabrîyʾêl,** *gab-ree-ale´*; from 1397 and 410; *man of God; Gabriel,* an archangel:—Gabriel.

1404. גְּבֶרֶת, g⁰bereth, *geb-eh´-reth*; feminine of 1376; *mistress*:—lady, mistress.

A noun meaning lady, queen, mistress. In many cases, this word refers to either a woman who is a mistress or to the servant of a mistress (Ge 16:4, 8, 9; 2Ki 5:3; Pr 30:23). Also, it refers to a lady of a kingdom, that is, the queen (Isa 47:5, 7).

1405. גִּבְּתוֹן, Gibb⁰thôwn, *gib-beth-one´*; intensive from 1389; a *hilly* spot; *Gibbethon*, a place in Palestine:—Gibbethon.

1406. גָּג, gâg, *gawg*; probably by reduplication from 1342; a *roof*; (by analogy) the *top* of an altar:—roof (of the house), (house) top (of the house).

1407. גַּד, gad, *gad*; from 1413 (in the sense of *cutting*); *coriander* seed (from its furrows):—coriander.

1408. גַּד, Gad, *gad*; a variation of 1409; *Fortune*, a Babylonian deity:—that troop.

1409. גָּד, gâd, *gawd*; from 1464 (in the sense of *distributing*); *fortune*:—troop.

1410. גָּד, Gâd, *gawd*; from 1464; *Gad*, a son of Jacob, includ. his tribe and its territory; also a prophet:—Gad.

1411. גְּדָבַר, g⁰dâbar, *ged-aw-bar´*; (Chaldee); corresponding to 1489; a *treasurer*:—treasurer.

1412. גֻּדְגֹּדָה, Gudgôdâh, *gud-go´-daw*; by reduplication from 1413 (in the sense of *cutting*) *cleft*; *Gudgodah*, a place in the Desert:—Gudgodah.

1413. גָּדַד, gâdad, *gaw-dad´*; a primitive root [compare 1464]; to *crowd*; also to *gash* (as if by *pressing* into):—assemble (selves by troops), gather (selves together, self in troops), cut selves.

A verb meaning to cut, to crowd together. In some cases, this verb is used to describe cutting the skin in mourning (Jer 16:6; 41:5; 47:5) or in pagan religious practices (1Ki 18:28). God prohibited such pagan rites (Dt 14:1). This Hebrew verb also means to gather together, such as troops (Mic 5:1[4:14]) or a crowd (Jer 5:7).

1414. גְּדַד, g⁰dad, *ged-ad´*; (Chaldee); corresponding to 1413; to *cut down*:—hew down.

1415. גָּדָה, gâdâh, *gaw-daw´*; from an unused root (meaning to *cut* off); a *border* of a river (as *cut* into by the stream):—bank.

1416. גְּדוּד, g⁰dûwd, *ged-ood´*; from 1413; a *crowd* (especially of soldiers):—army, band (of men), company, troop (of robbers).

A masculine noun meaning a band, a troop. It is used to indicate a marauding band, a raiding party, or a group that makes inroads into enemy territory. It sometimes refers to Israel's military (2Sa 4:2; 2Ch 22:1), but more often, it refers to the marauding enemies of Israel (Ge 49:19; 1Sa 30:8, 15, 23; 1Ki 11:24; 2Ki 5:2; 6:23; 24:2). In some instances, these marauding bands operate independently and are thus labeled as troops of robbers (Hos 6:9; 7:1). By extension, the word sometimes refers to the actual raid itself (2Sa 3:22). On other occasions, it indicates the army in general (Job 29:25) or some division of troops within the army (1Ch 7:4; 2Ch 25:9, 10, 13; 26:11; Mic 5:1[4:14]). It is used figuratively for God's chastisements (Job 19:12) and His attacking forces (Job 25:3).

1417. גְּדוּד, g⁰dûwd, *ged-ood´*; or (feminine) גְּדֻדָה, gedudâh, *ged-oo-daw´*; from 1413; a *furrow* (as *cut*):—furrow.

1418. גְּדוּדָה, g⁰dûwdâh, *ged-oo-daw´*; feminine participle passive of 1413; an *incision*:—cutting.

1419. גָּדוֹל, gâdôwl, *gaw-dole´*; or (shortened) גָּדֹל, gâdôl, *gaw-dole´*; from 1431; *great* (in any sense); hence *older*; also *insolent*:— + aloud, elder (-est), + exceeding (-ly), + far, (man of) great (man, matter, thing, -er, -ness), high, long, loud, mighty, more, much, noble, proud thing, × sore, (×) very.

1420. גְּדוּלָה, g⁰dûwlâh, *ged-oo-law´*; or (shortened) גְּדֻלָה, g⁰dullâh, *ged-ool-law´*; or (less accurately) גְּדוּלָּה, g⁰dûwllâh, *ged-ool-law´*; feminine of 1419; *greatness*; (concretely) *mighty acts*:—dignity, great things (-ness), majesty.

1421. גִּדּוּף, giddûwph, *gid-doof´*; or (shortened) גִּדֻּף, gidduph, *gid-doof´*; and (feminine) גִּדּוּפָה, giddûwphâh, *gid-doo-faw´*; or גִּדֻּפָה, gidduphâh, *gid-doo-faw´*; from 1422; *vilification*:—reproach, reviling.

1422. גְּדוּפָה, g⁰dûwphâh, *ged-oo-faw´*; feminine passive participle of 1442; a *revilement*:—taunt.

1423. גְּדִי, g⁰dîy, *ged-ee´*; from the same as 1415; a young *goat* (from *browsing*):—kid.

1424. גַּדִּי, Gâdîy, *gaw-dee´*; from 1409; *fortunate; Gadi*, an Israelite:—Gadi.

1425. גַּדִּי, Gâdîy, *gaw-dee´*; patronymic from 1410; a *Gadite* (collective) or descendants of Gad:—Gadites, children of Gad.

1426. גַּדִּי, Gaddîy, *gad-dee´*; intensive for 1424; *Gaddi*, an Israelite:—Gaddi.

1427. גַּדִּיאֵל, Gaddîy'êl, *gad-dee-ale´*; from 1409 and 410; *fortune of God; Gaddiel*, an Israelite:—Gaddiel.

1428. גִּדְיָה, gidyâh, *gid-yaw´*; or גַּדְיָה, gadyâh, *gad-yaw´*; the same as 1415; a river *brink*:—bank.

1429. גְּדִיָּה, g⁰dîyyâh, *ged-ee-yaw´*; feminine of 1423; a young female *goat*:—kid.

1430. גָּדִישׁ, gâdîysh, *gaw-deesh´*; from an unused root (meaning to *heap* up); a *stack* of sheaves; by analogy a *tomb*:—shock (stack) (of corn), tomb.

1431. גָּדַל, gâdal, *gaw-dal´*; a primitive root; (properly) to *twist* [compare 1434], i.e. to *be* (causative *make*) *large* (in various senses, as in body, mind, estate or honour, also in pride):—advance, boast, bring up, exceed, excellent, be (-come, do, give, make, wax), great (-er, come to … estate, + things), grow (up), increase, lift up, magnify (-ifical), be much set by, nourish (up), pass, promote, proudly [spoken], tower.

1432. גָּדֵל, gâdêl, *gaw-dale´*; from 1431; *large* (literal or figurative):—great, grew.

1433. גֹּדֶל, gôdel, *go´-del*; from 1431; *magnitude* (literal or figurative):—greatness, stout (-ness).

1434. גְּדִל, gâdil, *ged-eel´*; from 1431 (in the sense of *twisting*); *thread*, i.e. a *tassel* or *festoon*:—fringe, wreath.

1435. גִּדֵּל, Giddêl, *gid-dale´*; from 1431; *stout; Giddel*, the name of one of the Nethinim, also of one of "Solomon's servants":—Giddel.

1436. גְּדַלְיָה, G⁰dalyâh, *ged-al-yaw´*; or (prolonged) גְּדַלְיָהוּ, Gedalyâhûw, *ged-al-yaw´-hoo*; from 1431 and 3050; *Jah has become great; Gedaljah*, the name of five Israelites:—Gedaliah.

1437. גִּדַּלְתִּי, Giddaltîy, *gid-dal´-tee*; from 1431; *I have made great; Giddalti*, an Israelite:—Giddalti.

1438. גָּדַע, gâda‘, *gaw-dah´*; a primitive root; to *fell* a tree; (generally) to *destroy* anything:—cut (asunder, in sunder, down, off), hew down.

1439. גִּדְעוֹן, Gid‘ôwn, *gid-ohn´*; from 1438; *feller* (i.e. *warrior); Gidon*, an Israelite:—Gideon.

1440. גִּדְעֹם, Gid‘ôm, *gid-ohm´*; from 1438; a *cutting* (i.e. *desolation); Gidom*, a place in Palestine:—Gidom.

1441. גִּדְעֹנִי, Gid‘ônîy, *gid-o-nee´*; from 1438; *warlike* [compare 1439]; *Gidoni*, an Israelite:—Gideoni.

1442. גָּדַף, gâdaph, *gaw-daf´*; a primitive root; to *hack* (with words), i.e. *revile*:—blaspheme, reproach.

1443. גָּדַר, gâdar, *gaw-dar´*; a primitive root; to *wall* in or around:—close up, fence up, hedge, inclose, make up [a wall], mason, repairer.

1444. גֶּדֶר, geder, *geh´-der*; from 1443; a *circumvallation*:—wall.

1445. גֶּדֶר, Geder, *geh´-der*; the same as 1444; *Geder*, a place in Palestine:—Geder.

1446. גְּדֹר, G⁰dôr, *ged-ore´*; or (fully) גְּדוֹר, G⁰dôwr, *ged-ore´*; from 1443; *inclosure; Gedor*, a place in Palestine; also the name of three Israelites:—Gedor.

1447. גָּדֵר, gâdêr, *gaw-dare´*; from 1443; a *circumvallation*; (by implication) an *inclosure*:—fence, hedge, wall.

1448. גְּדֵרָה, g⁰dêrâh, *ged-ay-raw´*; feminine of 1447; *inclosure* (especially for flocks):—[sheep-] cote (fold) hedge, wall.

1449. גְּדֵרָה, G⁰dêrâh, *ged-ay-raw´*; the same as 1448; (with the article) *Gederah*, a place in Palestine:—Gederah, hedges.

1450. גְּדֵרוֹת, G⁰dêrôwth, *ged-ay-rohth´*; plural of 1448; *walls; Gederoth*, a place in Palestine:—Gederoth.

1451. גְּדֵרִי, G⁰dêrîy, *ged-ay-ree´*; patrial from 1445; a *Gederite*, or inhabitant of Geder:—Gederite.

1452. יְגֵדְרָתִי, Gᵉdêrâthîy, *ged-ay-raw-thee´*; patrial from 1449; a *Gederathite*, or inhabitant of Gederah:—Gederathite.

1453. גְּדֵרֹתַיִם, Gᵉdêrôthayim, *ged-ay-ro-thah´-yim*; dual of 1448; *double wall*; *Gederothajim*, a place in Palestine:—Gederothaim.

1454. גֵּה, gêh, *gay*; probably a clerical error for 2088; *this*:—this.

1455. גָּהָה, gâhâh, *gaw-haw´*; a primitive root; to *remove* (a bandage from a wound, i.e. *heal* it):—cure.

1456. גֵּהָה, gêhâh, *gay-haw´*; from 1455; a *cure*:—medicine.

1457. גָּהַר, gâhar, *gaw-har´*; a primitive root; to *prostrate* oneself:—cast self down, stretch self.

1458. גַּו, gav, *gav*; another form for 1460; the *back*:—back.

1459. גַּו, gav, *gav*; (Chaldee); corresponding to 1460; the *middle*:—midst, same, there- (where-) in.

1460. גֵּו, gêv, *gave*; from 1342 [corresponding to 1354]; the *back*; (by analogy) the *middle*:— + among, back, body.

I. A masculine noun meaning back. It depicts the back of a person's body. A fool's back is for lashes or a rod (Pr 10:13; 19:29; 26:3) so that he might learn wisdom. In a figure of speech, the Lord casts the sins of repentant persons behind His back (Isa 38:17). Walking on someone's back means to humiliate and denigrate him or her (Isa 51:23).

II. A masculine noun meaning midst, community. It indicates the fellowship or the midst of a community of persons (Job 30:5) from which the lowly in society are driven.

1461. גּוּב, gûwb, *goob*; a primitive root; to *dig*:—husbandman.

1462. גּוֹב, gôwb, *gobe*; from 1461; the *locust* (from its *grubbing* as a larve):—grasshopper, × great.

1463. גּוֹג, Gôwg, *gohg*; of uncertain derivation; *Gog*, the name of an Israelite, also of some northern nation:—Gog.

1464. גּוּד, gûwd, *goode*; a primitive root [akin to 1413]; to *crowd* upon, i.e. *attack*:—invade, overcome.

1465. גֵּוָה, gêvâh, *gay-vaw´*; feminine of 1460; the *back*, i.e. (by extension) the *person*:—body.

1466. גֵּוָה, gêvâh, *gay-vaw´*; the same as 1465; *exaltation*; (figurative) *arrogance*:—lifting up, pride.

1467. גֵּוָה, gêvâh, *gay-vaw´*; (Chaldee); corresponding to 1466:—pride.

1468. גּוּז, gûwz, *gooz*; a primitive root [compare 1494]; (properly) to *shear* off; but used only in the (figurative) sense of *passing* rapidly:—bring, cut off.

1469. גּוֹזָל, gôwzzâl, *goz-zawl´*; or (shortened) גֹּזָל, gôzâl, *go-zawl´*; from 1497; a *nestling* (as being comparatively *nude* of feathers):—young (pigeon).

1470. גּוֹזָן, Gôwzân, *go-zawn´*; probably from 1468; a *quarry* (as a place of *cutting* stones); *Gozan*, a province of Assyria:—Gozan.

1471. גּוֹי, gôwy, *go´ee*; rarely (shortened) גֹּי, gôy, *go´-ee*; apparently from the same root as 1465 (in the sense of *massing*); a foreign *nation*; hence a *Gentile*; also (figurative) a *troop* of animals, or a *flight* of locusts:—Gentile, heathen, nation, people.

A masculine noun meaning nation, people, Gentiles, country. The word is used to indicate a nation or nations in various contexts and settings: it especially indicates the offspring of Abraham that God made into a nation (Ge 12:2) and thereby set the stage for Israel's appearance in history as a nation (Ge 18:18; Ps 106:5). Israel was to be a holy nation (Ex 19:6). Even the descendants of Abraham that did not come from the seed of Isaac would develop into nations (Ge 21:13). God can create a nation, even a holy nation like Israel, through the descendants of the person whom He chooses, as He nearly does in the case of Moses when Israel rebels (Ex 32:10). Edom refers to Israel and Judah as two separate nations (Eze 35:10), but God planned for them to be united forever into one nation (Eze 37:22). Then they would become the head of the nations (Dt 28:12). In this overall literary, theological, and historical context, it is clear that Israel would share common ancestors, and would have a sufficient increase in numbers to be considered a nation. It would have a common place of habitation and a common origin, not only in flesh and blood, but in their religious heritage. It would share a common history, culture, society, religious worship, and purposes for the present and the future.

This noun is used to mean nations other than Israel as well; pagan, Gentile, or heathen nations (Ex 9:24; 34:10; Eze 5:6–8), for all the earth and all the nations belong to God (cf. Ex 19:5). Israel was to keep herself from the false religions, unclean practices, and views of these nations (Ezr 6:21). In the plural, the noun may indicate the generic humankind (Isa 42:6). In a few instances, the word refers to a group of people rather than to a nation (2Ki 6:18; Ps 43:1; Isa 26:2), although the exact translation is difficult in these cases.

The word is used in a figurative sense to refer to animals or insects, such as in Joel 1:6 where it depicts locusts.

1472. גְּוִיָּה, **gᵉvîyyâh,** *gev-ee-yaw´*; prolonged for 1465; a *body*, whether alive or dead:—(dead) body, carcase, corpse.

A feminine noun meaning body, corpse, carcass. Most often, this word is used to depict a dead body, either a human, such as Saul (1Sa 31:10), or an animal, such as Samson's lion (Jgs 14:8, 9). In the Bible, this word is used to describe the slaughter of a nation as dead bodies are scattered everywhere (Ps 110:6; Na 3:3). Sometimes the word refers to live bodies. But in these cases, the idea of defeat or humiliation is present (Ge 47:18; Ne 9:37). When the experience is visionary, however, the word depicts live beings with no humiliation implied (Eze 1:11, 23; Da 10:6).

1473. גּוֹלָה, **gôwlâh,** *go-law´*; or (shortened) גֹּלָה, **gôlâh,** *go-law´*; active participle feminine of 1540; *exile*; (concrete and collateral) *exiles*:— (carried away), captive (-ity), removing.

A feminine noun meaning captivity, exile, captives, exiles. This word is the feminine participle of *gâlâh* (1540). It most often refers to the Babylonian captivity and its captives (2Ki 24:16; Eze 1:1) but is also used of the Assyrian captivity (1Ch 5:22) and even of the exiles of foreign nations (Jer 48:7, 11; Am 1:15). The

phrase, children of the captivity, occurs in Ezra and describes those who returned from the captivity in Babylon (Ezr 4:1; 6:19, 20; 10:7, 16).

1474. גּוֹלָן, **Gôwlân,** *go-lawn´*; from 1473; *captive; Golan,* a place east of the Jordan:—Golan.

1475. גּוּמָּץ, **gûwmmâts,** *goom-mawts´*; of uncertain derivation; a *pit*:—pit.

A masculine noun meaning pit. Although this word is used only once in the OT, its meaning is derived from a related Aramaic word, which means to dig. Thus, a pit is the result of digging. The meaning is clear when it is used in Ecc 10:8: "He that diggeth a pit shall fall into it" (KJV). Furthermore, this meaning is further verified in a similar passage found in Pr 26:27, in which a parallel word, *shachath* (7845), meaning pit, is used.

1476. גּוּנִי, **Gûwnîy,** *goo-nee´*; probably from 1598; *protected; Guni,* the name of two Israelites:—Guni.

1477. גּוּנִי, **Gûwnîy,** *goo-nee´*; patronymic from 1476; a *Gunite* (collective with article prefix) or descendants of Guni:—Gunites.

1478. גָּוַע, **gâva',** *gaw-vah´*; a primitive root; to *breathe* out, i.e. (by implication) *expire*:—die, be dead, give up the ghost, perish.

A verb meaning to expire, to die. The word is apparently from a root meaning to breathe out. This word is used to describe the death of humans and animals in the flood (Ge 6:17; 7:21). It is used in a repeated formula (along with *mûth* [4191], meaning to die) to describe the death of the patriarchs and Ishmael (Ge 25:8, 17; 35:29; 49:33). Sometimes the context of the word refers to the root meaning of breathing out (Job 34:14; Ps 104:29). In Zec 13:8, the word is used to predict the deaths of two-thirds of the nation of Israel.

1479. גּוּף, **gûwph,** *goof*; a primitive root; (properly) to *hollow* or *arch*, i.e. (figurative) *close*; to *shut*:—shut.

1480. גּוּפָה, **gûwphâh,** *goo-faw´*; from 1479; a *corpse* (as *closed* to sense):—body.

A feminine noun meaning dead body, corpse. This word appears only twice in the OT and in the same verse. First Chronicles 10:12 describes Saul and his son's dead bodies. The word has a similar meaning to *gĕwiyyâh* (1472), meaning body, as is demonstrated when that word is used in a parallel passage, 1Sa 31:12.

1481. גּוּר, **gûwr,** *goor;* a primitive root; properly to *turn* aside from the road (for a lodging or any other purpose), i.e. *sojourn* (as a guest); also to *shrink, fear* (as in a *strange* place); also to *gather* for hostility (as *afraid*):—abide, assemble, be afraid, dwell, fear, gather (together), inhabitant, remain, sojourn, stand in awe, (be) stranger, × surely.

A verb meaning to sojourn, to dwell as a foreigner; in the reflexive sense, to seek hospitality with. The term is commonly used of the patriarchs who sojourned in Canaan (Ge 26:3; 35:27); places outside Canaan (Ge 12:10; 20:1; 21:23; 32:4[5]; 47:4); Naomi and her family in Moab (Ru 1:1); the exiles in Babylonia (Jer 42:15). Metaphorically, the term is used of one who worships in God's temple (Ps 15:1; 61:4[5]). It is used reflexively with the meaning to seek hospitality with in 1Ki 17:20.

1482. גּוּר, **gûwr,** *goor;* or (shortened) גֻּר, **gur,** *goor;* perhaps from 1481; a *cub* (as still *abiding* in the lair), especially of the lion:—whelp, young one.

1483. גּוּר, **Gûwr,** *goor;* the same as 1482; *Gur,* a place in Palestine:—Gur.

1484. גּוֹר, **gôwr,** *gore;* or (feminine) גֹּרה, **gôrâh,** *go-raw´;* a variation of 1482:—whelp.

1485. גּוּר־בַּעַל, **Gûwr-Ba‘al,** *goor-bah´-al;* from 1481 and 1168; *dwelling of Baal;* Gur-Baal, a place in Arabia:—Gur-baal.

1486. גּוֹרָל, **gôwrâl,** *go-rawl´;* or (shortened) גֹּרָל, **gôrâl,** *go-ral´;* from an unused root meaning to *be rough* (as stone); (properly) a *pebble,* i.e. a *lot* (small stones being used for that purpose); (figurative) a *portion* or *destiny* (as if determined by lot):—lot.

1487. גּוּשׁ, **gûwsh,** *goosh;* or rather (by permutation) גִּישׁ, **gîysh,** *geesh;* of uncertain derivation; a *mass* of earth:—clod.

1488. גֵּז, **gêz,** *gaze;* from 1494; a *fleece* (as *shorn*); also mown *grass:*—fleece, mowing, mown grass.

1489. גִּזְבָּר, **gizbâr,** *giz-bawr´;* of foreign derivation; *treasurer:*—treasurer.

1490. גִּזְבַּר, **gizbâr,** *giz-bawr´;* (Chaldee); corresponding to 1489:—treasurer.

1491. גָּזָה, **gâzâh,** *gaw-zaw´;* a primitive root [akin to 1468]; to *cut* off, i.e. *portion* out:—take.

1492. גִּזָּה, **gizzâh,** *giz-zaw´;* feminine from 1494; a *fleece:*—fleece.

1493. גִּזוֹנִי, **Gizôwnîy,** *gee-zo-nee´;* patrial from the unused name of a place apparently in Palestine; a *Gizonite* or inhabitant of Gizoh:—Gizonite.

1494. גָּזַז, **gâzaz,** *gaw-zaz´;* a primitive root [akin to 1468]; to *cut* off; specifically to *shear* a flock, or *shave* the hair; (figurative) to *destroy* an enemy:—cut off (down), poll, shave, ([sheep-]) shear (-er).

1495. גָּזֵז, **Gâzêz,** *gaw-zaze´;* from 1494; *shearer; Gazez,* the name of two Israelites:—Gazez.

1496. גָּזִית, **gâzîyth,** *gaw-zeeth´;* from 1491; something *cut,* i.e. *dressed* stone:—hewed, hewn stone, wrought.

1497. גָּזַל, **gâzal,** *gaw-zal´;* a primitive root; to *pluck* off; specifically to *flay, strip* or *rob:*—catch, consume, exercise [robbery], pluck (off), rob, spoil, take away (by force, violence), tear.

1498. גָּזֵל, **gâzêl,** *gaw-zale´;* from 1497; *robbery,* or (concrete) *plunder:*—robbery, thing taken away by violence.

1499. גֵּזֶל, **gêzel,** *ge´-zel;* from 1497; *plunder,* i.e. *violence:*—violence, violent perverting.

1500. גְּזֵלָה, **gᵉzêlâh,** *gez-ay-law´;* feminine of 1498 and meaning the same:—that (he had robbed) [which he took violently away], spoil, violence.

1501. גָּזָם, **gâzâm,** *gaw-zawm´;* from an unused root meaning to *devour;* a kind of *locust:*—palmer worm.

1502. גַּזָּם, **Gazzâm,** *gaz-zawm´;* from the same as 1501; *devourer; Gazzam,* one of the Nethinim:—Gazzam.

1503. גֶּזַע, **geza‘,** *geh´-zah;* from an unused root meaning to *cut* down (trees); the *trunk* or *stump* of a tree (as felled or as planted):—stem, stock.

1504. גָּזַר, **gâzar,** *gaw-zar´*; a primitive root; to *cut* down or off; (figurative) to *destroy, divide, exclude* or *decide*:—cut down (off), decree, divide, snatch.

A verb meaning to cut, to divide, to separate. The basic meaning of this word can be seen in Solomon's command to divide the baby in two pieces (1Ki 3:25, 26); in the act of cutting down trees (2Ki 6:4); or when God divided the Red Sea (Ps 136:13). The word also describes a person separated from God's temple (2Ch 26:21); from God's caring hand (Ps 88:5[6]); or from life itself (Isa 53:8). So great may be the separation that destruction may occur (La 3:54; Eze 37:11; Hab 3:17). In a few instances, this word means to decree (Est 2:1; Job 22:28). The meaning is related to the Hebrew idiom, to cut a covenant, which means to make a covenant. In that idiom, the synonym *kârath* (3772), meaning to cut, is used.

1505. גְּזַר, **gᵉzar,** *gez-ar´*; (Chaldee); corresponding to 1504; to *quarry; determine*:—cut out, soothsayer.

An Aramaic verb meaning to cut, to decide, to determine. The participle is used as a noun meaning soothsayer or astrologer. The verb occurs in Da 2:34 and 2:45 to describe a stone cut without hands—an image that symbolizes the kingdom of God. Apparently, the idea of future events being cut out led to the word being used to signify soothsayers or astrologers who could foretell the future (Da 2:27; 4:7[4]; 5:7, 11).

1506. גֶּזֶר, **gezer,** *geh´-zer*; from 1504; something *cut off*; a *portion*:—part, piece.

A masculine noun meaning part, portion, division, half. It is found only as a plural form. It refers to the halves of animals that Abraham prepared in the covenant ceremony of Ge 15:17 and the two halves of the Red Sea when God divided it (Ps 136:13).

1507. גֶּזֶר, **Gezer,** *geh´-zer*; the same as 1506; *Gezer*, a place in Palestine:—Gazer, Gezer.

1508. גִּזְרָה, **gizrâh,** *giz-raw´*; feminine of 1506; the *figure* or person (as if *cut* out); also an *inclosure* (as *separated*):—polishing, separate place.

1509. גְּזֵרָה, **gᵉzêrâh,** *gez-ay-raw´*; from 1504; a *desert* (as *separated*):—not inhabited.

1510. גְּזֵרָה, **gᵉzêrâh,** *gez-ay-raw´*; (Chaldee); from 1505 (as 1504); a *decree*:—decree.

1511. גִּזְרִי, **Gizrîy,** *giz-ree´*; (in the margin), patrial from 1507; a *Gezerite* (collective) or inhabitant of Gezer; but better (as in the text) by transpositon גִּרְזִי, **Girzîy,** *ger-zee´*; patrial of 1630; a *Girzite* (collective) or member of a native tribe in Palestine:—Gezrites.

1512. גָּחוֹן, **gâchôwn,** *gaw-khone´*; probably from 1518; the external *abdomen, belly* (as the *source* of the fetus [compare 1521]):—belly.

1513. גֶּחֶל, **gechel,** *geh´-khel*; or (feminine) גַּחֶלֶת, **gacheleth,** *gah-kheh´-leth*; from an unused root meaning to *glow* or *kindle*; an *ember*:—(burning) coal.

1514. גַּחַם, **Gacham,** *gah´-kham*; from an unused root meaning to *burn; flame; Gacham,* a son of Nahor:—Gaham.

1515. גַּחַר, **Gachar,** *gah´-khar*; from an unused root meaning to *hide; lurker; Gachar,* one of the Nethinim:—Gahar.

1516. גַּיְא, **gay',** *gah´ee*; or (shortened) גַּי, **gay,** *gah´ee*; probably (by transcription) from the same root as 1466 (abbreviation); a *gorge* (from its *lofty* sides; hence narrow, but not a gully or winter-torrent):—valley.

1517. גִּיד, **gîyd,** *geed*; probably from 1464; a *thong* (as *compressing*); (by analogy) a *tendon*:—sinew.

1518. גִּיחַ, **gîyach,** *gee´-akh*; or (shortened) גֹּחַ, **gôach,** *go´-akh*; a primitive root; to *gush* forth (as water), generally to *issue*:—break forth, labour to bring forth, come forth, draw up, take out.

1519. גִּיחַ, **gîyach,** *gee´-akh*; (Chaldee); or (shortened) גּוּחַ, **gûwach,** *goo´-akh*; (Chaldee); corresponding to 1518; to *rush* forth:—strive.

1520. גִּיחַ, **Gîyach,** *gee´-akh*; from 1518; a *fountain; Giach,* a place in Palestine:—Giah.

1521. גִּיחוֹן, **Gîychôwn,** *gee-khone´*; or (shortened) גִּחוֹן, **Gichôwn,** *gee-khone´*; from 1518; *stream; Gichon,* a river of Paradise; also a valley (or pool) near Jerusalem:—Gihon.

1522. גֵּיחֲזִי, **Gêychăzîy,** *gay-khah-zee´*; or גֵּחֲזִי, **Gêchă-zîy,** *gay-khah-zee´*; apparently from

1516 and 2372; *valley of a visionary; Gechazi,* the servant of Elisha:—Gehazi.

1523. גִּיל, **gîyl,** *geel*; or (by permutation) גּוּל, **gûwl,** *gool*; a primitive root; (properly) to *spin round* (under the influence of any violent emotion), i.e. usually *rejoice,* or (as *cringing*) *fear*:—be glad, joy, be joyful, rejoice.

1524. גִּיל, **gîyl,** *geel*; from 1523; a *revolution* (of time, i.e. an *age*); also *joy*:— × exceedingly, gladness, × greatly, joy, rejoice (-ing), sort.

1525. גִּילָה, **gîylâh,** *gee-law´*; or גִּילַת, **gîylath,** *gee-lath´*; feminine of 1524; *joy*:—joy, rejoicing.

1526. גִּילֹנִי, **Gîylônîy,** *gee-lo-nee´*; patrial from 1542; a *Gilonite* or inhabitant of Giloh:—Gilonite.

1527. גִּינַת, **Gîynath,** *gee-nath´*; of uncertain derivation; *Ginath,* an Israelite:—Ginath.

1528. גִּיר, **gîyr,** *geer*; (Chaldee); corresponding to 1615; *lime*:—plaster.

1529. גֵּישָׁן, **Gêyshân,** *gay-shawn´*; from the same as 1487; *lumpish; Geshan,* an Israelite:—Geshan.

1530. גַּל, **gal,** *gal*; from 1556; something *rolled,* i.e. a *heap* of stone or dung (plural *ruins*), (by analogy) a *spring* of water (plural *waves*):—billow, heap, spring, wave.

1531. גֹּל, **gôl,** *gole*; from 1556; a *cup* for oil (as *round*):—bowl.

1532. גַּלָּב, **gallâb,** *gal-lawb´*; from an unused root meaning to *shave*; a *barber*:—barber.

1533. גִּלְבֹּעַ, **Gilbôaʻ,** *gil-bo´-ah*; from 1530 and 1158; *fountain of ebullition; Gilboa,* a mountain of Palestine:—Gilboa.

1534. גַּלְגַּל, **galgal,** *gal-gal´*; by reduplication from 1556; a *wheel*; (by analogy) a *whirlwind*; also *dust* (as *whirled*):—heaven, rolling thing, wheel.

A masculine noun meaning a wheel, a whirl, a whirlwind. This word primarily describes an object circling or rotating around and around. This can be seen in the related verb *gâlal* (1556), meaning to roll. This word is often used to describe wheels, like those on a chariot (Eze 23:24; 26:10); an instrument used to draw water from a cistern (Ecc 12:6); or the objects in

Ezekiel's vision (Eze 10:2, 6, 13), which are similar to *ʼôwph ân* (212), meaning wheels. In most passages, a sense of a whirling movement is found in swift wheels (Isa 5:28); rumbling, noisy wheels (Jer 47:3); swirling chaff (Isa 17:13); thunder in the swirling storm (Ps 77:18[19]).

1535. גַּלְגַּל, **galgal,** *gal-gal´*; (Chaldee); corresponding to 1534; a *wheel*:—wheel.

An Aramaic masculine noun meaning wheel. The word occurs only in Da 7:9, where it describes fiery wheels on the blazing throne of the Ancient of Days. It is thought that the throne is seen as connected to a chariot. The wheeled cherubim (cf. Eze 10:15, 20) may be related to the wheels of this throne (cf. 1Ch 28:18; Ps 99:1).

1536. גִּלְגָּל, **gilgâl,** *gil-gawl´*; a variation of 1534:—wheel.

A masculine noun meaning a cart wheel. It is the cart wheel used in the process of threshing or crushing grain (Isa 28:28). This word is a variation of the Hebrew word *galgal* (1534).

1537. גִּלְגָּל, **Gilgâl,** *gil-gawl´*; the same as 1536 (with the article as a proper noun); *Gilgal,* the name of three places in Palestine:—Gilgal. See also 1019.

1538. גֻּלְגֹּלֶת, **gulgôleth,** *gul-go´-leth*; by reduplication from 1556; a *skull* (as *round*); (by implication) a *head* (in enumeration of persons):—head, every man, poll, skull.

A feminine noun meaning skull, head, and thus a person. The author of Judges used this word when he described Abimelech's skull being cracked when a woman dropped a millstone on it (Jgs 9:53). When Jezebel was killed, her skull was one of the few remnants of her body when people buried her (2Ki 9:35). The Philistines hung up Saul's head in the temple of Dagon (1Ch 10:10). At other times, this word is used more generically to mean person, as when Moses instructed the Israelites to gather an omer of manna per person (Ex 16:16); a beka of silver per person for the tabernacle (Ex 38:26); or to redeem the Levites (Nu 3:47). It is also used in passages concerning the taking of a census (Nu 1:2, 18, 20, 22; 1Ch 23:3, 24). This word means the same as the Aramaic word *Golgotha*—the name of the place where Jesus was crucified (Lk 23:33).

1539. גֶּלֶד, **gêled,** *gay´-led*; from an unused root probably meaning to *polish*; the (human) *skin* (as *smooth*):—*skin*.

A masculine noun meaning skin. It is an archaic Hebrew word, since it is found only one time in the book of Job. The word is used when the text describes Job expressing his grief by sewing sackcloth over his skin (Job 16:15)—a common custom of mourning in ancient Israel.

1540. גָּלָה, **gâlâh,** *gaw-law´*; a primitive root; to *denude* (especially in a disgraceful sense); (by implication) to *exile* (captives being usually *stripped*); (figurative) to *reveal*:— + advertise, appear, bewray, bring, (carry, lead, go) captive (into captivity), depart, disclose, discover, exile, be gone, open, × plainly, publish, remove, reveal, × shamelessly, shew, × surely, tell, uncover.

A verb meaning to reveal, to be revealed, to uncover, to remove, to go into exile, to reveal oneself, to expose, to disclose. It is used with the words ear (1Sa 9:15; 20:2, 12, 13) and eyes (Nu 24:4), meaning to reveal. On occasion, it is used in the expression to uncover the nakedness of, which often implies sexual relations (Le 18:6).

1541. גְּלָה, **gᵉlâh,** *gel-aw´*; (Chaldee); or גְּלָא, **gᵉlâ’,** *gel-aw´*; (Chaldee); corresponding to 1540:—bring over, carry away, reveal.

An Aramaic verb meaning to bring over, to take away (into exile), to reveal. This word is used of those who were deported to Babylonia (Ezr 4:10; 5:12). In the book of Daniel, the meaning is to uncover or to reveal. In the story of the dreams of Nebuchadnezzar, God is shown as the One who reveals hidden things, specifically the meanings of dreams (Da 2:22, 28, 29, 47).

1542. גִּלֹה, **Gilôh,** *gee-lo´*; or (fully) גִּילֹה, **Gîylôh,** *gee-lo´*; from 1540; *open*; *Giloh*, a place in Palestine:—Giloh.

1543. גֻּלָּה, **gullâh,** *gool-law´*; feminine from 1556; a *fountain*, *bowl* or *globe* (all as *round*):—bowl, pommel, spring.

1544. גִּלּוּל, **gillûwl,** *gil-lool´*; or (shortened) גִּלֻּל, **gillul,** *gil-lool´*; from 1556; (properly) a *log* (as *round*); (by implication) an *idol*:—idol.

A masculine noun meaning idols. The Hebrew word is always found in the plural form. The term is used thirty-eight times in

Ezekiel and nine times in the rest of the OT. The people are told to destroy, abandon, and remove their idols. Dt 29:17[16] implies idols can be made of wood, stone, silver, or gold. Ezekiel longs for a day when Israel will no longer worship idols (Eze 37:23).

1545. גְּלוֹם, **gᵉlôwm,** *gel-ome´*; from 1563; *clothing* (as *wrapped*):—clothes.

1546. גָּלוּת, **gâlûwth,** *gaw-looth´*; feminine from 1540; *captivity*; (concrete) *exiles* (collective):— (they that are carried away) captives (-ity).

A feminine singular noun meaning exiles, captives, captivity. This word is used with the meaning of exiles in the prophetic messages concerning the prisoners of the king of Assyria (Isa 20:4); those exiles whom the Lord will free (Isa 45:13); and those whom God would protect (Jer 24:5; 28:4). It is also used to refer to Jehoiachin's captivity (2Ki 25:27; Eze 1:2), and the exile of the Israelites as a whole (Eze 33:21). The word comes from the Hebrew root *gâlâh* (1540).

1547. גְּלוּ, **gâlûw,** *gaw-loo´*; (Chaldee); corresponding to 1546:—captivity.

An Aramaic feminine singular noun meaning captivity, exile. It is the equivalent of the Hebrew word *gâlûth* (1546). In Aramaic, it is commonly used in the phrase *sons of captivity*. In the book of Ezra, the word refers to the exiles who celebrated when the temple was rebuilt after King Darius's decree (Ezr 6:16). In the book of Daniel, it refers to Daniel's captivity (Da 2:25; 5:13; 6:13[14]).

1548. גָּלַח, **gâlach,** *gaw-lakh´*; a primitive root; (properly) to *be bald*, i.e. (causative) to *shave*; (figurative) to *lay waste*:—poll, shave (off).

1549. גִּלָּיוֹן, **gillâyôwn,** *gil-law-yone´*; or גִּלְיוֹן, **gilyôwn,** *gil-yone´*; from 1540; a *tablet* for writing (as *bare*); (by analogy) a *mirror* (as a *plate*):—glass, roll.

1550. גָּלִיל, **gâlîyl,** *gaw-leel´*; from 1556; a *valve* of a folding door (as *turning*); also a *ring* (as *round*):—folding, ring.

1551. גָּלִיל, **Gâlîyl,** *gaw-leel´*; or (prolonged) גְּלִילָה, **Gâlîylâh,** *gaw-lee-law´*; the same as 1550; a *circle* (with the article); *Galil* (as a special *circuit*) in the North of Palestine:—Galilee.

1552. גְּלִילָה, **geliylâh,** *gel-ee-law´;* feminine of 1550; a *circuit* or *region:*—border, coast, country.

1553. גְּלִילוֹת, **Geliylôwth,** *gel-ee-lowth´;* plural of 1552; *circles; Geliloth,* a place in Palestine:—Geliloth.

1554. גַּלִּים, **Gallîym,** *gal-leem´;* plural of 1530; *springs; Gallim,* a place in Palestine:—Gallim.

1555. גָּלְיַת, **Golyath,** *gol-yath´;* perhaps from 1540; *exile; Goljath,* a Philistine:—Goliath.

1556. גָּלַל, **gâlal,** *gaw-lal´;* a primitive root; to *roll* (literal or figurative):—commit, remove, roll (away, down, together), run down, seek occasion, trust, wallow.

A verb meaning to roll, to remove, to commit, to trust. The root idea of the word is to roll. The Hebrew word often refers to rolling stones (Ge 29:8; Jos 10:18; Pr 26:27) as well as other concrete objects. It can also describe abstract concepts, such as reproach being rolled off (removed) from someone (Ps 119:22) or one's ways and works rolled onto (committed, entrusted) to someone (especially God) (Ps 37:5; Pr 16:3). This important root word is used to form many other names and words (cf. Gilgal in Jos 5:9).

1557. גָּלָל, **gâlâl,** *gaw-lawl´;* from 1556; *dung* (as in *balls*):—dung.

1558. גָּלָל, **gâlâl,** *gaw-lawl´;* from 1556; a *circumstance* (as *rolled* around); only used adverbially, on *account* of:—because of, for (sake).

1559. גָּלָל, **Gâlâl,** *gaw-lawl´;* from 1556, in the sense of 1560; *great; Galal,* the name of two Israelites:—Galal.

1560. גְּלָל, **gelâl,** *gel-awl´;* (Chaldee); from a root corresponding to 1556; *weight* or *size* (as if *rolled*):—great.

1561. גֵּלֶל, **gêlel,** *gay´-lel;* a variation of 1557; *dung* (plural *balls* of dung):—dung.

1562. גִּלֲלַי, **Gilalay,** *ge-lal-ah´ee;* from 1561; *dungy; Gilalai,* an Israelite:—Gilalai.

1563. גָּלַם, **gâlam,** *gaw-lam´;* a primitive root; to *fold:*—wrap together.

1564. גֹּלֶם, **gôlem,** *go´-lem;* from 1563; a *wrapped* (and unformed *mass,* i.e. as the *embryo*):—substance yet being unperfect.

1565. גַּלְמוּד, **galmûwd,** *gal-mood´;* probably by prolongation from 1563; *sterile* (as *wrapped* up too hard); (figurative) *desolate:*—desolate, solitary.

1566. גָּלַע, **gâla‘,** *gaw-lah´;* a primitive root; to *be obstinate:*—(inter-) meddle (with).

1567. גַּלְעֵד, **Galyêd,** *gal-ade´;* from 1530 and 5707; *heap of testimony; Galed,* a memorial cairn East of the Jordan:—Galeed.

1568. גִּלְעָד, **Gil‘âd,** *gil-awd´;* probably from 1567; *Gilad,* a region East of the Jordan; also the name of three Israelites:—Gilead, Gileadite.

1569. גִּלְעָדִי, **Gil‘âdîy,** *gil-aw-dee´;* patronymic from 1568; a *Giladite* or descendant of Gilad:—Gileadite.

1570. גָּלַשׁ, **gâlash,** *gaw-lash´;* a primitive root; probably to *caper* (as a goat):—appear.

1571. גַּם, **gam,** *gam;* by contraction from an unused root meaning to *gather;* (properly) *assemblage;* used only adverbially *also, even, yea, though;* often repeated as correlation *both … and:*—again, alike, also, (so much) as (soon), both (so) … and, but, either … or, even, for all, (in) likewise (manner), moreover, nay … neither, one, then (-fore), though, what, with, yea.

1572. גָּמָא, **gâmâ’,** *gaw-maw´;* a primitive root (literal or figurative) to *absorb:*—swallow, drink.

1573. גֹּמֶא, **gôme’,** *go´-meh;* from 1572; (properly) an *absorbent,* i.e. the *bulrush* (from its *porosity*); specifically the *papyrus:*—(bul-) rush.

1574. גֹּמֶד, **gômed,** *go´-med;* from an unused root apparently meaning to *grasp;* (properly) a *span:*—cubit.

1575. גַּמָּדִים, **gammâdîym,** *gam-maw-deem´;* from the same as 1574; a *warrior* (as *grasping* weapons):—Gammadims.

1576. גְּמוּל, **gemûwl,** *gem-ool´;* from 1580; *treatment,* i.e. an *act* (of good or ill); (by implication) *service* or *requital:*— + as hast served, benefit, desert, deserving, that which he hath given, recompense, reward.

1577. גָּמוּל, **gâmûwl,** *gaw-mool´*; passive participle of 1580; *rewarded; Gamul,* an Israelite:— Gamul. See also 1014.

1578. גְּמוּלָה, **gᵉmûwlâh,** *gem-oo-law´*; feminine of 1576; meaning the same:—deed, recompense, such a reward.

1579. גִּמְזוֹ, **Gimzôw,** *gim-zo´*; of uncertain derivation; Gimzo, a place in Palestine:—Gimzo.

1580. גָּמַל, **gâmal,** *gaw-mal´*; a primitive root; to *treat* a person (well or ill), i.e. *benefit* or *requite*; by implication (of *toil*) to *ripen,* i.e. (specific) to *wean:*—bestow on, deal bountifully, do (good), recompense, requite, reward, ripen, + serve, mean, yield.

A verb meaning to recompense another, to bring to completion, to do good. This word has a broad spectrum of meanings. The predominant idea of this word is to recompense either with a benevolent reward (1Sa 24:17[18]; 2Sa 19:36[37]) or an evil recompense (Dt 32:6; 2Ch 20:11; Ps 137:8). The idea of bringing to an end is demonstrated in verses that describe a child who is weaned (Ge 21:8; 1Sa 1:22–24; Isa 11:8) or plants that have ripened (Nu 17:8[23]; Isa 18:5). At times this word is best translated to do good or to deal bountifully (Ps 119:17; Pr 11:17; Isa 63:7).

1581. גָּמָל, **gâmâl,** *gaw-mawl´*; apparently from 1580 (in the sense of *labour* or *burden-bearing*); a *camel:*—camel.

1582. גְּמַלִּי, **Gᵉmalliy,** *gem-al-lee´*; probably from 1581; *camel-driver; Gemalli,* an Israelite:— Gemalli.

1583. גַּמְלִיאֵל, **Gamliy'êl,** *gam-lee-ale´*; from 1580 and 410; *reward of God; Gamliel,* an Israelite:—Gamaliel.

1584. גָּמַר, **gâmar,** *gaw-mar´*; a primitive root; to *end* (in the sense of *completion* or *failure*):— cease, come to an end, fail, perfect, perform.

A verb meaning to complete, to perfect, to fail, to cease. The root idea of the word is to end. In three intransitive uses, the psalmist prayed for wickedness to end, cried out that the godly person fails, and asked if God's promise fails forever (Ps 7:9[10]; 12:1[2]; 77:8[9]). In two transitive uses, God is the subject. He will perfect that which concerns the psalmist and will

complete (or perform) all things for him (Ps 57:2[3]; 138:8).

1585. גְּמַר, **gᵉmar,** *gem-ar´*; (Chaldee); corresponding to 1584:—perfect.

A verb meaning to complete. This Aramaic word is used only once in the OT and is equivalent to the Hebrew word *gâmar* (1584), meaning to complete. It is found only in the introductory section of Artaxerxes' decree given to Ezra (Ezr 7:12). Although the exact meaning of this word is unclear, it is best to understand this word as an introductory comment similar to Ezr 5:7, where the Hebrew word *shĕlâm* (8001), meaning peace, is used.

1586. גֹּמֶר, **Gômer,** *go´-mer*; from 1584; *completion; Gomer,* the name of a son of Japheth and of his descendant; also of a Hebrewess:— Gomer.

1587. גְּמַרְיָה, **Gᵉmaryâh,** *gem-ar-yaw´*; or גְּמַרְיָהוּ, **Gᵉmaryâhûw,** *gem-ar-yaw´-hoo*; from 1584 and 3050; *Jah has perfected; Gemarjah,* the name of two Israelites:—Gemariah.

1588. גַּן, **gan,** *gan*; from 1598; a *garden* (as *fenced*):—garden.

1589. גָּנַב, **gânab,** *gaw-nab´*; a primitive root; to *thieve* (literal or figurative); (by implication) to *deceive:*—carry away, × indeed, secretly bring, steal (away), get by stealth.

1590. גַּנָּב, **gannâb,** *gan-nawb´*; from 1589; a *stealer:*—thief.

1591. גְּנֵבָה, **gᵉnêbâh,** *gen-ay-baw´*; from 1589; *stealing,* i.e. (concrete) something *stolen:*—theft.

1592. גְּנֻבַת, **Gᵉnubath,** *gen-oo-bath´*; from 1589; *theft; Genubath,* an Edomitish prince:—Genubath.

1593. גַּנָּה, **gannâh,** *gan-naw´*; feminine of 1588; a *garden:*—garden.

1594. גִּנָּה, **ginnâh,** *gin-naw´*; another form for 1593:—garden.

1595. גֶּנֶז, **genez,** *geh´-nez*; from an unused root meaning to *store; treasure*; (by implication) a *coffer:*—chest, treasury.

1596. גְּנַז, **gᵉnaz,** *gen-az´*; (Chaldee); corresponding to 1595; *treasure:*—treasure.

1597. גְּנְזַךְ, **ganzak,** *gan-zak´*; prolonged from 1595; a *treasury*:—treasury.

1598. גָּנַן, **gânan,** *gaw-nan´*; a primitive root; to *hedge* about, i.e. (generally) *protect*:—defend.

1599. גִּנְּתוֹן, **Ginnᵉthôwn,** *gin-neth-ōne´*; or גִּנְּתוֹ, **Ginnᵉthôw,** *gin-neth-o´*; from 1598; *gardener*; Ginnethon or Ginnetho, an Israelite:—Ginnetho, Ginnethon.

1600. גָּעָה, **gâ'âh,** *gaw-aw´*; a primitive root; to *bellow* (as cattle):—low.

1601. גֹּעָה, **Gô'âh,** *go-aw´*; feminine active participle of 1600; *lowing*; Goah, a place near Jerusalem:—Goath.

1602. גָּעַל, **gâ'al,** *gaw-al´*; a primitive root; to *detest*; (by implication) to *reject*:—abhor, fail, lothe, vilely cast away.

A verb meaning to detest, to abhor. It is used in Le 26:15, 43 to warn Israel not to abhor God's commandments. He would otherwise abhor them (Le 26:30), yet not to such an extent that He would destroy them completely (Le 26:44). This word also describes Israel as an unfaithful wife who loathes her husband (God) and her children (Eze 16:45). A bull that is not able to mate with a cow or whose seed is miscarried is said, literally, to cause loathing (Job 21:10). In 2Sa 1:21, a shield that failed to protect its owner, Saul, was cast away as detested rather than being oiled.

1603. גַּעַל, **Ga'al,** *gah´-al*; from 1602; *loathing*; Gaal, an Israelite:—Gaal.

1604. גֹּעַל, **gô'al,** *go´-al*; from 1602; *abhorrence*:—loathing.

1605. גָּעַר, **gâ'ar,** *gaw-ar´*; a primitive root; to *chide*:—corrupt, rebuke, reprove.

A verb meaning to rebuke. This word depicts the sharp criticism of one person to another: Jacob rebuked Joseph for telling his dream (Ge 37:10), and Boaz commanded his servants not to rebuke Ruth's gleaning activity (Ru 2:16). When depicting God's actions, this word is often used to describe the result of His righteous anger (Isa 54:9; Na 1:4) against those who rebel against Him, including wicked nations (Ps 9:5[6]; Isa 17:13); their offspring (Mal 2:3); the proud (Ps 119:21); and Satan (Zec 3:2). So

authoritative is the Lord's rebuke that even nature obeys His voice (Ps 106:9; Na 1:4).

1606. גְּעָרָה, **gᵉ'ârâh,** *geh-aw-raw´*; from 1605; a *chiding*:—rebuke (-ing), reproof.

A feminine singular noun meaning rebuke. It occurs fifteen times in the Bible, always in poetic passages. Both God and humans are the subject of such rebukes (2Sa 22:16; Isa 50:2).

1607. גָּעַשׁ, **gâ'ash,** *gaw-ash´*; a primitive root to *agitate* violently:—move, shake, toss, trouble.

1608. גַּעַשׁ, **Ga'ash,** *ga´-ash*; from 1607; a *quaking; Gaash*, a hill in Palestine:—Gaash.

1609. גַּעְתָּם, **Ga'tâm,** *gah-tawm´*; of uncertain derivation; *Gatam*, an Edomite:—Gatam.

1610. גַּף, **gaph,** *gaf*; from an unused root meaning to *arch*; the *back*; (by extension) the *body* or *self*:— + highest places, himself.

1611. גַּף, **gaph,** *gaf*; (Chaldee); corresponding to 1610; a *wing*:—wing.

1612. גֶּפֶן, **gephen,** *geh´-fen*; from an unused root meaning to *bend*; a *vine* (as *twining*), especially the grape:—vine, tree.

1613. גֹּפֶר, **gôpher,** *go´-fer*; from an unused root, probably meaning to *house in*; a kind of tree or wood (as used for *building*), apparently the *cypress*:—gopher.

1614. גָּפְרִית, **gophrîyth,** *gof-reeth´*; probably feminine of 1613; (properly) cypress *resin*; (by analogy) *sulphur* (as equally inflammable):—brimstone.

1615. גִּר, **gir,** *geer*; perhaps from 3564; *lime* (from being *burned* in a kiln):—chalk [-stone].

1616. גֵּר, **gêr,** *gare*; or (fully) גֵּיר, **gêyr,** *gare*; from 1481; (properly) a *guest*; (by implication) a *foreigner*:—alien, sojourner, stranger.

A masculine noun meaning sojourner, alien, stranger. The word indicates in general anyone who is not native to a given land or among a given people (Ex 12:19). The word is used most often to describe strangers or sojourners in Israel who were not native-born Israelites and were temporary dwellers or newcomers. A person, family, or group might leave their homeland and people to go elsewhere because of war or immediate danger as Moses had done (Ex 2:22; cf. 2Sa 4:3); Naomi and her family were forced to travel to Moab to sojourn because of a famine in Israel (Ru 1:1). God's call to Abraham to leave his own land of Ur of the Chaldees and made him a sojourner and an alien in the land of Canaan (Ge 12:1). Israel's divinely orchestrated descent into Egypt resulted in their becoming an alien people in a foreign land for four hundred years (Ge 15:13). Abraham considered himself an alien, although he was in the land of Canaan, the land of promise, because he was living among the Hittites at Hebron (Ge 23:4).

This evidence indicates that strangers or aliens were those living in a strange land among strange people. Their stay was temporary or they did not identify with the group among whom they were living, no matter how long they stayed. The transitory nature of aliens' status is indicated in passages that describe them as seeking overnight lodging or accommodations (Job 31:32; Jer 14:8).

Sojourners or strangers in Israel were not to be oppressed but were to receive special consideration for several reasons: Israel knew about being aliens, for they had been aliens in Egypt (Ex 23:9); aliens had a right to rest and cessation from labour just as the native Israelites did (Ex 20:10); aliens were to be loved, for God loved them (Dt 10:18) just as He loved widows and orphans; aliens had a right to food to satisfy their needs just as orphans and widows did (Dt 14:29). In Ezekiel's vision of a new temple and temple area, the children of aliens and sojourners were given an allotment of land (Eze 47:22), for they were to be considered as native children of Israel. However, this shows that sojourners had to receive special concessions because they did not have all the rights of native Israelites. Aliens could eat the Lord's Passover only if they and their entire household submitted to circumcision (Ex 12:48, 49). They were then not allowed to eat anything with yeast in it during the celebration of the Passover, just like native Israelites (Ex 12:19, 20). However, major distinctions did exist between sojourners or aliens and native Israelites. Unclean food could be given to aliens to eat, but the Israelites were prohibited from eating the same food. To have done so would violate their holiness and consecration to the Lord God. Unfortunately, David himself laid forced labour on the shoul-

ders of aliens in Israel to prepare to build the temple (1Ch 22:2; cf. 2Ch 8:7–9).

1617. גֵּרָא, **Gêrâ**, *gay-raw´*; perhaps from 1626; a *grain*; *Gera*, the name of six Israelites:—Gera.

1618. גָּרָב, **gârâb**, *gaw-rawb´*; from an unused root meaning to *scratch; scurf* (from *itching*):—scab, scurvy.

1619. גָּרֵב, **Gârêb**, *gaw-rabe´*; from the same as 1618; *scabby; Gareb*, the name of an Israelite, also of a hill near Jerusalem:—Gareb.

1620. גַּרְגַּר, **gargêr**, *gar-gayr´*; by reduplication from 1641; a *berry* (as if a pellet of *rumination*):—berry.

1621. גַּרְגְּרוֹת, **gargârôwth**, *gar-ghawr-owth´*; feminine plural from 1641; the *throat* (as used in *rumination*):—neck.

1622. גִּרְגָּשִׁי, **Girgâshîy**, *gir-gaw-shee´*; patrial from an unused name [of uncertain derivation]; a *Girgashite*, one of the native tribes of Canaan:—Girgashite, Girgasite.

1623. גָּרַד, **gârad**, *gaw-rad´*; a primitive root; to *abrade*:—scrape.

1624. גָּרָה, **gârâh**, *gaw-raw´*; a primitive root; (properly) to *grate*, i.e. (figurative) to *anger*:—contend, meddle, stir up, strive.

1625. גֵּרָה, **gêrâh**, *gay-raw´*; from 1641; the *cud* (as *scraping* the throat):—cud.

1626. גֵּרָה, **gêrâh**, *gay-raw´*; from 1641 (as in 1625); properly (like 1620) a *kernel* (round as if *scraped*), i.e. a *gerah* or small weight (and coin):—gerah.

1627. גָּרוֹן, **gârôwn**, *gaw-rone´*; or (shortened) גָּרֹן, **gârôn**, *gaw-rone´*; from 1641; the *throat* [compare 1621] (as *roughened* by swallowing):—× aloud, mouth, neck, throat.

1628. גֵּרוּת, **gêrûwth**, *gay-rooth´*; from 1481; a (temporary) *residence*:—habitation.

1629. גָּרַז, **gâraz**, *gaw-raz´*; a primitive root; to *cut* off:—cut off.

1630. גְּרִזִים, **Gᵉrizîym**, *ger-ee-zeem´*; plural of an unused noun from 1629 [compare 1511], *cut up* (i.e. *rocky*); *Gerizim*, a mountain of Palestine:—Gerizim.

1631. גַּרְזֶן, **garzen,** *gar-zen´*; from 1629; an *ax:*—ax.

1632. גָּרֹל, **gârôl,** *gaw-role´*; from the same as 1486; *harsh:*—man of great [*as in the margin which reads* 1419].

1633. גָּרַם, **gâram,** *gaw-ram´*; a primitive root; to *be spare* or *skeleton-like*; used only as a denominative from 1634; (causative) to *bone,* i.e. *denude* (by extension) *crunch* the bones:— gnaw the bones, break.

1634. גֶּרֶם, **gerem,** *geh´-rem*; from 1633; a *bone* (as the *skeleton* of the body); hence *self,* i.e. (figurative) *very:*—bone, strong, top.

1635. גְּרַם, **gᵉram,** *geh´-ram*; (Chaldee); corresponding to 1634; a *bone:*—bone.

1636. גַּרְמִי, **Garmîy,** *gar-mee´*; from 1634; *bony,* i.e. *strong:*—Garmite.

1637. גֹּרֶן, **gôren,** *go´-ren*; from an unused root meaning to *smooth*; a threshing-*floor* (as made *even*); (by analogy) any open *area:*—(barn, corn, threshing-) floor, (threshing-, void) place.

1638. גָּרַס, **gâras,** *gaw-ras´*; a primitive root; to *crush*; also (intransitive and figurative) to *dissolve:*—break.

1639. גָּרַע, **gâra‛,** *gaw-rah´*; a primitive root; to *scrape* off; (by implication) to *shave, remove, lessen* or *withhold:*—abate, clip, (di-) minish, do (take) away, keep back, restrain, make small, withdraw.

1640. גָּרַף, **gâraph,** *gaw-raf´*; a primitive root; to *bear* off violently:—sweep away.

1641. גָּרַר, **gârar,** *gaw-rar´*; a primitive root; to *drag* off roughly; (by implication) to *bring up* the cud (i.e. *ruminate*); (by analogy) to *saw:*—catch, chew, × continuing, destroy, saw.

A verb meaning to scrape, to drag, to ruminate, to saw. The idea of a noise made in the back of the throat seems to be the root idea so that the word is onomatopoetic like the English word gargle. The word is used once to signify rumination, an essential mark of a ceremonially clean animal (Le 11:7). It described hostile forces dragging people away (Pr 21:7) or catching them like fish in a net (Hab 1:15). The word also signifies sawing, as dragging a saw over wood (1Ki 7:9).

1642. גְּרָר, **Gᵉrâr,** *ger-awr´*; probably from 1641; a *rolling* country; *Gerar,* a Philistine city:— Gerar.

1643. גֶּרֶשׂ, **gereś,** *geh´-res*; from an unused root meaning to *husk*; a *kernel* (collective), i.e. *grain:*—beaten corn.

1644. גָּרַשׁ, **gârash,** *gaw-rash´*; a primitive root; to *drive* out from a possession; especially to *expatriate* or *divorce:*—cast up (out), divorced (woman), drive away (forth, out), expel, × surely put away, trouble, thrust out.

1645. גֶּרֶשׁ, **geresh,** *geh´-resh*; from 1644; *produce* (as if *expelled*):—put forth.

1646. גְּרֻשָׁה, **gᵉrushâh,** *ger-oo-shaw´*; feminine passive participle of 1644; (abstract) *dispossession:*—exaction.

1647. גֵּרְשֹׁם, **Gêrᵉshôm,** *gay-resh-ome´*; for 1648; *Gereshom,* the name of four Israelites:—Gershom.

1648. גֵּרְשׁוֹן, **Gêrᵉshôwn,** *gay-resh-one´*; or גֵּרְשׁוֹם, **Gêrᵉshôwm,** *gay-resh-ome´*; from 1644; a *refugee; Gereshon* or *Gereshom,* an Israelite:— Gershon, Gershom.

1649. גֵּרְשֻׁנִּי, **Gêrᵉshunnîy,** *gay-resh-oon-nee´*; patronymic from 1648; a *Gereshonite* or descendant of Gereshon:—Gershonite, sons of Gershon.

1650. גְּשׁוּר, **Gᵉshûwr,** *gesh-oor´*; from an unused root (meaning to *join*); *bridge; Geshur,* a district of Syria:—Geshur, Geshurite.

1651. גְּשׁוּרִי, **Gᵉshûwrîy,** *ge-shoo-ree´*; patrial from 1650; a *Geshurite* (also collective) or inhabitant of Geshur:—Geshuri, Geshurites.

1652. גָּשַׁם, **gâsham,** *gaw-sham´*; a primitive root; to *shower* violently:—(cause to) rain.

1653. גֶּשֶׁם, **geshem,** *geh´-shem*; from 1652; a *shower:*—rain, shower.

1654. גֶּשֶׁם, **Geshem,** *geh´-shem*; or (prolonged) גַּשְׁמוּ, **Gashmûw,** *gash-moo´*; the same as 1653; *Geshem* or *Gashmu,* an Arabian:—Geshem, Gashmu.

1655. גֶּשֶׁם, **gᵉshêm,** *geh´-shame*; (Chaldee); apparently the same as 1653; used in a peculiar sense, the *body* (probably for the [figurative] idea of a *hard* rain):—body.

A masculine noun meaning body. This is an Aramaic term and is found only in the book of Daniel. When Shadrach, Meshach, and Abednego emerged from the fiery furnace, this word was used to describe their unscathed bodies (Da 3:27). This term was also used to describe the nature of Nebuchadnezzar's being when he was turned into a beast (Da 5:21).

1656. גֹּשֶׁם, **gôshem,** *go´-shem;* from 1652; equivalent to 1653:—rained upon.

1657. גֹּשֶׁן, **Gôshen,** *go´-shen;* probably of Egyptian origin; *Goshen,* the residence of the Israelites in Egypt; also a place in Palestine:—Goshen.

1658. גִּשְׁפָּא, **Gishpâ',** *gish-paw´;* of uncertain derivation; *Gishpa,* an Israelite:—Gispa.

1659. גָּשַׁשׁ, **gâshash,** *gaw-shash´;* a primitive root; apparently to *feel* about:—grope.

1660. גַּת, **gath,** *gath;* probably from 5059 (in the sense of *treading* out grapes); a wine-*press* (or vat for holding the grapes in pressing them):— (wine-) press (fat).

1661. גַּת, **Gath,** *gath;* the same as 1660; *Gath,* a Philistine city:—Gath.

1662. גַּת־הַחֵפֶר, **Gath-ha-Chêpher,** *gath-hah-khay´-fer;* or (abridged) גִּתָּה־חֵפֶר, **Gittâh-Chêpher,** *git-taw-khay´-fer;* from 1660 and 2658 with the article inserted; *wine-press of (the) well; Gath-Chepher,* a place in Palestine:— Gath-kephr, Gittah-kephr.

1663. גִּתִּי, **Gittîy,** *git-tee´;* patrial from 1661; a *Gittite* or inhabitant of Gath:—Gittite.

1664. גִּתַּיִם, **Gittayim,** *git-tah´-yim;* dual of 1660; *double wine-press; Gittajim,* a place in Palestine:—Gittaim.

1665. גִּתִּית, **Gittîyth,** *git-teeth´;* feminine of 1663; a *Gittite* harp:—Gittith.

1666. גֶּתֶר, **Gether,** *geh´-ther;* of uncertain derivation; *Gether,* a son of Aram, and the region settled by him:—Gether.

1667. גַּת־רִמּוֹן, **Gath-Rimmôwn,** *gath-rim-mone´;* from 1660 and 7416; *wine-press of* (the) *pomegranate; Gath-Rimmon,* a place in Palestine:—Gath-rimmon.

ד (Daleth)

1668. דָּא, **dâ',** *daw*; (Chaldee); corresponding to 2088; *this:*—one ... another, this.

1669. דְּאַב, **dâ'ab,** *daw-ab'*; a primitive root; to *pine:*—mourn, sorrow (-ful).

1670. דְּאָבָה, **dᵉ'âbâh,** *dĕh-aw-baw'*; from 1669; (properly) *pining;* (by analogy) *fear:*—sorrow.

1671. דְּאָבוֹן, **dᵉ'âbôwn,** *dĕh-aw-bone'*; from 1669; *pining:*—sorrow.

1672. דָּאַג, **dâ'ag,** *daw-ag'*; a primitive root; *be anxious:*—be afraid (careful, sorry), sorrow, take thought.

A verb meaning to be anxious, to fear. This word describes uneasiness of mind as a result of the circumstances of life. It denotes the anxiety of Saul's father when Saul was away from home (1Sa 9:5; 10:2); the anxiety of David which resulted from his sin (Ps 38:18[19]); and the fear of famine (Jer 42:16). On the other hand, Jeremiah described the righteous person as one who would not be anxious in drought (Jer 17:8). This word is also used as a synonym for the Hebrew word *yârê'* (3372), meaning to fear when speaking of the anxiety of King Zedekiah (Jer 38:19) or fear in general (Isa 57:11).

1673. דֹּאֵג, **Dô'êg,** *do-ayg'*; or (fully) דּוֹאֵג, **Dôw'êg,** *do-ayg'*; active participle of 1672; *anxious; Doëg,* an Edomite:—Doeg.

1674. דְּאָגָה, **dᵉ'âgâh,** *dĕh-aw-gaw'*; from 1672; *anxiety:*—care (-fulness), fear, heaviness, sorrow.

A feminine noun meaning anxiety, care. This word refers to apprehension because of approaching trouble. In Joshua 22:24, it refers to a concern that Israel might forget God and prompted the building of a memorial altar. Elsewhere, it refers to anxiety over running out of food or an anxiety caused by God's judgment (Eze 4:16; 12:18, 19). This anxiety was sometimes roused by bad news (Jer 49:23) and sometimes relieved by good words (Pr 12:25).

1675. דָּאָה, **dâ'âh,** *daw-aw'*; a primitive root; to *dart,* i.e. *fly* rapidly:—fly.

1676. דָּאָה, **dâ'âh,** *daw-aw'*; from 1675; the *kite* (from its rapid *flight*):—vulture. See 7201.

1677. דֹּב, **dôb,** *dobe*; or (fully) דּוֹב, **dôwb,** *dobe*; from 1680; the *bear* (as slow):—bear.

1678. דֹּב, **dôb,** *dobe*; (Chaldee); corresponding to 1677:—bear.

1679. דֹּבֶא, **dôbe',** *do'-beh*; from an unused root (compare 1680) (probably meaning to be *sluggish,* i.e. *restful*); *quiet:*—strength.

1680. דְּבַב, **dâbab,** *daw-bab'*; a primitive root (compare 1679); to *move* slowly, i.e. *glide:*—cause to speak.

A verb meaning to move slowly, to glide over. It is used in late Hebrew to mean to flow slowly or to drop. In the OT, it suggests something that causes one to speak. In the discourse of the Shulamite and the beloved, this word identifies the way wine gently or slowly moves over the taster's lips and teeth (SS 7:9[10]).

1681. דִּבָּה, **dibbâh,** *dib-baw'*; from 1680 (in the sense of *furtive* motion); *slander:*—defaming, evil report, infamy, slander.

1682. דְּבוֹרָה, **dᵉbôwrâh,** *deb-o-raw'*; or (shortened) דְּבֹרָה, **dᵉbôrâh,** *deb-o-raw'*; from 1696 (in the sense of *orderly* motion); the *bee* (from its *systematic* instincts):—bee.

1683. דְּבוֹרָה, **Dᵉbôwrâh,** *deb-o-raw'*; or (shortened) דְּבֹרָה, **Dᵉbôrâh,** *deb-o-raw'*; the same as 1682; *Deborah,* the name of two Hebrewesses:—Deborah.

1684. דְּבַח, **dᵉbach,** *deb-akh'*; (Chaldee); corresponding to 2076; to *sacrifice* (an animal):—offer [sacrifice].

An Aramaic verb meaning to sacrifice, to offer sacrifices. When King Darius issued the decree permitting the rebuilding of the Temple, he specified that it would be a place to offer sacrifices (Ezr 6:3). This word is the equivalent of the Hebrew verb *zâbach* (2076).

1685. דְּבַח, **dᵉbach,** *deb-akh´*; (Chaldee); from 1684; a *sacrifice*:—sacrifice.

A masculine noun meaning sacrifice. This word comes from the Aramaic and is derived from the verb *dĕbach* (1684), meaning to sacrifice. It is the term used when King Cyrus ordered a decree for the rebuilding of the Temple, describing it as the place where the Israelites offered sacrifices (Ezr 6:3).

1686. דְּבֹנִים, **dibyônîym,** *dib-yo-neem´*; in the margin for the textual reading חֲרִיוֹן, **cheryôwn,** *kher-yone´*; both (in the plural only and) of uncertain derivation; probably some cheap vegetable, perhaps a bulbous root:—dove's dung.

1687. דְּבִיר, **dᵉbîyr,** *deb-eer´*; or (shortened) דְּבִר, **debir,** *deb-eer´*; from 1696 (apparently in the sense of *oracle*); the *shrine* or innermost part of the sanctuary:—oracle.

A masculine noun referring to the innermost part of Solomon's Temple, also called the Holy of Holies. This cubical room, which took up one-third of the space of the Temple, housed the Ark of the Covenant (1Ki 6:16, 19–23). The ark contained the original tablets of the Ten Commandments, was overarched by carved cherubim covered with gold, and was especially associated with God's presence. When it was first brought into the Holy of Holies, God's glory filled the Temple (1Ki 8:6; cf. 1Ki 8:10). In Ps 28:2, David spoke of lifting his hands to the *dĕbiyr.* Since the Temple had not yet been built, this likely referred to the heavenly reality that was the model for the Temple and earlier tabernacle (cf. Ps 18:6[7]; Heb 8:5; 9:3–5) or perhaps to the room in the tabernacle that housed the Ark of the Covenant.

1688. דְּבִיר, **Dᵉbîyr,** *deb-eer´*; or (shortened) דְּבִר, **Dᵉbir,** *deb-eer´*; (Jos 13:26 [but see 3810]), the same as 1687; *Debir,* the name of an Amoritish king and of two places in Palestine:—Debir.

1689. דִּבְלָה, **Diblâh,** *dib-law´*; probably an orthographical error for 7247; *Diblah,* a place in Syria:—Diblath.

1690. דְּבֵלָה, **dᵉbêlâh,** *deb-ay-law´*; from an unused root (akin to 2082) probably meaning to *press* together; a *cake* of pressed figs:—cake (lump) of figs.

1691. דִּבְלַיִם, **Diblayim,** *dib-lah´-yim*; dual from the masculine of 1690; *two cakes; Diblajim,* a symbol. name:—Diblaim.

1692. דָּבַק, **dâbaq,** *daw-bak´*; a primitive root; (properly) to *impinge,* i.e. *cling* or *adhere*; (figurative) to *catch* by pursuit:—abide fast, cleave (fast together), follow close (hard after), be joined (together), keep (fast), overtake, pursue hard, stick, take.

1693. דְּבַק, **dᵉbaq,** *deb-ak´*; (Chaldee); corresponding to 1692; to *stick* to:—cleave.

1694. דֶּבֶק, **debeq,** *deh´-bek*; from 1692; a *joint*; (by implication) *solder*:—joint, solder.

1695. דָּבֵק, **dâbêq,** *daw-bake´*; from 1692; *adhering*:—cleave, joining, stick closer.

1696. דָּבַר, **dâbar,** *daw-bar´*; a primitive root; (perhaps properly) to *arrange*; but used figuratively (of words) to *speak*; rarely (in a destructive sense) to *subdue*:—answer, appoint, bid, command, commune, declare, destroy, give, name, promise, pronounce, rehearse, say, speak, be spokesman, subdue, talk, teach, tell, think, use [entreaties], utter, × well, × work.

A verb meaning to speak, to say. God told Moses to tell Pharaoh what He said (Ex 6:29). It can mean to promise (Dt 1:11). When used with the word song, it can mean to sing or chant (Jgs 5:12). The word can also mean think, as when Solomon spoke in his heart (Ecc 2:15). In Jeremiah, it means to pronounce judgment (Jer 1:16). This verb also refers to speaking about or against someone (Mal 3:13) or someone speaking to someone else (Mal 3:16). It is closely related to the Hebrew noun *dâbar* (1697).

1697. דָּבָר, **dâbâr,** *daw-bawr´*; from 1696; a *word*; (by implication) a *matter* (as *spoken* of) or *thing*; (adverbial) a *cause*:—act, advice, affair, answer, × any such (thing), + because of, book, business, care, case, cause, certain rate, + chronicles, commandment, × commune (-ication), + concern [-ing], + confer, counsel, + dearth, decree, deed, × disease, due, duty, effect, + eloquent, errand, [evil favoured-] ness, + glory,

+ harm, hurt, + iniquity, + judgment, language, + lying, manner, matter, message, [no] thing, oracle, × ought, × parts, + pertaining, + please, portion, + power, promise, provision, purpose, question, rate, reason, report, request, × (as hast) said, sake, saying, sentence, + sign, + so, some [uncleanness], somewhat to say, + song, speech, × spoken, talk, task, + that, × there done, thing (concerning), thought, + thus, tidings, what [-soever], + wherewith, which, word, work.

A masculine noun meaning word, speech, matter. This frequent word has a wide range of meanings associated with it. It signified spoken words or speech (Ge 11:1; Isa 36:5; Jer 51:64); a command or royal decree (Est 1:12, 19); a report or tidings (Ex 33:4); advice (Jgs 20:7); poetic writings of David (2Ch 29:30); business affairs (1Ch 26:32); a legal cause (Ex 18:16); the custom or manner of activity (Est 1:13); and something indefinite (thing, Ge 22:16). Most important was the use of this word to convey divine communication. Often the word of the Lord signified the revelation given to prophets (2Sa 7:4; Jer 25:3; Hos 1:1). Similarly, the Ten Commandments were literally called the ten words of the Lord (Ex 34:28; Dt 4:13).

1698. דֶּבֶר, **deber,** *deh´-ber;* from 1696 (in the sense of *destroying*); a *pestilence:*—murrain, pestilence, plague.

A noun meaning plague or pestilence. This plague is a dreaded disease similar to the bubonic plague in the Middle Ages. It was likely carried by rat fleas and produced tumors on the infected person. First Samuel 5—6 describes the plague on the Philistines as a punishment from God. The word is also used as the most dreaded threat of the Lord against His people (Le 26:25; Nu 14:12). The prophets use this word frequently to predict coming judgment and destruction as in the common phrase, sword, famine, and plague (Jer 21:9; 38:2; Eze 6:11, NIV).

1699. דֹּבֶר, **dôber,** *do´-ber;* from 1696 (in its original sense); a *pasture* (from its *arrangement* of the flock):—fold, manner. דִּבֵּר, **dibbêr,** *dib-bare´,* for 1697:—word.

1700. דִּבְרָה, **dibrâh,** *dib-raw´;* feminine of 1697; a *reason, suit* or *style:*—cause, end, estate, order, regard.

A feminine singular noun meaning cause, end, regard, manner. In the book of Job, Elip-

haz used the word to describe how he was laying down his cause before God (Job 5:8). This word is also used in the Psalms when it describes the priest who would exercise his duties in the manner of Melchizedek (Ps 110:4). Sometimes, it is translated much more briefly than it reads in the original language, as the literal translation in Ecclesiastes would read, "concerning the situation of mankind," while the NIV translates it "as for men" (Ecc 3:18). It can also mean for this reason or because (Ecc 7:14; 8:2).

1701. דִּבְרָה, **dibrâh,** *dib-raw´;* (Chaldee); corresponding to 1700:—intent, sake.

An Aramaic feminine noun meaning purpose, end, cause. The word is similar to the Hebrew form of the same spelling (1700). The Aramaic form occurs in Da 2:30 and 4:17(14). In both places, it is used with other words to create a purpose clause which is translated in order that, for the purpose of, or for the sake of.

1702. דֹּבְרוֹת, **dôberôwth,** *do-ber-oth´;* feminine active participle of 1696 in the sense of *driving* [compare 1699]; a *raft:*—float.

1703. דַּבֶּרֶת, **dabbereth,** *dab-ber-eth´;* intensive from 1696; a *word:*—word.

A feminine noun meaning word. This word is found only once in the OT (Dt 33:3), where it is best translated words. In this context, it poetically describes the words God gave Moses to deliver to the people. It comes from the verb *dâbar* (1696), meaning to speak and is related to the much-used Hebrew noun *dâbâr* (1697).

1704. דִּבְרִי, **Dibrîy,** *dib-ree´;* from 1697; *wordy; Dibri,* an Israelite:—Dibri.

1705. דָּבְרַת, **Dâberath,** *daw-ber-ath´;* from 1697 (perhaps in the sense of 1699); *Daberath,* a place in Palestine:—Dabareh, Daberath.

1706. דְּבַשׁ, **debash,** *deb-ash´;* from an unused root meaning to *be gummy; honey* (from its *stickiness*); (by analogy) *syrup:*—honey ([-comb]).

1707. דַּבֶּשֶׁת, **dabbesheth,** *dab-beh´-sheth;* intensive from the same as 1706; a sticky *mass,* i.e. the *hump* of a camel:—hunch [of a camel].

1708. דַּבֶּשֶׁת, **Dabbesheth,** *dab-beh´-sheth;* the same as 1707; *Dabbesheth,* a place in Palestine:—Dabbesheth.

1709. דָּג, **dâg,** *dawg*; or (fully) דָּאג, **dâ'g,** *dawg*; (Ne 13:16), from 1711; a *fish* (as *prolific*); or perhaps rather from 1672 (as *timid*); but still better from 1672 (in the sense of *squirming,* i.e. moving by the vibratory action of the tail); a *fish* (often used collectively):—fish.

A masculine noun meaning fish. The word is derived from *dâgâh* (1711) based on the idea that fish multiply quickly. The word is used of fish in the sea, often occurring alongside birds of the heavens and beasts of the field (Ge 9:2; Ps 8:7[8], 8[9]; Eze 38:20). The word also signifies fish as food and thus gives the name fish gate to the gate where they were brought into Jerusalem to sell (2Ch 33:14; Ne 3:3; Zep 1:10). Further, it describes fish as an object of study (1Ki 4:33[5:13]); as a symbol of defenselessness (Hab 1:14); and as showing God's sovereign creative power (Job 12:8).

1710. דָּגָה, **dâgâh,** *daw-gaw'*; feminine of 1709, and meaning the same:—fish.

A feminine noun meaning fish. This word is identical in meaning to *dâg* (1709), which can be found in the book of Jonah, where the fish was called a *dâg* (Jnh 1:17[2:1]; 2:10[11]) but was called a *dâgâh* in Jnh 2:1[2]. In all other instances, this word was used in the collective sense to refer to the fish at creation (Ge 1:26, 28); the fish who died in the plague (Ex 7:18, 21; Ps 105:29); the fish eaten in Egypt (Nu 11:5); and the fish in the waters (Dt 4:18; Eze 29:4, 5; 47:9, 10).

1711. דָּגָה, **dâgâh,** *daw-gaw'*; a primitive root; to *move rapidly*; used only as a denominative from 1709; to *spawn,* i.e. *become numerous:*—grow.

A verb meaning to multiply, to grow. Its primary meaning is to cover. It is used only in Ge 48:16 where Jacob blessed Ephraim and Manasseh, the sons of Joseph. He desired that they multiply or grow into a multitude. Jacob prophesied that Ephraim, the younger brother, would be a multitude of nations, more populous than Manasseh (cf. Ge 48:17–19) but that both would be a model of blessedness (cf. Ge 48:20).

1712. דָּגוֹן, **Dâgôwn,** *daw-gohn'*; from 1709; the *fish-god; Dagon,* a Philistine deity:—Dagon.

1713. דָּגַל, **dâgal,** *daw-gal'*; a primitive root; to *flaunt,* i.e. *raise a flag;* (figurative) to *be conspicuous:*—(set up, with) banners, chiefest.

1714. דֶּגֶל, **degel,** *deh'-gel*; from 1713; a *flag:*—banner, standard.

1715. דָּגָן, **dâgân,** *daw-gawn'*; from 1711; (properly) *increase,* i.e. *grain:*—corn ([floor]), wheat.

1716. דָּגַר, **dâgar,** *daw-gar'*; a primitive root; to *brood* over eggs or young:—gather, sit.

1717. דַּד, **dad,** *dad*; apparently from the same as 1730; the *breast* (as the seat of *love,* or from its shape):—breast, teat.

1718. דָּדָה, **dâdâh,** *daw-daw'*; a doubtful root; to *walk gently:*—go (softly, with).

1719. דְּדָן, **D⁰dân,** *ded-awn'*; or (prolonged) דְּדָנֶה, **Dedâneh,** *deh-daw'-neh*; (Eze 25:13), of uncertain derivation; *Dedan,* the name of two Cushites and of their territory:—Dedan.

1720. דְּדָנִים, **D⁰dânîym,** *ded-aw-neem'*; plural of 1719 (as patrial); *Dedanites,* the descendant or inhabitant of Dedan:—Dedanim.

1721. דֹּדָנִים, **Dôdânîym,** *do-daw-neem'*; or (by orthographical error) רֹדָנִים, **Rôdânîym,** *ro-daw-neem'*; (1Ch 1:7), a plural of uncertain derivation; *Dodanites,* or descendant of a son of Javan:—Dodanim.

1722. דְּהַב, **d⁰hab,** *deh-hab'*; (Chaldee); corresponding to 2091; *gold:*—gold (-en).

1723. דַּהֲוָא, **Dehâvê',** *deh-hawv-ay'*; (Chaldee); of uncertain derivation; *Dahava,* a people colonized in Samaria:—Dehavites.

1724. דָּהַם, **dâham,** *daw-ham'*; a primitive root (compare 1740); to *be dumb,* i.e. (figurative) *dumbfounded:*—be astonished.

1725. דָּהַר, **dâhar,** *daw-har'*; a primitive root; to *curvet* or move irregularly:—pause.

1726. דַּהֲהַר, **dahăhar,** *dah-hah-har'*; by reduplication from 1725; a *gallop:*—pransing.

1727. דּוּב, **dûwb,** *doob*; a primitive root; to *mope,* i.e. (figurative) *pine:*—sorrow.

1728. דַּוָּג, **davvâg,** *dav-vawg'*; an orthographical variation of 1709 as a denominative [1771]; a *fisherman:*—fisher.

1729. דּוּגָה, **dûwgâh,** *doo-gaw´*; feminine from the same as 1728; (properly) *fishery,* i.e. a *hook* for fishing:—fish [hook].

1730. דּוֹד, **dôwd,** *dode*; or (shortened) דֹּד, **dôd,** *dode*; from an unused root meaning (properly) to *boil,* i.e. (figurative) to *love*; (by implication) a *love-token, lover, friend*; specifically an *uncle*:—(well-) beloved, father's brother, love, uncle.

A masculine noun meaning beloved, loved one, uncle. This word is used most often in the SS of Solomon and has three clear meanings: **(1)** the most frequent is an address to a lover, beloved (SS 5:4; 6:3; 7:9[10]); **(2)** love, used literally of an adulteress who seduced a naïve man (Pr 7:18), and of Solomon and his lover (SS 1:2, 4; 4:10) (This meaning of love is also used symbolically of Jerusalem reaching the age of love [Eze 16:8] and Jerusalem's adultery [bed of love] with the Babylonians [Eze 23:17]); and finally, **(3)** uncle (Le 10:4; 1Sa 10:14–16; Est 2:15).

1731. דּוּד, **dûwd,** *dood*; from the same as 1730; a *pot* (for *boiling*); also (by resemblance of shape) a *basket*:—basket, caldron, kettle, (seething) pot.

1732. דְּוִד, **Dâvid,** *daw-veed´*; rarely (fully) דְּוִיד, **Dâvîyd,** *daw-veed´*; from the same as 1730; *loving*; *David,* the youngest son of Jesse:—David.

1733. דּוֹדָה, **dôwdâh,** *do-daw´*; feminine of 1730; an *aunt*:—aunt, father's sister, uncle's wife.

1734. דּוֹדוֹ, **Dôwdôw,** *do-do´*; from 1730; *loving*; *Dodo,* the name of three Israelites:—Dodo.

1735. דּוֹדָוָהוּ, **Dôwdâvâhûw,** *do-daw-vaw´-hoo*; from 1730 and 3050; *love of Jah*; *Dodavah,* an Israelite:—Dodavah.

1736. דּוּדָאִים, **dûwdâ'îym,** *doo-daw´-eem*; from 1731; a *boiler* or *basket*; also the *mandrake* (as *aphrodisiac*):—basket, mandrake.

A masculine plural noun meaning mandrake. A fragrant plant (SS 7:13[14]), the mandrake was considered a potent aphrodisiac. This usage can be seen in Ge 30:14–16, where the text describes Leah using these plants to attract Jacob.

1737. דּוֹדַי, **Dôwday,** *do-dah´ee*; formed like 1736; *amatory*; *Dodai,* an Israelite:—Dodai.

1738. דָּוָה, **dâvâh,** *daw-vaw´*; a primitive root; to *be sick* (as if in menstruation):—infirmity.

1739. דָּוֶה, **dâveh,** *daw-veh´*; from 1738; *sick* (especially in menstruation):—faint, menstruous cloth, she that is sick, having sickness.

1740. דּוּחַ, **dûwach,** *doo´-akh*; a primitive root; to *thrust* away; (figurative) to *cleanse*:—cast out, purge, wash.

A verb meaning to rinse, to cleanse, to wash away. This word is used only four times in the OT. On two occasions, it is used within the sacrificial context to describe offerings that needed to be washed (2Ch 4:6; Eze 40:38). In other contexts, the word describes the washing away of the sins of those in Jerusalem (Isa 4:4) and Nebuchadnezzar's carrying away (or washing away) of Judah in the Babylonian exile (Jer 51:34).

1741. דְּוַי, **dᵉvay,** *dev-ah´ee*; from 1739; *sickness*; (figurative) *loathing*:—languishing, sorrowful.

1742. דַּוָּי, **davvây,** *dav-voy´*; from 1739; *sick*; (figurative) *troubled*:—faint.

1743. דּוּךְ, **dûwk,** *dook*; a primitive root; to *bruise* in a mortar:—beat.

1744. דּוּכִיפַת, **dûwkîyphath,** *doo-kee-fath´*; of uncertain derivation; the *hoopoe* or else the *grouse*:—lapwing.

1745. דּוּמָה, **dûwmâh,** *doo-maw´*; from an unused root meaning to *be dumb* (compare 1820); *silence*; (figurative) *death*:—silence.

1746. דּוּמָה, **Dûwmâh,** *doo-maw´*; the same as 1745; *Dumah,* a tribe and region of Arabia:—Dumah.

1747. דּוּמִיָּה, **dûwmîyyâh,** *doo-me-yaw´*; from 1820; *stillness*; (adverb) *silently*; (abstract) *quiet, trust*:—silence, silent, waiteth.

1748. דּוּמָם, **dûwmâm,** *doo-mawm´*; from 1826; *still*; (adverb) *silently*:—dumb, silent, quietly wait.

1749. דּוֹנַג, **dôwnag,** *do-nag´*; of uncertain derivation; *wax*:—wax.

1750. דּוּץ, **dûwts,** *doots*; a primitive root; to *leap*:—be turned.

1751. קְדַק, **dᵉqaq,** *de-kak´;* (Chaldee); corresponding to 1854; to *crumble*:—be broken to pieces.

1752. דּוּר, **dûwr,** *dure;* a primitive root; (properly) to *gyrate* (or move in a circle), i.e. to *remain*:—dwell.

1753. דּוּר, **dûwr,** *dure;* (Chaldee); corresponding to 1752; to *reside*:—dwell.

1754. דּוּר, **dûwr,** *dure;* from 1752; a *circle, ball* or *pile*:—ball, turn, round about.

1755. דּוֹר, **dôwr,** *dore;* or (shortened) דֹּר, **dôr,** *dore;* from 1752; (properly) a *revolution* of time, i.e. an *age* or generation; also a *dwelling*:—age, × evermore, generation, [n-]ever, posterity.

A masculine noun meaning generation, period of time, posterity, age, time, setting of life. In general, the word indicates the time from birth to death; the time from one's birth to the birth of one's first child; the living adults of a certain time or place; a period as it is defined through major events, persons, behaviour, and the spirit of the age. It also marks a duration of time. There is no agreed on length of time which may stretch from twenty to one hundred years, but the word is also used figuratively to mean an indefinite or unending length of time in the past or future. These basic observations can be illustrated from various passages and contexts: the generation of Noah was characterized by wickedness and violence, yet he was a righteous man in his generation (Ge 7:1); Moses spoke of a crooked generation in his day and in the future (Dt 32:5); however, the psalmist spoke of a generation of righteous people (Ps 14:5) and a generation of people who seek the Lord (Ps 24:6). These generations will be blessed by God (Ps 112:2). Generations come and go without interruption (Ecc 1:4).

Time can be measured by the passing of generations, as when the great deeds of the Lord are passed on from generation to generation, in effect forever (Ps 145:4; Isa 34:17); God's throne lasts forever, from generation to generation (La 5:19). Likewise, God's judgments can endure forever (Jer 50:39). The closing of an era can be marked by the death of all the persons belonging to that generation (Ex 1:6; Jgs 2:10), but persons can be taken from their own proper age, dwellings, or circles of existence, as Hezekiah

nearly was (Ps 102:24[25]; Isa 38:12), and a subgroup, such as fighting men, can pass away from an era (Dt 2:14). On the other hand, God's length of days spans all generations without end (Ps 102:24[25]).

The generation or generations mentioned may refer to the past, present, or future. Noah was perfect during the time of his contemporaries (Ge 6:9); the generations extended into the future when God established His covenant with Abraham and all future generations (Ge 17:7, 12; cf. Le 25:30) or when He gave His name as a memorial for all generations to come (Ex 3:15). The word often refers to past generations, such as the generation of the fathers (Ps 49:19[20]; Isa 51:9). God's constancy again stands out, for His days span all past eras as well as all future generations (Ps 102:24[25]). Israel was encouraged in Moses' song to remember the past generations of old (Dt 32:7) when God effected His foundational acts of deliverance for Israel and gave them the Law at Sinai. Present generations are to learn from past generations (Dt 32:7) and can affect future generations by declaring the Lord's power (Ps 71:18).

Certain generations were singled out for special note: the third and fourth generations of children are punished for the sins of their fathers (Ex 20:5; 34:7); the infamous generation that wandered in the wilderness for forty years experienced God's judgments until everyone in that generation died (Ps 95:10). Yet the love of God is not bound, for, in a figurative sense, it is passed on to thousands of generations (i.e. without limitation) forever and to every person (Ex 20:6; 34:7).

1756. דּוֹר, **Dôwr,** *dore;* or (by permutive) דֹּאר, **Dô'r,** *dore;* (Jos 17:11; 1Ki 4:11), from 1755; *dwelling; Dor,* a place in Palestine:—Dor.

1757. דּוּרָא, **Dûwrâ',** *doo-raw´;* (Chaldee); probably from 1753; *circle* or *dwelling; Dura,* a place in Babylon:—Dura.

1758. דּוּשׁ, **dûwsh,** *doosh;* or דּוֹשׁ, **dôwsh,** *dosh;* or דִּישׁ, **dîysh,** *deesh;* a primitive root; to *trample* or *thresh*:—break, tear, thresh, tread out (down), at grass [Jer 50:11, *by mistake for* 1877].

1759. דּוּשׁ, **dûwsh,** *doosh;* (Chaldee); corresponding to 1758; to *trample*:—tread down.

1760. דָּחָה, **dâchâh,** *daw-khaw´*; or דָּחַח, **dâchach,** *daw-khakh´*; (Jer 23:12), a primitive root; to *push* down:—chase, drive away (on), overthrow, outcast, × sore, thrust, totter.

1761. דַּחֲוָה, **dachăvâh,** *dakh-av-aw´*; (Chaldee); from the equivalent of 1760; probably a musical *instrument* (as being *struck*):—instrument of music.

1762. דְּחִי, **dᵉchîy,** *deh-khee´*; from 1760; a *push*, i.e. (by implication) a *fall*:—falling.

1763. דְּחַל, **dᵉchal,** *deh-khal´*; (Chaldee); corresponding to 2119; to *slink*, i.e. (by implication) to *fear*, or (causative) *be formidable*:—make afraid, dreadful, fear, terrible.

A verb meaning to fear, to slink. It comes from the Aramaic and corresponds to the Hebrew word *zâchal* (2119). The idea is one of slinking or crawling, such as a serpent or a worm; to back away or tremble in fear. People trembled before the greatness which God gave Nebuchadnezzar (Da 5:19). Darius turned this and focused on the Giver of the greatness, saying that people would tremble before God's awesome being (Da 6:26[27]).

1764. דֹּחַן, **dôchan,** *do´-khan*; of uncertain derivation; *millet*:—millet.

1765. דָּחַף, **dâchaph,** *daw-khaf´*; a primitive root; to *urge*, i.e. *hasten*:—(be) haste (-ned), pressed on.

1766. דָּחַק, **dâchaq,** *daw-khak´*; a primitive root; to *press*, i.e. *oppress*:—thrust, vex.

1767. דַּי, **day,** *dahee*; of uncertain derivation; *enough* (as noun or adverb), used chiefly with prepositional phrases:—able, according to, after (ability), among, as (oft as), (more than) enough, from, in, since, (much as is) sufficient (-ly), too much, very, when.

1768. דִּי, **dîy,** *dee*; (Chaldee); apparently for 1668; *that*, used as relative, conjunction, and especially (with preposition) in adverbial phrases; also as a preposition *of*:— × as, but, for (-asmuch), + now, of, seeing, than, that, therefore, until, + what (-soever), when, which, whom, whose.

1769. דִּיבוֹן, **Dîybôwn,** *dee-bone´*; or (shortened) דִּיבֹן, **Dîybôn,** *dee-bone´*; from 1727; *pining*;

Dibon, the name of three places in Palestine:—Dibon. [*Also, with* 1410 *added*, Dibon-gad.]

1770. דִּיג, **dîyg,** *deeg*; denominative from 1709; to *fish*:—fish.

1771. דַּיָּג, **dayyâg,** *dah-yawg´*; from 1770; a *fisherman*:—fisher.

1772. דַּיָּה, **dayyâh,** *dah-yaw´*; intensive from 1675; a *falcon* (from its *rapid* flight):—vulture.

1773. דְּיוֹ, **dᵉyôw,** *deh-yo´*; of uncertain derivation; *ink*:—ink.

1774. דִּי זָהָב, **Dîy zâhâb,** *dee zaw-hawb´*; as if from 1768 and 2091; *of gold*; *Dizahab*, a place in the Desert:—Dizahab.

1775. דִּימוֹן, **Dîymôwn,** *dee-mone´*; perhaps for 1769; *Dimon*, a place in Palestine:—Dimon.

1776. דִּימוֹנָה, **Dîymôwnâh,** *dee-mo-naw´*; feminine of 1775; *Dimonah*, a place in Palestine:—Dimonah.

1777. דִּין, **dîyn,** *deen*; or (Ge 6:3) דּוּן, **dûwn,** *doon*; a primitive root [compare 113]; to *rule*; (by implication) to *judge* (as umpire); also to *strive* (as at law):—contend, execute (judgment), judge, minister judgment, plead (the cause), at strife, strive.

A verb meaning to bring justice, to go to court, to pass sentence, to contend, to act as judge, to govern, to plead a cause, to be at strife, to quarrel. The verb regularly involves bringing justice or acting as judge; the Lord Himself is the chief judge over the whole earth and especially over those who oppose Him (1Sa 2:10). The tribe of Dan, whose name means "He provides justice" and is followed by this verb, will indeed provide justice for His people (Ge 30:6). The king of Israel was to deliver justice in righteousness (Ps 72:2). Israel's many sins included failure to obtain justice in the case of the orphan (Jer 5:28). The verb also signifies pleading a case: God's people often failed to plead the case of the orphan (Jer 5:28); this was a heinous sin for the house of David, for Judah was to administer justice every day for all those who needed it (Jer 21:12). Sometimes pleading a case resulted in vindication, as when God gave Rachel a son through her maidservant Bilhah, and Rachel in thanks named him Dan (Ge 30:6). At other times, it resulted in redress for evils done, as when God judges the nations in the day of His anger (Ps 110:6); Israel's plight because of their sin had become hopeless so they had no one to plead their cause (Jer 30:13).

The verb also signifies governance, contention, or going to law or court. It is hopeless for individuals to contend with persons who are far more powerful and advantaged than they are (Ecc 6:10). The high priest, Joshua, was given authority to govern, render justice, and judge the house of the Lord on the condition that he himself walked in the ways of the Lord (Zec 3:7).

In the passive-reflexive stem, the verb signifies to be at strife or to quarrel (2Sa 19:10).

1778. דִּין, **dîyn,** *deen*; (Chaldee); corresponding to 1777; to *judge*:—judge.

An Aramaic verb meaning to judge. It corresponds to the Hebrew word that is spelled the same or spelled as *diyn* (1777). The word occurs only in Ezr 7:25, where Artaxerxes commanded Ezra to appoint people to judge those beyond the river who knew God's laws.

1779. דִּין, **dîyn,** *deen*; or (Job 19:29) דּוּן, **dûwn,** *doon*; from 1777; *judgment* (the suit, justice, sentence or tribunal); (by implication) also *strife*:—cause, judgment, plea, strife.

A masculine noun meaning judgment, condemnation, plea, cause. This word carries a legal connotation and is found in poetic texts with most of its occurrences in the book of Job. The idea of judgment is often followed by justice (Job 36:17). Judah is called a wicked nation, one that does not plead the cause of the less fortunate (Jer 5:28). It also occurs in relation to strife in a legal case (Pr 22:10).

1780. דִּין, **dîyn,** *deen*; (Chaldee); corresponding to 1779:—judgment.

An Aramaic, masculine noun meaning justice, judgment. It is used to signify punishment (Ezr 7:26) or the justice of God (Da 4:37[34]). It is related to the Aramaic noun *dayyân* (1782) and the Aramaic verb *diyn* (1778). It is also similar to the Hebrew verb *diyn* (1777) and the Hebrew noun *diyn* (1779).

1781. דַּיָּן, **dayyân,** *dah-yawn´*; from 1777; a *judge* or *advocate*:—judge.

A masculine noun meaning judge, and more specifically, God as judge. David uses this word

to refer to God as his judge (1Sa 24:15[16]). The psalmist uses this term to describe God as the defender or judge of the widows (Ps 68:5[6]).

1782. דַּיָּן, **dayyân,** *dah-yawn´*; (Chaldee); corresponding to 1781:—judge.

An Aramaic masculine noun meaning judge. It corresponds to the Hebrew word of the same spelling and meaning. This word is used only in Ezr 7:25 where it refers to judges that Ezra was to appoint over those who knew God's laws. The judges were to judge diligently and had power to imprison, execute, and banish people in addition to confiscating property (cf. Ezr 7:26).

1783. דִּינָה, **Dîynâh,** *dee-naw´*; feminine of 1779; *justice; Dinah,* the daughter of Jacob:—Dinah.

1784. דִּינָיֵא, **Dîynâyê´,** *dee-naw´-yee*; (Chaldee); patrial from an uncertain primitive; a *Dinaite* or inhabitant of some unknown Assyrian province:—Dinaite.

1785. דָּיֵק, **dâyêq,** *daw-yake´*; from a root corresponding to 1751; a *battering*-tower:—fort.

1786. דַּיִשׁ, **dayish,** *dah´-yish*; from 1758; *threshing* time:—threshing.

1787. דִּישׁוֹן, **Dîyshôwn,** *dee-shone´*; דִּישֹׁן, **Dîyshôn,** *dee-shone´*; דִּישׁוֹן, **Dishôwn,** *dee-shone´*; or דִּשֹׁן, **Dishôn,** *dee-shone´*; the same as 1788; *Dishon,* the name of two Edomites:—Dishon.

1788. דִּישֹׁן, **dîyshôn,** *dee-shone´*; from 1758; the *leaper,* i.e. an *antelope*:—pygarg.

1789. דִּישָׁן, **Dîyshân,** *dee-shawn´*; another form of 1787; *Dishan,* an Edomite:—Dishan, Dishon.

1790. דַּךְ, **dak,** *dak*; from an unused root (compare 1794); *crushed,* i.e. (figurative) *injured*:—afflicted, oppressed.

1791. דֵּךְ, **dêk,** *dake*; (Chaldee); or דָּךְ, **dâk,** *dawk*; (Chaldee); prolonged from 1668; *this*:—the same, this.

1792. דָּכָא, **dâkâ´,** *daw-kaw´*; a primitive root (compare 1794); to *crumble*; transposed to *bruise* (literal or figurative):—beat to pieces, break (in pieces), bruise, contrite, crush, destroy, humble, oppress, smite.

A verb meaning to crush, to beat down, to bruise, to oppress. The Hebrew word is often used in a poetic or figurative sense. Eliphaz spoke of those who lived in houses of clay, whose foundations were crushed easily (Job 4:19). The psalmist prayed that the king would crush an oppressor (Ps 72:4) and accused the wicked of crushing the Lord's people (Ps 94:5). The wise man exhorted others not to crush the needy in court (Pr 22:22). Isaiah said that it was the Lord's will to crush the Servant (Isa 53:10). Metaphorically, this word can also be used in the same way the English word *crushed* is used to mean dejected or sad (Isa 19:10).

1793. אָכָּד, **dakkâ',** *dak-kaw';* from 1792; crushed, (literal) *powder* or (figurative) *contrite:*—contrite, destruction.

An adjective meaning destruction, a crumbled substance, an object crushed into a powder, or pulverized dust. Thus, by extension, *dakkâ'* can mean humble or contrite. God is the healer and rescuer of one who is crushed in spirit (Ps 34:18[19]). He also lives with those whose spirits are contrite and humble (Isa 57:15). It comes from the Hebrew verb *dâkâ'* (1792), meaning to crush or to beat to pieces.

1794. דָּכָה, **dâkâh,** *daw-kaw';* a primitive root (compare 1790, 1792); to *collapse* (physically or mentally):—break (sore), contrite, crouch.

1795. דָּכָה, **dakkâh,** *dak-kaw';* from 1794 like 1793; *mutilated:*— + wounded.

1796. דֳּכִי, **dŏkîy,** *dok-ee';* from 1794; a *dashing* of surf:—wave.

1797. דִּכֵּן, **dikkên,** *dik-kane';* (Chaldee); prolonged from 1791; *this:*—same, that, this.

1798. דְּכַר, **dᵉkar,** *dek-ar';* (Chaldee); corresponding to 2145; (properly) a *male,* i.e. of sheep:—ram.

1799. דִּכְרוֹן, **dikrôwn,** *dik-rone';* (Chaldee); or דָּכְרָן, **dokrân,** *dok-rawn';* (Chaldee); corresponding to 2146; a *register:*—record.

1800. דַּל, **dal,** *dal;* from 1809; (properly) *dangling,* i.e. (by implication) *weak* or *thin:*—lean, needy, poor (man), weaker.

1801. דָּלַג, **dâlag,** *daw-lag';* a primitive root; to *spring:*—leap.

1802. דָּלָה, **dâlâh,** *daw-law';* a primitive root (compare 1809); (properly) to *dangle,* i.e. to *let down* a bucket (for *drawing* out water); (figurative) to *deliver:*—draw (out), × enough, lift up.

1803. דַּלָּה, **dallâh,** *dal-law';* from 1802; (properly) something *dangling,* i.e. a loose *thread* or *hair;* (figurative) *indigent:*—hair, pining sickness, poor (-est sort).

1804. דָּלַח, **dâlach,** *daw-lakh';* a primitive root; to *roil* water:—trouble.

1805. דְּלִי, **dᵉlîy,** *del-ee';* or דֳּלִי, **dŏlîy,** *dol-ee';* from 1802; a *pail* or *jar* (for *drawing* water):—bucket.

1806. דְּלָיָה, **Dᵉlâyâh,** *del-aw-yaw';* or (prolonged) דְּלָיָהוּ, **Dᵉlâ-yâhûw,** *del-aw-yaw'-hoo;* from 1802 and 3050; *Jah has delivered; Delajah,* the name of five Israelites:—Dalaiah, Delaiah.

1807. דְּלִילָה, **Dᵉlîylâh,** *del-ee-law';* from 1809; *languishing; Delilah,* a Philistine woman:—Delilah.

1808. דָּלִית, **dâlîyth,** *daw-leeth';* from 1802; something *dangling,* i.e. a *bough:*—branch.

1809. דָּלַל, **dâlal,** *daw-lal';* a primitive root (compare 1802); to *slacken* or *be feeble;* (figurative) to *be oppressed:*—bring low, dry up, be emptied, be not equal, fail, be impoverished, be made thin.

1810. דִּלְעָן, **Dil‘ân,** *dil-awn';* of uncertain derivation; *Dilan,* a place in Palestine:—Dilean.

1811. דָּלַף, **dâlaph,** *daw-laf';* a primitive root; to *drip;* (by implication) to *weep:*—drop through, melt, pour out.

1812. דֶּלֶף, **deleph,** *deh'-lef;* from 1811; a *dripping:*—dropping.

1813. דַּלְפוֹן, **Dalphôwn,** *dal-fone';* from 1811; *dripping; Dalphon,* a son of Haman:—Dalphon.

1814. דָּלַק, **dâlaq,** *daw-lak';* a primitive root; to *flame* (literal or figurative):—burning, chase, inflame, kindle, persecute (-or), pursue hotly.

1815. דְּלַק, **dᵉlaq,** *del-ak';* (Chaldee); corresponding to 1814:—burn.

1816. דַּלֶּקֶת, **dalleqeth,** *dal-lek'-keth;* from 1814; a *burning* fever:—inflammation.

1817. דֶּלֶת, **deleth,** *deh´-leth*; from 1802 something *swinging*, i.e.. the *valve* of a door:—door (two-leaved), gate, leaf, lid. [In Ps 141:3, *dal*, irreg.]

1818. דָּם, **dâm,** *dawm*; from 1826 (compare 119); *blood* (as that which when shed causes *death*) of man or an animal; (by analogy) the *juice* of the grape; (figurative, especially in the plural) *bloodshed* (i.e. *drops* of blood):—blood (-y, -guiltiness, [-thirsty], + innocent.

A masculine singular noun meaning blood of either humans or animals. It is commonly used with the verb *shâphak* (8210) meaning to shed. Figuratively, it signifies violence and violent individuals: man of blood (2Sa 16:8); house of blood (2Sa 21:1); in wait for blood (Pr 1:11); shedder of blood (Eze 18:10). Blood also carries religious significance, having a major role in sacrificial rituals. The metaphor "blood of grapes" is used for wine (Ge 49:11).

1819. דָּמָה, **dâmâh,** *daw-maw´*; a primitive root; to *compare*; (by implication) to *resemble, liken, consider*:—compare, devise, (be) like (-n), mean, think, use similitudes.

1820. דָּמָה, **dâmâh,** *daw-maw´*; a primitive root; to *be dumb* or *silent*; hence to *fail* or *perish*; (transitive) to *destroy*:—cease, be cut down (off), destroy, be brought to silence, be undone, × utterly.

A verb meaning to cease, to cause to cease, to be silent, to destroy. It is used in reference to beasts that die (Ps 49:12[13]); a prophet who feels undone when he sees the Lord (Isa 6:5); Zion's destruction (Jer 6:2); eyes that weep without ceasing (La 3:49); the destruction of people who have no knowledge (Hos 4:6); the destruction of merchants (Zep 1:11); the destruction of the nation of Edom (Ob 1:5).

1821. דְּמָה, **dᵉmâh,** *dem-aw´*; (Chaldee); corresponding to 1819; to *resemble*:—be like.

1822. דֻּמָה, **dumâh,** *doom-aw´*; from 1820; *desolation*; (concrete) *desolate*:—destroy.

A feminine noun of debated meaning. If it derives from *dâmâh* (1820), it would mean destroyed one; if from *dâmam* (1826), it would mean silent one. It is used only in Eze 27:32 where it describes the wealthy and beautiful seaport of Tyre as having sunk into the sea, a symbol of being overrun by foreign armies (cf.

Eze 26:3–5). This judgment came on the people of Tyre because of their pride and because they rejoiced over the fall of Jerusalem (cf. Eze 26:2). The ruined city would be relatively silent (although fishermen would still spread their nets there), but in Eze 27:32 "destroyed one" seems to fit the context better.

1823. דְּמוּת, **dᵉmûwth,** *dem-ooth´*; from 1819; *resemblance*; (concrete) *model, shape*; (adverb) *like*:—fashion, like (-ness, as), manner, similitude.

A feminine noun meaning likeness. This word is often used to create a simile by comparing two unlike things, such as the wickedness of people and the venom of a snake (Ps 58:4[5]); the sound of God's gathering warriors and of many people (Isa 13:4); or the angelic messenger and a human being (Da 10:16). Additionally, this word is used in describing humans as being created in the image or likeness of God (Ge 1:26; 5:1); the likeness of Seth to Adam (Ge 5:3); the figures of oxen in the temple (2Ch 4:3); the pattern of the altar (2Ki 16:10). But most often, Ezekiel uses it as he describes his visions by comparing what he saw to something similar on earth (Eze 1:5, 16; 10:1).

1824. דְּמִי, **dᵉmîy,** *dem-ee´*; or דֳּמִי, **dŏmîy,** *dom-ee´*; from 1820; *quiet*:—cutting off, rest, silence.

1825. דִּמְיוֹן, **dimyôwn,** *dim-yone´*; from 1819; *resemblance*:— × like.

1826. דָּמַם, **dâmam,** *daw-mam´*; a primitive root [compare 1724, 1820]; to *be dumb*; (by implication) to *be astonished*, to *stop*; also to *perish*:—cease, be cut down (off), forbear, hold peace, quiet self, rest, be silent, keep (put to) silence, be (stand) still, tarry, wait.

1827. דְּמָמָה, **dᵉmâmâh,** *dem-aw-maw´*; feminine from 1826; *quiet*:—calm, silence, still.

1828. דֹּמֶן, **dômen,** *do´-men*; of uncertain derivation; *manure*:—dung.

1829. דִּמְנָה, **Dimnâh,** *dim-naw´*; feminine from the same as 1828; a *dung-heap; Dimnah*, a place in Palestine:—Dimnah.

1830. דָּמַע, **dâmaʿ,** *daw-mah´*; a primitive root; to *weep*:— × sore, weep.

1831. דֶּמַע, **demaʿ,** *deh´-mah*; from 1830; a *tear*; (figurative) *juice*:—liquor.

1832. דִּמְעָה, **dim'âh,** *dim-aw´*; feminine of 1831; *weeping*:—tears.

1833. דְּמֶשֶׁק, **d'emesheq,** *dem-eh´-shek*; by orthographical variation from 1834; *damask* (as a fabric of Damascus):—in Damascus.

1834. דַּמֶּשֶׂק, **Dammeśeq,** *dam-meh´-sek*; or דּוּמֶשֶׂק, **Dûwmeśeq,** *doo-meh´-sek*; or דַּרְמֶשֶׂק, **Darmeśeq,** *dar-meh´-sek*; of foreign origin; *Damascus*, a city of Syria:—Damascus.

1835. דָּן, **Dân,** *dawn*; from 1777; *judge*; *Dan*, one of the sons of Jacob; also the tribe descended from him, and its territory; likewise a place in Palestine colonized by them:—Dan.

1836. דְּנָה, **d'enâh,** *den-aw*; (Chaldee); an orthographical variation of 1791; *this*:—[afore-] time, + after this manner, here [-after], one ... another, such, there [-fore], these, this (matter), + thus, where [-fore], which.

1837. דַּנָּה, **Dannâh,** *dan-naw´*; of uncertain derivation; *Dannah*, a place in Palestine:—Dannah.

1838. דִּנְהָבָה, **Dinhâbâh,** *din-haw-baw´*; of uncertain derivation; *Dinhabah*, an Edomitish town:—Dinhabah.

1839. דָּנִי, **Dâniy,** *daw-nee´*; patronymic from 1835; a *Danite* (often collective) or descendant (or inhabitant) of Dan:—Danites, of Dan.

1840. דָּנִיֵּאל, **Dânîyyê'l,** *daw-nee-yale´*; in Ezekiel דָּנִאֵל, **Dâni'êl,** *daw-nee-ale´*; from 1835 and 410; *judge of God*; *Daniel* or *Danijel*, the name of two Israelites:—Daniel.

1841. דָּנִיֵּאל, **Dânîyyê'l,** *daw-nee-yale´*; (Chaldee); corresponding to 1840; *Danijel*, the Hebrew prophet:—Daniel.

1842. דָּן יַעַן, **Dân Ya'an,** *dawn yah´-an*; from 1835 and (apparently) 3282; *judge of purpose*; *Dan-Jaan*, a place in Palestine:—Dan-jaan.

1843. דֵּעַ, **dêa',** *day´-ah*; from 3045; *knowledge*:—knowledge, opinion.

A noun meaning knowledge. The word is possibly the masculine form of *dê'âh* (1844). It is used only by Elihu in the book of Job, where it refers to Elihu's opinion that he was about to make known to Job and his three friends (Job 32:6, 10, 17); knowledge as brought in from a distance, perhaps from heaven, since Elihu has

just claimed to speak for God (Job 36:3); and God's perfect knowledge demonstrated in the clouds and lightning (37:16). The phrase "perfect in knowledge" occurs also in Job 36:4, apparently describing Elihu but using *dê'âh* (1844). It might be thought that Elihu was using a more modest word in describing his own knowledge. The word *dê'âh*, however, is also used to refer to God's knowledge (cf. 1Sa 2:3), and it is difficult to find any distinction of meaning between the two forms.

1844. דֵּעָה, **dê'âh,** *day-aw´*; feminine of 1843; *knowledge*:—knowledge.

A feminine noun meaning knowledge. This word comes from the verb *yâda'* (3045), meaning to know, and is equivalent in meaning to the much more common form of this noun, *da'ath* (1847), meaning knowledge. This particular word refers to the knowledge within God (1Sa 2:3; Ps 73:11). The word also describes the knowledge of God that was known throughout the land (Isa 11:9) or taught either by God or by His faithful shepherds (Jer 3:15).

1845. דְּעוּאֵל, **D'e'ûw'êl,** *deh-oo-ale´*; from 3045 and 410; *known of God*; *Deüel*, an Israelite:—Deuel.

1846. דָּעַךְ, **dâ'ak,** *daw-ak´*; a primitive root; to *be extinguished*; (figurative) to *expire* or *be dried up*:—be extinct, consumed, put out, quenched.

1847. דַּעַת, **da'ath,** *dah´-ath*; from 3045; *knowledge*:—cunning, [ig-] norantly, know (-ledge), [un-] awares (wittingly).

A feminine noun meaning knowledge, knowing, learning, discernment, insight, and notion. The word occurs forty of its ninety-one times in Proverbs as one of the many words associated with the biblical concept of wisdom. The root meaning of the term is knowledge or knowing. In Pr 24:3, 4, it is the third word in a chain of three words describing the building of a house by wisdom, the establishment of that house by understanding, and finally, the filling of the rooms of the house by knowledge. The word describes God's gift of technical or specific knowledge along with wisdom and understanding to Bezalel so he could construct the tabernacle (Ex 31:3; 35:31; cf. Ps 94:10). It also describes the Israelites when they lacked the proper knowledge to please God (Isa 5:13; Hos 4:6). God holds both pagan unbelievers and Israelites responsible to know Him. On the other hand, a lack of knowledge also describes the absence of premeditation or intentionality. That lack of knowledge clears a person who has accidentally killed someone (Dt 4:42; Jos 20:3, 5).

The word is also used in the sense of knowing by experience, relationship, or encounter. For example, Balaam received knowledge from the Most High who met him in a vision (Nu 24:16); the knowledge gained by the suffering Servant of Isaiah justified many people (Isa 53:11); and to truly know the Holy God leads to real understanding (Pr 9:10). This moral, experiential knowledge of good and evil was forbidden to the human race in the Garden of Eden (Ge 2:9, 17). But the Messiah will have the Spirit of understanding in full measure as the Spirit of the Lord accompanied Him (Isa 11:2).

The term is also used to indicate insight or discernment. God imparted discernment to the psalmist when he trusted in God's commands (Ps 119:66). Job was guilty of speaking words without discernment (lit., words without knowledge, Job 34:35; 38:2).

God alone possesses all knowledge. No one can impart knowledge to God, for His knowledge, learning, and insight are perfect (Job 21:22); He alone has full knowledge about the guilt, innocence, or uprightness of a person (Job 10:7). God's knowledge of a human being is so profound and all-encompassing that the psalmist recognized that such knowledge is not attainable by people (Ps 139:6).

Some knowledge is empty and useless (Job 15:2), but God's people and a wise person are marked by true knowledge of life and the divine (Pr 2:5; 8:10; 10:14; 12:1). Knowledge affects behaviour, for persons who control their speech have true knowledge (Pr 17:27). While the preacher of Ecclesiastes admitted that knowledge may result in pain (Ecc 1:18), he also asserted that having knowledge is, in the end, better, for it protects the life of the one who has it (Ecc 7:12), and it is God's gift (Ecc 2:26).

1848. דֳפִי, **dŏphîy,** *daf´-ee;* from an unused root (meaning to *push* over); a *stumbling*-block:—slanderest.

1849. דָּפַק, **dâphaq,** *daw-fak´;* a primitive root; to *knock;* (by analogy) to *press* severely:—beat, knock, overdrive.

1850. דָּפְקָה, **Dophqâh,** *dof-kaw´;* from 1849; a *knock; Dophkah,* a place in the Desert:—Dophkah.

1851. דַּק, **daq,** *dak;* from 1854; *crushed,* i.e. (by implication) *small* or *thin:*—dwarf, lean [-fleshed], very little thing, small, thin.

1852. דֹּק, **dôq,** *doke;* from 1854; something *crumbling,* i.e. *fine* (as a *thin* cloth):—curtain.

1853. דִּקְלָה, **Diqlâh,** *dik-law´;* of foreign origin; *Diklah,* a region of Arabia:—Diklah.

1854. דָּקַק, **dâqaq,** *daw-kak´;* a primitive root [compare 1915]; to *crush* (or intransitive) *crumble:*—beat in pieces (small), bruise, make dust, (into) × powder, (be, very) small, stamp (small).

1855. דְּקַק, **deqaq,** *dek-ak´;* (Chaldee); corresponding to 1854; to *crumble* or (transposed) *crush:*—break to pieces.

1856. דָּקַר, **dâqar,** *daw-kar´;* a primitive root; to *stab;* (by analogy) to *starve;* (figurative) to *revile:*—pierce, strike (thrust) through, wound.

1857. דֶּקֶר, **Deqer,** *deh´-ker;* from 1856; a *stab; Deker,* an Israelite:—Dekar.

1858. דַּר, **dar,** *dar;* apparently from the same as 1865; (properly) a *pearl* (from its sheen as rapidly *turned*); (by analogy) *pearl-stone,* i.e. mother-of-pearl or alabaster:— × white.

1859. דָּר, **dâr,** *dawr;* (Chaldee); corresponding to 1755; an *age:*—generation.

An Aramaic masculine noun meaning generation. This word is used only twice in the OT and is equivalent to the Hebrew word *dôwr* (1755), meaning generation. In both instances, the word is used in a phrase that is literally translated "with generation and generation," the idea referring to God's kingdom enduring from generation to generation (Da 4:3[3:33]; 4:34[31]).

1860. דְּרָאוֹן, **derâ'ôwn,** *der-aw-one´;* or דֵּרָאוֹן, **dêrâ'-ôwn,** *day-raw-one´;* from an unused root (meaning to *repulse*); an object of *aversion:*—abhorring, contempt.

A masculine noun meaning abhorrence. This word is related to an Arabic verb, which means to repel. Thus, the object of repulsion is an abhorrence. It is used only twice in the OT and in both cases speaks about the eternal abhorrence of those who rebelled against the Lord. The prophet Isaiah ended his message by declaring the abhorrence of wicked men in the eternal state (Isa 66:24). Daniel, likewise, spoke about the everlasting abhorrence of the wicked who were resurrected (Da 12:2).

1861. דָּרְבוֹן, **dorbôwn,** *dor-bone´*; [also *dor-bawn´*]; of uncertain derivation; a *goad:*—goad.

1862. דַּרְדַּע, **Darda,** *dar-dah´*; apparently from 1858 and 1843; *pearl of knowledge; Darda,* an Israelite:—Darda.

1863. דַּרְדַּר, **dardar,** *dar-dar´*; of uncertain derivation; a *thorn:*—thistle.

1864. דָּרוֹם, **dârôwm,** *daw-rome´*; of uncertain derivation; the *south;* (poetic) the *south wind:*—south.

1865. דְּרוֹר, **derôwr,** *der-ore´*; from an unused root (meaning to *move rapidly*); *freedom;* hence *spontaneity* of outflow, and so *clear:*—liberty, pure.

1866. דְּרוֹר, **derôwr,** *der-ore´*; the same as 1865, applied to a bird; the *swift,* a kind of swallow:—swallow.

1867. דָּרְיָוֶשׁ, **Dâreyâvesh,** *daw-reh-yaw-vesh´*; of Persian origin; *Darejavesh,* a title (rather than name) of several Persian kings:—Darius.

1868. דָּרְיָוֶשׁ, **Dâreyâvesh,** *daw-reh-yaw-vesh´*; (Chaldee); corresponding to 1867:—Darius.

1869. דָּרַךְ, **dârak,** *daw-rak´*; a primitive root; to *tread;* (by implication) to *walk;* also to *string* a bow (by treading on it in bending):—archer, bend, come, draw, go (over), guide, lead (forth), thresh, tread (down), walk.

1870. דֶּרֶךְ, **derek,** *deh´-rek*; from 1869; a *road* (as *trodden*); (figurative) a *course* of life or *mode* of action, often adverbial:—along, away, because of, + by, conversation, custom, [east-] ward, journey, manner, passenger, through, toward, [high-] [path-] way [-side], whither [-soever].

A masculine noun meaning path, journey, way. This common word is derived from the

Hebrew verb *dârak* (1869), meaning to walk or to tread, from which the basic idea of this word comes: the path that is traveled. The word may refer to a physical path or road (Ge 3:24; Nu 22:23; 1Ki 13:24) or to a journey along a road (Ge 30:36; Ex 5:3; 1Sa 15:18). However, this word is most often used metaphorically to refer to the pathways of one's life, suggesting the pattern of life (Pr 3:6); the obedient life (Dt 8:6); the righteous life (2Sa 22:22; Jer 5:4); the wicked life (1Ki 22:52[53]). The ways are described as ways of darkness (Pr 2:13); pleasant ways (Pr 3:17); and wise ways (Pr 6:6).

1871. דַּרְכְּמוֹן, **darkemôwn,** *dar-kem-one´*; of Persian origin; a "*drachma,*" or coin:—dram.

A noun meaning weight, monetary value. The word may refer to the Greek drachma that weighed 4.3 grams or to the Persian daric that weighed about twice as much. It occurs in Ezr 2:69 describing gold given toward Temple construction. In Ne 7:70–72 [69–71], it also refers to gold given toward the work of revitalizing Jerusalem. This word apparently has the same meaning as *’ădarkôn* (150) but may have a different origin.

1872. דְּרַע, **dera,** *der-aw´*; (Chaldee); corresponding to 2220; an *arm:*—arm.

1873. דָּרַע, **Dâra,** *daw-rah´*; probably contracted from 1862; *Dara,* an Israelite:—Dara.

1874. דַּרְקוֹן, **Darqôwn,** *dar-kone´*; of uncertain derivation; *Darkon,* one of "Solomon's servants":—Darkon.

1875. דָּרַשׁ, **dârash,** *daw-rash´*; a primitive root; (properly) to *tread* or *frequent;* (usually) to *follow* (for pursuit or search); (by implication) to *seek* or *ask;* (specifically) to *worship:*—ask, × at all, care for, × diligently, inquire, make inquisition, [necro-] mancer, question, require, search, seek [for, out], × surely.

1876. דָּשָׁא, **dâshâ’,** *daw-shaw´*; a primitive root; to *sprout:*—bring forth, spring.

1877. דֶּשֶׁא, **deshe’,** *deh´-sheh*; from 1876; a *sprout;* (by analogy) *grass:*—(tender) grass, green, (tender) herb.

1878. דָּשֵׁן, **dâshên,** *daw-shane´*; a primitive root; to *be fat;* (transitive) to *fatten* (or regard as fat); (specifically) to *anoint;* (figurative) to *sat-*

isfy; denominative (from 1880) to *remove* (fat) *ashes* (of sacrifices):—accept, anoint, take away the (receive) ashes (from), make (wax) fat.

A verb meaning to be fat, to grow fat, to fatten, or in a figurative sense, to anoint, to satisfy. In Proverbs, the word is used for one's bones growing fat (that is, one being in good health) after receiving good news (Pr 15:30). Conversely, when Israel came to the Promised Land, she grew fat with the food of the pagan culture and turned away to other gods (Dt 31:20). In Isaiah, the word is used to describe the ground being covered with the fat of animals (Isa 34:7).

1879. דָּשֵׁן, **dâshên,** *daw-shane´*; from 1878; *fat*; (figurative) *rich, fertile*:—fat.

1880. דֶּשֶׁן, **deshen,** *deh´-shen*; from 1878; the *fat*; (abstract) *fatness*, i.e. (figurative) *abundance*; (specifically) the (fatty) *ashes* of sacrifices:—ashes, fatness.

1881. דָּת, **dâth,** *dawth*; of uncertain (perhaps foreign) derivation; a royal *edict* or statute:—commandment, commission, decree, law, manner.

A feminine noun meaning law, edict. This word is used to describe either a permanent law that governed a nation or an edict sent out with the king's authority. The first meaning can be seen in Est 1:13, 15, where the king counseled with those who knew the law (cf. Est 3:8). The second meaning appears in the several occasions where King Ahasuerus (Xerxes) sent out a decree (Est 2:8; 3:14, 15). At times, it is difficult to distinguish between these two meanings (Est 1:8), for the edict of the king became a written law among the Persians (Est 1:19). With several exceptions, this word occurs only in the book of Esther (Ezr 8:36; cf. Dt 33:2).

1882. דָּת, **dâth,** *dawth*; (Chaldee); corresponding to 1881; decree, law.

An Aramaic noun meaning decree, law. It corresponds to the Hebrew word of the same spelling (1881). The decrees imposed on humans may agree more or less with God's Law, but God is always presented as controlling human laws. The word describes God's changeless Law in Ezr 7:12 and Da 6:5(6). Elsewhere, it signifies a king's decree made in anger (Da 2:9, 13). In the case of the Medes and Persians, a king could make the law at his own will but could not change it even if it were wrong (Da 6:8[9], 12[13], 15[16]). In Ezr 7:26, God's Law and the king's law coincide. In Da 7:25, a ruler was prophesied to speak against the Most High God and to set up laws in opposition to Him, but the ruler could only do so for a period of time set by God.

1883. דֶּתֶא, **dethe',** *deh´-thay*; (Chaldee); corresponding to 1877:—tender grass.

1884. דְּתָבַר, **dethâbar,** *deth-aw-bar´*; (Chaldee); of Persian origin; meaning one *skilled in law*; a *judge*:—counsellor.

1885. דָּתָן, **Dâthân,** *daw-thawn´*; of uncertain derivation; *Dathan*, an Israelite:—Dathan.

1886. דֹּתָן, **Dôthân,** *do´-thawn*; or (Chaldaizing dual) דֹּתַיִן, **Dôthayin,** *do-thah´-yin*; (Ge 37:17), of uncertain derivation; *Dothan*, a place in Palestine:—Dothan.

ה (He)

1887. הֵא, **hê’**, *hay*; a primitive particle; *lo!*:—behold, lo.

1888. הֵא, **hê’**, *hay*; (Chaldee); or הָא, **hâ’**, *haw*; (Chaldee); corresponding to 1887:—even, lo.

1889. הֶאָח, **he’âch**, *heh-awkh´*; from 1887 and 253; *aha!*:—ah, aha, ha.

1890. הַבְהַב, **habhab**, *hab-hab´*; by reduplication from 3051; *gift* (in sacrifice), i.e. *holocaust*:—offering.

A masculine noun meaning gift in the sense of sacrifice or offering. This type of sacrifice is not made by one person but always occurs with a plural subject. Israel (collectively) sacrificed animals to God as gift offerings—gifts God did not accept (Hos 8:13). This word comes from the verb *yâhab* (3051), meaning to give.

1891. הָבַל, **hâbal**, *haw-bal´*; a primitive root; to *be vain* in act, word, or expectation; (specifically) to *lead astray*:—be (become, make) vain.

1892. הֶבֶל, **hebel**, *heh´-bel*; or (rarely in the abstract) הֲבֵל, **hăbêl**, *hab-ale´*; from 1891; *emptiness* or *vanity*; (figurative) something *transitory* and *unsatisfactory*; often used as an adverb:—× altogether, vain, vanity.

1893. הֶבֶל, **Hebel**, *heh´-bel*; the same as 1892; *Hebel*, the son of Adam:—Abel.

1894. הָבְנִים, **hobnîym**, *hob´-neem*; only in plural, from an unused root meaning to *be hard*; *ebony*:—ebony.

1895. הָבַר, **hâbar**, *haw-bar´*; a primitive root of uncertain (perhaps foreign) derivation; to *be a horoscopist*:— + (astro-) loger.

1896. הֵגֵא, **Hêgê’**, *hay-gay´*; or (by permutation) הֵגַי, **Hêgay**, *hay-gah´ee*; probably of Persian origin; *Hege* or *Hegai*, a eunuch of Xerxes:—Hegai, Hege.

1897. הָגָה, **hâgâh**, *haw-gaw´*; a primitive root [compare 1901]; to *murmur* (in pleasure or anger); (by implication) to *ponder*:—imagine, meditate, mourn, mutter, roar, × sore, speak, study, talk, utter.

A verb meaning to growl, to groan, to sigh, to mutter, to speak; used figuratively: to meditate, to ponder. The Lord told Joshua to meditate on the Law day and night (Jos 1:8), and the Psalms proclaimed people blessed if they meditate on the Law (Ps 1:2). Job promised not to speak wickedness (Job 27:4). The Hebrew verb can also refer to the mutterings of mediums and wizards (Isa 8:19); the moans of grief (Isa 16:7); the growl of a lion (Isa 31:4); the coos of a dove (Isa 38:14).

1898. הָגָה, **hâgâh**, *haw-gaw´*; a primitive root; to *remove*:—stay, take away.

1899. הֶגֶה, **hegeh**, *heh´-geh*; from 1897; a *muttering* (in sighing, thought, or as thunder):—mourning, sound, tale.

A masculine noun meaning a muttering, rumbling, growling, moaning, or sighing sound. It generally describes a sound that comes from deep within the body. The Lord's voice is also described as making a rumbling sound associated with thunder (Job 37:2). The idea of moaning or sighing depicts the sound uttered in mourning, lamentation, woe (Eze 2:10), or in deep resignation (Ps 90:9).

1900. הָגוּת, **hâgûwth**, *haw-gooth´*; from 1897; *musing*:—meditation.

A feminine noun denoting meditation or musing. The psalmist describes the pondering of his heart as meditation (Ps 49:3[4]). This word is derived from the Hebrew word *hâgâh* (1897), which means to moan or to growl.

1901. הָגִיג, **hâgîyg**, *haw-gheeg´*; from an unused root akin to 1897; (properly) a *murmur*, i.e. *complaint*:—meditation, musing.

1902. הִגָּיוֹן, **higgâyôwn,** *hig-gaw-yone´*; intensive from 1897; a *murmuring* sound, i.e. a musical notation (probably similar to the modern *affettuoso* to indicate solemnity of movement); (by implication) a *machination:*—device, Higgaion, meditation, solemn sound.

1903. הָגִין, **hâgîyn,** *haw-gheen´*; of uncertain derivation; perhaps *suitable* or *turning:*—directly.

1904. הָגָר, **Hâgâr,** *haw-gawr´*; of uncertain (perhaps foreign) derivation; *Hagar,* the mother of Ishmael:—Hagar.

1905. הַגְרִי, **Hagrîy,** *hag-ree´*; or (prolonged) הַגְרִיא, **Hagrîy’,** *hag-ree´*; perhaps patronymic from 1904; a *Hagrite* or member of a certain Arabian clan:—Hagarene, Hagarite, Haggeri.

1906. הֵד, **hêd,** *hade´*; for 1959; a *shout:*—sounding again.

1907. הַדָּבָר, **haddâbâr,** *had-daw-bawr´*; (Chaldee); probably of foreign origin; a *vizier:*—counsellor.

1908. הֲדַד, **Hădad,** *had-ad´*; probably of foreign origin [compare 111]; *Hadad,* the name of an idol, and of several kings of Edom:—Hadad.

1909. הֲדַדְעֶזֶר, **Hădad‘ezer,** *had-ad-eh´-zer*; from 1908 and 5828; *Hadad (is his) help; Hadadezer,* a Syrian king:—Hadadezer. Compare 1928.

1910. הֲדַדְרִמּוֹן, **Hădadrimmôwn,** *had-ad-rim-mone´*; from 1908 and 7417; *Hadad-Rimmon,* a place in Palestine:—Hadad-rimmon.

1911. הָדָה, **hâdâh,** *haw-daw´*; a primitive root [compare 3034]; to *stretch forth* the hand:—put.

1912. הֹדּוּ, **Hôddûw,** *hod´-doo*; of foreign origin; *Hodu* (i.e. Hindustan):—India.

1913. הֲדוֹרָם, **Hădôwrâm,** *had-o-rawm´*; or הֲדֹרָם, **Hădôrâm,** *had-o-rawm´*; probably of foreign derivation; *Hadoram,* a son of Joktan, and the tribe descended from him:—Hadoram.

1914. הִדַּי, **Hidday,** *hid-dah´ee*; of uncertain derivation; *Hiddai,* an Israelite:—Hiddai.

1915. הָדַךְ, **hâdak,** *haw-dak´*; a primitive root [compare 1854]; to *crush* with the foot:—tread down.

1916. הֲדֹם, **hădôm,** *had-ome´*; from an unused root meaning to *stamp* upon; a foot-*stool:*—[foot-] stool.

1917. הַדָּם, **haddâm,** *had-dawm´*; (Chaldee); from a root corresponding to that of 1916; something *stamped* to pieces, i.e. a *bit:*—piece.

1918. הֲדַס, **hădas,** *had-as´*; of uncertain derivation; the *myrtle:*—myrtle (tree).

1919. הֲדַסָּה, **Hădassâh,** *had-as-saw´*; feminine of 1918; *Hadassah* (or *Esther*):—Hadassah.

1920. הָדַף, **hâdaph,** *haw-daf´*; a primitive root; to *push* away or down:—cast away (out), drive, expel, thrust (away).

1921. הָדַר, **hâdar,** *haw-dar´*; a primitive root; to *swell* up (literal or figurative, active or passive); (by implication) to *favour* or *honour, be high* or *proud:*—countenance, crooked place, glorious, honour, put forth.

A verb meaning to honour, to make glorious. The Israelites were commanded not to show unjust bias toward the poor (Ex 23:3) and to honour older people (Le 19:32). This did not always happen (La 5:12), but Solomon said that a person should not honour himself (Pr 25:6). Isaiah used this word when he prophesied that the Lord would come dressed in glory (Isa 63:1).

1922. הֲדַר, **hădar,** *had-ar´*; (Chaldee); corresponding to 1921; to *magnify* (figurative):—glorify, honour.

An Aramaic verb meaning to glorify, to magnify. Nebuchadnezzar built up Babylon to glorify himself until God took his power away and showed him who was sovereign. Then Nebuchadnezzar glorified God (Da 4:34[31], 37[34]). Unfortunately, King Belshazzar did not learn from his ancestor's mistake and also decided to honour himself instead of God (Da 5:23).

1923. הֲדַר, **hădar,** *had-ar´*; (Chaldee); from 1922; *magnificence:*—honour, majesty.

An Aramaic masculine noun meaning honour, majesty. In a meeting between Daniel and King Belshazzar, Daniel reminded Belshazzar that the Lord gave his father Nebuchadnezzar kingship, majesty, glory, and honour (Da 5:18).

1924. הֲדַר, **Hădar,** *had-ar´*; the same as 1926; *Hadar,* an Edomite:—Hadar.

1925. הֶדֶר, **heder,** *heh´-der*; from 1921; *honour*; used (figurative) for the *capital* city (Jerusalem):—glory.

A masculine noun meaning splendor, ornament. This word is used once in Daniel, where it speaks of the splendor of the kingdom (Da 11:20). This word is difficult to translate. It has been translated "the glory of the kingdom" (KJV), "royal splendor" (NIV), or a particular place, such as "the Jewel [the heart or gem] of his kingdom" (NASB).

1926. הָדָר, **hâdâr,** *haw-dawr´*; from 1921; *magnificence,* i.e. ornament or splendor:—beauty, comeliness, excellency, glorious, glory, goodly, honour, majesty.

A noun meaning glory, splendor, majesty. It describes the impressive character of God in 1Ch 16:27 and His thunderous voice in Ps 29:4. Isaiah describes sinners fleeing from the *hâdâr* of the Lord (Isa 2:10, 19). Often the Psalms use this word in conjunction with others to describe God's glory, splendor, and majesty (Ps 96:6; 145:5). It also refers to the majesty of kings (Ps 21:5[6]; 45:3[4]). Ps 8:5[6] expresses the splendor of God's creation of humans in comparison to the rest of creation. In Isaiah's prophetic description of the Suffering Servant, he uses *hâdâr* to say that the Servant will have no splendor to attract people to Him (Isa 53:2).

1927. הֲדָרָה, **hădârâh,** *had-aw-raw´*; feminine of 1926; *decoration:*—beauty, honour.

A feminine noun meaning adornment, glory. This word comes from the verb *hâdar* (1921), meaning to honour or to adorn and is related to the Hebrew noun *hâdâr* (1926), meaning majesty. In four of the five occurrences of this word, it occurs in the context of worshiping the Lord, "the beauty of holiness" (KJV) (1Ch 16:29; 2Ch 20:21; Ps 29:2; 96:9). In other instances, the word expresses the glory kings find in a multitude of people (Pr 14:28).

1928. הֲדַרְעֶזֶר, **Hădar'ezer,** *had-ar-eh´-zer*; from 1924 and 5828; *Hadar* (i.e. *Hadad,* 1908) is his *help; Hadarezer* (i.e. Hadadezer, 1909), a Syrian king:—Hadarezer.

1929. הָהּ, **hâh,** *haw*; a shortened form of 162; *ah!* expressing grief:—woe worth.

1930. הוֹ, **hôw,** *ho*; by permutation from 1929; *oh!*:—alas.

1931. הוּא, **hûw',** *hoo*; of which the feminine (beyond the Pentateuch) is הִיא, **hîy',** *he*; a primitive word, the third person pronoun singular, *he* (*she* or *it*); only expressed when emphatic or without a verb; also (intensive) *self,* or (especially with the article) the *same*; sometimes (as demonstrative) *this* or *that*; occasionally (instead of copula) *as* or *are:*—he, as for her, him (-self), it, the same, she (herself), such, that (… it), these, they, this, those, which (is), who.

1932. הוּא, **hûw',** *hoo*; (Chaldee); or (feminine) הִיא, **hîy',** *he*; (Chaldee); corresponding to 1931:— × are, it, this.

1933. הָוָא, **hâvâ',** *haw-vaw´*; or הָוָה, **hâvâh,** *haw-vaw´*; a primitive root [compare 183, 1961] supposed to mean (properly) to *breathe*; to *be* (in the sense of existence):—be, × have.

1934. הָוָא, **hâvâ',** *hav-aw´*; (Chaldee); or הָוָה, **hâvâh,** *hav-aw´*; (Chaldee); corresponding to 1933; to *exist*; used in a great variety of applications (especially in connection with other words):—be, become, + behold, + came (to pass), + cease, + cleave, + consider, + do, + give, + have, + judge, + keep, + labour, + mingle (self), + put, + see, + seek, + set, + slay, + take heed, tremble, + walk, + would.

1935. הוֹד, **hôwd,** *hode*; from an unused root; *grandeur* (i.e. an imposing form and appearance):—beauty, comeliness, excellency, glorious, glory, goodly, honour, majesty.

A masculine noun meaning vigour, authority, majesty. It refers to human physical vigour (Pr 5:9; Da 10:8); the fighting vigour of a horse in battle (Zec 10:3); and the growing vigour of an olive plant (Hos 14:6[7]). The word also implies authority, such as what Moses bestowed on Joshua (Nu 27:20); and royal majesty (1Ch 29:25; Jer 22:18). Thus, it is used to describe God's majesty (Job 37:22; Ps 145:5; Zec 6:13). The word often describes God's glory as displayed above the heavens (Ps 8:1[2]; 148:13; Hab 3:3; cf. Ps 96:6; 104:1, where the word is related to God's creation of the heavens).

1936. הוֹד, **Hôwd,** *hode*; the same as 1935; *Hod,* an Israelite:—Hod.

1937. הוֹדְוָה, **Hôwdᵉvâh,** *ho-dev-aw´*; a form of 1938; *Hodevah* (or Hodevjah), an Israelite:— Hodevah.

1938. הוֹדַוְיָה, **Hôwdavyâh,** *ho-dav-yaw´*; from 1935 and 3050; *majesty of Jah; Hodavjah,* the name of three Israelites:—Hodaviah.

1939. הוֹדַוְיָהוּ, **Hôwdayvâhûw,** *ho-dah-vaw´-hoo*; a form of 1938; *Hodajvah,* an Israelite:— Hodaiah.

1940. הוֹדִיָה, **Hôwdîyyâh,** *ho-dee-yaw´*; a form for the feminine of 3064; a *Jewess:*—Hodiah.

1941. הוֹדִיָה, **Hôwdîyyâh,** *ho-dee-yaw´*; a form of 1938; *Hodijah,* the name of three Israelites:— Hodijah.

1942. הַוָּה, **havvâh,** *hav-vaw´*; from 1933 (in the sense of eagerly *coveting* and *rushing* upon; by implication of *falling*); *desire;* also *ruin:*— calamity, iniquity, mischief, mischievous (thing), naughtiness, naughty, noisome, perverse thing, substance, very wickedness.

A feminine noun meaning destruction, desire. This word usually describes an event associated with calamity, evil, or destruction. It can speak of the wickedness of evildoers (Ps 5:9[10]); the devastation a foolish son could cause his father (Pr 19:13); the destruction intended by the tongue (Ps 38:12[13]; 52:2[4]); the calamities of life which require refuge in God for protection (Ps 57:1[2]). In several places, this word depicts the evil desires of the wicked that resulted in destruction: God would cast away the wicked person's desire (Pr 10:3); the evil desires of transgressors would be their downfall (Pr 11:6); and destruction awaited the ones who trust in their own desires (Ps 52:7[9]).

1943. הוָה, **hôvâh,** *ho-vaw´*; another form for 1942; *ruin:*—mischief.

A feminine noun meaning disaster. The root idea is a pit or chasm, a symbol of disaster. The word describes a disaster coming on Babylon that it will not be able to prevent with its occult practices (Isa 47:11). The only other occurrence of this word describes a series of disasters (literally, disaster upon disaster) prophesied to come on Israel because of idolatry (Eze 7:26). In this passage, there will be no escape although Israel will look for a prophetic vision.

1944. הוֹהָם, **Hôwhâm,** *ho-hawm´*; of uncertain derivation; *Hoham,* a Canaanitish king:— Hoham.

1945. הוֹי, **hôwy,** *hoh´ee*; a prolonged form of 1930 [akin to 188]; *oh!:*—ah, alas, ho, O, woe.

1946. הוּךְ, **hûwk,** *hook*; (Chaldee); corresponding to 1981; *to go;* (causative) to *bring:*—bring again, come, go (up).

1947. הוֹלֵלוֹת, **hôwlêlôwth,** *ho-lay-loth´*; feminine active participle of 1984; *folly:*—madness.

1948. הוֹלֵלוּת, **hôwlêlûwth,** *ho-lay-looth´*; from active participle of 1984; *folly:*—madness.

1949. הוּם, **hûwm,** *hoom*; a primitive root [compare 2000]; to *make an uproar,* or *agitate* greatly:—destroy, move, make a noise, put, ring again.

A verb meaning to rouse, to roar, to confuse. This verb describes a stirring or rousing, such as occurred in Bethlehem when Ruth and Naomi returned from Moab (Ru 1:19), or would occur in the nations when God would confuse them before their destruction (Dt 7:23). On several occasions, the audible effects of the rousing was emphasized, such as when Solomon was anointed king, the roar of the city could be heard (1Ki 1:45; cf. 1Sa 4:5; Mic 2:12). In the only other occurrence of this verb, David described himself as restless and roused (Ps 55:2[3]).

1950. הוֹמָם, **Hôwmâm,** *ho-mawm´*; from 2000; *raging; Homam,* an Edomitish chieftain:— Homam. Compare 1967.

1951. הוּן, **hûwn,** *hoon*; a primitive root; (properly) to *be naught,* i.e. (figurative) to *be* (causative *act*) *light:*—be ready.

1952. הוֹן, **hôwn,** *hone*; from the same as 1951 in the sense of 202; *wealth;* (by implication) *enough:*—enough, + for nought, riches, substance, wealth.

1953. הוֹשָׁמָע, **Hôwshâmâ‘,** *ho-shaw-maw´*; from 3068 and 8085; *Jehovah has heard; Hoshama,* an Israelite:—Hoshama.

1954. הוֹשֵׁעַ, **Hôwshêa‘,** *ho-shay´-ah*; from 3467; *deliverer; Hosheä,* the name of five Israelites:— Hosea, Hoshea, Oshea.

1955. הוֹשַׁעְיָה, **Hôwshaʿyâh,** *ho-shah-yaw´*; from 3467 and 3050; *Jah has saved; Hoshajah,* the name of two Israelites:—Hoshaiah.

1956. הוֹתִיר, **Hôwthîyr,** *ho-theer´*; from 3498; *he has caused to remain; Hothir,* an Israelite:—Hothir.

1957. הָזָה, **hâzâh,** *haw-zaw´*; a primitive root [compare 2372]; to *dream:*—sleep.

1958. הִי, **hîy,** *he*; for 5092; *lamentation:*—woe.

1959. הֵידָד, **hêydâd,** *hay-dawd´*; from an unused root (meaning to *shout*); *acclamation:*—shout (-ing).

1960. הֵידוֹת, **huyyᵉdôwth,** *hoo-yed-oth´*; from the same as 1959; (properly) an *acclaim,* i.e. a *choir* of singers:—thanksgiving.

1961. הָיָה, **hâyâh,** *haw-yaw´*; a primitive root [compare 1933]; to *exist,* i.e. *be* or *become, come to pass* (always emphatic, and not a mere copula or auxiliary):—beacon, × altogether, be (-come, accomplished, committed, like), break, cause, come (to pass), do, faint, fall, + follow, happen, × have, last, pertain, quit (one-) self, require, × use.

A verb meaning to exist, to be, to become, to happen, to come to pass, to be done. It is used over 3,500 times in the OT. In the simple stem, the verb often means to become, to take place, to happen. It indicates that something has occurred or come about, such as events that have turned out a certain way (1Sa 4:16); something has happened to someone, such as Moses (Ex 32:1, 23; 2Ki 7:20); or something has occurred just as God said it would (Ge 1:7, 9). Often a special Hebrew construction using the imperfect form of the verb asserts that something came to pass (cf. Ge 1:7, 9). Less often, the construction is used with the perfect form of the verb to refer to something coming to pass in the future (Isa 7:18, 21; Hos 2:16).

The verb is used to describe something that comes into being or arises. For instance, a great cry arose in Egypt when the firstborn were killed in the tenth plague (Ex 12:30; cf. Ge 9:16; Mic 7:4); and when God commanded light to appear, and it did (Ge 1:3). It is used to join the subject and verb as in Ge 1:2 where the earth was desolate and void, or to say Adam and Eve were naked (Ge 2:25). With certain prepositions, it can mean to follow or to be in favour

of someone (Ps 124:1, 2). The verb is used with a variety of other words, normally prepositions, to express subtle differences in meaning, such as to be located somewhere (Ex 1:5); to serve or function as something (e.g., gods [Ex 20:3]); to become something or as something, as when a person becomes a living being (Ge 2:7); to be with or by someone (Dt 22:2); to be or come on someone or something (e.g., the fear of humans on the beasts [Ge 9:2]); to express the idea of better than or a comparison (Eze 15:2), as in the idea of too small (Ex 12:4).

1962. הַיָּה, **hayyâh,** *hah-yaw´*; another form for 1943; *ruin:*—calamity.

A feminine noun meaning destruction. This word occurs only once in the OT (Job 6:2) and is a slightly different form of *hawwâh* (1942), also meaning destruction.

1963. הֵיךְ, **hêyk,** *hake*; another form for 349; *how?:*—how.

1964. הֵיכָל, **hêykâl,** *hay-kawl´*; probably from 3201 (in the sense of *capacity*); a large public building, such as a *palace* or *temple:*—palace, temple.

A masculine noun meaning temple, palace. The word derives from the word *yâkôl* (3201), meaning to be able and comes from the idea of capacity. It refers to a king's palace or other royal buildings (1Ki 21:1; Isa 13:22) and, likely by extension, to the dwelling of God, whether on earth (Ps 79:1) or in heaven (Isa 6:1). The word is used of Solomon's Temple, the second Temple (Ezr 3:6; Ne 6:10) and also of the tabernacle. In reference to foreign buildings, it is sometimes difficult to say whether a palace or the temple of a false god is meant (2Ch 36:7; Joel 3:5[4:5]). A special usage of the word designates the holy place of the Temple as opposed to the Holy of Holies (1Ki 6:17; Eze 41:4, 15).

1965. הֵיכַל, **hêykal,** *hay-kal´*; (Chaldee); corresponding to 1964:—palace, temple.

A masculine noun meaning temple, palace. This is the Aramaic form of the Hebrew word *hêykâl* (1964). The word is used most often in relation to a king's palace (Ezr 4:14). When Belshazzar sees the handwriting on the wall of the palace, this is the word used (Da 5:5). It is also used in reference to the Temple of God in

Jerusalem (Ezr 5:14, 15), as well as the temple in Babylon (Ezr 5:14).

1966. הֵילֵל, **hêylêl,** *hay-lale´;* from 1984 (in the sense of *brightness*); the *morning-star:*—lucifer.

1967. הֵימָם, **Hêymâm,** *hey-mawm´;* another form for 1950; *Hemam,* an Idumæan:—Hemam.

1968. הֵימָן, **Hêymân,** *hay-mawn´;* probably from 539; *faithful; Heman,* the name of at least two Israelites:—Heman.

1969. הִין, **hîyn,** *heen;* probably of Egypt origin; a *hin* or liquid measure:—hin.

1970. הָכַר, **hâkar,** *haw-kar´;* a primitive root; apparently to *injure:*—make self strange.

1971. הַכָּרָה, **hakkârâh,** *hak-kaw-raw´;* from 5234; *respect,* i.e. partiality:—shew.

1972. הָלְא, **hâlâ',** *haw-law´;* probably denominative from 1973; to *remove* or be *remote:*—cast far off.

1973. הָלְאָה, **hâl°'âh,** *haw-leh-aw´;* from the primitive form of the article [הַל **hal**]; *to the distance,* i.e. *far away;* also (of time) *thus far:*—back, beyond, (hence-) forward, hitherto, thenceforth, yonder.

1974. הִלּוּל, **hillûwl,** *hil-lool´;* from 1984 (in the sense of *rejoicing*); a *celebration* of thanksgiving for harvest:—merry, praise.

1975. הַלָּז, **hallâz,** *hal-lawz´;* from 1976; *this* or *that:*—side, that, this.

1976. הַלָּזֶה, **hallâzeh,** *hal-law-zeh´;* from the article [see 1973] and 2088; *this very:*—this.

1977. הַלֵּזוּ, **hallêzûw,** *hal-lay-zoo´;* another form of 1976; *that:*—this.

1978. הָלִיךְ, **hâlîyk,** *haw-leek´;* from 1980; a *walk,* i.e. (by implication) a *step:*—step.

1979. הֲלִיכָה, **hălîykâh,** *hal-ee-kaw´;* feminine of 1978; a *walking;* (by implication) a *procession* or *march,* a *caravan:*—company, going, walk, way.

1980. הָלַךְ, **hâlak,** *haw-lak´;* akin to 3212; a primitive root; to *walk* (in a great variety of applications, literal and figurative):—(all) along, apace, behave (self), come, (on) continually, be conversant, depart, + be eased, enter, exercise (self), + follow, forth, forward, get, go (about, abroad, along, away, forward, on, out, up and down), + greater, grow, be wont to haunt, lead, march, × more and more, move (self), needs, on, pass (away), be at the point, quite, run (along), + send, speedily, spread, still, surely, + talebearer, + travel (-ler), walk (abroad, on, to and fro, up and down, to places), wander, wax, [way-] faring man, × be weak, whirl.

A verb meaning to go, to come, to walk. This common word carries with it the basic idea of movement: the flowing of a river (Ge 2:14); the descending of floods (Ge 8:3); the crawling of beasts (Le 11:27); the slithering of snakes (Le 11:42); the blowing of the wind (Ecc 1:6); the tossing of the sea (Jnh 1:13). Since it is usually a person who is moving, it is frequently translated "walk" (Ge 48:15; 2Sa 15:30). Like a similar verb *dârak* (1869), meaning to tread, this word is also used metaphorically to speak of the pathways (i.e. behaviour) of one's life. A son could walk in (i.e. follow after) the ways of his father (2Ch 17:3) or not (1Sa 8:3). Israel was commanded to walk in the ways of the Lord (Dt 28:9), but they often walked after other gods (2Ki 13:11).

1981. הֲלַךְ, **hălak,** *hal-ak´;* (Chaldee); corresponding to 1980 [compare 1946]; to *walk:*—walk.

1982. הֵלֶךְ, **hêlek,** *hay´-lek;* from 1980; (properly) a *journey,* i.e. (by implication) a *wayfarer;* also a *flowing:*— × dropped, traveller.

1983. הֲלָךְ, **hălâk,** *hal-awk´;* (Chaldee); from 1981; (properly) a *journey,* i.e. (by implication) *toll* on goods at a road:—custom.

1984. הָלַל, **hâlal,** *haw-lal´;* a primitive root; to *be clear* (origin of sound, but usually of colour); to *shine;* hence to *make a show,* to *boast;* and thus to be (clamorously) *foolish;* to *rave;* (causative) to *celebrate;* also to *stultify:*—(make) boast (self), celebrate, commend, (deal, make), fool (-ish, -ly), glory, give [light], be (make, feign self) mad (against), give in marriage, [sing, be worthy of] praise, rage, renowned, shine.

A verb meaning to praise, to commend, to boast, to shine. The root meaning may be to shine but could also be to shout. The word most often means praise and is associated with the ministry of the Levites who praised God morning and evening (1Ch 23:30). All creation, however, is urged to join in (Ps 148), and various instruments were used to increase the praise to God (Ps 150). The word hallelujah is a command to praise *Yah* (the Lord), derived from the word *hâlal* (Ps 105:45; 146:1). The reflexive form of the verb is often used to signify boasting, whether in a good object (Ps 34:2[3]) or a bad object (Ps 49:6[7]). Other forms of the word mean to act foolishly or to be mad (1Sa 21:13[14]; Ecc 7:7; Isa 44:25).

1985. הֵלֵל, **Hillêl,** *hil-layl´*; from 1984; *praising* (namely God); *Hillel,* an Israelite:—Hillel.

1986. הָלַם, **hâlam,** *haw-lam´*; a primitive root; to *strike* down; (by implication) to *hammer, stamp, conquer, disband*:—beat (down), break (down), overcome, smite (with the hammer).

A verb meaning to smite, to hammer, to strike down. It also carries the implication of conquering and disbanding. The author of Judges used this word to describe Jael hammering the tent peg through Sisera's head (Jgs 5:26). Isaiah employed this word figuratively to describe nations breaking down grapevines (Isa 16:8) and people overcome by wine (Isa 28:1).

1987. הֶלֶם, **Helem,** *hay´-lem*; from 1986; *smiter; Helem,* the name of two Israelites:—Helem.

1988. הֲלֹם, **hălôm,** *hal-ome´*; from the article [see 1973]; *hither*:—here, hither (-[to]), thither.

1989. הַלְמוּת, **halmûwth,** *hal-mooth´*; from 1986; a *hammer* (or *mallet*):—hammer.

1990. הָם, **Hâm,** *hawm*; of uncertain derivation; *Ham,* a region of Palestine:—Ham.

1991. הֵם, **hêm,** *haym*; from 1993; *abundance,* i.e. *wealth*:—any of theirs.

1992. הֵם, **hêm,** *haym*; or (prolonged) הֵמָּה, **hêmmâh,** *haym´-maw*; masculine plural from 1931; *they* (only used when emphatic):—it, like, × (how, so) many (soever, more as) they (be), (the) same, × so, × such, their, them, these, they, those, which, who, whom, withal, ye.

1993. הָמָה, **hâmâh,** *haw-maw´*; a primitive root [compare 1949]; to *make a loud sound* (like English "hum"); by implication to *be in great commotion* or *tumult,* to *rage, war, moan, clamour*:—clamorous, concourse, cry aloud, be disquieted, loud, mourn, be moved, make a noise,

rage, roar, sound, be troubled, make in tumult, tumultuous, be in an uproar.

1994. הִמּוֹ, **himmôw,** *him-mo´*; (Chaldee); or (prolonged) הִמּוֹן, **himmôwn,** *him-mone´*; (Chaldee); corresponding to 1992; *they*:— × are, them, those.

1995. הָמוֹן, **hâmôwn,** *haw-mone´*; or הָמֹן, **hâmôn,** *haw-mone´*; (Eze 5:7), from 1993; a *noise, tumult, crowd*; also *disquietude, wealth*:—abundance, company, many, multitude, multiply, noise, riches, rumbling, sounding, store, tumult.

1996. הֲמוֹן גּוֹג, **Hămôwn Gôwg,** *ham-one´ gohg*; from 1995 and 1463; the *multitude of Gog*; the fanciful name of an emblematic place in Palestine:—Hamon-gog.

1997. הֲמוֹנָה, **Hămôwnâh,** *ham-o-naw´*; feminine of 1995; *multitude; Hamonah,* the same as 1996:—Hamonah.

1998. הֶמְיָה, **hemyâh,** *hem-yaw´*; from 1993; *sound*:—noise.

1999. הֲמֻלָּה, **hămulâh,** *ham-ool-law´*; or (too fully) הֲמוּלָּה, **hămûwllâh,** *ham-ool-law´*; (Jer 11:16), feminine passive participle of an unused root meaning to *rush* (as rain with a windy roar); a *sound*:—speech, tumult.

A feminine noun meaning a rushing noise. The two occurrences of this word conjure up the sound of a great wind. The first is in the prophecy of Jeremiah, where Israel was called a strong olive tree, but the Lord would set the tree on fire with a great rushing sound as a sign of judgment (Jer 11:16). The word is also used in Ezekiel's vision, where the sound of the creatures' wings was like the roar of a rushing river (Eze 1:24).

2000. הָמַם, **hâmam,** *haw-mam´*; a primitive root [compare 1949, 1993]; (properly) to *put in commotion*; (by implication) to *disturb, drive, destroy*:—break, consume, crush, destroy, discomfit, trouble, vex.

A verb meaning to make a noise, to move noisily, to confuse, to put into commotion. When it means to move noisily, it often refers to the wheels of wagons or chariots (Isa 28:28). The idea of moving noisily or with commotion carries over into the idea of confusion: God confuses the Egyptians when they pursue Israel (Ex 14:24); and He sends confusion to the nations before the Israelites go into Canaan (Jos 10:10).

2001. הָמָן, **Hâmân,** *haw-mawn´*; of foreign derivation; *Haman*, a Persian vizier:—Haman.

2002. הַמְנִיךְ, **hamnîyk,** *ham-neek´*; (Chaldee); but the text is הֲמוּנַךְ, **hămûwnêk,** *ham-oo-nayk´*; of foreign origin; a *necklace*:—chain.

2003. הֲמָסִים, **hămâsîym,** *haw-maw-seem´*; from an unused root apparently meaning to *crackle*; a dry *twig* or *brushwood*:—melting.

2004. הֵן, **hên,** *hane*; feminine plural from 1931; *they* (only used when emphatic):— × in, such like, (with) them, thereby, therein, (more than) they, wherein, in which, whom, withal.

2005. הֵן, **hên,** *hane*; a primitive particle; *lo!*; also (as expressing surprise) *if*:—behold, if, lo, though.

2006. הֵן, **hên,** *hane*; (Chaldee); corresponding to 2005; *lo!* also *there* [-fore], [un-] *less, whether, but, if*:—(that) if, or, whether.

2007. הֵנָּה, **hênnâh,** *hane´-naw*; prolonged for 2004; *themselves* (often used emphatically for the copula, also in indirect relation):— × in, × such (and such things), their, (into) them, thence, therein, these, they (had), on this side, those, wherein.

2008. הֵנָּה, **hênnâh,** *hane´-naw*; from 2004; *hither* or *thither* (but used both of place and time):—here, hither [-to], now, on this (that) side, + since, this (that) way, thitherward, + thus far, to … fro, + yet.

2009. הִנֵּה, **hinnêh,** *hin-nay´*; prolonged for 2005; *lo!*:—behold, lo, see.

2010. הֲנָחָה, **hănâchâh,** *han-aw-khaw´*; from 5117; *permission* of rest, i.e. *quiet*:—release.

2011. הִנֹּם, **Hinnôm,** *hin-nome´*; probably of foreign origin; *Hinnom*, apparently a Jebusite:—Hinnom.

2012. הֵנַע, **Hêna‘,** *hay-nah´*; probably of foreign derivation; *Hena*, a place apparently in Mesopotamia:—Hena.

2013. הָסָה, **hâsâh,** *haw-saw´*; a primitive root; to *hush*:—hold peace (tongue), (keep) silence, be silent, still.

2014. הֲפֻגָה, **hăphugâh,** *haf-oo-gaw´*; from 6313; *relaxation*:—intermission.

2015. הָפַךְ, **hâphak,** *haw-vak´*; a primitive root; to *turn* about or over; (by implication) to *change, overturn, return, pervert*:— × become, change, come, be converted, give, make [a bed], overthrow (-turn), perverse, retire, tumble, turn (again, aside, back, to the contrary, every way).

A verb meaning to turn around, to change, to throw down, to overturn, to pervert, to destroy, to be turned against, to turn here and there, to wander. The verb is used to describe the simple act of turning something over (2Ki 21:13; Hos 7:8) but also to indicate turning back from something (Ps 78:9). These turnings indicate that Jerusalem would lose all its inhabitants by being turned over as a dish is turned over after wiping it; "Ephraim has become a cake not turned," that is, overdone on one side, uncooked on the other, and not edible (Hos 7:8 NASB).

The verb becomes more figurative when it describes the act of overthrowing or destroying. Second Kings 21:13 is relevant here also, but Haggai speaks of God overthrowing the thrones of kingdoms (Persia) as well as chariots and riders (Hag 2:22). Even more violently, the verb describes the overthrow of the enemies of God and His people; Sodom and Gomorrah were especially singled out (Ge 19:21, 25; Dt 29:23[22]; cf. 2Sa 10:3). The word also indicates a change or is used to indicate defeat in battle when an army turned in flight (Jos 7:8) or simply the change in direction of something (1Ki 22:34). Metaphorically, the word comes to mean to change (by turning). For example, the Lord changed the curse of Balaam into a blessing (Dt 23:5[6]); He will change the mourning of His people into joy and gladness (Jer 31:13). The simple stem is also found in a reflexive sense; the men of Israel turned themselves about in battle against the Benjamites (Jgs 20:39, 41; cf. 2Ki 5:26; 2Ch 9:12).

The verb is used a few times in the reflexive stems to indicate turning oneself about: The Israelites are pictured as having turned themselves back against their enemies (Jos 8:20); and Pharaoh changed his heart in himself (Ex 14:5; Hos 11:8), thus changing his mind. The word is used in the sense of being overwhelmed or overcome by pain (1Sa 4:19); the clouds rolled about (Job. 37:12); the sword placed by the Lord to guard the Garden of Eden turned itself about (Ge 3:24); and the earth's surface was shaped and moved like clay being impressed under a seal (Job 38:14).

2016. הֶפֶךְ, **hephek,** *heh´-fek*; or הֵפֶךְ, **hêphek,** *hay´-fek*; from 2015; a *turn*, i.e. the *reverse*:—contrary.

2017. הֹפֶךְ, **hôphek,** *ho´-fek*; from 2015; an *upset*, i.e. (abstract) *perversity*:—turning of things upside down.

2018. הֲפֵכָה, **hăphêkâh,** *haf-ay-kaw´*; feminine of 2016; *destruction*:—overthrow.

2019. הֲפַכְפַּךְ, **hăphakpak,** *haf-ak-pak´*; by reduplication from 2015; *very perverse*:—froward.

2020. הַצָּלָה, **hatstsâlâh,** *hats-tsaw-loaw´*; from 5337; *rescue*:—deliverance.

2021. הֹצֶן, **hôtsen,** *ho´-tsen*; from an unused root meaning apparently to *be sharp* or *strong*; a *weapon* of war:—chariot.

2022. הַר, **har,** *har*; a shorter form of 2042; a *mountain* or *range* of hills (sometimes used figuratively):—hill (country), mount (-ain), × promotion.

2023. הֹר, **Hôr,** *hore*; another form for 2022; *mountain; Hor,* the name of a peak in Idumæa and of one in Syria:—Hor.

2024. הָרָא, **Hârâ',** *haw-raw´*; perhaps from 2022; *mountainousness; Hara,* a region of Media:—Hara.

2025. הַרְאֵל, **har'êl,** *har-ale´*; from 2022 and 410; *mount of God*; (figurative) the *altar* of burnt offering:—altar. Compare 739.

2026. הָרַג, **hârag,** *haw-rag´*; a primitive root; to *smite* with deadly intent:—destroy, out of hand, kill, murder (-er), put to [death], make [slaughter], slay (-er), × surely.

A verb meaning to kill, murder, slay. It carries a wide variety of usages. Its first use in the Bible is in the fratricide of Cain and Abel (Ge 4:8). The word is employed for war and slaughter (Jos 8:24; 1Ki 9:16; Est 8:11); God's killing in judgment (Ge 20:4; Ex 13:15; Am 2:3); humans killing animals (Le 20:15; Nu 22:29); animals killing humans (2Ki 17:25; Job 20:16).

2027. הֶרֶג, **hereg,** *heh´-reg*; from 2026; *slaughter*:—be slain, slaughter.

A masculine noun meaning slaughter. The Jews had a great victory and struck down all their enemies (Est 9:5), while the book of Proverbs advises that one should rescue those unwise people heading for the slaughter (Pr 24:11). Isaiah uses the "day of the great slaughter" to refer to the time of Israel's deliverance (Isa 30:25). In the prophecy against Tyre, Ezekiel warns of the day when a slaughter will take place there (Eze 26:15).

2028. הֲרֵגָה, **hărêgâh,** *har-ay-gaw´*; feminine of 2027; *slaughter*:—slaughter.

A noun meaning slaughter. It is the feminine form of *hereg* (2027) and is used only five times in the OT. Two of these are found in the phrase "valley of slaughter" (Jer 7:32; 19:6). In both of these occurrences, the Lord renames the Hinnom Valley because of the slaughter He will bring on the Israelites who have done horrifying deeds by sacrificing their children to other gods. Jeremiah also uses the word when he pleads with the Lord for the wicked to be taken away for the "day of slaughter" (Jer 12:3 NIV). Zechariah uses this word twice in a metaphor describing Israel as the "flock marked for slaughter" (Zec 11:4 NIV).

2029. הָרָה, **hârâh,** *haw-raw´*; a primitive root; to *be* (or *become*) *pregnant, conceive* (literal or figurative):—been, be with child, conceive, progenitor.

2030. הָרֶה, **hâreh,** *haw-reh´*; or הָרִי, **hârîy,** *haw-ree´* (Hos 14:1), from 2029; *pregnant*:—(be, woman) with child, conceive, × great.

2031. הַרְהֹר, **harhôr,** *har-hor´*; (Chaldee); from a root corresponding to 2029; a mental *conception*:—thought.

2032. הֵרוֹן, **hêrôwn,** *hay-rone´*; or הֵרָיוֹן, **hêrâyôwn,** *hay-raw-yone´*; from 2029; *pregnancy*:—conception.

2033. הֲרוֹרִי, **Hărôwrîy,** *har-o-ree´*; another form for 2043; a *Harorite* or mountaineer:—Harorite.

2034. הֲרִיסָה, **hărîysâh,** *har-ee-saw´*; from 2040; something *demolished*:—ruin.

2035. הֲרִיסָה, **hărîysâh,** *har-ee-saw´*; from 2040; *demolition*:—destruction.

2036. הֹרָם, **Hôrâm,** *ho-rawm´*; from an unused root (meaning to *tower* up); *high; Horam,* a Canaanitish king:—Horam.

2037. הָרוּם, **Hârûwm,** *haw-room´*; passive participle of the same as 2036; *high; Harum,* an Israelite:—Harum.

2038. הַרְמוֹן, **harmôwn,** *har-mone´*; from the same as 2036; a *castle* (from its height):—palace.

2039. הָרָן, **Hârân,** *haw-rawn´*; perhaps from 2022; *mountaineer; Haran,* the name of two men:—Haran.

2040. הָרַס, **hâras,** *haw-ras´*; a primitive root; to *pull* down or in pieces, *break, destroy:*—beat down, break (down, through), destroy, overthrow, pluck down, pull down, ruin, throw down, × utterly.

A verb meaning to pull down, to break through, to overthrow, to destroy. In Miriam and Moses' song, God threw down His enemies (Ex 15:7). Elijah told God that the Israelites had pulled down God's altars (1Ki 19:10, 14). The psalmist wanted God to break out the teeth of the wicked (Ps 58:6[7]) and also said that God would tear down the wicked and not build them up again (Ps 28:5). The foolish woman tore down her own house (Pr 14:1). On Mount Sinai, God cautioned Moses to warn the people not to force their way through to see God and then perish (Ex 19:21). In Exodus, this word is used in an even stronger sense when God instructs the Israelites not to worship foreign gods but to utterly demolish them (Ex 23:24).

2041. הֶרֶס, **heres,** *heh´-res*; from 2040; *demolition:*—destruction.

2042. הָרָר, **hârâr,** *haw-rawr´*; from an unused root meaning to *loom* up; a *mountain:*—hill, mount (-ain).

2043. הֲרָרִי, **Hărârîy,** *hah-raw-ree´*; or הָרָרִי, **Hârârîy,** *haw-raw-ree´*; (2Sa 23:11), or הָאֱרָרִי, **Hâ'rârîy,** *haw-raw-ree´*; (2Sa 23:34, last clause), apparently from 2042; a *mountaineer:*—Hararite.

2044. הָשֵׁם, **Hâshêm,** *haw-shame´*; perhaps from the same as 2828; *wealthy; Hashem,* an Israelite:—Hashem.

2045. הַשְׁמָעוּת, **hashmâ‘ûwth,** *hashmaw-ooth´*; from 8085; *announcement:*—to cause to hear.

2046. הִתּוּךְ, **hittûwk,** *hit-took´*; from 5413; a *melting:*—is melted.

2047. הֲתָךְ, **Hăthâk,** *hath-awk´*; probably of foreign origin; *Hathak,* a Persian eunuch:—Hatach.

2048. הָתַל, **hâthal,** *haw-thal´*; a primitive root; to *deride*; (by implication) to *cheat:*—deal deceitfully, deceive, mock.

2049. הֲתֻלִים, **hăthulîym,** *haw-thoo-leem´*; from 2048 (only in plural collective); a *derision:*—mocker.

2050. הָתַת, **hâthath,** *haw-thath´*; a primitive root; (properly) to *break* in upon, i.e. to *assail:*—imagine mischief.

‎ו‎ (Waw)

2051. ‎וְדָן‎, **Vᵉdân**, *ved-awn´*; perhaps for 5730; *Vedan* (or Aden), a place in Arabia:—Dan also.

2052. ‎וָהֵב‎, **Vâhêb**, *vaw-habe´*; of uncertain derivation; *Vaheb*, a place in Moab:—what he did.

2053. ‎וָו‎, **vâv**, *vaw*; probably a *hook* (the name of the sixth Hebrew letter):—hook.

2054. ‎וָזָר‎, **vâzâr**, *vaw-zawr´*; presumed to be from an unused root meaning to *bear* guilt; *crime:*— × strange.

A noun meaning guilty one. It occurs only once in the OT (Pr 21:8), where the immoral path of the guilty is contrasted to the pure behaviour of the innocent. The translators for the King James Version understood the word to be a combination of the word *and* with the adjective meaning strange. Therefore, they translated this Hebrew word, "The way of man is froward and strange." But modern translators translate this word "guilty."

2055. ‎וַיְזָתָא‎, **Vayzâthâʾ**, *vah-zaw´-thaw*; of foreign origin; *Vajezatha*, a son of Haman:—Vajezatha.

2056. ‎וָלָד‎, **vâlâd**, *vaw-lawd´*; for 3206; a *boy:*—child.

2057. ‎וַנְיָה‎, **Vanyâh**, *van-yaw´*; perhaps for 6043; *Vanjah*, an Israelite:—Vaniah.

2058. ‎וָפְסִי‎, **Vophsîy**, *vof-see´*; probably from 3254; *additional*; *Vophsi*, an Israelite:—Vophsi.

2059. ‎וַשְׁנִי‎, **Vashnîy**, *vash-nee´*; probably from 3461; *weak*; *Vashni*, an Israelite:—Vashni.

2060. ‎וַשְׁתִּי‎, **Vashtîy**, *vash-tee´*; of Persian origin; *Vashti*, the queen of Xerxes:—Vashti.

ז (Zayin)

2061. זְאֵב, **zeʾêb,** *zeh-abe´*; from an unused root meaning to *be yellow*; a *wolf:*—wolf.

2062. זְאֵב, **Zeʾêb,** *zeh-abe´*; the same as 2061; *Zeëb,* a Midianitish prince:—Zeeb.

2063. זֹאת, **zôʾth,** *zothe´*; irregular feminine of 2089; *this* (often used adverbially):—hereby (-in, -with), it, likewise, the one (other, same), she, so (much), such (deed), that, therefore, these, this (thing), thus.

2064. זָבַד, **zâbad,** *zaw-bad´*; a primitive root; to *confer:*—endure.

2065. זֶבֶד, **zebed,** *zeh´-bed*; from 2064; a *gift:*—dowry.

2066. זָבָד, **Zâbâd,** *zaw-bawd´*; from 2064; *giver; Zabad,* the name of seven Israelites:—Zabad.

2067. זַבְדִּי, **Zabdîy,** *zab-dee´*; from 2065; *giving; Zabdi,* the name of four Israelites:—Zabdi.

2068. זַבְדִּיאֵל, **Zabdîyʾêl,** *zab-dee-ale´*; from 2065 and 410; *gift of God; Zabdiel,* the name of two Israelites:—Zabdiel.

2069. זְבַדְיָה, **Zᵉbadyâh,** *zeb-ad-yaw´*; or זְבַדְיָהוּ, **Zebadyâhûw,** *zeb-ad-yaw´-hoo*; from 2064 and 3050; *Jah has given; Zebadjah,* the name of nine Israelites:—Zebadiah.

2070. זְבוּב, **zᵉbûwb,** *zeb-oob´*; from an unused root (meaning to *flit*); a *fly* (especially one of a stinging nature):—fly.

2071. זָבוּד, **Zâbûwd,** *zaw-bood´*; from 2064; *given; Zabud,* an Israelite:—Zabud.

2072. זַבּוּד, **Zabbûwd,** *zab-bood´*; a form of 2071; *given; Zabbud,* an Israelite:—Zabbud.

2073. זְבוּל, **zᵉbûwl,** *ze-bool´*; or זְבֻל, **zebul,** *zeb-ool´*; from 2082; a *residence:*—dwell in, dwelling, habitation.

2074. זְבוּלוּן, **Zᵉbûwlûwn,** *zeb-oo-loon´*; or זְבֻלוּן, **Zebulûwn,** *zeb-oo-loon´*; or זְבוּלֻן, **Zebûwlun,** *zeb-oo-loon´*; from 2082; *habitation; Zebulon,* a son of Jacob; also his territory and tribe:—Zebulun.

2075. זְבוּלֹנִי, **Zᵉbûwlônîy,** *zeb-oo-lo-nee´*; patronymic from 2074; a *Zebulonite* or descendant of Zebulun:—Zebulonite.

2076. זָבַח, **zâbach,** *zaw-bakh´*; a primitive root; to *slaughter* an animal (usually in sacrifice):—kill, offer, (do) sacrifice, slay.

A verb meaning to slaughter, to kill, to offer, to sacrifice. The word is used in its broadest sense to indicate the slaughtering of various animals. It indicates the slaughter of animals for food (Dt 12:21; 1Sa 28:24) or for sacrifice with strong political implications (1Ki 1:9, 19); Elisha slaughtered his oxen to make his break with his past and establish his commitment to Elijah (1Ki 19:21). The word describes a sacrifice made to create communion or to seal a covenant. Jacob made a sacrificial meal to celebrate the peace between him and Laban (Ge 31:54); and the priests were to receive part of the bulls or sheep offered by the people (Dt 18:3). These slaughtered sacrificial animals were presented to gods or the true God; Jacob's sacrifice was to God (Ge 46:1) as were most of these sacrifices, but the nations sacrificed to other gods as well, such as Dagon (Jgs 16:23) or the gods of Damascus (2Ch 28:23).

Various kinds of sacrifices are given as the objects of this verb. For instance, sacrifices that open the womb (Ex 13:15); offerings of well-being, peace offerings, and burnt offerings (Ex 20:24); and animals of the flock and herd (Nu 22:40). Certain slaughtered sacrifices were prohibited, such as a sacrifice with blood and yeast in it (Ex 23:18; cf. Ex 12:15). In an exceptional setting, however, a prophet proclaimed the slaughter and sacrifice of the defiled priests who served at the forbidden high places (1Ki 13:2). God will exercise divine judgment on the enemies of His people, Gog and Magog, slaying and providing their carcasses as a great banquet for every kind of bird and animal (Eze 39:17, 19); Israel, in their rebellion, offered, although forbidden, their own sons as offerings (Eze 16:20).

2077. זֶבַח, **zebach,** *zeh´-bakh*; from 2076; (properly) a *slaughter*, i.e. the *flesh* of an animal; (by implication) a *sacrifice* (the victim or the act):—offer (-ing), sacrifice.

A masculine noun meaning sacrifice. This word refers to the kind of flesh sacrifice the offerer ate after it was given to God (parts of the flesh went to God and to the priests as well). This practice was ancient and did not solely apply to sacrifices to the true God of Israel (Ex 34:15; Nu 25:2). Other sacrifices of this type included the covenant between Jacob and Laban (Ge 31:54); the Passover Feast (Ex 34:25); the thank offering (Le 22:29); the annual sacrifice (1Sa 1:21); the sacrifice of a covenant with God (Ps 50:5). See the related Hebrew verb *zâbach* (2076).

2078. זֶבַח, **Zebach,** *zeh´-bakh*; the same as 2077; *sacrifice; Zebach*, a Midianitish prince:—Zebah.

2079. זַבַּי, **Zabbay,** *zab-bah´ee*; probably by orthographical error for 2140; *Zabbai* (or *Zaccai*), an Israelite:—Zabbai.

2080. זְבִידָה, **Zᵉbîydâh,** *zeb-ee-daw´*; feminine from 2064; *giving; Zebidah*, an Israelitess:—Zebudah.

2081. זְבִינָא, **Zᵉbîynâʼ,** *zeb-ee-naw´*; from an unused root (meaning to *purchase*); *gainfulness; Zebina*, an Israelite:—Zebina.

2082. זָבַל, **zâbal,** *zaw-bal´*; a primitive root; apparently (properly) to *inclose*, i.e. to *reside*:—dwell with.

2083. זְבֻל, **Zᵉbul,** *zeb-ool´*; the same as 2073; *dwelling; Zebul*, an Israelite:—Zebul. Compare 2073.

2084. זְבַן, **zᵉban,** *zeb-an´*; (Chaldee); corresponding to the root of 2081; to *acquire* by purchase:—gain.

2085. זָג, **zâg,** *zawg*; from an unused root probably meaning to *inclose*; the *skin* of a grape:—husk.

2086. זֵד, **zêd,** *zade´*; from 2102; *arrogant:*—presumptuous, proud.

An adjective meaning proud, arrogant. This word most often occurs in the Psalms where it is used in connection with sin (Ps 19:13[14]) or to describe the ungodly (Ps 86:14; 119:21, 85). Elsewhere in the OT, *zêd* describes the proud who will be judged (Isa 13:11; Mal 4:1[3:19]) and the disobedience of the proud (Jer 43:2).

2087. זָדוֹן, **zâdôwn,** *zaw-done´*; from 2102; *arrogance:*—presumptuously, pride, proud (man).

A noun meaning presumptuousness, pride. David's brothers accused him of being presumptuous when he wanted to challenge Goliath (1Sa 17:28). Ob 1:3 addresses the pride of the Edomites who fatally presumed that they had a safe place in the cliffs. Proverbs also describes the negative aspects of pride (Pr 11:2; 13:10; 21:24), while Ezekiel uses this word in his description of the day of judgment (Eze 7:10).

2088. זֶה, **zeh,** *zeh*; a primitive word; the masculine demonstrative pronoun, *this* or *that:*—he, × hence, × here, it (-self), × now, × of him, the one … the other, × than the other, (× out of) the (self) same, such (an one) that, these, this (hath, man), on this side … on that side, × thus, very, which. Compare 2063, 2090, 2097, 2098.

2089. זֶה, **zeh,** *zeh*; (1Sa 17:34), by permutation for 7716; a *sheep:*—lamb.

2090. זֹה, **zôh,** *zo*; for 2088; *this* or *that:*—as well as another, it, this, that, thus and thus.

2091. זָהָב, **zâhâb,** *zaw-hawb´*; from an unused root meaning to *shimmer; gold*; (figurative) something *gold-coloured* (i.e. *yellow*), as *oil*, a *clear sky:*—gold (-en), fair weather.

2092. זָהַם, **zâham,** *zaw-ham´*; a primitive root; to *be rancid*, i.e. (transposed) to *loathe:*—abhor.

2093. זַהַם, **Zaham,** *zah´-ham*; from 2092; *loathing; Zaham*, an Israelite:—Zaham.

2094. זָהַר, **zâhar,** *zaw-har´*; a primitive root; to *gleam*; (figurative) to *enlighten* (by caution):—admonish, shine, teach, (give) warn (-ing).

A verb meaning to teach, to warn, to shine. Ezekiel uses this verb more than any other OT writer. In chapter 3, he uses *zâhar* seven times consecutively when God commands him to warn the wicked and righteous about their sin

(Eze 3:17–21). Similarly, Eze 33 uses this word eight times to describe coming judgment for sin (Eze 33:3–9). Other books also use *zâhar* to mean warn (2Ki 6:10; 2Ch 19:10) or admonish (Ecc 4:13; 12:12). Exodus uses this word to mean teach (Ex 18:20). Daniel is the only book which uses the future tense of the word (Da 12:3).

2095. זְהַר, **zᵉhar**, *zeh-har´*; (Chaldee); corresponding to 2094; (passive) *be admonished*:—take heed.

An Aramaic verb meaning to take heed, to be admonished, to be cautious. The word *zĕhar* is used only once in Scripture. King Artaxerxes told his secretaries and other men under his command to be careful to obey his order (Ezr 4:22).

2096. זֹהַר, **zôhar**, *zo´-har*; from 2094; *brilliancy*:—brightness.

2097. זוֹ, **zôw**, *zo*; for 2088; *this* or *that*:—that, this.

2098. זוּ, **zûw**, *zoo*; for 2088; *this* or *that*:—that this, × wherein, which, whom.

2099. זִו, **Ziv**, *zeev´*; probably from an unused root meaning to *be prominent*; (properly) *brightness* [compare 2122], i.e. (figurative) the month of *flowers; Ziv* (corresponding to Ijar or May):—Zif.

2100. זוּב, **zûwb**, *zoob*; a primitive root; to *flow* freely (as water), i.e. (specifically) to *have a* (sexual) *flux*; (figurative) to *waste* away; also to *overflow*:—flow, gush out, have a (running) issue, pine away, run.

2101. זוֹב, **zôwb**, *zobe*; from 2100; a seminal or menstrual *flux*:—issue.

2102. זוּד, **zûwd**, *zood*; or (by permutation) זִיד, **zîyd**, *zeed*; a primitive root; to *seethe*; (figurative) to *be insolent*:—be proud, deal proudly, presume, (come) presumptuously, sod.

2103. זוּד, **zûwd**, *zood*; (Chaldee); corresponding to 2102; to *be proud*:—in pride.

2104. זוּזִים, **Zûwzîym**, *zoo-zeem´*; plural probably from the same as 2123; *prominent; Zuzites*, an aboriginal tribe of Palestine:—Zuzims.

2105. זוֹחֵת, **Zôwchêth**, *zo-khayth´*; of uncertain origin; *Zocheth*, an Israelite:—Zoheth.

2106. זָוִית, **zâvîyth**, *zaw-veeth´*; apparently from the same root as 2099 (in the sense of *prominence*); an *angle* (as projecting), i.e. (by implication) a *corner-column* (or *anta*):—corner (stone).

2107. זוּל, **zûwl**, *zool*; a primitive root [compare 2151]; probably to *shake* out, i.e. (by implication) to *scatter* profusely; (figurative) to *treat lightly*:—lavish, despise.

2108. זוּלָה, **zûwlâh**, *zoo-law´*; from 2107; (properly) *scattering*, i.e. *removal*; (used adverbially) *except*:—beside, but, only, save.

2109. זוּן, **zûwn**, *zoon*; a primitive root; perhaps (properly) to *be plump*, i.e. (transposed) to *nourish*:—feed.

2110. זוּן, **zûwn**, *zoon*; (Chaldee); corresponding to 2109:—feed.

2111. זוּעַ, **zûwaʻ**, *zoo´-ah*; a primitive root; (properly) to *shake* off, i.e. (figurative) to *agitate* (as with fear):—move, tremble, vex.

A verb meaning to tremble, to shake. Haman was angry when Mordecai did not tremble at his sight (Est 5:9). This word is also used to describe an old man (Ecc 12:3). In Habakkuk, it occurs in a causative sense, meaning to cause to tremble. This verse refers to the debtors of Israel (used figuratively for Babylon) who would make Israel tremble with fear (Hab 2:7). See the related Aramaic verb *zûʻa* (2112).

2112. זוּעַ, **zûwaʻ**, *zoo´-ah*; (Chaldee); corresponding to 2111; to *shake* (with fear):—tremble.

An Aramaic verb meaning to tremble. This word is used only twice in the OT and is equivalent to the Hebrew word *zûʻa* (2111), meaning to tremble or to shake. In Da 5:19, this word is used to describe the trembling fear of the people before the mighty Nebuchadnezzar. In Da 6:26[27], it describes the same trembling fear that people ought to have before the God of Daniel. In both instances, it is used synonymously with another Aramaic word meaning fear, *dĕchal* (1763).

2113. זְוָעָה, **zᵉvâʻâh**, *zev-aw-aw´*; from 2111; *agitation, fear*:—be removed, trouble, vexation. Compare 2189.

2114. זוּר, **zûwr,** *zoor*; a primitive root; to *turn* aside (especially for lodging); hence to *be a foreigner, strange, profane*; specifically (active participle) to *commit adultery*:—(come from) another (man, place), fanner, go away, (e-) strange (-r, thing, woman).

A verb meaning to be a stranger. The basic meaning of this word is to turn aside (particularly for lodging); therefore, it refers to being strange or foreign. It can mean to go astray, to be wayward (Ps 58:3[4]). The participle is used frequently as an adjective, signifying something outside the law of God (Ex 30:9; Le 10:1); a person outside the family (Dt 25:5); the estranged way Job's guests and servants viewed him (Job 19:15); hallucinations from drunkenness (Pr 23:33). This word is used several times in Proverbs of the adulterous woman (Pr 2:16; 5:3, 20; 7:5; 22:14).

2115. זוּר, **zûwr,** *zoor*; a primitive root [compare 6695]; to *press* together, *tighten*:—close, crush, thrust together.

2116. זוּרֶה, **zûwreh,** *zoo-reh´*; from 2115; *trodden* on:—that which is crushed.

2117. זָזָא, **zâzâʾ,** *zaw-zaw*; probably from the root of 2123; *prominent; Zaza,* an Israelite:—Zaza.

2118. זָחַח, **zâchach,** *zaw-khakh´*; a primitive root; to *shove* or *displace*:—loose.

2119. זָחַל, **zâchal,** *zaw-khal´*; a primitive root; to *crawl*; (by implication) to *fear*:—be afraid, serpent, worm.

A verb meaning to crawl, to fear, and to be afraid. It can refer to the movement of a snake on the ground (Dt 32:24; Mic 7:17). It can also be a metaphor for an individual who is afraid or one who creeps forward slowly and cautiously (Job 32:6).

2120. זֹחֶלֶת, **Zôcheleth,** *zo-kheh´-leth*; feminine active participle of 2119; *crawling* (i.e. *serpent); Zoche-leth,* a boundary stone in Palestine:—Zoheleth.

2121. זֵידוֹן, **zêydôwn,** *zay-dohn´*; from 2102; *boiling* of water, i.e. *wave*:—proud.

2122. זִיו, **zîyv,** *zeev*; (Chaldee); corresponding to 2099; (figurative) *cheerfulness*:—brightness, countenance.

2123. זִיז, **zîyz,** *zeez*; from an unused root apparently meaning to *be conspicuous; fulness* of the breast; also a moving *creature*:—abundance, wild beast.

2124. זִיזָא, **Zîyzâʾ,** *zee-zaw´*; apparently from the same as 2123; *prominence; Ziza,* the name of two Israelites:—Ziza.

2125. זִיזָה, **Zîyzâh,** *zee-zaw´*; another form for 2124; *Zizah,* an Israelite:—Zizah.

2126. זִינָא, **Zîynâʾ,** *zee-naw´*; from 2109; well *fed*; or perhaps an orthographical error for 2124; *Zina,* an Israelite:—Zina.

2127. זִיעַ, **Zîyaʿ,** *zee´-ah*; from 2111; *agitation; Zia,* an Israelite:—Zia.

2128. זִיף, **Zîyph,** *zeef*; from the same as 2203; *flowing; Ziph,* the name of a place in Palestine; also of an Israelite:—Ziph.

2129. זִיפָה, **Zîyphâh,** *zee-faw´*; feminine of 2128; a *flowing; Ziphah,* an Israelite:—Ziphah.

2130. זִיפִי, **Zîyphîy,** *zee-fee´*; patrial from 2128; a *Ziphite* or inhabitant of Ziph:—Ziphim, Ziphite.

2131. זִיקָה, **zîyqâh,** *zee-kaw´*; (Isa 50:11), (feminine) and זִק, **ziq,** *zeek*; or זֵק, **zêq,** *zake*; from 2187; (properly) what *leaps* forth, i.e. *flash* of fire, or a burning *arrow*; also (from the original sense of the root) a *bond*:—chain, fetter, firebrand, spark.

2132. זַיִת, **zayith,** *zah´-yith*; probably from an unused root [akin to 2099]; an *olive* (as yielding *illuminating* oil), the tree, the branch or the berry:—olive (tree, -yard), Olivet.

2133. זֵיתָן, **Zêythân,** *zay-thawn´*; from 2132; *olive* grove; *Zethan,* an Israelite:—Zethan.

2134. זַךְ, **zak,** *zak*; from 2141; *clear*:—clean, pure.

An adjective meaning pure, clean. It is derived from the related verbs *zâkâh* (2135), meaning to be clear or pure, and *zâkak* (2141), meaning to be clean or pure. This word is used to describe objects used in the worship of God, such as pure oil (Ex 27:20; Le 24:2) and pure frankincense (Ex 30:34; Le 24:7). It also denotes the purity of the righteous, such as Job (Job 8:6; 33:9), in contrast with one living a crooked life (Pr 21:8). This word can also speak about all aspects of one's life: one's actions in general (Pr 16:2; 20:11); one's teaching (Job 11:4); or one's prayer (Job 16:17).

2135. זָכָה, **zâkâh,** *zaw-kaw´*; a primitive root [compare 2141]; to *be translucent*; (figurative) to *be innocent*:—be (make) clean, cleanse, be clear, count pure.

A verb meaning to clean, to be clean, to cleanse. Job's friends used this word twice, questioning how one born of a woman could be clean or righteous before God (Job 15:14; 25:4). It is also used to describe the state of the heart (Ps 73:13; Pr 20:9). In other uses, it carries the connotation of being pure or cleansed from sin (Ps 119:9; Isa 1:16; Mic 6:11).

2136. זְכוּ, **zâkûw,** *zaw-koo´*; (Chaldee); from a root corresponding to 2135; *purity*:—innocency.

2137. זְכוּכִית, **zᵉkûwkîyth,** *zek-oo-keeth´*; from 2135; (properly) *transparency*, i.e. *glass*:—crystal.

2138. זְכוּר, **zᵉkûwr,** *zeh-koor´*; (properly) passive participle of 2142, but used for 2145; a *male* (of man or animals):—males, men-children.

2139. זַכּוּר, **Zakkûwr,** *zak-koor´*; from 2142; *mindful*; *Zakkur*, the name of seven Israelites:—Zaccur, Zacchur.

2140. זַכַּי, **Zakkay,** *zak-kah´ee*; from 2141; *pure*; *Zakkai*, an Israelite:—Zaccai.

2141. זָכַךְ, **zâkak,** *zaw-kak´*; a primitive root [compare 2135]; to *be transparent* or *clean* (physical or moral):—be (make) clean, be pure (-r).

A verb meaning to be clean, to be pure. This word is used only four times in the OT. Job uses it to describe washing his hands to make them clean (Job 9:30). On two occasions, it speaks of the purity of the heavens (Job 15:15) and the stars (Job 25:5). The final usage of the word describes certain people as being purer than snow (La 4:7) in contrast with the blackness of soot (La 4:8). See the related verb, *zâkâh* (2135), meaning to be clear or pure, and the related noun, *zak* (2134), meaning pure.

2142. זָכַר, **zâkar,** *zaw-kar´*; a primitive root; (properly) to *mark* (so as to be recognized), i.e. to *remember*; (by implication) to *mention*; also

(as denominative from 2145) to *be male*:— × burn [incense], × earnestly, be male, (make) mention (of), be mindful, recount, record (-er), remember, make to be remembered, bring (call, come, keep, put) to (in) remembrance, × still, think on, × well.

A verb meaning to remember, to mention, to recall, to think about, to think on, to be remembered, to recall, to acknowledge, to mention, to make known. The basic meaning indicates a process of mentioning or recalling either silently, verbally, or by means of a memorial sign or symbol. The verb often means to mention, to think about. The Lord warned the people and false prophets not to verbally mention the oracle of the Lord (Jer 23:36); the Lord thought about Ephraim in a good sense (Jer 31:20); and the psalmist thought or meditated on the Lord in his heart and mind without words (Ps 63:6[7]).

These meanings, of course, overlap with the primary translation of the verb, to remember. The psalmist remembered the Lord often, and 43 of the 165 uses of the simple stem are in the Book of Psalms. Remembering in ancient Israel was a major aspect of proper worship, as it is today.

Remembering involves many things, and various connotations are possible. God or people can be the subject that remembers. For example, because God had acted so often for His people, they were to remember Him and His acts on their behalf (Dt 5:15; 15:15; 24:18). They were to remember His covenant and commandments without fail (Ex 20:8; Mal 4:4[3:22]). Above all, they were to remember Him by His name. By remembering Him, they imitated the Lord, for He never forgot them (cf. Dt 4:29–31). He faithfully remembered His people (Ge 8:1), and they could beg Him to remember them, as Jeremiah did in his distress (Ne 13:31; Jer 15:15). The Lord especially remembered His covenant with the ancestors and fathers of Israel (Le 26:45; Dt 9:27; Jer 14:21) and with all humankind through Noah (Ge 9:15, 16).

In the passive stem, the word expresses similar meanings. For example, the psalmist prayed that the sins of his accuser's parents would be remembered against his accuser (Ps 109:14). Yet in an important passage on moral and religious responsibility before God, it was asserted that if righteous people abandoned their righteous ways and followed evil, their righteous deeds would not be remembered by the Lord. The opposite case is also true. None of the evil deeds people commit will be remembered against them if they turn to God (Eze 18:22), nor will the actions, good or evil, of their parents be held for or against them (Eze 18:22, 24). Righteous people will, in fact, be remembered throughout the ages (cf. Ps 112:6).

The causative stem indicates the act of bringing to memory or bringing to attention. It means to recall, as when the Lord challenged His people in Isaiah to recall their past in order to state their argument for their case (Ge 41:9; Isa 43:26). Eli, the high priest, recalled (i.e. mentioned) the ark and then died according to God's prophetic word (1Sa 4:18). The verb is used to indicate urging someone to remember something, such as sin (1Ki 17:18; Eze 21:23[28]; 29:16). It is also used to convey the idea of causing something to be acknowledged, as when the psalmist asserted that he would cause the Lord's righteousness to be acknowledged above all else (Ps 71:16). In the infinitive form, this word sometimes means petition, as found in the superscriptions of some Psalms (Ps 38:title[1], 70:title[1]). It may also mean performing an act of worship (Isa 66:3).

2143. זֵכֶר, **zêker**, *zay´-ker*; or זֶכֶר, **zeker**, *zeh´-ker*; from 2142; a *memento*, abstract *recollection* (rarely if ever); by implication *commemoration*:—memorial, memory, remembrance, scent.

A masculine noun meaning remembrance. This word comes from the verb *zâkar* (2142), meaning to remember. God has given His people many things as remembrances: Himself (Ps 102:12 [13]); His name (Ex 3:15; Hos 12:5[6]); His works (Ps 111:4); His goodness (Ps 145:7); His holiness (Ps 30:4[5]; 97:12); His deliverance of the Jews (Est 9:28). God also promises the remembrance of the righteous (Pr 10:7) but often cuts off the remembrance of the wicked (Job 18:17; Ps 34:16[17]; 109:15; Pr 10:7); wicked nations (Ex 17:14; Dt 25:19; 32:26); and the dead (Ecc 9:5; Isa 26:14). In several instances of this word, it is used synonymously with *shêm* (8034), meaning name, because one's name invokes the memory (Ex 3:15; Pr 10:7; Hos 12:5[6]).

2144. זֶכֶר, **Zeker**, *zeh´-ker*; the same as 2143; *Zeker*, an Israelite:—Zeker.

2145. זָכָר, **zâkâr**, *zaw-kawr´*; from 2142; (properly) *remembered*, i.e. a *male* (of man or animals, as being the most noteworthy sex):— × him, male, man (child, -kind).

2146. זִכְרוֹן, **zikkârôwn**, *zik-ka-rone´*; from 2142; a *memento* (or memorable thing, day or writing):—memorial, record.

A masculine noun meaning memorial, remembrance, record, reminder. This word conveys the essential quality of remembering something in the past that has a particular significance (Ecc 1:11). It signifies stone monuments (Jos 4:7); the shoulder ornamentation of the ephod (Ex 28:12; 39:7); a sacrifice calling for explicit retrospection (Nu 5:15); the securing of a progeny (Isa 57:8); a written record (Ex 17:14; Est 6:1); a memorable adage or quote (Job 13:12); some proof of an historic claim (Ne 2:20); a festival memorializing a pivotal event (Ex 12:14; 13:9).

2147. זִכְרִי, **Zikrîy**, *zik-ree´*; from 2142; *memorable*; *Zicri*, the name of twelve Israelites:—Zichri.

2148. זְכַרְיָה, **Zekaryâh**, *zek-ar-yaw´*; or זְכַרְיָהוּ, **Zekaryâhûw**, *zek-ar-yaw´-hoo*; from 2142 and 3050; *Jah has remembered*; *Zecarjah*, the name of twenty-nine Israelites:—Zachariah, Zechariah.

2149. זְלוּת, **zullûwth**, *zool-looth´*; from 2151; (properly) a *shaking*, i.e. perhaps a *tempest*:—vilest.

2150. זַלְזַל, **zalzal**, *zal-zal´*; by reduplication from 2151; *tremulous*, i.e. a *twig*:—sprig.

2151. זָלַל, **zâlal**, *zaw-lal´*; a primitive root [compare 2107]; to *shake* (as in the wind), i.e. to *quake*; (figurative) to *be loose* morally, *worthless* or *prodigal*:—blow down, glutton, riotous (eater), vile.

2152. זַלְעָפָה, **zal'âphâh**, *zal-aw-faw´*; or זִלְעָפָה, **zil'âphâh**, *zil-aw-faw´*; from 2196; a *glow* (of wind or anger); also a *famine* (as *consuming*):—horrible, horror, terrible.

A feminine noun meaning burning heat. This word occurs only three times in the OT. In two of the locations, the literal usage of this word is implied. In La 5:10, Jeremiah explains the hunger pangs as the burning heat of famine. In Ps 11:6, David describes how God will pour out His wrath with this burning heat, along with fire and brimstone. In Ps 119:53, the psalmist speaks figuratively about his righteous, burning zeal on account of those who forsake God's law.

2153. זִלְפָּה, **Zilpâh,** *zil-paw;* from an unused root apparently meaning to *trickle,* as myrrh; fragrant *dropping; Zilpah,* Leah's maid:—Zilpah.

2154. זִמָּה, **zimmâh,** *zim-maw´;* or זַמָּה, **zammâh,** *zam-maw´;* from 2161; a *plan,* especially a bad one:—heinous crime, lewd (-ly, -ness), mischief, purpose, thought, wicked (device, mind, -ness).

A feminine noun meaning plan, purpose, counsel, wickedness, lewdness, sin. The word refers to the plans and purposes of the mind which give rise to one's actions. Yet the word rarely pertains to good intentions (Job 17:11). It is used in reference to the evil plotting of the wicked (Isa 32:7); the thoughts of foolish people (Pr 24:9); and mischievous motivations (Ps 119:150). Moreover, it relates to sexual sins that spring from lustful intentions, such as incest (Le 18:17); prostitution (Le 19:29); adultery (Job 31:11); and rape (Jgs 20:6). Figuratively, the word represents the wickedness of the people of Israel in their idolatry, calling to mind the connection with adultery (Jer 13:27; Eze 16:27).

2155. זִמָּה, **Zimmâh,** *zim-maw´;* the same as 2154; *Zimmah,* the name of two Israelites:—Zimmah.

2156. זְמוֹרָה, **zᵉmôwrâh,** *zem-o-raw´;* or זְמֹרָה, **zᵉmôrâh,** *zem-o-raw´* (feminine); and זְמֹר, **zᵉmôr,** *zem-ore´* (masculine); from 2168; a *twig* (as *pruned*): —vine, branch, slip.

2157. זַמְזֻמִּים, **Zamzummîym,** *zam-zoom-meem´;* from 2161; *intriguing;* a *Zamzumite,* or native tribe of Palestine:—Zamzummim.

2158. זָמִיר, **zâmîyr,** *zaw-meer´;* or זָמִר, **zâmir,** *zaw-meer´;* and (feminine) זְמִרָה, **zᵉmirâh,** *zem-ee-raw´;* from 2167; a *song* to be accompanied with instrumental music:—psalm (-ist), singing, song.

2159. זָמִיר, **zâmîyr,** *zaw-meer´;* from 2168; a *twig* (as *pruned*):—branch.

2160. זְמִירָה, **Zᵉmîyrâh,** *zem-ee-raw´;* feminine of 2158; *song; Zemirah,* an Israelite:—Zemira.

2161. זָמַם, **zâmam,** *zaw-mam´;* a primitive root; to *plan,* usually in a bad sense:—consider, devise, imagine, plot, purpose, think (evil).

A verb meaning to consider, to purpose, to devise. This verb derives its meaning from the idea of talking to oneself in a low voice, as if arriving at some conclusion. It denotes the action of fixing thought on an object so as to acquire it (Pr 31:16); devising a plan or an agenda (La 2:17; Zec 8:15); conceiving an idea (Ge 11:6); and determining a course of action (Ps 17:3). In an adverse sense, it also denotes the plotting of evil against another (Ps 31:14; 37:12; Pr 30:32).

2162. זָמָם, **zâmâm,** *zaw-mawm´;* from 2161; a *plot:*—wicked device.

A masculine noun meaning plans. The Hebrew word occurs once in the OT. David uses this word as he pleads with the Lord to intercede in the plans of the wicked (Ps 140:8[9]).

2163. זָמַן, **zâman,** *zaw-man´;* a primitive root; to *fix* (a time):—appoint.

A verb meaning to fix, to appoint a time. In the book of Ezra, so many Israelites had violated the command not to marry foreign women that leaders had to set a fixed time for people to come by towns to repent (Ezr 10:14). In Nehemiah, the Levites, priests, and people worked out a time (by casting lots) for each family to contribute wood for the altar (Ne 10:34[35]). In the closing words of his book, Nehemiah reminded the Lord of his leadership in this matter (Ne 13:31). See the related Aramaic verb *zĕman* (2164).

2164. זְמַן, **zᵉman,** *zem-an´;* (Chaldee); corresponding to 2163; to *agree* (on a time and place):—prepare.

An Aramaic verb meaning to agree together. Nebuchadnezzar believed that his wise men were conspiring together, which is why he insisted they tell him both his dream and its interpretation (Da 2:9). See the related Hebrew verb *zâman* (2163).

2165. זְמָן, **zᵉmân,** *zem-awn´;* from 2163; an *appointed* occasion:—season, time.

A masculine noun meaning appointed time, season. This word occurs only four times in the OT. Two of these are in the book of Esther, referring to the time set for the Feast of Purim (Est 9:27, 31). In the book of Nehemiah, it refers to an appointed time to return from a journey (Ne 2:6). In Ecclesiastes, it occurs in an often-quoted verse, "To every thing there is a season" (Ecc 3:1) to say that everything has a predestined time. The word translated time throughout Ecc 3 is *ʿêth* (6256). Thus, *zĕman* bears a different sense, emphasizing the specificity in time.

2166. זְמָן, **zᵉmân,** *zem-awn´*; (Chaldee); from 2165; the same as 2165:—season, time.

An Aramaic noun meaning a specific time, a time period. This word is used in Daniel indicating a duration of time or a period of time (Da 2:16; 7:12) and also in reference to the feast times (Da 7:25). See the Hebrew cognate 2165.

2167. זָמַר, **zâmar,** *zaw-mar´*; a primitive root [perhaps identical with 2168 through the idea of *striking* with the fingers]; (properly) to *touch* the strings or parts of a musical instrument, i.e. *play* upon it; to make *music*, accompanied by the voice; hence to *celebrate* in song and music:—give praise, sing forth praises, psalms.

A verb meaning to play an instrument, to sing with musical accompaniment. Stringed instruments are commonly specified in connection with this word, and the tambourine is also mentioned once (Ps 33:2; 71:22, 23; 149:3). The term occurs frequently in a call to praise—usually a summons to oneself (2Sa 22:50; 1Ch 16:9; Ps 66:4; Isa 12:5). In the Bible, the object of this praise is always the Lord, who is lauded for both His attributes and His actions (Jgs 5:3; Ps 101:1; 105:2). Besides the above references, this verb appears exclusively in the Book of Psalms, contributing to a note of praise in psalms of various types: hymns (Ps 104:33); psalms of thanksgiving (Ps 138:1); and even psalms of lament (Ps 144:9).

2168. זָמַר, **zâmar,** *zaw-mar´*; a primitive root [compare 2167, 5568, 6785]; to *trim* (a vine):—prune.

2169. זֶמֶר, **zemer,** *zeh´-mer*; apparently from 2167 or 2168; a *gazelle* (from its lightly *touching* the ground):—chamois.

2170. זְמָר, **zᵉmâr,** *zem-awr´*; (Chaldee); from a root corresponding to 2167; instrumental *music*:—musick.

2171. זַמָּר, **zammâr,** *zam-mawr´*; (Chaldee); from the same as 2170; an instrumental *musician*:—singer.

2172. זִמְרָה, **zimrâh,** *zim-raw´*; from 2167; a *musical* piece or *song* to be accompanied by an instrument:—melody, psalm.

2173. זִמְרָה, **zimrâh,** *zim-raw´*; from 2168, *pruned* (i.e. *choice*) fruit:—best fruit.

2174. זִמְרִי, **Zimrîy,** *zim-ree´*; from 2167; *musical*; *Zimri*, the name of five Israelites, and of an Arabian tribe:—Zimri.

2175. זִמְרָן, **Zimrân,** *zim-rawn´*; from 2167; *musical*; *Zimran*, a son of Abraham by Keturah:—Zimran.

2176. זִמְרָת, **zimrâth,** *zim-rawth´*; from 2167; instrumental *music*; (by implication) *praise*:—song.

2177. זַן, **zan,** *zan*; from 2109; (properly) *nourished* (or fully *developed*), i.e. a *form* or *sort*:—divers kinds, × all manner of store.

2178. זַן, **zan,** *zan*; (Chaldee); corresponding to 2177; *sort*:—kind.

2179. זָנַב, **zânab,** *zaw-nab´*; a primitive root meaning to *wag*; used only as a denominative from 2180; to *curtail*, i.e. *cut* off the rear:—smite the hindmost.

2180. זָנָב, **zânâb,** *zaw-nawb´*; from 2179 (in the original sense of *flapping*); the *tail* (literal or figurative):—tail.

2181. זָנָה, **zânâh,** *zaw-naw´*; a primitive root [highly *fed* and therefore *wanton*]; to *commit adultery* (usually of the female, and less often of simple fornication, rarely of involuntary ravishment); (figurative) to *commit idolatry* (the Jewish people being regarded as the spouse of Jehovah):—(cause to) commit fornication, × continually, × great, (be an, play the) harlot, (cause to be, play the) whore, (commit, fall to) whoredom, (cause to) go a-whoring, whorish.

A verb meaning to fornicate, to prostitute. It is typically used for women and only twice in reference to men (Nu 25:1). This verb occurs in connection with prostitution (Le 21:7; Pr 7:10);

figuratively, Israel's improper relationships with other nations (Isa 23:17; Eze 23:30; Na 3:4); or other gods (Ex 34:15, 16; Dt 31:16; Eze 6:9; Hos 9:1). As a metaphor, it describes Israel's breach of the Lord's covenant relationship (Ex 34:16).

2182. זָנוֹחַ, **Zânôwach,** *zaw-no´-akh;* from 2186; *rejected; Zanoach,* the name of two places in Palestine:—Zanoah.

2183. זְנוּנִים, **z°nûwnîym,** *zeh-noo-neem´;* from 2181; *adultery;* (figurative) *idolatry:*—whoredom.

A masculine noun meaning fornication, prostitution, adultery, idolatry. Judah's daughter-in-law Tamar was accused of prostitution (Ge 38:24). This word can also be used to describe cities like Nineveh (Na 3:4). Most often, it is used in a religious sense to describe, for instance, the unfaithfulness of Israel. Jezebel practiced idolatry (2Ki 9:22); and Jerusalem's idolatry was portrayed in a story where she was the prostitute Aholibah (Eze 23:11, 29). God commanded Hosea to take an unfaithful wife (Hos 1:2), who was also a picture of Israel (Hos 2:2[4], 4[6]; 4:12; 5:4).

2184. זְנוּת, **z°nûwth,** *zen-ooth´;* from 2181; *adultery,* i.e. (figurative) *infidelity, idolatry:*—whoredom.

A feminine noun meaning fornication. In the literal sense, this word refers to sexual sin that violates the marriage covenant (Hos 4:11). Most often, however, this word is figuratively applied to God's nation Israel for their wickedness (Hos 6:10). This fornication is usually associated with the worship of other gods (Jer 3:2, 9; 13:27; Eze 23:27), but it can describe outright rebellion (Nu 14:33) or general iniquities (Eze 43:7, 9). This word comes from the common verb *zânâh* (2181), meaning to commit fornication.

2185. זְנוֹת, **zônôwth,** *zo-noth´;* regarded by some as if from 2109 or an unused root, and applied to military *equipments;* but evidently the feminine plural active participle of 2181; *harlots:*—armour.

2186. זָנַח, **zânach,** *zaw-nakh´;* a primitive root meaning to *push* aside, i.e. *reject, forsake, fail:*—cast away (off), remove far away (off).

2187. זָנַק, **zânaq,** *zaw-nak´;* a primitive root; (properly) to *draw together* the feet (as an animal about to dart upon its prey), i.e. to *spring* forward:—leap.

2188. זֵעָה, **zê°âh,** *zay-aw´;* from 2111 (in the sense of 3154); *perspiration:*—sweat.

2189. זַעֲוָה, **za°ăvâh,** *zah-av-aw´;* by transposition for 2113; *agitation, maltreatment:*— × removed, trouble.

2190. זַעֲוָן, **Za°ăvân,** *zah-av-awn´;* from 2111; *disquiet; Zaavan,* an Idumæan:—Zaavan.

2191. זְעֵיר, **z°°êyr,** *zeh-ayr´;* from an unused root [akin (by permutation) to 6819], meaning to *dwindle; small:*—little.

2192. זְעֵיר, **z°°êyr,** *zeh-ayr´;* (Chaldee); corresponding to 2191:—little.

2193. זָעַךְ, **zâ°ak,** *zaw-ak´;* a primitive root; to *extinguish:*—be extinct.

2194. זָעַם, **zâ°am,** *zaw-am´;* a primitive root; (properly) to *foam* at the mouth, i.e. to *be enraged:*—abhor, abominable, (be) angry, defy, (have) indignation.

A verb meaning to be indignant, to be enraged. The root means literally to foam at the mouth, to be enraged. It is used to describe the fury of the king of the North against the holy covenant in Daniel's vision (Da 11:30). Because God is a righteous judge, He shows indignation against evil every day (Ps 7:11[12]). This theme is picked up again in Isaiah (Isa 66:14). God was angry with the towns of Judah (Zec 1:12), and Edom was under the wrath of the Lord (Mal 1:4). This anger can also show in one's face (Pr 25:23).

2195. זַעַם, **za°am,** *zah´-am;* from 2194; strictly *froth* at the mouth, i.e. (figurative) *fury* (especially of God's displeasure with sin):—angry, indignation, rage.

A masculine noun meaning intense anger, indignation, denunciation, curse. Although this noun can refer to a state of being or actions of a human being (Jer 15:17; Hos 7:16), it usually refers to those of the Lord (Isa 26:20; 30:27; Hab 3:12). This word is also used in parallel with other words with the connotation of anger: *'aph* (639) (Ps 69:24[25]; Isa 10:5, 25; 30:27; Zep 3:8); *'ebrâh* (5678) (Ps 78:49; Eze 21:31[36];

22:31); and *qetseph* (7110) (Ps 102:10[11]; Jer 10:10).

2196. זָעַף, **zâ'aph,** *zaw-af'*; a primitive root; (properly) to *boil* up, i.e. (figurative) to *be peevish* or *angry*:—fret, sad, worse liking, be wroth.

A verb meaning to be dejected, to be enraged. The root idea of this word is to storm, which is seen in the use of the related noun *za'aph* (2197) to describe the raging sea in Jnh 1:15. The word describes an unsettled storm within a person that exhibits itself in either dejection or rage. The cupbearer and baker were dejected when they couldn't understand their dreams (Ge 40:6). The guard thought that Daniel and his friends would look downcast if denied the king's food (Da 1:10). King Uzziah was enraged when the priests attempted to remove him from the temple (2Ch 26:19).

2197. זַעַף, **za'aph,** *zah'-af*; from 2196; *anger*:—indignation, rage (-ing), wrath.

A noun meaning wrath, rage, indignation. This word is used to refer to the rage of kings (2Ch 28:9) or the stormy rage of the sea (Jnh 1:15).

2198. זָעֵף, **zâ'êph,** *zaw-afe'*; from 2196; *angry*:—displeased.

An adjective meaning dejected. This particular word is only used twice in the OT. In each instance, it describes the dejected attitude of King Ahab when the prophet told him bad news (1Ki 20:43) and when Naboth refused to sell his vineyard to Ahab (1Ki 21:4). See the related verb *zâ'aph* (2196), meaning to be dejected and the related noun *za'aph* (2197), meaning raging.

2199. זָעַק, **zâ'aq,** *zaw-ak'*; a primitive root; to *shriek* (from anguish or danger); by analogy (as a herald) to *announce* or *convene* publicly:—assemble, call (together), (make a) cry (out), come with such a company, gather (together), cause to be proclaimed.

A verb meaning to cry out, to exclaim, to call. The primary activity implied is that of crying out in pain or by reason of affliction (Ex 2:23; Job 35:9; Jer 25:34). The verb signifies the action of calling on the Lord in a time of need (Joel 1:14; Mic 3:4); uttering sounds of sorrow, distress, or alarm (2Sa 13:19; Isa 26:17; Eze 11:13); entreating for some favour (2Sa 19:28[29]); and

issuing a summons for help (Jgs 12:2). By inference, it also implies assembling together as in response to a call (Jgs 6:34, 35; 1Sa 14:20); and the making of a proclamation by a herald (Jnh 3:7).

2200. זְעִק, **ze'iq,** *zeh'-eek*; (Chaldee); corresponding to 2199; to *make an outcry*:—cry.

2201. זַעַק, **za'aq,** *zah'-ak*; and (feminine) זְעָקָה, **ze'âqâh,** *zeh-aw-kaw'*; from 2199; a *shriek* or *outcry*:—cry (-ing).

2202. זִפְרֹן, **Ziphrôn,** *zi-fron'*; from an unused root (meaning to *be fragrant*); *Ziphron*, a place in Palestine:—Ziphron.

2203. זֶפֶת, **zepheth,** *zeh'-feth*; from an unused root (meaning to *liquify*); *asphalt* (from its tendency to *soften* in the sun):—pitch.

2204. זָקֵן, **zâqên,** *zaw-kane'*; a primitive root; to *be old*:—aged man, be (wax) old (man).

A verb meaning to be old, to become old. This word is related to the adjective *zâqên* (2205), meaning old, and the noun *zâqân* (2206), meaning beard. In Ps 37:25, David described himself as an aged person as opposed to a youth, *na'ar* (5288), "I have been young, and now am old" (KJV). Solomon also used the same words to demonstrate the contrast between a person when young and when old (Pr 22:6). This word is used of men (Ge 24:1; Jos 13:1; 1Sa 12:2); of women (Ge 18:13; Pr 23:22); or even a tree (Job 14:8). When used of older people, this word is often used to describe the last days of their lives (Ge 27:1, 2; 1Ki 1:1; 2Ch 24:15).

2205. זָקֵן, **zâqên,** *zaw-kane'*; from 2204; *old*:—aged, ancient (man), elder (-est), old (man, men and … women), senator.

An adjective meaning elder, old, aged, old man, old woman (as a noun), leader(s). The word's basic meaning is old or aged. But from this basic meaning, several different meanings arise. The word means aged persons, but the ideas of dignity, rank, and privilege also became attached to this concept. The person referred to was usually an old man (Ge 19:4; Jgs 19:16, 17). One of the most famous was the old man in a robe (Samuel) that the witch of Endor saw (1Sa 28:14). Abraham and Sarah were both described as old in Genesis 18:11; the oldest servant in the master's house evidently had some prerogatives of seniority (Ge 24:2). Old men, women, and children were often spared in war and were given special care and protection (cf. Eze 9:6) but not in the corrupt city of Jerusalem at its fall.

The group of men called elders in Israel were a powerfully influential group. They represented the nation from the time of the wilderness period (Ex 19:7) and earlier (Ex 3:16; 4:29). Of the 180 times the phrase is found, it occurs thirty-four times in Exodus when Israel was being formed into a people. There were traditionally seventy elders, and they ate and drank before the Lord with Moses and Joshua on Mount Sinai (Ex 24:9, 11). The older priests held special respect among the priests (2Ki 19:2). The elders were equal to the judges in influence and regularly took part in making decisions (Dt 21:2, 19, 20). The elders of a city as a whole formed a major ruling group (Jos 20:4; Ru 4:2). For example, the elders of Jabesh tried to locate help and negotiated with the Ammonites who were besieging the city (1Sa 11:3). But the elders could lead in evil as well as good, for the picture Ezekiel painted of them was devastating and incriminating. The elders had become corrupt and helped lead the people astray. Their counsel would fail (Eze 7:26; 8:11, 12; 9:6).

2206. זָקָן, **zâqân,** zaw-kawn´; from 2204; the *beard* (as indicating *age*):—beard.

A feminine noun meaning beard. This word is usually used of the beards of men (1Ch 19:5; Isa 15:2) but once refers to the mane of a lion (1Sa 17:35). In biblical times, to have one's beard shaved was humbling. When shaved by another, it was an act of humiliation (2Sa 10:4, 5; Isa 7:20), but when pulled on (Ezr 9:3) or shaved by oneself, it was usually a sign of repentance (Jer 41:5; 48:37). The beard is mentioned in connection with infection (Le 13:29, 30) and was to be trimmed properly according to ceremonial requirements (Le 19:27; 21:5). Ezekiel shaved and divided up his beard as a sign against Jerusalem (Eze 5:1).

2207. זָקֵן, **zôqen,** zo´-ken; from 2204; old *age*:—age.

A masculine noun meaning extreme old age. The word is used only once in the OT (Ge 48:10), describing Jacob at the time he blessed Ephriam above Manasseh. By this time, he was well-advanced in years, so much so that his sight was extremely poor.

2208. זְקֻנִים, **zᵉqunîym,** zaw-koon´; (properly) passive participle of 2204 (used only in the plural as a noun); old age:—old age.

A passive participle, used only in the plural as a masculine noun, meaning old age. This word is used only four times in the OT, each time in the book of Genesis. It appears in reference to children born to parents late in life. Particularly, it is used of Isaac as the son of Abraham's old age (Ge 21:2, 7); and of Joseph (Ge 37:3) and Benjamin (Ge 44:20) as the sons of Jacob's old age.

2209. זִקְנָה, **ziqnâh,** zik-naw´; feminine of 2205; old *age*:—old (age).

A feminine noun meaning old, old age. This word is used most often to refer to people who are past their prime age. For example, it describes Sarah who is past the normal childbearing age (Ge 24:36). Ps 71 uses the word to ask the Lord not to turn away from the psalmist in his old age (Ps 71:9, 18). Isa 46:4 describes God's care for the aged, even though their bodies grow weak.

2210. זָקַף, **zâqaph,** zaw-kaf´; a primitive root; to *lift,* i.e. (figurative) *comfort:*—raise (up).

2211. זְקַף, **zᵉqaph,** zek-af´; (Chaldee); corresponding to 2210; to *hang,* i.e. *impale:*—set up.

2212. זָקַק, **zâqaq,** zaw-kak´; a primitive root; to *strain,* (figurative) *extract, clarify:*—fine, pour down, purge, purify, refine.

A verb meaning to refine, to purify. The literal meaning of this word is to strain or extract. It is used in reference to gold (1Ch 28:18); silver (1Ch 29:4; Ps 12:6[7]); water (Job 36:27); wine (Isa 25:6). It is also used of the purification of the Levites, comparing it to refining gold and silver (Mal 3:3).

2213. זֵר, **zêr,** zare; from 2237 (in the sense of *scattering*); a *chaplet* (as *spread* around the top), i.e. (specific) a border *moulding:*—crown.

2214. זָרָא, **zârâ’,** zaw-raw´; from 2114 (in the sense of *estrangement*) [compare 2219]; *disgust:*—loathsome.

2215. זָרַב, **zârab,** *zaw-rab´*; a primitive root; to *flow* away:—wax warm.

2216. זְרֻבָּבֶל, **Zᵉrubbâbel,** *zer-oob-baw-bel´*; from 2215 and 894; *descended of* (i.e. from) *Babylon,* i.e. born there; *Zerubbabel,* an Israelite:—Zerubbabel.

2217. זְרֻבָּבֶל, **Zᵉrubbâbel,** *zer-oob-baw-bel´*; (Chaldee); corresponding to 2216:—Zerubbabel.

2218. זֶרֶד, **Zered,** *zeh´-red*; from an unused root meaning to *be exuberant* in growth; lined with *shrubbery; Zered,* a brook East of the Dead Sea:—Zared, Zered.

2219. זָרָה, **zârâh,** *zaw-raw´*; a primitive root [compare 2114; to *toss* about; (by implication) to *diffuse, winnow:*—cast away, compass, disperse, fan, scatter (away), spread, strew, winnow.

2220. זְרוֹעַ, **zᵉrôwaʻ,** *zer-o´-ah*; or (shorter) זְרֹעַ, **zᵉrôaʻ,** *zer-o´-ah*; and (feminine) זְרוֹעָה, **zᵉrôwʻâh,** *zer-o-aw´*; or זְרֹעָה, **zᵉrôʻâh,** *zer-o-aw´*; from 2232; the *arm* (as *stretched* out), or (of animals) the *foreleg;* (figurative) *force:*—arm, + help, mighty, power, shoulder, strength.

2221. זֵרוּעַ, **zêrûwaʻ,** *zay-roo´-ah*; from 2232; something *sown,* i.e. a *plant:*—sowing, thing that is sown.

2222. זַרְזִיף, **zarzîyph,** *zar-zeef´*; by reduplication from an unused root meaning to *flow;* a *pouring rain:*—water.

2223. זַרְזִיר, **zarzîyr,** *zar-zeer´*; by reduplication from 2115; (properly) tightly *girt,* i.e. probably a *racer,* or some fleet animal (as being *slender* in the waist):— + greyhound.

2224. זָרַח, **zârach,** *zaw-rakh´*; a primitive root; (properly,) to *irradiate* (or shoot forth beams), i.e. to *rise* (as the sun); (specifically) to *appear* (as a symptom of leprosy):—arise, rise (up), as soon as it is up.

2225. זֶרַח, **zerach,** *zeh´-rakh*; from 2224; a *rising* of light:—rising.

2226. זֶרַח, **Zerach,** *zeh´-rakh*; the same as 2225; *Zerach,* the name of three Israelites, also of an Idumæan and an Ethiopian prince:—Zarah, Zerah.

2227. זַרְחִי, **Zarchîy,** *zar-khee´*; patronymic from 2226; a *Zarchite* or descendant of Zerach:—Zarchite.

2228. זְרַחְיָה, **Zᵉrachyâh,** *zer-akh-yaw´*; from 2225 and 3050; *Jah has risen; Zerachjah,* the name of two Israelites:—Zerahiah.

2229. זָרַם, **zâram,** *zaw-ram´*; a primitive root; to *gush* (as water):—carry away as with a flood, pour out.

2230. זֶרֶם, **zerem,** *zeh´-rem*; from 2229; a *gush* of water:—flood, overflowing, shower, storm, tempest.

2231. זִרְמָה, **zirmâh,** *zir-maw´*; feminine of 2230; a *gushing* of fluid (semen):—issue.

2232. זָרַע, **zâraʻ,** *zaw-rah´*; a primitive root; to *sow;* (figurative) to *disseminate, plant, fructify:*—bear, conceive seed, set with, sow (-er), yield.

2233. זֶרַע, **zeraʻ,** *zeh´-rah*; from 2232; *seed;* (figurative) *fruit, plant, sowing-time, posterity:*— × carnally, child, fruitful, seed (-time), sowing-time.

A masculine noun meaning sowing, seed, descendants, offspring, children, and posterity. The literal use of the word indicates seed of the field (i.e. seed planted in the field). When Israel entered Egypt, Joseph instructed the Israelites to keep four-fifths of the crop as seed to plant in their fields and to serve as food for them (Ge 47:24); the season for planting seed was guaranteed by God to continue without fail (Ge 8:22); and successful, abundant harvests were promised right up until the sowing season if Israel followed the Lord's laws and commands (Le 26:5). God had created the seed of the field by decreeing that plants and trees would be self-perpetuating, producing their own seed (Ge 1:11) and that the seed-producing plants would be edible (Ge 1:29). Manna, the heavenly food, resembled coriander seed (Ex 16:31). Any seed could be rendered unclean and not usable if a dead body fell on it after the seed had been moistened (Le 11:38).

The noun is used to describe the seed (i.e. the offspring) of both people and animals. The seed of Judah and Israel would be united and planted peacefully in the land together with animals in a pleasant setting (Jer 31:27). Seed can be translated as son (i.e. seed as when God gives Hannah a promise of a son [1Sa 1:11]). The seed of a woman mentioned in Ge 3:15 is her offspring.

The offspring of humans is described many times by this word. Hannah was given additional children to replace Samuel, whom she gave to the Lord's service (1Sa 2:20). The most important seed that the author of Genesis describes is the seed of Abraham, the promised seed, referring to Isaac, Jacob, and his twelve sons (Ge 12:7; 15:3). The author of Genesis uses the word twenty-one times in this setting (Ex 32:13; Dt 1:8). The seed of the royal line of David was crucial to Israel's existence, and the term is used nine times to refer to David's offspring or descendants (2Sa 7:12). In a figurative sense, seed refers to King Zedekiah and perhaps to Israelites of royal lineage, whom Nebuchadnezzar established in Jerusalem (Eze 17:5). Royal lines or seed were found outside Israel, such as in Edom, where Hadad belonged to the royal line (1Ki 11:14), and in Judah, where the wicked Athaliah attempted to destroy the royal seed (2Ki 11:1; 25:25; Jer 41:1).

The seed or offspring of a particular nation can be characterized in moral and religious terms as well. Three verses stand out: The seed of Israel was called a holy seed (Ezr 9:2; Isa 6:13); and, in the case of Ezr 9:2, the seed corrupted itself by mixing with the peoples around them. The seed of Israel is a seed of God or a divine seed (Mal 2:15) through its union with God (cf. 2Pe 1:4). An offspring could be described as deceitful and wicked (Ps 37:28; Isa 57:4). It was important in Israel to prove that one's origin or seed stemmed from an Israelite ancestor, for some Israelites and Israelite priests who returned from exile could not show their origin (Ezr 2:59). The word also refers to the seed or posterity of the Messiah (Isa 53:10).

2234. זְרַע, z⁰ra‘, *zer-ah´*; (Chaldee); corresponding to 2233; *posterity:*—seed.

An Aramaic noun meaning seed. This word is used only once in Da 2:43 in the idiomatic phrase "with the seed of men" (KJV). In this passage, Daniel interpreted King Nebuchadnezzar's dream about the gold, silver, bronze, iron, and clay statue. This mixing of people with the seed of men is a reference to other people groups joining a community or nation. Those who come afterward lack the national spirit to adhere to one another, just as iron does not mix with clay.

2235. זְרֹעַ, zêrôa‘, *zay-ro´-ah*; or זֵרָעֹן, zêrâ‘ôn, *zay-raw-ohn´*; from 2232; something *sown* (only in the plural), i.e. a *vegetable* (as food):—pulse.

2236. זָרַק, zâraq, *zaw-rak´*; a primitive root; to *sprinkle* (fluid or solid particles):—be here and there, scatter, sprinkle, strew.

A verb meaning to sprinkle, to scatter, to be sprinkled. This word is most often used to describe the actions of the priests performing the sacrificial rituals. They sprinkled the blood of the sacrifices (Le 1:5; 2Ki 16:13; 2Ch 29:22). It is also used of water (Nu 19:13; Eze 36:25). In a time of grief, Job's friends sprinkled dust on their heads (Job 2:12). King Josiah destroyed the false gods and scattered their pieces (powder, NASB) over the graves of those who had worshipped them (2Ch 34:4).

2237. זָרַר, zârar, *zaw-rar´*; a primitive root [compare 2114]; perhaps to *diffuse*, i.e. (specifically) to *sneeze:*—sneeze.

2238. זֶרֶשׁ, Zeresh, *zeh´-resh*; of Persian origin; *Zeresh*, Haman's wife:—Zeresh.

2239. זֶרֶת, zereth, *zeh´-reth*; from 2219; the *spread* of the fingers, i.e. a *span:*—span.

2240. זַתּוּא, Zattûw’, *zat-too´*; of uncertain derivation; *Zattu*, an Israelite:—Zattu.

2241. זֵתָם, Zêthâm, *zay-thawm´*; apparently a variation for 2133; *Zetham*, an Israelite:—Zetham.

2242. זֵתַר, Zêthar, *zay-thar´*; of Persian origin; *Zethar*, a eunuch of Xerxes:—Zethar.

ח (Heth)

2243. חֹב, **chôb,** *khobe;* by contraction from 2245; (properly) a *cherisher,* i.e. the *bosom:*—bosom.

2244. חָבָא, **châbâ',** *khaw-baw';* a primitive root [compare 2245]; to *secrete:*— × held, hide (self), do secretly.

2245. חָבַב, **châbab,** *khaw-bab';* a primitive root [compare 2244, 2247]; (properly) to *hide* (as in the bosom), i.e. to *cherish* (with affection):—love.

A verb meaning to love. This word occurs only once in the OT, in which it describes God's love for the people of Israel (Dt 33:3). This verse is in a poetical section of Scripture, which helps to explain why this word is used only once. It is related to *chôb* (2243), meaning bosom, which is used only in Job 31:33. Thus, the love expressed here probably signifies an embracing, motherly affection.

2246. חֹבָב, **Chôbâb,** *kho-bawb';* from 2245; *cherished; Chobab,* father-in-law of Moses:—Hobab.

2247. חָבָה, **châbâh,** *khaw-bah';* a primitive root [compare 2245]; to *secrete:*—hide (self).

2248. חֲבוּלָה, **chăbûwlâh,** *khab-oo-law';* (Chaldee); from 2255; (properly) *overthrown,* i.e. (moral) *crime:*—hurt.

2249. חָבוֹר, **Châbôwr,** *khaw-bore';* from 2266; *united; Chabor,* a river of Assyria:—Habor.

2250. חַבּוּרָה, **chabbûwrâh,** *khab-boo-raw';* or חַבֻּרָה, **chabburâh,** *khab-boo-raw';* or חֲבֻרָה, **chăburâh,** *khab-oo-raw';* from 2266; (properly) *bound* (with stripes), i.e. a *weal* (or black-and-blue mark itself):—blueness, bruise, hurt, stripe, wound.

2251. חָבַט, **châbaṭ,** *khaw-bat';* a primitive root; to *knock* out or off:—beat (off, out), thresh.

2252. חֲבַיָּה, **Chăbayyâh,** *khab-ah-yaw';* or חֲבָיָה, **Chăbâyâh,** *khab-aw-yaw';* from 2247 and 3050; *Jah has hidden; Chabajah,* an Israelite:—Habaiah.

2253. חֶבְיוֹן, **chebyôwn,** *kheb-yone';* from 2247; *concealment:*—hiding.

2254. חָבַל, **châbal,** *khaw-bal';* a primitive root; to *wind* tightly (as a rope), i.e. to *bind;* specifically by a *pledge;* (figurative) to *pervert, destroy;* also to *writhe* in pain (especially of parturition):— × at all, band, bring forth, (deal) corrupt (-ly), destroy, offend, lay to (take a) pledge, spoil, travail, × very, withhold.

A verb meaning to take a pledge, to destroy. This verb is translated in a variety of ways. Most commonly, it means taking a pledge for such things as a loan (Ex 22:26[25]; Dt 24:6; Eze 18:16; Am 2:8). The word is used in Job in reference to debts (Job 22:6; 24:3, 9). It also describes the destruction of the wicked (Pr 13:13; Isa 32:7) or destruction of property (Isa 10:27; 13:5). This word can also mean to corrupt (Ne 1:7; Job 17:1). Zechariah used it in a metaphor describing the union between Israel and Judah (Zec 11:7, 14).

2255. חֲבַל, **chăbal,** *khab-al';* (Chaldee); corresponding to 2254; to *ruin:*—destroy, hurt.

An Aramaic verb meaning to ruin, to hurt, to destroy. King Darius issued a decree that ended with a plea for God to overthrow anyone who tried to destroy the Temple (Ezr 6:12). The tree in Nebuchadnezzar's dream was cut down and destroyed (Da 4:23[20]). Because the angel shut the lions' mouths, they did not hurt Daniel (Da 6:22[23]). This word also refers to a kingdom that will never be destroyed. In the interpretation of one of Nebuchadnezzar's dreams, Daniel told of a kingdom that would never be destroyed (Da 2:44). King Darius praised God when Daniel was not eaten by lions, saying the kingdom of God would not be destroyed (Da 6:26[27]). Once again, Daniel saw a kingdom like this in his dream of the four beasts (Da 7:14).

2256. חֶבֶל, **chebel,** *kheh´-bel;* or חֵבֶל, **chêbel,** *khay´-bel;* from 2254; a *rope* (as *twisted*), especially a measuring *line;* (by implication) a *district* or *inheritance* (as *measured*); or a *noose* (as of *cords*); (figurative) a *company* (as if *tied* together); also a *throe* (especially of parturition); also *ruin:*—band, coast, company, cord, country, destruction, line, lot, pain, pang, portion, region, rope, snare, sorrow, tackling.

A masculine or feminine noun meaning cord, pangs, region, company. This word has many meanings, depending on the context. The most basic meaning is a rope or a cord, such as the rope the spies used to escape through Rahab's window (Jos 2:15) or the cords used to bind Jeremiah in the dungeon (Jer 38:11–13). Although these cords may be decorative (Est 1:6), they are usually used to bind and control objects, such as animals (Job 41:1[40:25]) or buildings (Isa 33:20). This word is also used symbolically to speak of the cords of sin and death (2Sa 22:6; Ps 18:4[5], 5[6]; Pr 5:22) or the pangs of childbirth (Isa 13:8; Jer 13:21; Hos 13:13). It can even be translated "destruction" (Job 21:17). This word is also used to describe a dividing line (2Sa 8:2; Am 7:17); a geographical region (Dt 3:13, 14; 1Ki 4:13; Zep 2:5, 6); or an allotment of an inheritance (Dt 32:9; Jos 17:5; Ps 105:11). In a few instances, this word describes a company of prophets (1Sa 10:5, 10).

2257. חֲבַל, **chăbâl,** *khab-awl´;* (Chaldee); from 2255; *harm* (personal or pecuniary):—damage, hurt.

2258. חֲבֹל, **chăbôl,** *khab-ole´;* or (feminine) חֲבֹלָה, **chăbôlâh,** *khab-o-law´;* from 2254; a *pawn* (as security for debt):—pledge.

A noun meaning pledge. This word is always used when speaking of those who do or do not return pledges, which were items taken to guarantee loans. These items were usually people's cloaks, and the Law stated that they were to be returned to the owners before the sun set because they were the only covering they had (cf. Ex 22:26[25], 27[26]). Righteous persons returned the pledges (Eze 18:7) or did not even require them (Eze 18:16), whereas wicked persons kept the items used for the pledge (Eze 18:12). But if they repented and returned them,

they would live instead of die for the evil they did (Eze 33:15).

2259. חֹבֵל, **chôbêl,** *kho-bale´;* active participle from 2254 (in the sense of handling *ropes*); a *sailor:*—pilot, shipmaster.

2260. חִבֵּל, **chibbêl,** *khib-bale´;* from 2254 (in the sense of furnished with *ropes*); a *mast:*—mast.

2261. חֲבַצֶּלֶת, **chăbatstseleth,** *khab-ats-tseh´-leth;* of uncertain derivation; probably *meadow-saffron:*—rose.

2262. חֲבַצִּנְיָה, **Chăbatstsinyâh,** *khab-ats-tsin-yaw´;* of uncertain derivation; *Chabatstsanjah,* a Rechabite:—Habazaniah.

2263. חָבַק, **châbaq,** *khaw-bak´;* a primitive root; to *clasp* (the hands or in embrace):—embrace, fold.

2264. חִבֻּק, **chibbuq,** *khib-book´;* from 2263; a *clasping* of the hands (in idleness):—fold.

2265. חֲבַקּוּק, **Chăbaqqûwq,** *khab-ak-kook´;* by reduplication from 2263; *embrace; Chabakkuk,* the prophet:—Habakkuk.

2266. חָבַר, **châbar,** *khaw-bar´;* a primitive root; to *join* (literal or figurative); specifically (by means of spells) to *fascinate:*—charm (-er), be compact, couple (together), have fellowship with, heap up, join (self, together), league.

2267. חֶבֶר, **cheber,** *kheh´-ber;* from 2266; a *society;* also a *spell:*— + charmer (-ing), company, enchantment, × wide.

A masculine noun meaning a company, an association, a spell. It is used to refer to a band of bad priests (Hos 6:9); a house of association, namely, a house shared with an antagonistic woman (Pr 21:9; 25:24); or a magical spell or incantation (Dt 18:11; Ps 58:5[6]; Isa 47:9, 12).

2268. חֶבֶר, **Cheber,** *kheh´-ber;* the same as 2267; *community; Cheber,* the name of a Kenite and of three Israelites:—Heber.

2269. חֲבַר, **chăbar,** *khab-ar´;* (Chaldee); from a root corresponding to 2266; an *associate:*—companion, fellow.

2270. חָבֵר, **châbêr,** *khaw-bare´;* from 2266; an *associate:*—companion, fellow, knit together.

2271. חַבָּר, **chabbâr,** *khab-bawr´*; from 2266; a *partner:*—companion.

2272. חֲבַרְבֻּרָה, **chăbarburâh,** *khab-ar-boo-raw´*; by reduplication from 2266; a *streak* (like a *line*), as on the tiger:—spot.

2273. חֲבְרָה, **chabrâh,** *khab-raw´*; (Chaldee); feminine of 2269; an *associate:*—other.

2274. חֶבְרָה, **chebrâh,** *kheb-raw´*; feminine of 2267; *association:*—company.

2275. חֶבְרוֹן, **Chebrôwn,** *kheb-rone´*; from 2267; seat of *association; Chebron,* a place in Palestine, also the name of two Israelites:—Hebron.

2276. חֶבְרוֹנִי, **Chebrôwnîy,** *kheb-ro-nee´*; or חֶבְרֹנִי, **Chebrônîy,** *kheb-ro-nee´*; patronymic from 2275; *Chebronite* (collective), an inhabitant of Chebron:—Hebronites.

2277. חֶבְרִי, **Chebrîy,** *kheb-ree´*; patronymic from 2268; a *Chebrite* (collective) or descendants of Cheber:—Heberites.

2278. חֶבֶרֶת, **chăbereth,** *khab-eh´-reth*; feminine of 2270; a *consort:*—companion.

2279. חֹבֶרֶת, **chôbereth,** *kho-beh´-reth*; feminine active participle of 2266; a *joint:*—which coupleth, coupling.

2280. חָבַשׁ, **châbash,** *khaw-bash´*; a primitive root; to *wrap* firmly (especially a turban, compress, or *saddle*); (figurative) to *stop,* to *rule:*—bind (up), gird about, govern, healer, put, saddle, wrap about.

A verb meaning to bind. This word is used primarily to describe a binding or wrapping of one object with another. It is frequently used of saddling a donkey (Ge 22:3; Jgs 19:10; 1 Kgs 2:40) but can be used to describe the binding of caps on the priests' heads (Ex 29:9; Le 8:13); the tying of garments and carpets in a roll (Eze 27:24); the wrapping of weeds around Jonah's head (Jnh 2:5[6]); God stopping the floods (Job 28:11). This word is often used to describe binding wounds (both physical and spiritual) with the result that healing occurs (Isa 61:1; Eze 30:21; Hos 6:1). In a few cases, this binding may refer to one's ability to control (or rule) another (Job 34:17; 40:13).

2281. חֲבִתִּים, **chăbittîym,** *khaw-bit-teem´*; from an unused root probably meaning to *cook* [compare 4227]; something *fried,* probably a griddle-*cake:*—pan.

2282. חַג, **chag,** *khag*; or חָג, **châg,** *khawg*; from 2287; a *festival,* or a *victim* therefor:—(solemn) feast (day), sacrifice, solemnity.

A noun meaning a feast, a festival. This word is used numerous times throughout the OT referring to the feasts of the Hebrew religious calendar. It is used of the major feasts, including the Feast of Unleavened Bread and the Passover Feast (Ex 34:18, 25; Le 23:6; Dt 16:16; Ezr 6:22); the Feast of Weeks (Dt 16:16; 2Ch 8:13); and the Feast of Tabernacles (Le 23:34; Nu 29:12; Dt 31:10; Zech 14:16). It was used in the Temple dedication during Solomon's reign (1Ki 8:2, 65). Evil King Jeroboam held a festival described in 1Ki 12:32, 33. The prophets often used this word to describe the negligence of the people in keeping the feasts commanded by Mosaic Law (Isa 29:1; Am 5:21; Mal 2:3).

2283. חָגָּא, **châggâ,** *khawg-gaw´*; from an unused root meaning to *revolve* [compare 2287]; (properly) *vertigo,* i.e. (figurative) *fear:*—terror.

A feminine noun meaning terror. This word occurs only once in the OT in Isa 19:17 and speaks of the reeling terror that Judah would cause in Egypt.

2284. חָגָב, **châgâb,** *khaw-gawb´*; of uncertain derivation; a *locust:*—locust.

2285. חָגָב, **Châgâb,** *khaw-gawb´*; the same as 2284; *locust; Chagab,* one of the Nethinim:—Hagab.

2286. חֲגָבָא, **Chăgâbâ,** *khag-aw-baw´*; or חֲגָבָה, **Chăgâbâh,** *khag-aw-baw´*; feminine of 2285; *locust; Chagaba* or *Chagabah,* one of the Nethinim:—Hagaba, Hagabah.

2287. חָגַג, **châgag,** *khaw-gag´*; a primitive root [compare 2283, 2328]; (properly) to *move* in a *circle,* i.e. (specifically) to *march* in a sacred procession, to *observe* a festival; (by implication) to *be giddy:*—celebrate, dance, (keep, hold) a (solemn) feast (holiday), reel to and fro.

2288. חָגוּ, **châgûw,** *khaw-goo´*; from an unused root meaning to take *refuge;* a *rift* in rocks:—cleft.

2289. חֲגוֹר, **chăgôwr,** *khaw-gore´*; from 2296; *belted:*—girded with.

2290. חֲגוֹר, **chăgôwr,** *khag-ore´*; or חֲגֹר **chăgôr,** *khag-ore´*; and (feminine) חֲגוֹרָה **chăgôwrâh,** *khag-o-raw´*; or חֲגֹרָה **chăgôrâh,** *khag-o-raw´*; from 2296; a *belt* (for the waist):—apron, armour, gird (-le).

2291. חַגִּי, **Chaggîy,** *khag-ghee´*; from 2287; *festive; Chaggi,* an Israelite; also (patronymic) a *Chaggite,* or descendant of the same:—Haggi, Haggites.

2292. חַגַּי, **Chaggay,** *khag-gah´ee*; from 2282; *festive; Chaggai,* a Hebrew prophet:—Haggai.

2293. חַגִּיָּה, **Chaggîyyâh,** *khag-ghee-yaw´*; from 2282 and 3050; *festival of Jah; Chaggijah,* an Israelite:—Haggiah.

2294. חַגִּית, **Chaggîyth,** *khag-gheeth´*; feminine of 2291; *festive; Chaggith,* a wife of David:—Haggith.

2295. חׇגְלָה, **Choglâh,** *khog-law´*; of uncertain derivation; probably a *partridge; Choglah,* an Israelitess:—Hoglah. See also 1031.

2296. חָגַר, **châgar,** *khaw-gar´*; a primitive root; to *gird* on (as a belt, armour, etc.):—be able to put on, be afraid, appointed, gird, restrain, × on every side.

2297. חַד, **chad,** *khad*; abridged from 259; *one:*—one.

2298. חַד, **chad,** *khad*; (Chaldee); corresponding to 2297; (as cardinal) *one*; (as article) *single*; (as ordinal) *first*; (adverbial) *at once:*—a, first, one, together.

2299. חַד, **chad,** *khad*; from 2300; *sharp:*—sharp.

2300. חָדַד, **châdad,** *khaw-dad´*; a primitive root; to *be* (causative *make*) *sharp* or (figurative) *severe:*—be fierce, sharpen.

2301. חֲדַד, **Chădad,** *khad-ad´*; from 2300; *fierce; Chadad,* an Ishmaelite:—Hadad.

2302. חָדָה, **châdâh,** *khaw-daw´*; a primitive root; to *rejoice:*—make glad, be joined, rejoice.

2303. חַדּוּד, **chaddûwd,** *khad-dood´*; from 2300; a *point:*—sharp.

2304. חֶדְוָה, **chedvâh,** *khed-vaw´*; from 2302; *rejoicing:*—gladness, joy.

2305. חֶדְוָה, **chedvâh,** *khed-vaw´*; (Chaldee); corresponding to 2304:—joy.

2306. חֲדֵה, **chădêh,** *khad-ay´*; (Chaldee); corresponding to 2373; a *breast:*—breast.

2307. חָדִיד, **Châdîyd,** *khaw-deed´*; from 2300; a *peak; Chadid,* a place in Palestine:—Hadid.

2308. חָדַל, **châdal,** *khaw-dal´*; a primitive root; (properly) to *be flabby,* i.e. (by implication) *desist*; (figurative) *be lacking* or *idle:*—cease, end, fail, forbear, forsake, leave (off), let alone, rest, be unoccupied, want.

2309. חֶדֶל, **chedel,** *kheh´-del*; from 2308; *rest,* i.e. the state of the *dead:*—world.

A masculine noun meaning cessation, rest. This word occurs only in Isa 38:11 in the lamentation of Hezekiah. Despite the fact it is translated "world," it conveys the idea of a place of termination or repose. By considering the context in the OT, one comes to understand that the word refers to the grave, or more exactly, Sheol (cf. Isa 38:10).

2310. חָדֵל, **châdêl,** *khaw-dale´*; from 2308; *vacant,* i.e. *ceasing* or *destitute:*—he that forbeareth, frail, rejected.

2311. חַדְלַי, **Chadlay,** *khad-lah´ee*; from 2309; *idle; Chadlai,* an Israelite:—Hadlai.

2312. חֵדֶק, **chêdeq,** *khay´-dek*; from an unused root meaning to *sting*; a *prickly* plant:—brier, thorn.

2313. חִדֶּקֶל, **Chiddeqel,** *khid-deh´-kel*; probably of foreign origin; the *Chiddekel* (or Tigris) river:—Hiddekel.

2314. חָדַר, **châdar,** *khaw-dar´*; a primitive root; (properly) to *inclose* (as a room), i.e. (by analogy) to *beset* (as in a siege):—enter a privy chamber.

2315. חֶדֶר, **cheder,** *kheh´-der*; from 2314; an *apartment* (usually literal):—([bed] inner) chamber, innermost (-ward) part, parlour, + south, × within.

2316. חֲדַר, **Chădar,** *khad-ar´*; another form for 2315; *chamber; Chadar,* an Ishmaelite:—Hadar.

2317. חֲדְרָךְ, **Chadrâk,** *khad-rawk´*; of uncertain derivation; *Chadrak,* a Syrian deity:—Hadrach.

2318. חָדַשׁ, **châdash,** *khaw-dash´*; a primitive root; to *be new;* (causative) to *rebuild:*—renew, repair.

2319. חָדָשׁ, **châdâsh,** *khaw-dawsh´*; from 2318; *new:*—fresh, new thing.

2320. חֹדֶשׁ, **chôdesh,** *kho´-desh*; from 2318; the *new* moon; (by implication) a *month:*—month (-ly), new moon.

2321. חֹדֶשׁ, **Chôdesh,** *kho´-desh*; the same as 2320; *Chodesh,* an Israelitess:—Hodesh.

2322. חֲדָשָׁה, **Chădâshâh,** *khad-aw-shaw´*; feminine of 2319; *new; Chadashah,* a place in Palestine:—Hadashah.

2323. חֲדָת, **chădâth,** *khad-ath´*; (Chaldee); corresponding to 2319; *new:*—new.

2324. חֲוָה, **chăvâh,** *khav-aw´*; (Chaldee); corresponding to 2331; to *show:*—shew.

2325. חוּב, **chûwb,** *khoob*; also חָיַב, **châyab,** *khaw-yab´*; a primitive root; (properly) perhaps to *tie,* i.e. (figurative and reflexive) to *owe,* or (by implication) to *forfeit:*—make endanger.

2326. חוֹב, **chôwb,** *khobe*; from 2325; *debt:*—debtor.

2327. חוֹבָה, **chôwbâh,** *kho-baw´*; feminine active participle of 2247; *hiding* place; *Chobah,* a place in Syria:—Hobah.

2328. חוּג, **chûwg,** *khoog*; a primitive root [compare 2287]; to *describe* a *circle:*—compass.

2329. חוּג, **chûwg,** *khoog*; from 2328; a *circle:*—circle, circuit, compass.

2330. חוּד, **chûwd,** *khood*; a primitive root; (properly) to *tie* a knot, i.e. (figurative) to *propound* a riddle:—put forth.

2331. חָוָה, **châvâh,** *khaw-vah´*; a primitive root; [compare 2324, 2421]; (properly) to *live;* (by implication) (intensive) to *declare* or *show:*—show.

2332. חַוָּה, **Chavvâh,** *khav-vaw´*; causative from 2331; *life-giver; Chavvah* (or Eve), the first woman:—Eve.

2333. חַוָּה, **chavvâh,** *khav-vaw´*; (properly) the same as 2332 (*life-giving,* i.e. *living-place*); (by implication) an *encampment* or *village:*—(small) town.

2334. חַוֹּת יָאִיר, **Chavvôth Yâ'îyr,** *khav-vothe´ yaw-eer´*; from the plural of 2333 and a modification of 3265; *hamlets of Jair,* a region of Palestine:—[Bashan-] Havoth-jair.

2335. חוֹזַי, **Chôwzay,** *kho-zah´ee*; from 2374; *visionary; Chozai,* an Israelite:—the seers.

2336. חוֹחַ, **chôwach,** *kho´-akh*; from an unused root apparently meaning to *pierce;* a *thorn;* (by analogy) a *ring* for the nose:—bramble, thistle, thorn.

2337. חָוָח, **châvâch,** *khaw-vawkh´*; perhaps the same as 2336; a *dell* or *crevice* (as if *pierced* in the earth):—thicket.

2338. חוּט, **chûwṭ,** *khoot*; (Chaldee); corresponding to the root of 2339, perhaps as a denominative; to *string* together, i.e. (figurative) to *repair:*—join.

2339. חוּט, **chûwṭ,** *khoot*; from an unused root probably meaning to *sew;* a *string;* (by implication) a *measuring* tape:—cord, fillet, line, thread.

2340. חִוִּי, **Chivvîy,** *khiv-vee´*; perhaps from 2333; a *villager;* a *Chivvite,* one of the aboriginal tribes of Palestine:—Hivite.

2341. חֲוִילָה, **Chăvîylâh,** *khav-ee-law´*; probably from 2342; *circular; Chavilah,* the name of two or three eastern regions; also perhaps of two men:—Havilah.

2342. חוּל, **chûwl,** *khool*; or חִיל, **chîyl,** *kheel*; a primitive root; (properly) to *twist* or *whirl* (in a circular or spiral manner), i.e. (specific) to *dance,* to *writhe* in pain (especially of parturition) or fear; (figurative) to *wait,* to *pervert:*—bear, (make to) bring forth, (make to) calve, dance, drive away, fall grievously (with pain), fear, form, great, grieve, (be) grievous, hope, look, make, be in pain, be much (sore) pained, rest, shake, shapen, (be) sorrow (-ful), stay, tarry, travail (with pain), tremble, trust, wait carefully (patiently), be wounded.

A verb meaning to whirl, to shake, to fear, to dance, to writhe, to grieve. This word has many different meanings, most of which derive from two basic ideas: to whirl in motion and to writhe in pain. The first of these ideas may be seen in the shaking of the earth (Ps 29:8); the stirring of the waters (Ps 77:16[17]); or the trembling of the mountains (Hab 3:10). At times, this word is used in a context of shaking with fear (Dt 2:25; Jer 5:22); worshiping in trembling awe (1Ch 16:30; Ps 96:9); or anxiously waiting (Ge 8:10; Ps 37:7). It is also used to describe dancing women (Jgs 21:21, 23). The second idea of writhing in pain can be either physical, as when Saul was wounded in battle (1Sa 31:3), or emotional, as when Jeremiah grieved in anguish over Jerusalem's refusal to grieve (Jer 4:19). This word is often used to describe the labour pains of giving birth (Ps 29:9; Isa 26:17, 18; 51:2) but can also imply God's creating work (Dt 32:18; Job 15:7; Ps 90:2; Pr 8:24, 25).

2343. חוּל, **Chûwl,** *khool;* from 2342; a *circle; Chul,* a son of Aram; also the region settled by him:—Hul.

2344. חוֹל, **chôwl,** *khole;* from 2342; *sand* (as *round* or whirling particles):—sand.

2345. חוּם, **chûwm,** *khoom;* from an unused root meaning to *be warm,* i.e. (by implication) *sunburnt* or *swarthy* (blackish):—brown.

2346. חוֹמָה, **chôwmâh,** *kho-maw´;* feminine active participle of an unused root apparently meaning to *join;* a *wall* of protection:—wall, walled.

2347. חוּס, **chûws,** *khoos;* a primitive root; (properly) to *cover,* i.e. (figurative) to *compassionate:*—pity, regard, spare.

2348. חוֹף, **chôwph,** *khofe;* from an unused root meaning to *cover;* a *cove* (as a *sheltered* bay):—coast [of the sea], haven, shore, [sea-] side.

2349. חוּפָם, **Chûwphâm,** *khoo-fawm´;* from the same as 2348; *protection; Chupham,* an Israelite:—Hupham.

2350. חוּפָמִי, **Chûwphâmîy,** *khoo-faw-mee´;* patronymic from 2349; a *Chuphamite* or descendant of Chupham:—Huphamites.

2351. חוּץ, **chûwts,** *khoots;* or (shortened) חֻץ, **chuts,** *khoots;* (both forms feminine in the plural) from an unused root meaning to *sever;* (properly) *separate* by a wall, i.e. *outside, out-* doors:—abroad, field, forth, highway, more, out (-side, -ward), street, without.

2352. חוּר, **chûwr,** *khoor;* or (shortened) חֻר, **chur,** *khoor;* from an unused root probably meaning to *bore;* the *crevice* of a serpent; the *cell* of a prison:—hole.

2353. חוּר, **chûwr,** *khoor;* from 2357; *white* linen:—white.

2354. חוּר, **Chûwr,** *khoor;* the same as 2353 or 2352; *Chur,* the name of four Israelites and one Midianite:—Hur.

2355. חוֹרָי, **chôwrây,** *kho-raw-ee´;* the same as 2353; *white* linen:—network. Compare 2715.

2356. חוֹר, **chôwr,** *khore;* or (shortened) חֹר, **chôr,** *khore;* the same as 2352; a *cavity, socket, den:*—cave, hole.

2357. חָוַר, **châvar,** *khaw-var´;* a primitive root; to *blanch* (as with shame):—wax pale.

2358. חִוָּר, **chivvâr,** *khiv-vawr´;* (Chaldee); from a root corresponding to 2357; *white:*—white.

2359. חוּרִי, **Chûwrîy,** *khoo-ree´;* probably from 2353; *linen*-worker; *Churi,* an Israelite:—Huri.

2360. חוּרַי, **Chûwray,** *khoo-rah´ee;* probably an orthographical variation for 2359; *Churai,* an Israelite:—Hurai.

2361. חוּרָם, **Chûwrâm,** *khoo-rawm´;* probably from 2353; *whiteness,* i.e. noble; *Churam,* the name of an Israelite and two Syrians:—Huram. Compare 2438.

2362. חַוְרָן, **Chavrân,** *khav-rawn´;* apparently from 2357 (in the sense of 2352); *cavernous; Chavran,* a region East of the Jordan:—Hauran.

2363. חוּשׁ, **chûwsh,** *koosh;* a primitive root; to *hurry;* (figurative) to *be eager* with excitement or enjoyment:—(make) haste (-n), ready.

2364. חוּשָׁה, **Chûwshâh,** *khoo-shaw´;* from 2363; *haste; Chushah,* an Israelite:—Hushah.

2365. חוּשַׁי, **Chûwshay,** *khoo-shah´ee;* from 2363; *hasty; Chushai,* an Israelite:—Hushai.

2366. חוּשִׁים, **Chûwshîym,** *khoo-sheem´;* or חֻשִׁים, **Chushîym,** *khoo-sheem´;* or חֻשִׁם, **Chushim,** *khoo-sheem´;* plural from 2363; *hasters; Chushim,* the name of three Israelites:—Hushim.

2367. חוּשָׁם, **Chûwshâm,** *khoo-shawm´*; or חֻשָׁם, **Chushâm,** *khoo-shawm´*; from 2363; *hastily; Chu-sham,* an Idumæan:—Husham.

2368. חוֹתָם, **chôwthâm,** *kho-thawm´*; or חֹתָם, **chô-thâm,** *kho-thawm´*; from 2856; a *signature-ring:*—seal, signet.

2369. חֹתָם, **Chôwthâm,** *kho-thawm´*; the same as 2368; *seal; Chotham,* the name of two Israelites:—Hotham, Hothan.

2370. חֲזָא, **chăzâ’,** *khaz-aw´*; (Chaldee); or חֲזָה, **chăzâh,** *khaz-aw´*; (Chaldee); corresponding to 2372; to *gaze* upon; (mentally) to *dream, be usual* (i.e. *seem*):—behold, have [a dream], see, be wont.

An Aramaic verb meaning to see, to behold, to witness, to observe. This word appears only in the books of Ezra and Daniel. It signifies the literal sense of sight (Da 5:23); the observation of something with the eye (Da 3:25; 5:5); the witnessing of a king's dishonour (Ezr 4:14); beholding something in a dream (Da 2:41; 4:20[17]); and having a dream (Da 7:1). On one occasion, the verb is used to imply the usual condition or customary state of the furnace set to receive Shadrach, Meshach, and Abednego (Da 3:19). This use probably stresses the difference in the appearance of the furnace, which would be obvious to the observer.

2371. חֲזָאֵל, **Chăzâ’êl,** *khaz-aw-ale´*; or חֲזָהאֵל, **Chăzâh’êl,** *khaz-aw-ale´*; from 2372 and 410; *God has seen; Chazaël,* a king of Syria:—Hazael.

2372. חָזָה, **châzâh,** *khaw-zaw*; a primitive root; to *gaze* at; (mentally) to *perceive, contemplate* (with pleasure); specifically to *have a vision of:*—behold, look, prophesy, provide, see.

A verb meaning to see, to perceive. This term is more poetic than the common *râ’âh* (7200). It refers to seeing God (Ex 24:11; Job 19:26, 27; Ps 11:7; 17:15); astrological observations (Isa 47:13); prophetic vision and insight (Isa 1:1; La 2:14; Eze 12:27; Hab 1:1; Zec 10:2).

2373. חָזֶה, **châzeh,** *khaw-zeh´*; from 2372; the *breast* (as most *seen* in front):—breast.

2374. חֹזֶה, **chôzeh,** *kho-zeh´*; active participle of 2372; a *beholder* in vision; also a *compact* (as *looked upon* with approval):—agreement, prophet, see that, seer, [star-] gazer.

A masculine noun meaning a seer, a prophet. It is used only seventeen times in the OT, always in the present active participle. The word means one who sees or perceives; it is used in parallel with the participle of the verb that means literally to see, to perceive. In Isaiah a rebellious people sought to curb the functions of these seers (Isa 30:10). In 1Sa 9:9, the author parenthetically states that the word for prophet in his day, *nâbiy’* (5030), was formerly called a seer. However, for seer, he did not use *chôwzeh* but a present participle of the verb *râ’âh* (7200), meaning to see, to perceive. It appears that the participles of *chôwzeh* and of *râ’âh* function synonymously. But, terminology aside, a seer functioned the same as a prophet, who was moved by God and had divinely given insight. This Hebrew word is also used in parallel with the word prophet (2Ki 17:13; Am 7:12, 14); hence, its meaning overlaps with that term as well (cf. 2Ch 33:18; Isa 29:10). Seers sometimes served a specific person: Gad served as King David's seer and did not hesitate to declare the words the Lord gave him for the king (2Sa 24:11). David had more than one seer (cf. 1Ch 25:5; 2Ch 29:25).

The functions of a seer as indicated by this term included, besides receiving and reporting the word of the Lord, writing about David's reign (1Ch 29:29); receiving and writing down visions (2Ch 9:29); writing genealogical records under Rehoboam's reign (2Ch 12:15). In general, the Lord forewarned His people through His prophets and seers (2Ki 17:13; 2Ch 33:18). In many cases, these warnings were recorded in writing (2Ch 33:19).

2375. חֲזוֹ, **Chăzôw,** *khaz-o´*; from 2372; *seer; Chazo,* a nephew of Abraham:—Hazo.

2376. חֱזוּ, **chĕzûw,** *kheh´-zoo*; (Chaldee); from 2370; a *sight:*—look, vision.

An Aramaic masculine noun meaning a vision, a revelation. This word appears exclusively in the book of Daniel and draws attention to the nature of revelation. It denotes the nighttime dreams of Nebuchadnezzar (Da 2:19, 28; 4:5[2], 13[10]) and Daniel (Da 7:2, 7, 13) that have prophetic significance. There appears to be some connection with the ominous or troubling nature of these revelations (Da 7:15; cf. 2:1). Once the word pertains to the outward appearance of an object in the vision of the fourth beast (Da 7:20).

2377. חָזוֹן, **châzôwn,** *khaw-zone´*; from 2372; a *sight* (mentally), i.e. a *dream, revelation,* or *oracle:*—vision.

A masculine noun meaning a revelation by means of a vision, an oracle, a divine communication. The primary essence of this word is not so much the vision or dream itself as the message conveyed. It signifies the direct, specific communication between God and people through the prophetic office (1Sa 3:1; 1Ch 17:15; Ps 89:19[20]) or the collection of such messages (2Ch 32:32; Isa 1:1; Ob 1:1; Na 1:1; Hab 2:2, 3). Also, the word is used of the messages of false prophets (Jer 14:14; 23:16); a guiding communication from the Lord, often restricted when a people are under judgment (La 2:9; Eze 7:26; Mic 3:6); and the revelation of future events on a grand scale (Da 9:24; 10:14). People who disregard this divine communication face certain doom (Pr 29:18).

2378. חָזוֹת, **châzôwth,** *khaw-zooth´*; from 2372; a *revelation:*—vision.

A feminine noun meaning a vision, a revelation. This particular word is used only once in the description of a book of prophetic writings called the visions of Iddo (2Ch 9:29). See the related Hebrew verb *châzâh* (2372).

2379. חֲזוֹת, **chǎzôwth,** *khaz-oth´*; (Chaldee) from 2370; a *view:*—sight.

2380. חָזוּת, **châzûwth,** *khaw-zooth´*; from 2372; a *look;* hence (figurative) striking *appearance, revelation,* or (by implication) *compact:*—agreement, notable (one), vision.

A feminine noun meaning a vision, a striking appearance. A difficult vision appeared to Isaiah (Isa 21:2); and another vision seemed to the Israelites to be words on a scroll (Isa 29:11). Daniel saw in his vision a goat with a visible (large) horn (Da 8:5). This word can also mean commitment or agreement, as in Isaiah's oracle against Ephraim (Isa 28:18). See the related Hebrew root *châzâh* (2372).

2381. חֲזִיאֵל, **Chǎzîy´êl,** *khaz-ee-ale´*; from 2372 and 410; *seen of God; Chaziel,* a Levite:—Haziel.

2382. חֲזָיָה, **Chǎzâyâh,** *khaz-aw-yaw´*; from 2372 and 3050; *Jah has seen; Chazajah,* an Israelite:—Hazaiah.

2383. חֶזְיוֹן, **Chezyôwn,** *khez-yone´*; from 2372; *vision; Chezjon,* a Syrian:—Hezion.

2384. חִזָּיוֹן, **chizzâyôwn,** *khiz-zaw-yone´*; from 2372; a *revelation,* especially by *dream:*—vision.

A masculine noun meaning a dream, a vision, a revelation. The primary stress of this word lies on the means and manner of divine revelation. It is used in reference to revelations that come in the night (2Sa 7:17; Job 4:13; 33:15); visions imparted (Zec 13:4); and dreams in a general sense (Job 7:14; 20:8). Metaphorically, Jerusalem is called the "valley of vision," alluding to the city as the center of prophetic activity (Isa 22:1, 5; cf. Lk 13:33).

2385. חֲזִיז, **chǎzîyz,** *khaw-zeez´*; from an unused root meaning to *glare;* a *flash* of lightning:—bright cloud, lightning.

2386. חֲזִיר, **chǎzîyr,** *khaz-eer´*; from an unused root probably meaning to *inclose;* a *hog* (perhaps as *penned*):—boar, swine.

2387. חֵזִיר, **Chêzîyr,** *khay-zeer´*; from the same as 2386; perhaps *protected; Chezir,* the name of two Israelites:—Hezir.

2388. חָזַק, **châzaq,** *khaw-zak´*; a primitive root; to *fasten* upon; hence to *seize, be strong* ([figurative] *courageous,* [causative] *strengthen, cure, help, repair, fortify*), *obstinate;* to *bind, restrain, conquer:*—aid, amend, × calker, catch, cleave, confirm, be constant, constrain, continue, be of good (take) courage (-ous, -ly), encourage (self), be established, fasten, force, fortify, make hard, harden, help, (lay) hold (fast), lean, maintain, play the man, mend, become (wax) mighty, prevail, be recovered, repair, retain, seize, be (wax) sore, strengthen (self), be stout, be (make, shew, wax) strong (-er), be sure, take (hold), be urgent, behave self valiantly, withstand.

A verb meaning to be strong, to strengthen, to be courageous, to overpower. This verb is widely used to express the strength of various phenomena, such as the severity of famine (2Ki 25:3; Jer 52:6); the strength of humans to overpower each other; the condition of Pharaoh's heart (Ex 7:13); David and Goliath (1Sa 17:50); Amnon and Tamar (2Sa 13:14); a battle situation (2Ch 8:3); Samson's strength for his last superhuman performance (Jgs 16:28). This word occurs in the commonly known charge, "Be strong and of good courage!" (Jos 1:9).

Moses urges Joshua (Dt 31:6, 7) to be strong. The Lord also bids Joshua to be strong in taking the Promised Land (Dt 31:23; Jos 1:6, 7, 9), after which Joshua encourages the people in the same way (Jos 10:25).

2389. חָזָק, **châzâq,** *khaw-zawk´*; from 2388; *strong* (usually in a bad sense, *hard, bold, violent*):—harder, hottest, + impudent, loud, mighty, sore, stiff [-hearted], strong (-er).

A masculine adjective meaning firmness, strength. The feminine form of this word is *chăzâqâh*. It can refer to human strength or power (Nu 13:18; Jos 14:11); to human persistence or stubbornness (Eze 2:4; 3:8, 9); or to divine strength or power (Ex 3:19; Isa 40:10). In addition, it can refer to the strength of things, but it must be translated to fit the context: a *loud* trumpet blast (Ex 19:16); a *sore* war (1Sa 14:52); the *hottest* battle (2Sa 11:15); a *sore* sickness (1Ki 17:17); a *severe* famine (1Ki 18:2); a *strong* wind (Ex 10:19). This adjective can also be used as a substantive for a strong or mighty person (Job 5:15; Isa 40:10; Eze 34:16).

2390. חָזֵק, **châzêq,** *khaw-zake´*; from 2388; *powerful:*— × wax louder, stronger.

An adjective meaning stronger. This word is used only twice in Scripture. In Ex 19:19, it described the trumpet blast on Mount Sinai as the Lord's presence descended around Moses. In 2Sa 3:1, it described the strength of David's house over the house of Saul.

2391. חֵזֶק, **chêzeq,** *khay´-zek*; from 2388; *help:*—strength.

A masculine noun meaning strength. This particular word is used only once in the OT, where God is the strength of the psalmist (Ps 18:1[2]). See the related Hebrew root *châzaq* (2388) and the feminine form of this noun, *chezqâh* (2393).

2392. חֹזֶק, **chôzeq,** *kho´-zek*; from 2388; *power:*—strength.

A masculine noun meaning strength. This word is used to describe the Lord's strength in delivering Israel out of Egyptian bondage (Ex 13:3, 14, 16). It is also used to describe the military strength of Israel (Am 6:13) and of other kingdoms (Hag 2:22). Although this particular word is used only five times in the OT, its related verb, *châzaq* (2388), meaning to be

strong, and its related adjective, *châzâq* (2389), meaning strong, are used many times.

2393. חֶזְקָה, **chezqâh,** *khez-kaw´*; feminine of 2391; *prevailing power:*—strength (-en self), (was) strong.

A feminine noun meaning strength, force. This word refers to the hand of the Lord on Isaiah as the Lord spoke to him (Isa 8:11). It is also used to describe the power of kings. When Rehoboam became strong and established his kingdom, he and his people abandoned the Law of the Lord (2Ch 12:1). When King Uzziah became strong, he became proud and went into the Temple to burn incense, even though that was the job of the priests (2Ch 26:16). In Daniel's vision, the fourth king gained power through his great wealth (Da 11:2). See the related Hebrew root *châzaq* (2388) and the masculine form of this noun *chêzeq* (2391).

2394. חָזְקָה, **chozqâh,** *khoz-kaw´*; feminine of 2392; *vehemence* (usually in a bad sense):— force, mightily, repair, sharply.

A feminine noun meaning strength, force. It always occurs with the preposition *bᵉ* (with or by). It can be used to modify oppression (Jgs 4:3); rebuke (Jgs 8:1); capture (1Sa 2:16); ruling (Eze 34:4); crying to God (Jnh 3:8). Only the last of these references has a positive connotation. All the others connote a harsh, cruel, and self-serving connotation of the use of one's strength and power.

2395. חִזְקִי, **Chizqîy,** *khiz-kee´*; from 2388; *strong; Chizki,* an Israelite:—Hezeki.

2396. חִזְקִיָּה, **Chizqîyyâh,** *khiz-kee-yaw´*; or חִזְקִיָּהוּ, **Chiz-qîyyâhûw,** *khiz-kee-yaw´-hoo;* also יְחִזְקִיָּה, **Yᵉchizqîyyâh,** *yekh-iz-kee-yaw´;* or יְחִזְקִיָּהוּ, **Yᵉchiz-qîyyâhûw,** *yekh-iz-kee-yaw´-hoo;* from 2388 and 3050; *strengthened of Jah; Chizkijah,* a king of Judah, also the name of two other Israelites:—Hezekiah, Hizkiah, Hizkijah. Compare 3169.

2397. חָח, **châch,** *khawkh*; once (Eze 29:4) חָחִי, **châchîy,** *khakh-ee´*; from the same as 2336; a *ring* for the nose (or lips):—bracelet, chain, hook.

2398. חָטָא, **châṭâ,** *khaw-taw´*; a primitive root; (properly) to *miss;* hence (figurative and general) to *sin;* (by inference) to *forfeit, lack, expiate,* *repent,* (causative) *lead astray, condemn:*—bear the blame, cleanse, commit [sin], by fault, harm he hath done, loss, miss, (make) offend (-er), offer for sin, purge, purify (self), make reconciliation, (cause, make) sin (-ful, -ness), trespass.

A verb meaning to miss the mark, to wrong, to sin, to lead into sin, to purify from sin, to free from sin. Four main Hebrew words express the idea of sin in the Hebrew Bible, with this word used most often. Its central meaning is to miss the mark or fail. It is used in a nonmoral or non-religious sense to indicate the simple idea of missing or failing in any task or endeavour. In Jgs 20:16, it indicated the idea of a slinger missing his target. The verb also indicated the situation that arose when something was missing (Job 5:24); or it described a failure to reach a certain goal or age (Pr 19:2; Isa 65:20). These are minor uses of the verb. The word is used the most to describe human failure and sin. It indicates failure to do what is expected; the one who fails to find God in this life destroys himself (Pr 8:36). Many times the word indicates being at fault (Ge 20:9; Ex 10:16; 2Ki 18:14; Ne 6:13) as Pharaoh was toward Moses or to be guilty or responsible (Ge 43:9; 44:32). It regularly means to sin; Pharaoh sinned against God (Ex 10:16). People can also sin against other human beings (Ge 42:22; 1Sa 19:4, 5) or against their own souls (Pr 20:2). The verb is used to indicate sin with no object given, as when Pharaoh admitted flatly that he had sinned (Ex 9:27; Jgs 10:15) or when Israel was described as a "sinful nation" (Isa 1:4). Sometimes the writer used the noun from this same verbal root as the object of the verb for emphasis, such as in Ex 32:30, 31, where Moses asserted that Israel had sinned a great sin (Le 4:3; Nu 12:11). Sinning, unfortunately, is a universal experience, for there is no one who does not sin (Ecc 7:20). Persons may sin with various parts of their bodies or in certain ways or attitudes. They may sin with their tongues or lips (Job 2:10; Ps 39:1[2]). Persons may sin innocently or in such a way as to bring guilt on others (Le 4:2, 3; Nu 15:27).

Three other stems of this verb are used less often. The intensive stem is used to indicate people bearing their own material losses or failures (Ge 31:39); one freeing oneself from sin or purifying an object or person (Le 8:15; Ps 51:7[9]); and one bringing a sin offering (Le 6:26[19]; 2Ch 29:24). The causative stem,

besides indicating failure to miss a literal target, means to lead into sin, to lead astray. Jeroboam was an infamous king who caused all Israel to walk in sin (1Ki 14:16; 15:26). The reflexive stem communicates the idea of freeing oneself from sin. The Levites purified themselves (i.e. set themselves apart from sin) so they could work at the sanctuary (Nu 8:21).

2399. אֵטְח, **chêt**, *khate*; from 2398; a *crime* or its *penalty:*—fault, × grievously, offence, (punishment of) sin.

A masculine noun meaning sin, an offence, a fault. The word suggests the accumulated shortcomings that lead to punishment (Ge 41:9); errors or offences that cause the wrath of a supervisor (Ecc 10:4); and the charge against an individual for his or her actions contrary to the Law (Le 24:15; Nu 9:13; Dt 15:9; 23:21[22]). Isaiah uses the word to reinforce the tremendous sinfulness of Judah in contrast to the Messiah's redemptive suffering (Isa 53:12).

2400. אֵטָּח, **chattâ**, *khat-taw´*; intensive from 2398; a *criminal*, or one accounted *guilty:*—offender, sinful, sinner.

A masculine noun meaning sinners and an adjective meaning sinful. This word comes from the common verb *châtâ'* (2398), meaning to sin, and is related to the common noun *chattâ'th* (2403), meaning sin or sin offering. As a noun, it is used to describe those who, by their actions, are under the wrath and judgment of God (Ps 1:5) and face ultimate destruction (Ge 13:13; Ps 104:35; Isa 1:28). The influence of these people is to be avoided (Ps 1:1; 26:9; Pr 1:10), but they are to be instructed in the way of righteousness (Ps 25:8; 51:13[15]). As an adjective, it describes the sinful people the tribes of Reuben and Gad were raising (Nu 32:14).

2401. הָאָטֲח, **chătâ'âh**, *khat-aw-aw´*; feminine of 2399; an *offence*, or a *sacrifice* for it:—sin (offering).

A feminine noun meaning sin, a sacrifice for sin. The word generally stands as a synonym for transgression (Ps 32:1). It is used to convey the evil committed by Abimelech in taking Sarah into his harem (Ge 20:9); the wickedness of idolatry committed by the Israelites at Sinai (Ex 32:21, 30, 31); and the perversion foisted on the Northern Kingdom by Jeroboam (2Ki 17:21).

Conversely, the psalmist uses the Hebrew word once to mean a sin offering (Ps 40:6[7]).

2402. הַטָּאָה, **chattā'âh,** *khat-taw-aw´;* (Chaldee); corresponding to 2401; an *offence,* and the *penalty* or *sacrifice* for it:—sin (offering).

A feminine noun meaning sin. This word is used only twice in the OT and is equivalent to the Hebrew word *chattâ'th* (2403), meaning sin. It is used in Ex 34:7 to speak of what God, in the greatness of His lovingkindness, will forgive. It is also used in Isa 5:18 to describe God's woe against those who sin greatly.

2403. הַטָּאָה, **chattā'âh,** *khat-taw-aw´;* or הַטָּאת, **chattā'th,** *khat-tawth´;* from 2398; an *offence* (sometimes habitual *sinfulness*), and its penalty, occasion, sacrifice, or expiation; also (concrete) an *offender:*—punishment (of sin), purifying (-fication for sin), sin (-ner, offering).

A feminine noun meaning sin, transgression, sin offering, punishment. The word denotes youthful indiscretions (Ps 25:7); evil committed against another (Ge 50:17); trespasses against God (2Ch 33:19; Ps 51:2[4]; Am 5:12); a general state of sinfulness (Isa 6:7); and the specific occasion of sin, particularly in reference to idolatry (Dt 9:21; Hos 10:8). It also implies an antidote to sin, including purification from ceremonial impurity (Nu 19:9, 17); the sacrificial offering for sin (Ex 29:14; Le 4:3); and the punishment for sin (La 4:6; Zec 14:19). In the story of Cain and Abel, sin appears as a creature, ready to pounce, lurking "at the door" of Cain's heart (Ge 4:7).

2404. הָטַב, **châṭab,** *khaw-tab´;* a primitive root; to *chop* or *carve* wood:—cut down, hew (-er), polish.

2405. הֲטֻבוֹת, **chăṭubôwth,** *khat-oo-both´;* feminine passive participle of 2404; (properly) a *carving;* hence a *tapestry* (as figured):—carved.

2406. הִטָּה, **chiṭṭâh,** *khit-taw´;* of uncertain derivation; *wheat,* whether the grain or the plant:—wheat (-en).

2407. הַטּוּשׁ, **Chaṭṭûwsh,** *khat-toosh´;* from an unused root of uncertain significance; *Chattush,* the name of four or five Israelites:—Hattush.

2408. הֲטָי, **chăṭây,** *khat-aw-ee´;* (Chaldee); from a root corresponding to 2398; an *offence:*—sin.

An Aramaic noun meaning sin. This word is used only once in the OT and is equivalent to the Hebrew word *chattâ'th* (2403), meaning sin or sin offering. Daniel advised King Nebuchadnezzar to turn from his sins (Da 4:27[24]).

2409. הֲטָיָא, **chaṭṭâyâ',** *khat-taw-yaw´;* (Chaldee); from the same as 2408; an *expiation:*—sin offering.

A feminine noun meaning an offering for sin. This Aramaic word appears only in Ezr 6:17, where it indicates the particular sacrifice made at the dedication of the rebuilt Temple, following the return from exile. The text states that the "sin offering" consisted of twelve rams for the sins of the twelve tribes of Israel.

2410. הֲטִיטָא, **Chăṭîyṭâ',** *khat-ee-taw´;* from an unused root apparently meaning to *dig* out; *explorer; Chatita,* a temple porter:—Hatita.

2411. הֲטִיל, **Chaṭṭîyl,** *khat-teel´;* from an unused root apparently meaning to *wave; fluctuating; Chattil,* one of "Solomon's servants":—Hattil.

2412. הֲטִיפָא, **Chăṭîyphâ',** *khat-ee-faw´;* from 2414; *robber; Chatipha,* one of the Nethinim:—Hatipha.

2413. הָטַם, **châtam,** *khaw-tam´;* a primitive root; to *stop:*—refrain.

2414. הָטַף, **châtaph,** *khaw-taf´;* a primitive root; to *clutch;* hence to *seize* as a prisoner:—catch.

2415. הֹטֶר, **chôṭer,** *kho´-ter;* from an unused root of uncertain significance; a *twig:*—rod.

2416. הַי, **chay,** *khah´ee;* from 2421; *alive;* hence *raw* (flesh); *fresh* (plant, water, year), *strong;* also (as noun, especially in the feminine singular and masculine plural) *life* (or living thing), whether literal or figurative:— + age, alive, appetite, (wild) beast, company, congregation, life (-time), live (-ly), living (creature, thing), maintenance, + merry, multitude, + (be) old, quick, raw, running, springing, troop.

A feminine noun meaning a living thing, an animal, a beast, a living thing. The basic meaning is living things, but its most common translation is animals or beasts. The word refers to all kinds of animals and beasts of the field or earth (Ge 1:24, 25; 1Sa 17:46) and sometimes stands in parallel with birds of the air (Eze 29:5). The nations, such as Egypt, were referred to metaphorically as beasts (Ps 68:30[31]). Beasts were categorized in various ways: beasts of burden (Isa 46:1); land animals (Ge 1:28; 8:19); cattle (Nu 35:3); sea creatures (Ps 104:25); clean, edible creatures (Le 11:47; 14:4); unclean, nonedible creatures (Le 5:2); large and small creatures (Ps 104:25).

Two further categories of animals are noted: wild animals or animals of prey and animal or beastlike beings. God made the wild animals of the field. Sometimes the Lord used wild beasts as instruments of His judgments (Eze 14:15; 33:27), but on other occasions He protected His people from ravenous beasts (Ge 37:20; Le 26:6). At any rate, vicious beasts will not inhabit the land of the Lord's restored people (Isa 35:9). The bizarre living beings mentioned in Eze 1:5, 13, 22; 3:13 were like birds and animals but were composite beings. They could not be described adequately by human language, for they also had the forms of humans, each with faces of a man, lion, ox, and eagle. However, they did not resemble flesh and blood in their appearance (Eze 1:13) and were tied to the movement of the Spirit (Eze 1:20).

2417. חַי, **chay,** *khah´ee*; (Chaldee); from 2418; *alive*; also (as noun in plural) *life*:—life, that liveth, living.

An Aramaic adjective meaning living, alive. In the book of Daniel, it is used of people (Da 2:30; 4:17[14]); and King Darius used this word in his description of God (Da 6:20[21], 26[27]).

2418. אֲיָא, **chăyâ’,** *khah-yaw´*; (Chaldee); or חֲיָה, **chăyâh,** *khah-yaw´*; (Chaldee); corresponding to 2421; to *live*:—live, keep alive.

An Aramaic verb meaning to live. The main usage of this word is the polite address for the king to live forever. The astrologers used this verb to address Nebuchadnezzar when they asked him to tell them his dream (Da 2:4) and again when they informed him that certain Jews were not bowing down to his golden image (Da 3:9). The queen used the verb to advise Belshazzar that Daniel could interpret the handwriting on the wall (Da 5:10). The king's advisors also used these words when they tricked King Darius into making a decree to worship only the king (Da 6:6[7]). Daniel also used this phrase when he explained to Darius that God saved him from the lions (Da 6:21[22]).

2419. חִיאֵל, **Chîy’êl,** *khee-ale´*; from 2416 and 410; *living of God; Chiel,* an Israelite:—Hiel.

2420. חִידָה, **chîydâh,** *khee-daw´*; from 2330; a *puzzle*; hence a *trick, conundrum,* sententious *maxim*:—dark saying (sentence, speech), hard question, proverb, riddle.

A feminine noun possibly meaning enigma. The Greek root of this English term is used in various contexts by the Septuagint (the Greek translation of the Hebrew OT) to translate the Hebrew word. Nearly half of this noun's occurrences refer to Samson's "riddle" when he tested the wits of the Philistines at his wedding feast (Jgs 14:12–19). The term is connected with several different words from the wisdom tradition, most notably the word frequently translated "proverb" (Ps 78:2; Pr 1:6; cf. 2Ch 9:1). The term is also associated with the prophetic tradition, where it was contrasted with clear speaking and compared with communication through more obscure means (Nu 12:8; Eze 17:2). Daniel prophesied of a future destructive king whose abilities include "understanding enigmas." A somewhat similar Aramaic expression is used of Daniel himself earlier in the book (cf. Da 5:12; 8:23).

2421. חָיָה, **châyâh,** *khaw-yaw´*; a primitive root [compare 2331, 2421]; to *live,* whether literal or figurative; (causative) to *revive*:—keep (leave, make) alive, × certainly, give (promise) life, (let, suffer to) live, nourish up, preserve (alive), quicken, recover, repair, restore (to life), revive, (× God) save (alive, life, lives), × surely, be whole.

A verb meaning to be alive, to live, to keep alive. This verb is used numerous times in Scripture. It is used in the sense of flourishing (Dt 8:1; 1Sa 10:24; Ps 22:26[27]); or to convey that an object is safe (Ge 12:13; Nu 14:38; Jos 6:17). It connotes reviving in Eze 37:5 and 1Ki 17:22 or healing in Joshua 5:8 and 2Ki 8:8. Genesis often uses the word when people are kept alive in danger (Ge 6:19, 20; 19:19; 47:25; 50:20). Also, the word is used in the genealogies of Genesis (Ge 5:3–30; 11:11–26). Ps 119 employs this word to say that God's Word preserves life (Ps 119:25, 37, 40, 88). Many verses instruct hearers to obey a command (either God's or a king's) in order to live (Ge 20:7; Pr 4:4; Jer 27:12).

2422. חָיֶה, **châyeh,** *khaw-yeh´*; from 2421; *vigorous:*—lively.

An adjective meaning strong, vigorous. It is found only in Ex 1:19, where the Egyptian midwives explained to Pharaoh that the Hebrew women were so vigorous in childbirth that they delivered before the midwives arrived.

2423. חֵיוָא, **chêyvâ’,** *khay-vaw´*; (Chaldee); from 2418; an *animal:*—beast.

2424. חַיּוּת, **chayyûwth,** *khah-yooth´*; from 2421; *life:*— × living.

A feminine abstract noun meaning lifetime. This word occurs only in 2Sa 20:3, where it states that David provided for the ten concubines who were left to watch the palace in Jerusalem (2Sa 15:16) and were later violated by David's son, Absalom (2Sa 16:21, 22). Although David kept them and provided for their needs, he did not lie with them; consequently, they were like widows during the lifetime of their husband.

2425. חָיַי, **châyay,** *khaw-yah´ee*; a primitive root [compare 2421]; to *live*; (causative) to *revive:*— live, save life.

A verb meaning to live. This verb is often used in reference to the length of a person's life (Ge 5:5; 11:12, 14; 25:7). Ge 3:22 employs this word to describe eternal life represented by the tree of life. It is used in reference to life which is a result of seeing God (Ex 33:20; Dt 5:24[21]) or looking at the bronze serpent (Nu 21:8, 9). It is also used to refer to living by the Law (Le 18:5; Eze 20:11, 13, 21). Cities of refuge were established to which people could flee and live (Dt 4:42; 19:4, 5). This verb is identical in form and meaning to the verb *châyâh* (2421).

2426. חֵיל, **chêyl,** *khale*; or (shorter) חֵל, **chêl,** *khale*; a collateral form of 2428; an *army*; also (by analogy) an *intrenchment:*—army, bulwark, host, + poor, rampart, trench, wall.

A masculine noun meaning entrenchment, fortress, army, defense, fortified wall. The wall of Jezreel was the location where the dogs would gnaw on Jezebel's dead body (1Ki 21:23). The psalmist prayed for peace within the walls of Jerusalem (Ps 122:7). The Lord decided to tear down the wall around Israel (La 2:8). A surrounding river was the defense of Thebes (Na 3:8). See the related noun *chayil* (2428).

2427. חִיל, **chîyl,** *kheel*; and (feminine) חִילָה, **chîylâh,** *khee-law´*; from 2342; a *throe* (especially of childbirth):—pain, pang, sorrow.

2428. חַיִל, **chayil,** *khah´-yil*; from 2342; probably a *force*, whether of men, means or other resources; an *army, wealth, virtue, valor, strength:*—able, activity, (+) army, band of men (soldiers), company, (great) forces, goods, host, might, power, riches, strength, strong, substance, train, (+) valiant (-ly), valour, virtuous (-ly), war, worthy (-ily).

A masculine noun meaning strength, wealth, army. This word has the basic idea of strength and influence. It can be used to speak of the strength of people (1Sa 2:4; 9:1; 2Sa 22:40); of horses (Ps 33:17); or of nations (Est 1:3). God is often seen as the supplier of this strength (2Sa 22:33; Hab 3:19). When describing men, it can speak of those who are strong for war (Dt 3:18; 2Ki 24:16; Jer 48:14); able to judge (Ex 18:21, 25); or are righteous in behaviour (1Ki 1:52). When describing women, it speaks of virtuous character (Ru 3:11; Pr 12:4; 31:10). This idea of strength is often used to imply a financial influence (i.e. wealth) (Job 31:25; Ps 49:6[7]; Zec 14:14); a military influence (i.e. an army) (Ex 14:9; 2Ch 14:8[7], 9[8]; Isa 43:17); or a numerical influence (i.e. a great company) (1Ki 10:2; 2Ch 9:1).

2429. חַיִל, **chayil,** *khah´-yil*; (Chaldee); corresponding to 2428; an *army*, or *strength:*—aloud, army, × most [mighty], power.

An Aramaic masculine noun meaning strength, power, army. In the book of Ezra, Rehum and Shimshai forced the Jews to stop rebuilding the city (Ezr 4:23). It can mean a loud or powerful voice, such as Nebuchadnezzar's herald (Da 3:4); a messenger from heaven (Da 4:14[11]); and King Belshazzar to his enchanters (Da 5:7). Nebuchadnezzar had the most powerful soldiers bind up Shadrach, Meshach, and Abednego (Da 3:20). See the related Hebrew noun *chayil* (2428).

2430. חֵילָה, **chêylâh,** *khay-law´*; feminine of 2428; an *intrenchment:*—bulwark.

2431. חֵילָם, **Chêylâm,** *khay-lawm´*; or חֵלְאָם, **Chê-l’âm,** *khay-lawm´*; from 2428; *fortress*; *Chelam*, a place East of Palestine:—Helam.

2432. חִילֵן, **Chîylên,** *khee-lane*; from 2428; *fortress*; *Chilen*, a place in Palestine:—Hilen.

2433. חִין, **chîyn**, *kheen*; another form for 2580; *beauty*:—comely.

2434. חַיִץ, **chayits**, *khah´-yits*; another form for 2351; a *wall*:—wall.

2435. חִיצׂון, **chîytsôwn**, *khee-tsone´*; from 2434; (properly) the (outer) *wall side*; hence *exterior*; (figurative) *secular* (as opposed to sacred):— outer, outward, utter, without.

2436. חֵיק, **chêyq**, *khake*; or חֵק, **chêq**, *khake*; and חׂוק, **chôwq**, *khoke*; from an unused root, apparently meaning to *inclose*; the *bosom* (literal or figurative):—bosom, bottom, lap, midst, within.

2437. חִירָה, **Chîyrâh**, *khee-raw´*; from 2357 in the sense of *splendor*; *Chirah*, an Adullamite:— Hirah.

2438. חִירָם, **Chîyrâm**, *khee-rawm´*; or חִירׂום, **Chîy-rôwm**, *khee-rome´*; another form of 2361; *Chiram* or *Chirom*, the name of two Tyrians:— Hiram, Huram.

2439. חִישׁ, **chîysh**, *kheesh*; another form for 2363; to *hurry*:—make haste.

2440. חִישׁ, **chîysh**, *kheesh*; from 2439; (properly) a *hurry*; hence (adverb) *quickly*:—soon.

2441. חֵךְ, **chêk**, *khake*; probably from 2596 in the sense of *tasting*; (properly) the *palate* or inside of the mouth; hence the *mouth* itself (as the organ of speech, taste and kissing):—(roof of the) mouth, taste.

2442. חָכָה, **châkâh**, *khaw-kaw´*; a primitive root [apparently akin to 2707 through the idea of *piercing*]; (properly) to *adhere* to; hence to *await*:—long, tarry, wait.

2443. חַכָּה, **chakkâh**, *khak-kaw´*; probably from 2442; a *hook* (as *adhering*):—angle, hook.

2444. חֲכִילָה, **Chăkîylâh**, *khak-ee-law´*; from the same as 2447; *dark*; *Chakilah*, a hill in Palestine:—Hachilah.

2445. חַכִּים, **chakkîym**, *khak-keem´*; (Chaldee); from a root corresponding to 2449; *wise*, i.e. a *Magian*:—wise.

2446. חֲכַלְיָה, **Chăkalyâh**, *khak-al-yaw´*; from the base of 2447 and 3050; *darkness of Jah*; *Chakaljah*, an Israelite:—Hachaliah.

2447. חַכְלִיל, **chaklîyl**, *khak-leel´*; by reduplication from an unused root apparently meaning to *be dark*; darkly *flashing* (only of the eyes); in a good sense, *brilliant* (as stimulated by wine):—red.

2448. חַכְלִלוּת, **chaklilûwth**, *khak-lee-looth´*; from 2447; *flash* (of the eyes); in a bad sense, *blearedness*:—redness.

2449. חָכַם, **châkam**, *khaw-kam´*; a primitive root, to *be wise* (in mind, word or act):— × exceeding, teach wisdom, be (make self, shew self) wise, deal (never so) wisely, make wiser.

A verb meaning to be wise, to act according to wisdom, to make wise decisions, to manifest wisdom. This word is used to convey the act of instructing which if received brings wisdom (Job 35:11; Ps 105:22); the wise activity that derives from such instruction (Pr 6:6; 8:33); the way of conduct contrary to that of the wicked (Pr 23:19); the wisdom manifested in the animal kingdom (Pr 30:24). In the reflexive sense, the verb implies the tangible manifestation of wisdom (Ecc 2:19); the exaggerated perception of one's own wisdom (Ecc 7:16); and the cunning activities of the deceiver (Ex 1:10). The psalmist declares that the Lord delights in dispensing wisdom to the simpleminded (Ps 19:7[8]).

2450. חָכָם, **châkâm**, *khaw-kawm´*; from 2449; *wise*, (i.e. intelligent, skilful or artful):—cunning (man), subtil, ([un-]), wise ([hearted], man).

An adjective meaning wise. This word is used to describe one who is skilled or experienced. It was used in the physical arena to describe those men who were skilled as builders (Ex 31:6; 36:1, 2); as craftsmen of all sorts (1Ch 22:15); as precious metal workers (2Ch 2:7[6]); those women who could spin fabrics (Ex 35:25). This word was used in the social arena to express those who were the leaders of the day (Jer 51:57); who could interpret dreams (Ge 41:8; Ex 7:11); who were able to rule (Dt 1:13, 15); who knew the law (Est 1:13); who were counselors (Est 6:13; Jer 18:18). In the personal arena, this word denoted skill in living, which was embodied in Solomon like no other before or since (1Ki 3:12). The wise person is the one who learns (Pr 1:5; 9:9; 13:1); who heeds a rebuke (Pr 9:8; 15:31); and who speaks properly (Pr 14:3; 15:2; 16:23). See the verb *châkam* (2449), meaning to be wise, and the noun *chokmâh* (2451), meaning wisdom.

2451. חָכְמָה, **chokmâh,** *khok-maw´*; from 2449; *wisdom* (in a good sense):—skilful, wisdom, wisely, wit.

A feminine noun meaning wisdom, skill, experience, shrewdness. This is one of the wisdom words that cluster in Proverbs, Ecclesiastes, Job, and other wisdom literature scattered throughout the OT. The high point of this word and its concept is reached in Pr 8:1, 11, 12. In Pr 8:22–31, wisdom is personified. It is God's gracious creation and is thus inherent in the created order. God alone knows where wisdom dwells and where it originates (Job 28:12, 20); no other living being possesses this knowledge about wisdom (see Job 28:21). For humans, the beginning of wisdom and the supreme wisdom is to properly fear and reverence God (Job 28:28; Pr 1:7; cf. Pr 8:13); God is the master, creator, and giver of wisdom (see Job 28:27; Pr 8:22, 23). He employed wisdom as His master craftsman to create all things (Ps 104:24; Jer 10:12). Rulers govern wisely by means of wisdom provided by God (1Ki 3:28; cf. Pr 8:15, 16). Wisdom keeps company with all the other virtues: prudence, knowledge, and discretion (Pr 8:12). The portrayal of wisdom in Pr 8:22–24 lies behind Paul's magnificent picture of Christ in Colossians 1:15, 16, for all the treasures of wisdom are lodged in Christ (cf. Col 2:3).

Wisdom, ordained and created by God, manifests itself in many ways in the created universe. It is expressed as a technical capability (Ex 28:3; 31:3, 6; 1Ki 7:14). It becomes evident in experience and prudence as evidenced in a wise woman (2Sa 20:22) who fears the Lord (see Pr 31:30) or in a wise king (1Ki 2:6). Wisdom in general, and worldly wisdom in particular, was universal to humankind created in the image of God; Babylonians, men of the East, Egyptians, and Edomites could obtain it or be found with it (Isa 47:10; Jer 49:7). Wrongly used, however, for self-adulation or self-aggrandizement, this wisdom could be deadly. For unbelievers, wisdom led to piety, holiness, and devotion to the Lord and His will. The psalmist asked God to give him a wise heart (Ps 90:12). God imparted wisdom to His people by His Spirit (Ex 31:3), but His Anointed One, the Messiah, the Branch, would have His Spirit rest

upon Him, the Spirit of wisdom (Isa 11:2), in abundance. Wisdom is also personified as a woman who seeks whoever will come and listen to her, thus receiving a blessing (Pr 1:20; 2:2; 3:13, 19). Wisdom ends its presentation in Pr 8 with the striking assertion that all who hate wisdom love death.

2452. חָכְמָה, **chokmâh,** *khok-maw´*; (Chaldee); corresponding to 2451; *wisdom:*—wisdom.

An Aramaic feminine noun meaning wisdom. This word is used only nine times in the OT and is equivalent to the Hebrew word *chokmâh* (2451), meaning wisdom. In these few instances, this word is used to speak of God's wisdom (Ezr 7:25; Da 2:20). It is God who gives this wisdom (Da 2:21, 23, 30) that was recognized by Belshazzar and the queen mother (Da 5:10, 11, 14).

2453. חַכְמוֹנִי, **Chakmôwnîy,** *khak-mo-nee´*; from 2449; *skilful; Chakmoni,* an Israelite:—Hachmoni, Hachmonite.

2454. חָכְמוֹת, **chokmôwth,** *khok-môth´*; or חַכְמוֹת, **chakmôwth,** *khak-môth´*; collateral forms of 2451; *wisdom:*—wisdom, every wise [woman].

A feminine noun meaning wisdom or that which is wise. Found exclusively in the wisdom literature of the OT, this word is a form of the Hebrew word *chokmâh* (2451). It denotes a wise woman (Pr 14:1); the feminine personification of wisdom (Pr 1:20; 9:1); and the wisdom that exceeds a fool's understanding (Pr 24:7); or wisdom that reveals deep understanding (Ps 49:3[4]).

2455. חֹל, **chôl,** *khole*; from 2490; (properly) *exposed*; hence *profane:*—common, profane (place), unholy.

A masculine noun meaning profane or common. This word comes from the verb *châlal* (2490), meaning to pollute or to profane and is always used in opposition to *qôdesh* (6944), meaning sacred or set apart. The priests were to make a distinction between the sacred and the common (Le 10:10). David discussed with the priest the difference between the common bread and the set–apart bread (1Sa 21:4[5], 5[6]). The priests would teach the difference between the sacred and the common (Eze 44:23)—a distinction the priests of Ezekiel's day failed to teach (Eze 22:26). The Temple, described by Ezekiel, had a wall separating the sacred and the common (Eze 42:20); there was to be a clear distinction between the land holy to the Lord and the common land (Eze 48:15).

2456. חָלָא, **châlâ'**, *khaw-law´*; a primitive root [compare 2470]; to *be sick*:—be diseased.

2457. חֶלְאָה, **chel'âh**, *khel-aw´*; from 2456; (properly) *disease*; hence *rust*:—scum.

2458. חֶלְאָה, **Chel'âh**, *khel-aw´*; the same as 2457; *Chelah*, an Israelitess:—Helah.

2459. חֶלֶב, **cheleb**, *kheh´-leb*; or חֵלֶב, **chêleb**, *khay´-leb*; from an unused root meaning to *be fat*; *fat*, whether literal or figurative.; hence the *richest* or *choice* part:— × best, fat (-ness), × finest, grease, marrow.

2460. חֵלֶב, **Chêleb**, *khay´-leb*; the same as 2459; *fatness*; *Cheleb*, an Israelite:—Heleb.

2461. חָלָב, **châlâb**, *khaw-lawb´*; from the same as 2459; *milk* (as the *richness* of kine):— + cheese, milk, sucking.

2462. חֶלְבָּה, **Chelbâh**, *khel-baw´*; feminine of 2459; *fertility*; *Chelbah*, a place in Palestine:—Helbah.

2463. חֶלְבּוֹן, **Chelbôwn**, *khel-bone´*; from 2459; *fruitful*; *Chelbon*, a place in Syria:—Helbon.

2464. חֶלְבְּנָה, **chelbinâh**, *khel-bin-aw´*; from 2459; *galbanum*, an odorous gum (as if *fatty*):—galbanum.

2465. חֶלֶד, **cheled**, *kheh´-led*; from an unused root apparently meaning to *glide* swiftly; *life* (as a *fleeting* portion of time); hence the *world* (as *transient*):—age, short time, world.

A masculine noun meaning age, duration of life, the world. The primary sense of the word is a duration or span of time. It signifies the world, that is, this present existence (Ps 17:14; 49:1[2]); life itself (Job 11:17); and the span of a person's life (Ps 39:5[6]).

2466. חֵלֶד, **Chêled**, *khay´-led*; the same as 2465; *Cheled*, an Israelite:—Heled.

2467. חֹלֶד, **chôled**, *kho´-led*; from the same as 2465; a *weasel* (from its *gliding* motion):—weasel.

2468. חֻלְדָּה, **Chuldâh**, *khool-daw´*; feminine of 2467; *Chuldah*, an Israelitess:—Huldah.

2469. חֶלְדַּי, **Chelday**, *khel-dah´-ee*; from 2466; *worldliness*; *Cheldai*, the name of two Israelites:—Heldai.

2470. חָלָה, **châlâh**, *khaw-law´*; a primitive root [compare 2342, 2470, 2490]; (properly) to *be rubbed* or *worn*; hence (figurative) to *be weak, sick, afflicted*; or (causative) to *grieve, make sick*; also to *stroke* (in flattering), *entreat*:—beseech, (be) diseased, (put to) grief, be grieved, (be) grievous; infirmity, intreat, lay to, put to pain, × pray, make prayer, be (fall, make) sick, sore, be sorry, make suit (× supplication), woman in travail, be (become) weak, be wounded.

2471. חַלָּה, **challâh**, *khal-law´*; from 2490; a *cake* (as usually *punctured*):—cake.

2472. חֲלוֹם, **chălôwm**, *khal-ome´*; or (shorter) חֲלֹם, **chălôm**, *khal-ome´*; from 2492; a *dream*:—dream (-er).

2473. חֹלוֹן, **Chôlôwn**, *kho-lone´*; or (shorter) חֹלֹן, **Chôlôn**, *kho-lone´*; probably from 2344; *sandy*; *Cholon*, the name of two places in Palestine:—Holon.

2474. חַלּוֹן, **challôwn**, *khal-lone´*; a *window* (as *perforated*):—window.

2475. חֲלוֹף, **chălôwph**, *khal-ofe´*; from 2498; (properly) *surviving*; (by implication and collective) *orphans*:— × destruction.

2476. חֲלוּשָׁה, **chălûwshâh**, *khal-oo-shaw´*; feminine passive participle of 2522; *defeat*:—being overcome.

2477. חֲלַח, **Chălach**, *khal-akh´*; probably of foreign origin; *Chalach*, a region of Assyria:—Halah.

2478. חַלְחוּל, **Chalchûwl**, *khal-khool´*; by reduplication from 2342; *contorted*; *Chalchul*, a place in Palestine:—Halhul.

2479. חַלְחָלָה, **chalchâlâh**, *khal-khaw-law´*; feminine from the same as 2478; *writhing* (in childbirth); (by implication) *terror*:—(great, much) pain.

2480. חָלַט, **châlaṭ**, *khaw-lat´*; a primitive root; to *snatch* at:—catch.

2481. חֲלִי, **chălîy,** *khal-ee´*; from 2470; a *trinket* (as *polished*):—jewel, ornament.

2482. חֲלִי, **Chălîy,** *khal-ee´*; the same as 2481; *Chali,* a place in Palestine:—Hali.

2483. חֳלִי, **chŏlîy,** *khol-ee´*; from 2470; *malady, anxiety, calamity*:—disease, grief, (is) sick (-ness).

2484. חֶלְיָה, **chelyâh,** *khel-yaw´*; feminine of 2481; a *trinket*:—jewel.

2485. חָלִיל, **châlîyl,** *khaw-leel´*; from 2490; a *flute* (as *perforated*):—pipe.

2486. חָלִילָה, **châlîylâh,** *khaw-lee´-law*; or חָלִלָה, **châlilâh,** *khaw-lee´-law*; a directive from 2490; (literal) *for a profaned* thing; used (interjectionally) *far be it!*:—be far, (× God) forbid.

2487. חֲלִיפָה, **chălîyphâh,** *khal-ee-faw´*; from 2498; *alternation*:—change, course.

2488. חֲלִיצָה, **chălîytsâh,** *khal-ee-tsaw´*; from 2503; *spoil*:—armour.

2489. חֵלְכָא, **chêlkâ’,** *khayl-kaw´*; or חֵלְכָה, **chêlkâh,** *khayl-kaw´*; apparently from an unused root probably meaning to *be dark* or (figurative) *unhappy*; a *wretch*, i.e. unfortunate:—poor.

2490. חָלַל, **châlal,** *khaw-lal´*; a primitive root [compare 2470]; (properly) to *bore*, i.e. (by implication) to *wound*, to *dissolve*; (figurative) to *profane* (a person, place or thing), to *break* (one's word), to *begin* (as if by an "opening wedge"); denominative (from 2485) to *play* (the flute):—begin (× men began), defile, × break, defile, × eat (as common things), × first, × gather the grape thereof, × take inheritance, pipe, player on instruments, pollute, (cast as) profane (self), prostitute, slay (slain), sorrow, stain, wound.

A verb meaning to pierce, to play the pipe, to profane. This word has three distinct meanings. The first meaning is to pierce or wound, either physically unto death (Isa 53:5; Eze 32:26) or figuratively unto despair (Ps 109:22). The second meaning of this word is to play the pipe, which is used only twice in the OT (1Ki 1:40; Ps 87:7). The third meaning is to profane or to defile, which is used primarily of the ceremonial objects of worship (Ex 20:25; Eze 44:7; Da 11:31); of the Sabbath (Ex 31:14; Ne 13:17; Eze

23:38); of God's name (Le 18:21; Jer 34:16); of God's priests (Le 21:4, 6). However, it also refers to sexual defilement (Ge 49:4; Le 21:9); the breaking of a covenant (Ps 89:31[32], 34[35]; Mal 2:10); and making a vineyard common (Dt 20:6; 28:30). In the causative form of this verb, it means to begin (Ge 4:26; 2Ch 3:2).

2491. חָלָל, **châlâl,** *khaw-lawl´*; from 2490; *pierced* (especially to death); (figurative) *polluted*:—kill, profane, slain (man), × slew, (deadly) wounded.

A masculine noun or adjective meaning slain, pierced, mortally wounded, profaned. This word denotes the carnage of battle; the dead, generally as a result of warfare (Ge 34:27; Jer 14:18; Eze 21:29[34]); and those having sustained some fatal injury (Jgs 9:40; 1Sa 17:52). Also, by extension, the word is used twice to indicate a state of defilement or perversion. In the first instance, it denotes a woman whose virginity has been violated or, as it were, pierced (Le 21:7, 14). The other applies to a wicked regent of Israel destined for punishment, emphasizing that he is already, in a prophetic sense, mortally wounded (Eze 21:25[30]).

2492. חָלַם, **châlam,** *khaw-lam´*; a primitive root; (properly) to *bind* firmly, i.e. (by implication) to *be* (causative to *make*) *plump*; also (through the figurative sense of *dumbness*) to *dream*:—(cause to) dream (-er), be in good liking, recover.

2493. חֵלֶם, **chêlem,** *khay´-lem*; (Chaldee); from a root corresponding to 2492; a *dream*:—dream.

2494. חֵלֶם, **Chêlem,** *khay´-lem*; from 2492; a *dream; Chelem,* an Israelite:—Helem. Compare 2469.

2495. חַלָּמוּת, **challâmûwth,** *khal-law-mooth´*; from 2492 (in the sense of *insipidity*); probably *purslain*:—egg.

2496. חַלָּמִישׁ, **challâmîysh,** *khal-law-meesh´*; probably from 2492 (in the sense of *hardness*); *flint*:—flint (-y), rock.

2497. חֵלֹן, **Chêlôn,** *khay-lone´*; from 2428; *strong; Chelon,* an Israelite:—Helon.

2498. חָלַף, **châlaph,** *khaw-laf´*; a primitive root; (properly) to *slide by*, i.e. (by implication) to *hasten* away, *pass* on, *spring* up, *pierce* or *change*:—abolish, alter, change, cut off, go on forward, grow up, be over, pass (away, on, through), renew, sprout, strike through.

2499. חֲלַף, **chălaph,** *khal-af´*; (Chaldee); corresponding to 2498; to *pass* on (of time):—pass.

2500. חֵלֶף, **chêleph,** *khay´-lef*; from 2498; (properly) *exchange*; hence (as preposition) *instead* of:— × for.

2501. חֵלֶף, **Chêleph,** *khay´-lef*; the same as 2500; *change; Cheleph,* a place in Palestine:— Heleph.

2502. חָלַץ, **châlats,** *khaw-lats´*; a primitive root; to *pull* off; hence (intensive) to *strip*, (reflexive) to *depart*; (by implication) to *deliver, equip* (for fight); *present, strengthen*:—arm (self), (go, ready) armed (× man, soldier), deliver, draw out, make fat, loose, (ready) prepared, put off, take away, withdraw self.

A verb meaning to draw out, to prepare, to deliver, to equip for war. The primary meaning of the word is that of strengthening or fortifying (Isa 58:11). It is used to convey the activity of drawing out, such as occurs in breast-feeding (La 4:3); removing a shoe (Dt 25:9, 10; Isa 20:2); dispatching to another location (Le 14:40, 43); withdrawing from a crowd (Hos 5:6); removing or delivering from danger (2Sa 22:20; Ps 6:4[5]; 50:15). Significantly, this word conveys the notion of taking up arms for battle (Nu 31:3; 32:17) or preparing for a general state of military readiness (Jos 4:13; 2Ch 17:18).

2503. חֶלֶץ, **Chelets,** *kheh´-lets*; or חָלֶץ, **Chêlets,** *khay´-lets*; from 2502; perhaps *strength; Chelets,* the name of two Israelites:—Helez.

2504. חֲלָצַיִם, **chălâtsayim,** *kha-law-tsa-yeem´*; from 2502 (in the sense of *strength*); only in the dual; the *loins* (as the seat of vigour):—loins, reins.

2505. חָלַק, **châlaq,** *khaw-lak´*; a primitive root; to *be smooth* (figurative); by implication (as smooth stones were used for *lots*) to *apportion* or *separate*:—deal, distribute, divide, flatter, give, (have, im-) part (-ner), take away a portion, receive, separate self, (be) smooth (-er).

2506. חֵלֶק, **chêleq,** *khay´-lek*; from 2505; (properly) *smoothness* (of the tongue); also an *allot-*

ment:—flattery, inheritance, part, × partake, portion.

2507. חֵלֶק, **Chêleq,** *khay´-lek*; the same as 2506; *portion; Chelek,* an Israelite:—Helek.

2508. חֲלָק, **chălâq,** *khal-awk´*; (Chaldee); from a root corresponding to 2505; a *part*:—portion.

2509. חָלָק, **châlâq,** *khaw-lawk´*; from 2505; *smooth* (especially of tongue):—flattering, smooth.

2510. חָלָק, **Châlâq,** *khaw-lawk´*; the same as 2509; *bare; Chalak,* a mountain of Idumæa:— Halak.

2511. חַלָּק, **challâq,** *khal-lawk´*; from 2505; *smooth*:—smooth.

2512. חַלֻּק, **challuq,** *khal-look´*; from 2505; *smooth*:—smooth.

2513. חֶלְקָה, **chelqâh,** *khel-kaw´*; feminine of 2506; (properly) *smoothness*; (figurative) *flattery*; also an *allotment*:—field, flattering (-ry), ground, parcel, part, piece of land ([ground]), plat, portion, slippery place, smooth (thing).

2514. חֲלַקָּה, **chălaqqâh,** *kal-ak-kaw´*; feminine from 2505; *flattery*:—flattery.

2515. חֲלֻקָּה, **chăluqqâh,** *khal-ook-kaw´*; feminine of 2512; a *distribution*:—division.

2516. חֶלְקִי, **Chelqây,** *khel-kaw-ee´*; patronymic from 2507; a *Chelkite* or descendant of Chelek:—Helkites.

2517. חֶלְקַי, **Chelqay,** *khel-kah´-ee*; from 2505; *apportioned; Chelkai,* an Israelite:—Helkai.

2518. חִלְקִיָּה, **Chilqîyyâh,** *khil-kee-yaw´*; or חִלְקִיָּהוּ, **Chilqîyyâhûw,** *khil-kee-yaw´-hoo*; from 2506 and 3050; *portion of Jah; Chilhijah,* the name of eight Israelites:—Hilkiah.

2519. חֲלַקְלַק, **chălaqlaq,** *khal-ak-lak´*; by reduplication from 2505; (properly) something *very smooth*; i.e. a *treacherous* spot; (figurative) *blandishment*:—flattery, slippery.

2520. חֶלְקַת, **Chelqath,** *khel-kath´*; a form of 2513; *smoothness; Chelkath,* a place in Palestine:—Helkath.

2521. חֶלְקַת הַצֻּרִים, **Chelqath hats-Tsurîym,** *khel-kath´ hats-tsoo-reem´*; from 2520 and the plural of 6697, with the article inserted; *smoothness of the rocks; Chelkath Hats-tsurim*, a place in Palestine:—Helkath-hazzurim.

2522. שָׁלַשׁ, **châlash**, *khaw-lash´*; a primitive root; to *prostrate*; (by implication) to *overthrow, decay*:—discomfit, waste away, weaken.

2523. שַׁלָּשׁ, **challâsh**, *khal-lawsh´*; from 2522; *frail*:—weak.

2524. חָם, **châm**, *khawm*; from the same as 2346; a *father-in-law* (as in *affinity*):—father in law.

2525. חָם, **châm**, *khawm*; from 2552; *hot*:—hot, warm.

2526. חָם, **Châm**, *khawm*; the same as 2525; *hot* (from the tropical habitat); *Cham*, a son of Noah; also (as a patronymic) his descendant or their country:—Ham.

2527. חֹם, **chôm**, *khome*; from 2552; *heat*:—heat, to be hot (warm).

2528. חֱמָא, **chĕmâ´**, *khem-aw´*; (Chaldee); or חֲמָה, **chămâh**, *kham-aw´*; (Chaldee); corresponding to 2534; *anger*:—fury.

2529. חֶמְאָה, **chem´âh**, *khem-aw´*; or (shortened) חֵמָה, **chêmâh**, *khay-maw´*; from the same root as 2346; curdled *milk* or *cheese*:—butter.

2530. חָמַד, **châmad**, *khaw-mad´*; a primitive root; to *delight* in:—beauty, greatly beloved, covet, delectable thing, (× great) delight, desire, goodly, lust, (be) pleasant (thing), precious (thing).

A verb meaning to take pleasure in, to desire, to lust, to covet, to be desirable, to desire passionately. The verb can mean to desire intensely even in its simple stem: the tenth commandment prohibits desiring to the point of coveting, such as a neighbour's house, wife, or other assets (Ex 20:17; cf. Ex 34:24). Israel was not to covet silver or gold (Dt 7:25; Jos 7:21) or the fields and lands of others (Mic 2:2). The word can also express slight variations in its basic meaning: the mountains of Bashan, including Mt. Hermon, looked in envy on the chosen mountains of Zion (Ps 68:16[17]); the simple fool delighted in his naïve, senseless way of life (Pr 1:22); and a man was not to lust after the beauty of an adulterous woman (Pr 6:25). The word expresses the idea of finding pleasure in something as when Israel took pleasure

in committing spiritual fornication among its sacred oaks (Isa 1:29). The passive participle of the simple stem indicates someone beloved or endearing (Isa 53:2) but has a negative meaning in Job 20:20, indicating excessive desiring or craving (cf. Ps 39:11[12]).

The passive stem indicates something that is worthy of being desired, desirable; the fruit of the tree of the knowledge of good and evil appeared inviting to make a person wise (Ge 2:9; 3:6; Pr 21:20) but proved to be destructive. The plural of this verbal stem expresses satisfaction or reward for keeping God's Law (Ps 19:10[11]).

2531. חֶמֶד, **chemed**, *kheh´-med*; from 2530; *delight*:—desirable, pleasant.

2532. חֶמְדָּה, **chemdâh**, *khem-daw´*; feminine of 2531; *delight*:—desire, goodly, pleasant, precious.

2533. חֶמְדָּן, **Chemdân**, *khem-dawn´*; from 2531; *pleasant*; *Chemdan*, an Idumæan:—Hemdan.

2534. חֵמָה, **chêmâh**, *khay-maw´*; or (Da 11:44) חֵמָא, **chêmâ´**, *khay-maw´*; from 3179; *heat*; (figurative) *anger, poison* (from its *fever*):—anger, bottles, hot displeasure, furious (-ly, -ry), heat, indignation, poison, rage, wrath (-ful). See 2529.

A noun meaning wrath, heat. The word is also synonymous with the feminine noun meaning heat or rage. Figuratively, it can signify anger, hot displeasure, indignation, poison, or rage. This noun describes the great fury that kings of the North executed in their utter destruction (Da 11:44); a person's burning anger (2Sa 11:20); and God's intense anger against Israel and those who practiced idolatry (2Ki 22:17).

2535. חַמָּה, **chammâh**, *kham-maw´*; from 2525; *heat*; (by implication) the *sun*:—heat, sun.

2536. חַמּוּאֵל, **Chammûw´êl**, *kham-moo-ale´*; from 2535 and 410; *anger of God; Chammuel*, an Israelite:—Hamuel.

2537. חֲמוּטַל, **Chămûwṭal**, *kham-oo-tal´*; or חֲמִיטַל, **Chămîyṭal**, *kham-ee-tal´*; from 2524 and 2919; *father-in-law of dew; Chamutal* or *Chamital*, an Israelitess:—Hamutal.

2538. חָמוּל, **Châmûwl,** *khaw-mool´*; from 2550; *pitied; Chamul,* an Israelite:—Hamul.

2539. חָמוּלִי, **Châmûwlîy,** *khaw-moo-lee´*; patronymic from 2538; a *Chamulite* (collective) or descendants of Chamul:—Hamulites.

2540. חַמּוֹן, **Chammôwn,** *kham-mone´*; from 2552; *warm spring; Chammon,* the name of two places in Palestine:—Hammon.

2541. חָמוֹץ, **châmôwts,** *khaw-motse´*; from 2556; (properly) *violent*; (by implication) a *robber*:—oppressed.

2542. חַמּוּק, **chammûwq,** *kham-mook´*; from 2559; a *wrapping,* i.e. *drawers*:—joints.

2543. חֲמוֹר, **chămôwr,** *kham-ore´*; or (shorter) חֲמֹר, **chămôr,** *kham-ore´*; from 2560; a male *ass* (from its dun *red*):—(he) ass.

2544. חֲמוֹר, **Chămôwr,** *kham-ore´*; the same as 2543; *ass; Chamor,* a Canaanite:—Hamor.

2545. חֲמוֹת, **chămôwth,** *kham-ōth´*; or (shorter) חֲמֹת, **chămôth,** *kham-ōth´*; feminine of 2524; a *mother-in-law*:—mother in law.

2546. חֹמֶט, **chômeṭ,** *kho´-met*; from an unused root probably meaning to *lie low*; a *lizard* (as *creeping*):—snail.

2547. חֻמְטָה, **Chumṭâh,** *khoom-taw´*; feminine of 2546; *low; Chumtah,* a place in Palestine:—Humtah.

2548. חָמִיץ, **châmîyts,** *khaw-meets´*; from 2556; *seasoned,* i.e. *salt* provender:—clean.

2549. חֲמִישׁ, **chămîyshîy,** *kham-ee-shee´*; or חֲמִשׁ, **chămishshîy,** *kham-ish-shee´*; ordinal from 2568; *fifth*; also a *fifth*:—fifth (part).

2550. חָמַל, **châmal,** *khaw-mal´*; a primitive root; to *commiserate*; (by implication) to *spare*:—have compassion, (have) pity, spare.

2551. חֶמְלָה, **chemlâh,** *khem-law´*; from 2550; *commiseration*:—merciful, pity.

A feminine noun meaning compassion, mercy. It describes the act of the angelic beings who led Lot and his family out of Sodom (Ge 19:16). It is also used in Isa 63:9 when retelling God's deeds of the past. In light of His angel saving the people in Egypt, the text refers to God showing mercy on them. Therefore, in its two uses, it denotes God's compassion which spares one from destruction or similar dismal fates.

2552. חָמַם, **châmam,** *khaw-mam´*; a primitive root; to *be hot* (literal or figurative):—enflame self, get (have) heat, be (wax) hot, (be, wax) warm (self, at).

2553. חַמָּן, **chammân,** *kham-mawn´*; from 2535; a *sun*-pillar:—idol, image.

A masculine noun meaning sun pillar. It also means idol or pillar in general. This is a pillar used in idolatrous worship of the solar deities, similar to the images Asa and Josiah tore down as part of their religious reforms (2Ch 14:5[4]; 34:4). Isaiah also condemned the worship of these images (Isa 17:8; 27:9).

2554. חָמַס, **châmas,** *khaw-mas´*; a primitive root; to *be violent*; (by implication) to *maltreat*:—make bare, shake off, violate, do violence, take away violently, wrong, imagine wrongfully.

A verb meaning to be violent, to act violently, to act wrongly. The term can be used to describe one who treats people badly. The prophet Jeremiah condemned the wrong treatment of widows and orphans (Jer 22:3). The word can also denote unethical behaviour in a construction that takes *tôwrâh* (8451) as an object (Eze 22:26; Zep 3:4) (lit., "do violence to the law"). God did violence to His dwelling when Jerusalem was sacked (La 2:6). Job thought his accusers treated him wrongly (Job 21:27).

2555. חָמָס, **châmâs,** *khaw-mawce´*; from 2554; *violence*; (by implication) *wrong*; (by metonymy) unjust *gain*:—cruel (-ty), damage, false, injustice, × oppressor, unrighteous, violence (against, done), violent (dealing), wrong.

A masculine noun meaning violence, wrong. It implies cruelty, damage, and injustice. Abraham's cohabiting with Hagar is described as a wrong done to Sarah (Ge 16:5). In relation to physical violence, cruelty is implied (Jgs 9:24). When coupled with the term instrument or weapon, it becomes an attributive noun describing weapons or instruments of violence (Ps 58:2[3]). When it describes a person, it can mean an oppressor or a violent man (Pr 3:31).

2556. חָמֵץ, **châmêts,** *khaw-mates´*; a primitive root; to *be pungent*; i.e. in taste (*sour,* i.e. [literal] *fermented,* or [figurative] *harsh*), in colour (*dazzling*):—cruel (man), dyed, be grieved, leavened.

A verb meaning to be sour, to be leavened. The verb occurs four times in the Hebrew Bible. In connection with the Exodus from Egypt, the Israelites were told not to leaven the bread before their departure (Ex 12:34, 39). In Hos 7:4, the prophet used the image of a baker kneading dough until it was leavened. This verb was also used metaphorically to refer to the heart being soured or embittered (Ps 73:21).

Another root, spelled exactly the same, is listed under this entry by Strong. It occurs in Isa 63:1 and means to be stained red.

2557. חָמֵץ, **châmêts,** *khaw-mates´*; from 2556; *ferment,* (figurative) *extortion*:—leaven, leavened (bread).

A masculine noun meaning leaven. The Hebrew word refers particularly to yeast that causes bread to rise. Bread was made without leaven when Israel went out of Egypt because there was not enough time to leaven it. Thus, unleavened bread is known as "the bread of affliction" and is eaten the week after Passover as a celebration of the Exodus (Dt 16:3). Leaven was later used in offerings (Le 7:13; 23:17) but was not allowed to be burned (Le 2:11). In Am 4:5, leaven is associated with hypocrisy and insincerity, an association made more explicitly in the NT (Lk 12:1; 1Co 5:6–8).

2558. חֹמֶץ, **chômets,** *kho´-mets*; from 2556; *vinegar*:—vinegar.

2559. חָמַק, **châmaq,** *khaw-mak´*; a primitive root; (properly) to *enwrap*; hence to *depart* (i.e. turn about):—go about, withdraw self.

2560. חָמַר, **châmar,** *khaw-mar´*; a primitive root; (properly) to *boil* up; hence to *ferment* (with scum); to *glow* (with redness); as denominative (from 2564) to *smear* with pitch:—daub, befoul, be red, trouble.

2561. חֶמֶר, **chemer,** *kheh´-mer*; from 2560; *wine* (as *fermenting*):— × pure, red wine.

2562. חֲמַר, **chămar,** *kham-ar´*; (Chaldee); corresponding to 2561; *wine*:—wine.

2563. חֹמֶר, **chômer,** *kho´-mer*; from 2560; (properly) a *bubbling* up, i.e. of water, a *wave*; of earth, *mire* or *clay* (cement); also a *heap*; hence

a *chomer* or dry measure:—clay, heap, homer, mire, motion.

2564. חֵמָר, **chêmâr,** *khay-mawr´*; from 2560; *bitumen* (as *rising* to the surface):—slime (-pit).

2565. חֲמֹרָה, **chămôrâh,** *kham-o-raw´*; from 2560 [compare 2563]; a *heap*:—heap.

2566. חַמְרָן, **Chamrân,** *kham-rawn´*; from 2560; *red; Chamran,* an Idumæan:—Amran.

2567. חָמַשׁ, **châmash,** *khaw-mash´*; a denominative from 2568; to *tax a fifth*:—take up the fifth part.

2568. חָמֵשׁ, **châmêsh,** *khaw-maysh´*; masculine חֲמִשָּׁה, **chămish-shâh,** *kham-ish-shaw´*; a primitive numeral; *five*:—fif [-teen], fifth, five (× apiece).

2569. חֹמֶשׁ, **chômesh,** *kho´-mesh*; from 2567; a *fifth* tax:—fifth part.

2570. חֹמֶשׁ, **chômesh,** *kho´-mesh*; from an unused root probably meaning to *be stout*; the *abdomen* (as *obese*):—fifth [rib].

2571. חָמֻשׁ, **châmush,** *khaw-moosh´*; passive participle of the same as 2570; *staunch*, i.e. able-bodied *soldiers*:—armed (men), harnessed.

2572. חֲמִשִּׁים, **chămishshîym,** *kham-ish-sheem´*; multiple of 2568; *fifty*:—fifty.

2573. חֵמֶת, **chêmeth,** *khay´-meth*; from the same as 2346; a skin *bottle* (as *tied* up):—bottle.

2574. חֲמָת, **Chămâth,** *kham-awth´*; from the same as 2346; *walled; Chamath,* a place in Syria:—Hamath, Hemath.

2575. חַמַּת, **Chammath,** *kham-math´*; a variation for the first part of 2576; *hot* springs; *Chammath,* a place in Palestine:—Hammath.

2576. חַמֹּת דֹּאר, **Chammôth Dô'r,** *kham-moth´ dore*; from the plural of 2535 and 1756; *hot* springs *of Dor; Chammath-Dor,* a place in Palestine:—Hamath-Dor.

2577. חֲמָתִי, **Chămâthîy,** *kham-aw-thee´*; patrial from 2574; a *Chamathite* or native of Chamath:—Hamathite.

2578. חֲמָת צוֹבָה, **Chămath Tsôwbâh,** *kham-ath´ tso-baw´*; from 2574 and 6678; *Chamath of Tsobah; Chamath-Tsobah*; probably the same as 2574:—Hamath-Zobah.

2579. חֲמַת רַבָּה, **Chămath Rabbâh,** *kham-ath´ rab-baw´*; from 2574 and 7237; *Chamath of Rabbah; Chamath-Rabbah,* probably the same as 2574.

2580. חֵן, **chên,** *khane*; from 2603; *graciousness,* i.e. subjectively (*kindness, favour*) or objective (*beauty*):—favour, grace (-ious), pleasant, precious, [well-] favoured.

A masculine noun meaning favour, grace, acceptance. Ge 6:8 stands as the fundamental application of this word, meaning an unmerited favour or regard in God's sight. Beyond this, however, the word conveys a sense of acceptance or preference in a more general manner as well, such as the enticement of a woman (Pr 31:30; Na 3:4); elegant speech (Ecc 10:12); and some special standing or privilege with God or people (Nu 32:5; Est 5:2; Zec 12:10).

2581. חֵן, **Chên,** *khane*; the same as 2580; *grace; Chen,* a figurative name for an Israelite:—Hen.

2582. חֵנָדָד, **Chênâdâd,** *khay-naw-dawd´*; probably from 2580 and 1908; *favour of Hadad; Chenadad,* an Israelite:—Henadad.

2583. חָנָה, **chânâh,** *khaw-naw´*; a primitive root [compare 2603]; (properly) to *incline*; (by implication) to *decline* (of the slanting rays of evening); (specifically) to *pitch* a tent; (generally) to *encamp* (for abode or siege):—abide (in tents), camp, dwell, encamp, grow to an end, lie, pitch (tent), rest in tent.

2584. חַנָּה, **Channâh,** *khan-naw´*; from 2603; *favoured; Channah,* an Israelitess:—Hannah.

2585. חֲנוֹךְ, **Chănôwk,** *khan-oke´*; from 2596; *initiated; Chanok,* an antediluvian patriarch:—Enoch.

2586. חָנוּן, **Chânûwn,** *khaw-noon´*; from 2603; *favoured; Chanun,* the name of an Ammonite and of two Israelites:—Hanun.

2587. חַנּוּן, **channûwn,** *khan-noon´*; from 2603; *gracious:*—gracious.

An adjective meaning gracious, merciful. This word is used solely as a descriptive term of God. The Lord used this word when He revealed Himself to Moses (Ex 34:6), as One who is, above all else, merciful and abounding in compassion (Ps 86:15; 103:8). Elsewhere, it expresses the Lord's response to the cry of the oppressed (Ex 22:27[26]); His treatment of those that reverence Him (Ps 111:4; 112:4); His attitude toward those who repent (Joel 2:13); His mercy in the face of rebellion (Ne 9:17, 31; Jnh 4:2); and His leniency toward His people in the midst of judgment (2Ch 30:9).

2588. חָנוּת, **chânûwth,** *khaw-nooth´*; from 2583; (properly) a *vault* or *cell* (with an arch); (by implication) a *prison:*—cabin.

2589. חֲנוֹת, **channôwth,** *khan-nōth´*; from 2603 (in the sense of *prayer*); *supplication:*—be gracious, intreated.

2590. חָנַט, **chânaṭ,** *khaw-nat´*; a primitive root; to *spice*; (by implication) to *embalm*; also to *ripen:*—embalm, put forth.

2591. חִנְטָא, **chinṭâ',** *khint-taw´*; (Chaldee); corresponding to 2406; *wheat:*—wheat.

2592. חַנִּיאֵל, **Channîy'êl,** *khan-nee-ale´*; from 2603 and 410; *favour of God; Channiel,* the name of two Israelites:—Hanniel.

2593. חָנִיךְ, **chânîyk,** *kaw-neek´*; from 2596; *initiated*; i.e. *practised:*—trained.

2594. חֲנִינָה, **chănîynâh,** *khan-ee-naw´*; from 2603; *graciousness:*—favour.

2595. חֲנִית, **chănîyth,** *khan-eeth´*; from 2583; a *lance* (for *thrusting,* like *pitching* a tent):—javelin, spear.

2596. חָנַךְ, **chânak,** *khaw-nak´*; a primitive root; (properly) to *narrow* [compare 2614]; (figurative) to *initiate* or *discipline:*—dedicate, train up.

A verb meaning to train, to dedicate. It is used once for training a child (Pr 22:6). Its other use is related to the dedication of a house or temple (Dt 20:5; 1Ki 8:63; 2Ch 7:5).

2597. חֲנֻכָּא, **chănukkâ',** *khan-ook-kaw´*; (Chaldee); corresponding to 2598; *consecration:*—dedication.

An Aramaic feminine noun meaning dedication, consecration. The word is used in relation to the dedication of Nebuchadnezzar's image (Da 3:2); and the dedication of the new Temple of God (Ezr 6:16, 17).

2598. חֲנֻכָּה, **chănukkâh,** *khan-ook-kaw´*; from 2596; *initiation,* i.e. *consecration:*—dedicating (-tion).

A feminine noun meaning dedication, ceremony. It was used to show that something was officially in service. The word describes the dedication of the wall of Jerusalem after it was rebuilt under Nehemiah (Ne 12:27). It also refers to the dedication of David's house (Ps 30:title[1]; cf. Dt 20:5). The word refers to an altar dedication in 2Ch 7:9 and also in Nu 7 where it appears to refer particularly to the offerings offered on the altar (Nu 7:10, 11, 84, 88). The word is best known in reference to the altar rededication described in the apocryphal books of Maccabees, which has since been celebrated as the Jewish festival, Hanukkah.

2599. חֲנֹכִי, **Chănôkîy**, *khan-o-kee´*; patronymic from 2585; a *Chanokite* (collective) or descendants of Chanok:—Hanochites.

2600. חִנָּם, **chinnâm**, *khin-nawm´*; from 2580; *gratis*, i.e. devoid of cost, reason or advantage:—without a cause (cost, wages), causeless, to cost nothing, free (-ly), innocent, for nothing (nought), in vain.

An adverb meaning freely, undeservedly, without cause, for no purpose, in vain. The primary meaning of this Hebrew word is related to the English word *gratis*. It appears in connection with goods exchanged without monetary charge (2Sa 24:24); services rendered without pay (Jer 22:13); innocence, as having no offence (1Ki 2:31); food without restriction or limit (Nu 11:5); faith without rational justification (Job 1:9); hostility without provocation (Ps 69:4[5]); religious activities done in vain (Mal 1:10).

2601. חֲנַמְאֵל, **Chănam'êl**, *khan-am-ale´*; probably by orthographical variation for 2606; *Chanamel*, an Israelite:— Hanameel.

2602. חֲנָמָל, **chănâmâl**, *khan-aw-mawl´*; of uncertain derivation; perhaps the *aphis* or plant-louse:—frost.

2603. חָנַן, **chânan**, *khaw-nan´*; a primitive root [compare 2583]; (properly) to *bend* or stoop in kindness to an inferior; to *favour, bestow*; (causative) to *implore* (i.e. move to favour by petition):—beseech, × fair, (be, find, shew) favour (-able), be (deal, give, grant) gracious (-ly), intreat, (be) merciful, have (shew) mercy (on, upon), have pity upon, pray, make supplication, × very.

A verb meaning to be gracious toward, to favour, to have mercy on. In the wisdom literature, this verb is used primarily with human relations to denote gracious acts toward someone in need (Job 19:21; Pr 19:17). Though the wicked may pretend to act graciously, they do not do so; neither should it be done so toward them (Ps 37:21; Pr 21:10; 26:25; Isa 26:10). Outside of the wisdom literature, the agent of graciousness is most frequently God, including the often repeated cry, "Have mercy on me!" (Ex 33:19; Nu 6:25; Ps 26:11; 27:7; 119:58). A mixture of divine and human agencies occurs when God, in judgment, sends nations that will show no mercy to punish other nations through warfare (Dt 7:2; 28:50; Isa 27:11).

2604. חֲנַן, **chănan**, *khan-an´*; (Chaldee); corresponding to 2603; to *favour* or (causative) to *entreat*:—shew mercy, make supplication.

An Aramaic verb meaning to show mercy, to ask for mercy. It corresponds to the Hebrew word *chânan* (2603). It refers to showing mercy to the poor, an action that would help Nebuchadnezzar break away from his iniquities (Da 4:27[24]). Daniel was discovered asking God for mercy even though it was against the new law of the Medes and Persians to do so (Da 6:11[12]). Here the word occurs alongside *be'â'* (1156), meaning to request.

2605. חָנָן, **Chânân**, *khaw-nawn´*; from 2603; *favour; Chanan*, the name of seven Israelites:—Canan.

2606. חֲנַנְאֵל, **Chănan'êl**, *khan-an-ale´*; from 2603 and 410; *God has favoured; Chananel*, probably an Israelite, from whom a tower of Jerusalem was named:—Hananeel.

2607. חֲנָנִי, **Chănânîy**, *khan-aw-nee´*; from 2603; *gracious; Chanani*, the name of six Israelites:—Hanani.

2608. חֲנַנְיָה, **Chănanyâh**, *khan-an-yaw´*; or חֲנַנְיָהוּ, **Chănanyâ-hûw**, *khan-an-yaw´-hoo*; from 2603 and 3050; *Jah has favoured; Chananjah*, the name of thirteen Israelites:—Hananiah.

2609. חָנֵס, **Chânês**, *khaw-nace´*; of Egyptian derivation; *Chanes*, a place in Egypt:—Hanes.

2610. חָנֵף, **chânêph**, *khaw-nafe´*; a primitive root; to *soil*, especially in a moral sense:—corrupt, defile, × greatly, pollute, profane.

A verb meaning to be defiled, to be profane, to pollute, to corrupt. This word most often appears in association with the defilement of the land, suggesting a tainting not by active commission but by passive contact with those committing sin. It denotes the pollution of the land through the shedding of blood (Nu 35:33); through divorce (Jer 3:1); and through breaking God's covenant (Isa 24:5). The prophets also used the term to define Zion's defilement by the Babylonians (Mic 4:11) and Israel by idolatry (Jer 3:9). Two notable exceptions to this linkage with the land further intensify the notion that the primary meaning is one of passive contamination. In Jeremiah, the Lord declared that the prophets and the priests were corrupted, seemingly by their association with the people's sin (Jer 23:11). Likewise, Daniel uses the word in reference to the corruption that comes from association with a deceiver (Da 11:32).

2611. חָנֵף, **chânêph,** *khaw-nafe´*; from 2610; *soiled* (i.e. with sin), *impious:*—hypocrite (-ical).

An adjective meaning profane, filthy, impious, godless. It is used as a substantive to refer to a person with such qualities. The root idea is to incline away (from God). The word refers to a person whom moral uncleanness separates him or her from God (Job 13:16). It commonly describes someone without hope after this life (Job 8:13; 20:5; 27:8), who can only expect anger from God (Job 36:13; Isa 33:14). Such people come into conflict with the righteous (Job 17:8; Pr 11:9) and are known by their cruelty to others (Ps 35:16; Pr 11:9).

2612. חֹנֶף, **chôneph,** *kho´-nef*; from 2610; moral *filth*, i.e. *wickedness:*—hypocrisy.

A masculine noun meaning hypocrisy, profaneness. This word is found only once in the Hebrew Bible. Isa 32:6 uses the word in reference to the ungodly practices of vile or foolish persons. Such individuals have little nobility as their hearts are inclined to ruthlessness and their mouths speak nonsense and error.

2613. חֲנֻפָּה, **chănuppâh,** *kha-noop-paw´*; feminine from 2610; *impiety:*—profaneness.

A feminine noun meaning filthiness, profaneness, godlessness. The word occurs only in Jer 23:15 where it describes the wickedness, including Baal worship, promoted by false prophets. The prophets' profaneness included substituting their own words for God's words. This led the people to hope for peace when they should have expected God's wrath.

2614. חָנַק, **chânaq,** *khaw-nak´*; a primitive root [compare 2596]; to *be narrow*; (by implication) to *throttle*, or (reflexive) to *choke* oneself to death (by a rope):—hang self, strangle.

2615. חֲנָתֹן, **Channâthôn,** *khan-naw-thone´*; probably from 2603; *favoured*; *Channathon*, a place in Palestine:—Hannathon.

2616. חָסַד, **châsad,** *khaw-sad´*; a primitive root; (properly) perhaps to *bow* (the neck only [compare 2603] in courtesy to an equal), i.e. to *be kind*; also (by euphemism [compare 1288], but rarely) to *reprove*:—shew self merciful, put to shame.

A verb which occurs twice in the Hebrew Bible with very different meanings. It is used reflexively as David sang to the Lord, meaning to show oneself as loyal or faithful to a covenant (2Sa 22:26; Ps 18:25[26]). This verb is related to the common noun *chesed* (2618). But in another context and in a different verbal stem, the same root carries the meaning to reproach or to bring shame upon (Pr 25:10).

2617. חֶסֶד, **chêsêd,** *kheh´-sed*; from 2616; *kindness*; by implication (toward God) *piety*; rarely (by opposition) *reproof*, or (subjective) *beauty:*—favour, good deed (-liness, -ness), kindly, (loving-) kindness, merciful (kindness), mercy, pity, reproach, wicked thing.

A masculine noun indicating kindness, lovingkindness, mercy, goodness, faithfulness, love, acts of kindness. This aspect of God is one of several important features of His character: truth; faithfulness; mercy; steadfastness; justice; righteousness; goodness. The classic text for understanding the significance of this word is Ps 136 where it is used twenty-six times to proclaim that God's kindness and love are eternal. The psalmist made it clear that God's kindness and faithfulness serves as the foundation for His actions and His character: it underlies His goodness (Ps 136:1); it supports His unchallenged position as God and Lord (Ps 136:2, 3); it is the basis for His great and wondrous acts in creation (Ps 136:4–9) and delivering and redeeming His people from Pharaoh and the Red Sea

(Ps 136:10–15); the reason for His guidance in the desert (Ps 136:16); His gift of the land to Israel and defeat of their enemies (Ps 136:17–22); His ancient as well as His continuing deliverance of His people (Ps 136:23–25); His rulership in heaven (Ps 136:26). The entire span of creation to God's redemption, preservation, and permanent establishment is touched upon in this psalm. It all happened, is happening, and will continue to happen because of the Lord's covenant faithfulness and kindness.

The other more specific uses of the term develop the ideas contained in Ps 136 in greater detail. Because of His kindness, He meets the needs of His creation by delivering them from enemies and despair (Ge 19:19; Ex 15:13; Ps 109:26; Jer 31:3); He preserves their lives and redeems them from sin (Ps 51:1[3]; 86:13). As Ps 136 demonstrates, God's kindness is abundant, exceedingly great, without end, and good (Ex 34:6; Nu 14:19; Ps 103:8; 109:21; Jer 33:11). The plural of the noun indicates the many acts of God on behalf of His people (Ge 32:10[11]; Isa 63:7). He is the covenant-keeping God who maintains kindness and mercy (Dt 7:9) to those who love Him.

People are to imitate God. They are to display kindness and faithfulness toward each other (1Sa 20:15; Ps 141:5; Pr 19:22), especially toward the poor, weak, and needy (Job 6:14; Pr 20:28). Israel was to show kindness and faithfulness toward the Lord but often failed. In its youth, Israel showed faithfulness to God, but its devotion lagged later (Jer 2:2). It was not constant (Hos 6:4), appearing and leaving as the morning mist even though God desired this from His people more than sacrifices (Hos 6:6; cf. 1Sa 15:22). He looked for pious people (Isa 57:1) who would perform deeds of piety, faithfulness, and kindness (2Ch 32:32; 35:26; Ne 13:14); the Lord desired people who would maintain covenant loyalty and responsibility so that He could build His righteous community.

2618. חֶסֶד, **Chesed,** *kheh´-sed*; the same as 2617; *favour*; *Chesed*, an Israelite:—Hesed.

2619. חֲסַדְיָה, **Chăsadyâh,** *khas-ad-yaw´*; from 2617 and 3050; *Jah has favoured*; *Chasadjah*, an Israelite:—Hasadiah.

2620. חָסָה, **châsâh,** *khaw-saw´*; a primitive root; to *flee* for protection [compare 982]; (figura-

tive) to *confide* in:—have hope, make refuge, (put) trust.

A verb meaning to seek, to take refuge. The word is used literally in reference to seeking a tree's shade (Jgs 9:15) and taking refuge in Zion (Isa 14:32). It is commonly used figuratively in relation to deities (Dt 32:37), particularly of Yahweh. He is a shield providing refuge (2Sa 22:31). Refuge is sought under His wings (Ru 2:12; Ps 36:7[8]; 57:1[2]; 61:4[5]; 91:4) and at the time of death (Pr 14:32).

2621. חֹסָה, **Chôsâh,** *kho-saw´*; from 2620; *hopeful*; *Chosah*, an Israelite; also a place in Palestine:—Hosah.

2622. חָסוּת, **châsûwth,** *khaw-sooth´*; from 2620; *confidence*:—trust.

A feminine noun meaning refuge, shelter, trust. It is not used frequently in the OT. Isaiah uses it to describe the false hope or trust that Israel put in Egypt (Isa 30:3). It comes from the Hebrew word *châsâh* (2620), meaning to take refuge.

2623. חָסִיד, **châsîyd,** *khaw-seed´*; from 2616; (properly) *kind*, i.e. (religiously) *pious* (a saint):—godly (man), good, holy (one), merciful, saint, [un-] godly.

An adjective meaning kind, benevolent, merciful, pious. The word carries the essential idea of the faithful kindness and piety that springs from mercy. It is used of the Lord twice: once to convey His holiness in the sense that His works are beyond reproach (Ps 145:17); and once to declare His tender mercy (Jer 3:12). Other occurrences of this word usually refer to those who reflect the character of God in their actions or personality. The word denotes those who share a personal relationship with the Lord (1Sa 2:9; Ps 4:3[4]; 97:10; 116:15); the state of one who fully trusts in God (Ps 86:2); and those who manifest the goodness or mercy of God in their conduct (2Sa 22:26; Ps 12:1, 2; Mic 7:2). More importantly, though, it signifies the nature of those who are specifically set apart by God to be the examples and mediators of His goodness and fidelity. Priests (Dt 33:8); prophets (Ps 89:19[20]); and the Messiah (Ps 16:10) all bear this "holy" mark and function.

2624. חֲסִידָה, **chăsîydâh,** *khas-ee-daw´*; feminine of 2623; the *kind* (maternal) bird, i.e. a *stork*:— × feather, stork.

2625. חָסִיל, **châsîyl,** *khaw-seel´*; from 2628; the *ravager*, i.e. a *locust*:—caterpillar.

2626. חָסִין, **chăsîyn,** *khas-een´*; from 2630; (properly) *firm*, i.e. (by implcation) *mighty*:— strong.

2627. חַסִּיר, **chassîyr,** *khas-seer´*; (Chaldee); from a root corresponding to 2637; *deficient*:— wanting.

2628. חָסַל, **châsal,** *khaw-sal´*; a primitive root; to *eat* off:—consume.

2629. חָסַם, **châsam,** *khaw-sam´*; a primitive root; to *muzzle*; (by analogy) to *stop* the nose:— muzzle, stop.

2630. חָסַן, **châsan,** *khaw-san´*; a primitive root; (properly) to (be) *compact*; (by implication) to *hoard*:—lay up.

2631. חֲסַן, **chăsan,** *khas-an´*; (Chaldee); corresponding to 2630; to *hold* in occupancy:— possess.

2632. חֶסֶן, **chĕsên,** *kheh´-sane*; (Chaldee); from 2631; *strength*:—power.

2633. חֹסֶן, **chôsen,** *kho´-sen*; from 2630; *wealth*:—riches, strength, treasure.

2634. חָסֹן, **châsôn,** *khaw-sone´*; from 2630; *powerful*:—strong.

2635. חֲסַף, **chăsaph,** *khas-af´*; (Chaldee); from a root corresponding to that of 2636; a *clod*:— clay.

2636. חַסְפַּס, **chaspas,** *khas-pas´*; reduplicated from an unused root meaning apparently to *peel*; a *shred* or *scale*:—round thing.

2637. חָסֵר, **châsêr,** *khaw-sare´*; a primitive root; to *lack*; (by implication) to *fail, want, lessen*:— be abated, bereave, decrease, (cause to) fail, (have) lack, make lower, want.

2638. חָסֵר, **châsêr,** *khaw-sare´*; from 2637; *lacking*; hence *without*:—destitute, fail, lack, have need, void, want.

2639. חֶסֶר, **cheser,** *kheh´-ser*; from 2637; *lack*; hence *destitution*:—poverty, want.

2640. חֹסֶר, **chôser,** *kho´-ser*; from 2637; *poverty*:—in want of.

2641. חַסְרָה, **Chasrâh,** *khas-raw´*; from 2637; *want*; *Chasrah*, an Israelite:—Hasrah.

2642. חֶסְרוֹן, **chesrôwn,** *khes-rone´*; from 2637; *deficiency*:—wanting.

2643. חַף, **chaph,** *khaf*; from 2653 (in the moral sense of *covered* from soil); *pure*:—innocent.

2644. חָפָא, **châphâ´,** *khaw-faw´*; an orthographical variation of 2645; (properly) to *cover*, i.e. (in a sinister sense) to *act covertly*:—do secretly.

2645. חָפָה, **châphâh,** *khaw-faw´*; a primitive root [compare 2644, 2653]; to *cover*; (by implication) to *veil*, to *incase, protect*:—ceil, cover, overlay.

2646. חֻפָּה, **chuppâh,** *khoop-paw´*; from 2645; a *canopy*:—chamber, closet, defence.

2647. חֻפָּה, **Chuppâh,** *khoop-paw´*; the same as 2646; *Chuppah*, an Israelite:—Huppah.

2648. חָפַז, **châphaz,** *khaw-faz´*; a primitive root; (properly) to *start* up suddenly, i.e. (by implication) to *hasten* away, to *fear*:—(make) haste (away), tremble.

2649. חִפָּזוֹן, **chippâzôwn,** *khip-paw-zone´*; from 2648; *hasty flight*:—haste.

2650. חֻפִּים, **Chuppîym,** *khoop-peem´*; plural of 2646 [compare 2349]; *Chuppim*, an Israelite:— Huppim.

2651. חֹפֶן, **chôphen,** *kho´-fen*; from an unused root of uncertain significance; a *fist* (only in the dual):—fists, (both) hands, hand [-ful].

2652. חָפְנִי, **Chophnîy,** *khof-nee´*; from 2651; perhaps *pugilist*; *Chophni*, an Israelite:— Hophni.

2653. חָפַף, **châphaph,** *khaw-faf´*; a primitive root [compare 2645, 3182]; to *cover* (in protection):—cover.

2654. חָפֵץ, **châphêts,** *khaw-fates´*; a primitive root; (properly) to *incline* to; (by implication, literal but rarely) to *bend*; (figurative) to be *pleased* with, *desire*:— × any at all, (have, take) delight, desire, favour, like, move, be (well) pleased, have pleasure, will, would.

A verb meaning to delight in, to have pleasure, to have favour, to be pleased. Shechem took delight in Dinah (Ge 34:19); King Ahasuerus also took delight in Esther (Est 2:14). This word describes Solomon's pleasure in building the Temple (1Ki 9:1). The Lord is described as taking pleasure in His people Israel (Isa 62:4). He is also pleased with those who practice justice and righteousness (Jer 9:24[23]).

2655. חָפֵץ, **châphêts,** *khaw-fates´*; from 2654; *pleased* with:—delight in, desire, favour, please, have pleasure, whosoever would, willing, wish.

An adjective meaning having delight in, having pleasure in. It modifies both humans and God. A good example is Ps 35:27, which refers to people who delighted in the psalmist's vindication and the Lord who delighted in His servant's well-being. Ps 5:4[5] notes that God does not take pleasure in wickedness. It can also mean simply to want or to desire, as in the men who wanted to be priests of the high places (1Ki 13:33). See the related verb *châphêts* (2654) and noun *chêphets* (2656).

2656. חֵפֶץ, **chêphets,** *khay´-fets*; from 2654; *pleasure*; hence (abstract) *desire*; (concrete) a *valuable* thing; hence (by extension) a *matter* (as something in mind):—acceptable, delight (-some), desire, things desired, matter, pleasant (-ure), purpose, willingly.

A masculine noun meaning delight, pleasure, desire, matter. The root idea is to incline toward something. The word signifies delight in or (in an unrealized sense) a desire for earthly goods, such as Solomon's desire for timber (1Ki 9:11); a delight in fruitful land (Mal 3:12); or the delight of hands in their labour (Pr 31:13). The word also refers to people's delight in God's Law (Ps 1:2); His works (Ps 111:2); God's own delight in His works (Isa 46:10; 48:14); His lack of delight in foolish or disrespectful people (Ecc 5:4[3]; Mal 1:10). Three times the word is used to liken a person or nation to an undesirable vessel (Jer 22:28; 48:38; Hos 8:8). In addition, the word is used in Ecclesiastes to refer to a matter without respect to its delightfulness (Ecc 3:1, 17).

2657. חֶפְצִי־בָהּ, **Chephtsîy-bâh,** *khef-tsee´ bah*; from 2656 with suffixes; *my delight* (is) *in her*; *Cheptsi-bah*, a fanciful name for Palestine:—Hephzi-bah.

2658. חָפַר, **châphar,** *khaw-far´*; a primitive root; (properly) to *pry* into; (by implication) to *delve*, to *explore*:—dig, paw, search out, seek.

2659. חָפֵר, **châphêr,** *khaw-fare´*; a primitive root [perhaps rather the same as 2658 through the idea of *detection*]; to *blush*; (figurative) to be *ashamed, disappointed*; (causative) to *shame, reproach*:—be ashamed, be confounded, be brought to confusion (unto shame), come (be put to) shame, bring reproach.

2660. חֵפֶר, **Chêpher,** *khay´-fer*; from 2658 or 2659; a *pit* or *shame*; *Chepher*, a place in Palestine; also the name of three Israelites:—Hepher.

2661. חֲפֹר, **chăphôr,** *khaf-ore´*; from 2658; a *hole*; only in connection with 6512, which ought rather to be joined as one word, thus חֲפַרְפָּרָה, **chăpharpârâh,** *khaf-ar-pay-raw´*; by reduplication from 2658; a *burrower*, i.e. probably a *rat*:— + mole.

2662. חֶפְרִי, **Chephrîy,** *khef-ree´*; patronymic from 2660; a *Chephrite* (collective) or descendants of *Chepher*:—Hepherites.

2663. חֲפָרַיִם, **Chăphârayim,** *khaf-aw-rah´-yim*; dual of 2660; *double pit*; *Chapharajim*, a place in Palestine:—Haphraim.

2664. חָפַשׂ, **châphaś,** *khaw-fas´*; a primitive root; to *seek*; (causative) to *conceal* oneself (i.e. let be sought), or *mask*:—change, (make) diligent (search), disguise self, hide, search (for, out).

2665. חֵפֶשׂ, **chêpheś,** *khay´-fes*; from 2664; something *covert*, i.e. a *trick*:—search.

2666. חָפַשׁ, **châphash,** *khaw-fash´*; a primitive root; to *spread* loose, (figurative) to *manumit*:—be free.

2667. חֹפֶשׁ, **Chôphesh,** *kho´-fesh*; from 2666; something *spread* loosely, i.e. a *carpet*:—precious.

2668. חֻפְשָׁה, **chuphshâh,** *khoof-shaw´*; from 2666; *liberty* (from slavery):—freedom.

2669. חָפְשׁוּת, **chophshûwth,** *khof-shooth´*; and חָפְשִׁית, **chophshîyth,** *khof-sheeth´*; from 2666; *prostration* by sickness (with 1004, a *hospital*):—several.

2670. חׇפְשִׁי, **chophshîy,** *khof-shee´*; from 2666; *exempt* (from bondage, tax or care):—free, liberty.

2671. חֵץ, **chêts,** *khayts*; from 2686; (properly) a *piercer*, i.e. an *arrow*; (by implication) a *wound*; (figurative, of God) thunder-*bolt*; (by interchange for 6086) the *shaft* of a spear:—+ archer, arrow, dart, shaft, staff, wound.

2672. חׇצַב, **châtsab,** *khaw-tsab´*; or חׇצֵב, **châtsêb,** *khaw-tsabe´*; a primitive root; to *cut* or carve (wood, stone or other material); (by implication) to *hew, split, square, quarry, engrave*:—cut, dig, divide, grave, hew (out, -er), make, mason.

2673. חׇצׇה, **châtsâh,** *khaw-tsaw´*; a primitive root [compare 2686]; to *cut* or *split* in two; to *halve*:—divide, × live out half, reach to the midst, part.

2674. חׇצוֹר, **Châtsôwr,** *khaw-tsore´*; a collective form of 2691; *village; Chatsor*, the name (thus simply) of two places in Palestine and of one in Arabia:—Hazor.

2675. חׇצוֹר חֲדַתׇּה, **Châtsôwr Chădattâh,** *khaw-tsore´ khad-at-taw´*; from 2674 and a Chaldaizing form of the feminine of 2319 [compare 2323]; *new Chatsor*, a place in Palestine:—Hazor, Hadattah [*as if two places*].

2676. חׇצוֹת, **chătsôwth,** *kha-tsoth´*; from 2673; the *middle* (of the night):—mid [-night].

2677. חֵצִי, **chătsîy,** *kha-tsee´*; from 2673; the *half* or *middle*:—half, middle, mid [-night], midst, part, two parts.

2678. חִצִּי, **chitstsîy,** *khits-tsee´*; or חֵצִי, **chêtsîy,** *khay-tsee´*; prolonged from 2671; an *arrow*:—arrow.

2679. חֲצִי הַמְּנֻחוֹת, **Chătsîy ham-Mᵉnuchôwth,** *khat-tsee´ ham-men-oo-khoth´*; from 2677 and the plural of 4496, with the article interposed; *midst of the resting-places; Chatsi-ham-Menuchoth*, an Israelite:—half of the Manahethites.

2680. חֲצִי הַמְּנַחְתִּי, **Chătsîy ham-Mᵉnachtîy,** *khat-see´ ham-men-akh-tee´*; patronymic from 2679; a *Chatsi-ham-Menachtite* or descendant of Chatsi-ham-Menuchoth:—half of the Manahethites.

2681. חׇצִיר, **châtsîyr,** *khaw-tseer´*; a collateral form of 2691; a *court* or *abode*:—court.

2682. חׇצִיר, **châtsîyr,** *khaw-tseer´*; perhaps originally the same as 2681, from the *greenness* of a court-yard; *grass*; also a *leek* (collective):—grass, hay, herb, leek.

2683. חֵצֶן, **chêtsen,** *khay´-tsen*; from an unused root meaning to hold *firmly*; the *bosom* (as *comprised* between the arms):—bosom.

2684. חֹצֶן, **chôtsen,** *kho´-tsen*; a collateral form of 2683, and meaning the same:—arm, lap.

2685. חֲצַף, **chătsaph,** *khats-af´*; (Chaldee); a primitive root; (properly) to *shear* or cut close; (figurative) to *be severe*:—hasty, be urgent.

2686. חׇצַץ, **châtsats,** *khaw-tsats´*; a primitive root [compare 2673]; (properly) to *chop* into, pierce or sever; hence to *curtail*, to *distribute* (into ranks); as denominative from 2671, to *shoot* an arrow:—archer, × bands, cut off in the midst.

2687. חׇצׇץ, **châtsâts,** *khaw-tsawts´*; from 2687; (properly) something *cutting*; hence *gravel* (as grit); also (like 2671) an *arrow*:—arrow, gravel (stone).

2688. חַצְצוֹן תׇּמׇר, **Chatstsôwn Tâmâr,** *khats-tsone´ taw-mawr´*; or חַצְצֹן תׇּמׇר, **Chatsătsôn Tâmâr,** *khats-ats-one´ taw-mawr´*; from 2686 and 8558; *division* [i.e. perhaps *row*] *of* (the) *palm-tree; Chatsetson-tamar*, a place in Palestine:—Hazezon-tamar.

2689. חֲצֹצְרׇה, **chătsôtsrâh,** *khats-ots-raw´*; by reduplication from 2690; a *trumpet* (from its *sundered* or quavering note):—trumpet (-er).

2690. חׇצְצַר, **chatstsar,** *khawts-tsar´*; a primitive root; (properly) to *surround* with a stockade, and thus *separate* from the open country; but used only in the reduplicated form חׇצֹצֵר, **châtsôtsêr,** *khast-o-tsare´*; or (2Ch 5:12) חׇצֹרֵר, **châtsôrêr,** *khats-o-rare´*; as deminished from 2689; to *trumpet*, i.e. blow on that instrument:—blow, sound, trumpeter.

2691. חׇצֵר, **châtsêr,** *khaw-tsare´*; (masculine and feminine); from 2690 in its original sense; a *yard* (as *inclosed* by a fence); also a *hamlet* (as similarly *surrounded* with walls):—court, tower, village.

2692. חֲצַר אַדָּר, **Chătsar ʾAddâr,** *khats-ar' ad-dawr';* from 2691 and 146; (the) *village of Addar; Chatsar-Addar,* a place in Palestine:—Hazar-addar.

2693. חֲצַר גַּדָּה, **Chătsar Gaddâh,** *khats-ar' gad-daw';* from 2691 and a feminine of 1408; (the) *village of* (female) *Fortune; Chatsar-Gaddah,* a place in Palestine:—Hazar-gaddah.

2694. חֲצַר הַתִּיכוֹן, **Chătsar hat-Tîykôwn,** *khats-ar' hat-tee-kone';* from 2691 and 8484 with the article interposed; *village of the middle; Chatsar-hat-Tikon,* a place in Palestine:—Hazar-hatticon.

2695. חֶצְרוֹ, **Chetsrôw,** *khets-ro';* by an orthographical variation for 2696; *inclosure; Chetsro,* an Israelite:—Hezro, Hezrai.

2696. חֶצְרוֹן, **Chetsrôwn,** *khets-rone';* from 2691; *court-yard; Chetsron,* the name of a place in Palestine; also of two Israelites:—Hezron.

2697. חֶצְרוֹנִי, **Chetsrôwnîy,** *khets-ro-nee';* patronymic from 2696; a *Chetsronite* or (collective) descendants of Chetsron:—Hezronites.

2698. חֲצֵרוֹת, **Chătsêrôwth,** *khats-ay-roth';* feminine plural of 2691; *yards; Chatseroth,* a place in Palestine:—Hazeroth.

2699. חֲצֵרִים, **Chătsêrîym,** *khats-ay-reem';* plural masculine of 2691; *yards; Chatserim,* a place in Palestine:—Hazerim.

2700. חֲצַרְמָוֶת, **Chătsarmâveth,** *khats-ar-maw'-veth;* from 2691 and 4194; *village of death; Chatsar-maveth,* a place in Arabia:—Hazar-maveth.

2701. חֲצַר סוּסָה, **Chătsar Sûwsâh,** *khats-ar' soo-saw';* from 2691 and 5484; *village of cavalry; Chatsar-Susah,* a place in Palestine:—Hazar-susah.

2702. חֲצַר סוּסִים, **Chătsar Sûwsîym,** *khats-ar' soo-seem';* from 2691 and the plural of 5483; *village of horses; Chatsar-Susim,* a place in Palestine:—Hazar-susim.

2703. חֲצַר עֵינוֹן, **Chătsar ʿÊynôwn,** *khats-ar' ay-nône';* from 2691 and a derivative of 5869; *village of springs; Chatsar-Enon,* a place in Palestine:—Hazar-enon.

2704. חֲצַר עֵינָן, **Chătsar ʿÊynân,** *khats-ar' ay-nawn';* from 2691 and the same as 5881; *village*

of springs; Chatsar-Enan, a place in Palestine:—Hazar-enan.

2705. חֲצַר שׁוּעָל, **Chătsar Shûwʿâl,** *khats-ar' shoo-awl';* from 2691 and 7776; *village of* (the) *fox; Chatsar-Shual,* a place in Palestine:—Hazar-shual.

2706. חֹק, **chôq,** *khoke;* from 2710; an *enactment;* hence an *appointment* (of time, space, quantity, labour or usage):—appointed, bound, commandment, convenient, custom, decree (-d), due, law, measure, × necessary, ordinance (-nary), portion, set time, statute, task.

A masculine noun meaning regulation, law, ordinance, decree, custom. Primarily, this word represents an expectation or mandate prescribed by decree or custom. It is used to speak of the general decrees of God (Jer 5:22; Am 2:4); the statutes of God given to Moses (Ex 15:26; Nu 30:16[17]; Mal 4:4[3:22]); the lawful share deserved by virtue of status (Ge 47:22; Le 10:13, 14); the declared boundaries or limits of something (Job 14:5; 26:10); the prevailing cultural norm (Jgs 11:39); the binding legislation made by a ruler (Ge 47:26); and that which must be observed by strict ritual (Ex 12:24).

2707. חָקָה, **châqâh,** *khaw-kaw';* a primitive root; to *carve;* (by implication) to *delineate;* also to *intrench:*—carved work, portrayed, set a print.

2708. חֻקָּה, **chuqqâh,** *khook-kaw';* feminine of 2706, and meaning substantially the same:—appointed, custom, manner, ordinance, site, statute.

A noun meaning a statute, an ordinance, anything prescribed. It serves as the feminine of *chôq.* Since its basic meaning is not specific, the word takes on different connotations in each context. Its most common meaning is decrees, statutes, or a synonym of these words. The decrees of the Lord could be oral or written; they made God's will known and gave divine directions to His people. Abraham kept them, evidently, before they were written down (Ge 26:5). Moses and his assistants were to teach the statutes of the Lord to Israel (Ex 18:20; Le 10:11) so that the Israelites could discern between the clean and the unclean. The decrees of the Lord, along with His laws, regulations, and commandments, covered all areas of life.

The Israelites were to follow His decrees so they would separate themselves from the practices of the pagan nations around them (Le 18:3, 4). Moses admonished the Israelites to keep God's decrees and statutes (Le 19:37; 20:22; 25:18). Blessing was the reward for keeping them (Le 26:3), but curses were promised for those who didn't obey them (Le 26:15, 43).

Throughout the passing of Israel's history, new decrees were added (Jos 24:25), and the people and leaders were judged with respect to their faithfulness in observing God's decrees, laws, statutes, and commandments. David was renowned for having observed them (2Sa 22:23). The Davidic covenant would be realized if later kings followed the Lord's decrees as David had (1Ki 6:12). However, most of the kings failed, including Solomon (1Ki 11:11; 2Ki 17:15, 34). Josiah renewed the covenant and exerted himself to follow the Lord's decrees (2Ki 23:3), but it was too late to save Judah from exile (see 2Ki 23:25–27).

The psalmist found great joy in the decrees, laws, commandments, precepts, ordinances, and instructions of the Lord; they were not burdensome (Ps 18:22[23]; 119:5). However, some leaders of Israel distorted God's decrees and established their own oppressive decrees on the people (see Isa 10:1).

God's issuance of a decree was effective and permanent: by His decree, He established the order of creation forever, the functions of the sun and the moon (Job 28:26; Jer 31:35). The prophets without fail condemned Israel and its leaders for not keeping the decrees of the Lord (Eze 11:12; 20:13; Am 2:4) but saw a future time when a redeemed people would follow them (Eze 36:27; 37:24).

2709. חֲקוּפָא, **Chăqûwphâ',** *khah-oo-faw';* from an unused root probably meaning to *bend; crooked; Chakupha,* one of the Nethinim:—Hakupha.

2710. חָקַק, **châqaq,** *khaw-kak';* a primitive root; (properly) to *hack,* i.e. *engrave* (Jgs 5:14, to *be a scribe* simply); (by implication) to *enact* (laws being *cut* in stone or metal tablets in primitive times) or (generally) *prescribe:*—appoint, decree, governor, grave, lawgiver, note, portray, print, set.

A verb meaning to cut, to inscribe, to engrave, to decree. The basic meaning, to cut, is used for

cutting a tomb out of rock (Isa 22:16), but it is used more commonly of engraving or writing (Isa 30:8; Eze 4:1; 23:14). It is employed for decreeing (i.e. inscribing) a law (Isa 10:1); and the word statute (*chôq*[2706]) is derived from it. Figuratively, God is said to have inscribed a boundary over the deep at creation (Pr 8:27). It also expresses the idea of a commander of decrees (Dt 33:21; Jgs 5:9).

2711. חֵקֶק, **chêqeq,** *khay'-kek;* from 2710; an *enactment,* a *resolution:*—decree, thought.

A masculine noun meaning something prescribed, a decree, a thought. This word is the construct of *chôwq* (2706) and is only found twice in the OT. When Deborah and Barak sang a song to commemorate the victory over the Canaanites, they sang of the "great thoughts of the heart" (KJV), referring to the thoughts and statues within a person (Jgs 5:15). In the other occurrence, Isaiah declared that the judgment of God was on those who enacted wicked statutes (Isa 10:1).

2712. חֻקֹּק, **Chuqqôq,** *khook-koke';* or (fully) חוּקֹק, **Chûwqôq,** *khoo-koke';* from 2710; *appointed; Chukkok* or *Chukok,* a place in Palestine:—Hukkok, Hukok.

2713. חָקַר, **châqar,** *khaw-kar';* a primitive root; (properly) to *penetrate;* hence to *examine* intimately:—find out, (make) search (out), seek (out), sound, try.

2714. חֵקֶר, **chêqer,** *khay'-ker;* from 2713; *examination, enumeration, deliberation:*—finding out, number, [un-] search (-able, -ed out, -ing).

2715. חֹר, **chôr,** *khore;* or (fully) חוֹר, **chôwr,** *khore;* from 2787; (properly) *white* or *pure* (from the *cleansing* or *shining* power of fire [compare 2751]); hence (figurative) *noble* (in rank):—noble.

A masculine noun meaning noble. It occurs only in the plural form and apparently comes from a root, unused in the OT, which means free. The nobles were a social order having power over the lower classes of people, a power which they sometimes misused, exacting usury (Ne 5:7), even following a royal order to kill innocent Naboth (1Ki 21:8, 11). In Nehemiah's time, they maintained strong family connections (Ne 6:17). Ecc 10:17 indicates that nobility was inherited and could not be instantly attained by election or force; otherwise, all kings would be nobility by definition. Thus, nobles made the best kings (Ecc 10:17), apparently because they came from a background of involvement in civic affairs and were not suddenly vaulted to such a high position.

2716. חֶרֶא, **chere᾿,** *kheh´-reh;* from an unused (and vulgar) root probably meaning to *evacuate* the bowels; *excrement:*—dung. Also חֲרִי, **chărîy,** *khar-ee´.*

2717. חָרַב, **chârab,** *khaw-rab´;* or חָרֵב, **chârêb,** *khaw-rabe´;* a primitive root; to *parch* (through drought), i.e. (by analogy) to *desolate, destroy, kill:*—decay, (be) desolate, destroy (-er), (be) dry (up), slay, × surely, (lay, lie, make) waste.

A verb meaning to be desolate, to be destroyed, to be dry, to dry up, to lay waste. Two related themes constitute the cardinal meaning of this word, devastation and drying up. Although each aspect is distinct from the other, both convey the notion of wasting away. The word is used to describe the drying of the earth after the flood (Ge 8:13); the drying of green vines (Jgs 16:7); the utter destruction of a physical structure (Eze 6:6); the devastation of war (Isa 37:18); the removal of human inhabitants (Eze 26:19); the slaughter of animals (Jer 50:27).

2718. חֲרַב, **chărab,** *khar-ab´;* (Chaldee); a root corresponding to 2717; to *demolish:*—destroy.

An Aramaic verb meaning to be utterly destroyed, to be laid waste. The only occurrence of this verb is preserved in a letter sent to Artaxerxes concerning the rebuilding of Jerusalem (Ezr 4:15). Certain antagonists of the Jewish people desired to hinder the rebuilding of the city and called to mind that it was due to wickedness that Jerusalem was destroyed by the Babylonians (cf. Jer 52:12–20). The result left the city in utter desolation and without defense (cf. Ne 2:17; Jer 9:11).

2719. חֶרֶב, **chereb,** *kheh´-reb;* from 2717; *drought;* also a *cutting* instrument (from its *destructive* effect), as a *knife, sword,* or other sharp implement:—axe, dagger, knife, mattock, sword, tool.

A feminine noun meaning a sword, a knife, a cutting tool. The word frequently pictures the sword, along with the bow and shield, as the standard fighting equipment of the times (Ge 48:22; Ps 76:3[4]; Hos 1:7). Warriors are referred to as those drawing the sword (Jgs 20; 1Ch 21:5). The sword may also stand for a larger unit of military power, sometimes pictured as coming on a people or land (Le 26:25; La 1:20; Eze 14:17). The cutting action of a sword is likened to eating, and its edges are literally referred to as mouths. Similarly, the mouths of people are likened to swords (Ps 59:7[8]; Pr 30:14; Isa 49:2). The sword is also a symbol of judgment executed by God (Ge 3:24; Dt 32:41; Jer 47:6); or His people (Ps 149:6). The word can refer to a knife (Jos 5:2, 3); or a tool for cutting stones (Ex 20:25).

2720. חָרֵב, **chârêb,** *khaw-rabe´;* from 2717; *parched* or *ruined:*—desolate, dry, waste.

An adjective meaning dry, desolate, wasted. Two connected ideas undergird the translation of this word. The first is the sense of dryness as opposed to wetness. In this line, it is used specifically of the grain offering (Le 7:10) or a morsel of food (Pr 17:1). The second is the sense of desolation. In this way, it is used to describe the wasted condition of Jerusalem after the Babylonian captivity (Ne 2:3); the emptiness of the land, which is comparable to the sparse population of the Garden of Eden (Eze 36:35); and the condition of the Temple in Haggai's day, as it still lay in ruins (Hag 1:4).

2721. חֹרֶב, **chôreb,** *kho´-reb;* a collateral form of 2719; *drought* or *desolation:*—desolation, drought, dry, heat, × utterly, waste.

2722. חֹרֵב, **Chôrêb,** *kho-rabe´;* from 2717; *desolate; Choreb,* a (generic) name for the Sinaitic mountains:—Horeb.

2723. חָרְבָּה, **chorbâh,** *khor-baw´;* feminine of 2721; (properly) *drought,* i.e. (by implication) a *desolation:*—decayed place, desolate (place, -tion), destruction, (laid) waste (place).

A feminine noun meaning ruin. The word almost always refers to an area ruined by the judgment of God. The destroyed area is usually a country or city but may also be individual property (Ps 109:10). Sometimes the ruins are referred to as being restored by God (Isa 51:3; 52:9; 58:12). The ruins of Job 3:14 may have been rebuilt by men; if so, the context makes clear that the rebuilding was unsuccessful. In

Mal 1:4, God would not allow Edom to rebuild his ruins successfully; similarly, Ps 9:6[7] seems to refer to an eternal state of ruin. Eze 26:20 and Isa 58:12 refer to ancient ruins, but it is difficult to identify them definitely. The ruins of the latter passage would be restored by those who seek God sincerely with fasting.

2724. חָרְבָה, **chârâbâh,** *khaw-raw-baw´*; feminine of 2720; a *desert*:—dry (ground, land).

A feminine noun meaning dry land, dry ground. The central principle of this word is the lack of moisture. It is used to refer to the habitable ground inundated by the flood (Ge 7:22); dry waterbeds (Eze 30:12); and land in general (Hag 2:6). Three times the word describes the condition of a path made in the miraculous parting of water: for Moses and Israel (Ex 14:21); for Joshua and Israel (Jos 3:17); and for Elijah and Elisha (2Ki 2:8).

2725. חָרָבוֹן, **chărâbôwn,** *khar-aw-bone´*; from 2717; parching *heat*:—drought.

2726. חַרְבוֹנָא, **Charbôwnâ’,** *khar-bo-naw´*; or חַרְבוֹנָה, **Charbôwnâh,** *khar-bo-naw´*; of Persian origin; *Charbona* or *Charbonah,* a eunuch of Xerxes:—Harbona, Harbonah.

2727. חָרַג, **chârag,** *khaw-rag´*; a primitive root; (properly) to *leap* suddenly, i.e. (by implication) to *be dismayed*:—be afraid.

A verb meaning to be afraid, to quake. The word occurs only in Ps 18:45[46] where foreigners came quaking from their strongholds. The idea of foreigners coming out derives from the word *min* (4480), meaning from. However, a similar passage in Mic 7:17 (using a different verb but dependent on *min* for the idea of coming out) justifies the translation "to come quaking." The passage thus pictures foreigners surrendering their strongholds to David and coming out.

2728. חַרְגֹּל, **chârgôl,** *khar-gole´*; from 2727; the *leaping* insect, i.e. a *locust*:—beetle.

2729. חָרַד, **chârad,** *khaw-rad´*; a primitive root; to *shudder* with terror; hence to *fear*; also to *hasten* (with anxiety):—be (make) afraid, be careful, discomfit, fray (away), quake, tremble.

A verb meaning to tremble, to quake, to be terrified. The term is used in reference to mountains (Ex 19:18); islands (Isa 41:5); birds

and beasts (Jer 7:33); and people (Eze 32:10). It can mark a disturbance, such as being startled from sleep (Ru 3:8); or terror brought on by a trumpet's sound (Am 3:6); or an act of God (1Sa 14:15). It is often connected with terrifying an enemy in battle. It is also used in the causative, meaning to terrify (Jgs 8:12; 2Sa 17:2; Zec 1:21[2:4]). See the word *chărâdâh* (2731).

2730. חָרֵד, **chârêd,** *khaw-rade´*; from 2729; *fearful*; also *reverential*:—afraid, trembling.

An adjective meaning trembling, reverential. God told Gideon to limit the number of warriors by telling those who were afraid or trembling to return to their camp at Gilead (Jgs 7:3). God honours and looks upon those who are contrite in spirit and tremble at His word (Isa 66:2). Those who tremble at God's words are also accounted as obedient (Ezr 9:4).

2731. חֲרָדָה, **chărâdâh,** *khar-aw-daw´*; feminine of 2730; *fear, anxiety*:—care, × exceedingly, fear, quaking, trembling.

A feminine noun meaning trembling, quaking, fear. This trembling is often brought on by acts of God. It is the terror of God that overcame the enemy (1Sa 14:15); and startled Daniel's friends in a vision (Da 10:7). Humans can also inspire fear (Pr 29:25). See the cognate verb *chârad* (2729).

2732. חֲרָדָה, **Chărâdâh,** *khar-aw-daw´*; the same as 2731; *Charadah,* a place in the Desert:—Haradah.

2733. חֲרֹדִי, **Chărôdîy,** *khar-o-dee´*; patrial from a derivative of 2729 [compare 5878]; a *Charodite,* or inhabitant of *Charod*:—Harodite.

2734. חָרָה, **chârâh,** *khaw-raw´*; a primitive root [compare 2787]; to *glow* or grow warm; figurative (usually) to *blaze* up, of anger, zeal, jealousy:—be angry, burn, be displeased, × earnestly, fret self, grieve, be (wax) hot, be incensed, kindle, × very, be wroth. See 8474.

A verb meaning to burn, to be kindled, to glow, to grow warm. Figuratively, it means to get angry or to become vexed. Anger can be between two people: Potiphar's anger was kindled against Joseph when his wife accused Joseph of rape (Ge 39:19). Anger can also be between God and a person: God's anger is against those who transgress His law (Jos

23:16). This word can also describe a future event of one becoming angry (Isa 41:11).

2735. חֹר הַגִּדְגָּד, **Chôr hag-Gidgâd,** *khore hag-ghid-gawd´*; from 2356 and a collateral (masculine) form of 1412, with the article interposed; *hole of the cleft; Chor-hag-Gidgad,* a place in the Desert:—Hor-hagidgad.

2736. חַרְהֲיָה, **Charhăyâh,** *khar-hah-yaw´*; from 2734 and 3050; *fearing Jah; Charhajah,* an Israelite:—Harhaiah.

2737. חָרוּז, **chârûwz,** *khaw-rooz´*; from an unused root meaning to *perforate;* (properly) *pierced,* i.e. a *bead* of pearl, gems or jewels (as strung):—chain.

2738. חָרוּל, **chârûwl,** *khaw-rool´*; or (shortened) חָרֻל, **chârul,** *khaw-rool´*; apparently passive participle of an unused root probably meaning to *be prickly;* (properly) *pointed,* i.e. a *bramble* or other thorny weed:—nettle.

2739. חֲרוּמַף, **chărûwmaph,** *khar-oo-maf´*; from passive participle of 2763 and 639; *snubnosed; Charumaph,* an Israelite:—Harumaph.

2740. חָרוֹן, **chârôwn,** *khaw-rone´*; or (shortened) חָרֹן, **chârôn,** *khaw-rone´*; from 2734; a *burning* of anger:—sore displeasure, fierce (-ness), fury, (fierce) wrath (-ful).

2741. חֲרוּפִי, **Chărûwphîy,** *khar-oo-fee´*; a patrial from (probably) a collateral form of 2756; a *Char-uphite* or inhabitant of Charuph (or Chariph):—Haruphite.

2742. חָרוּץ, **chârûwts,** *khaw-roots´*; or חָרֻץ, **châruts,** *khaw-roots´*; passive participle of 2782; (properly) *incised* or (active) *incisive;* hence (as noun masculine or feminine) a *trench* (as dug), *gold* (as mined), a *threshing-sledge* (having sharp teeth); (figurative) *determination;* also *eager:*—decision, diligent, (fine) gold, pointed things, sharp, threshing instrument, wall.

2743. חָרוּץ, **Chârûwts,** *khaw-roots´*; the same as 2742; *earnest; Charuts,* an Israelite:—Haruz.

2744. חַרְחוּר, **Charchûwr,** *khar-khoor´*; a fuller form of 2746; *inflammation; Charchur,* one of the Nethinim:—Harhur.

2745. חַרְחַס, **Charchas,** *khar-khas´*; from the same as 2775; perhaps *shining; Charchas,* an Israelite:—Harhas.

2746. חַרְחֻר, **charchur,** *khar-khoor´*; from 2787; *fever* (as *hot*):—extreme burning.

2747. חֶרֶט, **chereṭ,** *kheh´-ret*; from a primitive root meaning to *engrave;* a *chisel* or *graver;* also a *style* for writing:—graving tool, pen.

A masculine noun designating an engraving tool, a chisel. It is an instrument used by Aaron to "fashion" or "dress down" the golden calf (Ex 32:4). Its use implicated Aaron further into the guilt of the Israelites. The word is also used in Isa 8:1 as a writing utensil.

2748. חַרְטֹם, **charṭôm,** *khar-tome´*; from the same as 2747; a *horoscopist* (as *drawing* magical lines or circles):—magician.

A masculine noun meaning engraver, a writer associated with the occult. These people seem to have had knowledge of astrology or divination and were commonly associated with the magicians of Egypt in Pharaoh's court. Pharaoh could not find any magicians to interpret his dream, so he called Joseph (Ge 41:24). Moses caused plagues to come upon Egypt which the magicians could not reverse (Ex 9:11).

2749. חַרְטֹם, **charṭôm,** *khar-tome´*; (Chaldee); the same as 2748:—magician.

An Aramaic noun meaning magician. It occurs only in the book of Daniel (Da 2:10, 27; 4:7[4], 9[6]; 5:11). These people, who practiced sorcery and other occult practices, were advisors and counselors of kings.

2750. חֳרִי, **chŏrîy,** *khor-ee´*; from 2734; a *burning* (i.e. intense) anger:—fierce, × great, heat.

A masculine noun meaning burning. It is used to describe anger. The word occurs with *'aph* (639) which primarily means nose, but in this case, it means anger as derived from the snorting of an angry person. The anger may be righteous anger, such as God's anger at Israel's unfaithfulness (Dt 29:24[23]; La 2:3); Moses' anger aroused by Pharaoh's stubbornness (Ex 11:8); and Jonathan's anger at Saul's outburst against David (1Sa 20:34). It may also be unrighteous anger, such as the anger of troops dismissed with pay because of God's word (2Ch 25:10); and the anger of the kings of Israel and Syria against Judah (Isa 7:4). In all cases, the heat of the anger is evident whether expressed by leaving the room or by attempting to put to death the object of anger (2Ch 25:10; cf. v. 13).

2751. חֹרִי, **chôrîy,** *kho-ree´*; from the same as 2353; *white* bread:—white.

2752. חֹרִי, **Chôrîy,** *kho-ree´*; from 2356; *caved-weller* or troglodyte; a *Chorite* or aboriginal Idumæan:—Horims, Horites.

2753. חֹרִי, **Chôrîy,** *kho-ree´*; or חוֹרִי, **Chôwrîy,** *kho-ree´*; the same as 2752; *Chori*, the name of two men:—Hori.

2754. חָרִיט, **chârîyṭ,** *khaw-reet´*; or חָרִט, **chârit,** *khaw-reet´*; from the same as 2747; (properly) *cut* out (or *hollow*), i.e. (by implication) a *pocket*:—bag, crisping pin.

2755. חֲרִי־יוֹנִים, **chărêy-yôwnîym,** *khar-ay´-yo-neem´*; from the plural of 2716 and the plural of 3123; *excrements of doves* [or perhaps rather the plural of a single word חֲרָאיוֹן, **chărâ'yôwn,** *khar-aw-yone´*; of similar or uncertain derivation], probably a kind of vegetable:—doves' dung.

2756. חָרִיף, **Chârîyph,** *khaw-reef´*; from 2778; *autumnal*; *Chariph*, the name of two Israelites:—Hariph.

2757. חָרִיץ, **chârîyts,** *khaw-reets´*; or חָרִץ, **chârits,** *khaw-reets´*; from 2782; (properly) *incisure* or (passive) *incised* [compare 2742]; hence a *threshing-sledge* (with *sharp* teeth); also a *slice* (as cut):— + cheese, harrow.

2758. חָרִישׁ, **chârîysh,** *khaw-reesh´*; from 2790; *ploughing* or its season:—earing (time), ground.

2759. חֲרִישִׁי, **chărîyshîy,** *khar-ee-shee´*; from 2790 in the sense of *silence; quiet*, i.e. *sultry* (as noun feminine the sirocco or hot east wind):—vehement.

2760. חָרַךְ, **chârak,** *khaw-rak´*; a primitive root; to *braid* (i.e. to *entangle* or snare) or *catch* (game) in a net:—roast.

2761. חֲרַךְ, **chărak,** *khar-ak´*; (Chaldee); a root probably allied to the equivalent of 2787; to *scorch*:—singe.

2762. חֶרֶךְ, **chârâk,** *kheh´-rek*; from 2760; (properly) a *net*, i.e. (by analogy) *lattice*:—lattice.

2763. חָרַם, **châram,** *khaw-ram´*; a primitive root; to *seclude*; specifically (by a ban) to *devote* to religious uses (especially destruction); (phys-

ically and reflexively) to be *blunt* as to the nose:—make accursed, consecrate, (utterly) destroy, devote, forfeit, have a flat nose, utterly (slay, make away).

A verb meaning to destroy, to doom, to devote. This word is most commonly associated with the Israelites destroying the Canaanites upon their entry into the Promised Land (Dt 7:2; Jos 11:20). It indicates complete and utter destruction (Jgs 21:11; 1Sa 15:18); the severe judgment of God (Isa 11:15); the forfeiture of property (Ezr 10:8); being "accursed" or set apart for destruction (Jos 6:18). This latter application, being set apart, accounts for what appears to be a contradictory element in the verb. It is also used to mean devotion or consecration to the Lord (Le 27:28, 29; Mic 4:13). Just as something accursed is set apart for destruction, so something devoted to God is set apart for His use.

2764. חֵרֶם, **chêrem,** *khay´-rem*; or (Zec 14:11) חֶרֶם, **cherem,** *kheh´-rem*; from 2763; physically (as *shutting in*) a *net* (either literal or figurative); usually a *doomed* object; (abstract) *extermination*:—(ac-) curse (-d, -d thing), dedicated thing, things which should have been utterly destroyed, (appointed to) utter destruction, devoted (thing), net.

A masculine noun meaning devoted things, devoted to destruction, devotion, things under ban, cursed. The basic meaning of the word, to be set aside or devoted, is qualified in several ways. Things, including persons, were set aside or devoted to a special function or an area of service by a declaration of God or His servants. The entire city of Jericho was a deadly threat to the formation of God's people and fell under a ban, except for Rahab and her family (Jos 6:17, 18), and was set aside for destruction. A person could be set aside for destruction (1Ki 20:42) as well as an entire people, such as Edom (Isa 34:5). The Lord set the Israelites apart for destruction when they turned to other gods (Dt 13:17[18]; Isa 43:28); the Israelites could not take idols of the conquered pagans into their houses, even when acquired in battle. These items were set aside for destruction only (Dt 7:26). This term was the last word in the text of the Prophets (Mal 4:6[3:24]) and expressed a potential curse on the entire restored exilic community of Israel. Happily, the Lord also announced a time when the ban for destruction would be lifted from Jerusalem forever (Zec 14:11).

Various items could become holy, that is, devoted to cultic or holy use, as in the case of a field given to the Lord (Le 27:21); or the spoils of war could be set aside for religious use only (Nu 18:14; Jos 6:18; 1Sa 15:21), including gold, silver, items of bronze or iron, and animals. These items, set aside exclusively to holy use, could not be used for everyday purposes, for to use such items in this way was a grave sin. Achan and others died for this offence (Jos 7:1, 12, 15; 22:20).

2765. חָרֵם, **Chŏrêm,** *khor-ame´*; from 2763; *devoted; Chorem,* a place in Palestine:—Horem.

2766. חָרִם, **Chârim,** *khaw-reem´*; from 2763; *snub-nosed; Charim,* an Israelite:—Harim.

2767. חָרְמָה, **Chormâh,** *khor-maw´*; from 2763; *devoted; Chormah,* a place in Palestine:—Hormah.

2768. חֶרְמוֹן, **Chermôwn,** *kher-mone´*; from 2763; *abrupt; Chermon,* a mount of Palestine:—Hermon.

2769. חֶרְמוֹנִים, **Chermôwnîym,** *kher-mo-neem´*; plural of 2768; *Hermons,* i.e. its peaks:—the Hermonites.

2770. חֶרְמֵשׁ, **chermêsh,** *kher-mashe´*; from 2763; a *sickle* (as *cutting*):—sickle.

2771. חָרָן, **Chârân,** *khaw-rawn´*; from 2787; *parched; Charan,* the name of a man and also of a place:—Haran.

2772. חֹרֹנִי, **Chôrônîy,** *kho-ro-nee´*; patrial from 2773; a *Choronite* or inhabitant of Choronaim:—Horonite.

2773. חֹרֹנַיִם, **Chôrônayim,** *kho-ro-nah´-yim*; dual of a derivative from 2356; *double cave-town; Choro-najim,* a place in Moab:—Horonaim.

2774. חַרְנֶפֶר, **Charnepher,** *khar-neh´-fer*; of uncertain derivation; *Charnepher,* an Israelite:—Harnepher.

2775. חֶרֶס, **cheres,** *kheh´-res*; or (with a directive enclitic) חַרְסָה, **charsâh,** *khar´-saw*; from an unused root meaning to *scrape*; the *itch*; also [perhaps from the mediating idea of 2777] the *sun*:—itch, sun.

2776. חֶרֶס, **Cheres,** *kheh´-res*; the same as 2775; *shining; Cheres,* a mountain in Palestine:—Heres.

2777. חַרְסוּת, **charsûwth,** *khar-sooth´*; from 2775 (apparently in the sense of a red *tile* used for scraping); a *potsherd,* i.e. (by implication) a *pottery;* the name of a gate at Jerusalem:—east.

2778. חָרַף, **châraph,** *khaw-raf´*; a primitive root; to *pull* off, i.e. (by implication) to *expose* (as by *stripping*); specifically to *betroth* (as if a surrender); (figurative) to carp at, i.e. *defame;* (denominative [from 2779]) to spend the *winter:*—betroth, blaspheme, defy, jeopard, rail, reproach, upbraid.

2779. חֹרֶף, **chôreph,** *kho´-ref*; from 2778; (properly) the *crop* gathered, i.e. (by implication) the *autumn* (and winter) season; (figurative) *ripeness* of age:—cold, winter ([-house]), youth.

2780. חָרֵף, **Chârêph,** *khaw-rafe´*; from 2778; *reproachful; Chareph,* an Israelite:—Hareph.

2781. חֶרְפָּה, **cherpâh,** *kher-paw´*; from 2778; *contumely, disgrace,* the *pudenda:*—rebuke, reproach (-fully), shame.

A feminine noun meaning reproach, scorn, taunt. The term can be used for a taunt hurled at an enemy (1Sa 17:26; Ne 4:4 [3:36]) or for a state of shame that remains with an individual such as barrenness (Ge 30:23); uncircumcision (Ge 34:14); and widowhood (Isa 54:4).

2782. חָרַץ, **chârats,** *khaw-rats´*; a primitive root; (properly) to *point* sharply, i.e. (literal) to *wound;* (figurative) to *be alert,* to *decide:*—bestir self, decide, decree, determine, maim, move.

2783. חֲרַץ, **chărats,** *khar-ats´*; (Chaldee); from a root corresponding to 2782 in the sense of *vigour;* the *loin* (as the seat of strength):—loin.

2784. חַרְצֻבָּה, **chartsubbâh,** *khar-tsoob-baw´*; of uncertain derivation; a *fetter;* (figurative) a *pain:*—band.

2785. חַרְצָן, **chartsan,** *khar-tsan´*; from 2782; a *sour* grape (as *sharp* in taste):—kernel.

2786. חָרַק, **châraq,** *khaw-rak*; a primitive root; to *grate* the teeth:—gnash.

2787. חָרַר, **chârar,** *khaw-rar´*; a primitive root; to *glow,* i.e. literal (to *melt, burn, dry* up) or figurative (to *show* or *incite passion*):—be angry, burn, dry, kindle.

A verb meaning to be hot, to be scorched, to burn. Jerusalem is scorched under the figurative caldron that Ezekiel saw (Eze 24:11). It also describes the physical burning Job felt in his bones (Job 30:30). Figuratively, Jeremiah refers to Babylon as burning the bellows of Jerusalem (Jer 6:29). This word can also connote an angry person kindling strife (Pr 26:21).

2788. חָרֵר, **chârêr,** *khaw-rare´*; from 2787; *arid*:—parched place.

A noun meaning parched place, a scorched place. It occurs only in Jer 17:6 where it is plural and refers to places where lack of water keeps plants from prospering. This symbolizes the lives of those who trust in people rather than in God. In contrast, those who trust in God have enough water even in heat and drought (Jer 17:7, 8).

2789. חֶרֶשׂ, **chereś,** *kheh´-res*; a collateral form mediating between 2775 and 2791; a piece of *pottery*:—earth (-en), (pot-) sherd, + stone.

A masculine noun meaning earthenware, clay pottery, and potsherd. This word signifies any vessel made from clay (Le 15:12; Jer 19:1); the sharp fragments of broken pottery (Job 41:30[22]); and the larger potsherd useful to scoop burning coals from a fire (Isa 30:14); or to scrape boils (Job 2:8). Figuratively, David used the image of kiln-dried pottery to describe the depletion of his strength (Ps 22:15[16]).

2790. חָרַשׁ, **chârash,** *khaw-rash´*; a primitive root; to *scratch*, i.e. (by implication) to *engrave*, *plough*; hence (from the use of tools) to *fabricate* (of any material); (figurative) to *devise* (in a bad sense); hence (from the idea of secrecy) to be *silent*, to *let alone*; hence (by implication) to be *deaf* (as an accompaniment of dumbness):— × altogether, cease, conceal, be deaf, devise, ear, graven, imagine, leave off speaking, hold peace, plow (-er, -man), be quiet, rest, practise secretly, keep silence, be silent, speak not a word, be still, hold tongue, worker.

2791. חֶרֶשׁ, **cheresh,** *kheh´-resh*; from 2790; magical *craft*; also *silence*:—cunning, secretly.

2792. חֶרֶשׁ, **Cheresh,** *kheh´-resh*; the same as 2791; *Cheresh*, a Levite:—Heresh.

2793. חֹרֶשׁ, **chôresh,** *kho´-resh*; from 2790; a *forest* (perhaps as furnishing the material for fabric):—bough, forest, shroud, wood.

2794. חֹרֵשׁ, **chôrêsh,** *kho-rashe´*; active participle of 2790; a *fabricator* or mechanic:—artificer.

2795. חֵרֵשׁ, **chêrêsh,** *khay-rashe*; from 2790; *deaf* (whether literal or spiritual):—deaf.

2796. חָרָשׁ, **chârâsh,** *khaw-rawsh´*; from 2790; a *fabricator* of any material:—artificer, (+) carpenter, craftsman, engraver, maker, + mason, skilful, (+) smith, worker, workman, such as wrought.

A masculine noun meaning craftsman, artisan, and engraver. This Hebrew word denotes a craftsman who is skilled in a given medium. It appears in reference to one skilled in metalwork (1Ch 29:5; Hos 13:2); one skilled in woodwork (1Ch 14:1; Isa 40:20); and one skilled in stonework (Ex 28:11). More broadly, the term is applied to those who make their living by fashioning idols (Isa 45:16); or one highly skilled in his or her vocation (Eze 21:31[36]).

2797. חַרְשָׁא, **Charshâ’,** *khar-shaw´*; from 2792; *magician*; *Charsha*, one of the Nethinim:—Harsha.

2798. חֲרָשִׁים, **Chărâshîym,** *khar-aw-sheem´*; plural of 2796; *mechanics*, the name of a valley in Jerusalem:—Charashim, craftsmen.

2799. חֲרֹשֶׁת, **chărôsheth,** *khar-o´-sheth*; from 2790; mechanical *work*:—carving, cutting.

2800. חֲרֹשֶׁת, **Chărôsheth,** *khar-o´-sheth*; the same as 2799; *Charosheth*, a place in Palestine:—Harosheth.

2801. חָרַת, **chârath,** *khaw-rath´*; a primitive root; to *engrave*:—graven.

2802. חֶרֶת, **Chereth,** *kheh´-reth*; from 2801 [but equivalent to 2793]; *forest*; *Chereth*, a thicket in Palestine:—Hereth.

2803. חָשַׁב, **châshab,** *khaw-shab´*; a primitive root; (properly) to *plait* or interpenetrate, i.e. (literal) to *weave* or (generally) to *fabricate*; (figurative) to *plot* or contrive (usually in a malicious sense); hence (from the mental effort) to *think, regard, value, compute*:—(make) account (of), conceive, consider, count, cunning (man, work, workman), devise, esteem, find out, fore-cast, hold, imagine, impute, invent, be like, mean, purpose, reckon (-ing be made), regard, think.

A verb meaning to think, to devise, to reckon, to regard, to invent, to consider, to be accounted, to consider, to reckon oneself. When the subject of this verb is God, the verb means to consider, to devise, to plan, to reckon. Job cried out to God and asked why God considered him His enemy (Job 13:24; 33:10); however, Job was falsely accusing his Creator. Through the evil actions of Joseph's brothers, God had intended good for all of them (Ge 50:20; Ps 40:17[18]). Against a wicked people, the Lord planned destruction (Jer 18:11; Mic 2:3). God also "reckoned" Abraham's faith as righteousness (Ge 15:6).

When humans are the subjects of this verb, the word has similar meanings: the king of Assyria thought he would destroy many nations (Isa 10:7); people devised or planned evil (Ge 50:20; Ps 35:4; Eze 38:10); Shimei begged David not to reckon his behaviour as sin against him (2Sa 19:19[20]; Ps 32:2). In addition, the word is used to mean to regard or to invent: the Medes did not esteem gold or silver as the Persians did (Isa 13:17); and the Servant of Isaiah's passage was not highly esteemed by men (Isa 53:3). God endowed people with the ability to invent new things, such as artistic and practical devices (Ex 31:4; 35:32, 35; 2Ch 2:14[13]); and instruments for music (Am 6:5).

When the verb is passive, the word expresses being valuable or being considered. Silver was not considered valuable in Solomon's reign (1Ki 10:21). In the time of Israel's wandering, the Emites were reckoned to be Rephaites or Moabites (Dt 2:11, 20).

This verb can also mean to plot, to think upon, to think out something. A person could think out his or her course of life (Pr 16:9; Hos 7:15); the evil person in Da 11:24 plotted the overthrow of all resistance to him; the boat that Jonah shipped out in came to the point of destruction in the storm (Jnh 1:4, lit., "it was thinking to be destroyed").

2804. חֲשַׁב, **chăshab,** *khash-ab´*; (Chaldee); corresponding to 2803; to *regard:*—repute.

2805. חֵשֶׁב, **chêsheb,** *khay´-sheb*; from 2803; a *belt* or strap (as being interlaced):—curious girdle.

2806. חַשְׁבַּדָּנָה, **Chashbaddânâh,** *khash-bad-daw´-naw*; from 2803 and 1777; *considerate judge; Chas-baddanah,* an Israelite:—Hasbadana.

2807. חֲשֻׁבָה, **Chăshubâh,** *khash-oo-baw´*; from 2803; *estimation; Chashubah,* an Israelite:—Hashubah.

2808. חֶשְׁבּוֹן, **cheshbôwn,** *khesh-bone´*; from 2803; (properly) *contrivance;* (by implication) *intelligence:*—account, device, reason.

2809. חֶשְׁבּוֹן, **Cheshbôwn,** *khesh-bone´*; the same as 2808; *Cheshbon,* a place East of the Jordan:—Heshbon.

2810. חִשָּׁבוֹן, **chishshâbôwn,** *khish-shaw-bone´*; from 2803; a *contrivance,* i.e. actual (a warlike *machine*) or mental (a *machination*):—engine, invention.

2811. חֲשַׁבְיָה, **Chăshabyâh,** *khash-ab-yaw´*; or חֲשַׁבְיָהוּ, **Chăshab-yâhûw,** *khash-ab-yaw´-hoo;* from 2803 and 3050; *Jah has regarded; Chashabjah,* the name of nine Israelites:—Hashabiah.

2812. חֲשַׁבְנָה, **Chăshabnâh,** *khash-ab-naw´*; feminine of 2808; *inventiveness; Chashnah,* an Israelite:—Hashabnah.

2813. חֲשַׁבְנְיָה, **Chăshabnᵉyâh,** *khash-ab-neh-yaw´*; from 2808 and 3050; *thought of Jah; Chashabnejah,* the name of two Israelites:—Hashabniah.

2814. חָשָׁה, **châshâh,** *khaw-shaw´*; a primitive root; to *hush* or keep quiet:—hold peace, keep silence, be silent, (be) still.

2815. חַשּׁוּב, **Chashshûwb,** *khash-shoob´*; from 2803; *intelligent; Chashshub,* the name of two or three Israelites:—Hashub, Hasshub.

2816. חֲשׁוֹךְ, **chăshôwk,** *khash-oke´*; (Chaldee); from a root corresponding to 2821; the *dark:*—darkness.

2817. חֲשׂוּפָא, **Chăśûwphâ´,** *khas-oo-faw´*; or חֲשֻׂפָא, **Chăśuphâ´,** *khas-oo-faw´*; from 2834; *nakedness; Chasupha,* one of the Nethinim:—Hashupha, Hasupha.

2818. חֲשַׁח, **chăshach,** *khash-akh´*; (Chaldee); a collateral root to one corresponding to 2363 in the sense of *readiness*; to *be necessary* (from the idea of *convenience*) or (transitive) to *need*:— careful, have need of.

2819. חַשְׁחוּ, **chashchûw,** *khash-khoo´*; from a root corresponding to 2818; *necessity*:—be needful.

2820. חָשַׂךְ, **châśak,** *khaw-sak´*; a primitive root; to *restrain* or (reflexive) *refrain*; (by implication) to *refuse, spare, preserve*; also (by interch. with 2821) to *observe*:—assuage, × darken, forbear, hinder, hold back, keep (back), punish, refrain, reserve, spare, withhold.

2821. חָשַׁךְ, **châshak,** *khaw-shak´*; a primitive root; to *be dark* (as *withholding* light); (transitive) to *darken*:—be black, be (make) dark, darken, cause darkness, be dim, hide.

A verb meaning to be dark, to grow dim, to be black, to hide, to obscure. The primary meaning of the word is to darken. It is used to describe God's bringing about nightfall (Am 5:8); the deterioration of sight (La 5:17); the covering of the earth with insects so as to obscure the ground (Ex 10:15); the sullying of wisdom by foolishness (Job 38:2); the act of concealing from view (Ps 139:12). Poetically, the word denotes the change in one's countenance in response to abject fear or distress (Ecc 12:3).

2822. חֹשֶׁךְ, **chôshek,** *kho-shek´*; from 2821; the *dark*; hence (literal) *darkness*; (figurative) *misery, destruction, death, ignorance, sorrow, wickedness*:—dark (-ness), night, obscurity.

A masculine noun meaning darkness. As in English, the word has many symbolic uses. In its first occurrence, it is associated with disorder (Ge 1:2) and is distinguished and separated from light (Ge 1:4). In subsequent uses, whether used in a physical or a symbolic sense, it describes confusion and uncertainty (Job 12:25; 37:19); evil done in secret (Job 24:16; Pr 2:13; Eze 8:12); obscurity, vanity, things forgotten (Job 3:4; 10:21; Ecc 6:4); death (1Sa 2:9; Ps 88:12[13]). Although God created darkness (Isa 45:7) and uses it to judge His enemies (Ex 10:21, 22; figuratively, Ps 35:6), He enlightens the darkness of His people (Isa 9:2[1]); bringing them out of desperate situations (Ps 107:10, 14; Mic 7:8); observing secret

actions (Job 34:22; Ps 139:11, 12); and giving insight and freedom (Isa 29:18; 42:7).

2823. חָשֹׁךְ, **châshôk,** *khaw-shoke´*; from 2821; *dark* (figurative i.e. *obscure*):—mean.

2824. חֶשְׁכָה, **cheshkâh,** *khesh-kaw´*; from 2821; *darkness*:—dark.

A feminine noun meaning dark or obscure. This Hebrew word is the construct form of the word *chăshêkâh* (2825). The psalmist alone uses this word in reference to the "dark waters" surrounding the Lord's pavilion (Ps 18:11[12]). The vivid picture is that of the murky darkness of extremely deep water. This imagery suggests the mystical, almost ethereal, gulf between the supernatural presence of the Holy One of Israel and the natural order.

2825. חֲשֵׁכָה, **chăshêkâh,** *khash-ay-kaw´*; or חֲשֵׁיכָה, **chăshêykâh,** *khash-ay-kaw´*; from 2821; *darkness*; (figurative) *misery*:—darkness.

A feminine noun meaning darkness. The word is similar in meaning to *chôshek* (2822). It refers to the experience of Abraham when God revealed to him the coming slavery of his descendants (Ge 15:12); to the failure of the wicked to see God's standards and that results in disorder for them (Ps 82:5; Isa 8:22); to the darkness sometimes surrounding persons that requires them to trust in God (Isa 50:10); He can see through darkness as well as light (Ps 139:12).

2826. חָשַׁל, **châshal,** *khaw-shal´*; a primitive root; to *make* (intransitive *be*) *unsteady*, i.e. *weak*:—feeble.

2827. חֲשַׁל, **chăshal,** *khash-al´*; (Chaldee); a root corresponding to 2826; to *weaken*, i.e. *crush*:—subdue.

2828. חָשֻׁם, **Châshum,** *khaw-shoom´*; from the same as 2831; *enriched*; *Chashum*, the name of two or three Israelites:—Hashum.

2829. חֶשְׁמוֹן, **Cheshmôwn,** *khesh-mone´*; the same as 2831; *opulent*; *Cheshmon*, a place in Palestine:—Heshmon.

2830. חַשְׁמַל, **chashmal,** *khash-mal´*; of uncertian derivation; probably *bronze* or polished spectrum metal:—amber.

2831. חַשְׁמַן, **chashman,** *khash-man´*; from an unused root (probably meaning *firm* or *capacious* in resources); apparently *wealthy*:—princes.

A noun which occurs in the plural in Ps 68:31[32]. It is translated "ambassador," but its meaning and derivation are unknown.

2832. חַשְׁמֹנָה, **Chashmônâh**, *khash-mo-naw´*; feminine of 2831; *fertile*; *Chasmonah*, a place in the Desert:—Hashmonah.

2833. חֹשֶׁן, **chôshen**, *kho´-shen*; from an unused root probably meaning to *contain* or *sparkle*; perhaps a *pocket* (as holding the Urim and Thummim), or *rich* (as containing gems), used only of the *gorget* of the highpriest:—breastplate.

2834. חָשַׂף, **châsaph**, *khaw-saf´*; a primitive root; to *strip* off, i.e. generally to *make naked* (for exertion or in disgrace), to *drain* away or *bail* up (a liquid):—make bare, clean, discover, draw out, take, uncover.

2835. חָשִׂף, **châsiph**, *khaw-seef´*; from 2834; (properly) *drawn off*, i.e. separated; hence a small *company* (as divided from the rest):—little flock.

2836. חָשַׁק, **châshaq**, *khaw-shak´*; a primitive root; to *cling*, i.e. *join*, (figurative) to *love, delight* in; elliptically (or by interchanging for 2820) to *deliver*:—have a delight, (have a) desire, fillet, long, set (in) love.

A verb meaning to be attached to, to love, to delight in, to bind. Laws in Deuteronomy described the procedure for taking a slave woman to whom one has become attached as a wife (Dt 21:11). Shechem's soul longed after and delighted in Dinah, who was an Israelite (Ge 34:8). God's binding love for Israel is described as unmerited love (Dt 7:7). Hezekiah describes the figurative way in which God's love for his soul delivered him by casting all his sins behind His back (Isa 38:17).

2837. חֵשֶׁק, **chêsheq**, *khay´-shek*; from 2836; *delight*:—desire, pleasure.

A noun meaning a desired thing. Three of its uses referred to Solomon's building projects. He was able to build the Temple and the other constructions that he desired (1Ki 9:1, 19; 2Ch 8:6). Isa 21:4 implied that the prophet desired Babylon's destruction, but the passage goes on

to say that what he desired was so horrific that it terrified him.

2838. חָשֻׁק, **châshuq**, *khaw-shook´*; or חָשׁוּק, **châshûwq**, *khaw-shook´*; passive participle of 2836; *attached*, i.e. a fence-*rail* or rod connecting the posts or pillars:—fillet.

2839. חִשֻּׁק, **chishshuq**, *khish-shook´*; from 2836; *conjoined*, i.e. a wheel-*spoke* or rod connecting the hub with the rim:—felloe.

2840. חִשֻּׁר, **chishshur**, *khish-shoor´*; from an unused root meaning to *bind* together; *combined*, i.e. the *nave* or hub of a wheel (as holding the spokes together):—spoke.

2841. חַשְׁרָה, **chashrâh**, *khash-raw´*; from the same as 2840; (properly) a *combination* or gathering, i.e. of watery *clouds*:—dark.

2842. חָשַׁשׁ, **châshash**, *khaw-shash´*; by variation for 7179; dry *grass*:—chaff.

2843. חֻשָׁתִי, **Chushâthîy**, *khoo-shaw-thee´*; patronymic from 2364; a *Chushathite* or descendant of Chushah:—Hushathite.

2844. חַת, **chath**, *khath*; from 2865; (concrete) *crushed*; also *afraid*; (abstract) *terror*:—broken, dismayed, dread, fear.

2845. חֵת, **Chêth**, *khayth*; from 2865; *terror*; *Cheth*, an aboriginal Canaanite:—Heth.

2846. חָתָה, **châthâh**, *khaw-thaw´*; a primitive root; to *lay hold* of; especially to *pick* up fire:—heap, take (away).

2847. חִתָּה, **chittâh**, *khit-taw´*; from 2865; *fear*:—terror.

A feminine noun meaning terror, great fear. The Lord sent terror before Jacob into the land of Canaan as he returned from Mesopotamia so he and his family could pass through without being attacked by the native population (Ge 35:5).

2848. חִתּוּל, **chittûwl**, *khit-tool´*; from 2853; *swathed*, i.e. a *bandage*:—roller.

2849. חַתְחַת, **chathchath**, *khath-khath´*; from 2844; *terror*:—fear.

A noun meaning terror. It occurs in the plural in Ecc 12:5, referring to terrors on the road. It is part of a list of coming negative situations. The word is derived from the verbal root *châthath* (2865), meaning to be dismayed or to be shattered.

2850. יתִּח, **Chittîy,** *khit-tee´*; patronymic from 2845; a *Chittite,* or descendant of Cheth:—Hittite, Hittites.

2851. תיתִּח, **chittîyth,** *khit-teeth´*; from 2865; *fear:*—terror.

A feminine noun meaning terror. This word is found exclusively in Ezekiel's writings where he described the reign of terror that powerful nations and cities brought on the Promised Land. For example, in Ezekiel's oracles to the nations, he described the terror that would come on Tyre when it was destroyed (Eze 26:17). When Assyria's slain army fell to the sword, they could no longer cause terror in the land (Eze 32:23).

2852. ךְתַח, **chāthak,** *khaw-thak´*; a primitive root; (properly) to *cut* off, i.e. (figurative) to *decree:*—determine.

2853. לתַח, **chāthal,** *khaw-thal´*; a primitive root; to *swathe:*— × at all, swaddle.

2854. הלָּתֻח, **chăthullâh,** *khath-ool-law´*; from 2853; a *swathing* cloth (figurative):—swaddling band.

2855. לןֹתְח, **Chethlôn,** *kheth-lone´*; from 2853; *enswathed; Chethlon,* a place in Palestine:—Hethlon.

2856. םתַח, **chātham,** *khaw-tham´*; a primitive root; to *close* up; especially to *seal:*—make an end, mark, seal (up), stop.

2857. םתַח, **chătham,** *khath-am´*; (Chaldee); a root corresponding to 2856; to *seal:*—seal.

2858. תמֶתֹֽח, **chôthemeth,** *kho-the-meth*; feminine active participle of 2856; a *seal:*—signet.

2859. ןתַח, **châthan,** *khaw-than´*; a primitive root; to *give* (a daughter) *away* in marriage;

hence (general) to *contract affinity* by marriage:—join in affinity, father in law, make marriages, mother in law, son in law.

2860. ןתָח, **châthân,** *khaw-thawn´*; from 2859; a *relative* by marriage (especially through the bride); (figurative) a *circumcised* child (as a species of religious espousal):—bridegroom, husband, son in law.

2861. הנָּתֻח, **chăthunnâh,** *khath-oon-naw´*; from 2859; a *wedding:*—espousal.

2862. ףתַח, **châthaph,** *khaw-thaf´*; a primitive root; to *clutch:*—take away.

2863. ףתֶח, **chetheph,** *kheh´-thef*; from 2862; (properly) *rapine*; (figurative) *robbery:*—prey.

2864. רתַח, **châthar,** *khaw-thar´*; a primitive root; to *force* a passage, as by burglary; figuratively with oars:—dig (through), row.

2865. תתַח, **châthath,** *khaw-thath´*; a primitive root; (properly) to *prostrate*; hence to *break* down, either (literal) by violence, or (figurative) by confusion and fear:—abolish, affright, be (make) afraid, amaze, beat down, discourage, (cause to) dismay, go down, scare, terrify.

A verb meaning to be shattered, to be dismayed, to dismay, to shatter, to scare. The base meaning is probably breaking or shattering like a bow (Jer 51:56); or of the drought-cracked ground (Jer 14:4). Figuratively, it refers to nations shattered by God (Isa 7:8). It is also used with a intensive and causative meaning to scare, to terrify, or to dismay (Isa 30:31). Job said that God terrified him with dreams (Job 7:14). God's name can also cause dismay (Mal 2:5) where it is parallel to the word *yârê'* (3372).

2866. תחַת, **chăthath,** *khath-ath´*; from 2865; *dismay:*—casting down.

2867. תחַת, **Chăthath,** *khath-ath´*; the same as 2866; *Chathath,* an Israelite:—Hathath.

ט (Teth)

2868. טְאֵב, ṭeʾêb, teh-abeʹ; (Chaldee); a primitive root; to *rejoice*:—be glad.

2869. טָב, ṭâb, tawb; (Chaldee); from 2868; the same as 2896; *good*:—fine, good.

2870. טָבְאֵל, ṭâbeʾêl, taw-beh-aleʹ; from 2895 and 410; *pleasing* (to) *God; Tabeël,* the name of a Syrian and of a Persian:—Tabeal, Tabeel.

2871. טָבוּל, ṭâbûwl, taw-boolʹ; passive participle of 2881; (properly) *dyed,* i.e. a *turban* (probably as of *coloured* stuff):—dyed attire.

2872. טַבּוּר, ṭabbûwr, tab-boorʹ; from an unused root meaning to *pile* up; (properly) *accumulated;* i.e. (by implication) a *summit:*—middle, midst.

2873. טָבַח, ṭâbach, taw-bakhʹ; a primitive root; to *slaughter* (animals or men):—kill, (make) slaughter, slay.

A verb meaning to slaughter. It signifies the slaughter of livestock to prepare it for food (Ge 43:16; Ex 22:1[21:37]; 1Sa 25:11). The Hebrew word *zâbach* (2076), in contrast, signifies slaughtering livestock for sacrifice. Slaughter was used as a picture of destruction, whether attempted against righteous people (Ps 37:14; Jer 11:19) or brought on those being judged by God (La 2:21; Eze 21:10[15]). The slaughter of lambs, which do not comprehend or expect slaughter, symbolized an unexpected destruction (Jer 11:19). In Pr 9:2, the slaughtering of livestock symbolizes a feast prepared by wisdom.

2874. טֶבַח, ṭebach, tehʹ-bakh; from 2873; (properly) something *slaughtered;* hence a *beast* (or *meat,* as butchered); (abstract) *butchery* (or [concrete] a *place of slaughter*):— × beast, slaughter, × slay, × sore.

A masculine noun meaning slaughter. Originally, the term referred to the actual slaughtering of animals for food (Ge 43:16; Pr 9:2); however, this term has also been used metaphorically. It describes the condition of a man seduced by an adulteress (Pr 7:22), as well as the slaughter of the Suffering Servant (Isa 53:7). Furthermore, it characterizes the destinies of Edom (Isa 34:6); Moab (Jer 48:15); Babylon (Jer 50:27); and all those who forsake God (Isa 34:2; 65:12). A parallel term is *zebach* (2077), meaning slaughtering for a sacrifice.

2875. טֶבַח, Ṭebach, tehʹ-bakh; the same as 2874; *massacre; Tebach,* the name of a Mesopotamian and of an Israelite:—Tebah.

2876. טַבָּח, ṭabbâch, tab-bawkhʹ; from 2873; (properly) a *butcher;* hence a *lifeguardsman* (because acting as executioner); also a *cook* (as usually slaughtering the animal for food):—cook, guard.

2877. טַבָּח, ṭabbâch, tab-bawkhʹ; (Chaldee); the same as 2876; a *lifeguardsman:*—guard.

2878. טִבְחָה, ṭibchâh, tib-khawʹ; feminine of 2874 and meaning the same:—flesh, slaughter.

A feminine noun meaning slaughtered meat, a slaughter. In 1Sa, Nabal questioned why he should give his food to David and his men (1Sa 25:11). But in Ps 44:22[23] and Jer 12:3, it is a generic term for slaughter. In both passages, it compared the punishment of people to the slaughtering of sheep. See the cognate verb *ṭâbach* (2873).

2879. טַבָּחָה, ṭabbâchâh, tab-baw-khawʹ; feminine of 2876; a female *cook:*—cook.

2880. טִבְחַת, Ṭibchath, tib-khathʹ; from 2878; *slaughter; Tib-chath,* a place in Syria:—Tibhath.

2881. טָבַל, ṭâbal, taw-balʹ; a primitive root; to *dip:*—dip, plunge.

A verb meaning to dip. The term is often connected with ritual behaviour. The priest was to dip his fingers, a live bird, cedar wood, hyssop, and scarlet yarn into blood for various ceremonies (Le 4:6, 17; 9:9; 14:6, 51). The clean person was to dip hyssop in water and sprinkle it for purification on unclean persons or things (Nu 19:18). It is used intransitively with the preposition b^e when Naaman dipped himself in the Jordan to be healed of leprosy (2Ki 5:14).

2882. טְבַלְיָהוּ, **Tᵉbalyâhûw,** teb-al-yaw´-hoo; from 2881 and 3050; *Jah has dipped; Tebaljah,* an Israelite:—Tebaliah.

2883. טָבַע, **ṭâbaʿ,** taw-bah´; a primitive root; to *sink:*—drown, fasten, settle, sink.

2884. טַבָּעוֹת, **Ṭabbâʿôwth,** tab-baw-othe´; plural of 2885; *rings; Tabbaoth,* one of the Nethinim:—Tabbaoth.

2885. טַבַּעַת, **ṭabbaʿath,** tab-bah´-ath; from 2883; (properly) a *seal* (as *sunk* into the wax), i.e. *signet* (for sealing); hence (general) a *ring* of any kind:—ring.

2886. טַבְרִמּוֹן, **Ṭabrimmôwn,** tab-rim-mone´; from 2895 and 7417; *pleasing* (to) *Rimmon; Tabrimmon,* a Syrian:—Tabrimmon.

2887. טֵבֶת, **Ṭêbeth,** tay´-beth; probably of foreign derivation; *Tebeth,* the tenth Hebrew month:—Tebeth.

2888. טַבַּת, **Ṭabbath,** tab-bath´; of uncertain derivation; *Tabbath,* a place East of the Jordan:—Tabbath.

2889. טָהוֹר, **ṭâhôwr,** haw-hore´; or טָהֹר, **ṭâhôr,** taw-hore´; from 2891; *pure* (in a physical, chemical, ceremonial or moral sense):—clean, fair, pure (-ness).

An adjective meaning clean, pure, genuine. This word is used ninety times in the OT, primarily to distinguish things that were culturally pure, capable of being used in, or taking part in the religious rituals of Israel. The Lord decreed that Israel must mark off the clean from the unclean (Le 10:10; 11:47; Job 14:4). Persons could be ceremonially clean or unclean (Dt 12:15). A human corpse was especially defiling, and contact with it made a person unclean for seven days (Nu 19:11). When persons were clean, they could eat clean meat, but an unclean person could not (Le 7:19). Certain animals were considered ceremonially clean (Ge 7:2) and needed by Noah and his family for sacrifices after the flood (Ge 8:20). Ceremonially clean birds were used in various rituals (Le 14:4).

Clean things were considered normal; unclean things were considered polluted, but they could be restored to their state of purity (Le 11—15). Some things, however, were permanently unclean, such as unclean animals (Le 11:7, 26, 29–31). Other things were temporarily unclean. A woman in her period (Le 12:2) and a person with an infectious disease (Le 13:8) could be cleansed and be clean again (Le 12:4; 14:7); spring water could be considered as clean; even seed could be clean or unclean depending on whether a dead carcass had fallen on it while it was dry or wet (Le 11:36–38). Leprosy made a person unclean (Le 13:45, 46).

God expected His people to be morally pure and to imitate Him (Hab 1:13). This word served to express that state. Clean hands merited God's favour (Job 17:9), and pure words were pleasing to the Lord. God judged a sacrifice's value by the quality of the offerer's heart (Ps 51:10[12]); thus, David prayed for a pure heart.

The root meaning of the word shines through in its use to describe the quality of metals and other items. Pure gold was used in the construction of the Ark of the Covenant and many other items (Ex 25:11, 17; 28:14; 30:3); pure frankincense was prepared for use on the altar of incense (Ex 30:34, 35; 37:29). The fear of the Lord was proclaimed pure and therefore endured forever. It guided the psalmist to know God (Ps 19:9[10]).

2890. טְהוֹר, **ṭᵉhôwr,** teh-hore´; from 2891; *purity:*—pureness.

A masculine noun meaning cleanness. This word occurs only in Pr 22:11. As it is written in Hebrew, it is unpronounceable and appears to be a misspelling of the adjective *ṭâhôwr* (2889). However, the noun "cleanness," fits much better than the adjective "clean," both grammatically and contextually (cf. Pr 23:7, 8) and is the choice of the King James Version. Loving cleanness of heart (rather than "loving [the] clean of heart") results in graceful speech.

2891. טָהֵר, **ṭâhêr,** taw-hare´; a primitive root; (properly) to *be bright;* i.e. (by implication) to *be pure* ([physically] *sound, clear, unadulterated;* [Levitical] *uncontaminated;* [moral] *innocent* or *holy*):—be (make, make self, pronounce) clean, cleanse (self), purge, purify (-ier, self).

A verb meaning to be clean, to make clean, to be pure, to make pure. The term occurs most frequently in Leviticus where it was used for ritual cleansing of either things or persons (Le 14:48; 16:19; 22:7). The OT also speaks of ritual cleansing performed on persons within the sphere of false worship (Isa 66:17; Eze 22:24). Animals were not made clean (like people), for animals were either clean or unclean by nature; the concept did not apply to plants at all. Sometimes cleanness had a moral dimension that, of course, did not exclude the spiritual. One was not to think that persons made themselves clean nor that their cleanness exceeded that of their Maker (Job 4:17; Pr 20:9). Exilic and postexilic prophets prophesied of a future purification for God's people like the purifying of silver (Jer 33:8; Eze 36:25; Mal 3:3).

2892. טֹהַר, **ṭôhar,** *to'-har*; from 2891; (literal) *brightness*; (ceremonial) *purification*:—clearness, glory, purifying.

A masculine noun meaning purity, pureness, clarity, luster. This word is from a verb meaning to be pure or to be clean, both physically and ceremonially. It is used to denote the lustrous quality of a clear sky (Ex 24:10); the glory of an individual (Ps 89:44[45]); and the purification cycle after childbirth (Le 12:4, 6).

2893. טָהֳרָה, **ṭohŏrâh,** *toh-or-aw'*; feminine of 2892; (ceremonial) *purification*; (moral) *purity*:— × is cleansed, cleansing, purification (-fying).

A feminine noun meaning cleansing, purification. The word refers to a ceremonial cleansing pronounced by a priest on one formerly unclean (Le 13:7). The cleansing from such things as leprosy (Le 14:2, 23, 32); issues relating to genital organs (Le 15:13); touching a dead body (Nu 6:9); and childbirth (Le 12:4, 5) required additional procedures such as washing clothes and bathing. The birth of a child rendered a woman unclean, remaining in the blood of her purification (i.e. extra bleeding in the days following childbirth) for a set time after which she brought a sacrifice to the priest (cf. Lk 2:24). Cleansing from leprosy involved an extensive ceremony (Le 14:1–32). These ceremonies promoted good hygiene, but in the days of Hezekiah, God pardoned those who were seeking Him but failed to maintain ceremonial cleanness (2Ch 30:19).

2894. מַאֲטֵא, **ṭê'ṭê',** *tay-tay'*; a primitive root; to *sweep away*:—sweep.

2895. טוֹב, **ṭôwb,** *tobe*; a primitive root, to *be* (transitive *do* or *make*) *good* (or *well*) in the widest sense:—be (do) better, cheer, be (do, seem) good, (make) goodly, × please, (be, do, go, play) well.

A verb meaning to be happy, to please, to be loved, to be favoured, to seem good, to be acceptable, to endure, to be valuable, to do well, to do right. It means to be happy or glad, such as when Nabal, husband of Abigail, was joyous from drinking too much (1Sa 25:36; 2Sa 13:28; Est 1:10). The word naturally expresses the idea of being loved or enjoying the favour of someone. Samuel grew up in favour before the Lord and people (1Sa 2:26). It is used with the idiom "in the eyes of" to express the idea of seeming good or advisable; Abner informed David of everything that was good in the eyes of Israel (2Sa 3:19; 15:26). The word is used to express the meaning of good, as when the Israelites asserted they were better off in Egypt than in the wilderness (Nu 11:18; cf. Dt 5:29). The idea of being better or being valuable is expressed several times using this word: Jephthah asked the Ammonites whether they were better than Balak, son of Zippor (Jgs 11:25); while the psalmist asserted that it was good for him to have been afflicted, for thereby he learned the Lord's decrees (Ps 119:71).

The verb is used four times in the causative stem to mean to deal rightly or to deal justly. The Lord informed David that he had done well to plan to build a temple for God (2Ch 6:8) and informed Jehu that he had performed his assassination of Ahab's house well (2Ki 10:30).

2896. טוֹב, **ṭôwb,** *tobe*; from 2895; *good* (as an adjective) in the widest sense; used likewise as a noun, both in the masculine and the feminine, the singular and the plural (*good*, a *good* or *good* thing, a *good* man or woman; the *good*, *goods* or *good* things, *good* men or women), also as an adverb (*well*):—beautiful, best, better, bountiful, cheerful, at ease, × fair (word), (be in) favour, fine, glad, good (deed, -lier, -liest, -ly, -ness, -s), graciously, joyful, kindly, kindness, liketh (best), loving, merry, × most, pleasant, + pleaseth, pleasure, precious, prosperity, ready, sweet, wealth, welfare, (be) well ([-favoured]).

An adjective meaning good, well-pleasing, fruitful, morally correct, proper, convenient. This word is frequently encountered in the OT and is roughly equivalent to the English word *good* in terms of its function and scope of meaning. It describes that which is appealing and pleasant to the senses (Nu 14:7; Est 1:11; Ps 52:9[11]); is useful and profitable (Ge 2:18; Zec 11:12); is abundant and plentiful (Ge 41:22; Jgs 8:32); is kind and benevolent (1Sa 24:18[19]; 2Ch 5:13; Na 1:7); is good in a moral sense as opposed to evil (Ge 2:17; Le 27:14; Ps 37:27); is proper and becoming (Dt 1:14; 1Sa 1:23; Ps 92:1[2]); bears a general state of well-being or happiness (Dt 6:24; Ecc 2:24); is the better of two alternatives (Ge 29:19; Ex 14:12; Jnh 4:3). The creation narrative of Ge 1 best embodies all these various elements of meaning when the Lord declares each aspect of His handiwork to be "good."

2897. טוֹב, **Ṭôwb,** *tobe;* the same as 2896; *good; Tob,* a region apparently East of the Jordan:— Tob.

2898. טוּב, **ṭûwb,** *toob;* from 2895; *good* (as a noun), in the widest sense, especially *goodness* ([superlatively concrete] the *best*), *beauty, gladness, welfare:*—fair, gladness, good (-ness, thing, -s), joy, go well with.

A masculine noun meaning property, goods, goodness, fairness, and beauty. The root concept of this noun is that of desirability for enjoyment. It is used to identify the personal property of an individual (Ge 24:10); the plentiful harvest of the land (Ne 9:36; Jer 2:7); items of superior quality and desirability (2Ki 8:9); inward joy (Isa 65:14); the manifest goodness of the Lord (Ex 33:19; Ps 25:7). Notably, the psalmist employs the word to describe the state of spiritual blessing (Ps 31:19[20]; 65:4[5]).

2899. טוֹב אֲדֹנִיָּהוּ, **Ṭôwb 'Ădônîyyâhûw,** *tobe ado-nee-yah´-hoo;* from 2896 and 138; *pleasing* (to) *Adonijah; Tob-Adonijah,* an Israelite:— Tob-adonijah.

2900. טוֹבִיָּה, **Ṭôwbîyyâh,** *to-bee-yaw´;* or טוֹבִיָּהוּ, **Ṭôwbîyyâhûw,** *to-bee-yaw´-hoo;* from 2896 and 3050; *goodness of Jehovah; Tobijah,* the name of three Israelites and of one Samaritan:—Tobiah, Tobijah.

2901. טָוָה, **ṭâvâh,** *taw-vaw´;* a primitive root; to *spin:*—spin.

2902. טוּחַ, **ṭûwach,** *too´-akh;* a primitive root; to *smear,* especially with lime:—daub, overlay, plaister, smut.

2903. טוֹטָפוֹת, **ṭôwṭâphôwth,** *to-taw-foth´;* from an unused root meaning to *go around* or *bind;* a *fillet* for the forehead:—frontlet.

2904. טוּל, **ṭûwl,** *tool;* a primitive root; to *pitch* over or *reel;* hence (transitive) to *cast* down or out:—carry away, (utterly) cast (down, forth, out), send out.

2905. טוּר, **ṭûwr,** *toor;* from an unused root meaning to *range* in a regular manner; a *row;* hence a *wall:*—row.

2906. טוּר, **ṭûwr,** *toor;* (Chaldee); corresponding to 6697; a *rock* or hill:—mountain.

2907. טוּשׂ, **ṭûwś,** *toos;* a primitive root; to *pounce* as a bird of prey:—haste.

2908. טְוָת, **ṭᵉvâth,** *tev-awth´;* (Chaldee); from a root corresponding to 2901; *hunger* (as twisting):—fasting.

2909. טָחָה, **ṭâchâh,** *taw-khaw´;* a primitive root; to *stretch* a bow, as an *archer:*—[bow-] shot.

2910. טֻחוֹת, **ṭuchôwth,** *too-khoth´;* from 2909 (or 2902) in the sense of *overlaying;* (in the plural only) the *kidneys* (as being *covered*); hence (figurative) the inmost *thought:*—inward parts.

2911. טְחוֹן, **ṭᵉchôwn,** *tekh-one´;* from 2912; a hand *mill;* hence a *millstone:*—to grind.

2912. טָחַן, **ṭâchan,** *taw-khan´;* a primitive root; to *grind* meal; hence to *be a concubine* (that being their employment):—grind (-er).

2913. טַחֲנָה, **ṭachănâh,** *takh-an-aw´;* from 2912; a hand *mill;* hence (figurative) *chewing:*—grinding.

2914. טְחֹר, **ṭᵉchôr,** *tekh-ore´;* from an unused root meaning to *burn;* a *boil* or ulcer (from the inflammation), especially a tumor in the anus or pudenda (the piles):—emerod.

2915. טִיחַ, **ṭîyach,** *tee´-akh;* from (the equivalent of) 2902; *mortar* or *plaster:*—daubing.

2916. טִיט, **ṭîyṭ,** *teet*; from an unused root meaning apparently to *be sticky* [rather perhaps a denominative from 2894, through the idea of dirt to be *swept* away]; *mud* or *clay*; (figurative) *calamity*:—clay, dirt, mire.

2917. טִין, **ṭîyn,** *teen*; (Chaldee); perhaps by interchange for a word corresponding to 2916; *clay*:—miry.

2918. טִירָה, **ṭîyrâh,** *tee-raw´*; feminine of (an equivalent to) 2905; a *wall*; hence a *fortress* or a *hamlet*:—(goodly) castle, habitation, palace, row.

2919. טַל, **ṭal,** *tal*; from 2926; *dew* (as *covering* vegetation):—dew.

2920. טַל, **ṭal,** *tal*; (Chaldee); the same as 2919:—dew.

2921. טָלָא, **ṭâlâ’,** *taw-law´*; a primitive root; (properly) to *cover* with pieces; i.e. (by implication) to *spot* or *variegate* (as tapestry):—clouted, with divers colours, spotted.

2922. טְלָא, **ṭᵉlâ’,** *tel-aw´*; apparently from 2921 in the (original) sense of *covering* (for protection); a *lamb* [compare 2924]:—lamb.

2923. טְלָאִים, **Ṭᵉlâ’îym,** *tel-aw-eem´*; from the plural of 2922; *lambs; Telaim,* a place in Palestine:—Telaim.

2924. טָלֶה, **ṭâleh,** *taw-leh´*; by variation for 2922; a *lamb*:—lamb.

2925. טַלְטֵלָה, **ṭalṭêlâh,** *tal-tay-law´*; from 2904; *overthrow* or *rejection*:—captivity.

2926. טָלַל, **ṭâlal,** *taw-lal´*; a primitive root; (properly) to *strew* over, i.e. (by implication) to *cover* in or *plate* (with beams):—cover.

2927. טְלַל, **ṭᵉlal,** *tel-al´*; (Chaldee); corresponding to 2926; to *cover* with shade:—have a shadow.

2928. טֶלֶם, **Ṭelem,** *teh´-lem*; from an unused root meaning to *break* up or treat violently; *oppression; Telem,* the name of a place in Idumæa, also of a temple doorkeeper:—Telem.

2929. טַלְמוֹן, **Ṭalmôwn,** *tal-mone´*; from the same as 2728; *oppressive; Talmon,* a temple doorkeeper:—Talmon.

2930. טָמֵא, **ṭâmê’,** *taw-may´*; a primitive root; to *be foul,* especially in a ceremonial or moral sense (*contaminated*):—defile (self), pollute (self), be (make, make self, pronounce) unclean, × utterly.

A verb meaning to be unclean, to desecrate, to defile, to make impure. The main idea of the action was that of contaminating or corrupting, especially in the sight of God. The Levitical Law often spoke in terms of sexual, religious, or ceremonial uncleanness. Any object or individual who was not clean could not be acceptable to the Holy God of Israel. Examples of actions that caused a state of impurity would include eating forbidden food (Hos 9:4); worshiping idols (Ps 106:39; Hos 5:3); committing adultery or engaging in sexual relations outside of marriage (Ge 34:5; Nu 5:13; Eze 18:6); touching unclean objects or individuals (Le 5:3; 18:24; 19:31); and any action that violated the sacredness of the Lord (Jer 32:34). It was the duty of the priesthood to discern matters of impurity (Le 13:3; Hag 2:13) and to see that the strict rituals of purification were followed.

2931. טָמֵא, **ṭâmê’,** *taw-may´*; from 2930; *foul* in a religious sense:—defiled, + infamous, polluted (-tion), unclean.

An adjective meaning unclean. It can denote impurity or defilement (Isa 6:5; Eze 22:5). It can also refer to ritually unclean items such as people, things, foods, and places. The land east of the Jordan (Jos 22:19) and foreign lands (Am 7:17) were unclean in contrast to the land of Israel.

2932. טֻמְאָה, **ṭum’âh,** *toom-aw´*; from 2930; religious *impurity*:—filthiness, unclean (-ness).

A feminine noun meaning uncleanness, filthy. It refers to the sexual impurity of a woman during the menstrual cycle (Nu 5:19; La 1:9). It can also denote any unclean thing from which the temple needed to be purified (2Ch 29:16). Finally, both ethical and religious uncleanness were dealt with: in the laws referring to proper behaviour (Le 16:16); and in the heart, referring to an unclean spirit that causes one to lie (Eze 24:13).

2933. טָמָה, **ṭâmâh,** *taw-maw´*; a collateral form of 2930; to *be impure* in a religious sense:—be defiled, be reputed vile.

A verb which occurs once in the Hebrew Bible (Job 18:3). It is translated "stopped up," "stupid," or possibly "unclean."

2934. טָמַן, **ṭâman,** *taw-man´*; a primitive root; to *hide* (by *covering* over):—hide, lay privily, in secret.

2935. טֶנֶא, **ṭene',** *teh´-neh*; from an unused root probably meaning to *weave*; a *basket* (of interlaced osiers):—basket.

2936. טָנַף, **ṭânaph,** *taw-naf´*; a primitive root; to *soil*:—defile.

2937. טָעָה, **ṭâ'âh,** *taw-aw´*; a primitive root; to *wander*; (causative) to *lead astray*:—seduce.

2938. טָעַם, **ṭâ'am,** *taw-am´*; a primitive root; to *taste*; (figurative) to *perceive*:— × but, perceive, taste.

2939. טְעַם, **ṭᵉ'am,** *teh-am´*; (Chaldee); corresponding to 2938; to *taste*; (causative) to *feed*:— make to eat, feed.

2940. טַעַם, **ṭa'am,** *tah´-am*; from 2938; (properly) a *taste*, i.e. (figurative) *perception*; (by implication) *intelligence*; (transitive) a *mandate*:—advice, behaviour, decree, discretion, judgment, reason, taste, understanding.

A masculine noun meaning taste, judgment, discernment, discretion. The word is used only thirteen times in the OT but is a key word when considering the concept of taste, perception, or decree. It is used to describe the experience of taste: it describes the physical taste of manna as something like wafers or cakes made with honey (Ex 16:31); or as something made with olive oil (Nu 11:8); it also refers to tasteless food needing salt in order to be eaten (Job 6:6). The word has several abstract meanings. It can mean mental or spiritual perception, discretion, or discernment. David thanked Abigail for her good discretion that kept him from killing Nabal and his men (1Sa 25:33). This Hebrew word is ranked along with knowledge as something the psalmist wanted from the Lord (i.e. good discernment or judgment [Ps 119:66]); and in a famous proverb, the beautiful woman without discretion is unfavourably compared to a gold ring in a pig's snout (Pr 11:22). The word can also mean an oral or written proclamation (i.e. a decree). It depicts the proclamation of the king of Nineveh (Jnh

3:7). Finally, its Aramaic equivalent *ṭa'am* (2941) means decree or command.

2941. טְעֵם, **ṭa'am,** *tah´-am*; (Chaldee); from 2939; (properly) a *taste*, i.e. (as in 2940) a judicial *sentence*:—account, × to be commanded, commandment, matter.

An Aramaic noun meaning taste, judgment, command. It is closely related to the Hebrew word of the same spelling (*ṭa'am* [2940]) and is equivalent to the Aramaic noun *ṭᵉ'êm* (2942). In Ezr 6:14, the word refers to a command of God; and therefore some argue this vocalization is a theological scribal distinction to differentiate between it and *ṭᵉ'êm.* The determined use of *ṭa'ĕmâ'* in Ezr 5:5 could be declined from either *ṭa'am* or *ṭᵉ'êm.*

2942. טְעֵם, **ṭᵉ'êm,** *teh-ame´*; (Chaldee); from 2939, and equivalent to 2941; (properly) *flavor*; (figurative) *judgment* (both subjective and objective); hence *account* (both subjective and objective):— + chancellor, + command, commandment, decree, + regard, taste, wisdom.

An Aramaic masculine noun meaning taste, judgment, command, flavor. Belshazzar held a great feast and tasted wine from the consecrated vessels of God's Temple (Da 5:2). When used figuratively, the word has the meaning of judgment or discretion, such as Daniel's counsel and wisdom to Nebuchadnezzar's chief guard (Da 2:14). This word is also used in relaying a command of God, such as the rebuilding of the Temple (Ezr 6:14), or of a person, as in the decree to worship the golden image of Nebuchadnezzar (Da 3:10).

2943. טָעַן, **ṭâ'an,** *taw-an´*; a primitive root; to *load* a beast:—lade.

2944. טָעַן, **ṭâ'an,** *taw-an´*; a primitive root; to *stab*:—thrust through.

2945. טַף, **ṭaph,** *taf*; from 2952 (perhaps referring to the *tripping* gait of children); a *family* (mostly used collectively in the singular):—(little) children (ones), families.

A masculine singular noun meaning child, little one. Though the term is sometimes used in a parallel construction with *bâniym* (plural of 1121; Dt 1:39), elsewhere it often denotes younger children. It is distinguished from young men, virgins (Eze 9:6), and sons (2Ch 20:13, "children"). It is often used in the formulaic pattern "men, women, and children" (Dt 2:34; 3:6; 31:12; Jer 40:7; 43:6), meaning everyone.

2946. טָפַח, **tâphach,** *taw-fakh´*; a primitive root; to *flatten* out or *extend* (as a tent); (figurative) to *nurse* a child (as *promotive* of growth); or perhaps a denominative from 2947, from *dandling* on the palms:—span, swaddle.

2947. טֶפַח, **tephach,** *teh´-fakh*; from 2946; a *spread* of the hand, i.e. a *palm-breadth* (not "span" of the fingers); (architecture) a *corbel* (as a supporting palm):—coping, hand-breadth.

2948. טֹפַח, **tôphach,** *to´-fakh*; from 2946 (the same as 2947):—hand-breadth (broad).

2949. טִפֻּח, **tippuch,** *tip-pookh´*; from 2946; *nursing*:—span long.

2950. טָפַל, **tâphal,** *taw-fal´*; a primitive root; (properly) to *stick* on as a patch; (figurative) to *impute* falsely:—forge (-r), sew up.

2951. טִפְסַר, **tiphsar,** *tif-sar´*; of foreign derivation; a military *governor*:—captain.

A noun, probably masculine, meaning a military commander. In Jer 51:27, it appears to refer to the supreme commander of an army called to oppose Babylon. In the only other occurrence, Na 3:17, it is plural and has a slightly different spelling. Here it refers to commanders in the army of Nineveh, the capital of Assyria. Interestingly, in both passages, comparison is made between military power and different kinds of locusts.

2952. טָפַף, **tâphaph,** *taw-faf´*; a primitive root; apparently to *trip* (with short steps) coquettishly:—mince.

2953. טְפַר, **tᵉphar,** *tef-ar´*; (Chaldee); from a root corresponding to 6852, and meaning the same as 6856; a finger-*nail*; also a *hoof* or *claw*:—nail.

2954. טָפַשׁ, **tâphash,** *taw-fash´*; a primitive root; (properly) apparently to *be thick*; (figurative) to *be stupid*:—be fat.

2955. טָפַת, **Tâphath,** *taw-fath´*; probably from 5197; a *dropping* (of ointment); *Taphath*, an Israelitess:—Taphath.

2956. טָרַד, **târad,** *taw-rad´*; a primitive root; to *drive* on; (figurative) to *follow* close:—continual.

2957. טְרַד, **tᵉrad,** *ter-ad´*; (Chaldee); corresponding to 2956; to *expel*:—drive.

2958. טְרוֹם, **tᵉrôwm,** *ter-ome´*; a variation of 2962; *not yet*:—before.

2959. טָרַח, **târach,** *taw-rakh´*; a primitive root; to *overburden*:—weary.

2960. טֹרַח, **tôrach,** *to´-rakh*; from 2959; a *burden*:—cumbrance, trouble.

2961. טָרִי, **târîy,** *taw-ree´*; from an unused root apparently meaning to *be moist*; (properly) *dripping*; hence *fresh* (i.e. recently made such):—new, putrefying.

2962. טֶרֶם, **terem,** *teh´-rem*; from an unused root apparently meaning to *interrupt* or *suspend*; (properly) *non-occurrence*; (used adverbially) *not yet* or *before*:—before, ere, not yet.

2963. טָרַף, **târaph,** *taw-raf´*; a primitive root; to *pluck* off or *pull* to pieces; (causative) to *supply* with food (as in morsels):—catch, × without doubt, feed, ravin, rend in pieces, × surely, tear (in pieces).

2964. טֶרֶף, **tereph,** *teh´-ref*; from 2963; something *torn*, i.e. a fragment, e.g., a *fresh* leaf, *prey, food*:—leaf, meat, prey, spoil.

2965. טָרָף, **târâph,** *taw-rawf´*; from 2963; recently *torn* off, i.e. *fresh*:—plucked off.

2966. טְרֵפָה, **tᵉrêphâh,** *ter-ay-faw´*; feminine (collective) of 2964; *prey*, i.e. flocks devoured by animals:—ravin, (that which was) torn (of beasts, in pieces).

2967. טַרְפְּלַי, **Ţarpᵉlay,** *tar-pel-ah´ee*; (Chaldee); from a name of foreign derivation; a *Tarpelite* (collective) or inhabitant of Tarpel, a place in Assyria:—Tarpelites.

' (Yodh)

2968. אָב, **yâ'ab,** *yaw-ab´*; a primitive root; to *desire*:—long.

2969. יָאָה, **yâ'âh,** *yaw-aw´*; a primitive root; to *be suitable*:—appertain.

2970. יַאֲזַנְיָה, **Ya'ăzanyâh,** *yah-az-an-yaw´*; or יַאֲזַנְיָהוּ, **Ya'ăzanyâhûw,** *yah-az-an-yaw´-hoo*; from 238 and 3050; *heard of Jah; Jaazanjah,* the name of four Israelites:—Jaazaniah. Compare 3153.

2971. יָאִיר, **Yâ'îyr,** *yaw-ere´*; from 215; *enlightener; Jair,* the name of four Israelites:—Jair.

2972. יָאִרִי, **Yâ'irîy,** *yaw-ee-ree´*; patronymic from 2971; a *Jaïrite* or descendant of Jair:—Jairite.

2973. יָאַל, **yâ'al,** *yaw-al´*; a primitive root; (properly) to *be slack,* i.e. (figurative) to *be foolish*:—dote, be (become, do) foolish (-ly).

2974. יָאַל, **yâ'al,** *yaw-al´*; a primitive root [probably rather the same as 2973 through the idea of mental *weakness*]; (properly) to *yield,* especially *assent*; hence (positively) to *undertake* as an act of volition:—assay, begin, be content, please, take upon, × willingly, would.

A verb meaning to choose to do something. The focus of this verb is on the decision to act. This concept is expressed on three levels. On the first level, the individual shows a willingness to act a certain way, to accept an invitation (Ex 2:21; Jos 7:7; Jgs 19:6). On the next level, the individual is more active and voluntarily decides to act a certain way (Ge 18:27; Dt 1:5). On the final level, the individual is even more active and voluntarily decides to act a certain way with determination and resolve (Jos 17:12; Jgs 1:27, 35; Hos 5:11). This verb provides strong support for the theological concept of human free will because humanity is permitted to decide to act a certain way. God, however, will hold humanity responsible for those decisions and actions.

2975. יְאֹר, **y^e'ôr,** *yeh-ore´*; of Egyptian origin; a *channel,* i.e. a fosse, canal, shaft; specifically the *Nile,* as the one river of Egypt, including its collateral trenches; also the *Tigris,* as the main river of Assyria:—brook, flood, river, stream.

2976. יָאַשׁ, **yâ'ash,** *yaw-ash´*; a primitive root; to *desist,* i.e. (figurative) to *despond*:—(cause to) despair, one that is desperate, be no hope.

A verb meaning to despair. The word refers to despair in the sense that one concludes that something desirable is out of reach and usually stops working toward it. In 1Sa 27:1, David hoped Saul would despair of finding him when he fled to the Philistines. The word may refer to loss of hope in God or a false god (Isa 57:10; Jer 2:25; 18:12). It may also refer, similarly, to a loss of meaning in life (Ecc 2:20; cf. Php 1:21, 22). In Job 6:26, the word describes an emotional state of despair without immediately focusing on the cause of despair. In three passages, the word occurs in a passive sense as a statement or exclamation meaning "it is hopeless" (Isa 57:10; Jer 2:25; 18:12).

2977. יֹאשִׁיָּה, **Yô'shîyyâh,** *yo-she-yaw´*; or יֹאשִׁיָהוּ, **Yô'shîyyâhûw,** *yo-she-yaw´-hoo*; from the same root as 803 and 3050; *founded of Jah; Joshijah,* the name of two Israelites:—Josiah.

2978. יִאתוֹן, **yi'thôwn,** *yi-thone´*; from 857; an *entry*:—entrance.

2979. יְאָתְרַי, **y^e'âthray,** *yeh-awth-rah´ee*; from the same as 871; *stepping; Jeätherai,* an Israelite:—Jeaterai.

2980. יָבַב, **yâbab,** *yaw-bab*; a primitive root; to *bawl*:—cry out.

2981. יְבוּל, **y^ebûwl,** *yeb-ool´*; from 2986; *produce,* i.e. a *crop* or (figurative) *wealth*:—fruit, increase.

2982. יְבוּס, Yᵉbûws, *yeb-oos´*; from 947; *trodden,* i.e. threshing-place; *Jebus,* the aboriginal name of Jerusalem:—Jebus.

2983. יְבוּסִי, Yᵉbûwsîy, *yeb-oo-see´*; patrial from 2982; a *Jebusite* or inhabitant of Jebus:— Jebusite (-s).

2984. יִבְחַר, Yibchar, *yib-khar´*; from 977; *choice; Jibchar,* an Israelite:—Ibhar.

2985. יָבִין, Yâbîyn, *yaw-bene´*; from 995; *intelligent; Jabin,* the name of two Canaanitish kings:—Jabin.

2986. יָבַל, yâbal, *yaw-bal´*; a primitive root; (properly) to *flow;* (causative) to *bring* (especially with pomp):—bring (forth), carry, lead (forth).

2987. יְבַל, yᵉbal, *yeb-al´*; (Chaldee); corresponding to 2986; to *bring:*—bring, carry.

2988. יָבָל, yâbâl, *yaw-bawl;* from 2986; a *stream:*—[water-] course, stream.

2989. יָבָל, Yâbâl, *yaw-bawl´*; the same as 2988; *Jabal,* an antediluvian:—Jabal.

2990. יַבֶּלֶת, yabbeleth, *yab-bel-eth´*; from 2986; having *running* sores:—wen.

2991. יִבְלְעָם, Yiblᵉʿâm, *yib-leh-awm´*; from 1104 and 5971; *devouring people; Jibleäm,* a place in Palestine:—Ibleam.

2992. יָבַם, yâbam, *yaw-bam´*; a primitive root of doubtful meaning; used only as a denominative from 2993; to *marry* a (deceased) brother's widow:—perform the duty of a husband's brother, marry.

2993. יָבָם, yâbâm, *yaw-bawm´*; from (the original of) 2992; a *brother-in-law:*—husband's brother.

2994. יְבָמָה, yᵉbâmâh, *yeb-aw´-maw*; feminine participle of 2992; a *sister-in-law:*— brother's wife, sister in law.

2995. יַבְנְאֵל, Yabnᵉʾêl, *yab-neh-ale´*; from 1129 and 410; *built of God; Jabneël,* the name of two places in Palestine:—Jabneel.

2996. יַבְנֶה, Yabneh, *yab-neh´*; from 1129; a *building; Jabneh,* a place in Palestine:—Jabneh.

2997. יִבְנְיָה, Yibnᵉyâh, *yib-neh-yaw´*; from 1129 and 3050; *built of Jah; Jibnejah,* an Israelite:— Ibneiah.

2998. יִבְנִיָּה, Yibnîyyâh, *yib-nee-yaw´*; from 1129 and 3050; *building of Jah; Jibnijah,* an Israelite:—Ibnijah.

2999. יַבֹּק, Yabbôq, *yab-boke´*; probably from 1238; *pouring* forth; *Jabbok,* a river East of the Jordan:—Jabbok.

3000. יֶבֶרֶכְיָהוּ, Yᵉberekyâhûw, *yeb-eh-rek-yaw´-hoo*; from 1288 and 3050; *blessed of Jah; Jeberek-jah,* an Israelite:—Jeberechiah.

3001. יָבֵשׁ, yâbêsh, *yaw-bashe´*; a primitive root; to *be ashamed, confused* or *disappointed;* also (as failing) to *dry* up (as water) or *wither* (as herbage):—be ashamed, clean, be confounded, (make) dry (up), (do) shame (-fully), × utterly, wither (away).

A verb meaning to be dried up, to be dry, to be withered. This common intransitive verb refers to the drying up and withering of plants, trees, grass, crops, and the earth itself after the flood (Ge 8:14). It also occurs with an intensive and causative sense meaning to dry, to wither. *Yahweh* dried the waters, particularly the sea (Jos 2:10; Ps 74:15; Isa 42:15; Jer 51:36; Na 1:4). It is used figuratively to denote God destroying Babylon (Eze 17:24).

3002. יָבֵשׁ, yâbêsh, *yaw-bashe´*; from 3001; *dry:*—dried (away), dry.

An adjective meaning dry, dried. The Nazarite vow prohibited partaking of the fruit of the vine, including dried grapes (Nu 6:3). The Israelites complained in the desert because they had no food like they did in Egypt; all they had to eat was manna, and their souls were dried up (Nu 11:6). A second use of dry is when it refers to chaff that breaks in pieces. It is used figuratively of Job, who was weary and worn out (Job 13:25).

3003. יָבֵשׁ, Yâbêsh, *yaw-bashe´*; the same as 3002 (also יָבֵישׁ, Yâbêysh, *yaw-bashe´*; often with the addition of 1568, i.e. *Jabesh of Gilead*); *Jabesh,* the name of an Israelite and of a place in Palestine:—Jabesh ([-Gilead]).

3004. יַבָּשָׁה, yabbâshâh, *yab-baw-shaw´*; from 3001; *dry* ground:—dry (ground, land).

A feminine noun meaning dry land. This word can be an adjective as well. In all uses, it is contrasted with water. It often describes land formerly covered with water, such as the land appearing on the third day of creation; the land on which the people of Israel crossed the Red Sea (Ex 14:16, 22, 29; Ps 66:6); and the land on which they crossed the Jordan (Jos 4:22). It also describes land onto which water is poured both literally (Ex 4:9) and as a figure of the Holy Spirit being poured on the descendants of Jacob (Isa 44:3).

3005. יִבְשָׂם, **Yibśâm,** *yib-sawm´*; from the same as 1314; *fragrant*; *Jibsam*, an Israelite:—Jibsam.

3006. יַבֶּשֶׁת, **yabbesheth,** *yab-beh´-sheth*; a variation of 3004; *dry* ground:—dry land.

A feminine noun meaning dry land. It is apparently identical to *yabbâshâh* (3004). This word occurs only twice. In Ex 4:9, it refers to land upon which water had been poured and subsequently had turned to blood. In Ps 95:5, it refers to dry land (in contrast to the sea, which the Lord's hands formed.

3007. יַבֶּשֶׁת, **yabbesheth,** *yab-beh´-sheth*; (Chaldee); corresponding to 3006; *dry* land:—earth.

An Aramaic feminine noun meaning earth. This noun, appearing only in Da 2:10, suggests any patch of dry land on which a person can stand. Thus, the word is taken to imply the whole planet or the entire world.

3008. יִגְאָל, **Yig'âl,** *yig-awl´*; from 1350; *avenger*; *Jigal*, the name of three Israelites:—Igal, Igeal.

3009. יָגַב, **yâgab,** *yaw-gab´*; a primitive root; to *dig* or plough:—husbandman.

3010. יָגֵב, **yâgêb,** *yaw-gabe´*; from 3009; a ploughed *field*:—field.

3011. יָגְבְּהָה, **Yogbᵉhâh,** *yog-beh-haw´*; feminine from 1361; *hillock*; *Jogbehah*, a place East of the Jordan:—Jogbehah.

3012. יִגְדַּלְיָהוּ, **Yigdalyâhûw,** *yig-dal-yaw´-hoo*; from 1431 and 3050; *magnified of Jah*; *Jigdaljah*, an Israelite:—Igdaliah.

3013. יָגָה, **yâgâh,** *yaw-gaw´*; a primitive root; to *grieve*:—afflict, cause grief, grieve, sorrowful, vex.

3014. יָגָה, **yâgâh,** *yaw-gaw´*; a primitive root [probably rather the same as 3013 through the common idea of *dissatisfaction*]; to *push away*:—be removed.

3015. יָגוֹן, **yâgôwn,** *yaw-gohn´*; from 3013; *affliction*:—grief, sorrow.

3016. יָגוֹר, **yâgôwr,** *yaw-gore´*; from 3025; *fearful*:—afraid, fearest.

3017. יָגוּר, **Yâgûwr,** *yaw-goor´*; probably from 1481; a *lodging*; *Jagur*, a place in Palestine:—Jagur.

3018. יְגִיעַ, **yᵉgîyaʻ,** *yeg-ee´-ah*; from 3021; *toil*; hence a *work, produce, property* (as the result of labour):—labour, work.

3019. יָגִיעַ, **yâgîyaʻ,** *haw-ghee´-ah*; from 3021; *tired*:—weary.

3020. יָגְלִי, **Yoglîy,** *yog-lee´*; from 1540; *exiled*; *Jogli*, an Israelite:—Jogli.

3021. יָגַע, **yâgaʻ,** *yaw-gah´*; a primitive root; (properly) to *gasp*; hence to *be exhausted*, to *tire*, to *toil*:—faint, (make to) labour, (be) weary.

3022. יָגָע, **yâgâʻ,** *yaw-gaw´*; from 3021; *earnings* (as the product of toil):—that which he laboured for.

3023. יָגֵעַ, **yâgêaʻ,** *yaw-gay´-ah*; from 3021; *tired*; hence (transposed) *tiresome*:—full of labour, weary.

3024. יְגִיעָה, **yᵉgîyʻâh,** *yeg-ee-aw´*; feminine of 3019; *fatigue*:—weariness.

3025. יָגֹר, **yâgôr,** *yaw-gore´*; a primitive root; to *fear*:—be afraid, fear.

A verb meaning to fear, to be afraid. In comparison to the more common verb for fear, *yârê'* (3372), which often refers to a general sense of vulnerability (cf. Ge 15:1), *yâgôr* refers to fear of specific occurrences such as catching a disease (Dt 28:60); being reproached or scorned (Ps 119:39); or being delivered into the power of specific people (Jer 39:17). It describes the fear of God in Dt 9:19 but focuses on the specific possibility of God destroying Israel.

3026. יְגַר שָׂהֲדוּתָא, **Yᵉgar Śahăḏûwthâ',** *yegar´ sah-had-oo-thaw´*; (Chaldee); from a word derived from an unused root (meaning to *gather*) and a derivative of a root corresponding to 7717; *heap of the testimony; Jegar-Sahadutha,* a cairn East of the Jordan:—Jegar-Sahadutha.

3027. יָד, **yâd,** *yawd*; a primitive word; a *hand* (the *open* one [indicating *power, means, direction,* etc.], in distinction from 3709, the *closed* one); used (as noun, adverb, etc.) in a great variety of applications, both literal and figurative, both proximate and remote [as follow]:— (+ be) able, × about, + armholes, at, axletree, because of, beside, border, × bounty, + broad, [broken-] handed, × by, charge, coast, + consecrate, + creditor, custody, debt, dominion, × enough, + fellowship, force, × from, hand [-staves, -y work], × he, himself, × in, labour, + large, ledge, [left-] handed, means, × mine, ministry, near, × of, × order, ordinance, × our, parts, pain, power, × presumptuously, service, side, sore, state, stay, draw with strength, stroke, + swear, terror, × thee, × by them, × themselves, × thine own, × thou, through, × throwing, + thumb, times, × to, × under, × us, × wait on, [way-] side, where, + wide, × with (him, me, you), work, + yield, × yourselves.

A feminine noun meaning hand, strength. This word frequently appears in the OT with literal, figurative, and technical uses. Literally, it implies the hand of a human being (Le 14:28; Jer 36:14) and occasionally the wrist (Ge 38:28). Metaphorically, it signifies strength or power (Dt 32:36; Isa 37:27); authority or right of possession (Ge 16:9; 2Ch 13:16); location or direction (Nu 24:24; Ps 141:6); the side of an object (1Sa 4:18); a fractional portion of the whole (Ge 47:24; Ne 11:1). In a technical sense, the word is used to identify the upright supports for the bronze laver (1Ki 7:35, 36); the tenons for the tabernacle (Ex 26:17); and an axle (1Ki 7:32, 33).

3028. יַד, **yad,** *yad*; (Chaldee); corresponding to 3027:—hand, power.

An Aramaic noun meaning hand, power, control, possession. The word corresponds to the Hebrew noun of the same spelling (3027) and refers to a literal hand (although not a human one) as writing (Da 5:5). From the ability of the hand to hold and manipulate objects, the word is used figuratively to describe control, power, or possession, such as Nebuchadnezzar's power over Israel (Ezr 5:12) and other people and animals (Da 2:38); God's power to do whatever He wishes (Da 4:35[32]); the lions' power

to hurt a person (Da 6:27[28]; cf. 1Sa 17:37); the Jews' control over the rebuilding of the Temple (Ezr 5:8). The stone cut out without hands (Da 2:34) refers to a kingdom set up by God independently of human power (Da 2:45). In Ezr 6:12, the word refers to an attempt to gain power to change the edict of Darius.

3029. יְדָא, **yᵉdâ',** *yed-aw'*; (Chaldee); corresponding to 3034; to *praise:*—(give) thank (-s).

An Aramaic verb meaning to give thanks, to offer praise. Twice this word appears in the OT, both times in Daniel. It is solely directed to the Lord, signifying the thanks given to God for answered prayer (Da 2:23) and in reference to Daniel's daily devotional practice (Da 6:10[11]).

3030. יִדְאֲלָה, **Yid'ălâh,** *yid-al-aw'*; of uncertain derivation *Jidalah,* a place in Palestine:—Idalah.

3031. יִדְבָּשׁ, **Yidbâsh,** *yid-bawsh'*; from the same as 1706; perhaps *honeyed; Jidbash,* an Israelite:—Idbash.

3032. יָדַד, **yâdad,** *yaw-dad'*; a primitive root; (properly) to *handle* [compare 3034], i.e. to *throw,* e.g., lots:—cast.

3033. יְדִדוּת, **yᵉdidûwth,** *yed-ee-dooth'*; from 3039; (properly) *affection;* (concrete) a *darling* object:—dearly beloved.

A feminine noun meaning beloved, highly valued, dear one. It is derived from the word *yĕdiyd* (3039), which has a similar meaning. The word occurs only in Jer 12:7 where it describes Israel as beloved of God's soul but forsaken by Him and delivered to their enemies because they only pretended to return His love (Jer 12:1, 2).

3034. יָדָה, **yâdâh,** *yaw-daw'*; a primitive root; used only as denominative from 3027; (literal) to *use* (i.e. hold out) *the hand*; (physically) to *throw* (a stone, an arrow) at or away; especially to *revere* or *worship* (with extended hands); (intensive) to *bemoan* (by wringing the hands):—cast (out), (make) confess (-ion), praise, shoot, (give) thank (-ful, -s, -sgiving).

A verb meaning to acknowledge, to praise, to give thanks, to confess, to cast. The essential meaning is an act of acknowledging what is right about God in praise and thanksgiving (1Ch 16:34). It can also mean a right acknowledgment of self before God in confessing sin

(Le 26:40) or of others in their God-given positions (Ge 49:8). It is often linked with the word *hâlal* (1984) in a hymnic liturgy of "thanking and praising" (1Ch 16:4; 23:30; Ezr 3:11; Ne 12:24, 46). This rightful, heavenward acknowledgment is structured in corporate worship (Ps 100:4; 107:1, 8, 15, 21, 31), yet is also part of personal lament and deliverance (Ps 88:11[10]). Several uses of *yâdâh* evidence an essence of motion or action (as something given), intensively referring twice to cast or to throw down (La 3:53; Zec 1:21 [2:4]), and once it means to shoot (as an arrow; Jer 50:14).

3035. יִדּוֹ, **Yiddôw,** *yid-do´*; from 3034; *praised; Jiddo*, an Israelite:—Iddo.

3036. יָדוֹן, **Yâdôwn,** *yaw-done´*; from 3034; *thankful; Jadon*, an Israelite:—Jadon.

3037. יַדּוּעַ, **Yaddûwaʻ,** *yad-doo´-ah*; from 3045; *knowing; Jadduä*, the name of two Israelites:—Jaddua.

3038. יְדוּתוּן, **Yᵉdûwthûwn,** *yed-oo-thoon´*; or יְדֻתוּן, **Yeduthûwn,** *yed-oo-thoon´*; or יְדִיתוּן, **Yedîythûwn,** *yed-ee-thoon´*; probably from 3034; *laudatory; Jedu-thun*, an Israelite:—Jeduthun.

3039. יָדִיד, **yâdîyd,** *yawd-eed´*; from the same as 1730; *loved:*—amiable, (well-) beloved, loves.

An adjective meaning beloved, well-loved. This word is often used in poetry. It is used mainly to describe a person who is beloved; for example, Moses called Benjamin the beloved of the Lord (Dt 33:12). Another use is to describe the loveliness of the tabernacle of the Lord (Ps 84:1[2]). A third use is its literal meaning, love. The psalmist calls his poem (Ps 45) a song of love.

3040. יְדִידָה, **Yᵉdîydâh,** *yed-ee-daw´*; feminine of 3039; *beloved; Jedidah*, an Israelitess:—Jedidah.

3041. יְדִידְיָה, **Yᵉdîydᵉyâh,** *yed-ee-deh-yaw´*; from 3039 and 3050; *beloved of Jah; Jedidejah*, a name of Solomon:—Jedidiah.

3042. יְדָיָה, **Yᵉdâyâh,** *yed-aw-yaw´*; from 3034 and 3050; *praised of Jah; Jedajah*, the name of two Israelites:—Jedaiah.

3043. יְדִיעֲאֵל, **Yᵉdîyʻăʼêl,** *yed-ee-ah-ale´*; from 3045 and 410; *knowing God; Jediaël*, the name of three Israelites:—Jediael.

3044. יִדְלָף, **Yidlâph,** *yid-lawf´*; from 1811; *tearful; Jidlaph*, a Mesopotamian:—Jidlaph.

3045. יָדַע, **yâdaʻ,** *yaw-dah´*; a primitive root; to *know* (properly to ascertain by *seeing*); used in a great variety of senses, figurative, literal, euphemism and inference (including *observation, care, recognition*; and causative *instruction, designation, punishment*, etc.) [as follow]:—acknowledge, acquaintance (-ted with), advise, answer, appoint, assuredly, be aware, [un-] awares, can [-not], certainly, for a certainty, comprehend, consider, × could they, cunning, declare, be diligent, (can, cause to) discern, discover, endued with, familiar friend, famous, feel, can have, be [ig-] norant, instruct, kinsfolk, kinsman, (cause to, let, make) know, (come to give, have, take) knowledge, have [knowledge], (be, make, make to be, make self) known, + be learned, + lie by man, mark, perceive, privy to, × prognosticator, regard, have respect, skilful, shew, can (man of) skill, be sure, of a surety, teach, (can) tell, understand, have [understanding], × will be, wist, wit, wot.

A verb meaning to know, to learn, to perceive, to discern, to experience, to confess, to consider, to know people relationally, to know how, to be skillful, to be made known, to make oneself known, to make to know.

The simple meaning, to know, is its most common translation out of the eight hundred or more uses. One of the primary uses means to know relationally and experientially: it refers to knowing or not knowing persons (Ge 29:5; Ex 1:8) personally or by reputation (Job 19:13). The word also refers to knowing a person sexually (Ge 4:1; 19:5; 1Ki 1:4). It may even describe knowing or not knowing God or foreign gods (Ex 5:2; Dt 11:28; Hos 2:20[22]; 8:2), but it especially signifies knowing what to do or think in general, especially with respect to God (Isa 1:3; 56:10). One of its most important uses is depicting God's knowledge of people: The Lord knows their hearts entirely (Ex 33:12; 2Sa 7:20; Ps 139:4; Jer 17:9; Hos 5:3); God knows the suffering of His people (Ex 2:25), and He cares.

The word also describes knowing various other things: when Adam and Eve sinned, knowing good and evil (Ge 3:22); knowing nothing (1Sa 20:39); and knowing the way of wisdom (Job 28:23). One could know by observation (1Sa 23:22, 23), as when Israel and Pharaoh came to know God through the plagues He brought on Egypt (Ex 10:2). People knew by experience (Jos 23:14) that God kept His promises; this kind of experience could lead to knowing by confession (Jer 3:13; 14:20). Persons could be charged to know what they were about to do (Jgs 18:14) or what the situation implied (1Ki 20:7) so they would be able to discriminate between right and wrong, good and bad, what was not proper or advantageous (Dt 1:39; 2Sa 19:35[36]).

The word describes different aspects of knowing in its other forms. In the passive forms, it describes making something or someone known. The most famous illustration is Ex 6:3 when God asserted to Moses that He did not make himself known to the fathers as Yahweh.

3046. יְדַע, **yᵉda‘,** *yed-ah´*; (Chaldee); corresponding to 3045:—certify, know, make known, teach.

An Aramaic verb meaning to know, to communicate, to inform, to cause to know. The word primarily refers to knowledge sharing or awareness and occurs often in the books of Ezra and Daniel. In Ezra, the men opposed to the rebuilding of Jerusalem wanted it to be known to Artaxerxes (Ezr 4:12, 13), and when opposing the Temple, they made it known to Darius (Ezr 5:8, 10). The book of Daniel presents a theological subtheme of true knowledge. In the desired and hidden meanings of life, only the God of Heaven truly knows the end from the beginning, and only He can ultimately reveal and wisely inform (Da 2:5, 21–23, 28–30; 4:9[6]; 5:8, 15, 16). Fearing Him is true knowing (Da 5:17, 21–23), a sovereign awareness that removes crippling human fear in circumstantial knowing (Da 3:18; 6:10[11]). *Yĕda‘* compares with the Hebrew word *yâda‘* (3045), which is used with much broader variances of meaning in Scripture, ranging from cognitive to experiential to sexual relations.

3047. יָדָע, **Yâdâ‘,** *yaw-daw´*; from 3045; *knowing; Jada,* an Israelite:—Jada.

3048. יְדַעְיָה, **Yᵉda‘yâh,** *yed-ah-yaw´*; from 3045 and 3050; *Jah has known; Jedajah,* the name of two Israelites:—Jedaiah.

3049. יִדְּעֹנִי, **yiddᵉ‘ônîy,** *yid-deh-o-nee´*; from 3045; (properly) a *knowing* one; (specifically) a *conjurer;* (by implication) a *ghost:*—wizard.

A masculine noun meaning a familiar spirit, a conjurer, and a wizard. In Levitical Law, this type of person was considered an abomination to the Lord (Dt 18:11). King Saul consulted such a medium when he desired to know the outcome of his war against the Philistines (1Sa 28:9). King Manasseh's evil deeds included the practice of consulting mediums and wizards (2Ki 21:6). Isaiah condemned the people of Israel for turning to the way of the Canaanites, who sought out mediums and wizards in order to hear from their dead (Isa 8:19).

3050. יָהּ, **Yâh,** *yaw*; contraction for 3068, and meaning the same; *Jah,* the sacred name:—Jah, the Lord, most vehement. Cp. names in "-iah," "-jah."

A neuter pronoun of God, a shortened form of Yahweh, often translated "LORD." This abbreviated noun for Yahweh is used in poetry, especially in the Psalms. The word is found first in Ex 15:2 and 17:16; in both cases, the LORD is exalted after He delivered His people from possible annihilation, first by Egypt and then by the Amalekites. These two poetic passages are then quoted later (Ps 118:14; Isa 12:2). In a poetic prayer, Hezekiah used the endearing term also (Isa 38:11). All other uses of the shortened name are found in Psalms (Ps 68:18[19]; 77:11 [12]; 130:3). Many times it is found in the phrase, "Hallelujah, praise be to Yah!" (Ps 104:35; 105:45; 106:1, 48).

3051. יָהַב, **yâhab,** *yaw-hab´*; a primitive root; to *give* (whether literal or figurative); generally to *put;* imperative (reflexive) *come:*—ascribe, bring, come on, give, go, set, take.

3052. יְהַב, **yᵉhab,** *yeh-hab´*; (Chaldee); corresponding to 3051:—deliver, give, lay, + prolong, pay, yield.

3053. יְהָב, **yᵉhâb,** *yeh-hawb´*; from 3051; (properly) what is *given* (by Providence), i.e. a *lot:*—burden.

3054. יָהַד, **yâhad,** *yaw-had´*; denominative from a form corresponding to 3061; to *Judaize,* i.e. become Jewish:—become Jews.

3055. יְהֻד, **Yᵉhud,** *yeh-hood´*; a briefer form of one corresponding to 3061; *Jehud,* a place in Palestine:—Jehud.

3056. יֶהְדַּי, **Yehday,** *yeh-dah´ee;* perhaps from a form corresponding to 3061; *Judaistic; Jehdai,* an Israelite:—Jehdai.

3057. יְהֻדִיָּה, **Yᵉhudîyyâh,** *yeh-hoo-dee-yaw´;* feminine of 3064; *Jehudijah,* a Jewess:—Jehudijah.

3058. יֵהוּא, **Yêhûw’,** *yay-hoo´;* from 3068 and 1931; *Jehovah (is) He; Jehu,* the name of five Israelites:—Jehu.

3059. יְהוֹאָחָז, **Yᵉhôw’âchâz,** *yeh-ho-aw-khawz´;* from 3068 and 270; *Jehovah-seized; Jehoächaz,* the name of three Israelites:—Jehoahaz. Compare 3099.

3060. יְהוֹאָשׁ, **Yᵉhôw’âsh,** *yeh-ho-awsh´;* from 3068 and (perhaps) 784; *Jehovah-fired; Jehoäsh,* the name of two Israelite kings:—Jehoash. Compare 3101.

3061. יְהוּד, **Yᵉhûwd,** *yeh-hood´;* (Chaldee); contracted from a form corresponding to 3063; (properly) *Judah,* hence *Judæa:*—Jewry, Judah, Judea.

3062. יְהוּדָי, **Yᵉhûwdây,** *yeh-hoo-daw-ee´;* (Chaldee); patrial from 3061; a *Jehudaïte (or Judaite),* i.e. Jew:—Jew.

3063. יְהוּדָה, **Yᵉhûwdâh,** *yeh-hoo-daw´;* from 3034; *celebrated; Jehudah (or Judah),* the name of five Israelites; also of the tribe descended from the first, and of its territory:—Judah.

3064. יְהוּדִי, **Yᵉhûwdîy,** *yeh-hoo-dee´;* patronymic from 3063; a *Jehudite (i.e. Judaite or Jew),* or descendant of Jehudah (i.e. Judah):—Jew.

3065. יְהוּדִי, **Yᵉhûwdîy,** *yeh-hoo-dee´;* the same as 3064; *Jehudi,* an Israelite:—Jehudi.

3066. יְהוּדִית, **Yᵉhûwdîyth,** *yeh-hoo-deeth´;* feminine of 3064; the *Jewish* (used adverbially) language:—in the Jews' language.

3067. יְהוּדִית, **Yᵉhûwdîyth,** *yeh-hoo-deeth´;* the same as 3066; *Jewess; Jehudith,* a Canaanitess:—Judith.

3068. יְהֹוָה, **Yᵉhôvâh,** *yeh-ho-vaw´;* from 1961; (the) self-*Existent* or Eternal; *Jehovah,* Jewish national name of God:—Jehovah, the Lord. Compare 3050, 3069.

A noun meaning God. The word refers to the proper name of the God of Israel, particularly the name by which He revealed Himself to Moses (Ex 6:2, 3). The divine name has traditionally not been pronounced, primarily out of respect for its sacredness (cf. Ex 20:7; Dt 28:58). Until the Renaissance, it was written without vowels in the Hebrew text of the OT, being rendered as YHWH. However, since that time, the vowels of another word, *’ădônây* (136), have been supplied in hopes of reconstructing the pronunciation. Although the exact derivation of the name is uncertain, most scholars agree that its primary meaning should be understood in the context of God's existence, namely, that He is the "I AM THAT I AM" (Ex 3:14), the One who was, who is, and who always will be (cf. Rev 11:17). Older translations of the Bible and many newer ones employ the practice of rendering the divine name in capital letters, so as to distinguish it from other Hebrew words. It is most often rendered as Lord (Ge 4:1; Dt 6:18; Ps 18:31[32]; Jer 33:2; Jnh 1:9) but also as God (Ge 6:5; 2Sa 12:22) or JEHOVAH (Ps 83:18[19]; Isa 26:4). The frequent appearance of this name in relation to God's redemptive work underscores its tremendous importance (Le 26:45; Ps 19:14[15]). Also, it is sometimes compounded with another word to describe the character of the Lord in greater detail (see Ge 22:14; Ex 17:15; Jgs 6:24).

3069. יְהֹוִה, **Yᵉhôvih,** *yeh-ho-vee´;* a variation of 3068 [used after 136, and pronounced by Jews as 430, in order to prevent the repetition of the same sound, since they elsewhere pronounce 3068 as 136]:—God.

3070. יְהֹוָה יִרְאֶה, **Yᵉhôvâh yir’eh,** *yeh-ho-vaw´ yir-eh´;* from 3068 and 7200; *Jehovah will see* (to it); *Jehovah-Jireh,* a symbolical name for Mt. Moriah:—Jehovah-jireh.

3071. יְהֹוָה נִסִּי, **Yᵉhôvâh Nissîy,** *yeh-ho-vaw´ nis-see´;* from 3068 and 5251 with pronoun suffix; *Jehovah (is) my banner; Jehovah-Nissi,* a symbolical name of an altar in the Desert:—Jehovah-nissi.

3072. יְהֹוָה צִדְקֵנוּ, **Yᵉhôvâh Tsidqênûw,** *yeh-ho-vaw´ tsid-kay´-noo;* from 3068 and 6664 with pronoun suffix; *Jehovah (is) our right; Jehovah-Tsidkenu,* a symbolical epithet of the Messiah and of Jerusalem:—the Lord our righteousness.

3073. יְהוָֹה שָׁלוֹם, **Yᵉhôvâh shâlôwm,** *yeh-ho-vaw′ shaw-lome′;* from 3068 and 7965; *Jehovah* (is) *peace; Jehovah-Shalom,* a symbolical name of an altar in Palestine:—Jehovah-shalom.

3074. יְהוָֹה שָׁמָּה, **Yᵉhôvâh shâmmâh,** *yeh-ho-vaw′ shawm′-maw;* from 3068 and 8033 with directive enclitic; *Jehovah* (is) *thither; Jehovah-Shammah,* a symbolic title of Jerusalem:—Jehovah-shammah.

3075. יְהוֹזָבָד, **Yᵉhôwzâbâd,** *yeh-ho-zaw-bawd′;* from 3068 and 2064; *Jehovah-endowed; Jehozabad,* the name of three Israelites:—Jehozabad. Compare 3107.

3076. יְהוֹחָנָן, **Yᵉhôwchânân,** *yeh-ho-khaw-nawn′;* from 3068 and 2603; *Jehovah-favoured; Jehochanan,* the name of eight Israelites:—Jehohanan, Johanan. Compare 3110.

3077. יְהוֹיָדָע, **Yᵉhôwyâdâʿ,** *yeh-ho-yaw-daw′;* from 3068 and 3045; *Jehovah-known; Jehojada,* the name of three Israelites:—Jehoiada. Compare 3111.

3078. יְהוֹיָכִין, **Yᵉhôwyâkîyn,** *yeh-ho-yaw-keen′;* from 3068 and 3559; *Jehovah will establish; Jehojakin,* a Jewish king:—Jehoiachin. Compare 3112.

3079. יְהוֹיָקִים, **Yᵉhôwyâqîym,** *yeh-ho-yaw-keem′;* from 3068 abbreviation and 6965; *Jehovah will raise; Jehojakim,* a Jewish king:—Jehoiakim. Compare 3113.

3080. יְהוֹיָרִיב, **Yᵉhôwyârîyb,** *yeh-ho-yaw-reeb′;* from 3068 and 7378; *Jehovah will contend; Jehojarib,* the name of two Israelites:—Jehoiarib. Compare 3114.

3081. יְהוּכַל, **Yᵉhûwkal,** *yeh-hoo-kal′;* from 3201; *potent; Jehukal,* an Israelite:—Jehucal. Compare 3116.

3082. יְהוֹנָדָב, **Yᵉhôwnâdâb,** *yeh-ho-naw-dawb′;* from 3068 and 5068; *Jehovah-largessed; Jehonadab,* the name of an Israelite and of an Arab:—Jehonadab, Jonadab. Compare 3122.

3083. יְהוֹנָתָן, **Yᵉhôwnâthân,** *yeh-ho-naw-thawn′;* from 3068 and 5414; *Jehovah-given; Jehonathan,* the name of four Israelites:—Jonathan. Compare 3129.

3084. יְהוֹסֵף, **Yᵉhôwsêph,** *yeh-ho-safe′;* a fuller form of 3130; *Jehoseph* (i.e. Joseph), a son of Jacob:—Joseph.

3085. יְהוֹעַדָּה, **Yᵉhôwʿaddâh,** *yeh-ho-ad-daw′;* from 3068 and 5710; *Jehovah-adorned; Jehoäddah,* an Israelite:—Jehoada.

3086. יְהוֹעַדִּין, **Yᵉhôwʿaddîyn,** *yeh-ho-ad-deen′;* or יְהוֹעַדָּן, **Yᵉhôwʿaddân,** *yeh-ho-ad-dawn′;* from 3068 and 5727; *Jehovah-pleased; Jehoäddin* or *Jehoäddan,* an Israelitess:—Jehoaddan.

3087. יְהוֹצָדָק, **Yᵉhôwtsâdâq,** *yeh-ho-tsaw-dawk′;* from 3068 and 6663; *Jehovah-righted; Jehotsadak,* an Israelite:—Jehozadek, Josedech. Compare 3136.

3088. יְהוֹרָם, **Yᵉhôwrâm,** *yeh-ho-rawm′;* from 3068 and 7311; *Jehovah-raised; Jehoram,* the name of a Syrian and of three Israelites:—Jehoram, Joram. Compare 3141.

3089. יְהוֹשֶׁבַע, **Yᵉhôwsheba**ʿ**,** *yeh-ho-sheh′-bah;* from 3068 and 7650; *Jehovah-sworn; Jehosheba,* an Israelitess:—Jehosheba. Compare 3090.

3090. יְהוֹשַׁבְעַת, **Yᵉhôwshab**ʿ**ath,** *yeh-ho-shab-ath′;* a form of 3089; *Jehoshabath,* an Israelitess:—Jehoshabeath.

3091. יְהוֹשׁוּעַ, **Yᵉhôwshûwa**ʿ**,** *yeh-ho-shoo′-ah;* or יְהוֹשֻׁעַ, **Yᵉhôwshua**ʿ**,** *yeh-ho-shoo′-ah;* from 3068 and 3467; *Jehovah-saved; Jehoshuä* (i.e. Joshua), the Jewish leader:—Jehoshua, Jehoshuah, Joshua. Compare 1954, 3442.

3092. יְהוֹשָׁפָט, **Yᵉhôwshâphât,** *yeh-ho-shaw-fawt′;* from 3068 and 8199; *Jehovah-judged; Jehoshaphat,* the name of six Israelites; also of a valley near Jerusalem:—Jehoshaphat. Compare 3146.

3093. יָהִיר, **yâhîyr,** *yaw-here′;* probably from the same as 2022; *elated;* hence *arrogant:*—haughty, proud.

3094. יְהַלֶּלְאֵל, **Yᵉhallel'êl,** *yeh-hal-lel-ale′;* from 1984 and 410; *praising God; Jehallelel,* the name of two Israelites:—Jehaleleel, Jehalelel.

3095. יַהֲלֹם, **yahălôm,** *yah-hal-ome′;* from 1986 (in the sense of *hardness*); a precious stone, probably *onyx:*—diamond.

3096. יַהַץ, **Yahats,** *yah′-hats;* or יַהְצָה, **Yahtsâh,** *yah′-tsaw;* or (feminine) יָהְצָה, **Yahtsâh,** *yah-*

tsaw´; from an unused root meaning to *stamp*; perhaps *threshing*-floor; *Jahats* or *Jahtsah*, a place East of the Jordan:—Jahaz, Jahazah, Jahzah.

3097. יוֹאָב, **Yôw'âb,** *yo-awb´*; from 3068 and 1; *Jehovah-fathered; Joäb,* the name of three Israelites:—Joab.

3098. יוֹאָח, **Yôw'âch,** *yo-awkh´*; from 3068 and 251; *Jehovah-brothered; Joach,* the name of four Israelites:—Joah.

3099. יוֹאָחָז, **Yôw'âchâz,** *yo-aw-khawz´*; a form of 3059; *Joächaz,* the name of two Israelites:—Jehoahaz, Joahaz.

3100. יוֹאֵל, **Yôw'êl,** *yo-ale´*; from 3068 and 410; *Jehovah* (is his) *God; Joël,* the name of twelve Israelites:—Joel.

3101. יוֹאָשׁ, **Yôw'âsh,** *yo-awsh´*; or יֹאָשׁ, **Yô'âsh,** *yo-awsh´*; (2Ch 24:1), a form of 3060; *Joäsh,* the name of six Israelites:—Joash.

3102. יוֹב, **Yôwb,** *yobe*; perhaps a form of 3103, but more probably by erroneous transcription for 3437; *Job,* an Israelite:—Job.

3103. יוֹבָב, **Yôwbâb,** *yo-bawb´*; from 2980; *howler; Jobab,* the name of two Israelites and of three foreigners:—Jobab.

3104. יוֹבֵל, **yôwbêl,** *yo-bale´*; or יֹבֵל, **yôbêl,** *yo-bale´*; apparently from 2986; the *blast* of a horn (from its *continuous* sound); specifically the *signal* of the silver trumpets; hence the instrument itself and the festival thus introduced:—jubile, ram's horn, trumpet.

3105. יוּבַל, **yûwbal,** *yoo-bal´*; from 2986; a *stream:*—river.

3106. יוּבָל, **Yûwbâl,** *yoo-bawl´*; from 2986; *stream; Jubal,* an antediluvian:—Jubal.

3107. יוֹזָבָד, **Yôwzâbâd,** *yo-zaw-bawd´*; a form of 3075; *Jozabad,* the name of ten Israelites:—Josabad, Jozabad.

3108. יוֹזָכָר, **Yôwzâkâr,** *yo-zaw-kawr´*; from 3068 and 2142; *Jehovah-remembered; Jozacar,* an Israelite:—Jozachar.

3109. יוֹחָא, **Yôwchâ',** *yo-khaw´*; probably from 3068 and a variation of 2421; *Jehovah-revived; Jocha,* the name of two Israelites:—Joha.

3110. יוֹחָנָן, **Yôwchânân,** *yo-khaw-nawn´*; a form of 3076; *Jochanan,* the name of nine Israelites:—Johanan.

3111. יוֹיָדָע, **Yôwyâdâ',** *yo-yaw-daw´*; a form of 3077; *Jojada,* the name of two Israelites:—Jehoiada, Joiada.

3112. יוֹיָכִין, **Yôwyâkîyn,** *yo-yaw-keen´*; a form of 3078; *Jojakin,* an Israelite king:—Jehoiachin.

3113. יוֹיָקִים, **Yôwyâqîym,** *yo-yaw-keem´*; a form of 3079; *Jojakim,* an Israelite:—Joiakim. Compare 3137.

3114. יוֹיָרִיב, **Yôwyârîyb,** *yo-yaw-reeb´*; a form of 3080; *Jojarib,* the name of four Israelites:—Joiarib.

3115. יוֹכֶבֶד, **Yôwkebed,** *yo-keh´-bed*; from 3068 contracted and 3513; *Jehovah-gloried; Jokebed,* the mother of Moses:—Jochebed.

3116. יוּכַל, **Yûwkal,** *yoo-kal´*; a form of 3081; *Jukal,* an Israelite:—Jucal.

3117. יוֹם, **yôwm,** *yome*; from an unused root meaning to *be hot*; a *day* (as the *warm* hours), whether literal (from sunrise to sunset, or from one sunset to the next), or figurative (a space of time defined by an associated term), [often used adverbially]:—age, + always, + chronicles, continually (-ance), daily, ([birth-], each, to) day, (now a, two) days (agone), + elder, × end, + evening, + (for) ever (-lasting, -more), × full, life, as (so) long as (... live), (even) now, + old, + outlived, + perpetually, presently, + remaineth, × required, season, × since, space, then, (process of) time, + as at other times, + in trouble, weather, (as) when, (a, the, within a) while (that), × whole (+ age), (full) year (-ly), + younger.

A masculine noun meaning day, time, year. This word stands as the most basic conception of time in the OT. It designates such wide-ranging elements as the daylight hours from sunrise to sunset (Ge 1:5; 1Ki 19:4); a literal twenty-four hour cycle (Dt 16:8; 2Ki 25:30); a generic span of time (Ge 26:8; Nu 20:15); a given point in time (Ge 2:17; 47:29; Eze 33:12). In the plural, the word may also mean the span of life (Ps 102:3 [4]) or a year (Le 25:29; 1 Sam 27:7). The prophets often infuse the word with end–times meanings or connotations, using it in connection with a future period of consequential events, such as the "day of the LORD" (Jer 46:10;

Zec 14:1) or simply, "that day" (Isa 19:23; Zec 14:20, 21).

3118. יוֹם, **yôwm,** *yome*; (Chaldee); corresponding to 3117; a *day*:—day (by day), time.

A masculine Aramaic noun meaning day. The word corresponds to the Hebrew noun of the same spelling and meaning. It refers to a twenty-four hour period (in which Daniel prays three times) (Da 6:10[11], 13[14]. In the plural, it describes a time period marked by a particular state of affairs as, for example, the days of Nebuchadnezzar's madness (Da 4:34[31]) or the days of Belshazzar's father (Da 5:11). The number of days may be specified; in the book of Daniel, only King Darius could legally be worshipped for thirty days (Da 6:7[8], 12[13]). The word is used to refer to God as the Ancient of Days, emphasizing in human terms God's eternal existence (Da 7:9, 13, 22).

3119. יוֹמָם, **yôwmâm,** *yo-mawm´*; from 3117; *daily*:—daily, (by, in the) day (-time).

An adverb meaning in daytime, by day. It is used to mean during the day, such as the cloud of the Lord that led the Israelites by day in the wilderness (Nu 10:34; Ne 9:19). It is often also used in parallel to something occurring by night, such as the sun by day and the moon by night (Jer 31:35). It comes from the Hebrew word *yôwm* (3117).

3120. יָוָן, **Yâvân,** *yaw-vawn´*; probably from the same as 3196; *effervescing* (i.e. hot and active); *Javan*, the name of a son of Joktan, and of the race (*Ionians*, i.e. Greeks) descended from him, with their territory; also of a place in Arabia:—Javan.

3121. יָוֵן, **yâvên,** *yaw-ven´*; from the same as 3196; (properly) *dregs* (as *effervescing*); hence *mud*:—mire, miry.

3122. יוֹנָדָב, **Yôwnâdâb,** *yo-naw-dawb´*; a form of 3082; *Jonadab*, the name of an Israelite and of a Rechabite:—Jonadab.

3123. יוֹנָה, **yôwnâh,** *yo-naw´*; probably from the same as 3196; a *dove* (apparently from the *warmth* of their mating):—dove, pigeon.

3124. יוֹנָה, **Yôwnâh,** *yo-naw´*; the same as 3123; *Jonah*, an Israelite:—Jonah.

3125. יְוָנִי, **Yᵉvânîy,** *yev-aw-nee´*; patronymic from 3121; a *Jevanite*, or descendant of Javan:—Grecian.

3126. יוֹנֵק, **yôwnêq,** *yo-nake´*; active participle of 3243; a *sucker*; hence a *twig* (of a tree felled and sprouting):—tender plant.

3127. יוֹנֶקֶת, **yôwneqeth,** *yo-neh´-keth*; feminine of 3126; a *sprout*:—(tender) branch, young twig.

3128. יוֹנַת אֵלֶם רְחֹקִים, **yôwnath 'êlem rᵉchôqîym,** *yo-nath´ ay´-lem rekh-o-keem´*; from 3123 and 482 and the plural of 7350; *dove of* (the) *silence* (i.e. *dumb* Israel) *of* (i.e. among) *distances* (i.e. strangers); the title of a ditty (used for a name of its melody):—Jonath-elem-rechokim.

3129. יוֹנָתָן, **Yôwnâthân,** *yo-naw-thawn´*; a form of 3083; *Jonathan*, the name of ten Israelites:—Jonathan.

3130. יוֹסֵף, **Yôwsêph,** *yo-safe´*; future of 3254; *let him add* (or perhaps simply active participle *adding*); *Joseph*, the name of seven Israelites:—Joseph. Compare 3084.

3131. יוֹסִפְיָה, **Yôwsiphyâh,** *yo-sif-yaw´*; from active participle of 3254 and 3050; *Jah* (is) *adding*; *Josiph-jah*, an Israelite:—Josiphiah.

3132. יוֹעֵאלָה, **Yôw'ê'lâh,** *yo-ay-law´*; perhaps feminine active participle of 3276; *furthermore*; *Joelah*, an Israelite:—Joelah.

3133. יוֹעֵד, **Yôw'êd,** *yo-ade´*; apparently active participle of 3259; *appointer*; *Joed*, an Israelite:—Joed.

3134. יוֹעֶזֶר, **Yôw'ezer,** *yo-eh´-zer*; from 3068 and 5828; *Jehovah* (is his) *help*; *Joezer*, an Israelite:—Joezer.

3135. יוֹעָשׁ, **Yôw'âsh,** *yo-awsh´*; from 3068 and 5789; *Jehovah-hastened*; *Joash*, the name of two Israelites:—Joash.

3136. יוֹצָדָק, **Yôwtsâdâq,** *yo-tsaw-dawk´*; a form of 3087; *Jotsadak*, an Israelite:—Jozadak.

3137. יוֹקִים, **Yôwqîym,** *yo-keem´*; a form of 3113; *Jokim*, an Israelite:—Jokim.

3138. יוֹרֶה, **yôwreh,** *yo-reh´*; active participle of 3384; *sprinkling*; hence a *sprinkling* (or autumnal showers):—first rain, former [rain].

3139. יוֹרָה, **Yôwrâh,** *yo-raw´*; from 3384; *rainy; Jorah,* an Israelite:—Jorah.

3140. יוֹרַי, **Yôwray,** *yo-rah´-ee*; from 3384; *rainy; Jorai,* an Israelite:—Jorai.

3141. יוֹרָם, **Yôwrâm,** *yo-rawm´*; a form of 3088; *Joram,* the name of three Israelites and one Syrian:—Joram.

3142. יוֹשָׁב חֶסֶד, **Yûwshab Chesed,** *yoo-shab´ kheh´-sed*; from 7725 and 2617; *kindness will be returned; Jushab-Chesed,* an Israelite:—Jushab-hesed.

3143. יוֹשִׁבְיָה, **Yôwshibyâh,** *yo-shib-yaw´*; from 3427 and 3050; *Jehovah will cause to dwell; Joshibjah,* an Israelite:—Josibiah.

3144. יוֹשָׁה, **Yôwshâh,** *yo-shaw´*; probably a form of 3145; *Joshah,* an Israelite:—Joshah.

3145. יוֹשַׁוְיָה, **Yôwshavyâh,** *yo-shav-yaw´*; from 3068 and 7737; *Jehovah-set; Joshavjah,* an Israelite:—Joshaviah. Compare 3144.

3146. יוֹשָׁפָט, **Yôwshâphâṭ,** *yo-shaw-fawt´*; a form of 3092; *Joshaphat,* an Israelite:—Joshaphat.

3147. יוֹתָם, **Yôwthâm,** *yo-thawm´*; from 3068 and 8535; *Jehovah (is) perfect; Jotham,* the name of three Israelites:—Jotham.

3148. יוֹתֵר, **yôwthêr,** *yo-thare´*; active participle of 3498; (properly) *redundant;* hence *over and above,* as adjective, noun, adverb or conjunction [as follows]:—better, more (-over), over, profit.

3149. יְזִיאֵל, **Yᵉzîy'êl,** *yez-ee-ale´*; from an unused root (meaning to *sprinkle*) and 410; *sprinkled of God; Jezavel,* an Israelite:—Jeziel [*from the margin*].

3150. יִזִּיָּה, **Yizzîyyâh,** *yiz-zee-yaw´*; from the same as the first part of 3149 and 3050; *sprinkled of Jah; Jizzijah,* an Israelite:—Jeziah.

3151. יָזִיז, **Yâzîyz,** *yaw-zeez´*; from the same as 2123; *he will make prominent; Jaziz,* an Israelite:—Jaziz.

3152. יִזְלִיאָה, **Yizlîy'âh,** *yiz-lee-aw´*; perhaps from an unused root (meaning to *draw up*); *he will draw out; Jizliah,* an Israelite:—Jezliah.

3153. יְזַנְיָה, **Yᵉzanyâh,** *yez-an-yaw´*; or יְזַנְיָהוּ, **Yᵉzanyâhûw,** *yez-an-yaw´-hoo*; probably for 2970; *Jezanjah,* an Israelite:—Jezaniah.

3154. יֵזַע, **yeza',** *yeh´-zah*; from an unused root meaning to *ooze; sweat,* i.e. (by implication) a *sweating* dress:—any thing that causeth sweat.

3155. יִזְרָח, **Yizrâch,** *yiz-rawkh´*; a variation for 250; a *Jizrach* (i.e. Ezrachite or Zarchite) or descendant of Zerach:—Izrahite.

3156. יִזְרַחְיָה, **Yizrachyâh,** *yiz-rakh-yaw´*; from 2224 and 3050; *Jah will shine; Jizrachjah,* the name of two Israelites:—Izrahiah, Jezrahiah.

3157. יִזְרְעֶאל, **Yizrᵉ'e'l,** *yiz-reh-ell´*; from 2232 and 410; *God will sow; Jizreël,* the name of two places in Palestine and of two Israelites:—Jezreel.

3158. יִזְרְעֵאלִי, **Yizrᵉ'ê'lîy,** *yiz-reh-ay-lee´*; patronymic from 3157; a *Jizreëlite* or native of Jizreel:—Jezreelite.

3159. יִזְרְעֵאלִית, **Yizrᵉ'ê'lîyth,** *yiz-reh-ay-leeth´*; feminine of 3158; a *Jezreëlitess:*—Jezreelitess.

3160. יְחֻבָּה, **Yᵉchubbâh,** *yekh-oob-baw´*; from 2247; *hidden; Jechubbah,* an Israelite:—Jehubbah.

3161. יָחַד, **yâchad,** *yaw-khad´*; a primitive root; to *be* (or become) *one:*—join, unite.

3162. יַחַד, **yachad,** *yakh´-ad*; from 3161; (properly) a *unit,* i.e. (adverb) *unitedly:*—alike, at all (once), both, likewise, only, (al-) together, withal.

3163. יַחְדּוֹ, **Yachdôw,** *yakh-doe´*; from 3162 with pronoun suffix; *his unity,* i.e. (adverb) *together; Jachdo,* an Israelite:—Jahdo.

3164. יַחְדִּיאֵל, **Yachdîy'êl,** *yakh-dee-ale´*; from 3162 and 410; *unity of God; Jachdiel,* an Israelite:—Jahdiel.

3165. יֶחְדְּיָהוּ, **Yechdᵉyâhûw,** *yekh-deh-yaw´-hoo*; from 3162 and 3050; *unity of Jah; Jechdijah,* the name of two Israelites:—Jehdeiah.

3166. יַחֲזִיאֵל, **Yachăzîy'êl,** *yakh-az-ee-ale´*; from 2372 and 410; *beheld of God; Jachaziël,* the name of five Israelites:—Jahaziel, Jahziel.

3167. יַחְזְיָה, **Yachzᵉyâh,** *yakh-zeh-yaw´*; from 2372 and 3050; *Jah will behold; Jachzejah,* an Israelite:—Jahaziah.

3168. יְחֶזְקֵאל, **Yᵉchezqê'l,** *yekh-ez-kale´*; from 2388 and 410; *God will strengthen; Jechezkel,* the name of two Israelites:—Ezekiel, Jehezekel.

3169. יְחִזְקִיָּה, **Yᵉchizqîyyâh,** *yekh-iz-kee-yaw´*; or יְחִזְקִיָּהוּ, **Yᵉchizqîyyâhûw,** *yekh-iz-kee-yaw´-hoo*; from 3388 and 3050; *strengthened of Jah; Jechizkijah,* the name of five Israelites:—Hezekiah, Jehizkiah. Compare 2396.

3170. יַחְזֵרָה, **Yachzêrâh,** *yakh-zay-raw´*; from the same as 2386; perhaps *protection; Jachzerah,* an Israelite:—Jahzerah.

3171. יְחִיאֵל, **Yᵉchîy'êl,** *yekh-ee-ale´*; or (2Ch 29:14) יְחַוְאֵל, **Yᵉchav'êl,** *yekh-av-ale´*; from 2421 and 410; *God will live; Jechiël* (or *Jechavel*), the name of eight Israelites:—Jehiel.

3172. יְחִיאֵלִי, **Yᵉchîy'êlîy,** *yekh-ee-ay-lee´*; patronymic from 3171; a *Jechiëlite* or descendant of Jechiel:—Jehieli.

3173. יָחִיד, **yâchîyd,** *yaw-kheed´*; from 3161; (properly) *united,* i.e. *sole;* (by implication) *beloved;* also *lonely;* (feminine) the *life* (as not to be replaced):—darling, desolate, only (child, son), solitary.

An adjective meaning sole, only, solitary. This word is frequently used to refer to an only child. Isaac was Abraham's only son by Sarah (Ge 22:2, 12, 16). Jepthah's daughter was his only child, who came running out to greet him after his vow to sacrifice the first thing to come out of his door (Jgs 11:34). The father of an only child began teaching him wisdom when he was very young (Pr 4:3). Mourning an only child was considered an especially grievous sorrow (Jer 6:26; Am 8:10; Zec 12:10). The feminine form is used parallel to life or soul, portraying the precious, only life we are given (Ps 22:20[21]; 35:17). It is also used to mean lonely or alone (Ps 25:16; 68:6[7]). See the related Hebrew root *yâchad* (3161).

3174. יְחִיָּה, **Yᵉchîyyâh,** *yekh-ee-yaw´*; from 2421 and 3050; *Jah will live; Jechijah,* an Israelite:—Jehiah.

3175. יָחִיל, **yâchîyl,** *yaw-kheel´*; from 3176; *expectant:*—should hope.

This word occurs only in La 3:26, and its exact meaning is difficult to determine. It could be derived from *yâchal* (3176) and be an adjective meaning hopeful. Or it could also be a verb derived from *chûl* (2342) and thus refer to waiting (cf. Ps 37:7). In this case, the word might imply painful waiting as in childbirth, which would harmonize with the next verse. Whether hopefully or in pain (or both), the verse says it is good to wait in silence for the salvation of the Lord.

3176. יָחַל, **yâchal,** *yaw-chal´*; a primitive root; to *wait;* by implication to *be patient, hope:*—(cause to, have, make to) hope, be pained, stay, tarry, trust, wait.

A verb meaning to wait, to hope, to tarry. It is used of Noah (Ge 8:12); Saul (1Sa 10:8; 13:8); Joab (2Sa 18:14); the king of Aram (2Ki 6:33); Job (Job 6:11; 13:15; 14:14); Elihu (Job 32:11, 16). In the Psalms, it frequently means to wait with hope (Ps 31:24[25]; 33:18, 22; 38:15[16]); 42:5[6], 11[12]). This meaning also occurs in Isaiah (Isa 42:4; 51:5); Lamentations (La 3:21, 24); Ezekiel (Eze 19:5); and Micah (Mic 7:7).

3177. יַחְלְאֵל, **Yachlᵉ'êl,** *yakh-leh-ale´*; from 3176 and 410; *expectant of God; Jachleël,* an Israelite:—Jahleel.

3178. יַחְלְאֵלִי, **Yachlᵉ'êlîy,** *yakh-leh-ay-lee´*; patronymic from 3177; a *Jachleëlite* or descendant of Jachleel:—Jahleelites.

3179. יָחַם, **yâcham,** *yaw-kham´*; a primitive root; probably to *be hot;* (figurative) to *conceive:*—get heat, be hot, conceive, be warm.

3180. יַחְמוּר, **yachmûwr,** *yakh-moor´*; from 2560; a kind of *deer* (from the colour; compare 2543):—fallow deer.

3181. יַחְמַי, **Yachmay,** *yakh-mah´-ee*; probably from 3179; *hot; Jachmai,* an Israelite:—Jahmai.

3182. יָחֵף, **yâchêph,** *yaw-khafe´*; from an unused root meaning to *take off the shoes; unsandalled:*—barefoot, being unshod.

3183. יַחְצְאֵל, **Yachtsᵉ'êl,** *yakh-tseh-ale´*; from 2673 and 410; *God will allot; Jachtseël,* Israelite:—Jahzeel. Compare 3185.

3184. יַחְצְאֵלִי, **Yachtsᵉ'êlîy,** *yakh-tseh-ay-lee´*; patronymic from 3183; a *Jachtseëlite* (collective) or descendants of Jachtseel:—Jahzeelites.

3185. יַחְצִיאֵל, **Yachtsîy'êl,** *yakh-tsee-ale´*; from 2673 and 410; *allotted of God*; *Jachtsiël*, an Israelite:—Jahziel. Compare 3183.

3186. יָחַר, **yâchar,** *yaw-khar´*; a primitive root; to *delay*:—tarry longer.

3187. יָחַשׂ, **yâchaś,** *yaw-khas´*; a primitive root; to *sprout*; used only as denominative from 3188; to *enroll* by pedigree:—(number after, number throughout the) genealogy (to be reckoned), be reckoned by genealogies.

3188. יַחַשׂ, **yachaś,** *yakh´-as*; from 3187; a *pedigree* or family list (as *growing* spontaneously):—genealogy.

3189. יַחַת, **Yachath,** *yakh´-ath*; from 3161; *unity*; *Jachath*, the name of four Israelites:—Jahath.

3190. יָטַב, **yâtab,** *yaw-tab´*; a primitive root; to *be* (causative) *make well*, literal (*sound, beautiful*) or figurative (*happy, successful, right*):—be accepted, amend, use aright, benefit, be (make) better, seem best, make cheerful, be comely, + be content, diligent (-ly), dress, earnestly, find favour, give, be glad, do (be, make) good ([-ness]), be (make) merry, please (+ well), shew more [kindness], skilfully, × very small, surely, make sweet, thoroughly, tire, trim, very, be (can, deal, entreat, go, have) well [said, seen].

A verb meaning to be good, to be well, to be pleasing. In the causative stem, it means to do good, to do well, to please, to make pleasing. It is often used in idiomatic expressions with heart (*lêb* [3820]), meaning to be pleased or to be happy (Jgs 18:20; 19:6, 9; Ru 3:7); and with eyes, to be pleasing to someone else (i.e. pleasing or good in their eyes [Ge 34:18; 1Sa 18:5]). The term does not necessarily carry a moral weight but can be translated adverbially as "well." For instance, see Mic 7:3 where their hands do evil well (cf. 1Sa 16:17; Pr 30:29; Isa 23:16). The word can also imply morality (Ps 36:3[4]; 119:68).

3191. יְטַב, **y⁽e⁾tab,** *yet-ab´*; (Chaldee); corresponding to 3190:—seem good.

3192. יָטְבָה, **Yotbâh,** *yot-baw´*; from 3190; *pleasantness*; *Jotbah*, a place in Palestine:—Jotbah.

3193. יָטְבָתָה, **Yotbâthâh,** *yot-baw´-thaw*; from 3192; *Jotbathah*, a place in the Desert:—Jotbath, Jotbathah.

3194. יֻטָּה, **Yuttâh,** *yoot-taw´*; or יוּטָּה, **Yûwttâh,** *yoo-taw´*; from 5186; *extended*; *Juttah* (or *Jutah*), a place in Palestine:—Juttah.

3195. יְטוּר, **Y⁽e⁾tûwr,** *yet-oor´*; probably from the same as 2905; *encircled* (i.e. *inclosed*); *Jetur*, a son of Ishmael:—Jetur.

3196. יַיִן, **yayin,** *yah´-yin*; from an unused root meaning to *effervesce*; *wine* (as fermented); (by implication) *intoxication*:—banqueting, wine, wine [-bibber].

3197. יַךְ, **yak,** *yak*; by erroneous transcription for 3027; a *hand* or *side*:—[way-] side.

3198. יָכַח, **yâkach,** *yaw-kakh´*; a primitive root; to *be right* (i.e. correct); (reciprocal) to *argue*; (causative) to *decide, justify* or *convict*:appoint, argue, chasten, convince, correct (-ion), daysman, dispute, judge, maintain, plead, reason (together), rebuke, reprove (-r), surely, in any wise.

A verb meaning to argue, to convince, to convict, to judge, to reprove. The word usually refers to the clarification of people's moral standing, which may involve arguments being made for them (Job 13:15; Isa 11:4) or against them (Job 19:5; Ps 50:21). The word may refer to the judgment of a case between people (Ge 31:37, 42) or even (in the days before Christ) to someone desired to mediate between God and humankind (Job 9:33). The word may also refer to physical circumstances being used to reprove sin (2Sa 7:14; Hab 1:12). Reproving sin, whether done by God (Pr 3:12) or persons (Le 19:17), was pictured as a demonstration of love, but some people were too rebellious or scornful to be reproved (Pr 9:7; 15:12; Eze 3:26). In Genesis 24:14, 44, the word referred to God's appointment (or judgment) of Rebekah as the one to be married to Isaac.

3199. יָכִין, **Yâkîyn,** *yaw-keen´*; from 3559; *he* (or *it*) *will establish*; *Jakin*, the name of three Israelites and of a temple pillar:—Jachin.

3200. יָכִינִי, **Yâkîynîy,** *yaw-kee-nee´*; patronymic from 3199; a *Jakinite* (collective) or descendants of Jakin:—Jachinites.

3201. יָכֹל, **yâkôl,** *yaw-kole´*; or (fuller) יָכוֹל, **yâkôwl,** *yaw-kole´*; a primitive root; to *be able*, literal (*can, could*) or moral (*may, might*):—be able, any at all (ways), attain, can (away with,

[-not]), could, endure, might, overcome, have power, prevail, still, suffer.

3202. יְכֵל, yᵉkil, *yek-ill´*; (Chaldee); or יְכִיל, yᵉkîyl, *yek-eel´*; (Chaldee); corresponding to 3201:—be able, can, couldest, prevail.

3203. יְכָלְיָה, Yᵉkolyâh, *yek-ol-yaw´*; and יְכָלְיָהוּ, Yᵉkolyâhûw, *yek-ol-hoo´*; or (2Ch 26:3) יְכִילְיָה, Yᵉkîyleᵉyâh, *yek-ee-leh-yaw´*; from 3201 and 3050; *Jah will enable*; *Jekoljah* or *Jekiljah*, an Israelitess:—Jecholiah, Jecoliah.

3204. יְכָנְיָה, Yᵉkonyâh, *yek-on-yaw´(-hoo)*; and יְכָנְיָהוּ, Yᵉkonyâhûw, *yek-on-yaw´-hoo*; or (Jer 27:20) יְכוֹנְיָה, Yᵉkôw-neᵉyâh, *yek-o-neh-yaw´*; from 3559 and 3050; *Jah will establish*; *Jekonjah*, a Jewish king:—Jeconiah. Compare 3659.

3205. יָלַד, yâlad, *yaw-lad´*; a primitive root; to *bear* young; (causative) to *beget*; to *act as midwife*; specifically to *show lineage*:—bear, beget, birth ([-day]), born, (make to) bring forth (children, young), bring up, calve, child, come, be delivered (of a child), time of delivery, gender, hatch, labour, (do the office of a) midwife, declare pedigrees, be the son of, (woman in, woman that) travail (-eth, -ing woman).

3206. יֶלֶד, yeled, *yeh´-led*; from 3205; something *born*, i.e. a *lad* or *offspring*:—boy, child, fruit, son, young man (one).

3207. יַלְדָּה, yaldâh, *yal-daw´*; feminine of 3206; a *lass*:—damsel, girl.

3208. יַלְדוּת, yaldûwth, *yal-dooth´*; abstracted from 3206; *boyhood* (or *girlhood*):—childhood, youth.

3209. יִלּוֹד, yillôwd, *yil-lode´*; passive from 3205; *born*:—born.

3210. יָלוֹן, Yâlôwn, *yaw-lone´*; from 3885; *lodging*; *Jalon*, an Israelite:—Jalon.

3211. יָלִיד, yâlîyd, *yaw-leed´*; from 3205; *born*:—([home-]) born, child, son.

3212. יָלַךְ, yâlak, *yaw-lak´*; a primitive root [compare 1980]; to *walk* (literal or figurative); (causative) to *carry* (in various senses):—× again, away, bear, bring, carry (away), come (away), depart, flow, + follow (-ing), get (away, hence, him), (cause to, make) go (away, -ing, -ne, one's way, out), grow, lead (forth), let down, march, prosper, + pursue, cause to run, spread,

take away ([-journey]), vanish, (cause to) walk (-ing), wax, × be weak.

3213. יָלַל, yâlal, *yaw-lal´*; a primitive root; to *howl* (with a wailing tone) or *yell* (with a boisterous one):—(make to) howl, be howling.

3214. יְלֵל, yᵉlêl, *yel-ale´*; from 3213; a *howl*:—howling.

3215. יְלָלָה, yᵉlâlâh, *yel-aw-law´*; feminine of 3214; a *howling*:—howling.

3216. יָלַע, yâla‘, *yaw-lah´*; a primitive root; to *blurt* or utter inconsiderately:—devour.

3217. יַלֶּפֶת, yallepheth, *yal-leh´-feth*; from an unused root apparently meaning to *stick* or *scrape*; *scurf* or *tetter*:—scabbed.

3218. יֶלֶק, yeleq, *yeh´-lek*; from an unused root meaning to *lick* up; a *devourer*; specifically the young *locust*:—cankerworm, caterpillar.

3219. יַלְקוּט, yalqûwṭ, *yal-koot´*; from 3950; a *travelling pouch* (as if for gleanings):—scrip.

3220. יָם, yâm, *yawm*; from an unused root meaning to *roar*; a *sea* (as breaking in *noisy* surf) or large body of water; specifically (with the article) the *Mediter-ranean*; sometimes a large *river*, or an artificial *basin*; locally, the *west*, or (rarely) the *south*:—sea (× -faring man, [-shore]), south, west (-ern, side, -ward).

3221. יָם, yam, *yam*; (Chaldee); corresponding to 3220:—sea.

3222. יֵם, yêm, *yame*; from the same as 3117; a *warm* spring:—mule.

3223. יְמוּאֵל, Yᵉmûw’êl, *yem-oo-ale´*; from 3117 and 410; *day of God*; *Jemuel*, an Israelite:—Jemuel.

3224. יְמִימָה, Yᵉmîymâh, *yem-ee-maw´*; perhaps from the same as 3117; (properly) *warm*, i.e. *affectionate*; hence *dove* [compare 3123]; *Jemimah*, one of Job's daughters:—Jemimah.

3225. יָמִין, yâmîyn, *yaw-meen´*; from 3231; the *right* hand or side (leg, eye) of a person or other object (as the *stronger* and more dexterous); locally, the *south*:— + left-handed, right (hand, side), south.

3226. יָמִין, **Yâmîyn,** *yaw-meen´*; the same as 3225; *Jamin,* the name of three Israelites:— Jamin. See also 1144.

3227. יְמִינִי, **yᵉmîynîy,** *yem-ee-nee´*; for 3225; *right:*—(on the) right (hand).

3228. יְמִינִי, **Yᵉmîynîy,** *yem-ee-nee´*; patronymic from 3226; a *Jeminite* (collective) or descendants of Jamin:—Jaminites. See also 1145.

3229. יִמְלָא, **Yimlâ,** *yeem-law´*; or יִמְלָה, **Yimlâh,** *yim-law´*; from 4390; *full; Jimla* or *Jimlah,* an Israelite:—Imla, Imlah.

3230. יַמְלֵךְ, **Yamlêk,** *yam-lake´*; from 4427; *he will make king; Jamlek,* an Israelite:—Jamlech.

3231. יָמַן, **yâman,** *yaw-man´*; a primitive root; to *be* (physical) *right* (i.e. firm); but used only as denominative from 3225 and transitive, to *be right-handed* or *take the right-hand* side:—go (turn) to (on, use) the right hand.

3232. יִמְנָה, **Yimnâh,** *yim-naw´*; from 3231; *prosperity* (as betokened by the *right* hand); *Jimnah,* the name of two Israelites; also (with the article) of the posterity of one of them:—Imna, Imnah, Jimnah, Jimnites.

3233. יְמָנִי, **yᵉmânîy,** *yem-aw-nee´*; from 3231; *right* (i.e. at the right hand):—(on the) right (hand).

3234. יִמְנָע, **Yimnâ,** *yim-naw´*; from 4513; *he will restrain; Jimna,* an Israelite:—Imna.

3235. יָמַר, **yâmar,** *yaw-mar´*; a primitive root; to *exchange;* (by implication) to *change places:*— boast selves, change.

3236. יִמְרָה, **Yimrâh,** *yim-raw´*; probably from 3235; *interchange; Jimrah,* an Israelite:—Imrah.

3237. יָמַשׁ, **yâmash,** *yaw-mash´*; a primitive root; to *touch:*—feel.

3238. יָנָה, **yânâh,** *yaw-naw´*; a primitive root; to *rage* or *be violent;* (by implication) to *suppress,* to *maltreat:*—destroy, (thrust out by) oppress (-ing, -ion, -or), proud, vex, do violence.

A verb meaning to oppress, to treat violently. The term is used in Ex 22:21[20], Le 25:14, 17, and Dt 23:16 [17] to refer to improper treatment of strangers and the poor. The participle functions as a noun meaning oppressor (Jer

25:38; 46:16; 50:16). In the Prophets, the term is typically used of foreign oppressors.

3239. יָנוֹחַ, **Yânôwach,** *yaw-no´-akh;* or (with enclitic) יָנוֹחָה, **Yânôwchâh,** *yaw-no´-khaw;* from 3240; *quiet; Janoäch* or *Janochah,* a place in Palestine:—Janoah, Janohah.

3240. יָנַח, **yânach,** *yaw-nakh´*; a primitive root; to *deposit;* (by implication) to *allow to stay:*— bestow, cast down, lay (down, up), leave (off), let alone (remain), pacify, place, put, set (down), suffer, withdraw, withhold. (The Hiphil forms with the *dagesh* are here referred to, in accordance with the older grammarians; but if any distinction of the kind is to be made, these should rather be referred to 5117, and the others here.)

3241. יָנִים, **Yânîym,** *yaw-neem´*; from 5123; *asleep; Janim,* a place in Palestine:—Janum [*from the margin*].

3242. יְנִיקָה, **yᵉnîyqâh,** *yen-ee-kaw´*; from 3243; a *sucker* or *sapling:*—young twig.

3243. יָנַק, **yânaq,** *yaw-nak´*; a primitive root; to *suck;* (causative) to *give milk:*—milch, nurse (-ing mother), (give, make to) suck (-ing child, -ling).

3244. יַנְשׁוּף, **yanshûwph,** *yan-shoof´*; or יַנְשׁוֹף, **yanshôwph,** *yan-shofe´*; apparently from 5398; an unclean (aquatic) bird; probably the *heron* (perhaps from its *blowing* cry, or because the *night*-heron is meant [compare 5399]):—(great) owl.

3245. יָסַד, **yâsad,** *yaw-sad´*; a primitive root; to *set* (literal or figurative); (intensive) to *found;* (reflexive) to *sit* down together, i.e. *settle, consult:*—appoint, take counsel, establish, (lay the, lay for a) found (-ation), instruct, lay, ordain, set, × sure.

A verb meaning to establish, to found, to fix. In a literal sense, this term can refer to laying the foundation of a building, primarily the Temple (1Ki 5:17[31]; 6:37; Ezr 3:11; Isa 44:28); or to laying the foundation of a city like Jericho (Jos 6:26; 1Ki 16:34); or Zion (Isa 14:32). In a metaphorical sense, it can allude to the founding of Egypt (Ex 9:18); the earth (Isa 48:13). This word can also connote the appointment or ordination of an individual(s) to a task or position (1Ch 9:22; Est 1:8). Probably one of the most noteworthy occurrences of this word is in Isa 28:16, where God declares that He will "lay in Zion for a foundation a stone, a tried stone, a precious corner stone, a sure foundation: he that believeth shall not make haste" (KJV). The NT writers announce that that stone is Jesus Christ (Ro 9:33; 1Pe 2:6).

3246. יְסֻד, **yᵉsud,** *yes-ood´*; from 3245; a *foundation* (figuratively) *beginning:*— × began.

3247. יְסוֹד, **yᵉsôwd,** *yes-ode´*; from 3245; a *foundation* (literal or figurative):—bottom, foundation, repairing.

A noun meaning foundation. The word refers to a base on which people build structures. It is used several times to refer to the base of the sacrificial altar, where the blood of sacrifices was poured (Ex 29:12; Le 4:7, 18, 25, 30, 34). The Gate of the Foundation, mentioned in 2Ch 23:5, may have been named from its proximity to the altar. In reference to larger buildings, the word is usually used to express the extent of destruction which sometimes included razing a city down to its foundation (Ps 137:7; Mic 1:6) and sometimes even the destruction of the foundation itself (La 4:11; Eze 30:4). Egypt's foundations appear to symbolize its dependence on other nations (Eze 30:4, 5). Symbolically, the word refers to principles on which people build their lives, whether they be faulty (Job 4:19; 22:16) or sound (Pr 10:25; cf. Mt 7:24–27).

3248. יְסוּדָה, **yᵉsûwdâh,** *yes-oo-daw´*; feminine of 3246; a *foundation:*—foundation.

A feminine noun meaning foundation. This word occurs only in Ps 87:1. The words in Zec 4:9, 8:9, and 12:1, are forms of the verb *yâsad* (3245); the words in Isa 28:16, although difficult to analyze, also do not appear to belong under this reference. In Ps 87:1, the word refers to Jerusalem as God's foundation or base in the holy mountain. The psalm enlarges on this, saying that Jerusalem will be the place of His particular dwelling, the home of a large number of His people, and a source of blessing.

3249. יָסוּר, **yâsûwr,** *yaw-soor´*; from 5493; *departing:*—they that depart.

3250. יִסּוֹר, **yissôwr,** *yis-sore´*; from 3256; a *reprover:*—instruct.

A masculine singular noun meaning one who reproves. The word comes from the verb *yâsar* (3256). Its only occurrence is in Job 40:2.

3251. יָסַךְ, **yâsak,** *yaw-sak´*; a primitive root; to *pour* (intransitive):—be poured.

3252. יִסְכָּה, **Yiskâh,** *yis-kaw´*; from an unused root meaning to *watch; observant; Jiskah,* sister of Lot:—Iscah.

3253. יִסְמַכְיָהוּ, **Yismakyâhûw,** *yis-mak-yaw-hoo´*; from 5564 and 3050; *Jah will sustain; Jismakjah,* an Israelite:—Ismachiah.

3254. יָסַף, **yâsaph,** *yaw-saf´*; a primitive root; to *add* or *augment* (often adverbial) to *continue* to do a thing:—add, × again, × any more, × cease, × come more, + conceive again, continue, exceed, × further, × gather together, get more, give moreover, × henceforth, increase (more and more), join, × longer (bring, do, make, much, put), × (the, much, yet) more (and more), proceed (further), prolong, put, be [strong-] er, × yet, yield.

3255. יְסַף, **yᵉsaph,** *yes-af´*; (Chaldee); corresponding to 3254:—add.

3256. יָסַר, **yâsar,** *yaw-sar´*; a primitive root; to *chastise,* literal (with blows) or figurative (with words); hence to *instruct:*—bind, chasten, chastise, correct, instruct, punish, reform, reprove, sore, teach.

A verb meaning to discipline, to chasten, to instruct, to teach, to punish. It is used with two general poles of meaning (chastening or instructing) that at times merge. Both aspects are presented in Scripture in terms of God and humans. Others can instruct and teach (Job 4:3), as can the conscience (Ps 16:7). Still others can discipline, but God is the ultimate source of true instruction and chastening. He often chides toward an instructive end, especially for His covenant people (Le 26:18, 23; Jer 46:28); wisdom presents the disciplined one as blessed, even though the process is painful (Ps 94:12; 118:18). However, chastisement is not always presented as positive or instructive, for Rehoboam promised an evil chastening that eventually split the united kingdom (1Ki 12:11, 14); and God's just, unremitted punishment would bring desolation (Jer 6:8; 10:24).

3257. יָע, **yâʻ,** *yaw*; from 3261; a *shovel:*—shovel.

3258. יַעְבֵּץ, **Ya'bêts,** *yah-bates´*; from an unused root probably meaning to *grieve; sorrowful; Jabets,* the name of an Israelite, and also of a place in Palestine:—Jabez.

3259. יָעַד, **yâ'ad,** *yaw-ad´*; a primitive root; to *fix* upon (by agreement or appointment); (by implication) to *meet* (at a stated time), to *summon* (to trial), to *direct* (in a certain quarter or position), to *engage* (for marriage):—agree, (make an) appoint (-ment, a time), assemble (selves), betroth, gather (selves, together), meet (together), set (a time).

A verb meaning to appoint, to summon, to engage, to agree, to assemble. It also means allotted or appointed time, such as the amount of time David appointed to Amasa to assemble the men of Judah (2Sa 20:5). This word can also take the meaning of appointing or designating someone to be married (Ex 21:8, 9). Another meaning is to meet someone at an appointed time. Amos asked the question, How can two walk together unless they appoint a time at which to meet (Am 3:3)?

3260. יֶעְדִּי, **Ye'dîy,** *yed-ee´*; from 3259; *appointed; Jedi,* an Israelite:—Iddo [*from the margin*]. See 3035.

3261. יָעָה, **yâ'âh,** *yaw-aw´*; a primitive root; apparently to *brush* aside:—sweep away.

3262. יְעוּאֵל, **Ye'ûw'êl,** *yeh-oo-ale´*; from 3261 and 410; *carried away of God; Jeüel,* the name of four Israelites:—Jehiel, Jeiel, Jeuel. Compare 3273.

3263. יְעוּץ, **Ye'ûwts,** *yeh-oots´*; from 5779; *counsellor; Jeüts,* an Israelite:—Jeuz.

3264. יְעוֹרִים, **ye'ôwrîym,** *yeh-ow-reem´*; a variation of 3293; a *forest:*—wood.

3265. יָעוּר, **Yâ'ûwr,** *yaw-oor´*; apparently passive participle of the same as 3293; *wooded; Jaür,* an Israelite:—Jair [*from the margin*].

3266. יְעוּשׁ, **Ye'ûwsh,** *yeh-oosh´*; from 5789; *hasty; Jeüsh,* the name of an Edomite and of four Israelites:—Jehush, Jeush. Compare 3274.

3267. יָעַז, **yâ'az,** *yaw-az´*; a primitive root; to be *bold* or *obstinate:*—fierce.

3268. יַעֲזִיאֵל, **Ya'ăzîy'êl,** *yah-az-ee-ale´*; from 3267 and 410; *emboldened of God; Jaaziël,* an Israelite:—Jaaziel.

3269. יַעֲזִיָּהוּ, **Ya'ăzîyyâhûw,** *yah-az-ee-yaw´-hoo*; from 3267 and 3050; *emboldened of Jah; Jaazijah,* an Israelite:—Jaaziah.

3270. יַעְזֵיר, **Ya'ăzêyr,** *yah-az-ayr´*; or יַעְזֵר, **Ya'zêr,** *yah-zare´*; from 5826; *helpful; Jaazer* or *Jazer,* a place East of the Jordan:—Jaazer, Jazer.

3271. יָעַט, **yâ'aṭ,** *yaw-at´*; a primitive root; to *clothe:*—cover.

3272. יְעַט, **ye'aṭ,** *yeh-at´*; (Chaldee); corresponding to 3289; to *counsel;* (reflexive) to *consult:*—counsellor, consult together.

3273. יְעִיאֵל, **Ye'îy'êl,** *yeh-ee-ale´*; from 3261 and 410; *carried away of God; Jeïel,* the name of six Israelites:—Jeiel, Jehiel. Compare 3262.

3274. יְעִישׁ, **Ye'îysh,** *yeh-eesh´*; from 5789; *hasty; Jeïsh,* the name of an Edomite and of an Israelite:—Jeush [*from the margin*]. Compare 3266.

3275. יַעְכָּן, **Ya'kân,** *yah-kawn´*; from the same as 5912; *troublesome; Jakan,* an Israelite:—Jachan.

3276. יָעַל, **ya'al,** *yaw-al´*; a primitive root; (properly) to *ascend;* (figurative) to *be valuable* ([objective] *useful,* [subjective] *benefited*):—× at all, set forward, can do good, (be, have) profit (-able).

3277. יָעֵל, **yâ'êl,** *yaw-ale´*; from 3276; an *ibex* (as *climbing*):—wild goat.

3278. יָעֵל, **Yâ'êl,** *yaw-ale´*; the same as 3277; *Jaël,* a Canaanite:—Jael.

3279. יַעְלָא, **Ya'ălâ',** *yah-al-aw´*; or יַעְלָה, **Ya'ălâh,** *yah-al-aw´*; the same as 3280 or direct from 3276; *Jaala* or *Jaalah,* one of the Nethinim:—Jaala, Jaalah.

3280. יַעֲלָה, **ya'ălâh,** *yah-al-aw´*; feminine of 3277; wild goat:—roe.

3281. יַעְלָם, **Ya'lâm,** *yah-lawm´*; from 5956; *occult; Jalam,* an Edomite:—Jalam.

3282. יַעַן, **ya'an,** *yah´-an*; from an unused root meaning to *pay attention;* (properly) *heed;* (by implication) *purpose* (sake or account); used adverbially to indicate the *reason* or *cause*:—because (that), forasmuch (+ as), seeing then, + that, + whereas, + why.

3283. יָעֵן, **yâ'ên,** *yaw-ane'*; from the same as 3282; the *ostrich* (probably from its *answering* cry:—ostrich.

3284. יַעֲנָה, **ya'ănâh,** *yah-an-aw'*; feminine of 3283, and meaning the same:— + owl.

3285. יַעֲנַי, **Ya'nay,** *yah-nah'ee*; from the same as 3283; *responsive*; Jaanai, an Israelite:—Jaanai.

3286. יָעַף, **yâ'aph,** *yaw-af'*; a primitive root; to *tire* (as if from wearisome *flight*):—faint, cause to fly, (be) weary (self).

3287. יָעֵף, **yâ'êph,** *yaw-afe'*; from 3286; *fatigued*; (figurative) *exhausted*:—faint, weary.

3288. יְעָף, **y'âph,** *yeh-awf'*; from 3286; *fatigue* (adverbial) utterly *exhausted*:—swiftly.

3289. יָעַץ, **yâ'ats,** *yaw-ats'*; a primitive root; to *advise*; (reflexive) to *deliberate* or *resolve*:—advertise, take advice, advise (well), consult, (give, take) counsel (-lor), determine, devise, guide, purpose.

A verb meaning to advise, to consult, to counsel, to be advised, to deliberate, to conspire, to take counsel. Jethro, Moses' father-in-law, advised Moses about how to judge the people of Israel (Ex 18:19); and wise men, such as Hushai and Ahithophel, served as counselors to kings and other important people (2Sa 17:15; 1Ki 12:9); as did prophets (Jer 38:15). Many counselors help ensure that plans will succeed (Pr 15:22); God counseled His servants (Ps 16:7); the coming ruler of Israel will be the "Wonderful Counselor" (Isa 9:6[5]). The verb also means to decide, to make plans or decisions. These plans can be for or against someone or something with God or a human as a subject of the sentence (Isa 7:5; 14:24; Jer 49:20; Hab 2:10), but God's plans will never fail (Isa 14:24).

In the passive, this verb means to permit oneself to be counseled—wisdom is gained by a person who acts in this manner (Pr 13:10; cf. 1:5). More often, this stem expresses a reciprocal sense: Rehoboam consulted together with the elders (1Ki 12:6); and the enemies of the psalmist conspired against him (Ps 71:10). In the reflexive stem, it means to take counsel

against as when the Lord's enemies conspired against His people (Ps 83:3[4]).

3290. יַעֲקֹב, **Ya'ăqôb,** *yah-ak-obe'*; from 6117; *heel-catcher* (i.e. supplanter); Jaakob, the Israelite patriarch:—Jacob.

3291. יַעֲקֹבָה, **Ya'ăqôbâh,** *yah-ak-o'-baw*; from 3290; *Jaakobah,* an Israelite:—Jaakobah.

3292. יַעֲקָן, **Ya'ăqân,** *yah-ak-awn'*; from the same as 6130; *Jaakan,* an Idumæan:—Jaakan. Compare 1142.

3293. יַעַר, **ya'ar,** *yah'-ar*; from an unused root probably meaning to *thicken* with verdure; a *copse* of bushes; hence a *forest*; hence *honey* in the *comb* (as hived in trees):—[honey-] comb, forest, wood.

3294. יַעְרָה, **Ya'râh,** *yah-raw'*; a form of 3295; *Jarah,* an Israelite:—Jarah.

3295. יַעֲרָה, **ya'ărâh,** *yah-ar-aw'*; feminine of 3293, and meaning the same:—[honey-] comb, forest.

3296. יַעֲרֵי אֹרְגִים, **Ya'ărêy 'Ôr'gîym,** *yah-ar-ay' o-reg-eem'*; from the plural of 3293 and the masculine plural participle active of 707; *woods of weavers;* Jaare-Oregim, an Israelite:—Jaare-oregim.

3297. יְעָרִים, **Y'ârîym,** *yeh-aw-reem'*; plural of 3293; *forests;* Jeärim, a place in Palestine:—Jearim. Compare 7157.

3298. יַעֲרֶשְׁיָה, **Ya'ăreshyâh,** *yah-ar-esh-yaw'*; from an unused root of uncertain significance and 3050; *Jaareshjah,* an Israelite:—Jaresiah.

3299. יַעֲשׂוּ, **Ya'ăsâv,** *yah-as-awv'*; from 6213; *they will do;* Jaasu, an Israelite:—Jaasau.

3300. יַעֲשִׂיאֵל, **Ya'ăsîy'êl,** *yah-as-ee-ale'*; from 6213 and 410; *made of God;* Jaasiel, an Israelite:—Jaasiel, Jasiel.

3301. יִפְדְיָה, **Yiphd'yâh,** *yif-deh-yaw'*; from 6299 and 3050; *Jah will liberate;* Jiphdejah, an Israelite:—Iphedeiah.

3302. יָפָה, **yâphâh,** *yaw-faw'*; a primitive root; (properly) to *be bright,* i.e. (by implication) *beautiful*:—be beautiful, be (make self) fair (-r), deck.

3303. יָפֶה, **yâpheh,** *yaw-feh´*; from 3302; *beautiful* (literal or figurative):— + beautiful, beauty, comely, fair (-est, one), + goodly, pleasant, well.

3304. יְפֵה־פִיָּה, **yᵉphêh-phîyyâh,** *yef-eh´ fee-yaw´*; from 3302 by reduplication; *very beautiful*:—very fair.

3305. יָפוֹ, **Yâphôw,** *yaw-fo´*; or יָפוֹא, **Yâphôw',** *yaw-fo´*; (Ezr 3:7), from 3302; *beautiful; Japho,* a place in Palestine:—Japha, Joppa.

3306. יָפַח, **yâphach,** *yaw-fakh´*; a primitive root; (properly) to *breathe* hard, i.e. (by implication) to *sigh*:—bewail self.

3307. יָפֵחַ, **yâphêach,** *yaw-fay´-akh*; from 3306; (properly) *puffing,* i.e. (figurative) *meditating*:—such as breathe out.

3308. יֳפִי, **yŏphîy,** *yof-ee´*; from 3302; *beauty*:—beauty.

3309. יָפִיעַ, **Yâphîyaʻ,** *yaw-fee´-ah*; from 3313; *bright; Japhia,* the name of a Canaanite, an Israelite, and a place in Palestine:—Japhia.

3310. יַפְלֵט, **Yaphlêṭ,** *yaf-late´*; from 6403; *he will deliver; Japhlet,* an Israelite:—Japhlet.

3311. יַפְלֵטִי, **Yaphlêṭîy,** *yaf-lay-tee´*; patronymic from 3310; a *Japhletite* or descendant of Japhlet:—Japhleti.

3312. יְפֻנֶּה, **Yᵉphunneh,** *yef-oon-neh´*; from 6437; *he will be prepared; Jephunneh,* the name of two Israelites:—Jephunneh.

3313. יָפַע, **yâphaʻ,** *yaw-fah´*; a primitive root; to *shine*:—be light, shew self, (cause to) shine (forth).

3314. יִפְעָה, **yiphʻâh,** *yif-aw´*; from 3313; *splendor* or (figurative) *beauty*:—brightness.

3315. יֶפֶת, **Yepheth,** *yeh´-feth*; from 6601; *expansion; Jepheth,* a son of Noah; also his posterity:—Japheth.

3316. יִפְתָּח, **Yiphtâch,** *yif-tawkh´*; from 6605; *he will open; Jiphtach,* an Israelite; also a place in Palestine:—Jephthah, Jiphtah.

3317. יִפְתַּח־אֵל, **Yiphtach-'êl,** *yif-tach-ale´*; from 6605 and 410; *God will open; Jiphtach-el,* a place in Palestine:—Jiphthah-el.

3318. יָצָא, **yâtsâ',** *yaw-tsaw´*; a primitive root; to *go* (causatively, *bring*) *out,* in a great variety of applications, literal and figurative, direct and proximate:— × after, appear, × assuredly, bear out, × begotten, break out, bring forth (out, up), carry out, come (abroad, out, thereat, without), + be condemned, depart (-ing, -ure), draw forth, in the end, escape, exact, fail, fall (out), fetch forth (out), get away (forth, hence, out), (able to, cause to, let) go abroad (forth, on, out), going out, grow, have forth (out), issue out, lay (lie) out, lead out, pluck out, proceed, pull out, put away, be risen, × scarce, send with commandment, shoot forth, spread, spring out, stand out, × still, × surely, take forth (out), at any time, × to [and fro], utter.

3319. יְצָא, **yᵉtsa',** *yets-ah´*; (Chaldee); corresponding to 3318:—finish.

3320. יָצַב, **yâtsab,** *yaw-tsab´*; a primitive root; to *place* (any thing so as to stay); (reflexive) to *station, offer, continue*:—present selves, remaining, resort, set (selves), (be able to, can, with-) stand (fast, forth, -ing, still, up).

3321. יְצַב, **yᵉtsab,** *yets-ab´*; (Chaldee); corresponding to 3320; to *be firm;* hence to *speak surely*:—truth.

An Aramaic verb meaning to take, to make a stand, to gain certainty, to know the truth. It is used only once in the entire OT, in Da 7:19, where Daniel desired to know the truth of the fourth beast's identity. This corresponds with the Hebrew word *yâtsab* (3320), meaning to make one's stand, to take one's stand, or to present oneself.

3322. יָצַג, **yâtsag,** *yaw-tsag´*; a primitive root; to *place* permanently:—establish, leave, make, present, put, set, stay.

3323. יִצְהָר, **yitshâr,** *yits-hawr´*; from 6671; *oil* (as producing *light*); (figurative) *anointing*:— + anointed, oil.

A masculine noun meaning fresh oil, anointing oil. It most commonly refers to fresh oil produced from the land, most likely from olive trees (2Ki 18:32). This oil could be in an unprocessed state (Dt 7:13). Concerning religious uses, people gave this oil to the Levites and priests as a means of support (2Ch 31:5). The Hebrew word is also used once for the purpose of anointing (Zec 4:14).

3324. יִצְהָר, **Yitshâr,** *yits-hawr´*; the same as 3323; *Jitshar*, an Israelite:—Izhar.

3325. יִצְהָרִי, **Yitshârîy,** *yits-haw-ree´*; patronymic from 3324; a *Jitsharite* or descendant of Jitshar:—Izeharites, Izharites.

3326. יָצוּעַ, **yâtsûwa‘,** *yaw-tsoo´-ah*; passive participle of 3331; *spread*, i.e. a *bed*; (architecturally) an *extension*, i.e. *wing* or *lean-to* (a single story or collectively):—bed, chamber, couch.

3327. יִצְחָק, **Yitschâq,** *yits-khawk´*; from 6711; *laughter* (i.e. *mockery*); *Jitschak* (or Isaac), son of Abraham:—Isaac. Compare 3446.

3328. יִצְחַר, **Yitschar,** *yits-khar´*; from the same as 6713; *he will shine*; *Jitschar*, an Israelite:—and Zehoar [*from the margin*].

3329. יָצִיא, **yâtsîy’,** *yaw-tsee´*; from 3318; *issue*, i.e. *offspring*:—those that came forth.

3330. יַצִּיב, **yatstsîyb,** *yats-tseeb´*; (Chaldee); from 3321; *fixed, sure*; (concrete) *certainty*:—certain (-ty), true, truth.

3331. יָצַע, **yatsa‘,** *yaw-tsah´*; a primitive root; to *strew* as a surface:—make [one’s] bed, × lie, spread.

3332. יָצַק, **yâtsaq,** *yaw-tsak´*; a primitive root; (properly) to *pour* out (transitive or intransitive); (by implication) to *melt* or *cast* as metal; (by extension) to *place* firmly, to *stiffen* or grow hard:—cast, cleave fast, be (as) firm, grow, be hard, lay out, molten, overflow, pour (out), run out, set down, steadfast.

3333. יְצֻקָה, **yᵉtsuqâh,** *yets-oo-kaw´*; passive participle feminine of 3332; *poured* out, i.e. *run* into a mould:—when it was cast.

3334. יָצַר, **yâtsar,** *yaw-tsar´*; a primitive root; to *press* (intrans.), i.e. *be narrow*; (figurative) *be in distress*:—be distressed, be narrow, be straitened (in straits), be vexed.

3335. יָצַר, **yâtsar,** *yaw-tsar´*; probably identical with 3334 (through the *squeezing* into shape); ([compare 3331]); to *mould* into a form; especially as a *potter*; (figurative) to *determine* (i.e. form a resolution):— × earthen, fashion, form, frame, make (-r), potter, purpose.

A verb meaning to form, to fashion, to shape, to devise. The primary meaning of the word is

derived from the idea of cutting or framing. It is used of God’s fashioning man from the dust of the ground (Ge 2:7); God’s creative works in nature (Ps 95:5; Am 4:13); and in the womb (Ps 139:16; Jer 1:5; cf. Zec 12:1); the molding of clay (Isa 29:16; 45:9); the framing of seasons (Ps 74:17); the forging of metal (Isa 44:12); the crafting of weapons (Isa 54:17); the making of plans (Ps 94:20; Isa 46:11; Jer 18:11). It also signifies a potter (Ps 2:9; Isa 41:25); a sculptor (Isa 44:9); or the Creator (Isa 43:1; 44:2, 24). By extension, the word conveys the notion of predestination and election (2Ki 19:25; Isa 49:5).

3336. יֵצֶר, **yêtser,** *yay´-tser*; from 3335; a *form*; (figurative) *conception* (i.e. *purpose*):—frame, thing framed, imagination, mind, work.

A masculine noun meaning form, framing, purpose, imagination. One use of this word was to refer to a pottery vessel formed by a potter (i.e. that which was formed [Isa 29:16]). Another example of a formed object was a graven image (Hab 2:18). The psalmist said that man was formed from the dust (Ps 103:14). This word also carries the connotation of something thought of in the mind, such as wickedness in people’s hearts (Ge 6:5); or something treasured or stored in the heart (1Ch 29:18).

3337. יֵצֶר, **Yêtser,** *yay´-tser*; the same as 3336; *Jetser*, an Israelite:—Jezer.

3338. יָצֻר, **yâtsur,** *yaw-tsoor´*; passive participle of 3335; *structure*, i.e. limb or part:—member.

3339. יִצְרִי, **Yitsrîy,** *yits-ree´*; from 3335; *formative*; *Jitsri*, an Israelite:—Isri.

3340. יִצְרִי, **Yitsrîy,** *yits-ree´*; patron. from 3337; a *Jitsrite* (collectively) or descendant of Jetser:—Jezerites.

3341. יָצַת, **yâtsath,** *yaw-tsath´*; a primitive root; to *burn* or *set on fire*; (figurative) to *desolate*:—burn (up), be desolate, set (on) fire ([fire]), kindle.

3342. יֶקֶב, **yeqeb,** *yeh´-keb*; from an unused root meaning to *excavate*; a *trough* (as dug out); specifically a *wine-vat* (whether the lower one, into which the juice drains; or the upper, in which the grapes are crushed):—fats, presses, press-fat, wine (-press).

3343. יְקַבְצְאֵל, Yᵉqabtsᵉ'êl, *yek-ab-tseh-ale´*; from 6908 and 410; *God will gather; Jekabtseël,* a place in Palestine:—Jekabzeel. Compare 6909.

3344. יָקַד, yâqad, *yaw-kad´*; a primitive root; to *burn:*—(be) burn (-ing), × from the hearth, kindle.

3345. יְקַד, yᵉqad, *yek-ad´*; (Chaldee); corresponding to 3344:—burning.

3346. יְקֵדָה, yᵉqêdâh, *yek-ay-daw´*; (Chaldee); from 3345; a *conflagration:*—burning.

3347. יׇקְדְעָם, Yoqdᵉ'âm, *yok-deh-awm´*; from 3344 and 5971; *burning of* (the) *people; Jokdeäm,* a place in Palestine:—Jokdeam.

3348. יָקֶה, Yâqeh, *yaw-keh´*; from an unused root probably meaning to *obey; obedient; Jakeh,* a symbolical name (for Solomon):—Jakeh.

3349. יְקָהָה, yᵉqâhâh, *yek-aw-haw´*; from the same as 3348; *obedience:*—gathering, to obey.

A feminine noun meaning obedience. In Jacob's prophecy to Judah, he said that the kingship would not depart from Judah's descendants until one came who would have the obedience of the nations (Ge 49:10). This verse is considered by many to be prophetic of Jesus Christ. In the sayings of Agur, the disobedient child should have his eyes pecked out by ravens and vultures (Pr 30:17).

3350. יְקוֹד, yᵉqôwd, *yek-ode´*; from 3344; a *burning:*—burning.

3351. יְקוּם, yᵉqûwm, *yek-oom´*; from 6965; (properly) *standing* (extant), i.e. (by implication) a *living thing:*—(living) substance.

3352. יָקוֹשׁ, yâqôwsh, *yaw-koshe´*; from 3369; (properly) *entangling;* hence a *snarer:*—fowler.

3353. יָקוּשׁ, yâqûwsh, *yaw-koosh´*; passive participle of 3369; (properly) *entangled,* i.e. (by implication) (intransitive) a *snare,* or (transitive) a *snarer:*—fowler, snare.

3354. יְקוּתִיאֵל, Yᵉqûwthîy'êl, *yek-ooth-ee´-ale;* from the same as 3348 and 410; *obedience of God; Jekuthiël,* an Israelite:—Jekuthiel.

3355. יׇקְטָן, Yoqṭân, *yok-tawn´*; from 6994; *he will be made little; Joktan,* an Arabian patriarch:—Joktan.

3356. יָקִים, Yâqîym, *yaw-keem´*; from 6965; *he will raise; Jakim,* the name of two Israelites:—Jakim. Compare 3079.

3357. יַקִּיר, yaqqîyr, *yak-keer´*; from 3365; *precious:*—dear.

3358. יַקִּיר, yaqqîyr, *yak-keer´*; (Chaldee); corresponding to 3357:—noble, rare.

3359. יְקַמְיָה, Yᵉqamyâh, *yek-am-yaw´*; from 6965 and 3050; *Jah will rise; Jekamjah,* the name of two Israelites:—Jekamiah. Compare 3079.

3360. יְקַמְעָם, Yᵉqam'âm, *yek-am´-awm;* from 6965 and 5971; (the) *people will rise; Jekamam,* an Israelite:—Jekameam. Compare 3079, 3361.

3361. יׇקְמְעָם, Yoqmᵉ'âm, *yok-meh-awm´*; from 6965 and 5971; (the) *people will be raised; Jokmeäm,* a place in Palestine:—Jokmeam. Compare 3360, 3362.

3362. יׇקְנְעָם, Yoqnᵉ'âm, *yok-neh-awm´*; from 6969 and 5971; (the) *people will be lamented; Jokneäm,* a place in Palestine:—Jokneam.

3363. יָקַע, yâqa', *yaw-kah´*; a primitive root; (properly) to *sever* oneself, i.e. (by implication) to *be dislocated;* (figurative) to *abandon;* (causative) to *impale* (and thus allow to drop to pieces by *rotting):*—be alienated, depart, hang (up), be out of joint.

3364. יָקַץ, yâqats, *yaw-kats´*; a primitive root; to *awake* (intransitive):—(be) awake (-d).

3365. יָקַר, yâqar, *yaw-kar´*; a primitive root; (properly) apparently to *be heavy,* i.e. (figurative) *valuable;* (causative) to *make rare;* (figurative) to *inhibit:*—be (make) precious, be prized, be set by, withdraw.

3366. יְקָר, yᵉqâr, *yek-awr´*; from 3365; *value,* i.e. (concrete) *wealth;* (abstract) *costliness, dignity:*—honour, precious (things), price.

3367. יְקָר, yᵉqâr, *yek-awr´*; (Chaldee); corresponding to 3366:—glory, honour.

3368. יָקָר, yâqâr, *yaw-kawr´*; from 3365; *valuable* (objective or subjective):—brightness, clear, costly, excellent, fat, honourable women, precious, reputation.

3369. יָקֹשׁ, yâqôsh, *yaw-koshe´*; a primitive root; to *ensnare* (literal or figurative):—fowler (lay a) snare.

A verb meaning to snare. The word refers primarily to the snaring of animals, especially birds (Ps 124:7; Ecc 9:12). However, this word always refers figuratively to the catching of a person or people in an undesirable situation. The bait of these snares is people's desire for other gods (Dt 7:25; Ps 141:9, cf. Ps 141:4). Pride makes persons susceptible to snares (Jer 50:24[cf. Jer 50:31, 32]) while humility (Pr 6:2) and the help of God may deliver them. In two similar passages in Isaiah, Israel is snared by their rejection of God's word (Isa 8:15; 28:13).

3370. יָקְשָׁן, **Yoqshân,** *yok-shawn´*; from 3369; *insidious; Jokshan*, an Arabian patriarch:—Jokshan.

3371. יָקְתְאֵל, **Yoqthᵉ'êl,** *yok-theh-ale´*; probably from the same as 3348 and 410; *veneration of God* [compare 3354]; *Joktheël*, the name of a place in Palestine, and of one in Idumæa:—Joktheel.

3372. יָרֵא, **yârê',** *yaw-ray´*; a primitive root; to *fear*; (moral) to *revere*; (causative) to *frighten*:—affright, be (make) afraid, dread (-ful), (put in) fear (-ful, -fully, -ing), (be had in) reverence (-end), × see, terrible (act, -ness, thing).

A verb meaning to fear, to respect, to reverence, to be afraid, to be awesome, to be feared, to make afraid, to frighten. The most common translations are to be afraid, to fear, to fear God. "The fear of the LORD is the beginning of knowledge" is a famous use of the noun (Pr 1:7 NIV); the famous narrative of the near sacrifice of Isaac proved to God that Abraham feared Him above all (Ge 22:12); people who feared God were considered faithful and trustworthy for such fear constrained them to believe and act morally (Ex 18:21). The midwives of Pharaoh feared God and did not kill the newborn Hebrew males (Ex 1:17, 21). The fear of the Lord was closely tied to keeping God's decrees and laws (Dt 6:2); people who fear God delight in hearing of His deeds for His people (Ps 66:16). The God of Israel was an object of respectful fear (Le 19:30; 26:2) for Obadiah and Hezekiah (1Ki 18:3, 12; Jer 26:19). In addition, because Israel feared and worshipped other gods, they were destroyed by Assyria (Jgs 6:10; 2Ki 17:7, 35). They were to worship and fear only the Lord their God (Jos 24:14). Israel had an unnecessary and unhealthy fear of the

nations of Canaan (Dt 7:19). The verb describes the fear of men: Jacob feared Esau, his brother (Ge 32:7[8]); and the official in charge of Daniel feared the king (Da 1:10). In the sense of respectful fear, each person was to honour his mother and father (Le 19:3). As a stative verb, it describes a state of being or attitude, such as being afraid or fearful: a man afraid of war was to remove himself from the army of Israel (Dt 20:3, 8; Jgs 7:3); as a result of rebellion, Adam and Eve were afraid before the Lord (Ge 3:10).

In the passive form, the word expresses the idea of being feared, held in esteem: God was feared and awesome (Ex 15:11; Ps 130:4); His deeds were awe-inspiring (Dt 10:21; 2Sa 7:23); the Cushites were an aggressive people feared by many (Isa 18:2); even the threatening desert area was considered fearful or dreadful (Dt 8:15).

The factitive or intensive form means to frighten or to impart fear: the wise woman of Tekoa was frightened by the people (2Sa 14:15); and the governor of Samaria, Sanballat, attempted to frighten Nehemiah so that he would not rebuild the wall of Jerusalem (Ne 6:9).

3373. יָרֵא, **yârê',** *yaw-ray´*; from 3372; *fearing*; moral *reverent*:—afraid, fear (-ful).

An adjective meaning fearing, afraid. The Hebrew word is used when the author of Genesis speaks of Abraham fearing God because he did not hold back his only son (Ge 22:12). Jacob asked God to save him from Esau, because he was afraid that Esau would attack him (Ge 32:11[12]). Jethro told Moses to select as judges men who feared God (Ex 18:21). Proverbs says that a woman who fears the Lord is to be praised (Pr 31:30). Jeremiah told the Israelite army that God said not to fear the king of Babylon (Jer 42:11). See the primary verb *yârê'* (3372).

3374. יִרְאָה, **yir'âh,** *yir-aw´*; feminine of 3373; *fear* (also used as infinitive); moral *reverence*:—× dreadful, × exceedingly, fear (-fulness).

A feminine noun meaning fear. The word usually refers to the fear of God and is viewed as a positive quality. This fear acknowledges God's good intentions (Ex 20:20). It will motivate and delight even the Messiah (Isa 11:2, 3). This fear is produced by God's Word (Ps 119:38; Pr 2:5) and makes a person receptive to wisdom and knowledge (Pr 1:7; 9:10). It is even identified with wisdom (Job 28:28; Pr 15:33). The fear of the Lord may be lost by despair of one's own situation (Job 6:14) or envy of a sinner's (Pr 23:17). This fear restrains people from sin (Ge 20:11; Ex 20:20; Ne 5:9); gives confidence (Job 4:6; Pr 14:26); helps rulers and causes judges to act justly (2Sa 23:3; 2Ch 19:9; Ne 5:15); results in good sleep (Pr 19:23); with humility, leads to riches, honour, and life (Pr 22:4). The word also refers to the fear of briers and thorns (Isa 7:25); and the fear of Israel that would fall on other nations (Dt 2:25).

3375. יִרְאוֹן, **Yir'ôwn,** *yir-ohn´*; from 3372; *fearfulness; Jiron,* a place in Palestine:—Iron.

3376. יִרְאִיָּיה, **Yir'îyyâyh,** *yir-ee-yaw´*; from 3373 and 3050; *fearful of Jah; Jirijah,* an Israelite:—Irijah.

3377. יָרֵב, **Yârêb,** *yaw-rabe´*; from 7378; *he will contend; Jareb,* a symbolical name for Assyria:—Jareb. Compare 3402.

3378. יְרֻבַּעַל, **Yᵉrubba'al,** *yer-oob-bah´-al*; from 7378 and 1168; *Baal will contend; Jerubbaal,* a symbolical name of Gideon:—Jerubbaal.

3379. יָרָבְעָם, **Yârob'âm,** *yaw-rob-awm´*; from 7378 and 5971; (the) *people will contend; Jarobam,* the name of two Israelites kings:—Jeroboam.

3380. יְרֻבֶּשֶׁת, **Yᵉrubbesheth,** *yer-oob-beh´-sheth*; from 7378 and 1322; *shame* (i.e. the idol) *will contend; Jerubbesheth,* a symbolical name for Gideon:—Jerubbesheth.

3381. יָרַד, **yârad,** *yaw-rad´*; a primitive root; to *descend* (literally) to *go downwards;* or conventionally to a lower region, as the shore, a boundary, the enemy, etc.; (figuratively) to *fall;* (causative) to *bring down* (in all the above applications):— × abundantly, bring down, carry down, cast down, (cause to) come (-ing) down, fall (down), get down, go (-ing) down (-ward), hang down, × indeed, let down, light (down), put down (off), (cause to, let) run down, sink, subdue, take down.

3382. יֶרֶד, **Yered,** *yeh´-red*; from 3381; a *descent; Jered,* the name of an antediluvian, and of an Israelite:—Jared.

3383. יַרְדֵּן, **Yardên,** *yar-dane´*; from 3381; a *descender; Jarden,* the principal river of Palestine:—Jordan.

3384. יָרָה, **yârâh,** *yaw-raw´*; or (2Ch 26:15) יָרָא, **yârâ',** *yaw-raw´*; a primitive root; (properly) to *flow* as water (i.e. to *rain*); (transitive) to *lay* or *throw* (especially an arrow, i.e. to *shoot*); (figurative) to *point* out (as if by *aiming* the finger), to *teach:*—(+) archer, cast, direct, inform, instruct, lay, shew, shoot, teach (-er, -ing), through.

A verb meaning to shoot, to throw, to pour. God hurled Pharaoh's army into the sea (Ex 15:4); Joshua cast lots (Jos 18:6); and God asked Job who laid the cornerstone of the earth (Job 38:6). This word is used often in reference to shooting with arrows, as Jonathan (1Sa 20:36); and those who killed some of David's men (2Sa 11:24). King Uzziah made machines that shot arrows (2Ch 26:15); and the wicked shot arrows at the upright of heart (Ps 11:2; 64:4[5]). In the sense of throwing, people were overthrown (Nu 21:30); and Job said that God had thrown him in the mud (Job 30:19).

3385. יְרוּאֵל, **Yᵉrûw'êl,** *yer-oo-ale´*; from 3384 and 410; *founded of God; Jeruel,* a place in Palestine:—Jeruel.

3386. יָרוֹחַ, **Yârôwach,** *yaw-ro´-akh*; perhaps denominative from 3394; (born at the) *new moon; Jaroäch,* an Israelite:—Jaroah.

3387. יָרוֹק, **yârôwq,** *yaw-roke´*; from 3417; *green,* i.e. an herb:—green thing.

3388. יְרוּשָׁא, **Yᵉrûwshâ',** *yer-oo-shaw´*; or יְרוּשָׁה, **Yᵉrûwshâh,** *yer-oo-shaw´*; feminine passive participle of 3423; *possessed; Jerusha* or *Jerushàh,* an Israelitess:—Jerusha, Jerushah.

3389. יְרוּשָׁלַם, **Yᵉrûwshâlaim,** *yer-oo-shaw-lah´-im*; rarely יְרוּשָׁלַיִם, **Yᵉrûwshâlayim,** *yer-oo-shaw-lah´-yim;* a dual (in allusion to its two main hills [the true pointing, at least of the former reading, seems to be that of 3390]); probably from (the passive participle of) 3384 and 7999; *founded peaceful; Jerushalaïm* or *Jerushalem,* the capital city of Palestine:—Jerusalem.

3390. יְרוּשָׁלֶם, **Yᵉrûwshâlem,** *yer-oo-shaw-lem´*; (Chaldee); corresponding to 3389:—Jerusalem.

3391. יֶרַח, **yerach,** *yeh´-rakh*; from an unused root of uncertain significance; a *lunation*, i.e. *month*:—month, moon.

3392. יֶרַח, **Yerach,** *yeh´-rakh*; the same as 3391; *Jerach*, an Arabian patriarch:—Jerah.

3393. יְרַח, **yᵉrach,** *yeh-rakh´*; (Chaldee); corresponding to 3391; a *month*:—month.

3394. יָרֵחַ, **yârêach,** *yaw-ray´-akh*; from the same as 3391; the *moon*:—moon.

3395. יְרֹחָם, **Yᵉrôchâm,** *yer-o-khawm´*; from 7355; *compassionate; Jerocham*, the name of seven or eight Israelites:—Jeroham.

3396. יְרַחְמְאֵל, **Yᵉrachmᵉ’êl,** *yer-akh-meh-ale´*; from 7355 and 410; *God will compassionate; Jerachmeël*, the name of three Israelites:— Jerahmeel.

3397. יְרַחְמְאֵלִי, **Yᵉrachmᵉ’êlîy,** *yer-akh-meh-ay-lee´*; patronymic from 3396; a *Jerachmeëlite* or descendant of Jerachmeel:—Jerahmeelites.

3398. יַרְחָע, **Yarchâ‘,** *yar-khaw´*; probably of Egyptian origin; *Jarcha*, an Eggyptian:—Jarha.

3399. יָרַט, **yârat,** *yaw-rat´*; a primitive root; to *precipitate* or *hurl* (*rush*) headlong; (intransitive) to *be rash*:—be perverse, turn over.

3400. יְרִיאֵל, **Yᵉrîy’êl,** *yer-ee-ale´*; from 3384 and 410; *thrown of God; Jeriël*, an Israelite:—Jeriel. Compare 3385.

3401. יָרִיב, **yârîyb,** *yaw-rebe´*; from 7378; (literally) *he will contend*; proper adjective *contentious*; used as noun, an *adversary*:—that contend (-eth), that strive.

3402. יָרִיב, **Yârîyb,** *yaw-rebe´*; the same as 3401; *Jarib*, the name of three Israelites:—Jarib.

3403. יְרִיבַי, **Yᵉrîybay,** *yer-eeb-ah´ee*; from 3401; *contentious; Jeribai*, an Israelite:—Jeribai.

3404. יְרִיָּה, **Yᵉrîyyâh,** *yer-ee-yaw´*; or יְרִיָהוּ, **Yᵉrîy-yâhûw,** *yer-ee-yaw´-hoo*; from 3384 and 3050; *Jah will throw; Jerijah*, an Israelite:—Jeriah, Jerijah.

3405. יְרִיחוֹ, **Yᵉrîychôw,** *yer-ee-kho´*; or יְרֵחוֹ, **Yᵉrêchôw,** *yer-ay-kho´*; or variation (1Ki 16:34) יְרִיחֹה, **Yᵉrîychôh,** *yer-ee-kho´*; perhaps from 3394; *its month*; or else from 7306; *fragrant; Jericho* or *Jerecho*, a place in Palestine:—Jericho.

3406. יְרִימוֹת, **Yᵉrîymôwth,** *yer-ee-mohth´*; or יְרֵימוֹת, **Yᵉrêymôwth,** *yer-ay-mohth´*; or יְרֵמוֹת, **Yᵉrêmôwth,** *yer-ay-mohth´*; feminine plural from 7311; *elevations; Jerimoth* or *Jeremoth*, the name of twelve Israelites:—Jeremoth, Jerimoth, and Ramoth [*from the margin*].

3407. יְרִיעָה, **yᵉrîy‘âh,** *yer-ee-aw´*; from 3415; a *hanging* (as *tremulous*):—curtain.

3408. יְרִיעוֹת, **Yᵉrîy‘ôwth,** *yer-ee-ohth´*; plural of 3407; *curtains; Jerioth*, an Israelitess:—Jerioth.

3409. יָרֵךְ, **yârêk,** *yaw-rake´*; from an unused root meaning to *be soft*; the *thigh* (from its fleshy *softness*); (by euphemism) the *generative parts*; (figurative) a *shank, flank, side*:— × body, loins, shaft, side, thigh.

A feminine singular noun meaning a thigh, a side, a base. The word is used of Jacob's thigh in the story of his wrestling with God (Ge 32:25[26], 32[33]) and is most likely used euphemistically of genitals (Ge 46:26; Ex 1:5; Jgs 8:30). It is best translated side in the cultic language of Le 1:11 and Nu 3:29, 35. The Pentateuch also employs it with the meaning of a base (Ex 25:31).

3410. יַרְכָה, **yarkâh,** *yar-ka´*; (Chaldee); corresponding to 3411; a *thigh*:—thigh.

3411. יְרֵכָה, **yᵉrêkâh,** *yer-ay-kaw´*; feminine of 3409; (properly) the *flank*; but used only figuratively, the *rear* or *recess*:—border, coast, part, quarter, side.

3412. יַרְמוּת, **Yarmûwth,** *yar-mooth´*; from 7311; *elevation; Jarmuth*, the name of two places in Palestine:—Jarmuth.

3413. יְרֵמַי, **Yᵉrêmay,** *yer-ay-mah´ee*; from 7311; *elevated; Jeremai*, an Israelite:—Jeremai.

3414. יִרְמְיָה, **Yirmᵉyâh,** *yir-meh-yaw´*; or יִרְמְיָהוּ, **Yirmᵉyâhûw,** *yir-meh-yaw´-hoo*; from 7311 and 3050; *Jah will rise; Jirmejah*, the name of eight or nine Israelites:—Jeremiah.

3415. יָרַע, **yâra‘,** *yaw-rah´*; a primitive root; (properly) to *be broken* up (with any violent action), i.e. (figurative) to *fear*:—be grievous [*only Isa 15:4; the rest belong* to 7489].

A verb meaning to tremble. It occurs only in Isa 15:4. As the result of the sudden devastation of Moab, his (i.e. Moab's or possibly an individual soldier's) life (or soul) trembles. The sentence could refer to inner turmoil: his soul trembles within him; or it could refer to an objective sense that his prospects of surviving are shaky; his life trembles before him (cf. Dt 28:66). Of course, both meanings could be true; both could even be implied.

3416. יִרְפְּאֵל, **Yirpᵉʼêl,** *yir-peh-ale´*; from 7495 and 410; *God will heal; Jirpeël,* a place in Palestine:—Irpeel.

3417. יָרַק, **yâraq,** *yaw-rak´*; a primitive root; to *spit*:— × but, spit.

3418. יֶרֶק, **yereq,** *yeh´-rek*; from 3417 (in the sense of *vacuity* of colour); (properly) *pallor,* i.e. hence the yellowish *green* of young and sickly vegetation; (concrete) *verdure,* i.e. grass or vegetation:—grass, green (thing).

3419. יָרָק, **yârâq,** *yaw-rawk´*; from the same as 3418; (properly) *green;* (concrete) a *vegetable:*—green, herbs.

3420. יֵרָקוֹן, **yêrâqôwn,** *yay-raw-kone´*; from 3418; *paleness,* whether of persons (from fright), or of plants (from drought):—greenish, yellow.

3421. יָרְקְעָם, **Yorqŏʻâm,** *yor-ko-awm´*; from 7324 and 5971; *people will be poured forth; Jorkeäm,* a place in Palestine:—Jorkeam.

3422. יְרַקְרַק, **yᵉraqraq,** *yer-ak-rak´*; from the same as 3418; *yellowishness:*—greenish, yellow.

3423. יָרַשׁ, **yârash,** *yaw-rash´*; or יָרֵשׁ, **yârêsh,** *yaw-raysh´*; a primitive root; to *occupy* (by *driving* out previous tenants, and *possessing* in their place); (by implication) to *seize,* to *rob,* to *inherit;* also to *expel,* to *impoverish,* to *ruin:*—cast out, consume, destroy, disinherit, dispossess, drive (-ing) out, enjoy, expel, × without fail, (give to, leave for) inherit (-ance, -or), + magistrate, be (make) poor, come to poverty, (give to, make to) possess, get (have) in (take) possession, seize upon, succeed, × utterly.

A verb meaning to take possession, to inherit, to dispossess, to drive out. This term is sometimes used in the generic sense of inheriting possessions (Ge 15:3, 4). But the word is used usually in connection with the idea of conquering a land. This verb is a theme of Deuteronomy in particular where God's promise of covenantal relationship is directly related to Israelite posses-

sion (and thereby foreign dispossession) of the land of Israel. This theme continued throughout Israel's history and prophetic message. Possession of the land was directly connected to a person's relationship with the Lord; breaking the covenantal relationship led to dispossession. But even in exile, Israelites awaited the day when they would repossess the land (Jer 30:3).

3424. יְרֵשָׁה, **yᵉrêshâh,** *yer-ay-shaw´*; from 3423; *occupancy:*—possession.

A feminine noun meaning possession, property. It refers to a nation and is used only once in the Hebrew Bible. In Nu 24:18, Edom and Seir would become the possession of someone else (i.e. they would be defeated). This word comes from the root word *yârêsh* (3423).

3425. יְרֻשָּׁה, **yᵉrushshâh,** *yer-oosh-shaw´*; from 3423; something *occupied;* a *conquest;* also a *patrimony:*—heritage, inheritance, possession.

A feminine noun meaning possession, inheritance. The word refers to an inheritance given, to a possession taken by force, or both. The word describes the land God gave to the Edomites, Moabites, and Ammonites (Dt 2:5, 9, 19). The Edomites and Ammonites, however, seized land from other tribes (Dt 2:12, 19). The Israelites, likewise, had to fight to gain their inheritance (Dt 3:20; Jos 12:6, 7). However, God later protected Israel's inheritance against the unjust claims of discontent Edomites, Moabites, and Ammonites (2Ch 20:11). The word is also used to refer to the possession of wives (Jgs 21:17) and land (Jer 32:8), both of which still waited to be claimed (sinfully in the former passage). In Ps 61:5[6], the word refers to God's presence as the inheritance of those who fear God.

3426. יֵשׁ, **yêsh,** *yaysh*; perhaps from an unused root meaning to *stand* out, or *exist; entity;* used adverbially or as a copula for the substantive verb (1961); there *is* or *are* (or any other form of the verb to *be,* as may suit the connection):—(there) are, (he, it, shall, there, there may, there shall, there should) be, thou do, had, hast, (which) hath, (I, shalt, that) have, (he, it, there) is, substance, it (there) was, (there) were, ye will, thou wilt, wouldest.

3427. יָשַׁב, **yâshab,** *yaw-shab´*; a primitive root; (properly) to *sit* down (specifically as judge, in ambush, in quiet); (by implication) to *dwell,* to *remain*; (causative) to *settle*, to *marry*:—(make to) abide (-ing), continue, (cause to, make to) dwell (-ing), ease self, endure, establish, × fail, habitation, haunt, (make to) inhabit (-ant), make to keep [house], lurking, × marry (-ing), (bring again to) place, remain, return, seat, set (-tle), (down-) sit (-down, still, -ting down, -ting [place] -uate), take, tarry.

A verb meaning to sit, to dwell, to inhabit, to endure, to stay. Apparently, to sit is the root idea, and other meanings are derived from this. The subject of the verb may be God, human, animal (Jer 50:39), or inanimate matter. The word sometimes emphasizes the location of persons, whether they were sitting under a tree (Jgs 6:11; 1Ki 19:4) or in a house (2Ki 6:32). It could also reflect a person's position: one sat as a judge (Pr 20:8; Isa 28:6); as a widow (Ge 38:11); or on a throne as king (Ex 12:29; 2Ki 13:13). Sometimes it indicated one's companions; one sits with scoffers (Ps 1:1); or with the elders of the land (Pr 31:23). The word may signify "to dwell," either temporarily (Le 23:42) or in a permanent dwelling (Ge 4:16; Zep 2:15). Sometimes the word means that an object or person stays in a limited area (Ex 16:29); or abides for a period of time (Le 12:4, 5; 2Sa 6:11); or for eternity (Ps 9:7[8]; 102:12[13]; 125:1). The years are even said to sit, that is, to pass (1Ki 22:1).

3428. יֶשֶׁבְאָב, **Yesheb'âb,** *yeh-sheb-awb´*; from 3427 and 1; *seat of* (his) *father*; *Jeshebab*, an Israelite:—Jeshebeab.

3429. יֹשֵׁב בַּשֶּׁבֶת, **Yôshêb bash-Shebeth,** *yo-shabe´ bash-sheh´-beth*; from the active participle of 3427 and 7674, with a preposition and the article interposed; *sitting in the seat*; *Josheb-bash-Shebeth*, an Israelite:—that sat in the seat.

3430. יֹשְׁבִי בְּנֹב, **Yishbîy be-Nôb,** *yish-bee´ beh-nobe´*; from 3427 and 5011, with a pronoun suffix and a preposition interposed; *his dwelling* (is) *in Nob*; *Jishbo-be-Nob*, a Philistine:—Ishbibenob [*from the margin*].

3431. יִשְׁבַּח, **Yishbach,** *yish-bakh´*; from 7623; *he will praise*; *Jishbach*, an Israelite:—Ishbah.

3432. יָשֻׁבִי, **Yâshubîy,** *yaw-shoo-bee´*; patronymic from 3437; a *Jashubite*, or descendant of Jashub:—Jashubites.

3433. יֹשְׁבֵי לֶחֶם, **Yâshubîy Lechem,** *yaw-shoo´-bee leh´-khem*; from 7725 and 3899; *returner of bread*; *Jashubi-Lechem*, an Israelite:—Jashubilehem. [Probably the text should be pointed יֹשְׁבֵי לֶחֶם, **Yôshbêy Lechem,** *yosh-bay´ leh´-khem*, and rendered "(they were) inhabitants of Lechem," i.e. of Bethlehem (by contraction). Compare 3902].

3434. יָשָׁבְעָם, **Yâshob'âm,** *yaw-shob-awm´*; from 7725 and 5971; *people will return*; *Jashobam*, the name of two or three Israelites:—Jashobeam.

3435. יִשְׁבָּק, **Yishbâq,** *yish-bawk´*; from an unused root corresponding to 7662; *he will leave*; *Jishbak*, a son of Abraham:—Ishbak.

3436. יָשְׁבְּקָשָׁה, **Yoshbe qâshâh,** *yosh-bek-aw-shaw´*; from 3427 and 7186; a *hard seat*; *Joshbekashah*, an Israelite:—Joshbekashah.

3437. יָשׁוּב, **Yâshûwb,** *yaw-shoob´*; or יָשִׁיב, **Yâshîyb,** *yaw-sheeb´*; from 7725; *he will return*; *Jashub*, the name of two Israelites:—Jashub.

3438. יִשְׁוָה, **Yishvâh,** *yish-vaw´*; from 7737; *he will level*; *Jishvah*, an Israelite:—Ishvah, Isvah.

3439. יְשׁוֹחָיָה, **Ye shôwchâyâh,** *yesh-o-khaw-yaw´*; from the same as 3445 and 3050; *Jah will empty*; *Jeshochajah*, an Israelite:—Jeshoaiah.

3440. יִשְׁוִי, **Yishvîy,** *yish-vee´*; from 7737; *level*; *Jishvi*, the name of two Israelites:—Ishuai, Ishvi, Isui, Jesui.

3441. יִשְׁוִי, **Yishvîy,** *yish-vee´*; patronymic from 3440; a *Jishvite* (collective) or descendants of Jishvi:—Jesuites.

3442. יֵשׁוּעַ, **Yêshûwa',** *yah-shoo´-ah*; for 3091; *he will save*; *Jeshua*, the name of ten Israelites, also of a place in Palestine:—Jeshua.

3443. יֵשׁוּעַ, **Yêshûwa',** *yah-shoo´-ah*; (Chaldee) corresponding to 3442:—Jeshua.

3444. יְשׁוּעָה, **ye shûw'âh,** *yesh-oo´-aw*; feminine passive participle of 3467; something *saved*, i.e. (abstract) *deliverance*; hence *aid, victory, prosperity*:—deliverance, health, help (-ing), salvation, save, saving (health), welfare.

A feminine noun meaning salvation, deliverance, help, victory, prosperity. The primary meaning is to rescue from distress or danger. It is used to signify help given by other human beings (1Sa 14:45; 2Sa 10:11); help or security offered by fortified walls, delivering in the sense of preventing what would have happened if the walls were not there (Isa 26:1); one's welfare and safety (Job 30:15); salvation by God, with reference to being rescued by Him from physical harm (Ex 14:13; 2Ch 20:17); being rescued from the punishment due for sin (Ps 70:4[5]; Isa 33:6; 49:6; 52:7). Used in the plural, it signifies works of help (Ps 44:4[5]; 74:12); and God's salvation (2Sa 22:51; Ps 42:5[6]; 116:13).

3445. יֶשַׁח, **yeshach,** *yeh´-shakh*; from an unused root meaning to *gape* (as the empty stomach); *hunger*:—casting down.

3446. יִשְׂחָק, **Yiśchâq,** *yis-khawk´*; from 7831; *he will laugh; Jischak,* the heir of Abraham:—Isaac. Compare 3327.

3447. יָשַׁט, **yâshaṭ,** *yaw-shat´*; a primitive root; to *extend*:—hold out.

3448. יִשַׁי, **Yishay,** *yee-shah´ee*; by Chaldee אִישַׁי, **'îyshay,** *ee-shah´ee*; from the same as 3426; *extant; Jishai,* David's father:—Jesse.

3449. יִשִּׁיָּה, **Yishshîyyâh,** *yish-shee-yaw´*; or יִשִּׁיָהוּ, **Yishshîy-yâhûw,** *yish-shee-yaw´-hoo*; from 5383 and 3050; *Jah will lend; Jishshijah,* the name of five Israelites:—Ishiah, Isshiah, Ishijah, Jesiah.

3450. יְשִׂימָאֵל, **Yᵉśîymi'êl,** *yes-eem-aw-ale´*; from 7760 and 410; *God will place; Jesimaël,* an Israelite:—Jesimael.

3451. יְשִׁימָה, **yᵉshîymâh,** *yesh-ee-maw´*; from 3456; *desolation*:—let death seize [*from the margin*].

A feminine noun meaning desolation. It occurs in Ps 55:15[16] in an imprecatory sense, where desolation was to be the ultimate end of a wicked and false person. As such, it links with the developed wisdom theme of wickedness as consummating in nothingness. Here the word invoked the result of falsity and idolatry that the true believer would escape by steadfast loyalty to God (cf. Ps 55:16, 17, 22). Ezekiel used the verb from which this word is derived (*yâsham,* 3456) several times in describing the habitation of Israel due to idolatry and unbelief (Eze 6:6; 12:19; 19:7). The one who would falsely break the covenant (Ps 55:20[21],

21[22]) could expect desolation–a message Ezekiel preached to the people of the covenant.

3452. יְשִׁימוֹן, **yᵉshîymôwn,** *yesh-ee-mone´*; from 3456; a *desolation*:—desert, Jeshimon, solitary, wilderness.

3453. יָשִׁישׁ, **yâshîysh,** *yaw-sheesh´*; from 3486; an *old* man:—(very) aged (man), ancient, very old.

An adjective meaning aged. This word is found only in Job and referred to people who had gray hair; they were considered old or aged (Job 15:10; 32:6). It referred to a class of people, such as modern-day senior citizens (Job 12:12; 29:8).

3454. יְשִׁישַׁי, **Yᵉshîyshay,** *yesh-ee-shah´ee*; from 3453; *aged; Jeshishai,* an Israelite:—Jeshishai.

3455. יָשַׂם, **yâśam,** *yaw-sam´*; a primitive root; to *place*; (intransitive) to *be placed*:—be put (set).

3456. יָשַׁם, **yâsham,** *yaw-sham´*; a primitive root; to *lie waste*:—be desolate.

A verb meaning to be desolate, to lie waste. In most cases, the people affected were afraid famine would cause the land to lie waste. During the famine, the Egyptians asked Joseph to buy them and their land so they would not die and their land become desolate (Ge 47:19). The Israelites were commanded to tell the people of Canaan that they were to soon experience the fear and trembling of the Lord that would cause them to leave their land (Eze 12:19).

3457. יִשְׁמָא, **Yishmâ',** *yish-maw´*; from 3456; *desolate; Jishma,* an Israelite:—Ishma.

3458. יִשְׁמָעֵאל, **Yishmâ'ê'l,** *yish-maw-ale´*; from 8085 and 410; *God will hear; Jishmaël,* the name of Abraham's oldest son, and of five Israelites:—Ishmael.

3459. יִשְׁמְעֵאלִי, **Yishmᵉ'ê'lîy,** *yish-meh-ay-lee´*; patronymic from 3458; a *Jishmaëlite* or descendant of Jishmael:—Ishmaelite.

3460. יִשְׁמַעְיָה, **Yishma'yâh,** *yish-mah-yaw´*; or יִשְׁמַעְיָהוּ, **Yish-ma'yâhûw,** *yish-mah-yaw´-hoo*; from 8085 and 3050; *Jah will hear; Jishmajah,* the name of two Israelites:—Ishmaiah.

3461. יִשְׁמְרַי, **Yishmᵉray,** *yish-mer-ah´ee*; from 8104; *preservative; Jishmerai,* an Israelite:— Ishmerai.

3462. יָשֵׁן, **yâshên,** *yaw-shane´*; a primitive root; (properly) to *be slack* or *languid,* i.e. (by implication) to *sleep;* (figurative) to *die;* also to *grow old, stale* or *inveterate:*—old (store), remain long, (make to) sleep.

3463. יָשֵׁן, **yâshên,** *yaw-shane´*; from 3462; *sleepy:*—asleep, (one out of) sleep (-eth, -ing), slept.

3464. יָשֵׁן, **Yâshên,** *yaw-shane´*; the same as 3463; *Jashen,* an Israelite:—Jashen.

3465. יָשָׁן, **yâshân,** *yaw-shawn´*; from 3462; *old:*—old.

3466. יְשָׁנָה, **Yᵉshânâh,** *yesh-aw-naw´*; feminine of 3465; *Jeshanah,* a place in Palestine:— Jeshanah.

3467. יָשַׁע, **yâshaʿ,** *yaw-shah´*; a primitive root; (properly) to *be open, wide* or *free,* i.e. (by implication) to *be safe;* (causative) to *free* or *succor:*— × at all, avenging, defend, deliver (-er), help, preserve, rescue, be safe, bring (having) salvation, save (-iour), get victory.

A verb meaning to save, to help, to deliver, to defend. The underlying idea of this verb is bringing to a place of safety or broad pasture as opposed to a narrow strait, symbolic of distress and danger. The word conveys the notion of deliverance from tribulation (Jgs 10:13, 14); deliverance from certain death (Ps 22:21[22]); rescue from one's enemies (Dt 28:31; Jgs 6:14); victory in time of war (1Sa 14:6); the protective duty of a shepherd (Eze 34:22; cf. Jgs 10:1); avenging wrongs (1Sa 25:33); compassionate aid in a time of need (2Ki 6:26, 27; Ps 12:1[2]); the salvation that only comes from God (Isa 33:22; Zep 3:17).

3468. יֶשַׁע, **yeshaʿ,** *yeh´-shah*; or יֵשַׁע, **yêshaʿ,** *yay´-shah*; from 3467; *liberty, deliverance, prosperity:*—safety, salvation, saving.

A masculine noun meaning deliverance, rescue, liberty, welfare, salvation. David used the word salvation to describe the hope and welfare he had in the midst of strife due to his covenant with God (2Sa 23:5). God saves communities, as when He promised relief to Jerusalem (Isa 62:11) as well as individuals (see Mic 7:7).

3469. יִשְׁעִי, **Yishʿîy,** *yish-ee´*; from 3467; *saving; Jishi,* the name of four Israelites:—Ishi.

3470. יְשַׁעְיָה, **Yᵉshaʿyâh,** *yesh-ah-yaw´*; or יְשַׁעְיָהוּ, **Yᵉshaʿyâhûw,** *yesh-ah-yaw´-hoo*; from 3467 and 3050; *Jah has saved; Jeshajah,* the name of seven Israelites:—Isaiah, Jesaiah, Jeshaiah.

3471. יָשְׁפֵה, **yâshᵉphêh,** *yaw-shef-ay´*; from an unused root meaning to *polish;* a gem supposed to be *jasper* (from the resemblance in name):— jasper.

3472. יִשְׁפָּה, **Yishpâh,** *yish-paw´*; perhaps from 8192; *he will scratch; Jishpah,* an Israelite:— Ispah.

3473. יִשְׁפָּן, **Yishpân,** *yish-pawn´*; probably from the same as 8227; *he will hide; Jishpan,* an Israelite:—Ishpan.

3474. יָשַׁר, **yâshar,** *yaw-shar´*; a primitive root; to *be straight* or *even;* (figurative) to *be* (causative, to *make*) *right, pleasant, prosperous:*—direct, fit, seem good (meet), + please (well), be (esteem, go) right (on), bring (look, make, take the) straight (way), be upright (-ly).

A verb meaning to be straight, to be upright, to be smooth, to be pleasing. When it means straight, it applies in a physical and an ethical sense as in straightforward. Therefore, this word can be used to refer to a path (1Sa 6:12); water (2Ch 32:30); the commands of God (Ps 119:128); or of a person (Hab 2:4). This word is also used to mean pleasing, as Samson found a Philistine woman pleasing to him (Jgs 14:7); but the cities that Solomon gave to Hiram were not pleasing (1Ki 9:12). It can also mean to make (or be) smooth or even, as with gold (1Ki 6:35); or a level road (Isa 40:3).

3475. יֵשֶׁר, **Yêsher,** *yay´-sher*; from 3474; *right; Jesher,* an Israelite:—Jesher.

3476. יֹשֶׁר, **yôsher,** *yo´-sher*; from 3474; the *right:*—equity, meet, right, upright (-ness).

A masculine noun meaning straightness or uprightness, equity. The OT often talks of two paths in life and warns people to stay on the straight path and not to stray onto the crooked path (Pr 2:13). David was praised for walking in an upright manner before the Lord (1Ki 9:4). Uprightness was also praised as a good quality to possess (Pr 17:26). The word can also designate virtuous words that one speaks (Job 6:25).

Another meaning less common is related to equity: one should give to another what is due to him or her (Pr 11:24).

3477. יָשָׁר, **yâshâr,** *yaw-shawr´*; from 3474; *straight* (literal or figurative):—convenient, equity, Jasher, just, meet (-est), + pleased well right (-eous), straight, (most) upright (-ly, -ness).

An adjective meaning straight, just, right. This word can refer to something physical, such as a path (Ps 107:7; Isa 26:7), but it more often means right in an ethical or an emotional sense, as agreeable or pleasing. Examples of this include what is right in God's eyes (Ex 15:26; 1Ki 11:33, 38; 2Ki 10:30); or in the eyes of people (Pr 12:15; Jer 40:5). It also means upright, such as God (Ps 25:8); and His ways (Hos 14:9[10]). Some people were considered upright, such as David (1Sa 29:6); and Job (Job 1:1). An ancient history book was called the book of Jashar or the book of the Upright (Jos 10:13; 2Sa 1:18). See the Hebrew root *yâshar* (3474).

3478. יִשְׂרָאֵל, **Yiśrâ'êl,** *yis-raw-ale´*; from 8280 and 410; *he will rule as God; Jisraël,* a symbolical name of Jacob; also (typically) of his posterity:—Israel.

3479. יִשְׂרָאֵל, **Yiśrâ'êl,** *yis-raw-ale´*; (Chaldee); corresponding to 3478:—Israel.

3480. יְשַׂרְאֵלָה, **Yᵉśar'êlâh,** *yes-ar-ale´-aw*; by variation from 3477 and 410 with directive enclitic; *right toward God; Jesarelah,* an Israelite:—Jesharelah. Compare 841.

3481. יִשְׂרְאֵלִי, **Yiśrᵉ'êlîy,** *yish-reh-ay-lee´*; patronymic from 3478; a *Jisreëlite* or descendant of Jisrael:—of Israel, Israelite.

3482. יִשְׂרְאֵלִית, **Yiśrᵉ'êlîyth,** *yis-reh-ay-leeth´*; feminine of 3481; a *Jisreëlitess* or female descendant of Jisrael:—Israelite.

3483. יִשְׂרָה, **yishrâh,** *yish-raw´*; feminine of 3477; *rectitude:*—uprightness.

A feminine noun meaning uprightness. The word is derived from *yâshar* (3474). It occurs only in 1Ki 3:6 where Solomon's prayer referred to the uprightness of David's heart that was rewarded with lovingkindness, especially the lovingkindness of having his son reign after him. David's life ruled out any meaning of sinlessness and pointed to repentance, faith, and knowledge of God as central to his uprightness (cf. Ro 4:6–8).

3484. יְשֻׁרוּן, **Yᵉshurûwn,** *yesh-oo-roon´*; from 3474; *upright; Jeshurun,* a symbolical name for Israel:—Jeshurun.

3485. יִשָּׂשכָר, **Yiśśâkâr,** *yis-saw-kawr´*; (strictly יִשְׂשָׂכָר, **Yiśśâśkâr,** *yis-saws-kawr´*), from 5375 and 7939; *he will bring a reward; Jissaskar,* a son of Jacob:—Issachar.

3486. יָשֵׁשׁ, **yâshêsh,** *yaw-shaysh´*; from an unused root meaning to *blanch; gray*-haired, i.e. an *aged* man:—stoop for age.

An adjective meaning aged or decrepit. It is used only with the word *zâqên* (2204). When King Zedekiah rebelled, the Lord caused the king of the Chaldeans to destroy Jerusalem and all the people in it. The Chaldean king showed no mercy for any of the people, including the aged or old (2Ch 36:17).

3487. יָת, **yâth,** *yawth*; (Chaldee); corresponding to 853; a *sign* of the object of a verb:—+ whom.

3488. יְתִב, **yᵉthib,** *yeth-eeb´*; (Chaldee); corresponding to 3427; to *sit* or *dwell:*—dwell, (be) set, sit.

3489. יָתֵד, **yâthêd,** *yaw-thade´*; from an unused root meaning to *pin* through or fast; a *peg:*—nail, paddle, pin, stake.

3490. יָתוֹם, **yâthôwm,** *yaw-thome´*; from an unused root meaning to *be lonely;* a *bereaved* person:—fatherless (child), orphan.

3491. יָתוּר, **yᵉthûwr,** *yeh-thoor´*; passive participle of 3498; (properly) what is *left,* i.e. (by implication) a *gleaning:*—range.

3492. יַתִּיר, **Yattîyr,** *yat-teer´*; from 3498; *redundant; Jattir,* a place in Palestine:—Jattir.

3493. יַתִּיר, **yattîyr,** *yat-teer´*; (Chaldee); corresponding to 3492; *preeminent;* (adverb) *very:*—exceeding (-ly), excellent.

3494. יִתְלָה, **Yithlâh,** *yith-law´*; probably from 8518; it *will hang,* i.e. be high; *Jithlah,* a place in Palestine:—Jethlah.

3495. יִתְמָה, **Yithmâh,** *yith-maw´*; from the same as 3490; *orphanage; Jithmah,* an Israelite:—Ithmah.

3496. יְתַנְיְאֵל, **Yathnîy'êl,** *yath-nee-ale´*; from an unused root meaning to *endure*, and 410; *continued of God; Jathniël*, an Israelite:—Jathniel.

3497. יִתְנָן, **Yithnân,** *yith-nawn´*; from the same as 8577; *extensive; Jithnan*, a place in Palestine:—Ithnan.

3498. יָתַר, **yâthar,** *yaw-thar´*; a primitive root; to *jut* over or *exceed*; (by implication) to *excel*; (intransitive) to *remain* or *be left*; (causative) to *leave, cause to abound, preserve*:—excel, leave (a remnant), left behind, too much, make plenteous, preserve, (be, let) remain (-der, -ing, -nant), reserve, residue, rest.

A verb meaning to be left over, to remain. Jacob was left alone after he sent his family across the river (Ge 32:24[25]); nothing remained after the locusts came (Ex 10:15); Absalom was thought to have killed all the king's sons with not one remaining (2Sa 13:30); Isaiah prophesied to Hezekiah that nothing would be left of his kingdom (2Ki 20:17); God said that when He destroyed Judah, He would leave a remnant (Eze 6:8).

3499. יֶתֶר, **yether,** *yeh´-ther*; from 3498; (properly) an *overhanging*, i.e. (by implication) an *excess, superiority, remainder*; also a small *rope* (as hanging free):— + abundant, cord, exceeding, excellency (-ent), what they leave, that hath left, plentifully, remnant, residue, rest, string, with.

A masculine noun meaning remainder, the rest, abundance, excellence, a cord. The word refers to that which is left over: the produce of a field not used by people (and left for beasts) (Ex 23:11); the years of a life span not yet finished (Isa 38:10); temple vessels besides the ones specifically mentioned (Jer 27:19). The word also signifies abundance as what was left beyond the necessities of life (Job 22:20; Ps 17:14). In Genesis 49:3, the word means excellence, referring to the extra honour and power accorded to the firstborn. The word may refer to the cord of a tent or to a bowstring (Job 30:11; Ps 11:2), both apparently derived from the idea of a string hanging over something, being extra. The word may be used adverbially to mean abundantly or exceedingly (Da 8:9).

3500. יֶתֶר, **Yether,** *yeh´-ther*; the same as 3499; *Jether*, the name of five or six Israelites and of one Midianite:—Jether, Jethro. Compare 3503.

3501. יִתְרָא, **Yithrâ',** *yith-raw´*; by variation for 3502; *Jithra*, an Israelite (or Ishmaelite):—Ithra.

3502. יִתְרָה, **yithrâh,** *yith-raw´*; feminine of 3499; (properly) *excellence*, i.e. (by implication) *wealth*:—abundance, riches.

3503. יִתְרוֹ, **Yithrôw,** *yith-ro´*; from 3499 with pronoun suffix; *his excellence; Jethro*, Moses' father-in-law:—Jethro. Compare 3500.

3504. יִתְרוֹן, **yithrôwn,** *yith-rone´*; from 3498; *preeminence, gain*:—better, excellency (-leth), profit (-able).

3505. יִתְרִי, **Yithrîy,** *yith-ree´*; patronymic from 3500; a *Jithrite* or descendant of Jether:—Ithrite.

3506. יִתְרָן, **Yithrân,** *yith-rawn´*; from 3498; *excellent; Jithran*, the name of an Edomite and of an Israelite:—Ithran.

3507. יִתְרְעָם, **Yithre'âm,** *yith-reh-awm´*; from 3499 and 5971; *excellence of people; Jithreäm*, a son of David:—Ithream.

3508. יֹתֶרֶת, **yôthereth,** *yo-theh´-reth*; feminine active participle of 3498; the *lobe* or *flap* of the liver (as if redundant or outhanging):—caul.

3509. יְתֵת, **Y e thêth,** *yeh-thayth´*; of uncertain derivation; *Jetheth*, an Edomite:—Jetheth.

כ (Kaph)

3510. כָּאַב, **kâ'ab,** *kaw-ab´*; a primitive root; (properly) to feel *pain*; (by implication) to *grieve*; (figuratively) to *spoil*:—grieving, mar, have pain, make sad (sore), (be) sorrowful.

3511. כְּאֵב, **ke'êb,** *keh-abe´*; from 3510; *suffering* (physical or mental), *adversity*:—grief, pain, sorrow.

3512. כָּאָה, **kâ'âh,** *kaw-aw´*; a primitive root; to *despond*; (causative) to *deject*:—broken, be grieved, make sad.

3513. כָּבַד, **kâbad,** *kaw-bad*; or כָּבֵד, **kâbêd,** *kaw-bade´*; a primitive root; to *be heavy*, i.e. in a bad sense (*burdensome, severe, dull*) or in a good sense (*numerous, rich, honourable*); (causative) to *make weighty* (in the same two senses):—abounding with, more grievously afflict, boast, be chargeable, × be dim, glorify, be (make) glorious (things), glory, (very) great, be grievous, harden, be (make) heavy, be heavier, lay heavily, (bring to, come to, do, get, be had in) honour (self), (be) honourable (man), lade, × more be laid, make self many, nobles, prevail, promote (to honour), be rich, be (go) sore, stop.

A verb meaning to weigh heavily, to be heavy, to be honoured, to be made heavy, to get honour, to make dull, to let weigh down, to harden, to multiply.

In the simple form, the verb means to be heavy, to weigh heavily, to be honoured. The hands of both humans and God were described metaphorically as heavy, that is, powerful. The heavy hand of Joseph dispossessed the Amorites of their land, and the Lord's hand was heavy against the city of Ashdod (i.e. He brought devastation upon it [1Sa 5:6]). The Hebrew word refers to mere physical weight as well; the description of Absalom's hair is a celebrated example of this use (2Sa 14:26). The labour of the Israelites in Egypt became burdensome (Ex 5:9). The word's metaphorical use extended to the description of failing senses, such as Jacob's

eyes (Israel's) in old age (Ge 48:10; Isa 59:1). This is one of three words describing the dulling or hardening of Pharaoh's heart in the plagues. Pharaoh's heart became dull, obstinate, heavy (Ex 9:7) to the Lord's warnings. Yet the word also describes honour being bestowed on someone (Job 14:21; Isa 66:5).

In the passive form, the word expresses the idea of enjoying honour or glory. It describes the smug self-glorification of Amaziah (2Sa 6:22; 2Ki 14:10); God's honouring Himself through the defeat of Pharaoh is also expressed by this stem (Ex 14:4, 17, 18; Isa 26:15). In the factitive or intensive stem, the verb expresses the idea of causing or making something unfeeling (1Sa 6:6) but also the act of honouring people or God (Jgs 9:9; Ps 22:23[24]). God's people also honour some things: the Sabbath (Isa 58:13); Jerusalem; God's sanctuary (Isa 60:13); wisdom (Pr 4:8). The causative form carries the ideas of making something heavy (1Ki 12:10; Isa 47:6); or dull and heavy, especially Pharaoh's heart (Ex 8:15[11], 32[28]; 9:34). In two places, the word means to make into many or multiply (Jer 30:19); as when God's people multiplied (cf. 2Ch 25:19). It is used once in the reflexive form meaning to act deceptively (i.e. to pretend something [Pr 12:9]).

3514. כֹּבֶד, **kôbed,** *ko´-bed*; from 3513; *weight, multitude, vehemence*:—grievousness, heavy, great number.

3515. כָּבֵד, **kâbêd,** *kaw-bade´*; from 3513; *heavy*; (figurative) in a good sense (*numerous*) or in a bad sense (*severe, difficult, stupid*):—(so) great, grievous, hard (-ened), (too) heavy (-ier), laden, much, slow, sore, thick.

3516. כָּבֵד, **kâbêd,** *kaw-bade´*; the same as 3515; the *liver* (as the *heaviest* of the viscera):—liver.

3517. כְּבֵדֻת, **kebêduth,** *keb-ay-dooth´*; feminine of 3515; *difficulty*:— × heavily.

3518. כָּבָה, **kâbâh,** *kaw-baw´*; a primitive root; to *expire* or (causative) to *extinguish* (fire, light, anger):—go (put) out, quench.

3519. כָּבוֹד, **kâbôwd,** *kaw-bode´*; rarely כָּבֹד, **kâbôd,** *kaw-bode´*; from 3513; (properly) *weight*; but only figurative in a good sense, *splendor* or *copiousness*:—glorious (-ly), glory, honour (-able).

A masculine singular noun meaning honour, glory, majesty, wealth. This term is commonly used of God (Ex 33:18; Ps 72:19; Isa 3:8; Eze 1:28); humans (Ge 45:13; Job 19:9; Ps 8:5[6]; 21:5[6]); and objects (1Sa 2:8; Est 1:4; Isa 10:18), particularly of the Ark of the Covenant (1Sa 4:21, 22).

3520. כְּבוּדָּה, **kᵉbûwddâh,** *keb-ood-daw´*; irregular feminine passive participle of 3513; *weightiness*, i.e. *magnificence, wealth*:—carriage, all glorious, stately.

3521. כָּבוּל, **Kâbûwl,** *kaw-bool´*; from the same as 3525 in the sense of *limitation; sterile; Cabul*, the name of two places in Palestine:—Cabul.

3522. כַּבּוֹן, **Kabbôwn,** *kab-bone´*; from an unused root meaning to *heap* up; *hilly; Cabbon*, a place in Palestine:—Cabbon.

3523. כְּבִיר, **kᵉbîyr,** *kawb-eer*; from 3527 in the original sense of *plaiting; a matrass* (of intertwined materials):—pillow.

3524. כַּבִּיר, **kabbîyr,** *kab-beer´*; from 3527; *vast*, whether in extent (figurative of power, *mighty*; of time, *aged*), or in number, *many*:— + feeble, mighty, most, much, strong, valiant.

3525. כֶּבֶל, **kebel,** *keh´-bel*; from an unused root meaning to *twine* or braid together; a *fetter*:—fetter.

3526. כָּבַס, **kâbas,** *kaw-bas´*; a primitive root; to *trample*; hence to *wash* (properly, by stamping with the feet), whether literal (including the *fulling* process) or figurative:—fuller, wash (-ing).

A verb meaning to wash. The root meaning of the verb is to trample, which was the means of washing clothes. The word most often refers to washing clothes (Ge 49:11; 2Sa 19:24[25]), especially ceremonially (Ex 19:10; Le 15; Nu 19). As a participle, the word means fuller, one who left clothes to dry in the fuller's field (2Ki 18:17; Isa 7:3; 36:2). An intensive form of the

verb is used of the fuller in Mal 3:2, whose soap is a symbol of Christ's demand for purity. In Jer 2:22, the word may refer literally to ceremonial washings but also implies mere human effort used in an external attempt to overcome sin. In Ps 51:2[4], 7[9], the word refers to God's internal cleansing of the heart, making it as white as snow. Jer 4:14, however, showed that God's people must work to cleanse their hearts and avoid temporal destruction.

3527. כָּבַר, **kâbar,** *kaw-bar´*; a primitive root; (properly) to *plait* together, i.e. (figurative) to *augment* (especially in number or quantity, to *accumulate*):—in abundance, multiply.

3528. כְּבָר, **kᵉbâr,** *keb-awr´*; from 3527; (properly) *extent* of time, i.e. a *great while*; hence long ago, formerly, hitherto:—already, (seeing that which), now.

3529. כְּבָר, **Kᵉbâr,** *keb-awr´*; the same as 3528; length; *Kebar*, a river of Mesopotamia:—Chebar. Compare 2249.

3530. כִּבְרָה, **kibrâh,** *kib-raw´*; feminine of 3528; (properly) *length*, i.e. a *measure* (of uncertain dimension):— × little.

3531. כְּבָרָה, **kᵉbârâh,** *keb-aw-raw´*; from 3527 in its original sense; a *sieve* (as netted):—sieve.

3532. כֶּבֶשׂ, **kebeś,** *keh-bes´*; from an unused root meaning to *dominate*; a *ram* (just old enough to *butt*):—lamb, sheep.

3533. כָּבַשׁ, **kâbash,** *kaw-bash´*; a primitive root; to *tread* down; hence negative to *disregard*; positive to *conquer, subjugate, violate*:—bring into bondage, force, keep under, subdue, bring into subjection.

3534. כֶּבֶשׁ, **kebesh,** *keh´-besh*; from 3533; a *footstool* (as trodden upon):—footstool.

3535. כִּבְשָׂה, **kibśâh,** *kib-saw´*; or כַּבְשָׂה, **kabśâh,** *kab-saw´*; feminine of 3532; a *ewe*:—(ewe) lamb.

3536. כִּבְשָׁן, **kibshân,** *kib-shawn´*; from 3533; a smelting *furnace* (as *reducing* metals):—furnace.

3537. כַּד, **kad,** *kad*; from an unused root meaning to *deepen*; (properly) a *pail*; but generically of earthenware; a *jar* for domestic purposes:—barrel, pitcher.

3538. כְּדַב, k°dab, *ked-ab´*; (Chaldee); from a root corresponding to 3576; *false*:—lying.

3539. כַּדְכֹּד, **kadkôd,** *kad-kode´*; from the same as 3537 in the sense of *striking fire* from a metal forged; a *sparkling* gem, probably the ruby:—agate.

3540. כְּדָרְלָעֹמֶר, **K°dorlâ'ômer,** *ked-or-law-o´-mer*; of foreign origin; *Kedorlaomer,* an early Persian king:—Chedorlaomer.

3541. כֹּה, **kôh,** *ko*; from the prefix *k* and 1931; (properly) *like this,* i.e. (by implication, of manner) *thus* (or *so*); also (of place) *here* (or *hither*); or (of time) *now*:—also, here, + hitherto, like, on the other side, so (and much), such, on that manner, (on) this (manner, side, way, way and that way), + meanwhile, yonder.

3542. כָּה, **kâh,** *kaw*; (Chaldee); corresponding to 3541:—hitherto.

3543. כָּהָה, **kâhâh,** *kaw-haw´*; a primitive root; to *be weak,* i.e. (figurative) to *despond* (causative, to *rebuke*), or (of light, the eye) to *grow dull*:—darken, be dim, fail, faint, restrain, × utterly.

3544. כֵּהֶה, **kêheh,** *kay-heh´*; from 3543; *feeble, obscure*:—somewhat dark, darkish, wax dim, heaviness, smoking.

3545. כֵּהָה, **kêhâh,** *kay-haw´*; feminine of 3544; (properly) a *weakening*; (figurative) *alleviation,* i.e. *cure*:—healing.

3546. כְּהַל, **k°hal,** *ke-hal´*; (Chaldee); a root corresponding to 3201 and 3557; to *be able*:—be able, could.

3547. כָּהַן, **kâhan,** *kaw-han´*; a primitive root, apparently meaning to *mediate* in religious services; but used only as denominative from 3548; to *officiate* as a priest; (figurative) to *put on regalia*:—deck, be (do the office of a, execute the, minister in the) priest ('s office).

A verb meaning to act, to serve as a priest. This is a denominative verb from the noun *kôhên* (3548). The verb occurs twenty-three times in the Hebrew Bible, and twelve of them occur in Exodus. The most unusual usage is Isa 61:10 where it seems to refer to dressing in a priestly (i.e. ornate) manner.

3548. כֹּהֵן, **kôhên,** *ko-hane´*; active participle of 3547; literally one *officiating,* a *priest*; also (by courtesy) an *acting priest* (although a layman):—chief ruler, × own, priest, prince, principal officer.

A masculine noun meaning priest. The word is used to designate the various classes of priests in Israel. These people performed the function of mediators between God and His people. God called the nation of Israel to be a kingdom of priests (Ex 19:6), but God also appointed a priesthood to function within the nation. All the priests were to come from the tribe of Levi (Dt 17:9, 18). The Lord set up a high priest who was over all the priestly services. The high priest was literally the great priest or head priest: Jehoiada was described as a high or great priest (2Ki 12:10[11]). Joshua is called the high priest over the community that returned from the Babylonian exile (Hag 1:12; 2:2). God appointed Aaron to serve as high priest and his sons as priests when the entire priestly order was established (Le 21:10; Nu 35:25). The high point of the religious year was the atonement ritual the high priest performed on the Day of Atonement (Le 16). Aaron's family line produced the Aaronic priests or priesthood. Zadok became the ancestor of the legitimate priests from the time of Solomon's reign (1Ki 1:8, 38, 44); and the prophet Ezekiel approved of this line of priests from among the Levites (Eze 40:46; 43:19). The priests were in charge of all the holy things in Israel: they bore the ark (Jos 3:13, 14) and trumpets (Nu 10:8). They even counseled kings (1Sa 22:21; 1Ki 1:38, 44). However, there arose priests who were not appointed by the Lord and who functioned illegitimately, such as Micah's priests during the time of the judges (Jgs 17:5, 10, 12) or Jeroboam's priests who did not come from the sons of Levi (1Ki 12:31).

Some priests who functioned in other religions or nations are mentioned in Scripture. The most famous was Melchizedek, who was also a king in Canaan (Ge 14:18). His priesthood became the model for Christ's eternal priesthood (Heb 6:20). Jethro, Moses' father-in-law, was a priest among the Midianites (Ex 2:16; 3:1). Joseph married Asenath, the daughter of an Egyptian priest (Ge 41:45). There were priests of the Philistines (1Sa 6:2); and priests who served the false gods, the Baals, and the Asherim (2Ch 34:5) of the heathen nations.

3549. כָּהֵן, **kâhên,** *kaw-hane´*; (Chaldee); corresponding to 3548:—priest.

3550. כְּהֻנָּה, **keʻhunnâh,** *keh-hoon-naw´*; from 3547; *priesthood:*—priesthood, priest's office.

A feminine noun meaning priesthood, the priest's office. The priest's office belonged to Aaron and his sons and involved making sacrifices and entering the Holy of Holies (Nu 18:7), work from which the other Levites were excluded (Nu 18:1, 7). Because of the holiness of the priesthood, those without right who presumed to act in it (Nu 16:10), as well as priests who misused the office, faced severe judgments. Levites outside of Aaron's descendants were permitted to do other service in the tabernacle; and, thus, the priesthood was referred to as their inheritance in place of land (Jos 18:7). The ordination of priests was described in Ex 29 and included the use of anointing oil, special clothes, and sacrifices.

3551. כַּוָּה, **kavvâh,** *kav-vaw´*; (Chaldee); from a root corresponding to 3854 in the sense of *piercing*; a *window* (as a perforation):—window.

3552. כּוּב, **Kûwb,** *koob*; of foreign derivation; *Kub,* a country near Egypt:—Chub.

3553. כּוֹבַע, **kôwbaʻ,** *ko´-bah*; from an unused root meaning to be *high* or *rounded*; a *helmet* (as *arched*):—helmet. Compare 6959.

3554. כָּוָה, **kâvâh,** *kaw-vaw´*; a primitive root; (properly) to *prick* or *penetrate*; hence to *blister* (as smarting or eating into):—burn.

3555. כְּוִיָּה, **keʻvîyyâh,** *kev-ee-yaw´*; from 3554; a *branding:*—burning.

3556. כּוֹכָב, **kôwkâb,** *ko-kawb´*; probably from the same as 3522 (in the sense of *rolling*) or 3554 (in the sense of *blazing*); a *star* (as *round* or as *shining*); (figurative) a *prince:*—star ([-gazer]).

3557. כּוּל, **kûwl,** *kool*; a primitive root; (properly) to *keep in*; hence to *measure*; (figurative) to *maintain* (in various senses):—(be able to, can) abide, bear, comprehend, contain, feed, forbearing, guide, hold (-ing in), nourish (-er),

be present, make provision, receive, sustain, provide sustenance (victuals).

3558. כּוּמָז, **kûwmâz,** *koo-mawz´*; from an unused root meaning to *store* away; a *jewel* (probably gold beads):—tablet.

3559. כּוּן, **kûwn,** *koon*; a primitive root; (properly) to *be erect* (i.e. stand perpendicular); hence (causative) to *set up*, in a great variety of applications, whether literal (*establish, fix, prepare, apply*), or figurative (*appoint, render sure, proper* or *prosperous*):—certain (-ty), confirm, direct, faithfulness, fashion, fasten, firm, be fitted, be fixed, frame, be meet, ordain, order, perfect, (make) preparation, prepare (self), provide, make provision, (be, make) ready, right, set (aright, fast, forth), be stable, (e-) stablish, stand, tarry, × very deed.

A verb meaning to set up, to make firm, to establish, to prepare. The primary action of this verb is to cause to stand in an upright position, and thus the word also means fixed or steadfast. It signifies the action of setting in place or erecting an object (Isa 40:20; Mic 4:1); establishing a royal dynasty (2Sa 7:13; 1Ch 17:12); founding a city (Hab 2:12); creating the natural order (Dt 32:6; Ps 8:3[4]; Pr 8:27); fashioning a people for oneself (2Sa 7:24); adjusting weapons for targets (Ps 7:12[13]; 11:2); appointing to an office (Jos 4:4); confirming a position (1Ki 2:12); making ready or preparing for use (2Ch 31:11; Ps 103:19; Zep 1:7); attaining certainty (Dt 13:14[15]; 1Sa 23:23).

3560. כּוּן, **Kûwn,** *koon*; probably from 3559; *established*; *Kun,* a place in Syria:—Chun.

3561. כַּוָּן, **kavvân,** *kav-vawn´*; from 3559; something *prepared*, i.e. a sacrificial *wafer:*—cake.

3562. כּוֹנַנְיָהוּ, **Kôwnanyâhûw,** *ko-nan-yaw´-hoo*; from 3559 and 3050; *Jah has sustained; Conanjah,* the name of two Israelites:—Conaniah, Cononiah. Compare 3663.

3563. כּוֹס, **kôws,** *koce*; from an unused root meaning to *hold* together; a *cup* (as a container); (often figurative) a *lot* (as if a potion); also some unclean bird, probably an *owl* (perhaps from the cup-like cavity of its eye):—cup, (small) owl. Compare 3599.

3564. כּוּר, **kûwr,** *koor*; from an unused root meaning properly to *dig* through; a *pot* or *fur-*

nace (as if excavated):—furnace. Compare 3600.

3565. כּוּר עָשָׁן, **Kôwr 'Âshân,** *kore aw-shawn'*; from 3564 and 6227; *furnace of smoke; Cor-Ashan*, a place in Palestine:—Chor-ashan.

3566. כֹּרֶשׁ, **Kôwresh,** *ko'-resh*; or (Ezr 1:1 [last time], 2) כֹּרֶשׁ, **Kôresh,** *ko'-resh*; from the Persian; *Koresh* (or *Cyrus*), the Persian king:—Cyrus.

3567. כֹּרֶשׁ, **Kôwresh,** *ko'-resh*; (Chaldee); corresponding to 3566:—Cyrus.

3568. כּוּשׁ, **Kûwsh,** *koosh*; probably of foreign origin; *Cush* (or *Ethiopia*), the name of a son of Ham, and of his territory; also of an Israelite:—Chush, Cush, Ethiopia.

3569. כּוּשִׁי, **Kûwshîy,** *koo-shee'*; patronymic from 3568; a *Cushite*, or descendant of Cush:—Cushi, Cushite, Ethiopian (-s).

3570. כּוּשִׁי, **Kûwshîy,** *koo-shee'*; the same as 3569; *Cushi*, the name of two Israelites:—Cushi.

3571. כּוּשִׁית, **Kûwshîyth,** *koo-sheeth'*; feminine of 3569; a *Cushite woman*:—Ethiopian.

3572. כּוּשָׁן, **Kûwshân,** *koo-shawn'*; perhaps from 3568; *Cushan*, a region of Arabia:—Cushan.

3573. כּוּשַׁן רִשְׁעָתַיִם, **Kûwshan Rish'âthayim,** *koo-shan' rish-aw-thah'-yim*; apparently from 3572 and the dual of 7564; *Cushan of double wickedness; Cushan-Rishathajim*, a Mesopotamian king:—Chushan-rishathaim.

3574. כּוֹשָׁרָה, **kôwshârâh,** *ko-shaw-raw'*; from 3787; *prosperity*; in plural *freedom*:— × chain.

3575. כּוּת, **Kûwth,** *kooth*; or (feminine) כּוּתָה, **Kûwthâh,** *koo-thaw'*; of foreign origin; *Cuth* or *Cuthah*, a province of Assyria:—Cuth.

3576. כָּזַב, **kâzab,** *kaw-zab'*; a primitive root; to *lie* (i.e. *deceive*), literal or figurative:—fail, (be found a, make a) liar, lie, lying, be in vain.

A verb meaning to lie, to be a liar, to declare a liar, to make a liar of someone. This verb occurs sixteen times and refers to false witnesses (Pr 14:5); worshippers (Pr 30:6); and figuratively of water (Isa 58:11). The book of Job, filled with courtroom rhetoric, debating the trustworthiness of the speakers' accounts, uses

the verb four times (Job 6:28; 24:25; 34:6; 41:9[1]).

3577. כָּזָב, **kâzâb,** *kaw-zawb'*; from 3576; *falsehood*; literal (*untruth*) or figurative (*idol*):—deceitful, false, leasing, + liar, lie, lying.

A masculine noun meaning a lie, a deception, a falsehood. Indeed, the idea of nontruth is unequivocally presented as antithetical to God. He destroys liars (Ps 5:6[7]; 62:4[5]) and calls them an abomination (Pr 6:19). Lies and deceptions place one against God and guarantee His punishment (Pr 19:5, 9). Isaiah graphically depicted one taking shelter in lying and falsehood as equivalent to making a covenant with death and an agreement with hell—a contract that cannot save on Judgment Day (28:15, 17). Freedom from falsehood is both the character and heritage of God's children (Ps 40:4[5]; Zep 3:13). The verb *kâzab* (3576) also develops the anti-God theme of lying: God cannot lie (Nu 23:19); and His word will never deceive (Ps 89:35[36]), unlike false prophets and humans.

3578. כֹּזְבָא, **Kôzêbâ',** *ko-zeeb-aw'*; from 3576; *fallacious; Cozeba*, a place in Palestine:—Choseba.

3579. כָּזְבִּי, **Kozbîy,** *koz-bee'*; from 3576; *false; Cozbi*, a Midianitess:—Cozbi.

3580. כְּזִיב, **K^ezîyb,** *kez-eeb'*; from 3576; *falsified; Kezib*, a place in Palestine:—Chezib.

3581. כֹּחַ, **kôach,** *ko'-akh*; or (Da 11:6) כֹּוחַ, **kôwach,** *ko'-akh*; from an unused root meaning to *be firm; vigour*, literal (*force*, in a good or a bad sense) or figurative (*capacity, means, produce*); also (from its hardiness) a large *lizard*:—ability, able, chameleon, force, fruits, might, power (-ful), strength, substance, wealth.

3582. כָּחַד, **kâchad,** *kaw-khad'*; a primitive root; to *secrete*, by act or word; hence (intensive) to *destroy*:—conceal, cut down (off), desolate, hide.

3583. כָּחַל, **kâchal,** *kaw-khal'*; a primitive root; to *paint* (with stibium):—paint.

3584. כָּחַשׁ, **kâchash,** *kaw-khash'*; a primitive root; to *be untrue*, in word (to *lie, feign, disown*) or deed (to *disappoint, fail, cringe*):—deceive, deny, dissemble, fail, deal falsely, be found liars, (be-) lie, lying, submit selves.

3585. כַּחַשׁ, **kachash,** *kakh´-ash*; from 3584; (literal) a *failure* of flesh, i.e. *emaciation*; (figurative) *hypocrisy*:—leanness, lies, lying.

3586. כֶּחָשׁ, **kechâsh,** *kekh-awsh´*; from 3584; *faithless*:—lying.

An adjective meaning deceptive, false, lying. This word occurs only in Isa 30:9. The reference is to the deceitfulness of Israel. Their rebellious activities included urging prophets to prophesy falsely and to subvert the authority of the Lord (Isa 30:10, 11).

3587. כִּי, **kîy,** *kee*; from 3554; a *brand* or *scar*:—burning.

3588. כִּי, **kîy,** *kee*; a primitive particle [the full form of the prepositional prefix] indicating *causal* relations of all kinds, antecedent or consequent; (by implication) very widely used as a relative conjunction or adverb [as below]; often largely modified by other particles annexed:—and, + (forasmuch, inasmuch, where-) as, assured [-ly], + but, certainly, doubtless, + else, even, + except, for, how, (because, in, so, than) that, + nevertheless, now, rightly, seeing, since, surely, then, therefore, + (al-) though, + till, truly, + until, when, whether, while, whom, yea, yet.

3589. כִּיד, **kîyd,** *keed*; from a primitive root meaning to *strike*; a *crushing*; (figurative) *calamity*:—destruction.

A masculine noun of uncertain meaning. It comes from a primitive root word and most likely means a crushing, a calamity, or a misfortune. Job responded to Zophar and lamented about the wicked. Job wished that the wicked would see God's wrath and their own destruction (Job 21:20).

3590. כִּידוֹד, **kîydôwd,** *kee-dode´*; from the same as 3589 [compare 3539]; (properly) something *struck* off, i.e. a *spark* (as struck):—spark.

3591. כִּידוֹן, **kîydôwn,** *kee-dohn´*; from the same as 3589; (properly) something to *strike* with, i.e. a *dart* (perhaps smaller than 2595):—lance, shield, spear, target.

3592. כִּידֹן, **Kîydôn,** *kee-dohn´*; the same as 3591; *Kidon*, a place in Palestine:—Chidon.

3593. כִּידוֹר, **kîydôwr,** *kee-dore´*; of uncertain derivation; perhaps *tumult*:—battle.

3594. כִּיּוּן, **Kîyyûwn,** *kee-yoon´*; from 3559; (properly) a *statue*, i.e. idol; but used (by euphemism) for some heathen deity (perhaps corresponding to Priapus or Baal-peor):—Chiun.

3595. כִּיּוֹר, **kîyyôwr,** *kee-yore´*; or כִּיֹר, **kîyyôr,** *kee-yore´*; from the same as 3564; (properly) something *round* (as *excavated* or *bored*), i.e. a chafing-*dish* for coals or a *caldron* for cooking; hence (from similarity of form) a *washbowl*; also (for the same reason) a *pulpit* or platform:—hearth, laver, pan, scaffold.

3596. כִּילַי, **kîylay,** *kee-lah´ee*; or כֵּלַי, **kêlay,** *kay-lah´ee*; from 3557 in the sense of *withholding*; *niggardly*:—churl.

3597. כֵּילַף, **kêylaph,** *kay-laf´*; from an unused root meaning to *clap* or strike with noise; a *club* or sledge-hammer:—hammer.

3598. כִּימָה, **Kîymâh,** *kee-maw´*; from the same as 3558; a *cluster* of stars, i.e. the *Pleiades*:—Pleiades, seven stars.

3599. כִּיס, **kîys,** *keece*; a form for 3563; a *cup*; also a *bag* for money or weights:—bag, cup, purse.

3600. כִּיר, **kîyr,** *keer*; a form for 3564 (only in the dual); a cooking *range* (consisting of two parallel stones, across which the boiler is set):—ranges for pots.

3601. כִּישׁוֹר, **kîyshôwr,** *kee-shore´*; from 3787; (literal) a *director*, i.e. the *spindle* or shank of a distaff (6418), by which it is twirled:—spindle.

3602. כָּכָה, **kâkâh,** *kaw´-kaw*; from 3541; *just so*, referring to the previous or following context:—after that (this) manner, this matter, (even) so, in such a case, thus.

3603. כִּכָּר, **kikâr,** *kik-kawr´*; from 3769; a *circle*, i.e. (by implication) a circumjacent *tract* or region, especially the *Ghor* or valley of the Jordan; also a (round) *loaf*; also a *talent* (or large [round] coin):—loaf, morsel, piece, plain, talent.

3604. כִּכַּר, **kakkar,** *kak-kar´*; (Chaldee); corresponding to 3603; a *talent*:—talent.

3605. כֹּל, **kôl,** *kole*; or (Jer 33:8) כּוֹל, **kôwl,** *kole*; from 3634; (properly) the *whole*; hence *all, any* or *every* (in the singular only, but often in a plural sense):—(in) all (manner, [ye]), altogether, any (manner), enough, every (one, place, thing), howsoever, as many as, [no-] thing, ought, whatsoever, (the) whole, whoso (-ever).

3606. כֹּל, **kôl,** *kole*; (Chaldee); corresponding to 3605:—all, any, + (forasmuch) as, + be- (for this) cause, every, + no (manner, -ne), + there (where) -fore, + though, what (where, who) -soever, (the) whole.

3607. כָּלָא, **kâlâ',** *kaw-law'*; a primitive root; to *restrict,* by act (*hold* back or in) or word (*prohibit*):—finish, forbid, keep (back), refrain, restrain, retain, shut up, be stayed, withhold.

3608. כֶּלֶא, **kele',** *keh'-leh*; from 3607; a *prison:*—prison. Compare 3610, 3628.

3609. כִּלְאָב, **Kil'âb,** *kil-awb'*; apparently from 3607 and 1; *restraint of* (his) *father; Kilab,* an Israelite:—Chileab.

3610. כִּלְאַיִם, **kil'ayim,** *kil-ah'-yim*; dual of 3608 in the original sense of *separation; two heterogeneities:*—divers seeds (-e kinds), mingled (seed).

3611. כֶּלֶב, **keleb,** *keh'-leb*; from an unused root meaning to *yelp,* or else to *attack;* a *dog;* hence (by euphemism) a male *prostitute:*—dog.

3612. כָּלֵב, **Kâlêb,** *kaw-labe'*; perhaps a form of 3611, or else from the same root in the sense of *forcible; Caleb,* the name of three Israelites:—Caleb.

3613. כָּלֵב אֶפְרָתָה, **Kâlêb 'Ephrâthâh,** *kaw-labe' ef-raw'-thaw*; from 3612 and 672; *Caleb-Ephrathah,* a place in Egypt (if the text is correct):—Caleb-ephrathah.

3614. כָּלִבּוֹ, **Kâlibbôw,** *kaw-lib-bo'*; probably by erroneous transcription for כָּלִבִי, **Kâlêbîy,** *kaw-lay-bee'*; patronymic from 3612; a *Calebite* or descendant of Caleb:—of the house of Caleb.

3615. כָּלָה, **kâlâh,** *kaw-law'*; a primitive root; to *end,* whether intransitive (to *cease, be finished, perish*) or transitive (to *complete, prepare, consume*):—accomplish, cease, consume (away), determine, destroy (utterly), be (when … were) done, (be an) end (of), expire, (cause to) fail, faint, finish, fulfil, × fully, × have, leave (off), long, bring to pass, wholly reap, make clean riddance, spend, quite take away, waste.

A verb meaning to complete, to accomplish, to end, to finish, to fail, to exhaust. Its primary meaning is to consummate or to bring to completion. This occasionally occurs in a positive sense as in the awesome goodness of God's perfected and finished creation (Ge 2:1, 2). It also represents the favourable conclusion of meaningful human labour as in building the tabernacle (Ex 39:32); or preparing tithes (Dt 26:12). However, *kâlâh* is more often used with a negative connotation. God threatened to consume human unbelief (as in completing the life span), a promise terribly fulfilled at Korah's rebellion (Nu 16:21). Also, Israel was to be God's vehicle in consuming or finishing the heathen nations in the land (Dt 7:22), thus completing the ban. The verb also describes the transitory reality of fallen human nature. We finish our years like a sigh (Ps 90:9), passing away like an exhausted cloud (Job 7:9).

3616. כָּלֶה, **kâleh,** *kaw-leh'*; from 3615; *pining:*—fail.

3617. כָּלָה, **kâlâh,** *kaw-law'*; from 3615; a *completion;* adverb *completely;* also *destruction:*—altogether, (be, utterly) consume (-d), consummation (-ption), was determined, (full, utter) end, riddance.

A feminine noun meaning completion, complete destruction, annihilation. In the sense of completion, God told Moses that Pharaoh would let the Israelites go by driving them completely out of Egypt (Ex 11:1). Complete destruction or annihilation was most often attributed to God. Isaiah prophesied that the Lord would make a determined end to Israel (Isa 10:23); Nahum spoke of God's judgment by which He made an utter end of His enemies (Na 1:8). Destruction of such massive quantity is attributed to humans in Daniel's prophecy of Greece (Da 11:16).

3618. כַּלָּה, **kallâh,** *kal-law'*; from 3634; a *bride* (as if *perfect*); hence a *son's wife:*—bride, daughter-in-law, spouse.

3619. כְּלוּב, **kᵉlûwb,** *kel-oob'*; from the same as 3611; a bird-*trap* (as furnished with a *clap*-stick or treadle to spring it); hence a *basket* (as resembling a wicker cage):—basket, cage.

3620. כְּלוּב, **Kᵉlûwb,** *kel-oob'*; the same as 3619; *Kelub,* the name of two Israelites:—Chelub.

3621. כְּלוּבָי, Keluwbây, *kel-oo-baw´ee*; a form of 3612; *Kelubai*, an Israelite:—Chelubai.

3622. כְּלֻהִי, Keluhîy, *kel-oo-hee´*; from 3615; *completed*; an Israelite:—Chelluh.

3623. כְּלוּלָה, keluwlâh, *kel-oo-law´*; denominative passive participle from 3618; *bridehood* (only in the plural):—espousal.

3624. כֶּלַח, kelach, *keh´-lakh*; from an unused root meaning to *be complete*; *maturity*:—full (old) age.

3625. כֶּלַח, Kelach, *keh´-lakh*; the same as 3624; *Kelach*, a place in Assyria:—Calah.

3626. כָּל־חֹזֶה, Kol-Chôzeh, *kol-kho-zeh´*; from 3605 and 2374; *every seer*; *Col-Chozeh*, an Israelite:—Col-hozeh.

3627. כְּלִי, kelîy, *kel-ee´*; from 3615; something *prepared*, i.e. any *apparatus* (as an implement, utensil, dress, vessel or weapon):—armour ([-bearer]), artillery, bag, carriage, + furnish, furniture, instrument, jewel, that is made of, × one from another, that which pertaineth, pot, + psaltery, sack, stuff, thing, tool, vessel, ware, weapon, + whatsoever.

3628. כְּלִיא, kelîy’, *kel-ee´*; or כְּלוּא, keluw’, *kel-oo´*; from 3607 [compare 3608]; a *prison*:—prison.

3629. כִּלְיָה, kilyâh, *kil-yaw´*; feminine of 3627 (only in the plural); a *kidney* (as an essential *organ*); (figurative) the *mind* (as the interior self):—kidneys, reins.

3630. כִּלְיוֹן, Kilyôwn, *kil-yone´*; a form of 3631; *Kiljon*, an Israelite:—Chilion.

3631. כִּלָּיוֹן, killâyôwn, *kil-law-yone´*; from 3615; *pining, destruction*:—consumption, failing.

3632. כָּלִיל, kâlîyl, *kaw-leel´*; from 3634; *complete*; as noun, the *whole* (specifically a sacrifice *entirely consumed*); as adverb *fully*:—all, every whit, flame, perfect (-ion), utterly, whole burnt offering (sacrifice), wholly.

An adjective meaning whole, entire, perfect, complete. This word can refer to an offering that was entirely consumed (Dt 33:10; 1Sa 7:9); figuratively, it refers to burning a whole town that worshipped other gods (Dt 13:16 [17]). The ephod had to be all purple (Ex 28:31; 39:22);

Isaiah prophesied of a day when idols would completely disappear (Isa 2:18). This word also referred to Jerusalem's complete beauty (La 2:15; Eze 16:14); or Tyre's (Eze 27:3; 28:12). See the Hebrew root *kâlal* (3634).

3633. כַּלְכֹּל, Kalkôl, *kal-kole´*; from 3557; *sustenance*; *Calcol*, an Israelite:—Calcol, Chalcol.

3634. כָּלַל, kâlal, *kaw-lal´*; a primitive root; to *complete*:—(make) perfect.

A verb meaning to complete, to make perfect. Ezekiel lamented over Tyre's pride concerning her perfected beauty (Eze 27:4). Builders as well as war bounty came from all over the Near East to the port city of Tyre and added to the perfect beauty of the city (Eze 27:11).

3635. כְּלַל, kelal, *kel-al´*; (Chaldee); corresponding to 3634; to *complete*:—finish, make (set) up.

An Aramaic verb meaning to complete. This word described the completed Temple (Ezr 5:11). It also carries the meaning of to restore (Ezr 4:12, 13, 16; 5:3, 9). See the related Hebrew root *kâlal* (3634) and the related Hebrew adjective *kâliyl* (3632).

3636. כְּלָל, Kelâl, *kel-awl´*; from 3634; *complete*; *Kelal*, an Israelite:—Chelal.

3637. כָּלַם, kâlam, *kaw-lawm´*; a primitive root; (properly) to *wound*; but only figurative, to *taunt* or *insult*:—be (make) ashamed, blush, be confounded, be put to confusion, hurt, reproach, (do, put to) shame.

3638. כִּלְמַד, Kilmad, *kil-mad´*; of foreign derivation; *Kilmad*, a place apparently in the Assyrian empire:—Chilmad.

3639. כְּלִמָּה, kelimmâh, *kel-im-maw´*; from 3637; *disgrace*:—confusion, dishonour, reproach, shame.

3640. כְּלִמּוּת, kelimmûwth, *kel-im-mooth´*; from 3639; *disgrace*:—shame.

3641. כַּלְנֶה, Kalneh, *kal-neh´*; or כַּלְנֵה, Kalnêh, *kal-nay´*; also כַּלְנוֹ, Kalnôw, *kal-no´*; of foreign derivation; *Calneh* or *Calno*, a place in the Assyrian empire:—Calneh, Calno. Compare 3656.

3642. כָּמַהּ, **kâmah,** *kaw-mah´*; a primitive root; to *pine* after:—long.

3643. כִּמְהָם, **Kimhâm,** *kim-hawm´*; from 3642; *pining; Kimham,* an Israelite:—Chimham.

3644. כְּמוֹ, **kᵉmôw,** *kem-o´*; or כָּמוֹ, **kâmôw,** *kaw-mo´*; a form of the prefix *k,* but used separately [compare 3651]; *as, thus, so:*—according to, (such) as (it were, well as), in comparison of, like (as, to, unto), thus, when, worth.

3645. כְּמוֹשׁ, **Kᵉmôwsh,** *kem-oshe´*; or (Jer 48:7) כְּמִישׁ, **Kᵉmîysh,** *kem-eesh´*; from an unused root meaning to *subdue*; the *powerful; Kemosh,* the god of the Moabites:—Chemosh.

3646. כַּמֹּן, **kammôn,** *kam-mone´*; from an unused root meaning to *store* up or *preserve*; "*cummin*" (from its use as a *condiment*):—cummin.

3647. כָּמַס, **kâmas,** *kaw-mas´*; a primitive root; to *store* away, i.e. (figurative) in the memory:—lay up in store.

3648. כָּמַר, **kâmar,** *kaw-mar´*; a primitive root; (properly) to *intertwine* or *contract,* i.e. (by implication) to *shrivel* (as with heat); (figurative) to be deeply *affected* with passion (love or pity):—be black, be kindled, yearn.

3649. כֹּמֶר, **kômer,** *kow-mer´*; from 3648; (properly) an *ascetic* (as if *shrunk* with self-maceration), i.e. an idolatrous *priest* (only in plural):—Chemarims, (idolatrous) priests.

A masculine noun meaning a (pagan) priest. In the OT, this word occurs three times. In 2Ki 23:5, Josiah's reformation got rid of priests who burned incense in the idolatrous high places. In Hos 10:5, Hosea prophesied that priests would mourn over the calf statue they worshiped when it was carried off to Assyrian captivity. In Zep 1:4, God promised to cut off the names of unfaithful priests, along with His own priests (cf. Zep 1:5, 6).

3650. כִּמְרִיר, **kimrîyr,** *kim-reer´*; reduplication from 3648; *obscuration* (as if from *shrinkage* of light; i.e. an *eclipse* (only in plural):—blackness.

3651. כֵּן, **kên,** *kane*; from 3559; (properly) *set* upright; hence (figurative as adjective) *just*; but usually (as adverb or conjunction) *rightly* or *so* (in various applications to manner, time and relation; often with other particles):— + after

that (this, -ward, -wards), as … as, + [for-] asmuch as yet, + be (for which) cause, + following, howbeit, in (the) like (manner, -wise), × the more, right, (even) so, state, straightway, such (thing), surely, + there (where) -fore, this, thus, true, well, × you.

A word that is used either as an adverb or adjective, depending on the context of the sentence. The word is derived from the verb meaning to stand upright or to establish. As an adjective, it means correct, according to an established standard (Nu 27:7); upright and honest (Ge 42:11); it is used as a statement of general agreement (Ge 44:10; Jos 2:21). As an adverb, it is usually translated as "thus" or "so" but conveys quality (Est 4:16; Job 9:35; Na 1:12); quantity (Jgs 21:14); cause and effect (Jgs 10:13; Isa 5:24); or time (Ne 2:16).

3652. כֵּן, **kên,** *kane*; (Chaldee); corresponding to 3651; *so:*—thus.

3653. כֵּן, **kên,** *kane*; the same as 3651, used as a noun; a *stand,* i.e. pedestal or station:—base, estate, foot, office, place, well.

3654. כֵּן, **kên,** *kane*; from 3661, in the sense of *fastening*; a *gnat* (from infixing its sting; used only in plural [and irregular in Ex 8:17, 18; Hebrew 8:13, 14]):—lice, × manner.

3655. כָּנָה, **kânâh,** *kaw-naw´*; a primitive root; to *address* by an additional name; hence, to *eulogize*:—give flattering titles, surname (himself).

3656. כַּנֶּה, **Kanneh,** *kan-neh´*; for 3641; *Canneh,* a place in Assyria:—Canneh.

3657. כַּנָּה, **kannâh,** *kan-naw´*; from 3661; a *plant* (as *set*):— × vineyard.

3658. כִּנּוֹר, **kinnôwr,** *kin-nore´*; from an unused root meaning to *twang*; a *harp*:—harp.

3659. כָּנְיָהוּ, **Konyâhûw,** *kon-yaw´-hoo*; for 3204; *Conjah,* an Israelite king:—Coniah.

3660. כְּנֵמָא, **kᵉnêmâ',** *ken-ay-maw´*; (Chaldee); corresponding to 3644; *so* or *thus*:—so, (in) this manner (sort), thus.

3661. כָּנַן, **kânan,** *kaw-nan´*; a primitive root; to *set* out, i.e. *plant*:— × vineyard.

3662. כְּנָנִי, **Kᵉnânîy,** *ken-aw-nee´*; from 3661; *planted; Kenani,* an Israelite:—Chenani.

3663. כְּנַנְיָה, **Kᵉnanyâh,** *ken-an-yaw´*; or כְּנַנְיָהוּ, **Kᵉnanyâhûw,** *ken-an-yaw´-hoo*; from 3661 and 3050; *Jah has planted; Kenanjah,* an Israelite:— Chenaniah.

3664. כָּנַס, **kânas,** *kaw-nas´*; a primitive root; to *collect;* hence, to *enfold:*—gather (together), heap up, wrap self.

A verb meaning to gather, to collect. David assembled foreigners to be stonecutters (1Ch 22:2). Esther instructed Mordecai to gather the Jews and fast (Est 4:16). The Lord gathered the waters (Ps 33:7). The writer of Ecclesiastes collected silver and gold for himself (Ecc 2:8); there is a time to gather stones (Ecc 3:5). The Lord told Ezekiel that He would gather Jerusalem together for punishment (Eze 22:21).

3665. כָּנַע, **kâna',** *kaw-nah´*; a primitive root; (properly) to *bend* the knee; hence to *humiliate, vanquish:*—bring down (low), into subjection, under, humble (self), subdue.

3666. כִּנְעָה, **kin'âh,** *kin-aw´*; from 3665 in the sense of *folding* [compare 3664]; a *package:*— wares.

3667. כְּנַעַן, **Kᵉna'an,** *ken-ah´-an*; from 3665; *humiliated; Kenaan,* a son of Ham; also the country inhabited by him:—Canaan, merchant, traffick.

3668. כְּנַעֲנָה, **Kᵉna'ănâh,** *ken-ah-an-aw´*; feminine of 3667; *Kenaanah,* the name of two Israelites:—Chenaanah.

3669. כְּנַעֲנִי, **Kᵉna'ăniy,** *ken-ah-an-ee´*; patrial from 3667; a *Kenaanite* or inhabitant of Kenaan; (by implication) a *pedlar* (the Canaanites standing for their neighbours the Ishmaelites, who conducted mercantile caravans):—Canaanite, merchant, trafficker.

3670. כָּנַף, **kânaph,** *kaw-naf´*; a primitive root; (properly) to *project* laterally, i.e. probably (reflexive) to *withdraw:*—be removed.

3671. כָּנָף, **kânâph,** *kaw-nawf´*; from 3670; an *edge* or *extremity;* specifically (of a bird or army) a *wing,* (of a garment or bed-clothing) a *flap,* (of the earth) a *quarter,* (of a building) a *pinnacle:*— + bird, border, corner, end, feather [-ed], × flying, + (one an-) other, overspreading, × quarters, skirt, × sort, uttermost part, wing ([-ed]).

3672. כִּנֲרוֹת, **Kinnᵉrôwth,** *kin-ner-ōth´*; or כִּנֶּרֶת, **Kinnereth,** *kin-neh´-reth*; respectively plural and singular feminine from the same as 3658; perhaps *harp*-shaped; *Kinneroth* or *Kinnereth,* a place in Palestine:—Chinnereth, Chinneroth, Cinneroth.

3673. כְּנַשׁ, **kᵉnash,** *keh-nash´*; (Chaldee); corresponding to 3664; to *assemble:*—gather together.

An Aramaic verb meaning to assemble, to be assembled. It corresponds to the Hebrew word *kânas* (3664) and occurs only in Da 3:2, 3, and 27. It referred to the assembling of Babylonian officials, initiated by Nebuchadnezzar, to dedicate and worship an image. The assembly was apparently a formal occasion with high officials standing before the image, a herald proclaiming the purpose of the assembly, and musicians playing various instruments. Those assembled saw the Hebrews who refused to obey sentenced to the fiery furnace and subsequently delivered from it.

3674. כְּנָת, **kᵉnâth,** *ken-awth´*; from 3655; a *colleague* (as having the same title):—companion.

3675. כְּנָת, **kᵉnâth,** *ken-awth´*; (Chaldee); corresponding to 3674:—companion.

3676. כֵּס, **kês,** *kace*; apparently a contraction for 3678, but probably by erroneous transcription for 5251:—sworn.

3677. כֶּסֶא, **kese',** *keh´-seh*; or כֶּסֶה, **keseh,** *keh´-seh*; apparently from 3680; (properly) *fulness* or the *full moon,* i.e. its *festival:*—(time) appointed.

3678. כִּסֵּא, **kissê',** *kis-say´*; or כִּסֵּה, **kissêh,** *kis-say´*; from 3680; (properly) *covered,* i.e. a *throne* (as *canopied*):—seat, stool, throne.

A masculine noun meaning throne, a place of honour. Pharaoh put Joseph over everything in his kingdom except his throne (Ge 41:40). Other references to leaders on the throne include Pharaoh (Ex 11:5; 12:29); Solomon and Bathsheba (1Ki 2:19); King Ahasuerus (Est 5:1); departed kings (Isa 14:9); the princes of the coast (Eze 26:16); the prophetic one who will build the temple of the Lord (Zec 6:13). Scripture also depicts God as sitting on a throne (Isa 6:1; Eze 1:26). The throne can also be a symbol of a kingdom or power (2Sa 7:16; 14:9; Isa 16:5).

3679. כַּסְדָּי, **Kasdây,** *kas-daw´ee;* for 3778:—Chaldean.

3680. כָּסָה, **kâsâh,** *kaw-saw´;* a primitive root; (properly) to *plump,* i.e. *fill up* hollows; (by implication) to *cover* (for clothing or secrecy):—clad self, close, clothe, conceal, cover (self), (flee to) hide, overwhelm. Compare 3780.

A verb meaning to cover, to clothe, to conceal. The active meaning of this verb is to cover, to cover up. It is used in a literal sense to indicate that something is covering something else, as when the waters of the Red Sea covered the Egyptians or the cloud of God's glory covered Mount Sinai or the tabernacle (Ex 15:5; 24:15). In a metaphorical sense, the word describes shame covering the guilty (Ps 69:7[8]; Jer 3:25; Hab 2:17); the Israelites' covering the altar with tears (Mal 2:13); and the concealing of Joseph's blood to hide his brothers' guilt and sin (Ge 37:26). On the other hand, the psalmist found reconciliation with God by not concealing his sin but confessing it (Ps 32:5; Pr 10:11). The word sometimes means to cover oneself with clothing or sackcloth, to clothe oneself with something (Eze 16:18; Jnh 3:6).

The passive form of the verb means to be covered, such as when the mountains were covered by the waters of the great flood (Ge 7:19; Ps 80:10[11]). The reflexive form is used to mean to cover oneself; for example, when the people of Nineveh covered themselves in repentance at Jonah's preaching (Jnh 3:8). The word in Ecc 6:4 describes the name of a stillborn child covering itself in darkness.

3681. כָּסוּי, **kâsûwy,** *kaw-soo´ee;* passive participle of 3680; (properly) *covered,* i.e. (as noun) a *covering:*—covering.

3682. כְּסוּת, **keˢûwth,** *kes-ooth´;* from 3680; a *cover* (garment); (figurative) a *veiling:*—covering, raiment, vesture.

3683. כָּסַח, **kâsach,** *kaw-sakh´;* a primitive root; to *cut off:*—cut down (up).

3684. כְּסִיל, **keˢîyl,** *kes-eel´;* from 3688; (properly) *fat,* i.e. (figurative) *stupid* or *silly:*—fool (-ish).

3685. כְּסִיל, **Keˢîyl,** *kes-eel´;* the same as 3684; any notable *constellation;* specifically *Orion* (as if a *burly* one):—constellation, Orion.

3686. כְּסִיל, **Keˢîyl,** *kes-eel´;* the same as 3684; *Kesil,* a place in Palestine:—Chesil.

3687. כְּסִילוּת, **keˢîylûwth,** *kes-eel-ooth´;* from 3684; *silliness:*—foolish.

A feminine noun meaning foolishness, stupidity. This abstract noun is derived from the adjective *kĕsiyl* (3684), which means fat and, thus, (in a negative sense) stupid, foolish (or as a substantive, a foolish one). *Kĕsiylûth* occurs only in Pr 9:13, naming the woman of folly, a symbolic character who appealed to the evil desires of naive people in order to cause them to stray from right paths into paths that lead to death.

3688. כָּסַל, **kâsal,** *kaw-sal´;* a primitive root; (properly) to *be fat,* i.e. (figurative) *silly:*—be foolish.

A verb meaning to be stupid, to become stupid. It occurs once as a verb in Jer 10:8, referring to those taught by idols.

3689. כֶּסֶל, **kesel,** *keh´-sel;* from 3688; (properly) *fatness,* i.e. by implication (literal) the *loin* (as the seat of the leaf *fat*) or (generic) the *viscera;* also (figurative) *silliness* or (in a good sense) *trust:*—confidence, flank, folly, hope, loin.

A masculine noun meaning loins, confidence, stupidity. The first use can actually mean the waist area, the kidneys, etc. (Le 3:4, 10, 15; 4:9; 7:4; Job 15:27). The second use is more ambiguous, meaning that in which one puts trust or confidence (Job 8:14; 31:24; Ps 78:7; Pr 3:26). The final usage is a false self-trust or stupidity (Ps 49:13[14]; Ecc 7:25). See the related Hebrew verb *kâsal* (3688) and Hebrew noun *kislâh* (3690).

3690. כִּסְלָה, **kislâh,** *kis-law´;* feminine of 3689; in a good sense, *trust;* in a bad one, *silliness:*—confidence, folly.

A feminine noun meaning foolishness, stupidity, confidence. The root idea of fatness (see *kâsal* [3688]) may have two implications. In Job 4:6, *kĕsilâh* means the confidence of one who is fat and firm. Eliphaz cast doubt on Job's righteousness by asking why he was confused if he really feared God. In Ps 85:8[9], on the other hand, God warned His restored people not to return to their former folly. In that verse, the word refers to sluggish foolishness that is no longer alive to the fear of God.

3691. כִּסְלוֹ, **Kislêv,** *kis-lave´*; probably of foreign origin; *Kisleu*, the 9th Hebrew month:— Chisleu.

3692. כִּסְלוֹן, **Kislôwn,** *kis-lone´*; from 3688; *hopeful*; *Kislon*, an Israelite:—Chislon.

3693. כְּסָלוֹן, **Kᵉsâlôwn,** *kes-aw-lone´*; from 3688; *fertile*; *Kesalon*, a place in Palestine:— Chesalon.

3694. כְּסוּלּוֹת, **Kᵉsûwllôwth,** *kes-ool-lōth´*; feminine plural of passive participle of 3688; *fattened*, *Kesul-loth*, a place in Palestine:— Chesulloth.

3695. כַּסְלֻחִים, **Kasluchîym,** *kas-loo´-kheem*; a plural probably of foreign derivation; *Casluchim*, a people cognate to the Egyptian:— Casluhim.

3696. כִּסְלֹת תָּבֹר, **Kislôth Tâbôr,** *kis-lōth´ taw-bore´*; from the feminine plural of 3689 and 8396; *flanks of Tabor*; *Kisloth-Tabor*, a place in Palestine:—Chisloth-tabor.

3697. כָּסַם, **kâsam,** *kaw-sam´*; a primitive root; to *shear*:— × only, poll. Compare 3765.

3698. כֻּסֶּמֶת, **kussemeth,** *koos-seh´-meth*; from 3697; *spelt* (from its bristliness as if just *shorn*):—fitches, rie.

3699. כָּסַס, **kâsas,** *kaw-sas´*; a primitive root; to *estimate*:—make count.

3700. כָּסַף, **kâsaph,** *kaw-saf´*; a primitive root; (properly) to become *pale*, i.e. (by implication) to *pine* after; also to *fear*:—[have] desire, be greedy, long, sore.

3701. כֶּסֶף, **keseph,** *keh´-sef*; from 3700; *silver* (from its *pale* colour); (by implication) *money*:—money, price, silver (-ling).

3702. כְּסַף, **kᵉsaph,** *kes-af´*; (Chaldee); corresponding to 3701:—money, silver.

3703. כָּסְפְיָא, **Kâsiphyâʾ,** *kaw-sif-yaw´*; perhaps from 3701; *silvery*; *Casiphja*, a place in Babylon:—Casiphia.

3704. כֶּסֶת, **keseth,** *keh´-seth*; from 3680; a *cushion* or pillow (as *covering* a seat or bed):— pillow.

3705. כְּעַן, **kᵉan,** *keh-an´*; (Chaldee); probably from 3652; *now*:—now.

3706. כְּעֶנֶת, **kᵉeneth,** *keh-eh´-neth*; (Chaldee); or כְּעֶת, **kᵉeth,** *keh-eth´*; (Chaldee); feminine of 3705; *thus* (only in the formula "and *so forth*"):—at such a time.

3707. כָּעַס, **kâas,** *kaw-as´*; a primitive root; to *trouble*; (by implication) to *grieve, rage, be indignant*:—be angry, be grieved, take indignation, provoke (to anger, unto wrath), have sorrow, vex, be wroth.

A verb meaning to be angry, to provoke to anger. The causative sense of the verb occurs most often and frequently signifies idolatry provoking God to anger (cf. 1Ki 14:9; Ps 106:29; Eze 8:17). The result of provocation may be expressed as ʾaph, anger (639) (Dt 9:18; 2Ki 23:26; Jer 7:20). In a noncausative sense, the verb means to be angry; people were warned not to become angry hastily (Ecc 7:9); God says that after He punishes, He will not be angry (Eze 16:42). Three times it refers to the people's anger directed toward righteousness (2Ch 16:10; Ne 4:1[3:33]; Ps 112:10).

3708. כַּעַס, **kaas,** *kah´-as*; or (in Job) כַּעַשׂ, **kaaś,** *kah´-as*; from 3707; *vexation*:—anger, angry, grief, indignation, provocation, provoking, × sore, sorrow, spite, wrath.

A masculine singular noun meaning anger, provocation, vexation. The alternate spelling of the word occurs only in Job. The majority of occurrences are in poetic literature. Human sinfulness and idolatry (1Ki 15:30; Eze 20:28) cause God's anger, while fools, sons, wives, and rival wives can also cause vexation (1Sa 1:6; Pr 27:3; 17:25; 21:19, respectively).

3709. כַּף, **kaph,** *kaf*; from 3721; the hollow *hand* or palm (so of the *paw* of an animal, of the *sole*, and even of the *bowl* of a dish or sling, the *handle* of a bolt, the *leaves* of a palm-tree); (figurative) *power*:—branch, + foot, hand ([-ful], -dle [-led]), hollow, middle, palm, paw, power, sole, spoon.

A feminine noun meaning hand, the flat of the hand, the flat of the foot, hollow, bent. The principal meaning is hollow, often used of the hollow of the physical hand or foot. It also relates to cupped or bent objects such as spoons (Nu 7:80). In metaphysical overtones, Job declared his cleanness of hand (Job 9:30); and David linked clean hands with a pure heart (Ps 24:4). The righteous correctly lift up their hands in God's name (Ps 63:4[5]; 141:2), but the wicked are snared by their own hands' work (Ps 9:16). At wicked Jezebel's death, dogs devoured her but refused the palms of her hands (2Ki 9:35). The Israelites inherited every place on which their soles treaded in the Promised Land (Dt 11:24); the returning exiles were delivered from the hand of the enemy (Ezr 8:31). Ultimately, God is the skillful Shepherd, securely holding His own with a sovereign hand (Ps 139:5).

3710. כֵּף, **kêph,** *kafe*; from 3721; a hollow *rock:*—rock.

3711. כָּפָה, **kâphâh,** *kaw-faw´*; a primitive root; (properly) to *bend,* i.e. (figurative) to *tame* or *subdue:*—pacify.

3712. כִּפָּה, **kippâh,** *kip-paw´*; feminine of 3709; a *leaf* of a palm-tree:—branch.

3713. כְּפוֹר, **kᵉphôwr,** *kef-ore´*; from 3722; (properly) a *cover,* i.e. (by implication) a *tankard* (or *covered* goblet); also white *frost* (as *covering* the ground):—bason, hoar (-y) frost.

3714. כָּפִיס, **kâphîys,** *kaw-fece´*; from an unused root meaning to *connect*; a *girder:*—beam.

3715. כְּפִיר, **kᵉphîyr,** *kef-eer´*; from 3722; a *village* (as *covered* in by walls); also a young *lion* (perhaps as *covered* with a mane):—(young) lion, village. Compare 3723.

3716. כְּפִירָה, **Kᵉphîyrâh,** *kef-ee-raw´*; feminine of 3715; the *village* (always with the article); *Kephirah,* a place in Palestine:—Chephirah.

3717. כָּפַל, **kâphal,** *kaw-fal´*; a primitive root; to *fold* together; (figurative) to *repeat:*—double.

3718. כֶּפֶל, **kephel,** *keh´-fel*; from 3717; a *duplicate:*—double.

3719. כָּפַן, **kâphan,** *kaw-fan´*; a primitive root; to *bend:*—bend.

3720. כָּפָן, **kâphân,** *kaw-fawn´*; from 3719; *hunger* (as making to *stoop* with emptiness and pain):—famine.

3721. כָּפַף, **kâphaph,** *kaw-faf´*; a primitive root; to *curve:*—bow down (self).

3722. כָּפַר, **kâphar,** *kaw-far´*; a primitive root; to *cover* (specifically with bitumen); (figurative) to *expiate* or *condone,* to *placate* or *cancel:*—

appease, make (an) atonement, cleanse, disannul, forgive, be merciful, pacify, pardon, purge (away), put off, (make) reconcile (-liation).

A verb meaning to cover, to forgive, to expiate, to reconcile. This word is of supreme theological importance in the OT as it is central to an OT understanding of the remission of sin. At its most basic level, the word conveys the notion of covering but not in the sense of merely concealing. Rather, it suggests the imposing of something to change its appearance or nature. It is therefore employed to signify the cancellation or "writing over" of a contract (Isa 28:18); the appeasing of anger (Ge 32:20[21]; Pr 16:14); and the overlaying of wood with pitch so as to make it waterproof (Ge 6:14). The word also communicates God's covering of sin. Persons made reconciliation with God for their sins by imposing something that would appease the offended party (in this case the Lord) and cover the sinners with righteousness (Ex 32:30; Eze 45:17; cf. Da 9:24). In the OT, the blood of sacrifices was most notably imposed (Ex 30:10). By this imposition, sin was purged (Ps 79:9; Isa 6:7) and forgiven (Ps 78:38). The offences were removed, leaving the sinners clothed in righteousness (cf. Zec 3:3, 4). Of course, the imposition of the blood of bulls and of goats could never fully cover our sin (see Heb 10:4), but with the coming of Christ and the imposition of His shed blood, a perfect atonement was made (Ro 5:9–11).

3723. כָּפָר, **kâphâr,** *kaw-fawr´*; from 3722; a *village* (as *protected* by walls):—village. Compare 3715.

3724. כֹּפֶר, **kôpher,** *ko´-fer*; from 3722; (properly) a *cover,* i.e. (literal) a *village* (as *covered* in); (specific) *bitumen* (as used for *coating*), and the *henna* plant (as used for *dyeing*); (figurative) a *redemption*-price:—bribe, camphire, pitch, ransom, satisfaction, sum of money, village.

A masculine noun meaning a ransom, a bribe, a half-shekel. The most common translation of the word is ransom. It refers to the price demanded in order to redeem or rescue a person. The irresponsible owner of a bull that killed someone and was known to have gored people previously could be redeemed by the ransom that would be placed on him (Ex 21:30). When a census of people was taken in Israel, adult males had to pay a half-shekel ransom to keep the Lord's plague from striking them (Ex 30:12). A murderer could not be redeemed by a ransom (Nu 35:31). Yet money, without God's explicit approval, could not serve as a ransom for a human being (Ps 49:7[8]). On the other hand, money could serve as a ransom to buy off a person's human enemies (Pr 13:8). God sometimes used a wicked person as a ransom to redeem a righteous person (Pr 21:18); God ransomed Israel from Babylonian captivity for the ransom price of three nations (Isa 43:3): Egypt, Seba, and Cush.

The meaning of the word becomes a bribe when used in certain circumstances. For example, Samuel declared that he had never taken a bribe (1Sa 12:3); and Amos castigated the leaders of Israel for taking bribes (Am 5:12). Pr 6:35 describes a jealous husband whose fury would not allow him to take a bribe to lessen his anger.

3725. כִּפֻּר, **kippur,** *kip-poor´*; from 3722; *expiation* (only in plural):—atonement.

A masculine plural noun meaning atonement, the act of reconciliation, the Day of Atonement. It is used five times to indicate the act or process of reconciliation: a young bull was sacrificed each day for seven days during the ordination ceremony of Aaron and his sons to make atonement (Ex 29:36). Once a year, the blood of a sin offering was used to make atonement on the horns of the altar of incense located in front of the Holy of Holies (Ex 30:10). Ransom money of a half-shekel was used to effect atonement or reconciliation for male Israelites who were at least twenty years old (Ex 30:16). The money was then used to service the Tent of Meeting.

When a person had wronged the Lord or another person, a ram was presented to the priest, along with proper restitution (Nu 5:8); a sin offering for atonement was presented yearly on the Day of Atonement (Nu 29:11). Three times the noun is used to indicate the Day of Atonement itself (Le 23:27, 28; 25:9).

3726. כְּפַר הָעַמּוֹנִי, **Kᵉphar hâʻAmmôwnîy,** *kef-ar´ haw-am-mo-nee´*; from 3723 and 5984, with the article interposed; *village of the Ammonite; Kefar-ha-Ammoni,* a place in Palestine:—Chefar-haamonai.

3727. כַּפֹּרֶת, **kappôreth,** *kap-po´-reth*; from 3722; a *lid* (used only of the *cover* of the sacred Ark):—mercy seat.

A noun meaning a lid, propitiation. This word refers to the lid that covered the ark of the testimony. It was made of gold and was decorated with two cherubim. God resided above this mercy seat (Ex 25:17–22). Only at specific times could the high priest come before the mercy seat (Le 16:2). On the Day of Atonement, the high priest made atonement for himself, the tabernacle, and the people by a sin offering, which included sprinkling blood on this lid (Le 16:13–15).

3728. כָּפַשׁ, **kâphash,** *kaw-fash´*; a primitive root; to *tread* down; (figurative) to *humiliate*:—cover.

A verb meaning to bend, to trample down, to humiliate, to cover over. This word is a primary root, but it is used only once in the Hebrew Bible. There the writer of Lamentations felt like he was trampled in the dust (La 3:16).

3729. כְּפַת, **kᵉphath,** *kef-ath´*; (Chaldee); a root of uncertain correspondence; to *fetter*:—bind.

3730. כַּפְתֹּר, **kaphtôr,** *kaf-tore´*; or (Am 9:1) כַּפְתּוֹר, **kaphtôwr,** *kaf-tore´*; probably from an unused root meaning to *encircle*; a *chaplet*; but used only in an architectonic sense, i.e. the *capital* of a column, or a wreath-like *button* or *disk* on the candelabrum:—knop, (upper) lintel.

3731. כַּפְתֹּר, **Kaphtôr,** *kaf-tore´*; or (Am 9:7) כַּפְתּוֹר, **Kaphtôwr,** *kaf-tore´*; apparently the same as 3730; *Caphtor* (i.e. a *wreath*-shaped island), the original seat of the Philistines:—Caphtor.

3732. כַּפְתֹּרִי, **Kaphtôrîy,** *kaf-to-ree´*; patrial from 3731; a *Caphtorite* (collective) or native of Caphtor:—Caphthorim, Caphtorim (-s).

3733. כַּר, **kar,** *kar*; from 3769 in the sense of *plumpness*; a *ram* (as *full-grown* and *fat*), including a *battering-ram* (as *butting*); hence a *meadow* (as *for sheep*); also a *pad* or camel's saddle (as *puffed out*):—captain, furniture, lamb, (large) pasture, ram. See also 1033, 3746.

A masculine noun meaning pasture, a male lamb, and a battering ram. When used to mean pasture, it describes a bountiful restoration for the Israelites. Like sheep, they would have large pastures in which to graze (Isa 30:23). In reference to sheep, it means a male lamb as compared to ewes, lambs, or fatlings (1Sa 15:9). Tribute often came in the form of both ewes and rams, such as Mesha, king of Moab, paid to the king of Israel (2Ki 3:4). This word also connotes a battering ram such as those used in siege warfare (Eze 4:2). It is also interpreted as a saddle (Ge 31:34).

3734. כֹּר, **kôr,** *kore*; from the same as 3564; (properly) a deep round *vessel,* i.e. (specific) a *cor* or measure for things dry:—cor, measure. Chaldee the same.

3735. כְּרָא, **keʳrâʾ,** *keh-raw´*; (Chaldee); probably corresponding to 3738 in the sense of *piercing* (figurative); to *grieve*:—be grieved.

3736. כַּרְבֵּל, **karbêl,** *kar-bale´*; from the same as 3525; to *gird* or *clothe*:—clothed.

3737. כַּרְבְּלָה, **karbᵉlâh,** *kar-bel-aw´*; (Chaldee); from a verb corresponding to that of 3736; a *mantle*:—hat.

3738. כָּרָה, **kârâh,** *kaw-raw´*; a primitive root; (properly) to *dig*; (figurative) to *plot*; (generally) to *bore* or open:—dig, × make (a banquet), open.

3739. כָּרָה, **kârâh,** *kaw-raw´*; usually assigned as a primitive root, but probably only a special application of 3738 (through the common idea of *planning* implied in a bargain); to *purchase*:—buy, prepare.

3740. כֵּרָה, **kêrâh,** *kay-raw´*; from 3739; a *purchase*:—provision.

3741. כָּרָה, **kârâh,** *kaw-raw´*; feminine of 3733; a *meadow*:—cottage.

3742. כְּרוּב, **keʳrûwb,** *ker-oob´*; of uncertain derivation; a *cherub* or imaginary figure:—cherub, [*plural*] cherubims.

A masculine noun of uncertain derivation meaning an angelic being. It is commonly translated as cherub (plural, cherubim). The Bible provides scant details concerning the likeness of these winged creatures, except for the apocalyptic visions of Ezekiel in Eze 10. However, current pictures of cherubim as chubby infants with wings or as feminine creatures find no scriptural basis. The Bible portrays cherubim as the guardians of the Garden of Eden (Ge

3:24) and seemingly the glory of the Lord (cf. Eze 10:3, 4, 18–20); as flanking the throne of God (Ps 99:1; cf. Isa 37:16; though these may be poetic references to the mercy seat in the tabernacle [Nu 7:89]); as embroidered images on the tapestry of the tabernacle (Ex 26:1, 31); and as sculpted images arching above the mercy seat on the Ark of the Covenant (Ex 25:18–20, 22; 1Ki 6:23–28; 2Ch 3:10–13). Figuratively, the word is used to describe God's winged transport (2Sa 22:11; Ps 18:10[11]). Interestingly, Satan is described as being the anointed cherub (Eze 28:14) before he was cast out of heaven.

3743. כְּרוּב, **Keʳrûwb,** *ker-oob´*; the same as 3742; *Kerub*, a place in Babylon:—Cherub.

3744. כָּרוֹז, **kârôwz,** *kaw-roze´*; (Chaldee); from 3745; a *herald*:—herald.

3745. כְּרַז, **keʳraz,** *ker-az´*; (Chaldee); probably of Greek origin; to *proclaim*:—make a proclamation.

3746. כָּרִי, **kârîy,** *kaw-ree´*; perhaps an abridged plural of 3733 in the sense of *leader* (of the flock); a *life-guardsman*:—captains, Cherethites [*from the margin*].

A noun meaning a military order, the Kerethites or Cherethites. Under Benaiah (2Sa 20:23), the Kerethites or Cherethites, along with the Pelethites, remained loyal to David and Solomon when Adonijah attempted to become king. Joab, the commander of David's army, however, supported Adonijah (cf. 1Ki 1:18, 19).

The Karites or Carites again supported a king against treachery when they helped overthrow Athaliah and installed Joash as king (2Ki 11:19). It is possible that the Pelethites in 2Ki were a different group of Pelethites because the spelling of the Hebrew word is slightly different than in other references. What is clear is this term designates a special military unit.

3747. כְּרִית, **Keʳrîyth,** *ker-eeth´*; from 3772; a *cut*; *Kerith*, a brook of Palestine:—Cherith.

3748. כְּרִיתוּת, **keʳrîythûwth,** *ker-ee-thooth´*; from 3772; a *cutting* (of the matrimonial bond), i.e. *divorce*:—divorce (-ment).

A feminine noun meaning divorce. If a man was to find that his wife was unfaithful or any uncleanness in her, he was able to write a certificate of divorce that resulted in her expulsion from his house (Dt 24:1). Metaphorically, the Lord asked where Israel's certificate of divorce was. She should have had one to act so loosely (i.e. following other gods [Isa 50:1; Jer 3:8]).

3749. כַּרְכֹּב, **karkôb**, *kar-kobe´*; expanded from the same as 3522; a *rim* or top margin:—compass.

3750. כַּרְכֹּם, **karkôm**, *kar-kome´*; probably of foreign origin; the *crocus:*—saffron.

3751. כַּרְכְּמִישׁ, **Karkᵉmîysh**, *kar-kem-eesh´*; of foreign derivation; *Karkemish*, a place in Syria:—Carchemish.

3752. כַּרְכַּס, **Karkas**, *kar-kas´*; of Persian origin; *Karkas*, a eunuch of Xerxes:—Carcas.

3753. כִּרְכָּרָה, **kirkârâh**, *kir-kaw-raw´*; from 3769; a *dromedary* (from its *rapid* motion as if dancing):—swift beast.

3754. כֶּרֶם, **kerem**, *keh´-rem*; from an unused root of uncertain meaning; a *garden* or *vineyard:*—vines, (increase of the) vineyard (-s), vintage. See also 1021.

3755. כֹּרֵם, **kôrêm**, *ko-rame´*; active participle of an imaginary denominative from 3754; a *vinedresser:*—vine dresser [*as one or two words*].

3756. כַּרְמִי, **Karmîy**, *kar-mee´*; from 3754; *gardener; Karmi*, the name of three Israelites:—Carmi.

3757. כַּרְמִי, **Karmîy**, *kar-mee´*; patronymic from 3756; a *Karmite* or descendant of *Karmi:*—Carmites.

3758. כַּרְמִיל, **karmîyl**, *kar-mele´*; probably of foreign origin; *carmine*, a deep red:—crimson.

3759. כַּרְמֶל, **karmel**, *kar-mel´*; from 3754; a planted *field* (garden, orchard, vineyard or park); (by implication) garden *produce:*—full (green) ears (of corn), fruitful field (place), plentiful (field).

3760. כַּרְמֶל, **Karmel**, *kar-mel´*; the same as 3759; *Karmel*, the name of a hill and of a town in Palestine:—Carmel, fruitful (plentiful) field, (place).

3761. כַּרְמְלִי, **Karmᵉlîy**, *kar-mel-ee´*; patronymic from 3760; a *Karmelite* or inhabitant of Karmel (the town):—Carmelite.

3762. כַּרְמְלִית, **Karmᵉlîyth**, *kar-mel-eeth´*; feminine of 3761; a *Karmelitess* or female inhabitant of Karmel:—Carmelitess.

3763. כְּרָן, **Kᵉrân**, *ker-awn´*; of uncertain derivation; *Keran*, an aboriginal Idumæan:—Cheran.

3764. כָּרְסֵא, **korsê´**, *kor-say´*; (Chaldee); corresponding to 3678; a *throne:*—throne.

An Aramaic masculine noun meaning throne. Daniel reminded Belshazzer that Nebuchadnezzar had been deposed from his throne because of pride (Da 5:20). Daniel had a dream about a throne that belonged to the Ancient of Days (Da 7:9). See the related Hebrew nouns *kissê´* and *kissêh* (3678).

3765. כִּרְסֵם, **kirsêm**, *kir-same´*; from 3697; to *lay waste:*—waste.

3766. כָּרַע, **kâraʿ**, *kaw-rah´*; a primitive root; to *bend* the knee; (by implication) to *sink*, to *prostrate:*—bow (down, self), bring down (low), cast down, couch, fall, feeble, kneeling, sink, smite (stoop) down, subdue, × very.

A verb meaning to bow. The word signifies the crouching of a lion before going to sleep (Ge 49:9; Nu 24:9); the bowing of an animal (Job 39:3); or a woman in order to give birth (1Sa 4:19); the bowing down of a man over a woman in sexual intercourse (adulterous, in this case) (Job 31:10); the yielding of knees from weakness, sometimes after one has been wounded (Jgs 5:27; 2Ki 9:24); the bowing of knees under a heavy burden (Isa 10:4; 46:2); the bowing of knees in submission or subjugation (Est 3:2, 5; Isa 45:23); bowing in repentance (Ezr 9:5); to worship a false god (1Ki 19:18); or the true God (2Ch 29:29; Ps 95:6).

3767. כְּרָע, **kᵉrâʿ**, *keh-raw´*; from 3766; the *leg* (from the knee to the ankle) of men or locusts (only in the dual):—leg.

3768. כַּרְפַּס, **karpas**, *kar-pas´*; of foreign origin; *byssus* or fine vegetable wool:—green.

3769. כָּרַר, **kârar**, *kaw-rar´*; a primitive root; to *dance* (i.e. *whirl*):—dance (-ing).

3770. כֶּרֶשׂ, **kârêś**, *kaw-race´*; by variation from 7164; the *paunch* or belly (as *swelling* out):—belly.

3771. כַּרְשְׁנָא, **Karshᵉnâ’,** *kar-shen-aw´*; of foreign origin; *Carshena,* a courtier of Xerxes:— Carshena.

3772. כָּרַת, **kârath,** *kaw-rath´*; a primitive root; to *cut* (off, down or asunder); (by implication) to *destroy* or *consume*; specifically to *covenant* (i.e. make an alliance or bargain, originally by cutting flesh and passing between the pieces):— be chewed, be con- [feder-] ate, covenant, cut (down, off), destroy, fail, feller, be freed, hew (down), make a league ([covenant]), × lose, perish, × utterly, × want.

A verb meaning to cut off, to cut down, to make a covenant. This word can mean literally to cut something down or off, as grapes (Nu 13:23, 24); or branches (Jgs 9:48, 49). It can also be used figuratively, as with people (Jer 11:19; 50:16). Another important use of this word is to make a covenant (lit., to cut a covenant), perhaps deriving from the practice of cutting an animal in two in the covenant ceremony. God made a covenant with Abraham (Ge 15:18); Abraham made one with Abimelech (Ge 21:27). Finally, this word can also mean to destroy, as in Micah's prophecy (Mic 5:10).

3773. כְּרֻתוֹת, **kᵉruthôwth,** *keh-rooth-oth´*; passive participle feminine of 3772; something *cut,* i.e. a hewn *timber:*—beam.

3774. כְּרֵתִי, **Kᵉrêthîy,** *ker-ay-thee´*; probably from 3772 in the sense of *executioner*; a *Kerethite* or *life-guardsman* [compare 2876] (only collective in the singular as plural):— Cherethims, Cherethites.

3775. כֶּשֶׂב, **keśeb,** *keh´-seb*; apparently by transposition for 3532; a young *sheep:*—lamb.

3776. כִּשְׂבָּה, **kiśbâh,** *kis-baw´*; feminine of 3775; a young *ewe:*—lamb.

3777. כֶּשֶׂד, **Keśed,** *keh´-sed*; from an unused root of uncertain meaning; *Kesed,* a relative of Abraham:—Chesed.

3778. כַּשְׂדִּים, **Kaśdîym,** *kas-deem´*; (occasionally with enclitic כַּשְׂדִּימָה, **Kaśdîymâh,** *kas-dee´- maw*; *toward* the *Kasdites:*—into Chaldea), patronymic from 3777 (only in the plural); a *Kasdite,* or descendant of Kesed; (by implication) a *Chaldæan* (as if so descended); also an *astrologer* (as if proverbial of that people):— Chaldeans, Chaldees, inhabitants of Chaldea.

3779. כַּשְׂדָּי, **Kaśdây,** *kas-daw´ee*; (Chaldee); corresponding to 3778; a *Chaldæan* or inhabitant of Chaldæa; by implication a *Magian* or professional astrologer:—Chaldean.

3780. כָּשָׂה, **kâśâh,** *kaw-saw´*; a primitive root; to *grow fat* (i.e. be *covered* with flesh):—be covered. Compare 3680.

3781. כַּשִּׁיל, **kashshîyl,** *kash-sheel´*; from 3782; (properly) a *feller,* i.e. an *ax:*—ax.

3782. כָּשַׁל, **kâshal,** *kaw-shal´*; a primitive root; to *totter* or *waver* (through weakness of the legs, especially the ankle); (by implication) to *falter, stumble,* faint or fall:—bereave [*from the margin*], cast down, be decayed, (cause to) fail, (cause, make to) fall (down, -ing), feeble, be (the) ruin (-ed, of), (be) overthrown, (cause to) stumble, × utterly, be weak.

A verb meaning to stumble, to stagger, to totter, to cause to stumble, to overthrow, to make weak. This word is used literally of individuals falling or figuratively of cities and nations falling (Isa 3:8; Hos 14:1[2]). People can fall by the sword (Da 11:33); or because of evil (Pr 24:16); wickedness (Eze 33:12); and iniquity (Hos 5:5).

3783. כִּשָּׁלוֹן, **kishshâlôwn,** *kish-shaw-lone´*; from 3782; (properly) a *tottering,* i.e. *ruin:*—fall.

3784. כָּשַׁף, **kâshaph,** *kaw-shaf´*; a primitive root; (properly) to *whisper* a spell, i.e. to *inchant* or practise magic:—sorcerer, (use) witch (-craft).

A verb meaning to practice magic, to practice sorcery. It occurs with words of similar meaning in Dt 18:10 and 2Ch 33:6. While the exact meaning of the word is obscure, it involved the use of supernatural powers that hardened hearts against the truth (Ex 7:11). Those in Israel who used such powers were to be executed (Ex 22:18[17]). King Manasseh's involvement in sorcery to the point of making his children pass through fire, helped lead Judah to the breaking point of God's patience (2Ch 33:6; cf. 2Ki 24:3, 4). Judgment is promised against sorcerers when the Messiah returns (Mal 3:5). However, in a pagan country, where sorcery was practiced with greater ignorance, Daniel acted to save magicians from death while demonstrating that God's power exceeded that of the sorcerers (Da 2:2).

3785. כֶּשֶׁף, **kesheph,** *keh´-shef*; from 3784; *magic:*—sorcery, witchcraft.

A masculine noun meaning occult magic, sorcery. While specific practices included under this term cannot be established, the word occurs along with other similar terms such as enchantments and soothsaying, thus providing clues through association (Isa 47:9, 12; Mic 5:12[11]). This word always appears in a plural form, and half the time, it is modified by the word "numerous" (2Ki 9:22; Isa 47:9, 12). The plurals may indicate different manifestations, or they may represent plurals of intensification. Twice this term is linked with metaphorical harlotry (2Ki 9:22; Na 3:4). In the OT, magic was connected with several nations: Babylon, Nineveh, the Northern Kingdom and the Southern Kingdom (2Ki 9:22; Isa 47:9–12; Mic 5:12[11]; Na 3:4).

3786. כַּשָּׁף, **kashshâph,** *kash-shawf´*; from 3784; a *magician*:—sorcerer.

A masculine singular noun meaning sorcerer. It occurs once in the Hebrew Bible in Jer 27:9.

3787. כָּשֵׁר, **kâshêr,** *kaw-share´*; a primitive root; (properly) to be *straight* or *right*; (by implication) to *be acceptable*; also to *succeed* or *prosper*:—direct, be right, prosper.

A verb meaning to be successful, to cause to succeed. In Ecc 10:10, the word refers to success as the result of wisdom that enables one to go through difficult situations like a sharp ax through wood. In Ecc 11:6, the word refers to the success of seeds in growing, a matter beyond complete human control. Like other human ventures, successful farming calls for diligence and diversification. In Est 8:5, the word is used to confirm the king's opinion of Esther's proposal, whether in his view it would work smoothly.

3788. כִּשְׁרוֹן, **kishrôwn,** *kish-rone´*; from 3787; *success, advantage*:—equity, good, right.

A noun meaning profit, productivity. It occurs three times and refers to increase which brings no lasting satisfaction. In Ecc 2:21, it refers to the profit from labour which, at an owner's death, is given to one who did not labour for it. In Ecc 4:4, the word refers to the profit produced by hard work which is caused by or results in competition with and is the envy of one's neighbours. In Ecc 5:11[10], the word refers to the (lack of) profit in producing more than one can use.

3789. כָּתַב, **kâthab,** *kaw-thab´*; a primitive root; to *grave*; (by implication) to *write* (describe, inscribe, prescribe, subscribe):—describe, record, prescribe, subscribe, write (-ing, -ten).

3790. כְּתַב, **kethab,** *keth-ab´*; (Chaldee); corresponding to 3789:—write (-ten).

3791. כְּתָב, **kethâb,** *keh-thawb´*; from 3789; something *written*, i.e. a *writing, record* or *book*:—register, Scripture, writing.

3792. כְּתָב, **kethâb,** *keth-awb´*; (Chaldee); corresponding to 3791:—prescribing, writing (-ten).

3793. כְּתֹבֶת, **kethôbeth,** *keth-o´-beth*; from 3789; a *letter* or other *mark* branded on the skin:— × any [mark].

3794. כִּתִּי, **Kittîy,** *kit-tee´*; or כִּתִּיִּי, **Kittîyyîy,** *kit-tee-ee´*; patrial from an unused name denoting Cyprus (only in the plural); a *Kittite* or Cypriote; hence an *islander* in general, i.e. the Greeks or Romans on the shores opposite Palestine:—Chittim, Kittim.

3795. כָּתִית, **kâthîyth,** *kaw-theeth´*; from 3807; *beaten*, i.e. pure (oil):—beaten.

3796. כֹּתֶל, **kôthel,** *ko´-thel*; from an unused root meaning to *compact*; a *wall* (as *gathering* inmates):—wall.

3797. כְּתַל, **kethal,** *keth-al´*; (Chaldee); corresponding to 3796:—wall.

3798. כִּתְלִישׁ, **Kithlîysh,** *kith-leesh´*; from 3796 and 376; *wall of a man; Kithlish*, a place in Palestine:—Kithlish.

3799. כָּתַם, **kâtham,** *kaw-tham´*; a primitive root; (properly) to *carve* or *engrave*, i.e. (by implication) to *inscribe* indelibly:—mark.

3800. כֶּתֶם, **kethem,** *keh´-them*; from 3799; (properly) something *carved* out, i.e. *ore*; hence *gold* (pure as originally mined):—([most] fine, pure) gold (-en wedge).

3801. כֻּתֹּנֶת, **kuttôneth,** *koot-to´-neth*; from an unused root meaning to *cover* [compare 3802]; a *shirt*:—coat, garment, robe.

3802. כָּתֵף, **kâthêph,** *kaw-thafe´*; from an unused root meaning to *clothe*; the *shoulder* (properly, i.e. upper end of the arm; as being the spot where the garments hang); (figurative) *side-piece* or lateral projection of anything:— arm, corner, shoulder (-piece), side, undersetter.

3803. כָּתַר, **kâthar,** *kaw-thar´*; a primitive root; to *enclose*; hence (in a friendly sense) to *crown*, (in a hostile one) to *besiege*; also to *wait* (as restraining oneself):—beset round, compass about, be crowned, inclose round, suffer.

3804. כֶּתֶר, **kether,** *keh´-ther*; from 3803; (properly) a *circlet*, i.e. a *diadem*:—crown.

3805. כֹּתֶרֶת, **kôthereth,** *ko-theh´-reth*; feminine active participle of 3803; the *capital* of a column:—chapiter.

3806. כָּתַשׁ, **kâthash,** *kaw-thash´*; a primitive root; to *butt* or *pound*:—bray.

3807. כָּתַת, **kâthath,** *kaw-thath´*; a primitive root; to *bruise* or violently *strike*:—beat (down, to pieces), break in pieces, crushed, destroy, discomfit, smite, stamp.

A verb meaning to beat, to crush, to hammer. This term is used in reference to the destruction of the golden calf (Dt 9:21); and in the eschatological hope of hammering swords into plowshares (Isa 2:4; Mic 4:3). It can also be used figuratively for destroying an enemy (Dt 1:44).

ל (Lamedh)

3808. לֹא, **lô',** *lo;* or לוֹא, **lôw',** *lo;* or לֹה, **lôh,** *lo;* (Dt 3:11), a primitive particle; *not* (the simple or abstract negation); (by implication) *no;* often used with other particles (as follows):— × before, + or else, ere, + except, ig [-norant], much, less, nay, neither, never, no ([-ne], -r, [-thing]), (× as though … , [can-], for) not (out of), of nought, otherwise, out of, + surely, + as truly as, + of a truth, + verily, for want, + whether, without.

An adverb meaning no, not. The term is primarily utilized as an ordinary negation, as in Ge 3:4: "You will not surely die" (NIV cf. Jgs 14:4; Ps 16:10). Often it is used to express an unconditional prohibition, thus having the force of an imperative: "You shall not (= do not ever) steal" (Ex 20:15 NIV; cf. Jgs 13:5). Frequently, it functions as an absolute in answer to a question (Job 23:6; Zec 4:5). The word is also employed in questions to denote that an affirmative answer is expected (2Ki 5:26; Jnh 4:11). When it is prefixed to a noun or adjective, it negates that word, making it have an opposite or contrary meaning (e.g., god becomes non-god; strong becomes weak; cf. Dt 32:21; Pr 30:25). When prefixed by the preposition *bᵉ*, meaning in or by, the combined term carries the temporal meaning of beyond or before (Le 15:25); the meaning without is also not uncommon for this combination (Job 8:11). A prefixed preposition *lᵉ*, meaning to or for, gives the term the meaning of without (2Ch 15:3) or as though not (Job 39:16). Occasionally, the word suggests the meaning not only, on account of the context (Dt 5:3).

3809. לָא, **lâ',** *law;* (Chaldee); or לָה, **lâh,** *law;* (Chaldee) (Da 4:32), corresponding to 3808:— or even, neither, no (-ne, -r), ([can-]) not, as nothing, without.

3810. לֹא דְבַר, **Lô' Dᵉbar,** *lo deb-ar´;* or לוֹ דְבַר, **Lôw Dᵉbar,** *lo deb-ar´;* (2Sa 9:44, 5), or לִדְבַר, **Lidbir,** *lid-beer´;* (Jos 13:26), [probably rather

לִדְבַר, **Lôdᵉbar,** *lo-deb-ar´;* from 3808 and 1699; *pastureless; Lo-Debar,* a place in Palestine:— Debir, Lo-debar.

3811. לָאָה, **lâ'âh,** *law-aw´;* a primitive root; to *tire;* (figurative) to *be* (or *make*) *disgusted:*— faint, grieve, lothe, (be, make) weary (selves).

3812. לֵאָה, **Lê'âh,** *lay-aw´;* from 3811; *weary; Leah,* a wife of Jacob:— Leah.

3813. לָאַט, **lâ'aṭ,** *law-at´;* a primitive root; to *muffle:*— cover.

3814. לָאט, **lâ't,** *lawt;* from 3813 (or perhaps for active participle of 3874); (properly) *muffled,* i.e. *silently:*— softly.

3815. לָאֵל, **Lâ'êl,** *law-ale´;* from the prepositional prefix and 410; (belonging) *to God; Laël,* an Israelite:— Lael.

3816. לְאֹם, **lᵉôm,** *leh-ome´;* or לְאוֹם, **lᵉôwm,** *leh-ome´;* from an unused root meaning to *gather;* a *community:*— nation, people.

A masculine singular noun meaning people. This poetic term is used often as a synonym for people ('am [5971]) or nation (gôwy [1471]). It can refer to Israel or to humanity in general. A well-known passage (Ge 25:23) uses this term in regard to the two peoples in Rebekah's womb—Israel and Edom.

3817. לְאֻמִּים, **Lᵉ'ummîym,** *leh-oom-meem´;* plural of 3816; *communities; Leümmim,* an Arabian:— Leummim.

3818. לֹא עַמִּי, **Lô' 'Ammîy,** *lo am-mee´;* from 3808 and 5971 with pronoun suffix; *not my people; Lo-Ammi,* the symbolical name of a son of Hosea:— Lo-ammi.

3819. לֹא רֻחָמָה, **Lô' Ruchâmâh,** *lo roo-khaw-maw´;* from 3808 and 7355; *not pitied; Lo-Ruchamah,* the symbolical name of a son of Hosea:— Lo-ruhamah.

3820. לֵב, **lêb,** *labe*; a form of 3824; the *heart*; also used (figurative) very widely for the feelings, the will and even the intellect; likewise for the *centre* of anything:— + care for, comfortably, consent, × considered, courag [-eous], friend [-ly], ([broken-], [hard-], [merry-], [stiff-], [stout-], double) heart ([-ed]), × heed, × I, kindly, midst, mind (-ed), × regard ([-ed]), × themselves, × unawares, understanding, × well, willingly, wisdom.

A masculine noun usually rendered as heart but whose range of meaning is extensive. It can denote the heart as a human physical organ (Ex 28:29; 1Sa 25:37; 2Ki 9:24); or an animal (Job 41:24[16]). However, it usually refers to some aspect of the immaterial inner self or being since the heart is considered to be the seat of one's inner nature as well as one of its components. It can be used in a general sense (1Ki 8:23; Ps 84:2[3]; Jer 3:10); or it can be used of a specific aspect of personality: the mind (Ge 6:5; Dt 29:4[3]; Ne 6:8); the will (Ex 35:5; 2Ch 12:14; Job 11:13); the emotions (Ge 6:6[Note that God is the subject]; 1Sa 24:5[6]; 25:31). In addition, the word can also allude to the inside or middle (Ex 15:8; Dt 4:11).

3821. לֵב, **lêb,** *labe*; (Chaldee); corresponding to 3820:—heart.

An Aramaic masculine singular noun meaning heart. In this form, its only occurrence in the Hebrew Bible is in Da 7:28.

3822. לְבָאוֹת, **Lᵉbâ'ôwth,** *leb-aw-ōth'*; plural of 3833; *lionesses; Lebaoth,* a place in Palestine:— Lebaoth. See also 1034.

3823. לָבַב, **lâbab,** *law-bab'*; a primitive root; (properly) to *be enclosed* (as if with *fat*); (by implication, as denominative from 3824) to *unheart,* i.e. (in a good sense) *transport* (with love), or (in a bad sense) *stultify*; also (as denominative from 3834) to *make cakes:*— make cakes, ravish, be wise.

A verb meaning to stir the heart, to make cakes. This word is related to the common Hebrew nouns *lêb* (3820) and *lêbâb* (3824), which both mean heart, mind, or inner being. Solomon used this word twice in the same verse to express the stirring of his heart with affection for his lover (SS 4:9); Zophar used it to describe the mind of an idiot being made intelligent (Job 11:12). In the only other instances of this word,

it describes the making of bread or a cake that was kneaded and baked (2Sa 13:6, 8).

3824. לֵבָב, **lêbâb,** *lay-bawb'*; from 3823; the *heart* (as the most interior organ); used also like 3820:— + bethink themselves, breast, comfortably, courage, ([faint], [tender-] heart [-ed]), midst, mind, × unawares, understanding.

A masculine noun meaning heart, mind, inner person. The primary usage of this word describes the entire disposition of the inner person that God can discern (1Sa 16:7); be devoted to the Lord (1Ki 15:3); seek the Lord (2Ch 11:16); turn against people (Ex 14:5); be uncircumcised (Le 26:41); be hardened (1Sa 6:6); be totally committed to the Lord (Dt 6:5; 2Ch 15:15). It is also used to describe the place where the rational, thinking process occurs that allows a person to know God's blessings (Jos 23:14); to plan for the future (1Ki 8:18); to communicate (2Ch 9:1); and to understand God's message (Isa 6:10). Like our English usage, it often refers to the seat of emotions, whether it refers to joy (Dt 28:47); discouragement (Jos 2:11); comfort (Jgs 19:8); grief (1Sa 1:8); sorrow (Ps 13:2[3]); or gladness (Isa 30:29).

3825. לְבַב, **lᵉbab,** *leb-ab'*; (Chaldee); corresponding to 3824:—heart.

An Aramaic masculine noun meaning heart, mind, the inner person. This word is equivalent to the Hebrew word *lêbâb* (3824). It is used to describe the entire disposition of the inner person, which God can change (Da 4:16[13]; 5:21; 7:4). This inner person can be lifted up in pride (Da 5:20) or made low in humility (Da 5:22). The rational, thinking process is demonstrated when Daniel described the thoughts of the king's mind (Da 2:30).

3826. לִבָּה, **libbâh,** *lib-baw'*; feminine of 3820; the *heart:*—heart.

A feminine noun meaning heart. A variant of the word *lêb* (3820), it suggests the seat of emotions or the will (Eze 16:30).

3827. לַבָּה, **labbâh,** *lab-baw'*; for 3852; *flame:*— flame.

3828. לְבוֹנָה, **lᵉbôwnâh,** *leb-o-naw'*; or לְבֹנָה, **lebô-nâh,** *leb-o-naw'*; from 3836; *frankincense* (from its *whiteness* or perhaps that of its *smoke*):—(frank-) incense.

3829. לְבוֹנָה, **L^ebôwnâh,** *leb-o-naw´*; the same as 3828; *Lebonah,* a place in Palestine:—Lebonah.

3830. לְבוּשׁ, **l^ebûwsh,** *leb-oosh´*; or לְבֻשׁ, **l^ebush,** *leb-oosh´*; from 3847; a *garment* (literal or figurative); by implication (euphemistic) a *wife:*—apparel, clothed with, clothing, garment, raiment, vestment, vesture.

3831. לְבוּשׁ, **l^ebûwsh,** *leb-oosh´*; (Chaldee); corresponding to 3830:—garment.

3832. לָבַט, **lâbaṭ,** *law-bat´*; a primitive root; to *overthrow*; (intransitive) to *fall*:—fall.

3833. לָבִיא, **lâbîy’,** *law-bee´*; or (Eze 19:2) לְבִיָּא, **l^ebîyyâ’,** *leb-ee-yaw´*; irregular masculine plural לְבָאִים, **l^ebâ’îym,** *leb-aw-eem´*; irregular feminine plural לְבָאוֹת, **l^ebâ’ôwth,** *leb-aw-oth´*; from an unused root meaning to *roar*; a *lion* (properly, a *lioness* as the fiercer [although not a *roarer*; compare 738]):—(great, old, stout) lion, lioness, young [lion].

3834. לְבִיבָה, **lâbîybâh,** *law-bee-baw´*; or rather לְבִבָה, **l^ebibâh,** *leb-ee-baw´*; from 3823 in its original sense of *fatness* (or perhaps of *folding*); a *cake* (either as *fried* or *turned*):—cake.

3835. לָבַן, **lâban,** *law-ban´*; a primitive root; to *be* (or *become*) *white*; also (as denominative from 3843) to *make bricks*:—make brick, be (made, make) white (-r).

3836. לָבָן, **lâbân,** *law-bawn´*; or (Ge 49:12) לְבֵן, **lâbên,** *law-bane´*; from 3835; *white*:—white.

3837. לָבָן, **Lâbân,** *law-bawn´*; the same as 3836; *Laban,* a Mesopotamian; also a place in the Desert:—Laban.

3838. לְבָנָא, **L^ebânâ’,** *leb-aw-naw´*; or לְבָנָה, **Lebânâh,** *leb-aw-naw´*; the same as 3842; *Lebana* or *Lebanah,* one of the Nethinim:—Lebana, Lebanah.

3839. לִבְנֶה, **libneh,** *lib-neh´*; from 3835; some sort of *whitish* tree, perhaps the *storax*:—poplar.

3840. לִבְנָה, **libnâh,** *lib-naw´*; from 3835; (properly) *whiteness,* i.e. (by implication) *transparency*:—paved.

3841. לִבְנָה, **Libnâh,** *lib-naw´*; the same as 3839; *Libnah,* a place in the Desert and one in Palestine:—Libnah.

3842. לְבָנָה, **l^ebânâh,** *leb-aw-naw´*; from 3835; properly (the) *white,* i.e. the *moon*:—moon. See also 3838.

3843. לְבֵנָה, **l^ebênâh,** *leb-ay-naw´*; from 3835; a *brick* (from the *whiteness* of the clay):—(altar of) brick, tile.

3844. לְבָנוֹן, **L^ebânôwn,** *leb-aw-nohn´*; from 3825; (the) *white* mountain (from its snow); *Lebanon,* a mountain range in Palestine:—Lebanon.

3845. לִבְנִי, **Libnîy,** *lib-nee´*; from 3835; *white*; *Libni,* an Israelite:—Libni.

3846. לִבְנִי, **Libnîy,** *lib-nee´*; patronymic from 3845; a *Libnite* or descendant of Libni (collective):—Libnites.

3847. לָבַשׁ, **lâbash,** *law-bash´*; or לָבֵשׁ, **lâbêsh,** *law-bashe´*; a primitive root; (properly) *wrap around,* i.e. (by implication) to *put on* a garment or *clothe* (oneself, or another), literal or figurative:—(in) apparel, arm, array (self), clothe (self), come upon, put (on, upon), wear.

3848. לְבַשׁ, **l^ebash,** *leb-ash´*; (Chaldee); corresponding to 3847:—clothe.

3849. לֹג, **lôg,** *lohg*; from an unused root apparently meaning to *deepen* or *hollow* [like 3537]; a *log* or measure for liquids:—log [of oil].

3850. לֹד, **Lôd,** *lode*; from an unused root of uncertain significance; *Lod,* a place in Palestine:—Lod.

3851. לַהַב, **lahab,** *lah´-hab*; from an unused root meaning to *gleam*; a *flash*; (figurative) a sharply polished *blade* or *point* of a weapon:—blade, bright, flame, glittering.

3852. לְהָבָה, **lehâbâh,** *leh-aw-baw´*; or לַהֶבֶת, **lahebeth,** *lah-eh´-beth*; feminine of 3851, and meaning the same:—flame (-ming), head [of a spear].

3853. לְהָבִים, **L^ehâbîym,** *leh-haw-beem´*; plural of 3851; *flames; Lehabim,* a son of Mizrain, and his descendants:—Lehabim.

3854. לַהַג, **lahag,** *lah´-hag*; from an unused root meaning to *be eager*; intense mental *application*:—study.

3855. לַהַד, **Lâhad,** *law´-had*; from an unused root meaning to *glow* [compare 3851] or else to *be earnest* [compare 3854]; *Lahad,* an Israelite:—Lahad.

3856. לָהַהּ, **lâhah,** *law-hah´*; a primitive root meaning properly to *burn,* i.e. (by implication) to *be rabid;* (figurative) *insane;* also (from the *exhaustion* of frenzy) to *languish:*—faint, mad.

3857. לָהַט, **lâhat,** *law-hat´*; a primitive root; (properly) to *lick,* i.e. (by implication) to *blaze:*—burn (up), set on fire, flaming, kindle.

3858. לַהַט, **lahat,** *lah´-hat*; from 3857; a *blaze*; also (from the idea of *enwrapping*) *magic* (as *covert*):—flaming, enchantment.

A masculine noun meaning flame. This word is used only once in the OT. It describes the "flaming sword" of the cherubim stationed at the east side of the Garden of Eden (Ge 3:24). This word comes from the verb, *lâhat* (3857), meaning to flame or to set on fire.

3859. לָהַם, **lâham,** *law-ham´*; a primitive root; (properly) to *burn* in, i.e. (figurative) to *rankle:*—wound.

3860. לָהֵן, **lâhên,** *law-hane´*; from the prefix preposition meaning *to* or *for* and 2005; (properly) *for if*; hence *therefore:*—for them [*by mistake for prepositional suffix*].

3861. לָהֵן, **lâhên,** *law-hane´*; (Chaldee); corresponding to 3860; *therefore*; also *except:*—but, except, save, therefore, wherefore.

3862. לַהֲקָה, **lahăqâh,** *lah-hak-aw´*; probably from an unused root meaning to *gather*; an *assembly:*—company.

3863. לוּא, **lûw’,** *loo*; or לֻא, **lu’,** *loo*; or לוּ, **lûw,** *loo*; a conditional particle; *if*; by implication (interjection as a wish) *would that!:*—if (haply), peradventure, I pray thee, though, I would, would God (that).

3864. לוּבִי, **Lûwbîy,** *loo-bee´*; or לֻבִּי, **Lubbîy,** *loob-bee´*; (Da 11:43), patrial from a name probably derived from an unused root meaning to *thirst*, i.e. a *dry* region; apparently a *Libyan* or inhabitant of interior Africa (only in plural):—Lubim (-s), Libyans.

3865. לוּד, **Lûwd,** *lood*; probably of foreign derivation; *Lud,* the name of two nations:—Lud, Lydia.

3866. לוּדִי, **Lûwdîy,** *loo-dee´*; or לוּדִיִּ, **Lûwdîyyîy,** *loo-dee-ee´*; patrial from 3865; a *Ludite* or inhabitant of Lud (only in plural):—Ludim, Lydians.

3867. לָוָה, **lâvâh,** *law-vaw´*; a primitive root; (properly) to *twine*, i.e. (by implication) to *unite,* to *remain*; also to *borrow* (as a form of *obligation*) or (causative) to *lend:*—abide with, borrow (-er), cleave, join (self), lend (-er).

3868. לוּז, **lûwz,** *looz*; a primitive root; to *turn* aside [compare 3867, 3874 and 3885], i.e. (literal) to *depart,* (figurative) *be perverse:*—depart, froward, perverse (-ness).

3869. לוּז, **lûwz,** *looz*; probably of foreign origin; some kind of *nut*-tree, perhaps the *almond:*—hazel.

3870. לוּז, **Lûwz,** *looz*; probably from 3869 (as growing there); *Luz,* the name of two places in Palestine:—Luz.

3871. לוּחַ, **lûwach,** *loo´-akh*; or לֻחַ, **luach,** *loo´-akh*; from a primitive root; probably meaning to *glisten*; a *tablet* (as *polished*), of stone, wood or metal:—board, plate, table.

3872. לוּחִית, **Lûwchîyth,** *loo-kheeth´*; or לֻחוֹת, **Luchôwth,** *loo-khoth´*; (Jer 48:5), from the same as 3871; *floored*; *Luchith,* a place East of the Jordan:—Luhith.

3873. לוֹחֵשׁ, **Lôwchêsh,** *lo-khashe´*; active participle of 3907; (the) *enchanter*; *Lochesh,* an Israelite:—Hallohesh, Haloshesh [*including the art*].

3874. לוּט, **lûwt,** *loot*; a primitive root; to *wrap* up:—cast, wrap.

3875. לוֹט, **lôwt,** *lote*; from 3874; a *veil:*—covering.

3876. לוֹט, **Lôwt,** *lote*; the same as 3875; *Lot,* Abraham's nephew:—Lot.

3877. לוֹטָן, **Lôwtân,** *lo-tawn´*; from 3875; *covering*; *Lotan,* an Idumæan:—Lotan.

3878. לֵוִי, **Lêvîy,** *lay-vee´*; from 3867; *attached*; *Levi,* a son of Jacob:—Levi. See also 3879, 3881.

3879. לֵוִי, **Lêvây,** *lay-vaw´*; (Chaldee); corresponding to 3880:—Levite.

3880. לִוְיָה, **livyâh,** *liv-yaw´*; from 3867; something *attached*, i.e. a *wreath*:—ornament.

3881. לֵוִיִּי, **Lêvîyyîy,** *lay-vee-ee´*; or לֵוִי, **Lêvîy,** *lay-vee´*; patronymic from 3878; a *Leviite* or *descendant of Levi*:—Levite.

3882. לִוְיָתָן, **livyâthân,** *liv-yaw-thawn´*; from 3867; a *wreathed* animal, i.e. a *serpent* (especially the *crocodile* or some other large sea-monster); (figurative) the constellation of the *dragon*; also as a symbol of *Babylon*:—leviathan, mourning.

3883. לוּל, **lûwl,** *lool*; from an unused root meaning to *fold* back; a *spiral* step:—winding stair. Compare 3924.

3884. לוּלֵא, **lûwlê',** *loo-lay´*; or לוּלֵי, **lûwlêy,** *loo-lay´*; from 3863 and 3808; *if not*:—except, had not, if (… not), unless, were it not that.

3885. לוּן, **lûwn,** *loon*; or לִין, **lîyn,** *leen*; a primitive root; to *stop* (usually over night); (by implication) to *stay* permanently; hence (in a bad sense) to be *obstinate* (especially in words, to *complain*):—abide (all night), continue, dwell, endure, grudge, be left, lie all night, (cause to) lodge (all night, in, -ing, this night), (make to) murmur, remain, tarry (all night, that night).

3886. לָעַע, **lâ‘a‘,** *law´-ah*; a primitive root; to *gulp*; (figurative) to be *rash*:—swallow down (up).

3887. לוּץ, **lûwts,** *loots*; a primitive root; (properly) to *make mouths* at, i.e. to *scoff*; hence (from the effort to pronounce a foreign language) to *interpret*, or (generic) *intercede*:—ambassador, have in derision, interpreter, make a mock, mocker, scorn (-er, -ful), teacher.

A verb meaning to boast, to scorn, to mock, to deride, or to imitate. This Hebrew verb is frequently found in the book of Proverbs (Pr 9:7, 8; 13:1; 20:1), and means to deride or to boast so as to express utter contempt. The activity of the scornful is condemned as an abomination to people (Pr 24:9) and contrary to the Law of the Lord (Ps 1:1). Both Job (Job 16:20) and the psalmist (Ps 119:51) expressed the pain inflicted by the scornful, but in the end, the scorner will reap what he has sown (Pr 3:34). By extension the word is used to signify ambassadors (2Ch 32:31); interpreters (Ge 42:23); and spokesmen (Isa 43:27). These meanings arise from the

sense of speaking indirectly implied in the root word. Some grammarians view the participle of this verb as a separate noun. For a list of these references, see the division in the concordance.

3888. לוּשׁ, **lûwsh,** *loosh*; a primitive root; to *knead*:—knead.

3889. לוּשׁ, **Lûwsh,** *loosh*; from 3888; *kneading*; *Lush*, a place in Palestine:—Laish [*from the margin*]. Compare 3919.

3890. לְוָת, **lᵉvâth,** *lev-awth´*; (Chaldee); from a root corresponding to 3867; (properly) *adhesion*, i.e. (as prephaps) *with*:— × thee.

3891. לָזוּת, **lâzûwth,** *lawz-ooth´*; from 3868; *perverseness*:—perverse.

3892. לַח, **lach,** *lakh*; from an unused root meaning to be *new*; *fresh*, i.e. unused or undried:—green, moist.

3893. לֵחַ, **lêach,** *lay´-akh*; from the same as 3892; *freshness*, i.e. *vigour*:—natural force.

3894. לְחוּם, **lᵉchûwm,** *leh-khoom´*; or לָחֻם, **lâchum,** *law-khoom´*; passive participle of 3898; (properly) *eaten*, i.e. *food*; also *flesh*, i.e. *body*:—while … is eating, flesh.

A masculine noun meaning bowels, intestines. This word is of uncertain meaning, owing to its rare use in Scripture, but it is generally understood to mean the intestines or inward parts of the body. It is a derivative of the Hebrew word *lâcham* (3898), meaning to fight. Occurring only in Job 20:23 and Zep 1:17, the context is the outpouring of the Lord's wrath. In the latter text, the apocalyptic image is a most graphic picture of battle: "Their blood will be poured out like dust and their flesh [*lâchûm*, inner parts] like dung" (NASB).

3895. לְחִי, **lᵉchîy,** *lekh-ee´*; from an unused root meaning to be *soft*; the *cheek* (from its *fleshiness*); hence the *jaw*-bone:—cheek (bone), jaw (bone).

3896. לֶחִי, **Lechîy,** *lekh´-ee*; a form of 3895; *Lechi*, a place in Palestine:—Lehi. Compare also 7437.

3897. לָחַךְ, **lâchak,** *law-khak´*; a primitive root; to *lick*:—lick (up).

3898. לָחַם, **lâcham,** *law-kham´*; a primitive root; to *feed* on; (figurative) to *consume*; (by implication) to *battle* (as *destruction*):—devour, eat, × ever, fight (-ing), overcome, prevail, (make) war (-ring).

3899. לֶחֶם, **lechem,** *lekh´-em*; from 3898; *food* (for man or beast), especially *bread*, or *grain* (for making it):—([shew-]) bread, × eat, food, fruit, loaf, meat, victuals. See also 1036.

3900. לְחֵם, **lᵉchem,** *lekh-em´*; (Chaldee); corresponding to 3899:—feast.

3901. לָחֶם, **lâchem,** *law-khem´*; from 3898, *battle*:—war.

3902. לַחְמִי, **Lachmîy,** *lakh-mee´*; from 3899; *foodful*; *Lachmi*, an Israelite; or rather probably a brief form (or perhaps erroneous transcription) for 1022:—Lahmi. See also 3433.

3903. לַחְמָס, **Lachmâs,** *lakh-maws´*; probably by erroneous transcription for לַחְמָם, **Lachmâm,** *lakh-mawm´*; from 3899; *food-like*; *Lachmam* or *Lachmas*, a place in Palestine:—Lahmam.

3904. לְחֵנָה, **lᵉchênâh,** *lekh-ay-naw´*; (Chaldee); from an unused root of uncertain meaning; a *concubine*:—concubine.

3905. לָחַץ, **lâchats,** *law-khats´*; a primitive root; (properly) to *press*, i.e. (figurative) to *distress*:—afflict, crush, force, hold fast, oppress (-or), thrust self.

3906. לַחַץ, **lachats,** *lakh´-ats*; from 3905; *distress*:—affliction, oppression.

3907. לָחַשׁ, **lâchash,** *law-khash´*; a primitive root; to *whisper*; (by implication) to *mumble* a spell (as a magician):—charmer, whisper (together).

A verb meaning to whisper, to charm. This word is used only three times in the OT. In two of these cases, this word is best translated as whisper to describe the quiet talk of David's servants at the death of his child (2Sa 12:19); and the secretive talk of David's enemies (Ps 41:7[8]). The other instance of this word described the snake charmers (Ps 58:5[6]). See also the related noun, *lachash* (3908), meaning whispering or charming.

3908. לַחַשׁ, **lachash,** *lakh´-ash*; from 3907; (properly) a *whisper*, i.e. by implication (in a good sense) a private *prayer*, (in a bad one) an *incantation*; (concrete) an *amulet*:—charmed, earring, enchantment, orator, prayer.

A masculine noun meaning whispering, enchantment, and charm. The action of whispering, with the connotations of casting a spell, is the basis for this word. It is used in the Hebrew to signify charms or amulets worn by women (Isa 3:20); the charming of a snake (Ecc 10:11; Jer 8:17); one who crafts clever words so as to enchant (Isa 3:3); a prayer whispered in a time of sudden distress (Isa 26:16).

3909. לָט, **lât,** *lawt*; a form of 3814 or else participle from 3874; (properly) *covered*, i.e. *secret*; (by implication) *incantation*; also *secrecy* or (adverbial) *covertly*:—enchantment, privily, secretly, softly.

A masculine noun meaning secrecy, enchantment, mystery, privacy. A form of the Hebrew word *lâṭ* (3814), this word conveys the sense of a secret known to only a select group or to something done in secrecy. Three times the word is used in reference to the enchantments of the Egyptian sorcerers in Pharaoh's court (Ex 7:22; 8:7[13], 18[14]). The other occurrences in the OT signify an action done without another party's notice (Ru 3:7) or in private (1Sa 18:22).

3910. לֹט, **lôt,** *lote*; probably from 3874; a gum (from its *sticky* nature), probably *ladanum*:—myrrh.

3911. לְטָאָה, **lᵉtâ'âh,** *let-aw-aw´*; from an unused root meaning to *hide*; a kind of *lizard* (from its *covert* habits):—lizard.

3912. לְטוּשִׁם, **Lᵉtûwshim,** *let-oo-sheem´*; masculine plural of passive participle of 3913; *hammered* (i.e. *oppressed*) ones; *Letushim*, an Arabian tribe:—Letushim.

3913. לָטַשׁ, **lâtash,** *law-tash´*; a primitive root; (properly) to *hammer* out (an edge), i.e. to *sharpen*:—instructer, sharp (-en), whet.

3914. לֹיָה, **lôyâh,** *lo-yaw´*; a form of 3880; a *wreath*:—addition.

3915. לַיִל, **layil,** *lah´-yil*; or (Isa 21:11) לֵיל, **lêyl,** *lale*; also לַיְלָה, **layᵉlâh,** *lah´-yel-aw*; from the same as 3883; (properly) a *twist* (away of the light), i.e. *night*; (figurative) *adversity*:—([mid-]) night (season).

A masculine noun meaning night, midnight. This Hebrew word primarily describes the portion of day between sunset and sunrise (Ge 1:5; cf. Ps 136:9). Figuratively, it signifies the gloom or despair that sometimes engulfs the human heart from an absence of divine guidance (Mic 3:6); calamity (Job 36:20); or affliction (Job 30:17). Nevertheless, even in the dark night of the soul, the Lord gives His people a song of joy (Job 35:10; Ps 42:8[9]).

3916. לֵילְיָא**, lêylᵉyâʾ,** *lay-leh-yaw´*; (Chaldee); corresponding to 3915:—night.

An Aramaic masculine noun meaning night. All the undisputed instances occur in the book of Daniel. Most often, the term is utilized to declare the time in which several of Daniel's visions took place (Da 2:19; 7:2, 7, 13). However, it functions once to indicate when the assassination of the Babylonian king, Belshazzar, transpired (Da 5:30). The word closely corresponds with the Hebrew noun *layil* or *layᵉlâh* (3915).

3917. לִילִית**, lîylîyth,** *lee-leeth´*; from 3915; a *night* spectre:—screech owl.

3918. לַיִשׁ**, layish,** *lah´-yish*; from 3888 in the sense of *crushing*; a lion (from his destructive *blows*):—(old) lion.

3919. לַיִשׁ**, Layish,** *lah´-yish*; the same as 3918; *Laïsh,* the name of two places in Palestine:—Laish. Compare 3889.

3920. לָכַד**, lâkad,** *law-kad´*; a primitive root; to *catch* (in a net, trap or pit); (generally) to *capture* or occupy; also to *choose* (by lot); (figurative) to *cohere:*— × at all, catch (self), be frozen, be holden, stick together, take.

3921. לֶכֶד**, leked,** *leh´-ked*; from 3920; something to *capture* with, i.e. a *noose:*—being taken.

3922. לֵכָה**, lêkâh,** *lay-kaw´*; from 3212; a *journey*; *Lekah,* a place in Palestine:—Lecah.

3923. לָכִישׁ**, Lâkîysh,** *law-keesh´*; from an unused root of uncertain meaning; *Lakish,* a place in Palestine:—Lachish.

3924. לֻלָאוֹת**, lulâʾôwth,** *loo-law-oth´*; from the same as 3883; a *loop:*—loop.

3925. לָמַד**, lâmad,** *law-mad´*; a primitive root; (properly) to *goad,* i.e. (by implication) to *teach*

(the rod being an Oriental *incentive*):—[un-] accustomed, × diligently, expert, instruct, learn, skilful, teach (-er, -ing).

A verb meaning to learn, to study, to teach, to be taught, to be learned. The verb describes learning war, training for war, the lack of training (Isa 2:4; Mic 4:3), or the acquisition of instruction (Isa 29:24). God's people were warned not to learn the ways of the nations, that is, to acquire their corrupt and false practices and standards (Jer 10:2) but to learn the ways of God instead (Jer 12:16). The verb is sometimes used with an infinitive following it suggesting the meaning to learn to do something. Israel was not to learn to do the abominations of surrounding nations (Dt 18:9); it describes metaphorically the actions of Jehoahaz against his countrymen as he tore them as a lion would tear its prey (Eze 19:3).

In the intensive or factitive form, the root takes on the meaning of imparting learning (i.e. teaching). The verb simply means to teach (2Ch 17:7, 9) or to teach people or things; the Lord taught His people (Jer 31:34) His decrees and laws (Dt 4:1). The participle of this form often means teacher (Ps 119:99).

The passive forms of this verb mean to be teachable or to be knowledgeable or welltrained by the Lord (Jer 31:18) or people (Isa 29:13).

3926. לְמוֹ**, lᵉmôw,** *lem-o´*; a prolonged and separable form of the prefix preposition; *to* or *for:*—at, for, to, upon.

3927. לְמוּאֵל**, Lᵉmûwʾêl,** *lem-oo-ale´*; or לְמוֹאֵל**, Lᵉmôwʾêl,** *lem-o-ale´*; from 3926 and 410; (belonging) *to God; Lemuël* or *Lemoël,* a symbolical name of Solomon:—Lemuel.

3928. לִמּוּד**, limmûwd,** *lim-mood´*; or לִמֻּד**, limmud,** *lim-mood´*; from 3925; *instructed:*—accustomed, disciple, learned, taught, used.

A masculine adjective meaning accustomed, used to something, learned, practiced, an expert, one taught, a follower, a disciple. It was used to describe those who habitually practice evil (Jer 13:23). It was also employed to help portray Israel as a wild donkey in heat that was accustomed to life in the rugged wilderness (Jer 2:24). The Lord gave the Suffering Servant a "tongue of the learned," that is, the gift of inspirational and instructive speech and an ear that listens like those being taught (Isa 50:4). Isaiah says that the children of the desolate woman or widow will be taught by the Lord Himself (Isa 54:13). The word is also used once to denote Isaiah's disciples (Isa 8:16). It is derived from the verb *lâmad* (3925).

3929. לֶמֶךְ, **Lemek,** *leh´-mek*; from an unused root of uncertain meaning; *Lemek*, the name of two antediluvian patriarchs:—Lamech.

3930. לֹעַ, **lôaʻ,** *lo´ah*; from 3886; the *gullet*:—throat.

3931. לָעַב, **lâʻab,** *law-ab´*; a primitive root; to *deride*:—mock.

3932. לָעַג, **lâʻag,** *law-ag´*; a primitive root; to *deride*; by implication (as if imitating a foreigner) to *speak unintelligibly*:—have in derision, laugh (to scorn), mock (on), stammering.

3933. לַעַג, **laʻag,** *lah´-ag*; from 3932; *derision, scoffing*:—derision, scorn (-ing).

3934. לָעֵג, **lâʻêg,** *law-ayg´*; from 3932; a *buffoon*; also a *foreigner*:—mocker, stammering.

3935. לַעְדָּה, **Laʻdâh,** *lah-daw´*; from an unused root of uncertain meaning; *Ladah*, an Israelite:—Laadah.

3936. לַעְדָּן, **Laʻdân,** *lah-dawn´*; from the same as 3935; *Ladan*, the name of two Israelites:—Laadan.

3937. לָעֵז, **lâʻez,** *law-az´*; a primitive root; to *speak in a foreign tongue*:—strange language.

A verb meaning to speak in an incomprehensible foreign language. The term is used in a participial form to describe the Egyptians among whom the Hebrews lived for 430 years, a people who spoke a much different language (Ps 114:1). See the verb *lâ'ag* (3932) that appears to semantically overlap with this word.

3938. לָעַט, **lâʻaṭ,** *law-at´*; a primitive root; to *swallow* greedily; (causative) to *feed*:—feed.

3939. לַעֲנָה, **laʻănâh,** *lah-an-aw´*; from an unused root supposed to mean to *curse; wormwood* (regarded as *poisonous*, and therefore *accursed*):—hemlock, wormwood.

3940. לַפִּיד, **lappîyd,** *lap-peed´*; or לַפִּד, **lappid,** *lap-peed´*; from an unused root probably mean-

ing to *shine; a flambeau, lamp* or *flame*:—(fire-) brand, (burning) lamp, lightning, torch.

3941. לַפִּידוֹת, **Lappîydôwth,** *lap-pee-dōth´*; feminine plural of 3940; *Lappidoth*, the husband of Deborah:—Lappidoth.

3942. לִפְנַי, **liphnây,** *lif-naw´ee*; from the prefix preposition (*to* or *for*) and 6440; *anterior*:—before.

3943. לָפַת, **lâphath,** *law-fath´*; a primitive root; (properly) to *bend*, i.e. (by implication) to *clasp*; also (reflexive) to *turn* around or aside:—take hold, turn aside (self).

3944. לָצוֹן, **lâtsôwn,** *law-tsone´*; from 3887; *derision*:—scornful (-ning).

3945. לָצַץ, **lâtsats,** *law-tsats´*; a primitive root; to *deride*:—scorn.

3946. לַקּוּם, **Laqûwm,** *lak-koom´*; from an unused root thought to mean to *stop* up by a barricade; perhaps *fortification*; *Lakkum*, a place in Palestine:—Lakum.

3947. לָקַח, **lâqach,** *law-kakh´*; a primitive root; to *take* (in the widest variety of applications):—accept, bring, buy, carry away, drawn, fetch, get, infold, × many, mingle, place, receive (-ing), reserve, seize, send for, take (away, -ing, up), use, win.

3948. לֶקַח, **leqach,** *leh´-kakh*; from 3947; properly something *received*, i.e. (mentally) *instruction* (whether on the part of the teacher or hearer); also (in an active and sinister sense) *inveiglement*:—doctrine, learning, fair speech.

A masculine noun meaning something received, instruction. Having this basal sense, the word's usage can be divided further into three categories, each with its own distinctive variation of meaning. First, the word can signify the learning, insight, or understanding that a person receives, perceives, or learns through an instructor or some other means (Pr 1:5; 9:9; Isa 29:24). The second variation is similar to the first, yet only slightly different in that it arises from the perspective of the one dispensing the knowledge (i.e. a teacher or instructor), rather than that of the learner. It describes that which is being communicated to others, therefore giving the sense of teaching, instruction, or discourse (Dt 32:2; Pr 4:2). Finally, the term seems to have the force of persuasive speech, whether for a positive or a deceitful intent (Pr 7:21; 16:21). This noun derives from the verb *lâqach* (3947).

3949. לִקְחִי, **Liqchîy,** *lik-khee´*; from 3947; *learned; Likchi,* an Israelite:—Likhi.

3950. לָקַט, **lâqaṭ,** *law-kat´*; a primitive root; (properly) to *pick* up, i.e. (general) to *gather*; (specifically) to *glean*:—gather (up), glean.

A verb meaning to pick up, to gather. This word occurs with various objects such as manna, lilies, firewood, and people (Ex 16:4, 5; Jgs 11:3; SS 6:2; Jer 7:18); however, by far it is used most often with food, including once with grapes (Le 19:10; Isa 17:5). Even animals are able to gather the food God graciously provides (Ps 104:28). About half of the occurrences of this term relate to the provision of the Mosaic Law to take care of the needy by allowing them to glean the fields, a provision featured prominently in the story of Ruth (Le 19:9, 10; 23:22; Ru 2:2, 3, 7, 8, 15–19, 23). Isaiah used this term in both a picture of judgment and of restoration for the nation of Israel (Isa 17:5; 27:12).

3951. לֶקֶט, **leqeṭ,** *leh´-ket*; from 3950; the *gleaning*:—gleaning.

3952. לָקַק, **lâqaq,** *law-kak´*; a primitive root; to *lick* or *lap*:—lap, lick.

3953. לָקַשׁ, **lâqash,** *law-kash´*; a primitive root; to *gather* the *after* crop:—gather.

A verb of uncertain meaning, translated as to despoil, to take everything, to glean. Its only occurrence is in Job 24:6. It is most likely the denominative verb of the noun *leqesh* (3954), meaning spring crop or aftergrowth.

3954. לֶקֶשׁ, **leqesh,** *leh´-kesh*; from 3953; the *after crop*:—latter growth.

3955. לְשַׁד, **lâshâd,** *lawsh-awd´*; from an unused root of uncertain meaning; apparently *juice,* i.e. (figurative) *vigour*; also a sweet or fat *cake*:—fresh, moisture.

3956. לָשׁוֹן, **lâshôwn,** *law-shone´*; or לָשֹׁן, **lâshôn,** *law-shone´*; also (in plural) feminine לְשֹׁנָה, **lᵉshônâh,** *lesh-o-naw´*; from 3960; the *tongue* (of man or animals), used literal (as the instrument of licking, eating, or speech), and figurative (speech, an ingot, a fork of flame, a cove of water):— + babbler, bay, + evil speaker, language, talker, tongue, wedge.

3957. לִשְׁכָּה, **lishkâh,** *lish-kaw´*; from an unused root of uncertain meaning; a *room* in a building (whether for storage, eating, or lodging):—chamber, parlour. Compare 5393.

3958. לֶשֶׁם, **leshem,** *leh´-shem*; from an unused root of uncertain meaning; a *gem,* perhaps the *jacinth*:—ligure.

3959. לֶשֶׁם, **Leshem,** *leh´-shem*; the same as 3958; *Leshem,* a place in Palestine:—Leshem.

3960. לָשַׁן, **lâshan,** *law-shan´*; a primitive root; (properly) to *lick*; but used only as a denominative from 3956; to *wag the tongue,* i.e. to *calumniate*:—accuse, slander.

3961. לִשָּׁן, **lishshân,** *lish-shawn´*; (Chaldee); corresponding to 3956; *speech,* i.e. a *nation*:—language.

3962. לֶשַׁע, **Lesha´,** *leh´-shah*; from an unused root thought to mean to *break* through; a boiling *spring; Lesha,* a place probably East of the Jordan:—Lasha.

3963. לֶתֶךְ, **lethek,** *leh´-thek*; from an unused root of uncertain meaning; a *measure* for things dry:—half homer.

מ (Mem)

3964. מָא, **mâ’,** *maw*; (Chaldee); corresponding to 4100; (as indefinite) *that*:— + what.

3965. מַאֲבוּס, **ma’ăbûws,** *mah-ab-ooce´*; from 75; a *granary*:—storehouse.

3966. מְאֹד, **me’ôd,** *meh-ode´*; from the same as 181; (properly) *vehemence*, i.e. (with or without preposition) *vehemently*; (by implication) *wholly, speedily,* etc. (often with other words as an intensive or superlative; especially when repeated):—diligently, especially, exceeding (-ly), far, fast, good, great (-ly), × louder and louder, might (-ily, -y), (so) much, quickly, (so) sore, utterly, very (+ much, sore), well.

3967. מֵאָה, **mê’âh,** *may-aw´*; or מֵאיָה, **mê’yâh,** *may-yaw´*; probably a primitive numeral; a *hundred*; also as a multiplicative and a fraction:—hundred ([-fold], -th), + sixscore.

3968. מֵאָה, **Mê’âh,** *may-aw´*; the same as 3967; *Meäh*, a tower in Jerusalem:—Meah.

3969. מְאָה, **me’âh,** *meh-aw´*; (Chaldee); corresponding to 3967:—hundred.

3970. מַאֲוַיִּים, **ma’ăvayyîym,** *mah-av-ah´ee*; from 183; a *desire*:—desire.

3971. מאוּם, **m’ûwm,** *moom*; usually מוּם, **mûwm,** *moom*; as if passive participle from an unused root probably meaning to *stain*; a *blemish* (physical or moral):—blemish, blot, spot.

A masculine noun meaning blemish, defect. This word usually describes a physical characteristic that is deemed to be bad. A man with any sort of blemish could not be a priest (Le 21:17, 18, 21, 23) nor could an animal which had a blemish be sacrificed (Le 22:20, 21; Nu 19:2; Dt 17:1). The word is also used to describe an injury caused by another (Le 24:19, 20). On the other hand, the absence of any blemish was a sign of beauty (2Sa 14:25; SS 4:7) or potential (Da 1:4). In a figurative sense, the word is used to describe the effect of sin (Dt 32:5; Job 11:15; 31:7) or insult (Pr 9:7).

3972. מְאוּמָה, **me’ûwmâh,** *meh-oo´-maw*; apparently a form of 3971; (properly) a *speck* or *point*, i.e. (by implication) *something*; (with negative) *nothing*:—fault, + no (-ught), ought, somewhat, any ([no-]) thing.

3973. מָאוֹס, **mâ’ôws,** *maw-oce´*; from 3988; *refuse*:—refuse.

3974. מָאוֹר, **mâ’ôwr,** *maw-ore´*; or מָאֹר, **mâ’ôr,** *maw-ore´*; also (in plural) feminine מְאוֹרָה, **me’ôwrâh,** *meh-o-raw´*; or מְאֹרָה, **me’ôrâh,** *meh-o-raw´*; from 215; (properly) a *luminous body* or *luminary*, i.e. (abstract) *light* (as an element); (figurative) *brightness*, i.e. *cheerfulness*; (specifically) a *chandelier*:—bright, light.

A masculine singular noun meaning luminary, a light. This noun is employed in connection with the lamp in the tabernacle (Ex 35:14; Le 24:2; Nu 4:16). It is also used to describe the heavenly lights in the creation story of Ge 1:15, 16.

3975. מְאוּרָה, **me’ûwrâh,** *meh-oo-raw´*; feminine passive participle of 215; something *lighted*, i.e. an *aperture*; (by implication) a *crevice* or *hole* of a serpent:—den.

3976. מֹאזְנָיִם, **mô’zenayim,** *mo-ze-nah´-yim*; from 239; (only in the dual) a pair of *scales*:—balances.

3977. מֹאזְנֵא, **mô’zenê’,** *mo-zeh-nay´*; (Chaldee); corresponding to 3976:—balances.

3978. מַאֲכָל, **ma’ăkâl,** *mah-ak-awl´*; from 398; an *eatable* (including provender, flesh and fruit):—food, fruit, ([bake-] meat (-s), victual.

3979. מַאֲכֶלֶת, **ma’ăkeleth,** *mah-ak-eh´-leth*; from 398; something to *eat* with, i.e. a *knife*:—knife.

3980. מַאֲכֹלֶת, **ma'ăkôleth,** *mah-ak-o´-leth*; from 398; something *eaten* (by fire), i.e. *fuel:*—fuel.

3981. מַאֲמָץ, **ma'ămâts,** *mah-am-awts´*; from 553; *strength,* i.e. (plural) *resources:*—force.

3982. מַאֲמַר, **ma'ămar,** *mah-am-ar´*; from 559; something (authoritatively) *said,* i.e. an *edict:*—commandment, decree.

A masculine noun meaning word or command. In all three of its instances in the OT, this word is best translated, command (i.e. that which is spoken with authority). It referred to the command of King Ahasuerus that Queen Vashti ignored (Est 1:15). It described Mordecai's instructions to Esther to keep quiet about her nationality (Est 2:20). Finally, it referred to Esther's edict about the establishment of the days of Purim (Est 9:32). This word comes from the common verb 'âmar (559), meaning to say, which can be translated to command, depending on the context (2Ch 31:11; Est 1:10).

3983. מֵאמַר, **mê'mar,** *may-mar´*; (Chaldee); corresponding to 3982:—appointment, word.

An Aramaic masculine noun meaning word, command. This word is used only twice in the OT and is equivalent to the Hebrew word ma'ămar (3982). It describes the words the priests spoke to request supplies for rebuilding the temple (Ezr 6:9); and it also refers to the words of the holy ones that issued the edict in Nebuchadnezzar's dream (Da 4:17[14]). This word comes from the common Aramaic verb, 'ămar (560), meaning to say.

3984. מָאן, **ma'n,** *mawn*; (Chaldee); probably from a root corresponding to 579 in the sense of an *inclosure* by sides; a *utensil:*—vessel.

3985. מָאֵן, **mâ'an,** *maw-an´*; a primitive root; to *refuse:*—refuse, × utterly.

A verb meaning to refuse. The basic idea of this word is a refusal or rejection of an offer. It is used to describe the refusal to obey God (Ex 16:28; Ne 9:17; Isa 1:20; Jer 9:6[5]); His messengers, (1Sa 8:19); or other men (Est 1:12). Jacob refused comfort when he thought Joseph had died (Ge 37:35); Joseph refused Potiphar's wife's offer to sin (Ge 39:8); Pharaoh refused to let Israel go (Ex 4:23; 7:14); Balaam refused Balak's offer to curse Israel (Nu 22:13, 14); both Saul and Ammon refused to eat food offered to them (1Sa 28:23; 2Sa 13:9).

3986. מָאֵן, **mâ'ên,** *maw-ane´*; from 3985; *unwilling:*—refuse.

An adjective meaning refusing, disobeying. This word is found in the context of disobedience to a command. A prime example was that of the Israelites in bondage. God said that if Pharaoh refused to let His people go, He would bring various plagues on Egypt (Ex 8:2[7:27]; 9:2). King Zedekiah was warned that he would be captured by Babylon if he refused to surrender to the Lord (Jer 38:21).

3987. מֵאֵן, **mê'ên,** *may-ane´*; from 3985; *refractory:*—refuse.

An adjective meaning refusing. This word is used only once in the OT and comes from the verb mâ'ên (3985), meaning to refuse. In Jer 13:10, it described the people of Judah as those refusing to listen to God's words.

3988. מָאַס, **mâ'as,** *maw-as´*; a primitive root; to *spurn;* also (intransitive) to *disappear:*—abhor, cast away (off), contemn, despise, disdain, (become) loathe (-some), melt away, refuse, reject, reprobate, × utterly, vile person.

A verb meaning to reject, to despise, to abhor, to refuse. The primary meaning of this word is to reject or treat as loathsome. It designates people's actions in refusing to heed God or accept His authority (1Sa 10:19; Jer 8:9); esteeming God's commands lightly (Le 26:15; Isa 30:12); and despising one's spiritual condition in an act of repentance (Job 42:6). Scripture also speaks of the Lord rejecting His people (Hos 4:6) and their worship (Am 5:21) because of their rejection of Him. A secondary and more rare meaning of the word is to run or flow. This use appears in Ps 58:7[8] as David prayed for the wicked to melt away like a flowing river.

3989. מַאֲפֶה, **ma'ăpheh,** *mah-af-eh´*; from 644; something *baked,* i.e. a *batch:*—baken.

3990. מַאֲפֵל, **ma'ăphêl,** *mah-af-ale´*; from the same as 651; something *opaque:*—darkness.

3991. מַאְפֵלְיָה, **ma'pêlyâh,** *mah-pel-yaw´*; prolonged feminine of 3990; *opaqueness:*—darkness.

3992. מָאַר, **mâ'ar,** *maw-ar´*; a primitive root; to *be bitter* or (causative) to *embitter,* i.e. *be painful:*—fretting, picking.

3993. מַאֲרָב, **ma'ărâb,** *mah-ar-awb´*; from 693; an *ambuscade*:—lie in ambush, ambushment, lurking place, lying in wait.

3994. מְאֵרָה, **mᵉʼêrâh,** *meh-ay-raw´*; from 779; an *execration*:—curse.

3995. מִבְדָּלָה, **mibdâlâh,** *mib-daw-law´*; from 914; a *separation*, i.e. (concrete) a *separate* place:—separate.

3996. מָבוֹא, **mâbôw',** *maw-bo´*; from 935; an *entrance* (the place or the act); specifically (with or without 8121) *sunset* or the *west*; also (adverb with preposition) *toward*:—by which came, as cometh, in coming, as men enter into, entering, entrance into, entry, where goeth, going down, + westward. Compare 4126.

3997. מְבוֹאָה, **mᵉbôw'âh,** *meb-o-aw´*; feminine of 3996; a *haven*:—entry.

3998. מְבוּכָה, **mᵉbûwkâh,** *meb-oo-kaw´*; from 943; *perplexity*:—perplexity.

3999. מַבּוּל, **mabbûwl,** *mab-bool´*; from 2986 in the sense of *flowing*; a *deluge*:—flood.

4000. מְבוּנִים, **mᵉbûwnîym,** *meh-boo-neem´*; from 995; *instructing*:—taught.

4001. מְבוּסָה, **mᵉbûwsâh,** *meb-oo-saw´*; from 947; a *trampling*:—treading (trodden) down (under foot).

4002. מַבּוּעַ, **mabbûwaʻ,** *mab-boo´-ah*; from 5042; a *fountain*:—fountain, spring.

4003. מְבוּקָה, **mᵉbûwqâh,** *meb-oo-kaw´*; from the same as 950; *emptiness*:—void.

4004. מִבְחוֹר, **mâbchôwr,** *mib-khore´*; from 977; *select*, i.e. well fortified:—choice.

4005. מִבְחָר, **mibchâr,** *mib-khawr´*; from 977; *select*, i.e. best:—choice (-st), chosen.

4006. מִבְחָר, **Mibchâr,** *mib-khawr´*; the same as 4005; *Mibchar*, an Israelite:—Mibhar.

4007. מַבָּט, **mabbâṭ,** *mab-bawt´*; or מֶבָּט, **mebbâṭ,** *meb-bawt´*; from 5027; something *expected*, i.e. (abstract) *expectation*:—expectation.

4008. מִבְטָא, **mibṭâ',** *mib-taw´*; from 981; a rash *utterance* (hasty vow):—(that which ...) uttered (out of).

4009. מִבְטָח, **mibṭâch,** *mib-tawkh´*; from 982; (properly) a *refuge*, i.e. (objective) *security*, or (subjective) *assurance*:—confidence, hope, sure, trust.

4010. מַבְלִיגִית, **mablîygîyth,** *mab-leeg-eeth´*; from 1082; *desistance* (or rather *desolation*):—comfort self.

4011. מִבְנֶה, **mibneh,** *mib-neh´*; from 1129; a *building*:—frame.

4012. מְבֻנַּי, **Mᵉbunnay,** *meb-oon-nah´ee*; from 1129; *built* up; *Mebunnai*, an Israelite:—Mebunnai.

4013. מִבְצָר, **mibtsâr,** *mib-tsawr´*; also (in plural) feminine (Da 11:15) מִבְצָרָה, **mibtsârâh,** *mib-tsaw-raw´*; from 1219; a *fortification*, *castle*, or *fortified* city; (figurative) a *defender*:—(de-, most) fenced, fortress, (most) strong (hold).

4014. מִבְצָר, **Mibtsâr,** *mib-tsawr´*; the same as 4013; *Mibtsar*, an Idumæan:—Mibzar.

4015. מִבְרָח, **mibrâch,** *mib-rawkh´*; from 1272; a *refugee*:—fugitive.

4016. מְבוּשִׁים, **mᵉbûwshîym,** *meh-boo-sheem´*; from 954; (plural) the (male) *pudenda*:—secrets.

4017. מִבְשָׂם, **Mibśâm,** *mib-sawm´*; from the same as 1314; *fragrant*; *Mibsam*, the name of an Ishmaelite and of an Israelite:—Mibsam.

4018. מְבַשְּׁלוֹת, **mᵉbashshᵉlôwth,** *meb-ash-shel-oth´*; from 1310; a cooking *hearth*:—boiling-place.

4019. מַגְבִּישׁ, **Magbîysh,** *mag-beesh´*; from the same as 1378; *stiffening*; *Magbish*, an Israelite, or a place in Palestine:—Magbish.

4020. מִגְבָּלוֹת, **migbâlôwth,** *mig-bawl-oth´*; from 1379; a *border*:—end.

4021. מִגְבָּעָה, **migbâʻâh,** *mig-baw-aw´*; from the same as 1389; a *cap* (as *hemispherical*):—bonnet.

4022. מֶגֶד, **meged,** *meh´-ghed*; from an unused root (properly) meaning to *be eminent*; properly a *distinguished* thing; hence something *valuable*, as a product or fruit:—pleasant, precious fruit (thing).

4023. מְגִדּוֹן, **Mᵉgiddôwn,** *meg-id-done´*; (Zec 12:11), or מְגִדּוֹ, **Megiddôw,** *meg-id-do´*; from

1413; *rendezvous; Megiddon* or *Megiddo*, a place in Palestine:—Megiddo, Megiddon.

4024. מִגְדּוֹל, **Migdôwl,** *mig-dole´*; or מִגְדֹּל, **Migdôl,** *mig-dole´*; probably of Egyptian origin; *Migdol,* a place in Egypt:—Migdol, tower.

4025. מַגְדִּיאֵל, **Magdîy'êl,** *mag-dee-ale´*; from 4022 and 410; *preciousness of God; Magdiël,* an Idumæan:—Magdiel.

4026. מִגְדָּל, **migdâl,** *mig-dawl´*; also (in plural) feminine מִגְדָּלָה, **migdâlâh,** *mig-daw-law´*; from 1431; a *tower* (from its size or height); (by analogy) a *rostrum;* (figurative) a (pyramidal) *bed* of flowers:—castle, flower, tower. Compare the names following.

4027. מִגְדָּל־אֵל, **Migdal-'Êl,** *mig-dal-ale´*; from 4026 and 410; *tower of God; Migdal-El,* a place in Palestine:—Migdal-el.

4028. מִגְדָּל־גָּד, **Migdal-Gâd,** *mig-dal-gawd´*; from 4026 and 1408; *tower of Fortune; Migdal-Gad,* a place in Palestine:—Migdal-gad.

4029. מִגְדָּל־עֵדֶר, **Migdal-'Êder,** *mig-dal´-ay´-der;* from 4026 and 5739; *tower of a flock; Migdal-Eder,* a place in Palestine:—Migdal-eder, tower of the flock.

4030. מִגְדָּנָה, **migdânâh,** *mig-daw-naw´*; from the same as 4022; *preciousness,* i.e. a *gem:*—precious thing, present.

4031. מָגוֹג, **Mâgôwg,** *maw-gogue´*; from 1463; *Magog,* a son of Japheth; also a barbarous northern region:—Magog.

4032. מָגוֹר, **mâgôwr,** *maw-gore´*; or (La 2:22) מָגוּר, **mâgûwr,** *maw-goor´*; from 1481 in the sense of *fearing;* a *fright* (objective or subjective):—fear, terror. Compare 4036.

A masculine noun meaning fear, terror. The fundamental concept underlying this word is a sense of impending doom. It is used to signify the fear that surrounds one whose life is being plotted against (Ps 31:13[14]); the fear that causes a soldier to retreat in the face of an invincible foe (Isa 31:9; Jer 6:25); and the horrors that befall those facing God's judgment (La 2:22). Of interest is the prophecy of Jeremiah concerning Pashur after he had Jeremiah placed in the stocks for prophesying against the idolatry of Jerusalem (cf. Jer 20:1–6). The Lord would no longer call Pashur by his name. He gave him a new one, Magormissabib or Magor-Missabib ("fear on every side"), because the Lord would make him, as it were, afraid of his own shadow (Jer 20:4).

4033. מָגוֹר, **mâgôwr,** *maw-gor´*; or מָגֻר, **mâgur,** *maw-goor´*; from 1481 in the sense of *lodging;* a temporary *abode;* (by extension) a permanent *residence:*—dwelling, pilgrimage, where sojourn, be a stranger. Compare 4032.

A masculine noun meaning sojourning or a dwelling place. This word comes from the verb, *gûr* (1481), meaning to sojourn. Most often, this word is used to describe Israel as a sojourning people, who will inherit the land of Canaan, where they sojourned (Ge 17:8; 37:1; Ex 6:4). The psalmist described the preciousness of God's statutes in his sojourning (Ps 119:54). The wicked are described as having evil in their dwelling places (Ps 55:15[16]), which will result with God removing them from their dwelling places (Eze 20:38). As a result, the wicked will have no offspring in their dwelling places (Job 18:19).

4034. מְגוֹרָה, **mᵉgôwrâh,** *meg-o-raw´*; feminine of 4032; *affright:*—fear.

A feminine noun meaning fear, terror. The feminine form of *mâgôwr* (4032), this word occurs only once in the Bible. Pr 10:24 contrasts the fate of the wicked with that of the righteous. The ones serving the Lord will get their hearts' desires, but the wicked will get their worst nightmares—judgment.

4035. מְגוּרָה, **mᵉgûwrâh,** *meg-oo-raw´*; feminine of 4032 or of 4033; a *fright;* also a *granary:*—barn, fear.

A feminine noun meaning fear, terror. The use of this word for fear tends to imply the haunting apprehensions that one holds deep within. The Lord's judgments bring people's worst fears to reality (Isa 66:4), while His love frees us from them (Ps 34:4[5]; cf. 1Jn 4:18). Haggai, however, uses this word to signify a storage place or a barn (Hag 2:19). The link between the divergent ideas comes from the root word *gûr* (1481), which carries the connotation of dwelling as well as fear.

4036. מָגוֹר מִסָּבִיב, **Mâgôwr mis-Sâbîyb,** *maw-gore´ mis-saw-beeb´*; from 4032 and 5439 with the preposition inserted; *affright from around;*

Magor-mis-Sabib, a symbolical name of Pashur:—Magor-missabib.

4037. מַגְזֵרָה, **magzêrâh**, *mag-zay-raw´*; from 1504; a *cutting* implement, i.e. a *blade*:—axe.

4038. מַגָּל, **maggâl**, *mag-gawl´*; from an unused root meaning to *reap*; a *sickle*:—sickle.

4039. מְגִלָּה, **mᵉgillâh**, *meg-il-law´*; from 1556; a *roll*:—roll, volume.

A feminine noun meaning roll, volume, writing, scroll. This Hebrew word is approximately equivalent to the English word "book." In ancient Israel, instead of pages bound into a cover, "books" were written on scrolls of leather or other durable material and rolled together. All but one appearance of this word (Ps 40:7[8]) occurs in Jer 36. The importance of this word is found in its reference to the sacred volume recording God's own words (cf. Jer 36:2).

4040. מְגִלָּה, **mᵉgillâh**, *meg-il-law´*; (Chaldee); corresponding to 4039:—roll.

An Aramaic noun meaning roll, scroll. The term is used to describe the object upon which was written an official record of King Cyrus' decree concerning the rebuilding of the Temple at Jerusalem (Ezr 6:2).

4041. מְגַמָּה, **mᵉgammâh**, *meg-am-maw´*; from the same as 1571; (properly) *accumulation*, i.e. *impulse* or *direction*:—sup up.

4042. מָגַן, **mâgan**, *maw-gan´*; a denominative from 4043; (properly) to *shield*; *encompass* with; (figurative) to *rescue*, to *hand safely over* (i.e. *surrender*):—deliver.

4043. מָגֵן, **mâgên**, *maw-gane´*; also (in plural) feminine מְגִנָּה, **mᵉginnâh**, *meg-in-naw´*; from 1598; a *shield* (i.e. the small one or *buckler*); (figurative) a *protector*; also the scaly *hide* of the crocodile:— × armed, buckler, defence, ruler, + scale, shield.

4044. מְגִנָּה, **mᵉginnâh**, *meg-in-naw´*; from 4042; a *covering* (in a bad sense), i.e. *blindness* or obduracy:—sorrow. See also 4043.

4045. מִגְעֶרֶת, **migʻereth**, *mig-eh´-reth*; from 1605; *reproof* (i.e. curse):—rebuke.

4046. מַגֵּפָה, **maggêphâh**, *mag-gay-faw´*; from 5062; a *pestilence*; (by analogy) *defeat*:—(× be) plague (-d), slaughter, stroke.

4047. מַגְפִּיעָשׁ, **Magpîyʻâsh**, *mag-pee-awsh´*; apparently from 1479 or 5062 and 6211; *exterminator of* (the) *moth; Magpiash*, an Israelite:—Magpiash.

4048. מָגַר, **mâgar**, *maw-gar´*; a primitive root; to *yield up*; (intensive) to *precipitate*:—cast down, terror.

A verb meaning to cast before, to deliver over, to yield up. In a participial form, the term is used once to describe the people and princes of Israel who were being thrown to the sword because they stubbornly refused to heed God's discipline (Eze 21:12[17]). When used in its intensive form, the verb conveys the idea to cast down or to overthrow, as witnessed in Ps 89:44[45]: "You have made his splendor to cease and cast his throne to the ground" (NASB). See the verb *nâgar* (5064).

4049. מְגַר, **mᵉgar**, *meg-ar´*; (Chaldee); corresponding to 4048; to *overthrow*:—destroy.

An Aramaic verb meaning to overthrow, to cast down. In an edict decreed by King Darius, this verb describes what Darius hoped the God of heaven would do to any king or people who altered his edict or tried to destroy the Temple in Jerusalem (Ezr 6:12). The term is closely related to the Hebrew verb *mâgar* (4048).

4050. מְגֵרָה, **mᵉgêrâh**, *meg-ay-raw´*; from 1641; a *saw*:—axe, saw.

4051. מִגְרוֹן, **Migrôwn**, *mig-rone´*; from 4048; *preci-pice; Migron*, a place in Palestine:—Migron.

4052. מִגְרָעָה, **migrâʻâh**, *mig-raw-aw´*; from 1639; a *ledge* or offset:—narrowed rest.

4053. מִגְרָף, **migrâph**, *mig-rawf´*; from 1640; something *thrown off* (by the spade), i.e. a *clod*:—clod.

4054. מִגְרָשׁ, **migrâsh**, *mig-rawsh´*; also (in plural) feminine (Eze 27:28) מִגְרָשָׁה, **migrâshâh**, *mig-raw-shaw´*; from 1644; a *suburb* (i.e. open country whither flocks are *driven* for pasture); hence the *area* around a building, or the *margin* of the sea:—cast out, suburb.

4055. מַד, **mad**, *mad*; or מֵד, **mêd**, *made*; from 4058; (properly) *extent*, i.e. *height*; also a *measure*; (by implication) a *vesture* (as measured);

also a *carpet*:—armour, clothes, garment, judgment, measure, raiment, stature.

4056. מַדְבַּח, **madbach**, *mad-bakh´*; (Chaldee); from 1684; a sacrificial *altar*:—altar.

4057. מִדְבָּר, **midbâr**, *mid-bawr´*; from 1696 in the sense of *driving*; a *pasture* (i.e. open field, whither cattle are driven); (by implication) a *desert*; also *speech* (including its organs):—desert, south, speech, wilderness.

4058. מָדַד, **mâdad**, *maw-dad´*; a primitive root; (properly) to *stretch*; (by implication) to *measure* (as if by *stretching* a line); (figurative) to *be extended*:—measure, mete, stretch self.

4059. מִדַּד, **middad**, *mid-dad´*; from 5074; *flight*:—be gone.

4060. מִדָּה, **middâh**, *mid-daw´*; feminine of 4055; (properly) *extension*, i.e. height or breadth; also a *measure* (including its standard); hence a *portion* (as measured) or a *vestment*; specifically *tribute* (as measured):—garment, measure (-ing, meteyard, piece, size, (great) stature, tribute, wide.

4061. מִדָּה, **middâh**, *mid-daw´*; (Chaldee); or מִנְדָּה, **mindâh**, *min-daw´*; (Chaldee); corresponding to 4060; *tribute* in money:—toll, tribute.

4062. מַדְהֵבָה, **madhêbâh**, *mad-hay-baw´*; perhaps from the equivalent of 1722; *gold-making*, i.e. *exactress*:—golden city.

4063. מְדוּ, **mâdûw**, *maw´-doo*; from an unused root meaning to *stretch*; (properly) *extent*, i.e. *measure*; (by implication) a *dress* (as measured):—garment.

4064. מַדְוֶה, **madveh**, *mad-veh´*; from 1738; *sickness*:—disease.

4065. מַדּוּחַ, **maddûwach**, *mad-doo´-akh*; from 5080; *seduction*:—cause of banishment.

4066. מָדוֹן, **mâdôwn**, *maw-dohn´*; from 1777; a *contest* or quarrel:—brawling, contention (-ous), discord, strife. Compare 4079, 4090.

4067. מָדוֹן, **mâdôwn**, *maw-dohn´*; from the same as 4063; *extensiveness*, i.e. height:—stature.

4068. מָדוֹן, **Mâdôwn**, *maw-dohn´*; the same as 4067; *Madon*, a place in Palestine:—Madon.

4069. מַדּוּעַ, **maddûwa‛**, *mad-doo´-ah*; or מַדֻּעַ, **maddua‛**, *mad-doo´-ah*; from 4100 and the passive participle of 3045; *what* (is) *known*; i.e. (by implication) (adverb) *why*:—how, wherefore, why.

4070. מְדוֹר, **me̱dôwr**, *med-ore´*; (Chaldee); or מְדֹר, **me̱dôr**, *med-ore´*; (Chaldee); or מְדָר, **me̱dâr**, *med-awr´*; (Chaldee); from 1753; a *dwelling*:—dwelling.

4071. מְדוּרָה, **me̱dûwrâh**, *med-oo-raw´*; or מְדֻרָה, **me̱durâh**, *med-oo-raw´*; from 1752 in the sense of *accumulation*; a *pile* of fuel:—pile (for fire).

4072. מִדְחֶה, **midcheh**, *mid-kheh´*; from 1760; *overthrow*:—ruin.

4073. מַדְחֵפָה, **madchêphâh**, *mad-khay-faw´*; from 1765; a *push*, i.e. ruin:—overthrow.

4074. מָדַי, **Mâday**, *maw-dah´ee*; of foreign derivation; *Madai*, a country of central Asia:—Madai, Medes, Media.

4075. מָדִי, **Mâdîy**, *maw-dee´*; patrial from 4074; a *Madian* or native of Madai:—Mede.

4076. מָדַי, **Mâday**, *maw-dah´ee*; (Chaldee); corresponding to 4074:—Mede (-s).

4077. מָדָיָא, **Mâdây'â**, *maw-daw´-aw*; (Chaldee); corresponding to 4075:—Median.

4078. מַדַּי, **madday**, *mad-dah´ee*; from 4100 and 1767; *what* (is) *enough*, i.e. *sufficiently*:—sufficiently.

4079. מִדְיָנִים, **midyânîym**, *mid-yaw-neem´*; a variation for 4066:—brawling, contention (-ous).

4080. מִדְיָן, **Midyân**, *mid-yawn´*; the same as 4079; *Midjan*, a son of Abraham; also his country and (collective) his descendants:—Midian, Midianite.

4081. מִדִּין, **Middîyn**, *mid-deen´*; a variation for 4080:—Middin.

4082. מְדִינָה, **me̱dîynâh**, *med-ee-naw´*; from 1777; (properly) a *judgeship*, i.e. *jurisdiction*; (by implication) a *district* (as ruled by a judge); (generally) a *region*:—(× every) province.

4083. מְדִינָה, **me̱dîynâh**, *med-ee-naw´*; (Chaldee); corresponding to 4082:—province.

4084. מִדְיָנִי, **Midyânîy,** *mid-yaw-nee´*; patronymic or patrial from 4080; a *Midjanite* or descendant (native) of Midjan:—Midianite. Compare 4092.

4085. מִדֹּכָה, **mᵉdôkâh,** *med-o-kaw´*; from 1743; a *mortar:*—mortar.

4086. מַדְמֵן, **Madmên,** *mad-mane´*; from the same as 1828; *dunghill; Madmen,* a place in Palestine:—Madmen.

4087. מַדְמֵנָה, **madmênâh,** *mad-may-naw´*; feminine from the same as 1828; a *dunghill:*—dunghill.

4088. מַדְמֵנָה, **Madmênâh,** *mad-may-naw´*; the same as 4087; *Madmenah,* a place in Palestine:—Madmenah.

4089. מַדְמַנָּה, **Madmannâh,** *mad-man-naw´*; a variation for 4087; *Madmannah,* a place in Palestine:—Madmannah.

4090. מְדָנִים, **mᵉdânîym,** *med-aw-neem´*; a form of 4066:—discord, strife.

4091. מְדָן, **Mᵉdân,** *med-awn´*; the same as 4090; *Medan,* a son of Abraham:—Medan.

4092. מְדָנִי, **Mᵉdânîy,** *med-aw-nee´*; a variation of 4084:—Midianite.

4093. מַדָּע, **maddâ‘,** *mad-daw´*; or מַדַּע, **madda‘,** *mad-dah´*; from 3045; *intelligence* or *consciousness:*—knowledge, science, thought.

4094. מַדְקָרָה, **madqêrâh,** *mad-kay-raw´*; from 1856; a *wound:*—piercing.

4095. מַדְרֵגָה, **madrêgâh,** *mad-ray-gaw´*; from an unused root meaning to *step;* (properly) a *step;* (by implication) a *steep* or inaccessible place:—stair, steep place.

4096. מִדְרָךְ, **midrâk,** *mid-rawk´*; from 1869; a *treading,* i.e. a place for stepping on:—[foot-] breadth.

4097. מִדְרָשׁ, **midrâsh,** *mid-rawsh´*; from 1875; (properly) an *investigation,* i.e. (by implication) a *treatise* or elaborate compilation:—story.

4098. מְדֻשָׁה, **mᵉdushâh,** *meh-doo-shaw´*; from 1758; a *threshing,* i.e. (concrete and figurative) *down-trodden* people:—threshing.

4099. מְדָתָא, **Mᵉdâthâ’,** *med-aw-thaw´*; of Persian origin; *Medatha,* the father of Haman:—Hammedatha [*including the art.*].

4100. מָה, **mâh,** *maw;* or מַה, **mah,** *mah;* or מָ־, **mâ,** *maw;* or מַ־, **ma,** *mah;* also מֶה, **meh,** *meh;* a primitive particle; (properly) interrogative *what* (including *how why when*); but also exclamation *what!* (including *how!*), or indefinite *what* (including *whatever,* and even relative *that which*); often used with prefixes in various adverb or conjunction senses:—how (long, oft, [-soever]), [no-] thing, what (end, good, purpose, thing), whereby (-fore, -in, -to, -with), (for) why.

4101. מָה, **mâh,** *maw;* (Chaldee); corresponding to 4100:—how great (mighty), that which, what (-soever), why.

4102. מָהַהּ, **mâhah,** *maw-hah´*; apparently a denominative from 4100; (properly) to *question* or hesitate, i.e. (by implication) to *be reluctant:*—delay, linger, stay selves, tarry.

4103. מְהוּמָה, **mᵉhûwmâh,** *meh-hoo-maw´*; from 1949; *confusion* or uproar:—destruction, discomfiture, trouble, tumult, vexation, vexed.

A feminine noun meaning confusion, panic, tumult, disturbance. If the Israelites diligently observed God's covenant stipulations, He would throw the nations occupying Canaan into a great panic and give them over into the Israelites' hands (Dt 7:23). If, however, the Israelites did not obey and thus forsook the Lord their God, this same panic would be sent upon them instead (Dt 28:20). After the Philistines captured the ark of God and brought it to Gath (one of their five main cities), the Lord struck the people of that city with a great panic and severe tumors (1Sa 5:9, 11). Isaiah the prophet warned Jerusalem that a day of tumult, trampling, and confusion was at hand for it (Isa 22:5). The term also functions to describe daily life in certain geographical locations during troubled periods of time: Jerusalem (Eze 22:5); Israel and the surrounding lands (2Ch 15:5); and the mountains of Samaria (Am 3:9). Once the word describes the trouble wealth brings to a household that does not fear the Lord (Pr 15:16). The term derives from the verb *hûm* (1949).

4104. מְהוּמָן, **Mᵉhûwmân,** *meh-hoo-mawn´*; of Persian origin; *Mehuman,* a eunuch of Xerxes:—Mehuman.

4105. מְהֵיטַבְאֵל, **Mᵉhêytab'êl,** *meh-hay-tab-ale´*; from 3190 (augmented) and 410; *bettered of God; Mehetabel,* the name of an Edomitish man and woman:—Mehetabeel, Mehetabel.

4106. מָהִיר, **mâhîyr,** *maw-here´*; or מָהִר, **mâhir,** *maw-here´*; from 4116; *quick;* hence *skilful:*—diligent, hasty, ready.

4107. מָהַל, **mâhal,** *maw-hal´*; a primitive root; (properly) to *cut down* or *reduce,* i.e. (by implication) to *adulterate:*—mixed.

4108. מַהְלְכִים, **mahlᵉkîym,** *mah-leh-keem´*; from 1980; a *walking* (plural collective), i.e. *access:*—place to walk.

4109. מַהֲלָךְ, **mahălâk,** *mah-hal-awk´*; from 1980; a *walk,* i.e. a *passage* or a *distance:*—journey, walk.

4110. מַהֲלָל, **mahălâl,** *mah-hal-awl´*; from 1984; *fame:*—praise.

4111. מַהֲלַלְאֵל, **Mahălal'êl,** *mah-hal-al-ale´*; from 4110 and 410; *praise of God; Mahalalel,* the name of an antediluvian patriarch and of an Israelite:—Mahalaleel.

4112. מַהֲלֻמוֹת, **mahălumôwth,** *mah-hal-oo-moth´*; from 1986; a *blow:*—stripe, stroke.

4113. מַהֲמֹר, **mahămôr,** *mah-ha-mor´*; from an unused root of uncertain meaning; perhaps an *abyss:*—deep pit.

4114. מַהְפֵּכָה, **mahpêkâh,** *mah-pay-kaw´*; from 2015; a *destruction:*—when ... overthrew, overthrow (-n).

4115. מַהְפֶּכֶת, **mahpeketh,** *mah-peh´-keth*; from 2015; a *wrench,* i.e. the *stocks:*—prison, stocks.

4116. מָהַר, **mâhar,** *maw-har´*; a primitive root; (properly) to *be liquid* or *flow* easily, i.e. (by implication); to *hurry* (in a good or a bad sense); often used (with another verb) adverb *promptly:*—be carried headlong, fearful, (cause to make, in, make) haste (-n, -ily), (be) hasty, (fetch, make ready) × quickly, rash, × shortly, (be so) × soon, make speed, × speedily, × straightway, × suddenly, swift.

4117. מָהַר, **mâhar,** *maw-har´*; a primitive root (perhaps rather the same as 4116 through the idea of *readiness* in assent); to *bargain* (for a wife), i.e. to *wed:*—endow, × surely.

4118. מַהֵר, **mahêr,** *mah-hare´*; from 4116; (properly) *hurrying;* hence (adverb) *in a hurry:*—hasteth, hastily, at once, quickly, soon, speedily, suddenly.

4119. מֹהַר, **môhar,** *mo´-har*; from 4117; a *price* (for a wife):—dowry.

4120. מְהֵרָה, **mᵉhêrâh,** *meh-hay-raw´*; feminine of 4118; (properly) a *hurry;* hence (adverb) *promptly:*—hastily, quickly, shortly, soon, make (with) speed (-ily), swiftly.

4121. מַהֲרַי, **Mahăray,** *mah-har-ah´ee*; from 4116; *hasty; Maharai,* an Israelite:—Maharai.

4122. מַהֵר שָׁלָל חָשׁ בַּז, **Mahêr Shâlâl Châsh Baz,** *mah-hare´ shaw-lawl´ khawsh baz*; from 4118 and 7998 and 2363 and 957; *hasting* (is he [the enemy] to the) *booty,* swift (to the) *prey; Maher-Shalal-Chash-Baz;* the symbolic name of the son of Isaiah:—Maher-shalal-hash-baz.

4123. מְהִתַלָּה, **mahăthallâh,** *mah-hath-al-law´*; from 2048; a *delusion:*—deceit.

4124. מוֹאָב, **Môw'âb,** *mo-awb´*; from a prolonged form of the prepositional prefix *m*- and 1; *from* (her [the mother's]) *father; Moâb,* an incestuous son of Lot; also his territory and descendant:—Moab.

4125. מוֹאָבִי, **Môw'âbîy,** *mo-aw-bee´*; feminine מוֹאָבִיָּה, **Môw'âbîyyâh,** *mo-aw-bee-yaw´*; or מוֹאָבִית, **Môw'âbîyth,** *mo-aw-beeth´*; patronymic from 4124; a *Moâbite* or *Moâbitess,* i.e. a descendant from Moab:—(woman) of Moab, Moabite (-ish, -ss).

4126. מוֹבָא, **môwbâ',** *mo-baw´*; by transposition for 3996; an *entrance:*—coming.

4127. מוּג, **mûwg,** *moog*; a primitive root; to *melt,* i.e. literal (to *soften,* flow down, *disappear*), or figurative (to *fear, faint*):—consume, dissolve, (be) faint (-hearted), melt (away), make soft.

4128. מוּד, **môwd,** *mowd*; a primitive root; to *shake:*—measure.

4129. מוֹדַע, **môwdaʻ,** *mo-dah´*; or rather מֹדָע, **môdâʻ,** *mo-daw´*; from 3045; an *acquaintance:*—kinswoman.

4130. מוֹדַעַת, **môwdaʻath,** *mo-dah´-ath*; from 3045; *acquaintance:*—kindred.

4131. מוֹט, **môwṭ,** *mote´*; a primitive root; to *waver*; (by implication) to *slip, shake, fall*:—be carried, cast, be out of course, be fallen in decay, × exceedingly, fall (-ing down), be (re-) moved, be ready, shake, slide, slip.

4132. מוֹט, **môwṭ,** *mote´*; from 4131; a *wavering*, i.e. *fall*; (by implication) a *pole* (as shaking); hence a *yoke* (as essentially a bent pole):—bar, be moved, staff, yoke.

4133. מוֹטָה, **môwṭâh,** *mo-taw´*; feminine of 4132; a *pole*; (by implication) an ox-*bow*; hence a *yoke* (either literal or figurative):—bands, heavy, staves, yoke.

4134. מוּךְ, **mûwk,** *mook*; a primitive root; to *become thin*, i.e. (figurative) *be impoverished*:—be (waxen) poor (-er).

4135. מוּל, **mûwl,** *mool*; a primitive root; to *cut short*, i.e. *curtail* (specifically the prepuce, i.e. to *circumcise*); (by implication) to *blunt*; (figurative) to *destroy*:—circumcise (-ing, selves), cut down (in pieces), destroy, × must needs.

A verb meaning to cut short, to cut off, to circumcise. Abraham was commanded to circumcise both himself and his offspring as a sign of the covenant made between him and God (Ge 17:10–14). As a result, Abraham had his son Ishmael, all the male slaves in his house, and himself circumcised that same day (Ge 17:23–27). Later, when Isaac was born, Abraham circumcised him as well (Ge 21:4). Moses commanded the Israelites to circumcise their hearts, that is, to remove the hardness and to love God (Dt 10:16; cf. 30:6; Jer 4:4). When used in its intensive form, the verb carries the meaning to cut down, as seen in Ps 90:6: "In the morning it [the grass] flourisheth, and groweth up; in the evening it is cut down, and withereth" (KJV). Used in the causative sense, the verb gives the meaning to cut off, to destroy (Ps 118:10–12; lit., "I will cause them to be cut off"). See also the related verbs *mâhal* (4107), *mâlal* (4448), and *nâmal* (5243).

4136. מוּל, **mûwl,** *mool*; or מוֹל, **môwl,** *mole*; (Dt 1:1), or מוֹאל, **môw´l,** *mole*; (Ne 12:38), or מֻל, **mul,** *mool*; (Nu 22:5), from 4135; (properly) *abrupt*, i.e. a *precipice*; (by implication) the *front*; used only adverb (with prepositional prefix) *opposite*:—(over) against, before, [fore-] front, from, [God-] ward, toward, with.

4137. מוֹלָדָה, **Môwlâdâh,** *mo-law-daw´*; from 3205; *birth; Moladah*, a place in Palestine:—Moladah.

4138. מוֹלֶדֶת, **môwledeth,** *mo-leh´-deth*; from 3205; *nativity* (plural *birth-place*); (by implication) *lineage, native country*; also *offspring, family*:—begotten, born, issue, kindred, native (-ity).

4139. מוּלָה, **mûwlâh,** *moo-law´*; from 4135; *circumcision*:—circumcision.

A feminine noun meaning circumcision. Derived from the verb *mûl* (4135), the only undisputed occurrence of the term is found at the end of Ex 4:26.

4140. מוֹלִיד, **Môwlîyd,** *mo-leed´*; from 3205; *genitor; Molid*, an Israelite:—Molid.

4141. מוּסָב, **mûwsâb,** *moo-sawb´*; from 5437; a *turn*, i.e. *circuit* (of a building):—winding about.

4142. מוּסַבָּה, **mûwsabbâh,** *moo-sab-baw´*; or מֻסַבָּה, **musabbâh,** *moo-sab-baw´*; feminine of 4141; a *reversal*, i.e. the *backside* (of a gem), *fold* (of a double-leaved door), *transmutation* (of a name):—being changed, inclosed, be set, turning.

4143. מוּסָד, **mûwsâd,** *moo-sawd´*; from 3245; a *foundation*:—foundation.

A masculine singular noun meaning foundation, foundation laying. Its only occurrences are in Isa 28:16 and 2Ch 8:16 that refer to the foundations of Zion and the Temple, respectively.

4144. מוֹסָד, **môwsâd,** *mo-sawd´*; from 3245; a *foundation*:—foundation.

4145. מוּסָדָה, **mûwsâdâh,** *moo-saw-daw´*; feminine of 4143; a *foundation*; (figurative) an *appointment*:—foundation, grounded. Compare 4328.

A feminine noun meaning foundation or appointment. This word is used only twice in the OT and comes from the verb *yâsad* (3245), meaning to establish. Ezekiel used this word to describe the foundation of the Temple in his vision (Eze 41:8). Isaiah used it to describe the appointed rod of punishment by which the Lord would smite Assyria (Isa 30:32).

4146. מוֹסָדָה, **môwsâdâh,** *mo-saw-daw´*; or מֹסָדָה, **môsâdâh,** *mo-saw-daw´*; feminine of 4144; a *foundation*:—foundation.

A feminine singular noun meaning foundation. It always occurs in the plural. It often refers to the foundation of the world (2Sa 22:16; Ps 18:15[16]) or to the base of a man-made construction, such as a building or wall (Jer 51:26).

4147. מוֹסֵר, **môwsêr,** *mo-sare´*; also (in plural) feminine מוֹסֵרָה, **môwsêrâh,** *mo-say-raw´*; or מֹסְרָה, **môsʻrâh,** *mo-ser-aw´*; from 3256; (properly) *chastisement,* i.e. (by implication) a *halter;* (figurative) *restraint*:—band, bond.

4148. מוּסָר, **mûwsâr,** *moo-sawr´*; from 3256; (properly) *chastisement;* (figurative) *reproof, warning* or *instruction;* also *restraint*:—bond, chastening ([-eth]), chastisement, check, correction, discipline, doctrine, instruction, rebuke.

A masculine noun meaning instruction, discipline. It occurs almost exclusively in the poetic and prophetic literature. In Proverbs, instruction and discipline come primarily through the father (or a father figure such as a teacher) and usually are conveyed orally but may come via the rod (Pr 1:8; 13:1, 24). Those who are wise receive instruction, but fools reject it (Pr 1:7; 8:33; 13:1; 15:5). The reception of instruction brings life, wisdom, and the favour of the Lord (Pr 4:13; 8:33); however, rejection brings death, poverty, and shame (Pr 5:23; 13:18). Apart from Proverbs, this noun is always associated with God—with two exceptions (Job 20:3; Jer 10:8). When God's instruction is rejected, it results in punishments of various kinds (Job 36:10; Jer 7:28; 17:23; 32:33; Zep 3:2). The discipline of the Lord is not to be despised, for it is a demonstration of His love for His children (Job 5:17; Pr 3:11; cf. Heb 12:5, 6). The supreme demonstration of God's love came when Jesus Christ bore the "chastisement of our peace" (Isa 53:5).

4149. מוֹסֵרָה, **Môwsêrâh,** *mo-say-raw´*; or (plural) מֹסֵרוֹת, **Môsʻrôwth,** *mo-ser-othe´*; feminine of 4147; *correction* or *corrections; Moserah* or *Moseroth,* a place in the Desert:—Mosera, Moseroth.

4150. מוֹעֵד, **môwʻêd,** *mo-ade´*; or מֹעֵד, **môʻêd,** *mo-ade´*; or (feminine) מוֹעָדָה, **môwʻâdâh,** *mo-aw-daw´*; (2Ch 8:13), from 3259; (properly) an *appointment,* i.e. a fixed *time* or season; (specifically) a *festival;* conventionally a *year;* (by implication) an *assembly* (as convened for a definite purpose); (technically) the *congregation;* (by extension) the *place of meeting;* also a *signal* (as appointed beforehand):—appointed (sign, time), (place of, solemn) assembly, congregation, (set, solemn) feast, (appointed, due) season, solemn (-ity), synagogue, (set) time (appointed).

A masculine noun meaning an appointed time or place. It can signify an appointed meeting time in general (Ge 18:14; Ex 13:10); a specific appointed time, usually for a sacred feast or festival (Hos 9:5; 12:9[10]); the time of the birds' migration (Jer 8:7); the time of wine (Hos 2:9[11]); the same time next year (Ge 17:21). In addition to the concept of time, this word can also signify an appointed meeting place: "The mount of the congregation" identifies the meeting place of God or the gods (Isa 14:13), and "the house appointed for all living" identifies the meeting place of the dead—that is, the netherworld (Job 30:23). Moreover, the term is used to distinguish those places where God's people were to focus on God and their relationship with Him, which would include: the tent of meeting (Ex 33:7); the Temple (La 2:6); the synagogue (Ps 74:8).

4151. מוֹעָד, **môwʻâd,** *mo-awd´*; from 3259; (properly) an *assembly* [as in 4150]; (figurative) a *troop*:—appointed time.

A masculine noun meaning appointed place. This word is used only once in the OT and comes from the verb *yâʻad* (3259), meaning to appoint. It describes the appointed places for soldiers, often translated as ranks (Isa 14:31).

4152. מוּעָדָה, **mûwʻâdâh,** *moo-aw-daw´*; from 3259; an *appointed* place, i.e. *asylum*:—appointed.

4153. מוֹעַדְיָה, **Môwʻadyâh,** *mo-ad-yaw´*; from 4151 and 3050; *assembly of Jah; Moädjah,* an Israelite:—Moadiah. Compare 4573.

4154. מוּעֶדֶת, **mûwʻedeth,** *moo-eh´-deth;* feminine passive participle of 4571; (properly) *made to slip,* i.e. *dislocated*:—out of joint.

4155. מוּעָף, **mûwʻâph,** *moo-awf´*; from 5774; (properly) *covered,* i.e. *dark;* (abstract) *obscurity,* i.e. *distress*:—dimness.

4156. מוֹעֵצָה, **môw'êtsâh**, *mo-ay-tsaw´*; from 3289; a *purpose*:—counsel, device.

4157. מוּעָקָה, **mûw'âqâh**, *moo-aw-kaw´*; from 5781; *pressure*, i.e. (figurative) *distress*:—affliction.

4158. מוֹפַעַת, **Môwpha'ath**, *mo-fah´-ath*; (Jer 48:21), or מֵיפַעַת, **Mêypha'ath**, *may-fah´-ath*; or מֵפַעַת, **Mêpha'ath**, *may-fah´-ath*; from 3313; *illuminative; Mophaath* or *Mephaath*, a place in Palestine:—Mephaath.

4159. מוֹפֵת, **môwphêth**, *mo-faith´*; or מֹפֵת, **môphêth**, *mo-faith´*; from 3302 in the sense of *conspicuousness*; a *miracle*; (by implication) a *token* or *omen*:—miracle, sign, wonder (-ed at).

A masculine noun meaning a wonder, a sign, a portent, a token. It is often a phenomenon displaying God's power, used to describe some of the plagues God placed on Egypt (Ex 7:3; 11:9) directly or through Moses and Aaron (Ex 4:21; 11:10); the psalmists sang of these wonders (Ps 105:5); false prophets could work counterfeit wonders (Dt 13:1[2], 2[3]); God worked these signs in the heavens sometimes (Joel 2:30[3:3]). Even people can become signs and tokens. Both Isaiah and his children served as signs to Israel (Isa 8:18), as did Ezekiel (12:6, 11; Zec 3:8). The curses that God described in the Law would be signs and wonders to cause His people to see His activity in judging them if they broke His covenant (Dt 28:46).

4160. מֵץ, **mêts**, *mayts*; a primitive root; to *press*, i.e. (figurative) to *oppress*:—extortioner.

4161. מוֹצָא, **môwtsâ**, *mo-tsaw´*; or מֹצָא, **môtsâ**, *mo-tsaw´*; from 3318; a *going forth*, i.e. (the act) an *egress*, or (the place) an *exit*; hence a *source* or *product*; specifically *dawn*, the *rising* of the sun (the *East*), *exportation*, *utterance*, a *gate*, a *fountain*, a *mine*, a *meadow* (as producing grass):—brought out, bud, that which came out, east, going forth, goings out, that which (thing that) is gone out, outgoing, proceeded out, spring, vein, [water-] course [springs].

4162. מוֹצָא, **môwtsâ**, *mo-tsaw´*; the same as 4161; *Motsa*, the name of two Israelites:—Moza.

4163. מוֹצָאָה, **môwtsâ'âh**, *mo-tsaw-aw´*; feminine of 4161; a family *descent*; also a *sewer* [margin; compare 6675]:—draught house; going forth.

4164. מוּצַק, **mûwtsaq**, *moo-tsak´*; or מוּצָק, **mûwtsâq**, *moo-tsawk´*; from 3332; *narrowness*; (figurative) *distress*:—anguish, is straitened, straitness.

4165. מוּצָק, **mûwtsâq**, *moo-tsawk´*; from 5694; (properly) *fusion*, i.e. (literal) a *casting* (of metal); (figurative) a *mass* (of clay):—casting, hardness.

4166. מוּצָקָה, **mûwtsâqâh**, *moo-tsaw-kaw´*; or מֻצָקָה, **mutsâqâh**, *moo-tsaw-kaw´*; from 3332; (properly) something *poured* out, i.e. a *casting* (of metal); (by implication) a *tube* (as cast):—when it was cast, pipe.

4167. מוּק, **mûwq**, *mook*; a primitive root; to *jeer*, i.e. (intensive) *blaspheme*:—be corrupt.

A verb meaning to mock, to deride. This word is used only once in the OT. In Ps 73:8, it describes the proud, mocking speech of the wicked.

4168. מוֹקֵד, **môwqêd**, *mo-kade´*; from 3344; a *fire* or *fuel*; (abstract) a *conflagration*:—burning, hearth.

4169. מוֹקְדָה, **môwq^edâh**, *mo-ked-aw´*; feminine of 4168; *fuel*:—burning.

4170. מוֹקֵשׁ, **môwqêsh**, *mo-kashe´*; or מֹקֵשׁ, **môqêsh**, *mo-kashe´*; from 3369; a *noose* (for catching animals) (literal or figurative); (by implication) a *hook* (for the nose):—be ensnared, gin, (is) snare (-d), trap.

A masculine noun meaning a snare, a trap, bait. The proper understanding of this Hebrew word is the lure or bait placed in a hunter's trap. From this sense comes the primary use of the term to mean the snare itself. It is used to signify a trap by which birds or beasts are captured (Am 3:5); a moral pitfall (Pr 18:7; 20:25); and anything that lures one to ruin and disaster (Jgs 2:3; Pr 29:6).

4171. מוּר, **mûwr**, *moor*; a primitive root; to *alter*; (by implication) to *barter*, to *dispose of*:—× at all, (ex-) change, remove.

4172. מוֹרָא, **môwrâ**, *mo-raw´*; or מֹרָא, **môrâ**, *mo-raw´*; or מוֹרָה, **môwrâh**, *mo-raw´*; (Ps 9:20), from 3372; *fear*; (by implication) a *fearful thing* or deed:—dread, (that ought to be) fear (-ed), terribleness, terror.

A masculine noun meaning fear, terror, reverence. The primary concept underlying the meaning of this word is a sense of fear or awe that causes separation or brings respect. It is used to denote the fear animals have for humans (Ge 9:2); terror on the Canaanites as Israel entered the Promised Land (Dt 11:25); the reverence due those in authority (Mal 1:6); an object of reverence, which for Israel was to be God, yĕhôwâh (3068), alone (Isa 8:12, 13); a spectacle or event that inspires awe or horror (Dt 4:34; 34:12; Jer 32:21).

4173. מוֹרַג, **môwrag,** *mo-rag´*; or מֹרַג, **môrag,** *mo-rag´*; from an unused root meaning to *triturate*; a threshing *sledge*:—threshing instrument.

4174. מוֹרָד, **môwrâd,** *mo-rawd´*; from 3381; a *descent*; (architecturally) an ornamental *appendage*, perhaps a *festoon*:—going down, steep place, thin work.

4175. מוֹרֶה, **môwreh,** *mo-reh´*; from 3384; an *archer*; also *teacher* or *teaching*; also the *early rain* [see 3138]:—(early) rain.

4176. מוֹרֶה, **Môwreh,** *mo-reh´*; or מֹרֶה, **Môreh,** *mo-reh´*; the same as 4175; *Moreh*, a Canaanite; also a hill (perhaps named from him):—Moreh.

4177. מוֹרָה, **môwrâh,** *mo-raw´*; from 4171 in the sense of *shearing*; a *razor*:—razor.

4178. מוֹרָט, **môwrâṭ,** *mo-rawt´*; from 3399; *obstinate,* i.e. independent:—peeled.

4179. מוֹרִיָּה, **Môwrîyyâh,** *mo-ree-yaw´*; or מֹרִיָּה, **Môrîyyâh,** *mo-ree-yaw´*; from 7200 and 3050; *seen of Jah; Morijah,* a hill in Palestine:—Moriah.

4180. מוֹרָשׁ, **môwrâsh,** *mo-rawsh´*; from 3423; a *possession*; (figurative) *delight*:—possession, thought.

4181. מוֹרָשָׁה, **môwrâshâh,** *mo-raw-shaw´*; feminine of 4180; a *possession*:—heritage, inheritance, possession.

A feminine noun meaning a possession, an inheritance. This word comes from the verb *yârash* (3423), meaning to take possession of, to inherit. This word is used to refer to God giving land to Israel as an inheritance (Ex 6:8; Eze 11:15; 33:24), but it also refers to God giving the

land to other nations to possess (Eze 25:10). In one instance, the Edomites took land as a possession for themselves (Eze 36:5). In its other instances, God gave the Law as a possession (Dt 33:4); God delivered the people of Israel over to other nations for a possession (Eze 25:4; 36:3); and the people took the high places as possessions (Eze 36:2).

4182. מוֹרֶשֶׁת גַּת, **Môwresheth Gath,** *mo-reh´-sheth gath*; from 3423 and 1661; *possession of Gath; Moresheth-Gath,* a place in Palestine:—Moresheth-gath.

4183. מוֹרַשְׁתִּי, **Môwrashtîy,** *mo-rash-tee´*; patrial from 4182; a *Morashtite* or inhabitant of Moresheth-Gath:—Morashthite.

4184. מוּשׁ, **mûwsh,** *moosh*; a primitive root; to *touch*:—feel, handle.

4185. מוּשׁ, **mûwsh,** *moosh*; a primitive root [perhaps rather the same as 4184 through the idea of receding by *contact*]; to *withdraw* (both literal and figurative, whether intrans. or trans.):—cease, depart, go back, remove, take away.

4186. מוֹשָׁב, **môwshâb,** *mo-shawb´*; or מֹשָׁב, **môshâb,** *mo-shawb´*; from 3427; a *seat*; (figurative) a *site*; (abstract) a *session*; (by extension) an *abode* (the place or the time); (by implication) *population*:—assembly, dwell in, dwelling (-place), wherein (that) dwelt (in), inhabited place, seat, sitting, situation, sojourning.

A masculine noun meaning a seat, a habitation, a dwelling place, inhabitants. The primary notion giving rise to this word is that of remaining or abiding in a given location. It signifies a place to be seated (1Sa 20:18; Job 29:7); the sitting of an assembly (Ps 107:32); the location or situation of a city (2Ki 2:19); a place of habitation (Ge 27:39; Nu 24:21); the inhabitants of a particular residence (2Sa 9:12). The psalmist stated that the Lord Himself chose Zion as His dwelling place (Ps 132:13).

4187. מוּשִׁי, **Mûwshîy,** *moo-shee´*; or מֻשִׁי, **Mushshîy,** *mush-shee´*; from 4184; *sensitive; Mushi,* a Levite:—Mushi.

4188. מוּשִׁי, **Mûwshîy,** *moo-shee´*; patronymic from 4187; a *Mushite* (collective) or descendants of Mushi:—Mushites.

4189. מוֹשְׁכָה, **môwsh^ekâh,** *mo-shek-aw´*; active participle feminine of 4900; something *drawing*, i.e. (figurative) a *cord*:—band.

4190. מוֹשָׁעָה, **môwshâ‘âh,** *mo-shaw-aw´*; from 3467; *deliverance*:—salvation.

A feminine noun meaning salvation, deliverance. This word appears only once in the Bible, signifying the saving acts of the Lord (Ps 68:20[21]).

4191. מוּת, **mûwth,** *mooth*; a primitive root; to *die* (literal or figurative); (causative) to *kill*:— × at all, × crying, (be) dead (body, man, one), (put to, worthy of) death, destroy (-er), (cause to, be like to, must) die, kill, necro [-mancer], × must needs, slay, × surely, × very suddenly, × in [no] wise.

A verb meaning to die, to kill, to put to death, to execute. It occurs in the simple stem of the verb in 600 of its 809 occurrences, meaning to be dead or to die. It indicates a natural death in peace at an old age, as in the case of Abraham (Ge 25:8; Jgs 8:32). Dying, however, was not intended to be a natural aspect of being human. It came about through unbelief and rebellion against God (Ge 3:4) so that Adam and Eve died. The word describes dying because of failure to pursue a moral life (Pr 5:23; 10:21). It describes various kinds of death: at the hand of God—the Lord smote Nabal, and he died (1Sa 25:37); the execution of the offender in capital offence cases (Ge 2:17; 20:7); the sons of Job from the violence of a mighty storm (Job 1:19); a murderer could be handed over to die at the hand of the avenger of blood (Dt 19:12). The prophets declared that many people would die by the hand of the Lord when He would bring the sword, famine, and plagues upon them (Jer 11:22; cf. 14:12). The present participle of this form may indicate someone who is dying (Ge 20:3); dead or a corpse (Dt 25:5; Isa 22:2). People could also be put to death by legal or human authority (Ge 42:20; Ex 10:28).

The word indicates the dying of various non-human, nonanimal entities. A nation could die, such as Moab, Ephraim, or Israel (Eze 18:31; Hos 13:1; Am 2:2). A more powerful use of the verb is its description of the death of wisdom (Job 12:2) or courage (1Sa 25:37).

4192. מוּת, **Mûwth,** *mooth*; (Ps 48:14), or לְבֵן מוּת, **Mûwth Labbên,** *mooth lab-bane´*; from 4191 and 1121 with the preposition and article interposed; "*To die for the son*," probably the title of a popular song:—death, Muth-labben.

A phrase found only in the superscription at the top of Ps 9. It is part of the musical directions for the singing of this psalm, yet the meaning is ambiguous. Various renderings have been offered by interpreters, the most likely options being that the phrase is either a title of a tune to which the psalm was to be sung or that the phrase means "death to the son" or "to die for the son." Also possible is the combination of these two options, namely, that the phrase is a title of a tune called "Death to the Son"/ "To die for the Son" to which Ps 9 was to be sung.

4193. מוֹת, **môwth,** *mohth*; (Chaldee); corresponding to 4194; *death*:—death.

An Aramaic masculine noun meaning death. In writing a letter to Ezra the scribe, King Artaxerxes of Persia used this term to designate execution as one of the viable means of punishment available to Ezra in dealing with those who refused to obey the Law of God and the law of the king in the newly resettled land of Israel (Ezr 7:26). The term is the equivalent of the Hebrew noun mâweth (4194).

4194. מָוֶת, **mâveth,** *maw´-veth*; from 4191; *death* (natural or violent); (concrete) the *dead*, their place or state (*hades*); (figurative) *pestilence, ruin*:—(be) dead ([-ly]), death, die (-d).

A masculine noun meaning death. The term signifies death occurring by both natural and violent means (natural: Ge 27:7, 10; Nu 16:29; violent: Le 16:1; Jgs 16:30). In other texts, it designates the place where the dead dwell known as Sheol (sh^e´ôwl [7585]; Job 28:22; Ps 9:13[14]; Pr 7:27). Because death and disease are so intimately related and due to the context, the word suggests the intended meaning of deadly disease, plague, epidemic, or pestilence (Job 27:15; Jer 15:2, 18:21, 43:11). Figuratively, the term expresses the idea of ruin and destruction, especially when contrasted with the desirable notions of life, prosperity, and happiness (Pr 11:19; 12:28; cf. Ex 10:17). This noun is derived from the verb mûth (4191).

4195. מוֹתָר, **môwthâr,** *mo-thar´*; from 3498; (literal) *gain*; (figurative) *superiority*:—plenteousness, preeminence, profit.

4196. מִזְבֵּחַ, **mizbêach,** *miz-bay´-akh*; from 2076; an *altar*:—altar.

A masculine noun meaning the altar, the place of sacrifice. It is a noun formed from the verb *zâbach* (2076), which means to slaughter an animal, usually for a sacrifice. The sacrificial system was at the focal point of the pre-Israelite and Israelite systems of worship since the sacrifice and subsequent meal were used to solemnize a covenant or treaty and to symbolize a positive relationship between the two parties. Noah built an altar and offered sacrifices on exiting the ark (Ge 8:20); the patriarchs built altars and sacrificed at various points along their journeys: Abram (Ge 12:7, 8; 22:9); Isaac (Ge 26:25); Jacob (Ge 35:7); Moses (Ex 24:4). At Mount Sinai, God commanded that the Israelites build the tabernacle and include two altars: a bronze altar in the courtyard for the sacrificing of animals (Ex 27:1–8; 38:1–7) and a golden altar inside the tabernacle for the burning of incense (Ex 30:1–10; 37:25–29). Solomon (1Ki 6:20, 22; 8:64) and Ezekiel (Eze 41:22; 43:13–17) followed a similar pattern. God also commanded that the altar for burnt offerings be made of earth or undressed stones because human working of the stones would defile it. Moreover, God commanded that the altar should have no steps so that human nakedness would not be exposed on it (Ex 20:24–26).

4197. מֶזֶג, **mezeg,** *meh´-zeg*; from an unused root meaning to *mingle* (water with wine); *tempered* wine:—liquor.

4198. מָזֶה, **mâzeh,** *maw-zeh´*; from an unused root meaning to *suck* out; *exhausted*:—burnt.

4199. מִזָּה, **Mizzâh,** *miz-zaw´*; probably from an unused root meaning to *faint* with fear; *terror*; *Mizzah*, an Edomite:—Mizzah.

4200. מָזוּ, **mâzûw,** *maw´-zoo*; probably from an unused root meaning to *gather* in; a *granary*:—garner.

4201. מְזוּזָה, **mᵉzûwzâh,** *mez-oo-zaw´*; or מְזֻזָה, **mᵉzu-zâh,** *mez-oo-zaw´*; from the same as 2123; a *door-post* (as *prominent*):—(door, side) post.

4202. מָזוֹן, **mâzôwn,** *maw-zone´*; from 2109; *food*:—meat, victual.

4203. מָזוֹן, **mâzôwn,** *maw-zone´*; (Chaldee); corresponding to 4202:—meat.

4204. מָזוֹר, **mâzôwr,** *maw-zore´*; from 2114 in the sense of *turning aside* from truth; *treachery*, i.e. a *plot*:—wound.

4205. מָזוֹר, **mâzôwr,** *maw-zore´*; or מָזֹר, **mâzôr,** *maw-zore´*; from 2115 in the sense of *binding up*; a *bandage*, i.e. remedy; hence a *sore* (as needing a compress):—bound up, wound.

4206. מָזִיחַ, **mâzîyach,** *maw-zee´-akh*; or מֵזַח, **mê-zach,** *may-zakh´*; from 2118; a *belt* (as movable):—girdle, strength.

4207. מַזְלֵג, **mazlêg,** *maz-layg´*; or (feminine) מִזְלָגָה, **mizlâgâh,** *miz-law-gaw´*; from an unused root meaning to *draw* up; a *fork*:—fleshhook.

4208. מַזָּלָה, **mazzâlâh,** *maz-zaw-law´*; apparently from 5140 in the sense of *raining*; a *constellation*, i.e. Zodiacal sign (perhaps as affecting the weather):—planet. Compare 4216.

4209. מְזִמָּה, **mᵉzimmâh,** *mez-im-maw´*; from 2161; a *plan*, usually evil (*machination*), sometimes good (*sagacity*):—(wicked) device, discretion, intent, witty invention, lewdness, mischievous (device), thought, wickedly.

A feminine noun meaning a plan, a thought. Most often the term denotes the evil plans, schemes, or plots humanity devises that are contrary to God's righteous decrees. The Lord declared to Jeremiah that in carrying out their evil, idolatrous plans, His people forfeited their right to enter His house (i.e. the Temple, Jer 11:15). The psalmist prayed that the wicked might be ensnared by the very schemes they had planned to unleash on the poor (Ps 10:2). The cunning plans that God's enemies intend to execute against Him never succeed (Ps 21:11[12]; cf. Ps 37:7). Moreover, those who plot evil are condemned and hated by Him (Pr 12:2, 14:17). Often, the wicked are so blinded by pride that their only thought about God is that He doesn't exist (Ps 10:4). Another significant use of this word occurs when it describes an intention of God and so conveys the idea of purpose or plan. After the Lord confronted Job in the whirlwind, Job was deeply humbled and acknowledged that no purpose of the Lord's can be thwarted (Job 42:2). The Lord's anger so burned on account of the false prophets of Jeremiah's day that it would not be turned back until He had executed and accomplished the purpose of His heart against them (Jer 23:20; cf. Jer 30:24). The Lord's purpose for Babylon was to utterly destroy it for all the evil they had committed against Jerusalem and the Temple (Jer 51:11). In Proverbs, the word often conveys the sense of prudence, discretion, and wisdom. In his prologue to the book of Proverbs, Solomon expressed that one reason he was writing the work was to impart discretion to young men (Pr 1:4; cf. Pr 5:2). Solomon urged them to hold on to wisdom and not let it out of their sight once they acquired it (Pr 3:21). Wisdom and prudence go hand in hand (Pr 8:12). This noun derives from the verb *zâmam* (2161).

4210. מִזְמוֹר, **mizmôwr**, *miz-more´*; from 2167; (properly) instrumental *music*; (by implication) a *poem* set to notes:—psalm.

4211. מַזְמֵרָה, **mazmêrâh**, *maz-may-raw´*; from 2168; a *pruning-knife*:—pruning-hook.

4212. מְזַמֶּרֶת, **mᵉzammereth**, *mez-am-mer-eth´*; from 2168; a *tweezer* (only in the plural):—snuffers.

4213. מִזְעָר, **miz'âr**, *miz-awr´*; from the same as 2191; *fewness*; (by implication) as superlative *diminutiveness*:—few, × very.

4214. מִזְרֶה, **mizreh**, *miz-reh´*; from 2219; a *winnowing shovel* (as scattering the chaff):—fan.

4215. מְזָרֶה, **mᵉzâreh**, *mez-aw-reh´*; apparently from 2219; (properly) a *scatterer*, i.e. the north *wind* (as dispersing clouds; only in plural):—north.

4216. מַזָּרָה, **mazzârâh**, *maz-zaw-raw´*; apparently from 5144 in the sense of *distinction*; some noted *constellation* (only in the plural), (perhaps collectively) the *zodiac*:—Mazzaroth. Compare 4208.

4217. מִזְרָח, **mizrâch**, *miz-rawkh´*; from 2224; *sunrise*, i.e. the *east*:—east (side, -ward), (sun-)rising, (of the sun).

4218. מִזְרָע, **mizrâ'**, *miz-raw´*; from 2232; a planted *field*:—thing sown.

4219. מִזְרָק, **mizrâq**, *miz-rawk´*; from 2236; a *bowl* (as if for sprinkling):—bason, bowl.

4220. מֵחַ, **mêach**, *may´-akh*; from 4229 in the sense of *greasing; fat*; (figurative) *rich*:—fatling (one).

4221. מֹחַ, **môach**, *mo´-akh*; from the same as 4220; *fat*, i.e. marrow:—marrow.

4222. מָחָא, **mâchâ'**, *maw-khaw´*; a primitive root; to *rub* or *strike* the hands together (in exultation):—clap.

4223. מְחָא, **mᵉchâ'**, *mekh-aw´*; (Chaldee); corresponding to 4222; to *strike* in pieces; also to *arrest*; specifically to *impale*:—hang, smite, stay.

An Aramaic verb meaning to smite, to strike. The term corresponds closely with the Hebrew verbs *mâkâh* (4229) and *nâkâh* (5221). When combined with the prepositional phrase *bᵉyad* (3027) meaning on the hand, the term attains the idiomatic sense to restrain, to hinder, to prevent, or to stay (Da 4:35[32]). On one occasion, the word vividly described the penalty of impalement (on a beam) which awaited any individual who dared to alter King Darius' edict concerning the rebuilding of the Temple in Jerusalem (Ezr 6:11).

4224. מַחֲבֵא, **machăbê'**, *makh-ab-ay´*; or מַחֲבֹא, **machăbô'**, *makh-ab-o´*; from 2244; a *refuge*:—hiding (lurking) place.

4225. מַחְבֶּרֶת, **machbereth**, *makh-beh´-reth*; from 2266; a *junction*, i.e. seam or sewed piece:—coupling.

4226. מְחַבְּרָה, **mᵉchabbᵉrâh**, *mekh-ab-ber-aw´*; from 2266; a *joiner*, i.e. brace or cramp:—coupling, joining.

4227. מַחֲבַת, **machăbath**, *makh-ab-ath´*; from the same as 2281; a *pan* for baking in:—pan.

4228. מַחֲגֹרֶת, **machăgôreth**, *makh-ag-o´-reth*; from 2296; a *girdle*:—girding.

4229. מָחָה, **mâchâh**, *maw-khaw´*; a primitive root; (properly) to *stroke* or *rub*; (by implication) to *erase*; also to *smooth* (as if with oil), i.e. *grease* or make fat; also to *touch*, i.e. reach to:—abolish, blot out, destroy, full of marrow, put out, reach unto, × utterly, wipe (away, out).

A verb meaning to wipe, to wipe out. This term is often connected with divine judgment. It is used of God wiping out all life in the flood (Ge 7:23); destroying Jerusalem (2Ki 21:13); and threatening to wipe out Israel's name (Dt 9:14). God also wipes out sin (Ps 51:1[3]; Isa 43:25); and wipes away tears (Isa 25:8). Humans also act as the subject of this verb; the Israelites nearly wiped out the Benjamites (Jgs 21:17); and a prostitute wipes her mouth (Pr 30:20).

4230. מְחוּגָה, **mᵉchûwgâh,** *mekh-oo-gaw´*; from 2328; an instrument for marking a circle, i.e. *compasses:*—compass.

4231. מָחוֹז, **mâchôwz,** *maw-khoze´*; from an unused root meaning to *enclose;* a *harbor* (as *shut* in by the shore):—haven.

4232. מְחוּיָאֵל, **Mᵉchûwyâ´êl,** *mekh-oo-yaw-ale´*; or מְחִיָּיאֵל, **Mᵉchîyyây´êl,** *mekh-ee-yaw-ale´*; from 4229 and 410; *smitten of God; Mechujael* or *Mechijael,* an antediluvian patriarch:—Mehujael.

4233. מַחֲוִים, **Machăvîym,** *makh-av-eem´*; apparently a patrial, but from an unknown place (in the plural only for a singular); a *Machavite* or inhabitant of some place named Machaveh:—Mahavite.

4234. מָחוֹל, **mâchôwl,** *maw-khole´*; from 2342; a (round) *dance:*—dance (-cing).

4235. מָחוֹל, **Mâchôwl,** *maw-khole´*; the same as 4234; *dancing; Machol,* an Israelite:—Mahol.

4236. מַחֲזֶה, **machăzeh,** *makh-az-eh´*; from 2372; a *vision:*—vision.

A masculine noun meaning vision. This word is used only four times in the OT and comes from the verb *châzâh* (2372), meaning to see. God came to Abram in a vision (Ge 15:1); Balaam could rightly prophesy because he saw a vision of the Almighty (Nu 24:4, 16). However, false prophets saw a false vision and thus prophesied falsely (Eze 13:7).

4237. מֶחֱזָה, **mechĕzâh,** *mekh-ez-aw´*; from 2372; a *window:*—light.

4238. מַחֲזִיאוֹת, **Machăzîy´ôwth,** *makh-az-ee-oth´*; feminine plural from 2372; *visions; Machazioth,* an Israelite:—Mahazioth.

4239. מְחִי, **mᵉchîy,** *mekh-ee´*; from 4229; a *stroke,* i.e. battering-*ram:*—engines.

4240. מְחִידָא, **Mᵉchîydâ´,** *mekh-ee-daw´*; from 2330; *junction; Mechida,* one of the Nethinim:—Mehida.

4241. מִחְיָה, **michyâh,** *mikh-yaw´*; from 2421; *preservation of life;* hence *sustenance;* also the live flesh, i.e. the *quick:*—preserve life, quick, recover selves, reviving, sustenance, victuals.

A feminine singular noun meaning preservation of life, sustenance, raw flesh. Joseph said he was sent to Egypt for the preservation of life (Ge 45:5). The term is also used to mean food or sustenance (Jgs 6:4; 17:10). The Levitical Law used the term to refer to raw flesh because of a skin disease (Le 13:10, 24).

4242. מְחִיר, **mᵉchîyr,** *mekh-eer´*; from an unused root meaning to *buy; price, payment, wages:*—gain, hire, price, sold, worth.

4243. מְחִיר, **Mᵉchîyr,** *mekh-eer´*; the same as 4242; *price; Mechir,* an Israelite:—Mehir.

4244. מַחְלָה, **Machlâh,** *makh-law´*; from 2470; *sickness; Machlah,* the name apparently of two Israelitesses:—Mahlah.

4245. מַחֲלֶה, **machăleh,** *makh-al-eh´*; or (feminine) מַחֲלָה, **machălâh,** *makh-al-aw´*; from 2470; *sickness:*—disease, infirmity, sickness.

4246. מְחֹלָה, **mᵉchôlâh,** *mekh-o-law´*; feminine of 4234; a *dance:*—company, dances (-cing).

4247. מְחִלָּה, **mᵉchillâh,** *mekh-il-law´*; from 2490; a *cavern* (as if excavated):—cave.

4248. מַחְלוֹן, **Machlôwn,** *makh-lone´*; from 2470; *sick; Machlon,* an Israelite:—Mahlon.

4249. מַחְלִי, **Machlîy,** *makh-lee´*; from 2470; *sick; Machli,* the name of two Israelites:—Mahli.

4250. מַחְלִי, **Machlîy,** *makh-lee´*; patronymic from 4249; a *Machlite* or (collective) descendants of Machli:—Mahlites.

4251. מַחֲלָיִים, **machăluyîym,** *makh-ah-loo-yeem´*; from 2470; a *disease:*—disease.

4252. מַחֲלָף, **machălâph,** *makh-al-awf´*; from 2498; a (sacrificial) *knife* (as *gliding* through the flesh):—knife.

4253. מַחְלָפָה, **machlâphâh,** *makh-law-faw´*; from 2498; a *ringlet* of hair (as *gliding* over each other):—lock.

4254. מַחֲלָצָה, **machălâtsâh,** *makh-al-aw-tsaw´*; from 2502; a *mantle* (as easily *drawn off*):—changeable suit of apparel, change of raiment.

4255. מַחְלְקָה, **machlᵉqâh,** *makh-lek-aw´*; (Chaldee); corresponding to 4256; a *section* (of the Levites):—course.

4256. מַחֲלֹקֶת, **machălôqeth,** *makh-al-o´-keth*; from 2505; a *section* (of Levites, people or soldiers):—company, course, division, portion. See also 5555.

4257. מַחֲלַת, **mâchălath,** *mawkh-al-ath´*; from 2470; *sickness; Machalath,* probably the title (initial word) of a popular song:—Mahalath.

4258. מַחֲלַת, **Mâchălath,** *mawkh-al-ath´*; the same as 4257; *sickness; Machalath,* the name of an Ishmaelitess and of an Israelitess:—Mahalath.

4259. מְחֹלָתִי, **Mᵉchôlâthîy,** *mekh-o-law-thee´*; patrial from 65; a *Mecholathite* or inhabitant of Abel-Mecholah:—Mecho-lathite.

4260. מַחְמָאֹת, **machmâ'ôth,** *makh-maw-oth´*; a denominative from 2529; something *buttery* (i.e. unctuous and pleasant), as (figurative) *flattery*:— × than butter.

4261. מַחְמָד, **machmâd,** *makh-mawd´*; from 2530; *delightful;* hence a *delight,* i.e. object of affection or desire:—beloved, desire, goodly, lovely, pleasant (thing).

4262. מַחְמֹד, **machmôd,** *makh-mode´*; from 2530; *desired;* hence a *valuable:*—pleasant thing.

4263. מַחְמָל, **machmâl,** *makh-mawl´*; from 2550; (properly) *sympathy;* (by paronomasia with 4261) *delight:*—pitieth.

A masculine noun meaning an object of mercy. This word occurs only once in the OT and comes from the verb *châmal* (2550), meaning to spare. In Eze 24:21, this word is used to describe the compassion and delight that the Temple was to the Israelites. In this section of Scripture, Ezekiel's desire and delight for his wife is compared to Israel's desire and delight for the Temple (Eze 24:15–27).

4264. מַחֲנֶה, **machăneh,** *makh-an-eh´*; from 2583; an *encampment* (of travellers or troops); hence an *army,* whether literal (of soldiers) or figurative (of dancers, angels, cattle, locusts, stars; or even the sacred courts):—army, band, battle, camp, company, drove, host, tents.

A masculine noun meaning a camp, an army, and a company. This word comes from the verb *chânâh* (2583), meaning to encamp. The basic idea of this word is that of a multitude of people who have gathered together (Eze 1:24). This word is often used within the context of travel, like the wandering Israelites (Ex 14:19, 20; Nu 4:5); or within the context of war (1Sa 17:1; 2Ki 6:24; 19:35). This word is most often used of Israel but is also used to describe foreign nations (Jos 10:5; Jgs 7:8–11, 13–15; 1Sa 29:1); or even God's encampment (Ge 32:2[3]; 1Ch 12:22[23]).

4265. מַחֲנֵה־דָן, **Machănêh-Dân,** *makh-an-ay´-dawn*; from 4264 and 1835; *camp of Dan; Machaneh-Dan,* a place in Palestine:—Mahaneh-dan.

4266. מַחֲנַיִם, **Machănayim,** *makh-an-ah´-yim*; dual of 4264; *double camp; Machanajim,* a place in Palestine:—Mahanaim.

4267. מַחֲנַק, **machănaq,** *makh-an-ak´*; from 2614; *choking:*—strangling.

4268. מַחְסֶה, **machseh,** *makh-as-eh´*; or מַחְסֶה, **machseh,** *makh-seh´*; from 2620; a *shelter* (literal or figurative):—hope, (place of) refuge, shelter, trust.

4269. מַחְסֹום, **machsôwm,** *makh-sohm´*; from 2629; a *muzzle:*—bridle.

4270. מַחְסֹור, **machsôwr,** *makh-sore´*; or מַחְסֹר, **machsôr,** *makh-sore´*; from 2637; *deficiency;* hence *impoverishment:*—lack, need, penury, poor, poverty, want.

4271. מַחְסֵיָה, **Machsêyâh,** *makh-say-yaw´*; from 4268 and 3050; *refuge of* (i.e. *in*) *Jah; Machsejah,* an Israelite:—Maaseiah.

4272. מָחַץ, **machats,** *maw-khats´*; a primitive root; to *dash asunder;* (by implication) to *crush, smash* or violently *plunge;* (figurative) to *subdue* or *destroy:*—dip, pierce (through), smite (through), strike through, wound.

A verb meaning to wound severely, to pierce through, and to shatter. This word describes bodily destruction and is best illustrated in Jgs 5:26, where Jael pierced through Sisera's head from temple to temple with a tent peg. David used this word to describe some of his victories in which those wounded were not able to rise again (2Sa 22:39; Ps 18:38[39]). In all other instances of this word, God is in complete control (Dt 32:39; Job 5:18) and completely shatters His enemies (Ps 68:21[22]; 110:5, 6; Hab 3:13). This word occurs only in the poetical passages of the OT, which highlights the intensity of this word.

4273. מַחַץ, **machats,** *makh´-ats*; from 4272; a *contusion:*—stroke.

A masculine singular noun meaning a severe wound. It occurs only once in the Hebrew Bible (Isa 30:26), referring to God healing His wounded people.

4274. מַחְצֵב, **machtsêb,** *makh-tsabe´*; from 2672; (properly) a *hewing;* (concrete) a *quarry:*—hewed (-n).

4275. מֶחֱצָה, **mechĕtsâh,** *mekh-ets-aw´*; from 2673; a *halving:*—half.

4276. מַחֲצִית, **machătsîyth,** *makh-ats-eeth´*; from 2673; a *halving* or the *middle:*—half (so much), mid [-day].

4277. מָחַק, **mâchaq,** *maw-khak´*; a primitive root; to *crush:*—smite off.

A verb meaning to utterly destroy. This word is used only once in the OT, where it is used as a near synonym with *mâchats* (4272), meaning to wound severely, to pierce through, or to shatter. It describes Jael's actions in destroying Sisera by driving a tent peg between his temples (Jgs 5:26).

4278. מֶחְקָר, **mechqâr,** *mekh-kawr´*; from 2713; (properly) *scrutinized,* i.e. (by implication) a *recess:*—deep place.

4279. מָחָר, **mâchâr,** *maw-khar´*; probably from 309; (properly) *deferred,* i.e. the *morrow;* usually (adverb) *tomorrow;* (indefinite) *hereafter:*—time to come, tomorrow.

4280. מַחֲרָאָה, **machărâ'âh,** *makh-ar-aw-aw´*; from the same as 2716; a *sink:*—draught house.

4281. מַחֲרֵשָׁה, **machărêshâh,** *makh-ar-ay-shaw´*; from 2790; probably a *pick*-axe:—mattock.

4282. מַחֲרֶשֶׁת, **machăresheth,** *makh-ar-eh´-sheth*; from 2790; probably a *hoe:*—share.

4283. מָחֳרָת, **mochŏrâth,** *mokh-or-awth´*; or מָחֳרָתָם, **mochŏrâthâm,** *mokh-or-aw-thawm´*; (1Sa 30:17), feminine from the same as 4279; the *morrow* or (adverb) *tomorrow:*—morrow, next day.

4284. מַחֲשָׁבָה, **machăshâbâh,** *makh-ash-aw-baw´*; or מַחֲשֶׁבֶת, **machăshebeth,** *makh-ash-eh´-beth;* from 2803; a *contrivance,* i.e. (concrete) a *texture, machine,* or (abstract) *intention, plan* (whether bad, a *plot;* or good, *advice*):—cunning (work), curious work, device (-sed), imagination, invented, means, purpose, thought.

A feminine noun meaning a thought, a purpose, a device, an intention. Largely poetic in its use, this Hebrew word means thought or the inventions that spring from such thoughts. It denotes the thoughts of the mind, either belonging to people (1Ch 28:9; Ps 94:11); or God (Jer 29:11; Mic 4:12); the plans or intentions that arise from these thoughts (Pr 15:22; 19:21); the schemes of a wicked heart (La 3:60); skillful inventions coming from the mind of an artist (Ex 31:4; 2Ch 26:15).

4285. מַחְשָׁךְ, **machshâk,** *makh-shawk´*; from 2821; *darkness;* (concrete) a *dark place:*—dark (-ness, place).

A masculine noun meaning a dark place, a hiding place, secrecy. The primary meaning of this word is darkness that is both blinding and confining. Poetically, it is used to draw an image of the darkness and inescapability of the grave (Ps 88:6[7]; La 3:6). The range of meaning also extends to the unknown things the Lord makes plain (Isa 42:16); and the back alleys where deviant behaviour abounds (Ps 74:20).

4286. מַחְשֹׂף, **machśôph,** *makh-sofe´*; from 2834; a *peeling:*—made appear.

4287. מַחַת, **Machath,** *makh´-ath*; probably from 4229; *erasure; Machath,* the name of two Israelites:—Mahath.

4288. מְחִתָּה, **mᵉchittâh,** *mekh-it-taw´*; from 2846; (properly) a *dissolution;* (concrete) a *ruin,* or (abstract) *consternation:*—destruction, dismaying, ruin, terror.

A feminine noun meaning destruction, ruin, terror. This word comes from the verb *châthath* (2865), meaning to be broken or afraid. It is used most often in a figurative sense in Proverbs to describe the ruin of the foolish (Pr 10:14; 13:3; 18:7); and the workers of iniquity (Pr 10:29; 21:15). It also describes the result of poverty (Pr 10:15); and the failure to support a prince (Pr 14:28). Elsewhere, this word depicted the power of God bringing destruction (Ps 89:40[41]), which resulted in an object lesson to all around (Jer 48:39). It is the blessing of

God that people live without this terror (Isa 54:14; Jer 17:17).

4289. מַחְתָּה, **machtâh,** *makh-taw´*; the same as 4288 in the sense of *removal*; a *pan* for live coals:—censer, firepan, snuffdish.

4290. מַחְתֶּרֶת, **machtereth,** *makh-teh´-reth*; from 2864; a *burglary*; (figurative) *unexpected examination*:—breaking up, secret search.

4291. מְטָא, **m^etâ'**, *met-aw´*; (Chaldee); or מְטָה, **m^etâh,** *met-aw´*; (Chaldee); apparently corresponding to 4672 in the intransitive sense of being found *present*; to *arrive, extend* or *happen*:—come, reach.

4292. מַטְאֲטֵא, **mat'ătê'**, *mat-at-ay´*; apparently a denominative from 2916; a *broom* (as removing dirt [compare English "to dust," i.e. remove dust]):—besom.

4293. מַטְבֵּחַ, **matbêach,** *mat-bay´-akh*; from 2873; *slaughter*:—slaughter.

4294. מַטֶּה, **matteh,** *mat-teh´*; or (feminine) מַטָּה, **mattâh,** *mat-taw´*; from 5186; a *branch* (as *extending*); (figurative) a *tribe*; also a *rod*, whether for chastising (figurative, *correction*), ruling (a *sceptre*), throwing (a *lance*), or walking (a *staff*; [figurative] a *support* of life, e.g., bread):—rod, staff, tribe.

A masculine noun meaning a rod, a staff, a branch, a tribe. This word signifies, variously, a walking stick (Ex 4:2); a branch of a tree (Eze 19:11ff.); a spear used in battle (Hab 3:14); an instrument of chastisement (Isa 10:24); an instrument used in the threshing process (Isa 28:27). Metaphorically, the image of a staff symbolizes the supply of food (Le 26:26); strength (Isa 14:5); and authority (Ps 110:2). Uniquely, the word also signifies a tribe, such as one of the twelve tribes of Israel (Nu 36:3, 4; Jos 13:29). The origin of this use derives from the image of the leader of the tribe going before the company with his staff in hand (cf. Nu 17:2[17]).

4295. מַטָּה, **mattâh,** *mat´-taw*; from 5786 with directive enclitic appended; *downward, below* or *beneath*; often adverbial with or without prefixes:—beneath, down (-ward), less, very low, under (-neath).

4296. מִטָּה, **mittâh,** *mit-taw´*; from 5186; a *bed* (as *extended*) for sleeping or eating; (by analogy) a *sofa, litter* or *bier*:—bed ([-chamber]), bier.

4297. מֻטֶּה, **mutteh,** *moot-teh´*; from 5186; a *stretching*, i.e. *distortion;* (figurative) *iniquity*:—perverseness.

A masculine noun meaning something perverted, twisted, warped. Occurring only in Eze 9:9, this word derives its meaning from a primitive root meaning to stretch, to incline, or to bend (5186). It was used by the Lord to describe the perverseness of Judah in distorting His Law and justice.

4298. מֻטָּה, **muttâh,** *moot-taw´*; from 5186; *expansion*:—stretching out.

4299. מַטְוֶה, **matveh,** *mat-veh´*; from 2901; something *spun*:—spun.

4300. מְטִיל, **mâṭîyl,** *mawt-eel´*; from 2904 in the sense of *hammering* out; an iron *bar* (as *forged*):—bar.

4301. מַטְמוֹן, **matmôwn,** *mat-mone´*; or מַטְמֹן, **mat-môn,** *mat-mone´*; or מַטְמֻן, **matmun,** *mat-moon´*; from 2934; a *secret* storehouse; hence a *secreted* valuable (buried); generally *money*:—hidden riches, (hid) treasure (-s).

4302. מַטָּע, **matta‘**, *mat-taw´*; from 5193; something *planted*, i.e. the *place* (a *garden* or vineyard), or the *thing* (a *plant*, figurative of men); (by implication) the *act*, *planting*:—plant (-ation, -ing).

4303. מַטְעָם, **mat‘am,** *mat-am´*; or (feminine) מַטְעַמָּה, **mat‘am-mâh,** *mat-am-maw´*; from 2938; a *delicacy*:—dainty (meat), savoury meat.

4304. מִטְפַּחַת, **mitpachath,** *mit-pakh´-ath*; from 2946; a wide *cloak* (for a woman):—vail, wimple.

4305. מָטַר, **mâṭar,** *maw-tar´*; a primitive root; to *rain*:—(cause to) rain (upon).

4306. מָטָר, **mâṭâr,** *maw-tawr´*; from 4305; *rain*:—rain.

4307. מַטָּרָא, **mattârâ'**, *mat-taw-raw´*; or מַטָּרָה, **mattârâh,** *mat-taw-raw´*; from 5201; a *jail* (as a *guard*-house); also an *aim* (as being closely *watched*):—mark, prison.

4308. מַטְרֵד, **Maṭrêd,** *mat-rade´*; from 2956; *propulsive; Matred,* an Edomitess:—Matred.

4309. מַטְרִי, **Maṭrîy**, *mat-ree´*; from 4305; *rainy; Matri*, an Israelite:—Matri.

4310. מִי, **mîy**, *me*; an interrogative pronoun of persons, as 4100 is of things, *who* (occasionally, by a peculiar idiom, of things); also (indefinite) *whoever*; often used in oblique construction with prefix or suffix:—any (man), × he, × him, + O that! what, which, who (-m, -se, -soever), + would to God.

4311. מֵידְבָא, **Mêyd**^e**bâ’**, *may-deb-aw´*; from 4325 and 1679; *water of quiet; Medeba*, a place in Palestine:—Medeba.

4312. מֵידָד, **Mêydâd**, *may-dawd´*; from 3032 in the sense of *loving; affectionate; Medad*, an Israelite:—Medad.

4313. מֵי הַיַּרְקוֹן, **Mêy hay-Yarqôwn**, *may hah´-ee-yar-kone´*; from 4325 and 3420 with the article interposed; *water of the yellowness; Mehaj-Jarkon*, a place in Palestine:—Me-jarkon.

4314. מֵי זָהָב, **Mêy Zâhâb**, *may zaw-hawb´*; from 4325 and 2091, *water of gold; Me-Zahab*, an Edomite:—Mezahab.

4315. מֵיטָב, **mêyṭâb**, *may-tawb´*; from 3190; the *best* part:—best.

4316. מִיכָא, **Mîykâ’**, *mee-kaw´*; a variation for 4318; *Mica*, the name of two Israelites:—Micha.

4317. מִיכָאֵל, **Mîykâ’êl**, *me-kaw-ale´*; from 4310 and (the prefixed derivative from) 3588 and 410; *who (is) like God; Mikael*, the name of an archangel and of nine Israelites:—Michael.

4318. מִיכָה, **Mîykâh**, *mee-kaw´*; an abbreviation of 4320; *Micah*, the name of seven Israelites:—Micah, Micaiah, Michah.

4319. מִיכָהוּ, **Mîykâhûw**, *me-kaw´-hoo*; a contraction for 4321 *Mikehu*, an Israelite prophet:—Micaiah (2Ch 18:8).

4320. מִיכָיָה, **Mîykâyâh**, *me-kaw-yaw´*; from 4310 and (the prefixed derivative from) 3588 and 3050; *who (is) like Jah; Micajah*, the name of two Israelites:—Micah, Michaiah. Compare 4318.

4321. מִיכָיְהוּ, **Mîykây**^e**hûw**, *me-kaw-yeh-hoo´*; or מִכָיְהוּ, **Mikâ-y**^e**hûw**, *me-kaw-yeh-hoo´*; (Jer 36:11), abbreviation for 4322; *Mikajah*, the name of three Israelites:—Micah, Micaiah, Michaiah.

4322. מִיכָיְהוּ, **Mîykâyâhûw**, *me-kaw-yaw´-hoo*; for 4320; *Mikajah*, the name of an Israelite and an Israelitess:—Michaiah.

4323. מִיכָל, **mîykâl**, *me-kawl´*; from 3201; (properly) a *container*, i.e. a *streamlet*:—brook.

4324. מִיכַל, **Mîykal**, *me-kal´*; apparently the same as 4323; *rivulet; Mikal*, Saul's daughter:—Michal.

4325. מַיִם, **mayim**, *mah´-yim*; dual of a primitive noun (but used in a singular sense); *water*; (figurative) *juice*; (by euphemism) *urine, semen*:— + piss, wasting, water (-ing, [-course, -flood, -spring]).

4326. מִיָּמִן, **Mîyyâmin**, *me-yaw-meem´*; a form for 4509; *Mijamin*, the name of three Israelites:—Miamin, Mijamin.

4327. מִין, **mîyn**, *meen*; from an unused root meaning to *portion* out; a *sort*, i.e. *species*:—kind. Compare 4480.

4328. מְיֻסָּדָה, **m**^e**yussâdâh**, *meh-yoos-saw-daw´*; properly feminine passive participle of 3245; something *founded*, i.e. a *foundation*:—foundation.

4329. מוּסָךְ, **mûwsâk**, *moo-sawk´*; from 5526; a *portico* (as *covered*):—covert.

4330. מִיץ, **mîyts**, *meets*; from 4160; *pressure*:—churning, forcing, wringing.

4331. מֵישָׁא, **Mêyshâ’**, *may-shaw´*; from 4185; *departure; Mesha*, a place in Arabia; also an Israelite:—Mesha.

4332. מִישָׁאֵל, **Mîyshâ’êl**, *mee-shaw-ale*; from 4310 and 410 with the abbreviation inseparable relative [see 834] interposed; *who (is) what God (is); Mishaël*, the name of three Israelites:—Mishael.

4333. מִישָׁאֵל, **Mîyshâ’êl**, *mee-shaw-ale´*; (Chaldee); corresponding to 4332; *Mishaël*, an Israelite:—Mishael.

4334. מִישׁוֹר, **mîyshôwr**, *mee-shore´*; or מִישֹׁר, **mîyshôr**, *mee-shore´*; from 3474; a *level*, i.e. a *plain* (often used [with the article prefixed] as a proper name of certain districts); (figurative) *concord*; also *straightness*, i.e. (figurative) *justice*;

(sometimes adverbial) *justly*:—equity, even place, plain, right (-eously), (made) straight, uprightness.

A masculine noun meaning plain, evenness, straightness, righteousness, equity. Evenness is the fundamental sense of this word. It denotes straight, as opposed to crooked (Isa 40:4; 42:16); level land, such as a plain (Dt 3:10; 1Ki 20:23); and a safe, unobstructed path (Ps 27:11). By analogy, it is likewise used to imply a righteous lifestyle (Ps 143:10); and equitable leadership (Ps 45:6[7]; Isa 11:4).

4335. מֵישַׁךְ, **Mêyshak,** *may-shak´*; borrowed from 4336; *Meshak*, an Israelite:—Meshak.

4336. מֵישַׁךְ, **Mêyshak,** *may-shak´*; (Chaldee); of foreign origin and doubtful signification; *Meshak*, the Babylonian name of 4333:—Meshak.

4337. מֵישָׁע, **Mêyshâ‘,** *may-shah´*; from 3467; *safety*; *Mesha*, an Israelite:—Mesha.

4338. מֵישַׁע, **Mêysha‘,** *may-shaw´*; a variation for 4337; *safety*; *Mesha*, a Moabite:—Mesha.

4339. מֵישָׁר, **mêyshâr,** *may-shawr´*; from 3474; *evenness*, i.e. (figurative) *prosperity* or *concord*; also *straightness*, i.e. (figurative) *rectitude* (only in plural with singular sense; often adverbial):—agreement, aright, that are equal, equity, (things that are) right (-eously, things), sweetly, upright (-ly, -ness).

4340. מֵיתָר, **mêythâr,** *may-thawr´*; from 3498; a *cord* (of a tent) [compare 3499] or the *string* (of a bow):—cord, string.

4341. מַכְאֹב, **mak’ôb,** *mak-obe´*; sometimes מַכְאוֹב, **mak’ôwb,** *mak-obe´*; also (feminine Isa 53:3) מַכְאֹבָה, **mak’ôbâh,** *mak-o-baw´*; from 3510; *anguish* or (figurative) *affliction*:—grief, pain, sorrow.

4342. מַכְבִּיר, **makbîyr,** *mak-beer´*; transposed participle of 3527; *plenty*:—abundance.

4343. מַכְבֵּנָא, **Makbênâ’,** *mak-bay-naw´*; from the same as 3522; *knoll*; *Macbena*, a place in Palestine settled by him:—Machbenah.

4344. מַכְבַּנַּי, **Makbannay,** *mak-ban-nah´ee*; patrial from 4343; a *Macbannite* or native of Macbena:—Machbanai.

4345. מִכְבָּר, **mikbâr,** *mik-bawr´*; from 3527 in the sense of *covering* [compare 3531]; a *grate*:—grate.

4346. מִכְבֵּר, **mikbêr,** *mak-bare´*; from 3527 in the sense of *covering*; a *cloth* (as *netted* [compare 4345]):—thick cloth.

4347. מַכָּה, **makkâh,** *mak-kaw´*; or (masculine) מַכֶּה, **makkeh,** *mak-keh´*; (plural only) from 5221 a *blow* (in 2Ch 2:10, of the flail); (by implication) a *wound*; (figurative) *carnage*, also *pestilence*:—beaten, blow, plague, slaughter, smote, × sore, stripe, stroke, wound ([-ed]).

A feminine noun meaning a blow, a stroke. When the word carries this literal sense, often a weapon (sword, rod, whip) functions as the instrument by which the blow is delivered. The individual judged to be in the wrong in a legal case could receive as punishment a beating of up to forty blows or lashes (Dt 25:3). In accordance with the royal edict decreed in the name of Xerxes, King of Persia, the Jews struck down their enemies with the blow of the sword (Est 9:5). The Lord declared to Israel and Judah that He had dealt them their blows because their guilt was so great (Jer 30:14). Elsewhere, the term signifies the result of a blow: a wound. King Joram rested in Jezreel to recover from wounds incurred in battle against the Arameans (2Ki 9:15). In another battle, King Ahab died of a wound, having been pierced by an arrow (1Ki 22:35; cf. Isa 1:6; Jer 6:7; 30:17; Mic 1:9). In other passages, the word described calamities inflicted by God: affliction, misery, and plague. The Lord solemnly warned Israel that failing to diligently obey His commands would result in His overwhelming them with severe and lasting afflictions (Dt 28:59, 61). The Philistines remembered that the "gods" of the Hebrews struck the Egyptians with all kinds of miseries (1Sa 4:8; cf. Jer 10:19, 49:17). Finally, the term can convey the sense of defeat or slaughter. Joshua and his fighting men handed the Amorites a great defeat at Gibeon (Jos 10:10; cf. Jos 10:20). Samson took revenge on the Philistines, killing many in a terrible slaughter because they had burned his wife and father-in-law (Jgs 15:8; cf. Jgs 11:33; 1Sa 4:10; 14:14). This noun is related to the verb *nâkâh* (5221).

4348. מִכְוָה, **mikvâh,** *mik-vaw´*; from 3554; a *burn*:—that burneth, burning.

4349. מָכוֹן, **mâkôwn,** *maw-kone´*; from 3559; (properly) a *fixture,* i.e. a *basis;* (generically) a *place,* especially as an *abode:*—foundation, habitation, (dwelling-, settled) place.

4350. מְכוֹנָה, **mᵉkôwnâh,** *mek-o-naw´;* or מְכֹנָה, **mᵉkônâh,** *mek-o-naw´;* feminine of 4349; a *pedestal,* also a *spot:*—base.

4351. מְכוּרָה, **mᵉkûwrâh,** *mek-oo-raw´;* or מְכֹרָה, **mᵉkôrâh,** *mek-o-raw´;* from the same as 3564 in the sense of *digging; origin* (as if a mine):— birth, habitation, nativity.

4352. מָכִי, **Mâkîy,** *maw-kee´;* probably from 4134; *pining; Maki,* an Israelite:—Machi.

4353. מָכִיר, **Mâkîyr,** *maw-keer´;* from 4376; *salesman; Makir,* an Israelite:—Machir.

4354. מָכִירִי, **Mâkîyrîy,** *maw-kee-ree´;* patronymic from 4353; a *Makirite* or descendant of Makir:—of Machir.

4355. מָכַךְ, **mâkak,** *maw-kak´;* a primitive root; to *tumble* (in ruins); (figurative) to *perish:*— be brought low, decay.

4356. מִכְלָאָה, **miklâ'âh,** *mik-law-aw´;* or מִכְלָה, **miklâh,** *mik-law´;* from 3607; a *pen* (for flocks):—([sheep-]) fold. Compare 4357.

4357. מִכְלָה, **miklâh,** *mik-law´;* from 3615; *completion;* (in plural concrete adverb) *wholly:*— perfect. Compare 4356.

4358. מִכְלוֹל, **miklôwl,** *mik-lole´;* from 3634; *perfection,* i.e. (concrete adverb) *splendidly:*— most gorgeously, all sorts.

4359. מִכְלָל, **miklâl,** *mik-lawl´;* from 3634; *perfection* (of beauty):—perfection.

4360. מִכְלוּל, **maklûl,** *mak-lool´;* from 3634; something *perfect,* i.e. a splendid *garment:*—all sorts.

4361. מַכֹּלֶת, **makkôleth,** *mak-ko´-leth;* from 398; *nourishment:*—food.

4362. מִכְמָן, **mikman,** *mik-man´;* from the same as 3646 in the sense of *hiding; treasure* (as hidden):—treasure.

4363. מִכְמָס, **Mikmâs,** *mik-maws´;* (Ezr 2:27; Ne 7:31), or מִכְמָשׁ, **Mikmâsh,** *mik-mawsh´;* or מִכְמַשׁ, **Mikmash,** *mik-mash´;* (Ne 11:31), from

3647; *hidden; Mikmas* or *Mikmash,* a place in Palestine:—Mikmas, Mikmash.

4364. מַכְמֹר, **makmôr,** *mak-mor´;* or מִכְמֹר, **mikmâr,** *mik-mawr´;* from 3648 in the sense of *blackening* by heat; a (hunter's) *net* (as *dark* from concealment):—net.

4365. מִכְמֶרֶת, **mikmereth,** *mik-meh´-reth;* or מִכְמֹרֶת, **mikmôreth,** *mik-mo´-reth;* feminine of 4364; a (fisher's) *net:*—drag, net.

4366. מִכְמְתָת, **Mikmᵉthâth,** *mik-meth-awth´;* apparently from an unused root meaning to *hide; concealment; Mikmethath,* a place in Palestine:— Michmethath.

4367. מַכְנַדְבַי, **Maknadbay,** *mak-nad-bah´ee;* from 4100 and 5068 with a particle interposed; *what* (is) *like* (a) *liberal* (man); *Maknadbai,* an Israelite:—Machnadebai.

4368. מְכֹנָה, **Mᵉkônâh,** *mek-o-naw´;* the same as 4350; a *base; Mekonah,* a place in Palestine:— Mekonah.

4369. מְכֻנָה, **mᵉkunâh,** *mek-oo-naw´;* the same as 4350; a *spot:*—base.

4370. מִכְנָס, **miknâs,** *mik-nawce´;* from 3647 in the sense of *hiding;* (only in dual) *drawers* (from *concealing* the private parts):—breeches.

4371. מֶכֶס, **mekes,** *meh´-kes;* probably from an unused root meaning to *enumerate;* an *assessment* (as based upon a *census):*—tribute.

4372. מִכְסֶה, **mikseh,** *mik-seh´;* from 3680; a *covering,* i.e. weather-*boarding:*—covering.

4373. מִכְסָה, **miksâh,** *mik-saw´;* feminine of 4371; an *enumeration;* (by implication) a *valuation:*—number, worth.

4374. מְכַסֶּה, **mᵉkasseh,** *mek-as-seh´;* from 3680; a *covering,* i.e. *garment;* (specifically) a *coverlet* (for a bed), an *awning* (from the sun); also the *omentum* (as covering the intestines):—clothing, to cover, that which covereth.

4375. מַכְפֵּלָה, **Makpêlâh,** *mak-pay-law´;* from 3717; a *fold; Makpelah,* a place in Palestine:— Machpelah.

4376. מָכַר, **mâkar,** *maw-kar´;* a primitive root; to *sell,* literal (as merchandise, a daughter in marriage, into slavery), or figurative (to *surrender):*— × at all, sell (away, -er, self).

4377. מֶכֶר, **mekker,** *meh´-ker*; from 4376; *merchandise*; also *value*:—pay, price, ware.

4378. מַכָּר, **makkâr,** *mak-kawr´*; from 5234; an *acquaintance*:—acquaintance.

4379. מִכְרֶה, **mikreh,** *mik-reh´*; from 3738; a *pit* (for salt):—[salt-] pit.

4380. מְכֵרָה, **meʿkêrâh,** *mek-ay-raw´*; probably from the same as 3564 in the sense of *stabbing*; a *sword*:—habitation.

4381. מִכְרִי, **Mikrîy,** *mik-ree´*; from 4376; *salesman*; *Mikri*, an Israelite:—Michri.

4382. מְכֵרָתִי, **Meʿkêrâthîy,** *mek-ay-raw-thee´*; patrial from an unused name (the same as 4380) of a place in Palestine; a *Mekerathite*, or inhabitant of Mekerah:—Mecherathite.

4383. מִכְשׁוֹל, **mikshôwl,** *mik-shole´*; or מִכְשֹׁל, **mikshôl,** *mik-shole´*; masculine from 3782; a *stumbling-block*, literal or figurative (*obstacle, enticement* [specifically an idol], *scruple*):—caused to fall, offence, × [no-] thing offered, ruin, stumbling-block.

A masculine noun meaning a stumbling block, an obstacle. Sometimes the term refers to something an individual can literally stumble over. For instance, the Lord commanded the people of Israel not to put a stumbling block before the blind (Le 19:14). More often, however, it is used in a figurative sense. The Lord Himself will become the obstacle over which both houses of Israel will stumble (Isa 8:14). Much later in Isaiah, it is written that the Lord will demand that the obstacle be removed from His people's way (Isa 57:14). In other places, the word refers to that which causes people to stumble morally, that is, to sin: gold and silver (Eze 7:19); idols (Eze 14:3); the Levites (Eze 44:12). In other places, the term describes something that causes people to fall to their ruin. Because of Israel's persistent rejection of God's Law, He laid a stumbling block before them so they would trip and perish (Jer 6:21; cf. Ps 119:165; Eze 3:20; 18:30). This term is derived from the verb *kâshal* (3782).

4384. מַכְשֵׁלָה, **makshêlâh,** *mak-shay-law´*; feminine from 3782; a *stumbling-block*, but only figurative (*fall, enticement* [idol]):—ruin, stumbling-block.

A feminine noun meaning a heap of rubble, ruins. Isaiah prophesied to the people of Judah that because of their rebellion against the Lord, He was going to desolate their land so thoroughly that they would soon search for leaders to care for them and for the ruins of what remained, yet find none (Isa 3:6). This noun stems from the verb *kâshal* (3782).

4385. מִכְתָּב, **miktâb,** *mik-tawb´*; from 3789; a thing *written*, the *characters*, or a *document* (letter, copy, edict, poem):—writing.

4386. מְכִתָּה, **meʿkittâh,** *mek-it-taw´*; from 3807; a *fracture*:—bursting.

4387. מִכְתָּם, **miktâm,** *mik-tawm´*; from 3799; an *engraving*, i.e. (technical) a *poem*:—Michtam.

4388. מַכְתֵּשׁ, **maktêsh,** *mak-taysh´*; from 3806; a *mortar*; (by analogy) a *socket* (of a tooth):—hollow place, mortar.

4389. מַכְתֵּשׁ, **Maktêsh,** *mak-taysh´*; the same as 4388; *dell*; the *Maktesh*, a place in Jerusalem:—Maktesh.

4390. מָלֵא, **mâlêʾ,** *maw-lay´*; or מָלָא, **mâlâʾ,** *maw-law´*; (Est 7:5), a primitive root, to *fill* or (intransitive) *be full* of, in a wide application (literal and figurative):—accomplish, confirm, + consecrate, be at an end, be expired, be fenced, fill, fulfil, (be, become, × draw, give in, go) full (-ly, -ly set, tale), [over-] flow, fulness, furnish, gather (selves, together), presume, replenish, satisfy, set, space, take a [hand-] full, + have wholly.

A verb meaning to fill, to be full, to be complete, to fulfill, to finish, to satisfy. This word occurs 251 times in the OT and functions both in a spatial and temporal sense. Spatially, the term pictures the act of making that which was empty of a particular content no longer so. It can also express that state of being in which a certain container is holding to capacity a particular object or objects. God commanded the water creatures to fill the seas (Ge 1:22); and humanity to fill the earth (Ge 1:28). Elijah directed the people to fill four water jars; the trench was also filled (1Ki 18:34, 35). The word can also function in an abstract way: Judah filled the land with violence (Eze 8:17; cf. Le 19:29; Jer 51:5). Theologically, the glory of the Lord filled the Temple (1Ki 8:10,

11; cf. Isa 6:1); and Jeremiah declared that God fills heaven and earth (Jer 23:24). Temporally, the term refers to the completion of a specified segment of time. According to the Law, a woman who had given birth to a boy could not enter the sanctuary until the thirty-three days of her blood purification were completed (Le 12:4). The Lord promised to establish King David's kingdom after his days were fulfilled (i.e. he died: 2Sa 7:12; cf. La 4:18).

A final important use of the word entails the keeping of a vow or promise. The Lord fulfilled His promise to David that his son would build a house for His name (2Ch 6:4, 15; cf. 2Sa 7:12; 1Ki 2:27; 2Ch 36:21).

4391. מְלָא, **mᵉlâ'**, *mel-aw´*; (Chaldee); corresponding to 4390; to *fill*:—fill, be full.

4392. מָלֵא, **mâlê'**, *maw-lay´*; from 4390; *full* (literal or figurative) or *filling* (literal); also (concrete) *fulness*; (adverb) *fully*:— × she that was with child, fill (-ed, -ed with), full (-ly), multitude, as is worth.

4393. מְלֹא, **mᵉlô'**, *mel-o´*; rarely מְלוֹא, **mᵉlôw'**, *mel-o´*; or מְלוֹ, **mᵉlôw**, *mel-o´*; (Eze 41:8), from 4390; *fulness* (literal or figurative):— × all along, × all that is (there-) in, fill, (× that whereof ... was) full, fulness, [hand-] full, multitude.

4394. מִלֻּא, **millu'**, *mil-loo´*; from 4390; a *fulfilling* (only in plural), i.e. (literal) a *setting* (of gems), or (technical) *consecration;* (also concrete) a dedicatory *sacrifice*:—consecration, be set.

4395. מְלֵאָה, **mᵉlê'âh**, *mel-ay-aw´*; feminine of 4392; something *fulfilled*, i.e. *abundance* (of produce):—(first of ripe) fruit, fulness.

4396. מִלֻּאָה, **millu'âh**, *mil-loo-aw´*; feminine of 4394; a *filling*, i.e. *setting* (of gems):—inclosing, setting.

4397. מַלְאָךְ, **mal'âk,** *mal-awk´*; from an unused root meaning to *despatch* as a deputy; a *messenger*; specifically of God, i.e. an *angel* (also a prophet, priest or teacher):—ambassador, angel, king, messenger.

A masculine noun meaning a messenger, an angel. The term often denotes one sent on business or diplomacy by another (human) personage. Jacob sent messengers on ahead to his brother Esau in the hope of finding favour in his eyes (Ge 32:3[4], 6[7]). The elders of Jabesh sent messengers throughout Israel in a desperate attempt to locate someone who could rescue their town from the dire threat of the Ammonites (1Sa 11:3, 4, 9; cf. 2Sa 11:19; 1Ki 19:2; 2Ki 5:10). Very often, the term referred to messengers sent from God. Sometimes these were human messengers, whether prophets (Isa 44:26; Hag 1:13; Mal 3:1); priests (Ecc 5:6[5]; Mal 2:7); or the whole nation of Israel (Isa 42:19). More often, however, the term referred to heavenly beings who often assumed human form (Ge 19:1; Jgs 13:6, 15, 16) and appeared to people as bearers of the Lord's commands and tidings (Jgs 6:11, 12; 13:3). They were often responsible for aiding, protecting, and fighting for those who trusted in the Lord (Ge 24:7; Ex 23:20; 33:2; 1Ki 19:5; Ps 34:7[8]; 91:11). They also acted as instruments of divine judgment, meting out punishment on the rebellious and the guilty (2Sa 24:16, 17; Ps 35:5, 6; 78:49; Isa 37:36). Sometimes the angel of the Lord and his message are so closely identified with the Lord Himself that the text simply refers to the angel as "the Lord" or "God" (Ge 16:7; 22:11; 31:11; Ex 3:2; Jgs 13:18; cf. Ge 16:13; 22:12; 31:13, 16; Ex 3:4; Jgs 6:22; 13:22).

4398. מַלְאַךְ, **mal'ak,** *mal-ak´*; (Chaldee); corresponding to 4397; an *angel*:—angel.

An Aramaic noun meaning angel (Da 3:28; 6:22 [23]). The word is a cognate of the Hebrew noun *mal'âk* (4397).

4399. מְלָאכָה, **mᵉlâ'kâh**, *mel-aw-kaw´*; from the same as 4397; (properly) *deputyship*, i.e. ministry; (generally) *employment* (never servile) or work (abstract or concrete); also *property* (as the result of *labour*):—business, + cattle, + industrious, occupation, (+ -pied), + officer, thing (made), use, (manner of) work ([-man], -manship).

A feminine singular noun meaning work, occupation, business, something made, property, workmanship. This word is used for God's creative work (Ge 2:2, 3); as well as for human labour (Ex 20:9, 10); skilled craftsmanship (Le 13:48); and agricultural tasks (1Ch 27:26). It is used for livestock (Ge 33:14); property (Ex 22:8[7]); public and religious business. For instance, Ezr 10:13 employs the term in reference to the divorce of foreign wives.

4400. מַלְאָכוּת, **mal'âkûwth**, *mal-awk-ooth´*; from the same as 4397; a *message*:—message.

A feminine noun meaning message. This word is used only once in the OT, where it described Haggai's message from the Lord (Hag 1:13). This word is related to the common noun *mal'âk* (4397), meaning messenger, which is also used in Hag 1:13.

4401. מַלְאָכִי, **Mal'âkîy**, *mal-aw-kee'*; from the same as 4397; *ministrative; Malaki*, a prophet:— Malachi.

4402. מִלְאָת, **millê'th**, *mil-layth'*; from 4390; *fulness*, i.e. (concrete) a *plump* socket (of the eye):— × fitly.

4403. מַלְבּוּשׁ, **malbûwsh**, *mal-boosh'*; or מַלְבֻּשׁ, **malbush**, *mal-boosh'*; from 3847; a *garment*, or (collective) *clothing*:—apparel, raiment, vestment.

4404. מַלְבֵּן, **malbên**, *mal-bane'*; from 3835 (denominative); a *brick-kiln*:—brick kiln.

4405. מִלָּה, **millâh**, *mil-law'*; from 4448 (plural masculine as if from מִלֶּה, **milleh**, *mil-leh'*); a *word*; (collective) a *discourse*; (figurative) a *topic*:— + answer, byword, matter, any thing (what) to say, to speak (-ing), speak, talking, word.

A feminine singular noun meaning word, speech, utterance. It is the poetic equivalent of *dâbâr* (1697), carrying the same range of meaning (2Sa 23:2; Ps 19:4[5]; 139:4; Pr 23:9). Of its thirty-eight uses in the Hebrew portion of the OT, Job contains thirty-four (see concordance for references).

4406. מִלָּה, **millâh**, *mil-law'*; (Chaldee); corresponding to 4405; a *word, command, discourse*, or *subject*:—commandment, matter, thing, word.

An Aramaic feminine noun meaning word, command, matter. This word, used only in Daniel, is equivalent to the Hebrew word *millâh* (4405), meaning word or speech, and comes from the Hebrew verb *mâlal* (4448), meaning to speak or say. This word is used to describe words that were spoken (Da 4:31[28]; 7:11, 25), which, depending on the context, can be translated as command (Da 2:5; 3:22; 5:10). Often this word described an entire series of circumstances or matters (Da 2:9–11; 4:33[30]; 7:1).

4407. מִלּוֹא, **millôw'**, *mil-lo'*; or מִלֹּא, **millô'**, *mil-lo'*; (2Ki 12:20), from 4390; a *rampart* (as *filled* in), i.e. the *citadel*:—Millo. See also 1037.

4408. מַלּוּחַ, **mallûwach**, *mal-loo'-akh*; from 4414; *sea-purslain* (from its *saltness*):—mallows.

4409. מַלּוּךְ, **Mallûwk**, *mal-luke*; or מַלּוּכִי, **Malûw-kîy**, *mal-loo-kee'*; (Ne 12:14), from 4427; *regnant; Malluk*, the name of five Israelites:—Malluch, Melichu [*from the margin*].

4410. מְלוּכָה, **m^elûwkâh**, *mel-oo-kaw'*; feminine passive participle of 4427; something *ruled*, i.e. a *realm*:—kingdom, king's, × royal.

4411. מָלוֹן, **mâlôwn**, *maw-lone'*; from 3885; a *lodgment*, i.e. *caravanserai* or *encampment*:—inn, place where … lodge, lodging (place).

4412. מְלוּנָה, **m^elûwnâh**, *mel-oo-naw'*; feminine from 3885; a *hut*, a *hammock*:—cottage, lodge.

4413. מַלּוֹתִי, **Mallôwthîy**, *mal-lo'-thee*; apparently from 4448; *I have talked* (i.e. *loquacious*):—*Mallothi*, an Israelite:—Mallothi.

4414. מָלַח, **mâlach**, *maw-lakh'*; a primitive root; (properly) to *rub* to pieces or pulverize; (intransitive) to *disappear* as dust; also (as denominative from 4417) to *salt* whether internal (to *season* with salt) or external (to *rub* with salt):— × at all, salt, season, temper together, vanish away.

4415. מְלַח, **m^elach**, *mel-akh'*; (Chaldee); corresponding to 4414; to *eat* salt, i.e. (general) *subsist*:— + have maintenance.

4416. מְלַח, **m^elach**, *mel-akh'*; (Chaldee); from 4415; *salt*:— + maintenance, salt.

4417. מֶלַח, **melach**, *meh'-lakh*; from 4414; (properly) *powder*, i.e. (specific) *salt* (as easily pulverized and dissolved):—salt ([-pit]).

4418. מֶלַח, **melâch**, *meh-lakh'*; from 4414 in its original sense; a *rag* or old garment:—rotten rag.

4419. מַלָּח, **mallâch**, *mal-lawkh'*; from 4414 in its secondary sense; a *sailor* (as following "the salt"):—mariner.

4420. מְלֵחָה, **m^elêchâh**, *mel-ay-khaw'*; from 4414 (in its denominative sense); (properly) *salted* (i.e. land [776 being understood]), i.e. a *desert*:—barren land (-ness), salt [land].

4421. מִלְחָמָה, **milchâmâh,** *mil-khaw-maw´*; from 3898 (in the sense of *fighting*); a *battle* (i.e. the *engagement*); generally *war* (i.e. *warfare*):— battle, fight, (-ing), war ([-rior]).

4422. מָלַט, **mâlaṭ,** *maw-lat´*; a primitive root; (properly) to *be smooth*, i.e. (by implication) to *escape* (as if by *slipperiness*); (causative) to *release* or *rescue*; (specifically) to *bring forth* young, *emit* sparks:—deliver (self), escape, lay, leap out, let alone, let go, preserve, save, × speedily, × surely.

A verb meaning to escape. The picture of escape is as sparks leaping out of the fire (Job 41:19[11]); or like a bird escaping the fowlers (Ps 124:7). This word is usually used within the context of fleeing for one's life as Lot was urged to do (Ge 19:17, 19, 20, 22); as David did from the hands of Saul (1Sa 19:10–12; 27:1); or as Zedekiah could not do when facing the Chaldeans (Jer 32:4; 34:3). It is also used to describe rescue from death (Est 4:13; Ps 89:48[49]; Am 2:14, 15); calamity (Job 1:15–17, 19); or punishment (Pr 11:21; 19:5; 28:26). In a few instances, the word is used to describe protection (Ecc 9:15; Isa 31:5); in one instance, it means to give birth to a child (Isa 66:7).

4423. מֶלֶט, **meleṭ,** *meh´-let*; from 4422, *cement* (from its plastic *smoothness*):—clay.

4424. מְלַטְיָה, **Mᵉlaṭyâh,** *mel-at-yaw´*; from 4423 and 3050; (whom) *Jah has delivered; Melatjah,* a Gibeonite:—Melatiah.

4425. מְלִילָה, **mᵉlîylâh,** *mel-ee-law´*; from 4449 (in the sense of *cropping* [compare 4135]; a *head* of grain (as *cut* off):—ear.

4426. מְלִיצָה, **mᵉlîytsâh,** *mel-ee-tsaw´*; from 3887; an *aphorism*; also a *satire*:—interpretation, taunting.

4427. מָלַךְ, **mâlak,** *maw-lak´*; a primitive root; to *reign*; (inceptive) to *ascend the throne*; (causative) to *induct* into royalty; hence (by implication) to *take counsel*:—consult, × indeed, be (make, set a, set up) king, be (make) queen, (begin to, make to) reign (-ing), rule, × surely.

A verb meaning to rule, to be king, to make king. The verb is used approximately three hundred times in its simple form to mean to rule, to

be king, to have sway, power, and dominion over people and nations. God is King and will rule over the whole earth in the day when He judges the earth and establishes Mount Zion (Isa 24:23). Israel rejected God from ruling over them during the time of Samuel (1Sa 8:7; cf. Eze 20:33); the verb is used to proclaim the rulership of a king when he is installed, as when Adonijah prematurely attempted to usurp the throne of his father David (1Ki 1:11). The Lord reigns as the Lord Almighty over both earthly and divine subjects (Isa 24:23; Mic 4:7).

The verb also describes the rulership of human kings—the establishment of rulership and the process itself (Ge 36:31; Jgs 9:8; Pr 30:22). It describes the rule of Athaliah the queen over Judah for six years (2Ki 11:3). In the causative form, it depicts the installation of a king. It describes God's establishment of Saul as the first king over Israel (1Sa 15:35). Hos 8:4 indicates that the Israelites had set up kings without the Lord's approval.

4428. מֶלֶךְ, **melek,** *meh´-lek*; from 4427; a *king*:—king, royal.

A masculine noun meaning king. The feminine form is *malkâh* (4436), meaning queen, though the concept is more of a king's consort than a monarchical ruler. The word *melek* appears over 2,500 times in the OT. In many biblical contexts, this term is simply a general term, denoting an individual with power and authority. It is parallel with and conceptually related to a number of other Hebrew words that are usually translated as lord, captain, prince, chief, or ruler. It is used in reference to men and often with a genitive of people or place (Ge 14:1; Ex 1:15; 2Sa 2:4); the Lord who demonstrates His power and authority over Israel (Isa 41:21; 44:6); and over each individual (Ps 5:2[3]; 44:4[5]). In pagan worship, the worshippers attribute this term with its connotations to their idols (Isa 8:21; Am 5:26).

4429. מֶלֶךְ, **Melek,** *meh´-lek*; the same as 4428; *king; Melek,* the name of two Israelites:— Melech, Hammelech [*by including the article*].

4430. מֶלֶךְ, **melek,** *meh´-lek*; (Chaldee); corresponding to 4428; a *king*:—king, royal.

An Aramaic masculine noun meaning king. This very common word is equivalent to the Hebrew word *melek* (4428), meaning king. It is used to speak of the top government official. It is used to speak of the following kings: Artaxerxes (Ezr 4:8 ff.); Darius (Ezr 5:6ff; Da 6:2[3] ff.); Cyrus (Ezr 5:13 ff.); Nebuchadnezzar (Da 2:4 ff.); Belshazzar (Da 5:1 ff.); kings that will arise on the earth (Da 7:17, 24).

4431. מְלַךְ, **mᵉlak,** *mel-ak´*; (Chaldee); from a root corresponding to 4427 in the sense of *consultation; advice:*—counsel.

4432. מֹלֶךְ, **Môlek,** *mo´-lek*; from 4427; *Molek* (i.e. king), the chief deity of the Ammonites:— Molech. Compare 4445.

4433. מַלְכָּה, **malkâh,** *mal-kaw´*; (Chaldee); corresponding to 4436; a *queen:*—queen.

An Aramaic feminine noun meaning queen. This word, equivalent to the Hebrew word *malkâh* (4436), is used twice in Da 5:10. It designated the proper title of the wife of the king. Scholars disagree as to whether she was the wife or the mother of the last king of the neo-Babylonian Empire, Belshazzar.

4434. מַלְכֹּדֶת, **malkôdeth,** *mal-ko´-deth*; from 3920; a *snare:*—trap.

A feminine noun meaning a trap, a snare, a noose. This word is found only in Job 18:10. In his disputation with Job, Bildad the Shuhite used the word to describe the pitfalls that lay before the wicked.

4435. מִלְכָּה, **Milkâh,** *mil-kaw´*; a form of 4436; *queen; Milcah,* the name of a Hebrewess and of an Israelite:—Milcah.

4436. מַלְכָּה, **malkâh,** *mal-kaw´*; feminine of 4428; a *queen:*—queen.

A feminine noun meaning queen. The noun means queen exclusively, but the queen stands in several possible social positions. The queen is often merely the wife of the king; she was, for example, subordinate to the king, and was expected to do his bidding (Est 1:11, 12, 16, 17). She also had much court authority herself (Est 1:9). The only time the word is used to apply to Israelite women is in the plural, and they were part of Solomon's harem (SS 6:8, 9).

The term means queen without stressing the spousal relationship to the king, but it is not used in this way of any Israelite woman in the time of the monarchy. The queen of Sheba, from southwest Arabia, was a powerful monarch in her own right, traveled extensively (1Ki 10:1, 10), and was considered a wise woman and ruler (2Ch 9:1). Esther became queen in Persia because of her beauty but won over the king by gaining his approval and favour (see Est 2:17, 18).

4437. מַלְכוּ, **malkûw,** *mal-koo´*; (Chaldee); corresponding to 4438; *dominion* (abstract or concrete):—kingdom, kingly, realm, reign.

An Aramaic feminine noun meaning royalty, reign, kingdom, kingly authority. This word, corresponding to the word *malkûth* (4438), distinguishes the propriety of royalty from all else (e.g., Da 5:20). It is used to denote the reign of a particular sovereign (Da 6:28[29]); the extent of a king's authority (Ezr 7:13); the territorial or administrative dominion of a monarch (Da 6:3[4]); the nation or kingdom in a general sense (Da 5:31[6:1]).

4438. מַלְכוּת, **malkûwth,** *mal-kooth´*; or מַלְכֻת, **malkuth,** *mal-kooth´*; or (in plural) מַלְכֻיָּה, **malkuyyâh,** *mal-koo-yaw´*; from 4427; a *rule;* (concrete) a *dominion:*—empire, kingdom, realm, reign, royal.

A feminine noun meaning royalty, reign, dominion, kingdom. This term chiefly describes that which pertains to royalty or the natural outflow of power from the royal station. The book of Esther especially illustrates how this word is used to distinguish the royal from the ordinary, speaking of royal wine (Est 1:7); a royal command (Est 1:19); and royal clothing (Est 5:1). It is specifically used to signify the reign of a monarch (2Ch 15:10; Da 1:1); and the kingdom or territorial realm under the authority of a particular sovereign (1Ch 12:23 [24]; 2Ch 11:17; Da 10:13).

4439. מַלְכִּיאֵל, **Malkîy'êl,** *mal-kee-ale´*; from 4428 and 410; *king of* (i.e. appointed by) *God; Malkiël,* an Israelite:—Malchiel.

4440. מַלְכִּיאֵלִי, **Malkîy'êlîy,** *mal-kee-ay-lee´*; patronymic from 4439; a *Malkiëlite* or descendant of Malkiel:—Malchielite.

4441. מַלְכִּיָּה, **Malkîyyâh,** *mal-kee-yaw´*; or מַלְכִּיָהוּ, **Malkiyâhûw,** *mal-kee-yaw´-hoo*; (Jer 38:6), from 4428 and 3050; *king of* (i.e. appointed by) *Jah; Malkijah,* the name of ten Israelites:—Malchiah, Malchijah.

4442. מַלְכִּי־צֶדֶק, **Malkîy-Tsedeq,** *mal-kee-tseh´-dek*; from 4428 and 6664; *king of right; Malki-Tsedek,* an early king in Palestine:—Melchizedek.

4443. מַלְכִּירָם, **Malkîyrâm,** *mal-kee-rawm´*; from 4428 and 7311; *king of a high* one (i.e. of exaltation); *Malkiram,* an Israelite:—Malchiram.

4444. מַלְכִּישׁוּעַ, **Malkîyshûwaʿ,** *mal-kee-shoo´-ah*; from 4428 and 7769; *king of wealth; Malk-ishua,* an Israelite:—Malchishua.

4445. מַלְכָּם, **Malkâm,** *mal-kawm´*; or מִלְכֹּם, **Mil-kôm,** *mil-kome´*; from 4428 for 4432; *Malcam* or *Milcom,* the national idol of the Ammonites:—Malcham, Milcom.

4446. מְלֶכֶת, **mᵉleketh,** *mel-eh´-keth*; from 4427; a *queen:*—queen.

A feminine noun meaning queen. Rather than being just another term for a female regent, this word's significance is found in the chronicle of Judah's idolatry. It is used solely to designate a fertility goddess worshipped in Jeremiah's day, the queen of the heavens (*mĕleketh hashshâmayim* [8064]). Although the references are cryptic, it is believed that this queen of the heavens was either the goddess Ashtoreth, symbolized by the moon, or Astarte, symbolized by the planet Venus. Women baked cakes to offer to this goddess (Jer 7:18) and burned incense (Jer 44:17–19) in hopes of securing the blessings of fertility. However, the judgment of the Lord on this practice made it counterproductive (cf. Jer 44:25ff.).

4447. מֹלֶכֶת, **Môleketh,** *mo-leh´-keth*; feminine active participle of 4427; *queen; Moleketh,* an Israelitess:—Hammoleketh [*including the article*].

4448. מָלַל, **mâlal,** *maw-lal´*; a primitive root; to *speak* (mostly poetical) or *say:*—say, speak, utter.

A verb meaning to speak, to say, to declare, to utter. Except for an occurance found in Pr 6:13 (a wicked man "speaks" [that is, gives a sign] with his feet), the verb is utilized mostly with the intensive stem. Sarah said, "Who would have said to Abraham that Sarah would nurse children?" (Ge 21:7). Elihu stated that his lips would utter upright knowledge to Job (Job 33:3; cf. Job 8:2). The psalmist exclaimed that

no one can declare the mighty acts of God (Ps 106:2). The term compares closely in meaning with the Hebrew verb *dâbar* (1696).

4449. מְלַל, **mᵉlal,** *mel-al´*; (Chaldee); corresponding to 4448; to *speak:*—say, speak (-ing).

An Aramaic verb meaning to speak. All undisputed instances of this term occur in the Aramaic sections of the book of Daniel. In Daniel's vision of the four beasts, the fourth beast had a little horn upon which was a mouth speaking arrogantly (Da 7:8, 11, 20). This horn (symbolic of a king) spoke words against the Most High (Da 7:25). This term is closely related to the Hebrew verb *mâlal* (4448).

4450. מִלֲלַי, **Milălay,** *mee-lal-ah´ee*; from 4448; *talkative; Milalai,* an Israelite:—Milalai.

4451. מַלְמָד, **malmâd,** *mal-mawd´*; from 3925; a *goad* for oxen:—goad.

4452. מָלַץ, **mâlats,** *maw-lats´*; a primitive root; to *be smooth,* i.e. (figurative) *pleasant:*—be sweet.

4453. מֶלְצָר, **meltsâr,** *mel-tsawr´*; of Persian derivation; the *butler* or other officer in the Babylonian court:—Melzar.

4454. מָלַק, **mâlaq,** *maw-lak´*; a primitive root; to *crack* a joint; (by implication) to *wring* the neck of a fowl (without separating it):—wring off.

4455. מַלְקוֹחַ, **malqôwach,** *mal-ko´-akh*; from 3947; transposed (in dual) the *jaws* (as taking food); (intransitive) *spoil* [and captives] (as taken):—booty, jaws, prey.

4456. מַלְקוֹשׁ, **malqôwsh,** *mal-koshe´*; from 3953; the spring *rain* (compare 3954); (figurative) *eloquence:*—latter rain.

4457. מֶלְקָחַיִם, **melqâchayim,** *mel-kaw-kha-yim´*; from 3947; (only in dual) *tweezers:*—snuffers, tongs.

4458. מֶלְתָחָה, **meltâchâh,** *mel-taw-khaw´*; from an unused root meaning to *spread* out; a *wardrobe* (i.e. room where clothing is *spread*):—vestry.

4459. מַלְתָּעוֹת, **maltâʿôwth,** *mal-taw-oth´*; transposed for 4973; a *grinder,* i.e. back *tooth:*—great tooth.

4460. מְמְגוּרָה, **mamm^egûwrâh,** *mam-meg-oo-raw´*; from 4048 (in the sense of *depositing*); a *granary*:—barn.

4461. מֵמַד, **mêmad,** *may-mad´*; from 4058; a *measure*:—measure.

4462. מְמוּכָן, **M^emûwkân,** *mem-oo-kawn´*; or (transposed) מוֹמֻכָן, **Môwmukân,** *mo-moo-kawn´*; (Est 1:16), of Persian derivation; *Memucan* or *Momucan,* a Persian satrap:—Memucan.

4463. מָמוֹת, **mâmôwth,** *maw-mothe´*; from 4191; a mortal *disease*; (concrete) a *corpse*:—death.

4464. מַמְזֵר, **mamzêr,** *mam-zare´*; from an unused root meaning to *alienate*; a *mongrel*, i.e. born of a Jewish father and a heathen mother:—bastard.

4465. מִמְכָּר, **mimkâr,** *mim-kawr´*; from 4376; *merchandise*; (abstract) a *selling*:— × ought, (that which cometh of) sale, that which ... sold, ware.

4466. מִמְכֶּרֶת, **mimkereth,** *mim-keh´-reth*; feminine of 4465; a *sale*:— + sold as.

4467. מַמְלָכָה, **mamlâkâh,** *mam-law-kaw´*; from 4427; *dominion*, i.e. (abstract) the estate (*rule*) or (concrete) the country (*realm*):—kingdom, king's, reign, royal.

A feminine noun meaning kingdom. Often the term refers to the royal power an individual in sovereign authority possesses. Because Solomon did not keep the Lord's covenant and commandments, his kingdom (that is, his power to rule) was torn from his son (1Ki 11:11; cf. 1Sa 28:17; 1Ki 14:8). In many other places, however, the word is utilized concretely to denote a people under a king (that is, a realm). The kingdom (or realm) of King Sihon of the Amorites and the kingdom (realm) of King Og of Bashan were given to the Gadites, Reubenites, and the half-tribe of Manasseh (Nu 32:33; cf. Ex 19:6; Dt 28:25; 1Sa 24:20[21]). In some passages, the word functions as an adjective, meaning royal (e.g., city of the kingdom = royal city; Jos 10:2; 1Sa 27:5; cf. 2Ki 11:1; 2Ch 23:20; Am 7:13). This noun derives from the verb *mâlak* (4427), as does its synonym, *malkûth* (4438).

4468. מַמְלָכוּת, **mamlâkûwth,** *mam-law-kooth´*; a form of 4467 and equivalent to it:—kingdom, reign.

A feminine noun meaning kingdom, royal power. It is equivalent in meaning with the term *mamlâkâh* (4467) and occurs only in the construct form. Samuel told Saul that the Lord had torn the kingdom of Israel from him and given it to another better than he (1Sa 15:28). The Lord declared to Hosea that He was going to put an end to the kingdom of Israel (Hos 1:4; cf. Jos 13:12; 2Sa 16:3; Jer 26:1). This noun is derived from the verb *mâlak* (4427).

4469. מִמְסָךְ, **mimsâk,** *mim-sawk´*; from 4537; *mixture*, i.e. (specific) wine *mixed* (with water or spices):—drink-offering, mixed wine.

4470. מֶמֶר, **memer,** *meh´-mer*; from an unused root meaning to *grieve; sorrow*:—bitterness.

4471. מַמְרֵא, **Mamrê’,** *mam-ray´*; from 4754 (in the sense of *vigour*); *lusty*; *Mamre,* an Amorite:—Mamre.

4472. מַמְרֹר, **mamrôr,** *mam-rore´*; from 4843; a *bitterness*, i.e. (figurative) calamity:—bitterness.

4473. מִמְשַׁח, **mimshach,** *mim-shakh´*; from 4886, in the sense of *expansion; outspread* (i.e. with outstretched wings):—anointed.

A masculine noun possibly meaning expansion, extension. The word occurs only in Eze 28:14 and would, with this meaning, read "cherub of extension" (that is, a cherub with wings outstretched). However, this definition is now seriously questioned, largely because the term derives from the verb *mâshach* (4886), meaning to anoint. The term more likely expresses the sense of anointment or anointing. Taking the word this way, the phrase conveys the more satisfying expression "cherub of anointing," that is, the anointed cherub.

4474. מִמְשָׁל, **mimshâl,** *mim-shawl´*; from 4910; a *ruler* or (abstract) *rule*:—dominion, that ruled.

A masculine noun meaning dominion, sovereign authority, ruling power. One in human form spoke with Daniel, telling him about a warrior king and an officer who would soon rule their respective kingdoms with great authority (Da 11:3, 5). In 1Ch 26:6, the word describes the sons of Shemaiah as those who exercised ruling authority in their ancestral homes because of their great capabilities. The term stems from the verb *mâshal* (4910).

4475. מֶמְשָׁלָה, **memshâlâh,** *mem-shaw-law´;* feminine of 4474; *rule;* also (concrete in plural) a *realm* or a *ruler:*—dominion, government, power, to rule.

A feminine noun meaning dominion, rule, authority, province, realm. Often this term denotes the ruling power which one in authority exercises over his domain or kingdom. God made the sun to have authority over the day and the moon to have authority over the night (Ge 1:16; Ps 136:8). The Lord sent the prophet Isaiah to announce to Shebna that He was going to forcibly remove him from office and give his authority to Eliakim instead (Isa 22:21). In other places, the word refers to the territory over which one rules or governs. Hezekiah showed his whole realm to the king of Babylon's messengers (2Ki 20:13; cf. Ps 103:22; 114:2). Once it refers collectively to an envoy of powerful ambassadors, such as rulers, princes, or chief officers (2Ch 32:9). This term is derived from the verb *mâshal* (4910; see also the related word *mimshâl* [4474]).

4476. מִמְשָׁק, **mimshâq,** *mim-shawk´;* from the same as 4943; a *possession:*—breeding.

4477. מַמְתַקִּים, **mamtaqqîym,** *mam-tak-keem´;* from 4985; something *sweet* (literal or figurative):—(most) sweet.

4478. מָן, **man,** *man;* from 4100; (literal) a *whatness* (so to speak), i.e. *manna* (so called from the question about it):—manna.

A masculine noun meaning manna, who, or what. This is the reaction that the Israelites had to the substance that the Lord gave them to eat (Ex 16:15). They asked "What is it?" which translates into *mân.* This substance is described as wafers made with honey and like white coriander seeds in shape (Ex 16:31). The manna could be ground into grain and cooked into cakes (see Nu 11:7, 8). When the Israelites entered the Promised Land, God caused the manna to cease (Jos 5:12).

4479. מַן, **man,** *man;* (Chaldee); from 4101; *who* or *what* (properly interrogative, hence also indefinite and relative):—what, who (-msoever, + -so).

4480. מִן, **min,** *min;* or מִנִּי, **minnîy,** *min-nee´;* or מִנֵּי, **minnêy,** *min-nay´;* (constructive plural); (Isa 30:11), for 4482; (properly) a *part* of; hence (prepositional), *from* or *out of* in many senses (as follows):—above, after, among, at, because of, by, (reason of), from (among), in, × neither, × nor, (out) of, over, since, × then, through, × whether, with.

4481. מִן, **min,** *min;* (Chaldee); corresponding to 4480:—according, after, + because, + before, by, for, from, × him, × more than, (out) of, part, since, × these, to, upon, + when.

4482. מֵן, **mên,** *mane;* from an unused root meaning to *apportion;* a *part;* hence a musical *chord* (as parted into strings):—in [the same] (Ps 68:23), stringed instrument (Ps 150:4), whereby (Ps 45:8 *[defective plural]*).

4483. מְנָא, **me͏nâ',** *men-aw´;* (Chaldee); or מְנָה, **me͏nâh,** *men-aw´;* (Chaldee); corresponding to 4487; to *count, appoint:*—number, ordain, set.

4484. מְנֵא, **me͏nê',** *men-ay´;* (Chaldee); passive participle of 4483; *numbered:*—Mene.

4485. מַנְגִּינָה, **mangîynâh,** *man-ghee-naw´;* from 5059; a *satire:*—music.

4486. מַנְדַּע, **manda',** *man-dah´;* (Chaldee); corresponding to 4093; *wisdom* or *intelligence:*—knowledge, reason, understanding.

An Aramaic masculine noun meaning knowledge, reason, intelligence, power of knowing. This word is found only in Daniel. When King Nebuchadnezzar was turned into an animal, he was said to have lost his reason and understanding. Upon his restoration to his human body, his mind was also restored (Da 4:36[33]). Daniel himself was described as a man of understanding and knowledge with an excellent spirit (Da 5:12).

4487. מָנָה, **mânâh,** *maw-naw´;* a primitive root; (properly) to *weigh* out; (by implication) to *allot* or constitute officially; also to *enumerate* or enroll:—appoint, count, number, prepare, set, tell.

4488. מָנֶה, **mâneh,** *maw-neh´;* from 4487; (properly) a fixed *weight* or measured amount, i.e. (technical) a *maneh* or mina:—maneh, pound.

4489. מֹנֶה, **môneh,** *mo-neh´*; from 4487; (properly) something *weighed* out, i.e. (figurative) a *portion* of time, i.e. an *instance*:—time.

4490. מְנָה, **mânâh,** *maw-naw´*; from 4487; (properly) something *weighed* out, i.e. (general) a *division*; specifically (of food) a *ration*; also a *lot*:—such things as belonged, part, portion.

4491. מִנְהָג, **minhâg,** *min-hawg´*; from 5090; the *driving* (of a chariot):—driving.

4492. מִנְהָרָה, **minhârâh,** *min-haw-raw´*; from 5102; (properly) a *channel* or fissure, i.e. (by implication) a *cavern*:—den.

4493. מָנוֹד, **mânôwd,** *maw-node´*; from 5110; a *nodding* or *toss* (of the head in derision):—shaking.

4494. מָנוֹחַ, **mânôwach,** *maw-no´-akh*; from 5117; *quiet*, i.e. (concrete) a *settled spot*, or (figurative) a *home*:—(place of) rest.

4495. מָנוֹחַ, **Mânôwach,** *maw-no´-akh*; the same as 4494; *rest; Manoäch*, an Israelite:—Manoah.

4496. מְנוּחָה, **menûwchâh,** *men-oo-khaw´*; or מְנֻחָה, **menuchâh,** *men-oo-khaw´*; feminine of 4495; *repose* or (adverb) *peacefully*; (figurative) *consolation* (specifically) *matrimony*; hence (concrete) an *abode*:—comfortable, ease, quiet, rest (-ing place), still.

4497. מָנוֹן, **mânôwn,** *maw-nohn´*; from 5125; a *continuator*, i.e. *heir*:—son.

4498. מָנוֹס, **mânôws,** *maw-noce´*; from 5127; a *retreat* (literal or figurative); (abstract) a *fleeing*:—× apace, escape, way to flee, flight, refuge.

4499. מְנוּסָה, **menûwsâh,** *men-oo-saw´*; or מְנֻסָה, **menusâh,** *men-oo-saw´*; feminine of 4498; *retreat*:—fleeing, flight.

4500. מָנוֹר, **mânôwr,** *maw-nore´*; from 5214; a *yoke* (properly, for *ploughing*), i.e. the *frame* of a loom:—beam.

4501. מְנוֹרָה, **menôwrâh,** *men-o-raw´*; or מְנֹרָה, **menôrâh,** *men-o-raw´*; feminine of 4500 (in the original sense of 5216); a *chandelier*:—candlestick.

4502. מִנְזָר, **minnezâr,** *min-ez-awr´*; from 5144; a *prince*:—crowned.

4503. מִנְחָה, **minchâh,** *min-khaw´*; from an unused root meaning to *apportion*, i.e. *bestow*; a *donation*; (euphemism) *tribute*; specifically a sacrificial *offering* (usually bloodless and voluntary):—gift, oblation, (meat) offering, present, sacrifice.

A feminine noun meaning a gift, a tribute, an offering. This word is used to signify a gift as in the peace gifts that Jacob presented to Esau (Ge 32:13[14]). Secondly, it signifies a tribute. An example of the use of this word is Jgs 3:15, where Ehud was sent from Israel to Moab on the pretense of bringing a tribute. Perhaps the most frequent use of this word is to denote a grain offering. Grain offerings were brought on pans, suggesting cakes (Le 2:5) and mixed with oil and other substances (Nu 6:15).

4504. מִנְחָה, **minchâh,** *min-khaw´*; (Chaldee); corresponding to 4503; a sacrificial *offering*:—oblation, meat offering.

An Aramaic feminine noun meaning a gift, a sacrificial offering, an oblation, a meat offering. When Daniel was promoted to chief administrator of Babylon, the celebration included the presentation of an offering signified by this Aramaic word (Da 2:46). King Artaxerxes also used this Aramaic word to command Ezra to offer sacrificial gifts on the altar of God when he arrived in Jerusalem (Ezr 7:17). This word corresponds directly to *minchâh* (4503).

4505. מְנַחֵם, **Menachêm,** *men-akh-ame´*; from 5162; *comforter; Menachem*, an Israelite:—Menahem.

4506. מָנַחַת, **Mânachath,** *maw-nakh´-ath*; from 5117; *rest; Manachath*, the name of an Edomite and of a place in Moab:—Manahath.

4507. מְנִי, **Meniy,** *men-ee´*; from 4487; the *Appor-tioner*, i.e. Fate (as an idol):—number.

4508. מִנִּי, **Minniy,** *min-nee´*; of foreign derivation; *Minni*, an Armenian province:—Minni.

4509. מִנְיָמִין, **Minyâmiyn,** *min-yaw-meen´*; from 4480 and 3225; *from* (the) *right hand; Minjamin*, the name of two Israelites:—Miniamin. Compare 4326.

4510. מִנְיָן, **minyân,** *min-yawn´*; (Chaldee); from 4483; *enumeration*:—number.

4511. מִנִּית, **Minnîyth,** *min-neeth´*; from the same as 4482; *enumeration; Minnith,* a place East of the Jordan:—Minnith.

4512. מִנְלֶה, **minleh,** *min-leh´*; from 5239; *completion,* i.e. (in produce) *wealth*:—perfection.

4513. מָנַע, **mâna‘,** *maw-nah´*; a primitive root; to *debar* (negative or positive) from benefit or injury:—deny, keep (back), refrain, restrain, withhold.

4514. מַנְעוּל, **man‘ûwl,** *man-ool´*; or מַנְעֻל, **man‘ul,** *man-ool´*; from 5274; a *bolt*:—lock.

4515. מִנְעָל, **min‘âl,** *min-awl´*; from 5274; a *bolt*:—shoe.

4516. מַנְעַמִּים, **man‘ammîym,** *man-am-meem´*; from 5276; a *delicacy*:—dainty.

4517. מְנַעְנְעִים, **m^ena‘an‘îym,** *men-ah-ah-neem´*; from 5128; a *sistrum* (so called from its *rattling* sound):—cornet.

4518. מְנַקִּית, **m^enaqqîyth,** *men-ak-keeth´*; from 5352; a *sacrificial basin* (for holding blood):—bowl.

4519. מְנַשֶּׁה, **M^enashsheh,** *men-ash-sheh´*; from 5382; *causing to forget; Menashsheh,* a grandson of Jacob, also the tribe descendant from him, and its territory:—Manasseh.

4520. מְנַשִּׁי, **M^enashshîy,** *men-ash-shee´*; from 4519; a *Menash-shite* or descendant of Menashsheh:—of Manasseh, Manassites.

4521. מְנָת, **m^enâth,** *men-awth´*; from 4487; an *allotment* (by courtesy, law or providence):—portion.

4522. מַס, **mas,** *mas*; or מִס, **mis,** *mees*; from 4549; (properly) a *burden* (as causing to *faint*), i.e. a *tax* in the form of forced *labour*:—discomfited, levy, task [-master], tribute (-tary).

4523. מָס, **mâs,** *mawce*; from 4549; *fainting*, i.e. (figurative) *disconsolate*:—is afflicted.

4524. מֵסַב, **mêsab,** *may-sab´*; plural masculine מְסִבִּים, **mesibbîym,** *mes-ib-beem´*; or feminine מְסִבּוֹת, **mesibbôwth,** *mes-ib-bohth´*; from 5437; a *divan* (as *enclosing* the room); abstract (adverb) *around*:—that compass about, (place) round about, at table.

4525. מַסְגֵּר, **masgêr,** *mas-gare´*; from 5462; a *fastener*, i.e. (of a person) a *smith*, (of a thing) a *prison*:—prison, smith.

4526. מִסְגֶּרֶת, **misgereth,** *mis-gheh´-reth*; from 5462; something *enclosing*, i.e. a *margin* (of a region, of a panel); (concrete) a *stronghold*:—border, close place, hole.

4527. מַסַּד, **massad,** *mas-sad´*; from 3245; a *foundation*:—foundation.

4528. מִסְדְּרוֹן, **misd^erôwn,** *mis-der-ohn´*; from the same as 5468; a *colonnade* or internal portico (from its *rows* of pillars):—porch.

4529. מָסָה, **mâsâh,** *maw-saw´*; a primitive root; to *dissolve*:—make to consume away, (make to) melt, water.

4530. מִסָּה, **missâh,** *mis-saw´*; from 4549 (in the sense of *flowing*); *abundance*, i.e. (adverb) *liberally*:—tribute.

4531. מַסָּה, **massâh,** *mas-saw´*; from 5254; a *testing*, of men (judicial) or of God (querulous):—temptation, trial.

A feminine noun meaning despair, a test, a trial, proving. The Hebrew word is actually two homographs—words that are spelled the same yet have distinct origins and meanings. The first homograph is derived from the verb *mâsas* (4549), meaning to dissolve or melt, and it means despair. This word occurs only in Job 9:23. The second homograph is derived from the verb *nâsâh* (5254), meaning to test or try, and denotes a test, a trial, or proving. It is used in reference to the manifestations of God's power and handiwork before the Egyptians at the Exodus (Dt 4:34; 7:19; 29:3[2]). Furthermore, this term has become a proper noun, *massâh* (4532), to designate the place where the Israelites tested God (Ex 17:7; Dt 6:16; 9:22; Ps 95:8); and where Levi was tested (Dt 33:8).

4532. מַסָּה, **Massâh,** *mas-saw´*; the same as 4531; *Massah*, a place in the Desert:—Massah.

4533. מַסְוֶה, **masveh,** *mas-veh´*; apparently from an unused root meaning to *cover*; a *veil*:—vail.

4534. מְסוּכָה, **m^esûwkâh,** *mes-oo-kaw´*; for 4881; a *hedge*:—thorn hedge.

4535. מְסָח, **massâch,** *mas-sawkh´;* from 5255 in the sense of *staving* off; a *cordon,* (adverb) or (as a) military *barrier:*—broken down.

4536. מִסְחָר, **mischâr,** *mis-khawr´;* from 5503; *trade:*—traffic.

4537. מָסַךְ, **mâsak,** *maw-sak´;* a primitive root; to *mix,* especially wine (with spices):—mingle.

4538. מֶסֶךְ, **mesek,** *meh´-sek;* from 4537; a *mixture,* i.e. of wine with spices:—mixture.

4539. מָסָךְ, **mâsâk,** *maw-sawk;* from 5526; a *cover,* i.e. *veil:*—covering, curtain, hanging.

4540. מְסֻכָּה, **mᵉsukkâh,** *mes-ook-kaw´;* from 5526; a *covering,* i.e. garniture:—covering.

4541. מַסֵּכָה, **massêkâh,** *mas-say-kaw´;* from 5258; (properly) a *pouring* over, i.e. *fusion* of metal (especially a *cast* image); (by implication) a *libation,* i.e. league; (concrete) a *coverlet* (as if *poured* out):—covering, molten (image), vail.

A feminine noun meaning an image, molten metal, covering, an alliance. When the word means a libation or drink offering, it is associated with sacrifices that seal a covenant relationship (Isa 25:7; 28:20; 30:1); however, the word usually signifies an image or molten metal. In those cases, the word identifies an idol, which has been formed from molten metal and has been poured into a cast. The worship of such images is clearly prohibited by God (Ex 34:17; Le 19:4; Dt 27:15). The Israelites were commanded to destroy any idols they discovered in Canaan (Nu 33:52). The prophets proclaimed the futility of all idols, including those described as *massêkâh* (Isa 42:17); and God would punish those who worshiped them (Hos 13:2, 3; Na 1:14; Hab 2:18). In spite of all this, the Israelites formed and worshiped idols, including molten idols like Aaron's golden calf (Ex 32:4, 8; Dt 9:16; Ne 9:18); Micah's idols (Jgs 17:3, 4; 18:17, 18); and Jeroboam's idols (1Ki 14:9; cf. 1Ki 12:28–30).

4542. מִסְכֵּן, **miskên,** *mis-kane´;* from 5531; *indigent:*—poor (man).

4543. מִסְכְּנוֹת, **miskᵉnôwth,** *mis-ken-oth´;* by transposition from 3664; a *magazine:*—store (-house), treasure.

4544. מִסְכְּנֻת, **miskênuth,** *mis-kay-nooth´;* from 4542; *indigence:*—scarceness.

4545. מַסֶּכֶת, **masseketh,** *mas-seh´-keth;* from 5259 in the sense of *spreading* out; something *expanded,* i.e. the *warp* in a loom (as *stretched* out to receive the woof):—web.

4546. מְסִלָּה, **mᵉsillâh,** *mes-il-law´;* from 5549; a *thoroughfare* (as *turnpiked*), literal or figurative; specifically a *viaduct,* a *staircase:*—causeway, course, highway, path, terrace.

4547. מַסְלוּל, **maslûwl,** *mas-lool´;* from 5549; a *thoroughfare* (as turnpiked):—highway.

4548. מַסְמֵר, **masmêr,** *mas-mare´;* or מִסְמֵר, **mismêr,** *mis-mare´;* also (feminine) מַסְמְרָה, **masmᵉrâh,** *mas-mer-aw´;* or מִסְמְרָה, **mismᵉrâh,** *mis-mer-aw´;* or even מַשְׂמְרָה **maśmᵉrâh,** *mas-mer-aw´;* (Ecc 12:11), from 5568; a *peg* (as *bristling* from the surface):—nail.

4549. מָסַס, **mâsas,** *maw-sas´;* a primitive root; to *liquefy;* (figurative) to *waste* (with disease), to *faint* (with fatigue, fear or grief):—discourage, faint, be loosed, melt (away), refuse, × utterly.

4550. מַסַּע, **massa',** *mas-sah;* from 5265; a *departure* (from *striking* the tents), i.e. march (not necessarily a single day's travel); (by implication) a *station* (or point of *departure):*—journey (-ing).

4551. מַסָּע, **massâ',** *mas-saw´;* from 5265 in the sense of *projecting;* a *missile* (spear or arrow); also a *quarry* (whence stones are, as it were, *ejected):*—before it was brought, dart.

4552. מִסְעָד, **mis'âd,** *mis-awd´;* from 5582; a *balus-trade* (for stairs):—pillar.

4553. מִסְפֵּד, **mispêd,** *mis-pade´;* from 5594; a *lamentation:*—lamentation, one mourneth, mourning, wailing.

4554. מִסְפּוֹא, **mispôw',** *mis-po´;* from an unused root meaning to *collect; fodder:*—provender.

4555. מִסְפָּחָה, **mispâchâh,** *mis-paw-khaw´;* from 5596; a *veil* (as *spread* out):—kerchief.

4556. מִסְפַּחַת, **mispachath,** *mis-pakh´-ath;* from 5596; *scurf* (as *spreading* over the surface):—scab.

4557. מִסְפָּר, **mispâr,** *mis-pawr´;* from 5608; a *number,* definite (arithmetical) or indefinite (large, *innumerable;* small, a *few*); also (abstract) *narration:*— + abundance, account, × all, × few, [in-] finite, (certain) number (-ed), tale, telling, + time.

4558. מִסְפָּר, **Mispâr,** *mis-pawr´*; the same as 4457; *number; Mispar,* an Israelite:—Mizpar. Compare 4559.

4559. מִסְפֶּרֶת, **Mispereth,** *mis-peh´-reth*; feminine of 4457; *enumeration; Mispereth,* an Israelite:—Mispereth. Compare 4458.

4560. מָסַר, **mâsar,** *maw-sar´*; a primitive root; to *sunder,* i.e. (transitive) *set apart,* or (reflexive) *apostatize:*—commit, deliver.

4561. מֹסָר, **môsâr,** *mo-sawr´*; from 3256; *admonition:*—instruction.

4562. מֹסֶרֶת, **mâsôreth,** *maw-so´-reth*; from 631; a *band:*—bond.

4563. מִסְתּוֹר, **mistôwr,** *mis-tore´*; from 5641; a *refuge:*—covert.

4564. מַסְתֵּר, **mastêr,** *mas-tare´*; from 5641; (properly) a *hider,* i.e. (abstract) a *hiding,* i.e. *aversion:*—hid.

4565. מִסְתָּר, **mistâr,** *mis-tawr´*; from 5641; (properly) a *concealer,* i.e. a *covert:*—secret (-ly, place).

4566. מַעֲבָד, **ma‘âbâd,** *mah-ah-bawd´*; from 5647; an *act:*—work.

4567. מַעֲבָד, **ma‘âbâd,** *mah-ah-bawd´*; (Chaldee); corresponding to 4566; an *act:*—work.

4568. מַעֲבֶה, **ma‘âbeh,** *mah-ab-eh´*; from 5666; (properly) *compact* (part of soil), i.e. *loam:*—clay.

4569. מַעֲבָר, **ma‘âbâr,** *mah-ab-awr´*; or feminine מַעְבָּרָה, **ma‘bârâh,** *mah-baw-raw´*; from 5674; a *crossing*-place (of a river, a *ford;* of a mountain, a *pass*); (abstract) a *transit,* i.e. (figurative) *overwhelming:*—ford, place where … pass, passage.

4570. מַעְגָּל, **ma‘gâl,** *mah-gawl´*; or feminine מַעְגָּלָה, **ma‘gâlâh,** *mah-gaw-law´*; from the same as 5696; a *track* (literal or figurative); also a *rampart* (as *circular*):—going, path, trench, way ([-side]).

4571. מָעַד, **mâ‘ad,** *maw-ad´*; a primitive root; to *waver:*—make to shake, slide, slip.

4572. מַעֲדַי, **Ma‘ăday,** *mah-ad-ah´ee*; from 5710; *ornamental; Maadai,* an Israelite:—Maadai.

4573. מַעֲדְיָה, **Ma‘adyâh,** *mah-ad-yaw´*; from 5710 and 3050; *ornament of Jah; Maadjah,* an Israelite:—Maadiah. Compare 4153.

4574. מַעֲדָן, **ma‘ădân,** *mah-ad-awn´*; or (feminine) מַעֲדָנָה, **ma‘-ădannâh,** *mah-ad-an-naw´*; from 5727; a *delicacy* or (abstract) *pleasure* (adverb *cheerfully*):—dainty, delicately, delight.

4575. מַעֲדַנּוֹת, **ma‘ădannôwth,** *mah-ad-an-noth´*; by transposition from 6029; a *bond,* i.e. *group:*—influence.

4576. מַעְדֵּר, **ma‘dêr,** *mah-dare´*; from 5737; a (weeding) *hoe:*—mattock.

4577. מְעֵה, **m e ‘êh,** *meh-ay´*; (Chaldee); or מְעָא, **m e ‘â’,** *meh-aw´*; (Chaldee); corresponding to 4578; only in plural the *bowels:*—belly.

4578. מֵעֶה, **mê‘eh,** *may-aw´*; from an unused root probably meaning to *be soft*; used only in plural the *intestines,* or (collective) the *abdomen,* (figurative) *sympathy*; (by implication) a *vest*; (by extension) the *stomach,* the *uterus* (or of men, the seat of generation), the *heart* (figurative):—belly, bowels, × heart, womb.

A masculine noun meaning internal organs, intestines, belly, womb, sexual organs, sympathy. It refers to internal organs. When Joab stabbed Amasa, his entrails fell onto the ground (2Sa 20:10); the digestive tract; when a woman was suspected of infidelity, she was made to take an oath cursing the water that entered her stomach (Nu 5:22); and the sexual organs; God promised Abram that he would bear a son from his own loins (Ge 15:4). It can also be used figuratively to mean the seat of emotions or heart (Isa 16:11).

4579. מֵעָה, **mâ‘âh,** *maw-aw´*; feminine of 4578; the *belly,* i.e. (figurative) *interior:*—gravel.

4580. מָעוֹג, **mâ‘ôwg,** *maw-ogue´*; from 5746; a *cake* of bread (with 3934 a *table-buffoon,* i.e. *parasite*):—cake, feast.

4581. מָעוֹז, **mâ‘ôwz,** *maw-oze´*; (also מָעוּז, **mâ‘ûwz,** *maw-ooz´*; or מָעֹז, **mâ‘ôz,** *maw-oze´* (also מָעֻז, **mâ‘uz,** *maw-ooz´*; from 5810; a *fortified* place; (figurative) a *defence:*—force, fort (-ress), rock, strength (-en), (× most) strong (hold).

4582. מָעוּךְ, **Mâ'ôwk,** *maw-oke´*; from 4600; *oppressed; Maok,* a Philistine:—Maoch.

4583. מָעוֹן, **mâ'ôwn,** *maw-ohn´*; or מָעִין, **mâ'îyn,** *maw-een´*; (1Ch 4:41), from the same as 5772; an *abode,* of God (the tabernacle or the Temple), men (their home) or animals (their lair); hence a *retreat* (asylum):—den, dwelling ([-] place), habitation.

4584. מָעוֹן, **Mâ'ôwn,** *maw-ohn´*; the same as 4583; a *residence; Maon,* the name of an Israelite and of a place in Palestine:—Maon, Maonites. Compare 1010, 4586.

4585. מְעוֹנָה, **me'ôwnâh,** *meh-o-naw´*; or מְעֹנָה, **me'ônâh,** *meh-o-naw´*; feminine of 4583, and meaning the same:—den, habitation, (dwelling) place, refuge.

4586. מְעוּנִי, **Me'ûwnîy,** *meh-oo-nee´*; or מְעִינִי, **Me'îy-nîy,** *meh-ee-nee´*; probably patrial from 4584; a *Meünite,* or inhabitant of Maon (only in plural):—Mehunim (-s), Meunim.

4587. מְעוֹנֹתַי, **Me'ônôwthay,** *meh-o-no-thah´ee*; plural of 4585; *habitative; Meonothai,* an Israelite:—Meonothai.

4588. מָעוּף, **mâ'ûwph,** *maw-oof´*; from 5774 in the sense of *covering* with shade [compare 4155]; *darkness:*—dimness.

4589. מָעוֹר, **mâ'ôwr,** *maw-ore´*; from 5783; *nakedness,* i.e. (in plural) the *pudenda:*—nakedness.

4590. מַעַזְיָה, **Ma'azyâh,** *mah-az-yaw´*; or מַעַזְיָהוּ, **Ma'azyâhûw,** *mah-az-yaw´-hoo*; probably from 5756 (in the sense of *protection*) and 3050; *rescue of Jah; Maazjah,* the name of two Israelites:—Maaziah.

4591. מָעַט, **mâ'aṭ,** *maw-at´*; a primitive root; (properly) to *pare* off, i.e. *lessen;* (intransitive) to *be* (causative, to *make*) *small* or *few;* (figurative) *ineffective:*—suffer to decrease, diminish, (be, × borrow a, give, make) few (in number, -ness), gather least (little), be (seem) little, (× give the) less, be minished, bring to nothing.

4592. מְעַט, **me'aṭ,** *meh-at´*; or מְעָט, **me'âṭ,** *meh-awt´*; from 4591; a *little* or *few* (often adverbial or comparative):—almost, (some, very) few (-er, -est), lightly, little (while), (very) small (matter, thing), some, soon, × very.

4593. מְעֻטָּה, **me'uṭṭâh,** *maw-ote´*; passive adjective of 4591; *thinned* (as to the edge), i.e. *sharp:*—wrapped up.

4594. מַעֲטֶה, **ma'ăṭeh,** *mah-at-eh´*; from 5844; a *vestment:*—garment.

4595. מַעֲטָפָת, **ma'ăṭepheth,** *mah-at-aw-faw´*; from 5848; a *cloak:*—mantle.

4596. מְעִי, **me'îy,** *meh-ee´*; from 5753; a *pile* of rubbish (as *contorted*), i.e. a *ruin* (compare 5856):—heap.

4597. מָעַי, **Mâ'ay,** *maw-ah´ee*; probably from 4578; *sympathetic; Maai,* an Israelite:—Maai.

4598. מְעִיל, **me'îyl,** *meh-eel´*; from 4603 in the sense of *covering*; a *robe* (i.e. upper and outer *garment*):—cloke, coat, mantle, robe.

4599. מַעְיָן, **ma'yân,** *mah-yawn´*; or מַעְיְנוֹ, **ma'y e nôw,** *mah-yen-o´*; (Ps 114:8), or (feminine) מַעְיָנָה, **ma'yânâh,** *mah-yaw-naw´*; from 5869 (as a denominative in the sense of a *spring*); a *fountain* (also collective), (figurative) a *source* (of satisfaction):—fountain, spring, well.

4600. מָעַךְ, **mâ'ak,** *maw-ak´*; a primitive root; to *press,* i.e. to *pierce, emasculate, handle:*—bruised, stuck, be pressed.

4601. מַעֲכָה, **Ma'ăkâh,** *mah-ak-aw´*; or מַעֲכָת, **Ma'ă-kâth,** *mah-ak-awth´*; (Jos 13:13), from 4600; *depression; Maakah* (or *Maakath*), the name of a place in Syria, also of a Mesopotamian, of three Israelites, and of four Israelitesses and one Syrian woman:—Maachah, Maachathites. See also 1038.

4602. מַעֲכָתִי, **Ma'ăkâthîy,** *mah-ak-aw-thee´*; patrial from 4601; a *Maakathite,* or inhabitant of Maakah:—Maachathite.

4603. מָעַל, **mâ'al,** *maw-al´*; a primitive root; (properly) to *cover* up; (used only figurative) to *act covertly,* i.e. *treacherously:*—transgress, (commit, do a) trespass (-ing).

A verb meaning to violate one's duty. The term is used often as a synonym for sin; however, this word almost always denotes a willing act (Nu 5:6; Eze 14:13). It occurs principally in the later books of the OT and is almost exclusively a religious term. There are only two secular uses: one for a wife's unfaithfulness to her husband

and the other for a king's unfaithfulness in judgment (Nu 5:12, 27; Pr 16:10). Although the offence is usually against God Himself, three times the unfaithfulness is directed against something under divine ban and not directly against God (Jos 22:20; 1Ch 10:13; Eze 18:24). The writer of 1 and 2 Chronicles often connected national unfaithfulness with God's sending of punitive wars; ultimately, the outcome meant deportation for the Northern Kingdom and destruction and exile for the Southern Kingdom (1Ch 5:25; 2Ch 12:2; 28:19, 22; 36:14).

4604. מַעַל, **ma'al,** *mah´-al*; from 4603; *treachery,* i.e. sin:—falsehood, grievously, sore, transgression, trespass, × very.

A masculine noun meaning an unfaithful act, a treacherous act. Of its twenty-nine occurrences, it appears twenty times as a cognate accusative to the verb *mâ'al* (4603), meaning to act unfaithfully or treacherously. It can apply to actions against another person, such as a wife against her husband (Nu 5:12, 27); Job by his "comforters" (Job 21:34). However, it usually applies to actions against God, whether those actions be committed by an individual (Le 5:15; 6:2[5:21]; Jos 7:1; 22:20); or by the nation of Israel collectively (Jos 22:22; 1Ch 9:1; Ezr 9:2, 4; 10:6; Eze 39:26).

4605. מַעַל, **ma'al,** *mah´-al*; from 5927; (properly) the *upper* part, used only adverb with prefix *upward, above, overhead, from the top,* etc.:—above, exceeding (-ly), forward, on (× very) high, over, up (-on, -ward), very.

4606. מְעָל, **me'âl,** *meh-awl´*; (Chaldee); from 5954; (only in plural as singular) the *setting* (of the sun):—going down.

4607. מוֹעַל, **mô'al,** *mo´-al*; from 5927; a *raising* (of the hands):—lifting up.

4608. מַעֲלֶה, **ma'ăleh,** *mah-al-eh´*; from 5927; an *elevation,* i.e. (concrete) *acclivity* or *platform*; abstract (the relation or state) a *rise* or (figurative) *priority*:—ascent, before, chiefest, cliff, that goeth up, going up, hill, mounting up, stairs.

4609. מַעֲלָה, **ma'ălâh,** *mah-al-aw´*; feminine of 4608; *elevation,* i.e. the act; (literal) a *journey* to a higher place; (figurative) a *thought* arising; (concrete) the condition (literal) a *step* or *grade*-mark; (figurative) a *superiority* of station;

(specifically) a climactic *progression* (in certain Psalms):—things that come up, (high) degree, deal, go up, stair, step, story.

4610. מַעֲלֵה עַקְרַבִּים, **Ma'alêh 'Aqrabbîym,** *mah-al-ay´ ak-rab-beem´*; from 4608 and (the plural of) 6137; *Steep of Scorpions,* a place in the Desert:—Maaleh-accrabim, the ascent (going up) of Akrabbim.

4611. מַעֲלָל, **ma'ălâl,** *mah-al-awl´*; from 5953; an *act* (good or bad):—doing, endeavour, invention, work.

4612. מַעֲמָד, **ma'ămâd,** *mah-am-awd´*; from 5975; (figurative) a *position*:—attendance, office, place, state.

4613. מָעֳמָד, **mo'ŏmâd,** *moh-om-awd´*; from 5975; (literal) a *foothold*:—standing.

4614. מַעֲמָסָה, **ma'ămâsâh,** *mah-am-aw-saw´*; from 6006; *burdensomeness*:—burdensome.

4615. מַעֲמַקִּים, **ma'ămaqqîym,** *mah-am-ak-keem´*; from 6009; a *deep*:—deep, depth.

4616. מַעַן, **ma'an,** *mah´-an*; from 6030; (properly) *heed,* i.e. *purpose*; (used only adverbially) *on account of* (as a motive or an aim); (teleologically) *in order that*:—because of, to the end (intent) that, for (to, … 's sake), + lest, that, to.

4617. מַעֲנֶה, **ma'ăneh,** *mah-an-eh´*; from 6030; a *reply* (favourable or contradictory):—answer, × himself.

4618. מַעֲנָה, **ma'ănâh,** *mah-an-aw´*; from 6031, in the sense of *depression* or *tilling*; a *furrow*:—+ acre, furrow.

4619. מַעַץ, **Ma'ats,** *mah´-ats*; from 6095; *closure*; *Maats,* an Israelite:—Maaz.

4620. מַעֲצֵבָה, **ma'ătsêbâh,** *mah-ats-ay-baw´*; from 6087; *anguish*:—sorrow.

4621. מַעֲצָד, **ma'ătsâd,** *mah-ats-awd´*; from an unused root meaning to *hew*; an *ax*:—ax, tongs.

4622. מַעְצוֹר, **ma'tsôwr,** *mah-tsore´*; from 6113; (objective) a *hindrance*:—restraint.

A masculine noun meaning a restraint, a hindrance. This noun is derived from the verb *'âtsar* (6113), meaning to restrain or to retain. It occurs only one time, where Jonathan tells his armourbearer that "there is no restraint to the LORD to save by many or by few" (1Sa 14:6, KJV).

4623. מַעְצָר, **ma'tsâr,** *mah-tsawr´;* from 6113; (subjective) *control:*—rule.

A masculine noun meaning a restraint, a control. This noun is derived from the verb *'âtsar* (6113), meaning to restrain or retain. Its only occurrence is to characterize a person as one who is without self-control. This person is also compared to a ruined city without walls (Pr 25:28).

4624. מַעֲקֶה, **ma'ăqeh,** *mah-ak-eh´;* from an unused root meaning to *repress;* a *parapet:*—battlement.

4625. מַעֲקַשִׁים, **ma'ăqâshshîym,** *mah-ak-ash-sheem´;* from 6140; a *crook* (in a road):—crooked thing.

4626. מַעַר, **ma'ar,** *mah´-ar;* from 6168; a *nude* place, i.e. (literal) the *pudenda,* or (figurative) a vacant *space:*—nakedness, proportion.

4627. מַעֲרָב, **ma'ărâb,** *mah-ar-awb´;* from 6148, in the sense of *trading; traffic;* (by implication) mercantile *goods:*—market, merchandise.

4628. מַעֲרָב, **ma'ărâb,** *mah-ar-awb´;* or (feminine) מַעֲרָבָה, **ma'ărâbâh,** *mah-ar-aw-baw´;* from 6150, in the sense of *shading;* the *west* (as the region of the *evening* sun):—west.

4629. מַעֲרֶה, **ma'ăreh,** *mah-ar-eh´;* from 6168; a *nude* place, i.e. a *common:*—meadows.

4630. מַעֲרָה, **ma'ărâh,** *mah-ar-aw´;* feminine of 4629; an *open* spot:—army [*from the margin*].

4631. מְעָרָה, **mᵉ'ârâh,** *meh-aw-raw´;* from 5783; a *cavern* (as dark):—cave, den, hole.

4632. מְעָרָה, **Mᵉ'ârâh,** *meh-aw-raw´;* the same as 4631; *cave; Meärah,* a place in Palestine:—Mearah.

4633. מַעֲרָךְ, **ma'ărâk,** *mah-ar-awk´;* from 6186; an *arrangement,* i.e. (figurative) mental *disposition:*—preparation.

4634. מַעֲרָכָה, **ma'ărâkâh,** *mah-ar-aw-kaw´;* feminine of 4633; an *arrangement;* (concrete) a *pile;* (specifically) a military *array:*—army, fight, be set in order, ordered place, rank, row.

4635. מַעֲרֶכֶת, **ma'ăreketh,** *mah-ar-eh´-keth;* from 6186; an *arrangement,* i.e. (concrete) a *pile* (of loaves):—row, shewbread.

A feminine noun meaning a row, a line. This word comes from the verb *'ârak* (6186), meaning to arrange or to line up. The first time this word appears is in Le 24:6, 7, where it describes the arrangement of the showbread: two rows of bread with six pieces in a row. In the other seven instances of this word, it is best translated "showbread" (i.e. the bread that was lined up in a row) (1Ch 9:32; 23:29; 28:16; 2Ch 2:4; 13:11; 29:18; Ne 10:33[34]).

4636. מַעֲרֹם, **ma'ărôm,** *mah-ar-ome´;* from 6191, in the sense of *stripping; bare:*—naked.

4637. מַעֲרָצָה, **ma'ărâtsâh,** *mah-ar-aw-tsaw´;* from 6206; *violence:*—terror.

4638. מַעֲרָת, **Ma'ărâth,** *mah-ar-awth´;* a form of 4630; *waste; Maarath,* a place in Palestine:—Maarath.

4639. מַעֲשֶׂה, **ma'ăśeh,** *mah-as-eh´;* from 6213; an *action* (good or bad); (generally) a *transaction;* (abstract) *activity;* (by implication) a *product* (specifically) a *poem;* or (generic) *property:*—act, art, + bakemeat, business, deed, do (-ing), labour, thing made, ware of making, occupation, thing offered, operation, possession, × well, ([handy-, needle-, net-]) work (-ing, -manship), wrought.

4640. מַעֲשַׂי, **Ma'ăśay,** *mah-as-ah´ee;* from 6213; *operative; Maasai,* an Israelite:—Maasiai.

4641. מַעֲשֵׂיָה, **Ma'ăśêyâh,** *mah-as-ay-yaw´;* or מַעֲשֵׂיָהוּ, **Ma'ăśê-yâhûw,** *mah-as-ay-yaw´-hoo;* from 4639 and 3050; *work of Jah; Maasejah,* the name of sixteen Israelites:—Maaseiah.

4642. מַעֲשַׁקּוֹת, **ma'ăshaqqôth,** *mah-ash-ak-koth´;* from 6231; *oppression:*—oppression, × oppressor.

4643. מַעֲשֵׂר, **ma'ăśêr,** *mah-as-ayr´;* or מַעֲשַׂר, **ma'ăśar,** *mah-as-ar´;* and (in plural) feminine מַעֲשָׂרָה, **ma'aśrâh,** *mah-as-raw´;* from 6240; a *tenth;* especially a *tithe:*—tenth (part), tithe (-ing).

A masculine noun meaning tithe, tenth. This word is related to *'eśer* (6235), meaning ten, and often means tenth (Ge 14:20; Eze 45:11, 14). In the Levitical system of the OT, this word refers to the tenth part, which came to be known as the tithe. Israelites were to tithe from their land, herds, flocks, and other sources (Le 27:30–32).

Such tithes were intended to support the Levites in their priestly duties (Nu 18:21, 24, 26, 28); as well as strangers, orphans, and widows (Dt 26:12). When Israel failed to give the tithe, it was a demonstration of their disobedience (Mal 3:8, 10); when they reinstituted the tithe, it was a sign of reform, as in Hezekiah's (2Ch 31:5, 6, 12) and Nehemiah's times (Ne 10:37[38], 38[39]; 12:44).

4644. מֹף, **Môph,** *mofe*; of Egyptian origin; *Moph*, the capital of Lower Egypt:—Memphis. Compare 5297.

4645. מִפְגָּע, **miphgâ',** *mif-gaw'*; from 6293; an *object of attack*:—mark.

4646. מַפָּח, **mappâch,** *map-pawkh'*; from 5301; a *breathing out* (of life), i.e. expiring:—giving up.

A masculine noun meaning breathing out. This word comes from the verb *nâphach* (5301), meaning to breathe or to blow, and occurs only once in the OT. In Job 11:20, this word describes the soul that expires.

4647. מַפֻּחַ, **mappuach,** *map-poo'-akh*; from 5301; the *bellows* (i.e. *blower*) of a forge:—bellows.

4648. מְפִיבֹשֶׁת, **Mᵉphîybôsheth,** *mef-ee-bo'-sheth*; or מְפִבֹשֶׁת, **Mephibôsheth,** *mef-ee-bo'-sheth*; probably from 6284 and 1322; *dispeller of shame* (i.e. of Baal); *Mephibosheth*, the name of two Israelites:—Mephibosheth.

4649. מֻפִּים, **Muppîym,** *moop-peem'*; a plural apparently from 5130; *wavings; Muppim*, an Israelite:—Muppim. Compare 8206.

4650. מֵפִיץ, **mêphîyts,** *may-feets'*; from 6327; a *breaker*, i.e. mallet:—maul.

4651. מַפָּל, **mappâl,** *map-pawl'*; from 5307; a *falling off*, i.e. chaff; also something *pendulous*, i.e. a flap:—flake, refuse.

4652. מִפְלָאָה, **miphlâ'âh,** *mif-law-aw'*; from 6381; a *miracle*:—wondrous work.

4653. מִפְלַגָּה, **miphlaggâh,** *mif-lag-gaw'*; from 6385; a *classification*:—division.

A feminine noun meaning division. This word comes from the verb *pâlâh* (6395), meaning to separate, and occurs only once in the OT.

In 2Ch 35:12, this word is used to describe the household divisions among the Levites.

4654. מַפָּלָה, **mappâlâh,** *map-paw-law'*; or מַפֵּלָה, **mappêlâh,** *map-pay-law'*; from 5307; something *fallen*, i.e. a *ruin*:—ruin (-ous).

4655. מִפְלָט, **miphlât,** *mif-lawt'*; from 6403; an *escape*:—escape.

4656. מִפְלֶצֶת, **miphletseth,** *mif-leh'-tseth*; from 6426; a *terror*, i.e. an idol:—idol.

A feminine noun meaning horrid thing. This word comes from the verb *pâlats* (6426), meaning to shudder, and described something so horrible that one would shudder. It was used only to describe an image (perhaps some sort of idol) that Maacah had made as an object of worship (1Ki 15:13; 2Ch 15:16).

4657. מִפְלָשׂ, **miphlâs,** *mif-lawce'*; from an unused root meaning to *balance*; a *poising*:—balancing.

4658. מַפֶּלֶת, **mappeleth,** *map-peh'-leth*; from 5307; *fall*, i.e. decadence; (concrete) a *ruin*; (specifically) a *carcase*:—carcase, fall, ruin.

A feminine noun meaning a carcass, a ruin, overthrow. This word comes from the verb *nâphal* (5307), meaning to fall. It described the physical carcass of a dead animal (Jgs 14:8); and the practical ruin of the wicked (Pr 29:16). It also described the overthrow of two nations: Tyre (Eze 26:15, 18; 27:27); and Egypt (Eze 31:13, 16; 32:10).

4659. מִפְעָל, **miph'âl,** *mif-awl'*; or (feminine) מִפְעָלָה, **miph'âlâh,** *mif-aw-law'*; from 6466; a *performance*:—work.

4660. מַפָּץ, **mappâts,** *map-pawts'*; from 5310; a *smiting* to pieces:—slaughter.

A masculine noun meaning a smashing, a shattering. This word is used in this form only once and refers to a dangerous weapon for smashing (Eze 9:2). See the related Hebrew root *nâphats* (5310), as well as the Hebrew words *nephets* (5311) and *maphphêts* (4661).

4661. מַפֵּץ, **mappêts,** *map-pates'*; from 5310; a *smiter*, i.e. a war *club*:—battle ax.

4662. מִפְקָד, **miphqâd,** *mif-kawd'*; from 6485; an *appointment*, i.e. mandate; (concrete) a designated *spot*; (specifically) a *census*:—appointed place, commandment, number.

A masculine noun meaning a mandate, an appointment, a counting, a census; an appointed place. Ten men became assistant overseers for the management of offerings in the house of the Lord by the appointment of King Hezekiah (2Ch 31:13). King David ordered Joab to take a census of the number of people under his rule (2Sa 24:9; 1Ch 21:5). Twice the word functions to designate a location. In Eze 43:21, the bull of the sin offering was to be burnt in the appointed place of the Temple precincts. In Ne 3:31, the word was utilized (possibly as a proper name) to identify a particular gate in the city of Jerusalem. This term stems from the verb *pâqad* (6485).

4663. מִפְקָד, **Miphqâd,** *mif-kawd´;* the same as 4662; *assignment; Miphkad,* the name of a gate in Jerusalem:—Miphkad.

4664. מִפְרָץ, **miphrâts,** *mif-rawts´;* from 6555; a *break* (in the shore), i.e. a *haven:*—breach.

4665. מַפְרֶקֶת, **maphreqeth,** *maf-reh´-keth;* from 6561; (properly) a *fracture,* i.e. *joint* (*vertebra*) of the neck:—neck.

4666. מִפְרָשׂ, **miphrâs,** *mif-rawce´;* from 6566; an *expansion:*—that which ... spreadest forth, spreading.

4667. מִפְשָׂעָה, **miphsâ‘âh,** *mif-saw-aw´;* from 6585; a *stride,* i.e. (by euphemism) the *crotch:*—buttocks.

4668. מַפְתֵּחַ, **maphtêach,** *maf-tay´-akh;* from 6605; an *opener,* i.e. a *key:*—key.

4669. מִפְתָּח, **miphtâch,** *mif-tawkh´;* from 6605; an *aperture,* i.e. (figurative) *utterance:*—opening.

4670. מִפְתָּן, **miphtân,** *mif-tawn´;* from the same as 6620; a *stretcher,* i.e. a *sill:*—threshold.

4671. מֹץ, **môts,** *motes;* or מוֹץ, **môwts,** *motes;* (Zep 2:2), from 4160; *chaff* (as *pressed* out, i.e. *winnowed* or [rather] threshed loose):—chaff.

4672. מָצָא, **mâtsâ’,** *maw-tsaw´;* a primitive root; (properly) to *come* forth to, i.e. *appear* or *exist;* transposed to *attain,* i.e. *find* or *acquire;* (figurative) to *occur, meet* or *be present:*— + be able, befall, being, catch, × certainly, (cause to) come (on, to, to hand), deliver, be enough (cause to) find (-ing, occasion, out), get (hold upon), × have (here), be here, hit, be left, light (up-) on,

meet (with), × occasion serve, (be) present, ready, speed, suffice, take hold on.

4673. מַצָּב, **matstsâb,** *mats-tsawb´;* from 5324; a fixed *spot;* (figurative) an *office,* a military *post:*—garrison, station, place where ... stood.

4674. מֻצָּב, **mutstsâb,** *moots-tsawb´;* from 5324; a *station,* i.e. military *post:*—mount.

4675. מַצָּבָה, **matstsâbâh,** *mats-tsaw-baw´;* or מִצָּבָה, **mitstsâbâh,** *mits-tsaw-baw´;* feminine of 4673; a military *guard:*—army, garrison.

4676. מַצֵּבָה, **matstsêbâh,** *mats-tsay-baw´;* feminine (causative) participle of 5324; something *stationed,* i.e. a *column* or (memorial *stone*); (by analogy) an *idol:*—garrison, (standing) image, pillar.

A feminine noun meaning something set upright. The word most often refers to a standing, unhewn block of stone utilized for religious and memorial purposes. After a powerful experience of the Lord in a dream, Jacob set up as a pillar the stone on which he had laid his head, in commemoration of the event (Ge 28:18, 22; cf. Ge 31:45; 35:20). Moses set up an altar and also twelve pillars at the base of Mount Sinai to represent the twelve tribes of Israel (Ex 24:4). These pillars were erected as monuments to God (Hos 3:4); or, more commonly, to pagan deities (1Ki 14:23, Mic 5:13[12]). Many times in 2Ki, the term refers to a sacred pillar that aided people in their worship of pagan gods, especially the Canaanite god Baal. In most of these passages, the sacred columns were used by Israelites, contrary to the Lord's prohibition concerning the worship of any other god (2Ki 3:2; 10:26, 27; 18:4; 23:14; cf. Hos 10:1, 2; Mic 5:13[12]). This noun stems from the verb *nâtsab* (5324).

4677. מְצֹבָיָה, **Metsôbyâh,** *meh-tsob-yaw´;* apparently from 4672 and 3050; *found of Jah; Metsobajah,* a place in Palestine:—Mesobaite.

4678. מַצֶּבֶת, **matstsebeth,** *mats-tseh´-beth;* from 5324; something *stationary,* i.e. a monumental *stone;* also the *stock* of a tree:—pillar, substance.

A feminine noun meaning a pillar, a stump, a standing stone. A monument could be set up to commemorate a divine appearance, such as the pillar of stone Jacob set up at Bethel (Ge 35:14). The word can also refer to a pillar or monument set up to honour oneself, such as the one

Absalom set up for himself in order that his name would be remembered (2Sa 18:18).

4679. מֵצַד, **mᵉtsad,** *mets-ad´;* or מְצָד, **metsâd,** *mets-awd´;* or (feminine) מְצָדָה, **metsâdâh,** *mets-aw-daw´;* from 6679; a *fastness* (as a *covert* of ambush):—castle, fort, (strong) hold, munition.

4680. מָצָה, **mâtsâh,** *maw-tsaw´;* a primitive root; to *suck* out; (by implication) to *drain,* to *squeeze* out:—suck, wring (out).

4681. מֹצָה, **Môtsâh,** *mo-tsaw´;* active participle feminine of 4680; *drained; Motsah,* a place in Palestine:—Mozah.

4682. מַצָּה, **matstsâh,** *mats-tsaw´;* from 4711 in the sense of *greedily* devouring for sweetness; (properly) *sweetness;* (concrete) *sweet* (i.e. not soured or bittered with yeast); (specifically) an *unfermented cake* or loaf, or (elliptically) the festival of *Passover* (because no leaven was then used):—unleavened (bread, cake), without leaven.

A feminine noun meaning unleavened bread or cakes. This food was a staple in Israelite diets and could be prepared in a hurry for a meal (Ge 19:3, 1Sa 28:24). One of the three Israelite national feasts was the Feast of Unleavened Bread where the people ate flat bread for seven days to commemorate their deliverance from Egypt (Ex 23:15). Unleavened bread or cakes could also be anointed with oil and presented to the priests as a sacrifice (Ex 29:2).

4683. מַצָּה, **matstsâh,** *mats-tsaw´;* from 5327; a *quarrel:*—contention, debate, strife.

4684. מַצְהָלוֹת, **matshâlôwth,** *mats-haw-loth´;* from 6670; a *whinnying* (through impatience for battle or lust):—neighing.

4685. מָצוֹד, **mâtsôwd,** *maw-tsode´;* or (feminine) מְצוֹדָה, **mᵉtsôwdâh,** *mets-o-daw´;* or מְצֹדָה, **mᵉtsô-dâh,** *mets-o-daw´;* from 6679; a *net* (for *capturing* animals or fishes); also (by interch. for 4679) a *fastness* or (besieging) *tower:*—bulwark, hold, munition, net, snare.

A masculine noun meaning a net, a hunting implement, a siege tower. Job claimed that God had surrounded him with a net (Job 19:6). Used figuratively, a wicked person delighted in catching other evil ones (Pr 12:12); the seductress threw out nets to capture men (Ecc 7:26).

Siegeworks or bulwarks described the method of attack against a city (Ecc 9:14).

4686. מָצוּד, **mâtsûwd,** *maw-tsood´;* or (feminine) מְצוּדָה, **mᵉtsûwdâh,** *mets-oo-daw´;* or מְצֻדָה, **mᵉtsudâh,** *mets-oo-daw´;* for 4685; a *net,* or (abstract) *capture;* also a *fastness:*—castle, defence, fort (-ress), (strong) hold, be hunted, net, snare, strong place.

4687. מִצְוָה, **mitsvâh,** *mits-vaw´;* from 6680; a *command,* whether human or divine; (collective) the *Law:*—(which was) commanded (-ment), law, ordinance, precept.

A feminine noun meaning a commandment. It can apply to the edicts issued by a human being, most likely the king (1Ki 2:43; Est 3:3; Pr 6:20; Isa 36:21; Jer 35:18). It can also relate to a general corpus of human precepts (Isa 29:13); or a body of teachings (Pr 2:1; 3:1). On the other hand, this expression can reference God's commands. In the Pentateuch, this is its only usage. It does not refer to human commandments. In the singular, it may distinguish a certain commandment (1Ki 13:21); yet it appears most frequently in the plural to designate the entire corpus of divine law and instruction (Ge 26:5; Ex 16:28; Dt 6:2; 1Ki 2:3). It is also important to note that, in the plural, this word often appears in synonymous parallelism with such words as *chuqqîm* (2706); *mishpâṭîm* (4941); *'êdôth* (5715); *tôwrôwth* (8451).

4688. מְצוֹלָה, **mᵉtsôwlâh,** *mets-o-law´;* or מְצֹלָה, **mᵉtsôlâh,** *mets-o-law´;* also מְצוּלָה, **mᵉtsûwlâh,** *mets-oo-law´;* or מְצֻלָה, **mᵉtsulâh,** *mets-oo-law´;* from the same as 6683; a *deep* place (of water or mud):—bottom, deep, depth.

4689. מָצוֹק, **mâtsôwq,** *maw-tsoke´;* from 6693; a *narrow* place, i.e. (abstract and figurative) *confinement* or *disability:*—anguish, distress, straitness.

4690. מָצוּק, **mâtsûwq,** *maw-tsook´;* or מָצֻק, **mâtsuq,** *maw-tsook´;* from 6693; something *narrow,* i.e. a *column* or *hill*-top:—pillar, situate.

4691. מְצוּקָה, **mᵉtsûwqâh,** *mets-oo-kaw´;* or מְצֻקָה, **mᵉtsuqâh,** *mets-oo-kaw´;* feminine of 4690; *narrowness,* i.e. (figurative) *trouble:*—anguish, distress.

4692. מָצוֹר, **mâtsôwr,** *maw-tsore´;* or מָצוּר, **mâtsûwr,** *maw-tsoor´;* from 6696; something *hemming* in, i.e. (objective) a *mound* (of besiegers), (abstract) a *siege*, (figurative) *distress*; or (subjective) a *fastness*:—besieged, bulwark, defence, fenced, fortress, siege, strong (hold), tower.

4693. מָצֹור, **mâtsôwr**, *maw-tsore´*; the same as 4692 in the sense of a *limit; Egypt* (as the *border* of Palestine):—besieged places, defence, fortified.

4694. מְצוּרָה, **mᵉtsûwrâh**, *mets-oo-raw´*; or מְצֻרָה, **mᵉtsurâh**, *mets-oo-raw´*; feminine of 4692; a *hemming* in, i.e. (objective) a *mound* (of siege), or (subjective) a *rampart* (of protection), (abstract) *fortification*:—fenced (city), fort, munition, strong hold.

4695. מְצוּת, **matstsûwth**, *mats-tsooth´*; from 5327; a *quarrel*:—that contended.

4696. מֵצַח, **mêtsach**, *may´-tsakh*; from an unused root meaning to be *clear*, i.e. *conspicuous*; the *forehead* (as *open* and *prominent*):—brow, forehead, + impudent.

4697. מִצְחָה, **mitschâh**, *mits-khaw´*; from the same as 4696; a *shin-piece* of armour (as *prominent*), only plural:—greaves.

4698. מְצִלָּה, **mᵉtsillâh**, *mets-il-law´*; from 6750; a *tinkler*, i.e. a *bell*:—bell.

4699. מְצֻלָה, **mᵉtsulâh**, *mets-oo-law´*; from 6751; *shade*:—bottom.

4700. מְצִלְתַּיִם, **mᵉtsiltayim**, *mets-il´-ta-yeem*; from 6750; (only dual) double *tinklers*, i.e. cymbals:—cymbals.

4701. מִצְנֶפֶת, **mitsnepheth**, *mits-neh´-feth*; from 6801; a *tiara*, i.e. official *turban* (of a king or high priest):—diadem, mitre.

4702. מַצָּע, **matstsâʻ**, *mats-tsaw´*; from 3331; a *couch*:—bed.

4703. מִצְעָד, **mitsʻâd**, *mits-awd´*; from 6805; a *step*; (figurative) *companionship*:—going, step.

4704. מִצְעִירָה, **mitsʻᵉʻîyrâh**, *mits-tseh-ee-raw´*; feminine of 4705; (properly) *littleness*; (concrete) *diminutive*:—little.

4705. מִצְעָר, **mitsʻâr**, *mits-awr´*; from 6819; *petty* (in size or number); (adverbial) a *short* (time):—little one (while), small.

4706. מִצְעָר, **Mitsʻâr**, *mits-awr´*; the same as 4705; *Mitsar*, a peak of Lebanon:—Mizar.

4707. מִצְפֶּה, **mitspeh**, *mits-peh´*; from 6822; an *observatory*, especially for military purposes:—watch tower.

4708. מִצְפֶּה, **Mitspeh**, *mits-peh´*; the same as 4707; *Mitspeh*, the name of five places in Palestine:—Mizpeh, watch tower. Compare 4709.

4709. מִצְפָּה, **Mitspâh**, *mits-paw´*; feminine of 4708; *Mitspah*, the name of two places in Palestine:—Mitspah. [This seems rather to be only an orthographical variation of 4708 when "in pause".]

4710. מַצְפּוּן, **matspôwn**, *mits-pone´*; from 6845; a *secret* (place or thing, perhaps *treasure*):—hidden thing.

4711. מָצַץ, **mâtsats**, *maw-tsats´*; a primitive root; to *suck*:—milk.

4712. מֵצַר, **mêtsar**, *may-tsar´*; from 6896; something *tight*, i.e. (figurative) *trouble*:—distress, pain, strait.

4713. מִצְרִי, **Mitsrîy**, *mits-ree´*; from 4714; a *Mitsrite*, or inhabitant of Mitsrajim:—Egyptian, of Egypt.

4714. מִצְרַיִם, **Mitsrayim**, *mits-rah´-yim*; dual of 4693; *Mitsrajim*, i.e. Upper and Lower Egypt:—Egypt, Egyptians, Mizraim.

4715. מַצְרֵף, **matsrêph**, *mats-rafe´*; from 6884; a *crucible*:—refining pot.

4716. מַק, **maq**, *mak*; from 4743; (properly) a *melting*, i.e. *putridity*:—rottenness, stink.

4717. מַקֶּבֶת, **maqqebeth**, *mak-keh-beth´*; from 5344; (properly) a *perforatrix*, i.e. a *hammer* (as *piercing*):—hammer.

4718. מַקָּבֶת, **maqqebeth**, *mak-keh´-beth*; from 5344; (properly) a *perforator*, i.e. a *hammer* (as *piercing*); also (intransitive) a *perforation*, i.e. a *quarry*:—hammer, hole.

4719. מַקֵּדָה, **Maqqêdâh**, *mak-kay-daw´*; from the same as 5348 in the denominative sense of *herding* (compare 5349); *fold; Makkedah*, a place in Palestine:—Makkedah.

4720. מִקְדָּשׁ, **miqdâsh**, *mik-dawsh´*; or מִקְּדָשׁ, **miq-qᵉdâsh**, *mik-ked-awsh´*; (Ex 15:17), from

6942; a *consecrated* thing or place, especially a *palace, sanctuary* (whether of Jehovah or of idols) or *asylum*:—chapel, hallowed part, holy place, sanctuary.

A masculine noun meaning a holy or sacred place, a sanctuary. As a nominal form from the verb *qâdash* (6942), meaning to be set apart or to be consecrated, this noun designates that which has been sanctified or set apart as sacred and holy as opposed to the secular, common, or profane. It is a general term for anything sacred and holy, such as the articles of the tabernacle that were devoted for use during worship (Nu 10:21); or the best portion of the offerings given to the Lord (Nu 18:29). Most often, it connotes a sanctuary, the physical place of worship. In this sense, the word encompasses a variety of these concepts: the old Israelite sanctuaries (Jos 24:26); the tabernacle (Ex 25:8; Le 12:4; 21:12); the Temple (1Ch 22:19; 2Ch 29:21; Da 11:31); the sanctuaries dedicated to false worship (Le 26:31; Isa 16:12; Am 7:9). It can also denote a place of refuge or asylum because this status was accorded to sacred places among the Hebrews (Isa 8:14; Eze 11:16; cf. 1Ki 1:50; 2:28).

4721. מַקְהֵל, **maqhêl,** *mak-hale´*; or (feminine) מַקְהֵלָה, **maq-hêlâh,** *mak-hay-law´*; from 6950; an *assembly*:—congregation.

4722. מַקְהֵלֹת. **Maqhêlôth,** *mak-hay-loth´*; plural of 4721 (feminine); *assemblies; Makheloth,* a place in the Desert:—Makheloth.

4723. מִקְוֶה, **miqveh,** *mik-veh´*; or מִקְוֵה, **miqvêh,** *mik-vay´*; (1Ki 10:28), or מִקְוֵא, **miqvê',** *mik-vay´*; (2Ch 1:16), from 6960; something *waited* for, i.e. *confidence* (object or subject); also a *collection*, i.e. (of water) a *pond*, or (of men and horses) a *caravan* or *drove*:—abiding, gathering together, hope, linen yarn, plenty [of water], pool.

A masculine noun meaning hope. The word is used four times and is highly significant theologically. It is used twice as a designation for the Lord. King David, shortly before he died, asserted that as for humans, their days were without any hope in this life (1Ch 29:15). But Jeremiah answered this challenge in the midst of drought, famine, and sword. Jeremiah cried out to the Lord, calling Him the Hope of Israel in parallel with Saviour (Jer 14:8). He also viewed the day of the Lord prophetically at a

time when there was no positive outlook for Judah. Jeremiah asserted that the Lord was the only hope Judah had; to turn from Him would result in shame (Jer 17:13).

Those who returned from exile and established the community found themselves near the brink of rejection, but one brave soul was moved to assert that there was still some hope for Israel to be spared (Ezr 10:2). The word has within its root meaning the thought of waiting for the Lord to act.

4724. מִקְוָה, **miqvâh,** *mik-vaw´*; feminine of 4723; a *collection*, i.e. (of water) a *reservoir*:—ditch.

4725. מָקוֹם, **mâqôwm,** *maw-kome´*; or מָקֹם, **mâqôm,** *maw-kome´*; also (feminine) מְקוֹמָה, **mᵉqôwmâh,** *mek-o-mah´*; or מְקֹמָה, **mᵉqômâh,** *mek-o-mah´*; from 6965; (properly) a *standing*, i.e. a *spot*; but used widely of a *locality* (general or specific); also (figurative) of a *condition* (of body or mind):—country, × home, × open, place, room, space, × whither [-soever].

4726. מָקוֹר, **mâqôwr,** *maw-kore´*; or מָקֹר, **mâqôr,** *maw-kore´*; from 6979; (properly) something *dug*, i.e. a (general) *source* (of water, even when naturally flowing); also of tears, blood [by euphemism of the female *pudenda*]; figurative of happiness, wisdom, progeny):—fountain, issue, spring, well (-spring).

4727. מֶקַח, **miqqâch,** *mik-kawkh´*; from 3947; *reception*:—taking.

4728. מַקָּחוֹת. **maqqâchôwth,** *mak-kaw-khoth´*; from 3947; something *received*, i.e. *merchandise* (purchased):—ware.

4729. מִקְטָר, **miqtâr,** *mik-tawr´*; from 6999; something to *fume* (incense) on, i.e. a *hearth* place:—to burn ... upon.

4730. מִקְטֶרֶת, **miqtereth,** *mik-teh´-reth*; feminine of 4729; something to *fume* (incense) in, i.e. a *coal-pan*:—censer.

4731. מַקֵּל. **maqqêl,** *mak-kale´*; or (feminine) מַקְּלָה, **maqqᵉlâh,** *mak-kel-aw´*; from an unused root meaning apparently to *germinate*; a *shoot*, i.e. *stick* (with leaves on, or for walking, striking, guiding, divining):—rod, ([hand-]) staff.

4732. מִקְלוֹת, **Miqlôwth,** *mik-lohth´*; (or perhaps *mik-kel-ohth´*); plural of (feminine) 4731; *rods; Mikloth,* a place in the Desert:—Mikloth.

4733. מִקְלָט, **miqlât,** *mik-lawt´*; from 7038 in the sense of *taking* in; an *asylum* (as a *receptacle*):—refuge.

4734. מִקְלַעַת, **miqla'ath,** *mik-lah´-ath*; from 7049; a *sculpture* (probably in bass-relief):—carved (figure), carving, graving.

4735. מִקְנֶה, **miqneh,** *mik-neh´*; from 7069; something *bought,* i.e. *property,* but only live *stock*; (abstract) *acquisition*:—cattle, flock, herd, possession, purchase, substance.

4736. מִקְנָה, **miqnâh,** *mik-naw´*; feminine of 4735; (properly) a *buying,* i.e. *acquisition*; (concrete) a piece of *property* (land or living); also the *sum* paid:—(he that is) bought, possession, piece, purchase.

4737. מִקְנֵיָהוּ, **Miqnêyâhûw,** *mik-nay-yaw´-hoo*; from 4735 and 3050; *possession of Jah; Miknejah,* an Israelite:—Mikneiah.

4738. מִקְסָם, **miqsâm,** *mik-sawm´*; from 7080; an *augury*:—divination.

4739. מָקֵץ, **Mâqats,** *maw-kats´*; from 7112; *end; Makats,* a place in Palestine:—Makaz.

4740. מִקְצוֹעַ, **miqtsôwa',** *mik-tso´-ah*; or מִקְצֹעַ, **miqtsôa',** *mik-tso´-ah*; or (feminine) מִקְצֹעָה, **maqtsô'âh,** *mak-tso-aw´*; from 7106 in the denominative sense of *bending*; an *angle* or recess:—corner, turning.

4741. מַקְצֻעָה, **maqtsu'âh,** *mak-tsoo-aw´*; from 7106; a *scraper,* i.e. a carving *chisel*:—plane.

4742. מְקֻצְעָה, **m^equts'âh,** *mek-oots-aw´*; from 7106 in the denominative sense of *bending*; an *angle*:—corner.

4743. מָקַק, **mâqaq,** *maw-kak´*; a primitive root; to *melt*; (figurative) to *flow, dwindle, vanish*:—consume away, be corrupt, dissolve, pine away.

4744. מִקְרָא, **miqrâ',** *mik-raw´*; from 7121; something *called* out, i.e. a public *meeting* (the act, the persons, or the place); also a *rehearsal*:—assembly, calling, convocation, reading.

A masculine noun meaning a convocation, reading, a public meeting, and an assembly. This word usually refers to an assembly for religious purposes. The Passover included a holy convocation on the first and seventh days (Ex 12:16); other festivals also included the gathering of the people (Nu 28:18, 25, 26; 29:1, 7, 12). This word can also mean reading in the sense of a public reading or that which is read in such a meeting. For example, Ezra read the Law of God to a gathering of the Israelites, explaining so the people could understand (Ne 8:8).

4745. מִקְרֶה, **miqreh,** *mik-reh´*; from 7136; something *met* with, i.e. an *accident* or *fortune*:—something befallen, befalleth, chance, event, hap (-peneth).

4746. מְקָרֶה, **m^eqâreh,** *mek-aw-reh´*; from 7136; (properly) something *meeting,* i.e. a *frame* (of timbers):—building.

4747. מְקֵרָה, **m^eqêrâh,** *mek-ay-raw´*; from the same as 7119; a *cooling* off:—× summer.

4748. מִקְשֶׁה, **miqsheh,** *mik-sheh´*; from 7185 in the sense of *knotting* up round and hard; something *turned* (rounded), i.e. a *curl* (of tresses):—× well [set] hair.

4749. מִקְשָׁה, **miqshâh,** *mik-shaw´*; feminine of 4748; *rounded* work, i.e. moulded by *hammering* (*repoussé*):—beaten (out of one piece, work), upright, whole piece.

4750. מִקְשָׁה, **miqshâh,** *mik-shaw´*; denominative from 7180; (literal) a *cucumbered* field, i.e. a *cucumber* patch:—garden of cucumbers.

4751. מַר, **mar,** *mar*; or (feminine) מָרָה, **mârâh,** *maw-raw´*; from 4843; *bitter* (literal or figurative); also (as noun) *bitterness,* or (adverb) *bitterly*:— + angry, bitter (-ly, -ness), chafed, discontented, × great, heavy.

A masculine adjective meaning bitter. The feminine form is *mârâh.* As is common with Hebrew adjectives, it can modify another noun (Ex 15:23), or it can be a substantive, functioning alone as the noun bitterness (Isa 38:15, 17). This word can also operate as an adverb, meaning bitterly (Isa 33:7; Eze 27:30). Used literally, it may modify water (Ex 15:23) and food (Pr 27:7). The Hebrew word can also be used to describe the results of continued fighting (2Sa 2:26). It can be used metaphorically to modify a cry or mourning (Ge 27:34; Est 4:1; Eze 27:30); to represent a characteristic of death (1Sa 15:32); or to describe a person as hot-tempered (Jgs 18:25);

discontented (1Sa 22:2); provoked (2Sa 17:8); anguished (Eze 27:31); or ruthless (Hab 1:6). One instance of this word that deserves special attention is the "bitter water," that determined the legal status of a woman accused of infidelity (Nu 5:18, 19, 23, 24, 27). This was holy water that was combined with dust from the tabernacle floor and ink (see Nu 5:17, 23) and then was ingested by the accused. This water was literally "bitter" and would produce "bitterness" or punishment if the woman were guilty.

4752. מַר, **mar,** *mar;* from 4843 in its original sense of *distillation;* a *drop:*—drop.

4753. מֹר, **môr, more;** or מוֹר, **môwr, more;** from 4843; *myrrh* (as *distilling* in drops, and also as *bitter*):—myrrh.

4754. מָרָא, **mârâ',** *maw-raw´;* a primitive root; to *rebel;* hence (through the idea of *maltreating*) to *whip,* i.e. *lash* (self with wings, as the ostrich in running):—be filthy, lift up self.

4755. מָרָא, **Mârâ',** *maw-raw´;* for 4751 feminine; *bitter; Mara,* a symbolical name of Naomi:—Mara.

4756. מָרֵא, **mârê',** *maw-ray´;* (Chaldee); from a root corresponding to 4754 in the sense of *domineering;* a *master:*—lord, Lord.

An Aramaic noun meaning lord or king. It appears only four times, and all occurrences are found in the book of Daniel. It is applied to King Nebuchadnezzar (Da 4:19[16], 24[21]) and to God (Da 2:47; 5:23). This term appears in parallel with *melek* (4430), meaning king (Da 2:47; 4:24[21]) in two of the occurrences. It appears in reference to a human king (and in virtual parallelism with *melek* [4430]) in another occurrence (Da 4:19[16]). In the final occurrence (Da 5:23), it appears in the phrase, *mârê' shĕmayyâ'* (8065), "the Lord of heaven," which is a reference to the divine monarch. Therefore, it is clear that this is a term that represents an individual with much power, authority, and respect.

4757. מְרֹדַךְ־בַּלְאֲדָן, **Mᵉrôdak Bal'ădân,** *mer-o-dak´ bal-ah-dawn´;* of foreign derivation; *Merodak-Baladan,* a Babylonian king:—Merodach-baladan. Compare 4781.

4758. מַרְאֶה, **mar'eh,** *mar-eh´;* from 7200; a *view* (the act of seeing); also an *appearance* (the thing seen), whether (real) a *shape* (especially if

handsome, *comeliness;* often plural the *looks*), or (mental) a *vision:*— × apparently, appearance (-reth), × as soon as beautiful (-ly), countenance, fair, favoured, form, goodly, to look (up) on (to), look [-eth], pattern, to see, seem, sight, visage, vision.

A masculine noun meaning a sight, an appearance, a vision. Derived from the verb *râ'âh* (7200), meaning to see, this noun bears many of the same shades of meaning as the verb. It can represent the act of seeing (Ge 2:9; Le 13:12); the appearance of the object (Le 13:3; Da 1:13); the object which is seen (Ex 3:3); the face, being that part of the person which is visible (SS 2:14; 5:15); a supernatural vision (Eze 8:4; 11:24; Da 8:16, 27); the ability to see (Ecc 6:9); the shining light of a fire (Nu 9:15) or of lightning (Da 10:6).

4759. מַרְאָה, **mar'âh,** *mar-aw´;* feminine of 4758; a *vision;* also (causative) a *mirror:*—looking glass, vision.

A feminine noun meaning a supernatural vision, a mirror. This noun is derived from the verb *râ'âh* (7200), meaning to see. As a supernatural vision, it is a means of divine revelation (Nu 12:6). This term can stand by itself (1Sa 3:15); or it can function as a cognate accusative (Da 10:7, 8). The word is sometimes used in the expression *mar'ôth halaylâh* (3915), meaning visions of the night (Ge 46:2); and *mar'ôwth 'ĕlôhiym* (430), meaning visions of God (Eze 1:1; 8:3; 40:2). The word is only used once in the Hebrew Bible to signify a mirror or a polished metal plate (Ex 38:8).

4760. מֻרְאָה, **mur'âh,** *moor-aw´;* apparently feminine passive causative participle of 7200; something *conspicuous,* i.e. the *craw* of a bird (from its *prominence*):—crop.

4761. מַרְאָשׁוֹת, **mar'âshôth,** *mar-aw-shoth´;* denominative from 7218; (properly) *headship,* i.e. (plural for collective) *dominion:*—principality.

4762. מַרְאֵשָׁה, **Mârê'shâh,** *mawr-ay-shaw´;* or מַרֵשָׁה, **Mârêshâh,** *mawr-ay-shaw´;* formed like 4761; *summit; Mareshah,* the name of two Israelites and of a place in Palestine:—Mareshah.

4763. מְרַאֲשָׁה, **mᵉra'ăshâh,** *mer-ah-ash-aw´;* formed like 4761; (properly) a *headpiece,* i.e.

(plural for adverb) *at* (or *as*) the *head-rest* (or pillow):—bolster, head, pillow. Compare 4772.

4764. מֵרַב, **Mêrab,** *may-rab´*; from 7231; *increase; Merab,* a daughter of Saul:—Merab.

4765. מַרְבַד, **marbad,** *mar-bad´*; from 7234; a *coverlet:*—covering of tapestry.

4766. מַרְבֶּה, **marbeh,** *mar-beh´*; from 7235; (properly) *increasing;* as noun, *greatness,* or (adverb) *greatly:*—great, increase.

4767. מִרְבָּה, **mirbâh,** *meer-baw´*; from 7235; *abundance,* i.e. a great quantity:—much.

4768. מַרְבִית, **marbîyth,** *mar-beeth´*; from 7235; a *multitude;* also *offspring;* (specifically) *interest* (on capital):—greatest part, greatness, increase, multitude.

4769. מַרְבֵּץ, **marbêts,** *mar-bates´*; from 7257; a *reclining* place, i.e. *fold* (for flocks):—couching place, place to lie down.

4770. מַרְבֵּק, **marbêq,** *mar-bake´*; from an unused root meaning to *tie up;* a *stall* (for cattle):— × fat (-ted), stall.

4771. מַרְגּוֹעַ, **margôwa‘,** *mar-go´-ah*; from 7280; a *resting* place:—rest.

4772. מַרְגְּלוֹת, **margelôwth,** *mar-ghel-oth´*; denominative from 7272; (plural for collective) a *footpiece,* i.e. (adverb) *at the foot,* or (directive) the *foot* itself:—feet. Compare 4763.

4773. מַרְגֵּמָה, **margêmâh,** *mar-gay-maw´*; from 7275; a *stone*-heap:—sling.

4774. מַרְגֵּעָה, **margê‘âh,** *mar-gay-aw´*; from 7280; *rest:*—refreshing.

4775. מָרַד, **mârad,** *maw-rad´*; a primitive root; to *rebel:*—rebel (-lious).

A verb meaning to rebel. This word usually described the activity of resisting authority, whether against the Lord (Nu 14:9; Da 9:9) or against human kings (Ge 14:4; Ne 2:19). In one instance, it is used to describe those who rebel against the light (i.e. God's truth [Job 24:13]). This word is also used to describe a general, rebellious character of a nation (Eze 2:3; 20:38); as well as a specific act of rebellion, such as Hezekiah's rebellion against Sennacherib (2Ki 18:7, 20; Isa 36:5); or Zedekiah's rebellion

against Nebuchadnezzar (2Ki 24:20; Jer 52:3; Eze 17:15).

4776. מְרַד, **merad,** *mer-ad´*; (Chaldee); from a root corresponding to 4775; *rebellion:*—rebellion.

An Aramaic masculine noun meaning rebellion. This word is used only once in the OT and is related to the Hebrew word *mârad* (4775), meaning to rebel. In Ezr 4:19, this word described Jerusalem's past rebellion.

4777. מֶרֶד, **mered,** *meh´-red*; from 4775; *rebellion:*—rebellion.

A masculine noun meaning rebellion. This word comes from the verb *mârad* (4775), meaning to rebel, and occurs only once in the OT. In Jos 22:22, it was used to describe the act of building another altar on the east of the Jordan River as rebellious.

4778. מֶרֶד, **Mered,** *meh´-red*; the same as 4777; *Mered,* an Israelite:—Mered.

4779. מָרָד, **mârâd,** *maw-rawd´*; (Chaldee); from the same as 4776; *rebellious:*—rebellious.

An Aramaic adjective meaning rebellious. This word is used only twice in the OT and is related to the Hebrew word *mârad* (4775), meaning to rebel. In Ezr 4:12, 15, it described the historically rebellious character of Jerusalem.

4780. מַרְדּוּת, **mardûwth,** *mar-dooth´*; from 4775; *rebelliousness:*— × rebellious.

A feminine noun meaning rebelliousness. This word comes from the verb *mârad* (4775), meaning to rebel, and occurs only once in the OT. In 1Sa 20:30, Saul used it in his anger against Jonathan as a derogatory word to describe Jonathan's mother.

4781. מְרֹדָךְ, **Merôdâk,** *mer-o-dawk´*; of foreign derivation; *Merodak,* a Babylonian idol:—Merodach. Compare 4757.

4782. מָרְדְּכַי, **Mordekay,** *mor-dek-ah´ee*; of foreign derivation; *Mordecai,* an Israelite:—Mordecai.

4783. מֻרְדָּף, **murdâph,** *moor-dawf´*; from 7291; *persecuted:*—persecuted.

4784. מָרָה, **mârâh,** *maw-raw´*; a primitive root; to *be* (causative, *make*) *bitter* (or unpleasant); (figurative) to *rebel* or *resist;* (causative) to *provoke*:—bitter, change, be disobedient, disobey, grievously, provocation, provoke (-ing), (be) rebel (against, -lious).

A verb meaning to be rebellious. In one instance, this word spoke of a son's rebellion against his parents (Dt 21:18, 20). In all other instances, this word was used of rebellion against God, which provoked Him to action. This word is usually used as an indictment against a nation's rebellion, whether Israel's (Dt 9:23, 24; Ps 78:8; Jer 5:23); Samaria's (Hos 13:16[14:1]); or David's enemies (Ps 5:10[11]). In a few instances, it is used to indict specific people, as Moses (Nu 20:24; 27:14), or a man of God who disobeyed (1Ki 13:21, 26).

4785. מָרָה, **Mârâh,** *maw-raw´*; the same as 4751 feminine; *bitter; Marah,* a place in the Desert:—Marah.

4786. מֹרָה, **môrâh,** *mo-raw´*; from 4843; *bitterness,* i.e. (figurative) *trouble*:—grief.

4787. מֹרָה, **môrâh,** *mo-raw´*; from 4786; *trouble*:—bitterness.

4788. מָרוּד, **mârûwd,** *maw-rood´*; from 7300 in the sense of *maltreatment*; an *outcast*; (abstract) *destitution*:—cast out, misery.

4789. מֵרוֹז, **Mêrôwz,** *may-roze´*; of uncertain derivation; *Meroz,* a place in Palestine:—Meroz.

4790. מָרוֹחַ, **mârôwach,** *mawr-o-akh´*; from 4799; *bruised,* i.e. *emasculated*:—broken.

4791. מָרוֹם, **mârôwm,** *maw-rome´*; from 7311; *altitude,* i.e. concrete (an *elevated place*), abstract (*elevation*), figurative (*elation*), or adverb (*aloft*):—(far) above, dignity, haughty, height, (most, on) high (one, place), loftily, upward.

4792. מֵרוֹם, **Mêrôwm,** *may-rome´*; formed like 4791; *height; Merom,* a lake in Palestine:—Merom.

4793. מָרוֹץ, **mêrôwts,** *may-rotes´*; from 7323; a *run* (the trial of speed):—race.

4794. מְרוּצָה, **mᵉrûwtsâh,** *mer-oo-tsaw´*; or מְרֻצָה, **mᵉrutsâh,** *mer-oo-tsaw´*; feminine of 4793; a *race* (the act), whether the manner or the progress:—course, running. Compare 4835.

4795. מָרוּק, **mârûwq,** *maw-rook´*; from 4838; (properly) *rubbed*; but used abstractly, a *rubbing* (with perfumery):—purification.

A masculine noun meaning rubbing, purification. The one occurrence of this word is in the book of Esther and mentions the treatments the women underwent for a year prior to meeting King Ahasuerus. This entailed being cleansed and perfumed with various oils (Est 2:12). See the related Hebrew root *mâraq* (4838).

4796. מָרוֹת, **Mârôwth,** *maw-rohth´*; plural of 4751 feminine; *bitter* springs; *Maroth,* a place in Palestine:—Maroth.

4797. מִרְזַח, **mirzach,** *meer-zakh´*; from an unused root meaning to *scream*; a *cry,* i.e. (of joy), a *revel*:—banquet.

4798. מַרְזֵחַ, **marzêach,** *mar-zay´-akh*; formed like 4797; a *cry,* i.e. (of grief) a *lamentation*:—mourning.

4799. מָרַח, **mârach,** *maw-rakh´*; a primitive root; (properly) to *soften* by rubbing or pressure; hence (medicinally) to *apply* as an emollient:—lay for a plaister.

4800. מֶרְחָב, **merchâb,** *mer-khawb´*; from 7337; *enlargement,* either literal (an *open space,* usually in a good sense), or figurative (*liberty*):—breadth, large place (room).

4801. מֶרְחָק, **merchâq,** *mer-khawk´*; from 7368; *remoteness,* i.e. (concrete) a *distant* place; often (adverb) *from afar*:—(a-, dwell in, very) far (country, off). See also 1023.

4802. מַרְחֶשֶׁת, **marchesheth,** *mar-kheh´-sheth*; from 7370; a *stew-pan*:—frying pan.

4803. מָרַט, **mârat,** *maw-rat´*; a primitive root; to *polish*; (by implication) to *make bald* (the head), to *gall* (the shoulder); also, to *sharpen*:—bright, furbish, (have his) hair (be) fallen off, peeled, pluck off (hair).

4804. מְרַט, **mᵉrat,** *mer-at´*; (Chaldee); corresponding to 4803; to *pull* off:—be plucked.

4805. מְרִי, **mᵉrîy,** *mer-ee´*; from 4784; *bitterness,* i.e. (figurative) *rebellion*; (concrete) *bitter,* or *rebellious*:—bitter, (most) rebel (-lion, -lious).

A masculine noun meaning obstinacy, stubbornness, rebelliousness. The term consistently stays within this tight semantic range and most often describes the Israelites' determined refusal to obey the precepts laid down by the Lord in His Law or Torah. This characteristic attitude was a visible manifestation of their hard hearts. Moses had the Book of the Law placed beside the Ark of the Covenant to remain there as a witness against the Israelites' rebelliousness after he died (Dt 31:27; Nu 17:10[25]). The Lord rejected Saul as king over Israel because of his rebellion against the command the Lord had earlier given him (1Sa 15:23). Continually in Ezekiel, the Lord refers to Israel as the "house of rebelliousness" (= rebellious people; Eze 2:5–8; 3:9, 26, 27; 12:2, 3, 9). This noun is derived from the verb *mârâh* (4784).

4806. מְרִיא, **m^erîy',** *mer-ee´*; from 4754 in the sense of *grossness*, through the idea of *domineering* (compare 4756); *stall-fed*; often (as noun) a *beeve*:—fat (fed) beast (cattle, -ling).

4807. מְרִיב בַּעַל, **M^erîyb Ba'al,** *mer-eeb´ bah´-al*; from 7378 and 1168; *quarreller of Baal; Merib-Baal,* an epithet of Gideon:—Meribbaal. Compare 4810.

4808. מְרִיבָה, **m^erîybâh,** *mer-ee-baw´*; from 7378; *quarrel*:—provocation, strife.

4809. מְרִיבָה, **M^erîybâh,** *mer-ee-baw´*; the same as 4808; *Meribah,* the name of two places in the Desert:—Meribah.

4810. מְרִי בַּעַל, **M^erîy Ba'al,** *mer-ee´ bah´-al*; from 4805 and 1168; *rebellion of* (i.e. *against*) *Baal; Meri-Baal,* an epithet of Gideon:—Meribaal. Compare 4807.

4811. מְרָיָה, **M^erâyâh,** *mer-aw-yaw´*; from 4784; *rebellion; Merajah,* an Israelite:—Meraiah. Compare 3236.

4812. מְרָיוֹת, **M^erâyôwth,** *mer-aw-yohth´*; plural of 4811; *rebellious; Merajoth,* the name of two Israelites:—Meraioth.

4813. מִרְיָם, **Miryâm,** *meer-yawm´*; from 4805; *rebelliously; Mirjam,* the name of two Israelitesses:—Miriam.

4814. מְרִירוּת, **m^erîyrûwth,** *mer-ee-rooth´*; from 4843; *bitterness,* i.e. (figurative) *grief*:—bitterness.

4815. מְרִירִי, **m^erîyrîy,** *mer-ee-ree´*; from 4843; *bitter,* i.e. *poisonous*:—bitter.

4816. מֹרֶךְ, **môrek,** *mo´-rek*; perhaps from 7401; *softness,* i.e. (figurative) *fear*:—faintness.

4817. מֶרְכָּב, **merkâb,** *mer-kawb´*; from 7392; a *chariot*; also a *seat* (in a vehicle):—chariot, covering, saddle.

4818. מֶרְכָּבָה, **merkâbâh,** *mer-kaw-baw´*; feminine of 4817; a *chariot*:—chariot. See also 1024.

4819. מַרְכֹּלֶת, **markôleth,** *mar-ko´-leth*; from 7402; a *mart*:—merchandise.

4820. מִרְמָה, **mirmâh,** *meer-maw´*; from 7411 in the sense of *deceiving; fraud*:—craft, deceit (-ful, -fully), false, feigned, guile, subtilly, treachery.

A feminine noun meaning fraud, deceit. The term signifies the intentional misleading of someone else through distorting or withholding the truth. Jacob stole Esau's blessing through deceit (Ge 27:35; cf. Ge 34:13). Deceit fills the heart of those who plan evil (Pr 12:20; cf. Ps 36:3[4]; Pr 12:5, 17; 14:8). David exhorted his children to keep their tongues from evil and their lips from words of deceit (Ps 34:13[14]). The Lord cannot tolerate deceitful weights (Mic 6:11); and a false balance is an abomination to Him (Pr 11:1).

4821. מִרְמָה, **Mirmâh,** *meer-maw´*; the same as 4820; *Mirmah,* an Israelite:—Mirma.

4822. מְרֵמוֹת, **M^erêmôwth,** *mer-ay-mohth´*; plural from 7311; *heights; Meremoth,* the name of two Israelites:—Meremoth.

4823. מִרְמָס, **mirmâs,** *meer-mawce´*; from 7429; *abasement* (the act or the thing):—tread (down) -ing, (to be) trodden (down) under foot.

4824. מְרֹנֹתִי, **Mêrônôthîy,** *may-ro-no-thee´*; patrial from an unused noun; a *Meronothite,* or inhabitant of some (otherwise unknown) Meronoth:—Meronothite.

4825. מֶרֶס, **Meres,** *meh´-res*; of foreign derivation; *Meres,* a Persian:—Meres.

4826. מַרְסְנָא, **Mars^enâ,** *mar-sen-aw´*; of foreign derivation; *Marsena,* a Persian:—Marsena.

4827. מֵרַע, **mêra',** *may-rah´*; from 7489; used as (abstract) noun, *wickedness*:—do mischief.

4828. מֵרֵעַ, **mêrêaʻ,** *may-ray´-ah*; from 7462 in the sense of *companionship*; a *friend*:—companion, friend.

4829. מִרְעֶה, **mirʻeh,** *meer-eh´*; from 7462 in the sense of *feeding; pasture* (the place or the act); also the *haunt* of wild animals:—feeding place, pasture.

4830. מַרְעִית, **marʻîyth,** *mar-eeth´*; from 7462 in the sense of *feeding; pasturage*; (concrete) a *flock*:—flock, pasture.

4831. מַרְעֲלָה, **Marʻălâh,** *mar-al-aw´*; from 7477; perhaps *earthquake; Maralah,* a place in Palestine:—Maralah.

4832. מַרְפֵּא, **marpê',** *mar-pay´*; from 7495; (properly) *curative,* i.e. literal (concrete) a *medicine,* or (abstract) a *cure*; figurative (concrete) *deliverance,* or (abstract) *placidity*:—([in-]) cure (-able), healing (-lth), remedy, sound, wholesome, yielding.

4833. מִרְפָּשׂ, **mirpâs,** *meer-paws´*; from 7515; *muddled* water:—that which ... have fouled.

4834. מָרַץ, **mârats,** *maw-rats´*; a primitive root; (properly) to *press,* i.e. (figurative) to be *pungent* or vehement; to *irritate*:—embolden, be forcible, grievous, sore.

4835. מְרוּצָה, **mᵉrûwtsâh,** *mer-oo-tsaw´*; from 7533; *oppression*:—violence. See also 4794.

4836. מַרְצֵעַ, **martsêaʻ,** *mar-tsay´-ah*; from 7527; an *awl*:—aul.

4837. מַרְצֶפֶת, **martsepheth,** *mar-tseh´-feth*; from 7528; a *pavement*:—pavement.

4838. מָרַק, **mâraq,** *maw-rak´*; a primitive root; to *polish*; (by implication) to *sharpen*; also to *rinse*:—bright, furbish, scour.

4839. מָרָק, **mâraq,** *maw-rak´*; from 4838; *soup* (as if a *rinsing*):—broth. See also 6564.

4840. מֶרְקָח, **merqâch,** *mer-kawkh´*; from 7543; a *spicy* herb:—× sweet.

4841. מֶרְקָחָה, **merqâchâh,** *mer-kaw-khaw´*; feminine of 4840; (abstract) a *seasoning* (with spicery); (concrete) an *unguent-kettle* (for preparing spiced oil):—pot of ointment, × well.

4842. מִרְקַחַת, **mirqachath,** *meer-kakh´-ath*; from 7543; an aromatic *unguent*; also an *unguent-pot*:—prepared by the apothecaries' art, compound, ointment.

4843. מָרַר, **mârar,** *maw-rar´*; a primitive root; (properly) to *trickle* [see 4752]; but used only as a denominative from 4751; to *be* (causative, *make*) *bitter* (literal or figurative):—(be, be in, deal, have, make) bitter (-ly, -ness), be moved with choler, (be, have sorely, it) grieved (-eth), provoke, vex.

4844. מָרֹר, **mârôr,** *mawr-ore´*; or מָרוֹר, **mârôwr,** *mawr-ore´*; from 4843; a *bitter* herb:—bitter (-ness).

4845. מְרֵרָה, **mᵉrêrâh,** *mer-ay-raw´*; from 4843; *bile* (from its bitterness):—gall.

4846. מְרֹרָה, **mᵉrôrâh,** *mer-o-raw´*; or מְרוֹרָה, **mᵉrôwrâh,** *mer-o-raw´*; from 4843; (properly) *bitterness*; (concrete) a *bitter thing*; (specifically) *bile*; also *venom* (of a serpent):—bitter (thing), gall.

4847. מְרָרִי, **Mᵉrârîy,** *mer-aw-ree´*; from 4843; *bitter; Merari,* an Israelite:—Merari. See also 4848.

4848. מְרָרִי, **Mᵉrârîy,** *mer-aw-ree´*; from 4847; a *Merarite* (collective), or descendants of Merari:—Merarites.

4849. מִרְשַׁעַת, **mirshaʻath,** *meer-shah´-ath*; from 7561; a female *wicked doer*:—wicked woman.

4850. מְרָתַיִם, **Mᵉrâthayim,** *mer-aw-thah´-yim*; dual of 4751 feminine; *double bitterness; Merathajim,* an epithet of Babylon:—Merathaim.

4851. מַשׁ, **Mash,** *mash*; of foreign derivation; *Mash,* a son of Aram, and the people descendant from him:—Mash.

4852. מֵשָׁא, **Mêshâ',** *may-shaw´*; of foreign derivation; *Mesha,* a place in Arabia:—Mesha.

4853. מַשָּׂא, **maśśâ',** *mas-saw´*; from 5375; a *burden*; (specifically) *tribute,* or (abstract) *porterage*; (figurative) an *utterance,* chiefly a *doom,* especially *singing*; mental, *desire*:—burden, carry away, prophecy, × they set, song, tribute.

A masculine noun meaning a burden or load; by extension, a burden in the form of a prophetic utterance or oracle. It is derived from the verb *nâśâ'* (5375) meaning to lift, to bear, to carry. When used to express a burden or load, it is commonly used to describe that which is placed on the backs of pack animals, like donkeys (Ex 23:5); mules (2Ki 5:17); or camels (2Ki 8:9). Another common usage is in designating what parts of the tabernacle the sons of Kohath, Gershon, and Merari were to carry (Nu 4:15, 19, 24, 27, 31, 32, 47, 49). In Eze 24:25, it is interesting that the lifting of one's soul, *maśśâ'naphshâm* (5315), is used to mean the desires of the heart and that to which persons lift up their souls. By extension, this term is also applied to certain divine oracles that were negative proclamations. Isaiah used this formula to pronounce judgments against the nations of Babylon (Isa 13:1); Philistia (Isa 14:28); Moab (Isa 15:1); Damascus (Isa 17:1); Egypt (Isa 19:1); the desert of the sea (Isa 21:1); Dumah (Isa 21:11); Arabia (Isa 21:13); the Valley of Vision (Isa 22:1); Tyre (Isa 23:1). Other prophets used the same formula to pronounce judgments on Nineveh (Na 1:1); Judah (Hab 1:1); Damascus (Zec 9:1); Jerusalem (Zec 12:1); Israel (Mal 1:1). This formula was also employed to prophesy threats or judgments on individuals (2Ki 9:25; 2Ch 24:27; Pr 30:1; 31:1).

4854. מַשָּׂא, **Maśśâ'**, *mas-saw'*; the same as 4853; *burden; Massa*, a son of Ishmael:—Massa.

4855. מַשָּׁא, **mashshâ'**, *mash-shaw'*; from 5383; a *loan*; (by implication) *interest* on a debt:—exaction, usury.

4856. מַשּׂא, **maśśô'**, *mas-so'*; from 5375; *partiality* (as a *lifting* up):—respect.

4857. מַשְׁאָב, **mash'âb**, *mash-awb'*; from 7579; a *trough* for cattle to drink from:—place of drawing water.

4858. מַשָּׂאָה, **maśśâ'âh**, *mas-saw-aw'*; from 5375; a *conflagration* (from the *rising* of smoke):—burden.

4859. מַשָּׁאָה, **mashshâ'âh**, *mash-shaw-aw'*; feminine of 4855; a *loan*:— × any [-thing], debt.

4860. מַשָּׁאוֹן, **mashshâ'ôwn**, *mash-shaw-ohn'*; from 5377; *dissimulation*:—deceit.

4861. מִשְׁאָל, **Mish'âl**, *mish-awl'*; from 7592; *request; Mishal*, a place in Palestine:—Mishal, Misheal. Compare 4913.

4862. מִשְׁאָלָה, **mish'âlâh**, *mish-aw-law'*; from 7592; a *request*:—desire, petition.

4863. מִשְׁאֶרֶת, **mish'ereth**, *mish-eh'-reth*; from 7604 in the original sense of *swelling*; a *kneading-trough* (in which the dough *rises*):—kneading trough, store.

4864. מַשְׂאֵת, **maś'êth**, *mas-ayth'*; from 5375; properly (abstract) a *raising* (as of the hands in prayer), or *rising* (of flame); (figurative) an *utterance*; (concrete) a *beacon* (as *raised*); a *present* (as taken), *mess*, or *tribute*; (figurative) a *reproach* (as a burden):—burden, collection, sign of fire, (great) flame, gift, lifting up, mess, oblation, reward.

A feminine noun meaning an uprising, an utterance, a burden, a portion, a tribute, a reward. The main use connotes something that rises or is lifted up, such as smoke in a smoke signal (Jgs 20:38); or hands in a sacrifice of praise (Ps 141:2). Figuratively, a reproach could be lifted up as a burden (Zep 3:18). This word can also depict a portion or a gift that is carried to someone, often from the table of nobility. For example, David sent a gift of food to Uriah's house (2Sa 11:8); as part of the feast honouring Queen Esther, the king sent gifts to his subjects (Est 2:18).

4865. מִשְׁבְּצוֹת, **mishbᵉtsôwth**, *mish-bets-oth'*; from 7660; a *brocade*; (by analogy) a reticulated *setting* of a gem:—ouch, wrought.

4866. מַשְׁבֵּר, **mashbêr**, *mish-bare'*; from 7665; the *orifice* of the womb (from which the fetus *breaks* forth):—birth, breaking forth.

4867. מִשְׁבָּר, **mishbâr**, *mish-bawr'*; from 7665; a *breaker* (of the sea):—billow, wave.

4868. מִשְׁבָּת, **mishbâth**, *mish-bawth'*; from 7673; *cessation*, i.e. destruction, downfall:—sabbaths (KJV).

4869. מִשְׂגָּב, **miśgâb**, *mis-gawb'*; from 7682; (properly) a *cliff* (or other *lofty* or *inaccessible* place); (abstract) *altitude*; (figurative) a *refuge*:—defence, high fort (tower), refuge. 4869; *Misgab*, a place in Moab:—Misgab.

4870. מִשְׁגֶּה, **mishgeh**, *mish-gay'*, from 7686; an *error*:—oversight.

4871. מָשָׁה, **mâshâh**, *maw-shaw'*; a primitive root; to *pull* out (literal or figurative):—draw (out).

4872. מֹשֶׁה, **Môsheh,** *mo-sheh´*; from 4871; *drawing* out (of the water), i.e. *rescued; Mosheh,* the Israelite lawgiver:—Moses.

4873. מֹשֶׁה, **Môsheh,** *mo-sheh´*; (Chaldee); corresponding to 4872:—Moses.

4874. מַשֶּׁה, **mashsheh,** *mash-sheh´*; from 5383; a *debt:*— + creditor.

4875. מְשׁוֹאָה, **mᵉshôw’âh,** *mesh-o-aw´*; or מְשֹׁאָה, **mᵉshô’âh,** *mesh-o-aw´*; from the same as 7722; (a) *ruin,* abstract (the act) or concrete (the wreck):—desolation, waste.

4876. מַשּׁוּאָה, **mashshûw’âh,** *mash-shoo-aw´*; or מַשֻּׁאָה, **mash-shu’âh,** *mash-shoo-aw´*; for 4875; *ruin:*—desolation, destruction.

A plural feminine noun meaning deceptions, destructions, and desolations. The psalmist took solace in the fact that God would cause the destruction of the wicked (Ps 73:18). He also called on God to remember the righteous who had been in the depths of desolation (Ps 74:3).

4877. מְשׁוֹבָב, **Mᵉshôwbâb,** *mesh-o-bawb´*; from 7725; *returned; Meshobab,* an Israelite:—Meshobab.

4878. מְשׁוּבָה, **mᵉshûwbâh,** *mesh-oo-baw´*; or מְשֻׁבָה, **meshubâh,** *mesh-oo-baw´*; from 7725; *apostasy:*—backsliding, turning away.

4879. מְשׁוּגָה, **mᵉshûwgâh,** *mesh-oo-gaw´*; from an unused root meaning to *stray; mistake:*—error.

4880. מָשׁוֹט, **mâshôwṭ,** *maw-shote´*; or מִשּׁוֹט, **mish-shôwṭ,** *mish-shote´*; from 7751; an *oar:*—oar.

4881. מְשׂוּכָה, **mᵉśûwkkâh,** *mes-ook-kaw´*; or מְשֻׂכָה, **mᵉśukkâh,** *mes-oo-kaw´*; from 7753; a *hedge:*—hedge.

4882. מְשׁוּסָה, **mᵉshûwsâh,** *mesh-oo-saw´*; from an unused root meaning to *plunder; spoliation:*—spoil.

4883. מַשּׂוֹר, **maśśôwr,** *mas-sore´*; from an unused root meaning to *rasp;* a *saw:*—saw.

4884. מְשׂוּרָה, **mᵉśûwrâh,** *mes-oo-raw´*; from an unused root meaning apparently to *divide;* a *measure* (for liquids):—measure.

4885. מָשׂוֹשׂ, **mâśôwś,** *maw-soce´*; from 7797; *delight,* concrete (the cause or object) or abstract (the feeling):—joy, mirth, rejoice.

4886. מָשַׁח, **mâshach,** *maw-shakh´*; a primitive root; to *rub* with oil, i.e. to *anoint;* (by implication) to *consecrate;* also to *paint:*—anoint, paint.

A verb meaning to smear, to anoint. In its common usage, this verb can refer to the rubbing of a shield with oil (Isa 21:5); the painting of a house (Jer 22:14); the anointing of an individual with ointments or lotions (Am 6:6); the spreading of oil on wafers (Ex 29:2). If the verb is used in association with a religious ceremony, it connotes the sanctification of things or people for divine service. Once the tabernacle was erected, it and all its furnishings were anointed with oil to consecrate them (Ex 40:9–11). The most common usage of this verb is the ritual of divine installation of individuals into positions of leadership by the pouring oil on their heads. Most frequently, people were anointed for kingship: Saul (1Sa 10:1); David (1Sa 16:13); and Solomon (1Ki 1:34). The word is also used of people anointed as priests (Ex 28:41; Nu 35:25); and prophets (1Ki 19:16; Isa 61:1).

4887. מְשַׁח, **mᵉshach,** *mesh-akh´*; (Chaldee); from a root corresponding to 4886; *oil:*—oil.

An Aramaic noun meaning olive oil. This word appears only in two passages (Ezr 6:9; 7:22). These passages cite the provisions, including silver, livestock, wheat, salt, wine, and oil, that kings Darius and Artaxerxes supplied to the restoration priests at the Temple in Jerusalem.

4888. מִשְׁחָה, **mishchâh,** *meesh-khaw´*; or מָשְׁחָה, **moshchâh,** *mosh-khaw´*; from 4886; *unction* (the act); (by implication) a consecratory *gift:*—(to be) anointed (-ing), ointment.

A feminine noun meaning anointing, a priestly portion. When used in reference to the anointing, *mishchâh* is always used to modify *shemen* (8081), meaning olive oil (Ex 37:29). At times, this phrase is further qualified by the addition of another modifier, like *qôdesh* (6944), meaning holy (Ex 30:31); *yᵉhôwâh* (3068), the proper name of the God of Israel (Le 10:7); or *’ĕlôhym* (430), meaning his God (Le 21:12). This "oil of anointing" was made from a combination of olive oil and spices (Ex 30:25; 35:8, 28). It was then used to anoint someone or something and to consecrate the individual or item to

God, such as the Aaronic priests (Ex 29:7, 21; Le 8:2, 12, 30; 21:10); and the tabernacle (Ex 40:9; Le 8:10). It was also used in the customary ministrations of the tabernacle (Ex 31:11; 35:15; Nu 4:16). In addition, this term identified the portion of the sacrifices presented to God, then given to the priests (Le 7:35).

4889. מַשְׁחִית, **mashchîyth,** *mash-kheeth´*; from 7843; *destructive*, i.e. (as noun) *destruction*, literal (specifically a *snare*) or figurative (*corruption*):— corruption, (to) destroy (-ing), destruction, trap, × utterly.

A feminine noun meaning destruction, corruption (Ex 12:13; 2Ki 23:13; 2Ch 20:23; 22:4; Pr 18:9; 28:24; Isa 54:16; Jer 5:26; 22:7; 51:1; Eze 9:6; 21:31[36]; 25:15; Da 10:8.). See also 7843.

4890. מִשְׂחָק, **miśchâq,** *mis-khawk´*; from 7831; a *laughing-stock*:—scorn.

4891. מִשְׁחָר, **mishchâr,** *mish-khawr´*; from 7836 in the sense of day *breaking; dawn*:—morning.

4892. מַשְׁחֵת, **mashchêth,** *mash-khayth´*; for 4889; *destruction*:—destroying.

4893. מִשְׁחָת, **mishchâth,** *mish-khawth´*; or מָשְׁחָת, **moshchâth,** *mosh-khawth´*; from 7843; *disfigurement*:—corruption, marred.

4894. מִשְׁטוֹחַ, **mishṭôwach,** *mish-to´-akh*; or מִשְׁטַח, **mishṭach,** *mish-takh´*; from 7849; a *spreading*-place:—(to) spread (forth, -ing, upon).

4895. מַשְׂטֵמָה, **maśṭêmâh,** *mas-tay-maw´*; from the same as 7850; *enmity*:—hatred.

4896. מִשְׁטָר, **mishṭâr,** *mish-tawr´*; from 7860; *jurisdiction*:—dominion.

4897. מֶשִׁי, **meshîy,** *meh´-shee*; from 4871; *silk* (as *drawn* from the cocoon):—silk.

4898. מְשֵׁיזַבְאֵל, **Mᵉshêyzab'êl,** *mesh-ay-zab-ale´*; from an equivalent to 7804 and 410; *delivered of God*; *Meshezabel*, an Israelite:—Meshezabeel.

4899. מָשִׁיחַ, **mâshîyach,** *maw-shee´-akh*; from 4886; *anointed*; usually a *consecrated* person (as a king, priest, or saint); specifically the *Messiah*:—anointed, Messiah.

A masculine noun meaning anointed one. Although this word is a noun, it can function both as a substantive (1Sa 24:6[7], 10[11]); or an adjective (Le 4:3, 5, 16). Since it refers to an indi-

vidual who has been anointed by divine command (2Sa 1:14, 16), it can reference the high priest of Israel (Le 4:3, 5, 16; 6:22[15]); however, it is usually reserved as a marker for kingship, primarily the kings of Israel (1Sa 26:9, 11, 16, 23). In this way, the patriarchs were regarded as God's anointed kings (1Ch 16:22; Ps 105:15). One unique instance of this term is in reference to Cyrus the Persian, a non-Israelite who was regarded as God's anointed (Isa 45:1); therefore, one is forced to understand this characterization, not as a statement of the individual's inherent goodness and perfection, since Cyrus was a worshipper of pagan deities like Marduk. On the contrary, it is a statement of God's appointing or choosing an individual for a task. Furthermore, the concept of the *mâshiyach*, meaning Messiah, as a Saviour is not fully developed in the OT. The closest that one comes to this in the OT is Da 9:25, 26. This concept is developed later, during the NT period and fits better with the parallel Greek word *christos*.

4900. מָשַׁךְ, **mâshak,** *maw-shak´*; a primitive root; to *draw*, used in a great variety of applications (including to *sow*, to *sound*, to *prolong*, to *develop*, to *march*, to *remove*, to *delay*, to *be tall*, etc.):—draw (along, out), continue, defer, extend, forbear, × give, handle, make (pro-, sound) long, × sow, scatter, stretch out.

4901. מֶשֶׁךְ, **meshek,** *meh´-shek*; from 4900; a *sowing*; also a *possession*:—precious, price.

4902. מֶשֶׁךְ, **Meshek,** *meh´-shek*; the same in form as 4901, but probably of foreign derivation; *Meshek*, a son of Japheth, and the people descendant from him:—Mesech, Meshech.

4903. מִשְׁכַּב, **mishkab,** *mish-kab´*; (Chaldee); corresponding to 4904; a *bed*:—bed.

4904. מִשְׁכָּב, **mishkâb,** *mish-kawb´*; from 7901; a *bed*; (figurative) a *bier*; (abstract) *sleep*; (by euphemism) carnal *intercourse*:—bed ([-chamber]), couch, lieth (lying) with.

4905. מַשְׂכִּיל, **maśkîyl,** *mas-keel´*; from 7919; *instructive*, i.e. a *didactic* poem:—Maschil.

4906. מַשְׂכִּית, **maśkîyth,** *mas-keeth´*; from the same as 7906; a *figure* (carved on stone, the wall, or any object); (figurative) *imagination*:—conceit, image (-ry), picture, × wish.

A feminine noun meaning an image, the imagination. It is usually used of a carved image or sculpture, often idolatrous, whether of stone (Le 26:1); silver (Pr 25:11); or of unspecified material (Nu 33:52; Eze 8:12). It is also utilized as a metaphor for one's imagination or conceit (Ps 73:7 *maśkiyyôwthlêbâb* [3824], meaning images of the heart; cf. Pr 18:11).

4907. מִשְׁכָּן, **mishkan,** *mish-kan´*; (Chaldee); corresponding to 4908; *residence:*—habitation.

4908. מִשְׁכָּן, **mishkân,** *mish-kawn´*; from 7931; a *residence* (including a shepherd's *hut*, the *lair* of animals); (figurative) the *grave*; also the *Temple*; (specifically) the *tabernacle* (properly, its wooden walls):—dwelleth, dwelling (place), habitation, tabernacle, tent.

A masculine noun meaning dwelling, tabernacle, or sanctuary. The most significant meaning of the word indicates the dwelling place of the Lord, the tabernacle. The word is often used in Exodus to indicate the temporary lodging of God and His glory among His people, the tabernacle (Le 26:11; Ps 26:8). It is used parallel to the word meaning sanctuary or holy place in the preceding verse (Ex 25:9, cf. v. 8). The noun is formed from the verbal root *shâkan* (7931), which indicates temporary lodging (Ex 25:9; 26:1, 6; 2Sa 7:6). This noun is also often found in parallel with or described by the Hebrew word for tent (Ex 26:35; Jer 30:18).

The tabernacle was called the Tent of Meeting (1Ch 6:32[17]; see Ex 28:43; 30:20; 40:32), for there the Lord met with His people. It was also called the Tent of Testimony (Ex 38:21; Nu 9:15; cf. Nu 17:22, 23; 18:2), since the covenantal documents, the Ten Commandments, were lodged in the Holy of Holies. The Hebrew noun is used with the definite article in 74 of 130 times, indicating that the author expected the reader to know what tabernacle he meant. God gave Moses the pattern of the structure for the tabernacle (Ex 25:9; 26:30). The Lord had His tabernacle set up at Shiloh in Canaan, but it was later abandoned (Ps 78:60). The word is hardly ever used regarding the later Temple of Solomon, of Ezekiel's visionary Temple (2Ch 29:6; Ps 26:8; 46:4[5]; Eze 37:27); or the Lord's dwelling place in Zion (Ps 132:5, 7). The word used most often to describe Solomon's Temple

and the postexilic Temple is *bayith* (1004), meaning house.

The word also indicates the dwelling places of the Israelites and other peoples; it describes Korah's dwelling place (Nu 16:24, 27); Israel's dwelling place (Nu 24:5; Isa 32:18; Jer 30:18). Twice the word indicates the dwelling of the dead, i.e. the grave Jerusalem made for herself, and the abode of all classes of men (Ps 49:11[12]; Isa 22:16).

4909. מַשְׂכֹּרֶת, **maśkôreth,** *mas-koh´-reth*; from 7936; *wages* or a *reward:*—reward, wages.

4910. מָשַׁל, **mâshal,** *maw-shal´*; a primitive root; to *rule:*—(have, make to have) dominion, governor, × indeed, reign, (bear, cause to, have) rule (-ing, -r), have power.

A verb denoting to rule, to reign, or to have dominion over. Although its general tone communicates leadership and authority, its specific nuance and connotation are derived from the context in which it appears. In the creation narratives on the fourth day, God created the great luminaries. The greater luminary was to rule the day, and the lesser was to rule the night (Ge 1:18). It is also applied to people who rule: a servant over his master's household (Ge 24:2); a king over his country (Jos 12:5); or his people (Jgs 8:22, 23); a people over another people (Jgs 14:4). God is also said to rule over His people (Jgs 8:23); not over His adversaries (Isa 63:19); over the nations (2Ch 20:6; Ps 22:28[29]); over Jacob (Ps 59:13[14]); over all things (1Ch 29:12).

4911. מָשַׁל, **mâshal,** *maw-shal´*; denominative from 4912; to *liken*, i.e. (transposed) to use figurative language (an allegory, adage, song or the like); (intransitive) to *resemble:*—be (-come) like, compare, use (as a) proverb, speak (in proverbs), utter.

4912. מָשָׁל, **mâshâl,** *maw-shawl´*; apparently from 4910 in some original sense of *superiority* in mental action; (properly) a pithy *maxim*, usually of a metaphorical nature; hence a *simile* (as an adage, poem, discourse):—byword, like, parable, proverb.

4913. מָשָׁל, **Mâshâl,** *maw-shawl´*; for 4861; *Mashal*, a place in Palestine:—Mashal.

4914. מְשֹׁל, **mᵉshôl,** *mesh-ol´*; from 4911; a *satire*:—byword.

4915. מֹשֵׁל, **môshel,** *mo´-shel*; (1) from 4910; *empire*; (2) from 4911; a *parallel*:—dominion, like.

A masculine noun meaning likeness, dominion. This number in Strong's is associated with two words. The first comes from the verb *mâshal* (4911), meaning to represent or to be like, and is found only in Job 41:33[25], where it is translated "likeness." The second comes from the verb *mâshal* (4910), meaning to rule or to govern. This word is found in Da 11:4 and Zec 9:10, where it describes the dominion of Alexander and the coming Messiah.

4916. מִשְׁלוֹחַ, **mishlôwach,** *mish-lo´-akh*; or מִשְׁלֹחַ, **mishlôach,** *mish-lo´-akh*; also מִשְׁלָח, **mishlâch,** *mish-lawkh´*; from 7971; a *sending out,* i.e. (abstract) *presentation* (favourable), or *seizure* (unfavourable); also (concrete) a place of *dismissal,* or a *business* to be discharged:—to lay, to put, sending (forth), to set.

4917. מִשְׁלַחַת, **mishlachath,** *mish-lakh´-ath*; feminine of 4916; a *mission,* i.e. (abstract and favourable) *release,* or (concrete and unfavourable) an *army*:—discharge, sending.

4918. מְשֻׁלָּם, **Mᵉshullâm,** *mesh-ool-lawm´*; from 7999; *allied*; *Meshullam,* the name of seventeen Israelites:—Meshullam.

4919. מְשִׁלֵּמוֹת, **Mᵉshillêmôwth,** *mesh-il-lay-mohth´*; plural from 7999; *reconciliations*:—*Meshillemoth,* an Israelite:—Meshillemoth. Compare 4921.

4920. מְשֶׁלֶמְיָה, **Mᵉshelemyâh,** *mesh-eh-lem-yaw´*; or מְשֶׁלֶמְיָהוּ, **Mᵉshelemyâhûw,** *mesh-eh-lem-yaw´-hoo*; from 7999 and 3050; *ally of Jah*; *Meshelemjah,* an Israelite:—Meshelemiah.

4921. מְשִׁלֵּמִית, **Mᵉshillêmîyth,** *mesh-il-lay-meeth´*; from 7999; *reconciliation*; *Meshillemith,* an Israelite:—Meshillemith. Compare 4919.

4922. מְשֻׁלֶּמֶת, **Mᵉshullemeth,** *mesh-ool-leh´-meth*; feminine of 4918; *Meshullemeth,* an Israelitess:—Meshullemeth.

4923. מְשַׁמָּה, **mᵉshammâh,** *mesh-am-maw´*; from 8074; a *waste* or *amazement*:—astonishment, desolate.

4924. מִשְׁמָן, **mishmân,** *mish-mawn´*; from 8080; *fat,* i.e. (literal and abstract) *fatness*; but usually (figurative and concrete) a *rich* dish, a *fertile* field, a *robust* man:—fat (one, -ness, -test, -test place).

4925. מִשְׁמַנָּה, **Mishmannâh,** *mish-man-naw´*; from 8080; *fatness*; *Mashmannah,* an Israelite:—Mishmannah.

4926. מִשְׁמָע, **mishmâ‘,** *mish-maw´*; from 8085; a *report*:—hearing.

4927. מִשְׁמָע, **Mishmâ‘,** *mish-maw´*; the same as 4926; *Mishma,* the name of a son of Ishmael, and of an Israelite:—Mishma.

4928. מִשְׁמַעַת, **mishma‘ath,** *mish-mah´-ath*; feminine of 4926; *audience,* i.e. the royal *court*; also *obedience,* i.e. (concrete) a *subject*:—bidding, guard, obey.

A feminine noun meaning obedient subjects. This word comes from the verb *shâma‘* (8085), meaning to hear and obey, and describes a group of people who are bound to obey. In several instances of this word, it describes a king's personal guard (1Sa 22:14; 2Sa 23:23; 1Ch 11:25). In the only other instance, it depicts a conquered people who are bound to obey (Isa 11:14).

4929. מִשְׁמָר, **mishmâr,** *mish-mawr´*; from 8104; a *guard* (the man, the post, or the *prison*); (figurative) a *deposit*; also (as observed) a *usage* (abstract), or an *example* (concrete):—diligence, guard, office, prison, ward, watch.

4930. מַשְׂמֵרָה, **maśmêrâh,** *mas-mayr-aw´*; for 4548 feminine; a *peg*:—nail.

4931. מִשְׁמֶרֶת, **mishmereth,** *mish-meh´-reth*; feminine of 4929; *watch,* i.e. the act (*custody*) or (concrete) the *sentry,* the *post*; (objective) *preservation,* or (concrete) *safe*; (figurative) *observance,* i.e. (abstract) *duty,* or (objective) a *usage* or *party*:—charge, keep, to be kept, office, ordinance, safeguard, ward, watch.

A feminine noun meaning guard, charge, duty. This word comes from the verb *shâmar* (8104), meaning to watch, to keep, to protect, or to guard, and has a multiplicity of usages. In its most basic sense, it describes a guarded place (Nu 17:10[25]; 1Sa 22:23); keeping for later use (Ex 12:6; 16:32–34); or protection against enemies (2Ki 11:5–7). In several instances, it is used of a guard post (Isa 21:8; Hab 2:1). The idea of obedience (i.e. keeping the commandments) is often depicted, which leads to a translation of charge (Ge 26:5; Dt 11:1; Zec 3:7) or duty (Nu 3:7; 9:23; 2Ch 8:14).

4932. מִשְׁנֶה, **mishneh,** *mish-neh´*; from 8138; (properly) a *repetition*, i.e. a *duplicate* (*copy* of a document), or a *double* (in amount); (by implication) a *second* (in order, rank, age, quality or location):—college, copy, double, fatlings, next, second (ordinal), twice as much.

4933. מְשִׁסָּה, **mᵉshissâh,** *mesh-is-saw´*; from 8155; *plunder:*—booty, spoil.

4934. מִשְׁעוֹל, **mishʻôwl,** *mish-ole´*; from the same as 8168; a *hollow*, i.e. a narrow passage:—path.

4935. מִשְׁעִי, **mishʻîy,** *mish-ee´*; probably from 8159; *inspection:*—to supple.

4936. מִשְׁעָם, **Mishʻâm,** *mish-awm´*; apparently from 8159; *inspection; Misham*, an Israelite:—Misham.

4937. מַשְׁעֵן, **mashʻên,** *mash-ane´*; or מִשְׁעָן, **mishʻân,** *mish-awn´*; from 8172; a *support* (concrete), i.e. (figurative) a *protector* or *sustenance:*—stay.

4938. מַשְׁעֵנָה, **mashʻênâh,** *mash-ay-naw´*; or מִשְׁעֶנֶת, **mishʻeneth,** *mish-eh´-neth*; feminine of 4937; *support* (abstract), i.e. (figurative) *sustenance* or (concrete) a *walking-stick:*—staff.

4939. מִשְׂפָּח, **miśpâch,** *mis-pawkh´*; from 5596; *slaughter:*—oppression.

4940. מִשְׁפָּחָה, **mishpâchâh,** *mish-paw-khaw´*; from 8192 [compare 8198]; a *family*, i.e. circle of relatives; (figurative) a *class* (of persons), a *species* (of animals) or *sort* (of things); (by extension) a *tribe* or *people:*—family, kind (-red).

A feminine noun meaning an extended family, a tribe, a clan. It is a group in which there is a close blood relationship. In a technical sense, a *mishpâchâh* is the middle of the subdivisions of the Israelite peoples. The inhabitants of an individual household were identified as a *bayith* (1004), meaning house. Several households together constituted a *mishpâchâh* (Ge 10:31, 32; Ex 6:14, 15, 19, 25). Several families or clans together constituted a *shêbeṭ* (7626) or *maṭṭeh*

(4294), meaning tribe. This noun is also used in a less technical sense to indicate an entire people or nation (Eze 20:32; Mic 2:3); an ethnic or racial group (Ge 10:5; 12:3); a tribe (Jos 7:17; Jgs 13:2; 18:2, 11). It occurs in the sense of a guild of scribes in one verse (1Ch 2:55) because the scribal profession was originally a hereditary position. It can also represent a species or kind of animal (Ge 8:19); or a divine plague (Jer 15:3).

4941. מִשְׁפָּט, **mishpâṭ,** *mish-pawt´*; from 8199; (properly) a *verdict* (favourable or unfavourable) pronounced judicially, especially a *sentence* or formal decree (human or [participle] divine *law*, individual or collective), including the act, the place, the suit, the crime, and the penalty; (abstract) *justice*, including a participle *right*, or *privilege* (statutory or customary), or even a *style:*— + adversary, ceremony, charge, × crime, custom, desert, determination, discretion, disposing, due, fashion, form, to be judged, judgment, just (-ice, -ly), (manner of) law (-ful), manner, measure, (due) order, ordinance, right, sentence, usest, × worth, + wrong.

A masculine noun meaning a judgment, a legal decision, a legal case, a claim, proper, rectitude. The word connotes several variations in meanings depending on the context. It is used to describe a legal decision or judgment rendered: it describes a legal decision given by God to be followed by the people (Isa 58:2; Zep 2:3; Mal 2:17). These decisions could come through the use of the Urim and Thummim (Nu 27:21). The high priest wore a pouch called the breastpiece of justice, containing the Urim and Thummim by which decisions were obtained from the Lord (Ex 28:30). Doing what was right and just in the Lord's eyes was far more important than presenting sacrifices to Him (Ge 18:19; Pr 21:3, 15). God was declared to be the Judge of the whole earth who rendered justice faithfully (Ge 18:25; Isa 30:18). In the plural form, the word describes legal judgments, cases, examples, laws, and specifications.

The word describes the legal case or cause presented by someone. The Servant spoken of by Isaiah asked who brought his case of justice against him (Isa 50:8); Job brought his case to vindicate himself (Job 13:18; 23:4). The legal claim or control in a situation is also described by the word. Samuel warned the people of the civil and legal demands a king would place on them (1Sa 8:9); Moses gave legislation to protect the rightful claim of daughters (Ex 21:9). The Hebrew word also described the legal right to property (Jer 32:8). Not surprisingly, the place where judgments were rendered was also described by this word; disputes were to be taken to the place of judgment (Dt 25:1). Solomon built a hall of justice where he served as judge (1Ki 7:7).

The word also describes plans or instructions: it describes the building plans for the tabernacle (Ex 35—40); and the specifications for the Temple (1Ki 6:38); the instructions the angelic messenger gave to Samson's parents about how he was to be brought up (Jgs 13:12). In a more abstract sense, it depicts the manner of life a people followed, such as the Sidonians (Jgs 18:7; 1Sa 2:13).

The word means simple justice in some contexts, often in parallel with synonymous words, such as *chôq* (2706) or *tsedeq* (6664), meaning ordinance or righteousness. It describes justice as one thing Jerusalem was to be filled with along with righteousness (Isa 1:21). Justice and righteousness characterize the Lord's throne (Ps 89:14[15]); and these were coupled with love and faithfulness (cf. Ps 101:1; 111:7). Executing or doing justice was the central goal that Yahweh had for His people (Jer 7:5; Eze 18:8), for that equaled righteousness (Eze 18:9).

4942. מִשְׁפְּתַיִם, **mishpᵉthayim,** *mish-peh-tha-yeem´*; from 8192; a *stall* for cattle (only dual):—burden, sheepfold.

4943. מֶשֶׁק, **mesheq,** *meh´-shek*; from an unused root meaning to *hold; possession:*— + steward.

4944. מַשָּׁק, **mashshâq,** *mash-shawk´*; from 8264; a *traversing,* i.e. rapid *motion:*—running to and fro.

4945. מַשְׁקֶה, **mashqeh,** *mash-keh´*; from 8248; (properly) *causing to drink,* i.e. a *butler*; by implication (intransitive) *drink* (itself); (figurative) a *well-watered* region:—butler (-ship), cupbearer, drink (-ing), fat pasture, watered.

4946. מִשְׁקוֹל, **mishqôwl,** *mish-kole´*; from 8254; *weight:*—weight.

4947. מַשְׁקוֹף, **mashqôwph,** *mash-kofe´*; from 8259 in its original sense of *overhanging*; a *lintel:*—lintel.

4948. מִשְׁקָל, **mishqâl,** *mish-kawl´*; from 8254; *weight* (numerically estimated); hence, *weighing* (the act):—(full) weight.

4949. מִשְׁקֶלֶת, **mishqeleth,** *mish-keh´-leth*; or מִשְׁקֹלֶת, **mishqôleth,** *mish-ko´-leth*; feminine of 4948 or 4947; a *weight,* i.e. a *plummet* (with line attached):—plummet.

4950. מִשְׁקָע, **mishqâ‘,** *mish-kaw´*; from 8257; a *settling* place (of water), i.e. a *pond:*—deep.

4951. מִשְׂרָה, **miśrâh,** *mis-raw´*; from 8280; *empire:*—government.

4952. מִשְׁרָה, **mishrâh,** *mish-raw´*; from 8281 in the sense of *loosening; maceration,* i.e. steeped *juice:*—liquor.

4953. מַשְׁרוֹקִי, **mashrôwqîy,** *mash-ro-kee´*; (Chaldee); from a root corresponding to 8319; a (musical) *pipe* (from its *whistling* sound):—flute.

4954. מִשְׁרָעִי, **Mishrâ‘îy,** *mish-raw-ee´*; patrial from an unused noun from an unused root; probably meaning to *stretch* out; *extension*; a *Mishraite,* or inhabitant (collective) of Mishra:—Mishraites.

4955. מִשְׂרָפָה, **miśrâphâh,** *mis-raw-faw´*; from 8313; *combustion,* i.e. *cremation* (of a corpse), or *calcination* (of lime):—burning.

4956. מִשְׂרְפוֹת מַיִם, **Miśrᵉphôwth mayim,** *mis-ref-ohth´ mah´-yim*; from the plural of 4955 and 4325; *burnings of water; Misrephoth-Majim,* a place in Palestine:—Misrephoth-mayim.

4957. מַשְׂרֵקָה, **Maśrêqâh,** *mas-ray-kaw´*; a form for 7796 used denominatively; *vineyard; Masrekah,* a place in Idumæa:—Masrekah.

4958. מַשְׂרֵת, **maśrêth,** *mas-rayth´*; apparently from an unused root meaning to *perforate,* i.e. hollow out; a *pan:*—pan.

4959. מָשַׁשׁ, **mâshash,** *maw-shash´*; a primitive root; to *feel* of; (by implication) to *grope:*—feel, grope, search.

4960. מִשְׁתֶּה, **mishteh,** *mish-teh´*; from 8354; *drink*; (by implication) *drinking* (the act); also (by implication), a *banquet* or (general) *feast:*—banquet, drank, drink, feast ([-ed], -ing).

A masculine noun meaning a drink, a feast. This word comes from the verb *shâthâh* (8354), meaning to drink. In a few instances, this word referred specifically to drinks (Ezr 3:7; Da 1:5, 8, 10, 16), but it usually referred to feasts prepared for special occasions: hospitality (Ge 19:3); the weaning of a child (Ge 21:8); making peace (Ge 26:30; 2Sa 3:20); a wedding (Ge 29:22; Jgs 14:10, 12, 17; Est 2:18); merriment (Est 1:3; 9:17–19; Job 1:4, 5; Ecc 7:2). A feast was indicative of blessing (Pr 15:15; Isa 25:6).

4961. מִשְׁתֵּא, **mishtê',** *mish-tay´*; (Chaldee); corresponding to 4960; a *banquet:*—banquet.

4962. מַת, **math,** *math*; from the same as 4970; (properly) an *adult* (as of full length); (by implication) a *man* (only in the plural):— + few, × friends, men, persons, × small.

4963. מַתְבֵּן, **mathbên,** *math-bane´*; denominative from 8401; *straw in the heap:*—straw.

4964. מֶתֶג, **metheg,** *meh´-theg*; from an unused root meaning to *curb*; a *bit:*—bit, bridle.

4965. מֶתֶג הָאַמָּה, **Metheg hâ'Ammâh,** *meh´-theg haw-am-maw´*; from 4964 and 520 with the article interposed; *bit of the metropolis; Metheg-ha-Ammah,* an epithet of Gath:—Metheg-ammah.

4966. מָתוֹק, **mâthôwq,** *maw-thoke´*; or מָתוּק, **mâ-thûwq,** *maw-thook´*; from 4985; *sweet:*—sweet (-er, -ness).

4967. מְתוּשָׁאֵל, **Mᵉthûwshâ'êl,** *meth-oo-shaw-ale´*; from 4962 and 410, with the relative interposed; *man who* (is) *of God; Methushaël,* an antediluvian patriarch:—Methusael.

4968. מְתוּשֶׁלַח, **Mᵉthûwshelach,** *meth-oo-sheh´-lakh*; from 4962 and 7973; *man of a dart; Methushelach,* an antediluvian patriarch:—Methuselah.

4969. מָתַח, **mâthach,** *maw-thakh´*; a primitive root; to *stretch* out:—spread out.

4970. מָתַי, **mâthay,** *maw-thah´ee*; from an unused root meaning to *extend*; (properly) *extent* (of time); but used only adverb (especially with other particles prefixed), *when* (either relative or interrogitive):—long, when.

4971. מַתְכֹּנֶת, **mathkôneth,** *math-ko´-neth*; or מַתְכֻּנֶת, **mathkuneth,** *math-koo´-neth*; from 8505 in the transferred sense of *measuring; pro-*

portion (in size, number or ingredients):— composition, measure, state, tale.

4972. מַתְלָאָה, **mattᵉlâ'âh,** *mat-tel-aw-aw´*; from 4100 and 8513; *what a trouble!:*—what a weariness.

4973. מְתַלְּעוֹת, **mᵉthallᵉˁôwth,** *meth-al-leh-oth´*; contraction from 3216; (properly) a *biter,* i.e. a *tooth:*—cheek (jaw) tooth, jaw.

4974. מְתֹם, **mᵉthôm,** *meth-ohm´*; from 8552; *wholesomeness*; also (adverb) *completely:*—men [*by reading* 4962], soundness.

4975. מָתְנַיִם, **mothnayim,** *moth´-na-yim*; from an unused root meaning to *be slender*; (properly) the *waist* or small of the back; only in plural the *loins:*— + greyhound, loins, side.

4976. מַתָּן, **mattân,** *mat-tawn´*; from 5414; a *present:*—gift, to give, reward.

4977. מַתָּן, **Mattân,** *mat-tawn´*; the same as 4976; *Mattan,* the name of a priest of Baal, and of an Israelite:—Mattan.

4978. מַתְּנָא, **mattᵉnâ',** *mat-ten-aw´*; (Chaldee); corresponding to 4979:—gift.

4979. מַתָּנָה, **mattânâh,** *mat-taw-naw´*; feminine of 4976; a *present*; specifically (in a good sense) a sacrificial *offering,* (in a bad sense) a *bribe:*—gift.

4980. מַתָּנָה, **Mattânâh,** *mat-taw-naw´*; the same as 4979; *Mattanah,* a place in the Desert:—Mattanah.

4981. מִתְנִי, **Mithnîy,** *mith-nee´*; probably patrial from an unused noun meaning *slenderness*; a *Mith-nite,* or inhabitant of Methen:—Mithnite.

4982. מַתְּנַי, **Mattᵉnay,** *mat-ten-ah´ee*; from 4976; *liberal; Mattenai,* the name of three Israelites:—Mattenai.

4983. מַתַּנְיָה, **Mattanyâh,** *mat-tan-yaw´*; or מַתַּנְיָהוּ, **Mattanyâhûw,** *mat-tan-yaw´-hoo*; from 4976 and 3050; *gift of Jah; Mattanjah,* the name of ten Israelites:—Mattaniah.

4984. מִתְנַשֵּׂא, **mithnassê',** *mith-nas-say´*; from 5375; (used as abstract) supreme *exaltation:*—exalted.

4985. מָתַק, **mâthaq,** *maw-thak´*; a primitive root; to *suck*; (by implication) to *relish,* or (intransitive) *be sweet*:—be (made, × take) sweet.

4986. מֶתֶק, **metheq,** *meh´-thek*; from 4985; (figurative) *pleasantness* (of discourse):—sweetness.

4987. מֹתֶק, **môtheq,** *mo´-thek*; from 4985; *sweetness*:—sweetness.

4988. מְתָק, **mâthâq,** *maw-thawk´*; from 4985; a *dainty*, i.e. (general) *food*:—feed sweetly.

4989. מִתְקָה, **Mithqâh,** *mith-kaw´*; feminine of 4987; *sweetness; Mithkah*, a place in the Desert:—Mithcah.

4990. מִתְרְדָת, **Mithredâth,** *mith-red-awth´*; of Persian origin; *Mithredath*, the name of two Persians:—Mithredath.

4991. מַתָּת, **mattâth,** *mat-tawth´*; feminine of 4976 abbreviation; a *present*:—gift.

4992. מַתַּתָּה, **Mattattâh,** *mat-tat-taw´*; for 4993; *gift of Jah; Mattattah*, an Israelite:—Mattathah.

4993. מַתִּתְיָה, **Mattithyâh,** *mat-tith-yaw´*; or מַתִּתְיָהוּ, **Mattithyâhûw,** *mat-tith-yaw´-hoo*; from 4991 and 3050; *gift of Jah; Mattithjah*, the name of four Israelites:—Mattithiah.

נ (Nun)

4994. נָא, **nâ',** *naw;* a primitive particle of incitement and entreaty, which may usually be rendered *I pray, now* or *then;* added mostly to verbs (in the imperative or future), or to interject, occasionally to an adverb or conjuction:— I beseech (pray) thee (you), go to, now, oh.

A participle meaning please, now. The most common use of this word is similar to the antiquated use of pray as in pray tell. Since it was frequently used as a polite form of asking for something, it was often left untranslated in many English versions of the Bible. Abraham used this word when he asked Sarah to say she was his sister (Ge 12:13); Moses used the word when he asked the people to listen to him (Nu 20:10). It was often used to ask permission (Nu 20:17).

4995. נָא, **nâ',** *naw;* apparently from 5106 in the sense of *harshness* from refusal; (properly) *tough,* i.e. *uncooked* (flesh):—raw.

4996. נֹא, **Nô',** *no;* of Egyptian origin; *No* (i.e. *Thebes*), the capital of Upper Egypt:—No. Compare 528.

4997. נֹאד, **nô'd,** *node;* or נֹואד, **nôw'd,** *node;* also (feminine) נֹאדָה, **nô'dâh,** *no-daw´;* from an unused root of uncertain significance; a (skin or leather) *bag* (for fluids):—bottle.

4998. נָאָה, **nâ'âh,** *naw-aw´;* a primitive root; (properly) to *be at home,* i.e. (by implication) to be *pleasant* (or *suitable*), i.e. *beautiful:*—be beautiful, become, be comely.

4999. נָאָה, **nâ'âh,** *naw-aw´;* from 4998; a *home;* (figurative) a *pasture:*—habitation, house, pasture, pleasant place.

A feminine noun meaning a dwelling, an abode, a residence, a habitation, a pasture, a meadow. This word describes a place where humans permanently settle and live; or to an area where flocks and herds graze, reside, lie down, and rest. In His fierce anger for their iniquities, the Lord vented His wrath on Israel, destroying without mercy the dwellings found within its borders (La 2:2; cf. Jer 25:37). The Lord roars from Zion, and the pastures of the shepherds wither (Am 1:2). Painting a picture of abundant provisions, the psalmist praises God for the overflowing pastures of the wilderness (Ps 65:12[13]; cf. the description of wilderness pastures in Jer 9:10[9]). The most famous use of the term comes in Ps 23, where in vivid imagery the Lord is depicted as the great Shepherd who causes His sheep to lie down in green pastures (Ps 23:2). Once it is used in conjunction with the term used for God, forming the phrase pastures of God. In the context, the phrase refers to the land of Israel and recalls the idea of the people of Israel as God's flock (Ps 83:12[13]). This term stems from the verb nâ'âh (4998).

5000. נָאוֶה, **nâ'veh,** *naw-veh´;* from 4998 or 5116; *suitable,* or *beautiful:*—becometh, comely, seemly.

5001. נָאַם, **nâ'am,** *naw-am´;* a primitive root; (properly) to *whisper,* i.e. (by implication) to *utter* as an oracle:—say.

A verb meaning to murmur, to mutter, to whisper, to utter. The term is used once to describe the occupation which the false prophets of Jeremiah's day habitually practiced. They uttered false prophecies and claimed they were from the Lord, thus leading many people astray (Jer 23:31).

5002. נְאֻם, **n°um,** *nah-oom´;* from 5001; an *oracle:*—(hath) said, saith.

5003. נָאַף, **nâ'aph,** *naw-af´;* a primitive root; to *commit adultery;* (figurative) to *apostatize:*—adulterer (-ess), commit (-ing) adultery, woman that breaketh wedlock.

5004. נִאֻף, **ni'uph,** *nee-oof´;* from 5003; *adultery:*—adultery.

288

5005. נָאֲפוּף, **na'ăphûwph**, *nah-af-oof'*; from 5003; *adultery*:—adultery.

5006. נָאַץ, **nâ'ats**, *naw-ats'*; a primitive root; to *scorn*; or (Ecc 12:5) by interchange for 5132, to *bloom*:—abhor, (give occasion to) blaspheme, contemn, despise, flourish, × great, provoke.

A verb meaning to revile, to scorn, to reject. It is related to *nâtsats* (5340), meaning to scorn or to blaspheme. This word often refers to rejecting the counsel of a wise person. This scornful attitude results in an unhappy life: people live in affliction because they reject God's counsel (Ps 107:11). Another example of a passage that uses this word is Pr 1:30, where wisdom laments that people scorn her reproof. In another instance of this word, the Israelites were chastised because they had rejected God's Law (Isa 5:24).

5007. נְאָצָה, **n°âtsâh**, *neh-aw-tsaw'*; or נֶאָצָה, **ne'âtsâh**, *neh-aw-tsaw'*; from 5006; *scorn*:—blasphemy.

5008. נָאַק, **nâ'aq**, *naw-ak'*; a primitive root; to *groan*:—groan.

5009. נְאָקָה, **n°âqâh**, *neh-aw-kaw'*; from 5008; a *groan*:—groaning.

5010. נָאַר, **nâ'ar**, *naw-ar'*; a primitive root; to *reject*:—abhor, make void.

5011. נֹב, **Nôb**, *nobe*; the same as 5108; *fruit; Nob*, a place in Palestine:—Nob.

5012. נָבָא, **nâbâ'**, *naw-baw'*; a primitive root; to *prophesy*, i.e. speak (or sing) by inspiration (in prediction or simple discourse):—prophesy (-ing), make self a prophet.

A verb meaning to prophesy, to speak by inspiration, to predict. This most commonly refers to the way in which the word of the Lord came to the people (Jer 19:14; Eze 11:13). There were various means in which people came to prophesy. Eldad and Medad became ecstatic when they prophesied (Nu 11:25–27); whereas the sons of Asaph used songs and instruments when they prophesied (1Ch 25:1). False prophets were also known to prophesy (Zec 13:3).

5013. נְבָא, **n°bâ'**, *neb-aw'*; (Chaldee); corresponding to 5012:—prophesy.

An Aramaic verb meaning to prophesy. This word corresponds to the Hebrew word *nâbâ'*

(5012). It is possible that this word takes on the meaning of being carried away through prophecy. Only found once in the OT, this word is used to describe the means by which Haggai and Zechariah prophesied to the people of Israel (Ezr 5:1).

5014. נָבַב, **nâbab**, *naw-bab'*; a primitive root; to *pierce*; to *be hollow*, or (figurative) *foolish*:—hollow, vain.

5015. נְבוֹ, **N°bôw**, *neb-o'*; probably of foreign derivation; *Nebo*, the name of a Babylonian deity, also of a mountain in Moab, and of a place in Palestine:—Nebo.

5016. נְבוּאָה, **n°bûw'âh**, *neb-oo-aw'*; from 5012; a *prediction* (spoken or written):—prophecy.

A feminine noun meaning prophecy, a prophetic word. Shemaiah gave a false prophecy to Nehemiah in order to cause him to sin and to saddle him with a bad name (Ne 6:12). The prophecy of Azariah, son of Oded, encouraged King Asa of Judah to implement religious reform in the country, bringing the people back to the Lord their God (2Ch 15:8). Once the word refers to a written prophecy by a prophet named Ahijah (2Ch 9:29). This word stems from the verb *nâbâ'* (5012).

5017. נְבוּאָה, **n°bûw'âh**, *neb-oo-aw'*; (Chaldee); corresponding to 5016; inspired *teaching*:—prophesying.

An Aramaic feminine noun meaning prophesying. It refers to the role and functions of a prophet and appears only once in the OT, where it is recorded that the elders prospered through the prophesying of Haggai the prophet and Zechariah the son of Iddo (Ezr 6:14). It is probably closely related to the Hebrew word *něbû'âh* (5016).

5018. נְבוּזַרְאֲדָן, **N°bûwzar'ădân**, *neb-oo-zar-ad-awn'*; of foreign origin; *Nebuzaradan*, a Babylonian general:—Nebuzaradan.

5019. נְבוּכַדְנֶאצַּר, **N°bûwkadne'tstsar**, *neb-oo-kad-nets-tsar'*; or נְבֻכַדְנֶאצַּר, **N°bukadne'tstsar**, *neb-oo-kad-nets-tsar'*; or נְבֻכַדְנֶצַּר, **N°bukad-netstsar**, *neb-oo-kad-nets-tsar'*; or נְבוּכַדְנֶאצַּר, **N°bûw-kad Ne'tstsar**, *neb-oo-kad nets-tsar'*, (Jer 28:3); or נְבוּכַד נֶצַּר, **N°bûwkad Netstsar**, *neb-oo-kad nets-tsar'*; or נְבוּכַדְרֶאצּוֹר, **Nebûwkadre'tsôwr**, *neb-oo-kad-tsore*, (Jer 49:8); or

נְבוּכַדְרֶאצַּר, **Nebûwkadre'tstsar**, *neb-oo-kad-rets-tsar´*; of foreign derivation; *Nebukadnets-tsar* (or *-retstsar*, or *-retstsor*), king of Babylon:— Nebuchadnezzar, Nebuchadrezzar.

5020. נְבוּכַדְנֶצַּר, **Nᵉbûwkadnetstsar**, *neb-oo-kad-nets-tsar´*; (Chaldee); corresponding to 5019:—Nebuchadnezzar.

5021. נְבוּשַׁזְבָּן, **Nᵉbûwshazbân**, *neb-oo-shaz-bawn´*; of foreign derivation; *Nebushazban*, Nebuchadnezzar's chief eunuch:—Nebushazban.

5022. נָבוֹת, **Nâbôwth**, *naw-both´*; feminine plural from the same as 5011; *fruits*; *Naboth*, an Israelite:—Naboth.

5023. נְבִזְבָּה, **nᵉbizbâh**, *neb-iz-baw´*; (Chaldee); of uncertain derivation; a *largess*:—reward.

5024. נָבַח, **nâbach**, *naw-bakh*; a primitive root; to *bark* (as a dog):—bark.

5025. נֹבַח, **Nôbach**, *no´-bach*; from 5024; a *bark*; *Nobach*, the name of an Israelite, and of a place East of the Jordan:—Nobah.

5026. נִבְחַז, **Nibchaz**, *nib-khaz´*; of foreign origin; *Nibchaz*, a deity of the Avites:—Nibhaz.

5027. נָבַט, **nâbaṭ**, *naw-bat´*; a primitive root; to *scan*, i.e. look intently at; (by implication) to *regard* with pleasure, favour or care:—(cause to) behold, consider, look (down), regard, have respect, see.

5028. נְבָט, **Nᵉbâṭ**, *neb-awt´*; from 5027; *regard*; *Nebat*, the father of Jeroboam I:—Nebat.

5029. נְבִיא, **nᵉbîy'**, *neb-ee´*; (Chaldee); corresponding to 5030; a *prophet*:—prophet.

An Aramaic masculine noun meaning prophet. It refers to an individual that fulfilled the role and functions of a prophet (Ezr 5:1, 2; 6:14). The word is probably closely related to the biblical Hebrew word (if not the same word), *nâbiy'* (5030); as such, it would share similar, if not the same, variations in meaning.

5030. נָבִיא, **nâbiy'**, *naw-bee´*; from 5012; a *prophet* or (general) *inspired* man:—prophecy, that prophesy, prophet.

A masculine noun meaning a prophet, a spokesman. The meaning is consistently one of prophet and inspired spokesman. Moses was the greatest prophet of the OT (Dt 34:10) and the example for all later prophets. He displayed every aspect of a true prophet, both in his call, his work, his faithfulness, and, at times, his doubts. Only Abraham is called a prophet before Moses (Ge 20:7).

Moses received a call from God to speak His words and perform a specific task (see Ex 3:4, 10; 4:17, 29; 5:1) with the promise that the Lord would be with him and help him accomplish it (see Ex 3:12, 20; 4:12, 14–16). He responded, though reluctantly (see Ex 3:11, 13; 4:1), and God did what He had said He would do (see Ex 6:1; 14:30, 31; 40:34, 38). Moses' prophetic voice spoke to Israel of the past (see Dt 1—3), the present (see Dt 4:1; 26:18), and the future (see Dt 31:20–22), as would every major prophet after him. This pattern, or much of it, is found in the case of every true prophet (see Isa 6; Jer 1; Eze 1—3; Hos 1:2; Am 7:14, 15; Jnh 1:1). All the true prophets stood in the counsel of God to receive their messages (see 1Ki 22:19; Jer 23:22; Am 3:7).

This word describes one who was raised up by God and, as such, could only proclaim that which the Lord gave him to say. A prophet could not contradict the Law of the Lord or speak from his own mind or heart. To do so was to be a false prophet (Jer 14:14; 23:16, 26, 30). What a prophet declared had to come true, or he was false (Dt 18:22; Jer 23:9).

The noun is found parallel to two other words meaning a seer, a prophet (*chôzeh*[2374], *rô'eh*[1Sa 9:9; 2Sa 24:11]), which tends to stress the visionary or perceptive aspects of a prophet's experiences. There were "sons of the prophets," a phrase indicating bands or companies of prophets, "son" in this case meaning a member (1Ki 20:35; 2Ki 2:3, 5; 4:1). Kings sometimes had a group of prophets around them (1Ki 22:22; 2Ch 18:21, 22). Prophets were designated from Israel (Eze 13:2, 4); Samaria (Jer 23:13); and Jerusalem (Zep 3:4). In an unusual development, David set aside some of the sons of Asaph, Heman, and Jeduthun to serve as prophets. Their prophesying was accompanied with musical instruments and possibly was brought on and aided by these instruments. This phenomenon is described mainly in the book of 2 Chronicles (see 2Ch 20:14; 29:30). Evidently, Zechariah, the priest, also prophesied in that era. But Moses himself desired that all God's people have the Spirit of God on them, as did the prophets (Nu 11:29).

5031. נְבִיאָה, **nᵉbîy'âh**, *neb-ee-yaw'*; feminine of 5030; a *prophetess* or (generally) *inspired* woman; (by implication) a *poetess*; (by association) a *prophet's wife*:—prophetess.

A feminine noun meaning prophetess. It is the feminine form of the Hebrew *nâbî'* (5030), meaning a spokesman, a speaker, or a prophet. The ancient concept of a prophetess was a woman who had the gift of song, like Miriam (Ex 15:20) or Deborah (Jgs 4:4; cf. 5:1). The later concept of a prophetess, being more in line with the concept of a prophet, was one who was consulted in order to receive a word from the Lord, like Huldah (2Ki 22:14; 2Ch 34:22). It also described a false prophetess, Noadiah (Ne 6:14). A unique usage may be its reference to the wife of Isaiah as a prophetess (Isa 8:3). Is this because of her own position and work or because of her relationship with Isaiah, a prophet? It has been interpreted both ways.

5032. נְבָיוֹת, **Nᵉbâyôwth**, *neb-aw-yoth'*; or נְבָיֹת, **Nebâyôth**, *neb-aw-yoth'*; feminine plural from 5107; *fruitfulnesses; Nebajoth*, a son of Ishmael, and the country settled by him:—Nebaioth, Nebajoth.

5033. נֶבֶךְ, **nêbek**, *nay'-bek*; from an unused root meaning to *burst* forth; a *fountain*:—spring.

5034. נָבֵל, **nâbêl**, *naw-bale'*; a primitive root; to *wilt*; (generally) to *fall away, fail, faint*; (figurative) to *be foolish* or (moral) *wicked*; (causative) to *despise, disgrace*:—disgrace, dishonour, lightly esteem, fade (away, -ing), fall (down, -ling, off), do foolishly, come to nought, × surely, make vile, wither.

5035. נֶבֶל, **nebel**, *neh'-bel*; or נֵבֶל, **nêbel**, *nay'-bel*; from 5034; a skin-*bag* for liquids (from *collapsing* when empty); hence, a *vase* (as similar in shape when full); also a *lyre* (as having a body of like form):—bottle, pitcher, psaltery vessel, viol.

5036. נָבָל, **nâbâl**, *naw-bawl'*; from 5034; *stupid; wicked* (especially *impious*):—fool (-ish, -ish man, -ish woman), vile person.

5037. נָבָל, **Nâbâl**, *naw-bawl'*; the same as 5036; *dolt; Nabal*, an Israelite:—Nabal.

5038. נְבֵלָה, **nᵉbêlâh**, *neb-ay-law'*; from 5034; a *flabby* thing, i.e. a *carcase* or *carrion* (human or bestial, often collective); (figurative) an *idol*:—(dead) body, (dead) carcase, dead of itself, which died, (beast) that (which) dieth of itself.

A feminine noun meaning a carcass, a corpse. It describes a body devoid of life, whether human (Jos 8:29; Isa 5:25) or animal (Dt 14:8). The Law clearly stated that contact with the carcass of a dead animal (Le 5:2) or with the body of a dead person (cf. Nu 19:11) would render an individual unclean. Also, it was possible for the land to be defiled by the presence of an unburied corpse (Dt 21:23). Hence, Jeremiah used the word *nebêlâh* for idols. Pagan idols were devoid of life just like corpses and were a source of defilement for the people, priests, and land.

5039. נְבָלָה, **nᵉbâlâh**, *neb-aw-law'*; feminine of 5036; *foolishness*, i.e. (moral) *wickedness*; (concrete) a *crime*; (by extension) *punishment*:—folly, vile, villany.

5040. נַבְלוּת, **nablûwth**, *nab-looth'*; from 5036; (properly) *disgrace*, i.e. the (female) *pudenda*:—lewdness.

5041. נְבַלָּט, **Nᵉballâṭ**, *neb-al-lawt'*; apparently from 5036 and 3909; *foolish secrecy; Neballat*, a place in Palestine:—Neballat.

5042. נָבַע, **nâba'**, *naw-bah'*; a primitive root; to *gush* forth; (figurative) to *utter* (good or bad words); (specifically) to *emit* (a foul odor):—belch out, flowing, pour out, send forth, utter (abundantly).

5043. נֶבְרְשָׁא, **nebrᵉshâ'**, *neb-reh-shaw'*; (Chaldee); from an unused root meaning to *shine*; a *light*; plural (collective) a *chandelier*:—candlestick.

5044. נִבְשָׁן, **Nibshân**, *nib-shawn'*; of uncertain derivation; *Nibshan*, a place in Palestine:—Nibshan.

5045. נֶגֶב, **negeb**, *neh'-gheb*; from an unused root meaning to *be parched*; the *south* (from its drought); (specifically) the *Negeb* or southern district of Judah, occasionally, *Egypt* (as south to Palestine):—south (country, side, -ward).

5046. נָגַד, **nâgad**, *naw-gad'*; a primitive root; (properly) to *front*, i.e. stand boldly out opposite; by implication (causative), to *manifest*; (figurative) to *announce* (always by word of mouth to one present); (specifically) to *expose, predict, explain, praise*:—bewray, × certainly, certify, declare (-ing), denounce, expound, × fully, messenger, plainly, profess, rehearse, report, shew (forth), speak, × surely, tell, utter.

A verb meaning to tell, to report, to make known, to explain, to be reported. The root idea of the word and the causative form in which it is used is to declare something. The manner and context in which this is done creates the various shades of meaning of the verb. Its simplest use is to announce, to report, to share. Samuel, when a child, was afraid to report the vision he had to Eli (1Sa 3:15, 18; 1Ki 1:23). In some cases, it means to solve or explain, to make known. God asked Adam who had made him know he was naked (Ge 3:11; 12:18); it indicated the resolution of a riddle (Jgs 14:12, 15); or dream (Job 11:6; Da 2:2). Close to this is its meaning to share with or to inform someone of something, to speak out. People were responsible to speak out when they knew something relevant to a case (Le 5:1; Jos 2:14; Pr 29:24). It is used to proclaim or announce something, often proclaiming the character and attributes of the Lord. The psalmist proclaimed the great deeds of the Lord (Ps 9:11[12]); the posterity of the righteous psalmist would declare God's righteousness (Ps 22:31[32]); the Lord's love was regularly proclaimed (Ps 92:2[3]). The participle of the verb may indicate a messenger (Jer 51:31).

The passive use of the verb means to be told, to be announced. If an Israelite turned and followed false gods, this act of rebellion was to be brought to the attention of the leaders (Dt 17:4); anything that needed to be reported could be covered by this verb (Jgs 9:25; 2Sa 10:17). The Queen of Sheba used this verb when she declared that not even half the splendor of Solomon's wisdom and wealth had been told her (1Ki 10:7; Isa 21:2).

5047. נְגַד, **neʻgad,** *neg-ad´*; (Chaldee); corresponding to 5046; to *flow* (through the idea of *clearing* the way):—issue.

5048. נֶגֶד, **neged,** *neh´-ghed*; from 5046; a *front*, i.e. part opposite; (specifically) a *counterpart*, or mate; usually (adverb, especially with preposition) *over against* or *before*:—about, (over) against, × aloof, × far (off), × from, over, presence, × other side, sight, × to view.

5049. נְגֵד, **neged,** *neh´-ghed*; (Chaldee); corresponding to 5048; *opposite*:—toward.

5050. נָגַהּ, **nâgahh,** *naw-gah´*; a primitive root; to *glitter*; (causative) to *illuminate*:—(en-) lighten, (cause to) shine.

5051. נֹגַהּ, **nôgahh,** *no´-gah*; from 5050; *brilliancy* (literal or figurative):—bright (-ness), light, (clear) shining.

5052. נֹגַהּ, **Nôgahh,** *no´-gah*; the same as 5051; *Nogah*, a son of David:—Nogah.

5053. נֹגַהּ, **nôgahh,** *no´-gah*; (Chaldee); corresponding to 5051; *dawn*:—morning.

5054. נְגֹהָה, **neʻgôhâh,** *neg-o-haw´*; feminine of 5051; *splendor*:—brightness.

5055. נָגַח, **nâgach,** *naw-gakh´*; a primitive root; to *butt* with the horns; (figurative) to *war* against:—gore, push (down, -ing).

5056. נַגָּח, **naggâch,** *nag-gawkh´*; from 5055; *butting*, i.e. *vicious*:—used (wont) to push.

5057. נָגִיד, **nâgîyd,** *naw-gheed´*; or נָגִד, **nâgid,** *naw-gheed´*; from 5046; a *commander* (as occupying the *front*), civil, military or religious; generally (abstract plural), *honourable* themes:—captain, chief, excellent thing, (chief) governor, leader, noble, prince, (chief) ruler.

A masculine noun meaning a leader, a ruler, a prince. This term has a broad range of applications. At the top, it could allude to the king of Israel (1Sa 9:16; 13:14; 1Ki 1:35); a ruler from a foreign land like Tyre (Eze 28:2); or Assyria (2Ch 32:21). It could also be used regarding cultic leaders and officials from the high priest down (1Ch 9:11, 20; 2Ch 31:12, 13; 35:8; Jer 20:1). It could also be a label for various other lesser positions of leadership (1Ch 27:16; 2Ch 11:11, 22; 19:11; Job 29:10). The word is also used in an abstract sense to convey that which is princely, noble, and honourable (Pr 8:6).

5058. נְגִינָה, **neʻgîynâh,** *neg-ee-naw´*; or נְגִינַת, **neʻgîynath,** *neg-ee-nath´*; (Ps 611:title), from 5059; (properly) instrumental *music*; (by implication) a stringed *instrument*; (by extension) a *poem* set to music; (specifically) an *epigram*:—stringed instrument, musick, Neginoth [*plural*], song.

5059. נָגַן, **nâgan,** *naw-gan´*; a primitive root; (properly) to *thrum*, i.e. *beat* a tune with the fingers; especially to *play* on a stringed instrument; hence (general) to *make music*:—player on instruments, sing to the stringed instruments, melody, minstrel, play (-er, -ing).

5060. נָגַע, **nâga**ʻ, *naw-gah´*; a primitive root; (properly) to *touch*, i.e. *lay the hand upon* (for any purpose); (euphemism) to *lie with* a woman; (by implication) to *reach;* (figurative) to *arrive, acquire*; violently, to *strike* (punish, defeat, destroy, etc.):—beat, (× be able to) bring (down), cast, come (nigh), draw near (nigh), get up, happen, join, near, plague, reach (up), smite, strike, touch.

A verb meaning to touch, to reach, to strike. The basic import of this verb is physical contact from one person to another. Since interpersonal contact can come in one (or more) of many varieties, this verb carries a range of semantic possibilities. Its use could represent mere physical contact (Ge 3:3; 1Ki 6:27; Est 5:2). On a deeper level, it could designate striking (Job 1:19; Isa 53:4; Eze 17:10). Along these lines is the figurative use to identify God's judgment (1Sa 6:9; Job 1:11; 19:21). On an even deeper level, it indicates doing actual harm (Ge 26:11; Jos 9:19; 2Sa 14:10). In a metaphorical sense, this verb can also portray the concept to reach or extend (Isa 16:8; Jer 51:9; Jnh 3:6). In the passive form, it denotes the idea to allow oneself to be beaten in a military context (Jos 8:15). In the intensive form, this verb means to afflict or to be afflicted (Ge 12:17; 2Ki 15:5; Ps 73:5).

5061. נֶגַע, **nega**ʻ, *neh´-gah*; from 5060; a *blow;* (figurative) *infliction;* also (by implication) a *spot*; (concrete) a *leprous* person or dress:—plague, sore, stricken, stripe, stroke, wound.

A masculine noun meaning a blemish, a mark, a stroke, a plague. This word comes from the verb *nâga*ʻ (5060), meaning to touch or to strike, and is best understood as a blemish that has been created by touching or striking. In the majority of instances, it described a blemish inflicted by leprosy or a skin disease that the priest was to discern (used over sixty times in Le 13—14). It also referred to a physical injury inflicted by another person (Dt 17:8; 21:5; Isa 53:8); or by God Himself (Ps 89:32[33]). When describing land or property, it is best translated plague (Ge 12:17; Ex 11:1; 1Ki 8:37). At times, this word described a nonphysical blemish (1Ki 8:38; 2Ch 6:29; Pr 6:33).

5062. נָגַף, **nâgaph,** *naw-gaf´*; a primitive root; to *push, gore, defeat, stub* (the toe), *inflict* (a disease):—beat, dash, hurt, plague, slay, smite (down), strike, stumble, × surely, put to the worse.

A verb meaning to strike, to smite. This word is most often used within the context of warring nations when one nation struck another (Le 26:17; Nu 14:42; Dt 28:7, 25). At times, this was followed by the death of many (Jgs 20:35; 1Sa 4:10; 2Sa 18:7); at others, it merely signified defeat in war, with no mention of death (1Ki 8:33; 2Ki 14:12). God is often the One who smote, which led to incurable illness (2Ch 21:18; Zec 14:12, 18); or even death (1Sa 25:38; 2Sa 12:15). This word is also used to describe the stumbling of the foot (Pr 3:23; Jer 13:16); the causing of injury to another person (Ex 21:22); or to an animal (Ex 21:35).

5063. נֶגֶף, **negeph,** *neh´-ghef*; from 5062; a *trip* (of the foot); (figurative) an *infliction* (of disease):—plague, stumbling.

A masculine noun meaning a plague, stumbling. This word comes from the verb *nâgaph* (5062), meaning to strike or to smite, and described the effect of being struck or smitten. It usually described a plague that God sent on a disobedient people (Ex 12:13; 30:12; Nu 8:19; Jos 22:17). In one instance, it described the stone of stumbling (Isa 8:14).

5064. נָגַר, **nâgar,** *naw-gar´*; a primitive root; to *flow*; (figurative) to *stretch* out; (causative) to *pour* out or down; (figurative) to *deliver* over:—fall, flow away, pour down (out), run, shed, spilt, trickle down.

5065. נָגַשׂ, **nâgaś,** *naw-gas´*; a primitive root; to *drive* (an animal, a workman, a debtor, an army); (by implication) to *tax, harass, tyrannize*:—distress, driver, exact (-or), oppress (-or), × raiser of taxes, taskmaster.

5066. נָגַשׁ, **nâgash,** *naw-gash´*; a primitive root; to *be* or *come* (causative, *bring*) *near* (for any purpose); (euphemism) to *lie with* a woman; as an enemy, to *attack*; (religious) to *worship*; (causative) to *present*; (figurative) to *adduce* an argument; (by reversal) to *stand back*:—(make to) approach (nigh), bring (forth, hither, near), (cause to) come (hither, near, nigh), give place, go hard (up), (be, draw, go) near (nigh), offer, overtake, present, put, stand.

A verb meaning to come near, to approach, to draw near, to bring near, to be brought near. In the simple form of the verb, it indicates coming near, as when Jacob went near to Isaac his father who reached out and touched him (Ge 27:22); it simply describes approaching a person for whatever reason (Ge 43:19; Ex 19:15). It is used of priests approaching the Lord (Eze 44:13); or the altar to carry out their priestly duties (Ex 28:43; 30:20); and of armies drawing near for engagement in battle (Jgs 20:23; 2Sa 10:13). The word asserts close proximity in all these cases and can even describe the closeness of the scales of a crocodile (Job 41:16[8]).

In the reflexive form, it describes coming near. Dt 25:9 prescribed the action of a widow toward her brother-in-law who would not perform his Levitical duty toward her: She was to approach him, take off one of his sandals, and spit in his face (cf. Isa 45:20).

In the causative form, the verb means to bring near: a slave who decided to remain with his master perpetually was brought to the judges and to the doorpost so his ear could be bored with an awl (Ex 21:6; 1Sa 15:32); sacrifices were brought near as well (1Sa 13:9; 14:34). In a metaphorical sense, the word is used to call for the presentation of legal argumentation (Isa 41:21). The passive use of this form describes what is offered or presented, once to indicate that Abner's feet were not brought near, that is, they were not placed in chains (2Sa 3:34); and once to describe incense and pure offerings brought in the Lord's name (Mal 1:11).

5067. נֵד, **nêd,** *nade*; from 5110 in the sense of *piling* up; a *mound*, i.e. *wave:*—heap.

5068. נָדַב, **nâdab,** *naw-dab´*; a primitive root; to *impel*; hence to *volunteer* (as a soldier), to *present* spontaneously:—offer freely, be (give, make, offer self) willing (-ly).

A verb meaning to incite willingly. This word described the free, voluntary desire of the heart to give of oneself or of one's resources to the service of the Lord. It was used to describe the willing contributions that the people of Israel made to build the tabernacle (Ex 25:2; 35:21, 29); Solomon's Temple (1Ch 29:5, 6, 9, 14, 17);

and Zerubbabel's Temple (Ezr 1:6; 2:68; 3:5). In a few other instances, it spoke of the willing sacrifice of service that Amaziah made (2Ch 17:16); the returning exiles made (Ne 11:2); and Deborah commended (Jgs 5:2, 9). See the related noun *nĕdâbâh* (5071), meaning freewill offering.

5069. נְדַב, **nᵉdab,** *ned-ab´*; (Chaldee); corresponding to 5068; *be* (or *give*) *liberal* (*-ly*):—(be minded of ... own) freewill (offering), offer freely (willingly).

An Aramaic verb meaning to offer willingly, to make a freewill offering. This word is used exclusively in the book of Ezra and refers to those who could leave Babylon freely (Ezr 7:13). It also indicates the gifts given freely by a king (Ezr 7:15); and the Israelites (Ezr 7:16). See the related Hebrew verbs *nâdab* (5068) and *nĕdâbâh* (5071).

5070. נָדָב, **Nâdâb,** *naw-dawb´*; from 5068; *liberal*; *Nadab*, the name of four Israelites:—Nadab.

5071. נְדָבָה, **nᵉdâbâh,** *ned-aw-baw´*; from 5068; properly (abstract) *spontaneity*, or (adjective) *spontaneous*; also (concrete) a *spontaneous* or (by inference, in plural) *abundant* gift:—free (-will) offering, freely, plentiful, voluntary (-ily, offering), willing (-ly, offering).

A feminine noun meaning willingness, a freewill offering, a voluntary gift. As an adverb, it means willingly, freely, spontaneously, voluntarily. This term can denote that state of being which allows a person to offer a gift or a favour to someone else without any thought of return or payback. The favour is not given out of any obligation owed by the giver; rather, it is the result of an overflow from an abundance within the heart. The Lord declares that He loves Israel freely because His anger has turned away from them (Hos 14:4[5]). The Hebrews were commanded to diligently perform the vows they freely uttered to the Lord (Dt 23:23[24]). Most often, however, the term is utilized to signify an offering, a gift, or a sacrifice given voluntarily, as opposed to one offered in dutiful fulfillment of an obligation or vow (Le 22:23). Many from the congregation of Israel whose hearts were willing gave of their possessions as freewill offerings for the building of the Tent of Meeting and its services (Ex 35:29; 36:3; cf. Le 7:16;

Ezr 1:4; 3:5; 8:28; Eze 46:12; Am 4:5). Once the word possibly functions to convey an abundance, that is, of rain (Ps 68:9[10]). This term is derived from the verb *nâdab* (5068).

5072. נְדַבְיָה, **Nᵉdabyâh**, *ned-ab-yaw´*; from 5068 and 3050; *largess of Jah*; *Nedabjah*, an Israelite:—Nedabiah.

5073. נִדְבָּךְ, **nidbâk**, *nid-bawk´*; (Chaldee); from a root meaning to *stick*; a *layer* (of building materials):—row.

5074. נָדַד, **nâdad**, *naw-dad´*; a primitive root; (properly) to *wave* to and fro (rarely, to *flap* up and down); (figurative) to *rove*, *flee*, or (causative) to *drive* away:—chase (away), × could not, depart, flee (× apace, away), (re-) move, thrust away, wander (abroad, -er, -ing).

5075. נְדַד, **nᵉdad**, *ned-ad´*; (Chaldee); corresponding to 5074; to *depart*:—go from.

5076. נְדֻדִים, **nᵉdudîym**, *ned-oo-deem´*; passive participle of 5074; (properly) *tossed*; (abstract) a *rolling* (on the bed):—tossing to and fro.

5077. נָדָה, **nâdâh**, *naw-daw´*; or נָדָא, **nâdâ'**, *naw-daw´*; (2Ki 17:21), a primitive root; (properly) to *toss*; (figurative) to *exclude*, i.e. banish, postpone, prohibit:—cast out, drive, put far away.

5078. נֵדֶה, **nêdeh**, *nay´-deh*; from 5077 in the sense of freely *flinging* money; a *bounty* (for prostitution):—gifts.

5079. נִדָּה, **niddâh**, *nid-daw´*; from 5074; (properly) *rejection*; (by implication) *impurity*, especially personal (menstruation) or moral (idolatry, incest):— × far, filthiness, × flowers, menstruous (woman), put apart, × removed (woman), separation, set apart, unclean (-ness), thing, with filthiness).

5080. נָדַח, **nâdach**, *naw-dakh´*; a primitive root; to *push* off; used in a great variety of applications, literal and figurative (to expel, mislead, strike, inflict, etc.):—banish, bring, cast down (out), chase, compel, draw away, drive (away, out, quite), fetch a stroke, force, go away, outcast, thrust away (out), withdraw.

5081. נָדִיב, **nâdîyb**, *naw-deeb´*; from 5068; (properly) *voluntary*, i.e. generous; hence, *magnanimous*; as noun, a *grandee* (sometimes a

tyrant):—free, liberal (things), noble, prince, willing ([hearted]).

An adjective meaning willing, generous, noble; as a noun, those of noble birth. The word often denotes an attitude of heart which consents or agrees (often readily and cheerfully) to a course of action. The Hebrews who were of willing hearts gave as offerings to the Lord jewelry and gold for the construction of the tabernacle and its accessories (Ex 35:5, 22; cf. 2Ch 29:31; Ps 51:12[14]). In many other places, the term describes an individual as one of excellent moral character. Proverbs states that to punish the noble for their integrity is wrong (Pr 17:26; cf. Pr 17:7; Isa 32:5, 8). At other times, the word signifies those born into lineages of nobility. The Lord lifts the needy from the ash heap and causes them to sit with princes (1Sa 2:8; cf. Nu 21:18; Job 12:21; 34:18; Ps 47:9[10]; 107:40; 113:8; 118:9; Pr 25:7; Isa 13:2). This term is closely related to the verb *nâdab* (5068).

5082. נְדִיבָה, **nᵉdîybâh**, *ned-ee-baw´*; feminine of 5081; (properly) *nobility*, i.e. reputation:—soul.

5083. נָדָן, **nâdân**, *naw-dawn´*; probably from an unused root meaning to *give*; a *present* (for prostitution):—gift.

5084. נָדָן, **nâdân**, *naw-dawn´*; of uncertain derivation; a *sheath* (of a sword):—sheath.

5085. נִדְנֶה, **nidneh**, *nid-neh´*; (Chaldee); from the same as 5084; a *sheath*; (figurative) the *body* (as the receptacle of the soul):—body.

An Aramaic masculine noun meaning sheath for a sword. It is used only in the book of Daniel, where it figuratively described the relationship between Daniel's spirit and body. His spirit was within his body in the same way as a sword fits into its sheath (Da 7:15). The Hebrew counterpart of this word is *nâdân* (5084).

5086. נָדַף, **nâdaph**, *naw-daf´*; a primitive root; to *shove* asunder, i.e. *disperse*:—drive (away, to and fro), thrust down, shaken, tossed to and fro.

5087. נָדַר, **nâdar**, *naw-dar´*; a primitive root; to *promise* (positively, to do or give something to God):—(make a) vow.

A verb meaning to vow. The verbal concept denotes the making of an oral, voluntary promise to give or do something as an expression of consecration or devotion to the service of God. Jacob vowed to return a tenth of all that God bestowed on him if God would protect and preserve him on his journey (Ge 28:20). Le 27:8 discusses the special vow offerings to the Lord and the cost of redeeming someone or something which had been dedicated to the Lord. King David also made a vow that he would deny himself the pleasures of his house and his bed until the time came when he had established a resting place and a habitation for the Lord (Ps 132:2). The sailors, unable to save themselves and having cast Jonah into the sea with the resulting calm, greatly feared the Lord, offered sacrifices, and made vows to Him (Jnh 1:16).

5088. נֶדֶר, **neder,** *neh´-der;* or נֵדֶר, **nêder,** *nay´-der;* from 5087; a *promise* (to God); also (concrete) a thing *promised:*—vow ([-ed]).

A masculine noun meaning vow. The word is found twenty-five times in the OT and basically means a solemn promise to God or the thing promised. Several times, the word refers to the specific words given in a vow. Jacob vowed that the Lord would be his God and he would give Him a tenth of everything the Lord gave him (Ge 28:20; 31:13; Nu 21:2; Jgs 11:30). The word is used to describe the object or intent of vows: a Nazirite vow (Nu 6:2, 5, 21); a vow made by a wife (Nu 30:9[10]); or by people in a difficult situation who made a promise before the Lord (Jnh 1:16). The object of the vow can be a sacrifice (Le 7:16; 22:21); or a person dedicated to the Lord (Le 27:2). Neither money earned by prostitution nor deformed animals could be used as part of a vow (Le 22:23; Dt 23:18[19]). Once made, a vow had to be paid by the one who made it, for if he or she did not pay, it was considered a sin (Dt 23:21[22]; 2Sa 15:7; Ps 56:12[13]). Pr 20:25 warned against making a vow before carefully considering the wisdom of doing so. Jephthah made a rash vow without considering its implications and suffered greatly for it (Jgs 11:30, 39). The word also describes the vow of some of the Israelites and their wives to burn incense and give libation offerings to the Queen of Heaven in the time of Jeremiah (Jer 44:25).

5089. נֹהַּ, **nôah,** *no´-ah;* from an unused root meaning to *lament; lamentation:*—wailing.

5090. נָהַג, **nâhag,** *naw-hag´;* a primitive root; to *drive* forth (a person, an animal or chariot), i.e.

lead, carry away; (reflexive) to *proceed* (i.e. impel or guide oneself); also (from the *panting* induced by effort), to *sigh:*—acquaint, bring (away), carry away, drive (away), lead (away, forth), (be) guide, lead (away, forth).

5091. נָהָה, **nâhâh,** *naw-haw´;* a primitive root; to *groan,* i.e. *bewail;* hence (through the idea of *crying* aloud) to *assemble* (as if on proclamation):—lament, wail.

5092. נְהִי, **n^ehîy,** *neh-hee´;* from 5091; an *elegy:*—lamentation, wailing.

5093. נִהְיָה, **nihyâh,** *nih-yaw´;* feminine of 5092; *lamentation:*—doleful.

5094. נְהִיר, **n^ehîyr,** *neh-heere´;* (Chaldee); or יְרוּ נַה, **nahîyrûw,** *nah-hee-roo´;* (Chaldee); from the same as 5105; *illumination,* i.e. (figurative) *wisdom:*—light.

An Aramaic feminine noun meaning illumination, wisdom, or insight. This word is found only in Daniel. The story of the handwriting on the wall in Belshazzar's banquet hall established the fact that Daniel was able to discern things people found baffling. Belshazzar described Daniel's wisdom as light and understanding coming from the Spirit of God within him (Da 5:11, 14).

5095. נָהַל, **nâhal,** *naw-hal´;* a primitive root; (properly) to *run* with a *sparkle,* i.e. *flow;* hence (transitive) to *conduct,* and (by inference) to *protect, sustain:*—carry, feed, guide, lead (gently, on).

5096. נַהֲלָל, **Nahălâl,** *năh-hal-awl´;* or נַהֲלֹל, **Nahălôl,** *năh-hal-ole´;* the same as 5097; *Nahalal* or *Nahalol,* a place in Palestine:—Nahalal, Nahallal, Nahalol.

5097. נַהֲלֹל, **nahălôl,** *năh-hal-ole´;* from 5095; *pasture:*—bush.

5098. נָהַם, **nâham,** *naw-ham´;* a primitive root; to *growl:*—mourn, roar (-ing).

5099. נַהַם, **naham,** *năh´-ham;* from 5098; a *snarl:*—roaring.

5100. נְהָמָה, **n^ehâmâh,** *neh-haw-maw´;* feminine of 5099; *snarling:*—disquietness, roaring.

5101. נָהַק, **nâhaq,** *naw-hak´;* a primitive root; to *bray* (as an ass), *scream* (from hunger):—bray.

5102. נָהַר, **nâhar,** *naw-har´*; a primitive root; to *sparkle*, i.e. (figurative) *be cheerful*; hence (from the *sheen* of a running stream) to *flow*, i.e. (figurative) *assemble*:—flow (together), be lightened.

5103. נְהַר, **nᵉhar,** *neh-har´*; (Chaldee); from a root corresponding to 5102; a *river*, especially the Euphrates:—river, stream.

5104. נָהָר, **nâhâr,** *naw-hawr´*; from 5102; a *stream* (including the *sea*; especially the Nile, Euphrates, etc.); (figurative) *prosperity*:—flood, river.

5105. נְהָרָה, **nᵉhârâh,** *neh-haw-raw´*; from 5102 in its original sense; *daylight*:—light.

5106. נוּא, **nûw’,** *noo*; a primitive root; to *refuse*, *forbid*, *dissuade*, or *neutralise*:—break, disallow, discourage, make of no effect.

5107. נוּב, **nûwb,** *noob*; a primitive root; to *germinate*, i.e. (figurative) to (causative, *make*) *flourish*; also (of words), to *utter*:—bring forth (fruit), make cheerful, increase.

5108. נוֹב, **nôwb,** *nobe*; or נִיב, **nîyb,** *neeb*; from 5107; *produce*, literal or figurative:—fruit.

5109. נוֹבַי, **Nôwbay,** *no-bah´ee*; from 5108; *fruitful*; *Nobai*, an Israelite:—Nebai [*from the margin*].

5110. נוּד, **nûwd,** *nood*; a primitive root; to *nod*, i.e. *waver*; (figurative) to *wander, flee, disappear*; also (from *shaking* the head in sympathy), to *console, deplore*, or (from *tossing* the head in scorn) *taunt*:—bemoan, flee, get, mourn, make to move, take pity, remove, shake, skip for joy, be sorry, vagabond, way, wandering.

5111. נוּד, **nûwd,** *nood*; (Chaldee); corresponding to 5116; to *flee*:—get away.

5112. נוֹד, **nôwd,** *node*; [only defective נֹד, **nôd,** *node*]; from 5110; *exile*:—wandering.

5113. נוֹד, **Nôwd,** *node*; the same as 5112; *vagrancy*; *Nod*, the land of Cain:—Nod.

5114. נוֹדָב, **Nôwdâb,** *no-dawb´*; from 5068; *noble*; *Nodab*, an Arab tribe:—Nodab.

5115. נָוָה, **nâvâh,** *naw-vaw´*; a primitive root; to *rest* (as at home); causative (through the implied idea of *beauty* [compare 5116], to *celebrate* (with praises):—keep at home, prepare an habitation.

5116. נָוֶה, **nâveh,** *naw-veh´*; or (feminine) נָוָה, **nâvâh,** *naw-vaw´*; from 5115; (adjective) *at home*; hence (by implication of satisfaction) *lovely*; also (noun) a *home*, of God (temple), men (residence), flocks (pasture), or wild animals (*den*):—comely, dwelling (place), fold, habitation, pleasant place, sheepcote, stable, tarried.

5117. נוּחַ, **nûwach,** *noo´-akh*; a primitive root; to *rest*, i.e. *settle* down; used in a great variety of applications, literal and figurative, intransivitive, transitive and causative (to *dwell, stay, let fall, place, let alone, withdraw, give comfort*, etc.):—cease, be confederate, lay, let down, (be) quiet, remain, (cause to, be at, give, have, make to) rest, set down. Compare 3241.

5118. נוּחַ, **nûwach,** *noo´-akh*; or נוֹחַ, **nôwach,** *no´-akh*; from 5117; *quiet*:—rest (-ed, -ing place).

5119. נוֹחָה, **Nôwchâh,** *no-khaw´*; feminine of 5118; *quietude*; *Nochah*, an Israelite:—Nohah.

5120. נוּט, **nûwṭ,** *noot*; to *quake*:—be moved.

5121. נָווֹת, **Nâwôwth,** *naw-vowth´*; but in the Qere it is נָיוֹת, **Nâyôwth,** *naw-yoth´*; from 5115; *residence*; a place in Palestine:—Naioth [*from the margin*].

5122. נְוָלוּ, **nᵉvâlûw,** *nev-aw-loo´*; (Chaldee); or נְוָלִי, **nᵉvâlîy,** *nev-aw-lee´*; (Chaldee); from an unused root probably meaning to be *foul*; a *sink*:—dunghill.

5123. נוּם, **nûwm,** *noom*; a primitive root; to *slumber* (from drowsiness):—sleep, slumber.

5124. נוּמָה, **nûwmâh,** *noo-maw´*; from 5123; *sleepiness*:—drowsiness.

5125. נוּן, **nûwn,** *noon*; a primitive root; to *resprout*, i.e. propagate by shoots; (figurative) to *be perpetual*:—be continued.

5126. נוּן, **Nûwn,** *noon*; or נוֹן, **Nôwn,** *nohn*; (1Ch 7:27), from 5125; *perpetuity*; *Nun* or *Non*, the father of Joshua:—Non, Nun.

5127. נוּס, **nûws,** *noos*; a primitive root; to *flit*, i.e. *vanish* away (subside, escape); (causative) chase, impel, deliver:— × abate, away, be displayed, (make to) flee (away, -ing), put to flight, × hide, lift up a standard.

5128. נוּעַ, **nûwa',** *noo´-ah;* a primitive root; to *waver,* in a great variety of applications, literal and figurative (as subjoined):—continually, fugitive, × make to [go] up and down, be gone away, (be) move (-able, -d), be promoted, reel, remove, scatter, set, shake, sift, stagger, to and fro, be vagabond, wag, (make) wander (up and down).

5129. נוֹעַדְיָה, **Nôw'adyâh,** *no-ad-yaw´;* from 3259 and 3050; *convened of Jah; Noädjah,* the name of an Israelite, and a false prophetess:—Noadiah.

5130. נוּף, **nûwph,** *noof;* a primitive root; to *quiver* (i.e. *vibrate* up and down, or *rock* to and fro); used in a great variety of applications (including sprinkling, beckoning, rubbing, bastinadoing, sawing, waving, etc.):—lift up, move, offer, perfume, send, shake, sift, strike, wave.

A verb meaning to move back and forth, to sprinkle. This verb only occurs in the basic verbal form once, where it refers to sprinkling a bed with myrrh (Pr 7:17). Most often, it occurs in the causative form, where it can carry a similar semantic idea, namely making rain fall (Ps 68:9[10]). However, it usually carries the idea of moving back and forth or waving. It could be used to represent the reciprocating motion of a tool, like a sword (Ex 20:25); a sickle (Dt 23:25[26]); a tool for dressing stone (Dt 27:5); or a saw (Isa 10:15). It could also be used of the motion of one's hand as a healing ritual (2Ki 5:11); as retribution (Isa 11:15; 19:16); or as a signal (Isa 13:2). In a cultic context, this verb is a technical term that referenced the actions of the priest as he offered a sacrifice to God by waving it before the altar (Ex 29:24; Le 23:11; Nu 5:25).

5131. נוֹף, **nôwph,** *nofe;* from 5130; *elevation:*—situation. Compare 5297.

5132. נוּץ, **nûwts,** *noots;* a primitive root; (properly) to *flash;* hence, to *blossom* (from the brilliancy of colour); also, to *fly* away (from the quickness of motion):—flee away, bud (forth).

5133. נוֹצָה, **nôwtsâh,** *no-tsaw´;* or נֹצָה, **nôtsâh,** *no-tsaw´;* feminine active participle of 5327 in the sense of *flying;* a *pinion* (or wing feather); often (collective) *plumage:*—feather (-s), ostrich.

5134. נוּק, **nûwq,** *nook;* a primitive root; to *suckle:*—nurse.

5135. נוּר, **nûwr,** *noor;* (Chaldee); from an unused root (corresponding to that of 5216) meaning to *shine; fire:*—fiery, fire.

5136. נוּשׁ, **nûwsh,** *noosh;* a primitive root; to *be sick,* i.e. (figurative) *distressed:*—be full of heaviness.

5137. נָזָה, **nâzâh,** *naw-zaw´;* a primitive root; to *spirt,* i.e. *besprinkle* (especially in expiation):—sprinkle.

A verb meaning to spurt, to spatter, to sprinkle, to spring, to leap. This verb appears only a few times in the basic verbal form and carries the connotation of blood spurting or spattering (Le 6:27[20]; 2Ki 9:33; Isa 63:3). In the causative form, the verb connotes the sprinkling of a liquid as part of a ritual cleansing. The sprinkled liquid could be blood (Le 5:9; 14:7); oil (Le 8:11); water (Nu 19:18, 19); blood and oil (Ex 29:21); or blood and water (Le 14:51). Also in the causative form, this verb could signify to leap or to spring, especially with the connotation of surprise or joy (Isa 52:15).

5138. נָזִיד, **nâzîyd,** *naw-zeed´;* from 2102; something *boiled,* i.e. *soup:*—pottage.

5139. נָזִיר, **nâzîyr,** *naw-zeer´;* or נָזִר, **nâzir,** *naw-zeer´;* from 5144; *separate,* i.e. *consecrated* (as *prince,* a *Nazirite);* hence (figurative from the latter) an *unpruned* vine (like an unshorn Nazirite):—Nazarite [*by a false alliteration with Nazareth*], separate (-d), vine undressed.

A masculine noun meaning one consecrated, separated, devoted, a Nazarite. The term Nazarite means one who is consecrated to God. The Nazarite vow included abstinence from strong drink or the cutting of his hair, and no contact with dead bodies (Jgs 13:4–7). Samuel, as well as Samson, was dedicated before birth by his mother to be a Nazarite (cf. 1Sa 1:11). Less common is the meaning of a prince or ruler being consecrated, as was the case with Joseph, who was separated from his brothers (Ge 49:26). A third meaning of this word depicts an untrimmed vine (Le 25:5).

5140. נָזַל, **nâzal,** *naw-zal´*; a primitive root; to *drip,* or *shed* by trickling:—distil, drop, flood, (cause to) flow (-ing), gush out, melt, pour (down), running water, stream.

5141. נֶזֶם, **nezem,** *neh´-zem*; from an unused root of uncertain meaning; a nose-*ring*:—earring, jewel.

5142. נְזַק, **n**e**zaq,** *nez-ak´*; (Chaldee); corresponding to the root of 5143; to *suffer* (causative, *inflict*) *loss*:—have (en-) damage, hurt (-ful).

5143. נֶזֶק, **nêzeq,** *nay´-zek*; from an unused root meaning to *injure; loss*:—damage.

5144. נָזַר, **nâzar,** *naw-zar´*; a primitive root; to *hold aloof,* i.e. (intransitive) *abstain* (from food and drink, from impurity, and even from divine worship [i.e. *apostatize*]); (specifically) to *set apart* (to sacred purposes), i.e. *devote*:—consecrate, separate (-ing, self).

A verb meaning to dedicate, to consecrate. In the passive or reflexive form, it can signify a dedication to (Hos 9:10) or a separation from a deity (Eze 14:7). It can also indicate considering something as sacred and consecrated (Le 22:2). This verb also expresses the idea of consecrating oneself by fasting (Zec 7:3). In the causative form, it can denote to separate or to refrain from something (Le 15:31); or to take on the obligations of a Nazirite, a *nâziyr* (5139) (Nu 6:2, 5, 12).

5145. נֶזֶר, **nezer,** *neh´-zer*; or נֵזֶר, **nêzer,** *nay´-zer*; from 5144; (properly) something *set apart*, i.e. (abstract) *dedication* (of a priest or Nazirite); hence (concrete) unshorn *locks*; also (by implication) a *chaplet* (especially of royalty):—consecration, crown, hair, separation.

A masculine noun meaning a consecration, an ordination. This could be the consecration of the high priest (Le 21:12); or of a person taking a vow as a Nazirite (Nu 6:5, 7, 9, 12). This term is also used to identify a crown as the symbol of the wearer's consecration. This could be the king's crown (2Sa 1:10; 2Ki 11:12); or the golden crown of the high priest (Ex 29:6; 39:30). Jeremiah also used this term to refer to the hair of the personified Jerusalem (Jer 7:29). The basis of this extension could be the connection between the Nazirite and his long, uncut hair as his symbol of consecration (Nu 6:5); or to the idea that a woman's long hair itself is her "crown

of consecration." This would be similar to Paul's teaching in the NT (cf. 1Co 11:15).

5146. נֹחַ, **Nôach,** *no´-akh*; the same as 5118; *rest; Noäch,* the patriarch of the flood:—Noah.

5147. נַחְבִּי, **Nachbîy,** *nakh-bee´*; from 2247; *occult; Nachbi,* an Israelite:—Nakbi.

5148. נָחָה, **nâchâh,** *naw-khaw´*; a primitive root; to *guide*; (by implication) to *transport* (into exile, or as colonists):—bestow, bring, govern, guide, lead (forth), put, straiten.

A verb meaning to lead, to guide, usually in the right direction or on the proper path. The verb sometimes occurs with a human subject (Ex 32:34; Ps 60:9[11]; 108:10[11]); however, it usually appears with the Lord as the subject (Ge 24:27; Ex 13:17; 15:13). This term is also used metaphorically to represent spiritual guidance in righteousness (Ps 5:8[9]; 27:11; 139:24). This term also carries a connotation of treating kindly (Job 31:18); blessing (Ps 23:3); deliverance (Ps 31:3[4]); protection (Ps 61:2[3]); or wisdom (Ps 73:24).

5149. נְחוּם, **N**e**chûwm,** *neh-khoom´*; from 5162; *comforted; Nechum,* an Israelite:—Nehum.

5150. נִחוּם, **nichûwm,** *nee-khoom´*; or נִחֻם, **nichum,** *nee-khoom´*; from 5162; (properly) *consoled*; (abstract) *solace*:—comfort (-able), repenting.

5151. נַחוּם, **Nachûwm,** *nakh-oom´*; from 5162; *comfortable; Nachum,* an Israelite prophet:—Nahum.

5152. נָחוֹר, **Nâchôwr,** *naw-khore´*; from the same as 5170; *snorer; Nachor,* the name of the grandfather and a brother of Abraham:—Nahor.

5153. נָחוּשׁ, **nâchûwsh,** *naw-khoosh´*; apparently passive participle of 5172 (perhaps in the sense of *ringing,* i.e. bell-metal; or from the *red* colour of the throat of a serpent [5175, as denominative] when hissing; *coppery,* i.e. (figurative) hard:—of brass.

5154. נְחוּשָׁה, **n**e**chûwshâh,** *nekh-oo-shaw´*; or נְחֻשָׁה, **n**e**chushâh,** *nekh-oo-shaw´*; feminine of 5153; *copper*:—brass, steel. Compare 5176.

5155. נְחִילָה, **n^echîylâh,** *nekh-ee-law´*; probably denominative from 2485; a *flute:*—[plural] Nehiloth.

5156. נְחִיר, **nâchîyr,** *nawkh-eer´*; from the same as 5170; a *nostril:*—[dual] nostrils.

5157. נָחַל, **nâchal,** *naw-khal´*; a primitive root; to *inherit* (as a [figurative] mode of descent), or (generally) to *occupy*; (causative) to *bequeath*, or (generally) *distribute, instate:*—divide, have ([inheritance]), take as an heritage, (cause to, give to, make to) inherit, (distribute for, divide [for, for an, by], give for, have, leave for, take [for]) inheritance, (have in, cause to, be made to) possess (-ion).

A verb meaning to receive, to take property as a permanent possession. The verb was formed from the noun *nachălâh* (5159) which refers to a possession or inheritance. It can refer to the actual taking of the Promised Land, whether it was the entire land of Canaan as a gift from God (Ex 23:30; 32:13); a tribal allotment (Jos 16:4); or a familial portion (Jos 17:6). In addition to the taking of Canaan, God declared that Israel's remnant would possess the lands of Moab and Edom (Zep 2:9). It can also refer to the division and distribution of the land of Canaan to the tribal units (Jos 14:1). This verb is further used of God acquiring possession of Israel (Ex 34:9; Zec 2:12[16]); and the nations as His own private property (Ps 82:8). In the causative form, the verb denotes the giving of a possession (Dt 1:38; 3:28); or inheritance (Dt 21:16). This term is used figuratively to indicate the acquiring of things other than real property, like testimonies (Ps 119:111); glory (Pr 3:35); good things (Pr 28:10); lies (Jer 16:19); wind (Pr 11:29); simplicity (Pr 14:18); blessings (Zec 8:12).

5158. נַחַל, **nachal,** *nakh´-al*; or (feminine) נַחְלָה, **nachlâh,** *nakh´-law*; (Ps 124:4), or נַחֲלָה, **nachălâh,** *nakh-al-aw´*; (Eze 47:19; 48:28), from 5157 in its original sense; a *stream*, especially a winter *torrent*; (by implication) a (narrow) *valley* (in which a brook runs); also a *shaft* (of a mine):—brook, flood, river, stream, valley.

5159. נַחֲלָה, **nachălâh,** *nakh-al-aw´*; from 5157 (in its usual sense); (properly) something *inherited*, i.e. (abstract) *occupancy*, or (concrete) an *heirloom*; (generally) an *estate, patrimony* or *portion:*—heritage, to inherit, inheritance, possession. Compare 5158.

A feminine noun meaning possession, property, inheritance. This word implied property that was given by means of a will or as a heritage. It denoted the land of Canaan given to Israel and distributed among the tribes (Nu 26:53–56; Eze 48:29); a portion or state of blessing assigned by God to His people (Isa 54:17), or any possession presented by a father (Nu 27:8, 9; Job 42:15). The Lord Himself was declared to be the portion and inheritance of the Levites who served Him (Nu 18:20).

5160. נַחֲלִיאֵל, **Nachăliy'êl,** *nakh-al-ee-ale´*; from 5158 and 410; *valley of God*; *Nachaliël*, a place in the Desert:—Nahaliel.

5161. נֶחֱלָמִי, **Nechĕlâmîy,** *nekh-el-aw-mee´*; apparently a patronymic from an unused name (apparently passive participle of 2492); *dreamed*; a *Nechelamite*, or descend. of Nechlam:—Nehelamite.

5162. נָחַם, **nâcham,** *naw-kham´*; a primitive root; (properly) to *sigh*, i.e. *breathe* strongly; (by implication) to *be sorry*, i.e. (in a favourable sense) to *pity, console* or (reflexive) *rue*; or (unfavourably) to *avenge* (oneself):—comfort (self), ease [one's self], repent (-er, -ing, self).

A verb meaning to be sorry, to pity, to comfort, to avenge. The verb often means to be sorry or to regret: the Lord was sorry that He had made people (Ge 6:6); He led Israel in a direction to avoid war when they left Egypt, lest they became so sorry and grieved that they would turn back (Ex 13:17). The Lord had compassion on His people (i.e. He became sorry for them because of the oppression their enemies placed on them [Jgs 2:18]). While the Lord could be grieved, He did not grieve or become sorry so that He changed His mind as a human does (1Sa 15:29). The word also means to comfort or console oneself. Isaac was comforted after Sarah, his mother, died (Ge 24:67).

The verb always means to console or comfort. Jacob refused to be comforted when he believed that Joseph had been killed (Ge 37:35). To console is synonymous with showing kindness to someone, as when David consoled Hanun, king of the Ammonites, over the death of his father (2Sa 10:2). God refused to be consoled over the destruction of His people (Isa 22:4; 40:1); yet He comforts those who need it (Ps 119:82; Isa 12:1). The passive form of the word means to be comforted: the afflicted city of Zion would be comforted by the Lord (Isa 54:11; 66:13). In the reflexive stem, it can mean to get revenge for oneself (Ge 27:42; Eze 5:13); to let oneself be sorry or have compassion (Nu 23:19; Dt 32:36); and to let oneself be comforted (Ge 37:35; Ps 119:52).

5163. נַחַם, **Nacham,** *nakh´-am*; from 5162; *consolation; Nacham,* an Israelite:—Naham.

5164. נֹחַם, **nôcham,** *no´-kham*; from 5162; *ruefulness,* i.e. desistance:—repentance.

A masculine noun meaning sorrow, repentance, compassion. This word comes from the verb *nâcham* (5162), meaning to be sorry or to repent, and occurs only once in the OT. In Hos 13:14, it described the compassion that God would not have toward sinful Ephraim.

5165. נֶחָמָה, **nechâmâh,** *nekh-aw-maw´*; from 5162; *consolation:*—comfort.

A feminine noun meaning compassion, consolation. This word comes from the verb *nâcham* (5162), meaning to be sorry or to repent, and occurs twice in the OT. In Job 6:10, Job was comforted that in the midst of his trials, he did not deny the Holy One; the psalmist declared that his comfort in his affliction was God's Word, which revived him (Ps 119:50).

5166. נְחֶמְיָה, **Nᵉchemyâh,** *nekh-em-yaw´*; from 5162 and 3050; *consolation of Jah; Nechemjah,* the name of three Israelites:—Nehemiah.

5167. נַחֲמָנִי, **Nachămânîy,** *nakh-am-aw-nee´*; from 5162; *consolatory; Nachamani,* an Israelite:—Nahamani.

5168. נַחְנוּ, **nachnûw,** *nakh-noo´*; for 587; *we:*—we.

5169. נָחַץ, **nâchats,** *naw-khats´*; a primitive root; to *be urgent:*—require haste.

5170. נַחַר, **nachar,** *nakh´-ar*; and (feminine) נַחֲרָה, **nachărâh,** *nakh-ar-aw´*; from an unused root meaning to *snort* or *snore*; a *snorting:*—nostrils, snorting.

5171. נַחְרַי, **Nachăray,** *nakh-ar-ah´ee*; or נַחְרַי, **Nach-ray,** *nakh-rah´ee*; from the same as 5170; *snorer; Nacharai* or *Nachrai,* an Israelite:—Naharai, Nahari.

5172. נָחַשׁ, **nâchash,** *naw-khash´*; a primitive root; (properly) to *hiss,* i.e. *whisper* a (magic) spell; (generally) to *prognosticate:*— × certainly, divine, enchanter, (use) × enchantment, learn by experience, × indeed, diligently observe.

A verb meaning to practice divination, to observe omens. This verb described the pagan practice of seeking knowledge through divination, which was expressly forbidden in the Law of Moses (Le 19:26; Dt 18:10); and was used as an indication that the kings of Israel and Judah were wicked (2Ki 17:17; 21:6; 2Ch 33:6). In its other usages, Laban used divination to confirm that Jacob was a blessing to him (Ge 30:27); Joseph claimed that a cup helped him practice divination (Ge 44:5, 15); and the Arameans took Ahab's words as an omen (1Ki 20:33).

5173. נַחַשׁ, **nachash,** *nakh´-ash*; from 5172; an *incantation* or *augury:*—enchantment.

A masculine noun meaning divination, omen. This word comes from the verb *nâchash* (5172), meaning to practice divination or to observe omens, and is used only twice in the OT. In both instances of this word, it is used within the context of Balaam and his prophecies. In one discourse, Balaam declared that there was no omen against Jacob (Nu 23:23); and in preparing for another discourse, he did not seek omens (Nu 24:1).

5174. נְחָשׁ, **nᵉchâsh,** *nekh-awsh´*; (Chaldee); corresponding to 5154; *copper:*—brass.

5175. נָחָשׁ, **nâchâsh,** *naw-khawsh´*; from 5172; a *snake* (from its *hiss*):—serpent.

A masculine noun meaning snake. It is used to refer to an actual serpent (Ex 4:3; Nu 21:6; Dt 8:15; Ecc 10:8; Am 5:19); or an image of one (Nu 21:9), but it is also used figuratively. Some of these symbolic uses include the tempter (Ge 3:1, 2, 4, 13, 14); the tribe of Dan (Ge 49:17); wicked rulers (Ps 58:4[5]); and enemies (Isa 14:29; Jer 8:17; 46:22).

5176. נָחָשׁ, **Nâchâsh,** *naw-khawsh´*; the same as 5175; *Nachash,* the name of two persons apparently non-Israelite:—Nahash.

5177. נַחְשׁוֹן, **Nachshôwn,** *nakh-shone´*; from 5172; *enchanter; Nachshon,* an Israelite:—Naashon, Nahshon.

5178. נְחֹשֶׁת, n⁰chôsheth, *nekh-o´-sheth*; for 5154; *copper*; hence, something made of that metal, i.e. *coin*, a *fetter*; (figurative) *base* (as compared with gold or silver):—brasen, brass, chain, copper, fetter (of brass), filthiness, steel.

5179. נְחֻשְׁתָּא, N⁰chushtâ, *nekh-oosh-taw´*; from 5178; *copper*; *Nechushta*, an Israelitess:—Nehushta.

5180. נְחֻשְׁתָּן, N⁰chushtân, *nekh-oosh-tawn´*; from 5178; something made *of copper*, i.e. the copper *serpent* of the Desert:—Nehushtan.

5181. נָחַת, nâchath, *naw-khath´*; a primitive root; to *sink*, i.e. *descend*; (causative) to *press* or *lead* down:—be broken, (cause to) come down, enter, go down, press sore, settle, stick fast.

5182. נְחַת, n⁰chath, *nekh-ath´*; (Chaldee); corresponding to 5181; to *descend*; (causative) to *bring away, deposit, depose*:—carry, come down, depose, lay up, place.

5183. נַחַת, nachath, *nakh´-ath*; from 5182; a *descent*, i.e. imposition, unfavourable (*punishment*) or favourable (*food*); also (intransitive; perhaps from 5117), *restfulness*:—lighting down, quiet (-ness), to rest, be set on.

5184. נַחַת, Nachath, *nakh´-ath*; the same as 5183; *quiet*; *Nachath*, the name of an Edomite and of two Israelites:—Nahath.

5185. נָחֵת, nâchêth, *naw-khayth´*; from 5181; *descending*:—come down.

5186. נָטָה, nâṭâh, *naw-taw´*; a primitive root; to *stretch* or spread out; (by implication) to *bend* away (including moral deflection); used in a great variety of applications (as follows):— + afternoon, apply, bow (down, -ing), carry aside, decline, deliver, extend, go down, be gone, incline, intend, lay, let down, offer, outstretched, overthrown, pervert, pitch, prolong, put away, shew, spread (out), stretch (forth, out), take (aside), turn (aside, away), wrest, cause to yield.

5187. נָטִיל, nâṭîyl, *nawt-eel´*; from 5190; *laden*:—that bear.

5188. נְטִיפָה, n⁰ṭîyphâh, *net-ee-faw´*; from 5197; a *pendant* for the ears (especially of pearls):—chain, collar.

5189. נְטִישָׁה, n⁰ṭîyshâh, *net-ee-shaw´*; from 5203; a *tendril* (as an offshoot):—battlement, branch, plant.

5190. נָטַל, nâṭal, *naw-tal´*; a primitive root; to *lift*; (by implication) to *impose*:—bear, offer, take up.

5191. נְטַל, n⁰ṭal, *net-al´*; (Chaldee); corresponding to 5190; to *raise*:—take up.

5192. נֵטֶל, nêṭel, *nay´-tel*; from 5190; a *burden*:—weighty.

5193. נָטַע, nâṭa‘, *naw-tah´*; a primitive root; (properly) to *strike* in, i.e. *fix*; (specifically) to *plant* (literal or figurative):—fastened, plant (-er).

5194. נֶטַע, neṭa‘, *neh´-tah*; from 5193; a *plant*; (collective) a *plantation*; (abstract) a *planting*:—plant.

5195. נָטִיעַ, nâṭîya‘, *naw-tee´-ah*; from 5193; a *plant*:—plant.

5196. נְטָעִים, N⁰ṭâ‘îym, *net-aw-eem´*; plural of 5194; *Netaïm*, a place in Palestine:—plants.

5197. נָטַף, nâṭaph, *naw-taf´*; a primitive root; to *ooze*, i.e. *distil* gradually; (by implication) to *fall* in drops; (figurative) to *speak* by inspiration:—drop (-ping), prophesy (-et).

A verb meaning to drip, to drop, to flow. It is used to describe rain (Jgs 5:4; Ps 68:8[9]); and words which are like rain (Job 29:22). Lips may drip with honey (Pr 5:3); and hands may drip with myrrh (SS 5:5). This word can also be taken figuratively, meaning to prophesy (Eze 21:2[7]; Am 7:16). It is sometimes used to refer to false prophets (Mic 2:6).

5198. נָטָף, nâṭâph, *naw-tawf´*; from 5197; a *drop*; specifically, an aromatic *gum* (probably *stacte*):—drop, stacte.

5199. נְטֹפָה, N⁰ṭôphâh, *net-o-faw´*; from 5197; *distillation*; *Netophah*, a place in Palestine:—Netophah.

5200. נְטֹפָתִי, N⁰ṭôphâthîy, *net-o-faw-thee´*; patronymic from 5199; a *Netophathite*, or inhabitant of Netophah:—Neto-phathite.

5201. נָטַר, nâṭar, *naw-tar´*; a primitive root; to *guard*; (figurative) to *cherish* (anger):—bear grudge, keep (-er), reserve.

5202. נְטַר, **nᵉṭar,** *net-ar´*; (Chaldee); corresponding to 5201; to *retain*:—keep.

5203. נָטַשׁ, **nâṭash,** *naw-tash´*; a primitive root; (properly) to *pound*, i.e. *smite*; by implication (as if beating out, and thus expanding) to *disperse*; also, to *thrust* off, down, out or upon (including *reject, let alone, permit, remit,* etc.):— cast off, drawn, let fall, forsake, join [battle], leave (off), lie still, loose, spread (self) abroad, stretch out, suffer.

A verb meaning to forsake, to leave alone. The word occurs in relation to the land that should be unused ("forsaken") in the seventh year (Ex 23:11); the Israelites who abandoned God (Dt 32:15); Saul's father who forgot about the donkeys and began to worry about him (1Sa 10:2); David who left his flock with a shepherd (1Sa 17:20); the psalmist who pleaded with God not to turn from him (Ps 27:9). This word is used once to mean to not permit when Laban was not allowed to kiss his grandchildren good-bye (Ge 31:28).

5204. נִי, **nîy,** *nee*; a doubtful word; apparently from 5091; *lamentation*:—wailing.

5205. נִיד, **nîyd,** *need*; from 5110; *motion* (of the lips in speech):—moving.

5206. נִידָה, **nîydâh,** *nee-daw´*; feminine of 5205; *removal*, i.e. *exile*:—removed.

5207. נִיחוֹחַ, **nîychôwach,** *nee-kho´-akh*; or נִיחֹחַ, **nîychôach,** *nee-kho´-akh*; from 5117; (properly) *restful*, i.e. *pleasant*; (abstract) *delight*:— sweet (odour).

5208. נִיחוֹחַ, **nîychôwach,** *nee-kho´-akh*; (Chaldee); or (shorter) נִיחֹחַ, **nîychôach,** *nee-kho´-akh*; (Chaldee); corresponding to 5207; *pleasure*:—sweet odour (savour).

5209. נִין, **nîyn,** *neen*; from 5125; *progeny*:—son.

5210. נִינְוֵה, **Nîynᵉvêh,** *nee-nev-ay´*; of foreign origin; *Nineveh*, the capital of Assyria:—Nineveh.

5211. נִיס, **nîys,** *neece*; from 5127; *fugitive*:—that fleeth.

5212. נִיסָן, **Nîysân,** *nee-sawn´*; probably of foreign origin; *Nisan*, the first month of the Jewish sacred year:—Nisan.

5213. נִיצוֹץ, **nîytsôwts,** *nee-tsotes´*; from 5340; a *spark*:—spark.

5214. נִיר, **nîyr,** *neer*; a root probably identical with that of 5216, through the idea of the *gleam* of a fresh furrow; to *till* the soil:—break up.

5215. נִיר, **nîyr,** *neer*; or נִר, **nir,** *neer*; from 5214; (properly) *ploughing*, i.e. (concrete) freshly *ploughed* land:—fallow ground, ploughing, tillage.

5216. נִיר, **nîyr,** *neer*; or נִר, **nir,** *neer*; also נֵיר, **nêyr,** *nare*; or נֵר, **nêr,** *nare*; or (feminine) נֵרָה, **nêrâh,** *nay-raw´*; from a primitive root [see 5214; 5135] properly meaning to *glisten*; a *lamp* (i.e. the burner) or *light* (literal or figurative):— candle, lamp, light.

A masculine noun meaning lamp, light. This word referred to the lamps of the tabernacle (Ex 27:20); the lamp in the Temple with Samuel (1Sa 3:3); the Word of God that lights the way (Ps 119:105); and the noble wife that does not let her lamp go out at night (Pr 31:18). The lamp can be used figuratively, as when God promised that David would always have a lamp before Him in Jerusalem (1Ki 11:36; 2Ch 21:7). This word corresponds to the Aramaic noun *nûr* (5135), which can be masculine or feminine and means fire or flame. See the book of Daniel, where the fire does not harm the three Hebrews (see Da 3:27); and where fire describes the Ancient of Days (see Da 7:9, 10).

5217. נְכָא, **nâkâʾ,** *naw-kaw´*; a primitive root; to *smite*, i.e. *drive* away:—be viler.

5218. נָכֵא, **nâkêʾ,** *naw-kay´*; or נָכָא, **nâkâʾ,** *naw-kaw´*; from 5217; *smitten*, i.e. (figurative) *afflicted*:—broken, stricken, wounded.

5219. נְכֹאת, **nᵉkʾôth,** *nek-ohth´*; from 5218; (properly) a *smiting*, i.e. (concrete) an aromatic *gum* [perhaps *styrax*] (as *powdered*):—spicery (-ces).

5220. נֶכֶד, **neked,** *neh´-ked*; from an unused root meaning to *propagate*; *offspring*:—nephew, son's son.

5221. נָכָה, **nâkâh,** *naw-kaw´*; a primitive root; to *strike* (lightly or severely, literal or figurative):—beat, cast forth, clap, give [wounds], × go forward, × indeed, kill, make [slaughter], murderer, punish, slaughter, slay (-er, -ing), smite (-r, -ing), strike, be stricken, (give) stripes, × surely, wound.

A verb meaning to beat, to strike, to wound. There are many instances of striking physically (Ex 21:15, 19; Job 16:10; Ps 3:7[8]; SS 5:7). This word is also used in a different sense, as when the men of Sodom and Gomorrah were stricken blind by the two angels (Ge 19:11); when a priest stuck a fork into the kettle (1Sa 2:14); when people clapped their hands (2Ki 11:12); or when people verbally abused Jeremiah (Jer 18:18). God struck the Egyptians with plagues (Ex 3:20); and struck people down in judgment (Isa 5:25).

5222. נֵכֶה, **nêkeh,** *nay-keh´*; from 5221; a *smiter,* i.e. (figurative) *traducer:*—abject.

5223. נָכֶה, **nâkeh,** *naw-keh´*; *smitten,* i.e. (literal) maimed, or (figurative) dejected:—contrite, lame.

5224. נְכוֹ, **Nᵉkôw,** *nek-o´*; probably of Egyptian origin; *Neko* an Egyptian king:—Necho. Compare 6549.

5225. נָכוֹן, **Nâkôwn,** *naw-kone´*; from 3559; *prepared; Nakon,* probably an Israelite:—Nachon.

5226. נֵכַח, **nêkach,** *nay´-kakh*; from an unused root meaning to *be straightforward*; (properly) the *fore* part; (used adverbially) *opposite:*—before, over against.

5227. נֹכַח, **nôkach,** *no´-kakh*; from the same as 5226; (properly,) the *front* part; (used adverbially, especially with a preposition) *opposite, in front of, forward, in behalf of:*—(over) against, before, direct [-ly], for, right (on).

5228. נָכֹחַ, **nâkôach,** *naw-ko´-akh*; from the same as 5226; *straightforward,* i.e. (figurative) *equitable, correct,* or (abstract) *integrity:*—plain, right, uprightness.

An adjective meaning straightforward, honest. In 2Sa 15:3, it is used to describe a legal case as straightforward, obviously deserving amends. In Pr 8:9, it describes wisdom's words as straightforward, not perverted, to the one who has the right attitude to receive them. In Pr 24:26, the adjective describes words spoken honestly, without partiality (cf. Pr 24:23–25); lips speaking this way kiss the hearer. The word occurs as a noun in Isa 57:2 and means straightforwardness or

honesty. For the feminine form of the word, see *nĕkôchâh* (5229).

5229. נְכֹחָה, **nᵉkôchâh,** *nek-o-khaw´*; feminine of 5228; (properly) *straightforwardness,* i.e. (figurative) *integrity,* or (concrete) *a truth:*—equity, right (thing), uprightness.

5230. נָכַל, **nâkal,** *naw-kal´*; a primitive root; to *defraud,* i.e. *act treacherously:*—beguile, conspire, deceiver, deal subtilly.

5231. נֵכֶל, **nêkel,** *nay´-kel*; from 5230; *deceit:*—wile.

5232. נְכַס, **nᵉkas,** *nek-as´*; (Chaldee); corresponding to 5233:—goods.

5233. נֶכֶס, **nekes,** *neh´-kes*; from an unused root meaning to *accumulate; treasure:*—riches, wealth.

5234. נָכַר, **nâkar,** *naw-kar´*; a primitive root; (properly) to *scrutinize,* i.e. look intently at; hence (with *recognition* implied), to *acknowledge, be acquainted with, care for, respect, revere,* or (with *suspicion* implied), to *disregard, ignore, be strange* toward, *reject, resign, dissimulate* (as if ignorant or disowning):—acknowledge, × could, deliver, discern, dissemble, estrange, feign self to be another, know, take knowledge (notice), perceive, regard, (have) respect, behave (make) self strange (-ly).

A verb meaning to pretend, to consider carefully, to investigate, to acknowledge, to recognize, to make unrecognizable. This verb is used mainly in the causative stem to indicate the process of investigation, knowing something, or knowing how to do something. Jacob told Laban to investigate to see if he could recognize his gods in any of Jacob's tents (Ge 31:32); Tamar challenged Judah to investigate the seal and cord she had to see if he could recognize them (Ge 38:25, 26). The Hebrew word is also used to indicate someone already known previously (1Ki 18:7; 20:41). The word is found metaphorically meaning to acknowledge, to follow, or to refuse to do so: evildoers refused to acknowledge the light (God's laws) and did not walk according to God's laws (Job 24:13). When the word is used with an infinitive, it means to know how to do something or to know something so that a person acts in a certain way. Judeans, who had intermarried with foreigners, had children who did not know how to speak the language of Judah, which was Hebrew (Ne 13:24).

Finally, in the reflexive stem, the word means to present oneself in such a way as to fool others (1Ki 14:5, 6); or to hide one's identity, as Joseph hid his identity from his brothers (Ge 42:7). In the case of children, they reflected their characters by their actions, revealing their essential dispositions (Pr 20:11).

5235. נֶכֶר, **neker,** *neh´-ker;* or נֹכֶר, **nôker,** *no´-ker;* from 5234; something *strange*, i.e. unexpected *calamity*:—strange.

A masculine noun meaning disaster, calamity. The meaning derives from the idea of strangeness (cf. *nêkâr* [5236]); a calamity interrupts the normal flow of life. The word occurs in Job 31:3 where it refers to calamity as the punishment of iniquity. In Ob 1:12, the word occurs along with several words of similar meaning (cf. Ob 1:13, 14), describing a time in which Judah met with calamity.

5236. נֵכָר, **nêkâr,** *nay-kawr´;* from 5234; *foreign,* or (concrete) a *foreigner,* or (abstract) *heathendom*:—alien, strange (+ -er).

A masculine noun meaning foreign. The word comes from a root meaning to scrutinize, perhaps drawing on the idea that people look closely at something foreign or strange (see *nâkar*[5234]). The word modifies other nouns to signify a foreigner or a foreign god. Foreigners with their false gods posed a threat to Israel's service to the Lord (Dt 32:12; Jgs 10:16; Mal 2:11); sometimes even infiltrating the Temple service (Ne 13:30; Eze 44:9). They also posed a physical threat at times (Ps 144:7; Isa 62:8; Jer 5:19). However, foreigners sometimes turned to Israel's God (Isa 56:3, 6). The word also refers (with other words) to foreign land (Ps 137:4; Jer 5:19); and a foreign power (Ps 144:7).

5237. נְכְרִי, **nokrîy,** *nok-ree´;* from 5235 (second form); *strange,* in a variety of degrees and applications (*foreign, non-relative, adulterous, different, wonderful*):—alien, foreigner, outlandish, strange (-r, woman).

An adjective meaning strange, foreign, stranger, foreigner. It refers to someone who was not part of the family (Ge 31:15; cf. Ge 31:14; Ps 69:8[9]), especially the extended family of Israel (Dt 17:15). Under the Law, strangers

were not allowed to rule in Israel (Dt 17:15); they were not released from their debts every seven years as Hebrews were (Dt 15:3); and could be sold certain ceremonially unclean food (Dt 14:21). Strangers were regarded as unholy (Dt 14:21); and were often looked down on (Ru 2:10; Job 19:15). Some hope for the conversion of foreigners was offered (Ru 2:10; 1Ki 8:41, 43); but with this word, more emphasis was placed on avoiding the defilement of foreign women (1Ki 11:1; Ezr 10:2, 10, 11, 14, 17, 18, 44; Pr 6:24); and foreign ways (Isa 2:6; Jer 2:21; Zep 1:8). The word *gêr* (1616), meaning sojourner, focuses more sympathetically on foreigners in Israel.

5238. נְכֹת, **nᵉkôth,** *nek-ōth´;* probably for 5219; *spicery,* i.e. (generally) *valuables*:—precious things.

5239. נָלָה, **nâlâh,** *naw-law´;* apparently a primitive root; to *complete*:—make an end.

5240. נִמְבְזָה, **nᵉmibzâh,** *nem-ib-zaw´;* from 959; *despised*:—vile.

5241. נְמוּאֵל, **Nᵉmûw'êl,** *nem-oo-ale´;* apparently for 3223; *Nemuel,* the name of two Israelites:—Nemuel.

5242. נְמוּאֵלִי, **Nᵉmûw'êlîy,** *nem-oo-ay-lee´;* from 5241; a *Nemu-elite,* or descendant of Nemuel:—Nemuelite.

5243. נְמַל, **nâmal,** *naw-mal´;* a primitive root; to *become clipped* or (specific) *circumcised*:—(branch to) be cut down (off), circumcise.

A noun assumed to be the root for the Hebrew word *nᵉmâlâh* (5244), meaning ant (see Pr 6:6; 30:25). The actual word does not exist in Scripture. Scholars assume that the word means cut or circumcised (Ge 17:11; Job 14:2; 18:16; 24:24; Ps 37:2).

5244. נְמָלָה, **nᵉmâlâh,** *nem-aw-law´;* feminine from 5243; an *ant* (probably from its almost *bisected* form):—ant.

5245. נְמַר, **nᵉmar,** *nem-ar´;* (Chaldee); corresponding to 5246:—leopard.

5246. נָמֵר, **nâmêr,** *naw-mare´;* from an unused root meaning properly to *filtrate,* i.e. *be limpid* [compare 5247 and 5249]; and thus to *spot* or *stain* as if by dripping; a *leopard* (from its stripes):—leopard.

5247. נִמְרָה, **Nimrâh,** *nim-raw´*; from the same as 5246; *clear* water; *Nimrah*, a place East of the Jordan:—Nimrah. See also 1039, 5249.

5248. נִמְרוֹד, **Nimrôwd,** *nim-rode´*; or נִמְרֹד, **Nimrôd,** *nim-rode´*; probably of foreign origin; *Nimrod*, a son of Cush:—Nimrod.

5249. נִמְרִים, **Nimrîym,** *nim-reem´*; plural of a masculine corresponding to 5247; *clear* waters; *Nimrim*, a place East of the Jordan:—Nimrim. Compare 1039.

5250. נִמְשִׁי, **Nimshîy,** *nim-shee´*; probably from 4871; *extricated; Nimshi*, the (grand-) father of Jehu:—Nimshi.

5251. נֵס, **nês,** *nace*; from 5264; a *flag*; also a *sail*; (by implication) a *flagstaff*; (generally) a *signal*; (figurative) a *token*:—banner, pole, sail, (en-) sign, standard.

5252. נְסִבָּה, **nᵉsibbâh,** *nes-ib-baw´*; feminine participle passive of 5437; (properly) an *environment*, i.e. *circumstance* or *turn* of affairs:—cause.

5253. נָסַג, **nâsag,** *naw-sag´*; a primitive root; to *retreat*:—departing away, remove, take (hold), turn away.

5254. נָסָה, **nâsâh,** *naw-saw´*; a primitive root; to *test*; (by implication) to *attempt*:—adventure, assay, prove, tempt, try.

A verb meaning to test, to try, to prove. Appearing nearly forty times in the OT, this term often refers to God testing the faith and faithfulness of human beings, including Abraham (Ge 22:1); the nation of Israel (Ex 15:25; 16:4; 20:20; Dt 8:2, 16; 13:3[4]; Jgs 2:22; 3:1, 4); Hezekiah (2Ch 32:31); David (Ps 26:2). Although people were forbidden from putting God to the test, they often did so (Ex 17:2, 7; Nu 14:22; Dt 6:16; 33:8; Ps 78:18, 41, 56; 95:9; 106:14; Isa 7:12). Testing, however, does not always suggest tempting or enticing someone to sin, as when the Queen of Sheba tested Solomon's wisdom (1Ki 10:1; 2Ch 9:1); and Daniel's physical appearance was tested after a ten-day vegetarian diet (Da 1:12, 14). Finally, this term can refer to the testing of equipment, such as swords or armour (1Sa 17:39).

5255. נָסַח, **nâsach,** *naw-sakh´*; a primitive root; to *tear* away:—destroy, pluck, root.

A verb meaning to tear down, to tear out. In the Hebrew OT, this verb almost always occurs in poetical literature and always occurs in contexts of judgment. For example, as the result of disobedience to God's covenant, He promised to remove Israel from the land. According to the psalmist, God would snatch the unrighteous from the comforts of their homes for putting trust in material wealth rather than in Him (Ps 52:5[7]). Similarly, Pr 2:22 indicates that the righteous would remain in the land while the unrighteous would be removed from it. Finally, the Lord promised to tear down or destroy the house of the proud person (Pr 15:25).

5256. נְסַח, **nᵉsach,** *nes-akh´*; (Chaldee); corresponding to 5255:—pull down.

An Aramaic verb meaning to be pulled out. Found only once in the OT, this word refers to the removal of a beam of wood from the house of any person who altered the decree of King Cyrus. As punishment for disregarding the decree, the offending party would be hung or impaled on the wooden beam (Ezr 6:11).

5257. נְסִיךְ, **nᵉsîyk,** *nes-eek´*; from 5258; (properly) something *poured* out, i.e. a *libation*; also a molten *image*; (by implication) a *prince* (as *anointed*):—drink offering, duke, prince (-ipal).

A masculine noun meaning a drink offering, a molten image. Derived from a verb meaning to pour out, this term refers to the pouring out of a drink offering or libation (Dt 32:38). Here God mockingly inquires about the whereabouts of the gods that drank the drink offerings of wine offered by their pagan worshippers. In Da 11:8, this term refers to metal idols or images brought home by the Egyptian ruler Ptolemy after defeating the Syrian army.

5258. נָסַךְ, **nâsak,** *naw-sak´*; a primitive root; to *pour* out, especially a libation, or to *cast* (metal); (by analogy) to *anoint* a king:—cover, melt, offer, (cause to) pour (out), set (up).

A verb meaning to pour out. Frequently, this term refers to pouring out drink offerings or libations. These offerings usually employed wine (Hos 9:4); or another fermented drink (Nu 28:7). But David offered water as a drink offering to the Lord (2Sa 23:16; 1Ch 11:18). In the books of Moses (Nu 28:7), God clearly outlined instructions for making proper sacrifices. For example, He prohibited pouring a drink offering on the altar of incense (Ex 30:9). Scripture clearly condemned the practice of making drink offerings to false gods (Jer 19:13; 44:17–19, 25); a practice that angered God and incurred His judgment (Jer 7:18; 32:29; Eze 20:28). Infrequently, this Hebrew term referred to the casting of idols from metal (Isa 40:19; 44:10); and in one instance, to a deep sleep that the Lord poured over the inhabitants of Jerusalem (Isa 29:10).

5259. נָסַךְ, **nâsak,** *naw-sak´*; a primitive root [probably identical with 5258 through the idea of fusion]; to *interweave,* i.e. (figurative) to *overspread:*—that is spread.

5260. נְסַךְ, **nᵉsak,** *nes-ak´*; (Chaldee); corresponding to 5258; to *pour* out a libation:—offer.

5261. נְסַךְ, **nᵉsak,** *nes-ak´*; (Chaldee); corresponding to 5262; a *libation:*—drink offering.

An Aramaic masculine singular noun meaning drink offering, libation. Its only occurrence in the Hebrew Bible is in Ezr 7:17 where Artaxerxes provided offerings and sacrifices to be delivered for the Temple in Jerusalem. This term is related to the verb *nĕsak* (5260), meaning to pour out. For the Hebrew cognate of this noun, see *nesek* (5262).

5262. נֶסֶךְ, **nesek,** *neh´-sek*; or נֵסֶךְ, **nêsek,** *nay´-sek*; from 5258; a *libation*; also a *cast idol:*—cover, drink offering, molten image.

A masculine singular noun meaning drink offering, libation, molten image. The most common usage of the term referred to a liquid offering that was poured out (*nâsak* [5258]) (Ge 35:14; Le 23:37; Nu 15:5, 7, 10, 24). It is employed both for offerings made to *Yahweh* as well as to foreign deities (2Ki 16:13; Isa 57:6). In four passages, the term is used for a molten image (i.e. a "poured out" thing) (Isa 41:29; 48:5; Jer 10:14).

5263. נָסַס, **nâsas,** *naw-sas´*; a primitive root; to *wane,* i.e. *be sick:*—faint.

5264. נָסַס, **nâsas,** *naw-sas´*; a primitive root; to *gleam* from afar, i.e. to *be conspicuous* as a signal; or rather perhaps a denominative from 5251 [and identical with 5263, through the idea of a flag as *fluttering* in the wind]; to *raise a beacon:*—lift up as an ensign.

5265. נָסַע, **nâsaʻ,** *naw-sah´*; a primitive root; (properly) to *pull* up, especially the tent-pins, i.e. *start* on a journey:—cause to blow, bring, get, (make to) go (away, forth, forward, onward, out), (take) journey, march, remove, set aside (forward), × still, be on his (go their) way.

5266. נָסַק, **nâsaq,** *naw-sak´*; a primitive root; to *go* up:—ascend.

5267. נְסַק, **nᵉsaq,** *nes-ak´*; (Chaldee); corresponding to 5266:—take up.

5268. נִסְרֹךְ, **Nisrôk,** *nis-roke´*; of foreign origin; *Nisrok,* a Babylonian idol:—Nisroch.

5269. נֵעָה, **Nêʻâh,** *nay-aw´*; from 5128; *motion; Neäh,* a place in Palestine:—Neah.

5270. נֹעָה, **Nôʻâh,** *no-aw´*; from 5128; *movement; Noäh,* an Israelitess:—Noah.

5271. נְעוּרִים, **nᵉʻûwrîym,** *neh-oo-reem´*; properly passive participle from 5288 as denominative; (only in plural collective or emphatical) *youth,* the state (*juvenility*) or the persons (*young* people):—childhood, youth.

5272. נְעִיאֵל, **Nᵉʻîyʼêl,** *neh-ee-ale´*; from 5128 and 410; *moved of God; Neïel,* a place in Palestine:—Neiel.

5273. נָעִים, **nâʻîym,** *naw-eem´*; from 5276; *delightful* (objective or subjective, literal or figurative):—pleasant (-ure), sweet.

5274. נָעַל, **nâʻal,** *naw-al´*; a primitive root; (properly) to *fasten* up, i.e. with a bar or cord; hence (denominative from 5275), to *sandal,* i.e. furnish with slippers:—bolt, inclose, lock, shoe, shut up.

5275. נַעַל, **naʻal,** *nah´-al*; or (feminine) נַעֲלָה, **naʻălâh,** *nah-al-aw´*; from 5274; (properly) a sandal *tongue*; (by extension) a *sandal* or slipper (sometimes as a symbol of occupancy, a refusal to marry, or of something valueless):—dryshod, (pair of) shoe ([-latchet], -s).

5276. נָעֵם, **nâʻêm,** *naw-ame´*; a primitive root; to *be agreeable* (literal or figurative):—pass in beauty, be delight, be pleasant, be sweet.

5277. נַעַם, **Naʻam,** *nah´-am*; from 5276; *pleasure; Naam,* an Israelite:—Naam.

5278. נֹעַם, **nô'am,** *no´-am;* from 5276; *agreeableness,* i.e. *delight, suitableness, splendor* or *grace:*—beauty, pleasant (-ness).

5279. נַעֲמָה, **Na'ămâh,** *nah-am-aw´;* feminine of 5277; *pleasantness; Naamah,* the name of an antediluvian woman, of an Ammonitess, and of a place in Palestine:—Naamah.

5280. נַעֲמִי, **Na'ămîy,** *nah-am-ee´;* patronymic from 5283; a *Naamanite,* or descendant of Naaman (collective):—Naamites.

5281. נָעֳמִי, **No'ŏmîy,** *nŏ-om-ee´;* from 5278; *pleasant; Noömi,* an Israelitess:—Naomi.

5282. נַעֲמָן, **na'ămân,** *nah-am-awn´;* from 5276; *pleasantness* (plural as concrete):—pleasant.

5283. נַעֲמָן, **Na'ămân,** *nah-am-awn´;* the same as 5282; *Naaman,* the name of an Israelite and of a Damascene:—Naaman.

5284. נַעֲמָתִי, **Na'ămâthîy,** *nah-am-aw-thee´;* patrial from a place corresponding in name (but not identical) with 5279; a *Naamathite,* or inhabitant of Naamah:—Naamathite.

5285. נַעֲצוּץ, **na'ătsûwts,** *nah-ats-oots´;* from an unused root meaning to *prick;* probably a *brier;* (by implication) a *thicket* of thorny bushes:—thorn.

5286. נָעַר, **nâ'ar,** *naw-ar´;* a primitive root; to *growl:*—yell.

5287. נָעַר, **nâ'ar,** *naw-ar´;* a primitive root [probably identical with 5286, through the idea of the *rustling* of mane, which usually accompanies the lion's roar]; to *tumble* about:—shake (off, out, self), overthrow, toss up and down.

5288. נַעַר, **na'ar,** *nah´-ar;* from 5287; (concrete) a *boy* (as active), from the age of infancy to adolescence; (by implication) a *servant;* also (by interchange of sex), a *girl* (of similar latitude in age):—babe, boy, child, damsel [*from the margin*], lad, servant, young (man).

5289. נַעַר, **na'ar,** *nah´-ar;* from 5287 in its derivative sense of *tossing* about; a *wanderer:*—young one.

5290. נֹעַר, **nô'ar,** *no´-ar;* from 5287; (abstract) *boyhood* [compare 5288]:—child, youth.

5291. נַעֲרָה, **na'ărâh,** *nah-ar-aw´;* feminine of 5288; a *girl* (from infancy to adolescence):—damsel, maid (-en), young (woman).

5292. נַעֲרָה, **Na'ărâh,** *nah-ar-aw´;* the same as 5291; *Naarah,* the name of an Israelitess, and of a place in Palestine:—Naarah, Naarath.

5293. נַעֲרַי, **Na'ăray,** *nah-ar-ah´ee;* from 5288; *youthful; Naarai,* an Israelite:—Naarai.

5294. נְעַרְיָה, **Nᵉ'aryâh,** *neh-ar-yaw´;* from 5288 and 3050; *servant of Jah; Neärjah,* the name of two Israelites:—Neariah.

5295. נַעֲרָן, **Na'ărân,** *nah-ar-awn´;* from 5288; *juvenile; Naaran,* a place in Palestine:—Naaran.

5296. נְעֹרֶת, **nᵉ'ôreth,** *neh-o´-reth;* from 5287; something *shaken* out, i.e. *tow* (as the refuse of flax):—tow.

5297. נֹף, **Nôph,** *nofe;* a variation of 4644; *Noph,* the capital of Upper Egypt:—Noph.

5298. נֶפֶג, **Nepheg,** *neh´-feg;* from an unused root probably meaning to *spring* forth; a *sprout; Nepheg,* the name of two Israelites:—Nepheg.

5299. נָפָה, **nâphâh,** *naw-faw´;* from 5130 in the sense of *lifting;* a *height;* also a *sieve:*—border, coast, region, sieve.

5300. נְפוּשְׁסִים, **Nᵉphûwshᵉsîym,** *nef-oo-shes-eem´;* for 5304; *Nephushesim,* a Temple-servant:—Nephisesim [*from the margin*].

5301. נָפַח, **nâphach,** *naw-fakh´;* a primitive root; to *puff,* in various applications; (literal) to *inflate, blow* hard, *scatter, kindle, expire;* (figurative) to *disesteem:*—blow, breath, give up, cause to lose [life], seething, snuff.

5302. נֹפַח, **Nôphach,** *no´-fach;* from 5301; a *gust; Nophach,* a place in Moab:—Nophah.

5303. נְפִילִים, **nᵉphîylîym,** *nef-eel-eem´;* from 5307; (properly) a *feller,* i.e. a *bully* or *tyrant:*—giant.

A masculine noun used only in the plural meaning giants. The celebrated, puzzling passage where this term is first used is Ge 6:4 which merely transliterates the Hebrew word into English as Nephilim. These beings evidently appeared on the earth in the ancient past when divine beings cohabited with woman, and Nephilim, the mighty men or warriors of great fame, were the offspring. This huge race of Nephilim struck fear into the Israelite spies who had gone up to survey the land of Canaan (see Nu 13:31–33). The sons of Anak, a tall race of people, came from the Nephilim (Nu 13:33; cf. Dt 2:10, 11; 9:2; Jos 15:14). Eze 32:21, 27 may have the Nephilim in mind, possibly equating them with the mighty men or mighty warriors in the passage. These beings were not divine but only at best great, powerful men.

5304. נְפִיסִים, **Nᵉphîysîym,** *nef-ee-seem´*; plural from an unused root meaning to *scatter; expansions; Nephism,* a Temple-servant:—Nephusim [*from the margin*].

5305. נָפִישׁ, **Nâphîysh,** *naw-feesh´*; from 5314; *refreshed; Naphish,* a son of Ishmael, and his posterity:—Naphish.

5306. נֹפֶךְ, **nôphek,** *no´-fek*; from an unused root meaning to *glisten; shining*; a gem, probably the *garnet*:—emerald.

5307. נָפַל, **nâphal,** *naw-fal´*; a primitive root; to *fall*, in a great variety of applications (intransitive or causative, literal or figurative):—be accepted, cast (down, self, [lots], out), cease, die, divide (by lot), (let) fail, (cause to, let, make, ready to) fall (away, down, -en, -ing), fell (-ing), fugitive, have [inheritance], inferior, be judged [*by mistake for* 6419], lay (along), (cause to) lie down, light (down), be (× hast) lost, lying, overthrow, overwhelm, perish, present (-ed, -ing), (make to) rot, slay, smite out, × surely, throw down.

A verb meaning to fall, to lie, to prostrate oneself, to overthrow. This common Hebrew verb carries many possible variations in meaning, much like the English verb to fall. For instance, it can be used literally of someone or something falling down (Ge 14:10; 1Sa 4:18; 17:49; 2Ki 6:5); or into a pit (Ex 21:33; Dt 22:4). It is employed for inanimate objects like walls, towers, trees, and hailstones (1Ki 20:30; Ecc 11:3). It is used idiomatically for a violent death, especially in battle (Jgs 5:27; 1Sa 4:10; Am 7:17); and for the overthrow of a city (Jer 51:8). The word also describes those who fall prostrate before God or those in authority (Ge 50:18; 2Ch 20:18). With the preposition *'al* (5921), meaning upon, it carries the meaning to attack (literally, to fall upon) (Job 1:19); to desert (to fall away) (2Ki 25:11; Jer 21:9); to be overcome by sleep or emotion (to fall

into) (Ge 4:5; 15:12; Jos 2:9; 1Sa 17:32; Ne 6:16). It is used to express the idea of being bedridden or debilitated (Ex 21:18); to be overtaken (lit., to fall into the hands of) (Jgs 15:18; La 1:7); and to be born (Isa 26:18). In its causative usage, it also takes the meaning to cast lots (Ne 10:34[35]; Isa 34:17).

5308. נְפַל, **nᵉphal,** *nef-al´*; (Chaldee); corresponding to 5307:—fall (down), have occasion.

An Aramaic verb meaning to fall, to prostrate oneself, to die. The verb is commonly used in reference to paying homage to a human being (Da 2:46); or to an image (Da 3:5–7). It is also used to denote a violent death (Da 7:20). It carries the meaning of responsibility in Ezr 7:20, where it referred to taking responsibility for carrying out the king's order. See the Hebrew word *nâphal* (5307).

5309. נֶפֶל, **nephel,** *neh´-fel*; or נֵפֶל, **nêphel,** *nay´-fel*; from 5307; something *fallen*, i.e. an *abortion*:—untimely birth.

A masculine noun meaning an untimely birth, a miscarriage. This word is taken from the Hebrew root *nâphal* (5307), meaning to fall. Job thought it might have been better to have been stillborn than to be born and live with his trouble (Job 3:16). The psalmist hoped the wicked would be put away like a miscarried infant (Ps 58:8[9]). The teacher in Ecclesiastes thought it would have been better for people to never be born than not to be able to enjoy their riches and have proper burials (Ecc 6:3).

5310. נָפַץ, **nâphats,** *naw-fats´*; a primitive root; to *dash* to pieces, or *scatter*:—be beaten in sunder, break (in pieces), broken, dash (in pieces), cause to be discharged, dispersed, be overspread, scatter.

5311. נֶפֶץ, **nephets,** *neh´-fets*; from 5310; a *storm* (as dispersing):—scattering.

5312. נְפַק, **nᵉphaq,** *nef-ak´*; (Chaldee); a primitive root; to *issue*; (causative) to *bring out*:—come (go, take) forth (out).

5313. נִפְקָה, **niphqâh,** *nif-kaw´*; (Chaldee); from 5312; an *outgo*, i.e. expense:—expense.

5314. נָפַשׁ, **nâphash,** *naw-fash´*; a primitive root; to *breathe*; (passive) to *be breathed* upon, i.e. (figurative) *refreshed* (as if by a current of air):—(be) refresh selves (-ed).

5315. נֶפֶשׁ, **nephesh,** *neh´-fesh*; from 5314; (properly) a *breathing* creature, i.e. *animal* or (abstract) *vitality*; used very widely in a literal, accommodated or figurative sense (bodily or mental):—any, appetite, beast, body, breath, creature, × dead (-ly), desire, × [dis-] contented, × fish, ghost, + greedy, he, heart (-y), (hath, × jeopardy of) life (× in jeopardy), lust, man, me, mind, mortally, one, own, person, pleasure, (her-, him-, my-, thy-) self, them (your) -selves, + slay, soul, + tablet, they, thing, (× she) will, × would have it.

A feminine noun meaning breath, the inner being with its thoughts and emotions. It is used 753 times in the OT and has a broad range of meanings. Most of its uses fall into these categories: breath, literally or figuratively (Jer 15:9); the inner being with its thoughts and emotions (Jgs 10:16; Pr 14:10; Eze 25:6); and by extension, the whole person (Ge 12:5; Le 4:2; Eze 18:4). Moreover, the term can cover the animating force of a person or his or her dead body (Le 21:11; Nu 6:6; Jer 2:34). It is even applied to animals in a number of the above senses: the breath (Job 41:21[13]); the inner being (Jer 2:24); the whole creature (Ge 1:20); and the animating force (Le 17:11). When this word is applied to a person, it doesn't refer to a specific part of a human being. The Scriptures view a person as a composite whole, fully relating to God and not divided in any way (Dt 6:5; cf. 1Th 5:23).

5316. נֶפֶת, **nepheth,** *neh´-feth*; for 5299; a *height*:—country.

5317. נֹפֶת, **nôpheth,** *no´-feth*; from 5130 in the sense of *shaking* to pieces; a *dripping* i.e. of *honey* (from the comb):—honeycomb.

5318. נְפְתּוֹחַ, **Nephtôwach,** *nef-to´-akh*; from 6605; *opened*, i.e. a *spring*; *Nephtoäch*, a place in Palestine:—Neptoah.

5319. נַפְתּוּלִים, **naphtûwlîym,** *naf-too-leem´*; from 6617; (properly) *wrestled*; but used (in the plural) transposed, a *struggle*:—wrestling.

5320. נַפְתֻּחִים, **Naphtuchîym,** *naf-too-kheem´*; plural of foreign origin; *Naphtuchim*, an Egyptian tribe:—Naptuhim.

5321. נַפְתָּלִי, **Naphtâlîy,** *naf-taw-lee´*; from 6617; *my wrestling*; *Naphtali*, a son of Jacob, with the tribe descended from him, and its territory:—Naphtali.

5322. נֵץ, **nêts,** *nayts*; from 5340; a *flower* (from its *brilliancy*); also a *hawk* (from its *flashing* speed):—blossom, hawk.

5323. נָצָא, **nâtsâ',** *naw-tsaw´*; a primitive root; to *go away*:—flee.

5324. נָצַב, **nâtsab,** *naw-tsab´*; a primitive root; to *station*, in various applications (literal or figurative):—appointed, deputy, erect, establish, × Huzzah [*by mistake for a proper name*], lay, officer, pillar, present, rear up, set (over, up) settle, sharpen, stablish, (make to) stand (-ing, still, up, upright), best state.

A verb meaning to station, to appoint, to erect, to take a stand. Abraham's servant stationed himself beside the well to find a wife for Isaac (Ge 24:13); Jacob set up a stone pillar (Ge 35:14, 20); the people stood up when Moses went out to the tent to meet God (Ex 33:8); God established the boundaries for Israel (Dt 32:8); Boaz asked the work supervisor (the one who stands over) about Ruth (Ru 2:5, 6). See the related Hebrew noun *nitstsâb* (5325) and the Aramaic noun *nitsbâh* (5326).

5325. נִצָּב, **nitstsâb,** *nits-tsawb´*; passive participle of 5324; *fixed*, i.e. a *handle*:—haft.

5326. נִצְבָּה, **nitsbâh,** *nits-baw´*; (Chaldee); from a root corresponding to 5324; *fixedness*, i.e. *firmness*:—strength.

5327. נָצָה, **nâtsâh,** *naw-tsaw´*; a primitive root; (properly) to *go forth*, i.e. (by implication) to *be expelled*, and (consequently) *desolate*; (causative) to *lay waste*; also (specific), to *quarrel*:—be laid waste, ruinous, strive (together).

5328. נִצָּה, **nitstsâh,** *nits-tsaw´*; feminine of 5322; a *blossom*:—flower.

5329. נָצַח, **nâtsach,** *naw-tsakh´*; a primitive root; (properly) to *glitter* from afar, i.e. to be *eminent* (as a superintendent, especially of the Temple services and its music); also (as denominative from 5331), to be *permanent*:—excel, chief musician (singer), oversee (-r), set forward.

5330. נְצַח, **netsach,** *nets-akh´*; (Chaldee); corresponding to 5329; to *become chief*:—be preferred.

5331. נֵצַח, **netsach,** *neh´-tsakh*; or נֶצַח, **nêtsach,** *nay´-tsakh*; from 5329; (properly) a *goal*, i.e. the bright object at a distance travelled toward; hence (figurative), *splendor*, or (subjective) *truthfulness*, or (objective) *confidence*; but usually (adverb), *continually* (i.e. to the most distant point of view):—alway (-s), constantly, end, (+ n-) ever (more), perpetual, strength, victory.

A noun meaning ever, always, perpetual. The word is used especially in prayers to ask whether God has forgotten His people forever (Ps 13:1[2]; 77:8[9]; Jer 15:18); and to affirm that He has not (Ps 9:18[19]; 103:9). With a negative, the word may be translated never (Ps 10:11; Isa 13:20; Am 8:7). The word also describes as perpetual (or appearing so to the writer) such things as ruins (Ps 74:3); and pain (Jer 15:18). In some passages, the word points to God's eternal nature (Ps 68:16[17]; Isa 25:8); and in 1Ch 29:11, nêtsach is among those attributes ascribed to God, namely, the kingdom, power, and glory. God even refers to Himself as the nêtsach of Israel (1Sa 15:29), a usage that may indicate His glory (see nâtsach[5329]). It also points to His eternal, truthful nature that is contrary to lying or changing.

5332. נֵצַח, **nêtsach,** *nay´-tsakh*; probably identical with 5331, through the idea of *brilliancy* of colour; *juice* of the grape (as blood red):—blood, strength.

A masculine noun meaning grape juice. The word occurs only in Isa 63:3, 6. In this passage, God's treading of grapes is a picture of His judgment of Israel's enemies, particularly Edom (cf. Isa 63:1). Grape juice, as elsewhere in the OT (cf. Dt 32:14) and the NT, is a symbol of blood. In Isa 63, God returned from judgment with His garments stained with blood like the garments of a grape treader are stained with juice.

5333. נְצִיב, **netsîyb,** *nets-eeb´*; or נְצִב, **netsib,** *nets-eeb´*; from 5324; something *stationary*, i.e. a *prefect*, a military *post*, a *statue*:—garrison, officer, pillar.

5334. נְצִיב, **Netsîyb,** *nets-eeb´*; the same as 5333; *station; Netsib*, a place in Palestine:—Nezib.

5335. נְצִיחַ, **netsîyach,** *nets-ee´-akh*; from 5329; *conspicuous; Netsiach*, a Temple-servant:—Neziah.

5336. נָצִיר, **nâtsîyr,** *naw-tsere´*; from 5341; (properly) *conservative*; but used passively, *delivered*:—preserved.

5337. נָצַל, **nâtsal,** *naw-tsal´*; a primitive root; to *snatch* away, whether in a good or a bad sense:— × at all, defend, deliver (self), escape, × without fail, part, pluck, preserve, recover, rescue, rid, save, spoil, strip, × surely, take (out).

A verb meaning to deliver. Deliverance often indicated the power of one entity overcoming the power of another. It was frequently expressed as deliverance from the hand (i.e. power) of another (Ge 32:11[12]; Hos 2:10[12]). Thus, idols (1Sa 12:21) and mere human might (Ps 33:16) were belittled as unable to deliver. God was frequently honoured as delivering His people, whether from earthly enemies (2Sa 22:1; Jer 1:8); or from more abstract things like transgressions (Ps 39:8[9]); and death (Ps 33:19; 56:13[14]). The word also refers to the taking of objects from another's power and is thus translated to recover (Jgs 11:26; 1Sa 30:8); to strip (2Ch 20:25); or to spoil (Ex 3:22; 12:36). In a special usage, the word signifies warriors delivering one's eyes, that is, escaping from sight (2Sa 20:6). In 2Sa 14:6, a participle referred to one who would separate two men fighting each other. In Ps 119:43, the psalmist asked God not to take (or deliver) His word out of his mouth.

5338. נְצַל, **netsal,** *nets-al´*; (Chaldee); corresponding to 5337; to *extricate*:—deliver, rescue.

An Aramaic verb meaning to deliver. The word corresponds to the Hebrew word nâtsal (5337)and occurs three times in the OT. In Da 3:29, it referred to God's deliverance of the three Hebrews from the fiery furnace, an action Nebuchadnezzar recognized as beyond any other so-called god. In Da 6:14[15], the word referred to Daniel's deliverance from the lions' den, a feat that Darius unsuccessfully attempted. Da 6:27[28] referred to God's successful deliverance of Daniel from the hand (i.e. power) of the lions. As with the Hebrew form, this word acknowledges God as the deliverer of those who trust in Him.

5339. נִצָּן, **nitstsân,** *nits-tsawn´*; from 5322; a *blossom*:—flower.

5340. נָצַץ, **nâtsats,** *naw-tsats´*; a primitive root; to *glare*, i.e. *be bright*-coloured:—sparkle.

5341. נָצַר, **nâtsar**, *naw-tsar´*; a primitive root; to *guard*, in a good sense (to *protect, maintain, obey*, etc.) or a bad one (to *conceal*, etc.):— besieged, hidden thing, keep (-er, -ing), monument, observe, preserve (-r), subtil, watcher (-man).

A verb meaning to guard, to keep, to observe, to preserve, to hide. The word refers to people's maintaining things entrusted to them, especially to keeping the truths of God in both actions and mind (Ps 119:100, 115). God's Word is to be kept with our whole hearts (Ps 119:69); our hearts, in turn, ought to be maintained in a right state (Pr 4:23). The word also refers to keeping speech under control (Ps 34:13 [14]; 141:3); the maintenance of a tree (Pr 27:18); the work of God's character (Ps 40:11[12]); its reflection in humans as preserving them (Ps 25:21; Pr 2:11). Sometimes the word refers directly to God's preservation and maintenance of His people (Pr 24:12; Isa 49:8). The passive participle form of the verb describes an adulteress' heart as guarded or kept secret (Pr 7:10). It also describes a city as guarded or besieged (Isa 1:8). The active participle is used to signify a watchman (2Ki 17:9; Jer 31:6).

5342. נֵצֶר, **nêtser**, *nay´-tser*; from 5341 in the sense of *greenness* as a striking colour; a *shoot*; (figurative) a *descendant*:—branch.

5343. נְקֵא, **nᵉqê**, *nek-ay´*; (Chaldee); from a root corresponding to 5352; *clean*:—pure.

5344. נָקַב, **nâqab**, *naw-kab´*; a primitive root; to *puncture*, literal (to *perforate*, with more or less violence) or figurative (to *specify, designate, libel*):—appoint, blaspheme, bore, curse, express, with holes, name, pierce, strike through.

A verb meaning to pierce, to designate, to curse. The word signifies the piercing of an animal's head, jaw, or nose with a spear (Job 40:24; 41:2[40:26]; Hab 3:14). It also signifies the piercing of a person's hand by a reed, symbolic of pain. Egypt was charged with bringing such pain on its allies (2Ki 18:21; Isa 36:6). In Hag 1:6, the passive participle described a bag as being pierced. This word can also refer to wages being paid (Ge 30:28); and to men being singled out for some task or distinction (2Ch 28:15; Am 6:1). The meaning to curse may also be derived from a different root, *qâbab* (6895). It signified the cursing or blaspheming of God's name (Le 24:11, 16); the speaking of a negative spiritual sentence on people (Nu 23:8; Pr 11:26; 24:24); or things associated with people (Job 3:8; 5:3).

5345. נֶקֶב, **neqeb**, *nek´-keb*; a *bezel* (for a gem):—pipe.

5346. נֶקֶב, **Neqeb**, *nek´-keb*; the same as 5345; *dell; Nekeb*, a place in Palestine:—Nekeb.

5347. נְקֵבָה, **nᵉqêbâh**, *nek-ay-baw´*; from 5344; *female* (from the sexual form):—female.

A feminine noun meaning female. It can refer either to a woman (Ge 1:27; 5:2; Le 12:5, 7; 15:33; 27:4, 5, 6, 7; Nu 5:3; 31:15; Jer 31:22); or a female animal (Ge 6:19; 7:3, 9, 16; Le 3:1, 6; 4:28, 32; 5:6).

5348. נָקֹד, **nâqôd**, *naw-kode´*; from an unused root meaning to *mark* (by *puncturing* or *branding*); *spotted*:—speckled.

5349. נֹקֵד, **nôqêd**, *no-kade´*; active participle from the same as 5348; a *spotter* (of sheep or cattle), i.e. the owner or tender (who thus marks them):—herdman, sheepmaster.

5350. נִקֻּדִים, **niqqudîym**, *nik-koo-deem´*; from the same as 5348; a *crumb* (as *broken* to spots); also a *biscuit* (as *pricked*):—cracknel, mouldy.

5351. נְקֻדָּה, **nᵉquddâh**, *nek-ood-daw´*; feminine of 5348; a *boss*:—stud.

5352. נָקָה, **nâqâh**, *naw-kaw´*; a primitive root; to *be* (or *make*) *clean* (literal or figurative); by implication (in an adverse sense) to *be bare*, i.e. *extirpated*:—acquit × at all, × altogether, be blameless, cleanse, (be) clear (-ing), cut off, be desolate, be free, be (hold) guiltless, be (hold) innocent, × by no means, be quit, be (leave) unpunished, × utterly, × wholly.

A verb meaning to be free, to be clean, to be pure. Originally, this verb meant to be emptied; therefore, its most basic sentiment is to be poured out and can have a negative or positive connotation. In the negative sense, it refers to a city which has been deserted, emptied of people (Isa 3:26). In the positive sense, it is used to connote freedom from the obligations of an oath (Ge 24:8, 41); from guilt (Nu 5:31; Jgs 15:3; Jer 2:35); and from punishment (Ex 21:19; Nu 5:28; 1Sa 26:9). Regardless of whether the connotation is positive or negative, most occurrences of this verb have a moral or ethical implication. Aside from the passive or stative form, this verb also has a factitive form. (The factitive concept is to make something a certain state, in this instance, to make something clean or pure.) The factitive form has two aspects: (1) acquittal, the declaration of someone as innocent (Job 9:28; 10:14; Ps 19:12[13]); (2) leaving someone unpunished (Ex 20:7; 34:7; Jer 30:11).

5353. נְקוֹדָא, **Nᵉqôwdâ**, *nek-o-daw´*; feminine of 5348 (in the figurative sense of *marked*); *distinction; Nekoda,* a Temple-servant:—Nekoda.

5354. נָקַט, **nâqaṭ,** *naw-kat´*; a primitive root; to *loathe*:—weary.

5355. נָקִי, **nâqîy,** *naw-kee´*; or נָקִיא, **nâqîy',** *naw-kee´*; (Joel 4:19; Jnh 1:14), from 5352; *innocent*:—blameless, clean, clear, exempted, free, guiltless, innocent, quit.

An adjective meaning clean, free from, exempt. This term frequently refers to innocent blood, that is, the shed blood of an innocent individual (Dt 19:10, 13; 21:8, 9; 1Sa 19:5; 2Ki 21:16; 24:4; Ps 94:21; 106:38; Pr 6:17; Isa 59:7; Jer 7:6; 22:3, 17). It also refers to a person who is innocent (Job 4:7; 17:8; 22:19, 30; 27:17; Ps 10:8; 15:5; Pr 1:11). According to Ps 24:4, it is a necessary quality for those who will stand in the presence of the Lord. It also refers to those who are free from blame (Ge 44:10); free from liability or punishment (Ex 21:28; 2Sa 14:9); released from an oath (Ge 24:41; Jos 2:17, 19, 20); exempt from various obligations (Nu 32:22); or free from the obligation of military service (Dt 24:5).

5356. נִקָּיוֹן, **niqqâyôwn**, *nik-kaw-yone´*; or נִקָּיֹן, **niqqâyôn**, *nik-kaw-yone´*; from 5352; *clearness* (literal or figurative):—cleanness, innocency.

A masculine noun meaning cleanness, whiteness, innocence. The Hebrew word generally implies innocence or freedom from guilt applied in the realm of sexual morality (Ge 20:5); and ritual purification or personal conduct as it relates to worship (Ps 26:6; 73:13). Choosing to embrace idolatry rather than innocence in their worship, Israel faced God's judgment (Hos 8:5). In Am 4:6, this term appears in a phrase that literally means cleanness of teeth, which is an idiomatic expression implying empty stomachs or nothing to eat.

5357. נָקִיק, **nâqîyq,** *naw-keek´*; from an unused root meaning to *bore*; a *cleft*:—hole.

5358. נָקַם, **nâqam,** *naw-kam´*; a primitive root; to *grudge*, i.e. *avenge* or *punish*:—avenge (-r, self), punish, revenge (self), × surely, take vengeance.

A verb meaning to avenge, to take revenge, to be avenged, to suffer vengeance, to take one's revenge. In actual usage, the following ideas come out: in the simple, intensive, and reflexive stems, the word can mean to take vengeance, to avenge. The Lord instructed His people not to seek revenge against each other, for to do so was unworthy of them (Le 19:18); the Lord took vengeance on His enemies and the enemies of His people (Na 1:2); but He would also take vengeance on His own people if necessary (Le 26:25); and He would avenge the death of His servants, the prophets (2Ki 9:7); and His city, Jerusalem (Jer 51:36). The reflexive idea of taking one's vengeance is found in the Lord's avenging Himself on Judah (Jer 5:9).

5359. נָקָם, **nâqâm,** *naw-kawm´*; from 5358; *revenge*:— + avenged, quarrel, vengeance.

A masculine noun meaning revenge or vengeance. This term is employed to signify human vengeance. For example, Samson sought revenge against the Philistines for gouging out his eyes (Jgs 16:28). According to Proverbs, a jealous husband will show no mercy when he exacts vengeance on his wife's adulterous lover (Pr 6:34). More often, however, this Hebrew term refers to divine repayment (Le 26:25; Dt 32:35, 41, 43; Eze 24:8; Mic 5:15[14]). For example, the psalmist encouraged the righteous with the hope that someday they will be avenged, and God will redress the wrongs committed against them (Ps 58:10[11]). In fact, He will judge those who have acted with vengeance toward His people (Eze 25:12, 15). Ultimately, the judgment of God's enemies will mean redemption for His people (Isa 34:8; 35:4; 47:3; 59:17; 63:4).

5360. נְקָמָה, **nᵉqâmâh,** *nek-aw-maw´*; feminine of 5359; *avengement,* whether the act or the passion:— + avenge, revenge (-ing), vengeance.

A feminine singular noun meaning vengeance. Jeremiah employed this word most frequently, referring to the vengeance of God (Jer 11:20; 46:10; 50:15, 28; 51:6, 11, 36). The worship of false gods, improper sacrifices, and a plot against Jeremiah himself all stirred up the vengeance of God. But it is also used with Israel as the subject (Nu 31:2; Ps 149:7); and object (La 3:60; Eze 25:15). Even when Israel took vengeance on an enemy, it was God's vengeance that they delivered (Nu 31:2, 3).

5361. נָקַע, **nâqaʻ,** *naw-kah´*; a primitive root; to *feel aversion:*—be alienated.

5362. נָקַף, **nâqaph,** *naw-kaf´*; a primitive root; to *strike* with more or less violence (*beat, fell, corrode*); by implication (of attack) to *knock together,* i.e. *surround* or *circulate:*—compass (about, -ing), cut down, destroy, go round (about), inclose, round.

A verb meaning to strike off, to strip away. It occurs twice in the Hebrew Bible. It is used passively in Isa 10:34 where it referred to the stripping away the forest thicket, describing God's destruction of Lebanon with an ax. In Job 19:26, the word is employed figuratively to describe the effects of his disease on his skin.

5363. נֹקֶף, **nôqeph,** *no´-kef*; from 5362; a *threshing* (of olives):—shaking.

5364. נִקְפָּה, **niqpâh,** *nik-paw´*; from 5362; probably a *rope* (as *encircling*):—rent.

5365. נָקַר, **nâqar,** *naw-kar´*; a primitive root; to *bore* (*penetrate, quarry*):—dig pick out, pierce, put (thrust) out.

5366. נְקָרָה, **nᵉqârâh,** *nek-aw-raw´*; from 5365; a *fissure:*—cleft, clift.

5367. נָקַשׁ, **nâqash,** *naw-kash´*; a primitive root; to *entrap* (with a noose), literal or figurative:—catch, (lay a) snare.

A verb meaning to strike, to strike down, to knock, to bring down. This word is associated with hunting birds, and therefore it is often translated to ensnare. It occurs four times in the Hebrew Bible and is used with the connotation of a subject attempting to destroy the object. For instance, the witch of Endor asked why Saul was entrapping her (1Sa 28:9). Dt 12:30 warned of being ensnared by the worship of other gods. According to Ps 109:11, a creditor could also strike down one's estate.

5368. נְקַשׁ, **nᵉqash,** *nek-ash´*; (Chaldee); corresponding to 5367; but used in the sense of 5362; to *knock:*—smote.

An Aramaic verb meaning to knock. It occurs only once in the Hebrew Bible. Da 5:6 employed the idiomatic phase knocking knees to express Belshazzar's fear when he saw a finger mysteriously writing on the wall. See the Hebrew word *nâqash* (5367).

5369. נֵר, **Nêr,** *nare*; the same as 5216; *lamp; Ner,* an Israelite:—Ner.

5370. נֵרְגַל, **Nêrᵉgal,** *nay-re-gal´*; of foreign origin; *Nergal,* a Cuthite deity:—Nergal.

5371. נֵרְגַל שַׁרְאֶצֶר, **Nêrᵉgal Shar'etser,** *nay-re-gal´ shar-eh´-tser*; from 5370 and 8272; *Nergal-Sharetser,* the name of two Babylonians:—Nergal-sharezer.

5372. נִרְגָּן, **nirgân,** *neer-gawn´*; from an unused root meaning to *roll* to pieces; a *slanderer:*—talebearer, whisperer.

5373. נֵרְדְּ, **nêrd,** *nayrd*; of foreign origin; *nard,* an aromatic:—spikenard.

5374. נֵרִיָּה, **Nêrîyyâh,** *nay-ree-yaw´*; or נֵרִיָּהוּ, **Nêrîyyâhûw,** *nay-ree-yaw´-hoo*; from 5216 and 3050; *light of Jah; Nerijah,* an Israelite:—Neriah.

5375. נָשָׂא, **nâsâ',** *naw-saw´*; or נָסָה, **nâsâh,** *naw-saw´*; (Ps 4:6 [7]), a primitive root; to *lift,* in a great variety of applications, literal and figurative, absolutely and relatively (as follows):—accept, advance, arise, (able to, [armour], suffer to) bear (-er, up), bring (forth), burn, carry (away), cast, contain, desire, ease, exact, exalt (self), extol, fetch, forgive, furnish, further, give, go on, help, high, hold up, honourable (+ man), lade, lay, lift (self) up, lofty, marry, magnify, × needs, obtain, pardon, raise (up), receive, regard, respect, set (up), spare, stir up, + swear, take (away, up), × utterly, wear, yield.

A verb meaning to lift, to carry, to take away. This verb is used almost six hundred times in the Hebrew Bible and covers three distinct semantic ranges. The first range is to lift, which occurs in both literal (Ge 7:17; 29:1; Eze 10:16) and figurative statements: to lift the hand in taking an oath (Dt 32:40); in combat (2Sa 18:28); as a sign (Isa 49:22); in retribution (Ps 10:12). Other figurative statements include the lifting of: the head (Ge 40:13); the face (2Sa 2:22); the eyes (Ge 13:10); the voice (1Sa 30:4). It is also important to note that a person can take up or induce iniquity by a number of actions (Ex 28:43; Le 19:17; 22:9; Nu 18:32). The second semantic category is to bear or to carry and is used especially in reference to the bearing of guilt or punishment of sin (Ge 4:13; Le 5:1). This flows easily then into the concept of the representative or substitutionary bearing of one person's guilt by another (Le 10:17; 16:22). The final category is to take away. It can be used in the simple sense of taking something (Ge 27:3); to take a wife or to get married (Ru 1:4); to take away guilt or to forgive (Ge 50:17); to take away or to destroy (Job 32:22).

5376. אְשָׂנ, n⁵sâ', *nes-aw´*; (Chaldee); corresponding to 5375:—carry away, make insurrection, take.

5377. אָשָׁנ, **nâshâ'**, *naw-shaw´*; a primitive root; to *lead astray*, i.e. (mentally) to *delude*, or (morally) to *seduce*:—beguile, deceive, × greatly, × utterly.

5378. אָשָׁנ, **nâshâ'**, *naw-shaw´*; a primitive root [perhaps identical with 5377, through the idea of *imposition*]; to *lend* on interest; (by implication) to *dun* for debt:— × debt, exact, giver of usury.

5379. תאֵשַׁנ, **niśśê'th**, *nis-sayth´*; passive participle feminine of 5375; something *taken*, i.e. a *present*:—gift.

5380. בַשָׁנ, **nâshab**, *naw-shab´*; a primitive root; to *blow*; (by implication) to *disperse*:—(cause to) blow, drive away.

5381. גַשָׂנ, **nâśag**, *naw-sag´*; a primitive root; to *reach* (literal or figurative):—ability, be able, attain (unto), (be able to, can) get, lay at, put, reach, remove, wax rich, × surely, (over-) take (hold of, on, upon).

5382. הָשָׁנ, **nâshâh**, *naw-shaw´*; a primitive root; to *forget*; (figurative) to *neglect*; (causative) to *remit, remove*:—forget, deprive, exact.

5383. הָשָׁנ, **nâshâh**, *naw-shaw´*; a primitive root [rather identical with 5382, in the sense of 5378]; to *lend* or (by reciprocity) *borrow* on security or interest:—creditor, exact, extortioner, lend, usurer, lend on (taker of) usury.

5384. הֶשָׁנ, **nâsheh**, *naw-sheh´*; from 5382, in the sense of *failure*; *rheumatic* or *crippled* (from the incident to Jacob):—which shrank.

5385. הָאוּשְׂנ, n⁵śûw'âh, *nes-oo-aw´*; or rather הָאֻשְׂנ, n⁵śu'âh, *nes-oo-aw´*; feminine passive participle of 5375; something *borne*, i.e. a *load*:—carriage.

5386. יִשְׁנ, n⁵shîy, *nesh-ee´*; from 5383; a *debt*:—debt.

5387. איִשָׂנ, **nâśîy'**, *naw-see´*; or אִשָׂנ, **nâśi'**, *naw-see´*; from 5375; (properly) an *exalted* one, i.e. a *king* or *sheik*; also a rising *mist*:—captain, chief, cloud, governor, prince, ruler, vapour.

A noun meaning something that is lifted up, a prince, a mist. The Hebrew word is formed from the verb *nâsâ'* (5375), meaning to lift. It refers to a leader of the people (Ge 23:6; Ex 16:22; 22:28[27]). Although rare, it can refer to the king (1Ki 11:34); or to a non-Israelite leader (Ge 34:2; Nu 25:18; Jos 13:21). Some scholars have proposed that the term refers to elected officials, contending that these were common people who were elevated or lifted up. They often buttress their argument with Nu 1:16, which talks of these leaders as the ones called, chosen, or appointed from the congregation. In a few instances, this word also indicates mist or vapors that rise from the earth to form clouds and herald the coming of rain (Ps 135:7; Pr 25:14; Jer 10:13; 51:16).

5388. הָיִּשְׁנ, **n⁵shîyyâh**, *nesh-ee-yaw´*; from 5382; *oblivion*:—forgetfulness.

5389. ןיִשְׁנ, **n⁵shîyn**, *neh-sheen´*; (Chaldee); irregular plural feminine of 606:—women.

5390. הָקיִשְׁנ, **n⁵shîyqâh**, *nesh-ee-kaw´*; from 5401; a *kiss*:—kiss.

5391. ךַשָׁנ, **nâshak**, *naw-shak´*; a primitive root; to *strike* with a sting (as a serpent); (figurative) to *oppress* with interest on a loan:—bite, lend upon usury.

5392. ךֶשֶׁנ, **neshek**, *neh´-shek*; from 5391; *interest* on a debt:—usury.

5393. הָכְּשִׁנ, **nishkâh**, *nish-kaw´*; for 3957; a *cell*:—chamber.

5394. לַשָׁנ, **nâshal**, *naw-shal´*; a primitive root; to *pluck* off, i.e. *divest, eject*, or *drop*:—cast (out), drive, loose, put off (out), slip.

5395. נָשַׁם‎, **nâsham,** *naw-sham´*; a primitive root; (properly) to *blow* away, i.e. *destroy:*—destroy.

A verb meaning to breathe heavily, to pant. This particular form of the word is used only once in the Bible and describes the deep breathing and gasping of a woman in labour. God said that although He had been silent, He would cry out like a woman about to give birth (Isa 42:14). See the related Aramaic noun *nishmâ'* (5396) and Hebrew noun *něshâmâh* (5397).

5396. נִשְׁמָה‎, **nishmâh,** *nish-maw´*; (Chaldee); corresponding to 5397; vital *breath:*—breath.

5397. נְשָׁמָה‎, **nᵉshâmâh,** *nesh-aw-maw´*; from 5395; a *puff,* i.e. *wind,* angry or vital *breath,* divine *inspiration, intellect,* or (concrete) an *animal:*—blast, (that) breath (-eth), inspiration, soul, spirit.

A feminine noun meaning breath, wind, spirit. Its meaning is parallel to *nephesh* (5315) and *rûach* (7307). It refers to the breath of God as a destructive wind that kills and clears the foundations of the earth (2Sa 22:16; Job 4:9); a stream of brimstone that kindles a fire (Isa 30:33); a freezing wind that produces frost (Job 37:10); the source of life that vitalizes humanity (Job 33:4). The breath of humans is recognized as the source and center of life (1Ki 17:17; Job 27:3). It is also understood that such breath originates with God, and He can withhold it, thereby withholding life from humanity (Ge 2:7; Job 34:14; Isa 42:5). Therefore, people's breath is a symbol of their weakness and frailty (Isa 2:22). Since breath is the source of life, by extension, this word is also used to represent life and anything that is alive (Dt 20:16; Jos 10:40; 11:11, 14; Isa 57:16). Like *nephesh* (5315), this word also connotes the human mind or intellect (Pr 20:27).

5398. נָשַׁף‎, **nâshaph,** *naw-shaf´*; a primitive root; to *breeze,* i.e. *blow* up fresh (as the wind):—blow.

5399. נֶשֶׁף‎, **nesheph,** *neh´-shef*; from 5398; (properly) a *breeze,* i.e. (by implication) *dusk* (when the evening breeze prevails):—dark, dawning of the day (morning), night, twilight.

5400. נָשַׂק‎, **nâśaq,** *naw-sak´*; a primitive root; to *catch* fire:—burn, kindle.

5401. נָשַׁק‎, **nâshaq,** *naw-shak´*; a primitive root [identical with 5400, through the idea of fastening up; compare 2388, 2836]; to *kiss,* literal or figurative (*touch*); also (as a mode of *attachment*), to *equip* with weapons:—armed (men), rule, kiss, that touched.

A verb meaning to kiss, to touch lightly. The word rarely has romantic implications (Pr 7:13; SS 1:2). Often, along with tears and embraces, kisses expressed the dearness of relationships between friends and family, especially at a farewell (Ru 1:9, 14; 1Sa 20:41; 1Ki 19:20); or a reunion (Ge 45:15, cf. Ro 16:16; 1Pe 5:14). Kisses also expressed acceptance of a person (Ge 45:15; 2Sa 14:33); and even the mutual acceptance or harmony of moral qualities (Ps 85:10[11]). They also were associated with giving blessings (Ge 27:27; 2Sa 19:39[40]). Kisses sometimes expressed the worship of idols (1Ki 19:18; Hos 13:2); and the worship of the Messiah (Ps 2:12; cf. Ps 2:7; Heb 1:5). Some kisses, however, were deceitful (2Sa 20:9). The meaning of lightly touching occurs in Eze 3:13.

5402. נֶשֶׁק‎, **nesheq,** *neh´-shek*; or נֵשֶׁק‎, **nêsheq,** *nay´-shek*; from 5401; military *equipment,* i.e. (collective) *arms* (offensive or defensive), or (concrete) an *arsenal:*—armed men, armour (-y), battle, harness, weapon.

A noun meaning weapons, battle, armoury. The word refers to a variety of weapons, both offensive (bows, arrows, spears, and clubs) and defensive (shields). Weapons were sometimes given as gifts (1Ki 10:25; 2Ch 9:24); and were kept in the palace Solomon built (Isa 22:8); thus, they probably involved a high level of craftsmanship and were sometimes made of precious metals (cf. 1Ki 10:16, 17, shields of gold); as well as iron and bronze (Job 20:24). In Ne 3:19, the word means armoury, a place where weapons were kept. The word also referred to a battle (Job 39:21; Ps 140:7[8]) as a place where horses charged, weapons flew, and one's head needed God's protection.

5403. נְשַׁר‎, **nᵉshar,** *nesh-ar´*; (Chaldee); corresponding to 5404; an *eagle:*—eagle.

5404. נֶשֶׁר‎, **nesher,** *neh´-sher*; from an unused root meaning to *lacerate*; the *eagle* (or other large bird of prey):—eagle.

5405. נָשַׁת‎, **nâshath,** *naw-shath´*; a primitive root; (properly) to *eliminate,* i.e. (intransitive) to *dry* up:—fail.

5406. נִשְׁתְּוָן, **nisht°vân,** *nish-tev-awn´*; probably of Persian origin; an *epistle:*—letter.

5407. נִשְׁתְּוָן, **nisht°vân,** *nish-tev-awn´*; (Chaldee); corresponding to 5406:—letter.

5408. נָתַח, **nâthach,** *naw-thakh´*; a primitive root; to *dismember:*—cut (in pieces), divide, hew in pieces.

5409. נֵתַח, **nêthach,** *nay´-thakh*; from 5408; a *fragment:*—part, piece.

5410. נָתִיב, **nâthîyb,** *naw-theeb´*; or (feminine) נְתִיבָה, **n°thîybâh,** *neth-ee-baw´*; or נְתִבָה, **n°thibâh,** *neth-ee-baw´*; (Jer 6:16), from an unused root meaning to *tramp*; a (beaten) *track:*—path ([-way]), × travel [-ler], way.

5411. נָתִין, **Nâthîyn,** *naw-theen´*; or נָתוּן, **Nâthûwn,** *naw-thoon´*; (Ezr 8:17), (the proper form, as passive participle), from 5414; one *given*, i.e. (in the plural only) the *Nethinim*, or *Temple-servants* (as *given* up to that duty):—Nethinims.

5412. נְתִין, **N°thîyn,** *neth-een´*; (Chaldee); corresponding to 5411:—Nethinims.

5413. נָתַךְ, **nâthak,** *naw-thak´*; a primitive root; to *flow* forth (literal or figurative); (by implication) to *liquefy:*—drop, gather (together), melt, pour (forth, out).

5414. נָתַן, **nâthan,** *naw-than´*; a primitive root; to *give*, used with great latitude of application (*put, make*, etc.):—add, apply, appoint, ascribe, assign, × avenge, × be ([healed]), bestow, bring (forth, hither), cast, cause, charge, come, commit, consider, count, + cry, deliver (up), direct, distribute, do, × doubtless, × without fail, fasten, frame, × get, give (forth, over, up), grant, hang (up), × have, × indeed, lay (unto charge, up), (give) leave, lend, let (out), + lie, lift up, make, + O that, occupy, offer, ordain, pay, perform, place, pour, print, × pull, put (forth), recompense, render, requite, restore, send (out), set (forth), shew, shoot forth (up), + sing, + slander, strike, [sub-] mit, suffer, × surely, × take, thrust, trade, turn, utter, + weep, × willingly, + withdraw, + would (to) God, yield.

A verb meaning to give, to place. This verb is used approximately two thousand times in the OT; therefore, it is understandable that it should have a broad semantic range. However, it is pos-

sible to identify three general categories of semantic variation: (1) to give, whether it be the exchange of tangible property (Ge 3:6; Ex 5:18); the production of fruit (Ps 1:3); the presentation of an offering to the Lord (Ex 30:14); the passing on of knowledge and instruction (Pr 9:9); the granting of permission (Ge 20:6). Often, God provides either preservation (Le 26:4; Dt 11:14, 15; Jer 45:5); or plague (Ex 9:23). (2) This Hebrew word also means to put, to place, or something literally placed: the luminaries in the sky (Ge 1:17); God's bow in the clouds (Ge 9:13); the ark on a cart (1Sa 6:8); the abomination in the temple. It could also be something figuratively placed: an obstacle (Eze 3:20); God's Spirit (Isa 42:1); reproach (Jer 23:40); curses (Dt 30:7). (3) The word can also mean to make or to constitute, such as the prohibition against making incisions in one's flesh (Le 19:28); God making Abraham into a father of many nations (Ge 17:5); or Solomon making silver as stones (1Ki 10:27).

5415. נְתַן, **n°than,** *neth-an´*; (Chaldee); corresponding to 5414; *give:*—bestow, give, pay.

5416. נָתָן, **Nâthân,** *naw-thawn´*; from 5414; *given; Nathan*, the name of five Israelites:—Nathan.

5417. נְתַנְאֵל, **N°than'êl,** *neth-an-ale´*; from 5414 and 410; *given of God; Nethanel*, the name of ten Israelites:—Nethaneel.

5418. נְתַנְיָה, **N°thanyâh,** *neth-an-yaw´*; or נְתַנְיָהוּ, **N°thanyâhûw,** *neth-an-yaw´-hoo*; from 5414 and 3050; *given of Jah; Nethanjah*, the name of four Israelites:—Nethaniah.

5419. נְתַן־מֶלֶךְ, **N°than-Melek,** *neth-an´ meh´-lek*; from 5414 and 4428; *given of* (the) *king; Nethan-Melek*, an Israelite:—Nathan-melech.

5420. נָתַס, **nâthas,** *naw-thas´*; a primitive root; to *tear* up:—mar.

5421. נָתַע, **nâtha‘,** *naw-thah´*; for 5422; to *tear* out:—break.

5422. נָתַץ, **nâthats,** *naw-thats´*; a primitive root; to *tear* down:—beat down, break down (out), cast down, destroy, overthrow, pull down, throw down.

A verb meaning to tear down, to destroy. The idea is the breaking down of a structure so that it can no longer support its own weight. Most often the word signified the destruction of idolatrous religious structures such as the altars that Israel was commanded to tear down on entering the Promised Land (Dt 7:5; 12:3; Jgs 2:2; 2Ch 31:1). The word also signified the destruction of buildings: a tower (Jgs 8:9, 17; Eze 26:9); a leprous house (Le 14:45); or an entire city (Jgs 9:45). In a spiritual sense, the word signified the tearing down of an individual (Ps 52:5[7]); or a nation (Jer 18:7). In Ps 58:6[7], the word signified breaking the teeth of fierce lions.

5423. נָתַק, **nâthaq,** *naw-thak´*; a primitive root; to *tear* off:—break (off), burst, draw (away), lift up, pluck (away, off), pull (out), root out.

5424. נֶתֶק, **netheq,** *neh´-thek*; from 5423; *scurf*:—(dry) scall.

5425. נָתַר, **nâthar,** *naw-thar´*; a primitive root; to *jump*, i.e. *be* violently *agitated*; (causative) to *terrify, shake* off, *untie*:—drive asunder, leap, (let) loose, × make, move, undo.

5426. נְתַר, **nᵉthar,** *neth-ar´*; (Chaldee); corresponding to 5425:—shake off.

5427. נֶתֶר, **nether,** *neh´-ther*; from 5425; mineral *potash* (so called from *effervescing* with acid):—nitre.

5428. נָתַשׁ, **nâthash,** *naw-thash´*; a primitive root; to *tear* away:—destroy, forsake, pluck (out, up, by the roots), pull up, root out (up), × utterly.

ס (Samekh)

5429. סְאָה, se'âh, *seh-aw´*; from an unused root meaning to *define*; a *seäh*, or certain measure (as *determinative*) for grain:—measure.

5430. סְאוֹן, se'ôwn, *seh-own´*; from 5431; perhaps a military *boot* (as a protection from *mud*):—battle.

5431. סָאַן, sâ'an, *saw-an´*; a primitive root; to *be miry*; used only as denominative from 5430; to *shoe*, i.e. (active participle) a *soldier shod*:—warrior.

5432. סַאסְּאָה, sa'sse'âh, *sahs-seh-aw´*; from 5429; *measurement*, i.e. *moderation*:—measure.

5433. סָבָא, sâbâ', *saw-baw´*; a primitive root; to *quaff* to satiety, i.e. *become tipsy*:—drunkard, fill self, Sabean, [wine-] bibber.

5434. סְבָא, Seᵇâ', *seb-aw´*; of foreign origin; *Seba*, a son of Cush, and the country settled by him:—Seba.

5435. סֹבֶא, sôbe', *so´-beh*; from 5433; *potation*, concrete (*wine*), or abstract (*carousal*):—drink, drunken, wine.

5436. סְבָאִי, Seᵇâ'îy, *seb-aw-ee´*; patrial from 5434; a *Sebaite*, or inhabitant of Seba:—Sabean.

5437. סָבַב, sâbab, *saw-bab´*; a primitive root; to *revolve, surround* or *border*; used in various applications, literal and figurative (as follows):—bring, cast, fetch, lead, make, walk, × whirl, × round about, be about on every side, apply, avoid, beset (about), besiege, bring again, carry (about), change, cause to come about, × circuit, (fetch a) compass (about, round), drive, environ, × on every side, beset (close, come, compass, go, stand) round about, inclose, remove, return, set, sit down, turn (self) (about, aside, away, back).

5438. סִבָּה, sibbâh, *sib-baw´*; from 5437; a (providential) *turn* (of affairs):—cause.

5439. סָבִיב, sâbîyb, *saw-beeb´*; or (feminine) סְבִיבָה, sebîybâh, *seb-ee-baw´*; from 5437; (as noun) a *circle, neighbour,* or *environs*; but chiefly (as adverb, with or without preposition) *around*:—(place, round) about, circuit, compass, on every side.

5440. סָבַךְ, sâbak, *saw-bak´*; a primitive root; to *entwine*:—fold together, wrap.

5441. סְבֹךְ, seᵇôk, *seh´-bok*; from 5440; a *copse*:—thicket.

5442. סְבַךְ, seᵇak, *seb-ak´*; or סֹבֶךְ, seᵇâk, *seb-awk´*; from 5440; a *copse*:—thick (-et).

5443. סַבְּכָא, sabbeᵏâ', *sab-bek-aw´*; (Chaldee); or שַׂבְּכָא, śabbeᵏâ', *sab-bek-aw´*; (Chaldee); from a root corresponding to 5440; a *lyre*:—sackbut.

5444. סִבְּכַי, Sibbeᵏay, *sib-bek-ah´ee*; from 5440; *corpse-like*; *Sibbecai*, an Israelite:—Sibbecai, Sibbechai.

5445. סָבַל, sâbal, *saw-bal´*; a primitive root; to *carry* (literal or figurative), or (reflexive) *be burdensome*; (specifically) to *be gravid*:—bear, be a burden, carry, strong to labour.

5446. סְבַל, seᵇal, *seb-al´*; (Chaldee); corresponding to 5445; to *erect*:—strongly laid.

5447. סֵבֶל, sêbel, *say´-bel*; from 5445; a *load* (literal or figurative):—burden, charge.

5448. סֹבֶל, sôbel, *so´-bel*; [only in the form סֻבָּל, subbâl, *soob-bawl´*; from 5445; a *load* (figurative):—burden.

5449. סַבָּל, sabbâl, *sab-bawl´*; from 5445; a *porter*:—(to bear, bearer of) burden (-s).

5450. סְבָלָה, seᵇâlâh, *seb-aw-law´*; from 5447; *porterage*:—burden.

5451. סִבֹּלֶת, sibbôleth, *sib-bo´-leth*; for 7641; an *ear* of grain:—Sibboleth.

5452. סְבַר, s^ebar, *seb-ar´*; (Chaldee); a primitive root; to *bear in mind*, i.e. *hope*:—think.

5453. סִבְרַיִם, **Sibrayim**, *sib-rah´-yim*; dual from a root corresponding to 5452; *double hope; Sibrajim*, a place in Syria:—Sibraim.

5454. סַבְתָּא, **Sabtâ**, *sab-taw´*; or סַבְתָּה, **Sabtâh**, *sab-taw´*; probably of foreign derivative; *Sabta* or *Sabtah*, the name of a son of Cush, and the country occupied by his posterity:—Sabta, Sabtah.

5455. סַבְתְּכָא, **Sabt^ekâ**, *sab-tek-aw´*; probably of foreign derivation; *Sabteca*, the name of a son of Cush, and the region settled by him:—Sabtecha, Sabtechah.

5456. סָגַד, **sâgad**, *saw-gad´*; a primitive root; to *prostrate* oneself (in homage):—fall down.

A verb meaning to fall down, to bow down, to lie down in worship. The word occurs four times, only in Isaiah (Isa 44:15, 17, 19; 46:6). It refers to bowing or lying flat before a wooden or golden idol to worship, to pray, or to seek deliverance from it (Isa 44:17). Isaiah satirized those who lowered themselves in this way before an idol and did not recognize that an idol is only the work of human hands.

5457. סְגִד, s^e**gid**, *seg-eed´*; (Chaldee); corresponding to 5456:—worship.

An Aramaic verb meaning to worship, to bow, to lie in worship. The word corresponds to the Hebrew word *sâgad* (5456). It occurs in Da 2:46, referring to King Nebuchadnezzar's prostration before Daniel and his command that an offering and incense be offered to Daniel for interpreting his dream. The only other occurrences are the eleven uses in Da 3, referring to the worship of the gold image Nebuchadnezzar made. All these occurrences are accompanied by the words to fall (5308) or to serve (6399). The three Hebrew officials appointed by Nebuchadnezzar at Daniel's recommendation refused to fall and worship this foreign gods. Instead, they yielded their own bodies to God in the fiery furnace (Da 3:28; cf. Ro 12:1).

5458. סְגוֹר, s^e**gôwr**, *seg-ore´*; from 5462; (properly) *shut up*, i.e. the *breast* (as inclosing the heart); also *gold* (as generally *shut* up safely):—caul, gold.

5459. סְגֻלָּה, s^e**gullâh**, *seg-ool-law´*; feminine passive participle of an unused root meaning to *shut* up; *wealth* (as closely *shut* up):—jewel, peculiar (treasure), proper good, special.

A feminine noun meaning a personal possession, a special possession, property. This noun is used only six times, but it gives one of the most memorable depictions of the Lord's relationship to His people and the place established for them.

The primary meaning of the word theologically is its designation "unique possession." God has made Israel His own unique possession (Ex 19:5). Israel holds a special position among the nations of the world, although all nations belong to the Lord. Israel's position, function, character, responsibility, and calling create its uniqueness (Dt 7:6; 14:2; 26:18; Ps 135:4). Israel is to be a priestly community that honours and fears the Lord, to be His alone (Mal 3:17). In the NT, 1 Peter 2:9 quotes Ex 19:5, applying it to the church.

The word is used in a secular sense to indicate personal possessions, such as when David gave his own gold and silver to the Lord (1Ch 29:3; Ecc 2:8).

5460. סְגַן, s^e**gan**, *seg-an´*; (Chaldee); corresponding to 5461:—governor.

An Aramaic masculine noun meaning prefect, governor. King Nebuchadnezzar positioned Daniel to be the head of all the governors of Babylon (Da 2:48). Da 3:2 lists the various officers of the neo-Babylonian Empire, one of which was the office signified by this term. Later, King Nebuchadnezzar summoned these and other officials to the dedication of the golden image he had erected. At this dedication, all the officials were expected to fall down and worship the image. Later, Darius the Mede issued a similar edict (Da 6:7[8]). However, in both instances, some refused, including Daniel.

5461. סָגָן, **sâgân**, *saw-gawn´*; from an unused root meaning to *superintend*; a *præfect* of a province:—prince, ruler.

A masculine noun meaning prefect or ruler. Sometimes this term refers to an official of the Assyrian or Babylonian Empire (Isa 41:25; Jer 51:23, 28, 57; Eze 23:6, 12, 23). It can also refer to the head of a Jewish community (Ezr 9:2); as well as lesser officials of Judah (Ne 2:16; 4:14[8], 19[13]; 5:7, 17; 7:5; 12:40; 13:11).

5462. סָגַר, **sâgar,** *saw-gar´*; a primitive root; to *shut* up; (figurative) to *surrender:*—close up, deliver (up), give over (up), inclose, × pure, repair, shut (in, self, out, up, up together), stop, × straitly.

5463. סְגַר, **sᵉgar,** *seg-ar´*; (Chaldee); corresponding to 5462:—shut up.

5464. סַגְרִיר, **sagrîyr,** *sag-reer´*; probably from 5462 in the sense of *sweeping* away; a pouring rain:—very rainy.

5465. סַד, **sad,** *sad*; from an unused root meaning to *estop*; the *stocks:*—stocks.

5466. סָדִין, **sâdîyn,** *saw-deen´*; from an unused root meaning to *envelop*; a *wrapper,* i.e. *shirt:*—fine linen, sheet.

5467. סְדֹם, **Sᵉdôm,** *sed-ome´*; from an unused root meaning to *scorch; burnt* (i.e. *volcanic* or *bituminous*) district; *Sedom,* a place near the Dead Sea:—Sodom.

5468. סֶדֶר, **seder,** *seh´-der*; from an unused root meaning to *arrange; order:*—order.

5469. סַהַר, **sahar,** *sah´-har*; from an unused root meaning to *be round; roundness:*—round.

5470. סֹהַר, **sôhar,** *so´-har*; from the same as 5469; a *dungeon* (as *surrounded* by walls):—prison.

5471. סוֹא, **Sôw',** *so*; of foreign derivation; *So,* an Egyptian king:—So.

5472. סוּג, **sûwg,** *soog*; a primitive root; properly to *flinch,* i.e. (by implication) to *go back;* (literal) to *retreat;* (figurative) to *apostatize:*—backslider, drive, go back, turn (away, back).

5473. סוּג, **sûwg,** *soog*; a primitive root [probably rather identical with 5472 through the idea of *shrinking* from a hedge; compare 7735]; to *hem* in, i.e. *bind:*—set about.

5474. סוּגַר, **sûwgar,** *soo-gar´*; from 5462; an *inclosure,* i.e. *cage* (for an animal):—ward.

5475. סוֹד, **sôwd,** *sode*; from 3245; a *session,* i.e. *company* of persons (in close deliberation); (by implication) *intimacy, consultation,* a *secret:*—assembly, counsel, inward, secret (counsel).

A masculine noun meaning counsel. Confidentiality is at the heart of this term. According to Pr 25:9, information shared in confidence should remain confidential. Yet gossip makes it difficult to do this (Pr 11:13; 20:19). Elsewhere, this term reflects a more general meaning of counsel, which is viewed as essential to successful planning (Pr 15:22). When it means counsel, this term suggests the idea of intimacy. For example, Job used this term to refer to his close friendship with God (Job 29:4); and with individuals he thought of as his close friends (Job 19:19). David used this term to describe one of his close friendships (Ps 55:14[15]). God establishes a close, intimate relationship with those who revere Him and walk uprightly (Ps 25:14; Pr 3:32). Sometimes, however, human relationships involve less than ideal associations (Ge 49:6). Used in a negative sense, this term can denote evil plotting (Ps 64:2[3]; 83:3[4]).

5476. סוֹדִי, **Sôwdîy,** *so-dee´*; from 5475; a *confidant; Sodi,* an Israelite:—Sodi.

5477. סוּחַ, **Sûwach,** *soo´-akh*; from an unused root meaning to *wipe* away; *sweeping; Suäch,* an Israelite:—Suah.

5478. סוּחָה, **sûwchâh,** *soo-kahw´*; from the same as 5477; something *swept* away, i.e. *filth:*—torn.

5479. סוֹטַי, **Sôwṭay,** *so-tah´ee*; from 7750; *roving; Sotai,* one of the Nethinim:—Sotai.

5480. סוּךְ, **sûwk,** *sook*; a primitive root; (properly) to *smear* over (with oil), i.e. *anoint:*—anoint (self), × at all.

A verb meaning to anoint, to pour upon. Oil is frequently the substance used for anointing (Dt 28:40; 2Sa 14:2; Eze 16:9; Mic 6:15). This procedure could be performed on oneself (2Sa 12:20; Ru 3:3; Da 10:3) as well as on another person (2Ch 28:15; Eze 16:9). In several instances, the absence of anointing oil among God's people is an indication of divine judgment (Dt 28:40; Mic 6:15).

5481. סוּמְפּוֹנְיָה, **sûwmpôwnᵉyâh,** *soom-po-neh-yaw´*; (Chaldee); or סוּמְפֹּנְיָה, **sûwmpônᵉyâh,** *soom-po-neh-yaw´*; (Chaldee); or סִיפֹנְיָא, **sîyphônᵉyâ',** *see-fo-neh-yaw´*; (Da 3:10) (Chaldee), of Greek origin a *bagpipe* (with a double pipe):—dulcimer.

5482. סְוֵנֵה, Sᵉvênêh, *sev-ay-nay´*; [rather to be written סְוֵנָה, Sᵉvênâh, *sev-ay´-naw*; for סְוֵן, Sᵉvên, *sev-ane´*; i.e. *to Seven*]; of Egyptian derivation; *Seven*, a place in Upper Egypt:—Syene.

5483. סוּס, sûws, *soos*; or סֻס, sus, *soos*; from an unused root meaning to *skip* (properly for joy); a *horse* (as leaping); also a *swallow* (from its rapid *flight*):—crane, horse ([-back, -hoof]). Compare 6571.

5484. סוּסָה, sûwsâh, *soo-saw´*; feminine of 5483; a *mare*:—company of horses.

5485. סוּסִי, Sûwsîy, *soo-see´*; from 5483; *horse-like; Susi*, an Israelite:—Susi.

5486. סוּף, sûwph, *soof*; a primitive root; to *snatch* away, i.e. *terminate*:—consume, have an end, perish, × be utterly.

A verb meaning to come to an end, to cease, to terminate. The OT describes Purim as an annual observance whose celebration should not cease (Est 9:28). The psalmist used the term to describe how quickly the prosperity enjoyed by the wicked is brought to an end (Ps 73:19). Elsewhere, it is a general term that refers to the end of something as a result of God's judgment (Isa 66:17; Jer 8:13; Zep 1:2, 3).

5487. סוּף, sûwph, *soof*; (Chaldee); corresponding to 5486; to *come to an end*:—consume, fulfil.

An Aramaic verb meaning to be fulfilled, to be ended, to end. The word is used in Da 2:44 in connection with the divinely established kingdom that will never be destroyed and will bring all other kingdoms to an end. In Da 4:33[30], it referred to King Nebuchadnezzar, who finished speaking as God began to address him.

5488. סוּף, sûwph, *soof*; probably of Egyptian origin; a *reed*, especially the *papyrus*:—flag, Red [sea], weed. Compare 5489.

5489. סוּף, Sûwph, *soof*; for 5488 (by ellipsis of 3220); the *Reed (Sea)*:—Red sea.

5490. סוֹף, sôwph, *sofe*; from 5486; a *termination*:—conclusion, end, hinder part.

5491. סוֹף, sôwph, *sofe*; (Chaldee); corresponding to 5490:—end.

5492. סוּפָה, sûwphâh, *soo-faw´*; from 5486; a *hurricane*:—Red Sea, storm, tempest, whirlwind, Red sea.

5493. סוּר, sûwr, *soor*; or שׂוּר, śûwr, *soor*; (Hos 9:12), a primitive root; to *turn* off (literal or figurative):—be [-head], bring, call back, decline, depart, eschew, get [you], go (aside), × grievous, lay away (by), leave undone, be past, pluck away, put (away, down), rebel, remove (to and fro), revolt, × be sour, take (away, off), turn (aside, away, in), withdraw, be without.

A verb meaning to turn away, to go away, to desert, to quit, to keep far away, to stop, to take away, to remove, to be removed, to make depart. The word is used equally in the simple and causative stems. The basic meaning of the root, to turn away, takes on various connotations in the simple stem according to context. In the simple stem, the verb means to turn aside, as Moses turned aside to see why the bush was not being consumed by the fire (Ex 3:3, 4); it is used metaphorically to describe turning away from the Lord because of a rebellious heart (Jer 5:23); or taking time to turn aside and seek someone's welfare (Jer 15:5). The word describes leaving or going away literally (Ex 8:31[27]); or figuratively, the scepter would not leave Judah (Ge 49:10); but Samson's strength left him (Jgs 16:19). Its meaning extends further to indicate falling away, as when one is enticed to fall away from following the Lord to pursue other gods (Dt 11:16; 1Sa 12:20; Ps 14:3). It means to stop something; for example, the banqueting and carousing of Israel would cease at the time of exile (Hos 4:18; Am 6:7). It also indicates the act of keeping away from something, such as evil (Isa 59:15); or when the Lord kept Himself from His people (Hos 9:12). Wise teaching helps keep a person far from the dangers of death (Pr 13:14, 19).

The causative stem adds the idea of making something move, go away, turn away, or simply to put aside. The priests would set aside burnt offerings to be offered up (2Ch 35:12); and clothing was put aside as Tamar removed her widow's clothes to deceive Judah (Ge 38:14; 1Sa 17:39; 1Ki 20:41). God removed Israel from His presence because He was angry with them (2Ki 17:18, 23; 23:27); Jacob charged his entire clan to get rid of their strange gods (Ge 35:2; Jos 24:14, 23).

When the verb is passive, it means to be removed, such as when the fat of offerings was removed by the priests (Le 4:31, 35). In Da 12:11, the word expresses the idea that the daily sacrifice was removed.

5494. סוּר, **sûwr,** *soor;* probably passive participle of 5493; *turned off,* i.e. *deteriorated:*—degenerate.

5495. סוּר, **Sûwr,** *soor;* the same as 5494; *Sur,* a gate of the Temple:—Sur.

5496. סוּת, **sûwth,** *sooth;* perhaps denominative from 7898; (properly) to *prick,* i.e. (figurative) *stimulate;* (by implication) to *seduce:*—entice, move, persuade, provoke, remove, set on, stir up, take away.

5497. סוּת, **sûwth,** *sooth;* probably from the same root as 4533; *covering,* i.e. *clothing:*—clothes.

5498. סָחַב, **sâchab,** *saw-khab´;* a primitive root; to *trail* along:—draw (out), tear.

5499. סְחָבָה, **sᵉchâbâh,** *seh-khaw-baw´;* from 5498; a *rag:*—cast clout.

5500. סָחָה, **sâchâh,** *saw-khaw´;* a primitive root; to *sweep* away:—scrape.

5501. סְחִי, **sᵉchîy,** *seh-khee´;* from 5500; *refuse* (as *swept* off):—offscouring.

5502. סָחַף, **sâchaph,** *saw-khaf´;* a primitive root; to *scrape* off:—sweep (away).

5503. סָחַר, **sâchar,** *saw-khar´;* a primitive root; to *travel* round (specifically as a *pedlar*); (intensive) to *palpitate:*—go about, merchant (-man), occupy with, pant, trade, traffick.

5504. סַחַר, **sachar,** *sakh´-ar;* from 5503; *profit* (from trade):—merchandise.

5505. סְחַר, **sachar,** *sah-khar´;* from 5503; an *emporium;* (abstract) *profit* (from trade):—mart, merchandise.

5506. סְחֹרָה, **sᵉchôrâh,** *sekh-o-raw´;* from 5503; *traffic:*—merchandise.

5507. סֹחֵרָה, **sôchêrâh,** *so-khay-raw´;* properly active participle feminine of 5503; something *surrounding* the person, i.e. a *shield:*—buckler.

5508. סֹחֶרֶת, **sôchereth,** *so-kheh´-reth;* similar to 5507; probably a (black) *tile* (or *tessara*) for laying borders with:—black marble.

5509. סִיג, **sîyg,** *seeg;* or סוּג, **sûwg,** *soog;* (Eze 22:18), from 5472 in the sense of *refuse; scoria:*—dross.

5510. סִיוָן, **Sîyvân,** *see-vawn´;* probably of Persian origin; *Sivan,* the third Hebrew month:—Sivan.

5511. סִיחוֹן, **Sîychôwn,** *see-khone´;* or סִיחֹן, **Sîychôn,** *see-khone´;* from the same as 5477; *tempestuous; Sichon,* an Amoritish king:—Sihon.

5512. סִין, **Sîyn,** *seen;* of uncertain derivation; *Sin,* the name of an Egyptian town and (probably) desert adjoining:—Sin.

5513. סִינִי, **Sîynîy,** *see-nee´;* from an otherwise unknown name of a man; a *Sinite,* or descendant of one of the sons of Canaan:—Sinite.

5514. סִינַי, **Sîynay,** *see-nah´ee;* of uncertain derivation; *Sinai,* a mountain of Arabia:—Sinai.

5515. סִינִים, **Sîynîym,** *see-neem´;* plural of an otherwise unknown name; *Sinim,* a distant Oriental region:—Sinim.

5516. סִיסְרָא, **Sîysᵉrâ’,** *see-ser-aw´;* of uncertain derivation; *Sisera,* the name of a Canaanitish king and of one of the Nethinim:—Sisera.

5517. סִיעָא, **Sîy‘â’,** *see-ah´;* or סִיעֲהָא, **Sîy‘ăhâ’,** *see-ah-haw´;* from an unused root meaning to *converse; congregation; Sia,* or *Siaha,* one of the Nethinim:—Sia, Siaha.

5518. סִיר, **sîyr,** *seer;* or (feminine) סִירָה, **sîyrâh,** *see-raw´;* or סִרָה, **sirâh,** *see-raw´;* (Jer 52:18), from a primitive root meaning to *boil* up; a *pot;* also a *thorn* (as springing up rapidly); (by implication) a *hook:*—caldron, fishhook, pan, ([wash-]) pot, thorn.

5519. סָךְ, **sâk,** *sawk;* from 5526; (properly) a *thicket* of men, i.e. a *crowd:*—multitude.

5520. סֹךְ, **sôk,** *soke;* from 5526; a *hut* (as of entwined boughs); also a *lair:*—covert, den, pavilion, tabernacle.

5521. סֻכָּה, **sukkâh,** *sook-kaw´;* feminine of 5520; a *hut* or *lair:*—booth, cottage, covert, pavilion, tabernacle, tent.

A feminine singular noun meaning a booth, a thicket. This term is used for temporary shelters used to cover animals (Ge 33:17); warriors (2Sa 11:11); and the prophet Jonah (Jnh 4:5). It is used poetically to refer to the clouds (Job 36:29; Ps 18:11[12]). A specialized usage is employed for booths constructed for the fall harvest festival (Le 23:42, 43). The festival was known as the *chag hassukkôwth* (2282), the Feast of Booths (Dt 16:13, 16). This was to remind the Israelites that they lived in booths when the Lord brought them up from Egypt (Le 23:43).

5522. סֻכּוֹת, **sikkûwth,** *sik-kooth´*; feminine of 5519; an (idolatrous) *booth*:—tabernacle.

An obscure masculine singular noun that occurs only in Am 5:26 and may mean tabernacle. This passage clearly describes the Israelites' false and improper worship. The question is how detailed the prophet's charge was. Some have translated the phrase as booth or shrine, while the Septuagint (Greek OT) reads "shrine of Molech." Some have suggested that both terms represent Akkadian astral deities, Sakkut and Kaiwan.

5523. סֻכּוֹת, **Sukkôwth,** *sook-kohth´*; or סֻכֹּת, **Sukkôth,** *sook-kohth´*; plural of 5521; *booths*; *Succoth*, the name of a place in Egypt and of three in Palestine:—Succoth.

5524. סֻכּוֹת בְּנוֹת, **Sukkôwth bᵉnôwth,** *sook-kohth´ ben-ohth´*; from 5523 and the (irregular) plural of 1323; *booths of* (the) *daughters*; *brothels*, i.e. idolatrous *tents* for impure purposes:—Succoth-benoth.

5525. סֻכִּי, **Sukkîy,** *sook-kee´*; patrial from an unknown name (perhaps 5520); a *Sukkite*, or inhabitant of some place near Egypt (i.e. *hut-dwellers*):—Sukkiims.

5526. סָכַךְ, **sâkak,** *saw-kak´*; or שָׂכַךְ, **sâkak,** *saw-kak´*; (Ex 33:22), a primitive root; (properly) to *entwine* as a screen; (by implication) to *fence* in, *cover* over, (figurative) *protect*:—cover, defence, defend, hedge in, join together, set, shut up.

5527. סְכָכָה, **Sᵉkâkâh,** *sek-aw-kaw´*; from 5526; *inclosure*; *Secacah*, a place in Palestine:—Secacah.

5528. סָכַל, **sâkal,** *saw-kal´*; for 3688; to be *silly*:—do (make, play the, turn into) fool (-ish, -ishly, -ishness).

5529. סֶכֶל, **sekel,** *seh´-kel*; from 5528; *silliness*; (concrete and collective) *dolts*:—folly.

5530. סָכָל, **sâkâl,** *saw-kawl´*; from 5528; *silly*:—fool (-ish), sottish.

5531. סִכְלוּת, **siklûwth,** *sik-looth´*; or שִׂכְלוּת, **siklûwth,** *sik-looth´*; (Ecc 1:17), from 5528; *silliness*:—folly, foolishness.

5532. סָכַן, **sâkan,** *saw-kan´*; a primitive root; to *be familiar* with; (by implication) to *minister* to, *be serviceable* to, *be customary*:—acquaint (self), be advantage, × ever, (be, [un-]) profit (-able), treasurer, be wont.

5533. סָכַן, **sâkan,** *saw-kan´*; probably a denominative from 7915; (properly) *to cut*, i.e. *damage*; also to *grow* (causative, *make*) *poor*:—endanger, impoverish.

5534. סָכַר, **sâkar,** *saw-kar´*; a primitive root; *shut* up; (by implication) to *surrender*:—stop, give over. See also 5462; 7936.

5535. סָכַת, **sâkath,** *saw-kath´*; a primitive root; to *be silent*; (by implication) to *observe* quietly:—take heed.

5536. סַל, **sal,** *sal*; from 5549; (properly) a *willow twig* (as *pendulous*), i.e. an *osier*; but only as woven into a *basket*:—basket.

5537. סָלָא, **sâlâ’,** *saw-law´*; a primitive root; to *suspend* in a balance, i.e. *weigh*:—compare.

5538. סִלָּא, **Sillâ’,** *sil-law´*; from 5549; an *embankment*; *Silla*, a place in Jerusalem:—Silla.

5539. סָלַד, **sâlad,** *saw-lad´*; a primitive root; probably to *leap* (with joy), i.e. *exult*:—harden self.

5540. סֶלֶד, **Seled,** *seh´-led*; from 5539; *exultation*; *Seled*, an Israelite:—Seled.

5541. סָלָה, **sâlâh,** *saw-law´*; a primitive root; to *hang* up, i.e. *weigh*, or (figurative) *contemn*:—tread down (under foot), value.

5542. סֶלָה, **selâh,** *seh´-law*; from 5541; *suspension* (of music), i.e. *pause*:—Selah.

5543. סַלּוּ, **Sallûw,** *sal-loo´*; or סַלּוּא, **Sallûw’,** *sal-loo´*; or סַלּוּא, **Sâlûw’,** *saw-loo´*; or סַלָּא, **Sallu’,** *sal-loo´*; from 5541; *weighed*; *Sallu* or *Sallai*, the name of two Israelites:—Sallai, Sallu, Salu.

5544. סִלּוֹן, **sillôwn,** *sil-lone´*; or סַלּוֹן, **sallôwn,** *sal-lone´*; from 5541; a *prickle* (as if *pendulous*):—brier, thorn.

5545. סָלַח, **sâlach,** *saw-lakh´*; a primitive root; to *forgive*:—forgive, pardon, spare.

A verb meaning to forgive, to pardon, to spare, to be forgiven. The verb's subject is always God: He forgave the people of Israel after Moses interceded for them in the desert (Nu 14:20; Isa 55:7); Solomon prayed that the Lord would always hear and forgive His people (1Ki 8:30, 39; Da 9:19; Am 7:2). Some sins of Israel, however, were not forgiven. Jehoiachin had shed so much innocent blood that the Lord was not willing to forgive him (2Ki 24:4; La 3:42). The verb means to free from or release from something: the word describes the Lord pardoning or releasing a young woman from her vows in some instances (Nu 30:5[6], 8[9]); the Lord will not forgive an Israelite who in his heart approves of his own rebellious actions and continues in them (Dt 29:20[19]). The Lord forgives wickedness if it is repented of (Ex 34:9; Nu 14:19).

In the passive stem, the Hebrew word means to be forgiven; the people are forgiven (Le 4:20, 26; 5:10; 19:22) for their unintentional sins (Nu 15:25, 28) by turning away from them.

5546. סַלָּח, **sallâch,** *sal-lawkh´*; from 5545; *placable*:—ready to forgive.

An adjective meaning forgiving. This particular word is used only once in the Bible in a verse that describes the love and mercy of God (Ps 86:5). See the related Hebrew root *sâlach* (5545) and noun *sĕliychâh* (5547).

5547. סְלִיחָה, **sᵉlîychâh,** *sel-ee-khaw´*; from 5545; *pardon*:—forgiveness, pardon.

A feminine noun meaning forgiveness. God is a forgiving God (Ne 9:17). He does not keep a record of sin, but with Him there is forgiveness (Ps 130:4). Daniel also proclaimed that God is forgiving, even though the Hebrews had sinned greatly against Him (Da 9:9). See the related Hebrew root *sâlach* (5545) and the related Hebrew adjective *sallâch* (5546).

5548. סַלְכָה, **Salkâh,** *sal-kaw´*; from an unused root meaning to *walk; walking; Salcah,* a place East of the Jordan:—Salcah, Salchah.

5549. סָלַל, **sâlal,** *saw-lal´*; a primitive root; to *mound* up (especially a turnpike); (figurative) to *exalt*; reflex, to *oppose* (as by a dam):—cast up, exalt (self), extol, make plain, raise up.

5550. סֹלְלָה, **sôlᵉlâh,** *so-lel-aw´*; or סוֹלְלָה, **sôwlᵉlâh,** *so-lel-aw´*; active participle feminine of 5549, but used passively; a military *mound*, i.e. *rampart* of besiegers:—bank, mount.

5551. סֻלָּם, **sullâm,** *sool-lawm´*; from 5549; a *stair-case*:—ladder.

5552. סַלְסִלָּה, **salsillâh,** *sal-sil-law´*; from 5541; a *twig* (as *pendulous*):—basket.

5553. סֶלַע, **sela',** *seh´-lah*; from an unused root meaning to be *lofty*; a craggy *rock,* literal or figurative (a *fortress*):—(ragged) rock, stone (-ny), strong hold.

5554. סֶלַע, **Sela',** *seh´-lah*; the same as 5553; *Sela,* the rock-city of Idumæa:—rock, Sela (-h).

5555. סֶלַע הַמַּחְלְקוֹת, **Sela' ham-machlᵉqôwth,** *seh´-lah ham-makh-lek-ōth´*; from 5553 and the plural of 4256 with the article interposed; *rock of the divisions; Sela-ham-Machlekoth,* a place in Palestine:—Sela-hammalekoth.

5556. סָלְעָם, **sol'âm,** *sol-awm´*; apparently from the same as 5553 in the sense of *crushing* as with a rock, i.e. consuming; a kind of *locust* (from its *destructiveness*):—bald locust.

5557. סָלַף, **sâlaph,** *saw-laf´*; a primitive root; properly to *wrench,* i.e. (figurative) to *subvert*:—overthrow, pervert.

5558. סֶלֶף, **seleph,** *seh´-lef*; from 5557; *distortion,* i.e. (figurative) *viciousness*:—perverseness.

5559. סְלִק, **sᵉliq,** *sel-eek´*; (Chaldee); a primitive root; to *ascend*:—come (up).

5560. סֹלֶת, **sôleth,** *so´-leth*; from an unused root meaning to *strip; flour* (as *chipped* off):—(fine) flour, meal.

5561. סַם, **sam,** *sam*; from an unused root meaning to *smell* sweet; an *aroma*:—sweet (spice).

5562. סַמְגַּר נְבוֹ, **Samgar Nᵉbôw,** *sam-gar´ neb-o´*; of foreign origin; *Samgar-Nebo,* a Babylonian general:—Samgar-nebo.

5563. סְמָדַר, **sᵉmâdar,** *sem-aw-dar´*; of uncertain derivation; a vine *blossom;* used also adverbially *abloom*:—tender grape.

5564. סָמַךְ, **sâmak,** *saw-mak´*; a primitive root; to *prop* (literal or figurative); (reflexive) to *lean* upon or *take hold* of (in a favourable or unfavourable sense):—bear up, establish, (up-) hold, lay, lean, lie hard, put, rest self, set self, stand fast, stay (self), sustain.

5565. סְמַכְיָהוּ, **Sᵉmakyâhûw,** *sem-ak-yaw´-hoo*; from 5564 and 3050; *supported of Jah; Semak-jah,* an Israelite:—Semachiah.

5566. סֶמֶל, **semel,** *seh´-mel*; or סֵמֶל, **sêmel,** *say´-mel*; from an unused root meaning to *resemble*; a *likeness*:—figure, idol, image.

A masculine noun meaning statue, image, idol. Moses instructed the people to keep careful watch on themselves, lest they make an idol and worship it (Dt 4:16). Manasseh put a carved image in God's Temple but later humbled himself before God and removed it (2Ch 33:7, 15). In a vision, Ezekiel saw an idol of jealousy—an idol in the north gate that was standing near the glory of the God of Israel (Eze 8:3, 5).

5567. סָמַן, **sâman,** *saw-man´*; a primitive root; to *designate*:—appointed.

5568. סָמַר, **sâmar,** *saw-mar´*; a primitive root; to *be erect*, i.e. *bristle* as hair:—stand up, tremble.

5569. סָמָר, **sâmâr,** *saw-mawr´*; from 5568; *bristling*, i.e. *shaggy*:—rough.

5570. סְנָאָה, **Sᵉnâ'âh,** *sen-aw-aw´*; from an unused root meaning to *prick; thorny; Senaah,* a place in Palestine:—Senaah, Hassenaah [*with the article*].

5571. סַנְבַלַּט, **Sanballat,** *san-bal-lat´*; of foreign origin; *Sanballat,* a Persian satrap of Samaria:—Sanballat.

5572. סְנֶה, **sᵉneh,** *sen-eh´*; from an unused root meaning to *prick*; a *bramble*:—bush.

5573. סֶנֶּה, **Senneh,** *sehn´-neh*; the same as 5572; *thorn; Seneh,* a crag in Palestine:—Seneh.

5574. סְנוּאָה, **Sᵉnûw'âh,** *sen-oo-aw´*; or סְנָאָה, **Sᵉnu'âh,** *sen-oo-aw´*; from the same as 5570; *pointed*; (used with the article as a proper name) *Senuah,* the name of two Israelites:—Hasenuah [*including the article*], Senuah.

5575. סַנְוֵרִים, **sanvêrîym,** *san-vay-reem´*; of uncertain derivation; (in plural) *blindness*:—blindness.

5576. סַנְחֵרִיב, **Sanchêrîyb,** *san-khay-reeb´*; of foreign origin; *Sancherib,* an Assyrian king:—Sennacherib.

5577. סַנְסִנָּה, **sansinnâh,** *san-seen-aw´*; from an unused root meaning to be *pointed*; a *twig* (as *tapering*):—bough.

5578. סַנְסַנָּה, **Sansannâh,** *san-san-naw´*; feminine of a form of 5577; a *bough; Sansannah,* a place in Palestine:—Sansannah.

5579. סְנַפִּיר, **sᵉnappîyr,** *sen-ap-peer´*; of uncertain derivation; a *fin* (collective):—fins.

5580. סָס, **sâs,** *sawce*; from the same as 5483; a *moth* (from the *agility* of the fly):—moth.

5581. סִסְמַי, **Sismay,** *sis-mah´ee*; of uncertain derivation; *Sismai,* an Israelite:—Sisamai.

5582. סָעַד, **sâ'ad,** *saw-ad´*; a primitive root; to *support* (mostly figurative):—comfort, establish, hold up, refresh self, strengthen, be upholden.

5583. סְעַד, **sᵉ'ad,** *seh-ad´*; (Chaldee); corresponding to 5582; to *aid*:—helping.

5584. סָעָה, **sâ'âh,** *saw-aw´*; a primitive root; to *rush*:—storm.

5585. סָעִיף, **sâ'îyph,** *saw-eef´*; from 5586; a *fissure* (of rocks); also a *bough* (as *subdivided*):—(outmost) branch, clift, top.

5586. סָעַף, **sâ'aph,** *saw-af´*; a primitive root; (properly) to *divide* up; but used only as denominative from 5585, to *disbranch* (a tree):—top.

5587. סְעִפִּים, **sᵉ'ippîym,** *seh-ip-peem´*; from 5586; *divided* (in mind), i.e. (abstract) a *sentiment*:—opinion.

A noun meaning a division, an opinion, a belief. The word comes from a root meaning to divide. It occurs only in 1Ki 18:21, where Elijah asked the Israelites how long they would halt between two opinions. In context, the word refers to belief, whether in the Lord or in Baal.

5588. סֵעֵף, **sê'êph,** *say-afe´*; from 5586; *divided* (in mind), i.e. (concrete) a *skeptic*:—thought.

5589. סְעַפָּה, **sᵉ'appâh,** *seh-ap-paw´*; feminine of 5585; a *twig*:—bough, branch. Compare 5634.

5590. סָעַר, **sâ'ar,** *saw-ar´*; a primitive root; to *rush* upon; (by implication) to *toss* (transitive or intransitive, literal or figurative):—be (toss with) tempest (-uous), be sore troubled, come out as a (drive with the, scatter with a) whirl-wind.

5591. סַעַר, **sa'ar,** *sah´-ar*; or (feminine) סְעָרָה, **s'êrâh,** *seh-aw-raw´*; from 5590; a *hurricane*:—storm (-y), tempest, whirlwind.

5592. סַף, **saph,** *saf*; from 5605, in its original sense of *containing*; a *vestibule* (as a *limit*); also a *dish* (for holding blood or wine):—bason, bowl, cup, door (post), gate, post, threshold.

5593. סַף, **Saph,** *saf*; the same as 5592; *Saph,* a Philistine:—Saph. Compare 5598.

5594. סָפַד, **sâphad,** *saw-fad´*; a primitive root; (properly) to *tear* the hair and *beat* the breasts (as Orientals do in grief); (generally) to *lament*; (by implication) to *wail*:—lament, mourn (-er), wail.

5595. סָפָה, **sâphâh,** *saw-faw´*; a primitive root; properly to *scrape* (literally, to *shave*; but usually figurative) together (i.e. to *accumulate* or *increase*) or away (i.e. to *scatter, remove* or *ruin*; [intransitive] to *perish*):—add, augment, consume, destroy, heap, join, perish, put.

A verb meaning to scrape or sweep away, to destroy, to perish, to be captured. The word refers to the destruction or sweeping away of people (Ps 40:14[15]); or a city (Ge 18:23, 24); especially as the judgment of God. In Dt 29:19[18], the word refers to complete destruction: the destruction of the saturated with the dry. In Isa 13:15, it means captured as if swept up into another's possession. It is also used of the scraping away (i.e. shaving) of a beard (Isa 7:20).

5596. סָפַח, **sâphach,** *saw-fakh´*; or שָׂפַח, **śâphach,** *saw-fakh´*; (Isa 3:17), a primitive root; (properly) to *scrape* out, but in certain peculiar senses (of *removal* or *association*):—abiding, gather together, cleave, smite with the scab.

A verb meaning to join, to be gathered together, to be joined, to cleave, to join oneself, to abide in. The word refers to putting a priest into office, that is, joining him to the office (1Sa 2:36). It refers to David remaining in Israel's inheritance in spite of death threats from Saul (1Sa 26:19); similarly, it refers to the Gentiles being joined to Israel (Isa 14:1). In Job 30:7, it refers to the gathering of foolish poor people for

protection under a plant. It appears to refer to the joining of heat (that is, poison) to a drink meant to make someone drunk; but the word here may be a copyist's error for *saph* (5592), meaning goblet (Hab 2:15). In Isa 3:17, the word means to smite with a scab, but here it is spelled *śippach*. and may belong to another root of similar spelling.

5597. סַפַּחַת, **sappachath,** *sap-pakh´-ath*; from 5596; the *mange* (as making the hair fall off):—scab.

5598. סִפַּי, **Sippay,** *sip-pah´ee*; from 5592; *bason-like*; *Sippai,* a Philistine:—Sippai. Compare 5593.

5599. סָפִיחַ, **sâphîyach,** *saw-fee´-akh*; from 5596; something (spontaneously) *falling* off, i.e. a *self-sown* crop; (figurative) a *freshet*:—(such) things as (which) grow (of themselves), which groweth of its own accord (itself).

5600. סְפִינָה, **s'phîynâh,** *sef-ee-naw´*; from 5603; a (sea-going) *vessel* (as *ceiled* with a deck):—ship.

5601. סַפִּיר, **sappîyr,** *sap-peer´*; from 5608; a *gem* (perhaps as used for *scratching* other substances), probably the *sapphire*:—sapphire.

5602. סֵפֶל, **sêphel,** *say´-fel*; from an unused root meaning to *depress*; a *basin* (as *deepened* out):—bowl, dish.

5603. סָפַן, **sâphan,** *saw-fan´*; a primitive root; to *hide* by covering; (specifically) to *roof* (passive participle as noun, a *roof*) or *wainscot*; (figurative) to *reserve*:—cieled, cover, seated.

5604. סִפֻּן, **sippun,** *sip-poon´*; from 5603; a *wainscot*:—cieling.

5605. סָפַף, **sâphaph,** *saw-faf´*; a primitive root; (properly) to *snatch* away, i.e. *terminate*; but used only as denominative from 5592 (in the sense of a *vestibule*), to *wait* at the *threshold*:—be a doorkeeper.

5606. סָפַק, **sâphaq,** *saw-fak´*; or שָׂפַק, **śâphaq,** *saw-fak´*; (1Ki 20:10; Job 27:23; Isa 2:6), a primitive root; to *clap* the hands (in token of compact, derision, grief, indignation or punishment); (by implication of satisfaction) to *be enough*; (by implication of excess) to *vomit*:—clap, smite, strike, suffice, wallow.

A verb meaning to clap, to strike, to smite. It signifies the clapping of hands in derision or disrespect, sometimes accompanied by hissing (Job 27:23; 34:37; La 2:15); the clapping of the hand on the thigh as a sign of grief or shame (Jer 31:19; Eze 21:12[17]); or the clapping of the hands in anger (Nu 24:10). The word is used to refer to God's striking of people in public rebuke for backsliding (Job 34:26); and the wallowing or splashing of Moab in its vomit (Jer 48:26). In Isa 2:6, the word referred to the striking of hands, that is, making deals with foreigners. The meaning, "suffice," found in 1Ki 20:10, appears to belong under another root, and this may also be true of Isa 2:6 (both passages spell the word with *ś* instead of *s*).

5607. סֶפֶק, **sêpheq**, *say´-fek*; or שֶׂפֶק, **śepheq**, *seh´-fek*; (Job 20:22; 36:18), from 5606; *chastisement*; also *satiety*:—stroke, sufficiency.

5608. סָפַר, **sâphar**, *saw-far´*; a primitive root; (properly) to *score* with a mark as a tally or record, i.e. (by implication) to *inscribe*, and also to *enumerate*; (intensive) to *recount*, i.e. *celebrate*:—commune, (ac-) count, declare, number, + penknife, reckon, scribe, shew forth, speak, talk, tell (out), writer.

A verb meaning to number, to recount, to relate, to declare. It is used to signify the numbering or counting of objects (Ge 15:5; Ps 48:12[13]); and people, as in a census (1Ch 21:2; 2Ch 2:17[16]). It also refers to a quantity that is too great to number (Ge 16:10; Jer 33:22). God's numbering of one's steps is a sign of His care (Job 14:16; cf. Mt 10:30). The word also means to relate or to recount and is used often to refer to the communication of important information and truths to those who have not heard them, especially to foreign nations (Ex 9:16; 1Ch 16:24; Ps 96:3); or to the children in Israel (Ps 73:15; 78:4, 6; 79:13). The matter communicated included dreams (Ge 40:9; 41:8, 12; Jgs 7:13); God's works (Ex 18:8; Ps 73:28; Jer 51:10); and recounting one's own ways to God (Ps 119:26). The word also signifies the silent witness of the creation to its Creator and His wisdom and glory (Job 12:8; 28:27; Ps 19:1[2]).

The participle form of the word *sôphêr*, means scribe and occurs about fifty times in the OT. Scribes such as Ezra studied, practiced, and taught the Law (Ezr 7:11). Scribes also served kings, writing and sometimes carrying messages to and from court (2Ki 18:18; 19:2; Est 3:12; 8:9). In 2Ki 22:10, a scribe read the recovered scroll of the Law to King Josiah, bringing about a personal revival. Scribes, as people who could read and count, also acted militarily, gathering the troops (2Ki 25:19; Jer 52:25). The occupation of scribe could belong to a family (1Ch 2:55). Also, some Levites occupied the position as part of their job (2Ch 34:13).

5609. סְפַר, **sᵉphar**, *sef-ar´*; (Chaldee); from a root corresponding to 5608; a *book*:—book, roll.

An Aramaic masculine noun meaning a book, a scroll. The word refers to the book of Moses, the first five books of the Bible, that were used to instruct the priests and Levites in their duties (Ezr 6:18). It refers to books of national records that rulers in Babylon could check regarding Israeli-Babylonian relations (Ezr 4:15). It also refers to books that the Ancient of Days will use to judge in favour of His saints against the boastful little horn (Da 7:10, cf. Da 7:21ff.). The word is used to signify a library or archive, as a house of books in Ezr 6:1.

5610. סְפָר, **sᵉphâr**, *sef-awr´*; from 5608; a *census*:—numbering.

5611. סְפָר, **Sᵉphâr**, *sef-awr´*; the same as 5610; *Sephar*, a place in Arabia:—Sephar.

5612. סֵפֶר, **sêpher**, *say´-fer*; or (feminine) סִפְרָה, **siphrâh**, *sif-raw´*; (Ps 56:8 [99]), from 5608; (properly) *writing* (the art or a document); (by implication) a *book*:—bill, book, evidence, × learn [-ed] (-ing), letter, register, scroll.

A masculine noun meaning a document, a writing, a book, a scroll. Borrowed from an Assyrian word meaning missive or message, this word can refer to a letter (2Sa 11:14, 15; 1Ki 21:8, 9, 11; 2Ki 10:1, 2, 6, 7; Jer 29:1); a divorce decree (Dt 24:1, 3; Isa 50:1; Jer 3:8); a proof of purchase deed (Jer 32:10–12, 14, 16); a book in which things were written for a need in the future (Ex 17:14; 1Sa 10:25; Isa 30:8); a book of laws (Ex 24:7; Dt 30:10; Jos 1:8; Ne 8:1, 3; 13:1); a genealogical record (Ge 5:1; Ne 7:5); writing and language (Da 1:4, 17).

5613. סָפַר, **sâphar**, *saw-fare´*; (Chaldee); from the same as 5609; a *scribe* (secular or sacred):—scribe.

An Aramaic masculine noun meaning a clerk, a secretary, a scribe. This term can refer to someone who had the ability to read and write documents, but it can also refer to someone who held a special government office. A Persian official named Shimshai was identified as a scribe, whose duties probably included copying documents as well as translating documents from and into Aramaic (Ezr 4:8, 9, 17, 23). In the official Persian office of scribe, Ezra was especially qualified to interpret and teach the Law of God (Ezr 7:12, 21).

5614. סְפָרָד, **Sᵉphârâd,** *sef-aw-rawd´*; of foreign derivation; *Sepharad*, a region of Assyria:—Sepharad.

5615. סְפֹרָה, **sᵉphôrâh,** *sef-o-raw´*; from 5608; a *numeration:*—number.

5616. סְפַרְוִי, **Sᵉpharvîy,** *sef-ar-vee´*; patrial from 5617; a *Sepharvite* or inhabitant of Sepharvain:—Sepharvite.

5617. סְפַרְוַיִם, **Sᵉpharvayim,** *sef-ar-vah´-yim*; (dual) or סְפָרִים, **Sᵉphârîym,** *sef-aw-reem´*; (plural), of foreign derivation; *Sepharvajim* or *Sepharim*, a place in Assyria:—Sepharvaim.

5618. סֹפֶרֶת, **Sôphereth,** *so-feh´-reth*; feminine active participle of 5608; a *scribe* (properly female); *Sophereth*, a temple servant:—Sophereth.

5619. סָקַל, **sâqal,** *saw-kal´*; a primitive root; (properly) to *be weighty*; but used only in the sense of *lapidation* or its contrary (as if a *delapidation*):—(cast, gather out, throw) stone (-s), × surely.

5620. סַר, **sar,** *sar*; from 5637 contraction; *peevish:*—heavy, sad.

5621. סָרָב, **sârâb,** *saw-rawb´*; from an unused root meaning to *sting*; a *thistle:*—brier.

5622. סַרְבַּל, **sarbal,** *sar-bal´*; (Chaldee) of uncertain derivation; a *cloak:*—coat.

5623. סַרְגּוֹן, **Sargôwn,** *sar-gone´*; of foreign derivation; *Sargon*, an Assian king:—Sargon.

5624. סֶרֶד, **Sered,** *seh´-red*; from a primitive root meaning to *tremble*; *trembling*; *Sered*, an Israelite:—Sered.

5625. סַרְדִּי, **Sardîy,** *sar-dee´*; patronymic from 5624; a *Seredite* (collective) or descendants of Sered:—Sardites.

5626. סִרָה, **Sirâh,** *see-raw´*; from 5493; *departure; Sirah*, a cistern so-called:—Sirah. See also 5518.

5627. סָרָה, **sârâh,** *saw-raw´*; from 5493; *apostasy, crime*; (figurative) *remission:*—× continual, rebellion, revolt ([-ed]), turn away, wrong.

A feminine noun meaning a defection, a revolt, an apostasy. Derived from a verb that means to turn aside, this term refers to God's people turning away from Him to follow false gods (Dt 13:5[6]). Frequently, it describes those who chose to rebel against God (Isa 1:5; 31:6; 59:13; Jer 28:16; 29:32). Although some translations of this term in Dt 19:16 suggest it simply means a general offence, its use elsewhere in Deuteronomy and the rest of the OT indicates that this word refers to apostasy.

5628. סָרַח, **sârach,** *saw-rakh´*; a primitive root; to *extend* (even to *excess*):—exceeding, hand, spread, stretch self, banish.

5629. סֶרַח, **serach,** *seh´-rakh*; from 5628; a *redundancy:*—remnant.

A masculine noun meaning excess. Derived from a verbal form that means to hang over or overrun, this noun form occurs only once in the OT. In Ex 26:12, it refers to the remaining or excess material of the curtains in the tabernacle.

5630. סִרְיוֹן, **siryôn,** *sir-yone´*; for 8302; a coat of *mail:*—brigandine.

5631. סָרִיס, **sârîys,** *saw-reece´*; or סָרִס, **sâris,** *saw-reece´*; from an unused root meaning to *castrate*; a *eunuch*; (by implication) *valet* (especially of the female apartments), and thus a *minister* of state:—chamberlain, eunuch, officer. Compare 7249.

A masculine noun meaning a court official, a eunuch. Derived from an Assyrian phrase meaning one who is the head or chief, this word can refer to someone with a high-ranking military or political status (Ge 40:2, 7; 1Sa 8:15). Potiphar held an official post called the captain of the guard while working in the court of an Egyptian pharaoh (Ge 37:36; 39:1). The term eunuch comes from the custom of placing castrated males in certain key government positions (2Ki

20:18; Est 2:3, 14, 15, 21; 4:4, 5; Isa 39:7). According to Mosaic Law, males who had defective genital organs would have been excluded from the worshiping community of Israel (cf. Le 21:20; Dt 23:1). In 2Ki 18:17, the term appears in a phrase that probably does not denote a eunuch but simply means an important government official (Jer 39:3, 13).

5632. סָרַךְ, **sârak,** *saw-rak´*; (Chaldee); of foreign origin; an *emir:*—president.

An Aramaic masculine noun meaning an official, a president. A loanword from Persian for head or chief, this term appears in the OT only in Daniel. It is a title given to three high-ranking government officials, one of whom was Daniel (Da 6:2–4[3–5], 6[7], 7[8]). Appointed by Darius the Mede, the three officials oversaw the work of 120 satraps, whose function may have been to collect taxes for the king from throughout the empire.

5633. סֶרֶן, **seren,** *seh´-ren;* from an unused root of uncertain meaning; an *axle;* (figurative) a *peer:*—lord, plate.

A masculine singular noun meaning a lord, a tyrant. This term is a Philistine loan word and was applied only to Philistine rulers. Five rulers reigned in the five main cities of the Philistines: Ashdod, Gaza, Ashkelon, Gath, and Ekron (1Sa 6:16, 18). In one passage, the word is translated axle of brass, based on the Septuagint rendering (1Ki 7:30), but the etymology is unknown. David and his men were sent away by the *seren* and not allowed to fight for the Philistines (1Ch 12:19[20]).

5634. סַרְעַפָּה, **sar‘appâh,** *sar-ap-paw´;* for 5589; a *twig:*—bough.

5635. סָרַף, **sâraph,** *saw-raf´;* a primitive root; to *cremate,* i.e. to *be* (near) *of kin* (such being privileged to kindle the pyre):—burn.

5636. סַרְפָּד, **sirpâd,** *sir-pawd´;* from 5635; a *nettle* (as stinging like a *burn*):—brier.

5637. סָרַר, **sârar,** *saw-rar´;* a primitive root; to *turn away,* i.e. (moral) *be refractory:*— × away, backsliding, rebellious, revolter (-ing), slide back, stubborn, withdrew.

A verb meaning to be stubborn, to be rebellious. Israel was said to be stubborn for forming

an alliance with Egypt against God's ordained plan (Isa 30:1); performing improper sacrifices, eating unclean things, and worshiping ancestors (Isa 65:2). They were even compared to a stubborn heifer (Hos 4:16). They stubbornly turned their backs (lit., shoulders) on God and His words (Ne 9:29; Zec 7:11). The son who rebelled against his parents could be severely disciplined and was eventually stoned (Dt 21:18, 21). The term is also used of an immoral woman (Pr 7:11).

5638. סְתָו, **sᵉthâv,** *seth-awv´;* from an unused root meaning to *hide; winter* (as the dark season):—winter.

5639. סְתוּר, **Sᵉthûwr,** *seth-oor´;* from 5641; *hidden; Sethur,* an Israelite:—Sethur.

5640. סָתַם, **sâtham,** *saw-tham´;* or שָׂתַם, **sâtham,** *saw-tham´;* (Nu 24:15), a primitive root; to *stop* up; (by implication) to *repair;* (figurative) to *keep secret:*—closed up, hidden, secret, shut out (up), stop.

5641. סָתַר, **sâthar,** *saw-thar´;* a primitive root; to *hide* (by covering), literal or figurative:—be absent, keep close, conceal, hide (self), (keep) secret, × surely.

5642. סְתַר, **sᵉthar,** *seth-ar´;* (Chaldee); corresponding to 5641; to *conceal;* (figurative) to *demolish:*—destroy, secret thing.

An Aramaic verb derived from two separate roots. One of these means to hide. It occurs as a passive participle in Da 2:22 where it refers to hidden things that God reveals to the wise. See the Hebrew word *sâthar* (5641). The second means to destroy. Its one usage describes the actions of Nebuchadnezzar, the Chaldean, who destroyed God's Temple in Jerusalem (Ezr 5:12). It is possibly related to the Hebrew root *sâthar* (8368).

5643. סֵתֶר, **sêther,** *say´-ther;* or (feminine) סִתְרָה, **sithrâh,** *sith-raw´;* (Dt 32:38), from 5641; a *cover* (in a good or a bad, a literal or a figurative sense):—backbiting, covering, covert, × disguise [-th], hiding place, privily, protection, secret (-ly, place).

5644. סִתְרִי, **Sithrîy,** *sith-ree´;* from 5643; *protective; Sithri,* an Israelite:—Zithri.

ע (Ayin)

5645. עָב, **'âb,** *awb*; (masculine and feminine), from 5743; (properly) an *envelope*, i.e. *darkness* (or *density*, 2Ch 4:17); (specifically) a (scud) *cloud*; also a *copse*:—clay, (thick) cloud, × thick, thicket. Compare 5672.

5646. עָב, **'âb,** *awb*; or עֹב, **'ôb,** *obe*; from an unused root meaning to *cover*; properly equivalent to 5645; but used only as an architectural term, an *architrave* (as *shading* the pillars):—thick (beam, plant).

5647. עָבַד, **'âbad,** *aw-bad'*; a primitive root; to *work* (in any sense); (by implication) to *serve, till,* (causative) *enslave,* etc.:— × be, keep in bondage, be bondmen, bond-service, compel, do, dress, ear, execute, + husbandman, keep, labour (-ing man), bring to pass, (cause to, make to) serve (-ing, self), (be, become) servant (-s), do (use) service, till (-er), transgress [*from margin*], (set a) work, be wrought, worshipper.

A verb meaning to work, to serve. This labour may be focused on things, other people, or God. When it is used in reference to things, that item is usually expressed: to till the ground (Ge 2:5; 3:23; 4:2); to work in a garden (Ge 2:15); or to dress a vineyard (Dt 28:39). Similarly, this term is also applied to artisans and craftsmen, like workers in fine flax (Isa 19:9); and labourers of the city (Eze 48:19). When the focus of the labour is another person, that person is usually expressed: Jacob's service to Laban (Ge 29:15); the Israelites' service for the Egyptians (Ex 1:14); and a people's service to the king (Jgs 9:28; 1Sa 11:1). When the focus of the labour is the Lord, it is a religious service to worship Him. Moreover, in these cases, the word does not have connotations of toilsome labour but instead of a joyful experience of liberation (Ex 3:12; 4:23; 7:16; Jos 24:15, 18). Unfortunately, this worship service was often given to false gods (Dt 7:16; 2Ki 10:18, 19, 21–23).

5648. עֲבַד, **'ăbad,** *ab-ad'*; (Chaldee); corresponding to 5647; to *do, make, prepare, keep,* etc.:— × cut, do, execute, go on, make, move, work.

5649. עֲבַד, **'ăbad,** *ab-ad'*; (Chaldee); from 5648; a *servant*:—servant.

An Aramaic masculine singular noun meaning a slave, a servant. It is used for servants of God or of human beings. King Nebuchadnezzar refers to Shadrach, Meshach, and Abednego as servants of the Most High God (Da 3:26). Darius calls Daniel the servant of the living God (Da 6:20[21]). One could also be known as a servant of the king (Da 2:7). This noun is derived from the verb *'ăbad* (5648), meaning to do or make. See the Hebrew cognate *'ebed* (5650).

5650. עֶבֶד, **'ebed,** *eh'-bed*; from 5647; a *servant*:— × bondage, bondman, [bond-] servant, (man-) servant.

A masculine noun meaning a servant, a slave. Although the most basic concept of this term is that of a slave, slavery in the Bible was not the same as the slavery of modern times. The period of slavery was limited to six years (Ex 21:2). Slaves had rights and protection under the Law (Ex 21:20). It was also possible for slaves to attain positions of power and honour (Ge 24:2; 41:12). In addition, the people under the king were called his servants (Ge 21:25); as well as his officers (1Sa 19:1); officials (2Ki 22:12); ambassadors (Nu 22:18); vassal kings (2Sa 10:19); tributary nations (1Ch 18:2, 6, 13). This word is also a humble way of referring to one's self when speaking with another of equal or superior rank (Ge 33:5). The term is also applied to those who worship God (Ne 1:10); and to those who minister or serve Him (Isa 49:5, 6). The phrase, the servant of the Lord, is the most outstanding reference to the Messiah in the OT, and its teachings are concentrated at the end of Isaiah (Isa 42:1, 19; 43:10; 49:3, 5–7; 52:13; 53:11).

5651. עֶבֶד, **'Ebed,** *eh´-bed;* the same as 5650; *Ebed,* the name of two Israelites:—Ebed.

5652. עֲבָד, **'ăbâd,** *ab-awd´;* from 5647; a *deed:*—work.

5653. עַבְדָּא, **'Abdâ',** *ab-daw´;* from 5647; *work; Abda,* the name of two Israelites:—Abda.

5654. עֹבֵד אֱדוֹם, **'Ôbêd 'Ĕdôwm,** *o-bade´ ed-ome´;* from the active participle of 5647 and 123; *worker of Edom; Obed-Edom,* the name of five Israelites:—Obed-edom.

5655. עַבְדְּאֵל, **'Abde°'êl,** *ab-deh-ale´;* from 5647 and 410; *serving God; Abdeël,* an Israelite:—Abdeel. Compare 5661.

5656. עֲבֹדָה, **'ăbôdâh,** *ab-o-daw´;* or עֲבוֹדָה, **'ăbôwdâh,** *ab-o-daw´;* from 5647; *work* of any kind:—act, bondage, + bondservant, effect, labour, ministering (-try), office, service (-ile, -itude), tillage, use, work, × wrought.

A feminine noun meaning service, work. This word encompasses the wide variations of meaning of the English word "work"—from delicate artistry to forced labour. The Egyptians made the Israelites do slave labour (Ex 1:14); for certain feast days, the Israelites were not allowed to do any work (Le 23:7ff.); different parts of the tabernacle were considered to be in its service (Nu 4:26, 32); the descendants of Judah included workers of linen (1Ch 4:21). God handed the Israelites into the hand of Shishak so they would learn the difference between serving Him and serving other kings (2Ch 12:8). See the related Hebrew root *'âbad* (5647).

5657. עֲבֻדָּה, **'ăbuddâh,** *ab-ood-daw´;* passive participle of 5647; something *wrought,* i.e. (concrete) *service:*—household, store of servants.

A feminine noun meaning service, servants. This word usually refers to an entire household of servants. The Philistines were jealous of Isaac because of his wealth, including his livestock and servants (Ge 26:14). Job was considered the wealthiest man of the East because of all his possessions, including his multitude of servants (Job 1:3). See the related Hebrew root *'âbad* (5647), Aramaic root *'ăbad* (5648), Aramaic noun *'ăbêd* (5649), and Hebrew noun *'ebed* (5650).

5658. עַבְדוֹן, **'Abdôwn,** *ab-dohn´;* from 5647; *servitude; Abdon,* the name of a place in Palestine and of four Israelites:—Abdon. Compare 5683.

5659. עַבְדוּת, **'abdûwth,** *ab-dooth´;* from 5647; *servitude:*—bondage.

A feminine noun meaning bondage, slavery. This word is derived from the word *'âbad* (5647), meaning to serve. It occurs three times in the Hebrew Bible. In Ezr 9:8, 9, it refers twice to the bondage of the Hebrews under Babylon, a bondage where God revived them a little by allowing them to rebuild the wall and temple. In Ne 9:17, it refers to severe bondage in Egypt (see Ne 9:9), to which some rebellious Hebrews wanted to return.

5660. עַבְדִּי, **'Abdîy,** *ab-dee´;* from 5647; *serviceable; Abdi,* the name of two Israelites:—Abdi.

5661. עַבְדִּיאֵל, **'Abdîy'êl,** *ab-dee-ale´;* from 5650 and 410; *servant of God; Abdiël,* an Israelite:—Abdiel. Compare 5655.

5662. עֹבַדְיָה, **'Ôbadyâh,** *o-bad-yaw´;* or עֹבַדְיָהוּ, **'Ôbadyâhûw,** *o-bad-yaw´-hoo;* active participle of 5647 and 3050; *serving Jah; Obadjah,* the name of thirteen Israelites:—Obadiah.

5663. עֶבֶד מֶלֶךְ, **'Ebed Melek,** *eh´-bed meh´-lek;* from 5650 and 4428; *servant of a king; Ebed-Melek,* a eunuch of king Zedekeah:—Ebed-melech.

5664. עֲבֵד נְגוֹ, **'Ăbêd N°gôw,** *ab-ade´ neg-o´;* the same as 5665; *Abed-Nego,* the Babylonian name of one of Daniel's companions:—Abed-nego.

5665. עֲבֵד נְגוֹא, **'Ăbêd N°gôw',** *ab-ade´ neg-o´;* (Chaldee); of foreign origin; *Abed-Nego,* the name of Azariah:—Abed-nego.

5666. עָבָה, **'âbâh,** *aw-baw´;* a primitive root; to *be dense:*—be (grow) thick (-er).

5667. עֲבוֹט, **'ăbôwṭ,** *ab-ote´;* or עֲבֹט, **'ăbôṭ,** *ab-ote´;* from 5670; a *pawn:*—pledge.

5668. עָבוּר, **'âbûwr,** *aw-boor´;* or עָבֻר, **'âbur,** *aw-boor´;* passive participle of 5674; (properly) *crossed,* i.e. (abstract) *transit;* used only adverbially on *account* of, in *order* that:—because of, for (… 's sake), (intent) that, to.

5669. עָבוּר, **'âbûwr,** *a-boor´;* the same as 5668; *passed,* i.e. *kept* over; used only of *stored* grain:—old corn.

5670. עָבַט, **'âbaṭ,** *aw-bat´*; a primitive root; to *pawn*; (causative) to *lend* (on security); (figurative) to *entangle*:—borrow, break [*ranks*], fetch [*a pledge*], lend, × surely.

5671. עֲבְטִיט, **'abṭîyṭ,** *ab-teet´*; from 5670; something *pledged*, i.e. (collective) *pawned* goods:—thick clay [*by a false etymology*].

5672. עֳבִי, **'ăbîy,** *ab-ee´*; or עֳבִי, **'ŏbîy,** *ob-ee´*; from 5666; *density*, i.e. *depth* or *width*:—thick (-ness). Compare 5645.

5673. עֲבִידָה, **'ăbîydâh,** *ab-ee-daw´*; (Chaldee); from 5648; *labour* or *business*:—affairs, service, work.

5674. עָבַר, **'âbar,** *aw-bar´*; a primitive root; to *cross* over; used very widely of any *transition* (literal or figurative; transitive, intransitive, intensive or causative); specifically to *cover* (in copulation):—alienate, alter, × at all, beyond, bring (over, through), carry over, (over-) come (on, over), conduct (over), convey over, current, deliver, do away, enter, escape, fail, gender, get over, (make) go (away, beyond, by, forth, his way, in, on, over, through), have away (more), lay, meddle, overrun, make partition, (cause to, give, make to, over) pass (-age, along, away, beyond, by, -enger, on, out, over, through), (cause to, make) + proclaim (-amation), perish, provoke to anger, put away, rage, + raiser of taxes, remove, send over, set apart, + shave, cause to (make) sound, × speedily, × sweet smelling, take (away), (make to) transgress (-or), translate, turn away, [way-] faring man, be wrath.

A verb meaning to pass through or over, to cover, to go beyond, to go along, to be crossed over, to make to cross over, to go through, to go away. This verb indicates the physical act of crossing or passing over and takes on a figurative usage that exhibits many variations in meaning. Two figurative meanings are of primary importance theologically; the verb means going beyond, overstepping a covenant or a command of God or man. Moses uses the word when charging the people with disobeying and overstepping the Lord's commands (Nu 14:41; Jos 7:11, 15). Esther 3:3 depicts Mordecai's transgressing of the king's command. The word is used of God's passing over His people's rebellion (Mic 7:18); but also of His decision not to pass over or spare them any longer (Am 7:8;

8:2). The verb relates to the placement of a yoke of punishment on the neck of Ephraim, God's rebellious nation (Hos 10:11; cf. Job 13:13).

The word indicates the literal movement of material subjects and objects in time and space in various contexts: a stream or river is passed over (Jos 3:14); as are boundaries (Nu 20:17). An attacking army passes through its enemies' territories, conquering them like a flood (cf. Jos 18:9; Isa 8:8; Da 11:10, 40); and as the literal flood waters of Noah's day covered the earth (Ps 42:7[8]; 88:16[17]; Isa 54:9). In a figurative sense, the word describes the feeling of jealousy that can come over a suspecting or jealous husband (Nu 5:14, 30); or the movement of God's Spirit (1Ki 22:24; 2Ch 18:23; Jer 5:28). The location of an event could move or pass on, as when the Israelites routed the Philistines, and the battle, both in location and progress, passed by Beth Aven (1Sa 14:23; 2Sa 16:1; Jer 5:22).

The word indicates passing away or leaving (emigrating) from a certain territory (Mic 1:11). It indicates dying or perishing, as when the Lord described the perishing of Assyria's allies (Na 1:12); or the disappearance of Job's safety (Job 30:15; 33:18); it describes the passing of a law's validity or its passing out of use (Est 1:19; 9:27).

The causative stem adds the aspect of making these things happen as described in the simple stem. Jacob caused his family to cross over the Jabbok River (Ge 32:23[24]). The word is used of the heinous act of devoting children to pagan gods (Jer 32:35; Eze 23:37). A proclamation or the sound of the shofar can pass through the land (Ex 36:6; Le 25:9).

The word means to cause something to pass away. Many things could be noted: God caused Saul's kingdom to pass over to David (2Sa 3:10); evil could be put away, as when Asa, king of Judah, put away male prostitutes from the religions of Israel (1Ki 15:12); or holy persons turned away their eyes from vain things (Ps 119:37).

The word is used one time in the passive stem to indicate a river that cannot be crossed (Eze 47:5); and in the factitive or intensive stem to describe Solomon's stringing gold chains across the front area inside the Holy Place in the Temple (1Ki 6:21).

5675. עֲבַר, **'ăbar,** *ab-ar'*; (Chaldee); corresponding to 5676:—beyond, this side.

5676. עֵבֶר, **'êber,** *ay'-ber*; from 5674; (properly) a region *across*; but used only adverbially (with or without a preposition) on the *opposite* side (especially of the Jordan; usually meaning the *east*):— × against, beyond, by, × from, over, passage, quarter, (other, this) side, straight.

5677. עֵבֶר, **'Êber,** *ay'-ber*; the same as 5676; *Eber*, the name of two patriarchs and four Israelites:—Eber, Heber.

5678. עֶבְרָה, **'ebrâh,** *eb-raw'*; feminine of 5676; an *outburst* of passion:—anger, rage, wrath.

A feminine noun meaning wrath, fury. The word is derived from the word *'âbar* (5674) and thus implies an overflowing anger. When the word is used of people, it usually describes a fault of character, a cruel anger (Ge 49:7; Am 1:11); associated with pride (Pr 21:24; Isa 16:6). The wrath of a king toward shameful servants, however, is justifiable, representing God's anger (Pr 14:35, cf. Pr 14:34; Ro 13:4). The word most often signifies God's wrath, an attribute people generally fail to properly appreciate (Ps 90:11). God's wrath disregards a person's wealth (Pr 11:4); and brings fiery judgment, purging the sin of His people (Eze 22:21, cf. Eze 22:22); and ultimately bringing wickedness and wicked people to an end on earth (Zep 1:15, 18). The instrument of wrath is sometimes pictured as a rod (Pr 22:8; La 3:1).

5679. עֶבְרָה, **'ăbârâh,** *ab-aw-raw'*; from 5674; a *crossing*-place:—ferry, plain [*from the margin*].

5680. עִבְרִי, **'Ibrîy,** *ib-ree'*; patronymic from 5677; an *Eberite* (i.e. Hebrew) or descendant of Eber:—Hebrew (-ess, woman).

5681. עִבְרִי, **'Ibrîy,** *ib-ree'*; the same as 5680; *Ibri*, an Israelite:—Ibri.

5682. עֲבָרִים, **'Ăbârîym,** *ab-aw-reem'*; plural of 5676; regions *beyond*; *Abarim*, a place in Palestine:—Abarim, passages.

5683. עֶבְרֹן, **'Ebrôn,** *eb-rone'*; from 5676; *transitional*; *Ebron*, a place in Palestine:—Hebron. Perhaps a clerical error for 5658.

5684. עֶבְרֹנָה, **'Abrônâh,** *ab-roe-naw'*; or עֶבְרֹנָה, **'Ebrônâh,** *eb-roe-naw'*; feminine of 5683; *Ebronah*, a place in the Desert:—Ebronah.

5685. עָבַשׁ, **'âbash,** *aw-bash'*; a primitive root; to *dry* up:—be rotten.

5686. עָבַת, **'âbath,** *aw-bath'*; a primitive root; to *interlace*, i.e. (figurative) to *pervert*:—wrap up.

5687. עָבֹת, **'âbôth,** *aw-both'*; or עֲבוֹת, **'âbôwth,** *aw-both'*; from 5686; *intwined*, i.e. *dense*:—thick.

5688. עֲבֹת, **'ăbôth,** *ab-oth'*; or עֲבוֹת, **'ăbôwth,** *ab-oth'*; or (feminine) עֲבֹתָה, **'ăbôthâh,** *ab-oth-aw'*; the same as 5687; something *intwined*, i.e. a *string*, *wreath* or *foliage*:—band, cord, rope, thick bough (branch), wreathen (chain).

5689. עָגַב, **'âgab,** *aw-gab'*; a primitive root; to *breathe* after, i.e. to *love* (sensually):—dote, lover.

A verb meaning to lust after. The word occurs in Eze 23 six times where it refers to the desire of Jerusalem and Samaria for foreign ways under the figure of two sisters who lust after foreigners. Ezekiel warned that, just as Assyria, the object of Samaria's lust, had destroyed them, so sensual Babylon would destroy Jerusalem. The word also occurs as a participle in Jer 4:30 and means lovers. Again, the word is used figuratively in a warning that Jerusalem's foreign lovers would despise and destroy them.

5690. עֲגָבִים, **'âgâbîym,** *ag-aw-beem'*; from 5689; *love* (concrete), i.e. *amative* words:—much love, very lovely.

5691. עֲגָבָה, **'ăgâbâh,** *ag-aw-baw'*; from 5689; *love* (abstract), i.e. *amorousness*:—inordinate love.

5692. עֻגָה, **'ugâh,** *oo-gaw'*; from 5746; an *ash-cake* (as *round*):—cake (upon the hearth).

5693. עָגוּר, **'âgûwr,** *aw-goor'*; passive participle [but with active sense] of an unused root meaning to *twitter*; probably the *swallow*:—swallow.

5694. עָגִיל, **'âgîyl,** *aw-gheel'*; from the same as 5696; something *round*, i.e. a *ring* (for the ears):—earring.

5695. עֵגֶל, **'êgel,** *ay'-ghel*; from the same as 5696; a (male) *calf* (as *frisking* round), especially one nearly grown (i.e. a *steer*):—bullock, calf.

5696. עָגֹל, **'agôl,** *aw-gole´*; or עָגוֹל, **'agôwl,** *aw-gole´*; from an unused root meaning to *revolve, circular*:—round.

5697. עֶגְלָה, **'eglâh,** *eg-law´*; feminine of 5695; a (female) *calf*, especially one nearly grown (i.e. a *heifer*):—calf, cow, heifer.

5698. עֶגְלָה, **'Eglâh,** *eg-law´*; the same as 5697; *Eglah*, a wife of David:—Eglah.

5699. עֲגָלָה, **'ăgâlâh,** *ag-aw-law´*; from the same as 5696; something *revolving*, i.e. a wheeled *vehicle*:—cart, chariot, wagon.

5700. עֶגְלוֹן, **'Eglôwn,** *eg-lawn´*; from 5695; *vituline; Eglon*, the name of a place in Palestine and of a Moabitish king:—Eglon.

5701. עָגַם, **'âgam,** *aw-gam´*; a primitive root; to *be sad*:—grieve.

5702. עָגַן, **'âgan,** *aw-gan´*; a primitive root; to *debar*, i.e. from marriage:—stay.

5703. עַד, **'ad,** *ad*; from 5710; properly a (peremptory) *terminus*, i.e. (by implication) *duration*, in the sense of *advance* or *perpetuity* (substantially as a noun, either with or without a preposition):—eternity, ever (-lasting, -more), old, perpetually, + world without end.

A noun meaning eternity. The word signifies God's dwelling place (Isa 57:15). It also refers to the continuance of a king on the throne (Ex 15:18; 1Ch 28:9; Ps 132:12; Pr 29:14). The word can indicate continual joy (Ps 61:8[9]; Isa 65:18); or continual anger (Mic 7:18; Am 1:11). The word's references to mountains that would be shattered (Hab 3:6); the sun and the moon (Ps 148:6) may show that the word sometimes means less than eternity or only an apparent eternity. The word occurs with the word *'ôwlâm* (5769) (Ps 10:16; 45:6[7]; Da 12:3) and sometimes with the word *netsach* (5331) (Ps 9:18[19]; Am 1:11).

5704. עַד, **'ad,** *ad*; properly the same as 5703 (used as a preposition, adverb or conjunction; especially with a preposition); *as far* (or *long*, or *much*) *as*, whether of space (*even unto*) or time (*during, while, until*) or degree (*equally with*):—against, and, as, at, before, by (that), even (to), for (-asmuch as), [hither-] to, + how long, into, as long (much) as, (so) that, till, toward, until, when, while, (+ as) yet.

5705. עַד, **'ad,** *ad*; (Chaldee); corresponding to 5704:— × and, at, for, [hither-] to, on, till (un-) to, until, within.

5706. עַד, **'ad,** *ad*; the same as 5703 in the sense of the *aim* of an attack; *booty*:—prey.

5707. עֵד, **'êd,** *ayd*; from 5749 contraction; (concrete) *a witness*; (abstract) *testimony*; (specifically) a *recorder*, i.e. *prince*:—witness.

5708. עֵד, **'êd,** *ayd*; from an unused root meaning to *set* a period [compare 5710, 5749]; the *menstrual* flux (as periodical); by implication (in plural) *soiling*:—filthy.

5709. עֲדָה, **'ădâh,** *ad-aw´*; (Chaldee); corresponding to 5710:—alter, depart, pass (away), remove, take (away).

5710. עָדָה, **'âdâh,** *aw-daw´*; a primitive root; to *advance*, i.e. *pass* on or *continue*; (causative) to *remove*; (specifically) to *bedeck* (i.e. bring an ornament upon):—adorn, deck (self), pass by, take away.

5711. עָדָה, **'Âdâh,** *aw-daw´*; from 5710; *ornament; Adah*, the name of two women:—Adah.

5712. עֵדָה, **'êdâh,** *ay-daw´*; feminine of 5707 in the original sense of *fixture*; a stated *assemblage* (specifically, a *concourse*; or generically, a *family* or *crowd*):—assembly, company, congregation, multitude, people, swarm. Compare 5713.

A feminine noun meaning a congregation, an assembly, a band, an entourage, a pack. The word is modified to indicate various kinds of groups or communities. It is used to describe a congregation of heavenly or human beings; an assembly of divine beings over which God presides (Ps 82:1); a gathering of nations (Ps 7:7[8]); a community of the righteous (Ps 1:5); a group of evildoers (Nu 26:9; Ps 22:16[17]); ruthless people (Ps 86:14). It describes an entire circle of families and friends (Job 16:7).

Most often the word refers to Israel as a group in many settings. It describes all Israel gathered before Solomon (1Ki 8:5; 12:20); or as a total community in general (Hos 7:12); it refers to the community of Israel at the Exodus in phrases like the congregation of the Lord (Nu 27:17; 31:16; Jos 22:16); the community of Israel (Ex 12:3, 6; Nu 16:9); or the community of the sons of Israel (Ex 16:1, 2; 17:1). At times leaders in Israel were described as the leaders or elders of the congregation (Ex 16:22; Le 4:15; Nu 4:34).

The word is used to describe a swarm of bees (Jgs 14:8); and figuratively describes the people in Ps 68:30[31] as bulls, evidently supporters of foreign nations.

5713. עֵדָה, **ʻêdâh,** *ay-daw´*; feminine of 5707 in its technical sense; *testimony*:—testimony, witness. Compare 5712.

A feminine noun meaning a testimony, a witness. Derived from a word that denotes permanence, this term refers to the act of testifying to a fact or an event. For example, by accepting Abraham's gift of ewe lambs, Abimelech acknowledged the truth of Abraham's statement about the ownership of the well at Beersheba (Ge 21:30). Likewise, a heap of stones became a witness to the boundary agreement reached between Jacob and Laban (Ge 31:52). Within the context of a covenant renewal ceremony, Joshua placed a single large stone to function as a witness of the covenant established between the Lord and His people (Jos 24:27).

5714. עִדּוֹ, **ʻIddôw,** *id-do´*; or עִדּוֹא, **ʻIddôw´,** *id-do´*; from 5710; *timely; Iddo* (or *Iddi*), the name of five Israelites:—Iddo. Compare 3035, 3260.

5715. עֵדוּת, **ʻêdûwth,** *ay-dooth´*; feminine of 5707; *testimony*:—testimony, witness.

A feminine noun meaning testimony, precept, warning sign. It is always used in connection with the testimony of God and most frequently in association with the tabernacle (Ex 38:21; Nu 1:50, 53). The stone tablets containing the Ten Commandments are identified as God's testimony (Ex 25:16; 31:18; 32:15). Because the Ten Commandments represent the covenant that God made with Israel (see Ex 34:27, 28), they are also called the "tables of the covenant" (see Dt 9:9; 11:15); and they were preeminent in the tabernacle. As a result, the tabernacle is sometimes called the tabernacle of the testimony (Ex 38:21; Nu 1:50, 53); and the ark is sometimes called the ark of the testimony (Ex 25:22; 26:33, 34; 30:6, 26). This term is also used alone to represent the ark (Ex 16:34; 27:21; 30:36; Le 16:13). In time, this term came to stand for the laws or precepts that God had delivered to humanity (Ps 19:7[8]; 119:88; 122:4).

5716. עֲדִי, **ʻádîy,** *ad-ee´*; from 5710 in the sense of *trappings; finery*; (generically) an *outfit*; (specifically) a *headstall*:— × excellent, mouth, ornament.

5717. עֲדִיאֵל, **ʻÁdîyʼêl,** *ad-ee-ale´*; from 5716 and 410; *ornament of God; Adiël,* the name of three Israelites:—Adiel.

5718. עֲדָיָה, **ʻÁdâyâh,** *ad-aw-yaw´*; or עֲדָיָהוּ, **ʻÁdâ-yâhûw,** *ad-aw-yaw´-hoo*; from 5710 and 3050; *Jah has adorned; Adajah,* the name of eight Israelites:—Adaiah.

5719. עָדִין, **ʻádîyn,** *aw-deen´*; from 5727; *voluptuous*:—given to pleasures.

5720. עָדִין, **ʻÂdîyn,** *aw-deen´*; the same as 5719; *Adin,* the name of two Israelites:—Adin.

5721. עֲדִינָא, **ʻÁdîynâʼ,** *ad-ee-naw´*; from 5719; *effeminacy; Adina,* an Israelite:—Adina.

5722. עֲדִינוֹ, **ʻádîynôw,** *ad-ee-no´*; probably from 5719 in the original sense of *slender* (i.e. a *spear*); *his spear*:—Adino.

5723. עֲדִיתַיִם, **ʻÁdîythayim,** *ad-ee-thah´-yim*; dual of a feminine of 5706; *double prey; Adithajim,* a place in Palestine:—Adithaim.

5724. עַדְלָי, **ʻAdlay,** *ad-lah´ee*; probably from an unused root of uncertain meaning; *Adlai,* an Israelite:—Adlai.

5725. עֲדֻלָּם, **ʻÁdullâm,** *ad-ool-lawm´*; probably from the passive participle of the same as 5724; *Adullam,* a place in Palestine:—Adullam.

5726. עֲדֻלָּמִי, **ʻÁdullâmîy,** *ad-ool-law-mee´*; patrial from 5725; an *Adullamite* or native of Adullam:—Adullamite.

5727. עָדַן, **ʻâdan,** *aw-dan´*; a primitive root; to be *soft* or *pleasant*; (figurative and reflexive) to *live voluptuously*:—delight self.

5728. עֲדֶן, **ʻáden,** *ad-en´*; or עֲדֶנָּה, **ʻádennâh,** *ad-en´-naw*; from 5704 and 2004; *till now*:—yet.

5729. עֶדֶן, **ʻEden,** *eh´-den*; from 5727; *pleasure; Eden,* a place in Mesopotamia:—Eden.

5730. עֵדֶן, **ʻêden,** *ay´-den*; or (feminine) עֶדְנָה, **ʻednâh,** *ed-naw´*; from 5727; *pleasure*:—delicate, delight, pleasure. See also 1040.

5731. עֵדֶן, **'Êden,** *ay´-den*; the same as 5730 (masculine); *Eden*, the region of Adam's home:—Eden.

5732. עִדָּן, **'iddân,** *id-dawn´*; (Chaldee); from a root corresponding to that of 5708; a set *time*; (technical) a *year*:—time.

5733. עַדְנָא, **'Adnâ',** *ad-naw´*; from 5727; *pleasure; Adna,* the name of two Israelites:—Adna.

5734. עַדְנָה, **'Adnâh,** *ad-naw´*; from 5727; *pleasure; Adnah,* the name of two Israelites:—Adnah.

5735. עֲדָעָדָה, **'Ad'âdâh,** *ad-aw-daw´*; from 5712; *festival; Adadah,* a place in Palestine:—Adadah.

5736. עָדַף, **'âdaph,** *aw-daf´*; a primitive root; to *be* (causative, *have*) *redundant*:—be more, odd number, be (have) over (and above), overplus, remain.

5737. עָדַר, **'âdar,** *aw-dar´*; a primitive root; to *arrange,* as a battle, a vineyard (to *hoe*); hence to *muster,* and so to *miss* (or find *wanting*):—dig, fail, keep (rank), lack.

5738. עֵדֶר, **'Eder,** *eh´-der*; from 5737; an *arrangement* (i.e. drove); *Eder,* an Israelite:—Ader.

5739. עֵדֶר, **'êder,** *ay´-der*; from 5737; an *arrangement,* i.e. *muster* (of animals):—drove, flock, herd.

5740. עֵדֶר, **'Êder,** *ay´-der*; the same as 5739; *Eder,* the name of an Israelite and of two places in Palestine:—Edar, Eder.

5741. עַדְרִיאֵל, **'Adrîy'êl,** *ad-ree-ale´*; from 5739 and 410; *flock of God; Adriel,* an Israelite:—Adriel.

5742. עֲדָשָׁה, **'ădâshâh,** *ah-daw-shaw´*; from an unused root of uncertain meaning; a *lentil:*—lentile.

5743. עוּב, **'ûwb,** *oob*; a primitive root; to be *dense* or *dark,* i.e. to *becloud:*—cover with a cloud.

5744. עוֹבֵד, **'Ôwbêd,** *o-bade´*; active participle of 5647; *serving; Obed,* the name of five Israelites:—Obed.

5745. עוֹבָל, **'Ôwbâl,** *o-bawl´*; of foreign derivation; *Obal,* a son of Joktan:—Obal.

5746. עוּג, **'ûwg,** *oog*; a primitive root; (properly) to *gyrate*; but used only as denominative from 5692, to *bake* (round cakes on the hearth):—bake.

5747. עוֹג, **'Ôwg,** *ogue*; probably from 5746; *round; Og,* a king of Bashan:—Og.

5748. עוּגָב, **'ûwgâb,** *oo-gawb´*; or עֻגָּב, **'uggâb,** *oog-gawb´*; from 5689 in the original sense of *breathing*; a *reed*-instrument of music:—organ.

5749. עוּד, **'ûwd,** *ood*; a primitive root; to *duplicate* or *repeat*; (by implication) to *protest, testify* (as by reiteration); (intensive) to *encompass, restore* (as a sort of reduplication):—admonish, charge, earnestly, lift up, protest, call (take) to record, relieve, rob, solemnly, stand upright, testify, give warning, (bear, call to, give, take to) witness.

A verb meaning to bear witness, to testify. Specifically, it can signify either to serve as a witness or to testify against someone, albeit falsely (1Ki 21:10, 13); or in favour of someone (Job 29:11). It can also mean either to admonish someone (Ge 43:3; Ne 9:26, 30); or to warn solemnly (Ge 43:3; Ex 19:21; Dt 32:46; 1Sa 8:9; 1Ki 2:42; 2Ch 24:19; Ne 9:29; 13:15, 21; Jer 42:19; Am 3:13). Such warnings frequently came from the Lord (2Ki 17:13, 15; Jer 11:7); but they were also mediated through His prophets (2Ch 24:19; Jer 42:19). In the causative form, it can mean to call to witness, to take as a witness (Dt 4:26; Isa 8:2); or to obtain witnesses, that is, authentication (Jer 32:10, 25, 44).

5750. עוֹד, **'ôwd,** *ode*; or עֹד, **'ôd,** *ode*; from 5749; (properly) *iteration* or *continuance*; used only adverb (with or without preposition), *again, repeatedly, still, more*:—again, × all life long, at all, besides, but, else, further (-more), henceforth, (any) longer, (any) more (-over), × once, since, (be) still, when, (good, the) while (having being), (as, because, whether, while) yet (within).

5751. עוֹד, **'ôwd,** *ode*; (Chaldee); corresponding to 5750:—while.

5752. עוֹדֵד, **'Ôwdêd,** *o-dade´*; or עֹדֵד, **'Ôdêd,** *o-dade´*; from 5749; *reiteration; Oded,* the name of two Israelites:—Oded.

5753. עָוָה, **'âvâh,** *aw-vaw´*; a primitive root; to *crook*, literal or figurative (as follows):—do amiss, bow down, make crooked, commit iniquity, pervert, (do) perverse (-ly), trouble, × turn, do wickedly, do wrong.

A verb meaning to bend, to twist. In its various uses, the word means to do wrong, to commit iniquity (Est 1:16; Da 9:5); or to be physically or emotionally distressed (Isa 21:3). It is used with reference to a person with a disturbed mind (Pr 12:8). In the intensive form, it can mean to distort something, such as the face of the earth (Isa 24:1); or the path that one walks (La 3:9). In its causative form, it refers to perverting right behaviour (Job 33:27; Jer 3:21); or simply doing that which is wrong (2Sa 7:14; 19:19[20]; Jer 9:5[4]); referring to behaviour acknowledged as wrong by the psalmist (Ps 106:6); by David (2Sa 24:17); and by Solomon (1Ki 8:47; 2Ch 6:37).

5754. עַוָּה, **'avvâh,** *av-vaw´*; intensive from 5753 abbreviation; *overthrow:*— × overturn.

5755. עִוָּה, **'Ivvâh,** *iv-vaw´*; or עַוָּא, **'Avvâ',** *av-vaw´*; (2Ki 17:24), for 5754; *Ivvah* or *Avva,* a region of Assyria:—Ava, Ivah.

5756. עוּז, **'ûwz,** *ooz*; a primitive root; to *be strong*; (causative) to *strengthen,* i.e. (figurative) to *save* (by flight):—gather (self, self to flee), retire.

5757. עַוִּי, **'Avviy,** *av-vee´*; patrial from 5755; an *Avvite* or native of Avvah (only plural):—Avims, Avites.

5758. עֲוָיָה, **'ăvâyâh,** *ah-vaw-yaw´*; (Chaldee); from a root corresponding to 5753; *perverseness:*—iniquity.

An Aramaic feminine noun meaning offence, iniquity. Related to a Hebrew word whose root meaning is iniquity or guilt, this Aramaic term is found only once in the OT, in Daniel's interpretation of one of King Nebuchadnezzar's dreams (Da 4:27[24]). In his interpretation, Daniel warned the king that unless he repented of his sins and iniquities and began to act righteously and show mercy, judgment would fall on him.

5759. עֲוִיל, **'ăvîyl,** *av-eel´*; from 5764; a *babe:*— young child, little one.

5760. עֲוִיל, **'ăvîyl,** *av-eel´*; from 5765; *perverse* (moral):—ungodly.

A masculine noun meaning an unjust one, an evil one. Derived from a verb meaning to act wrongfully, this term appears once in the OT, where it has the sense of ungodly or evil people (Job 16:11). Job used the term to describe Bildad, Zophar, and Eliphaz, his accusers, whom he sarcastically referred to as his friends (cf. Job 16:20).

5761. עַוִּים, **'Avviym,** *av-veem´*; plural of 5757; *Avvim* (as inhabited by Avvites), a place in Palestine (with the article prefixed):—Avim.

5762. עַוִּית, **'Ăvîyth,** *av-veeth´*; or [perhaps עֲיוֹת, **'Ayyôwth,** *ah-yoth´*, as if plural of 5857] עֲיוּת, **'Ayûwth,** *ah-yooth´*; from 5753; *ruin; Avvith* (or *Avvoth*), a place in Palestine:—Avith.

5763. עוּל, **'ûwl,** *ool*; a primitive root; to *suckle,* i.e. *give milk:*—milch, (ewe great) with young.

5764. עוּל, **'ûwl,** *ool*; from 5763; a *babe:*—sucking child, infant.

5765. עָוַל, **'âval,** *aw-val´*; a primitive root; to *distort* (moral):—deal unjustly, unrighteous.

A verb meaning to act wrongfully, to act unjustly, to deviate from the moral standard. The word is derived from the noun meaning injustice or iniquity. It occurs in Isa 26:10, where the prophet bemoaned the fact that despite God's showing grace to the wicked, they continued to act wrongfully. The verb occurs as a substantive participle where the psalmist prayed for deliverance from the clutches of the unrighteous (Ps 71:4). See the noun *'âwel* (5766).

5766. עֶוֶל, **'evel,** *eh´-vel*; or עָוֶל, **'âvel,** *aw´-vel*; and (feminine) עַוְלָה, **'avlâh,** *av-law´*; or עוֹלָה, **'ôwlâh,** *o-law´*; or עֹלָה, **'ôlâh,** *o-law´*; from 5765; (moral) *evil:*—iniquity, perverseness, unjust (-ly), unrighteousness (-ly), wicked (-ness).

A masculine singular noun meaning injustice, unrighteousness. The word refers to anything that deviates from the right way of doing things. It is often the direct object of *'âśâh* (6213), meaning to do (Le 19:15; Dt 25:16; Ps 7:3[4]; Eze 3:20; 33:13); and is in direct contrast to words like righteous (Pr 29:27); upright (Ps 107:42); and justice (Dt 32:4). God has no part with injustice (Dt 32:4; 2Ch 19:7; Job 34:10; Jer 2:5). See the verb *'âwal* (5765).

5767. עַוָּל, **'avvâl,** *av-vawl´*; intensive from 5765; *evil* (moral):—unjust, unrighteous, wicked.

A masculine singular noun meaning an unjust person, an unrighteous person. This word occurs five times in the Hebrew Bible with four of them occurring in the Book of Job. Job said that an *'awwâl* deserved God's punishment (Job 31:3). But he countered the implications of his friends by stating adamantly that he was not such a person (Job 29:17). Likewise, Zephaniah argued that God is righteous and not an *'awwâl,* contrary to the corrupted leaders of Jerusalem (Zep 3:5).

5768. עוֹלֵל, **'ôwlêl,** *o-lale´*; or עֹלֵל, **'ôlâl,** *o-lawl´*; from 5763; a *suckling:*—babe, (young) child, infant, little one.

5769. עוֹלָם, **'ôwlâm,** *o-lawm´*; or עֹלָם, **'ôlâm,** *o-lawm´*; from 5956; (properly) *concealed,* i.e. the *vanishing* point; (generally) time *out of mind* (past or future), i.e. (practical) *eternity;* frequent adverb (especially with prepositional prefix) *always:*—alway (-s), ancient (time), any more, continuance, eternal, (for, [n-]) ever (-lasting, -more, of old), lasting, long (time), (of) old (time), perpetual, at any time, (beginning of the) world (+ without end). Compare 5331, 5703.

A masculine noun meaning a very long time. The word usually refers to looking forward but many times expresses the idea of looking backward. It may cover a given person's lifetime (Ex 21:6; 1Sa 1:22); a period of many generations (Jos 24:2; Pr 22:28); the time of the present created order (Dt 33:15; Ps 73:12); time beyond this temporal sphere, especially when used regarding God (Ge 21:33; Ps 90:2; Da 12:2, 7). The term also applies to many things associated with God, such as His decrees, His covenants, and the Messiah (Ge 9:16; Ex 12:14; Mic 5:2[1]). This word describes the span of time in which God is to be obeyed and praised (1Ch 16:36; Ps 89:1[2]; 119:112). In the age to come, there will be no need for sun or moon, for God Himself will be the everlasting light (Isa 60:19, 20; cf. Rev 22:5).

5770. עֲוַן, **'âvan,** *aw-van´*; denominative from 5869; to *watch* (with jealousy):—eye.

5771. עָוֹן, **'âvôwn,** *aw-vone´*; or עָווֹן, **'âvôwn,** *aw-vone´*; (2Ki 7:9; Ps 51:5 [77]), from 5753; *perversity,* i.e. (moral) *evil:*—fault, iniquity, mischief, punishment (of iniquity), sin.

A masculine noun meaning iniquity, evil, guilt, punishment. This is one of the four main words indicating sin in the OT. This word indicates sin that is particularly evil, since it strongly conveys the idea of twisting or perverting deliberately. The noun carries along with it the idea of guilt from conscious wrongdoing (Ge 44:16; Jer 2:22). The punishment that goes with this deliberate act as a consequence is indicated by the word also (Ge 4:13; Isa 53:11).

The Hebrew word means sin or transgression in a conscious sense, as when David kept (consciously) from transgression or sin (2Sa 22:24); Israel by choice returned to the sins their ancestors had committed (Jer 11:10; 13:22).

This word for sin can also indicate the guilt that results from the act of sin: Moses prayed that the Lord would forgive the guilt and sin of rebellious Israel (Nu 14:19); the guilt of the Amorites was not yet full in the time of Abraham (Ge 15:16); God would remove the guilt of His people when they returned from exile (Jer 50:20); the guilt of the fathers was a recurring phrase in the OT (Ex 20:5; 34:7).

The word also indicates in some contexts the punishment that results from sin and guilt; Cain's punishment was unbearable for him (Ge 4:13; Jer 51:6). Edom was condemned for not helping Israel in the time of Israel's punishment (Eze 35:5); and the Levites had to bear their punishment because they strayed from following the Lord (Ps 31:10[11]; Eze 44:10, 12).

5772. עוֹנָה, **'ôwnâh,** *o-naw´*; from an unused root apparently meaning to *dwell* together; (sexual) *cohabitation:*—duty of marriage.

5773. עְוְעִים, **'iv'îym,** *iv-eem´*; from 5753; *perversity:*— × perverse.

5774. עוּף, **'ûwph,** *oof*; a primitive root; to *cover* (with wings or obscurity); hence (as denominative from 5775) to *fly;* also (by implication of dimness) to *faint* (from the darkness of swooning):—brandish, be (wax) faint, flee away, fly (away), × set, shine forth, weary.

5775. עוֹף, **'ôwph,** *ofe*; from 5774; a *bird* (as *covered* with feathers, or rather as *covering* with wings), often collective:—bird, that flieth, flying, fowl.

5776. עוֹף, **'ôwph,** *ofe*; (Chaldee); corresponding to 5775:—fowl.

5777. עוֹפֶרֶת, **'ôwphereth,** *o-feh´-reth*; or עֹפֶרֶת, **'ôphereth,** *o-feh´-reth*; feminine participle active of 6080; *lead* (from its *dusty* colour):—lead.

5778. עֵיפָי, **'Êyphay,** *ay-fah´-ee*; from 5775; *bird-like*; *Ephai*, an Israelite:—Ephai [*from margin*].

5779. עוּץ, **'ûwts,** *oots*; a primitive root; to *consult*:—take advice ([counsel] together).

5780. עוּץ, **'Ûwts,** *oots*; apparently from 5779; *consultation*; *Uts*, a son of Aram, also a Seirite, and the regions settled by them:—Uz.

5781. עוּק, **'ûwq,** *ook*; a primitive root; to *pack*:—be pressed.

5782. עוּר, **'ûwr,** *oor*; a primitive root [rather identical with 5783 through the idea of *opening* the eyes]; to *wake* (literal or figurative):—(a-) wake (-n, up), lift up (self), × master, raise (up), stir up (self).

5783. עוּר, **'ûwr,** *oor*; a primitive root; to (*be*) *bare*:—be made naked.

5784. עוּר, **'ûwr,** *oor*; (Chaldee); *chaff* (as the *naked* husk):—chaff.

5785. עוֹר, **'ôwr,** *ore*; from 5783; *skin* (as *naked*); (by implication) *hide, leather*:—hide, leather, skin.

A masculine singular noun meaning skin. It is used literally of human skin, such as Moses' shining face (Ex 34:29); or in connection with regulations regarding leprosy or skin diseases (Le 13:2). It is employed figuratively in the expression, skin of my teeth (Job 19:20). It can also denote skins of animals, typically already skinned (with the exception of Job 41:7 [40:31]). Skins were used for the garments that God made for Adam and Eve (Ge 3:21); and for coverings of items like the tabernacle (Ex 25:5); and the ark (Nu 4:6).

5786. עָוַר, **'âvar,** *aw-var´*; a primitive root [rather denominative from 5785 through the idea of a *film* over the eyes]; to *blind*:—blind, put out. See also 5895.

5787. עִוֵּר, **'ivvêr,** *iv-vare´*; intensive from 5786; *blind* (literal or figurative):—blind (men, people).

5788. עִוָּרוֹן, **'ivvârôwn,** *iv-vaw-rone´*; and (feminine) עַוֶּרֶת, **'avvereth,** *av-veh´-reth*; from 5787; *blindness*:—blind (-ness).

5789. עוּשׁ, **'ûwsh,** *oosh*; a primitive root; to *hasten*:—assemble self.

A verb which occurs once in the Hebrew Bible (Joel 3:11 [4:11]). Recent translations have abandoned the former translation, to lend aid, to come to help, for a different Arabic cognate, meaning to hurry. Joel used the word with the verb to come to summon all the nations to prepare for battle in the Valley of Jehoshaphat. At that location, God will judge them, trampling them like grapes in a winepress.

5790. עוּת, **'ûwth,** *ooth*; for 5789; to *hasten*, i.e. *succor*:—speak in season.

A verb which occurs once in the Hebrew Bible (Isa 50:4). It is traditionally translated to help but the meaning is uncertain. In this context, Isaiah proclaimed that the Lord gave him a tongue to help the weary.

5791. עָוַת, **'âvath,** *aw-vath´*; a primitive root; to *wrest*:—bow self, (make) crooked, falsifying, overthrow, deal perversely, pervert, subvert, turn upside down.

A verb meaning to be bent, to be crooked. It is always used in the intensive stems with the meaning to bend, to subvert, or to pervert. Except for Ecc 12:3, where it refers to the strong men bending themselves (that is, bowing down), it is used figuratively of bending or perverting justice and righteousness. Bildad and Elihu told Job that God does not pervert justice (Job 8:3; 34:12); but Job thought God had been crooked with him (Job 19:6).

5792. עַוְּתָה, **'avvâthâh,** *av-vaw-thaw´*; from 5791; *oppression*:—wrong.

A feminine singular noun meaning a subversion, a perversion. It is used only in La 3:59 where the poet declared that God had seen the perversion of justice done to Jerusalem (that is, its destruction). This passage is interesting because the writer saw God's judgment as severe. See the verb *'âwath* (5791).

5793. עוּתַי, **'Ûwthay,** *oo-thah´-ee*; from 5790; *succoring*; *Uthai*, the name of two Israelites:—Uthai.

5794. עַז, **ʻaz,** *az;* from 5810; *strong, vehement, harsh:*—fierce, + greedy, mighty, power, roughly, strong.

5795. עֵז, **ʻêz,** *aze;* from 5810; a she-*goat* (as *strong*), but masculine in plural (which also is used elliptically for *goats' hair*):—(she) goat, kid.

5796. עֵז, **ʻêz,** *aze;* (Chaldee); corresponding to 5795:—goat.

5797. עֹז, **ʻôz,** *oze;* or (fully) עוֹז, **ʻôwz,** *oze;* from 5810; *strength* in various applications (*force, security, majesty, praise*):—boldness, loud, might, power, strength, strong.

5798. עֻזָּא, **ʻUzzâ',** *ooz-zaw´;* or עֻזָּה, **ʻUzzâh,** *ooz-zaw´;* feminine of 5797; *strength; Uzza* or *Uzzah,* the name of five Israelites:—Uzza, Uzzah.

5799. עֲזָאזֵל, **ʻázâ'zêl,** *az-aw-zale´;* from 5795 and 235; *goat of departure;* the *scapegoat:*—scapegoat.

5800. עָזַב, **ʻâzab,** *aw-zab´;* a primitive root; to *loosen,* i.e. *relinquish, permit,* etc.:—commit self, fail, forsake, fortify, help, leave (destitute, off), refuse, × surely.

A verb derived from two separate roots. The more common in the Hebrew Bible is *ʻâzab* I, meaning to leave, to abandon, to forsake, to loose. It can be used to designate going away to a new locale (2Ki 8:6); or to separate oneself from another person (Ge 44:22; Ru 1:16). When Zipporah's father found her without Moses, he asked, "Why did you leave him?" (Ex 2:20). A man is to leave his parents to marry (Ge 2:24). To leave in the hand of is an idiomatic expression meaning to entrust (Ge 39:6). The word can also carry a much more negative connotation. Israelites abandoned their towns after the army fled (1Sa 31:7); the ultimate sign of defeat (and often God's judgment) were abandoned cities (Isa 17:9; Jer 4:29; Zep 2:4). The Israelites often were warned and accused of forsaking God by sacrificing to other gods (Dt 28:20; Jgs 10:10; Jer 1:16). The prophets called on them to forsake idols and sin instead (Isa 55:7; Eze 20:8; 23:8). While the psalmist said that God would not abandon his soul (Ps 16:10), God does on occasion abandon humans because of their sin (Dt 31:17; Eze 8:12). But despite the psalmist's

cry which Jesus quoted from the cross (Ps 22:1[2]), most Biblical writers took heart because God would not abandon them (Ezr 9:9; Isa 42:16).The word *ʻâzab* can also mean to restore or repair. It occurs only in Ne 3:8 in reference to the walls of Jerusalem.

5801. עִזָּבוֹן, **ʻizzâbôwn,** *iz-zaw-bone´;* from 5800 in the sense of *letting go* (for a price, i.e. *selling*); *trade,* i.e. the place (*mart*) or the payment (*revenue*):—fair, ware.

5802. עַזְבּוּק, **ʻAzbûwq,** *az-book´;* from 5794 and the root of 950; *stern depopulator; Azbuk,* an Israelite:—Azbuk.

5803. עַזְגָּד, **ʻAzgâd,** *az-gawd´;* from 5794 and 1409; *stern troop; Azgad,* an Israelite:—Azgad.

5804. עַזָּה, **ʻAzzâh,** *az-zaw´;* feminine of 5794; *strong; Azzah,* a place in Palestine:—Azzah, Gaza.

5805. עֲזוּבָה, **ʻăzûwbâh,** *az-oo-baw´;* feminine passive participle of 5800; *desertion* (of inhabitants):—forsaking.

5806. עֲזוּבָה, **ʻĂzûwbâh,** *az-oo-baw´;* the same as 5805; *Azubah,* the name of two Israelitesses:—Azubah.

5807. עֱזוּז, **ʻĕzûwz,** *ez-ooz´;* from 5810; *forcibleness:*—might, strength.

5808. עִזּוּז, **ʻizzûwz,** *iz-zooz´;* from 5810; *forcible;* (collective and concrete) an *army:*—power, strong.

5809. עַזּוּר, **ʻAzzûwr,** *az-zoor´;* or עַזֻּר, **ʻAzzur,** *az-zoor´;* from 5826; *helpful; Azur,* the name of three Israelites:—Azur, Azzur.

5810. עָזַז, **ʻâzaz,** *aw-zaz´;* a primitive root; to *be stout* (literal or figurative):—harden, impudent, prevail, strengthen (self), be strong.

5811. עָזָז, **ʻÂzâz,** *aw-zawz´;* from 5810; *strong; Azaz,* an Israelite:—Azaz.

5812. עֲזַזְיָהוּ, **ʻĂzazyâhûw,** *az-az-yaw´-hoo;* from 5810 and 3050; *Jah has strengthened; Azaziah,* the name of three Israelites:—Azaziah.

5813. עֻזִּי, **ʻUzzîy,** *ooz-zee´;* from 5810; *forceful; Uzzi,* the name of six Israelites:—Uzzi.

5814. עֻזִּיָּה, **'Uzzîyyâh,** *ooz-zee-yaw´*; or עֻזִּיָּא, **'Uzîyyâ',** *oo-zee-yaw´*; perhaps for 5818; *Uzzija,* an Israelite:—Uzzia.

5815. עֲזִיאֵל, **'Ăzîy'êl,** *az-ee-ale´*; from 5756 and 410; *strengthened of God; Aziël,* an Israelite:—Aziel. Compare 3268.

5816. עֻזִּיאֵל, **'Uzzîy'êl,** *ooz-zee-ale´*; from 5797 and 410; *strength of God; Uzziël,* the name of six Israelites:—Uzziel.

5817. עֻזִּיאֵלִי, **'Ozzîy'êlîy,** *oz-zee-ay-lee´*; patronymic from 5816; an *Uzziëlite* (collective) or descendants of Uzziel:—Uzzielites.

5818. עֻזִּיָּה, **'Uzzîyyâh,** *ooz-zee-yaw´*; or עֻזִּיָּהוּ, **'Uz-zîyyâhûw,** *ooz-zee-yaw´-hoo*; from 5797 and 3050; *strength of Jah; Uzzijah,* the name of five Israelites:—Uzziah.

5819. עֲזִיזָא, **'Ăzîyzâ',** *az-ee-zaw´*; from 5756; *strengthfulness; Aziza,* an Israelite:—Aziza.

5820. עַזְמָוֶת, **'Azmâveth,** *az-maw´-veth*; from 5794 and 4194; *strong* one *of death; Azmaveth,* the name of three Israelites and of a place in Palestine:—Azmaveth. See also 1041.

5821. עַזָּן, **'Azzân,** *az-zawn´*; from 5794; *strong* one; *Azzan,* an Israelite:—Azzan.

5822. עָזְנִיָּה, **'oznîyyâh,** *oz-nee-yaw´*; probably feminine of 5797; probably the *sea-eagle* (from its *strength*):—ospray.

5823. עָזַק, **'âzaq,** *aw-zak´*; a primitive root; to *grub* over:—fence about.

5824. עִזְקָא, **'izqâ',** *iz-kaw´*; (Chaldee); from a root corresponding to 5823; a *signet*-ring (as engraved):—signet.

5825. עֲזֵקָה, **'Ăzêqâh,** *az-ay-kaw´*; from 5823; *tilled; Azekah,* a place in Palestine:—Azekah.

5826. עָזַר, **'âzar,** *aw-zar´*; a primitive root; to *surround,* i.e. *protect* or *aid:*—help, succour.

5827. עֶזֶר, **'Ezer,** *eh´-zer*; from 5826; *help; Ezer,* the name of two Israelites:—Ezer. Compare 5829.

5828. עֵזֶר, **'êzer,** *ay´-zer*; from 5826; *aid:*—help.

5829. עֵזֶר, **'Êzer,** *ay´-zer*; the same as 5828; *Ezer,* the name of four Israelites:—Ezer. Compare 5827.

5830. עֶזְרָא, **'Ezrâ',** *ez-raw´*; a variation of 5833; *Ezra,* an Israelite:—Ezra.

5831. עֶזְרָא, **'Ezrâ',** *ez-raw´*; (Chaldee); corresponding to 5830; *Ezra,* an Israelite:—Ezra.

5832. עֲזַרְאֵל, **'Ăzar'êl,** *az-ar-ale´*; from 5826 and 410; *God has helped; Azarel,* the name of five Israelites:—Azarael, Azareel.

5833. עֶזְרָה, **'ezrâh,** *ez-raw´*; or עֶזְרָת, **'ezrâth,** *ez-rawth´*; (Ps 60:11 [13]; 108:12 [133]), feminine of 5828; *aid:*—help (-ed, -er).

5834. עֶזְרָה, **'Ezrâh,** *ez-raw´*; the same as 5833; *Ezrah,* an Israelite:—Ezrah.

5835. עֲזָרָה, **'ăzârâh,** *az-aw-raw´*; from 5826 in its original meaning of *surrounding*; an *inclosure*; also a *border:*—court, settle.

5836. עֶזְרִי, **'Ezrîy,** *ez-ree´*; from 5828; *helpful; Ezri,* an Israelite:—Ezri.

5837. עַזְרִיאֵל, **'Azrîy'êl,** *az-ree-ale´*; from 5828 and 410; *help of God; Azriël,* the name of three Israelites:—Azriel.

5838. עֲזַרְיָה, **'Ăzaryâh,** *az-ar-yaw´*; or עֲזַרְיָהוּ, **'Ăzar-yâhûw,** *az-ar-yaw´-hoo*; from 5826 and 3050; *Jah has helped; Azarjah,* the name of nineteen Israelites:—Azariah.

5839. עֲזַרְיָה, **'Ăzaryâh,** *az-ar-yaw´*; (Chaldee); corresponding to 5838; *Azarjah,* one of Daniel's companions:—Azariah.

5840. עֲזְרִיקָם, **'Azrîyqâm,** *az-ree-kawm´*; from 5828 and active participle of 6965; *help of an enemy; Azrikam,* the name of four Israelites:—Azrikam.

5841. עַזָּתִי, **'Azzâthîy,** *az-zaw-thee´*; patrial from 5804; an *Azzathite* or inhabitant of Azzah:—Gazathite, Gazite.

5842. עֵט, **'êt,** *ate*; from 5860 (contraction) in the sense of *swooping,* i.e. *side-long stroke*; a *stylus* or marking stick:—pen.

5843. עֵטָה, **'êțâh,** *ay-taw´*; (Chaldee); from 3272; *prudence:*—counsel.

5844. עָטָה, **'âțâh,** *aw-taw´*; a primitive root; to *wrap,* i.e. *cover, veil, clothe* or *roll:*—array self, be clad, (put a) cover (-ing, self), fill, put on, × surely, turn aside.

5845. עָטִין, **'ăṭîyn,** *at-een´*; from an unused root meaning apparently to *contain*; a *receptacle* (for milk, i.e. *pail*; [figurative] *breast*):—breast.

5846. עֲטִישָׁה, **'ăṭîyshâh,** *at-ee-shaw´*; from an unused root meaning to *sneeze; sneezing*:—sneezing.

5847. עֲטַלֵּף, **'ăṭallêph,** *at-al-lafe´*; of uncertain derivation; a *bat*:—bat.

5848. עָטַף, **'âṭaph,** *aw-taf´*; a primitive root; to *shroud*, i.e. *clothe* (whether transitive or reflexive); hence (from the idea of *darkness*) to *languish*:—cover (over), fail, faint, feebler, hide self, be overwhelmed, swoon.

5849. עָטַר, **'âṭar,** *aw-tar´*; a primitive root; to *encircle* (for attack or protection); especially to *crown* (literal or figurative):—compass, crown.

5850. עֲטָרָה, **'ăṭârâh,** *at-aw-raw´*; from 5849; a *crown*:—crown.

5851. עֲטָרָה, **'Ăṭârâh,** *at-aw-raw´*; the same as 5850; *Atarah*, an Israelitess:—Atarah.

5852. עֲטָרוֹת, **'Ăṭârôwth,** *at-aw-rōth´*; or עֲטָרֹת, **'Ăṭârôth,** *at-aw-rōth´*; plural of 5850; *Ataroth*, the name (thus simply) of two places in Palestine:—Ataroth.

5853. עֲטְרוֹת אַדָּר, **'Ăṭrôwth 'Addâr,** *at-rōth´ ad-dawr´*; from the same as 5852 and 146; *crowns of Addar; Atroth-Addar*, a place in Palestine:—Ataroth-adar (-addar).

5854. עֲטְרוֹת בֵּית יוֹאָב, **'Ăṭrôth bêyth Yôw'âb,** *at-rōth´ bayth yo-awb´*; from the same as 5852 and 1004 and 3097; *crowns of* the *house of Joäb; Atroth-beth-Joäb*, a place in Palestine:—Ataroth the house of Joab.

5855. עֲטְרוֹת שׁוֹפָן, **'Ăṭrôwth Shôwphân,** *at-rōth´ sho-fawn´*; from the same as 5852 and a name otherwise unused [being from the same as 8226] meaning *hidden; crowns of Shophan; Atroth-Shophan*, a place in Palestine:—Atroth, Shophan [*as if two places*].

5856. עִי, **'îy,** *ee*; from 5753; a *ruin* (as if overturned):—heap.

5857. עַי, **'Ay,** *ah´ee*; or (feminine) עַיָּא, **'Ayyâ',** *ah-yaw´*; (Ne 11:31), or עַיָּת, **'Ayyâth,** *ah-yawth´*; (Isa 10:28), for 5856; *Ai, Aja* or *Ajath*, a place in Palestine:—Ai, Aija, Aijath, Hai.

5858. עֵיבָל, **'Êybâl,** *ay-bawl´*; perhaps from an unused root probably meaning to be *bald; bare; Ebal*, a mountain of Palestine:—Ebal.

5859. עִיּוֹן, **'Iyyôwn,** *ee-yone´*; from 5856; *ruin; Ijon*, a place in Palestine:—Ijon.

5860. עִיט, **'îyṭ,** *eet*; a primitive root; to *swoop down upon* (literal or figurative):—fly, rail.

5861. עַיִט, **'ayiṭ,** *ah´-yit*; from 5860; a *hawk* or other bird of prey:—bird, fowl, ravenous (bird).

5862. עֵיטָם, **'Êyṭâm,** *ay-tawm´*; from 5861; *hawk-ground; Etam*, a place in Palestine:—Etam.

5863. עִיֵּי הָעֲבָרִים, **'Iyyêy hâ'Ăbârîym,** *ee-yay´ haw-ab-aw-reem´*; from the plural of 5856 and the plural of the active participle of 5674 with the article interposed; *ruins of the passers; Ije-ha-Abarim*, a place near Palestine:—Ije-abarim.

5864. עִיִּים, **'Iyyîym,** *ee-yeem´*; plural of 5856; *ruins; Ijim*, a place in the Desert:—Iim.

5865. עֵילוֹם, **'êylôwm,** *ay-lome´*; for 5769:—ever.

5866. עִילַי, **'Îylay,** *ee-lah´ee*; from 5927; *elevated; Ilai*, an Israelite:—Ilai.

5867. עֵילָם, **'Êylâm,** *ay-lawm´*; or עוֹלָם, **'Ôwlâm,** *o-lawm´*; (Ezr 10:2; Jer 49:36), probably from 5956; *hidden*, i.e. *distant; Elam*, a son of Shem, and his descendant, with their country; also of six Israelites:—Elam.

5868. עֲיָם, **'ăyâm,** *ah-yawm´*; of doubtful origin and authenticity; probably meaning *strength*:—mighty.

5869. עַיִן, **'ayin,** *ah´-yin*; probably a primitive word; an *eye* (literal or figurative); (by analogy) a *fountain* (as the *eye* of the landscape):—affliction, outward appearance, + before, + think best, colour, conceit, + be content, countenance, + displease, eye ([brow], [-d], -sight), face, + favour, fountain, furrow [*from the margin*], × him, + humble, knowledge, look, (+ well), × me, open (-ly), + (not) please, presence, + regard, resemblance, sight, × thee, × them, + think, × us, well, × you (-rselves).

A feminine noun meaning an eye, a spring, a fountain. This Hebrew word is used to refer to either an aperture or a source. It is used to signify the physical organ of sight (Pr 20:12); the providential oversight of the Lord (Ps 33:18); and a water well (Ge 16:7; Ex 15:27). By extension, it refers to being in the presence of another (Jer 32:12); the visible surface of the earth (Nu 22:5); the human face (1Ki 20:38; 2Ki 9:30); and the general appearance of something (1Sa 16:7; Eze 1:4). In a figurative sense, the eye was seen as the avenue of temptation (Job 31:7); the scope of personal judgment or opinion (Jgs 17:6); and the source of self-assessment (Pr 26:5).

5870. עַיִן, **'ayin,** *ah´-yin;* (Chaldee); corresponding to 5869; an *eye:*—eye.

5871. עַיִן, **'Ayin,** *ah´-yin;* the same as 5869; *fountain; Ajin,* the name (thus simply) of two places in Palestine:—Ain.

5872. עֵין גֶּדִי, **'Êyn Gedîy,** *ane geh´-dee;* from 5869 and 1423; *fountain of a kid; En-Gedi,* a place in Palestine:—En-gedi.

5873. עֵין גַּנִּים, **'Êyn Gannîym,** *ane gan-neem´;* from 5869 and the plural of 1588; *fountain of gardens; En-Gannim,* a place in Palestine:—En-gannim.

5874. עֵין־דֹּאר, **'Êyn-D'ôr,** *ane-dore´;* or עֵין דּוֹר **'Êyn Dôwr,** *ane dore;* or עֵין־דֹּר, **'Êyn-Dôr,** *ane-dore´;* from 5869 and 1755; *fountain of dwelling; En-Dor,* a place in Palestine:—En-dor.

5875. עֵין הַקּוֹרֵא, **'Êyn haqQôwrê',** *ane hak-ko-ray´;* from 5869 and the active participle of 7121; *fountain of One calling; En-hak-Korè,* a place near Palestine:—En-hakkore.

5876. עֵין חַדָּה, **'Êyn Chaddâh,** *ane khad-daw´;* from 5869 and the feminine of a derivative from 2300; *fountain of sharpness; En-Chaddah,* a place in Palestine:—En-haddah.

5877. עֵין חָצוֹר, **'Êyn Châtsôwr,** *ane khaw-tsore´;* from 5869 and the same as 2674; *fountain of a village; En-Chatsor,* a place in Palestine:—En-hazor.

5878. עֵין חֲרֹד, **'Êyn Chărôd,** *ane khar-ode´;* from 5869 and a derivative of 2729; *fountain of trembling; En-Charod,* a place in Palestine:—well of Harod.

5879. עֵינָיִם, **'Êynayim,** *ay-nah´-yim;* or עֵינָם, **'Êynâm,** *ay-nawm´;* dual of 5869 *double foun-*

tain; *Enajim* or *Enam,* a place in Palestine:—Enaim, openly (Ge 38:21).

5880. עֵין מִשְׁפָּט, **'Êyn Mishpât,** *ayn mish-pawt´;* from 5869 and 4941; *fountain of judgment; En-Mishpat,* a place near Palestine:—Enmishpat.

5881. עֵינָן, **'Êynân,** *ay-nawn´;* from 5869; *having eyes; Enan,* an Israelite:—Enan. Compare 2704.

5882. עֵין עֶגְלַיִם, **'Êyn 'Eglayim,** *ayn eg-lah´-yim;* from 5869 and the dual of 5695; *fountain of two calves; En-Eglajim,* a place in Palestine:—En-eglaim.

5883. עֵין רֹגֵל, **'Êyn Rôgêl,** *ayn ro-gale´;* from 5869 and the active participle of 7270; *fountain of a traveller; En-Rogel,* a place near Jerusalem:—En-rogel.

5884. עֵין רִמּוֹן, **'Êyn Rimmôwn,** *ayn rim-mone´;* from 5869 and 7416; *fountain of a pomegranate; En-Rimmon,* a place in Palestine:—En-rimmon.

5885. עֵין שֶׁמֶשׁ, **'Êyn Shemesh,** *ayn sheh´-mesh;* from 5869 and 8121; *fountain of the sun; En-Shemesh,* a place in Palestine:—En-shemesh.

5886. עֵין הַתַּנִּים, **'Êyn hattannîym,** *ayn hat-tan-neem´;* from 5869 and the plural of 8565; *fountain of jackals; En-Tannim,* a pool near Jerusalem:—dragon well.

5887. עֵין תַּפּוּחַ, **'Êyn Tappûwach,** *ayn tappoo´-akh;* from 5869 and 8598; *fountain of an apple-*tree; *En-Tappuäch,* a place in Palestine:—En-tappuah.

5888. עָיֵף, **'âyêph,** *aw-yafe´;* a primitive root; to *languish:*—be wearied.

5889. עָיֵף, **'âyêph,** *aw-yafe´;* from 5888; *languid:*—faint, thirsty, weary.

5890. עֵיפָה, **'êyphâh,** *ay-faw´;* feminine from 5774; *obscurity* (as if from *covering*):—darkness.

A feminine noun meaning darkness. This word appears only twice in the OT in Job 10:22 and Am 4:13. In both instances, the word implies the darkness of night as opposed to the light of day. In Job, the word is used in parallel to the word *'ôphel* (652), meaning spiritual gloom or despair.

5891. עֵיפָה, **'Êyphâh,** *ay-faw´*; the same as 5890; *Ephah*, the name of a son of Midian, and of the region settled by him; also of an Israelite and of an Israelitess:—Ephah.

5892. עִיר, **'îyr,** *eer*; or (in the plural) עָר, **'âr,** *awr*; or עָיַר, **'âyar,** *aw-yar´*; (Jgs 10:4), from 5782 a *city* (a place guarded by *waking* or a *watch*) in the widest sense (even of a mere *encampment* or *post*):—Ai [*from margin*], city, court [*from margin*], town.

5893. עִיר, **'Îyr,** *eer*; the same as 5892; *Ir*, an Israelite:—Ir.

5894. עִיר, **'îyr,** *eer*; (Chaldee); from a root corresponding to 5782; a *watcher*, i.e. an *angel* (as guardian):—watcher.

5895. עַיִר, **'ayir,** *ah´-yeer*; from 5782 in the sense of *raising* (i.e. *bearing* a burden); (properly) a young *ass* (as just broken to a load); hence an ass-*colt*:—(ass) colt, foal, young ass.

5896. עִירָא, **'Îyrâ',** *ee-raw´*; from 5782; *wakefulness; Ira*, the name of three Israelites:—Ira.

5897. עִירָד, **'Îyrâd,** *ee-rawd´*; from the same as 6166; *fugitive; Irad*, an antediluvian:—Irad.

5898. עִיר הַמֶּלַח, **'Îyr hamMelach,** *eer hammeh´-lakh*; from 5892 and 4417 with the article of substance interpretation; *city of (the) salt; Ir-ham-Melach*, a place near Palestine:—the city of salt.

5899. עִיר הַתְּמָרִים, **'Îyr hatTᵉmârîym,** *err hattem-aw-reem´*; from 5892 and the plural of 8558 with the article interposed; *city of the palmtrees; Ir-hat-Temarim*, a place in Palestine:—the city of palmtrees.

5900. עִירוּ, **'Îyrûw,** *ee-roo´*; from 5892; a *citizen; Iru*, an Israelite:—Iru.

5901. עִירִי, **'Îyrîy,** *ee-ree´*; from 5892; *urbane; Iri*, an Israelite:—Iri.

5902. עִירָם, **'Îyrâm,** *ee-rawm´*; from 5892; *citywise; Iram*, an Idumæan:—Iram.

5903. עֵירֹם, **'êyrôm,** *ay-rome´*; or עֵרֹם, **'êrôm,** *ay-rome´*; from 6191; *nudity*:—naked (-ness).

5904. עִיר נָחָשׁ, **'Îyr Nâchâsh,** *eer naw-khawsh´*; from 5892 and 5175; *city of a serpent; Ir-Nachash*, a place in Palestine:—Ir-nahash.

5905. עִיר שֶׁמֶשׁ, **'Îyr Shemesh,** *err sheh´-mesh*; from 5892 and 8121; *city of the sun; Ir-Shemesh*, a place in Palestine:—Ir-shemesh.

5906. עַיִשׁ, **'Ayish,** *ah´-yish*; or עָשׁ, **'Âsh,** *awsh*; from 5789; the constellation of the Great *Bear* (perhaps from its *migration* through the heavens):—Arcturus.

5907. עַכְבּוֹר, **'Akbôwr,** *ak-bore´*; probably for 5909; *Akbor*, the name of an Idumæan and two Israelites:—Achbor.

5908. עַכָּבִישׁ, **'akkâbîysh,** *ak-kaw-beesh´*; probably from an unused root in the literal sense of *entangling*; a *spider* (as *weaving* a network):—spider.

5909. עַכְבָּר, **'akbâr,** *ak-bawr´*; probably from the same as 5908 in the secondary sense of *attacking*; a *mouse* (as *nibbling*):—mouse.

5910. עַכּוֹ, **'Akkôw,** *ak-ko´*; apparently from an unused root meaning to *hem* in; *Akko* (from its situation on a *bay*):—Accho.

5911. עָכוֹר, **'Âkôwr,** *aw-kore´*; from 5916; *troubled; Akor*, the name of a place in Palestine:—Achor.

5912. עָכָן, **'Âkân,** *aw-kawn´*; from an unused root meaning to *trouble; troublesome; Akan*, an Israelite:—Achan. Compare 5917.

5913. עָכַס, **'âkas,** *aw-kas´*; a primitive root; (properly) to *tie*, specifically with fetters; but used only as denominative from 5914; to *put on anklets*:—make a tinkling ornament.

5914. עֶכֶס, **'ekes,** *eh´-kes*; from 5913; a *fetter*; hence an *anklet*:—stocks, tinkling ornament.

5915. עַכְסָה, **'Aksâh,** *ak-saw´*; feminine of 5914; *anklet; Aksah*, an Israelitess:—Achsah.

5916. עָכַר, **'âkar,** *aw-kar´*; a primitive root; (properly) to *roil* water; (figurative) to *disturb* or *afflict*:—trouble, stir.

5917. עָכָר, **'Âkâr,** *aw-kawr´*; from 5916; *troublesome; Akar*, an Israelite:—Achar. Compare 5912.

5918. עָכְרָן, **'Okrân,** *ok-rawn´*; from 5916; *muddler; Okran*, an Israelite:—Ocran.

5919. עָכְשׁוּב, **'akshûwb,** *ak-shoob´*; probably from an unused root meaning to *coil*; an *asp* (from lurking *coiled* up):—adder.

5920. עַל, **'al,** *al*; from 5927; (properly) the *top*; (specifically) the *Highest* (i.e. *God*); also (adverb) *aloft, to Jehovah*:—above, high, most High.

5921. עַל, **'al,** *al*; properly the same as 5920 used as a preposition (in the singular or plural, often with prefix, or as conjunction with a particle following); *above, over, upon,* or *against* (yet always in this last relation with a downward aspect) in a great variety of applications (as follow):— above, according to (-ly), after, (as) against, among, and, × as, at, because of, beside (the rest of), between, beyond the time, × both and, by (reason of), × had the charge of, concerning for, in (that), (forth, out) of, (from) (off), (up-) on, over, than, through (-out), to touching, × with.

5922. עַל, **'al,** *al*; (Chaldee); corresponding to 5921:—about, against, concerning, for, [there-] fore, from, in, × more, of, (there-, up-) on, (in-) to, + why, with.

5923. עֹל, **'ôl,** *ole*; or עוֹל, **'ôwl,** *ole*; from 5953; a *yoke* (as *imposed* on the neck), literal or figurative:—yoke.

5924. עֵלָּא, **'êllâ',** *ale-law´*; (Chaldee); from 5922; *above*:—over.

5925. עֻלָּא, **'Ullâ',** *ool-law´*; feminine of 5923; *burden; Ulla,* an Israelite:—Ulla.

5926. עִלֵּג, **'illêg,** *il-layg´*; from an unused root meaning to *stutter; stuttering*:—stammerer.

5927. עָלָה, **'âlâh,** *aw-law´*; a primitive root; to *ascend,* intransitive (*be high*) or active (*mount*); used in a great variety of senses, primary and secondary, literal and figurative (as follow):— arise (up), (cause to) ascend up, at once, break [*the day*] (up), bring (up), (cause to) burn, carry up, cast up, + shew, climb (up), (cause to make to) come (up), cut off, dawn, depart, exalt, excel, fall, fetch up, get up, (make to) go (away, up), grow (over), increase, lay, leap, levy, lift (self) up, light, [make] up, × mention, mount up, offer, make to pay, + perfect, prefer, put (on), raise, recover, restore, (make to) rise (up), scale, set (up), shoot forth (up), (begin to) spring (up), stir up, take away (up), work.

A verb meaning to go up, to ascend, to take away, to lift, to offer. This Hebrew word carries with it the connotation of an upward motion. It is used generically to denote an ascension to a higher place (Nu 13:17); a departure in a northerly direction (Ge 45:25); the flight of a bird (Isa 40:31); the springing up of plants (Isa 34:13); the preference of one thing above another (Ps 137:6); and the offering of a sacrifice (Jgs 6:28; 2Ki 3:20). Theologically significant is the fact that this verb is used in relationship to a person's appearance before God. One must go up to stand before the Lord (Ex 34:24; see also Ge 35:1).

5928. עֲלָה, **'ălâh,** *al-aw´*; (Chaldee); corresponding to 5930; a *holocaust*:—burnt offering.

An Aramaic feminine noun meaning a burnt offering, a holocaust. This word parallels the Hebrew word 'ôlâh (5930). It is used only by Ezra in reference to the daily burnt sacrifices required under the Law (Ezr 6:9).

5929. עָלֶה, **'âleh,** *aw-leh´*; from 5927; a *leaf* (as *coming up* on a tree); (collective) *foliage*:— branch, leaf.

5930. עֹלָה, **'ôlâh,** *o-law´*; or עוֹלָה, **'ôwlâh,** *o-law´*; feminine active participle of 5927; a *step* or (collective) *stairs,* as *ascending*; usually a *holocaust* (as *going up* in smoke):—ascent, burnt offering (sacrifice), go up to. See also 5766.

A feminine noun meaning a whole burnt offering, that which goes up. The primary discussion of this offering is found in Le 1; 6:9[2], 10[3], 12[5]). The noun is a feminine participial form of the verb meaning to go up, to ascend. The offering was voluntary. The Israelites understood the animal or fowl that was being sacrificed as a gift to God and thus ascending to God as smoke from the altar (Le 1:9), hence its name. The sacrifice was a pleasing odor acceptable to the Lord (Le 1:9). Those presenting the animal laid hands on the sacrifice—possibly to indicate ownership or to indicate that the animal was a substitute for themselves (Le 1:4). The blood of the sacrifice was sprinkled against the altar (Le 1:6). The offering and its ritual properly carried out atoned for the offerers, and they became acceptable before the Lord.

The total burning of the sacrifice indicates the total consecration of the presenter to the

Lord. The animals that could be offered were bulls, sheep, rams, or male birds (Le 1:3, 10, 14). The ashes of the offering remained on the altar overnight. The priest removed them and deposited them in an approved location (Le 6:9[2], 10[3]).

The burnt offerings were presented often in conjunction with the peace and grain offerings (Jos 8:31; Jgs 6:26; 1Ki 3:4; 8:64). The burnt offerings, along with other offerings, were employed in the various feasts, festivals, and celebrations recorded in the prophetic books. Often, however, the burnt offerings were condemned as useless because the Israelites didn't have their hearts right before God (Jer 6:20; 7:21). Ezekiel foresaw renewed burnt offerings in a new Temple (Eze 40:38, 39). When Israel returned from exile, burnt offerings, along with others, were once again presented to the Lord (Ezr 3:2; 8:35). David's observation was correct and to the point, for he noted that whole burnt offerings did not satisfy or delight the Lord. Only an offering of a broken spirit and humble heart could do that (Ps 51:16[18]). Only then could acceptable sacrifices be given to the Lord (Ps 51:19[21]; 66:13).

5931. עִלָּה, **'illâh,** *il-law´*; (Chaldee); feminine from a root corresponding to 5927; a *pretext* (as *arising* artificially):—occasion.

5932. עַלְוָה, **'alvâh,** *al-vaw´*; for 5766; moral *perverseness*:—iniquity.

A feminine noun meaning injustice, unrighteousness, iniquity. Hos 10:9 is the sole occurrence of this word in the Bible. It is used to denote the supreme wickedness and depravity of Israel. The prophet relates the current situation to an episode at Gibeah during the time of the judges (cf. Jgs 19:1—20:28).

5933. עַלְוָה, **'Alvâh,** *al-vaw´*; or עַלְיָה, **'Alyâh,** *al-yaw´*; the same as 5932; *Alvah* or *Aljah*, an Idumæan:—Aliah, Alvah.

5934. עֲלוּמִים, **'ălûwmîym,** *aw-loom-eem´*; passive participle of 5956 in the denominative sense of 5958; (only in plural as abstract) *adolescence*; (figurative) *vigour*:—youth.

5935. עַלְוָן, **'Alvân,** *al-vawn´*; or עַלְיָן, **'Alyân,** *al-yawn´*; from 5927; *lofty*; *Alvan* or *Aljan*, an Idumæan:—Alian, Alvan.

5936. עֲלוּקָה, **'ălûwqâh,** *al-oo-kaw´*; feminine passive participle of an unused root meaning to *suck*; the *leech*:—horse-leech.

5937. עָלַז, **'âlaz,** *aw-laz´*; a primitive root; to *jump* for joy, i.e. *exult*:—be joyful, rejoice, triumph.

5938. עָלֵז, **'âlêz,** *aw-laze´*; from 5937; *exultant*:—that rejoiceth.

5939. עֲלָטָה, **'ălâṭâh,** *al-aw-taw´*; feminine from an unused root meaning to *cover; dusk*:—dark, twilight.

5940. עֱלִי, **'ĕlîy,** *el-ee´*; from 5927; a *pestle* (as *lifted*):—pestle.

5941. עֵלִי, **'Êlîy,** *ay-lee´*; from 5927; *lofty*; *Eli*, an Israelite high-priest:—Eli.

5942. עִלִּי, **'illîy,** *il-lee´*; from 5927; *high*, i.e. *compare*:—upper.

5943. עִלַּי, **'illay,** *il-lah´ee*; (Chaldee); corresponding to 5942; *supreme* (i.e. *God*):—(most) high.

An Aramaic masculine adjective meaning highest. This adjective always refers to God and shows the supremacy of God over humanity and other gods. It can occur as an adjective to modify *'ĕlâh* (426), meaning God. Nebuchadnezzar used this term of God to indicate His supremacy in general (Da 4:2 [3:32]). Daniel also used this term of God (Da 5:18, 21) to reveal the difference between God and Belshazzar, who had lifted up [himself] against the Lord of heaven (see Da 5:23). This term can also occur as a noun to represent God, especially in His role as the supreme Ruler of the kingdoms of humanity (Da 4:17[14], 24[21], 25[22], 32[29], 34[31]).

5944. עֲלִיָּה, **'ălîyyâh,** *al-ee-yaw´*; feminine from 5927; something *lofty*, i.e. a *stair-way*; also a *second-story* room (or even one on the roof); (figurative) the *sky*:—ascent, (upper) chamber, going up, loft, parlour.

5945. עֶלְיוֹן, **'elyôwn,** *el-yone´*; from 5927; an *elevation*, i.e. (adjective) *lofty* (comparative); as title, the *Supreme*:—(Most, on) high (-er, -est), upper (-most).

A masculine noun meaning Most High, the Highest. The word serves as an epithet for God and is used thirty-one times in the OT. The most celebrated use of this word is in Genesis 14:18—20: Melchizedek was priest of God Most High (*'êl 'elyôwn*), so the term in context defines the God whom he served. But in this same passage, Abraham equated the God Most High with the Lord his God, the Creator of heaven and earth (Ge 14:20). In Nu 24:16, this epithet stands in parallel to the epithet God and Shaddai; it depicts the God who gave Balaam his knowledge and visions. The term also stands in parallel with other names of God, such as the LORD (Dt 32:8; 2Sa 22:14; Ps 18:13[14]); and God (Ps 46:4[5]; 50:14).

5946. עֶלְיוֹן, **'elyôwn,** *el-yone'*; (Chaldee); corresponding to 5945; the *Supreme*:—Most high.

An Aramaic masculine adjective meaning Most High God. This term always appears in the plural of majesty, comparable to the Hebrew word *'ĕlôhiym* (430). Furthermore, it always occurs in the construct with *qaddiysh* (6922), meaning the holy ones or saints of the Most High God, and in the context of Daniel's interpretation of Nebuchadnezzar's dream of the four beasts, where four kingdoms were represented (Da 7:18, 22, 25, 27).

5947. עַלִּיז, **'alliyz,** *al-leez'*; from 5937; *exultant*:—joyous, (that) rejoice (-ing).

5948. עֲלִיל, **'ăliyl,** *al-eel'*; from 5953 in the sense of *completing*; probably a *crucible* (as *working* over the metal):—furnace.

5949. עֲלִילָה, **'ăliylâh,** *al-ee-law'*; or עֲלִלָה, **'ălilâh,** *al-ee-law'*; from 5953 in the sense of *effecting*; an *exploit* (of God), or a *performance* (of man, often in a bad sense); (by implication) an *opportunity*:—act (-ion), deed, doing, invention, occasion, work.

5950. עֲלִילִיָּה, **'ăliyliyyâh,** *al-ee-lee-yaw'*; for 5949; (miraculous) *execution*:—work.

5951. עֲלִיצוּת, **'ăliytsûwth,** *al-ee-tsooth'*; from 5970; *exultation*:—rejoicing.

5952. עִלִּי, **'illiy,** *il-lee'*; from 5927; a *second-story room*:—chamber. Compare 5944.

5953. עָלַל, **'âlal,** *aw-lal'*; a primitive root; to *effect* thoroughly; specifically to *glean* (also figurative); by implication (in a bad sense) to *overdo*, i.e. maltreat, be saucy to, pain, impose (also literal):—abuse, affect, × child, defile, do,

glean, mock, practise, thoroughly, work (wonderfully).

5954. עֲלַל, **'ălal,** *al-al'*; (Chaldee); corresponding to 5953 (in the sense of *thrusting* oneself in), to *enter*; (causative) to *introduce*:—bring in, come in, go in.

5955. עֹלֵלוֹת, **'ôlêlôwth,** *o-lay-loth'*; feminine active participle of 5953; only in plural *gleanings*; (by extension) *gleaning-time*:—(gleaning) (of the) grapes, grapegleanings.

5956. עָלַם, **'âlam,** *aw-lam'*; a primitive root; to *veil* from sight, i.e. *conceal* (literal or figurative):— × any ways, blind, dissembler, hide (self), secret (thing).

5957. עָלַם, **'ălam,** *aw-lam'*; (Chaldee); corresponding to 5769; *remote* time, i.e. the *future* or *past* indefinitely; often adverbial *forever*:—for ([n-]) ever (lasting), old.

An Aramaic masculine noun meaning perpetuity, antiquity. This word is related to the Hebrew word *'ôwlâm* (5769). It can mean a perpetual period in the future (Da 4:3[3:33]; 7:27); or a period of distant antiquity (Ezr 4:15, 19). It can also represent a period of time with no limits, either past or present (Da 4:34[31]). It can stand alone (Da 4:3[3:33]) or with the following prepositions, where it acts more like an adverb: *min* (4481) (Da 2:20); and *'ad* (5705) (Da 2:20; 7:18).

5958. עֶלֶם, **'elem,** *eh'-lem*; from 5956; (properly) something *kept out of sight* [compare 5959], i.e. a *lad*:—young man, stripling.

A masculine noun meaning a young man. Its feminine counterpart is found in the word *'almâh* (5959). The focus of this term is probably sexual maturity. It connotes an individual who has gone through puberty and is therefore sexually mature. Thus, *'elem* is the picture of an individual who has crossed (or is crossing) the threshold from boyhood or girlhood to manhood or womanhood, and, as such, is of marriageable age. Saul applied this term to David after he killed Goliath (1Sa 17:56); and Jonathan used it to refer to his armourbearer (1Sa 20:22).

5959. עַלְמָה, **'almâh,** *al-maw'*; feminine of 5958; a *lass* (as *veiled* or private):—damsel, maid, virgin.

A feminine noun meaning a maiden, a young woman, a girl, and a virgin. The word describes young women in different categories: Rebekah was understood to be a marriageable young woman by Abraham's servant (Ge 24:43); as was the maiden described in Pr 30:19, for in this case, the man was wooing her as a possible wife. Moses' sister was probably in this category (Ex 2:8). Sometimes it is unclear how old or mature these young maidens were (Ps 68:25[26]). The most famous passage where this term is used is Isa 7:14, where it asserts an 'almâh will give birth to a son. The author of Matthew 1:23 understood this woman to be a virgin.

5960. עַלְמוֹן, **'Almôwn,** *al-mone´*; from 5956; *hidden; Almon,* a place in Palestine:—Almon. See also 5963.

5961. עֲלָמוֹת, **'Âlâmôwth,** *al-aw-mōth´*; plural of 5959; (properly) *girls,* i.e. the *soprano* or female voice, perhaps *falsetto:*—Alamoth.

5962. עֵלְמָי, **'Êlmây,** *ayl-maw´ee*; (Chaldee); patrial from a name corresponding to 5867 contraction; an *Elamite* or inhabitant of Elam:—Elamite.

5963. עַלְמֹן דִּבְלָתָיְמָה, **'Almôn Diblâthây᷎mâh,** *al-mone´ dib-law-thaw´-yem-aw*; from the same as 5960 and the dual of 1690 [compare 1015] with enclitic of direction; *Almon toward Diblathajim; Almon-Diblathajemah,* a place in Moab:—Almon-dilathaim.

5964. עָלֶמֶת, **'Âlemeth,** *aw-leh´-meth*; from 5956; a *covering; Alemeth,* the name of a place in Palestine and of two Israelites:—Alameth, Alemeth.

5965. עָלַס, **'âlas,** *aw-las´*; a primitive root; to *leap* for joy, i.e. *exult, wave* joyously:— × peacock, rejoice, solace self.

5966. עָלַע, **'âla',** *aw-lah´*; a primitive root; to *sip* up:—suck up.

5967. עֲלַע, **'ăla',** *al-ah´*; (Chaldee); corresponding to 6763; a *rib:*—rib.

5968. עָלַף, **'âlaph,** *aw-laf´*; a primitive root; to *veil* or *cover;* (figurative) to *be languid:*—faint, overlaid, wrap self.

5969. עֻלְפֶּה, **'ulpeh,** *ool-peh´*; from 5968; an *envelope,* i.e. (figurative) *mourning:*—fainted.

5970. עָלַץ, **'âlats,** *aw-lats´*; a primitive root; to *jump* for joy, i.e. *exult:*—be joyful, rejoice, triumph.

5971. עַם, **'am,** *am*; from 6004; a *people* (as a congregated *unit*); (specifically) a *tribe* (as those of Israel); hence (collective) *troops* or *attendants*; (figurative) a *flock:*—folk, men, nation, people.

A masculine noun meaning a people, peoples, people of the land, citizens. The word is used over nineteen hundred times to indicate groups of people that can be categorized in various ways. The largest group of people is the one comprising the whole earth (see Ge 11:1); it constituted one people (Ge 11:6); who shared a common language (Ge 11:6; Eze 3:5); a common location (see Ge 11:2); and a common purpose and goal (see Ge 11:4). However, the Lord scattered the group and brought about multiple languages, thereby producing many groups who would then develop into new peoples united around common languages, including common ancestors, religious beliefs, traditions, and ongoing blood relationships.

The word is used to describe various groups that developed. The people of the sons of Israel (Ex 1:9; Ezr 9:1), was a term referring to all Israel. The people of Judah were a subgroup of Israel (2Sa 19:40[41]), as was northern Israel (2Ki 9:6). The people of Israel as a whole could be described in religious or moral terms as a holy, special people (Dt 7:6; 14:2; Da 8:24); or the Lord's inheritance (Dt 4:20). Above all, they were to be the Lord's people (Jgs 5:11; 1Sa 2:24); and the people of God (2Sa 14:13). They were the Lord's own people because He had rescued them from slavery to Pharaoh and his gods (Ex 6:7). But the Lord Himself characterized His people as stiff-necked (Ex 32:9; 33:3; 34:9; Dt 9:13). To be a member of the Lord's people was to have the Lord as one's God (Ru 1:16); if God's people rejected the Lord, they ceased to be His people. Therefore, it is clear that God's presence and ownership of His people gave them their identity (Ex 33:13, 16; Hos 1:9; cf. Dt 32:21).

In the plural form, the word refers to many peoples or nations. Jerusalem, destroyed and lamenting, called for the people of the world to look on it and its guilt (La 1:18). Israel was chosen from among all the peoples of the earth (Ex 19:5, 7; Dt 14:2). The Lord is in control of all the plans of the nations and peoples (Ps 33:10). The word is used in parallel with *gôwyim* (1471). Isaac prayed for Jacob's offspring to become a community of peoples that would include the twelve tribes of Israel (Ge 28:3).

The word described people in general—that is, nonethnic or national groups. It refers to all the people as individuals in the world (Isa 42:5). When persons died, they were gathered to their people (Ge 25:8, 17). It also referred to people from a particular city (Ru 4:9; 2Ch 32:18); or people from a specific land (e.g., Canaan [Zep 1:11]). Centuries earlier, Pharaoh referred to the Hebrews living in Egypt under slavery as the people of the land (Ex 5:5). This phrase could refer to the population at large in Solomon's time and later (2Ki 11:14, 18; 15:5); or to the population of Canaan in Abraham's time (Ge 23:7).

The term also depicted foreign peoples and nations. The Moabites were the people of the god Chemosh (Nu 21:29). The word designated foreigners in general as strange or alien people (Ex 21:8); the people of Egypt were considered the people of Pharaoh (Ex 1:9, 22).

The word is even used to describe a gathering of ants (Pr 30:25); or rock badgers (Pr 30:26).

5972. עַם, **'am**, *am*; (Chaldee); corresponding to 5971:—people.

An Aramaic masculine noun meaning people. It was not used in reference to a disparate group of individuals or to a specific ethnic group. This is seen especially in its parallel usage with *'ûmmâh* (524), meaning nation, and *lishshân* (3961), meaning tongue (Da 3:4, 7, 29). The specific ethnic group being identified could be either the Israelites (Ezr 5:12; Da 7:27); or the Gentiles (Ezr 6:12; Da 2:44).

5973. עִם, **'im**, *eem*; from 6004; adverb or preposition, *with* (i.e. in *conjunction* with), in varied applications; (specifically) *equally with*; often with prepositional prefix (and then usually unrepresented in English):—accompanying, against, and, as (× long as), before, beside, by (reason of), for all, from (among, between), in, like, more than, of, (un-) to, with (-al).

5974. עִם, **'im**, *eem*; (Chaldee); corresponding to 5973:—by, from, like, to (-ward), with.

5975. עָמַד, **'âmad**, *aw-mad´*; a primitive root; to *stand*, in various relations (literal and figurative, intransitive and transitive):—abide (behind), appoint, arise, cease, confirm, continue, dwell, be employed, endure, establish, leave, make, ordain, be [over], place, (be) present (self), raise up, remain, repair, + serve, set (forth, over, -tle, up), (make to, make to be at a, with-) stand (by, fast, firm, still, up), (be at a) stay (up), tarry.

5976. עָמַד, **'âmad**, *aw-mad´*; for 4571; to *shake*:—be at a stand.

5977. עֹמֶד, **'ômed**, *o´-med*; from 5975; a *spot* (as being *fixed*):—place, (+ where) stood, upright.

5978. עִמָּד, **'immâd**, *im-mawd´*; prolonged for 5973; along *with*:—against, by, from, in, + me, + mine, of, + that I take, unto, upon, with (-in).

5979. עֶמְדָּה, **'emdâh**, *em-daw´*; from 5975; a *station*, i.e. domicile:—standing.

5980. עֻמָּה, **'ummâh**, *oom-maw´*; from 6004; *conjunction*, i.e. *society*; mostly adverb or preposition (with prepositional prefix), *near, beside, along with*:—(over) against, at, beside, hard by, in points.

5981. עֻמָּה, **'Ummâh**, *oom-maw´*; the same as 5980; *association*; *Ummah*, a place in Palestine:—Ummah.

5982. עַמּוּד, **'ammûwd**, *am-mood´*; or עַמֻּד, **'ammud**, *am-mood´*; from 5975; a *column* (as *standing*); also a *stand*, i.e. platform:— × apiece, pillar.

5983. עַמּוֹן, **'Ammôwn**, *am-mone´*; from 5971; *tribal*, i.e. *inbred*; *Ammon*, a son of Lot; also his posterity and their country:—Ammon, Ammonites.

5984. עַמּוֹנִי, **'Ammôwnîy**, *am-mo-nee´*; patronymic from 5983; an *Ammonite* or (adjective) *Ammoni-tish*:—Ammonite (-s).

5985. עַמּוֹנִית, **'Ammôwnîyth**, *am-mo-neeth´*; feminine of 5984; an *Ammonitess*:—Ammonite (-ss).

5986. עָמוֹס, **'Âmôws**, *aw-moce´*; from 6006; *burdensome*; *Amos*, an Israelite prophet:—Amos.

5987. עֲמוֹק, **ʿÂmôwq,** *aw-moke´*; from 6009; *deep; Amok,* an Israelite:—Amok.

5988. עֲמִּיאֵל, **ʿAmmîyʾêl,** *am-mee-ale´*; from 5971 and 410; *people of God; Ammiël,* the name of three or four Israelites:—Ammiel.

5989. עֲמִּיהוּד, **ʿAmmîyhûwd,** *am-mee-hood´*; from 5971 and 1935; *people of splendor; Ammihud,* the name of three Israelites:—Ammihud.

5990. עֲמִּיזָבָד, **ʿAmmîyzâbâd,** *am-mee-zaw-bawd´*; from 5971 and 2064; *people of endowment; Ammi-zabad,* an Israelite:—Ammizabad.

5991. עֲמִּיחוּר, **ʿAmmîychûwr,** *am-mee-khoor´*; from 5971 and 2353; *people of nobility; Ammichur,* a Syrian prince:—Ammihud [*from the margin*].

5992. עֲמִּינָדָב, **ʿAmmîynâdâb,** *am-mee-naw-dawb´*; from 5971 and 5068; *people of liberality; Ammi-nadab,* the name of four Israelites:—Amminadab.

5993. עֲמִּי נָדִיב, **ʿAmmîy Nâdîyb,** *am-mee´ naw-deeb´*; from 5971 and 5081; *my people* (is) *liberal; Ammi-Nadib,* probably an Israelite:—Amminadib.

5994. עֲמִיק, **ʿămîyq,** *am-eek´*; (Chaldee); corresponding to 6012; *profound,* i.e. unsearchable:—deep.

5995. עָמִיר, **ʿâmîyr,** *aw-meer´*; from 6014; a *bunch* of grain:—handful, sheaf.

5996. עֲמִּישַׁדָּי, **ʿAmmîyshadday,** *am-mee-shaddah´ee*; from 5971 and 7706; *people of* (the) *Almighty; Ammishaddai,* an Israelite:—Ammishaddai.

5997. עָמִית, **ʿâmîyth,** *aw-meeth´*; from a primitive root meaning to *associate; companionship*; hence (concrete) a *comrade* or kindred man:—another, fellow, neighbour.

5998. עָמַל, **ʿâmal,** *aw-mal´*; a primitive root; to *toil,* i.e. *work severely* and with irksomeness:—[take] labour (in).

5999. עָמָל, **ʿâmâl,** *aw-mawl´*; from 5998; *toil,* i.e. *wearing effort*; hence *worry,* whether of body or mind:—grievance (-vousness), iniquity, labour, mischief, miserable (-sery), pain (-ful), perverseness, sorrow, toil, travail, trouble, wearisome, wickedness.

A masculine singular noun meaning trouble, labour, toil. This word can be used for the general difficulties and hardships of life, which can be seen by its use in conjunction with sorrow (Jer 20:18); affliction (Dt 26:7; Ps 25:18); and futility (Job 7:3). It can also refer to trouble or mischief directed at another person. The evil person talks of causing trouble (Pr 24:2); and God cannot look at the trouble caused by sin (Hab 1:3, 13). Its usage in Ecclesiastes and Ps 105:44 and 107:12 is best rendered labour. The Teacher in Ecclesiastes repeatedly asked what benefit toil was (Ecc 2:10, 11).

6000. עָמָל, **ʿÂmâl,** *aw-mawl´*; the same as 5999; *Amal,* an Israelite:—Amal.

6001. עָמֵל, **ʿâmêl,** *aw-male´*; from 5998; *toiling*; (concrete) a *labourer*; (figurative) *sorrowful*:—that laboureth, that is a misery, had taken [labour], wicked, workman.

A verbal adjective meaning toiling. This form is used exclusively in Ecclesiastes (Ecc 2:18, 22; 3:9; 4:8; 9:9) and always as a predicate adjective. The overall use of the word is to stress the meaninglessness of human efforts. Toiling under the sun appears to the writer to have no lasting value. One must leave the rewards to those who come afterward (Ecc 2:18). This working results in nothing more than pain and grief (Ecc 2:22). See the word ʿâmâl (5999).

6002. עֲמָלֵק, **ʿÂmâlêq,** *am-aw-lake´*; probably of foreign origin; *Amalek,* a descendant of Esau; also his posterity and their country:—Amalek.

6003. עֲמָלֵקִי, **ʿÂmâlêqîy,** *am-aw-lay-kee´*; patronymic from 6002; an *Amalekite* (collective, the *Amalekites*) or descendant of Amalek:—Amalekite (-s).

6004. עָמַם, **ʿâmam,** *aw-mam´*; a primitive root; to *associate*; (by implication) to *overshadow* (by *huddling* together):—become dim, hide.

6005. עִמָּנוּאֵל, **ʿImmânûwʾêl,** *im-maw-noo-ale´*; from 5973 and 410 with suffix pronoun inserted; *with us* (is) *God; Immanuel,* a typical name of Isaiah's son:—Immanuel.

6006. עָמַס, **ʿâmas,** *aw-mas´*; or עָמַשׂ, **ʿâmaś,** *aw-mas´*; a primitive root; to *load,* i.e. *impose* a burden; (figurative) *infliction*:—be borne, (heavy) burden (self), lade, load, put.

6007. עֲמַסְיָה, **'Ămasyâh,** *am-as-yaw´*; from 6006 and 3050; *Jah has loaded; Amasjah,* an Israelite:—Amasiah.

6008. עֲמָעָד, **'Am'âd,** *am-awd´*; from 5971 and 5703; *people of time; Amad,* a place in Palestine:—Amad.

6009. עָמֵק, **'âmaq,** *aw-mak´*; a primitive root; to be (causative, *make*) *deep* (literal or figurative):—(be, have, make, seek) deep (-ly), depth, be profound.

6010. עֵמֶק, **'êmeq,** *ay´-mek*; from 6009; a *vale* (i.e. broad *depression*):—dale, vale, valley [*often used as a part of proper names*]. See also 1025.

6011. עֹמֶק, **'ômeq,** *o´-mek*; from 6009; *depth*:—depth.

6012. עָמֵק, **'âmêq,** *aw-make´*; from 6009; *deep* (literal or figurative):—deeper, depth, strange.

An adjective meaning deep, unfathomable. Both times it is used to describe the speech of foreign peoples as unintelligible. Isaiah spoke of the return from Babylon, telling the people that they would no longer hear the unintelligible speech of foreigners (Isa 33:19). When God called Ezekiel, He told him that he was to speak to the house of Israel, not to people of unintelligible speech (Eze 3:5, 6).

6013. עָמֹק, **'âmoq,** *aw-moke´*; from 6009; *deep* (literal or figurative):—(× exceeding) deep (thing).

6014. עָמַר, **'âmar,** *aw-mar´*; a primitive root; (properly) apparently to *heap*; (figurative) to *chastise* (as if *piling* blows); specifically (as denominative from 6016) to *gather* grain:—bind sheaves, make merchandise of.

6015. עֲמַר, **'ămar,** *am-ar´*; (Chaldee); corresponding to 6785; *wool*:—wool.

6016. עֹמֶר, **'ômer,** *o´-mer*; from 6014; (properly) a *heap*, i.e. a *sheaf*; also an *omer*, as a dry measure:—omer, sheaf.

6017. עֲמֹרָה, **'Ămôrâh,** *am-o-raw´*; from 6014; a (ruined) *heap; Amorah,* a place in Palestine:—Gomorrah.

6018. עָמְרִי, **'Omrîy,** *om-ree´*; from 6014; *heaping; Omri,* an Israelite:—Omri.

6019. עַמְרָם, **'Amrâm,** *am-rawm´*; probably from 5971 and 7311; *high people; Amram,* the name of two Israelites:—Amram.

6020. עַמְרָמִי, **'Amrâmîy,** *am-raw-mee´*; patronymic from 6019; an *Amramite* or descendant of Amram:—Amramite.

6021. עֲמָשָׂא, **'Ămâsâ',** *am-aw-saw´*; from 6006; *burden; Amasa,* the name of two Israelites:—Amasa.

6022. עֲמָשַׂי, **'Ămâśay,** *am-aw-sah´ee*; from 6006; *burdensome; Amasai,* the name of three Israelites:—Amasai.

6023. עֲמַשְׁסַי, **'Ămashsay,** *am-ash-sah´ee*; probably from 6006; *burdensome; Amashsay,* an Israelite:—Amashai.

6024. עֲנָב, **'Ănâb,** *an-awb´*; from the same as 6025; *fruit; Anab,* a place in Palestine:—Anab.

6025. עֵנָב, **'ênâb,** *ay-nawb´*; from an unused root probably meaning to *bear* fruit; a *grape*:—(ripe) grape, wine.

6026. עָנַג, **'ânag,** *aw-nag´*; a primitive root; to be *soft* or pliable, i.e. (figurative) *effeminate* or luxurious:—delicate (-ness), (have) delight (self), sport self.

6027. עֹנֶג, **'ôneg,** *o´-neg*; from 6026; *luxury*:—delight, pleasant.

6028. עָנֹג, **'ânôg,** *aw-nogue´*; from 6026; *luxurious*:—delicate.

6029. עָנַד, **'ânad,** *aw-nad´*; a primitive root; to *lace* fast:—bind, tie.

6030. עָנָה, **'ânâh,** *aw-naw´*; a primitive root; (properly) to *eye* or (general) to *heed*, i.e. *pay attention*; (by implication) to *respond*; (by extension) to *begin* to speak; (specifically) to *sing, shout, testify, announce*:—give account, afflict [*by mistake for* 6031], (cause to, give) answer, bring low [*by mistake for* 6031], cry, hear, Leannoth, lift up, say, × scholar, (give a) shout, sing (together by course), speak, testify, utter, (bear) witness. See also 1042, 1043.

6031. עָנָה, **'ânâh,** *aw-naw´*; a primitive root [possibly rather identical with 6030 through the idea of *looking* down or *browbeating*]; to *depress* (literal or figurative, transitive or intransitive, in various applications, as follow):—abase self, afflict (-ion, self), answer [by mistake for 6030], chasten self, deal hardly with, defile, exercise, force, gentleness, humble (self), hurt, ravish, sing [by mistake for 6030], speak [by mistake for 6030], submit self, weaken, × in any wise.

6032. עֲנָה, **'ănâh,** *an-aw´*; (Chaldee); corresponding to 6030:—answer, speak.

6033. עֲנָה, **'ănâh,** *an-aw´*; (Chaldee); corresponding to 6031:—poor.

6034. עֲנָה, **'Ănâh,** *an-aw´*; probably from 6030; an *answer*; *Anah*, the name of two Edomites and one Edomitess:—Anah.

6035. עָנָו, **'ânâv,** *aw-nawv´*; or [by intermixture with 6041] עָנָיו, **'ânâyv,** *aw-nawv´*; from 6031; *depressed* (figurative), in mind (*gentle*) or circumstances (*needy*, especially *saintly*):—humble, lowly, meek, poor. Compare 6041.

6036. עָנוּב, **'Ănûwb,** *aw-noob´*; passive participle from the same as 6025; *borne* (as fruit); *Anub*, an Israelite:—Anub.

6037. עַנְוָה, **'anvâh,** *an-vaw´*; feminine of 6035; *mildness* (royal); also (concrete) *oppressed*:—gentleness, meekness.

6038. עֲנָוָה, **'ănâvâh,** *an-aw-vaw´*; from 6035; *condescension*, human and subjective (*modesty*), or divine and objective (*clemency*):—gentleness, humility, meekness.

6039. עֱנוּת, **'ĕnûwth,** *en-ooth´*; from 6031; *affliction*:—affliction.

6040. עֳנִי, **'ŏnîy,** *on-ee´*; from 6031; *depression*, i.e. *misery*:—afflicted (-ion), trouble.

6041. עָנִי, **'ânîy,** *aw-nee´*; from 6031; *depressed*, in mind or circumstances [practically the same as 6035, although the margin constantly disputes this, making 6035 subjective and 6041 objective]:—afflicted, humble, lowly, needy, poor.

6042. עֻנִּי, **'Unnîy,** *oon-nee´*; from 6031; *afflicted*; *Unni*, the name of two Israelites:—Unni.

6043. עֲנָיָה, **'Ănâyâh,** *an-aw-yaw´*; from 6030; *Jah has answered*; *Anajah*, the name of two Israelites:—Anaiah.

6044. עָנִים, **'Ânîym,** *aw-neem´*; for plural of 5869; *fountains*; *Anim*, a place in Palestine:—Anim.

6045. עִנְיָן, **'inyân,** *in-yawn´*; from 6031; *ado*, i.e. (general) *employment* or (specific) an *affair*:—business, travail.

6046. עָנֵם, **'Ânêm,** *aw-name´*; from the dual of 5869; *two fountains*; *Anem*, a place in Palestine:—Anem.

6047. עֲנָמִים, **'Ănâmîym,** *an-aw-meem´*; as if plural of some Egyptian word; *Anamim*, a son of Mizraim and his descendant, with their country:—Anamim.

6048. עֲנַמֶּלֶךְ, **'Ănammelek,** *an-am-meh´-lek*; of foreign origin; *Anammelek*, an Assyrian deity:—Anammelech.

6049. עָנַן, **'ânan,** *aw-nan´*; a primitive root; to *cover*; used only as denominative from 6051, to *cloud* over; (figurative) to *act covertly*, i.e. practise magic:— × bring, enchanter, Meonenim, observe (-r of) times, soothsayer, sorcerer.

A verb meaning to practice soothsaying, fortune-telling, divining, magic. While it is clear from the contexts and the versions that this term is used for some type of magic or witchcraft, its etymology is unclear. Therefore, the specifics of the practice it connotes are equally unclear. However, it is clear that it was strictly forbidden, and the one who practiced this act was detestable to God (Dt 18:10, 12). Isaiah appears to use the term figuratively to demean the idolatrous Israelites (Isa 57:3).

6050. עֲנָן, **'ănan,** *an-an´*; (Chaldee); corresponding to 6051:—cloud.

A masculine singular Aramaic noun meaning cloud. It occurs only in Da 7:13 in the phrase, clouds of heaven. In a night vision, Daniel saw the Son of Man coming with the clouds of heaven. This use of clouds in apocalyptic language is familiar to the writer of Revelation who echoes the same phrase, "Look, he is coming with the clouds" (Rev 1:7, NIV). See the Hebrew cognate 'ânân (6051).

6051. עָנָן, **'ânân,** *aw-nawn´*; from 6049; a *cloud* (as *covering* the sky), i.e. the *nimbus* or thundercloud:—cloud (-y).

A masculine singular noun meaning cloud. In the ancient world, clouds were often seen as the pedestal or shroud of the divine presence. This imagery is also present in the Hebrew Bible. God preceded the Israelites through the wilderness in a pillar of cloud (Ex 13:21, 22); and the same cloud rested over the tabernacle (Ex 33:10). The cloud was over Mount Sinai (Ex 19:9); and entered the Temple in Jerusalem (1Ki 8:10, 11). Clouds are typical of the apocalyptic language of the Day of God (Eze 30:3; Joel 2:2; Zep 1:15). Other poetic uses of cloud describe God's shelter (Isa 4:5); Israel's evaporating love (Hos 6:4); the transient nature of life (Job 7:9); and the breadth of a great army (Eze 38:9). See the Aramaic *ănân* (6050).

6052. עָנָן, **'Ânân,** *aw-nawn´*; the same as 6051; *cloud; Anan,* an Israelite:—Anan.

6053. עֲנָנָה, **'ănânâh,** *an-aw-naw´*; feminine of 6051; *cloudiness:*—cloud.

6054. עֲנָנִי, **'Ănânîy,** *an-aw-nee´*; from 6051; *cloudy; Anani,* an Israelite:—Anani.

6055. עֲנַנְיָה, **'Ănân°yâh,** *a-naw-ne-yaw´*; from 6049 and 3050; *Jah has covered; Ananjah,* the name of an Israelite and of a place in Palestine:—Ananiah.

6056. עֲנַף, **'ănaph,** *an-af´*; (Chaldee); or עֶנֶף, **'eneph,** *eh´-nef*; (Chaldee); corresponding to 6057:—bough, branch.

6057. עָנָף, **'ânâph,** *aw-nawf´*; from an unused root meaning to *cover;* a *twig* (as *covering* the limbs):—bough, branch.

6058. עָנֵף, **'ânêph,** *aw-nafe´*; from the same as 6057; *branching:*—full of branches.

6059. עָנַק, **'ânaq,** *aw-nak´*; a primitive root; (properly) to *choke;* used only as denominative from 6060, to *collar,* i.e. adorn with a necklace; (figurative) to *fit out* with supplies:—compass about as a chain, furnish, liberally.

6060. עֲנָק, **'ănâq,** *ah-nawk´*; from 6059; a *necklace* (as if *strangling*):—chain.

6061. עֲנָק, **'Ânâq,** *aw-nawk´*; the same as 6060; *Anak,* a Canaanite:—Anak.

6062. עֲנָקִי, **'Ănâqîy,** *an-aw-kee´*; patronymic from 6061; an *Anakite* or descendant of Anak:—Anakim.

6063. עָנֵר, **'Ânêr,** *aw-nare´*; probably for 5288; *Aner,* an Amorite, also a place in Palestine:—Aner.

6064. עָנַשׁ, **'ânash,** *aw-nash´*; a primitive root; (properly) to *urge;* (by implication) to *inflict* a penalty, (specifically) to *fine:*—amerce, condemn, punish, × surely.

A verb meaning to fine, to penalize with a fine. The primary meaning is the monetary assessment for a crime and is clearly seen in Dt 22:19 (see also Ex 21:22). Similarly, Amos used the word to denote the condemnation that rests on those under punishment (Am 2:8). In a practical sense, the writer of wisdom extolled the educational benefits of applying such a fine to the wicked (Pr 21:11); but he expressly warned against punishing the righteous (Pr 17:26).

6065. עֲנַשׁ, **'ănash,** *an-ash´*; (Chaldee); corresponding to 6066; a *mulct:*—confiscation.

An Aramaic masculine noun meaning confiscation, repossession. This word appears only once in Ezr 7:26 and simply refers to the seizure of goods as a legal penalty for crimes.

6066. עֹנֶשׁ, **'ônesh,** *o´-nesh*; from 6064; a *fine:*—punishment, tribute.

A masculine noun meaning a fine, a penalty, an indemnity. The basic meaning of the word is a monetary obligation placed on one who violated the Law or was under subjugation to a higher authority. It was used to refer to the tribute forced on Jehoahaz by the Egyptian pharaoh (2Ki 23:33); and the punishment facing unrestrained anger (Pr 19:19).

6067. עֲנָת, **'Ănâth,** *an-awth´*; from 6030; *answer; Anath,* an Israelite:—Anath.

6068. עֲנָתוֹת, **'Ănâthôwth,** *an-aw-thōth´*; plural of 6067; *Anathoth,* the name of two Israelites, also of a place in Palestine:—Anathoth.

6069. עֲנְתֹתִי, **'Ănôthôthîy,** *an-tho-thee´*; or עֶנְתוֹתִי, **'Ann°thôwthîy,** *an-ne-tho-thee´*; patrial from 6068; an *Antothite* or inhabitant of Anathoth:—of Anathoth, Anethothite, Anetothite, Antothite.

6070. עֲנְתֹתִיָּה, **'Anthôthîyyâh,** *an-tho-thee-yaw´*; from the same as 6068 and 3050; *answers of Jah; Anthothijah,* an Israelite:—Antothijah.

6071. עָסִיס, **'âsîys,** *aw-sees´*; from 6072; *must* or fresh grape juice (as just *trodden* out):—juice, new (sweet) wine.

6072. עָסַס, **'âsas,** *aw-sas'*; a primitive root; to *squeeze* out juice; (figurative) to *trample*:—tread down.

6073. עֳפָאִים, **'ŏphâ'îym,** *of-aw-yim'*; from an unused root meaning to *cover*; a *bough* (as covering the tree):—branch.

6074. עֳפִי, **'ŏphîy,** *of-ee'*; (Chaldee); corresponding to 6073; a *twig*; bough, i.e. (collective) *foliage*:—leaves.

6075. עָפַל, **'âphal,** *aw-fal'*; a primitive root; to *swell*; (figurative) to *be elated*:—be lifted up, presume.

6076. עֹפֶל, **'ôphel,** *o'-fel*; from 6075; a *tumor*; also a *mound*, i.e. fortress:—emerod, fort, strong hold, tower.

I. A masculine noun meaning hill, fort, citadel (2Ki 5:24; Isa 32:14; Mic 4:8).

II. A masculine noun meaning tumor (Dt 28:27; 1Sa 5:6, 9, 12; 6:4, 5).

6077. עֹפֶל, **'Ôphel,** *o'-fel*; the same as 6076; *Ophel*, a ridge in Jerusalem:—Ophel.

6078. עָפְנִי, **'Ophnîy,** *of-nee'*; from an unused noun [denoting a place in Palestine; from an unused root of uncertain meaning]; an *Ophnite* (collective) or inhabitant of Ophen:—Ophni.

6079. עַפְעַף, **'aph'aph,** *af-af'*; from 5774; an *eye-lash* (as *fluttering*); (figurative) morning *ray*:—dawning, eyelid.

6080. עָפַר, **'âphar,** *aw-far'*; a primitive root; meaning either to *be gray* or perhaps rather to *pulverize*; used only as denominative from 6083, to *be dust*:—cast [dust].

A verb meaning to powder, to dust. This word literally means to sprinkle dust or dirt and conveys the image of a dusty garment whose appearance is gray. It was used to describe the scornful action of Shimei as he threw dirt on David and his procession (2Sa 16:13).

6081. עֵפֶר, **'Êpher,** *ay'-fer*; probably a variation of 6082; *gazelle*; *Epher*, the name of an Arabian and of two Israelites:—Epher.

6082. עֹפֶר, **'ôpher,** *o'-fer*; from 6080; a *fawn* (from the *dusty* colour):—young roe [hart].

6083. עָפָר, **'âphâr,** *aw-fawr'*; from 6080; *dust* (as *powdered* or *gray*); hence *clay, earth, mud*:—ashes, dust, earth, ground, morter, powder, rubbish.

A masculine noun meaning dust, dry earth, loose dirt. The primary meaning of this word is the dry, loose dirt or dust that covers the ground (Am 2:7; Mic 1:10). It is used to imply earth or soil (Job 5:6; 28:2); the original material used to form the first man (Ge 2:7); the material used to plaster walls (Le 14:42); the remains of a destroyed city (Eze 26:4); and anything pulverized into powder (Dt 9:21). Figuratively, it signifies abundance (Ge 13:16); utter defeat (2Ki 13:7); and humiliation (Job 16:15).

6084. עָפְרָה, **'Ophrâh,** *of-raw'*; feminine of 6082; *female fawn; Ophrah*, the name of an Israelite and of two places in Palestine:—Ophrah.

6085. עֶפְרוֹן, **'Ephrôwn,** *ef-rone'*; from the same as 6081; *fawn-like; Ephron*, the name of a Canaanite and of two places in Palestine:—Ephron, Ephrain [*from the margin*].

6086. עֵץ, **'êts,** *ates*; from 6095; a *tree* (from its *firmness*); hence *wood* (plural *sticks*):— + carpenter, gallows, helve, + pine, plank, staff, stalk, stick, stock, timber, tree, wood.

6087. עָצַב, **'âtsab,** *aw-tsab'*; a primitive root; (properly) to *carve*, i.e. fabricate or fashion; hence (in a bad sense) to *worry, pain* or *anger*:—displease, grieve, hurt, make, be sorry, vex, worship, wrest.

A verb meaning to hurt, to pain, to grieve, to shape, to fashion. This word has two separate meanings. The first meaning deals with physical pain (Ecc 10:9); emotional pain (1Sa 20:34); or some combination of physical and emotional pain (1Ch 4:10). The word is also used of David's inaction when Adonijah attempted to usurp the throne (1Ki 1:6). The second meaning generally refers to creative activity, such as the kind God exercised when He created human bodies (Job 10:8); or the creative activity of people (Jer 44:19). In both these instances, the word occurs in parallel with the word *'âśâh* (6213), which means to make or to do.

6088. עֲצִיב, **'ătsîyb,** *ats-eeb'*; (Chaldee); corresponding to 6087; to *afflict*:—lamentable.

An Aramaic verb meaning to pain, to grieve. It is similar to the Hebrew word *'âtsab* (6087). It appears only one time in the form of a passive participle and is used as an adjective to modify *qôwl* (6963), meaning voice. In this instance, King Darius called into the lion's den for Daniel with a pained voice to see if God had preserved Daniel and kept him safe from harm (Da 6:20[21]).

6089. עֶצֶב, **'etseb,** *eh´-tseb*; from 6087; an earthen *vessel*; usually (painful) *toil*; also a *pang* (whether of body or mind):—grievous, idol, labour, sorrow.

A masculine noun meaning pain, hurt, toil. Since, like the noun *'ôtseb* (6090), it is derived from the verb *'âtsab* (6087), this noun carries the same variations of meaning. The word is used of physical pain, such as a woman's pain in childbirth (Ge 3:16); or of emotional pain, such as that caused by inappropriate words (Pr 15:1). The word can also express both meanings (cf. Pr 10:22); and can also refer to hard work or toil (Ps 127:2; Pr 5:10; 14:23).

6090. עֹצֶב, **'ôtseb,** *o´-tseb*; a variation of 6089; an *idol* (as fashioned); also *pain* (bodily or mental):—idol, sorrow, × wicked.

A masculine noun meaning pain, image, idol. Like the noun *'etseb* (6089), this word is derived from the verb *'âtsab* (6087). It can be used to depict the physical pain of childbirth (1Ch 4:9); a painful way, meaning a harmful habit like idolatry (Ps 139:24); and the sorrow and hardship of the Babylonian exile (Isa 14:3). In the final passage, this word is in parallel with *rôgez* (7267), meaning disquiet or turmoil.

6091. עָצָב, **'âtsâb,** *aw-tsawb´*; from 6087; an (idolatrous) *image*:—idol, image.

A masculine noun used to identify an idol. This term always appears in the plural. It is derived from the second meaning of the verb *'âtsab* (6087), meaning to form or fashion, and thereby highlights the fact that these idols ("gods") were formed by human hands. This term can allude to idols in general (Hos 4:17); idols of silver (Hos 13:2); or idols of gold and silver (Hos 8:4). It appears in parallel with *massêkâh* (4541), meaning a molten image (Hos 13:2); and *gillûl* (1544), meaning idols (Jer 50:2).

6092. עָצֵב, **'âtsêb,** *aw-tsabe´*; from 6087; a (hired) *workman*:—labour.

A masculine noun meaning a labourer, a worker. This noun is derived from the verb

'âtsab (6087), which conveys the idea of physical or emotional pain and suffering. This noun occurs only in Isa 58:3, where God condemned the people of Israel for not properly fasting because they sacrificed nothing personally while exploiting their labourers or workers.

6093. עִצָּבוֹן, **'itstsâbôwn,** *its-tsaw-bone´*; from 6087; *worrisomeness,* i.e. *labour* or *pain:*—sorrow, toil.

A masculine noun meaning pain, toil. This noun is derived from the verb *'âtsab* (6087) and occurs three times in Genesis, relating to the curse that God placed on fallen humanity. To the woman, God stated that she would have pain and toil during childbirth (Ge 3:16). To the man, God stated that he would have pain and toil in working the ground to produce food (Ge 3:17; 5:29).

6094. עַצֶּבֶת, **'atstsebeth,** *ats-tseh´-beth*; from 6087; an *idol*; also a *pain* or *wound:*—sorrow, wound.

A feminine noun meaning hurt, injury, pain. This noun is derived from the verb *'âtsab* (6087). This noun is used only in Hebrew poetry and refers to the grief or sorrow that causes fear of discipline (Job 9:28); the grief caused by idolatry (Ps 16:4); the grief that comes with being brokenhearted (Ps 147:3); the grief caused by one who winks with the eye (Pr 10:10); or grief that causes the spirit to be broken (Pr 15:13). Although sometimes portrayed in physical terms (Ps 147:3), this term clearly refers to emotional suffering and not physical pain or injury.

6095. עָצָה, **'âtsâh,** *aw-tsaw´*; a primitive root; (properly) to *fasten* (or *make firm*), i.e. to *close* (the eyes):—shut.

6096. עָצֶה, **'âtseh,** *aw-tseh´*; from 6095; the *spine* (as giving *firmness* to the body):—back bone.

6097. עֵצָה, **'êtsâh,** *ay-tsaw´*; feminine of 6086; *timber:*—trees.

6098. עֵצָה, **'êtsâh,** *ay-tsaw´*; from 3289; *advice*; (by implication) *plan*; also *prudence:*—advice, advisement, counsel ([-lor]), purpose.

A feminine noun meaning advice, a plan. It sometimes may suggest the idea of a plot (Ne 4:15[4:9]; Pr 21:30); of a judgment or decision (Jgs 20:7; 2Sa 16:20; Ezr 10:3, 8). The term occurs in a positive sense in association with wisdom and understanding (Job 12:13; Pr 8:14; 12:15). Thus, the meaning of advice came from the sages of Israel and the astrologers of Babylon who were viewed as wise in their communities (Isa 47:13; Jer 18:18). Kings and would-be kings sought out advice but did not always have the discernment to choose the good (2Sa 17:7, 14, 23; 1Ki 12:8, 13, 14). This term is used quite often as a possession of God and the promised Messiah (Pr 19:21; Isa 5:19; 11:2; Jer 32:19).

6099. עָצוּם, **'âtsûwm,** *aw-tsoom´*; or עָצֻם, **'âtsum,** *aw-tsoom´*; passive participle of 6105; *powerful* (specifically, a *paw*); (by implication) *numerous*:— + feeble, great, mighty, must, strong.

6100. עֶצְיוֹן גֶּבֶר, **'Etsyôwn Geber,** *ets-yone´ gheh´-ber*; (shorter עֶצְיֹן גֶּבֶר, **'Etsyôn Geber,** *ets-yone´ gheh´-ber*; Ezion-gaber, a place on the Red Sea:—Ezion-geber.

6101. עָצַל, **'âtsal,** *aw-tsal´*; a primitive root; to *lean* idly, i.e. to be *indolent* or *slack*:—be slothful.

6102. עָצֵל, **'âtsêl,** *aw-tsale*; from 6101; *indolent*:—slothful, sluggard.

6103. עַצְלָה, **'atslâh,** *ats-law´*; feminine of 6102; (as abstract) *indolence*:—slothfulness.

6104. עַצְלוּת, **'atslûwth,** *ats-looth´*; from 6101; *indolence*:—idleness.

6105. עָצַם, **'âtsam,** *aw-tsam´*; a primitive root; to *bind* fast, i.e. *close* (the eyes); (intransitive) to *be* (causative, *make*) *powerful* or *numerous*; denominative (from 6106) to *crunch* the bones:—break the bones, close, be great, be increased, be (wax) mighty (-ier), be more, shut, be (-come, make) strong (-er).

6106. עֶצֶם, **'etsem,** *eh´-tsem*; from 6105; a *bone* (as *strong*); (by extension) the *body*; (figurative) the *substance*, i.e. (as pronoun) *selfsame*:—body, bone, × life, (self-) same, strength, × very.

A feminine singular noun meaning bone, substance, self. The first use of the term in the Bible is in Genesis when Adam proclaimed Eve was bone of his bones (Ge 2:23). This phrase is echoed later as an idiom of close relationship (Jgs 9:2; 2Sa 19:13[14]). The word can also be employed for animal bones (Ex 12:46; Nu 9:12; Job 40:18). Speaking figuratively, Jeremiah said

that the Word of God was like fire shut in his bones (Jer 20:9). 'Etsem can also denote identity, as in the phrase *bᵉ'etsem hayyôwm hazzeh*, (in this very day; Ex 12:17). A similar construction is seen in Ex 24:10 (the sky itself).

6107. עֶצֶם, **'Etsem,** *eh´-tsem*; the same as 6106; *bone*; *Etsem*, a place in Palestine:—Azem, Ezem.

6108. עֹצֶם, **'ôtsem,** *o´-tsem*; from 6105; *power*; hence *body*:—might, strong, substance.

6109. עָצְמָה, **'otsmâh,** *ots-maw´*; feminine of 6108; *powerfulness*; (by extension) *numerousness*:—abundance, strength.

6110. עַצֻמוֹת, **'ǎtsumôwth,** *ah-tsoo-moth´*; feminine of 6099; a *bulwark*, i.e. (figurative) *argument*:—strong.

6111. עַצְמוֹן, **'Atsmôwn,** *ats-mone´*; or עַצְמֹן, **'Ats-môn,** *ats-mone´*; from 6107; *bone-like*; *Atsmon*, a place near Palestine:—Azmon.

6112. עֵצֶן, **'êtsen,** *ay´-tsen*; from an unused root meaning to *be sharp* or *strong*; a *spear*:—Eznite [*from the margin*].

6113. עָצַר, **'âtsar,** *aw-tsar´*; a primitive root; to *inclose*; (by analogy) to *hold back*; also to *maintain, rule, assemble*:— × be able, close up, detain, fast, keep (self close, still), prevail, recover, refrain, × reign, restrain, retain, shut (up), slack, stay, stop, withhold (self).

6114. עֶצֶר, **'etser,** *eh´-tser*; from 6113; *restraint*:— + magistrate.

6115. עֹצֶר, **'ôtser,** *o´-tser*; from 6113; *closure*; also *constraint*:— × barren, oppression, × prison.

6116. עֲצָרָה, **'ǎtsârâh,** *ats-aw-raw´*; or עֲצֶרֶת, **'ǎtsereth,** *ats-eh´-reth*; from 6113; an *assembly*, especially on a *festival* or *holiday*:—(solemn) assembly (meeting).

A feminine singular noun meaning assembly. This use of assembly usually has some religious or cultic connection; thus, it is often translated solemn assembly. These assemblies may be according to God's Law, such as the Feast of Passover (Dt 16:8); or the all-day gathering at the end of the Feast of Booths in Ne 8:18. But other assemblies were for the worship of other gods (2Ki 10:20); or were detestable to God because of Israel's wickedness (Isa 1:13; Am 5:21).

6117. עָקַב, **'âqab,** aw-kab'; a primitive root; (properly) to *swell* out or up; used only as denominative from 6119, to *seize by the heel*; (figurative) to *circumvent* (as if *tripping* up the heels); also to *restrain* (as if holding by the heel):—take by the heel, stay, supplant, × utterly.

A verb meaning to grasp at the heel, to supplant, to deceive. This verb is derived from the noun meaning heel ('âqêb [6119]) and is connected etymologically to the name Jacob (ya'ăqôb). The first occurrence sets the backdrop for the other uses. After Jacob tricked his brother Esau out of Isaac's blessing, Esau says, "He is rightly called 'Jacob'—for he has tricked (*Jacobed*) me twice" (Ge 27:36). In Jer 9:4[3], reflecting on the Jacob story, the prophet said every brother deceives. Hosea used the term in its more literal meaning when he recalled that Jacob grasped the heel of his brother in the womb (Hos 12:3[4]).

6118. עֵקֶב, **'êqeb,** ay'-keb; from 6117 in the sense of 6119; a *heel*, i.e. (figurative) the *last* of anything (used adverb *for ever*); also *result*, i.e. *compensation*; and so (adverb with preposition or relative) on *account* of:— × because, by, end, for, if, reward.

6119. עָקֵב, **'âqêb,** aw-kabe'; or (feminine) עִקְּבָה, **'iqq e bâh,** ik-keb-aw'; from 6117; a *heel* (as *protuberant*); hence a *track*; (figurative) the *rear* (of an army):—heel, [horse-] hoof, last, lier in wait [*by mistake for* 6120], (foot-) step.

A masculine singular noun meaning a heel, footprints, a back, a rear. The basic meaning of the word is heel and is seen in the passage where the serpent was told that he would strike at the heel of Eve's offspring (Ge 3:15). Jacob grasped Esau's heel in the womb (Ge 25:26). But the term can also be used to refer to the mark left by the heel (that is, a footprint) (Ps 56:6[7]; 77:19[20]; SS 1:8). It is also used in a military context to mean rear, that is, at the heels (Ge 49:19; Jos 8:13).

6120. עָקֵב, **'âqêb,** aw-kabe'; from 6117 in its denominative sense; a *lier in wait*:—heel [*by mistake for* 6119].

6121. עָקֹב, **'âqôb,** aw-kobe'; from 6117; in the original sense, a *knoll* (as *swelling* up); in the denominative sense (transitive) *fraudulent*

or (intransitive) *tracked*:—crooked, deceitful, polluted.

This form actually represents two adjectives. The first means deceitful, insidious, "footprinted." It is from the verb 'âqab (6117) and the noun 'âqêb (6119). As Jeremiah proclaimed God's efforts with sinful humanity, he also declared that the heart is more deceitful than anything (Jer 17:9). The other usage is related to the word for footprint. To describe the wickedness of Gilead, the prophet called it a town of bloody footprints (Hos 6:8). The second adjective means steep, hilly. Isaiah spoke of making a path for the exiles to return, making the hilly places like a plain (Isa 40:4). This famous passage is appropriated in the Gospels to describe John the Baptist's preparation for Jesus' ministry.

6122. עָקְבָה, **'oqbâh,** ok-baw'; feminine of an unused form from 6117 meaning a *trick*; *trickery*:—subtilty.

6123. עָקַד, **'âqad,** aw-kad'; a primitive root; to *tie* with thongs:—bind.

6124. עָקֹד, **'âqôd,** aw-kode'; from 6123; *striped* (with *bands*):—ring straked.

6125. עָקָה, **'âqâh,** aw-kaw'; from 5781; *constraint*:—oppression.

6126. עַקּוּב, **'Aqqûb,** ak-koob'; from 6117; *insidious*; *Akkub*, the name of five Israelites:—Akkub.

6127. עָקַל, **'âqal,** aw-kal'; a primitive root; to *wrest*:—wrong.

6128. עֲקַלְקַל, **'ăqalqal,** ak-al-kal'; from 6127; *winding*:—by [-way], crooked way.

6129. עֲקַלָּתוֹן, **'ăqallâthôwn,** ak-al-law-thone'; from 6127; *tortuous*:—crooked.

6130. עָקָן, **'Âqân,** ah-kawn'; from an unused root meaning to *twist*; *tortuous*; *Akan*, an Idumæan:—Akan. Compare 3292.

6131. עָקַר, **'âqar,** aw-kar'; a primitive root; to *pluck* up (especially by the roots); (specifically) to *hamstring*; (figurative) to *exterminate*:—dig down, hough, pluck up, root up.

6132. עֲקַר, **'ăqar,** ak-ar'; (Chaldee); corresponding to 6131:—pluck up by the roots.

6133. עֵקֶר, **'êqer,** *ay´-ker*; from 6131; (figurative) a *transplanted* person, i.e. naturalized citizen:—stock.

6134. עֵקֶר, **'Êqer,** *ay´-ker*; the same as 6133; *Eker,* an Israelite:—Eker.

6135. עָקָר, **'âqâr,** *aw-kawr´*; from 6131; *sterile* (as if *extirpated* in the generative organs):—(× male or female) barren (woman).

6136. עִקַּר, **'iqqar,** *ik-kar´*; (Chaldee); from 6132; a *stock*:—stump.

6137. עֶקְרָב, **'aqrâb,** *ak-rawb´*; of uncertain derivation; a *scorpion*; (figurative) a *scourge* or knotted whip:—scorpion.

6138. עֶקְרוֹן, **'Eqrôwn,** *ek-rone´*; from 6131; *eradication; Ekron,* a place in Palestine:—Ekron.

6139. עֶקְרוֹנִי, **'Eqrôwnîy,** *ek-ro-nee´*; or עֶקְרֹנִי, **'Eqrônîy,** *ek-ro-nee´*; patrial from 6138; an *Ekronite* or inhabitant of Ekron:—Ekronite.

6140. עָקַשׁ, **'âqash,** *aw-kash´*; a primitive root; to *knot* or *distort*; (figurative) to *pervert* (act or declare perverse):—make crooked, (prove, that is) perverse (-rt).

6141. עִקֵּשׁ, **'iqqêsh,** *ik-kashe´*; from 6140; *distorted*; hence *false*:—crooked, froward, perverse.

6142. עִקֵּשׁ, **'Iqqêsh,** *ik-kashe´*; the same as 6141; *perverse; Ikkesh,* an Israelite:—Ikkesh.

6143. עִקְּשׁוּת, **'iqqᵉshûwth,** *ik-kesh-ooth´*; from 6141; *perversity*:— × froward.

6144. עָר, **'Âr,** *awr*; the same as 5892; a *city; Ar,* a place in Moab:—Ar.

6145. עָר, **'âr,** *awr*; from 5782; a *foe* (as *watchful* for mischief):—enemy.

6146. עָר, **'âr,** *awr*; (Chaldee); corresponding to 6145:—enemy.

6147. עֵר, **'Êr,** *ayr*; from 5782; *watchful; Er,* the name of two Israelites:—Er.

6148. עָרַב, **'ârab,** *aw-rab´*; a primitive root; to *braid,* i.e. *intermix*; (technical) to *traffic* (as if by barter); also to *give* or *be security* (as a kind of exchange):—engage, (inter-) meddle (with), mingle (self), mortgage, occupy, give pledges, be (-come, put in) surety, undertake.

A verb meaning to exchange, to take as a pledge, to give as a pledge. This word denotes the action of giving a pledge or a guarantee (Ge 43:9); a pledge given in exchange for the delivery of material goods (2Ki 18:23); the action of taking possession of exchanged material (Eze 27:9); and the mortgage of property (Ne 5:3). By extension, it was used in reference to the scattering of the Jews among the nations (Ps 106:35); and implied sharing or association at a meaningful level (Pr 14:10; 20:19). In Jer 30:21, it conveyed the idea of purposing or engaging to meet with the Lord.

6149. עָרַב, **'ârab,** *aw-rab´*; a primitive root [rather identical with 6148 through the idea of close *association*]; to be *agreeable*:—be pleasant (-ing), take pleasure in, be sweet.

6150. עָרַב, **'ârab,** *aw-rab´*; a primitive root [rather identical with 6148 through the idea of *covering* with a texture]; to *grow dusky* at sundown:—be darkened, (toward) evening.

6151. עֲרַב, **'ărab,** *ar-ab´*; (Chaldee); corresponding to 6148; to *commingle*:—mingle (self), mix.

An Aramaic verb meaning to mix, to mingle, to join together. Daniel used this word to describe the feet of the image Nebuchadnezzar saw in his dream (Da 2:41, 43). They were a curious mixture of clay and iron. Thus, the word implies an amalgamation of two uncomplementary materials, which is at best unstable.

6152. עֲרָב, **'Ărâb,** *ar-ab´*; or עֲרַב, **'Ărab,** *ar-awb´*; from 6150 in the figurative sense of *sterility; Arab* (i.e. *Arabia*), a country East of Palestine:—Arabia.

6153. עֶרֶב, **'ereb,** *eh´-reb*; from 6150; *dusk*:—+ day, even (-ing, tide), night.

6154. עֵרֶב, **'êreb,** *ay´-reb*; or עֶרֶב, **'ereb,** *eh´-reb*; (1Ki 10:15), (with the article prefixed), from 6148; the *web* (or transverse threads of cloth); also a *mixture,* (or *mongrel* race):—Arabia, mingled people, mixed (multitude), woof.

A masculine noun meaning a mixture, a mixed company, interwoven. The primary meaning is a grouping of people from various ethnic and cultural backgrounds. It was used of any heterogeneous band associated with the nation of Israel as it departed Egypt (Ex 12:38);

the tribes not aligned with any specific culture (Jer 25:24); and the mingled people resulting from the Babylonian captivity (Jer 50:37). By extension, the word was also used of interwoven material of varying fibers (Le 13:48).

6155. עֲרָבָה, **ʻărâbâh,** *ah-raw-baw´*; from 6148; a *willow* (from the use of osiers as wattles):—willow.

6156. עָרֵב, **ʻârêb,** *aw-rabe´*; from 6149; *pleasant*:—sweet.

6157. עָרֹב, **ʻârôb,** *aw-robe´*; from 6148; a *mosquito* (from its *swarming*):—divers sorts of flies, swarm.

6158. עֹרֵב, **ʻôrêb,** *o-rabe´*; or עוֹרֵב, **ʻôwrêb,** *o-rabe´*; from 6150; a *raven* (from its *dusky* hue):—raven.

6159. עֹרֵב, **ʻÔrêb,** *o-rabe´*; or עוֹרֵב, **ʻÔwrêb,** *o-rabe´*; the same as 6158; *Oreb*, the name of a Midianite and of a cliff near the Jordan:—Oreb.

6160. עֲרָבָה, **ʻărâbâh,** *ar-aw-baw´*; from 6150 (in the sense of *sterility*); a *desert*; especially (with the article prefixed) the (general) sterile valley of the Jordan and its continuation to the Red Sea:—Arabah, champaign, desert, evening, heaven, plain, wilderness. See also 1026.

A feminine noun meaning a desert plain, a steppe, a wilderness. This word designates a prominent geographic feature of the Middle East. It is used to designate the arid plateau in south Judah (Isa 51:3; see also 1Sa 23:24); various portions of the Jordan River valley and the adjacent plains (Jos 12:1; 2Sa 2:29); the desert area in northern Arabia (Dt 1:1); and any generic land formation similar to these arid plateaus (Dt 1:7; Isa 40:3). There is some uncertainty as to the use of this word in Ps 68:4[5]. Most translations render the word as heavens or clouds, rather than the more literal meaning, desert.

6161. עֲרֻבָּה, **ʻărubbâh,** *ar-oob-baw´*; feminine passive participle of 6048 in the sense of a *bargain* or *exchange*; something given as *security*, i.e. (literal) a *token* (of safety) or (metaphorical) a *bondsman*:—pledge, surety.

A feminine noun meaning a pledge, a guarantee, a token. Occurring only twice in the Hebrew Bible, this word implies a tangible sign of a current or soon-expected reality. It was used specifically in reference to an assurance of well-

being brought from the battlefield (1Sa 17:18); and a collateral exchanged at the making of a pledge (Pr 17:18).

6162. עֵרָבוֹן, **ʻêrâbôwn,** *ay-raw-bone´*; from 6148 (in the sense of *exchange*); a *pawn* (given as security):—pledge.

A masculine noun meaning pledge. It is a deposit given as evidence and proof that something else will be done. When the act is accomplished, the pledge is returned. Judah gave his seal and staff to Tamar, whom he believed was a temple prostitute, as a guarantee that he would return the next day so he might give her a young goat as payment for her services and then reacquire his seal and staff (Ge 38:17, 18, 20). It is also probable that this word is what is meant in Job's reply to Eliphaz (see Job 17:3).

6163. עֲרָבִי, **ʻĂrâbîy,** *ar-aw-bee´*; or עַרְבִי, **ʻArbîy,** *ar-bee´*; patrial from 6152; an *Arabian* or inhabitant of Arab (i.e. Arabia):—Arabian.

6164. עַרְבָתִי, **ʻArbâthîy,** *ar-baw-thee´*; patrial from 1026; an *Arbathite* or inhabitant of (Beth-) Arabah:—Arbathite.

6165. עָרַג, **ʻârag,** *aw-rag´*; a primitive root; to *long* for:—cry, pant.

6166. עֲרָד, **ʻĂrâd,** *ar-awd´*; from an unused root meaning to *sequester* itself; *fugitive; Arad*, the name of a place near Palestine, also of a Canaanite and an Israelite:—Arad.

6167. עֲרָד, **ʻărâd,** *ar-awd´*; (Chaldee); corresponding to 6171; an *onager*:—wild ass.

6168. עֵרָבוֹן, **ʻêrâbôwn,** *ay-raw-bone´*; a primitive root; to *be* (causative, *make*) *bare*; hence to *empty, pour* out, *demolish*:—leave destitute, discover, empty, make naked, pour (out), rase, spread self, uncover.

6169. עָרָה, **ʻârâh,** *aw-raw´*; feminine from 6168; a *naked* (i.e. level) plot:—paper reed.

6170. עֲרוּגָה, **ʻărûwgâh,** *ar-oo-gaw´*; or עֲרֻגָה, **ʻăru-gâh,** *ar-oo-gaw´*; feminine passive participle of 6165; something *piled* up (as if [figurative] *raised* by mental aspiration), i.e. a *parterre*:—bed, furrow.

6171. עָרוֹד, **ʻârôwd,** *aw-rode´*; from the same as 6166; an *onager* (from his *lonesome* habits):—wild ass.

6172. עֶרְוָה, **'ervâh,** *er-vaw´*; from 6168; *nudity*, literal (especially the *pudenda*) or figurative (*disgrace, blemish*):—nakedness, shame, unclean (-ness).

A feminine noun expressing nakedness. This word can pertain to physical nakedness for either a man or a woman (Ge 9:22, 23; Ex 20:26); however, it is more often used in a figurative sense. When used with the verbs *gâlâh* (1540), meaning to uncover or remove, and *râ'âh* (7200), meaning to see, one finds a common euphemism for sexual relations—to uncover one's nakedness (Le 18:6; 20:17). On the other hand, when combined with the verb *kâsâh* (3680), meaning to cover, one finds a common idiom for entering into a marriage contract (Eze 16:8). Nakedness is also a symbol of the shame and disgrace of Egypt (Isa 20:4); Babylonia (Isa 47:3); and Jerusalem (Eze 16:37). Furthermore, when in construct with *dâbâr* (1697), meaning a word, matter, or thing, this term forms an idiom for indecent or improper behaviour (Dt 23:14[15]; 24:1). When in construct with the word *'erets* (776), it can refer to exposed or undefended areas (Ge 42:9, 12).

6173. עֶרְוָה, **'arvâh,** *ar-vaw´*; (Chaldee); corresponding to 6172; *nakedness*, i.e. (figurative) *impoverishment*:—dishonour.

6174. עָרוֹם, **'ârôwm,** *aw-rome´*; or עָרֹם, **'ârôm,** *aw-rome´*; from 6191 (in its orig. sense); *nude*, either partially or totally:—naked.

An adjective meaning naked. It can allude to physical nakedness (Ge 2:25; 1Sa 19:24; Isa 20:2–4). It can also be used figuratively to relate to one who has no possessions (Job 1:21; Ecc 5:15 [14]). Moreover, Sheol is described as being naked before God, a statement of its openness and vulnerability to God and His power (Job 26:6).

6175. עָרוּם, **'ârûwm,** *aw-room´*; passive participle of 6191; *cunning* (usually in a bad sense):—crafty, prudent, subtil.

An adjective meaning crafty, shrewd, sensible. This adjective can have either a positive or negative connotation. In a positive connotation, it is understood as being prudent. As such, a prudent individual takes no offence at an insult (Pr 12:16); does not flaunt his knowledge (Pr 12:23); takes careful thought of his ways (Pr 14:8); takes careful thought before action (Pr

14:15); is crowned with knowledge (Pr 14:18); and sees and avoids danger (Pr 22:3; 27:12). When the word has a negative meaning, it means being crafty (Job 5:12; 15:5). This word is used when the Bible describes the serpent in the Garden of Eden. The serpent was more subtle [crafty] than any beast of the field (Ge 3:1). This description is presented in stark contrast to the situation of Adam and Eve. They sought to be crafty like the serpent, but they only realized that they were *'êyrôm* (5903), meaning naked.

6176. עֲרוֹעֵר, **'ărôw'êr,** *ar-o-ayr´*; or עַרְעָר, **'ar'âr,** *ar-awr´*; from 6209 reduplication; a *juniper* (from its *nudity* of situation):—heath.

6177. עֲרוֹעֵר, **'Ărôw'êr,** *ar-o-ayr´*; or עֲרֹעֵר, **'Ărô'êr,** *ar-o-ayr´*; or עַרְעוֹר, **'Ar'ôwr,** *ar-ore´*; the same as 6176; *nudity* of situation; *Aroër*, the name of three places in or near Palestine:—Aroer.

6178. עָרוּץ, **'ărûwts,** *aw-roots´*; passive participle of 6206; *feared*, i.e. (concrete) a *horrible* place or *chasm*:—cliffs.

6179. עֵרִי, **'Êrîy,** *ay-ree´*; from 5782; *watchful*; *Eri*, an Israelite:—Eri.

6180. עֵרִי, **'Êrîy,** *ay-ree´*; patronymic of 6179; an *Erite* (collective) or descendants of Eri:—Erites.

6181. עֶרְיָה, **'eryâh,** *er-yaw´*; for 6172; *nudity*:—bare, naked, × quite.

A feminine noun meaning nakedness. This term is only used figuratively. It can function as a metaphor for shame and disgrace. In the allegory of unfaithful Jerusalem, God stated that Jerusalem was naked and bare, *'êrôm* (5903) *wĕ'eryâh* (Eze 16:7). The inhabitants of Shaphir were considered to be in the nakedness of shame, *'eryâh bôsheth* (1322) (Mic 1:11). It is also used to indicate the outpouring of God's wrath on the earth by the allusion to God's bow being naked or uncovered, meaning that it was taken from its storage place and put to use (Hab 3:9).

6182. עֲרִיסָה, **'ărîysâh,** *ar-ee-saw´*; from an unused root meaning to *comminute*; *meal*:—dough.

6183. עֲרִיפִים, **'ărîyphîym,** *aw-reef-eem´*; from 6201; the *sky* (as *drooping* at the horizon):—heaven.

A masculine noun meaning cloud. Isaiah used this word when he pronounced God's judgments on Israel by means of foreign nations. He stated that the judgment would be so severe that there would be only darkness and distress; there would be no light, as when storm clouds block out the light (Isa 5:30).

6184. עָרִיץ, **‘ârîyts,** aw-reets´; from 6206; *fearful*, i.e. *powerful* or *tyrannical*:—mighty, oppressor, in great power, strong, terrible, violent.

6185. עֲרִירִי, **‘ărîyrîy,** ar-ee-ree´; from 6209; *bare*, i.e. *destitute* (of children):—childless.

6186. עָרַךְ, **‘ârak,** aw-rak´; a primitive root; to set in a *row*, i.e. *arrange*, put in *order* (in a very wide variety of applications):—put (set) (the battle, self) in array, compare, direct, equal, esteem, estimate, expert [in war], furnish, handle, join [battle], ordain, (lay, put, reckon up, set) (in) order, prepare, tax, value.

6187. עֵרֶךְ, **‘erek,** eh´-rek; from 6186; a *pile*, *equipment*, *estimate*:—equal, estimation, (things that are set in) order, price, proportion, × set at, suit, taxation, × valuest.

6188. עָרֵל, **‘ârêl,** aw-rale´; a primitive root; (properly) to *strip*; but used only as denominative from 6189; to *expose* or *remove* the *prepuce*, whether literal (to *go naked*) or figurative (to *refrain* from using):—count uncircumcised, foreskin to be uncovered.

6189. עָרֵל, **‘ârêl,** aw-rale´; from 6188; (properly) *exposed*, i.e. projecting loose (as to the prepuce); (used only technically) *uncircumcised* (i.e. still having the prepuce uncurtailed):—uncircumcised (person).

A masculine adjective meaning uncircumcised. In the literal sense, it was used to designate a specific individual (Ge 17:14; Ex 12:48); a group (Jos 5:7); or a nation, especially the Philistines (1Sa 14:6; Isa 52:1). In addition to the simple statement of physical condition, the term could also convey an attitude of derision since the object was considered unclean and impure (Jgs 14:3; 15:18). Furthermore, the term could be used metaphorically to describe the corrupted nature of certain body parts: uncircumcised lips denoted an inability to speak effectively (Ex 6:12, 30; cf. Isa 6:5); uncircumcised in heart represented a flawed character and precluded

entrance to the Temple (Eze 44:7, 9); and uncircumcised in the ear signified an inability to hear (Jer 6:10). Also, the fruit of newly planted trees was considered uncircumcised (unclean) for the first three years (Le 19:23).

6190. עָרְלָה, **‘orlâh,** or-law´; feminine of 6189; the *prepuce*:—foreskin, + uncircumcised.

A feminine noun meaning foreskin. The word could represent just the foreskin (Ge 17:11; 1Sa 18:25, 27); the state of being uncircumcised (having a foreskin [Ge 34:14]); or the act of circumcision (cutting off the foreskin [Ex 4:25]). Like the word *‘ârêl* (6189), this term could be used figuratively to represent the impure nature of fruit trees (Le 19:23); or the human heart (Dt 10:16; Jer 4:4).

6191. עָרַם, **‘âram,** aw-ram´; a primitive root; (properly) to *be* (or *make*) *bare*; but used only in the derivative sense (through the idea perhaps of *smoothness*) to *be cunning* (usually in a bad sense):— × very, beware, take crafty [counsel], be prudent, deal subtilly.

A verb meaning to be shrewd, to be subtle. This verb has a neutral tone but can assume either a negative tone: crafty and tricky (1Sa 23:22; Ps 83:3[4]); or a positive tone: prudent and wise (Pr 15:5; 19:25).

6192. עָרַם, **‘âram,** aw-ram´; a primitive root; to *pile* up:—gather together.

A verb meaning to be heaped up. This verb occurs once in the Hebrew Bible in Ex 15:8. In Moses' song at the sea, he describes God's miraculous act by singing about how the waters were heaped up.

6193. עֹרֶם, **‘ôrem,** o´-rem; from 6191; a *stratagem*:—craftiness.

A masculine singular noun meaning craftiness. Its only use in the Hebrew Bible is in the book of Job. Eliphaz told Job that God catches the wise in their craftiness. He cannot be fooled (Job 5:13). See the verb *‘âram* (6191).

6194. עָרֵם, **‘ârêm,** aw-rame´; (Jer 50:26), or (feminine) עֲרֵמָה, **‘ărêmâh,** ar-ay-maw´; from 6192; a *heap*; (specifically) a *sheaf*:—heap (of corn), sheaf.

6195. עָרְמָה, **‘ormâh,** or-maw´; feminine of 6193; *trickery*; or (in a good sense) *discretion*:—guile, prudence, subtilty, wilily, wisdom.

A feminine singular noun meaning craftiness, prudence. Ex 21:14 employs it adverbially (schemes craftily) as does Jos 9:4, where the foreign kings tricked Joshua into making a treaty. In Proverbs, the word has a different connotation. Both in the instruction for a son (Pr 1:4) and in describing Lady Wisdom who has *'ormâh* with her (Pr 8:5, 12), the term is best translated prudence. See the verb *'âram* (6191).

6196. עַרְמוֹן, **'armôwn,** *ar-mone´*; probably from 6191; the *plane* tree (from its *smooth* and shed bark):—chestnut tree.

6197. עֵרָן, **'Êrân,** *ay-rawn´*; probably from 5782; *watchful; Eran,* an Israelite:—Eran.

6198. עֵרָנִי, **'Êrânîy,** *ay-raw-nee´*; patronymic from 6197; an *Eranite* or descendants (collective) of Eran:—Eranites.

6199. עַרְעָר, **'ar'âr,** *ar-awr´*; from 6209; *naked,* i.e. (figurative) *poor:*—destitute. See also 6176.

6200. עַרְעֵרִי, **'Ărô'êrîy,** *ar-o-ay-ree´*; patronymic from 6177; an *Aroërite* or inhabitant of Aroër:—Aroerite.

6201. עָרַף, **'âraph,** *aw-raf´*; a primitive root; to *droop*; hence to *drip:*—drop (down).

A verb translated to drip, to drop. In Moses' final blessing of Israel, he says they would experience God's security and bounty where His heavens drop dew (Dt 33:28). In Moses' final song, he prayed that his teaching would drop like rain on his listeners (Dt 32:2). See the nominal form of this root, *'ărâphel* (6205), which means cloud.

6202. עָרַף, **'âraph,** *aw-raf´*; a primitive root [rather identical with 6201 through the idea of *sloping*]; (properly) to *bend* downward; but used only as a denominative from 6203, to *break the neck*; hence (figurative) to *destroy:*—that is beheaded, break down, break (cut off), strike off) neck.

6203. עֹרֶף, **'ôreph,** *o-ref´*; from 6202; the *nape* or back of the neck (as *declining*); hence the *back* generally (whether literal or figurative):—back ([stiff-] neck ([-ed]).

6204. עָרְפָּה, **'Orpâh,** *or-paw´*; feminine of 6203; *mane; Orpah,* a Moabitess:—Orpah.

6205. עֲרָפֶל, **'ărâphel,** *ar-aw-fel´*; probably from 6201; *gloom* (as of a *lowering* sky):—(gross, thick) dark (cloud, -ness).

A masculine singular noun meaning cloud. A cloud enshrouded God (Ex 20:21; Job 22:13); and also served as His pedestal (2Sa 22:10; Ps 18:9[10]). The term is used figuratively to depict a stormy sea that has clouds for a garment (Job 38:9). Prophetic pictures of God's judgment are filled with clouds, darkening the ominous Day of the Lord (Jer 13:16; Eze 34:12; Joel 2:2; Zep 1:15).

6206. עָרַץ, **'ârats,** *aw-rats´*; a primitive root; to *awe* or (intrans.) to *dread*; hence to *harass:*—be affrighted (afraid, dread, feared, terrified), break, dread, fear, oppress, prevail, shake terribly.

A verb which means to tremble, to cause to tremble, to strike with awe, to strike with dread. The Lord's splendor can make the earth tremble (Isa 2:19, 21). Job wondered why God must overwhelm humans who are nothing more than driven leaves (Job 13:25). God and His leaders continually reminded the Israelites before battle not to be terrified by the enemy because God who would fight for them (Dt 1:29; 7:21; 20:3; 31:6; Jos 1:9). If God is with us, we have no need to dread humans and their conspiracies and plots (Isa 8:12).

6207. עָרַק, **'âraq,** *aw-rak´*; a primitive root; to *gnaw*, i.e. (figurative) *eat* (by hyperbole); also (participle) a *pain:*—fleeing, sinew.

6208. עַרְקִי, **'Arqîy,** *ar-kee´*; patrial from an unused name meaning a *tush*; an *Arkite* or inhabitant of Erek:—Arkite.

6209. עָרַר, **'ârar,** *aw-rar´*; a primitive root; to *bare*; (figurative) to *demolish:*—make bare, break, raise up [*perhaps by clerical error for* RAZE], × utterly.

6210. עֶרֶשׂ, **'ereś,** *eh´-res*; from an unused root meaning perhaps to *arch*; a *couch* (properly with a *canopy*):—bed (-stead), couch.

6211. עָשׁ, **'âsh,** *awsh*; from 6244; a *moth:*—moth. See also 5906. NOTE: Strong's has two words numbered 6211; the second definition follows: עֲשַׂב, **'ăśab,** *as-ab´*, (Chaldee); 6212:—grass.

6212. עֵשֶׂב, **'eśeb,** *eh´-seb*; from an unused root meaning to *glisten* (or *be green*); *grass* (or any tender shoot):—grass, herb.

6213. עָשָׂה, **'aśah,** *aw-saw´*; a primitive root; to *do* or *make*, in the broadest sense and widest application (as follows):—accomplish, advance, appoint, apt, be at, become, bear, bestow, bring forth, bruise, be busy, × certainly, have the charge of, commit, deal (with), deck, + displease, do, (ready) dress (-ed), (put in) execute (-ion), exercise, fashion, + feast, [fight-] ing man, + finish, fit, fly, follow, fulfil, furnish, gather, get, go about, govern, grant, great, + hinder, hold ([a feast]), × indeed, + be industrious, + journey, keep, labour, maintain, make, be meet, observe, be occupied, offer, + officer, pare, bring (come) to pass, perform, practise, prepare, procure, provide, put, requite, × sacrifice, serve, set, shew, × sin, spend, × surely, take, × throughly, trim, × very, + vex, be [warr-] ior, work (-man), yield, use.

A verb meaning to do, to make, to accomplish, to complete. This frequently used Hebrew verb conveys the central notion of performing an activity with a distinct purpose, a moral obligation, or a goal in view (cf. Ge 11:6). Particularly, it was used in conjunction with God's commands (Dt 16:12). It described the process of construction (Ge 13:4; Job 9:9; Pr 8:26); engaging in warfare (Jos 11:18); the yielding of grain (Hos 8:7); observing a religious ceremony (Ex 31:16; Nu 9:4); and the completion of something (Ezr 10:3; Isa 46:10). Provocatively, the word appears twice in Ezekiel to imply the intimate action of caressing or fondling the female breast (Eze 23:3, 8).

6214. עֲשָׂהאֵל, **'Ăśah'êl,** *as-aw-ale´*; from 6213 and 410; *God has made; Asahel*, the name of four Israelites:—Asahel.

6215. עֵשָׂו, **'Êśav,** *ay-sawv´*; apparently a form of the passive participle of 6213 in the original sense of *handling; rough* (i.e. sensibly *felt*); *Esav*, a son of Isaac, including his posterity:—Esau.

6216. עָשׁוֹק, **'ashôwq,** *aw-shoke´*; from 6231; *oppressive* (as noun, a *tyrant*):—oppressor.

6217. עֲשׁוּקִים, **'ăshûwqîym,** *aw-shoo-keem´*; passive participle of 6231; used in plural masculine as abstract *tyranny*:—oppressed (-ion). [*Doubtful.*]

6218. עָשׂוֹר, **'âśôwr,** *aw-sore´*; or עָשֹׂר, **'âśôr,** *aw-sore´*; from 6235; *ten*; by abbreviation ten *strings*, and so a *decachord*:—(instrument of) ten (strings, -th).

6219. עָשׁוֹת, **'âshôwth,** *aw-shōth´*; from 6245; *shining*, i.e. polished:—bright.

6220. עַשְׁוָת, **'Ashvâth,** *ash-vawth´*; for 6219; *bright; Ashvath*, an Israelite:—Ashvath.

6221. עֲשִׂיאֵל, **'Ăśîy'êl,** *as-ee-ale´*; from 6213 and 410; *made of God; Asiel*, an Israelite:—Asiel.

6222. עֲשָׂיָה, **'Ăśâyâh,** *aw-saw-yaw´*; from 6213 and 3050; *Jah has made; Asajah*, the name of three or four Israelites:—Asaiah.

6223. עָשִׁיר, **'âshîyr,** *aw-sheer´*; from 6238; *rich*, whether literal or figurative (*noble*):—rich (man).

6224. עֲשִׂירִי, **'ăśîyrîy,** *as-ee-ree´*; from 6235; *tenth*; (by abbreviation) *tenth month* or (feminine) *part*:—tenth (part).

6225. עָשַׁן, **'âshan,** *aw-shan´*; a primitive root; to *smoke*, whether literal or figurative:—be angry (be on a) smoke.

A verb meaning to smoke, to be angry, to be furious. The literal meaning of this Hebrew word is to smolder or smoke (Ex 19:18; Ps 144:5). Metaphorically, it was used by the psalmist to convey the idea of fuming anger (Ps 74:1; 80:4[5]).

6226. עָשֵׁן, **'âshên,** *aw-shane´*; from 6225; *smoky*:—smoking.

6227. עָשָׁן, **'âshân,** *aw-shawn´*; from 6225; *smoke*, literal or figurative (*vapor, dust, anger*):—smoke (-ing).

6228. עָשָׁן, **'Âshân,** *aw-shawn´*; the same as 6227; *Ashan*, a place in Palestine:—Ashan.

6229. עָשַׂק, **'âśaq,** *aw-sak´*; a primitive root (identical with 6231); to *press upon*, i.e. *quarrel*:—strive with.

6230. עֵשֶׂק, **'êśeq,** *ay´-sek*; from 6229; *strife*:—Esek.

6231. עָשַׁק, **'âshaq,** *aw-shak´*; a primitive root (compare 6229); to *press upon*, i.e. *oppress, defraud, violate, overflow*:—get deceitfully, deceive, defraud, drink up, (use) oppress ([-ion], -or), do violence (wrong).

6232. עֶשֶׁק, **'Êsheq,** *ay-shek´*; from 6231; *oppression*; *Eshek*, an Israelite:—Eshek.

6233. עֹשֶׁק, **'ôsheq,** *o´-shek*; from 6231; *injury, fraud,* (subjective) *distress,* (concrete) *unjust gain:*—cruelly, extortion, oppression, thing [deceitfully gotten].

6234. עָשְׁקָה, **'oshqâh,** *osh-kaw´*; feminine of 6233; *anguish:*—oppressed.

6235. עֶשֶׂר, **'eśer,** *eh´-ser*; masculine עֲשָׂרָה, **'ăśârâh,** *as-aw-raw´*; from 6237; *ten* (as an *accumulation* to the extent of the digits):—ten, [fif-, seven-] teen.

6236. עֲשַׂר, **'ăśar,** *as-ar´*; (Chaldee); masculine עֶשְׂרָה, **'aśrâh,** *as-raw´*; (Chaldee); corresponding to 6235; *ten:*—ten, + twelve.

6237. עָשַׂר, **'âśar,** *aw-sar´*; a primitive root (identical with 6238); to *accumulate*; but used only as denominative from 6235; to *tithe*, i.e. take or give a tenth:— × surely, give (take) the tenth, (have, take) tithe (-ing, -s), × truly.

A verb meaning to give a tenth part, to take a tenth part, to give the tithe, to receive the tithe. This pivotal Hebrew word first appears in reference to a vow made by Jacob (Ge 28:22). He promised to return one-tenth of his possessions to the Lord if the Lord would go with him. Under the Law given by Moses, this tithe was made mandatory on all increase (Dt 14:22; see also Dt 26:12). It was the duty of the priest to receive these tithes (Ne 10:37[38], 38[39]). Samuel also used this word to describe the taxes imposed by a king (1Sa 8:15, 17).

6238. עָשַׁר, **'âshar,** *aw-shar´*; a primitive root; (properly) to *accumulate*; chiefly (specific) to *grow* (causative, *make*) *rich:*—be (-come, en-, make, make self, wax) rich, make [1Ki 22:48 *margin*]. See 6240.

6239. עֹשֶׁר, **'ôsher,** *o´-sher*; from 6238; *wealth:*— × far [richer], riches.

6240. עָשָׂר, **'âśar,** *aw-sawr´*; for 6235; *ten* (only in combination), i.e. *-teen*; also (ordinal) *-teenth:*—[eigh-, fif-, four-, nine-, seven-, six-, thir-] teen (-th), + eleven (-th), + sixscore thousand, + twelve (-th).

6241. עִשָּׂרוֹן, **'iśśârôwn,** *is-saw-rone´*; or עִשָּׂרֹן, **'iśśârôn,** *is-saw-rone´*; from 6235; (fractional) a *tenth* part:—tenth deal.

6242. עֶשְׂרִים, **'esrîym,** *es-reem´*; from 6235; *twenty*; also (ordinal) *twentieth:*—[six-] score, twenty (-ieth).

6243. עֶשְׂרִין, **'eśrîyn,** *es-reen´*; (Chaldee); corresponding to 6242:—twenty.

6244. עָשֵׁשׁ, **'âshêsh,** *aw-shaysh´*; a primitive root; probably to *shrink*, i.e. *fail:*—be consumed.

6245. עָשַׁת, **'âshath,** *aw-shath´*; a primitive root; probably to be *sleek*, i.e. *glossy*; hence (through the idea of *polishing*) to *excogitate* (as if *forming* in the mind):—shine, think.

6246. עֲשִׁת, **'ăshith,** *ash-eeth´*; (Chaldee); corresponding to 6245; to *purpose:*—think.

6247. עֶשֶׁת, **'esheth,** *eh´-sheth*; from 6245; a *fabric:*—bright.

6248. עַשְׁתּוּת, **'ashtûwth,** *ash-tooth´*; from 6245; *cogitation:*—thought.

6249. עַשְׁתֵּי, **'ashtêy,** *ash-tay´*; apparently masculine plural construction of 6247 in the sense of an *afterthought*; (used only in connection with 6240 in lieu of 259) *eleven* or (ordinal) *eleventh:*— + eleven (-th).

6250. עַשְׁתֹּנָה, **'eshtônâh,** *esh-to-naw´*; from 6245; *thinking:*—thought.

6251. עַשְׁתֶּרֶת, **'ashtereth,** *ash-ter-eth´*; probably from 6238; *increase:*—flock.

6252. עַשְׁתָּרוֹת, **'Ashtârôwth,** *ash-taw-roth´*; or עַשְׁתָּרֹת, **'Ashtâ-rôth,** *ash-taw-rōth´*; plural of 6251; *Ashtaroth*, the name of a Sidonian deity, and of a place East of the Jordan:—Ashtaroth, Astaroth. See also 1045, 6253, 6255.

6253. עַשְׁתֹּרֶת, **'Ashtôreth,** *ash-to´-reth*; probably for 6251; *Ashtoreth*, the Phoenician goddess of love (and *increase*):—Ashtoreth.

6254. עַשְׁתְּרָתִי, **'Ashterâthîy,** *ash-ter-aw-thee´*; patrial from 6252; an *Ashterathite* or inhabitant of Ashtaroth:—Ashterathite.

6255. עַשְׁתְּרֹת קַרְנַיִם, **'Ashterôth Qarnayim,** *ash-ter-ōth´ kar-nah´-yim*; from 6252 and the dual of 7161; *Ashtaroth of* (the) *double horns* (a symbol of the deity); *Ashteroth-Karnaïm*, a place East of the Jordan:—Ashtoreth Karnaim.

6256. עֵת, **ʻêth**, *ayth*; from 5703; *time*, especially (adverb with preposition) *now, when,* etc.:— + after, [al-] ways, × certain, + continually, + evening, long, (due) season, so [long] as, [even-, evening-, noon-] tide, ([meal-], what) time, when.

A masculine or feminine noun meaning time. The word basically means time. But in context, it expresses many aspects of time and kinds of time. It is used most often to express the time of the occurrence of some event. The word means at that time in a general sense, as when Abimelech and Phicol spoke to Abraham during the days when Ishmael was growing up (Ge 21:22; 38:1). The time described can be more specific, such as when Moses refers to the time of crisis in the wilderness when the people wanted meat to eat (Dt 1:9). It may refer to a specific date (Ex 9:18; 1Sa 9:16); or a part of a day, as when the dove returned to Noah in the evening (Ge 8:11; 24:11). The word can refer to a duration of time, as for all time (Ex 18:22; Pr 8:30); or for any time in general (Le 16:2). The time referred to may be past, present, or future (Nu 23:23; Jgs 13:23; Isa 9:1[8:23]). The word can describe times of the Lord's anger (Ps 21:9[10]); or times of trouble (Ps 9:9[10]). In fact, this word can be made to refer to about any kind of time or duration of time by its modifying words and context.

It is used to describe the time when certain appropriate things took place in general. For example, kings customarily went forth to war in the spring (2Sa 11:1; 1Ch 20:1). It can depict times that are fitting or suitable for certain reasons, such as rain falling on the land in its season (Dt 11:14; Jer 5:24); and fruit trees bearing fruit at the proper time (Ps 1:3). The author of Pr 15:23 spoke of a proper time for fitting words. Ecc 3 described all of life as a grand mosaic of times and seasons; there is a time to do everything—to be born, to die, to plant, to uproot, to kill, to heal, to love, to hate (Ecc 3:1–3, 8). This word occurs nineteen times in these verses (Ecc 3:1–8), along with a synonym of this word, *zĕmân* (2165), to make twenty references to time.

The Hebrew word can be used to designate a time even more accurately. When the exiles returned, it was time for the house of the Lord to be rebuilt (Hag 1:2). The word designated the set time of marriage (1Sa 18:19). It pinpointed the time of God's judgments (Isa 13:22; Eze 7:7, 12); but also the many times in the past when He delivered them (Ne 9:28). The Lord stands in readiness to judge every nation when its time comes (Jer 27:7). There will be a time of the end for all the nations as well (Da 8:17; 11:35; 12:4, 9). In contrast, the word in context can be combined with chance to indicate uncertain time (Ecc 9:11); and, appropriately, it describes life in general and its content, whether good or bad (Ps 31:15[16]; Isa 33:6).

6257. עָתַד, **ʻâthad**, *aw-thad´*; a primitive root; to *prepare*:—make fit, be ready to become.

6258. עַתָּה, **ʻattâh**, *at-taw´*; from 6256; at *this time,* whether adverb, conjunction or expletive:—henceforth, now, straightway, this time, whereas.

6259. עָתוּד, **ʻâthûwd**, *aw-thood´*; passive participle of 6257; *prepared:*—ready.

6260. עַתּוּד, **ʻattûwd**, *at-tood´*; or עַתֻּד, **ʻattud**, *at-tood´*; from 6257; *prepared,* i.e. *full grown;* spoken only (in plural) of *he-goats,* or (figurative) *leaders* of the people:—chief one, (he) goat, ram.

6261. עִתִּי, **ʻittîy**, *it-tee´*; from 6256; *timely:*—fit.

6262. עַתַּי, **ʻAttay**, *at-tah´ee*; for 6261; *Attai,* the name of three Israelites:—Attai.

6263. עֲתִיד, **ʻăthîyd**, *ath-eed´*; (Chaldee); corresponding to 6264; *prepared:*—ready.

6264. עָתִיד, **ʻâthîyd**, *aw-theed´*; from 6257; *prepared;* (by implication) *skilful;* feminine plural the *future;* also *treasure:*—things that shall come, ready, treasures.

6265. עֲתָיָה, **ʻĂthâyâh**, *ath-aw-yaw´*; from 5790 and 3050; *Jah has helped;* Athajah, an Israelite:—Athaiah.

6266. עָתִיק, **ʻâthîyq**, *aw-theek´*; from 6275; (properly) *antique,* i.e. *venerable* or *splendid:*—durable.

6267. עַתִּיק, **ʻattîyq**, *at-teek´*; from 6275; *removed,* i.e. *weaned;* also *antique:*—ancient, drawn.

6268. עַתִּיק, **'attîyq,** *at-teek´*; (Chaldee); corresponding to 6267; *venerable:*—ancient.

6269. עֲתָךְ, **'Áthâk,** *ath-awk´*; from an unused root meaning to *sojourn; lodging; Athak,* a place in Palestine:—Athach.

6270. עַתְלַי, **'Athlay,** *ath-lah´ee*; from an unused root meaning to *compress; constringent; Athlai,* an Israelite:—Athlai.

6271. עֲתַלְיָה, **'Áthalyâh,** *ath-al-yaw´*; or עֲתַלְיָהוּ, **'Áthalyâhûw,** *ath-al-yaw´-hoo*; from the same as 6270 and 3050; *Jah has constrained; Athaljah,* the name of an Israelitess and two Israelites:—Athaliah.

6272. עָתַם, **'âtham,** *aw-tham´*; a primitive root; probably to *glow,* i.e. (figurative) *be desolated:*—be darkened.

6273. עָתְנִי, **'Othnîy,** *oth-nee´*; from an unused root meaning to *force; forcible; Othni,* an Israelite:—Othni.

6274. עָתְנִיאֵל, **'Othnîy'êl,** *oth-nee-ale´*; from the same as 6273 and 410; *force of God; Othniël,* an Israelite:—Othniel.

6275. עָתַק, **'âthaq,** *aw-thak´*; a primitive root; to *remove* (intransitive or transitive); (figurative) to *grow old;* (specifically) to *transcribe:*—copy out, leave off, become (wax) old, remove.

6276. עָתֵק, **'âthêq,** *aw-thake´*; from 6275; *antique,* i.e. *valued:*—durable.

6277. עָתָק, **'âthâq,** *aw-thawk´*; from 6275 in the sense of *license; impudent:*—arrogancy, grievous (hard) things, stiff.

6278. עֵת קָצִין, **'Êth Qâtsîyn,** *ayth kaw-tseen´*; from 6256 and 7011; *time of a judge; Eth-Katsin,* a place in Palestine:—Ittah-kazin [*by including directive enclitic*].

6279. עָתַר, **'âthar,** *aw-thar´*; a primitive root [rather denominative from 6281]; to *burn incense* in worship, i.e. *intercede* (reciprocal, *listen* to prayer):—intreat, (make) pray (-er).

A verb meaning to pray, to entreat, to supplicate. The fundamental meaning of this word is that of a cry to the Lord for deliverance. It was used in Isaac's prayer concerning his wife's barrenness (Ge 25:21); and the prayers of Moses to stop the plagues in Egypt (Ex 8:8[4]). Scripture says that the Lord is faithful to hear such prayers (Job 33:26).

6280. עָתַר, **'âthar,** *aw-thar´*; a primitive root; to *be* (causative, *make*) *abundant:*—deceitful, multiply.

6281. עֶתֶר, **'Ether,** *eh´-ther*; from 6280; *abundance; Ether,* a place in Palestine:—Ether.

6282. עָתָר, **'âthâr,** *aw-thawr´*; from 6280; *incense* (as increasing to a *volume* of smoke); hence (from 6279) a *worshipper:*—suppliant, thick.

6283. עֲתֶרֶת, **'áthereth,** *ath-eh´-reth*; from 6280; *copiousness:*—abundance.

פ (Pe)

6284. פָּאָה, **pâ'âh,** *paw-aw´*; a primitive root; to *puff*, i.e. *blow* away:—scatter into corners.

6285. פֵּאָה, **pê'âh,** *pay-aw´*; feminine of 6311; (properly) *mouth* in a figurative sense, i.e. *direction, region, extremity:*—corner, end, quarter, side.

6286. פָּאַר, **pâ'ar,** *paw-ar´*; a primitive root; to *gleam,* (causative) *embellish;* (figurative) to *boast;* also to *explain* (i.e. make clear) oneself; denominative from 6288, to *shake* a tree:—beautify, boast self, go over the boughs, glorify (self), glory, vaunt self.

A verb meaning to beautify, to glorify. In the factitive form, God brings beauty and glory to His chosen people (Ps 149:4; Isa 55:5; 60:9); and to His Temple (Ezr 7:27; Isa 60:7). In the reflexive form, one beautifies and glorifies one's self and not others. Gideon is instructed to reduce the number of men in his army so the Israelites could not give themselves the glory for the victory that was to come (Jgs 7:2). In God's judgment against Assyria—a country that was merely an instrument in God's hand—Isaiah rhetorically asked whether the ax and the saw could take credit for the work accomplished through them (Isa 10:15). Obviously, the answer is no. In the same way, people should not take glory in what God is doing through their lives. In several passages, Isaiah also states that God brings glory to Himself by His actions through His people (Isa 44:23; 49:3; 60:21; 61:3).

6287. פְּאֵר, **p°'êr,** *peh-ayr´*; from 6286; an *embellishment,* i.e. fancy *head-dress:*—beauty, bonnet, goodly, ornament, tire.

6288. פְּאֹרָה, **p°'ôrâh,** *peh-o-raw´*; or פֹּרָאה **pôrâ'h,** *po-raw´*; or פֻּארָה, **pu'râh,** *poo-raw´*; from 6286; (properly) *ornamentation,* i.e. (plural) *foliage* (including the limbs) as *bright green:*—bough, branch, sprig.

6289. פָּארוּר, **pâ'rûwr,** *paw-roor´*; from 6286; (properly) *illuminated,* i.e. a *glow;* as noun, a *flush* (of anxiety):—blackness.

A masculine noun whose meaning is assumed to be in dread or fear; however, the meaning of this word is uncertain. It occurs two times, each with the verb qâbats (6908), meaning to gather. From the context, it is clear that the term is a negative one. In Joel 2:6, the context is a warning against the Day of the Lord, when an imposing army will invade, and people will be struck with great fear. In Na 2:10[11], the context is a prophecy of judgment against and the impending doom of Nineveh, which was like a lion's den, a place of safety and sanctuary (yet no fear) but would soon be a place of destruction and devastation.

6290. פָּארָן, **Pâ'rân,** *paw-rawn´*; from 6286; *ornamental; Paran,* a desert of Arabia:—Paran.

6291. פַּג, **pag,** *pag;* from an unused root meaning to *be torpid,* i.e. *crude;* an *unripe* fig:—green fig.

6292. פִּגּוּל, **piggûwl,** *pig-gool´;* or פִּגֻּל, **piggul,** *pig-gool´;* from an unused root meaning to *stink;* (properly) *fetid,* i.e. (figurative) *unclean* (ceremonially):—abominable (-tion, thing).

A masculine noun meaning a foul thing, refuse. It is a technical term for a part of a sacrifice that has become or been rendered unclean. This was applied to the fellowship offering that was to be eaten the same day it was offered or the next day. If it remained until the third day, it was considered unclean (Le 7:18; 19:7). Isaiah recorded the prophecy of God where He defined the activities of people that rendered them unclean, including contact with the deceased and eating unclean food, namely pork (Isa 65:4). Ezekiel protested God's instruction to him because he had never eaten any unclean meat; however, he failed to define what unclean meat was (Eze 4:14).

6293. פָּגַע, **pâga‛**, *paw-gah´*; a primitive root; to *impinge*, by accident or violence, or (figurative) by importunity:—come (betwixt), cause to entreat, fall (upon), make intercession, intercessor, intreat, lay, light [upon], meet (together), pray, reach, run.

A verb meaning to meet, to encounter, to reach. It could simply mean to meet (Ex 5:20; 1Sa 10:5). It could also signify to meet someone with hostility, where it is usually rendered to fall upon (Jos 2:16; Jgs 8:21; Ru 2:22). In addition, it could convey the concept of meeting with a request or entreaty and is usually rendered as intercession (Jer 7:16). This verb is used to designate the establishment of a boundary, probably with the idea of extending the boundary to reach a certain point (Jos 16:7; 19:11, 22, 26, 27, 34).

6294. פֶּגַע, **pega‛**, *peh´-gah*; from 6293; *impact* (casual):—chance, occurrent.

6295. פַּגְעִיאֵל, **Pag‛îy’êl**, *pag-ee-ale´*; from 6294 and 410; *accident of God; Pagiël*, an Israelite:—Pagiel.

6296. פָּגַר, **pâgar**, *paw-gar´*; a primitive root; to *relax*, i.e. become *exhausted*:—be faint.

6297. פֶּגֶר, **peger**, *peh´-gher*; from 6296; a *carcase* (as *limp*), whether of man or beast; (figurative) an idolatrous *image*:—carcase, corpse, dead body.

A masculine noun meaning a corpse, a carcass. It can refer to the carcasses of animals (Ge 15:11); however, it is usually used in connection with human corpses. Though this term can refer to a single body (Isa 14:19), it is usually found in the plural (Isa 34:3; Jer 31:40; Eze 6:5). In several instances, the singular is used as a collective (1Sa 17:46; Am 8:3; Na 3:3). One occurrence of this word is a metaphor for the lifelessness of idols (Le 26:30).

6298. פָּגַשׁ, **pâgash**, *paw-gash´*; a primitive root; to *come in contact with*, whether by accident or violence; (figurative) to *concur*:—meet (with, together).

6299. פָּדָה, **pâdâh**, *paw-daw´*; a primitive root; to *sever*, i.e. *ransom*; (generally) to *release, preserve*:— × at all, deliver, × by any means, ransom, (that are to be, let be) redeem (-ed), rescue, × surely.

A verb meaning to ransom, to redeem, and to deliver. The word is used to depict God's act of redeeming; He redeemed His people with a mighty hand from Pharaoh and the slavery they were under in Egypt (Dt 7:8; Mic 6:4). Egypt was literally the house of slavery and became the symbol of slavery and oppression from which Israel was delivered (Dt 9:26; 24:18). After Israel was in exile in Babylon, the Lord redeemed them from their strong enemies (Jer 31:11). He had longed to redeem them from their apostasy before He gave them over to judgment, but they would not respond to His call (Hos 7:13; 13:14).

The Lord also redeemed individuals in the sense of rescuing them. He delivered David (2Sa 4:9; 1Ki 1:29); Abraham (Isa 29:22); Jeremiah (Jer 15:21); and the psalmist (Ps 26:11; 31:5[6]).

The word often describes the process of ransoming persons in the cultic setting of ancient Israel. The firstborn was ransomed or redeemed (Ex 13:13, 15; Nu 18:15); animals were redeemed by payment of a half-shekel of ransom money (Le 27:27; Nu 18:15). The firstborn of an ox, sheep, or goat could not be redeemed (Nu 18:17). The word described the action of both the community and friends to redeem individuals (1Sa 14:45; Job 6:23).

In the passive stem, the word means to be redeemed. The word is used to describe a female slave who has not been ransomed (Le 19:20). A person under the ban for destruction could not be ransomed either (Le 27:29). Zion would be redeemed through justice (Isa 1:27); one person could not be redeemed by the life of another (Ps 49:7[8]).

In the causative stem, it means to bring about deliverance or redemption; the master who did not accept his slave girl had to cause her to be redeemed (Ex 21:8); the firstborn male of unclean animals and humans had to be redeemed as well (Nu 18:15, 16).

6300. פְּדַהְאֵל, **Pᵉdah’êl**, *ped-ah-ale´*; from 6299 and 410; *God has ransomed; Pedahel*, an Israelite:—Pedahel.

6301. פְּדָהצוּר, **Pᵉdâhtsûwr**, *ped-aw-tsoor´*; from 6299 and 6697; a *rock* (i.e. God) *has ransomed; Pedahtsur*, an Israelite:—Pedahzur.

6302. פְּדוּיִם, **pᵉdûwyim,** *pe-doo´-yim;* passive participle of 6299; *ransomed* (and so occurring under 6299); as abstract (in plural masculine) a *ransom:*—(that are) to be (that were) redeemed.

A masculine noun meaning ransom. Like the word *pidyôwm* (6306), it is an abstract form of the basic passive participle derived from the verb *pâdâh* (6299), meaning to ransom. As such, it occurs three times in the context of Israel's ransoming their firstborn males. In this context, this term is parallel with the silver that was used to redeem firstborn males and then given to Aaron and his sons (Nu 3:46, 48; 51).

6303. פָּדוֹן, **Pâdôwn,** *paw-done´;* from 6299; *ransom; Padon,* one of the Nethinim:—Padon.

6304. פְּדוּת, **pᵉdûwth,** *ped-ooth´;* or פְּדֻת, **pᵉduth,** *ped-ooth´;* from 6929; *distinction;* also *deliverance:*—division, redeem, redemption.

A feminine noun meaning ransom, redemption. It is used four times in the OT and could refer to redemption in general (Ps 111:9); redemption from sins (Ps 130:7); or redemption from exile (Isa 50:2). The meaning of the fourth occurrence of this word (Ex 8:23[19]) is difficult to ascertain. The Septuagint renders the Hebrew with *diastole* (1293, NT), meaning a division or distinction, and English translations follow suit.

6305. פְּדָיָה, **Pᵉdâyâh,** *ped-aw-yaw´;* or פְּדָיָהוּ, **Pᵉdâ-yâhûw,** *ped-aw-yaw´-hoo;* from 6299 and 3050; *Jah has ransomed; Pedajah,* the name of six Israelites:—Pedaiah.

6306. פִּדְיוֹם, **pidyôwm,** *pid-yome´;* or פִּדְיֹם, **pidyôm,** *pid-yome´;* also פִּדְיוֹן, **pidyôwn,** *pid-yone´;* or פִּדְיֹן, **pidyôn,** *pid-yone´;* from 6299; a *ransom:*—ransom, that were redeemed, redemption.

A masculine noun meaning ransom, ransom money. Like the word *pâdûy* (6302), *pidyôwm* is an abstract form of the basic passive participle derived from the verb *pâdâh* (6299), meaning to ransom. As such, it occurs in the same context as *pâdûy,* referring to the ransoming of the Israelite firstborn males (Nu 3:49, 51).

Pidyôwn is a masculine noun meaning ransom money. The word is closely related to *pidyôwm* (see above paragraph) and *pâdûy* (6302); yet it is a substantive noun and not an abstract noun. It refers to the money exchanged as a ransom, not simply to the concept of ransoming. In addition, this term always occurs in connection with the term *nephesh* (5315), meaning life (Ex 21:30; Ps 49:8[9]).

6307. פַּדָּן, **Paddân,** *pad-dawn´;* from an unused root meaning to *extend;* a *plateau;* or פַּדַּן אֲרָם, **Paddan 'Ărâm,** *pad-dan´ ar-awm´;* from the same as 758; the *table-land of Aram; Paddan* or *Paddan-Aram,* a region of Syria:—Padan, Padan-aram.

6308. פָּדַע, **pâda‘,** *paw-dah´;* a primitive root; to *retrieve:*—deliver.

A verb derived from an unknown root. It occurs only in Job 33:24, and the context requires that it carry a meaning like to deliver, to rescue. The verse talks of delivering one from going down to the pit.

6309. פֶּדֶר, **peder,** *peh´-der;* from an unused root meaning to *be greasy; suet:*—fat.

6310. פֶּה, **peh,** *peh;* from 6284; the *mouth* (as the means of *blowing*), whether literal or figurative (particularly *speech*); (specifically) *edge, portion* or *side;* (adverbially, with preposition) *according to:*—accord (-ing as, -ing to), after, appointment, assent, collar, command (-ment), × eat, edge, end, entry, + file, hole, × in, mind, mouth, part, portion, × (should) say (-ing), sentence, skirt, sound, speech, × spoken, talk, tenor, × to, + two-edged, wish, word.

A masculine singular noun meaning mouth. Besides the literal meaning, this term is used as the instrument of speech and figuratively for speech itself. When Moses claimed to be an ineffective speaker, he was heavy of mouth (Ex 4:10); the psalmist also uses *peh* to mean speech (Ps 49:13[14]; Ecc 10:13; Isa 29:13). The word is rendered edge in the expression the mouth of the sword (Jgs 4:16; Pr 5:4); or in some measurements from edge to edge or end to end (2Ki 10:21; 21:16; Ezr 9:11). It is also used for other openings like those in caves, gates, wells, or sacks. In land and inheritance references, it is translated as share or portion (Dt 21:17; 2Ki 2:9; Zec 13:8). With the preposition *lᵉ,* it means in proportion to or according to.

6311. פֹּה, **pôh,** *po;* or פֹּא, **pô',** *po;* (Job 38:11), or פּוֹ, **pôw,** *po;* probably from a primitive inseparable particle פ **p** (of demonstrative force) and

1931; *this place* (French *ici*), i.e. *here* or *hence*:— here, hither, the one (other, this, that) side.

6312. פּוּאָה, **Pûw'âh**, *poo-aw´*; or פֻּוָּה, **Puvvâh**, *poov-vaw´*; from 6284; a *blast; Puäh* or *Puvvah*, the name of two Israelites:—Phuvah, Pua, Puah.

6313. פּוּג, **pûwg**, *poog*; a primitive root; to *be sluggish*:—cease, be feeble, faint, be slacked.

6314. פּוּגָה, **pûwgâh**, *poo-gaw´*; from 6313; *intermission*:—rest.

6315. פּוּחַ, **pûwach**, *poo´-akh*; a primitive root; to *puff*, i.e. blow with the breath or air; hence to *fan* (as a breeze), to *utter*, to *kindle* (a fire), to *scoff*:—blow (upon), break, puff, bring into a snare, speak, utter.

A verb translated to breathe, to blow. The word is only used in poetic contexts in the Hebrew Bible. In the Song of Songs, the expression until the day breathes refers to the early morning when shadows flee (SS 2:17; 4:6); and the north wind is told to blow on the garden (SS 4:16). But just as often, the word implies a negative connotation, such as to snort at an enemy (Ps 10:5); to incite a city (Pr 29:8); or the Lord to blow out His anger (Eze 21:31[36]). In a unique usage, Proverbs uses the verb to refer to speaking lies (Pr 6:19; 14:5, 25; 19:5, 9); but once for speaking truth (Pr 12:17).

6316. פּוּט, **Pûwṭ**, *poot*; of foreign origin; *Put*, a son of Ham, also the name of his descendants or their region, and of a Persian tribe:—Phut, Put.

6317. פּוּטִיאֵל, **Pûwṭiy'êl**, *poo-tee-ale´*; from an unused root (probably meaning to *disparage*) and 410; *contempt of God; Putiël*, an Israelite:—Putiel.

6318. פּוֹטִיפַר, **Pôwṭîyphar**, *po-tee-far´*; of Egyptian derivation; *Potiphar*, an Egyptian:—Potiphar.

6319. פּוֹטִי פֶרַע, **Pôwṭîy Phera‘**, *po´-tee feh´-rah*; of Egyptian derivation; *Poti-Phera*, an Egyptian:—Poti-pherah.

6320. פּוּךְ, **pûwk**, *pook*; from an unused root meaning to *paint; dye* (specifically *stibium* for the eyes):—fair colours, glistering, paint [-ed] (-ing).

6321. פּוֹל, **pôwl**, *pole*; from an unused root meaning to *be thick*; a *bean* (as *plump*):—beans.

6322. פּוּל, **Pûwl**, *pool*; of foreign origin; *Pul*, the name of an Assyrian king and of an Ethiopian tribe:—Pul.

6323. פּוּן, **pûwn**, *poon*; a primitive root meaning to *turn*, i.e. *be perplexed*:—be distracted.

6324. פּוּנִי, **Pûwnîy**, *poo-nee´*; patronymic from an unused name meaning a *turn*; a *Punite* (collective) or descendants of an unknown *Pun*:—Punites.

6325. פּוּנֹן, **Pûwnôn**, *poo-none´*; from 6323; *perplexity; Punon*, a place in the Desert:—Punon.

6326. פּוּעָה, **Pûw‘âh**, *poo-aw´*; from an unused root meaning to *glitter; brilliancy; Puäh*, an Israelitess:—Puah.

6327. פּוּץ, **pûwts**, *poots*; a primitive root; to *dash* in pieces, literal or figurative (especially to *disperse*):—break (dash, shake) in (to) pieces, cast (abroad), disperse (selves), drive, retire, scatter (abroad), spread abroad.

6328. פּוּק, **pûwq**, *pook*; a primitive root; to *waver*:—stumble, move.

6329. פּוּק, **pûwq**, *pook*; a primitive root [rather identical with 6328 through the idea of *dropping* out; compare 5312]; to *issue*, i.e. *furnish*; (causative) to *secure*; (figurative) to *succeed*:—afford, draw out, further, get, obtain.

6330. פּוּקָה, **pûwqâh**, *poo-kaw´*; from 6328; a *stumbling-block*:—grief.

6331. פּוּר, **pûwr**, *poor*; a primitive root; to *crush*:—break, bring to nought, × utterly take.

6332. פּוּר, **Pûwr**, *poor*; also (plural) פּוּרִים, **Pûwrîym**, *poo-reem´*; or פֻּרִים, **Purîym**, *poo-reem´*; from 6331; a *lot* (as by means of a *broken* piece):—Pur, Purim.

6333. פּוּרָה, **pûwrâh**, *poo-raw´*; from 6331; a *wine-press* (as *crushing* the grapes):—winepress.

6334. פּוֹרָתָה, **Pôwrâthâh**, *po-raw-thaw´*; of Persian origin; *Poratha*, a son of Haman:—Poratha.

6335. פּוּשׁ, **pûwsh**, *poosh*; a primitive root; to *spread*; (figurative) to *act proudly*:—grow up, be grown fat, spread selves, be scattered.

6336. פּוּתִי, **Pûwthîy,** *poo-thee´*; patronymic from an unused name meaning a *hinge*; a *Puthite* (collective) or descendant of an unknown Puth:—Puhites [*as if from* 6312].

6337. פָּז, **pâz,** *pawz*; from 6388; *pure* (gold); hence *gold* itself (as refined):—fine (pure) gold.

6338. פָּזַז, **pâzaz,** *paw-zaz´*; a primitive root; to *refine* (gold):—best [gold].

6339. פָּזַז, **pâzaz,** *paw-zaz´*; a primitive root [rather identical with 6338]; to *solidify* (as if by *refining*); also to *spring* (as if *separating* the limbs):—leap, be made strong.

6340. פָּזַר, **pâzar,** *paw-zar´*; a primitive root; to *scatter*, whether in enmity or bounty:—disperse, scatter (abroad).

6341. פַּח, **pach,** *pakh*; from 6351; a (metallic) *sheet* (as *pounded* thin); also a spring *net* (as spread out like a *lamina*):—gin, (thin) plate, snare.

A masculine singular noun translated bird trap. It is used in its literal sense in Am 3:5, Pr 7:23, and Ecc 9:12. But more often it is used figuratively for a human ensnarement. Jeremiah prophesied that a snare awaited Moab (Jer 48:43); while Proverbs said that snares were set for the wicked (Pr 22:5). Eliphaz told Job that snares surrounded him (Job 22:10). The psalmist's path was filled with the snares of his enemies (Ps 140:5[6]; 142:3[4]). But retribution was envisioned as the enemies' tables turned into a snare (Ps 69:22[23]).

6342. פָּחַד, **pâchad,** *paw-khad´*; a primitive root; to *be startled* (by a sudden alarm); hence to *fear* in general:—be afraid, stand in awe, (be in) fear, make to shake.

A verb meaning to dread, to be in dread, to be in awe. This verb occurs in poetry. Those who worship and trust God have no need to dread, but those who break the Law (Dt 28:66); sinners in Zion (Isa 33:14); and worshippers of idols (Isa 44:11) have reason to fear. It often takes a cognate accusative. For a positive use, in the eschatological perspective of Isa 60:5, the term is best translated to be awed.

6343. פַּחַד, **pachad,** *pakh´-ad*; from 6342; a (sudden) *alarm* (properly, the object feared; by implication, the feeling):—dread (-ful), fear, (thing) great [fear, -ly feared], terror.

A masculine singular noun translated dread, terror. This dread was often caused by the Lord (1Sa 11:7; Job 13:11; Isa 2:10, 19, 21). The dread could cause trembling (Job 13:11; Ps 119:120). The noun often occurs in a cognate accusative construction (see *pâchad* [6342]) (Dt 28:67; Job 3:25; Ps 14:5). A unique use of the term is found in Genesis 31:42, often translated the Dread or Fear of Isaac, parallel to the God of Abraham.

6344. פַּחַד, **pachad,** *pakh´-ad*; the same as 6343; a *testicle* (as a cause of *shame* akin to fear):—stone.

6345. פַּחְדָּה, **pachdâh,** *pakh-daw´*; feminine of 6343; *alarm* (i.e. *awe*):—fear.

A feminine noun meaning fear, religious awe. This Hebrew word appears only in Jer 2:19, where it refers to the proper respect and reverence due to the Lord, which is lacking when one forsakes God and His commands.

6346. פֶּחָה, **pechâh,** *peh-khaw´*; of foreign origin; a *prefect* (of a city or small district):—captain, deputy, governor.

A masculine noun meaning a governor, a captain. The primary meaning of this word is that of a lord over a given district or territory. It signified an office that is appointed and not received by virtue of birth or other right. It was generally used of the leader of the Jewish nation after the exile (Ne 12:26; Hag 1:14; Mal 1:8); but in other places it was used of a deputy bureaucrat in any given location (Est 8:9; Jer 51:23); or a military leader (1Ki 20:24).

6347. פֶּחָה, **pechâh,** *peh-khaw´*; (Chaldee); corresponding to 6346:—captain, governor.

An Aramaic masculine noun meaning a governor, a satrap, a captain. Corresponding to the Hebrew word *pechâh* (6346), this word means a governor or other similarly appointed authority. It was used particularly of a provincial governor in the Persian Empire (Ezr 5:6); the postexilic leader of the Jewish nation (Ezr 6:7); and various similar officers involved in the political structure (Da 6:7[8]).

6348. פָּחַז, **pâchaz,** *paw-khaz´*; a primitive root; to *bubble* up or *froth* (as boiling water), i.e. (figurative) to *be unimportant*:—light.

6349. פַּחַז, **pachaz,** *pakh´-az*; from 6348; *ebullition*, i.e. froth (figurative) *lust*:—unstable.

6350. פַּחֲזוּת, **pachăzûwth,** *pakh-az-ooth´*; from 6348; *frivolity*:—lightness.

6351. פָּחַח, **pâchach,** *paw-khakh´*; a primitive root; to *batter* out; but used only as denominative from 6341, to *spread a net*:—be snared.

6352. פֶּחָם, **pechâm,** *peh-khawm´*; perhaps from an unused root probably meaning to *be black*; a *coal*, whether charred or live:—coals.

6353. פֶּחָר, **pechâr,** *peh-khawr´*; (Chaldee); from an unused root probably meaning to *fashion*; a *potter*:—potter.

6354. פַּחַת, **pachath,** *pakh´-ath*; probably from an unused root apparently meaning to *dig*; a *pit*, especially for catching animals:—hole, pit, snare.

A masculine singular noun meaning a pit, a cave. Within the prophecies of Isaiah and Jeremiah, the term is used in judgment as a trap for the wicked enemies of the Lord and Israel (Isa 24:17, 18; Jer 48:28, 43, 44). In Lamentations, it was a place for sinful Jerusalem (La 3:47). The term is used for the cave where David and his men were hiding (2Sa 17:9); and for the pit in which Absalom's body was thrown (2Sa 18:17).

6355. פַּחַת מוֹאָב, **Pachath Môw'âb,** *pakh´-ath mo-awb´*; from 6354 and 4124; *pit of Moäb*; *Pachath-Moäb*, an Israelite:—Pahath-moab.

6356. פְּחֶתֶת, **pⁱchetheth,** *pekh-eh´-theth*; from the same as 6354; a *hole* (by mildew in a garment):—fret inward.

A feminine noun meaning bored out, eaten away. This word is used once to denote the condition of a decaying leprous garment (Le 13:55). The image underlying the word is similar to that of a wormhole or spot eaten away by a moth.

6357. פִּטְדָה, **piṭdâh,** *pit-daw´*; of foreign derivation; a *gem*, probably the *topaz*:—topaz.

6358. פָּטוּר, **pâṭûwr,** *paw-toor´*; passive participle of 6362; *opened*, i.e. (as noun) a *bud*:—open.

6359. פָּטִיר, **pâṭîyr,** *paw-teer´*; from 6362; *open*, i.e. *unoccupied*:—free.

6360. פַּטִּישׁ, **paṭṭîysh,** *pat-teesh´*; intensive from an unused root meaning to *pound*; a *hammer*:—hammer.

6361. פַּטִּישׁ, **paṭṭîysh,** *pat-teesh´*; (Chaldee); from a root corresponding to that of 6360; a *gown* (as if *hammered* out wide):—hose.

6362. פָּטַר, **pâṭar,** *paw-tar´*; a primitive root; to *cleave* or burst through, i.e. (causative) to *emit*, whether literal or figurative (*gape*):—dismiss, free, let (shoot) out, slip away.

6363. פֶּטֶר, **peṭer,** *peh´-ter*; or פִּטְרָה, **piṭrâh,** *pit-raw´*; from 6362; a *fissure*, i.e. (concrete) *firstling* (as *opening* the matrix):—firstling, openeth, such as open.

6364. פִּי־בֶסֶת, **Pîy-Beseth,** *pee beh´-seth*; of Egyptian origin; *Pi-Beseth*, a place in Egypt:—Pi-beseth.

6365. פִּיד, **pîyd,** *peed*; from an unused root probably meaning to *pierce*; (figurative) *misfortune*:—destruction, ruin.

A masculine noun meaning a ruin, a disaster. It is used of divine judgment (Job 30:24; 31:29), as when the father encouraged his son to avoid the wicked and focus on God because God's judgment will eventually come on the wicked (Pr 24:22).

6366. פֵּיוֹת, **pêyôwth,** *pay-oth´*; feminine of 6310; an *edge*:—(two-) edge (-d).

6367. פִּי הַחִרֹת, **Pîy ha-Chirôth,** *pee hah-khee-rōth´*; from 6310 and the feminine plural of a noun (from the same root as 2356, with the article internal; *mouth of the gorges*; *Pi-ha-Chiroth*, a place in Egypt:—Pi-hahiroth. [In Nu 14:19 without Pi-.]

6368. פִּיחַ, **pîyach,** *pee´-akh*; from 6315; a *powder* (as easily *puffed* away), i.e. *ashes* or *dust*:—ashes.

6369. פִּיכֹל, **Pîykôl,** *pee-kole´*; apparently from 6310 and 3605; *mouth of all*; *Picol*, a Philistine:—Phichol.

6370. פִּילֶגֶשׁ, **pîylegesh,** *pee-leh´-ghesh*; or פִּלֶגֶשׁ, **pilegesh,** *pee-leh´-ghesh*; of uncertain derivation; a *concubine*; also (masculine) a *paramour*:—concubine, paramour.

A feminine noun meaning a concubine. A concubine was a legitimate wife; however, she was of secondary rank. This is evident by the references to the concubine as having a husband (Jgs 19:2); and that this man and her father are considered to be son-in-law (cf. Jgs

19:5) and father-in-law (cf. Jgs 19:4), respectively. But concubines were presented opposite the wives of higher rank (1Ki 11:3; SS 6:8). The ability to have and to keep concubines was a sign of wealth, status, and often of royalty (1Ki 11:3; Est 2:14; SS 6:8). To sleep with a king's concubine would have indicated plans to usurp the throne (2Sa 3:7; 16:21, 22; cf. 1Ki 2:21–24).

6371. פִּימָה, **pîymâh,** *pee-maw´*; probably from an unused root meaning to *be plump; obesity:*— collops.

6372. פִּינְחָס, **Pîynᵉchâs,** *pee-nekh-aws´*; apparently from 6310 and a variation of 5175; *mouth of a serpent; Pinechas,* the name of three Israelites:—Phinehas.

6373. פִּינֹן, **pîynôn,** *pee-none´*; probably the same as 6325; *Pinon,* an Idumæan:—Pinon.

6374. פִּיפִיֹּות, **pîyphîyyôwth,** *pee-fee-yoth´*; for 6366; an *edge* or *tooth:*—tooth, × two-edged.

6375. פִּיק, **pîyq,** *peek*; from 6329; a *tottering:*— smite together.

A masculine noun meaning tottering. This noun only occurs in one passage, where the devastation of Nineveh is portrayed: "She is empty, and void, and waste: and the heart melteth, and the knees smite together, and much pain is in all loins, and the faces of them all gather blackness" (Na 2:10[11] KJV).

6376. פִּישֹׁון, **Pîyshôwn,** *pee-shone´*; from 6335; *dispersive; Pishon,* a river of Eden:—Pison.

6377. פִּיתֹון, **Pîythôwn,** *pee-thone´*; probably from the same as 6596; *expansive; Pithon,* an Israelite:—Pithon.

6378. פַּךְ, **pak,** *pak*; from 6379; a *flask* (from which a liquid may *flow*):—box, vial.

6379. פָּכָה, **pâkâh,** *paw-kaw´*; a primitive root; to *pour:*—run out.

6380. פֹּכֶרֶת הַצְּבָיִים, **Pôkereth hats-Tsᵉbâyîym,** *po-keh´-reth hats-tseb-aw-yeem´*; from the active participle (of the same form as the first word) feminine of an unused root (meaning to *entrap*) and plural of 6643; *trap of gazelles; Pokereth-Tsebajim,* one of the "servants of Solomon":—Pochereth of Zebaim.

6381. פָּלָא, **pâlâ',** *paw-law´*; a primitive root; (properly) perhaps to *separate,* i.e. *distinguish* (literal or figurative); (by implication) to *be* (causative, *make*) *great, difficult, wonderful:*— accomplish, (arise ... too, be too) hard, hidden, things too high, (be, do, do a, shew) marvelous (-ly, -els, things, work), miracles, perform, separate, make singular, (be, great, make) wonderful (-ers, -ly, things, works), wondrous (things, works, -ly).

A verb meaning to do something wonderful, to do something extraordinary, or difficult. It frequently signifies the wondrous works of God, especially His deliverance and judgments (Ex 3:20; Ps 106:22; 136:4; Mic 7:15). Because God's extraordinary deeds inspire thanksgiving and praise, this Hebrew word occurs often in the hymnic literature of the Bible and of the Dead Sea Scrolls (Ps 9:1[2]; 107:8; 145:5). While nothing is too extraordinary for God, various things are said to be beyond the abilities of some individuals to do or comprehend (Dt 17:8; Pr 30:18; Jer 32:17); however, obeying God's commandments is not too difficult a task (Dt 30:11). A rare use of this Hebrew word expresses the performance of a special vow beyond the ordinary commitment (Le 27:2; Nu 6:2; 15:3, 8).

6382. פֶּלֶא, **pele',** *peh´-leh*; from 6381; a *miracle:*—marvelous thing, wonder (-ful, -fully).

A masculine noun meaning a wonder, a miracle, a marvel. This word is used to represent something unusual or extraordinary. Except for La 1:9, this term always appears in the context of God's words or deeds. It is used of God's actions among His people (Isa 29:14); the Law of God (Ps 119:129); God's acts of judgment and deliverance (Ex 15:11; Ps 78:12; Isa 25:1); and the child to be born as the Messiah (Isa 9:6[5]). These things then become the focus of people's worship of God (Ps 77:11[12], 14[15]). This word is also used as an adverb to reveal how astounding, significant, and extreme was the fall of the city of Jerusalem (La 1:9).

6383. פִּלְאִי, **pil'îy,** *pil-ee´*; or פָּלְאִי, **pel'îy,** *pel-ee´*; from 6381; *remarkable:*—secret, wonderful.

A masculine adjective meaning wonderful, incomprehensible. The feminine form of this adjective is pᵉlî'âyh or pil'iyyâh. It was used as a description of the name of the angel of the Lord (Jgs 13:18); and as a description of the knowledge of the Lord (Ps 139:6).

6384. יאלִפְּ, **Pallu'îy,** *pal-loo-ee´*; patronymic from 6396; a *Palluïte* (collective) or descendants of Pallu:—Palluites.

6385. גלַפְּ, **pâlag,** *paw-lag´*; a primitive root; to *split* (literal or figurative):—divide.

A verb meaning to split, to divide. It is used in the passive form to refer to the earth being divided (Ge 10:25). In the factitive form, it refers to making or dividing a watercourse or cleaving a channel (Job 38:25). The factitive form is also used metaphorically of the Lord to cause dissension, that is, dividing their tongues (Ps 55:9[10]).

6386. גלַפְּ, **pᵉlag,** *pel-ag´*; (Chaldee); corresponding to 6385:—divided.

An Aramaic verb meaning to split, to divide. This word is the equivalent of the Hebrew verb *pâlag* (6385). It is used only once when Daniel was interpreting Nebuchadnezzar's dream. The feet of the statue in the dream were composed partly of clay and partly of iron, representing the idea that the kingdom would be divided (Da 2:41).

6387. גלַפְּ, **pᵉlag,** *pel-ag´*; (Chaldee); from 6386; a *half*:—dividing.

An Aramaic masculine noun meaning half. Like the word *pᵉluggâh* (6392), this noun is derived from the verb *pᵉlag* (6386), meaning to divide, and represented the results of that action, the production of parts or divisions. Unlike the word *pᵉluggâh*, this term seems to assume a single division into two equal parts or halves. This term is used only once in the famous passage stating that the saints will be delivered for a time, times and a half time (Da 7:25).

6388. גלֶפֶּ, **peleg,** *peh´-leg*; from 6385; a *rill* (i.e. small *channel* of water, as in irrigation):—river, stream.

6389. גלֶפֶּ, **Peleg,** *peh´-leg*; the same as 6388; *earthquake*; *Peleg*, a son of Shem:—Peleg.

6390. הגָּלַפְּ, **pᵉlaggâh,** *pel-ag-gaw´*; from 6385; a *runlet*, i.e. *gully*:—division, river.

A feminine noun meaning a stream, a division. This noun is derived from the verb *pâlag* (6385), whose basic idea is to divide and which, in the extensive-factitive form, can refer to making a watercourse. It can also denote a stream (Job 20:17). See the words *nâhâr* (5104),

meaning river, and *nachal* (6391), meaning a torrent or wadi.

6391. הגָּלֻפְּ, **pᵉluggâh,** *pel-oog-gaw´*; from 6385; a *section*:—division.

A feminine noun meaning division. It can only be found in 2Ch 35:5, where Josiah instructed the people of Israel to stand in the holy place by their family divisions.

6392. הגָּלֻפְּ, **pᵉluggâh,** *pel-oog-gaw´*; (Chaldee); corresponding to 6391:—division.

An Aramaic feminine noun meaning division. Like the word *pĕlag* (6387), this noun is derived from the verb *pĕlag* (6386), meaning to divide, and represented the results of that action: the production of parts or divisions. Unlike *pĕlag* (6387), this term seems to assume multiple divisions yielding several equal parts. It is only used once to refer to the apportionment of priests into the divisions that would share the responsibility for the restored Temple (Ezr 6:18).

6393. הדָלְפְּ, **pᵉlâdâh,** *pel-aw-daw´*; from an unused root meaning to *divide*; a *cleaver*, i.e. iron *armature* (of a chariot):—torch.

6394. שׁדָּלְפִּ, **Pildâsh,** *pil-dawsh´*; of uncertain derivation; *Pildash*, a relative of Abraham:—Pildash.

6395. הלָפָּ, **pâlâh,** *paw-law´*; a primitive root; to *distinguish* (literal or figurative):—put a difference, show marvelous, separate, set apart, sever, make wonderfully.

6396. אוּלַפַּ, **Pallûw',** *pal-loo´*; from 6395; *distinguished; Pallu*, an Israelite:—Pallu, Phallu.

6397. ינוֹלְפַּ, **Pᵉlôwnîy,** *pel-o-nee´*; patronymic from an unused name (from 6395) meaning *separate*; a *Pelonite* or inhabitant of an unknown Palon:—Pelonite.

6398. חלַפָּ, **pâlach,** *paw-lakh´*; a primitive root; to *slice*, i.e. *break* open or *pierce*:—bring forth, cleave, cut, shred, strike through.

6399. חלַפְּ, **pᵉlach,** *pel-akh´*; (Chaldee); corresponding to 6398; to *serve* or worship:—minister, serve.

An Aramaic verb meaning to serve, to revere, to worship. King Nebuchadnezzar was amazed when Daniel's three friends were not harmed in the furnace; he recognized their

God for rescuing them because they would not serve any other (Da 3:28). King Darius referred to God as the One Daniel served continually (Da 6:16[17], 20[21]). Later, Daniel wrote of his vision of the Ancient of Days and how all nations worshipped Him (Da 7:14). This thought is echoed later in the same passage (Da 7:27). This word was also used to denote servants of the Temple (Ezr 7:24).

6400. פֶּלַח, **pelach,** *peh´-lakh*; from 6398; a *slice:*—piece.

6401. פִּלְחָא, **Pilchâ',** *pil-khaw´*; from 6400; *slicing; Pilcha,* an Israelite:—Pilcha.

6402. פָּלְחָן, **polchân,** *pol-khawn´*; (Chaldee); from 6399; *worship:*—service.

6403. פָּלַט, **pâlaṭ,** *paw-lat´*; a primitive root; to *slip* out, i.e. *escape*; (causative) to *deliver:*—calve, carry away safe, deliver, (cause to) escape.

6404. פֶּלֶט, **Peleṭ,** *peh´-let*; from 6403; *escape*; *Pelet,* the name of two Israelites:—Pelet. See also 1046.

6405. פַּלֵּט, **pallêṭ,** *pal-late´*; from 6403; *escape:*—deliverance, escape.

6406. פַּלְטִי, **Palṭiy,** *pal-tee´*; from 6403; *delivered; Palti,* the name of two Israelites:—Palti, Phalti.

6407. פַּלְטִי, **Palṭiy,** *pal-tee´*; patronymic from 6406; a *Paltite* or descendant of Palti:—Paltite.

6408. פִּלְטַי, **Pilṭay,** *pil-tah´ee*; for 6407; *Piltai,* an Israelite:—Piltai.

6409. פַּלְטִיאֵל, **Palṭiy'êl,** *pal-tee-ale´*; from the same as 6404 and 410; *deliverance of God; Paltiël,* the name of two Israelites:—Paltiel, Phaltiel.

6410. פְּלַטְיָה, **Peleṭyâh,** *pel-at-yaw´*; or פְּלַטְיָהוּ, **Peleṭyâhûw,** *pel-at-yaw´-hoo*; from 6403 and 3050; *Jah has delivered; Pelatjah,* the name of four Israelites:—Pelatiah.

6411. פְּלָיָה, **Pelâyâh,** *pel-aw-yaw´*; or פְּלָאיָה, **Pelâ'yâh,** *pel-aw-yaw´*; from 6381 and 3050; *Jah has distinguished; Pelaiah,* the name of three Israelites:—Pelaiah.

6412. פָּלִיט, **pâliyṭ,** *paw-leet´*; or פָּלֵיט, **pâlêyṭ,** *paw-late´*; or פָּלֵט, **pâlêṭ,** *paw-late´*; from 6403; a *refugee:*—(that have) escape (-d, -th), fugitive.

6413. פְּלֵיטָה, **peleyṭâh,** *pel-ay-taw´*; or פְּלֵטָה, **peleṭâh,** *pel-ay-taw´*; feminine of 6412; *deliverance*; (concrete) an *escaped* portion:—deliverance, (that is) escape (-d), remnant.

A feminine noun meaning deliverance, something delivered, a remnant. Jacob split his group into two camps so that if Esau attacked one, the other could escape (Ge 32:8[9]). Joseph told his brothers that God used what they meant for evil to be deliverance for them (Ge 45:7). Moses told Pharaoh that the locusts would eat whatever was left from the hail (Ex 10:5). The Israelites looked for wives for the Benjamites who were left (Jgs 21:17). David had everyone flee, or no one would be safe from Absalom (2Sa 15:14).

6414. פָּלִיל, **pâliyl,** *paw-leel´*; from 6419; a *magistrate:*—judge.

A masculine noun meaning judge. This word is only used in the plural in the Hebrew OT. The song of Moses said that even the enemies of Israel judged the Israelite God to be different from other gods (Dt 32:31). As Job listed all the sins he had not committed, he mentioned that it would be shameful to be judged by those sins (Job 31:11). See the related Hebrew root *pâlal* (6419).

6415. פְּלִילָה, **peliylâh,** *pel-ee-law´*; feminine of 6414; *justice:*—judgment.

A feminine noun meaning a settlement, a judgment. This form of the word is used only once in the Hebrew OT in the book of Isaiah. In the oracle against Moab, the women cried out for a judgment or settlement to be made for them (Isa 16:3). See the masculine form of this word *pâliyl* (6414) and the related Hebrew root *pâlal* (6419).

6416. פְּלִילִי, **peliyliy,** *pel-ee-lee´*; from 6414; *judicial:*—judge.

6417. פְּלִילִיָּה, **peliyliyyâh,** *pel-ee-lee-yaw´*; feminine of 6416; *judicature:*—judgment.

6418. פֶּלֶךְ, **pelek,** *peh´-lek*; from an unused root meaning to *be round*; a *circuit* (i.e. *district*); also a *spindle* (as *whirled*); hence a *crutch:*—(di-) staff, part.

6419. פָּלַל, **pâlal,** *paw-lal´*; a primitive root; to *judge* (officially or mentally); (by extension) to *intercede, pray:*—intreat, judge (-ment), (make) pray (-er, -ing), make supplication.

A verb meaning to pray, to intercede. This is the most common Hebrew word used to describe the general act of prayer (Jer 29:7). It was often used to describe prayer offered in a time of distress, such as Hannah's prayer for a son (1Sa 1:10, 12); Elisha's prayer for the dead boy (2Ki 4:33); Hezekiah's prayer for protection and health (2Ki 19:15; 20:2); and Jonah's prayer from the fish (Jnh 2:1[2]). In some contexts, this word described a specific intercession of one person praying to the Lord for another, such as Abraham for Abimelech (Ge 20:7, 17); Moses and Samuel for Israel (Nu 11:2; 21:7; 1Sa 7:5); the man of God for the king (1Ki 13:6); or Ezra and Daniel for Israel's sins (Ezr 10:1; Da 9:4, 20). This prayer of intercession could also be made to a false god (Isa 44:17; 45:14).

6420. פָּלָל, **Pâlâl,** *paw-lawl´;* from 6419; *judge; Palal,* an Israelite:—Palal.

6421. פְּלַלְיָה, **Pᵉlalyâh,** *pel-al-yaw´;* from 6419 and 3050; *Jah has judged; Pelajah,* an Israelite:—Pelaliah.

6422. פַּלְמוֹנִי, **palmôwnîy,** *pal-mo-nee´;* probably for 6423; a *certain* one, i.e. so-and-so:—certain.

6423. פְּלֹנִי, **pᵉlônîy,** *pel-o-nee´;* from 6395; *such* a one, i.e. a specified *person:*—such.

6424. פָּלַס, **pâlas,** *paw-las´;* a primitive root; (properly) to *roll* flat, i.e. *prepare* (a road); also to *revolve,* i.e. *weigh* (mentally):—make, ponder, weigh.

6425. פֶּלֶס, **peles,** *peh´-les;* from 6424; a *balance:*—scales, weight.

6426. פָּלַץ, **pâlats,** *paw-lats´;* a primitive root; (properly, perhaps) to *rend,* i.e. (by implication) to *quiver:*—tremble.

6427. פַּלָּצוּת, **pallâtsûwth,** *pal-law-tsooth´;* from 6426; *affright:*—fearfulness, horror, trembling.

A feminine noun meaning shuddering. This word describes the physical reaction of the body in response to fear. Job shuddered at the fate of the wicked (Job 21:6); David shuddered in fear of his enemy (Ps 55:5[6]); Isaiah shuddered because of God's judgment (Isa 21:4);

and those about to be judged by God will shudder (Eze 7:18). See the word *miphletseth* (4656).

6428. פָּלַשׁ, **pâlash,** *paw-lash´;* a primitive root; to *roll* (in dust):—roll (wallow) self.

6429. פְּלֶשֶׁת, **Pᵉlesheth,** *pel-eh´-sheth;* from 6428; *rolling,* i.e. *migratory; Pelesheth,* a region of Syria:—Palestina, Palestine, Philistia, Philistines.

6430. פְּלִשְׁתִּי, **Pᵉlishtîy,** *pel-ish-tee´;* patrial from 6429; a *Pelishtite* or inhabitant of Pelesheth:—Philistine.

6431. פֶּלֶת, **Peleth,** *peh´-leth;* from an unused root meaning to *flee; swiftness; Peleth,* the name of two Israelites:—Peleth.

6432. פְּלֵתִי, **Pᵉlêthîy,** *pel-ay-thee´;* from the same form as 6431; a *courier* (collective) or official *messenger:*—Pelethites.

6433. פֻּם, **pum,** *poom;* (Chaldee); probably for 6310; the *mouth* (literal or figurative):—mouth.

6434. פֵּן, **pên,** *pane;* from an unused root meaning to *turn;* an *angle* (of a street or wall):—corner.

6435. פֶּן, **pen,** *pen;* from 6437; (properly) *removal;* used only (in the construct) adverb as conjunction *lest:*—(lest) (peradventure), that ... not.

6436. פַּנַּג, **pannag,** *pan-nag´;* of uncertain derivation; probably *pastry:*—Pannag.

6437. פָּנָה, **pânâh,** *paw-naw´;* a primitive root; to *turn;* (by implication) to *face,* i.e. *appear, look,* etc.:—appear, at [even-] tide, behold, cast out, come on, × corner, dawning, empty, go away, lie, look, mark, pass away, prepare, regard, (have) respect (to), (re-) turn (aside, away, back, face, self), × right [early].

6438. פִּנָּה, **pinnâh,** *pin-naw´;* feminine of 6434; an *angle;* (by implication) a *pinnacle;* (figurative) a *chieftain:*—bulwark, chief, corner, stay, tower.

6439. פְּנוּאֵל, **Pᵉnûw'êl,** *pen-oo-ale´;* or (more properly) פְּנִיאֵל, **Pᵉnîy'êl,** *pen-ee-ale´;* from 6437 and 410; *face of God; Penuël* or *Peniël,* a place East of Jordan; also (as Penuel) the name of two Israelites:—Peniel, Penuel.

6440. פָּנִים, **pânîym**, *paw-neem´*; plural (but always as singular) of an unused noun [פָּנֶה **pâneh**, *paw-neh´*; from 6437]; the *face* (as the part that *turns*); used in a great variety of applications (literal and figurative); also (with prepositional prefix) as a preposition (*before*, etc.):— + accept, a- (be-) fore (-time), against, anger, × as (long as), at, + battle, + because (of), + beseech, countenance, edge, + employ, endure, + enquire, face, favour, fear of, for, forefront (-part), form (-er time, -ward), from, front, heaviness, × him (-self), + honourable, + impudent, + in, it, look [-eth] (-s), × me, + meet, × more than, mouth, of, off, (of) old (time), × on, open, + out of, over against, the partial, person, + please, presence, propect, was purposed, by reason, of, + regard, right forth, + serve, × shewbread, sight, state, straight, + street, × thee, × them (-selves), through (+ -out), till, time (-s) past, (un-) to (-ward), + upon, upside (+ down), with (-in, + -stand), × ye, × you.

A masculine plural noun meaning a face. Although the literal meaning of face is possible (Ge 43:31; Le 13:41; 1Ki 19:13), most of the time this word occurs in a figurative, idiomatic phrase. Face can be a substitute for the entire person (Ex 33:14, 15); or it can be a reflection of the person's mood or attitude: defiant (Jer 5:3); ruthless (Dt 28:50); joyful (Job 29:24); humiliated (2Sa 19:5[6]); terrified (Isa 13:8); displeased (Ge 4:5). It is also used to indicate direction (Ge 31:21); or purpose (Jer 42:15, 17). This noun also designates the top or surface of something: the ground (Ge 2:6; 4:14); a field (Isa 28:25); or water (Ge 1:2). It also connotes the front of something, like a pot (Jer 1:13); or an army (Joel 2:20). With various prepositions, *pânîm* takes on the nature of a particle and expresses such concepts as upon (Ex 23:17; Le 14:53); before a place (Nu 8:22); before a time (Eze 42:12; Am 1:1); in the presence of (Est 1:10).

6441. פְּנִימָה, **p^enîymâh**, *pen-ee´-maw*; from 6440 with directive enclitic; *faceward*, i.e. *indoors:*—(with-) in (-ner part, -ward).

6442. פְּנִימִי, **p^enîymîy**, *pen-ee-mee´*; from 6440; *interior:*—(with-) in (-ner, -ward).

6443. פְּנִינִים, **p^enîynîym**, *pe-nee-neem´*; or פְּנִי, **pânîy**, *paw-nee´*; from the same as 6434; probably a *pearl* (as *round*):—ruby.

6444. פְּנִנָּה, **P^eninnâh**, *pen-in-naw´*; probably feminine from 6443 contracted; *Peninnah*, an Israelitess:—Peninnah.

6445. פָּנַק, **pânaq**, *paw-nak´*; a primitive root; to *enervate:*—bring up.

6446. פַּס, **pas**, *pas*; from 6461; (properly) the *palm* (of the hand) or *sole* (of the foot) [compare 6447]; by implication (plural) a *long and sleeved* tunic (perhaps simply a *wide* one; from the original sense of the root, i.e. of *many breadths*):—(divers) colours.

6447. פַּס, **pas**, *pas*; (Chaldee); from a root corresponding to 6461; the *palm* (of the hand, as being *spread* out):—part.

6448. פָּסַג, **pâsag**, *paw-sag´*; a primitive root; to *cut up*, i.e. (figurative) *contemplate:*—consider.

6449. פִּסְגָּה, **Pisgâh**, *pis-gaw´*; from 6448; a *cleft*; *Pisgah*, a mountain East of Jordan:—Pisgah.

6450. פַּס דַּמִּים, **Pas Dammîym**, *pas dam-meem´*; from 6446 and the plural of 1818; *palm* (i.e. *dell*) *of bloodshed*; *Pas-Dammim*, a place in Palestine:—Pas-dammim. Compare 658.

6451. פִּסָּה, **pissâh**, *pis-saw´*; from 6461; *expansion*, i.e. *abundance:*—handful.

6452. פָּסַח, **pâsach**, *paw-sakh´*; a primitive root; to *hop*, i.e. (figurative) *skip* over (or *spare*); (by implication) to *hesitate*; also (literal) to *limp*, to *dance:*—halt, become lame, leap, pass over.

A verb meaning to leap, to pass over, to halt, to limp, to be lame. The first occurrence of this verb is in Exodus, where God states that He will preserve the Israelites by passing over their homes when He goes through Egypt to kill the firstborn (Ex 12:13, 23, 27). This sentiment is echoed by the prophet Isaiah (Isa 31:5). In 2Sa 4:4, the word is used of Saul's grandson who became lame. Before Elijah confronted the prophets of Baal, he confronted the Israelites for their syncretism. He asked them how long they would bounce back and forth between the Lord and Baal (1Ki 18:21). Then during Elijah's confrontation, the prophets of Baal began to dance on the altar that they had constructed (1Ki 18:26). This was probably some sort of cultic dance performed as part of the sacrifice ritual.

6453. פֶּסַח, **pesach**, *peh´-sakh*; from 6452; a *pretermission*, i.e. *exemption*; used only technically of the Jewish *Passover* (the festival or the victim):—passover (offering).

A masculine noun meaning Passover, a Passover animal, a sacrifice. The word is used forty-nine times, usually referring to the Passover festival or celebration. It is first used to describe the Passover ritual while Israel was still in Egypt (Ex 12:11, 27, 43, 48; 34:25). The first Passover ideally was constituted as follows: on the human level, the Israelites killed the Passover sacrifice on the evening of the fourteenth day of the first month, Abib or Nisan (March or April). They then took some of the blood of the slain Passover animal (Dt 16:2, 5) and smeared it on the sides and tops of the doorframes of their houses (cf. Ex 12:7). The Passover ritual and the Passover animal were directed to and belonged to the Lord (Ex 12:11, 48; Dt 16:1). They then roasted the animal (lamb, kid, young ram, goat—a one-year-old without any defect) and ate it with their sandals on their feet and their staffs in their hands ready to move out in haste at any time. The angel of death passed through Egypt and passed over the Israelites' houses with the blood of the lambs on the doorposts, but the angel struck the firstborn of all the Egyptian households (cf. Ex 12:12, 13, 29). Later Passovers were held in commemoration of the historical event of Israel's deliverance from Egyptian bondage.

The animals eaten were also called the *pesach*, the Passover sacrifice (Ex 12:21; 2Ch 30:15; 35:1). The Passover was celebrated throughout Israel's history before and after the exile (Nu 9:4; Jos 5:10; 2Ki 23:22; Ezr 6:19, 20).

6454. פָּסֵחַ, **Pâsêach,** *paw-say´-akh*; from 6452; *limping*; *Paseäch*, the name of two Israelites:—Paseah, Phaseah.

6455. פִּסֵּחַ, **pissêach,** *pis-say´-akh*; from 6452; *lame*:—lame.

6456. פָּסִיל, **pâsîyl,** *paws-eel´*; from 6458; an *idol*:—carved (graven) image, quarry.

A masculine noun meaning idol. This word comes from the verb *pâsal* (6458), meaning to hew or to cut, which was done to create a carved image. In the Law of the OT, it was clear that such idols should be burned (Dt 7:5, 25); and cut down (Dt 12:3); for they provoked God to anger (Ps 78:58; Jer 8:19); and incited Him to judgment (Jer 51:47, 52; Mic 1:7; 5:13[12]). The presence of these idols were indicative of the sin

and rebellion of the people (2Ch 33:19, 22; Hos 11:2); while the removal of such idols was a sign of repentance (2Ch 34:3, 4, 7; Isa 30:22).

6457. פָּסַךְ, **Pâsak,** *paw-sak´*; from an unused root meaning to *divide; divider; Pasak*, an Israelite:—Pasach.

6458. פָּסַל, **pâsal,** *paw-sal´*; a primitive root; to *carve*, whether wood or stone:—grave, hew.

A verb meaning to hew, to cut. This word is used most often in the context of cutting stone. Moses cut two stone tablets so God could record His words on them (Ex 34:1, 4; Dt 10:1, 3); the builders cut stones in building the Temple (1Ki 5:18[32]); and an idol maker cut the material to create an idol (Hab 2:18). See the related nouns *pěsiyl* (6456) and *pesel* (6459), meaning idol.

6459. פֶּסֶל, **pesel,** *peh´-sel*; from 6458; an *idol*:—carved (graven) image.

A noun meaning idol, a graven image. This word comes from the verb *pâsal* (6458), meaning to hew or to cut, which was done to create an idol. In the Law of the OT, the Lord forbade Israel to create such images (Ex 20:4; Le 26:1; Dt 5:8); for they were an abomination to Him (Dt 27:15). Those who served idols would be ashamed in the judgment (Ps 97:7; Isa 42:17); and the Lord would cut them off from Him (Na 1:14). The presence of these idols were indicative of the sin and rebellion of the people (Dt 4:16, 23, 25; 2Ch 33:7). The prophets often demonstrated the folly of these idols: they were profitable for nothing (Isa 44:10; Hab 2:18); they could easily be burned (Isa 44:15); they had no breath (Jer 10:14); and they could not save (Isa 45:20). Idols could be made of metal (Jgs 17:3, 4; Isa 40:19); wood (Isa 40:20; 44:15, 17); or possibly stone (Hab 2:18; cf. Hab 2:19).

6460. פְּסַנְטֵרִין, **pĕsantêrîyn,** *pes-an-tay-reen´*; (Chaldee); or פְּסַנְתֵּרִין, **pĕsantêrîyn,** *pes-an-tay-reen´*; a transliteration of the Greek *psalterion*; a *lyre*:—psaltery.

6461. פָּסַס, **pâsas,** *paw-sas´*; a primitive root; probably to *disperse*, i.e. (intrans.) *disappear*:—cease.

6462. פִּסְפָּה, **Pispâh,** *pis-paw´*; perhaps from 6461; *dispersion*; *Pispah*, an Israelite:—Pispah.

6463. פָּעָה, **pâ'âh,** *paw-aw´*; a primitive root; to *scream*:—cry.

6464. פָּעוּ, **Pâ'ûw,** *paw-oo´*; or פָּעִי, **Pâ'îy,** *paw-ee´*; from 6463; *screaming; Paü* or *Paï,* a place in Edom:—Pai, Pau.

6465. פְּעוֹר, **Pᵉ'ôwr,** *peh-ore´*; from 6473; a *gap; Peör,* a mountain East of Jordan; also (for 1187) a deity worshipped there:—Peor. See also 1047.

6466. פָּעַל, **pâ'al,** *paw-al´*; a primitive root; to *do* or *make* (systematically and habitually), especially to *practise*:—commit, [evil-] do (-er), make (-r), ordain, work (-er).

6467. פֹּעַל, **pô'al,** *po´-al*; from 6466; an *act* or *work* (concrete):—act, deed, do, getting, maker, work.

6468. פְּעֻלָּה, **pᵉ'ullâh,** *peh-ool-law´*; feminine passive participle of 6466; (abstract) *work*:—labour, reward, wages, work.

6469. פְּעֻלְּתַי, **Pᵉ'ullᵉthay,** *peh-ool-leh-thah´ee*; from 6468; *laborious; Peüllethai,* an Israelite:—Peulthai.

6470. פָּעַם, **pâ'am,** *paw-am´*; a primitive root; to *tap,* i.e. beat regularly; hence (general) to *impel* or *agitate*:—move, trouble.

6471. פַּעַם, **pa'am,** *pah´-am*; or (feminine) פַּעֲמָה, **pa'ămâh,** *pah-am-aw´*; from 6470; a *stroke,* literal or figurative (in various applications, as follow):—anvil, corner, foot (-step), going, [hundred-] fold, × now, (this) + once, order, rank, step, + thrice, ([often-], second, this, two) time (-s), twice, wheel.

6472. פַּעֲמֹן, **pa'ămôn,** *pah-am-one´*; from 6471; a *bell* (as *struck*):—bell.

6473. פָּעַר, **pâ'ar,** *paw-ar´*; a primitive root; to *yawn,* i.e. *open* wide (literal or figurative):—gape, open (wide).

6474. פַּעֲרַי, **Pa'ăray,** *pah-ar-ah´ee*; from 6473; *yawning; Paarai,* an Israelite:—Paarai.

6475. פָּצָה, **pâtsâh,** *paw-tsaw´*; a primitive root; to *rend,* i.e. *open* (especially the mouth):—deliver, gape, open, rid, utter.

6476. פָּצַח, **pâtsach,** *paw-tsakh´*; a primitive root; to *break* out (in joyful sound):—break (forth, forth into joy), make a loud noise.

6477. פְּצִירָה, **pᵉtsîyrâh,** *pets-ee-raw´*; from 6484; *bluntness*:— + file.

6478. פָּצַל, **pâtsal,** *paw-tsal´*; a primitive root; to *peel*:—pill.

6479. פְּצָלָה, **pᵉtsâlâh,** *pets-aw-law´*; from 6478; a *peeling*:—strake.

6480. פָּצַם, **pâtsam,** *paw-tsam´*; a primitive root; to *rend* (by earthquake):—break.

6481. פָּצַע, **pâtsa',** *paw-tsah´*; a primitive root; to *split,* i.e. *wound*:—wound.

6482. פֶּצַע, **petsa',** *peh´-tsah*; from 6481; a *wound*:—wound (-ing).

6483. פִּצֵּץ, **Pitstsêts,** *pits-tsates´*; from an unused root meaning to *dissever; dispersive; Pitstsets,* a priest:—Apses [*including the article*].

6484. פָּצַר, **pâtsar,** *paw-tsar´*; a primitive root; to *peck* at, i.e. (figurative) *stun* or *dull*:—press, urge, stubbornness.

6485. פָּקַד, **pâqad,** *paw-kad´*; a primitive root; to *visit* (with friendly or hostile intent); (by analogy) to *oversee, muster, charge, care for, miss, deposit,* etc.:—appoint, × at all, avenge, bestow, (appoint to have the, give a) charge, commit, count, deliver to keep, be empty, enjoin, go see, hurt, do judgment, lack, lay up, look, make, × by any means, miss, number, officer, (make) overseer, have (the) oversight, punish, reckon, (call to) remember (-brance), set (over), sum, × surely, visit, want.

A verb meaning to attend, to visit, and to search out. The word refers to someone (usually God) paying attention to persons, either to do them good (Ge 50:24, 25; Ex 3:16; 1Sa 2:21; Jer 23:2); or to bring punishment or harm (Ex 20:5; Isa 10:12; Jer 23:2). The word also means, usually in a causative form, to appoint over or to commit to, that is, to cause people to attend to something placed under their care (Ge 39:4, 5; Jos 10:18; Isa 62:6). The passive causative form means to deposit, that is, to cause something to be attended to (Le 6:4[5:23]). The word also means to number or to be numbered, which is an activity requiring attention. This meaning occurs over ninety times in the book of Numbers. The word can also mean (usually in a passive form) lacking or missing, as if a quantity was numbered less than an original amount (Jgs 21:3; 1Sa 20:18; 1Ki 20:39).

6486. פְּקֻדָּה, **pᵉquddâh,** *pek-ood-daw´*; feminine passive participle of 6485; *visitation* (in many senses, chiefly official):—account, (that have the) charge, custody, that which … laid up, numbers, office (-r), ordering, oversight, + prison, reckoning, visitation.

A feminine noun meaning an arrangement, an office, an officer, accounting. The root idea is something that is attended to or set in order. The word signifies the arrangement of fighting men under an officer (2Ch 17:14), of priests or Levites in an order (1Ch 23:11; 24:19); or the arrangement of the tabernacle and its contents (Nu 4:16[2x]). It signifies the office of one in charge of something (Ps 109:8); and the officers themselves (2Ki 11:18; Isa 60:17). Most often, the word means accounting and refers to a time of accounting when God attended to people's actions, usually to call them to account for their sins (Nu 16:29; Jer 48:44). In Job 10:12, however, God's attention was for Job's good.

6487. פִּקָּדוֹן, **piqqâdôwn,** *pik-kaw-done´*; from 6485; a *deposit*:—that which was delivered (to keep), store.

A masculine noun meaning deposit. The root idea is that something is left under someone's care or attention. The word occurs three times in the OT. In Genesis 41:36, the word referred to a store of food that Joseph advised Pharaoh to store up for the coming famine. In Le 6:2[5:21], 4[5:23], the word signified any deposit left in someone's care. If the keeper of this deposit dealt dishonestly with it, he had to pay a 20 percent penalty in addition to the deposit.

6488. פְּקִדֻת, **pᵉqiduth,** *pek-ee-dooth´*; from 6496; *supervision*:—ward.

A feminine noun meaning supervision, oversight. It occurs only in Jer 37:13, where it refers with the word baʿal (1167), meaning master, to an official or policeman as a master of supervision. In this passage, the officer was stationed at the Gate of Benjamin where financial transactions took place (cf. Dt 21:19; Ru 4:1ff.); and where the king sometimes officiated (cf. Jer 38:7). The office gave its bearer the legal power to arrest Jeremiah (Jer 37:13).

6489. פְּקוֹד, **Pᵉqôwd,** *pek-ode´*; from 6485; *punishment; Pekod,* a symbolical name for Babylon:—Pekod.

6490. פִּקּוּד, **piqqûwd,** *pik-kood´*; or פִּקֻּד, **piqqud,** *pik-kood´*; from 6485; (properly) *appointed,* i.e. a *mandate* (of God; plural only, collective for the *Law*):—commandment, precept, statute.

A masculine noun meaning precept, instruction. The root expresses the idea that God is paying attention to how He wants things ordered (see *pâqad* [6485]). God's precepts strike those who love Him as right and delightful (Ps 19:8[9]). This word is always plural and is only found in the Psalms, mostly in Ps 119 (twenty-one times). This psalm talked of seeking (Ps 119:40, 45, 94); keeping (Ps 119:63, 69, 134); and not forgetting God's instructions (Ps 119:87, 93, 141); even when opposed by the proud (Ps 119:69, 78). The psalmist's diligence in obeying God's precepts was rewarded with understanding and the hatred of evil (Ps 119:100, 104); liberty (Ps 119:45); confidence in asking God's help (Ps 119:94, 173); and spiritual life (Ps 119:93).

6491. פָּקַח, **pâqach,** *paw-kakh´*; a primitive root; to *open* (the senses, especially the eyes); (figurative) to *be observant*:—open.

6492. פֶּקַח, **Peqach,** *peh´-kakh*; from 6491; *watch; Pekach,* an Israelite king:—Pekah.

6493. פִּקֵּחַ, **piqqêach,** *pik-kay´-akh*; from 6491; *clear-sighted;* (figurative) *intelligent*:—seeing, wise.

A masculine adjective meaning seeing, sight. This noun is derived from the verb *pâqach* (6491), meaning to open the eyes and ears. In a literal sense, it occurs in Ex 4:11 when God answered Moses' objections for leading the people out of Egypt. In a metaphorical sense, this term represented those who could see clearly but could be blinded by a gift (Ex 23:8).

6494. פְּקַחְיָה, **Pᵉqachyâh,** *pek-akh-yaw´*; from 6491 and 3050; *Jah has observed; Pekachjah,* an Israelite king:—Pekahiah.

6495. פְּקַח־קוֹחַ, **pᵉqach-qôwach,** *pek-akh-ko´-akh*; from 6491 redoubled; *opening* (of a dungeon), i.e. *jail-delivery;* (figurative) *salvation* from sin:—opening of the prison.

6496. פָּקִיד, **pâqîyd,** *paw-keed´*; from 6485; a *superintendent* (civil, military or religious):— which had the charge, governor, office, overseer, [that] was set.

A masculine noun meaning a commissioner, a deputy, and an overseer. Depending on the context, this term has a broad range of possible meanings. It could apply to government representatives whose positions are temporary, like the officers appointed by Pharaoh to collect grain during the seven plentiful years (Ge 41:34). It could also represent a permanent position of leadership for a king (Jgs 9:28); a high priest (2Ch 24:11); or a Levite (2Ch 31:13). It could further signify a general leader of men, such as a military officer (2Ki 25:19); a tribal leader (Ne 11:9); or a priestly leader (Ne 11:14).

6497. פְּקָעִים, **peqâ'îym,** *peh´-kah-eem*; from an unused root meaning to *burst*; only used as an architectural term of an ornament similar to 6498, a *semi-globe*:—knop.

6498. פַּקֻּעָה, **paqqu'âh,** *pak-koo-aw´*; from the same as 6497; the *wild cucumber* (from *splitting* open to shed its seeds):—gourd.

6499. פַּר, **par,** *par*; or פָּר, **pâr,** *pawr*; from 6565; a *bullock* (apparently as *breaking forth* in wild strength, or perhaps as *dividing* the hoof):— (+ young) bull (-ock), calf, ox.

6500. פָּרָא, **pârâ',** *paw-raw´*; a primitive root; to *bear fruit*:—be fruitful.

6501. פֶּרֶא, **pere',** *peh´-reh*; or פֶּרֶה, **pereh,** *peh´-reh*; (Jer 2:24), from 6500 in the secondary sense of *running* wild; the *onager*:—wild (ass).

6502. פִּרְאָם, **Pir'âm,** *pir-awm´*; from 6501; *wildly*; *Piram*, a Canaanite:—Piram.

6503. פַּרְבָּר, **Parbâr,** *par-bawr´*; or פַּרְוָר, **Parvâr,** *par-vawr´*; of foreign origin; *Parbar* or *Parvar*, a quarter of Jerusalem:—Parbar, suburb.

6504. פָּרַד, **pârad,** *paw-rad´*; a primitive root; to *break* through, i.e. *spread* or *separate* (oneself):—disperse, divide, be out of joint, part, scatter (abroad), separate (self), sever self, stretch, sunder.

6505. פֶּרֶד, **pered,** *peh´-red*; from 6504; a *mule* (perhaps from his *lonely* habits):—mule.

6506. פִּרְדָּה, **p**e**rudâh,** *per-oo-daw´*; feminine of 6505; a *she-mule*:—mule.

6507. פְּרֻדֹת, **p**e**rudôth,** *per-oo-doth´*; feminine passive participle of 6504; something *separated*, i.e. a *kernel*:—seed.

6508. פַּרְדֵּס, **pardês,** *par-dace´*; of foreign origin; a *park*:—forest, orchard.

6509. פָּרָה, **pârâh,** *paw-raw´*; a primitive root; to *bear fruit* (literal or figurative):—bear, bring forth (fruit), (be, cause to be, make) fruitful, grow, increase.

6510. פָּרָה, **pârâh,** *paw-raw´*; feminine of 6499; a *heifer*:—cow, heifer, kine.

6511. פָּרָה, **Pârâh,** *paw-raw´*; the same as 6510; *Parah*, a place in Palestine:—Parah.

6512. פֵּרָה, **pêrâh,** *pay-raw´*; from 6331; a *hole* (as *broken*, i.e. dug):— + mole. Compare 2661.

6513. פֻּרָה, **Purâh,** *poo-raw´*; for 6288; *foliage*; *Purah*, an Israelite:—Phurah.

6514. פְּרוּדָא, **P**e**rûdâ',** *per-oo-daw´*; or פְּרִידָא, **P**e**rîydâ',** *per-ee-daw´*; from 6504; *dispersion*; *Peruda* or *Perida*, one of "Solomon's servants":—Perida, Peruda.

6515. פָּרוּחַ, **Pârûwach,** *paw-roo´-akh*; passive participle of 6524; *blossomed*; *Paruäh*, an Israelite:—Paruah.

6516. פַּרְוַיִם, **Parvayim,** *par-vah´-yim*; of foreign origin; *Parvajim*, an Oriental region:—Parvaim.

6517. פָּרוּר, **pârûwr,** *paw-roor´*; passive participle of 6565 in the sense of *spreading* out [compare 6524]; a *skillet* (as *flat* or *deep*):—pan, pot.

6518. פָּרָז, **pârâz,** *paw-rawz´*; from an unused root meaning to *separate*, i.e. *decide*; a *chieftain*:—village.

6519. פְּרָזָה, **p**e**râzâh,** *per-aw-zaw´*; from the same as 6518; an *open* country:—(unwalled) town (without walls), unwalled village.

6520. פְּרָזוֹן, **p**e**râzôwn,** *per-aw-zone´*; from the same as 6518; *magistracy*, i.e. *leadership* (also [concrete] *chieftains*):—village.

6521. פְּרָזִי, **p**e**râzîy,** *per-aw-zee*; or פְּרוֹזִי, **p**e**rôwzîy,** *per-o-zee´*; from 6519; a *rustic*:—village.

6522. יִּזְרְפ, **Pᵉrizzîy,** *per-iz-zee´*; for 6521; inhabitant *of the open country*; a Perizzite, one of the Canaanitish tribes:—Perizzite.

6523. לֶזְרַפ, **parzel,** *par-zel´*; (Chaldee); corresponding to 1270; *iron*:—iron.

6524. חַרָפ, **pârach,** *paw-rakh´*; a primitive root; to *break* forth as a bud, i.e. *bloom*; (generally) to *spread*; (specifically) to *fly* (as extending the wings); (figurative) to *flourish*:— × abroad, × abundantly, blossom, break forth (out), bud, flourish, make fly, grow, spread, spring (up).

6525. חַרֶפ, **perach,** *peh´-rakh*; from 6524; a *calyx* (native or artificial); (general) *bloom*:—blossom, bud, flower.

6526. חַחְרִפ, **pirchach,** *pir-khakh´*; from 6524; *progeny*, i.e. a *brood*:—youth.

6527. טַרָפ, **pâraṭ,** *paw-rat´*; a primitive root; to *scatter* words, i.e. *prate* (or *hum*):—chant.

6528. טֶרֶפ, **pereṭ,** *peh´-ret*; from 6527; a *stray* or *single* berry:—grape.

6529. יִרְפ, **pᵉrîy,** *per-ee´*; from 6509; *fruit* (literal or figurative):—bough, ([first-]) fruit ([-full]), reward.

6530. ץיִרָפ, **pârîyts,** *pawr-eets´*; from 6555; *violent*, i.e. a *tyrant*:—destroyer, ravenous, robber.

A masculine noun meaning a violent individual. The term was usually applied to a person or people. David claimed to have refrained from the ways of the violent (Ps 17:4). God asked if the Temple had become the dwelling place of the violent (Jer 7:11). God proclaimed through the prophet Ezekiel that the end would come when the violent desecrate God's treasured place (Eze 7:22); they would be punished (Eze 18:10). The prophet Isaiah also applied this term to wild animals like the lion (Isa 35:9).

6531. ךֶרֶפ, **perek,** *peh´-rek*; from an unused root meaning to *break* apart; *fracture*, i.e. *severity*:—cruelty, rigour.

6532. תֶכֹרָפ, **pârôketh,** *paw-roh´-keth*; feminine active participle of the same as 6531; a *separatrix*, i.e. (the sacred) *screen*:—vail.

6533. םַרָפ, **pâram,** *paw-ram´*; a primitive root; to *tear*:—rend.

6534. אָתְּשַׁמְרַפ, **Parmashtâ’,** *par-mash-taw´*; of Persian origin; *Parmashta*, a son of Haman:—Parmasta.

6535. ךְַנְרַפ, **Parnak,** *par-nak´*; of uncertain derivation; *Parnak*, an Israelite:—Parnach.

6536. סַרָפ, **pâras,** *paw-ras´*; a primitive root; to *break* in pieces, i.e. (usually without violence) to *split, distribute*:—deal, divide, have hoofs, part, tear.

6537. סַרְפ, **pᵉras,** *per-as´*; (Chaldee); corresponding to 6536; to *split* up:—divide, [U-] pharsin.

6538. סֶרֶפ, **peres,** *peh´-res*; from 6536; a *claw*; also a kind of *eagle*:—claw, ossifrage.

6539. סַרָפ, **Pâras,** *paw-ras´*; of foreign origin; *Paras* (i.e. Persia), an Eastern country, including its inhabitants:—Persia, Persians.

6540. סַרָפ, **Pâras,** *paw-ras´*; (Chaldee); corresponding to 6539:—Persia, Persians.

6541. הָסְרַפ, **parsâh,** *par-saw´*; feminine of 6538; a *claw* or split *hoof*:—claw, [cloven-] footed, hoof.

6542. יִסְרַפ, **Parsîy,** *par-see´*; patrial from 6539; a *Parsite* (i.e. Persian), or inhabitant of Peres:—Persian.

6543. יָסְרַפ, **Parsây,** *par-saw´ee*; (Chaldee); corresponding to 6542:—Persian.

6544. עַרָפ, **pâra‘,** *paw-rah´*; a primitive root; to *loosen*; (by implication) to *expose, dismiss*; (figurative) to *absolve, begin*:—avenge, avoid, bare, go back, let, (make) naked, set at nought, perish, refuse, uncover.

A verb meaning to let go, to let loose, to unbind. Moses saw that Aaron had let the Israelites get out of hand when Moses was up on the mountain (Ex 32:25[2x]). This word can also apply to hair, as with those who were commanded not to let their hair down from their turbans. This warning was given to Aaron concerning mourning (Le 10:6); and to high priests in general (Le 21:10). However, lepers were to let their hair down to call attention to their condition (Le 13:45). A possible unfaithful wife had her hair loosened by the priest in connection with the drinking of bitter water to see if she was guilty (Nu 5:18). This word can also mean to ignore (Pr 1:25); to avoid (Pr 4:15); or to lead (Jgs 5:2).

6545. פֶּרַע, **pera',** *peh'-rah*; from 6544; the *hair* (as *dishevelled*):—locks.

6546. פֶּרַע, **pera',** *peh'-rah*; feminine of 6545 (in the sense of *beginning*); *leadership* (plural [concrete] *leaders*):— + avenging, revenge.

A feminine noun meaning leaders. This specific form of the word is not used in the Hebrew Bible, but the plural form is used. In the song of Moses, the Lord proclaimed that He would overcome the enemy leaders (Dt 32:42). See the Hebrew root *para'* (6544).

6547. פַּרְעֹה, **Par'ôh,** *par-o'*; of Egyptian derivation; *Paroh,* a generic title of Egyptian kings:—Pharaoh.

6548. פַּרְעֹה חָפְרַע, **Par'ôh Chophra',** *par-o' khof-rah'*; of Egyptian derivation; *Paroh-Chophra,* an Egyptian king:—Pharaoh-hophra.

6549. פַּרְעֹה נְכֹה, **Par'ôh Nᵉkôh,** *par-o' nek-o'*; or פַּרְעֹה נְכוֹ, **Par'ôh Nᵉkôw,** *par-o' nek-o'*; of Egyptian derivation; *Paroh-Nekoh* (or -*Neko*), an Egyptian king:—Pharaoh-necho, Pharaoh-nechoh.

6550. פַּרְעֹשׁ, **par'ôsh,** *par-oshe'*; probably from 6544 and 6211; a *flea* (as the *isolated insect*):—flea.

6551. פַּרְעֹשׁ, **Par'ôsh,** *par-oshe'*; the same as 6550; *Parosh,* the name of four Israelites:—Parosh, Pharosh.

6552. פִּרְעָתוֹן, **Pir'âthôwn,** *pir-aw-thone'*; from 6546; *chieftaincy; Pirathon,* a place in Palestine:—Pirathon.

6553. פִּרְעָתוֹנִי, **Pir'âthôwnîy,** *pir-aw-tho-nee'*; or פִּרְעָתֹנִי, **Pir'âthônîy,** *pir-aw-tho-nee'*; patrial from 6552; a *Pirathonite* or inhabitant of Pirathon:—Pirathonite.

6554. פַּרְפַּר, **Parpar,** *par-par'*; probably from 6565 in the sense of *rushing; rapid; Parpar,* a river of Syria:—Pharpar.

6555. פָּרַץ, **pârats,** *paw-rats'*; a primitive root; to *break* out (in many applications, direct and indirect, literal and figurative):— × abroad, (make a) breach, break (away, down, -er, forth, in, up), burst out, come (spread) abroad, com-

pel, disperse, grow, increase, open, press, scatter, urge.

6556. פֶּרֶץ, **perets,** *peh'-rets*; from 6555; a *break* (literal or figurative):—breach, breaking forth (in), × forth, gap.

6557. פֶּרֶץ, **Perets,** *peh'-rets*; the same as 6556; *Perets,* the name of two Israelites:—Perez, Pharez.

6558. פַּרְצִי, **Partsîy,** *par-tsee'*; patronymic from 6557; a *Partsite* (collective) or descendants of Perets:—Pharzites.

6559. פְּרָצִים, **pᵉrâtsîym,** *per-aw-tseem'*; plural of 6556; *breaks; Peratsim,* a mountain in Palestine:—Perazim.

6560. פֶּרֶץ עֻזָּא, **Perets 'Uzzâ',** *peh'-rets ooz-zaw'*; from 6556 and 5798; *break of Uzza; Perets-Uzza,* a place in Palestine:—Perez-uzza.

6561. פָּרַק, **pâraq,** *paw-rak'*; a primitive root; to *break* off or *crunch;* (figurative) to *deliver:*—break (off), deliver, redeem, rend (in pieces), tear in pieces.

6562. פְּרַק, **pᵉraq,** *per-ak'*; (Chaldee); corresponding to 6561; to *discontinue:*—break off.

6563. פֶּרֶק, **pereq,** *peh'-rek*; from 6561; *rapine;* also a *fork* (in roads):—crossway, robbery.

6564. פָּרָק, **pârâq,** *paw-rawk'*; from 6561; *soup* (as full of *crumbed* meat):—broth. See also 4832.

6565. פָּרַר, **pârar,** *paw-rar'*; a primitive root; to *break* up (usually figurative, i.e. to *violate, frustrate*):— × any ways, break (asunder), cast off, cause to cease, × clean, defeat, disannul, disappoint, dissolve, divide, make of no effect, fail, frustrate, bring (come) to nought, × utterly, make void.

A verb meaning to break, to divide, to frustrate. This word is often used in conjunction with a covenant or agreement. The Lord warned the Israelites what would happen if they broke the covenant with Him (Le 26:15); and pledged to them that He would not break it (Le 26:44). Asa, king of Judah, asked the king of Aram to break a covenant Aram had made with Israel (1Ki 15:19). This word is also used to refer to the frustration of plans, as the enemies of Israel did to the Israelites trying to rebuild the Temple (Ezr 4:5). However, the Lord's purposes cannot be frustrated (Isa 14:27).

6566. פָּרַשׂ, **pâraś,** *paw-ras´*; a primitive root; to *break* apart, *disperse,* etc.:—break, chop in pieces, lay open, scatter, spread (abroad, forth, selves, out), stretch (forth, out).

6567. פָּרַשׁ, **pârash,** *paw-rash´*; a primitive root; to *separate,* literal (to *disperse*) or figurative (to *specify*); also (by implication) to *wound:*—scatter, declare, distinctly, shew, sting.

6568. פְּרַשׁ, **pᵉrash,** *per-ash´*; (Chaldee); corresponding to 6567; to *specify:*—distinctly.

6569. פֶּרֶשׁ, **peresh,** *peh´-resh*; from 6567; *excrement* (as *eliminated*):—dung.

6570. פֶּרֶשׁ, **Peresh,** *peh´-resh*; the same as 6569; *Peresh,* an Israelite:—Peresh.

6571. פָּרָשׁ, **pârâsh,** *paw-rawsh´*; from 6567; a *steed* (as *stretched* out to a vehicle, not single nor for mounting [compare 5483]); also (by implication) a *driver* (in a chariot), i.e. (collective) *cavalry:*—horseman.

6572. פַּרְשֶׁגֶן, **parshegen,** *par-sheh´-ghen*; or פַּתְשֶׁגֶן, **pathshegen,** *path-sheh´-gen*; of foreign origin; a *transcript:*—copy.

6573. פַּרְשֶׁגֶן, **parshegen,** *par-sheh´-ghen*; (Chaldee); corresponding to 6572:—copy.

6574. פַּרְשְׁדֹן, **parshᵉdôn,** *par-shed-one´*; perhaps by compounding 6567 and 6504 (in the sense of *straddling*) [compare 6576]; the *crotch* (or *anus*):—dirt.

6575. פָּרָשָׁה, **pârâshâh,** *paw-raw-shaw´*; from 6567; *exposition:*—declaration, sum.

6576. פַּרְשֵׁז, **parshêz,** *par-shaze´*; a root apparently formed by compounding 6567 and that of 6518 [compare 6574]; to *expand:*—spread.

6577. פַּרְשַׁנְדָּתָא, **Parshandâthâ´,** *par-shan-daw-thaw´*; of Persian origin; *Parshandatha,* a son of Haman:—Parshandatha.

6578. פְּרָת, **Pᵉrâth,** *per-awth´*; from an unused root meaning to *break* forth; *rushing; Perath* (i.e. *Euphrates*), a river of the East:—Euphrates.

6579. פַּרְתְּמִים, **partᵉmîym,** *par-teh-meem´*; of Persian origin; a *grandee:*—(most) noble, prince.

A noun meaning a prince, a noble. This word is only used in the plural form in the Hebrew OT. The most important people in the kingdom were invited to King Xerxes' banquet (Est 1:3). Haman suggested to the king that the appropriate way to honour someone was to have a nobleman lead him around the kingdom in the king's robe and on the king's horse (Est 6:9). When Babylon captured Jerusalem, the young Israelite nobility were taken into Nebuchadnezzar's service (Da 1:3). Shadrach, Meshach, Abednego, and Daniel were part of this group.

6580. פַּשׁ, **pash,** *pash*; probably from an unused root meaning to *disintegrate; stupidity* (as a result of *grossness* or of *degeneracy*):—extremity.

6581. פָּשָׂה, **pâśâh,** *paw-saw´*; a primitive root; to *spread:*—spread.

6582. פָּשַׁח, **pâshach,** *paw-shakh´*; a primitive root; to *tear* in pieces:—pull in pieces.

6583. פַּשְׁחוּר, **Pashchûwr,** *pash-khoor´*; probably from 6582; *liberation; Pashchur,* the name of four Israelites:—Pashur.

6584. פָּשַׁט, **pâshaṭ,** *paw-shat´*; a primitive root; to *spread* out (i.e. *deploy* in hostile array); (by analogy) to *strip* (i.e. *unclothe, plunder, flay,* etc.):—fall upon, flay, invade, make an invasion, pull off, put off, make a road, run upon, rush, set, spoil, spread selves (abroad), strip (off, self).

6585. פָּשַׂע, **pâśa‘,** *paw-sah´*; a primitive root; to *stride* (from *spreading* the legs), i.e. *rush* upon:—go.

6586. פָּשַׁע, **pâsha‘,** *paw-shah´*; a primitive root [rather identical with 6585 through the idea of *expansion*]; to *break* away (from just authority), i.e. *trespass, apostatize, quarrel:*—offend, rebel, revolt, transgress (-ion, -or).

A verb meaning to rebel, to transgress, to revolt, to sin. This verb is used about forty times in the simple stem of the verb. It means to sin, but the sin involved is one of revolt or rebellion in nearly every case. It indicates rebellion against various parties; the people of Israel rebelled against their God (Isa 1:2; 66:24; Jer 2:29; 3:13); especially their leaders (Jer 2:8). Nations and peoples revolted or broke with one another: Israel broke from and rebelled against Judah (1Ki 12:19); Moab rebelled against Israel (2Ki 1:1; 3:5); and Edom revolted against Judah (2Ki

8:20). Revolt and rebellion against the Lord, Isaiah said, was a part of the character of Israel from its birth and throughout its history (Isa 48:8; 59:13). Amos described Israel's insistence to worship at the unapproved sanctuaries at Bethel and Gilgal as revolt and rebellion (Am 4:4). The postexilic community rebelled through intermarriages with pagans (Ezr 10:13). God asserted that He would restore His people, forgiving their sins of rebellion (Jer 33:8). Unrestrained rebellion seems to be a mark of the end times as noted by Da 8:23.

6587. עֶשַׂפ, **peśaʿ,** *peh´-sah;* from 6585; a *stride:*—step.

6588. עֶשַׁפ, **peshaʿ,** *peh´-shah;* from 6586; a *revolt* (national, moral or religious):—rebellion, sin, transgression, trespass.

A masculine noun meaning transgression, rebellion. Though it can be a transgression of one individual against another (Ge 31:36; 50:17; Ex 22:9[8]); or of one nation against another (Am 1:3, 6, 9, 11, 13; 2:1); this word primarily expresses a rebellion against God and His laws (Isa 58:1; 59:12; Am 5:12). Since it is possible for humanity to recognize this transgression (Ps 32:5; 51:3[5]), God's first step in dealing with it is to reveal it and call His people to accountability (Job 36:9; Mic 3:8). He then punishes the guilty (Isa 53:5, 8; Am 2:4, 6) in the hope of restoring the relationship and forgiving the transgressors who repent (Eze 18:30, 31). In addition to the act of transgression itself, this term can also be used to convey the guilt that comes from the transgression (Job 33:9; 34:6; Ps 59:3[4]); the punishment for the transgression (Da 8:12, 13; 9:24); or the offering that is presented to atone for the transgression (Mic 6:7).

6589. קֶשַׂפ, **pâśaq,** *paw-sak´;* a primitive root; to *dispart* (the feet or lips), i.e. *become licentious:*—open (wide).

6590. רֶשַׁפ, **pᵉshar,** *pesh-ar´;* (Chaldee); corresponding to 6622; to *interpret:*—make [interpretations], interpreting.

6591. רֶשַׁפ, **pᵉshar,** *pesh-ar´;* (Chaldee); from 6590; an *interpretation:*—interpretation.

6592. רֶשֵׁפ, **pêsher,** *pay´-sher;* corresponding to 6591:—interpretation.

6593. תֶשֵׁפ, **pêsheth,** *pay-sheth´;* from the same as 6580 as in the sense of *comminuting; linen* (i.e. the thread, as *carded*):—flax, linen.

6594. הָתְּשׁפ, **pishtâh,** *pish-taw´;* feminine of 6593; *flax;* (by implication) a *wick:*—flax, tow.

6595. תַפ, **path,** *path;* from 6626; a *bit:*—meat, morsel, piece.

6596. תֹפ, **pôth,** *pohth;* or הָתֹפ, **pôthâh,** *po-thaw´;* (Eze 13:19), from an unused root meaning to *open;* a *hole,* i.e. *hinge* or the female *pudenda:*—hinge, secret part.

6597. םֹאְתִפ, **pith'ôwm,** *pith-ome´;* or םֹאְתִפ, **pith'ôm,** *pith-ome´;* from 6621; *instantly:*—straightway, sudden (-ly).

6598. גַבְּתַפ, **pathbag,** *path-bag´;* of Persian origin; a *dainty:*—portion (provision) of meat.

6599. םָגְּתִפ, **pithgâm,** *pith-gawm´;* of Persian origin; a (judicial) *sentence:*—decree, sentence.

A masculine noun meaning an edict, a decree. This word is used only twice in the OT. In Est 1:20, it describes a king's authoritative edict (or law) that could not be repealed (cf. Est 1:19). In Ecc 8:11, it refers to a court sentence (or judgment) that should be executed against evil.

6600. םָגְּתִפ, **pithgâm,** *pith-gawm´;* (Chaldee); corresponding to 6599; a *word, answer, letter* or *decree:*—answer, letter, matter, word.

An Aramaic masculine noun meaning a written word, an affair. This word is related to the Hebrew word *pithgâm* (6599) and was used in Ezra to describe the written communication that was used between the kings, the Israelites, and their adversaries (Ezr 4:17; 5:7, 11; 6:11). In Daniel, this word described the affair surrounding the unwillingness of Shadrach, Meshach, and Abednego to bow to the golden image (Da 3:16); in addition to the matters contained in Nebuchadnezzar's dream (Da 4:17[14]).

6601. הָתָפ, **pâthâh,** *paw-thaw´;* a primitive root; to *open,* i.e. *be* (causative, *make*) *roomy;* usually figurative (in a mental or moral sense) to *be* (causative, *make*) *simple* or (in a sinister way) *delude:*—allure, deceive, enlarge, entice, flatter, persuade, silly (one).

6602. לֵאוּתְפ, **Pᵉthûw'êl,** *peth-oo-ale´;* from 6601 and 410; *enlarged of God;* Pethuel, an Israelite:—Pethuel.

6603. פִּתּוּחַ, **pittûwach,** *pit-too´-akh*; or פִּתֻּחַ, **pittuach,** *pit-too´-akh*; passive participle of 6605; *sculpture* (in low or high relief or even intaglio):—carved (work) (are, en-) grave (-ing, -n).

6604. פְּתוֹר, **P⁰thôwr,** *peth-ore´*; of foreign origin; *Pethor,* a place in Mesopotamia:—Pethor.

6605. פָּתַח, **pâthach,** *paw-thakh´*; a primitive root; to *open* wide (literal or figurative); (specifically) to *loosen, begin, plough, carve*:—appear, break forth, draw (out), let go free, (en-) grave (-n), loose (self), (be, be set) open (-ing), put off, ungird, unstop, have vent.

6606. פְּתַח, **p⁰thach,** *peth-akh´*; (Chaldee); corresponding to 6605; to *open*:—open.

6607. פֶּתַח, **pethach,** *peh´-thakh*; from 6605; an *opening* (literal), i.e. *door* (*gate*) or *entrance* way:—door, entering (in), entrance (-ry), gate, opening, place.

6608. פֵּתַח, **pêthach,** *pah´-thakh*; from 6605; *opening* (figurative) i.e. *disclosure*:—entrance.

6609. פְּתִיחָה, **p⁰thîychâh,** *peth-ee-khaw´*; from 6605; something *opened*, i.e. a *drawn* sword:—drawn sword.

6610. פִּתְחוֹן, **pithchôwn,** *pith-khone´*; from 6605; *opening* (the act):—open (-ing).

6611. פְּתַחְיָה, **P⁰thachyâh,** *peth-akh-yaw´*; from 6605 and 3050; *Jah has opened; Pethachjah,* the name of four Israelites:—Pethakiah.

6612. פְּתִי, **p⁰thîy,** *peth-ee´*; or פֶּתִי, **pethîy,** *peh´-thee;* or פְּתָאִי, **p⁰thâ'îy,** *peth-aw-ee´*; from 6601; *silly* (i.e. *seducible*):—foolish, simple (-icity, one).

6613. פְּתַי, **p⁰thây,** *peth-aw´ee*; (Chaldee); from a root corresponding to 6601; *open,* i.e. (as noun) *width*:—breadth.

6614. פְּתִיגִיל, **p⁰thîygîyl,** *peth-eeg-eel´*; of uncertain derivation; probably a figured *mantle* for holidays:—stomacher.

6615. פְּתַיּוּת, **p⁰thayyûwth,** *peth-ah-yooth´*; from 6612; *silliness* (i.e. *seducibility*):—simple.

6616. פָּתִיל, **pâthîyl,** *paw-theel´*; from 6617; *twine:*—bound, bracelet, lace, line, ribband, thread, wire.

6617. פָּתַל, **pâthal,** *paw-thal´*; a primitive root; to *twine,* i.e. (literal) to *struggle* or (figurative) *be* (moral) *tortuous*:—(shew self) froward, shew self unsavoury, wrestle.

6618. פְּתַלְתֹּל, **p⁰thaltôl,** *peth-al-tole´*; from 6617; *tortuous* (i.e. crafty):—crooked.

6619. פִּתֹם, **Pithôm,** *pee-thome´*; of Egyptian derivation; *Pithom,* a place in Egypt:—Pithom.

6620. פֶּתֶן, **pethen,** *peh´-then*; from an unused root meaning to *twist*; an *asp* (from its *contortions*):—adder.

6621. פֶּתַע, **petha‘,** *peh´-thah*; from an unused root meaning to *open* (the eyes); a *wink,* i.e. *moment* [compare 6597] (used only [with or without preposition] adverbially *quickly* or *unexpectedly*):—at an instant, suddenly, × very.

6622. פָּתַר, **pâthar,** *paw-thar´*; a primitive root; to *open* up, i.e. (figurative) *interpret* (a dream):—interpret (-ation, -er).

6623. פִּתְרוֹן, **pithrôwn,** *pith-rone´;* or פִּתְרֹן, **pithrôn,** *pith-rone´*; from 6622; *interpretation* (of a dream):—interpretation.

6624. פַּתְרוֹס, **Pathrôws,** *path-roce´*; of Egyptian derivation; *Pathros,* a part of Egypt:—Pathros.

6625. פַּתְרֻסִי, **Pathrusîy,** *path-roo-see´*; patrial from 6624; a *Pathrusite,* or inhabitant of Pathros:—Pathrusim.

6626. פָּתַת, **pâthath,** *paw-thath´*; a primitive root; to *open,* i.e. *break*:—part.

צ (Tsadhe)

6627. צֵאָה, **tsê'âh,** *tsay-aw´*; from 3318; *issue,* i.e. (human) *excrement:*—that (which) cometh from (out).

6628. צֶאֱלִים, **tse'ĕlîym,** *tseh´-el-eem*; from an unused root meaning to *be slender;* the *lotus* tree:—shady tree.

6629. צֹא, **tsô'n,** *tsone*; or צָאוֹן, **tsᵉ'ôwn,** *tseh-one´*; (Ps 144:13), from an unused root meaning to *migrate*; a collective name for a *flock* (of sheep or goats); also figurative (of men):— (small) cattle, flock (+ -s), lamb (+ -s), sheep ([- cote, -fold, -shearer, -herds]).

6630. צַאֲנָן, **Tsa'ănân,** *tsah-an-awn´*; from the same as 6629 used denominative; *sheep* pasture; *Zaanan,* a place in Palestine:—Zaanan.

6631. צֶאֱצָא, **tse'ĕtsâ',** *tseh-ets-aw´*; from 3318; *issue,* i.e. *produce, children:*—that which cometh forth (out), offspring.

6632. צָב, **tsâb,** *tsawb*; from an unused root meaning to *establish*; a *palanquin* or *canopy* (as a *fixture*); also a species of *lizard* (probably as clinging *fast*):—covered, litter, tortoise.

6633. צָבָא, **tsâbâ',** *tsaw-baw´*; a primitive root; to *mass* (an army or servants):—assemble, fight, perform, muster, wait upon, war.

A verb meaning to wage war, to muster into service, to serve. This word is primarily used to describe a gathering of people waging war against another city or country (Nu 31:7, 42; Isa 29:7, 8; Zec 14:12). In one instance, it was used to depict the Lord waging war (Isa 31:4). In several contexts, this word referred to the mustering of people into service (2Ki 25:19; Jer 52:25). Finally, this word described the religious service in the tabernacle (Ex 38:8; Nu 4:23; 8:24; 1Sa 2:22).

6634. צְבָא, **tsᵉbâ',** *tseb-aw´*; (Chaldee); corresponding to 6633 in the figurative sense of *summoning* one's wishes; to *please:*—will, would.

6635. צָבָא, **tsâbâ',** *tsaw-baw´*; or (feminine) צְבָאָה, **tsebâ'âh,** *tseb-aw-aw´*; from 6633; a *mass* of persons (or figurative things), especially reg. organized for war (an *army*); (by implication) a *campaign,* literal or figurative (specifically *hardship, worship*):—appointed time, (+) army, (+) battle, company, host, service, soldiers, waiting upon, war (-fare).

A masculine noun meaning service, servants. It may apply to military service (Nu 1:3; 1Sa 17:55); hard, difficult service (Job 7:1; Isa 40:2); or divine service (Nu 4:3; 8:24, 25; Ps 68:11[12]). The angels and the heavens alike are in divine service and therefore come under this term (Ge 2:1; 1Ki 22:19; Jer 33:22; cf. Lk 2:13). Over half of its nearly five hundred uses come in the phrase, the Lord [or God] of hosts. The phrase is absent from the first five books of the Bible. But frequently in the Prophets, the phrase introduces a divine declaration. At least once the hosts (always plural) in this expression are identified as human armies, but elsewhere they most likely refer to angelic forces (Jos 5:13–15; 1Sa 17:55; Ps 103:21; Isa 1:9). The title the LORD of hosts was often translated in the Septuagint as the LORD of powers or the LORD Almighty (Ps 24:10; Zec 4:6). On other occasions, the Hebrew word for hosts was transliterated into Greek (1Sa 1:3, 11). This Greek form of the Hebrew word shows up twice in the NT, once in a quotation from Isaiah (cf. Ro 9:29; Jas 5:4).

6636. צְבֹאִים, **Tsᵉbô'îym,** *tseb-o-eem´*; or (more correctly) צְבָאִים, **Tsᵉbô'yim,** *tse-bo-yeem´*; or צְבִים, **Tsᵉbôyim,** *tse-bo-yeem´*; plural of 6643; *gazelles; Tseboïm* or *Tsebijim,* a place in Palestine:—Zeboïm, Zeboim.

6637. צֹבֵבָה, **Tsôbêbâh,** *tso-bay-baw´*; feminine active participle of the same as 6632; the *canopier* (with the article); *Tsobebah,* an Israelitess:—Zobebah.

6638. צָבָה, **tsâbâh,** *tsaw-baw´*; a primitive root; to *amass,* i.e. *grow turgid;* (specifically) to *array* an army against:—fight, swell.

6639. צָבֶה, **tsâbeh,** *tsaw-beh´*; from 6638; *turgid:*—swell.

6640. צְבוּ, **ts͏ebûw,** *tseb-oo´*; (Chaldee); from 6634; (properly) *will;* (concrete) an *affair* (as a matter of *determination*):—purpose.

6641. צָבוּעַ, **tsâbûwaʻ,** *tsaw-boo´-ah*; passive participle of the same as 6648; *dyed* (in stripes), i.e. the *hyena:*—speckled.

6642. צָבַט, **tsâbaṭ,** *tsaw-bat´*; a primitive root; to *grasp,* i.e. *hand* out:—reach.

6643. צְבִי, **ts͏ebîy,** *tseb-ee´*; from 6638 in the sense of *prominence; splendor* (as *conspicuous*); also a *gazelle* (as *beautiful*):—beautiful (-ty), glorious (-ry), goodly, pleasant, roe (-buck).

A masculine noun meaning beauty, glory, a gazelle. This word has essentially two meanings. The first meaning describes something that is beautiful or glorious, such as the glorious land which God gave Israel that flowed with milk and honey (Eze 20:6, 15); or the beautiful flower of Ephraim (Isa 28:1). This word was normally used to depict the glory of a nation: Israel (2Sa 1:19); Babylon (Isa 13:19); Tyre (Isa 23:9); Ephraim (Isa 28:1, 4); a city (Eze 25:9); a mountain (Da 11:45); or a land in general (Da 8:9; 11:16, 41). In a few instances, it speaks of the Lord Himself (Isa 4:2; Isa 28:5). The second meaning of this word is a gazelle, which is described in the dietary laws of the OT (Dt 12:15, 22); used to describe the speed of a runner (2Sa 2:18; 1Ch 12:8[9]; Pr 6:5); and compared to a lover (SS 2:9, 17; 8:14).

6644. צִבְיָא, **Tsibyâ’,** *tsib-yaw´*; for 6645; *Tsibja,* an Israelite:—Zibia.

6645. צִבְיָה, **Tsibyâh,** *tsib-yaw´*; for 6646; *Tsibjah,* an Israelitess:—Zibiah.

6646. צְבִיָּה, **ts͏ebîyyâh,** *tseb-ee-yaw´*; feminine of 6643; a *female* gazelle:—roe.

6647. צְבַע, **ts͏ebaʻ,** *tseb-ah´*; (Chaldee); a root corresponding to that of 6648; to *dip:*—wet.

6648. צֶבַע, **tsebaʻ,** *tseh´-bah*; from an unused root meaning to *dip* (into colouring fluid); a *dye:*—divers, colours.

6649. צִבְעוֹן, **Tsibʻôwn,** *tsib-one´*; from the same as 6648; *variegated; Tsibon,* an Idumæan:—Zibeon.

6650. צְבֹעִים, **Ts͏ebôʻîym,** *tseb-o-eem´*; plural of 6641; *hyenas; Tseboïm,* a place in Palestine:—Zeboim.

6651. צָבַר, **tsâbar,** *tsaw-bar´*; a primitive root; to *aggregate:*—gather (together), heap (up), lay up.

6652. צִבֻּר, **tsibbur,** *tsib-boor´*; from 6551; a *pile:*—heap.

6653. צֶבֶת, **tsebeth,** *tseh´-beth*; from an unused root apparently meaning to *grip*; a *lock* of stalks:—handful.

6654. צַד, **tsad,** *tsad*; contracted from an unused root meaning to *sidle* off; a *side;* (figurative) an *adversary:*—(be-) side.

6655. צַד, **tsad,** *tsad*; (Chaldee); corresponding to 6654; used adverbially (with preposition) at or upon the *side* of:—against, concerning.

6656. צְדָא, **ts͏edâ’,** *tsed-aw´*; (Chaldee); from an unused root corresponding to 6658 in the sense of *intentness*; a (sinister) *design:*—true.

An Aramaic masculine noun meaning purpose. The word refers to doing something with malicious intent and is found once in the OT in the form of a question. Nebuchadnezzar approached Shadrach, Meshach, and Abednego, asking them if their intent was to defy him by not serving his gods or the golden image (Da 3:14).

6657. צְדָד, **Ts͏edâd,** *tsed-awd´*; from the same as 6654; a *siding; Tsedad,* a place near Palestine:—Zedad.

6658. צָדָה, **tsâdâh,** *tsaw-daw´*; a primitive root; to *chase;* (by implication) to *desolate:*—destroy, hunt, lie in wait.

A verb meaning to hunt, to lie in wait. The word occurs only twice in the OT. In Ex 21:13, it signified deliberation and planning before a murder; those who were lying in wait were to be executed. Those, however, who committed a murder without lying in wait could flee to a city of refuge and be protected within its borders (cf. Nu 35:9–34). In 1Sa 24:11[12], the word signified Saul's attempt to hunt down David and kill him.

6659. צָדוֹק, **Tsâdôwq,** *tsaw-doke´*; from 6663; *just; Tsadok,* the name of eight or nine Israelites:—Zadok.

6660. צְדִיָּה, **tseᵈdîyyâh,** *tsed-ee-yaw´*; from 6658; *design* [compare 6656]:—lying in wait.

6661. צִדִּים, **Tsiddîym,** *tsid-deem´*; plural of 6654; *sides; Tsiddim* (with the article), a place in Palestine:—Ziddim.

6662. צַדִּיק, **tsaddîyq,** *tsad-deek´*; from 6663; *just:*—just, lawful, righteous (man).

An adjective meaning just, righteous. The term bears primarily a moral or ethical significance. Someone or something is considered to be just or righteous because of conformity to a given standard. It could be used to describe people or actions in a legal context, indicating they were in accordance with the legal standards (2Ki 10:9); or in a religious context, that they were in accordance with God's standards (Ge 6:9). It is used of human beings, such as the Davidic king (2Sa 23:3); judges and rulers (Pr 29:2; Eze 23:45); and individuals (Ge 6:9). It is also often applied to God, who is the ultimate standard used to define justice and righteousness (Ex 9:27; Ezr 9:15; Ps 7:11[12]). As a substantive, the righteous is used to convey the ideal concept of those who follow God's standards (Mal 3:18). In this way, it is often in antithetic parallelism with the wicked, *râshâʿ* (7563), the epitome of those who reject God and His standards (Pr 29:7).

6663. צָדֵק, **tsâdaq,** *tsaw-dak´*; a primitive root; to *be* (causative, *make*) *right* (in a moral or forensic sense):—cleanse, clear self, (be, do) just (-ice, -ify, -ify self), (be, turn to) righteous (-ness).

A verb meaning to be right, to be righteous, to be just, to be innocent, to be put right, to justify, to declare right, to prove oneself innocent. The word is used twenty out of forty times in the simple stem. In this stem, it basically means to be right or just. God challenged His own people to show they were right in their claims (Isa 43:26). The verb can also connote being innocent, for God's people, through the Lord, will be found innocent (Ps 51:4[6]; Isa 45:25). Job argued his case effectively, proving himself right and vindicated (Job 11:2; 40:8). The ordinances of God were declared right by the psalmist (Ps 19:9[10]).

In the passive stem, it means to be put right. The verb refers to the altar in the second Temple being put right after its defilement (Da 8:14). In the intensive stem, the verb means to make or to declare righteous. Judah, because of her sin, made Samaria, her wicked sister, seem righteous (Eze 16:51, 52); the Lord asserted that northern Israel had been more just than Judah (Jer 3:11; cf. Job 32:2).

In the causative stem, the verb takes on the meaning of bringing about justice: Absalom began his conspiracy against David by declaring that he would administer justice for everyone (2Sa 15:4). The Lord vindicates His servant (Isa 50:8); every person of God is to declare the rights of the poor or oppressed (Ps 82:3). In Isa 53:11, it has the sense of the Servant helping other persons obtain their rights. Once in the reflexive stem, it means to justify oneself, as when Judah was at a loss as to how he and his brothers could possibly justify themselves before Pharaoh (Ge 44:16).

6664. צֶדֶק, **tsedeq,** *tseh´-dek*; from 6663; the *right* (natural, moral or legal); also (abstract) *equity* or (figurative) *prosperity:*— × even, (× that which is altogether) just (-ice), ([un-]) right (-eous) (cause, -ly, -ness).

A masculine noun meaning a right relation to an ethical or legal standard. The Hebrew word occurs most often in the Psalms and Isaiah. The word is frequently connected with the term justice (Ps 119:106; Isa 58:2). Kings, judges, and other leaders were to execute their duties based on righteous standards (Dt 1:16; Pr 8:15; Isa 32:1). God Himself acts in righteousness both in judgment and deliverance (Ps 119:75, 160; Isa 51:5; 62:1). Furthermore, God can be credited for generating human righteousness (Ps 4:1[2]; Jer 23:6). The concept of righteousness was so important in the OT period that the community that housed the Dead Sea scrolls called their most prominent leader the "Teacher of Righteousness," a person whom many regard as the founder of the sect.

6665. צִדְקָה, **tsidqâh,** *tsid-kaw´*; (Chaldee); corresponding to 6666; *beneficence:*—righteousness.

An Aramaic feminine noun meaning righteousness. The word occurs only in Da 4:27[24] where it signifies righteousness as positive action by which a person breaks off from sin.

The Hebrew word in that verse is parallel to a Hebrew word meaning to show mercy. Daniel warned Nebuchadnezzar that he would go insane because of his arrogance (see Da 4:25) but that righteousness might prolong his prosperous state. For the corresponding Hebrew noun, see *tsĕdâqâh* (6666).

6666. צְדָקָה, **tseʿdâqâh**, *tsed-aw-kaw´*; from 6663; *rightness* (abstract), subjective (*rectitude*), objective (*justice*), moral (*virtue*) or figurative (*prosperity*):—justice, moderately, right (-eous) (act, -ly, -ness).

A feminine noun meaning righteousness, blameless conduct, and integrity. The noun describes justice, right actions, and right attitudes, as expected from both God and people when they judge. God came speaking justice and righteousness as the divine Judge (Isa 63:1; Jer 9:24[23]; Mic 7:9); the Lord's holiness was made known by His righteousness in judgments (Isa 5:16; 10:22). Human judges were to imitate the divine Judge in righteousness and justice (Ge 18:19; 2Sa 8:15; Ps 72:3; Isa 56:1).

The word describes the attitude and actions God had and expected His people to maintain. He is unequivocally righteous; righteousness is entirely His prerogative. His people are to sow righteousness, and they will receive the same in return (Hos 10:12). He dealt with His people according to their righteousness and blamelessness (2Sa 22:21; Eze 3:20). Faith in God was counted as righteousness to Abraham (Ge 15:6); and obedience to the Lord's Law was further evidence of faith that God considered as righteousness (Dt 6:25). Returning a poor man's cloak was an act of obedience that was considered righteous and just before the Lord (Dt 24:13). Jacob declared that his integrity (honesty, righteousness) would speak for him in the future to Laban (Ge 30:33). The lives of people are to reflect righteousness and integrity (Pr 8:20; 15:9); even old age may be attained by living a life of righteousness (Pr 16:31).

The noun describes the justice of God or His will: persons are to act according to God's righteousness toward other persons (Dt 33:21; Isa 48:1). The word is also synonymous with truth or integrity. God declares His words are based on His own truthfulness (Isa 45:23). The word depicts God's salvation or deliverance, such as when Isaiah spoke of the Lord bringing near

His righteousness as equal to bringing near His salvation (Isa 46:13; 51:6; 56:1).

The word may indicate a just claim before the king (2Sa 19:28[29]); or the righteous claim for vindication God gives to His people (Ne 2:20; Isa 54:17). A person who was denied justice but was righteous was, in fact, innocent (Isa 5:23). In the plural, the word referred to the righteous acts that God performed for His people (1Sa 12:7); or, in the plural used in an abstract sense, it depicted people living righteously (Isa 33:15). The word was used to mean legitimate and blameless, referring to the Lord's righteous Branch (Jer 23:5; 33:15) who will act justly and righteously in the restored land.

6667. צִדְקִיָּה, **Tsidqîyyâh**, *tsid-kee-yaw´*; or צִדְקִיָהוּ, **Tsidqîy-yâhûw**, *tsid-kee-yaw´-hoo*; from 6664 and 3050; *right of Jah; Tsidkijah*, the name of six Israelites:—Zedekiah, Zidkijah.

6668. צָהַב, **tsâhab**, *tsaw-hab´*; a primitive root; to *glitter*, i.e. *be golden* in colour:— × fine.

6669. צָהֹב, **tsâhôb**, *tsaw-obe´*; from 6668; *golden* in colour:—yellow.

6670. צָהַל, **tsâhal**, *tsaw-hal´*; a primitive root; to *gleam*, i.e. (figuratively) *be cheerful*; (by transformation) to *sound* clear (of various animal or human expressions):—bellow, cry aloud (out), lift up, neigh, rejoice, make to shine, shout.

6671. צָהַר, **tsâhar**, *tsaw-har´*; a primitive root; to *glisten*; used only as denominative from 3323, to *press* out oil:—make oil.

6672. צֹהַר, **tsôhar**, *tso´-har*; from 6671; a *light* (i.e. *window*); dual *double light*, i.e. *noon*:—midday, noon (-day, -tide), window.

6673. צַו, **tsav**, *tsav*; or צָו, **tsâv**, *tsawv*; from 6680; an *injunction*:—commandment, precept.

6674. צוֹא, **tsôwʼ**, *tso*; or צֹא, **tsôʼ**, *tso*; from an unused root meaning to *issue*; *soiled* (as if *excrementitious*):—filthy.

6675. צוֹאָה, **tsôwʼâh**, *tso-aw´*; or צֹאָה, **tsôʼâh**, *tso-aw´*; feminine of 6674; *excrement*; (generic) *dirt*; (figurative) *pollution*:—dung, filth (-iness). Margin for 2716.

6676. צַוָּאר, **tsavvaʼr**, *tsav-var´*; (Chaldee); corresponding to 6677:—neck.

6677. צַוָּאר, **tsavvâ'r,** *tsav-vawr´*; or צַוָּר, **tsavvâr,** *-vawr´*; (Ne 3:5), or צַוָּרֹן, **tsavvârôn,** *-vaw-rone´*; (SS 4:9), or (feminine) צַוָּארָה, **tsavvâ'râh,** *-vaw-raw*; (Mic 2:3), intensive from 6696 in the sense of *binding*; the back of the *neck* (as that on which burdens are *bound*):—neck.

6678. צוֹבָא, **Tsôwbâ',** *tso-baw´*; or צוֹבָה, **Tsôwbâh,** *tso-baw´*; or צֹבָה, **Tsôbâh,** *tso-baw´*; from an unused root meaning to *station*; a *station*; *Zoba* or *Zobah*, a region of Syria:—Zoba, Zobah.

6679. צוּד, **tsûwd,** *tsood*; a primitive root; to *lie* alongside (i.e. in wait); (by implication) to *catch* an animal (figurative, men); (denominative from 6718) to *victual* (for a journey):—chase, hunt, sore, take (provision).

6680. צָוָה, **tsâvâh,** *tsaw-vaw´*; a primitive root; (intensive) to *constitute, enjoin:*—appoint, (for-) bid, (give a) charge, (give a, give in, send with) command (-er, -ment), send a messenger, put, (set) in order.

A verb meaning to order, to direct, to appoint, to command, to charge, to be ordered, to be commanded. The word means to give an order or to command, to direct someone; it indicates commands given to people in various situations. The Lord commanded Adam and Eve to eat from certain trees but to refrain from eating from the tree of the knowledge of good and evil (Ge 2:16; 3:17). He ordered Moses hundreds of times to do or say certain things as He established Israel's worship, feasts, festivals, and rituals (Ex 7:2; 16:34; Nu 15:23). Israel was to keep all the directives the Lord gave them (Dt 4:2; 1Ki 11:10). The Lord commanded His prophets to speak (Am 6:11; Na 1:14; Zec 1:6). People gave orders to others as well, as when Pharaoh ordered that all newborn Hebrew males should be drowned in the Nile River (Ex 1:22). Deborah ordered Barak to defeat Sisera (Jgs 4:6). Abraham ordered his family to follow the ways of the Lord (Ge 18:19). Kings commanded their people (1Ki 5:17[31]; Jer 36:26). Priests in Israel gave directives to the people about what to do under certain circumstances (Le 9:6; cf. Le 13:58). A person who was chosen for a task or position was commanded concerning his responsibilities by the priestly authorities (Nu 27:19, 23). The word may mean to give directives or to set in order as when the Lord told Hezekiah to order—that is,

to set things in order, in his household, for he was about to die (2Ki 20:1).

God commands not only people but creation: He created all things by His command (Ps 33:9; 148:5); He commanded the clouds not to send their rain on a disobedient vineyard (i.e. Israel [Ps 78:23; Isa 5:6]); He commands the entire heavenly realms (Isa 45:12). God commands historical processes; He will ultimately set up David, His ruler, as the one who commands (Isa 55:4).

6681. צָוַח, **tsâvach,** *tsaw-vakh´*; a primitive root; to *screech* (exultingly):—shout.

6682. צְוָחָה, **tsᵉvâchâh,** *tsev-aw-khaw´*; from 6681; a *screech* (of anguish):—cry (-ing).

6683. צוּלָה, **tsûwlâh,** *tsoo-law´*; from an unused root meaning to *sink*; an *abyss* (of the sea):—deep.

6684. צוּם, **tsûwm,** *tsoom*; a primitive root; to *cover* over (the mouth), i.e. to *fast:*— × at all, fast.

6685. צוֹם, **tsôwm,** *tsome*; or צֹם, **tsôm,** *tsome*; from 6684; a *fast:*—fast (-ing).

6686. צוּעָר, **Tsûw'âr,** *tsoo-awr´*; from 6819; *small*; *Tsuär*, an Israelite:—Zuar.

6687. צוּף, **tsûwph,** *tsoof*; a primitive root; to *overflow:*—(make to over-) flow, swim.

6688. צוּף, **tsûwph,** *tsoof*; from 6687; *comb* of honey (from *dripping*):—honeycomb.

6689. צוּף, **Tsûwph,** *tsoof*; or צוֹפַי, **Tsôwphay,** *tso-fah´ee*; or צִיף, **Tsîyph,** *tseef*; from 6688; *honey-comb*; *Tsuph* or *Tsophai* or *Tsiph*, the name of an Israelite and of a place in Palestine:—Zophai, Zuph.

6690. צוֹפַח, **Tsôwphach,** *tso-fakh´*; from an unused root meaning to *expand, breadth*; *Tsophach*, an Israelite:—Zophah.

6691. צוֹפַר, **Tsôwphar,** *tso-far´*; from 6852; *departing*; *Tsophar*, a friend of Job:—Zophar.

6692. צוּץ, **tsûwts,** *tsoots*; a primitive root; to *twinkle*, i.e. *glance*; (by analogy) to *blossom* (figurative) to *flourish:*—bloom, blossom, flourish, shew self.

6693. צוּק, **tsûwq,** *tsook;* a primitive root; to *compress,* i.e. (figurative) *oppress, distress:*—constrain, distress, lie sore, (op-) press (-or), straiten.

6694. צוּק, **tsûwq,** *tsook;* a primitive root [rather identical with 6693 through the idea of *narrowness* (of orifice)]; to *pour* out, i.e. (figurative) *smelt, utter:*—be molten, pour.

6695. צוֹק, **tsôwq,** *tsoke;* or (feminine) צוּקָה, **tsûw-qâh,** *tsoo-kaw´;* from 6693; a *strait,* i.e. (figurative) *distress:*—anguish, × troublous.

6696. צוּר, **tsûwr,** *tsoor;* a primitive root; to *cramp,* i.e. *confine* (in many applications, literal and figurative, formative or hostile):—adversary, assault, beset, besiege, bind (up), cast, distress, fashion, fortify, inclose, lay siege, put up in bags.

6697. צוּר, **tsûwr,** *tsoor;* or צֻר, **tsur,** *tsoor;* from 6696; (properly) a *cliff* (or sharp rock, as *compressed*); (generally) a *rock* or *boulder;* (figurative) a *refuge;* also an *edge* (as *precipitous*):—edge, × (mighty) God (one), rock, × sharp, stone, × strength, × strong. See also 1049.

6698. צוּר, **Tsûwr,** *tsoor;* the same as 6697; *rock; Tsur,* the name of a Midianite and of an Israelite:—Zur.

6699. צוּרָה, **tsûwrâh,** *tsoo-raw´;* feminine of 6697 a *rock* (Job 28:10); also a *form* (as if *pressed* out):—form, rock.

6700. צוּרִיאֵל, **Tsûwrîy'êl,** *tsoo-ree-ale´;* from 6697 and 410; *rock of God; Tsuriël,* an Israelite:—Zuriel.

6701. צוּרִישַׁדָּי, **Tsûwrîyshadday,** *tsoo-ree-shad-dah´ee;* from 6697 and 7706; *rock of* (the) *Almighty; Tsurishaddai,* an Israelite:—Zurishaddai.

6702. צוּת, **tsûwth,** *tsooth;* a primitive root; to *blaze:*—burn.

6703. צַח, **tsach,** *tsakh;* from 6705; *dazzling,* i.e. *sunny, bright,* (figurative) *evident:*—clear, dry, plainly, white.

6704. צִחֶה, **tsicheh,** *tsee-kheh´;* from an unused root meaning to *glow; parched:*—dried up.

6705. צָחַח, **tsâchach,** *tsaw-khakh´;* a primitive root; to *glare,* i.e. *be dazzling* white:—be whiter.

6706. צְחִיחַ, **tseᵉchîyach,** *tsekh-ee´-akh;* from 6705; *glaring,* i.e. *exposed* to the bright sun:—higher place, top.

6707. צְחִיחָה, **tseᵉchîychâh,** *tsekh-ee-khaw´;* feminine of 6706; a *parched* region, i.e. the *desert:*—dry land.

6708. צְחִיחִי, **tseᵉchîychîy,** *tsekh-ee-khee´;* from 6706; *bare* spot, i.e. in the *glaring* sun:—higher place.

6709. צַחֲנָה, **tsachănâh,** *tsakh-an-aw´;* from an unused root meaning to *putrefy; stench:*—ill savour.

6710. צִחְצָחָה, **tsachtsâchâh,** *tsakh-tsaw-khaw´;* from 6705; a *dry* place, i.e. *desert:*—drought.

6711. צָחַק, **tsâchaq,** *tsaw-khak´;* a primitive root; to *laugh* outright (in merriment or scorn); (by implication) to *sport:*—laugh, mock, play, make sport.

6712. צְחֹק, **tseᵉchôq,** *tsekh-oke´;* from 6711; *laughter* (in pleasure or derision):—laugh (-ed to scorn).

6713. צַחַר, **tsachar,** *tsakh´-ar;* from an unused root meaning to *dazzle; sheen,* i.e. *whiteness:*—white.

6714. צֹחַר, **Tsôchar,** *tso´-khar;* from the same as 6713; *whiteness; Tsochar,* the name of a Hittite and of an Israelite:—Zohar. Compare 3328.

6715. צָחֹר, **tsâchôr,** *tsaw-khore´;* from the same as 6713; *white:*—white.

6716. צִי, **tsîy,** *tsee;* from 6680; a *ship* (as a *fixture*):—ship.

6717. צִיבָא, **Tsîybâ',** *tsee-baw´;* from the same as 6678; *station; Tsiba,* an Israelite:—Ziba.

6718. צַיִד, **tsayid,** *tsah´-yid;* from a form of 6679 and meaning the same; the *chase;* also *game* (thus taken); (general) *lunch* (especially for a journey):— × catcheth, food, × hunter, (that which he took in) hunting, venison, victuals.

6719. צַיָּד, **tsayyâd,** *tsah´-yawd;* from the same as 6718; a *huntsman:*—hunter.

6720. צֵידָה, **tsêydâh,** *tsay-daw´;* or צֵדָה, **tsêdâh,** *tsay-daw´;* feminine of 6718; *food:*—meat, provision, venison, victuals.

6721. צִידוֹן, **Tsîydôwn,** *tsee-done´*; or צִידֹן, **Tsîy-dôn,** *tsee-done´*; from 6679 in the sense of *catching* fish; *fishery; Tsidon,* the name of a son of Canaan, and of a place in Palestine:—Sidon, Zidon.

6722. צִידֹנִי, **Tsîydônîy,** *tsee-do-nee´*; patrial from 6721; a *Tsidonian* or inhabitant of Tsidon:—Sidonian, of Sidon, Zidonian.

6723. צִיָּה, **tsîyyâh,** *tsee-yaw´*; from an unused root meaning to *parch; aridity;* (concrete) a *desert:*—barren, drought, dry (land, place), solitary place, wilderness.

6724. צָיוֹן, **tsâyôwn,** *tsaw-yone´*; from the same as 6723; a *desert:*—dry place.

6725. צִיּוּן, **tsîyyûwn,** *tsee-yoon´*; from the same as 6723 in the sense of *conspicuousness* [compare 5329]; a monumental or guiding *pillar:*—sign, title, waymark.

6726. צִיּוֹן, **Tsîyyôwn,** *tsee-yone´*; the same (regular) as 6725; *Tsijon* (as a permanent *capital*), a mountain of Jerusalem:—Zion.

6727. צִיחָא, **Tsîychâ’,** *tsee-kahw´*; or צִחָא, **Tsichâ’,** *tsee-khaw´*; as if feminine of 6704; *drought; Tsicha,* the name of two Nethinim:—Ziha.

6728. צִיִּים, **tsîyyîym,** *tsee-eem´*; from the same as 6723; a *desert-dweller,* i.e. *nomad* or wild *beast:*—wild beast of the desert, that dwell in (inhabiting) the wilderness.

6729. צִינֹק, **tsîynôq,** *tsee-noke´*; from an unused root meaning to *confine;* the *pillory:*—stocks.

6730. צִיעֹר, **Tsîy‘ôr,** *tsee-ore´*; from 6819; *small; Tsior,* a place in Palestine:—Zior.

6731. צִיץ, **tsîyts,** *tseets*; or צִץ, **tsits,** *tseets*; from 6692; (properly) *glistening,* i.e. a burnished *plate;* also a *flower* (as *bright* coloured); a *wing* (as *gleaming* in the air):—blossom, flower, plate, wing.

6732. צִיץ, **Tsîyts,** *tseets*; the same as 6731; *bloom; Tsits,* a place in Palestine:—Ziz.

6733. צִיצָה, **tsîytsâh,** *tsee-tsaw´*; feminine of 6731; a *flower:*—flower.

6734. צִיצִת, **tsîytsith,** *tsee-tseeth´*; feminine of 6731; a *floral* or *wing*-like projection, i.e. a *forelock* of hair, a *tassel:*—fringe, lock.

6735. צִיר, **tsîyr,** *tseer*; from 6696; a *hinge* (as *pressed* in turning); also a *throe* (as a physical or mental *pressure*); also a *herald* or errand-doer (as *constrained* by the principal):—ambassador, hinge, messenger, pain, pang, sorrow. Compare 6736.

6736. צִיר, **tsîyr,** *tseer*; the same as 6735; a *form* (of beauty; as if *pressed* out, i.e. *carved*); hence an (idolatrous) *image:*—beauty, idol.

A masculine noun meaning a form, an image. This noun focuses on the physical appearance of an item. That form and structure could be of the human body: the psalmist records how dead bodies decay in the grave (Ps 49:14[15]). That form and structure could also be that of an idol: Isaiah states that those who formed idols would be ashamed and confounded (Isa 45:16).

6737. צָיַר, **tsâyar,** *tsaw-yar´*; a denominative from 6735 in the sense of *ambassador;* to *make an errand,* i.e. *betake* oneself:—make as if ... had been ambassador.

6738. צֵל, **tsêl,** *tsale*; from 6751; *shade,* whether literal or figurative:—defence, shade (-ow).

A masculine noun meaning a shade, a shadow. This word is frequently used as a symbol for protection or refuge. This can be seen in the allegory of the trees (Jgs 9:15); and of the vine (Ps 80:10[11]). God protects in the shadow of His wings (Ps 17:8; 36:7[8]; 57:1[2]). The Lord is portrayed as the shade (Ps 121:5); and hid His servant in the shadow of His hand (Isa 49:2). The writer of Ecclesiastes taught that money and wisdom are both forms of protection, but wisdom could save one's life (Ecc 7:12).

6739. צְלָא, **tsᵉlâ’,** *tsel-aw´*; (Chaldee); probably corresponding to 6760 in the sense of *bowing; pray:*—pray.

An Aramaic verb meaning to pray. Daniel was praying to God when the royal administrators caught him after King Darius' edict petitions should only be made of the king (Da 6:10[11]). King Darius instructed his governors to give to the Israelites whatever they needed to rebuild the Temple so they could offer sacrifices to God and continue praying for him (Ezr 6:10).

6740. צָלָה, **tsâlâh,** *tsaw-law´*; a primitive root; to *roast:*—roast.

6741. צִלָּה, **Tsillâh,** *tsil-law´*; feminine of 6738; *Tsillah,* an antediluvian woman:—Zillah.

6742. צְלוּל, **ts⁰lûwl,** *tsel-ool´*; from 6749 in the sense of *rolling*; a (round or flattened) *cake*:—cake.

6743. צָלַח, **tsâlach,** *tsaw-lakh´*; or צָלֵחַ, **tsâlêach,** *tsaw-lay´-akh*; a primitive root; to *push* forward, in various senses (literal or figurative, transitive or intransitive):—break out, come (mightily), go over, be good, be meet, be profitable, (cause to, effect, make to, send) prosper (-ity, -ous, -ously).

6744. צְלַח, **ts⁰lach,** *tsel-akh´*; (Chaldee); corresponding to 6743; to *advance* (transitive or intransitive):—promote, prosper.

6745. צֵלָחָה, **tsêlâchâh,** *tsay-law-khaw´*; from 6743; something *protracted* or flattened out, i.e. a *platter*:—pan.

6746. צְלֹחִית, **ts⁰lôchîyth,** *tsel-o-kheeth´*; from 6743; something *prolonged* or tall, i.e. a *vial* or salt-*cellar*:—cruse.

6747. צַלַּחַת, **tsallachath,** *tsal-lakh´-ath*; from 6743; something *advanced* or deep, i.e. a *bowl*; (figurative) the *bosom*:—bosom, dish.

6748. צָלִי, **tsâlîy,** *tsaw-lee´*; passive participle of 6740; *roasted*:—roast.

6749. צָלַל, **tsâlal,** *tsaw-lal´*; a primitive root; (properly) to *tumble* down, i.e. *settle* by a waving motion:—sink. Compare 6750, 6751.

6750. צָלַל, **tsâlal,** *tsaw-lal´*; a primitive root [rather identical with 6749 through the idea of *vibration*]; to *tinkle*, i.e. *rattle* together (as the ears in *reddening* with shame, or the teeth in *chattering* with fear):—quiver, tingle.

6751. צָלַל, **tsâlal,** *tsaw-lal´*; a primitive root [rather identical with 6749 through the idea of *hovering* over (compare 6754)]; to *shade*, as twilight or an opaque object:—begin to be dark, shadowing.

A Hebrew verb meaning to be dark, to grow dim. This word is used only twice in the Hebrew OT. Nehemiah spoke of the gates of Jerusalem growing dim (in other words, evening came, and it grew dark) (Ne 13:19). Assyria was compared to a Lebanese cedar that

had such long, thick branches that it darkened the forest (Eze 31:3).

6752. צֵלֶל, **tsêlel,** *tsay´-lel*; from 6751; *shade*:—shadow.

A masculine noun meaning shadow. This word occurs only four times in the OT. In Job it described the shade of trees (Job 40:22). In the other instances, it depicted the time of day when the shadows fled (SS 2:17; 4:6) or lengthened (Jer 6:4).

6753. צְלֶלְפּוֹנִי, **Ts⁰lelpôwnîy,** *tsel-el-po-nee´*; from 6752 and the active participle of 6437; *shade-facing; Tselelponi,* an Israelitess:—Hazelelponi [*including the article*].

6754. צֶלֶם, **tselem,** *tseh´-lem*; from an unused root meaning to *shade*; a *phantom*, i.e. (figurative) *illusion, resemblance*; hence a representative *figure*, especially an *idol*:—image, vain shew.

A masculine noun meaning an image, a likeness, a statue, a model, a drawing, a shadow. The word means image or likeness; its most celebrated theological and anthropological use was to depict human beings as made in God's own image (Ge 1:26, 27; 5:3). People continue to be in His image even after the Fall, although the image is marred (Ge 9:6), and still serves as the basis of the prohibition not to kill human beings.

It is used metaphorically to depict persons as shadows, phantoms, or unknowing, senseless, fleeting beings carrying out the motions of life (Ps 39:6[7]); unless they have hope in God (see Ps 39:7[8]). In a similar vein, the wicked before the Lord are considered as mere dreams or fantasies (Ps 73:20).

The word is also used in a concrete sense to depict images cut out of or molded from various materials. The word describes the images or idols of foreign or strange gods (2Ki 11:18; Am 5:26). The people of Israel produced images used as idols from their own jewelry (Eze 7:20; 16:17). Israel was, on its entrance into Canaan, to destroy all the molten images of the heathen (Nu 33:52). In Ezekiel 23:14, this word refers to pictures of Babylonians that enticed the people of Israel into apostasy when they saw them (Eze 23:14).

6755. צֶלֶם, **tselem,** *tseh´-lem*; (Chaldee); or צְלֵם, **ts⁰lêm,** *tsel-ame´*; (Chaldee); corresponding to 6754; an idolatrous *figure*:—form, image.

An Aramaic masculine noun meaning a statue, an image. This word is related to the Hebrew word *tselem* (6754), meaning image. It was used to describe the statue in Nebuchadnezzar's dream (Da 2:31, 32, 34, 35); the image that Nebuchadnezzar built (Da 3:1–3, 5, 7); and the distortion of Nebuchadnezzar's face in anger when he heard the response of Shadrach, Meshach, and Abednego (Da 3:19).

6756. צַלְמוֹן, **Tsalmôwn,** *tsal-mone´*; from 6754; *shady; Tsalmon,* the name of a place in Palestine and of an Israelite:—Zalmon.

6757. צַלְמָוֶת, **tsalmâveth,** *tsal-maw´-veth*; from 6738 and 4194; *shade of death,* i.e. the *grave;* (figurative) *calamity:*—shadow of death.

A masculine noun meaning a death shadow, a deep shadow. This word is made up of two Hebrew words, *tsêl* (6738) or *tsêlel* (6752), meaning shadow, and *mâweth* (4194), meaning death, which gives rise to the translation of shadow of death (Ps 23:4). In some contexts, this word was used to describe death (Job 38:17); or those close to death (Ps 107:10, 14). In other contexts, it was used to describe a physical darkness (Job 24:17; Am 5:8); a spiritual darkness (Isa 9:2[1]); a darkness of understanding (Job 12:22); a gloomy countenance (Job 16:16); or a dangerous land (Jer 2:6). Occasionally, both elements of death and darkness are present in the context (Job 3:5; 10:21, 22).

6758. צַלְמֹנָה, **Tsalmônâh,** *tsal-mo-naw´*; feminine of 6757; *shadiness; Tsalmonah,* a place in the Desert:—Zalmonah.

6759. צַלְמֻנָּע, **Tsalmunnâ‘,** *tsal-moon-naw´*; from 6738 and 4513; *shade has been denied; Tsalmunna,* a Midianite:—Zalmunna.

6760. צָלַע, **tsâla‘,** *tsaw-lah´*; a primitive root; probably to *curve;* used only as denominative from 6763, to *limp* (as if *one-sided*):—halt.

6761. צֶלַע, **tsela‘,** *tseh´-lah*; from 6760; a *limping* or *fall* (figurative):—adversity, halt (-ing).

6762. צֶלַע, **Tsêla‘,** *tsay´-lah*; the same as 6761; *Tsela,* a place in Palestine:—Zelah.

6763. צֵלָע, **tsêlâ‘,** *tsay-law´*; or (feminine) צַלְעָה **tsal‘âh,** *tsal-aw´*; from 6760; a *rib* (as *curved*), literal (of the body), or figurative (of a door, i.e. *leaf*); hence a *side,* literal (of a person) or figu-

rative (of an object or the sky, i.e. *quarter*); architecturally a (especially floor or ceiling) *timber* or *plank* (single or collective, i.e. a *flooring*):—beam, board, chamber, corner, leaf, plank, rib, side (chamber).

6764. צָלָף, **Tsâlâph,** *tsaw-lawf´*; from an unused root of unknown meaning; *Tsalaph,* an Israelite:—Zalaph.

6765. צְלָפְחָד, **Tselophchâd,** *tsel-of-khawd´*; from the same as 6764 and 259; *Tselopchad,* an Israelite:—Zelophehad.

6766. צֶלְצַח, **Tseltsach,** *tsel-tsakh´*; from 6738 and 6703; *clear shade; Tseltsach,* a place in Palestine:—Zelzah.

6767. צְלָצַל, **tselâtsal,** *tsel-aw-tsal´*; from 6750 reduplication; a *clatter,* i.e. (abstract) *whirring* (of wings); (concrete) a *cricket;* also a *harpoon* (as *rattling*), a *cymbal* (as *clanging*):—cymbal, locust, shadowing, spear.

6768. צֶלֶק, **Tseleq,** *tseh´-lek*; from an unused root meaning to *split; fissure; Tselek,* an Israelite:—Zelek.

6769. צִלְּתַי, **Tsilletthay,** *tsil-leth-ah´ee*; from the feminine of 6738; *shady; Tsillethai,* the name of two Israelites:—Zilthai.

6770. צָמֵא, **tsâmê’,** *tsaw-may´*; a primitive root; to *thirst* (literal or figurative):—(be a-, suffer) thirst (-y).

6771. צָמֵא, **tsâmê’,** *tsaw-may´*; from 6770; *thirsty* (literal or figurative):—(that) thirst (-eth, -y).

6772. צָמָא, **tsâmâ’,** *tsaw-maw´*; from 6770; *thirst* (literal or figurative):—thirst (-y).

6773. צִמְאָה, **tsim’âh,** *tsim-aw´*; feminine of 6772; *thirst;* (figurative) *libidinousness:*—thirst.

6774. צִמָּאוֹן, **tsimmâ’ôwn,** *tsim-maw-one´*; from 6771; a *thirsty place,* i.e. *desert:*—drought, dry ground, thirsty land.

6775. צָמַד, **tsâmad,** *tsaw-mad´*; a primitive root; to *link,* i.e. *gird;* (figurative) to *serve,* (mentally) *contrive:*—fasten, frame, join (self).

6776. צֶמֶד, **tsemed,** *tseh´-med*; a *yoke* or *team* (i.e. pair); hence an *acre* (i.e. day's task for a yoke of cattle to plough):—acre, couple, × together, two [asses], yoke (of oxen).

6777. צַמָּה, **tsammâh,** *tsam-maw´*; from an unused root meaning to *fasten* on; a *veil:*— locks.

6778. צִמּוּקִים, **tsimmûwqîym,** *tsim-moo-keem´*; from 6784; a cake of *dried* grapes:—bunch (cluster) of raisins.

6779. צָמַח, **tsâmach,** *tsaw-makh´*; a primitive root; to *sprout* (transitive or intransitive, literal or figurative):—bear, bring forth, (cause to, make to) bud (forth), (cause to, make to) grow (again, up), (cause to) spring (forth, up).

6780. צֶמַח, **tsemach,** *tseh´-makh*; from 6779; a *sprout* (usually concrete), literal or figurative:— branch, bud, that which (where) grew (upon), spring (-ing).

6781. צָמִיד, **tsâmîyd,** *tsaw-meed´*; or צָמִד, **tsâmid,** *tsaw-meed´*; from 6775; a *bracelet* or *arm-clasp*; (generally) a *lid:*—bracelet, covering.

6782. צַמִּים, **tsammîym,** *tsam-meem´*; from the same as 6777; a *noose* (as *fastening*); (figurative) *destruction:*—robber.

6783. צְמִיתֻת, **ts͏ᵉmîythuth,** *tsem-ee-thooth´*; or צְמִתֻת, **ts͏ᵉmithuth,** *tsem-ee-thooth´*; from 6789; *excision,* i.e. *destruction;* used only (adverb) with prepositional prefix *to extinction,* i.e. *perpetually:*—ever.

A feminine noun meaning completion, finality. This word is used only twice in the OT and comes from the verb *tsâmath* (6789), meaning to put to an end. It was used in the Levitical Law to describe the duration of property ownership (Le 25:23, 30).

6784. צָמַק, **tsâmaq,** *tsaw-mak´*; a primitive root; to *dry* up:—dry.

6785. צֶמֶר, **tsemer,** *tseh´-mer*; from an unused root probably meaning to *be shaggy; wool:*— wool (-len).

6786. צְמָרִי, **Ts͏ᵉmârîy,** *tsem-aw-ree´*; patrial from an unused name of a place in Palestine; a *Tsemarite* or branch of the Canaanites:— Zemarite.

6787. צְמָרַיִם, **Ts͏ᵉmârayim,** *tsem-aw-rah´-yim*; dual of 6785; *double fleece; Tsemarajim,* a place in Palestine:—Zemaraim.

6788. צַמֶּרֶת, **tsammereth,** *tsam-meh´-reth*; from the same as 6785; *fleeciness,* i.e. *foliage:*—highest branch, top.

6789. צָמַת, **tsâmath,** *tsaw-math´*; a primitive root; to *extirpate* (literal or figurative):—consume, cut off, destroy, vanish.

A verb meaning to put to an end. This word appears most often in the imprecatory psalms—that is, the psalms that call down curses on one's enemies. The word occurs within the context of putting an end to the wicked (Ps 73:27; 101:8); or to one's enemies (2Sa 22:41; Ps 54:5[7]; 143:12). In both of these cases, this word alludes to the physical death of these people. But in other instances, this word describes the process of rendering powerless by putting persons in prison (La 3:53); the drying up of riverbeds (Job 6:17); or the wearying of the psalmist (Ps 119:139).

6790. צִן, **Tsin,** *tseen*; from an unused root meaning to *prick*; a *crag; Tsin,* a part of the Desert:—Zin.

6791. צֵן, **tsên,** *tsane*; from an unused root meaning to *be prickly*; a *thorn*; hence a *cactus-hedge:*—thorn.

6792. צֹנֵא, **tsônê’,** *tso-nay´*; or צֹנֶה, **tsôneh,** *tso-neh´*; for 6629; a *flock:*—sheep.

6793. צִנָּה, **tsinnâh,** *tsin-naw´*; feminine of 6791; a *hook* (as *pointed*); also a (large) *shield* (as if guarding by *prickliness*); also *cold* (as *piercing*):—buckler, cold, hook, shield, target.

6794. צִנּוֹר, **tsinnôwr,** *tsin-nor´*; from an unused root perhaps meaning to *be hollow;* a *culvert:*— gutter, water-spout.

6795. צָנַח, **tsânach,** *tsaw-nakh´*; a primitive root; to *alight;* (transitive) to *cause to descend,* i.e. *drive* down:—fasten, light [from off].

6796. צָנִין, **tsânîyn,** *tsaw-neen´*; or צָנִן, **tsânin,** *tsaw-neen*; from the same as 6791; a *thorn:*— thorn.

6797. צָנִיף, **tsânîyph,** *tsaw-neef´*; or צָנוֹף, **tsânôwph,** *tsaw-nofe´*; or (feminine) צָנִיפָה, **tsânîyphâh,** *tsaw-nee-faw´*; from 6801; a *head-dress* (i.e. piece of cloth *wrapped* around):— diadem, hood, mitre.

6798. צָנַם, **tsânam,** *tsaw-nam´*; a primitive root; to *blast* or *shrink*:—withered.

6799. צְנָן, **Tsᵉnân,** *tsen-awn´*; probably for 6630; *Tsenan,* a place near Palestine:—Zenan.

6800. צָנַע, **tsâna**ʻ, *tsaw-nah´*; a primitive root; to *humiliate*:—humbly, lowly.

6801. צָנַף, **tsânaph,** *tsaw-naf´*; a primitive root; to *wrap,* i.e. *roll* or *dress*:—be attired, × surely, violently turn.

6802. צְנֵפָה, **tsᵉnêphâh,** *tsen-ay-faw´*; from 6801; a *ball*:— × toss.

6803. צִנְצֶנֶת, **tsintseneth,** *tsin-tseh´-neth*; from the same as 6791; a *vase* (probably a vial *tapering* at the top):—pot.

6804. צַנְתָּרוֹת, **tsantᵉrôwth,** *tsan-teh-rowth´*; probably from the same as 6794; a *tube*:—pipe.

6805. צָעַד, **tsâʻad,** *tsaw-ad´*; a primitive root; to *pace,* i.e. *step* regularly; (upward) to *mount*; (along) to *march*; (down and causative) to *hurl*:—bring, go, march (through), run over.

6806. צַעַד, **tsaʻad,** *tsah´-ad*; from 6804; a *pace* or regular *step*:—pace, step.

6807. צְעָדָה, **tsᵉʻâdâh,** *tseh-aw-daw´*; feminine of 6806; a *march*; (concrete) an (ornamental) *ankle-chain*:—going, ornament of the legs.

6808. צָעָה, **tsâʻâh,** *tsaw-aw´*; a primitive root; to *tip* over (for the purpose of *spilling* or *pouring* out), i.e. (figurative) *depopulate*; (by implication) to *imprison* or *conquer*; (reflexive) to *lie down* (for coition):—captive exile, travelling, (cause to) wander (-er).

6809. צָעִיף, **tsâʻîyph,** *tsaw-eef´*; from an unused root meaning to *wrap* over; a *veil*:—vail.

6810. צָעִיר, **tsâʻîyr,** *tsaw-eer´*; or צָעוֹר, **tsâʻôwr,** *tsaw-ore´*; from 6819; *little*; (in number) *few*; (in age) *young,* (in value) *ignoble*:—least, little (one), small (one), + young (-er, -est).

6811. צָעִיר, **Tsâʻîyr,** *tsaw-eer´*; the same as 6810; *Tsaïr,* a place in Idumæa:—Zair.

6812. צְעִירָה, **tsᵉʻîyrâh,** *tseh-ee-raw´*; feminine of 6810; *smallness* (of age), i.e. *juvenility*:—youth.

6813. צָעַן, **tsâʻan,** *tsaw-an´*; a primitive root; to *load* up (beasts), i.e. to *migrate*:—be taken down.

6814. צֹעַן, **Tsôʻan,** *tso´-an*; of Egyptian derivation; *Tsoän,* a place in Egypt:—Zoan.

6815. צַעֲנַנִּים, **Tsaʻănannîym,** *tsah-an-an-neem´*; or (dual) צַעֲנַיִם, **Tsaʻănayim,** *tsah-an-ah´-yim*; plural from 6813; *removals*; *Tsaanannim* or *Tsaanajim,* a place in Palestine:—Zaannannim, Zaanaim.

6816. צַעֲצֻעִים, **tsaʻătsuʻîym,** *tsah-ah-tsoo´-eem*; from an unused root meaning to *bestrew* with carvings; *sculpture*:—image [work].

6817. צָעַק, **tsâʻaq,** *tsaw-ak´*; a primitive root; to *shriek*; (by implication) to *proclaim* (an assembly):— × at all, call together, cry (out), gather (selves) (together).

6818. צְעָקָה, **tsᵉʻâqâh,** *tseh-awk-aw´*; from 6817; a *shriek*:—cry (-ing).

6819. צָעַר, **tsâʻar,** *tsaw-ar´*; a primitive root; to *be small,* i.e. (figurative) *ignoble*:—be brought low, little one, be small.

6820. צֹעַר, **Tsôʻar,** *tso´-ar*; from 6819; *little*; *Tsoär,* a place East of the Jordan:—Zoar.

6821. צָפַד, **tsâphad,** *tsaw-fad´*; a primitive root; to *adhere*:—cleave.

6822. צָפָה, **tsâphâh,** *tsaw-faw´*; a primitive root; (properly) to *lean* forward, i.e. to *peer* into the distance; (by implication) to *observe, await*:—behold, espy, look up (well), wait for, (keep the) watch (-man).

6823. צָפָה, **tsâphâh,** *tsaw-faw´*; a primitive root [probably rather identical with 6822 through the idea of *expansion* in outlook transferred to act]; to *sheet* over (especially with metal):—cover, overlay.

6824. צָפָה, **tsâphâh,** *tsaw-faw´*; from 6823; an *inundation* (as *covering*):— × swimmest (KJV).

6825. צְפוֹ, **Tsᵉphôw,** *tsef-o´*; or צְפִי, **Tsᵉphîy,** *tsef-ee´*; from 6822; *observant*; *Tsepho* or *Tsephi,* an Idumæan:—Zephi, Zepho.

6826. צִפּוּי, **tsippûwy,** *tsip-poo´ee*; from 6823; *encasement* (with metal):—covering, overlaying.

6827. צְפוֹן, **Tsᵉphôwn,** *tsef-one´*; probably for 6837; *Tsephon,* an Israelite:—Zephon.

6828. צָפוֹן, **tsâphôwn,** *tsaw-fone'*; or צָפֹן, **tsâphôn,** *tsaw-fone'*; from 6845; (properly) *hidden,* i.e. *dark*; used only of the *north* as a quarter (*gloomy* and *unknown*):—north (-ern, side, -ward, wind).

6829. צָפוֹן, **Tsâphôwn,** *tsaw-fone'*; the same as 6828; *boreal*; *Tsaphon,* a place in Palestine:—Zaphon.

6830. צְפוֹנִי, **tsᵉphôwnîy,** *tsef-o-nee'*; from 6828; *northern*:—northern.

6831. צְפוֹנִי, **Tsᵉphôwnîy,** *tsef-o-nee'*; patronymic from 6827; a *Tsephonite,* or (collective) descendants of Tsephon:—Zephonites.

6832. צְפִיעַ, **tsâphîyaʻ,** *tsaw-fee'-ah*; from the same as 6848; *excrement* (as *protruded*):—dung.

6833. צִפּוֹר, **tsippôwr,** *tsip-pore'*; or צִפֹּר, **tsippôr,** *tsip-pore'*; from 6852; a little *bird* (as *hopping*):—bird, fowl, sparrow.

6834. צִפּוֹר, **Tsippôwr,** *tsip-pore'*; the same as 6833; *Tsippor,* a Moabite:—Zippor.

6835. צַפַּחַת, **tsappachath,** *tsap-pakh'-ath*; from an unused root meaning to *expand*; a *saucer* (as *flat*):—cruse.

6836. צְפִיָּה, **tsᵉphîyyâh,** *tsef-ee-yaw'*; from 6822; *watchfulness*:—watching.

6837. צִפְיוֹן, **Tsiphyôwn,** *tsif-yone'*; from 6822; *watch-*tower; *Tsiphjon,* an Israelite:—Ziphion. Compare 6827.

6838. צַפִּיחִת, **tsappîychith,** *tsap-pee-kheeth'*; from the same as 6835; a flat thin *cake*:—wafer.

6839. צֹפִים, **Tsôphîym,** *tso-feem'*; plural of active participle of 6822; *watchers*; *Tsophim,* a place East of the Jordan:—Zophim.

6840. צָפִין, **tsâphîyn,** *tsaw-feen'*; from 6845; a *treasure* (as *hidden*):—hid.

6841. צְפִיר, **tsᵉphîyr,** *tsef-eer'*; (Chaldee); corresponding to 6842; a he-*goat*:—he [goat].

6842. צָפִיר, **tsâphîyr,** *tsaw-feer'*; from 6852; a male *goat* (as *prancing*):—(he) goat.

6843. צְפִירָה, **tsᵉphîyrâh,** *tsef-ee-raw'*; feminine formed like 6842; a *crown* (as *encircling* the head); also a *turn* of affairs (i.e. *mishap*):—diadem, morning.

6844. צָפִית, **tsâphîyth,** *tsaw-feeth'*; from 6822; a *sentry*:—watchtower.

6845. צָפַן, **tsâphan,** *tsaw-fan'*; a primitive root; to *hide* (by *covering* over); (by implication) to *hoard* or *reserve*; (figurative) to *deny*; specifically (favourably) to *protect,* (unfavourably) to *lurk*:—esteem, hide (-den one, self), lay up, lurk (be set) privily, (keep) secret (-ly, place).

6846. צְפַנְיָה, **Tsᵉphanyâh,** *tsef-an-yaw'*; or צְפַנְיָהוּ, **Tsᵉphan-yâhûw,** *tsef-an-yaw'-hoo*; from 6845 and 3050; *Jah has secreted*; *Tsephanjah,* the name of four Israelites:—Zephaniah.

6847. צָפְנַת פַּעְנֵחַ, **Tsâphnath Paʻnêach,** *tsof-nath' pah-nay'-akh*; of Egyptian derivation; *Tsophnath-Paneäh,* Joseph's Egyptian name:—Zaphnath-paaneah.

6848. צֶפַע, **tsephaʻ,** *tseh'-fah*; or צִפְעֹנִי, **tsiphʻônîy,** *tsif-o-nee'*; from an unused root meaning to *extrude*; a *viper* (as *thrusting* out the tongue, i.e. *hissing*):—adder, cockatrice.

6849. צְפָעָה, **tsᵉphiʻâh,** *tsef-ee-aw'*; feminine from the same as 6848; an *outcast* thing:—issue.

6850. צָפַף, **tsâphaph,** *tsaw-faf'*; a primitive root; to *coo* or *chirp* (as a bird):—chatter, peep, whisper.

6851. צַפְצָפָה, **tsaphtsâphâh,** *tsaf-tsaw-faw'*; from 6687; a *willow* (as growing in *overflowed* places):—willow tree.

6852. צָפַר, **tsâphar,** *tsaw-far'*; a primitive root; to *skip* about, i.e. *return*:—depart early.

6853. צְפַר, **tsᵉphar,** *tsip-par'*; (Chaldee); corresponding to 6833; a *bird*:—bird.

6854. צְפַרְדֵּעַ, **tsᵉphardêaʻ,** *tsef-ar-day'-ah*; from 6852 and a word elsewhere unused meaning a *swamp*; a *marsh-leaper,* i.e. *frog*:—frog.

6855. צִפֹּרָה, **Tsippôrâh,** *tsip-po-raw'*; feminine of 6833; *bird*; *Tsipporah,* Moses' wife:—Zipporah.

6856. צִפֹּרֶן, **tsippôren,** *tsip-po'-ren*; from 6852 (in the denominative sense [from 6833] of *scratching*); (properly) a *claw,* i.e. (human) *nail*; also the *point* of a style (or pen, tipped with adamant):—nail, point.

6857. צְפַת, **Tsᵉphath,** *tsef-ath'*; from 6822; *watch-*tower; *Tsephath,* a place in Palestine:—Zephath.

6858. צֶפֶת, **tsepheth,** *tseh´-feth*; from an unused root meaning to *encircle*; a *capital* of a column:—chapiter.

6859. צְפָתָה, **Ts⁰phâthâh,** *tsef-aw´-thaw*; the same as 6857; *Tsephathah*, a place in Palestine:—Zephathah.

6860. צִקְלַג, **Tsiqlag,** *tsik-lag´*; or צִיקְלַג, **Tsîyq⁰-lag,** *tsee-kel-ag´*; (1Ch 12:1, 20), of uncertain derivation; *Tsiklag* or *Tsikelag*, a place in Palestine:—Ziklag.

6861. צִקְלוֹן, **tsiqqâlôwn,** *tsik-ka-lone´*; from an unused root meaning to *wind*; a *sack* (as *tied* at the mouth):—husk.

6862. צַר, **tsar,** *tsar*; or צָר, **tsâr,** *tsawr*; from 6887; *narrow*; (as a noun) a *tight* place (usually figurative, i.e. *trouble*); also a *pebble* (as in 6864); (transitive) an *opponent* (as *crowding*):—adversary, afflicted (-tion), anguish, close, distress, enemy, flint, foe, narrow, small, sorrow, strait, tribulation, trouble.

6863. צֵר, **Tsêr,** *tsare*; from 6887; *rock*; *Tser*, a place in Palestine:—Zer.

6864. צֹר, **tsôr,** *tsore*; from 6696; a *stone* (as if *pressed* hard or to a point); (by implication of use) a *knife*:—flint, sharp stone.

6865. צֹר, **Tsôr,** *tsore*; or צוֹר, **Tsôwr,** *tsore*; the same as 6864; a *rock*; *Tsor*, a place in Palestine:—Tyre, Tyrus.

6866. צָרַב, **tsârab,** *tsaw-rab´*; a primitive root; to *burn*:—burn.

6867. צָרֶבֶת, **tsârebeth,** *tsaw-reh´-beth*; from 6686; *conflagration* (of fire or disease):—burning, inflammation.

6868. צְרֵדָה, **Ts⁰rêdâh,** *tser-ay-daw´*; or צְרֵדָתָה, **Ts⁰rêdâthâh,** *tser-ay-daw´-thaw*; apparently from an unused root meaning to *pierce*; *puncture*; *Tseredah*, a place in Palestine:—Zereda, Zeredathah.

6869. צָרָה, **tsârâh,** *tsaw-raw´*; feminine of 6862; *tightness* (i.e. [figurative] *trouble*); (transitive) a female *rival*:—adversary, adversity, affliction, anguish, distress, tribulation, trouble.

6870. צְרוּיָה, **Ts⁰rûwyâh,** *tser-oo-yaw´*; feminine participle passive from the same as 6875; *wounded*; *Tserujah*, an Israelitess:—Zeruiah.

6871. צְרוּעָה, **Ts⁰rûw´âh,** *tser-oo-aw´*; feminine passive participle of 6879; *leprous*; *Tseruäh*, an Israelitess:—Zeruah.

6872. צְרוֹר, **ts⁰rôwr,** *tser-ore´*; or (shorter) צְרֹר, **ts⁰rôr,** *tser-ore´*; from 6887; a *parcel* (as *packed* up); also a *kernel* or *particle* (as if a *package*):—bag, × bendeth, bundle, least grain, small stone.

6873. צָרַח, **tsârach,** *tsaw-rakh´*; a primitive root; to *be clear* (in tone, i.e. *shrill*), i.e. to *whoop*:—cry, roar.

6874. צְרִי, **Ts⁰rîy,** *tser-ee´*; the same as 6875; *Tseri*, an Israelite:—Zeri. Compare 3340.

6875. צְרִי, **ts⁰rîy,** *tser-ee´*; or צֳרִי, **tsŏrîy,** *tsor-ee´*; from an unused root meaning to *crack* [as by *pressure*], hence to *leak; distillation,* i.e. *balsam*:—balm.

6876. צֹרִי, **Tsôrîy,** *tso-ree´*; patrial from 6865; a *Tsorite* or inhabitant of Tsor (i.e. *Syrian*):—(man) of Tyre.

6877. צְרִיחַ, **ts⁰rîyach,** *tser-ee´-akh*; from 6873 in the sense of *clearness* of vision; a *citadel*:—high place, hold.

6878. צֹרֶךְ, **tsôrek,** *tso´-rek*; from an unused root meaning to *need; need*:—need.

6879. צָרַע, **tsâra´,** *tsaw-rah´*; a primitive root; to *scourge*, i.e. (intransitive and figurative) to *be stricken with leprosy*:—leper, leprous.

6880. צִרְעָה, **tsir´âh,** *tsir-aw´*; from 6879; a *wasp* (as *stinging*):—hornet.

6881. צָרְעָה, **Tsor´âh,** *tsor-aw´*; apparently another form for 6880; *Tsorah*, a place in Palestine:—Zareah, Zorah, Zoreah.

6882. צָרְעִי, **Tsor´îy,** *tsor-ee´*; or צָרְעָתִי, **Tsor´âthîy,** *tsor-aw-thee´*; patrial from 6881; a *Tsorite* or *Tsorathite*, i.e. inhabitant of Tsorah:—Zorites, Zareathites, Zorathites.

6883. צָרַעַת, **tsâra´ath,** *tsaw-rah´-ath*; from 6879; *leprosy*:—leprosy.

6884. צָרַף, **tsâraph,** *tsaw-raf´*; a primitive root; to *fuse* (metal), i.e. *refine* (literal or figurative):—cast, (re-) fine (-er), founder, goldsmith, melt, pure, purge away, try.

A verb meaning to refine, to test. This word describes the purifying process of a refiner, who heats metal, takes away the dross, and is left with a pure substance (Pr 25:4). As a participle, this word refers to a tradesman (i.e. a goldsmith or silversmith) who does the refining work (Jgs 17:4; Ne 3:8; Isa 41:7). This word is also used to speak of the Word of God that is described as pure and refined (2Sa 22:31; Ps 12:6[7]; Pr 30:5). When applied to people, this word refers to the purifying effects of external trials (Ps 66:10; 105:19; Isa 48:10) that God often uses to purify His people from sin (Isa 1:25; Zec 13:9); or to remove the wicked from His people (Jer 6:29; Mal 3:2, 3).

6885. צֹרְפִי, **Tsôrᵉphîy,** *tso-ref-ee´*; from 6884; *refiner; Tsorephi* (with the article), an Israelite:—goldsmith's.

6886. צָרְפַת, **Tsârᵉphath,** *tsaw-ref-ath´*; from 6884; *refinement; Tsarephath,* a place in Palestine:—Zarephath.

6887. צָרַר, **tsârar,** *tsaw-rar´*; a primitive root; to *cramp,* literal or figurative, transitive or intransitive (as follows):—adversary, (be in) afflict (-ion), besiege, bind (up), (be in, bring) distress, enemy, narrower, oppress, pangs, shut up, be in a strait (trouble), vex.

6888. צְרֵרָה, **Tsᵉrêrâh,** *tser-ay-raw´*; apparently by erroneous transcription for 6868; *Tsererah* for *Tseredah:*—Zererath.

6889. צֶרֶת, **Tsereth,** *tseh´-reth*; perhaps from 6671; *splendor; Tsereth,* an Israelite:—Zereth.

6890. צֶרֶת הַשַּׁחַר, **Tsereth hash-Shachar,** *tseh´-reth hash-shakh´-ar*; from the same as 6889 and 7837 with the article interposed; *splendor of the dawn; Tsereth-hash-Shachar,* a place in Palestine:—Zareth-shahar.

6891. צָרְתָן, **Tsârᵉthân,** *tsaw-reth-awn´*; perhaps for 6868; *Tsarethan,* a place in Palestine:—Zarthan.

ק (Qoph)

6892. קֵא, qê’, *kay*; or קִיא, qîy’, *kee*; from 6958; *vomit*:—vomit.

6893. קָאַת, qâ’ath, *kaw-ath´*; from 6958; probably the *pelican* (from *vomiting*):—cormorant.

6894. קַב, qab, *kab*; from 6895; a *hollow*, i.e. vessel used as a (dry) *measure*:—cab.

6895. קָבַב, qâbab, *kaw-bab´*; a primitive root; to *scoop* out, i.e. (figurative) to *malign* or *execrate* (i.e. *stab* with words):— × at all, curse.

A verb meaning to curse. The general idea of this word is a pronouncement of bad fortune or ill favour bestowed on another. This word is used often in the story of Balaam and Balak, where Balak repeatedly requested that Balaam pronounce a curse on Israel (Nu 22:11; 23:13, 27). Rather than a curse, Balaam pronounced a blessing on them (Nu 23:8; 24:10). In other instances of this word, it describes cursing the Lord (Le 24:11); cursing the day of one's birth (Job 3:8); or cursing the home of the foolish (Job 5:3). It is used twice in the Proverbs in a general way (Pr 11:26; 24:24) as an opposite to the word *bĕrâkâh* (1293), meaning blessing, and similar to the much more frequent word *qâlal* (7043), meaning to curse.

6896. קֵבָה, qêbâh, *kay-baw´*; from 6895; the *paunch* (as a *cavity*) or first stomach of ruminants:—maw.

6897. קֹבָה, qôbâh, *ko´-baw*; from 6895; the *abdomen* (as a cavity):—belly.

6898. קֻבָּה, qubbâh, *koob-baw´*; from 6895; a *pavilion* (as a domed *cavity*):—tent.

A feminine noun meaning a large tent, a domed cavity, a pavilion. This word is not found often in the OT, but where it does appear, it refers to some sort of habitation. Phinehas chased a man and woman who were idolaters into one of these large tents and thrust them through with a javelin, thus ending a plague on Israel (Nu 25:8).

6899. קִבּוּץ, qibbûwts, *kib-boots´*; from 6908; a *throng*:—company.

6900. קְבוּרָה, qᵉbûwrâh, *keb-oo-raw´*; or קְבֻרָה, qeburâh, *keb-oo-raw´*; feminine passive participle of 6912; *sepulture*; (concrete) a *sepulchre*:—burial, burying place, grave, sepulchre.

A feminine noun meaning a grave, a burial place. It is the passive participle of *qâbar* (6912), meaning to bury. The word can signify various types of graves: the dignified grave of a king (2Ki 21:26; 23:30); the unknown burial place of Moses (Dt 34:6); and the burial place of a donkey where Jehoiakim would be buried (Jer 22:19). Burial was important to the Hebrews of the OT; the lack of a grave was considered a tragedy, the sign of an unwanted life that was best forgotten (Ecc 6:3; Isa 14:20). The meaning is similar to the word *qeber* (6913).

6901. קָבַל, qâbal, *kaw-bal´*; a primitive root; to *admit*, i.e. *take* (literal or figurative):—choose, (take) hold, receive, (under-) take.

6902. קְבַל, qᵉbal, *keb-al´*; (Chaldee); corresponding to 6901; to *acquire*:—receive, take.

6903. קְבֵל, qᵉbêl, *keb-ale´*; (Chaldee); or קֳבֵל, qŏbêl, *kob-ale´*; (Chaldee); corresponding to 6905; (adverb) *in front of*; usually (with other particles) *on account of*, so as, since, hence:— + according to, + as, + because, before, + for this cause, + forasmuch as, + by this means, over against, by reason of, + that, + therefore, + though, + wherefore.

6904. קֹבֵל, qôbel, *ko´-bel*; from 6901 in the sense of *confronting* (as standing *opposite* in order to receive); a *battering* ram:—war.

6905. קָבָל, qâbâl, *kaw-bawl´*; from 6901 in the sense of *opposite* [see 6904]; the *presence*, i.e. (adverb) *in front of*:—before.

6906. קָבַע, qâbaʻ, *kaw-bah´*; a primitive root; to *cover*, i.e. (figurative) *defraud*:—rob, spoil.

402

6907. קֻבַּעַת, **qubba'ath,** *koob-bah´-ath*; from 6906; a *goblet* (as deep like a *cover*):—dregs.

6908. קָבַץ, **qâbats,** *kaw-bats´*; a primitive root; to *grasp*, i.e. *collect*:—assemble (selves), gather (bring) (together, selves together, up), heap, resort, × surely, take up.

A verb meaning to gather, to collect, to assemble. The passive form is used to signify the gathering or assembling of people, especially for battle (Jos 9:2; Ne 4:20[14]; Jer 49:14); and for religious and national purposes (1Ch 11:1; Ezr 10:1, 7). The word in an active form often signifies the gathering of materials: food into storehouses (Ge 41:35); sheaves (Mic 4:12); money and wealth (2Ch 24:5; Pr 28:8); lambs by a shepherd (Isa 13:14; 40:11; Jer 23:3). The word also refers to God's gathering of nations for judgment in the end times (Isa 43:9; 66:18; Joel 3:2[4:2]); and especially to the gathering of His scattered people, Israel (Ps 106:47; Jer 29:14; 31:10; Hos 1:11[2:2]).

6909. קַבְצְאֵל, **Qabts°'êl,** *keb-tseh-ale´*; from 6908 and 410; *God has gathered; Kabtseël,* a place in Palestine:—Kabzeel. Compare 3343.

6910. קְבֻצָה, **q°butsâh,** *keb-oo-tsaw´*; feminine passive participle of 6908; a *hoard*:— × gather.

A feminine noun meaning gathering. This word is the feminine passive participle of *qâbats* (6908), meaning to gather. It occurs only in Eze 22:20 where it signifies the gathering of metals into a furnace, which is a picture of God gathering Israel to pour out His burning anger on them.

6911. קִבְצַיִם, **Qibtsayim,** *kib-tsah´-yim*; dual from 6908; a *double heap; Kibtsajim,* a place in Palestine:—Kibzaim.

6912. קָבַר, **qâbar,** *kaw-bar´*; a primitive root; to *inter*:— × in any wise, bury (-ier).

A verb meaning to bury, to entomb, to be buried. The word often refers to the placing of a body in a cave or a stone sepulchre rather than directly into the ground (Ge 23:4; 50:13; 2Sa 21:14; 1Ki 13:31; cf. Isa 22:16). Abraham stated that one goal of burial was to get the dead out of sight (Ge 23:4). Dead bodies were seen as polluting the land until they were buried (Eze 39:11–14). It was also a reproach to the dead to be buried in a foreign place or not to be buried at all (Ge 47:29, 30; 50:5; cf. 50:24–26; Jer 20:6).

Bones were sometimes specifically mentioned as the object of burial (Jos 24:32; 1Sa 31:13; 1Ki 13:31). Buried persons were said to sleep or be buried with their fathers, and they were often placed in the same tomb (Ge 47:30; 50:13; Jgs 16:31; 2Sa 2:32; 17:23).

6913. קֶבֶר, **qeber,** *keh´-ber*; or (feminine) קְבָרָה, **qibrâh,** *kib-raw´*; from 6912; a *sepulchre*:—burying place, grave, sepulchre.

A masculine noun meaning a grave, a sepulchre. The grave was a place of grief (2Sa 3:32; Ps 88:11[12]); the end of life in contrast to the womb (Job 10:19; Jer 20:17). The dead were laid to rest, often with previously deceased relatives (2Sa 19:37[38]). In the OT, graves were associated with uncleanness: one who touched a grave (or a bone, cf. 2Ch 34:5) had to be ceremonially cleansed (Nu 19:16–19). Josiah sprinkled the dust of crushed idolatrous paraphernalia on graves of idol worshippers to defile the idols (2Ki 23:6; 2Ch 34:4). In a figurative sense, Isaiah prophesied against his self-righteous countrymen as living among graves and eating the flesh of swine (Isa 65:4; cf. Mt 23:27, 28). Ezekiel prophesied that God would revive the Israelites from their graves, that is, from their exile and defilement among idolatrous nations (Eze 37:12, 13).

6914. קִבְרוֹת הַתַּאֲוָה, **Qibrôwth hat-Ta'ăvâh,** *kib-rōth´ hat-tah-av-aw´*; from the feminine plural of 6913 and 8378 with the article interposed; *graves of the longing; Kibroth-hat-Taavh,* a place in the Desert:—Kibroth-hattaavah.

6915. קָדַד, **qâdad,** *kaw-dad´*; a primitive root; to *shrivel* up, i.e. *contract* or *bend* the body (or neck) in deference:—bow (down) (the) head, stoop.

6916. קִדָּה, **qiddâh,** *kid-daw´*; from 6915; *cassia bark* (as in *shrivelled* rolls):—cassia.

6917. קְדוּמִים, **q°dûwmîym,** *keh-doo-meem´*; passive participle of 6923; a *pristine* hero:—ancient.

6918. קָדוֹשׁ, **qâdôwsh,** *kaw-doshe´*; or קָדֹשׁ, **qâdôsh,** *kaw-doshe´*; from 6942; *sacred* (ceremonially or morally); (as noun) *God* (by eminence), an *angel*, a *saint*, a *sanctuary*:—holy (One), saint.

An adjective meaning sacred, holy. It is used to denote someone or something that is inherently sacred or has been designated as sacred by divine rite or cultic ceremony. It designates that which is the opposite of common or profane. It could be said the *qâdôwsh* is a positive term regarding the character of its referent, where common is a neutral term and profane a very negative term. This word is often used to refer to God as being inherently holy, sacred, and set apart (Ps 22:3[4]; Isa 6:3; 57:15); and as being free from the attributes of fallen humanity (Hos 11:9). Therefore, in the OT, God is accorded the title "The Holy One of Israel" (2Ki 19:22; Ps 78:41; Isa 17:7; Jer 50:29). As such, God instructed that humanity should be holy because He is holy (Le 11:44, 45; 19:2). In addition to its divine references, this word can also modify places, like the court of the tabernacle (Ex 29:31); the camp of Israel (Dt 23:14[15]); Jerusalem (Ecc 8:10); heaven (Isa 57:15); people, like the priests (Le 21:7, 8); a Nazirite (Nu 6:5, 8); the prophet Elisha (2Ki 4:9); Levites (2Ch 35:3); saints [angels] (Job 5:1; 15:15; Da 8:13); water (Nu 5:17); time (Ne 8:9–11; Isa 58:13).

6919. קָדַח, **qâdach**, *kaw-dakh´*; a primitive root; to *inflame*:—burn, kindle.

6920. קַדַּחַת, **qaddachath**, *kad-dakh´-ath*; from 6919; *inflammation*, i.e. febrile disease:—burning ague, fever.

6921. קָדִים, **qâdîym**, *kaw-deem´*; or קָדִם, **qâdim**, *kaw-deem´*; from 6923; the *fore* or front part; hence (by orientation) the *East* ([often adverbial] *eastward*; [for brevity] the *east wind*):—east (-ward, wind).

6922. קַדִּישׁ, **qaddîysh**, *kad-deesh´*; (Chaldee); corresponding to 6918:—holy (One), saint.

An Aramaic masculine adjective meaning holy. It is the Aramaic equivalent of the Hebrew word *qâdôwsh* (6918). This term can modify the word *'ĕlâh* (426), meaning God or gods (Da 4:8[5], 9[6], 18[15]; 5:11). As a substantive, it could stand for angel(s), the supernatural holy one(s) (Da 4:13[10], 17[14], 23[20]). It could also refer to God's people, human holy ones, or saints (Da 7:18, 21, 22, 25, 27).

6923. קָדַם, **qâdam**, *kaw-dam´*; a primitive root; to *project* (one self), i.e. *precede*; hence to *antic-*ipate, *hasten, meet* (usually for help):—come (go, [flee]) before, + disappoint, meet, prevent.

6924. קֶדֶם, **qedem**, *keh´-dem*; or קֵדְמָה, **qêdmâh**, *kayd´-maw*; from 6923; the *front*, of place ([absolute] the *fore part*; [relative] the *East*) or time (*antiquity*); often used adverbially (*before, anciently, eastward*):—aforetime, ancient (time), before, east (end, part, side, -ward), eternal, × ever (-lasting), forward, old, past. Compare 6926.

A masculine noun meaning the east, earlier, formerly, long ago. The word is used regularly to mean east or eastern. The Lord planted the Garden of Eden in the east (Ge 2:8; 3:24); Abraham traveled toward the eastern hills (Ge 12:8; 13:11). The word describes the East as a place known for its wise men (Ge 29:1; Jgs 6:3; 1Ki 4:30 [5:10]); Job was the greatest among these people (Job 1:3). Isaiah, however, called the East a place of superstitions (Isa 2:6). One of Jeremiah's oracles was directed against the people of the East (Jer 49:28); but not, according to Ezekiel, until the Lord gave Judah to one of the peoples of the East—Babylon (Eze 25:4, 10). The famous movement of the whole earth's population to the east to build the Tower of Babel in the plain of Shinar is toward the area of Babylon (Ge 11:2).

The word is also used to refer to former times, times of old. It describes the works of God before the world was created (Pr 8:22, 23). The psalmist implored the Lord to remember the people He purchased long before (Ps 74:2; 77:11[12]; 143:5); for He was the psalmist's King from old (Ps 74:12). The psalmist of Ps 78:2 uttered wisdom and parables as a wise man from ancient times. God planned the fall of Assryia long before it happened (Isa 37:26; La 2:17). The word also refers to Tyre, describing it as an old, ancient city (Isa 23:7). In an important passage, Mic 5:2[1] describes the Lord's coming Ruler from Bethlehem whose origins were from eternity or from ancient days. This word describes the mountains and the heavens as old, of long ago (Dt 33:15; Ps 68:33[34]; Isa 46:10).

A few times the word means front or in front. The Lord knows His people before and behind—thus, altogether (Ps 139:5). The Lord spurred Rezin's foes against him (i.e. from the front) to confront him (Isa 9:12[11]).

6925. קְדָם, **qŏdâm,** *kod-awm´*; (Chaldee); or קְדָם, **qᵉdâm,** *ked-awm´*; (Chaldee) (Da 7:13), corresponding to 6924; *before:*—before, × from, × I (thought), × me, + of, × it pleased, presence.

6926. קִדְמָה, **qidmâh,** *kid-maw´*; feminine of 6924; the *forward* part (or relative) *East* (often adverbial *on* the *east* or *in front*):—east (-ward).

6927. קַדְמָה, **qadmâh,** *kad-maw´*; from 6923; *priority* (in time); also used adverbially (*before*):—afore, antiquity, former (old) estate.

A feminine noun meaning a beginning, a former time. In the oracle concerning Tyre, it was called the city of old (Isa 23:7). The Lord promised to restore Sodom, Samaria, and Jerusalem to what they were before in order to bring shame on Jerusalem (Eze 16:55). A prophecy to the mountains of Israel said that they would be populated as they were in the past (Eze 36:11). See the Hebrew noun *qedem* (6924) and Aramaic noun *qadmâh* (6928).

6928. קַדְמָה, **qadmâh,** *kad-maw´*; (Chaldee); corresponding to 6927; *former* time:—afore [-time], ago.

An Aramaic feminine noun meaning a former time. When the elders of Judah were questioned about rebuilding the Temple, they answered that they were restoring something built long ago (Ezr 5:11). Even after the edict from King Darius, Daniel continued to pray as he had done before (Da 6:10[11]). See the Hebrew noun *qadmâh* (6927).

6929. קֵדְמָה, **Qêdᵉmâh,** *kayd´-maw*; from 6923; *precedence; Kedemah,* a son of Ishmael:—Kedemah.

6930. קַדְמוֹן, **qadmôwn,** *kad-mone´*; from 6923; *eastern:*—east.

6931. קַדְמוֹנִי, **qadmôwnîy,** *kad-mo-nee´*; or קַדְמֹנִי, **qadmônîy,** *kad-mo-nee´*; from 6930; (of time) *anterior* or (of place) *oriental:*—ancient, they that went before, east, (thing of) old.

6932. קְדֵמוֹת, **Qᵉdêmôwth,** *ked-ay-mothe´*; from 6923; *beginnings; Kedemoth,* a place in eastern Palestine:—Kedemoth.

6933. קַדְמָי, **qadmây,** *kad-maw´ee*; (Chaldee); from a root corresponding to 6923; *first:*—first.

6934. קַדְמִיאֵל, **Qadmîy'êl,** *kad-mee-ale´*; from 6924 and 410; *presence of God; Kadmiël,* the name of three Israelites:—Kadmiel.

6935. קַדְמֹנִי, **Qadmônîy,** *kad-mo-nee´*; the same as 6931; *ancient,* i.e. aboriginal; *Kadmonite* (collective), the name of a tribe in Palestine:—Kadmonites.

6936. קָדְקֹד, **qodqôd,** *kod-kode´*; from 6915; the *crown* of the head (as the part most *bowed*):—crown (of the head), pate, scalp, top of the head.

6937. קָדַר, **qâdar,** *kaw-dar´*; a primitive root; to *be ashy,* i.e. *dark*-coloured; (by implication) to *mourn* (in sackcloth or sordid garments):—be black (-ish), be (make) dark (-en), × heavily, (cause to) mourn.

A verb meaning to be dark. This word can also mean to mourn in the sense of being dark with sadness or gloom (Job 5:11; Ps 35:14; Jer 8:21). Sometimes the sky grew dark due to an actual storm (1Ki 18:45). Other times, it was not a literal darkness, as when the prophet Ezekiel prophesied against Pharaoh, saying that the heavens would be darkened when God acted against him (Eze 32:7, 8). Another example of symbolism was when Micah warned the false prophets that dark days were coming for them due to a lack of revelation (Mic 3:6).

6938. קֵדָר, **Qêdâr,** *kay-dawr´*; from 6937; *dusky* (of the skin or the tent); *Kedar,* a son of Ishmael; also (collective) *bedawin* (as his descendants or representatives):—Kedar.

6939. קִדְרוֹן, **Qidrôwn,** *kid-rone´*; from 6937; *dusky place; Kidron,* a brook near Jerusalem:—Kidron.

6940. קַדְרוּת, **qadrûwth,** *kad-rooth´*; from 6937; *duskiness:*—blackness.

A feminine noun meaning blackness. This word is used only once in the OT and comes from the verb *qâdar* (6937), meaning to be dark. In Isa 50:3, this word described the ability of God to clothe the heavens with blackness (that is, make them dark).

6941. קְדֹרַנִּית, **qᵉdôrannîyth,** *ked-o-ran-neeth´*; adverb from 6937; *blackish ones* (i.e. *in sackcloth*); used adverbially in *mourning* weeds:—mournfully.

An adverb meaning mournfully. This word is used only once in the OT and comes from the verb *qâdar* (6937), meaning to be dark. In Mal 3:14, this word describes those who acted as mourners (i.e. those who were gloomy in their countenances).

6942. קָדַשׁ, **qâdash**, *kaw-dash´*; a primitive root; to *be* (causative, *make, pronounce* or *observe* as) *clean* (ceremonially or morally):—appoint, bid, consecrate, dedicate, defile, hallow, (be, keep) holy (-er, place), keep, prepare, proclaim, purify, sanctify (-ied one, self), × wholly.

A verb meaning to be set apart, to be holy, to show oneself holy, to be treated as holy, to consecrate, to treat as holy, to dedicate, to be made holy, to declare holy or consecrated, to behave, to act holy, to dedicate oneself. The verb, in the simple stem, declares the act of setting apart, being holy (i.e. withdrawing someone or something from profane or ordinary use). The Lord set aside Aaron and his sons, consecrated them, and made them holy for the priesthood (Ex 29:21). The altar was made holy, and anything coming into contact with it became holy (Ex 29:37). The tabernacle, the ark, the table of showbread, the altar of burnt offering, and all the smaller accessories and utensils used in the cult of Israel were anointed with a special anointing oil so they became holy. Whatever came in contact with them became holy (Ex 30:26–29). The men accompanying David as his military were declared holy (1Sa 21:5[6]).

The word is used most often in the intensive stem, meaning to pronounce or to make holy, to consecrate. The Lord pronounced the Sabbath day holy (Ge 2:3; Ex 20:8). Places could be dedicated as holy, such as a part of the courtyard of the Temple (1Ki 8:64); or Mount Sinai itself (Ex 19:23). The Year of Jubilee, the fiftieth year, was declared holy (Le 25:10). Persons could be consecrated to holy duties: Aaron and his sons were consecrated to serve as priests of the Lord (Ex 28:3, 41; 1Sa 7:1); the firstborn males of people or animals were consecrated to the Lord (Ex 13:2). Holy times were designated using this word in the factitive stem: Jehu deceitfully proclaimed a holy assembly to Baal (2Ki 10:20); a holy fast could be consecrated as Joel did (Joel 1:14). With the Lord as the subject, the word describes establishing something as holy. The Lord Himself consecrated or made holy His people (Ex 31:13; Le 20:8; 21:8); through His judgments on Israel and the nations, God proved the holiness of His name (Eze 36:23). The priests' holy garments serving in Ezekiel's restored Temple will make those who touch them holy (Eze 44:19; 46:20).

In the causative stem, the meanings overlap with the meanings in the intensive stem. It indicates designating something as consecrated or holy; Jeremiah was declared holy (Jer 1:5); as was the Temple (1Ki 9:3). The word means to treat as holy or dedicated. Gifts, fields, or money could be treated as holy (Le 27:16; 2Sa 8:11; 2Ki 12:18[19]). God declared things holy to Himself (1Ki 9:7); God Himself is to be treated as holy (Nu 20:12; 27:14; Isa 29:23).

In the passive stems, the word means to be consecrated, to be treated as holy, or to show oneself as holy. Ezekiel described the Zadokite priests as consecrated for service at a future Temple (Eze 48:11); Ezr 3:5 described the established holy feasts of the Lord in the return from exile. The entrance at the tabernacle was to be treated as consecrated and holy through the Lord's glory (Ex 29:43). The Lord showed Himself as holy (Le 10:3; 22:32; Eze 20:41).

In the reflexive stem, the verb means to show oneself holy or consecrated: the priests had to properly consecrate themselves before coming before the Lord (Ex 19:22; Le 11:44); the Lord would prove Himself holy before the nations and Israel (Eze 38:23). The word indicates putting oneself or another into a state of holiness to the Lord (Nu 11:18; Jos 3:5; 1Sa 16:5; 2Ch 31:18).

6943. קֶדֶשׁ, **Qedesh**, *keh´-desh*; from 6942; a *sanctum; Kedesh*, the name of four places in Palestine:—Kedesh.

6944. קֹדֶשׁ, **qôdesh**, *ko´-desh*; from 6942; a *sacred* place or thing; (rarely abstract) *sanctity*:—consecrated (thing), dedicated (thing), hallowed (thing), holiness, (× most) holy (× day, portion, thing), saint, sanctuary.

A masculine noun meaning a holy thing, holiness, and sacredness. The word indicates something consecrated and set aside for sacred use only; it was not to be put into common use, for if it was, it became profaned and common (*chôwl*), not holy. This noun described holy offerings or things used in Israel's cult; it described the holy offerings which only the priest or his family could eat (Le 22:10). Some of the offerings of the Lord were described as Most Holy (Le 2:3, 10; Nu 18:9); various things could be consecrated as holy: warriors (1Sa 21:6); food (Ex 29:33); and the places where the holy ark had been located (2Ch 8:11). Only holy priests could go into the Temple (2Ch 23:6). Many vessels and items used in the tabernacle or Temple areas were holy (Ezr 8:28; Ex 30:32, 35). The Sabbath was, of course, holy (Ex 31:14).

This word also designates divine holiness: the Lord alone can swear by His own holiness (Ps 89:35[36]; Am 4:2); and His ways are holy (Ps 77:13[14]). In fact, God is marvelous in holiness (Ex 15:11).

Since the Lord is holy, He expected Israel to be holy. This word described the essence of the Israelites: They were His holy people (Ex 22:31[30]; 28:36).

The word describes holiness when it relates to various things: holiness adhered to the Lord's house and beautified it (Ps 93:5). The Lord's name is holy (Le 20:3; 22:2; Eze 39:7, 25; Am 2:7). The Lord will establish His holy mountain when all the earth will know Him (Isa 11:9; 56:7). Zion is God's holy hill (Da 9:20; Joel 3:17[4:17]).

The word is also used when referring to holy places. God's presence is what makes any place, anything, or anyone holy (Ex 3:5). The Holy Place in the tabernacle (Ex 26:33; 28:29) was separated from the Most Holy Place by a curtain (Ex 26:33); it refers to the Most Holy Place in the Temple as well (1Ki 6:16). This word with the definite article refers to the entire tabernacle (Ex 36:1, 3, 4; 38:27) and later the Temple Solomon built (1Ki 8:8); literally, the Holy Place (Ps 60:6[8]; 63:2[3]).

6945. קָדֵשׁ, **qâdêsh,** *kaw-dashe´*; from 6942; a (quasi) *sacred* person, i.e. (technical) a (male) *devotee* (by prostitution) to licentious idolatry:—sodomite, unclean.

A masculine noun meaning male temple prostitute. The feminine form of this word is *qĕdêshâh* (6948). Although the term denotes one who was holy or sacred, the question must be asked, "Holy for what?" In the context of a pagan temple cult, which was the proper context for this word, it connotes a man who was set apart for pagan temple service, namely, male prostitution (Dt 23:17[18]; 1Ki 14:24; 15:12; 22:46 [47]). This term is sometimes translated as sodomite, which is an excellent expression of the likelihood that these were homosexual or at least bisexual prostitutes.

6946. קֶדֶשׁ, **Qâdêsh,** *kaw-dashe´*; the same as 6945; *sanctuary; Kadesh,* a place in the Desert:—Kadesh. Compare 6947.

6947. קָדֵשׁ בַּרְנֵעַ, **Qâdêsh Barnêaʻ,** *kaw-dashe´ bar-nay´-ah*; from the same as 6946 and an otherwise unused word (apparently compounded of a correspondent to 1251 and a derivitive of 5128) meaning *desert of a fugitive; Kadesh of* (the) *Wilderness of Wandering; Kadesh-Barneä,* a place in the Desert:—Kadesh-barnea.

6948. קְדֵשָׁה, **qĕdêshâh,** *ked-ay-shaw´*; feminine of 6945; a female *devotee* (i.e. *prostitute*):—harlot, whore.

A feminine noun meaning a female temple prostitute. The masculine form of this word is *qâdêsh* (6945). Although the term refers to a person that was holy or sacred, it is necessary to know what they were holy to. When referring to a pagan temple cult, it connotes a woman set apart for pagan temple service, namely, female prostitution (Dt 23:17[18]; Hos 4:14). It is also possible that this term was used as a general term for prostitution (Ge 38:21, 22) because of its parallel usage with *zânâh* (2181) (see Ge 38:15). However, it is at the same time possible that *zânâh* was merely the more general term for a prostitute, while *qĕdêshâh* was the exclusive term for a shrine prostitute.

6949. קָהָה, **qâhâh,** *kaw-haw´*; a primitive root; to be *dull*:—be set on edge, be blunt.

6950. קָהַל, **qâhal,** *kaw-hal´*; a primitive root; to *convoke*:—assemble (selves) (together), gather (selves) (together).

A verb meaning to gather, to assemble. The meaning of this verb is closely connected with that of *qâhâl* (6951), a Hebrew noun meaning a convocation, a congregation, or an assembly. It indicates an assembling together for a convocation or as a congregation, often for religious purposes. The word is used in reference to the act of congregating to fulfill a chiefly religious end (Jos 18:1); of assembling for battle (Jgs 20:1; 2Sa 20:14); and of summoning to an appointed religious assembly (Dt 31:28).

6951. קָהָל, **qâhâl,** *kaw-hawl*; from 6950; *assemblage* (usually concrete):—assembly, company, congregation, multitude.

A masculine noun meaning an assembly, a community, a congregation, a crowd, a company, a throng, a mob. The word describes various gatherings and assemblies called together. It can describe a gathering called for evil purposes—such as the deceitful assembly of the brothers Simeon and Levi to plan violence against the city of Shechem (Ge 49:6; Eze 23:47). The man of God abhors the gathering of evildoers (Ps 26:5); but he should proclaim the Lord's name in the worshiping congregation (Ps 22:22[23]). An assembly for war or a group of soldiers was common in the OT (Nu 22:4; Jgs 20:2; 1Sa 17:47); the various groups of exiles that traveled from Babylon to Jerusalem were a renewed community (Ezr 2:64; Ne 7:66; Jer 31:8). Many assemblies were convened for holy religious purposes: the congregation of Israel gathered at Sinai to hear the Lord's words (Dt 9:10); many feasts and holy convocations called for worship and fasting as noted by the author of Chronicles (2Ch 20:5; 30:25).

The word describes Israel as a congregation, an organized community. Israel was the Lord's community (Nu 16:3; 20:4). The word also describes the gathering of Israel before King Solomon when he dedicated the Temple (1Ki 8:14); the high priest atoned for the whole community of Israel on the Day of Atonement (Le 16:17; Dt 31:30). The word designates the community restored in Jerusalem after the Babylonian exile (Ezr 10:8, 12, 14); the gathering of the congregation of Israel when they killed the Passover lambs (Ex 12:6).

The word refers to gatherings of any assembled multitude: an assembly of nations (Ge 35:11); or of peoples (Ge 28:3), such as Abraham's descendants were to comprise. It refers to a great mass of people as mentioned by Balak, king of Moab (Nu 22:4).

6952. קְהִלָּה, **qᵉhillâh,** *keh-hil-law´*; from 6950; an *assemblage*:—assembly, congregation.

A feminine noun meaning an assembly, a congregation. This word expresses the gathering of a collection of people, such as the congregation of Jacob referred to by Moses in his blessing of the tribes (Dt 33:4). This word can also describe the gathering of people for legal action (Ne 5:7).

6953. קֹהֶלֶת, **qôheleth,** *ko-heh´-leth*; feminine of active participle from 6950; a (female) *assembler* (i.e. lecturer); (abstract) *preaching* (used as a "nom de plume," *Koheleth*):—preacher.

A noun meaning a collector of wisdom, a preacher. This word is the active feminine participle of the word *qâhal* (6950), meaning to gather or to assemble. Thus, the root meaning appears to indicate a person who gathered wisdom. The word has a feminine form because it referred to an office or position, but it was usually used with masculine verbs and always referred to a man. *Qôheleth* only occurs in Ecclesiastes: three times at the beginning and end of the book and once in the middle (Ecc 7:27). It is also the Hebrew name of the book. The word Ecclesiastes is a translation of this Hebrew word into Greek and referred to someone who addressed a public assembly. This is another meaning of the word based on the fact that the preacher had gathered knowledge to speak about life. Solomon used the word to describe himself as one who gathered wisdom (Ecc 12:9, 10; cf. 1Ki 4:32–34[5:12–14]); and as one who spoke to people about wisdom (Ecc 12:9; cf. 2Ch 9:23).

6954. קְהֵלָתָה, **Qᵉhêlâthâh,** *keh-hay-law´-thaw*; from 6950; *convocation; Kehelathah,* a place in the Desert:—Kehelathah.

6955. קְהָת, **Qᵉhâth,** *keh-hawth´*; from an unused root meaning to *ally* oneself; *allied; Kehath,* an Israelite:—Kohath.

6956. קְהָתִי, **Qᵉhâthîy,** *ko-haw-thee´*; patronymic from 6955; a *Kohathite* (collective) or descendants of Kehath:—Kohathites.

6957. קָו, **qav,** *kav*; or קָו, **qâv,** *kawv*; from 6960 [compare 6961]; a *cord* (as *connecting*), especially for measuring; (figurative) a *rule*; also a *rim,* a musical *string* or *accord*:—line. Compare 6978.

6958. קָיא, **qâya´,** *kaw-yah´*; (Jer 25:27), a primitive root; to *vomit*:—spue (out), vomit (out, up, up again).

6959. קוֹבַע, **qôwbaʿ,** *ko´-bah;* a form collateral to 3553; a *helmet:*—helmet.

6960. קָוָה, **qâvâh,** *kaw-vaw´;* a primitive root; to *bind* together (perhaps by *twisting*), i.e. *collect;* (figurative) to *expect:*—gather (together), look, patiently, tarry, wait (for, on, upon).

A verb meaning to wait for, to look for, to hope for. The root meaning is that of twisting or winding a strand of cord or rope, but it is uncertain how that root meaning relates to the idea of hope. The word is used to signify depending on and ordering activities around a future event (Job 7:2; Mic 5:7[6]). The hopes of someone can remain unfulfilled, especially when a person or a nation is sinning (Job 3:9; Ps 69:20[21]; Isa 5:2, 4, 7). Hoping, however, for what God has promised will not ultimately be disappointed, although it may not appear to succeed in the short run (Job 30:26; Isa 59:11; cf. Isa 59:15–21). The Lord will give strength to those who hope in Him (Ps 27:14[2x]; Isa 40:31). Because He is all-powerful (Jer 14:22), He will eventually bring His promises to pass (La 3:25). These promises include the establishing of His kingdom on earth (Ps 37:9, 34; Isa 25:9[2x]). The word also means to be gathered and refers to the gathering of waters (Ge 1:9) and of people (Jer 3:17).

6961. קָוֶה, **qâveh,** *kaw-veh´;* from 6960; a (measuring) *cord* (as if for *binding*):—line.

6962. קוּט, **qûwṭ,** *koot;* a primitive root; (properly) to *cut off,* i.e. (figurative) *detest:*—be grieved, lothe self.

6963. קוֹל, **qôwl,** *kole;* or קֹל, **qôl,** *kole;* from an unused root meaning to *call* aloud; a *voice* or *sound:*— + aloud, bleating, crackling, cry (+ out), fame, lightness, lowing, noise, + hold peace, [pro-] claim, proclamation, + sing, sound, + spark, thunder (-ing), voice, + yell.

6964. קוֹלָיָה, **Qôwlâyâh,** *ko-law-yaw´;* from 6963 and 3050; *voice of Jah; Kolajah,* the name of two Israelites:—Kolaiah.

6965. קוּם, **qûwm,** *koom;* a primitive root; to *rise* (in various applications, literal, figurative, intensive and causative):—abide, accomplish, × be clearer, confirm, continue, decree, × be dim, endure, × enemy, enjoin, get up, make good, help, hold, (help to) lift up (again), make, × but

newly, ordain, perform, pitch, raise (up), rear (up), remain, (a-) rise (up) (again, against), rouse up, set (up), (e-) stablish, (make to) stand (up), stir up, strengthen, succeed, (as-, make) sure (-ly), (be) up (-hold, -rising).

A verb meaning to arise, to stand, to stand up. The basic meaning of this word is the physical action of rising up (Ge 19:33, 35; Ru 3:14); or the resultant end of that action, standing (Jos 7:12, 13). However, a myriad of derived and figurative meanings for this term have developed. It can designate the following attributes: to show honour and respect (Ge 27:19; Ex 33:10; Nu 23:18); to move (Ex 10:23); to recover (Ex 21:19); to belong (Le 25:30); to cost (Le 27:14, 17); to be valid (Nu 30:5); to appear (Dt 13:1[2]); to follow (Dt 29:22[21]); to be hostile (Jgs 9:18); to endure (1Sa 13:14); to replace (1Ki 8:20). The word can also mean to ratify (Ru 4:7); to obligate (Est 9:21, 27, 31); to establish or strengthen (Ps 119:28); to fulfill (Eze 13:6). In the causative form, it means to provide (Ge 38:8; 2Sa 12:11); to rouse (Ge 49:9); to perform (Dt 9:5); to revive (Ru 4:5, 10); to keep one's word (1Sa 3:12); to erect (1Ki 7:21); to appoint (1Ki 11:14); to be victorious (Ps 89:43[44]); to bring to silence (Ps 107:29).

6966. קוּם, **qûwm,** *koom;* (Chaldee); corresponding to 6965:—appoint, establish, make, raise up self, (a-) rise (up), (make to) stand, set (up).

6967. קוֹמָה, **qôwmâh,** *ko-maw´;* from 6965; *height:*— × along, height, high, stature, tall.

6968. קוֹמְמִיּוּת, **qôwmᵉmîyyûwth,** *ko-mem-ee-yooth´;* from 6965; *elevation,* i.e. (adverb) *erectly* (figurative):—upright.

6969. קוּן, **qûwn,** *koon;* a primitive root; to *strike* a musical note, i.e. *chant* or *wail* (at a funeral):—lament, mourning woman.

6970. קוֹעַ, **Qôwaʿ,** *ko´-ah;* probably from 6972 in the original sense of *cutting* off; *curtailment; Koä,* a region of Babylon:—Koa.

6971. קוֹף, **qôwph,** *kofe;* or קֹף, **qôph,** *kofe;* probably of foreign origin; a *monkey:*—ape.

6972. קוּץ, **qûwts,** *koots;* a primitive root; to *clip* off; used only as denominative from 7019; to *spend the harvest* season:—summer.

6973. קוּץ, **qûwts,** *koots*; a primitive root [rather identical with 6972 through the idea of *severing* oneself from (compare 6962)]; to be (causative, *make*) *disgusted* or *anxious*:—abhor, be distressed, be grieved, loathe, vex, be weary.

A verb meaning to loathe, to be disgusted, to be sick of. The word signifies God's revulsion toward pagan practices (Le 20:23); by Israel toward manna (ungratefully and wrongly) after eating it for years (Nu 21:5; cf. Ps 78:22–25); by Rebekah toward her Hittite daughters-in-law (Ge 27:46); and by Solomon's son toward the Lord's rebuke (Pr 3:11). It also signified the loathing felt by enemies toward Israel's prosperity (Ex 1:12; Nu 22:3). In Isa 7:6, the causative sense means to vex. By taking over, the enemies planned to cause Judah to abhor them.

6974. קוּץ, **qûwts,** *koots*; a primitive root [rather identical with 6972 through the idea of *abruptness* in starting up from sleep (compare 3364)]; to *awake* (literal or figurative):—arise, (be) (a-) wake, watch.

6975. קוֹץ, **qôwts,** *kotse*; or קֹץ, **qôts,** *kotse*; from 6972 (in the sense of *pricking*); a *thorn*:—thorn.

6976. קוֹץ, **Qôwts,** *kotse*; the same as 6975; *Kots,* the name of two Israelites:—Koz, Hakkoz [*including the article*].

6977. קְוֻצָּה, **qᵉvutstsâh,** *kev-oots-tsaw´*; feminine passive participle of 6972 in its original sense; a *forelock* (as *shorn*):—lock.

6978. קַו־קָו, **qav-qav,** *kav-kav´*; from 6957 (in the sense of a *fastening*); *stalwart*:— × meted out.

6979. קוּר, **qûwr,** *koor*; a primitive root; to *trench*; (by implication) to *throw forth*; also (denominative from 7023) to *wall up*, whether literal (to *build* a wall) or figurative (to *estop*):—break down, cast out, destroy, dig.

6980. קוּר, **qûwr,** *koor*; from 6979; (only plural) *trenches*, i.e. a *web* (as if so formed):—web.

6981. קוֹרֵא, **Qôwrê',** *ko-ray´*; or קֹרֵא, **Qôrê',** *ko-ray´*; (1Ch 26:1), active participle of 7121; *crier; Korè,* the name of two Israelites:—Kore.

6982. קוֹרָה, **qôwrâh,** *ko-raw´*; or קֹרָה, **qôrâh,** *ko-raw´*; from 6979; a *rafter* (forming *trenches* as it were); (by implication) a *roof*:—beam, roof.

6983. קוּשׁ, **qûwsh,** *kooshe*; a primitive root; to *bend*; used only as denominative for 3369, to *set a trap*:—lay a snare.

A verb meaning to set a trap, to lay a snare. The root idea may be that of bending, as the energy stored in bent wood powers a snare. *Qôwsh* occurs only in Isa 29:21 where it figuratively refers to the laying of a snare to cause trouble and to silence the person who judges justly and thwarts the wicked.

6984. קוּשָׁיָהוּ, **qûwshâyâhûw,** *koo-shaw-yaw´-hoo*; from the passive participle of 6983 and 3050; *entrapped of Jah; Kushajah,* an Israelite:—Kushaiah.

6985. קָט, **qaṭ,** *kat´*; from 6990 in the sense of *abbreviation*; a *little*, i.e. (adverb) *merely*:—very.

6986. קֶטֶב, **qeṭeb,** *keh´-teb*; from an unused root meaning to *cut* off; *ruin*:—destroying, destruction.

A masculine noun meaning destruction. It is closely associated with the word *qôṭeb* (6987). God is always connected with this concept of destruction. It seems ironic that in two passages, God was the source of the destruction (Dt 32:24; Isa 28:2), while in another passage, He was the salvation from the destruction (Ps 91:6). On further reflection, though, it becomes evident that God is the source of this destruction, which was a means of divine retribution. The difference is that in Deuteronomy and Isaiah, God was brought His judgment on the wicked, but in Psalms, God preserved the righteous in the midst of His judgment on the wicked. The specific nature of the destruction is flexible. In each of the passages, it is set in a different context and is parallel with a different word: *reshep* (7566), meaning fire (Dt 32:24); *deber* (1698), meaning plague or pestilence (Ps 91:6); and *mayim* (4325), meaning water (Isa 28:2).

6987. קֹטֶב, **qôṭeb,** *ko´-teb*; from the same as 6986; *extermination*:—destruction.

A masculine noun meaning destruction. It is closely associated with the word *qeṭeb* (6986). It occurs only once where it refers to the judgment that God was going to bring against Samaria for its wickedness (Hos 13:14). See the word *deber* (1698), meaning plague or pestilence, as in Ps 91:6. Even though this word appears in the context of God's impending judgment for wickedness, the specific verse in which it appears is actually a vision of hope for a coming restoration. God is going to allow judgment for a time, but then He will remove it because, without His permission, death and Sheol have no power.

6988. קְטוֹרָה, **qᵉṭôwrâh,** *ket-o-raw´*; from 6999; *perfume:*—incense.

6989. קְטוּרָה, **Qᵉṭûwrâh,** *ket-oo-raw´*; feminine passive participle of 6999; *perfumed; Keturah,* a wife of Abraham:—Keturah.

6990. קָטַט, **qâṭaṭ,** *kaw-tat´*; a primitive root; to *clip* off, i.e. (figurative) *destroy:*—be cut off.

6991. קָטַל, **qâṭal,** *kaw-tal´*; a primitive root; (properly) to *cut* off, i.e. (figurative) *put to death:*—kill, slay.

6992. קְטַל, **qᵉṭal,** *ket-al´*; (Chaldee); corresponding to 6991; to *kill:*—slay.

6993. קֶטֶל, **qeṭel,** *keh´-tel*; from 6991; a violent *death:*—slaughter.

6994. קָטֹן, **qâṭôn,** *kaw-tone´*; a primitive root [rather denominative from 6996]; to *diminish,* i.e. *be* (causative, *make*) *diminutive* or (figurative) *of no account:*—be a (make) small (thing), be not worthy.

6995. קֹטֶן, **qôṭen,** *ko´-ten*; from 6994; a *pettiness,* i.e. the *little finger:*—little finger.

6996. קָטָן, **qâṭân,** *kaw-tawn´*; or קָטֹן, **qâṭôn,** *kaw-tone´*; from 6962; *abbreviated,* i.e. *diminutive,* literal (in quantity, size or number) or figurative (in age or importance):—least, less (-ser), little (one), small (-est, one, quantity, thing), young (-er, -est).

6997. קָטָן, **Qâṭân,** *kaw-tawn´*; the same as 6996; *small; Katan,* an Israelite:—Hakkatan [*including the article*].

6998. קָטַף, **qâṭaph,** *kaw-taf´*; a primitive root; to *strip* off:—crop off, cut down (up), pluck.

6999. קָטַר, **qâṭar,** *kaw-tar´*; a primitive root [rather identical with 7000 through the idea of fumigation in a *close* place and perhaps thus *driving* out the occupants]; to *smoke,* i.e. turn into fragrance by fire (especially as an act of worship):—burn (incense, sacrifice) (upon), (altar for) incense, kindle, offer (incense, a sacrifice).

A verb meaning to produce smoke. Often smoke is made by burning incense, but every major offering may also be associated with this word (Ex 30:7; Le 1:9; 2:2; 3:5; 4:10; 7:5). One unusual use of this term describes Solomon's carriage as perfumed with myrrh and incense (SS 3:6). Many times this verb is used of improper worship directed either to the true God or to false gods (1Ki 12:33; 2Ch 26:16, 18, 19; Jer 48:35). In the OT, the burning of incense was restricted to the Aaronic priesthood (Nu 16:40[17:5]; 2Ch 26:16, 18, 19). In the NT, Zacharias, a priest and the father of John the Baptist, burned incense; and prayers of saints are compared to burning incense (cf. Lk 1:10, 11; Rev 5:8; 8:3, 4).

7000. קָטַר, **qâṭar,** *kaw-tar´*; a primitive root; to *inclose:*—join.

7001. קְטַר, **qᵉṭar,** *ket-ar´*; (Chaldee); from a root corresponding to 7000; a *knot* (as *tied* up), i.e. (figurative) a *riddle;* also a *vertebra* (as if a knot):—doubt, joint.

7002. קִטֵּר, **qiṭṭêr,** *kit-tare´*; from 6999; *perfume:*—incense.

7003. קִטְרוֹן, **Qiṭrôwn,** *kit-rone´*; from 6999; *fumigative; Kitron,* a place in Palestine:—Kitron.

7004. קְטֹרֶת, **qᵉṭôreth,** *ket-o´-reth*; from 6999; a *fumigation:*—(sweet) incense, perfume.

A feminine noun meaning smoke, incense, the smell of a burning sacrifice. Incense was one of the valid gifts Moses was to ask from the people (Ex 25:6); and it played an important role in Aaron's atonement for the sin of his sons (Le 16:13). David's plans for the Temple included an altar for incense (1Ch 28:18); and David prayed that his prayers would be like incense to the Lord (Ps 141:2). God told Judah that the smell of worthless sacrifices was detestable (Isa 1:13). See the related Hebrew verb *qâṭar* (6999).

7005. קַטָּת, **Qaṭṭâth,** *kat-tawth´*; from 6996; *littleness, Kattath,* a place in Palestine:—Kattath.

7006. קָיָה, **qâyâh,** *kaw-yaw´*; a primitive root; to *vomit:*—spue.

7007. קַיִט, **qayiṭ,** *kah´-yit*; (Chaldee); corresponding to 7019; *harvest:*—summer.

7008. קִישׁוֹר, **qîytôwr,** *kee-tore´;* or קִיטֹר, **qîytôr,** *kee-tore´;* from 6999; a *fume,* i.e. *cloud:*—smoke, vapour.

7009. קִים, **qîym,** *keem;* from 6965; an *opponent* (as *rising* against one), i.e. (collective) enemies:—substance.

7010. קְיָם, **qᵉyâm,** *keh-yawm´;* (Chaldee); from 6966; an *edict* (as *arising* in law):—decree, statute.

An Aramaic masculine noun meaning a decree, a statute. A form of this word is only used twice in the Hebrew OT, both times in the book of Daniel. When King Darius' advisors wanted to get rid of Daniel, they persuaded Darius to make a law that forbade worship of anyone but himself (Da 6:7[8]). When Daniel broke this law, the advisors compelled Darius to enforce the punishment because the edict he issued could not be revoked (Da 6:15[16]).

7011. קַיָּם, **qayyâm,** *kah-yawm´;* (Chaldee); from 6966; *permanent* (as *rising* firmly):—steadfast, sure.

7012. קִימָה, **qîymâh,** *kee-maw´;* from 6965; an *arising:*—rising up.

7013. קַיִן, **qayin,** *kah´-yin;* from 6969 in the original sense of *fixity;* a *lance* (as *striking* fast):—spear.

7014. קַיִן, **Qayin,** *kah´-yin;* the same as 7013 (with a play upon the affinity to 7069); *Kajin,* the name of the first child, also of a place in Palestine, and of an Oriental tribe:—Cain, Kenite (-s).

7015. קִינָה, **qîynâh,** *kee-naw´;* from 6969; a *dirge* (as accompanied by *beating* the breasts or on instruments):—lamentation.

7016. קִינָה, **Qîynâh,** *kee-naw´;* the same as 7015; *Kinah,* a place in Palestine:—Kinah.

7017. קֵינִי, **Qêynîy,** *kay-nee´;* or קִינִי, **Qîynîy,** *kee-nee´;* (1Ch 2:55), patronymic from 7014; a *Kenite* or member of the tribe of Kajin:—Kenite.

7018. קֵינָן, **Qêynân,** *kay-nawn´;* from the same as 7064; *fixed; Kenan,* an antediluvian:—Cainan, Kenan.

7019. קַיִץ, **qayits,** *kah´-yits;* from 6972; *harvest* (as the *crop*), whether the product (grain or fruit) or the (dry) season:—summer (fruit, house).

7020. קִיצוֹן, **qîytsôwn,** *kee-tsone´;* from 6972; *terminal:*—out- (utter-) most.

7021. קִיקָיוֹן, **qîyqâyôwn,** *kee-kaw-yone´;* perhaps from 7006; the *gourd* (as *nauseous*):—gourd.

7022. קִיקָלוֹן, **qîyqâlôwn,** *kee-kaw-lone´;* from 7036; intense *disgrace:*—shameful spewing.

7023. קִיר, **qîyr,** *keer;* or קִר, **qir,** *keer;* (Isa 22:5), or (feminine) קִירָה, **qîyrâh,** *kee-raw´;* from 6979; a *wall* (as built in a *trench*):— + mason, side, town, × very, wall.

A masculine noun meaning wall. Balaam's donkey, afraid of the angel, pressed against a wall and crushed Balaam's foot (Nu 22:25). Saul wanted to pin David to a wall with his spear (1Sa 18:11). This word also was used to describe a place one thought was safe (Am 5:19). Solomon lined the interior walls of the Temple with cedar (1Ki 6:15); and Jezebel's blood splattered on a wall (2Ki 9:33). The Hebrew phrase, walls of one's heart, means something like the depths of one's soul in Jer 4:19. The King James Version translates that Hebrew phrase as, my very heart. In Ezekiel's vision of the new Temple, the walls were six cubits thick (Eze 41:5).

7024. קִיר, **Qîyr,** *keer;* the same as 7023; *fortress; Kir,* a place in Assyria; also one in Moab:—Kir. Compare 7025.

7025. קִיר חֶרֶשׂ, **Qîyr Chereś,** *(keer) kheh´-res;* or (feminine of the latter word) קִיר חֲרֶשֶׂת, **Qîyr Chăreśeth,** *khar-eh´-seth;* from 7023 and 2789; *fortress of earthenware; Kir-Cheres* or *Kir-Chareseth,* a place in Moab:—Kir-haraseth, Kir-hareseth, Kir-haresh, Kir-heres.

7026. קֵירֹס, **Qêyrôs,** *kay-roce´;* or קֵרֹס, **Qêrôs,** *kay-roce´;* from the same as 7166; *ankled; Keros,* one of the Nethinim:—Keros.

7027. קִישׁ, **Qîysh,** *keesh;* from 6983; a *bow; Kish,* the name of five Israelites:—Kish.

7028. קִישׁוֹן, **Qîyshôwn,** *kee-shone´;* from 6983; *winding; Kishon,* a river of Palestine:—Kishon, Kison.

7029. קִישִׁי, **Qîyshîy,** *kee-shee´;* from 6983; *bowed; Kishi,* an Israelite:—Kishi.

7030. קִיתָרֹס, **qîythârôs,** *kee-thaw-roce´;* (Chaldee); of Greek origin; a *lyre:*—harp.

7031. קַל, **qal,** *kal*; contracted from 7043; *light*; (by implication) *rapid* (also adverb):—light, swift (-ly).

7032. קָל, **qâl,** *kawl*; (Chaldee); corresponding to 6963:—sound, voice.

7033. קָלָה, **qâlâh,** *kaw-law´*; a primitive root [rather identical with 7034 through the idea of *shrinkage* by heat]; to *toast*, i.e. *scorch* partially or slowly:—dried, loathsome, parch, roast.

7034. קָלָה, **qâlâh,** *kaw-law´*; a primitive root; to *be light* (as implied in *rapid* motion), but figurative only (*be* [causative *hold*] *in contempt*):— base, contemn, despise, lightly esteem, set light, seem vile.

7035. קָלַה, **qâlah,** *kaw-lah´*; for 6950; to *assemble*:—gather together.

A verb meaning to assemble. This word is used only once in the OT. It occurs in 2Sa 20:14 where Joab gathered the people together.

7036. קָלוֹן, **qâlôwn,** *kaw-lone´*; from 7034; *disgrace*; (by implication) the *pudenda*:—confusion, dishonour, ignominy, reproach, shame.

7037. קַלַּחַת, **qallachath,** *kal-lakh´-ath*; apparently but a form for 6747; a *kettle*:—caldron.

7038. קָלַט, **qâlaṭ,** *kaw-lat´*; a primitive root; to *maim*:—lacking in his parts.

7039. קָלִי, **qâlîy,** *kaw-lee´*; or קָלִיא, **qâlîy’,** *kaw-lee´*; from 7033; *roasted* ears of grain:—parched corn.

7040. קַלָּי, **Qallay,** *kal-lah´ee*; from 7043; *frivolous; Kallai,* an Israelite:—Kallai.

7041. קֵלָיָה, **Qêlâyâh,** *kay-law-yaw´*; from 7034; *insignificance; Kelajah,* an Israelite:—Kelaiah.

7042. קְלִיטָא, **Qᵉlîyṭâ’,** *kel-ee-taw´*; from 7038; *maiming; Kelita,* the name of three Israelites:—Kelita.

7043. קָלַל, **qâlal,** *kaw-lal´*; a primitive root; to be (causative, *make*) *light,* literal (*swift, small, sharp,* etc.) or figurative (*easy, trifling, vile,* etc.):— abate, make bright, bring into contempt, (ac-) curse, despise, (be) ease (-y, -ier), (be a, make, make somewhat, move, seem a, set) light (-en, -er, -ly, -ly afflict, -ly esteem, thing), × slight [-ly], be swift (-er), (be, be more, make, re-) vile, whet.

A verb meaning to be slight, to be trivial, to be swift. This word is used in many different ways, but most uses trace back to the basic idea of this word, which is lightness. In its most simple meaning, it referred to the easing of a burden (Ex 18:22); lightening judgment (1Sa 6:5); lessening labour (1Ki 12:9, 10; 2Ch 10:9, 10); or the lightening of a ship (Jnh 1:5). This idea leads to its usage to describe people who were swifter than eagles (2Sa 1:23); swift animals (Hab 1:8); or days that pass quickly (Job 7:6; 9:25). When describing an event or a circumstance, it means trivial (1Sa 18:23; 1Ki 16:31; Isa 49:6). In many instances, it is used to describe speaking lightly of another or cursing another: a person cursing another person (Ex 21:17; 2Sa 16:9–11; Ne 13:2); people cursing God (Le 24:11); or God cursing people (Ge 12:3; 1Sa 2:30; Ps 37:22).

7044. קָלָל, **qâlâl,** *kaw-lawl´*; from 7043; *brightened* (as if *sharpened*):—burnished, polished.

7045. קְלָלָה, **qᵉlâlâh,** *kel-aw-law´*; from 7043; *vilification*:—(ac-) curse (-d, -ing).

A feminine noun meaning curse. This word comes from the verb *qâlal* (7043), meaning to curse. This noun describes the general speaking of ill-will against another (2Sa 16:12; Ps 109:17, 18); as well as the official pronouncement on a person, as Jacob feared he would receive from Isaac (Ge 27:12, 13); or on a nation, as Balaam gave to Moab (Dt 23:5[6]; Ne 13:2). God's curse is on the disobedient (Dt 11:28; 28:15; Jer 44:8); while His blessing, *bĕrâkâh* (1293), is on the righteous (Dt 11:26; 30:19). Jeremiah used several other words in close connection with this one to describe the undesirable nature of this word: reproach, proverb, taunt, curse, hissing, desolation, and imprecation (Jer 24:9; 25:18; 42:18).

7046. קָלַס, **qâlas,** *kaw-las´*; a primitive root; to *disparage*, i.e. *ridicule*:—mock, scoff, scorn.

7047. קֶלֶס, **qeles,** *keh´-les*; from 7046; a *laughingstock*:—derision.

7048. קַלָּסָה, **qallâsâh,** *kal-law-saw´*; intensive from 7046; *ridicule*:—mocking.

7049. קָלַע, **qâla‘,** *kaw-lah´*; a primitive root; to *sling*; also to *carve* (as if a *circular* motion, or into *light* forms):—carve, sling (out).

7050. קֶלַע, **qela',** *kah´-lah*; from 7049; a *sling*; also a (door) *screen* (as if *slung* across), or the *valve* (of the door) itself:—hanging, leaf, sling.

7051. קַלָּע, **qallâ',** *kal-law´*; intensive from 7049; a *slinger*:—slinger.

7052. קְלֹקֵל, **qᵉlôqêl,** *kel-o-kale´*; from 7043; *insubstantial*:—light.

7053. קִלְּשׁוֹן, **qillᵉshôwn,** *kil-lesh-one´*; from an unused root meaning to *prick*; a *prong*, i.e. hay-fork:—fork.

7054. קָמָה, **qâmâh,** *kaw-maw´*; feminine of active participle of 6965; something that *rises*, i.e. a *stalk* of grain:—(standing) corn, grown up, stalk.

7055. קְמוּאֵל, **Qᵉmûw'êl,** *kem-oo-ale´*; from 6965 and 410; *raised of God; Kemuël,* the name of a relative of Abraham, and of two Israelites:—Kemuel.

7056. קָמוֹן, **Qâmôwn,** *kaw-mone´*; from 6965; an *elevation; Kamon,* a place East of the Jordan:—Camon.

7057. קִמּוֹשׂ, **qimmôwś,** *kim-mos´*; from an unused root meaning to *sting*; a *prickly* plant:—nettle. Compare 7063.

7058. קֶמַח, **qemach,** *keh´-makh*; from an unused root probably meaning to *grind; flour*:—flour, meal.

7059. קָמַט, **qâmaṭ,** *kaw-mat´*; a primitive root; to *pluck*, i.e. destroy:—cut down, fill with wrinkles.

7060. קָמַל, **qâmal,** *kaw-mal´*; a primitive root; to *wither*:—hew down, wither.

7061. קָמַץ, **qâmats,** *kaw-mats´*; a primitive root; to *grasp* with the hand:—take an handful.

7062. קֹמֶץ, **qômets,** *ko´-mets*; from 7061; a *grasp*, i.e. *handful*:—handful.

7063. קִמָּשׂוֹן, **qimmâśôwn,** *kim-maw-sone´*; from the same as 7057; a *prickly* plant:—thorn.

7064. קֵן, **qên,** *kane*; contracted from 7077; a *nest* (as *fixed*), sometimes including the *nestlings*; (figurative) a *chamber* or *dwelling*:—nest, room.

7065. קָנָא, **qânâ',** *kaw-naw´*; a primitive root; to be (causative, *make*) *zealous*, i.e. (in a bad sense) *jealous* or *envious*:—(be) envy (-ious), be (move to, provoke to) jealous (-y), × very, (be) zeal (-ous).

A verb meaning to be jealous, to be envious, to be zealous. This is a verb derived from a noun and, as such, occurs in the extensive and causative forms only. The point of the verb is to express a strong emotion in which the subject is desirous of some aspect or possession of the object. It can express jealousy, where persons are zealous for their own property or positions for fear they might lose them (Nu 5:14, 30; Isa 11:13); or envy, where persons are zealous for the property or positions of others, hoping they might gain them (Ge 26:14; 30:1; 37:11). Furthermore, it can indicate someone being zealous on behalf of another (Nu 11:29; 2Sa 21:2); on behalf of God (Nu 25:13; 1Ki 19:10, 14); as well as God being zealous (Eze 39:25; Joel 2:18; Zec 1:14; 8:2). It is also used to denote the arousing of one's jealousy or zeal (Dt 32:16, 21; 1Ki 14:22; Ps 78:58).

7066. קְנָא, **qᵉnâ',** *ken-aw´*; (Chaldee); corresponding to 7069; to *purchase*:—buy.

7067. קַנָּא, **qannâ',** *kan-naw´*; from 7065; *jealous*:—jealous. Compare 7072.

An adjective meaning jealous. This word comes from the verb qânâ' (7065), meaning to be jealous or zealous. In every instance of this word, it is used to describe the character of the Lord. He is a jealous God who will not tolerate the worship of other gods (Ex 20:5; Dt 5:9). This word is always used to describe God's attitude toward the worship of false gods, which arouses His jealousy and anger in judgment against the idol worshippers (Dt 4:24; 6:15). So closely is this characteristic associated with God that His name is Jealous (Ex 34:14).

7068. קִנְאָה, **qin'âh,** *kin-aw´*; from 7065; *jealousy* or *envy*:—envy (-ied), jealousy, × sake, zeal.

A feminine noun meaning zeal, jealousy. This word comes from the verb qânâ' (7065), meaning to be jealous or zealous, and describes an intense fervor, passion, and emotion that is greater than a person's wrath and anger (Pr 27:4). It can be either good or bad: Phinehas was commended for taking up the Lord's jealousy (Nu 25:11); but such passion can also be rottenness to the bones (Pr 14:30). It is used to describe a spirit of jealousy, which comes on a man for his wife (Nu 5:14, 15, 29). Most often, however, this word describes God's zeal, which will accomplish His purpose (2Ki 19:31; Isa 9:7[6]; 37:32); and will be the instrument of His wrath in judgment (Ps 79:5; Eze 36:5, 6; Zep 3:8).

7069. קָנָה, **qânâh,** *kaw-naw´*; a primitive root; to *erect*, i.e. *create*; (by extension) to *procure*, especially by purchase (causative, *sell*); (by implication) to *own*:—attain, buy (-er), teach to keep cattle, get, provoke to jealousy, possess (-or), purchase, recover, redeem, × surely, × verily.

7070. קָנֶה, **qâneh,** *kaw-neh´*; from 7069; a *reed* (as *erect*); (by resemblance) a *rod* (especially for measuring), *shaft, tube, stem,* the *radius* (of the arm), *beam* (of a steelyard):—balance, bone, branch, calamus, cane, reed, × spearman, stalk.

7071. קָנָה, **Qânâh,** *kaw-naw´*; feminine of 7070; *reediness; Kanah,* the name of a stream and of a place in Palestine:—Kanah.

7072. קַנּוֹא, **qannôw',** *kan-no´*; for 7067; *jealous* or *angry*:—jealous.

7073. קְנַז, **Qᵉnaz,** *ken-az´*; probably from an unused root meaning to *hunt; hunter; Kenaz,* the name of an Edomite and of two Israelites:—Kenaz.

7074. קְנִזִּי, **Qᵉnizzîy,** *ken-iz-zee´*; patronymic from 7073, a *Kenizzite* or descendants of Kenaz:—Kenezite, Kenizzites.

7075. קִנְיָן, **qinyân,** *kin-yawn´*; from 7069; *creation,* i.e. (concrete) *creatures*; also *acquisition, purchase, wealth*:—getting, goods, × with money, riches, substance.

7076. קִנָּמוֹן, **qinnâmôwn,** *kin-naw-mone´*; from an unused root (meaning to *erect*); *cinnamon* bark (as in *upright* rolls):—cinnamon.

7077. קָנַן, **qânan,** *kaw-nan´*; a primitive root; to *erect*; but used only as denominative from 7064; to *nestle,* i.e. *build* or *occupy* as a nest:—make … nest.

7078. קֶנֶץ, **qenets,** *keh´-nets*; from an unused root probably meaning to *wrench; perversion*:—end.

7079. קְנָת, **Qᵉnâth,** *ken-awth´*; from 7069; *possession; Kenath,* a place East of the Jordan:—Kenath.

7080. קָסַם, **qâsam,** *kaw-sam´*; a primitive root; (properly) to *distribute,* i.e. *determine* by lot or magical scroll; (by implication) to *divine*:—divine (-r, -ation), prudent, soothsayer, use [divination].

A verb meaning to practice divination. It occurs most frequently in the prophetic books as God's prophets proclaimed the judgment this practice brings (Isa 3:2; Mic 3:6, 7). God had earlier established that He would guide His people through true prophets, not through diviners (Dt 18:10, 14). Thus, the falsity of divination is repeatedly pointed out by the prophets (Jer 29:8; Eze 13:9; 22:28; Zec 10:2). Nevertheless, divination was a problem for Israel as well as for other nations (1Sa 6:2; 28:8; 2Ki 17:17). This Hebrew term is broad enough to encompass necromancy, augury, and visions (1Sa 28:8; Eze 21:21–29; Mic 3:6, 7). Divination was quite profitable for some even in NT times (cf. Ac 16:16–18).

7081. קֶסֶם, **qesem,** *keh´-sem*; from 7080; a *lot*; also *divination* (including its *fee*), *oracle*:—(reward of) divination, divine sentence, witchcraft.

A masculine noun meaning divination. This word described the cultic practice of foreign nations that was prohibited in Israel (Dt 18:10); and considered a great sin (1Sa 15:23; 2Ki 17:17). False prophets used divination to prophesy in God's name, but God identified them as false (Jer 14:14; Eze 13:6); and pledged to remove such practices from Israel (Eze 13:23). Several verses give some insight into what this actual practice looked like: it was compared to a kingly sentence (Pr 16:10); and was used to discern between two choices (Eze 21:21[26], 22[27]).

7082. קָסַס, **qâsas,** *kaw-sas´*; a primitive root; to *lop* off:—cut off.

7083. קֶסֶת, **qeseth,** *keh´-seth*; from the same as 3563 (or as 7185); (properly) a *cup,* i.e. an *inkstand*:—inkhorn.

7084. קְעִילָה, **Qᵉʿîylâh,** *keh-ee-law´*; perhaps from 7049 in the sense of *inclosing; citadel; Keïlah,* a place in Palestine:—Keilah.

7085. קַעֲקַע, **qaʿăqaʿ,** *kah-ak-ah´*; from the same as 6970; an *incision* or gash:— + mark.

7086. קְעָרָה, **qeʿârâh,** *keh-aw-raw´*; probably from 7167; a *bowl* (as *cut* out hollow):—charger, dish.

7087. קָפָא, **qâphâʾ,** *kaw-faw´*; a primitive root; to *shrink*, i.e. *thicken* (as unracked wine, curdled milk, clouded sky, frozen water):—congeal, curdle, dark, settle.

7088. קָפַד, **qâphad,** *kaw-fad´*; a primitive root; to *contract*, i.e. roll together:—cut off.

7089. קְפָדָה, **qᵉphâdâh,** *kef-aw-daw´*; from 7088; *shrinking*, i.e. *terror*:—destruction.

A feminine noun meaning horror, terror. Early Jewish interpreters translated the word as destruction; however, terror follows better from the root, which means to roll up, to contract (*qâphad* [7088]). The word occurs only in Eze 7:25 where it refers to the fear that would come on Israel, causing them to seek peace they would not find. Ezekiel was prophesying of the coming Babylonian invasion, which led to the fall of Jerusalem in 586 B.C.

7090. קִפּוֹד, **qippôwd,** *kip-pode´*; or קִפֹּד, **qippôd,** *kip-pode´*; from 7088; a species of bird, perhaps the *bittern* (from its *contracted* form):—bittern.

7091. קִפּוֹז, **qippôwz,** *kip-poze´*; from an unused root meaning to *contract*, i.e. *spring* forward; an *arrow-snake* (as *darting* on its prey):—great owl.

7092. קָפַץ, **qâphats,** *kaw-fats´*; a primitive root; to *draw together*, i.e. close; (by implication) to *leap* (by *contracting* the limbs); specifically to *die* (from *gathering* up the feet):—shut (up), skip, stop, take out of the way.

7093. קֵץ, **qêts,** *kates*; contracted from 7112; an *extremity*; adverb (with prepositional prefix) *after*:— + after, (utmost) border, end, [in-] finite, × process.

7094. קָצַב, **qâtsab,** *kaw-tsab´*; a primitive root; to *clip*, or (general) *chop*:—cut down, shorn.

7095. קֶצֶב, **qetseb,** *keh´-tseb*; from 7094; *shape* (as if *cut* out); *base* (as if there *cut* off):—bottom, size.

7096. קָצָה, **qâtsâh,** *kaw-tsaw´*; a primitive root; to *cut* off; (figurative) to *destroy*; (partial) to *scrape* off:—cut off, cut short, scrape (off).

7097. קָצֶה, **qâtseh,** *kaw-tseh´*; or (negative only) קֵצֶה, **qêtseh,** *kay-tseh´*; from 7096; an *extremity* (used in a great variety of applications and idioms; compare 7093):— × after, border, brim, brink, edge, end, [in-] finite, frontier, outmost coast, quarter, shore, (out-) side, × some, ut (-ter) most (part).

7098. קָצָה, **qâtsâh,** *kaw-tsaw´*; feminine of 7097; a *termination* (used like 7097):—coast, corner, (selv-) edge, lowest, (uttermost) part.

7099. קָצוּ, **qâtsûw,** *kaw´-tsoo*; and (feminine) קִצְוָה, **qitsvâh,** *kits-vaw´*; from 7096; a *limit* (used like 7097, but with less variety):—end, edge, uttermost part.

7100. קֶצַח, **qetsach,** *keh´-tsakh*; from an unused root apparently meaning to *incise*; *fennel-flower* (from its *pungency*):—fitches.

7101. קָצִין, **qâtsîyn,** *kaw-tseen´*; from 7096 in the sense of *determining*; a *magistrate* (as *deciding*) or other *leader*:—captain, guide, prince, ruler. Compare 6278.

A masculine noun meaning a captain, a ruler. The root meaning is one who decides. Sometimes the word indicates military leadership (Jos 10:24; Jgs 11:6, 11; cf. Jgs 11:9; Da 11:18), but it can signify a nonmilitary authority (Isa 3:6, 7). A captain could be chosen by men (Jgs 11:6; Isa 3:6); but he was ultimately appointed by God (Jgs 11:11; cf. Jgs 2:16, 18; 11:29). Captains were sometimes subordinate to a higher human authority (Jos 10:24; Da 11:18); but not always (Jgs 11:6, 11; cf. Jgs 12:7, 8). They had responsibility before God for the moral state of their followers (Isa 1:10; Mic 3:1, 9); but their subordinates also had responsibility to influence their rulers positively (Pr 25:15).

7102. קְצִיעָה, **qᵉtsiyʿâh,** *kets-ee-aw´*; from 7106; *cassia* (as *peeled*; plural, the *bark*):—cassia.

7103. קְצִיעָה, **Qᵉtsiyʿâh,** *kets-ee-aw´*; the same as 7102; *Ketsiah*, a daughter of Job:—Kezia.

7104. קְצִיץ, **Qᵉtsîyts,** *kets-eets´*; from 7112; *abrupt*; *Keziz*, a valley in Palestine:—Keziz.

7105. קָצִיר, **qâtsîyr,** *kaw-tseer´*; from 7114; *severed*, i.e. *harvest* (as *reaped*), the crop, the time, the reaper, or figurative; also a *limb* (of a tree, or simply *foliage*):—bough, branch, harvest (man).

7106. עָצַ, **qâtsaʽ,** *kaw-tsah´*; a primitive root; to *strip* off, i.e. (partial) *scrape*; (by implication) to *segregate* (as an angle):—cause to scrape, corner.

7107. קָצַף, **qâtsaph,** *kaw-tsaf´*; a primitive root; to *crack* off, i.e. (figurative) *burst* out in rage:— (be) anger (-ry), displease, fret self, (provoke to) wrath (come), be wroth.

A verb meaning to be angry, to provoke to anger. The word refers to anger that arose because people failed to perform their duties properly. Pharaoh was angry with his baker and butcher (Ge 40:2; 41:10); while Moses was angry with the people for hoarding manna (Ex 16:20); Aaron's sons' apparent failure to follow rules of sacrifice (Le 10:16); and the captains' failure to finish off the enemy (Nu 31:14). King Ahasuerus was also angry with Vashti for failing to show off her beauty when summoned (Est 1:12). The word often expressed an authority being angry with a subject but not always (2Ki 13:19; Est 2:21). Sometimes the anger was not justified (2Ki 5:11; Jer 37:15). The word could also refer to God being angry or provoked (Dt 9:7, 8, 22; Zec 1:2; 8:14); an anger that could be aroused by a corporate failure to keep troublemakers in line (Nu 16:22; Jos 22:18). Isa 8:21 contains a reflexive form of the word, as if the anger was unable to find a reasonable object and thus caused the occult practitioners to fret themselves.

7108. קְצַף, **qᵉtsaph,** *kets-af´*; (Chaldee); corresponding to 7107; to *become enraged:*—be furious.

An Aramaic verb meaning to be angry. It corresponds to the Hebrew word *qâtsaph* (7107) and refers to anger aroused by someone's failure to fulfill a duty properly. It occurs only in Da 2:12 where Nebuchadnezzar became angry over the failure of the Babylonian wise men to tell him his dream with its interpretation.

7109. קְצַף, **qᵉtsaph,** *kets-af´*; (Chaldee); from 7108; *rage:*—wrath.

An Aramaic masculine noun meaning anger. Like the word *qĕtsaph* (7108), this word refers to anger aroused by someone's failure to fulfill a duty properly. The word occurs only in Ezr 7:23 where Artaxerxes commanded that work necessary for the second Temple was to be done diligently, lest God's wrath fall on Persia. Artaxerxes

understood that his responsibility was to see that his subjects did their duties.

7110. קֶצֶף, **qetseph,** *keh´-tsef*; from 7107; a *splinter* (as *chipped* off); (figurative) *rage* or *strife:*—foam, indignation, × sore, wrath.

A masculine noun meaning wrath. The word refers to anger aroused by someone's failure to do a duty. For example, a wife in Persia who showed contempt for her husband by not doing her duties would arouse his wrath (Est 1:18). This word usually refers to God's wrath aroused by people failing to do their duties (Dt 29:28[27]; Ps 38:1[2]; Isa 34:2). In some cases, this wrath was directed against sinful Gentile nations (Isa 34:2; Zec 1:15; cf. Ro 1:18). In Israel's case, this duty was expressed in the Law of Moses (2Ch 19:10; Zec 7:12; cf. Ro 4:15). Atonement performed by priests turned away God's wrath when laws were broken (Nu 16:46 [17:11]; 2Ch 29:8; 27:24; 2Ch 29:8).

7111. קְצָפָה, **qᵉtsâphâh,** *kets-aw-faw´*; from 7107; a *fragment:*—bark [-ed].

7112. קָצַץ, **qâtsats,** *kaw-tsats´*; a primitive root; to *chop* off (literal or figurative):—cut (asunder, in pieces, in sunder, off), × utmost.

7113. קְצַץ, **qᵉtsats,** *kets-ats´*; (Chaldee); corresponding to 7112:—cut off.

7114. קָצַר, **qâtsar,** *kaw-tsar´*; a primitive root; to *dock* off, i.e. *curtail* (transitive or intransitive, literal or figurative); especially to *harvest* (grass or grain):— × at all, cut down, much discouraged, grieve, harvestman, lothe, mourn, reap (-er), (be, wax) short (-en, -er), straiten, trouble, vex.

7115. קֹצֶר, **qôtser,** *ko´-tser*; from 7114; *shortness* (of spirit), i.e. *impatience:*—anguish.

7116. קָצֵר, **qâtsêr,** *kaw-tsare´*; from 7114; *short* (whether in size, number, life, strength or temper):—few, hasty, small, soon.

7117. קְצָת, **qᵉtsâth,** *kets-awth´*; from 7096; a *termination* (literal or figurative); also (by implication) a *portion;* adverb (with prepositional prefix) *after:*—end, part, × some.

7118. קְצָת, **qᵉtsâth,** *kets-awth´*; (Chaldee); corresponding to 7117:—end, partly.

7119. קַר, **qar,** *kar*; contracted from an unused root meaning to *chill; cool*; (figurative) *quiet*:—cold, excellent [*from the margin*].

7120. קֹר, **qôr,** *kore*; from the same as 7119; *cold*:—cold.

7121. קָרָא, **qârâ',** *kaw-raw'*; a primitive root [rather identical with 7122 through the idea of *accosting* a person met]; to *call* out to (i.e. [properly] *address* by name, but used in a wide variety of applications):—bewray [self], that are bidden, call (for, forth, self, upon), cry (unto), (be) famous, guest, invite, mention, (give) name, preach, (make) proclaim (-ation), pronounce, publish, read, renowned, say.

A verb meaning to call, to declare, to summon, to invite, to read, to be called, to be invoked, to be named. The verb means to call or to summon, but its context and surrounding grammatical setting determine the various shades of meaning given to the word. Abraham called on the name of the Lord (Ge 4:26; 12:8); the Lord called to Adam (Ge 3:9; Ex 3:4). With the Hebrew preposition meaning to, the verb means to name. Adam named all the animals and birds (Ge 2:20; 3:20); and God named the light day (Ge 1:5). The word may introduce a long message, as in Ex 34:6, that gives the moral and ethical definition of God. It can also mean to summon, such as when God summoned Bezalel to build the tabernacle (Ex 31:2).

In certain contexts, the verb has the sense of proclaiming or announcing. Jezebel urged Ahab to proclaim a holy day of fasting so Naboth could be killed (1Ki 21:9); the Servant of Isaiah proclaimed freedom for the captives and prisoners (Isa 61:1). The word may mean simply to call out or cry out, as Potiphar's wife said she did (Ge 39:15; 1Ki 18:27, 28).

The word means to read aloud from a scroll or a book: the king of Israel was to read aloud from a copy of the Law (Dt 17:19); just as Moses read the Book of the Covenant to all Israel at Sinai (Ex 24:7). Baruch read the scroll of Jeremiah to the people (Jer 36:6, 8).

In the passive stem, the word means to be called or summoned: Esther was called by name (Est 2:14); in the book of Esther, the secretaries who were to carry out the king's orders were summoned (Est 3:12; Isa 31:4). News that was delivered was called out or reported (Jer 4:20). In

Nehemiah's reform, the Book of Moses was read aloud in the audience of the people (Ne 13:1). Also, Eve was called, that is, named, woman (Ge 2:23). The word takes on the nuance of to be reckoned or called. Genesis 21:12 describes how Abraham's seed would be reckoned by the Lord through Isaac.

7122. קָרָא, **qârâ',** *kaw-raw'*; a primitive root; to *encounter*, whether accidentally or in a hostile manner:—befall, (by) chance, (cause to) come (upon), fall out, happen, meet.

7123. קְרָא, **qᵉrâ',** *ker-aw'*; (Chaldee); corresponding to 7121:—call, cry, read.

7124. קֹרֵא, **qôrê',** *ko-ray'*; properly active participle of 7121; a *caller*, i.e. *partridge* (from its *cry*):—partridge. See also 6981.

7125. קִרְאָה, **qir'âh,** *keer-aw'*; from 7122; an *encountering*, accidental, friendly or hostile (also adverb *opposite*):— × against (he come), help, meet, seek, × to, × in the way.

7126. קָרַב, **qârab,** *kaw-rab'*; a primitive root; to *approach* (causative, *bring near*) for whatever purpose:—(cause to) approach, (cause to) bring (forth, near), (cause to) come (near, nigh), (cause to) draw near (nigh), go (near), be at hand, join, be near, offer, present, produce, make ready, stand, take.

A verb meaning to come near, to approach. The basic concept is a close, spatial proximity of the subject and the object (Ge 37:18; Dt 4:11); although it is also possible for this word to introduce actual contact (Eze 37:7; cf. Ex 14:20; Jgs 19:13). This verb is also used in a temporal context to indicate the imminence of some event (Ge 27:41). This usage is common to communicate the impending doom of God's judgment, like Moses' day of calamity and the prophet's day of the Lord (La 4:18). This term has also developed several technical meanings. It can refer to armed conflict. Sometimes it is clarified by modifiers, such as to fight or unto battle (Dt 20:10). Other times, this word alone carries the full verbal idea of entering into battle. Some of these instances are clear by context (Dt 25:11; Jos 8:5); however, there are others where this meaning may be missed (Dt 2:37; Ps 27:2; 91:10; 119:150; cf. Dt 2:19). Another technical meaning refers to sexual relations (Ge 20:4; Dt 22:14; Isa 8:3). One other technical meaning refers to the protocol for presenting an offering to God (Ex 29:4; Le 1:5, 13, 14; Nu 16:9).

7127. קְרֵב, **qᵉrêb,** *ker-abe´*; (Chaldee); corresponding to 7126:—approach, come (near, nigh), draw near.

7128. קְרָב, **qᵉrâb,** *ker-awb´*; from 7126; hostile *encounter:*—battle, war.

7129. קְרָב, **qᵉrâb,** *ker-awb´*; (Chaldee); corresponding to 7128:—war.

7130. קֶרֶב, **qereb,** *keh´-reb*; from 7126; (properly) the *nearest* part, i.e. the *centre*, whether literal, figurative or adverbial (especially with preposition):— × among, × before, bowels, × unto charge, + eat (up), × heart, × him, × in, inward (× -ly, part, -s, thought), midst, + out of, purtenance, × therein, × through, × within self.

A masculine noun meaning midst, middle, interior, inner part, inner organs, bowels, inner being. The term occurs 222 times in the OT and denotes the center or inner part of anything, e.g., the middle of a battle (1Ki 20:39); middle of the streets (Isa 5:25); but especially the inner organs of the body. In the ceremony to ordain Aaron and his sons as priests for ministry to the Lord, all the fat that covered the inner organs of the sacrifices was to be burned on the altar (Ex 29:13, 22; see also Le 1:13, 9:14). On many other occasions, however, the word is utilized abstractly to describe the inner being of a person. This place was regarded as the home of the heart from which the emotions spring (Ps 39:3[4]; 55:4[5]; La 1:20). It was also viewed as the source of thoughts (Ge 18:12; Ps 62:4[5]; Jer 9:8[7]), which are often deceitful, wicked, and full of cursing. Yet wisdom from God can reside there also (1Ki 3:28). This inner being is also the seat of one's moral disposition and thus one's affections and desires. David, grieved over his sin with Bathsheba, pleaded with God to place a right or steadfast spirit within him (lit., in [his] inner being), so that he might always desire to stay close to God and obey His laws (Ps 51:10[12]). The Lord promised to place His Law in the inner beings of His people Israel (Jer 31:33; see also Eze 11:19, 36:26, 27).

7131. קָרֵב, **qârêb,** *kaw-rabe´*; from 7126; *near:*—approach, come (near, nigh), draw near.

7132. קִרְבָה, **qirbâh,** *kir-baw´*; from 7126; *approach:*—approaching, draw near.

7133. קָרְבָּן, **qorbân,** *kor-bawn´*; or קֻרְבָּן, **qurbân,** *koor-bawn´*; from 7126; something *brought near* the altar, i.e. a sacrificial *present:*—oblation, that is offered, offering.

A masculine noun meaning an offering, a gift. This is the most general term, used eighty times in the OT, for offerings and gifts of all kinds. The word is found in Leviticus referring to animal offerings of all permissible types (Le 1:2, 3); grain offerings of fine flour (Le 2:1, 5); gifts or votive offerings of gold vessels. It is found in Numbers referring to silver vessels and rings (Nu 7:13; 31:50) and jewelry (Nu 31:50).

Ezekiel uses the word to designate an offering. Israel corrupted the land by presenting their offerings at every high hill, leafy tree, and high place (Eze 20:28). Happily, the second use in Ezekiel depicts the table where the flesh offering would be properly presented within the restored Temple (Eze 40:43).

7134. קַרְדֹּם, **qardôm,** *kar-dome´*; perhaps from 6923 in the sense of *striking* upon; an *axe:*—ax.

7135. קָרָה, **qârâh,** *kaw-raw´*; feminine of 7119; *coolness:*—cold.

7136. קָרָה, **qârâh,** *kaw-raw´*; a primitive root; to *light upon* (chiefly by accident); (causative) to *bring about*; (specifically) to *impose* timbers (for roof or floor):—appoint, lay (make) beams, befall, bring, come (to pass unto), floor, [hap] was, happen (unto), meet, send good speed.

7137. קָרֶה, **qâreh,** *kaw-reh´*; from 7136; an (unfortunate) *occurrence*, i.e. some accidental (ceremonial) *disqualification:*—uncleanness that chanceth.

7138. קָרוֹב, **qârôwb,** *kaw-robe´*; or קָרֹב, **qârôb,** *kaw-robe´*; from 7126; *near* (in place, kindred or time):—allied, approach, at hand, + any of kin, kinsfolk (-sman), (that is) near (of kin), neighbour, (that is) next, (them that come) nigh (at hand), more ready, short (-ly).

7139. קָרַח, **qârach,** *kaw-rakh´*; a primitive root; to *depilate:*—make (self) bald.

7140. קֶרַח, **qerach,** *keh´-rakh*; or קֹרַח, **qôrach,** *ko´-rakh*; from 7139; *ice* (as if bald, i.e. *smooth*);

hence, *hail*; (by resemblance) rock *crystal*:—crystal, frost, ice.

7141. קֹרַח, **Qôrach,** *ko´-rakh*; from 7139; *ice*; *Korach*, the name of two Edomites and three Israelites:—Korah.

7142. קֵרֵחַ, **qêrêach,** *kay-ray´-akh*; from 7139; *bald* (on the back of the head):—bald (head).

7143. קָרֵחַ, **Qârêach,** *kaw-ray´-akh*; from 7139; *bald*; *Kareäch*, an Israelite:—Careah, Kareah.

7144. קָרְחָה, **qorchâh,** *kor-khaw´*; or קָרְחָא, **qorchâ’,** *kor-khaw´*; (Eze 27:31), from 7139; *baldness*:—bald (-ness), × utterly.

7145. קָרְחִי, **Qorchîy,** *kor-khee´*; patronymic from 7141; a *Korchite* (collective) or descendants of Korach:—Korahite, Korathite, sons of Kore, Korhite.

7146. קָרַחַת, **qârachath,** *kaw-rakh´-ath*; from 7139; a *bald* spot (on the back of the head); (figurative) a *threadbare* spot (on the back side of the cloth):—bald head, bare within.

7147. קְרִי, **qᵉrîy,** *ker-ee´*; from 7136; *hostile encounter*:—contrary.

7148. קָרִיא, **qârîy’,** *kaw-ree´*; from 7121; *called*, i.e. *select*:—famous, renowned.

7149. קִרְיָא, **qiryâ’,** *keer-yaw´*; (Chaldee); or קִרְיָה, **qiryâh,** *keer-yaw´*; (Chaldee); corresponding to 7151:—city.

7150. קְרִיאָה, **qᵉrîy’âh,** *ker-ee-aw´*; from 7121; a *proclamation*:—preaching.

7151. קִרְיָה, **qiryâh,** *kir-yaw´*; from 7136 in the sense of *flooring*, i.e. building; a *city*:—city.

7152. קְרִיּוֹת, **Qᵉrîyyôwth,** *ker-ee-yôth´*; plural of 7151; *buildings*; *Kerioth*, the name of two places in Palestine:—Kerioth, Kirioth.

7153. קִרְיַת אַרְבַּע, **Qiryath ’Arba‘,** *(keer-yath´) ar-bah´*; or (with the article interposed) הָאַרְבַּע קִרְיַת, **Qiryath Hâ’arba‘,** *haw-ar-bah´*; (Ne 11:25), from 7151 and 704 or 702; *city of Arba*, or *city of the four* (giants); *Kirjath-Arba* or *Kirjath-ha-Arba*, a place in Palestine:—Kirjath-arba.

7154. קִרְיַת בַּעַל, **Qiryath Ba‘al,** *keer-yath´ bah´-al*; from 7151 and 1168; *city of Baal*; *Kirjath-Baal*, a place in Palestine:—Kirjath-baal.

7155. קִרְיַת חֲצוֹת, **Qiryath Chutsôwth,** *keer-yath´ khoo-tsôth´*; from 7151 and the feminine plural of 2351; *city of streets*; *Kirjath-Chutsoth*, a place in Moab:—Kirjath-huzoth.

7156. קִרְיָתַיִם, **Qiryâthayim,** *keer-yaw-thah´-yim*; dual of 7151; *double city*; *Kirjathaïm*, the name of two places in Palestine:—Kiriathaim, Kirjathaim.

7157. קִרְיַת יְעָרִים, **Qiryath Yᵉ‘ârîym,** *(keer-yath´) yeh-aw-reem´*; or (Jer 26:20) with the article interposed; or (Jos 18:28) simply the former part of the word; or קִרְיַת עָרִים, **Qiryath ‘Ârîym,** *aw-reem´*; from 7151 and the plural of 3293 or 5892; *city of forests*, or *city of towns*; *Kirjath-Jeärim* or *Kirjath-Arim*, a place in Palestine:—Kirjath, Kirjath-jearim, Kirjath-arim.

7158. קִרְיַת סַנָּה, **Qiryath Sannâh,** *keer-yath´ san-naw´*; or קִרְיַת סֵפֶר, **Qiryath Sêpher,** *keer-yath´ say´-fer*; from 7151 and a simpler feminine from the same as 5577, or (for the latter name) 5612; *city of branches*, or *of a book*; *Kirjath-Sannah* or *Kirjath-Sepher*, a place in Palestine:—Kirjath-sannah, Kirjath-sepher.

7159. קָרַם, **qâram,** *kaw-ram´*; a primitive root; to *cover*:—cover.

7160. קָרַן, **qâran,** *kaw-ran´*; a primitive root; to *push* or gore; used only as denominative from 7161, to *shoot out horns*; (figurative) *rays*:—have horns, shine.

7161. קֶרֶן, **qeren,** *keh´-ren*; from 7160; a *horn* (as projecting); (by implication) a *flask, cornet*; (by resemblance) an elephant's *tooth* (i.e. *ivory*), a *corner* (of the altar), a *peak* (of a mountain), a *ray* (of light); (figurative) *power*:— × hill, horn.

7162. קֶרֶן, **qeren,** *keh´-ren*; (Chaldee); corresponding to 7161; a *horn* (literal or for sound):—horn, cornet.

7163. קֶרֶן הַפּוּךְ, **qeren happûwk,** *keh´-ren hap-pook´*; from 7161 and 6320; *horn of cosmetic*; *Keren-hap-Puk*, one of Job's daughters:—Keren-happuch.

7164. קָרַס, **qâras,** *kaw-ras´*; a primitive root; (properly) to *protrude*; used only as denominative from 7165 (for alliteration with 7167), to *hunch*, i.e. be humpbacked:—stoop.

7165. קֶרֶס, **qeres,** *keh´-res;* from 7164; a *knob* or belaying-pin (from its swelling form):—tache.

7166. קַרְסֹל, **qarsôl,** *kar-sole´;* from 7164; an *ankle* (as a *protuberance* or joint):—foot.

7167. קָרַע, **qâra‘,** *kaw-rah´;* a primitive root; to *rend,* literal or figurative (*revile, paint* the eyes, as if enlarging them):—cut out, rend, × surely, tear.

7168. קֶרַע, **qera‘,** *keh´-rah;* from 7167; a *rag:*— piece, rag.

7169. קָרַץ, **qârats,** *kaw-rats´;* a primitive root; to *pinch,* i.e. (partial) to *bite* the lips, *blink* the eyes (as a gesture of malice), or (fully) to *squeeze* off (a piece of clay in order to mould a vessel from it):—form, move, wink.

7170. קְרַץ, **qᵉrats,** *ker-ats´;* (Chaldee); corresponding to 7171 in the sense of a *bit* (to "eat the *morsels* of" any one, i.e. *chew* him up [figurative] by *slander*):— + accuse.

7171. קֶרֶץ, **qerets,** *keh´-rets;* from 7169; *extirpation* (as if by *constriction*):—destruction.

A masculine noun possibly meaning destruction. It is found only in Jer 46:20. Due to the immediate context of the passage, however, the more probable meaning is biter (i.e. a biting fly, such as a gadfly, a horsefly, or a mosquito). Egypt was described as a beautiful heifer, but a biting fly from the north (i.e. Babylon) was being sent to punish her. This noun is derived from the verb *qârats* (7169).

7172. קַרְקַע, **qarqa‘,** *kar-kah´;* from 7167; *floor* (as if a pavement of pieces or *tessaræ*), of a building or the sea:—bottom, (× one side of the) floor.

7173. קַרְקַע, **Qarqa‘,** *kar-kah´;* the same as 7172; *ground-floor; Karka* (with the article prefixed), a place in Palestine:—Karkaa.

7174. קַרְקֹר, **Qarqôr,** *kar-kore´;* from 6979; *foundation; Karkor,* a place East of the Jordan:—Karkor.

7175. קֶרֶשׁ, **qeresh,** *keh´-resh;* from an unused root meaning to *split* off; a *slab* or plank; (by implication) a *deck* of a ship:—bench, board.

7176. קֶרֶת, **qereth,** *keh´-reth;* from 7136 in the sense of building; a *city:*—city.

7177. קַרְתָּה, **Qartâh,** *kar-taw´;* from 7176; *city; Kartah,* a place in Palestine:—Kartah.

7178. קַרְתָּן, **Qartân,** *kar-tawn´;* from 7176; *city-plot; Kartan,* a place in Palestine:—Kartan.

7179. קַשׁ, **qash,** *kash;* from 7197; *straw* (as *dry*):—stubble.

7180. קִשֻּׁאָה, **qishshu’âh,** *kish-shoo´-aw;* from an unused root (meaning to be *hard*); a *cucumber* (from the difficulty of *digestion*):—cucumber.

7181. קָשַׁב, **qâshab,** *kaw-shab´;* a primitive root; to *prick up* the ears, i.e. *hearken:*—attend, (cause to) hear (-ken), give heed, incline, mark (well), regard.

A verb meaning to listen carefully, to pay attention, to give heed, to obey. The basic significance of the term is to denote the activity of paying close attention to something, usually another person's words or sometimes to something that can be seen (e.g., Isa 21:7). Job pleaded for his three friends to listen to his words (Job 13:6; see also Isa 32:3; Jer 23:18). Often the term functioned as an appeal to God to hear and respond to an urgent prayer (Ps 17:1; 61:1[2]; 66:19; cf. Ps 5:2[3]). At other times, it denoted the obedience that was expected after the hearing of the Lord's requirements (1Sa 15:22; Ne 9:34; Isa 48:18). Israel's history, however, was characterized by a life of hard-heartedness and rebellion. Jeremiah declared that this was due to the fact that Israel's ears were uncircumcised; therefore, they could not listen so they were able to obey (Jer 6:10).

7182. קֶשֶׁב, **qesheb,** *keh´-sheb;* from 7181; a *hearkening:*— × diligently, hearing, much heed, that regarded.

7183. קַשָּׁב, **qashshâb,** *kash-shawb´;* or קָשֻׁב, **qash-shub,** *kash-shoob´;* from 7181; *hearkening:*—attent (-ive).

7184. קָשָׂה, **qâśâh,** *kaw-saw´;* or קַשְׂוָה, **qasvâh,** *kas-vaw´;* from an unused root meaning to be *round;* a *jug* (from its shape):—cover, cup.

7185. קָשָׁה, **qâshâh,** *kaw-shaw´;* a primitive root; (properly) to *be dense,* i.e. tough or *severe* (in various applications):—be cruel, be fiercer, make grievous, be ([ask a], be in, have, seem, would) hard (-en, [labour], -ly, thing), be sore, (be, make) stiff (-en, [-necked]).

7186. קָשֶׁה, **qâsheh,** *kaw-sheh´*; from 7185; *severe* (in various applications):—churlish, cruel, grievous, hard ([-hearted], thing), heavy, + impudent, obstinate, prevailed, rough (-ly), sore, sorrowful, stiff ([-necked]), stubborn, + in trouble.

An adjective meaning hard, harsh, cruel, severe, strong, violent, fierce. This term's basic function is to describe something as hard. The word modifies a variety of different subjects and encompasses a fairly broad range of meanings. The labour the Egyptians imposed on the Hebrews was described as hard (i.e. harsh, Ex 1:14; 6:9). Joseph spoke hard words to his brothers at first (Ge 42:7, 30; cf. 1Sa 20:10). A Calebite named Nabal was labeled as being hard, i.e. cruel and evil (1Sa 25:3). The Israelites were often characterized as being hard or stiff of neck, i.e. stubborn, rebellious, obstinate (Ex 32:9, 33:3, 5; Dt 9:6, 13; cf. Eze 3:7). An experience could be hard, i.e. painful (Ps 60:3[5]); as could a vision or revelation (Isa 21:2). Hannah was hard of spirit, that is, deeply troubled (1Sa 1:15). Both battles and winds could be hard, i.e. fierce (2Sa 2:17; Isa 27:8). Moses chose capable men from all Israel to serve as judges; they judged minor cases while Moses himself judged the difficult ones (Ex 18:26).

7187. קְשׁוֹט, **qᵉshôwṭ,** *kesh-ote´*; (Chaldee); or קְשֹׁט, **qᵉshôṭ,** *kesh-ote´*; (Chaldee); corresponding to 7189; *fidelity:*—truth.

An Aramaic masculine noun meaning truth. The term is utilized twice, with both occurrences embedded within the book of Daniel. After being deeply humbled by the Lord, Nebuchadnezzar praised God and acknowledged that all His works were truth (Da 4:37[34]). Prior to this humbling, King Nebuchadnezzar had declared Daniel's God in truth to be the God of gods, i.e. truly (Da 2:47). Nevertheless, this knowledge failed to penetrate his proud heart, because in the very next section of text, Nebuchadnezzar built a monumental golden idol. This word is equivalent to the Hebrew term *qôshet* (7189).

7188. קָשַׁח, **qâshach,** *kaw-shakh´*; a primitive root; to *be* (causative, *make*) *unfeeling:*—harden.

A verb meaning to make hard, to treat roughly. Used twice in the OT, this word implies a hardening similar to the formation of a callous. It signifies the hardening of a mother's heart toward her offspring (Job 39:16); and is used by Isaiah to connote the spiritual dullness of the people toward God (Isa 63:17).

7189. קֹשֶׁט, **qoshet,** *ko´-shet;* or קֹשְׁט, **qosht,** *kosht;* from an unused root meaning to *balance; equity* (as evenly *weighed*), i.e. *reality:*—truth.

A masculine noun meaning truth, certainty. This word comes from an unused root meaning to balance, as in a scale. It appears twice in the Wisdom Literature, meaning the vindication of a true assessment by reality (Ps 60:4[6]); and the realization of a person's truthfulness by an intimate knowledge of the individual (Pr 22:21).

7190. קְשִׁי, **qᵉshîy,** *kesh-ee´*; from 7185; *obstinacy:*—stubbornness.

7191. קִשְׁיוֹן, **Qishyôwn,** *kish-yone´*; from 7190; *hard ground; Kishjon,* a place in Palestine:—Kishion, Keshon.

7192. קְשִׂיטָה, **qᵉśîyṭâh,** *kes-ee-taw´*; from an unused root (probably meaning to *weigh* out); an *ingot* (as definitely *estimated* and stamped for a coin):—piece of money (silver).

7193. קַשְׂקֶשֶׂת, **qaśqeśeth,** *kas-keh´-seth;* by reduplication from an unused root meaning to *shale* off as bark; a *scale* (of a fish); hence a coat of *mail* (as composed of or covered with jointed *plates* of metal):—mail, scale.

7194. קָשַׁר, **qâshar,** *kaw-shar´*; a primitive root; to *tie,* physical (*gird, confine, compact*) or mentally (in *love, league*):—bind (up), (make a) conspire (-acy, -ator), join together, knit, stronger, work [treason].

7195. קֶשֶׁר, **qesher,** *keh´-sher;* from 7194; an (unlawful) *alliance:*—confederacy, conspiracy, treason.

7196. קִשֻּׁרִים, **qishshurîym,** *kish-shoor-eem´*; from 7194; an (ornamental) *girdle* (for women):—attire, headband.

7197. קָשַׁשׁ, **qâshash,** *kaw-shash´*; a primitive root; to *become sapless* through drought; used only as denominative from 7179; to *forage* for straw, stubble or wood; (figurative) to *assemble*:—gather (selves) (together).

7198. קֶשֶׁת, **qesheth,** *keh´-sheth*; from 7185 in the original sense (of 6983) of *bending*; a *bow*, for *shooting* (hence [figurative] *strength*) or the *iris*:— × arch (-er), + arrow, bow ([-man, -shot]).

7199. קַשָּׁת, **qashshâth,** *kash-shawth´*; intensive (as denominative) from 7198; a *bowman*:— × archer.

ר (Resh)

7200. רָאָה, **râ'âh,** *raw-aw´*; a primitive root; to *see*, literal or figurative (in numerous applications, direct and implied, transitive, intransitive and causative):—advise self, appear, approve, behold, × certainly, consider, discern, (make to) enjoy, have experience, gaze, take heed, × indeed, × joyfully, lo, look (on, one another, one on another, one upon another, out, up, upon), mark, meet, × be near, perceive, present, provide, regard, (have) respect, (fore-, cause to, let) see (-r, -m, one another), shew (self), × sight of others, (e-) spy, stare, × surely, × think, view, visions.

A verb meaning to see. Its basic denotation is to see with the eyes (Ge 27:1). It can also have the following derived meanings, all of which require the individual to see physically outside of himself or herself: to see so that one can learn to know, whether it be another person (Dt 33:9) or God (Dt 1:31; 11:2); to experience (Jer 5:12; 14:13; 20:18; 42:14); to perceive (Ge 1:4, 10, 12, 18, 21, 25, 31; Ex 3:4); to see by volition (Ge 9:22, 23; 42:9, 12); to look after or to visit (Ge 37:14; 1Sa 20:29); to watch (1Sa 6:9); to find (1Sa 16:17); to select (2Ki 10:3); to be concerned with (Ge 39:23). It is also possible for this verb to require the individual to make a mental observation. As an imperative, it can function as an exclamation similar to *hinnêh* (2009), which means to behold (Ge 27:27; 31:50). Further, it can denote to give attention to (Jer 2:31); to look into or inquire (1Sa 24:15[16]); to take heed (Ex 10:10); to discern (Ecc 1:16; 3:13); to distinguish (Mal 3:18); to consider or reflect on (Ecc 7:14). It can also connote a spiritual observation and comprehension by means of seeing visions (Ge 41:22; Isa 30:10).

7201. רָאָה, **râ'âh,** *raw-aw´*; from 7200; a *bird* of prey (probably the *vulture*, from its sharp *sight*):—glede. Compare 1676.

7202. רָאֶה, **râ'eh,** *raw-eh´*; from 7200; *seeing*, i.e. experiencing:—see.

An adjective meaning seeing. This word appears in Job 10:15 in an idiomatic use, meaning to be drenched or utterly covered with affliction. The connection with the root meaning stems from the visible signs of being afflicted.

7203. רֹאֶה, **rô'eh,** *ro-eh´*; active participle of 7200; a *seer* (as often rendered); but also (abstract) a *vision*:—vision.

A masculine noun meaning a seer, prophetic vision. The word is the active participle of *râ'âh* (7200), which signifies a prophet (see 1Ch 9:22, Isa 30:10). It refers to the vision or insight that the prophet receives (Isa 28:7).

7204. רֹאֶה, **Rô'êh,** *ro-ay´*; for 7203; *prophet*; *Roëh*, an Israelite:—Haroeh [*including the article*].

7205. רְאוּבֵן, **R°'ûwbên,** *reh-oo-bane´*; from the imperative of 7200 and 1121; *see ye a son*; *Reüben*, a son of Jacob:—Reuben.

7206. רְאוּבֵנִי, **R°'ûwbênîy,** *reh-oo-bay-nee´*; patronymic from 7205; a *Reübenite* or descendant of Reüben:—children of Reuben, Reubenites.

7207. רַאֲוָה, **ra'ăvâh,** *rah-av-aw´*; from 7200; *sight*, i.e. satisfaction:—behold.

A verb infinitive meaning to behold, to see. Appearing only once in the OT, the word alludes to looking on the outward appearance and fondly admiring an object (Ecc 5:11[10]).

7208. רְאוּמָה, **R°'ûwmâh,** *reh-oo-maw´*; feminine passive participle of 7213; *raised*; *Reümah*, a Syrian woman:—Reumah.

7209. רְאִי, **r°'îy,** *reh-ee´*; from 7200; a *mirror* (as *seen*):—looking glass.

A masculine noun meaning mirror. The primary meaning is that of a looking glass used to see one's own reflection. Job uses the word metaphorically to refer to the sky (Job 37:18).

7210. רֳאִי, **rŏ'îy,** *ro-ee´*; from 7200; *sight,* whether abstract (*vision*) or concrete (a *spectacle*):— gazingstock, look to, (that) see (-th).

A masculine noun meaning sight, an appearance, a spectacle. The basic force of this word is that of a visible appearance. It is used in reference to God's ability to see (Ge 16:13); the outward look of an individual (1Sa 16:12); and a visual spectacle that drew attention to itself (Na 3:6).

7211. רְאָיָה, **Rᵉ'âyâh,** *reh-aw-yaw´*; from 7200 and 3050; *Jah has seen; Reäjah,* the name of three Israelites:—Reaia, Reaiah.

7212. רְאִית, **rᵉ'îyth,** *reh-eeth´*; from 7200; *sight:*—beholding.

A feminine noun meaning look, sight. The word is derived from the verb râ'âh (7200) and is used to denote a looking on of goods by their owner. The author of Ecclesiastes rhetorically inquired as to the good of increasing wealth and goods, if only for the owner merely to look on them (Ecc 5:11[10]).

7213. רָאַם, **râ'am,** *raw-am´*; a primitive root; to *rise:*—be lifted up.

7214. רְאֵם, **rᵉ'êm,** *reh-ame´*; or רְאֵים, **rᵉ'êym,** *reh-ame´*; or רֵים, **rêym,** *rame*; or רֵם, **rêm,** *rame*; from 7213; a wild *bull* (from its *conspicuousness*):—unicorn.

7215. רָאמוֹת, **râ'môwth,** *raw-moth´*; from 7213; something *high* in value, i.e. perhaps *coral:*—coral.

7216. רָאמוֹת, **Râ'môwth,** *raw-mōth´*; or רָאמֹת, **Râ'môth,** *raw-mōth´*; plural of 7215; *heights; Ramoth,* the name of two places in Palestine:—Ramoth.

7217. רֵאשׁ, **rê'sh,** *raysh*; (Chaldee); corresponding to 7218; the *head;* (figurative) the *sum:*—chief, head, sum.

An Aramaic masculine noun meaning head. The word is used to indicate the head of a man (Da 3:27); of an image constructed by Nebuchadnezzar (Da 2:32, 38); and a beast in Daniel's vision (Da 7:6, 20). This word is also used to denote a receptacle for dreams and visions (i.e. the head [Da 7:1]), and in the same verse it represents the sum total (i.e. essential matter). Ezra used this noun to indicate those

people who served in the capacity of leaders (Ezr 5:10).

7218. רֹאשׁ, **rô'sh,** *roshe*; from an unused root apparently meaning to *shake;* the *head* (as most easily *shaken*), whether literal or figurative (in many applications, of place, time, rank, etc.):— band, beginning, captain, chapiter, chief (-est place, man, things), company, end, × every [man], excellent, first, forefront, ([be-]) head, height, (on) high (-est part, [priest]), × lead, × poor, principal, ruler, sum, top.

A masculine noun meaning a head, hair, a person, a point, the top, the beginning, the best, a chief, a leader. It is clear from the multitude of legitimate translations of this word that it has many metaphorical meanings. In Scripture, the word is used to refer to a human head (Ge 40:16); it also refers to animal heads as well, such as the serpent's head (Ge 3:15); a dog; an ass; a living being (2Sa 3:8; 2Ki 6:25; Eze 1:22). It regularly indicates the heads of animals being sacrificed (Ex 12:9; 29:15, 19).

This word is used in several Hebrew idioms: to bring something down on someone's head is to get vengeance (Eze 9:10); and to sprinkle dust on one's head is to mourn and show despair (Jos 7:6; Eze 27:30).

The word can designate an individual person: It refers to Joseph's head as representative of his whole tribe (Ge 49:26; Dt 33:16). It refers to the top or peak of things and indicates the tops of mountains (Ge 8:5); such as the top of Mount Olives in 2Sa 15:32 or even the top of a bed (Ge 47:31).

This Hebrew word commonly designates the beginning of something: It refers to the head or beginning of the year (Eze 40:1); or month (Ex 12:2). Its use extends to describing the best of something. The best spices or myrrh were depicted by this word (Ex 30:23), as were the most influential persons: commanders (Dt 20:9; Eze 10:11); the heads or leaders of families and chiefs (1Ki 8:1; 1Ch 24:31); the chief priest of Israel (1Ch 27:5). It is used with a superlative connotation to describe the chief cornerstone (Ps 118:22); or the most lofty stars (Job 22:12).

In some places, the word is best translated to indicate the entire or complete amount of something: the Lord made the chief part of the dust of the earth, i.e. all of it (Pr 8:26). It also meant to take (or lift up) the total number of people, i.e. take a census (Ex 30:12). The psalmist asserted that the sum total of God's words are righteous forever (Ps 119:160).

It also indicates the source of a river or branch as its head (Ge 2:10). When combined with the noun dog, it expresses a major insult. Abner used the term of himself, a dog's head, as a term of disgust (2Sa 3:8).

7219. רֹאשׁ, **rô'sh,** *roshe*; or רוֹשׁ, **rôwsh,** *roshe*; (Dt 32:32), apparently the same as 7218; a poisonous *plant,* probably the *poppy* (from its conspicuous *head*); (generally) *poison* (even of serpents):—gall, hemlock, poison, venom.

7220. רֹאשׁ, **Rô'sh,** *roshe*; probably the same as 7218; *Rosh,* the name of an Israelite and of a foreign nation:—Rosh.

7221. רֹאשָׁה, **ri'shâh,** *ree-shaw´*; from the same as 7218; a *beginning:*—beginning.

A feminine noun meaning a beginning. Ezekiel used the word to denote an earlier time (Eze 36:11). He spoke figuratively, saying that the Lord would make the mountains of Israel more prosperous than before. The Lord would also increase the number of people and animals, who would in turn be fruitful and multiply.

7222. רֹאשָׁה, **rô'shâh,** *ro-shaw´*; feminine of 7218; the *head:*—head [-stone].

An adjective meaning head, chief. It occurs only in Zec 4:7 where it describes a stone. The adjective sometimes indicates that the stone is the cornerstone, the first stone laid (see *rô'sh* [7218]). However, it often refers to the top stone as being at a prominent place on the Temple structure (cf. Mt 4:5), like the head is atop the body. The latter makes better sense in context because the foundation was already laid at the time of the prophecies that use this word (cf. Ezr 5; Zec 1:1; 4:9). The stone may be the same stone mentioned in Zec 3:9 and 4:10, which is clearly a symbol of Christ (cf. Zec 4:10; Rev 5:6). It would make sense for Jesus, the Alpha and the Omega (Rev 1:8), to be both the first stone (cf. Isa 28:16; 1Pe 2:4–8) and the last stone laid in the Temple.

7223. רִאשׁוֹן, **ri'shôwn,** *ree-shone´*; or רִאשֹׁן, **ri'shôn,** *ree-shone´*; from 7221; *first,* in place, time or rank (as adjective or noun):—ancestor,

(that were) before (-time), beginning, eldest, first, fore [-father] (-most), former (thing), of old time, past.

An adjective meaning first, former, foremost, earlier, head, chief. This term occurs 182 times and denotes that which comes first among given items, whether in place, rank, or order (Ge 25:25, 32:17[18]; 2Ki 1:14) or (more frequently) in time. Moses had the tabernacle set up in the first month, just as the Lord commanded (Ex 40:2, 17; cf. Nu 9:5; Ezr 7:9; Eze 45:18, 21). Zechariah warned the exiles who returned to the Promised Land from the Babylonian captivity not to be like their ancestors who refused to listen to the former prophets (Zec 1:4, 7:7, 12). The Lord declares Himself to be the first and the last, the Eternal One (Isa 44:6, 48:12). In later Hebrew, the word came to signify the highest in rank or authority (i.e. chief, head). The archangel Michael is portrayed as holding the rank of chief prince (Da 10:13; cf. 1Ch 18:17; Est 1:14). This word is derived from the noun *rô'sh* (7218).

7224. רִאשֹׁנִי, **ri'shônîy,** *ree-sho-nee´*; from 7223; *first:*—first.

An adjective meaning first. The word is derived from the noun *rô'sh* (7218) and corresponds closely in meaning to the adjective *ri'shôwn* (7223). It occurs only in Jer 25:1. The word of the Lord concerning all the people of Judah came to Jeremiah in the first year of King Nebuchadnezzar's reign over all Babylon.

7225. רֵאשִׁית, **rê'shîyth,** *ray-sheeth´*; from the same as 7218; the *first,* in place, time, order or rank (specifically a *firstfruit*):—beginning, chief (-est), first (-fruits, part, time), principal thing.

A noun meaning the beginning, the first, the chief, the best, the firstfruits. Occurring fifty-one times in the OT, this term holds the honour of being the first word written in the entire Bible (Ge 1:1). Often, the term denotes the point in time or space at which something started, except when it specifies the point when time and space themselves were started (Isa 46:10). It conveys the beginning of strife (Pr 17:14); of a ruler's reign (Jer 26:1, 27:1; 28:1; 49:34); of a sin (Mic 1:13); of a kingdom (Ge 10:10); or of wisdom and knowledge (Ps 111:10; Pr 1:7). On other occasions, the term signifies the highest of anything, i.e. the best or most excellent, such as the choicest parts of offerings (1Sa 2:29); the best of the spoil (1Sa 15:21); or the finest in oils (Am 6:6). Elsewhere, the word designates the earliest or first products or results of something. It refers many times to the first products of a harvest (Le 23:10; Dt 18:4; Ne 12:44); and sometimes to the first product, i.e. the firstborn of a father (Ge 49:3; Dt 21:17). Both this term and the noun *rô'sh* (7218) are derived from the same unused verbal root.

7226. רַאֲשׁת, **ra'ăshôth,** *rah-ash-ōth´*; from 7218; a *pillow* (being for the *head*):—bolster.

7227. רַב, **rab,** *rab*; by contraction from 7231; *abundant* (in quantity, size, age, number, rank, quality):—(in) abound (-undance, -ant, -antly), captain, elder, enough, exceedingly, full, great (-ly, man, one), increase, long (enough, [time]), (do, have) many (-ifold, things, a time), ([ship-]) master, mighty, more, (too, very) much, multiply (-tude), officer, often [-times], plenteous, populous, prince, process [of time], suffice (-ient).

7228. רַב, **rab,** *rab*; by contraction from 7232; an *archer* [or perhaps the same as 7227]:—archer.

7229. רַב, **rab,** *rab*; (Chaldee); corresponding to 7227:—captain, chief, great, lord, master, stout.

7230. רֹב, **rôb,** *robe*; from 7231; *abundance* (in any respect):—abundance (-antly), all, × common [sort], excellent, great (-ly, -ness, number), huge, be increased, long, many, more in number, most, much, multitude, plenty (-ifully), × very [age].

7231. רָבַב, **râbab,** *raw-bab´*; a primitive root; (properly) to *cast together* [compare 7241], i.e. *increase,* especially in number; also (as denominative from 7233) to *multiply by the myriad:*—increase, be many (-ifold), be more, multiply, ten thousands.

7232. רָבַב, **râbab,** *raw-bab´*; a primitive root [rather identical with 7231 through the idea of *projection*]; to *shoot* an arrow:—shoot.

7233. רְבָבָה, **rᵉbâbâh,** *reb-aw-baw´*; from 7231; *abundance* (in number), i.e. (specific) a *myriad* (whether defensive or indefensive):—many, million, × multiply, ten thousand.

7234. רָבַד, **râbad,** *raw-bad´*; a primitive root; to *spread:*—deck.

7235. רָבָה, **râbâh,** *raw-baw´*; a primitive root; to *increase* (in whatever respect):—[bring in] abundance (× -antly), + archer [*by mistake for* 7232], be in authority, bring up, × continue, enlarge, excel, exceeding (-ly), be full of, (be, make) great (-er, -ly, × -ness), grow up, heap, increase, be long, (be, give, have, make, use) many (a time), (any, be, give, give the, have) more (in number), (as, be, be so, gather, over, take, yield) much (greater, more), (make to) multiply, nourish, plenty (-eous), × process [of time], sore, store, thoroughly, very.

7236. רְבָה, **rᵉbâh,** *reb-aw´*; (Chaldee); corresponding to 7235:—make a great man, grow.

7237. רַבָּה, **Rabbâh,** *rab-baw´*; feminine of 7227; *great*; *Rabbah*, the name of two places in Palestine, East and West:—Rabbah, Rabbath.

7238. רְבוּ, **rᵉbûw,** *reb-oo´*; (Chaldee); from a root corresponding to 7235; *increase* (of dignity):—greatness, majesty.

7239. רִבּוֹ, **ribbôw,** *rib-bo´*; from 7231; or רִבּוֹא, **ribbôw',** *rib-bo´*; from 7231; a *myriad*, i.e. indefensive *large number:*—great things, ten ([eight] -een, [for] -ty, + sixscore, + threescore, × twenty, [twen] -ty) thousand.

7240. רִבּוֹ, **ribbôw,** *rib-bo´*; (Chaldee); corresponding to 7239:— × ten thousand times ten thousand.

7241. רָבִיב, **râbîyb,** *raw-beeb´*; from 7231; a *rain* (as an *accumulation* of drops):—shower.

7242. רָבִיד, **râbîyd,** *raw-beed´*; from 7234; a *collar* (as *spread* around the neck):—chain.

7243. רְבִיעִי, **rᵉbîy'îy,** *reb-ee-ee´*; or רְבִעִי, **rebi'îy,** *reb-ee-ee´*; from 7251; *fourth*; also (fractional) a *fourth:*—four-square, fourth (part).

7244. רְבִיעִי, **rᵉbîy'îy,** *reb-ee-ee´*; (Chaldee); corresponding to 7243:—fourth.

7245. רַבִּית, **Rabbîyth,** *rab-beeth´*; from 7231; *multitude*; *Rabbith*, a place in Palestine:—Rabbith.

7246. רָבַך, **râbak,** *raw-bak´*; a primitive root; to *soak* (bread in oil):—baken, (that which is) fried.

7247. רִבְלָה, **Riblâh,** *rib-law´*; from an unused root meaning to *be fruitful; fertile; Riblah,* a place in Syria:—Riblah.

7248. רַב־מָג, **Rab-Mâg,** *rab-mawg´*; from 7227 and a foreign word for a Magian; *chief Magian; Rab-Mag,* a Babylonian official:—Rab-mag.

7249. רַב־סָרִיס, **Rab-Sârîys,** *rab-saw-reece´*; from 7227 and a foreign word for a eunuch; *chief chamberlain; Rab-Saris,* a Babylonian official:—Rab-saris.

7250. רָבַע, **râba‘,** *raw-bah´*; a primitive root; to *squat* or *lie* out flat, i.e. (specific) in copulation:—let gender, lie down.

7251. רָבַע, **râba‘,** *raw-bah´*; a primitive root [rather identical with 7250 through the idea of *sprawling* "at all fours" (or possibly the reverse is the order of derivation); compare 702]; (properly) to *be four* (sided); used only as denominative of 7253; to *be quadrate*:—(four-) square (-d).

7252. רֶבַע, **reba‘,** *reh´-bah*; from 7250; *prostration* (for sleep):—lying down.

7253. רֶבַע, **reba‘,** *reh´-bah*; from 7251; a *fourth* (part or side):—fourth part, side, square.

7254. רֶבַע, **Reba‘,** *reh´-bah*; the same as 7253; *Reba,* a Midianite:—Reba.

7255. רֹבַע, **rôba‘,** *ro´-bah*; from 7251; a *quarter*:—fourth part.

7256. רִבֵּעַ, **ribbêa‘,** *rib-bay´-ah*; from 7251; a descendant of the *fourth* generation, i.e. *great great grandchild*:—fourth.

7257. רָבַץ, **râbats,** *raw-bats´*; a primitive root; to *crouch* (on all four legs folded, like a recumbent animal); (by implication) to *recline, repose, brood, lurk, imbed*:—crouch (down), fall down, make a fold, lay, (cause to, make to) lie (down), make to rest, sit.

7258. רֶבֶץ, **rêbets,** *reh´-bets*; from 7257; a *couch* or place of repose:—where each lay, lie down in, resting place.

7259. רִבְקָה, **Ribqâh,** *rib-kaw´*; from an unused root probably meaning to *clog* by tying up the fetlock; *fettering* (by beauty); *Ribkah,* the wife of Isaac:—Rebekah.

7260. רַבְרַב, **rabrab,** *rab-rab´*; (Chaldee); from 7229; *huge* (in size); *domineering* (in character):—(very) great (things).

7261. רַבְרְבָן, **rabrebân,** *rab-reb-awn´*; (Chaldee); from 7260; a *magnate*:—lord, prince.

An Aramaic masculine noun meaning a noble, a lord. The term occurs only in the plural and is found only in the book of Daniel. Nebuchadnezzar and Belshazzar, both kings of Babylon at one point, were served and sought by a great host of these important officials (Da 4:36[33]; 5:1–3, 9, 10, 23; 6:17[18]).

7262. רַבְשָׁקֵה, **Rabshâqêh,** *rab-shaw-kay´*; from 7227 and 8248; *chief butler; Rabshakeh,* a Babylonian official:—Rabshakeh.

7263. רֶגֶב, **regeb,** *reh´-gheb*; from an unused root meaning to *pile* together; a *lump* of clay:—clod.

7264. רָגַז, **râgaz,** *raw-gaz´*; a primitive root; to *quiver* (with any violent emotion, especially anger or fear):—be afraid, stand in awe, disquiet, fall out, fret, move, provoke, quake, rage, shake, tremble, trouble, be wroth.

A verb meaning to shake, to tremble, to agitate, to disturb, to rouse up, to rage, to provoke. This term occurs forty-one times in the OT and is utilized most often to express the idea of the physical moving or shaking of someone or something. Lands (1Sa 14:15; Am 8:8); mountains (Ps 18:7[8]; Isa 5:25); the heavens (2Sa 22:8); kingdoms (Isa 23:11); and even the whole earth (Joel 2:10) are described as being shaken in this way, with the Lord's anger often given as the basis for the quaking. Often people, whether groups or individuals, would shake, i.e. were moved or stirred by deep emotions in response to specific circumstances. They trembled in fear (Ex 15:14; Dt 2:25; Isa 64:2[1]; Joel 2:1; Mic 7:17); or shook in agitation or anger (Pr 29:9; Eze 16:43); and even grief (2Sa 18:33[19:1]). Sometimes the word signifies the disturbing or rousing up of someone (1Sa 28:15; 2Sa 7:10; 1Ch 17:9). Occasionally, it conveys the act of rebelling or raging against another, literally, to shake oneself against someone (cf. 2Ki 19:27, 28; Isa 37:28, 29). This verb is related to the verbs *râga‘* and *râgash* (7283). The noun *rôgez* (7267) is directly derived from it.

7265. רְגַז, r⁽ᵉ⁾gaz, *reg-az´*; (Chaldee); corresponding to 7264:—provoke unto wrath.

An Aramaic verb meaning to provoke, to anger. The term occurs only once in the entire OT. In a report written to King Darius, the elders of the Jews were quoted as conceding to the fact that the Babylonian exile and destruction of Solomon's Temple (ca. 586 B.C.) took place because their ancestors had angered the God of heaven (Ezr 5:12). This verb corresponds to the Hebrew verb *râgaz* (7264).

7266. רְגַז, r⁽ᵉ⁾gaz, *reg-az´*; (Chaldee); from 7265; violent *anger*:—rage.

An Aramaic masculine noun meaning violent anger, rage. The term occurs only once in the entire OT. When King Nebuchadnezzar heard that three Jews—Shadrach, Meshach, and Abednego—refused to worship the image of gold that he had erected, he flew into a rage (Da 3:13). This term is derived from the Aramaic verb *r⁽ᵉ⁾gaz* (7265) and is related to the Hebrew noun *rôgez* (7267).

7267. רֹגֶז, rôgez, *ro´-ghez*; from 7264; *commotion, restlessness* (of a horse), *crash* (of thunder), *disquiet, anger*:—fear, noise, rage, trouble (-ing), wrath.

A masculine noun meaning commotion, raging, excitement. The primary meaning of this word is a state of agitation or uproar. It denotes the tumult that comes from fear (Isa 14:3); the fury of the Lord's judgment (Hab 3:2); a general state of upheaval (Job 3:26); and the chaos of ordinary life in this world (Job 14:1).

7268. רַגָּז, raggâz, *rag-gawz´*; intensive from 7264; *timid*:—trembling.

An adjective meaning trembling, shaking. Deuteronomy 28:65 records the sole occurrence of this word. It describes a fainting heart that is full of unease.

7269. רָגְזָה, rogzâh, *rog-zaw´*; feminine of 7267; *trepidation*:—trembling.

A feminine noun meaning a trembling, a quaking. In Eze 12:18, this word is used to imply a trembling or quivering hand. The suggestion is that of tremendous worry or unsteadiness even during routine activities.

7270. רָגַל, râgal, *raw-gal´*; a primitive root; to *walk* along; but only in specific applications, to *reconnoitre*, to *be a tale-bearer* (i.e. slander); also

(as denominative from 7272) to *lead about*:—backbite, search, slander, (e-) spy (out), teach to go, view.

7271. רְגַל, r⁽ᵉ⁾gal, *reg-al´*; (Chaldee); corresponding to 7272:—foot.

7272. רֶגֶל, regel, *reh´-gel*; from 7270; a *foot* (as used in *walking*); (by implication) a *step*; (by euphemism) the *pudenda*:— × be able to endure, × according as, × after, × coming, × follow, ([broken-]) foot ([-ed, -stool]), × great toe, × haunt, × journey, leg, + piss, + possession, time.

7273. רַגְלִי, raglîy, *rag-lee´*; from 7272; a *footman* (soldier):—(on) foot (-man).

7274. רֹגְלִים, Rôg⁽ᵉ⁾lîym, *ro-gel-eem´*; plural of active participle of 7270; *fullers* (as *tramping* the cloth in washing); *Rogelim*, a place East of the Jordan:—Rogelim.

7275. רָגַם, râgam, *raw-gam´*; a primitive root [compare 7263, 7321, 7551]; to *cast* together (stones), i.e. to *lapidate*:— × certainly, stone.

7276. רֶגֶם, Regem, *reh´-gem*; from 7275; stoneheap; *Regem*, an Israelite:—Regem.

7277. רִגְמָה, rigmâh, *rig-maw´*; feminine of the same as 7276; a *pile* (of stones), i.e. (figurative) a *throng*:—council.

7278. רֶגֶם מֶלֶךְ, Regem Melek, *reh´-gem meh´-lek*; from 7276 and 4428; *king's heap*; *Regem-Melek*, an Israelite:—Regem-melech.

7279. רָגַן, râgan, *raw-gan´*; a primitive root; to *grumble*, i.e. *rebel*:—murmur.

7280. רָגַע, râga‘, *raw-gah´*; a primitive root; (properly) to *toss* violently and suddenly (the sea with waves, the skin with boils); figurative (in a favourable manner) to *settle*, i.e. quiet; (specifically) to *wink* (from the motion of the eyelids):—break, divide, find ease, be a moment, (cause, give, make to) rest, make suddenly.

7281. רֶגַע, rega‘, *reh´-gah*; from 7280; a *wink* (of the eyes), i.e. a very *short space* of time:—instant, moment, space, suddenly.

7282. רָגֵעַ, râgêa‘, *raw-gay´-ah*; from 7280; *restful*, i.e. peaceable:—that are quiet.

7283. רָגַשׁ, râgash, *raw-gash´*; a primitive root; to *be tumultuous*:—rage.

A verb meaning to be in commotion, to rage against. This word appears only in Ps 2:1 where it denotes the uproar and plotting of the wicked against the righteous. The image of a gathering lynch mob conveys well the action suggested here.

7284. רְגַשׁ, **reᵉgash,** *reg-ash´*; (Chaldee); corresponding to 7283; to *gather* tumultuously:— assemble (together).

An Aramaic verb meaning to assemble in a throng, to be turbulent, to be in tumult. Occurring only in Daniel, this word describes the gathering of the men who conspired against the prophet (Da 6:6[7], 11[12], 15[16]).

7285. רֶגֶשׁ, **regesh,** *reh´-ghesh*; or (feminine) רִגְשָׁה, **rigshâh,** *rig-shaw´*; from 7283; a tumultuous *crowd*:—company, insurrection.

A noun meaning a crowd, a company, an insurrection. The basic meaning of this word is that of a thronging mass of people. The word refers to worshippers going to the Temple in a large group (Ps 55:14 [15]); and the riotous scheming that could result from a large gathering of people whose minds were not directed toward God (Ps 64:2[3]).

7286. רָדַד, **râdad,** *raw-dad´*; a primitive root; to *tread* in pieces, i.e. (figurative) to *conquer*, or (specific) to *overlay*:—spend, spread, subdue.

7287. רָדָה, **râdâh,** *raw-daw´*; a primitive root; to *tread* down, i.e. *subjugate*; (specifically) to *crumble* off:—(come to, make to) have dominion, prevail against, reign, (bear, make to) rule (-r, over), take.

A verb meaning to rule, to have dominion, to subjugate. This Hebrew word conveys the notion of exercising domain, whether legitimate or not, over those who are powerless or otherwise under one's control. It is related as the exercise of authority by the priesthood (Jer 5:31); by slave owners over their slaves (Le 25:43); by supervisors over their workers (1Ki 9:23); and by a king over his kingdom (1Ki 4:24[5:4]). Theologically significant is the use of this word to identify people's God-ordained relationship to the created world around them (Ge 1:26, 28).

7288. רַדַּי, **Radday,** *rad-dah´ee*; intensive from 7287; *domineering; Raddai,* an Israelite:— Raddai.

7289. רָדִיד, **râdîyd,** *raw-deed´*; from 7286 in the sense of *spreading*; a *veil* (as expanded):—vail, veil.

7290. רָדַם, **râdam,** *raw-dam´*; a primitive root; to *stun*, i.e. *stupefy* (with sleep or death):—(be fast a-, be in a deep, cast into a dead, that) sleep (-er, -eth).

7291. רָדַף, **râdaph,** *raw-daf´*; a primitive root; to *run after* (usually with hostile intent; figurative [of time] *gone by*):—chase, put to flight, follow (after, on), hunt, (be under) persecute (-ion, -or), pursue (-r).

7292. רָהַב, **râhab,** *raw-hab´*; a primitive root; to *urge* severely, i.e. (figurative) *importune, embolden, capture, act insolently*:—overcome, behave self proudly, make sure, strengthen.

7293. רַהַב, **rahab,** *rah´-hab*; from 7292; *bluster* (*-er*):—proud, strength.

7294. רַהַב, **Rahab,** *rah´-hab*; the same as 7293; *Rahab* (i.e. *boaster*), an epithet of Egypt:— Rahab.

7295. רָהָב, **râhâb,** *raw-hawb´*; from 7292; *insolent*:—proud.

7296. רֹהַב, **rôhab,** *ro´-hab*; from 7292; *pride*:—strength.

7297. רָהָה, **râhâh,** *raw-haw´*; a primitive root; to *fear*:—be afraid.

A verb meaning to be afraid, to fear. Occurring only in Isa 44:8, this word implies a fear that stems from uncertainty or a sense of being utterly alone. In the text, the Lord offered His assurance that He was still living and was in control of all situations.

7298. רַהַט, **rahaṭ,** *rah´-hat*; from an unused root apparently meaning to *hollow out*; a *channel* or watering-box; by resemblance a *ringlet* of hair (as forming parallel lines):—gallery, gutter, trough.

7299. רֵו, **rêv,** *rave*; (Chaldee); from a root corresponding to 7200; *aspect*:—form.

7300. רוּד, **rûwd,** *rood*; a primitive root; to *tramp* about, i.e. *ramble* (free or disconsolate):—have the dominion, be lord, mourn, rule.

A verb meaning to wander restlessly, to roam. Hosea uses the verb figuratively to refer to Judah's restlessness, that is, their lack of obedience to God (Hos 11:12[12:1]). The Lord uses the verb in Jeremiah to ask why His people felt they were free to roam (Jer 2:31). Esau, after Jacob deceived Isaac, was doomed to live by the sword and serve his brother. However, there would come a time when he would become restless and throw off his yoke (Ge 27:40).

7301. רָוָה, **râvâh,** *raw-vaw´*; a primitive root; to *slake* the thirst (occasionally of other appetites):—bathe, make drunk, (take the) fill, satiate, (abundantly) satisfy, soak, water (abundantly).

7302. רָוֶה, **râveh,** *raw-veh´*; from 7301; *sated* (with drink):—drunkenness, watered.

7303. רוֹהֲגָה, **Rôwhăgâh,** *ro-hag-aw´*; from an unused root probably meaning to *cry* out; *outcry; Rohagah,* an Israelite:—Rohgah.

7304. רָוַח, **râvach,** *raw-vakh´*; a primitive root [rather identical with 7306]; (properly) to *breathe* freely, i.e. *revive;* (by implication) to *have ample room:*—be refreshed, large.

A verb meaning to breathe freely, to be spacious, to smell. The primary meaning is to breathe freely by means of being spacious or revived. This word is used to indicate a relief that comes to a troubled mind or spirit (1Sa 16:23; Job 32:20). Shallem, son of Josiah, stated that he would build a great palace with spacious upper rooms (Jer 22:14). *Râwah* was also used to dictate the smelling of aromas of both the burnt offering and incense (see Ge 8:21; Ex 30:38). In Genesis, the burnt offerings had a pleasing aroma to God, which in turn prompted Him to state His covenant. In Exodus, the people were warned against making the special mixture of incense (meant only for the use of an incense offering to God) simply to enjoy its aroma. The punishment for disobeying this command was to be cut off from one's own people.

7305. רֶוַח, **revach,** *reh´-vakh*; from 7304; *room,* literal (an *interval*) or figurative (*deliverance*):—enlargement, space.

A masculine noun meaning a space, an interval, a respite, a relief, a liberation. In Genesis, the word is used in Jacob's command to keep a space between the herds that were given as gifts to his brother Esau (Ge 32:16[17]). This space gave Jacob more time to prepare, looked more

impressive to the receiver (i.e. controlled herds), and gave a better impression of the size or amount of the gift. In Esther, Mordecai indicated that if Esther kept silent, then relief for the Jews would arise from another place, and she and her father's family would die (Est 4:14).

7306. רוּחַ, **rûwach,** *roo´-akh*; a primitive root; (properly) to *blow,* i.e. *breathe;* only (literal) to *smell;*(by implication) to *perceive;* (figurative) to *anticipate, enjoy:*—accept, smell, × touch, make of quick understanding.

A verb meaning to feel relief, to be spacious, to smell. This verb is used rarely in the Hebrew Bible. In the simple stem, it occurs twice meaning to gain or feel relief. When David played the harp, Saul found relief (1Sa 16:23); the verbose Elihu had to speak in order to get relief from his anxiety (Job 32:20). In its single use in the passive intensive stem, it means roomy or spacious. The vain King Shallum proposed to build himself a palace with spacious, roomy, upper chambers (Jer 22:14).

The verb is used most often in the causative stem to mean to smell. Gods of wood cannot smell (Dt 4:28); nor can idols of gold or silver (Ps 115:6). Isaac smelled the clothes that Jacob wore to deceive him (Ge 27:27). In 1Sa 26:19, however, the verb refers to God being pleased by the aroma of an offering (Ge 8:21; Le 26:31). The verb evidently means to be burned with in Jgs 16:9, for the ropes holding Samson snapped as when they sensed (i.e. were burned) with fire. The Shoot of Jesse, the Branch, will respond (i.e. be sensitive) to the fear of the Lord (Isa 11:1, 2).

7307. רוּחַ, **rûwach,** *roo´-akh*; from 7306; *wind;* (by resemblance) *breath,* i.e. a sensible (or even violent) exhalation; (figurative) *life, anger, unsubstantiality;* (by extension) a *region* of the sky; (by resemblance) *spirit,* but only of a rational being (including its expression and functions):—air, anger, blast, breath, × cool, courage, mind, × quarter, × side, spirit ([-ual]), tempest, × vain, ([whirl-]) wind (-y).

A feminine noun meaning spirit, wind, breath. The word is used to refer to the Spirit of God or the Lord. The Spirit of the Lord inspired prophets to utter their prophecies (Nu 11:17, 25; 1Sa 10:6; 19:20); the Spirit of the Lord moved the prophets in time and space, as in the case of Elijah (1Ki 18:12; Eze 2:2). The word could be modified by an adjective to refer to an evil spirit from the Lord (1Sa 16:15, 16; 1Ki 22:22, 23). The Spirit of God is properly referred to as the Holy Spirit (Ps 51:11[13]; 106:33; Isa 63:10, 11). The Spirit produced and controlled the message of the prophets, even of a Mesopotamian prophet like Balaam (Nu 24:2). David was inspired to speak as a prophet by the Spirit (2Sa 23:2). The Spirit was present among the returned exiles in Jerusalem (Hag 2:5; Zec 4:6); and will be poured out in the latter days on all flesh, imparting prophecy, dreams, and visions (Joel 2:28[3:1]). The Spirit of God was grieved by the rebellion of God's people (Isa 63:10).

The Lord's Spirit imparted other gifts: giving Bezalel skill and ability in all kinds of work (Ex 31:3; 35:31); including the skill to teach others (see Ex 35:34); the Spirit gave understanding as well (Job 32:8). The Spirit of the Lord had a part in creating the universe; the Spirit hovered over the deep and imparted life to persons (Ge 1:2; Job 33:4); and even revived the dead (Eze 37:5, 10; 39:29).

The human spirit and the Spirit of God are closely linked with moral character and moral attributes. God will give His people a new spirit so they will follow His decrees and laws (Eze 11:19; 36:26). God's Spirit will rest on His people, transforming them (Isa 59:21). The Lord preserves those who have heavy spirits and broken hearts (Ps 34:18[19]; Isa 65:14).

The human spirit is sometimes depicted as the seat of emotion, the mind, and the will. In a song of praise, Isaiah asserted that the spirit desires the Lord (Isa 26:9; Job 7:11). The spirit imparts wisdom for understanding (Ex 28:3; Dt 34:9); and carrying out one's responsibilities. David prayed for a willing spirit to aid him (Ex 35:21; Ps 51:10[12]).

The spirit made flesh alive and is the life force of living humans and animals. The Lord makes the spirits of people that give them life (Zec 12:1). This spirit is from God and leaves at death (Ge 6:3; Ps 78:39; Ecc 3:21). The spirit is pictured as giving animation, agitation, or liveliness; the Queen of Sheba was overcome in her spirit when she saw the splendors of Solomon's world (1Ki 10:5). Not to have any spirit is to lose all courage; the Amorite kings had no spirit in them when they learned how Israel had crossed the Jordan. To be short of spirit is to be despondent or impatient (Ecc 6:9).

The word also describes the breath of a human being or the natural wind that blows. The idols of the goldsmith have no breath in them; they are inanimate (Jer 10:14; 51:17). Human speech is sometimes only words of wind that mean nothing (Job 16:3). By the gust of his nostrils, the Lord piled up the waters of the Red Sea (Ex 15:8). Often, the word refers to wind or a synonym of wind. The Lord sent a wind over the earth to dry up the floodwaters (Ge 8:1; Ex 15:10; Nu 11:31). Jeremiah spoke of the four winds, referring to the entire earth (Jer 49:36; Eze 37:9). The word is also used to mean wind in the sense of nothing (Ecc 1:14; 2:11; Isa 26:18). The wind, like the Spirit, cannot be caught, tamed, or found (Ecc 2:11).

7308. רוּחַ, *rûwach, roo´-akh*; (Chaldee); corresponding to 7307:—mind, spirit, wind.

An Aramaic noun meaning wind; spirit of a person, mind; spirit divine. All occurrences of the word are located in the book of Daniel. For the Hebrew mind, the term at its heart encapsulated the experience of any mysterious, invisible, awesome, living power. This included such forces as the wind (Da 2:35; 7:2); the active inner being of a person where attitudes, feelings, and intellect resided (Da 5:12, 20; 6:3[4]; 7:15); the divine Spirit that could come down from God and indwell individuals, often giving them supernatural abilities, such as Daniel's ability to interpret dreams (Da 4:8[5], 9[6], 18[15]; 5:11, 14). This term is identical in form and meaning to the Hebrew noun *rûah* (7307).

7309. רְוָחָה, *rᵉvâchâh, rev-aw-khaw´*; feminine of 7305; *relief*:—breathing, respite.

A feminine noun meaning breathing space, relief, respite. The term occurs only twice in the entire OT and is derived from the verb *râwah* (7304), meaning to breathe, to have breathing room, or to feel relief. In its first occurrence, the word denotes the alleviation that resulted from God's act of terminating the plague of frogs in Egypt (Ex 8:15[11]). The second use of the term involves a desperate cry to the Lord for deliverance and rest from merciless enemies (La 3:56).

7310. רְוָיָה, *rᵉvâyâh, rev-aw-yaw´*; from 7301; *satisfaction*:—runneth over, wealthy.

7311. רוּם, *rûwm, room*; a primitive root; to *be high;* (active) to *rise* or *raise* (in various applications, literal or figurative):—bring up, exalt (self), extol, give, go up, haughty; heave (up), (be, lift up on, make on, set up on, too) high (-er, one), hold up, levy, lift (-er) up, (be) lofty, (× a-) loud, mount up, offer (up), + presumptuously, (be) promote (-ion), proud, set up, tall (-er), take (away, off, up), breed worms.

7312. רוּם, **rûwm**, *room*; or רֻם, **rum**, *room*; from 7311; (literal) *elevation* or (figurative) *elation*:—haughtiness, height, × high.

7313. רוּם, **rûwm**, *room*; (Chaldee); corresponding to 7311; (figurative only):—extol, lift up (self), set up.

7314. רוּם, **rûwm**, *room*; (Chaldee); from 7313; (literal) *altitude*:—height.

7315. רוֹם, **rôwm**, *rome*; from 7311; *elevation*, i.e. (adverb) *aloft*:—on high.

7316. רוּמָה, **Rûwmâh**, *roo-maw´*; from 7311; *height*; *Rumah*, a place in Palestine:—Rumah.

7317. רוֹמָה, **rôwmâh**, *ro-maw´*; feminine of 7315; *elation*, i.e. (adverb) *proudly*:—haughtily.

7318. רוֹמָם, **rôwmam**, *ro-mam´*; from 7426; *exaltation*, i.e. (figurative and specific) *praise*:—be extolled.

7319. רוֹמְמָה, **rôwmᵉmâh**, *ro-mem-aw´*; feminine active participle of 7426; *exaltation*, i.e. *praise*:—high.

7320. רוֹמַמְתִּי עֶזֶר, **Rôwmamtîy 'Ezer** (or רֹמַמְתִּי **Rômamtîy**), *ro-mam´-tee eh´-zer*; from 7311 and 5828; *I have raised* up a *help*; *Romamti-Ezer*, an Israelite:—Romamti-ezer.

7321. רוּעַ, **rûwa'**, *roo-ah´*; a primitive root; to *mar* (especially by breaking); (figurative) to *split* the ears (with sound), i.e. *shout* (for alarm or joy):—blow an alarm, cry (alarm, aloud, out), destroy, make a joyful noise, smart, shout (for joy), sound an alarm, triumph.

A verb meaning to shout, to sound a blast. The term occurs thirty-three times in the OT and was utilized fundamentally to convey the action of shouting or the making of a loud noise. Shouting often took place just before a people or army rushed into battle against opposition; sometimes the war cry became the very signal used to commence engagement with the enemy (Jos 6:10, 16, 20; Jgs 15:14; 1Sa 4:5; 17:20;

2Ch 13:15). Many times the shout was a cry of joy, often in response to the Lord's creating or delivering activity on behalf of His people (Job 38:7; Ps 47:1[2]; 95:1, 2; Isa 44:23; Zep 3:14; Zec 9:9). In several other instances, the shout expressed triumph and victory over a foe (Ps 41:11[12]; 60:8[10]; 108:9[10]); and occasionally mourning (Isa 15:4; Mic 4:9). A few times, the term denotes the shout of a trumpet (i.e. the blast), usually as a signal to begin battle (Nu 10:9; 2Ch 13:12; cf. Hos 5:8; Joel 2:1).

7322. רוּף, **rûwph**, *roof*; a primitive root; (properly) to *triturate* (in a mortar), i.e. (figurative) to *agitate* (by concussion):—tremble.

7323. רוּץ, **rûwts**, *roots*; a primitive root; to *run* (for whatever reason, especially to *rush*):—break down, divide speedily, footman, guard, bring hastily, (make) run (away, through), post.

7324. רוּק, **rûwq**, *rook*; a primitive root; to *pour* out (literal or figurative), i.e. *empty*:— × arm, cast out, draw (out), (make) empty, pour forth (out).

7325. רוּר, **rûwr**, *roor*; a primitive root; to *slaver* (with spittle), i.e. (by analogy) to *emit* a fluid (ulcerous or natural):—run.

7326. רוּשׁ, **rûwsh**, *roosh*; a primitive root; to *be destitute*:—lack, needy, (make self) poor (man).

7327. רוּת, **Rûwth**, *rooth*; probably for 7468; *friend*; *Ruth*, a Moabitess:—Ruth.

7328. רָז, **râz**, *rawz*; (Chaldee); from an unused root probably meaning to *attenuate*, i.e. (figurative) *hide*; a *mystery*:—secret.

7329. רָזָה, **râzâh**, *raw-zaw´*; a primitive root; to *emaciate*, i.e. *make* (*become*) *thin* (literal or figurative):—famish, wax lean.

7330. רָזֶה, **râzeh**, *raw-zeh´*; from 7329; *thin*:—lean.

7331. רְזוֹן, **Rᵉzôwn**, *rez-one´*; from 7336; *prince*; *Rezon*, a Syrian:—Rezon.

7332. רָזוֹן, **râzôwn**, *raw-zone´*; from 7329; *thinness*:—leanness, × scant.

7333. רָזוֹן, **râzôwn**, *raw-zone´*; from 7336; a *dignitary*:—prince.

A masculine noun meaning a dignitary, a ruler, a prince. The term occurs once in the entire

OT in Pr 14:28 and is synonymous with the noun *melek* (4428), meaning king. The proverb states that what makes or breaks a prince is whether or not he has a multitude of subjects to rule over. The term is derived from the verb *râzan* (7336).

7334. רָזִי, **râzîy,** *raw-zee´*; from 7329; *thinness:*—leanness.

7335. רָזַם, **râzam,** *raw-zam´*; a primitive root; to *twinkle* the eye (in mockery):—wink.

7336. רָזַן, **râzan,** *raw-zan´*; a primitive root; probably to be *heavy,* i.e. (figurative) *honourable:*—prince, ruler.

A verb meaning to be heavy, to be weighty, to be honoured, to be mighty. The term also occurs six times as a noun, meaning rulers. Five times the word is used in conjunction with the Hebrew word for king (*melek* [4428]; Jgs 5:3; Ps 2:2; Pr 8:15; 31:4; Hab 1:10); and once with judge (a participle of the verb *shâphat*[8199]; Isa 40:23). Rulers were summoned to listen to Deborah's victory song (Jgs 5:3); warned to not conspire against the Lord and His anointed one (Ps 2:2); enabled by wisdom to decree just laws (Pr 8:15); abstained from strong drink (Pr 31:4); and were made as nothing by the Lord (Isa 40:23). The noun *râzôwn* (7333) is derived from this verb; also see the verb *kâbêd* (3513).

7337. רָחַב, **râchab,** *raw-khab´*; a primitive root; to *broaden* (intransitive or transitive, literal or figurative):—be an en- (make) large (-ing), make room, make (open) wide.

7338. רַחַב, **rachab,** *rakh´-ab*; from 7337; a *width:*—breadth, broad place.

7339. רְחֹב, **rᵉchôb,** *rekh-obe´*; or רְחוֹב, **rᵉchôwb,** *rekh-obe´*; from 7337; a *width,* i.e. (concrete) *avenue* or *area:*—broad place (way), street. See also 1050.

7340. רְחֹב, **Rᵉchôb,** *rekh-obe´*; or רְחוֹב, **Rᵉchôwb,** *rekh-obe´*; the same as 7339; *Rechob,* the name of a place in Syria, also of a Syrian and an Israelite:—Rehob.

7341. רֹחַב, **rôchab,** *ro´-khab*; from 7337; *width* (literal or figurative):—breadth, broad, largeness, thickness, wideness.

7342. רָחָב, **râchâb,** *raw-khawb´*; from 7337; *roomy,* in any (or every) direction, literal or figurative:—broad, large, at liberty, proud, wide.

7343. רָחָב, **Râchâb,** *raw-khawb´*; the same as 7342; *proud; Rachab,* a Canaanitess:—Rahab.

7344. רְחֹבוֹת, **Rᵉchôbôwth,** *rekh-o-bōth´*; or רְחֹבֹת, **Rechôbôth,** *rekh-o-bōth´*; plural of 7339; *streets; Rechoboth,* a place in Assyria and one in Palestine:—Rehoboth.

7345. רְחַבְיָה, **Rᵉchabyâh,** *rekh-ab-yaw´*; or רְחַבְיָהוּ, **Rechabyâhûw,** *rekh-ab-yaw´-hoo*; from 7337 and 3050; *Jah has enlarged; Rechabjah,* an Israelite:—Rehabiah.

7346. רְחַבְעָם, **Rᵉchab'âm,** *rekh-ab-awm´*; from 7337 and 5971; a *people has enlarged; Rechabam,* an Israelite king:—Rehoboam.

7347. רֵחֶה, **rêcheh,** *ray-kheh´*; from an unused root meaning to *pulverize;* a *mill*-stone:—mill (stone).

7348. רְחוּם, **Rᵉchûwm,** *rekh-oom´*; a form of 7349; *Rechum,* the name of a Persian and of three Israelites:—Rehum.

7349. רַחוּם, **rachûwm,** *rakh-oom´*; from 7355; *compassionate:*—full of compassion, merciful.

7350. רָחוֹק, **râchôwq,** *raw-khoke´*; or רָחֹק, **râchôq,** *raw-khoke´*; from 7368; *remote,* literal or figurative, of place or time; (specifically) *precious;* often used adverb (with preposition):—(a-) far (abroad, off), long ago, of old, space, great while to come.

7351. רְחִיט, **râchîyṭ,** *rekh-eet´*; from the same as 7298; a *panel* (as resembling a *trough*):—rafter.

7352. רַחִיק, **rachîyq,** *rakh-eek´*; (Chaldee); corresponding to 7350:—far.

7353. רָחֵל, **râchêl,** *raw-khale´*; from an unused root meaning to *journey;* a *ewe* [the *females* being the predominant element of a flock] (as a good *traveller*):—ewe, sheep.

7354. רָחֵל, **Râchêl,** *raw-khale´*; the same as 7353; *Rachel,* a wife of Jacob:—Rachel.

7355. רָחַם, **râcham,** *raw-kham´*; a primitive root; to *fondle;* (by implication) to *love,* especially to *compassionate:*—have compassion (on, upon), love, (find, have, obtain, shew) mercy (-iful, on, upon), (have) pity, Ruhamah, × surely.

A verb meaning to have compassion, to have mercy, to find mercy. The word pictures a deep, kindly sympathy and sorrow felt for another who has been struck with affliction or misfortune, accompanied with a desire to relieve the suffering. The word occurs forty-seven times in the OT, with God being by far the most common subject and His afflicted people the object (Dt 13:17[18]; 2Ki 13:23; Isa 14:1; 30:18; 60:10; Jer 12:15; 31:20; La 3:32). Though the Lord showed compassion, it was not because of any meritorious work the recipient had done; it was solely due to God's sovereign freedom to bestow it on whom He chose (Ex 33:19; cf. Ro 9:14–16). Two types of people God has sovereignly chosen to have mercy on include those who fear Him (Ps 103:13); and those who confess and forsake their sin (Pr 28:13).

7356. רֹחַם, **racham,** *rakh´-am*; from 7355; *compassion* (in the plural); (by extension) the *womb* (as *cherishing* the fetus); (by implication) a *maiden*:—bowels, compassion, damsel, tender love, (great, tender) mercy, pity, womb.

A feminine noun meaning womb, compassion, mercy, affection, maiden. The singular form of this word always signified the physical womb of a woman and was commonly used in this way (Ge 49:25). Yet when the plural form was used, the author had in mind the idea of compassion, tenderness, or mercy. The OT authors thought of the womb or bowels as the seat of warm and tender emotions. For example, when Joseph saw his brother Benjamin, he became overwhelmed with tender affection (lit., wombs [Ge 43:30]). Through the prophet Zechariah, the Lord commanded His people to show compassion to one another (Zec 7:9; cf. Dt 13:17 [18]; Ps 25:6; 103:4; Isa 47:6).

7357. רַחַם, **Racham,** *rakh´-am*; the same as 7356; *pity*; *Racham,* an Israelite:—Raham.

7358. רֶחֶם, **rechem,** *rekh´-em*; from 7355; the *womb* [compare 7356]:—matrix, womb.

7359. רַחֲמִין, **rachămîyn,** *ra-kha-meen´*; (Chaldee); corresponding to 7356; (plural) *pity*:—mercy.

7360. רָחָם, **râchâm,** *raw-khawm´*; or (feminine) רָחָמָה, **râchâmâh,** *raw-khaw-maw´*; from 7355; a kind of *vulture* (supposed to be *tender* toward its young):—gier-eagle.

7361. רַחֲמָה, **rachămâh,** *rakh-am-aw´*; feminine of 7356; a *maiden*:—damsel.

7362. רַחְמָנִי, **rachmânîy,** *rakh-maw-nee´*; from 7355; *compassionate*:—pitiful.

7363. רָחַף, **râchaph,** *raw-khaf´*; a primitive root; to *brood*; (by implication) to *be relaxed*:—flutter, move, shake.

7364. רָחַץ, **râchats,** *raw-khats´*; a primitive root; to *lave* (the whole or a part of a thing):—bathe (self), wash (self).

A verb meaning to wash off, to wash away, to bathe. This Hebrew word carries the connotation of washing with water in order to make clean. It describes the action involved in washing the hands or feet (Ex 30:19); the face (Ge 43:31); the body (2Sa 11:2); clothes (Le 14:9); or the parts of a sacrificial offering (Le 1:9). Symbolically, such a washing was declarative of innocence (Dt 21:6); and was figurative of cleansing from sin (Pr 30:12; Isa 4:4).

7365. רְחַץ, **rᵉchats,** *rekh-ats´*; (Chaldee); corresponding to 7364 [probably through the accessory idea of *ministering* as a servant at the bath]; to *attend* upon:—trust.

7366. רַחַץ, **rachats,** *rakh´-ats*; from 7364; a *bath*:—wash[-pot].

A masculine noun meaning washing. This word appears twice where it refers to a washing pot (Ps 60:8[10]; 108:9[10]). In both instances, it was a term of derision and was meant to convey a sense of utter contempt.

7367. רַחְצָה, **rachtsâh,** *rakh-tsaw´*; feminine of 7366; a *bathing* place:—washing.

A feminine noun meaning washing. The primary meaning of this word is found in its two uses in the SS of Solomon. Both times it referred to the bathing of sheep in water that caused them to be clean and white (SS 4:2; 6:6).

7368. רָחַק, **râchaq,** *raw-khak´*; a primitive root; to *widen* (in any direction), i.e. (intransitive) *recede* or (transitive) *remove* (literal or figurative, of place or relation):—(a-, be, cast, drive, get, go, keep [self], put, remove, be too, [wander], withdraw) far (away, off), loose, × refrain, very, (be) a good way (off).

7369. רָחֵק, **râchêq,** *raw-khake´*; from 7368; *remote*:—that are far.

7370. רָחַשׁ, **râchash,** *raw-khash´*; a primitive root; to *gush*:—indite.

7371. רַחַת, **rachath,** *rakh´-ath*; from 7306; a *winnowing*-fork (as *blowing* the chaff away):—shovel.

7372. רָטַב, **râṭab,** *raw-tab´*; a primitive root; to *be moist*:—be wet.

7373. רָטֹב, **râṭôb,** *raw-tobe´*; from 7372; *moist* (with sap):—green.

7374. רֶטֶט, **reṭeṭ,** *reh´-tet*; from an unused root meaning to *tremble; terror*:—fear.

A masculine noun meaning fear, trembling, panic. From an unused root meaning to tremble, this word is found only in Jer 49:24. It denoted fear or hysteria in the face of impending attack.

7375. רֻטֲפַשׁ, **ruṭăphash,** *roo-taf-ash´*; a root compounded from 7373 and 2954; to *be rejuvenated*:—be fresh.

7376. רָטַשׁ, **râṭash,** *raw-tash´*; a primitive root; to *dash* down:—dash (in pieces).

7377. רִי, **rîy,** *ree*; from 7301; *irrigation*, i.e. a shower:—watering.

7378. רִיב, **rîyb,** *reeb*; or רוּב, **rûwb,** *roob*; a primitive root; (properly) to *toss*, i.e. *grapple*; (mostly figurative) to *wrangle*, i.e. *hold a controversy*; (by implication) to *defend*:—adversary, chide, complain, contend, debate, × ever, × lay wait, plead, rebuke, strive, × thoroughly.

A verb meaning to strive, to contend, to dispute, and to conduct a lawsuit. The verb means to conduct a lawsuit or legal case and all that it involves. The Lord conducts His case against the leaders of His people (Isa 3:13). He relents in His case from accusing humankind, knowing how weak they are (Isa 57:16). David pleaded with the Lord to give him vindication in his case (1Sa 24:15[16]); as did Israel when God contended for them (Mic 7:9).

The word means to contend or to strive for some reason in a nonlegal setting as well. The servants of Isaac and Abimelech contended over wells they had dug or claimed to own (Ge 26:21). Two men could quarrel and come to blows (Ex 21:18; Jgs 11:25). Jacob and Laban disputed with one another (Ge 31:36). The peo-

ple of Israel complained bitterly against the Lord at Meribah (Nu 20:13).

The word means to raise complaints or accusations against others. The tribes of Israel complained because some of their women were taken and given as wives to the Benjamites (Jgs 21:22). An arrogant Israel would dare to bring charges against the Lord (Isa 45:9; Jer 2:29; 12:1). The tribe of Levi contended with the Lord at Meribah as well (Dt 33:8; cf. Nu 20:13).

The causative stem of this verb means to bring a case against (i.e. to oppose). The Lord will judge those who oppose Him (1Sa 2:10).

7379. רִיב, **rîyb,** *reeb*; or רִב, **rib,** *reeb*; from 7378; a *contest* (personal or legal):— + adversary, cause, chiding, contend (-tion), controversy, multitude [*from the margin*], pleading, strife, strive (-ing), suit.

A masculine noun meaning a strife, a controversy, a contention. The primary idea of this noun is that of a quarrel or dispute. It appears in reference to an argument over land-use rights (Ge 13:7); the logical dispute the Lord has with sinners (Jer 25:31); any general state of contention between individuals (Pr 20:3); the clamouring of people for station or possessions (2Sa 22:44); and open hostilities with an enemy (Jgs 12:2). Israel is commanded not to pervert justice in a lawsuit (Ex 23:2). Similarly, the word is used in a legal sense to refer to an argument or case made in one's defense (Dt 21:5; Pr 18:17; Mic 7:9).

7380. רִיבַי, **Rîybay,** *ree-bah´ee*; from 7378; *contentious; Ribai,* an Israelite:—Ribai.

7381. רֵיחַ, **rêyach,** *ray´-akh*; from 7306; *odor* (as if *blown*):—savour, scent, smell.

7382. רֵיחַ, **rêyach,** *ray´-akh*; (Chaldee); corresponding to 7381:—smell.

7383. רִיפָה, **rîyphâh,** *ree-faw´*; or רִפָה, **riphâh,** *ree-faw´*; from 7322; (only plural), *grits* (as *pounded*):—ground corn, wheat.

7384. רִיפַת, **Rîyphath,** *ree-fath´*; or (probably by orthographic error) דִּיפַת, **Dîyphath,** *dee-fath´*; of foreign origin; *Riphath,* a grandson of Japheth and his descendant:—Riphath.

7385. רִיק, **rîyq,** *reek*; from 7324; *emptiness*; (figurative) a *worthless* thing; (adverbial) *in vain*:—empty, to no purpose, (in) vain (thing), vanity.

7386. רִיק, **rêyq,** *rake;* or (shorter) רֵק, **rêq,** *rake;* from 7324; *empty;* (figurative) *worthless:*—emptied (-ty), vain (fellow, man).

7387. רֵיקָם, **rêyqâm,** *ray-kawm´;* from 7386; *emptily;* figurative (objective) *ineffectually,* (subjective) *undeservedly:*—without cause, empty, in vain, void.

7388. רִיר, **rîyr,** *reer;* from 7325; *saliva;* (by resemblance) *broth:*—spittle, white [of an egg].

7389. רֵישׁ, **rêysh,** *raysh;* or רֹאשׁ, **rê'sh,** *raysh;* or רִישׁ, **rîysh,** *reesh;* from 7326; *poverty:*—poverty.

7390. רַךְ, **rak,** *rak;* from 7401; *tender* (literal or figurative); (by implication) *weak:*—faint [-hearted], soft, tender ([-hearted], one), weak.

7391. רֹךְ, **rôk,** *roke;* from 7401; *softness* (figurative):—tenderness.

7392. רָכַב, **râkab,** *raw-kab´;* a primitive root; to *ride* (on an animal or in a vehicle); (causative) to *place upon* (for riding or general), to *despatch:*—bring (on [horse-] back), carry, get [oneself] up, on [horse-] back, put, (cause to, make to) ride (in a chariot, on, -r), set.

7393. רֶכֶב, **rekeb,** *reh´-keb;* from 7392; a *vehicle;* (by implication) a *team;* (by extension) *cavalry;* (by analogy) a *rider,* i.e. the upper millstone:—chariot, (upper) millstone, multitude [*from the margin*], wagon.

7394. רֵכָב, **Rêkâb,** *ray-kawb´;* from 7392; *rider; Rekab,* the name of two Arabs and of two Israelites:—Rechab.

7395. רַכָּב, **rakkâb,** *rak-kawb´;* from 7392; a *charioteer:*—chariot man, driver of a chariot, horseman.

7396. רִכְבָּה, **rikbâh,** *rik-baw´;* feminine of 7393; a *chariot* (collective):—chariots.

7397. רֵכָה, **Rêkâh,** *ray-kaw´;* probably feminine from 7401; *softness; Rekah,* a place in Palestine:—Rechah.

7398. רְכוּב, **rᵉkûwb,** *rek-oob´;* from passive participle of 7392; a *vehicle* (as *ridden* on):—chariot.

7399. רְכוּשׁ, **rᵉkûwsh,** *rek-oosh´;* or רְכֻשׁ, **rᵉkush,** *rek-oosh´;* from passive participle of 7408; *property* (as *gathered*):—good, riches, substance.

7400. רָכִיל, **râkîyl,** *raw-keel´;* from 7402; a *scandal-monger* (as *travelling* about):—slander, carry tales, talebearer.

7401. רָכַךְ, **râkak,** *raw-kak´;* a primitive root; to *soften* (intransitive or transitive), used figuratively:—(be) faint ([-hearted]), mollify, (be, make) soft (-er), be tender.

7402. רָכַל, **râkal,** *raw-kal´;* a primitive root; to *travel* for trading:—(spice) merchant.

7403. רָכָל, **Râkâl,** *raw-kawl´;* from 7402; *merchant; Rakal,* a place in Palestine:—Rachal.

7404. רְכֻלָּה, **rᵉkullâh,** *rek-ool-law´;* feminine passive participle of 7402; *trade* (as *peddled*):—merchandise, traffic.

7405. רָכַס, **râkas,** *raw-kas´;* a primitive root; to *tie:*—bind.

7406. רֶכֶס, **rekes,** *reh´-kes;* from 7405; a *mountain ridge* (as of *tied* summits):—rough place.

7407. רֹכֶס, **rôkes,** *ro´-kes;* from 7405; a *snare* (as of *tied* meshes):—pride.

7408. רָכַשׁ, **râkash,** *raw-kash´;* a primitive root; to *lay up,* i.e. collect:—gather, get.

7409. רֶכֶשׁ, **rekesh,** *reh´-kesh;* from 7408; a *relay* of animals on a post-route (as *stored* up for that purpose); (by implication) a *courser:*—dromedary, mule, swift beast.

7410. רָם, **Râm,** *rawm;* active participle of 7311; *high; Ram,* the name of an Arabian and of an Israelite:—Ram. See also 1027.

7411. רָמָה, **râmâh,** *raw-maw´;* a primitive root; to *hurl;* (specifically) to *shoot;* (figurative) to *delude* or *betray* (as if causing to *fall*):—beguile, betray, [bow-] man, carry, deceive, throw.

7412. רְמָה, **rᵉmâh,** *rem-aw´;* (Chaldee); corresponding to 7411; to *throw, set,* (figurative) *assess:*—cast (down), impose.

7413. רָמָה, **râmâh,** *raw-maw´;* feminine active participle of 7311; a *height* (as a seat of idolatry):—high place.

7414. רָמָה, **Râmâh,** *raw-maw´;* the same as 7413; *Ramah,* the name of four places in Palestine:—Ramah.

7415. רִמָּה, **rimmâh,** *rim-maw´*; from 7426 in the sense of *breeding* [compare 7311]; a *maggot* (as rapidly *bred*), literal or figurative:—worm.

7416. רִמּוֹן, **rimmôwn,** *rim-mone´*; or רִמֹּן, **rimmôn,** *rim-mone´*; from 7426; a *pomegranate*, the tree (from its *upright* growth) or the fruit (also an artificial ornament):—pomegranate.

7417. רִמּוֹן, **Rimmôwn,** *rim-mone´*; or (shorter) רִמֹּן, **Rimmôn,** *rim-mone´*; or רִמּוֹנוֹ, **Rimmôwnôw,** *rim-mo-no´*; (1Ch 6:62 [777]), the same as 7416 *Rimmon*, the name of a Syrian deity, also of five places in Palestine:—Remmon, Rimmon. The addition "-methoar" (Jos 19:13) is הַמְּתֹאָר **ham-mᵉthô´âr,** *ham-meth-o-awr´*; passive participle of 8388 with the article; *the* (one) *marked off*, i.e. *which pertains*; mistaken for part of the name.

7418. רָמוֹת־נֶגֶב, **Râmôwth-Negeb,** *raw-môth´neh´-gheb*; or רָמַת נֶגֶב, **Râmath Negeb,** *raw´-math neh´-gheb*; from the plural or construct of 7413 and 5045; *heights* (or *height*) *of* the *South*; *Ramoth-Negeb* or *Ramath-Negeb*, a place in Palestine:—south Ramoth, Ramath of the south.

7419. רָמוּת, **râmûwth,** *raw-mooth´*; from 7311; a *heap* (of carcases):—height.

7420. רֹמַח, **rômach,** *ro´-makh*; from an unused root meaning to *hurl*; a *lance* (as *thrown*); especially the iron *point*:—buckler, javelin, lancet, spear.

7421. רַמִּי, **rammîy,** *ram-mee´*; for 761; a *Ramite*, i.e. Aramæan:—Syrian.

7422. רִמְיָה, **Ramyâh,** *ram-yaw´*; from 7311 and 3050; *Jah has raised; Ramjah,* an Israelite:—Ramiah.

7423. רְמִיָּה, **rᵉmîyyâh,** *rem-ee-yaw´*; from 7411; *remissness, treachery*:—deceit (-ful, -fully), false, guile, idle, slack, slothful.

7424. רַמָּךְ, **rammâk,** *ram-mawk´*; of foreign origin; a brood *mare*:—dromedary.

7425. רְמַלְיָהוּ, **Rᵉmalyâhûw,** *rem-al-yaw´-hoo*; from an unused root and 3050 (perhaps meaning to *deck*); *Jah has bedecked; Remaljah,* an Israelite:—Remaliah.

7426. רָמַם, **râmam,** *raw-mam´*; a primitive root; to *rise* (literal or figurative):—exalt, get [oneself] up, lift up (self), mount up.

7427. רֹמֵמֻת, **rômêmuth,** *ro-may-mooth´*; from the active participle of 7426; *exaltation*:—lifting up of self.

7428. רִמֹּן פֶּרֶץ, **Rimmôn Perets,** *rim-mone´ peh´-rets*; from 7416 and 6556; *pomegranate of* the *breach; Rimmon-Perets,* a place in the Desert:—Rimmon-parez.

7429. רָמַס, **râmas,** *raw-mas´*; a primitive root; to *tread* upon (as a potter, in walking or abusively):—oppressor, stamp, upon, trample (under feet), tread (down, upon).

7430. רָמַשׂ, **râmaś,** *raw-mas´*; a primitive root; (properly) to *glide* swiftly, i.e. to *crawl* or *move* with short steps; (by analogy) to *swarm*:—creep, move.

7431. רֶמֶשׂ, **remeś,** *reh´-mes*; from 7430; a *reptile* or any other rapidly moving animal:—that creepeth, creeping (moving) thing.

7432. רֶמֶת, **Remeth,** *reh´-meth*; from 7411; *height; Remeth,* a place in Palestine:—Remeth.

7433. רָמֹת (or רָמוֹת **Râmôwth**) גִּלְעָד **Râmôth Gilʻâd** (2Ch 22:5), *raw-môth´ gil-awd´*; from the plural of 7413 and 1568; *heights of Gilad; Ramoth-Gilad,* a place East of the Jordan:—Ramoth-gilead, Ramoth in Gilead. See also 7216.

7434. רָמַת הַמִּצְפֶּה, **Râmath ham-Mitspeh,** *raw-math´ ham-mits-peh´*; from 7413 and 4707 with the article interposed; *height of the watch-tower; Ramath-ham-Mitspeh,* a place in Palestine:—Ramath-mizpeh.

7435. רָמָתִי, **Râmâthîy,** *raw-maw-thee´*; patronymic of 7414; a *Ramathite* or inhabitant of Ramah:—Ramathite.

7436. רָמָתַיִם צוֹפִים, **Râmâthayim Tsôwphîym,** *raw-maw-thah´-yim tso-feem´*; from the dual of 7413 and the plural of the active participle of 6822; *double height of watchers; Ramathajim-Tsophim,* a place in Palestine:—Ramathaim-zophim.

7437. רָמַת לֶחִי, **Râmath Lechîy,** *raw´-math lekh´-ee*; from 7413 and 3895; *height of* a *jawbone; Ramath-Lechi,* a place in Palestine:—Ramath-lehi.

7438. רֹן, **rôn,** *rone*; from 7442; a *shout* (of deliverance):—song.

7439. רָנָה, **rânâh,** *raw-naw´*; a primitive root; to *whiz:*—rattle.

7440. רִנָּה, **rinnâh,** *rin-naw´*; from 7442; (properly) a *creaking* (or shrill sound), i.e. *shout* (of joy or grief):—cry, gladness, joy, proclamation, rejoicing, shouting, sing (-ing), triumph.

7441. רִנָּה, **Rinnâh,** *rin-naw´*; the same as 7440; *Rinnah,* an Israelite:—Rinnah.

7442. רָנַן, **rânan,** *raw-nan´*; a primitive root; (properly) to *creak* (or emit a stridulous sound), i.e. to *shout* (usually for joy):—aloud for joy, cry out, be joyful, (greatly, make to) rejoice, (cause to) shout (for joy), (cause to) sing (aloud, for joy, out), triumph.

7443. רֶנֶן, **renen,** *reh´-nen*; from 7442; an *ostrich* (from its *wail*):— × goodly.

7444. רַנֵּן, **rannên,** *ran-nane´*; intensive from 7442; *shouting* (for joy):—singing.

7445. רְנָנָה, **reʻnânâh,** *ren-aw-naw´*; from 7442; a *shout* (for joy):—joyful (voice), singing, triumphing.

7446. רִסָּה, **Rissâh,** *ris-saw´*; from 7450; a *ruin* (as *dripping* to pieces); *Rissah,* a place in the Desert:—Rissah.

7447. רָסִיס, **râsîys,** *raw-sees´*; from 7450; (properly) *dripping* to pieces, i.e. a *ruin* also a dew-drop:—breach, drop.

7448. רֶסֶן, **resen,** *reh´-sen*; from an unused root meaning to *curb*; a *halter* (as *restraining*); (by implication) the *jaw:*—bridle.

7449. רֶסֶן, **Resen,** *reh´-sen*; the same as 7448; *Resen,* a place in Assyria:—Resen.

7450. רָסַס, **râsas,** *raw-sas´*; a primitive root; to *comminute;* used only as denominative from 7447, to *moisten* (with drops):—temper.

7451. רַע, **raʻ,** *rah*; from 7489; *bad* or (as noun) *evil* (natural or moral):—adversity, affliction, bad, calamity, + displease (-ure), distress, evil ([-favouredness], man, thing), + exceedingly, × great, grief (-vous), harm, heavy, hurt (-ful), ill (favoured), + mark, mischief (-vous), misery, naught (-ty), noisome, + not please, sad (-ly), sore, sorrow, trouble, vex, wicked (-ly, -ness, one), worse (-st), wretchedness, wrong.

[Including feminine רָעָה, **râ'âh,** *raw-aw´*; as adjective or noun.]

An adjective meaning bad, evil. The basic meaning of this word displays ten or more various shades of the meaning of evil according to its contextual usage. It means bad in a moral and ethical sense and is used to describe, along with good, the entire spectrum of good and evil; hence, it depicts evil in an absolute, negative sense, as when it describes the tree of the knowledge of good and evil (Ge 2:9; 3:5, 22). It was necessary for a wise king to be able to discern the evil or the good in the actions of his people (Ecc 12:14); men and women are characterized as evil (1Sa 30:22; Est 7:6; Jer 2:33). The human heart is evil all day long (Ge 6:5) from childhood (Ge 8:21); yet the people of God are to purge evil from among them (Dt 17:7). The Lord is the final arbiter of whether something was good or evil; if something was evil in the eyes of the Lord, there is no further court of appeals (Dt 9:18; 1Ki 14:22). The day of the Lord's judgment is called an evil day, a day of reckoning and condemnation (Am 6:3). Jacob would have undergone grave evil (i.e. pain, misery, and ultimate disaster) if he had lost Benjamin (Ge 44:34). The word can refer to circumstances as evil, as when the Israelite foremen were placed in a grave situation (Ex 5:19; 2Ki 14:10).

The word takes on the aspect of something disagreeable, unwholesome, or harmful. Jacob evaluated his life as evil and destructive (Ge 47:9; Nu 20:5); and the Israelites considered the wilderness as a threatening, terrifying place. The Canaanite women were evil in the eyes of Isaac (i.e. displeasing [Ge 28:8]). The rabble's cry within Israel for meat was displeasing in the eyes of Moses (Nu 11:10). This word describes the vicious animal that killed Joseph, so Jacob thought (Ge 37:33). The despondent countenances of persons can be described by this word; the baker's and the butler's faces were downcast because of their dreams (Ge 40:7). It can also describe one who is heavy in heart (Pr 25:20).

In a literal sense, the word depicts something that is of poor quality or even ugly in appearance. The weak, lean cows of Pharaoh's dream were decrepit, ugly-looking (Ge 41:3, 20, 27); poisonous drinking water was described as bad (2Ki 2:19; 4:41). From these observations, it is clear that the word can be used to attribute a negative aspect to nearly anything.

Used as a noun, the word indicates realities that are inherently evil, wicked, or bad; the psalmist feared no evil (Ps 23:4). The noun also depicts people of wickedness, that is, wicked people. Aaron characterized the people of Israel as inherently wicked in order to clear himself (Ex 32:22). Calamities, failures, and miseries are all connotations of this word when it is used as a noun.

7452. רֵעַ, **rêa‘**, rah´-ah; from 7321; a *crash* (of thunder), *noise* (of war), *shout* (of joy):— × aloud, noise, shouted.

7453. רֵעַ, **rêa‘**, ray´-ah; or רֵיעַ, **rêya‘**, ray´-ah; from 7462; an *associate* (more or less close):— brother, companion, fellow, friend, husband, lover, neighbour, × (an-) other.

A masculine noun meaning another person. Most frequently, this term is used to refer to the second party in a personal interaction without indicating any particular relationship (Ge 11:7; Jgs 7:13, 14; Ru 3:14). It is extremely broad, covering everyone from a lover (Hos 3:1); a close friend (Job 2:11); an acquaintance (Pr 6:1); an adversary in court (Ex 18:16); an enemy in combat (2Sa 2:16). Thus, this word is well-suited for its widely inclusive use in the Ten Commandments (see Ex 20:16, 17; Dt 5:20, 21; cf. Lk 10:29–37).

7454. רֵעַ, **rêa‘**, ray´-ah; from 7462; a *thought* (as *association* of ideas):—thought.

7455. רֹעַ, **rôa‘**, ro´-ah; from 7489; *badness* (as *marring*), physical or moral:— × be so bad, badness, (× be so) evil, naughtiness, sadness, sorrow, wickedness.

A masculine noun meaning badness, evil. This word is used to depict the quality of meat and produce (Ge 41:19, Jer 24:2, 3, 8). In Genesis, the word is used to describe cows, while in Jeremiah it describes figs. Eliab, David's oldest brother, describes David as conceited with a wicked heart, for he claims that David left the sheep only to come and watch the battle (1Sa 17:28). *Rôa‘* is also used as a reason for punishment or for the wrath of God (i.e. for evil that had been done [Dt 28:20; Isa 1:16; Jer 4:4; 21:12]). This word is also used to denote sadness or sorrow (Ecc 7:3). In Ecclesiastes, the

author states that sorrow is better than laughter, for a sad face is good for the heart.

7456. רָעֵב, **râ‘êb**, raw-abe´; a primitive root; to *hunger*:—(suffer to) famish, (be, have, suffer, suffer to) hunger (-ry).

7457. רָעֵב, **râ‘êb**, raw-abe´; from 7456; *hungry* (more or less intensely):—hunger bitten, hungry.

7458. רָעָב, **râ‘âb**, raw-awb´; from 7456; *hunger* (more or less extensive):—dearth, famine, + famished, hunger.

7459. רְעָבוֹן, **re‘âbôwn**, reh-aw-bone´; from 7456; *famine*:—famine.

7460. רָעַד, **râ‘ad**, raw-ad´; a primitive root; to *shudder* (more or less violently):—tremble.

A verb meaning to tremble, to quake. The psalmist uses the word in a description of the holiness, majesty, and power of God, where the earth is depicted as trembling at the mere gaze of the Lord (Ps 104:32). Daniel trembled in fear and reverence at the sight and presence of the vision before he heard the words that the messenger had been sent to deliver (Da 10:11).

7461. רַעַד, **ra‘ad**, rah´-ad; or (feminine) רְעָדָה, **re‘âdâh**, reh-aw-daw´; from 7460; a *shudder*:— trembling.

A masculine noun meaning trembling. In the song of Moses and Miriam, the leaders of Moab were described as being seized with trembling before the power of the Lord (Ex 15:15). In a cry to God, the psalmist uses the word to state that fear and trembling had bent him (Ps 55:5[6]). He cried out for God to come to his rescue and deliver him from his enemies.

7462. רָעָה, **râ‘âh**, raw-aw´; a primitive root; to *tend* a flock, i.e. *pasture* it; (intransitive) to *graze* (literal or figurative); (generally) to *rule*; (by extension) to *associate* with (as a friend):— × break, companion, keep company with, devour, eat up, evil entreat, feed, use as a friend, make friendship with, herdman, keep [sheep] (-er), pastor, + shearing house, shepherd, wander, waste.

7463. רֵעֶה, **rê‘eh**, ray-eh´; from 7462; a (male) *companion*:—friend.

7464. רֵעָה, **rê‘âh**, ray´-aw; feminine of 7453; a female *associate*:—companion, fellow.

7465. רֹעָה, **rô'âh,** *ro-aw´*; for 7455; *breakage:*—broken, utterly.

7466. רְעוּ, **Reʿûw,** *reh-oo´*; for 7471 in the sense of 7453; *friend; Reü,* a postdiluvian patriarch:—Reu.

7467. רְעוּאֵל, **Reʿûw'êl,** *reh-oo-ale´*; from the same as 7466 and 410; *friend of God; Reüel,* the name of Moses' father-in-law, also of an Edomite and an Israelite:—Raguel, Reuel.

7468. רְעוּת, **reʿûwth,** *reh-ooth´*; from 7462 in the sense of 7453; a female *associate*; (generally) an *additional* one:— + another, mate, neighbour.

A feminine noun meaning a fellow woman, an associate. In Jeremiah, the women were to teach one another (i.e. their associates or companions) a lament (Jer 19:20[19]). Isaiah used the word to denote the mates of falcons or birds of prey (Isa 34:15, 16). In a figurative use, Zechariah used the word to denote that the people who remained would be left to eat one another's flesh (Zec 11:9). In Esther, King Xerxes was advised to make a decree stating that Vashti was never again to enter his presence and that her position was to be given to one of her associates that was better than she was (Est 1:19).

7469. רְעוּת, **reʿûwth,** *reh-ooth´*; probably from 7462; a *feeding* upon, i.e. grasping after:—vexation.

7470. רְעוּ, **reʿûw,** *reh-oo´*; (Chaldee); corresponding to 7469; *desire:*—pleasure, will.

7471. רְעִי, **reʿîy,** *reh-ee´*; from 7462; *pasture:*—pasture.

7472. רֵעִי, **Rêʿîy,** *ray-ee´*; from 7453; *social; Reï,* an Israelite:—Rei.

7473. רֹעִי, **rôʿîy,** *ro-ee´*; from active participle of 7462; *pastoral*; as noun, a *shepherd:*—shepherd.

7474. רַעְיָה, **raʿyâh,** *rah-yaw´*; feminine of 7453; a female *associate:*—fellow, love.

7475. רַעְיוֹן, **raʿyôwn,** *rah-yone´*; from 7462 in the sense of 7469; *desire:*—vexation.

7476. רַעְיוֹן, **raʿyôwn,** *rah-yone´*; (Chaldee); corresponding to 7475; a *grasp,* i.e. (figurative) mental *conception:*—cogitation, thought.

7477. רָעַל, **râʿal,** *raw-al´*; a primitive root; to *reel,* i.e. (figurative) to *brandish:*—terribly shake.

7478. רַעַל, **raʿal,** *rah´-al*; from 7477; a *reeling* (from intoxication):—trembling.

7479. רַעֲלָה, **reʿâlâh,** *reh-aw-law´*; feminine of 7478; a long *veil* (as *fluttering*):—muffler.

7480. רְעֵלָיָה, **Reʿêlâyâh,** *reh-ay-law-yaw´*; from 7477 and 3050; *made to tremble* (i.e. *fearful*) of *Jah; Reëlajah,* an Israelite:—Reeliah.

7481. רָעַם, **râʿam,** *raw-am´*; a primitive root; to *tumble,* i.e. *be* violently *agitated*; (specifically) to *crash* (of thunder); (figurative) to *irritate* (with anger):—make to fret, roar, thunder, trouble.

7482. רַעַם, **raʿam,** *rah´-am*; from 7481; a *peal* of thunder:—thunder.

7483. רַעְמָה, **raʿmâh,** *rah-maw´*; feminine of 7482; the *mane* of a horse (as *quivering* in the wind):—thunder.

7484. רַעְמָה, **Raʿmâh,** *rah-maw´*; the same as 7483; *Ramah,* the name of a grandson of Ham, and of a place (perhaps founded by him):—Raamah.

7485. רַעַמְיָה, **Raʿamyâh,** *rah-am-yaw´*; from 7481 and 3050; *Jah has shaken; Ramjah,* an Israelite:—Raamiah.

7486. רַעְמְסֵס, **Raʿmesês,** *rah-mes-ace´*; or רַעַמְסֵס, **Raʿamsês,** *rah-am-sace´*; of Egyptian origin; *Rameses* or *Raamses,* a place in Egypt:—Raamses, Rameses.

7487. רַעֲנַן, **raʿănan,** *rah-aw-nan´*; (Chaldee); corresponding to 7488; *green,* i.e. (figurative) *prosperous:*—flourishing.

7488. רַעֲנָן, **raʿănân,** *rah-an-awn´*; from an unused root meaning to *be green; verdant*; (by analogy) *new*; (figurative) *prosperous:*—green, flourishing.

7489. רָעַע, **râʿaʿ,** *raw-ah´*; a primitive root; (properly) to *spoil* (literally, by *breaking* to pieces); (figurative) to *make* (or *be*) *good for nothing,* i.e. *bad* (physically, socially or morally):—afflict, associate selves [*by mistake for* 7462], break (down, in pieces), + displease, (be, bring, do) evil (doer, entreat, man), show self friendly [*by mistake for* 7462], do harm, (do) hurt, (behave self, deal) ill, × indeed, do mischief, punish, still, vex, (do) wicked (doer, -ly), be (deal, do) worse.

A verb meaning to be bad, to do wrong. The root of the word indicates breaking, in contrast to the word *tâmam* (8552), which means to be whole. For example, tree branches that break are bad (Jer 11:16). The word also refers to moral evil: an eye could be evil, that is, covetous (Dt 15:9); or a person could do evil (Ge 44:5; Pr 4:16; Jer 4:22). The word also refers to physical evil: God harmed or punished those who provoked Him (Zec 8:14); and Laban would have hurt Jacob without God's prevention (Ge 31:7). In addition, the word expresses sadness and describes the face or heart as being bad (1Sa 1:8; Ne 2:3). The causative participle signifies an evildoer (Ps 37:1; Isa 9:17[16]). The idiomatic phrase, to be evil in someone's eyes, means to displease (Ge 48:17; 2Sa 11:25; Jnh 4:1).

7490. רְעַע, **rᵉʿaʿ**, *reh-ah´*; (Chaldee); corresponding to 7489:—break, bruise.

An Aramaic verb meaning to break in pieces, to shatter, to crush. The term occurs only twice in the OT; both are located within the same passage in the book of Daniel. In interpreting King Nebuchadnezzar's dream, Daniel declared that the fourth kingdom, represented by the legs of iron and feet of iron mixed with clay of the statue, would be as strong as iron and would break the previously mentioned kingdoms into pieces (Da 2:40). This term is closely related to the Hebrew verb *râ'a'* (7489).

7491. רָעַף, **râ'aph**, *raw-af´*; a primitive root; to drip:—distil, drop (down).

7492. רָעַץ, **râ'ats**, *raw-ats´*; a primitive root; to break in pieces; (figurative) harass:—dash in pieces, vex.

7493. רָעַשׁ, **râ'ash**, *raw-ash*; a primitive root; to undulate (as the earth, the sky, etc.; also a field of grain), particularly through fear; (specifically) to spring (as a locust):—make afraid, (re-) move, quake, (make to) shake, (make to) tremble.

A verb meaning to quake, to tremble, to shake, to leap, to be abundant. The word occurs thirty times in the OT and most often refers to the physical, forceful (often violent), quick, back-and-forth movement of a physical body by an outside force. Frequently, the trembling or shaking takes place as nature's response to God's presence or to His activity of rendering divine judgment. Things shaken included the walls of a city (Eze 26:10); the thresholds of doors (Am 9:1); the heavens (Joel 2:10,

3:16[4:16]; Hag 2:6); the mountains (Jer 4:24; Na 1:5); coastlands or islands (Eze 26:15); kingdoms (Isa 14:16); the earth or lands (Jgs 5:4; 2Sa 22:8; Ps 60:2[4]; 68:8[9]; 77:18[19]; Isa 13:13; Jer 8:16; 10:10; 49:21); Gentile nations (Eze 31:16; Hag 2:7); and every living creature of creation (Eze 38:20). Twice the term conveys a much different action than the one related above. In the first rare usage, the verb portrays the leaping ability of a warhorse (Job 39:20). The second unique use expresses the psalmist's desire that there be an abundance of grain in the land (Ps 72:16).

7494. רַעַשׁ, **ra'ash**, *rah´-ash*; from 7493; vibration, bounding, uproar:—commotion, confused noise, earthquake, fierceness, quaking, rattling, rushing, shaking.

7495. רָפָא, **râphâ'**, *raw-faw´*; or רָפָה, **râphâh**, *raw-faw´*; a primitive root; (properly) to mend (by stitching), i.e. (figurative) to cure:—cure, (cause to) heal, physician, repair, × thoroughly, make whole. See 7503.

7496. רָפָא, **râphâ'**, *raw-faw´*; from 7495 in the sense of 7503; (properly) lax; i.e. (figurative) a ghost (as dead; in plural only):—dead, deceased.

A masculine noun meaning shades, departed spirits, deceased ones, dead ones. The term always occurs in the plural form (*rᵉphâ'iym*) and consistently denotes those who died and entered into a shadowy existence within *shᵉ'ôwl* (7585) (Job 26:5; Pr 9:18; Isa 14:9). Three times the word is employed in direct parallelism with the Hebrew term for dead ones (*mᵉthiym*, from *mûth* [4191], to die) (Ps 88:10[11]; Isa 26:14, 19). "Shades" or deceased ones do not rise (Isa 26:14). They reside in a place of darkness and oblivion (Ps 88:10[11]). They cannot praise God (Ps 88:10 [11]). The smooth words of the adulteress bring her victims down to death, to the place of the shades, never to return (Pr 21:16; cf. Pr 2:16–19; 9:13–18). Yet even in the OT, a confident resurrection hope was gloriously and joyously held out to those in Sheol who obeyed God while alive (Isa 26:19).

7497. רָפָא, **râphâ'**, *raw-faw´*; or רָפָה, **râphâh**, *raw-faw´*; from 7495 in the sense of invigorating; a giant:—giant, Rapha, Rephaim (-s). See also 1051.

A masculine noun meaning a giant, Rephaim (an ethnic people group), Valley of Rephaim. Frequently, the term (only with the plural form) designated a Canaanite tribe that inhabited the Promised Land prior to the Hebrew conquest and who were known for their unusually large size (Ge 14:5; 15:20; Dt 2:11, 20; 3:11, 13; Jos 12:4; 13:12; 17:15). In two accounts, the singular form was utilized to refer to a particular giant, perhaps an ancestor of the tribe of the Rephaim (2Sa 21:16, 18, 20, 22; 1Ch 20:6, 8). In a different vein, the word (also only in the plural form) acted as the proper name of a valley located southwest of Jerusalem (Jos 15:8; 18:16; 2Sa 5:18, 22; 23:13; 1Ch 11:15; 14:9; Isa 17:5).

7498. רָפָא, **Râphâ',** *raw-faw'*; or רָפָה, **Râphâh,** *raw-faw'*; probably the same as 7497; *giant; Rapha* or *Raphah,* the name of two Israelites:— Rapha.

7499. רְפוּאָה, **rᵉphûw'âh,** *ref-oo-aw'*; feminine passive participle of 7495; a *medicament:*—heal [-ed], medicine.

7500. רִפְאוּת, **riph'ûwth,** *rif-ooth'*; from 7495; a *cure:*—health.

7501. רְפָאֵל, **Rᵉphâ'êl,** *ref-aw-ale'*; from 7495 and 410; *God has cured; Rephaël,* an Israelite:— Rephael.

7502. רָפַד, **râphad,** *raw-fad'*; a primitive root; to *spread* (a bed); (by implication) to *refresh:*— comfort, make [a bed], spread.

7503. רָפָה, **râphâh,** *raw-faw'*; a primitive root; to *slacken* (in many applications, literal or figurative):—abate, cease, consume, draw [toward evening], fail, (be) faint, be (wax) feeble, forsake, idle, leave, let alone (go, down), (be) slack, stay, be still, be slothful, (be) weak (-en). See 7495.

A verb meaning to become slack, to relax, to cease, to desist, to become discouraged, to become disheartened, to become weak, to become feeble, to let drop, to discourage, to leave alone, to let go, to forsake, to abandon, to be lazy. The word occurs forty-five times, often with the word *yâd* (3027), meaning hand, forming an idiomatic phrase that requires careful translation within the context of a particular passage. For example, when Ish-Bosheth, Saul's son, heard that Abner had died, his hands

became feeble, i.e. his courage failed him (2Sa 4:1; cf. 2Ch 15:7; Isa 13:7; Jer 6:24, 50:43; Eze 7:17; 21:7[12]). The term was also employed to signify the act of ceasing from something (Jgs 8:3; 2Sa 24:16; Ne 6:9; Ps 37:8); of leaving some- one alone (Ex 4:26; Dt 9:14; Jgs 11:37; Job 7:19); of letting go (Job 27:6; Pr 4:13; SS 3:4); and of abandoning or forsaking someone (Dt 4:31; 31:6, 8; Jos 1:5; 10:6; Ps 138:8). On rare occa- sions, the term conveyed a state of laziness or complacency (Ex 5:8, 17; Jos 18:3; Pr 18:9).

7504. רָפֶה, **râpheh,** *raw-feh'*; from 7503; *slack* (in body or mind):—weak.

7505. רָפוּא, **Râphûw',** *raw-foo'*; passive partici- ple of 7495; *cured; Raphu,* an Israelite:—Raphu.

7506. רֶפַח, **Rephach,** *reh'-fakh*; from an unused root apparently meaning to *sustain; support; Rephach,* an Israelite:—Rephah.

7507. רְפִידָה, **rᵉphîydâh,** *ref-ee-daw'*; from 7502; a *railing* (as *spread* along):—bottom.

7508. רְפִידִים, **Rᵉphîydîym,** *ref-ee-deem'*; plural of the masculine of the same as 7507; *ballusters; Rephidim,* a place in the Desert:—Rephidim.

7509. רְפָיָה, **Rᵉphâyâh,** *ref-aw-yaw'*; from 7495 and 3050; *Jah has cured; Rephajah,* the name of five Israelites:—Rephaiah.

7510. רִפְיוֹן, **riphyôwn,** *rif-yone'*; from 7503; *slackness:*—feebleness.

7511. רָפַס, **râphas,** *raw-fas'*; a primitive root; to *trample,* i.e. *prostrate:*—humble self, submit self.

7512. רְפַס, **rᵉphas,** *ref-as'*; (Chaldee); corre- sponding to 7511:—stamp.

7513. רַפְסֹדָה, **raphsôdâh,** *raf-so-daw'*; from 7511; a *raft* (as *flat* on the water):—flote.

7514. רָפַק, **râphaq,** *raw-fak'*; a primitive root; to *recline:*—lean.

7515. רָפַשׂ, **râphaś,** *raw-fas'*; a primitive root; to *trample,* i.e. *roil* water:—foul, trouble.

7516. רֶפֶשׂ, **rephesh,** *reh'-fesh*; from 7515; *mud* (as *roiled*):—mire.

7517. רֶפֶת, **repheth,** *reh'-feth*; probably from 7503; a *stall* for cattle (from their *resting* there):—stall.

7518. רַץ, **rats,** *rats*; contracted from 7533; a *fragment:*—piece.

7519. רָצָא, **râtsâ',** *raw-tsaw'*; a primitive root; to *run*; also to *delight* in:—accept, run.

7520. רָצַד, **râtsad,** *raw-tsad'*; a primitive root; probably to *look askant,* i.e. (figurative) *be jealous:*—leap.

7521. רָצָה, **râtsâh,** *raw-tsaw'*; a primitive root; to *be pleased with*; (specifically) to *satisfy* a debt:—(be) accept (-able), accomplish, set affection, approve, consent with, delight (self), enjoy, (be, have a) favour (-able), like, observe, pardon, (be, have, take) please (-ure), reconcile self.

A verb meaning to delight, to take pleasure, to treat favourably, to favour, to accept, to pay off, to pay for, to make up for. Both humans (cf. Ge 33:10; Dt 33:24; 1Ch 29:3; Ps 50:18; Pr 3:12); and the Lord can be found as the subjects (1Ch 28:4; Ps 51:16[18]; 147:10; Mic 6:7; Hag 1:8). The Lord takes pleasure in uprightness (1Ch 29:17); in those who fear Him (Ps 147:11); and in His Servant (Isa 42:1). The word is also utilized within texts concerning sacrifices, offerings, and worship, denoting that which was acceptable or unacceptable to the Lord (Le 1:4; 7:18; Ps 119:108; Jer 14:12; Hos 8:13; Am 5:22; Mal 1:8). Less common is the employment of the term to communicate the satisfying of a debt (e.g., when the land must pay off or make up for the Sabbath years that it owes [Le 26:34; cf. Le 26:41, 43; 2Ch 36:21; Isa 40:2]).

7522. רָצוֹן, **râtsôwn,** *raw-tsone'*; or רָצֹן, **râtsôn,** *raw-tsone'*; from 7521; *delight* (especially as shown):—(be) acceptable (-ance, -ed), delight, desire, favour, (good) pleasure, (own, self, voluntary) will, as … (what) would.

A masculine noun meaning pleasure, delight, desire, will, favour, acceptance. This term is ascribed both to human agents and to God. For humans, the word often described what the heart was set on having or doing, whether for good or evil (Ge 49:6; 2Ch 15:15; Ne 9:24, 37; Est 1:8; Ps 145:16, 19; Da 8:4; 11:3). When attributed to God, the term expresses the divine goodwill which He extends to humanity as He sees fit (Dt 33:16, 23; Ps 5:12[13]; 69:13[14]; 106:4; Pr 12:2; 18:22; Isa 49:8; 60:10; 61:2). In passages pertaining to the offering of sacrifices,

offerings, or fasting in worship, the word designates the favourable reception of the worshippers (and thus their worship) by the Lord (Ex 28:38; Le 1:3; 19:5; 22:19–21, 29; 23:11; Isa 56:7; 58:5; 60:7; Jer 6:20). On a few occasions, the word denotes anything that is pleasing to God (i.e. His will [lit., His pleasure]; Ps 40:8[9]; 103:21; 143:10). This noun is derived from the verb *râsâh* (7521).

7523. רָצַח, **râtsach,** *raw-tsakh'*; a primitive root; (properly) to *dash* in pieces, i.e. *kill* (a human being), (especially) to *murder:*—put to death, kill, (man-) slay (-er), murder (-er).

A verb meaning to murder, to slay, to kill. The taking of a human life is the primary concept behind this word. It is used to indicate a premeditated murder (Dt 5:17; 1Ki 21:19; Jer 7:9); an accidental killing (Nu 35:11; Jos 20:3); the ultimate act of revenge (Nu 35:27); and death by means of an animal attack (Pr 22:13). Provocatively, Hosea refers to the lewdness of the priests that led people astray as being equal to murder (Hos 6:9).

7524. רֶצַח, **retsach,** *reh'-tsakh*; from 7523; a *crushing*; (specifically) a *murder*-cry:—slaughter, sword.

7525. רִצְיָא, **Ritsyâ',** *rits-yaw'*; from 7521; *delight*; *Ritsjah,* an Israelite:—Rezia.

7526. רְצִין, **R°tsîyn,** *rets-een'*; probably for 7522; *Retsin,* the name of a Syrian and of an Israelite:—Rezin.

7527. רָצַע, **râtsa',** *raw-tsah'*; a primitive root; to *pierce:*—bore.

7528. רָצַף, **râtsaph,** *raw-tsaf'*; a denominative from 7529; to *tessellate,* i.e. embroider (as if with bright stones):—pave.

7529. רֶצֶף, **retseph,** *reh'-tsef*; for 7565; a redhot *stone* (for baking):—coal.

7530. רֶצֶף, **Retseph,** *reh'-tsef*; the same as 7529; *Retseph,* a place in Assyria:—Rezeph.

7531. רִצְפָּה, **ritspâh,** *rits-paw'*; feminine of 7529; a hot *stone*; also a tessellated *pavement:*—live coal, pavement.

7532. רִצְפָּה, **Ritspâh,** *rits-paw'*; the same as 7531; *Ritspah,* an Israelitess:—Rizpah.

7533. רָצַץ, **râtsats,** *raw-tsats´*; a primitive root; to *crack* in pieces, literal or figurative:—break, bruise, crush, discourage, oppress, struggle together.

7534. רַק, **raq,** *rak*; from 7556 in its orig. sense; *emaciated* (as if *flattened* out):—lean ([-fleshed]), thin.

7535. רַק, **raq,** *rak*; the same as 7534 as a noun; (properly) *leanness,* i.e. (figurative) limitation; (only adverbial) *merely,* or (conjunctive) *although:*—but, even, except, howbeit, howsoever, at the least, nevertheless, nothing but, notwithstanding, only, save, so [that], surely, yet (so), in any wise.

7536. רֹק, **rôq,** *roke*; from 7556; *spittle:*—spit (-ting, -tle).

7537. רָקַב, **râqab,** *raw-kab´*; a primitive root; to *decay* (as by worm-eating):—rot.

7538. רָקָב, **râqâb,** *raw-kawb´*; from 7537; *decay* (by *caries*):—rottenness (thing).

7539. רִקָּבוֹן, **riqqâbôwn,** *rik-kaw-bone´*; from 7538; *decay* (by *caries*):—rotten.

7540. רָקַד, **râqad,** *raw-kad´*; a primitive root; (properly) to *stamp,* i.e. to *spring* about (wildly or for joy):—dance, jump, leap, skip.

7541. רַקָּה, **raqqâh,** *rak-kaw´*; feminine of 7534; (properly) *thinness,* i.e. the *side* of the head:—temple.

7542. רַקּוֹן, **Raqqôwn,** *rak-kone´*; from 7534; *thinness; Rakkon,* a place in Palestine:—Rakkon.

7543. רָקַח, **râqach,** *raw-kakh´*; a primitive root; to *perfume:*—apothecary, compound, make [ointment], prepare, spice.

7544. רֶקַח, **reqach,** *reh´-kakh*; from 7543; (properly) *perfumery,* i.e. (by implication) *spicery* (for flavor):—spiced.

7545. רֹקַח, **rôqach,** *ro´-kakh*; from 7542; an *aromatic:*—confection, ointment.

7546. רַקָּח, **raqqâch,** *rak-kawkh´*; from 7543; a male *perfumer:*—apothecary.

7547. רִקֻּחַ, **riqquach,** *rik-koo´-akh*; from 7543; a *scented* substance:—perfume.

7548. רִקָּחָה, **raqqâchâh,** *rak-kaw-khaw´*; feminine of 7547; a female *perfumer:*—confectioner.

7549. רָקִיעַ, **râqîya‘,** *raw-kee´-ah*; from 7554; (properly) an *expanse,* i.e. the *firmament* or (apparently) visible arch of the sky:—firmament.

A masculine noun meaning an expanse, the firmament, an extended surface. Literally, this word refers to a great expanse and, in particular, the vault of the heavens above the earth. It denotes the literal sky that stretches from horizon to horizon (Ge 1:6–8); the heavens above that contain the sun, moon, and stars (Ge 1:14); or any vaulted ceiling or expanse that stands above (Eze 10:1). By extension, the psalmist uses the word to refer to the infinite and sweeping power of the Lord (Ps 150:1).

7550. רָקִיק, **râqîyq,** *raw-keek´*; from 7556 in its original sense; a thin *cake:*—cake, wafer.

7551. רָקַם, **râqam,** *raw-kam´*; a primitive root; to *variegate* colour, i.e. *embroider;* (by implication) to *fabricate:*—embroiderer, needlework, curiously work.

7552. רֶקֶם, **Reqem,** *reh´-kem*; from 7551; *versicolor; Rekem,* the name of a place in Palestine, also of a Midianite and an Israelite:—Rekem.

7553. רִקְמָה, **riqmâh,** *rik-maw´*; from 7551; *variegation* of colour; (specifically) *embroidery:*—broidered (work), divers colours, (raiment of) needlework (on both sides).

7554. רָקַע, **râqa‘,** *raw-kah´*; a primitive root; to *pound* the earth (as a sign of passion); (by analogy) to *expand* (by hammering); (by implication) to *overlay* (with thin sheets of metal):—beat, make broad, spread abroad (forth, over, out, into plates), stamp, stretch.

A verb meaning to beat, to stamp, to stretch out. The fundamental picture is that of a smith pounding a piece of metal that in turn causes the metal to spread out as it flattens. This word conveys the action of flattening metal for some specific use (Ex 39:3); stamping one's foot on the ground as a symbol of displeasure (Eze 6:11); the laying out of the earth in creation (Isa 42:5); and the flattening of an enemy (2Sa 22:43).

7555. רִקֻּעַ, **riqqua‘,** *rik-koo´-ah*; from 7554; *beaten* out, i.e. a (metallic) *plate:*—broad.

A masculine noun meaning expansion, broad. Signifying the stretching effect produced when metal is beaten, this word appears only in reference to the plates covering the altar of the tabernacle (Nu 16:38[17:3]).

7556. רָקַק, **râqaq,** *raw-kak´*; a primitive root; to *spit*:—spit.

7557. רַקַּת, **Raqqath,** *rak-kath´*; from 7556 in its original sense of *diffusing*; a *beach* (as *expanded* shingle); *Rakkath*, a place in Palestine:—Rakkath.

7558. רִשְׁיוֹן, **rishyôwn,** *rish-yone´*; from an unused root meaning to *have leave*; a *permit*:—grant.

7559. רָשַׁם, **râsham,** *raw-sham´*; a primitive root; to *record*:—note.

7560. רְשַׁם, **rᵉsham,** *resh-am´*; (Chaldee); corresponding to 7559:—sign, write.

7561. רָשַׁע, **râshaʿ,** *raw-shah´*; a primitive root; to *be* (causative, *do* or *declare*) *wrong*; (by implication) to *disturb, violate*:—condemn, make trouble, vex, be (commit, deal, depart, do) wicked (-ly, -ness).

A verb meaning to be in the wrong, to be guilty, to be wicked, to do wickedly, to condemn. In the simple stem, this verb means to be or to become guilty, to act wickedly. When God's people confessed that they acted wickedly, then the Lord forgave them (1Ki 8:47; Ecc 7:17; Da 9:15); to depart from the Lord is an act of wickedness (2Sa 22:22; Ps 18:21[22]).

In the causative stem, the word carries the idea of condemning others or doing wickedness; the people confessed that they had done wickedness (Ne 9:33; Ps 106:6; Da 12:10). The verb also means to condemn. God declares who is guilty in cases of illegal possession (Ex 22:9[8]; Dt 25:1); when a moral or ethical offence has occurred, the Lord will judge in order to declare the guilty (1Ki 8:32; Job 9:20).

7562. רֶשַׁע, **reshaʿ,** *reh´-shah*; from 7561; a *wrong* (especially moral):—iniquity, wicked (-ness).

A masculine noun meaning wickedness, injustice, and unrighteousness. It embodies that character which is opposite the character of God (Job 34:10; Ps 5:4[5]; 84:10[11]). It is also placed in opposition to justice and righteousness, *tsedeq* (6664), which is often used to describe God's

character (Ps 45:7[8]). This word is presented as the bad and evil actions that are done by humanity (Job 34:8); and, as such, these actions became the object of God's judgment (see Job 34:26). It describes those actions that are violent. In Pr 4:17, this word is a parallel to *châmâs* (2555), meaning violence. In addition, the Hebrew word means violations of civil law, especially fraud and deceit (Pr 8:7; note the word's opposition to *'emeth*[571], which means truth; cf. Mic 6:10, 11). It can also denote the actions of enemy nations (Ps 125:3; note its opposition to *tsaddiyq* (6662), which means just or righteous; cf. Eze 31:11). In a general sense, it may represent wrongful deeds (Dt 9:27; note the parallel with *chaṭṭâ'th* (2403), which means sin).

7563. רָשָׁע, **râshâʿ,** *raw-shaw´*; from 7561; moral *wrong*; (concrete) an (actively) *bad* person:— + condemned, guilty, ungodly, wicked (man), that did wrong.

An adjective meaning wicked, guilty, in the wrong, criminal, transgressor. This adjective is used 264 times, many more times than the verb formed from it. It means essentially someone guilty or in the wrong and is an antonym to the Hebrew word *tsaddiyq* (6662), meaning righteous, in the right. Moses accused the Hebrew man who was in the wrong and was fighting with another Hebrew (Ex 2:13); no one was to aid wicked persons in their wickedness (Ex 23:1). A murderer worthy of death could not be ransomed (Nu 35:31); guilty, wicked persons accept bribes (Pr 17:23; 18:5). The word may describe wicked people as murderers (2Sa 4:11).

The word indicates people who are enemies of God and His people: the psalmist prayed to be rescued from the wicked (Ps 17:13). Those described by this word are evil and do not learn righteousness. Instead, they pursue their wicked ways among the righteous (Isa 26:10); but the Lord will eventually slay the wicked (Isa 11:4). Pharaoh admitted he was in the wrong in his attitude and actions against Moses, the Lord, and His people (Ex 9:27; Isa 14:5).

The word indicates the guilt engendered by sinning against others, including God. The Lord moved to destroy the leaders and the wicked people who revolted against Him in the desert (Nu 16:26); the wicked are those who do not serve God and are as a result wicked and guilty before Him (Mal 3:18). If wicked people continue in their ways toward God or others, they will die in their sins (Eze 3:18); but the righteous do not die with the wicked (Ge 18:23, 25). The counsel of the wicked is avoided by the persons blessed by God (Job 10:3; 21:16; Ps 1:1). Several phrases became idiomatic when talking about the wicked described by this word: the counsel of the wicked (Ps 1:1); the way of the wicked (Pr 15:9); the path of the wicked (Mic 6:10); the tent of the wicked (Job 8:22); the life (literally, candle) of the wicked (Job 21:7). All these terms describe things, people, and locations that God's people are to avoid so He will not destroy them in the end.

7564. רִשְׁעָה, **rish'âh,** *rish-aw´*; feminine of 7562; *wrong* (especially moral):—fault, wickedly (-ness).

A feminine noun meaning wickedness, guilt. This word for immorality refers to a wide range of evil. It indicates a crime worthy of punishment (Dt 25:2); the unrestrained evil that lurks in the human heart (Isa 9:18[17]); the vileness of surrounding enemies (Mal 1:4); the breach of a religious expectation (Mal 4:1[3:19]); or an unlawful act in general (Eze 33:19).

7565. רֶשֶׁף, **resheph,** *reh´-shef*; from 8313; a live *coal*; (by analogy) *lightning*; (figurative) an *arrow* (as *flashing* through the air); (specifically) *fever*:—arrow, (burning) coal, burning heat, + spark, hot thunderbolt.

7566. רֶשֶׁף, **Resheph,** *reh´-shef*; the same as 7565; *Resheph*, an Israelite:—Resheph.

7567. רָשַׁשׁ, **râshash,** *raw-shash´*; a primitive root; to *demolish*:—impoverish.

7568. רֶשֶׁת, **resheth,** *reh´-sheth*; from 3423; a *net* (as *catching* animals):—net [-work].

7569. רַתּוֹק, **rattôwq,** *rat-toke´*; from 7576; a *chain*:—chain.

7570. רָתַח, **râthach,** *raw-thakh´*; a primitive root; to *boil*:—boil.

7571. רֶתַח, **rethach,** *reh´-thakh*; from 7570; a *boiling*:— × [boil] well.

7572. רַתִּיקָה, **rattîyqâh,** *rat-tee-kaw´*; from 7576; a *chain*:—chain.

7573. רָתַם, **râtham,** *raw-tham´*; a primitive root; to *yoke* up (to the pole of a vehicle):—bind.

7574. רֶתֶם, **rethem,** *reh´-them*; or רֹתֶם, **rôthem,** *ro´-them*; from 7573; the Spanish *broom* (from its pole-like stems):—juniper (tree).

7575. רִתְמָה, **Rithmâh,** *rith-maw´*; feminine of 7574; *Rithmah*, a place in the Desert:—Rithmah.

7576. רָתַק, **râthaq,** *raw-thak´*; a primitive root; to *fasten*:—bind.

7577. רְתוּקָה, **rᵉthûwqâh,** *reth-oo-kaw´*; feminine passive participle of 7576; something *fastened*, i.e. a *chain*:—chain.

7578. רְתֵת, **rᵉthêth,** *reth-ayth´*; for 7374; *terror*:—trembling.

ש (Sin/Shin)

7579. שָׁאַב, **shâ'ab,** *shaw-ab´*; a primitive root; to *bale* up water:—(woman to) draw (-er, water).

7580. שָׁאַג, **shâ'ag,** *shaw-ag´*; a primitive root; to *rumble* or *moan:*— × mightily, roar.

7581. שְׁאָגָה, **sheʾâgâh,** *sheh-aw-gaw´*; from 7580; a *rumbling* or *moan:*—roaring.

7582. שָׁאָה, **shâ'âh,** *shaw-aw´*; a primitive root; to *rush*; (by implication) to *desolate:*—be desolate, (make a) rush (-ing), (lay) waste.

7583. שָׁאָה, **shâ'âh,** *shaw-aw´*; a primitive root [rather identical with 7582 through the idea of *whirling* to giddiness]; to *stun*, i.e. (intransitive) *be astonished:*—wonder.

7584. שַׁאֲוָה, **sha'ăvâh,** *shah-av-aw´*; from 7582; a *tempest* (as *rushing*):—desolation.

A feminine noun meaning a storm, a tempest. This type of storm is used to describe the aftermath of rejecting Lady Wisdom's advice on how to live wisely (Pr 1:27).

7585. שְׁאוֹל, **sheʾôwl,** *sheh-ole´*; or שְׁאֹל, **sheʾôl,** *sheh-ole´*; from 7592; *hades* or the world of the dead (as if a subterranean *retreat*), including its accessories and inmates:—grave, hell, pit.

A noun meaning the world of the dead, Sheol, the grave, death, the depths. The word describes the underworld but usually in the sense of the grave and is most often translated as grave. Jacob described himself as going to the grave upon Joseph's supposed death (Ge 37:35; 42:38); Korah, Dathan, and Abiram went down into the ground, which becomes their grave, when God judges them (Nu 16:30, 33; 1Sa 2:6). David described his brush with death at the hands of Saul as feeling the ropes or bands of the grave clutching him (2Sa 22:6). The Lord declares that He will ransom His people from the grave or Sheol (Hos 13:14). Habakkuk declared that the grave's desire for more victims is never satiated (Hab 2:5).

The word means depths or Sheol. Job called the ways of the Almighty higher than heaven and lower than Sheol or the depths of the earth (Job 11:8). The psalmist could not escape the Lord even in the lowest depths of the earth, in contrast to the high heavens (Ps 139:8; Am 9:2). It means the deepest valley or depths of the earth in Isa 7:11.

In a few cases, Sheol seems to mean death or a similar concept; that Abaddon (destruction) lies uncovered seems to be matched with Sheol's meaning of death (Job 26:6). It means death or the grave, for neither is ever satisfied (Pr 7:27; cf. Isa 38:10) The word is best translated as death or the depths in Dt 32:22.

Sheol or the grave is the place of the wicked (Ps 9:17[18]; 31:17[18]); Ezekiel pictured it as the place of the uncircumcised (Eze 31:15; 32:21, 27). Israel's search for more wickedness and apostasy took them to the depths of Sheol (Isa 57:9). On the other hand, the righteous were not made for the grave or Sheol; it was not their proper abode. They were not left in the grave or Sheol (Ps 16:10) but were rescued from that place (Ps 49:15[16]). Adulterers and fornicators were, metaphorically, described as in the lower parts of Sheol or the grave (Pr 9:18). Sheol and Abaddon (destruction) are as open to the eyes of God as are the hearts and thoughts of humankind; there is nothing mysterious about them to Him (Pr 15:11).

7586. שָׁאוּל, **Shâ'ûwl,** *shaw-ool´*; passive participle of 7592; *asked; Shaül,* the name of an Edomite and two Israelites:—Saul, Shaul.

7587. שָׁאוּלִי, **Shâ'ûwlîy,** *shaw-oo-lee´*; patronymic from 7856; a *Shaülite* or descendant of Shaul:—Shaulites.

7588. שָׁאוֹן, **shâ'ôwn,** *shaw-one´*; from 7582; *uproar* (as of *rushing*); (by implication) *destruction:*— × horrible, noise, pomp, rushing, tumult (× -uous).

A masculine noun meaning a roar, a din, a crash. This term is found mostly in the prophets and generally refers to the din of battle (Hos 10:14; Am 2:2); or the crash of waves (Isa 17:12). A less frequent use of the word describes the merriment or uproar of revelers (Isa 24:8).

7589. שְׁאָט, **shᵉ'âṭ,** *sheh-awt´*; from an unused root meaning to *push* aside; *contempt:*—despite (-ful).

7590. שָׁאט, **shâ'ṭ,** *shawt*; for active participle of 7750 [compare 7589]; one *contemning:*—that (which) despise (-d).

7591. שְׁאִיָּה, **shᵉ'îyyâh,** *sheh-ee-yaw´*; from 7582; *desolation:*—destruction.

A feminine noun meaning ruin. This word is used only once in the OT and comes from the verb *shâ'âh* (7582), meaning to crash into ruins. In Isa 24:12, it describes the destroyed gate of the city that had been battered into ruins.

7592. שָׁאַל, **shâ'al,** *shaw-al´*; or שָׁאֵל, **shâ'êl,** *shaw-ale´*; a primitive root; to *inquire*; (by implication) to *request*; (by extension) to *demand:*—ask (counsel, on), beg, borrow, lay to charge, consult, demand, desire, × earnestly, enquire, + greet, obtain leave, lend, pray, request, require, + salute, × straitly, × surely, wish.

A verb meaning to ask. One could ask another person or even God for something (1Sa 23:2; Ps 122:6; 137:3; Ecc 7:10). People sometimes sought information by asking Urim and Thummim (Nu 27:21), or an occult wooden object (Eze 21:21[26]; Hos 4:12). Asking could be done as a begging request or a stern demand (1Ki 2:16; Job 38:3; Ps 109:10; Mic 7:3). The Hebrew expression of asking about someone's peace is similar to the English expression, "How are you?" (Ge 43:27; Jgs 18:15; Jer 15:5). Very rarely, the term could refer to borrowing or lending. But this is certainly not the meaning when the people of Israel asked goods from the Egyptians they plundered (Ex 3:22; 22:14[13]; 1Sa 1:28; 2:20; 2Ki 4:3; 6:5).

7593. שְׁאֵל, **shᵉ'êl,** *sheh-ale´*; (Chaldee); corresponding to 7592:—ask, demand, require.

An Aramaic verb meaning to ask, to demand, to require. The word is closely related to the Hebrew verb *shâ'al* (7592), meaning to ask. Tattenai, the governor of the province beyond the river, asked the elders of the returned Jews for their names and for the name of the one who authorized their rebuilding of the Temple in Jerusalem (Ezr 5:9, 10). Later on, King Artaxerxes decreed that the treasurers in that same province had to provide whatever Ezra asked of them so that the priestly ministry at the newly rebuilt Temple could be maintained (Ezr 7:21; cf. Da 2:10, 11, 27).

7594. שְׁאָל, **Shᵉ'âl,** *sheh-awl´*; from 7592; *request*; *Sheäl*, an Israelite:—Sheal.

7595. שְׁאֵלָה, **shᵉ'êlâh,** *sheh-ay-law´*; (Chaldee); from 7593; (properly) a *question* (at law), i.e. judicial *decision* or mandate:—demand.

An Aramaic feminine noun meaning a decision, a verdict, a decree. The word occurs only in Da 4:17 (4:14) and is derived from the verbal root *shᵉ'êl* (7593). It is also related to the Hebrew noun *shᵉ'êlâh* (7596). The word denotes a question at law (i.e. a judicial decision or edict). In Nebuchadnezzar's second dream, he witnessed an angelic watchman crying out and announcing the verdict concerning the greatest tree in all the earth. Daniel later interpreted the dream, declaring that the great tree represented Nebuchadnezzar himself (cf. Da 4:4–27).

7596. שְׁאֵלָה, **shᵉ'êlâh,** *sheh-ay-law´*; or שֵׁלָה, **shêlâh,** *shay-law´*; (1Sa 1:17), from 7592; a *petition*; (by implication) a *loan:*—loan, petition, request.

A feminine noun meaning a request, a petition. The term is derived from the verb *shâ'al* (7592) and signifies what a person or group asks for from another party. The request can be made of another human: Gideon, for gold earrings from the Ishmaelites (Jgs 8:24); Adonijah, for Abishag the Shunammite from Solomon with Bathsheba as intermediary (1Ki 2:16, 20); Esther, for the king's presence at her banquet; also for the sparing of the Jews' and her own life (Est 5:6–8; 7:2, 3; 9:12); or of God: Hannah, for a son (1Sa 1:17, 27; 2:20); Job, for death (Job 6:8); the Israelites, for delicious food (Ps 106:15[cf. Nu 11:4–6, 31–35]).

7597. שְׁאַלְתִּיאֵל, **Shᵉ'altîy'êl,** *sheh-al-tee-ale´*; or שַׁלְתִּיאֵל, **Shaltîy'êl,** *shal-tee-ale´*; from 7592 and 410; *I have asked God*; *Sheältiël*, an Israelite:—Shalthiel, Shealtiel.

7598. שְׁאַלְתִּיאֵל, **Shᵉ'altîy'êl,** *sheh-al-tee-ale´*; (Chaldee); corresponding to 7597:—Shealtiel.

7599. שָׁאַן, **shâ'an,** *shaw-an´*; a primitive root; to *loll*, i.e. *be peaceful*:—be at ease, be quiet, rest. See also 1052.

7600. שַׁאֲנָן, **sha'ănân,** *shah-an-awn´*; from 7599; *secure*; in a bad sense, *haughty*:—that is at ease, quiet, tumult. Compare 7946.

7601. שָׁסַם, **shâ'as,** *shaw-as´*; a primitive root; to *plunder*:—spoil.

7602. שָׁאַף, **shâ'aph,** *shaw-af´*; a primitive root; to *inhale* eagerly; (figurative) to *covet*; (by implication) to *be angry*; also to *hasten*:—desire (earnestly), devour, haste, pant, snuff up, swallow up.

7603. שְׂאֹר, **śe'ôr,** *seh-ore´*; from 7604; *barm* or yeast-cake (as *swelling* by fermentation):—leaven.

7604. שָׁאַר, **shâ'ar,** *shaw-ar´*; a primitive root; (properly) to *swell* up, i.e. *be* (causative, *make*) *redundant*:—leave, (be) left, let, remain, remnant, reserve, the rest.

A verb meaning to remain, to be left over; to leave, to let remain, to spare. The term maintains a narrow semantic range throughout OT literature. The verb and the nouns that derive from it (see *shě'âr*[7605] and *shě 'êriyth*[7611]) play a key role in the development of the remnant theme that unfolds and evolves over the course of OT history. From the early beginnings of salvation history in Genesis and all the way through to the end of the OT and beyond, God has sovereignly acted to preserve for Himself a remnant of people who will worship Him alone (cf. Ge 7:23; 32:8[9]; 1Ki 19:18; Ezr 9:8; Isa 4:3; 11:11, 16; 37:31; Eze 9:8; Zep 3:12; see also Ro 11:5). Nevertheless, though this usage became the most significant function of the term, the verb was also employed in a variety of other contexts. For instance, the Egyptians came to Joseph for help because they had no remaining money to buy food (Ge 47:18). After the Israelites crossed the Red Sea, the waters caved in on Pharaoh's army. Not one person remained (Ex 14:28). The blood that remained from the sin offering was to be drained out at the base of the altar (Le 5:9).

7605. שְׁאָר, **shě'âr,** *sheh-awr´*; from 7604; a *remainder*:— × other, remnant, residue, rest.

A masculine noun meaning a remnant, a remainder, the rest. The term plays an important role in the development of the remnant theme concerning God's people. This theme is interwoven throughout Scripture, and a variety of words were employed to convey the idea (cf. Isa 10:20, 21, 22; 11:11, 16). However, this term is not limited to the designation of the remnant of God's people. For instance, it was also employed to denote the remnant of other nations: Assyria (Isa 10:19); Babylon (Isa 14:22); Moab (Isa 16:14); Aram (Isa 17:3); Kedar (Isa 21:17). Moreover, the word was always utilized as a collective, never referring to a single individual (cf. 1Ch 16:41; Ezr 3:8; 4:3, 7; Est 9:16; Zep 1:4). See also the verb *shâ'ar* (7604), from which this noun is derived, and its corresponding feminine cognate *shě'êriyth* (7611).

7606. שְׁאָר, **shě'âr,** *sheh-awr´*; (Chaldee); corresponding to 7605:— × whatsoever more, residue, rest.

An Aramaic masculine noun meaning the remainder, the rest. The word closely corresponds with the Hebrew noun *shě'âr* (7605). It signifies that which was left over after the removal of everything else. The fourth beast in Daniel's vision devoured, broke things in pieces, and stamped the remainder with its feet (Da 7:7, 19; cf. Da 2:18; 7:12). The people of Israel, the priests, the Levites, and the rest of the returned exiles joyfully celebrated the dedication of the newly rebuilt Temple (Ezr 6:16; cf. Ezr 4:9, 10, 17; 7:18, 20).

7607. שְׁאֵר, **shě'êr,** *sheh-ayr´*; from 7604; *flesh* (as *swelling* out), as living or for food; (generally) *food* of any kind; (figurative) *kindred* by blood:—body, flesh, food, (near) kin (-sman, -swoman), near (nigh) [of kin].

A masculine noun meaning flesh, food, meat, body, self, blood relative, blood kindred. The word is roughly synonymous with the noun *bâsâr* (1320), meaning flesh. The term connotes the meaty part of an animal which can be eaten: quail (Ps 78:20, 27; cf. Nu 11:31); or food in general (Ex 21:10). Frequently, on account of context, the term strongly implies the idea of close (blood) relative or kindred (Le 18:6, 12, 13, 17; 20:19; 21:2; 25:49; Nu 27:11). In two contexts, the word suggests the notion of physical strength (Ps 73:26; Pr 5:11); and in Mic 3:2, 3, it refers to the actual physical flesh of a human body.

7608. שַׁאֲרָה, **sha'ărâh**, *shah-ar-aw´*; feminine of 7607; female *kindred* by blood:—near kinswomen.

7609. שֶׁאֱרָה, **She'ĕrâh**, *sheh-er-aw´*; the same as 7608; *Sheërah*, an Israelitess:—Sherah.

7610. שְׁאָר יָשׁוּב, **Sh**e**'âr Yâshûwb**, *sheh-awr´ yaw-shoob´*; from 7605 and 7725; a *remnant will return; Sheär-Jashub*, the symbolical name of one of Isaiah's sons:—Shear-jashub.

7611. שְׁאֵרִית, **sh**e**'êrîyth**, *sheh-ay-reeth´*; from 7604; a *remainder* or residual (surviving, final) portion:—that had escaped, be left, posterity, remain (-der), remnant, residue, rest.

A feminine noun meaning a remnant, a residue, the remainder. The primary meaning conveyed by this word is that which is left over or remains. It was used with reference to scrap pieces of wood (Isa 44:17); undesignated territory (Isa 15:9); and any group of people that remained (Jer 15:9; Am 1:8). Most significant was the technical use of this word by the prophets to denote the few among Israel or Judah that remained faithful to God (Isa 37:32; Mic 5:7[6], 8[7]); or those who survived the calamity of the exile (Zec 8:11). Joseph declared that the purpose of his captivity was to preserve a remnant of Jacob's lineage (Ge 45:7).

7612. שְׁאֵת, **shê'th**, *shayth*; from 7582; *devastation*:—desolation.

7613. שְׂאֵת, **ś**e**'êth**, *seh-ayth´*; from 5375; an *elevation* or leprous scab; (figurative) *elation* or cheerfulness; *exaltation* in rank or character:—be accepted, dignity, excellency, highness, raise up self, rising.

7614. שְׁבָא, **Sh**e**bâ'**, *sheb-aw´*; of foreign origin; *Sheba*, the name of three early progenitors of tribes and of an Ethiopian district:—Sheba, Sabeans.

7615. שְׁבָאִי, **Sh**e**bâ'îy**, *sheb-aw-ee´*; patronymic from 7614; a *Shebaïte* or descendant of Sheba:—Sabean.

7616. שְׁבָבִים, **sh**e**bâbîym**, *she-baw-beem´*; from an unused root meaning to *break* up; a *fragment*, i.e. *ruin*:—broken in pieces.

7617. שָׁבָה, **shâbâh**, *shaw-baw´*; a primitive root; to *transport* into captivity:—(bring away, carry, carry away, lead, lead away, take) captive (-s), drive (take) away.

A verb meaning to take captive, to lead into captivity. The main idea behind this word is that of being taken prisoner as a spoil of war or other military raid. It signified the fate that befell Lot at the hands of Chedorlaomer and his compatriots (Ge 14:14); the threat that hung over the heads of any rebellious people (1Ki 8:46); and forced enslavement by a foreign military power (2Ki 5:2).

7618. שְׁבוֹ, **sh**e**bôw**, *sheb-oh´*; from an unused root (probably identical with that of 7617 through the idea of *subdivision* into flashes or streamers [compare 7632] meaning to *flame*; a *gem* (from its sparkle), probably the *agate*:—agate.

7619. שְׁבוּאֵל, **Sh**e**bûw'êl**, *sheb-oo-ale´*; or שׁוּבָאֵל, **Shûwbâ'êl**, *shoo-baw-ale´*; from 7617 (abbreviated) or 7725 and 410; *captive* (or *returned*) *of God; Shebuël*, the name of two Israelites:—Shebuel, Shubael.

7620. שָׁבוּעַ, **shâbûwa'**, *shaw-boo´-ah*; or שָׁבֻעַ, **shâbua'**, *shaw-boo´-ah*; also (feminine) שְׁבֻעָה, **shebu'âh**, *sheb-oo-aw´*; properly passive participle of 7650 as a denominative of 7651; (literal) *sevened*, i.e. a *week* (specifically of years):—seven, week.

7621. שְׁבוּעָה, **sh**e**bûw'âh**, *sheb-oo-aw´*; feminine passive participle of 7650; (properly something *sworn*, i.e. an *oath*:—curse, oath, × sworn.

A feminine noun meaning oath. An oath is a sacred promise attesting to what one has done or will do. God swore an oath to Abraham, Isaac, and Jacob that He would fulfill His covenant with them (Ge 26:3; Dt 7:8; 1Ch 16:16). An oath could also be sworn by a person to declare innocence (Ex 22:11[10]; Nu 5:21); to proclaim friendship (2Sa 21:7); to affirm a promise (Le 5:4; 1Ki 2:43); to ratify a peace treaty (Jos 9:20); to pledge loyalty to God (2Ch 15:15); or to another person (Ne 6:18). An oath was considered to be an unbreakable contract; however, in two instances, the Bible presents well-defined possibilities in which an oath could be nullified and the obligated party could be acquitted. Abraham provided for his servant to be released from his obligation to find a bride for Isaac if the woman refused to follow (Ge 24:8); and the spies provided for their own release from their oath to Rahab if she did not display the scarlet cord and stay in her house or if she revealed the intentions of the Israelites (Jos 2:17, 20).

7622. שְׁבוּת, **sheᶜbûwth,** *sheb-ooth´*; or שְׁבִית, **shebîyth,** *sheb-eeth´*; from 7617; *exile*; (concrete) *prisoners*; (figurative) a *former state* of prosperity:—captive (-ity).

A feminine noun meaning captivity, captives. This word conveys either a state of exile, such as being taken for a spoil of war, or the subjects of such captivity. The chief use was in declaring the liberating power of the Lord in releasing His people from such banishment (Dt 30:3; Jer 33:7; Hos 6:11). Interestingly, when Job's fortunes were restored, he was said to have been freed from captivity (Job 42:10).

7623. שָׁבַח, **shâbach,** *shaw-bakh´*; a primitive root; (properly) to *address* in a loud tone, i.e. (specifically) *loud*; (figurative) to *pacify* (as if by words):—commend, glory, keep in, praise, still, triumph.

A verb meaning to soothe, to stroke, to praise. The primary meaning of this word is to calm or still. It was used particularly in reference to the calming of the sea (Ps 65:7[8]). A secondary current of meaning associated with this word is that of praise. In this sense, it was employed to denote either the exaltation of God (Ps 63:3[4]); or the holding of something in higher esteem (Ecc 4:2). The connection between the two may stem from the soothing effect of praise on the ego.

7624. שְׁבַח, **sheᶜbach,** *sheb-akh´*; (Chaldee); corresponding to 7623; to *adulate*, i.e. *adore*:—praise.

An Aramaic verb meaning to praise, to adore. This word occurs five times in the book of Daniel. It denotes Daniel's praise of the Lord (Da 2:23); the praise of the Lord by a humbled Nebuchadnezzar (Da 4:37[34]); and the praise given to idols during Belshazzar's debaucherous feast (Da 5:4, 23).

7625. שְׁבַט, **sheᶜbaṭ,** *sheb-at´*; (Chaldee); corresponding to 7626; a *clan*:—tribe.

An Aramaic masculine noun meaning a clan, a tribe. This word occurs only in Ezr 6:17 and is used in reference to the tribal divisions of Israel (cf. Ge 49:28).

7626. שֵׁבֶט, **shebeṭ,** *shay´-bet*; from an unused root probably meaning to *branch* off; a *scion*, i.e. (literal) a *stick* (for punishing, writing, fighting, ruling, walking, etc.) or (figurative) a *clan*:— × correction, dart, rod, sceptre, staff, tribe.

A masculine noun meaning a rod, a scepter, and a tribe. It is presented in parallel with the word *maṭṭeh* (4294) that designates a rod or a tribe (Isa 10:15). As a rod, it represents a common tool used as a shepherd's staff (Le 27:32; Eze 20:37); a crude weapon (2Sa 23:21); or for beating out cumin (Isa 28:27). It also refers to the shaft of a spear (2Sa 18:14). The rod was also used in meting out discipline, both literally for a slave (Ex 21:20); a fool (Pr 10:13; 26:3); and a son (Pr 13:24; 22:15; 29:15); and figuratively of God against Solomon (2Sa 7:14); of God against Israel through Assyria (Isa 10:24); against Philistia (Isa 14:29); and of God against Assyria (Isa 30:31). Because of the association between smiting and ruling, the rod became a symbol of the authority of the one bearing it; thus, this word can also mean a scepter (Ge 49:10; Jgs 5:14; Isa 14:5). Also, the connotation of tribe is based on the connection between this term and the concept of rulership. It can connote the tribes of Israel collectively (Ge 49:16; Dt 33:5); or individually (Jos 7:16; Jgs 18:1). It can also represent a portion of one of the tribes (Nu 4:18; Jgs 20:12; 1Sa 9:21). Eventually, the term was used in the singular to denote Israel as a whole (Ps 74:2; Jer 10:16; 51:19). It is also interesting to note that this word was never used in reference to the tribes of other nations.

7627. שְׁבָט, **Sheᶜbâṭ,** *sheb-awt´*; of foreign origin; *Shebat*, a Jewish month:—Sebat.

7628. שְׁבִי, **sheᶜbîy,** *sheb-ee´*; from 7618; *exiled*; *captured*; as noun, *exile* (abstract or concrete and collective); (by extension) *booty*:—captive (-ity), prisoners, × take away, that was taken.

A masculine noun meaning captivity, captives. This word comes from the verb *shâbâh* (7617), meaning to take captive, and was normally used to describe those captured in war and taken back to the conquering country (Nu 21:1; Ezr 3:8; Ne 1:2). It could describe anything captured, such as booty (Nu 31:26); or horses (Am 4:10). The word could also be used to describe prisoners in a dungeon (Ex 12:29).

7629. שׁוֹבִי, **Shôbîy,** *sho-bee´*; from 7617; *captor; Shobi,* an Ammonite:—Shobi.

7630. שׁוֹבַי, **Shôbay,** *sho-bah´ee*; for 7629; *Shobai,* an Israelite:—Shobai.

7631. שְׁבִיב, **sheᵇîyb,** *sheb-eeb´*; (Chaldee); corresponding to 7632:—flame.

7632. שָׁבִיב, **shâbîyb,** *shaw-beeb´*; from the same as 7616; *flame* (as *split* into tongues):—spark.

7633. שִׁבְיָה, **shibyâh,** *shib-yaw´*; feminine of 7628; *exile* (abstract or concrete and collective):—captives (-ity).

A feminine noun meaning captives. This word comes from the verb *shâbâh* (7617), meaning to take captive. It always describes those who had been defeated in war and were taken captive into a foreign land. It was also used to describe the captives taken in victory by Israel (Dt 21:11); as well as those taken in defeat from Israel by a foreign nation (2Ch 28:11, 13–15; Ne 4:4[3:36]).

7634. שָׁבְיָה, **Shobyâh,** *shob-yaw´*; feminine of the same as 7629; *captivation; Shobjah,* an Israelite:—Shachia [*from the margin*].

7635. שְׁבִיל, **sheᵇîyl,** *she-beel´*; from the same as 7640; a *track* or passageway (as if *flowing* along):—path.

7636. שָׁבִיס, **shâbîys,** *shaw-beece´*; from an unused root meaning to *interweave;* a *netting* for the hair:—caul.

7637. שְׁבִיעִי, **sheᵇîy῾îy,** *sheb-ee-ee´*; or שְׁבִעִי, **shebi῾îy,** *sheb-ee-ee´*; ordinal from 7657; *seventh:*—seventh (time).

An adjective meaning seventh. This word is normally used in relation to time: the seventh day (Le 13:5, 6; Jos 6:4; Est 1:10); the seventh week (Le 23:16); the seventh month (Le 23:27; Jer 28:17; Hag 2:1); and the seventh year (Le 25:4; 2Ki 11:4; 2Ch 23:1). When this word refers to the seventh day, it can refer to the Sabbath (Ge 2:2; Ex 20:10, 11; Dt 16:8). In other usages, this word describes the seventh of a series of events (Jos 6:16; 1Ki 18:44); the seventh lot (Jos 19:40; 1Ch 24:10); the seventh son (1Ch 2:15; 26:3); the seventh mighty man (1Ch 12:11[12]); and the seventh commander (1Ch 27:10).

7638. שָׂבָךְ, **śâbâk,** *saw-bawk´*; from an unused root meaning to *intwine;* a *netting* (ornament to the capital of a column):—net.

7639. שְׂבָכָה, **śᵉbâkâh,** *seb-aw-kaw´*; feminine of 7638; a *net-work,* i.e. (in hunting) a *snare,* (in architecture) a *ballustrade;* also a *reticulated* ornament to a pillar:—checker, lattice, network, snare, wreath (-enwork).

7640. שֹׁבֶל, **shôbel,** *show´-bel*; from an unused root meaning to *flow;* a lady's *train* (as *trailing* after her):—leg.

7641. שִׁבֹּל, **shibbôl,** *shib-bole´*; or (feminine) שִׁבֹּלֶת, **shibbôleth,** *shib-bo´-leth*; from the same as 7640; a *stream* (as *flowing*); also an *ear* of grain (as *growing* out); (by analogy) a *branch:*—branch, channel, ear (of corn), ([water-]) flood, Shibboleth. Compare 5451.

7642. שַׁבְלוּל, **shablûwl,** *shab-lool´*; from the same as 7640; a *snail* (as if *floating* in its own slime):—snail.

7643. שְׂבָם, **Śᵉbâm,** *seb-awm´*; or (feminine) שִׂבְמָה, **Śibmâh,** *sib-maw´*; probably from 1313; *spice; Sebam* or *Sibmah,* a place in Moab:—Shebam, Shibmah, Sibmah.

7644. שֶׁבְנָא, **Shebnâ',** *sheb-naw´*; or שֶׁבְנָה, **Shebnâh,** *sheb-naw´*; from an unused root meaning to *grow; growth; Shebna* or *Shebnah,* an Israelite:—Shebna, Shebnah.

7645. שְׁבַנְיָה, **Sheᵇanyâh,** *sheb-an-yaw´*; or שְׁבַנְיָהוּ, **Shebanyâhûw,** *sheb-an-yaw´-hoo*; from the same as 7644 and 3050; *Jah has grown* (i.e. *prospered*); *Shebanjah,* the name of three or four Israelites:—Shebaniah.

7646. שָׂבַע, **śâba῾,** *saw-bah´*; or שָׂבֵעַ, **śâbêa῾,** *saw-bay´-ah*; a primitive root; to *sate,* i.e. *fill* to satisfaction (literal or figurative):—have enough, fill (full, self, with), be (to the) full (of), have plenty of, be satiate, satisfy (with), suffice, be weary of.

7647. שָׂבָע, **śâbâ῾,** *saw-baw´*; from 7646; *copiousness:*—abundance, plenteous (-ness, -ly).

7648. שֹׂבַע, **śôba῾,** *so´-bah*; from 7646; *satisfaction* (of food or [figurative] joy):—fill, full (-ness), satisfying, be satisfied.

7649. שָׂבֵעַ, **śâbêaʿ,** *saw-bay´-ah*; from 7646; *satiated* (in a pleasant or disagreeable sense):—full (of), satisfied (with).

7650. שָׁבַע, **shâbaʿ,** *shaw-bah´*; a primitive root; (properly) to *be complete*, but used only as a denominative from 7651; to *seven* oneself, i.e. *swear* (as if by repeating a declaration seven times):—adjure, charge (by an oath, with an oath), feed to the full [*by mistake for* 7646], take an oath, × straitly, (cause to, make to) swear.

A verb meaning to swear, to take an oath, to make to swear an oath. In the passive reflexive stem, the verb means to swear, to take an oath; Abimelech and Phicol asked Abraham to swear his kindness and integrity to them and their descendants (Ge 21:23; Jgs 21:1; 2Sa 21:2). The Lord swears by Himself, since there is nothing greater to swear by. God swore to multiply and bless Abraham's descendants (Ge 22:16; Jer 22:5). God also swore an oath to Abraham personally (Ge 24:7; Ex 13:11). God swore by His holiness to lead Israel into captivity (Am 4:2).

In the causative stem, the verb means to make, to cause someone to take an oath: Abraham made his servant swear an oath to get Isaac a wife from Abraham's own people (Ge 24:37). A wife suspected of adultery was forced to take an oath affirming the proposed curse on her if she were found guilty (Nu 5:21). Saul had ordered the people to take an oath not to eat honey or food while they were engaged in battle with the Philistines (1Sa 14:27; 1Ki 18:10). In this stem, the word can mean to charge someone or to adjure that person. David's men adjured him not to go into battle with them again (2Sa 21:17; 1Ki 22:16). The land of Canaan became the Promised Land the Lord gave to His people based on His oath. He brought them into the land as He had promised by oath to their fathers (Ex 13:5; Dt 1:8, 35; 6:10; Jos 1:6; Jgs 2:1; Jer 11:5).

7651. שֶׁבַע, **shebaʿ,** *sheh´-bah*; or (masculine) שִׁבְעָה, **shibʿâh,** *shib-aw´*; from 7650; a primitive cardinal number; *seven* (as the sacred *full* one); also (adverb) *seven times*; (by implication) a *week*; (by extension) an *indefinite* number:—(+ by) seven ([-fold], -s, [-teen, -teenth], -th, times). Compare 7658.

7652. שֶׁבַע, **shebaʿ,** *sheh´-bah*; the same as 7651; *seven; Sheba,* the name of a place in Palestine, and of two Israelites:—Sheba.

7653. שִׂבְעָה, **śibʿâh,** *sib-aw´*; feminine of 7647; *satiety*:—fulness.

7654. שׂבְעָה, **śobʿâh,** *sob-aw´*; feminine of 7648; *satiety*:—(to have) enough, × till … be full, [un-] satiable, satisfy, × sufficiently.

7655. שִׁבְעָה, **shibʿâh,** *shib-aw´*; (Chaldee); corresponding to 7651:—seven (times).

7656. שִׁבְעָה, **Shibʿâh,** *shib-aw´*; masculine of 7651; *seven* (*-th*); *Shebah,* a well in Palestine:—Shebah.

7657. שִׁבְעִים, **shibʿîym,** *shib-eem´*; multiple of 7651; *seventy*:—seventy, threescore and ten (+ -teen).

7658. שִׁבְעָנָה, **shibʿânâh,** *shib-aw-naw´*; prolonged for the masculine of 7651; *seven*:—seven.

7659. שִׁבְעָתַיִם, **shibʿâthayim,** *shib-aw-thah´-yim*; dual (adverb) of 7651; *seven-times*:—seven (-fold, times).

7660. שָׁבַץ, **shâbats,** *shaw-bats´*; a primitive root; to *interweave* (coloured) threads in squares; by implication (*of reticulation*) to *enchase* gems in gold:—embroider, set.

7661. שָׁבָץ, **shâbâts,** *shaw-bawts´*; from 7660; *intanglement,* i.e. (figurative) *perplexity*:—anguish.

7662. שְׁבַק, **shᵉbaq,** *sheb-ak´*; (Chaldee); corresponding to the root of 7733; to *quit,* i.e. allow to remain:—leave, let alone.

7663. שָׂבַר, **śâbar,** *saw-bar´*; erroneously שָׁבַר, **shâbar,** *shaw-bar´*; (Ne 2:13, 15), a primitive root; to *scrutinize*; by implication (of *watching*) to *expect* (with hope and patience):—hope, tarry, view, wait.

A verb meaning to scrutinize, to expect with hope and patience, to hope, to tarry, to view, to wait. Nehemiah used this word to express an examination of the broken walls of Jerusalem before the returning exiles began rebuilding (Ne 2:13–15). In this context, the verb did not only refer to Nehemiah's viewing of simply a broken wall but also a metaphorical viewing of

Israel's brokenness and need for the return of the presence of God to Jerusalem.

7664. שֶׁבֶר, **śeber,** *say´-ber;* from 7663; *expectation:*—hope.

7665. שָׁבַר, **shâbar,** *shaw-bar´;* a primitive root; to *burst* (literal or figurative):—break (down, off, in pieces, up), broken ([-hearted]), bring to the birth, crush, destroy, hurt, quench, × quite, tear, view [*by mistake for* 7663].

A verb meaning to break, to burst, to break in pieces, to break down, to break up, to smash, to shatter, to bring to birth. The word is most often used to express bursting or breaking. Other meanings include God's actions against stubborn pride (Le 26:19); or a metaphor for deliverance expressed figuratively by the breaking of a yoke (Jer 28:2). In a figurative sense, the word describes the breaking of Pharaoh's arms (Eze 30:21, 22). It also depicts the literal smashing or shattering of the tablets of the commandments (Ex 32:19). Further expressions of the word can mean to bring to the moment of birth (Isa 66:9); to break down or destroy a people (Isa 14:25); to break objects of material quality (Ge 19:9; Le 6:28[21]; Jer 49:35).

7666. שָׁבַר, **shâbar,** *shaw-bar´;* denominative from 7668; to *deal* in grain:—buy, sell.

7667. שֶׁבֶר, **sheber,** *sheh´-ber;* or שֵׁבֶר, **shêber,** *shay´-ber;* from 7665; a *fracture,* (figurative) *ruin;* (specifically) a *solution* (of a dream):—affliction, breach, breaking, broken [-footed, -handed], bruise, crashing, destruction, hurt, interpretation, vexation.

A masculine noun meaning destruction, ruin, affliction, fracture, solution of a dream, breach. This noun can be used to express the result from the breaking of a dream (i.e. its interpretation [Jgs 7:15]). Isaiah used this noun to express the possible result of sin by speaking metaphorically of the shattering of a wall (Isa 30:13). In Leviticus, this noun is used to designate a fracture of the foot or hand, indicating a cripple (Le 21:19). The noun can also be used to indicate the primary reason for suffering due to disobedience to God.

7668. שֶׁבֶר, **sheber,** *sheh´-ber;* the same as 7667; *grain* (as if *broken* into kernels):—corn, victuals.

A masculine noun meaning grain, i.e. that which is broken into kernels, corn, or food stuff. The word is used nine times in the OT as a general term for grain, with seven being used in the Joseph narratives of Genesis. This noun can connote grain that is for sale (Ge 42:1); especially that which is eaten during a famine (Ge 42:19). This word is the food stuff eaten when people are less particular about what they eat. In Nehemiah, it describes the food brought in by neighboring countries to sell on the Sabbath. The remnant that had returned promised God they would not buy it (Ne 10:31[32]). The noun is also used in reference to Israel's greed and disobedience when they were waiting impatiently for the end of the Sabbath that they might once again sell grain (Am 8:5).

7669. שֶׁבֶר, **Sheber,** *sheh´-ber;* the same as 7667; *Sheber,* an Israelite:—Sheber.

7670. שִׁבְרוֹן, **shibrôwn,** *shib-rone´;* from 7665; *rupture,* i.e. a *pang;* (figurative) *ruin:*—breaking, destruction.

A masculine noun meaning rupture (i.e. a pang). It is used figuratively for ruin, breaking, and destruction. This noun was used figuratively in Jeremiah to describe emotional distress by way of broken loins (Jer 17:18). It was used in reference to the coming exile, in which it would seem as if Israel had been cut off from the covenant of God, although God, being faithful and true, would provide a remnant or a branch of David. It was also used in Ezekiel as the reason for distress and sorrow (Eze 21:6[11]). This reference was also for the coming exile of Israel, in which God would give the Israelites over to those they hated.

7671. שְׁבָרִים, **Sh°bârîym,** *sheb-aw-reem´;* plural of 7667; *ruins; Shebarim,* a place in Palestine:—Shebarim.

7672. שְׁבַשׁ, **sh°bash,** *sheb-ash´;* (Chaldee); corresponding to 7660; to *intangle,* i.e. *perplex:*—be astonished.

7673. שָׁבַת, **shâbath,** *shaw-bath´;* a primitive root; to *repose,* i.e. *desist* from exertion; used in many implication relations (causative, figurative or specific):—(cause to, let, make to) cease, celebrate, cause (make) to fail, keep (sabbath), suffer to be lacking, leave, put away (down), (make to) rest, rid, still, take away.

A verb meaning to repose, to rest, to rid of, to still, to put away, to leave. Most often, the word expresses the idea of resting (i.e. abstaining from labour), especially on the seventh day (see Ex 20:8–11). It is from this root that the noun for *Sabbath* originates, a word designating the time to be set aside for rest. The verb is used of God to describe His resting after the completion of creation (Ge 2:2). This example of rest by God at creation set the requirement of rest that He desires for His people in order that they may live lives pleasing to Him, full of worship and adoration (Ex 31:17). In Joshua, the verb expresses a cessation of the provision of manna by God to the Israelites (Jos 5:12). The land was also depicted as enjoying a rest from the Israelite farmers while they were in exile (Le 26:34, 35).

Daniel uses this verb to indicate a ceasing of ritual sacrifice and offerings (Da 9:27). In that passage, Daniel was speaking of the Messiah's coming and the establishment of the New Covenant, when there would be no more need for ritual sacrifices. In another context, the verb can mean to exterminate or destroy a certain object, such as in Am 8:4 in which Amos addresses those who trampled the needy and did away with the poor. The verb means to cause, to desist from, as in God's declaration of action against the shepherds (Eze 34:10). The word suggests a removing of people or other objects (Ex 12:15; Eze 23:27, 48; Isa 30:11). In still other contexts, the causative stem means to fail or to leave lacking. In Ru 4:14, God was praised because He did not leave Naomi without a kinsman-redeemer.

7674. שֶׁבֶת, **shebeth,** *sheh´-beth*; from 7673; *rest, interruption, cessation*:—cease, sit, still, loss of time.

7675. שֶׁבֶת, **shebeth,** *sheh´-beth*; infinitive of 3427; (properly) *session*; but used also concretely an *abode* or *locality*:—place, seat. Compare 3429.

7676. שַׁבָּת, **shabbâth,** *shab-bawth´*; intensive from 7673; *intermission*, i.e. (specific) the *Sabbath*:—(+ every) sabbath.

A noun meaning Sabbath, Day of Atonement, Sabbath week or year, weeks. The word can be translated as Sabbath in practically every instance. The seventh day was set aside at cre-

ation, but the holy Sabbath was first given to Israel and first mentioned in the biblical text in Ex 16:23 as a gift to God's people (Ex 16:25, 26, 29). The word describes the day as it was officially established in the Ten Commandments at Sinai. It was the seventh day, and it was to be kept holy, set apart to the Lord (Ex 20:8, 10). That day was blessed by the Lord (Ex 20:11); and was to be observed by Israel forever (Ex 31:13–16; Eze 20:12). Not even a fire could be lit in any house on the Sabbath (Ex 35:3; Le 23:32; Ne 10:31[32]; Isa 58:13; Jer 17:22); nor could work, even on the tabernacle, be performed (Ex 35:2). Special offerings were presented on the Sabbath in addition to the regular daily burnt offerings, properly termed Sabbath offerings (Nu 28:9, 10). The purpose for the Sabbath was rest for all God's people; its basis was found in God's cessation from work at Creation (Ex 20:11; cf. Ex 31:17); and Israel's historic experience of forced labour in Egypt (Dt 5:15). Unfortunately, God's people chose to utterly desecrate the Lord's Sabbaths (Eze 20:13, 16, 20).

The high point of the religious year for Israel was the Day of Atonement which the author described as a Sabbath of Sabbaths (Le 16:31; 23:32), a Sabbath of rest. Every seventh year was described as a Sabbath to the Lord or, using the same term employed for the Day of Atonement, a Sabbath of Sabbaths (Le 25:4). During this time, the land was to remain unplowed; thus, the land itself was to enjoy its Sabbaths (Le 25:6; 26:34). When Israel was in exile, God remembered the land, giving it rest, so that it was refreshed by lying fallow for seventy years (Le 26:34, 35, 43); enjoying its Sabbaths that Israel had not observed (2Ch 36:21). Seven Sabbaths or seven weeks of years were equal to forty-nine years (Le 25:8). The produce of the land that grew of itself during the Sabbath year is described as the Sabbath (produce) of the land (Le 25:6).

7677. שַׁבָּתוֹן, **shabbâthôwn,** *shab-baw-thone´*; from 7676; a *sabbatism* or special holiday:—rest, sabbath.

A masculine noun meaning a time to rest, a special holiday, a day of rest, a Sabbath feast. The meaning most often denoted from this word is that of the day of rest (Ex 31:15). In Leviticus, this noun is used to refer to the Day of Atonement (Le 16:31); the sabbatical year

(Le 25:4); the Feast of Trumpets (Le 23:24); and the first and eighth days of the Feast of Tabernacles (Le 23:39).

During the sabbatical year, the land was not to be plowed but to be given a Sabbath rest, a time of refreshing to the Lord. This word was also used to describe the requirements of rest on the first and eighth days of the Feast of Tabernacles. In any context, however, the meaning of this noun is still one of a requirement for God's people to rest on the seventh day or any other holy day as directed.

7678. שַׁבְּתַי, **Shabbᵉthay,** *shab-beth-ah´ee;* from 7676; *restful; Shabbethai,* the name of three Israelites:—Shabbethai.

7679. שָׂגָא, **sâgâ',** *saw-gaw´;* a primitive root; to *grow,* i.e. (causative) to *enlarge,* (figurative) *laud:*—increase, magnify.

7680. שְׂגָא, **sᵉgâ',** *seg-aw´;* (Chaldee); corresponding to 7679; to *increase:*—grow, be multiplied.

7681. שָׁגֵא, **Shâgê',** *shaw-gay´;* probably from 7686; *erring; Shagè,* an Israelite:—Shage.

7682. שָׂגַב, **sâgab,** *saw-gab´;* a primitive root; to *be* (causative, *make*) *lofty,* especially *inaccessible;* (by implication) *safe, strong;* used literal and figurative:—defend, exalt, be excellent, (be, set on) high, lofty, be safe, set up (on high), be too strong.

7683. שָׁגַג, **shâgag,** *shaw-gag´;* a primitive root; to *stray,* i.e. (figurative) *sin* (with more or less apology):— × also for that, deceived, err, go astray, sin ignorantly.

A verb meaning to stray, to be deceived, to err, to go astray, to sin ignorantly. The primary meaning of this word is to commit an error, to sin inadvertently. In Leviticus, this word referred to the unintentional sin atoned for by the sacrifice of a ram, referred to as a guilt offering (Le 5:18). In addition to Leviticus, Nu 15:28 also described the priestly function in atonement for one's unintentional sin. Recognition of sin may result from a realization or awareness of covenant violations due to the work of the human consciousness. The psalmist used this word to describe an action before he was afflicted (i.e. he went astray [Ps 119:67]). This verb was also used to designate erring mentally

on the part of self or another person (i.e. being the deceived or the deceiver [Job 12:16]).

7684. שְׁגָגָה, **shᵉgâgâh,** *sheg-aw-gaw´;* from 7683; a *mistake* or inadvertent *transgression:*—error, ignorance, at unawares, unwittingly.

A feminine noun meaning mistake, inadvertent transgression, error, ignorance. The primary meaning is an inadvertent error performed in the daily routine of life that ranged from a slip of the tongue (Ecc 5:6[5]); to accidental manslaughter (Nu 35:11, 15; Jos 20:3, 9). When used with the word *châṭâ'* (2398), it describes a procedure or policy used by priests for the guilt offering that atones for inadvertent sin (Le 4:2, 22, 27; 5:15, 18). Unatoned sin breaks the order and peace between God and people, even if unintentional, and an atonement has to be made. The noun also describes acts in which the sinner is conscious, yet the sinfulness of those acts becomes known after the act takes place.

7685. שָׂגָה, **sâgâh,** *saw-gaw´;* a primitive root; to *enlarge* (especially upward, also figurative):— grow (up), increase.

7686. שָׁגָה, **shâgâh,** *shaw-gaw´;* a primitive root; to *stray* (causative, *mislead*), usually (figurative) to *mistake,* especially (moral) to *transgress;* by extension (through the idea of intoxication) to *reel,* (figurative) *be enraptured:*—(cause to) go astray, deceive, err, be ravished, sin through ignorance, (let, make to) wander.

A verb meaning to stray, to go astray, to err, to deceive, to wander, to make a mistake, to reel. It is primarily used to express the idea of straying or wandering. It is used frequently to describe a wandering or aimless flock, both figuratively and literally (Eze 34:6). Isaiah used this verb to suggest swerving, meandering, or reeling in drunkenness (Isa 28:7). At times, it could define intoxication, not only from wine or beer but also from love (Pr 5:19, 20). This verb also depicts moral corruption (Pr 5:23). Dt 27:18 describes it as a reason for being cursed (i.e. leading a blind man astray). Le 4:13 indicates a sin of ignorance of which the person is still guilty and must provide an atonement when knowledge of the sin is known. The word also expresses a misleading mentally (i.e. being a deceiver or the deceived). The idea of atonement for sin, even of that which is an inadvertent or unintentional sin, is a prevalent thought found in Scripture (Eze 45:20).

7687. שָׂגוּב, **Śᵉgûwb,** *seg-oob´*; from 7682; *aloft; Segub,* the name of two Israelites:—Segub.

7688. שָׂגַח, **shâgach,** *shaw-gakh´*; a primitive root; to *peep,* i.e. *glance* sharply at:—look (narrowly).

7689. שַׂגִּיא, **śaggîy’,** *sag-ghee´*; from 7679; (superlative) *mighty:*—excellent, great.

7690. שַׂגִּיא, **śaggîy’,** *sag-ghee´*; (Chaldee); corresponding to 7689; *large* (in size, quantity or number, also adverbial):—exceeding, great (-ly), many, much, sore, very.

7691. שְׁגִיאָה, **shᵉgîy’âh,** *sheg-ee-aw´*; from 7686; a moral *mistake:*—error.

A feminine noun meaning a moral mistake, an error. As written in Ps 19:12[13], the noun signifies an error or lapse that is hidden from the sight of others. The inclusion of this noun in the verse seems to indicate that only God can see or discern this type of error or moral mistake. In its plural absolute form, this noun indicates a willful sin (Ps 19:13).

7692. שִׁגָּיוֹן, **shiggâyôwn,** *shig-gaw-yone´*; or שִׁגָּיֹנָה, **shiggâyônâh,** *shig-gaw-yo-naw´*; from 7686; (properly) *aberration,* i.e. (technical) a *dithyramb* or rambling poem:—Shiggaion, Shigionoth.

7693. שָׁגַל, **shâgal,** *shaw-gal´*; a primitive root; to *copulate* with:—lie with, ravish.

7694. שֵׁגָל, **shêgal,** *shay-gal´*; from 7693; a *queen* (from cohabitation):—queen.

A feminine noun meaning a queen, a concubine, a harem favourite, a consort. The primary meaning of this noun is queen. This noun was used by Nehemiah to describe the queen who sat beside the king (Ne 2:6). In the book of Psalms, the psalmist used this noun to designate the queen who sat at the right hand of the king (Ps 45:9[10]). Concubine, harem favourite, and consort are also possible definitions due to the close connection of this word with *shâgal* (7693), which can mean to sleep or to have sexual intercourse with.

7695. שֵׁגָל, **shêgal,** *shay-gal´*; (Chaldee); corresponding to 7694; a (legitimate) *queen:*—wife.

7696. שָׁגַע, **shâga‘,** *shaw-gah´*; a primitive root; to *rave* through insanity:—(be, play the) mad (man).

7697. שִׁגָּעוֹן, **shiggâ‘ôwn,** *shig-gaw-yone´*; from 7696; *craziness:*—furiously, madness.

7698. שֶׁגֶר, **sheger,** *sheh´-ger;* from an unused root probably meaning to *eject;* the *fetus* (as finally *expelled*):—that cometh of, increase.

7699. שַׁד, **shad,** *shad;* or שֹׁד, **shôd,** *shode;* probably from 7736 (in its original sense) contraction; the *breast* of a woman or animal (as *bulging*):—breast, pap, teat.

7700. שֵׁד, **shêd,** *shade;* from 7736; a *demon* (as *malignant*):—devil.

A masculine noun meaning a demon, a devil. The primary or typical translation of this noun is demon or demons. This noun was used to describe the recipient of a sacrifice (i.e. a sacrifice that was not directed or given to God [Dt 32:17]). Certain sacrifices in which sons and daughters were sacrificed were also directed toward demons (Ps 106:37). This word is also used to designate the recipients of forbidden sacrifices.

7701. שֹׁד, **shôd,** *shode;* or שׁוֹד, **shôwd,** *shode;* (Job 5:21), from 7736; *violence, ravage:*—desolation, destruction, oppression, robbery, spoil (-ed, -er, -ing), wasting.

A masculine noun meaning violence, destruction, desolation, robbery, spoil, wasting. The primary meaning of this word is violence or destruction. In Job, the noun is used to describe an object or idea of which not to fear (Job 5:21). The word is also used in Psalms to designate a reason for God's arising to protect the weak (Ps 12:5[6]). Isaiah used the noun to depict the reason that God weeps bitterly (i.e. the destruction of His people due to their sin [Isa 22:4]). This word was also used by Jeremiah and Amos to describe violence and havoc as social sins (Jer 6:7; Am 3:10). The primary meaning of destruction was used by Hosea to express God's reason for the coming destruction of a nation (Hos 7:13).

7702. שָׂדַד, **sâdad,** *saw-dad´*; a primitive root; to *abrade,* i.e. *harrow* a field:—break clods, harrow.

7703. שָׁדַד, **shâdad,** *shaw-dad´*; a primitive root; (properly) to *be burly*, i.e. (figurative) *powerful* (passive, *impregnable*); (by implication) to *ravage*:—dead, destroy (-er), oppress, robber, spoil (-er), × utterly, (lay) waste.

A verb meaning to be burly, to ravage, to destroy, to oppress, to assault, to spoil, to lay waste, to devastate. The primary meaning of the verb is to devastate or to destroy. This word is used to describe the destruction of the unfaithful, an action taken due to their duplicity (Pr 11:3). The verb is also used in Isaiah's prophecy against Moab to describe the action that would result on its cities (Isa 15:1). The actions of an outlaw or thief are depicted by the verb concerning a righteous person's house (Pr 24:15). The word expresses God's judgment on Egypt and the overthrowing of its hordes (Eze 32:12). The verb is also used to describe the actions of subjects such as a lion, a wolf, or a leopard in the figurative sense as a response to the rebellions and backsliding of Jerusalem (Jer 5:6). Jeremiah uses the word to describe the destruction of the tabernacle and the barrenness when everything was taken away (Jer 10:20).

7704. שָׂדֶה, **śâdeh,** *saw-deh´*; or שָׂדַי, **śâday,** *saw-dah´ee*; from an unused root meaning to *spread* out; a *field* (as *flat*):—country, field, ground, land, soil, × wild.

A masculine noun meaning open country, a field, a domain, a plot (of land). The primary meaning of the word is a field, oftentimes defined more descriptively as an open field. The noun is used to describe pastureland in which flocks of sheep were fed (Ge 29:2). The word is also used to describe a field or a plot of land that was normally unfrequented and in which one could meditate without being disturbed (Ge 24:63, 65). Another meaning of the word is a field in which a slain man was found (Dt 21:1). The word is also used as a place opposite of the Tent of Meeting in which the Israelites had made sacrifices but were to no longer (Le 17:5). In Numbers, the noun is used to indicate a land or territory that belonged to a nation or tribe (Nu 21:20).

7705. שִׁדָּה, **shiddâh,** *shid-dah´*; from 7703; a *wife* (as *mistress* of the house):— × all sorts, musical instrument.

7706. שַׁדַּי, **Shadday,** *shad-dah´ee*; from 7703; the *Almighty*:—Almighty.

A masculine noun and name for God meaning Shaddai, Almighty. The word occurs only forty-eight times in the Hebrew Bible, thirty-one times in the book of Job. This is a name for the Lord—the OT people of faith referring to Him as El Shaddai, God Almighty. The term is found in the passages that report God's promises of fertility, land, and abundance to them, indicating that He, the Almighty, could fulfill His promises (Ge 17:1; 28:3; 35:11). The Lord appeared to Abraham when he was ninety-nine years old and identified himself as El Shaddai, God Almighty (Ge 17:1). All three patriarchs knew Him by this name (Ge 28:1–3; 35:11); as did Joseph (Ge 48:3; cf. Ex 6:3); Ezekiel the prophet knew the tradition of Shaddai as well (Eze 10:5). Balaam, Naomi, the psalmist, Joel, and Isaiah employed the term Shaddai, Almighty (Nu 24:4; Ru 1:20; Ps 68:14[15]; Isa 13:6; Joel 1:15). But it is especially Job who uses the term appropriately as a non-Israelite (Job 5:17; 13:3; 24:1; 37:23), since it is a universal term for God. It is always found in poetic sections of material. The book of Job also uses the name the LORD, Yahweh, twenty-seven times, and it is found all but five times in the prose sections (Job 1—2; 42:7–17; see concordance for specific references).

7707. שְׁדֵיאוּר, **Shᵉdêy´ûwr,** *shed-ay-oor´*; from the same as 7704 and 217; *spreader of light*; *Shedejur*, an Israelite:—Shedeur.

7708. שִׂדִּים, **Śiddîym,** *sid-deem´*; plural from the same as 7704; *flats*; *Siddim*, a valley in Palestine:—Siddim.

7709. שְׁדֵמָה, **shᵉdêmâh,** *shed-ay-maw´*; apparently from 7704; a cultivated *field*:—blasted, field.

7710. שָׁדַף, **shâdaph,** *shaw-daf´*; a primitive root; to *scorch*:—blast.

7711. שְׁדֵפָה, **shᵉdêphâh,** *shed-ay-faw´*; or שִׁדָּפוֹן, **shiddâphôwn,** *shid-daw-fone´*; from 7710; *blight*:—blasted (-ing).

7712. שְׁדַר, **shᵉdar,** *shed-ar´*; (Chaldee); a primitive root; to *endeavour*:—labour.

7713. שְׁדֵרָה, **s⁵derâh,** *sed-ay-raw´*; from an unused root meaning to *regulate*; a *row,* i.e. *rank* (of soldiers), *story* (of rooms):—board, range.

7714. שַׁדְרַךְ, **Shadrak,** *shad-rak´*; probably of foreign origin; *Shadrak,* the Babylonian name of one of Daniel's companions:—Shadrach.

7715. שַׁדְרַךְ, **Shadrak,** *shad-rak´*; (Chaldee); the same as 7714:—Shadrach.

7716. שֶׂה, **śeh,** *seh*; or שֵׂי, **śêy,** *say*; probably from 7582 through the idea of *pushing* out to graze; a member of a flock, i.e. a *sheep* or *goat:*— (lesser, small) cattle, ewe, goat, lamb, sheep. Compare 2089.

7717. שָׂהֵד, **śâhêd,** *saw-hade´*; from an unused root meaning to *testify*; a *witness:*—record.

7718. שֹׁהַם, **shôham,** *sho´-ham*; from an unused root probably meaning to *blanch*; a gem, probably the *beryl* (from its *pale* green colour):— onyx.

7719. שֹׁהַם, **Shôham,** *sho´-ham*; the same as 7718; *Shoham,* an Israelite:—Shoham.

7720. שַׂהֲרֹן, **śahărôn,** *sah-har-one´*; from the same as 5469; a round *pendant* for the neck:— ornament, round tire like the moon.

7721. שׂוֹא, **śôw',** *so*; from an unused root (akin to 5375 and 7722) meaning to *rise*; a *rising:*— arise.

7722. שׁוֹא, **shôw',** *sho*; or (feminine) שׁוֹאָה, **shôw'âh,** *sho-aw´*; or שֹׁאָה, **shô'âh,** *sho-aw´*; from an unused root meaning to *rush* over; a *tempest*; (by implication) *devastation:*—desolate (-ion), destroy, destruction, storm, wasteness.

A masculine noun meaning ravage. When used in the feminine form *shô'âh,* the noun means devastation, ruin, desolation, or noise. The primary meaning of the word is devastation. Often this word carries with it a sense of something sudden or unexpected like that of a devastating storm (Eze 38:9). In Isaiah, the word describes a coming disaster on the day of reckoning (Isa 10:3). The noun is used to depict a wasteland or a desert (Job 30:3; 38:27). Ps 35:17 uses the masculine form of the word to indicate the ravages that held the psalmist down.

7723. שָׁוְא, **shâv',** *shawv*; or שַׁו, **shav,** *shav*; from the same as 7722 in the sense of *desolating; evil* (as *destructive*), literal (*ruin*) or moral (especially *guile*); (figurative) *idolatry* (as false, subjective), *uselessness* (as deceptive, objective; also adverb in *vain*):—false (-ly), lie, lying, vain, vanity.

A masculine noun meaning emptiness, vanity, evil, ruin, uselessness, deception, worthless, without result, fraud, deceit. The primary meaning of the word is deceit, lie, or falsehood. God used the word to indicate that He punished Judah in vain. The word is used by the psalmist to state that all activities such as labouring, guarding, rising early, staying up late, and toiling for food were useless without God's assistance (Ps 127:1, 2). In the Ten Commandments, the word is used to describe what is prohibited (Dt 5:20). The word is used in Proverbs to indicate that which the author desires to be kept away from him: in this case, falsehood and lies (Pr 30:8). Idols were declared worthless with the usage of the noun in Jeremiah (Jer 18:15). These idols were those that led the people of God to forget Him.

7724. שְׁוָא, **Sh⁵vâ',** *shev-aw´*; from the same as 7723; *false*; *Sheva,* an Israelite:—Sheva.

7725. שׁוּב, **shûwb,** *shoob*; a primitive root; to *turn* back (hence, away) transitive or intransitive, literal or figurative (not necessarily with the idea of *return* to the starting point); (generally) to *retreat*; (often adverbial) *again:*— ([break, build, circumcise, dig, do anything, do evil, feed, lay down, lie down, lodge, make, rejoice, send, take, weep]) × again, (cause to) answer (+ again), × in any case (wise), × at all, averse, bring (again, back, home again), call [to mind], carry again (back), cease, × certainly, come again (back) × consider, + continually, convert, deliver (again), + deny, draw back, fetch home again, × fro, get [oneself] (back) again, × give (again), go again (back, home), [go] out, hinder, let, [see] more, × needs, be past, × pay, pervert, pull in again, put (again, up again), recall, recompense, recover, refresh, relieve, render (again), requite, rescue, restore, retrieve, (cause to, make to) return, reverse, reward, + say nay, send back, set again, slide back, still, × surely, take back (off), (cause to, make to) turn (again, self again, away, back, back again, backward, from, off), withdraw.

A verb meaning to turn, to return, to go back, to do again, to change, to withdraw, to bring back, to reestablish, to be returned, to bring back, to take, to restore, to recompense, to answer, to hinder. The verb is used over one thousand times and has various shades of meaning in its four stems. In the simple stem, it is used to describe divine and human reactions, attitudes, and feelings. The verb describes the possibility that Israel might change (turn) their minds and return to Egypt (Ex 13:17). Josiah the king turned back to the Lord with all his heart, soul, and strength (2Ki 23:25; Jer 34:15). Nevertheless, the Lord did not turn from the anger He held toward Judah (2Ki 23:26; Jer 4:28). Job pleaded with his miserable comforters to relent (i.e. turn away) from him (Job 6:29). God's people will return (repent) and seek Him in the last days (Dt 30:2; Isa 59:20; Hos 3:5) instead of turning away from Him as they are now; to return to Egypt (Isa 6:10; Hos 11:5). God's call was persistently for His people to return to Him (1Ki 8:33; Jer 4:1). Any nation can repent and turn to God for forgiveness (Jer 18:8).

The word is used metaphorically to describe things returning: God's Word will not be revoked (returned) once it has been uttered (Isa 45:23; 55:11); Jacob stayed with Laban until Esau's anger cooled off (turned back) (Ge 27:44, 45); blood guilt could return on one's own head (1Ki 2:33; Ps 7:16[17]). This word also describes the sword of Saul that did not return without success from the battlefield (2Sa 1:22).

The verb also indicates to returning to or to change into. For example, human beings return to the dust of the earth (Ge 3:19; Ecc 12:7); but a person cannot naturally return to life (2Sa 12:23); unless God's Spirit brings it about (1Ki 13:6). A land of great natural fertility can be reduced (turned into) to a farmer's cropland (Isa 29:17).

In its simplest sense, the word means to return, to restore, to go back. Abraham's descendants in their fourth generation would return to Canaan (Ge 15:16); God returned to visit His people (Ge 8:9; 18:10). It is also used to describe turning chariots about when needed (1Ki 22:33; Mic 2:8).

This verb is used with other verbs of motion, all in their infinitive or participial forms, to describe a back and forth motion; the ravens Noah sent out went back and forth (Ge 8:7). Used with another verb in general, *shûb* is either not translated or means to do again

whatever action is indicated by the other verb, such as when Isaac dug again the wells his father had previously dug (Ge 26:18). A similar meaning is to take back or recapture when this verb is used with the Hebrew verb *lâqach* (3947), meaning to take or to receive (2Ki 13:25; Mic 7:19). Finally, if this verb is used with a following infinitive of another verb, it means to do over and over or more and more; Israel angered the Lord more and more than they had already angered Him by performing pagan rituals (Eze 8:17).

7726. שׁוֹבָב, **shôwbâb,** *sho-bawb´*; from 7725; *apostate,* i.e. idolatrous:—backsliding, frowardly, turn away [*from margin*].

7727. שׁוֹבָב, **Shôwbâb,** *sho-bawb´*; the same as 7726; *rebellious; Shobab,* the name of two Israelites:—Shobab.

7728. שׁוֹבֵב, **shôwbêb,** *sho-babe´*; from 7725; *apostate,* i.e. heathenish or (actually) heathen:—backsliding.

7729. שׁוּבָה, **shûwbâh,** *shoo-baw´*; from 7725; a *return:*—returning.

7730. שׂוֹבֶךְ, **sôwbek,** *so´-bek*; for 5441; a *thicket,* i.e. interlaced branches:—thick boughs.

7731. שׂוֹבָךְ, **Shôwbâk,** *sho-bawk´*; perhaps for 7730; *Shobak,* a Syrian:—Shobach.

7732. שׁוֹבָל, **Shôwbâl,** *sho-bawl´*; from the same as 7640; *overflowing; Shobal,* the name of an Edomite and two Israelites:—Shobal.

7733. שׁוֹבֵק, **Shôwbêq,** *sho-bake´*; active participle from a primitive root meaning to *leave* (compare 7662); *forsaking; Shobek,* an Israelite:—Shobek.

7734. שׂוּג, **sûwg,** *soog*; a primitive root; to *retreat:*—turn back.

7735. שׂוּג, **sûwg,** *soog*; a primitive root; to *hedge in:*—make to grow.

7736. שׁוּד, **shûwd,** *shood*; a primitive root; (properly to) *swell* up, i.e. figurative (by implication of *insolence*) to *devastate:*—waste.

7737. שָׁוָה, **shâvâh,** *shaw-vaw´*; a primitive root; (properly) to *level,* i.e. *equalize;* (figurative) to *resemble;* (by implication) to *adjust* (i.e. counterbalance, be suitable, compose, place, yield, etc.):—avail, behave, bring forth, compare, countervail, (be, make) equal, lay, be (make, a-) like, make plain, profit, reckon.

7738. שָׁוָה, **shâvâh**, *shaw-vaw´*; a primitive root; to *destroy*:— × substance [*from the margin*].

7739. שְׁוָה, **shᵉvâh**, *shev-aw´*; (Chaldee); corresponding to 7737; to *resemble*:—make like.

7740. שָׁוֵה, **Shâvêh**, *shaw-vay´*; from 7737; *plain; Shaveh*, a place in Palestine:—Shaveh.

7741. שָׁוֵה קִרְיָתַיִם, **Shâvêh Qiryâthayim**, *shaw-vay´ kir-yaw-thah´-yim*; from the same as 7740 and the dual of 7151; *plain of a double city; Shaveh-Kirjathaim*, a place East of the Jordan:—Shaveh Kiriathaim.

7742. שׂוּחַ, **sûwach**, *soo´-akh*; a primitive root; to *muse* pensively:—meditate.

7743. שׁוּחַ, **shûwach**, *shoo´-akh*; a primitive root; to *sink*, literal or figurative:—bow down, incline, humble.

7744. שׁוּחַ, **Shûwach**, *shoo´-akh*; from 7743; *dell; Shuäch*, a son of Abraham:—Shuah.

7745. שׁוּחָה, **shûwchâh**, *shoo-khaw´*; from 7743; a *chasm*:—ditch, pit.

A feminine noun meaning a ditch, a pit, a chasm. The primary meaning of the word is pit. The verb is used primarily to describe figuratively a trap that leads to ruin. Proverbs uses this word in a figurative sense to describe a prostitute as a deep pit in comparison to a wayward wife as a narrow well (Pr 23:27). This word could also be used to describe plots against someone, as where Jeremiah stated that his accusers had dug pits for him (Jer 18:20). The word also describes the mouth of an adulteress (i.e. a deep pit [Pr 22:14]). Out of the six times that it is used in the OT, only one is used in its literal sense, describing a rift through which God led His people (Jer 2:6).

7746. שׁוּחָה, **Shûwchâh**, *shoo-khaw´*; the same as 7745; *Shuchah*, an Israelite:—Shuah.

7747. שׁוּחִי, **Shûwchîy**, *shoo-khee´*; patronymic from 7744; a *Shuchite* or descendant of Shuach:—Shuhite.

7748. שׁוּחָם, **Shûwchâm**, *shoo-khawm´*; from 7743; *humbly; Shucham*, an Israelite:—Shuham.

7749. שׁוּחָמִי, **Shûwchâmîy**, *shoo-khaw-mee´*; patronymic from 7748; a *Shuchamite* (collective):—Shuhamites.

7750. שׂוּט, **sûwt**, *soot*; or (by permutation) סוּט, **sûwt**, *soot*; a primitive root; to *detrude*, i.e. (intransitive and figurative) *become derelict* (wrongly practise; namely, idolatry):—turn aside to.

7751. שׁוּט, **shûwt**, *shoot*; a primitive root; (properly) to *push* forth; (but used only figurative) to *lash*, i.e. (the sea with oars) to *row*; (by implication) to *travel*:—go (about, through, to and fro), mariner, rower, run to and fro.

7752. שׁוֹט, **shôwt**, *shote*; from 7751; a *lash* (literal or figurative):—scourge, whip.

7753. שׂוּךְ, **sûwk**, *sook*; a primitive root; to *entwine*, i.e. *shut* in (for formation, protection or restraint):—fence, (make an) hedge (up).

7754. שׂוֹךְ, **sôwk**, *soke*; or (feminine) שׂוֹכָה, **sôwkâh**, *so-kaw´*; from 7753; a *branch* (as *interleaved*):—bough.

7755. שׂוֹכֹה, **Sôwkôh**, *so-ko´*; or שֹׂכֹה, **Sôkôh**, *so-ko´*; or שׂוֹכוֹ, **Sôwkôw**, *so-ko´*; from 7753; *Sokoh* or *Soko*, the name of two places in Palestine:—Shocho, Shochoh, Sochoh, Soco, Socoh.

7756. שׂוּכָתִי, **Sûwkâthîy**, *soo-kaw-thee´*; probably patronymic from a name corresponding to 7754 (feminine); a *Sukathite* or descendant of an unknown Israelite named Sukah:—Suchathite.

7757. שׁוּל, **shûwl**, *shool*; from an unused root meaning to *hang* down; a *skirt*; (by implication) a bottom *edge*:—hem, skirt, train.

7758. שׁוֹלָל, **shôwlâl**, *sho-lawl´*; or שֵׁילָל, **shêylâl**, *shay-lawl´*; (Mic 1:8); from 7997; *nude* (especially barefoot); (by implication) *captive*:—spoiled, stripped.

7759. שׁוּלַמִּית, **Shûwlammîyth**, *shoo-lam-meeth´*; from 7999; *peaceful* (with the article always prefixed, making it a pet name); the *Shulammith*, an epithet of Solomon's queen:—Shulamite.

7760. שׂוּם, **sûwm**, *soom*; or שִׂים, **sîym**, *seem*; a primitive root; to *put* (used in a great variety of applications, literal, figurative, inference and ellipsis):— × any wise, appoint, bring, call [a name], care, cast in, change, charge, commit, consider, convey, determine, + disguise, dispose, do, get, give, heap up, hold, impute, lay (down, up), leave, look, make (out), mark, + name, × on, ordain, order, + paint, place, preserve, purpose, put (on), + regard, rehearse, reward, (cause to) set (on, up), shew, + steadfastly, take, × tell, + tread down, ([over-]) turn, × wholly, work.

A verb meaning to appoint, to bring, to call, to put, to change, to charge, to commit, to consider, to convey, to determine. The primary meaning of the verb is to put, to set, or to place. The verb indicates that which God put on the earth, as noted in Genesis where God put the man and woman that He formed in the Garden of Eden (Ge 2:8). The usage of the verb in this sense indicates God's sovereignty over all creation, especially that of humankind. The verb is also used to describe Samuel's action concerning the stone he named Ebenezer (1Sa 7:12). This stone was set up between Mizpah and Shen to remember God's deliverance of the Israelites from the Philistines. The verb is used to describe a committing of one's cause before God (Job 5:8). The word is used in Exodus in response to an interaction between Moses and God, in which God gave a new decree and law to the Israelites (Ex 15:25). In this setting, the verb again emphasizes God's sovereignty, His ability to establish the order of things, and His ability to control the elements of nature and disease. In Deuteronomy, *śûm* is used to describe God's appointing of leaders over the different tribes of Israel, for their numbers were too great for Moses alone (Dt 1:13). The word is also used to indicate a charging of someone, as where a man charged his wife with premarital sex (Dt 22:14).

7761. שׂוּם, **sûwm,** *soom*; (Chaldee); corresponding to 7760:— + command, give, lay, make, + name, + regard, set.

7762. שׁוּם, **shûwm,** *shoom*; from an unused root meaning to *exhale*; *garlic* (from its rank *odor*):— garlic.

7763. שׁוֹמֵר, **Shôwmêr,** *sho-mare´*; or שֹׁמֵר, **Shômêr,** *sho-mare´*; active participle of 8104; *keeper*; *Shomer*, the name of two Israelites:— Shomer.

7764. שׁוּנִי, **Shûwnîy,** *shoo-nee´*; from an unused root meaning to *rest*; *quiet*; *Shuni*, an Israelite:— Shuni.

7765. שׁוּנִי, **Shûwnîy,** *shoo-nee´*; patronymic from 7764; a *Shunite* (collective) or descendants of Shuni:— Shunites.

7766. שׁוּנֵם, **Shûwnêm,** *shoo-name´*; probably from the same as 7764; *quietly*; *Shunem*, a place in Palestine:— Shunem.

7767. שׁוּנַמִּית, **Shûwnammîyth,** *shoo-nam-meeth´*; patrial from 7766; a *Shunammitess*, or female inhabitant of Shunem:— Shunamite.

7768. שָׁוַע, **shâva‘,** *shaw-vah´*; a primitive root; (properly) to *be free*; but used only causative and reflexive to *halloo* (for help, i.e. *freedom* from some trouble):— cry (aloud, out), shout.

7769. שׁוּעַ, **shûwa‘,** *shoo´-ah*; from 7768; a *halloo*:— cry, riches.

7770. שׁוּעַ, **Shûwa‘,** *shoo´-ah*; the same as 7769; *Shua*, a Canaanite:— Shua, Shuah.

7771. שׁוֹעַ, **shôwa‘,** *sho´-ah*; from 7768 in the original sense of *freedom*; a *noble*, i.e. *liberal, opulent*; also (as noun in the derived sense) a *halloo*:— bountiful, crying, rich.

7772. שׁוֹעַ, **Shôwa‘,** *sho´-ah*; the same as 7771; *rich*; *Shoa*, an Oriental people:— Shoa.

7773. שֶׁוַע, **sheva‘,** *sheh´-vah*; from 7768; a *halloo*:— cry.

7774. שׁוּעָא, **Shûwâ‘,** *shoo-aw´*; from 7768; *wealth*; *Shua*, an Israelitess:— Shua.

7775. שַׁוְעָה, **shav‘âh,** *shav-aw´*; feminine of 7773; a *hallooing*:— crying.

7776. שׁוּעָל, **shûw‘âl,** *shoo-awl´*; or שֻׁעָל, **shu‘âl,** *shoo-awl´*; from the same as 8168; a *jackal* (as a *burrower*):— fox.

7777. שׁוּעָל, **Shûw‘âl,** *shoo-awl´*; the same as 7776; *Shual*, the name of an Israelite and of a place in Palestine:— Shual.

7778. שׁוֹעֵר, **shôw‘êr,** *sho-are´*; or שֹׁעֵר, **shô‘êr,** *sho-are´*; active participle of 8176 (as denominative from 8179); a *janitor*:— door-keeper, porter.

7779. שׁוּף, **shûwph,** *shoof*; a primitive root; (properly) to *gape*, i.e. *snap* at; (figurative) to *overwhelm*:—break, bruise, cover.

7780. שׁוֹפָךְ, **Shôwphâk,** *sho-fawk´*; from 8210; *poured*; *Shophak*, a Syrian:—Shophach.

7781. שׁוּפָמִי, **Shûwphâmîy,** *shoo-faw-mee´*; patronymic from 8197; a *Shuphamite* (collective) or descendants of Shephu-pham:—Shuphamite.

7782. שׁוֹפָר, **shôwphâr,** *sho-far´*; or שֹׁפָר, **shôphâr,** *sho-far´*; from 8231 in the original sense of *incising*; a *cornet* (as giving a *clear* sound) or curved horn:—cornet, trumpet.

7783. שׁוּק, **shûwq,** *shook*; a primitive root; to *run* after or over, i.e. *overflow*:—overflow, water.

7784. שׁוּק, **shûwq,** *shook*; from 7783; a *street* (as *run* over):—street.

7785. שׁוֹק, **shôwq,** *shoke*; from 7783; the (lower) *leg* (as a *runner*):—hip, leg, shoulder, thigh.

7786. שׂוּר, **śûwr,** *soor*; a primitive root; (properly) to *vanquish*; (by implication) to *rule* (causative, *crown*):—make princes, have power, reign. See 5493.

A verb meaning to vanquish, to rule, to have power. The primary meaning of this word is to rule or to have power over. In Hosea, the verb denotes what will happen to the parents of children (i.e. they will be vanquished and bereaved of their children) when God turns away from them (see Hos 9:12).

The word is also used to describe Abimelech's ruling of Israel for three years (Jgs 9:22). God sent an evil spirit between Abimelech and the people of Shechem, and they acted treacherously against Abimelech. This was done so that the shedding of the blood of Jerub-Baal's seventy sons might be avenged on their brother Abimelech and the citizens of Shechem who helped him. The verb also denotes one of the reasons for Israel's upcoming punishment. Not only did they choose princes without Yahweh's approval, but Israel also made and worshipped idols in blatant disregard for the rulership and dominion of Yahweh over them (Hos 8:4).

7787. שׂוּר, **śûwr,** *soor*; a primitive root [rather identical with 7786 through the idea of *reducing* to pieces; compare 4883]; to *saw*:—cut.

7788. שׁוּר, **shûwr,** *shoor*; a primitive root; (properly) to *turn*, i.e. *travel* about (as a harlot or a merchant):—go, singular See also 7891.

7789. שׁוּר, **shûwr,** *shoor*; a primitive root [rather identical with 7788 through the idea of *going round* for inspection]; to *spy* out, i.e. (general) *survey*, (for evil) *lurk for*, (for good) *care for*:—behold, lay wait, look, observe, perceive, regard, see.

7790. שׁוּר, **shûwr,** *shoor*; from 7889; a *foe* (as *lying in wait*):—enemy.

7791. שׁוּר, **shûwr,** *shoor*; from 7788; a *wall* (as *going about*):—wall.

7792. שׁוּר, **shûwr,** *shoor*; (Chaldee); corresponding to 7791:—wall.

7793. שׁוּר, **Shûwr,** *shoor*; the same as 7791; *Shur*, a region of the Desert:—Shur.

7794. שׁוֹר, **shôwr,** *shore*; from 7788; a *bullock* (as a *traveller*):—bull (-ock), cow, ox, wall [by mistake for 7791].

7795. שׂוֹרָה, **śôwrâh,** *so-raw´*; from 7786 in the primitive sense of 5493; (properly) a *ring*, i.e. (by analogy) a *row* (adverb):—principal.

7796. שׂוֹרֵק, **Śôwrêq,** *so-rake´*; the same as 8321; a *vine*; *Sorek*, a valley in Palestine:—Sorek.

7797. שׂוּשׂ, **śûwś,** *soos*; or שִׂישׂ, **śîyś,** *sece*; a primitive root; to *be bright*, i.e. *cheerful*:—be glad, × greatly, joy, make mirth, rejoice.

7798. שַׁוְשָׁא, **Shavshâ’,** *shav-shaw´*; from 7797; *joyful*; *Shavsha*, an Israelite:—Shavsha.

7799. שׁוּשַׁן, **shûwshan,** *shoo-shan´*; or שׁוֹשָׁן, **shôwshân,** *sho-shawn´*; or שֹׁשָׁן, **shôshân,** *sho-shawn´*; and (feminine) שׁוֹשַׁנָּה, **shôwshannâh,** *sho-shan-naw´*; from 7797; a *lily* (from its *whiteness*), as a flower or architectural ornament; also a (straight) *trumpet* (from the *tubular* shape):—lily, Shoshannim.

7800. שׁוּשַׁן, **Shûwshan,** *shoo-shan´*; the same as 7799; *Shushan*, a place in Persia:—Shushan.

7801. שׁוּשַׁנְכִי, **Shûwshankîy,** *shoo-shan-kee´*; (Chaldee); of foreign origin; a *Shushankite* (collective) or inhabitant of some unknown place in Assyria:—Susanchites.

7802. שׁוּשַׁן עֵדוּת, **Shûwshan 'Êdûwth,** *shoo-shan´ ay-dooth´*; or (plural of former) שׁוֹשַׁנִּים עֵדוּת, **Shôwshannîym 'Êdûwth,** *sho-shan-neem´ ay-dooth´*; from 7799 and 5715; *lily* (or *trumpet*) *of assemblage; Shushan-Eduth* or *Shoshannim-Eduth,* the title of a popular song:—Shoshan-nim-Eduth, Shushan-eduth.

7803. שׁוּתֶלַח, **Shûwthelach,** *shoo-theh´-lakh*; probably from 7582 and the same as 8520; *crash of breakage; Shuthelach,* the name of two Israelites:—Shuthelah.

7804. שְׁזַב, **sheᶜzab,** *shez-ab´*; (Chaldee); corresponding to 5800; *to leave,* i.e. (causative) *free:*—deliver.

7805. שָׁזַף, **shâzaph,** *shaw-zaf´*; a primitive root; to *tan* (by sun-burning); figurative (as if by a piercing ray) to *scan:*—look up, see.

7806. שָׁזַר, **shâzar,** *shaw-zar´*; a primitive root; to *twist* (a thread of straw):—twine.

7807. שַׁח, **shach,** *shakh*; from 7817; *sunk,* i.e. *downcast:*— + humble.

7808. שֵׂחַ, **śêach,** *say´-akh*; for 7879; *communion,* i.e. (reflexive) *meditation:*—thought.

7809. שָׁחַד, **shâchad,** *shaw-khad´*; a primitive root; to *donate,* i.e. *bribe:*—hire, give a reward.

7810. שֹׁחַד, **shôchad,** *shokh´-ad*; from 7809; a *donation* (venal or redemptive):—bribe (-ry), gift, present, reward.

7811. שָׂחָה, **śâchâh,** *saw-khaw´*; a primitive root; to *swim*; (causative) to *inundate:*—(make to) swim.

7812. שָׁחָה, **shâchâh,** *shaw-khaw´*; a primitive root; to *depress,* i.e. *prostrate* (especially reflexive in homage to royalty or God):—bow (self) down, crouch, fall down (flat), humbly beseech, do (make) obeisance, do reverence, make to stoop, worship.

A verb meaning to bow down, to prostrate oneself, to crouch, to fall down, to humbly beseech, to do reverence, to worship. The primary meaning of the word is to bow down. This verb is used to indicate bowing before a monarch or a superior and paying homage to him or her (Ge 43:28). In contexts such as Genesis 24:26, *shâchâh* is used to indicate bowing down in worship to Yahweh. The psalmists used

this word to describe all the earth bowing down in worship to God as a response to His great power (Ps 66:4); or bowing down in worship and kneeling before the Lord (Ps 95:6). This act of worship is given to God because He deserves it and because those that are speaking are people of His pasture.

The word is also used of Joseph when he described the sheaves of his brothers and parents bowing down to his sheaf after it stood upright in a dream that he had (Ge 37:7). Gideon also interacted with a dream through which God spoke. When he overheard a man telling his friend a dream that the man had and its interpretation, he worshipped God (Jgs 7:15).

Joshua instructed the people of Israel not to associate with the nations remaining around them and not to bow down to or serve any of their gods. He instructed Israel to hold fast to the true God, Yahweh (Jos 23:7). In Zephaniah, the word is also used for worship. When Yahweh destroys all the gods of the land, the nations on every shore will worship Him (Zep 2:11).

7813. שָׂחוּ, **śâchûw,** *saw´-khoo*; from 7811; a *pond* (for *swimming*):—to swim in.

7814. שְׂחוֹק, **śeᶜchôwq,** *sekh-oke´*; or שְׂחֹק, **śeᶜchôq,** *sekh-oke´*; from 7832; *laughter* (in merriment or defiance):—derision, laughter (-ed to scorn, -ing), mocked, sport.

7815. שְׁחוֹר, **sheᶜchôwr,** *shekh-ore´*; from 7835; *dinginess,* i.e. perhaps *soot:*—coal.

A masculine noun meaning dinginess, blackness. This word is used to describe a punishment of Israel, i.e. they were blacker than soot, and their skin had shriveled on their bones (La 4:8). The people of different nations told the Israelites that they must leave for they were seen as unclean. This is similar to the descriptions of the results of the Day of the Lord, which will be a day of blackness (see Joel 2:2). This blackness figuratively represents an army of locusts with which Yahweh will punish those who live in the land for their sin. For this reason, the prophet declared that all who live in the land should and will tremble in fear.

7816. שְׁחוּת, **sheᶜchûwth,** *shekh-ooth´*; from 7812; *pit:*—pit.

A feminine noun meaning pit. Metaphorically speaking, it is a trap that is created as one leads the upright along the path of evil (Pr 28:10). This trap or pit will eventually ensnare its builder. As the wicked plot and scheme against the righteous, in the end, they will only succeed in being caught in their own traps.

7817. שָׁחַח, **shâchach,** *shaw-khakh´*; a primitive root; to *sink* or *depress* (reflexive or causative):— bend, bow (down), bring (cast) down, couch, humble self, be (bring) low, stoop.

7818. שָׂחַט, **sâchat,** *saw-khat´*; a primitive root; to *tread* out, i.e. *squeeze* (grapes):—press.

7819. שָׁחַט, **shâchat,** *shaw-khat´*; a primitive root; to *slaughter* (in sacrifice or massacre):— kill, offer, shoot out, slay, slaughter.

A verb meaning to slaughter, to kill, to offer, to shoot out, to slay. The primary meaning of the verb is to slaughter. In Leviticus, the word is used to indicate that the one who brings the sacrifice is the person who will slaughter the animal (Le 1:5). After the slaughtering, the priests brought the blood and other parts of the animal to the altar. In contrast to Leviticus, 2 Chronicles indicates that the worshippers could not slaughter their sacrifices because they did not consecrate themselves and were ceremonially unclean. In this case, the Levites (i.e. priests) had to slaughter the lambs for all who were ceremonially unclean (cf. 2Ch 30:17). This verb is also used to indicate an ineffective sacrifice where the offerers were only going through the motions of worship (Isa 66:3). Even though the object of their worship appears to be God, their hearts were still bent toward evil. This failure is the reason for their upcoming judgment. Another usage of the verb depicts Saul's army pouncing on the plunder, butchering sheep, cattle, and calves, and eating the meat together with the blood, which was forbidden in the Law (1Sa 14:32). This makes the actions of Saul's army in direct disobedience of God's Law.

The verb is also used to describe the process of a human sacrifice to Yahweh (i.e. the process used to test Abraham with his son Isaac [Ge 22:10]). Since He does not desire human sacrifices, God stopped Abraham from sacrificing his son Isaac. When used in the context of a human sacrifice to false gods, the verb describes the actual process being carried out rather than

the anticipated process such as that found with Abraham (Isa 57:5; Eze 16:21; 23:39).

7820. שָׁחַט, **shâchat,** *shaw-khat´*; a primitive root [rather identical with 7819 through the idea of *striking*]; to *hammer out*:—beat.

7821. שְׁחִיטָה, **shᵉchîytâh,** *shekh-ee-taw´*; from 7819; *slaughter*:—killing.

7822. שְׁחִין, **shᵉchîyn,** *shekh-een´*; from an unused root probably meaning to *burn; inflammation,* i.e. an *ulcer*:—boil, botch.

7823. שָׁחִיס, **shâchîys,** *shaw-khece´*; or סָחִישׁ, **sâchîysh,** *saw-kheesh´*; from an unused root apparently meaning to *sprout; after-growth:*— (that) which springeth of the same.

7824. שָׁחִיף, **sâchîyph,** *shaw-kheef´*; from the same as 7828; a *board* (as *chipped* thin):—cieled with.

7825. שְׁחִית, **shᵉchîyth,** *shekh-eeth´*; from 7812; a *pit-fall* (literal or figurative):—destruction, pit.

A feminine noun meaning a pit, destruction, and pitfall. In La 4:20, the Lord's anointed, King Zedekiah, was caught in the trap of the Babylonians. In Psalms, the noun is used to indicate the crisis from which Yahweh saves those who cry out to Him in their troubles (Ps 107:20). By simply a mere utterance and sending forth His word, God heals and rescues from destruction those who cry out to Him. The proper response of those rescued is to give thank offerings and tell of His works through songs of joy.

7826. שַׁחַל, **shachal,** *shakh´-al*; from an unused root probably meaning to *roar*; a *lion* (from his characteristic *roar*):—(fierce) lion.

7827. שְׁחֵלֶת, **shᵉchêleth,** *shekh-ay´-leth*; apparently from the same as 7826 through some obscure idea, perhaps that of *peeling* off by concussion of sound; a *scale* or shell, i.e. the aromatic *mussel*:—onycha.

7828. שַׁחַף, **shachaph,** *shakh´-af*; from an unused root meaning to *peel*, i.e. *emaciate*; the *gull* (as *thin*):—cuckoo.

7829. שַׁחֶפֶת, **shachepheth,** *shakh-eh´-feth*; from the same as 7828; *emaciation:*—consumption.

7830. שַׁחַץ, **shachats,** *shakh´-ats*; from an unused root apparently meaning to *strut; haughtiness* (as evinced by the attitude):— × lion, pride.

7831. שַׁחֲצוֹם, **Shachătsôwm,** *shakh-ats-ome´*; from the same as 7830; *proudly*; *Shachatsom,* a place in Palestine:—Shahazimah [*from the margin*].

7832. שָׂחַק, **śâchaq,** *saw-khak´*; a primitive root; to *laugh* (in pleasure or detraction); (by implication) to *play*:—deride, have in derision, laugh, make merry, mock (-er), play, rejoice, (laugh to) scorn, be in (make) sport.

7833. שָׁחַק, **shâchaq,** *shaw-khak´*; a primitive root; to *comminate* (by trituration or attrition):—beat, wear.

A verb meaning to beat, to wear, to rub away, to beat fine, to pulverize. The primary usage of the verb is to beat fine or to rub away. In Job, the word is used to describe water wearing away stones in conjunction with torrents washing away the soil. This definition was used as a simile for Job's accusation that Yahweh was destroying a person's hope (Job 14:19). Yahweh uses the verb to dictate to Moses how a blend of incense was to be made (Ex 30:36). This formula, which was placed in front of the Testimony in the Tent of Meeting, was to be regarded as holy and only meant for the Lord. Anyone who used it in another context would be cut off from his people. In a figurative sense, *shâchaq* is used to describe David's victory over his enemies in which he beat them down like fine dust (2Sa 22:43, Ps 18:42[Ps 18:43]).

7834. שַׁחַק, **shachaq,** *shakh´-ak*; from 7833; a *powder* (as *beaten* small); (by analogy) a thin *vapor*; (by extension) the *firmament*:—cloud, small dust, heaven, sky.

A masculine noun meaning dust, a fine cloud, a thin cloud. The primary usage of the word denotes a cloud. Often this word is used to depict a cloud or clouds (in the plural) in the sky (Job 35:5, Pr 8:28). In Psalms, this word is used to describe the heavens (Ps 36:5[Ps 36:6]). In a metaphorical sense, Moses described God as riding on the heavens and clouds in His majesty to help His people (Dt 33:26). Used in this sense, it denotes Yahweh as Ruler over the heavens and all that is in them. This word is used to depict dark rain clouds which form a canopy around Him (2Sa 22:12). The word can also be used to denote nations as fine dust (Isa 40:15).

7835. שָׁחַר, **shâchar,** *shaw-khar´*; a primitive root [rather identical with 7836 through the idea of the *duskiness* of early dawn]; to be *dim* or *dark* (in colour):—be black.

7836. שָׁחַר, **shâchar,** *shaw-khar´*; a primitive root; (properly) to *dawn*, i.e. (figurative) *be* (up) *early* at any task (with the implication of earnestness); (by extension) to *search* for (with painstaking):—[do something] betimes, enquire early, rise (seek) betimes, seek diligently (early, in the morning).

7837. שַׁחַר, **shachar,** *shakh´-ar*; from 7836; *dawn* (literal, figurative or adverb):—day (-spring), early, light, morning, whence riseth.

7838. שָׁחֹר, **shâchôr,** *shaw-khore´*; or שָׁחוֹר, **shâchôwr,** *shaw-khore´*; from 7835; (properly) *dusky,* but also (absolute) *jetty*:—black.

7839. שַׁחֲרוּת, **shachărûwth,** *shakh-ar-ooth´*; from 7836; a *dawning,* i.e. (figurative) *juvenescence*:—youth.

7840. שְׁחַרְחֹר, **sheꞏcharchôr,** *shekh-ar-khor´*; from 7835; *swarthy*:—black.

7841. שְׁחַרְיָה, **Sheꞏcharyâh,** *shekh-ar-yaw´*; from 7836 and 3050; *Jah has sought*; *Shecharjah,* an Israelite:—Shehariah.

7842. שַׁחֲרַיִם, **Shachărayim,** *shakh-ar-ah´-yim*; dual of 7837; *double dawn*; *Shacharajim,* an Israelite:—Shaharaim.

7843. שָׁחַת, **shâchath,** *shaw-khath´*; a primitive root; to *decay,* i.e. (causative) *ruin* (literal or figurative):—batter, cast off, corrupt (-er, thing), destroy (-er, -uction), lose, mar, perish, spill, spoiler, × utterly, waste (-r).

A verb meaning to spoil, to ruin, to destroy, to pervert, to corrupt, to become corrupt, to wipe out. The verb is used to denote the action(s) of the world (i.e. it is corrupt) and ultimately the reason for God's flooding it (Ge 6:11, 12). However, even in total destruction meant to punish the evil of humans, God was sure to save a remnant and therefore keep His part of the covenant. This idea of a saved remnant is predominant throughout the rest of the OT.

Another usage of the verb depicts disobedience to God's command to be fruitful and multiply by spoiling or wasting semen on the ground (Ge 38:9). In this case, Onan's disobedience led to his death, for what he did was wicked in the eyes of Yahweh. The verb is also used to describe violating the covenant in terms of being corrupt (Mal 2:8). As Lot looked over the valley of the Jordan, this word was used to depict what would happen to Sodom and Gomorrah in a future time because of their wickedness (Ge 13:10). In the context of the plagues, the smearing of blood on the lintels and doorposts protected Israel from the destruction of their firstborn (Ex 12:23). When the destroyer came, he would pass by those who had blood on the lintels and doorposts of their houses.

Jerusalem was saved from destruction in 2 Samuel when the Lord was grieved due to the calamity of His people (2Sa 24:16). This verb is used to denote the destruction of a slave's eye that allowed him to go free (Ex 21:26). In Deuteronomy, God prohibited the destruction of fruit trees, for their fruit could be eaten (Dt 20:19–20). He commanded this, for the trees were for the benefit of humans. He also prohibited the shaving (i.e. in terms of spoiling, destroying) of one's beard (Le 19:27).

7844. שְׁחַת, **sh°chath**, *shekh-ath´*; (Chaldee); corresponding to 7843:—corrupt, fault.

An Aramaic verb meaning to corrupt. This word can also function as a noun, in which is designates fault. The verb is used in Daniel to depict what the astrologers did to their words in an effort to gain more time from the king (Da 2:9). The inability of the astrologers and other wise men to interpret Nebuchadnezzar's dream set the stage for Daniel.

In Da 6:5, the word is used as a noun and designated the charge against Daniel. Since no fault could be found, the administrators and satraps persuaded King Darius to issue and enforce the decree that no one could pray to anyone or anything but him for a period of thirty days or be thrown into the lions' den.

7845. שַׁחַת, **shachath**, *shakh´-ath*; from 7743; a *pit* (especially as a trap); (figurative) *destruction*:—corruption, destruction, ditch, grave, pit.

A feminine noun denoting a pit, a ditch, a grave, a hollow place. Its prominent usage is pit. The word is used to describe the pit of destruction from which the Lord's love saves (Isa 38:17). The psalmist uses the word figuratively to designate a type of trap that those who are

seeking his life have dug for him (Ps 35:7). The occurrence of the word in Ezekiel metaphorically denotes a pit in which lions are caught (Eze 19:4). The term lion is used to represent Israel's Prince Jehoahaz and is a metaphorical representation of his policies. He learned to tear prey and devour people. The noun is also used to denote Sheol (Job 33:24; Eze 28:8). Job uses the word in a rhetorical sense to describe a situation in which there is no hope (Job 17:14). He stated that if he allowed himself to call corruption his father and the worm his mother and sister, where would his hope lie?

7846. שֵׂט, **sêt**, *sayte*; or סֵט, **sêt**, *sayt*; from 7750; a *departure* from right, i.e. *sin*:—revolter, that turn aside.

7847. שָׂטָה, **sâṭâh**, *saw-taw´*; a primitive root; to *deviate* from duty:—decline, go aside, turn.

7848. שִׁטָּה, **shiṭṭâh**, *shit-taw´*; feminine of a derivative [only in the plural שִׁטִּים, **shiṭṭîym**, *shit-teem´*, meaning the *sticks* of wood] from the same as 7850; the *acacia* (from its *scourging* thorns):—shittah, shittim. See also 1029.

7849. שָׁטַח, **shâṭach**, *shaw-takh´*; a primitive root; to *expand*:—all abroad, enlarge, spread, stretch out.

7850. שֹׁטֵט, **shôṭêṭ**, *sho-tate´*; active participle of an otherwise unused root meaning (properly, to *pierce*; but only as denominative from 7752) to *flog*; a *goad*:—scourge.

7851. שִׁטִּים, **Shiṭṭîym**, *shit-teem´*; the same as the plural of 7848; *acacia* trees; *Shittim*, a place East of the Jordan:—Shittim.

7852. שָׂטַם, **sâṭam**, *saw-tam´*; a primitive root; (properly) to *lurk* for, i.e. *persecute*:—hate, oppose self against.

7853. שָׂטַן, **sâṭan**, *saw-tan´*; a primitive root; to *attack*, (figurative) *accuse*:—(be an) adversary, resist.

A verb meaning to accuse, to slander, and to harbor animosity toward. The verb is used only six times and presents a negative attitude or bias against something. The psalmist complained about those who attacked or slandered him when he pursued what was good (Ps 38:20[21]); even accusing or attacking him in spite of his positive attitude toward them (Ps 109:4). The psalmist asked for his accusers to be destroyed by shame (Ps 71:13; 109:20, 29). Satan stood ready to accuse or to persecute Joshua, the high priest, in the postexilic community (Zec 3:1). Also, see the noun *śâṭân* (7854).

7854. שָׂטָן, **śâṭân,** *saw-tawn´*; from 7853; an *opponent*; especially (with the article prefixed) *Satan*, the arch-enemy of good:—adversary, Satan, withstand.

A masculine noun meaning an adversary, Satan, an accuser. This noun is used twenty-seven times. In Job it is found fourteen times meaning (the) Satan, the accuser. Satan presented himself among the sons of God and roundly accused Job of not loving or serving God with integrity (Job 1:6, 7; 2:1, 2, 4, 7); all of these uses are in the prologue of the book (Job 1—2). In Zechariah, this noun is used three times with the verb to accuse (*śâṭan* [7853]). Satan stood ready to accuse the high priest Joshua (Zec 3:1, 2). In 1Ch 21:1, Satan was depicted as the one who motivated David insolently to take a census of Israel's army (cf. 2Sa 24:1).

The noun is used in a general sense to indicate any adversary or someone who hinders or opposes. The angel of the Lord opposed Balaam and his donkey on their way to curse Israel, acting in opposition (Nu 22:22, 32); the Philistines feared that David might act in opposition to them in battle (1Sa 29:4; 2Sa 19:22[23]). In Solomon's day, the Lord had given him rest all around him (cf. 1Ki 4:24[5:4]); except for Rezon who reigned in Aram (1Ki 11:14, 23, 25). The psalmist's enemies appointed an accuser to attack him, a person who was wicked (Ps 109:6).

7855. שִׂטְנָה, **śiṭnâh,** *sit-naw´*; from 7853; *opposition* (by letter):—accusation.

A feminine noun meaning accusation, opposition, hostility. Its primary meaning of the word is accusation. In Ezra, the word is used to depict the accusation which those who opposed the rebuilding of the Temple in Jerusalem brought before the king (Ezr 4:6). This accusation stated that the Jews were a rebellious people and that if the completion of the Temple were allowed, they would not submit to the authority of Artaxerxes, king of Persia. This accusation resulted in stopping the building

process until the second year of the reign of Darius.

7856. שִׂטְנָה, **Śiṭnâh,** *sit-naw´*; the same as 7855; *Sitnah*, the name of a well in Palestine:—Sitnah.

7857. שָׁטַף, **shâṭaph,** *shaw-taf´*; a primitive root; to *gush*; (by implication) to *inundate, cleanse*; (by analogy) to *gallop, conquer*:—drown, (over-) flow (-whelm), rinse, run, rush, (thoroughly) wash (away).

A verb meaning to gush, to cleanse, to conquer, to drown, to overflow, to overwhelm, to rinse, to run, to rush, to wash away. In its prominent meaning, the word means to wash away. *Šâṭaph* is used to depict what the Lord will do to a hiding place, that is, He will overflow it (Isa 28:17). This word is used to describe God's power as a flooding downpour (Isa 28:2). It also describes a medium through which God delivers punishment (Jer 47:2). The Lord declared that the time had come to destroy the Philistines, and He would do so, metaphorically speaking, by raising up the waters into an overflowing torrent. If a man with a discharge touched another without rinsing his hands, the person touched had to wash the infected clothing and take a bath with water; he or she would be unclean until evening (Le 15:11). Ezekiel used *shâṭaph* metaphorically to describe the Lord cleansing His bride (Eze 16:9). The Song of Songs uses this word to depict what cannot be done to love, that is, waters cannot flood or quench it. True love withstands all tests (SS 8:7). The psalmist made use of *shâṭaph* to indicate a weariness of life and its trials, speaking metaphorically of sinking into the miry depths in which there is no foothold (Ps 69:2[3]). In Ps 124:4, the psalmist used the word to indicate a physical or material tragedy that is avoided with God on his side. Isaiah used the verb to indicate divine judgment against Judah (Isa 8:8); and Ephraim (Isa 28:2, 15, 17, 18). The usage of this word can also indicate a flooding over or utter destruction at the hands of another nation, sometimes dictated by God and at other times simply by the nature of people (Jer 47:2; Da 11:10, 22, 40).

7858. שֶׁטֶף, **sheṭeph,** *sheh´-tef*; or שֵׁטֶף, **shêṭeph,** *shay´-tef*; from 7857; a *deluge* (literal or figurative):—flood, outrageous, overflowing.

A masculine noun meaning a flood, mighty waters, a torrent. Its primary usage is flood. The noun is used figuratively to indicate coming judgment (Da 9:26; Na 1:8). In Job, the Lord is depicted as being able to cut channels for torrents of rain (Job 38:25). The psalmist indicates that through prayer, one can avoid the mighty waters (Ps 32:6). The word is also used figuratively to depict the intensity of anger (Pr 27:4).

7859. שְׁטַר, **sheᵗtar,** *shet-ar´*; (Chaldee); of uncertain derivation; a *side*:—side.

7860. שֹׁטֵר, **shôṭêr,** *sho-tare´*; active participle of an otherwise unused root probably meaning to *write*; (properly) a *scribe*, i.e. (by analogy or implication) an official *superintendent* or *magistrate*:—officer, overseer, ruler.

A masculine noun meaning a scribe, an official, a magistrate, a record keeper, and an officer. The word is used primarily to denote an officer or overseer. Proverbs contrasts the ant with the sluggard. While the ant has no overseer or ruler, it stores up in the summer and gathers at harvest in contrast to the sluggard who does not (Pr 6:7). The word is also used to denote an officer in the military (2Ch 26:11). In Joshua, the word denoted the person that was responsible for organizing the camp for departure (Jos 1:10; 3:2). In addition, *shôṭêr* denoted those that organized the army and appointed its officers (Dt 20:5, 8, 9). In Exodus, the slave drivers appointed Israelite foremen over the other workers (Ex 5:14). The word is used to denote the officials appointed over Israel (Nu 11:16); and the designation of the Levites as officials (2Ch 19:11).

7861. שִׁטְרַי, **Shiṭray,** *shit-rah´ee*; from the same as 7860; *magisterial; Shitrai,* an Israelite:—Shitrai.

7862. שַׁי, **shay,** *shah´ee*; probably from 7737; a *gift* (as *available*):—present.

7863. שִׂיא, **sîy’,** *see*; from the same as 7721 by permutation; *elevation*:—excellency.

7864. שְׁיָא, **Sheᵗyâ’,** *sheh-yaw´*; for 7724; *Sheja,* an Israelite:—Sheva [*from the margin*].

7865. שִׂיאֹן, **Sîy’ôn,** *see-ohn´*; from 7863; *peak; Sion,* the summit of Mount Hermon:—Sion.

7866. שִׁיאֹן, **Shîy’ôn,** *shee-ohn´*; from the same as 7722; *ruin; Shijon,* a place in Palestine:—Shihon.

7867. שִׂיב, **sîyb,** *seeb*; a primitive root; (properly) to *become aged,* i.e. (by implication) to *grow gray:*—(be) grayheaded.

A verb meaning to grow gray. In Samuel's farewell speech, he stated that it was time for him to step down, for he was old and gray (1Sa 12:2). Eliphaz used the word in Job to designate those that have grown gray-haired and aged, in his somewhat skewed argument to Job. These people are denoted as having wisdom above anyone else of a younger age (Job 15:10).

7868. שִׂיב, **sîyb,** *seeb*; (Chaldee); corresponding to 7867:—elder.

An Aramaic verb meaning to become aged, to grow gray. The word is used in Ezra to denote those appointed as leaders over Israel (Ezr 5:5). It is again used in Ezra to depict the elders of the Jews, in whom the responsibility for rebuilding the Temple lay, according to Darius (Ezr 6:7, 8, 14).

7869. שֵׂיב, **sêyb,** *sabe*; from 7867; old *age:*—age.

A masculine noun meaning old age. In 1Ki, Ahijah is described as being aged, and his eyesight has failed (1Ki 14:4). The usage of this word for Ahijah designates his wisdom. To have a head of gray hair is to have a crown of wisdom.

7870. שִׁיבָה, **shîybâh,** *shee-baw´*; by permutation from 7725; a *return* (of property):—captivity.

7871. שִׁיבָה, **shîybâh,** *shee-baw´*; from 3427; *residence:*—while ... lay.

7872. שֵׂיבָה, **sêybâh,** *say-baw´*; feminine of 7869; old *age:*—(be) gray (grey, hoar, -y) hairs (head, -ed), old age.

A feminine noun meaning old age or gray hair. The word is used to denote that Joseph's brothers would bring to the grave the gray head of their father (Ge 44:31). Hosea uses the word figuratively to depict Ephraim being old before its natural time, that is, its hair was sprinkled with gray (Hos 7:9). In Proverbs, gray hair is a crown of splendor (Pr 16:31); while 1Ki denotes the gray head, not as wise, but simply old (1Ki 2:6, 9). The psalmist uses the word to depict a point in life in which he could not perform the same deeds as before. On account of this, the psalmist asked God not to forsake him until he was able to declare God's glory to the coming generation (Ps 71:18). Genesis uses the word to denote the time Abraham will be buried, that is, a good old age (Ge 15:15; 25:8). Naomi's friends predicted that her grandson Obed would renew her life and sustain her in her old age (Ru 4:15).

7873. שִׂיג, **śîyg,** *seeg*; from 7734; a *withdrawal* (into a private place):—pursuing.

7874. שִׂד, **śîyd,** *seed*; a primitive root probably meaning to *boil* up (compare 7736); used only as denominative from 7875; to *plaster*:—plaister.

7875. שִׂיד, **śîyd,** *seed*; from 7874; *lime* (as *boiling* when slacked):—lime, plaister.

7876. שָׁיָה, **shâyâh,** *shaw-yaw´*; a primitive root; to *keep* in memory:—be unmindful. [Render Dt 32:18, "A Rock bore thee, *thou must recollect*; and (yet) thou hast forgotten," etc.]

7877. שֵׁיזָא, **Shîyzâ',** *shee-zaw´*; of unknown derivation; *Shiza,* an Israelite:—Shiza.

7878. שִׂיחַ, **śîyach,** *see´-akh*; a primitive root; to *ponder,* i.e. (by implication) *converse* (with oneself, and hence aloud) or (transitive) *utter:*—commune, complain, declare, meditate, muse, pray, speak, talk (with).

A verb meaning to ponder, to converse, to utter, to complain, to meditate, to pray, to speak. Its primary use is to complain. In Job, the word denotes the action that Job took against the bitterness in his soul, that is, his complaints (Job 7:11). God's people were instructed to sing praises to Him (1Ch 16:9; Ps 105:2). This singing tells of all His wondrous acts. The word is used in Job to denote speaking to the earth (Job 12:8); while Isaiah used it to depict Christ's dying without children, that is, descendants (Isa 53:8). Isaiah's rhetorical question denoted that an absence of descendants was normally a shameful thing in the culture.

7879. שִׂיחַ, **śîyach,** *see´-akh*; from 7878; a *contemplation*; (by implication) an *utterance:*—babbling, communication, complaint, meditation, prayer, talk.

A masculine noun meaning contemplation, meditation, prayer, talk, utterance, babbling.

The primary meaning of the word is a complaint. In Job's narrative, he stated that even his couch would not ease his complaint (Job 7:13); that even if he were to forget his complaint, he would still dread all of his sufferings (Job 9:27); and because he loathed his very life, he would give free reign to his complaint (Job 10:1). Elijah mocked the prophets of Baal, telling them to cry louder because their god might be deep in thought (1Ki 18:27). The word is also used to denote Hannah's prayer containing words of great anguish (1Sa 1:16). The psalmist used the word to depict meditation that he hoped would be pleasing to the Lord (Ps 104:34).

7880. שִׂיחַ, **śîyach,** *see´-akh*; from 7878; a *shoot* (as if *uttered* or put forth), i.e. (general) *shrubbery:*—bush, plant, shrub.

A masculine noun meaning a shoot, brush, a plant, a shrub. The most common usage of this word is a shrub or brush. It is used to denote that when the Lord made the heavens and earth, no shrub of the field had yet appeared nor had any plant sprung up (Ge 2:5). *Śiyach* designates the bushes under which Hagar placed Ishmael to die (Ge 21:15). The two were dying due to lack of water, and therefore Hagar placed Ishmael underneath bushes, walked out of sight, still in hearing distance, and sat down. She did not want to watch her son die. In his discourse, Job designated the brush as the place where fathers of the sons who mocked him gathered salt herbs (Job 30:4). The bushes were also the place in which these fathers brayed (Job 30:7).

7881. שִׂיחָה, **śîychâh,** *see-khaw´*; feminine of 7879; *reflection*; (by extension) *devotion:*—meditation, prayer.

A feminine noun meaning meditation, reflection, concern of one's thoughts, musing, reflection. The word is primarily used to indicate meditation. The psalmist indicated the proper procedure for an individual's response to God's Law. Because of his love for God's Law, the psalmist was prompted to meditate on it all day long. Due to his practice of meditation, the psalmist received more understanding than his elders (Ps 119:97, 99). As Job expressed his feelings and frustrations, Eliphaz responded condemningly, stating that what Job was feeling and saying was hindering devotion to God (Job 15:4). Eliphaz's response was that of an ignorant man who did not realize the true nature of devotion to God.

7882. שִׁיחָה, **shîychâh,** *shee-khaw´*; for 7745; a *pit*-fall:—pit.

A feminine noun meaning a pit. Jeremiah used a metaphorical rendering of the word to describe his enemies' actions against him, they had dug a pit to capture him (Jer 18:22). The psalmist also used a similar rendering of the word to describe what his enemies had done. They had dug a pit for him but had fallen into it themselves (Ps 57:6[7]). In Ps 119:85, the word was used to indicate attempts on the part of the arrogant to cause the psalmist to act contrary to God's Law. However, the psalmist's firm grounding in the laws and precepts of *Yahweh* kept him from falling into their traps.

7883. שִׁיחוֹר, **Shîychôwr,** *shee-khore´*; or שְׁחוֹר, **Shi-chôwr,** *shee-khore´*; or שִׁחֹר, **Shichôr,** *shee-khore´*; probably from 7835; *dark*, i.e. *turbid; Shichor,* a stream of Egypt:—Shihor, Sihor.

7884. שִׁיחוֹר לִבְנָת, **Shîychôwr Libenâth,** *shee-khore´ lib-nawth´*; from the same as 7883 and 3835; *darkish whiteness; Shichor-Libnath,* a stream of Palestine:—Shihor-libnath.

7885. שַׁיִט, **shayiṭ,** *shah´-yit*; from 7751; an *oar*; also (compare 7752) a *scourge* (figurative):—oar, scourge.

7886. שִׁילֹה, **Shîylôh,** *shee-lo´*; from 7951; *tranquil; Shiloh,* an epithet of the Messiah:—Shiloh.

7887. שִׁילֹה, **Shîylôh,** *shee-lo´*; or שִׁלֹה, **Shilôh,** *shee-lo´*; or שִׁילוֹ, **Shîylôw,** *shee-lo´*; or שִׁלוֹ, **Shilôw,** *shee-lo´*; from the same as 7886; *Shiloh,* a place in Palestine:—Shiloh.

7888. שִׁילוֹנִי, **Shîylôwnîy,** *shee-lo-nee´*; or שִׁילֹנִי, **Shîylônîy,** *shee-lo-nee´*; or שִׁלֹנִי, **Shilônîy,** *shee-lo-nee´*; from 7887; a *Shilonite* or inhabitant of Shiloh:—Shilonite.

7889. שִׁימוֹן, **Shîymôwn,** *shee-mone´*; apparently for 3452; *desert; Shimon,* an Israelite:—Shimon.

7890. שַׁיִן, **shayin,** *shah´-yin*; from an unused root meaning to *urinate; urine*:—piss.

7891. שִׁיר, **shîyr,** *sheer*; or (the original form) שׁוּר, **shûwr,** *shoor*; (1Sa 18:6), a primitive root [rather identical with 7788 through the idea of

strolling minstrelsy]; to *sing*:—behold [*by mistake for* 7789], sing (-er, -ing man, -ing woman).

A verb meaning to sing. This word occurs often in a call to praise the Lord; the call may be directed toward oneself or others (Ps 27:6; 96:1, 2; 101:1; Jer 20:13). This term is frequently associated with the Levitical worship established by David and emphasized by postexilic writers (1Ch 15:16; Ezr 2:41; Ne 7:1). Although the Levitical singers were all men, women also were singers in ancient Israel both in religious and secular settings (Ex 15:21; Jgs 5:1–3; Ecc 2:8). Secular occasions for singing included celebration of victory in battle (1Sa 18:6); mourning over death (2Ch 35:25); entertainment (2Sa 19:35[36]); and an expression of love (Isa 5:1). The Bible once mentions the singing of birds (Zep 2:14).

7892. שִׁיר, **shîyr,** *sheer*; or feminine שִׁירָה, **shîyrâh,** *shee-raw´*; from 7891; a *song;* (abstract) *singing*:—musical (-ick), × sing (-er, -ing), song.

A masculine noun meaning a song. This word is used to indicate a type of lyrical song, a religious song, or a specific song of Levitical choirs. In Amos, God uses the word to indicate that He will turn their joyful singing into mourning because of their unfaithfulness to Him (Am 8:10). This time of mourning will be like that of mourning for an only son, and it will end in a bitter day. In a similar usage, Laban asks Jacob why he ran off secretly without telling Laban. If Jacob would have stated he wanted to leave, Laban would have sent him off with joy and singing (Ge 31:27). Isaiah uses the word to indicate the type of songs that will no longer be sung when the Lord lays waste the earth (Isa 24:9). The type of drunken revels associated with drinking wine and beer will no longer be heard.

This word is also used in Nehemiah to denote songs of praise (Ne 12:46). In this particular context, Nehemiah indicates that the music directors in the days of David and Asaph led songs of praise. The noun is also used to indicate specific songs of Levitical choirs accompanied by musical instruments. When David and the Israelites brought the ark of the Lord from Baalah of Judah (Kiriath Jearim), they celebrated with songs (1Ch 13:8). Amos uses the word to denote complacency and apathy. Many Israelites lay on ivory couches and strummed their musical instruments while dining on fattened calves and choice lambs. These people were so caught up in themselves that they did not even give thought to the threat of destruction by the Lord.

7893. שַׁיִשׁ, **shayish,** *shah´-yish*; from an unused root meaning to *bleach*, i.e. *whiten; white*, i.e. *marble*:—marble. See 8336.

7894. שִׁישָׁא, **Shîyshâ'**, *shee-shaw´*; from the same as 7893; *whiteness; Shisha,* an Israelite:—Shisha.

7895. שִׁישַׁק, **Shîyshaq,** *shee-shak´*; or שׁוּשַׁק, **Shûw-shaq,** *shoo-shak´*; of Egyptian derivation; *Shishak,* an Egyptian king:—Shishak.

7896. שִׁית, **shîyth,** *sheeth*; a primitive root; to *place* (in a very wide application):—apply, appoint, array, bring, consider, lay (up), let alone, × look, make, mark, put (on), + regard, set, shew, be stayed, × take.

7897. שִׁית, **shîyth,** *sheeth*; from 7896; a *dress* (as *put* on):—attire.

7898. שַׁיִת, **shayith,** *shah´-yith*; from 7896; *scrub* or *trash,* i.e. wild *growth* of weeds or briers (as if *put* on the field):—thorns.

7899. שֵׂךְ, **sêk,** *sake*; from 5526 in the sense of 7753; a *brier* (as of a hedge):—prick.

7900. שֹׂךְ, **sôk,** *soke*; from 5526 in the sense of 7753; a *booth* (as *interlaced*):—tabernacle.

7901. שָׁכַב, **shâkab,** *shaw-kab´*; a primitive root; to *lie* down (for rest, sexual connection, decease or any other purpose):— × at all, cast down, ([over-]) lay (self) (down), (make to) lie (down, down to sleep, still, with), lodge, ravish, take rest, sleep, stay.

7902. שְׁכָבָה, **shekâbâh,** *shek-aw-baw´*; from 7901; a *lying* down (of dew, or for the sexual act):— × carnally, copulation, × lay, seed.

7903. שְׁכֹבֶת, **shekôbeth,** *shek-o´-beth*; from 7901; a (sexual) *lying* with:— × lie.

7904. שָׁכָה, **shâkâh,** *shaw-kaw´*; a primitive root; to *roam* (through lust):—in the morning [*by mistake for* 7925].

7905. שֻׂכָּה, **śukkâh,** *sook-kaw´*; feminine of 7900 in the sense of 7899; a *dart* (as pointed like a *thorn*):—barbed iron.

7906. שֵׂכוּ, **Śêkûw,** *say´-koo*; from an unused root apparently meaning to *surmount*; an *observatory* (with the article); *Seku,* a place in Palestine:—Sechu.

7907. שֶׂכְוִי, **śekvîy,** *sek-vee´*; from the same as 7906; *observant,* i.e. (concrete) the *mind*:—heart.

A masculine noun meaning a celestial appearance or phenomenon, the mind. This word is used in Job to denote the mind that has been given understanding (Job 38:36). In a rhetorical question, the Lord indicated His sovereignty over all, including the lives of His servants. The exact meaning of this word is unclear.

7908. שְׁכוֹל, **shekôwl,** *shek-ole´*; infinitive of 7921; *bereavement*:—loss of children, spoiling.

A masculine noun meaning bereavement. This word primarily indicates a loss of children. In Isaiah's oracle against Babylon, he stated that the woman who thought of herself as lasting forever would become a widow and suffer the loss of her children. The Virgin Daughter of Babylon, who once thought that there was none like her, would suffer the fate of a common person (Isa 47:8). The word is also used to denote how the soul is left after a ruthless witness repays evil for good (Ps 35:12).

7909. שַׁכּוּל, **shakkûwl,** *shak-kool´*; or שַׁכֻּל, **shakkul,** *shak-kool´*; from 7921; *bereaved*:—barren, bereaved (robbed) of children (whelps).

An adjective meaning bereaved. The word is used figuratively to describe the fierceness of David and his men by comparing them to a wild bear robbed of her cubs (2Sa 17:8). In another analogy, the intensity of God's punishment is described as a bear robbed of her cubs. God would attack the Israelites for their sins and rip them open (Hos 13:8). Proverbs used the same figurative language, stating that it is better to meet a bear robbed of her cubs than a fool in his folly (Pr 17:12). In a different sense, Jeremiah used this word to describe a punishment in which wives would be made childless and widows (Jer 18:21).

7910. שִׁכּוֹר, **shikkôwr,** *shik-kore´*; or שִׁכֹּר, **shikkôr,** *shik-kore´*; from 7937; *intoxicated,* as a state or a habit:—drunk (-ard, -en, -en man).

7911. שָׁכַח, **shâkach,** *shaw-kakh´*; or שָׁכֵחַ, **shâkêach,** *shaw-kay´-akh*; a primitive root; to *mislay,* i.e. to *be oblivious* of, from want of memory or attention:— × at all, (cause to) forget.

7912. שְׁכַח, **shekach,** *shek-akh´*; (Chaldee); corresponding to 7911 through the idea of disclosure of a *covered* or *forgotten* thing; to *discover* (literal or figurative):—find.

7913. שָׁכֵחַ, **shâkêach,** *shaw-kay´-akh*; from 7911; *oblivious:*—forget.

7914. שְׂכִיָּה, **sekîyyâh,** *sek-ee-yaw´*; feminine from the same as 7906; a *conspicuous* object:—picture.

7915. שַׂכִּין, **sakkîyn,** *sak-keen´*; intensive perhaps from the same as 7906 in the sense of 7753; a *knife* (as *pointed* or edged):—knife.

7916. שָׂכִיר, **sâkîyr,** *saw-keer´*; from 7936; a man *at wages* by the day or year:—hired (man, servant), hireling.

7917. שְׂכִירָה, **sekîyrâh,** *sek-ee-raw´*; feminine of 7916; a *hiring:*—that is hired.

7918. שָׁכַךְ, **shâkak,** *shaw-kak´*; a primitive root; to *weave* (i.e. *lay*) a trap; figurative (through the idea of *secreting*) to *allay* (passions; [physical] *abate* a flood):—appease, assuage, make to cease, pacify, set.

7919. שָׂכַל, **sâkal,** *saw-kal´*; a primitive root; to *be* (causative, *make* or *act*) *circumspect* and hence *intelligent:*—consider, expert, instruct, prosper, (deal) prudent (-ly), (give) skill (-ful), have good success, teach, (have, make to) understand (-ing), wisdom, (be, behave self, consider, make) wise (-ly), guide wittingly.

A verb meaning to act with insight, to be prudent, to give insight, to teach, to prosper, to consider, to ponder, to understand, to act prudently, to act with devotion. The primary meaning of the word is to be prudent. The word is used in Isaiah to denote what was hoped and expected of Israel, i.e. that they would consider and understand that the hand of the Lord had acted (Isa 41:20). The word is also used in Deuteronomy to denote a lack of understanding on the part of the people. If they were wise and would understand, they would know what their end would be (Dt 32:29). Jeremiah used this word to denote wisdom in

terms of insight and comprehension (Jer 9:24[23]). In a similar usage of the word, fools are to take heed and become wise (Ps 94:8). The wisdom of comprehension will open their eyes to the Lord, who sees and punishes wrong actions. In a confession of sins, the Holy Spirit is remembered as having been sent to instruct (Ne 9:20); the prudent person keeps quiet in evil times (Am 5:13); those who meditate on the Book of the Law day and night, being careful to do everything in it, will be prosperous and successful (Jos 1:8). In the causative form, *sâkal* denoted God's actions to Solomon if he observed what the Lord required and walked in His ways. If this pattern were followed, the Lord would prosper Solomon (1Ki 2:3).

7920. שְׂכַל, **sekal,** *sek-al´*; (Chaldee); corresponding to 7919:—consider.

An Aramaic verb meaning to consider. The reflexive form of the word is used in Daniel to depict the state of mind that Daniel was in while he was shown the vision. While Daniel was contemplating the horns that he had previously seen, a smaller horn appeared and brought his attention back to the vision itself (Da 7:8).

7921. שָׁכֹל, **shâkôl,** *shaw-kole´*; a primitive root; (properly) to *miscarry,* i.e. *suffer abortion;* (by analogy) to *bereave* (literal or figurative):—bereave (of children), barren, cast calf (fruit, young), be (make) childless, deprive, destroy, × expect, lose children, miscarry, rob of children, spoil.

7922. שֶׂכֶל, **sekel,** *seh´-kel*; or שֵׂכֶל, **sêkel,** *say´-kel*; from 7919; *intelligence;* (by implication) *success:*—discretion, knowledge, policy, prudence, sense, understanding, wisdom, wise.

A masculine noun meaning intelligence, good sense. This intelligence is more than just mere book knowledge or learning about a particular subject. It has a greater significance and means insight or understanding. This insight is a gift from God (1Ch 22:12); and God holds the freedom to give it or to take it away whenever He chooses (Job 17:4). The results from having this intelligence and insight is that it gives a person patience (Pr 19:11); and wins praise from others (Pr 12:8). Only fools despise this intelligence (Pr 23:9). This noun is used once with a negative connotation in Da 8:25 where it stands for cunning, requiring much intelligence.

7923. שִׂכֻּלִים, **shikkulîym,** *shik-koo-leem´*; plural from 7921; *childlessness* (by continued bereavements):—to have after loss of others.

7924. שָׂכְלְתָנוּ, **śokl͏ͤthânûw,** *sok-leth-aw-noo´*; (Chaldee); from 7920; *intelligence*:—understanding.

An Aramaic feminine noun meaning wisdom, insight. It is used in Da 5:11, 12, and 14. In this context, it described Daniel's wisdom and insight into the interpretation of dreams. It was obvious to the people around Daniel that his wisdom was not merely human wisdom, for they said he had the spirit of the gods living in him and that he was like the gods. Thus, this wisdom cannot be gained by mere human training. It comes as a gift from God. The pagan culture did not attribute it to the one true God but to their gods.

7925. שָׁכַם, **shâkam,** *shaw-kam´*; a primitive root; (properly) to *incline* (the shoulder to a burden); but used only as denominative from 7926; (literal) to *load up* (on the back of man or beast), i.e. to *start early* in the morning:—(arise, be up, get [oneself] up, rise up) early (betimes), morning.

7926. שְׁכֶם, **sh͏ͤkem,** *shek-em´*; from 7925; the *neck* (between the shoulders) as the place of burdens; (figurative) the *spur* of a hill:—back, × consent, portion, shoulder.

7927. שְׁכֶם, **Sh͏ͤkem,** *shek-em´*; the same as 7926; *ridge; Shekem*, a place in Palestine:—Shechem.

7928. שֶׁכֶם, **Shekem,** *sheh´-kem*; for 7926; *Shekem*, the name of a Hivite and two Israelites:—Shechem.

7929. שִׁכְמָה, **shikmâh,** *shik-maw´*; feminine of 7926; the *shoulder*-bone:—shoulder blade.

7930. שִׁכְמִי, **Shikmîy,** *shik-mee´*; patronymic from 7928; a *Shikmite* (collective), or descendants of Shekem:—Shichemites.

7931. שָׁכַן, **shâkan,** *shaw-kan´*; a primitive root [apparently akin (by transmission) to 7901 through the idea of *lodging*; compare 5531, 7925]; to *reside* or permanently stay (literal or figurative):—abide, continue, (cause to, make

to) dwell (-er), have habitation, inhabit, lay, place, (cause to) remain, rest, set (up).

A verb meaning to settle down, to dwell. In its most simple form, three slight variations of meaning are found for this verb. First, it simply means to settle down (Ex 24:16; Nu 24:2; Ps 102:28[29]). Second, it can mean to lie down or rest. When used this way, it can refer to objects (Nu 9:17; Job 3:5); animals (Isa 13:21); and people (Jer 23:6; 33:16). When people are the object of the verb, it means that they are resting in peace and security. Third, it may mean to dwell or abide. Again, this can have several referents such as people (Ps 37:27; Pr 2:21); the dead (Job 26:5); God (1Ki 8:12; Isa 8:18); or objects such as the tabernacle (Jos 22:19). In the intensive form, it means to establish. The word is used in this way in Dt 12:11 and Ps 78:60 to describe how God set up a dwelling place for His name, establishing Himself in Israel. Finally, the causative form means to lay, to place, to set (Ge 3:24; Jos 18:1); or to cause to dwell (Job 11:14; Ps 78:55).

7932. שְׁכַן, **sh͏ͤkan,** *shek-an´*; (Chaldee); corresponding to 7931:—cause to dwell, have habitation.

7933. שֶׁכֶן, **sheken,** *sheh´-ken*; from 7931; a *residence*:—habitation.

7934. שָׁכֵן, **shâkên,** *shaw-kane´*; from 7931; a *resident*; (by extension) a fellow-*citizen*:—inhabitant, neighbour, nigh.

An adjective meaning inhabitant. This word usually refers to an inhabitant of a city (Isa 33:24; Hos 10:5). It can also have the more specific meaning of neighbour. These neighbours can either be people who are friends or enemies (Ex 3:22; Ru 4:17); or nations (Dt 1:7). Neighbours can also be extremely influential (Eze 16:26). Israel was said to have engaged in prostitution with her neighbour Egypt, meaning that she followed the gods and religions of Egypt rather than following the one true God.

7935. שְׁכַנְיָה, **Sh͏ͤkanyâh,** *shek-an-yaw´*; or (prolonged) שְׁכַנְיָהוּ, **Sh͏ͤkanyâhûw,** *shek-an-yaw´-hoo*; from 7931 and 3050; *Jah has dwelt; Shekanjah*, the name of nine Israelites:—Shecaniah, Shechaniah.

7936. שָׂכַר, **śâkar,** *saw-kar´*; or (by permutation) סָכַר, **sâkar,** *saw-kar´*; (Ezr 4:5), a primitive root [apparently akin (by prosthesis) to 3739 through the idea of temporary *purchase*; compare 7937]; to *hire*:—earn wages, hire (out self), reward, × surely.

7937. שָׁכַר, **shâkar,** *shaw-kar´*; a primitive root; to *become tipsy*; in a qualified sense, to *satiate* with a stimulating drink or (figurative) influence:—(be filled with) drink (abundantly), (be, make) drunk (-en), be merry. [Superlative of 8248.]

7938. שֵׂכֶר, **śeker,** *seh´-ker*; from 7936; *wages*:—reward, sluices.

7939. שָׂכָר, **śâkâr,** *saw-kawr´*; from 7936; *payment* of contract; (concrete) *salary, fare, maintenance*; (by implication) *compensation, benefit*:—hire, price, reward [-ed], wages, worth.

7940. שָׂכָר, **Śâkâr,** *saw-kawr´*; the same as 7939; *recompense*; *Sakar*, the name of two Israelites:—Sacar.

7941. שֵׁכָר, **shêkâr,** *shay-kawr´*; from 7937; an *intoxicant*, i.e. intensely alcoholic *liquor*:—strong drink, + drunkard, strong wine.

7942. שִׁכְּרוֹן, **Shikkᵉrôwn,** *shik-ker-one´*; for 7943; *drunkenness; Shikkeron*, a place in Palestine:—Shicron.

7943. שִׁכָּרוֹן, **shikkârôwn,** *shik-kaw-rone´*; from 7937; *intoxication*:—(be) drunken (-ness).

7944. שָׁל, **shal,** *shal*; from 7952 abbreviated; a *fault*:—error.

A masculine noun meaning a sin, an error. It comes from the verb *shâlâh* (7952), meaning to sin. This noun is used only once in the OT in 2Sa 6:7, but from this usage, we can gain the insight that the error described by this word is a great one. The context is that of Uzzah, whom God struck down because he touched the ark: this error cost him his life. This word has strong connotations of a great sin or error deserving of death.

7945. שֶׁל, **shel,** *shel*; for the relative 834; used with prepositional prefix, and often followed by some pronoun affixed; on *account* of, *whatso-ever, which*soever:—cause, sake.

7946. שַׁלְאֲנָן, **shal'ănân,** *shal-an-awn´*; for 7600; *tranquil*:—being at ease.

7947. שָׁלַב, **shâlab,** *shaw-lab´*; a primitive root; to *space* off; intensive (*evenly*) to *make equidistant*:—equally distant, set in order.

7948. שָׁלָב, **shâlâb,** *shaw-lawb´*; from 7947; a *spacer* or raised *interval*, i.e. the *stile* in a frame or panel:—ledge.

7949. שָׁלַג, **shâlag,** *shaw-lag´*; a primitive root; (properly) meaning to be *white*; used only as denominative from 7950; to be *snow-white* (with the linen clothing of the slain):—be as snow.

7950. שֶׁלֶג, **sheleg,** *sheh´-leg*; from 7949; *snow* (probably from its *whiteness*):—snow (-y).

7951. שָׁלָה, **shâlâh,** *shaw-law´*; or שָׁלַו, **shâlav,** *shaw-lav´*; (Job 3:26), a primitive root; to be *tranquil*, i.e. *secure* or *successful*:—be happy, prosper, be in safety.

7952. שָׁלָה, **shâlâh,** *shaw-law´*; a primitive root [probably rather identical with 7953 through the idea of *educing*]; to *mislead*:—deceive, be negligent.

A verb meaning to be careless, to be thoughtless, to sin. The sin described by this verb does not seem to be a deliberate sin but rather one that is committed by ignorance or inadvertence. The verb is used only in the passive and causative forms. In the passive form, it holds the meaning of being negligent or being careless of duties (2Ch 29:11). The causative form means to lead astray or to deceive. It is used in 2Ki 4:28 when the Shunammite woman felt deceived that she had been promised a son who later died. Although the sins described by this verb were not intentional, they were still deserving of punishment in God's sight.

7953. שָׁלָה, **shâlâh,** *shaw-law´*; a primitive root [rather cognate (by contrete) to the base of 5394, 7997 and their congeners through the idea of *extracting*]; to *draw* out or off, i.e. *remove* (the soul by death):—take away.

7954. שְׁלֵה, **shᵉlêh,** *shel-ay´*; (Chaldee); corresponding to 7951; to be *secure*:—at rest.

7955. שָׁלָה, **shâluh,** *shaw-loo´*; (Chaldee); from a root corresponding to 7952; a *wrong*:—thing amiss.

7956. שֵׁלָה, **Shêlâh,** *shay-law´*; the same as 7596 (shortened); *request; Shelah,* the name of a postdiluvian patriarch and of an Israelite:— Shelah.

7957. שַׁלְהֶבֶת, **shalhebeth,** *shal-heh´-beth*; from the same as 3851 with sibilant prefix; a *flare* of fire:—(flaming) flame.

7958. שְׂלָו, **śelâv,** *sel-awv´*; or שְׂלָיו, **śelâyv,** *sel-awv´*; by orthographic variation from 7951 through the idea of *sluggishness*; the *quail* collective (as *slow* in flight from its weight):— quails.

7959. שְׁלֵו, **shâlûw,** *shaw´-loo*; from 7951; *security:*—prosperity.

7960. שָׁלוּ, **shâlûw,** *shaw-loo´*; (Chaldee); or שָׁלוּת, **shâlûwth,** *shaw-looth´*; (Chaldee); from the same as 7955; a *fault:*—error, × fail, thing amiss.

7961. שָׁלֵו, **shâlêv,** *shaw-lave´*; or שָׁלֵיו, **shâlêyv,** *shaw-lave´*; feminine שְׁלֵוָה, **shelêvâh,** *shel-ay-vaw´*; from 7951; *tranquil;* (in a bad sense) *careless;* (abstract) *security:*—(being) at ease, peaceable, (in) prosper (-ity), quiet (-ness), wealthy.

7962. שַׁלְוָה, **shalvâh,** *shal-vaw´*; from 7951; *security* (genuine or false):—abundance, peace (-ably), prosperity, quietness.

7963. שְׁלֵוָה, **shelêvâh,** *shel-ay-vaw´*; (Chaldee); corresponding to 7962; *safety:*—tranquillity. See also 7961.

7964. שִׁלּוּחִים, **shillûwchîym,** *shil-loo´-kheem*; or שִׁלֻּחִים, **shilluchîym,** *shil-loo´-kheem*; from 7971; (only in plural) a *dismissal,* i.e. (of a wife) *divorce* (especially the document); also (of a daughter) *dower:*—presents, have sent back.

7965. שָׁלוֹם, **shâlôwm,** *shaw-lome´*; or שָׁלֹם, **shâlôm,** *shaw-lome´*; from 7999; *safe,* i.e. (figurative) *well, happy, friendly;* also (abstract) *welfare,* i.e. health, prosperity, peace:— × do, familiar, × fare, favour, + friend, × great, (good) health, (× perfect, such as be at) peace (-able, -ably), prosper (-ity, -ous), rest, safe (-ty), salute, welfare, (× all is, be) well, × wholly.

A masculine noun meaning peace or tranquility. This Hebrew term is used 237 times in the OT and is used to greet someone (Jgs 19:20; 1Ch 12:18[19]; Da 10:19). It is common in Hebrew to ask how one's peace is (Ge 43:27; Ex 18:7; Jgs 18:15), which is equivalent to asking "How are you?" Moreover, this word was often used to describe someone's manner of coming or going; sometimes this took the form of a blessing: Go in peace (Jgs 8:9; 1Sa 1:17; Mal 2:6). Another common expression involved dying or being buried in peace (Ge 15:15; 2Ch 34:28; Jer 34:5) Peace is present with the wise but absent from the wicked (Pr 3:2, 17; Isa 57:21; 59:8). It is often pictured as coming from God; Gideon built an altar and called the altar *Yahweh-shalom* (the Lord Is Peace; Nu 6:26; Jgs 6:24; Isa 26:3).

7966. שִׁלּוּם, **shillûwm,** *shil-loom´*; or שִׁלֻּם, **shillum,** *shil-loom´*; from 7999; a *requital,* i.e. (secure) *retribution,* (venal) a *fee:*—recompense, reward.

A masculine noun meaning a requital, a retribution. It is derived from the verb *shâlam* (7999). In context, this noun is used as God's punishment of Israel for their repeated disobedience (Isa 34:8; Hos 9:7). It is not something given on a whim but is deserved. This noun can also mean a reward, or more accurately, a bribe (Mic 7:3). Only the corrupt accept these bribes, which are used to distort justice. Such people have no care for what is right or wrong but only in what they will receive. Ultimately, they will receive their retribution from God for their wrongdoings.

7967. שַׁלּוּם, **Shallûwm,** *shal-loom´*; or (shorter) שַׁלֻּם, **Shallum,** *shal-loom´*; the same as 7966; *Shallum,* the name of fourteen Israelites:— Shallum.

7968. שַׁלּוּן, **Shallûwn,** *shal-loon´*; probably for 7967; *Shallun,* an Israelite:—Shallum.

7969. שָׁלוֹשׁ, **shâlôwsh,** *shaw-loshe´*; or שָׁלֹשׁ, **shâlôsh,** *shaw-loshe´*; masculine שְׁלוֹשָׁה, **shelôwshâh,** *shel-o-shaw´*; or שְׁלֹשָׁה, **shelôshâh,** *shel-o-shaw´*; a primitive number; *three;* occasionally (ordinal) *third,* or (multiple) *thrice:*— + fork, + often [-times], third, thir [-teen, -teenth], three, + thrice. Compare 7991.

7970. שְׁלוֹשִׁים, **shelôwshîym,** *shel-o-sheem´*; or שְׁלֹשִׁים, **shelô-shîym,** *shel-o-sheem´*; multiple of 7969; *thirty;* or (ordinal) *thirtieth:*—thirty, thirtieth. Compare 7991.

7971. שָׁלַח, **shâlach,** *shaw-lakh´*; a primitive root; to *send* away, for, or out (in a great variety of applications):— × any wise, appoint, bring (on the way), cast (away, out), conduct, × earnestly, forsake, give (up), grow long, lay, leave, let depart (down, go, loose), push away, put (away, forth, in, out), reach forth, send (away, forth, out), set, shoot (forth, out), sow, spread, stretch forth (out).

7972. שְׁלַח, **sheʿlach,** *shel-akh´*; (Chaldee); corresponding to 7971:—put, send.

7973. שֶׁלַח, **shelach,** *sheh´-lakh*; from 7971; a *missile* of attack, i.e. *spear*; also (figurative) a *shoot* of growth, i.e. *branch*:—dart, plant, × put off, sword, weapon.

7974. שֶׁלַח, **Shelach,** *sheh´-lakh*; the same as 7973; *Shelach,* a postdiluvian patriarch:—Salah, Shelah. Compare 7975.

7975. שִׁלֹחַ, **Shilôach,** *shee-lo´-akh*; or (in imitation of 7974 שֶׁלַח, **Shelach,** *sheh´-lakh*; (Ne 3:15), from 7971; *rill;* Shiloäch, a fountain of Jerusalem:—Shiloah, Siloah.

7976. שִׁלְחָה, **shilluchâh,** *shil-loo-kahw´*; feminine of 7964; a *shoot:*—branch.

7977. שִׁלְחִי, **Shilchîy,** *shil-khee´*; from 7973; *missive,* i.e. *armed; Shilchi,* an Israelite:—Shilhi.

7978. שִׁלְחִים, **Shilchîym,** *shil-kheem´*; plural of 7973; *javelins* or *sprouts; Shilchim,* a place in Palestine:—Shilhim.

7979. שֻׁלְחָן, **shulchân,** *shool-khawn´*; from 7971; a *table* (as *spread* out); (by implication) a *meal:*—table.

7980. שָׁלַט, **shâlaṭ,** *shaw-lat´*; a primitive root; to *dominate,* i.e. *govern;* by implication to *permit:*—(bear, have) rule, have dominion, give (have) power.

A verb meaning to domineer, to be master of. In the simple form, it takes the connotation of ruling. This can be ruling over people (Ne 5:15; Ecc 8:9); or possessions which one has been given control of (Ecc 2:19). It can also mean to obtain power or to get mastery over something. Examples of this would be how sin can have power over a person (Ps 119:133); or people can have power over each other (Est 9:1). This verb is also used in the causative form, meaning to give power (Ecc 5:19[18]; 6:2). In these con-

texts, God gives people power over their lives, possessions, honour, and wealth. God is the only legitimate source of power, and all power flows from Him.

7981. שְׁלֵט, **sheʿlêṭ,** *shel-ate´*; (Chaldee); corresponding to 7980:—have the mastery, have power, bear rule, be (make) ruler.

An Aramaic verb meaning to have power, to rule over. It is found in the intensive and causative forms only. In the causative form, it means to make rule or to cause to rule, referring to someone in power who gives that power to another (Da 2:38, 48). In the intensive form, it may mean merely to have power in the sense of controlling other people (Da 3:27, 6:24[25]), or to rule or be a ruler. In this sense, it is used in the context of King Belshazzar, who promised that whoever could interpret his dream would become a ruler (Da 5:7, 16).

7982. שֶׁלֶט, **sheleṭ,** *sheh´-let*; from 7980; probably a *shield* (as *controlling,* i.e. protecting the person):—shield.

A masculine noun meaning a shield. Most commonly, this word is used to refer to shields used for protection in battle. In Eze 27:11, they were hung on walls; in Jer 51:11, they were to be taken up as warriors prepared to defend themselves. Another context in which this word is used is in describing the gold shields that King David took from people he defeated (2Sa 8:7). They were then kept in the Temple and used when Jehoida presented Joash as king (2Ki 11:10).

7983. שִׁלְטוֹן, **shilṭôwn,** *shil-tone´*; from 7980; a *potentate:*—power.

A masculine noun meaning mastery. It can be used to mean powerful, as in the words of a king that are described as being supreme (Ecc 8:4). It can also mean having power over. It is used in Ecc 8:8 to say that no one has power over the day of his or her death. This word carries the connotation of legitimate authority, not just power that persons claim they have or have taken from others. A king's words had legitimate authority, for he was the ruler of his people; and no one except God has legitimate authority over death.

7984. שִׁלְטוֹן, **shiltôwn,** *shil-tone´*; (Chaldee); or שִׁלְטֹן, **shiltôn,** *shil-tone´*; corresponding to 7983:—ruler.

An Aramaic noun meaning a lord, a magistrate, an official. This noun is used only once in Da 3:2, where it is found at the end of a long list of officials whom King Nebuchadnezzar called together before him. This noun is the last word used and seems to be a catchall phrase to account for any official who was missed in the specific titles given before. Due to the lack of specificity, it would appear that this is a general noun used to name anyone who holds a position of authority.

7985. שָׁלְטָן, **sholtân,** *shol-tawn´*; (Chaldee); from 7981; *empire* (abstract or concrete):— dominion.

An Aramaic masculine noun meaning dominion, sovereignty. Most frequently, this noun is used in conjunction with God, showing that He has dominion over everything that exists (Da 4:3[3:33]; 4:34[31]). His dominion is greater than that of a person's many ways, one being that it is an everlasting dominion that can never be destroyed (Da 7:14). This noun can also be used of kings (Da 4:22[19]). It was used in Daniel's dream of the four beasts to describe the dominion they have (Da 7:6, 12, 26). God both gives and takes away the dominion of all human rulers. Much less frequently, this word can be used in the concrete sense of a physical kingdom (Da 6:26[27]).

7986. שַׁלֶּתֶת, **shalleteth,** *shal-leh´-teth*; feminine from 7980; a *vixen:*—imperious.

7987. שְׁלִי, **sheliy,** *shel-ee´*; from 7951; *privacy:*— + quietly.

7988. שִׁלְיָה, **shilyâh,** *shil-yaw´*; feminine from 7953; a *fetus* or *babe* (as *extruded* in birth):— young one.

7989. שַׁלִּיט, **shalliyt,** *shal-leet´*; from 7980; *potent*; (concrete) a *prince* or *warrior:*—governor, mighty, that hath power, ruler.

An adjective meaning mastery, power. This could be used to describe power over anything, but it is used in a limited context in the OT. With this meaning, it is only found in Ecc 8:8, where people are said to have no power over the wind. It can also be used as a noun meaning a ruler or one who has mastery (Ge 42:6). Rulers can also be a cause of evil (Ecc 10:5).

7990. שַׁלִּיט, **shalliyt,** *shal-leet´*; (Chaldee); corresponding to 7989; *mighty*; (abstract) *permission*; (concrete) a *premier:*—captain, be lawful, rule (-r).

An Aramaic masculine adjective meaning mastery. It is commonly used of God and His sovereignty that gives Him mastery over everything. There is nothing that is not under His authority, including the kingdoms of people (Da 4:17[14]; 5:21). God's mastery covers everything that exists. This adjective can also be used in describing the power that kings have (Ezr 4:20); and the authority they can exercise (Ezr 7:24). This word can also be used as a noun meaning captain or one who has authority and mastery over others (Da 2:15).

7991. שָׁלִישׁ, **shâliysh,** *shaw-leesh´*; or שָׁלוֹשׁ, **shâlôwsh,** *shaw-loshe´*; (1Ch 11:11; 12:18), or שָׁלֹשׁ, **shâlôsh,** *shaw-loshe´*; (2Sa 23:13), from 7969; a *triple*, i.e. (as a musical instrument) a *triangle* (or perhaps rather *three*-stringed lute); also (as an indefinite great quantity) a *three*-fold measure (perhaps a *treble* ephah); also (as an officer) a general of the *third* rank (upward, i.e. the highest):—captain, instrument of musick, (great) lord, (great) measure, prince, three [*from the margin*].

A masculine noun carrying many different meanings associated with the number three. First of all, it can be used to signify a measure, perhaps originally a third or an ephah. From the contexts in which it is used, it is clear the word stands for a large measure (Ps 80:5[6]; Isa 40:12). It is also used once as a noun for a type of musical instrument—perhaps a three-cornered one with strings, such as a lute. This instrument was played with songs of celebration (1Sa 18:6). Finally, this word can signify a particular type of high–ranking officer or the third man in a chariot during battle (Ex 14:7; 2Sa 23:8; 2Ki 9:25).

7992. שְׁלִישִׁי, **sheliyshiy,** *shel-ee-shee´*; ordinal from 7969; *third*; feminine a *third* (part); (by extension) a *third* (day, year or time); (specifically) a *third*-story cell:—third (part, rank, time), three (years old).

7993. שָׁלַךְ, **shâlak,** *shaw-lak´*; a primitive root; to *throw* out, down or away (literal or figurative):—adventure, cast (away, down, forth, off, out), hurl, pluck, throw.

A verb meaning to throw, to cast. In the causative form, several different variations of meaning are associated with this verb. The basic meaning to cast or throw is found in Ge 21:15 and Nu 35:20. It can also mean to cast away in the sense of getting rid of something that hinders, such as sin (Eze 18:31); or fetters (Ps 2:3). This verb is also used to describe God's rejection of someone (2Ki 17:20; 24:20). In a good sense, God will sustain those who cast their cares on Him (Ps 55:22[23]). In the passive causative form, this verb means to be cast, to be thrown or to be cast out. Usually, this is used in a negative sense, as when someone was cast out of his or her burial site (Isa 14:19; Jer 36:30); or when people were cast away because of their disobedience to God (Jer 14:16). Yet it can also be used in a good sense. In Ps 22:10[11], the writer says that from birth he had been cast on God. So this verb can have either positive or negative connotations.

7994. שָׁלָךְ, **shâlâk,** *shaw-lawk´*; from 7993; *bird of prey,* usually thought to be the *pelican* (from *casting* itself into the sea):—cormorant.

7995. שַׁלֶּכֶת, **shalleketh,** *shal-leh´-keth*; from 7993; a *felling* (of trees):—when cast.

7996. שַׁלֶּכֶת, **Shalleketh,** *shal-leh´-keth*; the same as 7995; *Shalleketh,* a gate in Jerusalem:—Shalleketh.

7997. שָׁלַל, **shâlal,** *shaw-lal´*; a primitive root; to *drop* or *strip*; (by implication) to *plunder*:—let fall, make self a prey, × of purpose, (make a, [take]) spoil.

7998. שָׁלָל, **shâlâl,** *shaw-lawl´*; from 7997; *booty:*—prey, spoil.

7999. שָׁלַם, **shâlam,** *shaw-lam´*; a primitive root; to *be safe* (in mind, body or estate); (figurative) to *be* (causative, *make*) *completed*; (by implication) to *be friendly*; (by extension) to *reciprocate* (in various applications):—make amends, (make an) end, finish, full, give again, make good, (re-) pay (again), (make) (to) (be at) peace (-able), that is perfect, perform, (make)

prosper (-ous), recompense, render, requite, make restitution, restore, reward, × surely.

A verb meaning to be safe, to be completed. The primary meaning is to be safe or uninjured in mind or body (Job 8:6; 9:4). This word is normally used when God is keeping His people safe. In its simple form, this verb also means to be completed or to be finished. This could refer to something concrete such as a building (1Ki 7:51); or things more abstract, such as plans (Job 23:14). Other meanings of this verb include to be at peace with another person (Ps 7:4[5]); to make a treaty of peace (Jos 11:19; Job 5:23); to pay, to give a reward (Ps 62:12[13]); to restore, repay, or make retribution (Ex 21:36; Ps 37:21).

8000. שְׁלַם, **shᵉlam,** *shel-am´*; (Chaldee); corresponding to 7999; to *complete,* to *restore*:—deliver, finish.

An Aramaic verb meaning to complete, to finish. This word corresponds to the Hebrew verb *shâlam* (7999). It refers to work being done, such as rebuilding the Temple in Jerusalem (Ezr 5:16). Closely related to this meaning is the secondary meaning, to make an end. In Da 5:26, this word is used to say that God would bring the days of Belshazzar's reign to an end. This word could also mean to restore in the sense of delivering something from captivity and returning it to the rightful owner. It was used when discussing the restoration of the temple furnishings in Jerusalem (Ezr 7:19).

8001. שְׁלָם, **shᵉlâm,** *shel-awm´*; (Chaldee); corresponding to 7965; *prosperity*:—peace.

A masculine singular noun meaning peace. This word is most frequently used in the context of a greeting and may be used in both the singular and plural forms with the same meaning. As a greeting, these words signified a wish for peace, prosperity, and general good welfare to those who were being greeted. This seems to have been a common way to begin letters in ancient biblical times. In Nebuchadnezzar's letter to his subjects, he started by wishing prosperity to all his subjects (Da 4:1[3:31]); and in the letter which Tatnai sent to King Darius, he used this word as a greeting of well-wishing (Ezr 5:7).

8002. שֶׁלֶם, **shelem,** *sheh´-lem;* from 7999; (properly) *requital,* i.e. a (voluntary) sacrifice in *thanks:*—peace offering.

A noun meaning thanksgiving offerings, also called peace offerings. These offerings were voluntary, given to God in thanks or in praise to Him. These offerings were first described in the book of Leviticus, and the word is used many times after that, especially in the remaining sections of the Law dealing with sacrifices (Le 3:1; 7:11; Nu 7:17). This noun is also used in the plural form, which has a wider significance (Am 5:22). In this context, the thanksgiving offerings were offered in great distress, not out of thankful hearts. They were offered to try to gain God's favour, but God rejected them because they were not given out of love and thankfulness to Him.

8003. שָׁלֵם, **shâlêm,** *shaw-lame´;* from 7999; *complete* (literal or figurative); especially *friendly:*—full, just, made ready, peaceable, perfect (-ed), quiet, Shalem [*by mistake for a name*], whole.

An adjective meaning full, complete, safe, whole, peaceful. This adjective has several uses when it means complete, safe, unharmed, natural. Moses instructed the Israelites to build the altar on Mount Ebal of natural, unhewn or whole stones (Dt 27:6; Jos 8:31). Stones that were whole, finished, and from a rock quarry could be used to build the Temple (1Ki 6:7). The word describes the work on the Lord's Temple as finished, complete (2Ch 8:16). The word describes weights that had to be solid, accurate, and fair for use in the marketplace (Dt 25:15; Pr 11:1); it described wages paid as full, complete, rich (Ru 2:12). It described Jacob traveling safely to the city of Shechem (Ge 33:18). When referring to groups of people, it means entire or whole, such as whole communities taken captive in Amos's day (Am 1:6, 9). Something could be described as not yet complete or full; the sin of the Amorites was not yet complete (Ge 15:16).

The word connotes the idea of whole or undivided; the hearts of the Israelites were to be wholly centered on the Lord and His decrees (1Ki 8:61), but Solomon's heart was not so committed (1Ki 11:4; 2Ki 20:3; Isa 38:3).

The word means peaceful or peaceable when used of persons in certain relationships; the people of Shechem believed the Israelites intended to live in a peaceful relationship with them (Ge 34:21).

8004. שָׁלֵם, **Shâlêm,** *shaw-lame´;* the same as 8003; *peaceful; Shalem,* an early name of Jerusalem:—Salem.

8005. שִׁלֵּם, **shillêm,** *shil-lame´;* from 7999; *requital:*—recompense.

A masculine singular noun meaning retribution, requital, recompense. It is used when speaking of a deserved punishment, in the sense of a repayment for whatever wrong was done by a person (Dt 32:35). In addition, it can also signify rewards for good that has been done. The idea behind this word is that it is a reward or punishment that is deserved and is in conjunction with what was done beforehand. Ultimately, only God has the power of retribution. It is His right only to avenge wrongdoers and give those persons what they deserve or to reward those who have done right.

8006. שִׁלֵּם, **Shillêm,** *shil-lame´;* the same as 8005; *Shillem,* an Israelite:—Shillem.

8007. שַׂלְמָא, **Śalmâʾ,** *sal-maw´;* probably for 8008; *clothing; Salma,* the name of two Israelites:—Salma.

8008. שַׂלְמָה, **śalmâh,** *sal-maw´;* transposed for 8071; a *dress:*—clothes, garment, raiment.

8009. שַׂלְמָה, **Śalmâh,** *sal-maw´;* the same as 8008; *clothing; Salmah,* an Israelite:—Salmon. Compare 8012.

8010. שְׁלֹמֹה, **Shᵉlômôh,** *shel-o-mo´;* from 7965; *peaceful; Shelomoh,* David's successor:—Solomon.

8011. שִׁלֻּמָה, **shillumâh,** *shil-loo-maw´;* feminine of 7966; *retribution:*—recompense.

A feminine singular noun meaning retribution, punishment, penalty. This word has negative meanings when it is used in Scripture, for example, persons were punished or repaid for whatever evil they did. The word does not seem to have anything to do with repayment in the sense of receiving rewards for doing what is right, but this could be because of its limited use in the OT. The righteous remained safe in God's protection, but the wicked received their punishment before the eyes of the righteous

(Ps 91:8). God Himself is the giver of this retribution.

8012. שַׁלְמוֹן, **Šalmôwn,** *sal-mone´*; from 8008; *investiture; Salmon,* an Israelite:—Salmon. Compare 8009.

8013. שְׁלֹמוֹת, **Shᵉlômôwth,** *shel-o-mōth´*; feminine plural of 7965; *pacifications; Shelomoth,* the name of two Israelites:—Shelomith [*from the margin*], Shelomoth. Compare 8019.

8014. שַׁלְמַי, **Šalmay,** *sal-mah´ee*; from 8008; *clothed; Salmai,* an Israelite:—Shalmai.

8015. שְׁלֹמִי, **Shᵉlômîy,** *shel-o-mee´*; from 7965; *peaceable; Shelomi,* an Israelite:—Shelomi.

8016. שִׁלֵּמִי, **Shillêmîy,** *shil-lay-mee*; patronymic from 8006; a *Shilemite* (collective) or descendants of Shillem:—Shillemites.

8017. שְׁלֻמִיאֵל, **Shᵉlumîy'êl,** *shel-oo-mee-ale´*; from 7965 and 410; *peace of God; Shelumiël,* an Israelite:—Shelumiel.

8018. שֶׁלֶמְיָה, **Shelemyâh,** *shel-em-yaw´*; or שֶׁלֶמְיָהוּ, **Shelem-yâhûw,** *shel-em-yaw´-hoo*; from 8002 and 3050; *thank-offering of Jah; Shelemjah,* the name of nine Israelites:—Shelemiah.

8019. שְׁלֹמִית, **Shᵉlômîyth,** *shel-o-meeth´*; or שְׁלוֹמִית, **Shᵉlôw-mîyth,** *shel-o-meeth´*; (Ezr 8:10), from 7965; *peaceableness; Shelomith,* the name of five Israelites and three Israelitesses:—Shelomith.

8020. שַׁלְמָן, **Shalman,** *shal-man´*; of foreign derivation; *Shalman,* a king apparently of Assyria:—Shalman. Compare 8022.

8021. שַׁלְמֹן, **shalmôn,** *shal-mone´*; from 7999; a *bribe:*—reward.

A masculine noun meaning a gift. It is used only in its plural form of *shalmôniym.* This word is not used to describe simple gifts given out of goodwill but gifts given as bribes to try to sway persons in authority to do what the giver wants them to do (Isa 1:23). These bribes are accepted only by corrupt people and end up corrupting people even further. Those who are totally corrupt even seek out bribes. Along with these bribes went the idea of a lack of justice and righteousness as a result of God's will not being done in those matters.

8022. שַׁלְמַנְאֶסֶר, **Shalman'eser,** *shal-man-eh´-ser*; of foreign derivation; *Shalmaneser,* an Assyrian king:—Shalmaneser. Compare 8020.

8023. שִׁלֹנִי, **Shilônîy,** *shee-lo-nee´*; the same as 7888; *Shiloni,* an Israelite:—Shiloni.

8024. שֵׁלָנִי, **Shêlânîy,** *shay-law-nee´*; from 7956; a *Shelanite* (collective), or descendants of Shelah:—Shelanites.

8025. שָׁלַף, **shâlaph,** *shaw-laf´*; a primitive root; to *pull* out, up or off:—draw (off), grow up, pluck off.

8026. שֶׁלֶף, **sheleph,** *sheh´-lef*; from 8025; *extract; Sheleph,* a son of Jokthan:—Sheleph.

8027. שָׁלַשׁ, **shâlash,** *shaw-lash´*; a primitive root perhaps originally to *intensify,* i.e. *treble;* but apparently used only as denominative from 7969, to be (causative, *make*) *triplicate* (by restoration, in portions, strands, days or years):—do the third time, (divide into, stay) three (days, -fold, parts, years old).

8028. שֶׁלֶשׁ, **Shêlesh,** *shay´-lesh*; from 8027; *triplet; Shelesh,* an Israelite:—Shelesh.

8029. שִׁלֵּשׁ, **shillêsh,** *shil-laysh´*; from 8027; a descendant of the *third* degree, i.e. *great grandchild:*—third [generation].

8030. שִׁלְשָׁה, **Shilshâh,** *shil-shaw´*; feminine from the same as 8028; *triplication; Shilshah,* an Israelite:—Shilshah.

8031. שָׁלִשָׁה, **Shâlishâh,** *shaw-lee-shaw´*; feminine from 8027; *trebled* land; *Shalishah,* a place in Palestine:—Shalisha.

8032. שִׁלְשׁוֹם, **shilshôwm,** *shil-shome´*; or שִׁלְשֹׁם, **shilshôm,** *shil-shome´*; from the same as 8028; *trebly,* i.e. (in time) *day before yesterday:*— + before (that time, -time), excellent things [*from the margin*], + heretofore, three days, + time past.

8033. שָׁם, **shâm,** *shawm*; a primitive particle [rather from the relative 834]; *there* (transferred to time) *then;* often *thither,* or *thence:*—in it, + thence, there (-in, + of, + out), + thither, + whither.

8034. שֵׁם, **shêm,** *shame*; a primitive word [perhaps rather from 7760 through the idea of definite and conspicuous *position;* compare 8064];

an *appellation*, as a mark or memorial of individuality; (by implication) *honour, authority, character*:— + base, [in-] fame [-ous], name (-d), renown, report.

8035. שֵׁם, **Shêm**, *shame*; the same as 8034; *name; Shem*, a son of Noah (often including his posterity):—Sem, Shem.

8036. שֻׁם, **shum**, *shoom*; (Chaldee); corresponding to 8034:—name.

8037. שַׁמָּא, **Shammâ'**, *sham-maw'*; from 8074; *desolation; Shamma*, an Israelite:—Shamma.

8038. שְׁמְאֵבֶר, **Shem'êber**, *shem-ay'-ber*; apparently from 8034 and 83; *name of pinion*, i.e. *illustrious; Shemeber*, a king of Zeboim:—Shemeber.

8039. שִׁמְאָה, **Shim'âh**, *shim-aw'*; perhaps for 8093; *Shimah*, an Israelite:—Shimah. Compare 8043.

8040. שְׂמֹאול, **s͏ᵉmô'l**, *sem-ole'*; or שְׂמֹאל, **s͏ᵉm'ôl**, *sem-ole'*; a primitive word [rather perhaps from the same as 8071 (by insertion of aleph) through the idea of *wrapping* up]; (properly) *dark* (as *enveloped*), i.e. the *north*; hence (by orientation) the *left* hand:—left (hand, side).

8041. שְׂמֹאל, **s͏ᵉmô'l**, *seh-mol'*; a primitive root [rather denominative from 8040]; to use the *left* hand or pass in that direction):—(go, turn) (on the, to the) left.

8042. שְׂמָאלִי, **s͏ᵉmâ'lîy**, *sem-aw-lee'*; from 8040; situated on the *left* side:—left.

8043. שִׁמְאָם, **Shim'âm**, *shim-awm'*; for 8039 [compare 38]; *Shimam*, an Israelite:—Shimeam.

8044. שַׁמְגַּר, **Shamgar**, *sham-gar'*; of uncertain derivation; *Shamgar*, an Israelite judge:—Shamgar.

8045. שָׁמַד, **shâmad**, *shaw-mad'*; a primitive root; to *desolate*:—destroy (-uction), bring to nought, overthrow, perish, pluck down, × utterly.

A verb meaning to be destroyed. This verb is not used in its simple form and is only used in the passive and causative stems of the verb. The primary passive meaning is to be destroyed, to be exterminated, or to be annihilated, referring to individual people, households, or nations (Ge 34:30; Pr 14:11; Eze 32:12). It can also sig-

nify the devastation of land and places (Hos 10:8). The causative forms have the same root meanings as the passive forms. It can mean to annihilate, to exterminate people (Dt 1:27, 2:22); or to destroy objects such as cities, fortresses, or idols (Isa 23:11; Mic 5:14[13]). The difference between these two verb forms lies in who is destroying and who is being destroyed.

8046. שְׁמַד, **sh͏ᵉmad**, *shem-ad'*; (Chaldee); corresponding to 8045:—consume.

An Aramaic verb meaning to destroy. The word corresponds to the Hebrew verb *shâmad* (8045). It signifies more than simply ruining or destroying something but described a destruction that could not be reversed or fixed. Its connotations go far beyond mere destruction to mean to consume, to destroy completely without hope of restoration. In Da 7:26, this verb was used to signify a total destruction of a ruler's power. This verb is used only to describe a final destruction. God is the power behind this ultimate destruction.

8047. שַׁמָּה, **shammâh**, *sham-maw'*; from 8074; *ruin*; (by implication) *consternation*:—astonishment, desolate (-ion), waste, wonderful thing.

A feminine singular noun meaning ruin, astonishment. The primary meaning is that of ruin and wasting. This noun can be used to refer to evil people and their households who deserved to be destroyed because of their sins (Ps 73:19; Isa 5:9); also of land, towns, and buildings that were destroyed as a result of the evil people who lived there (Jer 2:15). A second meaning of astonishment, dismay, and horror is not clearly related to the primary meaning, but it is used to describe feelings toward Israel and its cities in their times of disobedience. Israel is seen as a horror, an object of scorn to all who saw her (Dt 28:37; Jer 19:8). It is also used to describe the extreme dismay people can feel at seeing destruction, a horror that fills persons (Jer 8:21).

8048. שַׁמָּה, **Shammâh**, *sham-maw'*; the same as 8047; *Sham-mah*, the name of an Edomite and four Israelites:—Shammah.

8049. שִׁמְהוּת, **Shamhûwth,** *sham-hooth´*; for 8048; *desolation; Shamhuth,* an Israelite:— Shamhuth.

8050. שְׁמוּאֵל, **Shemûw'êl,** *shem-oo-ale´*; from the passive participle of 8085 and 410; *heard of God; Shemuël,* the name of three Israelites:— Samuel, Shemuel.

8051. שַׁמּוּעַ, **Shammûwa',** *sham-moo´-ah*; from 8074; *renowned; Shammua,* the name of four Israelites:—Shammua, Shammuah.

8052. שְׁמוּעָה, **shemûw'âh,** *shem-oo-aw´*; feminine passive participle of 8074; *something heard,* i.e. an *announcement:*—bruit, doctrine, fame, mentioned, news, report, rumor, tidings.

8053. שָׁמוּר, **Shâmûwr,** *shaw-moor´*; passive participle of 8103; *observed; Shamur,* an Israelite:—Shamir [*from the margin*].

8054. שַׁמּוֹת, **Shammôwth,** *sham-môth´*; plural of 8047; *ruins; Shammoth,* an Israelite:— Shamoth.

8055. שָׂמַח, **sâmach,** *saw-makh´*; a primitive root; probably to *brighten* up, i.e. (figurative) *be* (causative, make) *blithe* or *gleesome:*—cheer up, be (make) glad, (have, make) joy (-ful), be (make) merry, (cause to, make to) rejoice, × very.

8056. שָׂמֵחַ, **sâmêach,** *saw-may´-akh*; from 8055; *blithe* or *gleeful:*—(be) glad, joyful, (making) merry ([-hearted], -ily), rejoice (-ing).

8057. שִׂמְחָה, **simchâh,** *sim-khaw´*; from 8056; *blithesomeness* or *glee,* (religious or festival):— × exceeding (-ly), gladness, joy (-fulness), mirth, pleasure, rejoice (-ing).

8058. שָׁמַט, **shâmaṭ,** *shaw-mat´*; a primitive root; to *fling* down; (incipiently) to *jostle;* (figurative) to *let alone, desist, remit:*—discontinue, overthrow, release, let rest, shake, stumble, throw down.

8059. שְׁמִטָּה, **shemiṭṭâh,** *shem-it-taw´*; from 8058; *remission* (of debt) or *suspension* (of labour):—release.

A feminine noun meaning a remission, a release, a suspension. This word signifies the cancellation of a debt that was owed to another person. This was a debt which a person would, under ordinary circumstances, be obligated to

pay back. In Israel, at the end of every seven years, the people were to release and forgive their fellow people from debts owed to them. This word was used in this context of the seventh year to show that the debtor was released from any obligation to pay back what had been loaned to him before that time (Dt 15:1, 2, 9; 31:10). In the OT, this noun was used only in the context of forgiving debts at the end of every seven years.

8060. שַׁמַּי, **Shammay,** *sham-mah´ee*; from 8073; *destructive; Shammai,* the name of three Israelites:—Shammai.

8061. שְׁמִידָע, **Shemîydâ',** *shem-ee-daw´*; apparently from 8034 and 3045; *name of knowing; Shemida,* an Israelite:—Shemida, Shemidah.

8062. שְׁמִידָעִי, **Shemîydâ'îy,** *shem-ee-daw-ee´*; patronymic from 8061; a *Shemidaïte* (collective) or descendants of Shemida:—Shemidaites.

8063. שְׂמִיכָה, **semîykâh,** *sem-ee-kaw´*; from 5564; a *rug* (as *sustaining* the Oriental sitter):— mantle.

8064. שָׁמַיִם, **shâmayim,** *shaw-mah´-yim*; dual of an unused singular שָׁמֶה, **shâmeh,** *shaw-meh´*; from an unused root meaning to *be lofty;* the *sky* (as *aloft;* the dual perhaps alluding to the visible arch in which the clouds move, as well as to the higher ether where the celestial bodies revolve):— air, × astrologer, heaven (-s).

A masculine noun meaning sky, heaven, abode, firmament, air, stars. Although the word is plural or dual in form, it can be translated into English as singular or plural depending on the context. The word describes everything God made besides the earth: God made the heavens of the universe (Ge 1:1; 14:19); the firmament or expanse which He created around the earth was named sky or heaven as well (Ge 1:8). He stretched out the heavens (Isa 40:22); creating them (Isa 42:5; 45:18).

The heavens that humans observe with their senses are indicated by this word. The stars are part of the heavens (Ge 15:5) and are personified in some cases (Jgs 5:20); the sun and the moon, along with the stars, make up a major part of the hosts of heaven (Dt 4:19). Unfortunately, these things were worshipped as gods by even the Israelites (Jer 8:2). The heavens became a source of knowing the future and life in general, for scanners of the heavens and astrologers searched the heavens for signs (Isa 47:13). A favourite pagan deity was the Queen of Heaven whom the people worshipped (Jer 7:18; 44:17). God created waters above and below the heavens (Ge 1:8, 9). The clouds are a feature of the sky (Ge 8:2; Jgs 5:4; 1Ki 18:45; Job 26:13). The word indicates the total inhabited earth when it speaks of from under heaven, as when the Amalekites were to be destroyed from under heaven (Ge 6:17; Ex 17:14). The teacher of Ecclesiastes spoke of examining everything under heaven, i.e. everything done in the world in which humans live (Ecc 1:13; 2:3; 3:1); birds and other fowl fly in the sky (Ge 1:20). In God's new world, there will be a new heaven and a new earth (Isa 65:17; 66:22).

The invisible heavens are the abode of God. Heaven is the Lord's throne, the earth is the resting place of His feet—a beautiful metaphor of God's sovereignty over the universe (Isa 66:1). He extends the heavens as the tent roof of the universe (Isa 40:22); He dwells in heaven (1Ki 8:30, 32); yet He is not contained in even the heaven of heavens, the most exclusive part of the heavens (1Ki 8:27).

Heaven describes the place from which God operates: He calls to people from heaven (Ge 21:17; 22:11). The Ten Commandments were spoken from heaven (Ex 20:22; Ne 9:13). He sent down manna from heaven for His people in the desert (Ex 16:4). He is not merely a dweller in heaven, but He is the God of heaven (Ge 24:3; 2Ch 36:23; Ezr 1:2). The heavens grow old and pass away, but God is eternal (Job 14:12; Isa 13:10; 65:17). Satan aspired to usurp God's reign in heaven and was cast out (Isa 14:12, 13). Elijah the prophet, because he faithfully followed the Lord, was taken up into heaven in a whirlwind (2Ki 2:1, 11).

8065. שְׁמַיִן, **shᵉmayin,** *sheh-mah´-yin*; (Chaldee); corresponding to 8064:—heaven.

An Aramaic noun meaning sky, heavens. This word has several different connotations, but the basic meaning is that of the sky (Da 4:11[8]; 7:2). Reaching beyond the simple meaning of sky, this word also referred to heaven, the dwelling place of God that is much higher than any other place (Da 2:28; 4:34[31]). The heavens are great not because of what they are but because of who lives there. Not only

does God dwell in heaven, but His messengers, the angels, also dwell there and are sent down to earth to do His work (Da 4:13[10]). This word also signifies the whole universe where God showed His mighty signs and made His works known to all (Da 6:27[28]). It is combined to form phrases such as the God of heaven (Ezr 5:11, 12; Da 2:18, 19, 28, 37, 44); birds of the sky (Da 2:38); winds of heaven (Da 7:2, 13). This noun corresponds to the Hebrew noun *shâmayim* (8064), that is very similar in meaning.

8066. שְׁמִינִי, **shᵉmîynîy,** *shem-ee-nee´*; from 8083; *eight:*—eight.

8067. שְׁמִינִית, **shᵉmîynîyth,** *shem-ee-neeth´*; feminine of 8066; probably an *eight*-stringed lyre:—Sheminith.

8068. שָׁמִיר, **shâmîyr,** *shaw-meer´*; from 8104 in the original sense of *pricking*; a *thorn*; also (from its *keenness* for scratching) a gem, probably the *diamond:*—adamant (stone), brier, diamond.

8069. שָׁמִיר, **Shâmîyr,** *shaw-meer´*; the same as 8068; *Shamir*, the name of two places in Palestine:—Shamir. Compare 8053.

8070. שְׁמִירָמוֹת, **Shᵉmîyrâmôwth,** *shem-ee-raw-môth´*; or שְׁמָרִימוֹת, **Shᵉmârîymôwth,** *shem-aw-ree-môth´*; probably from 8034 and plural of 7413; *name of heights; Shemiramoth,* the name of two Israelites:—Shemiramoth.

8071. שִׂמְלָה, **śimlâh,** *sim-law´*; perhaps by permutation for the feminine of 5566 (through the idea of a *cover* assuming the shape of the object beneath); a *dress*, especially a *mantle:*—apparel, cloth (-es, -ing), garment, raiment. Compare 8008.

8072. שַׂמְלָה, **Śamlâh,** *sam-law´*; probably for the same as 8071; *Samlah,* an Edomite:—Samlah.

8073. שַׁמְלַי, **Shamlay,** *sham-lah´ee*; for 8014; *Shamlai,* one of the Nethinim:—Shalmai [*from the margin*].

8074. שָׁמֵם, **shâmêm,** *shaw-mame´*; a primitive root; to *stun* (or [intransitive] *grow numb*), i.e. *devastate* or (figurative) *stupefy* (both usually in a passive sense):—make amazed, be astonied, (be an) astonish (-ment), (be, bring into, unto, lay, lie, make) desolate (-ion, places), be destitute, destroy (self), (lay, lie, make) waste, wonder.

A verb meaning to be desolated, to be destroyed. The desolation or destruction that this verb refers to can be used of both people (2Sa 13:20; La 1:13, 16); and places (Le 26:31, 32; Isa 61:4; Eze 35:12) and is used in both its simple and causative forms. A second meaning of this verb, which is extremely common, is to be appalled or astonished and is used in the simple, passive, and passive causative stems (Job 18:20; Isa 52:14; Jer 18:16). The connection between these two meanings is not entirely clear; yet they are both used with great frequency. When this verb is used in the second meaning, it often describes a person's reaction on seeing desolation and destruction. For example, in 1Ki 9:8, the reaction of people to a destroyed land was described with this verb. A much less common use of this verb is in the reflexive stem. Here it meant to be disheartened or dismayed (Ps 143:4).

8075. שְׁמַם, **sh⁰mam,** *shem-am´*; (Chaldee); corresponding to 8074:—be astonied.

8076. שָׁמֵם, **shâmêm,** *shaw-mame´*; from 8074; *ruined:*—desolate.

A masculine adjective meaning ruined, wasted, desolate. This adjective corresponds to the verb *shâmêm* (8074). This adjective can be used to describe both land and objects that have been destroyed. The connotations here are of an extreme destruction that has lasting effects and causes all people to stand up and take notice of what has happened. When Jerusalem fell, the Temple was torn apart and utterly destroyed, and this adjective was used to describe the condition of the Temple (Da 9:17). In Jer 12:11, it is also used to prophesy what the land would be like after the fall of Jerusalem. This adjective paints a picture of harsh destruction. In these contexts, this destruction is indicative of God's judgment on His people.

8077. שְׁמָמָה, **sh⁰mâmâh,** *shem-aw-maw´*; feminine of 8076; *devastation*; (figurative) *astonishment:*—(laid, × most) desolate (-ion), waste.

A feminine singular noun meaning desolation, waste. This noun can be used to refer to many things such as land, cities, or houses (Ex 23:29; Le 26:33; Isa 1:7). Most often it is used in conjunction with a passage describing what did happen to the land of Israel after God judged His people and sent them into exile. This shows

the totality of the destruction that Israel endured. Nothing was to be saved from this destruction. Fields and vineyards were turned into wastelands and desolate fields after God's judgment (Jer 12:10). God allowed such desolation as a punishment for the sins of His people because they refused to repent. This punishment could even fall on people of other nations, such as the Edomites (Eze 33:28, 29; 35:3).

8078. שִׁמָּמוֹן, **shimmâmôwn,** *shim-maw-mone´*; from 8074; *stupefaction:*—astonishment.

8079. שְׂמָמִית, **s⁰mâmîyth,** *sem-aw-meeth´*; probably from 8074 (in the sense of *poisoning*); a *lizard* (from the superstition of its *noxiousness*):—spider.

8080. שָׁמֵן, **shâman,** *shaw-man´*; a primitive root; to *shine,* i.e. (by analogy) *be* (causative. *make*) *oily* or *gross:*—become (make, wax) fat.

8081. שֶׁמֶן, **shemen,** *sheh´-men*; from 8080; *grease,* especially liquid (as from the olive, often perfumed); (figurative) *richness:*—anointing, × fat (things), × fruitful, oil ([-ed]), ointment, olive, + pine.

A masculine noun meaning fat, oil. This word has a wide range of figurative meanings relating to richness and plenty. Most simply, it is used of food, relating to feasts of good, rich food (Isa 25:6). It is also used frequently of oil. This can be oil used for food and cooking (Dt 8:8; 32:13); for oil which was used to anoint holy objects or kings (Ex 30:25; 1Sa 10:1); or for oil used as an ointment to soothe and cleanse, leading to healing (Ps 133:2; Isa 1:6). The figurative meanings are also important. This word can be used to signify strength, such as in Isa 10:27 where growing fat meant growing strong. It also frequently relates to fruitfulness and fertile places where good things grew (Isa 5:1; 28:1). The overall picture one gets from this word is that of richness, strength, and fertility.

8082. שָׁמֵן, **shâmên,** *shaw-mane´*; from 8080; *greasy,* i.e. *gross;* (figurative) *rich:*—fat, lusty, plenteous.

8083. שְׁמֹנֶה, **sh⁰môneh,** *shem-o-neh´*; or שְׁמוֹנֶה, **sh⁰môwneh,** *shem-o-neh´*; feminine שְׁמֹנָה, **sh⁰mô-nâh,** *shem-o-naw´*; or שְׁמוֹנָה, **sh⁰môwnâh,** *shem-o-naw´*; apparently from 8082 through the idea of *plumpness*; a cardinal number, *eight* (as if a *surplus* above the "perfect" seven); also (as ordinal) *eighth*:—eight ([-een, -eenth]), eighth.

8084. שְׁמֹנִים, **shᵉmônîym,** *shem-o-neem´*; or שְׁמוֹנִים, **shᵉmôw-nîym,** *shem-o-neem´*; mult. from 8083; *eighty*; also *eightieth*:—eighty (-ieth), fourscore.

8085. שָׁמַע, **shâma',** *shaw-mah´*; a primitive root; to *hear* intelligently (often with implication of attention, obedience, etc.; [causative] to *tell*, etc.):— × attentively, call (gather) together, × carefully, × certainly, consent, consider, be content, declare, × diligently, discern, give ear, (cause to, let, make to) hear (-ken, tell), × indeed, listen, make (a) noise, (be) obedient, obey, perceive, (make a) proclaim (-ation), publish, regard, report, shew (forth), (make a) sound, × surely, tell, understand, whosoever [heareth], witness.

A verb meaning to hear, to obey, to listen, to be heard of, to be regarded, to cause to hear, to proclaim, to sound aloud. The verb basically means to hear and in context expresses various connotations of this. The most famous use of this word is to introduce the Shema, "Hear, O, Israel," followed by the content of what the Israelites are to understand about the Lord their God and how they are to respond to Him (Dt 6:4). In a parallel usage, the heavens are commanded to "Hear, Oh heavens!" to the prophet's message about Israel (Isa 1:2). The word calls attention to hear various things: It means to hear another person speaking (Ge 27:6); the Lord's voice (Ge 3:10); or anything that can be perceived by the ear. Used with or without the preposition *'el* (413) following, the word means to listen to someone. The house of Israel was not willing to listen to Ezekiel (Eze 3:7); the Lord was not willing to listen to the beautiful worship services of God's people, for they were not following justice (Ge 27:5; Am 5:23).

The word takes on the connotation of obedience in certain contexts and with certain Hebrew constructions: It can mean to heed a request or command, such as Abraham's request concerning Ishmael (Ge 17:20). The Lord listened to Hagar's prayer and gave her a son (Ge 16:11; 30:6). It means to obey in certain contexts (Ge 3:17; 22:18; Ex 24:7; 2Ki 14:11).

The word is used to connote the idea of understanding. God confused the speech of the people at the Tower of Babel so they could not understand each other (Ge 11:7; Isa 33:19). Solomon wanted a heart of discernment and understanding (hearing) to govern his people (Dt 1:16; 1Ki 3:9); to be able to decide between good and evil (2Sa 14:17).

In the passive stem, the word means to be heard. Pharaoh heard the news that Joseph's brothers had arrived in Egypt (Ge 45:16). No sound of a tool was heard as the Temple was being built (Dt 4:32; 1Ki 6:7). It also meant to be obedient to King David (2Sa 22:45); or to make hear, to call, or to summon as when Saul summoned his soldiers (1Sa 15:4; 23:8).

The word is used often in the causative stem to mean to cause to listen, to proclaim, to announce. When Israel assembled at Mount Horeb (Sinai), the Lord caused them to hear His words (Dt 4:10; Jos 6:10). It also means to proclaim, to summon; Isaiah spoke of those who proclaim peace (1Ki 15:22; Isa 52:7); and the psalmist proclaimed the praise of the Lord (Ps 26:7).

8086. שְׁמַע, **shᵉma',** *shem-ah´*; (Chaldee); corresponding to 8085:—hear, obey.

An Aramaic verb meaning to hear. This verb is used only in the book of Daniel and is used when speaking of words that have been heard from another person (Da 5:14, 16); or when hearing sounds, such as the sounds of music from many instruments (Da 3:5, 7, 10). In a broader perspective, it can also mean to have a sense of hearing as opposed to being deaf (Da 5:23). This verb can also be used in the reflexive form and means that one shows one's obedience to what has been heard (Da 7:27).

8087. שֶׁמַע, **Shema',** *sheh´-mah*; for the same as 8088; *Shema*, the name of a place in Palestine and of four Israelites:—Shema.

8088. שֵׁמַע, **shêma',** *shay´-mah*; from 8085; something *heard*, i.e. a *sound, rumor, announcement*; (abstract) *audience*:—bruit, fame, hear (-ing), loud, report, speech, tidings.

A masculine noun meaning hearing. This word can mean hearing as opposed to or in addition to seeing (Job 42:5; Ps 18:44[45]). This word can also be used to represent a rumor, a report, or an announcement, as these are things that have been announced and heard by others. These reports may be good news to be greeted joyously, such as a report of fame and good deeds (Ge 29:13; 1Ki 10:1); bad news to be concerned about (Isa 23:5); or even lies and malicious rumors causing others to suffer (Ex 23:1).

8089. שֹׁמַע, **shôma‘,** *sho´-mah*; from 8085; a *report*:—fame.

8090. שְׁמָע, **Shᵉmâ‘,** *shem-aw´*; for 8087; *Shema,* a place in Palestine:—Shema.

8091. שָׁמָע, **Shâmâ‘,** *shaw-maw´*; from 8085; *obedient; Shama,* an Israelite:—Shama.

8092. שִׁמְאָא, **Shim‘â’,** *shim-aw´*; for 8093; *Shima,* the name of four Israelites:—Shimea, Shimei, Shamma.

8093. שִׁמְעָה, **Shim‘âh,** *shim-aw´*; feminine of 8088; *annunciation; Shimah,* an Israelite:—Shimeah.

8094. שְׁמָעָה, **Shᵉmâ‘âh,** *shem-aw-aw´*; for 8093; *Shemaah,* an Israelite:—Shemaah.

8095. שִׁמְעוֹן, **Shim‘ôwn,** *shim-ōne´*; from 8085; *hearing; Shimon,* one of Jacob's sons, also the tribe descendants from him:—Simeon.

8096. שִׁמְעִי, **Shim‘iy,** *shim-ee´*; from 8088; *famous; Shimi,* the name of twenty Israelites:—Shimeah [*from the margin*], Shimei, Shimhi, Shimi.

8097. שִׁמְעִי, **Shim‘iy,** *shim-ee´*; patronymic from 8096; a *Shimite* (collective) or descendants of Shimi:—of Shimi, Shimites.

8098. שְׁמַעְיָה, **Shᵉma‘yâh,** *shem-aw-yaw´*; or שְׁמַעְיָהוּ, **Shᵉma‘-yâhûw,** *shem-aw-yaw´-hoo*; from 8085 and 3050; *Jah has heard; Shemajah,* the name of twenty-five Israelites:—Shemaiah.

8099. שִׁמְעֹנִי, **Shim‘ôniy,** *shim-o-nee´*; patronymic from 8095; a *Shimonite* (collective) or descendants of Shimon:—tribe of Simeon, Simeonites.

8100. שִׁמְעָת, **Shim‘âth,** *shim-awth´*; feminine of 8088; *annunciation; Shimath,* an Ammonitess:—Shimath.

8101. שִׁמְעָתִי, **Shim‘âthiy,** *shim-aw-thee´*; patronymic from 8093; a *Shimathite* (collective) or descendants of Shimah:—Shimeathites.

8102. שֶׁמֶץ, **shemets,** *sheh´-mets*; from an unused root meaning to *emit* a sound; an *inkling*:—a little.

8103. שִׁמְצָה, **shimtsâh,** *shim-tsaw´*; feminine of 8102; scornful *whispering* (of hostile spectators):—shame.

8104. שָׁמַר, **shâmar,** *shaw-mar´*; a primitive root; (properly) to *hedge* about (as with thorns), i.e. *guard*; (generally) to *protect, attend to,* etc.:—beware, be circumspect, take heed (to self), keep (-er, self), mark, look narrowly, observe, preserve, regard, reserve, save (self), sure, (that lay) wait (for), watch (-man).

A verb meaning to watch, to keep, to preserve, to guard, to be careful, to watch over, to watch carefully over, to be on one's guard. The verb means to watch, to guard, to care for. Adam and Eve were to watch over and care for the Garden of Eden where the Lord had placed them (Ge 2:15); cultic and holy things were to be taken care of dutifully by priests (2Ki 22:14). The word can suggest the idea of protecting: David gave orders to keep Absalom safe (1Sa 26:15; 2Sa 18:12); the Lord keeps those who look to Him (Ps 121:7). The word can mean to simply save or to preserve certain items; objects could be delivered to another person for safekeeping (Ge 41:35; Ex 22:7[6]). The word also means to pay close attention to: Eli the priest continued to observe Hannah's lips closely as she prayed (1Sa 1:12; Isa 42:20). Closely related to this meaning is the connotation to continue to do something, as when Joab maintained his siege of the city of Rabbah (2Sa 11:16). The verb also indicates caring for sheep (1Sa 17:20).

The Hebrew word means to maintain or to observe something for a purpose and is followed by another verb indicating the purpose or manner, as in the following examples: Israel was to observe the laws of the Lord, so as to do them (Dt 4:6; 5:1); Balaam had to observe accurately what he had been charged with (Nu 23:12); and Israel was responsible to keep the way of the Lord and walk in it (Ge 17:9; 18:19).

The word naturally means to watch over some physical object, to keep an eye on it. In its participial form, the word means human guards, those who watch for people or over designated objects (Jgs 1:24; Ne 12:25). The Lord, as the moral Governor of the world, watches over the moral and spiritual behaviour of people (Job 10:14).

In the passive reflexive stem, it means to be taken care of. To take care in the passive aspect, the verb was used to assert that Israel was watched over (Hos 12:13[14]). Most often it means to take care, as when the Lord instructed Laban to take care not to harm Jacob (Ge 31:29). Amasa did not guard himself carefully and was killed by Joab (2Sa 20:10). Pharaoh warned Moses to take care not to come into his presence again or he would die (Ex 10:28; cf. Ge 24:6; 2Ki 6:10; Jer 17:21).

The word in its intensive stem means to pay regard to or attach oneself to. In the participial form of this verb, it means those who give heed to useless vanities (Jnh 2:8[9]). In the reflexive stem, it means to keep oneself. David declared he was blameless since he had kept himself from sin (2Sa 22:24; Ps 18:23[24]).

8105. שֶׁמֶר, **shemer,** *sheh´-mer*; from 8104; something *preserved*, i.e. the *settlings* (plural only) of wine:—dregs, (wines on the) lees.

8106. שֶׁמֶר, **Shemer,** *sheh´-mer*; the same as 8105; *Shemer*, the name of three Israelites:—Shamer, Shemer.

8107. שִׁמֻּר, **shimmur,** *shim-moor´*; from 8104; an *observance*:— × be (much) observed.

8108. שָׁמְרָה, **shomrâh,** *shom-raw´*; feminine of an unused noun from 8104 meaning a *guard*; *watchfulness*:—watch.

8109. שְׁמֻרָה, **shᵉmurâh,** *shem-oo-raw´*; feminine of passive participle of 8104; something *guarded*, i.e. an *eye-lid*:—waking.

8110. שִׁמְרוֹן, **Shimrôwn,** *shim-rone´*; from 8105 in its original sense; *guardianship*; *Shimron*, the name of an Israelite and of a place in Palestine:—Shimron.

8111. שֹׁמְרוֹן, **Shômᵉrôwn,** *sho-mer-ōne´*; from the active participle of 8104; *watch-station*; *Shomeron*, a place in Palestine:—Samaria.

8112. שִׁמְרוֹן מְראֹאוֹן, **Shimrôwn Mᵉrôʾôwn,** *shim-rone´ mer-oh-one´*; from 8110 and a derivative of 4754; *guard of lashing*; *Shimron-Meron*, a place in Palestine:—Shimon-meron.

8113. שִׁמְרִי, **Shimrîy,** *shim-ree´*; from 8105 in its original sense; *watchful*; *Shimri*, the name of four Israelites:—Shimri.

8114. שְׁמַרְיָה, **Shᵉmaryâh,** *shem-ar-yaw´*; or שְׁמַרְיָהוּ, **Shᵉmaryâ-hûw,** *shem-ar-yaw´-hoo*; from 8104 and 3050; *Jah has guarded*; *Shemarjah*, the name of four Israelites:—Shamariah, Shemariah.

8115. שָׁמְרַיִן, **Shâmᵉrayin,** *shaw-meh-rah´-yin*; (Chaldee); corresponding to 8111; *Shomraïn*, a place in Palestine:—Samaria.

8116. שִׁמְרִית, **Shimrîyth,** *shim-reeth´*; feminine of 8113; *female guard*; *Shimrith*, a Moabitess:—Shimrith.

8117. שִׁמְרֹנִי, **Shimrônîy,** *shim-ro-nee´*; patronymic from 8110; a *Shimronite* (collective) or descendants of Shimron:—Shimronites.

8118. שֹׁמְרֹנִי, **Shômᵉrônîy,** *sho-mer-o-nee´*; patrial from 8111; a *Shomeronite* (collective) or inhabitant of Shomeron:—Samaritans.

8119. שִׁמְרָת, **Shimrâth,** *shim-rawth´*; from 8104; *guardship*; *Shimrath*, an Israelite:—Shimrath.

8120. שְׁמַשׁ, **shᵉmash,** *shem-ash´*; (Chaldee); corresponding to the root of 8121 through the idea of *activity* implied in day-light; to *serve*:—minister.

An Aramaic verb meaning to serve, to minister to, and to attend to. This word is used only in Da 7:10 in a stunning vision of God, the Ancient of Days, on His throne. Thousands attend God, serving Him only. In this limited context, we get the idea that this verb is one that signifies much more than just serving or attending someone as a paid servant or a slave would do out of necessity. The connotation here seems to be that of having absolute devotion to the person, just as all who serve God must be wholeheartedly devoted to Him. This serving is voluntary for those who love God.

8121. שֶׁמֶשׁ, **shemesh,** *sheh´-mesh*; from an unused root meaning to be *brilliant*; the *sun*; (by implication) the *east*; (figurative) a *ray*, i.e. (architectural) a notched *battlement*:— + east side (-ward), sun ([rising]), + west (-ward), window. See also 1053.

8122. שֶׁמֶשׁ, **shemesh,** *sheh´-mesh*; (Chaldee); corresponding to 8121; the *sun*:—sun.

8123. שִׁמְשׁוֹן, **Shimshôwn,** *shim-shone´*; from 8121; *sunlight*; *Shimshon*, an Israelite:—Samson.

8124. שַׁמְשַׁי, **Shimshay,** *shim-shah´ee*; (Chaldee); from 8122; *sunny*; *Shimshai*, a Samaritan:—Shimshai.

8125. שַׁמְשְׁרַי, **Shamsheray,** *sham-sher-ah´ee*; apparently from 8121; *sunlike*; *Shamsherai*, an Israelite:—Shamsherai.

8126. שֻׁמָתִי, **Shumâthîy,** *shoo-maw-thee´*; patronymic from an unused name from 7762 probably meaning *garlic*-smell; a *Shumathite* (collective) or descendants of Shumah:—Shumathites.

8127. שֵׁן, **shên,** *shane´*; from 8150; a *tooth* (as *sharp*); specifically (for 8143) *ivory*; (figurative) a *cliff*:—crag, × forefront, ivory, × sharp, tooth.

8128. שֵׁן, **shên,** *shane*; (Chaldee); corresponding to 8127; a *tooth*:—tooth.

8129. שֵׁן, **Shên,** *shane*; the same as 8127; *crag*; *Shen*, a place in Palestine:—Shen.

8130. שָׂנֵא, **sânê’,** *saw-nay´*; a primitive root; to *hate* (personal):—enemy, foe, (be) hate (-ful, -r), odious, × utterly.

A verb meaning to hate, to be unwilling, to be hated. This verb is the antonym of the Hebrew verb *’âhab* (157), meaning to love. The verb means to hate God or persons; God punishes children for the sins of their fathers to the third and fourth generation of those who hate Him, but He shows kindness instead of punishment to those who love (*’âhab*) Him (Ex 20:5). God hates as His enemies those who love cruelty and wickedness (Ps 11:5); they do not keep His covenant and are not loyal to Him (Ex 20:5). God's people were not to become allied to those who hated the Lord (2Ch 19:2; Ps 139:21). God or persons can be the subject of the verb; God came to hate the palaces of Jacob (Am 6:8; Hos 9:15); and even the religious services of His own people because they were false (Am 5:21). In fact, God hates all who do evil (Ps 5:5[6]); and wickedness (Ps 45:7[8]); thus, to fear God means to hate evil (Pr 8:13).

God is different from all other so-called gods, so much so that He hates the corrupt things the heathen do when they worship these gods (Dt 12:31). The word describes the haters or enemies of persons. David's enemies were those whom his soul hated (2Sa 5:8); the enemies of Rebekah would be those who might hate her descendants (Ge 24:60). The lack of hatred toward a person cleared someone who accidentally killed another person without planning to do so and did not previously hate the person (Dt 4:42). Absalom, on the other hand, hated his brother Ammon for humiliating his sister and planned his death because he hated him (2Sa 13:22). The negative rendition of love your neighbour as yourself asserted that you should not hate your brother in your heart (Le 19:17).

The word means to dislike, to be hostile to, or to loathe someone or something in some contexts: Isaac accused Abimelech of rejecting him or acting hostile toward him when he asked Isaac to move away from him (Ge 26:27; Jgs 11:7); Joseph's brothers became bitter and hostile toward him and his dreams (Ge 37:5); Malachi asserted that God hated Esau but loved Jacob to explain how God had dealt with their descendants (Mal 1:3); God cared for Esau and gave him offspring. A similar use of this word is found concerning Jacob's love for Rachel and the hyperbolic statement that he hated Leah (Ge 29:31, 33; Dt 21:16, 17); Jethro instructed Moses to choose faithful men who despised increasing their wealth in dishonest ways (Ex 18:21). In the passive stem of the verb, it is used once to refer to the poor who are despised by their friends or neighbours in contrast to the rich who have many friends (Pr 14:20).

In the intensive stem, the word means one who radiates hatred (i.e. an enemy); Moses prayed for the Lord to strike the enemies of Levi (Dt 33:11; 2Sa 22:41). The word described the enemies of the Lord (Nu 10:35; Dt 32:41). The word also described the person who hates wisdom; such a person loves death (Pr 8:36).

8131. שְׂנָא, **senê’,** *sen-ay´*; (Chaldee); corresponding to 8130:—hate.

An Aramaic verb meaning an enemy. This word only occurs once in the Hebrew Bible and refers to those who hate a person. In Da 4:19[16], this word is used when Daniel is speaking to King Nebuchadnezzar about the interpretation of his dream. The interpretation is so unfavourable that Daniel says he wishes it were for the king's enemies instead of being for the king himself.

8132. שְׁנָא, **shânâ',** *shaw-naw'*; a primitive root; to *alter*:—change.

8133. שְׁנָא, **sheʿnâ',** *shen-aw'*; (Chaldee); corresponding to 8132:—alter, change, (be) diverse.

8134. שִׁנְאָב, **Shin'âb,** *shin-awb'*; probably from 8132 and 1; a *father has turned*; Shinab, a Canaanite:—Shinab.

8135. שִׂנְאָה, **śin'âh,** *sin-aw'*; from 8130; *hate*:— + exceedingly, hate (-ful, -red).

A feminine noun meaning hating, hatred. The word is derived from the verb *śânê'* (8130) and signifies a strong feeling of hatred. It is most commonly used to describe hatred that one human feels toward another. This hate can be so strong that it leads to murder (Nu 35:20); or it can be a hate that causes unrest and dissension between people, yet not necessarily leading to violence (Pr 10:12; 15:17). In one place, this noun is even used to describe sexual revulsion and is indicative of a strong hate (2Sa 13:15). This word can be used as a verb at times, such as in Dt 1:27 and 9:28. Here God is the subject, and the people were complaining that He hated them, although this was not true. The connotations the people had with this word showed through because they felt that God hated them so much that He would hand them over to be killed by their enemies.

8136. שִׁנְאָן, **shin'ân,** *shin-awn'*; from 8132; *change*, i.e. *repetition*:— × angels.

A masculine noun meaning repeating, repetition. This word is used only once in the OT, in Ps 68:17[18], where it is preceded by the word that means a thousand. Therefore, it means a thousand in repetition or thousands of thousands. Here it is in reference to the chariots of God, which shows how mighty and powerful God is because He is the ruler over so much. Chariots were also a sign of wealth; and since God had so many chariots, it showed that all the wealth in the world belongs to Him alone.

8137. שֶׁנְאַצַּר, **Shen'atstsar,** *shen-ats-tsar'*; apparently of Babylonian origin; *Shenatstsar*, an Israelite:—Senazar.

8138. שָׁנָה, **shânâh,** *shaw-naw'*; a primitive root; to *fold*, i.e. *duplicate* (literal or figurative); (by implication) to *transmute* (transitive or intransitive):—do (speak, strike) again, alter, double, (be given to) change, disguise, (be) diverse, pervert, prefer, repeat, return, do the second time.

8139. שְׁנָה, **sheʿnâh,** *shen-aw'*; (Chaldee); corresponding to 8142:—sleep.

8140. שְׁנָה, **sheʿnâh,** *shen-aw'*; (Chaldee); corresponding to 8141:—year.

8141. שָׁנָה, **shânâh,** *shaw-naw'*; from 8138; a *year* (as a *revolution* of time):— + whole age, × long, + old, year (× -ly).

8142. שֵׁנָה, **shênâh,** *shay-naw'*; or שֵׁנָא, **shênâ',** *shay-naw'*; (Ps 127:2), from 3462; *sleep*:—sleep.

8143. שֶׁנְהַבִּים, **shenhabbîym,** *shen-hab-beem'*; from 8127 and the plural apparently of a foreign word; probably *tooth of elephants*, i.e. *ivory tusk*:—ivory.

8144. שָׁנִי, **shânîy,** *shaw-nee'*; of uncertain derivation; *crimson*, (properly) the insect or its colour, also stuff dyed with it:—crimson, scarlet (thread).

8145. שֵׁנִי, **shênîy,** *shay-nee'*; from 8138; (properly) *double*, i.e. *second*; (also adverb) *again*:—again, either [of them], (an-) other, second (time).

8146. שָׂנִיא, **śânîy',** *saw-nee'*; from 8130; *hated*:—hated.

A feminine adjective meaning one who is hated or held in aversion. It is used in Dt 21:15 contrasting a wife who is loved with a wife who is hated. There does not seem to be a connotation of extreme hate here but rather of dislike, preferring one wife to the other. The terms are used as opposites, but the strength of opposition cannot be determined accurately. In this limited context, it is difficult to tell how strong of a connotation the word really holds, but here it seems to connote more dislike or neglect than strong hate that would lead to overtly hateful actions toward that person.

8147. שְׁנַיִם, **shenayim,** *shen-ah'-yim*; dual of 8145; feminine שְׁתַּיִם, **shettayim,** *shet-tah'-yim*; *two*; also (as ordinal) *twofold*:—both, couple, double, second, twain, + twelfth, + twelve, + twenty (sixscore) thousand, twice, two.

8148. שְׁנִינָה, **sh⁶nîynâh,** *shen-ee-naw´*; from 8150; something *pointed,* i.e. a *gibe:*—byword, taunt.

8149. שְׂנִיר, **Sh⁶nîyr,** *shen-eer´*; or שְׂנִיר, **Ś⁶nîyr,** *sen-eer´*; from an unused root meaning to be *pointed; peak; Shenir* or *Senir,* a summit of Lebanon:—Senir, Shenir.

8150. שָׁנַן, **shânan,** *shaw-nan´*; a primitive root; to *point* (transitive or intransitive); (intensive) to *pierce;* (figurative) to *inculcate:*—prick, sharp (-en), teach diligently, whet.

A verb meaning to whet, to sharpen. This word is used in three of the basic stems. In its simple meaning of sharpen, it can be used to refer to the sharpening of a sword. In context it refers to God sharpening His sword of judgment (Dt 32:41). Also, it can be used in reference to sharp arrows (Ps 45:5[6]; Isa 5:28). Figuratively, this verb can be used to signify sharp words that a person says in order to hurt someone else (Ps 64:3[4]; 140:3[4]). In the intensive form of the verb, it means to teach incisively (Dt 6:7). The idea here is that just as words are cut into a stone tablet with a sharp object, so the Law should be impressed on the hearts of the children of every generation. Finally, in the reflexive stem, this verb means to be pierced by grief or envy or to be wounded (Ps 73:21).

8151. שָׁנַס, **shânas,** *shaw-nas´*; a primitive root; to *compress* (with a belt):—gird up.

8152. שִׁנְעָר, **Shin'âr,** *shin-awr´*; probably of foreign derivation; *Shinar,* a plain in Babylon:—Shinar.

8153. שְׁנָת, **sh⁶nâth,** *shen-awth´*; from 3462; *sleep:*—sleep.

8154. שָׁסָה, **shâsâh,** *shaw-saw´*; or שָׁשָׂה, **shâśâh,** *shaw-saw´*; (Isa 10:13), a primitive root; to *plunder:*—destroyer, rob, spoil (-er).

A verb that means to spoil, to plunder. This verb is used only in the simple stem and in the participle form. It can refer to the plundering of both land and objects (Jgs 2:14; 1Sa 14:48; Hos 13:15). In almost every reference where this word is found, enemies were plundering the land and the people of Israel. God allowed this in judgment on the sins of the Israelites after they had been warned and refused to

repent or as a warning to call them to repentance. The participle form of this verb refers to people who do the plundering (Isa 10:13; 42:22). Ultimately, God allowed any persons to be plunderers. But if they overstepped their boundaries, they too would be plundered as the punishment for their sins.

8155. שָׁסַס, **shâsas,** *shaw-sas´*; a primitive root; to *plunder:*—rifle, spoil.

8156. שָׁסַע, **shâsa',** *shaw-sah´*; a primitive root; to *split* or *tear;* (figurative) to *upbraid:*—cleave, (be) cloven ([footed]), rend, stay.

8157. שֶׁסַע, **shesa',** *sheh´-sah;* from 8156; a *fissure:*—cleft, clovenfooted.

8158. שָׁסַף, **shâsaph,** *shaw-saf´*; a primitive root; to *cut* in pieces, i.e. *slaughter:*—hew in pieces.

8159. שָׁעָה, **shâ'âh,** *shaw-aw´*; a primitive root; to *gaze* at or about (properly, for help); (by implication) to *inspect, consider, compassionate, be nonplussed* (as looking around in amazement) or *bewildered:*—depart, be dim, be dismayed, look (away), regard, have respect, spare, turn.

8160. שָׁעָה, **shâ'âh,** *shaw-aw´*; (Chaldee); from a root corresponding to 8159; (properly) a *look,* i.e. a *moment:*—hour.

8161. שַׁעֲטָה, **sha'ăṭâh,** *shah´-at-aw;* feminine from an unused root meaning to *stamp;* a *clatter* (of hoofs):—stamping.

8162. שַׁעַטְנֵז, **sha'aṭnêz,** *shah-at-naze´*; probably of foreign derivative; *linsey-woolsey,* i.e. cloth of linen and wool carded and spun together:—garment of divers sorts, linen and woollen.

8163. שָׂעִיר, **sâ'îyr,** *saw-eer´*; or שָׂעִר, **sâ'ir,** *saw-eer´*; from 8175; *shaggy;* as noun, a *he-goat;* (by analogy) a *faun:*—devil, goat, hairy, kid, rough, satyr.

A masculine noun meaning a male goat, a buck. Occasionally, the word can be used figuratively to mean a hairy one. Under the Israelite sacrificial system, a male goat was an acceptable sin offering. This noun is used many times in conjunction with the sin offering, in which a male goat without any defects was offered by the priest to atone for the sins of himself and the people (Le 9:15; 2Ch 29:23; Eze 43:25). On the negative side, the Israelites worshiped the goat as an idol in times of rebellion against God; the same noun is used in these references (Le 17:7; 2Ch 11:15).

8164. שָׂעִיר, **sâ'îyr**, *saw-eer´*; formed the same as 8163; a *shower* (as *tempestuous*):—small rain.

8165. שֵׂעִיר, **Sê'îyr**, *say-eer´*; formed like 8163; *rough; Seïr*, a mountain of Idumæa and its aboriginal occupants, also one in Palestine:—Seir.

8166. שְׂעִירָה, **s^e'îyrâh**, *seh-ee-raw´*; feminine of 8163; a *she-goat*:—kid.

8167. שְׂעִירָה, **S^e'îyrâh**, *seh-ee-raw´*; formed as 8166; *roughness; Seïrah*, a place in Palestine:—Seirath.

8168. שֹׁעַל, **shô'al**, *sho´-al*; from an unused root meaning to *hollow* out; the *palm*; (by extension) a *handful*:—handful, hollow of the hand.

8169. שַׁעַלְבִים, **Sha'albîym**, *shah-al-beem´*; or שַׁעֲלַבִּין, **Sha'ălabbîyn**, *shah-al-ab-been´*; plural from 7776; *fox-holes; Shaalbim* or *Shaalabbin*, a place in Palestine:—Shaalabbin, Shaalbim.

8170. שַׁעַלְבֹנִי, **Sha'albônîy**, *shah-al-bo-nee´*; patrial from 8169; a *Shaalbonite* or inhabitant of Shaalbin:—Shaalbonite.

8171. שַׁעֲלִים, **Sha'alîym**, *shah-al-eem´*; plural of 7776; *foxes; Shaalim*, a place in Palestine:—Shalim.

8172. שָׁעַן, **shâ'an**, *shaw-an´*; a primitive root; to *support* one's self:—lean, lie, rely, rest (on, self), stay.

A verb meaning to lean, to rely, to support oneself. This verb is found only in the passive form, but it is active in meaning. In its simplest meaning, it refers to leaning on things for support, such as trees (Ge 18:4) and pillars (Jgs 16:26). The idea conveyed here is simply that of resting one's weight against something to give it support, but not all things leaned on will actually support (Job 8:15). This verb is also used in the sense of a king leaning or relying on his closest friends and advisors. This may mean literally leaning on someone's arm or trusting in his or her counsel (2Ki 5:18; 7:2, 17). Leaning on can also mean trusting in persons, whether it be God (Mic 3:11); other people (Eze 29:7); or oneself (Pr 3:5). Ultimately, God should be trusted and leaned on, for He will never fail.

8173. שָׁעַע, **shâ'a'**, *shaw-ah´*; a primitive root; (in a good acceptation) to *look* upon (with complacency), i.e. *fondle, please* or *amuse* (self); (in a bad one) to *look* about (in dismay), i.e. *stare:*—cry (out) *[by confusion with 7768]*, dandle, delight (self), play, shut.

8174. שַׁעַף, **Sha'aph**, *shah´-af*; from 5586; *fluctuation; Shaaph*, the name of two Israelites:—Shaaph.

8175. שָׂעַר, **sâ'ar**, *saw-ar´*; a primitive root; to *storm*; (by implication) to *shiver*, i.e. *fear*:—be (horribly) afraid, fear, hurl as a storm, be tempestuous, come like (take away as with) a whirlwind.

A verb meaning to sweep away, to whirl away. The image brought to mind when this verb is used is that of a stormy wind sweeping things away that cannot stand against its power. It appears in the simple, passive, intensive, and reflexive stems of the verb, but the meanings in each stem are all comparable. This verb is often used to describe the fate of evil persons (Job 27:21; Ps 58:9[10]). Their punishment from God is that they will be swept away suddenly, just as a stormy wind arises suddenly to sweep things away. Another use of this word is to describe God in all His power and glory, the Ruler of the universe (Ps 50:3); and it can also be used to describe a battle where one ruler storms out against another (Da 11:40).

8176. שָׁעַר, **shâ'ar**, *shaw-ar´*; a primitive root; to *split* or *open*, i.e. (literal, but only as denominative from 8179) to *act as gate-keeper* (see 7778); (figurative) to *estimate*:—think.

A verb possibly meaning to cleave, to divide, but it took on the meaning of to calculate, to estimate, to set a price on. The meaning was transferred to the sense of judging something, thereby setting a price to it. There are no references to the verb meaning to cleave in the OT, but in Pr 23:7, this verb is used to mean to calculate or to set a price on. The context here is that of misers who count the cost of everything that their guests eat or drink. They find no enjoyment in their guests but only worry about the cost of it all.

8177. שְׂעַר, **s^e'ar**, *seh-ar´*; (Chaldee); corresponding to 8181; *hair*:—hair.

8178. שַׂעַר, **śaʿar,** *sah´-ar;* from 8175; a *tempest;* also a *terror:*—affrighted, × horribly, × sore, storm. See 8181.

A masculine noun meaning horror. The horror described by the use of this noun is what people feel when witnessing the destruction that God allows to happen to evil people of this world. In Job 18:20, it is said that people were seized with horror at the fate of an evil person. In Eze 27:35 and 32:10, this word is used in the context of laments composed for the land of Tyre and Pharaoh of Egypt, who were both destroyed. When people see the destruction wrought on them, they are filled with horror at their fate. A less common use of this word holds the meaning of storm (Isa 28:2).

8179. שַׁעַר, **shaʿar,** *shah´-ar;* from 8176 in its original sense; an *opening,* i.e. *door* or *gate:*—city, door, gate, port (× -er).

8180. שַׁעַר, **shaʿar,** *shah´-ar;* from 8176; a *measure* (as a *section*):—[hundred-] fold.

8181. שֵׂעָר, **śêʿār,** *say-awr´;* or שַׂעַר, **śaʿar,** *sah´-ar;* (Isa 7:20), from 8175 in the sense of *dishevelling; hair* (as if *tossed* or *bristling*):—hair (-y), × rough.

8182. שֹׁעָר, **shôʿār,** *sho-awr´;* from 8176; *harsh* or *horrid,* i.e. *offensive:*—vile.

An adjective meaning horrid, bad, disagreeable. This word is used only once in the OT in Jer 29:17 when describing figs that are so bad they cannot be eaten. There is absolutely no use for them but to be thrown away. This is used to explain what would become of the Israelites who remained in their land instead of going into exile. God would send the sword, famine, and plague against them so that in the end they too would be as worthless as bad figs. They would not be slightly disagreeable but would be so ruined and so horrid that they would simply be destroyed.

8183. שְׁעָרָה, **śeʿārâh,** *seh-aw-raw´;* feminine of 8178; a *hurricane:*—storm, tempest.

8184. שְׂעֹרָה, **śeʿôrâh,** *seh-o-raw´;* or שְׂעוֹרָה, **śeʿôwrâh,** *seh-o-raw´;* (feminine meaning the *plant*); and (masculine meaning the *grain*); also שְׂעֹר, **śeʿôr,** *seh-ore´;* or שְׂעוֹר, **śeʿôwr,** *seh-ore´;* from 8175 in the sense of *roughness; barley* (as *villose*):—barley.

8185. שַׂעֲרָה, **śaʿărâh,** *sah-ar-aw´;* feminine of 8181; *hairiness:*—hair.

8186. שַׁעֲרוּרָה, **shaʿărûwrâh,** *shah-ar-oo-raw´;* or שַׁעֲרִירִיָּה, **shaʿăriyrîyyâh,** *shah-ar-ee-ree-yaw´;* or שַׁעֲרֻרִת, **shaʿărurith,** *shah-ar-oo-reeth´;* feminine from 8176 in the sense of 8175; something *fearful:*—horrible thing.

A feminine noun meaning horror, a horrible thing. It is used to describe how bad the apostasy and apathy of the Israelites was. What they did in worshiping idols and prophesying falsely were truly horrible things in the eyes of God and the prophets who denounced them (Jer 5:30; 23:14). There are two variant spellings of this word. One, *shaʿărurı̂y-yâh,* is found in Hos 6:10 and another, *shaʿărurith,* is found in Jer 18:13. The uses of these variant spellings are exactly the same as the most common spelling. In every instance of the use of this word, it refers to the horror of the things that Israel was doing and the sins they were committing against the Lord.

8187. שְׁעַרְיָה, **Sheʿaryâh,** *sheh-ar-yaw´;* from 8176 and 3050; *Jah has stormed; Sheärjah,* an Israelite:—Sheariah.

8188. שְׂעֹרִים, **Śeʿôrîym,** *seh-o-reem´;* masculine plural of 8184; *barley* grains; *Seörim,* an Israelite:—Seorim.

8189. שַׁעֲרַיִם, **Shaʿărayim,** *shah-ar-ah´-yim;* dual of 8179; *double gates; Shaarajim,* a place in Palestine:—Shaaraim.

8190. שַׁעַשְׁגַּז, **Shaʿashgaz,** *shah-ash-gaz´;* of Persian derivation; *Shaashgaz,* a eunuch of Xerxes:—Shaashgaz.

8191. שַׁעֲשֻׁעִים, **shaʿăshuʿîym,** *sha-ah-shoo´-eem;* from 8173; *enjoyment:*—delight, pleasure.

8192. שָׁפָה, **shâphâh,** *shaw-faw´;* a primitive root; to *abrade,* i.e. *bare:*—high, stick out.

8193. שָׂפָה, **śâphâh,** *saw-faw´;* or (in dual and plural) שֶׂפֶת, **śepheth,** *sef-eth´;* probably from 5595 or 8192 through the idea of *termination* (compare 5490); the *lip* (as a natural boundary); (by implication) *language;* (by analogy) a *margin* (of a vessel, water, cloth, etc.):—band, bank, binding, border, brim, brink, edge, language, lip, prating, ([sea-]) shore, side, speech, talk, [vain] words.

A feminine noun meaning a lip, a language, an edge, a border. The most common use of this word is that of lip. It can be used merely to describe the organ of speech (Ex 6:12, 30; Ps 63:5[6]); and the place from where laughter comes (Job 8:21). Yet it can also be used as a feature of beauty in descriptions of a beautiful person (SS 4:3, 11). Finally, it can refer to the place from where divine speech comes, from the lips of God (Job 23:12; Ps 17:4). A more general meaning is that of language that originates from the lips (Ge 11:6, 7; Ps 81:5[6]; Isa 33:19). When an edge or a border is the meaning of this word, it can refer to a wide variety of things such as the shore of a sea (Ge 22:17); the edge or brim of a variety of objects (1Ki 7:23; Eze 43:13); or the boundary between geographical sites (Jgs 7:22).

8194. שָׁפָה, **shâphâh,** *shaw-faw´*; from 8192 in the sense of *clarifying*; a *cheese* (as *strained* from the whey):—cheese.

8195. שְׁפוֹ, **Sh⁰phôw,** *shef-o´*; or שְׁפִי, **Sh⁰phîy,** *shef-ee´*; from 8192; *baldness* [compare 8205]; *Shepho* or *Shephi,* an Idumæan:—Shephi, Shepho.

8196. שְׁפוֹט, **sh⁰phôwṭ,** *shef-ote´*; or שְׁפוּט, **sh⁰phûwṭ,** *shef-oot´*; from 8199; a judicial *sentence,* i.e. *punishment:*—judgment.

8197. שְׁפוּפָם, **Sh⁰phûwphâm,** *shef-oo-fawm´*; or שְׁפוּפָן, **Sh⁰-phûwphân,** *shef-oo-fawn´*; from the same as 8207; *serpent-like; Shephupham* or *Shephuphan,* an Israelite:—Shephuphan, Shupham.

8198. שִׁפְחָה, **shiphchâh,** *shif-khaw´*; feminine from an unused root meaning to *spread* out (as a *family*; see 4940); a *female slave* (as a member of the *household*):—(bond-, hand-) maid (-en, -servant), wench, bondwoman, womanservant.

8199. שָׁפַט, **shâphaṭ,** *shaw-fat´*; a primitive root; to *judge,* i.e. pronounce *sentence* (for or against); (by implication) to *vindicate* or *punish*; (by extension) to *govern*; (passive) to *litigate* (literal or figurative):— + avenge, × that condemn, contend, defend, execute (judgment), (be a) judge (-ment), × needs, plead, reason, rule.

A verb meaning to judge, to govern. This word, though often translated as judge, is much more inclusive than the modern concept of

judging and encompasses all the facets and functions of government: executive, legislative, and judicial. Consequently, this term can be understood in any one of the following ways. It could designate, in its broadest sense, to function as ruler or governor. This function could be fulfilled by individual judges (Jgs 16:31; 1Sa 7:16); the king (1Ki 3:9); or even God Himself (Ps 50:6; 75:7[8]); since He is the source of authority (cf. Ro 13:1) and will eventually conduct all judgments (Ps 96:13). In a judicial sense, the word could also indicate, because of the exalted status of the ruler, the arbitration of civil, domestic, and religious disputes (Dt 25:1). As before, this function could be fulfilled by the congregation of Israel (Nu 35:24); individual judges (Ex 18:16; Dt 1:16); the king (1Sa 8:5, 6, 20); or even God Himself (Ge 16:5; 1Sa 24:12[13], 15[16]). In the executive sense, it could denote to execute judgment, to bring about what had been decided. This could be in the form of a vindication (Ps 10:18; Isa 1:17, 23); or a condemnation and punishment (Eze 7:3, 8; 23:45).

8200. שְׁפַט, **sh⁰phaṭ,** *shef-at´*; (Chaldee); corresponding to 8199; to *judge:*—magistrate.

An Aramaic verb meaning to judge, to govern. This word is used only once in the OT and is related to the Hebrew word *shâphaṭ* (8199), meaning to judge or to govern. In Ezr 7:25, this word is used to describe one of the governing rulers that Ezra was to appoint. These rulers were to perform similar functions as the *dayyân* (1782) or judges that Ezra was also to appoint.

8201. שֶׁפֶט, **shepheṭ,** *sheh´-fet*; from 8199; a *sentence,* i.e. *infliction:*—judgment.

A masculine noun meaning judgment. This word comes from the verb *shâphaṭ* (8199), meaning to judge, and usually describes the active role of God in punishing. In several instances, such judgment is described as the sword, famine, wild beasts, plagues, stoning, and burning (Eze 14:21; 16:41). The plagues that God inflicted on Egypt are described as judgments (Ex 6:6; 7:4; 12:12; Nu 33:4). This word describes both the defeat of Israel (2Ch 24:24; Eze 5:10, 15); as well as the defeat of other nations (Eze 25:11; 28:22, 26). In one instance, this word speaks more generally, not of specific nations, but of unruly scoffers who will receive physical chastisement (Pr 19:29).

8202. שָׁפָט, **Shâphâṭ,** *shaw-fawt´*; from 8199; *judge; Shaphat,* the name of four Israelites:— Shaphat.

8203. שְׁפַטְיָה, **Shᵉphaṭyâh,** *shef-at-yaw´*; or שְׁפַטְיָהוּ, **Shᵉphaṭ-yâhûw,** *shef-at-yaw´-hoo*; from 8199 and 3050; *Jah has judged; Shephatjah,* the name of ten Israelites:—Shephatiah.

8204. שִׁפְטָן, **Shiphṭân,** *shif-tawn´*; from 8199; *judge-like; Shiphtan,* an Israelite:—Shiphtan.

8205. שְׁפִי, **shᵉphîy,** *shef-ee´*; from 8192; *bareness;* (concrete) a *bare* hill or plain:—high place, stick out.

A masculine noun meaning bare. This word carries the idea of a barren or smooth place and is used to describe dry places where God will open rivers (Isa 41:18); and infertile places where God will create pastures (Isa 49:9). The donkeys could not find grass in such places (Jer 14:6). The barren place was where Balaam went to meet God (Nu 23:3); and where Israel was to lament their destruction (Jer 7:29). At times, it could describe the bare hills (Jer 3:2, 21) from which the dry winds originated in the barren wilderness (Jer 4:11; 12:12).

8206. שֻׁפִּים, **Shuppîym,** *shoop-peem´*; plural of an unused noun from the same as 8207 and meaning the same; *serpents; Shuppim,* an Israelite:—Shuppim.

8207. שְׁפִיפֹן, **shᵉphîyphôn,** *shef-ee-fone´*; from an unused root meaning the same as 7779; a kind of *serpent* (as *snapping*), probably the *cerastes* or horned adder:—adder.

8208. שָׁפִיר, **Shâphîyr,** *shaf-eer´*; from 8231; *beautiful; Shaphir,* a place in Palestine:—Saphir.

8209. שַׁפִּיר, **shappîyr,** *shap-peer´*; (Chaldee); intensive of a form corresponding to 8208; *beautiful:*—fair.

8210. שָׁפַךְ, **shâphak,** *shaw-fak´*; a primitive root; to *spill* forth (blood, a libation, liquid metal; or even a solid, i.e. to *mound* up); also (figurative) to *expend* (life, soul, complaint, money, etc.); (intensive) to *sprawl* out:—cast (up), gush out, pour (out), shed (-der, out), slip.

A verb meaning to pour out. In its most basic sense, this word refers to the pouring out of something, for example, fluid on the ground (Ex 4:9; Dt 12:16; 1Sa 7:6); or blood on an altar (Ex 29:12; Le 4:7; Dt 12:27). In several instances, it describes the casting up of a mound against a city to form a siege ramp for attacking it (2Sa 20:15; Eze 4:2; Da 11:15). This word is also used idiomatically to refer to the shedding of blood (Ge 9:6; 1Ki 2:31); especially of innocent blood (2Ki 21:16; Pr 6:17). A dependent prayer is described as the pouring out of one's soul (1Sa 1:15; Ps 42:4[5]); one's heart (Ps 62:8[9]; La 2:19); or one's inner parts before the Lord (La 2:11). God poured out both His wrath (Ps 69:24[25]; Isa 42:25; Jer 6:11; Hos 5:10); and His grace (Joel 2:28[3:1], 29[3:2]; Zec 12:10) from heaven on people.

8211. שֶׁפֶךְ, **shephek,** *sheh´-fek*; from 8210; an *emptying* place, e.g., an ash-*heap:*—are poured out.

A masculine noun meaning a place of pouring, a place of emptying. It comes from the word *shâphak* (8210), meaning to spill forth, and is used in Leviticus to describe the place where the priest was to burn the remains of the bull sacrifice, i.e. next to the place where the ashes were poured out (Le 4:12).

8212. שָׁפְכָה, **shophkâh,** *shof-kaw´*; feminine of a derivative from 8210; a *pipe* (for *pouring* forth, e.g., wine), i.e. the *penis:*—privy member.

8213. שָׁפֵל, **shâphêl,** *shaw-fale´*; a primitive root; to *depress* or *sink* (especially figurative, to *humiliate,* intransitive or trans.):—abase, bring (cast, put) down, debase, humble (self), be (bring, lay, make, put) low (-er).

8214. שְׁפַל, **shᵉphal,** *shef-al´*; (Chaldee); corresponding to 8213:—abase, humble, put down, subdue.

8215. שְׁפַל, **shᵉphal,** *shef-al´*; (Chaldee); from 8214; *low:*—basest.

8216. שֵׁפֶל, **shêphel,** *shay´-fel*; from 8213; an *humble* rank:—low estate (place).

8217. שָׁפָל, **shâphâl,** *shaw-fawl´*; from 8213; *depressed,* literal or figurative:—base (-st), humble, low (-er, -ly).

8218. שִׁפְלָה, **shiphlâh,** *shif-law´*; feminine of 8216; *depression:*—low place.

8219. שְׁפֵלָה, **shᵉphêlâh,** *shef-ay-law´*; from 8213; *Lowland,* i.e. (with the article) the maritime slope of Palestine:—low country, (low) plain, vale (-ley).

8220. שִׁפְלוּת, **shiphlûwth**, *shif-looth´*; from 8213; *remissness:*—idleness.

8221. שְׁפָם, **Shᵉphâm**, *shef-awm´*; probably from 8192; *bare* spot; *Shepham*, a place in or near Palestine:—Shepham.

8222. שָׂפָם, **śâphâm**, *saw-fawm´*; from 8193; the *beard* (as a *lip-piece*):—beard, (upper) lip.

A masculine noun meaning a mustache, a beard. The most basic understanding of this word is evident in 2Sa 19:24 [25], where the text refers to the proper grooming of one's mustache or beard. By extension, this word is also used to imply the upper lip where a mustache grows (Le 13:45); and the mouth in general (Eze 24:17; Mic 3:7).

8223. שְׁפָם, **Shâphâm**, *shaw-fawm´*; formed like 8221; *baldly*; *Shapham*, an Israelite:—Shapham.

8224. שִׂפְמוֹת, **Śiphmôwth**, *sif-môth´*; feminine plural of 8221; *Siphmoth*, a place in Palestine:—Siphmoth.

8225. שִׁפְמִי, **Shiphmîy**, *shif-mee´*; patrial from 8221; a *Shiphmite* or inhabitant of Shepham:—Shiphmite.

8226. שָׂפַן, **śâphan**, *saw-fan´*; a primitive root; to *conceal* (as a valuable):—treasure.

8227. שָׁפָן, **shâphân**, *shaw-fawn´*; from 8226; a species of *rock-rabbit* (from its *hiding*), i.e. probably the *hyrax*:—coney.

8228. שֶׁפַע, **shephaʻ**, *sheh´-fah*; from an unused root meaning to *abound*; *resources:*—abundance.

8229. שִׁפְעָה, **shiphʻâh**, *shif-aw´*; feminine of 8228; *copiousness:*—abundance, company, multitude.

8230. שִׁפְעִי, **Shiphʻîy**, *shif-ee´*; from 8228; *copious; Shiphi*, an Israelite:—Shiphi.

8231. שָׁפַר, **shâphar**, *shaw-far´*; a primitive root; to *glisten*, i.e. (figurative) *be* (causative, *make*) *fair:*— × goodly.

8232. שְׁפַר, **shᵉphar**, *shef-ar´*; (Chaldee); corresponding to 8231; to *be beautiful:*—be acceptable, please, + think good.

8233. שֶׁפֶר, **shepher**, *sheh´-fer*; from 8231; *beauty:*— × goodly.

8234. שֶׁפֶר, **Shepher**, *sheh´-fer*; the same as 8233; *Shepher*, a place in the Desert:—Shapper.

8235. שִׁפְרָה, **shiphrâh**, *shif-raw´*; from 8231; *brightness:*—garnish.

8236. שִׁפְרָה, **Shiphrâh**, *shif-raw´*; the same as 8235; *Shiphrah*, an Israelitess:—Shiphrah.

8237. שַׁפְרִיר, **shaphrîyr**, *shaf-reer´*; from 8231; *splendid*, i.e. a *tapestry* or *canopy:*—royal pavilion.

8238. שְׁפַרְפָּר, **shᵉpharpâr**, *shef-ar-pawr´*; (Chaldee); from 8231; the *dawn* (as *brilliant* with aurora):— × very early in the morning.

8239. שָׁפַת, **shâphath**, *shaw-fath´*; a primitive root; to *locate*, i.e. (general) *hang* on or (figurative) *establish*, *reduce:*—bring, ordain, set on.

8240. שְׁפַתַּיִם, **shᵉphatayim**, *shef-ah-tah´-yeem*; from 8239; a (double) *stall* (for cattle); also a (two-pronged) *hook* (for flaying animals on):—hook, pot.

8241. שֶׁצֶף, **shetseph**, *sheh´-tsef*; from 7857 (for alliteration with 7110); an *outburst* (of anger):—little.

8242. שַׂק, **śaq**, *sak*; from 8264; (properly) a *mesh* (as allowing a liquid to *run* through), i.e. coarse loose cloth or *sacking* (used in mourning and for bagging); hence a *bag* (for grain, etc.):—sack (-cloth, -clothes).

8243. שָׁק, **shâq**, *shawk*; (Chaldee); corresponding to 7785; the *leg:*—leg.

8244. שָׂקַד, **śâqad**, *saw-kad´*; a primitive root; to *fasten:*—bind.

8245. שָׁקַד, **shâqad**, *shaw-kad´*; a primitive root; to *be alert*, i.e. *sleepless*; hence to *be on the lookout* (whether for good or ill):—hasten, remain, wake, watch (for).

8246. שָׁקַד, **shâqad**, *shaw-kad´*; a denominative from 8247; to *be* (intensive, *make*) *almond-shaped:*—make like (unto, after the fashion of) almonds.

8247. שָׁקֵד, **shâqêd**, *shaw-kade´*; from 8245; the *almond* (tree or nut; as being the *earliest* in bloom):—almond (tree).

8248. שָׁקָה, **shâqâh,** *shaw-kaw´*; a primitive root; to *quaff*, i.e. (causative) to *irrigate* or *furnish a potion* to:—cause to (give, give to, let, make to) drink, drown, moisten, water. See 7937, 8354.

8249. שִׁקֻּו, **shiqquv,** *shik-koov´*; from 8248; (plural collective) a *draught*:—drink.

8250. שִׁקּוּי, **shiqqûwy,** *shik-koo´ee*; from 8248; a *beverage; moisture,* i.e. (figurative) *refreshment*:—drink, marrow.

8251. שִׁקּוּץ, **shiqqûwts,** *shik-koots´*; or שִׁקֻּץ, **shiq-quts,** *shik-koots´*; from 8262; *disgusting,* i.e. *filthy*; especially *idolatrous* or (concrete) an *idol*:—abominable filth (idol, -ation), detestable (thing).

A masculine noun meaning a detestable thing, an abomination, and an idol. This Hebrew word identifies an object that is abhorrent or blasphemous. It is used to denote filth (Na 3:6); forbidden food (Zec 9:7); and a blasphemous activity (Da 9:27). Most often, it is used as a synonym for an idol or idolatry (Jer 7:30; Hos 9:10).

8252. שָׁקַט, **shâqat,** *shaw-kat´*; a primitive root; to *repose* (usually figurative):—appease, idleness, (at, be at, be in, give) quiet (-ness), (be at, be in, give, have, take) rest, settle, be still.

A verb meaning to be still, to be quiet, to be undisturbed. The primary meaning of this verb is the state or condition of tranquility (cf. Job 37:17). It signifies the condition during the absence of war (Jgs 3:30; 2Ch 20:30); a sense of safety and security (Eze 38:11); inactivity or passivity (Ps 83:1[2]; Isa 18:4); keeping silent (Ru 3:18; Isa 62:1); and an inner confidence or peace (Isa 7:4). Scripture declares that righteousness brings true security and tranquility (Isa 32:17); but also warns of the false security that comes to the unrighteous (Eze 16:49).

8253. שֶׁקֶט, **sheqet,** *sheh´-ket*; from 8252; *tranquillity*:—quietness.

A masculine noun meaning quietness, tranquility. The only occurrence of this word is found in 1Ch 22:9 and is parallel to the Hebrew word for peace (*shâlôwm,* 7965). It is used to describe the state of tranquility during the reign of Solomon when all enemies were defeated and the united kingdom was at its height.

8254. שָׁקַל, **shâqal,** *shaw-kal´*; a primitive root; to *suspend* or *poise* (especially in trade):—pay, receive (-r), spend, × thoroughly, weigh.

8255. שֶׁקֶל, **sheqel,** *sheh´-kel*; from 8254; probably a *weight*; used as a commercial standard:—shekel.

8256. שָׁקָם, **shâqâm,** *shaw-kawm´*; or (feminine) שִׁקְמָה, **shiq-mâh,** *shik-maw´*; of uncertain derivation; a *sycamore* (usually the tree):—sycamore (fruit, tree).

8257. שָׁקַע, **shâqa,** *shaw-kah´*; (abbreviated in Am 8:8), a primitive root; to *subside*; (by implication) to *be overflowed, cease*; (causative) to *abate, subdue*:—make deep, let down, drown, quench, sink.

8258. שְׁקַעֲרוּרָה, **sheqa‘ărûwrâh,** *she-kah-ah-roo-raw´*; from 8257; a *depression*:—hollow strake.

8259. שָׁקַף, **shâqaph,** *shaw-kaf´*; a primitive root; (properly) to *lean out* (of a window), i.e. (by implication) *peep* or *gaze* (passive *be a spectacle*):—appear, look (down, forth, out).

8260. שֶׁקֶף, **sheqeph,** *sheh´-kef*; from 8259; a *loophole* (for *looking out*), to admit light and air:—window.

8261. שָׁקֻף, **shâquph,** *shaw-koof´*; passive participle of 8259; an *embrasure* or opening [compare 8260] with bevelled jam:—light, window.

8262. שָׁקַץ, **shâqats,** *shaw-kats´*; a primitive root; to *be filthy,* i.e. (intensive) to *loathe, pollute*:—abhor, make abominable, have in abomination, detest, × utterly.

A verb meaning to detest, to make abominable. The primary meaning of this word is to make or to consider something odious. It is used to describe the attitude the Israelites were to have toward a graven image or idol (Dt 7:26); and certain nonkosher foods (Le 11:11, 13). If the Israelites failed to observe this command by partaking of unclean food, they would become detestable to the Lord (Le 20:25). On the other hand, the psalmist stated that this was never the Lord's attitude toward the cries of the afflicted (Ps 22:24[25]).

8263. שֶׁקֶץ, **sheqets,** *sheh´-kets*; from 8262; *filth,* i.e. (figurative and specific) an *idolatrous* object:—abominable (-tion).

A masculine noun meaning a detestation, an abomination, and a detestable thing. Chiefly, this Hebrew word marks those things that were ceremonially unclean and forbidden (Le 7:21). It is used of certain sea creatures (Le 11:10); birds of prey (Le 11:13ff.); and various creeping things (Le 11:20, 23, 41, 42).

8264. שָׁקַק, **shâqaq,** *shaw-kak´*; a primitive root; to *course* (like a beast of prey); by implication to *seek* greedily:—have appetite, justle one against another, long, range, run (to and fro).

8265. שָׂקַר, **śâqar,** *saw-kar´*; a primitive root; to *ogle*, i.e. *blink* coquettishly:—wanton.

8266. שָׁקַר, **shâqar,** *shaw-kar´*; a primitive root; to *cheat*, i.e. *be untrue* (usually in words):—fail, deal falsely, lie.

A verb meaning to engage in deceit, to deal falsely. The notion of a treacherous or deceptive activity forms the fundamental meaning of this word. It is used to describe an agreement entered into with deceitful intentions (Ge 21:23); outright lying (Le 19:11); and the violation of a covenant (Ps 44:17[18]). Scripture states clearly that such activity is the domain of humans, not of God (1Sa 15:29).

8267. שֶׁקֶר, **sheqer,** *sheh´-ker*; from 8266; an *untruth*; (by implication) a *sham* (often adverbial):—without a cause, deceit (-ful), false (-hood, -ly), feignedly, liar, + lie, lying, vain (thing), wrongfully.

A noun meaning a lie, vanity, without cause. This word is used of a lying witness (Dt 19:18); of false prophets (Jer 5:31; 20:6; 29:9); of telling lies (Le 19:12; Jer 37:14); and of a liar (Pr 17:4). In other cases, it describes something done in vain (1Sa 25:21; Ps 33:17); or an action without cause (Ps 38:19[20]; 119:78, 86).

8268. שֹׁקֶת, **shôqeth,** *sho´-keth*; from 8248; a *trough* (for *watering*):—trough.

8269. שַׂר, **śar,** *sar*; from 8323; a *head* person (of any rank or class):—captain (that had rule), chief (captain), general, governor, keeper, lord, ([-task-]) master, prince (-ipal), ruler, steward.

A masculine noun meaning a chieftain, a chief, a ruler, an official, a captain, a prince. The primary usage is official in the sense that this individual has immediate authority as the leader. While he was at Gath, David became the leader for those who were in distress, in debt, or were discontented (1Sa 22:2). The word describes the powers of a magistrate when a man posed a sarcastic question to Moses (Ex 2:14). In Genesis, the noun refers to Phicol as the commander of Abimelech's forces (Ge 21:22). In a similar usage of the word, Joshua was met by the commander of the Lord's army. This commander was so entrusted by God that Joshua had to take off his shoes due to the glory of God surrounding the man (Jos 5:14).

In terms of priesthood, *śar* designates a leading priest, i.e. a priest that is above the others (Ezr 8:24, 29). In this situation with Ezra, the leading priest was entrusted with the articles of the Temple and had to guard them with his life. The noun depicts Michael as one of the chief princes who came to Daniel's aid (Da 10:13). In Da 8:11, the word is used to denote the little horn setting itself up to be as great as the Prince of the host. This horn would set itself up, take away the daily sacrifice, and desecrate the Temple of God.

8270. שֹׁר, **shôr,** *shore*; from 8324; a *string* (as *twisted* [compare 8306]), i.e. (specific) the *umbilical cord* (also figurative as the centre of strength):—navel.

8271. שְׁרֵא, **shᵉrê’,** *sher-ay´*; (Chaldee); a root corresponding to that of 8293; to *free, separate*; (figurative) to *unravel, commence*; by implication (of unloading beasts) to *reside*:—begin dissolve, dwell, loose.

8272. שַׁרְאֶצֶר, **Shar’etser,** *shar-eh´-tser*; of foreign derivation; *Sharetser*, the name of an Assyrian and an Israelite:—Sharezer.

8273. שָׁרָב, **shârâb,** *shaw-rawb´*; from an unused root meaning to *glare*; quivering *glow* (of the air), especially the *mirage*:—heat, parched ground.

8274. שֵׁרֵבְיָה, **Shêrêbyâh,** *shay-rayb-yaw´*; from 8273 and 3050; *Jah has brought heat; Sherebjah*, the name of two Israelites:—Sherebiah.

8275. שַׁרְבִיט, **sharbîṭ,** *shar-beet´*; for 7626; a *rod* of empire:—sceptre.

A masculine noun meaning a scepter. This word is only found in the book of Esther. In Esther's response to Mordecai, she stated that anyone who went to see the king without being summoned would die unless the king extended the gold scepter in a symbolic act that saved the life of the individual (Est 4:11). In Est 5:2, Esther went before the king, touched the scepter that was extended to her, then stated her request that Haman come to a feast that she had provided for him and the king. Finally, Esther went again before the king and fell at his feet weeping and begging that he would stop Haman's evil plan. King Xerxes again extended the scepter to Esther, who in turn stood and restated her request (Est 8:4).

8276. שָׂרַג, **śârag,** *saw-rag´;* a primitive root; to *intwine:*—wrap together, wreath.

8277. שָׂרַד, **śârad,** *saw-rad´;* a primitive root; (properly) to *puncture* [compare 8279], i.e. (figurative, through the idea of *slipping* out) to *escape* or survive:—remain.

8278. שְׂרָד, **śᵉrâd,** *ser-awd´;* from 8277; *stitching* (as *pierced* with a needle):—service.

8279. שֶׂרֶד, **śered,** *seh´-red;* from 8277; a (carpenter's) *scribing-awl* (for *pricking* or scratching measurements):—line.

8280. שָׂרָה, **śârâh,** *saw-raw´;* a primitive root; to *prevail:*—have power (as a prince).

A verb meaning to persist, to exert oneself, to persevere. The primary meaning is to exert oneself. In Genesis, the word depicts Jacob, who had struggled with God and persons and prevailed. This achievement resulted in a name change to Israel (Ge 32:28[29]). The word is used figuratively in Hosea, recollecting on the memory of Jacob's struggle with God at Peniel to describe a reason for Ephraim's punishment (Hos 12:4[5]). This comparison relates Ephraim back to Jacob, the father of their tribe, as a call to repentance.

8281. שָׂרָה, **shârâh,** *shaw-raw´;* a primitive root; to *free:*—direct.

A verb meaning to let loose. This word occurs in the OT only once. In Job 37:3, it describes God's loosing of thunder and lightning.

8282. שָׂרָה, **śârâh,** *saw-raw´;* feminine of 8269; a *mistress*, i.e. female noble:—lady, princess, queen.

A feminine noun meaning a princess, a royal lady. This word comes from the verb *śârar* (8323), meaning to rule or to act as prince, and is the feminine form of the word *śar* (8269),

meaning prince, captain, or ruler. This word always refers to women who had access to the royal court. It is used of the particular princesses who associated with Deborah, Solomon, and the nation of Persia (Jgs 5:29; 1Ki 11:3; Est 1:18). It is also used in a general sense to describe princesses who were humbled to become nurses and servants (Isa 49:23; La 1:1).

8283. שָׂרָה, **Śârâh,** *saw-raw´;* the same as 8282; *Sarah*, Abraham's wife:—Sarah.

8284. שָׂרָה, **shârâh,** *shaw-raw´;* probably feminine of 7791; a *fortification* (literal or figurative):—sing [*by mistake for* 7891], wall.

8285. שֵׂרָה, **shêrâh,** *shay-raw´;* from 8324 in its original sense of *pressing;* a wrist-*band* (as *compact* or *clasping*):—bracelet.

8286. שְׂרוּג, **Śᵉrûwg,** *ser-oog´;* from 8276; *tendril; Serug*, a postdiluvian patriarch:—Serug.

8287. שָׂרוּחֶן, **Shârûwchen,** *shaw-roo-khen´;* probably from 8281 (in the sense of *dwelling* [compare 8271] and 2580; *abode of pleasure; Sharuchen*, a place in Palestine:—Sharuhen.

8288. שְׂרוֹךְ, **śᵉrôwk,** *ser-oke´;* from 8308; a *thong* (as *laced* or *tied*):—([shoe-]) latchet.

8289. שָׂרוֹן, **Shârôwn,** *shaw-rone´;* probably abridged from 3474; *plain; Sharon*, the name of a place in Palestine:—Lasharon, Sharon.

8290. שָׂרוֹנִי, **Shârôwnîy,** *shaw-ro-nee´;* patrial from 8289; a *Sharonite* or inhabitant of Sharon:—Sharonite.

8291. שָׂרֻק, **śârôq,** *sar-ook´;* passive participle from the same as 8321; a *grapevine:*—principal plant. See 8320, 8321.

8292. שְׂרוּקָה, **shᵉrûwqâh,** *sher-oo-kaw´;* or (by permutation) שְׂרִיקָה, **shᵉrîyqâh,** *sher-ee-kaw´;* feminine passive participle of 8319; a *whistling* (in scorn); (by analogy) a *piping:*—bleating, hissing.

8293. שֵׂרוּת, **shêrûwth,** *shay-rooth´;* from 8281 abbreviated; *freedom:*—remnant.

A feminine noun meaning a beginning. This word is another form of the word *shârâh* (8281). In Jer 15:11, this word refers to God setting Jeremiah free.

8294. שֶׂרַח, **śerach,** *seh´-rakh;* (by permutation) for 5629; *superfluity; Serach,* an Israelitess:— Sarah, Serah.

8295. שָׂרַט, **śâraṭ,** *saw-rat´;* a primitive root; to *gash:*—cut in pieces, make [cuttings] pieces.

8296. שֶׂרֶט, **śereṭ,** *seh´-ret;* and שָׂרֶטֶת, **śâreṭeth,** *saw-reh´-teth;* from 8295; an *incision:*—cutting.

8297. שָׂרַי, **Śâray,** *saw-rah´ee;* from 8269; *dominative; Sarai,* the wife of Abraham:—Sarai.

8298. שָׂרַי, **Shâray,** *shaw-rah´ee;* probably from 8324; *hostile; Sharay,* an Israelite:—Sharai.

8299. שָׂרִיג, **śârîyg,** *saw-reeg´;* from 8276; a *tendril* (as *intwining*):—branch.

8300. שָׂרִיד, **śârîyd,** *saw-reed´;* from 8277; a *survivor:*—× alive, left, remain (-ing), remnant, rest.

A masculine noun meaning a survivor. This word comes from the verb *śârad* (8277), meaning an escape. In one instance of this word, it is used to describe physical things that had not been devoured (Job 20:21). In all other instances, it is used to describe people who had survived the onslaught of an enemy (Nu 24:19; Jos 10:20; Jer 31:2). It is often used with the negative to describe total desolation, i.e. there were no survivors (Nu 21:35; Jos 10:28; Jer 42:17).

8301. שָׂרִיד, **Śârîyd,** *saw-reed´;* the same as 8300; *Sarid,* a place in Palestine:—Sarid.

8302. שִׁרְיוֹן, **shiryôwn,** *shir-yone´;* or שִׁרְיֹן, **shiryôn,** *shir-yone´;* and שִׁרְיָן, **shiryân,** *shir-yawn´;* also (feminine) שִׁרְיָה, **shiryâh,** *shir-yaw´;* and שִׁרְיֹנָה, **shir-yônâh,** *shir-yo-naw´;* from 8281 in the orig. sense of *turning;* a *corslet* (as if *twisted*):—breastplate, coat of mail, habergeon, harness. See 5630.

8303. שִׁרְיוֹן, **Shiryôwn,** *shir-yone´;* and שִׂרְיֹן, **Śiryôn,** *sir-yone´;* the same as 8304 (i.e. *sheeted* with snow); *Shirjon* or *Sirjon,* a peak of the Lebanon:—Sirion.

8304. שְׂרָיָה, **Śᵉrâyâh,** *ser-aw-yaw´;* or שְׂרָיָהוּ, **Śᵉrâ-yâhûw,** *ser-aw-yaw´-hoo;* from 8280 and 3050; *Jah has prevailed;* the name of nine Israelites:—Seraiah.

8305. שְׂרִיק, **śârîyq,** *saw-reek´;* from the same as 8321 in the original sense of *piercing; hetchelling*

(or combing flax), i.e. (concrete) *tow;* (by extension) *linen* cloth:—fine.

8306. שָׂרִיר, **shârîyr,** *shaw-reer´;* from 8324 in the original sense as in 8270 (compare 8326); a *cord,* i.e. (by analogy) *sinew:*—navel.

8307. שְׂרִירוּת, **shᵉrîyrûwth,** *sher-ee-rooth´;* from 8324 in the sense of *twisted,* i.e. *firm; obstinacy:*—imagination, lust.

A feminine noun meaning hardness, stubbornness. This word has the basic idea of firmness or hardness, but in its ten usages in the OT, it is always used in conjunction with the word *lêb* (3820), meaning heart, to describe disobedient Israel. Thus, it is best to translate this word stubbornness. It is used to describe those who did evil (Jer 16:12); who walked after their own plans (Jer 18:12); who refused to listen to God's words (Jer 13:10); who did not obey God's counsel (Jer 7:24; 9:14[13]; 11:8); and who were deluded to think they were at peace (Dt 29:19[18]; Jer 23:17). God gave such people over to their own devices (Ps 81:12[13]).

8308. שָׂרַךְ, **śârak,** *saw-rak´;* a primitive root; to *interlace:*—traverse.

8309. שְׂרֵמָה, **shᵉrêmâh,** *sher-ay-maw´;* probably by orthographic error for 7709; a *common:*— field.

8310. שַׂרְסְכִים, **Śarsᵉkîym,** *sar-seh-keem´;* of foreign derivation; *Sarsekim,* a Babylonian general:—Sarsechim.

8311. שָׂרַע, **śâra‘,** *saw-rah´;* a primitive root; to *prolong,* i.e. (reflexive) *be deformed* by excess of members:—stretch out self, (have any) superfluous thing.

8312. שַׂרְעַפִּים, **śar‘appîym,** *sar-ap-peem´;* for 5587; *cogitation:*—thought.

A masculine noun meaning a disquieting thought, an anxious feeling. The psalmist rejoiced that the Lord calmed his inner anxieties (Ps 94:19). This is the same word used by the psalmist when he asked God to search him and know his anxieties (Ps 139:23).

8313. שָׂרַף, **śâraph,** *saw-raf´;* a primitive root; to *be* (causative, *set*) *on fire:*—(cause to, make a) burn ([-ing], up), kindle, × utterly.

A verb meaning to burn. Most often, this word is used to mean to burn with intent, to destroy, or to consume. It is normally used to refer to sacrifices. Many sacrificial laws prescribed specific ways for offerings to be burnt (Ex 29:14). Burning could also be a form of punishment, as in the story of Achan (Jos 7:25). Buildings and cities were other common objects of burning: Men of Ephraim threatened to burn down Jephthah's house with fire (Jgs 12:1). Less frequently, this word refers to the process of firing bricks (Ge 11:3).

8314. שָׂרָף, **śârâph,** *saw-rawf´*; from 8313; *burning,* i.e. (figurative) *poisonous* (serpent); (specifically) a *saraph* or symbolic creature (from their copper colour):—fiery (serpent), seraph.

A masculine noun meaning a serpent. This word generally refers to a poisonous snake, deriving its origin from the burning sensation of the serpent's bite (see Dt 8:15). It is used specifically of the fiery serpents that were sent as judgment. The likeness of a serpent was made of brass at the Lord's command (Nu 21:8). The word is used twice by Isaiah to apparently denote a dragon (Isa 14:29; 30:6).

8315. שָׂרָף, **Śârâph,** *saw-rawf´*; the same as 8314; *Saraph,* an Israelite:—Saraph.

8316. שְׂרֵפָה, **śᵉrêphâh,** *ser-ay-faw´*; from 8313; *cremation:*—burning.

A feminine noun meaning burning, thoroughly burnt. The connotation of this word is that of being thoroughly consumed with fire. It is used to refer to kiln-firing brick (Ge 11:3); a destructive flame (Am 4:11); an inactive volcano (Jer 51:25); divine judgment (Le 10:6); and the burning of the red heifer (Nu 19:6). This word vividly portrays the state of the Temple during the Babylonian captivity (Isa 64:11[10]).

8317. שָׁרַץ, **shârats,** *shaw-rats´*; a primitive root; to *wriggle,* i.e. (by implication) *swarm* or *abound:*—breed (bring forth, increase) abundantly (in abundance), creep, move.

8318. שֶׁרֶץ, **sherets,** *sheh´-rets*; from 8317; a *swarm,* i.e. active mass of minute animals:—creep (-ing thing), move (-ing creature).

8319. שָׁרַק, **shâraq,** *shaw-rak´*; a primitive root; (properly) to *be shrill,* i.e. to whistle or *hiss* (as a call or in scorn):—hiss.

8320. שָׂרֹק, **śârôq,** *saw-rok´*; from 8319; *bright red* (as *piercing* to the sight), i.e. *bay:*—speckled. See 8291.

8321. שֹׂרֵק, **śôrêq,** *so-rake´*; or שׂוֹרֵק, **śôwrêq,** *so-rake´*; and (feminine) שֹׂרֵקָה, **śôrêqâh,** *so-ray-kaw´*; from 8319 in the sense of *redness* (compare 8320); a *vine* stock (properly, one yielding *purple* grapes, the richest variety):—choice (-st, noble) wine. Compare 8291.

8322. שְׁרֵקָה, **shᵉrêqâh,** *sher-ay-kaw´*; from 8319; a *derision:*—hissing.

8323. שָׂרַר, **śârar,** *saw-rar´*; a primitive root; to *have* (transitive, *exercise;* reflexive, *get*) *dominion:*— × altogether, make self a prince, (bear) rule.

A verb meaning to reign as a prince, to be a prince, to rule. This Hebrew word means literally to rule or to govern as a prince, as is evident in Isa 32:1. This word also may imply an unwelcome exercise of authority over another, as the protest against Moses in Nu 16:13 suggests.

8324. שָׁרַר, **shârar,** *shaw-rar´*; a primitive root; to *be hostile* (only active participle, an *opponent*):—enemy.

8325. שָׁרָר, **Shârâr,** *shaw-rawr´*; from 8324; *hostile; Sharar,* an Israelite:—Sharar.

8326. שֹׁרֶר, **shôrer,** *sho´-rer*; from 8324 in the sense of *twisting* (compare 8270); the umbilical *cord,* i.e. (by extension) a *bodice:*—navel.

8327. שָׁרַשׁ, **shârash,** *shaw-rash´*; a primitive root; to *root,* i.e. strike into the soil, or (by implication) to pluck from it:—(take, cause to take) root (out).

8328. שֶׁרֶשׁ, **sheresh,** *sheh´-resh*; from 8327; a *root* (literal or figurative):—bottom, deep, heel, root.

8329. שֶׁרֶשׁ, **Sheresh,** *sheh´-resh*; the same as 8328; *Sheresh,* an Israelite:—Sharesh.

8330. שֹׁרֶשׁ, **shôresh,** *sho´-resh*; (Chaldee); corresponding to 8328:—root.

8331. שְׁרָשָׁה, **sharshâh,** *shar-shaw´*; from 8327; a *chain* (as *rooted,* i.e. *linked*):—chain. Compare 8333.

8332. שְׁרֹשׁוּ, **sherôshûw,** *sher-o-shoo´*; (Chaldee); from a root corresponding to 8327; *eradication,* i.e. (figurative) *exile*:—banishment.

8333. שְׁרָשְׁרָה, **sharsherâh,** *shar-sher-aw´*; from 8327 [compare 8331]; a *chain*; (architecture) probably a *garland*:—chain.

8334. שָׁרַת, **shârath,** *shaw-rath´*; a primitive root; to *attend* as a menial or worshipper; (figurative) to *contribute* to:—minister (unto), (do) serve (-ant, -ice, -itor), wait on.

A verb meaning to minister, to serve. This Hebrew word was utilized in a generic sense to describe various activities, including that of a domestic servant serving a ranking official (Ge 39:4; 2Sa 13:17, 18); a chief assistant to an authority figure, such as Joshua was to Moses (Ex 24:13); the angelic host to God (Ps 103:21); and assistants to kings (Isa 60:10). More particularly, the word is used in the context of religious service before the Lord, such as that required of the priests (Ex 28:35; 1Ki 8:11); or Levites (Nu 3:6).

8335. שָׁרֵת, **shârêth,** *shaw-rayth´*; infinitive of 8334; *service* (in the Temple):—minister (-ry).

A masculine noun meaning religious ministry, service. Service in the place of worship underlies the primary meaning of this word. It is used twice in reference to the instruments used by those ministering in the tabernacle (Nu 4:12); and the vessels used for ritual in the Temple (2Ch 24:14). The stress was upon the connection to the functions of the priestly office.

8336. שֵׁשׁ, **shêsh,** *shaysh*; or (for alliteration with 4897) שְׁשִׁי, **sheshîy,** *shesh-ee´*; for 7893; *bleached stuff,* i.e. *white* linen or (by analogy) *marble*:— × blue, fine ([twined]) linen, marble, silk.

8337. שֵׁשׁ, **shêsh,** *shaysh*; masculine שִׁשָּׁה, **shishshâh,** *shish-shaw´*; a primitive number; *six* (as an overplus [see 7797] beyond five or the fingers of the hand); as ordinal *sixth*:—six ([-teen, -teenth]), sixth.

8338. שָׁשָׁא, **shâshâ’,** *shaw-shaw´*; a primitive root; apparently to *annihilate*:—leave but the sixth part [*by confusion with* 8341].

8339. שֵׁשְׁבַּצַּר, **Shêshbatstsar,** *shaysh-bats-tsar´*; of foreign derivation; *Sheshbatstsar,* Zerubbabel's Persian name:—Sheshbazzar.

8340. שֵׁשְׁבַּצַּר, **Shêshbatstsar,** *shaysh-bats-tsar´*; (Chaldee); corresponding to 8339:—Sheshbazzar.

8341. שָׁשָׁה, **shâshâh,** *shaw-shaw´*; a denominative from 8337; to *sixth* or divide into sixths:—give the sixth part.

8342. שָׂשׂוֹן, **sâsôwn,** *saw-sone´*; or שָׂשֹׂן, **sâsôn,** *saw-sone´*; from 7797; *cheerfulness*; (specifically) *welcome*:—gladness, joy, mirth, rejoicing.

8343. שָׁשַׁי, **Shâshay,** *shaw-shah´ee*; perhaps from 8336; *whitish*; *Shashai,* an Israelite:—Shashai.

8344. שֵׁשַׁי, **Shêshay,** *shay-shah´ee*; probably for 8343; *Sheshai,* a Canaanite:—Sheshai.

8345. שִׁשִּׁי, **shishshîy,** *shish-shee´*; from 8337; *sixth,* ordinal or (feminine) fractional:—sixth (part).

8346. שִׁשִּׁים, **shishshîym,** *shish-sheem´*; multiple of 8337; *sixty*:—sixty, three score.

8347. שֵׁשַׁךְ, **Shêshak,** *shay-shak´*; of foreign derivation; *Sheshak,* a symbolic name of Babylon:—Sheshach.

8348. שֵׁשָׁן, **Shêshân,** *shay-shawn´*; perhaps for 7799; *lily*; *Sheshan,* an Israelite:—Sheshan.

8349. שָׁשָׁק, **Shâshâq,** *shaw-shawk´*; probably from the base of 7785; *pedestrian*; *Shashak,* an Israelite:—Shashak.

8350. שָׁשָׁר, **shâshar,** *shaw-shar´*; perhaps from the base of 8324 in the sense of that of 8320; *red ochre* (from its *piercing* colour):—vermillion.

8351. שֵׁת, **shêth,** *shayth*; (Nu 24:17), from 7582; *tumult*:—Sheth.

8352. שֵׁת, **Shêth,** *shayth*; from 7896; *put,* i.e. *substituted*; *Sheth,* third son of Adam:—Seth, Sheth.

8353. שֵׁת, **shêth,** *shayth*; (Chaldee); or שִׁת, **shith,** *sheeth*; (Chaldee); corresponding to 8337:—six (-th).

8354. שָׁתָה, **shâthâh,** *shaw-thaw´*; a primitive root; to *imbibe* (literal or figurative):— × assuredly, banquet, × certainly, drink (-er, -ing), drunk (× -ard), surely. [Properly intensive of 8248.]

8355. שְׁתָה, she**thâh,** *sheth-aw´*; (Chaldee); corresponding to 8354:—drink.

8356. שָׁתָה, **shâthâh,** *shaw-thaw´*; from 7896; a *basis,* i.e. (figurative) political or moral *support:*—foundation, purpose.

8357. שֵׁתָה, **shêthâh,** *shay-thaw´*; from 7896; the *seat* (of the person):—buttock.

8358. שְׁתִי, she**thîy,** *sheth-ee´*; from 8354; *intoxication:*—drunkenness.

8359. שְׁתִי, she**thîy,** *sheth-ee´*; from 7896; a *fixture,* i.e. the *warp* in weaving:—warp.

8360. שְׁתִיָּה, she**thîyyâh,** *sheth-ee-yaw´*; feminine of 8358; *potation:*—drinking.

8361. שִׁתִּין, **shittîyn,** *shit-teen´*; (Chaldee); corresponding to 8346 [compare 8353]; *sixty:*—threescore.

8362. שָׁתַל, **shâthal,** *shaw-thal´*; a primitive root; to *transplant:*—plant.

8363. שְׁתִיל, she**thîyl,** *sheth-eel´*; from 8362; a *sprig* (as if *transplanted*), i.e. *sucker:*—plant.

8364. שֻׁתַלְחִי, **Shuthalchîy,** *shoo-thal-khee´*; patronymic from 7803; a *Shuthalchite* (collective) or descendants of Shuthelach:—Shuthalhites.

8365. שָׁתַם, **shâtham,** *shaw-tham´*; a primitive root; to *unveil* (figurative):—be open.

8366. שָׁתַן, **shâthan,** *shaw-than´*; a primitive root; (causative) to *make water,* i.e. *urinate:*—piss.

8367. שָׁתַק, **shâthaq,** *shaw-thak´*; a primitive root; to *subside:*—be calm, cease, be quiet.

8368. שָׂתַר, **sâthar,** *saw-thar´*; a primitive root; to *break* out (as an eruption):—have in [one's] secret parts.

8369. שֵׁתָר, **Shêthâr,** *shay-thawr´*; of foreign derivation; *Shethar,* a Persian satrap:—Shethar.

8370. שְׁתַר בּוֹזְנַי, **She**thar Bôwze**nay,** *sheth-ar´ bo-zen-ah´ee*; of foreign derivation; *Shethar-Bozenai,* a Persian officer:—Shethar-boznai.

8371. שָׁתַת, **shâthath,** *shaw-thath´*; a primitive root; to *place,* i.e. *array;* (reflexive) to *lie:*—be laid, set.

8372. תָא, **tâ',** *taw*; and (feminine) תָאָה, **tâ'âh,** *taw-aw'*; (Eze 40:12), from (the base of) 8376; a *room* (as *circumscribed*):—(little) chamber.

8373. תָאַב, **tâ'ab,** *taw-ab'*; a primitive root; to *desire*:—long.

8374. תָאַב, **tâ'ab,** *taw-ab'*; a primitive root [probably rather identical with 8373 through the idea of *puffing* disdainfully at; compare 340]; to *loathe* (moral):—abhor.

A verb meaning to loathe, to abhor. This unquestionably strong term of detest is used only in Am 6:8. The Lord employed it to convey His utter contempt for the pride of the people of Jacob.

8375. תַאֲבָה, **ta'ăbâh,** *tah-ab-aw'*; from 8374 [compare 15]; *desire*:—longing.

8376. תָאָה, **tâ'âh,** *taw-aw'*; a primitive root; to *mark* off, i.e. (intensive) *designate*:—point out.

8377. תְאוֹ, **t°'ôw,** *teh-o'*; and תּוֹא, **tôw',** *toh*; (the original form), from 8376; a species of *antelope* (probably from the white *stripe* on the cheek):—wild bull (ox).

8378. תַאֲוָה, **ta'ăvâh,** *tah-av-aw'*; from 183 (abbreviated); a *longing*; (by implication) a *delight* (subjective, *satisfaction*; objective, a *charm*):—dainty, desire, × exceedingly, × greedily, lust (-ing), pleasant. See also 6914.

8379. תַאֲוָה, **ta'ăvâh,** *tah-av-aw'*; from 8376; a *limit*, i.e. full extent:—utmost bound.

8380. תְאוֹמִים, **tâ'ôwm,** *taw-ome'*; or תָאֹם, **tâ'ôm,** *taw-ome'*; from 8382; a *twin* (in plural only), literal or figurative:—twins.

8381. תַאֲלָה, **ta'ălâh,** *tah-al-aw'*; from 422; an *imprecation*:—curse.

8382. תָאַם, **tâ'am,** *taw-am'*; a primitive root; to *be complete*; but used only as denominative from 8380, to *be* (causative, *make*) twinned, i.e.

(figurative) *duplicate* or (architecture) *jointed*:—coupled (together), bear twins.

A verb meaning to be double, to couple, to be joined. The primary thrust of this word is that of joining in a matched pair. It is used only in two contexts: to describe the action of linking two corners of a curtain together (Ex 26:24; 36:29); and poetically, to describe the birthing of twins (SS 4:2; 6:6).

8383. תְאֻן, **t°'un,** *teh-oon'*; from 205; *naughtiness*, i.e. *toil*:—lie.

8384. תְאֵן, **t°'ên,** *teh-ane'*; or (in the singular, feminine) תְאֵנָה, **t°'ênâh,** *teh-ay-naw'*; perhaps of foreign derivation; the *fig* (tree or fruit):—fig (tree).

8385. תַאֲנָה, **ta'ănâh,** *tah-an-aw'*; or תֹאֲנָה, **tô'ănâh,** *to-an-aw'*; from 579; an *opportunity* or (subjective) *purpose*:—occasion.

8386. תַאֲנִיָּה, **ta'ănîyyâh,** *tah-an-ee-yaw'*; from 578; *lamentation*:—heaviness, mourning.

8387. תַאֲנַת שִׁלֹה, **Ta'ănath Shilôh,** *tah-an-ath' shee-lo'*; from 8385 and 7887; *approach of Shiloh*; Taanath-Shiloh, a place in Palestine:—Taanath-shiloh.

8388. תָאַר, **tâ'ar,** *taw-ar'*; a primitive root; to *delineate*; (reflexive) to *extend*:—be drawn, mark out, [Rimmon-] methoar [*by union with* 7417].

8389. תֹאַר, **tô'ar,** *to'-ar*; from 8388; *outline*, i.e. *figure* or *appearance*:— + beautiful, × comely, countenance, + fair, × favoured, form, × goodly, × resemble, visage.

8390. תַאְרֵעַ, **Ta'ărêa‘,** *tah-ar-ay'-ah*; perhaps from 772; *Taareä*, an Israelite:—Tarea. See 8475.

8391. תְאַשּׁוּר, **t°'ashshûwr,** *teh-ash-shoor'*; from 833; a species of *cedar* (from its *erectness*):—box (tree).

505

8392. תֵּבָה, **têbâh,** *tay-baw´*; perhaps of foreign derivation; a *box*:—ark.

8393. תְּבוּאָה, **tᵉbûw'âh,** *teb-oo-aw´*; from 935; *income*, i.e. *produce* (literal or figurative):—fruit, gain, increase, revenue.

8394. תָּבוּן, **tâbûwn,** *taw-boon´*; and (feminine) תְּבוּנָה, **tebûw-nâh,** *teb-oo-naw´*; or תּוֹבֻנָה, **tôw-bunâh,** *to-boo-naw´*; from 995; *intelligence*; (by implication) an *argument*; (by extension) *caprice*:—discretion, reason, skilfulness, understanding, wisdom.

A feminine noun meaning understanding, insight. It occurs primarily in the Wisdom Literature and is associated with both wisdom and knowledge (Ex 35:31; Pr 8:1; 21:30); and is contrasted with foolishness (Pr 15:21; 18:2). A person of understanding is slow to wrath and walks uprightly (Pr 14:29; 15:21). God has understanding and gives it (Job 12:13; Ps 147:5; Pr 2:6; Isa 40:28). On the other hand, idolaters, who fashion idols by their own understanding, have no understanding at all (Isa 44:19; Hos 13:2).

8395. תְּבוּסָה, **tᵉbûwsâh,** *teb-oo-saw´*; from 947; a *treading down*, i.e. *ruin*:—destruction.

A feminine noun meaning ruin, downfall. The word is used in 2 Chronicles to depict God's judgment on Ahaziah and more generally the house of Ahab (2Ch 22:7). Jehu, God's chosen instrument, killed Ahaziah and Joram, the princes of Judah, in addition to the sons of Ahaziah's relatives.

8396. תָּבוֹר, **Tâbôwr,** *taw-bore´*; from a root corresponding to 8406; *broken region*; *Tabor*, a mountain in Palestine, also a city adjacent:—Tabor.

8397. תֵּבֵל, **tebel,** *teh´-bel*; apparently from 1101; *mixture*, i.e. *unnatural* bestiality:—confusion.

8398. תֵּבֵל, **têbêl,** *tay-bale´*; from 2986; the *earth* (as *moist* and therefore inhabited); (by extension) the *globe*; (by implication) its *inhabitants*; (specifically) a particular *land*, as Babylonia, Palestine:—habitable part, world.

A feminine noun meaning world, earth. The word is used in a description of the clouds responding to the command of God, i.e. they swirled over the face of the whole earth (Job 37:12). In Proverbs, the created world was a reason for rejoicing (Pr 8:31). This word is also used to indicate the foundations of the earth, as in 2 Samuel where the foundations of the earth were laid bare at the rebuke of the Lord (2Sa 22:16). *Têbêl* is also used to denote what was firmly established, i.e. the world (Ps 93:1; 96:10); something that would be punished for its evil (Isa 13:11); and what will be filled by Israel upon their blossoming (Isa 27:6). In Nahum, the world and all who live in it will tremble at the presence of the Lord (Na 1:5).

8399. תַּבְלִית, **tablîyth,** *tab-leeth´*; from 1086; *consumption*:—destruction.

A feminine noun meaning destruction. In Isaiah, the word is used to denote the end result of the direction of the wrath of the Lord, i.e. the destruction of the Assyrians (Isa 10:25). Even though disobedient, Israel was still loved and protected by the Lord, who maintained a remnant.

8400. תְּבַלֻּל, **tᵉballul,** *teb-al-lool´*; from 1101 in the original sense of *flowing*; a *cataract* (in the eye):—blemish.

A masculine noun meaning confusion, obscurity. This word comes from the verb *bâlal* (1101), meaning to mix or to confuse, and is used only once in the OT. In Le 21:20, it is used to describe an obscurity or some sort of defect in the eye that would prohibit a man from being a priest.

8401. תֶּבֶן, **teben,** *teh´-ben*; probably from 1129; (properly) *material*, i.e. (specific) refuse *haum* or stalks of grain (as *chopped* in threshing and used for fodder):—chaff, straw, stubble.

8402. תִּבְנִי, **Tibnîy,** *tib-nee´*; from 8401; *strawy*; *Tibni*, an Israelite:—Tibni.

8403. תַּבְנִית, **tabnîyth,** *tab-neeth´*; from 1129; *structure*; (by implication) a *model, resemblance*:—figure, form, likeness, pattern, similitude.

A feminine noun meaning a plan, a pattern, a form. This noun comes from the verb *bânâh* (1129), meaning to build, and refers to the plans of a building or an object, such as the pattern of the tabernacle and its contents (Ex 25:9, 40); an altar (Jos 22:28; 2Ki 16:10); and the Temple and its contents (1Ch 28:11, 12, 18, 19). However, in other contexts, it refers to an image that was patterned after something else, such as a graven image of a god (Dt 4:16–18); the calf at Horeb (Ps 106:20); pillars (Ps 144:12); or a person (Isa 44:13). In a few contexts, it refers to something in the form of an animal (Eze 8:10); or a hand (Eze 8:3; 10:8). Synonyms for this word are *temûnâh* (8544), meaning likeness or form, and *demût* (1823), meaning likeness.

8404. תַּבְעֵרָה, **Tab'êrâh**, *tab-ay-raw´*; from 1197; *burning*; *Taberah*, a place in the Desert:— Taberah.

8405. תֵּבֵץ, **Têbêts**, *tay-bates´*; from the same as 948; *whiteness*; *Tebets*, a place in Palestine:— Thebez.

8406. תְּבַר, **t**ᵉ**bar**, *teb-ar´*; (Chaldee); corresponding to 7665; to *be fragile* (figurative):—broken.

8407. תִּגְלַת פִּלְאֶסֶר, **Tiglath Pil'eser**, *tig-lath´ pil-eh´-ser*; or תִּגְלַת פְּלֶסֶר **Tiglath P**ᵉ**leser**, *tig-lath pel-eh-ser*; or תִּלְגַת פִּלְנְאֶסֶר **Tilgath Pil-n**ᵉ**'eser**, *til-gath´ pil-neh-eh´-ser*; תִּלְגַת פִּלְנֶסֶר **Tilgath Pilneser**, *til-gath´ pil-neh´-ser*; of foreign derivation; *Tiglath-Pileser* or *Tilgath-pilneser*, an Assyrian king:—Tiglath-pileser, Tilgath-pilneser.

8408. תַּגְמוּל, **tagmûwl**, *tag-mool´*; from 1580; a *bestowment*:—benefit.

8409. תִּגְרָה, **tigrâh**, *tig-raw´*; from 1624; *strife*, i.e. *infliction*:—blow.

8410. תִּדְהָר, **tidhâr**, *tid-hawr´*; apparently from 1725; *enduring*; a species of hardwood or *lasting* tree (perhaps *oak*):—pine (tree).

8411. תְּדִירָא, **t**ᵉ**dîyrâ'**, *ted-ee-raw´*; (Chaldee); from 1753 in the original sense of *enduring*; *permanence*, i.e. (adverb) *constantly*:—continually.

8412. תַּדְמֹר, **Tadmôr**, *tad-more´*; or תַּמֹּר, **Tammôr**, *tam-more´*; (1Ki 9:18), apparently from 8558; *palm*-city; *Tadmor*, a place near Palestine:—Tadmor.

8413. תִּדְעָל, **Tid'âl**, *tid-awl´*; perhaps from 1763; *fearfulness*; *Tidal*, a Canaanite:—Tidal.

8414. תֹּהוּ, **tôhûw**, *to´-hoo*; from an unused root meaning to lie *waste*; a *desolation* (of surface), i.e. *desert*; (figurative) a *worthless* thing; (adverbial) in *vain*:—confusion, empty place, without

form, nothing, (thing of) nought, vain, vanity, waste, wilderness.

A masculine noun meaning formlessness, confusion. The exact meaning of this term is difficult at best since its study is limited to its relatively few OT occurrences. It is used to describe primeval earth before the seven creative days (Ge 1:2); a land reduced to primeval chaos and formlessness (Isa 34:11; 45:18; Jer 4:23); a destroyed city (Isa 24:10); nothingness or empty space (Job 26:7); a barren wasteland (Dt 32:10; Job 6:18; 12:24; Ps 107:40); that which is vain and futile (1Sa 12:21; Isa 45:19; 49:4); like idolatry (Isa 41:29; 44:9); unfounded allegations (Isa 29:21; 59:4); the nations compared to God (Isa 40:17); or human rulers (Isa 40:23). Although it is impossible to grasp the full import of this word, it is obvious that it has a negative and disparaging tone. It represents chaos, confusion, and disorder, all things that are opposed to the organization, direction, and order that God has demonstrated.

8415. תְּהוֹם, **t**ᵉ**hôwm**, *teh-home´*; or תְּהֹם, **t**ᵉ**hôm**, *teh-home´*; (usually feminine) from 1949; an *abyss* (as a *surging* mass of water), especially the *deep* (the *main* sea or the subterranean *water-supply*):—deep (place), depth.

8416. תְּהִלָּה, **t**ᵉ**hillâh**, *teh-hil-law´*; from 1984; *laudation*; specifically (concrete) a *hymn*:— praise.

A feminine noun meaning praise, a song of praise. This word is a noun derived from the verb *hâlal* (1984), which connotes genuine appreciation for the great actions or the character of its object. It is used especially of the adoration and thanksgiving that humanity renders to God (Ps 34:1[2]). By extension, it also represents the character of God that deserves praise (Ps 111:10); and the specific divine acts that elicit human veneration (Ex 15:11). It can also refer to the condition of fame and renown that comes with receiving this sort of praise and, as such, was applied to God (Dt 10:21; Hab 3:3); Israel (Dt 26:19; Jer 13:11); Jerusalem (Isa 62:7; Zep 3:19, 20); Damascus (Jer 49:25); Moab (Jer 48:2); Babylon (Jer 51:41). In late Hebrew, this term became a technical term for a psalm of praise. In this capacity, it is used in the title of Ps 145 to designate it as David's Psalm of Praise. It has also become the Hebrew title for the entire book of Psalms.

8417. תְּהִלָּה, **tohŏlâh,** *to-hol-aw´*; feminine of an unused noun (apparently from 1984) meaning *bluster; braggadocio,* i.e. (by implication) *fatuity:*—folly.

8418. תַּהֲלֻכָה, **tahălukâh,** *tah-hal-oo-kaw´*; from 1980; a *procession:*— × went.

8419. תַּהְפֻּכָה, **tahpukâh,** *tah-poo-kaw´*; from 2015; a *perversity* or *fraud:*—(very) froward (-ness, thing), perverse thing.

8420. תָּו, **tâv,** *tawv*; from 8427; a *mark*; (by implication) a *signature:*—desire, mark.

8421. תּוּב, **tûwb,** *toob*; (Chaldee); corresponding to 7725; to *come back*; specifically (transitive and ellipsis) to *reply:*—answer, restore, return (an answer).

8422. תּוּבַל, **Tûwbal,** *too-bal´*; or תֻּבַל, **Tubal,** *too-bal´*; probably of foreign derivation; *Tubal,* a postdiluvian patriarch and his posterity:—Tubal.

8423. תּוּבַל קַיִן, **Tûwbal Qayin,** *too-bal´ kah´-yin*; apparently from 2986 (compare 2981) and 7014; *offspring of Cain*; *Tubal-Kajin,* an antediluvian patriarch:—Tubal-cain.

8424. תּוּגָה, **tûwgâh,** *too-gaw´*; from 3013; *depression* (of spirits); (concrete) a *grief:*—heaviness, sorrow.

8425. תּוֹגַרְמָה, **Tôwgarmâh,** *to-gar-maw´*; or תֹּגַרְמָה, **Tôgarmâh,** *to-gar-maw´*; probably of foreign derivation; *Togarmah,* a son of Gomer and his posterity:—Togarmah.

8426. תּוֹדָה, **tôwdâh,** *to-daw´*; from 3034; (properly) an *extension* of the hand, i.e. (by implication) *avowal,* or (usually) *adoration*; specifically a *choir* of worshippers:—confession, (sacrifice of) praise, thanks (-giving, offering).

A feminine noun meaning praise, thanksgiving. The word describes an offering of thanks or a sacrifice of thanksgiving, It is a subcategory of the fellowship offering or the offering of well-being; the fellowship offering could be presented as a thank offering (Le 7:12, 13, 15; 22:29; 2Ch 29:31; Am 4:5). The word depicts worship by the presentation of songs of thanksgiving and praise that extolled the mighty wonders of the Lord (Ne 12:27; Ps 26:7; Isa 51:3). It refers to shouts of jubilation and thanksgiving (Ps 42:4[5]; Jnh 2:9[10]). It describes the purpose of the choirs

used by Nehemiah, i.e. they were choirs of praise (Ne 12:31, 38). The goodness and praise of God were to be on the lips of even an enemy of the Lord, such as Achan, in the sense of proclaiming the glory of God while confessing and abandoning sin (Jos 7:19).

8427. תָּוָה, **tâvâh,** *taw-vaw´*; a primitive root; to *mark* out, i.e. (primitive) *scratch* or (defensive) *imprint:*—scrabble, set [a mark].

8428. תָּוָה, **tâvâh,** *taw-vaw´*; a primitive root [or perhaps identical with 8427 through a similar idea from *scraping* to pieces]; to *grieve:*—limit [*by confusion with* 8427].

8429. תְּוַה, **tᵉvah,** *tev-ah´*; (Chaldee); corresponding to 8539 or perhaps to 7582 through the idea of *sweeping* to ruin [compare 8428]; to *amaze,* i.e. (reflexive by implication) *take alarm:*—be astonied.

8430. תּוֹחַ, **Tôwach,** *to´-akh*; from an unused root meaning to *depress*; *humble*; *Toäch,* an Israelite:—Toah.

8431. תּוֹחֶלֶת, **tôwcheleth,** *to-kheh´-leth*; from 3176; *expectation:*—hope.

A feminine noun meaning hope. This word is found most often in the Wisdom Literature of Proverbs. Hope is associated with the prosperity of the righteous (Pr 10:28; 11:7); and is seen as the spring from which the desire for life flows (Pr 13:12). Jeremiah lamented that his soul was destitute because his hope in the Lord had perished (La 3:18).

8432. תָּוֶךְ, **tâvek,** *taw´-vek*; from an unused root meaning to *sever*; a *bisection,* i.e. (by implication) the *centre:*—among (-st), × between, half, × (there-, where-) in (-to), middle, mid [-night], midst (among), × out (of), × through, × with (-in).

A substantive meaning in the midst, in the middle, at the heart. The word can have the implication of something being surrounded on all sides, as when God made a firmament in the midst of the waters (Ge 1:6). It can also refer to something in the middle of a line: Samson destroyed the Temple by pushing over two middle pillars that supported it (Jgs 16:29). In relation to people, it can mean dwelling among (1 Sam 10:10); or taken from among a group (Nu 3:12).

8433. תּוֹכֵחָה, **tôwkêchâh,** *to-kay-khaw´*; and תּוֹכַחַת, **tôwka-chath,** *to-kakh´-ath*; from 3198; *chastisement*; figurative (by words) *correction, refutation, proof* (even in defence):—argument, × chastened, correction, reasoning, rebuke, reproof, × be (often) reproved.

A feminine noun meaning a rebuke, a correction, a reproof, an argument. The primary thrust of this word is that of correcting some wrong. It is employed to express the concept of rebuking (Pr 15:10); judgment (Hos 5:9); reckoning (2Ki 19:3); or the argument of a claim (Job 13:6; Hab 2:1).

8434. תּוֹלָד, **Tôwlâd,** *to-lawd´*; from 3205; *posterity*; *Tolad*, a place in Palestine:—Tolad. Compare 513.

8435. תּוֹלְדוֹת, **tôwlêdôwth,** *to-lay-doth´*; from 3205; (plural only) *descent*, i.e. *family*; (figurative) *history*:—birth, generations.

A feminine noun meaning a generation. This key Hebrew word carries with it the notion of everything entailed in a person's life and that of his or her progeny (Ge 5:1; 6:9). In the plural, it is used to denote the chronological procession of history as humans shape it. It refers to the successive generations in one family (Ge 10:32); or a broader division by lineage (Nu 1:20ff.). In Ge 2:4, the word accounts for the history of the created world.

8436. תִּילוֹן, **Tîylôwn,** *tee-lone´*; from 8524; *suspension*; *Tulon*, an Israelite:—Tilon [*from the margin*].

8437. תּוֹלָל, **tôwlâl,** *to-lawl´*; from 3213; *causing to howl*, i.e. an *oppressor*:—that wasted.

8438. תּוֹלָע, **tôwlâ‘,** *to-law´*; and (feminine) תּוֹלֵעָה, **tôwlê‘âh,** *to-lay-aw´*; or תּוֹלַעַת, **tôwla‘ath,** *to-lah´-ath*; or תֹּלַעַת, **tôla‘ath,** *to-lah´-ath*; from 3216; a *maggot* (as *voracious*); specifically (often with ellipsis of 8144) the crimson-*grub*, but used only (in this connection) of the colour from it, and cloths dyed therewith:—crimson, scarlet, worm.

8439. תּוֹלָע, **Tôwlâ‘,** *to-law´*; the same as 8438; *worm*; *Tola*, the name of two Israelites:—Tola.

8440. תּוֹלָעִי, **Tôwlâ‘îy,** *to-law-ee´*; patronymic from 8439; a *Tolaïte* (collective) or descendants of Tola:—Tolaites.

8441. תּוֹעֵבַה, **tôw‘êbah,** *to-ay-baw´*; or תֹּעֵבַה, **tô‘ê-bah,** *to-ay-baw´*; feminine active participle of 8581; (properly) something *disgusting* (moral), i.e. (as noun) an *abhorrence*; especially *idolatry* or (concrete) an *idol*:—abominable (custom, thing), abomination.

A feminine noun meaning an abomination. This word is primarily understood in the context of the Law. It identifies unclean food (Dt 14:3); the activity of the idolater (Isa 41:24); the practice of child sacrifice (Dt 12:31); intermarriage by the Israelites (Mal 2:11); the religious activities of the wicked (Pr 21:27); and homosexual behaviour (Le 18:22). In a broader sense, the word is used to identify anything offensive (Pr 8:7).

8442. תּוֹעָה, **tôw‘âh,** *to-aw´*; feminine active participle of 8582; *mistake*, i.e. (moral) *impiety*, or (political) *injury*:—error, hinder.

8443. תּוֹעָפָה, **tôw‘âphâh,** *to-aw-faw´*; from 3286; (only in plural collective) *weariness*, i.e. (by implication) *toil* (*treasure* so obtained) or *speed*:—plenty, strength.

8444. תּוֹצָאָה, **tôwtsâ’âh,** *to-tsaw-aw´*; or תֹּצָאָה, **tôtsâ’âh,** *to-tsaw-aw´*; from 3318; (only in plural collective) *exit*, i.e. (geographical) *boundary*, or (figurative) *deliverance*, (active) *source*:—border (-s), going (-s) forth (out), issues, outgoings.

8445. תּוֹקַהַת, **Tôwqahath,** *to-kah´-ath*; from the same as 3349; *obedience*; *Tokahath*, an Israelite:—Tikvath [*by correction for 8616*].

8446. תּוּר, **tûwr,** *toor*; a primitive root; to *meander* (causative, *guide*) about, especially for trade or reconnoitring:—chap [-man], sent to descry, be excellent, merchant [-man], search (out), seek, (e-) spy (out).

8447. תּוֹר, **tôwr,** *tore*; or תֹּר, **tôr,** *tore*; from 8446; a *succession*, i.e. a *string* or (abstract) *order*:—border, row, turn.

8448. תּוֹר, **tôwr,** *tore*; probably the same as 8447; a *manner* (as a sort of *turn*):—estate.

8449. תּוֹר, **tôwr,** *tore*; or תֹּר, **tôr,** *tore*; probably the same as 8447; a *ring-dove*, often (figurative) as a term of endearment:—(turtle) dove.

8450. תּוֹר, **tôwr,** *tore*; (Chaldee); corresponding (by permutation) to 7794; a *bull*:—bullock, ox.

8451. תּוֹרָה, **tôwrâh,** *to-raw´*; or תֹּרָה, **tôrâh,** *to-raw´*; from 3384; a *precept* or *statute,* especially the *Decalogue* or *Pentateuch:*—law.

A feminine noun meaning instruction, direction, law, Torah, the whole Law. This noun comes from the verb *yârâh* (3384), which has, as one of its major meanings, to teach, to instruct. The noun means instruction in a general way from God; for example, Eliphaz uttered truth when he encouraged Job and his readers to be willing to receive instruction from God, the Almighty (Job 22:22). In Israel, a father and mother were sources of instruction for life (Pr 1:8; 6:20); along with wise persons (Pr 13:14; 28:4). In contrast, rebellious people were not willing to accept God's instructions in any manner (Isa 30:8, 9); the scribes handled the instructions of the Lord deceitfully and falsely (Jer 8:8). Various words are found in synonyms parallel with this term: It is paralleled by the sayings of the Holy One (Isa 5:24); the word of the Lord (Isa 1:10); and the testimony or witness (Isa 8:20). It is used regularly to depict priestly instructions in general or as a whole. The Lord rejected the priests of Israel for they had disregarded (lit., forgotten) the Law (Jer 2:8; Hos 4:6). They had been charged to carry out and teach all the instructions of the Lord (Dt 17:11).

The term takes on the meaning of law in certain settings, although it is still currently debated about how to translate the various words that describe the laws, ordinances, commands, decrees, and requirements of the Lord. This word *tôwrâh* is used as a summary term of various bodies of legal, cultic, or civil instructions. The word refers to the entire book of Deuteronomy and Moses' exposition of the Torah found in it (Dt 1:5). By implication, the word here also refers to the laws given in Exodus, Leviticus, and Numbers. Numerous times this word refers to the whole Law of Moses, the Book of the Law of Moses, the Book of the Law of God, the Law of the Lord, and the Law of God given at Sinai (in order of titles listed, 1Ki 2:3; Ne 8:1; Jos 24:26; Ps 1:2; Ne 10:28[29], 29[30]). The kings of Israel were held to the standard of the Law of Moses (1Ki 2:3; 2Ki 10:31; 14:6; 23:25). The word can also refer to a single law, for example, the law of the burnt offering (Le 6:9[2]; 7:7; Ne 12:44).

It is used of special laws for the Feast of Unleavened Bread (Ex 13:9); the Passover (Ex 12:49); of decisions by Moses (Ex 18:16, 20); for the content of the Book of the Covenant (Ex 24:12). The Law or Torah of God is pursued diligently by the psalmist; this word is found twenty-five times in Ps 119 in parallel with various near synonyms. The word means the usual way, custom, or manner of God as David addressed his surprise to the Lord about the way He had dealt with him (2Sa 7:19).

8452. תּוֹרָה, **tôwrâh,** *to-raw´*; probably feminine of 8448; a *custom:*—manner.

8453. תּוֹשָׁב, **tôwshâb,** *to-shawb´*; or תֹּשָׁב, **tôshâb,** *to-shawb´*; (1Ki 17:1), from 3427; a *dweller* (but not outlandish [5237]); especially (as distinguished from a native citizen [active participle of 3427] and a temporary inmate [1616] or mere lodger [3885]) resident *alien:*—foreigner, inhabitant, sojourner, stranger.

A masculine noun meaning a sojourner, a foreigner. This word implies temporary visitors who were dependent in some way on the nation in which they were residing. It denotes a sojourner who received shelter from a priest (Le 22:10); foreigners who were closely linked to the economy of the people (Le 25:40, 47); and a wanderer with close ties to the land occupied by another people (Ge 23:4). David proclaimed himself to be such a sojourner with the Lord (Ps 39:12[13]).

8454. תּוּשִׁיָּה, **tûwshîyyâh,** *too-shee-yaw´*; or תֻּשִׁיָּה, **tushîyyâh,** *too-shee-yaw´*; from an unused root probably meaning to *substantiate; support* or (by implication) *ability,* i.e. (direct) *help,* (in purpose) an *undertaking,* (intellectual) *understanding:*—enterprise, that which (thing as it) is, substance, (sound) wisdom, working.

A feminine noun meaning sound wisdom, continuing success. The primary meaning of this Hebrew word is wisdom or ability that brings continued advancement. Used in the Wisdom Literature of the OT, it describes the wisdom of the Lord that keeps a person on the right path (Pr 3:21; Isa 28:29); the wisdom that recognizes the things of God (Mic 6:9); and the success that comes from heeding wise counsel (Job 5:12; 6:13).

8455. תּוֹתָח, **tôwthâch,** *to-thawkh´*; from an unused root meaning to *smite*; a *club*:—darts.

8456. תָּזַז, **tâzaz,** *taw-zaz´*; a primitive root; to *lop* off:—cut down.

8457. תַּזְנוּת, **taznûwth,** *taz-nooth´*; or תַּזְנֻת, **taznuth,** *taz-nooth´*; from 2181; *harlotry,* i.e. (figurative) *idolatry:*—fornication, whoredom.

A noun meaning whoredom, prostitution. This word is found only in Eze 16 and 23. Chapter sixteen is an allegorical story about Jerusalem's faithlessness to the Lord (Eze 16:26). In this chapter, the Lord indicts Jerusalem for acting like a prostitute, throwing herself to the gods of foreign nations (Eze 16:15, 20, 33, 36). Chapter twenty-three is a similar story about Judah and Israel portrayed as two sisters in whoredom with the foreign nations (Eze 23:7, 14, 18, 35). These passages expose the vileness of the Israelites' sin.

8458. תַּחְבֻּלָה, **tachbulâh,** *takh-boo-law´*; or תַּחְבּוּלָה, **tachbûwlâh,** *takh-boo-law´*; from 2254 as denominative from 2256; (only in plural) properly *steerage* (as a management of *ropes*), i.e. (figurative) *guidance* or (by implication) a *plan:*—good advice, (wise) counsels.

8459. תֹּחוּ, **Tôchûw,** *to´-khoo*; from an unused root meaning to *depress; abasement; Tochu,* an Israelite:—Tohu.

8460. תְּחוֹת, **t^echôwth,** *tekh-ōth´*; (Chaldee); or תְּחֹת, **t^echôth,** *tekh-ōth´*; (Chaldee); corresponding to 8478; *beneath:*—under.

8461. תַּחְכְּמֹנִי, **Tachk^emônîy,** *takh-kem-o-nee´*; probably for 2453; *sagacious; Tachkemoni,* an Israelite:—Tachmonite.

8462. תְּחִלָּה, **t^echillâh,** *tekh-il-law´*; from 2490 in the sense of *opening*; a *commencement*; (relative) *original*; (adverb) *originally:*—begin (-ning), first (time).

8463. תַּחֲלוּא, **tachălûw',** *takh-al-oo´*; or תַּחֲלֻא, **tachălu',** *takh-al-oo´*; from 2456; a *malady:*—disease, × grievous, (that are) sick (-ness).

8464. תַּחְמָס, **tachmâs,** *takh-mawce´*; from 2554; a species of unclean bird (from its *violence*), perhaps an *owl:*—night hawk.

8465. תַּחַן, **Tachan,** *takh´-an*; probably from 2583; *station; Tachan,* the name of two Israelites:—Tahan.

8466. תַּחֲנָה, **tachănâh,** *takh-an-aw´*; from 2583; (only plural collateral) an *encampment:*—camp.

8467. תְּחִנָּה, **t^echinnâh,** *tekh-in-naw´*; from 2603; *graciousness*; (causative) *entreaty:*—favour, grace, supplication.

A feminine noun meaning a request for favour. The request for favour is always directed toward God—with two exceptions when the request is made to the king (Jer 37:20; 38:26). This seldom-used term occurred predominately in connection with Solomon's dedication of the Temple (1Ki 8:28, 30, 38, 45, 49, 52, 54; 2Ch 6:14–42). In these passages, the request was often connected with prayer and associated with a distinct relationship to God. On two occasions, the word was used to refer to favour itself (Jos 11:20; Ezr 9:8).

8468. תְּחִנָּה, **T^echinnâh,** *tekh-in-naw´*; the same as 8467; *Techinnah,* an Israelite:—Tehinnah.

8469. תַּחֲנוּן, **tachănûwn,** *takh-an-oon´*; or (feminine) תַּחֲנוּנָה, **tachănûwnâh,** *takh-an-oo-naw´*; from 2603; earnest *prayer:*—intreaty, supplication.

A masculine noun meaning supplication. The word refers to asking for favour and is used in a comparison of a rich man with a poor man. The rich man answers harshly, while the poor man pleads for mercy (Pr 18:23). Daniel used the word to indicate how he turned to the Lord in a prayer of petition, i.e. he pleaded with Him in prayers of petition with fasting and in sackcloth and ashes (Da 9:3). He also called to God to hear the prayers and petitions of His servant (Da 9:17). The noun was also used by the psalmist, who made a plea to God to hear his cry for mercy (Ps 28:2; 31:22[23]; 86:6). In Jeremiah, a cry was heard on the barren heights, along with weeping and pleading by the people of Israel (Jer 3:21). The word was also used to inform Daniel that as soon as he began his prayer or petition, an answer would be given to him (Da 9:23).

8470. תַּחֲנִי, **Tachănîy,** *takh-an-ee´*; patronymic from 8465; a *Tachanite* (collective) or descendants of Tachan:—Tahanites.

8471. תַּחְפַּנְחֵס, **Tachpanchês,** *takh-pan-khace´*; or תְּחַפְנְחֵס, **T^echaphn^echês,** *tekh-af-nekh-ace´*; (Eze 30:18), or תַּחְפְּנֵס, **Tachp^enês,** *takh-pen-ace´*; (Jer 2:16), of Egyptian derivative; *Tachpan* ches, *Techaph-neches* or *Tachpenes*, a place in Egypt:— Tahapanes, Tahpanhes, Tehaphnehes.

8472. תַּחְפְּנֵיס, **Tachpᵉnêys**, *takh-pen-ace´*; of Egyptian derivation; *Tachpenes*, an Egyptian woman:—Tahpenes.

8473. תַּחֲרָא, **tachărâ’**, *takh-ar-aw´*; from 2734 in the original sense of 2352 or 2353; a linen *corslet* (as *white* or *hollow*):—habergeon.

8474. תַּחֲרָה, **tachârâh**, *takh-aw-raw´*; a factitious root from 2734 through the idea of the *heat* of jealousy; to *vie* with a rival:—close, contend.

8475. תַּחְרֵעַ, **Tachrêaʻ**, *takh-ray´-ah*; for 8390; *Tachreä*, an Israelite:—Tahrea.

8476. תַּחַשׁ, **tachash**, *takh´-ash*; probably of foreign derivation; a (clean) animal with fur, probably a species of *antelope*:—badger.

8477. תַּחַשׁ, **Tachash**, *takh´-ash*; the same as 8476; *Tachash*, a relative of Abraham:—Thahash.

8478. תַּחַת, **tachath**, *takh´-ath*; from the same as 8430; the *bottom* (as *depressed*); (only adverb) *below* (often with prepositional prefix *underneath*), in *lieu of*, etc.:—as, beneath, × flat, in (-stead), (same) place (where ... is), room, for ... sake, stead of, under, × unto, × when ... was mine, whereas, [where-] fore, with.

8479. תַּחַת, **tachath**, *takh´-ath*; (Chaldee); corresponding to 8478:—under.

8480. תַּחַת, **Tachath**, *takh´-ath*; the same as 8478; *Tachath*, the name of a place in the Desert, also of three Israelites:—Tahath.

8481. תַּחְתּוֹן, **tachtôwn**, *takh-tone´*; or תַּחְתֹּן, **tach-tôn**, *takh-tone´*; from 8478; *bottommost*:—lower (-est), nether (-most).

8482. תַּחְתִּי, **tachtîy**, *takh-tee´*; from 8478; *lowermost*; as noun (feminine plural) the *depths* (figurative, a *pit*, the *womb*):—low (parts, -er, -er parts, -est), nether (part).

8483. תַּחְתִּים חָדְשִׁי, **Tachtîym Chodshîy**, *takh-teem´ khod-shee´*; apparently from the plural masculine of 8482 or 8478 and 2320; *lower* (ones) *monthly*; *Tachtim-Chodshi*, a place in Palestine:—Tahtim-hodshi.

8484. תִּיכוֹן, **tîykôwn**, *tee-kone´*; or תִּיכֹן, **tîykôn**, *tee-kone´*; from 8432; *central*:—middle (-most), midst.

8485. תֵּימָא, **Têymâ’**, *tay-maw´*; or תֵּמָא, **Têmâ’**, *tay-maw´*; probably of foreign derivation; *Tema*, a son of Ishmael, and the region settled by him:—Tema.

8486. תֵּימָן, **têymân**, *tay-mawn´*; or תֵּמָן, **têmân**, *tay-mawn´*; denominative from 3225; the *south* (as being on the *right* hand of a person facing the east):—south (side, -ward, wind).

8487. תֵּימָן, **Têymân**, *tay-mawn´*; or תֵּמָן, **Têmân**, *tay-mawn´*; the same as 8486; *Teman*, the name of two Edomites, and of the region and descendant of one of them:—south, Teman.

8488. תֵּימְנִי, **Têymᵉnîy**, *tay-men-ee´*; probably for 8489; *Temeni*, an Israelite:—Temeni.

8489. תֵּימָנִי, **Têymânîy**, *tay-maw-nee´*; patronymic from 8487; a *Temanite* or descendant of Teman:—Temani, Temanite.

8490. תִּימָרָה, **tîymârâh**, *tee-maw-raw´*; or תִּמָרָה, **timârâh**, *tee-maw-raw´*; from the same as 8558; a *column*, i.e. cloud:—pillar.

8491. תִּיצִי, **Tîytsîy**, *tee-tsee´*; patrial or patronymic from an unused noun of uncertain meaning; a *Titsite* or descendant or inhabitant of an unknown Tits:—Tizite.

8492. תִּירוֹשׁ, **tîyrôwsh**, *tee-roshe´*; or תִּירֹשׁ, **tîyrôsh**, *tee-roshe´*; from 3423 in the sense of *expulsion*; *must* or fresh grape juice (as just *squeezed* out); by implication (rarely) fermented *wine*:—(new, sweet) wine.

8493. תִּירְיָא, **Tîyrᵉyâ’**, *tee-reh-yaw´*; probably from 3372; *fearful*; *Tirja*, an Israelite:—Tiria.

8494. תִּירָס, **Tîyrâs**, *tee-rawce´*; probably of foreign derivative; *Tiras*, a son of Japheth:—Tiras.

8495. תַּיִשׁ, **tayish**, *tah´-yeesh*; from an unused root meaning to *butt*; a *buck* or he-goat (as given to *butting*):—he goat.

8496. תֹּךְ, **tôk**, *toke*; or תּוֹךְ, **tôwk**, *toke*; (Ps 72:14), from the same base as 8432 (in the sense of *cutting* to pieces); *oppression*:—deceit, fraud.

8497. תָּכָה, **tâkâh**, *taw-kaw´*; a primitive root; to *strew*, i.e. *encamp*:—sit down.

8498. תְּכוּנָה, t⁰kûwnâh, *tek-oo-naw´*; feminine passive participle of 8505; *adjustment*, i.e. *structure*; (by implication) *equipage*:—fashion, store.

8499. תְּכוּנָה, t⁰kûwnâh, *tek-oo-naw´*; from 3559; or probably identical with 8498; something *arranged* or *fixed*, i.e. a *place*:—seat.

8500. תֻּכִּיִּים, tukkîyyîym, *took-kee-yeem´*; or תּוּכִּיִּים, tûwk-kîyîym, *took-kee-eem´*; probably of foreign derivation; some imported creature, probably a *peacock*:—peacock.

8501. תָּכָךְ, tâkâk, *taw-kawk´*; from an unused root meaning to *dissever*, i.e. *crush*:—deceitful.

8502. תִּכְלָה, tiklâh, *tik-law´*; from 3615; *completeness*:—perfection.

8503. תַּכְלִית, taklîyth, *tak-leeth´*; from 3615; *completion*; (by implication) an *extremity*:—end, perfect (-ion).

8504. תְּכֵלֶת, t⁰kêleth, *tek-ay´-leth*; probably for 7827; the cerulean *mussel*, i.e. the colour (*violet*) obtained therefrom or stuff dyed therewith:—blue.

8505. תָּכַן, tâkan, *taw-kan´*; a primitive root; to *balance*, i.e. *measure* out (by weight or dimension); (figurative) to *arrange, equalize*, through the idea of *levelling* (mentally *estimate, test*):—bear up, direct, be ([un-]) equal, mete, ponder, tell, weigh.

8506. תֹּכֶן, tôken, *to´-ken*; from 8505; a fixed *quantity*:—measure, tale.

8507. תֹּכֶן, Tôken, *to´-ken*; the same as 8506; *Token*, a place in Palestine:—Tochen.

8508. תָּכְנִית, toknîyth, *tok-neeth´*; from 8506; *admeasurement*, i.e. *consummation*:—pattern, sum.

8509. תַּכְרִיךְ, takrîyk, *tak-reek´*; apparently from an unused root meaning to *encompass*; a *wrapper* or robe:—garment.

8510. תֵּל, têl, *tale*; (by contraction) from 8524; a *mound*:—heap, × strength.

8511. תָּלָא, tâlâ’, *taw-law´*; a primitive root; to *suspend*; figurative (through *hesitation*) to be *uncertain*; by implication (of mental *dependence*) to *habituate*:—be bent, hang (in doubt).

8512. תֵּל אָבִיב, Têl ’Âbîyb, *tale aw-beeb´*; from 8510 and 24; *mound* of green growth; *Tel-Abib*, a place in Chaldæa:—Tel-abib.

8513. תְּלָאָה, t⁰lâ’âh, *tel-aw-aw´*; from 3811; *distress*:—travail, travel, trouble.

8514. תַּלְאוּבָה, tal’ûwbâh, *tal-oo-baw´*; from 3851; *desiccation*:—great drought.

8515. תְּלַאשַּׂר, T⁰la’śśâr, *tel-as-sawr´*; or תְּלַשָּׂר, T⁰laś-śâr, *tel-as-sawr´*; of foreign derivation; *Telassar*, a region of Assyria:—Telassar.

8516. תִּלְבֹּשֶׁת, tilbôsheth, *til-bo´-sheth*; from 3847; a *garment*:—clothing.

8517. תְּלַג, t⁰lag, *tel-ag´*; (Chaldee); corresponding to 7950; *snow*:—snow.

8518. תָּלָה, tâlâh, *taw-law´*; a primitive root; to *suspend* (especially to *gibbet*):—hang (up).

8519. תְּלוּנָה, t⁰lûwnâh, *tel-oo-naw´*; or תְּלֻנָה, t⁰lunnâh, *tel-oon-naw´*; from 3885 in the sense of *obstinacy*; a *grumbling*:—murmuring.

8520. תֶּלַח, Telach, *teh´-lakh*; probably from an unused root meaning to *dissever; breach; Telach*, an Israelite:—Telah.

8521. תֵּל חַרְשָׁא, Têl Charshâ’, *tale khar-shaw´*; from 8510 and the feminine of 2798; *mound of workmanship; Tel-Charsha*, a place in Babylon:—Tel-haresha, Tel-harsa.

8522. תְּלִי, t⁰lîy, *tel-ee´*; probably from 8518; a *quiver* (as *slung*):—quiver.

8523. תְּלִיתָי, t⁰lîythây, *tel-ee-thaw´ee*; (Chaldee); or תַּלְתִּי, taltîy, *tal-tee´*; (Chaldee); ordinal from 8532; *third*:—third.

8524. תָּלוּל, tâlûwl, *taw-lool´*; a primitive root; to *pile* up, i.e. *elevate*:—eminent. Compare 2048.

8525. תֶּלֶם, telem, *teh´-lem*; from an unused root meaning to *accumulate*; a *bank* or *terrace*:—furrow, ridge.

8526. תַּלְמַי, Talmay, *tal-mah´ee*; from 8525; *ridged; Talmai*, the name of a Canaanite and a Syrian:—Talmai.

8527. תַּלְמִיד, talmîyd, *tal-meed´*; from 3925; a *pupil*:—scholar.

8528. תֵּל מֶלַח, **Têl Melach,** *tale meh´-lakh;* from 8510 and 4417; *mound of salt; Tel-Melach,* a place in Babylon:—Tel-melah.

8529. תָּלַע, **tâla',** *taw-law´;* a denominative from 8438; to *crimson,* i.e. dye that colour:— × scarlet.

8530. תַּלְפִּיּוֹת, **talpîyôwth,** *tal-pee-yoth´;* feminine from an unused root meaning to *tower;* something *tall,* i.e. (plural collective) *slenderness:*—armoury.

8531. תְּלַת, **te·lath,** *tel-ath´;* (Chaldee); from 8532; a *tertiary* rank:—third.

8532. תְּלָת, **te·lâth,** *tel-awth´;* (Chaldee); masculine תְּלָתָה, **te·lâthâh,** *tel-aw-thaw´;* (Chaldee); or תְּלָתָא, **te·lâthâ',** *tel-aw-thaw´;* (Chaldee); corresponding to 7969; *three* or *third:*—third, three.

8533. תְּלָתִין, **te·lâthîyn,** *tel-aw-theen´;* (Chaldee); multiple of 8532; *ten times three:*—thirty.

8534. תַּלְתַּל, **taltal,** *tal-tal´;* by reduplication from 8524 through the idea of *vibration;* a *trailing bough* (as *pendulous*):—bushy.

8535. תָּם, **tâm,** *tawm;* from 8552; *complete;* usually (moral) *pious;* (specifically) *gentle, dear:*—coupled together, perfect, plain, undefiled, upright.

An adjective meaning integrity, completeness. This is a rare, almost exclusively poetic term often translated perfect but not carrying the sense of totally free from fault, for it was used of quite flawed people. It describes the mild manner of Jacob in contrast to his brother Esau, who was characterized by shedding blood (Ge 25:27; see also Pr 29:10). The term often carries a rather strong moral component in certain contexts (Job 1:1; 9:20–22; Ps 37:37; 64:4[5]). This word appears among a list of glowing terms describing the admirable qualities of the Shulamite lover (SS 5:2; 6:9).

8536. תָּם, **tâm,** *tawm;* (Chaldee); corresponding to 8033; *there:*— × thence, there, × where.

8537. תֹּם, **tôm,** *tome;* from 8552; *completeness;* (figurative) *prosperity;* usually (moral) *innocence:*—full, integrity, perfect (-ion), simplicity, upright (-ly, -ness), at a venture. See 8550.

A masculine noun meaning completeness, integrity. This word is used in Job to describe how a man could die, i.e. in complete security

(Job 21:23). When Absalom invited two hundred men from Jerusalem to his party, the word denoted that the men did not have any idea of what was about to happen (2Sa 15:11). In Genesis, Abimelech acted with a clear conscience after Abraham stated that Sarah was his sister (Ge 20:5, 6). In a statement of wisdom, Proverbs uses the word to indicate that righteousness guards the person of integrity (Pr 13:6); while the psalmist asks that his integrity and uprightness protect him because his hope is in the Lord (Ps 25:21).

8538. תֻּמָּה, **tummâh,** *toom-maw´;* feminine of 8537; *innocence:*—integrity.

A feminine noun meaning integrity. This comes from the verb *tâmam* (8552), meaning to be complete, and is the feminine equivalent of the word *tôm* (8537), meaning completeness or integrity. This word is used only five times in the OT and is only found in the Wisdom Literature of Job and the Psalms. In four of these instances, it is used by God, Job, and Job's wife to refer to Job's integrity (Job 2:3, 9; 27:5; 31:6). In Pr 11:3, integrity guides the upright person. See the related adjective *tâm* (8535), meaning complete.

8539. תָּמַהּ, **tâmah,** *taw-mah´;* a primitive root; to *be in consternation:*—be amazed, be astonished, marvel (-lously), wonder.

8540. תְּמַהּ, **te·mah,** *tem-ah´;* (Chaldee); from a root corresponding to 8539; a *miracle:*—wonder.

An Aramaic masculine noun meaning wonder. This word is related to the Hebrew verb *tâmah* (8539), meaning to be astonished. In its only three instances, this word speaks of the wondrous and perhaps miraculous deeds of God (Da 4:2[3:32], 3[3:33]; 6:27[28]). In every instance, it is used in close connection with 'âth (852), meaning signs.

8541. תִּמָּהוֹן, **timmâhôwn,** *tim-maw-hone´;* from 8539; *consternation:*—astonishment.

8542. תַּמּוּז, **Tammûwz,** *tam-mooz´;* of uncertain derivation; *Tammuz,* a Phoenician deity:—Tammuz.

8543. תְּמוֹל, **te·môwl,** *tem-ole´;* or תְּמֹל, **te·môl,** *tem-ole´;* probably for 865; (properly) *ago,* i.e. a (short or long) *time since;* especially *yesterday,* or (with 8032) *day before* yesterday: + before (- time), + these [three] days, + heretofore, + time past, yesterday.

8544. תְּמוּנָה, **tᵉmûwnâh,** *tem-oo-naw´*; or תְּמֻנָה, **tᵉmunâh,** *tem-oo-naw´*; from 4327; *something portioned* (i.e. *fashioned*) out, as a *shape*, i.e. (indefinite) *phantom*, or (specific) *embodiment*, or (figurative) *manifestation* (of favour):— image, likeness, similitude.

A feminine noun meaning a likeness or a form. This word is related to the noun *miyn* (4327), meaning kind or species. The main idea of this word is one of likeness or similarity. It is normally used to describe God's ban on creating images of anything that would attempt to resemble (or be like) Him (Ex 20:4; Dt 4:15, 16; 5:8). This word can also describe the form or likeness of a visible image (Job 4:16; Ps 17:15). Synonyms for this word are *tabniyt* (8403) meaning plan, pattern, or form, and *demût* (1823), meaning likeness.

8545. תְּמוּרָה, **tᵉmûwrâh,** *tem-oo-raw´*; from 4171; *barter, compensation:*—(ex-) change (-ing), recompense, restitution.

A feminine noun meaning an exchange. This word comes from the verb *mûr* (4171), meaning to change or to exchange. The word usually refers to the exchanging of one item for another. In Leviticus, it is used to give rules for the exchange of animals and land that were dedicated to the Lord (Le 27:10, 33). In Ruth, the word indicates the Israelite custom of exchanging items to confirm a vow (Ru 4:7). In Job, this word describes financial transactions (Job 20:18; 28:17). This word may be translated recompense in Job 15:31, where it describes the natural result of a life trusting in vanity.

8546. תְּמוּתָה, **tᵉmûwthâh,** *tem-oo-thaw´*; from 4191; *execution* (as a doom):—death, die.

A feminine noun meaning death. This word comes from the verb *mûth* (4191), meaning to die. In its only two occurrences in the OT, it is used to describe those who were appointed to and deserving of death. More literally, it was those who were appointed to death (Ps 79:11; 102:20[21]).

8547. תֶּמַח, **Temach,** *teh´-makh*; of uncertain derivation; *Temach*, one of the Nethinim:— Tamah, Thamah.

8548. תָּמִיד, **tâmîyd,** *taw-meed´*; from an unused root meaning to *stretch*; (properly) *continuance* (as indefinite *extension*); but used only (attributively as adjective) *constant* (or adverb *constantly*); elliptically the *regular* (daily) sacrifice:— alway (-s), continual (employment, -ly), daily, ([n-]) ever (-more), perpetual.

A masculine noun meaning continuity. This word commonly refers to actions concerning religious rituals: God commanded that the Israelites always set showbread on a table in the tabernacle (Ex 25:30). Similarly, special bread was to be set on the table continually every Sabbath (Le 24:8). Mealtime could also be seen as following a set pattern: David commanded that Mephibosheth always eat with him (2Sa 9:7). In another light, the psalmist referred to God as One he could continually turn to in times of need (Ps 71:3).

8549. תָּמִים, **tâmîym,** *taw-meem´*; from 8552; *entire* (literal, figurative or moral); also (as noun) *integrity, truth:*—without blemish, complete, full, perfect, sincerely (-ity), sound, without spot, undefiled, upright (-ly), whole.

An adjective meaning blameless, complete. In over half of its occurrences, it describes an animal to be sacrificed to the Lord, whether a ram, a bull, or a lamb (Ex 29:1; Le 4:3; 14:10). With respect to time, the term is used to refer to a complete day, a complete seven Sabbaths (weeks), and a complete year (Le 23:15; 25:30; Jos 10:13). When used in a moral sense, this word is linked with truth, virtue, uprightness, and righteousness (Jos 24:14; Ps 18:23[24]; Pr 2:21; 11:5). The term is used of one's relationship with another person (Jgs 9:19; Pr 28:18; Am 5:10); and of one's relationship with God (Ge 17:1; Dt 18:13; 2Sa 22:24, 26). Moreover, this word described the blamelessness of God's way, knowledge, and Law (2Sa 22:31; Job 37:16; Ps 19:7[8]).

8550. תֻּמִּים, **Tummîym,** *toom-meem´*; plural of 8537; *perfections*, i.e. (technical) one of the epithets of the objects in the high-priest's breastplate as an emblem of *complete* Truth:— Thummim.

8551. תָּמַךְ, **tâmak,** *taw-mak´*; a primitive root; to *sustain*; (by implication) to *obtain, keep fast*; (figurative) to *help, follow close:*—(take, up-) hold (up), maintain, retain, stay (up).

8552. תָּמַם, **tâmam,** *taw-mam´*; a primitive root; to *complete,* in a good or a bad sense, literal or figurative, transitive or intransitive (as follows):—accomplish, cease, be clean [pass-] ed, consume, have done, (come to an, have an, make an) end, fail, come to the full, be all gone, × be all here, be (make) perfect, be spent, sum, be (shew self) upright, be wasted, whole.

A verb meaning to be complete, to finish, to conclude. At its root, this word carries the connotation of finishing or bringing closure. It is used to signify the concluding of an oration (Dt 31:30); the completing of a building project (1Ki 6:22); the exhausting of resources (Ge 47:15; Le 26:20); the utter destruction of something (Nu 14:33); and the fulfilling of an established period of time (Dt 34:8).

8553. תִּמְנָה, **Timnâh,** *tim-naw´*; from 4487; a *portion* assigned; *Timnah,* the name of two places in Palestine:—Timnah, Timnath, Thimnathah.

8554. תִּמְנִי, **Timnîy,** *tim-nee´*; patrial from 8553; a *Timnite* or inhabitant of Timnah:—Timnite.

8555. תִּמְנָע, **Timnâ',** *tim-naw´*; from 4513; *restraint; Timna,* the name of two Edomites:—Timna, Timnah.

8556. תִּמְנַת חֶרֶס, **Timnath Cheres,** *tim-nath kheh´-res*; or תִּמְנַת סֶרַח, **Timnath Serach,** *tim-nath seh´-rakh*; from 8553 and 2775; *portion of* (the) *sun; Timnath-Cheres,* a place in Palestine:—Timnath-heres, Timnath-serah.

8557. תֶּמֶס, **temes,** *teh´-mes*; from 4529; *liquefaction,* i.e. *disappearance:*—melt.

8558. תָּמָר, **tâmar,** *taw-mawr´*; from an unused root meaning to *be erect;* a *palm* tree:—palm (tree).

8559. תָּמָר, **Tâmar,** *taw-mawr´*; the same as 8558; *Tamar,* the name of three women and a place:—Tamar.

8560. תֹּמֶר, **tômer,** *to´-mer*; from the same root as 8558; a *palm* trunk:—palm tree.

8561. תִּמֹּר, **timmôr,** *tim-more´*; (plural only) or (feminine) תִּמֹּרָה, **timmôrâh,** *tim-mo-raw´*; (singular and plural), from the same root as 8558; (architecture) a *palm*-like pilaster (i.e. umbellate):—palm tree.

8562. תַּמְרוּק, **tamrûwq,** *tam-rook´*; or תַּמְרֻק, **tamruq,** *tam-rook´*; or תַּמְרִיק, **tamrîyq,** *tam-reek´*; from 4838; (properly) a *scouring,* i.e. *soap* or *perfumery* for the bath; (figurative) a *detergent:*— × cleanse, (thing for) purification (-fying).

A masculine noun meaning scraping, rubbing, purifying. This Hebrew word carries the connotation of scraping away that which is impure or harmful. This word appears three times in reference to ritual purification following menstruation (Est 2:3, 9, 12). Figuratively, it is used to imply a remedy for an illness (Pr 20:30).

8563. תַּמְרוּר, **tamrûwr,** *tam-roor´*; from 4843; *bitterness* (plural as collective):— × most bitter (-ly).

8564. תַּמְרוּר, **tamrûwr,** *tam-roor´*; from the same root as 8558; an *erection,* i.e. *pillar* (probably for a guide-board):—high heap.

8565. תַּן, **tan,** *tan*; from an unused root probably meaning to *elongate;* a *monster* (as preternaturally formed), i.e. a *sea-serpent* (or other huge marine animal); also a *jackal* (or other hideous land animal):—dragon, whale. Compare 8577.

8566. תָּנָה, **tânâh,** *taw-naw´*; a primitive root; to *present* (a mercenary inducement), i.e. *bargain* with (a harlot):—hire.

8567. תָּנָה, **tânâh,** *taw-naw´*; a primitive root [rather identical with 8566 through the idea of *attributing* honour]; to *ascribe* (praise), i.e. *celebrate, commemorate:*—lament, rehearse.

8568. תַּנָּה, **tannâh,** *tan-naw´*; probably feminine of 8565; a female *jackal:*—dragon.

8569. תְּנוּאָה, **tᵉnûw'âh,** *ten-oo-aw´*; from 5106; *alienation;* (by implication) *enmity:*—breach of promise, occasion.

8570. תְּנוּבָה, **tᵉnûwbâh,** *ten-oo-baw´*; from 5107; *produce:*—fruit, increase.

8571. תְּנוּךְ, **tᵉnûwk,** *ten-ook´*; perhaps from the same as 594 through the idea of *protraction;* a *pinnacle,* i.e. *extremity:*—tip.

8572. תְּנוּמָה, **tᵉnûwmâh,** *ten-oo-maw´*; from 5123; *drowsiness,* i.e. *sleep:*—slumber (-ing).

8573. תְּנוּפָה, **tᵉnûwphâh**, *ten-oo-faw´*; from 5130; a *brandishing* (in threat); (by implication) *tumult*; specifically the official *undulation* of sacrificial offerings:—offering, shaking, wave (offering).

A feminine noun meaning swinging, waving, a wave offering, an offering. In a general sense, this word implies the side to side motion involved in waving. It is used specifically as a technical term for the wave offering (Ex 29:24; Le 8:27). Twice the word is taken to mean an offering in general (Ex 38:24, 29).

8574. תַּנּוּר, **tannûwr**, *tan-noor´*; from 5216; a *fire-pot*:—furnace, oven.

8575. תַּנְחוּם, **tanchûwm**, *tan-khoom´*; or תַּנְחֻם, **tanchum**, *tan-khoom´*; and (feminine) תַּנְחוּמָה, **tanchûwmâh**, *tan-khoo-maw´*; from 5162; *compassion, solace*:—comfort, consolation.

8576. תַּנְחֶמֶת, **Tanchumeth**, *tan-khoo´-meth*; for 8575 (feminine); *Tanchumeth*, an Israelite:—Tanhumeth.

8577. תַּנִּין, **tannîyn**, *tan-neen´*; or תַּנִּים, **tannîym**, *tan-neem´*; (Eze 29:3), intensive from the same as 8565; a marine or land *monster*, i.e. *sea-serpent* or *jackal*:—dragon, sea-monster, serpent, whale.

A masculine noun meaning a serpent, a dragon, and a sea monster. It can connote a creature living in the water (Ge 1:21; Job 7:12; Ps 148:7). When the word is used this way, it is also used figuratively to represent the crocodile, which was the symbol of Pharaoh and Egypt (Ps 74:13; Isa 27:1; 51:9; Eze 29:3). This imagery may help us better understand the confrontation between Moses and Pharaoh, when Aaron's staff became a serpent and then swallowed the staff-serpents of Pharaoh's magicians (Ex 7:9, 10, 12). God was providing a graphic sign of what was to come. It can also connote a creature that lives on the land (Dt 32:33; Ps 91:13; Jer 51:34). There is one other occurrence of this term in the OT where it is used as a descriptor or part of a proper name for a well or a spring (Ne 2:13). In all its occurrences, this term has either a neutral (Ge 1:21; Ps 148:7); or a negative meaning (Isa 27:1; 51:9; Jer 51:34). In a few instances, the negative meaning is somewhat lessened, as when God provides a serpent to save

His people (Ex 7:9, 10, 12); or when a serpent was divinely restrained (Ps 91:13).

8578. תִּנְיָן, **tinyân**, *tin-yawn´*; (Chaldee); corresponding to 8147; *second*:—second.

8579. תִּנְיָנוּת, **tinyânûwth**, *tin-yaw-nooth´*; (Chaldee); from 8578; a *second time*:—again.

8580. תִּנְשֶׁמֶת, **tinshemeth**, *tan-sheh´-meth*; from 5395; (properly) a hard *breather*, i.e. the name of two unclean creatures, a lizard and a bird (both perhaps from changing colour through their *irascibility*), probably the *tree-toad* and the *water-hen*:—mole, swan.

8581. תָּעַב, **tâ'ab**, *taw-ab´*; a primitive root; to *loathe*, i.e. (moral) *detest*:—(make to be) abhor (-red), (be, commit more, do) abominable (-y), × utterly.

A verb meaning to abhor, to be abhorrent, to do abominably. This word expresses a strongly detestable activity or the logical response to such an activity. It is associated with a severe sense of loathing (Dt 23:7[8]; 1Ch 21:6); the condition of sinful people (Job 15:16); the activity of idol worship (1Ki 21:26); and the Lord's opposition to sin (Ps 5:6[7]).

8582. תָּעָה, **tâ'âh**, *taw-aw´*; a primitive root; to *vacillate*, i.e. *reel* or *stray* (literal or figurative); also causative of both:—(cause to) go astray, deceive, dissemble, (cause to, make to) err, pant, seduce, (make to) stagger, (cause to) wander, be out of the way.

A verb meaning to err, to wander, and to go astray. The meaning of this Hebrew word primarily rests in the notion of wandering about (Ex 23:4; Job 38:41). Figuratively, it is used in reference to one who is intoxicated (Isa 28:7). Most often, however, it refers to erring or being misled in a moral or religious sense (Isa 53:6; Eze 44:10[2x]; Hos 4:12).

8583. תֹּעוּ, **Tô'ûw**, *to´-oo*; or תֹּעִי, **Tô'îy**, *to´-ee*; from 8582; *error*; *Toü* or *Toï*, a Syrian king:—Toi, Tou.

8584. תְּעוּדָה, **tᵉ'ûwdâh**, *teh-oo-daw´*; from 5749; *attestation*, i.e. a *precept, usage*:—testimony.

A noun meaning a testimony, a custom. This noun is used in Isa 8:16, 20 in combination with the word law. In these verses, the testimony was the law of God's people that instructed them on how to live. In Ru 4:7, this word refers to the common custom of sealing a legal agreement.

8585. תְּעָלָה, **teʻâlâh,** *teh-aw-law´*; from 5927; a *channel* (into which water is *raised* for irrigation); also a *bandage* or *plaster* (as placed *upon* a wound):—conduit, cured, healing, little river, trench, watercourse.

8586. תַּעֲלוּלִים, **taʻălûwlîym,** *tah-al-ool-eem´*; from 5953; *caprice* (as a fit *coming on*), i.e. *vexation*; (concrete) a *tyrant*:—babe, delusion.

8587. תַּעֲלֻמָה, **taʻălumâh,** *tah-al-oo-maw´*; from 5956; a *secret*:—thing that is hid, secret.

8588. תַּעֲנוּג, **taʻănûwg,** *tah-an-oog´*; or תַּעֲנֻג, **taʻănug,** *tah-an-oog´*; and (feminine) תַּעֲנֻגָה, **taʻănugâh,** *tah-an-oog-aw´*; from 6026; *luxury*:—delicate, delight, pleasant.

8589. תַּעֲנִית, **taʻănîyth,** *tah-an-eeth´*; from 6031; *affliction* (of self), i.e. *fasting*:—heaviness.

8590. תַּעֲנָךְ, **Taʻănâk,** *tah-an-awk´*; or תַּעְנָךְ, **Taʻnâk,** *tah-nawk´*; of uncertain derivation; *Taanak* or *Tanak*, a place in Palestine:—Taanach, Tanach.

8591. תָּעַע, **tâʻaʻ,** *taw-ah´*; a primitive root; to *cheat*; (by analogy) to *maltreat*:—deceive, misuse.

8592. תַּעֲצֻמָה, **taʻătsumâh,** *tah-ats-oo-maw´*; from 6105; *might* (plural collective):—power.

8593. תַּעַר, **taʻar,** *tah´-ar*; from 6168; a *knife* or *razor* (as *making* bare); also a *scabbard* (as *being* bare, i.e. *empty*):—[pen-] knife, rasor, scabbard, shave, sheath.

8594. תַּעֲרֻבָה, **taʻărubâh,** *tah-ar-oo-baw´*; from 6148; *suretyship*, i.e. (concrete) a *pledge*:— + hostage.

8595. תַּעְתֻּעִים, **taʻtuʻîym,** *tah-too´-eem*; from 8591; a *fraud*:—error.

A masculine plural noun meaning mockings, errors. Jeremiah used this word twice when he ridiculed the idols of the Israelites (Jer 10:15; 51:18). These two verses are identical and are found in identical passages. Jeremiah assaulted the idols, saying how worthless they were and that they were works of mockery whose end will be judgment.

8596. תֹּף, **tôph,** *tofe*; from 8608 contraction; a *tambourine*:—tabret, timbrel.

8597. תִּפְאָרָה, **tiphʼârâh,** *tif-aw-raw´*; or תִּפְאֶרֶת, **tiphʼereth,** *tif-eh´-reth*; from 6286; *ornament* (abstract or concrete, literal or figurative):—beauty (-iful), bravery, comely, fair, glory (-ious), honour, majesty.

A feminine noun meaning beauty, glory. Isaiah used the word to denote the so-called beauty of finery that would be snatched away by the Lord (Isa 3:18). The word was used in a similar manner in Ezekiel to denote that which the people trusted in other than God, in addition to what would be stripped away (Eze 16:17; 23:26). The making of priestly garments and other apparel brought glory to Aaron and his sons, giving them dignity and honour (Ex 28:2, 40). Wisdom was portrayed as giving a garland of grace and a crown of splendor in Proverbs (Pr 4:9); Zion was told that it will be a crown of splendor in the Lord's hand (Isa 62:3); and in the book of Jeremiah, the king and queen were told that the crowns would fall from their heads (Jer 13:18). The word was used in Deuteronomy to describe how God would recognize His people (Dt 26:19). In Lamentations, it was used in an opposite manner to describe the splendor of Israel that was thrown down from heaven to earth in the Lord's anger (La 2:1). Deborah used the word to describe the honour or glory of a warrior which would not be Barak's because he handled the situation wrongly (Jgs 4:9).

8598. תַּפּוּחַ, **tappûwach,** *tap-poo´-akh*; from 5301; an *apple* (from its *fragrance*), i.e. the fruit or the tree (probably including others of the *pome* order, as the quince, the orange, etc.):—apple (tree). See also 1054.

8599. תַּפּוּחַ, **Tappûwach,** *tap-poo´-akh*; the same as 8598; *Tappuäch*, the name of two places in Palestine, also of an Israelite:—Tappuah.

8600. תְּפוֹצָה, **tephôwtsâh,** *tef-o-tsaw´*; from 6327; a *dispersal*:—dispersion.

8601. תֻּפִינִים, **tuppîynîym,** *toop-peen-eem´*; from 644; *cookery*, i.e. (concrete) a *cake*:—baked piece.

8602. תָּפֵל, **tâphêl,** *taw-fale´*; from an unused root meaning to *smear*; *plaster* (as *gummy*) or *slime*; (figurative) *frivolity*:—foolish things, unsavoury, untempered.

8603. תֹּפֶל, **Tôphel,** *to´-fel*; from the same as 8602; *quagmire*; *Tophel*, a place near the Desert:—Tophel.

8604. תִּפְלָה, **tiphlâh,** *tif-law´*; from the same as 8602; *frivolity*:—folly, foolishly.

8605. תְּפִלָּה, **tᵉphillâh,** *tef-il-law´*; from 6419; *intercession, supplication*; (by implication) a *hymn*:—prayer.

A feminine noun meaning prayer. The word is used to describe a prayer that was similar to a plea (1Ki 8:38; 2Ch 6:29). In Samuel, David is described as having the courage to offer his prayer to God (2Sa 7:27). King Hezekiah was instructed to pray for the remnant that still survived (2Ki 19:4); and in Jeremiah, the word is used to denote what not to do, i.e. do not pray with any plea or petition (Jer 7:16). The word is used by the psalmist as he cried to God to hear his prayer (Ps 4:1[2]). He asked God not to be deaf to his weeping but to take heed to the turmoil His servant was in. In a similar manner, the psalmist again uses the word in a plea to God to hear his prayer and to know that it did not come from deceitful lips (Ps 17:1[2]). The word is also used in Habakkuk as an introduction to the rest of the chapter, indicating that what followed was his prayer (Hab 3:1).

8606. תִּפְלֶצֶת, **tiphletseth,** *tif-leh´-tseth*; from 6426; *fearfulness*:—terrible.

8607. תִּפְסַח, **Tiphsach,** *tif-sakh´*; from 6452; *ford*; *Tiphsach*, a place in Mesopotamia:—Tipsah.

8608. תָּפַף, **tâphaph,** *taw-faf´*; a primitive root; to *drum*, i.e. play (as) on the tambourine:—taber, play with timbrels.

8609. תָּפַר, **tâphar,** *taw-far´*; a primitive root; to *sew*:—(women that) sew (together).

8610. תָּפַשׂ, **tâphaś,** *taw-fas´*; a primitive root; to *manipulate*, i.e. *seize*; (chiefly) to *capture, wield*; (specifically) to *overlay*; (figurative) to *use* unwarrantably:—catch, handle, (lay, take) hold (on, over), stop, × surely, surprise, take.

8611. תֹּפֶת, **tôpheth,** *to´-feth*; from the base of 8608; a *smiting*, i.e. (figurative) *contempt*:—tabret.

8612. תֹּפֶת, **Tôpheth,** *to´-feth*; the same as 8611; *Topheth*, a place near Jerusalem:—Tophet, Topheth.

8613. תָּפְתֶּה, **Tophteh,** *tof-teh´*; probably a form of 8612; *Tophteh*, a place of cremation:—Tophet.

8614. תִּפְתָּי, **tiphtây,** *tif-taw´ee*; (Chaldee); perhaps from 8199; *judicial*, i.e. a *lawyer*:—sheriff.

8615. תִּקְוָה, **tiqvâh,** *tik-vaw´*; from 6960; (literal) a *cord* (as an *attachment* [compare 6961]); (figurative) *expectancy*:—expectation ([-ted]), hope, live, thing that I long for.

8616. תִּקְוָה, **Tiqvâh,** *tik-vaw´*; the same as 8615; *Tikvah*, the name of two Israelites:—Tikvah.

8617. תְּקוּמָה, **tᵉqûwmâh,** *tek-oo-maw´*; from 6965; *resistfulness*:—power to stand.

8618. תְּקוֹמֵם, **tᵉqôwmêm,** *tek-o-mame´*; from 6965; an *opponent*:—rise up against.

8619. תָּקוֹעַ, **tâqôwaʻ,** *taw-ko´-ah*; from 8628 (in the musical sense); a *trumpet*:—trumpet.

8620. תְּקוֹעַ, **Tᵉqôwaʻ,** *tek-o´-ah*; a form of 8619; *Tekoä*, a place in Palestine:—Tekoa, Tekoah.

8621. תְּקוֹעִי, **Tᵉqôwʻîy,** *tek-o-ee´*; or תְּקֹעִי, **Tᵉqôʻîy,** *tek-o-ee´*; patronymic from 8620; a *Tekoïte* or inhabitant of Tekoah:—Tekoite.

8622. תְּקוּפָה, **tᵉqûwphâh,** *tek-oo-faw´*; or תְּקֻפָה, **tᵉquphâh,** *tek-oo-faw´*; from 5362; a *revolution*, i.e. (of the sun) *course*, (of time) *lapse*:—circuit, come about, end.

8623. תַּקִּיף, **taqqîyph,** *tak-keef´*; from 8630; *powerful*:—mightier.

8624. תַּקִּיף, **taqqîyph,** *tak-keef´*; (Chaldee); corresponding to 8623:—mighty, strong.

8625. תְּקַל, **tᵉqal,** *tek-al´*; (Chaldee); corresponding to 8254; to *balance*:—Tekel, be weighed.

8626. תָּקַן, **tâqan,** *taw-kan´*; a primitive root; to *equalize*, i.e. *straighten* (intransitive or transitive); (figurative) to *compose*:—set in order, make straight.

8627. תְּקַן, **tᵉqan,** *tek-an´*; (Chaldee); corresponding to 8626; to *straighten up*, i.e. *confirm*:—establish.

8628. תָּקַע, **tâqaʿ,** *taw-kah´*; a primitive root; to *clatter*, i.e. *slap* (the hands together), *clang* (an instrument); (by analogy) to *drive* (a nail or tent-pin, a dart, etc.); (by implication) to *become bondsman* (by hand-clasping):—blow ([a trumpet]), cast, clap, fasten, pitch [tent], smite, sound, strike, × suretiship, thrust.

A verb meaning to thrust, to fasten, to clap, to blow. The basic idea of this word is a thrust or a burst, such as the wind blowing away locusts (Ex 10:19); the thrusting of a spear through a body (2Sa 18:14); or the driving of a nail into the ground to secure an object, such as a tent (Ge 31:25; Jgs 4:21; Jer 6:3). At times, this word has the connotation of fastening as a pin fastens hair (Jgs 16:14); a nail fastens to a secure place (Isa 22:23, 25); or the fastening of Saul's body to the wall of a pagan temple (1Sa 31:10; 1Ch 10:10). When describing hands, it can denote the clapping of hands in victory (Ps 47:1[2]; Na 3:19); or the clasping of hands in an agreement (Job 17:3; Pr 11:15; 17:18). In the majority of usages, it refers to the blowing of trumpets (Nu 10:3–8; Jos 6:8, 9; Jgs 7:18–20; Joel 2:15).

8629. תְּקַע, **têqaʿ,** *tay-kah´*; from 8628; a *blast* of a trumpet:—sound.

8630. תָּקַף, **tâqaph,** *taw-kaf´*; a primitive root; to *overpower*:—prevail (against).

8631. תְּקֵף, **tᵉqêph,** *tek-afe´*; (Chaldee); corresponding to 8630; to *become* (causative, *make*) *mighty* or (figurative) *obstinate*:—make firm, harden, be (-come) strong.

An Aramaic verb meaning to be strong, to grow strong. This word is related to the Hebrew verb *tâqaêph* (8630), meaning to prevail over. It describes the growing strength of the tree in Nebuchadnezzar's dream (Da 4:11[8], 20[17]) that referred to the growing strength of the king (Da 4:22[19]). It was also used to describe the growing arrogance of Belshazzar (Da 5:20). In its only other instance, it describes a strong enforcement of an edict (Da 6:7[8]).

8632. תְּקֹף, **tᵉqôph,** *tek-ofe´*; (Chaldee); corresponding to 8633; *power*:—might, strength.

8633. תֹּקֶף, **tôqeph,** *to´-kef*; from 8630; *might* or (figurative) *positiveness*:—authority, power, strength.

8634. תַּרְאֲלָה, **Tarʾălâh,** *tar-al-aw´*; probably for 8653; a *reeling*; *Taralah*, a place in Palestine:—Taralah.

8635. תַּרְבּוּת, **tarbûwth,** *tar-booth´*; from 7235; *multiplication*, i.e. *progeny*:—increase.

8636. תַּרְבִּית, **tarbîyth,** *tar-beeth´*; from 7235; *multiplication*, i.e. *percentage* or *bonus* in addition to principal:—increase, unjust gain.

8637. תִּרְגַּל, **tirgal,** *teer-gal´*; a denominative from 7270; to *cause to walk*:—teach to go.

8638. תִּרְגַּם, **tirgam,** *teer-gam´*; a denominative from 7275 in the sense of *throwing* over; to *transfer*, i.e. *translate*:—interpret.

8639. תַּרְדֵּמָה, **tardêmâh,** *tar-day-maw´*; from 7290; a *lethargy* or (by implication) *trance*:—deep sleep.

8640. תִּרְהָקָה, **Tirhâqâh,** *teer-haw´-kaw*; of foreign derivation; *Tirhakah*, a king of Kush:—Tirhakah.

8641. תְּרוּמָה, **tᵉrûwmâh,** *ter-oo-maw´*; or תְּרֻמָה, **tᵉrumâh,** *ter-oo-maw´*; (Dt 12:11), from 7311; a *present* (as offered *up*), especially in *sacrifice* or as *tribute*:—gift, heave offering ([shoulder]), oblation, offered (-ing).

A feminine noun meaning offering. This word comes from the verb *rûm* (7311), meaning to be high or to lift up. The basic idea of this Hebrew noun is something being lifted up, i.e. an offering. It is normally used to describe a variety of offerings: a contribution of materials for building (Ex 25:2; 35:5); an offering of an animal for sacrifice (Ex 29:27; Nu 6:20); a financial offering for the priests (Nu 31:52); an allotment of land for the priests (Eze 45:6, 7); or even the materials for an idol (Isa 40:20). In one instance, this word is used to describe a ruler who received bribes (Pr 29:4).

8642. תְּרוּמִיָּה, **tᵉrûwmîyyâh,** *ter-oo-mee-yaw´*; formed as 8641; a sacrificial *offering*:—oblation.

A feminine noun meaning an offering, an allotment. This word occurs only once in the OT and is a slightly different form of the word *tĕrûmâh* (8641), meaning offering. In Eze 48:12, it describes the allotment (*tĕrû-miyyâh*) of the allotment of land (*tĕrûmâh*) that will be given to the Levites.

8643. תְּרוּעָה, **terûw'âh,** *ter-oo-aw´*; from 7321; *clamour,* i.e. *acclamation* of joy or a *battle-cry;* especially *clangor* of trumpets, as an *alarum:*— alarm, blow (-ing) (of, the) (trumpets), joy, jubile, loud noise, rejoicing, shout (-ing), (high, joyful) sound (-ing).

8644. תְּרוּפָה, **terûwphâh,** *ter-oo-faw´*; from 7322 in the sense of its congener 7495; a *remedy:*—medicine.

8645. תִּרְזָה, **tirzâh,** *teer-zaw´*; probably from 7329; a species of *tree* (apparently from its *slenderness*), perhaps the *cypress:*—cypress.

8646. תֶּרַח, **Terach,** *teh´-rakh*; of uncertain derivation; *Terach,* the father of Abraham; also a place in the Desert:—Tarah, Terah.

8647. תִּרְחֲנָה, **Tirchănâh,** *teer-khan-aw´*; of uncertain derivation; *Tirchanah,* an Israelite:— Tirhanah.

8648. תְּרֵין, **terêyn,** *ter-ane´*; (Chaldee); feminine תַּרְתֵּין, **tartêyn,** *tar-tane´*; corresponding to 8147; *two:*—second, + twelve, two.

8649. תָּרְמָה, **tormâh,** *tor-maw´*; and תַּרְמוּת, **tarmûwth,** *tar-mooth´*; or תַּרְמִית, **tarmîyth,** *tar-meeth´*; from 7411; *fraud:*—deceit (-ful), privily.

8650. תֹּרֶן, **tôren,** *to´-ren*; probably for 766; a *pole* (as a mast or flag-staff):—beacon, mast.

8651. תְּרַע, **tera',** *ter-ah´*; (Chaldee); corresponding to 8179; a *door;* (by implication) a *palace:*—gate mouth.

8652. תָּרָע, **târâ',** *taw-raw´*; (Chaldee); from 8651; a *doorkeeper:*—porter.

8653. תַּרְעֵלָה, **tar'êlâh,** *tar-ay-law´*; from 7477; *reeling:*—astonishment, trembling.

8654. תִּרְעָתִי, **Tir'âthîy,** *teer-aw-thee´*; patrial from an unused name meaning *gate;* a *Tirathite* or inhabitant of an unknown Tirah:—Tirathite.

8655. תְּרָפִים, **terâphîym,** *ter-aw-feme´*; plural person from 7495; a *healer; Teraphim* (singular or plural) a family idol:—idols (-atry), images, teraphim.

A masculine plural noun meaning household gods, cultic objects, teraphim. This word refers to a kind of idols or objects of worship whose ownership was possibly tied to inheritance rights. They were employed in divination.

Rachel stole these objects from her father Laban for some reason not entirely clear to us now, but they were probably not tied to ancestor worship (Ge 31:19, 34). These objects seemed to have had the shape of persons. But in one case, the word refers to something larger than the objects Rachel stole from Laban (1Sa 19:13, 16). Some have suggested that the teraphim used here were old pieces of cloth. The word refers to idols owned by Micah during the time of the judges (Jgs 17:5).

These objects are more strongly condemned in other passages: the wickedness of consulting teraphim is asserted in 1Sa 15:23 (see Eze 21:21[26]; Zec 10:2). Josiah cast them out when he got rid of the mediums and spiritists, literally, the ghosts and familiar spirits (2Ki 23:24).

8656. תִּרְצָה, **Tirtsâh,** *teer-tsaw´*; from 7521; *delightsomeness; Tirtsah,* a place in Palestine; also an Israelitess:—Tirzah.

8657. תֶּרֶשׁ, **Teresh,** *teh´-resh*; of foreign derivation; *Teresh,* a eunuch of Xerxes:—Teresh.

8658. תַּרְשִׁישׁ, **tarshîysh,** *tar-sheesh´*; probably of foreign derivation [compare 8659]; a gem, perhaps the *topaz:*—beryl.

8659. תַּרְשִׁישׁ, **Tarshîysh,** *tar-sheesh´*; probably the same as 8658 (as the region of the stone, or the reverse); *Tarshish,* a place on the Mediterranean, hence the epithet of a *merchant* vessel (as if for or from that port); also the name of a Persian and of an Israelite:—Tarshish, Tharshish.

8660. תִּרְשָׁתָא, **Tirshâthâ',** *teer-shaw-thaw´*; of foreign derivation; the title of a Persian deputy or *governor:*—Tirshatha.

8661. תַּרְתָּן, **Tartân,** *tar-tawn´*; of foreign derivation; *Tartan,* an Assyrian:—Tartan.

8662. תַּרְתָּק, **Tartâq,** *tar-tawk´*; of foreign derivation; *Tartak,* a deity of the Avvites:—Tartak.

8663. תְּשֻׁאָה, **teshu'âh,** *tesh-oo-aw´*; from 7722; a *crashing* or loud *clamour:*—crying, noise, shouting, stir.

8664. תִּשְׁבִּי, **Tishbîy,** *tish-bee´*; patrial from an unused name meaning *recourse;* a *Tishbite* or inhabitant of Tishbeh (in Gilead):—Tishbite.

8665. תַּשְׁבֵּץ, **tashbêts,** *tash-bates´*; from 7660; *checkered* stuff (as *reticulated*):—broidered.

8666. תְּשׁוּבָה, **tᵉshûwbâh,** *tesh-oo-baw´*; or תְּשֻׁבָה, **teshubâh,** *tesh-oo-baw´*; from 7725; a *recurrence* (of time or place); a *reply* (as *returned*):—answer, be expired, return.

8667. תְּשׂוּמֶת, **tᵉśûwmeth,** *tes-oo-meth´*; from 7760; a *deposit,* i.e. *pledging:*— + fellowship.

8668. תְּשׁוּעָה, **tᵉshûw‛âh,** *tesh-oo-aw´*; or תְּשֻׁעָה, **tᵉshu‛âh,** *tesh-oo-aw´*; from 7768 in the sense of 3467; *rescue* (literal or figurative, person, national or spirit):—deliverance, help, safety, salvation, victory.

A feminine noun meaning a deliverance, a victory, safety. Typically, the term is used in the context of military conflict (Jgs 15:18; 1Sa 11:13; 1Ch 11:14). While victory was usually not obtained through human means (Ps 33:17; 108:12[13]; 146:3; Pr 21:31), safety came through a multitude of counselors (Pr 11:14; 24:6). Principally, however, deliverance was to be found only in God (2Ch 6:41; Ps 119:81; 144:10). The deliverance of the Lord was on the minds of both Isaiah and Jeremiah during the troubled times in which they lived (Isa 45:17; 46:13; Jer 3:23; La 3:26).

8669. תְּשׁוּקָה, **tᵉshûwqâh,** *tesh-oo-kaw´*; from 7783 in the original sense of *stretching* out after; a *longing:*—desire.

A feminine noun meaning longing. It was used to describe the strong feelings of desire that one person had for another, but it was not always a healthy desire. As part of the judgment after Adam and Eve's sin, God said that a woman would long for her husband (Ge 3:16). People are not the only thing that can long: God told Cain that sin was lying at his door, desiring to enter (Ge 4:7).

8670. תְּשׁוּרָה, **tᵉshûwrâh,** *tesh-oo-raw´*; from 7788 in the sense of *arrival*; a *gift*:—present.

8671. תְּשִׁיעִי, **tᵉshîy‛îy,** *tesh-ee-ee´*; ordinal from 8672; *ninth*:—ninth.

8672. תֵּשַׁע, **têsha‛,** *tay´-shah*; or (masculine) תִּשְׁעָה, **tish‛âh,** *tish-aw´*; perhaps from 8159 through the idea of a *turn* to the next or full number ten; *nine* or (ordinal) *ninth*:—nine (+ -teen, + -teenth, -th).

8673. תִּשְׁעִים, **tish‛îym,** *tish-eem´*; multiple from 8672; *ninety*:—ninety.

8674. תַּתְּנַי, **Tattᵉnay,** *tat-ten-ah´ee*; of foreign derivation; *Tattenai,* a Persian:—Tatnai.

AMG's Annotated
Strong's Greek Dictionary
Of the New Testament

Additional materials in this dictionary were taken from
The Complete Word Study Dictionary: New Testament compiled by Spiros Zodhiates.
©1992 by AMG Publishers. All Rights Reserved.

Transliteration of Greek Alphabet

Capital Letter	Lowercase Letter	Greek Name	Trans–literation	Phonetic Sound	Example
A	α	alpha	a	a	as in father
B	β	bēta	b	v	as in victory
Γ	γ	gamma	g	y	as in yell (soft gutteral)
Δ	δ	delta	d	th	as in there
E	ε	epsilon	e	e	as in met
Z	ζ	zēta	z	z	as in zebra
H	η	ēta	ē	ee	as in see
Θ	θ	thēta	th	th	as in thin
I	ι	iōta	i	i	as in machine
K	κ	kappa	k	k	as in kill (soft accent)
Λ	λ	lambda	l	l	as in land
M	μ	mē	m	m	as in mother
N	ν	nē	n	n	as in now
Ξ	ξ	xi	x	x	as in wax
O	o	omicron	o	o	as in obey
Π	π	pi	p	p	as in pet (soft accent)
P	ρ	ro	r	r	as in courage
Σ	σ, ς*	sigma	s	s	as in sit
T	τ	tau	t	t	as in tell (soft accent)
Υ	υ	ēpsilon	u	ee	as in see
Φ	φ	phi	ph	ph	as in graphic
X	χ	chi	ch	h	as in heel
Ψ	ψ	psi	ps	ps	as in ships
Ω	ω	omega	ō	o	as in obey

*At the end of words

Combinations of Consonants

γγ	gamma + gamma	gg		g	as in go
γκ	gamma + kappa	gk		g	as in go
γχ	gamma + chi	gch		gh	as in ghost
μπ	mē + pi	mp		b	as in boy
ντ	nē + tau	nt		d	as in dog
τζ	tau + zēta	tz		g	as in gym

Transliteration of Greek Alphabet

Diphthongs (double vowels)

αι	alpha + iōta	ai	ai	as in hair
αυ	alpha + ēpsilon	au	af, av	as in waft or lava
ει	epsilon + iōta	ei	ee	as in see
ευ	epsilon + ēpsilon	eu	ef, ev	as in effort or every
ηυ	ēta + ēpsilon	ēu	eef, eev	as in reef or sleeve
οι	omicron + iōta	oi	ee	as in see
ου	omicron + ēpsilon	ou	ou	as in group
υι	ēpsilon + iōta	ui	ee	as in see

Breathing Marks

The smooth breathing mark (') is not transliterated or pronounced. When words begin with vowels, it may occur at the beginning of words with every vowel or double vowel (diphthong). ἔργον—*ergon*, work; εὐχή—*euchē*, vow.

The rough breathing mark (ʻ) is represented by an "h" in the transliteration. When words begin with vowels, it may occur at the beginning of words with every vowel or double vowel (diphthong). In modern Greek there is no distinction in pronunciation from the smooth breathing.

When rho or ēpsilon begin a word, they always have the rough breathing. There they are transliterated rh, hu, respectively. ῥέω—*rheō*, flow; ὑπομονή—*hupomonē*, patience.

Special Symbols

:— (*colon and one-em dash*) are used within each entry to mark the end of the discussion of syntax and meaning of the word under consideration, and to mark the beginning of the list of word(s) used to render it in translation.

() (*parentheses*) denote, in the translation renderings only, a word or syllable given in connection with the principal word it follows.

+ (*addition symbol*) denotes a rendering in translation of one or more Hebrew words in connection with the one under consideration.

× (*multiplication symbol*) denotes a rendering within translation that results from an idiom peculiar to the Greek.

A (Alpha)

NT Numbers 1–895

1. A, a, *al´-fah*; of Hebrew origin; the first letter of the alphabet; figurative only (from its use as a numeral) the *first*:—Alpha. Often used (usually **ἀν** *an*, before a vowel) also in composition (as a contraction from 427) in the sense of *privation*; so in many words beginning with this letter; occasionally in the sense of *union* (as a contraction of 260).

2. Ἀαρών, Aarōn, *ah-ar-ohn´*; of Hebrew origin [175]; *Aaron*, the brother of Moses: — Aaron.

3. Ἀβαδδών, Abaddōn, *ab-ad-dohn´*; of Hebrew origin [11]; a destroying *angel*:—Abaddon.

4. ἀβαρής, abarēs, *ab-ar-ace´*; from 1 (as a negative particle) and 922; *weightless*, i.e. (figurative) *not burdensome*:—from being burdensome.

5. Ἀββᾶ, Abba, *ab-bah´*; of Chaldee origin [2]; *father* (as a vocative):—Abba.

6. Ἄβελ, Abel, *ab´-el*; of Hebrew origin [1893]; *Abel*, the son of Adam:—Abel.

7. Ἀβιά, Abia, *ab-ee-ah´*; of Hebrew origin [29]; *Abijah*, the name of two Israelites:—Abia.

8. Ἀβιάθαρ, Abiathar, *ab-ee-ath´-ar*; of Hebrew origin [54]; *Abiathar*, an Israelite:—Abiathar.

9. Ἀβιληνή, Abilēnē, *ab-ee-lay-nay´*; of foreign origin [compare 58]; *Abilene*, a region of Syria:—Abilene.

10. Ἀβιούδ, Abioud, *ab-ee-ood´*; of Hebrew origin [31]; *Abihud*, an Israelite:—Abiud.

11. Ἀβραάμ, Abraam, *ab-rah-am´*; of Hebrew origin [85; *Abraham*, the Hebrew patriarch:—Abraham. [In Ac 7:16 the text should probably read *Jacob*.]

12. ἄβυσσος, abussos, *ab´-us-sos*; from 1 (as a negative particle) and a variation of 1037; *depthless*, i.e. (special) (infernal) "*abyss*":—deep, (bottomless) pit.

13. Ἄγαβος, Agabos, *ag´-ab-os*; of Hebrew origin [compare 2285]; *Agabus*, an Israelite:—Agabus.

14. ἀγαθοεργέω, agathoergeō, *ag-ath-er-gheh´-o*; from 18 and 2041; to *work good*:—do good.

From *agathoergós* (n.f.), doing good, which is from *agathós* (18), benevolent, and *érgon* (2041), work. To do good to others, to work good, i.e. to act for someone's advantage or benefit (Mk 3:4; Lk 6:9, 35; Ac 6:33; 14:7); also to do well, to act virtuously (1Pe 2:15, 20; 3:6, 17; 3Jn 11).

In Ac 14:17, the UBS text has *agathourgón* instead of *agathopoión* as in the TR.

Syn.: *sumphéro* (4851), to cause things to be brought together for the glory of God and the benefit of oneself and others; *kalopoiéō* (2569), to do well and thus show one's good nature; *euergetéō* (2109), to do acts of benevolence instead of just having a benevolent attitude.

15. ἀγαθοποιέω, agathopoieō, *ag-ath-op-oy-eh´-o*; from 17; to *be a well-doer* (as a favour or a duty):—(when) do good (well).

From *agathós* (18), benevolent, and *poiéō* (4160), to make or do. To do good to others (Mk 3:4; Lk 6:9, 33, 35; Ac 14:17; 1Pe 2:15, 20; 3:6, 17).

Deriv.: *agathopoiía* (16), benevolence; *agathopoiós* (17), one that does well.

Syn.: *agathoergéo* (14), to do good works; *kalopoiéō* (2569), to do well or show one's good nature by doing good; *euergetéō* (2109), to do an act of benevolence; *sumphéro* (4851), to cause things to be brought together for the glory of God and the benefit of oneself and others.

16. ἀγαθοποιΐα, agathopoiia, *ag-ath-op-oy-ee´-ah*; from 17; *well-doing*, i.e. *virtue:—*well-doing.

17. ἀγαθοποιός, agathopoios, *ag-ath-op-oy-os´*; from 18 and 4160; a *well-doer*, i.e. *virtuous:—*them that do well.

18. ἀγαθός, agathos, *ag-ath-os´*; a primary word; *"good"* (in any sense, often as noun):—benefit, good (-s, things), well. Compare 2570.

Adjective meaning good and benevolent, profitable, useful.

(**I**) Good, excellent, distinguished, best, of persons (Mt 19:16, 17; Mk 10:17, 18; Lk 18:18, 19; Sept.: 1Sa 9:2); of things (Lk 10:42; Jn 1:46; 2Th 2:16; Sept.: Ezr 8:27).

(**II**) Good, i.e. of good character, disposition, quality.

(**A**) Of persons: upright, virtuous (Mt 5:45; 12:35; 25:21, 23; Lk 6:45; 19:17; 23:50; Jn 7:12; Ac 11:24; Sept.: 2Ch 21:13; Pr 13:2, where *agathós* is used as opposed to *paránomos*, unlawful; Pr 15:3; Isa 63:7, a benevolent judge). Of their external conditions, appearance, dress (Mt 22:10).

(**B**) Of things: (**1**) in a physical sense, e.g., a tree (Mt 7:17, 18); ground (Lk 8:8; Sept.: Ex 3:8). (**2**) in a moral sense, good, upright, virtuous; e.g., heart (Lk 8:15); commandment (Ro 7:12); word (2Th 2:17); will of God (Ro 12:2); the Spirit (Sept.: Ne 9:20; Ps 143:10); good conscience, i.e. conscious of integrity (Ac 23:1; 1Ti 1:5, 19; 1Pe 3:16, 21); good works, deeds, virtue, rectitude (Ro 2:7; 13:3; Eph 2:10; Col 1:10; 2Ti 2:21; 3:17; Tit 1:16; 3:1; Heb 13:21; Sept.: 1Sa 19:4).

(**C**) Of abstract things: *agathón* (sing.) and *agathá* (pl.), meaning virtue, rectitude, love of virtue (Mt 12:34, 35; 19:16; Lk 6:45; Jn 5:29; Ro 2:10; 3:8; 7:18, 19; 9:11; 12:9; 13:3; 16:19; 2Co 5:10; 1Pe 3:11, 13; 3Jn 11). In Ro 7:13 *tó agathón* means that which is in itself good; Ro 14:16, the good cause, the gospel of Christ; Sept.: Ps 34:14; 53:1, 3.

(**III**) Good, in respect to operation or influence on others, i.e. useful, beneficial, profitable.

(**A**) Of persons: benevolent, beneficent (Mt 20:15; Ro 5:7; 1Th 3:6; Tit 2:5; 1Pe 2:18; Sept.: 2Ch 30:19; Ps 73:1).

(**B**) Of things: e.g., *dómata* (1390), gifts (Mt 7:11; Lk 11:13); *dósis* (1394), gift (Jas 1:17); work (Php 1:6); conduct (1Pe 3:16); fruit (Jas 3:17); fidelity (Tit 2:10); benevolent way (Sept.: 1Sa 12:23); benevolent commandments (Sept.:

Ne 9:13). Benevolent treasure or treasure of good things (Mt 12:35; Lk 6:45); good deeds, benefits (Ac 9:36; 2Co 9:8; 1Ti 2:10; 5:10). With the meaning of suitable or adapted to (Ro 15:2; Eph 4:29, word suitable for education).

(**C**) Of abstract things: *tó agathón*, something useful and profitable, beneficial (Ro 8:28; 12:21; 13:4; Gal 6:10; Eph 4:28; 6:8; 1Th 5:15; Phm 6, 14). In the plural *tá agathá*, things good and useful, benefits, blessings (Mt 7:11; Lk 1:53; 16:25; Gal 6:6; Heb 9:11; 10:1). With the meaning of goods, wealth (Lk 12:18, 19; Sept.: Ge 24:10; 45:18, 20; Dt 6:11).

(**IV**) Good in respect to the feelings, excited, i.e. pleasant, joyful, happy (1Pe 3:10; Ro 10:15, blessed times; Sept.: Ps 34:12; Zec 8:19).

Deriv.: *agathopoiéo* (15), to do good to others; *agathōsúnē* (19), goodness; *philágathos* (5358), love of good men.

Syn.: *kalós* (2570), constitutionally good but not necessarily benefiting others; *chrēstós* (5543), useful, kind.

19. ἀγαθωσύνη, agathōsunē, *ag-ath-o-soo´-nay*; from 18; *goodness*, i.e. *virtue* or *beneficence:—*goodness.

Noun from *agathós* (18), benevolent. Active goodness.

(**I**) Of disposition and character, virtue (Ro 15:14; Eph 5:9; 2Th 1:11; Sept.: 2Ch 24:16).

(**II**) Beneficence, in Gal 5:22 referred to as goodness.

Syn.: *euergesía* (2108), good deed; *cháris* (5485), grace, benefit; *tó agathón* (from *agathós* [18], benevolent), the good action or deed, benefit; *eúnoia* (2133), that which is owed to someone; *eupoiÍa* (2140), the good deeds done; *philanthrōpía* (5363), love for human beings, philanthropy.

20. ἀγαλλίασις, agalliasis, *ag-al-lee´-as-is*; from 21; *exultation*; specially *welcome:—*gladness, (exceeding) joy.

Noun from *agalliáō* (21), to exult. Exultation, exuberant joy. Not found in Gr. writers but often meaning joy, exultation (Sept.: Ps 30:5; 45:15; 65:12, rejoicing with song, dancing. See Ps 126:2, 6); great joy (Ps 45:7; 51:8, 12). In the NT, joy, gladness, rejoicing (Lk 1:14, 44; Ac 2:46; Heb 1:9 from Ps 45:7, oil of gladness with which guests were anointed at feasts, where used as an emblem of the highest honours [cf. Jude 24]).

Syn.: *chará* (5479), joy, delight, the feeling experienced in one's heart, especially a result of God's grace (*cháris* [5485]), whereas *agallíasis* is the demonstration of that joy; *euphrosúnē* (2167), good cheer, joy.

21. ἀγαλλιάω, agalliaō, *ag-al-lee-ah´-o*; from ἄγαν, *agan* (*much*) and 242; properly to *jump for joy*, i.e. *exult*:—be (exceeding) glad, with exceeding joy, rejoice (greatly).

From *ágan* (n.f.), much, and *hállomai* (242), to leap. To exult, leap for joy, to show one's joy by leaping and skipping denoting excessive or ecstatic joy and delight. Hence in the NT to rejoice, exult. Often spoken of rejoicing with song and dance (Sept.: Ps 2:11; 20:5; 40:16; 68:3). Usually found in the middle deponent *agalliáomai*.

(**I**) Used in an absolute sense (Ac 2:26, "my tongue was glad," meaning I rejoiced in words, sang aloud; Lk 10:21; Ac 16:34). It is sometimes put after *chaírō* (5463), to rejoice, which is of less intense significance, and produces an expression meaning to rejoice exceedingly (Mt 5:12; 1Pe 4:13; Rev 19:7; see Ps 40:16; 90:14).

(**II**) With a noun of the same significance in an adverb sense (1 Pet 1:8 with *chará* [5479], joy, "rejoice with joy unspeakable").

(**III**) Followed by *hína* (2443), so that, with the subjunctive (Jn 8:56, "he rejoiced that he should see my day" [a.t.]).

(**IV**) Followed by *epí* (1909), upon, with the dat. (Lk 1:47).

(**V**) Followed by *en* (1722), in, with the dat. where a simple dat. might stand (Jn 5:35; Ac 16:34; 1Pe 1:16; Sept.: Ps 13:5; 89:16).

Deriv.: *agallíasis* (20), exultation.

Syn.: *euphraínō* (2165), to cheer, gladden; *chaírō* (5463), to rejoice; *kaucháomai* (2744), to boast, glory, rejoice; *katakaucháomai* (2620), to glory against.

22. ἄγαμος, agamos, *ag´-am-os*; from 1 (as a negative particle) and 1062; *unmarried*:—unmarried.

23. ἀγανακτέω, aganakteō, *ag-an-ak-teh´-o*; from ἄγαν, *agan* (*much*) and ἄχθος, *achhós* (*grief*; akin to the base of 43); to *be greatly afflicted*, i.e. (figurative) *indignant*:—be much (sore) displeased, have (be moved with, with) indignation.

24. ἀγανάκτησις, aganaktēsis, *ag-an-ak´-tay-sis*; from 23; *indignation*:—indignation.

25. ἀγαπάω, agapaō, *ag-ap-ah´-o*; perhaps from ἄγαν, *agan* (*much*) [or compare 5689]; to *love* (in a social or moral sense):—(be-) love (-ed). Compare 5368.

To love. It differs from *philéō* (5368), to love, indicating feelings, warm affection, the kind of love expressed by a kiss (*phílēma* [5370]).

(**I**) To love, to regard with strong affection (Lk 7:42; Jn 3:35; 8:42; 21:15; 2Co 9:7; Rev 3:9; Sept.: Ge 24:67; Ru 4:15). With the accusative of the corresponding noun, "his great love wherewith he loved us" (Eph 2:4 [cf. 2Sa 13:15]). Perf. pass. part. *ēgapēménos*, beloved (Eph 1:6; Col 3:12).

(**II**) As referring to superiors and including the idea of duty, respect, veneration, meaning to love and serve with fidelity (Mt 6:24; 22:37; Mk 12:30, 33; Lk 16:13; Ro 8:28; Sept.: 1Sa 18:16). The present act. part. used substantively of those loving the Lord, meaning faithful disciples or followers of the Lord (Eph 6:24; Jas 1:12; 2:5; Sept.: Ex 20:6; Dt 5:10).

(**III**) To love, i.e. to regard with favour, goodwill, benevolence (Mk 10:21; Lk 7:5; Jn 10:17). In other passages the effects of benevolence are expressed as to wish well to or do good to. To love one's neighbour, one's enemies (Mt 5:43; 19:19; 22:39; Lk 6:32). The fut. imper., *agapéseis*, especially in regard to one's enemies, should not necessarily be taken to mean doing that which will please them, but choosing to show them favour and goodwill (Mt 5:43, 44). In 2Co 12:15 it means, "even if, having conferred greater benefits on you, I receive less from you" (a.t.).

(**IV**) Spoken of things: to love, i.e. to delight in (Lk 11:43; Jn 3:19; Heb 1:9; 1Jn 2:15). The expression "not to love" means to neglect, disregard, condemn (Rev 12:11, meaning they condemned their lives even unto death, i.e. they willingly exposed themselves to death).

Deriv.: *agápē* (26), love; *agapētós* (27), beloved, dear.

Syn.: *philéō* (5368), to befriend, love.

26. ἀγάπη, agapē, *ag-ah´-pay*; from 25; *love*, i.e. *affection* or *benevolence*; specially (plural) a *love-feast*:—(feast of) charity ([-ably]), dear, love.

Noun from *agapáō* (25), to love. Love, affectionate regard, goodwill, benevolence.

(**I**) Generally, love as in 1Co 4:21, "Shall I come unto you with a rod, or in love," meaning full of love, all love; Col 1:13, "the kingdom of his dear Son [the Son of His love]," is the same as *ho agapētós*, beloved son. Spoken especially of goodwill toward others, the love of our neighbour, brotherly affection, which the Lord Jesus commands and inspires (Jn 15:13; 17:26; Ro 13:10; 1Co 13:1; 2Co 2:4, 8; 2Th 1:3; Heb 6:10; 1Pe 4:8; 1Jn 4:7). In 2Co 13:11, "the God of love" means the author and source of love, who Himself is love. In Ro 15:30, "the love of the Spirit" means that love which the Spirit inspires.

(II) Specifically "the love of God" or "of Christ":

(A) Subj. or act., means the love which God or Christ exercises toward Christians. The love that is derived from God (Ro 5:5; Eph 2:4; 2Th 3:5). Followed by *eis* (1519), unto someone (Ro 5:8), and by *en* (1722), in someone (1Jn 4:9, 16). The love of Christ means the love which is derived from Christ (2Co 5:14).

(B) Obj. or pass., that love of which God or Christ is the object in the hearts of Christians. Of God (Lk 11:42; Jn 5:42; 1Jn 2:5). Also used in an absolute sense (1Jn 4:16, 18; 2Jn 6; 3Jn 6). Of Christ (Jn 15:10; Ro 8:35).

(III) Metaphorically, the effect or proof of love, benevolence, benefit conferred (Eph 1:15; 3:19; 1Jn 3:1; 2Th 2:10, "the love of the truth," meaning the true love, the true and real benefits conferred by God through Christ).

(IV) In the plural, *agápai*, love feasts, public banquets of a frugal kind instituted by the early Christian church and connected with the celebration of the Lord's Supper. The provisions were contributed by the more wealthy individuals and were made common to all Christians, whether rich or poor, who chose to partake. Portions were also sent to the sick and absent members. These love feasts were intended as an exhibition of that mutual love which is required by the Christian faith, but as they became subject to abuses, they were discontinued.

Syn.: *philía* (5373), friendship based on common interests; *philanthrōpía* (5363), love for man, philanthropy; *agápai heortē* (1859), a feast or festival; *deípnon* (1173), the chief meal of the day, dinner; *dochē* (1403), a reception, feast, banquet.

27. ἀγαπητός, agapētos, *ag-ap-ay-tos´*; from 25; *beloved*:—(dearly, well) beloved, dear.

Adjective from *agapáō* (25), to love. Beloved, dear.

(I) Spoken of Christians as united with God or with each other in the bonds of holy love. *Agapētoí*, the plural (Ac 15:25; Ro 12:19; 2Co 7:1; 12:19; Col 1:7; 4:14; 1Th 2:8; 1Ti 6:2; Heb 6:9; 1Pe 2:11; 4:12; 2Pe 3:1, 8, 14, 15, 17; 1Jn 3:2, 21; 4:1, 7, 11; 2Jn 1, 2, 5, 11; Jude 3, 17, 20), meaning conjoined in the bonds of faith and love. In 1Co 15:58, "beloved brethren," i.e. Christians. See Eph 6:21; Php 4:1; Col 4:7, 9; Phm 1, 2, 16; Jas 1:16, 19; 2:5. *Agapētoí Theoú*, beloved of God, means chosen by Him to salvation (Ro 1:7; 11:28; Eph 5:1). *Agapētoí sou*, your beloved, refers to the worshippers of God (Sept.: Ps 60:5; 108:6; 127:2). Paul seems to apply the term particularly to those converted under his ministry when he speaks of *Epaíneton tón agapēton mou* in Ro 16:5. Also see Ro 16:8, 9, 12, "Timotheus, who is my beloved son . . . in the Lord" (cf. 1Co 4:17; 2Ti 1:2). Spoken also of a whole church gathered by Paul (1Co 4:14, "My beloved sons"). See 1Co 10:14; Php 2:12.

(II) The phrase *huiós agapētós* (*huiós* [5207], son; *agapētós*, inherently beloved) means the only son as being the object of peculiar love. In the NT, spoken only of Christ, the Son beloved of God (Mt 3:17; 12:18; 17:5; Mk 1:11; 9:7; Lk 3:22; 9:35; 2Pe 1:17). In Mk 12:6, "one son, his well-beloved," meaning his only son. See Lk 20:13; Sept.: Ge 22:2, 12. The phrase *pénthos agapētoú* (*pénthos* [3997], mourning; *agapētoú*, of a beloved one) e.g., mourning for an only son, i.e. deep sorrow (Jer 6:26; Am 8:10; Zec 12:10).

28. Ἄγαρ, Agar, *ag´-ar*; of Hebrew origin [1904]; *Hagar*, the concubine of Abraham:— Hagar.

29. ἀγγαρεύω, aggareuō, *ang-ar-yew´-o*; of foreign origin [compare 104]; properly to *be a courier*, i.e. (by implication) to *press* into public service:—compel (to go).

To press into service, to send off an *ággaros* or public courier. This word is of Persian origin, and after being received into the Gr. language, passed also into use among the Jews and Romans. The *ággaroi*, couriers, had authority to press into their service men, horses, ships or anything which came in their way and which might serve to hasten their journey. Afterwards *aggareúō* came to mean to press into service for a journey in the manner of an *ággaros*. In the NT, to compel, to press, to accompany one (Mt 5:41; 27:32; Mk 15:21).

Syn.: *anagkázō* (315), to constrain, whether by threat, entreaty, force or persuasion.

30. ἀγγεῖον, aggeion, *ang-eye´-on*; from ἄγκάλη, *aggŏs* (a *pail*, perhaps as *bent*; compare the base of 43); a *receptacle*:—vessel.

31. ἀγγελία, aggelia, *ang-el-ee´-ah*; from 32; an *announcement*, i.e. (by implication) *precept*:—message.

Noun from *ággelos* (32), messenger. Message (1Jn 3:11; Sept.: Pr 12:25).

Syn.: *akoé* (189), the thing heard; *kérugma* (2782), proclamation, preaching.

32. ἄγγελος, aggelos, *ang´-el-os*; from ἀγγέλλω, *aggellō*; [probable derivative from 71; compare 34] (to *bring tidings*); a *messenger*; especially an "*angel*"; (by implication) a *pastor*:—angel, messenger.

A noun meaning messenger, one sent to announce or proclaim.

(I) A messenger, one who is sent in order to announce, teach, perform, or explore something (Mt 11:10; Lk 7:24; 9:52; Gal 4:14; Jas 2:25; Sept.: Jos 6:17; Mal 2:7). In 1Co 11:10, *aggélous*, accusative plural, is interpreted variably as spies or angels, good or evil, even demons. The angels of the seven churches are probably the bishops or pastors of those churches, who were the delegates or messengers of the churches to God in the offering of prayer, etc. Others refer this to guardian angels (Rev 1:20; 2:1, 8, 12, 18; 3:1, 7, 14).

(II) An angel, a celestial messenger, a being superior to man. God is represented as surrounded by a host of beings of a higher order than man. These He uses as His messengers and agents in administering the affairs of the world and in promoting the welfare of humans (Mt 1:20; 18:10; 22:30; Ac 7:30). As to the numbers of the angels, see Heb 12:22; Rev 5:11. See *archággelos* (743), archangel. In 2Pe 2:4; Jude 6, some of the angels that sinned are said to have been cast down to hell. They are called the angels of the devil or Satan (Mt 25:41; 2Co 12:7; Rev 12:9). In Rev 9:11, the angel of the bottomless pit is the destroying angel *Abaddṓn* (3), Abaddon.

Deriv.: *aggelía* (31), message; *archággelos*

(743), archangel; *isággelos* (2465), like or equal to an angel.

Syn.: *apóstolos* (652), apostle, messenger.

33. ἄγε, age, *ag´-eh*; imperative of 71; properly *lead*, i.e. *come* on:—go to.

34. ἀγέλη, agelē, *ag-el´-ay*; from 71 [compare 32]; a *drove*:—herd.

35. ἀγενεαλόγητος, agenealogētos, *ag-en-eh-al-og´-ay-tos*; from 1 (as negative particle) and 1075; *unregistered* as to birth:—without descent.

Adjective from the priv. *a* (1), without, and *genealogéō* (1075), to trace a genealogy. Without a genealogy or pedigree. Melchizedec was said to be without genealogy (Heb 7:3) because, being a Canaanite, and not standing in the public genealogical registers as belonging to the family of Aaron, he was a priest not by right of sacerdotal descent, but by the grace of God (cf. Ex 40:15; Nu 3:10).

Syn.: *amḗtōr* (282), without the record of a mother; *apátōr* (540), without the record of a father.

36. ἀγενής, agenēs, *ag-en-ace´*; from 1 (as negative particle) and 1085; properly *without kin*, i.e. (of unknown descent, and by implication) *ignoble*:—base things.

37. ἁγιάζω, hagiazō, *hag-ee-ad´-zo*; from 40; to *make holy*, i.e. (ceremony) *purify* or *consecrate*; (mentally) to *venerate*:—hallow, be holy, sanctify.

From *hágios* (40), holy. To make holy, sanctify.

(I) To make clean, render pure.

(A) Particularly in Heb 9:13.

(B) Metaphorically, to render clean in a moral sense, to purify, sanctify (Ro 15:16, "being sanctified by the Holy Ghost," meaning by the sanctifying influences of the Holy Spirit on the heart. See 1Co 6:11; Eph 5:26; 1Th 5:23; 1Ti 4:5; Heb 2:11; 10:10, 14, 29; 13:12; Rev 22:11). *Hoi hēgiasménoi*, those who are sanctified, is a reference to Christians in general (Ac 20:32; 26:18; 1Co 1:2; Jude 1). In 1Co 7:14, the perf. tense *hēgíastai*, has been sanctified, refers to an unbelieving husband or wife who is sanctified by a believing spouse and is to be regarded, not as unclean or as an idolater, but as belonging to the Christian community.

(II) To consecrate, devote, set apart from a common to a sacred use since in the Jewish ritual, this was one great object of the purifications:

(A) Spoken of things (Mt 23:17; 23:19; 2Ti 2:21; Sept.: Le 8:10f., 30).

(B) Spoken of persons: to consecrate as being set apart of God and sent by Him for the performance of His will (Jn 10:36, "whom the father hath sanctified, and sent into the world"; 17:17, "Sanctify them through [or in the promulgation of] thy truth" [cf. Jn 17:18, 19]).

(III) To regard and venerate as holy, to hallow (Mt 6:9; Lk 11:2; 1Pe 3:15; Sept.: Isa 8:13; 10:17; 29:23). Thus the verb *hagiázō*, to sanctify, when its object is something that is filthy or common, can only be accomplished by separation (*aphorízō* [873]) or withdrawal. It also refers to the withdrawal from fellowship with the world and selfishness by gaining fellowship with God.

Deriv.: *hagiasmós* (38), sanctification.

38. ἁγιασμός, hagiasmos, *hag-ee-as-mos´*; from 37; properly *purification*, i.e. (the state) *purity*; concrete (by Hebrew) a *purifier:*—holiness, sanctification.

Noun from *hagiázō* (37), to sanctify. Sanctification, translated "holiness" (Ro 6:19, 22; 1Th 4:7; 1Ti 2:15; Heb 12:14). Separation unto God (in 1Co 1:30, cause or author of sanctification; 2Th 2:13, "sanctification of the Spirit," meaning produced by the Holy Spirit; 1Pe 1:2). The resultant state, the behaviour befitting those so separated (1Th 4:3, 4, resulting in abstention from fornication). There are two other Gr. words which are translated "holiness" but they must be distinguished from *hagiasmós*, sanctification. They are *hagiótēs* (41), the attribute of holiness, and *hagiōsúnē* (42), the state of being sanctified, i.e. sanctification not as a process but as the result of a process. *Hagiasmós* is similar to *dikaíōsis* (1347), justification, which denotes not only the act of God's free grace in justifying sinners, but also the result of that justification upon the sinner in making him just and equipping him to recognize the rights of God on his life. *Hagiasmós* refers not only to the activity of the Holy Spirit in setting man apart unto salvation and transferring him into the ranks of the redeemed, but also to enabling him to be holy even as God is holy (2Th 2:13).

Syn.: *hosiótēs* (3742), the quality of ceremo-nial conformity; *eusébeia* (2150), piety, godliness; *eilikríneia* (1505), sincerity.

39. ἅγιον, hagion, *hag´-ee-on*; neuter of 40; a *sacred* thing (i.e. spot):—holiest (of all), holy place, sanctuary.

Neuter of the adj. *hágios* (40), holy. Used of those structures set apart for God:

(I) Generally (Ac 6:13; 21:28; Heb 9:1).

(II) Specifically, the sanctuary of the temple of Jerusalem, either terrestrial (Heb 9:2), or heavenly (Heb 9:8, 12, 24; 10:19). Also, *tá hágia hagíōn*, the holy of holies, the inner sanctuary (Heb 9:3).

Syn.: *naós* (3485), the inner part of the temple in Jerusalem; *hierón* (2411), a sacred place, the entire area of the temple.

40. ἅγιος, hagios, *hag´-ee-os*; from ἅγος, *hagos* (an *awful* thing) [compare 53, 2282]; *sacred* (physical *pure*, moral *blameless* or *religious*, ceremony *consecrated*):—(most) holy (one, thing), saint.

Adjective from *hágos* (n.f.), any matter of religious awe, expiation, sacrifice. Primarily, pure, clean, including the notion of respect and veneration. Holy.

(I) Pure, clean, i.e. ceremonially or morally clean, including the idea of deserved respect, reverence:

(A) Particularly, perfect, without blemish (Ro 12:1).

(B) Metaphorically, morally pure, upright, blameless in heart and life, virtuous, holy: (1) Generally (Mk 6:20; Ro 7:12; 1Co 7:34; Eph 1:4; 5:27; 1Pe 1:16; Sept.: Le 11:44). (2) Spoken of those who are purified and sanctified by the influences of the Spirit, a saint. This is assumed of all who profess the Christian name, hence *hágios*, saint, *hágioi*, saints, Christians (Ac 9:13, 14, 32, 41; 26:10; Ro 1:7; 8:27; 1Th 3:13). Spoken of those who are to be in any way included in the Christian community (1Co 7:14).

(II) Consecrated, devoted, sacred, holy, i.e. set apart from a common to a sacred use; spoken of places, temples, cities, the priesthood, men (Mt 4:5; 7:6; 24:15; 27:53; Ac 6:13; 7:33; 1Pe 2:5); of persons (Lk 2:23; Ro 11:16); of apostles (Eph 3:5); of prophets (Lk 1:70; Ac 3:21; 2Pe 1:21); of angels (Mt 25:31).

(III) Holy, hallowed, worthy of reverence and veneration. Spoken of God (Jn 17:11; Rev 4:8;

6:10; Sept.: Isa 5:16; 6:3); of His Name (Lk 1:49; Sept.: Le 22:2); of the Holy Spirit (Mt 1:18); of holy covenant (Lk 1:72); of the Holy Scriptures (Ro 1:2; Sept.: Da 11:28, 30).

Deriv.: *hagiázō* (37), to sanctify; *hagiótēs* (41), holiness; *hagiōsúnē* (42), holiness, the quality of sanctification.

Syn.: *hieroprepés* (2412), a fitting sanctity; *eusebēs* (2152), godly, pious; *hósios* (3741), pure from evil contact, ceremonially pure; *áspilos* (784), without spot; *hierós* (2413), sacred, outwardly associated with God; *eilikrinēs* (1506), sincere, pure.

41. ἁγιότης, hagiotēs, *hag-ee-ot´-ace*; from 40; *sanctity* (i.e. properly the state):—holiness.

Noun from *hágios* (40), holy. Holiness. In the NT, used figuratively: sanctity of living, virtue, holiness. Only in Heb 12:10.

Syn.: *hagiōsúnē* (42), the attribute of holiness.

42. ἁγιωσύνη, hagiōsunē, *hag-ee-o-soo´-nay*; from 40; *sacredness* (i.e. properly the quality):—holiness.

Noun from *hágios* (40), holy. Sanctity, virtue (2Co 7:1; 1Th 3:13); the state of him who is deserving of veneration and worship, i.e. sanctity, majesty (Ro 1:4, speaking of Christ's spiritual state of exultation and majesty as Messiah, in contrast to *sárka* [*sárx* {4561} flesh] in the preceding verse).

Syn.: *hagiasmós* (38), sanctification; *hosiótēs* (41), the quality of ceremonial compliance; *eusébeia* (2150), piety, godliness.

43. ἀγκάλη, agkalē, *ang-kal´-ay*; from **ἄγκος, agkos** (a *bend*, "ache"); an *arm* (as *curved*):—arm.

44. ἄγκιστρον, agkistron, *ang´-kis-tron*; from the same as 43; a *hook* (as *bent*):—hook.

45. ἄγκυρα, agkura, *ang´-koo-rah*; from the same as 43; an "*anchor*" (as *crooked*):—anchor.

46. ἄγναφος, agnaphos, *ag´-naf-os*; from 1 (as a negative particle) and the same as 1102; properly *unfulled*, i.e. (by implication) *new* (cloth):—new.

47. ἁγνεία, hagneia, *hag-ni´-ah*; from 53; *cleanliness* (the quality), i.e. (special) *chastity*:—purity.

Noun from *hagnós* (53), pure from defilement, not contaminated. Purity, referring to chastity. Used only in 1Ti 4:12; 5:2.

Syn.: *katharótēs* (2514), the state of remaining clean; *katharismós* (2512), the act or process of cleansing, corresponding to *hagnismós* (49), ceremonial purification.

48. ἁγνίζω, hagnizo, *hag-nid´-zo*; from 53; to *make clean*, i.e. (figurative) *sanctify* (ceremony or moral):—purify (self).

From *hagnós* (53), pure. To make clean, purify.

(I) To consecrate, purify (Jn 11:55, to prepare one's self by purification for the sacred festivals, which was done by visiting the temple, offering up prayers, abstaining from certain kinds of food, washing the clothes, bathing, shaving the head, etc. [cf. Sept.: Ex 19:10, 14ff.; 2Ch 29:16, 18]).

(II) It is used in the middle, *hagnízomai*, perf. and aor. pass. *hḗgnismai, hḗgnísthēn* with middle meaning to live as one under a vow of abstinence, i.e. like a Nazarite (Ac 21:24, 26; 24:18). The Jews were accustomed, when under a vow of this kind, to abstain for a certain time from the better kinds of food, to let their hair grow, to keep themselves from all pollution, and so forth. When this time had expired, they were freed from the obligation of their vow by a particular sacrifice (Nu 6:2–21).

(III) Metaphorically, to render pure in a moral sense, to reform (Jas 4:8; 1Pe 1:22; 1Jn 3:3).

Deriv.: *hagnismós* (49), ceremonial purification.

Syn.: *katharízō* (2511), to cleanse; *kathaírō* (2508), to cleanse, purge; *ekkathaírō* (1571), to cleanse out, purge from; *diakatharízō* (1245), to cleanse thoroughly.

49. ἁγνισμός, hagnismos, *hag-nis-mos´*; from 48; a *cleansing* (the act), i.e. (ceremony) *lustration*:—purification.

Noun from *hagnízō* (48), to consecrate. Act of consecration, purification of the Levites (Nu 8:7; 31:23; see 6:9–13). In the NT, religious abstinence in consequence of a vow. Only in Ac 21:26.

Syn.: *katharismós* (2512), the act of cleansing; *katharótēs* (2514), the result or state of cleansing.

50. ἀγνοέω, agnoeō, *ag-no-eh´-o*; from 1 (as a negative particle) and 3539; *not to know* (through lack of information or intelligence); (by implication) to *ignore* (through disinclination):—(be) ignorant (-ly), not know, not understand, unknown.

From the priv. *a* (1), not, and *noéō* (3539), to perceive, understand. Not to recognize or know.

(I) To be ignorant of, unacquainted with (Ac 17:23; Ro 6:3; 7:1; 10:3; 11:25; 2Co 2:11; Gal 1:22); spoken of voluntary ignorance (1Co 14:38), where others prefer the meaning "to act foolishly," as in Sept.: Nu 12:11; not to understand or comprehend (Mk 9:32; Lk 9:45; Ro 2:4; 10:3); not to acknowledge or receive, i.e. to reject (Ac 13:27; 17:23), pass. unknown, i.e. rejected (2Co 6:9).

(II) To sin, to do wrong, originally with the idea of its being done ignorantly and involuntarily, but in the NT this idea no longer remains (Heb 5:2, those who commit sin; 2Pe 2:12, things they know not).

Deriv.: *agnóēma* (51), mistake, oversight, sin resulting from ignorance; *ágnoia* (52), ignorance.

Syn.: *lanthánō* (2990), to be hidden, concealed, unknown.

51. ἀγνόημα, agnoēma, *ag-no´-ay-mah*; from 50; a thing *ignored*, i.e. *shortcoming*:—error.

Noun from *agnoéō* (50) not to know, ignore. Error, ignorance, involuntary error (Sept.: Ge 43:12). In the NT, sin, error. Only in Heb 9:7.

Syn.: *hamartía* (266), sin.

52. ἄγνοια, agnoia, *ag´-noy-ah*; from 50; *ignorance* (properly the quality):—ignorance.

Noun from *agnoéō* (50), not to know. Want of knowledge, ignorance (Ac 3:17). Spoken of ignorance of God and divine things (Ac 17:30; Eph 4:18; 1Pe 1:14).

53. ἀγνός, hagnos, *hag-nos´*; from the same as 40; properly *clean*, i.e. (figurative) *innocent, modest, perfect*:—chaste, clean, pure.

Adjective. Akin to *hágios* (40), holy. Pure, clean. In the NT, used figuratively:

(I) Pure, perfect, holy. Of God (1Jn 3:3); of His wisdom (Jas 3:17; Sept.: Ps 12:1; 19:11).

(II) Innocent, blameless (2Co 7:11; Php 4:8; 1Ti 5:22).

(III) Modest, chaste (2Co 11:2; Tit 2:5; 1Pe 3:2).

Deriv.: *hagneía* (47), purity, cleanliness; *hagnízō* (48), to make clean, purify; *hagnótēs* (54), cleanness, pureness; *hagnós* (55), purely, sincerely.

Syn.: *alēthinós* (228), true; *gnésios* (1103), genuine; *apseudés* (893), true; *ádolos* (97), unadulterated; *katharós* (2513), clean; *amíantos* (283), undefiled; *áspilos* (784), unspotted; *haploús* (573), single, clear; *eilikrinés* (1506), sincere; *akéraios* (185), harmless, innocent; *ádolos* (97), without deceit.

54. ἀγνότης, hagnotēs, *hag-not´-ace*; from 53; *cleanness* (the state), i.e. (figurative) *blamelessness*:—pureness.

Noun from *hagnós* (53), pure. Purity, sincerity (2Co 6:6). In 2Co 11:3 UBS *hagnótēs* occurs with *haplótēs* (572), sincerity, simpleness, the opposite of duplicity, whereas the TR has only *haplótēs*. *Haplótēs* refers to sincerity, *eilikríneia* (1505), as part of the character of a person and not necessarily its influence on others.

Syn.: *hagneía* (47), purity; *katharótēs* (2514), cleanness, purification.

55. ἀγνῶς, hagnos, *hag-noce´*; adverb from 53; *purely*, i.e. *honestly*:—sincerely.

Adverb from *hagnós* (53), chaste. Purely, sincerely. In Php 1:16, it refers to the simplicity of spirit with the absence of selfish motives. Therefore, *hagnós* can really mean without duplicity.

Syn.: *haplós* (5740), simply, without duplicity).

56. ἀγνωσία, agnōsia, *ag-no-see´-ah*; from 1 (as negative particle) and 1108; *ignorance* (properly the state):—ignorance, not the knowledge.

Noun from the priv. *a* (1), without, and *gnósis* (1108), knowledge. Ignorance. In Class. Gr., it meant not being acquainted with something. In the NT, used figuratively: willful ignorance, blindness (1Co 15:34, contempt of God [cf. Eph 2:12; 1Pe 2:15; Sept.: Job 35:16]).

Syn.: *ágnoia* (52), ignorance.

57. ἄγνωστος, agnōstos, *ag´-noce-tos*; from 1 (as negative particle) and 1110; *unknown*:—unknown.

Adjective from the priv. *a* (1), not, and *gnōstós* (1110), known. Unknown (Ac 17:23).

Syn.: *apókruphos* (614), hidden, kept secret; *kruptós* (2927), private, concealed secret; *ádēlos*

(82), indistinct, uncertain; *aphanḗs* (852), unapparent; *árrētos* (731), unsaid, unspeakable, inexpressible.

58. ἀγορά, agora, *ag-or-ah´*; from ἀγείρω, *ageiro* (to *gather*; probably akin to 1453); properly the *town-square* (as a place of public resort); (by implication) a *market* or *thoroughfare*:—market (-place), street.

Noun from *ageírō* (n.f.), to collect, gather. A place in which the people assemble, assembly.

(I) The place of meeting, a public place, a broad street, and so forth (Mt 11:16; 20:3; 23:7; Mk 6:56; 12:38; Lk 7:32; 11:43; 20:46; see Sept.: Ecc 12:4, 5).

(II) A forum, a marketplace where things were exposed for sale and where assemblies and public trials were held (Mk 7:4; Ac 16:19; 17:17).

Deriv.: *agorázō* (59), to buy; *agoraíos* (60), relating to the marketplace, a vulgar person.

Syn.: *plateía* (4113), broadway, square; *ámphodon* (296), an open place where two streets meet, the open street.

59. ἀγοράζω, agorazō, *ag-or-ad´-zo*; from 58; properly to *go to market*, i.e. (by implication) to *purchase*; specially to *redeem*:—buy, redeem.

From *agorá* (58), marketplace. To buy, to purchase:

(I) Particularly (Mt 13:44, 46; 14:15; 25:9, 10; 27:7; Mk 6:36, 37; 15:46; 16:1; Lk 9:13; 14:18, 19; 22:36; Jn 4:8; 6:5; Sept.: Ge 41:57; Isa 24:2).

(II) Metaphorically, to redeem, to acquire for one's self by a ransom or price paid; in the NT, spoken of those whom Christ has redeemed by his blood from the bondage of sin and death (1Co 6:20; 7:23; 2Pe 2:1; Rev 14:3, 4).

Deriv.: *exagorázō* (1805), to buy out, especially to purchase a slave for his freedom.

Syn.: *ōnéomai* (5608), to buy; *emporeúomai* (1710), to trade, both buying and selling; *ktáomai* (2932), to obtain; *peripoiéō* (4046), to gain, possess, purchase; *lutróō* (3084), to release on receipt of ransom, redeem.

60. ἀγοραῖος, agoraios, *ag-or-ah´-yos*; from 58; *relating to the market-place*, i.e. *forensic* (times); (by implication) *vulgar*:—baser sort, low.

61. ἄγρα, agra, *ag´-rah*; from 71; (abstract) a *catching* (of fish); also (concrete) a *haul* (of fish):—draught.

62. ἀγράμματος, agrammatos, *ag-ram-mat-os*; from 1 (as negative particle) and 1121; *unlettered*, i.e. *illiterate*:—unlearned.

63. ἀγραυλέω, agrauleō, *ag-row-leh´-o*; from 68 and 832 (in the sense of 833); to *camp out*:—abide in the field.

64. ἀγρεύω, agreuō, *ag-rew-´o*; from 61; to *hunt*, i.e. (figurative) to *entrap*:—catch.

65. ἀγριέλαιος, agrielaios, *ag-ree-el´-ah-yos*; from 66 and 1636; an *oleaster*:—olive tree (which is) wild.

66. ἄγριος, agrios, *ag´-ree-os*; from 68; *wild* (as pertaining to the *country*), literal (*natural*) or figurative (*fierce*):—wild, raging.

67. Ἀγρίππας, Agrippas, *ag-rip´-pas*; apparently from 66 and 2462; *wild-horse* tamer; *Agrippas*, one of the Herods:—Agrippa.

68. ἀγρός, agros, *ag-ros´*; from 71; a *field* (as a *drive* for cattle); generically the *country*; specially a *farm*, i.e. *hamlet*:—country, farm, piece of ground, land.

69. ἀγρυπνέω, agrupneō, *ag-roop-neh´-o*; ultimately from 1 (as negative particle) and 5258; to *be sleepless*, i.e. *keep awake*:—watch.

70. ἀγρυπνία, agrupnia, *ag-roop-nee´-ah*; from 69; *sleeplessness*, i.e. a *keeping awake*:—watch.

71. ἄγω, agō, *ag´-o*; a primary verb; properly to *lead*; (by implication) to *bring*, *drive*, (reflexive) *go*, (special) *pass* (time), or (figurative) *induce*:—be, bring (forth), carry, (let) go, keep, lead away, be open.

To lead, lead along, bring, carry, remove.

(I) Transitively or in an absolute sense, to lead, conduct, bring:

(A) Used in a variety of modifications which are determined by adjuncts. (1) *Ágō éxō* (1854) out, to lead out, bring forth (Jn 19:4, 13). (2) Followed by *héōs* (2193), until (Lk 4:29; Ac 17:15). (3) Used with *epí* (1909), upon, with the accusative of person or place, to lead or conduct, bring before (Mt 10:18; Lk 21:12; 23:1; Ac 17:19; 18:12; Sept.: Ex 22:13; Jer 25:9; Eze 43:1).

See in Ac 8:32, *epí sphagḗn* (*sphagḗn* [4967], slaughter), for the purpose of slaughtering, in fulfillment of Isa 53:7. **(4)** Followed by *hṓde* (5602), hither, to bring hither (Lk 19:27; Sept.: Jgs 18:3). **(5)** To lead or bring to anyone, followed by *prós* (4314), toward (Lk 4:40; 18:40; 19:35; Jn 1:42; 8:3; 9:13; Ac 9:27; 23:18; Sept.: Ge 2:19, 22). Used in the same sense with the dat. in Mt 21:2, *agageté moi*, bring to me. The verb is also used by itself in the same sense as to bring (Mt 21:7; Mk 11:2, 7; Lk 19:30; Jn 7:45; 10:16; Ac 5:21, 26, 27; 19:37; 20:12; 25:6, 17, 23). **(6)** To bring with one (Ac 21:16, "brought with them one Mnason of Cyprus"; 1Th 4:14, "will God bring with him" meaning into heaven, see 1Th 4:17; 2Ti 4:11, "bring him with thee"). **(7)** To lead out or away; either simply (Mk 13:11; Lk 22:54; 23:32); or followed by *eis* (1519), unto, with the accusative of place, and so forth, lead away to, conduct to (Lk 4:1, 9; 10:34; Jn 18:28; Ac 6:12; 9:2; 11:26; 21:34; 22:5; 23:10, 31). In Ac 17:5, "to bring them out to the people"; Heb 2:10, "unto glory." Followed by *epí* (1909), upon, unto (Ac 9:21, "bring them bound unto the chief priests"). **(8)** Similar to the Hebrew *bō* (935, OT), to bring forth, i.e. to cause to come, cause to arise as in Ac 13:23 UBS, "raised unto Israel a Saviour, Jesus," instead of *égeire*, the aor. of *egeírō* (1453), to raise, as in the TR. Also Sept.: Isa 46:11; Zec 3:8.

(B) Metaphorically, to lead, induce, incite, guide (Ro 2:4, "to repentance"; 1Co 12:2, "even as ye were led," meaning to idolatry, the figure being drawn from pastoral life [cf. Ex 3:1; Isa 11:6]). Also, to be led by the Spirit of God (Ro 8:14; Gal 5:18); by lusts (2Ti 3:6).

(II) Transitively spoken of time:

(A) To pass, to spend. Lk 24:21, "today is the third day," where *ágei* is either impersonal or the word *chrónos* (5550), time, is implied.

(B) To celebrate, hold, e.g., a birthday (Mt 14:6); judicial days (Ac 19:38), which were held in the marketplace; see Sept.: Est 9:18, 19, 21, 22.

(III) Intransitively or reflexively, to go, depart, with *hēmás heautoús* implied meaning "Let us go" (Mk 14:42 [cf. Mt 26:46; Jn 11:16]). Followed by *enteúthen* (1782), hence, from here (Jn 14:31); followed by *eis* (1519), unto (Mk 1:38; Jn 11:7); followed by *prós* (4314), toward (Jn 11:15).

Deriv.: *agélē* (34), a herd; *agōgḗ* (72), course

of life, manner of leading or spending it; *anágō* (321), to bring, lead, carry, or take up; *áxios* (514), to estimate or value; *apágō* (520), to lead, carry or take away; *diágō* (1236), to lead one's life, to live; *doulagōgéō* (1396), to bring into subjection; *eiságō* (1521), to bring in, introduce; *exágō* (1806), to lead forth or bring out; *epágō* (1863), to bring upon; *hēgéomai* (2233), to lead, consider; *katágō* (2609), to bring down; *metágō* (3329), to turn about; *parágō* (3855), to depart, pass away; *periágō* (4013), to lead about; *proágō* (4254), to go before, lead, precede; *proságō* (4317), to bring or come to, to bring; *stratēgós* (4755), the leader, commander of an army; *sulagōgéō* (4812), to lead off as prey; *sunágō* (4863), to bring together, assemble; *hupágō* (5217), to depart, go away; *chalinagōgéō* (5468), to bridle; *cheiragōgós* (5497), one who leads another by the hand.

Syn.: *phérō* (5342), to carry, bear, lead; *hodēgéō* (3594), to lead the way, guide; *komízō* (2865), to receive, bring in; *aírō* (142), to take away; *anaphérō* (399), to offer up; *eisphérō* (1533), to carry or bring in.

72. ἀγωγή, agōgē, *ag-o-gay´*; reduplication from 71; a *bringing* up, i.e. *mode of living*:— manner of life.

73. ἀγών, agōn, *ag-one´*; from 71; properly a place of *assembly* (as if *led*), i.e. (by implication) a *contest* (held there); (figurative) an *effort* or *anxiety*:—conflict, contention, fight, race.

A noun meaning place of assembly, where games were often celebrated; a stadium, course, place of contest. In the NT:

(1) Metaphorically, a stadium, a place of contest, used to mean a course of life full of toil and conflict (Heb 12:1).

(II) A contest, combat; particularly a conflict in the public games. In the NT, metaphorically, spoken of unwearied zeal in promoting the spread of the gospel; generally (1Ti 6:12; 2Ti 4:7), and with the accessory idea of peril, toil, affliction (Php 1:30; Col 2:1; 1Th 2:2 [cf. Mt 26:37, 38; Jn 12:27]).

Deriv.: *agōnía* (74), agony; verb: *agōnízomai* (75), to contend.

Syn.: *áthlēsis* (119), combat, contest of athletes, a struggle or fight; *pólemos* (4171), war; *máchē* (3163), a fight, strife; *pálē* (3823), wrestling; *kópos* (2873), labour, weariness; *móch-*

thos (3449), painfulness, travail; *talaipōría* (5004), misery.

74. ἀγωνία, agōnia, *ag-o-nee´-ah*; from 73; a *struggle* (properly the state), i.e. (figurative) *anguish*:—agony.

Noun from *agṓn* (73), contest. In the NT, used metaphorically for anguish, agony, or perturbation of mind (Lk 22:44).

Syn.: *stenochōría* (4730), anguish, distress; *sunochḗ* (4928), anxiety, anguish; *phóbos* (5401), fear; *tarachḗ* (5016), disturbance, trouble; *súgchusis* (4799), riotous disturbance, confusion; *thórubos* (2351), disturbance, uproar; *anágkē* (318), distress.

75. ἀγωνίζομαι, agōnizomai, *ag-o-nid´-zom-ahee*; from 73; to *struggle*, literally (to *compete* for a prize), figurativ (to *contend* with an adversary), or genitive (to *endeavour* to accomplish something):—fight, labour fervently, strive.

From *agṓn* (73), conflict. To be a combatant in the public games (1Co 9:25); to fight, to contend with an adversary (Jn 18:36); to exert oneself, to strive earnestly (Lk 13:24; Col 1:29; 4:12); also used metaphorically, with the idea of labour and toil in behalf of the cause of Christ (1Ti 6:12; 2Ti 4:7).

Deriv.: *antagōnízomai* (464), to antagonize, strive against; *epagō-nízomai* (1864), to contend; *katagōnízomai* (2610), to subdue; *sunagō-nízomai* (4865), to struggle in company with, strive together with.

Syn.: *epilambánomai* (1949), to lay hold upon, take hold of, help; *kópiáō* (2872), to toil, feel fatigue; *ergázomai* (2038), to work; *kóptomai* (2875), to beat the breast in grief, lament; *máchomai* (3164), to fight, strive; *poleméō* (4170), to carry on a war, fight; *athléō* (118), to contend in competitive games, strive; *strateúomai* (4754), to contend, be a soldier, go to war; *hoplízomai* (3695), to equip with weapons, arm oneself.

76. Ἀδάμ, Adam, *ad-am´*; of Hebrew origin [121]; *Adam*, the first man; typical (of Jesus) *man* (as his representative):—Adam.

77. ἀδάπανος, adapanos, *ad-ap´-an-os*; from 1 (as negative particle) and 1160; *costless*, i.e. *gratuitous*:—without expense.

78. Ἀδδί, Addi, *ad-dee´*; probably of Hebrew origin [compare 5716]; *Addi*, an Israelite:—Addi.

79. ἀδελφή, adelphē, *ad-el-fay´*; feminine of 80; a *sister* (native or ecclesiastical):—sister.

80. ἀδελφός, adelphos, *ad-el-fos´*; from 1 (as a connective particle) and δελφύς, *delphus* (the *womb*); a *brother* (literal or figurative) near or remote [much like 1]:—brother.

Noun from the collative *a* (1), denoting unity, and *delphús* (n.f.), a womb.

(I) A brother, whether derived from the same father (Mt 1:2; Lk 3:1, 19) or also born of the same mother (Lk 6:14).

(II) Metaphorically, one who is connected with another in any kind of intimacy or fellowship:

(A) A near relative, a kinsman by blood, cousin (Mt 12:46; Jn 7:3; Ac 1:14; Gal 1:19; Sept.: Ge 13:8; 14:16).

(B) One born in the same country, descended from the same stock; a fellow countryman (Mt 5:47; Ac 3:22; Heb 7:5; Sept.: Ex 2:11; 4:18).

(C) One of equal rank and dignity (Mt 23:8; cf. Sept.: Pr 18:9).

(D) Spoken of disciples, followers, etc. (Mt 25:40; Heb 2:11, 12).

(E) One of the same faith, a fellow Christian (Ac 9:30; 1Co 5:11).

(F) An associate, colleague, in office or dignity (1Co 1:1; 2Co 1:1; 2:12; Sept.: Ezr 3:2).

(G) One of the same nature, fellow man (Mt 5:22–24; 7:5; Heb 2:17; 8:11; Sept.: Ge 13:11; 26:31).

(H) By implication, one beloved as a brother (Ac 2:29; 6:3; 1Th 5:1).

Deriv.: *adelphótēs* (81), brotherhood; *philádelphos* (5361), one who loves his brother; *pseudádelphos* (5569), false brother.

Syn.: *súntrophos* (4939), companion; *suggenḗs* (4773), relative.

81. ἀδελφότης, adelphotēs, *ad-el-fot´-ace*; from 80; *brotherhood* (properly the feeling of *brotherliness*), i.e. the (Christian) *fraternity*:—brethren, brotherhood.

Noun from *adelphós* (80), brother. Brotherly affection. In the NT, a fraternity, the Christian brotherhood (1Pe 2:17; 5:9).

82. ἄδηλος, adēlos, *ad´-ay-los*; from 1 (as a negative particle) and 1212; *hidden*, (figurative) *indistinct*:—appear not, uncertain.

83. ἀδηλότης, adēlotēs, *ad-ay-lot´-ace*; from 82; *uncertainty*:— × uncertain.

84. ἀδήλως, adēlōs, *ad-ay´-loce*; adverb from 82; *uncertainly*:—uncertainly.

85. ἀδημονέω, adēmoneō, *ad-ay-mon-eh´-o*; from a derivative of **ἀδέω, adeō** (to be *sated* to loathing); to *be in distress* (of mind):—be full of heaviness, be very heavy.

86. ᾅδης, haidēs, *hah´-dace*; from 1 (as a negative particle) and 1492; properly *unseen*, i.e. "*Hades*" or the place (state) of departed souls:—grave, hell.

Noun from the priv. *a* (1), not, and *ideín*, the inf. of the 2d aor. *eídō* (1492), to see. What is in darkness; hence in Class. Gr., orcus, the infernal regions. Used very frequently in the Sept. to translate the Heb še'ôl ([7585, OT] e.g., Sept.: Isa 14:9). So also in the NT, the abode or world of the dead, hades, orcus. According to the notions of the Hebrews, hades was a vast subterranean receptacle where the souls of the dead existed in a separate state until the resurrection of their bodies. The region of the blessed during this interval, the inferior paradise, they supposed to be in the upper part of this receptacle; while beneath was the abyss or Gehenna, Tartarus, in which the souls of the wicked were subjected to punishment.

(**I**) Generally (Ac 2:27, 31; Rev 1:18). In this sense *hádēs* is personified (1Co 15:55; Rev 6:8; 20:13, 14). In a metaphorical sense, to be cast down to the very lowest place (Mt 11:23; Lk 10:15).

(**II**) By metonymy of the whole for a part, the abyss of hades, place of punishment (Lk 16:23).

Syn.: *Géenna* (1067), the final destiny of the wicked, hell; *tartaróō* (5020), the prison of the fallen angels or evil spirits; *ábussos* (12), abyss, the place where the dragon (*drákōn* [1404]), i.e. Satan, is bound during the millennial reign (cf. Lk 8:31; Rev 9:11); *límnē* (3041) and *toú purós* (4442), lake of fire, the place into which the beast and the false prophet are cast after their defeat by Christ. An additional statement in Rev 21:8 describes those who have their part in the lake of fire, compare the description of those who are outside the city (Rev 22:15).

87. ἀδιάκριτος, adiakritos, *ad-ee-ak´-ree-tos*; from 1 (as a negative particle) and a derivative of 1252; properly *undistinguished*, i.e. (active) *impartial*:—without partiality.

Adjective from *a* (1), without, and *diakrínō* (1252), to separate, distinguish, judge. Indistinguishable. In the NT, used metaphorically: not open to distinction or doubt, unambiguous. Only in Jas 3:17, translated "without partiality."

Syn.: *díkaios* (1342), just.

88. ἀδιάλειπτος, adialeiptos, *ad-ee-al´-ipe-tos*; from 1 (as a negative particle) and a derivative of a compound of 1223 and 3007; *unintermitted*, i.e. *permanent*:—without ceasing, continual.

89. ἀδιαλείπτως, adialeiptōs, *ad-ee-al-ipe´-toce*; adverb from 88; *uninterruptedly*, i.e. *without omission* (on an appropriate occasion):—without ceasing.

90. ἀδιαφθορία, adiaphthoria, *ad-ee-af-thor-ee´-ah*; from a derivative of a compound of 1 (as a negative particle) and a derivative of 1311; *incorruptibleness*, i.e. (figurative) *purity* (of doctrine):—uncorruptness.

91. ἀδικέω, adikeō, *ad-ee-keh´-o*; from 94; to *be unjust*, i.e. (active) *do wrong* (moral, socially or physical):—hurt, injure, be an offender, be unjust, (do, suffer, take) wrong.

From *ádikos* (94), unjust. To do wrong, to act unjustly; to hurt, damage, harm.

(**I**) To do wrong:

(**A**) In respect to law, to break the law, to transgress (Ac 25:10, 11; 2Co 7:12; Col 3:25; Rev 22:11; Sept.: 1Ki 8:47; 2Ch 26:16; Ps 106:6; Jer 37:18).

(**B**) In respect to others, to wrong, to injure (Mt 20:13; Ac 7:26, 27; 1Co 6:8; 2Co 7:2; Gal 4:12; Phm 18). In a pass. sense, to be wronged, to suffer wrong or injury (Ac 7:24; 2Co 7:12). In the middle voice, to suffer one's self to be wronged (1Co 6:7).

(**II**) By metonymy, to hurt, damage, harm (Lk 10:19; Rev 2:11; 6:6; 7:2, 3; 9:4, 10, 19; 11:5; Sept.: Le 6:2; Isa 3:15; 10:20; 51:23).

Deriv.: *adíkēma* (92), a misdeed, an injury.

Syn.: *bláptō* (984), to injure, damage; *kakóō* (2559), to harm; *kakouchéō* (2558), to mistreat; *parabaínō* (3845), to transgress; *paranoméō*

(3891), to act contrary to law; *zēmióō* (2210), to suffer loss; *lumaínomai* (3705), to cause havoc; *páschō* (3958), to suffer.

92. ἀδίκημα, adikēma, *ad-eek´-ay-mah*; from 91; a *wrong* done:—evil doing, iniquity, matter of wrong.

Noun from *adikéō* (91), to act unjustly. Wrong, transgression, iniquity (Ac 18:14; 24:20; Rev 18:5; Sept.: 1Sa 20:1; 26:18; 2Sa 22:49; Isa 59:12).

Syn.: *adikía* (93), wrong, the act of injustice; *húbris* (5196), injurious treatment, hurt; *tó kakón* (the neuter of *kakós* [2556] with the article), an evil thing, harm; *anomía* (458), violation of law.

93. ἀδικία, adikia, *ad-ee-kee´-ah*; from 94; (legal) *injustice* (properly, the quality; by implication, the act); moral *wrongfulness* (of character, life or act):—iniquity, unjust, unrighteousness, wrong.

Noun from *ádikos* (94), unjust. Injustice.

(I) Wrong, injustice, unrighteousness: generally (Lk 18:6; Ro 9:14); as done to others, wrong, injury (2Co 12:13; Sept.: Ps 7:3; Mic 3:10).

(II) As related to *dikaiosúnē* (1343), righteousness, which is often used to describe character of life, *adikía* takes by antithesis the sense of impropriety, iniquity, unrighteousness, wickedness (Lk 13:27; Ac 1:18; Ro 1:29; 3:5; 6:13; 2Ti 2:19; Heb 8:12; Jas 3:6; 2Pe 2:13; 1Jn 1:9; 5:17). This wickedness or unrighteousness is seen more particularly in the neglect of the true God and His laws and in an adherence to the world or to idolatry; hence, *adikía* may mean impiety, ungodliness, contempt of God, as opposed to *alḗtheia* ([225], truth), piety toward God. In Ro 1:18, those "who hold the truth in unrighteousness," are those who impede the worship of the true God by their obstinate adherence to worldliness or to idolatry (Ro 2:8; 2Th 2:10, 12; 2Pe 2:15).

(III) In the sense of fraud, deceit, guile (Jn 7:18); a dishonest steward (Lk 16:8); wealth fraudulently acquired (Lk 16:9).

Syn.: *hamartía* (266), sin, missing the mark, *ponēría* (4189), wickedness; *kríma* (2917), condemnation, judgement; *égklēma* (1462), crime; *anomía* (458), lawlessness; *paranomía* (3892), transgression, iniquity.

94. ἄδικος, adikos, *ad´-ee-kos*; from 1 (as a negative particle) and 1349; *unjust*; by extension *wicked*; (by implication) *treacherous*; specially *heathen*:—unjust, unrighteous.

Adjective from the priv. *a* (1), without, and *díkē* (1349), justice. Unjust.

(I) Unjust toward others (Lk 18:11; Ro 3:5; Heb 6:10)

(II) As a characteristic of life, wicked, impious, ungodly (Mt 5:45; Ac 24:15; 1Co 6:9; 1Pe 3:18; 2Pe 2:9). So also an unbeliever, a pagan (1Co 6:1).

(III) Fraudulent, false, deceitful (Lk 16:10, 11; Sept.: Dt 19:18; Jer 5:31; 29:9).

Deriv.: *adikéō* (91), to act unjustly; *adikía* (93), injustice; *adíkōs* (95), unjustly.

Syn.: *athémitos* (111), unlawful; *skoliós* (4646), warped; *dólios* (1386), deceitful; *ponērós* (4190), evil; *kakós* (2556), bad; *phaúlos* (5337), foul, trivial; *hamartōlós* (268), sinful.

95. ἀδίκως, adikōs, *ad-ee´-koce*; adverb from 94; *unjustly*:—wrongfully.

96. ἀδόκιμος, adokimos, *ad-ok´-ee-mos*; from 1 (as a negative particle) and 1384; *unapproved*, i.e. *rejected*; (by implication) *worthless* (literal or moral):—castaway, rejected, reprobate.

Adjective from the priv. *a* (1), without, and *dókimos* (1384), acceptable. Not approved, rejected. Spoken of metals (Sept.: Pr 25:4; Isa 1:22). In the NT, used metaphorically: worthy of condemnation, reprobate (Ro 1:28; 1Co 9:27; 2Co 13:5–7; 2Ti 3:8); by implication, useless, worthless (Tit 1:16; Heb 6:8).

Syn.: *anáxios* (370), unworthy; *dólios* (1386), deceitful; *pseudḗs* (5571), false; *ásēmos* (767), mean, ignoble, one not bearing the mark; *koinós* (2839), common; *eleeinós* (1652), pitiable, miserable; *apóblētos* (579), cast away, rejected one; *achreíos* (888), useless; *áchrēstos* (890), inefficient.

97. ἄδολος, adolos, *ad´-ol-os*; from 1 (as a negative particle) and 1388; *undeceitful*, i.e. (figurative) *unadulterated*:—sincere.

Adjective from the priv. *a* (1), without, and *dólos* (1388), guile. Without deceit, sincere. In the NT, used only of milk in 1Pe 2:2, meaning unadulterated, pure, genuine, metaphorically for pure doctrine.

Syn.: *alēthinós* (228), true; *apseudḗs* (893), veracious, incapable of lying; *haploús* (573), single, without duplicity; *ákakos* (172), constitutionally harmless; *akéraios* (185), without admixture; *gnḗsios* (1103), true, genuine; *eilikrinḗs* (1506), sincere; *hagnós* (53), pure, undefiled.

98. Ἀδραμυττηνός, Adramuttēnos, *ad-ram-oot-tay-nos´*; from Ἀδραμύττειον, *Adramutteion* (a place in Asia Minor); *Adramyttene* or belonging to Adramyttium:—of Adramyttium.

99. Ἀδρίας, Adrias, *ad-ree´-as*; from Ἀδρία, *Adria* (a place near its shore); the *Adriatic* sea (including the Ionian):—Adria.

100. ἁδρότης, hadrotēs, *had-rot´-ace*; from ἁδρός, *hadros* (*stout*); *plumpness*, i.e. (figurative) *liberality*:—abundance.

Noun from *hadrós* (n.f.), full-grown, ripe. Maturity, fullness. In the NT, abundance, copiousness (2Co 8:20).

Syn.: *perisseía* (4050), overflowing, and *perísseuma* (4051), abundance; *huperbolḗ* (5236), exceeding greatness; *eulogía* (2129), a blessing; *haplótēs* (572), bountifulness, liberality.

101. ἀδυνατέω, adunateō, *ad-oo-nat-eh´-o*; from 102; to *be unable*, i.e. (passive) *impossible*:—be impossible.

102. ἀδύνατος, adunatos, *ad-oo´-nat-os*; from 1 (as a negative particle) and 1415; *unable*, i.e. *weak* (literal or figurative); passive *impossible*:—could not do, impossible, impotent, not possible, weak.

103. ᾄδω, aidō, *ad´-o*; a primary verb; to *sing*:—sing.

104. ἀεί, aei, *ah-eye´*; from an obsolete primary noun (apparently meaning continued *duration*); "*ever;*" by qualification *regularly*; (by implication) *earnestly*:—always, ever.

105. ἀετός, aetos, *ah-et-os´*; from the same as 109; an *eagle* (from its *wind*-like flight):—eagle.

106. ἄζυμος, azumos, *ad´-zoo-mos*; from 1 (as a negative particle) and 2219; *unleavened*, i.e. (figurative) *uncorrupted*; (in the neuter plural) specially (by implication) the *Passover* week:—unleavened (bread).

Adjective from the priv. *a* (1), without, and *zúmē* (2219), leaven. Unleavened.

(I) Spoken of bread: unleavened cakes or bread; hence the "feast of unleavened bread" or

"day of unleavened bread," indicating the festival day or days in which the Jews were to eat unleavened bread in commemoration of their departure from Egypt, i.e. the Passover (Mt 26:17; Mk 14:1, 12; Lk 22:1, 7; Ac 12:3; 20:6).

(II) Metaphorically, unmixed, unadulterated, uncorrupted (1Co 5:7, 8).

Syn.: *alēthinós* (228), true; *gnḗsios* (1103), genuine; *apseudḗs*, (893), without falsehood; *ádolos* (97), without deceit.

107. Ἀζώρ, Azōr, *ad-zore´*; of Hebrew origin [compare 5809]; *Azor*, an Israelite:—Azor.

108. Ἄζωτος, Azōtos, *ad´-zo-tos*; of Hebrew origin [795]; *Azotus* (i.e. Ashdod), a place in Palestine:—Azotus.

109. ἀήρ, aēr, *ah-ayr´*; from ἄημι, *aēmi* (to *breathe* unconsciously, i.e. *respire*; by analogy to *blow*); "*air*" (as naturally *circumambient*):—air. Compare 5594.

110. ἀθανασία, athanasia, *ath-an-as-ee´-ah*; from a compound of 1 (as a negative particle) and 2288; *deathlessness*:—immortality.

Noun from *athánatos* (n.f.), immortal, which is from the priv. *a* (1), without, and *thánatos* (2288), death. Immortality (1Co 15:53, 54; 1Ti 6:16).

Syn.: *aphtharsía* (861) incorruptibility.

111. ἀθέμιτος, athemitos, *ath-em´-ee-tos*; from 1 (as a negative particle) and a derivative of θέμις, *themis* (*statute*; from the base of 5087); *illegal*; (by implication) *flagitious*:—abominable, unlawful thing.

Adjective from the priv. *a* (1), not, and *themitós* (n.f.), lawful. Unlawful, forbidden (Ac 10:28; 1Pe 4:3).

Syn.: *ánomos* (459), lawless; *áthesmos* (113), lawless; *bdeluktós* (947), abominable; *ádikos* (94), unjust; *ponē-rós* (4190), evil; *kakós* (2556), bad; *phaúlos* (5337), foul.

112. ἄθεος, atheos, *ath´-eh-os*; from 1 (as a negative particle) and 2316; *godless*:—without God.

Adjective from the priv. *a* (1), without, and *Theós* (2316), God. Godless, impious. In the NT, estranged from the knowledge and worship of the true God. Only in Eph 2:12.

Syn.: *asebḗs* (765), impious, ungodly; *anósios* (462), unholy, profane.

113. ἄθεσμος, **athesmos,** *ath´-es-mos*; from 1 (as a negative particle) and a derivative of 5087 (in the sense of *enacting*); *lawless,* i.e. (by implication) *criminal:*—wicked.

114. ἀθετέω, **atheteō,** *ath-et-eh´-o*; from a compound of 1 (as a negative particle) and a derivative of 5087; to *set aside,* i.e. (by implication) to *disesteem, neutralize* or *violate:*—cast off, despise, disannul, frustrate, bring to nought, reject.

115. ἀθέτησις, **athetēsis,** *ath-et´-ay-sis*; from 114; *cancellation* (literal or figurative):—disannulling, put away.

116. Ἀθῆναι, **Athēnai,** *ath-ay´-nahee*; plural of Ἀθήνη, **Athēnē** (the goddess of wisdom, who was reputed to have founded the city); *Athenæ,* the capital of Greece:—Athens.

117. Ἀθηναῖος, **Athēnaios,** *ath-ay-nah´-yos*; from 116; an *Athenæan* or inhabitant of Athenæ:—Athenian.

118. ἀθλέω, **athleō,** *ath-leh´-o*; from ἄθλος, **athlos** (a *contest* in the public lists); to *contend* in the competitive games:—strive.

119. ἄθλησις, **athlēsis,** *ath´-lay-sis*; from 118; a *struggle* (figurative):—fight.

120. ἀθυμέω, **athumeō,** *ath-oo-meh´-o*; from a compound of 1 (as a negative particle) and 2372; to *be spiritless,* i.e. *disheartened:*—be dismayed.

121. ἄθωος, **athōos,** *ath´-o-os*; from 1 (as a negative particle) and a probable derivative of 5087 (meaning a *penalty*); *not guilty:*—innocent.

122. αἴγειος, **aigeios,** *ah´ee-ghi-os*; from αἴξ, **aix** (a *goat*); belonging to a *goat:*—goat.

123. αἰγιαλός, **aigialos,** *ahee-ghee-al-os´*; from ἀΐσσω, **aïssō** (to *rush*) and 251 (in the sense of the *sea*); a *beach* (on which the *waves dash*):—shore.

124. Αἰγύπτιος, **Aiguptios,** *ahee-goop´-tee-os*; from 125; an *Ægyptian* or inhabitant of Ægyptus:—Egyptian.

125. Αἴγυπτος, **Aiguptos,** *ah´ee-goop-tos*; of uncertain derivative; *Ægyptus,* the land of the Nile:—Egypt.

126. ἀΐδιος, **aïdios,** *ah-id´-ee-os*; from 104; *everduring* (forward and backward, or forward only):—eternal, everlasting.

Adjective from *aeí* (104), ever, always. Always existing, eternal, everlasting (Ro 1:20; Jude 6).

Syn.: *aiōnios* (166), eternal, primarily without end but possibly with a beginning such as eternal life.

127. αἰδώς, **aidōs,** *ahee-doce´*; perhaps from 1 (as a negative particle) and 1492 (through the idea of *downcast* eyes); *bashfulness,* i.e. (toward men), *modesty* or (toward God) *awe:*—reverence, shamefacedness.

A noun meaning modesty (1Ti 2:9); reverence, veneration (Heb 12:28).

Syn.: *entropē* (1791), withdrawal into oneself, recoiling; *aischúnē* (152) is subjective confusion, a feeling of shame felt by oneself or by others; *eulábeia* (2124), reverence.

128. Αἰθίοψ, **Aithiops,** *ahee-thee´-ops*; from αἴθω, **Aithō** (to *scorch*) and ὤψ, **Ōps** (the *face,* from 3700); an *Æthiopian* (as a *blackamoor*):—Ethiopian.

129. αἷμα, **aima,** *hah´ee-mah*; of uncertain derivative; *blood,* literal (of men or animals), figurative (the *juice* of grapes) or special (the atoning *blood* of Christ); (by implication) *bloodshed,* also *kindred:*—blood.

A noun meaning blood, bloodshed, blood-guiltiness, blood-relationship, kindred.

(I) Blood, either human or animal:

(A) Generally (Mk 5:25, 29; Lk 8:43, 44; 13:1).

(B) Figuratively, something may be said to be or become blood, or as blood, from its dark colour (Ac 2:19; Rev 8:7, 8; 11:6).

(II) Spoken of blood which has been shed:

(A) Of victims and other slaughtered animals (Heb 9:7, 12, 13, 18–25; 10:4; 11:28; 13:11). The Jews regarded the blood as the seat and principle of life; hence they were to offer it in sacrifice to God, but were forbidden to eat it (Le 17:10–14; Dt 12:23); so James charged early Gentile believers living among the Jews (Ac 15:20, 29; 21:25).

(B) Of men: generally (Lk 13:1; Jn 19:34; Rev 14:20); of the innocent, of martyrs (Mt 23:35; 27:4; Rev 17:6).

(C) Of the blood of Christ shed on the cross: in relation to the sacred supper (Mt 26:28; Mk 14:24; Lk 22:20; 1Co 10:16; 11:25, 27; 1Jn 6:53–

58), in relation to his church (Ac 20:28; Col 1:20; Eph 2:13); to the atonement made by his death (Ro 3:25; 5:9; Eph 1:7; Heb 9:12, 14; 1Pe 1:2, 19; Rev 5:9), and to the new covenant (Heb 10:29; 12:24; 13:20).

(D) In conjunction with *sárx* ([4561], flesh), flesh and blood, i.e. the human body, mortal man (Mt 16:17; 1Co 15:50; Gal 1:16; Eph 6:12; Heb 2:14).

(E) With the verb *ekchéō* ([1632], spill, pour forth), to shed blood, i.e. to kill, put to death (Lk 11:50; Ac 22:20; Ro 3:15; Rev 16:6).

(III) By metonymy, bloodshed, i.e. death, violent death, slaughter, murder (Mt 23:30; 27:6, 8, 24; Ac 1:19; Rev 6:10; 18:24; 19:2).

(IV) From the Hebrew, blood-guiltiness, i.e. the guilt and punishment of shedding blood (Mt 23:35; 27:25; Ac 5:28; 18:6; 20:26; Sept.: Nu 35:27; Jos 2:19; Eze 9:9; 33:4; 2Sa 1:16).

(V) Figuratively, blood-relationship, kindred, lineage, progeny, seed (Jn 1:13; Ac 17:26).

Deriv.: *haimatekchusía* (130), shedding of blood; *haimorroéō* (131), to hemorrhage.

130. αἱματεκχυσία, **aihmatekchusia,** *hahee-mat-ek-khoo-see'-ah*; from 129 and a derivative of 1632; an *effusion of blood:*—shedding of blood.

Noun from *haíma* (129), blood, and *ekchéō* (1632), to pour out. Shedding of blood. Only in Heb 9:22.

131. αἱμορῥέω, **aihmorrheō,** *hahee-mor-hreh'-o*; from 129 and 4482; to *flow blood,* i.e. *have a hæmorrhage:*—diseased with an issue of blood.

132. Αἰνέας, **Aineas,** *ahee-neh'-as*; of uncertain derivative; *Æneas,* an Israelite:—Æneas.

133. αἴνεσις, **ainesis,** *ah'ee-nes-is*; from 134; a *praising* (the act), i.e. (special) a *thank* (-offering):—praise.

Noun from *ainéō* (134), to praise. The act of praise (Heb 13:15).

Syn.: *húmnos* (5215), hymn; *psalmós* (5568), a sacred ode or poem, music accompanied with the voice, harp, or other instrument; *ōdḗ* (5603), a religious metrical composition, a song; *eulogía* (2129), blessing, praise.

134. αἰνέω, **aineō,** *ahee-neh'-o*; from 136; to *praise* (God):—praise.

To praise, to celebrate. Spoken in the NT only of God (Lk 2:13, 20; 19:37; 24:53; Ac 2:47; 3:8, 9; Ro 15:11; Rev 19:5; Sept.: Ge 49:8; 1Ch 16:4, 10; Ps 100:4).

Deriv.: *aínesis* (133), the act of praise; *aínos* (136), a tale or narration which came to denote praise; *epainéō* (1867), to commend; *parainéō* (3867), to exhort, admonish.

Syn.: *humnéō* (5214), to laud, to sing a hymn; *psállō* (5567), to twitch or twang as a bowstring, to play a stringed instrument with the fingers; *eulogéō* (2127), to speak well of, praise.

135. αἴνιγμα, **ainigma,** *ah'ee-nig-ma*; from a derivative of 136 (in its primary sense); an *obscure* saying ("enigma"), i.e. (abstract) *obscureness:*—× darkly.

136. αἶνος, **ainos,** *ah'ee-nos*; apparently a primary word; properly a *story,* but used in the sense of 1868; *praise* (of God):—praise.

Noun from *ainéō* (134), to praise. Praise (Mt 21:16; Lk 18:43; Sept.: Ps 8:3).

Deriv.: *épainos* (1868), approval, commendation.

137. Αἰνών, **Ainōn,** *ahee-nohn'*; of Hebrew origin [a derivative of 5869, *place of springs*]; *Ænon,* a place in Palestine:—Ænon.

138. αἱρέομαι, **aihreomai,** *hahee-reh'-om-ahee*; probably akin to 142; to *take for oneself,* i.e. to *prefer:*—choose. Some of the forms are borrowed from a cognate ἕλλομαι, **hellomai,** *hel'-lom-ahee*; which is otherwise obsolete.

To take. In the NT, only in the middle: to take for oneself, i.e. to choose, elect, prefer (Php 1:22; 2Th 2:13; Heb 11:25; Sept.: 2Sa 15:15; Job 34:42).

Deriv.: *haíresis* (139), heresy; *hairetízō* (140), to choose, akin to *hairetós,* that which may be taken; *hairetikós* (141), heretic; *anairéō* (337), to take up or away, abolish; *authaíretos* (830), of one's own accord; *aphairéō* (851), to take away; *diairéō* (1244), to separate, divide, distribute; *exairéō* (1807), to tear out, to select, to release, deliver, pluck out, rescue; *kathairéō* (2507), to take down; *periairéō* (4014), to take away that which surrounds; *proairéomai* (4255), prefer, propose, intend, purpose.

Syn.: *eklégomai* (1586), to choose out, elect; *epilégomai* (1951), to be called or named.

139. αἵρεσις, hairesis, *hah´ee-res-is*; from 138; properly a *choice*, i.e. (special) a *party* or (abstract) *disunion:*—heresy [*which is the Greek word itself*], sect.

Noun from *hairéō* (138), to choose, select. In the NT, a chosen way of life: a sect, school, party (Ac 5:17; 15:5; 24:5, 14; 26:5; 28:22); by implication, discord, dissension (1Co 11:19; Gal 5:20; 2Pe 2:1).

140. αἱρετίζω, aihretizō, *hahee-ret-id´-zo*; from a derivative of 138; to *make a choice:*—choose.

From *hairéō* (138), to take. To choose. In the NT, to prefer, to love. Only in Mt 12:18.

Syn.: *chōrízō* (5563), to separate; *anadeíknumi* (322), to indicate, appoint; *egkrínō* (1469), to accept as approved; *eklégomai* (1586), to choose because of love; *epilégomai* (1951), to select; *hairéomai* (138), to take for oneself, prefer; *aírō* (142), to take up or away.

141. αἱρετικός, aihretikos, *hahee-ret-ee-kos´*; from the same as 140; a *schismatic:*—heretic [*the Greek word itself*].

Noun from *hairéō* (138), to take. One who creates dissension, introduces errors, etc. a factious person. Only in Tit 3:10.

Syn.: *ápistos* (571), unfaithful.

142. αἴρω, airō, *ah´ee-ro*; a primary verb; to *lift*; (by implication) to *take up* or *away*; (figurative) to *raise* (the voice), *keep in suspense* (the mind); specially to *sail* away (i.e. *weigh anchor*); by Hebrew [compare 5375] to *expiate* sin:—away with, bear (up), carry, lift up, loose, make to doubt, put away, remove, take (away, up).

To take up, carry, remove.

(I) To take up, to lift up, to raise:

(A) Particularly, as stones from the ground (Jn 8:59); serpents (Mk 16:18); anchors (Ac 27:13); the hand (Rev 10:5); see also Sept.: Dt 32:40; Isa 49:22. Pass. *árthēti* (Mt 21:21).

(B) Figuratively, to raise, elevate; the eyes (Jn 11:41; see also Sept.: Ps 121:1; 123:1); the voice, meaning, to cry out, to sing (Lk 17:13; Ac 4:24; see also Sept.: Jgs 21:2; 1Sa 11:4). To hold the mind or soul of someone suspended, i.e. in suspense or doubt (Jn 10:24).

(II) To take up and place on oneself, to take up and bear, meaning to bear, carry (Mt 4:6; Sept.: Ps 91:12); my yoke (Mt 11:29; see also Sept.: La 3:27); the cross (Mt 16:24; 27:32; Mk

15:21); to take or carry with one (Mk 6:8; Lk 9:3; Sept.: Ge 44:1; 2Ki 7:8).

(III) To take up and carry away, meaning to take away, to remove by carrying: spoken of a bed (Mt 9:6; Jn 5:8); a dead body, a person, etc. (Mt 14:12; 22:13; Ac 20:9); bread, with the idea of laying up, making use of (Mt 14:20; 15:37; Mk 8:8, 19, 20). Generally (Mt 17:27; Ac 21:11). In a metaphorical sense, to take away sin, meaning the imputation or punishment of sin (Jn 1:29; 1Jn 3:5; 1Sa 15:25); to bear the punishment of sin (Le 5:17; Nu 5:31; 14:33); to take away by taking upon oneself (Mt 8:17; 1Pe 2:24).

(IV) To take away, remove, lift away from, usually with the idea of violence and authority:

(A) Particularly (Lk 6:29, 30; 11:22); of branches, meaning to cut off, prune (Jn 15:2); spoken of persons: to take away or remove from a church, excommunicate (1Co 5:2, in some MSS *exarthē* [1808]). To take away or remove out of the world by death (Mt 24:39; Ac 8:33; Isa 53:8; 57:1, 2). In the imper., "away with!" meaning put out of the way, kill (Lk 23:18; Jn 19:15; Ac 21:36; 22:22).

(B) Figuratively, to destroy (Jn 11:48); to deprive of, as the kingdom of heaven (Mt 21:43), the word of God (Mk 4:15; Lk 8:12, 18), gifts (Mk 4:25), joy (Jn 16:22; see also Sept.: Isa 16:10). Spoken of vices: to put away (Eph 4:31); of a law: to abrogate (Col 2:14).

Deriv.: *apaírō* (522), to lift off; *exaírō* (1808), to put away from the midst; *epaírō* (1869), to lift up, as in the eyes, the head, the hands or the heel; *sunaírō* (4868), to take up together, to reckon; *huperaírō* (5229), to be exalted above measure.

Syn.: *bastázō* (941), to bear; *phérō* (5342), to bring, carry; *methístēmi* (3179), to remove; *lambánō* (2983), to take, lay hold of; *piázō* (4084), to lay hold of forcefully; *airéō* (138), to take; *komízō* (2865), to bring.

143. αἰσθάνομαι, aisthanomai, *ahee-sthan´-om-ahee*; of uncertain derivative; to *apprehend* (properly, by the senses):—perceive.

From *aíō* (n.f.), to perceive. To perceive, primarily with the external senses. In the NT, used metaphorically of spiritual perception: to understand (Lk 9:45; Sept.: Job 23:5; Pr 24:14).

Deriv.: *aísthēsis* (144), perception, discernment; *aisthētḗrion* (145), organ of perception.

Syn.: *krínō* (2919), to judge, conclude; *suníēmi* (4920), to comprehend; *sōphronéō* (4993), to exercise a sound mind; *diakrínō* (1252), to discern.

144. αἴσθησις, aisthēsis, *ah´ee-sthay-sis*; from 143; *perception,* i.e. (figurative) *discernment:*—judgement.

Noun from *aisthánomai* (143), to perceive with the external senses. Perception by the external senses. In the NT, used metaphorically: understanding, the power of discerning (Php 1:9; Sept.: Pr 1:4, 22; Ex 28:3).

Syn.: *krísis* (2920), decision, judgement, evaluation; *gnṓmē* (1106), opinion, purpose.

145. αἰσθητήριον, aisthētērion, *ahee-sthay-tay´-ree-on*; from a derivative of 143; properly an *organ of perception,* i.e. (figurative) *judgement:*—senses.

Noun from *aisthánomai* (143), to perceive with the external senses. The seat of the senses. In the NT, used metaphorically: internal sense, faculty of perception. Only in Heb 5:14.

146. αἰσχροκερδής, aischrokerdēs, *ahee-skhrok-er-dace´*; from 150 and **κέρδος, kerdos** (*gain*); *sordid:*—given to (greedy of) filthy lucre.

147. αἰσχροκερδῶς, aischrokerdōs, *ahee-skhrok-er-doce´*; adverb from 146; *sordidly:*—for filthy lucre's sake.

148. αἰσχρολογία, aischrologia, *ahee-skhrol-og-ee´-ah*; from 150 and 3056; *vile conversation:*—filthy communication.

149. αἰσχρόν, aischron, *ahee-skhron´*; neuter of 150; a *shameful* thing, i.e. *indecorum:*—shame.

150. αἰσχρός, aischros, *ahee-skhros´*; from the same as 153; *shameful,* i.e. *base* (specially *venal*):—filthy.

151. αἰσχρότης, aischrotēs, *ahee-skhrot´-ace*; from 150; *shamefulness,* i.e. *obscenity:*—filthiness.

152. αἰσχύνη, aischunē, *ahee-skhoo´-nay*; from 153; *shame* or *disgrace* (abstract or concrete):—dishonesty, shame.

Noun from *aíschos* (n.f.), shame. Disgrace, shame.

(I) Subjectively: a sense of shame, fear of disgrace (Lk 14:9).

(II) Objectively: disgrace, reproach (Heb 12:2; Sept.: Job 8:22; Ps 69:20; Isa 50:6).

(III) Cause of shame, i.e. a shameful thing or action, disgraceful conduct. (2Co 4:2; Php 3:19; Heb 12:2; Jude 13; Rev 3:18; Sept.: 1Sa 20:30).

Syn.: *atimía* (819), dishonour; *entropḗ* (1791), hidden shame; *aschēmosúnē* (808), unseemliness; *aidṓs* (127), shame arising from conviction of others.

153. αἰσχύνομαι, aischunomai, *ahee-skhoo´-nom-ahee*; from **αἰσχος, aischos** (*disfigurement,* i.e. *disgrace*); to feel *shame* (for oneself):—be ashamed.

154. αἰτέω, aiteō, *ahee-teh´-o*; of uncertain derivative; to *ask* (in general):—ask, beg, call for, crave, desire, require. Compare 4441.

To ask, request, beg.

(I) Generally (Mt 5:42; 7:9, 10; Mk 6:22–25; Lk 11:9–13; 1Jn 5:14–16; Sept.: Jos 15:18; 19:50). Spoken in respect to God, to supplicate, to pray for (Mt 6:8; 7:7, 8, 11; 18:19; Col 1:9; Jas 1:5, 6; Sept.: Isa 7:11, 12).

(II) To ask or call for, require, demand (Lk 1:63; 12:48; 23:23; Ac 3:14; 25:15; 1Pe 3:15; Sept.: Job 6:22; Da 2:49).

(III) By Hebraism, to desire (Ac 7:46; Sept.: 1Ki 19:4; Ecc 2:10; Dt 14:26).

Deriv.: *aítēma* (155), request, petition; *aitía* (156), an accusation; *apaitéō* (523), to require; *exaitéomai* (1809), to ask to have; *epaitéō* (1871), to beg; *paraitéomai* (3868), to refuse, give up; *prosaitéō* (4319), to ask earnestly.

Syn.: *punthánomai* (4441), to ask by way of inquiry; *zētéō* (2212), to seek; *parakaléō* (3870), to beseech; *déomai* (1189), to make a specific request; *epithuméō* (1937), desire, long for; *epizētéō* (1934), to demand; *diṓkō* (1377), to pursue; *erōtáō* (2065), to ask.

155. αἴτημα, aitēma, *ah´ee-tay-mah*; from 154; a *thing asked* or (abstract) an *asking:*—petition, request, required.

Noun from *aitéō* (154), to ask. Thing asked for, object sought, request (Lk 23:24; 1Jn 5:15). From the Hebrew, desire (Php 4:6).

Syn.: *déēsis* (1162), supplication or prayer for particular benefits; *énteuxis* (1783), intercession; *eucharistía* (2169), thanksgiving; *hiketēría* (2428), entreaty, supplication; *boúlēma* (1013), will, purpose; *boulḗ* (1012) will; *epithumía*

(1939), a longing; *théléma* (2307), volition, determination; *paráklēsis* (3874), request.

156. αἰτία, aitia, *ahee-tee´-a*; from the same as 154; a *cause* (as if *asked* for), i.e. (logical) *reason* (motive, matter), (legal) *crime* (alleged or proved):—accusation, case, cause, crime, fault, [wh-] ere [-fore].

Noun from *aitéō* (154), to ask or require. Efficient cause, motive, reason, ground (Mt 19:3; Lk 8:47; Ac 22:24; 28:20; 2Ti 1:6, 12; Tit 1:13; Heb 2:11). Also in the sense of affair, matter, case (Mt 19:10; Ac 10:21; 23:28). In a forensic sense, an accusation of crime, charge (Mt 27:37; Mk 15:26; Ac 25:18, 27); fault, guilt, crime (Jn 18:38; 19:4, 6; Ac 13:28; 28:18; Sept.: Ge 4:13; Pr 28:17).

Deriv.: *anaítios* (338), innocent.

Syn.: *katēgoría* (2724), an accusation; *lógos* (3056), reason.

157. αἰτίαμα, aitiama, *ahee-tee´-am-ah*; from a derivative of 156; a *thing charged*:—complaint.

158. αἴτιον, aition, *ah´ee-tee-on*; neuter of 159; a *reason* or *crime* [like 156]:—cause, fault.

159. αἴτιος, aitios, *ah´ee-tee-os*; from the same as 154; *causative*, i.e. (concrete) a *causer*:—author.

160. αἰφνίδιος, aiphnidios, *aheef-nid´-ee-os*; from a compound of 1 (as a negative particle) and 5316 [compare 1810] (meaning *non-apparent*); *unexpected*, i.e. (adverb) *suddenly*:—sudden, unawares.

161. αἰχμαλωσία, aichmalōsia, *aheekh-mal-o-see´-ah*; from 164; *captivity*:—captivity.

162. αἰχμαλωτεύω, aichmalōteuō, *aheekh-mal-o-tew´-o*; from 164; to *capture* [like 163]:—lead captive.

163. αἰχμαλωτίζω, aichmalōtizō, *aheekh-mal-o-tid´-zo*; from 164; to *make captive*:—lead away captive, bring into captivity.

164. αἰχμαλωτός, aichmalōtos, *aheekh-mal-o-tos´*; from αἰχμή, *aichmē* (a spear) and a derivative of the same as 259; properly a *prisoner of war*, i.e. (generally) a *captive*:—captive.

165. αἰών, aiōn, *ahee-ohn´*; from the same as 104; properly an *age*; by extension *perpetuity* (also past); (by implication) the *world*; specially (Jewish) a Messianic period (present or future):—age, course, eternal, (for) ever (-more), [n-]ever, (beginning of the, while the) world (began, without end). Compare 5550.

A noun meaning age, the world.

(**I**) Age, an indefinitely long period or lapse of time, perpetuity, ever, forever, eternity:

(**A**) Spoken of time future in the following phrases: (**1**) *Eis tón aiōna*, lit. "unto the age," i.e. forever, without end, to the remotest time (Mk 11:14; Lk 1:55; Jn 6:51, 58; 8:35; 12:34; 13:8; 14:16; 1Co 8:13; Heb 5:6, 21; 1Pe 1:25; 2Jn 2); spoken of Christ (Heb 6:20; 7:17; 7:24, 28); spoken of the blessedness of the righteous (Jn 6:51, 58; 2Co 9:9; 1Jn 2:17; 2Pe 2:17); of the punishment of the wicked (Jude 13). With a neg., meaning never (Mt 21:19; Mk 3:29; Jn 4:14; 8:51, 52; 10:28; 11:26; Sept.: Dt 29:29; Isa 28:28; 40:8; 51:6, 8; Jer 50:39). (**2**) *Eis toús aiōnas*, lit. "unto the ages," i.e. ever, forever, to all eternity (Mt 6:13; Lk 1:33; Ro 16:27; Heb 13:8); spoken of God (Ro 1:25; 9:5; 11:36; 2Co 11:31); of Christ (Lk 1:33; Heb 13:8; Sept.: Ps 77:8). (**3**) *Eis toús aiōnas tōn aiōnōn*, lit. "unto the ages of the ages," an intensive form meaning forever and ever (2Ti 4:18; Heb 13:21; 1Pe 4:11; Rev 1:6; 5:13; 7:12; 19:3; 22:5); spoken of God (Gal 1:5; Php 4:20; 1Ti 1:17; 1Pe 5:11). Also in the expression *eis pásas tás geneás toú aiōnos tōn aiōnōn*, lit. "unto all generations of the age of the ages," meaning throughout all ages (see *pás* [3956], every, all; *geneá* [1074], generation), spoken of Christ (2Pe 3:18; Rev 1:18; 5:13; 11:15); of the blessedness of the saints (Rev 22:5); of the punishment of the wicked (Rev 14:11; 19:3; 20:10).

(**B**) Spoken of time past in the following phrases: (**1**) *Ap' aiōnos*, lit. "from the age" (see *apó* [575], from), often translated of old, from ancient times, from the beginning of the world (Lk 1:70; Ac 3:21; 15:18). (**2**) *Apó tōn aiōnōn*, lit. "from the ages" (Eph 3:9; Col 1:26). (**3**) *Ek toú aiōnos ou*, lit. "from the ages not" (see *ek* [1537], from; *ou* [3756], not), i.e. never (Jn 9:32). (**4**) *Pró tōn aiōnōn*, lit. "from the ages" (*pró* [4253], before), translated before the ages, before the world (1Co 2:7).

(**II**) The world, i.e. this present world or the world to come, understood either in the sense of the time after the destruction of the present world and resurrection of the dead, or as the earthly reign of the Messiah, awaited by the

Jews. In the NT, *aiṓn* is used of the future world chiefly in the first of these senses.

(A) This world and the next: **(1)** As implying duration (Mt 12:32, "neither in this world nor the next" [a.t.], meaning never; Mk 10:30; Lk 18:30). **(2)** The present world, with its cares, temptations, and desires; the idea of evil, both moral and physical, being everywhere implied (Mt 13:22; Lk 16:8; 20:34; Ro 12:2; 1Co 1:20; 2:6, 8; 2Ti 4:10; Tit 2:12). Hence this world is called *aiṓn ponērós*, "evil world" (Gal 1:4; see *ponērós*, [4190], evil). Satan is called the "god of this world" (2Co 4:4; Sept.: Ecc 3:11). **(3)** By metonymy, the men of this world, wicked generation, etc. (Eph 2:2). *Huioí toú aiṓnos toútou*, translated "the children of this world," is literally rendered "the sons of this age" (Lk 16:8; 20:34; see *huioí*, the plural of *huiós* [5207], son). **(4)** By metonymy, the world itself as an object of creation and existence (Mt 13:40; 24:3; 1Ti 1:17; Heb 1:2; 11:3).

(B) Spoken in reference to the advent of the Messiah, meaning age: **(1)** The age or world before the Messiah, the Jewish dispensation (1Co 10:11, "the ends of the world"). **(2)** The age or world after the Messiah, the gospel dispensation, the kingdom of the Messiah (Eph 2:7; Heb 6:5; see also Heb 2:5).

Deriv.: *aiṓnios* (166), eternal.

Syn.: *geneá* (1074), generation, the people of a certain period of time; *hēméra* (2250), day or period of time.

166. αἰώνιος, aiōnios, *ahee-o´-nee-os*; from 165; *perpetual* (also used of past time, or past and future as well):—eternal, for ever, everlasting, world (began).

Adjective from *aiṓn* (165), age. Eternal, perpetual, denoting those things which are not transitory.

(I) Spoken chiefly of future time:

(A) Of God (Ro 16:26; 1Ti 6:16; Sept.: Ge 21:33; Isa 40:28).

(B) Of the blessedness of the righteous (Mt 19:29; 25:46; Mk 10:30; Jn 3:15, 16, 36; Ro 2:7; 2Co 4:17). In some passages this *zōḗ aiṓnios*, lit. "life eternal" (see *zōḗ* [2222], life), is equivalent to entrance into the kingdom of God (Mt 19:16; Jn 3:3, 5, 15; Ac 13:46).

(C) Of the punishment of the wicked (Mt 18:8; 25:41, 46; Mk 3:29; 2Th 1:9; Heb 6:2; Jude 7; Sept.: Da 12:2).

(D) Generally (2Co 4:18; 5:1; Heb 9:14;

13:20; 1Jn 1:2; Rev 14:6). In the Sept.: *diathḗkē aiṓnios*, "eternal covenant" (Ge 9:16; 17:7; see *diathḗkē* [1242], testament, covenant).

(II) Spoken of time past (Ro 16:25), *chrónois aiōníois*, meaning times eternal, ancient ages, of old (2Ti 1:9; Tit 1:2; see *chrónos* [5550], time).

Syn.: *aḯdios* (126), having no beginning and no ending, everlasting.

167. ἀκαθαρσία, akatharsia, *ak-ath-ar-see´-ah*; from 169; *impurity* (the quality), physical or moral:—uncleanness.

Noun from *akáthartos* (169), unclean. Uncleanness, impurity, filth in a physical sense (Mt 23:27; Sept.: 2Sa 11:4). Moral uncleanness, lewdness, pollution, as opposed to chastity (Ro 1:24; 6:19; 2Co 12:21; Eph 4:19; 5:3; 1Th 2:3; 4:7; Sept.: Eze 22:15; 36:25).

Syn.: *miasmós* (3394), a defilement; *rhúpos* (4509), dirt, filth; *aischrótēs* (151), obscenity, impurity; *rhuparía* (4507), moral defilement; *molusmós* (3436), a soiling, defilement; *asélgeia* (766), lasciviousness, wantonness; *miasmós* (3394), contamination, uncleanness; *míasma* (3393), foulness, pollution; *spílos* (4696), stain, blemish defect, spot; *stígma* (4742), stigma, mark, scar.

168. ἀκαθάρτης, akathartēs, *ak-ath-ar´-tace*; from 169; *impurity* (the state moral:—filthiness.

Noun from the priv. *a* (1), without, and *katharótēs* (2514), cleanness. Uncleanness, filthiness, i.e. lewdness; used figuratively of idolatry, only in Rev 17:4.

Syn.: *akatharsía* (167), uncleanness.

169. ἀκάθαρτος, akathartos, *ak-ath´-ar-tos*; from 1 (as a negative particle) and a presumed derivative of 2508 (meaning *cleansed*); *impure* (ceremonial, moral [*lewd*] or special [*dæmonic*]):—foul, unclean.

Adjective from the priv. *a* (1), without, and *kathaírō* (2508), to cleanse. Unclean, impure.

(I) In the Levitical sense, i.e. ceremonially unclean (Ac 10:14, 28; 11:8; Rev 18:2 [cf. Le 5:2; 11:4, 25; 13:45; Dt 14:7]); so of persons who are not Jews, or who do not belong to the Christian community (Ac 10:28; 1Co 7:14; 2Co 6:17; Sept.: Isa 52:1; Am 7:17).

(II) In the sense of lewd, lascivious (Eph 5:5); spoken figuratively of idolatry (Rev 17:4); in this sense, partly, the devils or demons are called *pneúmata akátharta,* unclean spirits (Mt 10:1; 12:43; Mk 1:23, 26; Lk 4:33; 9:42; Ac 5:16; 8:7; Rev 16:13; 18:2; see also *pneúma* [4151], spirit). They are also probably so called as being impious, wicked (Mt 12:45; Ac 19:13, 15).

Deriv.: *akatharsía* (167), uncleanness.

Syn.: *bébēlos* (952), profane; *rhuparós* (4508), vile; *ponērós* (4190), evil, but sometimes used as unclean; *koinós* (2839), common, defiled.

170. ἀκαιρέομαι, akairēomai, *ak-ahee-reh´-om-ahee*; from a compound of 1 (as a negative particle) and 2540 (meaning *unseasonable*); to *be inopportune* (for oneself), i.e. to *fail of a proper occasion:*—lack opportunity.

171. ἀκαίρως, akairōs, *ak-ah´ee-roce;* adverb from the same as 170; *inopportunely:*—out of season.

172. ἄκακος, akakos, *ak´-ak-os;* from 1 (as a negative particle) and 2556; *not bad,* i.e. (objective) *innocent* or (subjective) *unsuspecting:*—harmless, simple.

Adjective from the priv. *a* (1), without, and *kakós* (2556), constitutionally bad. Harmless, well disposed, blameless (Heb 7:26); also in the sense of simple-hearted, confiding (Ro 16:18).

Syn.: *haploús* (573), single or without duplicity; *ádolos* (97), without guile; *akéraios* (185), without any foreign matter or without admixture; *athóos* (121), unpunished, innocent; *kalós* (2570), good; *agathós* (18), benevolent; *chrēstós* (5543), gentle, mellow.

173. ἄκανθα, akantha, *ak´-an-thah;* probably from the same as 188; a *thorn:*—thorn.

174. ἀκάνθινος, akanthinos, *ak-an´-thee-nos;* from 173; *thorny:*—of thorns.

175. ἄκαρπος, akarpos, *ak´-ar-pos;* from 1 (as a negative particle) and 2590; *barren* (literal or figurative):—without fruit, unfruitful.

176. ἀκατάγνωστος, akatagnōstos, *ak-at-ag´-noce-tos;* from 1 (as a negative particle) and a derivative of 2607; *unblameable:*—that cannot be condemned.

Adjective from the priv. *a* (1), without, and *kataginóskō* (2607), condemn. Irreprehensible, not worthy of condemnation, not to be condemned or blamed (Tit 2:8).

177. ἀκατακάλυπτος, akatakaluptos, *ak-at-ak-al´-oop-tos;* from 1 (as a negative particle) and a derivative of a compound of 2596 and 2572; *unveiled:*—uncovered.

178. ἀκατάκριτος, akatakritos, *ak-at-ak´-ree-tos;* from 1 (as a negative particle) and a derivative of 2632; *without* (legal) *trial:*—uncondemned.

179. ἀκατάλυτος, akatalutos, *ak-at-al´-oo-tos;* from 1 (as a negative particle) and a derivative of 2647; *indissoluble,* i.e. (figurative) *permanent:*—endless.

180. ἀκατάπαυστος, akatapaustos, *ak-at-ap´-ow-stos;* from 1 (as a negative particle) and a derivative of 2664; *unrefraining:*—that cannot cease.

181. ἀκαταστασία, akatastasia, *ak-at-as-tah-see´-ah;* from 182; *instability,* i.e. *disorder:*—commotion, confusion, tumult.

Noun from *akatástatos* (182), unstable. Commotion, tumult (Lk 21:9; 1Co 14:33; 2Co 6:5, "uncertainty of residence" [a.t.], i.e. exile ["tumults"]; 2Co 12:20; Jas 3:16; Sept.: Pr 26:28).

Syn.: *súgchusis* (4799), confusion; *thórubos* (2351), noise, tumult; *tarachē* (5016), disturbance.

182. ἀκατάστατος, akatastatos, *ak-at-as´-tat-os;* from 1 (as a negative particle) and a derivative of 2525; *inconstant:*—unstable.

Adjective from the priv. *a* (1), not, and *kathístēmi* (2525), to settle. Unsettled, unsteady, unstable (Jas 1:8).

Deriv.: *akatastasía* (181), instability.

Syn.: *akatáschetos* (183), one that cannot be restrained; *astēriktos* (793), unstable; *átaktos* (813), insubordinate, unruly.

183. ἀκατάσχετος, akataschetos, *ak-at-as´-khet-os;* from 1 (as a negative particle) and a derivative of 2722; *unrestrainable:*—unruly.

184. Ἀκελδαμά, Akeldama, *ak-el-dam-ah´;* of Chaldee origin [meaning *field of blood;* corresponding to 2506 and 1818]; *Akeldama,* a place near Jerus.:—Aceldama.

185. ἀκέραιος, akeraios, *ak-er´-ah-yos;* from 1 (as a negative particle) and a presumed derivative of 2767: *unmixed*, i.e. (figurative) *innocent:*—harmless, simple.

Adjective from the priv. *a* (1), without, and *keránnumi* (2767), to mix. Unmixed. In the NT, used metaphorically: without guile, cunning, or deceit; blameless (Mt 10:16; Ro 16:19; Php 2:15).

Syn.: *euschēmōn* (2158), comely, honourable; *téleios* (185), perfect, one who has reached the goal; *ártios* (739), complete; *holóklēros* (3648), entire, whole; *plérēs* (4134), complete, full; *tímios* (5093), honest; *éntimos* (1784), reputable, honourable; *euthús* (2117), straight; *chrēstós* (5543), of good and useful morals; *áxios* (514), worthy; *ákakos* (172), not bad, innocent; *ádolos* (97), without guile; *haploús* (573), without wrinkles or duplicity, single or simple.

186. ἀκλινής, aklinēs, *ak-lee-nace´*; from 1 (as a negative particle) and 2827; *not leaning*, i.e. (figurative) *firm:*—without wavering.

187. ἀκμάζω, akmazō, *ak-mad´-zo*; from the same as 188; to *make a point*, i.e. (figurative) *mature:*—be fully ripe.

188. ἀκμήν, akmēn, *ak-mane´*; accusative of a noun ("*acme*") akin to **ἀκή, akē** (a *point*) and meaning the same; adverb *just now*, i.e. *still:*—yet.

189. ἀκοή, akoē, *ak-o-ay´*; from 191; *hearing* (the act, the sense or the thing heard):—audience, ear, fame, which ye heard, hearing, preached, report, rumoural.

Noun from *akoúō* (191), to hear. Hearing, as the sense of hearing, or referring to that which is heard.

(I) The sense of hearing (1Co 12:17); also spoken of the organ or instrument of hearing, the ear (Mk 7:35; Ac 17:20; 2Ti 4:3, 4). Thus the expression *akoé akoúein*, "to hear with the ears" (with *akoúō* [191], to hear), meaning to listen attentively (Mt 13:14; Ac 28:26).

(II) That which is or may be heard: a thing announced, instruction, teaching (Jn 12:38; Ro 10:16, 17; Gal 3:2, 5; 1Th 2:13; Heb 4:2; 2Pe 2:8); a rumour, report (Mt 4:24; 14:1; 24:6; Mk 1:28; 13:7).

Syn.: *oús* (3775), ear; *ōtíon* (5621), a diminutive of *oús*, ear; *phémē* (5346), fame, report; *lógos* (3056), a word, report, account; *échos* (2279), noise, sound, rumour, echo; *aggelía*

(31), a message, proclamation, news; *presbeía* (4242), embassy, a message, messengers; *kḗrugma* (2782), proclamation, preaching; *marturía* (3141), witness, report; *diágnōsis* (1233), diagnosis, hearing for the purpose of discerning; *akroatḗrion* (201), a place of hearing.

190. ἀκολουθέω, akoutheō, *ak-ol-oo-theh´-o*; from 1 (as a particle of union) and **κέλευθος, keleuthos** (a *road*); properly to *be in the same way with*, i.e. to *accompany* (specially as a disciple):—follow, reach.

From *akólouthos* (n.f.), attendant, follower, which is from the coll. *a* (1), together, and *kéleuthos* (n.f.), a way. To accompany, to go with, to follow.

(I) Generally (Mt 8:1; 9:19, 27; Mk 5:24; 10:32; Lk 22:54; Jn 11:31; 1Co 10:4; Sept.: Ru 1:14; 1Sa 25:42).

(II) Specifically, to follow a teacher, i.e. to be or become the disciple of someone:

(A) To accompany him personally, as was usual with the followers of Jewish doctors and Greek philosophers (Mt 4:20, 22, 25; 9:9; 19:27, 28; 27:55; Mk 1:18; 9:38; Jn 1:41; 12:26; Lk 9:49; Sept.: 1Ki 19:20, 21; Isa 45:14).

(B) To be or become the disciple of anyone as to faith and practice, to follow his teaching, etc. (Mt 10:38; 16:24; Mk 8:34; Lk 9:23; Jn 8:12; 12:26).

(III) Of time, to follow in succession, to succeed (Rev 14:8, 9).

(IV) Spoken of things, or actions: to accompany, follow (Rev 14:13).

Deriv.: *exakolouthéō* (1811), to follow up, to continue to the end; *epakolouthéō* (1872), to follow after, close upon; *katakolouthéō* (2628), to follow behind or intently after; *parakolouthéō* (3877), to follow close up or side by side, hence to accompany, conform to, follow intending to practice; *sunakolouthéō* (4870), to follow along with, to accompany a leader.

Syn.: *hupakoúō* (5219), to obey; *diṓkō* (1377), to pursue without hostility, to follow; *miméomai* (3401), to imitate; *epioúsios* (1967), the following.

191. ἀκούω, akouō, *ak-oo´-o*; a primary verb; to *hear* (in various senses):—give (in the) audience (of), come (to the ears), ([shall]) hear (-er, -ken), be noised, be reported, understand.

To hear, also to learn by hearing, be informed.

(I) To hear, to perceive with the ears:

(A) Generally (Mt 2:3, 9, 18; 9:12; 10:27; 11:5; 12:19; Mk 7:25; 10:41; 14:64; Lk 7:3, 9; Jn 3:8; Sept.: Ge 3:8, 10).

(B) To hear with attention, to give ear to, listen to (Mk 4:3; 7:14; 12:29, 37; Lk 5:1; 10:39; 11:31; Ac 2:22; 15:7); in respect to a teacher (Mk 6:20; Lk 15:1; 19:48), hence *hoi akoúontes*, hearers, i.e. disciples.

(C) By implication, to give heed to, to obey (Mt 10:14; Lk 10:16; 16:29, 31 [cf. Jn 5:24; 8:47; 18:37; Ac 3:22, 23; 4:19; 1Jn 4:5, 6]; Sept.: Ge 3:17; Ex 16:20; Dt 11:27; 2Ch 20:14; Isa 48:18). Here belongs the phrase "he who hath ears, let him hear," i.e. give heed, obey (Mt 11:15; 13:9, 13; Rev 2:7, 11, 17, 29). In the writings of John as spoken of God: to heed, regard, i.e. to hear and answer prayer (Jn 9:31; 11:41, 42; 1Jn 5:15).

(II) To hear, i.e. to learn by hearing, be informed, know:

(A) Generally (Mt 2:3, 22; 4:12; 5:21, 27; 11:2; Mk 5:27; 6:14; Ac 14:14; 15:24); spoken of instruction, doctrines (Jn 8:40; 15:15; Ac 1:4; 4:20; Ro 10:14, 18; Heb 2:1; 1Jn 2:7, 24). Pass. meaning, to be heard of, to be reported (Mt 28:14; Mk 2:1; Lk 12:3; Ac 11:22; 1Co 5:1; Sept.: 2Ch 26:15).

(B) In a forensic sense, to hear as a judge or magistrate, i.e. to try, examine judicially (Ac 25:22; Jn 7:51).

(C) In the sense of to understand, comprehend (Mk 4:33; Jn 6:60; 1Co 14:2; Gal 4:21; Sept.: Ge 11:7; 42:23).

Deriv.: *akoē* (189), hearing; *diakoúō* (1251), to hear through, hear fully; *eisakoúō* (1522), to listen to, to hear and obey; *epakoúō* (1873), to listen to, hear with favour on an occasion; *parakoúō* (3878), to overhear or hear amiss; *proakoúō* (4257), to hear before; *hupakoúō* (5219), to obey.

Syn.: *epakroáomai* (1874), to listen attentively to; *enōtízomai* (1801), to give ear to, to listen; *peitharchéō* (3980), to obey one in authority, be obedient; *peíthomai* (3982), to be persuaded.

192. ἀκρασία, akrasia, *ak-ras-ee´-a*; from 193; *want of self-restraint:*—excess, incontinency.

193. ἀκράτης, akratēs, *ak-rat´-ace*; from 1 (as a negative particle) and 2904; *powerless,* i.e. *without self-control:*—incontinent.

194. ἄκρατος, akratos, *ak´-rat-os*; from 1 (as a negative particle) and a presumed derivative of 2767; *undiluted:*—without mixture.

195. ἀκρίβεια, akribeia, *ak-ree´-bi-ah*; from the same as 196; *exactness:*—perfect manner.

196. ἀκριβέστατος, akribestatos, *ak-ree-bes´-ta-tos*; superlative of **ἀκριβής, akribēs** (a derivative of the same as 206); *most exact:*—most straitest.

197. ἀκριβέστερον, akribesteron, *ak-ree-bes´-ter-on*; neuter of the comparative of the same as 196; (adverb) *more exactly:*—more perfect (-ly).

198. ἀκριβόω, akriboō, *ak-ree-bo´-o*; from the same as 196; to *be exact,* i.e. *ascertain:*—enquire diligently.

199. ἀκριβῶς, akribōs, *ak-ree-boce´*; adverb from the same as 196; *exactly:*—circumspectly, diligently, perfect (-ly).

200. ἀκρίς, akris, *ak-rece´*; apparently from the same as 206; a *locust* (as *pointed*, or as *lighting* on the *top* of vegetation):—locust.

201. ἀκροατήριον, akroaterion, *ak-ro-at-ay´-ree-on*; from 202; an *audience-room:*—place of hearing.

202. ἀκροατής, akroatēs, *ak-ro-at-ace´*; from **ἀκροάομαι, akroaomai** (to *listen*; apparently an intensive of 191); a *hearer* (merely):—hearer.

203. ἀκροβυστία, akrobustia, *ak-rob-oos-tee´-ah*; from 206 and probably a modified form of **πόσθη, posthē** (the *penis* or male sexual organ); the *prepuce*; (by implication) an *uncircumcised* (i.e. *Gentile*; figurative, *unregenerate*) state or person:—not circumcised, uncircumcised [*with* 2192], uncircumcision.

Noun from *ákron* (206), the extreme, and *búō* (n.f.), to cover. The foreskin. In Ac 11:3, "uncircumcised men" is lit. *ándras akrobustían échontas*, "men having foreskins" (*ándras* [*anér* {435}, man] *échontas* [*échō* {2192}, to have]), thus the term may be translated as uncircumcision (Ro 2:25, 26; 1Co 7:18, 19; Gal 5:6; 6:15; Col 2:13). By metonymy, uncircumcised refers to Gentiles or pagans, as opposed to the circumcision (*peritomé* [4061]), i.e. the Jews (Ro 2:26, 27; 3:30; 4:9–12; Gal 2:7; Eph 2:11; Col 3:11). The Jews in scorn called all other nations "uncircumcised" (Jgs 14:3; 15:18; Isa 52:1).

Syn.: *aperítmētos* (564), uncircumcised; verb: *epispáomai* (1986), to draw over, to become uncircumcised, as if to efface Judaism.

204. ἀκρογωνιαῖος, akrogōniaios, *ak-rog-o-nee-ah´-yos*; from 206 and 1137; belonging to the extreme *corner*:—chief corner.

205. ἀκροθίνιον, akrothinion, *ak-roth-in´-ee-on*; from 206 and θίς, *this* (a *heap*); properly (in the plural) the *top of the heap*, i.e. (by implication) *best of the booty*:—spoils.

206. ἄκρον, akron, *ak´-ron*; neuter of an adjective probably akin to the base of 188; the *extremity*:—one end ... other, tip, top, uttermost part.

207. Ἀκύλας, Akulas, *ak-oo´-las*; probably for Latin *aquila* (an *eagle*); *Akulas*, an Israelite:—Aquila.

208. ἀκυρόω, akuroō, *ak-oo-ro´-o*; from 1 (as a negative particle) and 2964; to *invalidate*:—disannul, make of no effect.

209. ἀκωλύτως, akōlutōs, *ak-o-loo´-toce*; adverb from a compound of 1 (as a negative particle) and a derivative of 2967; in *an unhindered manner*, i.e. *freely*:—no man forbidding him.

210. ἄκων, akōn, *ak´-ohn*; from 1 (as a negative particle) and 1635; *unwilling*:—against the will.

From the priv. *a* (1), without, and *hekṓn* (1635), willing. Unwillingly, against one's will, forced. Occurs only in 1Co 9:17.

Syn.: *akousíōs*, unwillingly, often used in the Sept., but not in the NT; *anagkastós* (317), by compulsion.

211. ἀλάβαστρον, alabastron, *al-ab´-as-tron*; neuter of ἀλά-βαστρος, *alabastros* (of uncertain derivative), the name of a stone; properly an "*alabaster*" box, i.e. (by extension) a perfume *vase* (of any material):—(alabaster) box.

212. ἀλαζονεία, alazoneia, *al-ad-zon-i´-a*; from 213; *braggadocio*, i.e. (by implication) *self-confidence*:—boasting, pride.

213. ἀλαζών, alazōn, *al-ad-zone´*; from ἄλη, *alē* (*vagrancy*); *braggart*:—boaster.

Masculine noun from *álē* (n.f.), a wandering about. A boaster, braggart (Ro 1:30; 2Ti 3:2; Sept.: Hab 2:5).

Deriv.: *alazoneía* (212), vaunting in those things one does not possess.

Syn.: *huperēphanos* (5244), proud, one who shows himself above his fellows; *hubristḗs* (5197), insolent wrongdoer to others for the pleasure which the affliction imparts.

214. ἀλαλάζω, alalazō, *al-al-ad´-zo*; from ἀλαλή, *alalē* (a *shout*, "*halloo*"); to *vociferate*, i.e. (by implication) to *wail*; (figurative) to *clang*:—tinkle, wail.

215. ἀλάλητος, alalētos, *al-al´-ay-tos*; from 1 (as a negative particle) and a derivative of 2980; *unspeakable*:—unutterable, which cannot be uttered.

216. ἄλαλος, alalos, *al´-al-os*; from 1 (as a negative particle) and 2980; *mute*:—dumb.

217. ἅλας, halas, *hal´-as*; from 251; *salt*; (figurative) *prudence*:—salt.

218. ἀλείφω, aleiphō, *al-i´-fo*; from 1 (as particle of union) and the base of 3045; to *oil* (with perfume):—anoint.

To rub, to cover over, besmear. In the NT: to anoint (Mt 6:17; Mk 6:13; 16:1; Lk 7:38, 46; Jn 11:2; 12:3; Jas 5:14; Sept.: Ge 31:13; Eze 13:10–12). The Jews were accustomed not only to anoint the head at their feasts in token of joy, but also both the head and the feet of those whom they wished to distinguish by special honour. In the case of sick persons and also of the dead, they anointed the whole body (see Ge 50:2; Ps 23:5; 45:7; 104:15; Ecc 9:8; Lk 7:37, 38; Jn 19:40).

Deriv.: *exaleíphō* (1813), to blot out, wipe away.

Syn.: *chríō* (5548), more limited in its use of sacred and symbolical anointing; *murízō* (3642), to anoint the body for burial.

219. ἀλεκτοροφωνία, alektorophōnia, *al-ek-tor-of-o-nee´-ah*; from 220 and 5456; *cock-crow*, i.e. the third night-watch:—cockcrowing.

220. ἀλέκτωρ, alektōr, *al-ek´-tore*; from ἀλέκω, *alekō* (to *ward* off); a *cock* or male fowl:—cock.

221. Ἀλεξανδρεύς, Alexandreus, *al-ex-and-reuce´*; from Ἀλεξάνδρεια, *Alexandreia* (the city so called); an *Alexandreian* or inhabitant of Alexandria:—of Alexandria, Alexandrian.

222. Ἀλεξανδρίνος, Alexandrinos, *al-ex-an-dree´-nos*; from the same as 221; *Alexandrine,* or belonging to Alexandria:—of Alexandria.

223. Ἀλέξανδρος, Alexandros, *al-ex´-an-dros*; from the same as (the first part of) 220 and 435; *mandefender*; *Alexander,* the name of three Israelites and one other man:—Alexander.

224. ἄλευρον, aleuron, *al´-yoo-ron*; from ἀλέω, *aleō* (to *grind*); *flour:*—meal.

225. ἀλήθεια, alētheia, *al-ay´-thi-a*; from 227; *truth:*—true, × truly, truth, verity.

Noun from *alēthḗs* (227), true. What is not concealed, but open and known; hence truth.

(I) Truth, verity, reality, conformity to the nature and reality of things:

(A) As evidenced in relation to facts (Mk 5:33; Jn 5:33; 16:7; Ac 26:25; Ro 9:1; 2Co 6:7; 12:6; Eph 4:25; 1Ti 2:7; Sept.: 1Ki 22:16; 2Ch 18:15). Prefixed by *epí* (1909), upon, *epí alētheías,* of a truth, as the fact or event shows (Lk 4:25; 22:59; Ac 4:27; 10:34; Sept.: Job 9:2; Isa 37:18).

(B) Spoken of what is true in itself, purity from all error or falsehood (Mk 12:32; Ac 26:25; Ro 2:20; 2Co 7:14; 12:6; Col 1:6; 2Ti 2:18; 3:7, 8; 4:4). "The truth of the gospel" (Gal 2:5), "the word of truth," the true doctrine (Eph 1:13; Col 1:5; 2Ti 2:15; Jas 1:18).

(II) Truth, i.e. love of truth, both in words and conduct, sincerity, veracity (Mt 22:16; Mk 12:14; Lk 20:21; Jn 4:23, 24; Jn 8:44; Eph 4:24; 5:9; 6:14; Php 1:18; 1Jn 1:6, 8; 2:4; 3:18, 19; 5:6; 2Jn 3; 3Jn 3; Sept.: Jos 2:14; 1Sa 12:24; 2Sa 2:6; 1Ki 2:4; 3:6; 2Ch 19:9; Ps 35:6).

(III) In the NT especially, divine truth or the faith and practice of the true religion is called "truth" either as being true in itself and derived from the true God, or as declaring the existence and will of the one true God, in opposition to the worship of false idols. Hence *alētheia* comes to mean divine truth, gospel truth, as opposed to heathen and Jewish fables (Jn 1:14, 17; 8:32, 40; 16:13; 18:37; Ro 1:18, 25; 2Co 4:2; 13:8; Gal 3:1; 5:7; 2Th 2:10; 1Ti 2:4; 3:15; 2Ti 2:25; Tit 1:1, 14; Heb 10:26; Jas 1:18; 3:14; 1Pe 1:22; 2Pe 1:12; 2:2; 1Jn 2:21; 2Jn 2, 4; 3Jn 8). Hence the Lord Jesus is called "the truth," i.e. truth incarnate, the teacher of divine truth (Jn 14:6). So also

"the Spirit of truth," who declares or reveals divine truth (Jn 14:17; 15:26; 16:13).

(IV) Conduct conformed to the truth, integrity, probity, virtue, a life conformed to the precepts of the gospel. In Jn 3:21, *ho poiṓn tḗn alḗtheian,* lit. "he who does truth" (see *poiéō* [4160], to make or to do), meaning someone who lives uprightly. See also Jn 8:44; Ro 2:8; 1Co 13:6; Eph 4:21; 1Ti 6:5; Jas 5:19; 3Jn 3, 4, 12; Sept.: Ps 119:30; Pr 28:6; Isa 26:10.

Syn.: *hupóstasis* (5287), substance; *bebaíōsis* (951), confirmation; *plḗrōma* (4138), fulfillment.

226. ἀληθεύω, alētheuō, *al-ayth-yoo´-o*; from 227; to *be true* (in doctrine and profession):— speak (tell) the truth.

From *alēthḗs* (227), real, actual, not counterfeit. To act truly, speak the truth, be sincere (Eph 4:15; Gal 4:16; Sept.: Ge 42:16; Pr 21:3).

Syn.: *bebaióō* (950), to confirm; *plēróō* (4137), to accomplish.

227. ἀληθής, alēthēs, *al-ay-thace´*; from 1 (as a negative particle) and 2990; *true* (as *not concealing*):—true, truly, truth.

Adjective from the priv. *a* (1), without, and *léthō,* an older form of *lanthánō* (2990), to be hid, unawares. Unconcealed, open; hence true.

(I) True, real, conformed to the nature and reality of things (Jn 8:16; 19:35; Ac 12:9; Sept.: Pr 22:21). Also, true as shown by the result or event (Jn 10:41; Tit 1:13, 2Pe 2:22), thus credible, not to be rejected as a witness (Jn 5:31, 32; 8:13, 14, 17; 21:24; a teacher [2Co 6:8]; grace [1Pe 5:12]; 1Jn 2:27; 3Jn 12; Sept.: Job 42:7, 8; Da 8:26).

(II) True, loving truth, sincere, veracious (Mt 22:16; Mk 12:14; Jn 3:33; 8:26; Ro 3:4).

(III) True in conduct, sincere, upright, honest, just (Jn 7:18; Php 4:8; Sept.: Isa 41:26).

Deriv.: *alḗtheia* (225), truth; *alētheúō* (226), to deal faithfully or truly; *alēthinós* (228), real, ideal, genuine (*alēthḗs* denotes the reality of the thing while *alēthinós* defines the relation of the concept to the corresponding thing, genuine); *alēthṓs* (230), truly, surely, indeed.

228. ἀληθινός, alēthinos, *al-ay-thee-nos´*; from 227; *truthful:*—true.

From *alēthḗs* (227), true. Real, genuine.

(I) True, conformed to truth (Jn 4:37; 19:35). In the sense of real, unfeigned, not fictitious (Jn 17:3; 1Th 1:9; 1Jn 5:20; Rev 3:7; Sept.: 2Ch 15:3; Isa 65:16). Spoken of what is true in itself, genuine, real, as opposed to that which is false or pretended (Jn 1:9; 4:23; 1Jn 2:8); of the vine (Jn 15:1; Sept.: Jer 2:21); of Jerusalem (Sept.: Zec 8:3); of the bread coming down from heaven (Jn 6:32, of which the manna was the type); so in Heb 8:2, *skēnē̂ alēthinē̂*, the true tabernacle (*skēnē̂* [4633], tabernacle), i.e. the heavenly temple, after the model of which the Jews regarded the temple of Jerusalem as built; also *tá alēthiná hágia*, the true holy place alluded to in Heb 9:24 (*hágion* [39], holy place, sanctuary), as opposed to the earthly copy. See Rev 11:19; 15:5.

(II) True, i.e. loving truth, veracious and hence worthy of credit (Jn 7:28; Rev 3:14; 19:9, 11; 21:5; 22:6; Sept.: Pr 12:19).

(III) True, i.e. sincere, upright of the heart (Heb 10:22; Sept.: Job 2:3; 8:6; 27:17; Isa 38:3); of a judge or judgement, meaning upright, just (Rev 6:10; 15:3; 16:7; 19:2; Sept.: Dt 25:15; Isa 25:1; 59:4).

Syn.: *gnḗsios* (1103), true, genuine, sincere; *pistós* (4103), faithful, true; *ádolos* (97), sincere, without guile; *apseudḗs* (893), veracious, one who cannot lie; *eilikrinḗs* (1506), sincere, tested as genuine.

229. ἀλήθω, alēthō, *al-ay´-tho*; from the same as 224; to *grind:*—grind.

230. ἀληθῶς, alēthōs, *al-ay-thoce´*; adverb from 227; *truly:*—indeed, surely, of a surety, truly, of a (in) truth, verily, very.

231. ἁλιεύς, halieus, *hal-ee-yoos´*; from 251; a *sailor* (as engaged on the *salt* water), i.e. (by implication) a *fisher* (-man).

232. ἁλιεύω, halieuō, *hal-ee-yoo´-o*; from 231; to *be a fisher*, i.e. (by implication) to *fish:*—go a fishing.

233. ἁλίζω, halizō, *hal-id´-zo*; from 251; to *salt:*—salt.

234. ἀλίσγεμα, alisgema, *al-is´-ghem-ah*; from ἀλισγέω, *alisgeō* (to *soil*); (ceremonial) *defilement:*—pollution.

235. ἀλλά, alla, *al-lah´*; neuter plural of 243; properly *other* things, i.e. (adverb) *contrariwise* (in many relations):—and, but (even), howbeit,

indeed, nay, nevertheless, no, notwithstanding, save, therefore, yea, yet.

236. ἀλλάσσω, allassō, *al-las´-so*; from 243; to *make different:*—change.

From *állos* (243), other, another. To change.

(I) To change the form or nature of a thing, to transform the voice or tone (Gal 4:20). To change for the better, in the pass. (1Co 15:51, 52; Sept.: Jer 13:23). To change for the worse, to corrupt, cause to decay, e.g., the heavens (Heb 1:10–12 [cf. Ps 102:26; Isa 51:6]). In Ac 6:14, to "change the customs," i.e. do away with them (Sept.: Ezr 6:11, 12).

(II) To change one thing for another, to exchange (Ro 1:23; Sept.: Ge 41:14, of garments; Le 27:10, 33; 2Sa 12:20; Ps 106:20).

Deriv.: *apallássō* (525), to change, to free from, release, deliver; *diallássō* (1259), to reconcile in cases of mutual hostility yielding to mutual concession; *katallássō* (2644), to reconcile to God in His relationship to sinful man; *metallássō* (3337), exchange one thing for another or into another.

Syn.: *metabállō* (3328), change; *metastréphō* (3344), to turn about; *katargéō* (2673), to abolish; *rhúomai* (4506), to rescue from; *antibállō* (474), to exchange, spoken usually of words that can be exchanged one with another.

237. ἀλλαχόθεν, allachothen, *al-lakh-oth´-en*; from 243; *from elsewhere:*—some other way.

238. ἀλληγορέω, allēgoreō, *al-lay-gor-eh´-o*; from 243 and ἀγορέω, *agoreō* (to *harangue* [compare 58]); to *allegorize:*—be an allegory [*the Greek word itself*].

From *állos* (243), another, and *agoreúō* (n.f.), to speak in a place of assembly, which is from *agorá* (58), marketplace. To allegorize, to speak allegorically where the thing spoken of is emblematic or representative. Only in Gal 4:24.

Syn.: *túpos* (5179), type; *múthos* (3454), a fable; *analogía* (356), analogy; *mustḗrion* (3466), mystery. All these may be classified as allegorical or figurative, insofar as they point to a meaning different from that contained in the word or words used.

239. ἀλληλούϊα, allēlouïa, *al-lay-loo´-ee-ah*; of Hebrew origin [imperative of 1984 and 3050]; *praise ye Jah!*, an adoring exclamation:—alleluiah.

240. ἀλλήλων, allēlōn, *al-lay´-lone*; Genitive plural from 243 reduplication; *one another*:— each other, mutual, one another, (the other), (them-, your-) selves, (selves) together [*sometimes with 3326 or 4314*].

Form of the reciprocal pron. *allḗlous*, one another, from *állos* (243), another. One another (Mt 24:10; Jn 15:12, 17).

241. ἀλλογενής, allogenēs, *al-log-en-ace´*; from 243 and 1085; *foreign*, i.e. not a Jew:— stranger.

Adjective from *állos* (243), other, and *génos* (1085), a nation, race. Used as a substantive, one of another nation, a stranger, foreigner, i.e. not a Jew (Lk 17:18, see Lk 17:16; Sept.: Ex 12:43; 29:33; Job 15:19; Isa 56:3, 6).

Syn.: *allóphulos* (246), one of another race, nation; *xénos* (3581), stranger, foreigner; *allótrios* (245), stranger; *pároikos* (3941), a pilgrim; *héteros* (2087), another of a different kind, a stranger; *parepídēmos* (3927), pilgrim or sojourner.

242. ἅλλομαι, hallomai, *hal´-lom-ahee*; middle of apparently a primary verb; to *jump*; (figurative) to *gush*:—leap, spring up.

243. ἄλλος, allos, *al´-los*; a primary word; "*else*," i.e. *different* (in many applications):— more, one (another), (an-, some an-) other (-s, -wise).

Adjective. Another, but of the same kind; another numerically; in contrast to *éteros* (2087), another qualitatively, another of a different kind.

(I) Without the article: other, another, some other:

(A) Simply (Mt 2:12; 13:33; 26:71; 27:42; Gal 1:7); another of the same kind (Mk 7:4, 8; Jn 21:25); another besides (Mt 25:16, 17; Mk 12:32; 15:41; Jn 6:22; 14:16); marking succession, i.e. in the second or third place (Mk 12:4, 5; Jn 20:30; Rev 12:3; 13:11).

(B) Distributively, when repeated or joined with other pronouns, e.g., *hoútos—állos*, meaning this or that, one or another (Mt 8:9; see *hoútos* [3778], this one); *hoi mén—álloi dé*, some or others (Mt 16:14; see *mén—dé* [3303, 1161], on the one hand or on the other); *álloi—álloi*, some or others (Mt 13:5–8; Mk 4:7, 8; 6:15; 8:28; 1Co 12:8–10); *állos prós állon*, one to another (Ac 2:12; see *prós* [4314], to); *álloi mén oún állo ti ékrazon*,

"Some therefore cried one thing, and some another" (Ac 19:32; see *oún* [3767] therefore; *ti* [5100], something; *krázō* [2896], to cry).

(II) With the article, *ho állos*, the other (Mt 5:39; 10:23; 12:13; Jn 18:16; Rev 17:10). *Hoi álloi*, the others, the rest (Jn 21:8; 1Co 14:29).

Deriv.: *allá* (235), but; *allássō / alláttō* (236), to change; *allachóthen* (237), from another place; *allēgoréō* (238), to allegorize; *allēlōn* (240), of one another; *allogenḗs* (241), one of another nation; *allótrios* (245), another's; *allóphulos* (246), one of another race or nation; *állōs* (247), an adverb meaning otherwise.

Syn.: *diáphoros* (1313), different.

244. ἀλλοτριεπίσκοπος, allotriepiskopos, *al-lot-ree-ep-is´-kop-os*; from 245 and 1985; *overseeing others' affairs*, i.e. a *meddler* (specially in Gentile customs):—busybody in other men's matters.

Noun from *allótrios* (245), another's, and *epískopos* (1985), superintendent, overseer, bishop. An inspector of foreign or strange things, one who busies himself with what does not concern him, a busybody. Found only in the NT, 1Pe 4:15.

245. ἀλλότριος, allotrios, *al-lot´-ree-os*; from 243; *another's*, i.e. not one's own; by extension *foreign*, *not akin*, *hostile*:—alien, (an-) other (man's, men's), strange (-r).

From *állos* (243), other. Another's, belonging to another, different (Lk 16:12; Ro 14:4; 15:20; 2Co 10:15, 16; 1Ti 5:22; Heb 9:25). Spoken of a country, strange, foreign (Ac 7:6; Heb 11:9); of persons, strangers, not belonging to one's own family (Mt 17:25, 26). By implication, hostile, an enemy; in the NT with the idea of impiety, i.e. heathen enemy, Gentile (Heb 11:34; Sept.: Ps 54:3; 1Ki 8:41; Ezr 10:2).

Deriv.: *allotrioepískopos* (244), busybody.

Syn.: Distinguished from *allóphulos* (246), one of another race or nation; *allogenḗs* (241), one of another nation, not a Jew, a stranger, foreigner (Lk 17:18); *héteros* (2087), another of a different kind; *xénos* (3581), alien, foreign, foreigner; *parádoxos* (3861), contrary to prevailing opinion or custom.

246. ἀλλόφυλος, allophulos, *al-lof´-oo-los*; from 243 and 5443; *foreign*, i.e. (special) *Gentile*:—one of another nation.

Adjective from *állos* (243), other, and *phulē* (5443), a tribe or race. Not a Jew, one of another race or nation (Ac 10:28; Sept.: 2Ki 8:28; Isa 2:6; 61:5).

Syn.: *éthnos* (1484), nation, not Jewish; *ethnikós* (1482), Gentile, non-Jewish; *allogenēs* (241), of another nation or race; *allótrios* (245), belonging to another.

247. ἄλλως, allōs, *al´-loce*; adverb from 243; *differently:*—
otherwise.

Adverb from *állos* (243), other. Otherwise. Only in 1Ti 5:25, also Sept.: Job 11:12; Est 1:19; 9:27.

Syn.: *hetérōs* (2088), otherwise, of a different frame of mind; *ei dé mēge* (1490), not indeed, otherwise.

248. ἀλοάω, aloaō, *al-o-ah´-o*; from the same as 257; to *tread* out grain:—thresh, tread out the corn.

249. ἄλογος, alogos, *al´-og-os*; from 1 (as a negative particle) and 3056; *irrational:*—brute, unreasonable.

250. ἀλοή, aloē, *al´-o-ay´*; of foreign origin [compare 174]; *aloes* (the gum):—aloes.

251. ἅλς, hals, *halce*; a primary word; "*salt*":—salt.

252. ἁλυκός, halukos, *hal-oo-kos´*; from 251; *briny:*—salt.

253. ἀλυπότερος, alupoteros, *al-oo-pot´-er-os*; comparative of a compound of 1 (as a negative particle) and 3077; *more without grief:*—less sorrowful.

254. ἅλυσις, halusis, *hal´-oo-sis*; of uncertain derivative; a *fetter* or *manacle:*—bonds, chain.

255. ἀλυσιτελής, alusitelēs, *al-oo-sit-el-ace´*; from 1 (as a negative particle) and the base of 3081; *gainless*, i.e. (by implication) *pernicious:*—unprofitable.

256. Ἀλφαῖος, Alphaios, *al-fah´-yos*; of Hebrew origin [compare 2501]; *Alphæus*, an Israelite:—Alpheus.

257. ἅλων, halōn, *hal´-ohn*; probably from the base of 1507; a threshing-*floor* (as *rolled* hard), i.e. (figurative) the *grain* (and chaff, as just threshed):—floor.

258. ἀλώπηξ, alōpex, *al-o´-pakes*; of uncertain derivative; a *fox*, i.e. (figurative) a *cunning* person:—fox.

259. ἅλωσις, halōsis, *hal´-o-sis*; from a collateral form of 138; *capture:*—be taken.

260. ἅμα, hama, *ham´-ah*; a primary particle; properly at the "*same*" time, but freely used as a preposition or adverb denoting close association:—also, and, together, with (-al).

261. ἀμαθής, amathēs, *am-ath-ace´*; from 1 (as a negative particle) and 3129; *ignorant:*—unlearned.

262. ἀμαράντινος, amarantinos, *am-ar-an´-tee-nos*; from 263; "*amaranthine*," i.e. (by implication) *fadeless:*—that fadeth not away.

Adjective corresponding to *amárantos* (263), unfading; hence, enduring. Only in 1Pe 5:4.

Syn.: *amárantos* (263), unfading; *áphthartos* (862), incorruptible; *amíantos* (283), unsoiled, undefiled.

263. ἀμάραντος, amarantos, *am-ar´-an-tos*; from 1 (as a negative particle) and a presumed derivative of 3133; *unfading*, i.e. (by implication) *perpetual:*—that fadeth not away.

Adjective from the priv. *a* (1), without, and *maraínō* (3133), to fade. Unfading; hence, enduring. Only in 1Pe 1:4.

264. ἁμαρτάνω, hamartanō, *ham-ar-tan´-o*; perhaps from 1 (as a negative particle) and the base of 3313; properly to *miss* the mark (and so *not share* in the prize), i.e. (figurative) to *err*, especially (moral) to *sin:*—for your faults, offend, sin, trespass.

To miss the mark, swerve from the way. In the NT, used metaphorically:

(I) To err, swerve from the truth, go wrong; speaking of errors of doctrine or faith (1Co 15:34; Tit 3:11).

(II) To err in action, in respect to a prescribed law, i.e. to commit errors, to do wrong, sin:

(A) Generally, to sin, spoken of any sin, used in an absolute sense (Mt 27:4; Jn 5:14; 8:11; 9:2, 3; Ro 2:12; 3:23; 5:12, 14, 16; 6:15; 1Co 7:28, 36; Eph 4:26; 1Ti 5:20; Heb 3:17; 10:26; 1Pe 2:20; 2Pe 2:4; 1Jn 1:10; 2:1; 3:6, 8, 9; 5:16, 18; Sept.: Ex 32:30; Le 4:14, 23, 28).

(B) With the prep. *eis* (1519), unto, to sin against anyone, to offend, wrong (Mt 18:15, 21;

Lk 15:18, 21; 17:3, 4; Ac 25:8; 1Co 6:18; 8:12; Sept.: Ge 20:6, 9; 43:9; 1Sa 2:25).

(C) The Hebraism *hamartánein enópion*, lit. "to sin in the face of [someone]" (see *enópion* [1799], in the face of), is usually translated "to do evil in the sight of someone," i.e. to sin against, to wrong, as above (Lk 15:21; Sept.: Ge 39:9; Dt 1:41; 20:18; 1Sa 7:6; 12:23; 14:33, 34).

Deriv.: *amártēma* (265), sin; *hamartía* (266), sin, sinful; *hamartōlós* (268), a sinner; *anamártētos* (361), without sin; *proamartánō* (4258), to sin previously.

Syn.: *ptaíō* (4417), to stumble, offend; *adikéō* (91), to do wrong; *skandalízō* (4624), to offend, be a stumbling block to someone, trip someone; *astochéō* (795), to miss the goal; *parabaínō* (3845), to transgress; *píptō* (4098), to fall; *parapíptō* (3895), to fall away; *paranoméō* (3891), to go contrary to law; *peripíptō* (4045), to fall by the side; *planáomai* (4105), to go astray.

265. ἁμάρτημα, hamartēma, *ham-ar´-tay-mah*; from 264; a *sin* (properly concrete):—sin.

Noun from *hamartánō* (264), to sin. A mistake, miss; in the NT, used metaphorically: an error, transgression, sin (Mk 3:28; 4:12; Ro 3:25; 1Co 6:18; Sept.: Ge 31:36; Isa 58:1).

Syn.: *paráptōma* (3900), the deed of trespassing, a trespass; *adíkēma* (92), a wrong, an iniquity perpetrated; *agnóēma* (51), shortcoming, error, a thing ignored; *opheílēma* (3783), that which one owes, a debt; *héttēma* (2275), a loss, defeat, defect; *plánē* (4106), deceit, delusion.

266. ἁμαρτία, hamartia, *ham-ar-tee´-ah*; from 264; *sin* (properly abstract):—offence, sin (-ful).

Noun from *hamartánō* (264), to sin. Miss, failure; in the NT, used metaphorically:

(I) Aberration from the truth, error (Jn 8:46; 16:8, 9).

(II) Sin, i.e. aberration from a prescribed law or rule of duty, whether in general or of particular sins:

(A) Generally (Mt 3:6; 9:2, 5, 6; Mk 1:4, 5; Jn 9:34; Ro 7:5; 1Co 15:3; 2Co 11:7; Heb 4:15; 10:26; Jas 2:9; 1Pe 2:22; Sept.: Ge 15:16; 18:20; Isa 53:5).

(B) Spoken of particular sins, which are to be gathered from the context; e.g., of unbelief (Jn 8:21, 24); of lewdness (2Pe 2:14); of defection from the gospel of Christ (Heb 11:25; 12:1).

(C) By metonymy of abstract for concrete,

hamartía for *hamartōlós* ([268], sinner), meaning sinful, i.e. either as causing sin (Ro 7:7, i.e. "Is the law the cause of sin?"), or as committing sin (2Co 5:21, i.e. "He has been treated as if He were a sinner").

(D) By metonymy, the practice of sinning, habit of sin (Ro 3:9; 5:12, 20, 21; Gal 3:22).

(E) By metonymy, proneness to sin, sinful desire or propensity (Jn 8:34; Ro 6:1, 2, 6, 12, 14; 7:7ff.; Heb 3:13).

(III) From the Hebrew, the imputation or consequences of sin, the guilt and punishment of sin as in the phrase "to take away [or bear] sin," i.e. the imputation of it (Jn 1:29; Ro 11:27; Heb 9:26; 10:11; 1Pe 2:24; 1Jn 3:5). So also to remit (*aphíemi* [863]) sins and the remission (*áphesis* [859]) of sins means to remove the guilt, punishment, and power of sin (Mt 9:2, 5, 6; 26:28; Lk 7:47–49; Jn 20:23; Heb 10:4); thus in Jn 9:41, "your sin remaineth" means your guilt and exposure to punishment remain (cf. Jn 15:22, 24; 1Jn 1:9). The same may be said of 1Co 15:17, where "ye are yet in your sins" indicates one is still under the guilt and power of sin (Heb 9:26, 28; Sept.: Le 22:9; Nu 9:13; Pr 10:16; Isa 5:18; 53:6, 11; La 3:39; Eze 3:20; Zec 14:19).

Syn.: *agnóēma* (51), a sin of ignorance; *opheílēma* ([3783] akin to *opheilē* [3782], a debt), that which is legally due; *adikía* (93), unrighteousness; *adíkēma* (92), a wrong, an injury; *ponēría* (4189), wickedness; *paranomía* (3892), law-breaking; *anomía* (458), lawlessness; *parábasis* (3847), violation, transgression; *kríma* (2917), condemnation; *égklēma* (1462), crime which is tried in court; *sunōmosía* (4945), a plot, conspiracy; *asébeia* (763), impiety, ungodliness; *parakoē* (3876), disobedience; *apeítheia* (543), obstinate rejection of God's will; *paráptōma* (3900), a false step, a blunder; *ptōsis* (4431), a fall; *apostasía* (646), a standing away from, although not necessarily a departure from a position in which one stood; *aitía* (156) and *aítion* (158), a crime, a legal ground for punishment, fault; *héttēma* (2275), a loss, defeat, defect; *hamártēma* (265), an act of sin or disobedience to divine requirement and expectation.

267. ἁμάρτυρος, amarturos, *am-ar´-too-ros*; from 1 (as a negative particle) and a form of 3144; *unattested*:—without witness.

268. ἁμαρτωλός, hamartōlos, *ham-ar-to-los´*; from 264; *sinful*, i.e. a *sinner*:—sinful, sinner.

Adjective from *hamartánō* (264), to deviate, miss the mark, sin. Erring from the way or mark. In the NT, used metaphorically:

(I) As adj.: erring from the divine law, sinful, wicked, impious:

(A) Generally: a sinful generation (Mk 8:38); a sinful man, a sinner (Lk 5:8; 19:7; 24:7; Jn 9:16, 24); a sinful woman (Lk 7:37, 39; Sept.: Nu 32:14; Isa 1:4); "more wicked than all others" (a.t.; Lk 13:2); a sinner (Lk 18:13; Ro 3:7); sinful, sinners (Ro 5:8; Gal 2:17; Jas 4:8).

(B) Oblivious to the consequences of sin, guilty and exposed to punishment (Ro 5:19; 7:13; Gal 2:15; Jude 15).

(II) As substantive, a sinner, transgressor, impious person:

(A) Generally (Mt 9:10, 11, 13; 11:19; Mk 2:15–17; Lk 5:30, 32; 6:32–34; 7:34; 15:1, 2, 7, 10; Jn 9:25, 31; 1Ti 1:9, 15; Heb 7:26; 12:3; Jas 5:20; 1Pe 4:18; Sept.: Ps 1:1, 5; 37:12, 20; Isa 13:9; Eze 33:8, 19; Am 9:8).

(B) Sinners, despisers of God; used by the Jews to refer to the Gentiles, heathen or pagan nations (Mt 26:45 [cf. Mt 20:19; Mk 10:33; Lk 18:32; Sept.: Isa 14:5]).

Syn.: *asebḗs* (765), impious, ungodly; *ápistos* (571), an unbeliever; *opheilétēs* (3781), a debtor; *énochos* (177), guilty of something; *aítios* (159), one to be blamed; *ádikos* (94), unjust.

269. ἄμαχος, amachos, *am´-akh-os*; from 1 (as a negative particle) and 3163; *peaceable*:— not a brawler.

270. ἀμάω, amaō, *am-ah´-o*; from 260; properly to *collect*, i.e. (by implication) *reap*:—reap down.

271. ἀμέθυστος, amethustos, *am-eth´-oos-tos*; from 1 (as a negative particle) and a derivative of 3184; the "*amethyst*" (supposed to *prevent intoxication*):—amethyst.

272. ἀμελέω, ameleo, *am-el-eh´-o*; from 1 (as a negative particle) and 3199; to *be careless* of:— make light of, neglect, be negligent, not regard.

273. ἄμεμπτος, amemptos, *am´-emp-tos*; from 1 (as a negative particle) and a derivative of 3201; *irreproachable*:—blameless, faultless, unblameable.

Adjective from the priv. *a* (1), without, and *mémphomai* (3201), to find fault. Blameless (Lk 1:6; Php 2:15; 3:6; 1Th 3:13; Heb 8:7).

Deriv.: *amémptōs* (274), unblamably.

Syn.: *ámōmos* (299), unblemished, unspotted. The *ámōmos*, the unblemished, may be *ámemptos*, unblamed; *áspilos* (784), without spot; *anégklētos* (410), legally irreproachable; *anepílēptos* (423), irreprehensible, one who cannot be caught and accused; *anaítios* (338), guiltless, blameless; *ádolos* (97), without guile; *ákakos* (172), without being bad in oneself; *akéraios* (185), without foreign mixture, sincere, harmless; *haploús* (573), single, without duplicity; *amṓmētos* (298), without blemish.

274. ἀμέμπτως, amemptōs, *am-emp´-toce*; adverb from 273; *faultlessly*:—blameless, unblamably.

275. ἀμέριμνος, amerimnos, *am-er´-im-nos*; from 1 (as a negative particle) and 3308; *not anxious*:—without care (-fulness), secure.

276. ἀμετάθετος, ametathetos, *am-et-ath´-et-os*; from 1 (as a negative particle) and a derivative of 3346; *unchangeable*, or (neuter as abstract) *unchangeability*:—immutable (-ility).

277. ἀμετακίνητος, ametakinētos, *am-et-ak-in´-ay-tos*; from 1 (as a negative particle) and a derivative of 3334; *immovable*:—unmovable.

278. ἀμεταμέλητος, ametamelētos, *am-et-am-el´-ay-tos*; from 1 (as a negative particle) and a presumed derivative of 3338; *irrevocable*:— without repentance, not to be repented of.

279. ἀμετανόητος, ametanoētos, *am-et-an-o´-ay-tos*; from 1 (as negative particle) and a presumed derivative of 3340; *unrepentant*:— impenitent.

Adjective from the priv. *a* (1), without, and *metanoéō* (3340), to repent or change one's mind. Inflexible, impenitent (Ro 2:5).

Syn.: *ametamélētos* (278), not to be concerned after an act has been committed (Ro 11:29; 2Co 7:10).

280. ἄμετρος, ametros, *am´-et-ros*; from 1 (as a negative particle) and 3358; *immoderate*:— (thing) without measure.

281. ἀμήν, amēn, *am-ane´*; of Hebrew origin [543]; properly *firm*, i.e. (figurative) *trustworthy*; adverb *surely* (often as interjection *so be it*):—amen, verily.

282. ἀμήτωρ, amētōr, *am-ay´-tore*; from 1 (as a negative particle) and 3384; *motherless*, i.e. *of unknown maternity*:—without mother.

283. ἀμίαντος, amiantos, *am-ee´-an-tos*; from 1 (as a negative particle) and a derivative of 3392; *unsoiled*, i.e. (figurative) *pure*:—undefiled.

Adjective from the priv. *a* (1), not or without, and *miaínō* (3392), to defile. That which has nothing in it that defiles; unpolluted, unstained, unsoiled, undefiled by sin (Heb 7:26); of marriage (Heb 13:4), chaste; of the worship of God (Jas 1:27), pure, sincere; of the heavenly inheritance (1Pe 1:4), inviolate.

Syn.: *hagnós* (53), pure from defilement; *katharós* (2513), cleansed; *eilikrinḗs* (1506), sincere, unalloyed; *hágios* (40), holy as being free from admixture of evil; *hósios* (3741), one who observes duties toward God, Godlike; *tímios* (5093), honourable; *hierós* (2413), sacred, outwardly associated with God.

284. Ἀμιναδάβ, Aminadab, *am-ee-nad-ab´*; of Hebrew origin [5992]; *Aminadab*, an Israelite:—Aminadab.

285. ἄμμος, ammos, *am´-mos*; perhaps from 260; *sand* (as *heaped* on the beach):—sand.

286. ἀμνός, amnos, *am-nos´*; apparently a primary word; a *lamb*:—lamb.

A noun meaning lamb. In the NT, used metaphorically of Christ delivered over to death as a lamb to the sacrifice (Jn 1:29, 36; Ac 8:32; 1Pe 1:19; Sept.: Ex 12:5; Le 14:10, 12, 13; Isa 16:1).

287. ἀμοιβή, amoibē, *am-oy-bay´*; from ἀμείβω, *ameibō* (to *exchange*); *requital*:—requite.

288. ἄμπελος, ampelos, *am´-pel-os*; probably from the base of 297 and that of 257; a *vine* (as *coiling about* a support):—vine.

289. ἀμπελουργός, ampelourgos, *am-pel-oor-gos´*; from 288 and 2041; a *vine-worker*, i.e. *pruner*:—vine-dresser.

290. ἀμπελών, ampelōn, *am-pel-ohn´*; from 288; a *vineyard*:—vineyard.

291. Ἀμπλίας, Amplias, *am-plee´-as*; contracted from Latin *ampliatus* [*enlarged*]; *Amplias*, a Roman Christian:—Amplias.

292. ἀμύνομαι, amunomai, *am-oo´-nom-ahee*; middle of a primary verb; to *ward off* (for oneself), i.e. *protect*:—defend.

293. ἀμφίβληστρον, amphiblēstron, *am-fib´-lace-tron*; from a compound of the base of 297 and 906; a (fishing) *net* (as *thrown about* the fish):—net.

Noun from *amphibállō* (n.f.), to throw around, which is from the prefix *amphí*, round about, and *bállō* (906), to throw. In the NT, a fish net, a casting net (Mt 4:18; Mk 1:16; Sept.: Ps 141:10; Ecc 9:12; Hab 1:15–17).

Syn.: *díktuon* (1350), a general term for net; *sagḗnē* (4522), a dragnet; *ágkistron* (44), a hook.

294. ἀμφιέννυμι, amphiennumi, *am-fee-en´-noo-mee*; from the base of 297 and ἕννυμι, *hennumi* (to *invest*); to *enrobe*:—clothe.

295. Ἀμφίπολις, Amphipolis, *am-fip´-ol-is*; from the base of 297 and 4172; a *city surrounded* by a river; *Amphipolis*, a place in Macedonia:—Amphipolis.

296. ἄμφοδον, amphodon, *am´-fod-on*; from the base of 297 and 3598; a *fork* in the road:—where two ways meet.

297. ἀμφότερος, amphoteros, *am-fot´-er-os*; comparative of ἀμφί, *amphi* (*around*); (in plural) *both*:—both.

298. ἀμώμητος, amōmētos, *am-o´-may-tos*; from 1 (as a negative particle) and a derivative of 3469; *unblameable*:—blameless.

299. ἄμωμος, amōmos, *am´-o-mos*; from 1 (as a negative particle) and 3470; *unblemished* (literal or figurative):—without blame (blemish, fault, spot), faultless, unblameable.

Adjective from the priv. *a* (1), without, and *mṓmos* (3470), spot, blemish. Spotless, without blemish. In the NT, spoken metaphorically of Christ, a lamb without blemish, as was required by Levitical law in regard to all victims (Heb 9:14; 1Pe 1:19; see Le 1:10; 22:19–22); also generally, blameless (Eph 1:4; 5:27; Col 1:22; Heb 9:14; Jude 24; Rev 14:5)

Syn.: *ámemptos* (273), unblameable, related to *mémphomai* (3201), to blame, find fault; *anaítios* (338), guiltless; *anepíleptos* (423), irreproachable; *anégklētos* (410), not chargeable in court; *díkaios* (1342), just; *euthús* (2117), straight; *orthós* (3717), straight, upright; *akatákritos* (178), uncondemned; *anepaís-chuntos* (422), irreprehensible.

300. Ἀμών, Amōn, *am-one´*; of Hebrew origin [526]; *Amon,* an Israelite:—Amon.

301. Ἀμώς, Amōs, *am-oce´*; of Hebrew origin [531]; *Amos,* an Israelite:—Amos.

302. ἄν, an, *an*; a primary particle, denoting a *supposition, wish, possibility* or *uncertainty:—* [what-, where-, whither-, who-] soever. Usually unexpressed except by the subjunctive or potential mood. Also contracted from 1437.

Particle, sometimes properly rendered by "perhaps"; more commonly not translated in Eng. by any corresponding particle, but only giving to a proposition or sentence a stamp of uncertainty and mere possibility, and indicating a dependence on circumstances.

(I) Indicating that a supposition or possibility will be realized, under the circumstances implied by *án:*

(A) In vows or wishes, as in Ac 26:29, where it gives the sense of "I could pray to God, and under the circumstances do pray to Him."

(B) Where the thing inquired about is possible, or certain, but the inquirer is uncertain when or how it is to take place. Lk 1:62, "how he might wish him to be called" (a.t.), i.e. since he was to have a name, what that name should be. See also Lk 9:46; Jn 13:24; Ac 2:12; 5:24; 17:18; 21:33.

(II) Used with relative words, rendering them more general and indicating mere possibility:

(A) With relative pronouns or particles, *án* implies some condition or uncertainty whether or where the thing will take place; equivalent to -ever, -soever. Thus in conjunction with *hós* [(3739), rel. pron; he who], for example, *hós án* becomes translated whoever, whosoever (Mt 5:21, 31, 32; 10:11; 12:32; Mk 3:29; Jn 1:33; Sept.: Da 3:5, 6). Again, combined with a word like *hópou* ([3699], where, at whichever spot), i.e. *hópou án*, the expression is translated wheresoever (Mk 9:18; 14:9; Lk 9:57; Rev 14:4).

(B) With particles of time, *án* indicates an element of uncertainty, not to the occurrence of an event, but to the time that event will occur. For example, in Mt 2:13, *án* appears with *héōs* ([2193], until); "be thou there until (*héōs án*) I bring thee word." The uncertainty lies not in whether or not they will be informed, but in the

time of that occurrence (see also Mt 2:13; 5:18, 26; 10:11, 23; Mk 6:10; Lk 20:43; Ac 2:35). In the same way, combined with *hós* ([5613], as), in 1Co 11:34, *án* conveys the meaning when, as soon as: "And the rest will I set in order when (*hós án*) I come." Paul will come; the time of his coming, however, is uncertain.

(C) Used with the particle *hópōs* [(3704), that, in order that], *án* again brings the idea of indefiniteness. Ac 15:16, 17 says, for example, "After this I will return, and will build again the tabernacle of David, ... that (*hópōs án*) the residue of men might seek after the Lord." The resulting seeking that occurs after the Lord's return will certainly take place; the time, however, is indefinite, as is the duration of this seeking. So *hópōs án* carries the sense of "at some time or another" or "sooner or later." By contrast, *hópōs* occurs by itself in Mt 6:16, "for they disfigure their faces, that (*hópōs*) they may appear unto men to fast." Here, the effect is much more immediate and definite. Other occurrences of *hópōs án* are in Lk 2:35; Ac 3:19; Ro 3:4.

(III) With the indic. in the historical tenses (but not in the primary ones), *án* is used in the apodosis (the result) of a conditional sentence in which *ei* ([1487], if) precedes and indicates that the thing in question would have taken place, if that contingency which is the subject of the protasis (the proposition) had also taken place; but that in fact neither the one nor the other has taken place. In Mt 11:21, it means that if these miracles had been done in Tyre, they would have repented; but the miracles were not done, and they did not repent (see also Lk 10:13; Jn 4:10; 9:41; Heb 4:8; Jn 8:42, where the meaning is, if God were your Father, you would love me; however, neither is true [similarly in Mt 11:23; 12:7; 23:30; 24:22, 43; Mk 13:20; Jn 11:21; Ro 9:29; 1Co 2:8; 11:31; Gal 1:10; 1Jn 2:19]).

(IV) When, in relative clauses, a relative pron. with *án* is followed by the indic., Class. Gr. writers employed the subjunctive or optative. This occurs in the NT when a thing is spoken of as actually taking place, not at a definite time or in a definite manner, but as often as opportunity arises. It is thus found only with a preterite, a verb tense that indicates action in the past without reference to duration, continuance, or repetition. Used in Mk 6:56, meaning, "as many as" or "however many"; Ac 2:45; 4:35; 1Co 12:2, meaning led away to idol worship, just as he happened to be led, i.e. I do not say by whom or how; see also Sept.: Ge 2:19; Le 5:3. Once with the present indic. in Mk 11:24, where some MSS have the indic. verb *aiteísthe* in the subjunctive (*aitésthe*, from *aitéomai* [154], to ask, beg). See also Lk 8:18; 10:8.

(V) As an adverb or in a false construction, meaning perhaps, possibly. Thus the translation in 2Co 10:9, "as if I would terrify you." In 1Co 7:5, the idea is "except perhaps by consent."

303. ἀνά, ana, *an-ah´*; a primary preposition and adverb; properly *up*; but (by extension) used (distributively) *severally*, or (locally) *at* (etc.):— and, apiece, by, each, every (man), in, through. In compounds (as a prefix) it often means (by implication) *repetition, intensity, reversal,* etc.

Preposition meaning on, upon, in.

(I) In the NT, used with other words, it forms a periphrase (a longer phrasing in place of a possible shorter and plainer form of expression) for an adverb; e.g., *aná méros* ([3313], part), by turns, alternately (1Co 14:27); *aná méson* ([3319], midst, middle), in the midst of, through the midst of, between. So with this use spoken of place (Mt 13:25; Mk 7:31; Rev 7:17; Sept.: Isa 57:5; 2Ki 16:14); spoken of persons (1Co 6:5). In Mt 20:9, 10 *aná dēnárion* (*aná* [303], to each, *dēnárion* [1220], dinar), "to each a dinar" (a.t.).

(II) With numerical words it marks distribution, e.g., "and sent them two and two (*aná dúo*) before his face" (Lk 10:1; see also Mk 6:40; Lk 9:3, 14; Jn 2:6; Rev 4:8; 21:21; Sept.: Isa 6:2).

In composition, *aná* denotes: (a) up or upward, as *anabaínō* (305), I go up; (b) back or again, equal to the Eng. prefix re-, implying repetition, increase, intensity, as *anakainízō* (340), to renew; *anachōréō* (402), to depart; *anaginóskō* (314), to know again, to read.

304. ἀναβαθμός, anabathmos, *an-ab-ath-mos´*; from 305 [compare 898]; a *stairway*:— stairs.

305. ἀναβαίνω, anabaino, *an-ab-ah´ee-no*; from 303 and the base of 939; to *go up* (literal or figurative):—arise, ascend (up), climb (go, grow, rise, spring) up, come (up).

From *aná* (303), up, and *baínō* (n.f.), to go. To go or come up, to ascend, cause to ascend from a lower to a higher place.

(I) Spoken of persons, animals: to go or come up (Mt 5:1; Mk 3:13; Lk 5:19; Sept.: Ge 49:4). Specifically, to climb (Lk 19:4); to enter into a boat, to embark (Mk 6:51); climbing up or entering some other way (Jn 10:1); to get up into a chariot (Ac 8:31); from the water (Mt 3:16); out of the water, from the water, upon the land (Ac 8:39; see Ac 8:38); of those who go from a lower to a higher region of country, e.g., from Galilee or Caesarea to Judea (Lk 2:4; Ac 18:22) and especially to Jerusalem (Mt 20:17, 18; Jn 7:8, 10; 12:20); of those who ascend into heaven or to the heights, either to have communion with God or to dwell there (Jn 3:13; 6:62; 20:17; Ro 10:6; Eph 4:8–10; Rev 4:1; 11:12); spoken of angels who are said to ascend and descend upon the Son of man (Jn 1:51).

(II) Spoken of inanimate things which are said to go up, ascend, rise, e.g., smoke (Rev 8:4; 9:2; 14:11; 19:3; Sept.: Ex 19:18; Isa 34:10); of plants, fruit: to spring up, grow (Mt 13:7; Mk 4:8, 32; Sept.: Isa 5:24; 32:13; 55:13); of a rumour (Ac 21:31, lit. "word was brought up to the chief captain"); of thoughts, actions, which come up into one's mind: to spring up, arise in the heart (Lk 24:38); upon the heart (Ac 7:23; 1Co 2:9); of prayers (Ac 10:4). See also Isa 65:17; Jer 3:16; 32:35; 44:21.

Deriv.: *anabathmós* (304), the act of ascending; *prosanabaínō* (4320), to go up higher; *sunanabaínō* (4872), to come up with.

Syn.: *anatéllō* (393), to arise, spring up; *érchomai* (2064), to come or go; *hḗkō* (2240), to come or be present; *katantáō* (2658), to come to; *anérchomai* (424), to go up; *phúō* (5453), to germinate, spring up, sprout; *blastánō* (985), to sprout.

306. ἀναβάλλομαι, anaballomai, *an-ab-al´-lom-ahee*; middle from 303 and 906; to *put off* (for oneself):—defer.

307. ἀναβιβάζω, anabibazo, *an-ab-ee-bad´-zo*; from 303 and a derivative of the base of 939; to *cause to go up*, i.e. *haul* (a net):—draw.

308. ἀναβλέπω, anablepo, *an-ab-lep´-o*; from 303 and 991; to *look up*; (by implication) to *recover sight*:—look (up), see, receive sight.

309. ἀνάβλεψις, anablepsis, *an-ab´-lep-sis*; from 308; *restoration of sight*:—recovering of sight.

310. ἀναβοάω, anaboaō, *an-ab-o-ah´-o*; from 303 and 994; to *halloo:*—cry (aloud, out).

311. ἀναβολή, anabolē, *an-ab-ol-ay´*; from 306; a *putting off:*—delay.

312. ἀναγγέλλω, anaggellō, *an-ang-el´-lo*; from 303 and the base of 32; to *announce* (in detail):—declare, rehearse, report, show, speak, tell.

From *aná* (303), on, upon, and *aggéllō* (n.f., see below), to tell, declare, which is from *ággelos* (32), messenger. To announce, make known, declare, tell of things done (Mk 5:14, 19; Ac 14:27; 15:4; 16:38; 2Co 7:7). To bring word, inform (Jn 5:15); of things fut., to show beforehand, foretell (Jn 16:13; Sept.: Isa 41:22, 23; 46:10); of the Christian doctrine, to declare, show forth, teach (Jn 4:25; 16:14, 15, 25; Ac 20:20, 27; Ro 15:21; 1Pe 1:12; 1Jn 1:5; Sept.: Dt 8:3; 26:3; Da 2:9); of evil deeds, meaning to declare, confess (Ac 19:18; Sept.: Job 33:23; Ps 38:18; Isa 3:8).

Deriv. of *angéllō* (n.f.): *apaggéllō* (518), to announce; *diaggéllō* (1229), to declare; *exaggéllō* (1804), to publish, show forth; *epaggéllō* (1861), to proclaim; *kataggéllō* (2605), to declare plainly, *paraggéllō* (3853), charge, command.

Syn.: *diēgéomai* (1334), to relate in full; *ekdiēgéomai* (1555), to narrate in full; *exēgéomai* (1834), to make known, explain, declare; *dēlóō* (1213), to make plain; *phrázō* (5419), to explain, declare; *gnōrízō* (1107), to make known; *emphanízō* (1718), to declare plainly; *phaneróō* (5319), to manifest; *anatíthēmi* (394), to make known, to place before, declare to someone; *martnréō* (3140), to testify; *diaphēmízō* (1310), to spread abroad; *mēnúō* (3377), to disclose, make known; *légō* (3004), to tell; *laléō* (2980), to speak; *apophthéggomai* (669), to speak forth, give utterance; *prosphōnéō* (4377), to address, call to; *eréō* (2046), to speak; *dialégomai* (1256), to discuss, reason, speak; *chrēmatízō* (5537), to warn, instruct as if through an oracle; *apologéomai* (626), to make a defence; *eklaléō* (1583), to speak out; *diasaphéō* (1285), to make clear.

313. ἀναγεννάω, anagennaō, *an-ag-en-nah´-o*; from 303 and 1080; to *beget* or (by extension) *bear* (again):—beget, (bear) × again.

From *aná* (303), again, and *gennáō* (1080), to beget. To beget again. In the NT, used metaphorically for a change of carnal nature to a Christian life; to regenerate. In the pass. *anagennáomai*, to be begotten again, regenerated (1Pe 1:3, 23). It is equivalent to being a child of God (Gal 3:26), being born of God (Jn 1:12, 13; 1Jn 3:9), being born from above (*ánōthen* [509], Jn 3:3), or becoming a new (*kainós* [2537]) creation or creature (*ktísis* [2937]), as in 2Co 5:17.

Syn.: *apokuéō* (616), to give birth to; *tíktō* (5088), to bring forth.

314. ἀναγινώσκω, anaginōskō, *an-ag-in-oce´-ko*; from 303 and 1097; to *know again*, i.e. (by extension) to *read:*—read.

From *aná* (303), an emphatic, and *ginōskō* (1097), to know. To know accurately, to distinguish. In the NT, to know by reading, to read:
(I) To read for oneself, to learn by reading (Mt 12:3, 5; 21:16, 42; 22:31; 24:15; Mk 2:25; 13:14; Lk 6:3; 10:26; Jn 19:20; Ac 8:28, 30, 32; 15:31; 23:34; 2Co 1:13; Eph 3:4; Rev 1:3; 5:4; Sept.: Dt 17:19; 2Ki 5:7; Isa 29:11, 12). Metaphorically in 2Co 3:2, "our epistle … read of all men," i.e. open, manifest.
(II) To read aloud before others (Lk 4:16; Ac 13:27; 15:21; 2Co 3:15; Col 4:16; 1Th 5:27; Sept.: Dt 31:11; 2Ki 22:11; Ne 13:1).

Deriv.: *anágnōsis* (320), reading.

315. ἀναγκάζω, anagkazo, *an-ang-kad´-zo*; from 318; to *necessitate*; compel, constrain.

To necessitate, to compel, to constrain. To compel by force, threats, circumstances, etc. (Ac 26:11; 28:19; 2Co 12:11; Gal 2:3, 14). To constrain by entreaty, invitations, etc.; to persuade (Mt 14:22; Mk 6:45; Lk 14:23; Gal 6:12).

Syn.: *aggareúō* (29), to press into service; *parabiázomai* (3849), to employ force contrary to nature and right, to compel by using force; *sunéchō* (4912), to constrain.

316. ἀναγκαῖος, anagkaios, *an-ang-kah´-yos*; from 318; *necessary*; (by implication) *close* (of kin):—near, necessary, necessity, needful.

Adjective from *anágkē* (318), necessity. Compulsive, compelled. In the NT, necessary. Used of things required by nature (1Co 12:22; Tit 3:14); necessary from natural ties of relationship or affinity (Ac 10:24); and necessary from a moral or spiritual standpoint, i.e. right, proper (Ac 13:46; 2Co 9:5; Php 1:24; 2:25; Heb 8:3).

Syn.: *epitḗdeios* (2006), suitable, convenient, necessary; *eúkairos* (2121), timely, seasonable;

chrḗsimos (5539), useful; *eúchrēstos* (2173), serviceable; *ōphélimos* (5624), profitable.

317. ἀναγκαστῶς, anagkastōs, *an-ang-kas-toce´*; adverb from a derivative of 315; *compulsorily:*—by constraint.

318. ἀναγκή, anagkē, *an-ang-kay´*; from 303 and the base of 43; *constraint* (literal or figurative); (by implication) *distress:*—distress, must needs, (of) necessity (-sary), needeth, needful.

(I) Spoken of as arising from the influence of other persons: constraint, compulsion (1Co 7:37; 2Co 9:7; Phm 14); as arising from the good or bad disposition of a person or persons, or from the nature and circumstances of the case (Mt 18:7; Heb 7:12, 27; 9:16, 23); spoken of the obligation of duty: to be right, proper, just; I must (Ro 13:5; 1Co 9:16; Jude 3).

(II) Unavoidable distress, calamity (Lk 21:23; 1Co 7:26; 2Co 6:4; 12:10; 1Th 3:7; Sept.: Ps 25:17; 107:6; 109:143; Job 27:9).

Deriv.: *anagkázō* (315), to force; *anagkaíos* (316), needful; *anagkastṓs* (317), of necessity, by constraint; *epánagkes* (1876), of necessity.

Syn.: *stenochōría* (4730), narrowness of place, distress; *thlípsis* (2347), affliction; *sunochḗ* (4928), a compressing together, distress, anguish; *chreía* (5532), a need, necessity; *deí* (1163), it is necessary; *déon*, from *déomai* (1189), to petition, related to *deí* (1163), it is necessary, used as a noun meaning that which is needful, due, proper; *prépō* (4241), I must; *epitagḗ* (2003), an injunction, decree, commandment.

319. ἀναγνωρίζομαι, anagnōrizomai, *an-ag-no-rid´-zom-ahee*; middle from 303 and 1107; to *make* (oneself) *known:*—be made known.

From *aná* (303), again, and *gnōrízō* (1107), to know. To know again, to recognize. Pass.: *anagnōrízomai*, to be made known again (Ac 7:13; Sept.: Ge 45:1); *anegnōrísthēn*, aor. pass. with reflexive meaning, to make oneself known.

Syn.: the phrase *phanerós gínomai* (*phanerós* [5318], manifest; *gínomai* [1096], become), to become manifest; *epiginṓskō* (1921), to fully know; *epístamai* (1987), to understand; *manthánō* (3129), to learn; *homologéō* (3670), to acknowledge, confess; *paradéchomai* (3858), to admit; *apodéchomai* (588), approve, accept; *egkrínō* (1469), approve; *sumphōnéō* (4856), to agree with.

320. ἀνάγνωσις, anagnōsis, *an-ag´-no-sis*; from 314; (the act of) *reading:*—reading.

Noun from *anaginṓskō* (314), to know accurately, to read. Reading, whether public or private (Ac 13:15; 2Co 3:14; 1Ti 4:13; Sept.: Ne 8:3).

321. ἀνάγω, anagō, *an-ag´-o*; from 303 and 71; to *lead up*; by extension to *bring out*; specially to *sail* away:—bring (again, forth, up again), depart, launch (forth), lead (up), loose, offer, sail, set forth, take up.

322. ἀναδείκνυμι, anadeiknumi, *an-ad-ike´-noo-mee*; from 303 and 1166; to *exhibit*, i.e. (by implication) to *indicate, appoint:*—appoint, shew.

323. ἀνάδειξις, anadeixis, *an-ad´-ike-sis*; from 322; (the act of) *exhibition:*—shewing.

324. ἀναδέχομαι, anadechomai, *an-ad-ekh´-om-ahee*; from 303 and 1209; to *entertain* (as a guest):—receive.

From *aná* (303), an emphatic, and *déchomai* (1209), to receive. To take upon oneself. In the NT, to receive, in the sense of to embrace, trust in (Heb 10:17); also, to receive a guest, i.e. to entertain (Ac 28:7).

Syn.: *lambánō* (2983), to receive; *analambánō* (353), to take to oneself, receive; *apolambánō* (618), to receive from another; *hupolambánō* (5274), to receive.

325. ἀναδίδωμι, anadidōmi, *an-ad-eed´-om-ee*; from 303 and 1325; to *hand over:*—deliver.

326. ἀναζάω, anazaō, *an-ad-zah´-o*; from 303 and 2198; to *recover life* (literal or figurative):—(be a-) live again, revive.

327. ἀναζητέω, anazēteō, *an-ad-zay-teh´-o*; from 303 and 2212; to *search* out:—seek.

328. ἀναζώννυμι, anazōnnumi, *an-ad-zone´-noo-mee*; from 303 and 2224; to *gird afresh:*—gird up.

329. ἀναζωπυρέω, anazōpureō, *an-ad-zo-poor-eh´-o*; from 303 and a compound of the base of 2226 and 4442; to *re-enkindle:*—stir up.

330. ἀναθάλλω, anathallō, *an-ath-al´-lo*; from 303 and **θάλλω, thallō** (to *flourish*); to *revive:*—flourish again.

331. ἀνάθεμα, anathema, *an-ath´-em-ah*; from 394; a (religious) *ban* or (concrete) *excommunicated* (thing or person):—accused, anathema, curse, × great.

Noun from *anatíthēmi* (394), to place, lay up. Anything laid up or suspended as an offering in the temple of a god, anything consecrated to God. In the Sept., *anáthema* is used to translate the Heb *ḥērem* (2764, OT), which is spoken in like manner of animals, persons, etc. (Le 27:28). Because every living thing thus consecrated to God could not be redeemed, but was to be put to death (Le 27:29), both *ḥērem* and Sept. *anáthema* are used to denote anything irrevocably devoted to death, destruction, etc., or anything on which a curse is laid, as cities and their inhabitants (Jos 6:17, 18; 7:1), and therefore anything abominable and detestable (Dt 7:26).

In the NT, *anáthema* is used to indicate an accursed thing, or, spoken of persons, one accursed; someone excluded from the favour of God and devoted to destruction (1Co 12:13; 16:22; Gal 1:8, 9; Ac 23:14; Ro 9:3).

Deriv.: *anathematízō* (332), to declare anathema, to curse; *katanáthema* (2652), an accursed thing.

Syn.: *ará* (685), a malediction, cursing; *katára* (2671), a curse.

332. ἀναθεματίζω, anathematizō, *an-ath-em-at-id´-zo*; from 331; to *declare* or *vow* under penalty of execration:—(bind under a) curse, bind with an oath.

From *anáthema* (331), a curse. To declare one to be accursed, to curse, to bind by a curse (Mk 14:71; Ac 23:12, 14, 21).

Deriv.: *katanathematízō* (2653), to utterly curse.

Syn.: *kataráomai* (2672), to pray or wish evil against a person or thing; *kakologéō* (2551), to speak evil.

333. ἀναθεωρέω, anatheōreō, *an-ath-eh-o-reh´-o*; from 303 and 2334; to *look again* (i.e. *attentively*) at (literal or figurative):—behold, consider.

334. ἀνάθημα, anathēma, *an-ath´-ay-mah*; from 394 [like 331, but in a good sense]; a *votive offering*:—gift.

From *anatíthēmi* (394), to separate, lay up. Anything consecrated to God and laid up or suspended in the temple; a gift, an offering (Lk 21:5). Votive offerings, such as shields, chaplets, golden chains, candlesticks, etc. were common in the temples of the heathen; the same custom was imitated in the Jewish temple.

Syn.: *dṓron* (1435), a gift; *dōreá* (1431), a gift emphasizing the freeness of the gift; *dṓrēma* (1434), that which is given as a gift, boon; *dóma* (1390), a gift as such without any benefit necessarily derived from it; *dósis* (1394), the act of giving; *chárisma* (5486), the gift resulting from grace or *cháris* (5485); *prosphorá* (4376), an offering; *holokaútōma* (3646), a burnt offering.

335. ἀναίδεια, anaideia, *an-ah´ee-die-ah´*; from a compound of 1 (as a negative particle [compare 427]) and 127; *impudence*, i.e. (by implication) *importunity*:—importunity.

Noun from *anaidḗs* (n.f.), impudent, which is from the priv. *a* (1), without, and *aidṓs* (127), shame. Want of modesty, shamelessness, insolence. Recklessness or disregard of consideration by the one making the request (Lk 11:8).

Syn.: *atimía* (819), shame, disgrace, dishonour; *aschēmosúnē* (808), unseemliness, shame.

336. ἀναίρεσις, anairesis, *an-ah´ee-res-is*; from 337; (the act of) *killing*:—death.

337. ἀναιρέω, anaireō, *an-ahee-reh´-o*; from 303 and (the active of) 138; to *take up*, i.e. *adopt*; (by implication) to *take away* (violently), i.e. *abolish, murder*:—put to death, kill, slay, take away, take up.

338. ἀναίτιος, anaitios, *an-ah´ee-tee-os*; from 1 (as a negative particle) and 159 (in the sense of 156); *innocent*:—blameless, guiltless.

339. ἀνακαθίζω, anakathizō, *an-ak-ath-id´-zo*; from 303 and 2523; properly to *set up*, i.e. (reflex.) to *sit up*:—sit up.

340. ἀνακαινίζω, anakainizō, *an-ak-ahee-nid´-zo*; from 303 and a derivative of 2537; to *restore*:—renew.

From *aná* (303), again, and *kainízō* (n.f.), to renew, which is from *kainós* (2537), qualitatively *new*. To renew, to restore to its former state. In the NT, used metaphorically, spoken of those who have fallen from the true faith: to bring back to repentance and former faith (Heb 6:6; Sept.: Ps 103:5).

Syn.: *ananeóō* (365), to renew in the sense of making young or replacing numerically. See both *néos* (3501), new, either numerically or one coming later, and *kainós* (2537), qualitatively new.

341. ἀνακαινόω, anakainoō, *an-ak-ahee-no´-o*; from 303 and a derivative of 2537; to *renovate:*—renew.

From *aná* (303), again, and *kainóō* (n.f.), to make new, which is from *kainós* (2537), qualitatively new. In the NT, found only in the writings of Paul: to renew; to renovate, in the sense of to change from a carnal to a Christian life; to increase in faith, hope, virtue, etc. (2Co 4:16; Col 3:10, cf. Eph 4:23).

Deriv.: *anakaínōsis* (342), renewal.

Syn.: *ananeóō* (365), to reform, renew with the same kind of experience as in the past; *neótēs* (3503), youth with reference simply to age and not quality of life.

342. ἀνακαίνωσις, anakainōsis, *an-ak-ah´ee-no-sis*; from 341; *renovation:*—renewing.

From *anakainóō* (341), to renew qualitatively. Therefore, a renewing or a renovation which makes a person different than in the past. Occurs in Ro 12:2; Tit 3:5 (cf. Jn 3:5). See also *anakainízō* (340), to renew qualitatively.

Syn.: *paliggenesía* (3824), rebirth, renewal.

343. ἀνακαλύπτω, anakaluptō, *an-ak-aloop´-to*; from 303 (in the sense of *reversal*) and 2572; to *unveil:*—open, ([un-]) taken away.

344. ἀνακάμπτω, anakamptō, *an-ak-amp´-to*; from 303 and 2578; to *turn back:*—(re-) turn.

345. ἀνακεῖμαι, anakeimai, *an-ak-i´-mahee*; from 303 and 2749; to *recline* (as a corpse or at a meal):—guest, lean, lie, sit (down, at meat), at the table.

346. ἀνακεφαλαίομαι, anakephalaiomai, *an-ak-ef-al-ah´ee-om-ahee*; from 303 and 2775 (in its original sense); to *sum up:*—briefly comprehend, gather together in one.

From *aná* (303), an emphatic meaning again, and *kephalaióō* (2775), to sum up, recapitulate. To sum up, as an orator at the close of his discourse. In the NT, to comprehend several things under one, to reduce under one head (Ro 13:9; Eph 1:10; 2:14, 15).

347. ἀνακλίνω, anaklinō, *an-ak-lee´-no*; from 303 and 2827; to *lean back:*—lay, (make) sit down.

348. ἀνακόπτω, anakoptō, *an-ak-op´-to*; from 303 and 2875; to *beat back,* i.e. *check:*—hinder.

349. ἀνακράζω, anakrazō, *an-ak-rad´-zo*; from 303 and 2896; to *scream up* (aloud):—cry out.

350. ἀνακρίνω, anakrinō, *an-ak-ree´-no*; from 303 and 2919; properly to *scrutinize,* i.e. (by implication) *investigate, interrogate, determine:*—ask, question, discern, examine, judge, search.

351. ἀνάκρισις, anakrisis, *an-ak´-ree-sis*; from 350; a (judicial) *investigation:*—examination.

352. ἀνακύπτω, anakuptō, *an-ak-oop´-to*; from 303 (in the sense of *reversal*) and 2955; to *unbend,* i.e. *rise;* (figurative) *be elated:*—lift up, look up.

353. ἀναλαμβάνω, analambanō, *an-al-am-ban´-o*; from 303 and 2983; to *take up:*—receive up, take (in, unto, up).

354. ἀνάληψις, analēpsis, *an-al´-ape-sis*; from 353; *ascension:*—taking up.

355. ἀναλίσκω, analiskō, *an-al-is´-ko*; from 303 and a form of the alternate of 138; properly to *use up,* i.e. *destroy:*—consume.

356. ἀναλογία, analogia, *an-al-og-ee´-ah*; from a compound of 303 and 3056; *proportion:*—proportion.

Noun from *aná* (303), denoting distribution, and *lógos* (3056), account. Proportion, ratio. Only in Ro 12:6.

Syn.: *métron* (3358), measure.

357. ἀναλογίζομαι, analogizomai, *an-al-og-id´-zom-ahee*; middle from 356; to *estimate,* i.e. (figurative) *contemplate:*—consider.

358. ἄναλος, analos, *an´-al-os*; from 1 (as a negative particle) and 251; *saltless,* i.e. *insipid:*—× lose saltness.

359. ἀνάλυσις, analusis, *an-al´-oo-sis*; from 360; *departure:*—departure.

360. ἀναλύω, analuō, *an-al-oo´-o*; from 303 and 3089; to *break up,* i.e. *depart* (literal or figurative):—depart, return.

361. ἀναμάρτητος, anamartētos, *an-am-ar´-tay-tos*; from 1 (as a negative particle) and a presumed derivative of 264; *sinless:*—that is without sin.

Adjective from the priv. *a* (1), without, and *hamartánō* (264), to sin, miss the mark. Without sin, sinless, faultless. Occurs only in Jn 8:7.

Syn.: *ámemptos* (273), unblameable; *athóos* (121), innocent; *anaítios* (338), blameless, guiltless; *anepílēmptos* or *anepílēptos* (423), irreproachable; *hágios* (40), saint, holy; *díkaios* (1342), righteous.

362. ἀναμένω, anamenō, *an-am-en´-o*; from 303 and 3306; to *await:*—wait for.

363. ἀναμιμνήσκω, anamimnēskō, *an-am-im-nace´-ko*; from 303 and 3403; to *remind*; reflexive to *recollect:*—call to mind, (bring to, call to, put in) remember (-brance).

364. ἀνάμνησις, anamnēsis, *an-am´-nay-sis*; from 363; *recollection:*—remembrance (again).

Noun from *anamimnēskō* (363), to remind. Remembrance (Lk 22:19; 1Co 11:24, 25; Heb 10:3).

365. ἀνανεόω, ananeoō, *an-an-neh-o´-o*; from 303 and a derivative of 3501; to *renovate,* i.e. *reform:*—renew.

From *aná* (303), again, and *neóō*, to renew (n.f.), which is from *néos* (3501), new, another. In the NT, to renew oneself; to be renewed in spirit, i.e. changed from a carnal to a Christian life. Only in Eph 4:3.

Syn.: *anakainízō* (340) and *anakainóō* (341), to make qualitatively new; *kainós* (2537), qualitatively new.

366. ἀνανήφω, ananēphō, *an-an-ay´-fo*; from 303 and 3525; to become *sober again,* i.e. (figurative) *regain* (one's) *senses:*—recover self.

367. Ἀνανίας, Ananias, *an-an-ee´-as*; of Hebrew origin [2608]; *Ananias,* the name of three Israelites:—Ananias.

368. ἀναντίρρητος, anantirrhētos, *an-an-tir´-hray-tos*; from 1 (as a negative particle) and a presumed derivative of a compound of 473 and 4483; *indisputable:*—cannot be spoken against.

369. ἀναντιρρήτως, anantirrhētōs, *an-an-tir-hray´-toce*; adverb from 368; *promptly:*—without gainsaying.

370. ἀνάξιος, anaxios, *an-ax´-ee-os*; from 1 (as a negative particle) and 514; *unfit:*—unworthy.

371. ἀναξίως, anaxiōs, *an-ax-ee´-oce*; adverb from 370; *irreverently:*—unworthily.

372. ἀνάπαυσις, anapausis, *an-ap´-ow-sis*; from 373; *intermission*; (by implication) *recreation:*—rest.

Noun from *anapaúō* (373), act., to give rest. Rest, quiet, from occupation, oppression, or torment (Mt 11:29; Rev 4:8; 14:11; Sept.: Ex 16:23; Le 25:8; Jer 14:3). By metonymy: place of rest, fixed habitation (Mt 12:43; Lk 11:24; Sept.: Ge 8:9; Ru 3:1; 1Ch 28:2).

Syn.: *anápsuxis* (403), recovery of breath; *ánesis* (425) relief; *katápausis* (2663), rest, cessation of labour; *sabbatismós* (4520), a sabbath keeping, sabbath rest; *koímēsis* (2838), a resting, reclining; *eirḗnē* (1515), peace.

373. ἀναπαύω, anapauō, *an-ap-ow´-o*; from 303 and 3973; (reflexive) to *repose* (literal or figurative [*be exempt*], *remain*); (by implication) to *refresh:*—take ease, refresh, (give, take) rest.

374. ἀναπείθω, anapeithō, *an-ap-i´-tho*; from 303 and 3982; to *incite:*—persuade.

375. ἀναπέμπω, anapempō, *an-ap-em´-po*; from 303 and 3992; to *send up* or *back:*—send (again).

376. ἀνάπηρος, anapēros, *an-ap´-ay-ros*; from 303 (in the sense of *intensity*) and πῆρος, *pēros* (*maimed*); *crippled:*—maimed.

377. ἀναπίπτω, anapipto, *an-ap-ip´-to*; from 303 and 4098; to *fall back,* i.e. *lie down, lean back:*—lean, sit down (to meat).

378. ἀναπληρόω, anaplēroō, *an-ap-lay-ro´-o*; from 303 and 4137; to *complete*; (by implication) to *occupy, supply*; (figurative) to *accomplish* (by coincidence or obedience):—fill up, fulfil, occupy, supply.

From *aná* (303), up, or as an emphatic, and *plēróō* (4137), to fill. To fill up, to fulfil, to complete. Spoken of measure: to fill up (Mt 23:32; 1Th 2:16); spoken of prophecy: to fulfil (Mt 13:14); spoken of a work or duty: to fulfil, to perform (Gal 6:2); spoken of persons: to fill the place of someone, i.e. to sustain his character (1Co 14:16).

Deriv.: *antanaplēróō* (466), to fill up, supplement; *prosanaplēróō* (4322), to supply abundantly.

Syn.: *pímplēmi* (4130), to fill; *empíplēmi* (1705), to fill full; *gemízō* (1072), to fill or load full; *korénnumi* (2880), to fill or to satisfy; *mestóō* (3325), to fill full; *teléō* (5055), to fulfill, to bring to its intended end; *sunteléō* (4931), to complete; *teleióō* (5048), to bring to an end.

379. ἀναπολόγητος, **anapologētos**, *an-ap-olog´-ay-tos*; from 1 (as a negative particle) and a presumed derivative of 626; *indefensible*:—without excuse, inexcusable.

380. ἀναπτύσσω, **anaptussō**, *an-ap-toos´-so*; from 303 (in the sense of *reversal*) and 4428; to *unroll* (a scroll or volume):—open.

381. ἀνάπτω, **anaptō**, *an-ap´-to*; from 303 and 681; to *enkindle*:—kindle, light.

382. ἀναρίθμητος, **anarithmētos**, *an-ar-ith´-may-tos*; from 1 (as a negative particle) and a derivative of 705; *unnumbered*, i.e. *without number*:—innumerable.

383. ἀνασείω, **anaseiō**, *an-as-i´-o*; from 303 and 4579; (figurative) to *excite*:—move, stir up.

384. ἀνασκευάζω, **anaskeuazō**, *an-ask-yoo-ad´-zo*; from 303 (in the sense of *reversal*) and a derivative of 4632; properly to *pack up* (baggage), i.e. (by implication and figurative) to *upset*:—subvert.

385. ἀνασπάω, **anaspaō**, *an-as-pah´-o*; from 303 and 4685; to *take up* or *extricate*:—draw up, pull out.

386. ἀνάστασις, **anastasis**, *an-as´-tas-is*; from 450; a *standing up* again, i.e. (literal) a *resurrection* from death (individual, genitive or by implication [its author]), or (figurative) a (moral) *recovery* (of spiritual truth):—raised to life again, resurrection, rise from the dead, that should rise, rising again.

Noun from *anístēmi* (450), to stand up. A rising up:

(I) A rising up as opposed to falling. By metonymy, the author or cause of rising up; so metaphorically, the author of a better state, of higher prosperity, of eternal happiness (Lk 2:34).

(II) Resurrection of the body from death, return to life:

(A) Spoken of individuals who have returned to life (Heb 11:35; Sept.: 1Ki 17:17f.; 2Ki 4:20f.); of the resurrection of Jesus (Ac 1:22; 2:31; 4:33; 17:18; Ro 1:4; 6:5; Php 3:10; 1Pe 1:3; 3:21).

(B) Spoken of the future and general resurrection at the end of all things (Jn 11:24; Ac 17:32; 24:15, 21; 26:23; 1Co 15:12, 13, 21, 42; Heb 6:2); of both the resurrection of life (*anástasin zōēs*, form *zōē* [2222], life), and the resurrection of damnation (*anástasin kríseōs*, from *krísis* [2920], judgement, condemnation) in Jn 5:29. This general resurrection was denied by the Sadducees (Mt 22:23, 28, 30, 31; Mk 12:18, 23; Lk 20:27, 33; Ac 23:8), and also certain Christians (2Ti 2:18).

(C) Spoken of the resurrection of the righteous (Mt 22:30; Lk 14:14; 20:35, 36), also called the first resurrection (Rev 20:5, 6, cf. 1Co 15:23, 24; 1Th 4:16).

(D) By metonymy, the author of resurrection (Jn 11:25).

Syn.: *égersis* (1454), a rousing, resurrection (Mt 27:53).

387. ἀναστατόω, **anastatoō**, *an-as-tat-o´-o*; from a derivative of 450 (in the sense of *removal*); properly to *drive out* of home, i.e. (by implication) to *disturb* (literal or figurative):—trouble, turn upside down, make an uproar.

From *anástatos* (n.f.), made to rise up and depart, which is from *anístēmi* (450), to stand up. To disturb, agitate, put in commotion. Spoken of cities (Ac 17:6; 21:38); of the minds of Christians (Gal 5:12).

Syn.: *epegeírō* (1892), to stir up; *diegeírō* (1326), to arouse or stir up; *anaseíō* (383), to shake out, move to and fro, stir up; *saleúō* (4531), to shake, stir up; *paroxúnō* (3947), to provoke; *erethízō* (2042), to stir up, provoke; *tarássō* (5015), to trouble; *diatarássō* (1298), to agitate greatly, and *ektarássō* (1613), to throw into great trouble; *enochléō* (1776), to disturb, vex; *parenochléō* (3926), to annoy, trouble; *skúllō* (4660), to annoy; *thorubéō* (2350), to make noise or an uproar; *throéō* (2360), to make an outcry; *thorubéō* (2350), to disturb, trouble, or turbázō (5182), to trouble.

388. ἀνασταυρόω, **anastauroō**, *an-as-tow-ro´-o*; from 303 and 4717; to *recrucify* (figurative):—crucify afresh.

From *aná* (303), again or up, and *stauróō* (4717), to crucify. To crucify again or afresh (Heb 6:6).

389. ἀναστενάζω, anastenazō, *an-as-ten-ad´-zo*; from 303 and 4727; to *sigh deeply*:—sigh deeply.

390. ἀναστρέφω, anastrepho, *an-as-tref´-o*; from 303 and 4762; to *overturn*; also to *return*; (by implication) to *busy* oneself, i.e. *remain, live*:—abide, behave self, have conversation, live, overthrow, pass, return, be used.

391. ἀναστροφή, anastrophē, *an-as-trof-ay´*; from 390; *behaviour*:—conversation.

392. ἀνατάσσομαι, anatassomai, *an-at-as´-som-ahee*; from 303 and the middle of 5021; to *arrange*:—set in order.

From *aná* (303), an intensive, and *tássō* (5021), to place in one's proper category. To set in order, to arrange. Only in Lk 1:1.

Syn.: *horízō* (3724), to determine, define; *títhēmi* (5087), to place; *paratíthēmi* (3908), to place alongside; *apokathístēmi* (600), to restore.

393. ἀνατέλλω, anatellō, *an-at-el´-lo*; from 303 and the base of 5056; to *(cause* to) *arise*:—(a-, make to) rise, at the rising of, spring (up), be up.

394. ἀνατίθεμαι, anatithemai, *an-at-ith´-em-ahee*; from 303 and the middle of 5087; to *set forth* (for oneself), i.e. *propound*:—communicate, declare.

395. ἀνατολή, anatolē, *an-at-ol-ay´*; from 393; a *rising* of light, i.e. *dawn* (figurative); (by implication) the *east* (also in plural):—dayspring, east, rising.

396. ἀνατρέπω, anatrepō, *an-at-rep´-o*; from 303 and the base of 5157; to *overturn* (figurative):—overthrow, subvert.

397. ἀνατρέφω, anatrephō, *an-at-ref´-o*; from 303 and 5142; to *rear* (physical or mental):—bring up, nourish (up).

398. ἀναφαίνω, anaphainō, *an-af-ah´ee-no*; from 303 and 5316; to *show*, i.e. (reflexive) *appear*, or (passive) *have pointed* out:—(should) appear, discover.

399. ἀναφέρω, anaphero, *an-af-er´-o*; from 303 and 5342; to *take up* (literal or figurative):—bear, bring (carry, lead) up, offer (up).

400. ἀναφωνέω, anaphōneō, *an-af-o-neh´-o*; from 303 and 5455; to *exclaim*:—speak out.

401. ἀνάχυσις, anachusis, *an-akh´-oo-sis*; from a compound of 303 and χέω, *cheō* (to *pour*); properly *effusion*, i.e. (figurative) *license*:—excess.

402. ἀναχωρέω, anachōreō, *an-akh-o-reh´-o*; from 303 and 5562; to *retire*:—depart, give place, go (turn) aside, withdraw self.

403. ἀνάψυξις, anapsuxis, *an-aps´-ook-sis*; from 404; properly a *recovery of breath*, i.e. (figurative) *revival*:—revival.

404. ἀναψύχω, anapsuchō, *an-aps-oo´-kho*; from 303 and 5594; properly to *cool off*, i.e. (figurative) *relieve*:—refresh.

From *aná* (303), again, and *psúchō* (5594), to breathe, to cool. To draw breath again, to take breath, i.e. to revive, be refreshed. In the NT, to refresh, recreate. Only in 2Ti 1:16.

Deriv.: *anápsuxis* (403), refreshing.

Syn.: *anapaúō* (373), to give inner rest; *sunanapaúonai* (4875), to rest with; *katapaúō* (2664), to cause to rest by ceasing from labour; *hēsucházō* (2270), to be still, rest from labour; *epanapaúomai* (1879), to rest upon; *aníēmi* (447), to refresh.

405. ἀνδραποδιστής, andrapodistēs, *an-drap-od-is-tace´*; from a derivative of a compound of 435 and 4228; an *enslaver* (as bringing *men* to his *feet*):—menstealer.

406. Ἀνδρέας, Andreas, *an-dreh´-as*; from 435; *manly*; *Andreas*, an Israelite:—Andrew.

407. ἀνδρίζομαι, andrizomai, *an-drid´-zom-ahee*; middle from 435; to *act manly*:—quit like men.

408. Ἀνδρόνικος, Andronikos, *an-dron´-ee-kos*; from 435 and 3534; *man of victory*; *Andronicos*, an Israelite:—Andronicus.

409. ἀνδροφόνος, androphonos, *an-drof-on´-os*; from 435 and 5408; a *murderer*:—manslayer.

410. ἀνέγκλητος, anegklētos, *an-eng´-klay-tos*; from 1 (as a negative particle) and a derivative of 1458; *unaccused*, i.e. (by implication) *irreproachable*:—blameless.

Adjective from the priv. *a* (1), without, and *egkaléō* (1458), to accuse in court. Not arraignable; hence in the NT, unblameable, irreprehensible (1Co 1:8; Col 1:22; 1Ti 3:10; Tit 1:6, 7).

Syn.: *ámemptos* (273), unblameable; *ámōmos* (299), unblemished; *anepíléptos* (423), irreproachable; *áspilos* (784), unspotted; *amómētos* (298), without blemish; *anaítios* (338), guiltless.

411. ἀνεκδιήγητος, anekdiēgētos, *an-ek-dee-ay´-gay-tos*; from 1 (as a negative particle) and a presumed derivative of 1555; *not expounded* in full, i.e. *indescribable*:—unspeakable.

412. ἀνεκλάλητος, aneklalētos, *an-ek-lal´-ay-tos*; from 1 (as a negative particle) and a presumed derivative of 1583; *not spoken out*, i.e. (by implication) *unutterable*:—unspeakable.

413. ἀνέκλειπτος, anekleiptos, *an-ek´-lipe-tos*; from 1 (as a negative particle) and a presumed derivative of 1587; *not left out*, i.e. (by implication) *inexhaustible*:—that faileth not.

414. ἀνεκτότερος, anektoteros, *an-ek-tot´-er-os*; comparative of a derivative of 430; *more endurable*:—more tolerable.

415. ἀνελεήμων, aneleēmōn, *an-eleh-ay´-mone*; from 1 (as a negative particle) and 1655; *merciless*:—unmerciful.

Adjective from the priv. *a* (1), without, and *eleémōn* (1655), merciful. Unmerciful, cruel, not compassionate (Ro 1:31; Sept.: Pr 5:9).

Syn.: *aníleōs* (448), unmerciful, merciless.

416. ἀνεμίζω, anemizō, *an-em-id´-zo*; from 417; to *toss with the wind*:—drive with the wind.

417. ἄνεμος, anemos, *an´-em-os*; from the base of 109; *wind*; (plural) by implication (the four) *quarters* (of the earth):—wind.

A noun meaning wind, i.e. air in motion:

(I) Spoken particularly of wind (Mt 11:7; Mk 4:41; Lk 7:24; Rev 7:1); of violent, stormy winds (Mt 7:25, 27; Mk 4:37, 39; Lk 8:23, 24; Ac 28:4, 7, 14, 15; Jas 3:4); of the four cardinal winds (Rev 7:1; Sept.: Jer 49:36).

(II) By metonymy, the four quarters of the earth or heavens, whence the cardinal winds blow (Mt 24:31; Mk 13:27, cf. Lk 13:29; Sept.: 1Ch 9:24; Da 11:4).

(III) Metaphorically, "wind of doctrine," i.e. empty doctrine, unstable opinion (Eph 4:14).

Deriv.: *anemízō* (416), to toss or drive with the wind.

Syn.: *pnoḗ* (4157), breath, used of the rushing wind at Pentecost (Ac 2:2); *pneúma* (4151), spirit (Jn 3:8); *thúella* (2366), tempest; *laílaps* (2978), whirlwind.

418. ἀνένδεκτος, anendektos, *an-en´-dek-tos*; from 1 (as a negative particle) and a derivative of the same as 1735; *unadmitted*, i.e. (by implication) *not supposable*:—impossible.

419. ἀνεξερεύνητος, anexereunētos, *an-ex-er-yoo´-nay-tos*; from 1 (as a negative particle) and a presumed derivative of 1830; *not searched out*, i.e. (by implication) *inscrutable*:—unsearchable.

420. ἀνεξίκακος, anexikakos, *an-ex-ik´-ak-os*; from 430 and 2556; *enduring of ill*, i.e. *forbearing*:—patient.

Adjective from *anéchō* (430), to bear, and *kakós* (2556), bad. Patient under evils and injuries. Only in 2Ti 2:24.

Syn.: *epieikḗs* (1933), tolerant. This stresses the positive attitude in contrast to *anexíkakos*, which stresses the negative attitude of being patient regarding wrong; *anektóteros* (414), more tolerable.

421. ἀνεξιχνίαστος, anexichniastos, *an-ex-ikh-nee´-as-tos*; from 1 (as a negative particle) and a presumed derivative of a compound of 1537 and a derivative of 2487; *not tracked out*, i.e. (by implication) *untraceable*:—past finding out, unsearchable.

422. ἀνεπαίσχυντος, anepaischuntos, *an-ep-ah´ee-skhoon-tos*; from 1 (as a negative particle) and a presumed derivative of a compound of 1909 and 153; *not ashamed*, i.e. (by implication) *irreprehensible*:—that needeth not to be ashamed.

423. ἀνεπίληπτος, anepilēptos, *an-ep-eel´-ape-tos*; from 1 (as a negative particle) and a derivative of 1949; *not arrested*, i.e. (by implication) *inculpable*:—blameless, unrebukeable.

Adjective from the priv. *a* (1), without, and *epilambánō* (1949), to seize. Not to be apprehended. In the NT, used metaphorically: irreprehensible, unblameable (1Ti 3:2 [cf. Tit 1:7, *anégklētos* {410}]; 5:7; 6:14).

Syn.: *anégklētos* (410), legally unaccused. *Anepílēptos* demonstrates a higher morality on which no blame can be found to base an accusation, while *anégklētos* indicates that one cannot be legally charged; *ámōmos* (299), without blemish; *amómētos* (298), unblameable; *ámemptos* (273), one in whom no fault can be found; *eúphēmos* (2163), of good report; *anaítios* (338), guiltless; *akatákritos* (178), uncondemned; *áspilos* (784), unspotted; *dókimos* (1384), approved; *áxios* (514), worthy.

424. ἀνέρχομαι, anerchomai, *an-erkh´-om-ahee*; from 303 and 2064; to *ascend*:—go up.

425. ἄνεσις, anesis, *an´-es-is*; from 447; *relaxation* or (figurative) *relief*:—eased, liberty, rest.

Noun from *aníēmi* (447), to loose. A letting loose, remission, relaxation: from bonds, imprisonment (Ac 24:23; Sept.: 2Ch 23:15); from active exertion, labour (2Co 8:13); figuratively, remission, rest, quiet, either internal (2Co 2:12) or external (2Th 1:7).

Syn.: *anápausis* (372), inward rest while labouring, whereas *ánesis* indicates a relaxation brought about by a source other than oneself; *chará* (5479), joy; *agallíasis* (20), exuberance; *euphrosúnē* (2167), rejoicing; *áphesis* (859), release, liberty, forgiveness; *eleuthería* (1657), freedom; *katápausis* (2663), rest by ceasing to work.

426. ἀνετάζω, anetazō, *an-et-ad´-zo*; from 303 and ἐτάζω, *etazō* (to *test*); to *investigate* (judicially):—(should have) examine (-d).

427. ἄνευ, aneu, *an´-yoo*; a primary particle; *without*:—without. Compare 1.

428. ἀνεύθετος, aneuthetos, *an-yoo´-the-tos*; from 1 (as a negative particle) and 2111; *not well set*, i.e. *inconvenient*:—not commodious.

429. ἀνευρίσκω, aneuriskō, *an-yoo-ris´-ko*; from 303 and 2147; to *find out*:—find.

430. ἀνέχομαι, anechomai, *an-ekh´-om-ahee*; middle from 303 and 2192; to *hold oneself up* against, i.e. (figurative) *put up* with:—bear with, endure, forbear, suffer.

From *aná* (303), in, and *échō* (2192), to have. To hold up or back from falling, to hold in or back, restrain, stop. In the NT, to hold oneself upright, to bear up, hold out, endure:

(I) Spoken of things: to endure, bear patiently, as afflictions (2Th 1:4). See Sept.: Isa 42:14. Used in an absolute sense (1Co 4:12; 2Co 11:20).

(II) Spoken of persons: to bear with, have patience with in regard to the errors or weaknesses of anyone (Mt 17:17; Mk 9:19; Lk 9:41; 2Co 11:1, 19; Eph 4:2; Col 3:13; Sept.: Isa 46:4; 63:15).

(III) By implication, to admit, receive, i.e. to listen to, spoken of persons (Ac 18:14); of doctrine (2Co 11:4, see 2Ti 4:3; Heb 13:22).

Deriv.: *anektóteros* (414), more tolerable; *anexíkakos* (420), forbearing; *anoché* (463), forbearance, tolerance.

Syn.: *bastázō* (941), to support, carry, take up; *phérō* (5342), to bring or bear; *hupophérō* (5297), to bear up under, endure; *phoréō* (5409), to bear or endure habitually; *tropophoréō* (5159), to bear as a matter of permanent attitude; *stégō* (4722), to bear up against; *metriopathéō* (3356), to treat with mildness or moderation, bear gently with; *karteréō* (2594), to be steadfast, patient (Heb 11:27); *kakopathéō* (2553), to suffer evil; *páschō* (3958), to suffer; *hupéchō* (5254), to hold under; *hupoménō* (5278), to endure as far as things or circumstances are concerned; *maktrothuméō* (3114), enduring or being longsuffering toward people.

431. ἀνέψιος, anepsios, *an-eps´-ee-os*; from 1 (as a particle of union) and an obsolete νέπος, *nepos* (a *brood*); properly *akin*, i.e. (special) a *cousin*:—sister's son.

432. ἄνηθον, anēthon, *an´-ay-thon*; probably of foreign origin; *dill*:—anise.

433. ἀνήκω, anēkō, *an-ay´-ko*; from 303 and 2240; to *attain to*, i.e. (figurative) *be proper*:—convenient, be fit.

434. ἀνήμερος, anēmeros, *an-ay´-mer-os*; from 1 (as a negative particle) and ἥμερος, *hēmeros* (*lame*); *savage*:—fierce.

435. ἀνήρ, anēr, *an´-ayr*; a primary word [compare 444]; a *man* (properly as an individual male):—fellow, husband, man, sir.

(I) A man, i.e. an adult male person:

(A) Males as distinguished from females (Mt 14:21; 15:38; Lk 1:34). Spoken of men in various relations and circumstances where the context determines the proper meaning; e.g., husband (Mt 1:16; Mk 10:2, 12; Lk 2:36; Ro 7:2,

3; 1Co 7:2–4, ff.; 2Co 11:2; Gal 4:27; Eph 5:22–25, 28, 33; Col 3:18, 19; 1Ti 2:8, 12; 3:2, 12; 5:9; Tit 1:6; 2:5; 1Pe 3:1, 5, 7; Sept.: Ge 2:23; 3:6); a bridegroom betrothed (Mt 1:19; Rev 21:2; Sept.: Dt 22:23); a soldier (Lk 22:63). In a direct address, *ándres*, men!, sirs! (Ac 14:15; 19:25; 27:10, 21, 25); in this sense, it also expresses respect and deference, and so implies a man of importance (Lk 24:19; Jn 1:30; Jas 2:2).

(B) Joined with an adj. or noun, it forms a periphrasis for a subst., e.g., *anér hamartōlós* ([268], sinner), a sinner (Lk 5:8, cf. Mt 7:24, 26); *anér phoneús* ([5406], murderer), a murderer (Ac 3:14); *anér Ioudaíos* ([2453], Jewish), a Jew (Ac 10:28; see Mt 12:41; Ac 8:27; 11:20; 16:9). With other adj. in a direct address, *ándres Athēnaíoi*, men of Athens, i.e. Athenians (Ac 17:22); Ephesians (Ac 19:35); Israelites (Ac 2:22; 3:12; 5:35; 13:16; 21:28); Galileans (Ac 1:11); brethren (Ac 1:16).

(C) Figuratively, a man of mature understanding, as opposed to a child (1Co 13:11). So in Eph 4:13 the progress of a Christian is likened to the growth of a child into a "perfect man," i.e. in understanding and true wisdom.

(II) Indefinitely, a man, one of the human race, a person (Mk 6:44; Lk 5:12, 18; 8:27; 9:38; 11:29, 31; Ac 6:11; Jas 1:8, 20, 23; 3:2; Sept.: Pr 16:27–29; Ne 4:18).

Deriv.: *andrízō* (407), to act manly; *androphónos* (409), murderer; *húpandros* (5220), one under the authority of a man.

Syn.: *árrēn* (730), male; *téleios* (5046), perfect, one of mature or ripe age; *súzugos* (4805), a yokefellow, hence a husband or wife.

436. ἀνθίστημι, anthistēmi, *anth-is´-tay-mee*; from 473 and 2476; to *stand against*, i.e. *oppose*:—resist, withstand.

437. ἀνθομολογέομαι, anthomologeomai, *anth-om-ol-og-eh´-om-ahee*; from 473 and the middle of 3670; to *confess in turn*, i.e. *respond* in praise:—give thanks.

438. ἄνθος, anthos, *anth´-os*; a primary word; a *blossom*:—flower.

439. ἀνθρακιά, anthrakia, *anth-rak-ee-ah´*; from 440; a bed of burning *coals*:—fire of coals.

440. ἄνθραξ, anthrax, *anth´-rax*; of uncertain derivative; a live *coal*:—coal of fire.

441. ἀνθρωπάρεσκος, anthrōpareskos, *anthro-par´-es-kos*; from 444 and 700; *man-courting*, i.e. *fawning*:—men-pleaser.

Adjective from *ánthrōpos* (444), man, and *aréskō* (700), to please. Desirous to please men, without regard to God (Eph 6:6; Col 3:22).

442. ἀνθρώπινος, anthrōpinos, *anth-ro´-pee-nos*; from 444; *human*:—human, common to man, man [-kind], [man-]kind, men's, after the manner of men.

443. ἀνθρωποκτόνος, anthrōpoktonos, *anthro-pok-ton´-os*; from 444 and κτείνω, kteinē (to *kill*); a *manslayer*:—murderer. Compare 5406.

Adjective from *ánthrōpos* (444), man and *kteínō* (n.f.), to kill. A murderer; spoken of Satan as the author of sin and death (Jn 8:44); a murderer in heart, in purpose (1Jn 3:15).

Syn.: *phoneús* (5406), murderer, a more general word; *sikários* (4607), an assassin; *patrolóas* (3964), a murderer of one's father; *mētralóas* (3389), a murderer of one's mother.

444. ἄνθρωπος, anthrōpos, *anth´-ro-pos*; from 435 and ὤψ, *ōps* (the *countenance*; from 3700); *man-faced*, i.e. a *human* being:—certain, man.

A noun meaning man, i.e. an individual of the human race, a man or woman, a person:

(I) Generally and universally (Mt 4:19; 12:12; Mk 7:21; Lk 2:52; 5:10; Jn 1:4; 1Co 4:9). In a direct address, "O man" (*ó ánthrōpe*) implies an inferior or common person (Lk 5:20; 12:14; 22:58, 60; Ro 2:1, 3; 9:20; Jas 2:20; Sept.: Isa 2:9; 5:15). *Hoi ánthrōpoi*, men, i.e. the living, are those with whom we live, people (Mt 5:13, 16, 19; 6:1; 8:27; 13:25; Mk 8:24, 27; Rev 9:10, 15, 18, 20); men of this world or generation, i.e. wicked men (Mt 10:17; 17:22; Lk 6:22, 26).

(A) Spoken in reference to his human nature, a man, i.e. a human being, a mortal: **(1)** With the idea of human infirmity and imperfection, especially when spoken in contrast to God and divine things (1Co 1:25; 3:21; Gal 1:11, 12; Php 2:7; 1Ti 2:5; Jas 5:17; Rev 4:7; 9:7). Used with this sense in the expression "to speak after the manner of men," i.e. in accordance with human views, and so forth, to illustrate by human example or institutions, to use a popular manner of speaking (Ro 3:5; 1Co 9:8; Gal 3:15). **(2)** Metaphorically, used of the internal man, meaning the mind, soul, the rational man (Ro 7:22; Eph 3:16); "the hidden man of the heart,"

(1Pe 3:4) to which is opposed the outward or external, visible man (2Co 4:16). So the old man (*ho palaiós* [3820]) or heart, and the new man (*kainós*, 2537), the disposition which is created and cherished by the new nature that Jesus Christ gives to the believer (Ro 6:6; Eph 2:15; 4:22, 24; Col 3:9).

(**B**) Spoken with reference to the character and condition of a person and applied in various senses according to the context: (**1**) A man, a male person of maturity and ripe age (Mt 8:9; 11:8; 25:24; Mk 3:3; Lk 19:21; Jn 1:6; 3:1; Ac 4:13). The expression "man of God" (*ánthrōpos toú Theoú*), i.e. a minister or messenger of God, one devoted to His service (1Ti 6:11; 2Ti 3:17; 2Pe 1:21; Sept.: 1Ki 13:1; 2Ki 1:9–13; 4:7, 9, 21). The "man of sin," i.e. the Antichrist (2Th 2:3; so named in 1Jn 2:18, 22; 4:3; 2Jn 7). (**2**) A husband as contrasted to a wife (Mt 19:3, 10; 1Co 7:1; Sept.: Dt 22:30). (**3**) A son as contrasted to a father (Mt 10:35), or a male child generally (Jn 7:23; 16:21). (**4**) A master as contrasted to servants (Mt 10:36). (**5**) A servant (Lk 12:36; Rev 18:13; Sept.: Eze 27:13).

(**II**) Used with *tis* (5100), an enclitic indefinite pron. meaning any man, a certain man, i.e. one, someone, anyone:

(**A**) Generally *ánthrōpós tis*, a certain man (Lk 10:30; 12:16; 14:2; Jn 5:5); *heís ánthrōpos*, "one man" (*heís* [1520], one), meaning a man, anyone out of a number (Jn 11:50; 18:14). In Ro 3:28, "a man is justified by faith" means anyone who has faith, irrespective of who he is (see also 1Co 11:28).

(**B**) Joined with an adj. or noun, it forms a periphrase for a substantive, e.g., *anthrṓpō basileí* (*basileús* [935]), king (Mt 18:23); *ánthrōpos oikodespótēs* (*oikodespótēs* [3617]), householder (Mt 21:33); *hoi ánthrōpoi hoi poiménes* (*poimḗn* [4166]), shepherds (Lk 2:15).

(**III**) *Ho ánthrōpos* with the article, meaning this or that man, he (Mt 12:13, 45; 26:72), this man of whom you speak (Mk 14:71. See Mk 3:3, 5; 14:21; Lk 6:10; 23:4, 6; Jn 4:50; 19:5; Sept.: Ge 24:29, 30, 32). Sometimes *ekeínos* (1565), that one, is added, as in Mt 26:24, *ho ánthrōpos ekeínos* (Mk 14:21; Jas 1:7).

(**IV**) *Huiós* (5207) *toú anthrṓpou*, son of man, from the Hebrew:

(**A**) Equivalent to *ánthrōpos*, a man; so "sons of men" are simply men (Mt 12:31; Mk 3:28; Heb 2:6; Rev 1:13).

(**B**) As a proper name for the Messiah, with the article, *ho huiós toú anthrṓpou*, drawn from Da 7:13, where the phrase appears in the Sept. for the Aram. *bar 'enāš* (*bar* [1247, OT], son; *'enāš* [606, OT], man). It is used by Jesus of Himself, but is applied to Him by no other person except Stephen (Ac 7:56). It would seem to refer not so much to His human nature as to the fact of His being the Messiah, who is described as coming from heaven in human form (Da 7:13; 10:16; Rev 1:13; 14:14). Often, the names "Son of Man," "Son of God," and "Christ" are used interchangeably (Mt 16:13, 16, 20; Lk 22:69, 70; Jn 12:34); by using this name of Himself before His judges, Jesus openly professed Himself to be the Messiah, and was so understood by all present (Mt 26:64; Mk 14:62; Lk 22:69, 70).

Deriv.: *anthrōpáreskos* (441), man-pleaser; *anthrṓpinos* (442), human; *anthrōpoktónos* (443), murderer.

445. ἀνθυπατεύω, anthupateuō, anth-oo-pat-yoo´-o; from 446; to *act as proconsul*:—be the deputy.

446. ἀνθύπατος, anthupatos, anth-oo´-pat-os; from 473 and a superlative of 5228; *instead of* the *highest* officer, i.e. (special) a Roman *proconsul*:—deputy.

447. ἀνίημι, aniēmi, an-ee´-ay-mee; from 303 and ἵημι, *hiēmi* (to *send*); to *let up*, i.e. (literal) *slacken*, or (figurative) *desert, desist* from:—forbear, leave, loose.

448. ἀνίλεως, anileōs, an-ee´-leh-oce; from 1 (as a negative particle) and 2436; *inexorable*:—without mercy.

Adjective from *a* (1), not, and *híleōs* (2436), merciful. Unmerciful, uncompassionate, stern. Only in Jas 2:13.

Syn.: *aneleḗmōn* (415), without mercy.

449. ἄνιπτος, aniptos, an´-ip-tos; from 1 (as a negative particle) and a presumed derivative of 3538; *without ablution*:—unwashen.

450. ἀνίστημι, anistēmi, an-is´-tay-mee; from 303 and 2476; to *stand up* (literal or figurative, transitive or intransitive):—arise, lift up, raise up (again), rise (again), stand up (-right).

From *aná* (303), again, and *hístēmi* (2476), to stand. To stand again. This verb may have a transitive or an intransitive meaning, as *hístēmi* (2476):

(I) Transitively, meaning to cause to rise up, to raise up, cause to stand:

(A) Spoken of those lying down (Ac 9:41; Sept.: Le 26:1; Nu 7:1); of the dead, meaning to raise up, recall to life (Jn 6:39, 40, 44, 54; Ac 2:32; 13:33); *ek nekrṓn* (*ek* [1537], out of; *nekrṓn* [3498], of the dead [pl.]) as in Ac 13:34; 17:31.

(B) Metaphorically, to raise up, to cause to exist, cause to appear (Mt 22:24 [cf. Ge 38:8]; Ac 2:30; 3:22, 26; 7:37; Sept.: Dt 18:18).

(II) Intransitively, to rise up, arise:

(A) Particularly spoken of those who are sitting or lying down (Mt 26:62; Mk 5:42; 9:27; 14:60; Lk 4:16; 5:25; 6:8; 22:45); rising up from prayer, i.e. from a kneeling or recumbent posture (Lk 17:19); rising from bed or from sleep (Lk 11:7, 8; 22:46); arising from the dead, returning to life (Mt 17:9; Mk 9:9, 10; Lk 16:31; Jn 20:9; Ac 17:3); without *ek nekrṓn* from among the dead (Mt 20:19; Mk 8:31; 9:31; 10:34; Lk 9:8, 19; 18:33; 1Th 4:14, 16). Metaphorically in Eph 5:14, to arise from the death of sin and put on the new man in Christ.

(B) Metaphorically, to arise, come into existence, to be (Ac 7:18; 20:30; Sept.: Ex 1:8; Da 8:22; 11:2).

(C) Meaning to stand forth, come forward, appear (Mt 12:41; Mk 14:57; Lk 10:25; 11:32; Ac 5:36, 37; 6:9; Sept.: 2Ch 20:5). Followed by *epí* ([1909], upon), meaning to rise up against any one, assault (Mk 3:26; Sept.: Ge 4:8; 2Ch 24:13).

(D) Followed by verbs of going or doing (Mt 9:9, "he arose, and followed him"; Mk 1:35; 2:14; 7:24; 10:1, 50; Lk 1:39; 5:28; 15:18, 20; Ac 8:26, 27; 9:6, 11; Sept.: 1Sa 24:5; 2Sa 13:31. See Ro 15:12 [cf. Isa 11:10]; 1Co 10:7 [cf. Ex 32:6]).

Deriv.: *anástasis* (386), resurrection; *exanístēmi* (1817), to rise out of or from among; *epanístamai* (1881), to rise up or against, to arise.

Syn.: *egeírō* (1453), to raise; *anatéllō* (393), to arise; *aírō* (142), to raise, take up, lift; *epaírō* (1869), to lift up, raise; *hupsóō* (5312), to lift or raise up; *anorthóō* (461), to set upright; *anakúptō* (352), to lift oneself up; *exegeírō* (1825), to raise up from; *sunegeírō* (4891), to raise together; *epegeírō* (1892), to rouse up, excite; *stékō* (4739), to stand fast.

451. Ἄννα, **Anna,** *an´-nah*; of Hebrew origin [2584]; *Anna*, an Israelitess:—Anna.

452. Ἄννας, **Annas,** *an´-nas*; of Hebrew origin [2608]; *Annas* (i.e. 367), an Israelite:—Annas.

453. ἀνόητος, **anoētos,** *an-o´-ay-tos*; from 1 (as a negative particle) and a derivative of 3539; *unintelligent*; (by implication) *sensual*:—fool (-ish), unwise.

Adjective from the priv. *a* (1), without, and *noéō* (3539), to comprehend. Lacking intelligence, unwise; spoken of those who are slow to understand and receive moral and religious truth (Lk 24:25; Ro 1:14; Gal 3:1, 3; Tit 3:3). Spoken of lusts: imprudent, brutal (1Ti 6:9; Sept.: Dt 32:31; Ps 49:13; Pr 15:21; 17:28).

Syn.: *áphrōn* (878), without reason; *mōrós* (3474), foolish; *asúnetos* (801), without discernment; *ásophos* (781), unwise.

454. ἄνοια, **anoia,** *an´-oy-ah*; from a compound of 1 (as a negative particle) and 3563; *stupidity*; (by implication) *rage*:—folly, madness.

Noun from *ánous* (n.f.), mad, foolish, from the priv. *a* (1), without, and *noús* (3563), mind, understanding. Want of understanding, folly. In the NT, spoken of rage, malignity (Lk 6:11; 2Ti 3:9).

Syn.: *mōría* (3472), foolishness; *aphrosúnē* (877), senselessness; *manía* (3130), madness, mania; *paraphronía* (3913), mind aberration.

455. ἀνοίγω, **anoigō,** *an-oy´-go*; from 303 and οἴγω, *oigō* (to *open*); to *open up* (literal or figurative, in various applications):—open.

456. ἀνοικοδομέω, **anoikodomeō,** *an-oy-kod-om-eh´-o*; from 303 and 3618; to *rebuild*:—build again.

457. ἄνοιξις, **anoixis,** *an´-oix-is*; from 455; *opening* (throat):— × open.

458. ἀνομία, **anomia,** *an-om-ee´-ah*; from 459; *illegality*, i.e. *violation of law* or (genitive) *wickedness*:—iniquity, × transgress (-ion of) the law, unrighteousness.

From *ánomos* (459), lawless. Lawlessness, violation of law, transgression. In the NT, spoken chiefly of the divine law:

(I) Particularly, in 1Jn 3:4, where lawlessness is joined with sin: "Whosoever committeth sin transgresseth also the law [*anomían*]:

for sin is the [*anomía*] transgression of the law."

(II) By implication, therefore, *anomía* is used of sin, iniquity, unrighteousness (Mt 23:28; 24:12; Ro 4:7; 6:19; 2Co 6:14; Tit 2:14); hence *ho poión anomían*, a "worker of iniquity" (*poiéo* [4160], to make, to do), i.e. wicked, impious (Mt 7:23; 13:41; Sept.: Job 31:3; Ps 5:6). Also spoken of defection from Christianity to idolatry, apostasy (2Th 2:7).

Syn.: *paranomía* (3892), transgression; *hamártēma* (265), individual sin; *hamartía* (266), sin; *kríma* (2917), condemnation; *opheílēma* (3783), debt; *égklēma* (1462), indictable crime; *athétēsis* (115), acting contrary to accepted custom; *adikía* (93), unrighteousness *adíkēma* (92), a wrong, injury, misdeed; *ponēría* (4189), wickedness, *ho ponērós* (4190) one of the designations of the devil; *parábasis* (3847), an overstepping, transgression; *paráptōma* (3900), sidestepping; *plánē* (4106), a wandering or forsaking of the right path; *agnóēma* (51), a sin of ignorance; *hamártēma* (265), evil deed; *asébeia* (763), impiety; *parábasis* (3847), transgression.

459. ἄνομος, anomos, *an´-om-os*; from 1 (as a negative particle) and 3551; *lawless,* i.e. (negative) *not subject to* (the Jewish) *law*; (by implication, a *Gentile*), or (positive) *wicked*:— without law, lawless, transgressor, unlawful, wicked.

Adjective from the priv. *a* (1), without, and *nómos* (3551), law. Lawless. Without law, not subject to the law of Moses (1Co 9:21); hence put for Gentile, pagan (Ac 2:23). By implication, a violator of the divine law, a transgressor, impious, wicked (Mk 15:28; Lk 22:37; Ac 2:23; 2Th 2:8; 1Ti 1:9; 2Pe 2:8; Sept.: Isa 53:12; 55:7; Eze 18:24; 33:8, 12).

Deriv.: *anomía* (458), lawlessness; *anómōs* (460), lawlessly.

Syn.: *ékthetos* (1570), exposed to perish, cast out; *ádikos* (94), unjust; *athémitos* (111), contrary to accepted customs; *anósios* (462), wicked, unholy, the strongest term denoting presumptuous and wicked self-assertion.

460. ἀνόμως, anomōs, *an-om´-oce*; adverb from 459; *lawlessly,* i.e. (special) *not amenable to* (the Jewish) *law*:—without law.

461. ἀνορθόω, anorthoō, *an-orth-o´-o*; from 303 and a derivative of the base of 3717; to *straighten up*:—lift (set) up, make straight.

From *aná* (303), again or up, and *orthóō* (n.f.), to erect, which is from *orthós* (3717), right, upright, erect. To make straight or upright again, to stand erect (Lk 13:13; Sept.: Ps 20:8). In the sense of to confirm, strengthen, establish (Heb 12:12 quoted from Isa 35:3; Sept.: 2Sa 7:13, 16; Ps 145:14; 146:8; Jer 33:2). To erect again, to rebuild (Ac 15:16).

Syn.: *egeírō* (1453), to raise up; *stékō* (4739), to stand fast, persevere; *exanístēmi* (1817), to raise or rise up; *exegeírō* (1825), to raise up; *aírō* (142), to raise or take up, lift; *epaírō* (1869), to raise, used of lifting up the eyes; *hupsóō* (5312), to lift or raise up; *anístēmi* (450), to lift or raise up; *anakúptō* (352), to lift oneself up.

462. ἀνόσιος, anosios, *an-os´-ee-os*; from 1 (as a negative particle) and 3741; *wicked*:—unholy.

463. ἀνοχή, anochē, *an-okh-ay´*; from 430; *self-restraint,* i.e. *tolerance*:—forbearance.

From *anéchō* (430), to bear with, suffer. Forbearance, a holding back, delay. In the NT, self-restraint, forbearance, patience (Ro 2:4; 3:25).

Syn.: *epieíkeia* (1932), clemency; *hupomoné* (5281), patience; *makrothumía* (3115), longsuffering toward people.

464. ἀνταγωνίζομαι, antagōnizomai, *an-tag-o-nid´-zom-ahee*; from 473 and 75; to *struggle against* (figurative) ["antagonize"]:—strive against.

From *antí* (473), against, and *agōnízomai* (75), to fight against a person. To be an antagonist, to contend with, strive against. Only in Heb 12:4.

Syn.: *pukteúō* (4438), to box, fight; *máchomai* (3164), to fight, strive; *poleméō* (4170), to war; *diamáchomai* (1264), to struggle against; *erízō* (2051), to wrangle, strive; *athléō* (118), to contend in games, wrestle.

465. ἀντάλλαγμα, antallagma, *an-tal´-ag-mah*; from a compound of 473 and 236; an *equivalent* or *ransom*:—in exchange.

Noun from *antallássō* (n.f.), to exchange, barter, which is from *antí* (473), against or instead of, and *allássō* (236), to change, make other than it is. That which is exchanged for anything, compensation, equivalent, generally

the price paid for something (Mt 16:26; Mk 8:37; Sept.: Ru 4:7; Jer 15:13; Job 28:15).
Syn.: *antapódosis* (469), reward.

466. ἀνταναπληρόω, antanaplēroō, *an-tan-ap-lay-ro´-o*; from 473 and 378; to *supplement*:—fill up.

467. ἀνταποδίδωμι, antapodidōmi, *an-tap-od-ee´-do-mee*; from 473 and 591; to *requite* (good or evil):—recompense, render, repay.

468. ἀνταπόδομα, antapodoma, *an-tap-od´-om-ah*; from 467; a *requital* (properly the thing):—recompense.

469. ἀνταπόδοσις, antapodosis, *an-tap-od´-os-is*; from 467; *requital* (properly the act):—reward.

470. ἀνταποκρίνομαι, antapokrinomai, *an-tap-ok-ree´-nom-ahee*; from 473 and 611; to *contradict* or *dispute*:—answer again, reply against.
From *antí* (473), against, and *apokrínomai* (611), to answer. To answer again, to reply against (Lk 14:6; Ro 9:20; Sept.: Jgs 5:29; Job 16:8; 32:12).
Syn.: *apologéomai* (626), to apologize, to speak for oneself; *antilégō* (483), to speak against.

471. ἀντέπω, antepō, *an-tep´-o*; from 473 and 2036; to *refute* or *deny*:—gainsay, say against.

472. ἀντέχομαι, antechomai, *an-tekh´-om-ahee*; from 473 and the middle of 2192; to *hold* oneself *opposite* to, i.e. (by implication) *adhere to*; by extension to *care for*:—hold fast, hold to, support.
From *antí* (473), against or to, and *échō* (2192), have. In the NT, to hold fast to, cleave to, i.e. to be faithfully attached to any person or thing (Mt 6:24; Lk 16:13; Tit 1:9); faithfully to care for (1Th 5:14; Sept.: Pr 3:18; 4:6; Isa 56:2, 4, 6; Jer 2:8; 8:2; Zep 1:6).
Syn.: *kratéō* (2902), to take hold of, keep, retain; *epilambánomai* (1949), to take hold of; *antilambánomai* (482), to help, support; *tēréō* (5083), to keep, give heed to, observe; *phulássō* (5442), to guard, hold.

473. ἀντί, anti, *an-tee´*; a primary particle; *opposite*, i.e. *instead* or *because* of (rarely *in addition* to):—for, in the room of. Often used

in composition to denote *contrast, requital, substitution, correspondence*, etc.
Preposition with the general meaning of over against, in the presence of, in lieu of. Spoken metaphorically either in a hostile sense, meaning against, or by way of comparison, where it implies something of equivalent value, and denotes substitution, exchange, requital. In the NT used in the following:
(I) By way of substitution, in place of, instead of (Lk 11:11; 1Co 11:15; Jas 4:15). As implying succession (Mt 2:22; so Jn 1:16, "and grace for grace," meaning grace upon grace, most abundant grace, one favour after another.
(II) By way of exchange, requital, equivalent, meaning in consideration of, on account of: spoken of price: for (Heb 12:16; Sept.: Nu 18:21, 31); of persons: for whom or for the sake of whom, in behalf of (Mt 17:27; 20:28; Mk 10:45); of retribution: for (Mt 5:38; Ro 12:17; 1Th 5:15; 1Pe 3:9); of the cause, motive, occasion: on account of, because of (Lk 12:3; Eph 5:31; Heb 12:2. See also Sept. for Jer 11:17).
In composition *antí* denotes: **(a)** over against, as *antitássomai* (498), to resist, oppose; **(b)** contrary to, as *antilégō* (483), to gainsay or speak against; **(c)** reciprocity, as *antapodídōmi* (467), to recompense or requite; **(d)** Substitution, as *anthúpatos* (446), a deputy, proconsul; **(e)** Similarity or correspondence, as *antíthesis* (477), opposition.
Deriv.: *antikrú* (481), opposite to, over against.

474. ἀντιβάλλω, antiballō, *an-tee-bal´-lo*; from 473 and 906; to *bandy*:—have.

475. ἀντιδιατίθεμαι, antidiatithemai, *an-tee-dee-at-eeth´-em-ahee*; from 473 and 1303; to *set oneself opposite*, i.e. *be disputatious*:—that oppose themselves.

476. ἀντίδικος, antidikos, *an-tid´-ee-kos*; from 473 and 1349; an *opponent* (in a lawsuit); specially *Satan* (as the arch-enemy):—adversary.
Noun from *antí* (473), against, and *díkē* (1349), a cause or suit at law. An opponent, accuser, e.g., the plaintiff in a suit at law (Mt 5:25; Lk 12:58). Hence generally, an adversary, enemy (Lk 18:3); also alluding to the Jewish notion that Satan is the accuser of men before God (1Pe 5:8 [cf. Job 1:6; Zec 3:1; Rev 12:10]; Sept.: 1Sa 2:10; Isa 41:11; Jer 50:34; 51:36).

Syn.: *hupenantíos* (5227), one who is contrary to; *ho antikeímenos* (480), the one lying in opposition, the adversary; *diábolos*, the devil, the false accuser; *Satanás* (4567), the adversary, Satan; *ho ponērós* (4190), the wicked one, the devil.

477. ἀντίθεσις, antithesis, *an-tith´-es-is*; from a compound of 473 and 5087; *opposition,* i.e. a *conflict* (of theories):—opposition.

478. ἀντικαθίστημι, antikathistēmi, *an-tee-kath-is´-tay-mee*; from 473 and 2525; to *set down* (troops) *against,* i.e. *withstand:*—resist.

479. ἀντικαλέω, antikaleō, *an-tee-kal-eh´-o*; from 473 and 2564; to *invite in return:*—bid again.

480. ἀντίκειμαι, antikeimai, *an-tik´-i-mahee*; from 473 and 2749; to *lie opposite,* i.e. *be adverse* (figurative, *repugnant*) *to:*—adversary, be contrary, oppose.

481. ἀντικρύ, antikru, *an-tee-kroo´*; prolonged from 473; *opposite:*—over against.

482. ἀντιλαμβάνομαι, antilambanomai, *an-tee-lam-ban´-om-ahee*; from 473 and the middle of 2983; to *take* hold of *in turn,* i.e. *succor;* also to *participate:*—help, partaker, support.

From *antí* (473), mutually or against, and *lambánō* (2983), to take, to hold. In the NT, to take hold of in one's turn, to take part in, to interest one's self for. Spoken of things (1Ti 6:2, "partakers of the benefit"); of persons: to aid, protect, relieve (Lk 1:54; Ac 20:35).

Deriv.: *antílepsis* (484), a help, assistance; *sunantilambánō* (4878), to help.

Syn.: *sunantilambánomai* (4878), to take hold of; *boēthéō* (997), aid, help, succor; *sumbállō* (4820), to throw together, helping or benefiting; *sunupourgéō* (4943), to help together, to serve with anyone; *sunergéō* (4903), to help in work, cooperate; *parístēmi* (3936), to stand by for help; *antéchomai* (472), to support, hold.

483. ἀντιλέγω, antilegō, *an-til´-eg-o*; from 473 and 3004; to *dispute, refuse:*—answer again, contradict, deny, gainsay (-er), speak against.

484. ἀντίληψις, antilēpsis, *an-til´-ape-sis*; from 482; *relief:*—help.

Noun from *antilambánō* (482), help, relief. In the NT, by metonymy of abstract for concrete: a helper, reliever. Only in 1Co 12:28, where it refers to those appointed to take care of the poor and sick.

Syn.: *boḗtheia* (996), help; *epikouría* (1947), help or assistance; *ōphéleia* (5622), usefulness; *euergesía* (2108), well-doing; *eupoiía* (2140), benefiting others; *chrēstótes* (5544), usefulness, kindness; *sumphéron* (4851), benefit.

485. ἀντιλογία, antilogia, *an-tee-log-ee´-ah*; from a derivative of 483; *dispute, disobedience:*—contradiction, gainsaying, strife.

486. ἀντιλοιδορέω, antiloidoreō, *an-tee-loy-dor-eh´-o*; from 473 and 3058; to *rail in reply:*—revile again.

487. ἀντίλυτρον, antilutron, *an-til´-oo-tron*; from 473 and 3083; a *redemption-price:*—ransom.

Noun from *antí* (473), in return, or correspondence, and *lútron* (3083), a ransom. A ransom, a price of redemption (Mt 20:28; 1Ti 2:6).

Syn.: *eleuthería* (1657), freedom; *sōtería* (4991), salvation; *sōtḗrion* (4992), means of salvation.

488. ἀντιμετρέω, antimetreō, *an-tee-met-reh´-o*; from 473 and 3354; to *mete in return:*—measure again.

489. ἀντιμισθία, antimisthia, *an-tee-mis-thee´-ah*; from a compound of 473 and 3408; *requital, correspondence:*—recompense.

490. Ἀντιόχεια, Antiocheia, *an-tee-okh´-i-ah*; from Ἀντίο-χος, *Antiochos* (a Syrian king); *Antiochia,* a place in Syria:—Antioch.

491. Ἀντιοχεύς, Antiocheus, *an-tee-okh-yoos´*; from 490; an *Antiochian* or inhabitant of *Antiochia:*—of Antioch.

492. ἀντιπαρέρχομαι, antiparerchomai, *an-tee-par-er´-khom-ahee*; from 473 and 3928; to *go along opposite:*—pass by on the other side.

493. Ἀντίπας, Antipas, *an-tee´-pas*; contracted from a compound of 473 and a derivative of 3962; *Antipas,* a Christian:—Antipas.

494. Ἀντιπατρίς, Antipatris, *an-tip-at-rece´*; from the same as 493; *Antipatris,* a place in Palestine:—Antipatris.

495. ἀντιπέραν, antiperan, *an-tee-per´-an*; from 473 and 4008; *on the opposite side:*—over against.

496. ἀντιπίπτω, antipiptō, *an-tee-pip´-to*; from 473 and 4098 (including its alternate); to *oppose*:—resist.

497. ἀντιστρατεύομαι, antistrateuomai, *an-tee-strat-yoo´-om-ahee*; from 473 and 4754; (figurative) to *attack*, i.e. (by implication) *destroy*:—war against.

498. ἀντιτάσσομαι, antitassomai, *an-tee-tas´-som-ahee*; from 473 and the middle of 5021; to *range oneself against*, i.e. *oppose*:—oppose themselves, resist.

499. ἀντίτυπον, antitupon, *an-teet´-oo-pon*; neuter of a compound of 473 and 5179; *correspond-ing* ["antitype"], i.e. a *representative, counterpart*:—(like) figure (whereunto).

The neuter of the adj. *antítupos* (n.f.), from *antí* (473), against, instead of, corresponding to, and *túpos* (5179), a type, model, figure, form, impression, print. In the NT, *antí* (473) in composition implies resemblance, correspondence; hence, formed after a type or model, like unto, corresponding. Used as a substantive meaning antitype, that which corresponds to a type (Heb 9:24; 1Pe 3:21).

Syn.: *parabolḗ* (3850), a parable; *hupódeigma* (5262), a pattern that is placed under for tracing; *homoíōma* (3667), something which is made to resemble something else; *eikṓn* (1504), an image representing something which has reality; *deígma* (1164), sample, example; *homoíōsis* (3669), making something to look like something else; *homoiótēs* (3665), likeness.

500. ἀντίχριστος, antichristos, *an-tee´-khris-tos*; from 473 and 5547; an *opponent of the Messiah*:—antichrist.

Noun from *antí* (473), instead of or against, and *Christós* (5547), Christ, anointed. Antichrist, literally an opposer of Christ. Found only in John's epistles, and there defined to be, collectively, all who deny that Jesus is the Messiah and that the Messiah is come in the flesh (1Jn 2:18, 22; 4:3; 2Jn 7). What class of persons the apostle had in mind is unknown; probably Jewish adversaries.

Syn.: *pseudóchristos* (5580), a false christ.

501. ἀντλέω, antleō, *ant-leh´-o*; from **ἄντλος,** *antlos* (the *hold* of a ship); to *bale* up (properly bilge water), i.e. *dip* water (with a bucket, pitcher, etc.):—draw (out).

502. ἄντλημα, antlēma, *ant´-lay-mah*; from 501; a *baling-vessel*:—thing to draw with.

503. ἀντοφθαλμέω, antophthalmeō, *ant-of-thal-meh´-o*; from a compound of 473 and 3788; to *face*:—bear up into.

504. ἄνυδρος, anudros, *an´-oo-dros*; from 1 (as a negative particle) and 5204; *waterless*, i.e. *dry*:—dry, without water.

505. ἀνυπόκριτος, anupokritos, *an-oo-pok´-ree-tos*; from 1 (as a negative particle) and a presumed derivative of 5271; *undissembled*, i.e. *sincere*:—without dissimulation (hypocrisy), unfeigned.

Adjective from the priv. *a* (1), without, and *hupokrínomai* (5271), to pretend, simulate. Unfeigned, genuine, real, true, sincere (Ro 12:9; 2Co 6:6; 1Ti 1:5; 2Ti 1:5; Jas 3:17; 1Pe 1:22).

Syn.: *ádolos* (97), pure, sincere; *gnḗsios* (1103), genuine; *eilikrinḗs* (1506), pure, sincere; *hagnós* (53), pure, chaste.

506. ἀνυπότακτος, anupotaktos, *an-oo-pot´-ak-tos*; from 1 (as a negative particle) and a presumed derivative of 5293; *unsubdued*, i.e. *insubordinate* (in fact or temper):—disobedient, that is not put under, unruly.

From the priv. *a* (1), without, and *hupotássō* (5293), to subject, sit under in an orderly manner. Spoken of things: not subject (Heb 2:8); spoken of persons: disobedient to authority, disorderly (1Ti 1:9; Tit 1:6, 10).

Syn.: *apeithḗs* (545), unwilling to be persuaded, disobedient.

507. ἄνω, anō, *an´-o*; adverb from 473; *upward* or *on the top*:—above, brim, high, up.

Adverb meaning above, in a higher place (Ac 2:19; Rev 5:3, Majority Text); With the article, what is above, upper, referred to heaven, and therefore heavenly, celestial (Gal 4:26; Php 3:14). So for heaven (Jn 8:23 [cf. 3:13, 31; 6:38]); and things above, heavenly or divine things (Col 3:1, 2). Also, motion to a higher place, upwards (Jn 11:41; Heb 12:15; Sept.: 1Ch 22:5; Ecc 3:21; Isa 8:21; 37:21).

Deriv.: *anṓgeon* (508), an upper room or chamber; *ánōthen* (509), from above, from the beginning, again; *epánō* (1883), above, more than; *huperánō* (5231), high above.

Syn.: *hupsēlós* (5308), high, lofty; *húpsistos* (5310), most high; *mégas* (3173), great, high;

húpsos (5311), height; *húpsōma* (5313), high thing or height.

508. ἀνώγεον, anōgeon, *an-ogue´-eh-on*; from 507 and 1093; *above the ground*, i.e. (properly) the *second floor* of a building; used for a *dome* or a *balcony* on the upper story:—upper room.

509. ἄνωθεν, anōthen, *an´-o-then*; from 507; *from above*; (by analogy) *from the first*; (by implication) *anew*:—from above, again, from the beginning (very first), the top.

Adverb from *ánō* (507), above, and the suffix *-then* denoting from. From above:

(I) Of place: from above, from a higher place (Mt 27:51; Mk 15:38; Jn 19:23). Hence spoken of whatever is heavenly or from heaven, and since God dwells in heaven, it signifies from God, in a divine manner (Jn 3:31; 19:11; Jas 1:17; 3:17).

(II) Of time, meaning from the first, from the beginning (Lk 1:3; Ac 26:5; Gal 4:9). Also, again, another time, as in Jn 3:3, 7, *gennēthḗ ánōthen,* translated "be born again" (*gennáō* [1080], to bear, be born). This could also be translated "to be born from above," doubtless equal to being "born of God" in Jn 1:13. In Jn 3:4, however, Nicodemus clearly takes it as synonymous with *deúteron* (1208), a second time.

Syn.: *dís* (1364), twice; *pálin* (3825), again; *próteron* (4386), before, first; *prṓtos* (4413), first; *prṓton* (4412), firstly, of time; *en archḗ* (*en* [1722], in; *archḗ* [746], beginning) from the beginning; *ap' archḗs* (*apó* [575], from, *archḗs* [n.f.], beginning), from the beginning.

510. ἀνωτερικός, anōterikos, *an-o-ter-ee-kos´*; from 511; *superior,* i.e. (locally) *more remote*:—upper.

511. ἀνώτερος, anōteros, *an-o´-ter-os*; comparative degree of 507; *upper,* i.e. (neuter as adverb) to a *more conspicuous* place, in a *former* part of the book:—above, higher.

512. ἀνωφέλες, anōpheles, *an-o-fel´-ace*; from 1 (as a negative particle) and the base of 5624; *useless* or (neuter) *inutility*:—unprofitable (-ness).

513. ἀξίνη, axinē, *ax-ee´-nay*; probably from ἄγνυμι, *agnumi* (to *break*; compare 4486); an *axe*:—axe.

514. ἄξιος, axios, *ax´-ee-os*; probably from 71; *deserving, comparable* or *suitable* (as if *drawing* praise):—due reward, meet, [un-] worthy.

515. ἀξιόω, axioō, *ax-ee-o´-o*; from 514; to *deem entitled* or *fit*:—desire, think good, count (think) worthy.

516. ἀξίως, axiōs, *ax-ee´-oce*; adverb from 514; *appropriately*:—as becometh, after a godly sort, worthily (-thy).

517. ἀόρατος, aoratos, *ah-or´-at-os*; from 1 (as a negative particle) and 3707; *invisible*:—invisible (thing).

518. ἀπαγγέλλω, apaggellō, *ap-ang-el´-lo*; from 575 and the base of 32; to *announce*:—bring word (again), declare, report, shew (again), tell.

From *apó* (575), from, and *aggéllō* (n.f., see *anaggéllō* [312]), to tell, declare. To announce:

(I) To bring a message from any person or place:

(A) To relate, inform, tell what has occurred (Mt 8:33; 14:12; Mk 6:30; 16:10, 13; Lk 8:20, 36; Jn 4:51; 20:18; Ac 11:13; Ac 4:23; 1Th 1:9; Sept.: Jgs 13:10).

(B) To announce, make known, declare, tell what is done or to be done (Mt 12:18; Ac 5:25; 15:27; 16:36; 28:21; Heb 2:12; 1Jn 1:2, 3; Sept.: Ge 24:49; 29:15; Jos 2:2; Jgs 13:6; Ps 78:4, 6 quoted from 22:23). To praise, celebrate (Sept.: Ps 89:1; 105:1). By implication, to confess (Lk 8:47; 1Co 14:25; Sept.: Ge 12:18).

(II) To bring back word from anyone, report (Mt 2:8; 11:4; Lk 7:22; 14:21; Ac 22:26; Sept.: Ge 27:42; 29:12).

Syn.: *diēgéomai* (1334), to narrate, relate; *ekdiēgéomai* (1555), to narrate in full; *exēgéomai* (1834), to lead out, make known, rehearse; *dēlóō* (1213), to declare; *phrázō* (5419), to express, declare; *gnōrízō* (1107), to make known; *marturéō* (3140), to testify; *diaphēmízō* (1310), to report to the public; *phaneróō* (5319), to make manifest; *légō* (3004), to tell; *laléō* (2980), to speak; *eklaléō* (1583), to speak out; *eréō* (2046), to say; *diasaphéō* (1285), to make clear; *mēnúō* (3377), to show or make known.

519. ἀπάγχομαι, apagchomai, *ap-ang´-khom-ahee*; from 575 and ἄγχω, *agchō* (to *choke*; akin to the base of 43); to *strangle oneself off* (i.e. to death):—hang himself.

520. ἀπάγω, apagō, *ap-ag´-o*; from 575 and 71; to *take off* (in various senses):—bring, carry away, lead (away), put to death, take away.

521. ἀπαίδευτος, apaideutos, *ap-ah´ee-dyoo-tos*; from 1 (as a negative particle) and a derivative of 3811; *uninstructed,* i.e. (figurative) *stupid:*—unlearned.

Adjective from the priv. *a* (1), without, and *paideúō* (3811), to instruct, chastise, correct. Unlearned, untaught, ignorant, stupid, foolish. Of persons (Sept.: Pr 8:5; 15:15; 17:21). In the NT, nonsensical, i.e. inept, trifling, absurd disputations. Only in 2Ti 2:23.

Syn.: *agrámmatos* (62), unlettered, unlearned; *amathḗs* (261), unlearned, ignorant; *idiṓtēs* (2399), a private citizen, an ignorant person; *áphrōn* (878), without reason; *anóētos* (453), without understanding; *mōrós* (3474), dull, sluggish in understanding; *asúnetos* (801), without discernment; *agoraíos* (60), one relating to the marketplace, a commoner.

522. ἀπαίρω, apairō, *ap-ah´ee-ro*; from 575 and 142; to *lift off,* i.e. *remove:*—take (away).

523. ἀπαιτέω, apaiteō, *ap-ah´ee-teh-o*; from 575 and 154; to *demand back:*—ask again, require.

From *apó* (575), again, and *aitéō* (154), to ask. To recall, demand back what is one's own, require (Lk 6:30; 12:20).

Syn.: *zētéō* (2212), to seek, inquire, desire; *epizētéō* (1934), to seek after or for; *ekzētéō* (1567), to seek out.

524. ἀπαλγέω, apalgeō, *ap-alg-eh´-o*; from 575 and ἀλγέω, *algeō* (to *smart*); to *grieve out,* i.e. *become apathetic:*—be past feeling.

525. ἀπαλλάσσω, apallassō, *ap-al-las´-so*; from 575 and 236; to *change away,* i.e. *release,* (reflexive) *remove:*—deliver, depart.

From *apó* (575), from, and *allássō* (236), to change. To remove from. In the NT: to remove one's self from, to depart, to leave (Ac 19:12; Sept.: Ex 19:22). By implication, to set free, to dismiss; to be set free (Lk 12:58); used metaphorically in Heb 2:15.

Syn.: *eleutheróō* (1659), to set free, deliver; *apolúō* (630), to loose from; *aphíēmi* (863), to remit, forgive; *lutróō* (3084), to ransom, redeem; *apolúō* (630), to release.

526. ἀπαλλοτριόω, apallotrioō, *ap-al-lot-ree-o´-o*; from 575 and a derivative of 245; to *estrange away,* i.e. (passive and figurative) to *be non-participant:*—alienate, be alien.

From *apó* (575), from, and *allotrióō* (n.f.), to alienate. To estrange, to be alienated from, to be a stranger (Eph 2:12; 4:18; Col 1:21). It denotes the state prior to man's reconciliation to God. See Sept.: Job 21:29; Ps 58:3; Eze 14:5.

527. ἀπαλός, apalos, *ap-al-os´*; of uncertain derivative; *soft:*—tender.

528. ἀπαντάω, apantaō, *ap-an-tah´-o*; from 575 and a derivative of 473; to *meet away,* i.e. *encounter:*—meet.

529. ἀπάντησις, apantēsis, *ap-an´-tay-sis*; from 528; a (friendly) *encounter:*—meet.

530. ἅπαξ, hapax, *hap´-ax*; probably from 537; *one* (or a *single*) *time* (numerically or conclusively):—once.

531. ἀπαράβατος, aparabatos, *ap-ar-ab´-at-os*; from 1 (as a negative particle) and a derivative of 3845; *not passing away,* i.e. *untransferable* (perpetual):—unchangeable.

Adjective from the priv. *a* (1), without, and *parabaínō* (3845), to go beyond, transgress. Not passing over, i.e. not transgressing; in the pass., not violated, inviolate. In the NT, spoken of Christ's priesthood as not transient, perpetual or immutable, unchanging, only in Heb 7:24.

Syn.: *hedraíos* (1476) and *ametakínētos* (277), immovable; *ametáthetos* (276), unchangeable; *stereós* (4731), solid, stable, steadfast; *bébaios* (949), firm.

532. ἀπαρασκεύαστος, aparaskeuastos, *ap-ar-ask-yoo´-as-tos*; from 1 (as a negative particle) and a derivative of 3903; *unready:*—unprepared.

533. ἀπαρνέομαι, aparneomai, *ap-ar-neh´-om-ahee*; from 575 and 720; to *deny utterly,* i.e. *disown, abstain:*—deny.

From *apó* (575), from, and *arnéomai* (720), to deny, refuse. Spoken of persons, to deny, disown, abjure:

(I) Of Christ and his religion (Mt 26:34, 35, 75; Mk 14:30, 31, 72; Lk 22:34 [TR], 61; Jn 13:38 [TR]); of persons denied by Christ (Lk 12:9).

(II) Followed by *heautón* (1438), oneself: to deny oneself, i.e. to disown and renounce self, to disregard all personal interests and enjoyments (Mt 16:24; Mk 8:34).

Syn.: *antilégō* (483), to speak against, contradict; *paraitéomai* (3868), to avoid, reject; *apodokimázō* (513), to reject, disapprove; *athetéō* (114), to make void, nullify, disallow; *anthístēmi* (436), to set against; *antikathístēmi* (478), to stand firm against; *antitássō* (498), to set oneself against, oppose; *antipíptō* (496), to strive against, resist.

534. ἀπάρτι, aparti, *ap-ar´-tee*; from 575 and 737; *from now*, i.e. *henceforth (already):*—from henceforth.

535. ἀπαρτισμός, apartismos, *ap-ar-tis-mos´*; from a derivative of 534; *completion:*—finishing.

536. ἀπαρχή, aparchē, *ap-ar-khay´*; from a compound of 575 and 756; a *beginning* of sacrifice, i.e. the (Jewish) *first-fruit* (figurative):—first-fruits.

Noun from *apárchomai* (n.f.), from *apó* (575), from, and *árchomai* (756), to begin. An offering of firstfruits; then, an offering generally. In the NT, the firstfruits, which were usually consecrated to God:

(I) The first part of something. In Ro 11:16, the firstfruits, the first portion, metaphorically spoken of the patriarchs and ancestors of the Jewish nation. Used figuratively in Ro 8:23, "the firstfruits of the Spirit," i.e. the first gifts of the Spirit, the earnest, the pledge of future and still higher gifts.

(II) Spoken of persons: first in time, the first of whom any particular thing may be predicated (Ro 16:5; 1Co 15:20, 23; 16:15; Jas 1:18; Rev 14:4).

Syn.: *prōtos* (4413), beginning, first.

537. ἅπας, hapas, *hap´-as*; from 1 (as a particle of union) and 3956; absolutely *all* or (singular) *every* one:—all (things), every (one), whole.

538. ἀπατάω, apataō, *ap-at-ah´-o*; of uncertain derivative; to *cheat*, i.e. *delude:*—deceive.

539. ἀπάτη, apatē, *ap-at´-ay*; from 538; *delusion:*—deceit (-ful, -fulness), deceivableness (-ving).

540. ἀπάτωρ, apatōr, *ap-at´-ore*; from 1 (as a negative particle) and 3962; *fatherless*, i.e. *of unrecorded paternity:*—without father.

541. ἀπαύγασμα, apaugasma, *ap-ow´-gas-mah*; from a compound of 575 and 826; an *off-flash*, i.e. *effulgence:*—brightness.

Noun from *apaugázō* (n.f.), to emit light or splendour, which is from *apó* (575), from, and *augázō* (826), to shine. Reflected splendour or brightness. Only in Heb 1:3, used figuratively, meaning in whom the divine majesty is conspicuous.

Syn.: *phṓs* (5457), light; *phéggos* (5338), brightness, lustre.

542. ἀπείδω, apeidō, *ap-i´-do*; from 575 and the same as 1492; to *see* fully:—see.

543. ἀπείθεια, apeitheia, *ap-i´-thi-ah*; from 545; *disbelief* (obstinate and rebellious):—disobedience, unbelief.

Noun from *apeithḗs* (545), disobedient. Disobedience, unwillingness to be persuaded, willful unbelief, obstinacy (Ro 11:30, 32; Eph 2:2; 5:6; Heb 4:6, 11); by Hebraism, *huioí tḗs apatheías*, "children of disobedience" (*huiós* [5207], son, child), i.e. heathen, pagans (Col 3:6 [TR]).

Syn.: *parakoḗ* (3876), hearing amiss, hence disobedience; *apistía* (570), unbelief; *parábasis* (3847), transgression; *paranomía* (3892), law-breaking.

544. ἀπειθέω, apeitheō, *ap-i-theh´-o*; from 545; to *disbelieve* (wilfully and perversely):—not believe, disobedient, obey not, unbelieving.

From *apeithḗs* (545), disobedient. Not to allow oneself to be persuaded or believe, to disbelieve, be disobedient:

(I) Spoken of disbelievers in Christ (Ac 14:2; 17:5; 19:9; Ro 15:31; 1Pe 2:8); of those who are disobedient to God (Ro 10:21; 11:31; Heb 3:18; 1Pe 3:20; Sept.: Dt 9:7; Isa 50:5; 63:10; 65:2). In Heb 11:31 *hoi apeithḗsantes*, those who did disobey, unbelievers, heathen. See Sept.: Isa 66:14.

(II) Of those disobedient to the Son (Jn 3:36); to God (Ro 11:30; Sept.: Nu 14:43); to the truth (Ro 2:8); to the Word (1Pe 2:8; 3:1); to the gospel (1Pe 4:17 [cf. Dt 1:26; 9:23; 32:51]).

Syn.: *apistéō* (569), to disbelieve; *parakoúō* (3878), to hear imperfectly and thus to disobey; *parabaínō* (3845), to transgress; *anthístēmi* (436), to stand against; *exanístēmi* (1817), to object; *epanístamai* (1881), to rise up against; *aphístēmi* (868), to stand afar, desist; *ataktéō* (812), to behave in a disorderly manner.

545. ἀπειθής, apeithēs, *ap-i-thace´*; from 1 (as a negative particle) and 3982; *unpersuadable*, i.e. *contumacious*:—disobedient.

Adjective from the priv. *a* (1), without, and *peíthō* (3982), to persuade. Unwilling to be persuaded, unbelieving, disobedient (Lk 1:17; Ac 26:19; Ro 1:30; 2Ti 3:2; Tit 1:16; 3:3).

Deriv.: *apeítheia* (543), disobedience; *apeithéō* (544), to be disobedient.

Syn.: *anupótaktos* (506), disobedient; *átaktos* (313), unruly; *sklērós* (4642), hard, not pliable.

546. ἀπειλέω, apeileō, *ap-i-leh´-o*; of uncertain derivative; to *menace*; (by implication) to *forbid*:—threaten.

547. ἀπειλή, apeilē, *ap-i-lay´*; from 546; a *menace*:— × straitly, threatening.

548. ἄπειμι, apeimi, *ap´-i-mee*; from 575 and 1510; to *be away*:—be absent. Compare 549.

From *apó* (575), from, and *eimí* (1510), to be. To be absent (1Co 5:3; 2Co 10:1, 11; 13:2, 10; Php 1:27; Col 2:5).

Deriv.: *apousía* (666), absence.

Syn.: *aphístēmi* (868), to stand away from, desist; *ekdēméō* (1553), to vacate, exit, be absent; *analúō* (360), to depart; *chōrízomai* (5563), to separate oneself.

549. ἄπειμι, apeimi, *ap´-i-mee*; from 575 and εἶμι, *eimi* (to go); to *go away*:—go. Compare 548.

550. ἀπειπόμην, apeipomēn, *ap-i-pom´-ane*; reflexive past of a compound of 575 and 2036; to *say off* for oneself, i.e. *disown*:—renounce.

551. ἀπείραστος, apeirastos, *ap-i´-ras-tos*; from 1 (as a negative particle) and a presumed derivative of 3987; *untried*, i.e. *not temptable*:—not to be tempted.

Adjective from the priv. *a* (1), without, and *peirázō* (3985), to tempt or test. Untried, untempted, i.e. incapable of being tempted. Only in Jas 1:13.

552. ἄπειρος, apeiros, *ap´-i-ros*; from 1 (as a negative particle) and 3984; *inexperienced*, i.e. *ignorant*:—unskilful.

553. ἀπεκδέχομαι, apekdechomai, *ap-ek-dekh´-om-ahee*; from 575 and 1551; to *expect fully*:—look (wait) for.

From *apó* (575), an intensive, and *ekdéchomai* (1551), to expect, look for. To wait out, i.e. to wait long for, to await ardently, to expect (Ro 8:19, 23, 25; 1Co 1:7; Gal 5:5; Php 3:20; Heb 9:28 [cf. 1Pe 3:20]).

Syn.: *prosdokáō* (4328), to await, expect; *prosdéchomai* (4327), to expect, look for; *anaménō* (362), to wait for with patience and confident expectancy; *periménō* (4037), to wait around for the fulfillment of an event; *proskarteréō* (4342), to wait around looking forward to the fulfillment of something one expects to take place; *elpízō* (1679), to hope; *prosménō* (4357), to tarry, wait with patience and steadfastness; *apoblépō* (578), to look away from all else at one object, to look steadfastly.

554. ἀπεκδύομαι, apekduomai, *ap-ek-doo´-om-ahee*; middle from 575 and 1562; to *divest wholly* oneself, or (for oneself) *despoil*:—put off, spoil.

555. ἀπέκδυσις, apekdusis, *ap-ek´-doo-sis*; from 554; *divestment*:—putting off.

556. ἀπελαύνω, apelaunō, *ap-el-ow´-no*; from 575 and 1643; to *dismiss*:—drive.

557. ἀπελεγμός, apelegmos, *ap-el-eg-mos´*; from a compound of 575 and 1651; *refutation*, i.e. (by implication) *contempt*:—nought.

558. ἀπελεύθερος, apeleutheros, *ap-el-yoo´-ther-os*; from 575 and 1658; one *freed away*, i.e. a *freedman*:—freeman.

Noun from *apó* (575), from, and *eleútheros* (1658), free. A freedman. Only in 1Co 7:22.

559. Ἀπελλῆς, Apellēs, *ap-el-lace´*; of Latin origin; *Apelles*, a Christian:—Apelles.

560. ἀπελπίζω, apelpizō, *ap-el-pid´-zo*; from 575 and 1679; to *hope out*, i.e. *fully expect*:—hope for again.

From *apó* (575), from, and *elpízō* (1679), to hope.

Syn.: *exaporéō* (1820), to be wholly without resource, to despair utterly; *aporéō* (639), despair or be perplexed. To have done hoping, to despair. Only in Lk 6:35, cf. 6:34.

561. ἀπέναντι, apenanti, *ap-en´-an-tee*; from 575 and 1725; *from in front*, i.e. *opposite, before* or *against*:—before, contrary, over against, in the presence of.

562. ἀπέραντος, aperantos, *ap-er´-an-tos*; from 1 (as a negative particle) and a secondary derivative of 4008; *unfinished*, i.e. (by implication) *interminable*:—endless.

563. ἀπερισπάστως, aperispastōs, *ap-er-is-pas´-toce*; adverb from a compound of 1 (as a negative particle) and a presumed derivative of 4049; *undistractedly*, i.e. *free from* (domestic) *solicitude*:—without distraction.

564. ἀπερίτμητος, aperitmētos, *ap-er-eet´-may-tos*; from 1 (as a negative particle) and a presumed derivative of 4059; *uncircumcised* (figurative):—uncircumcised.

Adjective from the priv. *a* (1), without, and *peritémnō* (4059), to circumcise. Uncircumcised. In the NT, used metaphorically in Ac 7:51, "uncircumcised in heart and ears," those who do not listen or obey the divine precepts. See Sept.: Ge 17:14; Ex 12:48; Le 26:41; Jer 6:10; 9:26; Eze 44:7, 9.

565. ἀπέρχομαι, aperchomai, *ap-erkh´-om-ahee*; from 575 and 2064; to *go off* (i.e. *depart*), *aside* (i.e. *apart*) or *behind* (i.e. *follow*), literal or figurative:—come, depart, go (aside, away, back, out, … ways), pass away, be past.

566. ἀπέχει, apechei, *ap-ekh´-i*; third person singular present indicative active of 568 used impersonally; *it is sufficient*:—it is enough.

Used impersonally, from the verb *apéchō* (568), to have, receive. Literally, "to have off or out," meaning to have all that is one's due so as to cease from demanding or having any more. Thus, used in this manner, *apéchei* means it is enough as in Mk 14:41, meaning you have slept enough.

567. ἀπέχομαι, apechomai, *ap-ekh´-om-ahee*; middle (reflexive) of 568; to *hold oneself off*, i.e. *refrain*:—abstain.

The middle voice of *apéchō* (568), to keep oneself from. To abstain or refrain (Ac 15:20, 29; 1Th 4:3; 5:22; 1Ti 4:3; 1Pe 2:11; Sept.: Job 1:1, 8; Pr 23:4).

Syn.: *egkrateúomai* (1467), to exercise self-restraint; *néphō* (3525), to be sober; *sōphronéō* (4993), to exercise soundness of mind, to think soberly, use self-control.

568. ἀπέχω, apechō, *ap-ekh´-o*; from 575 and 2192; (active) to *have out*, i.e. *receive in full*; (intransitive) to *keep* (oneself) *away*, i.e. *be distant* (literal or figurative):—be, have, receive.

From *apó* (575), from, and *échō* (2192), to have, be. To hold off from, as a ship from the shore; to be distant from, absent (Lk 7:6; 15:20; 24:13; Sept.: Isa 55:9); used figuratively, of the heart (Mt 15:8; Mk 7:6). Also, to have all that is one's due, to have received in full, spoken of reward, or wages (Mt 6:2, 15, 16; Lk 6:24; Php 4:18); spoken of a person: to have for good and all (Phm 15).

Deriv.: *apéchei* (566), it is enough.

Syn.: *aphístēmi* (868), to desist, stand off; *apotrépomai* (665), to turn away from.

569. ἀπιστέω, apisteō, *ap-is-teh´-o*; from 571; to *be unbelieving*, i.e. (transitive) *disbelieve*, or (by implication) *disobey*:—believe not.

From *ápistos* (571), untrustworthy. To withhold belief, to doubt, to distrust (Mk 16:11; Lk 24:11; Ac 28:24). Hence, to disbelieve, to be unbelieving, i.e. without faith in God and Christ (Mk 16:16; Ro 3:3); to break one's faith, to prove false (2Ti 2:13).

Syn.: *apeithéō* (544), to refuse to be persuaded or believe.

570. ἀπιστία, apistia, *ap-is-tee´-ah*; from 571; *faithlessness*, i.e. (negative) *disbelief* (*want of Christian faith*), or (positive) *unfaithfulness* (*disobedience*):—unbelief.

Noun from *ápistos* (571), untrustworthy. Faithlessness or uncertainty, distrust, unbelief. In respect to declarations, doctrines, promises, etc. (Mt 13:58; 17:20; Mk 9:24; Ro 3:3; 11; 20, 23). A state of unbelief, before embracing the gospel (1Ti 1:13). A violation of faith, apostasy (Heb 3:12, 19).

Syn.: *apeítheia* (543), disobedience; *parakoē* (3876), hearing amiss, an act of disobedience.

571. ἄπιστος, apistos, *ap´-is-tos*; from 1 (as a negative particle) and 4103; (active) *disbelieving*, i.e. *without* Christian *faith* (specially a *heathen*); (passive) *untrustworthy* (person), or *incredible* (thing):—that believeth not, faithless, incredible thing, infidel, unbeliever (-ing).

Adjective from *a* (1), without, and *pistós* (4103), believing, faithful. Not worthy of confidence, untrustworthy. Spoken of things: incredible, unbelievable (Ac 26:8); spoken of persons: withholding belief, incredulous, distrustful (Mt 17:17; Mk 9:19; Lk 9:41; Jn 20:27; 2Co 4:4). By implication, heathen, pagan, i.e. those who have not believed on Christ (1Co 6:6; 7:12, 13, 14; 14:22). So with the idea of impiety (2Co 6:14, 15; 1Ti 5:8; Tit 1:15).

Deriv.: *apistéō* (569), to disbelieve; *apistía* (570), unbelief.

Syn.: *apeithés* (545), spurning belief, disobedient; *anupótaktos* (506), insubordinate, disobedient.

572. ἁπλότης, haplotēs, *hap-lot´-ace*; from 573; *singleness,* i.e. (subjective) *sincerity* (*without dissimulation* or *self-seeking*), or (objective) *generosity* (*copious bestowal*):—bountifulness, liberal (-ity), simplicity, singleness.

Noun from *haplóos* contracted *haploús* (573), simplicity. Generally, sincerity, candor (2Co 1:12; Sept.: 2Sa 15:11; Pr 19:1); simplicity of heart (Eph 6:5; Col 3:22; Sept.: 1Ch 29:17). Specifically spoken of Christian simplicity, frankness, integrity, fidelity, etc. (Ro 12:8; 2Co 8:2; 9:11, 13; 11:3).

Syn.: *aphelótēs* (858), simplicity, singleness; *eulogía* (2129), a blessing, indicating abundance; *cháris* (5485), grace, with the meaning of bounty; *hadrótēs* (100), fatness, indicating abundance; *perisseía* (4050), an exceeding measure; *huperbolḗ* (5236), beyond measure.

573. ἁπλοῦς, haplous, *hap-looce´*; probably from 1 (as a particle of union) and the base of 4120; properly *folded together,* i.e. *single* (figurative, *clear*):—single.

Simple, sound, perfect (Mt 6:22; Lk 11:34).

Deriv.: *haplótēs* (572), singleness; *haplós* (574), bountifully.

Syn.: *ákakos* (172), harmless, unwilling to do harm; *akéraios* (185), harmless; *ádolos* (97), without guile; *gnḗsios* (1103), sincere, genuine; *eilikrinés* (1506), pure, sincere; *agathós* (18), benevolent; *kalós* (2570), good; *chrēstós* (5443), kindly.

574. ἁπλῶς, haplōs, *hap-loce´*; adverb from 573 (in the objective sense of 572); *bountifully:*—liberally.

575. ἀπό, apo, *apo´*; a primary particle; "*off,*" i.e. *away* (from something near), in various senses (of place, time, or relation; literal or figurative):—(× here-) after, ago, at, because of, before, by (the space of), for (-th), from, in, (out) of, off, (up-) on (-ce), since, with. In com-

position (as a prefix) it usually denotes *separation, departure, cessation, completion, reversal,* etc.

576. ἀποβαίνω, apobainō, *ap-ob-ah´ee-no*; from 575 and the base of 939; literal to *disembark*; (figurative) to *eventuate*:—become, go out, turn.

577. ἀποβάλλω, apoballō, *ap-ob-al´-lo*; from 575 and 906; to *throw off*; (figurative) to *lose*:—cast away.

578. ἀποβλέπω, apoblepō, *ap-ob-lep´-o*; from 575 and 991; to *look away* from everything else, i.e. (figurative) intently *regard*:—have respect.

579. ἀπόβλητος, apoblētos, *ap-ob´-lay-tos*; from 577; *cast off,* i.e. (figurative) such as to *be rejected*:—be refused.

580. ἀποβολή, apobolē, *ap-ob-ol-ay´*; from 577; *rejection*; (figurative) *loss*:—casting away, loss.

581. ἀπογενόμενος, apogenomenos, *ap-og-en-om´-en-os*; past participle of a compound of 575 and 1096; *absent,* i.e. *deceased* (figurative, *renounced*):—being dead.

Second aor. middle part. of *apogínomai* (n.f.), from *apó* (575), from, and *gínomai* (1096), to become. To be absent from, to depart, i.e. to die. In the NT, used metaphorically: to die to something, i.e. to renounce. Only in 1Pe 2:24.

Syn.: *thnḗskō* (2348), to die; *apothnḗskō* (599), to die off; *teleutáō* (5053), to end one's life; *ekleípō* (1587), to cease, die; *suntríbō* (4937), to break in pieces; *sbénnumi* (4570), to extinguish; *apóllumi* (622), to destroy, die, lose; *leípō* (3007), to be wanting, lacking; *apoleípō* (620), to leave behind; *phtheírō* (5351), to corrupt, destroy.

582. ἀπογραφή, apographē, *ap-og-raf-ay´*; from 583; an *enrollment*; (by implication) an *assessment*:—taxing.

583. ἀπογράφω, apographō, *ap-og-raf´-o*; from 575 and 1125; to *write off* (a copy or list), i.e. *enroll*:—tax, write.

584. ἀποδείκνυμι, apodeiknumi, *ap-od-ike´-noo-mee*; from 575 and 1166; to *show off,* i.e. *exhibit*; (figurative) to *demonstrate,* i.e. *accredit*:—(ap-) prove, set forth, shew.

585. ἀπόδειξις, apodeixis, *ap-od´-ike-sis*; from 584; *manifestation:*—demonstration.

586. ἀποδεκατόω, apodekatoō, *ap-od-ek-at-o´-o*; from 575 and 1183; to *tithe* (as debtor or creditor):—(give, pay, take) tithe.

587. ἀπόδεκτος, apodektos, *ap-od´-ek-tos*; from 588; *accepted,* i.e. *agreeable:*—acceptable.

Adjective from *apodéchomai* (588), to welcome. Acceptable (1Ti 2:3; 5:4).

Syn.: *euárestos* (2101), well-pleasing; *euprósdektos* (2144), acceptable, favourable; *dókimos* (1384), approved, acceptable.

588. ἀποδέχομαι, apodechomai, *ap-od-ekh´-om-ahee*; from 575 and 1209; to *take fully,* i.e. *welcome* (persons), *approve* (things):—accept, receive (gladly).

From *apó* (575), an intensive, and *déchomai* (1209), to take from another for oneself, to receive. Spoken of persons, to receive as a friend or guest, to bid welcome (Lk 8:40; Ac 15:4; 28:30). Figuratively, of doctrine: to admit, to embrace (Ac 2:41). To accept with joy, to welcome, and by implication to applaud, extol (Ac 24:3).

Deriv.: *apódektós* (587), acceptable; *apodoché* (594), a receiving back.

Syn.: *lambánō* (2983), to receive without necessarily indicating a favourable reception; *paralambánō* (3880), to receive from another; *apolambánō* (618), to receive from another as one's due; *proslambánō* (4355), to take to oneself; *eudokéō* (2106), to approve; *sugkatatíthemai* (4784), to consent; *euarestéō* (2100), to please or be pleased; *paradéchomai* (3858), to accept with delight, receive; *prosdéchomai* (4327), to accept, to look for; *egkrínō* (1469), to reckon on, approve; *homologéō* (3670), to assent, confess, accept, accept together.

589. ἀποδημέω, apodēmeō, *ap-od-ay-meh´-o*; from 590; to *go abroad,* i.e. *visit a foreign land:*—go (travel) into a far country, journey.

590. ἀπόδημος, apodēmos, *ap-od´-ay-mos*; from 575 and 1218; *absent from* one's own *people,* i.e. *a foreign traveller:*—taking a far journey.

591. ἀποδίδωμι, apodidōmi, *ap-od-eed´-o-mee*; from 575 and 1325; to *give away,* i.e. *up, over, back,* etc. (in various applications):—deliver (again), give (again), (re-) pay (-ment be made), perform, recompense, render, requite, restore, reward, sell, yield.

592. ἀποδιορίζω, apodiorizō, *ap-od-ee-or-id´-zo*; from 575 and a compound of 1223 and 3724; to *disjoin* (by a boundary, figuratively, a party):—separate.

From *apó* (575), from, and *diorízō* (n.f.), to divide, separate. To set bounds. In the NT, used metaphorically: to divide off, separate. Only in Jude 19.

Syn.: *aphorízō* (873), to mark off by bounds; *chōrízō* (5563), to separate.

593. ἀποδοκιμάζω, apodokimazō, *ap-od-ok-ee-mad´-zo*; from 575 and 1381; to *disapprove,* i.e. (by implication) to *repudiate:*—disallow, reject.

From *apó* (575), from, and *dokimázō* (1381), to prove. To disapprove, to reject. Spoken of a stone rejected or worthless (Mt 21:42; Mk 12:10; Lk 20:17; 1Pe 4:7; Sept.: Jer 6:30); of Jesus rejected as the Messiah by the Jews (Mk 8:31; Lk 9:22; 17:25); of Esau (Heb 12:17; Sept.: Jer 6:30; 7:28; 14:19; 31:36).

Syn.: *athetéō* (114), to make void, nullify, reject; *ekptúō* (1609), to spit out, spurn; *paraitéomai* (3868), to refuse; *akuróō* (208), to disannul, render of no effect; *aporríptō* (641), to reject.

594. ἀποδοχή, apodochē, *ap-od-okh-ay´*; from 588; *acceptance:*—acceptation.

Noun from *apodéchomai* (588), to receive from. Reception, particularly of a guest. In the NT, used metaphorically: assent, approbation, praise. Only in 1Ti 1:15; 4:9.

Syn.: *sugkatáthesis* (4783), agreement; *eudokía* (2107), good pleasure; *homología* (3671), acknowledgement, confession; *bebaíōsis* (951), confirmation; *anoché* (463), forbearance.

595. ἀπόθεσις, apothesis, *ap-oth´-es-is*; from 659; a *laying aside* (literal or figurative):—putting away (off).

596. ἀποθήκη, apothēkē, *ap-oth-ay´-kay*; from 659; a *repository,* i.e. *granary:*—barn, garner.

597. ἀποθησαυρίζω, apothēsaurizō, *ap-oth-ay-sow-rid´-zo*; from 575 and 2343; to *treasure away:*—lay up in store.

598. ἀποθλίβω, apothlibō, *ap-oth-lee´-bo*; from 575 and 2346; to *crowd* from (every side):—press.

599. ἀποθνήσκω, apothnēskō, *ap-oth-nace´-ko*; from 575 and 2348; to *die* off (literal or figurative):—be dead, death, die, lie a-dying, be slain (× with).

From *apó* (575) an intensive, and *thnḗskō* (2348), to die. To die; through the force of *apó*, to die out, to become quite dead. Hence it is stronger than *thnḗskō*, though generally used synonymously with it and instead of it:

(**I**) Spoken of persons (Mt 9:24; Mk 5:35, 39; Lk 8:42; Jn 21:23; Ac 9:37; Ro 6:10; 7:2, 3; 14:7, 8; Heb 11:4; Rev 14:13). Spoken of a violent death: to be put to death, to be killed, to perish (Mt 26:35; Ac 21:13; Ro 5:6–8; Rev 8:9, 11). So of animals, to perish (Mt 8:32; Rev 16:3); spoken of the punishment of death (Jn 19:7; Heb 10:28).

(**II**) Of vegetable life: to rot (Jn 12:24; 1Co 15:36); of trees: to wither, to die (Jude 12, figuratively).

(**III**) In an inchoative sense: to be dying, to be near death (Lk 8:42); to be exposed to death, to be in danger of death (1Co 15:31; 2Co 6:9). Also, to be subject to death, to be mortal (Ro 5:15; 1Co 15:22; Heb 7:8).

(**IV**) Metaphorically, referring to religious faith, works, etc.: to be ready to expire, become extinct (Rev 3:2). Also, to die to or from something, i.e. to renounce, to forsake (Ro 6:2; Gal 2:19; Col 2:20).

(**V**) Figuratively, to die forever, to come under condemnation of eternal death, i.e. exclusion from the Messiah's kingdom, and subjection to eternal punishment for sin (Jn 6:50; 8:21, 24; Ro 7:10; 8:13).

Deriv.: *sunapothnḗskō* (4880), to die with.

Syn.: *teleutáō* (5053), to end one's life; *koimáō* (2837), to fall asleep, figuratively, to die; *apogínomai* (581), to be away from, to die; *apóllumi* (622), to destroy, die.

600. ἀποκαθίστημι, apokathistēmi, *ap-ok-ath-is´-tay-mee*; from 575 and 2525; to *reconstitute* (in health, home or organization):—restore (again).

From *apó* (575), back again, and *kathístēmi* (2525), to constitute. To put back into a former state, to restore. Spoken of restoration to health

(Mt 12:13; Mk 3:5; 8:25; Lk 6:10; Sept.: Ex 4:7; Le 13:16); of the Jewish kingdom and government, which the Messiah was expected to restore and enlarge (Mt 17:11; Mk 9:12 [cf. Mal 4:6; Lk 1:16, 17]); of restoration of one's friends and country, e.g., from prison (Heb 13:19; Sept.: Jer 16:15; 24:6).

Deriv.: *apokatástasis* (605), restitution of a thing to its former condition.

Syn.: *epistréphō* (1994) and *epanágō* (1877), to return; *epanérchomai* (1880), to come again; *therapeúō* (2323), to cure, restore health.

601. ἀποκαλύπτω, apokaluptō, *ap-ok-al-oop´-to*; from 575 and 2572; to *take off the cover*, i.e. *disclose*:—reveal.

From *apó* (575), from, and *kalúptō* (2572), to cover, conceal. To uncover. In the NT, used metaphorically: to reveal, to disclose, to bring to light:

(**I**) Generally (Mt 10:26; Lk 12:2). In the pass., of things which become known by their effects (Lk 2:35; Jn 12:38; Ro 1:17, 18; 1Pe 5:1).

(**II**) Spoken of things revealed from God, i.e. taught, communicated, made known, by his Spirit and influences (Mt 11:25; 16:17; Lk 10:21; 1Co 2:10; 14:30; Eph 3:5; Php 3:15; 1Pe 1:12). Spoken of things revealed from God through Christ (Mt 11:27; Lk 10:22); through Paul (Gal 1:16).

(**III**) Spoken of persons, in the pass.: to be revealed, to appear; spoken of Christ's appearing from heaven (Lk 17:30); spoken of Antichrist (2Th 2:3, 6, 8).

Deriv.: *apokálupsis* (602), disclosure, revelation.

Syn.: *chrēmatízō* (5537), to give divine instruction; *apostegázō* (648), to unroof, uncover; *anakalúptō* (343), to unveil, discover, open up; *emphanízō* (1718), to manifest; *anaptússō* (380), to unroll, open up.

602. ἀποκάλυψις, apokalupsis, *ap-ok-al´-oop-sis*; from 601; *disclosure*:—appearing, coming, lighten, manifestation, be revealed, revelation.

Noun from *apokalúptō* (601), to reveal. An uncovering, nakedness (Sept.: 1Sa 20:30). In the NT, used metaphorically:

(**I**) Of the removal of the veil of ignorance and darkness by the communication of light and knowledge; illumination, instruction (Lk 2:32).

(II) In the sense of revelation, disclosure, manifestation (Ro 2:5; 8:19). So of that which before was unknown and concealed, especially the divine mysteries, purposes, doctrines, etc. (Ro 16:25; 1Co 14:6, 26); of revelations from God or Christ (2Co 12:1, 7; Gal 1:12; 2:2; Eph 3:3). Spoken of future events in Rev 1:1, where it makes part of the title of the book.

(III) In the sense of appearance, and spoken of Christ's appearance from heaven (2Th 1:7; 1Co 1:7; 1Pe 1:7, 13; 4:13).

Syn.: *gumnótēs* (1132), nakedness; *phanérōsis* (5321), manifestation; *éleusis* (1660), coming (Ac 7:32).

603. ἀποκαραδοκία, apokaradokia, *ap-ok-ar-ad-ok-ee´-ah*; from a compound of 575 and a compound of **κάρα, kara** (the *head*) and 1380 (in the sense of *watching*); *intense anticipation*:—earnest expectation.

Noun from *apokaradokéō* (n.f.), to expect earnestly. Earnest expectation (Ro 8:19; Php 1:20, where it is *karadokía* in some MSS; Sept.: Ps 37:7).

Syn.: *prosdokía* (4329), expectation; *ekdochḗ* (1561), the looking for, expectation.

604. ἀποκαταλλάσσω, apokatallassō, *ap-ok-at-al-las´-so*; from 575 and 2644; to *reconcile fully*:—reconcile.

From *apó* (575), from, indicating the state to be left behind, and *katallássō* (2644), to reconcile. To change from one state of feeling to another, i.e. to reconcile (Eph 2:16; Col 1:20, 21).

Syn.: *diallássō* (1259), to reconcile in cases of mutual hostility; *eirēnopoiéō* (1517), to make peace; *sumbibázō* (4822), to drive together.

605. ἀποκατάστασις, apokatastasis, *ap-ok-at-as´-tas-is*; from 600; *reconstitution*:—restitution.

Noun from *apokathístēmi* (600), to restore. A restoration of a thing to its former state. Only in Ac 3:21, "the times of restitution of all things," i.e. the Messiah's future kingdom.

606. ἀπόκειμαι, apokeimai, *ap-ok´-i-mahee*; from 575 and 2749; to *be reserved*; (figurative) to *await*:—be appointed, (be) laid up.

607. ἀποκεφαλίζω, apokephalizō, *ap-ok-ef-al-id´-zo*; from 575 and 2776; to *decapitate*:—behead.

608. ἀποκλείω, apokleiō, *ap-ok-li´-o*; from 575 and 2808; to *close fully*:—shut up.

609. ἀποκόπτω, apokoptō, *ap-ok-op´-to*; from 575 and 2875; to *amputate*; reflexive (by irony) to *mutilate* (the privy parts):—cut off. Compare 2699.

610. ἀπόκριμα, apokrima, *ap-ok´-ree-mah*; from 611 (in its original sense of *judging*); a judicial *decision*:—sentence.

Noun from *apokrínomai* (611), to answer. An answer, judicial response, sentence. In the NT, sentence of death (1Co 1:9), i.e. constant exposure to death, despair of life.

Syn.: *chrēmatismós* (5538), a divine response through an oracle; *apología:* (627), a verbal defence; *eperōtēma* (1906), a legal questioning or appeal; *katadíkē* (UBS) or *díkē* (TR) (1349), a judicial sentence, condemnation; *katákrisis* (2633), sentencing adversely.

611. ἀποκρίνομαι, apokrinomai, *ap-ok-ree´-nom-ahee*; from 575 and **κρίνω, krino;** to *conclude for oneself*, i.e. (by implication) to *respond*; by Hebrew [compare 6030] to *begin to speak* (where an address is expected):—answer.

From *apó* (575), from, and *krínō* (2919), to separate, discern, judge. To give a judicial answer. Generally, to answer, to respond:

(I) Particularly, to a question (Mt 11:4; 13:11; 19:4; Mk 12:34); to a judicial interrogation or accusation (Mt 26:62; 27:12, 14; Mk 14:61); to an entreaty, exhortation, proposition (Mt 4:4; Lk 22:68); by way of contradiction or denial (Mt 3:15; 12:48; Mk 7:28; Jn 2:18; Ac 25:4).

(II) By way of Hebraism, to proceed to speak, either to continue the discourse (Mt 11:25; 22:1; Mk 9:19; 10:24), or more frequently, to begin to speak, probably with reference to what another had already said (Mt 17:4, 17; Mk 9:5; 10:51; Ac 3:12). So of an interrogation (Mt 27:21; Rev 7:13).

Deriv.: *antapokrínomai* (470), to answer in contradiction, to answer back; *apókrima* (610), answer or judicial sentence; *apókrisis* (612), the act of answering.

Syn.: *hupolambánō* (5274), to catch up in speech, to answer; *apologéomai* (626), to speak back, to answer in making a defence for oneself; *antilégō* (483), to speak or answer against; *proslaléō* (4354), to speak to; *phthéggomai* (5350), to utter a sound or voice; *apophthég-*

gomai (669), to speak forth; *chrēmatízō* (5537), to utter an oracle.

612. ἀπόκρισις, apokrisis, *ap-ok´-ree-sis*; from 611; a *response*:—answer.

Noun from *apokrínomai* (611), answer. An answer, a reply (Lk 2:47; 20:26; Jn 1:22; 19:9; Sept.: Dt 1:22; Job 32:5; Ps 15:1). For syn. and ant. see *apókrima* (610), answer, sentence. The distinction between *apókrisis* and *apókrima* is that the first is the act of answering and the second is the answer itself.

613. ἀποκρύπτω, apokruptō, *ap-ok-roop´-to*; from 575 and 2928; to *conceal away* (i.e. *fully*); (figurative) to *keep secret*:—hide.

614. ἀπόκρυφος, apokruphos, *ap-ok´-roo-fos*; from 613; *secret*; (by implication) *treasured*:—hid, kept secret.

615. ἀποκτείνω, apokteinō, *ap-ok-ti´-no*; from 575 and κτείνω, *kteinō* (to *slay*); to *kill* outright; (figurative) to *destroy*:—put to death, kill, slay.

616. ἀποκυέω, apokueō, *ap-ok-oo-eh´o*; from 575 and the base of 2949; to *breed forth*, i.e. (by transfer) to *generate* (figurative):—beget, produce.

From *apó* (575), from, and *kuéō* (n.f.), to swell, be pregnant. To beget, bear. In the NT, used metaphorically (Jas 1:15, 18 [cf. 1Co 4:15; 1Pe 1:3, 23]).

Deriv.: of *kúō*, to swell (n.f.): *égkuos* (1471), pregnant; *kúma* (2949), a wave.

Syn.: *tíktō* (5088), to bring forth; *gennáō* (1080), to beget, give birth.

617. ἀποκυλίω, apokuliō, *ap-ok-oo-lee´-o*; from 575 and 2947; to *roll away*:—roll away (back).

618. ἀπολαμβάνω, apolambanō, *ap-ol-am-ban´-o*; from 575 and 2983; to *receive* (specially in *full*, or as a host); also to *take aside*:—receive, take.

619. ἀπόλαυσις, apolausis, *ap-ol´-ow-sis*; from a compound of 575 and λαύω, *lauō* (to *enjoy*); full *enjoyment*:—enjoy (-ment).

620. ἀπολείπω, apoleipō, *ap-ol-ipe´-o*; from 575 and 3007; to *leave* behind (passive *remain*); (by implication) to *forsake*:—leave, remain.

621. ἀπολείχω, apoleichō, *ap-ol-i´-kho*; from 575 and λείχω, *leichō* (to "*lick*"); to *lick* clean:—lick.

622. ἀπόλλυμι, apollumi, *ap-ol´-loo-mee*; from 575 and the base of 3639; to *destroy* fully (reflexive to *perish*, or *lose*), literal or figurative:—destroy, die, lose, mar, perish.

From *apó* (575) an intensive, the middle *óllumi* (n.f.), to destroy. The force of *apó* here is away or wholly; therefore, the verb is stronger than the simple *óllumi*. To destroy, middle be destroyed, perish. Also from *óllumi* (n.f.): *ólethros* (3639), rain, destruction.

(I) To destroy, cause to perish, transitively:

(A) Spoken of things figuratively (1Co 1:19, meaning to bring to naught, render void the wisdom of the wise, quoted from Isa 29:14).

(B) Of persons, to destroy, put to death, cause to perish: **(1)** Spoken of physical death (Mt 2:13; 12:14; 21:41; 22:7; Mk 3:6; 9:22; 11:18; 12:9; Lk 6:9 [TR]; 17:27, 29; 19:47; 20:16; Jn 10:10; Jude 5; Sept.: Ge 20:4; Dt 11:4; Est 4:9; 9:16). In a judicial sense, to sentence to death (Mt 27:20; Jas 4:12). **(2)** Spoken of eternal death, i.e. future punishment, exclusion from the Messiah's kingdom. In this sense it has the same meaning as *apothnḗskō* (599), to die (Mt 10:28; Mk 1:24; Lk 4:34; 9:56). This eternal death is called the second death (Rev 20:14). In Lk 9:25, to "destroy himself" (a.t.) means to subject himself to eternal death.

(II) To lose, be deprived of, transitively of such things as reward (Mk 9:41); a sheep (Lk 15:4); a drachma or coin (Lk 15:8, 9). See Jn 6:39; 2Jn 8; Sept.: Pr 29:3. To lose one's life or soul (Mt 10:39; 16:25; Mk 8:35; Lk 9:24; 17:33; Jn 12:25).

(III) In the middle and pass. forms, to be destroyed, perish; spoken of:

(A) Things (Mt 5:29, 30; 9:17; Mk 2:22; Lk 5:37; Jn 6:27; Heb 1:11; Jas 1:11; 1Pe 1:7).

(B) Persons, to be put to death, to die, perish, relating to physical death (Mt 8:25; 26:52; Mk 4:38; Lk 8:24; 11:51; 13:33; 15:17; Jn 18:14; Ac 5:37; 1Co 10:9, 10; 2Co 4:9; 2Pe 3:6; Jude 11; Sept.: Le 23:30; Est 9:12). Spoken of eternal death (see I, B, 2), to perish eternally, i.e. to be deprived of eternal life (Lk 13:3, 5; Jn 3:15, 16; 10:28; 17:12; Ro 2:12; 1Co 15:18; 2Pe 3:9).

(C) To be lost to the owner (Lk 21:18; Jn 6:12). Spoken of those who wander away and are lost, e.g., the prodigal son (Lk 15:24); sheep straying in the desert (Lk 15:4, 6). Metaphorically (Mt 10:6; 15:24; Sept.: Ps 119:176; Jer 50:6; Eze 34:4).

Deriv.: *Apollúōn* (623), destroyer; *apóleia* (684), destruction; *sun-apóllumi* (4881), to destroy with.

Syn.: *katargéō* (2673), abolish; *kathairéō* (2507), to cast down; *lúō* (3089), to loose; *katalúō* (2647), to destroy utterly; *olothreúō* (2645), to destroy; *exolothreúō* (1842), to destroy utterly; *phtheírō* (5351), to corrupt; *porthéō* (4199), to ruin by laying waste, to make havoc; *thnḗskō* (2348), to die; *apothnḗskō* (599), to die off or out; *teleutáō* (5053), to end, to die; *apogínomai* (581), to die, to become something else.

623. Ἀπολλύων, Apolluōn, *ap-ol-loo´-ohn;* active participle of 622; a *destroyer* (i.e. *Satan*):—Apollyon.

Masculine part. from *apóllumi* (622), to destroy, corrupt. The destroyer (Rev 9:11). A Greek name for the demon of the abyss (*ábussos* [12]). The Hebrew name is transliterated *Abaddón* (3).

Syn.: *olothreutḗs* (3644), a destroyer.

624. Ἀπολλωνία, Apollōnia, *ap-ol-lo-nee´-ah;* from the pagan deity Ἀπόλλων, *Apollōn* (i.e. the *sun*; from 622); *Apollonia,* a place in Macedonia:—Apollonia.

625. Ἀπολλώς, Apollōs, *ap-ol-loce´;* probably from the same as 624; *Apollos,* an Israelite:—Apollos.

626. ἀπολογέομαι, apologeomai, *ap-ol-og-eh´-om-ahee;* middle from a compound of 575 and 3056; to give an *account* (legal *plea*) of oneself, i.e. *exculpate* (self):—answer (for self), make defence, excuse (self), speak for self.

627. ἀπολογία, apologia, *ap-ol-og-ee´-ah;* from the same as 626; a *plea* ("apology"):—answer (for self), clearing of self, defence.

628. ἀπολούω, apolouō, *ap-ol-oo´-o;* from 575 and 3068; to *wash* fully, i.e. (figurative) *have remitted* (reflexive):—wash (away).

From *apó* (575), from, and *loúō* (3068), to wash, bathe. In the NT, used in the middle voice: to wash oneself clean from, i.e. to wash away; metaphorically, to be freed from the consequences of sin (Ac 22:16; 1Co 6:11; Sept.: Job 9:30; cf. Ps 51:4; Isa 1:16; Jer 4:14).

Syn.: *níptō* (3538), to wash part of the body; *aponíptō* (633), to wash off; *plúnō* (4150), to wash inanimate objects; *apoplúnō* (637) used of garments and figuratively; *rhantízō* (4472), to sprinkle; *bréchō* (1026), to wet; *baptízō* (907), to baptize.

629. ἀπολύτρωσις, apolutrōsis, *ap-ol-oo´-tro-sis;* from a compound of 575 and 3083; (the act) *ransom* in full, i.e. (figurative) *riddance,* or (specifically) Christian *salvation:*—deliverance, redemption.

Noun from *apolutróō* (n.f.), to let go free for a ransom. Redemption:

(I) Deliverance on account of the ransom paid; spoken of the deliverance from the power and consequences of sin which Christ procured by laying down His life as a ransom (*lútron* [3083]) for those who believe (Ro 3:24; 1Co 1:30; Eph 1:7, 14; Col 1:14; Heb 9:15 [cf. Mt 20:28; Ac 20:28]).

(II) Deliverance without the idea of ransom, i.e. from calamities and death (Lk 21:28; Heb 11:35). So also of the soul from the body as its prison (Ro 8:23 at the coming of the Lord; Eph 4:30 [cf. Ro 7:24]).

Syn.: *áphesis* (859), remission, forgiveness; *hilasmós* (2434), propitiation; *katallagḗ* (2643), reconciliation, atonement.

630. ἀπολύω, apoluō, *ap-ol-oo´-o;* from 575 and 3089; to *free* fully, i.e. (literal) *relieve, release, dismiss* (reflexive *depart*), or (figurative) *let die, pardon,* or (specifically) *divorce:*—(let) depart, dismiss, divorce, forgive, let go, loose, put (send) away, release, set at liberty.

From *apó* (575), from, and *lúō* (3089), to loose. To let loose from, to loose or unbind a person or thing:

(I) To free or relieve from sickness (Lk 13:12).

(II) To release, let go free, set at liberty, such as a debtor (Mt 18:27) or persons accused or imprisoned (Mt 27:15; Mk 15:6; Lk 22:68; Jn 19:10; Ac 4:21; 26:32; 28:18). Metaphorically: to overlook, forgive (Lk 6:37).

(III) Spoken of a wife, to let go free, put away, divorce (Mt 1:19; 5:31, 32; 19:3). So also of a husband (Mk 10:12).

(IV) To dismiss, i.e. simply to let go, send away, transitively (Mt 14:15, 22, 23; 15:32, 39;

Lk 8:38; 9:12; 14:4; Ac 13:3; 15:30; 19:41; 23:22). Middle *apolúomai*, to depart, go away (Ac 15:33; 28:25; Sept.: Ex 33:11).

(V) To dismiss from life, let depart, die (Lk 2:29; Sept.: Nu 20:29).

Syn.: *chōrízō* (5563), to put apart, separate; *apochōrízō* (673), to separate off; *diachōrízomai* (1316), to be separated through or completely; *analúō* (360), to depart, unloose; *aphístēmi* (868), to cause to depart; *aphíēmi* (863), to send away; *ápeimi* (548), to go away; *aníēmi* (447), to let up, forbear.

631. ἀπομάσσομαι, apomassomai, *ap-om-as'-som-ahee*; middle from 575 and **μάσσω, massō** (to *squeeze, knead, smear*); to *scrape away*:—wipe off.

632. ἀπονέμω, aponemō, *ap-on-em'-o*; from 575 and the base of 3551; to *apportion*, i.e. *bestow*:—give.

633. ἀπονίπτω, aponiptō, *ap-on-ip'-to*; from 575 and 3538; to *wash off* (reflexive one's own hands symbolically):—wash.

634. ἀποπίπτω, apopiptō, *ap-op-ip'-to*; from 575 and 4098; to *fall off*:—fall.

635. ἀποπλανάω, apoplanaō, *ap-op-lan-ah'-o*; from 575 and 4105; to *lead astray* (figurative) passive to *stray* (from truth):—err, seduce.

636. ἀποπλέω, apopleō, *ap-op-leh'-o*; from 575 and 4126; to *set sail*:—sail away.

637. ἀποπλύνω, apoplunō, *ap-op-loo'-no*; from 575 and 4150; to *rinse off*:—wash.

638. ἀποπνίγω, apopnigō, *ap-op-nee'-go*; from 575 and 4155; to *stifle* (by drowning or overgrowth):—choke.

639. ἀπορέω, aporeō, *ap-or-eh'-o*; from a compound of 1 (as a negative particle) and the base of 4198; to *have no way* out, i.e. *be at a loss* (mentally):—(stand in) doubt, be perplexed.

640. ἀπορία, aporia, *ap-or-ee'-a*; from the same as 639; a (state of) *quandary*:—perplexity.

641. ἀπορρίπτω, aporrhiptō, *ap-or-hrip'-to*; from 575 and 4496; to *hurl off*, i.e. *precipitate* (oneself):—cast.

642. ἀπορφανίζω, aporphanizō, *ap-or-fan-id'-zo*; from 575 and a derivative of 3737; to

bereave wholly, i.e. (figurative) *separate* (from intercourse):—take.

643. ἀποσκευάζω, aposkeuazō, *ap-osk-yoo-ad'-zo*; from 575 and a derivative of 4632; to *pack up* (one's) *baggage*:—take up … carriages.

644. ἀποσκίασμα, aposkiasma, *ap-os-kee'-as-mah*; from a compound of 575 and a derivative of 4639; a *shading off*, i.e. *obscuration*:—shadow.

645. ἀποσπάω, apospaō, *ap-os-pah'-o*; from 575 and 4685; to *drag forth*, i.e. (lit.) *unsheathe* (a sword), or relative (with a degree of force implied) *retire* (person or factiously):—(with-) draw (away), after we were gotten from.

646. ἀποστασία, apostasia, *ap-os-tas-ee'-ah*; feminine of the same as 647; *defection* from truth (properly the state) ["apostasy"]:—falling away, forsake.

Noun from *aphístēmi* (868), to depart. Defection, apostasy. Occurs in Ac 21:21 translated "forsake" and in 2Th 2:3, "a falling away"; Sept.: 2Ch 29:19; Jer 29:32.

647. ἀποστάσιον, apostasion, *ap-os-tas'-ee-on*; neuter of a (presumed) adjective from a derivative of 868; properly something *separative*, i.e. (special) *divorce*:—(writing of) divorcement.

648. ἀποστεγάζω, apostegazō, *ap-os-teg-ad'-zo*; from 575 and a derivative of 4721; to *unroof*:—uncover.

649. ἀποστέλλω, apostellō, *ap-os-tel'-lo*; from 575 and 4724; *set apart*, i.e. (by implication) to *send out* (properly on a mission) literal or figurative:—put in, send (away, forth, out), set [at liberty].

From *apó* (575), from, and *stéllō* (4724), to withdraw from, avoid. To send off, forth, out:

(I) Spoken of persons sent as agents, messengers, etc. (Mt 10:5, 16; 21:1; Mk 6:7; Lk 14:32); of prophets, messengers, teachers, angels, sent from God (Mt 10:40; 15:24; Lk 1:26; Jn 1:6; 3:17; Ac 3:26; Heb 1:14; Rev 1:1). Also in the sense of to expel, to drive away (Mk 5:10; 12:3, 4).

(II) Figuratively, spoken of things: to send forth, i.e. to proclaim, to bestow (Lk 24:49; Ac 10:36; 13:26; 28:28); so of physical things (Mk 4:29; Ac 11:30).

(III) In the sense of to dismiss, to let go (Mk 8:26; Lk 4:18).

Deriv.: *apostolḗ* (651), dispatching or sending forth; *apóstolos* (652), one sent, apostle, ambassador; *exapostéllō* (1821), to send away, forth; *sunapostéllō* (4882), to send along with.

Syn.: *ekbállō* (1544), to send out; *apotássomai* (657), to send forth; *ekpémpō* (1599), to send forth; *pémpō* (3992), to send.

650. ἀποστερέω, apostereō, *ap-os-ter-eh´-o*; from 575 and **στερέω, stereō** (to *deprive*); to *despoil*:—defraud, destitute, kept back by fraud.

651. ἀποστολή, apostolē, *ap-os-tol-ay´*; from 649; *commission*, i.e. (special) *apostolate*:—apostleship.

Noun from *apostéllō* (649), to send. Dispatching or sending forth, also that which is sent, e.g., a present. In the NT, apostleship (Ac 1:25; Ro 1:5; 1Co 9:2; Gal 2:8).

Syn.: *presbeía* (4242), persons sent as ambassadors.

652. ἀπόστολος, apostolos, *ap-os´-tol-os*; from 649; a *delegate*; specially an *ambassador* of the gospel; officially a *commissioner* of Christ ["*apostle*"] (with miraculous powers):—apostle, messenger, he that is sent.

Noun from *apostéllō* (649), to send. Used as a substantive, one sent, apostle, ambassador:

(I) Generally, a messenger (Jn 13:16; Php 2:25).

(II) Spoken of messengers or ambassadors sent from God (Lk 11:49; Eph 3:15; Rev 2:2; 28:20).

(III) Of the twelve apostles of Christ (Mt 10:2; Lk 6:13; Ac 1:26; Jude 17; Rev 21:14), so of Paul, reckoned as the "apostle of the gentiles" (1Ti 2:17; 2Ti 1:11). Also, in a wider sense, spoken of the helpers and companions of the twelve, as aiding to gather churches (2Co 8:23; so of Paul and Barnabas (Ac 14:4, 14); and of Andronicus and Junias (Ro 16:7).

Deriv.: *pseudapóstolos* (5570), a false apostle. **Syn.**: *ággelos* (32), a messenger, an angel.

653. ἀποστοματίζω, apostomatizō, *ap-os-tom-at-id´-zo*; from 575 and a (presumed) derivative of 4750; to *speak off-hand* (properly *dictate*), i.e. to *catechize* (in an invidious manner):—provoke to speak.

654. ἀποστρέφω, apostrephō, *ap-os-tref´-o*; from 575 and 4762; to *turn away* or *back* (literal or figurative):—bring again, pervert, turn away (from).

From *apó* (575), from or back again, and *stréphō* (4762), to turn. To turn away from, to turn aside, to avert:

(I) Particularly, turning aside ears from the truth (2Ti 4:4); turning away from iniquities (Ac 3:26); "preverteth the people," i.e. turning aside the people, inciting rebellion (Lk 23:14). In the sense of to put away from, to remove (Ro 11:26).

(II) In the middle, to turn oneself away from, i.e. either to forsake, to desert (2Ti 1:15), or to refuse, reject (Mt 5:42; Tit 1:14; Heb 12:25).

(III) To turn back, i.e. to return, to restore (Mt 27:3; Sept.: Ge 24:5, 6). Spoken of a sword: to put back, to replace (Mt 26:52).

Syn.: *apotíthēmi* (659), to put away; *apōthéō* (683), to thrust away; *apobaínō* (576), to turn out, to go; *metatíthēmi* (3346), to change, remove; *ektrépō* (1624), to cause to turn aside; *apotrépō* (665), to cause to turn away; *ekklínō* (1578), to turn aside; *anachōréō* (402), to withdraw; *apéchomai* (567), to hold oneself off, refrain; *bdelússomai* (948), to detest, abhor.

655. ἀποστυγέω, apostugeō, *ap-os-toog-eh´-o*; from 575 and the base of 4767; to *detest* utterly:—abhor.

From *apó* (575), from, or an intensive, and *stugéō* (n.f., see below), to hate. To hate, abhor, detest (Ro 12:9).

Deriv. of *stugéō* (n.f.): *theostugḗs* (2319), haters of God; *stugētós* (4767) hateful, detestable.

Syn.: *apostréphomai* (654), to turn away from; *apotrépō* (665), to deflect; *apophérō* (667), to bear off; *apéchomai* (567), to hold oneself off, refrain; *bdelússomai* (948), to abhor, detest; *phríssō* (5425), to shudder; *apōthéomai* (683), to push off.

656. ἀποσυνάγωγος, aposunagōgos, *ap-os-oon-ag´-o-gos*; from 575 and 4864; *excommunicated*:—(put) out of the synagogue (-s).

Adjective from *apó* (575), from, and *sunagōgḗ* (4864), synagogue. Excluded from the synagogue, excommunicated (John 9:22; 12:42; 16:2). There were three degrees of excommunication or banishment among the Jews. The first continued for one month, and prohibited a person from bathing, from shaving his head, or from approaching any person nearer than four cubits; but if he submitted to this, he was not debarred the privilege of attending the sacred rites. The second involved an exclusion from the sacred assemblies, was accompanied with heavy maledictions, and prohibited all communication with the person subjected to it. The last was a perpetual exclusion from all the rights and privileges of the Jewish people, both civil and religious.

Syn.: *apóbletos* (579), a rejected or cast off one.

657. ἀποτάσσομαι, apotassomai, *ap-ot-as´-som-ahee*; middle from 575 and 5021; literal to *say adieu* (by departing or dismissing); (figurative) to *renounce*:—bid farewell, forsake, take leave, send away.

From *apó* (575), from, and *tássō* (5021), to place in order. To assign to different places, to separate. In the NT, only in the middle meaning to take leave of, bid farewell; to dismiss, forsake, or renounce (Lk 9:61; Ac 18:18, 21; 2Co 2:13). In the sense of to dismiss, send away (Mk 6:46, cf. Mt 14:23). Used figuratively: to renounce, to forsake (Lk 14:33).

Syn.: *kataleípō* (2641), to leave behind; *egkataleípō* (1459), to abandon, leave; *aphíēmi* (863), to leave, forsake; *aniēmi* (447), to let go, to go up; *apoleípō* (620), to leave behind; *apaspázomai* in Ac 21:6 (UBS) and *aspázomai* (782 [TR]) to enfold in the arms, embrace, take leave.

658. ἀποτελέω, apoteleō, *ap-ot-el-eh´-o*; from 575 and 5055; to *complete entirely*, i.e. *consummate*:—finish.

659. ἀποτίθημι, apotithēmi, *ap-ot-eeth´-ay-mee*; from 575 and 5087; to *put away* (literal or figurative):—cast off, lay apart (aside, down), put away (off).

660. ἀποτινάσσω, apotinassō, *ap-ot-in-as´-so*; from 575 and τινάσσω, *tinassō* (to *jostle*); to *brush off*:—shake off.

661. ἀποτίνω, apotinō, *ap-ot-ee´-no*; from 575 and 5099; to *pay in full*:—repay.

662. ἀποτολμάω, apotolmaō, *ap-ot-ol-mah´-o*; from 575 and 5111; to *venture plainly*:—be very bold.

663. ἀποτομία, apotomia, *ap-ot-om-ee´-ah*; from the base of 664; (figurative) *decisiveness*, i.e. *rigour*:—severity.

664. ἀποτόμως, apotomōs, *ap-ot-om´-oce*; adverb from a derivative of a compound of 575 and τέμνω, *temnō* (to *cut*); *abruptly*, i.e. *peremptorily*:—sharply (-ness).

665. ἀποτρέπω, apotrepō, *ap-ot-rep´-o*; from 575 and the base of 5157; to *deflect*, i.e. (reflexive) *avoid*:—turn away.

666. ἀπουσία, apousia, *ap-oo-see´-ah*; from the participle of 548; a *being away*:—absence.

667. ἀποφέρω, apopherō, *ap-of-er´-o*; from 575 and 5342; to *bear off* (literal or relative):—bring, carry (away).

668. ἀποφεύγω, apopheugō, *ap-of-yoo´-go*; from 575 and 5343; (figurative) to *escape*:—escape.

669. ἀποφθέγγομαι, apophtheggomai, *ap-of-theng´-om-ahee*; from 575 and 5350; to *enunciate* plainly, i.e. *declare*:—say, speak forth, utterance.

670. ἀποφορτίζομαι, apophortizomai, *ap-of-or-tid´-zom-ahee*; from 575 and the middle of 5412; to *unload*:—unlade.

671. ἀπόχρησις, apochrēsis, *ap-okh´-ray-sis*; from a compound of 575 and 5530; the act of *using up*, i.e. *consumption*:—using.

672. ἀποχωρέω, apochōreō, *ap-okh-o-reh´-o*; from 575 and 5562; to *go away*:—depart.

673. ἀποχωρίζω, apochōrizō, *ap-okh-o-rid´-zo*; from 575 and 5563; to *rend apart*; reflexive to *separate*:—depart (asunder).

674. ἀποψύχω, apopsuchō, *ap-ops-oo´-kho*; from 575 and 5594; to *breathe out*, i.e. *faint*:—hearts failing.

From *apó* (575) denoting privation, and *psúchō* (5594), to breathe, wax cold. In the NT, to be faint of heart due to fear or terror. Only in Lk 21:26 (cf. Mt 28:4).

Syn.: *kámnō* (2577), to faint or be weary as a result of continuous labour.

675. Ἄππιος, Appios, *ap´-pee-os*; of Latin origin; (in the genitive, i.e. possessive case) *of Appius*, the name of a Roman:—Appii.

676. ἀπρόσιτος, aprositos, *ap-ros´-ee-tos*; from 1 (as a negative particle) and a derivative of a compound of 4314 and **εἶμι,** *eimi* (to *go*); *inaccessible*:—which no man can approach.

677. ἀπρόσκοπος, aproskopos, *ap-ros´-kop-os*; from 1 (as a negative particle) and a presumed derivative of 4350; act. *inoffensive*, i.e. *not leading into sin*; passive *faultless*, i.e. *not led into sin*:—none (void of, without) offence.

Adjective from the priv. *a* (1), not, and *proskóptō* (4350), to strike at, to trip. Not stumbling, i.e. not causing to stumble. In the NT, used metaphorically: giving no offence, not causing to sin (1Co 10:32). Also, not stumbling, i.e. not falling into sin, pure (Ac 24:16).

Syn.: *áptaistos* (679), not stumbling; *eleútheros* (1658), free, at liberty.

678. ἀπροσωπολήπτως, aprosōpolēptōs, *ap-ros-o-pol-ape´-toce*; adverb from a compound of 1 (as a negative particle) and a presumed derivative of a presumed compound of 4383 and 2983 [compare 4381]; in a way *not accepting* the *person*, i.e. *impartially*:—without respect of persons.

679. ἄπταιστος, aptaistos, *ap-tah´ee-stos*; from 1 (as a negative particle) and a derivative of 4417; *not stumbling*, i.e. (figurative) *without sin*:—from falling.

680. ἅπτομαι, haptomai, *hap´-tom-ahee*; reflexive of 681; properly to *attach* oneself to, i.e. to *touch* (in many implied relations):—touch.

From *háptō* (681), to connect, bind. To apply oneself to, to touch; generally (Mt 8:3, 15; 9:20; Mk 1:41; Lk 7:14); in the Levitical sense (2Co 6:17; Col 2:21); figuratively, to have sexual intercourse (1Co 7:1); by implication, to harm, to injure (1Jn 5:18).

Syn.: *prospsaúō* (4379), to touch upon, touch slightly (Lk 11:46); *eggízō* (1448), to come near; *piázō* (4084), to lay hand on; *kolláō* (2853), to glue; *proseggízō* (4331), to approach.

681. ἅπτω, haptō, *hap´-to*; a primary verb; properly to *fasten* to, i.e. (special) to *set on fire*:—kindle, light.

To put one thing to another, to adjoin, to apply. In the NT, spoken of fire as applied to things: to set fire to, kindle, light (Lk 8:16; 11:33; 15:8; 22:55).

Deriv.: *anáptō* (381), to light up, kindle; *háp-*

tomai (680), to touch; *aphḗ* (860), a joint; *katháptō* (2510), to bind, fasten.

Syn.: with the meaning of to light: *phōtízō* (5461), to shine, give light; *epiphaúō* (2017), to shine forth; *lámpō* (2989), to give forth the light of a torch; *epiphaínō* (2014), to show forth; *kaíō* (2545), to burn, a light. With the meaning to touch: *thiggánō* (2345), to touch.

682. Ἀπφία, Apphia, *ap-fee´-a*; probably of foreign origin; *Apphia*, a woman of Colossæ:—Apphia.

683. ἀπωθέομαι, apōtheomai, *ap-o-theh´-om-ahee*; or **ἀπω-ομαι,** *apōthomai, ap-o´-thom-ahee*; from 575 and the middle of **ὠθέω,** *ōtheō*; or **ὤθω,** *ōthō* (to *shove*); to *push off*, (figurative) to *reject*:—cast away, put away (from), thrust away (from).

684. ἀπώλεια, apōleia, *ap-o´-li-a*; from a presumed derivative of 622; *ruin* or *loss* (physical, spiritual or eternal):—damnable (-nation), destruction, die, perdition, × perish, pernicious ways, waste.

Noun from *apóllumi* (622), to destroy fully. Loss, destruction. Spoken of things: waste (Mt 26:8; Mk 14:4). Spoken of persons: destruction, death (Ac 25:16); the second death, perdition, i.e. exclusion from the Messiah's kingdom (Mt 7:13; Ac 8:20; Ro 9:22; Php 1:28; 1Ti 6:9; Heb 10:39; 2Pe 2:1, 3; 3:7, 16; Rev 17:8, 11).

Syn.: *phthorá* (5356), destruction that comes with corruption, consumption by using up; *súntrimma* (4938), a breaking in pieces; *thánatos* (2288), death; *anaíresis* (336), a taking up or off, usually used in regard to life; *teleutḗ* (5054), an end of life, death; *zēmía* (2209), loss; *apobolḗ* (580), a casting away; *hḗttēma* (2275), defeat, loss, defect; *kathaíresis* (2506), a taking or pulling down, hence destruction; *ólethros* (3639), an eschatological destruction surprising people like labour pains coming upon a pregnant woman.

685. ἀρά, ara, *ar-ah´*; probably from 142; properly *prayer* (as *lifted* to Heaven), i.e. (by implication) *imprecation*:—curse.

In the NT, implication, curse. Only in Ro 3:14.

Deriv.: *katára* (2671), a curse.

Syn.: *anáthema* (331), a curse, disfavour of God; *katanáthema* (2652), an accursed thing.

686. ἄρα, ara, *ar´-ah*; probably from 142 (through the idea of *drawing* a conclusion); a particle denoting an *inference* more or less decisive (as follows):—haply, (what) manner (of man), no doubt, perhaps, so be, then, therefore, truly, wherefore. Often used in connection with other particles, especially 1065 or 3767 (after) or 1487 (before). Compare also 687.

687. ἆρα, ara, *ar´-ah*; a form of 686, denoting an *interrogation* to which a negative answer is presumed:—therefore.

688. Ἀραβία, Arabia, *ar-ab-ee´-ah*; of Hebrew origin [6152]; *Arabia*, a region of Asia:—Arabia.

689. Ἀράμ, Aram, *ar-am´*; of Hebrew origin [7410]; *Aram* (i.e. *Ram*), an Israelite:—Aram.

690. Ἄραψ, Araps, *ar´-aps*; from 688; an *Arab* or native of Arabia:—Arabian.

691. ἀργέω, argeō, *arg-eh´-o*; from 692; to be *idle*, i.e. (figurative) to *delay*:—linger.

From *argós* (692), idle. In the NT, to be inactive, idle; metaphorically, to be still, to linger. Only in 2Pe 2:3.

Deriv.: *katargéō* (2673), entirely idle, abolish, cease.

Syn.: *scholázō* (4980), to be at leisure.

692. ἀργός, argos, *ar-gos´*; from 1 (as a negative particle) and 2041; *inactive*, i.e. *unemployed*; (by implication) *lazy, useless*:—barren, idle, slow.

Adjective from the priv. *a* (1), without, and *érgon* (2041), work. Not at work, idle, not employed, inactive (Mt 20:3, 6); with the idea of choice (1Ti 5:13). By implication: indolent, slothful, slow (2Pe 1:8); *gastéres argaí*, lit. "slow bellies" (see *gastér* [1064], stomach), i.e. lazy gluttons (Tit 1:12). Also by implication: idle, insincere, false, unprofitable (Mt 12:36, cf. 2Pe 1:8).

Deriv.: *argéō* (691), to be idle.

Syn.: *bradús* (1021), slow; *oknērós* (3636), indolent, slothful.

693. ἀργύρεος, argureos, *ar-goo´-reh-os*; from 696; made *of silver*:—(of) silver.

694. ἀργύριον, argurion, *ar-goo´-ree-on*; neuter of a presumed derivative of 696; *silvery*, i.e. (by implication) *cash*; specially a *silverling* (i.e. *drachma* or *shekel*):—money, (piece of) silver (piece).

695. ἀργυροκόπος, argurokopos, *ar-goo-rok-op´-os*; from 696 and 2875; a *beater* (i.e. *worker*) *of silver*:—silversmith.

696. ἄργυρος, arguros, *ar´-goo-ros*; from ἀργός, *argos* (*shining*); *silver* (the metal, in the articles or coin):—silver.

697. Ἄρειος Πάγος, Areios Pagos, *ar´-i-os pag´-os*; from Ἄρης, *Arēs* (the name of the Greek deity of war) and a derivative of 4078; *rock of Ares*, a place in Athens:—Areopagus, Mars' Hill.

698. Ἀρεοπαγίτης, Areopagitēs, *ar-eh-op-ag-ee´-tace*; from 697; an *Areopagite* or member of the court held on Mars' Hill:—Areopagite.

699. ἀρέσκεια, areskeia, *ar-es´-ki-ah*; from a derivative of 700; *complaisance*:—pleasing.

Noun from *aréskō* (700), to please. Desire of pleasing. Only in Col 1:10.

Syn.: *hēdoné* (2237), pleasure; *eudokía* (2107), good pleasure; *thélēma* (2307), will, pleasure, favour; *euphrosúnē* (2167), joyfulness, gladness; *chará* (5479), joy; *apólausis* (619), enjoyment; *agallíasis* (20), exuberance.

700. ἀρέσκω, areskō, *ar-es´-ko*; probably from 142 (through the idea of *exciting* emotion); to *be agreeable* (or, by implication, to seek to be so):—please.

From *áro* (n.f., see *podḗrēs* [4158]), to fit, adapt. To please. In the sense of to be pleasing, acceptable to (Mt 14:6; Mk 6:22; Ro 8:8; 1Co 7:33, 34; Gal 1:10; 1Th 2:15; 2Ti 2:4). In the sense of to seek to please or gratify, to accommodate oneself to (Ro 15:1–3; 1Co 10:33; Gal 1:10; 1Th 2:4).

Deriv.: *anthrōpáreskos* (441), one who endeavours to please men; *aréskeia* (699), the endeavour to please; *arestós* (701), dear, pleasant, well-pleasing; *euárestos* (2101), pleasing, agreeable.

Syn.: *eudokéō* (2106), to think well of; *thélō* (2309), to wish, desire; *dokimázō* (1381), to approve; *eucharistéō* (2168), to express gratitude, give thanks; *apolambánō* (618), to receive; *entrupháō* (1792), to revel in; *euphraínō* (2165), to rejoice, make glad.

701. ἀρεστός, arestos, *ar-es-tos´*; from 700; *agreeable*; (by implication) *fit*:—(things that) please (-ing), reason.

Adjective from *aréskō* (700), to please or to be content with. Pleasing, acceptable, grateful (Jn 8:29; Ac 12:3; 1Jn 3:22).

Syn.: *eúthetos* (2111), fit, proper; *kalós* (2570), good; *sumpathḗs* (4835), sympathetic; *euprósdektos* (2144), well-received, approved, favourable; *glukús* (1099), sweet; *dektós* (1184), approved, referring to relationship. *Arestós* presupposes man's relationship with God, but it also tells about God's judgement to man's conduct.

702. Ἀρέτας, Aretas, *ar-et´-as*; of foreign origin; *Aretas*, an Arabian:—Aretas.

703. ἀρέτη, aretē, *ar-et´-ay*; from the same as 730; properly *manliness* (*valor*), i.e. *excellence* (intrinsic or attributed):—praise, virtue.

A noun meaning virtue, i.e. good quality, excellence of any kind. In the NT, spoken of the divine power (2Pe 1:3); of goodness of action, virtuous deeds (Php 4:8; 2Pe 1:5). Spoken of God: wondrous deeds, as displays of divine power and goodness (1Pe 2:9; Sept.: Isa 42:12; 63:7; Hab 3:3).

Syn.: *huperbolḗ* (5236), a throwing beyond, surpassing, an excellence; *huperochḗ* (5247), the act of overhanging, hence superiority, preeminence, excellency; *aínos* (136), praise; *épainos* (1868), approbation, commendation; *dóxa* (1391), glory; *dúnamis* (1411), power; *chárisma* (5486), gift; *ōphéleia* (5622), usefulness, benefit.

704. ἀρήν, arēn, *ar-ane´*; perhaps the same as 730; a *lamb* (as a *male*):—lamb.

705. ἀριθμέω, arithmeō, *ar-ith-meh´-o*; from 706; to *enumerate* or *count*:—number.

706. ἀριθμός, arithmos, *ar-ith-mos´*; from 142; a *number* (as reckoned *up*):—number.

707. Ἀριμαθαία, Arimathaia, *ar-ee-math-ah´ee-ah*; of Hebrew origin [7414]; *Arimathæa* (or *Ramah*), a place in Palestine:—Arimathæa.

708. Ἀρίσταρχος, Aristarchos, *ar-is´-tar-khos*; from the same as 712 and 757; *best ruling*; *Aristar-chus*, a Macedonian:—Aristarchus.

709. ἀρισταω, aristaō, *ar-is-tah´-o*; from 712; to *take the principal meal*:—dine.

710. ἀριστερός, aristeros, *ar-is-ter-os´*; apparently a compound of the same as 712; the *left* hand (as *second-best*):—left [hand].

711. Ἀριστόβουλος, Aristoboulos, *ar-is-tob´-oo-los*; from the same as 712 and 1012; *best counseling*; *Aristoboulus*, a Christian:—Aristobulus.

712. ἀριστον, ariston, *ar´-is-ton*; apparently neuter of a superlative from the same as 730; the *best* meal [or *breakfast*; perhaps from ἦρι, ēri ("*early*")], i.e. *luncheon*:—dinner.

713. ἀρκετός, arketos, *ar-ket-os´*; from 714; *satisfactory*:—enough, suffice (-ient).

714. ἀρκέω, arkeō, *ar-keh´-o*; apparently a primary verb [but probably akin to 142 through the idea of *raising* a barrier]; properly to *ward off*, i.e. (by implication) to *avail* (figurative, *be satisfactory*):—be content, be enough, suffice, be sufficient.

715. ἄρκτος, arktos, *ark´-tos*; probably from 714; a *bear* (as *obstructing* by ferocity):—bear.

716. ἄρμα, harma, *har´-mah*; probably from 142 [perhaps with 1 (as a particle of union) prefixed]; a *chariot* (as *raised* or fitted *together* [compare 719]):—chariot.

717. Ἀρμαγεδδών, Armageddōn, *ar-mag-ed-dohn´*; of Hebrew origin [2022 and 4023]; *Armageddon* (or *Har-Megiddon*), a symbolical name:—Armageddon.

718. ἀρμόζω, harmozō, *har-mod´-zo*; from 719; to *joint*, i.e. (figurative) to *woo* (reflexive to *betroth*):—espouse.

719. ἀρμός, harmos, *har-mos´*; from the same as 716; an *articulation* (of the body):—joint.

720. ἀρνέομαι, arneomai, *ar-neh´-om-ahee*; perhaps from 1 (as a negative particle) and the middle of 4483; to *contradict*, i.e. *disavow, reject, abnegate*:—deny, refuse.

Deponent verb meaning to deny:

(I) To contradict, to affirm not to be (Mt 26:70, 72; Mk 14:68, 70; Jn 1:20; 18:25, 27; Lk 8:45; 22:57; Ac 4:16; Tit 1:16; 1Jn 2:22, 23). To refuse (Heb 9:24).

(II) To renounce, to reject, e.g., to reject Christ (Mt 10:33; Lk 12:9; Ac 3:13, 14; 2Ti 2:12; 2Pe 2:1; Jude 4); to desert the Christian faith, to apostatize (1Ti 5:8; Rev 2:13; 3:8); spoken of Christ as rejecting men (Mt 10:33; 2Ti 2:13). Used figuratively: to deny onself, i.e. disregard personal interests and enjoyments (Lk 9:23); to deny oneself, i.e. to renounce one's own character, to be inconsistent with oneself (2Ti 2:13). Also figuratively in Tit 2:12; 2Ti 3:5.

Deriv.: *aparnéomai* (533), to deny.

Syn.: *antitássomai* (498), to place oneself against, oppose, resist; *aporríptō* (641), to hurl off, reject; *aposteréō* (650), to despoil, keep back; *periphronéō* (4065), to despise, depreciate; *apōthéomai* (683), to reject, push away; *apotrépō* (665), to deflect, avoid, turn away; *apophérō* (667), to bear off, carry away; *aparnéomai* (533), to deny completely; *apotássomai* (657), to renounce; *paraitéomai* (3868), to avoid, reject; *apodokimázō* (593), to disapprove; *athetéō* (114), to break faith with, reject; *ekptúō* (1609), to spit out.

721. ἀρνίον, arnion, *ar-nee´-on*; diminutive from 704; a *lambkin*:—lamb.

A noun meaning lamb. In the NT, used figuratively for the followers of Christ (Jn 21:15), and of Christ Himself (Rev 5:6, 8, 12, 13; 6:1, 16; 7:9, 10, 14, 17; 12:11; 13:8; 14:1, 4, 10; 15:3; 17:14; 19:7, 9; 21:9, 14, 22, 23, 27; 22:1, 3).

722. ἀροτριόω, arotrioō, *ar-ot-ree-o´-o*; from 723; to *plough*:—plow.

723. ἄροτρον, arotron, *ar´-ot-ron*; from ἀρόω, *aroō* (to *till*); a *plough*:—plow.

724. ἁρπαγή, harpagē, *har-pag-ay´*; from 726; *pillage* (properly abstract):—extortion, ravening, spoiling.

From *harpázō* (726), to seize upon with force. Plundering, pillage, i.e. the act of spoiling (Heb 10:34). Used metaphorically of a disposition to plunder, ravening (Mt 23:25; Lk 11:39).

Syn.: *pleonexía* (4124), covetousness, extortion; *skúlon* (4661), in the plural meaning spoils, arms stripped from an enemy; *akrothínion* (205), the top of a heap, the choicest spoils in war.

725. ἁρπαγμός, harpagmos, *har-pag-mos´*; from 726; *plunder* (properly concrete):—robbery.

Noun from *harpázō* (726), to seize upon with force. Robbery. In the NT, used figuratively of

the object of plunder, something to be eagerly coveted. Only in Php 2:6.

Syn.: *klopé* (2829), theft; *klémma* (2809), a thing stolen.

726. ἁρπάζω, harpazō, *har-pad´-zo*; from a derivative of 138; to *seize* (in various applications):—catch (away, up), pluck, pull, take (by force).

A verb meaning to seize upon, spoil, snatch away:

(I) Spoken of beasts of prey (Jn 10:12; Sept.: Ge 37:33; Eze 22:25, 27). Used metaphorically: to seize with eagerness or greed (Mt 11:12, cf. Lk 16:16).

(II) Spoken of what is snatched suddenly away (Mt 13:19; Jude 23); in the sense of to rob, plunder (Jn 10:28, 29).

(III) To carry away, to hurry off; spoken of persons (Jn 6:15; Ac 8:39; 23:10; 2Co 12:2, 4; 1Th 4:17; Rev 12:5).

Deriv.: *harpagé* (724), robbery, plundering; *harpagmós* (725), robbery; *hárpax* (727), a rapacious person; *diarpázō* (1282), to seize, plunder; *sunarpázō* (4884), to seize or grasp with great violence.

Syn.: *paralambánō* (3880), to receive; *proslambánō* (4355), to receive unto; *apospáō* (645), to draw away; *aphairéō* (851), to remove; *exaírō* (1808), to take away; *exairéō* (1807), to pluck out, deliver, rescue; *aníēmi* (447), to let go; *apotássō* (657), to take away from and place in proper order.

727. ἅρπαξ, harpax, *har´-pax*; from 726; *rapacious*:—extortion, ravening.

728. ἀρραβών, arrhabōn, *ar-hrab-ohn´*; of Hebrew origin [6162]; a *pledge*, i.e. part of the purchase money or property given in advance as *security* for the rest:—earnest.

Noun transliterated from the Hebrew *'arabōn* (6162, OT). Earnest money, a pledge given to ratify a contract (Sept.: Ge 38:17, 18, 20). In the NT, used metaphorically, spoken of the privileges of Christians in this life, especially the gift of the Holy Spirit, as being an earnest, a pledge of future bliss in the Messiah's kingdom (2Co 1:22; 5:5; Eph 1:14).

Syn.: *aparché* (536), translated "firstfruits"; *parakatathékē* (3872), a deposit.

729. ἄρραφος, arrhaphos, *ar´-hraf-os*; from 1 (as a negative particle) and a presumed derivative of the same as 4476; *unsewed*, i.e. of a single piece:—without seam.

730. ἄρρην, arrhēn, *ar´-hrane*; or **αρσην, arsēn**; *ar´-sane*; probably from 142; *male* (as stronger for *lifting*):—male, man.

731. ἄρρητος, arrhētos, *ar´-hray-tos*; from 1 (as a negative particle) and the same as 4490; *unsaid*, i.e. (by implication) *inexpressible*:—unspeakable.

732. ἄρρωστος, arrhōstos, *ar´-hroce-tos*; from 1 (as a negative particle) and a presumed derivative of 4517; *infirm*:—sick (folk, -ly).

Adjective from *a* (1), without, and *rhónnumi* (4517), to strengthen. Infirm, feeble, sick, invalid (Mt 14:14; Mk 6:5, 13; 16:18; 1Co 11:30; Sept.: Mal 1:8).

Syn.: *asthenḗs* (772), without strength, feeble, hence sick.

733. ἀρσενοκοίτης, arsenokoitēs, *ar-sen-ok-oy´-tace*; from 730 and 2845; a *sodomite*:—abuser of (that defile) self with mankind.

734. Ἀρτεμάς, Artemas, *ar-tem-as´*; contracted from a compound of 735 and 1435; *gift of Artemis; Artemas* (or *Artemidorus*), a Christian:—Artemas.

735. Ἄρτεμις, Artemis, *ar´-tem-is*; probably from the same as 736; *prompt; Artemis*, the name of a Grecian goddess borrowed by certain Asian peoples for one of their deities:—Diana.

736. ἀρτέμων, artemōn, *ar-tem´-ohn*; from a derivative of 737; properly something *ready* [or else more remotely from 142 (compare 740); something *hung* up], i.e. (special) the *topsail* (rather *foresail* or *jib*) of a vessel:—mainsail.

737. ἄρτι, arti, *ar´-tee*; adverb from a derivative of 142 (compare 740) through the idea of *suspension*; just *now*:—this day (hour), hence [-forth], here [-after], hither [-to], (even) now, (this) present.

738. ἀρτιγέννητος, artigennētos, *ar-teeg-en´-nay-tos*; from 737 and 1084; *just born*, i.e. (figurative) a *young convert*:—newborn.

Adjective from *árti* (737), now, lately, and *gennētós* (1084), born. Lately born, newborn. In the NT, used metaphorically of those who

have just embraced the Christian faith. Only in 1Pe 2:2.

Syn.: *neossós* (3502), a youngling, used only of birds.

739. ἄρτιος, artios, *ar´-tee-os*; from 737; *fresh*, i.e. (by implication) *complete*:—perfect.

Adjective from *árti* (737), now, exactly. Complete, perfect. Spoken of a religious teacher, who should be wanting in nothing. Only in 2Ti 3:17.

Syn.: *téleios* (5046), perfect, complete; *pantelḗs* (3838), entire, complete; *akéraios* (185), unmixed, blameless, without guile; *plḗrēs* (4134), complete; *ámemptos* (273), faultless, blameless; *áptaistos* (679), not stumbling, without sin; *holotelḗs* (3651), complete to the end.

740. ἄρτος, artos, *ar´-tos*; from 142; *bread* (as *raised*) or a *loaf*:—(shew-) bread, loaf.

741. ἀρτύω, artuō, *ar-too´-o*; from a presumed derivative of 142; to *prepare*, i.e. *spice* (with *stimulating* condiments):—season.

742. Ἀρφαξάδ, Arphaxad, *ar-fax-ad´*; of Hebrew origin [775]; *Arphaxad*, a post-diluvian patriarch:—Arphaxad.

743. ἀρχάγγελος, archaggelos, *ar-khang´-el-os*; from 757 and 32; a *chief angel*:—archangel.

Noun from *árchōn* (758), chief, and *ággelos* (32), angel or messenger. An archangel, i.e. a chief angel (1Th 4:16; Jude 9). Of these there are said to be seven, who stand immediately before the throne of God (Lk 1:19; Rev 8:2), who have authority over other angels (Rev 12:7), and are the patrons of particular nations (Da 10:13; 12:1). The names of only two are found in Scripture: Michael, the patron of the Jewish nation (Da 10:13; 12:1; Jude 9; Rev 12:7), and Gabriel (Da 8:16; 9:21; Lk 1:19, 26).

744. ἀρχαῖος, archaios, *ar-khah´-yos*; from 746; *original* or *primeval*:—(them of) old (time).

Adjective from *archḗ* (746), beginning. Ancient, of former days, of old time (Mt 5:21, 27, 33; Lk 9:8, 19; Ac 15:7, 21; 2Co 5:17; 2Pe 2:5; Rev 12:9).

Syn.: *progínomai* (4266), to be already or to have previously come to exist; *patroparádotos* (3970), traditional; *patrṓos* (3971), hereditary.

745. Ἀρχέλαος, **Archelaos**, *ar-khel´-ah-os*; from 757 and 2994; *people-ruling; Archelaus*, a Jewish king:—Archelaus.

746. ἀρχή, **archē**, *ar-khay´*; from 756; (properly abstract) a *commencement*, or (concrete) *chief* (in various applications of order, time, place or rank):—beginning, corner, (at the, the) first (estate), magistrate, power, principality, principle, rule.

A noun meaning beginning:

(I) Spoken of time: the beginning, commencement (Mt 24:8; Mk 1:1; 13:9; Jn 2:11; Heb 3:14; 7:3). Used in conjunction with various prepositions:

(A) *Ap' archēs*, from the beginning (see *apó* [575]); of all things (Mt 19:4, 8; Jn 8:44; 1Jn 3:8); of any particular thing, e.g., of the gospel dispensation, or of the Christian experience (Lk 1:2; Jn 15:27; 2Th 2:13; 1Jn 1:1; 2:7); of life (Ac 26:4).

(B) *En archē*, in the beginning (see *en* [1722]); of all things, of the world (Jn 1:1, 2); of any particular thing, e.g., of the gospel dispensation, or of the Christian experience (Ac 11:15; Php 4:15).

(C) *Ex archēs*, from the beginning, from the first (see *ek* [1537]), e.g., of Christ's ministry (Jn 6:64; 16:4).

(D) *Kat' archás*, at the beginning, i.e. of old (Heb 1:10); see *katá* (2596).

(E) The accusative form, *tēn archēn* may be used adverbially, meaning at the beginning, at first; hence in the NT: from the very beginning on, throughout, wholly (Jn 8:25).

(II) By metonymy of abstract for concrete, spoken of persons: the first (Col 1:18). So the expression *archē kaí télos*, the first and the last (see *télos* [5056], last), i.e. the beginning and the end (Rev 1:8 [TR]; 21:6; 22:13).

(III) Spoken of place: the extremity; corner, e.g., of a sheet (Ac 10:11; 11:5).

(IV) Spoken of dignity, meaning the first place, power, dominion (Lk 20:20; Sept.: Ge 1:16; Jer 34:1; Mic 4:8); in the sense of preeminence, precedence, princedom (Jude 6). By metonymy of abstract for concrete: rulers, magistrates, princes, i.e. persons of influence and authority (Lk 12:11; Tit 3:1); spoken of the princes or chiefs among angels (Eph 1:21; 3:10; Col 2:10); among demons (1Co 15:24; Eph 6:12; Col 2:15); the powers of the other world

(Ro 8:38; Col 1:16 [cf. *exousía* {1849}, authority]).

Deriv.: *archaíos* (744), of old, original; *archēgós* (747), a leader; *árchō* (757), to be first or to rule; *patriárchēs* (3966), patriarch, progenitor.

Syn.: *gōnía* (1137), corner; *prōtos* (4413), first, preeminent; *dúnamis* (1411), ruling power; *exousía* (1849), authority; *krátos* (2904), dominion; *hēgemōn* (2232), a leader, ruler; *megistán* (3175), used usually in the plural *megistánes* meaning, great ones, magnates, chiefs; *kanōn* (2583), a rule; with the meaning of ruler: *kosmokrátōr* (2888), a ruler of this world; *pantokrátōr* (3841), universal ruler or ruler of all things, sovereign; *politárchēs* (4173), a ruler of a city; *architríklinos* (755), a superintendent of a banquet.

747. ἀρχηγός, **archēgos**, *ar-khay-gos´*; from 746 and 71; a *chief leader*:—author, captain, prince.

Noun from *archē* (746), beginning or rule, and *ágō* (71), to lead. One who makes a beginning, i.e. the author, source, cause of anything (Ac 3:15; Heb 2:10; 12:2; Sept.: Mic 1:13). Also, a leader, chief, prince, etc. (Ac 5:31 [cf. Ac 2:36; Eph 1:20]; Sept.: Jgs 5:15; 2Ch 23:14; Isa 30:4).

Syn.: *aítios* (159), he who causes something, the author; *chilíarchos* (5506), commander of a thousand soldiers; *stratēgós* (4755), commander of an army; *stratopedárchēs* (4759), camp commander; *árchōn* (758), he who rules but may not be a ruler per se, *hēgemōn* (2232), a leader, ruler; *megistánes* (3175), the great ones, princes, lords.

748. ἀρχιερατικός, **archieratikos**, *ar-khee-er-at-ee-kos´*; from 746 and a derivative of 2413; *high-priestly*:—of the high-priest.

749. ἀρχιερεύς, **archiereus**, *ar-khee-er-yuce´*; from 746 and 2409; the *high-priest* (literal of the Jews, typical Christ); by extension a *chief priest*:—chief (high) priest, chief of the priests.

Noun from *archí-*, denoting rank or degree, and *hiereús* (2409), a priest. A high priest, chief priest (Sept.: Le 4:3); more usually called the great priest (Sept.: Le 21:10; Nu 35:25).

(I) The high priest of the Jews (Mt 26:3, 62, 63, 65; Mk 2:26; Lk 22:50). By the original divine appointment he was to be of the family of Aaron (Ex 29:9), but by the time of the

Roman Empire, the office had become venal and was given even to foreign Jews. It was also no longer for life, so that there were often several persons living at one time who had borne the office, and still retained the title of high priest. There appears also to have been a *sāgān* (5461, OT), i.e. vicar or substitute for the high priest, to perform his duties on various occasions. Such a substitute is not expressly mentioned in the Scriptures, though such a person seems to be implied by the title "second priest" in 2Ki 25:18 and Jer 52:24. In one of these senses Annas is called high priest (Lk 3:2; Jn 18:13; Ac 4:6).

(II) A chief priest, as spoken of those who were at the head of the twenty-four classes of priests mentioned in 1Ch 24, and who are there called "the chief[s] of the fathers of the priests and Levites" (1Ch 24:6 [cf. Mt 2:4; 26:3; Mk 14:1; Lk 22:2]). These were members of the Sanhedrin, and indeed the expressions "chief priests and scribes" (Mt 2:4) and "chief priests and Pharisees" (Jn 7:32, 45) seem to be put by way of circumlocution for "the Sanhedrin," and in some instances the word *archiereús* appears to be used by itself in a general sense to denote the same council (Jn 12:10, cf. 11:47).

(III) In the epistle to the Hebrews (e.g., Heb 2:17; 3:1; 4:14; 5:5; 6:20), Christ is called *archiereús* and compared to the high priest of the Jews, as having offered Himself as a sacrifice for sin (cf. Heb 9:7, 11, 12).

Deriv.: *archieratikós* (748), high-priestly.

750. ἀρχιποίμην, **archipoimēn,** *ar-khee-poy´-mane*; from 746 and 4166; a *head shepherd:*—chief shepherd.

Noun from *archí-*, denoting rank or degree, and *poimén* (4166), a shepherd. Chief shepherd, applied to Christ (1Pe 5:4; cf. Heb 13:20).

Syn.: *archiereús* (749), chief priest; *árchōn* (758), a ruler; *archisunágōgos* (752), a ruler of a synagogue.

751. Ἄρχιππος, **Archippos,** *ar´-khip-pos*; from 746 and 2462; *horse-ruler; Archippus,* a Christian:—Archippus.

752. ἀρχισυνάγωγος, **archisunagōgos,** *ar-khee-soon-ag´-o-gos*; from 746 and 4864; *director of* the *synagogue* services:—(chief) ruler of the synagogue.

753. ἀρχιτέκτων, **architektōn,** *ar-khee-tek´-tone*; from 746 and 5045; a *chief constructor,* i.e. "*architect*":—masterbuilder.

754. ἀρχιτελώνης, **architelōnēs,** *ar-khee-tel-o´-nace*; from 746 and 5057; a *principal tax-gatherer:*—chief among the publicans.

755. ἀρχιτρίκλινος, **architriklinos,** *ar-khee-tree´-klee-nos*; from 746 and a compound of 5140 and 2827 (a *dinner-bed,* because composed of three couches); *director of* the *entertainment:*—governor (ruler) of the feast.

756. ἄρχομαι, **archomai,** *ar´-khom-ahee*; middle of 757 (through the implication of *precedence*); to *commence* (in order of time):—(rehearse from the) begin (-ning).

757. ἄρχω, **archō,** *ar´-kho*; a primary verb; to be *first* (in political rank or power):—reign (rule) over.

From *archḗ* (746), beginning, first. To begin, to be first:

(I) To be first in rank, dignity, etc., i.e. to rule, to reign (Mk 10:42; Ro 15:12; Sept.: Ge 1:18; Dt 15:6).

(II) Used in the middle voice, *árchomai,* to begin. Generally (Mt 4:17; 11:7, 20; Mk 1:45; Lk 4:21; Ac 1:1); by Hebraism, used emphatically implying difficulty: to attempt, to undertake, to venture (Mk 10:28, 32; Lk 3:8).

(III) As a participle, *arxámenos,* beginning from, expressing the point of departure in a narration, transaction, etc. (Mt 20:8; Lk 23:5; 24:27; Jn 8:9; Ac 1:22; 8:35; 10:37).

Deriv.: *árchomai* (756), beginning; *Asiárchēs* (775), a ruler of Asia; *ethnárchēs* (1481), the governor of a district; *hekatontárchēs* (1543), centurion; *politárchēs* (4173), ruler of the city; *stratopedárchēs* (4759), captain of the guard; *tetrárchēs* (5076), tetrarch; *hupárchō* (5225), to behave, live; *chilíarchos* (5506), captain.

Syn.: *basileúō* (936), to reign; *hēgemoneúō* (2230), to act as a ruler; *hēgéomai* (2233), to lead; *oikodespotéō* (3616), to rule a house; *proḯstēmi* (4291), to stand before, to rule; *poimaínō* (4165), to act as a shepherd; *exousiázō* (1850), to exercise authority upon; *katexousiázō* (2715), to exercise full authority; *kurieúō* (2961), to exercise lordship over; *katakurieúō* (2634), to lord it over completely; *prōteúō* (4409), to be first.

758. ἄρχων, **archōn,** *ar´-khone*; present participle of 757; a *first* (in rank or power):—chief (ruler), magistrate, prince, ruler.

Masculine part. of *árchō* (757), to rule. One first in power, authority, dominion; hence a ruler, lord, prince, a chief person. Generally (Mt 20:25; Ac 4:26; Ro 13:3; 1Co 2:6, 8; Sept.: Ge 49:20; Nu 23:21; 2Ch 8:9). Spoken of the Messiah as King of kings (Rev 1:5); of Moses as a ruler and leader of Israel (Ac 7:27, 35); of magistrates of any kind such as the high priest (Ac 23:5); of civil judges (Lk 12:58; Ac 16:19); of persons of weight and influence among the Pharisees and other sects at Jerusalem who also were members of the Sanhedrin (Lk 14:1; 18:18; 23:13, 35; 24:20; Jn 3:1 [cf. 7:45, 50; Jn 7:26, 48; 12:42; Ac 3:17; 4:5, 8; 13:27; 14:5]); of magnates (Sept.: Ne 5:7); of the chief of the fallen angels, Satan, "the prince of devils" (Mt 9:34; 12:24; Mk 3:22; Lk 11:15), called also "the ruler of this world," as ruling in the hearts of worldly and wicked men (Jn 12:31; 14:30; 16:11), also "the prince of the power of the air" (Eph 2:2).

Deriv.: *archággelos* (743), archangel.

Syn.: *stratēgós* (4755), captain, magistrate; *megistán* (3175), a great man; *kosmokrátōr* (2888), a ruler of the world; *pantokrátōr* (3841), almighty; *politárchēs* (4173), a ruler of a city; *architríklinos* (755), superintendent of a banquet; *hēgemṓn* (2232), a leader.

759. ἄρωμα, **arōma,** *ar´-o-mah*; from 142 (in the sense of *sending* off scent); an *aromatic*:— (sweet) spice.

760. Ἀσά, **Asa,** *as-ah´*; of Hebrew origin [609]; *Asa*, an Israelite:—Asa.

761. ἀσάλευτος, **asaleutos,** *as-al´-yoo-tos*; from 1 (as a negative particle) and a derivative of 4531; *unshaken*, i.e. (by implication) *immovable* (figurative):—which cannot be moved, unmovable.

762. ἄσβεστος, **asbestos,** *as´-bes-tos*; from 1 (as a negative particle) and a derivative of 4570; *not extinguished*, i.e. (by implication) *perpetual*:—not to be quenched, unquenchable.

763. ἀσέβεια, **asebeia,** *as-eb´-i-ah*; from 765; *impiety*, i.e. (by implication) *wickedness*:— ungodly (-liness).

Noun from *asebḗs* (765), impious, ungodly, wicked. Impiety toward God, ungodliness,

either in thought or action (Ro 1:18; 11:26; 2Ti 2:16; Tit 2:12; Jude 15, 18; Sept.: Pr 4:17; Ecc 8:8; Jer 5:6; Eze 16:58; 21:24).

Syn.: *adikía* (93), injustice, unrighteousness, iniquity; *anomía* (458), illegality, violation of law, wickedness; *hamartía* (266), sin; *ponēría* (4189), wickedness, malevolence; *kakía* (2549), wickedness, badness; *paranomía* (3892), law breaking; *anaídeia* (335), impudence, insolence; *kakoḗtheia* (2550), mischievousness, depravity of heart.

764. ἀσεβέω, **asebeō,** *as-eb-eh´-o*; from 765; to *be* (by implication, *act*) *impious* or *wicked*:— commit (live, that after should live) ungodly.

From *asebḗs* (765), impious, ungodly, wicked. To be ungodly, to live impiously (2Pe 2:6; Jude 15).

Syn.: *adikéō* (91), to be unjust, to do wrong; *hamartánō* (264), to sin, offend; *kataphronéō* (2706), to despise; *periphronéō* (4065), to depreciate, not to give due respect.

765. ἀσεβής, **asebēs,** *as-eb-ace´*; from 1 (as a negative particle) and a presumed derivative of 4576; *irreverent*, i.e. (by extension) *impious* or *wicked*:—ungodly (man).

Adjective from the priv. *a* (1), without, and *sébomai* (4576), to worship, venerate. Impious, ungodly, wicked (1Ti 1:9; 2Pe 2:5; 3:7; Jude 4, 15). Also implying exposure to punishment (Ro 4:5; 5:6).

Deriv.: *asébeia* (763), impiety; *asebéō* (764), to act impiously.

Syn.: *hamartōlós* (268), sinful, sinner; *anósios* (462), wicked, unholy; *bébēlos* (952), wicked, profane; *theostugḗs* (2319), impious, hater of God; *hubristḗs* (5197), an insulter.

766. ἀσέλγεια, **aselgeia,** *as-elg´-i-a*; from a compound of 1 (as a negative particle) and a presumed σελγής, *selgḗs* (of uncertain derivative, but apparently meaning *continent*); *licentiousness* (sometimes including other vices):— filthy, lasciviousness, wantonness.

Noun, from *aselgḗs* (n.f.), licentious, brutal. Excess, immoderation, intemperance in anything, e.g.: in language, speech: arrogance, insolence (Mk 7:22); in general conduct: licentiousness, madness (2Pe 2:2); particularly: wantonness, lasciviousness (Ro 13:13; 2Co 12:21; Gal 5:19; 2Pe 2:7, 18); in a wider sense: debauchery, perversion in general (Eph 4:19; 1Pe 4:3; Jude 4).

Syn.: *asōtía* (810), wastefulness and riotous excess; *epithumía* (1939), lust; *aischrótēs* (151), impropriety, all that is contrary to purity; *rhuparía* (4507), filth; *molusmós* (3436), defilement; *strḗnos* (4764), insolent luxury; *porneía* (4202), fornication; *akrasía* (192), lack of self-restraint, incontinency; *hēdonḗ* (2237), lust, pleasure; *kraipálē* (2897), debauchery, glut, drunkenness.

767. ἄσημος, asēmos, *as´-ay-mos*; from 1 (as a negative particle) and the base of 4591; *unmarked*, i.e. (figurative) *ignoble*:—mean.

768. Ἀσήρ, Asēr, *as-ayr´*; of Hebrew origin [836]; *Aser* (i.e. *Asher*), an Israelite tribe:—Aser.

769. ἀσθένεια, astheneia, *as-then´-i-ah*; from 772; *feebleness* (of body or mind); (by implication) *malady*; moral *frailty*:—disease, infirmity, sickness, weakness.

Noun from *asthenḗs* (772), weak, sick. Want of strength, infirmity, weakness:

(I) Generally (Ro 6:19; 1Co 15:43; 2Co 11:30; 12:5, 9, 10); spoken of the general weakness and infirmity of human nature (2Co 13:4; Heb 4:15; 5:2; 7:28).

(II) Specifically, infirmity of the body, i.e. disease, sickness (Mt 8:17; Lk 5:15; 9:2; 13:12; Jn 5:5; 11:4; Ac 28:9; 1Ti 5:23; Heb 11:34).

(III) Figuratively, of the mind: feebleness, depression, want of energy (1Co 2:3); by implication: sorrow, affliction, distress producing depression and perplexity of mind (Ro 8:26; Gal 4:13; Sept.: Ps 16:4).

Syn.: *árrōstos* (732), infirm, without robustness; *Malakía* (3119), weakness, softness; *nósos* (3554), disease, malady.

770. ἀσθενέω, astheneō, *as-then-eh´-o*; from 772; to *be feeble* (in any sense):—be diseased, impotent folk (man), (be) sick, (be, be made) weak.

From *asthenḗs* (772), without strength, powerless, sick. To lack strength, be infirm, weak, feeble:

(I) To be weak (Ro 8:3; 2Co 13:3, 4, 9; Sept.: 1Sa 2:5; 2Sa 3:1; La 2:8).

(II) Specifically, to be infirm in the body, i.e. to be sick, to suffer from disease or the consequences thereof (Mt 10:8; 25:36; Mk 6:56; Lk 4:40; 7:10; Jn 4:46; Ac 9:37; Php 2:26; Jas 5:14).

(III) Figuratively, of the mind: to be feeble-minded, faint-hearted, timid (2Co 11:21). By Hebraism, implying a want of firmness and decision of mind: to be weak-minded, to hesitate, to vacillate, spoken of those whose minds are easily disturbed (Ro 14:2, 21; 1Co 8:9, 11, 12). Also, to be weak, not settled in the faith (Ro 4:19), or in opinion (Ro 14:1).

(IV) By implication: to be afflicted, to be distressed by want, oppression, calamity, etc. (Ac 20:35; 2Co 11:29; Sept.: Job 4:4).

Deriv.: *asthénēma* (771), infirmity.

Syn.: *noséō* (3552), to be sick; *échō kakṓs* (*échō* [2192], to have; *kakṓs* [2560], badly), to have it badly, to be ill; *páschō* (3958), to suffer; *hupophérō* (5297), to endure, to bear from underneath; *basanízō* (928), to suffer pain; *phtheírō* (5351), to pine or waste away, to corrupt in the sense of degeneration; *sunéchō* (4912), to be sick, confined.

771. ἀσθένημα, asthenēma, *as-then´-ay-mah*; from 770; a *scruple* of conscience:—infirmity.

Noun from *astheneō* (770), to be weak or powerless. Infirmity. Used metaphorically: doubt, hesitation, scruple. Only in Ro 15:1.

772. ἀσθενής, asthenēs, *as-then-ace´*; from 1 (as a negative particle) and the base of 4599; *strengthless* (in various applications, literal, figurative and moral):—more feeble, impotent, sick, without strength, weak (-er, -ness, thing).

Adjective from the priv. *a* (1), without, and *sthénos* (n.f.), strength. Without strength, infirm, weak, feeble:

(I) Generally (Mt 26:41; Mk 14:38; 1Pe 3:7; Sept.: Nu 13:19; Job 4:3; Eze 17:14). Including the idea of imperfection (1Co 12:22; Gal 4:9; Heb 7:18).

(II) Infirm in body; sick, sickly, diseased (Mt 25:39, 43, 44; Lk 10:9; Ac 4:9; 5:15, 16; 1Co 11:30).

(III) Figuratively, of the mind: faint-hearted, timid (2Co 10:10 [cf. 11:21; 1Co 2:3]). Implying a want of decision and firmness of mind: weak-minded, i.e. doubting, hesitating, vacillating, in opinion or faith (1Co 8:7, 10; 9:22; 1Th 5:14).

(IV) By implication: afflicted, distressed by oppression, calamity, etc. (1Co 4:10). In a moral sense: wretched, diseased, i.e. in a state of sin and wretchedness (Ro 5:6).

Deriv.: *asthéneia* (769), lack of strength, powerlessness, weakness; *astheneō* (770), to be weak or powerless, sick.

Syn.: *árrōstos* (732), sick, without strength or robustness; *adúnatos* (102), weak, without strength.

773. Ἀσία, **Asia,** *as-ee´-ah*; of uncertain derivative; *Asia*, i.e. *Asia Minor*, or (usually) only its western shore:—Asia.

774. Ἀσιανός, **Asianos,** *as-ee-an-os´*; from 773; an *Asian* (i.e. *Asiatic*) or inhabitant of Asia:—of Asia.

775. Ἀσιάρχης, **Asiarchēs,** *as-ee-ar´-khace*; from 773 and 746; an *Asiarch* or president of the public festivities in a city of Asia Minor:—chief of Asia.

776. ἀσιτία, **asitia,** *as-ee-tee´-ah*; from 777; *fasting* (the state):—abstinence.

777. ἄσιτος, **asitos,** *as´-ee-tos*; from 1 (as a negative particle) and 4621; *without* (taking) *food*:—fasting.

778. ἀσκέω, **askeō,** *as-keh´-o*; probably from the same as 4632; to *elaborate*, i.e. (figurative) *train* (by implication, *strive*):—exercise.

779. ἀσκός, **askos,** *as-kos´*; from the same as 778; a leathern (or skin) *bag* used as a bottle:—bottle.

780. ἀσμένως, **asmenōs,** *as-men´-oce*; adverb from a derivative of the base of 2237; *with pleasure*:—gladly.

781. ἄσοφος, **asophos,** *as´-of-os*; from 1 (as a negative particle) and 4680; *unwise*:—fool.

782. ἀσπάζομαι, **aspazomai,** *as-pad´-zom-ahee*; from 1 (as a particle of union) and a presumed form of 4685; to *enfold* in the arms, i.e. (by implication) to *salute*, (figurative) to *welcome*:—embrace, greet, salute, take leave.

783. ἀσπασμός, **aspasmos,** *as-pas-mos´*; from 782; a *greeting* (in person or by letter):—greeting, salutation.

784. ἄσπιλος, **aspilos,** *as´-pee-los*; from 1 (as a negative particle) and 4695; *unblemished* (physical or moral):—without spot, unspotted.

Adjective from the priv. *a* (1), without, and *spílos* (4696), spot. Without blemish or spot, free from spot, unblemished, pure. Spoken of Christ in 1Pe 1:19; of doctrine in 1Ti 6:14; of moral conduct in Jas 1:27; 2Pe 3:14.

Syn.: *katharós* (2513), clean, pure; *amíantos* (283), pure, undefiled; *hagnós* (53), clean, chaste; *kalós* (2570), good; *chrēstós* (5543), useful, kind, gracious; *hierós* (2413), sacred, holy; *hágios* (40), holy, blameless; *hósios* (3741), consecrated, holy; *tímios* (5093), valuable, honored, of good reputation.

785. ἀσπίς, **aspis,** *as-pece´*; of uncertain derivative; a *buckler* (or *round* shield); used of a serpent (as *coiling* itself), probably the "*asp*":—asp.

786. ἄσπονδος, **aspondos,** *as´-pon-dos*; from 1 (as a negative particle) and a derivative of 4689; literal *without libation* (which usually accompanied a treaty), i.e. (by implication) *truceless*:—implacable, truce-breaker.

Adjective from the priv. *a* (1), without, and *spondḗ* (n.f.), libation or drink offering. In the NT, averse to any compact, i.e. implacable (Ro 1:31; 2Ti 3:3).

Syn.: *asúmphōnos* (800), one not agreeing; *philóneikos* (5380), quarrelsome, born of strife.

787. ἀσσάριον, **assarion,** *as-sar´-ee-on*; of Latin origin; an *assarius* or *as*, a Roman coin:—farthing.

788. ἄσσον, **asson,** *as´-son*; neuter comparative of the base of 1451; *more nearly*, i.e. *very near*:—close.

789. Ἄσσος, **Assos,** *as´-sos*; probably of foreign origin; *Assus*, a city of Asia Minor:—Assos.

790. ἀστατέω, **astateō,** *as-tat-eh´-o*; from 1 (as a negative particle) and a derivative of 2476; to *be non-stationary*, i.e. (figurative) *homeless*:—have no certain dwelling-place.

From *ástatos* (n.f.), unstable, which is from the priv. *a* (1), not, and *hístēmi* (2476), to stand, be fixed. To be unsettled, have no certain or fixed abode (1Co 4:11).

Syn.: *kinéō* (2795), to move; *metakinéō* (3334), to remove.

791. ἀστεῖος, **asteios,** *as-ti´-os*; from ἄστυ, *astu* (a *city*); *urbane*, i.e. (by implication) *handsome*:—fair.

Adjective from *ástu* (n.f.), a city. Urbane, polished. In the NT, elegant, and spoken of external form: fair, beautiful (Heb 11:23). By Hebraism, the phrase *asteíos tō theō*, lit. "beautiful to God" (see *theós* [2316]), translated "exceeding fair" (Ac 7:20).

Syn.: *hōraíos* (5611), beautiful; *kalós* (2570), good, beautiful.

792. ἀστήρ, astēr, *as-tare´*; probably from the base of 4766; a *star* (as *strown* over the sky), literal or figurative:—star.

793. ἀστήρικτος, astēriktos, *as-tay´-rik-tos*; from 1 (as a negative particle) and a presumed derivative of 4741; *unfixed*, i.e. (figurative) *vacillating*:—unstable.

794. ἄστοργος, astorgos, *as´-tor-gos*; from 1 (as a negative particle) and a presumed derivative of **στέργω, stergō** (to *cherish* affectionately); *hard-hearted* toward kindred:—without natural affection.

Adjective from the priv. *a* (1), without, and the noun *storgé* (n.f.), family love. Without natural affection; inhuman (Ro 1:31; 2Ti 3:3).

Syn.: *aphilágathos* (865), hostile to benevolence; *stugnētós* (4767), odious, hateful.

795. ἀστοχέω, astocheō, *as-tokh-eh´-o*; from a compound of 1 (as a negative particle) and **στόιχος, stoichos** (an *aim*); to *miss* the mark, i.e. (figurative) *deviate* from truth:—err, swerve.

796. ἀστραπή, astrapē, *as-trap-ay´*; from 797; *lightning*; (by analogy) *glare*:—lightning, bright shining.

797. ἀστράπτω, astraptō, *as-trap´-to*; probably from 792; to *flash* as lightning:—lighten, shine.

798. ἄστρον, astron, *as´-tron*; neuter from 792; properly a *constellation*; put for a single *star* (natural or artificial):—star.

799. Ἀσύγκριτος, Asugkritos, *as-oong´-kree-tos*; from 1 (as a negative particle) and a derivative of 4793; *incomparable*; *Asyncritus*, a Christian:—Asyncritus.

800. ἀσύμφωνος, asumphōnos, *as-oom´-fo-nos*; from 1 (as a negative particle) and 4859; *inharmonious* (figurative):—agree not.

801. ἀσύνετος, asunetos, *as-oon´-ay-tos*; from 1 (as a negative particle) and 4908; *unintelligent*; (by implication) *wicked*:—foolish, without understanding.

Adjective from the priv. *a* (1), without, and *sunetós* (4908), discerning. Void of understanding, dull of apprehension, foolish (Mt 15:16;

Mk 7:18; Sept.: Ps 92:7). From the Hebrew, with the accessory idea of impiety: ungodly, as neglecting the true wisdom and continuing in sin, heathenism, etc. (Ro 1:21, 31; 10:19; Sept.: Dt 32:1 [cf. Job 2:10; Ps 14:1]).

Syn.: *áphrōn* (878), without reason, mental insanity; *mátaios* (3152), vain; *anóētos* (453), thinking incorrectly; *mōrós* (3474), stupid, morally worthless, sluggish.

802. ἀσύνθετος, asunthetos, *as-oon´-thet-os*; from 1 (as a negative particle) and a derivative of 4934; properly *not agreed*, i.e. *treacherous* to compacts:—covenant-breaker.

Adjective from the priv. *a* (1), not, and the pass. of *suntíthēmi* (4934), to consent, make agreement. Not put together nor made up of several parts. In the NT, a breaker of a covenant or agreement, faithless, treacherous (Ro 1:31; Sept.: Jer 3:7, 8, 10, 11).

Syn.: *áspondos* (786), implacable (although *asúnthetos* presupposes a state of peace or an agreement interrupted by the unrighteous, while *áspondos* presupposes a broken treaty and a state of war involving a refusal to terminate the hostilities); *asúnetos* (801), foolish, without insight.

803. ἀσφάλεια, asphaleia, *as-fal´-i-ah*; from 804; *security* (literal or figurative):—certainty, safety.

804. ἀσφαλής, asphalēs, *as-fal-ace´*; from 1 (as a negative particle) and **σφάλλω, sphallō** (to "*fail*"); *secure* (literal or figurative):—certain (-ty), safe, sure.

805. ἀσφαλίζω, asphalizō, *as-fal-id´-zo*; from 804; to *render secure*:—make fast (sure).

806. ἀσφαλῶς, asphalōs, *as-fal-oce´*; adverb from 804; *securely* (literal or figurative):—assuredly, safely.

807. ἀσχημονέω, aschēmoneō, *as-kay-mon-eh´-o*; from 809; to *be* (i.e. *act*) *unbecoming*:—behave self uncomely (unseemly).

808. ἀσχημοσύνη, aschēmosunē, *as-kay-mos-oo´-nay*; from 809; an *indecency*; (by implication) the *pudenda*:—shame, that which is unseemly.

809. ἀσχήμων, aschēmōn, *as-kay´-mone*; from 1 (as a negative particle) and a presumed derivative of 2192 (in the sense of its congener 4976); properly *shapeless*, i.e. (figurative) *inelegant:*—uncomely.

810. ἀσωτία, asōtia, *as-o-tee´-ah*; from a compound of 1 (as a negative particle) and a presumed derivative of 4982; properly *unsavedness*, i.e. (by implication) *profligacy:*—excess, riot.

Noun from *ásōtos* (n.f.), not saveable, incorrigible, dissolute, past hope; which is from the priv. *a* (1), and *sōzō* (4982), to save. Dissoluteness, debauchery, revelry (Eph 5:18; Tit 1:6; 1Pe 4:4; Sept.: Pr 28:7).

Syn.: *akrasía* (192), lack of self-restraint; *hēdonē* (2237), lust, pleasure; *kraipálē* (2897), drunkenness, debauchery; *dapánē* (1160), expense, prodigality.

811. ἀσώτως, asōtōs, *as-o´-toce*; adverb from the same as 810; *dissolutely:*—riotous.

812. ἀτακτέω, atakteō, *at-ak-teh´-o*; from 813; to *be* (i.e. *act*) *irregular:*—behave self disorderly.

From *átaktos* (813), one out of order. To break the ranks (as of soldiers), to behave irregularly or in a disorderly manner, to neglect one's duties (2Th 3:7).

Syn.: *apeithéō* (544), to disbelieve, be disobedient; *anthístēmi* (436), to oppose, resist; *parabaínō* (3845), to transgress; *epanístamai* (1881), to rise up against; *parakoúō* (3878), to disobey, neglect to hear.

813. ἄτακτος, ataktos, *at´-ak-tos*; from 1 (as a negative particle) and a derivative of 5021; *unarranged*, i.e. (by implication) *insubordinate* (religiously):—unruly.

Adjective from the priv. *a* (1), and *tássō* (5021), to set in order. Disorderly, irregular, neglectful of duties. Only in 1Th 5:14.

Deriv.: *ataktéō* (812), to behave irregularly; *atáktōs* (814), irregularly and in a disorderly fashion.

Syn.: *akatástatos* (182), inconstant, unstable; *apeithés* (545), disobedient; *anupótaktos* (506), insubordinate.

814. ἀτάκτως, ataktōs, *at-ak´-toce*; adverb from 813; *irregularly* (moral):—disorderly.

815. ἄτεκνος, ateknos, *at´-ek-nos*; from 1 (as a negative particle) and 5043; *childless:*—childless, without children.

816. ἀτενίζω, atenizō, *at-en-id´-zo*; from a compound of 1 (as a particle of union) and τείνω, *teinō* (to *stretch*); to *gaze* intently:—behold earnestly (steadfastly), fasten (eyes), look (earnestly, steadfastly, up steadfastly), set eyes.

From *atenés* (n.f.), strained, intent, which is from the intensive *a* (1), and *teínō* (n.f.), stretch, strain. To look fixedly, gaze intently (Lk 4:20; 22:56; Ac 1:10; 3:4, 12; 6:15; 7:55; 10:4; 11:6; 13:9; 14:9; 23:1; 2Co 3:7, 13).

Syn.: *horáō* (3708), to perceive, see; *blépō* (991), to look, see,; *emblépō* (1689), to look earnestly; *theōréō* (2334), to carefully observe; *theáomai* (2300), to look with wonder; *elpízō* (1679), to hope; *prosdokáō* (4328), to expect, look for; *apekdéchomai* (553), to expect fully, look for; *anaménō* (362), to wait for; *skopéō* (4648), to look at, take heed.

817. ἄτερ, ater, *at´-er*; a particle probably akin to 427; *aloof*, i.e. *apart* from (literal or figurative):—in the absence of, without.

818. ἀτιμάζω, atimazō, *at-im-ad´-zo*; from 820; to *render infamous*, i.e. (by implication) *contemn* or *maltreat:*—despise, dishonour, suffer shame, entreat shamefully.

819. ἀτιμία, atimia, *at-ee-mee´-ah*; from 820; *infamy*, i.e. (subjective) comparative *indignity*, (objective) *disgrace:*—dishonour, reproach, shame, vile.

820. ἄτιμος, atimos, *at´-ee-mos*; from 1 (as a negative particle) and 5092; (negative) *unhonoured* or (positive) *dishonoured:*—despised, without honour, less honourable [*comparative degree*].

821. ἀτιμόω, atimoō, *at-ee-mo´-o*; from 820; used like 818, to *maltreat:*—handle shamefully.

822. ἀτμίς, atmis, *at-mece´*; from the same as 109; *mist:*—vapour.

823. ἄτομος, atomos, *at´-om-os*; from 1 (as a negative particle) and the base of 5114; *uncut*, i.e. (by implication) *indivisible* [an "atom" of time]:—moment.

824. ἄτοπος, atopos, *at´-op-os*; from 1 (as a negative particle) and 5117; *out of place*, i.e. (figurative) *improper, injurious, wicked:*—amiss, harm, unreasonable.

825. Ἀττάλεια, Attaleia, *at-tal´-i-ah*; from Ἄτταλος, *Attalos* (a king of Pergamus); *Attaleia,* a place in Pamphylia:—Attalia.

826. αὐγάζω, augazō, *ow-gad´-zo*; from 827; to *beam* forth (figurative):—shine.

From *augḗ* (827), dawn. Used transitively: to illuminate; intransitively: to shine (2Co 4:4; irradiate, beam, shine forth; Sept.: Le 13:24–26, 28).

Deriv.: *diaugázō* (1306), to shine through.

Syn.: *phaínō* (5316), to cause to appear, to shine; *epiphaínō* (2014), to shine upon, give light; *lámpō* (2989), to shine as a torch; *eklámpō* (1584), to shine forth; *astráptō* (797), to flash as lightning; *periastráptō* (4015), to flash around; *epiphaúskō* or *epiphaúō* (2017), to shine forth; *phōtízō* (5461), to illuminate; *anáptō* (381), to kindle, light.

827. αὐγή, augḗ, *owg-ay´*; of uncertain derivative; a *ray* of light, i.e. (by implication) *radiance, dawn:*—break of day.

A noun meaning brightness, light; spoken of the light of day, the sun, etc. (Ac 20:11; Sept.: Isa 59:9).

Deriv.: *augázō* (826), to shine.

Syn.: *órthros* (3722), dawn.

828. Αὔγουστος, Augoustos, *ow´-goos-tos*; from Latin ["august"]; *Augustus,* a title of the Roman emperor:—Augustus.

829. αὐθάδης, authadēs, *ow-thad´-ace*; from 846 and the base of 2237; *self-pleasing,* i.e. *arrogant:*—self-willed.

Adjective from *autós* (846), himself, and *hḗdomai* (n.f.), to please. Self-complacent; by implication: assuming, arrogant, imperious (Tit 1:7; 2Pe 2:10; Sept.: Ge 49:3, 7; Pr 21:24). Also from *hḗdomai* (n.f.): *asménōs* (780): gladly, with joy.

Syn.: *phílautos* (5367), loving self, selfish; *propetḗs* (4312), precipitous, headlong, heady, rash; *hubristḗs* (5197), an insulter.

830. αὐθαίρετος, authairetos, *ow-thah´ee-ret-os*; from 846 and the same as 140; *self-chosen,* i.e. (by implication) *voluntary:*—of own accord, willing of self.

831. αὐθεντέω, authenteō, *ow-then-teh´-o*; from a compound of 846 and an obsolete ἕν-της, *hentēs* (a *worker*); to *act of oneself,* i.e. (figurative) *dominate:*—usurp authority over.

832. αὐλέω, auleō, *ow-leh´-o*; from 836; to play the *flute:*—pipe.

833. αὐλή, aulē, *ow-lay´*; from the same as 109; a *yard* (as open to the *wind*); (by implication) a *mansion:*—court, ([sheep-]) fold, hall, palace.

834. αὐλητής, aulētēs, *ow-lay-tace´*; from 832; a *flute-player:*—minstrel, piper.

835. αὐλίζομαι, aulizomai, *ow-lid´-zom-ahee*; middle from 833; to *pass the night* (properly in the open air):—abide, lodge.

836. αὐλός, aulos, *ow-los´*; from the same as 109, a *flute* (as *blown*):—pipe.

837. αὐξάνω, auxanō, *owx-an´-o*; a prolonged form of a primary verb; to *grow* ("*wax*"), i.e. *enlarge* (literal or figurative, active or passive):—grow (up), (give the) increase.

838. αὔξησις, auxēsis, *owx´-ay-sis*; from 837; *growth:*—increase.

839. αὔριον, aurion, *ow´-ree-on*; from a derivative of the same as 109 (meaning a *breeze*, i.e. the morning *air*); properly *fresh,* i.e. (adverb with ellipsis of 2250) *to-morrow:*—(to-) morrow, next day.

840. αὐστηρός, austeros, *ow-stay-ros´*; from a (presumed) derivative of the same as 109 (meaning *blown*); *rough* (properly as a *gale*), i.e. (figurative) *severe:*—austere.

Adjective meaning austere, exacting (Lk 19:21, 22).

Syn.: *chalepós* (5467), difficult, furious, perilous; *oxús* (3691), sharp; *pikrós* (4089), bitter.

841. αὐτάρκεια, autarkeia, *ow-tar´-ki-ah*; from 842; *self-satisfaction,* i.e. (abstract) *contentedness,* or (concrete) a *competence:*—contentment, sufficiency.

842. αὐτάρκης, autarkēs, *ow-tar´-kace*; from 846 and 714; *self-complacent,* i.e. *contented:*—content.

843. αὐτοκατάκριτος, autokatakritos, *ow-tok-at-ak´-ree-tos*; from 846 and a derivative of 2632; *self-condemned:*—con-demned of self.

Adjective from *autós* (846), himself, and *katakrínō* (2632), to condemn. Self-condemned, condemned by one's own decision (Tit 3:11).

844. αὐτόματος, automatos, *ow-tom´-at-os*; from 846 and the same as 3155; *self-moved* ["automatic"], i.e. *spontaneous:*—of own accord, of self.

845. αὐτόπτης, autoptēs, *ow-top´-tace*; from 846 and 3700; *self-seeing,* i.e. an *eyewitness:*—eyewitness.

846. αὐτός, autos, *ow-tos´*; from the particle **αὖ,** *au*; [perhaps akin to the base of 109 through the idea of a *baffling* wind] (*backward*); the reflexive pronoun *self,* used (alone or in the compound 1438) of the third person, and, (with the properly personal pronoun) of the other persons:—her, it (-self), one, the other, (mine) own, said, ([self-], the) same, ([him-, my-, thy-]) self, [your-] selves, she, that, their (-s), them ([-selves]), there [-at, -by, -in, -into, -of, -on, -with], they, (these) things, this (man), those, together, very, which. Compare 848.

847. αὐτοῦ, autou, *ow-too´*; genitive (i.e. possessive) of 846, used as an adverb of location; properly belonging to the *same* spot, i.e. *in this* (or *that*) *place:*—(t-) here.

848. αὑτοῦ, hautou, *how-too´*; contracted from 1438; *self* (in some oblique case or reflexive relation):—her (own), (of) him (-self), his (own), of it, thee, their (own), them (-selves), they.

849. αὐτόχειρ, autocheir, *ow-tokh´-ire*; from 846 and 5495; *self-handed,* i.e. doing *personally:*—with … own hands.

850. αὐχμηρός, auchmēros, *owkh-may-ros´*; from **αὐχμός,** *auchmos*; [probably from a base akin to that of 109] (*dust,* as *dried* by wind); properly *dirty,* i.e. (by implication) *obscure:*—dark.

851. ἀφαιρέω, aphaireō, *af-ahee-reh´-o*; from 575 and 138; to *remove* (literal or figurative):—cut (smite) off, take away.

852. ἀφανής, aphanēs, *af-an-ace´*; from 1 (as a negative particle) and 5316; *non-apparent:*—that is not manifest.

853. ἀφανίζω, aphanizō, *af-an-id´-zo*; from 852; to *render unapparent,* i.e. (active) *consume* (*becloud*), or (passive) *disappear* (*be destroyed*):—corrupt, disfigure, perish, vanish away.

854. ἀφανισμός, aphanismos, *af-an-is-mos´*; from 853; *disappearance,* i.e. (figurative) *abrogation:*—vanish away.

855. ἄφαντος, aphantos, *af´-an-tos*; from 1 (as a negative particle) and a derivative of 5316; *non-manifested,* i.e. *invisible:*—vanished out of sight.

856. ἀφεδρών, aphedrōn, *af-ed-rone´*; from a compound of 575 and the base of 1476; a place of *sitting apart,* i.e. a *privy:*—draught.

857. ἀφειδία, apheidia, *af-i-dee´-ah*; from a compound of 1 (as a negative particle) and 5339; *unsparingness,* i.e. *austerity* (*ascetism*):—neglecting.

858. ἀφελότης, aphelotēs, *af-el-ot´-ace*; from a compound of 1 (as a negative particle) and **φέλλος,** *phellos* (in the sense of a *stone* as *stubbing* the foot); *smoothness,* i.e. (figurative) *simplicity:*—singleness.

859. ἄφεσις, aphesis, *af´-es-is*; from 863; *freedom*; (figurative) *pardon:*—deliverance, forgiveness, liberty, remission.

Noun from *aphíēmi* (863), to cause to stand away, to release one's sins from the sinner. Dismission, i.e. deliverance from service, captivity, etc. (Lk 4:18; Sept.: Isa 63:6; Le 25:10). Also remission, i.e. forgiveness, pardon of sins (Mk 1:4; 3:29; Lk 1:77; 3:3; 4:18; 24:47; Ac 2:38; 5:31; 10:43; 13:38; 26:18; Eph 1:7; Col 1:14; Heb 9:22; 10:18; Sept.: Le 25:11; Dt 15:3; Est 2:18; Isa 61:1).

Syn.: *apolútrōsis* (629), redemption; *ánesis* (425), a relaxing, letting loose; *aníēmi* (441), to stand up or to provide liberty or rest; *eleuthería* (1657), freedom, which is the resultant effect of forgiveness or *áphesis*; *hilasmós* (2434), atonement, propitiation; *cháris* (5485), grace (indicating the disposition of the one forgiving, while *áphesis* expresses the result of the acceptance of that grace; *sōtēría* (4991), salvation, deliverance; *dikaíōsis* (1347), justification, being more than acquittal since it also renders a person just.

860. ἀφή, haphē, *haf-ay´*; from 680; probably a *ligament* (as *fastening*):—joint.

861. ἀφθαρσία, aphtharsia, *af-thar-see´-ah*; from 862; *incorruptibility*; genitive *unending existence*; (figurative) *genuineness:*—immortality, incorruption, sincerity.

862. ἄφθαρτος, aphthartos, *af´-thar-tos*; from 1 (as a negative particle) and a derivative of 5351; *undecaying* (in essence or continuance):—not (in-, un-) corruptible, immortal.

Adjective from the priv. *a* (1), not, and *phthartós* (n.f.), corruptible, which is from *phtheírō* (5351), to corrupt. Incorruptible, i.e. spoken of persons: immortal, as God (Ro 1:23; 1Ti 1:17); the future bodies of saints (1Co 15:52). Spoken also of things: imperishable, enduring (1Co 9:25; 1Pe 1:4, 23; 3:4).

Deriv.: *aphtharsía* (861), incorruptibility.

Syn.: *akatálutos* (179), indissoluble, permanent, endless; *aiṓnios* (166), eternal, perpetual; *akéraios* (185), unmixed, unaffected.

863. ἀφίημι, aphiēmi, *af-ee´-ay-mee*; from 575 and ἵημι, *hiēmi* (to *send*; an intensive form of εἶμι, *eimi*; to *go*); to *send forth*, in various applications (as follow):—cry, forgive, forsake, lay aside, leave, let (alone, be, go, have), omit, put (send) away, remit, suffer, yield up.

From *apó* (575), from, and *hiēmi* (n.f., see *iós* [2447]), to send. To send forth or away, let go from oneself:

(I) To dismiss, e.g., the multitudes (Mt 13:36); to give up or let go (Mt 27:50; Mk 15:37); of a wife: to put her away (1Co 7:11–13).

(II) To let go from one's power, possession, to let go free, let escape (Mt 24:40, 41; Lk 17:34–36; Sept.: Pr 4:13). Metaphorically: to let go from obligation toward oneself, to remit, e.g., a debt, offence (Mt 18:27, 32, 35; Mk 11:25; Sept.: Dt 15:2). Of sins: to remit the penalty of sins, i.e. to pardon, forgive, e.g., *opheilḗmata* (3783), debts, faults (Mt 6:12); *hamartías* (266), sins (Mt 9:2, 5, 6; 12:31; Mk 2:5, 7, 9, 10); *blasphēmían* (988), blasphemy, evil speaking (Mt 12:31, 32); *paraptṓmata* (3900), trespasses, offenses (Mt 6:14, 15; Mk 11:25); *hamartḗmata* (265), individual sins (Mk 3:28; 4:12); *anomías* (458), iniquities, acts of lawlessness (Ro 4:7). Also Sept.: Ge 50:17; Ex 32:32; Le 4:20; 5:10, 13; Ps 25:18; 32:5; Isa 22:14; 55:7.

(III) To let go from one's further notice, care, attendance, occupancy, i.e. to leave or let alone:

(A) Spoken of persons: to quit, forsake or abandon (Mt 4:11; 8:15; 15:14; 26:44, 56; Mk 4:36; Jn 10:12). Of things: to leave, abandon, e.g., the nets (Mt 4:20); the house (Mk 13:34); Judea (Jn 4:3); all things (Mt 19:27, 29). See also Sept.: 1Sa 17:20, 28; Jer 12:7. To leave in any

place or state, let remain (Mt 5:24; 18:12; Mk 1:20; Lk 10:30; Jn 4:28; 8:29; 14:18, 27; 16:32; Ac 14:17; Sept.: Ge 42:33; Ex 9:21; 2Sa 15:16; 1Ki 19:3; 1Ch 16:21). To leave to anyone, i.e. to let him have or take (Mt 5:40). To leave behind, as at death (Mt 22:25; Mk 12:19–22; Sept.: Ps 17:14; Ecc 2:18). To leave remaining, and in the pass., to be left, remain (Mt 23:38; 24:2; Mk 13:2; Lk 13:35; 19:44; 21:6; Heb 2:8; Sept.: Jgs 2:23; 3:1).

(B) Metaphorically, in various senses: to leave, desert, quit (Ro 1:27, "the natural use"; Rev 2:4). To omit, pass by (Heb 6:1, leaving the word of the beginning). To neglect, to omit (Mt 23:23; Mk 7:8; Lk 11:42; Sept.: Ecc 11:6).

(IV) To let go, i.e. to let pass, permit (Mt 8:22; 13:30; 19:14; Mk 1:34; 5:37). Followed by *hína* (2443), so that, after verbs of command (Mk 11:16). The imper. *áphes* (sing.) and *áphete* (pl.) are followed by the subjunctive without *hína*, e.g., *áphes ídōmen* (first person plural 2d aor. subjunctive of *horáō* [3708], to see, let us see, suffer us to see [Mt 27:49; Mk 15:36]); Mt 7:4, "Let me pull out"; Lk 6:42.

Deriv.: *áphesis* (859), remission, forgiveness.

Syn.: *paúō* (3973), to stop, quit; *katapaúō* (2664), to cease; *katargéō* (2673), to render inactive; *charízomai* (5483), to bestow a favour, to forgive; *apolúō* (630), to release, dismiss; *kataleípō* (2641), to leave behind; *egkataleípō* (1459), to forsake, abandon; *apotássō* (657), to place in order away from oneself; *apotíthēmi* (659), to put off from oneself; *apoleípō* (620), to remain; *perileípō* (4035), to leave around; *eáō* (1439), to let, permit; *hupolimpánō* (5277), a late form of *leípō* (3007), to leave; *epitrépō* (2010), to permit; *apotíthēmi* (659), to put away; *chōrízō* (5563), to separate; *apostréphō* (654), to turn away; *apōthéomai* (683), to thrust away; *lúō* (3089), to loose; *pémpō* (3992), to send.

864. ἀφικνέομαι, aphikneomai, *af-ik-neh´-om-ahee*; from 575 and the base of 2425; to *go* (i.e. *spread*) *forth* (by rumour):—come abroad.

865. ἀφιλάγαθος, aphilagathos, *af-il-ag´-ath-os*; from 1 (as a negative particle) and 5358; *hostile to virtue*:—despiser of those that are good.

Adjective from the priv. *a* (1), and *philágathos* (5358), a lover of being good. Unfriendly, hostile to good men. Only in 2Ti 3:3.

Syn.: *kakós* (2556), bad; *phaúlos* (5337), foul, trivial; *aischrós* (150), shameful; *átimos* (820), without honour; *achreíos* (888), useless, unprofitable; *kataphronetés* (2707), a despiser.

866. ἀφιλάργυρος, aphilarguros, *af-il-ar´-goo-ros*; from 1 (as a negative particle) and 5366; *unavaricious:*—without covetousness, not greedy of filthy lucre.

867. ἄφιξις, aphixis, *af´-ix-is*; from 864; properly *arrival*, i.e. (by implication) *departure:*—departing.

868. ἀφίστημι, aphistēmi, *af-is´-tay-mee*; from 575 and 2476; to *remove*, i.e. (active) *instigate* to revolt; usually (reflexive) to *desist, desert*, etc.:—depart, draw (fall) away, refrain, withdraw self.

From *apó*, from, and *hístēmi* (2476), to stand, to place:

(**I**) Transitively: to place away from, to separate, i.e. to remove, to cause to depart. In the NT, to lead away, to seduce, as a people from their allegiance (Ac 5:37).

(**II**) Intransitively: to separate oneself, to depart:

(**A**) Generally: to go away from, to leave (Lk 2:37; 4:13; Ac 12:10; 19:9). In the sense of to forsake, to desert (Ac 15:38). In the sense of to withdraw from, to avoid (1Ti 6:5; 2Ti 2:19).

(**B**) Metaphorically: to desist from, to refrain from, to let alone (Ac 5:38; 22:29; 2Co 12:8; Sept.: Job 7:16; 1Sa 6:3).

(**C**) To make defection from, to revolt, to apostatize (Lk 8:13; 1Ti 4:1; Heb 3:12).

Deriv.: *apostasía* (646), apostasy, staying away from; *apostásion* (647), separative, divorce.

Syn.: *apolúō* (630), to depart, dismiss; *apospáō* (645), to draw away; *apochōrízō* (673), to separate, depart from; *apochōréō* (672), to depart from; *hupágō* (5217), to depart, go; *apérchomai* (565), to depart; *apopíptō* (634), to fall from.

869. ἄφνω, aphnō, *af´-no*; adverb from 852 (contraction); *unawares*, i.e. *unexpectedly:*—suddenly.

870. ἀφόβως, aphobōs, *af-ob´-oce*; adverb from a compound of 1 (as a negative particle) and 5401; *fearlessly:*—without fear.

871. ἀφομοιόω, aphomoioō, *af-om-oy-o´-o*; from 575 and 3666; to *assimilate* closely:—make like.

872. ἀφοράω, aphoraō, *af-or-ah´-o*; from 575 and 3708; to *consider* attentively:—look.

873. ἀφορίζω, aphorizō, *af-or-id´-zo*; from 575 and 3724; to *set off* by boundary, i.e. (figurative) *limit, exclude, appoint*, etc.:—divide, separate, sever.

From *apó* (575), from, and *horízō* (3724), to define. To set off by bounds. In the NT, to set off apart, to separate (Mt 13:49; 25:32 [cf. Ac 19:9]; 2Co 6:17; Gal 2:12; Sept.: Le 20:25; Isa 56:3); to set apart for something, to select, to choose (Ac 13:2; Ro 1:1; Gal 1:15). In the sense of to excommunicate (Lk 6:22).

Syn.: *diakrínō* (1252), to separate; *chōrízō* (5563), to separate; *apodiorízō* (592), to mark off, separate; *katargéō* (2673), to reduce to inactivity; *diachōrízō* (1316), to remove completely; *arnéomai* (720), to disavow; *antitássō* (498), to oppose; *aporríptō* (641), to reject; *periphronéō* (4065), despise; *apōthéomai* (683), to push off, reject; *periphronéō* (4065), to depreciate, despise; *apotrépō* (665), to avoid, turn away; *apophérō* (667), to bear off; *aparnéomai* (533), to deny utterly, disown; *apotássomai* (657), to put in one's proper category away from self.

874. ἀφορμή, aphormē, *af-or-may´*; from a compound of 575 and 3729; a *starting*-point, i.e. (figurative) an *opportunity:*—occasion.

875. ἀφρίζω, aphrizō, *af-rid´-zo*; from 876; to *froth* at the mouth (in epilepsy):—foam.

876. ἀφρός, aphros, *af-ros´*; apparently a primary word; *froth*, i.e. *slaver:*—foaming.

877. ἀφροσύνη, aphrosunē, *af-ros-oo´-nay*; from 878; *senselessness*, i.e. (euphemistic) *egotism*; (moral) *recklessness:*—folly, foolishly (-ness).

878. ἄφρων, aphrōn, *af´-rone*; from 1 (as a negative particle) and 5424; properly *mindless*, i.e. *stupid*, (by implication) *ignorant*, (special) *egotistic*, (practically) *rash*, or (moral) *unbelieving:*—fool (-ish), unwise.

879. ἀφυπνόω, aphupnoō, *af-oop-no´-o*; from a compound of 575 and 5258; properly to *become awake*, i.e. (by implication) to *drop* (off) in slumber:—fall asleep.

880. ἄφωνος, aphōnos, *af´-o-nos*; from 1 (as a negative particle) and 5456; *voiceless*, i.e. *mute* (by nature or choice); (figurative) *unmeaning*:—dumb, without signification.

881. Ἀχάζ, Achaz, *akh-adz´*; of Hebrew origin [271]; *Achaz,* an Israelite:—Achaz.

882. Ἀχαΐα, Achaïa, *ach-ah-ee´-ah*; of uncertain derivative; *Achaïa* (i.e. *Greece*), a country of Europe:—Achaia.

883. Ἀχαϊκός, Achaïkos, *ach-ah-ee-kos´*; from 882; an *Achaïan; Achaïus,* a Christian:—Achaicus.

884. ἀχάριστος, acharistos, *ach-ar´-is-tos*; from 1 (as a negative particle) and a presumed derivative of 5483; *thankless,* i.e. *ungrateful*:—unthankful.

885. Ἀχείμ, Acheim, *akh-ime´*; probably of Hebrew origin [compare 3137]; *Achim,* an Israelite:—Achim.

886. ἀχειροποίητος, acheiropoiētos, *akh-i-rop-oy´-ay-tos*; from 1 (as a negative particle) and 5499; *unmanufactured,* i.e. *inartificial*:—made without (not made with) hands.

887. ἀχλύς, achlus, *akh-looce´*; of uncertain derivative; *dimness* of sight, i.e. (probably) a *cataract*:—mist.

A noun meaning thick mist, cloud, darkness, which shrouds objects from view. In the NT, spoken of the eyes: a mist before the eyes (Ac 13:11).

Syn.: *skótos* (4655), darkness; *gnóphos* (1105), a thick dark cloud; *zóphos* (2217), thick darkness resulting from foggy weather or smoke; *néphos* (3509), cloud; *nephélē* (3507), a definitely shaped cloud.

888. ἀχρεῖος, achreios, *akh-ri´-os*; from 1 (as a negative particle) and a derivative of 5534 [compare 5532]; *useless,* i.e. (euphemism) *unmeritorious*:—unprofitable.

Adjective from the priv. *a* (1), without, and *chreía* (5532), utility, usefulness. Unprofitable, useless. In the NT, by implication: slothful, wicked (Mt 25:30 [cf. Mt 25:26]); spoken in humility: humble, of little value (Lk 17:10, humble, of little value; Sept.: 2Sa 6:22).

Deriv.: *achreióō* (889), to render useless, to become unprofitable.

Syn.: *áchrēstos* (890), unprofitable, useless; *alusitelḗs* (255), not advantageous, not useful; *anōphelḗs* (512), not serviceable, unprofitable, useless; *kenós* (2756), empty, vain; *mátaios* (3152), vain, empty, profitless; *adókimos* (96), unapproved, unfit; *alusitelḗs* (255), unprofitable, useless.

889. ἀχρειόω, achreioō, *akh-ri-o´-o*; from 888; to *render useless,* i.e. *spoil*:—become unprofitable.

890. ἄχρηστος, achrēstos, *akh´-race-tos*; from 1 (as a negative particle) and 5543; *inefficient,* i.e. (by implication) *detrimental*:—unprofitable.

Adjective from the priv. *a* (1), without, and *chrēstós* (5543), profitable. Unprofitable, useless. In the NT, metaphorically and by implication: worse than useless, wicked, detrimental (Phm 11 [see Phm 18]).

Syn.: *achreíos* (888), unprofitable.

891. ἄχρι, achri, *akh´-ree*; or ἄχρις, *achris, akh´-rece*; akin to 206 (through the idea of a *terminus*); (of time) *until* or (of place) *up to*:—as far as, for, in (-to), till, (even, un-) to, until, while. Compare 3360.

892. ἄχυρον, achuron, *akh´-oo-ron*; perhaps remotely from χέω, *cheō* (to *shed* forth); *chaff* (as *diffusive*):—chaff.

893. ἀψευδής, apseudēs, *aps-yoo-dace´*; from 1 (as a negative particle) and 5579; *veracious*:—that cannot lie.

894. ἄψινθος, apsinthos, *ap´-sin-thos*; of uncertain derivative; *wormwood* (as a type of *bitterness,* i.e. [figurative] *calamity*):—wormwood.

895. ἄψυχος, apsuchos, *ap´-soo-khos*; from 1 (as a negative particle) and 5590; *lifeless,* i.e. *inanimate* (mechanical):—without life.

Adjective from the priv. *a* (1), without, and *psuchḗ* (5590), soul or the breath of life. Lifeless, inanimate, void of sense and life (1Co 14:7).

Syn.: *adúnatos* (102), weak; *asthenḗs* (772), without strength, sick; *nekrós* (3498), dead.

β (Beta)

NT Numbers 896–1041

896. Βάαλ, Baal, *bah´-al*; of Hebrew origin [1168]; *Baal*, a Phoenician deity (used as a symbol of idolatry):—Baal.

897. Βαβυλών, Babulōn, *bab-oo-lone´*; of Hebrew origin [894]; *Babylon*, the capital of Chaldæa (literal or figurative [as a type of tyranny]):—Babylon.

898. βαθμός, bathmos, *bath-mos´*; from the same as 899; a *step*, i.e. (figurative) *grade* (of dignity):—degree.

899. βάθος, bathos, *bath´-os*; from the same as 901; *profundity*, i.e. (by implication) *extent*; (figurative) *mystery*:—deep (-ness, things), depth.

900. βαθύνω, bathunō, *bath-oo´-no*; from 901; to *deepen*:—deep.

901. βαθύς, bathus, *bath-oos´*; from the base of 939; *profound* (as *going* down), literal or figurative:—deep, very early.

902. βαΐον, baïon, *bah-ee´-on*; a diminutive of a derivative probably of the base of 939; a palm *twig* (as *going* out far):—branch.

903. Βαλαάμ, Balaam, *bal-ah-am´*; of Hebrew origin [1109]; *Balaam*, a Mesopotamian (symbolic of a false teacher):—Balaam.

904. Βαλάκ, Balak, *bal-ak´*; of Hebrew origin [1111]; *Balak*, a Moabite:—Balac.

905. βαλάντιον, balantion, *bal-an´-tee-on*; probably remotely from 906 (as a *depository*); a *pouch* (for money):—bag, purse.

906. βάλλω, ballō, *bal´-lo*; a primary verb; to *throw* (in various applications, more or less violent or intense):—arise, cast (out), × dung, lay, lie, pour, put (up), send, strike, throw (down), thrust. Compare 4496.

To cast, throw:

(I) To cast lots (Mt 27:35; Mk 15:24; Lk 23:25; Sept.: 1Sa 14:42; Ne 10:34; 11:1). Spoken of a tree: to cast its fruit (Rev 6:13). To cast oneself, and with *kátō* (2736), down, to cast oneself down (Mt 4:6; Lk 4:9). Followed by the dat. as in Mt 15:26; Mk 7:27, to cast to or before anyone; Mt 25:27, to put out or place out money with the brokers. When used with different prep. and particles, the meaning is altered accordingly, but with the idea of throwing always maintained:

(A) Followed by *apó* (575), from: to throw from one, cast away (Mt 5:29; 18:8, 9).

(B) Followed by *ek* (1537), out of: to cast out of the mouth, to vomit (Rev 12:15, 16).

(C) Followed by *éxō* (1854), away, forth, out, out of: to cast out or throw away, reject (Mt 5:13; 13:48; Lk 14:35; Jn 15:6).

(D) Followed by *eis* (1519), into: to cast into, i.e. a bed (Rev 2:22); the fire (Mt 3:10; 5:29; 6:30; 13:42; Mk 9:22, 45; Sept.: Da 3:21, 24); the sea (Mt 21:21; Mk 11:23; Rev 18:21); of nets: to cast into or let down into the sea (Mt 4:18; 13:47; Sept.: Isa 19:8); to cast into prison (Mt 18:30; Lk 12:58; Ac 16:37); to cast contributions of money into a treasury (Mk 12:41, 43; Lk 21:1, 4); to deposit (Mt 27:6); of a sword: to thrust into the sheath, to put away (Jn 18:11); of a sickle (Rev 14:19); of the finger, hand: to thrust into, put into (Mk 7:33; Jn 20:27 [cf. Sept.: Job 28:9]; Da 11:42 [*ekteínō* {1614}, to stretch forth]); to put or place bits in horses' mouths (Jas 3:3). Spoken of liquids as wine and water where we can only translate by saying to put or pour into (Mt 9:17; Mk 2:22; Lk 5:37; Jn 13:5; Sept.: Jgs 6:19). Metaphorically: to put into one's heart, suggest to one's mind (Jn 13:2).

(E) Followed by *émprosthen* (1715), in front of, or *enṓpion* (1799), before, meaning to cast before anyone or anything (Mt 7:6; Rev 2:14; 4:10).

(F) Followed by *epí* (1909), upon: to cast upon, as the seed upon the earth, to sow, scatter seed (Mk 4:26; Sept.: Ps 126:6); to cast stones at anyone (Jn 8:7, 59; Sept.: Ecc 3:5; Isa 37:33;

Eze 21:22); to send peace upon the earth (Mt 10:34); to put upon, impose (Rev 2:24). Spoken of a sickle: to thrust in (Rev 14:16). Spoken of liquids: to pour (Mt 26:12 [see also Mt 26:7]).

(II) Perf. and pluperf. pass., *béblēmai*, to be cast, meaning to be laid down, to lie, equivalent to *keímai* (2749), to lie outstretched (Mt 8:6, a paralytic was lying in the house [see Mt 8:14]); laid on a bed (Mt 9:2; Mk 7:30) laid at a gate (Lk 16:20).

(III) With the accusative of person, to throw at anyone (Mk 14:65, "they threw at him with blows" [a.t.], means they gave him blows). See Sept.: 2Ch 26:15; Ps 78:9.

(IV) Intransitively or with *heautón* [(1438), himself] implied: to cast oneself, to rush forward; as spoken of a wind: to blow (Ac 27:14).

Deriv.: *anabállō* (306), to defer, put off; *antibállō* (474), to have; *apobállō* (577), to throw off from, lay aside; *bélos* (956), a missile; *blētéos* (992), that which one must put out; *bolé* (1000), a throw; *bolís* (1002), dart; *diabállō* (1225), to throw in between; *ekbállō* (1544), to cast out of or from; *embállō* (1685), to cast into; *epibállō* (1911), to cast upon; *katabállō* (2598), to cast down or around; *lithoboléō* (3036), to cast stones; *metabállō* (3328), to throw over, change mind; *parabállō* (3846), to arrive, compare; *peribállō* (4016), to cast about; *probállō* (4261), to put forward; *sumbállō* (4820), to confer, encounter; *huperbállō* (5235), to excel, pass; *hupobállō* (5260), to suborn.

Syn.: With the meaning of to cast: *rhíptō* (4496), to throw with a certain motion; *apōthéō* (683), to thrust away; *apotíthēmi* (659), to put off; *ektíthēmi* (1620), to expose, cast out; *kathairéō* (2507), to cast down, demolish. With the meaning of to lay down: *títhēmi* (5087), to put or place, set; *anaklínō* (347), to lay down; *keímai* (2749), to lie; *apókeimai* (606), to be laid away or up, as money in a box or purse; *katákeimai* (2621), to lie down; *epíkeimai* (1945), to lie upon; *epipíptō* (1968), to fall upon; *anákeimai* (345), to be laid up, to lie. With the meaning of to pour as liquids: *katachéō* (2708), to pour down upon; *ekchéō* (1632), to pour out of; *ekchúnō* (1632), to pour out, shed; *epichéō* (2022), to pour upon. With the meaning of to put: *títhēmi* (5087), to place, lay, set; *apolúō* (630), to let go, dismiss; *aphíēmi* (863), to send away; *periairéō* (4014), to take away; *exaírō* (1808), to put away from; *apekdúō* (554), to strip off clothes

or arms; *methístēmi* (3179), to remove; *anágō* (321), to lead or bring up; *endúō* (1746), to put on oneself; *embibázō* (1688), to put in; *probibázō* (4264), to put forward; *apostréphō* (654), to turn away, remove; *ekteínō* (1614), to stretch forth; *lúō* (3089), to loose. With the meaning of to send: *apostéllō* (649), to send forth; *pémpō* (3992), to send; *apotássomai* (657), to place in a proper order away from oneself. With the meaning of thrust: *katatoxeúō* (2700), to strike down with an arrow; *exōthéō* (1856), to drive out.

907. βαπτίζω, baptizō, *bap-tid´-zo*; from a derivative of 911; to *make whelmed* (i.e. *fully wet*); used only (in the NT) of ceremonial *ablution*, especially (technical) of the ordinance of Christian *baptism*:—baptist, baptize, wash.

From *báptō* (911), to dip. Immerse, submerge for a religious purpose, to overwhelm, saturate, baptize:

(I) To wash, to cleanse by washing; in the middle, to wash oneself, to bathe, to perform ablution (Mk 7:4 [cf. v. 3, where the phrase "wash their hands" is the translation of *níptō* (3538), to wash part of the body]).

(II) To baptize, to administer the rite of baptism, either that of John or Christ. Pass. and middle: to be baptized or to cause oneself to be baptized. In the early churches, where, according to oriental habits, bathing was to them what washing is to us, the rite appears to have been ordinarily, though not necessarily, performed by immersion.

(A) Spoken of simply (Mt 3:6, 11; Mk 1:4, 5, 8, 9; Lk 3:7, 12, 16, 21; 7:30; Jn 1:25, 28; 3:22, 23, 26; 4:1, 2; 10:40; Ac 2:38, 41; 8:12, 13, 36, 38; 9:18; 10:47; 16:15, 33; 18:8; 22:16; 1Co 1:14, 16, 17).

(B) With adjuncts marking the object and effect of baptism: especially *eis* (1519), into, unto: to baptize or to be baptized into anything, meaning into the belief, profession, or observance of anything (Mt 3:11, "unto repentance"; Ac 2:38; 19:3; Ro 6:3; 1Co 12:13). Spoken of persons, it means to baptize or be baptized into a profession of faith or into anyone, in sincere obedience to him. Also in 1Co 10:2, "unto Moses"; Gal 3:27, "unto Christ"; also "into the name of someone" means to be identified with what the name of that one stands for (Mt 28:19; Ac 8:16; 19:5; 1Co 1:13, 15). The same sense is understood when the prep. *epí* [(1909), upon], or *en* [(1722), in], followed by *onómati* [(3686), name], is used (Ac

2:38, *epí*; 10:48, *en*). With *hupér* (5228), on behalf of or for (1Co 15:29, those being "baptized for [or on account of] the dead," i.e. on a belief of the resurrection of the dead).

(III) Metaphorically and in direct allusion to the practice of water baptism: to baptize in or with the Holy Spirit and in or with fire, the baptism in the Holy Spirit being the spiritual counterpart of the water baptism (Mt 3:11; Mk 1:8; Lk 3:16; Jn 1:33; Ac 1:5; 11:16).

(IV) Metaphorically, in connection with calamities: to baptize with calamities, i.e. to be overwhelmed with sufferings (Mt 20:22, 23; Mk 10:38, 39). In 1Co 15:29, "What shall those being baptized for the dead do? Why therefore are they baptized on their behalf?" (a.t.) means if the dead do not rise, why expose ourselves to so much danger and suffering in the hope of a resurrection?

Deriv.: *báptisma* (908), baptism, the result of baptizing; *baptismós* (909), the ceremonial washing of articles; *baptistḗs* (910), baptist, used of John to qualify him as one baptizing.

Syn.: *buthízō* (1036), to sink, but not necessarily to drown; *katapontízō* (2670), to plunge down, submerge; *embáptō* (1686), to dip.

908. βάπτισμα, baptisma, *bap´-tis-mah*; from 907; *baptism* (technical or figurative):—baptism.

Noun from *báptō* (911), to dip. Something immersed. In the NT, baptism, spoken of the rite, e.g., of John's baptism (Mt 3:7; 21:25; Mk 1:4; 11:30; Lk 3:3; 7:29; 20:4; Ac 1:22; 10:37; 13:24; 18:25; 19:3, 4); of the baptism instituted by Jesus (Ro 6:4; Eph 4:5; Col 2:12; 1Pe 3:21). Metaphorically: baptism into calamity, i.e. afflictions with which one is oppressed or overwhelmed (Mt 20:22, 23; Mk 10:38, 39; Lk 12:50).

909. βαπτισμός, baptismos, *bap-tis-mos´*; from 907; *ablution* (ceremony or Christian):—baptism, washing.

Noun from *baptízō* (907), to baptize. Washing, ablution of vessels, etc. (Mk 7:4, 8; Heb 6:2; Sept.: Le 11:32). Baptism, i.e. the Christian rite (Heb 6:2).

Syn.: *loutrón* (3067), a bath, metaphorically meaning the Word of God which, when believed, brings spiritual cleansing.

910. Βαπτιστής, Baptistēs, *bap-tis-tace´*; from 907; a *baptizer*, as an epithet of Christ's forerunner:—Baptist.

Noun from *baptízō* (907), to baptize. A baptizer or baptist, referring to John the Baptist (Mt 3:1; 11:11, 12; 14:2, 8; 16:14; 17:13; Mk 6:24, 25; 8:28; Lk 7:20, 28, 33; 9:19).

911. βάπτω, baptō, *bap´-to*; a primary verb; to *whelm*, i.e. cover wholly with a fluid; in the NT only in a qualified or special sense, i.e. (literal) to *moisten* (a part of one's person), or (by implication) to *stain* (as with dye):—dip.

To immerse, dip, transitively (Lk 16:24 of the thing touched; Jn 13:26). To dye by dipping (Rev 19:13, to tinge, dye). As a compound with the prep. *en*, in, *embáptō* (1686), to dip in (Mt 26:23; Mk 14:20; Sept.: Le 4:6; 14:6; Nu 19:18; Ru 2:14; 2Ki 8:15; Job 9:31).

Deriv.: *baptízō* (907), to baptize; *embáptō* (1686), to dip in.

912. Βαραββᾶς, Barabbas, *bar-ab-bas´*; of Chaldee origin [1347 and 5]; *son of Abba*; *Barabbas*, an Israelite:—Barabbas.

913. Βαράκ, Barak, *bar-ak´*; of Hebrew origin [1301]; *Barak*, an Israelite:—Barak.

914. Βαραχίας, Barachias, *bar-akh-ee´-as*; of Hebrew origin [1296]; *Barachias* (i.e. *Berechijah*), an Israelite:—Barachias.

915. βάρβαρος, barbaros, *bar´-bar-os*; of uncertain derivative; a *foreigner* (i.e. *non-Greek*):—barbarian (-rous).

916. βαρέω, bareō, *bar-eh´-o*; from 926; to *weigh* down (figurative):—burden, charge, heavy, press.

917. βαρέως, bareōs, *bar-eh´-oce*; adverb from 926; *heavily* (figurative):—dull.

918. Βαρθολομαῖος, Bartholomaios, *bar-thol-om-ah´-yos*; of Chaldee origin [1247 and 8526]; *son of Tolmai*; *Bar-tholomæus*, a Christian apostle:—Bartholomeus.

919. βαριησοῦς, Bariēsous, *bar-ee-ay-sooce´*; of Chaldee origin [1247 and 3091]; *son of Jesus* (or *Joshua*); *Bar-jesus*, an Israelite:—Barjesus.

920. Βαριωνᾶς, Bariōnas, *bar-ee-oo-nas´*; of Chaldee origin [1247 and 3124]; *son of Jonas* (or *Jonah*); *Bar-jonas*, an Israelite:—Bar-jona.

921. Βαρνάβας, Barnabas, *bar-nab´-as*; of Chaldee origin [1247 and 5029]; *son of Nabas* (i.e. *prophecy*); *Barnabas*, an Israelite:—Barnabas.

922. βάρος, baros, *bar´-os*; probably from the same as 939 (through the notion of *going* down; compare 899); *weight*; in the NT only figurative, a *load, abundance, authority*:—burden (-some), weight.

923. Βαρσαβᾶς, Barsabas, *bar-sab-as´*; of Chaldee origin [1247 and probably 6634]; *son of Sabas* (or *Tsaba*); *Bar-sabas*, the name of two Israelites:—Barsabas.

924. Βαρτιμαῖος, Bartimaios, *bar-tim-ah´-yos*; of Chaldee origin [1247 and 2931]; *son of Timæus* (or the *unclean*); *Bar-timæus*, an Israelite:—Bartimæus.

925. βαρύνω, barunō, *bar-oo´-no*; from 926; to *burden* (figurative):—overcharge.

926. βαρύς, barus, *bar-ooce´*; from the same as 922; *weighty*, i.e. (figurative) *burdensome, grave*:—grievous, heavy, weightier.

927. βαρύτιμος, barutimos, *bar-oo´-tim-os*; from 926 and 5092; highly *valuable*:—very precious.

928. βασανίζω, basanizō, *bas-an-id´-zo*; from 931; to *torture*:—pain, toil, torment, toss, vex.

929. βασανισμός, basanismos, *bas-an-is-mos´*; from 928; *torture*:—torment.

930. βασανιστής, basanistēs, *bas-an-is-tace´*; from 928; a *torturer*:—tormentor.

931. βάσανος, basanos, *bas´-an-os*; perhaps remotely from the same as 939 (through the notion of *going* to the bottom); a *touch-stone*, i.e. (by analogy) *torture*:—torment.

932. βασιλεία, basileia, *bas-il-i´-ah*; from 935; properly *royalty*, i.e. (abstract) *rule*, or (concrete) a *realm* (literal or figurative):—kingdom, + reign.

(I) Dominion, reign, the exercise of kingly power (Mt 6:13; Lk 1:33; 19:12, 15; Heb 1:8; Rev 17:12, 17, 18; Sept.: 1Sa 10:16, 25; 13:13; 28:17). In Rev 1:6, the TR has *basileís* (935), kings.

(II) Dominions, realm, i.e. a people in a territory under kingly rule (Mt 4:8; 12:25, 26; 24:7; Mk 3:24; 6:23; 13:8; Lk 4:5; 11:17, 18; 21:10; Heb

11:33; Rev 11:15; 16:10; Sept.: Ge 10:10; Nu 32:33; Jos 11:10; Est 2:3).

(III) The phrases *hē basileía toú Theoú* (2316), "the kingdom of God" (Mt 6:33; Mk 1:15; Lk 4:43; 6:20; Jn 3:5); "his kingdom," referring to Christ (Mt 13:41 [cf. 20:21]); "the kingdom of our father David" (Mk 11:10); "the kingdom of Christ and of God" (Eph 5:5); "the kingdom ... of Jesus Christ" (Rev 1:9); "heavenly kingdom" (2Ti 4:18); and *he basileía*, "the kingdom" (Mt 8:12; 9:35) are all syn. in the NT and mean the divine spiritual kingdom, the glorious reign of the Messiah. The idea of the kingdom has its basis in the prophecies of the OT where the coming of the Messiah and His triumphs are foretold (e.g., Ps 2; 110; Isa 2:1–4; 11:1ff.; Jer 23:5ff.; 31:31ff.; 32:37ff.; 33:14ff.; Eze 34:23ff.; 37:24ff.; Mic 4:1ff., and especially Da 2:44; 7:14, 27; 9:25ff.). His reign is described as a golden age when true righteousness will be established, and with it the theocracy will be established bringing peace and happiness. Prior to the visible manifestation of this kingdom and its extension to the material and natural realms of the world, it exists spiritually in the hearts of men, and thus it was understood by Zacharias (Lk 1:67ff.); Simeon (Lk 2:25ff.); Anna (Lk 2:36ff.); Joseph (Lk 23:50, 51).

The Jews, however, generally gave to these prophecies a temporal meaning and expected a Messiah who should come in the clouds of heaven. As king of the Jewish people, He was expected to restore the ancient Jewish religion and worship, reform the corrupt morals of the people, make expiation for their sins, give freedom from the yoke of foreign dominion, and at length reign over the whole earth in peace and glory.

The concept of the kingdom in the OT is partly fulfilled in the NT. First we have the Christian dispensation. The kingdom of heaven or God on earth, consisting of the community of those who receive Jesus as their Saviour, and who, through the Holy Spirit, form His Church with Him as its head. This spiritual kingdom has both an internal and external form. As internal, it already exists and rules in the hearts of all Christians and is therefore present. As external, it is either embodied both in the visible and invisible Church, and thus is present and progressive; or it is to be perfected in the coming of the Son of Man to judge and reign in bliss and glory. This is the further realization of the kingdom of God in the future.

However, these different aspects are not always distinguished. The expression often embraces both the internal and external kingdom and refers both to its commencement in this world and its completion in the world to come. Hence, in the NT we find it spoken about in the Jewish temporal sense by Jews and the apostles before the day of Pentecost (Mt 18:1; 20:21; Lk 17:20; 19:11; Ac 1:6); in the Christian sense as announced by John, where perhaps something of the Jewish view was intermingled (Mt 3:2 [cf. Lk 23:51]); as announced by Jesus and others (Mt 4:17, 23; 9:35; 10:7; Mk 1:14, 15; Lk 10:9, 11; Ac 28:31); in the internal spiritual sense (Mt 6:33; Mk 10:15; Lk 17:21; 18:17; Jn 3:3, 5; Ro 14:17; 1Co 4:20); in the external sense, i.e. as embodied in the visible church and the universal spread of the gospel (Mt 6:10; 12:28; 13:24, 31, 33, 44, 47; 16:28; Mk 4:30; 11:10; Lk 13:18, 20; Ac 19:8); as perfected in the future world (Mt 13:43; 16:19; 26:29; Mk 14:25; Lk 22:29, 30; 2Pe 1:11; Rev 12:10). In this latter view it denotes especially the bliss of heaven which is to be enjoyed in the Redeemer's kingdom, i.e. eternal life (Mt 8:11; 25:34; Mk 9:47; Lk 13:28, 29; Ac 14:22; 1Co 6:9, 10; 15:50; Gal 5:21; Eph 5:5; 2Th 1:5; 2Ti 4:18; Heb 12:28; Jas 2:5). The kingdom spoken of generally (Mt 5:19). In Mt 8:12, "the sons of the kingdom" (a.t.) means the Jews who thought that the Messiah's reign was destined only for them and that by ancestry alone, which claimed belief in the God of Abraham, they had the right to be called the sons of the kingdom (Jn 8:33, 37, 39). However, "the children of the kingdom" in Mt 13:38 are the true citizens of the kingdom of God. See also Mt 11:11, 12; 13:11, 19, 44, 45, 52; 18:4, 23; 19:12, 24; 20:1. Spoken also generally of the privileges and rewards of the divine kingdom, both here and hereafter (Mt 5:3, 10, 20; 7:21; 18:3; Col 1:13; 1Th 2:12).

Syn.: *hēgemonía* (2231), reign; *thrónos* (2362), throne, and by implication the power that the throne represents, kingdom; *aulé* (833), palace, as standing for kingdom; *krátos* (2904), dominion; *arché* (746), rule; *exousía* (1849), authority.

933. βασίλειον, basileion, *bas-il´-i-on;* neuter of 934; a *palace:*—king's court.

934. βασίλειος, basileios, *bas-il´-i-os;* from 935; *kingly* (in nature):—royal.

Adjective meaning royal, regal. Particularly (1Pe 2:9, "a royal priesthood," consecrated to God as kings and priests, i.e. in a distinguished manner). As a subst.: a royal mansion, palace (Lk 7:25).

Syn.: *baslikós* (937), royal.

935. βασιλεύς, basileus, *bas-il-yooce´;* probably from 939 (through the notion of a *foundation* of power); a *sovereign* (abstract, relative or figurative):—king.

Masculine noun meaning king, monarch, i.e. one who exercises royal authority and sovereignty:

(I) Of David (Mt 1:6; Ac 13:22); of Pharaoh (Ac 7:10, 18; Heb 11:23, 27); of the Roman emperor (Jn 19:15); of ancient Jewish kings (Lk 10:24); of Jesus as the Messiah who is often called King, King of Israel or of the Jews (Mt 2:2; 21:5; 25:34, 40; Lk 19:38; Jn 1:49; 12:13, 15; Sept.: Ps 2:6); spoken of God (1Ti 1:17; 6:15; Rev 15:3; 17:14, "King of kings" by way of emphasis; Sept.: Ps 5:2; 29:10; 47:2; 95:3). "The city of the great King" (Mt 5:35) means of God, Jerusalem as the seat of His worship (Ps 47:2).

(II) In a more general and lower sense, as a title of distinguished honour, e.g., viceroy, prince, leader, chief. Herod the Great and his successors had the title of king, but were dependent for the name and power on the Romans (Mt 2:1, 3, 9; Lk 1:5; Ac 12:1; 25:13ff.; 26:2ff.), and Herod Antipas was in fact only a tetrarch, meaning ruler of only a fourth of the kingdom (Mt 14:1; Lk 3:1, 19; 9:7), though he is called "king" in Mt 14:9; Mk 6:14. See also Aretas, king of Arabia, Petraea (2Co 11:32). Also used when joined with *hēgemónes* (2232), leaders, rulers (Mt 10:18; Mk 13:9; Lk 21:12; Sept.: Ps 2:2; 102:15). Generally (Mt 17:25; 18:23; Ac 9:15; 2Ti 2:2; 1Pe 2:13, 17; Rev 9:11). Figuratively spoken of Christians as about to reign with the Messiah over the nations (Rev 1:6 [{TR} cf. 5:10; 20:6]).

Deriv.: *basileía* (932), kingdom; *basíleios* (934), royal, kingly in nature; *basileúō* (936), to reign; *basilikós* (937), belonging to a king, such as a courtier or something kingly; *basílissa* (938), queen.

Syn.: *árchōn* (758), ruler; *politárchēs* (4173), ruler of a city; *despótēs* (1203), despot, an absolute ruler; *kúrios* (2962), lord; *pantokrátōr* (3841), the all-ruling, almighty, omnipotent; *hēgemṓn* (2232), a leader, ruler, governor; *Kaísar* (2541), Caesar, a title of the Roman emperor; *dunástēs* (1413), mighty potentate.

936. βασιλεύω, basileuō, *bas-il-yoo´-o*; from 935; to *rule* (literal or figurative):—king, reign.

From *basileús* (935), a king. To reign, rule, be king:

(I) To reign over (Lk 19:4, 17; 1Ti 6:15). Spoken of Archelaus, who for a time had the title of king (Mt 2:22; Sept.: Jgs 9:8, 10; 1Sa 8:9, 11). Spoken of the Messiah (Lk 1:33; 1Co 15:25; Rev 11:15).

(II) Absolutely: to reign, i.e. to possess and to exercise dominion; spoken of God as vindicating to himself his regal power (Rev 11:17; 19:6). Figuratively, spoken of Christians who are to reign with Christ, i.e. enjoy the high privileges, honours, and felicity of the Messiah's kingdom (Ro 5:17; Rev 5:10; 20:4, 6; 22:5). So of Christians on earth: to enjoy the honour and prosperity of kings (1Co 4:8). Figuratively: to have dominion, to prevail, to be predominant, e.g., death (Ro 5:14, 17); sin and grace (Ro 5:21; 6:12).

Deriv.: *sumbasileúō* (4821), to reign with someone.

Syn.: *huperéchō* (5242), to hold oneself above, be superior; *proéchō* (4284), to excel; *diakrínomai* (1252), to distinguish oneself as superior; *prōteúō* (4409), to have preeminence; *kurieúō* (2961), to exercise lordship, have dominion over; *árchō* (757), to reign, rule over; *sumbasileúō* (4821), to reign together; *hēgéomai* (2233), to rule over; *hēgemoneúō* (2230), to act as a ruler.

937. βασιλικός, basilikos, *bas-il-ee-kos´*; from 935; *regal* (in relation), i.e. (literal) belonging to (or befitting) the sovereign (as land, dress, or a *courtier*), or (figurative) *preeminent*:—king's, nobleman, royal.

Adjective from *basileús* (935), king. Kingly, royal, i.e. belonging to a king (Ac 12:20, a territory; Jn 4:46, 49, a nobleman, a person attached to a court; Sept.: Nu 20:17; 21:22; 2Sa 14:26; Est 8:15). Befitting a king, of kingly dignity (Ac 12:21, a robe; Jas 2:8, noble, excellent, preeminent, referring to law).

Syn.: *basíleios* (934), royal.

938. βασίλισσα, basilissa, *bas-il´-is-sah*; feminine from 936; a *queen:*—queen.

939. βάσις, basis, *bas´-ece*; from βαίνω, *bainō* (to *walk*); a *pace* ("base"), i.e. (by implication) the *foot:*—foot.

940. βασκαίνω, baskainō, *bas-kah´ee-no*; akin to 5335; to *malign*, i.e. (by extension) to *fascinate* (by false representations):—bewitch.

941. βαστάζω, bastazō, *bas-tad´-zo*; perhaps remotely derivative from the base of 939 (through the idea of *removal*); to *lift*, literal or figurative (*endure, declare, sustain, receive,* etc.):—bear, carry, take up.

942. βάτος, batos, *bat´-os*; of uncertain derivative; a *brier* shrub:—bramble, bush.

943. βάτος, batos, *bat´-os*; of Hebrew origin [1324]; a *bath*, or measure for liquids:—measure.

944. βάτραχος, batrachos, *bat´-rakh-os*; of uncertain derivative; a *frog:*—frog.

945. βαττολογέω, battologeō, *bat-tol-og-eh´-o*; from Βάττος, *Battos* (a proverbial stammerer) and 3056; to *stutter*, i.e. (by implication) to *prate* tediously:—use vain repetitions.

From *báttos* (n.f.), a proverbial stammerer, and *lógos* (3056), word. To speak foolishly, babble, chatter (see Le 5:4; Job 11:2, 3; Isa 16:6; 44:25). Not to be confused with *battarízō*, to stutter. Characterizes *polulogía* (4180), wordiness. Much talk without content, repeating the same thing over and over again (Mt 6:7), useless speaking without distinct expression of purpose as contrasted to succinct, knowledgeable speech, thus foolish speaking.

Syn.: *phluaréō* (5396), to be a babbler; *phlúaros* (5397), to be a tattler or one who talks unnecessarily and too much; *mōrología* (3473), foolish talking.

946. βδέλυγμα, bdelugma, *bdel´-oog-mah*; from 948; a *detestation*, i.e. (special) *idolatry:*—abomination.

Noun from *bdelússō* (948), to emit a foul odour, to turn away through loathing or disgust, abhor. An abomination, i.e. something abominable, detestable.

(I) Generally: that which is detestable to God (Lk 16:15; Sept.: Pr 11:1; 15:8, 9; 20:23; 21:27).

(II) That which was unclean in the Jewish tradition, and especially of impure idol worship; hence idolatry, licentiousness, abominable impurity (Rev 17:4, 5; 21:27; Sept.: 2Ki 16:3; 21:2 [cf. Le 18:22; also Le 11:10, 12, 13; Jer 11:15]).

(III) In connection with (II) is the expression "the abomination of desolation" (*to bdélugma tḗs erēmṓseōs* [2050], robbery, desolation, emptying out). This expression is found in the Olivet Discourse of our Lord (Mt 24:15; Mk 13:14), and applied to what was to take place at the destruction of Jerusalem by the Romans (cf. Lk 21:20). It is probably to be referred to the pollution of the temple by idol worship or the setting up of images, though express historical testimony is lacking (cf. Mt 24:15; 2Th 2:4; Sept.: 1Ki 11:5; 21:26; Isa 17:8).

947. βδελυκτός, bdeluktos, *bdel-ook-tos´*; from 948; *detestable,* i.e. (special) *idolatrous:*—abominable.

Adjective from *bdelússō* (948), to abominate. Abominable, detestable (Tit 1:16; Sept.: Pr 17:15).

Syn.: *anósios* (462), unholy; *bébēlos* (952), wicked, profane; *theostugḗs* (2319), impious, hater of God; *stugnētós* (4767), odious.

948. βδελύσσω, bdelussō, *bdel-oos´-so*; from a (presumed) derivative of **βδέω, bdeō** (to *stink*); to *be disgusted,* i.e. (by implication) *detest* (especially of idolatry):—abhor, abominable.

From *bdéō* (n.f.), to stink. To emit a stench, to excite disgust. In the NT, used in the middle: to feel disgust, to abhor (Ro 2:22; Rev 21:8; Sept.: Le 26:11; Dt 23:7; Am 5:10). In the perf. pass. part. *ebdelugménos*: abominable, detestable, i.e. polluted with crimes (Sept.: Le 18:30; Job 15:16; Pr 8:7; Isa 14:19; Hos 9:10).

Deriv.: *bdélugma* (946), an abomination; *bdeluktós* (947), abominable.

Syn.: *apostréphō* (654), to turn away.

949. βέβαιος, bebaios, *beb´-ah-yos*; from the base of 939 (through the idea of *basality*); *stable* (literal or figurative):—firm, of force, steadfast, sure.

Adjective from *baínō* (n.f.), to go. Fixed, firm, sure, certain, steadfast (see Ro 4:16; 2Co 1:7; Heb 2:2; 3:6, 14; 9:17; 2Pe 1:10, 19). In the NT, of objects (Heb 6:19), that which does not fail or waver, immovable, and on which one may rely.

Deriv.: *bebaióō* (950), to establish.

Syn.: *alēthḗs* (227), true; *asphalḗs* (804), safe, sure; *pistós* (4103), faithful, trustworthy; *hedraíos* (1476), steadfast, equivalent to *stereós* (4731), fast, firm, hard.

950. βεβαιόω, bebaioō, *beb-ah-yo´-o*; from 949; to *stabilitate* (figurative):—confirm, (e-) stablish.

From *bébaios* (949), sure, fixed. To make firm or steadfast, to confirm; spoken of persons (1Co 1:8; 2Co 1:21; Col 2:7; Heb 13:9; Sept.: Ps 41:13; 119:28); spoken of things: to corroborate, to ratify, to establish by arguments, proofs, etc. (Mk 16:20; Ro 15:8; 1Co 1:6; Heb 2:3).

Deriv.: *bebaíōsis* (951), confirmation; *diabebaióomai* (1226), to make firm.

Syn.: *stērízō* (4741), to set steadfastly; *epistērízō* (1991), to strengthen; *kuróō* (2964), to make valid, ratify; *stereóō* (4732), to make firm; *marturéō* (3140), to testify; *dēlóō* (1213), to declare; *apodeíknumi* (584), to prove.

951. βεβαίωσις, bebaiōsis, *beb-ah´-yo-sis*; from 950; *stabiliment:*—confirmation.

Noun from *bebaióō* (950), to establish. Ratification, confirmation, corroboration, firm establishment (Php 1:7; Heb 6:16).

Syn.: *stērigmós* (4740), stability; *asphâleia* (803), certainty, safety; *pepoíthēsis* (4006), confidence, trust; *apódeixis* (585), manifestation; *plērophoría* (4136), entire confidence, assurance.

952. βέβηλος, bebēlos, *beb´-ay-los*; from the base of 939 and **βηλός, bēlos** (a *threshold*); *accessible* (as by *crossing the door-way*), i.e. (by implication, of Jewish notions) *heathenish, wicked:*—profane (person).

Adjective from *baínō* (n.f.), to go, and *bēlos* (n.f.), a threshold. Particularly, of place: accessible to all; hence, common, profane, in opposition to *hágios* (40), holy. In the NT, spoken of persons: profane, i.e. impious, a scoffer (2Ti 1:9; Heb 12:16; Sept.: Eze 21:25); spoken of things, as disputes, etc.: common, unholy, unsanctified (1Ti 4:7; 6:20; 2Ti 2:16).

Deriv.: *bebēlóō* (953), to profane, pollute.

Syn.: *anósios* (462), unholy; *theostugḗs* (2319), hateful to God, impious.

953. βεβηλόω, bebēloō, *beb-ay-lo´-o*; from 952; to *desecrate:*—profane.

From *bébēlos* (952), profane. To profane, to cross the threshold (Mt 12:5; Ac 24:6; Sept.: Ex 31:14; Le 19:8, 12; Eze 43:7, 8).

Syn.: *miaínō* (3392), to taint, contaminate, defile; *molúnō* (3435), to soil; *asebéō* (764), to act impiously; *hierosuléō* (2416), to be a temple-robber, commit sacrilege; *blasphēméō* (987), to blaspheme, revile, speak evil; *koinóō* (2840), to defile, pollute; *spilóō* (4695), to stain, soil, spot.

954. Βεελζεβούλ, **Beelzeboul,** *beh-el-zeb-ool´*; of Chaldee origin [by parody upon 1176]; *dung-god; Beelzebul,* a name of Satan:—Beelzebub.

955. Βελίαλ, **Belial,** *bel-ee´-al*; of Hebrew origin [1100], *worthlessness; Belial,* as an epithet of Satan:—Belial.

956. βέλος, **belos,** *bel´-os*; from 906; a *missile,* i.e. *spear* or *arrow:*—dart.

957. βελτίον, **beltion,** *bel-tee´-on*; neuter of a compound of a derivative of 906 (used for the comparative of 18); *better:*—very well.

958. Βενιαμίν, **Beniamin,** *ben-ee-am-een´*; of Hebrew origin [1144]; *Benjamin,* an Israelite:—Benjamin.

959. Βερνίκη, **Bernikē,** *ber-nee´-kay*; from a provincial form of 5342 and 3529; *victorious; Bernicè,* a member of the Herodian family:—Bernice.

960. Βέροια, **Beroia,** *ber´-oy-ah*; perhaps a provincial from a derivative of 4008 [*Peræa,* i.e. the region *beyond* the coastline]; *Beroea,* a place in Macedonia:—Berea.

961. Βεροιαῖος, **Beroiaios,** *ber-oy-ah´-yos*; from 960; a *Beroeæan* or native of Berœea:—of Berea.

962. Βηθαβαρά, **Bēthabara,** *bay-thab-ar-ah´*; of Hebrew origin [1004 and 5679]; *ferry-house; Beth-abara* (i.e. *Bethabarah*), a place on the Jordan:—Bethabara.

963. Βηθανία, **Bēthania,** *bay-than-ee´-ah*; of Chaldee origin; *date-house; Beth-any,* a place in Palestine:—Bethany.

964. Βηθεσδά, **Bēthesda,** *bay-thes-dah´*; of Chaldee origin [compare 1004 and 2617]; *house of kindness; Beth-esda,* a pool in Jerusalem:—Bethesda.

965. Βηθλεέμ, **Bēthleem,** *bayth-leh-em´*; of Hebrew origin [1036]; *Bethleem* (i.e. *Beth-lechem*), a place in Palestine:—Bethlehem.

966. Βηθσαϊδά, **Bēthsaïda,** *bayth-sahee-dah´*; of Chaldee origin [compare 1004 and 6719]; *fishing-house; Bethsaïda,* a place in Palestine:—Bethsaida.

967. Βηθφαγή, **Bēthphagē,** *bayth-fag-ay´*; of Chaldee origin [compare 1004 and 6291]; *fig-house; Bethphagè,* a place in Palestine:—Bethphage.

968. βῆμα, **bēma,** *bay´-ma*; from the base of 939; a *step,* i.e. *foot-breath;* (by implication) a *rostrum,* i.e. *tribunal:*—judgement seat, set [foot] on, throne.

969. βήρυλλος, **bērullos,** *bay´-rool-los*; of uncertain derivative; a "*beryl*":—beryl.

970. βία, **bia,** *bee´-ah*; probably akin to 979 (through the idea of *vital* activity); *force:*—violence.

971. βιάζω, **biazō,** *bee-ad´-zo*; from 970; to *force,* i.e. (reflex.) to *crowd oneself* (into), or (passive) to *be seized:*—press, suffer violence.

From *bía* (970), violence. To force, to urge. In the NT, used in the middle: to use force, to force, to press (Lk 16:16); in the pass.: to suffer violence, be taken by force (Mt 11:12). Both of these occurrences imply the eagerness with which the gospel was received in the agitated state of men's minds.

Deriv.: *biastḗs* (973), a person who is violent; *parabiázomai* (3849), to coerce, persuade.

Syn.: *hormáō* (3729), to rush.

972. βίαιος, **biaios,** *bee´-ah-yos*; from 970; *violent:*—mighty.

973. βιαστής, **biastēs,** *bee-as-tace´*; from 971; a *forcer,* i.e. (figurative) *energetic:*—violent.

974. βιβλιαρίδιον, **bibliaridion,** *bib-lee-ar-id´-ee-on*; a diminutive of 975; a *booklet:*—little book.

975. βιβλίον, **biblion,** *bib-lee´-on*; a diminutive of 976; a *roll:*—bill, book, scroll, writing.

976. βίβλος, **biblos,** *bib´-los*; properly the inner *bark* of the papyrus plant, i.e. (by implication) a *sheet* or *scroll* of writing:—book.

A noun meaning inner rind of the papyrus, anciently used for writing. In the NT, a roll, volume, scroll, i.e. a book (Mk 12:26, "in the book of Moses" meaning the Law; Lk 3:4; 20:42; Ac 1:20; 7:42; 19:19; Sept.: Jos 1:8; 1Sa 10:25; Ezr 6:18). Spoken of a genealogical table or catalog (Mt 1:1; Sept.: Ge 5:1). The phrase, "the book of life [*bíblos tḗs zōḗs* {2222}, life]" is equal in the Sept. to the book of the living ones (Ps 69:28 [cf. Ex 32:32, 33]), where God is shown as having the names of the righteous who are to inherit eternal life inscribed in a book. See also Php 4:3; Rev 3:5; 20:15. This is the same phrase as *tó biblíon* (975), a diminutive of *bíblos* (Rev 17:8; 20:12; 21:27; Sept.: Da 12:1). Different from this is the book in which God has from eternity inscribed the destinies of men (Ps 139:16 [cf. Job 14:5]). The plural and the diminutive *biblía* are twice mentioned in Rev 20:12 referring to the books of judgement in which the actions of men are recorded (see Da 7:10).

Deriv.: *bibliarídion* (974), a little scroll; *biblíon* (975), a roll, scroll.

977. βιβρώσκω, bibrōskō, *bib-ro´-sko*; a reduplicated and prolonged form of an obsolete primary verb [perhaps causative of 1006]; to *eat*:—eat.

978. Βιθυνία, Bithunia, *bee-thoo-nee´-ah*; of uncertain derivative; *Bithynia,* a region of Asia:—Bithynia.

979. βίος, bios, *bee´-os*; a primary word; *life,* i.e. (literal) the present state of existence; (by implication) the means of *livelihood:*—good life, living.

A noun meaning life. Particularly, the present life (Lk 8:14; 1Th 2:2; 2Ti 2:4; 1Pe 4:3). Used figuratively: means of life, living, sustenance (Mk 12:44; Lk 8:43; 15:12, 30; 21:4).

Deriv.: *bióō* (980), to live, to pass one's life without reference to its quality.

Syn.: with the meaning of goods, wealth: *húparxis* (5223), subsistence, goods, and also as a plural part. noun, *tá hupárchonta; skeúos* (4632), primarily a vessel, but also goods; *psuchḗ* (5590), with the meaning of natural life, breath of life, the seat of personality; *agōgḗ* (72), a manner of life, conduct; *anastrophḗ* (391), behaviour, conduct.

980. βιόω, bioō, *bee-o´-o*; from 979; to *spend* existence:—live.

981. Βίωσις, Biōsis, *bee´-o-sis*; from 980; *living* (properly, the act; by implication, the mode):—manner of life.

982. βιωτικός, biōtikos, *bee-o-tee-kos´*; from a derivative of 980; *relating to* the present *existence:*—of (pertaining to, things that pertain to) this life.

983. βλαβερός, blaberos, *blab-er-os´*; from 984; *injurious:*—hurtful.

984. βλάπτω, blaptō, *blap´-to*; a primary verb; properly to *hinder,* i.e. (by implication) to *injure:*—hurt.

985. βλαστάνω, blastanō, *blas-tan´-o*; from **βλαστός, blastos** (a *sprout*); to *germinate*; (by implication) to *yield* fruit:—bring forth, bud, spring (up).

986. Βλάστος, Blastos, *blas´-tos*; perhaps the same as the base of 985; *Blastus,* an officer of Herod Agrippa:—Blastus.

987. βλασφημέω, blasphēmeō, *blas-fay-meh´-o*; from 989; to *vilify*; specially to *speak impiously:*—(speak) blaspheme (-er, -mously, -my), defame, rail on, revile, speak evil.

From *blásphēmos* (989), blasphemous or a blasphemer. To blaspheme, revile:

(I) Generally, spoken of men and things: to speak evil of, to slander, to defame, to revile (Mk 3:28; 15:29; Lk 23:39; Jn 10:36; Ac 18:6; 19:37; 26:11 [cf. Ac 26:9]; Ro 3:8; 14:16; 1Co 4:13; 10:30; 1Ti 1:20; 6:1; Tit 3:2; Jas 2:7; 1Pe 4:4, 14; 2Pe 2:2, 10, 12; Jude 8, 10; Sept.: 2Ki 19:6, 23).

(II) Spoken of God and his spirit, or of divine things: to revile, to treat with irreverence and scornful insolence (Mt 9:3; 26:65; Ac 13:45; Ro 2:24; Tit 2:5; Rev 16:9, 11, 21). In the NT generally syn. with *oneidízō* (3679), revile, and *loidoréō* (3058), to reproach (Mt 27:39; Mk 15:29; Lk 22:65; 23:39; Ro 3:8; 14:16; 1Co 4:13; Tit 3:2; 2Pe 2:10; Jude 8); especially to revile God and divine things (Rev 13:6).

Syn.: *hēttáō* (2274), to make inferior; *hubrízō* (5195), to insult; *kataráomai* (2672), to curse; *anathematízō* (332), to curse with an oath; *asebéō* (764), to be impious, disrespectful; *hierosuléō* (2416), to commit sacrilege.

988. βλασφημία, blasphēmia, *blas-fay-me´-ah*; from 989; *vilification* (especially against God):—blasphemy, evil speaking, railing.

From *blásphēmos* (989), blasphemous or a blasphemer. Blasphemy:

Generally, spoken of men and things: evil speakings, slander, reviling (Mt 12:31; 15:19; Mk 3:28; 7:22; Eph 4:31; Col 3:8; 1Ti 6:4; Rev 2:9). Spoken of God and His Spirit, or divine things: reviling, impious irreverence (Mt 12:31; Mk 2:7; 14:64; Lk 5:21; Jn 10:33; Rev 13:5, 6); against the Holy Spirit (Mt 12:31; Mk 3:28; Lk 12:10).

Syn.: *katalalía* (2636), evil speaking, backbiting; *loidoría* (3059), abuse, railing, reviling; *apistía* (570), unbelief; *asébeia* (763), impiety; *húbris* (5196), insult, hurt, reproach; *dusphēmía* (1426), defamation.

989. βλάσφημος, blasphēmos, *blas´-fay-mos*; from a derivative of 984 and 5345; *scurrilous*, i.e. *calumnious* (against man), or (special) *impious* (against God):—blasphemer (-mous), railing.

Adjective from *bláx* (n.f.), sluggish, slow, stupid, and *phḗmē* (5345), rumour, fame. Blasphemous, spoken of words uttered against God and divine things (Ac 6:11, 13). So of words against men: slanderous, haughtily contemptuous, insulting (2Pe 2:11). Used as a substantive, in respect to God: a blasphemer (1Ti 1:13); in respect to men: a slanderer, reviler (2Ti 3:2).

Deriv.: *blasphēméō* (987), to blaspheme; *blasphēmía* (988), blaspheming abuse against someone.

Syn.: *loídoros* (3060), reviling, railing, or a railer; *hubristḗs* (5197), an insulter; *empaíktēs* (1703), a derider, mocker.

990. βλέμμα, blemma, *blem´-mah*; from 991; *vision* (properly, concrete; by implication, abstract):—seeing.

991. βλέπω, blepō, *blep´-o*; a primary verb; to *look* at (literal or figurative):—behold, beware, lie, look (on, to), perceive, regard, see, sight, take heed. Compare 3700.

(I) To be able to see, i.e. to have the faculty of sight, and as spoken of the blind, to recover sight (Mt 12:22). In Ac 9:9, "without sight" means blind. See Rev 3:18; 9:20; Sept.: Ex 4:11; 23:8; 1Sa 3:2; Ps 69:23. The present inf. with the neuter article *tó blépein*, used as a substantive means sight, the faculty of seeing (Lk 7:21). Used figuratively in Jn 9:39: "that they which see not might see; and that they which see might be made blind" or may not see (cf. Jn

9:41). So by Hebraism, with a part. of the same verb for emphasis, e.g., "seeing ye shall see" in (Mt 13:14; Mk 4:12; Ac 28:26 [cf. Isa 6:9]).

(II) To perceive as with the eyes, meaning to discern, to understand (Mt 7:3; 11:4; 14:30; 24:2; Mk 8:24; Lk 11:33; Jn 1:29; 21:9; Sept.: 2Ki 9:17; Am 8:1). In Rev 1:12, "to see the voice," means to see where it came from. By implication: to have before the eyes, spoken of what is present (Ro 8:24, cf. v. 25]). Hence, the part. *blepómenos*, seen, may mean present (Ro 8:24). So *tá blepómena*, things seen, meaning present things; and *tá mḗ blepómena*, things not seen, meaning future things (2Co 4:18; Heb 11:1, 7). Spoken of a vision: to see in vision (Rev 1:11; 6:1, 3, 5, 7 [TR], where other texts read *íde*, the imper. of *eídō* [1492], to see).

(III) Metaphorically: to perceive with the mind, be aware of, observe (Ro 7:23; 2Co 7:8; Heb 3:19; 10:25; Jas 2:22; Sept.: Ne 2:17).

(IV) To look, i.e. to look at or upon, to direct the eyes upon, to behold:

(A) Spoken of persons (Mt 5:28; Rev 5:3, 4; Sept.: Hag 2:4). In Mt 18:10, "their angels do always behold the face of my Father," i.e. in accordance with the customs of oriental monarchs, they have constant access to him, are admitted to his privacy as his friends. See 2Ki 25:19; Est 1:14; Jer 52:25. Followed by *eis* [(1519), unto], meaning to look upon, behold (Ac 3:4). In Jn 13:22; Lk 9:62, *eis* [(1519), unto] *tá opísō* [(3694), behind], to look back (Sept.: Ge 19:17). Spoken of a place: to look, i.e. to be situated (Ac 27:12; Sept.: 2Ch 4:4; Eze 40:6, 21–23, 46; 46:1, 13, 20).

(B) Metaphorically: to look to, direct the mind upon, consider, take heed (Mt 22:16; 1Co 1:26; 10:18; Php 3:2; Col 2:5; Sept.: Ge 39:23; Ps 37:37; Isa 22:11). Spoken by way of caution, in the imper. *blepétō* or *blépete*: look to it, take heed, be on the watch, beware (Mk 13:23, 33; Mk 13:9; 2Jn 8). Also *blépete mḗ* [(3361), not], meaning watch out, take heed lest (Lk 21:8; Ac 13:40; 1Co 10:12; Gal 5:15).

Deriv.: *anablépō* (308), to look up, and when spoken of the blind, to receive their sight; *apoblépō* (578), to look away from all else and toward one object, to look steadfastly; *blémma* (990), a look, glance, sight; *diablépō* (1227), to see clearly or to see through; *emblépō* (1689), to look earnestly, with the object of learning lessons of faith from, e.g., the birds; *epiblépō*

(1914), to look upon or with favour; *periblépō* (4017), to look around; *problépō* (4265), to foresee, provide.

Syn.: *atenízō* (816), to gaze upon, behold earnestly; *katoptrízō* (2734), to look in a mirror; *aphoráō* (872), to look away from one thing so as to see another; *kathoráō* (2529), to look down upon, discern clearly. With the meaning of to heed: *proséchō* (4337), to pay attention to, beware; *phulássō* (5442), to guard, watch; *epéchō* (1907), to give attention to; *skopéō* (4648), to take heed; *muōpázō* (3467), to be shortsighted; *phaínō* (5316), to cause to appear.

992. βλητέος, blēteos, *blay-teh´-os*; from 906; fit *to be cast* (i.e. *applied*):—must be put.

993. Βοανεργές, Boanerges, *bo-an-erg-es´*; of Chaldee origin [1123 and 7266]; *sons of commotion; Boänerges,* an epithet of two of the apostles:—Boanerges.

994. βοάω, boaō, *bo-ah´-o*; apparently a prolonged form of a primary verb; to *halloo,* i.e. *shout* (for help or in a tumultuous way):—cry.

995. βοή, boē, *bo-ay´*; from 994; a *halloo,* i.e. *call* (for aid, etc.):—cry.

996. βοήθεια, boētheia, *bo-ay´-thi-ah*; from 998; *aid*; specially a rope or chain for *frapping* a vessel:—help.

997. βοηθέω, boētheō, *bo-ay-theh´-o*; from 998; to *aid* or *relieve*:—help, succour.

998. βοηθός, boēthos, *bo-ay-thos´*; from 995 and θέω, *theō* (to *run*); a *succourer*:—helper.

999. βόθυνος, bothunos, *both´-oo-nos*; akin to 900; a *hole* (in the ground); specially a *cistern*:—ditch, pit.

1000. βολή, bolē, *bol-ay´*; from 906; a *throw* (as a measure of distance):—cast.

1001. βολίζω, bolizō, *bol-id´-zo*; from 1002; to *heave* the lead:—sound.

1002. βολίς, bolis, *bol-ece´*; from 906; a *missile,* i.e. *javelin*:—dart.

1003. Βοόζ, Booz, *bo-oz´*; of Hebrew origin [1162]; *Boöz* (i.e. *Boäz*), an Israelite:—Booz.

1004. βόρβορος, borboros, *bor´-bor-os*; of uncertain derivative; *mud*:—mire.

1005. βορρᾶς, borrhas, *bor-hras´*; of uncertain derivative; the *north* (properly wind):—north.

1006. βόσκω, boskō, *bos´-ko*; a prolonged form of a primary verb [compare 977, 1016]; to *pasture*; by extension to *fodder*; reflexive to *graze*:—feed, keep.

To feed sheep, to pasture or tend while grazing. Middle *bóskomai,* to feed, i.e. to be feeding or grazing (Mt 8:30, 33; Mk 5:11, 14; Lk 8:32, 34; 15:15; Sept.: Ge 29:7, 9; 37:12, 16). Used metaphorically of a Christian teacher: to instruct (Jn 21:15, 17; Sept.: Eze 34:2, 3, 8, 10).

Deriv.: *botánē* (1008), herbage, plants.

Syn.: *poimaínō* (4165), to shepherd, to act as shepherd, tend, involving much more than feeding

1007. Βοσόρ, Bosor, *bos-or´*; of Hebrew origin [1160]; *Bosor* (i.e. *Beör*), a Moabite:—Bosor.

1008. βοτάνη, botanē, *bot-an´-ay*; from 1006; *herbage* (as if for *grazing*):—herb.

1009. βότρυς, botrus, *bot´-rooce*; of uncertain derivative; a *bunch* (of grapes):—(vine) cluster (of the vine).

1010. βουλευτής, bouleutēs, *bool-yoo-tace´*; from 1011; an *adviser,* i.e. (special) a *councillor* or member of the Jewish Sanhedrin:—counsellor.

1011. βουλεύω, bouleuō, *bool-yoo´-o*; from 1012; to *advise,* i.e. (reflexive) *deliberate,* or (by implication) *resolve*:—consult, take counsel, determine, be minded, purpose.

1012. βουλή, boulē, *boo-lay´*; from 1014; *volition,* i.e. (object) *advice,* or (by implication) *purpose*:— + advise, counsel, will.

A noun meaning counsel, senate. In the NT, counsel, i.e. determination, decision, decree; spoken of God (Lk 7:30; Ac 2:23; 13:36; 20:27; Eph 1:11; Heb 6:17); of men (Lk 23:51; Ac 27:12; Sept.: Pr 19:21; Isa 5:19; Jer 49:20, 30). By implication: purpose, plan, etc. (Ac 4:28; 5:38; 27:42; Sept.: Ezr 4:5; Ne 4:15); spoken of secret thoughts, purpose (1Co 4:5; Sept.: Job 5:12; Isa 55:7, 8 [cf. Ezr 6:22]).

Deriv.: *bouleúō* (1011), to take counsel; *epiboulé* (1917), a plot, conspiracy; *súmboulos* (4825), a councilman, council member.

Syn.: *gnốmē* (1106), the faculty of knowledge, reason, opinion, resolve, purpose; *krísis*

(2920), judgement, decision; *kritērion* (2922), a tribunal or the place or assembly where a judgement or decision is made; *phrónēma* (5427), thought or the object of thought; *phrónēsis* (5428), the ability to make a decision, prudence; *próthesis* (4286), purpose.

1013. βούλημα, boulēma, *boo´-lay-mah*; from 1014; a *resolve*:—purpose, will.

Noun from *boúlomai* (1014), to will. That which is willed, i.e. will (Ac 27:43; Ro 9:19).

1014. βούλομαι, boulomai, *boo´-lom-ahee*; middle of a primary verb; to *"will,"* i.e. (reflexive) *be willing*:—be disposed, minded, intend, list, (be, of own) will (-ing). Compare 2309.

To will, be willing, wish, desire. *Boúlomai* expresses a merely passive desire, propensity, willingness, while *thélō* (2309) expresses an active volition and purpose. *Boúlomai* expresses also the inward predisposition and bent from which active volition proceeds. In speaking of the gods, Homer uses *boúlomai* in the sense of *thélō* (2309).

(I) As spoken of men: to be willing, inclined, disposed (Mk 15:15; Ac 17:20; 18:27; 19:30; 22:30; 23:28; 25:22; 27:43; 28:18; Phm 13; 3Jn 10; Sept.: Le 26:21; Dt 25:7, 8; Job 9:3; 39:9); to intend, purpose, have in mind (Mt 1:19; Ac 5:28; 12:4; 2Co 1:15; Sept.: Ezr 4:5). Also in a stronger sense: to desire, to aim at (1Ti 6:9; Jas 4:4). With the meaning of to choose, prefer, decide (Jn 18:39; Ac 18:15; 25:20; Jas 3:4; 2Jn 12). As implying command or direction: to will, that is, to direct (Php 1:12, "It is my will" [a.t.]; 1Ti 2:8; 5:14; Tit 3:8; Jude 5, "I will that ye call to mind" [a.t.]).

(II) Spoken of God: equivalent to *thélō* (2309), to will, that is, to please, appoint, decree (Lk 22:42; Heb 6:17; Jas 1:18; 2Pe 3:9); of Jesus as the Son of God (Mt 11:27; Lk 10:22); of the Spirit (1Co 12:11).

Deriv.: *boúlēma* (1013), purpose, will.

Syn.: *axióō* (515), to desire worthily; *epithuméō* (1937), to desire earnestly stressing an inward impulse rather than an object desired, equivalent to covet; *orégomai* (3713), to long after something; *epizētéō* (1934), to seek earnestly; *epipothéō* (1971), to long after, usually in a bad sense meaning to lust; *parakaléō* (3870), to beseech; *bouleúō* (1011), to take counsel; *eúchomai* (2172), to wish.

1015. βουνός, bounos, *boo-nos´*; probably of foreign origin; a *hillock*:—hill.

1016. βοῦς, bous, *booce*; probably from the base of 1006; an *ox* (as *grazing*), i.e. an animal of that species ("beef"):—ox.

1017. βραβεῖον, brabeion, *brab-i´-on*; from **βραβεύς, brabeus** (an *umpire*; of uncertain derivative); an *award* (of arbitration), i.e. (special) a *prize* in the public games:—prize.

1018. βραβεύω, brabeuō, *brab-yoo´-o*; from the same as 1017; to *arbitrate*, i.e. (genitive) to *govern* (figurative, *prevail*):—rule.

1019. βραδύνω, bradunō, *brad-oo´-no*; from 1021; to *delay*:—be slack, tarry.

1020. βραδυπλοέω, braduploeō, *brad-oo-plo-eh´-o*; from 1021 and a prolonged form of 4126; to *sail slowly*:—sail slowly.

1021. βραδύς, bradus, *brad-ooce´*; of uncertain affinity; *slow*; (figurative) *dull*:—slow.

Adjective meaning slow, i.e. not hasty (Jas 1:19). Metaphorically: "slow of understanding," heavy, stupid (Lk 24:25).

Deriv.: *bradúnō* (1019), to be slow, delay; *braduploéō* (1020), to sail slowly; *bradútēs* (1022), slackness.

Syn.: *nōthrós* (3576), sluggish; *argós* (692), inactive; *oknērós* (3636), shrinking, irksome.

1022. βραδύτης, bradutēs, *brad-oo´-tace*; from 1021; *tardiness*:—slackness.

1023. βραχίων, brachiōn, *brakh-ee´-own*; properly, comparative of 1024, but apparently in the sense of **βράσσω, brassō** (to *wield*); the *arm*, i.e. (figurative) *strength*:—arm.

1024. βραχύς, brachus, *brakh-ooce´*; of uncertain affinity; *short* (of time, place, quantity, or number):—few words, little (space, while).

1025. βρέφος, brephos, *bref´-os*; of uncertain affinity; an *infant* (properly unborn) literal or figurative:—babe, (young) child, infant.

A noun meaning child. Spoken of a child yet unborn, a fetus (Lk 1:41, 44); usually an infant, babe, suckling (Lk 2:12, 16; 18:15; Ac 7:19; 2Ti 3:15). Used metaphorically of those who have just embraced the Christian religion (1Pe 2:2 [cf. 1Co 3:2; Heb 5:12, 13]).

Syn.: *népios* (3516), a little child; *tekníon* (5040), a little child; *téknon* (5043), child; *paidíon* (3813), a little or young child, an infant just born; *país* (3816), child; *paidárion* (3808), a little boy or girl; *korásion* (2877), a little girl, damsel; *paidískē* (3814), a little girl.

1026. βρέχω, brechō, *brekh´-o*; a primary verb; to *moisten* (especially by a shower):—(send) rain, wash.

1027. βροντή, brontē, *bron-tay´*; akin to **βρέμω, bremō** (to *roar*); *thunder*:—thunder (-ing).

1028. βροχή, brochē, *brokh-ay´*; from 1026; *rain*:—rain.

1029. βρόχος, brochos, *brokh´-os*; of uncertain derivative; a *noose*:—snare.

1030. βρυγμός, brugmos, *broog-mos´*; from 1031; a *grating* (of the teeth):—gnashing.

1031. βρύχω, bruchō, *broo´-kho*; a primary verb; to *grate* the teeth (in pain or rage):—gnash.

1032. βρύω, bruō, *broo´-o*; a primary verb; to *swell* out, i.e. (by implication) to *gush*:—send forth.

1033. βρῶμα, brōma, *bro´-mah*; from the base of 977; *food* (literal or figurative), especially (ceremonial) articles allowed or forbidden by the Jewish law:—meat, victuals.

1034. βρώσιμος, brōsimos, *bro´-sim-os*; from 1035; *eatable*:—meat.

1035. βρῶσις, brōsis, *bro´-sis*; from the base of 977; (abstract) *eating* (literal or figurative); by extension (concrete) *food* (literal or figurative):—eating, food, meat.

1036. βυθίζω, buthizo, *boo-thid´-zo*; from 1037; to *sink*; (by implication) to *drown*:—begin to sink, drown.

1037. βυθός, buthos, *boo-thos´*; a variation of 899; *depth*, i.e. (by implication) the *sea*:—deep.

1038. βυρσεύς, burseus, *boorce-yooce´*; from **βύρσα, bursa** (a *hide*); a *tanner*:—tanner.

1039. βύσσινος, bussinos, *boos´-see-nos*; from 1040; made of *linen* (neuter a linen *cloth*):—fine linen.

1040. βύσσος, bussos, *boos´-sos*; of Hebrew origin [948]; white *linen*:—fine linen.

1041. βῶμος, bōmos, *bo´-mos*; from the base of 939; properly a *stand*, i.e. (specifcally) an *altar*:—altar.

Noun from *baínō* (n.f.), to go, step. A step, base, pedestal. In the NT, it is used of idolatrous altars (Ac 17:23; Sept.: Ex 34:13; Nu 23:1). Contrast *thusiastérion* (2379), an altar of the true God.

Γ (Gamma)

NT Numbers 1042–1137

1042. γαββαθά, gabbatha, *gab-bath-ah´*; of Chaldee origin [compare 1355]; *the knoll; gabbatha,* a vernacular term for the Roman tribunal in Jerusalem:—Gabbatha.

1043. Γαβριήλ, Gabriēl, *gab-ree-ale´*; of Hebrew origin [1403]; *Gabriel,* an archangel:—Gabriel.

1044. γάγγραινα, gaggraina, *gang´-grahee-nah*; from **γραίνω,** *grainō* (to *gnaw*); an *ulcer* ("gangrene"):—canker.

1045. Γάδ, Gad, *gad*; of Hebrew origin [1410]; *Gad,* a tribe of Israel:—Gad.

1046. Γαδαρηνός, Gadarēnos, *gad-ar-ay-nos´*; from **Γαδαρά,** *Gadara* (a town East of the Jordan); a *Gadarene* or inhabitant of Gadara:—Gadarene.

1047. γάζα, gaza, *gad´-zah*; of foreign origin; a *treasure*:—treasure.

1048. Γάζα, Gaza, *gad´-zah*; of Hebrew origin [5804]; *Gazah* (i.e. *Azzah*), a place in Palestine:—Gaza.

1049. γαζοφυλάκιον, gazophulakion, *gad-zof-oo-lak´-ee-on*; from 1047 and 5438; a *treasure-house,* i.e. a court in the temple for the collection-boxes:—treasury.

1050. Γάϊος, Gaïos, *gah´-ee-os*; of Latin origin; *Gaïus* (i.e. *Caius*), a Christian:—Gaius.

1051. γάλα, gala, *gal´-ah*; of uncertain affinity; *milk* (figurative):—milk.

A noun meaning milk (1Co 9:7; Sept.: Ge 18:8; 49:12). Used figuratively for the first elements of Christian instruction (1Co 3:2; Heb 5:12, 13). In 1Pe 2:2, milk is put as the emblem of pure spiritual nourishment, or of Christian instruction in general.

1052. Γαλάτης, Galatēs, *gal-at´-ace*; from 1053; a *Galatian* or inhabitant of Galatia:—Galatian.

1053. Γαλατία, Galatia, *gal-at-ee´-ah*; of foreign origin; *Galatia,* a region of Asia:—Galatia.

1054. Γαλατικός, Galatikos, *gal-at-ee-kos´*; from 1053; *Galatic* or relating to Galatia:—of Galatia.

1055. γαλήνη, galēnē, *gal-ay´-nay*; of uncertain derivative; *tranquillity*:—calm.

1056. Γαλιλαία, Galilaia, *gal-il-ah-yah*; of Hebrew origin [1551]; *Galilæa* (i.e. the heathen *circle*), a region of Palestine:—Galilee.

1057. Γαλιλαῖος, Galilaios, *gal-ee-lah´-yos*; from 1056; *Galilæan* or belonging to Galilæa:—Galilæan, of Galilee.

1058. Γαλλίων, Galliōn, *gal-lee´-own*; of Latin origin; *Gallion* (i.e. *Gallio*), a Roman officer:—Gallio.

1059. Γαμαλιήλ, Gamaliēl, *gam-al-ee-ale´*; of Hebrew origin [1583]; *Gamaliel* (i.e. *Gamliel*), an Israelite:—Gamaliel.

1060. γαμέω, gameō, *gam-eh´-o*; from 1062; to *wed* (of either sex):—marry (a wife).

1061. γαμίσκω, gamiskō, *gam-is´-ko*; from 1062; to *espouse* (a daughter to a husband):—give in marriage.

1062. γάμος, gamos, *gam´-os*; of uncertain affinity; *nuptials*:—marriage, wedding.

A noun meaning wedding, nuptials, i.e. the nuptial solemnities, etc.:

(I) Spoken particularly of a wedding garment (Mt 22:11, 12); a nuptial banquet (Mt 22:10–12; Lk 14:8; Jn 2:1, 2; Rev 19:9). The happiness of the Messiah's kingdom is represented under the figure of a nuptial feast (Rev 19:7, 9, cf. Mt 25:1). Also, by metonymy, the place or hall where the nuptial feast is held (Mt 22:10).

(II) In common parlance, any festive banquet (Lk 12:36; 14:8; Sept.: Est 9:22).

(III) By metonymy: marriage, i.e. the marriage state (Heb 13:4).

Deriv.: *ágamos* (22), unmarried; *gaméō* (1060), to marry; *gamískō* (1061), to give in marriage.

1063. γάρ, gar, *gar*; a primary particle; properly assigning a *reason* (used in argument, explanation or intensification; often with other particles):—and, as, because (that), but, even, for, indeed, no doubt, seeing, then, therefore, verily, what, why, yet.

1064. γαστήρ, gastēr, *gas-tare´*; of uncertain derivative; the *stomach*; (by analogy) the *matrix*; (figurative) a *gourmand*:—belly, + with child, womb.

1065. γέ, ge, *gheh*; a primary particle of *emphasis* or *qualification* (often used with other particles prefixed):—and besides, doubtless, at least, yet.

1066. Γεδεών, Gedeōn, *ghed-eh-own´*; of Hebrew origin [1439]; *Gedeon* (i.e. *Gid[e]on*), an Israelite:—Gedeon.

1067. γέεννα, geenna, *gheh´-en-nah*; of Hebrew origin [1516 and 2011]; *valley of* (the son of) *Hinnom*; *gehenna* (or *Ge-Hinnom*), a valley of Jerusalem, used (figurative) as a name for the place (or state) of everlasting punishment:—hell.

A noun meaning Gehenna, i.e. the place of punishment in hades or the world of the dead, equivalent to *Tártaros* (2Pe 2:4, where it appears as the verb *tartaróō* [5020], to cast into hell), the lake of fire (Rev 20:14, 15), the everlasting fire (Mt 25:41; Jude 7). So simply for hell (Mt 5:29, 30; 10:28; Lk 12:5; Jas 3:6); with *púr* (4442, fire): hellfire, the fire of hell (Mt 5:22; 18:9; Mk 9:47); spoken of as *tó púr tó ásbeston* (*ásbestos* [762], unquenchable), the unquenchable fire, the fire that never shall be quenched (Mk 9:43, 45, cf. vv. 44, 46, 48). So the expression *huión géennēs*, son of Gehenna, son of hell (*huiós* [5207], son), i.e. worthy of punishment in hell (Mt 23:15); also *krísis tēs génnēs* (*krísis* [2920], condemnation, judgement), condemnation to Gehenna (Mt 23:33).

cf. Jude 7). It is therefore a place of eternal fire, and of thick darkness (cf. Jude 6, 13).

The name Gehenna is the Hebrew *gēy' hinnōm* (1516/2011, OT), valley of Hinnom (Jos 15:8), the narrow valley skirting Jerusalem on the south, running westward from the valley of Jehoshaphat under Mount Zion. Here the ancient Israelites established the idolatrous worship of Moloch, to whom they burned infants in sacrifice (1Ki 11:7; 2Ki 16:3; Jer 7:31; 32:35). This worship was broken up and the place desecrated by Josiah (2Ki 23:10, 14), after which it seems to have become the receptacle for all the filth of the city, and also for the carcasses of animals and the dead bodies of malefactors left unburied, to consume which fires would appear to have been from time to time kept up. It was also called Tophet (8612, OT [Jer 7:31]), i.e. abomination, place to be spit upon, from *tûp* (n.f., to spit), or more probably, since it had this name among idolaters, from *tāpeteh* (8613, OT), a place of burning, cremation. By an easy metaphor the Jews transferred the name to the place of punishment in the other world, the abode of demons and the souls of wicked men.

1068. Γεθσημανῆ, Gethsēmanē, *gheth-say-man-ay´*; of Chaldee origin [compare 1660 and 8081]; *oil-press*; *Gethsemane*, a garden near Jerusalem:—Gethsemane.

1069. γείτων, geitōn, *ghi´-tone*; from 1093; a *neighbour* (as adjoining one's *ground*); (by implication) a *friend*:—neighbour.

1070. γελάω, gelaō, *ghel-ah´-o*; of uncertain affinity; to *laugh* (as a sign of joy or satisfaction):—laugh.

1071. γέλως, gelōs, *ghel´-oce*; from 1070; *laughter* (as a mark of gratification):—laughter.

1072. γεμίζω, gemizō, *ghem-id´-zo*; transitive from 1073; to *fill* entirely:—fill (be) full.

1073. γέμω, gemō, *ghem´-o*; a primary verb; to *swell* out, i.e. *be full*:—be full.

1074. γενεά, genea, *ghen-eh-ah´*; from (a presumed derivative of) 1085; a *generation*; by implication an *age* (the period or the persons):—age, generation, nation, time.

Collective noun from *gínomai* (1096), to become. Birth. In the NT: generation, in the following senses:

(I) Offspring, progeny; generally and figuratively (Ac 8:33, quoted from Isa 53:8; Sept.: Ge 17:12; Nu 13:22; Est 9:28).

(II) A descent, a degree in a genealogical line of ancestors or descendants. Generation (Mt 1:17; Sept.: Ge 15:16; 25:13; Dt 23:3).

(III) Spoken of the period of time from one descendant to another, i.e. the average duration of human life, reckoned apparently by the ancient Jews at one hundred years (cf. Ge 15:16 with Ex 12:40, 41); by the Greeks at three generations for every one hundred years, that is, thirty-three and a half years each. Hence, in the NT of a less definite period: an age, time, period, day, as ancient generations, i.e. times of old (Lk 1:50 [cf. Rev 1:6; Ac 14:16; 15:21; Eph 3:5, 21; Col 1:26. See Sept.: Ge 9:12; Ps 72:5; Pr 27:24; Isa 34:17; Joel 3:20]). In Lk 16:8, "in their very own generation" (a.t.), means they are wiser in their day, so far as it concerns this life.

(IV) Metaphorically, spoken of the people of any generation or age, those living in any one period, a race or class, e.g., "this generation," meaning the present generation (Mt 11:16; 12:39, 41, 42, 45; 16:4; 17:17; 23:36; 24:34; Mk 8:12, 38; 9:19; 13:30; Lk 7:31; 9:41; 11:29–32, 50, 51; 17:25; 21:32; Ac 2:40; Php 2:15). Spoken of a former generation (Ac 13:36; Heb 3:10); of the future (Lk 1:48; Sept.: Dt 32:5, 20; Ps 12:8; 14:5; 24:6; 78:6, 8).

Deriv.: *genealogéō* (1075), to reckon by generations; *genetḗ* (1079), from his birth or the beginning of his life.

Syn.: *génos* (1085), kind, family, generation; *génnēma* (1081), generation, but with the idea of having had birth from; *éthnos* (1484), nation or people of the same kind; *aiṓn* (165), an age, era.

1075. γενεαλογέω, genealogeō, *ghen-eh-al-og-eh´-o*; from 1074 and 3056; to *reckon by generations*, i.e. *trace in genealogy*:—count by descent.

From *geneá* (1074), generation, and *légō* (3004), to reckon. In the NT in the middle/pass., *genealogéomai* or *genealogoúmai*, fut. *genealogḗsomai*: to be traced or inscribed in a genealogy, to be reckoned by descent (Heb 7:6, to trace one's descent or to derive one's origin; Sept.: 1Ch 5:1; 9:1; Ezr 2:61).

Deriv.: *agenealógētos* (35), one without

recorded pedigree or genealogy; *genealogía* (1076), genealogy.

1076. γενεαλογία, genealogia, *ghen-eh-al-og-ee´-ah*; from the same as 1075; *tracing by generations,* i.e. *"genealogy"*:—genealogy.

Noun from *genealogéō* (1075), to make a genealogical register. Genealogy, genealogical table of ancestors, etc. (1Ti 1:4; Tit 1:10; 3:9; Sept.: 1Ch 7:5, 7; 9:22).

1077. γενέσια, genesia, *ghen-es´-ee-ah*; neuter plural of a derivative of 1078; *birthday* ceremonies:—birthday.

1078. γένεσις, genesis, *ghen´-es-is*; from the same as 1074; *nativity*; (figurative) *nature*:—generation, nature (-ral).

Noun from *gínomai* (1096), to form. In the NT, birth, nativity:

(I) Particularly (Mt 1:18; Lk 1:14; Jas 1:23). Used figuratively in Jas 3:6, *tróchos tḗs genéseōs,* lit. "the wheel of birth" (*tróchos* [5164], wheel), set in motion at birth and rolls on through life, i.e. course of life.

(II) In the sense of descent, lineage, and *bíblos genéseōs,* book of descent (*bíblos* [976], book), i.e. genealogy, genealogical table (Mt 1:1).

Deriv.: *genésia* (1077), birthday; *paliggenesía* (3824), regeneration.

1079. γενετή, genetē, *ghen-et-ay´*; feminine of a presumed derivative of the base of 1074; *birth*:—birth.

1080. γεννάω, gennaō, *ghen-nah´-o*; from a variation of 1085; to *procreate* (properly of the father, but by extension of the mother); (figurative) to *regenerate*:—bear, beget, be born, bring forth, conceive, be delivered of, gender, make, spring.

From *génos* (1085), generation, kind, offspring. To beget as spoken of men; to bear as spoken of women; pass., to be begotten or be born:

(I) In the act. sense:

(A) Spoken of men, to beget (Mt 1:2–16; Ac 7:8, 29; Sept.: Ge 5:3ff.). Metaphorically, to generate, to occasion, e.g., strifes (2Ti 2:23).

(B) Spoken in the Jewish manner of the relation between a teacher and his disciples, to beget in a spiritual sense, to be the spiritual father of someone, i.e. the instrument of his conversion to a new spiritual life (1Co 4:15; Phm 10).

(C) Spoken of God begetting in a spiritual sense which consists in regenerating, sanctifying, quickening anew, and ennobling the powers of the natural man by imparting to him a new life and a new spirit in Christ (1Jn 5:1). Hence, Christians are said to be born of God and to be the sons of God (Ro 8:14; Gal 3:26; 4:6). Spoken of the relationship between God and the Messiah, called His Son (Ac 13:33; Ro 1:4; Heb 1:5; 5:5; Sept.: Ps 2:6–8 [cf. *huiós* {5207}, son]).

(D) Spoken of women, to bear, bring forth (Lk 1:13, 57; 23:29; Jn 16:21; figuratively Gal 4:24; Sept.: Ge 46:15; Ex 6:20; Ezr 10:44).

(II) In the pass. sense *gennáomai*, contracted *gennōmai*:

(A) To be begotten (Mt 1:20, "that which is conceived in her" or begotten, i.e. in her womb, the fetus; Heb 11:12).

(B) To be born as used generally (Mt 2:1, 4; 19:12; 26:24; Mk 14:21; Jn 3:4, blind; 9:2, 19, 20, 32; 16:21, "into the world"; Ac 7:20; 22:28, I have been born a Roman; Ro 9:11; Heb 11:23; Gal 4:23, 29, "after the flesh," in the course of nature). With *eis* (1510), unto, denoting finality, destination (Jn 18:37; 2Pe 2:12). In Mt 1:16, "of whom [fem. gen.]" meaning of the mother. See Lk 1:35. In Jn 3:6, with *ek* (1537), "out of the flesh" (a.t.), indicating the source. See also Jn 8:41. With *en* (1722), in, and the dat. of place (Ac 22:3). With the dat. of state or condition (Jn 9:34, in the state of sinfulness or sins). In Ac 2:8, "wherein we were born," meaning the dialect, the native tongue. Metaphorically, *ek* (1537), out of God or of the Spirit, only in the writings of John, meaning to be born of God or of the Spirit, in a spiritual sense, to have received from God a new spiritual life. See also Jn 1:13; 3:5, 6, 8; 1Jn 2:29; 3:9; 4:7; 5:1, 4, 18, and to be "born again" or from above which is equivalent to be born of God (Jn 3:3, 7); also *ánōthen* (509), from above.

Deriv.: *anagennáō* (313), to give new birth; *génnēma* (1081), offspring; *génnēsis* (1083), birth; *gennētós* (1084), born.

Syn.: *apokuéō* (616), to give birth to, bring forth. Used in a spiritual sense: *tíktō* (5088), to bring forth, give birth to a child, also used metaphorically in regard to sin in Jas 1:15.

1081. γέννημα, **gennēma,** *ghen´-nay-mah;* from 1080; *offspring;* (by analogy) *produce* (literal or figurative):—fruit, generation.

1082. Γεννησαρέτ, **Gennēsaret,** *ghen-nay-sar-et´;* of Hebrew origin [compare 3672]; *Gennesaret* (i.e. *Kinnereth*), a lake and plain in Palestine:—Gennesaret.

1083. γέννησις, **gennēsis,** *ghen´-nay-sis;* from 1080; *nativity:*—birth.

1084. γεννητός, **gennētos,** *ghen-nay-tos´;* from 1080; *born:*—they that are born.

1085. γένος, **genos,** *ghen´-os;* from 1096; "*kin*" (abstract or concrete, literal or figurative, individual or collective):—born, country (-man), diversity, generation, kind (-red), nation, offspring, stock.

1086. Γεργεσηνός, **Gergesēnos,** *gher-ghes-ay-nos´;* of Hebrew origin [1622]; a *Gergesene* (i.e. *Girgashite*) or one of the aborigines of Palestine:—Gergesene.

1087. γερουσία, **gerousia,** *gher-oo-see´-ah;* from 1088; the *eldership,* i.e. (collective) the Jewish *Sanhedrin:*—senate.

1088. γέρων, **gerōn,** *gher´-own;* of uncertain affinity [compare 1094]; *aged:*—old.

1089. γεύομαι, **geuomai,** *ghyoo´-om-ahee;* a primary verb; to *taste;* (by implication) to *eat;* (figurative) to *experience* (good or ill):—eat, taste.

To cause to taste, to let taste (Sept.: Ge 25:30). With the meaning of to eat, partake (Lk 14:24; Ac 10:10; 20:11; 23:14; Sept.: 1Sa 14:24 of bread; 2Sa 3:35). Metaphorically: to experience, prove, partake of (Mt 16:28; Mk 9:1; Lk 9:27; Jn 8:52; Heb 2:9; 6:5).

Syn.: With the meaning of to eat: *esthíō* (2068), to eat; *phágō* (5315), to eat, devour, consume; *trṓgō* (5176), to chew, eat; *bibrṓskō* (977), to eat, devour.

1090. γεωργέω, **geōrgeō,** *gheh-ore-gheh´-o;* from 1092; to *till* (the soil):—dress.

1091. γεώργιον, **geōrgion,** *gheh-ore´-ghee-on;* neuter of a (presumed) derivative of 1092; *cultivable,* i.e. a *farm:*—husbandry.

1092. γεωργός, geōrgos, *gheh-ore-gos´*; from 1093 and the base of 2041; a *land-worker,* i.e. *farmer:*—husbandman.

1093. γῆ, gē, *ghay;* contrete from a primary word; *soil;* by extension a *region,* or the solid part or the whole of the *terrene* globe (including the occupants in each application):—country, earth (-ly), ground, land, world.

(I) In reference to its vegetative power: earth, soil (Mt 13:5, 8, 23; Mk 4:5, 8, 20; Lk 14:35; Jn 12:24; Ge 1:11, 12; 3:14, 19; Sept.: Ge 4:2, 3).

(II) As that on which we tread, the ground (Mt 10:29; 15:35; Lk 6:49; 22:44; 24:5; Jn 8:6, 8; Ac 9:4, 8; Sept.: Ex 3:5; 9:33; 1Sa 26:7, 8; 2Sa 17:12).

(III) In distinction from the sea or a lake: the land, solid ground (Mk 4:1; 6:47; Jn 6:21; Ac 27:39, 43, 44; Sept.: Ge 8:7, 9; Jnh 1:13).

(IV) Of a country, region, territory, as the land of Israel (Mt 2:20, 21); Canaan (Ac 13:19); Egypt (Ac 7:11, 36, 40; 13:17); Judah (Mt 2:6); Zebulon (Mt 4:15); Gennesareth (Mt 14:34; Mk 6:53). Of the country adjacent to any place or city (Mt 9:26, 31). With a gen. of person, one's native land (Ac 7:3). Spoken particularly of and used in an absolute sense of the land of the Jews, Palestine (Mt 23:35; 27:45; Mk 15:33; Lk 4:25; 21:23; Ro 9:28; Jas 5:17; Isa 10:23). Also in the expression to "inherit the earth" (Mt 5:5 quoted from Ps 37:11; see Ps 37:9, 22, 29; 25:13; Isa 60:21 [cf. Le 20:24; Dt 16:20]). Figuratively used for the inhabitants of a country (Mt 10:15; 11:24).

(V) The earth, in distinction from *ho ouranós* (3772), heaven (Mt 5:18, 35; 6:10, 19; Lk 2:14; Ac 2:19; 7:49; Sept.: Ge 1:1, 2; 2:4; 4:11; 7:4; 1Ch 16:30); hence, "all things … that are in heaven, and that are in earth" means the universe (Col 1:16, 20). "A new earth" (2Pe 3:13; Rev 21:1) means qualitatively new (*kainē* [2537]), not just another earth.

(VI) Spoken of the habitable earth (*hē oikouménē* [3625]) (Lk 11:31; 21:35; Ac 10:12; 11:6; 17:26; Heb 11:13; Rev 3:10; Sept.: Ge 6:1, 5, 7, 11, 12; Isa 24:1), hence the expression *tá epí tḗs gḗs* (*tá epí* [1909], those upon; *tḗs gḗs,* of the earth), upon earthly things or pertaining to this life (Col 3:2); "all the earth" (Ro 9:17; 10:18); "upon the earth" (Col 3:5); the inhabitants of the earth, men (Rev 6:8; 11:6; 13:3; 19:2; Sept.: Ge 9:19; 11:1; 19:31). Also where things are said to be

done or take place on earth, which have reference chiefly to men (Mt 5:13; 6:10; 10:34; Lk 12:49; Jn 17:4). In Jn 3:31, "he being of the earth" (a.t.), means he who is of human birth and speaks only of worldly things.

Deriv.: *geōrgós* (1092); a farmer; *epígeios* (1919), of this earth, earthly.

Syn.: *agrós* (68), a field; *patrís* (3968), native country or one's fatherland; *chṓra* (5561), country, land; *períchōros* (4066), country round about; *oikouménē* (3625), the inhabited earth; *katachthónios* (2709), under the earth; *choïkós* (5517), of the soil or earthy; *édaphos* (1475), the ground; *chōríon* (5564), a piece of land; *kósmos* (2889), the earth, but primarily the people who dwell on the earth.

1094. γῆρας, gēras, *ghay´-ras;* akin to 1088; *senil-ity:*—old age.

1095. γηράσκω, gēraskō, *ghay-ras´-ko;* from 1094; to *be senescent:*—be (wax) old.

1096. γίνομαι, ginomai, *ghin´-om-ahee;* a prolonged and middle form of a primary verb; to *cause to be* ("*gen*"-*erate*), i.e. (reflexive) to *become* (*come into being*), used with great latitude (literal, figurative, intensive, etc.):—arise, be assembled, be (-come, -fall, -have self), be brought (to pass), (be) come (to pass), continue, be divided, draw, be ended, fall, be finished, follow, be found, be fulfilled, + God forbid, grow, happen, have, be kept, be made, be married, be ordained to be, partake, pass, be performed, be published, require, seem, be showed, × soon as it was, sound, be taken, be turned, use, wax, will, would, be wrought.

To begin to be, that is, to come into existence or into any state; and in the aor. and 2d perf. to have come into existence or simply to be:

(I) To begin to be, to come into existence, as implying origin (either from natural causes or through special agencies), result, change of state, place, and so forth:

(A) As implying origin in the ordinary course of nature: (1) Spoken of persons, to be born (Jn 8:58; Jas 3:9), to be born of, descended from (Ro 1:3; Gal 4:4; 1Pe 3:6; Sept.: Ge 21:3, 5). (2) Of plants and fruits: to be produced, grow (Mt 21:19; 1Co 15:37). (3) Of the phenomena, occurrences of nature: to arise, to come on, occur, e.g., *seismós* (4578), earthquake (Mt 8:24); *laílaps* (2978), storm, tempest (Mk 4:37); *galḗnē*

(1055), tranquillity (Mt 8:26; Mk 4:39); *skótos* (4655), darkness (Mt 27:45; Mk 15:33); *nephélē* (3507), cloudiness (Mk 9:7; Lk 9:34); *brontḗ* (1027), thunder (Jn 12:29). So also of a voice or cry, tumult as *phōnḗ* (5456), voice (Jn 12:30); *kraugḗ* (2906), clamor, cry (Mt 25:6); *thórubos* (2351), disturbance, uproar (Mt 26:5; 27:24); *stásis* (4714), an uprising (Lk 23:19); *schísma* (4978), division (Jn 7:43); *zḗtēsis* (2214), questioning (Jn 3:25); *sigḗ* (4602), silence (Ac 21:40; Rev 8:1). Also of emotions as *thlípsis* (2347), tribulation, affliction (Mt 13:21; see also Lk 15:10; 22:24; 1Ti 6:4). **(4)** Spoken of time such as day, night, evening: to come or come on, approach (Mt 8:16; 14:15, 23; 27:1; Mk 6:2; 11:19; 15:33; Lk 22:14; Jn 6:16; 21:4; Ac 27:27).

(II) As implying origin through an agency specially exerted: to be made, created, equal to *poioúmai*, the middle pass. of *poiéō* (4160), to make or to do:

(A) Spoken of the works of creation (Jn 1:3, 10; 1Co 15:45; Heb 4:3; 11:3; Sept.: Ge 2:4; Isa 48:7).

(B) Of works of art (Ac 19:26, "with hands").

(C) Of miracles and the like: to be wrought, performed (Mt 11:20; Ac 4:22; 8:13); with *diá*, through or with (Mk 6:2; Ac 2:43; 4:16); with *hupó* (5259), by (Lk 9:7; 13:17).

(D) Of a promise, plot: to be made (Ac 26:6; 20:3); of waste, *apṓleia* (684), loss, waste (Mk 14:4).

(E) Of the will or desire of someone: to be done, fulfilled (Mt 6:10; 26:42; Lk 11:2; 23:24; Ac 21:14).

(F) Of a meal: to be prepared, made ready (Jn 13:2); of a judicial investigation: to be made, initiated (Ac 25:26); so also of a change of law (Heb 7:12, 18).

(G) Of particular days, festivals to be held or celebrated (Mt 26:2; Jn 2:1; 10:22; Sept.: 2Ki 23:22).

(H) Of persons advanced to any station or office: to be made, constituted, appointed (1Co 1:30; Col 1:23, 25; Heb 5:5; 6:20); so also with *epánō* (1883), upon (Lk 19:19).

(I) Of customs, institutes: to be appointed, instituted (Mk 2:27, the Sabbath; Gal 3:17, the existing law).

(J) Of what is done to or in someone (Lk 23:31; Gal 3:13).

(III) As implying a result, event to take place or come to pass: occur, be done:

(A) Generally (Mt 1:22, "And all this took place" [a.t.]; Mk 5:14; Lk 1:20, "until these things take place" [a.t.]; 2:15; Jn 3:9; Ac 4:21; 5:24; 1Co 15:54; 1Th 3:4; Rev 1:19). In Heb 9:15, "death having taken place" (a.t.), that is, through His death. See also Mt 18:31; Lk 8:34; Jas 3:10; 2Pe 1:20. So also in the phrase *mḗ génoito* (*mḗ* [3361], not; *génoito* [1096], it be): let it not happen, God forbid, an exclamation of aversion (Lk 20:16; Ro 3:4, 6, 31; 6:2, 15; 7:7 [cf. Sept.: Ge 44:7, 17; Jos 22:29; 1Ki 21:3]).

(B) Of persons: to happen to someone (Mk 9:21; Lk 14:12; Jn 5:14; 1Pe 4:12). With the inf. as subj. (Ac 20:16; Gal 6:14; Sept.: Ge 44:7, 17). With an adverb of manner (Mk 5:16; Eph 6:3).

(C) With a prep. in the same sense as *eis* (1519), unto, followed by *tiná*, someone (Ac 28:6). In Mk 5:33, *epí* (1909), upon, with the dat. *tiní*, someone.

(D) With an inf. and accusative expressed or implied: to come to pass that (Mt 18:13, "if it comes to pass that he find it" [a.t.]; Mk 2:23; Ac 27:44, "it came to pass, that they escaped"; 28:8).

(IV) As implying a change of state, condition, or the passing from one state to another: to become, to enter upon any state, condition:

(A) Spoken of persons or things which receive any new character or form: **(1)** Where the predicate is a noun (Mt 4:3, "that these stones become bread" [a.t.]; 5:45, "that ye may become the sons of the father" [a.t.]; 13:32, "becomes a tree" [a.t.]; Mk 1:17, "that you may become fishers of men" [a.t.]; Lk 4:3; 6:16; 23:12; Jn 1:12, 14; 2:9; Ac 12:18, "what was become of Peter"; 26:28; Ro 4:18; Heb 2:17; Rev 8:8). **(2)** Construed with *eis* (1519), unto something as the predicate (Mt 21:42, He "became unto a cornerstone" [a.t.] or "He became a cornerstone" [a.t.]; Mk 12:10; Lk 13:19; Jn 16:20; Ac 5:36; Sept.: Ge 2:7; 1Sa 30:25). **(3)** When the predicate is an adj. (Mt 6:16, "do not ... become of a sad countenance" [a.t.], do not put on or affect sadness; 10:16, "therefore become prudent" [a.t.]; 12:45, "last ... shall be worse" [a.t.]; 13:22, "becomes fruitless" [a.t.]; 23:26; 24:32, 44, become ready, prepare yourselves; Jn 9:39; Ac 7:32; 10:4; Ro 3:19). With a particle of manner (Mt 10:25, "so that he become as his teachers" [a.t.]; 18:3; 28:4, "they became as if they were dead" [a.t.]). In 1Co 9:20, 22, with the dat. of person, for or in respect to whom. **(4)** With the gen. of possession or relation (Lk 20:14, "that the inheritance become ours" [a.t.]; 20:33; Rev 11:15). (5) With the dat. of person as possessor (Ro 7:3, 4, to become married to another man; Sept.: Le 22:12; Jer 3:1).

(B) Construed with prep. or adverb implying motion, it denotes change or transition to another place, to come. (1) With the prep. *eis* (1519), unto: to come to or into, to arrive at (Ac 20:16; 21:17; 25:15). Figuratively: the voice (Lk 1:44); the blessing (Gal 3:14); the gospel (1Th 1:5); sore or ulcer (Rev 16:2). (2) With *ek* (1537), out of: to come from a place, as the voice (Mk 1:11; Lk 3:22; 9:35), but *ek mésou* [(3319), from the midst] with *gínomai*: to be put out of the way (2Th 2:7). (3) With *en* (1722), in, used metaphorically (Ac 12:11, "being come to himself" [a.t. {cf. Lk 15:17}]). (4) With *epí* (1909), upon: to come upon, arrive at (Lk 22:40; Jn 6:21; Ac 21:35). With the accusative (Lk 1:65, fear; 4:36; 24:22; Ac 8:1); of an oracle (Lk 3:2). (5) With *katá* (2596), upon: to come throughout (Ac 10:37); to come to (Lk 10:32; Ac 27:7). (6) With *prós* (4314), toward: to come to (2Jn 12); of oracles (Ac 7:31; 10:13; Sept.: Ge 15:1, 4; Jer 1:2, 4). (7) With the adverb *eggús* (1451), near: to come or draw near (Jn 6:19; metaphorically Eph 2:13); *hóde* (5602), hither (Jn 6:25); *ekeí* (1563), thither (Ac 19:21).

(V) In the aor. and perf.: to have begun to be, to have come into existence, meaning simply to be, to exist.

(A) Generally: to be, to exist (Jn 1:6, "there came to be a man" [a.t.]; Ro 11:5; 1Jn 2:18). With *en* (1722), in (2Pe 2:1); *émprosthen* (1715), before someone (Jn 1:15, 30); *epí* (1909), upon the earth (Rev 16:18).

(B) As a copula connecting a subj. and predicate: (1) Of quality, with the nom. (Lk 1:2, those who "from the beginning became eyewitnesses ... of the word" [a.t.]; 2:2; Jn 14:22; Ac 4:4; 1Co 4:16; 2Co 1:18, 19; 1Th 2:8; Tit 3:7). With the dat. of advantage: to be anything to, for, or in behalf of (Ac 1:16; Lk 11:30; Col 4:11; 1Th 1:7). With an adverb (1Th 2:10). With a gen. of age (Lk 2:42; 1Ti 5:9). (2) Implying propriety (Mt 11:26; Lk 10:21, "such was thy good pleasure" [a.t.]). (3) Joined with the part. of another verb, it forms patterns like *eínai* (1511), to be, a periphrasis for a finite tense of that verb (Mk 1:4, literally, "it came to be John baptizing," which really stands for the verb "was baptizing"; see also 9:3, 7; Heb 5:12; Rev 16:10; Sept.: Ne 1:4.

(C) Joined with a prep. it implies locality or state, disposition of mind: (1) With *en* (1722), in, spoken of place: to be in a place (Mt 26:6, "when Jesus was in Bethany"; Mk 9:33, "in the house"; Ac 13:5; 2Ti 1:17; Rev 1:9). Spoken of condition or state: to be in any state (Lk 22:44, "when he came to be in agony" [a.t.]; Ac 22:17, "in ecstasy" [a.t.]; Ro 16:7, "in Christ," i.e. to be in the number of Christ's followers, Christians; Php 2:7, "having become the likeness" [a.t.], equal to "having likened himself" [a.t.]; 1Ti 2:14, "having placed herself in the state of the transgression" [a.t.]; Rev 1:10; 4:2). (2) With *metá* (3326), with, followed by the gen. of person: to be with someone (Ac 9:19; 20:18). In Mk 16:10, "those who had been with him" (a.t.), means His friends, companions. (3) Followed by *prós* (4314), to or toward, with an accusative: to be toward, that is, disposed toward someone (1Co 2:3; 16:10). (4) Followed by *sún* (4862), with: to be with (Lk 2:13).

Deriv.: *geneá* (1074), age, generation, nation; *génesis* (1078), generation, nature; *génos* (1085), generation, kind, offspring; *goneús* (1118), a parent; *diagínomai* (1230), to intervene, to elapse, pass; *epigínomai* (1920), to spring up, blow; *paragínomai* (3854), to be present; *progínomai* (4266), to happen before.

Syn.: *érchomai* (2064), to come; *apérchomai* (565), to come away from; *hḗkō* (2240), to come, be present; *aphiknéomai* (864), to arrive at a place; *enístēmi* (1764), to stand in, be present; *ephístēmi* (2186), to stand by or over; *katantáō* (2658), to come to, over against; *parístēmi* (3936), to stand by or near; *phérō* (5342), to come, to bring; *phthánō* (5348), to come upon, arrive at; *proseggízō* (4331), to come near; *diateléō* (1300), to bring through to an end; *ménō* (3306), to abide; *epioúsa* (1966), the next day, used as a verb meaning to come, arrive; *auxánō* (837), to grow or increase, to become something that one was not; *phúō* (5453), to produce, grow; *hupárchō* (5225), to exist, to continue to be what one was before; *eimí* (1510), to be; *diérchomai* (1330), to pass through or over; *apérchomai* (5656), to go away; *diabaínō* (1224), to step across or over; *metabaínō* (3327), to pass over from one place to another; *parágō* (3855), to pass by or away; *diaperáō* (1276), to pass over; *diodeúō* (1353), to travel through or along; *chōráō* (5562), to pass, retire; *katargéō* (2673), to do away with, abolish; *paroíchomai* (3944), to have passed by, be gone; *anachōréō* (402), to withdraw; *chōréō*

(5562), to have place; *phthánō* (5348), to arrive, catch up; *parístēmi* (3936), to be pressed, arrive; *sumbaínō* (4819), to come to pass; *prokóptō* (4298), to advance from within.

1097. γινώσκω, ginōskō, *ghin-oce´-ko*; a prolonged form of a primary verb; to "*know*" (absolute), in a great variety of applications and with many implication (as follows, with others not thus clearly expressed):—allow, be aware (of), feel, (have) know (-ledge), perceive, be resolved, can speak, be sure, understand.

To know, in a beginning or a completed sense:

(I) To know, in a beginning sense: that is, to come to know, to gain or receive a knowledge of:

(A) Generally (Mt 12:7; Mk 6:38; Lk 12:47; Jn 7:26; 8:32, 52; Ac 1:7; Ro 1:21; 1Co 4:19; 13:9; 2Co 2:9; Jas 2:20; 1Jn 3:16, 19, 24; 4:13). In the pass.: to be known or distinguished (1Co 14:7).

(B) In a judicial sense: to know by trial, to inquire into or examine the reason or cause (Jn 7:51; Ac 23:28).

(C) In the sense of to know from others, learn, find out. In the pass.: to be made known, disclosed (Mt 10:26; Mk 5:43; Ac 9:24; 21:34; Col 4:8; Mt 9:30; Lk 9:11; Sept.: 1Sa 21:2).

(D) In the sense of to perceive, observe, be aware of (Mt 16:8; 22:18; 26:10; Mk 5:29; Ac 23:6; Sept.: Ru 3:4).

(E) In the sense of to understand or comprehend (Mt 13:11; Mk 4:13; Lk 18:34; Jn 3:10; 7:49; 1Co 2:8, 14; Jn 10:6; 12:16; 13:12; Ac 8:30; Ro 11:34; Sept.: 1Sa 20:39; Pr 1:2).

(F) By euphemism: to lie with a person of another sex as spoken of a man or men (Mt 1:25; Sept.: Ge 4:1, 17; 24:16); of a woman or women (Lk 1:34; Sept.: Ge 19:8; Nu 31:17, 35).

(II) To know in a completed sense, that is, to have the knowledge of:

(A) Generally (Mt 6:3; 24:43; Lk 2:43; 7:39; 16:15; Jn 2:25; Ac 19:35; Ro 2:18; 10:19; 2Co 5:21; Eph 5:5; 1Jn 3:20). With persons: to know as by sight or person (Jn 1:48; 2Co 5:16); to know one's character (Jn 1:10; 2:24; 14:7, 9; 16:3; Ac 19:15; Sept.: Dt 34:10; Ps 87:4; 139:1).

(B) In the sense of to know, as being what one is or professes to be, to acknowledge (Mt 7:23). Passive tense (1Co 8:3; Gal 4:9; Sept.: Isa 33:13; 61:9; 63:16).

(C) With the idea of volition or goodwill: to know and approve or love, to care for, spoken of persons (Jn 10:14, 15, 27; 1Ti 2:18; Sept.: Ps

144:3; Am 3:2; Na 1:7); of things (Ro 7:15; Sept.: Ps 1:6).

Deriv.: *anaginōskō* (314), to read; *gnōmē* (1106), cognition; *gnōsis* (1108), knowledge; *gnōstēs* (1109), a knower, expert; *gnōstós* (1110), well-known, acquaintance; *diaginōskō* (1231), to know thoroughly; *epiginōskō* (1921), to observe, fully perceive, notice attentively, discern; *kardiognōstēs* (2589), heart-knower; *kataginōskō* (2607), to blame condemn; *proginōskō* (4267), to know beforehand.

Syn.: *epístamai* (1987), to know or acquire knowledge; *sunoída* (4894), to know together, be conscious of; *theōréō* (2334), to be a spectator and thus to understand or perceive; *aisthánomai* (143), to perceive with the senses, while *ginōskō* is to perceive through the mind; *noéō* (3539), to perceive with the mind, to understand; *katanoéō* (2657), to understand more fully; *katalambánō* (2638), to lay hold of, apprehend, perceive; *blépō* (991), to see and perceive; *suníēmi* (4920), to mentally put it together, to perceive, understand; *punthánomai* (4441), to inquire in order to know; *parakolouthéō* (3877), to follow, observe, understand; *gnōrízō* (1107), to come to know, know; *diagnōrízō* (1232), to make known widely; *gnōstós* (1110), known; *ágnōstos* (57), unknown; *agnōsía* (56), ignorance; *kardiognōstēs* (2589), one who knows the heart; *anagnōrízō* (319), to recognize, to make oneself known; *diagnōrízō* (1232), to make known; *diaginōskō* (1231), to determine by thorough examination; *gnōrízō* (1107), to make known, understand.

1098. γλεῦκος, gleukos, *glyoo´-kos*; akin to 1099; *sweet* wine, i.e. (properly) *must* (fresh juice), but used of the more saccharine (and therefore highly inebriating) fermented *wine*:— new wine.

Noun from *glukús* (1099), sweet. Musk; new or sweet wine (Ac 2:13; Sept.: Job 32:19).

1099. γλυκύς, glukus, *gloo-koos´*; of uncertain affinity; *sweet* (i.e. not bitter nor salt):—sweet, fresh.

1100. γλῶσσα, glōssa, *gloce´-sah*; of uncertain affinity; the *tongue*; (by implication) a *language* (specially one naturally unacquired):—tongue.

A noun meaning tongue:

(I) An organ of the body (Rev 16:10); as of taste (Lk 16:24); of speech (Mk 7:33, 35; Lk 1:64; 1Co 14:9; Jas 3:5, 6); personified (Ro

14:11; Php 2:11, "every tongue" means every person [cf. Ac 2:26; Sept.: Isa 45:23 {see also Ps 16:9}). To bridle the tongue (Jas 1:26; 3:8; 1Pe 3:10; Sept.: Jgs 7:5; Job 29:10; 33:2).

(II) Metaphorically, speech or language:

(A) Generally (1Jn 3:18; Sept.: Pr 25:15; 31:26).

(B) Of a particular language or dialect as spoken by a particular people (Ac 2:11; 1Co 13:1; Sept.: Ge 10:5, 20; Da 1:4). Used for the people who speak a particular language, e.g., tribes, people, and tongues (Rev 5:9; 7:9; 10:11; 11:9; 13:7; 14:6; 17:15; Sept.: Isa 66:18; Da 3:4, 7, 30, 32).

(C) In the phrases *glṓssais hetérais* (2083), different tongues (Ac 2:4); *glṓssais kainaís* (2537), new tongues (Mk 16:17); *glṓssais laleín* (2980), to speak in tongues (Ac 10:46; 19:6; 1Co 12:30; 14:2, 4–6, 13, 18, 23, 27, 39); *proseuchésthai glṓssē* (4336), to pray in a tongue (1Co 14:14); *lógoi en glṓssē* (3056), discourse in a tongue (1Co 14:19); or simply *glṓssai*, tongues (1Co 12:10, 28; 13:8; 14:22, 26). Here, according to the two passages in Mark and Acts, the sense would seem to be to speak in other living languages. But if the passages in 1 Corinthians are taken as the basis, these phrases would seem to mean to speak another kind of language, i.e. referring perhaps to a state of high spiritual excitement or ecstasy from inspiration, unconscious of external things and wholly absorbed in adoring communication with God, breaking forth into abrupt expressions of praise and devotion which are not coherent and therefore not always intelligible to others (cf. 1Co 14:2, 4, 6, 7). Most interpreters have adopted the first meaning; some prefer the latter. Others suppose there is a reference to two distinct gifts.

(III) Figuratively, for anything resembling a tongue in shape (Ac 2:3).

Deriv.: *glōssókomon* (1101), a bag, case; *heteróglōssos* (2084), a person speaking a tongue other than one's native tongue.

Syn.: *diálektos* (1258), dialect, an ethnic language.

1101. γλωσσόκομον, glōssokomon, *gloce-sok´-om-on;* from 1100 and the base of 2889; properly a *case* (to keep mouthpieces of wind-instruments in), i.e. (by extension) a *casket* or (special) *purse*:—bag.

1102. γναφεύς, gnapheus, *gnaf-yuce´;* by variation for a derivative from **κνάπτω, knaptō** (to *tease* cloth); a cloth-*dresser*:—fuller.

1103. γνήσιος, gnēsios, *gnay´-see-os;* from the same as 1077; *legitimate* (of birth), i.e. *genuine*:—own, sincerity, true.

1104. γνησίως, gnēsiōs, *gnay-see´-oce;* adverb from 1103; *genuinely*, i.e. *really*:—naturally.

1105. γνόφος, gnophos, *gnof´-os;* akin to 3509; *gloom* (as of a storm):—blackness.

Noun from *néphos* (3509), a cloud. A thick dark cloud (Heb 12:18; Sept.: Ex 20:21; Dt 4:11; 5:22; 2Sa 22:10).

Syn.: *skótos* (4655), darkness; *zóphos* (2217), darkness, foggy weather, smoke which is used to imply infernal darkness; *achlús* (887), a thick mist or a fog.

1106. γνώμη, gnōmē, *gnо´-may;* from 1097; *cognition*, i.e. (subject) *opinion*, or (object) *resolve* (*counsel, consent,* etc.):—advice, + agree, judgement, mind, purpose, will.

Noun from *ginóskō* (1097), to discern, know. Generally it means capacity of judgement, faculty of discernment as far as conduct is determined:

(I) As implying will: in the sense of accord, consent (Phm 14). In the sense of purpose, counsel, determination (Ac 20:3; Rev 17:17); in the sense of bent, inclination, desire (1Co 1:10; Rev 17:13).

(II) As implying opinion: judgement, in reference to oneself (1Co 7:40, "according to my opinion" [a.t.]); in reference to others: advice (1Co 7:25; 2Co 8:10).

Syn.: *boulḗ* (1012), a piece of advice, counsel; *krísis* (2920), legal decision, judgement; *kríma* (2917), condemnatory judgement; *aísthēsis* (144), perception resulting from the senses; *phrónēma* (5427), thought; *phrónēsis* (5428), the thought process, understanding; *boúlēma* (1013), deliberate intention or purpose; *thélēma* (2307), a desire expressive of the will; *próthesis* (4286), purpose; *thélēsis* (2308), the act of willing or wishing; *eudokía* (2107), good pleasure or will; *eúnoia* (2133), goodwill; *diánoia* (1271), intelligence, understanding; *dianóēma* (1270), something thought through, a thought, consideration.

1107. γνωρίζω, gnōrizō, *gno-rid´-zo;* from a derivative of 1097; to *make known;* subject to *know:*—certify, declare, make known, give to understand, do to wit, wot.

(I) To others:

(A) Generally to make known, declare, reveal (Ro 9:22, 23); with the dat. (Lk 2:15; Ac 2:28 quoted from Ps 16:11; Eph 3:3, 5, 10; Col 1:27; Gal 1:11); with the prep. *pros* (4314), to (Php 4:6; Sept.: 1Sa 16:3; 1Ch 16:8; Ps 25:4).

(B) In the sense of to narrate, tell, inform (Eph 6:21; Col 4:7, 9; 2Co 8:1).

(C) Spoken of a teacher who unfolds divine things, to announce, declare, proclaim (Jn 15:15; 17:26; Ro 16:26; Eph 1:9; 6:19; 2Pe 1:16; Sept.: Eze 20:11).

(D) In the sense of to put in mind of, impress upon, confirm (1Co 12:3; 15:1).

(II) To make known to oneself, to ascertain, find out (Php 1:22; Sept.: Job 34:25).

Deriv.: *anagnōrízomai* (319), to make known; *diagnōrízō* (1232), to tell abroad.

Syn.: *epístamai* (1987), to know, understand; *apokalúptō* (601), to reveal.

1108. γνῶσις, **gnōsis**, *gno´-sis*; from 1097; *knowing* (the act), i.e. (by implication) *knowledge*:—knowledge, science.

(I) The power of knowing, intelligence, comprehension (Ro 8:35; 1Co 12:31; 13:2; Eph 3:19).

(II) Subjectively spoken of what one knows: knowledge (Lk 1:77; Ro 11:33; Php 3:8; Sept.: Ps 73:11; 139:6; Hos 4:6); of the knowledge of Christianity generally (Ro 15:14; 1Co 1:5; 8:1; 2Pe 3:18); of a deeper and better Christian knowledge, both theoretical and experimental (1Co 8:7, 10, 11; 2Co 11:6). Spoken of practical knowledge, discretion, prudence (2Co 6:6; 1Pe 3:7; 2Pe 1:5, 6; Sept.: Pr 13:16).

(III) Objectively spoken of what is known: the object of knowledge, generally knowledge, doctrine, science (2Co 2:14; 4:6; Col 2:3; Sept.: Da 1:4; Mal 2:7); of religious knowledge, i.e. doctrine, science as spoken of Jewish teachers (Lk 11:52; Ro 2:20; 1Ti 6:20); of a deeper Christian knowledge, Christian doctrine (1Co 12:8; 1Co 13:2, 8; 14:6; 2Co 8:7). Hence in 2Co 10:5, "against the true doctrine of God" (a.t.), i.e. against the Christian religion. From *gnōsis* is derived "gnosticism," a cult of pre-Christian and early Christian centuries distinguished by the conviction that matter is evil and that emancipation comes through *gnōsis*, knowledge.

Deriv.: *agnōsía* (56), without knowledge.

1109. γνώστης, **gnōstēs**, *gnoce´-tace*; from 1097; a *knower*:—expert.

Noun from *ginōskō* (1097), to know. One who knows. Only in Ac 26:3.

1110. γνωστός, **gnōstos**, *gnoce-tos´*; from 1097; well *known*:—acquaintance, (which may be) known, notable.

Adjective from *ginōskō* (1097), to know. Known:

(I) Generally (Jn 18:15, 16; Ac 1:19; 9:42; 15:18; 19:17; 28:22). *Gnōstón éstō* (present imper. of *eimí* [1510], to be), be it known (Ac 2:14; 4:10; 13:38; 28:28; Sept.: Eze 36:32; Ezr 4:12, 13). In the sense of knowable, *tó gnōstón toú Theoú*, what may be known of God or the knowledge of God, equal to *gnōsis* (1108) as in Ro 1:19. God is knowable or known by man because of the demonstration of His power in His creation. Here reference is made not to the knowledge possessed by God, but to man's knowledge of God (Sept.: Ge 2:9). In an emphatic sense, known of all, i.e. notable, incontrovertible (Ac 4:16).

(II) As a substantive with the article *ho gnōstós*, it means an acquaintance (Lk 2:44; 23:49; Sept.: 2Ki 10:11; Ps 88:8, 18).

Deriv.: *ágnōstos* (57), unknown.

Syn.: *phanerós* (5318), visible, manifest, known.

1111. γογγύζω, **gogguzō**, *gong-good´-zo*; of uncertain derivative; to *grumble*:—murmur.

1112. γογγυσμός, **goggusmos**, *gong-goos-mos´*; from 1111; a *grumbling*:—grudging, murmuring.

1113. γογγυστής, **goggustēs**, *gong-goos-tace´*; from 1111; a *grumbler*:—murmurer.

1114. γόης, **goēs**, *go´-ace*; from γοάω, *goaō* (to *wail*); properly a *wizard* (as *muttering* spells), i.e. (by implication) an *imposter*:—seducer.

1115. Γολγοθᾶ, **Golgotha**, *gol-goth-ah´*; of Chaldee origin [compare 1538]; *the skull; Golgotha*, a knoll near Jerusalem:—Golgotha.

1116. Γόμορρα, **Gomorrha**, *gom´-or-hrhah*; of Hebrew origin [6017]; *Gomorrha* (i.e. *Amorah*), a place near the Dead Sea:—Gomorrha.

1117. γόμος, **gomos**, *gom´-os*; from 1073; a *load* (as *filling*), i.e. (special) a *cargo*, or (by extension) *wares*:—burden, merchandise.

1118. γονεύς, **goneus**, *gon-yooce´*; from the base of 1096; a *parent*:—parent.

1119. γονύ, gonu, *gon-oo´*; of uncertain affinity; the "*knee*":—knee (× -l).

1120. γονυπετέω, gonupeteō, *gon-oo-pet-eh´-o*; from a compound of 1119 and the alternative of 4098; to *fall* on the *knee*:—bow the knee, kneel down.

1121. γράμμα, gramma, *gram´-mah*; from 1125; a *writing*, i.e. a *letter, note, epistle, book,* etc.; plural *learning*:—bill, learning, letter, Scripture, writing, written.

Noun from *gráphō* (1125), to write. In the NT, lit. "the written," i.e. something written or cut in with the stylus, in the ancient manner of writing. Used of a letter of the alphabet (Lk 23:38; Gal 6:11); a letter, epistle (Ac 28:21; Gal 6:11); a bill, bond, note (Lk 16:6, 7); writings, a book, etc., e.g., of Moses (Jn 5:47); of the OT, i.e. the Scriptures (2Ti 3:15), so Jn 7:15, since the Jews had no other literature; used figuratively: the writing, the letter, i.e. the literal or verbal meaning, in antithesis to the spirit, spoken of the Mosaic Law (Ro 2:27, 29; 7:6; 2Co 3:6, 7). Also used of letters, learning, as contained in books (Ac 26:24).

Deriv.: *agrámmatos* (62), unlearned.

Syn.: *biblíon* (975), a small book, any scroll or sheet on which something is written; *didaskalía* (1319), teaching instruction, doctrine; *epistolé* (1992), epistle, letter; *pinakídion* (4093), a tablet on which one can write.

1122. γραμματεύς, grammateus, *gram-mat-yooce´*; from 1121; a *writer*, i.e. (professionally) *scribe* or *secretary*:—scribe, town-clerk.

Noun from *gráphō* (1125), to write. A scribe or writer:

(I) In the Greek sense, a public officer in the cities of Asia Minor, whose duty it seems to have been to preside in the senate, to enroll and have charge of the laws and decrees, and to read what was to be made known to the people; a public clerk, secretary (Ac 19:35). The office varied much in different places.

(II) In the Jewish sense, in the Sept. like the Hebrew *sōpēr* (from 5608, OT), the king's scribe, secretary of state (2Sa 8:17; 20:25); military clerk (2Ki 25:19; 2Ch 26:11). Later, in Sept. and in NT: a scribe, i.e. one skilled in the Jewish law, an interpreter of the Scriptures, a lawyer. The scribes had the charge of transcribing the sacred books, of interpreting difficult passages, and of deciding in cases which grew out of the ceremonial law. Their

influence was of course great; and since many of them were members of the Sanhedrin, we often find them mentioned with the elders and the chief priests (Mt 2:4; 5:20; 7:29; 12:38; 20:18; 21:15). They are also called *nomikoí* (3544), experts in the law, lawyers, and *nomodidáskaloi* (3547), a teacher of the law (cf. Mk 12:28 with Mt 22:35). Hence, the term is used also of one instructed, a scholar, a learned teacher of religion (Mt 13:52; 23:34; 1Co 1:20).

Syn.: *nomikós* (3544), lawyer; *nomodidáskalos* (3547), teacher of the law.

1123. γραπτός, graptos, *grap-tos´*; from 1125; *inscribed* (figurative):—written.

1124. γραφή, graphē, *graf-ay´*; from 1125; a *document*, i.e. holy *Writ* (or its contents or a statement in it):—Scripture.

Noun from *gráphō* (1125), to write. In the NT: Scripture, the Scriptures, i.e. of the Jews. The Old Testament (Mt 21:42; Jn 5:39; Ac 8:32; Ro 1:2; 9:17); Holy Scriptures (Ro 1:2; Sept.: Ezr 6:18). Put for the contents of Scripture, i.e. scriptural declaration, promise, etc. (Mt 22:29; Mk 12:24; Jn 10:35; Ac 1:16; Jas 2:23), scriptural prophecy (Mt 26:54, 56; Lk 4:21; Ro 16:26). In 2Pe 3:16, some think the writings of Paul and other apostles are meant.

1125. γράφω, graphō, *graf´-o*; a primary verb; to "*grave*," especially to *write*; (figurative) to *describe*:—describe, write (-ing, -ten).

To engrave or cut in, to insculp (Sept.: 1Ki 6:28). To sketch, picture. In the NT, to write:

(I) Particularly, to form letters with a stylus, in the ancient manner, so that the letters were cut in or graven upon the material (Jn 8:6, 8; 2Th 3:17). In the sense of to write upon, i.e. to fill with writing (Rev 5:1).

(II) To commit to writing, to express by writing (Lk 1:63; 16:6, 7; Jn 19:21, 22; 20:30, 31; 21:24, 25; Ro 16:22; Rev 1:11; 10:4). Spoken of what is written or contained in the Scriptures (Mk 1:2; Lk 3:4; Jn 8:17); so the expression "it is written" as a formula of citation (Mt 4:4, 6, 7, 10; Lk 4:4, 8, 10; Ro 1:17; 2:24). In the sense of to write about, to describe (Jn 1:46; Ro 10:5).

(III) To compose or prepare in writing (Mk 10:4; Lk 23:38; Ac 23:25; 2Pe 3:1).

(IV) To write to someone, i.e. to make known by writing (Ro 15:15; 2Co 1:13; 2:4; Php 3:1; 1Jn 2:12–14; Rev 2:1). So of written directions, instructions, information, etc. (Ac 15:23; 18:27; 1Co 5:9; 7:1; 2Co 9:1). Hence used in the expression "to write a command, precept" (Mk 10:5; 12:19; Lk 20:28; 1Jn 2:7).

(V) To inscribe, e.g., one's name in a book, register, etc. (Lk 10:20; Rev 13:8; 17:8).

Deriv.: *apográphō* (583), to write, tax; *grámma* (1121), bill, letter, Scripture; *grammateús* (1122), scribe, town clerk; *graptós* (1123), written; *graphḗ* (1124), Scripture; *eggráphō* (1449), engrave; *epigráphō* (1924), to inscribe; *prográphō* (4270), to write previously, before ordain; *cheirógraphon* (5498), handwriting.

1126. γραώδης, graōdēs, *grah-o´-dace*; from **γραῦς, graus** (an *old woman*) and 1491; *cronelike,* i.e. *silly*:—old wives'.

1127. γρηγορεύω, grēgoreuō, *gray-gor-yoo´-o*; from 1453; to *keep awake,* i.e. *watch* (literal or figurative):—be vigilant, wake, (be) watch (-ful).

From *egeírō* (1453) to arise, arouse. To wake, to keep awake, to watch. Particularly (Mt 24:43; 26:38, 40, 41; Mk 13:34; 14:34, 37, 38; Lk 12:37, 39). Used figuratively: to watch, i.e. be vigilant, attentive (Mt 24:42; 25:13; Mk 13:35, 37; Ac 20:31; 1Co 16:13; 1Pe 5:8; Rev 3:2, 3); also to wake, i.e. to live (1Th 5:10, where *katheúdō* [2518], to sleep, is referred to death).

Deriv.: *diagrēgoréō* (1235), to be awake.

Syn.: *agrupnéō* (69), keep awake; *blépō* (991), to take heed, beware; *horáō* (3708), behold, take heed; *proséchō* (4337), turn one's attention to, take heed; *epéchō* (1907), to give attention to, give heed; *skopéō* (4648), to watch, look, take heed; *phulássō* (5442), to guard.

1128. γυμνάζω, gumnazō, *goom-nad´-zo*; from 1131; to *practise naked* (in the games), i.e. *train* (figurative):—exercise.

1129. γυμνασία, gumnasia, *goom-nas-ee´-ah*; from 1128; *training,* i.e. (figurative) *asceticism*:—exercise.

1130. γυμνητεύω, gumnēteuō, *goom-nayt-yoo´-o*; from a derivative of 1131; to *strip,* i.e. (reflexive) *go poorly clad*:—be naked.

1131. γυμνός, gumnos, *goom-nos´*; of uncertain affinity; *nude* (absolute or relative, literal or figurative):—naked.

(I) In respect to the body: wholly nude, without any clothing (perhaps Mk 14:51, 52; figura-

tively, Rev 16:15; 17:16); also spoken of one who has no outer garment and is clad only in a tunic, which is fitted close to the body (Jn 21:7; Ac 19:16; probably Mk 14:51; Sept.: 1Sa 19:24; Isa 20:2). As in Eng., half-naked, i.e. poorly clad, destitute as to clothing, implying poverty and want (Mt 25:36, 38, 43, 44; Jas 2:15; Sept.: Job 31:19; 24:7; Isa 58:7). Figuratively: destitute of spiritual goods (Rev 3:17).

(II) Figuratively spoken of the soul as disencumbered of the body in which it had been clothed (2Co 5:3, cf. v. 4 and 15:51).

(III) Spoken of any thing as taken alone, abstractly, separate from everything else: naked, mere, bare (1Co 15:37).

(IV) Metaphorically: uncovered, open, manifest (Heb 4:13).

Deriv.: *gumnázō* (1128), to exercise; *gumnēteúō* (1130), to be naked or scantily clothed; *gumnótēs* (1132), nakedness, lack of sufficient clothing, metaphorically lack of spirituality.

1132. γυμνότης, gumnotēs, *goom-not´-ace*; from 1131; *nudity* (absolute or comparative):—nakedness.

Noun from *gumnós* (1131), naked. Nakedness, i.e. spoken of the state of one who is poorly clad (Ro 8:35; 2Co 11:27; Sept.: Dt 28:48); by euphemism, for the parts of shame (figuratively, Rev 3:18; Sept.: Ge 9:22, 23).

Syn.: *apobolé* (580), a casting off; *apékdusis* (555), a divestment, putting off.

1133. γυναικάριον, gunaikarion, *goo-nahee-kar´-ee-on*; a diminutive from 1135; a *little* (i.e. *foolish*) *woman*:—silly woman.

1134. γυναικεῖος, gunaikeios, *goo-nahee-ki´-os*; from 1135; *feminine*:—wife.

1135. γυνή, gunē, *goo-nay´*; probably from the base of 1096; a *woman*; specially a *wife*:—wife, woman.

1136. Γώγ, Gōg, *gogue*; of Hebrew origin [1463]; *Gog,* a symbolical name for some future Antichrist:—Gog.

1137. γωνία, gōnia, *go-nee´-ah*; probably akin to 1119; an *angle*:—corner, quarter.

Δ (Delta)

NT Numbers 1138–1436

1138. Δαβίδ, **Dabid,** *dab-eed´*; of Hebrew origin [1732]; *Dabid* (i.e. *David*), the Israelites king:—David.

1139. δαιμονίζομαι, **daimonizomai,** *dahee-mon-id´-zom-ahee*; middle from 1142; to *be exercised by a dæmon:*—have a (be vexed with, be possessed with) devil (-s).

From *daímōn* (1142), demon. To be afflicted, vexed, possessed, with an evil spirit; to be a demoniac (Mt 8:16, 28, 33; 9:32; 12:22; 15:22; Mk 1:32; 5:15, 16, 18; Lk 8:36; Jn 10:21, see Jn 10:20). It is much disputed whether the writers of the NT used this word to denote the actual presence of evil spirits in the persons affected, or whether they employed it only in compliance with popular usage and belief, just as we now use the word "lunatic" without assenting to the old opinion of the influence of the moon. A serious difficulty in the way of this latter supposition is that the demoniacs everywhere at once address Jesus as the Messiah (e.g., Mt 8:29; Mk 1:24; Lk 4:34; 8:28).

1140. δαιμόνιον, **daimonion,** *dahee-mon´-ee-on*; neuter of a derivative of 1142; a *dæmonic being*; by extension a *deity:*—devil, god.

1141. δαιμονιώδης, **daimoniōdēs,** *dahee-mon-ee-o´-dace*; from 1140 and 1142; *dæmon-like:*—devilish.

1142. δαίμων, **daimon,** *dah´ee-mown*; from δαίω, *daiō* (to *distribute* fortunes); a *dæmon* or supernatural spirit (of a bad nature):—devil.

A noun meaning demon, an evil spirit (Mt 8:31; Mk 5:12; Lk 8:29; Rev 16:14 [TR]; 18:2 [TR]).

Deriv.: *daimonízomai* (1139), to be possessed of a demon; *daimónion* (1140), a little demon.

1143. δάκνω, **daknō,** *dak´-no*; a prolonged form of a primary root; to *bite,* i.e. (figurative) *thwart:*—bite.

1144. δάκρυ, **dakru,** *dak´-roo*; or δάκρυον, **dakruon,** *dak´-roo-on*; of uncertain affinity; a *tear:*—tear.

1145. δακρύω, **dakruō,** *dak-roo´-o*; from 1144; to *shed tears:*—weep. Compare 2799.

1146. δακτύλιος, **daktulios,** *dak-too´-lee-os*; from 1147; a *finger-ring:*—ring.

1147. δάκτυλος, **daktulos,** *dak´-too-los*; probably from 1176; a *finger:*—finger.

1148. Δαλμανουθά, **Dalmanoutha,** *dal-man-oo-thah´*; probably of Chaldee origin; *Dalmanutha,* a place in Palestine:—Dalmanutha.

1149. Δαλματία, **Dalmatia,** *dal-mat-ee´-ah*; probably of foreign derivative; *Dalmatia,* a region of Europe:—Dalmatia.

1150. δαμάζω, **damazō,** *dam-ad´-zo*; a variation of an obsolete primary of the same meaning; to *tame:*—tame.

1151. δάμαλις, **damalis,** *dam´-al-is*; probably from the base of 1150; a *heifer* (as *tame*):—heifer.

1152. Δάμαρις, **Damaris,** *dam´-ar-is*; probably from the base of 1150; perhaps *gentle; Damaris,* an Athenian woman:—Damaris.

1153. Δαμασκηνός, **Damaskēnos,** *dam-as-kay-nos´*; from 1154; a *Damascene* or inhabitant of Damascus:—Damascene.

1154. Δαμασκός, **Damaskos,** *dam-as-kos´*; of Hebrew origin [1834]; *Damascus,* a city of Syria:—Damascus.

1155. δανείζω, **daneizō,** *dan-ide´-zo*; from 1156; to *loan* on interest; reflexive to *borrow:*—borrow, lend.

1156. δάνειον, **daneion,** *dan´-i-on*; from δάνος, *danos* (a *gift*); probably akin to the base of 1325; a *loan:*—debt.

1157. δανειστής, daneistēs, *dan-ice-tace´*; from 1155; a *lender*:—creditor.

1158. Δανιήλ, Daniēl, *dan-ee-ale´*; of Hebrew origin [1840]; *Daniel,* an Israelite:—Daniel.

1159. δαπανάω, dapanaō, *dap-an-ah´-o*; from 1160; to *expend,* i.e. (in a good sense) to *incur cost,* or (in a bad one) to *waste*:—be at charges, consume, spend.

1160. δαπάνη, dapanē, *dap-an´-ay*; from **δάπτω, daptō** (to *devour*); *expense* (as *consuming*):—cost.

1161. δέ, de, *deh*; a primary particle (adversative or continuative); *but, and,* etc.:—also, and, but, moreover, now [*often unexpressed in English*].

1162. δέησις, deēsis, *deh´-ay-sis*; from 1189; a *petition*:—prayer, request, supplication.

Noun from *déomai* (1189), to make known one's particular need. Want, need. In the NT: prayer, as the expression of need, desire, etc.; supplication, petition for oneself (Lk 1:13; Php 4:6; Heb 5:7; 1Pe 3:12; Sept.: Job 27:9; Ps 39:12; 40:2; 1Ki 8:28, 30); in behalf of others (Php 1:19; Jas 5:16); with *hupér* (5228), on behalf of (Ro 10:1; 2Co 1:11; 9:14; Php 1:4; 2Ti 2:1); with *perí* (4012), concerning (Eph 6:18). Generally, spoken of any prayer (Lk 2:37; 5:33; Ac 1:14; Eph 6:18; Php 1:4; 2Ti 5:5; 2Ti 1:3; Sept.: 1Ki 8:45; 2Ch 6:40).

Syn.: *proseuchḗ* (4335), a more general word for prayer to God in particular which is a more sacred word than *déēsis*; *euchḗ* (2171), translated "prayer," but in reality meaning a vow or wish; *énteuxis* (1783), intercession, a petition to a superior; *aítēma* (155), something asked for; *hiketēría* (2428), originally an olive branch carried by a suppliant.

1163. δεῖ, dei, *die*; third person singular active present of 1210; also **δεόν, deon,** *deh-on´*; neuter active participle of the same; both used impersonal; *it is* (*was,* etc.) *necessary* (as *binding*):—behoved, be meet, must (needs), (be) need (-ful), ought, should.

In the NT: it needs, it is necessary:

(**I**) Particularly, from the nature of the case, from a sense of duty, etc.: one must (Mt 16:21; 26:35; Mk 14:31; Lk 2:49; 4:43; Jn 3:7, 30; 1Co 11:19; Heb 9:26). So spoken of what is made

necessary by divine appointment (Jn 3:14; 20:9; Ac 4:2). Of things unavoidable (Mt 24:6; Mk 13:7; Ac 1:16; Ro 1:27; 2Co 11:30).

(**II**) Spoken of what is right and proper in itself, or prescribed by law, duty, custom, etc.: it is right or proper, one must, it ought, it should (Mt 18:33; 25:27; Mk 13:14; Lk 13:14, 16; Jn 4:20; Ac 5:29; 2Ti 2:6; Sept.: Job 15:3). Also that which prudence would dictate (Ac 27:21).

Syn.: *opheílō* (3784), morally obliged or personally obliged; *chrézō* (5535), to need; *chrē* (5534), if needs be; *opheilē* (3782), obligation, duty; *áxios* (514), worthy, fit; *hikanós* (2425), sufficient, competent, fit; *kalós* (2570), proper, meet; *eúthetos* (2111), correct, well-placed; *díkaios* (1342), just, meet; *anagkaíos* (316), necessary; *anágkē* (318), a necessity; *epánagkes* (1876), of necessity; *chreía* (5532), a need; *kathékon*, that which is necessary, becoming; *kathékō* (2520), to reach down to do what is right and necessary.

1164. δεῖγμα, deigma, *digh´-mah*; from the base of 1166; a *specimen* (as *shown*):—example.

1165. δειγματίζω, deigmatizō, *digh-mat-id´-zo*; from 1164; to *exhibit*:—make a shew.

1166. δεικνύω, deiknuō, *dike-noo´-o*; a prolonged form of an obstract primary of the same meaning; to *show* (literal or figurative):—shew.

1167. δειλία, deilia, *di-lee´-ah*; from 1169; *timid-ity*:—fear.

Noun from *deilós* (1169), fearful, timid. Cowardice, timidity, reticence, fearfulness (2Ti 1:7; Sept.: Ps 54:5).

Syn.: *Deilía* is always in a bad sense as contrasted with *phóbos* (5401), fear.

1168. δειλιάω, deiliaō, *di-lee-ah´-o*; from 1167; to *be timid*:—be afraid.

1169. δειλός, deilos, *di-los´*; from **δέος, deos** (*dread*); *timid,* i.e. (by implication) *faithless*:—fearful.

1170. δεῖνα, deina, *di´-nah*; probably from the same as 1171 (through the idea of forgetting the name as *fearful,* i.e. *strange*); *so and so* (when the person is not specified):—such a man.

1171. δεινῶς, deinōs, *di-noce´*; adverb from a derivative of the same as 1169; *terribly,* i.e. *excessively*:—grievously, vehemently.

1172. δειπνέω, deipneō, *dipe-neh´-o*; from 1173; to *dine*, i.e. take the principal (or evening) meal:—sup (× -per).

1173. δεῖπνον, deipnon, *dipe´-non*; from the same as 1160; *dinner*, i.e. the chief meal (usually in the evening):—feast, supper.

1174. δεισιδαιμονέστερος, deisidaimones-teros, *dice-ee-dahee-mon-es´-ter-os*; the compound of a derivative of the base of 1169 and 1142; *more religious* than others:—too superstitious.

The comparative of *deisidaímōn* (n.f.), fearing the gods. Fearing the gods, i.e. in a good sense: religiously disposed; in a bad sense: superstitious. In the NT, in the first sense, spoken of the Athenians (Ac 17:22).

1175. δεισιδαιμονία, deisidaimonia, *dice-ee-dahee-mon-ee´-ah*; from the same as 1174; *religion*:—superstition.

Noun from *deisidaímōn* (n.f.), fearing the gods. Fear of the gods, i.e. religiousness, i.e. religious (Ac 25:19).

Syn.: *thrēskeía* (2356), religion in its external aspect, religious worship, especially the ceremonial service of religion; *theosébeia* (2317), reverential worship of God; *eusébeia* (2150), piety; *eulábeia* (2124), the devotion arising from godly fear.

1176. δέκα, deka, *dek´-ah*; a primary number; *ten*:—[eight-] een, ten.

1177. δεκαδύο, dekaduo, *dek-ad-oo´-o*; from 1176 and 1417; *two* and *ten*, i.e. *twelve*:—twelve.

1178. δεκαπέντε, dekapente, *dek-ap-en´-teh*; from 1176 and 4002; *ten* and *five*, i.e. *fifteen*:—fifteen.

1179. Δεκάπολις, Dekapolis, *dek-ap´-ol-is*; from 1176 and 4172; the *ten-city* region; the *Decapolis*, a district in Syria:—Decapolis.

1180. δεκατέσσαρες, dekatessares, *dek-at-es´-sar-es*; from 1176 and 5064; *ten* and *four*, i.e. *fourteen*:—fourteen.

1181. δεκάτη, dekatē, *dek-at´-ay*; feminine of 1182; a *tenth*, i.e. as a percentage or (technical) *tithe*:—tenth (part), tithe.

1182. δέκατος, dekatos, *dek´-at-os*; ordinal from 1176; *tenth*:—tenth.

1183. δεκατόω, dekatoō, *dek-at-o´-o*; from 1181; to *tithe*, i.e. to *give* or *take a tenth*:—pay (receive) tithes.

1184. δεκτός, dektos, *dek-tos´*; from 1209; *approved*; (figurative) *propitious*:—accepted (-table).

Verbal adj. from *déchomai* (1209), to accept, decide fabourably. Accepted, i.e. metaphorically: acceptable, approved (Lk 4:24; Ac 10:35; Php 4:18). By implication: favourable, gracious; spoken of a time, i.e. a time of favour (Lk 4:19; 2Co 4:2, cf. Isa 49:8).

Syn.: *euárestos* (2101), well-pleasing, acceptable.

1185. δελεάζω, deleazō, *del-eh-ad´-zo*; from the base of 1388; to *entrap*, i.e. (figurative) *delude*:—allure, beguile, entice.

1186. δένδρον, dendron, *den´-dron*; probably from δρῦς, **drus** (an *oak*); a *tree*:—tree.

1187. δεξιολάβος, dexiolabos, *dex-ee-ol-ab´-os*; from 1188 and 2983; a *guardsman* (as if *taking the right*) or light-armed soldier:—spearman.

1188. δεξιός, dexios, *dex-ee-os´*; from 1209; the *right* side or (feminine) *hand* (as that which usually *takes*):—right (hand, side).

Adjective meaning right as opposed to left, right hand or side:

(I) With a substantive expressed, e.g., hand (Mt 5:30; Lk 6:6; Ac 3:7; Rev 1:16, 17); foot (Rev 10:2); eye (Mt 5:29); ear (Lk 22:50; Jn 18:10); cheek (Mt 5:39); the right side (Jn 21:6).

(II) Without a substantive expressed:

(A) Meaning "right hand" (Mt 6:3; 27:29; Rev 1:20; 2:1; 5:1, 7). The "right hand" of fellowship (Gal 3:9). Put for the right hand or side in general: the right (Heb 1:3; 8:1; 12:2); so the "right hand of God" (Ac 2:33; 5:31; Ro 8:34; Eph 1:20; Col 3:1; Heb 10:12; 1Pe 3:22).

(B) Meaning "the right parts," i.e. the right in general, e.g., "on the right" (Mt 27:38; Mk 15:27; Lk 23:33); so in the expression to sit or stand on the right of the Messiah or God, i.e. to be next in rank and power, to have the highest seat of honour and distinction (Mt 20:21, 23; 22:44; Mk 10:37, 40; 12:36; Lk 20:42; Ac 2:34; 7:55, 56; Heb 1:13); also "to be at one's right hand," i.e. to be one's helper, protector (Ac 2:25).

Deriv.: *dexiolábos* (1187), spearman, body-guard.

1189. δέομαι, deomai, *deh´-om-ahee*; middle of 1210; to *beg* (as *binding oneself*), i.e. *petition*:—beseech, pray (to), make request. Compare 4441.

To lack for oneself, to need. Hence in the NT: to make one's need known, to beseech, ask. *Déēsis* (1162), prayer for a particular need, supplication. Used with the gen. of the person (Lk 8:38; 9:40 [cf. Ac 26:3; 2Co 10:2]). With the accusative (2Co 8:4). Followed by *hópōs* (3704), so that (Mt 9:38; Lk 10:2 [cf. Ac 8:24]). Followed by *hína* (2443), in order (Lk 9:40 [cf. Lk 21:36; 22:32]). Followed by *mḗ* (3378), an interrogative neg. meaning never, not (Lk 8:28). Spoken of prayer to God in general (Ac 8:22, with the gen. of God, "I beseech of God" [a.t.]; 10:2). With the prep. *prós* (4314), and the accusative *tón Kúrion* ([3588], [2962]), the Lord (Ac 8:24). Used in an absolute sense in Lk 21:36; 22:32; Ac 4:31; 1Th 3:10; Sept.: Da 6:11; Job 8:5; Ps 30:8; Isa 37:4. Used generally and in an absolute sense in Ro 1:10, "making request"; 2Co 5:20. Followed by the gen. of person (Lk 5:12; 9:38, 40; Ac 8:34, "I pray thee"; 21:39; 26:3; Gal 4:12; Sept.: Dt 3:23; 2Ki 1:13; Pr 26:25). Followed by the accusative of thing or inf. for accusative (2Co 8:4; 10:2). While *proseuché* (4335) refers to prayer in general, *déēsis* refers to a particular need for which one prays. Thus *déomai* is related to *aitéō* (154), to make a request, ask as an inferior of a superior.

Deriv.: *déēsis* (1162), prayer, request; *prosdéomai* (4326), to require additionally.

Syn.: *chrḗzō* (5535), to have need; *parakaléō* (3870), literally to call to one's side, hence to call to one's aid, being the most commonly used word with this sense; *erōtáō* (2065), to beseech, to ask; *eúchomai* (2172), translated "pray," but in reality it means to wish.

1190. Δερβαῖος, Derbaios, *der-bah´ee-os*; from 1191; a *Derbæan* or inhabitant of Derbe:—of Derbe.

1191. Δέρβη, Derbē, *der´-bay*; of foreign origin; *Derbè*, a place in Asia Minor:—Derbe.

1192. δέρμα, derma, *der´-mah*; from 1194; a *hide*:—skin.

1193. δερμάτινος, dermatinos, *der-mat´-ee-nos*; from 1192; made of *hide*:—leathern, of a skin.

1194. δέρω, derō, *der´-o*; a primary verb; properly to *flay*, i.e. (by implication) to *scourge*, or (by analogy) to *thrash*:—beat, smite.

1195. δεσμεύω, desmeuō, *des-myoo´-o*; from a (presumed) derivative of 1196; to *be a binder* (*captor*), i.e. to *enchain* (a prisoner), to *tie on* (a load):—bind.

1196. δεσμέω, desmeō, *des-meh´-o*; from 1199; to *tie*, i.e. *shackle*:—bind.

1197. δεσμή, desmē, *des-may´*; from 1196; a *bundle*:—bundle.

1198. δέσμιος, desmios, *des´-mee-os*; from 1199; a *captive* (as *bound*):—in bonds, prisoner.

1199. δεσμόν, desmon, *des-mon´*; or **δεσμός, desmos,** *des-mos´*; neuter and masculine respectively from 1210; a *band*, i.e. *ligament* (of the body) or *shackle* (of a prisoner); (figurative) an *impediment* or *disability*:—band, bond, chain, string.

1200. δεσμοφύλαξ, desmophulax, *des-mof-oo´-lax*; from 1199 and 5441; a *jailer* (as *guarding* the *prisoners*):—jailor, keeper of the prison.

1201. δεσμωτήριον, desmōtērion, *des-mo-tay´-ree-on*; from a derivative of 1199 (equivalent to 1196); a *place of bondage*, i.e. a *dungeon*:—prison.

1202. δεσμώτης, desmōtēs, *des-mo´-tace*; from the same as 1201; (passive) a *captive*:—prisoner.

1203. δεσπότης, despotēs, *des-pot´-ace*; perhaps from 1210 and **πόσις, posis** (a *husband*); an absolute *ruler* ("despot"):—Lord, master.

A noun meaning master, as opposed to servant; the head of a family (1Ti 6:1, 2; 2Ti 2:21; Tit 2:9; 1Pe 2:18). By implication, as denoting supreme authority: Lord; spoken of God (Lk 2:29; Ac 4:24; Rev 6:10); of Christ (2Pe 2:1; Jude 4).

Deriv.: *oikodespótēs* (3617), householder, master of the house.

Syn.: *megistán* (3175), great, denoting chief men, nobles; *hēgemón* (2232), a chief person, ruler; *prōtótokos* (4416), in the sense of being the first over, supreme, in which case it is equivalent to *prōteúōn* (4409), having the preeminence; *árchōn* (758), chief ruler, prince; *kubernḗtēs* (2942), captain, master of a ship; *dunástēs* (1413), a ruler or officer, potentate, one who possesses great power (*dúnamis* [1411]). *Kúrios* (2962), lord, master. *Despótēs* wields unlimited authority, while *kúrios* exercises morally restricted authority for good. Jesus is predominantly called *Kúrios*, Lord, because of His omnipotent concern. God is *Kúrios*, Lord, because He is *despótēs* of all things (cf. Job 5:8ff.).

1204. δεῦρο, deuro, *dyoo´-ro*; of uncertain affinity; *here*; used also imperative *hither!*; and of time, *hitherto*:—come (hither), hither [-to].

1205. δεῦτε, deute, *dyoo´-teh*; from 1204 and an imperative form of **εἶμι, eimi** (to *go*); *come hither!*:—come, × follow.

1206. δευτεραῖος, deuteraios, *dyoo-ter-ah´-yos*; from 1208; *secondary*, i.e. (special) on the *second* day:—next day.

1207. δευτερόπρωτος, deuteroprōtos, *dyoo-ter-op´-ro-tos*; from 1208 and 4413; *second-first*, i.e. (special) a designation of the Sabbath immediately after the Paschal week (being the *second* after Passover day, and the *first* of the seven Sabbaths intervening before Pentecost):—second … after the first.

1208. δεύτερος, deuteros, *dyoo´-ter-os*; as the comparative of 1417; (ordinal) *second* (in time, place or rank; also adverbial):—afterward, again, second (-arily, time).

1209. δέχομαι, dechomai, *dekh´-om-ahee*; middle of a primary verb; to *receive* (in various applications, literal or figurative):—accept, receive, take. Compare 2983.

To take to oneself what is presented or brought by another, to receive:

(I) Of things:

(A) To take, receive, receive into one's hands (Lk 2:28; Lk 16:6, 7; Lk 22:17; Eph 6:17; Sept.: 2Ch 29:16, 22).

(B) Generally: to receive, accept, e.g., letters (Ac 22:5; 28:21); the grace or the collection (2Co 8:4); whatever was sent from the Philippians (Php 4:18). See Sept.: Ge 33:10; Ex 29:25; 32:4.

(C) Metaphorically: to receive the kingdom of God (Mk 10:15; Lk 18:17); living words (Ac

7:38); the grace of God (2Co 6:1; Sept.: Jer 9:20; 17:23). Also of what is received by the ear: to hear of, learn, as the gospel (2Co 11:4). To receive, admit with the mind and heart, i.e. by implication: to approve, embrace, follow (Mt 11:14; Lk 8:13; Ac 8:14; 11:1; 17:11; 1Th 1:6; 2:13; Jas 1:21); the things of the Spirit (1Co 2:14); the exhortation or teaching (2Co 8:17); the love of the truth (2Th 2:10). Also Sept.: Pr 10:8; Zep 3:7.

(II) Of persons: to receive, admit, accept. To receive kindly, welcome as a teacher, friend, or guest into the house (Lk 16:4); into the eternal habitations or heaven (Lk 16:9; Ac 7:59). In the sense of to admit to one's presence, to the house where one is, as the multitudes (Lk 9:11). By implication in 2Co 11:16, to bear with.

Deriv.: *anadéchomai* (324), to entertain anyone hospitality; *apodéchomai* (588), to receive heartily, welcome; *dektós* (1184), accepted, acceptable, agreeable; *diadéchomai* (1237), to come after; *dókimos* (1384), to prove, try; *dochḗ* (1403), a feast, acceptance, reception; *eisdéchomai* (1523), to receive into; *ekdéchomai* (1551), to take or receive from, to await, expect; *endéchomai* (1735), to accept; *epidéchomai* (1926), to receive; *paradéchomai* (3858), to receive, to admit; *prosdéchomai* (4327), to take, accept, receive, expect; *hupodéchomai* (5264), to entertain hospitably.

Syn.: *lambánō* (2983) to receive; *apéchō* (568), to have in full, to have received all that is due; *chōréō* (5562), to make room for, receive with the mind; *lagchánō* (2975), to obtain by lot.

1210. δέω, deō, *deh´-o*; a primary verb; to *bind* (in various applications, literal or figurative):—bind, be in bonds, knit, tie, wind. See also 1163, 1189.

To bind:

(I) Of things: to bind together or to anything, to bind around, fasten (Mt 13:30; 21:2; Mk 11:2, 4; Lk 19:30; Ac 10:11; Sept.: Jos 2:21; Jgs 15:4). Spoken of dead bodies which are bound or wound around with graveclothes (Jn 11:44; 19:40). Here also belong Mt 16:19; 18:18, where the allusion is to the ancient manner of binding together the doors of houses with a chain to which a padlock was sometimes suspended. Others here translate to interdict, to prohibit, i.e. to exclude, like Aram. *'āsar* (631, OT), decree (Da 8, 9, 13, 15).

(II) Of persons: to bind the hands, feet, etc.; to put in bonds, i.e. to deprive of liberty. Generally (Mt 12:29; 14:3; 22:13; Mk 3:27; 15:1; Jn 18:12; Ac 9:14; 21:11; Rev 20:2). Pass.: to be bound, to be in bonds, in prison, etc. (Mk 15:7; Jn 18:24; Ac 9:2, 21; 21:13; 24:27; Col 4:3; Rev 9:14). Figuratively in Lk 13:16, "whom Satan hath bound," i.e. deprived of the use of her limbs (v. 11); Satan being here represented as the author of physical evil. Also in 2Ti 2:9, i.e. the preaching of the word is not hindered because I am in bonds.

(III) Perf. pass.: to be bound, metaphorically spoken of the conjugal bond: to be bound to someone (Ro 7:2; 1Co 7:27, 39). Also used metaphorically in the expression "bound in spirit" (Ac 20:22), i.e. impelled in mind, compelled (cf. 18:5).

Deriv.: *désmē* (1197), a bundle; *desmós* (1199), a band, bond, fetter; *katadéō* (2611), to bind or tie down; *peridéō* (4019), to bind around; *sundéō* (4887), to bind together; *hupodéō* (5265), to bind underneath, used of binding of sandals.

Syn.: *sunistáō* or *sunístēmi* (4921), to set or hold together; *suntássō* (4929), to arrange jointly; *katartízō* (2675), to fit, join together; *sunéchō* (4912), to hold together.

1211. **δή, dē,** *day*; probably akin to 1161; a particle of emphasis or explicitness; *now, then,* etc.:—also, and, doubtless, now, therefore.

1212. **δῆλος, dēlos,** *day´-los*; of uncertain derivative; *clear:*— + bewray, certain, evident, manifest.

1213. **δηλόω, dēloō,** *day-lo´-o*; from 1212; to *make plain* (by words):—declare, shew, signify.

1214. **Δημᾶς, Dēmas,** *day-mas´*; probably for 1216; *Demas,* a Christian:—Demas.

1215. **δημηγορέω, dēmēgoreō,** *day-may-gor-eh´-o*; from a compound of 1218 and 58; to *be a people-gatherer,* i.e. to *address* a public assembly:—make an oration.

1216. **Δημήτριος, Dēmētrios,** *day-may´-tree-os*; from **Δημήτηρ**, *Dēmētēr* (*Ceres*); *Demetrius,* the name of an Ephesian and of a Christian:—Demetrius.

1217. **δημιουργός, dēmiourgos,** *day-me-oor-gos´*; from 1218 and 2041; a *worker* for the *people,* i.e. *mechanic* (spoken of the *Creator*):—maker.

Adjective from *démos* (1218), a people, and *érgon* (2041), work. Used as a substantive to denote one who works for the public or performs public works such as an architect. Hence generally and in the NT: an artist or artificer, maker, author. Only in Heb 11:10.

Syn.: *ktístēs* (2939), founder of a city, creator; *poiētḗs* (4162), a poet (Ac 17:28), a maker, doer (Ro 2:13; Jas 1:22, 23, 25; 4:11); *plástēs* (n.f.), a molder, an artist who works in clay or wax (see *plássō* [4111]).

1218. **δῆμος, dēmos,** *day´-mos*; from 1210; the *public* (as *bound* together socially):—people.

Noun from *déō* (1210), to bind. The people, *populus* (Ac 12:22; 17:5; 19:30, 33). From this word is derived "democracy" where the people or the public rules.

Deriv.: *apódēmos* (590), taking a far journey; *dēmēgoréō* (1215), to make an oration; *dēmiourgós* (1217), maker; *dēmósios* (1219), public, common.

Syn.: *laós* (2992), people; *óchlos* (3793), a crowd, throng; *éthnos* (1484), a nation; *kósmos* (2889), world, people; *koinōnía* (2842), partnership, communion, fellowship.

1219. **δημόσιος, dēmosios,** *day-mos´-ee-os*; from 1218; *public*; (feminine singular dative as adverb) *in public:*—common, openly, publickly.

1220. **δηνάριον, dēnarion,** *day-nar´-ee-on*; of Latin origin; a *denarius* (or *ten asses*):—pence, penny [-worth].

1221. **δήποτε, dēpote,** *day´-pot-eh*; from 1211 and 4218; a particle of generalization; *indeed, at any time:*—(what-) soever.

1222. **δήπου, dēpou,** *day´-poo*; from 1211 and 4225; a particle of asseveration; *indeed doubtless:*—verily.

1223. **διά, dia,** *dee-ah´*; a primary preposition denoting the *channel* of an act; *through* (in very wide applications, local, causal or occasional):—after, always, among, at, to avoid, because of (that), briefly, by, for (cause) ... fore, from, in, by occasion of, of, by reason of, for sake, that, thereby, therefore, × though, through (-out), to, wherefore, with (-in). In composition it retains the same general import.

1224. διαβαίνω, diabainō, *dee-ab-ah´ee-no*; from 1223 and the base of 939; to *cross:*—come over, pass (through).

1225. διαβάλλω, diaballō, *dee-ab-al´-lo*; from 1223 and 906; (figurative) to *traduce:*—accuse.

From *diá* (1223), through, and *bállō* (906), to cast, throw. To accuse falsely. Hence metaphorically and in the NT: to carry or deliver over to someone in words, i.e. to report or inform against, to disgrace, to accuse. Used only in Lk 16:1.

Deriv.: *diábolos* (1228), false accuser.

Syn.: *egkaléō* (1458), to bring a charge against, usually in court; *epēreázō* (1908), to insult, misuse, treat despitefully; *katēgoréō* (2723), to accuse; *sukophantéō* (4811), to accuse wrongfully; *proaitiáomai* (4256), to bring a previous charge against; *katalaléō* (2635), to speak against; *kakologéō* (2551), to speak evil.

1226. διαβεβαιόομαι, diabebaioomai, *dee-ab-eb-ahee-o´-om-ahee*; middle of a compound of 1223 and 950; to *confirm thoroughly* (by words), i.e. *asseverate:*—affirm constantly.

Deponent from *diá* (1223), an intensive, and *bebaióō* (950), to confirm. To assure firmly, affirm, make firm (1Ti 1:7; Tit 3:8).

Syn.: *diïschurízomai* (1340), to assert vehemently; *pháskō* (5335), to show or make known one's thoughts, to affirm by way of alleging or professing.

1227. διαβλέπω, diablepō, *dee-ab-lep´-o*; from 1223 and 991; to *look through*, i.e. *recover* full *vision:*—see clearly.

1228. διάβολος, diabolos, *dee-ab´-ol-os*; from 1225; a *traducer*; specially *Satan* [compare 7854]:—false accuser, devil, slanderer.

Noun from *diabállō* (1225), to accuse. A false accuser, slanderer:

(I) Generally (1Ti 3:11; 2Ti 3:3; Tit 2:3; Sept.: Est 7:4; 8:1).

(II) With the article *ho diábolos*, the devil, i.e. the accuser; the same as Hebrew *śāṭān* (adversary; 7854, OT) with the article, i.e. the adversary, Satan. According to the later Hebrews, he acts as the accuser and calumniator of men before God (Job 1:7, 12; Zec 3:1, 2, cf. Rev 12:9, 10), seduces them to sin (1Ch 21:1), and is the author of evil, both physical and moral, by which the human race is afflicted. In the NT, *ho*

diábolos appears as the constant enemy of God, of Christ, of the divine kingdom, of the followers of Christ, and of all truth; full of falsehood and malice, and seducing to evil in every possible way (Mt 4:1, 5, 8, 11; 25:41; Lk 4:2, 3, 5, 6, 13; 8:12; Jn 13:2; Ac 10:38; Eph 4:27; 6:11; 1Ti 3:6, 7; 2Ti 2:26; Heb 2:14; Jas 4:7; 1Pe 5:8; Jude 9; Rev 2:10; 20:2, 10). Hence the expression "child of the devil" (Jn 8:44; Ac 13:10, cf. Jn 6:70).

Syn.: *ho katégoros* (2725), the accuser; *Satanás* (4567), Satan or adversary; *apollúōn* (623), the destroyer.

1229. διαγγέλλω, diaggellō, *de-ang-gel´-lo*; from 1223 and the base of 32; to *herald thoroughly:*—declare, preach, signify.

From *diá* (1223), through, and *aggéllō* (n.f., see *anaggéllō* [312]), to tell, declare. To announce throughout, to publish, to proclaim (Lk 9:60; Ro 9:17, pass.; Sept.: Ex 9:16; Ps 2:7). Implying completeness: to declare plainly, fully, exactly (Ac 21:26; Sept.: Jos 6:10).

Syn.: *diēgéomai* (1334), to conduct a narration through to the end; *ekdiēgéomai* (1555), to narrate in full; *exēgéomai* (1834), to lead out, make known, declare; *dēlóō* (1213), to make plain, declare plainly; *phrázō* (5419), to declare by making it clear; *gnōrízō* (1107), to make known; *emphanízō* (1718), to declare plainly; *phaneróō* (5319), to manifest; *kērússō* (2784), to preach; *parrēsiázomai* (3955), to be bold in speech, to preach boldly; *laléō* (2980), to speak; *dialégomai* (1256), to give a reasoned discourse or to discuss.

1230. διαγίνομαι, diaginomai, *dee-ag-in´-om-ahee*; from 1223 and 1096; to *elapse meanwhile:*— × after, be past, be spent.

1231. διαγινώσκω, diaginōskō, *dee-ag-in-o´-sko*; from 1223 and 1097; to *know thoroughly*, i.e. *ascertain exactly:*—(would) enquire, know the uttermost.

From *diá* (1223), denoting separation or emphasis, and *ginóskō* (1097), to know experientially. To know throughout, i.e. accurately; to distinguish (Sept.: Dt 2:7). In the NT: to inquire fully into, to examine, to investigate (Ac 23:15; 24:22).

Deriv.: *diágnōsis* (1233), discernment.

Syn.: *oída* (1492), to know intuitively, to perceive; *epístamai* (1987), to understand; *suníēmi* (4920), to bring or set together, to put it together, understand; *noéō* (3539), to perceive with the mind; *punthánomai* (4441), to inquire, to understand; *gnōrízō* (1107), to make known; *manthánō* (3129), to learn; *phronéō* (5426), to mind, understand; *parakolouthéō* (3877), to follow up, to trace, have understanding; *plērophoréō* (4135), used in the pass., to be fully assured; *anagnōrízō* (319), to recognize; *diagnōrízō* (1232), to make known; *krínō* (2919), to be of an opinion, to determine; *horízō* (3724) to declare, determine, specify; *epilúō* (1956), to solve.

1232. διαγνωρίζω, diagnōrizō, *dee-ag-norid´-zo*; from 1123 and 1107; to *tell abroad:*— make known.

From *diá* (1223), denoting separation, and *gnōrízō* (1107), to know. To make known throughout, i.e. everywhere; to tell abroad, to publish. Only in Lk 2:17.

Syn.: *plērophoréō* (4135), to make fully known; *diaggéllō* (1229), to declare fully; *exaggéllō* (1804), to tell out, proclaim abroad; *diēgéomai* (1334), to relate in full; *anaggéllō* (312), to report, declare; *phaneróō* (5319), to manifest; *dēlóō* (1213), to make plain; *apaggéllō* (518), to announce, declare.

1233. διάγνωσις, diagnōsis, *dee-ag´-no-sis*; from 1231; (magisterial) *examination* ("diagnosis"):—hearing.

Noun from *diaginōskō* (1231), to know thoroughly. Exact knowledge. In the NT, in a judicial sense: examination, trial, hearing. Only in Ac 25:21.

Syn.: *diákrisis* (1253), a distinguishing, a decision, discerning.

1234. διαγογγύζω, diagogguzō, *dee-ag-onggood´-zo*; from 1223 and 1111; to *complain throughout* a crowd:—murmur.

1235. διαγρηγορέω, diagrēgoreō, *dee-ag-raygor-eh´-o*; from 1223 and 1127; to *waken thoroughly:*—be awake.

1236. διάγω, diagō, *dee-ag´-o*; from 1223 and 71; to *pass* time or life:—lead life, living.

1237. διαδέχομαι, diadechomai, *dee-adekh´-om-ahee*; from 1223 and 1209; to *receive in turn,* i.e. (figurative) *succeed to:*—come after.

From *diá* (1223), denoting transition, and *déchomai* (1209), to receive. To receive by succession from another or former possessor. Only in Ac 7:45.

Deriv.: *diádochos* (1240), a successor.

Syn.: *akolouthéō* (190), to follow, come after.

1238. διάδημα, diadēma, *dee-ad´-ay-mah*; from a compound of 1223 and 1210; a "*diadem*" (as *bound about* the head):—crown. Compare 4735.

Noun from *diadéō* (n.f.), to bind around, which is from the prep. *diá* (1223), around, and *déō* (1210), to bind. A diadem, the symbol of royal dignity. (Rev 12:3; 13:1; 19:12; Sept.: Est 1:11; 2:17; Isa 62:3).

Syn.: *stéphanos* (4735), crown.

1239. διαδίδωμι, diadidōmi, *dee-ad-id´-omee*; from 1223 and 1325; to *give throughout* a crowd, i.e. *deal out*; also to *deliver* over (as to a successor):—(make) distribute (-ion), divide, give.

1240. διάδοχος, diadochos, *dee-ad´-okh-os*; from 1237; a *successor* in office:—room.

Noun from *diadéchomai* (1237), to succeed, follow after. A successor. Only in Ac 24:27.

Syn.: *hústeros* (5306), latter; *opísō* (3694), one who follows.

1241. διαζώννυμι, diazōnnumi, *dee-az-own´noo-mee*; from 1223 and 2224; to *gird tightly:*— gird.

1242. διαθήκη, diathēkē, *dee-ath-ay´-kay*; from 1303; properly a *disposition,* i.e. (special) a *contract* (especially a devisory *will*):—covenant, testament.

Noun from *diatíthēmi* (1303), to set out in order, to dispose in a certain order. A disposition, arrangement:

(I) Spoken of a testamentary disposition: a testament, a will (Heb 9:16, 17).

(II) A covenant, i.e. a mutual agreement or mutual promises on mutual conditions (Gal 3:15; Sept.: 1Sa 18:3; 23; 18). In the NT, spoken of God's covenants with men, i.e. the divine promises conditioned on obedience:

(A) Of the Abrahamic covenant, confirmed also to the other patriarchs, of which circumcision was the sign (Ge 15:1–18; 17:1–19). So Lk 1:72; Ac 3:25; Gal 3:17).

(B) Of the Mosaic covenant, entered into at Mount Sinai, with sacrifice and blood of victims (Ex 24:3–12; Dt 5:2; Heb 8:9; 9:20); also called "the first covenant," i.e. the Old or Jewish dispensation, in reference to the gospel (Heb 9:15). So also in Heb 9:4, "the ark of the covenant," and "the tables of the covenant," i.e. the Ark that was the symbol of God's presence under the Mosaic covenant, and the tables of the Law which the people had covenanted to obey (Rev 11:19, cf. Heb 8:5). The Mosaic covenant was strictly the renewal of the Abrahamic; hence Paul uses the plural in Ro 9:4 and Eph 2:12. Since the ancient covenant is contained in the Mosaic books, *diathḗkē* is used by metonymy for the book of the covenant, the Mosaic writings, i.e. the Law (2Co 3:14).

(C) Of the new covenant promised of old and sanctioned by the blood of Christ: the gospel dispensation (Ro 11:27; Heb 8:10; 10:16, 29); also called the "new covenant" (with *néos* [3501], Heb 12:24; with *kainós* [2537], Lk 22:20; 1Co 11:25; 2Co 3:6; Heb 9:15), "better testament" (Heb 7:22; 8:6; see *kreíttōn* [2909], better), and "everlasting covenant" (Heb 13:20; see *aiṓnios* [166], everlasting).

1243. διαίρεσις, diairesis, *dee-ah´ee-res-is*; from 1244; a *distinction* or (concrete) *variety*:—difference, diversity.

Noun from *diairéō* (1244), to divide. Division, act of dividing. Used only in 1Co 12:4–6, speaking of diversities, differences, classes of gifts.

Syn.: *diastolḗ* (1293), a setting asunder, distinction; *merismós* (3311), division, partition, distribution.

1244. διαιρέω, diaireō, *dee-ahee-reh´-o*; from 1223 and 138; to *separate*, i.e. *distribute*:—divide.

From *diá* (1223), through or denoting separation, and *hairéō* (138), to take, grasp, seize. To take from, divide, partition, apportion, assign. In the NT, it means to distribute among (Lk 15:12; 1Co 12:11; Sept.: Jos 18:5; 1Ch 23:6).

Deriv.: *diaíresis* (1243), diversity.

Syn.: *aphorízō* (873), to mark off by boundaries, separate, divide; *apodiorízō* (592), to mark off, make separations or divisions; *diadídōmi* (1239), to deal out, distribute; *diakrínō* (1252), to separate, discriminate; *merízō* (3307), to divide into; *diamerízō* (1266), to divide up; *kataklērodotéō* (2624), to distribute lots; *chōrízō* (5563), to separate; *apochōrízō* (673), to separate, tear apart; *schízō* (4977), to split or sever.

1245. διακαθαρίζω, diakatharizō, *dee-ak-ath-ar-id´-zo*; from 1223 and 2511; to *cleanse perfectly*, i.e. (special) *winnow*:—thoroughly purge.

1246. διακατελέγχομαι, diakatelegchomai, *dee-ak-at-el-eng´-khom-ahee*; middle from 1223 and a compound of 2596 and 1651; to *prove downright*, i.e. *confute*:—convince.

1247. διακονέω, diakoneō, *dee-ak-on-eh´-o*; from 1249; to *be an attendant*, i.e. *wait upon* (menially or as a host, friend or [figurative] teacher); techn. to *act as a* Christian *deacon*:—(ad-) minister (unto), serve, use the office of a deacon.

From *diákonos* (1249), servant, deacon. To serve, wait upon, minister to:

(I) To serve at a table, to wait upon (Mt 8:15; 20:28; 27:55; Mk 1:31; 10:45; 15:41; Lk 4:39; 10:40; 12:37; 17:8; 22:26, 27; Jn 12:2). In Ac 6:2, to serve over money tables, i.e. have charge of the alms and other pecuniary matters.

(II) To minister to the wants of someone, to supply someone's needs (Mt 4:11; 25:44; Mk 1:13; Lk 8:3).

(III) Used also of the alms collected by the churches, the distribution of alms (Ro 15:25; Heb 6:10; 1Pe 4:11).

(IV) To be an attendant or assistant to someone, as Timothy and Erastos were said to be ministering to Paul (Ac 19:22). Spoken of service in the early church: to fill the office of a deacon, i.e. to have charge over the poor and sick (1Ti 3:10, 13).

(V) Of things: to administer, provide something for someone. Spoken of prophets who minister, i.e. announce, deliver the divine will (1Pe 1:12). Also to minister something to someone; to administer, provide (2Co 3:3; 2Ti 1:18). By implication: to minister to one's wants (1Pe 4:10).

Syn.: *leitourgéō* (3008), to render public service; *hupēretéō* (5256), to toil, render service; *therapeúō* (2323), to wait upon menially, relieve, cure; *hierourgéō* (2418), to minister in priestly service; *ergázomai* (2038), to work; *prosedreúō* (4332), to attend as a servant; *proskarteréō* (4342), to serve in a close personal relationship.

1248. διακονία, diakonia, *dee-ak-on-ee´-ah*; from 1249; *attendance* (as a servant, etc.); figurative (eleemosynary) *aid*, (official) *service* (especially of the Christian teacher, or technical of the *diaconate*):—(ad-) minister (-ing, -tration, -try), office, relief, service (-ing).

Noun from *diákonos* (1249), deacon, servant. Service, attendance, ministry:

(I) Service toward a master or guest, at table or in hospitality (Lk 10:40; 1Co 16:15).

(II) Ministry, ministration, i.e. the office of ministering in divine things, spoken chiefly of apostles and teachers (Ac 1:17, 25; 6:4; 20:24; 21:19; Ro 11:13; 1Co 12:5; 2Co 3:7–9; 4:1; 5:18; 6:3; Eph 4:12; Col 4:17; 1Ti 1:12; 2Ti 4:5, 11). Used once of the office of a *diákonos* (1249), deacon (Ro 12:7). Some, however, take this to have a wider sense as above.

(III) In the sense of aid or relief as spoken of alms, contributions (Ac 11:29; Ro 15:31 [see Ro 15:26]; 2Co 8:4; 9:1, 13; 11:8; Rev 2:19). Spoken of the distribution or ministration of alms collected (Ac 6:1; 12:25, see 11:30; 2Co 9:12).

Syn.: *ōpheleía* (5622), advantage, profit; *euergesía* (2108), benevolence; *chrēstótēs* (5544), usefulness, kindness; *sumphéron* (4851), profit, expedience; *therapeía* (2322), attendance, service or healing with tenderness; *leitourgía* (3009), a sacred or priestly ministration; *latreía* (2999), primarily hired service; *episkopé* (1984), inspection, the office of a bishop, visitation; *episústasis* (1999), responsibility for oversight based upon authority; *prónoia* (4307), forethought, provision, providence; *epiméleia* (1958), kind attention, care.

1249. διάκονος, diakonos, *dee-ak´-on-os*; probably from an obsolete **διάκω, diakō** (to *run* on errands; compare 1377); an *attendant*, i.e. (genitive) a *waiter* (at table or in other menial duties); specially a Christian *teacher* and *pastor* (technically a *deacon* or *deaconess*):—deacon, minister, servant.

A noun meaning minister, servant, attendant:

(I) Spoken of those who wait at table (Jn 2:5, 9); of the servants or attendants of a king (Mt 22:13; Ro 13:4); of an attendant, disciple (Jn 12:26); of ministers, teachers of divine things who act for God (1Co 3:5; 2Co 3:6; 11:23; Eph 6:21; 1Th 3:2).

(II) As an officer in the early church: one who has charge of the alms and money of the church, an overseer of the poor and sick (Php 1:1; 1Ti 3:8, 12; 4:6; see Ac 6:1–6); also of a female who had charge of the female poor and

sick (Ro 16:1). Hence the Eng. word "deacon," but in a different sense.

Deriv.: *diakonéō* (1247), to minister, adjust, regulate, set in order; *diakonía* (1248), ministry, service.

Syn.: *doúlos* (1401), a slave; *therápōn* (2324), attendant; *hupērétēs* (5257), servant; *leitourgós* (3011), a public servant, usually one serving at the temple or one who performs religious public duties; *místhios* (3407) and *misthōtós* (3411), a hired servant; *oikétēs* (3610), a household servant; *país* (3816), basically a child, but is also an attendant; *epískopos* (1985), a bishop, supervisor, one who serves as a leader in a church.

1250. διακόσιοι, diakosioi, *dee-ak-os´-ee-oy*; from 1364 and 1540; *two hundred*:—two hundred.

1251. διακούομαι, diakouomai, *dee-ak-oo´-om-ahee*; middle from 1223 and 191; to *hear throughout*, i.e. *patiently listen* (to a prisoner's plea):—hear.

1252. διακρίνω, diakrinō, *dee-ak-ree´-no*; from 1223 and 2919; to *separate thoroughly* i.e. (literal and reflexive) to *withdraw* from, or (by implication) *oppose*; (figurative) to *discriminate*, (by implication) *decide*, or (reflexive) *hesitate*:—contend, make (to) differ (-ence), discern, doubt, judge, be partial, stagger, waver.

From *diá* (1223), denoting separation, and *krínō* (2919), to distinguish, decide, judge. To separate throughout, completely. In the middle, to separate oneself:

(I) Particularly, spoken of physical separation in Jude 22: "And on some [i.e. those not Christians] have compassion, making a difference," i.e. separating yourselves from them. (TR only; for NASB, see IV, B, below.)

(II) By implication: to distinguish, make a distinction, cause to differ (Ac 15:9; 1Co 11:29); with the idea of preference or prerogative (1Co 4:7). In the middle, to make a distinction within a group, to be partial (Jas 2:4). Figuratively it means to distinguish, discern clearly, note accurately (Mt 16:3; 1Co 11:31; 14:29; 1Jn 4:1; Sept.: Job 12:11).

(III) To consider accurately, judge, decide (1Co 6:5; Sept.: Ex 18:16; 1Ki 3:9; Ps 50:4; Pr 31:9).

(IV) In the middle *diakrínomai*, to separate oneself from, i.e. to contend with. In the NT used metaphorically:

(A) To contend or strive with, dispute with (Ac 11:2; Jude 9; Sept.: Jer 15:10; Eze 20:35).

(B) To be in strife with oneself, i.e. to doubt, hesitate, waver (Mt 21:21; Mk 11:23; Ro 4:20; 14:23; Jas 1:6; Jude 22 [NASB only, following the syntax of the UBS text; for TR, see I, above]).

Deriv.: *adiákritos* (87), undistinguished, without partiality; *diákrisis* (1253), a distinguishing.

Syn.: *epagōnízomai* (1864), to contend; *diaginōskō* (1231), to distinguish, judge; *diaphérō* (1308), to be different from or superior to; *dokimázō* (1381), to test, prove; *aporéō* (639), to be in doubt, perplexity; *diaporéomai* (1280), to be in utter perplexity; *distázō* (1365), to hesitate, to stand at a crossroad with uncertainty as to which way to take; *meteōrízō* (3349), make doubtful; *apostréphomai* (654), to withdraw; *apōthéomai* (683), to thrust oneself away.

1253. **διάκρισις, diakrisis,** *dee-ak´-ree-sis*; from 1252; judicial *estimation:*—discern (-ing), disputation.

Noun from *diakrínō* (1252), to distinguish, decide, judge. A distinguishing, discerning clearly, i.e. spoken of the act or power (1Co 12:10; Heb 5:14). By implication Ro 14:1, literally meaning not for scrutinizing of thoughts, i.e. not with searching out and pronouncing judgement on their opinions (cf. Ro 14:5, 13). This also could be rendered as doubts, scruples.

Syn.: *diágnōsis* (1233), diagnosis, judgement, thorough understanding; *gnōmē* (1106), opinion.

1254. **διακωλύω, diakōluō,** *dee-ak-o-loo´-o*; from 1223 and 2967; to *hinder altogether*, i.e. *utterly prohibit:*—forbid.

1255. **διαλαλέω, dialaleō,** *dee-al-al-eh´-o*; from 1223 and 2980; to *talk throughout* a company, i.e. *converse* or (genitive) *publish:*—commune, noise abroad.

1256. **διαλέγομαι, dialegomai,** *dee-al-eg´-om-ahee*; middle from 1223 and 3004; to *say thoroughly*, i.e. *discuss* (in argument or exhortation):—dispute, preach (unto), reason (with), speak.

1257. **διαλείπω, dialeipō,** *dee-al-i´-po*; from 1223 and 3007; to *leave off in the middle*, i.e. *intermit:*—cease.

From *diá* (1223), between, and *leípō* (3007), to leave. To intermit, desist, cease; to leave an interval of space or time between (Lk 7:45; Sept.: Jer 17:8; 44:18).

Deriv.: *adiáleiptos* (88), unceasing, continual.

Syn.: *paúō* (3973), to stop, make an end, rest; *hēsucházō* (2270), to be quiet, still, at rest; *kopázō* (2869), to stop raging; *aphíēmi* (863), to let go; *katapaúō* (2664), to rest, cease.

1258. **διάλεκτος, dialektos,** *dee-al´-ek-tos*; from 1256; a (mode of) *discourse*, i.e. "*dialect*":—language, tongue.

1259. **διαλλάσσω, diallassō,** *dee-al-las´-so*; from 1223 and 236; to *change thoroughly*, i.e. (mental) to *conciliate:*—reconcile.

From *diá* (1223), denoting transition, and *allássō* (236), to change. To change one's own feelings toward, to reconcile oneself, become reconciled. In the middle voice, *diallássomai* or *dialáttomai*, to be reconciled, only in Mt 5:24.

Syn.: *eirēnopoiéō* (1517), to cause a state of peace or reconciliation between two persons.

1260. **διαλογίζομαι, dialogizomai,** *dee-al-og-id´-zom-ahee*; from 1223 and 3049; to *reckon thoroughly*, i.e. (genitive) to *deliberate* (by reflection or discussion):—cast in mind, consider, dispute, muse, reason, think.

From *diá* (1223), an intensive, and *logízomai* (3049), to reckon, reason. To reckon through, to settle an account. In the NT: to consider, reflect, ponder (Mt 21:25; Mk 2:6, 8; Lk 1:29; 3:15; 5:21, 22; 12:17; see Sept.: Ps 77:6; 119:59). Also, to consider together, deliberate, debate (Mt 16:7, 8; Mk 8:16, 17; Lk 20:14).

Deriv.: *dialogismós* (1261), word, account, reasoning.

Syn.: *noéō* (3539), to perceive; *katanoéō* (2657), to perceive clearly, consider carefully; *analogízomai* (357), to consider; *skopéō* (4648), to mark, consider, focus; *suníēmi* (4920), understand, put things together; *suzētéō* (4802), to discuss, examine together; *sullogízomai* (4817), to reason, compute; *dokéō* (1380), to think; *hēgéomai* (2233), to account, consider; *huponoéō* (5282), to surmise; *nomízō* (3543), to suppose; *phronéō* (5426), to think; *sōphronéō* (4993), to exercise sound mind or judgement; *krínō* (2919), to reckon, judge.

1261. **διαλογισμός, dialogismos,** *dee-al-og-is-mos´*; from 1260; *discussion*, i.e. (internal) *consideration* (by implication, *purpose*), or (external) *debate*:—dispute, doubtful (-ing), imagination, reasoning, thought.

Noun from *dialogízomai* (1260), to reason. Reflection, thought:

(I) Used generally (Lk 2:35; 5:22; 6:8; 9:47; Jas 2:4; Sept.: Ps 92:6; Isa 59:7; Da 2:29, 30). Reasoning, opinion (Ro 1:21; 1Co 3:20; Ro 14:1; Sept.: Ps 94:11). Mind, purpose, intention (Lk 6:8). Especially evil thoughts, purposes (Mt 15:19; Mk 7:21; Sept.: Ps 56:6, evil; Isa 59:7), doubts (Lk 24:38, doubtful thoughts, suspense).

(II) In the sense of dispute, debate, contention (Mk 9:33, 34; Lk 9:46; Php 2:14; 1Ti 2:8).

Syn.: *suzḗtēsis* (4803), a dispute, questioning; *antilogía* (485), contradiction, gainsaying; *logismós* (3053), a thought suggestive of evil intent, imagination; *enthúmēsis* (1761), deliberation, device; *epínoia* (1963), a design of the mind; *nóēma* (3540), a perception, thought; *dianóēma* (1270), a thought, plot, machination, sentiment.

1262. διαλύω, dialuō, *dee-al-oo´-o*; from 1223 and 3089; to *dissolve utterly*:—scatter.

1263. διαμαρτύρομαι, diamarturomai, *dee-am-ar-too´-rom-ahee*; from 1223 and 3140; to *attest* or *protest earnestly*, or (by implication) *hortatively*:—charge, testify (unto), witness.

From *diá* (1223), an intensive, and *martúromai* (3143), to witness, bear witness. To testify through and through, to bear full and complete witness. To admonish solemnly, to charge earnestly, to urge upon (Lk 16:28; Ac 2:40; 1Th 4:6; 1Ti 5:21; 2Ti 2:14; 4:1). Also, to testify fully, i.e. to declare fully, to teach earnestly, to enforce (Ac 8:25; 18:5; 20:21, 24; Heb 2:6).

Syn.: *diastéllomai* (1291), to admonish, literally to draw asunder; *embrimáomai* (1690), to charge strictly; *egkaléō* (1458), to accuse; *entéllomai* (1781), to command, give charge; *epitimáō* (2008), to rebuke; *paraggéllō* (3853), to command, give charge; *dierōtáō* (1331), to question so as to make sure.

1264. διαμάχομαι, diamachomai, *dee-am-akh´-om-ahee*; from 1223 and 3164; to *fight fiercely* (in altercation):—strive.

1265. διαμένω, diamenō, *dee-am-en´-o*; from 1223 and 3306; to *stay constantly* (in being or relation):—continue, remain.

1266. διαμερίζω, diamerizō, *dee-am-er-id´-zo*; from 1223 and 3307; to *partition thoroughly* (literal in distribution, figurative in dissension):—cloven, divide, part.

1267. διαμερισμός, diamerismos, *dee-am-er-is-mos´*; from 1266; *disunion* (of opinion and conduct):—division.

1268. διανέμω, dianemō, *dee-an-em´-o*; from 1223 and the base of 3551; to *distribute*, i.e. (of information) to *disseminate*:—spread.

1269. διανεύω, dianeuō, *dee-an-yoo´-o*; from 1223 and 3506; to *nod* (or *express* by signs) *across* an intervening space:—beckon.

1270. διανόημα, dianoēma, *dee-an-o´-ay-mah*; from a compound of 1223 and 3539; something *thought through*, i.e. a *sentiment*:—thought.

Noun from *dianoéomai* (n.f.), to agitate in mind, which is from *diá* (1223), denoting separation, and *noéō* (3539), to think over. Thought (Lk 11:17; Sept.: Isa 55:9).

Syn.: *enthúmēsis* (1761), an inward reasoning, generally evil surmising or supposition, device, usually imaginary; *énnoia* (1771), thoughtfulness, denoting inward intentions that involve moral understanding without any evil connotations; *logismós* (3053), the art of reckoning, reasoning; *dialogismós* (1261) refers to a more thorough reflection, thought, thinking something through; *phrónēsis* (5428), mental action or activity, intellectual insight, prudence; *phrónēma* (5427), that which one has in the mind, thought, an object of thought with a bad or good connotation.

1271. διάνοια, dianoia, *dee-an´-oy-ah*; from 1223 and 3563; *deep thought*, (properly) the faculty (*mind* or its *disposition*); (by implication) its exercise:—imagination, mind, understanding.

Noun from *dianoéomai* (n.f.), to agitate in mind, which is from *diá* (1223), denoting separation, and *noéō* (3539), to think over. Thought, mind, i.e. the power of thought:

(I) By metonymy: the mind, thoughts, intellect, i.e. the thinking faculty (Mt 22:37; Mk 12:30; Lk 10:27; Eph 1:18, only in some MSS; 4:18; Heb 8:10; 10:16 quoted from Jer 31:33; 1Pe 1:13; 2Pe 3:1; Sept.: Ge 17:17; 24:45).

(II) Intelligence, insight (1Jn 5:20; Sept.: Ex 35:25; 36:1).

(III) Mind, i.e. mode of thinking and feeling; the feelings, affections, disposition of mind (Eph 2:3; Col 1:21).

Syn.: *lógos* (3056), reason, intelligence; *phrónēma* (5427), the thought of the mind and the process of thinking and understanding; *phrónēsis* (5428), prudence; *epínoia* (1963), a thought or design for evil purposes; *nóēma* (3540), the product of the mind or thought; *dianóēma* (1270) an evil device; *enthúmēsis* (1761) a thought that involves the agitation of passion; *thumós* (2372), wrath; *logismós* (3053), the working out of the mind, imagination; *dialogismós* (1261), the results of the thorough exercise of the mind; *súnesis* (4907), discernment, understanding.

1272. διανοίγω, dianoigō, *dee-an-oy´-go*; from 1223 and 455; to *open thoroughly,* literal (as a firstborn) or figurative (to *expound*):—open.

1273. διανυκτερεύω, dianuktereuō, *dee-an-ook-ter-yoo´-o*; from 1223 and a derivative of 3571; to *sit up the whole night:*—continue all night.

1274. διανύω, dianuō, *dee-an-oo´-o*; from 1223 and ἀνύω, *anuō* (to *effect*); to *accomplish thoroughly:*—finish.

1275. διαπαντός, diapantos, *dee-ap-an-tos´*; from 1223 and the genitive of 3956; *through all* time, i.e. (adverb) *constantly:*—alway (-s), continually.

1276. διαπεράω, diaperaō, *dee-ap-er-ah´-o*; from 1223 and a derivative of the base of 4008; to *cross entirely:*—go over, pass (over), sail over.

1277. διαπλέω, diapleō, *dee-ap-leh´-o*; from 1223 and 4126; to *sail through:*—sail over.

1278. διαπονέω, diaponeō, *dee-ap-on-eh´-o*; from 1223 and a derivative of 4192; to *toil through,* i.e. (passive) *be worried:*—be grieved.

1279. διαπορεύομαι, diaporeuomai, *dee-ap-or-yoo´-om-ahee*; from 1223 and 4198; to *travel through:*—go through, journey in, pass by.

1280. διαπορέω, diaporeō, *dee-ap-or-eh´-o*; from 1223 and 639; to *be thoroughly nonplussed:*—(be in) doubt, be (much) perplexed.

1281. διαπραγματεύομαι, diapragmateuomai, *dee-ap-rag-mat-yoo´-om-ahee*; from 1223 and 4231; to *thoroughly occupy oneself,* i.e. (transitive and by implication) to *earn* in business:—gain by trading.

1282. διαπρίω, diapriō, *dee-ap-ree´-o*; from 1223 and the base of 4249; to *saw asunder,* i.e. (figurative) to *exasperate:*—cut (to the heart).

1283. διαρπάζω, diarpazō, *dee-ar-pad´-zo*; from 1223 and 726; to *seize asunder,* i.e. *plunder:*—spoil.

1284. διαρρήσσω, diarrhēssō, *dee-ar-hrayce´-so*; from 1223 and 4486; to *tear asunder:*—break, rend.

1285. διασαφέω, diasapheō, *dee-as-af-eh´-o*; from 1223 and σαφής, *saphēs* (*clear*); to *clear thoroughly,* i.e. (figurative) *declare:*—tell unto.

1286. διασείω, diaseiō, *dee-as-i´-o*; from 1223 and 4579; to *shake thoroughly,* i.e. (figurative) to *intimidate:*—do violence to.

1287. διασκορπίζω, diaskorpizō, *dee-as-kor-pid´-zo*; from 1223 and 4650; to *dissipate,* i.e. (genitive) to *rout* or *separate;* special to *winnow;* (figurative) to *squander:*—disperse, scatter (abroad), strew, waste.

1288. δεασπάω, deaspaō, *dee-as-pah´-o*; from 1223 and 4685; to *draw apart,* i.e. *sever* or *dismember:*—pluck asunder, pull in pieces.

1289. διασπείρω, diaspeirō, *dee-as-pi´-ro*; from 1223 and 4687; to *sow throughout,* i.e. (figurative) *distribute* in foreign lands:—scatter abroad.

1290. διασπορά, diaspora, *dee-as-por-ah´*; from 1289; *dispersion,* i.e. (special and concrete) the (converted) Israelite *resident* in Gentile countries:—(which are) scattered (abroad).

1291. διαστέλλομαι, diastellomai, *dee-as-tel´-lom-ahee*; middle from 1223 and 4724; to *set* (oneself) *apart* (figurative, *distinguish*), i.e. (by implication) to *enjoin:*—charge, that which was (give) commanded (-ment).

1292. διάστημα, diastēma, *dee-as´-tay-mah*; from 1339; an *interval:*—space.

1293. διαστολή, diastolē, *dee-as-tol-ay´*; from 1291; a *variation:*—difference, distinction.

1294. διαστρέφω, diastrephō, *dee-as-tref´-o*; from 1223 and 4762; to *distort,* i.e. (figurative) *misinterpret*, or (moral) *corrupt*:—perverse (-rt), turn away.

1295. διασώζω, diasōzō, *dee-as-odze'-o*; from 1223 and 4982; to *save thoroughly*, i.e. (by implication or analogy) to *cure, preserve, rescue*, etc.:—bring safe, escape (safe), heal, make perfectly whole, save.

From *diá* (1223), through, and *sōzō* (4982), to save. To save through, to bring safely through danger or sickness; to preserve (Ac 27:43; 28:1, 4; 1Pe 3:20; Sept.: Nu 10:9; Dt 20:4; Job 29:12; Da 11:41). With the idea of motion, to bring safely through to any place or person; in the pass., to come to or reach safely (Ac 23:24; 27:44; Sept.: Ge 19:19; Isa 37:38). Of the sick, to bring safely through, to heal (Mt 14:36; Lk 7:3; Sept.: Jer 8:20).

Syn.: *exairéomai* (1807), to rescue; *diaphulássō* (1314), to protect; *rhúomai* (4506) to rescue; *peripoiéomai* (4046), to preserve; *therapeúō* (2323), to care for the sick, heal; *iáomai* (2390), to heal.

1296. διαταγή, diatagē, *dee-at-ag-ay'*; from 1299; *arrangement*, i.e. *institution*:—instrumentality.

Noun from *diatássō* (1299), to appoint. An ordering of things, a disposition, ordinance, arrangement:

(I) Particularly, referring to the dispositions or arrangements of angels (Ac 7:53, cf. Gal 3:19; Heb 2:2). The OT makes no mention of angels at the giving of the Law (Ex 20:1, 19, 22), but the above passages of the NT assume their instrumentality, in accordance also with Jewish tradition (Sept.: Dt 33:2).

(II) In the sense of ordinance, institute (Ro 13:2; Sept.: Ezr 4:11).

Syn.: *diátagma* (1297), an arrangement, edict, mandate, the result of *diatagē*.

1297. διάταγμα, diatagma, *dee-at'-ag-mah*; from 1299; an *arrangement*, i.e. (authoritative) *edict*:—commandment.

Noun from *diatássō* (1299), to command, arrange in its proper order. Ordinance, mandate, edict. Only in Heb 11:23; Sept.: Ezr 7:11.

1298. διαταράσσω, diatarassō, *dee-at-ar-as'-so*; from 1223 and 5015; to *disturb wholly*, i.e. *agitate* (with alarm):—trouble.

1299. διατάσσω, diatassō, *dee-at-as'-so*; from 1223 and 5021; to *arrange thoroughly*, i.e. (special) *institute, prescribe*, etc.:—appoint, command, give, (set in) order, ordain.

From *diá* (1223), through, and *tássō* (5021), to appoint, order. To arrange throughout, to place in order, as troops. In the NT, used figuratively: to set fully in order, to arrange, to appoint, to ordain (Gal 3:19). Also in the sense of to direct, to prescribe, to order (Mt 11:1; Lk 8:55; Ac 18:2; 1Co 9:14; 16:1).

Deriv.: *diatagē* (1296), an ordinance; *diátagma* (1297), that which is imposed by decree or law; *epidiatássomai* (1928), to arrange, appoint.

1300. διατελέω, diateleō, *dee-at-el-eh'-o*; from 1223 and 5055; to *accomplish thoroughly*, i.e. (subject) to *persist*:—continue.

1301. διατηρέω, diatēreō, *dee-at-ay-reh'-o*; from 1223 and 5083; to *watch thoroughly*, i.e. (positive and transitive) to *observe* strictly, or (negative and reflexive) to *avoid* wholly:—keep.

From *diá* (1223), an intensive, and *tēréō* (5083), to guard, watch. To watch carefully, keep with care. In the NT, used figuratively: to guard with care, to lay up, to retain (Lk 2:51; Sept.: Ge 37:11); to guard or keep oneself from something, to abstain from something (Ac 15:29).

Syn.: *phulássō* (5442), to guard; *diaphulássō* (1314), guard thoroughly or carefully; *phrouréō* (5432), to keep as if with a military guard; *kratéō* (2902), to hold fast.

1302. διατί, diati, *dee-at-ee'*; from 1223 and 5101; *through what* cause?, i.e. *why?*:—wherefore, why.

1303. διατίθεμαι, diatithemai, *dee-at-ith'-em-ahee*; middle from 1223 and 5087; to *put apart*, i.e. (figurative) *dispose* (by assignment, compact or bequest):—appoint, make, testator.

From *diá* (1223), an intensive, and *títhēmi* (5087), to place. To set out in order, to arrange. In the NT, used only in the middle: to arrange in one's own behalf.

(I) Generally: to appoint, to make over (Lk 22:29); so of a testamentary disposition: to devise, to bequeath by will, hence used of a testator, i.e. the one making the will (Heb 9:16, 17).

(II) Spoken of a covenant: to make an arrangement with, to institute or make a covenant with

(Ac 3:25; Heb 8:10; 10:16; Sept.: Dt 5:3; Jos 9:6, 7; 2Sa 3:13).

Deriv.: *antidiatíthēmi* (475), to set oneself opposite; *diathḗkē* (1242), a contract, covenant.

Syn.: *protíthemai* (4388), to propose, purpose; *skopéō* (4648), to aim, look at, mark; *apoblépō* (578), to intensely regard; *atenízō* (816), to set eyes on; *bouleúomai* (1011), to purpose; *thélō* (2309), to will; *logízomai* (3049), to reckon; *prooorízō* (4309), to determine before.

1304. διατρίβω, diatribō, *dee-at-ree´-bo*; from 1223 and the base of 5147; to *wear through* (time), i.e. *remain*:—abide, be, continue, tarry.

1305. διατροφή, diatrophē, *dee-at-rof-ay´*; from a compound of 1223 and 5142; *nourishment*:—food.

1306. διαυγάζω, diaugazō, *dee-ow-gad´-zo*; from 1223 and 826; to *glimmer through*, i.e. *break* (as day):—dawn.

1307. διαφανής, diaphanēs, *dee-af-an-ace´*; from 1223 and 5316; *appearing through*, i.e. *"diapha-nous"*:—transparent.

1308. διαφέρω, diapherō, *dee-af-er´-o*; from 1223 and 5342; to *bear through*, i.e. (literal) *transport*; usually to *bear apart*, i.e. (objective) to *toss about* (figurative) *report*; subject to *"differ,"* or (by implication) *surpass*:—be better, carry, differ from, drive up and down, be (more) excellent, make matter, publish, be of more value.

1309. διαφεύγω, diapheugō, *dee-af-yoo´-go*; from 1223 and 5343; to *flee through*, i.e. *escape*:—escape.

1310. διαφημίζω, diaphēmizō, *dee-af-ay-mid´-zo*; from 1223 and a derivative of 5345; to *report thoroughly*, i.e. *divulgate*:—blaze abroad, commonly report, spread abroad, fame.

1311. διαφθείρω, diaphtheirō, *dee-af-thi´-ro*; from 1225 and 5351; to *rot thoroughly*, i.e. (by implication) to *ruin* (passive, *decay* utterly, figurative, *pervert*):—corrupt, destroy, perish.

1312. διαφθορά, diaphthora, *dee-af-thor-ah´*; from 1311; *decay*:—corruption.

1313. διάφορος, diaphoros, *dee-af´-or-os*; from 1308; *varying*; also *surpassing*:—differing, divers, more excellent.

1314. διαφυλάσσω, diaphulassō, *dee-af-oo-las´-so*; from 1223 and 5442; to *guard thoroughly*, i.e. *protect*:—keep.

1315. διαχειρίζομαι, diacheirizomai, *dee-akh-i-rid´-zom-ahee*; from 1223 and a derivative of 5495; to *handle thoroughly*, i.e. *lay* violent *hands* upon:—kill, slay.

1316. διαχωρίζομαι, diachōrizomai, *dee-akh-o-rid´-zom-ahee*; from 1223 and the middle of 5563; to *remove* (oneself) *wholly*, i.e. *retire*:—depart.

1317. διδακτικός, didaktikos, *did-ak-tik-os´*; from 1318; *instructive* ("didactic"):—apt to teach.

Adjective from *didáskō* (1321), to teach. Didactic, able to communicate Christian teaching, apt or skilled in teaching (1Ti 3:2; 2Ti 2:24).

1318. διδακτός, didaktos, *did-ak-tos´*; from 1321; (subject) *instructed* or (object) *communicated* by teaching:—taught, which ... teacheth.

1319. διδασκαλία, didaskalia, *did-as-kal-ee´-ah*; from 1320; *instruction* (the function or the information):—doctrine, learning, teaching.

Noun from *didáskō* (1321), to teach. Teaching or instruction:

(I) The art or manner of teaching (Ro 12:7; 1Ti 4:13, 16; 5:17; Tit 2:7). With the sense of warning or admonition (Ro 15:4; 2Ti 3:16 [cf. 1Co 10:11]).

(II) The thing taught, instruction, precept, doctrine: as coming from men, perverse (Mt 15:9; Mk 7:7; Eph 4:14; Col 2:22; 1Ti 4:1; Sept.: Isa 29:13); from God: divine teaching (1Ti 1:10; 4:6; 6:1, 3; 2Ti 3:10; 4:3; Tit 1:9; 2:1, 10).

Syn.: *paideía* (3809), education or training; *kḗrugma* (2782), preaching; *lógos* (3056), word, speech, utterance, doctrine, precept, teaching; *parádosis* (3862), delivery, the act of delivering over from one to another, that delivery being in some instances instruction, teaching, precept, ordinance.

1320. διδάσκαλος, didaskalos, *did-as´-kal-os*; from 1321; an *instructor* (genitive or special):—doctor, master, teacher.

Noun from *didáskō* (1321), to teach. Instructor, master, teacher (Ro 2:20; Heb 5:12). So of Jewish doctors or lawyers (Mt 9:11; 10:24, 25;

Lk 2:46; 6:40; Jn 3:10); hence equivalent to the title Rabbi (Jn 1:38; 20:16). Spoken of John the Baptist (Lk 3:12); of Jesus (Mt 8:19; 12:38; 17:24; Mk 5:35; 14:14; Jn 11:28); of the apostle Paul (1Ti 2:7); and of other Christian teachers (1Co 12:28, 29).

Deriv.: *heterodidaskaléō* (2085), to teach another doctrine; *kalodidáskalos* (2567), good teacher or teacher of good things; *nomodidáskalos* (3547), an expounder or teacher of the Jewish law; *pseudodidáskalos* (5572), a false teacher.

1321. διδάσκω, didaskō, *did-as´-ko*; a prolonged (causative) form of a primary verb **δάω,** *daō* (to *learn*); to *teach* (in the same broad application):—teach.

From *dáō* (n.f.), to know or teach. To teach, instruct:

(I) Generally and in an absolute sense (Mt 4:23; 5:2; 9:35; Mk 1:21; 9:31; Lk 4:15; Jn 7:35; 1Co 4:17; 11:14; Eph 4:21; 1Ti 4:11; Tit 1:11; Heb 5:12; 1Jn 2:27).

(II) In the sense of to tutor, to direct, to advise, to put in mind (Mt 28:15; Jn 9:34; Ac 21:21; Heb 8:11; Rev 2:20).

Deriv.: *didaktikós* (1317), instructive, didactic, skilled in teaching, communicative; *didaktós* (1318), capable of being taught, instructed; *didaskalía* (1319), instruction, teaching, either the manner of teaching or the content of teaching; *didáskalos* (1320), a teacher; *didachḗ* (1322), doctrine, instruction, the act or content of teaching which depends on the context in which it is found; *theodídaktos* (2312), taught by God.

Syn.: *paideúō* (3811), to instruct with discipline; *katēchéō* (2727), to teach orally, the word from which we derive our Eng. "catechize" and "catechism" which is religious instruction; *mathēteúō* (3100), to disciple, teach with the expectation of one's learning and appropriating; *muéō* (3453), to initiate into certain mysteries, learn a secret.

1322. διδαχή, didachē, *did-akh-ay´*; from 1321; *instruction* (the act or the matter):—doctrine, hath been taught.

Noun from *didáskō* (1321), to teach. The act of teaching, instructing, tutoring (Mk 4:2; 12:38; 1Co 14:6, 26; 2Ti 4:2); the manner or character of one's teaching (Mt 7:28; 22:33; Mk 1:22, 27; 11:18; Lk 4:32); the things taught, pre-

cept, doctrine (Mt 16:12; Jn 7:16, 17; Ac 17:19; Ro 6:17; Heb 6:2; 13:9).

Syn.: *lógos* (3056), word, doctrine or a discourse.

1323. δίδραχμον, didrachmon, *did´-rakh-mon*; from 1364 and 1406; a *double drachma* (*didrachm*):—tribute.

1324. Δίδυμος, Didumos, *did´-oo-mos*; prolonged from 1364; *double*, i.e. *twin*; *Didymus,* a Christian:—Didymus.

1325. δίδωμι, didōmi, *did´-o-mee*; a prolonged form of a primary verb (which is used as an alternative in most of the tenses); to *give* (used in a very wide application, properly or by implication, literal or figurative; greatly modified by the connection):—adventure, bestow, bring forth, commit, deliver (up), give, grant, hinder, make, minister, number, offer, have power, put, receive, set, shew, smite (+ with the hand), strike (+ with the palm of the hand), suffer, take, utter, yield.

1326. διεγείρω, diegeirō, *dee-eg-i´-ro*; from 1223 and 1453; to *wake fully,* i.e. *arouse* (literal or figurative):—arise, awake, raise, stir up.

1327. διέξοδος, diexodos, *dee-ex´-od-os*; from 1223 and 1841; an *outlet through,* i.e. probably an open *square* (from which roads diverge):—highway.

1328. διερμηνευτής, diermēneutēs, *dee-er-main-yoo-tace´*; from 1329; an *explainer*:—interpreter.

1329. διερμηνεύω, diermēneuō, *dee-er-main-yoo´-o*; from 1223 and 2059; to *explain thoroughly*; (by implication) to *translate*:—expound, interpret (-ation).

1330. διέρχομαι, dierchomai, *dee-er´-khom-ahee*; from 1223 and 2064; to *traverse* (literal):—come, depart, go (about, abroad, everywhere, over, through, throughout), pass (by, over, through, throughout), pierce through, travel, walk through.

1331. διερωτάω, dierōtaō, *dee-er-o-tah´-o*; from 1223 and 2065; to *question throughout,* i.e. *ascertain* by interrogation:—make enquiry for.

1332. διετής, dietēs, *dee-et-ace´*; from 1364 and 2094; *of two years* (in age):—two years old.

1333. διετία, dietia, *dee-et-ee´-a*; from 1332; a space of *two years* (*biennium*):—two years.

1334. διηγέομαι, diēgeomai, *dee-ayg-eh´-om-ahee*; from 1223 and 2233; to *relate fully*:—declare, shew, tell.

From *diá* (1223), through or an intensive, and *hēgéomai* (2233), to lead. To lead or conduct through to the end. To recount, tell, relate in full (Mk 5:16; 9:9; Lk 8:39; 9:10; Ac 8:33 [quoted from Isa 53:8]; 9:27; 12:17; Heb 11:32).

Deriv.: *diēgēsis* (1335), a narrative and not a declaration; *ekdiēgéomai* (1555), to recount, rehearse or relate particularly.

Syn.: *anaggéllō* (312), to announce, report; *apaggéllō* (518), to announce or report from a person or place, declare; *diaggéllō* (1229), to announce thoroughly, declare fully; *kataggéllō* (2605), to proclaim; *dēlóō* (1213), to make plain, declare; *phrázō* (5419), to declare; *gnōrízō* (1107), to make known; *emphanízō* (1718), to declare plainly; *phaneróō* (5319), to manifest; *anatíthemai* (394), to declare, communicate; *mēnúō* (3377), to disclose something before unknown; *exaggéllō* (1804), to tell out, proclaim abroad; *légō* (3004), to tell; *megalúnō* (3170), to magnify; *exēgéomai* (1834), to declare by making plain; *diasaphéō*, (1285) to make clear.

1335. διήγεσις, diēgesis, *dee-ayg´-es-is*; from 1334; a *recital*:—declaration.

1336. διηνεκές, diēnekes, *dee-ah-nek-es´*; neuter of a compound of 1223 and a derivative of an alternate of 5342; *carried through*, i.e. (adverb with 1519 and 3588 prefix) *perpetually*:— + continually, for ever.

1337. διθάλασσος, dithalassos, *dee-thal´-as-sos*; from 1364 and 2281; *having two seas*, i.e. a *sound* with a double outlet:—where two seas meet.

1338. διϊκνέομαι, diïkneomai, *dee-ik-neh´-om-ahee*; from 1223 and the base of 2425; to *reach through*, i.e. *penetrate*:—pierce.

1339. διΐστημι, diïstēme, *dee-is´-tay-mee*; from 1223 and 2476; to *stand apart*, i.e. (reflex.) to *remove, intervene*:—go further, be parted, after the space of.

1340. διϊσχυρίζομαι, diïschurizomai, *dee-is-khoo-rid´-zom-ahee*; from 1223 and a derivative of 2478; to *stout* it *through*, i.e. *asseverate*:—confidently (constantly) affirm.

1341. δικαιοκρισία, dikaiokrisia, *dik-ah-yok-ris-ee´-ah*; from 1342 and 2920; a *just sentence*:—righteous judgement.

Noun from *díkaios* (1342), just, righteous, and *krísis* (2920), judgement. Righteous judgement (Ro 2:5 [cf. Hos 6:5; 2Th 1:5]).

1342. δίκαιος, dikaios, *dik´-ah-yos*; from 1349; *equitable* (in character or act); (by implication) *innocent, holy* (absolute or relative):—just, meet, right (-eous).

Adjective from *díkē* (1349), right, just. Right, just, i.e. physically: like, even, equal, e.g., numbers. Also just as it should be, i.e. fit, proper, good. Hence usually and in the NT, in a moral sense: righteous, just; spoken:

(I) Of one who acts alike to all, who practices even-handed justice: just, equitable, impartial. Spoken of God (2Ti 4:8; Rev 16:5); of a judgement or decision (Jn 5:30; 7:24; Lk 12:57; 2Th 1:5, 6; Rev 16:7; 19:2; Sept.: Jer 42:5; Ps 12:2).

(II) Of character, conduct: just as it should be, i.e. upright, righteous, virtuous. Also, good in a general sense; however, *ho díkaios* is strictly one who does right, while *ho agathós* (18) is one who does good, a benefactor.

(A) Spoken of things righteous, just (Ro 7:12; 1Jn 3:12); what is right, proper (Mt 20:4, 7; Col 4:1).

(B) Spoken of persons: **(1)** In the usage of common life (Mt 5:45; Mk 2:17; Lk 5:32; 18:9; 20:20; Ac 10:22; Ro 5:7; 2Pe 2:7, 8); including the idea of innocent (Mt 27:19, 24); including the idea of mild, clement, kind (Mt 1:19; 1Jn 1:9). **(2)** Especially of those whose hearts are right with God: righteous, pious, godly (Mt 13:43; 23:29; 25:46; Mk 6:20; Lk 14:14; Ro 2:13; 3:10). **(3)** Spoken in the highest and most perfect sense of God (Jn 17:25; Ro 3:26; 1Jn 2:29); of Christ (Ac 3:14; 7:52; 1Jn 2:1; 3:7; Sept.: Ex 9:27; Dt 32:4; Ezr 9:15).

Deriv.: *dikaiokrisía* (1341), righteous judgement; *dikaiosúnē* (1343), righteousness; *dikaióō* (1344), to justify; *dikaíōs* (1346), justly.

Syn.: *agathós* (18), good; *hágios* (40), holy in the sense of blameless in character; *hósios* (3741), sacred, the performer of the ordinances. See *dikaiosúnē* (1343), righteousness, and *euthús* (2117), straight, true.

1343. δικαιοσύνη, dikaiosunē, *dik-ah-yos-oo´-nay*; from 1342; *equity* (of character or act); specially (Christian) *justification*:—righteousness.

Noun from *díkaios* (1342), just, righteous. Justice, righteousness:

(I) Doing alike to all, justice, equity, impartiality; spoken of a judge (Ac 17:31; Heb 11:33; Rev 19:11).

(II) Of character, conduct, etc.: being just as one should be, i.e. rectitude, uprightness, righteousness, virtue; equivalent to the adj. *díkaios* (1342), just, righteous.

(A) Of actions, duties, equivalent to *tó díkaion*, what is right, proper, fit (Mt 3:15).

(B) Of disposition or conduct in common life (Eph 5:9; 2Ti 6:11; 2Ti 2:22; Heb 1:9; 7:2; Rev 19:11; Sept.: 1Sa 26:23; Job 29:14; Ps 15:2; 50:6; Pr 8:18, 20). Including the idea of kindness, graciousness, liberality (2Co 9:9, 10; 2Pe 1:1 [cf. *díkaios*, just, righteous]).

(C) Spoken of that righteousness which has regard to God and the divine law: **(1)** Merely external, consisting of the observance of external precepts (Php 3:6). **(2)** Internal, where the heart is right with God, piety toward God, and hence righteousness, godliness (Mt 5:6, 10, 20; 6:33; 21:32; Lk 1:75; Ac 10:35; 24:25; Ro 6:16, 18f.; Heb 1:9; 5:13; Jas 3:18; Sept.: Ge 18:19; 1Ki 3:6; Ps 17:15; Eze 14:14). So used in the expression "to count or impute as righteousness," i.e. to regard as evidence of piety (Ro 4:3, 5, 6, 9, 22; Gal 3:6; Jas 2:23, all quoted from Ge 15:6). Spoken of the righteousness which is of (*ek* [1537], out of) or through (*diá* [1223]) faith in Christ, i.e. where faith is counted or imputed as righteousness or as evidence of piety (Ro 9:30; 10:6; Php 3:9; Heb 11:7); of Christ as the source or author of righteousness (1Co 1:30); of the righteousness of God, i.e. the righteousness which God approves, requires, bestows (Ro 1:17; 3:21, 22, 25, 26). Those on whom God bestows His righteousness become righteous before God (2Co 5:21; Sept.: Ps 5:8). **(3)** In the highest and most perfect sense, of God subjectively, i.e. as an attribute of His character (Ro 3:5); of Christ (Jn 16:8, 10).

(III) By metonymy, in the sense of being regarded as just, i.e. imputation of righteousness, justification, *dikaíōsis* (1347) being the act of justification (Ro 5:17, 21; 10:4, 5; 2Co 3:9).

Syn.: *euthútēs* (2118), rectitude, righteousness.

1344. δικαιόω, dikaioō, *dik-ah-yo´-o*; from 1342; to *render* (i.e. *show* or *regard* as) *just* or *innocent*:—free, justify (-ier), be righteous.

From *díkaios* (1342), just, righteous. To justify, i.e. to regard as just, to declare one to be just:

(I) As a matter of right or justice: to absolve, acquit, clear from any charge or imputation. (Mt 12:37; 1Co 4:4; Ac 13:39; Ro 6:7; Sept.: Ex 23:7; Dt 25:1; 1Ki 8:32). With *eautón* (*eautoú* [1438], oneself), to justify oneself, to excuse oneself (Lk 10:29).

(II) Spoken of character: to declare to be just as one should be, to pronounce right; of things, to regard as right and proper. In the NT, used only of persons: to acknowledge and declare anyone to be righteous, virtuous, good:

(A) By implication, to vindicate, approve, honour, glorify, and in the pass. to receive honour (Mt 11:19; Lk 7:29, 35; 1Ti 3:16).

(B) In relation to God and the divine Law: to declare righteous, to regard as pious. Spoken of the Pharisees, those who "justify themselves before men," i.e. those who profess themselves righteous and pious before men (Lk 16:15). Spoken especially of the justification bestowed by God on men through Christ, in which he is said to regard and treat them as righteous, i.e. to absolve from the consequences of sin and admit to the enjoyment of the divine favour (Ro 3:26, 30; 4:5; 8:30, 33; Gal 3:8). So in the pass.: to be justified (Ro 3:20, 24, 28; Gal 2:16; 3:11; Jas 2:21, 24, 25).

(III) In the sense of to make or cause to be upright. In the middle, to make oneself upright, i.e. to be upright, virtuous (Rev 22:11).

Deriv.: *dikaíōma* (1345), judgement, ordinance; *dikaíōsis* (1347), justification.

Syn.: *aphíēmi* (863), to forgive; *charízomai* (5483), to pardon; *charitóō* (5487), to supply with grace, make acceptable; *apallássō* (525), to deliver in a legal sense from the claims of an opponent; *lutróō* (3084), to redeem by paying ransom; *lúō* (3089), to loose, let go, and the compound *apolúō* (630), to dismiss, forgive, set at liberty; *rhúomai* (4506), to rescue. For further syn., see *dikaiosúnē* (1343), righteousness.

1345. δικαίωμα, dikaiōma, *dik-ah´-yo-mah*; from 1344; an *equitable deed*; (by implication) a *statute* or *decision*:—judgement, justification, ordinance, righteousness.

Noun from *dikaióō* (1344), to justify. Anything justly or rightly done, hence right, justice, equity:

(I) Spoken of a doing right or justice to someone, in a favourable sense: justification, acquittal (Ro 5:16); in an unfavourable sense: condemnation, judgement (Rev 15:4).

(II) Generally: a decree, as defining and establishing what is right and just, i.e. precept, law, ordinance (Lk 1:6; Ro 1:32; 2:26; 8:4; Heb 9:1, 10).

(III) Spoken of character: righteousness, virtue, piety toward God, e.g., of saints (Rev 19:8); of Christ, as manifested in his obedience (Ro 5:18).

Syn.: *diatagḗ* (1296), ordinance; *dógma* (1378), decree.

1346. δικαίως, dikaiōs, *dik-ah´-yoce*; adverb from 1342; *equitably*:—justly, (to) righteously (-ness).

Adverb from *díkaios* (1342), just. Justly, rightly (1Pe 2:23; Sept.: Dt 1:16; Pr 31:9); righteously, piously (1Th 2:10; Tit 2:12); with strict justice (Lk 23:41); as it is fit, proper, right (1Co 15:34).

Syn.: *eutheōs* (2112), straightly; *orthōs* (3723), rightly.

1347. δικαίωσις, dikaiōsis, *dik-ah´-yo-sis*; from 1344; *acquittal* (for Christ's sake):—justification.

From *dikaióō* (1344), to justify. Justification, which God bestows on men through Christ (Ro 4:25; 5:18).

Syn.: *áphesis* (859), remission; *lútrōsis* (3085), redemption, deliverance from the guilt and power of sin; *apolútrōsis* (629), a releasing on payment of ransom; *hilastḗrion* (2435), propitiation; *hilasmós* (2434), expiation; *sōtēría* (4991), salvation.

1348. δικαστής, dikastēs, *dik-as-tace´*; from a derivative of 1349; a *judger*:—judge.

Noun from *dikázō* (n.f.), to give judgement, which is from *díkē* (1349), justice. A judge (Lk 12:14; Ac 7:27, 35; Sept.: Ex 2:14; 1Sa 8:1).

1349. δίκη, dikē, *dee´-kay*; probably from 1166; *right* (as self-*evident*), i.e. *justice* (the principle, a decision, or its execution):—judgement, punish, vengeance.

A noun meaning judgement, sentence, implying punishment (Ac 25:15 [TR]; 2Th 1:9; Jude 7). Justice, personified as *Díkē*, the daughter of the mythological Greek god Zeus and goddess Themis (Ac 28:4).

Deriv.: *ádikos* (94), unjust or unrighteous; *antídikos* (476), an opponent, adversary; *díkaios* (1342), just; *ékdikos* (1558), a punisher or one who carries out the verdict of an issue, an avenger; *éndikos* (1738), one who acts within his rights, fair, just; *hupódikos* (5267), under sentence, one who comes under judgement.

1350. δίκτυον, diktuon, *dik´-too-on*; probably from a primary verb **δίκω, dikō** (to *cast*); a *seine* (for fishing):—net.

A noun meaning net, a fish-net (Mt 4:20, 21; Mk 1:18, 19; Lk 5:2, 4–6; Jn 21:6, 8, 11).

1351. δίλογος, dilogos, *dil´-og-os*; from 1364 and 3056; *equivocal*, i.e. telling a different story:—double-tongued.

1352. διό, dio, *dee-o´*; from 1223 and 3739; *through which* thing, i.e. *consequently*:—for which cause, therefore, wherefore.

1353. διοδεύω, diodeuō, *dee-od-yoo´-o*; from 1223 and 3593; to *travel through*:—go throughout, pass through.

1354. Διονύσιος, Dionusios, *dee-on-oo´-see-os*; from **Διό-νυσος, Dionusos** (*Bacchus*); *reveller; Dionysius*, an Athenian:—Dionysius.

1355. διόπερ, dioper, *dee-op´-er*; from 1352 and 4007; *on which very account*:—wherefore.

1356. διοπετής, diopetēs, *dee-op-et-ace´*; from the alternate of 2203 and the alternate of 4098; *sky-fallen* (i.e. an *aerolite*):—which fell down from Jupiter.

1357. διόρθωσις, diorthōsis, *dee-or´-tho-sis*; from a compound of 1223 and a derivative of 3717, meaning to *straighten thoroughly; rectification*, i.e. (special) the Messianic *restauration*:—reformation.

Noun from *diorthóō* (n.f.), to correct, amend. Amendment, correction, reformation, only in Heb 9:10, the time of a new and better dispensation under the Messiah.

Syn.: *táxis* (5010), order; *euprépeia* (2143), good suitableness.

1358. διορύσσω, **diorussō,** *dee-or-oos´-so*; from 1223 and 3736; to *penetrate* burglariously:—break through (up).

1359. Διόσκουροι, **Dioskouroi,** *dee-os´-koo-roy*; from the alternate of 2203 and a form of the base of 2877; *sons of Jupiter*, i.e. the twins *Dioscuri:*—Castor and Pollux.

1360. διότι, **dioti,** *dee-ot´-ee*; from 1223 and 3754; *on the very account that*, or *inasmuch as:*—because (that), for, therefore.

1361. Διοτρεφής, **Diotrephēs,** *dee-ot-ref-ace´*; from the alternate of 2203 and 5142; *Jove-nourished; Diotrephes*, an opponent of Christianity:—Diotrephes.

1362. διπλοῦς, **diplous,** *dip-looce´*; from 1364 and (probably) the base of 4119; *two-fold:*—double, two-fold more.

1363. διπλόω, **diploō,** *dip-lo´-o*; from 1362; to *render two-fold:*—double.

1364. δίς, **dis,** *dece*; adverb from 1417; *twice:*—again, twice.

1365. διστάζω, **distazō,** *dis-tad´-zo*; from 1364; properly to *duplicate*, i.e. (mental) to *waver* (in opinion):—doubt.

1366. δίστομος, **distomos,** *dis´-tom-os*; from 1364 and 4750; *double-edged:*—with two edges, two-edged.

1367. δισχίλιοι, **dischilïoi,** *dis-khil´-ee-oy*; from 1364 and 5507; *two thousand:*—two thousand.

1368. διϋλίζω, **diulizō,** *dee-oo-lid´-zo*; from 1223 and ὑλίζω, **hulizō,** *hoo-lid´-zo* (to *filter*); to *strain out:*—strain at [*probably by misprint*].

1369. διχάζω, **dichazō,** *dee-khad´-zo*; from a derivative of 1364; to *make apart*, i.e. *sunder* (figurative) *alienate:*—set at variance.

1370. διχοστασία, **dichostasia,** *dee-khos-tas-ee´-ah*; from a derivative of 1364 and 4714; *disunion*, i.e. (figurative) *dissension:*—division, sedition.

Noun from *dícha* (n.f.), separately, and *stásis* (4714), dissension. Dissention, discord (Ro 16:17; 1Co 3:3; Gal 5:20).

Syn.: *diamerismós* (1267), dissension, division, discord; *schísma* (4978), schism, division,

tearing apart; *haíresis* (139), heresy, disunion; *merismós* (3311), a division, partition, separation.

1371. διχοτομέω, **dichotomeō,** *dee-khot-om-eh´-o*; from a compound of a derivative of 1364 and a derivative of τέμνω, **temnō** (to *cut*); to *bisect*, i.e. (by extension) to *flog* severely:—cut asunder (in sunder).

1372. διψάω, **dipsaō,** *dip-sah´-o*; from a variation of 1373; to *thirst* for (literal or figurative):—(be, be a-) thirst (-y).

1373. δίψος, **dipsos,** *dip´-sos*; of uncertain affinity; *thirst:*—thirst.

1374. δίψυχος, **dipsuchos,** *dip´-soo-khos*; from 1364 and 5590; *two-spirited*, i.e. *vacillating* (in opinion or purpose):—double minded.

Adjective from *dís* (1364), twice, and *psuché* (5590), soul, mind. Double-minded, inconstant, wavering (Jas 1:8; 4:8).

Syn.: *akatástatos* (182), unstable.

1375. διωγμός, **diōgmos,** *dee-ogue-mos´*; from 1377; *persecution:*—persecution.

1376. διώκτης, **diōktēs,** *dee-oke´-tace*; from 1377; a *persecutor:*—persecutor.

1377. διώκω, **diōkō,** *dee-o´-ko*; a prolonged (and causative) form of a primary verb δίω, **dio** (to *flee*; compare the base of 1169 and 1249); to *pursue* (literal or figurative); (by implication) to *persecute:*—ensue, follow (after), given to, (suffer) persecute (-ion), press forward.

1378. δόγμα, **dogma,** *dog´-mah*; from the base of 1380; a *law* (civil, ceremonial or ecclesiastical):—decree, ordinance.

Noun from *dokéō* (1380), to think. A decree, edict, ordinance, e.g., of a prince (Lk 2:1; Ac 17:7); of the apostles (Ac 16:4); of the Mosaic Law, i.e. external precepts (Eph 2:15; Col 2:14; Sept.: Da 2:13; 3:10; 6:8, 13, 15).

Deriv.: *dogmatízō* (1379), to decree.

Syn.: *diatagé* (1296), ordinance; *parádosis* (3862), tradition, that which has been handed down; *arché* (746), principle; *kanón* (2583), rule, canon; *nómos* (3551), law; *alétheia* (225), truth; *pístis* (4102), faith.

1379. δογματίζω, **dogmatizō,** *dog-mat-id´-zo*; from 1378; to *prescribe* by statute, i.e. (reflexive) to *submit to* ceremonial *rule:*—be subject to ordinances.

From *dógma* (1378), decree, ordinance. To make a decree, to prescribe an ordinance. In the middle voice, *dogmatízomai*, to let oneself fall into a certain order, subject oneself to ordinances (Col 2:20).

Syn.: *kuróō* (2964), to ratify, confirm.

1380. δοκέω, dokeō, *dok-eh´-o*; a prolonged form of a primary verb **δόκω, dokō,** *dok´-o* (used only as an alternate in certain tenses; compare the base of 1166) of the same meaning; to *think*; (by implication) to *seem* (truthfully or uncertainly):—be accounted, (of own) please (-ure), be of reputation, seem (good), suppose, think, trow.

To seem, appear:

(I) With a reflexive pron. expressed or implied: to seem to oneself, i.e. to be of opinion, to think, suppose, believe (Mt 6:7; Lk 8:18; Ac 26:9; Heb 10:29).

(II) In reference to others: to seem, to appear (Lk 10:36; Ac 17:18; 1Co 12:22; 2Co 10:9; Heb 12:11). Spoken also, in the moderation and urbanity of the Greek manner, of what is real and certain (Mk 10:42; Lk 22:24; 1Co 11:16; Gal 2:9; Heb 4:1).

(III) Impersonally, *dokeí moi* ([3427], to me), it seems to me, that is:

(A) Personally to think, suppose. Used interrogatively in the expression "what do you think?" (Mt 17:25; 18:12; 21:28; 22:17, 42; 26:66; Jn 11:56). Without the interrogative (Ac 25:27).

(B) It seems good to me, it is my pleasure, equivalent to "determine" or "resolve" (Lk 1:3; Ac 15:22, 25, 28, 34). As a part.: what seems good to them, i.e. what seems their pleasure or will (Heb 12:10).

Deriv.: *dógma* (1378), a decree, ordinance; *dóxa* (1391), glory, esteem; *eudokéō* (2106), to think well of.

Syn.: *nomízō* (3543), to consider, suppose, think; *hupolambánō* (5274), to suppose; *huponoéō* (5282), to suspect, conjecture; *oíomai* (3633), to expect, imagine, suppose; *logízomai* (3049), to reckon, suppose; *hēgéomai* (2233), to account, to think; *noéō* (3539), to perceive, understand; *phronéō* (5426), to think; *ginōskō* (1097), to come to know, recognize; *oída* (1492), to perceive; *epístamai* (1987), to know, understand; *gnōrízō* (1107), to discover, know.

1381. δοκιμάζω, dokimazō, *dok-im-ad´-zo*; from 1384; to *test* (literal or figurative); (by implication) to *approve:*—allow, discern, examine, × like, (ap-) prove, try.

From *dókimos* (1384), tested, approved. To try, prove:

(I) To make trial of, put to the proof, examine, e.g., metals, by fire (1Co 3:13; 1Pe 1:7; Sept.: Pr 17:3; Zec 13:9); other things, by use (Lk 14:19); generally, by any method (Ro 12:2; 1Co 11:28; 2Co 8:8, 22; 13:5; Gal 6:4; Eph 5:10; 1Th 2:4; 5:21; 2Ti 3:10; 1Jn 4:1; Sept.: Ps 17:3; 139:1, 23; Jer 11:20). By implication, to examine and judge, i.e. to estimate, distinguish (Lk 12:56; see Mt 16:3; Ro 2:18; Php 1:10; Sept.: Zec 11:13). Spoken with reference to God meaning to put to the proof, i.e. to tempt (Heb 3:9 [cf. Mal 3:15]).

(II) In the sense of to have proved, i.e. to hold as tried, to regard as proved, and generally to approve, judge fit and proper, e.g., persons (1Co 16:3; 1Th 2:4); things (Ro 14:22).

Deriv.: *apodokimázō* (593), to disapprove, reject.

Syn.: *apodeíknumi* (584), to show forth, approve; *anakrínō* (350), to investigate, usually judicially; *diakrínō* (1252), to discriminate, determine, decide.

1382. δοκιμή, dokimē, *dok-ee-may´*; from the same as 1384; *test* (abstract or concrete); (by implication) *trustiness:*—experience (-riment), proof, trial.

Noun from *dókimos* (1384), approved, tried. Proof, trial. The state of being tried (2Co 8:2); the state of having been tried, tried uprightness, approved integrity (Ro 5:4; 2Co 2:9; 9:13). Also, proof, in the sense of evidence, sign, token (2Co 13:3; 12:12).

Syn.: *éndeigma* (1730), the result of proving, the token; *tekmḗrion* (5039), the mark or sign which provides positive proof of the trial.

1383. δοκίμιον, dokimion, *dok-im´-ee-on*; neuter of a presumed derivative of 1382; a *testing*; (by implication) *trustworthiness:*—trial, trying.

Noun from *dókimos* (1384), approved, tried. Proof, trial; a trying or testing (Jas 1:3; 1Pe 1:7).

1384. δόκιμος, dokimos, *dok´-ee-mos*; from 1380; properly *acceptable* (*current* after assayal), i.e. *approved:*—approved, tried.

Adjective from *déchomai* (1209), to accept, receive. Receivable, current; spoken of money, etc. as having been tried and refined (Sept.: Ge 23:16; 1Ch 29:4; 2Ch 9:17). Hence in the NT: tried, proved; approved, and therefore genuine (Ro 14:18; 16:10; 1Co 11:19; 2Co 10:18; 13:7; 2Ti 2:15; Jas 1:12);

Deriv.: *adókimos* (96), unapproved, reprobate; *dokimázō* (1381), to prove, try; *dokimé* (1382), trial, proof; *dokímion* (1383), test.

Syn.: *áxios* (514), worthy; *hikanós* (2425), able; *eklektós* (1588), chosen; *akatákritos* (178), uncondemned; *ámemptos* (273), unblameable; *anepíleptos* (423), blameless; *amómētos* (298), unblameable; *ámōmos* (299), faultless; *áspilos* (784), spotless.

1385. δοκός, dokos, *dok-os´*; from 1209 (through the idea of *holding* up); a *stick* of timber:—beam.

1386. δόλιος, dolios, *dol´-ee-os*; from 1388; *guileful*:—deceitful.

1387. δολιόω, dolioō, *dol-ee-o´-o*; from 1386; to *be guileful*:—use deceit.

1388. δόλος, dolos, *dol´-os*; from an obsolete primary **δέλλω, dellō** (probably meaning to *decoy*; compare 1185); a *trick* (*bait*), i.e. (figurative) *wile*:—craft, deceit, guile, subtilty.

1389. δολόω, doloō, *dol-o´-o*; from 1388; to *ensnare*, i.e. (figurative) *adulterate*:—handle deceitfully.

From *dólos* (1388), deceit. To adulterate, to corrupt. Only in 2Co 4:2.

Syn.: *apatáō* (538), to beguile, deceive; *exapatáō* (1818), to beguile thoroughly, deceive wholly; *phrenapatáō* (5422), to cause deceit in the mind; *planáō* (4105), to cause to go astray, wander; *paralogízomai* (3884), to deceive by false reasoning; *deleázō* (1185), to catch by a bait (*délear*); *apoplanáō* (635), to cause to wander away from, lead astray.

1390. δόμα, doma, *dom´-ah*; from the base of 1325; a *present*:—gift.

Noun from *dídōmi* (1325), to give. A gift (Mt 7:11; Lk 11:13; Eph 4:8; Php 4:17; see Sept.: Ge 25:6; Ps 68:18; Pr 18:16; Da 2:48).

1391. δόξα, doxa, *dox´-ah*; from the base of 1380; *glory* (as very *apparent*), in a wide application (literal or figurative, object or subject):—dignity, glory (-ious), honour, praise, worship.

Noun from *dokéō* (1380), to think, recognize. A seeming, an appearance. In the NT, honour, glory:

(I) Spoken of honour due or rendered, i.e. praise, applause (Lk 14:10; Jn 5:41, 44; 7:18; 8:50, 54; 2Co 6:8; 1Th 2:6); of God, e.g., to the honour and glory of God, i.e. that God may be honored, glorified (Jn 11:4; Ro 3:7; 15:7; Php 1:11; Rev 4:11). In ascriptions of glory or praise to God (Lk 2:14; Ro 11:36; Gal 1:5; 1Pe 4:11; Sept.: 1Ch 16:28, 29 [cf. Ps 29:9; 104:35; 106:48]). By metonymy, spoken of the occasion or source of honour or glory (1Co 11:15; 2Co 8:23; Eph 3:13; 1Th 2:20).

(II) In the NT, spoken also of that which excites admiration or to which honour is ascribed:

(A) Of external conditions: dignity, splendour, glory (Heb 2:7, quoted from Ps 8:5; 1Pe 1:24). By metonymy: that which reflects, expresses or exhibits dignity (1Co 11:7). Spoken of kings: regal majesty, splendour, pomp, magnificence, e.g., of the expected temporal reign of the Messiah (Mk 10:37); of the glory of His Second Coming (Mt 19:28; 24:30; Mk 13:26; Lk 9:26; 21:27; Tit 2:13; Sept.: 1Sa 2:8; 1Ch 29:25; Isa 8:7; Da 11:21); of the accompaniments of royalty, e.g., splendid apparel (Mt 6:29; Lk 12:27; Sept.: Ex 28:2, 36; Est 5:1; Isa 61:3); of wealth, treasures (Mt 4:8; Lk 4:6; Rev 21:24, 26; Sept.: Ge 31:1; Isa 10:3). By metonymy spoken in the plural of persons in high honour, e.g., *dóxai*, dignitaries, i.e. kings, princes, magistrates (2Pe 2:10; Jude 8 [cf. Isa 5:13]).

(B) Of an external appearance: luster, brightness, dazzling light (Ac 22:14; 1Pe 5:4); the sun, stars (1Co 15:40, 41); Moses' face (2Co 3:7; Sept.: Ex 34:29, 30, 35); the celestial light which surrounds angels (Rev 18:1), or glorified saints (Lk 9:31, 32; 1Co 15:43; Php 3:21; Col 3:4). Spoken especially of the celestial splendour in which God sits enthroned and His divine effulgence, dazzling majesty, radiant glory (2Th 1:9; 2Pe 1:17; Rev 15:8; 21:11, 23 [cf. 22:5]); as visible to mortals (Lk 2:9; Jn 12:41, see Isa 6:1; Ac 7:55); as manifested in the Messiah's Second Coming (Mt 16:27; Mk 8:38; Sept.: Ex 16:10; 24:17; 1Ki 8:11 [cf. Ps 104:1ff.; Eze 1:26–28]).

(C) Of internal character: glorious moral attributes, excellence, perfection. As spoken of

God: infinite perfection, divine majesty and holiness (Ac 7:2; Ro 1:23; Eph 1:17; Heb 1:3); of the divine perfections as manifested in the power of God (Jn 11:40; Ro 6:4; 9:23; Eph 1:12, 14, 18; 3:16; Col 1:11; 2Pe 1:3); of Jesus, as the brightness (*apaúgasma* [541]) of the divine character (Jn 1:14; 2:11; Heb 1:3); of things, in place of an adj.: excellent, splendid, glorious (2Co 3:7–9; Eph 1:6).

(D) Of that exalted state of blissful perfection which is the portion of those who dwell with God in heaven. As spoken of Christ and including the idea of His royal majesty as Messiah (Lk 24:26; Jn 17:5, 22, 24; 2Th 2:14; 1Ti 3:16; 1Pe 1:11); of glorified saints, i.e. salvation, eternal life (Ro 2:7, 10; 8:18; 1Co 2:7; 2Co 4:17; 1Th 2:12; 2Ti 2:10; Heb 2:10; 1Pe 5:1). By metonymy: the author or procurer of this glory for anyone, i.e. the author of salvation (Lk 2:32), the same as the Lord of glory (1Co 2:8 [see v. 7]).

Deriv.: *doxázō* (1392), to glorify; *éndoxos* (1741), glorious; *kenódoxos* (2755), self-conceited; *parádoxos* (3861), strange, contrary to expected appearance, equivalent to a miraculous manifestation.

Syn.: *agallíasis* (20), exultation; *chará* (5479), joy; *euphrosúnē* (2167), having a joyful attitude; *kléos* (2811), renown; *kaucháomai* (2744), to boast; *kaúchēsis* (2746), the act of boasting; *kaúchēma* (2745), the boast or the reason for boasting.

1392. δοξάζω, doxazō, *dox-ad´-zo*; from 1391; to *render* (or *esteem*) *glorious* (in a wide application):—(make) glorify (-ious), full of (have) glory, honour, magnify.

From *dóxa* (1391), glory. To glorify:

(I) To ascribe glory or honour to anyone, praise, celebrate (Mt 6:2; Lk 4:15; Jn 8:54; Ac 13:48; Heb 5:5; Rev 18:7; Sept.: 2Sa 6:22; La 1:8). To glorify God, meaning to render glory to Him; to celebrate with praises, worship, adoration (Mt 5:16; 9:8; 15:31; Mk 2:12; Lk 2:20; 5:25, 26; 7:16; 13:13; 17:15; 18:43; 23:47; Jn 13:31, 32; 14:13; 15:8; 17:4; 21:19; Ac 4:21; 11:18; 21:20; Ro 1:21; 15:6, 9; 1Co 6:20; 2Co 9:13; Gal 1:24; 1Pe 2:12; 4:11, 16); the name of God (Jn 12:28; Rev 15:4).

(II) To honour, bestow honour upon, exalt in dignity, render glorious:

(A) Used generally: to render excellent, splendid (1Co 12:26; 2Th 3:1; Sept.: 1Ch 19:3; Est 6:6, 7, 9, 11; Pr 13:18); in the pass. voice: to be excellent, splendid, glorious (Ro 11:13; 2Co 3:10; 1Pe 1:8; Sept.: Ex 34:29, 30, 35).

(B) Spoken of God and Christ, meaning to glorify, i.e. to render conspicuous and glorious the divine character and attributes; e.g., of God as glorified by the Son (Jn 12:28; 13:31, 32; 14:13; 17:1, 4); by Christians (Jn 15:8; 21:19); of Christ as glorified by the Father (Jn 8:54; 13:32; 17:1, 5; Ac 3:13); by the Spirit (Jn 16:14); by Christians (Jn 17:10); generally (Jn 11:4; 13:31; Sept.: Ex 15:6, 11; Le 10:3; Isa 5:16).

(C) Spoken of Christ and His followers: to glorify, i.e. to advance to that state of bliss and glory which is the portion of those who dwell with God in heaven, e.g., of Christ as the Messiah (Jn 7:39; 12:16, 23 [cf. Isa 52:13]).

Deriv.: *sundoxázō* (4888), to glorify together.

Syn.: *timáō* (5091), to honour; *megalúnō* (3170), to make great, magnify.

1393. Δορκάς, Dorkas, *dor-kas´*; *gazelle*; Dorcas, a Christian woman:—Dorcas.

1394. δόσις, dosis, *dos´-is*; from the base of 1325; a *giving*; by implication (concrete) a *gift*:—gift, giving.

Noun from *dídōmi* (1325), to give. A gift; the act of giving (Php 4:15; Jas 1:17). For a full discussion of all the cognate words see *dōron* (1435), a gift.

1395. δότης, dotēs, *dot´-ace*; from the base of 1325; a *giver*:—giver.

1396. δουλαγωγέω, doulagōgeō, *doo-lag-ogue-eh´-o*; from a presumed compound of 1401 and 71; to *be a slave-driver*, i.e. to *enslave* (figurative, *subdue*):—bring into subjection.

From *doúlos* (1401), servant, and *ágō* (71), to lead, bring. To bring into subjection, to subdue. Only in 1Co 9:27.

Syn.: *doulóō* (1402), to make a slave, enslave; *katadoulóō* (2615), to bring into bondage; *hupotássō* (5293), to subject.

1397. δουλεία, douleia, *doo-li´-ah*; from 1398; *slavery* (ceremonial or figurative):—bondage.

Noun from *douleúō* (1398), to be a slave, to serve. Slavery, bondage. Spoken of the condition of those under the Mosaic Law (Gal 4:24). Used figuratively: a slavish spirit, in contrast to the spirit of sonship (Ro 8:15); of the condition of those who are subject to death (Ro 8:21); of those subject to the fear of death (Heb 2:15).

Deriv.: *ophthalmodouleía* (3787), eyeservice, implying an outward service only.

1398. δουλεύω, **douleuō**, *dool-yoo´-o*; from 1401; to *be a slave* to (literal or figurative, involuntary or voluntary):—be in bondage, (do) serve (-ice).

From *doúlos* (1401), servant. To be a slave or servant:

(**I**) Spoken of involuntary service (Mt 6:24; Lk 16:13; Eph 6:7; 1Ti 6:2; Sept.: Le 25:39; Dt 15:12); of a people meaning to be subject to (Jn 8:33; Ac 7:7; Ro 9:12 [cf. Ge 25:23; 27:40]; Sept.: Ge 14:4; Jgs 3:8, 14). Metaphorically, of those subject to the Mosaic Law (Gal 4:25).

(**II**) Metaphorically spoken of voluntary service: to obey, be devoted to (Lk 15:29; Ro 12:11; Gal 5:13; Php 2:22; Sept.: Ge 29:15, 18, 20, 25, 30). In a moral sense: to obey or be devoted to God (Mt 6:24; Lk 16:13; Ac 20:19; Ro 7:6; 1Th 1:9); to Christ (Ro 14:18; 16:18; Col 3:24); to the law of God (Ro 7:25; Sept.: Dt 13:4; Jgs 2:7; Mal 3:18). Spoken of false gods (Gal 4:8; Sept.: Ex 23:33); of things: to obey, follow, indulge in, e.g., mammon (Mt 6:24; Lk 16:13); sin (Ro 6:6); the belly, i.e. one's appetite (Ro 16:18); the elements (Gal 4:9). To indulge in one's lusts (Tit 3:3).

Deriv.: *douleía* (1397), slavery, bondage.

Syn.: *diakonéō* (1247), to minister; *leitourgéō* (3008), to render public service, do service to the gods; *latreúō* (3000), to serve for hire; *hupēretéō* (5256), to serve as an underling; *hierourgéō* (2418), to minister in priestly service; *ergázomai* (2038), to work.

1399. δούλη, **doulē**, *doo´-lay*; feminine of 1401; a *female slave* (involuntary or voluntary):— handmaid (-en).

1400. δοῦλον, **doulon**, *doo´-lon*; neuter of 1401; *subservient*:—servant.

1401. δοῦλος, **doulos**, *doo´-los*; from 1210; a *slave* (literal or figurative, involuntary or voluntary; frequently therefore in a qualified sense of *subjection* or *subserviency*):—bond (-man), servant.

A noun meaning slave, servant:

(**I**) Spoken of involuntary service: a slave as opposed to a free man (1Co 7:21; Gal 3:28; Col 3:11; Rev 6:15). Also generally: a servant (Mt 13:27, 28; Jn 4:51; Ac 2:18; Eph 6:5; 1Ti 6:1; Sept.: Le 25:44; Jos 9:23; Jgs 6:27). In Php 2:7,

having taken "the form of a servant," means appearing in a humble and despised condition.

(**II**) Metaphorically, spoken of voluntary service: a servant, implying obedience, devotion (Jn 15:15; Ro 6:16). Implying modesty (2Co 4:5); in praise of modesty (Mt 20:27; Mk 10:44). Spoken of the true followers and worshippers of God, e.g., a servant of God: either of agents sent from God, as Moses (Rev 15:3; see Jos 1:1), prophets (Rev 10:7; 11:18; Sept.: Jos 24:29; Jer 7:25), or simply of the worshippers of God (Rev 2:20; 7:3; 19:5; Sept.: Ps 34:22; 134:1); the followers and ministers of Christ (Eph 6:6; 2Ti 2:24), especially applied to the apostles (Ro 1:1; Gal 1:10; 2Pe 1:1; Jude 1). Used instead of the personal pron. in the oriental style of addressing a superior (Lk 2:29; Ac 4:29; Sept.: 1Sa 3:9, 10; Ps 19:12). In respect of things, of one who indulges in or is addicted to something (Jn 8:34; Ro 6:16, 17; 2Pe 2:19).

(**III**) In the sense of minister, attendant; spoken of the officers of an oriental court (Mt 18:23, 26–28, 32; 22:3, 4, 6, 8, 10).

Deriv.: *doulagōgéō* (1396), to be a slave driver; *douleúō* (1398), to be a slave to, to serve; *doulóō* (1402), to make a slave or bring someone into slavery; *súndoulos* (4889), fellow slave.

Syn.: *diákonos* (1249), a deacon, servant, minister; *país* (3816), literally "a child," but also an attendant, servant; *oikétēs* (3610), a house servant; *hupērétēs* (5257), a servant; *therápōn* (2324), a healer, an attendant servant; *místhios* (3407) and *misthōtós* (3411), a hired servant.

1402. δουλόω, **doulóō**, *doo-lo´-o*; from 1401; to *enslave* (literal or figurative):—bring into (be under) bondage, × given, become (make) servant.

From *doúlos* (1401), slave. To make a slave or servant, to bring into bondage (Ac 7:6; 1Co 9:19; Sept.: Ge 15:13); in the pass., to be subjugated, subdued (Ro 6:18, 22); in the perf. tense, to be dependent (Gal 4:3).

Deriv.: *katadoulóō* (2615), to enslave.

Syn.: *kurieúō* (2961), to exercise lordship over.

1403. δοχή, **dochē**, *dokh-ay´*; from 1209; a *reception*, i.e. convivial *entertainment*:—feast.

Noun from *déchomai* (1209), to receive. A reception, entertainment, banquet (Lk 5:29; 14:13; Sept.: Ge 26:30; Est 1:3; 5:4).

Syn.: *heortē* (1859), a feast or festival; *deípnon* (1173), the chief meal of the day, dinner or supper; *gámos* (1062), a wedding or a wedding feast; *agápē* (26), a love feast.

1404. δράκων, drakōn, *drak´-ōn*; probably from an alternate form of **δέρκομαι,** *derkomai* (to *look*); a fabulous kind of *serpent* (perhaps as supposed to *fascinate*):—dragon.

1405. δράσσομαι, drassomai, *dras´-som-ahee*; perhaps akin to the base of 1404 (through the idea of *capturing*); to *grasp*, i.e. (figurative) *entrap*:—take.

1406. δραχμή, drachmē, *drakh-may´*; from 1405; a *drachma* or (silver) coin (as *handled*):— piece (of silver).

1407. δρέπανον, drepanon, *drep´-an-on*; from **δρέπω,** *drepō* (to *pluck*); a gathering *hook* (especially for harvesting):—sickle.

1408. δρόμος, dromos, *drom´-os*; from the alternate of 5143; a *race*, i.e. (figurative) *career*:— course.

1409. Δρούσιλλα, Drousilla, *droo´-sil-lah*; a feminine diminutive of *Drusus* (a Roman name); *Drusilla*, a member of the Herodian family:—Drusilla.

1410. δύναμαι, dunamai, *doo´-nam-ahee*; of uncertain affinity; to *be able* or *possible*:—be able, can (do, + -not), could, may, might, be possible, be of power.

To be able, have power, both in a physical and moral sense (Mt 3:9; 2Ti 3:15), as depending either on the disposition or faculties of mind (1Th 2:6), the degree of strength or skill (Ro 15:14), or the nature and external circumstances of the case (Ac 24:8, 11).

Deriv.: *dúnamis* (1411), power, ability, strength; *dunástēs* (1413), ruler; *dunatós* (1415), powerful, strong.

Syn.: *ischúō* (2480), to be strong, prevail, but indicating a more forceful strength or ability than is involved in *dúnamai; exischúō* (1840), to be thoroughly strong; *katischúō* (2729), to overpower, prevail; *krataióō* (2901), to strengthen, sustain; *sthenóō* (4599), to strengthen.

1411. δύναμις, dunamis, *doo´-nam-is*; from 1410; *force* (literal or figurative); specially miraculous *power* (usually by implication, a *miracle* itself):—ability, abundance, meaning, might

(-ily, -y, -y deed), (worker of) miracle (-s), power, strength, violence, might (wonderful) work.

Noun from *dúnamai* (1410), to be able. Power, ability, strength, force:

(**I**) Spoken of intrinsic power, either physical or moral, as in the verb *dúnamai* (1410):

(**A**) Of the body (1Co 15:43; Heb 11:11; Sept.: Job 39:19, *dúnamis*; Job 40:11, *ischús*; Ps 29:4, *ischús* [2479], strength).

(**B**) Generally (Mt 25:15; Ac 6:8; 1Co 15:56; 2Ti 1:7); a spirit of strength, meaning manly vigour in opposition to a spirit of cowardice (Heb 1:3; 7:16; 11:34; Rev 1:16; Sept.: 2Ki 18:20; 1Ch 13:8; 29:2; Ezr 2:69; 10:13; Job 12:13). Also in various constructions with *katá* (2596): according to one's strength, meaning as far as one can (2Co 8:3). With *hupér* (5228), beyond: above one's strength (2Co 1:8; 8:3). With *en* (1722), in: with power, powerfully, mightily (Col 1:29; 2Th 1:11).

(**C**) Spoken of God: the great power of God, meaning His almighty energy (Mt 22:29; Mk 12:24; Lk 1:35; 5:17; Ro 1:20; 9:17; 1Co 6:14; 2Co 4:7; 13:4; Eph 1:19; 3:7, 20; 2Ti 1:8; 1Pe 1:5; 2Pe 1:3). Joined with *dóxa* [(1391), glory] it implies the greatness, omnipotence, and majesty of God (Rev 15:8. See Mt 26:64; Mk 14:62; Lk 22:69; Heb 1:3, "on the right hand of the Majesty"). By metonymy, spoken of a person or thing in whom the power of God is manifested, i.e. the manifestation of the power of God (Ac 8:10; see Ro 1:16; 1Co 1:18, 24). With phrase "of God" it expresses the source, i.e. power imparted from God (1Co 2:5; 2Co 6:7). Spoken of Jesus as exercising the power to heal (Mk 5:30; Lk 6:19; 8:46; 2Co 12:9). In the sense of power, omnipotent majesty (Mt 24:30; Mk 9:1; 13:26; Lk 21:27; 2Th 1:7; 2Pe 1:16); as spoken of the power of the Spirit, meaning the power imparted by the Spirit (Lk 4:14; Ro 15:13, 19); of prophets and apostles as empowered by the Holy Spirit (Lk 1:17; 24:49; Ac 1:8 [cf. Ac 2:4]).

(**D**) By metonymy of effect for cause, the plural *dunámeis*, powers, is often used for mighty deeds, miracles (Mt 7:22; 11:20, 21, 23; 13:54, 58; 14:2; Mk 6:2, 5, 14; Lk 10:13; 19:37; Ac 2:22; 8:13; 19:11; 1Co 12:10; 2Co 12:12; Gal 3:5; Heb 2:4; Sept.: Job 37:14; Ps 106:2). Hence, as abstract for concrete: a worker of miracles (1Co 12:28, 29).

(**E**) Spoken of the essential power, true nature or reality of something (Php 3:10; 2Ti

3:5). As opposed to *lógos* (3056), speech merely (1Co 4:19, 20; 1Th 1:5). Metaphorically of language: the power of a word, i.e. meaning, significance (1Co 14:11).

(**II**) Spoken of power as resulting from external sources and circumstances:

(**A**) Power, authority, might (Lk 4:36; 9:1; Ac 3:12; 2Pe 2:11; Rev 13:2; 17:13). Spoken of omnipotent sovereignty as due to God, e.g., in ascriptions (Mt 6:13; Rev 4:11; 5:12; 7:12; 11:17; 12:10; 19:1; Sept.: 1Ch 29:11). Joined with *ónoma* (3686), name (Ac 4:7; 1Co 5:4). By metonymy of abstract for concrete, put for "the one in authority," similar to the Eng. authorities, i.e. persons in authority, the mighty, the powerful (Ro 8:38; 1Co 15:24; Eph 1:21; 1Pe 3:22; Sept.: Est 2:18).

(**B**) With the meaning of number, quantity, abundance, wealth (in Rev 3:8, a small number of members or perhaps true believers [cf. Rev 18:3]). Metaphorically for enjoyment, happiness (Heb 6:5).

(**C**) Of warlike power, like the Eng. force, forces, i.e. host, army (Lk 10:19; Sept.: Ex 14:28; 15:4; 2Sa 10:7; 17:25; 20:23). By Hebraism, *dunámeis tṓn ouranṓn*, "the hosts of heaven" (see *ouranós* [3772], heaven), i.e. the sun, moon, and stars (Mt 24:29; Mk 13:25; Lk 21:26 [cf. Rev 6:13; Sept.: Isa 34:4; Da 8:10]).

Deriv.: *dunamóō* (1412), to strengthen.

Syn.: *ischús* (2479), strength, ability, force, somewhat stronger than *dúnamis*; *krátos* (2904), dominion, enduring strength; *exousía* (1849), authority; *archḗ* (746), rule, power; *megaleiótēs* (3168), majesty; with the meaning of miracle: *sēmeíon* (4592), sign, token; *téras* (5059), something strange, a marvel, wonder; *megaleíon* (3167), a great work; *éndoxon* (1741), a glorious work; *parádoxon* (3861), a strange work; *thaumásion* (2297), a marvelous work; *thaúma* (2295), a wonder, marvel; *érgon* (2041), work when referring to Christ's work.

1412. δυναμόω, dunamoō, *doo-nam-o´-o*; from 1411; to *enable*:—strengthen.

From *dúnamis* (1411), strength. To strengthen. In the NT, used in the pass., to be strengthened, grow strong morally (Col 1:11 [cf. Eph 3:16]).

Deriv.: *endunamóō* (1743), to make strong.

Syn.: *ischúō* (2480), to have strength; *enischúō* (1765), to strengthen; *krataióō* (2901), to strengthen; *sthenóō* (4599), to strengthen; *stereóō*

(4732), to establish; *epistērízō* (1991), to establish, confirm; *stērízō* (4741), to establish, strengthen.

1413. δυνάστης, dunastēs, *doo-nas´-tace*; from 1410; a *ruler* or *officer*:—of great authority, mighty, potentate.

Noun from *dúnamai* (1410), to be able. One in power; a potentate, prince (Lk 1:52; 1Ti 6:15; Sept.: Pr 8:16; 14:28; 23:1); one in authority under a prince, a minister of a court (Ac 8:27; Sept.: Ge 50:4; Jer 34:19; Le 19:15).

Syn.: *dunatós* (1415), powerful, mighty, and *ischurós* (2478), strong; *krataiós* (2900), one who has dominion; *kúrios* (2962), lord, master; *despótēs* (1203), despot, master, lord; *megistán* (3175), great man, prince, lord.

1414. δυνατέω, dunateō, *doo-nat-eh´-o*; from 1415; to *be efficient* (figurative):—be mighty.

1415. δυνατός, dunatos, *doo-nat-os´*; from 1410; *powerful* or *capable* (literal or figurative); neuter *possible*:—able, could, (that is) mighty (man), possible, power, strong.

1416. δύνω, dunō, *doo´-no*; or **δῦμι, dumi,** *doo´-mee*; prolonged forms of an obsolete primary **δύω, duō;** *doo´-o* (to *sink*); to go "*down*":—set.

1417. δύο, duo, *doo´-o*; a primary numeral; "*two*":—both, twain, two.

1418. δυς, dus, *doos*; a primary inseparable particle of uncertain derivative; used only in composition as a prefix; *hard*, i.e. *with difficulty*:—+ hard, + grievous, *etc.*

1419. δυσβάστακτος, dusbastaktos, *doosbas´-tak-tos*; from 1418 and a derivative of 941; *oppressive*:—grievous to be borne.

1420. δυσεντερία, dusenteria, *doos-en-teree´-ah*; from 1418 and a compound of 1787 (meaning a *bowel*); a "*dysentery*":—bloody flux.

1421. δυσερμήνευτος, dusermēneutos, *dooser-mane´-yoo-tos*; from 1418 and a presumed derivative of 2059; *difficult of explanation*:—hard to be uttered.

1422. δύσκολος, duskolos, *doos´-kol-os*; from 1418 and **κόλον, kolon** (*food*); properly *fastidious about eating* (*peevish*), i.e. (genitive) *impracticable*:—hard.

1423. δυσκόλως, duskolōs, *doos-kol´-oce*; adverb from 1422; *impracticably:*—hardly.

1424. δυσμή, dusmē, *doos-may´*; from 1416; the sun-*set*, i.e. (by implication) the *western* region:—west.

1425. δυσνόητος, dusnoētos, *doos-no´-ay-tos*; from 1418 and a derivative of 3539; *difficult of perception:*—hard to be understood.
Adjective from *dus* (1418), hard, and *noētós* (n.f.), understood, which is from *noéō* (3539), to understand. Hard to be understood. Only in 2Pe 3:16.
Syn.: *dusermḗneutos* (1421), difficult to explain, hard to understand; *dúskolos* (1422), difficult; *sklērós* (4642), hard, difficult.

1426. δυσφημία, dusphēmia, *doos-fay-mee´-ah*; from a compound of 1418 and 5345; *defamation:*—evil report.

1427. δώδεκα, dōdeka, *do´-dek-ah*; from 1417 and 1176; *two* and *ten*, i.e. a *dozen:*—twelve.

1428. δωδέκατος, dōdekatos, *do-dek´-at-os*; from 1427; *twelfth:*—twelfth.

1429. δωδεκάφυλον, dōdekaphulon, *do-dek-af´-oo-lon*; from 1427 and 5443; the *commonwealth* of Israel:—twelve tribes.

1430. δῶμα, dōma, *do´-mah*; from **δέμο, demō** (to *build*); properly an *edifice*, i.e. (special) a *roof:*—housetop.

1431. δωρεά, dōrea, *do-reh-ah´*; from 1435; a *gratuity:*—gift.
Noun from *dídōmi* (1325), to give. A gift (Jn 4:10; Ac 2:38; 8:20; 10:45; 11:17; Ro 5:15, 17; 2Co 9:15; Eph 3:7; 4:7; Heb 6:4; Sept.: Da 2:6).
Deriv.: *dōreán* (1432), freely; *dōréomai* (1433), to make a gift of.

1432. δωρεάν, dōrean, *do-reh-an´*; accusative of 1431 as adverb; *gratuitously* (literal or figurative):—without a cause, freely, for naught, in vain.

1433. δωρέομαι, dōreomai, *do-reh´-om-ahee*; middle from 1435; to *bestow* gratuitously:—give.

1434. δώρημα, dōrēma, *do´-ray-mah*; from 1433; a *bestowment:*—gift.
Noun from *dōréō* (1433), to make a gift. A gift (Ro 5:16; Jas 1:17).

1435. δῶρον, dōron, *do´-ron*; a *present*; specially a *sacrifice:*—gift, offering.
Noun from *dídōmi* (1325), to give. Gift. Used of gifts given as an expression of honour (Mt 2:11); for support of the temple (Mt 15:5; Mk 7:11; Lk 21:1, 4); to God (Mt 5:23, 24; 8:4; 23:18, 19; Heb 5:1; 8:3, 4; 9:9; 11:4); as the gift of salvation (Eph 2:8); for celebrating (Rev 11:10).

E (Epsilon)

NT Numbers 1436–2193

1436. ἔα, **ea,** *eh´-ah*; apparently imperative of 1439; properly *let* it *be*, i.e. (as interject) *aha!*:—let alone.

1437. ἐάν, **ean,** *eh-an´*; from 1487 and 302; a *conditional* particle; *in case* that, *provided*, etc.; often used in connection with other particles to denote *indefiniteness* or *uncertainty*:—before, but, except, (and) if, (if) so, (what-, whither-) soever, though, when (-soever), whether (or), to whom, [who-] so (-ever). See 3361.

1438. ἑαυτοῦ, **heautou,** *heh-ow-too´* (including all the other cases); from a reflexive pronoun otherwise obsolete and the generic (dative or accusative) of 846; *him-* (*her-, it-, them-*, also [in conjunction with the personal pronoun of the other persons] *my-, thy-, our-, your-*) *self* (*selves*), etc.:—alone, her (own, -self), (he) himself, his (own), itself, one (to) another, our (thine) own (-selves), + that she had, their (own, own selves), (of) them (-selves), they, thyself, you, your (own, own conceits, own selves, -selves).

1439. ἐάω, **eaō,** *eh-ah´-o*; of uncertain affinity; to *let be*, i.e. *permit* or *leave* alone:—commit, leave, let (alone), suffer. See also 1436.

1440. ἑβδομήκοντα, **hebdomēkonta,** *heb-dom-ay´-kon-tah*; from 1442 and a modified form of 1176, *seventy*:—seventy, three score and ten.

1441. ἑβδομηκοντάκις, **hebdomēkontakis,** *heb-dom-ay-kon-tak-is´*; multiple adverb from 1440; *seventy times*:—seventy times.

1442. ἕβδομος, **hebdomos,** *heb´-dom-os*; ordinal from 2033; *seventh*:—seventh.

1443. Ἐβέρ, **Eber,** *eb-er´*; of Hebrew origin [5677]; *Eber*, a patriarch:—Eber.

1444. Ἑβραϊκός, **Hebraïkos,** *heb-rah-ee-kos´*; from 1443; *Hebraïc* or the *Jewish* language:—Hebrew.

1445. Ἑβραῖος, **Hebraios,** *heb-rah´-yos*; from 1443; a *Hebræan* (i.e. Hebrew) or *Jew*:—Hebrew.

1446. Ἑβραΐς, **Hebraïs,** *heb-rah-is´*; from 1443; the *Hebraistic* (i.e. Hebrew) or *Jewish* (*Chaldee*) language:—Hebrew.

1447. Ἑβραϊστί, **Hebraïsti,** *heb-rah-is-tee´*; adverb from 1446; *Hebraistically* or in the Jewish (Chaldee) language:—in (the) Hebrew (tongue).

1448. ἐγγίζω, **eggizō,** *eng-id´-zo*; from 1451; to *make near*, i.e. (reflexive) *approach*:—approach, be at hand, come (draw) near, be (come, draw) nigh.

From *eggús* (1451), near. To bring near, cause to approach. In the NT, used intransitively: to come near, approach (Lk 7:12; 15:1, 25; 22:47; Ac 10:9); in the perf., *éggika*, to be near, to be at hand (Mt 3:2; 4:17; 10:7; Mk 1:15; Lk 10:11).

(I) Spoken of persons (Mt 21:1; 26:46; Mk 11:1; 14:42; Lk 7:12; 12:33; 18:40; 19:37, 41; 24:15; Ac 10:9; 21:33; 23:15).

(II) Spoken of things, time (Mt 3:2; 4:17; 10:7; 21:34; 26:45; Mk 1:15; Lk 21:8, 20, 28; 22:1; Ac 7:17; Ro 13:12; Heb 10:25; Jas 5:8; 1Pe 4:7).

(III) Metaphorically (Php 2:30; Sept.: Job 33:22; Ps 88:3; 107:18).

(IV) The expression *eggízō tō Theō*, "to draw near to God" was often connected with offering sacrifices in the temple (Sept.: Ex 19:22; Eze 44:13). In the NT, it means to worship God with a pious heart (Mt 15:8; Heb 7:19; Jas 4:8, quoted from Isa 29:13). God is said to "approach men," which means to draw near to Christians, by the aid of His Spirit, grace (Jas 4:8; Sept.: Dt 4:7 [cf. Ps 145:18]).

Deriv.: *proseggízō* (4331), approaching, coming close to.

Syn.: *paraplēsion* (3897), near; *plēsíon* (4139), near, neighbour; *pará* (3844), beside, along side, near; *prós* (4314), toward, on the side, near;

ephístēmi (2186), to come near, be at hand; *prosérchomai* (4334), to draw near; *proságō* (4317), to draw near; *érchomai* (2064), to come, as contrasted to *hēkō* (2240), to arrive and be present; *paragínomai* (3854), to arrive and be present; *aphiknéomai* (864), to arrive at a place; *katantáō* (2658), to come to; *parístēmi* (3936), to stand by or near; *phthánō* (5348), to come upon, arrive.

1449. ἐγγράφω, eggraphō, *eng-graf´-o*; from 1722 and 1125; to *"engrave,"* i.e. *inscribe:*—write (in).

1450. ἔγγυος, egguos, *eng´-goo-os*; from 1722 and **γυῖον, guion** (a *limb*); *pledged* (as if *articulated* by a member), i.e. a *bondsman:*—surety.

Adjective from *eggúē* (n.f.), pledge, bail, security. Yielding a pledge. Only in Heb 7:22 (cf. Heb 7:21, 24, 25).

Syn.: *bebaíōsis* (951), confirmation; *plērophoría* (4136), assurance; *marturía* (3141), evidence; *apódeixis* (585), proof.

1451. ἐγγύς, eggus, *eng-goos´*; from a primary verb **ἄγχω, agchō** (to *squeeze* or *throttle*; akin to the base of 43); *near* (literal or figurative, of place or time):—from, at hand, near, nigh (at hand, unto), ready.

Adverb meaning close, near:

(I) Of place (Jn 3:23; 6:19, 23; 11:18, 54; 19:42; Lk 19:11; Ac 1:12; Sept.: Ge 45:10; Eze 23:12). Metaphorically: near, nigh (Php 4:5 [cf. Php 4:6 {see also Ps 34:18; 145:18}]; Heb 6:8; 8:13). Spoken of the Jews, "those who are near," i.e. having the knowledge and worship of the true God, as opposed to those who are far, the Gentiles (Eph 2:17; Sept.: Isa 57:19). Thus, to become near to God, by embracing the gospel (Eph 2:13).

(II) Of time: to be near, at hand (Mt 24:32, 33; Mk 13:28, 29; Rev 1:3; 22:10). Used of the Passover (Jn 2:13; 6:4; 11:55); the feast (Jn 7:2); the kingdom of God (Lk 21:31); the Lord (Php 4:5 [cf. Heb 10:37]). Used in the Sept. for *qārôb* (7138, OT): Eze 30:3; Joel 1:15; 2:1.

Deriv.: *eggízō* (1448), to bring near; *eggúteron* (1452), nearer.

1452. ἐγγύτερον, egguteron, *eng-goo´-ter-on*; neuter of the comparative of 1451; *nearer:*—nearer.

1453. ἐγείρω, egeirō, *eg-i´-ro*; probably akin to the base of 58 (through the idea of *collecting* one's faculties); to *waken* (transitive or intransitive), i.e. *rouse* (literal from sleep, from sitting or lying, from disease, from death; or figurative from obscurity, inactivity, ruins, nonexistence):—awake, lift (up), raise (again, up), rear up, (a-) rise (again, up), stand, take up.

To rise, to have risen:

(I) To rise from sleep, implying also the idea of rising up from the posture of sleep, i.e. from lying down (Mt 8:25; 25:7; Mk 4:27; Ac 12:7; Sept.: Ge 41:4, 7; Pr 6:9). Metaphorically, to wake up from sluggishness, lethargy (Ro 13:11 [cf. Eph 5:14]); from death, of which sleep is the emblem (Mt 27:52 [cf. Job 14:12; Da 12:2]). To raise the dead (Mt 10:8; Jn 5:21; Ac 26:8; 1Co 15:15, 16; 2Co 1:9). To rise from the dead (Mk 6:14, 16; Lk 9:7; Jn 2:22; see also Mt 16:21; 17:23; 27:63; Mk 16:14; Ac 5:30; Ro 4:25; 2Co 4:14; Sept.: 2Ki 4:31; Isa 26:19).

(II) The idea of sleep not being involved, it also means to cause to rise up, raise up, set upright, and in the middle to rise up, arise:

(A) Spoken of persons who are sitting (Ac 3:7) or reclining at a table (Jn 13:4), or prostrate or lying down (Mt 17:7; Lk 11:8; Ac 9:8; 10:26; Sept.: 2Sa 12:17); also of sick persons (Mt 8:15; Mk 1:31; 2:12), including the idea of convalescence, to set up again, i.e. to heal (Jas 5:15).

(B) By an oriental pleonasm, prefixed to verbs of going, of undertaking, or doing something (Mt 2:13, 14, "having risen take the child" [a.t.]; also Mt 2:20, 21; 9:19; Jn 11:29; Sept.: 1Ch 22:19).

(C) Metaphorically of persons, in the middle, to rise up against as does an adversary (Mt 24:7; Mk 13:8; Lk 21:10; Sept.: Isa 10:26; Jer 50:9). Also "to rise in the judgement with this generation" (a.t. [Mt 12:42; Lk 11:31]).

(D) Spoken of things, to raise up, e.g., out of a pit (Mt 12:11 [cf. Lk 14:5]). In Jn 2:19, 20, to erect, build.

(III) Metaphorically: to raise up, to cause to arise or exist; in the middle to arise, to appear (Lk 1:69; Ac 13:22, 23). In the middle, spoken of prophets (Mt 11:11; 24:11, 24; Mk 13:22; Lk 7:16; Jn 7:52; Sept.: Jgs 3:9, 15; Isa 41:25; 45:13). In the sense of to cause to be born, to create (Mt 3:9; Lk 3:8).

(IV) Intransitively: to awake, to arise; thus to awake from sleep or, figuratively, from sluggishness (Eph 5:14); also to rise up, arise from a sitting or reclining posture (Mk 2:9, 11; 3:3; 5:41; 10:49; Lk 5:23, 24; 6:8; Jn 5:8).

Deriv.: *grēgoréō* (1127), to watch, be vigilant; *diegeírō* (1326), awake from natural sleep; *égersis* (1454), stimulation, erection, awakening; *exegeírō* (1825), to raise from out of; *epegeírō* (1892), to rouse up, excite; *sunegeírō* (4891), to raise together.

Syn.: *diagrēgoréō* (1235), to be fully watchful by being wide awake; *agrupnéō* (69), to be awake, watchful; *agrupnía* (70), sleeplessness; *anístēmi* (450), to stand up or arise; *eknḗphō* (1594), to return to one's senses from drunkenness, become sober; *exupnízō* (1852), to arouse a person from sleep (Jn 11:11); *aírō* (142), to raise, take up, lift; *epaírō* (1869), to lift up, raise; *hupsóō* (5312), to lift or raise up; *anorthóō* (461), to set upright; *anakúptō* (352), to lift oneself up; *anabibázō* (307), to cause to go up or ascend; *exanístēmi* (1817), to raise up from among or to rise up; *anabaínō* (305), to go up; *anatéllō* (393), to rise, speaking of the sun; *katephístēmi* (2721), to rise up as in insurrection; *epanístamai* (1881), to rise up against; *hístēmi* (2476), to cause to stand; *stḗkō* (4739), to stand upright; *anakathízō* (339), to set up, intransitively to sit up.

1454. ἔγερσις, egersis, *eg´-er-sis*; from 1453; a *resurgence* (from death):—resurrection.

Noun from *egeírō* (1453), to wake up. Resurrection, reanimation of the dead (Mt 27:53).

Syn.: *anástasis* (386), resurrection; *exanástasis* (1815), resurrection out of.

1455. ἐγκάθετος, egkathetos, *eng-kath´-et-os*; from 1722 and a derivative of 2524; *subinduced*, i.e. surreptitiously *suborned* as a lier-in-wait:—spy.

1456. ἐγκαίνια, egkainia, *eng-kah´ee-nee-ah*; neuter plural of a presumed compound from 1722 and 2537; *innovatives*, i.e. (special) *renewal* (of religious services after the Antiochian interruption):—dedication.

Noun from *en* (1722), in or at, and *kainós* (2537), qualitatively new. Festival of dedication, only in Jn 10:22. This festival was instituted by Judas Maccabaeus to commemorate the purification of the temple and the renewal of the temple worship after the three years of profanation by Antiochus Epiphanes. It was held for eight days, beginning on the twenty-fifth day of the month of Kislev, which began the new moon of

December. Josephus calls it *phṓta* (5457), i.e. the festival of lights or lanterns.

1457. ἐγκαινίζω, egkainizō, *eng-kahee-nid´-zo*; from 1456; to *renew*, i.e. *inaugurate*:—consecrate, dedicate.

From *en* (1722), in or at, and *kainízō* (n.f.), to make new. To dedicate, consecrate (Heb 9:18; 10:20; Sept.: Dt 20:5; 1Ki 8:64 [cf. 1Sa 11:14]). Also from *kainízō* (n.f.): *anakainízō* (340), to renew.

Syn.: *ananeóō* (365), to renew.

1458. ἐγκαλέω, egkaleō, *eng-kal-eh´-o*; from 1722 and 2564; to *call in* (as a debt or demand), i.e. *bring to account* (*charge, criminate*, etc.):—accuse, call in question, implead, lay to the charge.

From *en* (1722), in, and *kaléō* (2564), to call. To bring a charge against, call to account, accuse, arraign (Ac 19:38, 40; 23:28, 29; 26:2, 7; Ro 8:33).

Deriv.: *anégkalētos* (410), unaccused, blameless; *égklēma* (1462), a public accusation.

Syn.: *katēgoréō* (2723), to accuse; *diabállō* (1225), to accuse, defame; *katakrínō* (2632), to condemn; *elégchō* (1651), to reprove; *mémphomai* (3201), to find fault.

1459. ἐγκαταλείπω, egkataleipō, *eng-kat-al-i´-po*; from 1722 and 2641; to *leave behind in* some place, i.e. (in a good sense) *let remain over*, or (in a bad one) to *desert*:—forsake, leave.

1460. ἐγκατοικέω, egkatoikeō, *eng-kat-oy-keh´-o*; from 1722 and 2730; to *settle down in* a place, i.e. *reside*:—dwell among.

1461. ἐγκεντρίζω, egkentrizō, *eng-ken-trid´-zo*; from 1722 and a derivative of 2759; to *prick in*, i.e. *ingraft*:—graff in (-to).

1462. ἔγκλημα, egklēma, *eng´-klay-mah*; from 1458; an *accusation*, i.e. *offence* alleged:—crime laid against, laid to charge.

Noun from *egkaléō* (1458), to arraign. Charge, accusation (Ac 23:29), complaint, charge (Ac 25:16).

Syn.: *katēgoría* (2724), a criminal charge, an accusation.

1463. ἐγκομβόομαι, egkomboomai, *eng-kom-bo´-om-ahee*; middle from 1722 and **κομβόω, komboō** (to *gird*); to *engirdle* oneself (for labour), i.e. figurative (the apron being a badge of servitude) to *wear* (in token of mutual deference):—be clothed with.

1464. ἐγκοπή, egkopē, *eng-kop-ay´*; from 1465; a *hindrance:*— × hinder.

1465. ἐγκόπτω, egkoptō, *eng-kop´-to*; from 1722 and 2875; to *cut into*, i.e. (figurative) *impede, detain:*—hinder, be tedious unto.

1466. ἐγκράτεια, egkrateia, *eng-krat´-i-ah*; from 1468; *self-control* (especially *continence*):—temperance.

1467. ἐγκρατεύομαι, egkrateuomai, *eng-krat-yoo´-om-ahee*; middle from 1468; to *exercise self-restraint* (in diet and chastity):—can ([-not]) contain, be temperate.

1468. ἐγκρατής, egkratēs, *eng-krat-ace´*; from 1722 and 2904; *strong* in a thing (*masterful*), i.e. (figurative and reflex.) *self-controlled* (in appetite, etc.):—temperate.

1469. ἐγκρίνω, egkrinō, *eng-kree´-no*; from 1722 and 2919; to *judge in*, i.e. *count* among:—make of the number.

From *en* (1722), in or among, and *krínō* (2919), to judge, reckon, classify. To judge or classify among. Only in 2Co 10:12.

Syn.: *psēphízō* (5585), to compute, count; *logízomai* (3049), to reckon; *katalégō* (2639), to enroll, take into the number; *anagnōrízō* (319), to recognize; *paradéchomai* (3858), to accept, receive.

1470. ἐγκρύπτω, egkruptō, *eng-kroop´-to*; from 1722 and 2928; to *conceal in*, i.e. *incorporate with:*—hid in.

1471. ἔγκυος, egkuos, *eng´-koo-os*; from 1722 and the base of 2949; *swelling* in*side*, i.e. *pregnant:*—great with child.

1472. ἐγκρίω, egchriō, *eng-khree´-o*; from 1722 and 5548; to *rub in* (oil), i.e. *besmear:*—anoint.

1473. ἐγώ, egō, *eg-o´*; a primary pronoun of the first person *I* (only expressed when emphatic):—I, me. For the other cases and the plural see 1691, 1698, 1700, 2248, 2249, 2254, 2257, etc.

1474. ἐδαφίζω, edaphizō, *ed-af-id´-zo*; from 1475; to *raze:*—lay even with the ground.

1475. ἔδαφος, edaphos, *ed´-af-os*; from the base of 1476; a *basis* (*bottom*), i.e. the *soil:*—ground.

1476. ἑδραῖος, hedraios, *hed-rah´-yos*; from a derivative of ἕζομαι, *hezomai* (to *sit*); *sedentary*, i.e. (by implication) *immovable:*—settled, steadfast.

1477. ἑδραίωμα, hedraiōma, *hed-rah´-yo-mah*; from a derivative of 1476; a *support*, i.e. (figurative) *basis:*—ground.

1478. Ἐζεκίας, Ezekias, *ed-zek-ee´-as*; of Hebrew origin [2396]; *Ezekias* (i.e. *Hezekiah*), an Israelite:—Ezekias.

1479. ἐθελοθρησκεία, ethelothrēskeia, *eth-el-oth-race-ki´-ah*; from 2309 and 2356; *voluntary* (*arbitrary* and *unwarranted*) *piety*, i.e. *sanctimony:*—will worship.

1480. ἐθίζω, ethizō, *eth-id´-zo*; from 1485; to *accustom*, i.e. (neuter passive participle) *customary:*—custom.

1481. ἐθνάρχης, ethnarchēs, *eth-nar´-khace*; from 1484 and 746; the *governor* [not king] *of a district:*—ethnarch.

1482. ἐθνικός, ethnikos, *eth-nee-kos´*; from 1484; *national* ("*ethnic*"), i.e. (special) a *Gentile:*—heathen (man).

Adjective from *éthnos* (1484), nation. National, popular. In the NT, used in the Jewish sense of Gentile, heathen, spoken of all who are not Israelites (Mt 6:7; 18:17).

Deriv.: *ethnikós* (1483), in a manner of the Gentiles.

1483. ἐθνικῶς, ethnikōs, *eth-nee-koce´*; adverb from 1482; *as a Gentile:*—after the manner of Gentiles.

Adverb from *ethnikós* (1482), a heathen, Gentile. After the manner of the heathen or the Gentiles. Only in Gal 2:14.

1484. ἔθνος, ethnos, *eth´-nos*; probably from 1486; a *race* (as of the same *habit*), i.e. a *tribe*; specially a *foreign* (*non-Jewish*) one (usually by implication, *pagan*):—Gentile, heathen, nation, people.

A noun meaning multitude, people, race, belonging and living together.

(**I**) Generally, the people or inhabitants of Samaria (Ac 8:9, cf. v. 5); the whole race of mankind (Ac 17:26). See also 1Pe 2:9; Sept.: 2Ch 32:7; Isa 13:4.

(II) In the sense of nation, people, as distinct from all others (Mt 20:25; Mk 10:42; Lk 7:5; Jn 11:48, 50; Ac 7:7; 10:22; Sept.: Ge 12:2; Ex 1:9; 33:13; Dt 1:28).

(III) In the Jewish sense, *tá éthnē*, the nations, means the Gentile nations or the Gentiles in general as spoken of all who are not Israelites and implying idolatry and ignorance of the true God, i.e. the heathen, pagan nations (Mt 4:15; 10:5; Mk 10:33; Lk 2:32; Ac 4:27; 26:17; Ro 2:14; 3:29; Sept.: Ne 5:8, 9; Isa 9:1; Eze 4:13; 27:33, 36; 34:13; Jer 10:3).

Deriv.: *ethnárchēs* (1481), the governor of a district; *ethnikós* (1482), a heathen.

1485. ἔθος, ethos, *eth´-os*; from 1486; a *usage* (prescribed by habit or law):—custom, manner, be wont.

1486. ἔθω, ethō, *eth´-o*; a primary verb; to *be used* (by habit or conventionality); neuter perfect participle *usage*:—be custom (manner, wont).

1487. εἰ, ei, *i*; a primary particle of conditionality; *if, whether, that*, etc.:—forasmuch as, if, that, ([al-]) though, whether. Often used in connection or composition with other particles, especially as in 1489, 1490, 1499, 1508, 1509, 1512, 1513, 1536, 1537. See also 1437.

1488. εἶ, ei, *i*; second personal singular present of 1510; thou *art*:—art, be.

1489. εἴγε, eige, *i´-gheh*; from 1487 and 1065; *if indeed, seeing that, unless,* (with negative) *otherwise*:—if (so be that, yet).

1490. εἰ δὲ μή(γε), ei de mē(ge), *i deh may´-(gheh)*; from 1487, 1161 and 3361 (sometimes with 1065 added); *but if not*:—(or) else, if (not, otherwise), otherwise.

1491. εἶδος, eidos, *i´-dos*; from 1492; a *view*, i.e. *form* (literal or figurative):—appearance, fashion, shape, sight.

Noun from *eidō* (1492), to see. The act of seeing, the thing seen, external appearance. The object of sight, form, appearance (Lk 3:22; 9:29; Jn 5:37; Sept.: Ge 41:2f.; Ex 24:17; Nu 9:16; 1Sa 25:3; Est 2:7); manner, kind, species (1Th 5:22, Sept.: Jer 15:3).

Deriv.: *eidōlon* (1497), idol; *petrṓdēs* (4075), rock-like, stone-like.

Syn.: *schḗma* (4976), figure, fashion; *morphḗ* (3444), form, makeup; *homoíōma* (3667), likeness; *theōría* (2335), gaze, spectacle; *hórama* (3705), that which is seen, appearance.

1492. εἴδω, eidō, *i´-do*; a primary verb; used only in certain past tenses, the others being borrowed from the equivalent 3700 and 3708; properly to *see* (literal or figurative); by implication (in the perf. only) to *know*:—be aware, behold, × can (+ not tell), consider, (have) know (-ledge), look (on), perceive, see, be sure, tell, understand, wish, wot. Compare 3700.

To see. This verb is obsolete in the present act. for which *horáō* (3708), to see with perception, is used. The tenses derived from the meaning of *eidō* form two families, one of which has exclusively the meaning of to see, the other that of to know:

(I) To see, implying not the mere act of seeing but the actual perception of some object, and thus differing from *blépō* (991), to see:

(A) Particularily, spoken of persons or things (Mt 2:2; 5:1; Mk 9:9; 11:13, 20; Jn 1:48; Ac 8:39; Heb 3:9; Rev 1:2), and also in various modified senses: (1) To behold, look upon, contemplate (Mt 9:36; 28:6; Mk 8:33; Lk 24:39; Jn 20:27; Sept.: Nu 12:8). (2) To see in order to know, to look at or into, examine (Mk 5:14; 6:38; 12:15; Lk 8:35; 14:18; Jn 1:39, 46). (3) To see face to face, to see and talk with, to visit, i.e. to have personal acquaintance and relationship with (Lk 8:20; 9:9; Jn 12:21; Ac 16:40; Ro 1:11; 1Co 16:7; Gal 1:19; Php 1:27; 2:28). Also of a city, such as Rome (Ac 19:21). (4) To wait to see, watch, observe (Mt 26:58; 27:49; Mk 15:36). (5) To see take place, witness, to live to see (Mt 13:17; 24:33; Mk 2:12). Also "to see one's day," meaning to witness the events of his life and times (Lk 17:22; Jn 8:56).

(B) Metaphorically, spoken of the mind: to perceive by the senses, to be aware of, to remark (Mt 9:2, 4; Lk 17:15; Jn 7:52; Ro 11:22).

(C) To see, i.e. to experience either good (meaning to enjoy) or evil (meaning to suffer), referring to death in (Lk 2:26; Jn 3:3; Ac 2:27, 31; 13:35; Heb 11:5; Rev 18:7; 1Pe 3:10; Sept.: Ps 89:48).

(II) To know, i.e. to have seen, perceived, apprehended:

(A) To be acquainted with, spoken of things (Mt 25:13; Mk 10:19; Lk 18:20; Jn 4:22; Ro 7:7;

13:11; Jude 5, 10; Sept.: Ex 3:7; Job 8:9. See also 1Co 16:15; 1Th 2:1); of persons (Mt 25:12; Mk 1:34; Jn 6:42; Ac 7:18; Heb 10:30; 1Pe 1:8). Used in an absolute sense (Lk 11:44; 2Co 11:11). Before an indirect question (Mt 24:43; Mk 13:35; Lk 12:39; Col 4:6; 1Th 4:2; 2Th 3:7).

(B) In the sense of to perceive, be aware of, understand (Mt 12:25; Mk 4:13; 12:15; Lk 11:17).

(C) By implication: to know how, i.e. to be able (Mt 7:11; Lk 12:56; Php 4:12; 1Th 4:4; 1Ti 3:5; Jas 4:17; 2Pe 2:9).

(D) From the Hebrew, with the idea of volition: to know and approve or love; hence spoken of men: to care for, take an interest in (1Th 5:12; Sept.: Ge 39:6). Of God: to know God, i.e. to acknowledge and adore God (Gal 4:8; 1Th 4:5; 2Th 1:8; Tit 1:16; Heb 8:11; Sept.: 1Sa 2:12; Job 18:21; Jer 31:34).

Deriv.: *Hádēs* (86), Hades; *apeídō* (542), to see fully; *eídos* (1491), appearance, shape, sight; *íde* (2396) and *epeídon* (1896), behold, look upon; *idéa* or *eidéa* (2397), aspect, countenance, idea; *ísēmi* (2467), to confirm; *proeídō* (4275), foresee; *suneídō* (4894), to understand together, metaphorically meaning to become aware; *hupereídon* (5237), to overlook.

Syn.: *blépō* (991), to see, to perceive, take heed; *horáō* (3708), to see; *emblépō* (1689), to look earnestly; *theōréō* (2334), to scrutinize; *theáomai* (2300), to behold with wonder; *epopteúō* (2029), to witness as a spectator or overseer; *atenízō* (816), to gaze upon; *katanoéō* (2657), to comprehend, apprehend, perceive fully; *óptomai* (3700), to see, both objectively and subjectively, sometimes *optánō*, to allow oneself to be seen; *noéō* (3539), to perceive with the mind; *katanoéō* (2657), to perceive clearly; *logízomai* (3049), to consider, use one's mind, take into account; *analogízomai* (357), to consider well; *suníēmi* (4920), to understand, consider; *ginóskō* (1097), to know; *proséchō* (4337), to pay attention to, take heed.

1493. **εἰδωλεῖον**, eidōleion, *i-do-li´-on*; neuter of a presumed derivative of 1497; an *image-fane*:—idol's temple.

1494. **εἰδωλόθυτον**, eidōlothuton, *i-do-loth´-oo-ton*; neuter of a compound of 1497 and a presumed derivative of 2380; an *image-sacrifice*, i.e. part of an *idolatrous offering*:—(meat, thing

that is) offered (in sacrifice, sacrificed) to (unto) idols.

Noun from *eídōlon* (1497), idol, and *thúō* (2380), to sacrifice. Whatever is sacrificed or offered to an idol, such as flesh or heathen sacrifices (Ac 15:29; 21:25; 1Co 8:1, 4, 7, 10; 10:19, 28; Rev 2:14, 20).

1495. **εἰδωλολατρεία**, eidōlolatreia, *i-do-lol-at-rí´-ah*; from 1497 and 2999; *image-worship* (literal or figurative):—idolatry.

Noun from *eídōlon* (1497), idol, and *latreía* (2999), service, worship. Idolatry, idol worship. Used only in the NT and Patristic Gr. (1Co 10:14; Gal 5:20; Col 3:5; 1Pe 4:3).

1496. **εἰδωλολάτρης**, eidōlolatrēs, *i-do-lol-at´-race*; from 1497 and the base of 3000; an *image-* (*servant* or) *worshipper* (literal or figurative):—idolater.

Noun from *eídōlon* (1497), idol, and *látris* (n.f.), a servant, worshipper. Idolater, a worshipper of idols (1Co 5:10, 11; 6:9; 10:7; Eph 5:5; Rev 21:8; 22:15).

Syn.: *ethnikós* (1482), heathen, Gentile; *proskunētēs* (4353), worshipper.

1497. **εἴδωλον**, eidōlon, *i´-do-lon*; from 1491; an *image* (i.e. for worship); (by implication) a heathen *god*, or (plural) the *worship* of such:—idol.

Noun from *eídos* (1491), a form, appearance. In Class. Gr., any image or figure. In the NT, an idol, either an idol-image (Ac 7:41; 1Co 12:2; Rev 9:20; Sept.: 2Ch 33:22; Isa 30:22), or an idol-god, a heathen deity (1Co 8:4, 7; 10:19; Sept.: Nu 25:2; 2Ki 17:12, 33; 21:11, 20). By implication: idol-worship, idolatry (Ro 2:22; 2Co 6:16; 1Th 1:9; 1Jn 5:21).

Deriv.: *eidōleíon* (1493), idol temple; *eidōlóthuton* (1494), that which is sacrificed to idols; *eidōlolatreía* (1495), idolatry; *eidōlolátrēs* (1496), an idolater; *kateídōlos* (2712), utterly idolatrous, given to idolatry.

Syn.: *eikōn* (1504), statue, icon, resemblance, image, representation.

1498. **εἴην**, eiēn, *i´-ane*; optative (i.e. English subjunctive) present of 1510 (including the other person); *might* (*could, would* or *should*) *be*:—mean, + perish, should be, was, were.

1499. **εἰ καί**, ei kai, *i kahee*; from 1487 and 2532; *if also* (or *even*):—if (that), though.

1500. εἰκῆ, eikē, *i-kay´*; probably from 1502 (through the idea of *failure*); *idly,* i.e. *without reason* (or *effect*):—without a cause, (in) vain (-ly).

1501. εἴκοσι, eikosi, *i´-kos-ee*; of uncertain affinity; a *score:*—twenty.

1502. εἴκω, eikō, *i´-ko*; apparently a primary verb; properly to *be weak,* i.e. *yield:*—give place.

1503. εἴκω, eikō, *i´-ko*; apparently a primary verb [perhaps akin to 1502 through the idea of *faintness* as a copy]; to *resemble:*—be like.

1504. εἰκών, eikōn, *i-kone´*; from 1503; a *likeness,* i.e. (literal) *statue, profile,* or (figurative) *representation, resemblance:*—image.

Noun from *eíkō* (1503), to be like, resemble. Likeness, image, effigy, figure (Mt 22:20; Mk 12:16; Lk 20:24; Ro 1:23), an idol-image, statue (Rev 13:14, 15; 14:9, 11; 15:2; 16:2; 19:20; Sept.: Dt 4:16; Isa 40:18, 20; Eze 23:14). In the sense of copy, representation (1Co 11:7; 2Co 4:4; Col 1:15; Heb 10:1). A likeness to anyone, resemblance, similitude (Ro 8:29; 1Co 15:49; Col 3:10).

1505. εἰλικρίνεια, eilikrineia, *i-lik-ree´-ni-ah*; from 1506; *clearness,* i.e. (by implication) *purity* (figurative):—sincerity.

Noun from *eilikrinḗs* (1506), pure, sincere. Clearness. Used metaphorically: pureness, sincerity (1Co 5:8; 2Co 1:12; 2:17).

Syn.: *euthútēs* (2118), rectitude; *haplótēs* (572), sincerity.

1506. εἰλικρινής, eilikrinēs, *i-lik-ree-nace´*; from εἴλη, *heilē* (the sun's *ray*) and 2919; *judged by sunlight,* i.e. tested as *genuine* (figurative):—pure, sincere.

Adjective from *heílē* (n.f.), the shining or splendour of the sun, and *krínō* (2919), to judge, discern. Judged of in sunshine; by implication: clear as light, manifest. In the NT, pure, sincere (Php 1:10; 2Pe 3:1).

Deriv.: *eilikríneia* (1505), sincerity.

Syn.: *ádolos* (97), guileless, pure; *ákakos* (172), without evil; *gnḗsios* (1103), true, genuine, sincere; *alēthḗs* (227), manifest, unconcealed; *alēthinós* (228), genuine, real; *hagnós* (53), pure; *katharós* (2513), pure, cleansed; *haploús* (573), sincere; *anupókritos* (505), unhypocritical.

1507. εἰλίσσω, heilissō, *hi-lis´-so*; a prolonged form of a primary but defective verb εἴλω, *heilō* (of the same meaning); to *coil* or *wrap:*—roll together. See also 1667.

1508. εἰ μή, ei mē, *i may*; from 1487 and 3361; *if not:*—but, except (that), if, not, more than, save (only) that, saving, till.

1509. εἰ μή τι, ei mē ti, *i may tee*; from 1508 and the neuter of 5100; *if not somewhat:*—except.

1510. εἰμί, eimi, *i-mee´*; first person singular presumed indicative; a prolonged form of a primary and defective verb; *I exist* (used only when emphatic):—am, have been, × it is I, was. See also 1488, 1498, 1511, 1527, 2070, 2071, 2075, 2076, 2258, 2468, 2771, 5600.

To be is the usual verb of existence, and also the usual logical copula or link, connecting subj. and predicate:

(I) As a verb of existence, to be, to have existence:

(A) Particularly and generally: (1) In the metaphysical sense (Mk 12:32; Jn 1:1; 8:50, 58; Ac 19:2; Heb 11:6). Spoken of life: to exist, to live (Mt 2:18; 23:30); not to die (Ac 17:28). (2) Generally: to be, to exist, to be found, as of persons (Mt 12:11; Lk 4:25, 27; Jn 3:1; Ro 3:10, 11). Of things: to be, to exist, to have place (Mt 6:30; 22:23; Mk 7:15; Lk 6:43; Ac 2:29; Ro 13:1). (3) Spoken of time, generally (Mk 11:13; Lk 23:44; Jn 1:40; Ac 2:15; 2Ti 4:3); of festivals (Mk 15:42; Ac 12:3).

(B) By implication and by force of the adjuncts, *eimí* means to come to be, come into existence, similar to *gínomai* (1096), to come about: (1) To come to pass, take place, occur, be done. The fut. *éstai* and other tenses also have similar meaning (Lk 12:55 [cf. 21:11, 25; Ac 11:28; 27:25]). (2) To become something (Mt 19:5; 2Co 6:18; Eph 5:31; Heb 8:10; Jas 5:3).

(C) It is proper, in one's power or convenient (1Co 11:20; Heb 9:5).

(II) As a logical copula or link connecting the subj. and predicate: to be, where the predicate specifies who or what a person or thing is in respect to nature, origin, office, condition, circumstances, state, place, habits, disposition of mind. But this all lies in the predicate and not in the copula, which merely connects the predicate with the subj., e.g., Mt 2:6; Ac 2:32. *Eimí* is also used in this sense to construct metaphorical expressions (Mt 5:13, 14; 12:50; Lk 8:11; 12:1; Jn 1:4). When used as a copula, the forms of *eimí* are often omitted (Mt 9:37; 13:54; Mk 9:23; 1Co 10:26; 11:12).

Deriv.: *ápeimi* (548), to be absent; *éneimi* (1751), to be within; *páreimi* (3918), to be present; *súneimi* (4895), to be with.

Syn.: *gínomai* (1096), to begin to be, to come to pass; *hupárchō* (5225), to be in existence.

1511. εἶναι, **einai,** *i´-nahee*; presumed infinitive from 1510; *to exist*:—am, are, come, is, × lust after, × please well, there is, to be, was.

1512. εἴ περ, **ei per,** *i per*; from 1487 and 4007; *if perhaps*:—if so be (that), seeing, though.

1513. εἴ πως, **ei pōs,** *i poce*; from 1487 and 4458; *if somehow*:—if by any means.

1514. εἰρηνεύω, **eirēneuō,** *i-rane-yoo´-o*; from 1515; to *be* (*act*) *peaceful*:—be at (have, live in) peace, live peaceably.

From *eirēnē* (1515), peace. To make peace, be at peace (Sept.: 1Ki 22:44). In the NT, used metaphorically: to live in peace, harmony, accord. Used in an absolute sense in 2Co 13:11. In 1Th 5:13, "be at peace among yourselves"; Mk 9:50, "with each other" (a.t.); Ro 12:18, "with all."

Syn.: *sigáō* (4601), to be silent, to hold one's peace; *hēsucházō* (2270), hold one's peace; *phimóō* (5392), to muzzle, hold one's peace.

1515. εἰρήνη, **eirēnē,** *i-rah´-nay*; probably from a primary verb εἴρω, *eirō* (to *join*); *peace* (literal or figurative); (by implication) *prosperity*:—one, peace, quietness, rest, + set at one again.

(I) Peace, particularly in a civil sense, the opposite of war and dissension (Lk 14:32; Ac 12:20; Rev 6:4). Among individuals, peace, harmony (Mt 10:34; Lk 12:51; Ac 7:26; Ro 14:19; Heb 7:2). Metaphorically: peace of mind, tranquillity, arising from reconciliation with God and a sense of a divine favour (Ro 5:1; 15:13; Php 4:7 [cf. Isa 53:5]).

(II) By implication, a state of peace, tranquillity (Lk 2:29; 11:21; Jn 16:33; Ac 9:31; 1Co 14:33; 1Th 5:3; Sept.: Jgs 6:23; Isa 14:30; Eze 38:8, 11).

(III) Peace, meaning health, welfare, prosperity, every kind of good. In Lk 1:79, "the way of peace" means the way of happiness; 2:14; 10:6, "son of peace" means son of happiness, i.e. one worthy of it; 19:42; Ro 8:6; Eph 6:15, "gospel of peace" means gospel of bliss, i.e. which leads to bliss; 2Th 3:16. "The God of peace" means the author and giver of blessedness (Ro 15:33; 16:20; Php 4:9; 1Th 5:23; Heb 13:20 [cf. Sept.: Isa 9:6, "the Prince of Peace"]). "Your peace" means the good or blessing which you have in Christ and share through salutation and benediction (Mt 10:13; Lk 10:6; Jn 14:27). The expression "with peace" means with good wishes, benediction, kindness (Ac 15:33; Heb 11:31). Simply "in peace" (1Co 16:11; Sept.: Ge 26:29; Ex 18:23). As used in formulas of salutation, either at meeting or parting, see *aspázomai* (782), to embrace, to greet. Thus on meeting, the salutation is "Peace be unto you [*eirēnē humín*]," meaning every good wish (Lk 24:36; Jn 20:19, 21, 26; Da 10:19). Also in letters (Ro 1:7; 2:10; 1Co 1:3; 2Co 1:2; Gal 1:3). In Lk 10:5, "Peace unto this house" (a.t.) means every good wish for this house; Sept.: Jgs 19:20; 1Ch 12:18. At parting, *húpage* (5217), go, meaning to go away in peace (Mk 5:34; Jas 2:16). The same with the verb *poreúou* from *poreúomai* (4198), to go in peace (Lk 7:50; 8:48; Ac 16:36; Sept.: Jgs 18:6; 1Sa 1:17; 20:42).

Deriv.: *eirēneúō* (1514), to bring peace, reconcile; *eirēnikós* (1516), peaceful; *eirēnopoiéō* (1517), to make peace without necessarily effecting a change in the person or persons involved.

Syn.: *hēsuchía* (2271), quietness; *galēnē* (1055), tranquillity, calm.

1516. εἰρηνικός, **eirēnikos,** *i-ray-nee-kos´*; from 1515; *pacific*; (by implication) *salutary*:—peaceable.

Adjective from *eirēnē* (1515), peace. Pertaining to peace, peaceable or peaceful (Heb 12:11, healthful, wholesome; Jas 3:17, peaceful, disposed to peace; Sept.: Dt 2:26; Ps 37:37; 120:7). The reference is to *eirēnē* (1515), peace, as the blessing of salvation.

Syn.: *hēsúchios* (2272), quiet, peaceful; *homóphrōn* (3675), harmonious, of one mind; *isópsuchos* (2473), of one soul, agreeable, likeminded; *éremos* (2263), tranquil.

1517. εἰρηνοποιέω, **eirēnopoieō,** *i-ray-nop-oy-eh´-o*; from 1518; to *be a peace-maker*, i.e. (figurative) to *harmonize*:—make peace.

From *eirénē* (1515), peace, and *poiéō* (4160), to make. To make peace, reconciliation (Col 1:20; Sept.: Pr 10:10).

Deriv.: *eirēnopoiós* (1518), peacemaking or a peacemaker.

Syn.: *diallássō* (1259), to conciliate, reconcile; *katallássō* (2644), to reconcile man to God when the change occurs in man; *apokatallássō* (604), to reconcile fully.

1518. εἰρηνοποιός, eirēnopoios, *i-ray-nop-oy-os´*; from 1518 and 4160; *pacificatory*, i.e. (subjective) *peaceable:*—peacemaker.

Noun from *eirēnopoiéō* (1517), to make peace. Peacemaker, an ambassador who comes to bring peace. In the NT, used metaphorically. Only in Mt 5:9.

1519. εἰς, eis, *ice*; a primary preposition; *to* or *into* (indicating the point reached or entered), of place, time, or (figurative) purpose (result, etc.); also in adverbial phrases:—[abundant-] ly, against, among, as, at, [back-] ward, before, by, concerning, + continual, + far more exceeding, for [intent, purpose], fore, + forth, in (among, at, unto, -so much that, -to), to the intent that, + of one mind, + never, of, (up-) on, + perish, + set at one again, (so) that, therefore (-unto), throughout, till, to (be, the end, -ward), (here-) until (-to), … ward, [where-] fore, with. Often used in composition with the same general import, but only with verbs (etc.) expressing motion (literal or figurative).

Preposition with the primary idea of motion into any place or thing; also of motion or direction to, toward or upon any place, thing. The antithesis is expressed by *ek* (1537), out of.

(**I**) Of place, which is the primary and most frequent use, meaning into, to:

(**A**) After verbs implying motion of any kind: into or to, toward, upon any place or object, e.g., verbs of going, coming, leading, following, sending, growing, placing, delivering over to and the like (Mt 2:12; 4:8; 5:1; 6:6; 8:18; 12:44; 15:11, 17; 20:17; 21:18; Mk 1:38; 5:21; 6:45; 9:31; 13:14; Lk 8:23, 26; Jn 1:9; 7:14; 16:21, "is born into the world"; Ac 16:16; 26:14; Ro 5:12; 10:18; Rev 2:22).

(**B**) After verbs implying duration: upon, or toward any place or object, e.g., verbs of hearing, calling, announcing, showing (Mt 10:27; 22:3, 4; Mk 5:14; 13:10; Lk 7:1; 24:47; Jn 8:26;

Ac 11:22, "hearing in the ears" [a.t.]; 1Co 14:9; 2Co 8:24; 11:6). Especially after verbs of looking (Mt 5:35, "toward Jerusalem" [a.t.], i.e. turning or looking toward it; Mt 22:16; Jn 13:22; Ac 1:10, 11; 3:4; Heb 11:26). After nouns (Ac 9:2, "letters [directed] to Damascus"; Ro 15:31, "my service which I have for Jerusalem").

(**C**) Metaphorically of a state or condition into which one comes, after verbs of motion, duration (Mt 25:46; Mk 5:26; 9:43; Lk 22:33; 24:20; Jn 4:38; 5:24; 16:13; Ac 26:18; 2Co 10:5; Gal 1:6; Php 1:12; 3:11; 2Ti 2:4; 3:6; Heb 2:10).

(**II**) Of time:

(**A**) Time meaning when, implying a term, limit, i.e. to, up to, until (Mt 10:22; Ac 4:3; 13:42; Php 1:10; 2:16; 1Th 4:15; 2Th 2:6; 2Pe 2:4; 3:7).

(**B**) Time, indicating how long, or marking duration, commonly translated for or from (Lk 1:50; 12:19). A frequent occurrence of this use in the NT is in the phrase *eis tón aióna*, lit. "until the age" (see *aión* [165]), which is often translated forever or everlasting (Mt 12:19; Mk 11:14; Jn 6:58; Ro 9:5; Heb 5:6; Rev 1:6), and in some cases, never (Mk 3:29; Jn 10:28).

(**III**) Figuratively, as marking the object or point to or toward which anything ends:

(**A**) Spoken of a result, effect, consequence, marking that which any person or thing inclines toward or becomes (Mt 13:30, "bind them in bundles"; Jn 17:23 "perfect in one"; Ac 2:20; 10:4, "Thy prayers and thine alms are come up for [*eis*] a memorial before God"; Ro 10:10; 1Co 11:17; 15:54; Eph 2:21, 22; Heb 6:6, 8; 1Pe 1:22; Rev 11:6).

(**B**) Spoken of measure, degree, extent, chiefly by way of periphrasis for an adverb as in Lk 13:11, *eis tó pantelés* (3838), i.e. entirely, at all. In Heb 7:25, with the idea of perpetuity. In 2Co 4:17, *eis huperbolén* (5236), hyperbole, exceeding or exceedingly. In 2Co 10:13, *eis tá ámetra* (280), beyond the measure, i.e. immoderately, extravagantly. In 2Co 13:2, *eis tó pálin* (3825), means simply again. Also *eis kenón* (2756), empty, vain, means in vain (2Co 6:1; Gal 2:2; Php 2:16).

(**C**) Spoken of a direction of mind, i.e. as marking an object of desire, goodwill, also aversion (**1**) In a good sense, toward, for, on behalf of (Mt 26:10, "she did a good work for my benefit" [a.t.]; Ro 10:1, "unto salvation" [a.t.] or for or toward salvation; Ro 12:16; 14:19; 2Co 10:1;

Php 1:23, "desire to depart" or to die; 1Th 4:10; 5:15; 2Pe 3:9). Also after nouns, e.g., love on behalf of someone (Ro 5:8; 2Co 2:4, 8; Eph 1:15); the gift bestowed upon someone or for the good of someone (2Co 1:11). After an adj. (Eph 4:32 "kind one to another"; 1Pe 4:9 "hospitable one to another"). With the verbs *elpízō* (1679), to hope, and *pisteúō* (4100), to believe, with *eis*, usually with a dat., in which case these verbs imply an affection or direction of mind toward a person or thing, i.e. to place hope or confidence in or upon (Mt 18:6, those "which believe [or place confidence] in me"; Jn 2:11; 5:45; 2Co 1:10 [cf. Ac 24:15]). The substantive *elpís* (1680), hope, or *pístis* (4102), faith, *eis* followed by the accusative, hope or faith in someone (Ac 20:21; 24:24; 1Pe 1:21). With *pepoíthēsis* (4006), confidence (2Co 8:22). **(2)** In an unfriendly sense, "against" (Mt 18:15; Mk 3:29; Lk 12:10, "whosoever shall speak a word against the Son of man," against the Holy Spirit, indicated by *eis*; Ac 9:1; 1Co 6:18, to sin against; Col 3:9). Also after nouns as in Ac 23:30 with *epiboulé* (1917), a plan against; Ro 8:7 with *échthra* (2189), enmity against God; Heb 12:3 with *antilogía* (485), contradiction against him.

(D) Spoken of an intention, purpose, aim, end: **(1)** In the sense of unto, in order to or for, i.e. for the purpose of, for the sake of, on account of (Mt 8:4, 34; 27:7, 10; Mk 1:4; Lk 5:4; 22:19; 24:20; Jn 1:7; 9:39; Ac 4:30; 11:29; 14:26; Ro 1:16, 17; 5:21; 6:19; 9:21; 10:4; 15:18; 1Co 2:7; 2Co 2:12; Eph 4:12; 2Ti 1:16). In Mt 18:20, "gathered together in my name," means on My account, because of Me, for My sake, in order to promote My cause. Also before an inf. with the article, in order to, in order that (Mt 20:19; Mk 14:55; Lk 20:20; Ro 1:11; 11:11; Jas 1:18). With the accusative meaning to what end? wherefore? why? (Mt 14:31; Mk 15:34). With *toúto* (5124), this, *eis toúto*, meaning to this end, for this purpose, therefore (Mk 1:38; Ac 9:21; Ro 9:17). Followed by the relative pron. *hó, eis hó*, meaning to which end, whereunto (2Th 1:11; 1Pe 2:8). **(2)** In the sense of to or for, implying use, advantage (Mt 5:13; 10:10; 20:1, "to hire labourers into his vineyard"; Mk 8:19, 20; Lk 7:30, "against themselves," i.e. to their own detriment; 9:13; 14:35, "neither for serving the land nor for the dunghill" [a.t.]; Jn 6:9; Ac 2:22; Ro 11:36; 15:26; 16:6; 1Co 8:6, unto him, for him, i.e. for his honour and glory; 2Co 8:6; Gal 4:11; Eph 1:5; 3:2; 1Pe 1:4).

(E) Generally as marking the obj. of any reference, relation, allusion unto or toward, i.e. with reference to: **(1)** In accordance with, conformable to (Mt 10:41, 42, "He that receiveth a prophet in the name of a prophet" means in accordance with the character of a prophet, or as a prophet, or with the honour due of a prophet). In Mt 12:41; Lk 11:32, "they repented at [*eis*] the preaching of Jonah," where *eis*, into, means conformable to or at the preaching of Jonah. In Ac 7:53, "received the law by the disposition of angels," *eis* means conformable to or in consequence of the arrangements of angels. (See *diatagé* (1296), arrangement.) **(2)** In the sense meaning as, as to, in respect to, concerning (Lk 12:21, "not rich toward [*eis*] God" means in respect to God; Ac 2:25, "For David speaketh concerning [*eis*] him"; 25:20, "because I doubted of such manner of questions," *eis tēn … zétēsin* [2214], searching, question, where *eis* [TR] means concerning; Ro 4:20; 13:14; 16:5, 19; 2Co 2:9; 9:8; Gal 6:4; Eph 3:16; 5:32; 1Th 5:18; 2Ti 2:14; Heb 7:14; 1Pe 3:21).

In composition, *eis* implies: **(a)** motion into, as *eisdéchomai* (1523), to take into one's favour, receive; *eíseimi* (1524), to enter into; *eisérchomai* (1525), to enter in; *eisphérō* (1533), to bring in; **(b)** motion or direction, direction to, toward, as *eisakoúō* (1522), to listen to, hear.

1520. εἰς, heis, *hice*; (including the neuter [etc.] **ἕν, hen**); a primary numeral; *one*:—a (-n, -ny, certain), + abundantly, man, one (another), only, other, some. See also 1527, 3367, 3391, 3762.

Masculine form *heís;* feminine *mía;* neuter *hén*. One, the first cardinal numeral:

(I) Without the substantive (Lk 18:19, "No one is good except one, God" [a.t.]; 1Co 9:24; Gal 3:20). In Mt 25:15, "to one he gave five talents, to the one two, to the other one [omitting the substantive talent repeated]" (a.t.). With a substantive (Mt 5:41, "one mile" [a.t.]; 6:27, "one cubit"; Mk 10:8, the two into one flesh; Jn 11:50; Ac 17:26; 1Co 10:8. With a neg., equivalent to not one, none (Mt 5:18, "one jot or one tittle shall in no wise pass"; Ro 3:12, "not so much as one" [a.t.], not even one, quoted from Ps 14:3; 53:4; Sept.: Jgs 4:16 [cf. Ex 9:7]). The expression *oudé* (3761), nor, followed by *heís* in the masc. or in the neuter *oudé hén*, not one, not even one, more emphatic than *oudeís* (3762), not even one. See

Mt 27:14; Jn 1:3; Ac 4:32; Ro 3:10; 1Co 6:5. With the article *ho heís*, masc., and *tó hén*, neuter, the one (Mt 25:18, 24; 1Co 10:17). In Mt 5:19, "one of these least commandments"; Mk 6:15, "one of the prophets"; Lk 5:3; Jn 12:2. Also with *ek* (1537), of, followed by the gen. (Mt 18:12, "one of them"; Mk 9:17; Ac 11:28; Rev 5:5).

(II) Used distributively:

(A) *Heís* / *heís*, one / one, i.e. one / the other (Mt 20:21; 24:41; 27:38; Jn 20:12), fem. *mía* / *mía*. Also with the article *ho heís* / *ho heís*, the one / the other (Mt 24:40). In 1Th 5:11, *heís tón héna*, one another. In 1Co 4:6, *heís hupér* (5228), above, *toú henós*, the one above the other. In Mt 17:4, *mían* / *mían* / *mían*, one tent for each of the three, Jesus, Moses, and Elijah. See Mk 4:8; Lk 9:33; Sept.: Le 12:8; 1Sa 10:3; 13:17, 18; 2Ch 3:17. With the article *ho heís* / *ho héteros*, the one / the other (Mt 6:24; Lk 7:41; Ac 23:6). In Rev 17:10, *ho heís* / *ho állos* (243), other, the one / the other.

(B) *Heís hékastos* (1538), each one, every one (Ac 2:6; 20:31; Col 4:6). Followed by the gen. partitively (Lk 4:40; Ac 2:3; Eph 4:7). In Rev 21:21, *aná* (303), on, upon, *heís hékastos* means each one of the gates. See *aná* (303, II).

(C) The expression *kath' héna* or *kath' hén*, one by one, singly (Jn 21:25; 1Co 14:31). In Eph 5:33, *hoi kath' héna*, every one of you. In Ac 21:19, *kath' hén hékaston*, each one singly, where *kath' hén* here qualifies *hékaston*, each one. The expression *hén kath' hén*, one by one, one after another, singly (Rev 4:8 [UBS]). The expression *heís kath' heís*, one by one, is irregularly used in the NT for *heís kath' héna* (Mk 14:19; Jn 8:9). In Ro 12:5, *ho dé kath' heís*, and every one.

(III) Emphatic, one, i.e.:

(A) Even one, one single, only one (Mt 5:36; 21:24; Mk 8:14; 10:21; 12:6; Jn 7:21; 1Co 10:17; 2Pe 3:8). The expression *apó* (575), from, *miás* in Lk 14:18 means with one accord or voice. In the sense of only, alone (Mk 2:7; Jas 4:12). In Jn 20:7, "in only one place" (a.t.).

(B) One and the same (Ro 3:30; 1Co 3:8; Gal 3:28; Php 2:2; Heb 2:11; Rev 17:13; Sept.: Ge 41:25, 26). Fully written, *hén kaí tó autó* (1Co 11:5; 12:11).

(IV) Indefinitely meaning one, someone, anyone, the same as *tis* (5100), someone (Mt 19:16). With the substantive (Mt 8:19, "a ... scribe"; Mk 12:42, "a ... widow"; Jn 6:9; Ro 9:10). Followed by the gen. partitive, one of many (Lk 5:3; 20:1; Sept.: Ge 22:2; 27:45; 42:16). *Heís tis*, a certain one (Mk 14:51, "a certain young man," followed by the gen. [see Mk 14:47]). Followed by *ek* (1537), of, from (Lk 22:50; Jn 11:49). In this use, *heís* sometimes has the force of our indefinite article "a" or "an" as in Mt 21:19, "a fig tree"; Jas 4:13, "a year"; Rev 8:13; 9:13; Sept.: Ezr 4:8; Da 2:31; 8:3.

(V) As an ordinal, the first, mostly spoken of the first day of the week as in Mt 28:1 where the noun *hēméra* (2250), day, is understood. See Mk 16:2; Lk 24:1; Ac 20:7; 1Co 16:2. In the Sept. used for the first of the month (Ge 1:5; 8:13; Ex 40:2, 17). In Rev 9:12, the "one" means the first.

Deriv.: *héndeka* (1733), eleven; *henótēs* (1775), oneness, unity.

1521. εἰσάγω, eisagō, *ice-ag´-o*; from 1519 and 71; to *introduce* (literal or figurative):—bring in (-to), (+ was to) lead into.

1522. εἰσακούω, eisakouō, *ice-ak-oo´-o*; from 1519 and 191; to *listen* to:—hear.

1523. εἰσδέχομαι, eisdechomai, *ice-dekh´-om-ahee*; from 1519 and 1209; to *take into* one's favour:—receive.

From *eis* (1519), into, and *déchomai* (1209), to receive. To receive into favour or communion (only in 2Co 6:17, "and I will gather you" [a.t.], quoted apparently from Jer 32:37, 38. See Jer 23:3; Eze 11:17; 20:34, 41, of God gathering the exiles of Israel into their own land).

Syn.: *lambánō* (2983), to receive; *paralambánō* (3880), to receive from another; *prosdéchomai* (4327), to accept fabourably; *proslambánō* (4355), to receive, take to oneself; *apodéchomai* (588), to receive gladly.

1524. εἴσειμι, eiseimi, *ice´-i-mee*; from 1519 and εἶμι, eimi (to *go*); to *enter*:—enter (go) into.

1525. εἰσέρχομαι, eiserchomai, *ice-er´-khom-ahee*; from 1519 and 2064; to *enter* (literal or figurative):— × arise, come (in, into), enter in (-to), go in (through).

1526. εἰσί, eisi, *i-see´*; third person plural presumed indicative of 1510; they *are*:—agree, are, be, dure, × is, were.

1527. εἶς καθ εἶς, heis kath heis, *hice kath hice*; from 1520 repeated with 2596 inserted; *severally*:—one by one.

1528. εἰσκαλέω, eiskaleō, *ice-kal-eh´-o*; from 1519 and 2564; to *invite* in:—call in.

1529. εἴσοδος, eisodos, *ice´-od-os*; from 1519 and 3598; an *entrance* (literal or figurative):—coming, enter (-ing) in (to).

1530. εἰσπηδάω, eispēdaō, *ice-pay-dah´-o*; from 1519 and πηδάω, *pēdaō* (to *leap*); to *rush in*:—run (spring) in.

1531. εἰσπορεύομαι, eisporeuomai, *ice-por-yoo´-om-ahee*; from 1519 and 4198; to *enter* (literal or figurative):—come (enter) in, go into.

1532. εἰστρέχω, eistrechō, *ice-trekh´-o*; from 1519 and 5143; to *hasten inward*:—run in.

1533. εἰσφέρω, eispherō, *ice-fer´-o*; from 1519 and 5342; to *carry inward* (literal or figurative):—bring (in), lead into.

1534. εἶτα, eita, *i´-tah*; of uncertain affinity; a particle of *succession* (in time or logical enumeration), *then, moreover*:—after that (-ward), furthermore, then. See also 1899.

1535. εἴτε, eite, *i´-teh*; from 1487 and 5037; *if too*:—if, or, whether.

1536. εἴ τις, ei tis, *i tis*; from 1487 and 5100; *if any*:—he that, if a (-ny) man ('s, thing, from any, ought), whether any, whosoever.

1537. ἐκ, ek, *ek*; or ἐξ, *ex, ex*; a primary preposition denoting *origin* (the point *whence* motion or action proceeds), *from, out* (of place, time or cause; literal or figurative; direct or remote):—after, among, × are, at, betwixt (-yond), by (the means of), exceedingly, (+ abundantly above), for (-th), from (among, forth, up), + grudgingly, + heartily, × heavenly, × hereby, + very highly, in, ... ly, (because, by reason) of, off (from), on, out among (from, of), over, since, × thenceforth, through, × unto, × vehemently, with (-out). Often used in composition, with the same general import; often of *completion*.

Before a vowel, it is spelled *ex*. Prep., primarily meaning out of, from, of, as spoken of such objects which before were in another, but are now seperated from it, either in respect of place, time, source, or origin. It is the direct opposite of *eis* (1519), into or in.

(I) Of place, which is the primary and most frequent use, meaning out of, from:

(A) After verbs implying motion of any kind, out of or from any place or object, e.g., verbs of going, coming, sending, throwing, following, gathering, separating, removing, and the like (Mt 2:6, 15, "out of Egypt"; 7:5; 13:49, "the wicked from among the just" [also Mt 13:52; 17:5; 24:17]; Mk 1:11; 9:7; 11:8; 13:15 [also Mk 13:27; 16:3]; Lk 2:4; 10:18; 17:24; 23:55; Jn 1:19; 2:15; 13:1; Ac 23:10; 27:29, 30; Ro 11:24; 2Th 2:7; Heb 3:16; Rev 2:5).

(B) After verbs implying direction, out of or from any place, thus marking the point from which the direction sets off or tends (Lk 5:3, "taught the people out of the ship," i.e. from the boat or while in the boat; Mk 11:20 [cf. Job 28:9; Jn 19:23; Ac 28:4]). As implying the direction in which one is placed in respect to a person or thing, as to sit, stand, or be *ek dexiás* (1188), right hand side, or *ex euōnúmōn* (2176), the left hand side, where in Eng. we use at or on (Mt 20:21, 23; 22:44; 25:33; 26:64; Mk 10:37; Lk 1:11; Ac 2:25, 34; Heb 1:13; Sept.: Ex 14:22, 29; 1Sa 23:19, 24; Ps 16:8).

(C) Metaphorically, of a state or condition out of which one comes or is brought. After verbs of motion or direction as in Jn 10:28, 39, "out of his hand"; Ac 4:2; 17:3, "resurrection from the dead"; Ro 6:4, 9, 13; 7:4, 24; 11:15; 13:11; Col 1:18.

(II) Of time, of the beginning of a period of time, a point from which onward anything takes place (Mt 19:12, "from their mother's womb"; 19:20, "from my youth"; Lk 8:27, for a "long time" is lit. "from years"; Jn 6:64; 9:1, 32; Ac 9:33; 15:21; 24:10; Sept.: Ps 22:10; 71:6).

(III) Of the origin or source of anything, i.e. the primary, direct, immediate source, in distinction from *apó* (575), which marks the secondary, indirect origin, and *hupó* (5259), by, which denotes the immediate efficient agent.

(A) Of persons: of the place, stock, family, condition, meaning out of which one is derived or to which he belongs, e.g.: **(1)** Of the place from which one is, where one resides (Lk 8:27, "out of the city"; 23:7, "that he belonged unto Herod's jurisdiction"; Jn 1:46; Ac 23:34). In Col 4:9, 12, *ho ex humṓn*, "of you" means of your city; Lk 11:13, *ho patḗr ho ex ouranoú*, "heavenly Father"; elsewhere usually *en* (1722), in, *ouranō̂*, in heaven (Mt 5:45; 6:9; 7:21). **(2)** Of family, race, ancestors (Lk 1:5, "a ... priest of the course of Abijah," 27; 2:4, "of the house of David"; Ac

4:6; 13:21; Ro 9:5, 6, 24; Heb 7:14). *Ek spérmatos* (4690), seed, followed by the gen., means of or from the seed, i.e. family or race of someone (Jn 7:42; Ro 1:3; 2Ti 2:8; Sept.: Ru 4:12; 1Ki 11:14). Followed by the gen., of the mother, to be born of a woman (Mt 1:3, 5, 6, 16; Gal 4:4, 22, 23). **(3)** Of condition or state (Jn 8:41, "We be not born of [*ek*] fornication"). *Hoi ek peritomḗs pistoí*, "they of the circumcision which believed" (see *peritomḗs* (4061), circumcision; *pistoí* (4103), believing), i.e. the Jewish Christians (Ac 10:45; cf. Ro 4:12; Gal 2:12).

(B) Of the source, i.e. the person or thing, out of or from which anything proceeds, is derived, or to which it pertains. **(1)** Used generally (Mt 21:19; Mk 11:30, "The baptism of John, was it from [*ek*] heaven, or of [*ek*] men?"; Lk 1:78; 10:11; Jn 1:13; 3:25, 27, 31; 4:22; 7:22; 10:16, 32; Ac 5:38; 19:25; Ro 2:29; 10:17; 1Co 2:12; 15:47; 2Co 5:2; 8:7; 9:2; Heb 2:11; 7:6; 1Jn 4:7; Rev 15:8). Spoken of an affection or state of mind out of which an emotion flows (2Co 2:4, "out of much affliction"; 2Ti 1:5; 1Pe 1:22); of any source of knowledge (Mt 12:33; Lk 6:44; Jn 12:34; Ro 2:18); of proof (Jas 2:18, "I shall show you my faith by [*ek*] my works," thus proving it; 3:13); of the source from which any judgement is drawn: from, out of, whereas in Eng. we would translate it "by" or "according to" (Mt 12:37, "by thy words thou shalt be justified"; Lk 19:22; Rev 20:12; Sept.: Nu 26:56). **(2)** As marking not only the source and origin, but also the character of any person or thing as derived from that source, implying connection, dependence, adherence, devotion, likeness (Jn 3:6, 8, "of the flesh"; 3:31, "of the earth"; 7:17, "he shall know of the doctrine, whether it be of God"; 8:23; 8:44; 8:47, "He that is of God, heareth God's words," i.e. character shows origin; 17:14, 16, "not of the world"; 1Jn 2:16, 29; 3:8–10; 4:1–7). Metaphorically, used of the source of character or quality, implying adherence to, connection with (Jn 18:37, "everyone that is of the truth," i.e. whose source is truth; Gal 3:10, 12; 1Jn 2:21; 3:19). Hence, *ek* forms a periphrasis for an adj. or part., e.g., *ho ek písteōs*, literally "a person of faith," a believer, (Ro 3:26; 4:16, a person "of the faith of Abraham," who believes as he did; Gal 3:7, 9); *ho ek nómou* (3551), law, one of the law, i.e. one under the law, an adherent of it (Ro 4:14, 16).

(C) Of the motive, ground, occasion from whence anything proceeds, the incidental cause,

"from," "out of," i.e. by reason of, because of, in consequence of (Jn 4:6, being tired as a result of walking; 2Co 13:4, "He was crucified because of weakness [physical], but He lives by reason of the power of God" [a.t.]; Php 1:16, 17; 2Ti 6:4; Heb 7:12; Jas 4:1; Rev 8:11, 13; 16:10, 11, 21). With the verb *dikaióō* (1344), to justify, or *dikaioúmai ek písteōs*, to justify or to be justified by, from, on account of, or through faith (Ro 3:30; 5:1; Gal 2:16; 3:24). Elsewhere with the gen. (Ro 3:20; 4:2; Gal 2:16), with the adj. *díkaios* (1342), just or righteous, *ek písteōs*, just or righteous by or on account of faith (Ro 1:17). With the noun *dikaiosúnē* (1343), righteousness, *ek písteōs* (Ro 3:26; 9:30; 10:6, righteousness out of or resulting from faith).

(D) Of the efficient cause or agent, that from which any action or thing proceeds, is produced or effected, i.e. from, by (Mt 1:18, 20; Jn 6:65, "except it were given to him of my Father," i.e. if the efficient cause is not the Father; 12:49, *ex emautoú* (1683), "of myself"; Ro 9:10; 1Co 8:6; 2Co 1:11; 2:2; 7:9; Gal 5:8; Eph 4:16; Php 1:23; Rev 2:11; 9:2, 18).

(E) Of the manner or mode in which anything is done, out of, from, or, as we would express in Eng., in, with (Mt 12:34; Mk 12:30, 33, "to love him with [*ek*] all the heart ... and with all the soul"; Lk 10:27; Jn 3:31; 8:44; Ac 8:37; Ro 6:17, heartily; 14:23, "not out of faith" [a.t.], i.e. not in or with faith; 2Co 8:11, "out of that which ye have"; 8:14; Eph 6:6; 1Th 2:3; 1Pe 4:11; 1Jn 4:5). In an adverb sense, e.g., *ek perissoú* (4053), abundance, meaning abundantly, exceedingly (Mk 6:51; 14:31); *ek mérous* (3313), part, meaning in part, partly (1Co 12:27; 13:9, 10, 12); *ek métrou* (3358), measure, meaning measurably, moderately (Jn 3:34); *ek sumphṓnou* (4859), agreement, meaning by mutual consent (1Co 7:5).

(F) Of the means, instrument, instrumental cause: from, i.e. by means of, by, through, with (Lk 16:9, "by means of" [a.t.]; Jn 3:5, "out of water" [a.t.]; 9:6; 1Co 9:13, 14, "live of the gospel," i.e. to live by means of the gospel; Heb 11:35; Rev 3:18, "gold tried by means of fire [*ek purós* (4442)]" [a.t.]; 17:2, 6; 18:3, 19). Also with verbs of filling, being full (Mt 23:25; Jn 12:3; Rev 8:5); also of a price as a means of acquiring anything (Mt 20:2, 13, for one dinar; 27:7, "and by means of them [silver coins] they bought the field" [a.t.]; Ac 1:18, where *ek* with the gen. is equivalent to the simple gen. which is the usual construction).

(**G**) Of the material, of, out of, from (Mt 27:29, "crown made of thorns" [a.t.]; Jn 2:15; Ro 9:21; 1Co 11:8; Eph 5:30; Heb 11:3; Rev 18:12; 21:21).

(**H**) Of the whole in relation to a part, a whole from which a part is spoken of, i.e. partitively (1Co 12:15, 16, "I am not [part] of the body"; Ac 10:1). After *esthíō* (2068) or *phágomai* (5315), to eat, *pínō* (4095), to drink, meaning to eat or drink of anything, i.e. part of it (Mt 26:27, 29; Lk 22:16; Jn 4:12–14; 6:26; 1Co 9:7; 11:28; Rev 2:7; 14:10; 18:3). Spoken of a class or number out of which one is separated, of which he forms part (Mk 14:69, "He is out of them" [a.t.], he belongs to them but he is separated from them; Lk 22:3; Jn 1:24; Ac 6:9; 21:8; Ro 16:10; Php 4:22; 2Ti 3:6). See *eimí* (1510, IX, C). After a numeral or pron., e.g., *heís* (1520), one (Mt 10:29, "one of them" [a.t.]; Mk 9:17; Lk 15:4); two (Mt 25:2, "five of them" [a.t.]; Mk 16:12; Jn 1:35, "two of his disciples" [a.t.]; Ac 26:23, "first of those from the resurrection of the dead" [a.t.]; Heb 7:4, "the tenth of the spoils"). After *tis* (5100), one, indefinite (Heb 4:1, "if any of you" [a.t.]); *tinés*, plural (Lk 11:15; Ac 11:20; Ro 11:14; Jas 2:16). After *tis* (5101) as an interrogative, who, which (Mt 21:31, "who of the two" [a.t.]; Lk 11:5; Jn 8:46). After *oudeís* (3762), none (Jn 7:19). Also with *tis* (sing.) and *tinés* (pl. implied) (Mt 23:34; Lk 21:16; Jn 9:40; 16:17; Rev 3:9).

In composition *ek* implies: (**a**) removal out, from, off, or away, as *ekbállō* (1544), to eject or to put away or out of; *ekphérō* (1627), to bring forth or out; (**b**) continuance, as *ekteínō* (1614), to extend, put or stretch forth; *ektréphō* (1625), to nourish, bring up; (**c**) completion, meaning "in full," as *ekdapanáō* (1550), to spend everything, all that one has; (**d**) intensiveness, as *ékdēlos* (1552), wholly evident or manifest; *exapatáō* (1818), to completely deceive; *ektarássō* (1613), to disturb completely.

1538. ἕκαστος, **hekastos,** *hek´-as-tos*; as if a superlative of ἕκας, **hekas** (*afar*); *each* or *every*:—any, both, each (one), every (man, one, woman), particularly.

Adjective from *hékas* (n.f.), separate. Each, every one, of any number separately, as in Mt 16:27, "every man," i.e. each one separately (Mt

26:22; Lk 6:44; Jn 7:53; Ro 2:6). This idea of separation or singling out is expressed still more strongly by *heís hékastos*, each one (Lk 4:40; Ac 2:3; 20:31; Eph 4:16; Rev 21:21).

Deriv.: *hekástote* (1539), each time, always.

Syn.: *pás* (3956), every one, any and every; *idía*, the dat. of *ídios* (2398), self, individual, individually.

1539. ἑκάστοτε, **hekastote,** *hek-as´-tot-eh*; as if from 1538 and 5119; at *every time*:—always.

1540. ἑκατόν, **hekaton,** *hek-at-on´*; of uncertain affinity; a *hundred*:—hundred.

1541. ἑκατονταέτης, **hekatontaetēs,** *hek-at-on-tah-et´-ace*; from 1540 and 2094; *centenarian*:—hundred years old.

1542. ἑκατονταπλασίων, **hekatontaplasiōn,** *hek-at-on-ta-plah-see´-own*; from 1540 and a presumed derivative of 4111; a *hundred times*:—hundredfold.

1543. ἑκατοντάρχης, **hekatontarchēs,** *hek-at-on-tar´-khace*; or ἑκατόνταρχος, **hekatontarchos**; *hek-at-on´-tar-khos*; from 1540 and 757; the *captain of one hundred men*:—centurion.

1544. ἐκβάλλω, **ekballō,** *ek-bal´-lo*; from 1537 and 906; to *eject* (literal or figurative):—bring forth, cast (forth, out), drive (out), expel, leave, pluck (pull, take, thrust) out, put forth (out), send away (forth, out).

1545. ἔκβασις, **ekbasis,** *ek´-bas-is*; from a compound of 1537 and the base of 939 (meaning to *go out*); an *exit* (literal or figurative):—end, way to escape.

1546. ἐκβολή, **ekbolē,** *ek-bol-ay´*; from 1544; *ejection*, i.e. (special) a *throwing overboard* of the cargo:— + lighten the ship.

1547. ἐκγαμίζω, **ekgamizō,** *ek-gam-id´-zo*; from 1537 and a form of 1061 [compare 1548]; to *marry off* a daughter:—give in marriage.

1548. ἐκγαμίσκω, **ekgamiskō,** *ek-gam-is´-ko*; from 1537 and 1061; the same as 1547:—give in marriage.

1549. ἔκγονον, **ekgonon,** *ek´-gon-on*; neuter of a derivative of a compound of 1537 and 1096; a *descendant*, i.e. (special) *grandchild*:—nephew.

1550. ἐκδαπανάω, **ekdapanaō,** *ek-dap-an-ah´-o*; from 1537 and 1159; to *expend* (wholly), i.e. (figurative) *exhaust*:—spend.

1551. ἐκδέχομαι, **ekdechomai,** *ek-dekh´-om-ahee*; from 1537 and 1209; to *accept from* some source, i.e. (by implication) to *await*:—expect, look (tarry) for, wait (for).

From *ek* (1537), out, and *déchomai* (1209), to receive. To watch for, expect, to be about to receive from any quarter (Jn 5:3; 1Co 16:11; Heb 11:10; Jas 5:7); expect, wait for (Ac 17:16; 1Co 11:33; Heb 10:13; 1Pe 3:20).

Deriv.: *apekdéchomai* (553), to look for, expect fully; *ekdoché* (1561), expectation.

Syn.: *anaménō* (362), to wait for in confident expectancy; *apekdéchomai* (553), to await or expect eagerly; *elpízō* (1679), to hope for; *periménō* (4037), to wait for; *prosdokáō* (4328), to watch toward, look for; *paredreúō* (4332), to wait upon with steadfastness; *proskarteréō* (4342), to wait on; *prosdéchomai* (4367), to expect, look for.

1552. ἔκδηλος, **ekdēlos,** *ek´-day-los*; from 1537 and 1212; *wholly evident*:—manifest.

1553. ἐκδημέω, **ekdēmeō,** *ek-day-meh´-o*; from a compound of 1537 and 1218; to *emigrate*, i.e. (figurative) *vacate* or *quit*:—be absent.

From *ékdēmos* (n.f.), away from home, which is from *ek* (1537), from or out of, and *démos* (1218), people. To go out from one's people, to be absent from one's country. In the NT, generally to be absent from any place or person (2Co 5:6, 8, 9).

Deriv.: *sunékdēmos* (4898), absent or traveling.

Syn.: *apogínomai* (581), to be away from; *apodēméō* (589), to go abroad, go away from where one is; *apothnéskō* (599), to die off or out; *thnéskō* (2348), to die; *teleutáō* (5053), to reach the end of the present state of being.

1554. ἐκδίδωμι, **ekdidōmi,** *ek-did´-o-mee*; from 1537 and 1325; to *give forth*, i.e. (special) to *lease*:—let forth (out).

1555. ἐκδιηγέομαι, **ekdiēgeomai,** *ek-dee-ayg-eh´-om-ahee*; from 1537 and a compound of 1223 and 2233; to *narrate* through wholly:—declare.

1556. ἐκδικέω, **ekdikeō,** *ek-dik-eh´-o*; from 1558; to *vindicate, retaliate, punish*:—a (re-) venge.

From *ékdikos* (1558), avenger. To execute justice, defend one's cause, maintain one's right (Lk 18:3, 5; Sept.: Ps 37:28). To avenge, i.e. to make penal satisfaction (Ro 12:19; cf. Ro 12:17, 20). To take vengeance on, to punish, e.g., in the constructions "avenge the blood on" or "at the hand of" (a.t.) someone (Rev 6:10; 19:2. See Sept.: 2Ki 9:7 [cf. Dt 18:19; Hos 1:4]). In the sense of simply to punish (2Co 10:6; Sept.: Ex 21:20).

Deriv.: *ekdíkēsis* (1557), vengeance, the bringing forth of justice.

Syn.: *antapodídōmi* (467), to repay; *apodídōmi* (591), to requite.

1557. ἐκδίκησις, **ekdikēsis,** *ek-dik´-ay-sis*; from 1556; *vindication, retribution*:—(a-, re-) venge (-ance), punishment.

Noun from *ekdikéō* (1556), to execute justice. Execution of right, justice:

(I) Maintenance of right, support, protection, hence, *poiéō ekdíkēsin* (*poiéō* [4160], to do) is the same as *ekdikéō*, to maintain one's right, defend one's cause, followed by the gen. of person, meaning for whom (Lk 18:7, 8). Followed by the dat. of person, meaning against whom (Ac 7:24 [cf. Sept.: Jgs 11:36; 2Sa 22:48]).

(II) Vengeance, i.e. penal retribution (Ro 12:19; Heb 10:30; Sept.: 2Sa 4:8; Ps 79:10; Jer 11:20; Hos 9:7). In the sense of vindictive justice: punishment (Lk 21:22; 2Th 1:8; 1Pe 2:14). Referring to the evildoer (2Co 7:11 [cf. 2Co 7:12; Sept.: Mic 5:15]).

Syn.: *epitimía* (2009), penalty, punishment; *kólasis* (2851), punishment; *kríma* (2917), condemnation; *krísis* (2920), judgement; *timōría* (5098), vengeance, punishment which vindicates one's honour.

1558. ἔκδικος, **ekdikos,** *ek´-dik-os*; from 1537 and 1349; carrying *justice out*, i.e. a *punisher*:—a (re-) venger.

Noun from *ek* (1537), from, out, and *díkē* (1349), justice. Executing right and justice, hence an avenger, punisher (Ro 13:4; 1Th 4:6).

Deriv.: *ekdikéō* (1556), to execute justice.

Syn.: *dikastés* (1348), one who brings justice among people; *krités* (2923), judge; *misthapodótēs* (3406), rewarder.

1559. ἐκδιώκω, ekdiōkō, *ek-dee-o´-ko*; from 1537 and 1377; to *pursue out*, i.e. *expel* or *persecute* implacably:—persecute.

1560. ἔκδοτος, ekdotos, *ek´-dot-os*; from 1537 and a derivative of 1325; *given out* or *over*, i.e. *surrendered*:—delivered.

1561. ἐκδοχή, ekdochē, *ek-dokh-ay´*; from 1551; *expectation*:—looking for.

Noun from *ekdéchomai* (1551), to expect. A looking for, expectation (Heb 10:27).

Syn.: *apokaradokía* (603), intense anticipation; *prosdokía* (4329), watching for, expectation; *elpís* (1680), hope.

1562. ἐκδύω, ekduō, *ek-doo´-o*; from 1537 and the base of 1416; to cause to *sink out* of, i.e. (specially as of clothing) to *divest*:—strip, take off from, unclothe.

1563. ἐκεῖ, ekei, *ek-i´*; of uncertain affinity; *there*; by extension *thither*:—there, thither (-ward), (to) yonder (place).

1564. ἐκεῖθεν, ekeithen, *ek-i´-then*; from 1563; *thence*:—from that place, (from) thence, there.

1565. ἐκεῖνος, ekeinos, *ek-i´-nos*; from 1563; *that* one (or [neuter] thing); often intensified by the article prefixed:—he, it, the other (same), selfsame, that (same, very), × their, × them, they, this, those. See also 3778.

1566. ἐκεῖσε, ekeise, *ek-i´-seh*; from 1563; *thither*:—there.

1567. ἐκζητέω, ekzēteō, *ek-zay-teh´-o*; from 1537 and 2212; to *search out*, i.e. (figurative) *investigate*, *crave*, *demand*, (by Hebrew) *worship*:—en- (re-) quire, seek after (carefully, diligently).

1568. ἐκθαμβέω, ekthambeō, *ek-tham-beh´-o*; from 1569; to *astonish* utterly:—affright, greatly (sore) amaze.

1569. ἔκθαμβος, ekthambos, *ek´-tham-bos*; from 1537 and 2285; *utterly astounded*:—greatly wondering.

1570. ἔκθετος, ekthetos, *ek´-thet-os*; from 1537 and a derivative of 5087; *put out*, i.e. *exposed* to perish:—cast out.

1571. ἐκκαθαίρω, ekkathairō, *ek-kath-ah´-ee-ro*; from 1537 and 2508; to *cleanse thoroughly*:—purge (out).

1572. ἐκκαίω, ekkaiō, *ek-kah´-yo*; from 1537 and 2545; to *inflame* deeply:—burn.

1573. ἐκκακέω, ekkakeō, *ek-kak-eh´-o*; from 1537 and 2556; to *be* (*bad* or) *weak*, i.e. (by implication) to *fail* (in heart):—faint, be weary.

From *ek* (1537), out of, or an intensive, and *kakós* (2556), bad. To turn out to be a coward, to lose one's courage. In the NT, generally: to be fainthearted, to faint or despond in view of trial, difficulty. Intransitively (2Co 4:1, 16; Eph 3:13). In the sense of to be remiss or slothful in duty (Lk 18:1; Gal 6:9; 2Th 3:13).

Syn.: *apopsúchō* (674), to lose soul or heart, faint; *eklúō* (1590), to be faint, grow weary; *kámnō* (2577), to be weary.

1574. ἐκκεντέω, ekkenteō, *ek-ken-teh´-o*; from 1537 and the base of 2759; to *transfix*:—pierce.

1575. ἐκκλάω, ekklaō, *ek-klah´-o*; from 1537 and 2806; to *exscind*:—break off.

1576. ἐκκλείω, ekkleiō, *ek-kli´-o*; from 1537 and 2808; to *shut out* (literal or figurative):—exclude.

1577. ἐκκλησία, ekklēsia, *ek-klay-see´-ah*; from a compound of 1537 and a derivative of 2564; a *calling out*, i.e. (concretely) a popular *meeting*, especially a religious *congregation* (Jewish *synagogue*, or Christian community of members on earth or saints in heaven or both):—assembly, church.

Noun from *ekklētos* (n.f.), called out, which is from *ekkaléō* (n.f.), to call out. A convocation, assembly, congregation:

(I) Of persons legally called out or summoned (Ac 19:39, of the people); and hence also of a tumultuous assembly not necessarily legal (Ac 19:32, 41). In the Jewish sense: a congregation, assembly of the people for worship, e.g., in a synagogue (Mt 18:17), or generally (Ac 7:38; Heb 2:12 quoted from Ps 22:22; Sept.: Dt 18:16; 2Ch 1:3, 5).

(II) In the Christian sense: an assembly of Christians, generally (1Co 11:18, a church, the Christian church).

(A) A particular church, e.g., in Jerusalem (Ac

8:1; 11:22); Antioch (Ac 11:26; 13:1); Corinth (1Co 1:2; 2Co 1:1); Asia Minor (1Co 16:19); Galatia (Gal 1:2); Thessalonica (1Th 1:1; 2Th 1:1); Cenchrea (Ro 16:1). Also, "the churches of the nations" (a.t.) means churches of Gentile Christians (Ro 16:4); the church which meets at the house of someone (Ro 16:5; 1Co 16:19; Phm 2); the churches of Christ (Ro 16:16); the church of God at Corinth (1Co 1:2).

(B) The universal church (Mt 16:18; 1Co 12:28; Gal 1:13; Eph 1:22; 3:10; Heb 12:23); church of God (1Co 10:32; 11:22; 15:9; 2Ti 3:15 [cf. in the Sept. the church of the Lord {Dt 23:2, 3}]).

1578. ἐκκλίνω, ekklinō, *ek-klee´-no*; from 1537 and 2827; to *deviate*, i.e. (absolute) to *shun* (literal or figurative), or (relative) to *decline* (from piety):—avoid, eschew, go out of the way.

1579. ἐκκολυμβάω, ekkolumbaō, *ek-kol-oom-bah´-o*; from 1537 and 2860; to *escape* by *swimming*:—swim out.

1580. ἐκκομίζω, ekkomizō, *ek-kom-id´-zo*; from 1537 and 2865; to *bear forth* (to burial):—carry out.

1581. ἐκκόπτω, ekkoptō, *ek-kop´-to*; from 1537 and 2875; to *exscind*; (figurative) to *frustrate*:—cut down (off, out), hew down, hinder.

1582. ἐκκρέμαμαι, ekkremamai, *ek-krem´-am-ahee*; middle from 1537 and 2910; to *hang upon* the lips of a speaker, i.e. *listen closely*:—be very attentive.

1583. ἐκλαλέω, eklaleō, *ek-lal-eh´-o*; from 1537 and 2980; to *divulge*:—tell.

1584. ἐκλάμπω, eklampō, *ek-lam´-po*; from 1537 and 2989; to *be resplendent*:—shine forth.

1585. ἐκλανθάνομαι, eklanthanomai, *ek-lan-than´-om-ahee*; middle from 1537 and 2990; to *be* utterly *oblivious* of:—forget.

1586. ἐκλέγομαι, eklegomai, *ek-leg´-om-ahee*; middle from 1537 and 3004 (in its primary sense); to *select*:—make choice, choose (out), chosen.

From *ek* (1537), out, and *légō* (3004), to select, choose. To choose, select, choose for oneself. In the NT found only in the middle *eklégomai*:

(I) Generally, of things (Lk 10:42; 14:7). Followed by *hína* (2443), so that, of purpose (1Co

1:27, 28; Sept.: Ge 13:11); of persons (Jn 6:70; 15:16; Ac 1:2, 24; 6:5; 15:22, 25; Sept.: 1Sa 8:18; 10:24); followed by *ek* (1537), from (Jn 15:19); followed by *apó* (575), of (Lk 6:13). With an inf. implied (Jas 2:5 where the implied inf. is *eínai* [1511], to be). Followed by *en* (1722), among (Ac 15:7, "God made choice among us").

(II) By implication: to choose out, with the accessory idea of kindness, favour, love (Mk 13:20; Jn 13:18; Ac 13:17; Eph 1:4; Sept.: Dt 4:37; Ps 65:4; Zec 3:2). In some MSS, Lk 9:35 (TR) has *eklelegménos*, chosen, instead of *agapetós* (27), beloved.

Deriv.: *eklektós* (1588), chosen, elect.

Syn.: *hairéomai* (138), to prefer; *hairetízō* (140), to prefer, choose; *epilégomai* (1951), to select, choose for oneself.

1587. ἐκλείπω, ekleipō, *ek-li´-po*; from 1537 and 3007; to *omit*, i.e. (by implication) *cease* (*die*):—fail.

1588. ἐκλεκτός, eklektos, *ek-lek-tos´*; from 1586; *select*; (by implication) *favorite*:—chosen, elect.

Adjective from *eklégō* (1586), to choose, select. Chosen, select:

(I) Select, choice, excellent. Used as an adj. in regard to stone as in 1Pe 2:4, 6 quoted from Isa 28:16; see Ezr 5:8. Of persons, chosen or distinguished as in 1Pe 2:9, *génos eklektón* (*génos* [1085], generation), "a chosen generation," referring to the believers in Christ. See Sept.: Isa 43:20. Of angels in 2Ti 5:21, referring to them as chosen by God to minister to the special needs of believers.

(II) By implication meaning chosen, with the accessory idea of kindness, favour, love, equivalent to cherished, beloved (Lk 23:35, "the chosen of God"; Ro 16:13; Sept.: Ps 105:6; 1Ch 16:13). Hence *hoi eklektoí*, the elect, i.e. those chosen of God for salvation or as members of the kingdom of heaven, and who therefore enjoy his favour, and lead a holy life in communion with him. They are also called saints (Ro 1:7; 15:31); Christians (Ac 11:26; 26:28; 1Pe 4:16).

Deriv.: *suneklektós* (4899), elected together with.

1589. ἐκλογή, eklogē, *ek-log-ay´*; from 1586; (divine) *selection* (abstract or concrete):—chosen, election.

Noun from *eklégō* (1586), to choose, select. Election, choice, selection:

(I) Generally as in Ac 9:15, a chosen vessel, an instrument of usefulness.

(II) Election, the benevolent purpose of God by which any are chosen unto salvation so that they are led to embrace and persevere in Christ's bestowed grace and the enjoyment of its privileges and blessings here and hereafter (Ro 11:15, 28; 1Th 1:4; 2Pe 2:10).

(III) By implication meaning free choice, free will, election. In Ro 9:11 we have the expression, "that the purpose of God according to election might stand." This means that God's intention (*próthesis* [4286]) was according to the principle of election which is God's free choice without being affected by any outside circumstances or the worth of the individuals concerned.

Syn.: *haíresis* (139), choice.

1590. ἐκλύω, **ekluō**, *ek-loo´-o*; from 1537 and 3089; to *relax* (literal or figurative):—faint.

1591. ἐκμάσσω, **ekmassō**, *ek-mas´-so*; from 1537 and the base of 3145; to *knead out*, i.e. (by analogy) to *wipe dry*:—wipe.

1592. ἐκμυκτερίζω, **ekmukterizō**, *ek-mook-ter-id´-zo*; from 1537 and 3456; to *sneer* outright at:—deride.

1593. ἐκνεύω, **ekneuō**, *ek-nyoo´-o*; from 1537 and 3506; (by analogy) to *slip off*, i.e. quietly *withdraw*:—convey self away.

1594. ἐκνήφω, **eknēphō**, *ek-nay´-fo*; from 1537 and 3525; (figurative) to *rouse* (oneself) *out* of stupor:—awake.

1595. ἐκούσιον, **hekousion**, *hek-oo´-see-on*; neuter of a derivative from 1635; *voluntariness*:—willingly.

Adjective from *hekōn* (1635), willingly. Voluntary, willing. Only in Phm 14 where it means willingly, uncompelled, gladly (Sept.: Nu 15:3).

Deriv.: *hekousíōs* (1596), voluntarily.

Syn.: *authaíretos* (830), voluntary, willing; *hétoimos* (2092), ready; *próthumos* (4289), willing.

1596. ἐκουσίως, **hekousiōs**, *hek-oo-see´-oce*; adverb from the same as 1595; *voluntarily*:—wilfully, willingly.

Adverb from *hekoúsios* (1595), voluntary. Voluntarily, intentionally (Heb 10:26; 1Pe 5:2; Sept.: Ps 54:6).

Syn.: *hekōn* (1635), voluntarily, willingly.

1597. ἔκπαλαι, **ekpalai**, *ek´-pal-ahee*; from 1537 and 3819; *long ago, for a long while*:—of a long time, of old.

1598. ἐκπειράζω, **ekpeirazō**, *ek-pi-rad´-zo*; from 1537 and 3985; to *test thoroughly*:—tempt.

From *ek* (1537), an intensive, and *peirázō* (3985), tempt. Try, prove, tempt, put to the test (Mt 4:7; Lk 4:12; 10:25; 1Co 10:9; Sept.: Dt 6:16; 8:16; Ps 78:18).

Syn.: *peirázō* (3985), to test; *dokimázō* (1381), to test, prove.

1599. ἐκπέμπω, **ekpempō**, *ek-pem´-po*; from 1537 and 3992; to *despatch*:—send away (forth).

1600. ἐκπετάννυμι, **ekpetannumi**, *ek-pet-an´-noo-mee*; from 1537 and a form of 4072; to *fly out*, i.e. (by analogy) *extend*:—stretch forth.

1601. ἐκπίπτω, **ekpiptō**, *ek-pip´-to*; from 1537 and 4098; to *drop away*; specially *be driven out* of one's course; (figurative) to *lose, become inefficient*:—be cast, fail, fall (away, off), take no effect.

1602. ἐκπλέω, **ekpleō**, *ek-pleh´-o*; from 1537 and 4126; to *depart* by ship:—sail (away, thence).

1603. ἐκπληρόω, **ekplēroō**, *ek-play-ro´-o*; from 1537 and 4137; to *accomplish* entirely:—fulfill.

From *ek* (1537), an intensive, and *pleróō* (4137), to fill, fulfill. To fulfill entirely, completely (Ac 13:33, "the promise").

Deriv.: *ekplērōsis* (1604), accomplishment.

Syn.: *anaplēróō* (378), to fill up, fill completely; *empíplēmi* (1705), to fill full; *epiteléō* (2005), to fill further, finish; *plēthō* (4130), to fill; *suntelēō* (4931), to complete, bring to completion; *teleióō* (5048), to bring to an end, fulfill; *teléō* (5055), to fulfill.

1604. ἐκπλήρωσις, **ekplērōsis**, *ek-play´-ro-sis*; from 1603; *completion*:—accomplishment.

Noun from *ekplēróō* (1603), to fulfill. A fulfilling, accomplishment (only in Ac 21:26 announcing the fulfillment [full observance] of the days, i.e. that he was about to keep in full the proper number of days; see Nu 6:9).

Syn.: *plērōma* (4138), a filling up, fulfillment; *teleíōsis* (5050), performance, fulfillment.

1605. ἐκπλήσσω, ekplēssō, *ek-place´-so*; from 1537 and 4141; to *strike* with astonishment:—amaze, astonish.

1606. ἐκπνέω, ekpneō, *ek-pneh´-o*; from 1537 and 4154; to *expire*:—give up the ghost.

1607. ἐκπορεύομαι, ekporeuomai, *ek-por-yoo´-om-ahee*; from 1537 and 4198; to *depart, be discharged, proceed, project*:—come (forth, out of), depart, go (forth, out), issue, proceed (out of).

1608. ἐκπορνεύω, ekporneuō, *ek-porn-yoo´-o*; from 1537 and 4203; to *be utterly unchaste*:—give self over to fornication.

1609. ἐκπτύω, ekptuō, *ek-ptoo´-o*; from 1537 and 4429; to *spit out*, i.e. (figurative) *spurn*:—reject.

1610. ἐκριζόω, ekrizoō, *ek-rid-zo´-o*; from 1537 and 4492; to *uproot*:—pluck up by the root, root up.

1611. ἔκστασις, ekstasis, *ek´-stas-is*; from 1839; a *displacement* of the mind, i.e. *bewilderment*, "*ecstasy*":— + be amazed, amazement, astonishment, trance.

From *exístēmi* (1839), to remove out of its place or state. A putting away, removal of anything out of a place. In the NT, used metaphorically: ecstasy, i.e. the state of being out of one's usual mind:

(I) Arising from any strong emotion, e.g., astonishment, amazement (Mk 5:42; 16:8; Lk 5:26; Ac 3:10; Sept.: Ge 27:33; Dt 28:28; 2Ch 14:14; Eze 27:35).

(II) A trance, i.e. a state in which the soul is unconscious of present objects, being rapt into visions of distant or future things (Ac 10:10; 11:5; 22:17 [cf. 2Co 12:2; Eze 1:1 {cf. Sept.: Ge 2:21}]).

Syn.: *aporía* (640), bewilderment; *thámbos* (2285), astonishment; *hórasis* (3706), gazing, vision; *phóbos* (5401), fear.

1612. ἐκστρέφω, ekstrephō, *ek-stref´-o*; from 1537 and 4762; to *pervert* (figurative):—subvert.

1613. ἐκταράσσω, ektarassō, *ek-tar-as´-so*; from 1537 and 5015; to *disturb wholly*:—exceedingly trouble.

1614. ἐκτείνω, ekteinō, *ek-ti´-no*; from 1537 and τείνω, teinō (to *stretch*); to *extend*:—cast, put forth, stretch forth (out).

1615. ἐκτελέω, ekteleō, *ek-tel-eh´-o*; from 1537 and 5055; to *complete* fully:—finish.

1616. ἐκτένεια, ekteneia, *ek-ten´-i-ah*; from 1618; *intentness*:— × instantly.

1617. ἐκτενέστερον, ektenesteron, *ek-ten-es´-ter-on*; neuter of the comparative of 1618; *more intently*:—more earnestly.

1618. ἐκτενής, ektenēs, *ek-ten-ace´*; from 1614; *intent*:—without ceasing, fervent.

Adjective from *ekteínō* (1614), to stretch out, extend. Stretched out, continual, intense (Ac 12:5 [TR]; 1Pe 4:8). The comparative: *ektenésteron* (1617), more intensely, earnestly.

Deriv.: *ektenós* (1619), intensely, earnestly.

Syn.: *adiáleiptos* (88), unceasing; *makrós* (3117), long; *spoudaíos* (4705), diligent, earnest.

1619. ἐκτενῶς, ektenōs, *ek-ten-oce´*; adverb from 1618; *intently*:—fervently.

1620. ἐκτίθημι, ektithēmi, *ek-tith´-ay-mee*; from 1537 and 5087; to *expose*; (figurative) to *declare*:—cast out, expound.

1621. ἐκτινάσσω, ektinassō, *ek-tin-as´-so*; from 1537 and τινάσσω, tinassō (to *swing*); to *shake* violently:—shake (off).

1622. ἐκτός, ektos, *ek-tos´*; from 1537; the *exterior*; figurative (as a preposition) *aside from, besides*:—but, except (-ed), other than, out of, outside, unless, without.

1623. ἕκτος, hektos, *hek´-tos*; ordinal from 1803; *sixth*:—sixth.

1624. ἐκτρέπω, ektrepō, *ek-trep´-o*; from 1537 and the base of 5157; to *deflect*, i.e. *turn away* (literal or figurative):—avoid, turn (aside, out of the way).

1625. ἐκτρέφω, ektrephō, *ek-tref´-o*; from 1537 and 5142; to *rear up* to maturity, i.e. (genitive) to *cherish* or *train*:—bring up, nourish.

1626. ἔκτρωμα, ektrōma, *ek´-tro-mah*; from a compound of 1537 and τιτρώσκω, titrōskō (to *wound*); a *miscarriage* (*abortion*), i.e. (by analogy) *untimely birth*:—born out of due time.

1627. ἐκφέρω, ekpherō, *ek-fer´-o*; from 1537 and 5342; to *bear out* (literal or figurative):— bear, bring forth, carry forth (out).

1628. ἐκφεύγω, ekpheugō, *ek-fyoo´-go*; from 1537 and 5343; to *flee out*:—escape, flee.

1629. ἐκφοβέω, ekphobeō, *ek-fob-eh´-o*; from 1537 and 5399; to *frighten utterly*:—terrify.

1630. ἔκφοβος, ekphobos, *ek´-fob-os*; from 1537 and 5401; *frightened out* of one's wits:— sore afraid, exceedingly fearful.

1631. ἐκφύω, ekphuō, *ek-foo´-o*; from 1537 and 5453; to *sprout up*:—put forth.

1632. ἐκχέω, ekcheō, *ek-kheh´-o*; or (by variation) ἐκχύνω, ekchunō, *ek-khoo´-no*; from 1537 and χέω, cheō (to *pour*); to *pour forth*; (figurative) to *bestow*:—gush (pour) out, run greedily (out), shed (abroad, forth), spill.

1633. ἐκχωρέω, ekchōreō, *ek-kho-reh´-o*; from 1537 and 5562; to *depart*:—depart out.

1634. ἐκψύχω, ekpsuchō, *ek-psoo´-kho*; from 1537 and 5594; to *expire*:—give (yield) up the ghost.

From *ek* (1537), out, and *psúchō* (5594), to breathe. To expire, die, used intransitively (Ac 5:5, 10; 12:23; Sept.: Jgs 4:21; Eze 21:7).

Syn.: *apogínomai* (581), to be away from; *thnēskō* (2348), to die; *apothnēskō* (599), to die off or out; *koimáomai* (2837), to fall asleep; *teleutáō* (5053) and *apóllumi* (622) to die, expire.

1635. ἑκών, hekōn, *hek-own´*; of uncertain affinity; *voluntary*:—willingly.

Adjective meaning willing, voluntary (Ro 8:20; 1Co 9:17).

Deriv.: *ákōn* (210), unwillingly; *ekoúsios* (1595), willing, voluntary.

Syn.: *hekousíōs* (1596), willingly.

1636. ἐλαία, elaia, *el-ah´-yah*; feminine of a presumed derivative from an obsolete primary; an *olive* (the tree or the fruit):—olive (berry, tree).

1637. ἔλαιον, elaion, *el´-ah-yon*; neuter of the same as 1636; olive *oil*:—oil.

Noun from *elaía* (1636), olive tree. Olive oil. Used for lamps (Mt 25:3, 4, 8); for wounds and anointing the sick (Mk 6:13; Lk 10:34; Jas 5:14);

as mixed with spices for anointing the head and body in token of honour (Lk 7:46; Heb 1:9); also an article of trade (Lk 16:6; Rev 8:13).

1638. ἐλαιών, elaiōn, *el-ah-yone´*; from 1636; an *olive-orchard*, i.e. (special) the *Mt. of Olives*:—Olivet.

1639. Ἐλαμίτης, Elamitēs, *el-am-ee´-tace*; of Hebrew origin [5867]; an *Elamite* or Persian:— Elamite.

1640. ἐλάσσων, elassōn, *el-as´-sone*; or ἐλάττων, elattōn, *el-at-tone´*; comparative of the same as 1646; *smaller* (in size, quantity, age or quality):—less, under, worse, younger.

1641. ἐλαττονέω, elattoneō, *el-at-ton-eh´-o*; from 1640; to *diminish*, i.e. *fall short*:—have lack.

1642. ἐλαττόω, elattoō, *el-at-to´-o*; from 1640; to *lessen* (in rank or influence):—decrease, make lower.

1643. ἐλαύνω, elaunō, *el-ow´-no*; a prolonged form of a primary verb (obsolete except in certain tenses as an alternative of this) of uncertain affinity; to *push* (as wind, oars or dæmoniacal power):—carry, drive, row.

1644. ἐλαφρία, elaphria, *el-af-ree´-ah*; from 1645; *levity* (figurative), i.e. *fickleness*:—lightness.

1645. ἐλαφρός, elaphros, *el-af-ros´*; probably akin to 1643 and the base of 1640; *light*, i.e. *easy*:—light.

1646. ἐλάχιστος, elachistos, *el-akh´-is-tos*; superlative of ἔλαχυς, elachus (*short*); used as equivalent to 3398; *least* (in size, amount, dignity, etc.):—least, very little (small), smallest.

1647. ἐλαχιστότερος, elachistoteros, *el-akh-is-tot´-er-os*; comparative of 1646; *far less*:—less than the least.

1648. Ἐλεάζαρ, Eleazar, *el-eh-ad´-zar*; of Hebrew origin [499]; *Eleazar*, an Israelite:— Eleazar.

1649. ἔλεγξις, elegxis, *el´-eng-xis*; from 1651; *refutation*, i.e. *reproof*:—rebuke.

1650. ἔλεγχος, elegchos, *el´-eng-khos*; from 1651; *proof, conviction*:—evidence, reproof.

Noun from *elégchō* (1651), to convict. Conviction. Metonymically, meaning certain persuasion (Heb 11:1). In the sense of refutation of adversaries (2Ti 3:16; see Sept.: Job 13:6; 23:4; Hos 5:9).

Syn.: *dokimḗ* (1382), proof; *krísis* (2920), judgement; *momphḗ* (3437), fault.

1651. ἐλέγχω, elegchō, *el-eng´-kho*; of uncertain affinity; to *confute, admonish*:—convict, convince, tell a fault, rebuke, reprove.

To shame, disgrace, but only in Class. Gr. In the NT, to convict, to prove one in the wrong and thus to shame him. Transitively:

(I) To convict, to show to be wrong (Jn 8:9, 46; 16:8; 1Co 14:24; Jas 2:9). To convince of error, refute, confute (Tit 1:9, 13; 2:15; Sept.: Job 32:12; Pr 18:17).

(II) By implication: to reprove, rebuke, admonish (Mt 18:15; Lk 3:19; 1Ti 5:20; 2Ti 4:2; Sept.: Ge 21:25; Pr 9:8). To reprove by chastisement, correct, chastise in a moral sense (Rev 3:19); with *paideúō* (3811), train (Heb 12:5 from Pr 3:11, 12. See Sept.: Job 5:17; Ps 6:1; 38:1).

(III) By implication spoken of hidden things: to detect, demonstrate, make manifest (Jn 3:20 where *elegchthḗ* is parallel with *phanerōthḗ* [5319], to manifest in Jn 3:21 [Eph 5:11, 13]).

Deriv.: *élegxis* (1649), the act of rebuking; *élegchos* (1650), reproof; *exelégchō* (1827), to convict thoroughly.

Syn.: *apodokimázō* (593), to repudiate; *epikrínō* (1948), to adjudge; *kakologéō* (2551), to speak evil of; *katakrínō* (2632) or *katadikázō* (2613), to condemn; *katalaléō* (2635), to slander; *katēgoréō* (2723), to accuse; *krínō* (2919), to judge; *mémphomai* (3201), to find fault.

1652. ἐλεεινός, eleeinos, *el-eh-i-nos´*; from 1656; *pitiable*:—miserable.

Adjective from *éleos* (1656), mercy. Worthy of pity, pitiable, full of misery, wretched, miserable. In the NT used only in 1Co 15:19; Rev 3:17.

Syn.: *kakós* (2556), bad in character; *ponērós* (4190), evil, harmful; *saprós* (4550), corrupt, rotten; *phaúlos* (5337), slight, trivial.

1653. ἐλεέω, eleeō, *el-eh-eh´-o*; from 1656; to *compassionate* (by word or deed, specially by divine grace):—have compassion (pity on), have (obtain, receive, shew) mercy (on).

From *éleos* (1656), mercy. To show mercy, to show compassion. The general meaning is to have compassion or mercy on a person in unhappy circumstances. Used transitively in the pass., to be pitied, obtain mercy, implying not merely a feeling for the misfortunes of others involving sympathy (*oiktirmós* [3628], pity), but also an active desire to remove those miseries.

(I) Generally (Mt 5:7; 9:27; 15:22; 17:15; 18:33; 20:30, 31; Mk 5:19; 10:47, 48; Lk 16:24; 17:13; 18:38, 39; Php 2:27; Jude 22; Sept.: Dt 13:17; 2Sa 12:22; 2Ki 13:23; Ps 6:2; Isa 13:18). Spoken of those who had charge of the poor (Ro 12:8 [cf. Pr 14:21, 31; 28:8]); of those who are freed from deserved punishment, in the pass.: to obtain mercy, be spared (1Ti 1:13, 16; Sept.: Dt 7:2; Isa 9:19; Eze 7:4, 9). By implication: to be gracious toward, bestow kindness on (Ro 9:15, 16, 18 quoted from Ex 33:19; Sept.: Ge 43:29).

(II) Spoken of the mercy of God through Christ or salvation in Christ: to bestow salvation on; in the pass.: to obtain salvation (Ro 11:30–32; 1Co 7:25; 2Co 4:1; 1Pe 2:10).

Syn.: *hiláskomai* (2433), to be propitious, merciful, make reconciliation for; *lupéō* (3076), to be sad, sorry; *splagchnízomai* (4697), to have bowels of mercy or a yearning heart, feel sympathy, pity; *sumpathéō* (4834), to have sympathy, compassion; *sumpáschō* (4841), to suffer with.

1654. ἐλεημοσύνη, eleēmosunē, *el-eh-ay-mos-oo´-nay*; from 1656; *compassionateness*, i.e. (as exercised toward the poor) *beneficence*, or (concretely) a *benefaction*:—alms (-deeds).

From *eleḗmōn* (1655), merciful. Mercy, compassion (Sept.: Pr 21:21; Isa 38:18). In the NT by metonymy of effect for cause: alms, charity, money given to the poor (Mt 6:1 [TR]; 6:2–4; Lk 11:41; 12:33; Ac 3:2, 3, 10; 9:36; 10:2, 4, 31; 24:17; Sept.: Da 4:24).

1655. ἐλεήμων, eleēmōn, *el-eh-ay´-mone*; from 1653; *compassionate* (actively):—merciful.

Adjective from *éleos* (1656), mercy. Compassionate, merciful; benevolently merciful, involving thought and action (Mt 5:7; Sept.: Ex 22:27; Ps 103:8; 145:8; Jer 3:12).

Deriv.: *aneleḗmōn* (415), unmerciful; *eleēmosúnē* (1654), merciful.

Syn.: *oiktírmōn* (3629) feelings of compassion.

1656. ἔλεος, **eleos,** *el´-eh-os*; of uncertain affinity; *compassion* (human or divine, especially active):—(+ tender) mercy.

A noun meaning mercy, compassion:

(**I**) *Ho éleos*, gen. *éleou*, masc. noun:

(**A**) Mercy, compassion, active pity (Mt 23:23; Tit 3:5; Heb 4:16; Sept.: Isa 60:10).

(**B**) With the sense of goodness in general, especially piety (Mt 9:13; 12:7 quoted from Hos 6:6).

(**II**) *To éleos*, gen. *eléous*, neuter noun, found only in the Sept., the NT, and church writers in contrast to the noun in the masc. *ho éleos* which alone is used by Class. Gr. writers. Mercy, compassion, active pity:

(**A**) Generally (Lk 1:50, 78; Ro 9:23; 15:9; Eph 2:4; 1Pe 1:3; Jas 3:17; Sept.: Dt 13:17; Ne 13:22; Ps 51:1; Isa 63:7). With the verb *poiéō* (4160), to do mercy for someone, meaning to show mercy to, equivalent to the verb *eleéō* (1653), to have compassion on, show mercy (Lk 1:72; 10:37; Jas 2:13; Sept.: Ge 24:12; 1Sa 15:6). With the verb *megalúnō* (3170), to make great, magnify, show great mercy on someone (Lk 1:58). In the phrase, *mnēsthḗnai eléous*, lit. "to remember mercy" (from *mimnḗskō* [3403], to remember), meaning to give a new proof of mercy and favour to Israel, in reference to God's ancient mercies to that people (Lk 1:54 [cf. Ps 25:6; 89:28, 50; Sept.: 2Ch 6:42; Jer 2:2]). Spoken of mercy as a passing over of deserved punishment (Jas 2:13 [cf. Sept.: Nu 14:19]).

(**B**) Spoken of the mercy of God through Christ, i.e. salvation in the Christian sense from sin and misery (Jude 21, "the mercy of our Lord Jesus Christ" means salvation through Christ; see Ro 11:31). In benedictions, including the idea of mercies and blessings of every kind, e.g., "the Lord give mercy" (2Ti 1:16, 18). Also joined with *eirḗnē* (1515), peace (Gal 6:16; 1Ti 1:2; 2Ti 1:2; Tit 1:4; 2Jn 3; Jude 2).

Deriv.: *eleeinós* (1652), worthy of pity; *eleéō* (1653), to be merciful; *eleḗmōn* (1655), merciful.

Syn.: *oiktirmós* (3628), pity; *lúpē* (3077), sorrow; *splágchnon* (4698), affection, sympathy; *hilasmós* (2434), propitiation.

1657. ἐλευθερία, **eleutheria,** *el-yoo-ther-ee´-ah*; from 1658; *freedom* (legitimate or licentious, chiefly moral or ceremonial):—liberty.

Noun from *eleútheros* (1658), a free person. Freedom, as liberty to do as one pleases (1Co 10:29; 2Pe 2:19); freedom from the yoke of the Mosaic Law (2Co 3:17; Gal 2:4; 5:1, 13), so from the yoke of external observances in general (1Pe 2:16); from the dominion of sinful appetites and passions (Jas 1:25; 2:12); from a state of calamity and death (Ro 8:21).

Syn.: *politeía* (4174), citizenship, referring to the fact that a citizen was a free man; *cháris* (5485), grace.

1658. ἐλεύθερος, **eleutheros,** *el-yoo´-ther-os*; probably from the alternative of 2064; *unrestrained* (to *go* at pleasure), i.e. (as a citizen) *not a slave* (whether *freeborn* or *manumitted*), or (genitive) *exempt* (from obligation or liability):—free (man, woman), at liberty.

Adjective meaning "one who can go where he will," free, at liberty:

(**I**) In a civil sense:

(**A**) Freeborn (1Co 12:13; Gal 3:28; 4:22, 23, 30, 31; Eph 6:8; Col 3:11; Rev 6:15; 13:16; 19:18). Figuratively of the heavenly Jerusalem, meaning nobler (Gal 4:26; Sept.: Ne 13:17; Ecc 10:17).

(**B**) Freed, made free (Jn 8:33; 1Co 7:21, 22; Sept.: Ex 21:2, 26, 27).

(**C**) Free, exempt from an obligation or law (Mt 17:26; Ro 7:3; 1Co 7:39 [cf. Sept.: Dt 21:14]); free from external obligations in general, so as to act as one pleases (1Co 9:1, 19); in respect to the exercise of piety (1Pe 2:16).

(**II**) Metaphorically: free from the slavery of sin (Jn 8:36; Ro 6:18 [cf. Ro 6:20, "free from righteousness"]).

Deriv.: *apeleútheros* (558) free man; *eleuthería* (1657), freedom; *eleutheróō* (1659), to make free.

1659. ἐλευθερόω, **eleutheroō,** *el-yoo-ther-o´-o*; from 1658; to *liberate*, i.e. (figurative) to *exempt* (from moral, ceremonial or mortal liability):—deliver, make free.

From *eleútheros* (1658), free. To make free, liberate from the power and punishment of sin, the result of redemption (Jn 8:32, 36; Ro 6:18, 22); from a state of calamity and death (Ro 8:2, 21); from the power of condemnation by the Mosaic Law (Gal 5:1). For a full discussion, see *eleuthería* (1657), freedom, liberty.

Syn.: *charízō* (5483), to deliver; *apolúō* (630), to set free; *apallássō* (525), to release.

1660. ἔλευσις, eleusis, *el´-yoo-sis*; from the alternative of 2064; an *advent*:—coming.

1661. ἐλεφάντινος, elephantinos, *el-ef-an´-tee-nos*; from ἔλεφας, *elephas* (an "*elephant*"); *elephantine*, i.e. (by implication) composed of *ivory*:—of ivory.

1662. ᾽Ελιακείμ, Eliakeim, *el-ee-ak-ime´*; of Hebrew origin [471]; *Eliakim*, an Israelite:— Eliakim.

1663. ᾽Ελιέζερ, Eliezer, *el-ee-ed´-zer*; of Hebrew origin [461]; *Eliezer*, an Israelite:—Eliezer.

1664. ᾽Ελιούδ, Elioud, *el-ee-ood´*; of Hebrew origin [410 and 1935]; *God of majesty; Eliud*, an Israelite:—Eliud.

1665. ᾽Ελισάβετ, Elisabet, *el-ee-sab´-et*; of Hebrew origin [472]; *Elisabet*, an Israelitess:— Elisabeth.

1666. ᾽Ελισσαῖος, Elissaios, *el-is-sah´-yos*; of Hebrew origin [477]; *Elissæus*, an Israelite:— Elissæus.

1667. ἑλίσσω, helissō, *hel-is´-so*; a form of 1507; to *coil* or *wrap*:—fold up.

1668. ἕλκος, helkos, *hel´-kos*; probably from 1670; an *ulcer* (as if drawn together):—sore.

1669. ἑλκόω, helkoō, *hel-ko´-o*; from 1668; to *cause to ulcerate*, i.e. (passive) *be ulcerous*:—full of sores.

1670. ἑλκύω, helkuō, *hel-koo´-o*; or ἕλκω, *helkō*, *hel´-ko*; probably akin to 138; to *drag* (literal or figurative):—draw. Compare 1667.

To draw, to drag (Jn 21:6, 11; 18:10). Of persons: to drag, to force before magistrates (Ac 16:19; Jas 2:6), or out of a place (Ac 21:30). Metaphorically: to draw, induce to come (Jn 6:44; 12:32).

Deriv.: *exélkō* (1828), to draw away.

1671. ῾Ελλάς, Hellas, *hel-las´*; of uncertain affinity; *Hellas* (or *Greece*), a country of Europe:—Greece.

1672. ῞Ελλην, Hellēn, *hel´-lane*; from 1671; a *Hellen* (*Grecian*) or inhabitant of Hellas; by extension a *Greek-speaking* person, especially a *non-Jew*:—Gentile, Greek.

1673. ῾Ελληνικός, Hellēnikos, *hel-lay-nee-kos´*; from 1672; *Hellenic*, i.e. *Grecian* (in language):—Greek.

1674. ῾Ελληνίς, Hellēnis, *hel-lay-nis´*; feminine of 1672; a *Grecian* (i.e. *non-Jewish*) woman:—Greek.

1675. ῾Ελληνιστής, Hellēnistēs, *hel-lay-nis-tace´*; from a derivative of 1672; a *Hellenist* or *Greek-speaking* Jew:—Grecian.

1676. ῾Ελληνιστί, Hellēnisti, *hel-lay-nis-tee´*; adverb from the same as 1675; *Hellenistically*, i.e. in the Grecian language:—Greek.

1677. ἐλλογέω, ellogeō, *el-log-eh´-o*; from 1722 and 3056 (in the sense of *account*); to *reckon in*, i.e. *attribute*:—impute, put on account.

From *en* (1722), in, and *lógos* (3056), word. To reckon in, to put to one's account (Phm 18). Metaphorically of sin: to impute (Ro 5:13).

Syn.: *logízomai* (3049), to reckon by calculation or imputation.

1678. ᾽Ελμωδάμ, Elmōdam, *el-mo-dam´*; of Hebrew origin [perhaps for 486]; *Elmodam*, an Israelite:—Elmodam.

1679. ἐλπίζω, elpizō, *el-pid´-zo*; from 1680; to *expect* or *confide*:—(have, thing) hope (-d) (for), trust.

From *elpís* (1680), hope. To hope, expect with desire (Lk 6:34; 23:8; Ac 26:7; Ro 15:24; 1Co 16:7; Php 2:19, 23; 1Ti 3:14; 2Jn 12; 3Jn 14); followed by the accusative of thing, to hope for (Ro 8:24, 25; 1Co 13:7). In the construction meaning to hope in someone, i.e. to trust in, confide in (Mt 12:21; Jn 5:45; Ro 15:12; 1Ti 6:17); spoken of those who put their trust in God (2Co 1:10; 1Ti 4:10; 5:5; 1Pe 3:5; Sept.: Ps 26:1; Isa 11:10); spoken of trusting in Christ (1Co 15:19; Sept.: 2Ki 18:5; Ps 33:21).

Deriv.: *apelpízō* (560), to bring to despair; *proelpízō* (4276), to hope before.

Syn.: *prosdokáō* (4328), to expect; *prosménō* (4357), to abide still, with an element of hope; *apekdéchomai* (553), to expect fully; *anaménō* (362), to wait for; *ekdéchomai* (1551), to await, expect, anticipate.

1680. ἐλπίς, elpis, *el-pece´*; from a primary ἔλπω, *elpō* (to *anticipate*, usually with pleasure); *expectation* (abstract or concrete) or *confidence*:—faith, hope.

A noun meaning hope, confident expectation of good:

(I) Generally (Ro 8:24; 2Co 10:15; Php 1:20). With a gen. of the thing hoped for (Ac 27:20). See Ac 16:19; 23:6, "of the hope and resurrection"; 26:6, 7. Of the person hoping (Ac 28:20; 2Co 1:7; Sept.: Job 14:7; 17:15; Isa 31:2; Eze 37:11). With *pará* (3844), against or in spite of, with the accusative *par' elpída*, against hope, i.e. without ground of hope (Ro 4:18). With *epí* (1909), upon, and the dat., *ep' elpídi*, literally on hope or in hope, i.e. with hope, full of hope and confidence (Ac 2:26; see Ro 4:18; 8:20; 1Co 9:10; Sept.: Ps 4:8; 16:9). By metonymy, spoken of the object of hope (Ro 8:24, "hope that is seen is not hope" [see *blépō* {991, I, B}, to see]). In 1Co 9:10 (TR), "should be partaker of his hope." See Sept.: Job 6:8.

(II) Spoken especially of those who experience the hope of salvation through Christ, eternal life, and blessedness (Ro 5:2, 4, 5; 12:12; 15:4, 13, "the God of hope," i.e. the author and source of hope, not the one who needs hope; see 1Co 13:13; 2Co 3:12; Eph 2:12; 4:4; 1Th 4:13; 5:8; 2Th 2:16; Tit 1:2; 3:7; Heb 3:6; 6:11; 10:23; 1Pe 1:3; 3:15). Followed by the gen. of the thing or person on which this hope rests (Eph 1:18; Col 1:23; 1Th 1:3). By metonymy, spoken of the object of this hope, i.e. salvation (Col 1:5). The hope or salvation resulting from justification by faith (Gal 5:5; see Tit 2:13; Heb 6:18; 7:19). By metonymy, also of the source, ground, author of hope, i.e. Christ (Col 1:27; 1Ti 1:1).

(III) Of a hope in or on someone, i.e. trust, confidence (Ac 24:15; 1Pe 1:21; 1Jn 3:3).

Deriv.: *elpízō* (1679), to trust, hope.

Syn.: *apokaradokía* (603), intense anticipation, earnest expectation; *ekdoché* (1561), expectation.

1681. Ἐλύμας, **Elumas**, *el-oo´-mas*; of foreign origin; *Elymas*, a wizard:—Elymas.

1682. ἐλοΐ, **eloï**, *el-o-ee´*; of Chaldee origin [426 with pronoun suffix]; *my God*:—Eloi.

1683. ἐμαυτοῦ, **emautou**, *em-ow-too´*; general compound of 1700 and 846; *of myself* (so likewise the dative ἐμαυτῷ, *emautōi*, *em-ow-to´*; and accusative ἐμαυτόν, *emauton*, *em-ow-ton´*):—me, mine own (self), myself.

1684. ἐμβαίνω, **embainō**, *em-ba´hee-no*; from 1722 and the base of 939; to *walk on*, i.e. *embark* (aboard a vessel), *reach* (a pool):—come (get) into, enter (into), go (up) into, step in, take ship.

1685. ἐμβάλλω, **emballō**, *em-bal´-lo*; from 1722 and 906; to *throw on*, i.e. (figurative) *subject to* (eternal punishment):—cast into.

1686. ἐμβάπτω, **embaptō**, *em-bap´-to*; from 1722 and 911; to *whelm on*, i.e. *wet* (a part of the person, etc.) by contact with a fluid:—dip.

1687. ἐμβατεύω, **embateuō**, *em-bat-yoo´-o*; from 1722 and a presumed derivative of the base of 939; equivalent to 1684; to *intrude on* (figurative):—intrude into.

1688. ἐμβιβάζω, **embibazō**, *em-bib-ad´-zo*; from 1722 and βιβάζω, *bibazō* (to *mount*; causative of 1684); to *place on*, i.e. *transfer* (aboard a vessel):—put in.

1689. ἐμβλέπω, **emblepō**, *em-blep´-o*; from 1722 and 991; to *look on*, i.e. (relative) to *observe* fixedly, or (absolute) to *discern* clearly:—behold, gaze up, look upon, (could) see.

1690. ἐμβριμάομαι, **embrimaomai**, *em-brim-ah´-om-ahee*; from 1722 and βριμάομαι, *brimaomai* (to *snort* with anger); to have *indignation on*, i.e. (transitive) to *blame*, (intransitive) to *sigh* with chagrin, (special) to sternly *enjoin*:—straitly charge, groan, murmur against.

1691. ἐμέ, **eme**, *em-eh´*; a prolonged form of 3165; *me*:—I, me, my (-self).

1692. ἐμέω, **emeō**, *em-eh´-o*; of uncertain affinity; to *vomit*:—(will) spue.

1693. ἐμμαίνομαι, **emmainomai**, *em-mah´ee-nom-ahee*; from 1722 and 3105; to *rave on*, i.e. *rage at*:—be mad against.

1694. Ἐμμανουήλ, **Emmanouēl**, *em-man-oo-ale´*; of Hebrew origin [6005]; *God with us*; *Emmanuel*, a name of Christ:—Emmanuel.

1695. Ἐμμαούς, **Emmaous**, *em-mah-ooce´*; probably of Hebrew origin [compare 3222]; *Emmaüs*, a place in Palestine:—Emmaus.

1696. ἐμμένω, **emmenō**, *em-men´-o*; from 1722 and 3306; to *stay in* the same place, i.e. (figurative) to *persevere*:—continue.

From *en* (1722), in, and *ménō* (3306), to remain. To remain, persevere in (Ac 14:22; Gal 3:10; Heb 8:9; Sept.: Dt 27:26).

Syn.: *epiménō* (1961), to continue in, metaphorically to persevere; *katartéō* (2594), to endure; *diaménō* (1265), to stay through, remain; *paraménō* (3887), to persevere; *diateléō* (1300), to persist, continue.

1697. Ἐμμόρ, **Emmor,** *em-mor´*; of Hebrew origin [2544]; *Emmor* (i.e. *Chamor*), a Canaanite:—Emmoral.

1698. ἐμοί, **emoi,** *em-oy´*; a prolonged form of 3427; *to me*:—I, me, mine, my.

1699. ἐμός, **emos,** *em-os´*; from the oblique cases of 1473 (1698, 1700, 1691); *my*:—of me, mine (own), my.

1700. ἐμοῦ, **emou,** *em-oo´*; a prolonged form of 3449; *of me*:—me, mine, my.

1701. ἐμπαιγμός, **empaigmos,** *emp-aheeg-mos´*; from 1702; *derision*:—mocking.

1702. ἐμπαίζω, **empaizō,** *emp-aheed´-zo*; from 1722 and 3815; to *jeer at*, i.e. *deride*:—mock.

1703. ἐμπαίκτης, **empaiktēs,** *emp-aheek-tace´*; from 1702; a *derider*, i.e. (by implication) a *false teacher*:—mocker, scoffer.

1704. ἐμπεριπατέω, **emperipateō,** *em-per-ee-pat-eh´-o*; from 1722 and 4043; to *perambulate on* a place, i.e. (figurative) to *be occupied among* persons:—walk in.

1705. ἐμπίπλημι, **empiplēmi,** *em-pip´-lay-mee*; or ἐμπλήθω, **emplēthō,** *em-play´-tho*; from 1722 and the base of 4118; to *fill in* (*up*), i.e. (by implication) to *satisfy* (literal or figurative):—fill.

1706. ἐμπίπτω, **empiptō,** *em-pip´-to*; from 1722 and 4098; to *fall on*, i.e. (literal) *be entrapped by*, or (figurative) *be overwhelmed with*:—fall among (into).

1707. ἐμπλέκω, **emplekō,** *em-plek´-o*; from 1722 and 4120; to *entwine*, i.e. (figurative) *involve* with:—entangle (in, self with).

1708. ἐμπλοκή, **emplokē,** *em-plok-ay´*; from 1707; elaborate *braiding* of the hair:—plaiting.

1709. ἐμπνέω, **empneō,** *emp-neh´-o*; from 1722 and 4154; to *inhale*, i.e. (figurative) to *be animated by* (*bent upon*):—breathe.

1710. ἐμπορεύομαι, **emporeuomai,** *em-por-yoo´-om-ahee*; from 1722 and 4198; to *travel in* (a country as a pedlar), i.e. (by implication) to *trade*:—buy and sell, make merchandise.

1711. ἐμπορία, **emporia,** *em-por-ee´-ah*; feminine from 1713; *traffic*:—merchandise.

1712. ἐμπόριον, **emporion,** *em-por´-ee-on*; neuter from 1713; a *mart* ("*emporium*"):—merchandise.

1713. ἔμπορος, **emporos,** *em´-por-os*; from 1722 and the base of 4198; a (wholesale) *tradesman*:—merchant.

1714. ἐμπρήθω, **emprēthō,** *em-pray´-tho*; from 1722 and πρήθω, *prēthō* (to *blow* a flame); to *enkindle*, i.e. *set on fire*:—burn up.

1715. ἔμπροσθεν, **emprosthen,** *em´-pros-then*; from 1722 and 4314; *in front of* (in place [literal or figurative] or time):—against, at, before, (in presence, sight) of.

1716. ἐμπτύω, **emptuō,** *em-too´-o*; from 1722 and 4429; to *spit at* or *on*:—spit (upon).

1717. ἐμφανής, **emphanēs,** *em-fan-ace´*; from a compound of 1722 and 5316; *apparent in* self:—manifest, openly.

1718. ἐμφανίζω, **emphanizō,** *em-fan-id´-zo*; from 1717; to *exhibit* (in person) or *disclose* (by words):—appear, declare (plainly), inform, (will) manifest, shew, signify.

1719. ἔμφοβος, **emphobos,** *em´-fob-os*; from 1722 and 5401; *in fear*, i.e. *alarmed*:—affrighted, afraid, tremble.

1720. ἐμφυσάω, **emphusaō,** *em-foo-sah´-o*; from 1722 and φυσάω, *phusaō* (to *puff*) [compare 5453]; to *blow at* or *on*:—breathe on.

1721. ἔμφυτος, **emphutos,** *em´-foo-tos*; from 1722 and a derivative of 5453; *implanted* (figurative):—engrafted.

1722. ἐν, **en,** *en*; a primary preposition denoting (fixed) *position* (in place, time or state), and (by implication) *instrumentality* (medially or constructively), i.e. a relation of *rest* (intermediate between 1519 and 1537); "*in*," at, (up-) *on*, *by*, etc.:—about, after, against, + almost, × altogether, among, × as, at, before, between, (here-) by (+ all means), for (… sake of), + give self wholly to, (here-) in (-to, -wardly), × mightily, (because) of, (up-) on, [open-] ly, × outwardly, one, × quickly, × shortly, [speedi-] ly, × that, × there (-in, -on), through (-out), (un-) to (-ward), under, when, where (-with), while, with (-in). Often used in compounds, with substantially the same import; rarely with verbs of motion, and then not to indicate direction, except (elliptically) by a separate (and different) preposition.

Preposition meaning in, on, at, by any place or thing, with the primary idea of rest. As compared with *eis* (1519), into or unto, and *ek* (1537), out of or from, it stands between the two; *eis* implies motion into, and *ek* motion out of, while *en* means remaining in place.

(I) Of place, which is the primary and most frequent use and spoken of everything which is conceived as being, remaining, taking place, meaning within some definite space or limits: in, on, at, by:

(A) Particularly with the meaning of in or within (Mt 4:21) as in a ship; in the synagogues (Mt 4:23); in the corners of the streets (Mt 6:5); at home (Mt 8:67); in the prison (Mt 11:2); in the market (Mt 11:16; Lk 7:32); in his field (Mt 13:24, 27); in the tomb (Mk 5:3; Jn 5:28; 11:17; 19:41); in a certain place (Lk 11:1); in their midst (Lk 22:5); in the temple (Ac 2:46); in the praetorium (Php 1:13). With the names of cities, countries, places (Mt 2:1, 5, 19; 3:1, 3; 4:13; 9:31; Ac 7:36; 9:36; 10:1; Ro 1:7; 1Th 1:7, 8). In hell (*Hádēs* [86]) (Lk 16:23 [cf. Mt 10:28; Rev 21:8]); in earth, in heaven (Mt 5:12; 6:10, 20; 16:19; Lk 15:7); your Father which is in heaven (Mt 5:45; 7:11 [cf. 18:35]); in the kingdom of heaven (Mt 5:19; 8:11); in the earth (Mt 25:18, 25; Jn 13:1; Ro 9:17; Col 1:6); in the sea (Mk 5:13; Mk 6:47; 2Co 11:25). Of a book, writing (Mk 12:26; Lk 2:23; 20:42; Jn 6:45; Ac 13:33; Ro 11:2, in the section respecting Elijah; Heb 4:5, 7; 5:6). Of the body and its parts (Mt 1:18, 23; 3:12; 7:3, 4; Lk 1:44; Ro 6:12; 2Co 12:2; 1Pe 2:22; Rev 6:5). Spoken of persons, particularly in one's body (Mt 1:20; Ac 19:16; 20:10; figuratively, Mt 6:23; Ro 7:17, 18, 20; 1Pe 2:22).

(B) Spoken of elevated objects, a surface, meaning in, i.e. on, upon, as a fig tree (Mk 11:13); a mountain (Lk 8:32; Jn 4:20; Heb 8:5;

Sept.: Ex 31:18); "engraven in stones" (2Co 3:7); "in my throne" (Rev 3:21); See Lk 12:51; Jn 20:25; Ac 7:33; Rev 13:12; 18:19. Figuratively, Jude 12.

(C) In a somewhat wider sense, simply implying contact, close proximity, meaning in, at, on, by, near, with, equivalent to *pará* (3844), near (Mt 6:5; 7:6, at or under the feet; Lk 13:4; 16:23; Jn 11:10; 15:4, remains on, attached to the vine; 19:41; Ac 2:19; Ro 8:34; Heb 1:3; 8:1; 10:12; Rev 9:10). (1) Of those with whom someone is in near connection, intimate union, oneness of heart, mind, purpose, especially of Christians, in union with Christ by faith and who are become as branches in the true vine (Jn 15:2, 4, 5; see Jn 6:56; 14:20; Ro 16:7, 11; 1Co 1:30; 9:1, 2; 2Co 5:17; Eph 2:13; 1Th 4:16, those who died in union with Christ by faith, as Christians [cf. 1Co 15:18; Rev 14:13]). Hence, those "in Christ" means Christians (2Co 12:2; Gal 1:22; 1Pe 5:14). Generally those in connection with Christ, in the Christian faith (Ro 12:5; Gal 3:28; 5:6; 6:15; Php 4:1; 1Th 3:8; 1Jn 2:24). Christ is in the believer and vice versa, in consequence of faith in Him (Jn 6:56; 14:20; 15:4, 5; 17:23, 26; Ro 8:9; Gal 2:20); of the believer's union with God (1Th 1:1; 1Jn 2:24; 3:6, 24; 4:13, 15, 16); of the mutual union of God and Christ (Jn 10:38; 14:10, 11, 20); of the Holy Spirit in Christians (Jn 14:17; Ro 8:9, 11; 1Co 3:16; 6:19). (2) Of those in, with, on whom, i.e. in whose person or character anything exists, is done (cf. *pará* [3844], near), e.g., in one's external life and conduct (Jn 18:38; 19:4, 6; Ac 24:20; 25:5; 1Co 4:2; 1Jn 2:10). Generally of any power, influence, efficiency, e.g., from God, the Spirit (Mt 14:2; Jn 1:4; 14:13, 30; 17:26; 1Co 12:6; 2Co 4:4, 12; 6:12; Gal 4:19; Php 2:5, 13; Col 1:19; Heb 13:21; 1Jn 3:9, 15); also *en heautō* ([1438], himself, in the dat.), meaning in, with, or of oneself (Mt 13:21; Jn 5:26; 6:53; 2Co 1:9). (3) Of those in or with whom, i.e. in whose mind, heart, soul, anything exists or takes place (cf. *pará* [3844], near) as virtues, vices, faculties (Jn 1:47; 4:14, meaning in his soul; 17:13; Ro 7:8; 1Co 2:11; 8:7; 2Co 11:10; Eph 4:18). "Your life is hid with Christ in God" (Col 3:3) means in the mind and counsels of God. See Eph 3:9. The expression *en heautō, en heautoís*, in or with oneself or themselves, means in one's heart (Mt 3:9; Lk 7:39, 49; Ro 8:23; Jas 2:4).

(D) Of a number or multitude, as indicating place, meaning in, among, with, equivalent to *en mésō* (3319), in the midst (Mt 2:6). With the same meaning of among (Mt 11:11, 21; 20:27; Mk 10:43; Lk 1:1; Jn 1:14; 11:54; Ac 2:29; 20:32; Ro 1:5, 6; 1Co 11:18; Eph 5:3; 1Pe 5:1, 2; 2Pe 2:8). Also in the dat. plural *en heautoís* (1438), in themselves, meaning among themselves (Mt 9:3; 21:38; Ac 28:29); *en allḗlois* (240), one another, meaning with one another (Mk 9:50; Jn 13:35; Ro 15:5). With the dat. sing. of a coll. noun (Lk 1:61; 2:44; 4:25, 27, "in Israel"; Jn 7:43; Ac 10:35; Eph 3:21; 2Pe 2:1; Sept.: Ge 23:6; Le 16:29; 2Ki 18:5). Hence with dat. plural of person by whom one is accompanied, escorted (Lk 14:31; Jude 14; Sept.: Nu 20:19). With the dat. plural of thing (1Co 15:3, adverb, "first of all," among the first).

(**E**) Of persons, by implication meaning before, in the presence of (Mk 8:38; Lk 1:25; Ac 6:8; 24:21, as before judges; 1Co 2:6; 2Co 10:1). Figuratively (Lk 4:21 [cf. Sept.: Dt 5:1]), hence metaphorically, meaning in the sight of someone, he being judge (Lk 16:15, "in the sight of," or judgement of men; 1Co 14:11; Col 3:20). Also, by Hebraism, *en ophthalmoís humṓn* (see *ophthalmós* [3788], eye; *humṓn* [5216], of you), meaning before your eyes, i.e. in your judgement (Mt 21:42; Mk 12:11; Sept.: Ps 118:23).

(**F**) Spoken of that by which one is surrounded or enveloped, meaning in, with (Mt 16:27; 25:31; Mk 13:26; Lk 21:27; Ac 7:30); of clothing (Mt 7:15; 11:8; Mk 12:38; Heb 11:37; Jas 2:2); ornaments (1Ti 2:9); bonds (Eph 6:20). Also *en sarkí* (4561), flesh, meaning in the flesh, clothed in flesh, in the body (1Jn 4:2; 2Jn 7); to live in the flesh (Gal 2:20; Php 1:22; Sept.: Dt 22:12; Ps 147:8). Hence of that with which one is furnished, which he carries with him (1Co 4:21; Heb 9:25). Metaphorically (Lk 1:17; Ro 15:29; Eph 6:2; Sept.: Jos 22:8; 1Sa 1:24; Ps 66:13).

(**II**) Of time:

(**A**) When, i.e. a definite point or period in, during, on, at which anything takes place (Mt 2:1; 3:1; 8:13; 12:1, 2; Ac 20:7; 1Co 11:23; Jn 11:9, 10, by day, by night). With a neuter adj. (Ac 7:13; 2Co 11:6; Php 4:6). With a pron. used in an absolute sense, *en hṓ* (3739), in which, in the dat. sing. implying *chrónō*, the dat. sing. of *chrónos* (5550), time (Mk 2:19; Jn 5:7). With the article and adverb (Lk 7:11; 8:1; Jn 4:31). Spoken of an action or event which serves to mark a definite time (Mt 22:28; Lk 11:31, 32; Jn 21:20; 1Co 15:52; 2Th 1:7; 1Jn 2:28). With *en hoís* (see *hós*

[3739], which) implying *prágmasi* (*prágma* [4229], affair, matter, thing), meaning during which things, meanwhile (Lk 12:1). Especially with the dat. article and inf., *en* is used to mean on or at an action or event, while it is taking place (Lk 1:8; 2:6; 5:1; 9:36; 24:51; Ac 8:6; Sept.: 1Sa 1:7).

(**B**) Meaning how long a space or period which anything takes place in or within, such as within or in three days (Mt 27:40; Mk 15:29; Sept.: Isa 16:14).

(**III**) Figuratively of the state, condition or manner in which one is, moves, acts; of the ground, occasion, means, on, in, by, or through which one is affected, moved, acted upon:

(**A**) Of the state, condition, or circumstances in which a person or thing is: (**1**) Generally, of an external state (Lk 2:29; 8:43; 11:21 [cf. Lk 16:23; 23:12, 40; Ro 1:4; 8:37; 1Co 7:18, 20, 24; 15:42, 43; 2Co 6:4, 5; Gal 1:14; Php 2:7]; 2Th 3:16, in every state, at every turn; 1Ti 2:2); of an internal state of the mind or feelings (Ac 11:5; Ro 15:32; 1Co 1:10; 2:3; 14:6, in the state or condition of one who receives and utters a revelation; 2Co 11:17, 21; Eph 3:12; 5:21; 1Th 2:17; 1Ti 1:13; 2:11; Heb 3:11; Jas 1:21; 2:1; Jude 24). In this usage *en* with its dat. is often equivalent to an adj. (Ro 4:10; 2Co 3:7, 8; Php 4:19; 1Ti 2:7, 12, 14; Tit 1:6; 3:5); an adverb (Ac 5:23; Ro 2:28, 29; Eph 6:24). (**2**) Of the business, employment or actions in which one is engaged (Mt 20:15, *en toís emoís*, lit. "in my own things, affairs"; 21:22; 22:15; 23:30; Mk 4:2; 8:27; Lk 16:10; 24:35; Jn 8:3; Ac 6:1; 24:16; Ro 1:9, "labouring in the gospel" [a.t.]; 14:18; 1Co 15:58; 2Co 7:11; Col 1:10; 4:2; 1Ti 4:15; 5:17; Heb 6:18; 11:34; Jas 1:8; 4:3). Also with the dat. of person, meaning in the work, business, cause of someone (Ro 16:12; 1Co 4:17; Eph 6:21). (**3**) Implying in the power of someone (Ac 4:12; 5:4 [cf. 1:7; Jn 3:35]); in the power or under the influence of the Spirit (*en pneúmati*, the dat. sing. of *pneúma* [4151], spirit) in Mt 12:28; 22:43; Mk 12:36; Lk 2:27; 4:1; 1Co 12:3; Rev 1:10; 4:2; 17:3; of demoniacs, *en pneúmati akathártō* (dat. sing. of *akáthartos* [169], unclean), in the power of or possessed by an unclean spirit (Mk 1:23; 5:2); of one's sound mind, *genómenos en heautō̂* (*gínomai* [1096], to become; *heautō̂* [1438] in the dat. sing., himself), having come to himself (Ac 12:11).

(B) Of manner or mode, i.e. the external or internal state or circumstances by which any action is accompanied, in, with or in reference to which it is performed: **(1)** Generally of manner (cf. *ek* [1537, III, E]; Mt 22:37, quoted from Dt 6:5; Mk 4:2; Lk 2:36; 21:25; Jn 16:25; Ac 2:46; 10:48 [cf. *baptízō* {907, III}; Ro 1:9; 9:22; 15:6; 1Co 2:4, 7; 14:21; 2Co 3:7; Col 3:22; 1Pe 2:24; 2Pe 2:3; 1Jn 5:6]). In an adverb sense (Mt 22:16, *en alētheía didáskeis*, lit. "in truth you teach," i.e. you teach truly; Mk 9:1; Ac 12:7; 22:18; Eph 6:19, *en parrēsía*, lit. "with/in boldness," i.e. boldly; Col 4:5; Rev 18:2; 19:11). **(2)** Of a rule, law, standard, in, by, according to, conformable to (Mt 7:2; Lk 1:8; 1Co 15:23; Php 1:8; 1Th 4:15; 1Ti 1:18; Heb 4:11). Of a rule of life (Lk 1:6). With the dat. of person (2Co 10:12). In conformity with the will, law or precept of someone (Jn 3:21; 1Co 7:39; Eph 6:1). **(3)** In the sense meaning in respect to, as to (Lk 1:7, 18; Eph 2:11; Tit 1:13; Jas 2:10; 3:2). Also *en pantí* (dat. sing. of *pás* [3956], all), in every respect (2Co 8:7; 9:8, 11); *en mēdení* (dat. sing. of *mēdén*, the neuter of *mēdeís* [3367], no one) meaning in no respect (2Co 7:9; Jas 1:4); and *en oudení* (dat. sing. of *oudén*, the neuter of *oudeís* [3762], no one), in a more absolute way, meaning in no way or respect (Php 1:20). After words meaning plenty or want (Ro 15:13; 1Co 1:5, 7; 2Co 3:9; 8:7; Eph 2:4; Col 2:7; 1Ti 6:18).

(C) Of the ground, basis, occasion, in, on or upon which anything rests, exists, takes place. **(1)** Of a person or thing (1Co 2:5, *en sophía anthrópōn*, "in the wisdom of men"; 2Co 4:10; Gal 4:14; Eph 2:11); in the person or case of someone: in or by his example (Lk 22:37; Jn 9:3; Ac 4:2; Ro 9:17; 1Co 4:6; 2Co 4:3; Eph 1:20; Php 1:30). After verbs implying to do anything in one's case, i.e. to or for one where the accusative or dat. might stand (Mt 17:12; Lk 23:31; 1Co 9:15; 1Th 5:12, for your benefit). With the verb *homologéō* (3670), to confess, followed by *en* and the dat. means to confess in one's case or cause, to acknowledge (Mt 10:32; Lk 12:8). With the verb *skandalízomai* (4624), to be offended, followed by *en* and the dat. sing. meaning to take offence in someone, in his case or cause (Mt 11:6; 13:57; 26:31, 33). Spoken of that in which anything consists, is comprised, fulfilled, manifested (Jn 9:30; Ro 13:9; Gal 5:14; Eph 2:7; 5:9; Heb 3:12; 1Pe 3:4; 1Jn 3:10; 4:9, 10, 17). After verbs of swearing, to mark the

ground, basis, or object on which the oath rests, expressed in Eng. as "by," or "upon" (Mt 5:34–36; 23:16, 18, 20; Rev 10:6; Sept.: 1Sa 24:22; 2Sa 19:7; 1Ki 2:8). **(2)** Of the ground, motive or exciting cause in consequence of which any action is performed, in, on, at, by, i.e. because of, on account of (Mt 6:7; Ac 7:29; 1Co 11:22; 2Co 6:12; 1Pe 4:14, 16 [cf. Mk 9:41; Sept.: 2Ch 16:7]). *En toútō*, sing. dat. of *toúto* (5124), this, meaning herein, hereby, on this account, therefore (Jn 15:8; 16:30; Ac 24:16; 1Co 4:4, to know herein, hereby, by this. See Jn 13:35; 1Jn 2:3, 5). When the relative pron. *en hō̂* is used, it is equivalent to *en toútō* followed by *hóti* (3754), that, meaning herein that, in that, because (Ro 8:3; Heb 2:18; 6:17, wherefore; 1Pe 2:12). In this sense, *en* does not occur with the dat. of person. Spoken also of the authority in consequence of which anything is done, in, by, under, i.e. by virtue of (Mt 21:9; Lk 20:2; Jn 5:43; 10:25; 12:13; 14:26; Ac 4:7; 1Co 5:4; 2Th 3:6). **(3)** Of the ground or occasion of an emotion of mind, after words expressing joy, wonder, hope, confidence, and the reverse. With the dat. of thing (Mt 12:21; Mk 1:15; Lk 10:20; Ac 7:41; Ro 2:23; Eph 3:13; Php 3:3, 4; Sept.: Ps 33:21; Jer 48:7); of person (Ro 5:11; 1Co 15:19; 2Co 7:16; Eph 1:12; 1Ti 6:17; Sept.: 2Ki 18:5; Hos 10:13).

(D) Of the means, by the aid or intervention of which anything takes place, is done, meaning in, by means of. **(1)** With the dat. of person, by whose aid or intervention, in, by, with, through whom, anything is done (Mt 9:34; Ac 4:9; 17:28, 31; 1Co 15:22; Gal 3:8, lit. "shall be blessed in you all nations," i.e. in and through you [cf. Ac 3:25; Heb 1:1; 1Jn 5:11]). **(2)** With the dat. of thing, but used strictly only of such means as imply that the obj. affected is actually in, among, surrounded by them, particularly in and through (Mt 8:32, "in [and by] the waters"; 1Co 3:13; Rev 14:10; 16:8; Sept.: Le 8:32). Hence generally where the obj. is conceived as being in or in contact or connection with the means (Mt 3:11, "baptize you in water" [a.t.]; 5:13; 17:21; 25:16; Lk 21:34; Ac 7:35, in or "by the hand" of someone; 11:14; 20:19; Ro 10:5, 9; 12:21; 1Co 6:20; Gal 3:19; Heb 10:29; 13:20; Rev 1:5; Sept.: Nu 36:2; Jgs 16:7; Job 18:8). Hence in the NT and later writers, simply of the instrument, where Class. Gr. writers usually use the dat. alone (Lk 22:49; Ro 16:16; Jas 3:9; Rev 6:8; 12:5; 13:10; Sept.: Ge 48:22; Dt 15:19; Jer 14:12; Hos

1:7). **(3)** Spoken of price or exchange, of that by means by which or with which anything is purchased or exchanged (Ro 1:23, "exchanged the glory of God for [*en*] an image," 25; Rev 5:9; Sept.: 1Sa 24:20; Ecc 4:9; La 5:4).

(IV) Sometimes *en* with the dat. is where the natural construction would seem to require *eis* (1519), unto, into, with the accusative as after verbs which imply, not rest in a place or state, but motion or direction into or toward an object. In such cases, the idea of arrival and subsequent rest in that place or state is either actually expressed or is implied in the context. See the converse of this in *eis* (1519, V). After verbs of motion (Mt 10:16, "in the midst of wolves," by whom you are already surrounded; 14:3, to put in prison or into prison; Mk 1:16; 15:46 [cf. Lk 23:53, they placed him in the tomb]; Lk 5:16, He withdrew and abode in deserts; 7:17, went out, spread abroad, in the whole land; Jn 3:35; 5:4; Rev 11:12; Sept.: Jgs 6:35; Ezr 7:10). Metaphorically, after words expressing an affection of mind toward someone (2Co 8:7; 1Jn 4:9, 16); wrath upon the people (Lk 21:23 [{TR} cf. Sept.: 2Sa 24:17]).

In composition *en* implies: **(a)** A being or resting in, as *éneimi* (1751), to be within; *emménō* (1696), to stay in the same place, persevere; **(b)** Into, when compounded with verbs of motion, as *embaínō* (1684), to walk on, embark, come into, step in; **(c)** Conformity, as *éndikos* (1738), equitable, just; *énnomos* (1772), lawful; **(d)** Participation, as *énochos* (1777), guilty of.

1723. ἐναγκαλίζομαι, **enagkalizomai,** *en-ang-kal-id´-zom-ahee*; from 1722 and a derivative of 43; to *take in* one's *arms*, i.e. *embrace*:—take up in arms.

1724. ἐνάλιος, **enalios,** *en-al´-ee-os*; from 1722 and 251; *in the sea*, i.e. *marine*:—thing in the sea.

1725. ἔναντι, **enanti,** *en´-an-tee*; from 1722 and 473; *in front* (i.e. figurative, *presence*) *of*:—before.

1726. ἐναντίον, **enantion,** *en-an-tee´-on*; neuter of 1727; (adverb) *in the presence* (*view*) *of*:—before, in the presence of.

1727. ἐναντίος, **enantios,** *en-an-tee´-os*; from 1725; *opposite*; (figurative) *antagonistic*:—(over) against, contrary.

1728. ἐνάρχομαι, **enarchomai,** *en-ar´-khom-ahee*; from 1722 and 756; to *commence on*:—rule [*by mistake* for 757].

1729. ἐνδεής, **endeēs,** *en-deh-ace´*; from a compound of 1722 and 1210 (in the sense of *lacking*); *deficient in*:—lacking.

1730. ἔνδειγμα, **endeigma,** *en´-dighe-mah*; from 1731; an *indication* (concrete):—manifest token.

1731. ἐνδείκνυμι, **endeiknumi,** *en-dike´-noo-mee*; from 1722 and 1166; to *indicate* (by word or act):—do, show (forth).

1732. ἔνδειξις, **endeixis,** *en´-dike-sis*; from 1731; *indication* (abstract):—declare, evident token, proof.

1733. ἔνδεκα, **hendeka,** *hen´-dek-ah*; from (the neuter of) 1520 and 1176; *one* and *ten*, i.e. *eleven*:—eleven.

1734. ἐνδέκατος, **hendekatos,** *hen-dek´-at-os*; order from 1733; *eleventh*:—eleventh.

1735. ἐνδέχεται, **endechetai,** *en-dekh´-et-ahee*; third person singular presumed of a compound of 1722 and 1209; (impersonally) *it is accepted in*, i.e. *admitted* (*possible*):—can (+ not) be.

From the prep. *en* (1722), in, upon, and *déchomai* (1209), to receive. As an impersonal verb *endéchetai*, used with the neg., it is not possible, it may not be (Lk 13:33).

Deriv.: *anéndektos* (418), impossible.

Syn.: *dúnamai* (1410), to be able; *ischúō* (2480), to be strong.

1736. ἐνδημέω, **endēmeō,** *en-day-meh´-o*; from a compound of 1722 and 1218; to *be in* one's own *country*, i.e. *home* (figurative):—be at home (present).

1737. ἐνδιδύσκω, **endiduskō,** *en-did-oos´-ko*; a prolonged form of 1746; to *invest* (with a garment):—clothe in, wear.

1738. ἔνδικος, **endikos,** *en´-dee-kos*; from 1722 and 1349; *in the right*, i.e. *equitable*:—just.

Adjective from *en* (1722), in, and *díkē* (1349), justice. Conformable to right, i.e. right, just (Heb 2:2). In Ro 3:8, *éndikon* presupposes that which has been decided justly.

Syn.: *díkaios* (1342), just; *dikaíōs* (1346), justly, is that which leads to the just sentence.

1739. ἐνδόμησις, endomēsis, *en-dom´-ay-sis*; from a compound of 1722 and a derivative of the base of 1218; a *housing in* (*residence*), i.e. *structure:*—building.

1740. ἐνδοξάζω, endoxazō, *en-dox-ad´-zo*; from 1741; to *glorify:*—glorify.

From *éndoxos* (1741), glorious. To glorify. Used only in 2Th 1:10, 12.

Syn.: *megalúnō* (3170), to make great; *peripoiéomai* (4046), to make something of oneself.

1741. ἔνδοξος, endoxos, *en´-dox-os*; from 1722 and 1391; *in glory,* i.e. *splendid,* (figurative) *noble:*—glorious, gorgeous [-ly], honourable.

Adjective from *en* (1722), in, and *dóxa* (1391), glory. Glorious, splendid:

(I) Of persons: honored, respected, noble (1Co 4:10; Sept.: 1Sa 9:6; Isa 23:8). Of deeds, in the neuter plural *tá éndoxa,* glorious, memorable (Lk 13:17; Sept.: Ex 34:10; Job 5:9; Isa 12:4).

(II) Of external appearance: splendid, glorious, as of raiment (Lk 7:25; Sept.: 2Ch 2:9; Isa 22:17; 23:9). Metaphorically: a glorious Church, signifying the Church adorned in pure and splendid raiment as a bride (Eph 5:27 [cf. Eph 5:25, as well as Rev 19:7, 8; 21:9]).

Deriv.: *endoxázō* (1740), to glorify.

Syn.: *tá éndoxa* implying glorious things, miracles, unusual acts; *sēmeía* (4592), signs; *dunámeis* (1411), mighty works; *megaleía* (3167), great works; *parádoxa* (3861), strange works; *thaumásia* (2297), admirable works; *tímios* (5093), precious, valuable, honourable; *éntimos* (1784), honourable; *euschémōn* (2158), comely, honourable; *kalós* (2570), good; *semnós* (4586), honourable, grave, modest.

1742. ἔνδυμα, enduma, *en´-doo-mah*; from 1746; *apparel* (especially the outer *robe*):—clothing, garment, raiment.

1743. ἐνδυναμόω, endunamoō, *en-doo-nam-o´-o*; from 1722 and 1412; to *empower:*—enable, (increase in) strength (-en), be (make) strong.

From *en* (1722), in, and *dunamóō* (1412), to strengthen. Found only in biblical and ecclesiastical Gr. meaning to make strong, vigorous, to strengthen. Used in the pass., to be strengthened, become strong. Of the body, as made strong out of weakness (Heb 11:34 [TR]). Metaphorically, of the mind (Ac 9:22; Ro 4:20; Eph 6:10; Php 4:13; 1Ti 1:12; 2Ti 2:1; 4:17; Sept.: Ps 52:9).

Syn.: *ischúō* (2480), to strengthen, enable; *enischúō* (1765), to strengthen fully; *epischúō* (2001), to make strong; *krataióō* (2901), to strengthen with the implied meaning of to establish; *sthenóō* (4599), to strengthen; *stērízō* (4741), to establish; *epistērízō* (1991), to confirm, establish; *stereóō* (4732), to make stable.

1744. ἐνδύνω, endunō, *en-doo´-no*; from 1772 and 1416; to *sink* (by implication, *wrap* [compare 1746] *on,* i.e. (figurative) *sneak:*—creep.

1745. ἔνδυσις, endusis, *en´-doo-sis*; from 1746; *investment* with clothing:—putting on.

1746. ἐνδύω, enduō, *en-doo´-o*; from 1722 and 1416 (in the sense of *sinking* into a garment); to *invest* with clothing (literal or figurative):—array, clothe (with), endue, have (put) on.

1747. ἐνέδρα, enedra, *en-ed´-rah*; feminine from 1722 and the base of 1476; an *ambuscade,* i.e. (figurative) murderous *purpose:*—lay wait. See also 1749.

1748. ἐνεδρεύω, enedreuō, *en-ed-ryoo´-o*; from 1747; to *lurk,* i.e. (figurative) *plot* assassination:—lay wait for.

1749. ἔνεδρον, enedron, *en´-ed-ron*; neuter of the same as 1747; an *ambush,* i.e. (figurative) murderous *design:*—lying in wait.

1750. ἐνειλέω, eneileō, *en-i-leh´-o*; from 1772 and the base of 1507; to *enwrap:*—wrap in.

1751. ἔνειμι, eneimi, *en´-i-mee*; from 1772 and 1510; to *be within* (neuter participle plural):—such things as … have. See also 1762.

1752. ἕνεκα, heneka, *hen´-ek-ah*; or **ἕνεκεν, heneken,** *hen´-ek-en*; or **εἵνεκεν, heineken,** *hi´-nek-en*; of uncertain affinity; *on account of:*—because, for (cause, sake), (where-) fore, by reason of, that.

1753. ἐνέργεια, energeia, *en-erg´-i-ah*; from 1756; *efficiency* ("energy"):—operation, strong, (effectual) working.

1754. ἐνεργέω, energeō, *en-erg-eh´-o*; from 1756; to *be active, efficient:*—do, (be) effectual (fervent), be mighty in, shew forth self, work (effectually in).

From *energés* (1756), in work, operative, active. To be at work, to be effective, operative:

(I) To work, be active, produce an effect, spoken of things (Mt 14:2; Mk 6:14, "mighty works do show forth themselves in him"; see Eph 1:20; 2:2; Php 2:13); of persons (Gal 2:8, "he that wrought effectually in Peter."

(II) Transitively: to work, to effect, produce, spoken of persons (1Co 12:6, "which worketh all"; see 1Co 12:11; Gal 3:5; Eph 1:11; Php 2:13; Sept.: Pr 21:6; Isa 41:4).

(III) Middle: to show activity, i.e. to work, be active, operate, spoken only of things (Ro 7:5; 2Co 1:6; 4:12; Gal 5:6; Eph 3:20; Col 1:29; 1Th 2:13; 2Th 2:7). In the part. *energoumené* as adj., working, effective (Jas 5:16, "an effective supplication" [a.t.]).

Deriv.: *enérgēma* (1755), operation, working, an effect.

Syn.: *ergázomai* (2038), work; *katergázomai* (2716), to achieve, effect by toil; *douleúō* (1398), work; *poiéō* (4160), to do; *dunatéō* (1414), to be powerful, be able; *ischúō* (2480), to prevail, able to do; *epiteléō* (2005), accomplish, perform; *prássō* (4238), to execute, accomplish; *kámnō* (2577), to toil.

1755. ἐνέργημα, energēma, *en-erg´-ay-mah*; from 1754; an *effect:*—operation, working.

Noun from *energéō* (1754), to effect. Effect produced, operation. In the NT, used only in 1Co 12:6, 10 of the results of the energy of God in the believer. Though *enérgēma* is translated "operation," it is actually the results energized by God's grace.

1756. ἐνεργής, energēs, *en-er-gace´*; from 1722 and 2041; *active, operative:*—effectual, powerful.

Adjective from *en* (1722), in, and *érgon* (2041), work. Working, operative, active, effective (1Co 16:9; Phm 6; Heb 4:12).

Deriv.: *enérgeia* (1753), operation, working; *energéō* (1754), to be active, efficient.

1757. ἐνευλογέω, eneulogeō, *en-yoo-log-eh´-o*; from 1722 and 2127; to *confer a benefit on:*—bless.

1758. ἐνέχω, enechō, *en-ekh´-o*; from 1722 and 2192; to *hold in* or *upon*, i.e. *ensnare*; (by implication) to *keep a grudge:*—entangle with, have a quarrel against, urge.

From *en* (1722), in or upon, and *échō* (2192), to have. To have in oneself, implying a disposition of mind toward a person or thing, either favourable or unfavourable (Mk 6:19; Lk 11:53). In the pass.: to be held in or by something; figuratively, to be entangled in, subject to (Gal 5:1).

Deriv.: *énochos* (1777), to be held fast, bound, obliged.

Syn.: *pagideúō* (3802), to ensnare; *emplékō* (1707), to entangle.

1759. ἐνθάδε, enthade, *en-thad´-eh*; from a prolonged form of 1722; properly *within*, i.e. (of place) *here, hither:*—(t-) here, hither.

1760. ἐνθυμέομαι, enthumeomai, *en-thoo-meh´-om-ahee*; from a compound of 1722 and 2372; to *be inspirited*, i.e. *ponder:*—think.

1761. ἐνθύμησις, enthumēsis, *en-thoo´-may-sis*; from 1760; *deliberation:*—device, thought.

1762. ἔνι, eni, *en´-ee*; contracted from third person singular presumed indicative of 1751; impersonal *there is* in or among:—be, (there) is.

1763. ἐνιαυτός, eniautos, *en-ee-ow-tos´*; prolonged from a primary ἔνος, *enos* (a *year*); a *year:*—year.

1764. ἐνίστημι, enistēmi, *en-is´-tay-mee*; from 1722 and 2476; to *place on* hand, i.e. (reflexive) *impend*, (participle) be *instant:*—come, be at hand, present.

From *en* (1722), in, with, and *hístēmi* (2476), to stand. In the NT, used metaphorically: to stand near, i.e. to be at hand, to impend (2Th 2:2; 2Ti 3:1). Instant, present (Ro 8:38; 1Co 3:22; 7:26; Gal 1:4; Heb 9:9).

Syn.: *hḗkō* (2240), to come, be present; *ephístēmi* (2186), to arrive; *parístēmi* (3936), to be near at hand; *proseggízō* (4331), to come near; *páreimi* (3918), to be near.

1765. ἐνισχύω, enischuō, *en-is-khoo´-o*; from 1722 and 2480; to *invigorate* (transitive or reflexive):—strengthen.

1766. ἔννατος, ennatos, *en´-nat-os*; order from 1767; *ninth*:—ninth.

1767. ἐννέα, ennea, *en-neh´-ah*; a primary number; *nine*:—nine.

1768. ἐννενηκονταεννέα, ennenēkontaennea, *en-nen-ay-kon-tah-en-neh´-ah*; from a (tenth) multiple of 1767 and 1767 itself; *ninety-nine*:—ninety and nine.

1769. ἐννεός, enneos, *en-neh-os´*; from 1770; *dumb* (as *making signs*), i.e. *silent* from astonishment:—speechless.

1770. ἐννεύω, enneuō, *en-nyoo´-o*; from 1722 and 3506; to *nod at*, i.e. *beckon* or *communicate by gesture*:—make signs.

1771. ἔννοια, ennoia, *en´-noy-ah*; from a compound of 1722 and 3563; *thoughtfulness*, i.e. moral *understanding*:—intent, mind.

Noun from *en* (1722), in, and *noús* (3563), mind. What is in the mind, e.g., idea, notion, intention, purpose (Heb 4:12; 1Pe 4:1; Sept.: Pr 3:21 [cf. Pr 23:19]).

Syn.: *lógos* (3056), reason, cause, intent; *aitía* (156), cause; *aítion* (158), fault; *enthúmēsis* (1761), device, thought; *epínoia* (1963), a thought by way of design; *nóēma* (3540), a purpose, a device of the mind; *dianóēma* (1270), a thought, machination; *logismós* (3053), imagination; *dialogismós* (1261), reasoning.

1772. ἔννομος, ennomos, *en´-nom-os*; from 1722 and 3551; (subject) *legal*, or (object) *subject to*:—lawful, under law.

Adjective from *en* (1722), in, and *nómos* (3551), law. What is within range of law or conformable to law. Legal, legitimate (Ac 19:39); subject to law (1Co 9:21).

Syn.: *éndikos* (1738), equitable, just.

1773. ἔννυχον, ennuchon, *en´-noo-khon*; neuter of a compound of 1722 and 3571; (adverb) *by night*:—before day.

1774. ἐνοικέω, enoikeō, *en-oy-keh´-o*; from 1722 and 3611; to *inhabit* (figurative):—dwell in.

1775. ἑνότης, henotēs, *hen-ot´-ace*; from 1520; *oneness*, i.e. (figurative) *unanimity*:—unity.

1776. ἐνοχλέω, enochleō, *en-okh-leh´-o*; from 1722 and 3791; to *crowd in*, i.e. (figurative) to *annoy*:—trouble.

1777. ἔνοχος, enochos, *en´-okh-os*; from 1758; *liable* to (a condition, penalty or imputation):—in danger of, guilty of, subject to.

1778. ἔνταλμα, entalma, *en´-tal-mah*; from 1781; an *injunction*, i.e. religious *precept*:—commandment.

Noun from *entéllomai* (1781), to charge, command. A mandate, precept, ordinance (Mt 15:9; Mk 7:7; Col 2:22; Sept.: Job 23:11, 12; Isa 29:13).

Syn.: *diátagma* (1297), that which is imposed by decree or law; *diatagē* (1296), a decree; *epitagē* (2003), command; *paraggelía* (3852), a proclamation, charge; *nómos* (3851), law.

1779. ἐνταφιάζω, entaphiazō, *en-taf-ee-ad´-zo*; from a compound of 1722 and 5028; to *inswathe* with cerements for interment:—bury.

1780. ἐνταφιασμός, entaphiasmos, *en-taf-ee-as-mos´*; from 1779; *preparation* for interment:—burying.

1781. ἐντέλλομαι, entellomai, *en-tel´-lom-ahee*; from 1722 and the base of 5056; to *enjoin*:—(give) charge, (give) command (-ments), injoin.

1782. ἐντεῦθεν, enteuthen, *ent-yoo´-then*; from the same as 1759; *hence* (literal or figurative); (repeated) *on both sides*:—(from) hence, on either side.

1783. ἔντευξις, enteuxis, *ent´-yook-sis*; from 1793; an *interview*, i.e. (special) *supplication*:—intercession, prayer.

Noun from *entugchánō* (1793), to chance upon, to entreat. A falling in with, meeting with, coming together. In the NT, intercession, prayer (1Ti 2:1; 4:5, prayer according to God's will).

1784. ἔντιμος, entimos, *en´-tee-mos*; from 1722 and 5092; *valued* (figurative):—dear, more honourable, precious, in reputation.

1785. ἐντολή, entolē, *en-tol-ay´*; from 1781; *injunction*, i.e. an authoritative *prescription*:—commandment, precept.

Noun from *entéllomai* (1781), to charge, command. Commandment, whether of God or man:

(**I**) Charge, commission, direction (Jn 10:18; 12:49, 50; Ac 17:15; Col 4:10; Heb 7:5; Sept.: 2Ki 18:36; 2Ch 8:15). With the meaning of a public charge or edict from magistrates (Jn 11:57; Sept.: 2Ch 35:16).

(**II**) In the sense of precept, commandment, law as spoken of:

(**A**) The traditions of the rabbis (Tit 1:14).

(**B**) The precepts and teachings of Jesus (Jn 13:34; 15:12; 1Co 14:37; 1Jn 2:8).

(**C**) The precepts and commandments of God in general (1Co 7:19; 1Jn 3:22, 23; Sept.: Dt 4:2, 40).

(**D**) The precepts of the Mosaic Law, in whole or in part (Mt 5:19; 19:17; 22:36, 38, 40; Mk 10:5, 19; Ro 7:8–13).

(**E**) Generally and collectively, *hē entolé* or *hē entolé Theoú*, the commandment of God, used either for the Mosaic Law (Mt 15:3, 6; Mk 7:8, 9; Lk 23:56; Sept.: 2Ki 21:8; 2Ch 12:1) or for the precepts given to Christians, Christian doctrines and duties (1Ti 6:14; 2Pe 2:21; 3:2). **Syn.**: *prostássō* (4367), to charge; *éntalma* (1778), a religious commandment; *diátagma*, (1297), edict, decree; *diatagḗ* (1296), ordinance, disposition; *epitagḗ* (2003), commanding authority, order, command; *paraggelía* (3852), charge.

1786. ἐντόπιος, **entopios**, *en-top´-ee-os*; from 1722 and 5117; a *resident:*—of that place.

1787. ἐντός, **entos**, *en-tos´*; from 1722; *inside* (adverb or noun):—within.

1788. ἐντρέπω, **entrepō**, *en-trep´-o*; from 1722 and the base of 5157; to *invert*, i.e. (figurative and reflexive) in a good sense, to *respect*; or in a bad one, to *confound:*—regard, (give) reverence, shame.

1789. ἐντρέφω, **entrephō**, *en-tref´-o*; from 1722 and 5142; (figurative) to *educate:*—nourish up in.

1790. ἔντρομος, **entromos**, *en´-trom-os*; from 1722 and 5156; *terrified:*— × quake, × trembled.

1791. ἐντροπή, **entropē**, *en-trop-ay´*; from 1788; *confusion:*—shame.

Noun from *entrépō* (1788), to withdraw. Shame, a putting to shame (1Co 6:5; 15:34; Sept.: Ps 35:26; 69:8, 20).

Syn.: *óneidos* (3681), reproach; *atimía* (819), dishonour, shame; *spílos* (4696), disgrace, spot; *stígma* (4742), scar; *skándalon* (4625), scandal, offence; *aischúnē* (152), shame.

1792. ἐντρυφάω, **entruphaō**, *en-troo-fah´-o*; from 1722 and 5171; to *revel in:*—sporting selves.

1793. ἐντυγχάνω, **entugchanō**, *en-toong-khan´-o*; from 1722 and 5177; to *chance upon*, i.e. (by implication) *confer with*; by extension to *entreat* (in favour or against):—deal with, make intercession.

1794. ἐντυλίσσω, **entulissō**, *en-too-lis´-so*; from 1722 and τυλίσσω, *tulissō* (to *twist*; probably akin to 1507); to *entwine*, i.e. *wind* up in:—wrap in (together).

1795. ἐντυπόω, **entupoō**, *en-too-po´-o*; from 1722 and a derivative of 5179; to *enstamp*, i.e. *engrave:*—engrave.

1796. ἐνυβρίζω, **enubrizō**, *en-oo-brid´-zo*; from 1722 and 5195; to *insult:*—do despite unto.

1797. ἐνυπνιάζομαι, **enupniazomai**, *en-oop-nee-ad´-zom-ahee*; middle from 1798; to *dream:*—dream (-er).

1798. ἐνύπνιον, **enupnion**, *en-oop´-nee-on*; from 1722 and 5258; something seen *in sleep*, i.e. a *dream* (*vision* in a dream):—dream.

1799. ἐνώπιον, **enōpion**, *en-o´-pee-on*; neuter of a compound of 1722 and a derivative of 3700; *in the face* of (literal or figurative):—before, in the presence (sight) of, to.

1800. Ἐνώς, **Enōs**, *en-oce´*; of Hebrew origin [583]; *Enos* (i.e. *Enosh*), a patriarch:—Enos.

1801. ἐνωτίζομαι, **enōtizomai**, *en-o-tid´-zom-ahee*; middle from a compound of 1722 and 3775; to *take in one's ear*, i.e. to *listen:*—hearken.

1802. Ἐνώχ, **Enōch**, *en-oke´*; of Hebrew origin [2585]; *Enoch* (i.e. *Chanok*), an antediluvian:—Enoch.

1803. ἕξ, hex, *hex;* a primary numeral; *six:*— six.

1804. ἐξαγγέλλω, exaggellō, *ex-ang-el´-lo;* from 1537 and the base of 32; to *publish* i.e. *celebrate:*—shew forth.

From *ek* (1537), out, and *aggéllō* (n.f., see *anaggéllō* [312]), to tell, declare. To declare abroad, make widely known (1Pe 2:9; Sept.: Ps 9:14; 79:13).

Syn.: *phaneróō* (5319), to manifest; *dēlóō* (1213), to make plain; *diēgéomai* (1334), to declare; *légō* (3004), to tell; *apaggéllō* (518), to declare, tell; *kērússō* (2784), to proclaim, preach; *kataggéllō* (2605), to proclaim; *marturéō* (3140), to witness.

1805. ἐξαγοράζω, exagorazō, *ex-ag-or-ad´-zo;* from 1537 and 59; to *buy up,* i.e. *ransom;* (figurative) to *rescue* from loss (*improve* opportunity):—redeem.

From *ek* (1537), out or from, and *agorázō* (59), to buy. To purchase out, to buy up from the possession or power of someone. In the NT, to redeem, to set free from service or bondage (Gal 3:13; 4:5); in the middle voice, to redeem for one's use, used metaphorically in Eph 5:16; Col 4:5.

Syn.: *lutróō* (3084), to release on receipt of ransom, redeem.

1806. ἐξάγω, exagō, *ex-ag´-o;* from 1537 and 71; to *lead forth:*—bring forth (out), fetch (lead) out.

1807. ἐξαιρέω, exaireō, *ex-ahee-reh´-o;* from 1537 and 138; active to *tear out;* middle to *select;* (figurative) to *release:*—deliver, pluck out, rescue.

1808. ἐξαίρω, exairō, *ex-ah´ee-ro;* from 1537 and 142; to *remove:*—put (take) away.

1809. ἐξαιτέομαι, exaiteomai, *ex-ahee-teh´-om-ahee;* middle from 1537 and 154; to *demand* (for trial):—desire.

From *ek* (1537), out, and *aitéō* (154), to ask, require or demand. To claim back, require something to be delivered up. In the middle voice as a deponent verb, *exaitéomai,* to claim back for oneself (Lk 22:31).

Syn.: *epithuméō* (1937), to covet, desire; *zētéō* (2212), to require; *epizētéō* (1934), to crave;

diṓkō (1377), to seek; *axióō* (515), to deem entitled; *apaitéō* (523), to demand back.

1810. ἐξαίφνης, exaiphnēs, *ex-ah´eef-nace;* from 1537 and the base of 160; *of a sudden* (*unexpectedly*):—suddenly. Compare 1819.

1811. ἐξακολουθέω, exakoloutheō, *ex-ak-ol-oo-theh´-o;* from 1537 and 190; to *follow out,* i.e. (figurative) to *imitate, obey,* yield to:—follow.

1812. ἐξακόσιοι, hexakosioi, *hex-ak-os´-ee-oy;* plural ordinal from 1803 and 1540; *six hundred:*—six hundred.

1813. ἐξαλείφω, exaleiphō, *ex-al-i´-fo;* from 1537 and 218; to *smear out,* i.e. *obliterate* (*erase* tears; figurative, *pardon* sin):—blot out, wipe away.

1814. ἐξάλλομαι, exallomai, *ex-al´-lom-ahee;* from 1537 and 242; to *spring forth:*—leap up.

1815. ἐξανάστασις, exanastasis, *ex-an-as´-tas-is;* from 1817; a *rising from* death:—resurrection.

Noun from *exanístēmi* (1817), to rise up. The resurrection from among the dead (Php 3:11).

1816. ἐξανατέλλω, exanatellō, *ex-an-at-el´-lo;* from 1537 and 393; to *start up out* of the ground, i.e. *germinate:*—spring up.

1817. ἐξανίστημι, exanistēmi, *ex-an-is´-tay-mee;* from 1537 and 450; objective to *produce,* i.e. (figurative) *beget;* subject to *arise,* i.e. (figurative) *object:*—raise (rise) up.

From *ek* (1537), out of or from, and *anístēmi* (450), to rise up. To rise up from among others (Ac 15:5; Sept.: Ge 18:16; 19:1; Jgs 3:20); transitively, to raise up seed from a woman (Mk 12:19; Lk 20:28; Sept.: Ge 4:25; 19:32, 34).

Deriv.: *exanástasis* (1815), resurrection.

Syn.: *exegeírō* (1825), to arouse fully, awaken; *anorthóō* (461), to straighten up; *stḗkō* (4739), to stand; *exanatéllō* (1816), to spring from.

1818. ἐξαπατάω, exapataō, *ex-ap-at-ah´-o;* from 1537 and 538; to *seduce wholly:*—beguile, deceive.

1819. ἐξάπινα, exapina, *ex-ap´-ee-nah;* from 1537 and a derivative of the same as 160; *of a sudden,* i.e. *unexpectedly:*—suddenly. Compare 1810.

1820. ἐξαπορέομαι, exaporeomai, *ex-ap-or-eh´-om-ahee*; middle from 1537 and 639; to *be utterly at a loss*, i.e. *despond*:—(in) despair.

1821. ἐξαποστέλλω, exapostellō, *ex-ap-os-tel´-lo*; from 1537 and 649; to *send away forth*, i.e. (on a mission) to *despatch*, or (peremptorily) to *dismiss*:—send (away, forth, out).

1822. ἐξαρτίζω, exartizō, *ex-ar-tid´-zo*; from 1537 and a derivative of 739; to *finish out* (time); (figurative) to *equip fully* (a teacher):—accomplish, thoroughly furnish.

From *ek* (1537), an intensive, and *artízō* (n.f.), to put in appropriate condition. To complete entirely. Spoken of time: to finish, to bring to an end (Ac 21:5); of a religious teacher: to make thoroughly perfect, to furnish out (2Ti 3:17).

Syn.: *kataskeuázō* (2680), to make, fit, prepare; *katartízō* (2675), to fit, frame, prepare; *sunistéō* (4921), to set together; *sunarmologéō* (4883), to fit together; *plēróō* (4137), to bring to completion; *teléō* (5055), to accomplish, complete.

1823. ἐξαστράπτω, exastraptō, *ex-as-trap´-to*; from 1537 and 797; to *lighten forth*, i.e. (figurative) to *be radiant* (of very white garments):—glistening.

1824. ἐξαύτης, exautēs, *ex-ow´-tace*; from 1537 and the generic singular feminine of 846 (5610 being understood); *from that* hour, i.e. *instantly*:—by and by, immediately, presently, straightway.

1825. ἐξεγείρω, exegeirō, *ex-eg-i´-ro*; from 1537 and 1453; to *rouse fully*, i.e. (figurative) to *resuscitate* (from death), *release* (from infliction):—raise up.

From *ek* (1537), out, and *egeírō* (1453), to raise. To raise up, wake out of sleep. In the NT, used metaphorically: to raise up out of death (1Co 6:14); to raise up, i.e. to cause to arise or exist (Ro 9:17, quoted from Ex 9:16).

Syn.: *anorthóō* (461), to raise up; *exanístēmi* (1817), to rise up.

1826. ἔξειμι, exeimi, *ex´-i-mee*; from 1537 and εἶμι, eimi (to go); to *issue*, i.e. *leave* (a place), *escape* (to the shore):—depart, get [to land], go out.

1827. ἐξελέγχω, exelegchō, *ex-el-eng´-kho*; from 1537 and 1651; to *convict fully*, i.e. (by implication) to *punish*:—convince.

1828. ἐξέλκω, exelkō, *ex-el´-ko*; from 1537 and 1670; to *drag forth*, i.e. (figurative) to *entice* (to sin):—draw away.

1829. ἐξέραμα, exerama, *ex-er´-am-ah*; from a compound of 1537 and a presumed ἐράω, eraō (to spew); *vomit*, i.e. *food disgorged*:—vomit.

1830. ἐξερευνάω, exereunaō, *ex-er-yoo-nah´-o*; from 1537 and 2045; to *explore* (figurative):—search diligently.

1831. ἐξέρχομαι, exerchomai, *ex-er´-khom-ahee*; from 1537 and 2064; to *issue* (literal or figurative):—come (forth, out), depart (out of), escape, get out, go (abroad, away, forth, out, thence), proceed (forth), spread abroad.

1832. ἔξεστι, exesti, *ex´-es-tee*; third person singular presumed indicative of a compound of 1537 and 1510; so also ἐξόν, exon, *ex-on´*; neuter presumed participle of the same (with or without some form of 1510 expressed); impersonal *it is right* (through the figurative idea of *being out* in public):—be lawful, let, × may (-est).

1833. ἐξετάζω, exetazō, *ex-et-ad´-zo*; from 1537 and ἐτάζω, etazō (to examine); to *test thoroughly* (by questions), i.e. *ascertain* or *interrogate*:—ask, enquire, search.

1834. ἐξηγέομαι, exēgeomai, *ex-ayg-eh´-om-ahee*; from 1537 and 2233; to *consider out* (aloud), i.e. *rehearse, unfold*:—declare, tell.

Middle deponent from *ek* (1537), out, or an intensive, and *hēgéomai* (2233), to tell, lead forward. To bring or lead out, to take the lead, be the leader. In the NT, to bring out, i.e. to make known, to declare:

(I) To unfold, reveal, make known, as a teacher (Jn 1:18 [cf. Mt 11:27; Sept.: Le 14:57]).

(II) To tell, narrate, recount (Lk 24:35; Ac 10:8; 15:12, 14; 21:19; Sept.: Jgs 7:13).

Syn.: *diasaphéō* (1285), to make clear; *phaneróō* (5319), to manifest.

1835. ἐξήκοντα, hexēkonta, *hex-ay´-kon-tah*; the tenth multiple of 1803; *sixty*:—sixty [-fold], threescore.

1836. ἑξῆς, hexēs, *hex-ace´*; from 2192 (in the sense of *taking hold* of, i.e. *adjoining*); *successive*:—after, following, × morrow, next.

1837. ἐξηχέομαι, exēcheomai, *ex-ah-kheh´-om-ahee*; middle from 1537 and 2278; to "*echo*" *forth*, i.e. *resound* (*be* generally *reported*):—sound forth.

1838. ἕξις, hexis, *hex´-is*; from 2192; *habit*, i.e. (by implication) *practice*:—use.

1839. ἐξίστημι, existēmi, *ex-is´-tay-mee*; from 1537 and 2476; to *put* (*stand*) *out* of wits, i.e. *astound*, or (reflexive) *become astounded, insane*:—amaze, be (make) astonished, be beside self (selves), bewitch, wonder.

From *ek* (1537), out, and *hístēmi* (2476), to stand. To put out of place. In the NT, used only metaphorically: to put out of oneself, i.e. to astonish, fill with wonder (Lk 24:22; Ac 8:9, 11); to be beside oneself, to be put out of one's mind (Mk 3:21; 2Co 5:13; Sept.: Job 12:17); to be astonished, amazed, filled with wonder (Mt 12:23; Mk 2:12; 5:42; 6:51; Lk 8:56; Sept.: Ge 27:33).

Deriv.: *ékstasis* (1611), bewilderment, wonder.

Syn.: *ekpléssomai* (1605), to be astonished; *thambéomaī* (2284), to be amazed; *ekthambéomai* (1568), to be utterly amazed; *maínomai* (3105), to rave; *paraphronéō* (3912), to act as a fool; *thaumázō* (2296), to marvel.

1840. ἐξισχύω, exischuō, *ex-is-khoo´-o*; from 1537 and 2480; to *have full strength*, i.e. *be entirely competent*:—be able.

1841. ἔξοδος, exodos, *ex´-od-os*; from 1537 and 3598; an *exit*, i.e. (figurative) *death*:—decease, departing.

1842. ἐξολοθρεύω, exolothreuō, *ex-ol-oth-ryoo´-o*; from 1537 and 3645; to *extirpate*:—destroy.

1843. ἐξομολογέω, exomologeō, *ex-om-ol-og-eh´-o*; from 1537 and 3670; to *acknowledge* or (by implication of *assent*) *agree fully*:—confess, profess, promise.

From *ek* (1537), out, and *homologéō* (3670), to assent. Similar to *homologéō*, but stronger: to speak out the same things as another; hence in the NT:

(I) To concede, to acknowledge, to confess fully (Mt 3:6; Mk 1:5; Ac 19:18; Jas 5:16; Sept.:

Da 9:4); to acknowledge openly, to profess (Php 2:11; Rev 3:5). In the middle, to make acknowledgement for benefits, i.e. to give thanks, to praise (Mt 11:25; Lk 10:21; Ro 14:11; 15:9 quoted from Ps 18:49, 50; Sept.: 1Ch 16:4; 2Ch 30:22; Ps 57:9, 10).

(II) To assent fully, to agree, to promise (Lk 22:6).

Syn.: *homologéō* (3670), to speak the same thing, confess, declare, admit; *epineúō* (1962), to nod to, express approval; *sumphōnéō* (4856), to agree; *egkrínō* (1469), judge in; *apodéchomai* (588), to accept; *anagnōrízō* (319), to recognize.

1844. ἐξορκίζω, exorkizō, *ex-or-kid´-zo*; from 1537 and 3726; to *exact an oath*, i.e. *conjure*:—adjure.

1845. ἐξορκιστής, exorkistēs, *ex-or-kis-tace´*; from 1844; *one that binds by an oath* (or *spell*), i.e. (by implication) an "*exorcist*" (*conjurer*):—exorcist.

1846. ἐξορύσσω, exorussō, *ex-or-oos´-so*; from 1537 and 3736; to *dig out*, i.e. (by extension) to *extract* (an eye), *remove* (a roofing):—break up, pluck out.

1847. ἐξουδενόω, exoudenoō, *ex-oo-den-o´-o*; from 1537 and a derivative of the neuter of 3762; to *make utterly nothing of*, i.e. *despise*:—set at nought. See also 1848.

1848. ἐξουθενέω, exoutheneō, *ex-oo-then-eh´-o*; a variation of 1847 and meaning the same:—contemptible, despise, least esteemed, set at nought.

1849. ἐξουσία, exousia, *ex-oo-see´-ah*; from 1832 (in the sense of *ability*); *privilege*, i.e. (subject) *force, capacity, competency, freedom*, or (object) *mastery* (concrete *magistrate, superhuman, potentate, token of control*), delegated *influence*:—authority, jurisdiction, liberty, power, right, strength.

Noun from *éxesti* (1832), it is permissible, allowed. Power:

(I) The power of doing something, ability, faculty (Mt 9:6, 8; Mk 2:10; Lk 5:24; 10:19; 12:5; Jn 10:18; 19:11; Ac 8:19; Rev 13:12). With the meaning of strength, force, efficiency (Mt 7:29; Mk 1:22; Rev 9:3, 19), with the prep. *en* (1722), in, and the dat., *en exousía* as adjunct, powerful (Lk 4:32); with the prep. *katá* (2596), according to, *kat' exousían* being equivalent to *en exousía*, as adverb, i.e. with intensive strength, with point and effect (Mk 1:27 [cf. Lk 4:36]).

(II) Power of doing or not doing, i.e. license, liberty, free choice (Ac 1:7; 5:4; Ro 9:21; 1Co 7:37; 8:9; 9:4–6, 12, 18; 2Th 3:9; Rev 22:14).

(III) Power as entrusted, i.e. commission, authority, right, full power (Mt 8:9; 21:23, 24, 27; Mk 3:15; 11:28, 29, 33; Lk 20:2, 8; Jn 1:12; Ac 9:14; 26:10, 12; 2Co 10:8; 13:10; Heb 13:10; Rev 13:5).

(IV) Power over persons and things, dominion, authority, rule.

(A) Particularly and generally (Mt 28:18; Mk 13:34; Lk 7:8; Jude 25; Rev 13:2, 4; 17:12, 13; 18:1; Sept.: Ps 136:8, 9; Da 3:33; 4:31). Before the gen. of person to whom the power belongs (Lk 20:20; 22:53; Ac 26:18; Col 1:13; Rev 12:10). Followed by the gen. of the object subjected to the power (Mt 10:1; Mk 6:7, "power over unclean spirits"; Jn 17:2).

(B) As a metonym used for: (1) What is subject to one's rule, dominion, domain, jurisdiction (Lk 4:6; 23:7; Sept.: 2Ki 20:13; Ps 114:2). (2) In plural or coll., those invested with power, as rulers, magistrates (Lk 12:11; Ro 13:1–3; Tit 3:1). For the celestial and infernal powers, princes, potentates, e.g., angels, archangels (Eph 1:21; 3:10; Col 1:16; 2:10; 1Pe 3:22); demons (Eph 6:12; Col 2:15). Generally, of the powerful adversaries of the gospel (1Co 15:24 [cf. *arché* {746}, principality]). (3) In 1Co 11:10, where *exousía* is used as an emblem of power, i.e. a veil or covering (cf. 1Co 11:13, 16) as an emblem of subjection to the power of a husband, a token of modest adherence to duties and usages established by law or custom lest spies or evil-minded persons should take advantage of any impropriety in the meetings of the Christians (cf. *timē* [5092], honour).

Syn.: *krátos* (2904), dominion; *dúnamis* (1411), power. *Exousía* denotes the executive power while *arché* (746), rule, represents the authority granting the power.

Deriv.: *exousiázō* (1850), to exercise authority.

1850. ἐξουσιάζω, **exousiazo,** *ex-oo-see-ad´-zo*; from 1849; to *control*:—exercise authority upon, bring under the (have) power of.

1851. ἐξοχή, **exochē,** *ex-okh-ay´*; from a compound of 1537 and 2192 (meaning to *stand out*); *prominence* (figurative):—principal.

1852. ἐξυπνίζω, **exupnizō,** *ex-oop-nid´-zo*; from 1853; to *waken*:—awake out of sleep.

1853. ἔξυπνος, **exupnos,** *ex´-oop-nos*; from 1537 and 5258; *awake*:— × out of sleep.

1854. ἔξω, **exō,** *ex´-o*; adverb from 1537; *out* (*-side, of doors*), literal or figurative:—away, forth, (with-) out (of, -ward), strange.

1855. ἔξωθεν, **exōthen,** *ex´-o-then*; from 1854; *external* (*-ly*):—out (-side, -ward, -wardly), (from) without.

1856. ἐξωθέω, **exōtheō,** *ex-o-theh´-o*; or ἐξώθω, *exōthō, ex-o´-tho*; from 1537 and ὠθέω, *ōtheō* (to *push*); to *expel*; (by implication) to *propel*:—drive out, thrust in.

1857. ἐξώτερος, **exōteros,** *ex-o´-ter-os*; comparative of 1854; *exterior*:—outer.

1858. ἑορτάζω, **heortazō,** *heh-or-tad´-zo*; from 1859; to *observe a festival*:—keep the feast.

1859. ἑορτή, **heortē,** *heh-or-tay´*; of uncertain affinity; a *festival*:—feast, holy day.

1860. ἐπαγγελία, **epaggelia,** *ep-ang-el-ee´-ah*; from 1861; an *announcement* (for information, assent or pledge; especially a divine *assurance* of good):—message, promise.

Noun from *epaggéllō* (1861), to announce. Annunciation, announcement:

(I) Particularly in 1Jn 1:5 (TR), where later editions have *aggelía* (31), message (Sept.: Eze 7:26).

(II) By implication, a promise:

(A) Particularly a promise given (2Co 1:20; Eph 1:13; 6:2; 1Ti 4:8; 2Pe 3:4, 9; Sept.: Est 4:7). Of special promises, e.g., made to Abraham (Ac 7:6, 17; Ro 4:16, 20; Heb 6:12, 15; 7:6; 11:9, Promised Land); in respect to Isaac (Ro 9:9; Gal 4:23); of a spiritual seed (Ro 9:8; Gal 4:28); as made to Abraham and the Jewish patriarchs and prophets in general, e.g., of a future Saviour (Ac 13:23, 32; 26:6); of future blessings and the enjoyment of God's favour (Ac 2:39; Ro 4:13, 14, 16; 9:4; 15:8; 2Co 7:1; Gal 3:16–18, 21, 22, 29; Eph 2:12; 3:6; Heb 6:12, 17; 11:17); of salvation in Christ (2Ti 1:1); an apostle in respect to the promise of eternal life in Christ, that is, appointed to announce it (Heb 4:1; 8:6; 9:15; 1Jn 2:25).

(B) Metonymically, used for the thing promised (Heb 11:13, 33, 39); of salvation in Christ (Heb 10:36); of the Holy Spirit (Lk 24:49; Ac 1:4). In Ac 2:33; Gal 3:14, "having received the promise of the Spirit" (a.t.) means having received the promised effusions of the Spirit.

1861. ἐπαγγέλλω, epaggellō, *ep-ang-el´-lo*; from 1909 and the base of 32; to *announce upon* (reflexive), i.e. (by implication) to *engage* to do something, to *assert* something respecting oneself:—profess, (make) promise.

From *epí* (1909), an intensive, and *aggéllō* (n.f., see *anaggéllō* [312]), to tell, declare. To proclaim, to announce a message. In the NT, used only in the middle voice, *epaggéllomai*, meaning to announce oneself, offer oneself for a responsibility or service. Used primarily as "to promise" in Mk 14:11; Ac 7:5; Ro 4:21, *apéggelmai*, with middle meaning; 2Pe 2:19, and "to profess" in 1Ti 2:10; 6:21 with the meaning of pretending. When used with this special meaning, the word and its deriv. refer to God's divine promise of spontaneous salvation. To render a service. (See Ac 1:4, *epaggelían* [1860] "the promise"; 7:5; Ro 4:21; Tit 1:2; Heb 12:26; Jas 1:12; 2:5; 1Jn 2:25.) Used in an absolute sense, meaning to give a promise (Gal 3:19 with pass. meaning; Heb 6:13; 10:23; 11:11;   Sept.:   Est   4:7).

Deriv.: *epaggelía* (1860), an announcement, message; *epággelma* (1862), promise; *proepaggéllō* (4279), to promise before.

1862. ἐπάγγελμα, epaggelma, *ep-ang´-el-mah*; from 1861; a *self-committal* (by *assurance* of conferring some good):—promise.

Noun from *epaggéllō* (1861), to proclaim. A promise. Found only in 2Pe 1:4; 3:13.

1863. ἐπάγω, epagō, *ep-ag´-o*; from 1909 and 71; to *superinduce,* i.e. *inflict* (an evil), *charge* (a crime):—bring upon.

1864. ἐπαγωνίζομαι, epagōnizomai, *ep-ag-o-nid´-zom-ahee*; from 1909 and 75; to *struggle for:*—earnestly contend for.

From *epí* (1909), for, and *agōnízomai* (75), to strive, contend earnestly. To fight for or in reference to something, with the dat. of that which gives the occasion (Jude 3).

Syn.: *máchomai* (3164), to fight; *diamáchomai* (1264), to struggle against; *erízō* (2051), to strive; *athléō* (118), to contend in games; *poleméō* (4170), to fight in war.

1865. ἐπαθροίζω, epathroizō, *ep-ath-roid´-zo*; from 1909 and ἀθροίζω, *athroizō* (to *assemble*); to *accumulate:*—gather thick together.

1866. Ἐπαίνετος, Epainetos, *ep-a´hee-net-os*; from 1867; *praised; Epænetus,* a Christian:—Epenetus.

1867. ἐπαινέω, epaineō, *ep-ahee-neh´-o*; from 1909 and 134; to *applaud:*—commend, laud, praise.

1868. ἔπαινος, epainos, *ep´-ahee-nos*; from 1909 and the base of 134; *laudation;* concretely a *commendable* thing:—praise.

1869. ἐπαίρω, epairō, *ep-ahee´-ro*; from 1909 and 142; to *raise up* (literal or figurative):—exalt self, poise (lift, take) up.

1870. ἐπαισχύνομαι, epaischunomai, *ep-ahee-skhoo´-nom-ahee*; from 1909 and 153; to *feel shame for* something:—be ashamed.

1871. ἐπαιτέω, epaiteō, *ep-ahee-teh´-o*; from 1909 and 154; to *ask for:*—beg.

From *epí* (1909), an intensive, and *aitéō* (154), to ask, implore, claim. To beg, ask for alms (Lk 16:3; Sept.: Ps 109:10).

Syn.: *zētéō* (2212), to ask; *epithuméō* (1937), to desire; *exaitéomai* (1809), to desire, demand; *axióō* (515), to consider oneself entitled to; *apaitéō* (523), to demand back, ask again, require; *epizētéō* (1934), to inquire for.

1872. ἐπακολουθέω, epakoloutheō, *ep-ak-ol-oo-theh´-o*; from 1909 and 190; to *accompany:*—follow (after).

1873. ἐπακούω, epakouō, *ep-ak-oo´-o*; from 1909 and 191; to *hearken* (fabourably) *to:*—hear.

1874. ἐπακροάομαι, epakroaomai, *ep-ak-ro-ah´-om-ahee*; from 1909 and the base of 202; to *listen* (intently) *to:*—hear.

1875. ἐπάν, epan, *ep-an´*; from 1909 and 302; a particle of indefinite contemporaneousness; *whenever, as soon as:*—when.

1876. ἐπάναγκες, **epanagkes,** *ep-an´-ang-kes*; neuter of a presumed compound of 1909 and 318; (adverb) *on necessity,* i.e. *necessarily:*— necessary.

Adverb from *epí* (1909), upon, on account of, and *anágkē* (318), necessity. Necessarily. With the article it assumes the meaning of a noun, *tó epánagkes,* necessities or things of necessity (Ac 15:28).

Syn.: *anagkaíos* (316), necessary; *deí* (1163), that which must be; *prépon* (4241), that which is proper; *chreía* (5532), need, necessity.

1877. ἐπανάγω, **epanagō,** *ep-an-ag´-o*; from 1909 and 321; to *lead up on,* i.e. (technical) to *put out* (to sea); (intransitive) to *return:*— launch (thrust) out, return.

1878. ἐπαναμιμνήσκω, **epanamimnēskō,** *ep-an-ah-mim-nace´-ko*; from 1909 and 363; to *remind of:*—put in mind.

1879. ἐπαναπαύομαι, **epanapauomai,** *ep-an-ah-pow´-om-ahee*; middle from 1909 and 373; to *settle on*; literal (*remain*) or figurative (*rely*):—rest in (upon).

From *epí* (1909), upon, and *anapaúomai* (373), to rest. In the NT, only in the middle *epanapaúomai.* To rely, rest, repose oneself upon (Ro 2:17; Sept.: Mic 3:11); to rest with the sense of remaining upon (Lk 10:6; Sept.: Nu 11:25, 26; 2Ki 2:15).

1880. ἐπανέρχομαι, **epanerchomai,** *ep-an-er´-khom-ahee*; from 1909 and 424; to *come up on,* i.e. *return:*—come again, return.

1881. ἐπανίσταμαι, **epanistamai,** *ep-an-is´-tam-ahee*; middle from 1909 and 450; to *stand up on,* i.e. (figurative) to *attack:*—rise up against.

1882. ἐπανόρθωσις, **epanorthōsis,** *ep-an-or´-tho-sis*; from a compound of 1909 and 461; a *straightening up again,* i.e. (figurative) *rectification* (*reformation*):—correction.

Noun from *epanorthóō* (n.f.), to set right again, correct, which is from *epí* (1909), upon, and *anorthóō* (461), to make straight. A setting to rights, reparation, restitution. Only in 2Ti 3:16.

Syn.: *nouthesía* (3559), admonition; *paideía* (3809), instruction; *apokatástasis* (605), restitution.

1883. ἐπάνω, **epanō,** *ep-an´-o*; from 1909 and 507; *up above,* i.e. *over* or *on* (of place, amount, rank, etc.):—above, more than, (up-) on, over.

1884. ἐπαρκέω, **eparkeō,** *ep-ar-keh´-o*; from 1909 and 714; to *avail for,* i.e. *help:*—relieve.

1885. ἐπαρχία, **eparchia,** *ep-ar-khee´-ah*; from a compound of 1909 and 757 (meaning a *governor* of a district, "eparch"); a special *region* of government, i.e. a Roman *præfecture:*—province.

1886. ἔπαυλις, **epaulis,** *ep´-ow-lis*; from 1909 and an equivalent of 833; a *hut over* the head, i.e. a *dwelling.*

1887. ἐπαύριον, **epaurion,** *ep-ow´-ree-on*; from 1909 and 839; occurring *on* the *succeeding* day, i.e. (2250 being implied) *to-morrow:*—day following, morrow, next day (after).

1888. ἐπαυτοφώρῳ, **epautophōrōi,** *ep-ow-tof-o´-ro*; from 1909 and 846 and (the dative singular of) a derivative of φώρ, *phōr* (a *thief*); *in theft itself,* i.e. (by analogy) *in actual crime:*—in the very act.

1889. Ἐπαφρᾶς, **Epaphras,** *ep-af-ras´*; contrete from 1891; *Epaphras,* a Christian:—Epaphras.

1890. ἐπαφρίζω, **epaphrizō,** *ep-af-rid´-zo*; from 1909 and 875; to *foam upon,* i.e. (figurative) to *exhibit* (a vile passion):—foam out.

1891. Ἐπαφρόδιτος, **Epaphroditos,** *ep-af-rod´-ee-tos*; from 1909 (in the sense of *devoted* to) and Ἀφροδίτη, *Aphroditē* (*Venus*); *Epaphroditus,* a Christian:—Epaphroditus. Compare 1889.

1892. ἐπεγείρω, **epegeirō,** *ep-eg-i´-ro*; from 1909 and 1453; to *rouse upon,* i.e. (figurative) to *excite* against:—raise, stir up.

1893. ἐπεί, **epei,** *ep-i´*; from 1909 and 1487; *thereupon,* i.e. *since* (of time or cause):—because, else, for that (then, -asmuch as), otherwise, seeing that, since, when.

1894. ἐπειδή, **epeidē,** *ep-i-day´*; from 1893 and 1211; *since now,* i.e. (of time) *when* or (of cause) *whereas:*—after that, because, for (that, -asmuch as), seeing, since.

1895. ἐπειδήπερ, **epeidēper,** *ep-i-day´-per*; from 1894 and 4007; *since indeed* (of cause):—forasmuch.

1896. ἐπεῖδον, epeidon, *ep-i´-don*; and other moods and persons of the same tense; from 1909 and 1492; to *regard* (fabourably or otherwise):—behold, look upon.

Second aor. 1st person of *ephoráō* ([n.f.], to look upon fabourably), from *epí* (1909), upon, and or *eídō* (1492), to look. In the NT, from the Hebrew: to look upon, to regard, to attend to, especially with kindness (Lk 1:25; Sept.: Ex 2:25; Ps 31:7); or unfabourably, for evil (Ac 4:29).

1897. ἐπείπερ, epeiper, *ep-i´-per*; from 1893 and 4007; *since indeed* (of cause):—seeing.

1898. ἐπεισαγωγή, epeisagōgē, *ep-ice-ag-o-gay´*; from a compound of 1909 and 1521; a *superintroduction*:—bringing in.

1899. ἔπειτα, epeita, *ep´-i-tah*; from 1909 and 1534; *thereafter*:—after that (-ward), then.

1900. ἐπέκεινα, epekeina, *ep-ek´-i-nah*; from 1909 and (the accusative plural neuter of) 1565; *upon those* parts of, i.e. *on the further side of*:—beyond.

1901. ἐπεκτείνομαι, epekteinomai, *ep-ek-ti´-nom-ahee*; middle from 1909 and 1614; to *stretch* (oneself) forward *upon*:—reach forth.

1902. ἐπενδύομαι, ependuomai, *ep-en-doo´-om-ahee*; middle from 1909 and 1746; to *invest upon* oneself:—be clothed upon.

1903. ἐπενδύτης, ependutēs, *ep-en-doo´-tace*; from 1902; a *wrapper*, i.e. outer garment:—fisher's coat.

1904. ἐπέρχομαι, eperchomai, *ep-er´-khom-ahee*; from 1909 and 2064; to *supervene*, i.e. *arrive, occur, impend, attack,* (figurative) *influence*:—come (in, upon).

1905. ἐπερωτάω, eperōtaō, *ep-er-o-tah´-o*; from 1909 and 2065; to *ask for*, i.e. *inquire, seek*:—ask (after, questions), demand, desire, question.

From *epí* (1909), an intensive, and *erōtáō* (2065), to ask, inquire of, beg of:

(I) Generally (Mk 7:17; 11:29; Lk 20:40; Sept.: 2Sa 14:18); to speak, say, saying, or the question itself (Mt 12:10; Mk 5:9; Lk 3:10, 14; Ac 1:6; 1Co 14:35). Used in an absolute sense (Mt 22:35; Ac 23:34; Sept.: Ge 38:21; 43:7). In the sense of to require, demand (Mt 16:1; Sept.: Ps 137:3).

(II) In a judicial sense: to question, interrogate (Mt 27:11; Jn 18:21; Ac 5:27). Used in an absolute sense (Lk 23:6).

(III) To ask or inquire after God, i.e. to seek God, the same as *ekzētéō* (1567), to seek after (Ro 10:20 quoted from Isa 65:1).

Deriv.: *eperótēma* (1906), inquiry.

Syn.: *ereunáō* (2045), to investigate.

1906. ἐπερώτημα, eperōtēma, *ep-er-o´-tay-mah*; from 1905; an *inquiry*:—answer.

1907. ἐπέχω, epechō, *ep-ekh´-o*; from 1909 and 2192; to *hold upon*, i.e. (by implication) to *retain*; (by extension) to *detain*; (with implication of 3563) to *pay attention to*:—give (take) heed unto, hold forth, mark, stay.

1908. ἐπηρεάζω, epēreazō, *ep-ay-reh-ad´-zo*; from a compound of 1909 and (probably) ἀρειά, *areia* (*threats*); to *insult, slander*:—use despitefully, falsely accuse.

1909. ἐπί, epi, *ep-ee´*; a primary preposition properly meaning *superimposition* (of time, place, order, etc.), as a relation of *distribution* [with the genitive], i.e. *over, upon,* etc.; of *rest* (with the dative) *at, on,* etc.; of *direction* (with the accusative) *toward, upon,* etc.:—about (the times), above, after, against, among, as long as (touching), at, beside, × have charge of, (be-, [where-]) fore, in (a place, as much as, the time of, -to), (because) of, (up-) on (behalf of), over, (by, for) the space of, through (-out), (un-) to (-ward), with. In compounds it retains essentially the same import, *at, upon,* etc. (literal or figurative).

1910. ἐπιβαίνω, epibainō, *ep-ee-bah´ee-no*; from 1909 and the base of 939; to *walk upon*, i.e. *mount, ascend, embark, arrive*:—come (into), enter into, go abroad, sit upon, take ship.

From *epí* (1909), upon, to, and *baínō* (n.f.), to go. To go upon, mount, as upon a donkey (Mt 21:5); aboard ship (Ac 21:2, 6 [TR]; 27:2); to set foot upon, to come upon or, enter into (Ac 20:18; 25:1).

Syn.: *epérchomai* (1904), to come or go upon; *ephístēmi* (2186), to come up; *eíseimi* (1524) and *eisporeúomai* (1531), to go into; *eisérchomai* (1525), to come into; *embaínō* (1684), to go into, step in; *embibázō* (1688), to place on, transfer, put on board ship.

1911. ἐπιβάλλω, epiballō, *ep-ee-bal´-lo*; from 1909 and 906; to *throw upon* (literal or figurative, transitive or reflexive; usually with more or less force); specially (with 1438 implied) to *reflect*; impersonally to *belong to:*—beat into, cast (up-) on, fall, lay (on), put (unto), stretch forth, think on.

1912. ἐπιβαρέω, epibareō, *ep-ee-bar-eh´-o*; from 1909 and 916; to *be heavy upon,* i.e. (pecuniarily) to *be expensive to;* (figurative) to *be severe toward:*—be chargeable to, overcharge.

1913. ἐπιβιβάζω, epibibazō, *ep-ee-bee-bad´-zo*; from 1909 and a reduplicated derivative of the base of 939 [compare 307]; to *cause to mount* (an animal):—set on.

1914. ἐπιβλέπω, epiblepō, *ep-ee-blep´-o*; from 1909 and 991; to *gaze at* (with favour, pity or partiality):—look upon, regard, have respect to.

1915. ἐπίβλημα, epiblēma, *ep-ib´-lay-mah*; from 1911; a *patch:*—piece.

1916. ἐπιβοάω, epiboaō, *ep-ee-bo-ah´-o*; from 1909 and 994; to *exclaim against:*—cry.

1917. ἐπιβουλή, epiboulē, *ep-ee-boo-lay´*; from a presumed compound of 1909 and 1014; a *plan against* someone, i.e. a *plot:*—laying (lying) in wait.

1918. ἐπιγαμβρεύω, epigambreuō, *ep-ee-gam-bryoo´-o*; from 1909 and a derivative of 1062; to *form affinity with,* i.e. (special) in a levirate way:—marry.

1919. ἐπίγειος, epigeios, *ep-ig´-i-os*; from 1909 and 1093; *worldly* (physical or moral):—earthly, in earth, terrestrial.

Adjective from *epí* (1909), upon, and *gē* (1093), the earth. Earthly, terrestrial; belonging on earth or to earth (1Co 15:40; 2Co 5:1 [cf. Job 4:19]); spoken of persons (Php 2:10); *tá epígeia,* earthly things, things relating to this life (Jn 3:12; Php 3:19); *sophía epígeios* (*sophía* [4678], wisdom), earthly wisdom, i.e. imperfect and perverse (Jas 3:15).

1920. ἐπιγίνομαι, epiginomai, *ep-ig-in´-om-ahee*; from 1909 and 1096; to *arrive upon,* i.e. *spring up* (as a wind):—blow.

1921. ἐπιγινώσκω, epiginōskō, *ep-ig-in-oce´-ko*; from 1909 and 1097; to *know upon* some mark, i.e. *recognise;* (by implication) to *become fully acquainted with,* to *acknowledge:*—(ac-, have, take) know (-ledge, well), perceive.

1922. ἐπίγνωσις, epignōsis, *ip-ig´-no-sis*; from 1921; *recognition,* i.e. (by implication) full *discernment, acknowledgment:*—(ac-) knowledge (-ing, -ment).

Noun from *epiginṓskō* (1921), to recognize. Full knowledge; the act of coming to a full knowledge of something; cognition, acknowledgement (1Ti 2:4; 2Ti 2:25; 3:7; Tit 1:1; Phm 6 [UBS]; 2Pe 1:3; 2:20); full knowledge, as spoken of what is known in the NT of God, Christ, divine things (Ro 1:28; 10:2; Eph 1:17; 4:13; Col 1:9, 10; 2:2; 1Ti 2:4; 2Ti 2:25; 3:7; Tit 1:1; Heb 10:26; 2Pe 1:2, 3).

Syn.: *pístis* (4102), faith, since it is the means of the acceptance of divine revelation as *epígnōsis* can be said to be the comprehension of divine revelation to man; *gnōsis* (1108), knowledge. See the contrasting use of *ginṓskō* in Ro 1:21 and *epígnōsis* in Ro 1:28.

1923. ἐπιγραφή, epigraphē, *ep-ig-raf-ay´*; from 1924; an *inscription:*—superscription.

1924. ἐπιγράφω, epigraphō, *ep-ee-graf´-o*; from 1909 and 1125; to *inscribe* (physical or mental):—inscription, write in (over, thereon).

1925. ἐπιδείκνυμι, epideiknumi, *ep-ee-dike´-noo-mee*; from 1909 and 1166; to *exhibit* (physical or mental):—shew.

1926. ἐπιδέχομαι, epidechomai, *ep-ee-dekh´-om-ahee*; from 1909 and 1209; to *admit* (as a guest or [figurative] teacher):—receive.

1927. ἐπιδημέω, epidēmeō, *ep-ee-day-meh´-o*; from a compound of 1909 and 1218; to *make oneself at home,* i.e. (by extension) to *reside* (in a foreign country):—[be] dwelling (which were) there, stranger.

1928. ἐπιδιατάσσομαι, epidiatassomai, *ep-ee-dee-ah-tas´-som-ahee*; middle from 1909 and 1299; to *appoint besides,* i.e. *supplement* (as a codicil):—add to.

1929. ἐπιδίδωμι, epididōmi, *ep-ee-did´-o-mee*; from 1909 and 1325; to *give over* (by hand or surrender):—deliver unto, give, let (+ [her drive]), offer.

1930. ἐπιδιορθόω, epidiorthoō, *ep-ee-dee-or-tho´-o*; from 1909 and a derivative of 3717; to *straighten further,* i.e. (figurative) *arrange additionally*:—set in order.

From *epí* (1909), besides, above, and *diorthóō* (n.f.), to correct. Only in Tit 1:5, meaning to proceed in correcting or setting in order. See *diórthōsis* (1357), an amendment, restoration.

Syn.: *paideúō* (3811), to train up, correct; *morphóō* (3445), to fashion.

1931. ἐπιδύω, epiduō, *ep-ee-doo´-o*; from 1909 and 1416; to *set* fully (as the sun):—go down.

1932. ἐπιείκεια, epieikeia, *ep-ee-i´-ki-ah*; from 1933; *suitableness,* i.e. (by implication) *equity, mildness*:—clemency, gentleness.

Noun from *epieikḗs* (1933), fitting, appropriate. Clemency or gentleness (Ac 24:4; 2Co 10:1).

Syn.: contrast *épios* (2261), mild; *anochḗ* (463), forbearance; *makrothumía* (3115), longsuffering; *hupomonḗ* (5281), patience; *praótēs* (4236), meekness.

1933. ἐπιεικής, epieikēs, *ep-ee-i-kace´*; from 1909 and 1503; *appropriate,* i.e. (by implication) *mild*:—gentle, moderation, patient.

1934. ἐπιζητέω, epizēteō, *ep-eed´-zay-teh´-o*; from 1909 and 2212; to *search* (inquire) *for*; intensive to *demand,* to *crave*:—desire, enquire, seek (after, for).

1935. ἐπιθανάτιος, epithanatios, *ep-ee-than-at´-ee-os*; from 1909 and 2288; doomed *to death*:—appointed to death.

1936. ἐπίθεσις, epithesis, *ep-ith´-es-is*; from 2007; an *imposition* (of hands officially):—laying (putting) on.

1937. ἐπιθυμέω, epithumeō, *ep-ee-thoo-meh´-o*; from 1909 and 2372; to *set the heart upon,* i.e. *long* for (rightfully or otherwise):—covet, desire, would fain, lust (after).

From *epí* (1909), in, and *thumós* (2372), the mind. To fix the desire on, to desire earnestly, to long for. Generally (Lk 17:22; Gal 5:17; Rev 9:6). To desire in a good sense (Mt 13:17; Lk 22:15; 1Ti 3:1; Heb 6:11; 1Pe 1:12); as a result of physical needs (Lk 15:16; 16:21); in a bad sense of coveting and lusting after (Mt 5:28; Ro 7:7; 13:9; 1Co 10:6 [cf. Jas 4:2; Sept.: Ex 20:17; Dt 5:21; 14:26; 2Sa 3:21; Pr 21:26]).

Deriv.: *epithumētḗs* (1938), one who desires; *epithumía* (1939), desire.

Syn.: *sumpathéō* (4834), to like, sympathize; *agapáō* (25), to love; *homeíromai* or *himeíromai* (2442), to have a strong affection for, yearn after; *orégomai* (3713) or *epipothéō* (1971), to long after; *thélō* (2309), to wish, implying volition and purpose; *boúlomai* (1014), to will deliberately, design; *thélō; zēlóō* (2206), to have a zeal for; *aitéō* (154), to ask, desire; *epizētéō* (1934), to seek earnestly; *exaitéomai* (1809), to desire earnestly.

1938. ἐπιθυμητής, epithumētēs, *ep-ee-thoo-may-tace´*; from 1937; a *craver*:— + lust after.

1939. ἐπιθυμία, epithumia, *ep-ee-thoo-mee´-ah*; from 1937; a *longing* (especially for what is forbidden):—concupiscence, desire, lust (after).

Noun from *epithuméō* (1937), to desire greatly. Strong desire, longing, lust:

(I) Generally: longing (Lk 22:15; Php 1:23; 1Th 2:17; Rev 18:14; Sept.: Pr 10:24; 11:23; Da 9:23; 10:3, 11).

(II) More frequently in a bad sense: irregular and inordinate desire, appetite, lust.

(A) Generally (Mk 4:19; Ro 6:12; 7:7, 8; 13:14; Col 3:5; 1Ti 6:9; 2Ti 3:6; 4:3; Tit 3:3; Jas 1:14, 15; 1Pe 1:14; 4:2, 3; 2Pe 1:4; 3:3; Jude 16, 18). The lust of the flesh means carnal desires, appetites (Gal 5:16, 24; Eph 2:3; 2Pe 2:18; 1Jn 2:16). Also *epithumíai sarkikaí* (4559), carnal, fleshly (1Pe 2:11) referring to worldly desires; desires of the eyes (1Jn 2:16); polluted desires (2Pe 2:10); "lusts of deceit" (a.t.) means "deceitful lusts" (Eph 4:22); "youthful lusts" (2Ti 2:22); see Sept.: Pr 21:25, 26. All these refer to the desires which are fixed on sensual objects as pleasures, profits, honours.

(B) Spoken of impure desire: lewdness (Ro 1:24; 1Th 4:5).

(C) By metonymy: lust, i.e. an object of impure desire, that which is lusted after (Jn 8:44; 1Jn 2:17; Sept.: Da 11:37).

Syn.: *eudokía* (2107), good pleasure or will; *epipóthēsis* (1972), an earnest desire; *epipothía* (1974), a great desire; *thélēma* (2307), a will; *boúlēma* (1013), desire, purpose; *órexis* (3715), desire of any kind with an evil connotation; *hēdonḗ* (2237), lust, pleasure; *páthēma* (3804), passion.

1940. ἐπικαθίζω, epikathizō, *ep-ee-kath-id´-zo*; from 1909 and 2523; to *seat upon:*—set upon.

1941. ἐπικαλέομαι, epikaleomai, *ep-ee-kal-eh´-om-ahee*; middle from 1909 and 2564; to *entitle*; (by implication) to *invoke* (for aid, worship, testimony, decision, etc.):—appeal (unto), call (on, upon), surname.

From *epí* (1909), upon, and *kaléō* (2564), to call, to surname. To call upon:

(**I**) To call upon for aid. In the NT, only in the middle: to call upon for aid in one's own behalf, to invoke:

(**A**) Particularly of invocation addressed to Christ for aid (Ac 7:59; see Sept.: 1Sa 12:17, 18; 2Sa 22:7). Generally: to invoke, pray to, worship, spoken of God (Ro 10:12, 14; 2Ti 2:22); followed by "the name" (Ac 2:21; 9:14; Ro 10:13; Sept.: Ge 4:26; 26:25; Dt 33:19; Joel 2:32); of Christ, followed by "the name," implying the Lord Jesus Christ (Ac 9:21; 22:16; 1Co 1:2).

(**B**) In adjurations, imprecations: to call upon, invoke, as a witness (2Co 1:23).

(**C**) In a judicial sense: to call upon, invoke a higher tribunal or judge, i.e. to appeal to, e.g., Caesar (Ac 25:11, 12, 25; 26:32; 28:19). Followed by an inf. (Ac 25:21, "demanding by appeal that" [a.t.]).

(**II**) To call a name upon, i.e. to name in addition, to surname (Mt 10:25 [UBS]; Sept.: Nu 21:3; Jgs 6:32, the simple verb *ekálesen*). In the middle, in 1Pe 1:17, "if ye call him your Father" (a.t. [cf. Jer 3:19]).

(**A**) Particularly in Mt 10:3; Lk 22:3; Ac 1:23; 4:36; 10:5, 18, 32; 11:13; 12:12, 25; 15:22; Heb 11:16; Sept.: Da 10:1; Mal 1:4.

(**B**) "Upon whom my name is called" (Ac 15:17, i.e. who are called or surnamed by my name, implying property, relation, quoted from Am 9:12; Jas 2:7; see 2Sa 12:28, the simple verb *klēthḗ*, Jer 14:9).

Syn.: *aitéō* (154), to ask, call for; *phōnéō* (5455), to cry out; *krázō* (2896), to call aloud, cry; *kraugázō* (2905), to shout; *onomázō* (3687), to name; *eponomázō* (2028), to surname; *prosagoreúō* (4316), to salute or call upon by name; *prosphōnéō* (4377), to call unto.

1942. ἐπικάλυμα, epikaluma, *ep-ee-kal´-oo-mah*; from 1943; a *covering*, i.e. (figurative) *pretext:*—cloke.

1943. ἐπικαλύπτω, epikaluptō, *ep-ee-kal-oop´-to*; from 1909 and 2572; to *conceal*, i.e. (figurative) *forgive:*—cover.

1944. ἐπικατάρατος, epikataratos, *ep-ee-kat-ar´-at-os*; from 1909 and a derivative of 2672; *imprecated*, i.e. *execrable:*—accursed.

Adjective from *epí* (1909), upon, and *katáratos* (n.f.), cursed. Accursed, under a curse, doomed to punishment (Jn 7:49; Gal 3:10 quoted from Dt 27:26; Sept.: Ge 9:25; Dt 27:15).

Syn.: *epáratos*, accursed.

1945. ἐπίκειμαι, epikeimai, *ep-ik´-i-mahee*; from 1909 and 2749; to *rest upon* (literal or figurative):—impose, be instant, (be) laid (there-, up-) on, (when) lay (on), lie (on), press upon.

1946. Ἐπικούρειος, Epikoureios, *ep-ee-koo´-ri-os*; from Ἐπίκουρος, *Epikouros*; [compare 1947] (a noted philosopher); an *Epicurean* or follower of Epicurus:—Epicurean.

1947. ἐπικουρία, epikouria, *ep-ee-koo-ree´-ah*; from a compound of 1909 and a (prolonged) form of the base of 2877 (in the sense of *servant*); *assistance:*—help.

1948. ἐπικρίνω, epikrinō, *ep-ee-kree´-no*; from 1909 and 2919; to *adjudge:*—give sentence.

1949. ἐπιλαμβάνομαι, epilambanomai, *ep-ee-lam-ban´-om-ahee*; middle from 1909 and 2983; to *seize* (for help, injury, attainment or any other purpose; literal or figurative):—catch, lay hold (up-) on, take (by, hold of, on).

From *epí* (1909), upon, and *lambánō* (2983), to take. To take hold upon, lay hold of in order to hold or detain oneself:

(**I**) Generally: to take hold of, e.g., to take the hand or take by the hand (Mk 8:23; Ac 23:19). Metaphorically (Heb 8:9; Sept.: Jer 31:32; Zec 14:13). To lay hold on, e.g., in order to lead, conduct (Lk 9:47; Ac 9:27; 17:19); in order to succor, heal (Mt 14:31; Lk 14:4). With the idea of violence: to lay hold on, to seize by force as a prisoner (Lk 23:26; Ac 16:19; 18:17; 21:30, 33). Figuratively spoken of language: to lay hold on another's words, i.e. to censure (Lk 20:20, 26).

(**II**) Metaphorically: to lay hold of in order to obtain and possess (1Ti 6:12, 19).

Deriv.: *anepílēptos* (423), blameless.

Syn.: *sullambánō* (4815), to seize; *harpázō* (726), to snatch or catch away; *sunarpázō* (4884), to snatch, seize, keep a firm grip on; *katéchō* (2722), to hold firmly, fast; *kratéō* (2902), to prevail; *tēréō* (5083), to keep; *bastázō* (941), to bear; *epiphérō* (2018), to bring against.

1950. ἐπιλανθάνομαι, epilanthanomai, *ep-ee-lan-than´-om-ahee*; middle from 1909 and 2990; to *lose out* of mind; (by implication) to *neglect:*—(be) forget (-ful of).

1951. ἐπιλέγομαι, epilegomai, *ep-ee-leg´-om-ahee*; middle from 1909 and 3004; to *surname, select:*—call, choose.

From *epí* (1909), upon, moreover, and *légō* (3004), to say. To speak or say upon, i.e. moreover, besides, in addition to. To say or speak upon, i.e. by implication, to name, call (Jn 5:2). To choose, either in addition to or in succession to another (Ac 15:40, to choose for oneself, with the accusative; Sept.: 2Sa 10:9).

Syn.: *eklégomai* (1586), to select out of; *hairéomai* (138), to choose in preference; *hairetízō* (140), to elect in preference; *kaléō* (2564), to call.

1952. ἐπιλείπω, epileipō, *ep-ee-li´-po*; from 1909 and 3007; to *leave upon,* i.e. (figurative) to *be insufficient for:*—fail.

1953. ἐπιλησμονή, epilēsmonē, *ep-ee-lace-mon-ay´*; from a derivative of 1950; *negligence:*— × forgetful.

1954. ἐπίλοιπος, epiloipos, *ep-il´-oy-pos*; from 1909 and 3062; *left over,* i.e. *remaining:*—rest.

1955. ἐπίλυσις, epilusis, *ep-il´-oo-sis*; from 1956; *explanation,* i.e. *application:*—interpretation.

1956. ἐπιλύω, epiluō, *ep-ee-loo´-o*; from 1909 and 3089; to *solve further,* i.e. (figurative) to *explain, decide:*—determine, expound.

1957. ἐπιμαρτυρέω, epimartureō, *ep-ee-mar-too-reh´-o*; from 1909 and 3140; to *attest further,* i.e. *corroborate:*—testify.

From *epí* (1909), an intensive, and *martureō* (3140), to witness. To testify, to attest (1Pe 5:12).

Deriv.: *sunepimartureō* (4901), to bear further witness with someone.

Syn.: *bebaióō* (950), to assure; *kuróō* (2964), to ratify, confirm.

1958. ἐπιμέλεια, epimeleia, *ep-ee-mel´-i-ah*; from 1959; *carefulness,* i.e. kind *attention* (*hospitality*):— + refresh self.

1959. ἐπιμελέομαι, epimeleomai, *ep-ee-mel-eh´-om-ahee*; middle from 1909 and the same as 3199; to *care for* (physical or otherwise):—take care of.

1960. ἐπιμελῶς, epimelōs, *ep-ee-mel-oce´*; adverb from a derivative of 1959; *carefully:*—diligently.

1961. ἐπιμένω, epimenō, *ep-ee-men´-o*; from 1909 and 3306; to *stay over,* i.e. *remain* (figurative, *persevere*):—abide (in), continue (in), tarry.

1962. ἐπινεύω, epineuō, *ep-een-yoo´-o*; from 1909 and 3506; to *nod at,* i.e. (by implication) to *assent:*—consent.

1963. ἐπίνοια, epinoia, *ep-in´-oy-ah*; from 1909 and 3563; *attention* of the mind, i.e. (by implication) *purpose:*—thought.

Noun from *epinoéō* (n.f.), to think upon, from *epí* (1909), upon, and *noús* (3563), mind. A thought, purpose, cogitation (Ac 8:22).

Syn.: *nóēma* (3540), a purpose, device of the mind; *dianóēma* (1270), a plan, machination; *enthúmēsis* (1761), thought, device; *logismós* (3053), thought, imagination; *dialogismós* (1261), reasoning.

1964. ἐπιορκέω, epiorkeō, *ep-ee-or-keh´-o*; from 1965; to *commit perjury:*—forswear self.

1965. ἐπίορκος, epiorkos, *ep-ee´-or-kos*; from 1909 and 3727; *on oath,* i.e. (falsely) a *forswearer:*—perjured person.

1966. ἐπιοῦσα, epiousa, *ep-ee-oo´-sah*; feminine singular participle of a compound of 1909 and **εἶμι, heimi** (to go); *supervening,* i.e. (2250 or 3571 being expressed or implied) the *ensuing* day or night:—following, next.

1967. ἐπιούσιος, epiousios, *ep-ee-oo´-see-os*; perhaps from the same as 1966; *to-morrow's*; but more probably from 1909 and a derivative of the presumed participle feminine of 1510; *for subsistence,* i.e. *needful:*—daily.

Adjective from *epí* (1909), for or into, and *ousía* (3776), being, substance. Daily, used as an adj. Occurs only in the Lord's Prayer (Mt 6:11; Lk 11:3). The Greek Church Father, Chrysostom, explains the *epioúsion árton* (740) as that bread which is needed for our daily support of life. It is that bread which is needful to the *ousía*, substance, of our being, that will sustain us. Other interpreters derive it from *epioúsa* (1966), the next, fem. referring to *hēméra* (2250), day, but in the masc. for *ártos* (740), bread, bread for the coming day.

Syn.: *ephḗmeros* (2184), for the day; *kathēmerinós* (2522), daily; *sḗmeron* (4594), today, this day; *tḗs sḗmeron hēméras*, unto this very day; *tás hēméras*, every day, in the daytime; *pásan hēméran*, every day; *kath' hekástēn hēméran*, literally according to each day, day by day.

1968. ἐπιπίπτω, **epipiptō**, *ep-ee-pip´-to*; from 1909 and 4098; to *embrace* (with affection) or *seize* (with more or less violence; literal or figurative):—fall into (on, upon), lie on, press upon.

1969. ἐπιπλήσσω, **epiplēssō**, *ep-ee-place´-so*; from 1909 and 4141; to *chastise*, i.e. (with words) to *upbraid*:—rebuke.

1970. ἐπιπνίγω, **epipnigō**, *ep-ee-pnee´-go*; from 1909 and 4155; to *throttle upon*, i.e. (figurative) *overgrow*:—choke.

1971. ἐπιποθέω, **epipotheō**, *ep-ee-poth-eh´-o*; from 1909 and ποθέω, *potheō* (to *yearn*); to *dote upon*, i.e. *intensely crave* possession (lawfully or wrongfully):—(earnestly) desire (greatly), (greatly) long (after), lust.

1972. ἐπιπόθησις, **epipothēsis**, *ep-ee-poth´-ay-sis*; from 1971; a *longing for*:—earnest (vehement) desire.

1973. ἐπιπόθητος, **epipothētos**, *ep-ee-poth´-ay-tos*; from 1909 and a derivative of the latter part of 1971; *yearned upon*, i.e. *greatly loved*:—longed for.

1974. ἐπιποθία, **epipothia**, *ep-ee-poth-ee´-ah*; from 1971; *intense longing*:—great desire.

1975. ἐπιπορεύομαι, **epiporeuomai**, *ep-ee-por-yoo´-om-ahee*; from 1909 and 4198; to *journey further*, i.e. *travel on* (*reach*):—come.

1976. ἐπιρράπτω, **epirrhaptō**, *ep-ir-hrap´-to*; from 1909 and the base of 4476; to *stitch upon*, i.e. *fasten* with the needle:—sew on.

1977. ἐπιρρίπτω, **epirrhiptō**, *ep-ir-hrip´-to*; from 1909 and 4496; to *throw upon* (literal or figurative):—cast upon.

1978. ἐπίσημος, **episēmos**, *ep-is´-ay-mos*; from 1909 and some form of the base of 4591; *remarkable*, i.e. (figurative) *eminent*:—notable, of note.

1979. ἐπισιτισμός, **episitismos**, *ep-ee-sit-is-mos´*; from a compound of 1909 and a derivative of 4621; a *provisioning*, i.e. (concretely) *food*:—victuals.

1980. ἐπισκέπτομαι, **episkeptomai**, *ep-ee-skep´-tom-ahee*; middle from 1909 and the base of 4649; to *inspect*, i.e. (by implication) to *select*; by extension to *go to see*, *relieve*:—look out, visit.

From *epí* (1909), upon, and *sképtomai* (n.f.), to look. To look at something, examine closely, inspect, observe:

(I) To look upon with mercy, favour, regard (Lk 1:68, 78; 7:16; Ac 15:14; Heb 2:6 quoted from Ps 8:5; see Ge 50:24, 25; Ps 106:4).

(II) To visit in order to punish (Sept.: Ps 89:32).

(III) To look after, take care of, tend (Ac 7:23; 15:36; Sept.: Jgs 15:1). Frequently used in the Class. Gr. for taking care of or nursing the sick (Mt 25:36, 43; Jas 1:27).

(IV) To look at accurately or diligently, with the meaning to look for, seek out, as persons for office, transitively (Ac 6:3; Sept.: Le 13:36; Ezr 6:1; Eze 20:40).

Syn.: *historéō* (2477), to visit, in order to be acquainted with; *epiphérō* (2018), to bear upon, add, bring against.

1981. ἐπισκηνόω, **episkēnoō**, *ep-ee-skay-no´-o*; from 1909 and 4637; to *tent upon*, i.e. (figurative) *abide with*:—rest upon.

1982. ἐπισκιάζω, **episkiazō**, *ep-ee-skee-ad´-zo*; from 1909 and a derivative of 4639; to *cast a shade upon*, i.e. (by analogy) to *envelop* in a haze of brilliancy; (figurative) to *invest* with preternatural influence:—overshadow.

1983. ἐπισκοπέω, **episkopeō**, *ep-ee-skop-eh´-o*; from 1909 and 4648; to *oversee*; (by implication) to *beware*:—look diligently, take the oversight.

From *epí* (1909), upon, and *skopéō* (4648), to regard, give attention to. To look upon, observe, examine the state of affairs of something, look after, oversee. In the NT, to look after, to see to, to take care of (Heb 12:15; 1Pe 5:2; Sept.: Dt 11:12).

Deriv.: *episkopḗ* (1984), the office of a bishop.

Syn.: *poimaínō* (4165), to shepherd, tend a flock; *bóskō* (1006), to lead to pasture, fodder; *epimeléomai* (1959), to show concern over; *merimnáō* (3309) to be concerned.

1984. ἐπισκοπή, episkopē, *ep-is-kop-ay´*; from 1980; *inspection* (for relief); (by implication) *superintendence*; specially the Christian "*episcopate*":—the office of a "bishop," bishoprick, visitation.

Noun from *episkopéō* (1983), to look after. Visitation, or the act of visiting or being visited or inspected. In the NT, used metaphorically of God, who is said to visit men for good (Lk 19:44; 1Pe 2:12; Sept.: Job 10:12; 34:9). Of the duty of visiting or inspecting, i.e. charge, office (Ac 1:20, quoted from Ps 109:8). Spoken of the office of an *epískopos*, overseer, i.e. the care and oversight of a Christian church (1Ti 3:1).

1985. ἐπίσκοπος, episkopos, *ep-is´-kop-os*; from 1909 and 4649 (in the sense of 1983); a *superintendent*, i.e. Christian officer in general charge of a (or the) church (literal or figurative):—bishop, overseer.

Noun from *epí* (1909), upon, and *skopós* (4649), a watchman. Superintendent, overseer. The overseer of public works (Sept.: 2Ch 34:12, 17); of cities, e.g., a prefect (Isa 60:17). In Athens *epískopoi* (pl.) were magistrates sent to outlying cities to organize and govern them. In the NT, used of officers in the local churches, overseers, superintendents (Ac 20:28; Php 1:1; 1Ti 3:2; Tit 1:7). Used figuratively of Jesus (1Pe 2:25). This name was originally simply the Greek term equal to *presbúteros* (4245), which was derived from the Jewish polity.

Deriv.: *allotrioepískopos* (244), a busybody.

Syn.: *presbúteros* (4245), elder; *poimḗn* (4166), shepherd; *diákonos* (1249), minister.

1986. ἐπισπάομαι, epispaomai, *ep-ee-spah´-om-ahee*; from 1909 and 4685; to *draw over*, i.e. (with 203 implied) *efface* the mark of *circum-*

cision (by recovering with the foreskin):—become uncircumcised.

1987. ἐπίσταμαι, epistamai, *ep-is´-tam-ahee*; apparently a middle of 2186 (with 3563 implied); to *put* the mind *upon*, i.e. *comprehend*, or *be acquainted with*:—know, understand.

1988. ἐπιστάτης, epistatēs, *ep-is-tat´-ace*; from 1909 and a presumed derivative of 2476; an *appointee over*, i.e. *commander* (*teacher*):—master.

1989. ἐπιστέλλω, epistellō, *ep-ee-stel´-lo*; from 1909 and 4724; to *enjoin* (by writing), i.e. (genitive) to *communicate by letter* (for any purpose):—write (a letter, unto).

1990. ἐπιστήμων, epistēmōn, *ep-ee-stay´-mone*; from 1987; *intelligent*:—endued with knowledge.

1991. ἐπιστηρίζω, epistērizō, *ep-ee-stay-rid´-zo*; from 1909 and 4741; to *support further*, i.e. *reëstablish*:—confirm, strengthen.

1992. ἐπιστολή, epistolē, *ep-is-tol-ay´*; from 1989; a *written message*:—"epistle," letter.

1993. ἐπιστομίζω, epistomizō, *ep-ee-stom-id´-zo*; from 1909 and 4750; to *put something over* the *mouth*, i.e. (figurative) to *silence*:—stop mouths.

1994. ἐπιστρέφω, epistrephō, *ep-ee-stref´-o*; from 1909 and 4762; to *revert* (literal, figurative or moral):—come (go) again, convert, (re-) turn (about, again).

From *epí* (1909), to, and *stréphō* (4762), to turn. To turn upon, toward:

(**I**) In a moral sense: to turn upon or convert unto (Lk 1:16, 17; Sept.: Ezr 6:22). In the sense of to turn back again upon, to cause to return from error (Jas 5:19, 20; Sept.: 1Ki 13:18–20).

(**II**) To turn oneself upon or toward, i.e. to turn toward or unto:

(**A**) Act. intransitively (Ac 9:40): (**1**) Figuratively: to turn to the service and worship of the true God (Ac 9:35; 11:21; 14:15; 15:19; 26:18, 20); to the Lord (2Co 3:16; 1Th 1:9); to the shepherd (1Pe 2:25; Sept.: Ge 24:49; Dt 31:18, where is found the verb *apostréphō* [654], to turn away; Jos 19:34; 1Ch 12:19; Hos 5:4; Am 4:6, 8). (**2**) By implication, to turn about, upon or toward (Rev 1:12). Used in an absolute sense

(Ac 16:18; Sept.: Jgs 18:21). **(3)** To turn back upon, return unto, and followed by *opísō* (3694), back (Mt 24:18); *eis tá opísō*, backward (Mk 13:16; Lk 17:31); by *eis* (1519), unto, with the accusative (Mt 12:44); by *epí* (1909), upon, with the accusative (Lk 17:4; 2Pe 2:22). Used in an absolute sense (Lk 2:20 [TR]; Ac 15:36). Of the breath or spirit returning to a dead body (Lk 8:55; Sept.: Ru 1:7, 10; 2Sa 6:20; 1Ki 2:30). Metaphorically, spoken of a return to good: to return, be converted, used in an absolute sense (Lk 22:32; Ac 3:19; also Mt 13:15; Mk 4:12; Ac 28:27, all quoted from Isa 6:10); also to turn back unto evil (Gal 4:9; 2Pe 2:21).

(B) Middle, intransitively: **(1)** By implication: to turn about, upon or toward (Mt 9:22; Mk 8:33; Jn 21:20); by *en* (1722), in (Mk 5:30; Sept.: Nu 23:5). **(2)** To turn back upon, return unto (Mt 10:13; Sept.: Ru 1:11, 12, 15). Metaphorically, to return to good, be converted (Jn 12:40 [cf. Isa 6:10]).

Deriv.: *epistrophḗ* (1995), conversion.

Syn.: *epanérchomai* (1880), to come back again; *anakámptō* (344), to return; *metastréphō* (3344), to change into something different.

1995. ἐπιστροφή, epistrophē, *ep-is-trof-ay´*; from 1994; *reversion*, i.e. moral *revolution*:— conversion.

Noun from *epistréphō* (1994), to turn about. A turning around, conversion. Occurs only in Ac 15:3.

1996. ἐπισυνάγω, episunagō, *ep-ee-soon-ag´-o*; from 1909 and 4863; to *collect upon* the same place:—gather (together).

1997. ἐπισυναγωγή, episunagōgē, *ep-ee-soon-ag-o-gay´*; from 1996; a complete *collection*; specially a Christian *meeting* (for worship):— assembling (gathering) together.

Noun from *episunágō* (1996), to gather together. The act of gathering or assembling together (2Th 2:1 [cf. 1Th 4:17]; Heb 10:25).

Syn.: *sunagōgḗ* (4864), a gathering of Jews for worship, a synagogue; *ekklēsía* (1577), an assembly, church; *sunédrion* (4892), a council; *panḗguris* (3831), a festive assembly; *sunodía* (4923), synod, companionship on a journey.

1998. ἐπισυντρέχω, episuntrechō, *ep-ee-soon-trekh´-o*; from 1909 and 4936; to *hasten*

together upon one place (or a participle occasion):—come running together.

1999. ἐπισύστασις, episustasis, *ep-ee-soo´-stas-is*; from the middle of a compound of 1909 and 4921; a *conspiracy*, i.e. *concourse* (riotous or friendly):—that which cometh upon, + raising up.

Noun from *episunístēmi* (n.f.), to come together upon, which is from *epí* (1909), an intensive, and *sunístēmi* (4921), to approve. A concourse, crowd. In Ac 24:12, *poieín episústasin*, to excite a crowd, raise a tumult (see *poiéō* [4160], to make, do). Spoken of a crowd: constant ingress of persons coming to someone (2Co 11:28).

Syn.: *próskomma* (4348), stumbling; *proskopḗ* (4349), offence; *phragmós* (5418), a barrier.

2000. ἐπισφαλής, episphalēs, *ep-ee-sfal-ace´*; from a compound of 1909 and σφάλλω, *sphallō* (to *trip*); (figurative) *insecure*:—dangerous.

2001. ἐπισχύω, epischuō, *ep-is-khoo´-o*; from 1909 and 2480; to *avail further*, i.e. (figurative) *insist stoutly*:—be the more fierce.

2002. ἐπισωρεύω, episōreuō, *ep-ee-so-ryoo´-o*; from 1909 and 4987; to *accumulate further*, i.e. (figurative) *seek* additionally:—heap.

2003. ἐπιταγή, epitagē, *ep-ee-tag-ay´*; from 2004; an *injunction* or *decree*; (by implication) *authoritativeness*:—authority, commandment.

Noun from *epitássō* (2004), to command, arrange upon. Authority, command imposed upon someone. Command of Christ (1Co 7:6, 25; 2Co 8:8); of God, will, decree (Ro 16:26 [TR]; 1Ti 1:1; Tit 1:3); generally (Tit 2:15, "with all injunction" [a.t.], i.e. strongly, severely).

Syn.: *diatagé* (1296), an order, ordinance, disposition; *diátagma* (1297), commandment, that which is imposed by decree or law; *entolḗ* (1785), a general injunction, charge, precept of moral and religious nature; *éntalma* (1778), the thing commanded, a commission, precept.

2004. ἐπιτάσσω, epitassō, *ep-ee-tas´-so*; from 1909 and 5021; to *arrange upon*, i.e. *order*:— charge, command, injoin.

From *epí* (1909), upon, over, and *tássō* (5021), to arrange, appoint or place appropriately. To give an order; put upon one as a duty, enjoin

(Mk 1:27; 6:27, 39; 9:25; Lk 4:36; 8:25, 31; 14:22; Ac 23:2; Phm 8).

Deriv.: *epitagḗ* (2003), injunction, command.

Syn.: *diastéllomai* (1291), to charge, enjoin; *diatássō* (1299), to set in order, command; *entéllomai* (1781), to order, command, enjoin; *keleúō* (2753), to order, bid; *paraggéllō* (3853), to order, give a charge; *prostássō* (4367), to prescribe, give command.

2005. ἐπιτελέω, epiteleō, *ep-ee-tel-eh´-o*; from 1909 and 5055; to *fulfill further* (or *completely*), i.e. *execute*; (by implication) to *terminate*, *undergo*:—accomplish, do, finish, (make) (perfect), perform (× -ance).

From *epí* (1909), an intensive, and *teléō* (5055), to complete. To bring through to an end, to finish, to perform. Spoken of a work, business, course, etc. (Lk 13:32; Ro 15:28; 2Co 7:1; 8:6, 11; Php 1:6; Heb 8:5; 9:6). In the middle: to come to an end, to finish (Gal 3:3). Figuratively, spoken of sufferings: to accomplish, i.e. to undergo, to endure (1Pe 5:9).

Syn.: *apoteléō* (658), to perfect, finish; *ekplēróō* (1603), to fulfill, accomplish entirely; *ekteléō* (1615), to finish out or complete; *plēróō* (4137), to complete, fulfill, carry out; *sunteléō* (4931), to bring to fulfillment, effect in concord with; *teleióō* (5048), to make perfect, complete, accomplish.

2006. ἐπιτήδειος, epitēdeios, *ep-ee-tay´-di-os*; from ἐπιτηδές, *epitēdes* (*enough*); *serviceable*, i.e. (by implication) *requisite*:—things which are needful.

2007. ἐπιτίθημι, epitithēmi, *ep-ee-tith´-ay-mee*; from 1909 and 5087; to *impose* (in a friendly or hostile sense):—add unto, lade, lay upon, put (up) on, set on (up), + surname, × wound.

2008. ἐπιτιμάω, epitimaō, *ep-ee-tee-mah´-o*; from 1909 and 5091; to *tax upon*, i.e. *censure* or *admonish*; (by implication) *forbid*:—(straitly) charge, rebuke.

From *epí* (1909), upon, and *timáō* (5091), to evaluate. In the NT, to punish, rebuke, charge:

(I) Generally (Mt 16:22; 19:13; 20:31; Mk 8:32; 10:13, 48; Lk 18:15, 39; 19:39). With the idea of punishment (Jude 9). With the idea of restraining: spoken of winds and waves (Mt 8:26; Mk 4:39; Lk 8:24); of a fever (Lk 4:39).

(II) By implication, to admonish strongly, with urgency, authority, i.e. to enjoin upon, charge strictly: e.g., not to tell something (Mt 12:16; Mk 3:12; 8:30; Lk 9:21); with the idea of censure implied, e.g., demons (Mt 17:18; Mk 1:25; 9:25; Lk 4:35, 41; 9:42).

Deriv.: *epitimía* (2009), punishment.

Syn.: *elégchō* (1651), to reprove with conviction; *embrimáomai* (1690), to charge strictly, rebuke sternly; *epiplḗssō* (1969), to strike at, rebuke.

2009. ἐπιτιμία, epitimia, *ep-ee-tee-mee´-ah*; from a compound of 1909 and 5092; properly *esteem*, i.e. *citizenship*; used (in the sense of 2008) of a *penalty*:—punishment.

2010. ἐπιτρέπω, epitrepō, *ep-ee-trep´-o*; from 1909 and the base of 5157; to *turn over* (*transfer*), i.e. *allow*:—give leave (liberty, license), let, permit, suffer.

2011. ἐπιτροπή, epitropē, *ep-ee-trop-ay´*; from 2010; *permission*, i.e. (by implication) full *power*:—commission.

2012. ἐπίτροπος, epitropos, *ep-it´-rop-os*; from 1909 and 5158 (in the sense of 2011); a *commissioner*, i.e. domestic *manager*, *guardian*:—steward, tutor.

2013. ἐπιτυγχάνω, epitugchanō, *ep-ee-toong-khan´-o*; from 1909 and 5177; to *chance upon*, i.e. (by implication) *attain*:—obtain.

2014. ἐπιφαίνω, epiphainō, *ep-ee-fah´ee-no*; from 1909 and 5316; to *shine upon*, i.e. *become* (literal) *visible* or (figurative) *known*:—appear, give light.

From *epí* (1909), over, upon or to, and *phaínō* (5316), to shine. To cause to appear upon or to; to show before, to exhibit. In the NT, to show oneself upon or to, i.e. to appear upon or to. Spoken of light: to shine upon (Lk 1:79; Ac 27:20). Metaphorically: to be conscious, to be known and manifest; spoken of God's grace (Tit 2:11); spoken of God's love (Tit 3:4).

Deriv.: *epipháneia* (2015), appearing; *epiphanḗs* (2016), memorable, notable.

Syn.: *emphanízō* (1718), to cause to appear; *óptomai, optánomai* (3700), to appear; *phaneróō* (5319), to manifest.

2015. ἐπιφάνεια, **epiphaneia,** *ep-if-an´-i-ah*; from 2016; a *manifestation,* i.e. (special) the *advent* of Christ (past or future):—appearing, brightness.

Noun from *epiphaínō* (2014), to appear. An appearing, appearance. Spoken of the advent of Jesus (2Ti 1:10); of his future advent (2Th 2:8; 1Ti 6:14; 2Ti 4:1, 8; Tit 2:13).

Syn.: *apokálupsis* (602), revelation, unveiling; *parousía* (3952), appearance, appearing, presence.

2016. ἐπιφανής, **epiphanēs,** *ep-if-an-ace´*; from 2014; *conspicuous,* i.e. (figurative) *memorable:*—notable.

2017. ἐπιφαύω, **epiphauō,** *ep-ee-fow´-o*; a form of 2014; to *illuminate* (figurative):—give light.

2018. ἐπιφέρω, **epipherō,** *ep-ee-fer´-o*; from 1909 and 5342; to *bear upon* (or *further*), i.e. *adduce* (personally or judicially [*accuse, inflict*]), *superinduce:*—add, bring (against), take.

2019. ἐπιφωνέω, **epiphōneō,** *ep-ee-fo-neh´-o*; from 1909 and 5455; to *call at* something, i.e. *exclaim:*—cry (against), give a shout.

2020. ἐπιφώσκω, **epiphōskō,** *ep-ee-foce´-ko*; a form of 2017; to begin to *grow light:*—begin to dawn, × draw on.

2021. ἐπιχειρέω, **epicheireō,** *ep-ee-khi-reh´-o*; from 1909 and 5495; to put the *hand upon,* i.e. *undertake:*—go about, take in hand (upon).

2022. ἐπιχέω, **epicheō,** *ep-ee-kheh´-o*; from 1909 and χέω, *cheō* (to *pour*); to *pour upon:*—pour in.

2023. ἐπιχορηγέω, **epichorēgeō,** *ep-ee-khor-ayg-eh´-o*; from 1909 and 5524; to *furnish besides,* i.e. fully *supply,* (figurative) *aid* or *contribute:*—add, minister (nourishment, unto).

2024. ἐπιχορηγία, **epichorēgia,** *ep-ee-khor-ayg-ee´-ah*; from 2023; *contribution:*—supply.

2025. ἐπιχρίω, **epichriō,** *ep-ee-khree´-o*; from 1909 and 5548; to *smear over:*—anoint.

2026. ἐποικοδομέω, **epoikodomeō,** *ep-oy-kod-om-eh´-o*; from 1909 and 3618; to *build upon,* i.e. (figurative) to *rear up:*—build thereon (thereupon, on, upon).

From *epí* (1909), upon, and *oikodoméō* (3618), to build. To build upon, to erect a foundation. In the NT, only figuratively: to build upon, spoken of the Christian faith and Christian life, both the whole church and its individual members as built upon the only foundation, Christ, and implying the constant internal development of the kingdom of God and the visible church, like a holy temple progressively and unceasingly built up from the foundation (1Co 3:10, 12, 14; Eph 2:20; Col 2:7). By implication: to build up further in the faith and upon Christ (Ac 20:32; Jude 20).

Syn.: *anoikodoméō* (456), to rebuild; *epoikodoméō* (2026), to build upon, edify; *kataskeuázō* (2680), to construct, build.

2027. ἐποκέλλω, **epokellō,** *ep-ok-el´-lo*; from 1909 and ὀκέλλω, *okellō* (to *urge*); to *drive upon* the shore, i.e. to *beach* a vessel:—run aground.

2028. ἐπονομάζω, **eponomazō,** *ep-on-om-ad´-zo*; from 1909 and 3687; to *name further,* i.e. *denominate:*—call.

2029. ἐποπτεύω, **epopteuō,** *ep-opt-yoo´-o*; from 1909 and a derivative of 3700; to *inspect,* i.e. *watch:*—behold.

2030. ἐπόπτης, **epoptēs,** *ep-op´-tace*; from 1909 and a presumed derivative of 3700; a *looker- on:*—eyewitness.

2031. ἔπος, **epos,** *ep´-os*; from 2036; a *word:*—× say.

2032. ἐπουράνιος, **epouranios,** *ep-oo-ran´-ee-os*; from 1909 and 3772; *above the sky:*—celestial, (in) heaven (-ly), high.

Adjective from *epí* (1909), upon, in, and *ouranós* (3772), heaven. Heavenly, celestial. Spoken of those who dwell in heaven (Mt 18:35; Php 2:10); of those who come from heaven (1Co 15:48, 49); of heavenly or celestial bodies, the sun, moon (1Co 15:40 [see 1Co 15:44]). The neuter plural with the definite article: the heavens, heaven (Eph 1:20; 2:6; 3:10). Of the lower heavens, the sky or air as the seat of evil spirits (Eph 6:12). Spoken of the kingdom of heaven and whatever pertains to it (2Ti 4:18). Also Jn 3:12; Eph 1:3; Heb 3:1; 6:4; 8:5; 9:23; 11:16; 12:22.

2033. ἑπτά, **hepta,** *hep-tah´*; a primary number; *seven:*—seven.

2034. ἑπτάκις, heptakis, *hep-tak-is´*; adverb from 2033; *seven times:*—seven times.

2035. ἑπτακισχίλιοι, heptakischilioi, *hep-tak-is-khil´-ee-oy*; from 2034 and 5507; *seven times a thousand:*—seven thousand.

2036. ἔπω, epō, *ep´-o*; a primary verb (used only in the definite past tense, the others being borrowed from 2046, 4483 and 5346); to *speak* or *say* (by word or writing):—answer, bid, bring word, call, command, grant, say (on), speak, tell. Compare 3004.

2037. Ἔραστος, Erastos, *er´-as-tos*; from ἐράω, *Eraō* (to *love*); *beloved*; *Erastus*, a Christian:—Erastus.

2038. ἐργάζομαι, ergazomai, *er-gad´-zom-ahee*; middle from 2041; to *toil* (as a task, occupation, etc.), (by implication) *effect, be engaged in* or *with*, etc.:—commit, do, labour for, minister about, trade (by), work.

Middle deponent from *érgon* (2041), work. To work, labour:

(I) Intransitively, to work, labour, that is:

(A) Particularly in a field (Mt 21:28); at a trade (Ac 18:3; 1Co 4:12; 1Th 2:9; 2Th 3:8); generally (Lk 13:14; Jn 9:4; 1Co 9:6; 1Th 4:11; 2Th 3:10–12).

(B) In the sense of being active, i.e. to exert one's powers and faculties (Jn 5:17; Ro 4:5).

(C) Also to do business, i.e. to trade, to deal (Mt 25:16).

(II) Transitively, to work, perform by labour, to do, produce:

(A) Of things wrought, done, performed, e.g., miracles (Jn 6:30; Ac 13:41); of sacred rites (1Co 9:13); generally (Eph 4:28; Col 3:23). To work the works of God, or a good work (Mt 26:10; Mk 14:6; Jn 3:21; 6:28; 9:4; 1Co 16:10; 3Jn 5). Also Mt 7:23; Ac 10:35; Ro 2:10; 13:10; Gal 6:10; Heb 11:33; Jas 2:9).

(B) In the sense of to till, cultivate, e.g., the earth (Sept.: Ge 2:5, 15). In the NT, metaphorically spoken only of the sea: to cultivate the sea, i.e. to ply or follow the sea as an occupation as sailors, mariners (Rev 18:17).

(C) In the sense of to work for, labour for, earn, e.g., one's food (Jn 6:27; 2Jn 8).

Deriv.: *ergasía* (2039), craft, diligence, gain; *ergátēs* (2040), labourer; *katergázomai* (2716), to work fully, accomplish; *periergázomai* (4020),

to be a busybody; *prosergázomai* (4333), to gain, acquire besides.

Syn.: *energéō* (1754), to work in; *epiteléō* (2005), to perform; *katergázomai* (2716), to work; *kopiáō* (2872), to toil; *poiéō* (4160), to do; *pragmateúomai* (4231), to trade; *prássō* (4238), to do work; *prosergázomai* (4333), to work out in addition.

2039. ἐργασία, ergasia, *er-gas-ee´-ah*; from 2040; *occupation*; (by implication) *profit, pains:*—craft, diligence, gain, work.

2040. ἐργάτης, ergatēs, *er-gat´-ace*; from 2041; a *toiler*; (figurative) a *teacher:*—labourer, worker (-men).

2041. ἔργον, ergon, *er´-gon*; from a primary (but obsolete) ἔργω, *ergō* (to *work*); *toil* (as an effort or occupation); (by implication) an *act:*—deed, doing, labour, work.

Noun from *érgō* (n.f.), to work. Work, performance, the result or object of employment, making or working:

(I) A labour, business, employment, something to be done.

(A) Generally (Mk 13:34; Eph 4:12; 1Ti 3:1); of the work which Jesus was sent to fulfill on earth (Jn 5:20, 36; 10:38; 17:4); that which one has been called or ordained to accomplish (Jn 4:34; 6:28, 29; 9:4; 17:4; Ac 13:2; 14:26; 15:38; 1Co 15:58; 16:10; Php 1:22; 2:30; Rev 2:26).

(B) In the sense of undertaking, attempt (Ac 5:38).

(II) Work, i.e. deed, act, action, something done:

(A) Generally: to work a work, do a deed (Ac 13:41 quoted from Hab 1:5); of the works of Jesus: miracles, mighty deeds (Mt 11:2; Jn 7:3, 21; 14:10–12; 15:24); of God (Heb 3:9 from Ps 95:9).

(B) An action or deed as contrasted to *lógos* (3056), word (Lk 24:19; Ac 7:22; Ro 15:18; 2Co 10:11; Col 3:17; Tit 1:16). By implication in Jas 1:25, a hearer, "but a doer of the work" or the deed.

(C) Of the works of men in reference to right and wrong as judged by the moral law, the precepts of the gospel: **(1)** Generally (Mt 23:3, 5; Jn 3:20, 21; Ac 26:20; Ro 2:6; 3:27; 2Co 11:15; Gal 6:4; 1Pe 1:17; Rev 20:12). **(2)** Of good works, with various adjectives (Mt 5:16; Mk 14:6; Ac 9:36; Ro 2:7; Eph 2:10; 2Th 2:17; 1Ti 6:18; Tit 2:7; 3:5; Heb 13:21; Jas 1:4). **(3)** Of evil works with various adjectives (Jn 3:19; Ro 13:12; Gal 5:19; Col 1:21; 2Ti 4:18; Heb 6:1; 2Pe 2:8; 1Jn 3:12; Jude 15). **(4)** Of works of the law, meaning works required or conformable to the Mosaic moral law and required by this law (Ro 2:15; 3:20; 4:2, 6; 9:11; 11:6; Gal 2:16; Eph 2:9; 2Ti 1:9). **(5)** Of works of faith, meaning springing from faith, combined with faith (1Th 1:3; 2Th 1:11; Heb 6:10; Jas 2:14, 17–26). **(III)** Work, i.e. the thing wrought, something made or created generally by men, such as an idol (Ac 7:41). Of the works of God, generally (Ac 15:18; Ro 14:20; Php 1:6; Heb 1:10; Rev 15:3). Also of works implying power, and used for power or might, e.g., of God (Jn 9:3); of Satan (1Jn 3:8).

Deriv.: *ampelourgós* (289), vine-dresser; *argós* (692), idle, barren; *geōrgós* (1092), husbandman; *dēmiourgós* (1217), one who works for the public; *energés* (1756), active; *ergázomai* (2038), to work; *euergétēs* (2110), benefactor; *leitourgós* (3011), public servant, minister; *panoúrgos* (3835), crafty; *períergos* (4021), busybody; *sunergós* (4904), workfellow.

Syn.: *dúnamis* (1411), miracle, a powerful deed or act; *ergasía* (2039), a working, business; *ktísma* (2938), product, creature; *poíēsis* (4162), a doing, deed; *prágma* (4229), an accomplished act, deed; *práxis* (4234), transaction, a deed; *téchnē* (5078) craft, occupation.

2042. ἐρεθίζω, **erethizō**, *er-eth-id´-zo*; from a presumed prolonged form of 2054; to *stimulate* (especially to anger):—provoke.

2043. ἐρείδω, **ereidō**, *er-i´-do*; of obscure affinity; to *prop*, i.e. (reflexive) *get fast*:—stick fast.

2044. ἐρεύγομαι, **ereugomai**, *er-yoog´-om-ahee*; of uncertain affinity; to *belch*, i.e. (figurative) to *speak out*:—utter.

2045. ἐρευνάω, **ereunaō**, *er-yoo-nah´-o*; apparently from 2046 (through the idea of *inquiry*); to *seek*, i.e. (figurative) to *investigate*:—search.

2046. ἐρέω, **ereō**, *er-eh´-o*; probably a fuller form of 4483; an alternate for 2036 in certain tenses; to *utter*, i.e. *speak* or *say*:—call, say, speak (of), tell.

Some tenses use *rhéō* (4483) or *épō* (2036). To say, declare (Mt 26:75; Lk 2:24; 22:13; Jn 4:18; Ro 4:1). To promise (Heb 13:5); to call (Jn 15:15).

Deriv.: *proeréō* (4280), to say before, foretell.
Syn.: *laléō* (2980), to talk; *phēmí* (5346), to speak, affirm.

2047. ἐρημία, **erēmia**, *er-ay-mee´-ah*; from 2048; *solitude* (concrete):—desert, wilderness.

2048. ἔρημος, **erēmos**, *er´-ay-mos*; of uncertain affinity; *lonesome*, i.e. (by implication) *waste* (usually as a noun, 5561 being implied):—desert, desolate, solitary, wilderness.

2049. ἐρημόω, **erēmoō**, *er-ay-mo´-o*; from 2048; to *lay waste* (literal or figurative):—(bring to, make) desolate (-ion), come to nought.

2050. ἐρήμωσις, **erēmōsis**, *er-ay´-mo-sis*; from 2049; *despoliation*:—desolation.

2051. ἐρίζω, **erizō**, *er-id´-zo*; from 2054; to *wrangle*:—strive.

2052. ἐριθεία, **eritheia**, *er-ith-i´-ah*; perhaps from the same as 2042; properly *intrigue*, i.e. (by implication) *faction*:—contention (-ious), strife.

Noun from *eritheúō* (n.f.), to work for hire. Contention, party-strife, rivalry (Php 1:16; 2:3). It also means canvassing for public office, scheming, promoting political factions (Ro 2:8; 2Co 12:20; Gal 5:20; Jas 3:14, 16).

Syn.: *éris* (2054), strife, quarrel, rivalry; *logomachía* (3055), strife of words; *paroxusmós* (3948), paroxysm, contention, irritation; *philoneikía* (5379), dispute, quarrelsomeness.

2053. ἔριον, **erion**, *er´-ee-on*; of obscure affinity; *wool*:—wool.

2054. ἔρις, **eris**, *er´-is*; of uncertain affinity; a *quarrel*, i.e. (by implication) *wrangling*:—contention, debate, strife, variance.

2055. ἐρίφιον, **eriphion**, *er-if´-ee-on*; from 2056; a *kidling*, i.e. (genitive) *goat* (symbolical wicked person):—goat.

2056. ἔριφος, **eriphos**, *er´-if-os*; perhaps from the same as 2053 (through the idea of *hairiness*); a *kid* or (generic) *goat*:—goat, kid.

2057. Ἑρμᾶς, **Hermas**, *her-mas´*; probably from 2060; *Hermas*, a Christian:—Hermas.

2058. ἑρμηνεία, **hermēneia**, *her-may-ni´-ah*; from the same as 2059; *translation*:—interpretation.

2059. ἑρμηνεύω, hermēneuō, *her-mayn-yoo´- o*; from a presumed derivative of 2060 (as the god of language); to *translate*:—interpret.

2060. Ἑρμῆς, Hermēs, *her-mace´*; perhaps from 2046; *Hermes*, the name of the messenger of the Greek deities; also of a Christian:—Hermes, Mercury.

2061. Ἑρμογενης, Hermōgenēs, *her-mogen´-ace*; from 2060 and 1096; *born of Hermes*; *Hermogenes*, an apostate Christian:—Hermogenes.

2062. ἑρπετόν, herpeton, *her-pet-on´*; neuter of a derivative of ἕρπω, herpō (to *creep*); a *reptile*, i.e. (by Hebrew [compare 7431]) a small *animal*:—creeping thing, serpent.

2063. ἐρυθρός, eruthros, *er-oo-thros´*; of uncertain affinity; *red*, i.e. (with 2281) the *Red* Sea:—red.

2064. ἔρχομαι, erchomai, *er´-khom-ahee*; middle of a primary verb (used only in the present and imperfect tenses, the others being supplied by a kindred [middle] ἐλεύθομαι, eleuthomai, *el-yoo´-thom-ahee*; or [active] ἔλθω, elthō, el´-tho; which do not otherwise occur); to *come* or *go* (in a great variety of applications, literal and figurative):—accompany, appear, bring, come, enter, fall out, go, grow, × light, × next, pass, resort, be set.

To come, to go, move or pass along in any direction, as marked by the adjuncts or often simply by the context. The forms of the 2d aor., however, more frequently signify to come, and are rarely used of one who goes from or away.

(**I**) To go, with adjuncts implying motion from a place or person to another: to go, to go to (Mk 11:13; Lk 2:44; Jn 6:17; Ac 9:17; Heb 11:8).

(**II**) To come, with adjuncts implying motion to or toward any person or place:

(**A**) As spoken of persons: in an absolute sense (Mt 8:9; Mk 4:4; Jn 1:39). In the present in a historical sense, that is, instead of the aor. (Mt 25:11, 19; Mk 2:18; Jn 20:18; 3Jn 3); in a fut. sense, apparently, but only of what is certain to take place (Jn 4:25; 14:3, 30; Rev 1:7). Especially in the phrase *ho erchómenos*, the coming One, i.e. the future One, He who shall come, the Messiah (Mt 11:3; 21:9; Lk 7:19, 20; Jn 6:14; 11:27; 12:13).

(**B**) In the sense of to come forth before the public: to appear, make one's appearance (Mt 11:14, 19; 17:11; 24:5; Mk 9:11, 12; Jn 1:31; Gal 3:19; 2Pe 3:3; 1Jn 4:2).

(**C**) In the sense of to come again, come back, to return: (Mt 2:21; 5:24; Lk 15:30; 19:13; Jn 7:45; 9:7; 14:18, 28; 21:22; Ro 9:9; 2Th 1:10; Heb 13:25).

(**D**) Metaphorically spoken of things, for example: (**1**) Of time (Mt 9:15; Lk 23:29; Jn 4:35; 9:4; 16:4, 32; Ac 2:20; 3:19; Heb 8:8). (**2**) Of the kingdom of God, to come, i.e. to be established (Mt 6:10; Mk 11:10).

Deriv.: *anérchomai* (424), to go up; *apérchomai* (565), to go away or from; *diérchomai* (1330), to come or go through; *eisérchomai* (1525), to go or come into; *éleusis* (1660), advent, coming; *exérchomai* (1831), to come out; *epérchomai* (1904), to come or go upon; *katérchomai* (2718), to come down; *parérchomai* (3928), to pass by; *periérchomai* (4022), to come or go all around; *proérchomai* (4281), to go before, precede; *prosérchomai* (4334), to come or go near; *sunérchomai* (4905), to come together.

Syn.: *paragínomai* (3854), to arrive, be present. Also *aphiknéomai* (864), to arrive at a place; *hḗkō* (2240), to come, with the emphasis of being present.

2065. ἐρωτάω, erōtaō, *er-o-tah´-o*; apparently from 2046 [compare 2045]; to *interrogate*; (by implication) to *request*:—ask, beseech, desire, intreat, pray. Compare 4441.

From *éromai* (n.f.), to ask, inquire. To ask:

(**I**) To interrogate, inquire of (Mt 16:13; 21:24; Mk 4:10; Lk 9:45; 20:3; 22:68; Jn 1:19; 16:5).

(**II**) To request, entreat, beseech (Mt 15:23; Lk 5:3; 7:3, 36; 14:18, 19; Jn 4:40, 47; 12:21; Ac 3:3; 23:20; Php 4:3; 1Th 4:1; 5:12; 2Th 2:1).

Deriv.: *dierōtáō* (1331), to inquire; *eperōtáō* (1905), to interrogate, inquire of.

Syn.: *akribóō* (198), to learn by diligent or exact inquiry; *déomai* (1189), to beseech; *parakaléō* (3870), to beseech; *diaginṓskō* (1231), to inquire; *exaitéomai* (1809), to demand, desire; *exetázō* (1833), to search out; *epaitéō* (1871), to ask for, beg; *punthánomai* (4441), to ask by way of inquiry.

2066. ἐσθής, esthēs, *es-thace´*; from ἕννυμι, hennumi (to *clothe*); *dress*:—apparel, clothing, raiment, robe.

2067. ἔσθησις, esthēsis, *es´-thay-sis*; from a derivative of 2066; *clothing* (concrete):—government.

2068. ἐσθίω, esthiō, *es-thee´-o*; strengthened for a primary ἔδω, edō (to *eat*); used only in certain tenses, the rest being supplied by 5315; to *eat* (usually literal):—devour, eat, live.

2069. Ἐσλί, Esli, *es-lee´*; of Hebrew origin [probably for 454]; *Esli*, an Israelite:—Esli.

2070. ἐσμέν, esmen, *es-men´*; first person plural indicative of 1510; we *are*:—are, be, have our being, × have hope, + [the gospel] was [preached unto] us.

2071. ἔσομαι, esomai, *es´-om-ahee*; future of 1510; *will be*:—shall (should) be (have), (shall) come (to pass), × may have, × fall, what would follow, × live long, × sojourn.

2072. ἔσοπτρον, esoptron, *es´-op-tron*; from 1519 and a presumed derivative of 3700; a *mirror* (for *looking into*):—glass. Compare 2734.

2073. ἑσπέρα, hespera, *hes-per´-ah*; feminine of an adjective ἑσπερός, hesperos (*evening*); the *eve* (5610 being implication):—evening (-tide).

2074. Ἐσρώμ, Esrōm, *es-rome´*; of Hebrew origin [2696]; *Esrom* (i.e. *Chetsron*), an Israelite:—Esrom.

2075. ἐστέ, este, *es-teh´*; second person plural presumed indicative of 1510; ye *are*:—be, have been, belong.

2076. ἐστί, esti, *es-tee´*; third person singular presumed indicative of 1510; he (she or it) *is*; also (with neuter plural) they *are*:—are, be (-long), call, × can [-not], come, consisteth, × dure for awhile, + follow, × have, (that) is (to say), make, meaneth, × must needs, + profit, + remaineth, + wrestle.

2077. ἔστω, estō, *es´-to*; second person singular presumed imperative of 1510; *be* thou; also ἔστωσαν, estōsan, *es´-to-san*; third person of the same; *let them be*:—be.

2078. ἔσχατος, eschatos, *es´-khat-os*; a superlative probably from 2192 (in the sense of *contiguity*); *farthest, final* (of place or time):—ends of, last, latter end, lowest, uttermost.

Noun probably from *ek* (1537), from, in the sense of farthest. The extreme, most remote, spoken of place and time:

(I) Of place:

(A) Particularly extreme, most remote, the neuter as substantive, the extremity (Ac 1:8; 13:47; Sept.: Dt 28:49; Isa 48:20; Jer 16:19).

(B) Metaphorically implying rank or dignity, the last, lowest, least (Lk 14:9, 10). Generally (Mt 19:30; Mk 9:35; 10:31; Lk 13:30; Jn 8:9; 1Co 4:9).

(C) Of order or number, the last, utmost (Mt 5:26; Lk 12:59).

(II) Of time, the last or latest:

(A) Generally of persons (Mt 20:8, 12, 14, 16; Mk 12:6, 22; 1Co 15:26, 45). In an adverb sense (Mk 12:6, 22, "the last to die being the woman" [a.t.]). Of things, the last or the latter one or thing (1Co 15:52; Rev 2:19; 15:1; 21:9); the latter state or condition of anyone or anything (Mt 12:45; 27:64; Lk 11:26; 2Pe 2:20). In the neuter as an adverb, "last of all" (1Co 15:8).

(B) With a noun of time, as the last day, e.g., of a festival (Jn 7:37); of the world, the day of judgement (Jn 6:39, 40, 44, 54; 11:24; 12:48). The last days, the last time, the last hour (Ac 2:17; 2Ti 3:1; Heb 1:2; Jas 5:3; 1Pe 1:5, 20; 2Pe 3:3; 1Jn 2:18; Jude 18). All the above refer to the last times of this age. These are the times since the coming of Christ in which the power of this world is in part broken, and will be wholly destroyed only at Christ's Second Advent, designated in 1Co 10:11 as the ends of the ages or the end of the age. These expressions cover the whole interval between the first and the final advent of Christ; but they sometimes refer more particularly to the period in which the sacred writers lived, adjacent to the first coming (Ac 2:17; Heb 1:2; 1Pe 1:20; Jude 18), and elsewhere more to later times, before the Second Coming (2Ti 3:1; Jas 5:3; 1Pe 1:5; 2Pe 3:3).

(C) The phrase *ho prōtos kaí ho éschatos* (*ho* [3588], the; *prōtos* [4413], first; *kaí* [2532], and), the first and the last, is spoken of the Messiah in glory (Rev 1:17; 2:8; 22:13) in the sense of eternal, the beginning and the end.

Deriv.: *eschátōs* (2079), extremely, used idiomatically of being at the point of death.

Syn.: *péras* (4009), extremity, end; *télos* (5056), end.

2079. ἐσχάτως, **eschatōs,** *es-khat´-oce*; adverb from 2078; *finally,* i.e. (with 2192) *at the extremity* of life:—point of death.

2080. ἔσω, **esō,** *es´-o*; from 1519; *inside* (as preposition or adjective):—(with-) in (-ner, -to, -ward).

2081. ἔσωθεν, **esōthen,** *es´-o-then*; from 2080; *from inside*; also used as equivalent to 2080 (*inside*):—inward (-ly), (from) within, without.

2082. ἐσώτερος, **esōteros,** *es-o´-ter-os*; comparative of 2080; *interior*:—inner, within.

2083. ἑταῖρος, **hetairos,** *het-ah´ee-ros*; from ἔτης, **etēs** (a *clansman*); a *comrade*:—fellow, friend.

2084. ἑτερόγλωσσος, **heteroglōssos,** *het-er-og´-loce-sos*; from 2087 and 1100; *other-tongued,* i.e. a *foreigner*:—man of other tongue.

Adjective from *héteros* (2087), another of a different kind, and *glóssa* (1100), a tongue, language. One of another tongue or language (1Co 14:21, equal to *glóssais hetérais* [pl. of *héteros* {2087}]), with other languages, an allusion to Isa 28:11).

2085. ἑτεροδιδασκαλέω, **heterodidaskaleō,** *het-er-od-id-as-kal-eh´-o*; from 2087 and 1320; to *instruct differently*:—teach other doctrine (-wise).

From *héteros* (2087), another of a different kind, and *didáskalos* (1320), teacher. To teach a doctrine different from one's own (1Ti 1:3; 6:3). Equal to the phrase *hétera didáskō* ([1321], to teach), to teach differently. The context implies that the doctrine taught is false.

2086. ἑτεροζυγέω, **heterozugeō,** *het-er-od-zoog-eh´-o*; from a compound of 2087 and 2218; to *yoke* up *differently,* i.e. (figurative) to *associate discordantly*:—unequally yoke together with.

From *héteros* (2087), another of a different kind, and *zugóō* (2218), to yoke. To yoke unequally, that is, to yoke two different kinds of animals together to pull a load (see Dt 22:10). In the NT, only figuratively of Christians living in improper alliances with pagan idolators. Used only in 2Co 6:14.

2087. ἕτερος, **heteros,** *het´-er-os*; of uncertain affinity; (an-, the) *other* or *different*:—altered, else, next (day), one, (an-) other, some, strange.

Correlative pronoun. The other:

(I) Particularly and definitely with the article, *ho héteros*: the other of two where one has been already mentioned (Mt 6:24; Lk 5:7; 7:41; 23:40; 1Co 14:17; Gal 6:4). In Lk 4:43, in those "other [*hetérais*] cities" where the gospel has not yet been preached. In distinction from oneself, another person (Ro 2:1; 1Co 4:6; 14:17).

(II) Indefinite and without the article: other, another, some other, equivalent to *állos* (243), another, but with a stronger expression of difference.

(A) Another, with limited emphasis on dissimilarities (Mt 8:21; 16:14; Lk 8:3; 11:16; 14:19, 20; Jn 19:37; Ac 1:20; 7:18; 8:34; 27:1; Ro 8:39; 1Co 12:9; 15:40; Eph 3:5; 1Ti 1:10).

(B) With more emphasis on dissimilarities, of another kind, another, different, in another form (Mk 16:12; Ro 7:23; Gal 1:6; Jas 2:25); of a priest from a different line or family (Heb 7:11, 15). In the sense of foreign, strange (Jude 7; of other languages (Ac 2:4; 1Co 14:21). Different, altered (Lk 9:29).

Deriv.: *heteróglōssos* (2084), one of a different tongue; *heterozugéō* (2086), to yoke unequally; *heterodidaskaléō* (2085), to teach a doctrine different than one's own; *heterozugéō hetérōs* (2088), otherwise, differently.

2088. ἑτέρως, **heterōs,** *het-er´-oce*; adverb from 2087; *differently*:—otherwise.

Adverb from *héteros* (2087), a different one, another of a different quality. Otherwise. Only in Php 3:15.

2089. ἔτι, **eti,** *et´-ee*; perhaps akin to 2094; "*yet,*" *still* (of time or degree):—after that, also, ever, (any) further, (t-) henceforth (more), hereafter, (any) longer, (any) more (-one), now, still, yet.

2090. ἑτοιμάζω, **hetoimazō,** *het-oy-mad´-zo*; from 2092; to *prepare*:—prepare, provide, make ready. Compare 2680.

2091. ἑτοιμασία, **hetoimasia,** *het-oy-mas-ee´-ah*; from 2090; *preparation*:—preparation.

2092. ἕτοιμος, **hetoimos,** *het-oy´-mos*; from an old noun ἔτεος, **heteos** (*fitness*); *adjusted,* i.e. *ready*:—prepared, (made) ready (-iness, to our hand).

2093. ἑτοίμως, **hetoimōs,** *het-toy´-moce*; adverb from 2092; *in readiness*:—ready.

2094. ἔτος, **etos,** *et´-os*; apparently a primary word; a *year*:—year.

2095. εὖ, **eu,** *yoo*; neuter of a primary εὖς, *eus* (*good*); (adverb) *well*:—good, well (done).

Adverb, neuter of *eús* (n.f.), good, brave, noble. Well, good.

(I) Particularly with verbs, with the verb *gínomai* (1096), to become, to be prosperous (Eph 6:3); with verbs of doing: to do good, to do right (Mk 14:7; Ac 15:29).

(II) In commendations, the equivalent of "Well done!" (Mt 25:21, 23; Lk 19:17).

(III) Used extensively as a prefix to compound verbs with the meaning of well, good, and hence often used as an intensive, e.g., *eulogéō* (2127), to eulogise, bless; *eukairía* (2120), good or appropriate opportunity.

Syn.: *kalós* (2573), well.

2096. Εὖα, **Eua,** *yoo´-ah*; of Hebrew origin [2332]; *Eua* (or *Eva*, i.e. *Chavvah*), the first woman:—Eve.

2097. εὐαγγελίζω, **euaggelizō,** *yoo-ang-ghel-id´-zo*; from 2095 and 32; to *announce good news* ("evangelize") especially the gospel:—declare, bring (declare, show) glad (good) tidings, preach (the gospel).

From *euággelos* (n.f.), bringing good news, which is from *eu* (2095), good, well, and *aggéllō* (n.f.), to proclaim, tell. To bring glad tidings, declare as a matter of joy:

(I) To announce, publish, as glad tidings (Lk 1:19; 4:18; Ac 10:36; 13:32; Ro 10:15; Eph 2:17; 1Th 3:6).

(II) Spoken of the annunciation of the gospel of Christ and all that pertains to it: to preach, proclaim, the idea of glad tidings being implied:

(A) To preach the kingdom of God, meaning the things concerning the kingdom of God (Lk 4:43; 8:1; Ac 8:12). With the kingdom implied (Lk 3:18; 9:6; 20:1).

(B) To preach Jesus Christ or the Lord Jesus (Ac 5:42; 8:35; 11:20; 17:18; Gal 1:16; Eph 3:8).

(C) Generally, to preach the gospel, the Word, the faith (Ac 8:4, 25, 40; 14:7, 15, 21; 15:35; 16:10; Ro 1:15; 15:20; 1Co 1:17; 9:16, 18;

15:1, 2; 2Co 10:16; 11:7; Gal 1:8, 9, 23; 4:13; 1Pe 1:12).

Deriv.: *euaggelistḗs* (2099), evangelist; *proeuaggelízomai* (4283), announce good news beforehand.

2098. εὐαγγέλιον, **euaggelion,** *yoo-ang-ghel´-ee-on*; from the same as 2097; a *good message*, i.e. the *gospel*:—gospel.

Noun from *euággelos* (n.f.), bringing good news, which is from *eú* (2095), good, well, and *aggéllō* (n.f.), to proclaim, tell. Originally a reward for good news, later becoming good news. In the NT, spoken only of the glad tidings of Christ and His salvation, the gospel.

(I) In the books of the NT, outside the writings of Paul, in the sense of glad tidings:

(A) The gospel of the kingdom of God (Mt 4:23; 9:35; 24:14; Mk 1:14). By implication (Mt 26:13; Mk 1:15; 13:10; 14:9; Rev 14:6).

(B) The glad tidings of the coming and life of Jesus as the Messiah (Mk 8:35; 10:29; 16:15; Ac 15:7). Later, *euaggélion* came to mean "gospel" in the sense of "a history of Jesus' life" such as we have in the Gospels of Matthew, Mark, Luke and John.

(II) In the writings of Paul, and once in the writings of Peter, the gospel, that is:

(A) Generally, the gospel plan of salvation, its doctrines, declarations, precepts, promises (Ro 2:16; 11:28; 16:25; 1Co 9:14, 18; 15:1; 2Co 4:3, 4; 9:13; 10:14; Gal 1:11; 2:2, 5, 14; Eph 1:13; 3:6; 6:19; Php 1:5, 7, 17, 27; 2:22; Col 1:5, 23; 1Th 1:5; 2:4; 2Ti 1:10; 2:8). The gospel of Christ made known by Him as its founder and chief cornerstone (Ro 15:19, 29; 1Co 9:12, 18; Gal 1:7; 1Th 3:2; 2Th 1:8). The gospel of God, of which God is the Author through Christ (Ro 15:16; 2Co 11:7; 1Th 2:2, 8, 9; 1Ti 1:11; 1Pe 4:17). By antithesis, *héteron* (2087), another but different gospel, including other precepts (2Co 11:4; Gal 1:6).

(B) By metonymy: the gospel work, i.e. the preaching of the gospel, labour in the gospel (Ro 1:1, 9, 16; 1Co 4:15; 9:14, 23; 2Co 2:12; 8:18; Gal 2:2; Eph 6:15; Php 1:12; 4:3, 15; 2Th 2:14; 2Ti 1:8; Phm 13).

2099. εὐαγγελιστής, **euaggelistēs,** *yoo-ang-ghel-is-tace´*; from 2097; a *preacher* of the gospel:—evangelist.

Noun from *eauggelízō* (2097), to evangelize. An evangelist, a preacher of the gospel. He was

often not located in any particular place but traveled as a missionary to preach the gospel and establish churches (Ac 21:8; Eph 4:11; 2Ti 4:5).
Syn.: *kḗrux* (2783), preacher. Also *ággelos* (32), messenger.

2100. ε**ὐαρεστέω, euaresteō,** *yoo-ar-es-teh´-o*; from 2101; to *gratify entirely*:—please (well).
From *euárestos* (2101), well pleasing. To please well as Enoch pleased God through his faith (Heb 11:5, 6; see Ge 5:22, 24). In the middle, to take pleasure in, to be pleased with (Heb 13:16).

2101. ε**ὐάρεστος, euarestos,** *yoo-ar´-es-tos*; from 2095 and 701; *fully agreeable*:—acceptable (-ted), well-pleasing.
Adjective from *eu* (2095), well, and *aréskō* (700), to please. Well-pleasing, acceptable. We are to strive to make our lives acceptable and well-pleasing to God (Ro 12:1, 2; 14:18; 2Co 5:9; Eph 5:10; Php 4:18; Col 3:20; Heb 13:21); slaves are to strive to please their masters (Tit 2:9).
Deriv.: *euarestéō* (2100), to please well; *euaréstōs* (2102), acceptably.
Syn.: *euprósdektos* (2144), acceptable.

2102. ε**ὐαρέστως, euarestōs,** *yoo-ar-es´-toce*; adverb from 2101; *quite agreeably*:—acceptably, + please well.
Adverb from *euárestos* (2101), pleasing, well-pleasing. Pleasingly, acceptably (Heb 12:28).

2103. Ε**ὔβουλος, Euboulos,** *yoo´-boo-los*; from 2095 and 1014; *good-willer*; *Eubulus*, a Christian:—Eubulus.

2104. ε**ὐγένης, eugenēs,** *yoog-en´-ace*; from 2095 and 1096; *well born*, i.e. (literal) *high* in rank, or (figurative) *generous*:—more noble, nobleman.

2105. ε**ὐδία, eudia,** *yoo-dee´-ah*; feminine from 2095 and the alternate of 2203 (as the god of the weather); a *clear sky*, i.e. *fine weather*:—fair weather.

2106. ε**ὐδοκέω, eudokeō,** *yoo-dok-eh´-o*; from 2095 and 1380; to *think well* of, i.e. *approve* (an act); specially to *approbate* (a person or thing):—think good, (be well) please (-d), be the good (have, take) pleasure, be willing.
From *eú* (2095), well, good, and *dokéō* (1380), to think. In the NT, to think good, i.e. to please, like, take pleasure in:

(I) Generally: to view with favour (Mt 3:17; 12:18; 17:5; Mk 1:11; Lk 3:22; 1Co 10:5; 2Co 12:10; 2Th 2:12; Heb 10:6, 8, 38; 2Pe 1:17).
(II) In the sense of to will, desire, followed by the inf. expressed or implied:
(A) Generally, to be willing, ready (2Co 5:8; 1Th 2:8).
(B) By implication to determine, resolve, choose with pleasure to do something, with the idea of benevolence being implied (Ro 15:26, 27; 1Th 3:1). Spoken of God (Lk 12:32; 1Co 1:21; Gal 1:15; Col 1:19).
Deriv.: *eudokía* (2107), goodwill, pleasure; *suneudokéō* (4909), to think well of with others.
Syn.: *euarestéō* (2100), gratify, please.

2107. ε**ὐδοκία, eudokia,** *yoo-dok-ee´-ah*; from a presumed compound of 2095 and the base of 1380; *satisfaction*, i.e. (subject) *delight*, or (object) *kindness*, *wish*, *purpose*:—desire, good pleasure (will), × seem good.
Noun from *eudokéō* (2106), to please, favour. goodwill, good pleasure:
(I) Particular delight in any person or thing and hence goodwill, favour (Lk 2:14, "goodwill toward men" on the part of God). See *eudokéō* (2106, I). Of men, goodwill, kind intention (Php 1:15). By implication, desire, longing (Ro 10:1).
(II) In the sense of good pleasure, will, purpose, the idea of benevolence being included. Spoken of God (Mt 11:26; Lk 10:21; Eph 1:5, 9; Php 2:13; 2Th 1:11).
Syn.: *apólausis* (619), enjoyment in regard to pleasures; *boúlēma* (1013), deliberate design, purpose; *epipóthēsis* (1972), an earnest desire, and with the same meaning *epipothía* (1974); *eúnoia* (2133), goodwill; *hēdonḗ* (2237), pleasure, but only in respect to lust; *thélēma* (2307), will, pleasure, favour.

2108. ε**ὐεργεσία, euergesia,** *yoo-erg-es-ee´-ah*; from 2110; *beneficence* (genitive or special):—benefit, good deed done.

2109. ε**ὐεργετέω, euergeteō,** *yoo-erg-et-eh´-o*; from 2110; to *be philanthropic*:—do good.

2110. ε**ὐεργέτης, euergetēs,** *yoo-erg-et´-ace*; from 2095 and the base of 2041; a *worker of good*, i.e. (special) a *philanthropist*:—benefactor.

2111. ε**ὔθετος, euthetos,** *yoo´-thet-os*; from 2095 and a derivative of 5087; *well placed*, i.e. (figurative) *appropriate*:—fit, meet.

2112. εὐθέως, eutheōs, *yoo-theh´-oce*; adverb from 2117; *directly*, i.e. *at once* or *soon*:—anon, as soon as, forthwith, immediately, shortly, straightway.

2113. εὐθυδρομέω, euthudromeō, *yoo-thoo-drom-eh´-o*; from 2117 and 1408; to *lay a straight course*, i.e. *sail direct*:—(come) with a straight course.

2114. εὐθυμέω, euthumeō, *yoo-thoo-meh´-o*; from 2115; to *cheer up*, i.e. (intransitive) be *cheerful*; neuter comparative (adverb) *more cheerfully*:—be of good cheer (merry).

2115. εὔθυμος, euthumos, *yoo´-thoo-mos*; from 2095 and 2372; in *fine spirits*, i.e. *cheerful*:—of good cheer, the more cheerfully.

2116. εὐθύνω, euthunō, *yoo-thoo´-no*; from 2117; to *straighten* (*level*); technically to *steer*:—governor, make straight.

2117. εὐθύς, euthus, *yoo-thoos´*; perhaps from 2095 and 5087; *straight*, i.e. (literal) *level*, or (figurative) *true*; adverb (of time) *at once*:—anon, by and by, forthwith, immediately, straightway.

2118. εὐθύτης, euthutēs, *yoo-thoo´-tace*; from 2117; *rectitude*:—righteousness.

2119. εὐκαιρέω, eukaireō, *yoo-kahee-reh´-o*; from 2121; to *have good time*, i.e. *opportunity* or *leisure*:—have leisure (convenient time), spend time.

2120. εὐκαιρία, eukairia, *yoo-kahee-ree´-ah*; from 2121; a favourable *occasion*:—opportunity.

Noun from *eúkairos* (2121), convenient, which is from *eú* (2095), good, well, and *kairós* (2540), time, season. The right and suitable time or convenient opportunity; used in the NT only of Judas seeking a good opportunity to betray Jesus (Mt 26:16; Lk 22:6).

2121. εὔκαιρος, eukairos, *yoo´-kahee-ros*; from 2095 and 2540; *well-timed*, i.e. *opportune*:—convenient, in time of need.

2122. εὐκαίρως, eukairōs, *yoo-kah´ee-roce*; adverb from 2121; *opportunely*:—conveniently, in season.

2123. εὐκοπώτερος, eukopōteros, *yoo-kop-o´-ter-os*; comparative of a compound of 2095 and 2873; *better for toil*, i.e. *more facile*:—easier.

2124. εὐλάβεια, eulabeia, *yoo-lab´-i-ah*; from 2126; properly *caution*, i.e. (religiously) *reverence* (*piety*); (by implication) *dread* (concrete):—fear (-ed).

Noun from *eulabḗs* (2126), devout, pious. In the NT, fear of God, reverence, piety. Spoken of Jesus (Heb 5:7); spoken as a challenge to us (Heb 12:28).

2125. εὐλαβέομαι, eulabeomai, *yoo-lab-eh´-om-ahee*; middle from 2126; to *be circumspect*, i.e. (by implication) to *be apprehensive*; religiously, to *reverence*:—(moved with) fear.

From *eulabḗs* (2126), devout, pious. To act with caution, to be circumspect. In the NT, to fear (Ac 23:10). In respect of God: to fear, to reverence spoken of Noah (Heb 11:7).

2126. εὐλαβής, eulabēs, *yoo-lab-ace´*; from 2095 and 2983; *taking well* (*carefully*), i.e. *circumspect* (religiously, *pious*):—devout.

Adjective from *eú* (2095), good, well, right, rightly, and *lambánō* (2983), to take. Cautious, circumspect. In the NT, spoken only in reference to God: God fearing, pious, devout (Lk 2:25; Ac 2:5; 8:2).

Deriv.: *eulábeia* (2124), right attitude, reverence; *eulabéomai* (2125), to act with caution, to fear.

2127. εὐλογέω, eulogeō, *yoo-log-eh´-o*; from a compound of 2095 and 3056; to *speak well of*, i.e. (religiously) to *bless* (*thank* or *invoke a benediction upon, prosper*):—bless, praise.

From *eú* (2095), good, well, and *lógos* (3056), word. To bless, speak well of:

(I) Of men toward God: to bless, i.e. to praise, speak well of with praise and thanksgiving (Lk 1:64; 2:28; 24:53; 1Co 14:16; Jas 3:9).

(II) Of men toward men and things: to bless, speak well of with praise and thanksgiving, to invoke God's blessing upon:

(A) To pray for one's welfare as God perceives it for His actions in their lives (Mt 5:44; Mk 10:16; Lk 6:28; Ro 12:14; 1Co 4:12; 1Pe 3:9).

(B) Spoken of food: to bless, i.e. to ask God's blessing upon (Mt 14:19; Mk 6:41; 8:7; Lk 9:16). Of the Lord's Supper where we may render by implication the meaning of to consecrate (Mt 26:26; Mk 14:22; Lk 24:30; 1Co 10:16).

(III) Of God toward men: to bless, i.e. to distinguish with favour, to prosper, to make happy (Ac 3:26; Eph 1:3; Heb 6:14). Blessed, favored of

God, happy; used in joyful salutations, of the Messiah and his reign (Mt 21:9; 23:39; Mk 11:9, 10; Lk 13:35; 19:38; Jn 12:13).

Deriv.: *eneulogéō* (1757), to bless, blessed; *eulogētós* (2128), blessed; *eulogía* (2129), blessing.

Syn.: *makarízō* (3106), to pronounce as blessed; *humnéō* (5214), to sing, laud, praise.

2128. εὐλογητός, eulogētos, *yoo-log-ay-tos´*; from 2127; *adorable*:—blessed.

Adjective from *eulogéō* (2127), to bless. Blessed. In the NT, only of God, i.e. worthy of praise. Used as a doxology: blessed be God (Lk 1:68; 2Co 1:3; Eph 1:3; 1Pe 1:3); spoken of Christ as God (Ro 9:5). Also Mk 14:61; Ro 1:25; 2Co 11:31.

2129. εὐλογία, eulogia, *yoo-log-ee´-ah*; from the same as 2127; *fine speaking*, i.e. *elegance of language*; *commendation* ("*eulogy*"), i.e. (reverentially) *adoration*; religiously, *benediction*; (by implication) *consecration*; by extension *benefit* or *largess*:—blessing (a matter of) bounty (× -tifully), fair speech.

Noun from *eulogéō* (2127), to bless. Commendation, blessing:

(I) In the NT, only once in a bad sense, spoken of as used by false teachers, flattering words (Ro 16:18). Elsewhere in the NT, blessing.

(II) Blessing God or ascribing praise, implying also thanksgiving (Rev 5:12, 13; 7:12), speaking well of and glorifying our God.

(III) From men toward men, i.e. blessing, benediction, petition for good from God upon persons (Heb 12:17); upon things: the cup of the Lord's Supper (1Co 10:16, see Mt 26:27).

(IV) By metonymy, blessing, favour conferred, gift, benefit, bounty:

(A) From God to men (Ro 15:29; Gal 3:14; Eph 1:3; Heb 6:7; 1Pe 3:9; Sept.: Ge 49:25; Isa 65:8).

(B) From men to men: a gift, bounty, present (2Co 9:5). Hence, by implication, for liberality, generosity (2Co 9:5, 6).

Syn.: *makarismós* (3108), blessedness or the action of becoming blessed.

2130. εὐμετάδοτος, eumetadotos, *yoo-met-ad´-ot-os*; from 2095 and a presumed derivative of 3330; *good at imparting*, i.e. *liberal*:—ready to distribute.

2131. Εὐνίκη, Eunikē, *yoo-nee´-kay*; from 2095 and 3529; *victorious*; *Eunice*, a Jewess:—Eunice.

2132. εὐνοέω, eunoeō, *yoo-no-eh´-o*; from a compound of 2095 and 3563; to *be well-minded*, i.e. *reconcile*:—agree.

From *eúnoos* (n.f.), benevolent, kindly, which is from *eú* (2095), well, and *noús* (3563), mind. To be well-disposed or well-intentioned toward another (Mt 5:25).

Deriv.: *eúnoia* (2133), benevolence.

Syn.: *eudokéō* (2106), to think well of.

2133. εὔνοια, eunoia, *yoo´-noy-ah*; from the same as 2132; *kindness*; euphemism *conjugal duty*:—benevolence, goodwill.

Noun from *eunoéō* (2132), to favour. Benevolence, goodwill (1Co 7:3; Eph 6:7).

Syn.: *eudokía* (2107), pleasure, good thought.

2134. εὐνουχίζω, eunouchizō, *yoo-noo-khid´-zo*; from 2135; to *castrate* (figurative, *live unmarried*):—make … eunuch.

2135. εὐνοῦχος, eunouchos, *yoo-noo´-khos*; from εὐνή, *eunē* (a *bed*) and 2192; a *castrated* person (such being employed in Oriental bed-chambers); by extension an *impotent* or *unmarried* man; (by implication) a *chamberlain* (*state-officer*):—eunuch.

2136. Εὐοδία, Euodia, *yoo-od-ee´-ah*; from the same as 2137; *fine travelling*; *Euodia*, a Christian woman:—Euodias.

2137. εὐοδόω, euodoō, *yoo-od-o´-o*; from a compound of 2095 and 3598; to *help* on the *road*, i.e. (passive) *succeed in reaching*; (figurative) to *succeed* in business affairs:—(have a) prosper (-ous journey).

2138. εὐπειθής, eupeithēs, *yoo-pi-thace´*; from 2095 and 3982; *good* for *persuasion*, i.e. (intransitive) *compliant*:—easy to be intreated.

2139. εὐπερίστατος, euperistatos, *yoo-per-is´-tat-os*; from 2095 and a derivative of a presumed compound of 4012 and 2476; *well standing around*, i.e. (a *competitor*) *thwarting* (a racer) in every direction (figurative, of sin in general):—which doth so easily beset.

2140. εὐποιΐα, eupoiïa, *yoo-poy-ee´-ah*; from a compound of 2095 and 4160; *well doing*, i.e. *beneficence*:—to do good.

2141. εὐπορέω, euporeō, *yoo-por-eh´-o*; from a compound of 2090 and the base of 4197; (intransitive) to *be good* for *passing* through, i.e. (figurative) *have* pecuniary *means:*—ability.

From *eúporos* (n.f.), prosperous, which is from *eú* (2095), good, well, and *poreía* (4197), journey. To prosper. Used only in Ac 11:29.

Deriv.: *euporía* (2142), pecuniary resources, abundance, wealth.

Syn.: *perisseúō* (4052), to abound; *pleonázō* (4121), to have more, increase.

2142. εὐπορία, euporia, *yoo-por-ee´-ah*; from the same as 2141; pecuniary *resources:*—wealth.

2143. εὐπρέπεια, euprepeia, *yoo-prep´-i-ah*; from a compound of 2095 and 4241; *good suitableness,* i.e. *gracefulness:*—grace.

2144. εὐπρόσδεκτος, euprosdektos, *yoo-pros´-dek-tos*; from 2095 and a derivative of 4327; *well-received,* i.e. *approved, favourable:*—acceptable (-ted).

Adjective from *eú* (2095), well, and *prosdéchomai* (4327), to receive, accept. Well-received, acceptable, approved: spoken concerning gifts (Ro 15:16, 31; 2Co 8:12); spoken concerning the present time (2Co 6:2); spoken concerning our spiritual sacrifices (1Pe 2:5).

Syn.: *apodektós* (587), acceptable; *arestós* (701), pleasing, agreeable; *dektós* (1184), acceptable, favourable; *euárestos* (2101), well-pleasing, acceptable.

2145. εὐπρόσεδρος, euprosedros, *yoo-pros´-ed-ros*; from 2095 and the same as 4332; *sitting well toward,* i.e. (figurative) *assiduous* (neuter *diligent service*):— × attend upon.

2146. εὐπροσωπέω, euprosōpeō, *yoo-pros-o-peh´-o*; from a compound of 2095 and 4383; to *be of good countenance,* i.e. (figurative) to *make a display:*—make a fair show.

From *euprósōpos* (n.f.), good-looking, pleasant in appearance, which is from *eú* (2095), well, and *prósōpon* (4383), a face, appearance. Only in Gal 6:12, meaning to make a fair show, to strive to please. In this case, desiring to please other men, not God.

2147. εὑρίσκω, heuriskō, *hyoo-ris´-ko*; a prolonged form of a primary εὕρω, **heurō,** *hyoo´-ro*; which (together with another cognate form εὑρέω, **heureō,** *hyoo-reh´-o*) is used for it in all the tenses except the present and imperfect; to *find* (literal or figurative):—find, get, obtain, perceive, see.

To find:

(I) Generally: to find without seeking, meet with, light upon:

(A) Particularly (Mt 13:44; Lk 4:17; 18:8; Jn 12:14; Ac 9:33; 21:2; 28:14).

(B) Metaphorically: to find, i.e. to perceive or learn by experience that a person or thing is or does a particular thing (Mt 12:44; Mk 7:30; Lk 8:35; 24:2; Jn 11:17; Ac 5:10; 9:2; 2Co 9:4; 1Pe 1:7; Rev 5:4).

(II) To find by search, inquiry, to find out, discover:

(A) Particularly and in an absolute sense (Mt 7:7, 8, 14; 12:43; 13:46; Mk 1:37; 11:13; Lk 2:45; 15:4; Jn 7:34, 35; 10:9; Ac 5:22; 7:11). Of a judge: to find innocent after examination (Jn 18:38; 19:4, 6; Ac 13:28; 23:9).

(B) In various figurative senses: **(1)** To find God, be accepted by Him when humbly and sincerely turning to Him (Ac 17:27; Ro 10:20). **(2)** Spoken of computation, measurement, to find, figure out a value, a distance, etc. (Ac 19:19; 27:28). **(3)** To find out mentally, i.e. to invent, contrive, to find a way to do something (Lk 5:19; 19:48; Ac 4:21).

(III) Middle, to find for oneself, i.e. to acquire, obtain, get for oneself or another (Mt 10:39; 11:29; Lk 9:12; Jn 21:6; Ac 7:46; Ro 4:1; Heb 9:12; 12:17; Rev 9:6; 18:14). To find grace or mercy, meaning to obtain favour with God (Lk 1:30; 2Ti 1:18; Heb 4:16).

Deriv.: *aneurískō* (429), to find out by search, discover.

Syn.: *ktáomai* (2932), to acquire.

2148. Εὐροκλύδων, Eurokludōn, *yoo-rok-loo´-dohn*; from Εὖρος, **Euros** (the *east* wind) and 2830; a *storm from the East* (or Southeast), i.e. (in modern phrase) a *Levanter:*—Euroklydon.

2149. εὐρύχωρος, euruchōros, *yoo-roo´-kho-ros*; from εὐρύς, **eurus** (*wide*) and 5561; *spacious:*—broad.

2150. εὐσέβεια, eusebeia, *yoo-seb´-i-ah*; from 2152; *piety;* specially the *gospel* scheme:—godliness, holiness.

Noun from *eusebḗs* (2152), devout, godly. Piety, reverence, in the NT, only as directed toward God and denoting the spontaneous feeling of the heart (Ac 3:12; 1Ti 2:2; 4:7, 8; 6:3, 5, 6, 11; Tit 1:1; 2Pe 1:3, 6, 7; 3:11). By metonymy: religion, the gospel plan (1Ti 3:16).

Syn.: *eulábeia* (2124), piety, reverence motivated by the fear of God or caution, more than by love for God, as *eusébeia*.

2151. εὐσεβέω, eusebeō, *yoo-seb-eh´-o*; from 2152; to *be pious*, i.e. (toward God) to *worship*, or (toward parents) to *respect* (*support*):—show piety, worship.

From *eusebés* (2152), devout, godly.

(I) To be reverent, pious: spoken of the attitude of the Athenians toward the Unknown God (Ac 17:23).

(II) To respect, honour: spoken of the proper attitude toward parents (1Ti 5:4).

Syn.: *latreúō* (3000), to serve religiously, worship; *proskunéō* (4352), to make obeisance, do reverence to; *sebázomai* (4573), to honour, worship.

2152. εὐσεβής, eusebes, *yoo-seb-ace´*; from 2095 and 4576; *well-reverent*, i.e. *pious*:—devout, godly.

Adjective from *eú* (2095), well, and *sébomai* (4576), to revere. Pious. In the NT, toward God: religious, devout (2Pe 2:9). Spoken as an attribute of Cornelius (Ac 10:2, 7). Spoken as an attribute of Ananias (Ac 22:12).

Deriv.: *eusébeia* (2150), piety, reverence; *eusebéō* (2151), to be pious; *eusebōs* (2153), in a godly manner.

2153. εὐσεβῶς, eusebōs, *yoo-seb-oce´*; adverb from 2152; *piously*:—godly.

2154. εὔσημος, eusēmos, *yoo´-say-mos*; from 2095 and the base of 4591; *well indicated*, i.e. (figurative) *significant*:—easy to be understood.

2155. εὔσπλαγχνος, eusplagchnos, *yoo´-splangkh-nos*; from 2095 and 4698; *well compassioned*, i.e. *sympathetic*:—pitiful, tenderhearted.

2156. εὐσχημόνως, euschēmonōs, *yoo-skhay-mon´-oce*; adverb from 2158; *decorously*:—decently, honestly.

2157. εὐσχημοσύνη, euschēmosunē, *yoo-skhay-mos-oo´-nay*; from 2158; *decorousness*:—comeliness.

2158. εὐσχήμων, euschēmōn, *yoo-skhay´-mone*; from 2095 and 4976; *well-formed*, i.e. (figurative) *decorous*, *noble* (in rank):—comely, honourable.

2159. εὐτόνως, eutonōs, *yoo-ton´-oce*; adverb from a compound of 2095 and a derivative of τείνω, *teinō* (to stretch); *in a well-strung manner*, i.e. (figurative) *intensely* (in a good sense, *cogently*; in a bad one, *fiercely*):—mightily, vehemently.

2160. εὐτραπελία, eutrapelia, *yoo-trap-el-ee´-ah*; from a compound of 2095 and a derivative of the base of 5157 (meaning *well-turned*, i.e. *ready at repartee, jocose*); *witticism*, i.e. (in a vulgar sense) *ribaldry*:—jesting.

Noun from *eutrápelos* (n.f.), courteous, sportive, which is from *eú* (2095), easily, and *trépō* (n.f.), to turn. Humor, wit. In the NT used in a bad sense: levity, jesting; frivolous and indecent discourse. Only in Eph 5:4.

2161. Εὔτυχος, Eutuchos, *yoo´-too-khos*; from 2095 and a derivative of 5177; *well-fated*, i.e. *fortunate*; *Eutychus*, a young man:—Eutychus.

2162. εὐφημία, euphēmia, *yoo-fay-mee´-ah*; from 2163; *good language* ("*euphemy*"), i.e. *praise* (*repute*):—good report.

2163. εὔφημος, euphēmos, *yoo´-fay-mos*; from 2095 and 5345; *well spoken of*, i.e. *reputable*:—of good report.

2164. εὐφορέω, euphoreō, *yoo-for-eh´-o*; from 2095 and 5409; to *bear well*, i.e. *be fertile*:—bring forth abundantly.

2165. εὐφραίνω, euphrainō, *yoo-frah´-ee-no*; from 2095 and 5424; to *put* (middle or passive *be*) *in a good* frame of *mind*, i.e. *rejoice*:—fare, make glad, be (make) merry, rejoice.

From *eú* (2095), good, well, and *phrēn* (5424), mind. To make glad-minded, to make glad, to cause to rejoice (2Co 2:2); in the middle, to be glad, joyful (Ac 2:26; Ro 15:10; Gal 4:27). As connected with feasting: to be joyful or merry, in a natural sense (Lk 15:23, 24, 29, 32) or in a bad sense (Lk 12:19; Ac 7:41).

Deriv.: *euphrosúnē* (2167), gladness.

Syn.: *agalliáō* (21), to exult, rejoice greatly; *euthuméō* (2114), to make cheerful; *chaírō* (5463), to rejoice.

2166. Εὐφράτης, **Euphratēs,** *yoo-frat´-ace*; of foreign origin [compare 6578]; *Euphrates*, a river of Asia:—Euphrates.

2167. εὐφροσύνη, **euphrosunē,** *yoo-fros-oo´-nay*; from the same as 2165; *joyfulness*:—gladness, joy.

Noun from *eúphron* (n.f.), gladsome, cheerful, which is from *eu* (2095), well, and *phrḗn* (5424), mind. Joy, joyfulness, gladness (Ac 2:28; 14:17). Also from *eúphrōn* (n.f.): *euphraínō* (2165), to rejoice.

Syn.: *agallíasis* (20), exultation, exuberant joy; *chará* (5479), joy, delight.

2168. εὐχαριστέω, **eucharisteō,** *yoo-khar-is-teh´-o*; from 2170; to *be grateful*, i.e. (active) to *express gratitude* (toward); specially to *say grace* at a meal:—(give) thank (-ful, -s).

From *eucháristos* (2170), thankful, grateful, well-pleasing. To show oneself grateful, to be thankful, to give thanks (Lk 17:16; Ro 16:4). Elsewhere in the NT, used only in reference to God: to give thanks to God (Lk 18:11; Jn 11:41; Ac 28:15; Ro 7:25; 1Co 1:14; 14:18; 2Co 1:11; Eph 1:16; 5:20; Col 1:3, 12; 3:17; 1Th 2:13; 5:18; Phm 4; Rev 11:17). Spoken of giving thanks before meals (Mt 15:36; 26:27; Mk 8:6; 14:23; Lk 22:17, 19; Jn 6:11, 23; Ac 27:35; Ro 14:6; 1Co 10:30; 11:24).

Syn.: *eulogéō* (2127), to bless, praise.

2169. εὐχαριστία, **eucharistia,** *yoo-khar-is-tee´-ah*; from 2170; *gratitude*; active *grateful language* (to God, as an act of worship):—thankfulness, (giving of) thanks (-giving).

Noun from *eucháristos* (2170), thankful, grateful, well-pleasing. Gratitude, thankfulness (Ac 24:3). In Paul's writings and in the Book of the Revelation, it means the giving of thanks, the expression of gratitude to God (1Co 14:16; 2Co 4:15; 9:11, 12; Eph 5:4; Php 4:6; Col 2:7; 4:2; 1Th 3:9; 1Ti 2:1; 4:3, 4; Rev 7:12).

2170. εὐχάριστος, **eucharistos,** *yoo-khar´-is-tos*; from 2095 and a derivative of 5483; *well favored*, i.e. (by implication) *grateful*:—thankful.

Adjective from *eú* (2095), well, and *charízomai* (5483), to grant, give. Thankful, grateful, well-pleasing (Col 3:15; Sept.: Pr 11:16). Some attribute to it, by implication, the meaning of well-pleasing, acceptable to God, and others the meaning of generous.

Deriv.: *eucharistéō* (2168), to be thankful; *eucharistía* (2169), thankfulness, giving of thanks.

2171. εὐχή, **euchē,** *yoo-khay´*; from 2172; properly a *wish*, expressed as a *petition* to God, or in *votive* obligation:—prayer, vow.

2172. εὔχομαι, **euchomai,** *yoo´-khom-ahee*; middle of a primary verb; to *wish*; (by implication) to *pray* to God:—pray, will, wish.

2173. εὔχρηστος, **euchrēstos,** *yoo´-khrays-tos*; from 2095 and 5543; *easily used*, i.e. *useful*:—profitable, meet for use.

Adjective from *eú* (2095), well, and *chráomai* (5530), to furnish what is needful. Useful or very useful. Spoken in the NT of Christian service (2Ti 2:21; 4:11; Phm 11).

Syn.: *chrḗsimos* (5539), serviceable, profitable, useful.

2174. εὐψυχέω, **eupsucheō,** *yoo-psoo-kheh´-o*; from a compound of 2095 and 5590; to *be in good spirits*, i.e. *feel encouraged*:—be of good comfort.

2175. εὐωδία, **euōdia,** *yoo-o-dee´-ah*; from a compound of 2095 and a derivative of 3605; *good-scentedness*, i.e. *fragrance*:—sweet savour (smell, -smelling).

2176. εὐώνυμος, **euōnumos,** *yoo-o´-noo-mos*; from 2095 and 3686; properly *well-named* (*good-omened*), i.e. the *left* (which was the *lucky* side among the pagan Greeks); neuter as adverb *at the left* hand:—(on the) left.

2177. ἐφάλλομαι, **ephallomai,** *ef-al´-lom-ahee*; from 1909 and 242; to *spring upon*:—leap on.

2178. ἐφάπαξ, **ephapax,** *ef-ap´-ax*; from 1909 and 530; *upon one occasion* (only):—(at) once (for all).

2179. Ἐφεσῖνος, **Ephesinos,** *ef-es-ee´-nos*; from 2181; *Ephesine*, or situated at Ephesus:—of Ephesus.

2180. Ἐφέσιος, **Ephesios,** *ef-es´-ee-os*; from 2181; an *Ephesian* or inhabitant of Ephesus:—Ephesian, of Ephesus.

2181. Ἔφεσος, **Ephesos,** *ef´-es-os*; probably of foreign origin; *Ephesus*, a city of Asia Minor:—Ephesus.

2182. ἐφευρέτης, epheuretēs, *ef-yoo-ret´-ace*; from a compound of 1909 and 2147; a *discoverer,* i.e. *contriver:*—inventor.

2183. ἐφημερία, ephēmeria, *ef-ay-mer-ee´-ah*; from 2184; *diurnality,* i.e. (special) the quotidian *rotation* or *class* of the Jewish priests' service at the temple, as distributed by families:—course.

2184. ἐφήμερος, ephēmeros, *ef-ay´-mer-os*; from 1909 and 2250; *for a day* ("ephemeral"), i.e. *diurnal:*—daily.

2185. ἐφικνέομαι, ephikneomai, *ef-ik-neh´-om-ahee*; from 1909 and a cognate of 2240; to *arrive upon,* i.e. *extend to:*—reach.

2186. ἐφίστημι, ephistēmi, *ef-is´-tay-mee*; from 1909 and 2476; to *stand upon,* i.e. *be present* (in various applications, friendly or otherwise, usually literal):—assault, come (in, to, unto, upon), be at hand (instant), present, stand (before, by, over).

2187. Ἐφραΐμ, Ephraïm, *ef-rah-im´*; of Hebrew origin [669 or better 6085]; *Ephraïm,* a place in Palestine:—Ephraim.

2188. ἐφφαθά, ephphatha, *ef-fath-ah´*; of Chaldee origin [6606]; *be opened!:*—Ephphatha.

2189. ἔχθρα, echthra, *ekh´-thrah*; feminine of 2190; *hostility;* (by implication) a reason for *opposition:*—enmity, hatred.

2190. ἐχθρός, echthros, *ekh-thros´*; from a primary ἔχθω, *echthō* (to *hate*); *hateful* (passive *odious,* or active *hostile*); usually as a noun, an *adversary* (especially Satan):—enemy, foe.

2191. ἔχιδνα, echidna, *ekh´-id-nah*; of uncertain origin; an *adder* or other poisonous snake (literal or figurative):—viper.

2192. ἔχω, echō, *ekh´-o*; (including an alternate form σχέω, *scheō,* *skheh´-o*; used in certain tenses only); a primary verb; to *hold* (used in very various applications, literal or figurative, direct or remote; such as *possession, ability, contiguity, relation* or *condition*):—be (able, × hold, possessed with), accompany, + begin to amend, can (+ -not), × conceive, count, diseased, do, + eat, + enjoy, + fear, following, have, hold, keep, + lack, + go to law, lie, + must needs, + of neces-

sity, + need, next, + recover, + reign, + rest, return, × sick, take for, + tremble, + uncircumcised, use.

To have, to hold, i.e. to have and hold, implying continued possession:

(I) Particularly and primarily to have in one's hands, to hold in the hand (Mt 26:7; Heb 8:3; Rev 1:16; 5:8; 6:2, 5; 8:3, 6; 9:14; 10:2; 17:4).

(II) Generally and most frequently, to have, to possess externally, to have in one's possession, power, charge, control: for example, property (Mt 13:12; 19:21, 22; Mk 10:22, 23; Lk 18:24; 21:4). In figurative phrases: to have years means to be so many years old (Jn 8:57); to have a certain distance means to be a certain distance away (Ac 1:12).

(III) Spoken of what one is said to have in, on, by, or with himself, i.e. of any condition, circumstance, or state either external or internal in which one is:

(A) Generally of any obligation, duty, course (Lk 12:50; Ac 18:18; 21:23; Ro 12:4; 2Co 4:1); of sin, guilt (Jn 9:41; 15:22; Ac 23:29; 1Ti 5:12); lawsuits (1Co 6:4, 7; see Ac 28:29).

(B) Of any condition or affection of body or mind: **(1)** Of the body, to have disease, infirmity (Mk 3:10; Ac 28:9; Heb 7:28; Rev 13:14, wounds); to have a demon or devil, meaning to be possessed (Mt 11:18; Mk 3:22, 30; 9:17; Lk 13:11; Ac 16:16; 19:13). **(2)** Of the mind, e.g., to have love (Jn 5:42; 13:35). Also Lk 17:9; Php 1:23; Col 4:13; 1Ti 5:20; 2Ti 1:12; 3Jn 4). An affection or emotion in Gr. writings is often said to have or to possess a person. In the NT, only in Mk 16:8, literally: "fear and trembling had them."

(C) Particularly of things which one has in, on, or about himself, including the idea of to bear, carry, e.g., in oneself, as in the womb, to be pregnant (Mt 1:18; Rev 12:2).

(IV) Metaphorically and intensively: to have firmly in mind, to hold to, hold fast:

(A) Generally, of things, e.g., Christ's commandments (Jn 14:21). Also 1Co 11:16; Php 3:9; 1Ti 3:9; 2Ti 1:13; Heb 6:19; 1Pe 2:12; Rev 2:24, 25. To have God and Christ, to hold fast to Them, i.e. to acknowledge with love and devotion (1Jn 2:23; 5:12; 2Jn 9).

(B) By implication: to hold for or as, to regard someone as something, e.g., to regard John the Baptist as a prophet (Mt 14:5; 21:26; Mk 11:32).

(V) In the middle, to be near to, adjacent, contiguous. In the NT, only in the participle, meaning near, next, e.g., of place (Mk 1:38, adjacent to, next); of time, with *hēméra* (2250), day, stated or implied, the next day (Lk 13:33; Ac 20:15; 21:26).

Deriv.: *anéchomai* (430), to tolerate, put up with, bear with, endure; *antéchō* (472), to hold firmly, cleave to, support; *apéchō* (568), to have in full; *enéchō* (1758), to hold fast, entangle; *hexés* (1836), next; *héxis* (1838), habit, practice; *epéchō* (1907), to hold fast, heed; *eunoúchos* (2135), a eunuch; *kakouchéō* (2558), to mistreat; *katéchō* (2722), to hold firmly, hold down, hold fast; *metéchō* (3348), to be partaker of, share, participate; *paréchō* (3930), to give from one to another; *periéchō* (4023), to include, contain; *pleonektéō* (4122), to take advantage, defraud; *pleonexía* (4124), covetousness, greediness; *proéchō* (4284), to excel, be better; *proséchō* (4337), to take heed; *rhabdoúchos* (4465), a rod-holder, officer; *sunéchō* (4912), to hold together, compress, arrest, afflict, be in a strait; *schedón* (4975), nigh, almost; *schéma* (4976), shape, fashion, figure; *huperéchō* (5242), to be superior; *hupéchō* (5254), to suffer, endure.

2193. ἕως, **heōs,** *heh´-oce*; of uncertain affinity; a conjunction, preposition and adverb of continuance, *until* (of time and place):—even (until, unto), (as) far (as), how long, (un-) til (-l), (hither-, un-, up) to, while (-s).

Z (Zeta)
NT Numbers 2194–2228

2194. Ζαβουλών, Zaboulōn, *dzab-oo-lone´*; of Hebrew origin [2074]; *Zabulon* (i.e. *Zebulon*), a region of Palestine:—Zabulon.

2195. Ζακχαῖος, Zakchaios, *dzak-chah´ee-os*; of Hebrew origin [compare 2140]; *Zacchæus,* an Israelite:—Zacchæus.

2196. Ζαρά, Zara, *dzar-ah´*; of Hebrew origin [2226]; *Zara* (i.e. *Zerach*), an Israelite:—Zara.

2197. Ζαχαρίας, Zacharias, *dzakh-ar-ee´-as*; of Hebrew origin [2148]; *Zacharias* (i.e. *Zechariah*), the name of two Israelites:—Zacharias.

2198. ζάω, zaō, *dzah´-o*; a primary verb; to *live* (literal or figurative):—life (-time), (a-) live (-ly), quick.

(I) To live, have life, spoken of physical life and existence as opposed to death or nonexistence, and implying always some duration:

(A) Generally, of human life (Ac 10:42; 17:28; 22:22; Ro 7:1–3; 14:9; 1Co 15:45; Heb 9:17; 1Pe 4:5). Of persons raised from the dead (Mt 9:18; Mk 16:11; Jn 5:25; Ac 1:3; 9:41; Rev 20:4); of those restored from sickness, not to die; by implication to be well (Jn 4:50, 51, 53).

(B) In the sense of to exist, in an absolute sense and without end, now and hereafter: to live forever; of human beings (Mt 22:32; Mk 12:27; Lk 20:38; Jn 11:25; 1Th 5:10; 1Pe 4:6); of Jesus (Jn 6:57; 14:19; Ro 6:10; 2Co 13:4; Heb 7:8, 25; Rev 1:18; 2:8); of God (Mt 16:16; Jn 6:57; Ac 14:15; Ro 9:26; 14:11; 1Th 1:9; 1Ti 6:17; Heb 3:12; 12:22; Rev 4:9, 10; 10:6).

(C) Metaphorically, of things, only in the part. *zōn*: living, lively, active, also enduring, opposed to what is dead, inactive, or transient (Ro 12:1; Heb 4:12; 1Pe 1:3, 23; 2:4, 5). "Living water" means the water of running streams and fountains, as opposed to that of stagnant cisterns, pools or marshes (Jn 4:10, 11; 7:38; Rev 7:17).

(II) To live, to sustain life, to live on or by anything (Mt 4:4; 1Co 9:14).

(III) To live in a certain way, to pass one's life in a certain manner (Lk 15:13; Ac 26:5; Ro 7:9; Gal 2:14; 2Ti 3:12; Tit 2:12).

Deriv.: *anazáō* (326), to revive; *zōé* (2222), life; *suzáō* (4800), to live with.

Syn.: *bióō* (980), to live; *diágō* (1236), to spend one's life; *hupárchō* (5225), to be in existence.

2199. Ζεβεδαῖος, Zebedaios, *dzeb-ed-ah´-yos*; of Hebrew origin [compare 2067]; *Zebedæus,* an Israelite:—Zebedee.

2200. ζεστός, zestos, *dzes-tos´*; from 2204; *boiled,* i.e. (by implication) *calid* (figurative, *fervent*):—hot.

Adjective from *zéō* (2204), to be hot. Hot, used figuratively, meaning fervent in Rev 3:15, 16.

Syn.: *ektenḗs* (1618), strained, stretched, fervent; *thérmē* (2329), heat.

2201. ζεῦγος, zeugos, *dzyoo´-gos*; from the same as 2218; a *couple,* i.e. a *team* (of oxen yoked together) or *brace* (of birds tied together):—yoke, pair.

2202. ζευκτηρία, zeuktēria, *dzyook-tay-ree´-ah*; feminine of a derivative (at the second stage) from the same as 2218; a *fastening* (*tiller-rope*):—band.

2203. Ζεύς, Zeus, *dzyooce*; of uncertain affinity; in the oblique cases there is used instead of it a (probably cognate) name **Δίς, Dis,** *deece*; which is otherwise obsolete; *Zeus* or *Dis* (among the Latins *Jupiter* or *Jove*), the supreme deity of the Greeks:—Jupiter.

2204. ζέω, zeō, *dzeh´-o*; a primary verb; to *be hot* (*boil,* of liquids; or *glow,* of solids), i.e. (figurative) *be fervid* (*earnest*):—be fervent.

To seethe, bubble, boil, from the sound of boiling water. In the NT, only applied spiritually, meaning to be fervent (Ac 18:25; Ro 12:11).

Deriv.: *zestós* (2200), fervent, hot; *zélos* (2205), zeal.

2205. ζῆλος, zēlos, *dzay´-los*; from 2204; properly *heat*, i.e. (figurative) *"zeal"* (in a favourable sense, *ardor*; in an unfavourable one, *jealousy*, as of a husband [figurative of God], or an enemy, *malice*):—emulation, envy (-ing), fervent mind, indignation, jealousy, zeal.

Noun from *zéō* (2204), to be hot, fervent. Zeal, used in a good sense (Jn 2:17; Ro 10:2; 2Co 7:7, 11; 11:2; Col 4:13), but often in an evil sense, meaning envy, jealousy, anger (Ac 5:17; 13:45; Ro 13:13; 1Co 3:3; Gal 5:20; Php 3:6; Heb 10:27; Jas 3:14, 16).

Deriv.: *zēlóō* (2206), to be zealous or jealous.

Syn.: *órexis* (3715), excitement of the mind, a longing after; *prothumía* (4288), willingness, readiness of mind; *spoudé* (4710), diligence, forwardness.

2206. ζηλόω, zēloō, *dzay-lo´-o*; from 2205; to *have warmth* of feeling for or against:—affect, covet (earnestly), (have) desire, (move with) envy, be jealous over, (be) zealous (-ly affect).

2207. ζηλωτής, zēlōtēs, *dzay-lo-tace´*; from 2206; a *"zealot"*:—zealous.

2208. Ζηλωτής, Zēlōtēs, *dzay-lo-tace´*; the same as 2208; a *Zealot*, i.e. (special) *partisan* for Jewish political independence:—Zelotes.

2209. ζημία, zēmia, *dzay-mee´-ah*; probably akin to the base of 1150 (through the idea of *violence*); *detriment*:—damage, loss.

2210. ζημιόω, zēmioō, *dzay-mee-o´-o*; from 2209; to *injure*, i.e. (reflexive or passive) to *experience detriment*:—be cast away, receive damage, lose, suffer loss.

2211. Ζηνᾶς, Zēnas, *dzay-nas´*; probably contrete from a poetic form of 2203 and 1435; *Jove-given*; *Zenas*, a Christian:—Zenas.

2212. ζητέω, zēteō, *dzay-teh´-o*; of uncertain affinity; to *seek* (literal or figurative); specially (by Hebrew) to *worship* (God), or (in a bad sense) to *plot* (against life):—be (go) about, desire, endeavour, enquire (for), require, (× will) seek (after, for, means). Compare 4441.

2213. ζήτημα, zētēma, *dzay´-tay-mah*; from 2212; a *search* (properly concrete), i.e. (in words) a *debate*:—question.

2214. ζήτησις, zētēsis, *dzay´-tay-sis*; from 2212; a *searching* (properly the act), i.e. a *dispute* or its *theme*:—question.

2215. ζιζάνιον, zizanion, *dziz-an´-ee-on*; of uncertain origin; *darnel* or false grain:—tares.

2216. Ζοροβάβελ, Zorobabel, *dzor-ob-ab´-el*; of Hebrew origin [2216]; *Zorobabel* (i.e. *Zerubbabel*), an Israelite:—Zorobabel.

2217. ζόφος, zophos, *dzof´-os*; akin to the base of 3509; *gloom* (as shrouding like a *cloud*):—blackness, darkness, mist.

2218. ζυγός, zugos, *dzoo-gos´*; from the root of ζεύγνυμι, zeugnumi (to *join*, especially by a "yoke"); a *coupling*, i.e. (figurative) *servitude* (a *law* or *obligation*); also (literal) the *beam* of the balance (as *connecting* the scales):—pair of balances, yoke.

2219. ζύμη, zumē, *dzoo´-may*; probably from 2204; *ferment* (as if *boiling* up):—leaven.

A noun meaning leaven, sourdough (Mt 13:33; Lk 13:21). As leaven causes to ferment and turn sour, spoken proverbially: "a little leaven leaveneth the whole lump" (1Co 5:7; Gal 5:9), i.e. a few bad men corrupt a multitude. Used figuratively of corruptness, perverseness of life, doctrine, heart, etc. (Mt 16:6, 11; Mk 8:15; Lk 12:1; 1Co 5:7, 8).

Deriv.: *ázumos* (106), unleavened; *zumóō* (2220), to leaven, mix with leaven.

2220. ζυμόω, zumoō, *dzoo-mo´-o*; from 2219; to *cause to ferment*:—leaven.

From *zúmē* (2219), leaven. To leaven, mix with leaven (Mt 13:33; Lk 13:21; 1Co 5:6; Gal 5:9). See *zúme* (2219), leaven.

2221. ζωγρέω, zōgreō, *dzogue-reh´-o*; from the same as 2226 and 64; to *take alive* (*make a prisoner of war*), i.e. (figurative) to *capture* or *ensnare*:—take captive, catch.

2222. ζωή, zōē, *dzo-ay´*; from 2198; *life* (literal or figurative):—life (-time). Compare 5590.

Noun from *záō* (2198), to live. Life:

(I) Generally, physical life and existence as opposed to death and nonexistence:

(A) Particularly and generally of human life (Lk 16:25; Ac 17:25; 1Co 3:22; 15:19; Heb 7:3; Jas 4:14; Rev 11:11). Of life or existence after rising from the dead, only of Christ (Ro 5:10; 2Co

4:10–12). Metaphorically of the Jewish people (Ro 11:15).

(B) In the sense of existence, life, in an absolute sense and without end (Jn 1:4; 5:26; Ro 6:4; Eph 4:18; Heb 7:16; 2Pe 1:3; 1Jn 1:1, 2; Rev 2:7; 21:6; 22:1, 2, 14, 17).

(II) Life, i.e. blessed life, life that satisfies:

(A) Generally (Lk 12:15; Jn 6:51; Ac 2:28; 2Co 2:16; 1Pe 3:10).

(B) In the Christian sense of eternal life, i.e. that life of bliss and glory in the kingdom of God which awaits the true disciples of Christ after the resurrection (Mt 7:14; 18:8, 9; 19:16, 17; Jn 3:15, 16; 5:24; Ro 5:17, 18; 8:2, 6, 10; Php 2:16; 1Ti 4:8; 6:19; 2Ti 1:1; 1Jn 3:14; 5:12, 13, 16).

Syn.: *bíos* (979), the period or duration of life; *psuchē* (5590), literally soul, the breath of life, natural life, the seat of personality. Also *bíosis* (981), manner of life.

2223. ζώνη, **zōnē**, *dzo´-nay*; probably akin to the base of 2218; a *belt*; (by implication) a *pocket*:—girdle, purse.

2224. ζώννυμι, **zōnnumi,** *dzone´-noo-mi*; from 2223; to *bind about* (especially with a belt):—gird.

2225. ζωογονέω, **zōogoneō,** *dzo-og-on-eh´-o*; from the same as 2226 and a derivative of 1096; to *engender alive*, i.e. (by analogy) to *rescue* (passive *be saved*) from death:—live, preserve.

From *zōogónos* (n.f.), life-giving. To give birth to living creatures, give life, make alive. In the NT, to retain, preserve life (Lk 17:33; Ac 7:19).

Syn.: *zōopoiéō* (2227), to cause to live; *suzōopoiéō* (4806), to quicken together or make alive with; *anazōpuréō* (329), to revive.

2226. ζῶον, **zōon,** *dzo´-on*; neuter of a derivative of 2198; a *live* thing, i.e. an *animal*:—beast.

Noun from *zōós* (n.f.), alive. A living creature, an animal (Heb 13:11; 2Pe 2:12; Jude 10). One of four angelic beings which John saw serving and praising God in heaven with the twenty-four elders (Rev 4:6–9; 5:6, 8, 11, 14; 6:1, 3, 5–7; 7:11; 14:3; 15:7; 19:4).

Syn.: *thēríon* (2342), a wild beast; *ktēnos* (2934), a pack animal or beast of any kind; *tetrápous* (5074), a four-footed beast.

2227. ζωοποιέω, **zōopoieō,** *dzo-op-oy-eh´-o*; from the same as 2226 and 4160; to (*re-*) *vitalize* (literal or figurative):—make alive, give life, quicken.

From *zōós* (n.f.), alive, and *poiéō* (4160), to make. To make alive, endue with life, to quicken:

(I) Particularly (1Ti 6:13); of the dead: to recall to life, to quicken, to reanimate (Jn 5:21; Ro 4:17; 8:11; 1Co 15:22; 1Pe 3:18); of seeds: to quicken, to germinate (1Co 15:36).

(II) By implication: to give eternal life, to make alive forever in the bliss and privileges of the Redeemer's kingdom (Jn 6:63; 1Co 15:45; 2Co 3:6; Gal 3:21).

Deriv.: *suzōopoiéō* (4806), to quicken together or make alive with.

Syn.: *zōogoneō* (2225), to give life, produce or preserve alive.

H (Eta)

NT Numbers 2228–2280

2228. ἤ, ē, *ay*; a primary particle of distinction between two connected terms; disjunctive, *or*; comparative, *than*:—and, but (either), (n-) either, except it be, (n-) or (else), rather, save, than, that, what, yea. Often used in connection with other particles. Compare especially 2235, 2260, 2273.

2229. ἦ, ē, *ay*; an adverb of *confirmation*; perhaps intensive of 2228; used only (in the NT) before 3303; *assuredly*:—surely.

2230. ἡγεμονεύω, hēgemoneuō, *hayg-em-on-yoo´-o*; from 2232; to *act as ruler*:—be governor.

2231. ἡγεμονία, hēgemonia, *hayg-em-on-ee´-ah*; from 2232; *government*, i.e. (in time) official *term*:—reign.

2232. ἡγεμών, hēgemōn, *hayg-em-ohn´*; from 2233; a *leader*, i.e. *chief* person (or figurative, place) of a province:—governor, prince, ruler.

2233. ἡγέομαι, hēgeomai, *hayg-eh´-om-ahee*; middle of a (presumed) strengthened form of 71; to *lead*, i.e. *command* (with official authority); (figurative) to *deem*, i.e. *consider*:—account, (be) chief, count, esteem, governor, judge, have the rule over, suppose, think.

Middle deponent of *ágō* (71), to lead. To lead or go before, go first, lead the way. In the NT:

(I) To be a leader, chief, generally only in the participle with the article, a leader, chief, equivalent to *hēgemṓn* (2232), leader, chief (Ac 14:12). Spoken generally of those who have influence and authority (Lk 22:26; Ac 15:22); of officers and teachers in the churches (Heb 13:7, 17, 24); of a chief magistrate such as Joseph in Egypt (Ac 7:10); the Messiah, a ruler, prince (Mt 2:6).

(II) Figuratively, to lead out before the mind, i.e. to view, regard, esteem, consider (2Co 9:5; Php 2:3, 6; 3:7, 8; 1Th 5:13; 2Th 3:15; 1Ti 1:12; 6:1; Heb 10:29; 11:11, 26; Jas 1:2; 2Pe 1:13; 2:13; 3:9, 15).

Deriv.: *diēgéomai* (1334), to declare, show; *exēgéomai* (1834), to bring forth, thoroughly explain; *hēgemṓn* (2232), governor; *proēgéomai* (4285), to prefer or go before another; *hodēgós* (3595), a guide.

Syn.: For **(I)**: *árchō* (757), to rule; *hēgemoneúō* (2230), to be a ruler; *oikodespotéō* (3616), to be ruler of the house; *proḯstēmi* (4291), to stand over or before, to rule; *poimaínō* (4165), to shepherd. For **(II)**: *dokéō* (1380), to be of an opinion, think; *krínō* (2919), to judge, esteem; *logízomai* (3049), to reckon; *nomízō* (3543), to suppose, think; *phronéō* (5426), to think.

2234. ἡδέως, hēdeōs, *hay-deh´-oce*; adverb from a derivative of the base of 2237; *sweetly*, i.e. (figurative) *with pleasure*:—gladly.

2235. ἤδη, ēdē, *ay´-day*; apparently from 2228 (or possibly 2229) and 1211; *even now*:—already, (even) now (already), by this time.

2236. ἥδιστα, hēdista, *hay´-dis-tah*; neuter plural of the superlative of the same as 2234; *with great pleasure*:—most (very) gladly.

2237. ἡδονή, hēdonē, *hay-don-ay´*; from ἁνδάνω, handanō (to *please*); sensual *delight*; (by implication) *desire*:—lust, pleasure.

2238. ἡδύοσμον, hēduosmon, *hay-doo´-os-mon*; neuter of a compound of the same as 2234 and 3744; a *sweet-scented* plant, i.e. *mint*:—mint.

2239. ἦθος, ethos, *ay´-thos*; a strengthened form of 1485; *usage*, i.e. (plural) moral *habits*:—manners.

2240. ἥκω, hēkō, *hay´-ko*; a primary verb; to *arrive*, i.e. *be present* (literal or figurative):—come.

2241. ἠλί, ēli, *ay-lee´*; of Hebrew origin [410 with pronoun suffix]; *my God*:—Eli.

2242. Ἡλί, **Hēli**, *hay-lee´*; of Hebrew origin [5941]; *Heli* (i.e. *Eli*), an Israelite:—Heli.

2243. Ἡλίας, **Hēlias**, *hay-lee´-as*; of Hebrew origin [452]; *Helias* (i.e. *Elijah*), an Israelite:—Elias.

2244. ἡλικία, **hēlikia**, *hay-lik-ee´-ah*; from the same as 2245; *maturity* (in years or size):—age, stature.

2245. ἡλίκος, **hēlikos**, *hay-lee´-kos*; from ἧλιξ, *hēlix* (a *comrade*, i.e. one of the same age); *as big as*, i.e. (interjectively) *how much*:—how (what) great.

2246. ἥλιος, **hēlios**, *hay´-lee-os*; from ἕλη, *helē* (a *ray*; perhaps akin to the alternate of 138); the *sun*; (by implication) *light*:— + east, sun.

2247. ἧλος, **hēlos**, *hay´-los*; of uncertain affinity; a *stud*, i.e. *spike*:—nail.

2248. ἡμᾶς, **hēmas**, *hay-mas´*; accusative plural of 1473; *us*:—our, us, we.

2249. ἡμεῖς, **hēmeis**, *hay-mice´*; nominal plural of 1473; *we* (only used when emphatic):—us, we (ourselves).

2250. ἡμέρα, **hēmera**, *hay-mer´-ah*; feminine (with 5610 implied) of a derivative of ἧμαι, *hēmai* (to *sit*; akin to the base of 1476) meaning *tame*, i.e. *gentle; day*, i.e. (literal) the time space between dawn and dark, or the whole twenty-four hours (but several days were usually reckoned by the Jews as inclusive of the parts of both extremes); (figurative) a *period* (always defined more or less clearly by the context):—age, + alway, (mid-) day (by day, [-ly]), + for ever, judgement, (day) time, while, years.

A noun meaning day, daytime, occasion, time:

(**I**) Day, particularly the time from one sunrise or sunset to another, equal to *nuchthēmeron* (3574), a day and a night, a full twenty-four-hour day or only a part of it.

(**A**) Generally (Mk 6:21; Lk 4:16; 9:28; 22:7; 24:21; Ac 21:26; Ro 14:5, 6; 1Co 15:31; Jas 5:5; Rev 2:10).

(**B**) Emphatically, a certain or set day (Ac 17:31; 1Co 4:3, "man's judgement," lit. "man's day," i.e. human day of trial, meaning a court day; Heb 4:7).

(**C**) Specifically, *hēméra toú kuríou* (*toú*

[3588], the; *kuríou* [2962], Lord), Day of the Lord when Christ will return to judge the world and fully establish His kingdom (1Co 1:8; 5:5; 2Co 1:14; 1Th 5:2, 4; 2Pe 3:10); the great day of judgement (Mt 7:22; 10:15; 11:22, 24; 12:36; Mk 13:32; Ac 2:20; Ro 2:16; 2Th 1:10; Jude 6); the day of wrath (Ro 2:5; Rev 6:17); "the day of redemption" (Eph 4:30); "the last day" (Jn 6:39, 40); "the day of God," by whose authority Christ sits as judge (2Pe 3:12).

(**D**) Day, daylight, from sunrise to sunset: in antithesis with *núx* (3571), night (Lk 4:42; 21:37; Jn 9:4; Ac 12:18; 16:35; 26:13; Rev 8:12); night and day, meaning continually (Mk 4:27; 5:5; Lk 2:37; 18:7; Ac 9:24; 20:31; 26:7; 1Th 2:9); metaphorically for the light of true and higher knowledge, moral light (Ro 13:12; 1Th 5:5, 8; 2Pe 1:19).

(**II**) Time in general, nearly equivalent to *chrónos* (5550), time:

(**A**) In the singular, of a point or period of time (Eph 6:13). Followed by the gen. of person (Lk 19:42, "in this thy time" [a.t.], meaning while you yet are living); followed by the possessive pronoun and the article (Jn 8:56, "so that he may see my day" [a.t.], meaning my time, the time of my manifestation).

(**B**) In the plural, *hēmérai*, days, i.e. time: (**1**) Generally (Mt 9:15; Lk 17:22); "the last days" (Ac 2:17; Jas 5:3); "these days" (Ac 3:24); "those days" (Mt 3:1; Mk 13:24; Rev 9:6); "the former days" (Heb 10:32). Followed by the gen. of person, e.g., "the days of John the Baptist" (Mt 11:12). Also see Lk 4:25; Ac 7:45. (**2**) Specifically the time of one's life, i.e. one's days, years, age, life, e.g., fully (Lk 1:75 [cf. Ge 47:8, 9]). Elizabeth is spoken of three times as being advanced in her days, meaning old (Lk 1:7, 18; 2:36).

Deriv.: *ephēmeros* (2184), for a day, daily; *kathēmerinós* (2522), daily; *mesēmbría* (3314), midday, noon; *nuchthēmeron* (3574), a day and night; *oktaēmeros* (3637), eighth day.

Syn.: *kairós* (2540), season; *chrónos* (5550), time; *hōra* (5610), hour.

2251. ἡμέτερος, **hēmeteros**, *hay-met´-er-os*; from 2349; *our*:—our, your [*by a different reading*].

2252. ἤμην, **ēmēn**, *ay´-mane*; a prolonged form of 2358; *I was*:—be, was. [*Sometimes unexpressed*].

2253. ἡμιθανής, hēmithanēs, *hay-mee-than-ace´*; from a presumed compound of the base of 2255 and 2348; *half dead*, i.e. *entirely exhausted*:—half dead.

2254. ἡμῖν, hēmin, *hay-meen´*; dative plural of 1473; *to* (or *for, with, by*) *us*:—our, (for) us, we.

2255. ἥμισυ, hēmisu, *hay´-mee-soo*; neuter of a derivative from an inseparable prefix akin to 260 (through the idea of *partition* involved in *connection*) and meaning *semi-*; (as noun) *half*:—half.

2256. ἡμιώριον, hēmiōrion, *hay-mee-o´-ree-on*; from the base of 2255 and 5610; a *half hour*:—half an hour.

2257. ἡμῶν, hēmōn, *hay-mone´*; generic plural of 1473; *of* (or *from*) *us*:—our (company), us, we.

2258. ἦν, ēn, *ane*; imperfect of 1510, *I* (*thou*, etc.) *was* (*wast* or *were*):— + agree, be, × have (+ charge of), hold, use, was (-t), were.

2259. ἡνίκα, hēnika, *hay-nee´-kah*; of uncertain affinity; *at which time*:—when.

2260. ἤπερ, ēper, *ay´-per*; from 2228 and 4007; *than at all* (or *than perhaps, than indeed*):—than.

2261. ἤπιος, ēpios, *ay´-pee-os*; probably from 2031; properly *affable*, i.e. *mild* or *kind*:—gentle.

Adjective meaning placid, gentle, mild, easy, compliant (1Th 2:7); given as an attribute of any good servant of God (2Ti 2:24).

Syn.: *práos* (4235), meek; *praús* (4239), meek; *epieikēs* (1933), gentle, tolerant; *hēsúchios* (2272), peaceable, quiet; *éremos* (2263), composed, peaceful.

2262. Ἤρ, Ēr, *ayr*; of Hebrew origin [6147]; *Er*, an Israelite:—Er.

2263. ἤρεμος, ēremos, *ay´-rem-os*; perhaps by transposition from 2048 (through the idea of *stillness*); *tranquil*:—quiet.

2264. Ἡρώδης, Hērōdēs, *hay-ro´-dace*; compound of ἥρως, Hērōs (a "*hero*") and 1491; *heroic*; *Herodes*, the name of four Jewish kings:—Herod.

2265. Ἡρωδιανοί, Hērōdianoi, *hay-ro-dee-an-oy´*; plural of a derivative of 2264; *Herodians*, i.e. partisans of Herodes:—Herodians.

2266. Ἡρωδιάς, Hērōdias, *hay-ro-dee-as´*; from 2264; *Herodias*, a woman of the Herodian family:—Herodias.

2267. Ἡροδίων, Hērōdiōn, *hay-ro-dee´-ohn*; from 2264; *Herodion*, a Christian:—Herodion.

2268. Ἡσαΐας, Hēsaïas, *hay-sah-ee´-as*; of Hebrew origin [3470]; *Hesaias* (i.e. *Jeshajah*), an Israelite:—Esaias.

2269. Ἡσαῦ, Ēsau, *ay-sow´*; of Hebrew origin [6215]; *Esau*, an Edomite:—Esau.

2270. ἡσυχάζω, hēsuchazō, *hay-soo-khad´-zo*; from the same as 2272; to *keep still* (intransitive), i.e. *refrain* from labour, meddlesomeness or speech:—cease, hold peace, be quiet, rest.

From *hēsuchos* (n.f.), quiet, still. To be quiet, live quietly (1Th 4:11). By implication: to rest from labour (Lk 23:56); to be silent, not speaking, keep one's self from speaking out (Lk 14:4); to acquiesce (Ac 11:18; 21:14).

Syn.: *katapaúō* (2664), to rest, restrain; *paúō* (3973), to stop; *sigáō* (4601), to be silent; *siōpáō* (4623), to keep silence.

2271. ἡσυχία, hēsuchia, *hay-soo-khee´-ah*; feminine of 2272; (as noun) *stillness*, i.e. desistance from bustle or language:—quietness, silence.

2272. ἡσύχιος, hēsuchios, *hay-soo´-khee-os*; a prolonged form of a compound probably of a derivative of the base of 1476 and perhaps 2192; properly *keeping* one's *seat* (*sedentary*), i.e. (by implication) *still* (*undisturbed, undisturbing*):—peaceable, quiet.

2273. ἤτοι, ētoi, *ay´-toy*; from 2228 and 5104; *either indeed*:—whether.

2274. ἡττάω, hēttaō, *hayt-tah´-o*; from the same as 2276; to *make worse*, i.e. *vanquish* (literal or figurative); (by implication) to *rate lower*:—be inferior, overcome.

2275. ἥττημα, hēttēma, *hayt´-tay-mah*; from 2274; a *deterioration*, i.e. (object) *failure* or (subject) *loss*:—diminishing, fault.

2276. ἧττον, hētton, *hate´-ton*; neuter of comparative of ἧκα, hēka (*slightly*) used for that of

2556; *worse* (as noun); (by implication) *less* (as adverb):—less, worse.

2277. ἤτω, **ētō,** *ay´-to*; third person singular imperative of 1510; *let him* (or *it*) *be*:—let ... be.

2278. ἠχέω, **ēcheō,** *ay-kheh´-o*; from 2279; to *make a* loud *noise*, i.e. *reverberate*:—roar, sound.

2279. ἦχος, **ēchos,** *ay´-khos*; of uncertain affinity; a loud or confused *noise* ("*echo*"), i.e. *roar*; (figurative) a *rumour*:—fame, sound.

Θ (Theta)

2280. Θαδδαῖος, **Thaddaios**, *thad-dah´-yos*; of uncertain origin; *Thaddæus*, one of the apostles:—Thaddæus.

2281. θάλασσα, **thalassa**, *thal´-as-sah*; probably prolonged from 251; the *sea* (general or special):—sea.

Noun probably from *háls* (251), salt. The sea, a sea:

(I) Generally, and as implying the vicinity of land (Mt 13:47; 18:6, "expanse of the sea" [a.t.]; Mk 9:42; Lk 21:25; Ro 9:27; 2Co 11:26; Rev 18:17; 20:13; 21:1); the land and sea standing for the whole earth (Rev 7:1–3; 12:12). The heaven, the earth, and the sea standing for the universe (Ac 4:24; 14:15; Rev 5:13). Poetically, because of the appearance of that upon which the throne of God is said to be founded, a crystal sea (Rev 4:6; 15:2).

(II) Of particular seas and lakes:

(A) By implication the Mediterranean (Ac 10:6, 32; 17:14).

(B) The Red Sea (Ac 7:36; 1Co 10:1, 2).

(C) The Sea of Galilee or Tiberias (Mt 4:15, 18; Mk 1:16; Jn 6:6–19; 21:1).

Deriv.: *dithálassos* (1337), between two seas; *parathalássios* (3864), along the sea.

Syn.: *límnē* (3041), lake.

2282. θάλπω, **thalpō**, *thal´-po*; probably akin to θάλλω, **thallō** (to *warm*); to *brood*, i.e. (figurative) to *foster*:—cherish.

2283. Θάμαρ, **Thamar**, *tham´-ar*; of Hebrew origin [8559]; *Thamar* (i.e. *Tamar*), an Israelitess:—Thamar.

2284. θαμβέω, **thambeō**, *tham-beh´-o*; from 2285; to *stupefy* (with surprise), i.e. *astound*:—amaze, astonish.

2285. θάμβος, **thambos**, *tham´-bos*; akin to an obsolete τάφω, **taphō** (to *dumbfound*); *stupefaction* (by surprise), i.e. *astonishment*:—× amazed, + astonished, wonder.

2286. θανάσιμος, **thanasimos**, *than-as´-ee-mos*; from 2288; *fatal*, i.e. *poisonous*:—deadly.

2287. θανατήφορος, **thanatēphoros**, *than-at-ay´-for-os*; from (the feminine form of) 2288 and 5342; *death-bearing*, i.e. *fatal*:—deadly.

2288. θάνατος, **thanatos**, *than´-at-os*; from 2348; (properly an adjective used as a noun) *death* (literal or figurative):—× deadly, (be ...) death.

Noun from *thnḗskō* (2348), to die. Death, the extinction of life, naturally or by violence:

(I) Generally, and of natural death (Jn 11:4, 13; Ro 8:38; Php 1:20; Heb 7:23). To taste or to experience death (Mt 26:38; Mk 14:34; Jn 12:33; 18:32; 21:19; Rev 13:3). Figuratively, exposure to death (2Co 11:23). Used by metonymy for plague, pestilence (Rev 6:8; 18:8).

(II) Spoken of a violent death.

(A) Of punishment: guilty of death (Mt 26:66; Mk 14:64); worthy of death (Lk 23:15; Ac 23:29); to sentence someone to death (Mt 20:18; Mk 10:33); death on the cross (Php 2:8). Also Mt 10:21; 15:4; Mk 7:10; 13:12; Lk 23:22; 24:20; Ac 22:4; 2Co 1:9, 10; Rev 2:10, 23.

(B) Of the death of Jesus (Ro 5:10; 1Co 11:26; Php 2:8; Col 1:22; Heb 2:9, 14; 9:15).

(III) Often in the Sept., *thánatos* has the sense of destruction, perdition, misery, implying both physical death and exclusion from the presence and favour of God in consequence of sin and disobedience. Opposed to *zōḗ* (2222), life and blessedness (Sept.: Dt 30:19; Pr 11:19; 12:28). In the NT, this sense is applied with more definitiveness to the gospel plan of salvation, and as *zōḗ* is used to denote the bliss and glory of the kingdom of God including the idea of a joyful resurrection, so *thánatos* is used for the opposite, i.e. rejection from the kingdom of God. This includes the idea of physical death as aggravated by eternal condemnation; sometimes with the idea of physical death being more prominent, and other times subsequent perdition being more prominent (Jn 8:51; Ro 6:16, 21, 23; 7:5, 10; 8:2, 6; 2Co 2:16; 3:7; 2Ti 1:10; Heb 2:15; Jas 5:20; 1Jn 3:14; 5:16, 17). Called also the second death (Rev 2:11; 20:6, 14; 21:8), referring to eternal spiritual separation from God. In this sense *ho thánatos* is used as a kind of personification, the idea of physical death being prominent (Ro 5:12, 14, 17, 21; 1Co 15:26, 54–56).

(IV) Poetically, death as the king of Hades (86), *ho thánatos* being personified (Rev 6:8; 20:13). See Rev 1:18.

Deriv.: *epithanátios* (1935), appointed to die; *thanásimos* (2286), deadly; *thanatēphóros* (2287), death-bearing, deadly; *thanatóō* (2289), to put to death.

Syn.: *nékrōsis* (3500), a deadness; *teleutē* (5054), an end, death.

2289. θανατόω, thanatoō, *than-at-o´-o*; from 2288; to *kill* (literal or figurative):—become dead, (cause to be) put to death, kill, mortify.

2290. θάπτω, thaptō, *thap´-to*; a primary verb; to *celebrate funeral rites*, i.e. *inter*:—bury.

2291. Θάρα, Thara, *thar´-ah*; of Hebrew origin [8646]; *Thara* (i.e. *Terach*), the father of Abraham:—Thara.

2292. θαρρέω, tharrheō, *thar-hreh´-o*; another form for 2293; to *exercise courage*:—be bold, × boldly, have confidence, be confident. Compare 5111.

2293. θαρσέω, tharseō, *thar-seh´-o*; from 2294; to *have courage*:—be of good cheer (comfort). Compare 2292.

2294. θάρσος, tharsos, *thar´-sos*; akin (by transposition) to **θράσος, thrasos** (*daring*); *boldness* (subjective):—courage.

2295. θαῦμα, thauma, *thou´-mah*; apparently from a form of 2300; *wonder* (properly, concrete; but by implication, abstract):—admiration.

2296. θαυμάζω, thaumazō, *thou-mad´-zo*; from 2295; to *wonder*; (by implication) to *admire*:—admire, have in admiration, marvel, wonder.

2297. θαυμάσιος, thaumasios, *thow-mas´-ee-os*; from 2295; *wondrous*, i.e. (neuter as noun) a *miracle*:—wonderful thing.

Adjective from *thaumázō* (2296), to admire. Wonderful, admirable. In the NT, a wonder, miracle. Only in Mt 21:15.

Syn.: *éndoxos* (1741), glorious; *thaumastós* (2298), wonderful, marvelous, worthy of admiration; *parádoxos* (3861), strange, astonishing work.

2298. θαυμαστός, thaumastos, *thow-mas-tos´*; from 2296; *wondered* at, i.e. (by implication) *wonderful*:—marvel (-lous).

2299. θεά, thea, *theh-ah´*; feminine of 2316; a female *deity*:—goddess.

2300. θεάομαι, theaomai, *theh-ah´-om-ahee*; a prolonged form of a primary verb; to *look* closely at, i.e. (by implication) to *perceive* (literal or figurative); by extension to *visit*:—behold, look (upon), see. Compare 3700.

Middle deponent from *tháomai* (n.f.) to wonder. To behold, to see, to look at:

(I) Simply to see, perceive with the eyes (Mk 16:11, 14; Lk 5:27; Jn 8:10; Ac 1:11; 21:27; 22:9; 1Jn 4:12, 14).

(II) Involving more than merely seeing and including the idea of desire, interest, pleasure (Mt 6:1; 11:7; 22:11; 23:5; Lk 7:24; 23:55; Jn 1:14; 4:35).

Deriv.: *théatron* (2302), theater.

Syn.: *atenízō* (816), to gaze intently; *blépō* (991) to see; *emblépō* (1689), to look earnestly upon and learn from; *epopteúō* (2029), to oversee; *theōréō* (2334), to look at a thing with interest and attention to details, to consider; *katanoéō* (2657), to comprehend with the mind.

2301. θεατρίζω, theatrizō, *theh-at-rid´-zo*; from 2302; to *expose as a spectacle*:—make a gazing stock.

2302. θέατρον, theatron, *theh´-at-ron*; from 2300; *a place for public show* ("*theatre*"), i.e. general *audience-room*; (by implication) a *show* itself (figurative):—spectacle, theatre.

2303. θεῖον, theion, *thi´-on*; probably neuter of 2304 (in its origin sense of *flashing*); *sulphur*:—brimstone.

2304. θεῖος, theios, *thi´-os*; from 2316; *godlike* (neuter as noun, *divinity*):—divine, godhead.

Adjective from *Theós* (2316), God. Divine, what is uniquely God's and proceeds from Him

(2Pe 1:3, 4); the divine nature, divinity (Ac 17:29).

2305. θειότης, theiotēs, *thi-ot´-ace*; from 2304; *divinity* (abstract):—godhead.

Noun from *Theíos* (2304), divine. Divinity, divine nature. Used only in Ro 1:20.

2306. θειώδης, theiōdēs, *thi-o´-dace*; from 2303 and 1491; *sulphur-like*, i.e. *sulphurous:*—brimstone.

2307. θέλημα, thelēma, *thel´-ay-mah*; from the prolonged form of 2309; a *determination* (properly the thing), i.e. (active) *choice* (special *purpose, decree*; abstract *volition*) or (passive) *inclination:*—desire, pleasure, will.

Noun from *thélō* (2309), to will. Will, active volition:

(I) Will, the act of willing, what one wills or prefers, wish, good pleasure (Mt 26:42; Jn 1:13; Ac 21:14; 1Co 16:12; Eph 5:17; 1Pe 2:15; 4:2, 3, 19; 1Jn 5:14).

(II) By metonymy: will, what one wills or determines to do or have done (Mt 7:21; 12:50; 21:31; Mk 3:35; Jn 5:30; 6:38; Ac 13:22; Ro 12:2; Eph 6:6; Heb 13:21); the desires of the flesh (Eph 2:3; Sept.: 1Ki 5:8, 9; Ps 103:21; 143:10). By implication: will, i.e. purpose, counsel, decree, law (Mt 18:14; Jn 6:39, 40; Ac 22:14; Heb 10:7, 9, 10, 36). Hence, the will of God, i.e. the counsels or eternal purposes of God (Mt 6:10; Lk 11:2).

(III) By metonymy: will, the faculty of willing, free will (Lk 23:25; 1Co 7:37; 2Pe 1:21); of God (Eph 1:5, 11; 1Pe 3:17).

Syn.: *boulé* (1012), counsel, purpose, will. Also *boúlēma* (1013), resolve, purpose, will; *epithumía* (1939), longing, desire, passion; *epipóthēsis* (1972), earnest desire; *thélēsis* (2308), determination, act of will.

2308. θέλησις, thelēsis, *thel´-ay-sis*; from 2309; *determination* (properly the act), i.e. *option:*—will.

2309. θέλω, thelō, *thel´-o*; or ἐθέλω, ethelō, *eth-el´-o*; in certain tenses θελέω, *theleō, thel-eh´-o*; and ἐθελέω, *etheleō, eth-el-eh´-o*; which are otherwise obsolete; apparently strengthened from the alternate form of 138; to *determine* (as an active *option* from subjective impulse; whereas 1014 properly denotes rather a passive *acquiescence* in objective considerations), i.e. *choose* or

prefer (literal or figurative); (by implication) to *wish*, i.e. *be inclined* to (sometimes adverbially *gladly*); impersonally for the future tense, to *be about to*; by Hebrew to *delight in*:—desire, be disposed (forward), intend, list, love, mean, please, have rather, (be) will (have, -ling, -ling [ly]).

To will, wish, desire, implying active volition and purpose; differing from *boúlomai* (1014), to wish, desire, in that *boúlomai* expresses a more passive desire or willingness.

(I) To will, i.e. to have in mind, to purpose, intend, be pleased:

(A) Of God and Christ (Jn 5:21; Ac 18:21; Ro 9:22; 1Co 4:19; Col 1:27; 1Ti 2:4; Jas 4:15).

(B) Of men (Mt 2:18; 5:40; 19:21; Mk 3:13; 6:19, 26; 7:24; Lk 8:20; 15:28; Ac 10:10; Gal 4:20; Rev 11:6).

(C) Used metaphorically of the wind (Jn 3:8).

(II) Generally: to wish, desire, choose (Mt 5:42; 7:12; 19:17; 20:32; Mk 6:25; Jn 16:19; 17:24; 1Co 7:7; 11:3; Gal 4:20). Sometimes *thélō* is rendered as an adverb, i.e. "willingly," "gladly," (Jn 6:21).

(III) By implication: to be disposed or inclined toward anything, delight in, love, in which case it is a syn. of *philéō* (5368), to love (Mt 9:13; 12:7; 27:43; Lk 20:46; Jn 3:8). Followed by *en* ([1722], in), to delight in anything (Col 2:18).

(IV) By implication: to be of a particular mind or opinion, to affirm (2Pe 3:5, "for they want to be ignorant" [a.t. {cf. 2Pe 3:4}]).

Deriv.: *ethelothrēskeía* (1479), voluntary; *thélēma* (2307), will; *thélēsis* (2308), the act of the will, pleasure, desire.

Syn.: *aitéō* (154), to ask, desire; *exaitéomai* (1809), to demand, desire; *epithuméō* (1937), to desire earnestly; *epipothéō* (1971), to long after; *erōtáō* (2065), to request, ask; *zēlóō* (2206), to have a zeal for, be jealous, desire earnestly; *himeíromai* (2442), to have a strong desire for; *orégomai* (3713), to desire.

2310. θεμέλιος, themelios, *them-el´-ee-os*; from a derivative of 5087; something *put* down, i.e. a *substruction* (of a building, etc.), (literal or figurative):—foundation.

2311. θεμελιόω, themelioō, *them-el-ee-o´-o*; from 2310; to *lay a basis* for, i.e. (literal) *erect,* or (figurative) *consolidate*:—(lay the) found (-ation), ground, settle.

2312. θεοδίδακτος, theodidaktos, *theh-od-id´-ak-tos*; from 2316 and 1321; *divinely instructed*:—taught of God. **θεολόγος** *theologos, theh-ol-og´-os*, from 2316 and 3004; a "*theologian*":—divine.

2313. θεομαχέω, theomacheō, *theh-o-makh-eh´-o*; from 2314; to *resist deity*:—fight against God.

2314. θεόμαχος, theomachos, *theh-om´-akh-os*; from 2316 and 3164; an *opponent of deity*:—to fight against God.

2315. θεόπνευστος, theopneustos, *theh-op´-nyoo-stos*; from 2316 and a presumed derivative of 4154; *divinely breathed* in:—given by inspiration of God.

Adjective from *theós* (2316), God, and *pnéō* (4154), to breathe or blow. Literally, "breathed by God." Given by God, divinely inspired. Occurs only in 2Ti 3:16.

2316. θεός, theos, *theh´-os*; of uncertain affinity; a *deity*, especially (with 3588) *the* supreme *Divinity*; (figurative) a *magistrate*; by Hebrew *very*:— × exceeding, God, god [-ly, -ward].

(I) God of all, Jehovah (Mt 1:23; 6:24; Lk 2:14, 52; Jn 3:2; 4:24; Ro 16:26; 1Co 4:1). Also "the Lord God" (Mt 4:10; 22:37; Mk 12:29, 30; Lk 1:16, 32; 1Pe 3:15; Rev 4:8). In construction:

(A) Of persons: the God of someone, i.e. his protector, benefactor, the object of his worship (Mt 22:32; Mk 12:26; Lk 1:68; Ac 5:30); of things, i.e. God as the author and giver, the source (Ro 15:5; Php 4:9; Heb 13:20; 1Pe 5:10).

(B) Spoken of what comes forth, is sent, given, appointed from God (Mt 3:16; Lk 11:49; Ac 23:4; 2Ti 3:17).

(II) Spoken of Christ, the logos, who is declared to be God (Jn 1:1; 20:28; Ro 9:5; Php 2:6; 1Ti 3:16; Heb 1:8; 1Jn 5:20).

(III) From the Hebrew, spoken of the leaders of Israel as representatives of God in the Jewish theocracy (Jn 10:34, 35, quoted from Ps 82:1, 6).

(IV) In the Greek sense: a god, a deity (Ac 7:43; 12:22; 14:11; 19:26; 1Co 8:4, 5; Gal 4:8). So Satan is called "the god of this world," its leader, etc. (2Co 4:4).

Deriv.: *átheos* (112), without God; *theá* (2299), goddess; *theíos* (2304), divine; *theiótēs* (2305), divinity, referring to the power of God but not to His essential character and nature; *theodídaktos* (2312), taught of God; *theomáchos* (2314), one fighting against God; *theópneustos* (2315), inspired of God; *theosebés* (2318), reverent of God; *theostugés* (2319), one hating God; *theótēs* (2320), divinity, referring to the essence and nature of God; *philótheos* (5377), fond of God, lover or friend of God.

Syn.: *kúrios* (2962), God, Lord, master, supreme in authority; *pantokrátōr* (3841), Omnipotent, Almighty.

2317. θεοσέβεια, theosebeia, *theh-os-eb´-i-ah*; from 2318; *devoutness*, i.e. *piety*:—godliness.

2318. θεοσεβής, theosebēs, *theh-os-eb-ace´*; from 2316 and 4576; *reverent of God*, i.e. *pious*:—worshipper of God.

Adjective from *theós* (2316), God, and *sébomai* (4576), to reverence. Godly, devout, translated "worshipper of God" (Jn 9:31).

Deriv.: *theosébeia* (2317), godliness.

Syn.: *eulabés* (2126), one who receives something well, devout but in a more passive way than *eusebés*; *eusebés* (2152), pious, reverent, devout, showing one's reverence in a worshipful attitude; *philótheos* (5377), fond or a friend of God. Also *theóphilos* (2321), a friend of God, used only as the proper name Theophilus.

2319. θεοστυγής, theostugēs, *theh-os-too-gace´*; from 2316 and the base of 4767; *hateful to God*, i.e. *impious*:—hater of God.

Adjective from *theós* (2316), God, and *stugéō* (n.f., see *apostugéō* [655]), to hate, abhor. In the NT: hating God, impious. Occurs only in Ro 1:30.

2320. θεότης, theotēs, *theh-ot´-ace*; from 2316; *divinity* (abstract):—godhead.

Noun from *Theós* (2316), God. Deity, the divine nature and perfections. Only in Col 2:9.

2321. Θεόφιλος, Theophilos, *theh-of´-il-os*; from 2316 and 5384; *friend of God*; Theophilus, a Christian:—Theophilus.

2322. θεραπεία, therapeia, *ther-ap-i´-ah*; from 2323; *attendance* (specially medical, i.e. *cure*); (figurative and collective) *domestics*:—healing, household.

2323. θεραπεύω, therapeuō, *ther-ap-yoo´-o*; from the same as 2324; to *wait upon* menially, i.e. (figurative) to *adore* (God), or (special) to *relieve* (of disease):—cure, heal, worship.

From *therápōn* (2324), attendant, servant. To wait upon, minister to, render voluntary service:
(I) With the root idea: only once, in the passive: to be served, ministered to (Ac 17:25).
(II) With the derived idea of to take care of the sick, to tend, with the more general meaning of to heal, cure (Mt 4:23, 24; 10:1, 8; 12:10; Mk 1:34; Lk 6:7; 7:21; 8:2; Ac 4:14; Rev 13:3, 12).
Deriv.: *therapeía* (2322), service, healing.
Syn.: *iáomai* (2390), to heal; *sṓzō* (4982), to save, heal.

2324. θεράπων, therapōn, *ther-ap´-ohn*; apparently a participle from an otherwise obsolete derivative of the base of 2330; a menial *attendant* (as if *cherishing*):—servant.

A noun meaning servant, attendant, minister, implying always voluntary service and attendance, and therefore different from *doúlos* (1401), a slave, which is often used to refer to involuntary service. Used once, of Moses (Heb 3:5).
Deriv.: *therapeúō* (2323), to voluntarily serve.

2325. θερίζω, therizō, *ther-id´-zo*; from 2330 (in the sense of the *crop*); to *harvest*:—reap.

2326. θερισμός, therismos, *ther-is-mos´*; from 2325; *reaping*, i.e. the *crop*:—harvest.

2327. θεριστής, theristēs, *ther-is-tace´*; from 2325; a *harvester*:—reaper.

2328. θερμαίνω, thermainō, *ther-mah´ee-no*; from 2329; to *heat* (oneself):—(be) warm (-ed, self).

2329. θέρμη, thermē, *ther´-may*; from the base of 2330; *warmth*:—heat.

2330. θέρος, theros, *ther´-os*; from a primary **θέρω, therō** (to *heat*); properly *heat*, i.e. *summer*:—summer.

2331. Θεσσαλονικεύς, Thessalonikeus, *thessal-on-ik-yoos´*; from 2332; a *Thessalonican*, i.e. inhabitant of Thessalonice:—Thessalonian.

2332. Θεσσαλονίκη, Thessalonikē, *thes-sal-on-ee´-kay*; from **Θεσσαλός, Thessalos** (a *Thessalian*) and 3529; *Thessalonice*, a place in Asia Minor:—Thessalonica.

2333. Θευδᾶς, Theudas, *thyoo-das´*; of uncertain origin; *Theudas*, an Israelite:—Theudas.

2334. θεωρέω, theōreō, *theh-o-reh´-o*; from a derivative of 2300 (perhaps by addition of 3708); to *be a spectator* of, i.e. *discern* (literal, figurative [*experience*] or intensive [*acknowledge*]):—behold, consider, look on, perceive, see. Compare 3700.

From *theōrós* (n.f.), a spectator, from *theáomai* (2300), to look closely at. To be a spectator of, i.e. to look on or at, to behold:
(I) Simply to see, perceive with the eyes, behold, nearly equivalent to *blépō* (991), to look.
(A) Generally: to see a person or thing (Mk 3:11; 5:15; Lk 10:18; 21:6; 24:37; Jn 7:3; 9:8; 14:19; 16:10, 16, 17, 19; Ac 3:16; 9:7; 20:38; 25:24).
(B) To see something happening (Mk 5:38; 16:4; Jn 10:12; 20:6; Ac 7:56; 10:11; 1Jn 3:17).
(II) Figuratively, to perceive with the mind:
(A) To recognize a present situation (Jn 4:19; Ac 17:16; 21:20).
(B) To perceive a danger, future reality (Ac 27:10).
(III) Metaphorically, to comprehend, consider, experience:
(A) To see in the sense of comprehending, recognizing, acknowledging (Jn 6:40; 12:45; 14:17).
(B) To consider (Heb 7:4).
(C) To experience, e.g., death (Jn 8:51); to experience in the sense of partaking of something, e.g., Christ's glory (Jn 17:24).
Deriv.: *anatheōréō* (333), to look again; *theōría* (2335), spectacle, sight; *paratheōréo* (3865), to overlook, neglect.
Syn.: *atenízō* (816), to gaze intently; *blépō* (991), to look; *diablépō* (1227), to see through clearly; *eídō* (1492), to know, consider, perceive; *emblépō* (1689), to look earnestly; *epopteúō* (2029), to oversee; *kathoráō* (2529), to discern clearly; *katalambánō* (2638), to comprehend, perceive; *katanoéō* (2657), to perceive.

2335. θεωρία, theōria, *theh-o-ree´-ah*; from the same as 2334; *spectatorship*, i.e. (concrete) a *spectacle*:—sight.

2336. θήκη, thēkē, *thay´-kay*; from 5087; a *receptacle*, i.e. *scabbard*:—sheath.

2337. θηλάζω, thēlazō, *thay-lad´-zo*; from θηλή, *thēlē* (the *nipple*); to *suckle*; (by implication) to *suck*:—(give) suck (-ling).

2338. θῆλυς, thēlus, *thay´-loos*; from the same as 2337; *female*:—female, woman.

Adjective meaning female, as contrasted with *arsēn* (730), male. God created the human race, male and female (Mt 19:4; Mk 10:6); in one sense, male and female are equal in Christ (Gal 3:28). Also used two times in referring to homosexual abuses of God's plan for marriage (Ro 1:26, 27).

Syn.: *gunē* (1135), woman or wife.

2339. θήρα, thēra, *thay´-rah*; from θήρ, *thēr* (a wild *animal*, as *game*); *hunting*, i.e. (figurative) *destruction*:—trap.

2340. θηρεύω, thēreuō, *thay-ryoo´-o*; from 2339; to *hunt* (an animal), i.e. (figurative) to *carp at*:—catch.

2341. θηριομαχέω, thēriomacheō, *thay-ree-om-akh-eh´-o*; from a compound of 2342 and 3164; to *be a beast-fighter* (in the gladiatorial show), i.e. (figurative) to *encounter* (furious men):—fight with wild beasts.

2342. θηρίον, thērion, *thay-ree´-on*; diminutive from the same as 2339; a *dangerous animal*:—(venomous, wild) beast.

Noun meaning wild beast (Mk 1:13; Ac 10:12; 11:6; Rev 6:8). Used metaphorically of brutal, savage men (Tit 1:12); used symbolically in the Apocalypse (Rev 11:7; 13:1ff.; 14:9; 17:3ff.; 19:19, 20; 20:4, 10).

Deriv.: *thēriomacheō* (2341), to fight with wild beasts.

2343. θησαυρίζω, thēsaurizō, *thay-sow-rid´-zo*; from 2344; to *amass* or *reserve* (literal or figurative):—lay up (treasure), (keep) in store, (heap) treasure (together, up).

2344. θησαυρός, thēsauros, *thay-sow-ros´*; from 5087; a *deposit*, i.e. *wealth* (literal or figurative):—treasure.

2345. θιγγάνω, thigganō, *thing-gan´-o*; a prolonged form of an obsolete primary θίγω, *thigō* (to *finger*); to *manipulate*, i.e. *have to do with*; (by implication) to *injure*:—handle, touch.

Verb meaning to touch. Spoken of ascetic prohibitions not to handle (Col 2:21); spoken of animals forbidden to touch Mt. Sinai while God gave the Law (Heb 12:20). Intensive: to touch forcibly, i.e. to smite, to harm (Heb 11:28).

Syn.: *háptomai* (680), to touch; *prospsaúō* (4379), to touch upon, touch slightly; *psēlapháō* (5584), to touch lightly, to search for.

2346. θλίβω, thlibō, *thlee´-bo*; akin to the base of 5147; to *crowd* (literal or figurative):—afflict, narrow, throng, suffer tribulation, trouble.

2347. θλίψις, thlipsis, *thlip´-sis*; from 2346; *pressure* (literal or figurative):—afflicted (-tion), anguish, burdened, persecution, tribulation, trouble.

Noun from *thlíbō* (2346), to crush, press, compress, squeeze, which is from *thláō* (n.f.), to break. Pressure, compression. In the NT, only figuratively: pressure from evils, i.e. affliction, distress (Jn 16:21; 2Co 2:4; Php 1:16). More often, by metonymy: evils by which one is pressed, affliction, distress, calamity, persecution; tribulation (Mt 13:21; Ac 7:10, 11; Ro 5:3; 2Co 1:4; Heb 10:33).

Syn.: *báros* (922), heavy, burdensome weight; *diōgmós* (1375), persecution; *kakopátheia* (2552), the suffering of affliction; *kákōsis* (2561), ill treatment; *páthēma* (3804), affliction, that which one suffers; *sunoché* (4928), anguish, distress; *tarachē* (5016), agitation, disturbance, trouble; *phortíon* (5413), a weight which one may bear without it becoming a burden or causing distress.

2348. θνήσκω, thnēskō, *thnay´-sko*; a strengthened form of a simpler primary θάνω, *thanō*, *than´-o* (which is used for it only in certain tenses); to *die* (literal or figurative):—be dead, die.

To die; naturally (Mt 2:20; Mk 15:44; Lk 7:12; 8:49; Jn 11:21, 39, 41, 44; 12:1; 19:33; Ac 14:19; 25:19; Sept.: 2Sa 12:18). Figuratively, to be dead spiritually, though physically alive (1Ti 5:6).

Deriv.: *apothnēskō* (599), to die off; *hēmithanēs* (2253), half dead; *thánatos* (2288), death; *thnētós* (2349), mortal.

Syn.: *apogenómenos* (581), to no longer be in one's present existence; *koimáō* (2837), to sleep, metaphorically used with the meaning of to die; *teleutáō* (5053), to end one's life.

2349. θνητός, thnētos, *thnay-tos´*; from 2348; *liable to die*:—mortal (-ity).

Adjective from *thnḗskō* (2348), to die. Mortal, subject to death (Ro 6:12; 8:11; 2Co 4:11); as a substantive with the article: mortal nature, mortality (1Co 15:53, 54; 2Co 5:4).

Syn.: *phthartós* (5349), corruptible.

2350. θορυβέω, thorubeō, *thor-oo-beh´-o*; from 2351; to *be in tumult*, i.e. *disturb, clamor*:—make ado (a noise), trouble self, set on an uproar.

2351. θόρυβος, thorubos, *thor´-oo-bos*; from the base of 2360; a *disturbance*:—tumult, uproar.

2352. θραύω, thrauō, *throw´-o*; a primary verb; to *crush*:—bruise. Compare 4486.

2353. θρέμμα, thremma, *threm´-mah*; from 5142; *stock* (as *raised* on a farm):—cattle.

2354. θρηνέω, thrēneō, *thray-neh´-o*; from 2355; to *bewail*:—lament, mourn.

From *thrḗnos* (2355), lamentation. To weep aloud, wail, mourn, as at a funeral:

(I) Intransitively (Mt 11:17; Lk 7:32; Jn 16:20).

(II) Transitively, to mourn for someone (Lk 23:27).

Syn.: *dakrúō* (1145), to shed tears; *klaíō* (2799), to weep; *stenázō* (4727), to groan.

2355. θρῆνος, thrēnos, *thray´-nos*; from the base of 2360; *wailing*:—lamentation.

2356. θρησκεία, thrēskeia, *thrace-ki´-ah*; from a derivative of 2357; ceremonial *observance*:—religion, worshipping.

2357. θρῆσκος, thrēskos, *thrace´-kos*; probably from the base of 2360; *ceremonious* in worship (as *demonstrative*), i.e. *pious*:—religious.

Adjective meaning fearing God, pious, religious. Only in Jas 1:26.

Syn.: *eulabḗs* (2126), reverent [toward God], one who accepts God's will; *eusebḗs* (2152), pious, devout; *theosebḗs* (2318), reverent toward God, pious, worshipful; *philótheos* (5377) and *theóphilos* (2321), a friend of God.

2358. θριαμβεύω, thriambeuō, *three-am-byoo´-o*; from a prolonged compound of the base of 2360 and a derivative of 680 (meaning a *noisy iambus*, sung in honour of Bacchus); to *make an acclamatory procession*, i.e. (figurative) to *conquer* or (by Hebrew) to *give victory*:—(cause) to triumph (over).

2359. θρίξ, thrix, *threeks*; generic **τριχός, trichos,** etc.; of uncertain derivative; *hair*:—hair. Compare 2864.

2360. θροέω, throeō, *thro-eh´-o*; from **θρέομαι, threomai** (to *wail*); to *clamor*, i.e. (by implication) to *frighten*:—trouble.

2361. θρόμβος, thrombos, *throm´-bos*; perhaps from 5142 (in the sense of *thickening*); a *clot*:—great drop.

2362. θρόνος, thronos, *thron´-os*; from **θράω, thraō** (to *sit*); a stately *seat* (*"throne"*); (by implication) *power* or (concrete) a *potentate*:—seat, throne.

2363. Θυάτειρα, Thuateira, *thoo-at´-i-rah*; of uncertain derivative; *Thyatira*, a place in Asia Minor:—Thyatira.

2364. θυγάτηρ, thugatēr, *thoo-gat´-air*; apparently a primary word [compare "daughter"]; a *female child*, or (by Hebrew) *descendant* (or *inhabitant*):—daughter.

2365. θυγάτριον, thugatrion, *thoo-gat´-ree-on*; from 2364; a *daughterling*:—little (young) daughter.

2366. θύελλα, thuella, *thoo´-el-lah*; from 2380 (in the sense of *blowing*) a *storm*:—tempest.

Noun from *thúō* (n.f.), to rush on or along, spoken of wind or a storm. Tempest. Only in Heb 12:18. Also from *thúō* (n.f.): *thumós* (2372), anger, wrath.

Syn.: *pnoḗ* (4157), wind; *laílaps* (2978), storm, tempest.

2367. θύϊνος, thuïnos, *thoo´-ee-nos*; from a derivative of 2380 (in the sense of *blowing*; denoting a certain *fragrant* tree); made of *citron*-wood:—thyine.

2368. θυμίαμα, thumiama, *thoo-mee´-am-ah*; from 2370; an *aroma*, i.e. fragrant *powder* burnt in religious service; (by implication) the *burning* itself:—incense, odour.

2369. θυμιαστήριον, thumiastērion, *thoo-mee-as-tay´-ree-on*; from a derivative of 2370; a *place of fumigation*, i.e. the *altar of incense* (in the temple):—censer.

2370. θυμιάω, thumiaō, *thoo-mee-ah´-o;* from a derivative of 2380 (in the sense of *smoking*); to *fumigate,* i.e. *offer* aromatic *fumes:*—burn incense.

2371. θυμομαχέω, thumomacheō, *thoo-mom-akh-eh´-o;* from a presumed compound of 2372 and 3164; to *be in a furious fight,* i.e. (figurative) to *be exasperated:*—be highly displeased.

2372. θυμός, thumos, *thoo-mos´;* from 2380; *passion* (as if *breathing* hard):—fierceness, indignation, wrath. Compare 5590.

Noun from *thúō* (n.f.), to move impetuously. In Classical Greek: mind, soul, e.g., as the principle of life, as the seat of the will, desire, emotions, passions, etc. Hence generally, and in the NT: passion, i.e. violent commotion of mind, indignation, anger, wrath; differing from *orgē* (3709) in the mode of conception rather than in the thing signified, with *thumós* picturing the inward feeling, and *orgē* representing the outward emotion (Lk 4:28; Ac 19:28; Eph 4:31; Col 3:8; Heb 11:27; Rev 12:12). In the plural, "bursts of anger" (2Co 12:20; Gal 5:20). Spoken of God, and including the idea of punishment, punitive judgements (Ro 2:8; Rev 15:1). Further, by the Hebrew prophets Jehovah is represented as giving to the nations in His wrath an intoxicating cup, so that they reel and stagger to destruction; hence also in the NT, the expression "the wine of the wrath (*thumós*) of God" (Rev 14:10; 16:19; with "wine" implied, 15:7; 16:1). By a similar figure, "the wine press of the wrath of God" (Rev 14:19; 19:15, in allusion to Isa 63:3).

Deriv.: *enthuméomai* (1760), to think upon; *epithuméō* (1937), to desire; *eúthumos* (2115), cheerful; *thumomachéō* (2371), to fight fiercely; *thumóō* (2373), to provoke to anger; *próthumos* (4289), predisposed, ready, willing; *prothúmōs* (4290), readily, willingly.

Syn.: *aganáktēsis* (24), irritation, indignation; *parorgismós* (3950), wrath.

2373. θυμόω, thumoō, *thoo-mo´-o;* from 2372; to *put in a passion,* i.e. *enrage:*—be wroth.

2374. θύρα, thura, *thoo´-rah;* apparently a primary word [compare "door"]; a *portal* or *entrance* (the opening or the closure, literal or figurative):—door, gate.

2375. θυρεός, thureos, *thoo-reh-os´;* from 2374; a large *shield* (as *door*-shaped):—shield.

2376. θυρίς, thuris, *thoo-rece´;* from 2374; an *aperture,* i.e. *window:*—window.

2377. θυρωρός, thurōros, *Thoo-ro-ros´;* from 2374 and *oὖρος, ouros* (a *watcher*); a *gate-warden:*—that kept the door, porter.

2378. θυσία, thusia, *thoo-see´-ah;* from 2380; *sacrifice* (the act or the victim, literal or figurative):—sacrifice.

Noun from *thúō* (2380), to sacrifice. Sacrifice:
(I) The act and rite of sacrificing (Mt 9:13; 12:7; Heb 9:26; 10:5, 8, quoted from Ps 40:6, 7).
(II) By metonymy: the thing sacrificed, victim, the flesh of victims, part of which was burned on the altar and part given to the priests (Mk 9:49 [cf. Le 2:13]; Mk 12:33; Lk 13:1; Ac 7:41, 42; 1Co 10:18); of an expiatory sacrifice for sin (Eph 5:2; Heb 5:1; 7:27; 8:3; 9:9, 23; 10:1, 11, 12, 26).
(III) Metaphorically, of service, obedience, praise offered to God, an offering, oblation (Ro 12:1; Php 2:17; 4:18; Heb 13:15, 16; 1Pe 2:5).

2379. θυσιαστήριον, thusiastērion, *thoo-see-as-tay´-ree-on;* from a derivative of 2378; a *place of sacrifice,* i.e. an *altar* (special or genitive, literal or figurative):—altar.

Noun from *thusiázō* (n.f.), to sacrifice. An altar (Mt 5:23, 24; 23:18–20; Ro 11:3; Heb 7:13; Jas 2:21). Used specifically of the altar for burnt offerings in the temple (Mt 23:35; Lk 11:51; 1Co 9:13; 10:18; Heb 13:10). Symbolically, in heaven (Rev 6:9; 8:3, 5; 9:13; 11:1; 14:18; 16:7); of the altar of incense in the temple, made of gold (Lk 1:11).

Syn.: *bōmós* (1041), an altar.

2380. θύω, thuō, *thoo´-o;* a primary verb; properly to *rush* (*breathe* hard, *blow, smoke*), i.e. (by implication) to *sacrifice* (properly by fire, but genitive); by extension to *immolate* (*slaughter* for any purpose):—kill, (do) sacrifice, slay.

To sacrifice, to kill and offer in sacrifice (Ac 14:13, 18; 1Co 10:20). "To sacrifice the passover" means to kill the Paschal Lamb as a species of sacrifice (Mk 14:12; Lk 22:7; 1Co 5:7). In a derived sense: to slay (Mt 22:4; Lk 15:23, 27, 30; Jn 10:10; Ac 10:13; 11:7).

Deriv.: *eidōlóthuton* (1494), sacrifice; *thusía* (2378), sacrifice.

Syn.: *anairéō* (337), to kill, used physically only; *apokteínō* (615), to kill; *diacheirízō* (1315), to lay violent hands upon, to kill; *thanatóō* (2289), to put to death; *spházō* (4969), to slay, slaughter.

2381. Θωμᾶς, Thōmas, *tho-mas´*; of Chaldee origin [compare 8380]; *the twin; Thomas*, a Christian:—Thomas.

2382. θώραξ, thōrax, *tho´-rax*; of uncertain affinity; the *chest* ("*thorax*"), i.e. (by implication) a *corslet*:—breastplate.

I (Iota)

2383. Ἰάειρος, Iaeiros, *ee-ah´-i-ros*; of Hebrew origin (2971, i.e. *Jair*), an Israelite:—Jairus.

2384. Ἰακώβ, Iakōb, *ee-ak-obe´*; of Hebrew origin [3290]; *Jacob* (i.e. *Ja'akob*), the progenitor of the Israelite; also an Israelite:—Jacob.

2385. Ἰάκωβος, Iakōbos, *ee-ak´-o-bos*; the same as 2384 Græcized; *Jacobus*, the name of three Israelites:—James.

2386. ἴαμα, iama, *ee´-am-ah*; from 2390; a *cure* (the effect):—healing.

2387. Ἰαμβρῆς, Iambrēs, *ee-am-brace´*; of Egyptian origin; *Jambres*, an Egyptian:—Jambres.

2388. Ἰαννά, Ianna, *ee-an-nah´*; probably of Hebrew origin [compare 3238]; *Janna*, an Israelite:—Janna.

2389. Ἰαννῆς, Iannēs, *ee-an-nace´*; of Egyptian origin; *Jannes*, an Egyptian:—Jannes.

2390. ἰάομαι, iaomai, *ee-ah´-om-ahee*; middle of apparently a primary verb; to *cure* (literal or figurative):—heal, make whole.

Verb meaning to heal, cure, restore to bodily health (Mt 8:8, 13; Lk 5:17; 6:19; 9:2, 11, 42; 14:4; 22:51; Jn 4:47; 5:13; Ac 10:38; 28:8; Jas 5:16). Metaphorically, of moral diseases: to heal or save from the consequences of sin (Mt 13:15; Jn 12:40; Ac 28:27; Lk 4:18 [cf. Isa 61:1]; Heb 12:13; 1Pe 2:24).

Deriv.: *íama* (2386), the means of healing; *íasis* (2392), the act or process of healing; *iatrós* (2395), physician.

Syn.: *therapeúō* (2323), to heal with the additional meaning of caring for; *sōzō* (4982), to save, with the additional meaning of rescuing from the effects of disease.

2391. Ἰάρεδ, Iared, *ee-ar´-ed*; of Hebrew origin [3382]; *Jared* (i.e. *Jered*), an antediluvian:—Jared.

2392. ἴασις, iasis, *ee´-as-is*; from 2390; *curing* (the act):—cure, heal (-ing).

2393. ἴασπις, iaspis, *ee´-as-pis*; probably of foreign origin [see 3471]; "*jasper*," a gem:—jasper.

2394. Ἰάσων, Iasōn, *ee-as´-oan*; future active participle masculine of 2390; *about to cure*; *Jason*, a Christian:—Jason.

2395. ἰατρός, iatros, *ee-at-ros´*; from 2390; a *physician*:—physician.

2396. ἴδε, ide, *id´-eh*; second person singular imperfect active of 1492; used as interjection to denote *surprise; lo!:*—behold, lo, see.

The later form for *idé*, 2d aor. of imper. of *eídō* (1492), to see, calling attention to what may be seen or heard or mentally apprehended in any way. In the NT, often as a particle of exclamation: see, lo, behold!, calling attention to something present (Mt 25:20, 22, 25; Mk 3:34; 11:21; Jn 1:29; 7:26; 11:36; 19:4, 5, 14). In the sense of behold, observe, consider (Mk 15:4; Jn 5:14; Ro 2:17; Gal 5:2).

Syn.: *atenízō* (816), to gaze intently; *blépō* (991), to see; *emblépō* (1689), to earnestly look; *epopteúō* (2029), to be an eyewitness; *theáomai* (2300), to view attentively, contemplate; *theōréō* (2334), to look with careful observation to details; *katanoéō* (2657), to perceive; *paratēréō* (3906), to note, observe.

2397. ἰδέα, idea, *id-eh´-ah*; from 1492; a *sight* [compare figurative "idea"], i.e. *aspect:*—countenance.

Noun from *eídō* (1492), to see. Aspect, appearance, countenance. Only in Mt 28:3.

2398. ἴδιος, idios, *id´-ee-os*; of uncertain affinity; *pertaining to self*, i.e. one's *own*; (by implication) *private* or *separate:*— × his acquaintance, when they were alone, apart, aside, due, his (own, proper, several), home, (her, our, thine, your) own (business), private (-ly), proper, severally, their (own).

Adjective meaning properly one's own:

(I) As belonging to oneself and not to another, one's own, peculiar:

(A) Denoting ownership, that of which one is himself the owner, possessor, producer, as: my own, your own, his own. Of things (Mt 22:5; 25:15; Mk 15:20; Lk 6:41, 44; Jn 5:43; 7:18; 10:3, 4; Ac 20:28; 28:30; Ro 10:3; 14:5; 1Ti 3:4, 5; 2Pe 1:20; 3:17). Hence, with the plural neuter article *tá ídia*, generally possessions, property, specifically one's own house or home (Jn 16:32; 19:27; Ac 21:6); own nation, people (Jn 1:11 which also includes the world, the total humanity that Christ made). Spoken of persons, e.g., denoting one's brother, father, etc. (Jn 1:41; 5:18). Also Mt 25:14; Jn 1:11; 13:1; Ro 8:32; 14:4; 1Co 7:2; 1Ti 6:1; 5:8).

(B) In the sense of peculiar, particular, as distinguishing one person from others, e.g., one's own dialect (Ac 1:19; 2:6, 8) or superstition (Ac 25:19).

(C) As denoting that which in its nature or by appointment pertains in any way to a person or thing, e.g., in Ac 1:25, "to his own place," i.e. proper and appointed for him; "his own generation" in which he lived (Ac 13:36); "his own reward" (1Co 3:8); see 1Co 15:23; Jude 6. Also *kairós* ([2540], occasion, opportunity, appropriate time) *ídios*, or in the plural *kairoí ídioi*, own times or opportunities, i.e. due or proper time as determined by God (Gal 6:9; 1Ti 2:6; 6:15; Tit 1:3).

(II) As pertaining to a private person and not to the public: private, particular, individual, as opposed to *démósios* (1219), public, open, and *koinós* (2839), common. Hence, in the NT, used adverbially:

(A) *Idía*, individually, severally, to each one (1Co 12:11).

(B) *Kat' idían* with the prep. *katá* (2596), according to, meaning privately, by oneself, apart from others (Mt 14:13, 23; 17:1, 19; Mk 4:34; 6:31; 9:2, 28; Ac 23:19; Gal 2:2).

Deriv.: *idiótēs* (2399), a common or private man.

2399. ἰδιώτης, idiōtēs, *id-ee-o´-tace*; from 2398; a *private* person, i.e. (by implication) an *ignoramus* (compare "idiot"):—ignorant, rude, unlearned.

Noun from *ídios* (2398), one's own. A private citizen, as opposed to someone in a public office. In the NT: plebeian, i.e. unlettered, unlearned, an amateur rather than a professional (Ac 4:13; 2Co 11:6). One who has not been initiated into Christian truth (1Co 14:16, 23, 24).

2400. ἰδού, idou, *id-oo´*; second person singular imperative middle of 1492; used as imperonal *lo!*:—behold, lo, see.

2401. Ἰδουμαία, Idoumaia, *id-oo-mah´-yah*; of Hebrew origin [123]; *Idumæa* (i.e. *Edom*), a region East (and South) of Palestine:—Idumæa.

2402. ἱδρός, hidros, *hid-roce´*; a strengthened form of a primary ἴδος, *idos* (*sweat*); *perspiration*:—sweat.

2403. Ἰεζαβήλ, Iezabēl, *ee-ed-zab-ale´*; of Hebrew origin [348]; *Jezabel* (i.e. *Jezebel*), a Tyrian woman (used as a synonym of a termagant or false teacher):—Jezabel.

2404. Ἱεράπολις, Hierapolis, *hee-er-ap´-ol-is*; from 2413 and 4172; *holy city*; *Hierapolis*, a place in Asia Minor:—Hierapolis.

2405. ἱερατεία, hierateia, *hee-er-at-i´-ah*; from 2407; *priestliness*, i.e. the *sacerdotal function*:—office of the priesthood, priest's office.

2406. ἱεράτευμα, hierateuma, *hee-er-at´-yoo-mah*; from 2407; the *priestly fraternity*, i.e. a *sacerdotal order* (figurative):—priesthood.

2407. ἱερατεύω, hierateuō, *hee-er-at-yoo´-o*; prolonged from 2409; to *be a priest*, i.e. *perform his functions*:—execute the priest's office.

2408. Ἱερεμίας, Hieremias, *hee-er-em-ee´-as*; of Hebrew origin [3414]; *Hieremias* (i.e. *Jermijah*), an Israelite:—Jeremiah.

2409. ἱερεύς, hiereus, *hee-er-yooce´*; from 2413; a *priest* (literal or figurative):—(high) priest.

Noun from *hierós* (2413), sacred. A priest, one who performs the sacred rites:

(I) Used of heathen priests (Ac 14:13).

(II) Used also to denote the Jewish priests, the descendants of Aaron generally (Mt 8:4; 12:4, 5; Mk 1:44; 2:26; Lk 1:5; 5:14; 6:4; 10:31; 17:14; Jn 1:19; Ac 6:7; Heb 9:6). They were divided into twenty-four classes for the service of the temple (1Ch 24), and the heads of these classes were sometimes called *archiereís* (749), chief priests. These seem to be referred to in Ac 4:1. See Le 1:5. Spoken of the high priest (Heb 7:21, 23; 8:4; 10:11, 21).

(III) Of Melchizedek as a high priest of God (Heb 7:1, 3; see Ge 14:18; Ps 110:4); of Jesus as the spiritual High Priest (Heb 5:6; 7:11, 15, 17, 21; 10:21).

(IV) Figuratively, Christians are also called priests unto God as offering Him spiritual sacrifices (Rev 1:6; 5:10; 20:6 [cf. 1Pe 2:5]).

Deriv.: *archiereús* (749), high priest; *hierateúō* (2407), to officiate as a priest.

Syn.: *Levítēs* (3019), Levite, a servant of the priests.

2410. Ἱεριχώ, **Hierichō,** *hee-er-ee-kho´*; of Hebrew origin [3405]; *Jericho,* a place in Palestine:—Jericho.

2411. ἱερόν, **hieron,** *hee-er-on´*; neuter of 2413; a *sacred* place, i.e. the entire precincts (whereas 3485 denotes the central *sanctuary* itself) of the *temple* (at Jerusalem or elsewhere):—temple.

Noun from *hierós* (2413), sacred. temple.

(I) A temple, whether of the true God (Mt 12:5, 6) or an idol (Ac 19:27). It often includes not only the building but the courts and all the sacred ground or enclosure.

(II) In the NT, it always refers to the temple as rebuilt by Herod the Great, and minutely described by Josephus (Ant. 15.11.3). According to him, the temple consisted of three parts or enclosures with the temple proper or *naós* (3485) in the center and two circular courts or areas around it, one exterior to the other. Only the priests could enter the *naós,* which was divided into two parts (*tó hágion* [39], the sanctuary, and *tó Hágion Hagíōn,* the Holy of Holies). The whole temple, therefore, consisted strictly of two parts: the physical structure (*ho naós*) and the courts leading into it. Hence, *tó hierón* is used for the whole and also for the courts, but not for the *naós* exclusively.

(A) Generally, and for the whole (Mt 24:1; Mk 13:1, 3; Lk 21:5; 22:52).

(B) Of the courts (Mt 12:5; Mk 11:11; Lk 2:27, 37; 18:10; Ac 2:46; 3:1; 21:26).

(C) Of the outer court where things were bought and sold (Mt 21:12, 14, 15; Mk 11:15, 16). It was here that Jesus disputed and taught (Mt 21:23; 26:55; Mk 11:27; Lk 2:46; Jn 5:14;

7:14, 28); also the apostles (Ac 5:20, 21, 25, 42). The pinnacle of the temple (Mt 4:5; Lk 4:9) is probably a reference to the apex or summit of Solomon's porch which Josephus describes as being exterior to the temple itself on the east side and built up to the height of 400 cubits (600 feet) from the foundation in the Valley of Kidron below.

Deriv.: *hierósulos* (2417), one who robs churches or temples.

Syn.: *naós* (3485), temple.

2412. ἱεροπρεπής, **hieroprepēs,** *hee-er-op-rep-ace´*; from 2413 and the same as 4241; *reverent:*—as becometh holiness.

Adjective from *hierós* (2413), sacred, and *prépō* (4241), to suit, become. Fitting or appropriate for a sacred place or person, venerable. Only in Tit 2:3, older women ought to adorn their profession of Christ with their behaviour.

Syn.: *sebastós* (4575), venerable, august; *eulabḗs* (2126), pious, devout; *semnós* (4586), honourable, venerable.

2413. ἱερός, **hieros,** *hee-er-os´*; of uncertain affinity; *sacred:*—holy.

Adjective meaning sacred, dedicated to God:

(I) Used of the sacred Scriptures (2Ti 3:15).

(II) Used of the sacred services, sacred rites (1Co 9:13).

Deriv.: *hiereús* (2409), priest.

Syn.: *hósios* (3741), sacred.

2414. Ἱεροσόλυμα, **Hierosoluma,** *hee-er-os-ol´-oo-mah*; of Hebrew origin [3389]; *Hierosolyma* (i.e. *Jerushalaïm*), the capital of Palestine:—Jerusalem. Compare 2419.

2415. Ἱεροσολυμίτης, **Hierosolumitēs,** *hee-er-os-ol-oo-mee´-tace*; from 2414; a *Hierosolymite,* i.e. inhabitant of Hierosolyma:—of Jerusalem.

2416. ἱεροσυλέω, **hierosuleō,** *hee-er-os-ool-eh´-o*; from 2417; to *be a temple-robber* (figurative):—commit sacrilege.

From *hierósulos* (2417), a sacrilegious person, which is from *hierón* (2411), the temple, and *suláō* (4813), to rob. To rob temples, commit sacrilege. Only in Ro 2:22, where some believe it refers to robbing idol temples with no concern for the defilement caused by coming into contact with idolatry, while others believe it refs to a profaning of the temple of God (see Ne 13:10; Mal 3:8; Mt 21:12).

2417. ἱερόσυλος, **hierosulos**, *hee-er-os´-oo-los*; from 2411 and 4813; a *temple-despoiler:—robber of churches.*

Adjective from *hierón* (2411), temple, and *suláō* (4813), to rob, spoil. A robber of a temple, a sacrilegious person. Only in Ac 19:37.

Deriv.: *hierosuléō* (2416), to commit sacrilege.

2418. ἱερουργέω, **hierourgeō**, *hee-er-oorg-eh´-o*; from a compound of 2411 and the base of 2041; to *be a temple-worker*, i.e. *officiate as a priest* (figurative):—*minister.*

From *hierourgós* (n.f.), sacrificing, which is from *hierón* (2411), temple, and *érgon* (2041), work. To perform sacred rites, especially sacrifice; to officiate as a priest. Occurs only in Ro 15:16.

2419. Ἰερουσαλήμ, **Hierousalēm**, *hee-er-oo-sal-ame´*; of Hebrew origin [3389]; *Hierusalem* (i.e. *Jerushalem*), the capital of Palestine:—Jerusalem. Compare 2414.

2420. ἱερωσύνη, **hierōsunē**, *hee-er-o-soo´-nay*; from 2413; *sacredness*, i.e. (by implication) the *priestly office:*—priesthood.

2421. Ἰεσσαί, **Iessai**, *es-es-sah´ee*; of Hebrew origin [3448]; *Jessæ* (i.e. *Jishai*), an Israelite:—Jesse.

2422. Ἰεφθάε, **Iephthae**, *ee-ef-thah´-eh*; of Hebrew origin [3316]; *Jephthaë* (i.e. *Jiphtach*), an Israelite:—Jephthah.

2423. Ἰεχονίας, **Iechonias**, *ee-ekh-on-ee´-as*; of Hebrew origin [3204]; *Jechonias* (i.e. *Jekonjah*), an Israelite:—Jechonias.

2424. Ἰησοῦς, **Iēsous**, *ee-ay-sooce´*; of Hebrew origin [3091]; *Jesus* (i.e. *Jehoshua*), the name of our Lord and two (three) other Israelites:—Jesus.

2425. ἱκανός, **hikanos**, *hik-an-os´*; from ἵκω *hikō* [ἱκάνω or ἱκνέομαι; akin to 2240] (to *arrive*); *competent* (as if *coming* in season), i.e. *ample* (in amount) or *fit* (in character):—able, + content, enough, good, great, large, long (while), many, meet, much, security, sore, sufficient, worthy.

Adjective from *hiknéomai* (n.f.), to come. Sufficient:

(I) Of things: enough (Lk 22:38). Hence *tó hikanón*, satisfaction, as in to do or make satisfaction, to satisfy (Mk 15:15); to take satisfaction or security (Ac 17:9).

(II) Of persons: sufficient, adequate, capable (2Co 2:16; 3:5; 2Ti 2:2). With the meaning of worthy (Mt 3:11; 8:8; Mk 1:7; Lk 3:16; 7:6; 1Co 15:9).

(III) Referring to number: many (Mt 28:12, literally many pieces of silver; Lk 8:32; 23:9; Ac 12:12; 14:21; 19:19; 20:8; 1Co 11:30); with the plural of *hēméra* (2250), day, many days (Ac 9:23, 43; 18:18).

(IV) Referring to magnitude: abundant, great, much (Ac 22:6); with *óchlos* (3793), crowd, a great crowd, many people (Mk 10:46; Lk 7:12; Ac 11:24, 26; 19:26); with *chrónos* (5550), time, a long time (Lk 8:27; 23:8; Ac 8:11; 27:9).

Deriv.: *hikanótēs* (2426), sufficiency, ability, fitness; *hikanóō* (2427), to make sufficient or fit, equip.

Syn.: *arketós* (713), enough.

2426. ἱκανότης, **hikanotēs**, *hik-an-ot´-ace*; from 2425; *ability:*—sufficiency.

2427. ἱκανόω, **hikanoō**, *hik-an-o´-o*; from 2425; to *enable*, i.e. *qualify:*—make able (meet).

2428. ἱκετηρία, **hiketēria**, *hik-et-ay-ree´-ah*; from a derivative of the base of 2425 (through the idea of *approaching* for a favour); *intreaty:*—supplication.

Noun from *hikétēs* (n.f.), a suppliant. Supplication. Only in Heb 5:7.

Syn.: *déēsis* (1162), supplication for a particular need; *énteuxis* (1783), intercession; *paráklēsis* (3874), entreaty; *proseuchē* (4335), prayer to God.

2429. ἱκμάς, **hikmas**, *hik-mas´*; of uncertain affinity; *dampness:*—moisture.

2430. Ἰκόνιον, **Ikonion**, *ee-kon´-ee-on*; perhaps from 1504; *image-like*; Iconium, a place in Asia Minor:—Iconium.

2431. ἱλαρός, **hilaros**, *hil-ar-os´*; from the same as 2436; *propitious* or *merry* ("*hilarious*"), i.e. *prompt* or *willing:*—cheerful.

2432. ἱλαρότης, **hilarotēs,** *hil-ar-ot´-ace;* from 2431; *alacrity:*—cheerfulness.

2433. ἱλάσκομαι, **hilaskomai,** *hil-as´-kom-ahee;* middle from the same as 2436; to *conciliate,* i.e. (transitive) to *atone* for (sin), or (intransitive) *be propitious:*—be merciful, make reconciliation for.

From *hílaos* (n.f., see *híleōs* [2436]), propitious. To reconcile to oneself, to be propitious, gracious, as of gods; of men: to be kind, gentle, gracious. In the NT: to propitiate, make propitiation for sins (Heb 2:17). In the passive sense, to be propitious, merciful (Lk 18:13).

Deriv.: *hilasmós* (2434), propitiation; *hilastérion* (2435), propitiation, mercy seat.

Syn.: *eleéō* (1653), to show mercy; *oikteírō* (3627), to have compassion on.

2434. ἱλασμός, **hilasmos,** *hil-as-mos´; atonement,* i.e. (concretely) an *expiator:*—propitiation.

Noun from *hiláskomai* (2433), to propitiate, expiate. Propitiation, that which appeases anger and brings reconciliation with someone who has reason to be angry with one (1Jn 2:2; 4:10).

2435. ἱλαστήριον, **hilastērion,** *hil-as-tay´-ree-on;* neuter of a derivative of 2433; an *expiatory* (place or thing), i.e. (concretely) an atoning *victim,* or (special) the *lid* of the Ark (in the temple):—mercyseat, propitiation.

From *hiláskomai* (2433), to propitiate, expiate. Propitiatory, expiatory. In the NT in the neuter: a propitiator, one who makes propitiation (Ro 3:25); with the article, mercy seat (Heb 9:5), the lid or cover of the Ark of the Covenant, where the high priest would make propitiation once a year by sprinkling blood upon the mercy seat (Ex 25:17–22; Le 16:11–15).

2436. ἵλεως, **hileōs,** *hil´-eh-oce;* perhaps from the alternate form of 138; *cheerful* (as *attractive*), i.e. *propitious;* adverb (by Hebrew) God be *gracious!,* i.e. (in averting some calamity) *far* be it:—be it far, merciful.

Adjective, the Attic for *hílaos* (n.f.). Appeased, merciful, as of gods; cheerful, propitious, favourable, merciful. In the NT, of God: propitious, merciful (Heb 8:12). Used by Peter in Mt 16:22 as an exclamation, *híleōs soi,* literally "mercy to you" (see *soi* [4671], to you), mean-

ing "May God have mercy on you and never allow this to happen."

Deriv.: *aníleōs* (448), unmerciful.

2437. Ἰλλυρικόν, **Illurikon,** *il-loo-ree-kon´;* neuter of an adjective from a name of uncertain derivative; (the) *Illyrican* (shore), i.e. (as a name itself) *Illyricum,* a region of Europe:—Illyricum.

2438. ἱμάς, **himas,** *hee-mas´;* perhaps from the same as 260; a *strap,* i.e. (special) the *tie* (of a sandal) or the *lash* (of a scourge):—latchet, thong.

2439. ἱματίζω, **himatizō,** *him-at-id´-zo;* from 2440; to *dress:*—clothe.

2440. ἱμάτιον, **himation,** *him-at´-ee-on;* neuter of a presumed derivative of ἕννυμι, **ennumi** (to *put on*); a *dress* (inner or outer):—apparel, cloke, clothes, garment, raiment, robe, vesture.

(I) Generally any garment (Mt 9:16; 11:8; Mk 2:21; Lk 5:36; 7:25; Heb 1:11). Plural with article: one's garments, clothing, raiment including the outer and inner garment, cape and shirt or coat (Mt 17:2; 24:18; 26:65; 27:31, 35; Mk 15:24; Jn 13:4, 12; Ac 14:14; 16:22; 22:23; Jas 5:2; Rev 4:4).

(II) The outer garment, mantle, cape (different from the tunic or *chitōn* [5509]), a shirt over which the *himátion* is worn (cf. Ac 9:39). The *himátion* seems to have been a large piece of woolen cloth nearly square, which was wrapped around the body or fastened about the shoulders, and served also to wrap oneself in at night (Ex 22:26, 27); hence it might not be taken by a creditor, though the tunic could be (cf. Mt 5:40; Lk 6:29). See also Mt 9:20, 21; 21:7, 8; 14:36; Jn 19:2; Ac 7:58; 12:8; 22:20.

Deriv.: *himatízō* (2439), to clothe.

Syn.: *énduma* (1742), a garment of any kind; *ependútēs* (1903), an upper or outer garment which sometimes fishermen wore when at work; *esthḗs* (2066) and *ésthēsis* (2067), clothing; *himatismós* (2441), clothing, apparel; *katastolḗ* (2689), long robe of dignity; *peribólaion* (4018), a wrap or cape, a garment thrown around one; *podḗrēs* (4158), an outer garment reaching to the feet; *népasma* (4629), a covering, raiment; *stolḗ* (4749), a stately robe or uniform, a long gown worn as a mark of dignity; *phelónēs* (5341), a mantle, traveling robe for protection against stormy weather, overcoat;

chlamús (5511), a military cloak worn over the *chitón* by emperors, kings, magistrates, military officers; *chitón* (5509), tunic.

2441. ἱματισμός, himatismos, *him-at-is-mos´*; from 2439; *clothing:*—apparel (× -led), array, raiment, vesture.

Noun from *himatízō* (2439), to clothe. Clothing, raiment. Garments stately and costly (Mt 27:35; Lk 7:25; 9:29; Jn 19:24; Ac 20:33; 1Ti 2:9).

Syn.: For a list of various types of clothing, see the synonyms under *himátion* (2440), garment.

2442. ἱμείρομαι, himeiromai, *him-i´-rom-ahee*; middle from ἵμερος, *himeros* (a *yearning*; of uncertain affinity); to *long for:*—be affectionately desirous.

2443. ἵνα, hina, *hin´-ah*; probably from the same as the former part of 1438 (through the *demonstrative* idea; compare 3588); in order *that* (denoting the *purpose* or the *result*):—albeit, because, to the intent (that), lest, so as, (so) that, (for) to. Compare 3363.

2444. ἱνατί, hinati, *hin-at-ee´*; from 2443 and 5101; *for what* reason?, i.e. *why?:*—wherefore, why.

2445. Ἰόππη, Ioppē, *ee-op´-pay*; of Hebrew origin [3305]; *Joppe* (i.e. *Japho*), a place in Palestine:—Joppa.

2446. Ἰορδάνης, Iordanēs, *ee-or-dan´-ace*; of Hebrew origin [3383]; the *Jordanes* (i.e. *Jarden*), a river of Palestine:—Jordan.

2447. ἰός, ios, *ee-os´*; perhaps from εἶμι, *eimi* (to *go*) or ἵημι, *hiēmi* (to *send*); *rust* (as if *emitted* by metals); also *venom* (as *emitted* by serpents):—poison, rust.

2448. Ἰουδά, Iouda, *ee-oo-dah´*; of Hebrew origin [3063 or perhaps 3194]; *Judah* (i.e. *Jehudah* or *Juttah*), a part of (or place in) Palestine:—Judah.

2449. Ἰουδαία, Ioudaia, *ee-oo-dah´-yah*; feminine of 2453 (with 1093 implication); the *Judæan* land (i.e. *Judæa*), a region of Palestine:—Judæa.

2450. Ἰουδαΐζω, Ioudaïzō, *ee-oo-dah-id´-zo*; from 2453; to *become a Judæan*, i.e. *"Judaize":*—live as the Jews.

2451. Ἰουδαϊκός, Ioudaïkos, *ee-oo-dah-ee-kos´*; from 2453; *Judaïc*, i.e. *resembling a Judæan:*—Jewish.

2452. Ἰουδαϊκῶς, Ioudaïkōs, *ee-oo-dah-ee-koce´*; adverb from 2451; *Judaïcally* or *in a manner resembling a Judæan:*—as do the Jews.

2453. Ἰουδαῖος, Ioudaios, *ee-oo-dah´-yos*; from 2448 (in the sense of 2455 as a country); *Judæan*, i.e. *belonging to Jehudah:*—Jew (-ess), of Judæa.

2454. Ἰουδαϊσμός, Ioudaismos, *ee-oo-dah-is-mos´*; from 2450; *"Judaïsm,"* i.e. the *Jewish faith and usages:*—Jews' religion.

2455. Ἰουδάς, Ioudas, *ee-oo-das´*; of Hebrew origin [3063]; *Judas* (i.e. *Jehudah*), the name of ten Israelites; also of the posterity of one of them and its region:—Juda (-h, -s); Jude.

2456. Ἰουλία, Ioulia, *ee-oo-lee´-ah*; feminine of the same as 2457; *Julia*, a Christian woman:—Julia.

2457. Ἰούλιος, Ioulios, *ee-oo´-lee-os*; of Latin origin; *Julius*, a centurion:—Julius.

2458. Ἰουνίας, Iounias, *ee-oo-nee´-as*; of Latin origin; *Junias*, a Christian:—Junias.

2459. Ἰοῦστος, Ioustos, *ee-ooce´-tos*; of Latin origin (*"just"*); *Justus*, the name of three Christians:—Justus.

2460. ἱππεύς, hippeus, *hip-yooce´*; from 2462; an *equestrian*, i.e. member of a *cavalry* corps:—horseman.

2461. ἱππικόν, hippikon, *hip-pee-kon´*; neuter of a derivative of 2462; the *cavalry* force:—horse [-men].

2462. ἵππος, hippos, *hip´-pos*; of uncertain affinity; a *horse:*—horse.

2463. ἶρις, iris, *ee´-ris*; perhaps from 2046 (as a symbol of the female *messenger* of the pagan deities); a *rainbow* (*"iris"*):—rainbow.

2464. Ἰσαάκ, Isaak, *ee-sah-ak´*; of Hebrew origin [3327]; *Isaac* (i.e. *Jitschak*), the son of Abraham:—Isaac.

2465. ἰσάγγελος, isaggelos, *ee-sang´-el-los*; from 2470 and 32; *like an angel*, i.e. *angelic:*—equal unto the angels.

Adjective from *ísos* (2470), similar or equal, and *ággelos* (32) angel. Angel-like. Only in Lk 20:36.

2466. Ἰσαχάρ, **Isachar,** *ee-sakh-ar´*; of Hebrew origin [3485]; *Isachar* (i.e. *Jissaskar*), a son of Jacob (figurative, his descendant):—Issachar.

2467. ἴσημι, **isēmi,** *is´-ay-mee*; assumed by some as the base of certain irregular forms of 1942; to *know*:—know.

2468. ἴσθι, **isthi,** *is´-thee*; second person imperfect preson of 1510; *be* thou:— + agree, be, × give thyself wholly to.

2469. Ἰσκαριώτης, **Iskariōtēs,** *is-kar-ee-o´-tace*; of Hebrew origin [probably 377 and 7149]; *inhabitant of Kerioth*; *Iscariotes* (i.e. *Keriothite*), an epithet of Judas the traitor:—Iscariot.

2470. ἴσος, **isos,** *ee´-sos*; probably from 1492 (through the idea of *seeming*); *similar* (in amount or kind):— + agree, as much, equal, like.

2471. ἰσότης, **isotēs,** *ee-sot´-ace*; *likeness* (in condition or proportion); (by implication) *equity*:—equal (-ity).

2472. ἰσότιμος, **isotimos,** *ee-sot´-ee-mos*; from 2470 and 5092; *of equal value* or *honour*:—like precious.

2473. ἰσόψυχος, **isopsuchos,** *ee-sop´-soo-khos*; from 2470 and 5590; *of similar spirit*:—likeminded.

Adjective from *ísos* (2470), equal, and *psuchē* (5590), soul, mind. Like-minded. Only in Php 2:20.

Syn.: *homóphrōn* (3675), like-minded.

2474. Ἰσραήλ, **Israēl,** *is-rah-ale´*; of Hebrew origin [3478]; *Israel* (i.e. *Jisrael*), the adopted name of Jacob, including his descendant (literal or figurative):—Israel.

2475. Ἰσραηλίτης, **Israēlitēs,** *is-rah-ale-ee´-tace*; from 2474; an "*Israelite,*" i.e. descendant of Israel (literal or figurative):—Israelite.

2476. ἵστημι, **histēmi,** *his´-tay-mee*; a prolonged form of a primary στάω, **staō,** *stah´-o* (of the same meaning, and used for it in certain tenses); to *stand* (transitive or intransitive), used in various applications (literal or figura-

tive):—abide, appoint, bring, continue, covenant, establish, hold up, lay, present, set (up), stanch, stand (by, forth, still, up). Compare 5087.

To stand, to place:

(I) Transitively: to cause to stand, to set or place:

(A) With adjuncts implying the place where (Mt 4:5; 25:33; Lk 9:47; Ac 5:27; 22:30). Generally: to cause to stand forth (Ac 1:23; 6:13; Ro 14:4).

(B) To establish, confirm (Ro 3:31; 10:3; Heb 10:9). Of time: to fix, appoint (Ac 17:31).

(C) To place in a balance, i.e. to weigh out (Mt 26:15). Metaphorically: to impute, e.g., sin unto someone (Ac 7:60).

(D) In the passive: to be established, stand firm, stand (Mt 12:25, 26; Mk 3:25); to be confirmed (Mt 18:16; 2Co 13:1).

(II) Intransitively: to stand:

(A) As opposed to falling (1Co 10:12); also standing in prayer or sacrifice (Mt 6:5; Heb 10:11). With adjuncts implying the place where (Mt 12:46; 13:2; Mk 11:5; Lk 1:11; 6:17; 9:27; Jn 20:11, 19; Ac 5:20, 23; 24:21; Rev 7:9, 11; 10:5). Without an adjunct of place expressed, but in the sense of to stand by, near, there, according to the context, i.e. to be present (Mt 26:73; Lk 19:8; 23:35; Jn 1:35; 3:29; 7:37; 18:18; Ac 2:14). Of persons standing before a judge, either as accusers (Lk 23:10) or as accused (Ac 26:6). Also before Christ as Judge, where it is (by implication) to stand firm in the consciousness of acquittal and final approval (Lk 21:36). Spoken of fishing boats: to stand or be stationed, lie (Lk 5:2).

(B) Figuratively: to stand fast, i.e. to continue, endure, persist, e.g., of things (Mt 12:25; Lk 11:18; 2Ti 2:19); of persons (Ac 26:22; 1Co 7:37; Col 4:12; Rev 6:17). To stand fast against an enemy, as opposed to *pheúgō* (5343), to run away (Eph 6:11, 13). In the sense of to be established, confirmed (Mt 18:16; 2Co 13:1).

(C) In the aorist tense, to stand still, stop, e.g., of persons (Mt 20:32; Mk 10:49; Lk 7:14; 18:40); of things (Mt 2:9; Ac 8:38); to cease (Lk 8:44); to remain, abide, continue (Jn 8:44).

Deriv.: *anthístēmi* (436), to oppose; *anístēmi* (450), to raise (transitively), and to rise (intransitively); *aphístēmi* (868), to withdraw from or stand away from; *diḯstēmi* (1339), to remove; *enístēmi* (1764), to be present; *exístēmi* (1839), to be amazed; *epístamai* (1987), to understand; *ephístēmi* (2186), to approach, be present; *kathístēmi* (2525), to appoint a person to a position; *methístēmi* or *methistánō* (3179), to remove; *parístēmi* or *paristánō* (3936), to stand by or beside; *periístēmi* (4026), to stand around; *proístēmi* (4291), to preside, rule; *prōtostátēs* (4414), a leader or captain; *stádios* (4712), furlong, race; *stámnos* (4713), a jar, earthen pot; *stásis* (4714), an uprising; *statḗr* (4715), piece of money; *staurós* (4716), stake, cross; *stḗthos* (4738), the breast; *stḗkō* (4739), to stand firm; *stērízō* (4741), to set fast, to fix firmly; *stoá* (4745), a pillar, column; *sunistánō* (4921), to commend, consist.

Syn.: *anorthóō* (461), to set straight or up; *bebaióō* (950), to confirm, establish; *egeírō* (1453), to raise; *keímai* (2749), to lie, set; *ménō* (3306), abide, continue, stand; *paragínomai* (3854), to be beside, present; *stereóō* (4732), to make firm; *stērízō* (4741), to fix, make fast, set; *tássō* (5021), to place in order.

2477. ἱστορέω, historeō, *his-tor-eh´-o*; from a derivative of 1492; to *be knowing* (*learned*), i.e. (by implication) to *visit* for information (*interview*):—see.

2478. ἰσχυρός, ischuros, *is-khoo-ros´*; from 2479; *forcible* (literal or figurative):—boisterous, mighty (-ier), powerful, strong (-er, man), valiant.

2479. ἰσχύς, ischus, *is-khoos´*; from a derivative of ἴς, *his* (*force*; compare ἔσχον, *eschon*, a form of 2192); *forcefulness* (literal or figurative):—ability, might ([-ily]), power, strength.

Noun from *is* (n.f.), strength, and *échō* (2192), to have. Strength, might, power, both of body and mind. Physical (Rev 18:2, literally, "with a mighty voice"); mental and moral (Mk 12:30, 33; Lk 10:27; 1Pe 4:11). Also generally: power, potency, preeminence (Eph 1:19; 2Th 1:9; 2Pe 2:11). So in ascriptions to God (Rev 5:12; 7:12).

Deriv.: *ischúō* (2480), to be strong.

Syn.: *dúnamis* (1411), power; *enérgeia* (1753), energy, efficiency, effectual working; *exousía* (1849), authority or the right to exercise power; *krátos* (2904), dominion, the outward manifestation of power; *megaleiótēs* (3168), greatness, mighty power.

2480. ἰσχύω, ischuō, *is-khoo´-o*; from 2479; to *have* (or *exercise*) *force* (literal or figurative):— be able, avail, can do ([-not]), could, be good, might, prevail, be of strength, be whole, + much work.

From *ischús* (2479), strength. To be strong, i.e. to have strength, ability, power, both physical and moral:

(I) Physically: to be strong, robust (Mt 9:12; Mk 2:17).

(II) Generally: to be able, followed by the inf. (Mt 8:28; 26:40; Mk 5:4; 14:37; Lk 6:48; 8:43; 14:6, 29, 30; 16:3; 20:26; Jn 21:6; Ac 6:10; 15:10; 25:7; 27:16). With the inf. implied (Mk 9:18; Lk 13:24; Php 4:13, either "I can do all things" or "I can endure all things").

(III) To have efficacy, to avail, have force and value (Gal 5:6; 6:15; Heb 9:17; Jas 5:16).

(IV) To prevail against or over anyone (Ac 19:16; Rev 12:8). Figuratively: to spread abroad, to acquire strength and be effective (Ac 19:20).

Deriv.: *enischúō* (1765), to be strong; *exischúō* (1840), to be able; *epischúō* (2001), to be stronger; *ischurós* (2478), strong, powerful; *katischúō* (2729), to overpower, prevail against.

Syn.: *dúnamai* (1410), to be able, have power; *dunatéō* (1414), to show oneself powerful; *krataióō* (2901), to become strong; *nikáō* (3528), to conquer, prevail; *stereóō* (4732), to confirm, make firm; *hugiaínō* (5198), to be in good health.

2481. ἴσως, isōs, *ee´-soce*; adverb from 2470; *likely*, i.e. *perhaps*:—it may be.

2482. Ἰταλία, Italia, *ee-tal-ee´-ah*; probably of foreign origin; *Italia*, a region of Europe:—Italy.

2483. Ἰταλικός, Italikos, *ee-tal-ee-kos´*; from 2482; *Italic*, i.e. belonging to Italia:—Italian.

2484. Ἰτουραία, Itouraia, *ee-too-rah´-yah*; of Hebrew origin [3195]; *Ituræa* (i.e. *Jetur*), a region of Palestine:—Ituræa.

2485. ἰχθύδιον, ichthudion, *ikh-thoo´-dee-on*; diminutive from 2486; a *petty fish*:—little (small) fish.

2486. ἰχθύς, ichthus, *ikh-thoos´*; of uncertain affinity; a *fish*:—fish.

2487. ἴχνος, ichnos, *ikh´-nos*; from ἱκνέομαι, *ikneomai* (to *arrive*; compare 2240); a *track* (figurative):—step.

2488. 'Ιωαθαμ, Iōatham, *ee-o-ath´-am*; of Hebrew origin [3147]; *Joatham* (i.e. *Jotham*), an Israelite:—Joatham.

2489. 'Ιωάννα, Iōanna, *ee-o-an´-nah*; feminine of the same as 2491; *Joanna*, a Christian:—Joanna.

2490. 'Ιωαννᾶς, Iōannas, *ee-o-an-nas´*; a form of 2491; *Joannas*, an Israelite:—Joannas.

2491. 'Ιωάννης, Iōannēs, *ee-o-an´-nace*; of Hebrew origin [3110]; *Joannes* (i.e. *Jochanan*), the name of four Israelites:—John.

2492. 'Ιώβ, Iōb, *ee-obe´*; of Hebrew origin [347]; *Job* (i.e. *Ijob*), a patriarch:—Job.

2493. 'Ιωήλ, Iōēl, *ee-o-ale´*; of Hebrew origin [3100]; *Joel*, an Israelite:—Joel.

2494. 'Ιωνάν, Iōnan, *ee-o-nan´*; probably for 2491 or 2495; *Jonan*, an Israelite:—Jonan.

2495. 'Ιωνᾶς, Iōnas, *ee-o-nas´*; of Hebrew origin [3124]; *Jonas* (i.e. *Jonah*), the name of two Israelites:—Jonas.

2496. 'Ιωράμ, Iōram, *ee-o-ram´*; of Hebrew origin [3141]; *Joram*, an Israelite:—Joram.

2497. 'Ιωρείμ, Iōreim, *ee-o-rime´*; perhaps for 2496; *Jorim*, an Israelite:—Jorim.

2498. 'Ιωσαφάτ, Iōsaphat, *ee-o-saf-at´*; of Hebrew origin [3092]; *Josaphat* (i.e. *Jehoshaphat*), an Israelite:—Josaphat.

2499. 'Ιωσή, Iōsē, *ee-o-say´*; genitive of 2500; *Jose*, an Israelite:—Jose.

2500. 'Ιωσῆς, Iōsēs, *ee-o-sace´*; perhaps for 2501; *Joses*, the name of two Israelites:—Joses. Compare 2499.

2501. 'Ιωσήφ, Iōsēph, *ee-o-safe´*; of Hebrew origin [3130]; *Joseph*, the name of seven Israelites:—Joseph.

2502. 'Ιωσίας, Iōsias, *ee-o-see´-as*; of Hebrew origin [2977]; *Josias* (i.e. *Joshiah*), an Israelite:—Josias.

2503. ἰῶτα, iōta, *ee-o´-tah*; of Hebrew origin [the tenth letter of the Hebrew alphabet]; "*iota*," the name of the eighth letter of the Greek alphabet, put (figurative) for a very small part of anything:—jot.

K (Kappa)

NT Numbers 2504–2974

2504. κἀγώ, **kago,** *kag-o´*; from 2532 and 1473 (so also the dative κἀμοί, *kamoi, kam-oy´*; and accusative κἀμέ, *kame, kam-eh´*); *and* (or *also, even,* etc.) *I,* (*to*) *me:*—(and, even, even so, so) I (also, in like wise), both me, me also.

2505. καθά, **katha,** *kath-ah´*; from 2596 and the neuter plural of 3739; *according to which things,* i.e. *just as:*—as.

2506. καθαίρεσις, **kathairesis,** *kath-ah´ee-res-is*; from 2507; *demolition;* (figurative) *extinction:*—destruction, pulling down.

2507. καθαιρέω, **kathaireō,** *kath-ahee-reh´-o*; from 2596 and 138 (including its alternate); to *lower* (or with violence) *demolish* (literal or figurative):—cast (pull, put, take) down, destroy.

2508. καθαίρω, **kathairō,** *kath-ah´ee-ro*; from 2513; to *cleanse,* i.e. (special) to *prune;* (figurative) to *expiate:*—purge.

From *katharós* (2513), pure, clean, without stain or spot. To cleanse from filth, purify. In the NT: to cleanse a tree or vine from useless branches, to prune (Jn 15:2). Figuratively, to cleanse from sin, to purify by making atonement (Heb 10:2).

Deriv.: *akáthartos* (169), unclean; *ekkathaírō* (1571), to purge out, cleanse thoroughly.

Syn.: *katharízō* (2511), to cleanse, make free from admixture. Also *hagnízō* (48), to cleanse from defilement, to purify ceremonially or morally.

2509. καθάπερ, **kathaper,** *kath-ap´-er*; from 2505 and 4007; *exactly as:*—(even, as well) as.

2510. καθάπτω, **kathaptō,** *kath-ap´-to*; from 2596 and 680; to *seize upon:*—fasten on.

2511. καθαρίζω, **katharizō,** *kath-ar-id´-zo*; from 2513; to *cleanse* (literal or figurative):—(make) clean (-se), purge, purify.

From *katharós* (2513), pure. To cleanse, free from filth:

(I) Particularly (Mt 23:25, 26; Lk 11:39). Spoken of lepers afflicted with a filthy disease and accounted as unclean: to cleanse, i.e. to heal (Mt 8:2, 3; 10:8; 11:5; Mk 1:40–42; Lk 4:27; 17:14, 17).

(II) Figuratively: to cleanse in a moral sense, i.e. from sin or pollution, by blood atonement (Heb 9:14, 22, 23; 1Jn 1:7); with no reference to blood atonement: to purify (Ac 15:9; 2Co 7:1; Jas 4:8); in the sense of to declare clean, i.e. Levitically: to make lawful (Mk 7:19; Ac 10:15; 11:9).

Deriv.: *diakatharízō* (1245), to cleanse thoroughly; *katharismós* (2512), the action or the result of cleansing, purification.

2512. καθαρισμός, **katharismos,** *kath-ar-is-mos´*; from 2511; a *washing* off, i.e. (ceremonial) *ablution,* (moral) *expiation:*—cleansing, + purge, purification, (-fying).

Noun from *katharízō* (2511), to make clean. Purification:

(I) Particularly, e.g., of the Jewish washings before meals (Jn 2:6); figuratively, of the ceremonial purification of lepers (Mk 1:44; Lk 5:14). Also of a woman after childbirth (Lk 2:22) and of baptism as a rite of purification (Jn 3:25).

(II) Metaphorically: purification from sin, expiation (Heb 1:3; 2Pe 1:9).

Syn.: *hagnismós* (49), ceremonial cleansing, purification; *baptismós* (909), ablution.

2513. καθαρός, **katharos,** *kath-ar-os´*; of uncertain affininity; *clean* (literal or figurative):—clean, clear, pure.

Adjective meaning clean, pure, in a natural sense: unsoiled, unalloyed:

(I) Particularly (Mt 27:59; Jn 13:10; Heb 10:22; Rev 15:6; 19:8, 14; 21:18, 21; 22:1). Used figuratively, in the Levitical sense (Jn 13:10); by implication: lawful, not forbidden (Ro 14:20; Tit 1:15).

(II) Metaphorically: clean, pure, in a moral sense, i.e. guiltless, innocent (Ac 18:6; 20:26);

sincere, upright, void of evil (Mt 5:8; Jn 13:11; 1Ti 1:5; 3:9; 2Ti 1:3; 2:22; 1Pe 1:22).

Deriv.: *kathaírō* (2508), to cleanse; *katharízō* (2511) to make clean; *katharótēs* (2514), purity.

2514. καθαρότης, katharotēs, *kath-ar-ot´-ace*; from 2513; *cleanness* (ceremonial):—purification.

Noun from *katharós* (2513), pure. Purity. Only in Heb 9:13.

Deriv.: *akathártēs* (168), uncleanness.

2515. καθέδρα, kathedra, *kath-ed´-rah*; from 2596 and the same as 1476; a *bench* (literal or figurative):—seat.

2516. καθέζομαι, kathezomai, *kath-ed´-zom-ahee*; from 2596 and the base of 1476; to *sit down*:—sit.

2517. καθεξῆς, kathexēs, *kath-ex-ace´*; from 2596 and 1836; *thereafter*, i.e. *consecutively*; as a noun (by ellipsis of noun) a *subsequent* person or time:—after (-ward), by (in) order.

2518. καθεύδω, katheudō, *kath-yoo´-do*; from 2596 and εὕδω, *heudō* (to *sleep*); to lie *down* to *rest*, i.e. (by implication) to *fall asleep* (literal or figurative):—(be a-) sleep.

2519. καθηγητής, kathēgētēs, *kath-ayg-ay-tace´*; from a compound of 2596 and 2233; a *guide*, i.e. (figurative) a *teacher*:—master.

2520. καθήκω, kathēkō, *kath-ay´-ko*; from 2596 and 2240; to *reach to*, i.e. (neuter of presumed active participle, figurative as adjective) *becoming*:—convenient, fit.

2521. κάθημαι, kathēmai, *kath´-ay-mahee*; from 2596 and ἧμαι, *hēmai* (to *sit*; akin to the base of 1476); to *sit down*; (figurative) to *remain*, *reside*:—dwell, sit (by, down).

2522. καθημερινός, kathēmerinos, *kath-ay-mer-ee-nos´*; from 2596 and 2250; *quotidian*:—daily.

2523. καθίζω, kathizō, *kath-id´-zo*; another (active) form for 2516; to *seat down*, i.e. *set* (figurative, *appoint*); intransitive to *sit* (down); (figurative) to *settle* (*hover, dwell*):—continue, set, sit (down), tarry.

2524. καθίημι, kathiēmi, *kath-ee´-ay-mee*; from 2596 and ἵημι, *hiēmi* (to *send*); to *lower*:—let down.

2525. καθίστημι, kathistēmi, *kath-is´-tay-mee*; from 2596 and 2476; to *place down* (permanently), i.e. (figurative) to *designate, constitute, convoy*:—appoint, be, conduct, make, ordain, set.

From *katá* (2596), down, and *hístēmi* (2476), to stand. To set, set down, place:

(**I**) To set, place. Transitively: to set down, bring to pass, cause to stand (Ac 17:15). Metaphorically: to stand, to be set, i.e. to be (Jas 3:6; 4:4). To cause to be, to make (2Pe 1:8); pass.: to be made, to become, Ro 5:19).

(**II**) Of persons: to set, to appoint, to place in charge of something (Mt 24:45, 47; 25:21, 23; Lk 12:42, 44; Ac 6:3); with double accusative: to appoint someone to a position, to put in a situation or position (Lk 12:14; Ac 7:10, 27, 35; Heb 7:28).

Deriv.: *akatástatos* (182), unstable; *antikathístēmi* (478), to resist; *apokathístēmi* (600), to restore; *katástēma* (2688), behaviour.

Syn.: *anadeíknumi* (322), to appoint to a position or a service; *diatássō* (1299), to appoint, prescribe; *tássō* (5021), to place in order; *títhēmi* (5087), to put; *cheirotonéō* (5500), to appoint by placing hands on as in the appointment of elders.

2526. καθό, katho, *kath-o´*; from 2596 and 3739; *according to which* thing, i.e. *precisely as*, *in proportion as*:—according to that, (inasmuch) as. And **καθολικός katholikos,** *kath-ol-ee-kos´*, from 2527; *universal*:—general.

2527. καθόλου, katholou, *kath-ol´-oo*; from 2596 and 3650; *on the whole*, i.e. *entirely*:—at all.

2528. καθοπλίζω, kathoplizō, *kath-op-lid´-zo*; from 2596 and 3695; to *equip fully* with armour:—arm.

2529. καθοράω, kathoraō, *kath-or-ah´-o*; from 2596 and 3708; to *behold fully*, i.e. (figurative) *distinctly apprehend*:—clearly see.

2530. καθότι, kathoti, *kath-ot´-ee*; from 2596 and 3739 and 5100; *according to which certain* thing, i.e. *as far* (or *inasmuch*) *as*:—(according, forasmuch) as, because (that).

2531. καθώς, kathōs, *kath-oce´*; from 2596 and 5613; *just* (or *inasmuch*) *as, that*:—according to, (according, even) as, how, when.

2532. καί, kai, *kahee;* apparently a primary particle, having a *copulative* and sometimes also a *cumulative* force; *and, also, even, so, then, too,* etc.; often used in connection (or composition) with other particles or small words:—and, also, both, but, even, for, if, or, so, that, then, therefore, when, yet.

2533. Καϊάφας, Kaïaphas, *kah-ee-af´-as;* of Chaldee origin; *the dell; Caïaphas* (i.e. *Cajepha*), an Israelite:—Caiaphas.

2534. καίγε, kaige, *ka´hee-gheh;* from 2532 and 1065; *and at least* (or *even, indeed*):—and, at least.

2535. Κάϊν, Kaïn, *kah´-in;* of Hebrew origin [7014]; *Caïn* (i.e. *Cajin*), the son of Adam:—Cain.

2536. Καϊνάν, Kaïnan, *Kah-ee-nan´;* of Hebrew origin [7018]; *Caïnan* (i.e. *Kenan*), the name of two patriarchs:—Cainan.

2537. καινός, kainos, *kahee-nos´;* of uncertain affinity; *new* (especially in *freshness;* while 3501 is properly so with respect to *age*):—new.

(I) Newly made, not impaired by time or use, spoken of: new skins used as containers (Mt 9:17; Mk 2:22; Lk 5:38); a grave or sepulchre (Mt 27:60; Jn 19:41); a garment (Lk 5:36). Also Mt 13:52, "treasures new and old."

(II) New, i.e. current or not before known, newly introduced. Spoken of a new: doctrine (Mk 1:27; Ac 17:19); commandment or precept (Jn 13:34; 1Jn 2:7, 8; 2Jn 5); name (Rev 2:17; 3:12). In the comparative degree, i.e. newer (Ac 17:21). In the sense of other, i.e. foreign or different, spoken of tongues or languages (Mk 16:17).

(III) New, as opposed to old or former and hence also implying better, as *kainḗ diathḗkē* ([1242] testament), a new and better covenant (Mt 26:28; Mk 14:24; Lk 22:20; 1Co 11:25; Heb 8:8, 13); "a new song," i.e. a nobler, loftier strain (Rev 5:9; 14:3). Also for renewed, made new, and therefore superior, more splendid, e.g. "new heavens and a new earth" (2Pe 3:13; Rev 21:1); the "new Jerusalem" (Rev 3:12; 21:2). Meta-phorically, speaking of Christians who are renewed and changed from evil to good by the Spirit of God: a new creation (2Co 5:17; Gal 6:15), a new man (Eph 2:15; 4:24).

Deriv.: *egkaínia* (1456), dedication; *kainótēs* (2538), newness.
Syn.: *néos* (3501), new.

2538. καινότης, kainotēs, *kahee-not´-ace;* from 2537; *renewal* (figurative):—newness.
Noun from *kainós* (2537), new. Newness. In the NT used in a moral sense (Ro 6:4; 7:6). See *kainós* (2537, III).
Syn.: *neótēs* (3503), newness, youthfulness; *anakaínōsis* (342), renewing.

2539. καίπερ, kaiper, *kah´ee-per;* from 2532 and 4007; *and indeed,* i.e. *nevertheless* or *notwithstanding:*—and yet, although.

2540. καιρός, kairos, *kahee-ros´;* of uncertain affinity; an *occasion,* i.e. *set* or *proper* time:— × always, opportunity, (convenient, due) season, (due, short, while) time, a while. Compare 5550.
Right proportion, just measure. In the NT, used only of time, season:

(I) Fit time, proper season:
(A) Generally equivalent to opportunity, occasion (Ac 24:25; 2Co 6:2; Gal 6:10; Eph 5:16; Col 4:5; Heb 11:15).
(B) Appointed time, set time, certain season, equivalent to a fixed and definite time or season (Mt 13:30; 21:34, 41; 26:18; Mk 11:13; Lk 8:13; 19:44; Jn 7:6; Ac 3:19; Gal 6:9; 2Ti 4:6; Heb 9:10; 11:11; Rev 11:18). With a demonstrative article or pron., e.g., this present time, that time, definitely marked out and expressed (Mt 11:25; 12:1; 14:1; Mk 10:30; Lk 13:1; 18:30; Ro 11:5; 2Co 8:14). Generally (Mk 12:2; Ac 17:26; Gal 4:10; 2Ti 4:3; Rev 12:12). So in allusion to the set time for the coming of the Messiah in His kingdom or for judgement (Mt 8:29; 16:3; Mk 1:15; 13:33; Lk 12:56; 21:8; Ac 1:7; Ro 13:11; 1Co 7:29; Eph 1:10; 1Th 5:1; 1Pe 1:11; 4:17; Rev 1:3; 22:10).
(II) Generally meaning time, season, equivalent to *chrónos* (5550):
(A) Particularly (Lk 21:36; Eph 6:18); a season of the year (Ac 14:17); in a prophetic style as used for a year (Rev 12:14).
Deriv.: *akairéomai* (170), to lack opportunity; *akaírōs* (171), inopportunely, out of season; *eúkairos* (2121), well-timed; *próskairos* (4340), recent, temporary, temporal, for a season.
Syn.: *chrónos* (5550), time, duration of a period; *hēméra* (2250), day as a point in time,

era; *hốra* (5610), hour, used sometimes with the meaning of season, opportunity.

2541. Καῖσαρ, Kaisar, *Kah´ee-sar;* of Latin origin; *Cæsar,* a title of the Roman emperor:—Cæsar.

2542. Καισάρεια, Kaisareia, *kahee-sar´-i-a;* from 2541; *Cæsaria,* the name of two places in Palestine:—Cæsarea.

2543. καίτοι, kaitoi, *kah´ee-toy;* from 2532 and 5104; *and yet,* i.e. *nevertheless:*—although.

2544. καίτοιγε, kaitoige, *kah´ee-toyg-eh;* from 2543 and 1065; *and yet indeed,* i.e. *although really:*—nevertheless, though.

2545. καίω, kaiō, *kah´-yo;* apparently a primary verb; *to set on fire,* i.e. *kindle* or (by implication) *consume:*—burn, light.

2546. κἀκεῖ, kakei, *kak-i´;* from 2532 and 1563; *likewise in that place:*—and there, there (thither) also.

2547. κἀκεῖθεν, kakeithen, *kak-i´-then;* from 2532 and 1564; *likewise from that place* (or *time*):—and afterward (from) (thence), thence also.

2548. κἀκεῖνος, kakeinos, *kak-i´-nos;* from 2532 and 1565; *likewise that* (or *those*):—and him (other, them), even he, him also, them (also), (and) they.

2549. κακία, kakia, *kak-ee´-ah;* from 2556; *badness,* i.e. (subject) *depravity,* or (active) *malignity,* or (passive) *trouble:*—evil, malice (-iousness), naughtiness, wickedness.

Noun from *kakós* (2556), bad. Badness. In the NT: evil in a moral sense:

(**I**) Wickedness of heart, life, and character (Ac 8:22; 1Co 14:20; Jas 1:21; 1Pe 2:16).

(**II**) In an act. sense: malice, the desire to do evil to others (1Co 5:8; Eph 4:31; Col 3:8; Tit 3:3; 1Pe 2:1).

(**III**) Evil, i.e. trouble, affliction (Mt 6:34).

Syn.: *adíkēma* (92), injustice, iniquity; *adikía* (93), unrighteousness; *hamartía* (266), sin; *anomía* (458), lawlessness; *paranomía* (3892), transgression.

2550. κακοήθεια, kakoētheia, *kak-o-ay´-thi-ah;* from a compound of 2556 and 2239; *bad*

character, i.e. (special) *mischievousness:*—malignity.

Noun from *kakoḗthēs* (n.f.), mischievous, which is from *kakós* (2556), bad, evil, and *ḗthos* (2239), disposition, custom. Mischief, malignity, evil habit, the desire to do evil to others. Occurs only in Ro 1:29.

2551. κακολογέω, kakologeō, *kak-ol-og-eh´-o;* from a compound of 2556 and 3056; to *revile:*—curse, speak evil of.

2552. κακοπάθεια, kakopatheia, *kak-op-ath´-i-ah;* from a compound of 2556 and 3806; *hardship:*—suffering affliction.

Noun from *kakopathéō* (2553), to suffer misfortune, hardship. A suffering of evil, i.e. suffering, affliction (Jas 5:10).

Syn.: *diōgmós* (1375), persecution; *thlípsis* (2347), pressure and hence affliction, being squeezed from the outside, constriction; *kákōsis* (2561), affliction, ill-treatment; *páthēma* (3804), suffering, affliction; *stenochōría* (4730), anguish; *sunochế* (4928), being in straits, distress; *tarachế* (5016), agitation, disturbance, trouble.

2553. κακοπαθέω, kakopatheō, *kak-op-ath-eh´-o;* from the same as 2552; to *undergo hardship:*—be afflicted, endure afflictions (hardness), suffer trouble.

From *kakopathḗs* (n.f.), suffering ill, which is from *kakós* (2556), evil, and *páthos* (3806), passion. To suffer evil or afflictions, to be afflicted (2Ti 2:9; Jas 5:13). Especially of soldiers and others: to endure hardships (2Ti 2:3; 4:5).

Deriv.: *kakopátheia* (2552), suffering, affliction; *sugkakopathéō* (4777), to suffer hardship with someone.

Syn.: *basanízō* (928), to toil, be tormented; *odunáō* (3600) to be tormented; *talaipōréō* (5003), to be afflicted, suffer hardship, be miserable.

2554. κακοποιέω, kakopoieō, *kak-op-oy-eh´-o;* from 2555; to *be a bad-doer,* i.e. (object) to *injure,* or (genitive) to *sin:*—do (-ing) evil.

From *kakopoiós* (2555), evildoer. To do evil to others, i.e. to injure, to harm (Mk 3:4; Lk 6:9); generally: to commit sin (1Pe 3:17; 3Jn 11).

Syn.: *kakóō* (2559), to ill-treat, exasperate, vex, afflict; *basanízo* (928), to torment; *bláptō* (984), to injure, hurt.

2555. κακοποιός, kakopoios, *kak-op-oy-os´*; from 2556 and 4160; a *bad-doer*; (special) a *criminal*:—evildoer, malefactor.

Adjective from *kakós* (2556), evil, and *poiéō* (4160), to do or make. An evildoer (1Pe 2:12, 14; 3:16; 4:15). Spoken falsely of Christ (Jn 18:30).

Deriv.: *kakopoiéō* (2554), to do evil.

Syn.: *kakoúrgos* (2557), evil worker, malefactor; *ponērós* (4190), one of the names attributed to Satan, malevolent.

2556. κακός, kakos, *kak-os´*; apparently a primary word; *worthless* (*intrinsically* such; whereas 4190 properly refers to *effects*), i.e. (subject) *depraved*, or (object) *injurious*:—bad, evil, harm, ill, noisome, wicked.

Adjective meaning bad, worthless externally. Of a soldier, cowardly. In the NT evil, wicked:

(I) In a moral sense: wicked, vicious, bad in heart, conduct, and character (Mt 21:41; 24:48; Php 3:2; Rev 2:2). Of things such as thoughts and works (Mk 7:21; Ro 13:3; 1Co 15:33; Col 3:5). In the neuter, evil, evil things, wickedness, fault, crime (Mt 27:23; Mk 15:14; Lk 23:22; Jn 18:23; Ac 23:9; Ro 1:30; 2:9; 3:8; 7:19, 21; 13:4; 16:19; 1Co 10:6; 2Co 13:7; 1Ti 6:10; Heb 5:14; Jas 1:13; 1Pe 3:12; 3Jn 11).

(II) Actively causing evil, i.e. hurtful, harmful (Ro 14:20; Tit 1:12; Rev 16:2). In the neuter, evil, i.e. cause or source of evil (Jas 3:8); evil done to anyone, harm, injury (Ac 16:28; 28:5; Ro 12:17, 21; 13:10; 1Co 13:5; 1Th 5:15; 1Pe 3:9). In words, evil speaking (1Pe 3:10). In the plural, evils, i.e. troubles, afflictions (Lk 16:25; Ac 9:13; 2Ti 4:14).

Deriv.: *ákakos* (172), one without evil, upright; *anexíkakos* (420), without evil, long-suffering; *ekkakéō* or *egkakéō* (1573), to become discouraged; *kakía* (2549), wickedness, trouble; *kakopoiós* (2555), evildoer; *kakoúrgos* (2557), one who works evil; *kakouchéō* (2558), to suffer adversity; *kakóō* (2559), to ill-treat; *kakṓs* (2560), badly.

Syn.: *ánomos* (459), lawless as a characterization of the person himself in regard to obedience to the law; *kakía* (2549), wickedness, iniquity, evil, affliction; *ponērós* (4190), malicious with willful harm to others, an element not necessarily found in *kakós*.; *saprós* (4550), corrupt, rotten, unfit for use, putrid; *phaúlos* (5337), trivial, bad in the sense of being worthless.

2557. κακοῦργος, kakourgos, *kak-oor´-gos*; from 2556 and the base of 2041; a *wrong-doer*, i.e. *criminal*:—evildoer, malefactor.

Noun from *kakós* (2556), bad, and *érgō* (n.f.), to work, which is the obsolete root of *érgon* (2041), work. An evildoer, malefactor; spoken of the two thieves who were crucified beside Jesus (Lk 23:32, 33, 39); spoken of Paul suffering wrongly as an evildoer (2Ti 2:9).

Syn.: *kakopoiós* (2555), an evildoer; *lēstḗs* (3027), a robber, plunderer.

2558. κακουχέω, kakoucheō, *kak-oo-kheh´-o*; from a presumed compound of 2556 and 2192; to *maltreat*:—which suffer adversity, torment.

2559. κακόω, kakoō, *kak-o´-o*; from 2556; to *injure*; (figurative) to *exasperate*:—make evil affected, entreat evil, harm, hurt, vex.

From *kakós* (2556), bad, evil. Physically, to do evil to someone, to maltreat, to harm, afflict (Ac 7:6, 19; 12:1; 18:10; 1Pe 3:13); also, in the NT, in a moral sense: to make evil-affected, i.e. to embitter (Ac 14:2).

Deriv.: *kákōsis* (2561), distress, affliction.

Syn.: *kakopoiéō* (2554), to do evil.

2560. κακῶς, kakōs, *kak-oce´*; adverb from 2556; *badly* (physical or moral):—amiss, diseased, evil, grievously, miserably, sick, sore.

Adverb from *kakós* (2556), bad, evil. Badly:

(I) Physically: with *échō* (2192), to have, meaning to be ill (Mt 4:24; 8:16; 9:12; 14:35; Mk 1:32, 34; 2:17; 6:55; Lk 5:31; 7:2).

(II) Used with various action verbs: badly, grievously, miserably (Mt 15:22; 17:15; 21:41).

(III) Used with verbs denoting speech: to speak evil of anyone, revile (Ac 23:5); to speak evil words (Jn 18:23); to ask amiss, badly, improperly (Jas 4:3).

Syn.: *árrōstos* (732), infirm, sick; *asthenḗs* (772), without strength, weak; *deinós* (1171), grievously, severely.

2561. κάκωσις, kakōsis, *kak´-o-sis*; from 2559; *maltreatment*:—affliction.

2562. καλάμη, kalamē, *kal-am´-ay*; feminine of 2563; a *stalk* of grain, i.e. (collective) *stubble*:—stubble.

2563. κάλαμος, kalamos, *kal´-am-os*; of uncertain affinity; a *reed* (the plant or its stem, or that of a similar plant); (by implication) a *pen:*—pen, reed.

2564. καλέω, kaleō, *kal-eh´-o*; akin to the base of 2753; to "*call*" (properly aloud, but used in a variety of applications, dirivative or otherwise):—bid, call (forth), (whose, whose sur-) name (was [called]).

To call:

(**I**) To call to someone in order that he may come or go somewhere:

(**A**) Particularly with the actual voice (Mt 4:21; 20:8; Mk 1:20; Lk 19:13); as a shepherd calls his flock (Jn 10:3).

(**B**) Generally: to call in some way, send for, direct to come (Mt 2:7, 15; Heb 11:8).

(**C**) To call authoritatively, to call forth, summon, e.g., before a judge (Ac 4:18; 24:2). Figuratively, of God calling forth and disposing of things that are not, even as though they were, i.e. calling them into existence (Ro 4:17).

(**D**) In the sense of to invite, particularly to a banquet (Mt 22:3, 8, 9; Lk 7:39; 14:8, 17; Jn 2:2; 1Co 10:27). Metaphorically: to call or invite to anything, e.g., of Jesus, to call to repentance, etc. (Mt 9:13; Mk 2:17); of God (Ro 9:24; 1Co 1:9; 7:15, 17ff.; Gal 5:8, 13; 1Th 2:12; 2Th 2:14; 1Ti 6:12; 2Ti 1:9; Heb 9:15; 1Pe 2:9, 21; 5:10; Rev 19:9).

(**E**) In the sense of to call to any position, i.e. to appoint, choose (Gal 1:15; Heb 5:4).

(**II**) To call, i.e. to name, to give a name to any person or thing:

(**A**) Particularly as spoken of: (**1**) A proper name or surname, e.g., of persons (Mt 1:21, 23, 25; Lk 1:13; 2:21; Ac 1:23; Ro 9:7; Heb 11:18; Rev 19:13). Of places (Mt 27:8; Lk 2:4; Ac 3:11; 28:1; Rev 1:9). (**2**) An epithet, descriptive adj., or appellation, e.g., a Nazarene (Mt 2:23). Also Mt 22:43; 23:7, 8, 10; Lk 6:15; 15:19, 21; Ac 10:1; Ro 9:26; Jas 2:23; 1Jn 3:1).

(**B**) Passive, in the sense of to be regarded, accounted, meaning to be (Mt 5:9, 19; 21:13; Mk 11:17; Lk 1:32, 35; 2:23; Heb 3:13).

Deriv.: *antikaléō* (479), to invite in return; *egkaléō* (1458), to accuse; *eiskaléō* (1528), to invite; *epikaléomai* (1941), to call upon, to be surnamed; *klésis* (2821), calling; *klētós* (2822), called; *metakaléō* (3333), to call; *parakaléō* (3870), to call near, to comfort; *prokaléō* (4292), to provoke; *proskaléō* (4341), to invite; *sugkaléō* (4779), to call together.

Syn.: *eponomázō* (2028), to surname; *onomázō* (3687), to name, call, command; *prosphōnéō* (4377), to call unto; *phōnéō* (5455), to call with a loud voice.

2565. καλλιέλαιος, kallielaios, *kal-le-el´-ah-yos*; from the base of 2566 and 1636; a *cultivated* olive tree, i.e. a *domesticated* or *improved* one:—good olive tree.

2566. καλλίον, kallion, *kal-lee´-on*; neuter of the (irregular) comparative of 2570; (adverb) *better* than many:—very well.

2567. καλοδιδάσκαλος, kalodidaskalos, *kal-od-id-as´-kal-os*; from 2570 and 1320; a *teacher of* the *right:*—teacher of good things.

2568. Καλοὶ Λιμένες, Kaloi Limenes, *kal-oy´ lee-man´-es*; plural of 2570 and 3040; *Good Harbors,* i.e. *Fairhaven,* a bay of Crete:—fair havens.

2569. καλοποιέω, kalopoieō, *kal-op-oy-eh´-o*; from 2570 and 4160; to *do well,* i.e. live virtuously:—well doing.

2570. καλός, kalos, *kal-os´*; of uncertain affinity; properly *beautiful,* but chiefly (figurative) *good* (literal or moral), i.e. *valuable* or *virtuous* (for *appearance* or *use,* and thus distinguished from 18, which is properly *intrinsic*):— × better, fair, good (-ly), honest, meet, well, worthy.

Adjective meaning handsome, beautiful, primarily as to external form and appearance. In the NT, of quality: good, handsome, excellent:

(**I**) Good as to quality and character:

(**A**) Generally, the soil of the earth (Mt 13:8, 23; Mk 4:8, 20; Lk 8:15); a tree (Mt 12:33; Lk 6:43); seed (Mt 13:24, 27, 37, 38); a measure, i.e. bountiful, proper measure (Lk 6:38).

(**B**) By implication: choice, excellent, e.g., fruit (Mt 3:10; 7:17–19; Lk 3:9; 6:43); wine (Jn 2:10); pearls (Mt 13:45); stones (Lk 21:5). See Mt 13:48; Ro 7:16; 1Th 5:21; 1Ti 3:1, 13; 4:6, "good doctrine"; 6:12, 13, 19; 2Ti 1:14; Heb 6:5).

(**C**) With a meaning of honourable, distinguished (1Ti 1:18; 3:7; Jas 2:7).

(**II**) Good as to effect or influence, useful, profitable (Mk 9:50; Lk 14:34). Hence the expression *kalón ésti* (1510), meaning it is good, profitable, and in some contexts, it is better (Mt 17:4; 18:8, 9; 26:24; Mk 9:5, 42; 14:21; Lk 9:33; 1Co 7:1, 8; 9:15).

(III) Good in a moral sense, virtuous: **(A)** Spoken of thoughts, feelings, actions, e.g., a good conscience (Heb 13:18); good conduct (Jas 3:13; 1Pe 2:12); "the good fight" (1Ti 6:12; 2Ti 4:7). In 1Ti 2:3; 5:4, "it is good in the sight of [*enōpion* {1799}, before] God" (a.t.); in Lk 8:15 of the heart being both *kalē* (2570), inherently good, and *agathē* (18), benevolent, able to externalize its qualities. Also used of work or works: **(1)** Generally meaning well-doing, virtue, as in Eng., a good or noble deed or deeds (Mt 5:16; 1Ti 5:25; Tit 2:7, 14; 3:8; Heb 10:24; 1Pe 2:12); **(2)** In the sense of useful work, i.e. benefit (Mt 26:10; Mk 14:6; Jn 10:32, 33; 1Ti 5:10; 6:18; Tit 3:8, 14). Hence, *kalón esti* (1510), it is good, meaning it is right (Mt 15:26; Mk 7:27; Ro 14:21; Gal 4:18; Heb 13:9).

(B) Spoken of persons in reference to the performance of duty, e.g., "the good shepherd" (Jn 10:11, 14). See also 1Ti 4:6; 2Ti 2:3; 1Pe 4:10.

Deriv.: *kállion* (2566), very well; *kalopoiéō* (2569), to do well, excellently; *kalós* (2573), well.

Syn.: *agathós* (18), good, benevolent; *áxios* (514), worthy; *arestós* (701), agreeable, pleasing; *chrēstós* (5543), good, kind.

2571. κάλυμα, kaluma, *kal´-oo-mah*; from 2572; a *cover*, i.e. *veil*:—vail.

2572. καλύπτω, kaluptō, *kal-oop´-to*; akin to 2813 and 2928; to *cover* up (literal or figurative):—cover, hide.

To envelop, to cover over:

(I) To cover (Mt 8:24; Lk 8:16; 23:30).

(II) By implication: to hide, the same as *krúptō* (2928), to hide (Mt 10:26; 2Co 4:3; Jas 5:20; 1Pe 4:8; in the two latter cases, it means to cause a multitude of sins to be overlooked and not punished.

Deriv.: *anakalúptō* (343), to uncover; *apokalúptō* (601), to disclose, reveal; *epikalúptō* (1943), to cover up or over; *kálumma* (2571), covering, veil; *katakalúptō* (2619), to cover completely; *parakalúptō* (3871), to hide; *perikalúptō* (4028), to cover around; *sugkalúptō* (4780), to cover up, conceal.

Syn.: *apokrúptō* (613), to conceal from; *egkrúptō* (1470), to hide in something; *krúptō* (2928), to keep secret, hide; *parakalúptō* (3871), to cover with a veil, hide.

2573. καλῶς, kalōs, *kal-oce´*; adverb from 2570; *well* (usually moral):—(in a) good (place), honestly, + recover, (full) well.

2574. κάμηλος, kamēlos, *kam´-ay-los*; of Hebrew origin [1581]; a "*camel*":—camel.

2575. κάμινος, kaminos, *kam´-ee-nos*; probably from 2545; a *furnace*:—furnace.

2576. καμμύω, kammuō, *kam-moo´-o*; for a compound of 2596 and the base of 3466; to *shut down*, i.e. *close* the eyes:—close.

2577. κάμνω, kamnō, *kam´-no*; apparently a primary verb; properly to *toil*, i.e. (by implication) to *tire* (figurative, *faint, sicken*):—faint, sick, be wearied.

Primarily to be weary from constant work (Heb 12:3). Also, to be sick (Jas 5:15; Rev 2:3).

Syn.: *apopsúchō* (674), to be faint at heart; *asthenéō* (770), to be weak, sick; *ekkakéō* or *egkakéō* (1573), to be faint-hearted, weary; *eklúō* (1590), to become feeble, grow weary; the expression *échō kakṓs* (*échō* [2192], to have; *kakṓs* [2560], bad) to have it badly or to be sick; *kopiáō* (2872), to grow weary, to toil; *noséō* (3552), to be sick.

2578. κάμπτω, kamptō, *kamp´-to*; apparently a primary verb; to *bend*:—bow.

2579. κἄν, kan, *kan*; from 2532 and 1437; *and (or even) if*:—and (also) if (so much as), if but, at the least, though, yet.

2580. Κανᾶ, Kana, *kan-ah´*; of Hebrew origin [compare 7071]; *Cana*, a place in Palestine:—Cana.

2581. Κανανίτης, Kananitēs, *kan-an-ee´-tace*; of Chaldee origin [compare 7067]; *zealous*; *Cananitès*, an epithet:—Canaanite [*by mistake for a derivative from* 5477].

2582. Κανδάκη, Kandakē, *kan-dak´-ay*; of foreign origin; *Candacè*, an Egyptian queen:—Candace.

2583. κανών, kanōn, *kan-ohn´*; from **κάνη, kanē** (a straight *reed*, i.e. *rod*); a *rule* ("*canon*"), i.e. (figurative) a *standard* (of faith and practice); (by implication) a *boundary*, i.e. (figurative) a *sphere* (of activity):—line, rule.

2584. Καπερναούμ, Kapernaoum, *cap-er-nah-oom´*; of Hebrew origin [probably 3723 and

5151]; *Capernaüm*, i.e. *Capha-nachum*), a place in Palestine:—Capernaum.

2585. καπηλεύω, kapēleuō, *kap-ale-yoo´-o*; from **κάπηλος,** *kapēlos* (a *huckster*); to *retail,* i.e. (by implication) to *adulterate* (figurative):— corrupt.

From *kápēlos* (n.f.), a retailer, huckster, vintner, inn-keeper. To peddle; for profit. Only in 2Co 2:17. The *kápēloi* were notorious for adulterating their commodities, and *kapēleúō,* may have a figurative implication here, meaning, to adulterate, to corrupt.

Syn.: *phtheírō* (5351), to corrupt; *kataphtheírō* (2704), to corrupt; *diaphtheírō* (1311), to corrupt.

2586. καπνός, kapnos, *kap-nos´*; of uncertain affinity; *smoke:*—smoke.

2587. Καππαδοκία, Kappadokia, *kap-pad-ok-ee´-ah*; of foreign origin; *Cappadocia,* a region of Asia Minor:—Cappadocia.

2588. καρδία, kardia, *kar-dee´-ah*; prolonged from a primary **κάρ,** *kar* (Latin *cor,* "*heart*"); the *heart,* i.e. (figurative) the *thoughts* or *feelings* (*mind*); also (by analogy) the *middle:*— (+ broken-) heart (-ed).

Noun meaning heart. The seat and center of circulation, and therefore of human life. In the NT, used only figuratively:

(I) As the seat of the desires, feelings, affections, passions, impulses, i.e. the heart or mind:

(A) Generally (Mt 5:8, 28; 6:21; Mk 4:15; Lk 1:17; Jn 14:1; Ac 11:23; 2Ti 2:22; Heb 3:8; 10:22).

(B) In phrases: as out of or from the heart, meaning willingly (Mt 18:35; Ro 6:17); with the whole heart (Mt 22:37; Mk 12:30; Sept.: Dt 6:5; Ps 119:34); of one heart and soul, i.e. entire unanimity (Ac 4:32).

(C) Used for the person himself in cases where values, affections or passions are attributed to the heart or mind (Mt 24:48; Jn 16:22; Ac 2:26; 14:17; Ro 10:6; Col 2:2; 2Th 2:17; Jas 1:26; 5:5; Rev 18:7).

(II) As the seat of the intellect meaning the mind, understanding (Mt 13:15; Mk 6:52; Lk 1:66; 2:51; 24:25; Jn 12:40; Ro 1:21; Eph 4:18; 2Pe 1:19). In the sense of conscience (Ro 2:15; 1Jn 3:20, 21).

(III) Figuratively: the heart of something,

the middle or central part, i.e. the heart of the earth (Mt 12:40).

Deriv.: *kardiognōstēs* (2589), heart-knower, heart-searcher; *sklērokardía* (4641), hardening of the heart, stubbornness.

Syn.: *noús* (3563), mind; *súnesis* (4907), understanding, prudence; *psuchḗ* (5590), soul.

2589. καρδιογνώστης, kardiognōstēs, *kar-dee-og-noce´-tace*; from 2588 and 1097; a *heart-knower:*—which knowest the hearts.

Noun from *kardía* (2588), heart, and *ginṓskō* (1097), to know. One who knows the heart, searcher of hearts (Ac 1:24; 15:8).

2590. καρπός, karpos, *kar-pos´*; probably from the base of 726; *fruit* (as *plucked*), literal or figurative:—fruit.

2591. Κάρπος, Karpos, *kar´-pos*; perhaps for 2590; *Carpus,* probably a Christian:—Carpus.

2592. καρποφορέω, karpophoreō, *kar-pof-or-eh´-o*; from 2593; to *be fertile* (literal or figurative):—be (bear, bring forth) fruit (-ful).

2593. καρποφόρος, karpophoros, *kar-pof-or´-os*; from 2590 and 5342; *fruitbearing* (figurative):—fruitful.

2594. καρτερέω, kartereō, *kar-ter-eh´-o*; from a derivative of 2904 (transposed); to *be strong,* i.e. (figurative) *steadfast* (*patient*):—endure.

From *karterós* (n.f.), strength. To be strong, steadfast, firm, to endure, hold out, bear the burden. Only in Heb 11:27.

Deriv.: *proskarteréō* (4342), to persist, hold fast.

Syn.: *anéchō* (430), to hold up; *makrothuméō* (3114) to be long-suffering toward people; *ménō* (3306), to abide, endure; *hupoménō* (5278), to abide under, endure circumstances; *hupophérō* (5297), to bear up under, to endure trial or suffering.

2595. κάρφος, karphos, *kar´-fos*; from **κάρφω,** *karpho* (to *wither*); a dry *twig* or *straw:*—mote.

2596. κατά, kata, *kat-ah´*; a primary particle; (preposition) *down* (in place or time), in varied relations (according to the case [general, dative or accusative] with which it is joined):—about, according as (to), after, against, (when they were) × alone, among, and, × apart, (even, like) as (concerning, pertaining to, touching), × aside, at, before, beyond, by, to the charge of, [charita-] bly, concerning, + covered, [dai-] ly, down, every, (+ far more) exceeding, × more excellent, for, from … to, godly, in (-asmuch, divers, every, -to, respect of), … by, after the manner of, + by any means, beyond (out of) measure, × mightily, more, × natural, of (up-) on (× part), out (of every), over against, (+ your) × own, + particularly, so, through (-out, -out every), thus, (un-) to (-gether, -ward), × uttermost, where (-by), with. In composition it retains many of these applications, and frequently denotes *opposition, distribution* or *intensity.*

Preposition with the primary meaning of down. Down from, down upon, down in:

(I) With the gen.:

(A) Of place: **(1)** Indicating motion meaning down from a higher to a lower place, e.g., down a precipice into the sea (Mt 8:32; Mk 5:13; Lk 8:33). **(2)** Generally of motion or direction upon, toward or through any place or object: **(a)** Particularly in the sense of upon, against (Ac 27:14). **(b)** In the sense of through, throughout (Lk 4:14; 23:5; Ac 9:31, 42; 10:37). **(c)** After verbs of swearing, i.e. to swear upon or by anything, at the same time stretching out the hand over, upon, or toward it (Mt 26:63; Heb 6:13, 16).

(B) Figuratively, of the object toward or upon which something tends or aims: upon, in respect to (1Co 15:15; Jude 15). More usually in a hostile sense: against; or after words of speaking, accusing, warring, and the like (Mt 5:11, 23; 10:35; 12:14; 26:59; Mk 11:25; 14:55ff.; Ac 4:26; 16:22; 2Co 13:8; Gal 5:17).

(II) With the accusative, where the primary and general idea is down upon, out over:

(A) Of place, that is: **(1)** Of motion expressed or implied or of extension out over, through, or throughout a place (Lk 8:39; 15:14; Ac 5:15; 8:1; 11:1; 15:23; 24:12). With *hodós* (3598), way, meaning along or by the way, while traveling upon it (Lk 10:4; Ac 25:3; 26:13). Hence, from the idea of motion throughout every part of the whole arises the distributive sense of *katá*, e.g., *katá pólin kaí kṓmēn*, "throughout every city and village" (Lk 8:1; see *pólis* (4172), city; *kai* (2532), and, *kṓmē* (2968), village. *Kat' oíkon*, "from house to house" (*katá*; *oikos* [3624], house). See also Lk 8:4; 9:6; 13:22; Ac 8:3; 14:23; 15:21; 22:19). **(2)** Of motion referring to situation upon, at, near to, or adja-

cent to (Lk 10:32, 33; Ac 2:10; 16:7; 27:2; 27:7). **(3)** Of motion or direction, upon, i.e. toward any place (Ac 8:26; 27:12; Php 3:14).

(B) Of time, i.e. of a period or point of time: down upon which, e.g., in, at, or during which anything takes place; *katá kairón* ([2540], occasion, season, opportune time), in due time (Jn 5:4; Ro 5:6); about midnight (Ac 16:25; 27:27); *kat' archás* ([746], beginning) in the beginning (Heb 1:10). Also used in a distributive sense with various designations of time. Thus: every day (Mt 26:55; Mk 14:49; Lk 11:3; 19:47; Ac 2:46; 17:17); every year (Lk 2:41; Heb 9:25; 10:1, 3); every feast (Mt 27:15; Lk 23:17); every Sabbath (Ac 18:4); every first day of the week (1Co 16:2).

(C) In a distributive sense, derived strictly from the idea of pervading all the parts of the whole; as of place, see I, A above, and of time, see I, B. Also generally of any parts, number, e.g., *katá méros* ([3313], part), i.e. part for part, particularly (Heb 9:5). Of number, *kath' héna* ([1520], one), meaning one by one (1Co 14:31). Also *katá dúo* ([1417], two), meaning two at a time, in a session (1Co 14:27).

(D) Metaphorically, as expressing the relation in which one thing stands toward another, thus also everywhere implying manner. Spoken of: **(1)** Accordance, conformity, e.g., **(a)** Of a norm, rule, standard of comparison: according to, conformable to, after: "According to your faith be it unto you" (Mt 9:29; 23:3; Mk 7:5; Lk 2:22, 39; 23:56; Jn 8:15; 19:7; Ac 22:12; 23:31; 26:5; Ro 2:2; 8:4, 5, 27; 10:2; Eph 4:22; Col 2:8; 3:22; Heb 5:6, 10). In composition, *katá* denotes: **(a)** motion downwards, as *katabaínō* (2597), to descend; *kathairéō* (2507), to demolish, put down, destroy; *katapíptō* (2667), to fall down **(b)** opposition against in a hostile sense as *kataginṓskō* (2607), to blame; *katēgoréō* (2723), to accuse; *katalaléō* (2635), to slander **(c)** distribution as *kataklērodotéō* (2624), to apportion an estate by casting lots.

2597. καταβαίνω, katabaínō, kat-ab-ah´ee-no; from 2596 and the base of 939; to *descend* (literal or figurative):—come (get, go, step) down, fall (down).

From *katá* (2596), down, and *baínō* (n.f.), to go or come. To come or go down, descend from a higher to a lower place:

(I) Spoken of persons, followed by *apó* ([575], from): to descend from somewhere (Mt 8:1; 14:29; 17:9; Mk 9:9; 15:30). Spoken of those who descend or come down from heaven, e.g.: of God as affording aid to the oppressed (Ac 7:34); of the Son of Man (Jn 6:38, 42; 1Th 4:16); of the Holy Spirit (Lk 3:22; Jn 1:32, 33); of angels (Mt 28:2; Jn 1:51; 5:4); of Satan as cast down from heaven (Rev 12:12).

(II) Spoken of things: a way leading down from a higher to a lower tract of country as the way coming down from Jerusalem unto Gaza (Ac 8:26). Of things descending from heaven, i.e. let down or sent down from God as a vessel (Ac 10:11; 11:5); spiritual gifts (Jas 1:17); the New Jerusalem, the one descending out of heaven from God (Rev 3:12).

Deriv.: *katábasis* (2600), descent; *sukatabaínō* (4782), to go down with.

Syn.: *katérchomai* (2718), to come down.

2598. καταβάλλω, kataballō, *kat-ab-al´-lo*; from 2596 and 906; to *throw down*:—cast down, lay.

2599. καταβαρέω, katabareō, *kat-ab-ar-eh´-o*; from 2596 and 916; to *impose upon*:—burden.

2600. κατάβασις, katabasis, *kat-ab´-as-is*; from 2597; a *declivity*:—descent.

2601. καταβιβάζω, katabibazō, *kat-ab-ib-ad´-zo*; from 2596 and a derivative of the base of 939; to *cause to go down*, i.e. *precipitate*:—bring (thrust) down.

2602. καταβολή, katabolē, *kat-ab-ol-ay´*; from 2598; a *deposition*, i.e. *founding*; (figurative) *conception*:—conceive, foundation.

Noun from *katabállō* (2598), to cast down. A casting or laying down:

(I) A laying down, founding, foundation. In the phrase, *katabolḗ toú kósmou*, the foundation of the world (*kósmos* [2889], world), i.e. the beginning of creation (Mt 13:35; 25:34; Lk 11:50; Jn 17:24; Eph 1:4; Heb 4:3; 9:26; 1Pe 1:20; Rev 13:8; 17:8).

(II) Of seed, a casting in; used metaphorically in Heb 11:11, conception.

Syn.: For (I): *archḗ* (746), beginning (a syn. for foundation); *ktísis* (2937), creation. For (II): *sullambánō* (4815), to take together.

2603. καταβραβεύω, katabrabeuō, *kat-ab-rab-yoo´-o*; from 2596 and 1018 (in its original sense); to *award* the price *against*, i.e. (figurative) to *defraud* (of salvation):—beguile of reward.

2604. καταγγελεύς, kataggeleus, *kat-ang-gel-yooce´*; from 2605; a *proclaimer*:—setter forth.

Noun from *kataggéllō* (2605) to proclaim. A proclaimer, publisher. Only in Ac 17:18.

Syn.: *kḗrux* (2783), a herald, preacher.

2605. καταγγέλλω, kataggellō, *kat-ang-gel´-lo*; from 2596 and the base of 32; to *proclaim, promulgate*:—declare, preach, shew, speak of, teach.

From *katá* (2596), an intensive, and *aggéllō* (n.f., see *anaggéllō* [312]), to tell, declare. To declare plainly, openly, or aloud:

(I) To announce, proclaim (Ac 13:38). To celebrate (Ro 1:8; 1Co 11:26).

(II) By implication: to preach, set forth, to implant in the mind by repetition (Ac 4:2; 13:5, 38; 15:36; 16:17, 21; 17:3, 13, 23; 26:23; 1Co 2:1; 9:14; Php 1:16, 18; Col 1:28).

Deriv.: *kataggeleús* (2604), a proclaimer, publisher; *prokataggéllō* (4293), to foretell.

Syn.: *kērússō* (2784), to preach, proclaim.

2606. καταγελάω, katagelaō, *kat-ag-el-ah´-o*; to *laugh down*, i.e. *deride*:—laugh to scorn.

2607. καταγινώσκω, kataginōskō, *kat-ag-in-o´-sko*; from 2596 and 1097; to *note against*, i.e. *find fault with*:—blame, condemn.

From *katá* (2596), against, and *ginṓskō* (1097), to know. To think ill of, to condemn, to blame (1Jn 3:20, 21). In the passive, to incur blame, be worthy of blame, spoken of Peter's withdrawing from the fellowship of Gentile Christians in Antioch (Gal 2:11).

Deriv.: *akatágnōstos* (176), unblameable.

Syn.: *katadikázō* (2613), to pronounce judgement, condemn; *katakrínō* (2632), to condemn; *mémphomai* (3201), to find fault; *mōmáomai* (3469), to find fault with, blame.

2608. κατάγνυμι, katagnumi, *kat-ag´-noo-mee*; from 2596 and the base of 4486; to *rend in pieces*, i.e. *crack apart*:—break.

2609. κατάγω, katagō, *kat-ag´-o*; from 2596 and 71; to *lead down*; specially to *moor* a vessel:—bring (down, forth), (bring to) land, touch.

2610. καταγωνίζομαι, katagōnizomai, *kat-ag-o-nid´-zom-ahee*; from 2596 and 75; to *struggle against,* i.e. (by implication) to *overcome:*—subdue.

From *katá* (2596), against, and *agōnízomai* (75), to contend for victory in the public games. To contend against; and by implication, to conquer, subdue. Only in Heb 11:33.

Syn.: *nikáō* (3528), to be victorious; *hupotássō* (5293), to subdue or bring into subjection. Also, *katakurieúō* (2634), to conquer, master; *hupernikáō* (5245), to be more than a conqueror.

2611. καταδέω, katadeō, *kat-ad-eh´-o*; from 2596 and 1210; to *tie down,* i.e. *bandage* (a wound):—bind up.

2612. κατάδηλος, katadēlos, *kat-ad´-ay-los*; from 2596 intensive and 1212; *manifest:*—far more evident.

2613. καταδικάζω, katadikazō, *kat-ad-ik-ad´-zo*; from 2596 and a derivative of 1349; to *adjudge against,* i.e. *pronounce guilty:*—condemn.

From *katá* (2596), against, and *dikázō* (n.f.), to judge, pronounce sentence, which is from *díkē* (1349), judgement. To give judgement against a person, pass sentence, condemn (Mt 12:7, 37; Lk 6:37; Jas 5:6).

Syn.: *kataginṓskō* (2607), to know something against, to condemn; *katakrínō* (2632), to give judgement against, pass sentence on, condemn; *krínō* (2919), to judge, distinguish, to condemn.

2614. καταδιώκω, katadiōkō, *kat-ad-ee-o´-ko*; from 2596 and 1377; to *hunt down,* i.e. *search for:*—follow after.

2615. καταδουλόω, katadouloō, *kat-ad-oo-lo´-o*; from 2596 and 1402; to *enslave utterly:*—bring into bondage.

From *katá* (2596), an intensive, and *doulóō* (1402), to enslave. To enslave utterly, reduce to absolute slavery (2Co 11:20); in the middle to make a slave for oneself (Gal 2:4).

Syn.: *doulagōgéō* (1396), to lead into slavery, bondage, or subject.

2616. καταδυναστεύω, katadunasteuō, *kat-ad-oo-nas-tyoo´-o*; from 2596 and a derivative of 1413; to *exercise dominion against,* i.e. *oppress:*—oppress.

2617. καταισχύνω, kataischunō, *kat-ahee-skhoo´-no*; from 2596 and 153; to *shame down,* i.e. *disgrace* or (by implication) *put to the blush:*—confound, dishonour, (be a-, make a-) shame (-d).

2618. κατακαίω, katakaiō, *kat-ak-ah´ee-o*; from 2596 and 2545; to *burn down* (to the ground), i.e. *consume wholly:*—burn (up, utterly).

2619. κατακαλύπτω, katakaluptō, *kat-ak-al-oop´-to*; from 2596 and 2572; to *cover wholly,* i.e. *veil:*—cover, hide.

2620. κατακαυχάομαι, katakauchaomai, *kat-ak-ow-khah´-om-ahee*; from 2596 and 2744; to *exult against* (i.e. *over*):—boast (against), glory, rejoice against.

2621. κατάκειμαι, katakeimai, *kat-ak´-i-mahee*; from 2596 and 2749; to *lie down,* i.e. (by implication) *be sick;* specially to *recline* at a meal:—keep, lie, sit at meat (down).

2622. κατακλάω, kataklaō, *kat-ak-lah´-o*; from 2596 and 2806; to *break down,* i.e. *divide:*—break.

2623. κατακλείω, katakleiō, *kat-ak-li´-o*; from 2596 and 2808; to *shut down* (in a dungeon), i.e. *incarcerate:*—shut up.

2624. κατακληροδοτέω, kataklērodoteō, *kat-ak-lay-rod-ot-eh´-o*; from 2596 and a derivative of a compound of 2819 and 1325; to *be a giver of lots to each,* i.e. (by implication) to *apportion an estate:*—divide by lot.

From *katá* (2596), according to, a distributive, and *klērodotéō* (n.f.), to distribute by lot, which is from *klēros* (2819), part, lot, and *dídōmi* (1325), to give. To distribute by lot (Ac 13:19).

Syn.: *diadídōmi* (1239), to distribute; *diairéō* (1244), to divide into parts, distribute; *merízō* (3307), to divide into parts.

2625. κατακλίνω, kataklinō, *kat-ak-lee´-no*; from 2596 and 2827; to *recline down,* i.e. (special) to *take a place* at table:—(make) sit down (at meat).

2626. κατακλύζω, katakluzō, *kat-ak-lood´-zo*; from 2596 and the base of 2830; to *dash* (*wash*) *down,* i.e. (by implication) to *deluge:*—overflow.

2627. κατακλυσμός, kataklusmos, *kat-ak-looce-mos´*; from 2626; an *inundation*:—flood.

2628. κατακολουθέω, katakoltheō, *kat-ak-ol-oo-theh´-o*; from 2596 and 190; to *accompany closely*:—follow (after).

2629. κατακόπτω, katakoptō, *kat-ak-op´-to*; from 2596 and 2875; to *chop down*, i.e. *mangle*:—cut.

2630. κατακρημνίζω, katakrēmnizō, *kat-ak-rame-nid´-zo*; from 2596 and a derivative of 2911; to *precipitate down*:—cast down headlong.

2631. κατάκριμα, katakrima, *kat-ak´-ree-mah*; from 2632; an *adverse sentence* (the verdict):—condemnation.

From *katakrínō* (2632), to condemn. Judgement against, condemnation. Spoken of as the result of Adam's fall (Ro 5:16, 18). Spoken of as being completely absent for the Christian walking after the spirit (Ro 8:1).

Syn.: *katákrisis* (2633), the process of judging which leads to condemnation; *kríma* (2917), the verdict or sentence pronounced, condemnation; *krísis* (2920), the process of investigation in the execution of justice.

2632. κατακρίνω, katakrinō, *kat-ak-ree´-no*; from 2596 and 2919; to *judge against*, i.e. *sentence*:—condemn, damn.

From *katá* (2596), against, and *krínō* (2919), to judge. To pronounce sentence against, condemn:

(I) Of persons, with an explicit punishment (Mt 20:18; Mk 10:33; 14:64; 2Pe 2:6); with the crime or punishment implied (Jn 8:10, 11; Ro 2:1). Used in an absolute sense (Mt 27:3; Ro 8:34). Of the last judgement (Mk 16:16; 1Co 11:32). Figuratively (Ro 8:3).

(II) By implication: to condemn by contrast, i.e. to show by one's good conduct that others are guilty of misconduct and deserve condemnation (Mt 12:41, 42; Lk 11:31, 32; Heb 11:7).

Deriv.: *akatákritos* (178), without trial, uncondemned; *autokatákritos* (843), self-condemned; *katákrima* (2631), condemnation; *katákrisis* (2633), the act of condemning.

Syn.: *kataginóskō* (2607), to know something against, to condemn; *katadikázō* (2613), to pronounce judgement, condemn.

2633. κατάκρισις, katakrisis, *kat-ak´-ree-sis*; from 2632; *sentencing adversely* (the act):—condemn (-ation).

Noun from *katakrínō* (2632), to condemn. Condemnation, as brought by the Mosaic Law (2Co 3:9); in the sense of censure, blame (2Co 7:3).

2634. κατακυριεύω, katakurieuō, *kat-ak-oo-ree-yoo´-o*; from 2596 and 2961; to *lord against*, i.e. *control, subjugate*:—exercise dominion over (lordship), be lord over, overcome.

2635. καταλαλέω, katalaleō, *kat-al-al-eh´-o*; from 2637; to *be a traducer*, i.e. to *slander*:—speak against (evil of).

From *katá* (2596), against, and *laléō* (2980), to speak. To speak against, to speak evil of, to slander (1Pe 2:12; 3:16). Forbidden for Christians (Jas 4:11).

Deriv.: *katalalía* (2636), backbiting, defamation; *katálalos* (2637), a backbiter.

Syn.: *blasphēméō* (987), to blaspheme, revile; *diabállō* (1225), to falsely accuse; *egkaléō* (1458), to accuse in court; *kakologéō* (2551), to speak evil; *kataginóskō* (2607), to blame, condemn; *katēgoréō* (2723), to accuse; *sukophantéō* (4811), to accuse falsely.

2636. καταλαλία, katalalia, *kat-al-al-ee´-ah*; from 2637; *defamation*:—backbiting, evil speaking.

2637. κατάλαλος, katalalos, *kat-al´-al-os*; from 2596 and the base of 2980; *talkative against*, i.e. a *slanderer*:—backbiter.

Adjective, from *katalaléō* (2635), to speak against. Slanderous. Used as a substantive, a slanderer, backbiter (Ro 1:30).

Syn.: *blásphēmos* (989), blasphemer; *diábolos* (1228), devil, slanderer; *katégoros* (2725), accuser; *kritikós* (2924), critical; *hubristés* (5197), insulter.

2638. καταλαμβάνω, katalambanō, *kat-al-am-ban´-o*; from 2596 and 2983; to *take eagerly*, i.e. *seize, possess*, etc. (literal or figurative):—apprehend, attain, come upon, comprehend, find, obtain, perceive, (over-) take.

From *katá* (2596), an intensive, and *lambánō* (2983), to take. To take; to receive, with the idea of eagerness:

(I) To lay hold of, seize, with eagerness, suddenness: spoken of the taking of the woman caught in adultery (Jn 8:3, 4); spoken of an evil spirit taking possession of a person (Mk 9:18). Spoken figuratively of darkness or evil suddenly coming upon someone (Jn 12:35; 1Th 5:4).

(II) In allusion to the public games: to obtain the prize with the idea of eager and strenuous exertion, to grasp, seize upon (Ro 9:30; 1Co 9:24; Php 3:12, 13).

(III) Figuratively: to seize with the mind, to comprehend, to perceive (Jn 1:5; Ac 4:13; 10:34; 25:25; Eph 3:18).

Syn.: *aisthánomai* (143) to understand, perceive through the senses; *harpázō* (726), to pluck, seize, take by force; *ginōskō* (1097), to know by experience and observation; *epiginōskō* (1921), to gain full knowledge; *katanoéō* (2657), to perceive fully; *kratéō* (2902), to get possession of, to hold; *noéō* (3539), to perceive with the mind; *piázō* (4084), to seize; *phthánō* (5348), to attain.

2639. καταλέγω, katalegō, *kat-al-eg´-o*; from 2596 and 3004 (in its original meaning); to *lay down*, i.e. (figurative) to *enroll:*—take into the number.

2640. κατάλειμμα, kataleimma, *kat-al´-ime-mah*; from 2641; a *remainder*, i.e. (by implication) a *few*:—remnant.

2641. καταλείπω, kataleipō, *kat-al-i´-po*; from 2596 and 3007; to *leave down*, i.e. *behind*; (by implication) to *abandon, have remaining*:—forsake, leave, reserve.

2642. καταλιθάζω, katalithazō, *kat-al-ith-ad´-zo*; from 2596 and 3034; to *stone down*, i.e. *to death*:—stone.

2643. καταλλαγή, katallagē, *kat-al-lag-ay´*; from 2644; *exchange* (figurative, *adjustment*), i.e. *restoration* to (the divine) favour:—atonement, reconciliation (-ing).

Noun from *katallássō* (2644), to reconcile. Reconciliation, restoration to the divine favour (Ro 5:11; 2Co 5:18, 19); the means, occasion of reconciling the world to God (Ro 11:15).

2644. καταλλάσσω, katallassō, *kat-al-las´-so*; from 2596 and 236; to *change mutually*, i.e. (figurative) to *compound* a difference:—reconcile.

From *katá* (2596), an intensive, and *allássō* (236), to change. In the NT, to change toward, i.e. one person toward another; to reconcile to

someone, differing from *diallássō* (1259), reconcile, which implies mutual change (Ro 5:10; 1Co 7:11; 2Co 5:20). Spoken also of God reconciling the world to Himself (2Co 5:18, 19).

Deriv.: *apokatallássō* (604), to reconcile fully; *katallagē* (2643), reconciliation.

Syn.: *diallássō* (1259), to reconcile when the fault may lie on the part of both parties concerned; *apokatallássō* (604), to reconcile completely and change from one condition to another; *apokathístēmi* (600), to restore, reclaim.

2645. κατάλοιπος, kataloipos, *kat-al´-oy-pos*; from 2596 and 3062; *left down (behind)* i.e. *remaining* (plural the *rest*):—residue.

2646. κατάλυμα, kataluma, *kat-al´-oo-mah*; from 2647; properly a *dissolution* (breaking up of a journey), i.e. (by implication) a *lodging-place*:—guestchamber, inn.

2647. καταλύω, kataluō, *kat-al-oo´-o*; from 2596 and 3089; to *loosen down (disintegrate)*, i.e. (by implication) to *demolish* (literal or figurative); specially [compare 2646] to *halt* for the night:—destroy, dissolve, be guest, lodge, come to nought, overthrow, throw down.

From *katá* (2596), an intensive, and *lúō* (3089), to loose. To loosen:

(I) Particularly: to dissolve, to disunite the parts of something; hence spoken of buildings: to pull down, to destroy (Mt 26:61; 27:40; Mk 13:2; 14:58; 15:29; Lk 21:6; Ac 5:38, 39; 6:14). Used figuratively in Gal 2:18.

(II) In the Septuagint OT, to unbind; hence of caravans, travelers, etc.: to halt for rest or for the night, to put up for the night, i.e. when the beasts of burden are unharnessed and unloaded (Sept.: Ge 42:27; 43:21). In the NT, generally: to lodge, to take lodging (Lk 9:12; 19:7).

Deriv.: *akatálutos* (179), indissoluble; *katáluma* (2646), lodging place.

Syn.: *analískō* (355), to destroy, consume; *anatrépō* (396), to overthrow, upset; *apóllumi* (622), to destroy; *dialúō* (1262), to dissolve utterly, scatter; *diaphtheírō* (1311), to utterly destroy; *erēmóō* (2049), to make desolate; *kathairéō* (2507), to put down; *katastréphō* (2690), to overthrow, ruin; *katastrṓnnumi* (2693), to overthrow.

2648. καταμανθάνω, katamanthanō, *kat-am-an-than´-o*; from 2596 and 3129; to *learn thor-*

oughly, i.e. (by implication) to *note carefully*:—consider.

2649. καταμαρτυρέω, katamartureō, *kat-am-ar-too-reh´-o*; from 2596 and 3140; to *testify against*:—witness against.

2650. καταμένω, katamenō, *kat-am-en´-o*; from 2596 and 3306; to *stay fully*, i.e. *reside*:—abide.

2651. καταμόνας, katamonas, *kat-am-on´-as*; from 2596 and accusative plural feminine of 3441 (with 5561 implied); *according to sole* places, i.e. (adverb) *separately*:—alone.

2652. κατανάθεμα, katanathema, *kat-an-ath´-em-ah*; from 2596 (intensive) and 331; an *imprecation*:—curse.

2653. καταναθεματίζω, katanathematizō, *kat-an-ath-em-at-id´-zo*; from 2596 (intensive) and 332; to *imprecate*:—curse.

2654. καταναλίσκω, katanaliskō, *kat-an-al-is´-ko*; from 2596 and 355; to *consume utterly*:—consume.

2655. καταναρκάω, katanarkaō, *kat-an-ar-kah´-o*; from 2596 and **ναρκάω, narkaō** (to *be numb*); to *grow utterly torpid*, i.e. (by implication) *slothful* (figurative, *expensive*):—be burdensome (chargeable).

2656. κατανεύω, kataneuō, *kat-an-yoo´-o*; from 2596 and 3506; to *nod down* (*toward*), i.e. (by analogy) to *make signs* to:—beckon.

2657. κατανοέω, katanoeō, *kat-an-o-eh´-o*; from 2596 and 3539; to *observe fully*:—behold, consider, discover, perceive.

From *katá* (2596), an intensive, and *noéō* (3539), to think. To see or discern distinctly, to perceive clearly (Mt 7:3; Lk 6:41; Ac 27:39); to take notice accurately, to observe, to consider (Lk 12:24, 27; 20:23; Ac 7:31, 32; 11:6; Heb 3:1; Jas 1:23, 24). In the sense of having respect for, to regard (Ro 4:19; Heb 10:24).

Syn.: *theōréō* (2334), discern; *katalambánō* (2638), to apprehend, comprehend, perceive; *katamanthánō* (2648), to learn thoroughly or consider accurately.

2658. καταντάω, katantaō, *kat-an-tah´-o*; from 2596 and a derivative of 473; to *meet against*, i.e. *arrive* at (literal or figurative):—attain, come.

2659. κατάνυξις, katanuxis, *kat-an´-oox-is*; from 2660; a *prickling* (sensation, as of the limbs *asleep*), i.e. (by implication [perhaps by some confusion with 3506 or even with 3571]) *stupor* (*lethargy*):—slumber.

2660. κατανύσσω, katanussō, *kat-an-oos´-so*; from 2596 and 3572; to *pierce thoroughly*, i.e. (figurative) to *agitate* violently ("sting to the quick"):—prick.

2661. καταξιόω, kataxioō, *kat-ax-ee-o´-o*; from 2596 and 515; to *deem entirely deserving*:—(ac-) count worthy.

2662. καταπατέω, katapateō, *kat-ap-at-eh´-o*; from 2596 and 3961; to *trample down*; (figurative) to *reject* with disdain:—trample, tread (down, underfoot).

2663. κατάπαυσις, katapausis, *kat-ap´-ow-sis*; from 2664; *reposing down*, i.e. (by Hebrew) *abode*:—rest.

Noun from *katapaúō* (2664), to make to cease. The act of resting, rest. From the Hebrew rest, i.e. place of rest, fixed abode, dwelling (Ac 7:49, alluding to a temple). Also of the rest or fixed abode of the Israelites in the Promised Land after their wanderings (Heb 3:11, 18; 4:3, 5). Hence, figuratively, the quiet abode of those who will dwell with God in heaven, in allusion to the Sabbath rest (Heb 4:1, 3, 10, 11).

Syn.: *hēsuchía* (2271), quietness.

2664. καταπαύω, katapauō, *kat-ap-ow´-o*; from 2596 and 3973; to *settle down*, i.e. (literal) to *colonize*, or (figurative) to (*cause to*) *desist*:—cease, (give) rest (-rain).

From *katá* (2596), an intensive, and *paúō* (3973), to make to cease. To quiet down:

(I) Transitively, to cause to rest, give rest (Heb 4:8 [cf. Heb 4:1, 9]).

(II) To restrain (Ac 14:18).

(III) Intransitively, to rest entirely (Heb 4:4, 10).

Deriv.: *akatápaustos* (180), incessant; *katápausis* (2663), cessation from work, rest.

Syn.: *anapaúō* (373), to rest inwardly, but not necessarily from a cessation of work as is expressed by *katapaúō*; *aniēmi* (447), to rest from endurance and suffering or persecution;

dialeípō (1257), to pause awhile, intermit, desist, cease; *hēsucházō* (2270), to be quiet, still, at rest; *kopázō* (2869), to relax from toil, to cease raging.

2665. καταπέτασμα, katapetasma, *kat-ap-et´-as-mah*; from a compound of 2596 and a congener of 4072; something *spread thoroughly*, i.e. (special) the door *screen* (to the Most Holy Place) in the Jewish Temple:—vail.

2666. καταπίνω, katapinō, *kat-ap-ee´-no*; from 2596 and 4095; to *drink down*, i.e. *gulp entire* (literal or figurative):—devour, drown, swallow (up).

2667. καταπίπτω, katapiptō, *kat-ap-ip´-to*; from 2596 and 4098; to *fall down*:—fall (down).

2668. καταπλέω, katapleō, *kat-ap-leh´-o*; from 2596 and 4126; to *sail down* upon a place, i.e. to *land* at:—arrive.

2669. καταπονέω, kataponeō, *kat-ap-on-eh´-o*; from 2596 and a derivative of 4192; to *labour down* i.e. *wear with toil* (figurative, *harass*):—oppress, vex.

2670. καταποντίζω, katapontizō, *kat-ap-on-tid´-zo*; from 2596 and a derivative of the same as 4195; to *plunge down*, i.e. *submerge*:—drown, sink.

2671. κατάρα, katara, *kat-ar´-ah*; from 2596 (intensive) and 685; *imprecation, execration*:—curse (-d, -ing).

Noun from *katá* (2596), against, and *ará* (685), a curse. To invoke evil upon, to curse:

(I) Particularly and generally: cursing (Jas 3:10).

(II) From the Hebrew curse, i.e. a devoting or dooming to utter destruction (see *anáthema* [331], curse); hence condemnation, doom, punishment (Gal 3:10, 13); by metonymy: accursed (2Pe 2:14). Also of the earth: accursed, i.e. doomed to sterility (Heb 6:8).

Syn.: *anáthema* (331) which translates the Hebrew *chērem* (2764, OT), a thing devoted to God such as sacrifices; a votive offering, gift, or for its destruction as an idol, a city. In the NT, it is used with this latter meaning as also *anathematízō* (332), to curse; *katáthema* (2652), sometimes *katanáthema*, an accursed thing from which is derived *katanathematízō* (2653), to utter a curse against.

2672. καταράομαι, kataraomai, *kat-ar-ah´-om-ahee*; middle from 2671; to *execrate*; (by analogy) to *doom*:—curse.

From *katára* (2671), a curse. To wish anyone evil or ruin, the opposite of *eulogéō* (Mt 5:44; Lk 6:28; Ro 12:14; Jas 3:9). To devote to destruction, as with *anáthema* (331), accursed thing (Mk 11:21). In the perf. pass., to be cursed (Mt 25:41).

Syn.: *anathematízō* (332), to declare something to be devoted to destruction, to curse; *kakologéō* (2551), to speak evil; *katanathematízō* (2653), to utter curses against.

2673. καταργέω, katargeō, *kat-arg-eh´-o*; from 2596 and 691; to *be* (*render*) *entirely idle* (*useless*), literal or figurative:—abolish, cease, cumber, deliver, destroy, do away, become (make) of no (none, without) effect, fail, loose, bring (come) to nought, put away (down), vanish away, make void.

From *katá* (2596), an intensive, and *argéō* (691), to be idle. To render inactive, idle, useless, ineffective:

(I) Particularly of land: to use up ineffectively (Lk 13:7); metaphorically: to make without effect, to make vain, void, fruitless (Ro 3:3, 31; 4:14; 1Co 1:28; Gal 3:17; Eph 2:15).

(II) By implication: to cause to cease, to do away, to put an end to (1Co 6:13). Hence to abolish, to destroy (Ro 6:6; 1Co 15:24, 26; 2Th 2:8; 2Ti 1:10; Heb 2:14). In the pass.: to cease, to be done away (1Co 2:6; 13:8, 10; 2Co 3:7, 11, 13, 14; Gal 5:11); to cease being under or connected with some person or thing (Ro 7:2, 6).

Syn.: *athetéō* (114), to set aside, reject; *akuróō* (208), to render void, deprive of force or authority; *kenóō* (2758), to make empty, of no effect; *lúō* (3089), to loose, dissolve, sever.

2674. καταριθμέω, katarithmeō, *kat-ar-ith-meh´-o*; from 2596 and 705; to *reckon among*:—number with.

2675. καταρτίζω, katartizō, *kat-ar-tid´-zo*; from 2596 and a derivative of 739; to *complete thoroughly*, i.e. *repair* (literal or figurative) or *adjust*:—fit, frame, mend, (make) perfect (-ly join together), prepare, restore.

From *katá* (2596), with, and *artízō* (n.f.), to adjust, fit, finish, which is from *ártios* (739), fit, complete. To put in full order, to make fully ready, to make complete:

(I) To refit, repair, mend that which is broken, e.g., nets (Mt 4:21; Mk 1:19). Spoken figuratively of a person in error, to restore, set right (Gal 6:1). To be suitable, such as one should be, deficient in no part: spoken of persons (Lk 6:40; 1Co 1:10; 2Co 13:11; Heb 13:21; 1Pe 5:10); spoken of things, to fill out, supply (1Th 3:10).

(II) Generally to prepare, set in order, constitute, only in the pass. and middle (Mt 21:16; Ro 9:22; Heb 10:5; 11:3).

Deriv.: *katártisis* (2676), the act of completion, making fit; *katartismós* (2677), complete furnishing, fitting; *prokatartízō* (4294), to perfect or make fit beforehand, make right, equip beforehand.

Syn.: *exartízō* (1822), to accomplish, equip fully; *sunarmologéō* (4883), to fit or frame together.

2676. κατάρτισις, katartisis, *kat-ar´-tis-is*; from 2675; *thorough equipment* (subject):— perfection.

Noun from *katartízō* (2675), to make fully ready, put in order. The act of completing, perfecting (2Co 13:9).

Syn.: *teleíōsis* (5050), a fulfillment, completion, perfection, an end accomplished as the effect of a process.

2677. καταρτισμός, katartismos, *kat-ar-tis-mos´*; from 2675; *complete furnishing* (object):— perfecting.

Noun from *katartízō* (2675), to make fully ready. A perfecting, i.e. the act of making perfect. Used only in Eph 4:12.

Syn.: *teleíōsis* (5050), a fulfillment, completion, perfection, an end accomplished as the effect of a process.

2678. κατασείω, kataseiō, *kat-as-i´-o*; from 2596 and 4579; to *sway downward*, i.e. *make a signal*:—beckon.

2679. κατασκάπτω, kataskaptō, *kat-as-kap´-to*; from 2596 and 4626; to *undermine*, i.e. (by implication) *destroy*:—dig down, ruin.

2680. κατασκευάζω, kataskeuazō, *kat-ask-yoo-ad´-zo*; from 2596 and a derivative of 4632; to *prepare thoroughly* (properly by external *equipment*; whereas 2090 refers rather to internal *fitness*); (by implication) to *construct, create*:—build, make, ordain, prepare.

2681. κατασκηνόω, kataskēnoō, *kat-as-kay-no´-o*; from 2596 and 4637; to *camp down*, i.e. *haunt*; (figurative) to *remain*:—lodge, rest.

2682. κατασκήνωσις, kataskēnōsis, *kat-as-kay´-no-sis*; from 2681; an *encamping*, i.e. (figurative) a *perch*:—nest.

2683. κατασκιάζω, kataskiazō, *kat-as-kee-ad´-zo*; from 2596 and a derivative of 4639; to *overshade*, i.e. *cover*:—shadow.

2684. κατασκοπέω, kataskopeō, *kat-as-kop-eh´-o*; from 2685; to *be a sentinel*, i.e. to *inspect insidiously*:—spy out.

2685. κατάσκοπος, kataskopos, *kat-as´-kop-os*; from 2596 (intensive) and 4649 (in the sense of a *watcher*); a *reconnoiterer*:—spy.

2686. κατασοφίζομαι, katasophizomai, *kat-as-of-id´-zom-ahee*; middle from 2596 and 4679; to *be crafty against*, i.e. *circumvent*:—deal subtilly with.

2687. καταστέλλω, katastellō, *kat-as-tel´-lo*; from 2596 and 4724; to *put down*, i.e. *quell*:—appease, quiet.

2688. κατάστημα, katastēma, *kat-as´-tay-mah*; from 2525; properly a *position* or *condition*, i.e. (subject) *demeanour*:—behaviour.

2689. καταστολή, katastolē, *kat-as-tol-ay´*; from 2687; a *deposit*, i.e. (special) *costume*:—apparel.

2690. καταστρέφω, katastrephō, *kat-as-tref´-o*; from 2596 and 4762; to *turn* upside *down*, i.e. *upset*:—overthrow.

2691. καταστρηνιάω, katastrēniaō, *kat-as-tray-nee-ah´-o*; from 2596 and 4763; to *become voluptuous against*:—begin to wax wanton against.

2692. καταστροφή, katastrophē, *kat-as-trof-ay´*; from 2690; an *overturn* ("*catastrophe*"), i.e. *demolition*; (figurative) *apostasy*:—overthrow, subverting.

2693. καταστρώννυμι, katastrōnnumi, *kat-as-trone´-noo-mee*; from 2596 and 4766; to *strew down*, i.e. (by implication) to *prostrate* (*slay*):—overthrow.

2694. κατασύρω, katasurō, *kat-as-oo´-ro*; from 2596 and 4951; to *drag down*, i.e. *arrest* judicially:—hale.

2695. κατασφάττω, katasphattō, *kat-as-fat´-to*; from 2596 and 4969; to *kill down*, i.e. *slaughter:*—slay.

2696. κατασφραγίζω, katasphragizō, *kat-as-frag-id´-zo*; from 2596 and 4972; to *seal closely:*—seal.

2697. κατάσχεσις, kataschesis, *kat-as´-khes-is*; from 2722; a *holding down*, i.e. *occupancy:*—possession.

2698. κατατίθημι, katatithēmi, *kat-at-ith´-ay-mee*; from 2596 and 5087; to *place down*, i.e. *deposit* (literal or figurative):—do, lay, shew.

2699. κατατομή, katatomē, *kat-at-om-ay´*; from a compound of 2596 and τέμνω, *temnō* (to *cut*); a *cutting down* (*off*), i.e. *mutilation* (ironically):—concision. Compare 609.

Noun from *katatémnō* (n.f.), to cut through or off. A cutting off, mutilation. Used contemptuously in Php 3:2, of the Jewish circumcision in contrast with the true spiritual circumcision in v. 3.

2700. κατατοξεύω, katatoxeuō, *kat-at-ox-yoo´-o*; from 2596 and a derivative of 5115; to *shoot down* with an arrow or other missile:—thrust through.

2701. κατατρέχω, katatrechō, *kat-at-rekh´-o*; from 2596 and 5143; to *run down*, i.e. *hasten* from a tower:—run down.

2702. καταφέρω, katapherō, *kat-af-er´-o*; from 2596 and 5342 (including its alternate); to *bear down*, i.e. (figurative) *overcome* (with drowsiness); specially to *cast* a vote:—fall, give, sink down.

2703. καταφευγω, katapheugō, *kat-af-yoo´-go*; from 2596 and 5343; to *flee down* (*away*):—flee.

2704. καταφθείρω, kataphtheirō, *kat-af-thi´-ro*; from 2596 and 5351; to *spoil entirely*, i.e. (literal) to *destroy*; or (figurative) to *deprave:*—corrupt, utterly perish.

2705. καταφιλέω, kataphileō, *kat-af-ee-leh´-o*; from 2596 and 5368; to *kiss earnestly:*—kiss.

2706. καταφρονέω, kataphroneō, *kat-af-ron-eh´-o*; from 2596 and 5426; to *think against*, i.e. *disesteem:*—despise.

2707. καταφροντής, kataphrontēs, *kat-af-ron-tace´*; from 2706; a *contemner:*—despiser.

2708. καταχέω, katacheō, *kat-akh-eh´-o*; from 2596 and χέω, *cheō* (to *pour*); to *pour down* (*out*):—pour.

2709. καταχθόνιος, katachthonios, *kat-akh-thon´-ee-os*; from 2596 and χθών, *chthōn* (the *ground*); *subterranean*, i.e. *infernal* (belonging to the world of departed spirits):—under the earth.

2710. καταχράομαι, katachraomai, *kat-akh-rah´-om-ahee*; from 2596 and 5530; to *overuse* i.e. *misuse:*—abuse.

From *katá* (2596), against, denoting wrong, or an intensive, denoting excess, and *chráomai* (5530), to use. To fail to use thoroughly, or to overuse, thus to misuse, abuse (1Co 7:31; 9:18).

2711. καταψύχω, katapsuchō, *kat-ap-soo´-kho*; from 2596 and 5594; to *cool down* (*off*), i.e. *refresh:*—cool.

From *katá* (2596), an intensive, and *psúchō* (5594), to cool. To cool, refresh. Used only in Lk 16:24.

Syn.: *anapsúchō* (404), to refresh.

2712. κατείδωλος, kateidōlos, *kat-i´-do-los*; from 2596 (intensive) and 1497; *utter idolatrous:*—wholly given to idolatry.

Adjective from *katá* (2596), an intensive, and *eídōlon* (1497), idol. Full of idols. Used only in Ac 17:16.

2713. κατέναντι, katenanti, *kat-en´-an-tee*; from 2596 and 1725; *directly opposite:*—before, over against.

2714. κατενώπιον, katenōpion, *kat-en-o´-pee-on*; from 2596 and 1799; *directly in front of:*—before (the presence of), in the sight of.

2715. κατεξουσιάζω, katexousiazō, *kat-ex-oo-see-ad´-zo*; from 2596 and 1850; to *have* (*wield*) *full privilege over:*—exercise authority.

2716. κατεργάζομαι, katergazomai, *kat-er-gad´-zom-ahee*; from 2596 and 2038; to *work fully*, i.e. *accomplish*; (by implication) to *finish*, *fashion:*—cause, do (deed), perform, work (out).

2717. *This number was omitted in Strong's Dictionary of the Greek Testament.*

2718. κατέρχομαι, katerchomai, *kat-er´-khom-ahee*; from 2596 and 2064 (including its alternate); to *come* (or *go*) *down* (literal or figurative):—come (down), depart, descend, go down, land.

2719. κατεσθίω, katesthiō, *kat-es-thee´-o*; from 2596 and 2068 (including its alternate); to *eat down,* i.e. *devour* (literal or figurative):—devour.

2720. κατευθύνω, kateuthunō, *kat-yoo-thoo´-no*; from 2596 and 2116; to *straighten fully,* i.e. (figurative) *direct:*—guide, direct.

2721. κατεφίστημι, katephistēmi, *kat-ef-is´-tay-mee*; from 2596 and 2186; to *stand over against,* i.e. *rush upon* (*assault*):—make insurrection against.

2722. κατέχω, katechō, *kat-ekh´-o*; from 2596 and 2192; to *hold down* (*fast*), in various applications (literal or figurative):—have, hold (fast), keep (in memory), let, × make toward, possess, retain, seize on, stay, take, withhold.

From *katá* (2596), an intensive, and *échō* (2192), to have, hold. Hold fast, retain, or hold down:

(I) To retain, detain a person (Lk 4:42; Phm 13). Used in the sense of to hinder, to repress (2Th 2:6, 7).

(II) To possess, i.e. to hold in secure possession (1Co 7:30; 2Co 6:10). Romans 1:18 is probably to be understood as possessing a knowledge of the truth, but living in unrighteousness.

(III) Figuratively: to hold fast in one's mind and heart (Lk 8:15; 1Co 11:2; 15:2; 1Th 5:21; Heb 3:6, 14; 10:23 [cf. Ro 7:6]). In the passive: to be held fast, bound, e.g., by a law (Ro 7:6), by a disease (Jn 5:4).

(IV) As a nautical term, to hold a ship firm toward the land, i.e. to steer toward land (Ac 27:40).

(V) By implication: to lay fast hold of, to seize (Mt 21:38; Lk 14:9).

Deriv.: *akatáschetos* (183), unrestrainable, unruly; *katáschesis* (2697), possession.

Syn.: *katalambánō* (2638), to comprehend, to apprehend; *kratéō* (2902), to hold fast; *lambánō* (2983), to lay hold of; *piázō* (4084), to lay hold of forcefully.

2723. κατηγορέω, katēgoreō, *kat-ay-gor-eh´-o*; from 2725; to *be a plaintiff,* i.e. to *charge* with some offence:—accuse, object.

From *katá* (2596), against, and *agoreúō* (n.f.), to speak. To speak openly against, to condemn or accuse mainly in a legal sense (Mt 12:10; Mk 3:2; 15:3; Lk 23:2, 10, 14; Jn 5:45; 8:6; Ac 22:30; 24:2, 8, 19; 25:5, 11; 28:19; Ro 2:15; Rev 12:10).

Deriv.: *katēgoría* (2724), accusation, incrimination; *katégoros* (2725), accuser.

2724. κατηγορία, katēgoria, *kat-ay-gor-ee´-ah*; from 2725; a *complaint* ("category"), i.e. criminal *charge:*—accusation (× -ed).

Noun from *katēgoréō* (2723), to accuse. Accusation, incrimination of a person (Lk 6:7; Jn 18:29; 1Ti 5:19; Tit 1:6).

Syn.: *aitía* (156), cause, accusation; *aitíama* (157), a complaint or accusation; *égklēma* (1462), accusation.

2725. κατήγορος, katēgoros, *kat-ay´-gor-os*; from 2596 and 58; *against* one in the *assembly,* i.e. a *complainant* at law; specially *Satan:*—accuser.

Noun from *katēgoréō* (2723), to accuse. Accuser (Jn 8:10; Ac 23:30, 35; 24:8; 25:16, 18; Rev 12:10).

Syn.: *diábolos* (1228), slanderer, the devil.

2726. κατήφεια, katēpheia, *kat-ay´-fi-ah*; from a compound of 2596 and perhaps a derivative of the base of 5316 (meaning *downcast* in look); *demureness,* i.e. (by implication) *sadness:*—heaviness.

2727. κατηχέω, katēcheō, *kat-ay-kheh´-o*; from 2596 and 2279; to *sound down* into the ears, i.e. (by implication) to *indoctrinate* ("catechize") or (genitive) to *apprise* of:—inform, instruct, teach.

2728. κατιόω, katioō, *kat-ee-o´-o*; from 2596 and a derivative of 2447; to *rust down,* i.e. *corrode:*—canker.

2729. κατισχύω, katischuō, *kat-is-khoo´-o*; from 2596 and 2480; to *overpower:*—prevail (against).

2730. κατοικέω, katoikeō, *kat-oy-keh´-o*; from 2596 and 3611; to *house permanently*, i.e. *reside* (literal or figurative):—dwell (-er), inhabitant (-ter).

From *katá* (2596), an intensive, and *oikéō* (3611), to dwell. To settle down in a fixed dwelling, to dwell permanently:

(I) To dwell permanently in, inhabit a house or place (Mt 2:23; 4:13; 12:45; Lk 13:4; Ac 1:20; 7:4; Heb 11:9; Rev 3:10; 6:10; 17:8).

(II) Metaphorically of God (Ac 7:48; 17:24); of Christ as being ever present by His Spirit in the hearts of Christians (Eph 3:17); of the fullness of the Godhead which was in Jesus (Col 1:19; 2:9); of the Spirit dwelling in man (Jas 4:5); of the righteousness dwelling in the new heavens and the new earth (2Pe 3:13).

Deriv.: *egkatoikéō* (1460), to dwell among; *katoíkēsis* (2731), the act of coming to dwell, a dwelling, habitation; *katoikētérion* (2732), a habitation; *katoikía* (2733), habitation, house.

Syn.: *enoikéō* (1774), to dwell in; *kataskēnóō* (2681), to pitch one's tent and lodge in it; *ménō* (3306), to abide, remain; *perioikéō* (4039), to dwell around; *skēnóō* (4637), to live in a tent; *sunoikéō* (4924), to dwell with.

2731. κατοίκησις, katoikēsis, *kat-oy´-kay-sis*; from 2730; *residence* (properly, the act; but by implication concretely, the mansion):—dwelling.

2732. κατοικητήριον, katoikētērion, *kat-oy-kay-tay´-ree-on*; from a derivative of 2730; a *dwelling-place*:—habitation.

2733. κατοικία, katoikia, *kat-oy-kee´-ah*; *residence* (properly, the condition; but by implication, the abode itself):—habitation.

2734. κατοπτρίζομαι, katoptrizomai, *kat-op-trid´-zom-ahee*; middle from a compound of 2596 and a derivative of 3700 [compare 2072]; to *mirror oneself*, i.e. to *see reflected* (figurative):—behold as in a glass.

2735. κατόρθωμα, katorthōma, *kat-or´-tho-mah*; from a compound of 2596 and a derivative of 3717 [compare 1357]; something *made fully upright*, i.e. (figurative) *rectification* (specially *good* public *administration*):—very worthy deed.

2736. κάτω, katō, *kat´-o*; also (comparative) **κατωτέρω, katōterō,** *kat-o-ter´-o* [compare 2737]; adverb from 2596; *downwards:*—beneath, bottom, down, under.

Adverb of place, from *katá* (2596), down. Downwards, below. The comparative is *katóteros* (2737), lower:

(I) Of place, implying motion: down (Mt 4:6; Lk 4:9; Jn 8:6; Ac 20:9; Sept.: Ecc 3:21; Isa 37:31); below, underneath (Mt 27:51; Mk 14:66; 15:38; Ac 2:19). Used as an adj.: that which is below, i.e. earthly (Jn 8:23).

(II) Of time: comparatively, *katōtérō*, below a certain age (Mt 2:16).

Deriv.: *hupokátō* (5270), under.

2737. κατώτερος, katōteros, *kat-o´-ter-os*; comparative from 2736; *inferior* (locally, of Hades):—lower.

2738. καῦμα, kauma, *kow´-mah*; from 2545; properly a *burn* (concrete), but used (abstract) of a *glow:*—heat.

2739. καυματίζω, kaumatizō, *kow-mat-id´-zo*; from 2738; to *burn:*—scorch.

2740. καῦσις, kausis, *kow´-sis*; from 2545; *burning* (the act):—be burned.

2741. καυσόω, kausoō, *kow-so´-o*; from 2740; to *set on fire:*—with fervent heat.

2742. καύσων, kausōn, *kow´-sone*; from 2741; a *glare:*—(burning) heat.

2743. καυτηριάζω, kautēriazō, *kow-tay-ree-ad´-zo*; from a derivative of 2545; to *brand* ("cauterize"), i.e. (by implication) to *render unsensitive* (figurative):—sear with a hot iron.

2744. καυχάομαι, kauchaomai, *kow-khah´-om-ahee*; from some (obsolete) base akin to that of **αὐχέω, aucheō** (to *boast*) and 2172; to *vaunt* (in a good or a bad sense):—(make) boast, glory, joy, rejoice.

2745. καύχημα, kauchēma, *kow´-khay-mah*; from 2744; a *boast* (properly, the object; by implication, the act) in a good or a bad sense:—boasting, (whereof) to glory (of), glorying, rejoice (-ing).

2746. καύχησις, kauchēsis, *kow´-khay-sis*; from 2744; *boasting* (properly, the act; by implication, the object), in a good or a bad sense:—boasting, whereof I may glory, glorying, rejoicing.

2747. Κεγχρεαί, Kegchreai, *keng-khreh-a´hee*; probably from **κέγχρος,** *Kegchros* (*millet*); *Cenchre´*, a port of Corinth:—Cenchrea.

2748. Κεδρών, Kedrōn, *ked-rone´*; of Hebrew origin [6939]; *Cedron* (i.e. *Kidron*), a brook near Jerusalem:—Cedron.

2749. κεῖμαι, keimai, *ki´-mahee*; middle of a primary verb; to *lie* outstretched (literal or figurative):—be (appointed, laid up, made, set), lay, lie. Compare 5087.

To lie, be laid down:

(**I**) To lie down, be laid down (Mt 28:6; Lk 2:12, 16; 23:53; 24:12; Jn 11:41; 20:5–7, 12; 21:9).

(**II**) To be placed or set (Mt 5:14; Jn 2:6; 19:29; 2Co 3:15; Rev 4:2); to be laid, applied, e.g., an ax laid to a tree (Mt 3:10; Lk 3:9); to be laid, as a foundation (1Co 3:11); to be stored up (Lk 12:19); to be set, appointed (Lk 2:34; Php 1:17; 1Th 3:3); to be made or promulgated as a law (1Ti 1:9).

(**III**) To be in the power of someone (1Jn 5:19).

Deriv.: *anákeimai* (345), to rest on; *antíkeimai* (480), to lie over against or to oppose; *apókeimai* (606), to be laid, reserved, appointed; *epíkeimai* (1945), to rest upon, impose, be instant, press upon; *katákeimai* (2621), to lie down; *kṓmē* (2968), a village; *parákeimai* (3873), to lie ready; *períkeimai* (4029), to lie around; *prókeimai* (4295), to lie before, set forth, to lie in front of.

Syn.: *kataklínō* (2625), to recline, sit down to eat.

2750. κειρία, keiria, *ki-ree´-ah*; of uncertain affinity; a *swathe*, i.e. *winding-sheet*:—graveclothes.

2751. κείρω, keirō, *ki´-ro*; a primary verb; to *shear*:—shear (-er).

2752. κέλευμα, keleuma, *kel´-yoo-mah*; from 2753; a *cry* of incitement:—shout.

2753. κελεύω, keleuō, *kel-yoo´-o*; from a primary **κέλλω,** *kellō* (to *urge* on); "hail"; to *incite* by word, i.e. *order*:—bid, (at, give) command (-ment).

2754. κενοδοξία, kenodoxia, *ken-od-ox-ee´-ah*; from 2755; *empty glorying*, i.e. *self-conceit*:—vain-glory.

2755. κενόδοξος, kenodoxos, *ken-od´-ox-os*; from 2756 and 1391; *vainly glorifying*, i.e. *self-conceited*:—desirous of vain-glory.

2756. κενός, kenos, *ken-os´*; apparently a primary word; *empty* (literal or figurative):—empty, (in) vain.

(**I**) Empty, the opposite of *pleres* (4134), full (Mk 12:3; Lk 1:53; 20:10, 11).

(**II**) Figuratively, meaning empty, vain: fruitless, without usefulness or success (Ac 4:25; 1Co 15:10, 14, 58; 2Co 6:1; Gal 2:2; Php 2:16; 1Th 2:1; 3:5).

(**III**) Of that in which there is nothing of truth or reality, false, fallacious, e.g., empty words meaning false words, deceitful (Eph 5:6; Col 2:8); of persons, meaning empty, foolish (Jas 2:20).

Deriv.: *kenódoxos* (2755), self-conceited; *kenophōnía* (2757), empty speaking; *kenóō* (2758), to be in vain; *kenós* (2761), in vain.

2757. κενοφωνία, kenophōnia, *ken-of-o-nee´-ah*; from a presumed compound of 2756 and 5456; *empty sounding*, i.e. *fruitless discussion*:—vain.

Noun from *kenós* (2756), vain, and *phōnē* (5456), a voice. Empty or fruitless speaking (1Ti 6:20; 2Ti 2:16).

2758. κενόω, kenoō, *ken-o´-o*; from 2756; to *make empty*, i.e. (figurative) to *abase, neutralize, falsify*:—make (of no effect, of no reputation, void), be in vain.

From *kenós* (2756), empty, void. To make empty, to empty. In the NT, used figuratively:

(**I**) To empty oneself, i.e. divest oneself of rightful dignity by descending to an inferior condition, to abase oneself (Php 2:7).

(**II**) To make empty, vain, fruitless (Ro 4:14; 1Co 1:17). Hence to show that something is without ground, fallacious (1Co 9:15; 2Co 9:3).

Syn.: *mataióō* (3154), to render vain, without meaning or fulfillment.

2759. κέντρον, kentron, *ken´-tron*; from **κεντέω,** *kenteō* (to *prick*); a *point* ("centre"), i.e. a *sting* (figurative, *poison*) or *goad* (figurative, divine *impulse*):—prick, sting.

2760. κεντυρίων, kenturiōn, *ken-too-ree´-ohn*; of Latin origin; a *centurion*, i.e. *captain* of one hundred soldiers:—centurion.

2761. κενῶς, kenōs, *ken-oce´*; adverb from 2756; *vainly*, i.e. *to no purpose*:—in vain.

2762. κεραία, keraia, *ker-ah´-yah*; feminine of a presumed derivative of the base of 2768; something *horn-like*, i.e. (special) the *apex* of a Hebrew letter (figurative, the least *particle*):—tittle.

2763. κεραμεύς, kerameus, *ker-am-yooce´*; from 2766; a *potter*:—potter.

2764. κεραμικός, keramikos, *ker-am-ik-os´*; from 2766; *made of clay*, i.e. *earthen*:—of a potter.

2765. κεράμιον, keramion, *ker-am´-ee-on*; neuter of a presumed derivative of 2766; an *earthenware* vessel, i.e. *jar*:—pitcher.

2766. κέραμος, keramos, *ker´-am-os*; probably from the base of 2767 (through the idea of *mixing* clay and water); *earthenware*, i.e. a *tile* (by analogy, a thin *roof* or *awning*):—tiling.

2767. κεράννυμι, kerannumi, *ker-an´-noo-mee*; a prolonged form of a more primary κεράω, keraō, *ker-ah´-o* (which is used in certain tenses); to *mingle*, i.e. (by implication) to *pour* out (for drinking):—fill, pour out. Compare 3396.

2768. κέρας, keras, *ker´-as*; from a primary κάρ, kar (the *hair* of the head); a *horn* (literal or figurative):—horn.

2769. κεράτιον, keration, *ker-at´-ee-on*; neuter of a presumed derivative of 2768; something *horned*, i.e. (special) the *pod* of the carob-tree:—husk.

2770. κερδαίνω, kerdainō, *ker-dah´ee-no*; from 2771; to *gain* (literal or figurative):—(get) gain, win.

2771. κέρδος, kerdos, *ker´-dos*; of uncertain affinity; *gain* (pecuniary or genitive):—gain, lucre.

2772. κέρμα, kerma, *ker´-mah*; from 2751; a *clipping* (*bit*), i.e. (special) a *coin*:—money.

2773. κερματιστής, kermatistēs, *ker-mat-is-tace´*; from a derivative of 2772; a *handler of coins*, i.e. *money-broker*:—changer of money.

2774. κεφάλαιον, kephalaion, *kef-al´-ah-yon*; neuter of a derivative of 2776; a *principal thing*, i.e. *main point*; specially an *amount* (of money):—sum.

2775. κεφαλαιόω, kephalaioō, *kef-al-ahee-o´-o*; from the same as 2774; (special) to *strike on the head*:—wound in the head.

2776. κεφαλή, kephalē, *kef-al-ay´*; probably from the primary κάπτω, kaptō (in the sense of *seizing*); the *head* (as the part most readily *taken* hold of), literal or figurative:—head.

Noun meaning the head:

(I) Particularly of a man or woman (Mt 6:17; 8:20; 27:30; Lk 7:38); as cut off (Mt 14:11; Mk 6:27); of animals (Rev 9:17, 19; 12:3); as the principal part, but emphatically for the whole person (Ac 18:6, "Your blood be upon your own heads," meaning the guilt for your destruction rests upon yourselves; Ro 12:20). Figuratively of things: the head, top, summit, e.g., the head of the corner, meaning the chief stone of the corner, the cornerstone, the same as *akrogōniaíos* (204), belonging to the extreme corner, chief corner (Mt 21:42; Mk 12:10; Lk 20:17; Ac 4:11; 1Pe 2:7).

(II) Figuratively of persons, i.e. the head, chief, one to whom others are subordinate, e.g., the husband in relation to his wife (1Co 11:3; Eph 5:23); of Christ in relation to His Church which is His body, and its members are His members (Eph 1:22; 4:15; 5:23; Col 1:18; 2:10, 19); of God in relation to Christ (1Co 11:3).

Deriv.: *apokephalízō* (607), to decapitate, behead; *kephalís* (2777), a knob, roll, volume; *perikephalaía* (4030), helmet.

Syn.: *hēgemṓn* (2232), a leader, ruler.

2777. κεφαλίς, kephalis, *kef-al-is´*; from 2776; properly a *knob*, i.e. (by implication) a *roll* (by extension from the *end* of a stick on which the manuscript was rolled):—volume.

2778. κῆνσος, kēnsos, *kane´-sos*; of Latin origin; properly an *enrollment* ("*census*"), i.e. (by implication) a *tax*:—tribute.

2779. κῆπος, kēpos, *kay´-pos*; of uncertain affinity; a *garden*:—garden.

2780. κηπουρός, **kēpouros,** *kay-poo-ros´*; from 2779 and οὖρος, *ouros* (a warden); a *garden-keeper,* i.e. *gardener:*—gardener.

2781. κηρίον, **kērion,** *kay-ree´-on*; diminutive from κηός, *kēos* (wax); a *cell* for honey, i.e. (collective) the *comb:*—[honey-] comb.

2782. κήρυγμα, **kērugma,** *kay´-roog-mah*; from 2784; a *proclamation* (especially of the gospel; (by implication) the *gospel* itself):—preaching.

Noun from *kērússō* (2784), to preach, discharge a herald's office, cry out, proclaim. Proclamation by a herald. In the NT, annunciation, preaching, spoken of prophets (Mt 12:41; Lk 11:32); of Christ and his apostles: preaching the gospel, public instruction (1Co 1:21; 2:4; 15:14; Tit 1:3); used by metonymy for the gospel preached (Ro 16:25; 2Ti 4:17).

Syn.: *aggelía* (31), a message, proclamation, news; *epaggelía* (1860), a promise, message.

2783. κῆρυξ, **kērux,** *kay´-roox*; from 2784; a *herald,* i.e. of divine truth (especially of the gospel):—preacher.

Noun from *kērússō* (2784), to preach. A herald, public crier. In the NT: a preacher, public instructor of the divine will and precepts, as Noah (2Pe 2:5), of the gospel, as Paul (1Ti 2:7; 2Ti 1:11).

2784. κηρύσσω, **kērussō,** *kay-roos´-so*; of uncertain affinity; to *herald* (as a public *crier*), especially divine truth (the gospel):—preach (-er), proclaim, publish.

To preach, to herald, proclaim:

(I) Generally, to proclaim, announce publicly (Mt 10:27; Lk 12:3; Ac 10:42; Rev 5:2). In the sense of to publish abroad, announce publicly (Mk 1:45; 5:20; 7:36; Lk 8:39).

(II) Especially to preach, publish, or announce religious truth, the gospel with its attendant privileges and obligations, the gospel dispensation:

(A) Generally of John the Baptist (Mt 3:1; Mk 1:4, 7; Lk 3:3; Ac 10:37); of Jesus (Mt 4:17, 23; 9:35; 11:1; Mk 1:14, 38, 39; Lk 4:44; 8:1; 1Pe 3:19); of apostles and teachers (Mt 10:7; 24:14; 26:13; Mk 3:14; 6:12; 13:10; 14:9; 16:15, 20; Lk 9:2; 24:47; Ac 20:25; 28:31; Ro 10:8, 14, 15; 1Co 9:27; 15:11; Gal 2:2; Col 1:23; 1Th 2:9; 2Ti 4:2). "To preach Christ" means to announce Him as

the Messiah and urge the reception of His gospel (Ac 8:5; 9:20; 19:13; 1Co 1:23; 15:12; 2Co 1:19; 4:5; 11:4; Php 1:15; 1Ti 3:16).

(B) In allusion to the Mosaic and prophetic institutions, to preach, teach (Lk 4:18, 19; Ac 15:21; Ro 2:21; Gal 5:11).

Deriv.: *kḗrugma* (2782), the message of a herald, denotes preaching, the substance of which is distinct from the act; *kḗrux* (2783), a herald, a preacher; *prokērússō* (4296), to proclaim before or ahead.

Syn.: *diaggéllō* (1229), to herald thoroughly, declare, preach, signify; *diamartúromai* (1263), to testify thoroughly; *euaggelízō* (2097), to proclaim the good news, evangelize; *kataggéllō* (2605), to proclaim, promulgate, declare; *parrēsiázomai* (3955), to speak or preach boldly.

2785. κῆτος, **kētos,** *kay´-tos*; probably from the base of 5490; a huge *fish* (as *gaping* for prey):—whale.

2786. Κηφᾶς, **Kēphas,** *kay-fas´*; of Chaldee origin [compare 3710]; *the Rock; Cephas* (i.e. *Kepha*), a surname of Peter:—Cephas.

2787. κιβωτός, **kibōtos,** *kib-o-tos´*; of uncertain derivative; a *box,* i.e. the sacred *ark* and that of Noah:—ark.

2788. κιθάρα, **kithara,** *kith-ar´-ah*; of uncertain affinity; a *lyre:*—harp.

2789. κιθαρίζω, **kitharizō,** *kith-ar-id´-zo*; from 2788; to *play on a lyre:*—harp.

2790. κιθαρῳδός, **kitharōidos,** *kith-ar-o-dos´*; from 2788 and a derivative of the same as 5603; a *lyre-singer* (*-player*), i.e. *harpist:*—harper.

2791. Κιλικία, **Kilikia,** *kil-ik-ee´-ah*; probably of foreign origin; *Cilicia,* a region of Asia Minor:—Cilicia.

2792. κινάμωμον, **kinamōmon,** *kin-am´-o-mon*; of foreign origin [compare 7076]; *cinnamon:*—cinnamon.

2793. κινδυνεύω, **kinduneuō,** *kin-doon-yoo´-o*; from 2794; to *undergo peril:*—be in danger, be (stand) in jeopardy.

2794. κίνδυνος, **kindunos,** *kin´-doo-nos*; of uncertain derivative; *danger:*—peril.

2795. κινέω, kineō, *kin-eh´-o*; from **κίω,** *kiō* (poetic for **εἶμι,** *eimi*, to go); to *stir* (transitive), literal or figurative:—(re-) move (-r), way.

2796. κίνησις, kinēsis, *kin´-ay-sis*; from 2795; a *stirring*:—moving.

2797. Κίς, Kis, *kis*; of Hebrew origin [7027]; *Cis* (i.e. *Kish*), an Israelite:—Cis.

2798. κλάδος, klados, *klad´-os*; from 2806; a *twig* or *bough* (as if broken off):—branch.

2799. κλαίω, klaiō, *klah´-yo*; of uncertain affinity; to *sob*, i.e. *wail* aloud (whereas 1145 is rather to *cry* silently):—bewail, weep.

2800. κλάσις, klasis, *klas´-is*; from 2806; *fracture* (the act):—breaking.

Noun from *kláō* (2806), to break. The act of breaking, particularly with reference to the bread in the Lord's Supper (Lk 24:35; Ac 2:42).

2801. κλάσμα, klasma, *klas´-mah*; from 2806; a *piece* (*bit*):—broken, fragment.

Noun from *kláō* (2806), to break. That which is broken off, a fragment, crumb; used of the fragments collected after the miraculous feedings (Mt 14:20; 15:37; Mk 6:43; 8:8, 19, 20; Lk 9:17; Jn 6:12, 13).

2802. Κλαύδη, Klaudē, *klow´-day*; of uncertain derivative; *Claude*, an island near Crete:—Clauda.

2803. Κλαυδία, Klaudia, *klow-dee´-ah*; feminine of 2804; *Claudia*, a Christian woman:—Claudia.

2804. Κλαύδιος, Klaudios, *klow´-dee-os*; of Latin origin; *Claudius*, the name of two Romans:—Claudius.

2805. κλαυθμός, klauthmos, *klowth-mos´*; from 2799; *lamentation*:—wailing, weeping, × wept.

2806. κλάω, klaō, *klah´-o*; a primary verb; to *break* (specially of bread):—break.

Verb meaning to break. In the NT, used only of the breaking of bread for distribution before a meal, the Jewish bread being in the form of thin cakes (Mt 14:19; 15:36; Mk 8:6, 19; Lk 24:30; Ac 27:35; Sept.: Jer 16:7); used in the Lord's Supper and *agápē* (26), love feast (Mt 26:26; Mk 14:22; Lk 22:19; Ac 2:46; 20:7, 11; 1Co 10:16; 11:24).

Deriv.: *ekkláō* (1575), to break off; *katakláō* (2622), to break bread; *kládos* (2798), branch; *klásis* (2800), the breaking; *klásma* (2801), that which is broken off, fragment, crumb; *kléma* (2814), branch.

Syn.: *katágnumi* (2608), to break, crack apart; *suntríbō* (4937), to shatter, break in pieces by crushing.

2807. κλείς, kleis, *klice*; from 2808; a *key* (as *shutting* a lock), literal or figurative:—key.

2808. κλείω, kleiō, *kli´-o*; a primary verb; to *close* (literal or figurative):—shut (up).

2809. κλέμμα, klemma, *klem´-mah*; from 2813; *stealing* (properly the thing stolen, but used of the act):—theft.

2810. Κλεόπας, Kleopas, *kleh-op´-as*; probably contrete from **Κλεόπατρος,** *Kleopatros* (compound of 2811 and 3962); *Cleopas*, a Christian:—Cleopas.

2811. κλέος, kleos, *kleh´-os*; from a shorter form of 2564; *renown* (as if *being called*):—glory.

2812. κλέπτης, kleptēs, *klep´-tace*; from 2813; a *stealer* (literal or figurative):—thief. Compare 3027.

From *kléptō* (2813), to steal. Thief (Mt 6:19, 20; Lk 12:33, 39; 1Co 6:10; 1Th 5:2, 4; 1Pe 4:15; 2Pe 3:10; Rev 3:3; 16:15). Occurring along with *lēstḗs* (3027), robber (Jn 10:1, 8). The *kléptēs* steals secretly, as would a burglar (Mt 24:43) or an embezzler (Jn 12:6), while the *lēstḗs* robs forcefully with violence. Figuratively, of false teachers or deceivers who steal men away from the truth (Jn 10:8, 10).

Syn.: *hárpax* (727), extortioner.

2813. κλέπτω, kleptō, *klep´-to*; a primary verb; to *filch*:—steal.

2814. κλῆμα, klēma, *klay´-mah*; from 2806; a *limb* or *shoot* (as if *broken* off):—branch.

Noun from *kláō* (2806), to break. A shoot, sprout, branch, such as are easily broken off. In the NT, of the vine: a shoot, tendril (Jn 15:2, 4–6; Sept.: Eze 15:2; 17:6, 7).

Syn.: *kládos* (2798), young tender shoot, branch; *stoibás* (4746), a branch full of leaves or a layer of leaves.

2815. Κλήμης, Klēmēs, *klay´-mace*; of Latin origin; *merciful; Clemes* (i.e. *Clemens*), a Christian:—Clement.

2816. κληρονομέω, klēronomeō, *klay-ron-om-eh´-o*; from 2818; to *be* an *heir* to (literal or figurative):—be heir, (obtain by) inherit (-ance).

From *klēronómos* (2818), an heir. To be an heir, to inherit. In the Septuagint OT, used originally of receiving an inheritance by lot, of the division of the land of Canaan among the twelve tribes (Nu 26:55; Jos 16:4). Hence, in the NT generally:

(I) To inherit, to be heir, in an absolute sense (Gal 4:30).

(II) To obtain, acquire, possess. In the NT, spoken of the friends of God as receiving admission to the kingdom of heaven and its attendant privileges (Mt 5:5; 25:34). To inherit eternal life (Mt 19:29; Mk 10:17; Lk 10:25; 18:18). Used with the negative to describe those who will not inherit (1Co 6:9, 10; 15:50; Gal 5:21). See also Heb 1:4, 14; 6:12; 12:17; 1Pe 3:9; Rev 21:7.

Syn.: *klēróō* (2820), to determine by lot.

2817. κληρονομία, klēronomia, *klay-ron-om-ee´-ah*; from 2818; *heirship*, i.e. (concrete) a *patrimony* or (genitive) a *possession*:—inheritance.

Noun from *klēronómos* (2818), an heir. Inheritance (Mt 21:38; Mk 12:7; Lk 12:13; 20:14). Generally: portion, possession, especially of the land of Canaan as the possession of Abraham and his descendants (Ac 7:5; Heb 11:8); hence figuratively of admission to the kingdom of God and its attendant privileges (Ac 20:32; Gal 3:18; Eph 1:14, 18; 5:5; Col 3:24; Heb 9:15; 1Pe 1:4). See *klēronoméō* (2816), to be an heir.

2818. κληρονόμος, klēronomos, *klay-ron-om´-os*; from 2819 and the base of 3551 (in its original sense of *partitioning*, i.e. [reflexive] *getting* by apportionment); a *sharer by lot*, i.e. an *inheritor* (literal or figurative); (by implication) a *possessor*:—heir.

Noun from *klḗros* (2819), lot, and *nómos* (3551), law, anything established. An heir, originally of an inheritance divided by lot, but later spoken of any heir (Mt 21:38; Mk 12:7; Lk 20:14; Gal 4:1). Figuratively, a partaker of the blessings which God bestows upon His children, implying admission to the kingdom of heaven and its privileges (Ro 4:13, 14; 8:17; Gal 3:29; 4:7; Tit 3:7; Heb 1:2; 6:17; 11:7; Jas 2:5). See *klēronoméō* (2816), to be an heir.

Deriv.: *klēronoméō* (2816), to be an heir; *klēronomía* (2817), that which constitutes one as heir, inheritance; *sugklēronómos* (4789), he who participates in the same inheritance or lot, joint-heir.

2819. κλῆρος, klēros, *klay´-ros*; probably from 2806 (through the idea of using *bits* of wood, etc., for the purpose); a *die* (for drawing chances); (by implication) a *portion* (as if so secured); by extension an *acquisition* (especially a *patrimony*, figurative):—heritage, inheritance, lot, part.

Noun probably from *kláō* (2806), to break. A lot:

(I) A lot, die, anything used in determining chances. Spoken of the lot cast by the soldiers gambling for Christ's clothing at the cross (Mt 27:35; Mk 15:24; Lk 23:34; Jn 19:24); spoken of the lot used to choose Judas's successor (Ac 1:26).

(II) A lot, allotment, portion, or share to which one is appointed by lot or otherwise (Ac 1:17, 25; 8:21). Hence, generally, a portion, possession, heritage (Ac 26:18; Col 1:12; 1Pe 5:3).

Deriv.: *klēronómos* (2818), one who has an inheritance, a lot; *klēróō* (2820), to cast lots, determine by lot; *naúklēros* (3490), an owner of a ship; *holóklēros* (3648), an entire portion, intact.

Syn.: *merís* (3310), part, share; *méros* (3313), a part, portion of the whole.

2820. κληρόω, klēroō, *klay-ro´-o*; from 2819; to *allot*, i.e. (figurative) to *assign* (a privilege):—obtain an inheritance.

From *klḗros* (2819), a lot. In the passive, to obtain an inheritance, as through the casting of lots. Only in Eph 1:11. See *klēronoméō* (2816), to be an heir.

Deriv.: *prosklēróō* (4345), to give or assign by lot.

2821. κλῆσις, klēsis, *klay´-sis*; from a shorter form of 2564; an *invitation* (figurative):—calling.

Noun from *kaléō* (2564), to call. A call, an invitation to a banquet.

In the NT, used metaphorically: a call, invitation to the kingdom of God and its privileges, i.e. the divine call by which Christians are introduced into the privileges of the gospel (Ro 11:29; 1Co 1:26; 7:20; Eph 1:18; 4:1, 4; Php 3:14; 2Th 1:11; 2Ti 1:9; Heb 3:1; 2Pe 1:10).

2822. κλητός, klētos, *klay-tos'*; from the same as 2821; *invited,* i.e. *appointed,* or (special) a *saint:*—called.

Verbal adj. from *kaléō* (2564), to call. Called, invited, e.g., to a banquet as guests. Hence In the NT, used figuratively: called, invited to the kingdom of heaven and its privileges: generally (Mt 20:16; 22:14); also emphatically of those who have obeyed this call, i.e. saints, Christians (Ro 1:6, 7; 1Co 1:2, 24; Jude 1; Rev 17:14). In the sense of appointed, chosen to an office (Ro 1:1; 1Co 1:1).

2823. κλίβανος, klibanos, *klib'-an-os*; of uncertain derivative; an earthen *pot* used for baking in:—oven.

2824. κλίμα, klima, *klee'-mah*; from 2827; a *slope,* i.e. (special) a *"clime"* or *tract* of country:—part, region.

2825. κλίνη, klinē, *klee'-nay*; from 2827; a *couch* (for sleep, sickness, sitting or eating):—bed, table.

2826. κλινίδιον, klinidion, *klin-id'-ee-on*; neuter of a presumed derivative of 2825; a *pallet* or *little couch:*—bed.

2827. κλίνω, klinō, *klee'-no*; a primary verb; to *slant* or *slope,* i.e. *incline* or *recline* (literal or figurative):—bow (down), be far spent, lay, turn to flight, wear away.

2828. κλισία, klisia, *klee-see'-ah*; from a derivative of 2827; properly *reclination,* i.e. (concrete and specific) a *party* at a meal:—company.

2829. κλοπή, klopē, *klop-ay'*; from 2813; *stealing:*—theft.

2830. κλύδων, kludōn, *kloo'-dohn*; from κλύζω, *kluzō* (to *billow* or *dash* over); a *surge* of the sea (literal or figurative):—raging, wave.

2831. κλυδωνίζομαι, kludōnizomai, *kloo-do-nid'-zom-ahee*; middle from 2830; to *surge,* i.e. (figurative) to *fluctuate:*—toss to and fro.

2832. Κλωπᾶς, Klōpas, *klo-pas'*; of Chaldee origin (corresponding to 256); *Clopas,* an Israelite:—Clopas.

2833. κνήθω, knēthō, *knay'-tho*; from a primary κνάω, *knaō* (to *scrape*); to *scratch,* i.e. (by implication) to *tickle:*— × itching.

2834. Κνίδος, Knidos, *knee'-dos*; probably of foreign origin; *Cnidus,* a place in Asia Minor:—Cnidus.

2835. κοδράντης, kodrantēs, *kod-ran'-tace*; of Latin origin; a *quadrans,* i.e. the fourth part of an *assarius* (787):—farthing.

2836. κοιλία, koilia, *koy-lee'-ah*; from κοῖλος, *koilos* (*"hollow"*); a *cavity,* i.e. (special) the *abdomen;* (by implication) the *matrix;* (figurative) the *heart:*—belly, womb.

2837. κοιμάω, koimaō, *koy-mah'-o*; from 2749; to *put to sleep,* i.e. (passive or reflexive) to *slumber;* (figurative) to *decease:*—(be a-, fall a-, fall on) sleep, be dead.

2838. κοίμησις, koimēsis, *koy'-may-sis*; from 2837; *sleeping,* i.e. (by implication) *repose:*—taking of rest.

2839. κοινός, koinos, *koy-nos'*; probably from 4862; *common,* i.e. (literally) *shared* by all or several, or (ceremonial) *profane:*—common, defiled, unclean, unholy.

Adjective meaning common.

(**I**) Particularly, pertaining equally to all (Ac 2:44; 4:32); spoken of the common faith (Tit 1:4) and of the common salvation (Jude 3).

(**II**) In the Levitical sense: not permitted by the Mosaic precepts, and therefore common, i.e. not sacred; hence the same as ceremonially unclean, unholy, profane (Mk 7:2; Ac 10:14, 28; 11:8; Ro 14:14). Figuratively, unholy, unconsecrated (Heb 10:29).

Deriv.: *koinóō* (2840), to make common, unclean; *koinōnós* (2844), an associate, companion, partner, participant.

Syn.: *akáthartos* (169), unclean; *anósios* (462), unholy, profane.

2840. κοινόω, koinoō, *koy-no'-o*; from 2839; to *make* (or *consider*) *profane* (ceremonial):—call common, defile, pollute, unclean.

From *koinós* (2839), common. To make common, unclean, pollute or defile (Mt 15:11, 18, 20; Mk 7:15, 18, 20, 23; Ac 21:28; Heb 9:13; Rev 21:27); to pronounce or call common or unclean (Ac 10:15; 11:9). See *koinós* (2839, II), common.

Syn.: *miaínō* (3392), to stain, defile; *molúnō* (3435), to besmear; *spilóō* (4695), to defile, spot.

2841. κοινωνέω, koinōneō, *koy-no-neh´-o*; from 2844; to *share* with others (object or subject):—communicate, distribute, be partaker.

From *koinōnós* (2844), an associate, partaker. To be a partaker of or in anything with someone else, i.e. to share in common (Ro 15:27; Heb 2:14); to share resources with others (Ro 12:13; Gal 6:6; Php 4:15); in an adverse sense, to share guilt (1Ti 5:22; 2Jn 11).

Deriv.: *koinōnía* (2842), fellowship; *sugkoinōnéō* (4790), to share with.

Syn.: *metéchō* (3348), to partake of, share; *summerízomai* (4829), to have a share in, be a partaker with.

2842. κοινωνία, koinōnia, *koy-nohn-ee´-ah*; from 2844; *partnership*, i.e. (literal) *participation*, or (social) *intercourse*, or (pecuniary) *benefaction*:—(to) communicate (-ation), communion, (contri-) distribution, fellowship.

Noun from *koinōnéō* (2841), to share in. Act of partaking, sharing, because of a common interest:

(I) Participation, communion, fellowship (Ac 2:42; 1Co 1:9; 10:16; 2Co 6:14; 13:14; Gal 2:9; Eph 3:9; Php 1:5; 2:1; 3:10; Phm 6; 1Jn 1:3, 6, 7).

(II) Sharing, distribution. In the NT, a metonym for contribution, collection of money in behalf of poorer churches (Ro 15:26; 2Co 8:4; 9:13; Heb 13:16).

Syn.: *eleēmosúnē* (1654), compassion, beneficence, alms; *metochḗ* (3352), partnership.

2843. κοινωνικός, koinōnikos, *koy-no-nee-kos´*; from 2844; *communicative*, i.e. (pecuniarily) *liberal*:—willing to communicate.

2844. κοινωνός, koinōnos, *koy-no-nos´*; from 2839; a *sharer*, i.e. *associate*:—companion, × fellowship, partaker, partner.

Adjective from *koinós* (2839), common. A partaker, partner, companion:

(I) Generally, of partners (Mt 23:20; Lk 5:10; 2Co 8:23; Phm 17).

(II) Figuratively, of those who eat meats offered to idols, partakers or companions either with God or with demons (1Co 10:18, 20).

(III) Figuratively, of those who serve Christ, partakers of divine blessings (2Co 1:7; 1Pe 5:1; 2Pe 1:4).

Deriv.: *koinōnéō* (2841), to share in; *koinōnikós* (2843), communicative, generous; *sugkoinōnós* (4791), joint participator, companion.

Syn.: *métochos* (3353), partner.

2845. κοίτη, koitē, *koy´-tay*; from 2749; a *couch*; by extension *cohabitation*; (by implication) the male *sperm*:—bed, chambering, × conceive.

2846. κοιτών, koitōn, *koy-tone´*; from 2845; a *bedroom*:— + chamberlain.

2847. κόκκινος, kokkinos, *kok´-kee-nos*; from 2848 (from the *kernel*-shape of the insect); *crimson*-coloured:—scarlet (colour, coloured).

2848. κόκκος, kokkos, *kok´-kos*; apparently a primary word; a *kernel* of seed:—corn, grain.

2849. κολάζω, kolazō, *kol-ad´-zo*; from **κόλος, kolos** (*dwarf*); properly to *curtail*, i.e. (figurative) to *chastise* (or *reserve* for infliction):—punish.

2850. κολακεία, kolakeia, *kol-ak-i´-ah*; from a derivative of **κόλαξ, kolax** (a *fawner*); *flattery*:— × flattering.

2851. κόλασις, kolasis, *kol´-as-is*; from 2849; penal *infliction*:—punishment, torment.

Noun from *kolázō* (2849), to punish. Mutilation, pruning. In the NT, punishment. Spoken of eternal punishment for those condemned by Christ (Mt 25:46); spoken of the temporary torment produced by fear in the soul of one conscious of sin before the love of God brings peace at salvation (1Jn 4:18).

Syn.: *díkē* (1349), judgement, the execution of a sentence; *ekdíkēsis* (1557), vengeance, punishment; *epitimía* (2009), penalty.

2852. κολαφίζω, kolaphizō, *kol-af-id´-zo*; from a derivative of the base of 2849; to *rap* with the fist:—buffet.

2853. κολλάω, kollaō, *kol-lah´-o*; from **κόλλα, kolla** ("*glue*"); to *glue*, i.e. (passive or reflexive) to *stick* (figurative):—cleave, join (self), keep company.

2854. κολλούριον, kollourion, *kol-loo´-ree-on*; neuter of a presumed derivative of **κολλύρα, kollura** (a *cake*; probably akin to the base of 2853); properly a *poultice* (as made of or in the form of *crackers*), i.e. (by analogy) a *plaster*:—eyesalve.

2855. κολλυβιστής, **kollubistēs,** *kol-loo-bis-tace´*; from a presumed derivative of κόλλυβος, *kollubos* (a small *coin*; probably akin to 2854); a *coin-dealer*:—(money-) changer.

2856. κολοβόω, **koloboō,** *kol-ob-o´-o*; from a derivative of the base of 2849; to *dock,* i.e. (figurative) *abridge*:—shorten.

2857. Κολοσσαί, **Kolossai,** *kol-os-sah´ee*; apparently feminine plural of κολοσσός, *Kolossos* ("*colossal*"); *Colossæ,* a place in Asia Minor:—Colosse.

2858. Κολοσσαεύς, **Kolossaeus,** *kol-os-sayoos´*; from 2857; a *Colossæan,* i.e. inhabitant of Colossæ:—Colossian.

2859. κόλπος, **kolpos,** *kol´-pos*; apparently a primary word; the *bosom*; (by analogy) a *bay*:—bosom, creek.

2860. κολυμβάω, **kolumbaō,** *kol-oom-bah´-o*; from κόλυμβος, *kolumbos* (a *diver*); to *plunge* into water:—swim.

2861. κολυμβήθρα, **kolumbēthra,** *kol-oom-bay´-thrah*; from 2860; a *diving-place,* i.e. *pond* for bathing (or swimming):—pool.

2862. κολωνία, **kolōnia,** *kol-o-nee´-ah*; of Latin origin; a Roman "*colony*" for veterans:—colony.

2863. κομάω, **komaō,** *kom-ah´-o*; from 2864; to *wear tresses* of hair:—have long hair.

2864. κόμη, **komē,** *kom´-ay*; apparently from the same as 2865; the *hair* of the head (*locks,* as *ornamental,* and thus differing from 2359, which properly denotes merely the *scalp*):—hair.

2865. κομίζω, **komizō,** *kom-id´-zo*; from a primary κομέω, *komeō* (to *tend,* i.e. take care of); properly to *provide* for, i.e. (by implication) to *carry* off (as if from harm; genitive *obtain*):—bring, receive.

2866. κομψότερον, **kompsoteron,** *komp-sot´-er-on*; neuter comparative of a derivative of the base of 2865 (meaning properly *well dressed,* i.e. *nice*); (figurative) *convalescent*:— + began to amend.

2867. κονιάω, **koniaō,** *kon-ee-ah´-o*; from κονία, *konia* (*dust*; by analogy, *lime*); to *whitewash*:—whiten.

2868. κονιορτός, **koniortos,** *kon-ee-or-tos´*; from the base of 2867 and ὄρνυμι, *ornumi* (to "*rouse*"); *pulverulence* (as *blown* about):—dust.

2869. κοπάζω, **kopazō,** *kop-ad´-zo*; from 2873; to *tire,* i.e. (figurative) to *relax*:—cease.

From *kópos* (2873), labour, fatigue. To be weary; hence to relax, to remit, to cease. In the NT, of the wind: to become calm (Mt 14:32; Mk 4:39; 6:51).

Syn.: *katapaúō* (2664), to cease or rest completely; *paúō* (3973), to stop.

2870. κοπετός, **kopetos,** *kop-et-os´*; from 2875; *mourning* (properly by *beating* the breast):—lamentation.

2871. κοπή, **kopē,** *kop-ay´*; from 2875; *cutting,* i.e. *carnage*:—slaughter.

2872. κοπιάω, **kopiaō,** *kop-ee-ah´-o*; from a derivative of 2873; to *feel fatigue*; (by implication) to *work hard*:—(bestow) labour, toil, be wearied.

2873. κόπος, **kopos,** *kop´-os*; from 2875; a *cut,* i.e. (by analogy) *toil* (as *reducing* the strength), literal or figurative; (by implication) *pains*:—labour, + trouble, weariness.

From *kóptō* (2875), to strike. Toil, labour, from an original meaning of beating, wailing, grief with beating the breast. In the NT, toil, labour, i.e. wearisome effort (Jn 4:38; 1Co 3:8; 15:58; 2Co 6:5; 10:15; 11:23, 27; 1Th 1:3; 2:9; 3:5; 2Th 3:8; Heb 6:10; Rev 2:2; 14:13). In the sense of trouble, vexation (Mt 26:10; Mk 14:6; Lk 11:7; 18:5; Gal 6:17).

Deriv.: *eukopóteros* (2123), easier, lighter; *kopázō* (2869), to tire, cease; *kopiáō* (2872), to feel fatigue from labour.

Syn.: *móchthos* (3449), the everyday word for human labour; *pónos* (4192), pain, work.

2874. κοπρία, **kopria,** *kop-ree´-ah*; from κόπρος, *kopros* (*ordure*; perhaps akin to 2875); *manure*:—dung (-hill).

2875. κόπτω, **koptō,** *kop´-to*; a primary verb; to *"chop"*; specially to *beat* the breast in grief:—cut down, lament, mourn, (be-) wail. Compare the base of 5114.

To cut, to strike, to smite.

(I) To cut off or down, as branches of a tree (Mt 21:8; Mk 11:8).

(II) In the middle: to strike or beat one's body, particularly the breast, with the hands in lamentation, to lament, wail (Mt 11:17; 24:30; Lk 23:27; Rev 1:7; 18:9).

Deriv.: *anakóptō* (348), to hinder, beat back; *apokóptō* (609), to cut off; *argurokópos* (695), silversmith; *egkóptō* (1465), to cut into, hinder; *ekkóptō* (1581), to cut or strike out; *katakóptō* (2629), to cut down; *kopetós* (2870), beating, mourning; *kopé* (2871), slaughter; *kópos* (2873), labour, weariness; *kōphós* (2974), deaf, dumb, speechless; *prokóptō* (4298), to advance, increase; *próskomma* (4348), offence, stumbling block; *proskóptō* (4350), to strike at, trip.

Syn.: *thrēnéō* (2354), to mourn, wail; *klaíō* (2799), to weep; *penthéō* (3996), to mourn; *stenázō* (4727), to groan.

2876. κόραξ, korax, *kor´-ax*; perhaps from 2880; a *crow* (from its *voracity*):—raven.

2877. κοράσιον, korasion, *kor-as´-ee-on*; neuter of a presumed derivative of **κόρη,** *korē* (a *maiden*); a (little) *girl*:—damsel, maid.

2878. κορβᾶν, korban, *kor-ban´*; and **κορβανᾶς, korbanas,** *kor-ban-as´*; of Hebrew and Chaldee origin respectively [7133]; a votive *offering* and *the offering*; a *consecrated present* (to the temple fund); by extension (the latter term) the *Treasury* itself, i.e. the room where the contribution boxes stood:—Corban, treasury.

2879. Κορέ, Kore, *kor-eh´*; of Hebrew origin [7141]; *Corè* (i.e. *Korach*), an Israelite:—Core.

2880. κορέννυμι, korennumi, *kor-en´-noo-mee*; a primary verb; to *cram*, i.e. *glut* or *sate*:—eat enough, full.

To sate, satisfy with food and drink. Passive: to be sated, to be full (Ac 27:38; 1Co 4:8).

Syn.: *gemízō* (1072), to fill; *empíplēmi* (1705), to fill full, satisfy, fill the hungry; *mestóō* (3325), to fill to the brim; *plḗthō* (4130), to fill; *plēróō* (4137), to make full, to fill; *chortázō* (5526), to fill or satisfy with food.

2881. Κορίνθιος, Korinthios, *kor-in´-thee-os*; from 2882; a *Corinthian*, i.e. inhabitant of Corinth:—Corinthian.

2882. Κόρινθος, Korinthos, *kor´-in-thos*; of uncertain derivative; *Corinthus*, a city of Greece:—Corinth.

2883. Κορνήλιος, Kornēlios, *kor-nay´-lee-os*; of Latin origin; *Cornelius*, a Roman:—Cornelius.

2884. κόρος, koros, *kor´-os*; of Hebrew origin [3734]; a *cor*, i.e. a specific measure:—measure.

2885. κοσμέω, kosmeō, *kos-meh´-o*; from 2889; to *put in* proper *order*, i.e. *decorate* (literal or figurative); specially to *snuff* (a wick):—adorn, garnish, trim.

2886. κοσμικός, kosmikos, *kos-mee-kos´*; from 2889 (in its secondary sense); *terrene* ("*cosmic*"), literal (*mundane*) or figurative (*corrupt*):—worldly.

From *kósmos* (2889), world. Worldly, terrestrial, that which belongs to the world. In the NT, it corresponds to the idea of *kósmos* (2889), world, as the opposite of heavenly and spiritual (Heb 9:1). Used figuratively in the sense of worldly, conforming to this world, belonging to the men of this world (Tit 2:12).

Syn.: *sarkikós* (4559), fleshly, carnal; *sōmatikós* (4984), bodily; *phusikós* (5446), physical.

2887. κόσμιος, kosmios, *kos´-mee-os*; from 2889 (in its primary sense); *orderly*, i.e. *decorous*:—of good behaviour, modest.

Adjective from *kósmos* (2889), order, arrangement. Well-ordered, decorous, modest, in a moral sense. Spoken of modest clothing (1Ti 2:9); spoken of modest behaviour (1Ti 3:2).

Syn.: *eulabḗs* (2126), reverent, circumspect; *hieroprepḗs* (2412), acting in a way befitting holiness; *euschḗmōn* (2158), decorous, honourable.

2888. κοσμοκράτωρ, kosmokratōr, *kos-mok-rat´-ore*; from 2889 and 2902; a *world-ruler*, an epithet of Satan:—ruler.

Noun from *kósmos* (2889), world, and *kratéō* (2902), to hold. Lord of the world. Used in the NT of Satan as the prince of this world. Only in Eph 6:12, in the plural, referring to Satan and his angels.

Syn.: *pantokrátōr* (3841), the Almighty, the ruler of everything, a title used only of God. Also *árchōn* (758), ruler; *basileús* (935), king; *despótēs* (1203), master, absolute ruler; *kúrios* (2962), God, Lord, master.

2889. κόσμος, kosmos, *kos´-mos*; probably from the base of 2865; orderly *arrangement*, i.e. *decoration*; (by implication) the *world* (in a wide or narrow sense, including its inhabitant, literal or figurative [moral]):—adorning, world.

Noun probably from *koméō* (n.f.), to tend, to take care of. Order, regular disposition and arrangement:

(**I**) Order of the universe, the world:

(**A**) The universe, heavens and earth (Mt 13:35; 24:21; Lk 11:50; Jn 17:5, 24; Ac 17:24; Ro 1:20; Heb 4:3). Used as a metonym for the inhabitants of the universe (1Co 4:9). Figuratively and symbolically: a world of something, as an aggregate such as in Jas 3:6, "a world of iniquity."

(**B**) The earth, this lower world as the abode of man: (**1**) The then-known world and particularly the people who lived in it (Mt 4:8; Mk 16:15; Jn 3:17, 19; 16:21, 28; 21:25; 1Ti 3:16; 1Pe 5:9; 2Pe 3:6). (**2**) Metonymically, inhabitants of the earth, men, mankind (Mt 5:14; 13:38; Jn 1:29; 3:16; Ro 3:6, 19; 1Co 4:13; 2Co 5:19; Heb 11:7; 2Pe 2:5; 1Jn 2:2). As a hyperbole, the world, everybody, when in fact, a smaller group is visualized (Jn 7:4; 12:19). It also stands for the heathen world, the same as *tá éthnē* (1484), "the nations" (Ro 11:12, 15).

(**C**) In the Jewish mode of speaking: the present world, the present order of things, as opposed to the kingdom of Christ; and hence, always with the idea of transience, worthlessness, and evil both physical and moral, the seat of cares, temptations, irregular desires. (**1**) Generally (Jn 12:25; 18:36; 1Co 5:10; Eph 2:2; 1Jn 4:17). Specifically: the wealth and enjoyments of this world, this life's goods (Mt 16:26; Mk 8:36; Lk 9:25; 1Co 3:22; 7:31, 33, 34; Gal 6:14; Jas 4:4; 1Jn 2:17). (**2**) Used metonymically for the men of this world as opposed to those who seek the kingdom of God (Jn 7:7; 14:17; 16:8; 17:6, 9; 1Co 1:20, 21; 3:19; 2Co 7:10; Php 2:15; Jas 1:27); as subject to Satan, the ruler of this world (Jn 12:31; 14:30; 16:11).

(**II**) Adornment, adorning (1Pe 3:3).

Deriv.: *kosméō* (2885), to order, put in order, decorate, adorn; *kosmikós* (2886), worldly, earthly; *kósmios* (2887), well-ordered, well-mannered, decorous; *kosmokrátor* (2888), a world ruler.

Syn.: *aiṓn* (165), age; *oikouménē* (3625), the inhabited earth, civilization; *gē̄* (1093), earth as

arable land, but also the earth as a whole, the world in contrast to the heavens.

2890. Κούαρτος, Kouartos, *koo´-ar-tos*; of Latin origin (*fourth*); *Quartus*, a Christian:—Quartus.

2891. κοῦμι, koumi, *koo´-mee*; of Chaldee origin [6966]; *cumi* (i.e. *rise!*):—cumi.

2892. κουστωδία, koustōdia, *koos-to-dee´-ah*; of Latin origin; "*custody*," i.e. a Roman *sentry*:—watch.

2893. κουφίζω, kouphizō, *koo-fid´-zo*; from **κοῦφος,** *kouphos* (*light* in weight); to *unload*:—lighten.

2894. κόφινος, kophinos, *kof´-ee-nos*; of uncertain derivative; a (small) *basket*:—basket.

2895. κράββατος, krabbatos, *krab´-bat-os*; probably of foreign origin; a *mattress*:—bed.

2896. κράζω, krazō, *krad´-zo*; a primary verb; properly to "*croak*" (as a raven) or *scream*, i.e. (genitive) to *call* aloud (*shriek, exclaim, intreat*):—cry (out).

2897. κραιπάλη, kraipalē, *krahee-pal´-ay*; probably from the same as 726; properly a *headache* (as a *seizure* of pain) from drunkenness, i.e. (by implication) a *debauch* (by analogy, a *glut*):—surfeiting.

Noun meaning headache, a hangover, a shooting pain or a confusion in the head arising from intoxication and its consequences. Constant reveling, carousing. Only in Lk 21:34.

Syn.: *kṓmos* (2970), revelings and riotings; *méthē* (3178), drunkenness; *oinophlugía* (3632), excess of wine; *pótos* (4224), a drinking bout leading possibly to excess.

2898. κρανίον, kranion, *kran-ee´-on*; diminutive of a derivative of the base of 2768; a *skull* ("*cranium*"):—Calvary, skull.

2899. κράσπεδον, kraspedon, *kras´-ped-on*; of uncertain derivative; a *margin*, i.e. (special) a *fringe* or *tassel*:—border, hem.

2900. κραταιός, krataios, *krat-ah-yos´*; from 2904; *powerful*:—mighty.

2901. κραταιόω, krataioō, *krat-ah-yo´-o*; from 2900; to *empower*, i.e. (passive) *increase in vigour*:—be strengthened, be (wax) strong.

2902. κρατέω, krateō, *krat-eh´-o;* from 2904; to *use strength,* i.e. *seize* or *retain* (literal or figurative):—hold (by, fast), keep, lay hand (hold) on, obtain, retain, take (by).

From *krátos* (2904), strength. To be strong, mighty, powerful; to have power over, to rule over:

(I) To have power over, to gain, attain to (Ac 27:13); to hold fast (Heb 4:14). To take the hand of someone (Mt 9:25; Mk 1:31; 5:41; 9:27; Lk 8:54) to hold by the feet (Mt 28:9).

(II) To have power over, to be or become the master of, always implying a certain degree of force with which one brings a person or thing wholly under his power, even when resistance is encountered. Generally: to bring under one's power, lay hold of, seize, or take a person (Mt 14:3; 18:28; 21:46; 22:6; 26:4, 48, 50, 55, 57; Mk 3:21; 6:17; 12:12; 14:1, 44, 46, 49, 51; Ac 24:6; Rev 20:2); an animal (Mt 12:11).

(III) To have in one's power, be master of, i.e. to hold, hold fast, not to let go, e.g., of things (Rev 2:1; 7:1); of persons: to hold in subjection (pass., Ac 2:24). To hold one fast, i.e. to hold fast to someone, cleave to him, for example, in person (Ac 3:11), or in faith hold on to Christ (Col 2:19). Metaphorically spoken of sins: to retain, not to forgive (Jn 20:23). To keep to oneself, e.g., the word (Mk 9:10). Generally: to hold fast in mind, observe (Mk 7:3, 4, 8; 2Th 2:15; Rev 2:13–15, 25; 3:11). In the passive, concerning the eyes: "to be held," i.e. prevented from recognizing (Lk 24:16).

Deriv.: *kosmokrátōr* (2888), a world ruler.

Syn.: *antéchomai* (472), to hold firmly to; *harpázō* (726), to take by force suddenly; *epilambánō* (1949), to lay hold of; *katéchō* (2722), to hold firmly; *piázō* (4084), to take hold, apprehend; *sunéchō* (4912), to hold a prisoner.

2903. κράτιστος, kratistos, *krat´-is-tos;* superl. of a derivative of 2904; *strongest,* i.e. (in dignity) *very honourable:*—most excellent (noble).

2904. κράτος, kratos, *krat´-os;* perhaps a primary word; *vigour* ["great"] (literal or figurative):—dominion, might [-ily], power, strength.

Noun meaning strength, might:

(I) Generally: might or power, strength (Ac 19:20; Eph 1:19; 6:10; Col 1:11). Used metonymically for might, for mighty deeds (Lk 1:51).

(II) Power, dominion, ruling control. Spoken of God (1Ti 6:16; 1Pe 4:11; 5:11; Jude 25; Rev 1:6; 5:13); spoken of the devil having temporary dominion over death (Heb 2:14).

Deriv.: *akratḗs* (193), without self-control; *egkratḗs* (1468), temperate; *kratéō* (2902), to be strong, to seize; *krátistos* (2903), most excellent; *pantokrátōr* (3841), ruler over all, Almighty.

Syn.: *dúnamis* (1411), strength, power and its execution; *exousía* (1849), authority; *ischús* (2479), strength possessed.

2905. κραυγάζω, kraugazō, *krow-gad´-zo;* from 2906; to *clamor:*—cry out.

2906. κραυγή, kraugē, *krow-gay´;* from 2896; an *outcry* (in notification, tumult or grief):—clamour, cry (-ing).

2907. κρέας, kreas, *kreh´-as;* perhaps a primary word; (butcher's) *meat:*—flesh.

2908. κρεῖσσον, kreisson, *krice´-son;* neuter of an alternate form of 2909; (as noun) *better,* i.e. *greater advantage:*—better.

The neuter of *kreíssōn* (2909) used as an adverb. Better, in the sense of more useful, more profitable. Used only in 1Co 7:38.

2909. κρείττων, kreittōn, *krite´-tohn;* comparative of a derivative of 2904; *stronger,* i.e. (figurative) *better,* i.e. *nobler:*—best, better.

Adjective, the comparative of *kratús* (n.f.), strong, which is from *krátos* (2904), power, and used as a comparative of *agathós* (18), benevolently good. Better in value or dignity, nobler, more excellent (1Co 7:9; 11:17; 12:31; Php 1:23; Heb 1:4; 6:9; 7:7, 19, 22; 8:6; 9:23; 10:34; 11:16, 35, 40; 12:24; 1Pe 3:17; 2Pe 2:21).

Syn.: *meízōn* (3187), greater.

2910. κρεμάννυμι, kremannumi, *krem-an´-noo-mee;* a prolonged form of a primary verb; to *hang:*—hang.

2911. κρημνός, krēmnos, *krame-nos´;* from 2910; *overhanging,* i.e. a *precipice:*—steep place.

2912. Κρής, Krēs, *krace;* from 2914; a *Cretan,* i.e. inhabitant of Crete:—Crete, Cretian.

2913. Κρήσκης, Krēskēs, *krace´-kace;* of Latin origin; *growing; Cresces* (i.e. *Crescens*), a Christian:—Crescens.

2914. Κρήτη, Krētē, *kray´-tay*; of uncertain derivative; *Cretè,* an island in the Mediterranean:—Crete.

2915. κριθή, krithē, *kree-thay´*; of uncertain derivative; *barley:*—barley.

2916. κρίθινος, krithinos, *kree´-thee-nos*; from 2915; consisting *of barley*:—barley.

2917. κρίμα, krima, *kree´-mah*; from 2919; a *decision* (the function or the effect, for or against ["crime"]):—avenge, condemned, condemnation, damnation, + go to law, judgement.

Noun from *krínō* (2919), to judge. Judgement, sentence, the reason for judgement:

(I) The act of judging, giving judgement, equivalent to *krísis* (2920), judgement (1Pe 4:17). Spoken in reference to future reward and punishment (Jn 9:39); of the judgement of the last day (Ac 24:25; Heb 6:2). Used metonymically for the power of judgement (Rev 20:4).

(II) Judgement given, decision, award, sentence:

(A) Generally (Mt 7:2; Ro 5:16; 11:33).

(B) More often, a sentence of punishment or condemnation, implying also the punishment itself as a certain consequence (Mt 23:14; Mk 12:40; Lk 20:47; 23:40; 24:20; Ro 2:2, 3; 3:8; 13:2; 1Co 11:29, 34; Gal 5:10; 1Ti 3:6; 5:12; Jas 3:1; 2Pe 2:3; Jude 4; Rev 17:1; 18:20).

(C) Lawsuit, cause, something to be judged (1Co 6:7).

Syn.: *apókrima* (610), sentence; *díkē* (1349), judgement, a decision or its execution.

2918. κρίνον, krinon, *kree´-non*; perhaps a primary word; a *lily:*—lily.

2919. κρίνω, krinō, *kree´-no*; properly to *distinguish,* i.e. *decide* (mentally or judicially); (by implication) to *try, condemn, punish*:—avenge, conclude, condemn, damn, decree, determine, esteem, judge, go to (sue at the) law, ordain, call in question, sentence to, think.

To separate, distinguish, discriminate between good and evil, select, choose out the good. In the NT, it means to judge, to form or give an opinion after separating and considering the particulars of a case:

(I) To judge in one's own mind as to what is right, proper, expedient; to deem, decide, determine (Lk 7:43; 12:57; Ac 3:13; 4:19; 15:19; 20:16;

25:25; 27:1; Ro 14:5; 1Co 2:2; 10:15; Tit 3:12; Rev 16:5).

(II) To form and express a judgement or opinion as to any person or thing, more commonly unfavourable (Jn 7:24; 8:15; Ro 2:1, 3, 27; 14:3, 4, 10, 13, 22; 1Co 4:5; 10:29; Col 2:16; Jas 4:11, 12); in an absolute sense (Mt 7:1, 2; Lk 6:37; Jn 8:16).

(III) To judge in a judicial sense:

(A) To sit in judgement on any person, to try (Jn 18:31; Ac 23:3; 24:6; 1Co 5:12). In the pass. *krínomai*: to be judged, tried, be on trial (Ac 23:6; 24:21; 25:9, 10; 26:6; Ro 3:4). Spoken in reference to the gospel dispensation, to the judgement of the great day of God's judging the world through Christ (Jn 5:22; 8:50; Ac 17:31; Ro 2:16; 3:6; 1Co 5:13; 2Ti 4:1; 1Pe 1:17; 2:23; 4:5; Rev 11:18; 19:11; 20:12, 13).

(B) In the sense of to pass judgement upon, condemn (Lk 19:22; Jn 7:51; Ac 13:27). As also implying punishment (1Co 11:31, 32; 1Pe 4:6). Of the condemnation of the wicked and including the idea of punishment as a certain consequence, meaning to punish, take vengeance on. Spoken of God as judge (Ac 7:7 quoted from Ge 15:14; Ro 2:12; 2Th 2:12; Heb 13:4; Rev 6:10; 18:8, 20; 19:2).

(C) To vindicate, avenge (Heb 10:30).

(IV) In the passive, particularly: to let oneself be judged, i.e. to have a lawsuit, go to law (Mt 5:40); to be judged before someone (1Co 6:1, 6).

Deriv.: *anakrínō* (350), to judicially investigate, examine; *apokrínomai* (611), to answer, respond; *diakrínō* (1252), to discriminate, make to differ, judge thoroughly; *egkrínō* (1469), to class with, count among, approve; *eilikrinḗs* (1506), pure, sincere; *epikrínō* (1948), to give sentence; *katakrínō* (2632), to judge against, condemn; *kríma* (2917), judicial decision; *krísis* (2920), judgement; *kritḗs* (2923), judge; *sugkrínō* (4793), to judge one thing comparing it with another, to interpret; *hupokrínomai* (5271), to speak or act under false identity.

Syn.: *diaginṓskō* (1231), to ascertain exactly; *diakrínō* (1252), to discern; *kataginṓskō* (2607), to think ill of, condemn, find fault with; *katadikázō* (2613), to pronounce judgement, condemn.

2920. κρίσις, krisis, *kree´-sis*; *decision* (subject or object, for or against); by extension a *tribunal*;

(by implication) *justice* (specially divine *law*):—accusation, condemnation, damnation, judgement.

Noun from *krínō* (2919), to judge. Judgement:

(I) Generally: an opinion formed and expressed (Jn 7:24; 8:16).

(II) Judgement, in a judicial sense:

(A) The act of judging in reference to the final judgement, as the day of judgement (Mt 10:15; 11:22, 24; 12:36; Mk 6:11; 2Pe 2:9; 3:7; 1Jn 4:17); as the hour of judgement (Rev 14:7); as the judgement of the great day (Jude 6). Simply *krísis* standing for the judgement of the great day (Mt 12:41, 42; Lk 10:14; 11:31, 32; Heb 9:27). Used metonymically for the power of judgement (Jn 5:22).

(B) Judgement given, sentence pronounced (Jn 5:30; 2Pe 2:11; Jude 9). Specifically: sentence of punishment or condemnation, e.g., to death (Ac 8:33). Usually implying also punishment as a certain consequence (Mt 23:33; Mk 3:29; Jn 3:19; 5:24, 29; 1Ti 5:24; Heb 10:27; Jas 2:13; 2Pe 2:4; Rev 16:7; 18:10; 19:2).

(C) Used metonymically for a court of justice, a tribunal, judges, i.e. the smaller tribunals established in the cities of Palestine and subordinate to the Sanhedrin (Mt 5:21, 22).

(III) Right, justice, equity (Mt 23:23; Lk 11:42). Also for law, statutes, i.e. the divine law, the religion of Jehovah as developed in the gospels (Mt 12:18, 20).

Syn.: *aísthēsis* (144), discernment, judgement as through the senses.

2921. Κρίσπος, Krispos, *kris´-pos*; of Latin origin; "*crisp*"; *Crispus*, a Corinthian:—Crispus.

2922. κριτήριον, kritērion, *kree-tay´-ree-on*; neuter of a presumed derivative of 2923; a *rule* of judging ("*criterion*"), i.e. (by implication) a *tribunal*:—to judge, judgement (seat)

Noun from *krités* (2923), a judge. Criterion, rule of judging. In the NT, used metaphorically: court of justice, tribunal (1Co 6:2; Jas 2:6); by implication: cause, lawsuit (1Co 6:4).

Syn.: *bḗma* (968), judgement seat, tribunal.

2923. κριτής, krités, *kree-tace´*; from 2919; a *judge* (general or special):—judge.

Noun from *krínō* (2919), to judge. He who decides, a judge:

(I) Generally (Mt 12:27; Lk 11:19; Jas 2:4); in an unfavourable sense (Jas 4:11).

(II) In a judicial sense: one who sits to render justice (Mt 5:25; Lk 12:58; 18:2, 6; Ac 18:15; 24:10). Of Christ the final judge (Ac 10:42; 2Ti 4:8; Jas 5:9); of God (Heb 12:23).

(III) A leader, ruler, chief, spoken of the Hebrew judges from Joshua to Samuel (Ac 13:20).

Deriv.: *kritérion* (2922), judgement, tribunal; *kritikós* (2924), discerner.

Syn.: *dikastḗs* (1348), a judicial judge.

2924. κριτικός, kritikos, *krit-ee-kos´*; from 2923; *decisive* ("*critical*"), i.e. *discriminative*:—discerner.

Adjective from *krités* (2923), a judge. Able to discern or decide correctly, skilled in judging. Used only in Heb 4:12.

2925. κρούω, krouō, *kroo´-o*; apparently a primary verb; to *rap*:—knock.

2926. κρυπτή, kruptē, *kroop-tay´*; feminine of 2927; a *hidden* place, i.e. *cellar* ("*crypt*"):—secret.

2927. κρυπτός, kruptos, *kroop-tos´*; from 2928; *concealed*, i.e. *private*:—hid (-den), inward [-ly], secret.

2928. κρύπτω, kruptō, *kroop´-to*; a primary verb; to *conceal* (properly by *covering*):—hide (self), keep secret, secret [-ly].

2929. κρυσταλλίζω, krustallizō, *kroos-tal-lid´-zo*; from 2930; to *make* (i.e. intransitive *resemble*) *ice* ("*crystallize*"):—be clear as crystal.

2930. κρύσταλλος, krustallos, *kroos´-tal-los*; from a derivative of **κρύος, kruos** (*frost*); *ice*, i.e. (by analogy) rock "*crystal*":—crystal.

2931. κρυφῇ, kruphē, *kroo-fay´*; adverb from 2928; *privately*:—in secret.

2932. κτάομαι, ktaomai, *ktah´-om-ahee*; a primary verb; to *get*, i.e. *acquire* (by any means; *own*):—obtain, possess, provide, purchase.

2933. κτῆμα, ktēma, *ktay´-mah*; from 2932; an *acquirement*, i.e. *estate*:—possession.

2934. κτῆνος, ktēnos, *ktay´-nos*; from 2932; *property*, i.e. (special) a domestic *animal*:—beast.

2935. κτήτωρ, ktētōr, *ktay´-tore*; from 2932; an *owner:*—possessor.

2936. κτίζω, ktizō, *ktid´-zo*; probably akin to 2932 (through the idea of the *proprietorship* of the *manufacturer*); to *fabricate*, i.e. *found* (*form* originally):—create, Creator, make.

To bring under tillage and settlement. In the NT: to establish, to create, produce from nothing (Mk 13:19; Ro 1:25; Eph 3:9; Col 1:16; 3:10; 1Ti 4:3; Rev 4:11; 10:6); to form out of preexistent matter (1Co 11:9); to make, compose (Eph 2:15); to create and form in a spiritual sense, regeneration or renewal (Eph 2:10; 4:24).

Deriv.: *ktísis* (2937), creation; *ktísma* (2938), creature; *ktístēs* (2939), creator, founder, inventor.

Syn.: *kataskeuázō* (2680), to prepare, make ready, build; *poiéō* (4160), to make.

2937. κτίσις, ktisis, *ktis´-is*; from 2936; original *formation* (properly, the act; by implication, the thing, literal or figurative):—building, creation, creature, ordinance.

Noun from *ktízō* (2936), to create, form or found. A founding of cities. In the NT: creation, i.e. the act of creation (Ro 1:20). Generally: a created thing, and collectively: created things (Ro 1:25; 8:39; Heb 4:13). Also in the sense of creation in general, the universe (Mk 10:6; 13:19; Col 1:15; 2Pe 3:4; Rev 3:14); specifically: the visible creation (Heb 9:11). Used metonymically for man, mankind (Mk 16:15; Ro 8:19–22; 2Co 5:17; Gal 6:15; Col 1:23). By implication: ordinance, institution (1Pe 2:13).

2938. κτίσμα, ktisma, *ktis´-mah*; from 2936; an original *formation* (concrete), i.e. *product* (created thing):—creature.

Noun from *ktízō* (2936), to create, form or found. In the NT: creature, created thing. Spoken of animals as a source of food (1Ti 4:4); spoken of mankind (Jas 1:18); spoken of every living being in the sea (Rev 8:9); spoken of every living being in the universe (Rev 5:13).

Syn.: *plásma* (4110), something molded or formed; *poíēma* (4161), a product.

2939. κτιστής, ktistēs, *ktis-tace´*; from 2936; a *founder*, i.e. *God* (as author of all things):—Creator.

Noun from *ktízō* (2936), to create, form or found. Creator, founder, inventor. Only in 1Pe 4:19, a creator.

Syn.: *dēmiourgós* (1217), builder, maker; *technítēs* (5079), architect, designer.

2940. κυβεία, kubeia, *koo-bi´-ah*; from **κύβος,** *kubos* (a "*cube*," i.e. die for playing); *gambling*, i.e. (figurative) *artifice* or *fraud:*—sleight.

2941. κυβέρνησις, kubernēsis, *koo-ber´-nay-sis*; from **κυβερνάω,** *kubernaō* (of Latin origin, to *steer*); *pilotage*, i.e. (figurative) *directorship* (in the church):—government.

2942. κυβερνήτης, kubernētēs, *koo-ber-nay´-tace*; from the same as 2941; *helmsman*, i.e. (by implication) *captain:*—(ship) master.

2943. κυκλόθεν, kuklothen, *koo-kloth´-en*; adverb from the same as 2945; *from the circle*, i.e. *all around:*—(round) about.

2944. κυκλόω, kukloō, *koo-klo´-o*; from the same as 2945; to *encircle*, i.e. *surround:*—compass (about), come (stand) round about.

2945. κύκλῳ, kuklōi, *koo´-klo*; as if dative of **κύκλος,** *kuklos* (a *ring*, "*cycle*"; akin to 2947); i.e. *in a circle* (by implication of 1722), i.e. (adverb) *all around:*—round about.

2946. κύλισμα, kulisma, *koo´-lis-mah*; from 2947; a *wallow* (the effect of *rolling*), i.e. *filth:*—wallowing.

2947. κυλιόω, kulioō, *koo-lee-o´-o*; from the base of 2949 (through the idea of *circularity*; compare 2945, 1507); to *roll about:*—wallow.

2948. κυλλός, kullos, *kool-los´*; from the same as 2947; *rocking* about, i.e. *crippled* (*maimed*, in feet or hands):—maimed.

2949. κῦμα, kuma, *koo´-mah*; from **κύω,** *kuō* (to *swell* [with young], i.e. bend, curve); a *billow* (as bursting or toppling):—wave.

2950. κύμβαλον, kumbalon, *koom´-bal-on*; from a derivative of the base of 2949; a "*cymbal*" (as hollow):—cymbal.

2951. κύμινον, kuminon, *koo´-min-on*; of foreign origin [compare 3646]; *dill* or *fennel* ("cummin"):—cummin.

2952. κυνάριον, kunarion, *koo-nar´-ee-on*; neuter of a presumed derivative of 2965; a *puppy:*—dog.

2953. Κύπριος, Kuprios, *koo´-pree-os*; from 2954; a *Cyprian* (*Cypriot*), i.e. inhabitant of Cyprus:—of Cyprus.

2954. Κύπρος, Kupros, *koo´-pros*; of uncertain origin; *Cyprus*, an island in the Mediterranean:—Cyprus.

2955. κύπτω, kuptō, *koop´-to*; probably from the base of 2949; to *bend* forward:—stoop (down).

To stoop, to bow down oneself. To stoop in subservience to tie another's sandal strings (Mk 1:7); to stoop to write on the ground (Mk 1:7; Jn 8:6, 8).

Deriv.: *anakúptō* (352), to lift up; *parakúptō* (3879), to stoop to look into; *sugkúptō* (4794), to bend or bow down over.

Syn.: *klínō* (2827), to bow down.

2956. Κυρηναῖος, Kurēnaios, *koo-ray-nah´-yos*; from 2957; a *Cyrenæan*, i.e. inhabitant of Cyrene:—of Cyrene, Cyrenian.

2957. Κυρήνη, Kurēnē, *koo-ray´-nay*; of uncertain derivative; *Cyrenè*, a region of Africa:—Cyrene.

2958. Κυρήνιος, Kurēnios, *koo-ray´-nee-os*; of Latin origin; *Cyrenius* (i.e. *Quirinus*), a Roman:—Cyrenius.

2959. Κυρία, Kuria, *koo-ree´-ah*; feminine of 2962; *Cyria*, a Christian woman:—lady.

2960. κυριακός, kuriakos, *koo-ree-ak-os´*; from 2962; *belonging to* the Lord (Jehovah or Jesus):—Lord's.

From *kúrios* (2962), God, Lord, master. Belonging to a lord or ruler. Spoken of the Lord's Supper (1Co 11:20), and of the Lord's day (Rev 1:10), as belonging to Christ, to the Lord, having special reference to Him.

2961. κυριεύω, kurieuō, *koo-ree-yoo´-o*; from 2962; to *rule*:—have dominion over, lord, be lord of, exercise lordship over.

2962. κύριος, kurios, *koo´-ree-os*; from κῦρος, *kuros* (*supremacy*); *supreme* in authority, i.e. (as noun) *controller*; (by implication) *Mr.* (as a respectful title):—God, Lord, master, Sir.

Noun from *kúros* (n.f.), might, power. Lord, master, owner:

(I) Generally:

(A) As the possessor, owner, master, e.g., of

property (Mt 20:8; 21:40; Gal 4:1); master or head of a house (Mt 15:27; Mk 13:35); of persons, servants, slaves (Mt 10:24; 24:45, 46, 48, 50; Ac 16:16, 19; Ro 14:4; Eph 6:5, 9; Col 3:22; 4:1). Spoken of a husband (1Pe 3:6). Lord, master of something and having absolute authority over it, e.g., master of the harvest (Mt 9:38; Lk 10:2); master of the Sabbath (Mt 12:8; Mk 2:28).

(B) Of a supreme lord, sovereign, e.g., the Roman emperor (Ac 25:26); the heathen gods (1Co 8:5).

(C) As an honorary title of address, especially to superiors, equivalent to mister, sir, as a servant to his master (Mt 13:27; Lk 13:8); a son to his father (Mt 21:30); a student or follower to a teacher, master (Mt 8:25; Lk 9:54). See also Mt 7:21, 22; Lk 6:46. Spoken to a person of dignity and authority (Mk 7:28; Jn 4:11, 15, 19, 49); to a Roman procurator (Mt 27:63). Spoken when addressing someone respectfully (Jn 12:21; 20:15; Ac 16:30).

(II) Spoken of God and Christ:

(A) Of God as the supreme Lord and Sovereign of the universe, usually in the Sept. for the Hebrew *Yehōwāh* (3068, OT), Jehovah, Lord. With the article *ho Kúrios* (Mt 1:22; 5:33; Mk 5:19; Lk 1:6, 28; Ac 7:33; Heb 8:2; Jas 4:15). Without the article *Kúrios* (Mt 27:10; Mk 13:20; Lk 1:58; Ac 7:49; Ro 4:8; Heb 7:21; 1Pe 1:25). With adjuncts, e.g., *Kúrios ho Theós* ([2316], God), the Lord God (Mt 4:7, 10; 22:37; Lk 1:16); *Kúrios Sabaōth* ([4519], armies), Lord of hosts, armies; a military appellation of God (Ro 9:29; Jas 5:4); *Kúrios Pantokrátōr* (3841), Lord Almighty or ruler of all (2Co 6:18); *Kúrios ho Theós ho Pantokrátōr*, Lord, the God, the Almighty (Rev 4:8; 11:17); *Kúrios tōn kurieuóntōn* (2961), Lord of lords, referring to those who are ruling (1Ti 6:15); Lord of heaven and earth (Mt 11:25; Lk 10:21; Ac 17:24).

(B) Of the Lord Jesus Christ: **(1)** In reference to His abode on earth as a master and teacher, equivalent to *rhabbí* (4461), rabbi, and *epistátēs* (1988), master, superintendent (Mt 17:4 [cf. Mk 9:5; Lk 9:33]. See also Jn 13:13, 14). Chiefly in the gospels before the resurrection of Christ (Mt 21:3; 28:6; Lk 7:13; 10:1; Jn 4:1; 20:2, 13; Ac 9:5; 1Co 9:5). With adjuncts, e.g., *ho Kúrios kaí ho didáskalos* ([1320], teacher), the Lord and teacher (Jn 13:13, 14); *ho Kúrios Iēsoús* (2424), the Lord Jesus (Lk 24:3; Ac 1:21; 4:33; 1Co 11:23). **(2)** As the supreme Lord of the gospel dispensation, "head over all things to the church" (Ro 10:12; Rev 17:14); as simply "Lord" or "the Lord" (Mt 22:44; Mk 16:20; Ac 8:25; 19:10; 2Co 3:16, 17; Eph 5:10; Col 3:23; 4:1; 2Th 3:1, 5; 2Ti 4:8; Heb 7:14; Jas 5:7; 2Pe 3:10; Rev 11:8). With adjuncts, e.g. "the Lord Jesus" (Ro 4:24; 10:9; 1Co 5:5; Php 2:19; Heb 13:20); "the Lord Jesus Christ" or "Jesus Christ the Lord" (Ac 16:31; Ro 1:3, 7; 13:14; 16:18; 1Co 1:2, 9, 10; Gal 6:18; Eph 3:11; Php 1:2; 1Ti 1:2); *Christós Kúrios*, meaning the Messiah (Lk 2:11).

Deriv.: *kuría* (2959), lady; *kuriakós* (2960), the Lord's; *kurieúō* (2961), to be lord; *kuriótēs* (2963), lordship, dominion.

Syn.: *archēgós* (747), leader; *árchōn* (758), ruler; *despótēs* (1203), master; *ethnárchēs* (1481), leader of a nation; *hēgemṓn* (2232), governor, ruler; *kosmokrátōr* (2888), world ruler; *pantokrátōr* (3841), Almighty.

2963. κυριότης, kuriotēs, *koo-ree-ot´-ace*; from 2962; *mastery*, i.e. (concrete and collective) *rulers*:—dominion, government.

Noun from *kúrios* (2962), God, Lord, master. Dominion, civil power, authority. Spoken of as despised by wicked men (2Pe 2:10; Jude 8); spoken of as created by Christ (Col 1:16), who has been placed above them (Eph 1:21).

Syn.: *archḗ* (746), rule; *exousía* (1849), authority; *hēgemonía* (2231), government; *krátos* (2904), dominion; *kubérnēsis* (2941), government.

2964. κυρόω, kuroō, *koo-ro´-o*; from the same as 2962; to *make authoritative*, i.e. *ratify*:—confirm.

2965. κύων, kuōn, *koo´-ohn*; a primary word; a *dog* ["*hound*"] (literal or figurative):—dog.

2966. κῶλον, kōlon, *ko´-lon*; from the base of 2849; a *limb* of the body (as if *lopped*):—carcase.

2967. κωλύω, kōluō, *ko-loo´-o*; from the base of 2849; to *estop*, i.e. *prevent* (by word or act):—forbid, hinder, keep from, let, not suffer, withstand.

2968. κώμη, kōmē, *ko´-may*; from 2749; a *hamlet* (as if *laid* down):—town, village.

2969. κωμόπολις, kōmopolis, *ko-mop´-ol-is*; from 2968 and 4172; an unwalled *city*:—town.

2970. κῶμος, kōmos, *ko´-mos*; from 2749; a *carousal* (as if a *letting loose*):—reveling, rioting.

Noun meaning feasting. In the NT: reveling and carousing (Ro 13:13; Gal 5:21; 1Pe 4:3); a carousing or merrymaking after supper, the guests often moving out into the streets and going through the city with torches, music, and songs in honour of Bacchus, etc.

Syn.: *kraipálē* (2897), giddiness caused by overindulgence in wine; *méthē* (3178), drunkenness; *oinophlugía* (3632), excess of wine; *pótos* (4224), a drinking bout or banquet.

2971. κώνωψ, kōnōps, *ko´-nopes*; apparently from a derivative of the base of 2759 and a derivative of 3700; a *mosquito* (from its *stinging proboscis*):—gnat.

2972. Κῶς, Kōs, *koce*; of uncertain origin; *Cos*, an island in the Mediterranean:—Cos.

2973. Κωσάμ, Kōsam, *ko-sam´*; of Hebrew origin [compare 7081]; *Cosam* (i.e. *Kosam*), an Israelite:—Cosam.

2974. κωφός, kōphos, *ko-fos´*; from 2875; *blunted*, i.e. (figurative) of hearing (*deaf*) or speech (*dumb*):—deaf, dumb, speechless.

Λ (Lambda)

NT Numbers 2975–3091

2975. λαγχάνω, **lagchanō,** *lang-khan´-o*; a prolonged form of a primary verb, which is only used as an alternate in certain tenses; to *lot*, i.e. *determine* (by implication, *receive*) especially by lot:—his lot be, cast lots, obtain.

2976. Λάζαρος, **Lazaros,** *lad´-zar-os*; probably of Hebrew origin [499]; *Lazarus* (i.e. *Elazar*), the name of two Israelites (one imaginary):—Lazarus.

2977. λάθρα, **lathra,** *lath´-rah*; adverb from 2990; *privately:*—privily, secretly.

2978. λαῖλαψ, **lailaps,** *lah´ee-laps*; of uncertain derivative; a *whirlwind* (*squall*):—storm, tempest.

Noun meaning fierce tempest with driving wind and rain, a whirlwind, hurricane. Spoken of storms on the sea of Galilee (Mk 4:37; Lk 8:23); used metaphorically to describe wicked false teachers (2Pe 2:17).

Syn.: *thúella* (2366), hurricane, cyclone; *cheimṓn* (5494), winter storm.

2979. λακτίζω, **laktizo,** *lak-tid´-zo*; from adverb λάξ, *lax* (*heelwise*); to *recalcitrate:*—kick.

2980. λαλέω, **laleō,** *lal-eh´-o*; a prolonged form of an otherwise obsolete verb; to *talk*, i.e. *utter* words:—preach, say, speak (after), talk, tell, utter. Compare 3004.

To speak, to talk; to use the voice without any necessary reference to the words spoken, thus differing from *légō* (3004). In Class. Gr., especially of children: to talk too much, to prattle. In the NT, generally: to speak, to talk:

(**I**) Particularly, simply to speak, e.g., spoken of those formerly deaf and dumb (Mt 9:33; 12:22; 15:31). See also Mk 7:35; Lk 7:15; Jn 7:26; Ac 2:6; 7:6; 18:9; 1Co 12:3; 14:9; Jas 1:19). To speak to or with someone (Mt 12:47; Mk 6:50; Lk 1:22; Jn 4:27; 9:29, 37; 19:10; Ac 7:38; Ro 7:1; 2Jn 12; Rev 21:9).

(**II**) As modified by the context where the meaning lies not so much in the verb itself, *laléō*, as in the adjuncts:

(**A**) To teach, preach (Mt 13:10; Lk 5:4; Jn 7:17; 12:50; Ac 14:1; 1Co 3:1; 14:34, 35; 1Pe 4:11).

(**B**) To tell, relate, declare, announce something (Mt 26:13; Lk 2:20; Jn 1:37; Ac 4:20; 27:25).

(**C**) To foretell, declare (Lk 1:55, 70; 24:25; Jn 16:1, 4; Ac 3:24; 26:22; 28:25; Jas 5:10; 2Pe 1:21).

(**D**) Figuratively: to speak by writing or letter (2Co 11:17; Heb 2:5; 2Pe 3:16); also spoken of one dead who speaks or exhorts by his example (Heb 11:4).

(**III**) By metonymy of things, e.g.:

(**A**) Spoken of the law in the sense of to prescribe (Ro 3:19).

(**B**) Spoken of the expiatory blood of Jesus in the sense of to accomplish (Heb 12:24).

Deriv.: *alálētos* (215), unspeakable; *álalos* (216), unable to speak; *dialaléō* (1255), to converse; *eklaléō* (1583), to speak out; *katalaléō* (2635), to speak against; *laliá* (2981), saying, speech; *mogilálos* (3424), speaking with difficulty, a stutterer; *proslaléō* (4354), to speak to or with; *sullaléō* (4814), to speak with.

Syn.: *anaggéllō* (312), to announce, declare; *apaggéllō* (518), to announce, declare, report; *apophthéggomai* (669), to speak forth; *diēgéomai* (1334), to declare, report, narrate; *eréō* (2046), to speak; *légō* (3004), to speak thoughtfully; *homiléō* (3656), to talk, converse; *phēmí* (5346), to declare; *phthéggomai* (5350), to utter a sound or voice, to proclaim.

2981. λαλιά, **lalia,** *lal-ee-ah´*; from 2980; *talk:*—saying, speech.

2982. λαμά, **lama,** *lam-ah´*; or λαμμᾶ, **lamma,** *lam-mah´*; of Hebrew origin [4100 with prepositional prefix]; *lama* (i.e. *why*):—lama.

2983. λαμβάνω, lambanō, *lam-ban´-o*; a prolonged form of a primary verb, which is used only as an alternate in certain tenses; to *take* (in very many applications, literal and figurative [properly object or active, to *get hold* of; whereas 1209 is rather subject or passive, to *have offered* to one; while 138 is more violent, to *seize* or *remove*]):—accept, + be amazed, assay, attain, bring, × when I call, catch, come on (× unto), + forget, have, hold, obtain, receive (× after), take (away, up).

To take in whatever manner:

(**I**) To take:

(**A**) Particularly with the hand: (**1**) Generally (Mt 14:19; 25:1; 26:26, 52; 27:6, 30, 48; Mk 9:36; Lk 22:17; Jn 12:3, 13; 13:4, 12, 30; 1Co 11:23; Rev 5:8; 22:17). Figuratively: to receive honour unto oneself (Heb 5:4); power (Rev 11:17). (**2**) Of taking food or drink (Mk 15:23; Jn 19:30; Ac 9:19; 1Ti 4:4). (**3**) With the meaning of to make provision for or take with (Mt 16:5, 7; 25:4; Jn 18:3). To take a wife (Mk 12:19, 21; Lk 20:28). (**4**) Figuratively, to take upon oneself, to bear, e.g., the cross (Mt 10:38); our sicknesses (Mt 8:17). (**5**) To take up, gather up (Mt 16:9, 10). Figuratively, to take the soul, as opposed to *títhēmi* (5087), to place, lay down (Jn 10:17, 18).

(**B**) To take out from a number, i.e. to choose (Ac 15:14).

(**C**) To take, i.e. to seize, lay hold of, with the idea of force or violence. (**1**) Particularly (Mt 21:35, 39; Mk 12:3, 8; 2Co 11:20). In hunting or fishing: to take, catch (Lk 5:5); metaphorically (2Co 12:16). (**2**) Figuratively: to seize, to come or to fall upon someone, spoken of temptation (1Co 10:13); spoken of an evil spirit, demon (Lk 9:39). Also, of a strong affection or emotion, e.g., ecstasy fell upon all (Lk 5:26); fear (Lk 7:16).

(**D**) To take away, e.g., from someone by force (Mt 5:40; Rev 3:11; 6:4).

(**E**) To take up with a person, i.e. to receive him as a friend or guest into one's house or society, equivalent to *déchomai* (1209), to accept: (**1**) Generally (Jn 19:27; 2Jn 10). Metaphorically of a teacher: to receive, acknowledge, embrace and follow his instructions (Jn 1:12; 5:43; 13:20; 14:17); of doctrine: to embrace, admit, e.g., the word (Mt 13:20; Mk 4:16); the witness (Jn 3:11, 32, 33); the words (Jn 12:48; 17:8; 1Jn 5:9). (**2**) To receive the person of someone, used only in a bad sense in the NT: to accept one's person, meaning to be partial toward him (Lk 20:21; Gal 2:6).

(**F**) Figuratively, with *léthēn* [3024], forgetfulness, "to take forgetfulness," i.e. to forget (2Pe 1:9); with *peíran* ([3984], trial, attempt, "to take an attempt," i.e. to make an attempt (Heb 11:29).

(**II**) To receive what is given or imparted or imposed, to obtain, partake of:

(**A**) Generally (Mt 7:8; 10:8; Mk 10:30; Jn 16:24; Ac 2:33; Ro 4:11; 1Co 4:7; Gal 3:14; Jas 1:7; 1Jn 2:27; Rev 18:4).

(**B**) Of those who receive an office, station, position (Lk 19:12, 15; Ac 1:20, 25; Heb 7:5).

(**C**) Of persons appointed to receive tribute, rent, etc.: to collect, exact (Mt 17:24, 25; 21:34; Heb 7:8).

(**D**) Figuratively: to receive instruction, i.e. to be instructed, to learn (Rev 3:3).

Deriv.: *analambánō* (353), to take up; *antilambánō* (482), to take hold of, support; *apolambánō* (618), to receive, take back; *dexiolábos* (1187), a spearman; *epilambánomai* (1949), to grasp; *eulabḗs* (2126), devout; *katalambánō* (2638), to seize, comprehend, attain; *lḗpsis* (3028), a receiving; *metalambánō* (3335), to take part, share; *paralambánō* (3880), to take or receive from another; *prolambánō* (4301), to anticipate; *proslambánō* (4355), to receive or take to oneself; *prosōpolḗptēs* (4381), a respector of persons; *sullambánō* (4815), to seize, catch; *hupolambánō* (5274), to assume.

Syn.: *déchomai* (1209), to receive. Also *anadéchomai* (324), to receive; *apéchō* (568), to receive, to have in full; *apodéchomai* (588), to receive, to accept gladly; *eisdéchomai* (1523), to receive into favour; *epidéchomai* (1926), to accept; *komízō* (2865), to receive; *paradéchomai* (3858), to receive or admit with approval; *prosdéchomai* (4327), to receive to oneself; *hupodéchomai* (5264), to receive as a guest.

2984. Λάμεχ, Lamech, *lam´-ekh*; of Hebrew origin [3929]; *Lamech* (i.e. *Lemek*), a patriarch:—Lamech.

2985. λαμπάς, lampas, *lam-pas´*; from 2989; a "*lamp*" or *flambeau*:—lamp, light, torch.

Noun from *lámpō* (2989), to light, shine. A torch, lamp. Spoken of torches (Jn 18:3); spoken of lights, where the context implies lamps on lampstands (Ac 20:8; Rev 4:5); spoken of lamps or special torches fed with oil (Mt 25:1,

3, 4, 7, 8); used figuratively of a burning star (Rev 8:10).

2986. λαμπρός, lampros, *lam-pros´*; from the same as 2985; *radiant*; (by analogy) *limpid*; (figurative) *magnificent* or *sumptuous* (in appearance):—bright, clear, gay, goodly, gorgeous, white.

2987. λαμπρότης, lamprotēs, *lam-prot´-ace*; from 2896; *brilliancy*:—brightness.

2988. λαμπρῶς, lamprōs, *lam-proce´*; adverb from 2986; *brilliantly*, i.e. (figurative) *luxuriously*:—sumptuously.

2989. λάμπω, lampō, *lam´-po*; a primary verb; to *beam*, i.e. *radiate* brilliancy (literal or figurative):—give light, shine.

2990. λανθάνω, lanthanō, *lan-than´-o*; a prolonged form of a primary verb, which is used only as an alternate in certain tenses; to *lie hid* (literal or figurative); often used adverb *unwittingly*:—be hid, be ignorant of, unawares.

2991. λαξευτός, laxeutos, *lax-yoo-tos´*; from a compound of **λᾶς,** *las* (a *stone*) and the base of 3584 (in its origin sense of *scraping*); *rock-quarried*:—hewn in stone.

2992. λαός, laos, *lah-os´*; apparently a primary word; a *people* (in genitive; thus differing from 1218, which denotes one's *own* populace):—people.

Noun meaning people:

(I) A people, nation, tribe, i.e. the mass of any people, and not like *démos* (1218), which would be limited to a community of free citizens (Lk 2:10; Ac 4:25; Rev 5:9). Specifically of the Jews as the people of God's choice (Mt 1:21; 2:4, 6; Mk 7:6; Lk 2:32; Jn 11:50; Heb 7:5). Figuratively, of Christians as God's spiritual Israel (Tit 2:14; Heb 2:17; 4:9; 13:12).

(II) Generally: the people, i.e. the multitude, the public, either indefinitely or of a multitude collected in one place (Lk 7:29; 8:47; 9:13; Ac 3:9, 11, 12); especially the common people, the populace, the inhabitants of any city or territory, e.g., Jerusalem (Ac 2:47; 21:30, 36); of Galilee (Mt 4:23; 9:35); as distinguished from magistrates, etc. (Mt 26:5; 27:25, 64; Mk 11:32; Lk 19:48; 23:13; Ac 6:12).

Syn.: *éthnos* (1484), nation, used in the plural to signify the heathen or Gentiles as distin-

guished from the Jews or believers. Also, *démos* (1218) a community of free citizens, a people commonly bound together; *óchlos* (3793), a disorganized crowd or multitude.

2993. Λαοδίκεια, Laodikeia, *Lah-od-ik´-i-ah*; from a compound of 2992 and 1349; *Laodicia*, a place in Asia Minor:—Laodicea.

2994. Λαοδικεύς, Laodikeus, *lah-od-ik-yooce´*; from 2993; a *Laodicean*, i.e. inhabitant of Laodicia:—Laodicean.

2995. λάρυγξ, larugx, *lar´-oongks*; of uncertain derivative; the *throat* ("larynx"):—throat.

2996. Λασαία, Lasaia, *las-ah´-yah*; of uncertain origin; *Lasæa*, a place in Crete:—Lasea.

2997. λάσχω, laschō, *las´-kho*; a strengthened form of a primary verb, which only occurs in this and another prolonged form as alternate in certain tenses; to *crack* open (from a fall):—burst asunder.

2998. λατομέω, latomeō, *lat-om-eh´-o*; from the same as the first part of 2991 and the base of 5114; to *quarry*:—hew.

2999. λατρεία, latreia, *lat-ri´-ah*; from 3000; *ministration* of God, i.e. *worship*:—(divine) service.

Noun from *latreúō* (3000), to serve for hire, to worship. Service for hire or as a slave. In the NT, only in respect to God, divine service (Jn 16:2); spoken of the priest's service in the sacrifices (Ro 9:4; Heb 9:1, 6); used figuratively of the Christian's offering himself as a living sacrifice (Ro 12:1).

Deriv.: *eidōlolatreía* (1495), idolatry.

Syn.: *diakonía* (1248), service, ministry; *thrēskeía* (2356), religion, worship; *leitourgía* (3009), public ministry.

3000. λατρεύω, latreuō, *lat-ryoo´-o*; from **λάτρις,** *latris* (a hired *menial*); to *minister* (to God), i.e. *render* religious *homage*:—serve, do the service, worship (-per).

From *latrís* (n.f.), one hired. To serve, in a religious sense to serve and to worship God (Mt 4:10; Lk 1:74; 2:37; 4:8; Ac 7:7; 24:14; 26:7; 27:23; Ro 1:9; Php 3:3; 2Ti 1:3; Heb 9:14; 12:28; Rev 22:3); used in a negative sense: to worship the host of heaven, i.e. the sun, moon, and stars (Ac 7:42); to worship the creature rather than the Creator (Ro 1:25). Used of those who served in offering the OT sacrifices (Heb 8:5; 9:9; 10:2; 13:10) and of those serving the celestial temple (Rev 7:15).

Deriv.: *latreía* (2999), service, worship.

Syn.: *eusebéō* (2151), to act piously toward, worship; *proskunéō* (4352), to make obeisance, do reverence to, worship, do homage; *sebázomai* (4573), to honour religiously, render reverence; *sébomai* (4576), to revere, render devotion. With the meaning of rendering service: *diakonéō* (1247), to minister; *leitourgéō* (3008), to minister publicly in sacred service.

3001. λάχανον, lachanon, *lakh´-an-on*; from **λαχαίνω,** *lachainō* (to *dig*); a *vegetable*:—herb.

3002. Λεββαῖος, Lebbaios, *leb-bah´-yos*; of uncertain origin; *Lebbæus*, a Christian:—Lebbæus.

3003. λεγεών, legeōn, *leg-eh-ohn´*; of Latin origin; a "*legion*," i.e. Roman *regiment* (figurative):—legion.

3004. λέγω, legō, *leg´-o*; a primary verb; properly to "*lay*" forth, i.e. (figurative) *relate* (in words [usually of systematic or set *discourse*; whereas 2036 and 5346 generally refer to an *individual* expression or speech respectively; while 4483 is properly to *break silence* merely, and 2980 means an *extended* or random harangue]); (by implication) to *mean*:—ask, bid, boast, call, describe, give out, name, put forth, say (-ing, on), shew, speak, tell, utter.

Originally: to lay or let lie down for sleep, to lay together, i.e. to collect; later: to relate, recount; and hence the meaning of to say, speak, i.e. to utter definite words, connected and significant discourse. It thus differs from *laléō* (2980), which refers primarily to words spoken and not to their connected sense. In the NT:

(**I**) To lay before, i.e. to relate, e.g., a parable, to put forth, propound (Lk 12:41; 13:6; 14:7; 18:1). Of events: to narrate, tell (Lk 24:10).

(**II**) To say, speak, discourse:

(**A**) Generally (Mt 16:13; 27:11; 21:16; Mk 9:11; 11:23; Lk 8:8; 9:7; Jn 4:20; 5:34; 18:37; Ac 4:32; 8:6; Ro 10:8; Eph 5:12).

(**B**) As modified by the context, where the meaning lies not so much in *légō*, as in the adjuncts, e.g.: (**1**) Before questions: to ask, inquire (Mt 9:14; Mk 5:30; 6:37; 14:14; Lk 7:20; 16:5; 22:11; Jn 7:11; Ac 25:20; Ro 10:19). (**2**)

Before replies: to answer, reply (Mt 17:25; 18:22; 20:7, 21; Jn 18:17). (**3**) In affirmations: to affirm, maintain (Mt 22:23; Mk 14:31; Lk 24:23; Gal 4:1; Jas 2:14; 1Jn 2:4, 6, 9). In the formulas "I say unto thee" (or unto you), in solemn affirmations, generally (Mt 11:9, 22; Mk 11:24; Lk 4:25; 7:14; 15:10; Jn 3:11). (**4**) Figuratively: to say or speak by writing, by letter, e.g., with the words written (Lk 1:63; 20:42; 1Co 7:6; 15:51; 2Co 6:13; Php 4:11; 1Th 4:15; Phm 21).

(**III**) To call, to name, similar to *kaléō* [(2564), to call)]; particularly: to speak of as being something or being called something (Mt 19:17; Mk 15:12; Lk 20:37; Jn 5:18; 15:15; Ac 10:28; Heb 11:24). Passive participle: called, named (Mt 2:23; 9:9; 26:3, 14; Mk 15:7; Jn 4:5; 9:11; 21:2; Ac 3:2; Eph 2:11). Also surnamed (Mt 4:18; 10:2; Col 4:11). With the idea of translation into another language (Jn 1:38; 4:25; 11:16; 19:17; 20:16; Ac 9:36).

Deriv.: *antilégō* (483), to contradict, speak against; *genealogéō* (1075), to reckon by generation; *dialégomai* (1256), to discuss, reason; *dílogos* (1351), double-tongued; *eklégomai* (1586), to choose, elect; *epilégō* (1951), to call, select; *katalégō* (2639), to reckon among, to count in; *logía* (3048), collection, gathering; *lógos* (3056), word, reason, expression; *mataiológos* (3151), one talking lightly; *paralégō* (3881), to pass, sail by; *prolégō* (4302), to tell before, foretell; *spermológos* (4691), babbler; *stratologéō* (4758), to enlist; *sullégō* (4816), to collect; *Philólogos* (5378), a proper name: lover of the word; *pseudológos* (5573), one speaking lies.

Syn.: *laléō* (2980), to say something (sometimes in contrast with *légō*, the former indicating a mere utterance of sounds, breaking silence, or speaking). Also, *anaggéllō* (312), to announce, report; *antapokrínomai* (470), to reply against; *apaggéllō* (518), to announce, report; *apokrínomai* (611), to give an answer to a question; *dēlóō* (1213), to make plain; *diēgéomai* (1334), to narrate; *diaggéllō* (1229), to announce, declare; *diasaphéō* (1285), to make clear; *ekdiēgéomai* (1555), to narrate in full; *exaggéllō* (1804), to publish, proclaim; *exēgéomai* (1834), to declare, bring out the meaning; *epaggéllō* (1861), to announce, proclaim; *eréō* (2046), to tell, say; *euaggelízō* (2097), to evangelize; *kataggéllō* (2605), to declare, proclaim; *kērússō* (2784), to preach, herald; *homiléō* (3656), to converse with; *paraggéllō* (3853), to charge, command; *parrēsiázomai*

(3955), to be bold in speech; *plērophoréō* (4135), to inform fully; *prophēteúō* (4395), to prophesy; *suzētéō* (4802), to discuss; *pháskō* (5335), to affirm; *phēmí* (5346), to say by way of enlightening, explaining, affirming; *phrázō* (5419), to declare.

3005. λεῖμμα, leimma, *lime´-mah*; from 3007; a *remainder:*—remnant.

3006. λεῖος, leios, *li´-os*; apparently a primary word; *smooth*, i.e. "*level*":—smooth.

3007. λείπω, leipō, *li´-po*; a primary verb; to *leave*, i.e. (intransitive or passive) to *fail* or *be absent:*—be destitute (wanting), lack.

3008. λειτουργέω, leitourgeō, *li-toorg-eh´-o*; from 3011; to be a *public servant*, i.e. (by analogy) to *perform* religious or charitable *functions* (*worship, obey, relieve*):—minister.

From *leitourgós* (3011), public servant. To perform a public service. In the NT: to minister, to serve publicly in religious worship, e.g., the priests of the OT (Heb 10:11), Christian teachers (Ac 13:2). By implication, in a more private sense: to minister to anyone, to supply monetary aid (Ro 15:27).

Syn.: *diakonéō* (1247), to minister voluntarily; *douleúō* (1398), to serve as a slave, and therefore to serve by compulsion; *latreúō* (3000), primarily to work for hire, but when it involves service to God, it is also part of worship; *hupēretéō* (5256), to serve.

3009. λειτουργία, leitourgia, *li-toorg-ee´-ah*; from 3008; *public function* (as priest ["liturgy"] or almsgiver):—ministration (-try), service.

3010. λειτουργικός, leitourgikos, *li-toorg-ik-os´*; from the same as 3008; *functional publicly* ("liturgic"), i.e. *beneficent:*—ministering.

3011. λειτουργός, leitourgos, *li-toorg-os´*; from a derivative of 2992 and 2041; a *public servant*, i.e. a *functionary* in the temple or gospel, or (genitive) a *worshipper* (of God) or *benefactor* (of man):—minister (-ed).

3012. λέντιον, lention, *len´-tee-on*; of Latin origin; a "*linen*" cloth, i.e. *apron:*—towel.

3013. λεπίς, lepis, *lep-is´*; from λέπω, *lepō* (to *peel*); a *flake*):—scale.

3014. λέπρα, lepra, *lep´-rah*; from the same as 3013; *scaliness*, i.e. "*leprosy*":—leprosy.

3015. λεπρός, lepros, *lep-ros´*; from the same as 3014; *scaly*, i.e. *leprous* (a *leper*):—leper.

3016. λεπτόν, lepton, *lep-ton´*; neuter of a derivative of the same as 3013; something *scaled* (*light*), i.e. a small *coin:*—mite.

3017. Λευΐ, Leuï, *lyoo-ee´*; of Hebrew origin [3878]; *Levi*, the name of three Israelites:—Levi. Compare 3018.

3018. Λευΐς, Leuïs, *lyoo-is´*; a form of 3017; *Lewis* (i.e. *Levi*), a Christian:—Levi.

3019. Λευΐτης, Leuïtēs, *lyoo-ee´-tace*; from 3017; a *Levite*, i.e. descendant of Levi:—Levite.

3020. Λευϊτικός, Leuïtikos, *lyoo-it´-ee-kos´*; from 3019; *Levitic*, i.e. relating to the Levites:—Levitical.

3021. λευκαίνω, leukainō, *lyoo-kah´ee-no*; from 3022; to *whiten:*—make white, whiten.

3022. λευκός, leukos, *lyoo-kos´*; from λύκη, *lukē* ("*light*"); *white:*—white.

3023. λεών, leōn, *leh-ohn´*; a primary word; a "*lion*":—lion.

3024. λήθη, lēthē, *lay´-thay*; from 2990; *forgetfulness:*— + forget.

3025. ληνός, lēnos, *lay-nos´*; apparently a primary word; a *trough*, i.e. wine-*vat:*—winepress.

3026. λῆρος, lēros, *lay´-ros*; apparently a primary word; *twaddle*, i.e. an *incredible* story:—idle tale.

3027. ληστής, lēistēs, *lace-tace´*; from ληΐζομαι, *lēizomai* (to *plunder*); a *brigand:*—robber, thief.

Noun from *leízomai* (n.f.), to plunder. A plunderer, robber (Mt 21:13; 26:55; 27:38, 44; Mk 11:17; 14:48; 15:27; Lk 10:30, 36; 19:46; 22:52; Jn 10:1; 18:40; 2Co 11:26; Sept.: Jer 7:11); metaphorically of false teachers (Jn 10:8). See *kléptēs* (2812), thief.

Syn.: *kléptēs* (2812), thief. Also, *hierósulos* (2417), a robber of temples; *kakopoiós* (2555), an evildoer; *kakoúrgos* (2557), an evil worker, malefactor.

3028. λῆψις, lēpsis, *lape´-sis*; from 2983; *receipt* (the act):—receiving.

3029. λίαν, lian, *lee´-an*; of uncertain affinity; *much* (adverb):—exceeding, great (-ly), sore, very (+ chiefest).

3030. λίβανος, libanos, *lib´-an-os*; of foreign origin [3828]; the *incense*-tree, i.e. (by implication) *incense* itself:—frankincense.

3031. λιβανωτός, libanōtos, *lib-an-o-tos´*; from 3030; *frankincense,* i.e. (by extension) a *censer* for burning it:—censer.

3032. Λιβερτῖνος, Libertinos, *lib-er-tee´-nos*; of Latin origin; a Roman *freedman:*—Libertine.

3033. Λιβύη, Libuē, *lib-oo´-ay*; probably from 3047; *Libye,* a region of Africa:—Libya.

3034. λιθάζω, lithazō, *lith-ad´-zo*; from 3037; to *lapidate:*—stone.

3035. λίθινος, lithinos, *lith´-ee-nos*; from 3037; *stony,* i.e. made of *stone:*—of stone.

3036. λιθοβολέω, lithoboleō, *lith-ob-ol-eh´-o*; from a compound of 3037 and 906; to *throw stones,* i.e. *lapidate:*—stone, cast stones.

3037. λίθος, lithos, *lee´-thos*; apparently a primary word; a *stone* (literal or figurative):— (mill-, stumbling-) stone.

3038. λιθόστρωτος, lithostrōtos, *lith-os´-tro-tos*; from 3037 and a derivative of 4766; *stone-strewed,* i.e. a tessellated *mosaic* on which the Roman tribunal was placed:—Pavement.

3039. λικμάω, likmaō, *lik-mah´-o*; from λικ-μός, *likmos,* the equivalent of λίκνον, *liknon* (a winnowing *fan* or basket); to *winnow,* i.e. (by analogy) to *triturate:*—grind to powder.

3040. λιμήν, limēn, *lee-mane´*; apparently a primary word; a *harbor:*—haven. Compare 2568.

3041. λίμνη, limnē, *lim´-nay*; probably from 3040 (through the idea of the nearness of shore); a *pond* (large or small):—lake.

3042. λιμός, limos, *lee-mos´*; probably from 3007 (through the idea of *destitution*); a *scarcity* of food:—dearth, famine, hunger.

3043. λίνον, linon, *lee´-non*; probably a primary word; *flax,* i.e. (by implication) *"linen"*:—linen.

3044. Λῖνος, Linos, *lee´-nos*; perhaps from 3043; *Linus,* a Christian:—Linus.

3045. λιπαρός, liparos, *lip-ar-os´*; from λίπος, *lipos* (*grease*); *fat,* i.e. (figurative) *sumptuous:*—dainty.

3046. λίτρα, litra, *lee´-trah*; of Latin origin [*libra*]; a *pound* in weight:—pound.

3047. λίψ, lips, *leeps*; probably from λείβω, *leibō* (to *pour* a "libation"); the *south* (-west) wind (as bringing rain, i.e. (by extension) the *south* quarter:—southwest.

3048. λογία, logia, *log-ee´-ah*; from 3056 (in the commercial sense); a *contribution:*—collection, gathering.

3049. λογίζομαι, logizomai, *log-id´-zom-ahee*; middle from 3056; to *take an inventory,* i.e. *estimate* (literal or figurative):—conclude, (ac-) count (of), + despise, esteem, impute, lay, number, reason, reckon, suppose, think (on).

From *lógos* (3056), reason, word, account. To reason, to think, consider, reckon:

(I) Generally to think upon, to consider (Mk 11:31; 2Co 10:7; Php 4:8; Heb 11:19). In the sense of to reason out, to think out, to find out by thinking (2Co 3:5).

(II) Of the result of reasoning: to conclude, to judge, to suppose, to hold (Ro 3:28; 2Co 11:5; 12:6; Php 3:13; 1Pe 5:12). So generally: to reason, to judge (1Co 13:11); also in the sense of to purpose (2Co 10:2).

(III) To reckon someone to be in a particular group: e.g., to consider Christ as a transgressor (Mk 15:28; Lk 22:37). To count, regard, to hold (Ac 19:27; Ro 8:36; 1Co 4:1; 2Co 10:2).

(IV) To reckon or count to someone, particularly: to put to one's account (Ro 4:4); hence figuratively: to impute, to attribute:

(A) Generally, of God's imputing righteousness (Ro 4:6, 11). So of evil: to impute, to lay to one's charge; and with a neg., not to impute, i.e. to overlook, to forgive (Ro 4:8; 2Co 5:19; 2Ti 4:16).

(B) Also followed by that which is imputed, laid to one's charge, e.g., imputing Abraham's faith to him as righteousness; i.e. treating him as righteous on account of his faith (Ro 4:3, 9, 22; Gal 3:6; Jas 2:23).

Deriv.: *analogízomai* (357), to consider; *dialogízomai* (1260), to reckon distributively, to settle with one, to consider, deliberate; *logismós* (3053), a thought; *paralogízomai* (3884), to beguile, deceive; *sullogízomai* (4817), to reason with.

Syn.: *dialégomai* (1256), to dispute or reason with; *dokéō* (1380), to think, suppose; *egkrínō* (1469), to judge, to classify; *ellogéō* (1677), to put to a person's account, to reckon, impute; *katalégō* (2639), to count in; *kataxióō* (2661), to count worthy; *katarithméō* (2674), to number with, count among; *krínō* (2919), to judge, reckon; *nomízō* (3543), to suppose; *oíomai* (3633) I suppose, think; *sugkatapsēphízō* (4785), to reckon together with; *sullogízomai* (4817), to reckon, reason; *huponoéō* (5282), to suppose, surmise, think; *phronéō* (5426), to think.

3050. λογικός, **logikos**, *log-ik-os´*; from 3056; *rational* ("*logical*"):—reasonable, of the word.

Adjective from *lógos* (3056), reason, word. Literally, "of the Word": rational, pertaining to the reason, mind, understanding. Used in Ro 12:1 concerning the presentation of our bodies to be a living sacrifice to God as our *logikḗn latreían,* "rational service," i.e. the service or worship which is made by our mind (see *latreía* [2999], service or worship), stressing the inner motive and desires of our sacrifice more than outward deeds. Also used in 1Pe 2:2 in the phrase, *logikón ádolon gála,* which can be rendered either "the pure milk of the word" or "the pure milk for [or fitted for] the mind" (see *ádolos* [97], pure; *gála* [1051], milk).

3051. λόγιον, **logion**, *log´-ee-on*; neuter of 3052; an *utterance* (of God):—oracle.

Noun from *lógios* (3052) eloquent. Something uttered or spoken. Of God: an oracle, divine communication, e.g., of the oracles in the OT (Ac 7:38; Ro 3:2). So through Christ, the doctrines of the gospel (Heb 5:12; 1Pe 4:11).

3052. λόγιος, **logios**, *log´-ee-os*; from 3056; *fluent,* i.e. an *orator:*—eloquent.

3053. λογισμός, **logismos**, *log-is-mos´*; from 3049; *computation,* i.e. (figurative) *reasoning* (*conscience, conceit*):—imagination, thought.

Noun from *logízomai* (3049), to count, reckon, take an inventory. A reckoning, calculation. In the NT: reasoning, thought, meditation (Ro 2:15). Also in the sense of devices, counsels against God (2Co 10:5).

Syn.: *boulḗ* (1012), purpose, plan; *nóema* (3540), thought.

3054. λογομαχέω, **logomacheō**, *log-om-akh-eh´-o*; from a compound of 3056 and 3164; to *be disputatious* (on trifles):—strive about words.

3055. λογομαχία, **logomachia**, *log-om-akh-ee´-ah*; from the same as 3054; *disputation* about trifles ("*logomachy*"):—strife of words.

3056. λόγος, **logos**, *log´-os*; from 3004; something *said* (including the *thought*); (by implication) a *topic* (subject of discourse), also *reasoning* (the mental faculty or *motive*; by extension a *computation*; specially (with the art. in John) the Divine *Expression* (i.e. *Christ*):—account, cause, communication, × concerning, doctrine, fame, × have to do, intent, matter, mouth, preaching, question, reason, + reckon, remove, say (-ing), shew, × speaker, speech, talk, thing, + none of these things move me, tidings, treatise, utterance, word, work.

Noun from *légō* (3004), to speak intelligently. A word, as spoken; anything spoken; also reason as manifesting itself in the power of speech:

(I) A word, both the act of speaking and the thing spoken:

(A) A word, as uttered by the living voice, a speaking, speech, utterance (Mt 8:8; Lk 7:7; 23:9; 1Co 14:9; Heb 12:19); a saying, discourse, conversation (Mt 12:37; 15:12; 19:22; 22:15; 26:1; Ac 5:24). Metonymically, the power of speech, delivery, oratory, eloquence (1Co 12:8; 2Co 11:6; Eph 6:19). The Word of God, meaning His omnipotent voice, decree (2Pe 3:5, 7; Sept.: Ps 32:6 [cf. Ge 1:3; Ps 148:5]).

(B) A saying, declaration, sentiment uttered:

(1) Generally (Mt 10:14; Lk 4:22; 20:20; Jn 6:60). In reference to words or declarations, e.g., which precede (Mt 7:24, 26; Mk 7:29; Jn 2:22; 6:60; 7:40; 10:19; 12:38; Ac 5:24; 20:35; Ro 9:9; 13:9; 1Co 15:54; 1Ti 3:1; Tit 3:8; Rev 19:9). The word, declaration of a prophet, meaning prediction, prophecy (Lk 3:4; Jn 12:38; Ac 15:15; 2Pe 1:19; Rev 1:3); a proverb, maxim (Jn 4:37).

(2) In reference to religion, religious duties, i.e.

doctrine, precept (Ac 15:24; 18:15; 1Ti 4:6; Tit 1:9; Heb 2:2); especially of God, the Word of God, meaning divine revelation and declaration, oracle (Mk 7:13; Lk 5:1; Jn 5:38; 10:35; 17:6; Ac 4:29; Ro 9:6, 28; 1Co 14:36; 2Co 4:2; Col 1:25; 1Th 2:13; Tit 1:3; Heb 4:2, 12; 13:7).

(II) Reason, the reasoning faculty as that power of the soul which is the basis of speech. In the NT:

(A) A reason, ground, cause (Mt 5:32; Ac 10:29; 18:14).

(B) Reason as demanded or assigned, i.e. a reckoning, an account (Mt 18:23; 25:19; Lk 16:2; Ac 19:40; 20:24; Heb 13:17; 1Pe 3:15; 4:5).

(III) The Word, the *Lógos* in the writings of John (Jn 1:1, 14; 1Jn 1:1; Rev 19:13); it here stands for the preexistent nature of Christ, i.e. that spiritual and divine nature spoken of in the Jewish writings before and about the time of Christ, under various names, e.g., Son of Man (Da 7:13); Word of Jehovah (used in the Aramaic Targums, the translations which were used in the Jewish synagogues along with the Hebrew Scriptures). On this divine word, the Jews of that age would appear to have had much subtle discussion; and therefore probably the apostle sets out with affirming, "In the beginning was the Word, and the Word was with God, and the Word was God" (Jn 1:1); and then also declares that this Word became flesh and was thus the Messiah (Jn 1:14).

Deriv.: *álogos* (249), irrational, without intelligence; *analogía* (356), analogy; *analogízomai* (357), to contemplate, consider; *apologéomai* (626), to answer back, defend oneself; *battologéō* (945), to use vain repetitions; *ellogéō* (1677), to account, reckon in; *eulogéō* (2127), to speak well of, bless; *logízomai* (3049), to reckon, impute; *logikós* (3050), reasonable; *lógios* (3052), fluent, orator, intelligent person; *polulogía* (4180), much speaking.

Syn.: *rhēma* (4487), word, utterance. Also, *aggelía* (31), message, announcement; *eperótēma* (1906), an inquiry, answer; *laliá* (2981), speech; *homilía* (3657), homily, communication, speech; *propheteía* (4394), prophecy, something spoken ahead of its occurrence or spoken forth; *suzētēsis* (4803), mutual questioning; *phēmē* (5345), fame, report, that which is being said about someone.

3057. **λόγχη, logchē,** *long'-khay*; perhaps a primary word; a "*lance*":—spear.

3058. **λοιδορέω, loidoreō,** *loy-dor-eh'-o*; from 3060; to *reproach*, i.e. *vilify*:—revile.

From *loídoros* (3060), a reviler. To revile, reproach (Jn 9:28; Ac 23:4; 1Co 4:12; 1Pe 2:23).

Deriv.: *antiloidoréō* (486), to revile again.

Syn.: *atimázō* (818), to dishonour; *blasphēméō* (987), to revile, blaspheme; *empaízō* (1702), to mock, jeer; *theatrízō* (2301), to expose as a spectacle; *katageláō* (2606), to deride, laugh to scorn; *muktērízō* (3456), to ridicule; *oneidízō* (3679), to reproach; *hubrízō* (5195), to insult, to use despitefully or shamefully; *chleuázō* (5512), to mock.

3059. **λοιδορία, loidoria,** *loy-dor-ee'-ah*; from 3060; *slander* or *vituperation*:—railing, reproach [-fully].

3060. **λοίδορος, loidoros,** *loy'-dor-os*; from **λοιδός,** *loidos* (*mischief*); *abusive*, i.e. a *blackguard*:—railer, reviler.

3061. **λοιμός, loimos,** *loy-mos'*; of uncertain affinity; a *plague* (literal, the *disease*; or figurative, a *pest*):—pestilence (-t).

3062. **λοιποί, loipoi,** *loy-poy'*; masculine plural of a derivative of 3007; *remaining* ones:—other, which remain, remnant, residue, rest.

3063. **λοιπόν, loipon,** *loy-pon'*; neuter singular of the same as 3062; something *remaining* (adverb):—besides, finally, furthermore, (from) henceforth, moreover, now, + it remaineth, then.

3064. **λοιποῦ, loipou,** *loy-poo'*; generic singular of the same as 3062; *remaining* time:—from henceforth.

3065. **Λουκᾶς, Loukas,** *loo-kas'*; contracted from Latin *Lucanus*; *Lucas*, a Christian:—Lucas, Luke.

3066. **Λούκιος, Loukios,** *loo'-kee-os*; of Latin origin; *illuminative*; *Lucius*, a Christian:—Lucius.

3067. **λουτρόν, loutron,** *loo-tron'*; from 3068; a *bath*, i.e. (figurative) *baptism*:—washing.

Noun from *loúō* (3068), to bathe. The act of bathing, washing, ablution. Spoken of the washing of the word of God as a cleansing instrument (Eph 5:26); spoken of the cleansing which takes place at salvation (Tit 3:5).

Syn.: *katharismós* (2512), cleansing.

3068. λούω, louō, *loo'-o*; a primary verb; to *bathe* (the *whole* person; whereas 3538 means to wet a *part* only, and 4150 to wash, cleanse *garments* exclusively):—wash.

To bathe, to wash (Jn 13:10; Ac 9:37; 16:33; Heb 10:22; 2Pe 2:22). Metaphorically: to cleanse and purify from sin, as in being washed by Christ's blood (Rev 1:5).

Deriv.: *apoloúō* (628), to wash away; *loutrón* (3067), bath.

Syn.: *katharízō* (2511), to cleanse.

3069. Λύδδα, Ludda, *lud'-dah*; of Hebrew origin [3850]; *Lydda* (i.e. *Lod*), a place in Palestine:—Lydda.

3070. Λυδία, Ludia, *loo-dee'-ah*; properly feminine of **Λύδιος, Ludios**; [of foreign origin] (a *Lydian*, in Asia Minor); *Lydia*, a Christian woman:—Lydia.

3071. Λυκαονία, Lukaonia, *loo-kah-on-ee'-ah*; perhaps remotely from 3074; *Lycaonia*, a region of Asia Minor:—Lycaonia.

3072. Λυκαονιστί, Lukaonisti, *loo-kah-on-is-tee'*; adverb from a derivative of 3071; *Lycaonistically*, i.e. in the language of the Lycaonians:—in the speech of Lycaonia.

3073. Λυκία, Lukia, *loo-kee'-ah*; probably remotely from 3074; *Lycia*, a province of Asia Minor:—Lycia.

3074. λύκος, lukos, *loo'-kos*; perhaps akin to the base of 3022 (from the *whitish* hair); a *wolf*:—wolf.

3075. λυμαίνομαι, lumainomai, *loo-mah'-ee-nom-ahee*; middle from a probable derivative of 3089 (meaning *filth*); properly to *soil*, i.e. (figurative) *insult* (*maltreat*):—make havock of.

3076. λυπέω, lupeō, *loo-peh'-o*; from 3077; to *distress*; reflexive or passive to *be sad*:—cause grief, grieve, be in heaviness, (be) sorrow (-ful), be (make) sorry.

From *lúpē* (3077), sorrow. To grieve, afflict with sorrow; middle or passive, to be grieved, sad, sorrowful (Mt 14:9; 17:23; 18:31; 19:22; 26:22, 37; Mk 10:22; 14:19; Jn 16:20; 21:17; Ro 14:15; 2Co 2:2, 4; 6:10; 7:9, 11; 1Th 4:13; 1Pe 1:6). With the meaning of to cause grief, offend (2Co 2:5; 7:8; Eph 4:30).

Deriv.: *sullupéō* (4818), to sorrow together.

Syn.: *adēmonéō* (85), to be in distress; *diaponéō* (1278), in the pass., to be troubled as the result of pain and toil; *enochléō* (1776), to vex; *thlíbō* (2346), to squeeze, to afflict; *thrēnéō* (2354), bewail; *kóptō* (2875), to beat the breast, an outward sign of an inward grief; *odunáō* (3600), to cause pain, be in anguish; *penthéō* (3996), mourn; *tarássō* (5015), to trouble; *turbázō* (5182), to disturb, trouble.

3077. λύπη, lupē, *loo'-pay*; apparently a primative word; *sadness*:—grief, grievous, + grudgingly, heaviness, sorrow.

3078. Λυσανίας, Lusanias, *loo-san-ee'-as*; from 3080 and **ἀνία, Ania** (*trouble*); *grief-dispelling*; *Lysanias*, a governor of Abilene:—Lysanias.

3079. Λυσίας, Lusias, *loo-see'-as*; of uncertain affinity; *Lysias*, a Roman:—Lysias.

3080. λύσις, lusis, *loo'-sis*; from 3089; a *loosening*, i.e. (special) *divorce*:—to be loosed.

3081. λυσιτελεῖ, lusitelei, *loo-sit-el-i'*; third person singular present indicative active of a derivative of a composition of 3080 and 5056; impersonal it *answers the purpose*, i.e. is *advantageous*:—it is better.

3082. Λύστρα, Lustra, *loos'-trah*; of uncertain origin; *Lystra*, a place in Asia Minor:—Lystra.

3083. λύτρον, lutron, *loo'-tron*; from 3089; something to *loosen* with, i.e. a redemption *price* (figurative, *atonement*):—ransom.

Noun from *lúō* (3089), to loose. Ransom, lit. "loosing-money," i.e. price paid for redeeming captives. Used metaphorically for the ransom paid by Christ for the delivering of men from the bondage of sin and death (Mt 20:28; Mk 10:45).

Deriv.: *antílutron* (487), ransom; *lutróō* (3084), to ransom.

Syn.: *timḗ* (5092), price.

3084. λυτρόω, lutroō, *loo-tro'-o*; from 3083; to *ransom* (literal or figurative):—redeem.

From *lútron* (3083), a ransom. To ransom, i.e. to let go free for a ransom. In the NT, used in the middle voice: to ransom, to redeem, to deliver; used metaphorically of Christ's purchasing our salvation (Lk 24:21; Tit 2:14; 1Pe 1:18).

Deriv.: *lútrōsis* (3085), the act of redemption or deliverance; *lutrōtḗs* (3086), redeemer.

Syn.: *apallássō* (525), to release, deliver; *diasṓzō* (1295), to rescue, bring through safely; *eleutheróō* (1659), to free; *sṓzō* (4982), to save, deliver.

3085. λύτρωσις, **lutrōsis**, *loo´-tro-sis*; from 3084; a *ransoming* (figurative):— + redeemed, redemption.

Noun from *lutróō* (3084), to release on receipt of a ransom. Redemption, deliverance; spoken of the redemption of Israel (Lk 1:68; 2:38). Used metaphorically: redemption from sin and its consequences (Heb 9:12).

Syn.: *áphesis* (859), release, forgiveness; *dikaíōsis* (1347), justification; *sōtēría* (4991), salvation, rescuing; *sōtḗrion* (4992), the means of salvation.

3086. λυτρωτής, **lutrōtēs**, *loo-tro-tace´*; from 3084; a *redeemer* (figurative):—deliverer.

Noun from *lutróō* (3084), to release on receipt of a ransom. Redeemer, liberator. In the NT, used only in Ac 7:35 of Moses.

Syn.: *sōtḗr* (4990), savior.

3087. λυχνία, **luchnia**, *lookh-nee´-ah*; from 3088; a *lamp-stand* (literal or figurative):—candlestick.

3088. λύχνος, **luchnos**, *lookh´-nos*; from the base of 3022; a portable *lamp* or other *illuminator* (literal or figurative):—candle, light.

Noun meaning portable light, as a candle, lamp, lantern, etc. (Mt 5:15; Mk 4:21; Lk 8:16; 11:33, 36; 12:35; 15:8; 2Pe 1:19; Rev 18:23; 22:5). "The lamp of the body" (a.t.) represents the eye (Mt 6:22; Lk 11:34). Metaphorically, of John the Baptist as a distinguished teacher (Jn 5:35); of the Messiah, the Lamb in the new Jerusalem (Rev 21:23).

Deriv.: *luchnía* (3087), lampstand.

Syn.: *lampás* (2985), a torch, but frequently fed like a lamp with oil from a little vessel used for the purpose; *phanós* (5322), a lantern or torch.

3089. λύω, **luō**, *loo´-o*; a primary verb; to "*loosen*" (literal or figurative):—break (up),

destroy, dissolve, (un-) loose, melt, put off. Compare 4486.

To loose, loosen what is bound, meaning to unbind, untie:

(I) Particularly, of loosing something fastened; e.g., sandal straps (Mk 1:7; Lk 3:16; Jn 1:27; Ac 7:33; 13:25); figuratively, the impediment of the tongue (Mk 7:35); the pains of death (Ac 2:24); also, of animals tied, e.g., a colt (Mt 21:2; Mk 11:2, 4; Lk 19:30, 31, 33); of a person swathed in bandages or graveclothes (Jn 11:44); of persons bound in sin and wickedness, who are loosed through the preaching of and a saving relationship with Jesus Christ and are judged or disciplined by the church based on their works (Mt 16:19; 18:18).

(II) Spoken of persons bound: to let go, loose, set free, e.g., prisoners (Ac 22:30; 24:26; Rev 20:3, 7); figuratively (Lk 13:16; 1Co 7:27).

(III) To loosen, dissolve, i.e. to sever, break (Ac 27:41; Rev 5:2, 5); figuratively of an assembly: to dissolve or break up (Ac 13:43).

(IV) By implication: to destroy, e.g., buildings, to demolish (Jn 2:19; Eph 2:14); figuratively (1Jn 3:8); of the world: to be destroyed by fire, to dissolve, melt (2Pe 3:10–12); figuratively of a law or institution: to loosen its obligation, i.e. either to make void, to do away (Mt 5:19; Jn 10:35), or to break, to violate (Jn 7:23).

Deriv.: *analúō* (360), to return; *apolúō* (630), to dismiss, release; *dialúō* (1262), to dissolve, scatter; *eklúō* (1590), to set free from; *epilúō* (1956), to unloose, explain, dissolve; *katalúō* (2647), to destroy, throw down; *lúsis* (3080), a loosening, divorce; *lútron* (3083), ransom; *paralúō* (3886), to loosen, become feeble, paralyzed.

Syn.: *apallássō* (525), to release, deliver; *apekdúō* (554), to strip off clothes, put off; *apochōrízō* (673), to separate off; *diachōrízō* (1316), to depart, remove oneself; *methístēmi* (3179), to remove; *chōrízō* (5563), to separate.

3090. Λωΐς, **Lōïs**, *lo-ece´*; of uncertain origin; *Loïs*, a Christian woman:—Lois.

3091. Λώτ, **Lōt**, *lote*; of Hebrew origin [3876]; *Lot*, a patriarch:—Lot.

M (Mu)

NT Numbers 3092–3475

3092. Μαάθ, Maath, *mah-ath´*; probably of Hebrew origin; *Maath*, an Israelite:—Maath.

3093. Μαγδαλά, Magdala, *mag-dal-ah´*; of Chaldee origin [compare 4026]; *the tower; Magdala* (i.e. *Migdala*), a place in Palestine:—Magdala.

3094. Μαγδαληνή, Magdalēnē, *mag-dal-ay-nay´*; feminine of a derivative of 3093; a female *Magda-lene*, i.e. inhabitant of Magdala:—Magdalene.

3095. μαγεία, mageia, *mag-i´-ah*; from 3096; *"magic"*:—sorcery.

3096. μαγεύω, mageuō, *mag-yoo´-o*; from 3097; to *practice magic*:—use sorcery.

3097. μάγος, magos, *mag´-os*; of foreign origin [7248]; a *Magian*, i.e. Oriental *scientist*; (by implication) a *magician*:—sorcerer, wise man.

3098. Μαγώγ, Magōg, *mag-ogue´*; of Hebrew origin [4031]; *Magog*, a foreign nation, i.e. (figurative) an Antichristian party:—Magog.

3099. Μαδιάν, Madian, *mad-ee-an´*; of Hebrew origin [4080]; *Madian* (i.e. *Midian*), a region of Arabia:—Madian.

3100. μαθητεύω, mathēteuō, *math-ayt-yoo´-o*; from 3101; intransitive to *become a pupil*; transitive to *disciple*, i.e. enroll as scholar:—be disciple, instruct, teach.

From *mathētés* (3101), disciple. To be the disciple of someone (Mt 27:57); to train as a disciple; to teach, to instruct; e.g., the Great Commission (Mt 28:19). Also Mt 13:52; Ac 14:21.

Syn.: *didáskō* (1321), to give instruction, teach; *heterodidaskaléō* (2085), to teach a different doctrine; *katēchéō* (2727), to teach orally, instruct, catechize; *paideúō* (3811), to instruct and train, to discipline.

3101. μαθητής, mathētēs, *math-ay-tes´*; from 3129; a *learner*, i.e. *pupil*:—disciple.

Noun from *manthánō* (3129), to learn, to understand. A disciple, scholar, follower of a teacher; generally (Mt 10:24); of the Pharisees (Mt 22:16); of John the Baptist (Mt 9:14; Mk 2:18; Lk 5:33; Jn 3:25); of Jesus (Mt 5:1; Mk 8:27; Lk 8:9; Jn 3:22); specifically of the twelve apostles (Mt 10:1; 11:1; 20:17; Lk 9:1); emphatically for true disciples (Jn 13:35; 15:8). After Christ's death, the term disciple takes the broader sense of follower, believer, i.e. Christian (Ac 6:1, 2; 11:26).

Deriv.: *mathēteúō* (3100), to disciple; *summathētés* (4827), a fellow disciple.

3102. μαθήτρια, mathētria, *math-ay´-tree-ah*; feminine from 3101; a female *pupil*:—disciple.

3103. Μαθουσάλα, Mathousala, *math-oo-sal´-ah*; of Hebrew origin [4968]; *Mathusala* (i.e. *Methu-shelach*), an antediluvian:—Mathusala.

3104. Μαϊνάν, Maïnan, *mahee-nan´*; probably of Hebrew origin; *Maïnan*, an Israelite:—Mainan.

3105. μαίνομαι, mainomai, *mah´ee-nom-ahee*; middle from a primary **μάω, maō** (to *long* for; through the idea of insensate *craving*); to *rave* as a "maniac":—be beside self (mad).

3106. μακαρίζω, makarizō, *mak-ar-id´-zo*; from 3107; to *beatify*, i.e. *pronounce* (or *esteem*) *fortunate*:—call blessed, count happy.

From *mákar* (n.f.), the poetic form of *makários* (3107), blessed. To call happy, blessed, to congratulate (Lk 1:48; Jas 5:11).

Deriv.: *makarismós* (3108), a state of blessedness.

Syn.: *eulogéō* (2127), to speak well of, bless.

3107. μακάριος, makarios, *mak-ar´-ee-os*; a prolonged form of the poetical **μάκαρ, makar**

(meaning the same); supremely *blest*; by extension *fortunate, well off*:—blessed, happy (× -ier). A prose form of the poetic *mákar* (n.f.), blessed one. Happy, fortunate, blessed. Spoken in the Beatitudes of those receiving God's favour, regardless of what their circumstances may be (Mt 5:3–11). See also Lk 1:45; 6:20–22; Ac 20:35; Ro 4:7; 1Co 7:40. Used to refer to God as being well-spoken of, praised (1Ti 1:11).
Deriv.: *makarízō* (3106), to declare blessed.
Syn.: *eulogētós* (2128), blessed, well-spoken of; *eulogēménos*, blessed, passive participle of *eulogéō* (2127), to eulogise, bless, thank.

3108. μακαρισμός, makarismos, *mak-ar-is-mos´*; from 3106; *beatification*, i.e. *attribution of good fortune*:—blessedness.

3109. Μακεδονία, Makedonia, *mak-ed-on-ee´-ah*; from 3110; *Macedonia*, a region of Greece:—Macedonia.

3110. Μακεδών, Makedōn, *mak-ed-ohn´*; of uncertain derivative; a *Macedon* (*Macedonian*), i.e. inhabitant of Macedonia:—of Macedonia, Macedonian.

3111. μάκελλον, makellon, *mak´-el-lon*; of Latin origin [*macellum*]; a *butcher's stall, meat market* or *provision-shop*:—shambles.

3112. μακράν, makran, *mak-ran´*; feminine accusative singular of 3117 (3598 being implied); *at a distance* (literal or figurative):—(a-) far (off), good (great) way off.

3113. μακρόθεν, makrothen, *mak-roth´-en*; adverb from 3117; *from a distance* or *afar*:—afar off, from far.

3114. μακροθυμέω, makrothumeō, *mak-roth-oo-meh´-o*; from the same as 3116; *to be long-spirited*, i.e. (objective) *forbearing* or (subjective) *patient*:—bear (suffer) long, be long-suffering, have (long) patience, be patient, patiently endure.
From *makróthumos* (n.f.), long-suffering, which is from *makrós* (3117), long, and *thumós* (2372), wrath, anger. To be long-minded, i.e. slow to anger; to be long-suffering, to be patient (Mt 18:26, 29; 1Co 13:4; 1Th 5:14; 2Pe 3:9), to wait patiently (Heb 6:15; Jas 5:7, 8).
Deriv.: *makrothumía* (3115), long-suffering.
Syn.: *hupoménō* (5278), to endure. Also, *ané-*

chomai (430), to tolerate, endure; *karteréō* (2594), to endure; *pheídomai* (5339), to spare.

3115. μακροθυμία, makrothumia, *mak-roth-oo-mee´-ah*; from the same as 3116; *longanimity*, i.e. (objective) *forbearance* or (subjective) *fortitude*:—long-suffering, patience.
Noun from *makrothuméō* (3114), to be long-suffering. Forbearance, long-suffering, patient endurance when others attack or make our lives difficult. *Makrothumía* describes patience with people, while *hupomonē* (5281), patience, describes more patience with circumstances. Used of God (Ro 2:4; 9:22; 1Pe 3:20; 2Pe 3:15). Spoken of as one of the fruits of the Spirit (Gal 5:22). Also 2Co 6:6; Eph 4:2; Col 1:11; 3:12; 1Ti 1:16; 2Ti 3:10; 4:2; Heb 6:12; Jas 5:10).
Syn.: *anochḗ* (463), tolerance; *epieíkeia* (1932), gentleness.

3116. μακροθυμώς, makrothumōs, *mak-roth-oo-moce´*; adverb of a compound of 3117 and 2372; *with long (enduring) temper*, i.e. *leniently*:—patiently.
Adverb from *makróthumos* (n.f.), long-suffering, which is from *makrós* (3117), long, and *thumós* (2372), wrath, anger. Patiently, i.e. with forbearance, with clemency. Used only in Ac 26:3. See *makrothumía* (3115), long-suffering.

3117. μακρός, makros, *mak-ros´*; from 3372; *long* (in place [*distant*] or time [neuter plural]):—far, long.

3118. μακροχρόνιος, makrochronios, *mak-rokh-ron´-ee-os*; from 3117 and 5550; *long-timed*, i.e. *long-lived*:—live long.

3119. μαλακία, malakia, *mal-ak-ee´-ah*; from 3120; *softness*, i.e. *enervation (debility)*:—disease.
Noun from *malakós* (3120), soft. Softness, used figuratively for timidity, effeminacy, luxury. In the NT: weakness, disease (Mt 4:23; 9:35; 10:1).
Syn.: *asthéneia* (769), disease, weakness; *nósēma* (3553), ailment, disease; *nósos* (3554), malady, infirmity.

3120. μαλακός, malakos, *mal-ak-os´*; of uncertain affinity.; *soft*, i.e. *fine* (clothing); (figurative) a *catamite*:—effeminate, soft.

3121. Μαλελεήλ, **Maleleēl,** *mal-el-eh-ale´*; of Hebrew origin [4111]; *Maleleēl* (i.e. *Mahalalel*), an antediluvian:—Maleleel.

3122. μάλιστα, **malista,** *mal´-is-tah*; neuter plural of the superlative of an apparently primary adverb μάλα, *mala* (*very*); (adverb) *most* (*in the greatest degree*) or *particularly*:—chiefly, most of all, (e-) specially.

3123. μᾶλλον, **mallon,** *mal´-lon*; neuter of the comparative of the same as 3122; (adverb) *more* (*in a greater degree*) or *rather*:— + better, × far, (the) more (and more), (so) much (the more), rather.

3124. Μάλχος, **Malchos,** *mal´-khos*; of Hebrew origin [4429]; *Malchus,* an Israelite:—Malchus.

3125. μάμμη, **mammē,** *mam´-may*; of native origin ["mammy"]; a *grandmother*:—grandmother.

3126. μαμμωνᾶς, **mammōnas,** *mam-mo-nas´*; of Chaldee origin (*confidence*; i.e. figurative, *wealth,* personified); *mammonas,* i.e. *avarice* (deified):—mammon.

From the Aramaic *māmôn* (n.f.), mammon, the comprehensive word for all kinds of possessions, earnings, and gains; wealth, riches (Lk 16:9, 11). Also personified, like the Gr. *ploútos* (4149), wealth, as that which one serves if he doesn't serve God (Mt 6:24; Lk 16:13).

3127. Μαναήν, **Manaēn,** *man-ah-ane´*; of uncertain origin; *Manaēn,* a Christian:—Manaen.

3128. Μανασσῆς, **Manassēs,** *man-as-sace´*; of Hebrew origin [4519]; *Manasses* (i.e. *Menashsheh*), an Israelite:—Manasses.

3129. μανθάνω, **manthanō,** *man-than´-o*; prolonged from a primary verb, another form of which, μαθέω, *matheō,* is used as an alternate in certain tenses; to *learn* (in any way):—learn, understand.

(I) Particularly: intellectually, from others or from study and observation (Mt 9:13; 11:29; 24:32; Mk 13:28; 1Ti 5:4, 13; 2Ti 3:14). To learn someone, i.e. his doctrines, precepts (Eph 4:20). In the sense of to learn by information, to be informed (Ac 23:27; Gal 3:2); also to understand, to comprehend (Rev 14:3).

(II) Morally: to learn from experience, with the idea of to do habitually, to be wont (Php 4:11; Tit 3:14; Heb 5:8).

Deriv.: *amathḗs* (261), unlearned; *katamanthánō* (2648), to learn, to understand thoroughly; *mathētḗs* (3101), disciple.

3130. μανία, **mania,** *man-ee´-ah*; from 3105; *craziness*:— [+ make] × mad.

3131. μάννα, **manna,** *man´-nah*; of Hebrew origin [4478]; *manna* (i.e. *man*), an edible gum:—manna.

3132. μαντεύομαι, **manteuomai,** *mant-yoo´-om-ahee*; from a derivative of 3105 (meaning a *prophet,* as supposed to *rave* through *inspiration*); to *divine,* i.e. *utter spells* (under pretence of foretelling):—by soothsaying.

From *mántis* (n.f.), a soothsayer, diviner, which is from *maínomai* (3105), to be mad, beside oneself. To utter responses from an oracle, to divine, foretell. Only in Ac 16:16.

Syn.: *proginṓskō* (4267), to foreknow; *prolégō* (4302), to foretell; *prooráō* (4308), to behold in advance; *prophēteúō* (4395), to prophesy.

3133. μαραίνω, **marainō,** *mar-ah´ee-no*; of uncertain affinity; to *extinguish* (as fire), i.e. (figurative and passive) to *pass away*:—fade away.

3134. μαρὰν ἀθά, **maran atha,** *mar´-an ath´-ah*; of Chaldee origin (meaning *our Lord has come*); *maranatha,* i.e. an exclamation of the approaching *divine judgement*:—Maranatha.

3135. μαργαρίτης, **margaritēs,** *mar-gar-ee´-tace*; from μάργαρος, *margaros* (a pearl-*oyster*); a *pearl*:—pearl.

3136. Μάρθα, **Martha,** *mar´-thah*; probably of Chaldee origin (meaning *mistress*); *Martha,* a Christian woman:—Martha.

3137. Μαρία, **Maria,** *mar-ee´-ah*; or Μαριάμ, **Mariam,** *mar-ee-am´*; of Hebrew origin [4813]; *Maria* or *Mariam* (i.e. *Mirjam*), the name of six Christian females:—Mary.

3138. Μάρκος, **Markos,** *mar´-kos*; of Latin origin; *Marcus,* a Christian:—Marcus, Mark.

3139. μάρμαρος, **marmaros,** *mar´-mar-os*; from μαρμαίρω, *marmairō* (to *glisten*); *marble* (as sparkling *white*):—marble.

μάρτυρ, *martur.* See 3144.

3140. μαρτυρέω, martureō, *mar-too-reh´-o;*
from 3144; to *be a witness,* i.e. *testify* (literal or
figurative):—charge, give [*evidence*], bear
record, have (obtain, of) good (honest) report,
be well reported of, testify, give (have) testimony, (be, bear, give, obtain) witness.

From *mártus* (3144), witness. To be a witness, bear witness:

(I) To bear witness, to testify to the truth of
what one has seen, heard, or knows:

(A) Particularly and generally: to bear witness concerning a person or thing (Jn 1:7, 8, 15;
2:25; 8:13, 14, 18; 21:24; 1Co 15:15; 1Jn 4:14);
to testify something (Jn 3:11; 3:32; Ac 26:5; Heb
10:15; 1Jn 1:2; 5:6–8; Rev 1:2; 22:16, 20); to
prove by testimony (Jn 18:23).

(B) Figuratively: of God as testifying by His
Spirit through signs and miracles. (Jn 5:37;
8:18; 1Jn 5:9, 10). Of the Scriptures or prophets
(Jn 5:39; Ac 10:43). Of one's deeds, works (Jn
5:36; 10:25).

(II) Emphatically: to testify strongly, bear
honourable testimony; and pass., to be well-tes-
tified about, to have good witness (Heb 7:8;
11:4, 5). Generally: to speak well of, applaud (Lk
4:22; Ac 15:8; Heb 11:4; 3Jn 12). In the pass.,
meaning to be lauded, to be of good report (Ac
6:3; 10:22; 16:2; 22:12; 1Ti 5:10; Heb 11:2; 3Jn
12).

Deriv.: *epimarturéō* (1957), to bear witness
to; *katamarturéō* (2649), to bear witness against;
marturía (3141), a testimony; *martúrion* (3142),
a declaration of facts, proof, a testimony; *sum-
marturéō* (4828), to bear witness with; *pseudo-
marturéō* (5576), to bear false witness.

Syn.: *bebaióō* (950), to assure; *plērophoréō*
(4135), to inform fully; *phanéroō* (5319), to
manifestly declare.

3141. μαρτυρία, marturia, *mar-too-ree´-ah;*
from 3144; *evidence* given (judicially or
generic):—record, report, testimony, witness.

Noun from *marturéō* (3140), to witness. Witness, testimony, as borne, given:

(I) Particularly: judicial testimony in court
(Mk 14:55, 56, 59; Lk 22:71; Jn 8:17).

(II) Generally, testimony to the truth of anything (Jn 19:35; 21:24; 3Jn 12). So of a poet (Tit
1:13). Elsewhere only in reference to Jesus and
his doctrines, i.e. to the truth of his mission and

gospel (Jn 5:34); so from John the Baptist (Jn
1:7, 19; 5:36), from other teachers (Ac 22:18; Rev
11:7; 12:11), also from God (Jn 5:32; 1Jn 5:9–
11). Of Christ's testimony respecting himself (Jn
3:11, 32, 33; 5:31; 8:13, 14).

(III) Emphatically: honourable testimony,
good report (1Ti 3:7).

Deriv.: *pseudomarturía* (5577), a false witness.

Syn.: *martúrion* (3142), testimony.

3142. μαρτύριον, marturion, *mar-too´-ree-
on;* neuter of a presumed derivative of 3144;
something *evidential,* i.e. (genitive) *evidence*
given or (special) the *Decalogue* (in the sacred
tabernacle):—to be testified, testimony, witness.

Noun from *marturéō* (3140), to witness. Witness, testimony, as borne, given, equivalent to
marturía (3141):

(I) Generally (2Co 1:12). So historically (Ac
4:33). In reference to Jesus and his doctrines
(1Co 1:6; 2:1; 2Th 1:10; 2Ti 1:8). Generally in
the sense of testimony, evidence, proof (Mt 8:4;
10:18; 24:14; Mk 1:44; 6:11; Lk 5:14; 21:13; Jas
5:3).

(II) Used as a designation of the Mosaic tabernacle (Ac 7:44; Rev 15:5).

Syn.: *bebaíōsis* (951), confirmation; *marturía*
(3141), testimony.

3143. μαρτύρομαι, marturomai, *mar-too´-
rom-ahee;* middle from 3144; to *be adduced* as *a
witness,* i.e. (figurative) to *obtest* (in affirmation
or exhortation):—take to record, testify.

From *mártus* (3144), witness. To call to witness, to invoke as witness. In the NT: to testify,
to solemnly affirm, to make an earnest and
solemn appeal (Ac 20:26; Gal 5:3); also to exhort
solemnly (Eph 4:17).

Deriv.: *diamartúromai* (1263), to bear witness, to charge; *promartúromai* (4303), to witness beforehand.

Syn.: *bebaióō* (950), to confirm; *dēlóō* (1213),
to declare.

3144. μάρτυς, martus, *mar´-toos;* of uncertain
affinity; a *witness* (literal [judicially] or figurative [genitive]); (by analogy) a *"martyr":*—
martyr, record, witness.

(I) Particularly, in a judicial sense (Mt 18:16;
26:65; Mk 14:63; Ac 6:13; 7:58; 2Co 13:1; Heb
10:28).

(II) Generally, one who testifies or can testify to the truth of what he has seen, heard, knows (Ro 1:9; 2Co 1:23; Php 1:8; 1Th 2:10; 1Ti 6:12); so in allusion to those who witness a public game (Heb 12:1). Especially of those who witnessed the life, death, and resurrection of Jesus, who bear witness to the truth as it is in Jesus (Lk 24:48; Ac 1:8, 22; 2:32; 5:32; 26:16; 2Ti 2:2); so of one who bears witness for God, and testifies to the world what God reveals through him, i.e. a teacher, prophet (Rev 1:5; 3:14; 11:3).

(III) A martyr, one who by his death bears witness to the truth (Ac 22:20; Rev 2:13; 17:6).

Deriv.: *amárturos* (267), without a witness; *marturéō* (3140), to witness; *martúromai* (3143), to summon as a witness, adjure; *pseudomártur* (5575), a person who bears false witness.

Syn.: *autóptēs* (845), eyewitness.

3145. μασσάομαι, massaomai, *mas-sah´-om-ahee*; from a primary **μάσσω, massō** (to *handle* or *squeeze*); to *chew*:—gnaw.

3146. μαστιγόω, mastigoō, *mas-tig-o´-o*; from 3148; to *flog* (literal or figurative):—scourge.

3147. μαστίζω, mastizō, *mas-tid´-zo*; from 3149; to *whip* (literal):—scourge.

3148. μάστιξ, mastix, *mas´-tix*; probably from the base of 3145 (through the idea of *contact*); a *whip* (literal, the Roman *flagellum* for criminals; figurative, a *disease*):—plague, scourging.

3149. μαστός, mastos, *mas-tos´*; from the base of 3145; a (properly female) *breast* (as if *kneaded* up):—pap.

3150. ματαιολογία, mataiologia, *mat-ah-yol-og-ee´-ah*; from 3151; *random talk*, i.e. *babble*:—vain jangling.

3151. ματαιολόγος, mataiologos, *mat-ah-yol-og´-os*; from 3152 and 3004; an *idle* (i.e. *senseless* or *mischievous*) *talker*, i.e. a *wrangler*:—vain talker.

Adjective from *mátaios* (3152), vain, and *légō* (3004), to speak. Given to vain talking; vain talker, empty wrangler. Used only in Tit 1:10.

Deriv.: *mataiología* (3150), vain talk.

3152. μάταιος, mataios, *mat´-ah-yos*; from the base of 3155; *empty*, i.e. (literal) *profitless*, or (special) an *idol*:—vain, vanity.

Adjective from *mátēn* (3155), to no purpose, in vain. Useless, worthless, vain, empty (1Co 3:20; 15:17; Tit 3:9; Jas 1:26; 1Pe 1:18). *Mátios* carries the idea of aimless, fruitless, and misleading, whereas *kenós* (2756), vain, emphasizes something's emptiness and hollowness. As a substantive in the plural: "vanities, nothings," for idols, idolatry (Ac 14:15).

Deriv.: *mataiológos* (3151), one who talks vainly; *mataiótēs* (3153), vanity; *mataióō* (3154), to become vain.

Syn.: *kenós* (2756), empty, vacant, inane. Also, *ákarpos* (175), unfruitful; *alazón* (213), braggart, boastful; *alusitelḗs* (255) and *anōphelḗs* (512), unprofitable; *kenódoxos* (2755), self-centered, conceited, vain.

3153. ματαιότης, mataiotēs, *mat-ah-yot´-ace*; from 3152; *inutility*; (figurative) *transientness*; (moral) *depravity*:—vanity.

Noun from *mátaios* (3152), vain. Vanity, emptiness (2Pe 2:18). In the sense of frailty, transientness (Ro 8:20). From the Hebrew for folly, perverseness, wickedness (Eph 4:17).

3154. ματαιόω, mataioō, *mat-ah-yo´-o*; from 3152; to *render* (passive *become*) *foolish*, i.e. (moral) *wicked* or (special) *idolatrous*:—become vain.

From *mátaios* (3152), vain. To make vain or worthless. In the NT, only passive: to become vain, i.e. foolish, perverse, wicked. Used only in Ro 1:21. See *mátaios* (3152), vain.

Syn.: *paraphronéō* (3912), to act foolishly, thoughtlessly.

3155. μάτην, matēn, *mat´-ane*; accusative of a derivative of the base of 3145 (through the idea of tentative *manipulation*, i.e. unsuccessful *search*, or else of *punishment*); *folly*, i.e. (adverb) *to no purpose*:—in vain.

Adverb meaning in vain, to no purpose, fruitlessly (Mt 15:9; Mk 7:7). See *mátaios* (3152), vain.

Deriv.: *mátaios* (3152), vain.

Syn.: *kenós* (2761), in vain.

3156. Ματθαῖος, Matthaios, *mat-thah´-yos*; a shorter form of 3161; *Matthæus* (i.e. *Matthitjah*), an Israelite and Christian:—Matthew.

3157. Ματθάν, Matthan, *mat-than´*; of Hebrew origin [4977]; *Matthan* (i.e. *Mattan*), an Israelite:—Matthan.

3158. Ματθάτ, Matthat, *mat-that´*; probably a shortened form of 3161; *Matthat* (i.e. *Mattithjah*), the name of two Israelites:—Mathat.

3159. Ματθίας, Matthias, *mat-thee´-as*; apparently a shortened form of 3161; *Matthias* (i.e. *Mattithjah*), an Israelite:—Matthias.

3160. Ματταθά, Mattatha, *mat-tath-ah´*; probably a shortened form of 3161 [compare 4992]; *Mattatha* (i.e. *Mattithjah*), an Israelite:—Mattatha.

3161. Ματταθίας, Mattathias, *mat-tath-ee´-as*; of Hebrew origin [4993]; *Mattathias* (i.e. *Mattithjah*), an Israelite and Christian:—Mattathias.

3162. μάχαιρα, machaira, *makh´-ahee-rah*; probably feminine of a presumed derivative of 3163; a *knife*, i.e. *dirk*; (figurative) *war*, judicial *punishment*:—sword.

3163. μάχη, mache, *makh´-ay*; from 3164; a *battle*, i.e. (figurative) *controversy*:—fighting, strive, striving.

Noun from *máchomai* (3164), to fight. A fight, battle. In the NT, generally: strife, contest, controversy (2Co 7:5; 2Ti 2:23; Jas 4:1); controversies respecting the Mosaic Law (Tit 3:9).

Deriv.: *ámachos* (269), not contentious.

Syn.: *agón* (73), strife, fight; *logomachía* (3055), strife of words; *pálē* (3823), wrestling; *pólemos* (4171), war; *stásis* (4714), insurrection or sedition as a civil war.

3164. μάχομαι, machomai, *makh´-om-ahee*; middle of an apparently primary verb; to *war*, i.e. (figurative) to *quarrel, dispute*:—fight, strive.

3165. μέ, me, *meh*; a shorter (and probably original) form of 1691; *me*:—I, me, my.

3166. μεγαλαυχέω, megalaucheo, *meg-al-ow-kheh´-o*; from a compound of 3173 and αὐχέω, *aucheo* (to *boast*; akin to 837 and 2744); to *talk big*, i.e. *be grandiloquent* (*arrogant, egotistic*):—boast great things.

3167. μεγαλεῖος, megaleios, *meg-al-i´-os*; from 3173; *magnificent*, i.e. (neuter plural as noun) a conspicuous *favour*, or (subject) *perfection*:—great things, wonderful works.

Adjective from *mégas* (3173), great, indicating great works or miracles. Great, glorious, wonderful. As a substantive: great things, wonderful works (Lk 1:49; Ac 2:11).

Deriv.: *megaleiótēs* (3168), majesty.

Syn.: In the plural as great things, miracles: *sēmeía* (4592), signs. Also, *dunámeis* (1411), mighty works; *éndoxa* (1741), glorious things; *thaumásia* (2297), astonishing things; *parádoxa* (3861), strange or extraordinary things; *térata* (5059), wonders.

3168. μεγαλειότης, megaleiotēs, *meg-al-i-ot´-ace*; from 3167; *superbness*, i.e. *glory* or *splendour*:—magnificence, majesty, mighty power.

3169. μεγαλοπρεπής, megaloprepēs, *meg-al-op-rep-ace´*; from 3173 and 4241; *befitting greatness* or *magnificence* (*majestic*):—excellent.

3170. μεγαλύνω, megaluno, *meg-al-oo´-no*; from 3173; to *make* (or *declare*) *great*, i.e. *increase* or (figurative) *extol*:—enlarge, magnify, shew great.

3171. μεγάλως, megalos, *meg-al´-oce*; adverb from 3173; *much*:—greatly.

3172. μεγαλωσύνη, megalōsunē, *meg-al-o-soo´-nay*; from 3173; *greatness*, i.e. (figurative) *divinity* (often *God* himself):—majesty.

3173. μέγας, megas, *meg´-as*; [including the prolonged forms, feminine μεγάλη, *megalē*, plural μέγάλοι, *megaloi*, etc.; compare also 3176, 3187]; *big* (literal or figurative, in a very wide application):—(+ fear) exceedingly, great (-est), high, large, loud, mighty, + (be) sore (afraid), strong, × to years.

3174. μέγεθος, megethos, *meg´-eth-os*; from 3173; *magnitude* (figurative):—greatness.

3175. μεγιστᾶνες, megistanes, *meg-is-tan´-es*; plural from 3176; *grandees*:—great men, lords.

3176. μέγιστος, megistos, *meg´-is-tos*; superlative of 3173; *greatest* or *very great*:—exceeding great.

3177. μεθερμηνεύω, methermēneuo, *meth-er-mane-yoo´-o*; from 3326 and 2059; to *explain over*, i.e. *translate*:—(by) interpret (-ation).

3178. μέθη, methe, *meth´-ay*; apparently a primary word; an *intoxicant*, i.e. (by implication) *intoxication*:—drunkenness.

Noun from *méthu* (n.f., see below). Drunkenness (Lk 21:34; Ro 13:13; Gal 5:21).

Deriv. of *méthu* (n.f.): *methúskō* (3182), to make or become drunk; *méthusos* (3183), a drunkard; *methúō* (3184), to be drunk.

Syn.: *oinophlugía* (3632), excess of wine. Also, *kraipálē* (2897), dissipation, excess, a headache from drunkenness; *pósis* (4213), the act of drinking; *pótos* (4224), banqueting or a drinking party.

3179. μεθίστημι, methistēmi, *meth-is´-tay-mee*; or (1Co 13:2) **μεθιστάνω, methistanō,** *meth-is-tan´-o*; from 3326 and 2476; to *transfer,* i.e. *carry away, depose* or (figurative) *exchange, seduce*:—put out, remove, translate, turn away.

From *metá* (3326), denoting change of place or condition, and *hístēmi* (2476), to place, stand. To set or move over from one place to another, to transfer, to remove. In the NT, to move physically (1Co 13:2); in a spiritual sense: to move into the kingdom of God (Col 1:13). Metaphorically: to draw over to another side or party, to seduce (Ac 19:26). Of persons: to remove from office, to depose (Ac 13:22); of a steward: to dismiss (Lk 16:4).

Syn.: *ekchōréō* (1633), to depart; *metakinéō* (3334), to move away; *metatíthēmi* (3346), to transport, change, remove.

3180. μεθοδεία, methodeia, *meth-od-i´-ah*; from a compound of 3326 and 3593 [compare "method"]; *travelling over,* i.e. *travesty* (*trickery*):—wile, lie in wait.

Noun from *methodeúō* (n.f.), to work by method. To trace out with method and skill, to treat methodically; to use art, to deal artfully; hence method, in the sense of art, wile (Eph 4:14; 6:11).

Syn.: *apátē* (539), deceit; *dólos* (1388), wile, craft; *panourgía* (3834), trickery, craftiness.

3181. μεθόριος, methorios, *meth-or´-ee-os*; from 3326 and 3725; *bounded alongside,* i.e. *contiguous* (neuter plural as noun, *frontier*):—border.

3182. μεθύσκω, methuskō, *meth-oos´-ko*; a prolonged (transitive) form of 3184; to *intoxicate*:—be drunk (-en).

3183. μέθυσος, methusos, *meth´-oo-sos*; from 3184; *tipsy,* i.e. (as noun) a *sot*:—drunkard.

3184. μεθύω, methuō, *meth-oo´-o*; from another form of 3178; to *drink* to *intoxication,* i.e. *get drunk*:—drink well, make (be) drunk (-en).

3185. μεῖζον, meizon, *mide´-zon*; neuter of 3187; (adverb) in a *greater* degree:—the more.

3186. μειζότερος, meizoteros, *mide-zot´-er-os*; continued comparative of 3187; *still larger* (figurative):—greater.

3187. μείζων, meizōn, *mide´-zone*; irregular comparative of 3173; *larger* (literal or figurative, specially in age):—elder, greater (-est), more.

3188. μέλαν, melan, *mel´-an*; neuter of 3189 as noun; *ink*:—ink.

3189. μέλας, melas, *mel´-as*; apparently a primary word; *black*:—black.

3190. Μελεᾶς, Meleas, *mel-eh-as´*; of uncertain origin; *Meleas,* an Israelite:—Meleas.

3191. μελετάω, meletaō, *mel-et-ah´-o*; from a presumed derivative of 3199; to *take care of,* i.e. (by implication) *revolve* in the mind:—imagine, (pre-) meditate.

3192. μέλι, meli, *mel´-ee*; apparently a primary word; *honey*:—honey.

3193. μελίσσιος, melissios, *mel-is´-see-os*; from 3192; *relating to honey,* i.e. *bee* (comb):—honeycomb.

3194. Μελίτη, Melitē, *mel-ee´-tay*; of uncertain origin; *Melita,* an island in the Mediterranean:—Melita.

3195. μέλλω, mellō, *mel´-lo*; a strengthened form of 3199 (through the idea of *expectation*); to *intend,* i.e. *be about* to be, do, or suffer something (of persons or things, especially events; in the sense of *purpose, duty, necessity, probability, possibility,* or *hesitation*):—about, after that, be (almost), (that which is, things, + which was for) to come, intend, was to (be), mean, mind, be at the point, (be) ready, + return, shall (begin), (which, that) should (after, afterwards, hereafter) tarry, which was for, will, would, be yet.

To be about to do or suffer anything; to be on the point of doing, usually followed by an infinitive expressing what one is going to do:

(I) Generally (Lk 7:2; Jn 4:47; Ac 21:27; 27:33; Rev 3:2). Also implying purpose, i.e. to have in mind, to intend, to will (Ac 12:6). Also Mt 2:13; Lk 10:1; Jn 6:6; Ac 3:3; Rev 10:4.

(II) With the idea of ought, should, must; implying necessity, accordance with the nature of things or with divine appointment, and therefore certain, destined to take place (Mt 11:14; Mk 10:32; Lk 9:31, 44; Jn 11:51; Ac 28:6; Heb 1:14; Rev 2:10); hence the participle without an infinitive: impending, future (Mt 3:7; 12:32; Lk 13:9; Ro 5:14; 8:38; 1Co 3:22; 1Ti 4:8; Heb 9:11).

(III) To be ever about to do a thing, i.e. to linger, to delay (Ac 22:16).

3196. μέλος, melos, *mel´-os*; of uncertain affinity; a *limb* or *part* of the body:—member.

3197. Μελχί, Melchi, *mel-khee´*; of Hebrew origin [4428 with pronoun suffix, *my king*]; *Melchi* (i.e. *Malki*), the name of two Israelites:—Melchi.

3198. Μελχισεδέκ, Melchisedek, *mel-khis-ed-ek´*; of Hebrew origin [4442]; *Melchisedek* (i.e. *Malkitsedek*), a patriarch:—Melchisedec.

3199. μέλω, melō, *mel´-o*; a primary verb; to *be of interest* to, i.e. to *concern* (only third person singular presumed indicative used impersonal *it matters*):—(take) care.

3200. μεμβράνα, membrana, *mem-bran´-ah*; of Latin origin ("*membrane*"); a (written) sheep-*skin*:—parchment.

3201. μέμφομαι, memphomai, *mem´-fom-ahee*; middle of an apparently primary verb; to *blame*:—find fault.

3202. μεμψίμοιρος, mempsimoiros, *mem-psim´-oy-ros*; from a presumed derivative of 3201 and **μοῖρα, moira** (*fate*; akin to the base of 3313); *blaming fate*, i.e. *querulous* (*discontented*):—complainer.

3203–3302. *These numbers were omitted in Strong's Dictionary of the Greek Testament.*

3303. μέν, men, *men*; a primary particle; properly indicative of *affirmation* or *concession* (*in fact*); usually followed by a *contrasted* clause with 1161 (*this* one, the *former*, etc.):—even, indeed, so, some, truly, verily. Often compounded with other particles in an *intensive* or *asseverative* sense.

3304. μενοῦνγε, menounge, *men-oon´-geh*; from 3303 and 3767 and 1065; *so then at least*:—nay but, yea doubtless (rather, verily).

3305. μέντοι, mentoi, *men´-toy*; from 3303 and 5104; *indeed though*, i.e. *however*:—also, but, howbeit, nevertheless, yet.

3306. μένω, menō, *men´-o*; a primary verb; to *stay* (in a given place, state, relation or expectancy):—abide, continue, dwell, endure, be present, remain, stand, tarry (for), × thine own.

To remain, abide, dwell, live.

(I) Intransitively, to remain, dwell:

(A) Of place, i.e. of a person dwelling or lodging in a place (Mt 10:11; 26:38; Lk 8:27; 19:5; 24:29; Jn 1:38, 39; 2:12; 7:9; 8:35; Ac 16:15; 20:15; 28:16; 2Ti 4:20). With the meaning of staying in one place (Mt 26:38; Ac 27:31). Of bodies remaining (Jn 19:31). Figuratively of a veil remaining over the eyes (2Co 3:14).

(B) Of a state or condition, i.e. of a person remaining in a state or condition (Jn 12:46; Ac 5:4; 1Co 7:8, 40; Php 1:25; 2Ti 2:13; Heb 7:3; 1Jn 3:14). To continue to exist, to remain in force, to endure, with the adjunct of time during or to which a person or thing remains, continues, endures (Jn 21:22, 23; 1Co 15:6; 2Co 9:9; 1Pe 1:25; Rev 17:10). Used in an absolute sense, with the idea of perpetuity, i.e. to remain or endure forever, to be perpetual, e.g., Christian graces, "faith, hope, love" (1Co 13:13). See Jn 15:16; 2Co 3:11; Heb 10:34; 12:27; 13:1.

(C) Of the relation in which one person or thing stands with another, chiefly in John's writings; thus to remain in or with someone, i.e. to be and remain united with him, one with him in heart, mind, and will (Jn 6:56; 14:10; 15:4–7; 1Jn 2:6; 3:24; 4:15, 16). Also: to remain in something, equivalent to remaining steadfast, persevering in it (Jn 8:31; 15:9; 1Ti 2:15; 1Jn 2:10; 4:16; 2Jn 9). Conversely and in a like general sense, something may be said to remain in a person (Jn 5:38; 15:11; 1Jn 2:14; 3:15, 17; 2Jn 2).

(II) Transitively: to remain for someone, wait for, await (Ac 20:5, 23).

Deriv.: *anamenō* (362), to await; *diamenō* (1265), to continue abiding; *emmenō* (1696), to persevere; *epimenō* (1961), to continue in, tarry; *katamenō* (2650), to remain or abide; *monē* (3438), an abode, place to stay; *paramenō* (3887), to remain beside, endure; *periménō* (4037), to stay around, wait for; *prosménō* (4357), to abide with, continue with; *hupoménō* (5278), to be patient, endure trials and afflictions.

Syn.: *agrauléō* (63), to lodge in a fold or in a field; *anastréphō* (390), to abide; *apoleípō* (620), to remain; *aulízomai* (835), to pass the night in the open air; *dianuktereúō* (1273), to pass the night; *diatríbō* (1304), to spend or pass time, stay.

3307. μερίζω, merizō, *mer-id´-zo*; from 3313; to *part,* i.e. (literal) to *apportion, bestow, share,* or (figurative) to *disunite, differ:*—deal, be difference between, distribute, divide, give part.

3308. μέριμνα, merimna, *mer´-im-nah*; from 3307 (through the idea of *distraction*); *solicitude:*—care.

3309. μεριμνάω, merimnaō, *mer-im-nah´-o*; from 3308; to *be anxious* about:—(be, have) care (-ful), take thought.

3310. μερίς, meris, *mer-ece´*; feminine of 3313; a *portion,* i.e. *province, share* or (abstract) *participation:*—part (× -akers).

3311. μερισμός, merismos, *mer-is-mos´*; from 3307; a *separation* or *distribution:*—dividing asunder, gift.

Noun from *merízō* (3307), to divide into parts. Partition, division, i.e. separation (Heb 4:12); also distribution, and so put for a gift which is distributed (Heb 2:4).

Syn.: *analogía* (356), analogy, proportion; *diaíresis* (1243), division, distribution; *klēronomía* (2817), inheritance, heirship.

3312. μεριστής, meristēs, *mer-is-tace´*; from 3307; an *apportioner* (*administrator*):—divider.

3313. μέρος, meros, *mer´-os*; from an obsolete but more primary form of **μείρομαι, meiromai** (to *get* as a *section* or *allotment*); a *division* or *share* (literal or figurative, in a wide application):—behalf, coast, course, craft, particular (+ -ly), part (+ -ly), piece, portion, respect, side, some sort (-what).

3314. μεσημβρία, mesēmbria, *mes-ame-bree´-ah*; from 3319 and 2250; *midday*; (by implication) the *south:*—noon, south.

3315. μεσιτεύω, mesiteuō, *mes-it-yoo´-o*; from 3316; to *interpose* (as arbiter), i.e. (by implication) to *ratify* (as surety):—confirm.

From *mesítēs* (3316), mediator. To be a mediator between two contending parties. Only in Heb 6:17, where it has the idea of pledging oneself as surety.

3316. μεσίτης, mesitēs, *mes-ee´-tace*; from 3319; a *go-between,* i.e. (simply) an *internunciator,* or (by implication) a *reconciler* (*intercessor*):—mediator.

Noun from *mésos* (3319), middle, in the midst. A go-between, a mediator; one who intervenes between two parties, i.e. an interpreter, a medium of communication (Gal 3:19, 20), an intercessor, reconciler, especially used of Christ (1Ti 2:5; Heb 8:6; 9:15; 12:24).

Deriv.: *mesiteúō* (3315), to mediate, intercede.

3317. μεσονύκτιον, mesonuktion, *mes-on-ook´-tee-on*; neuter of a compound of 3319 and 3571; *midnight* (especially as a watch):—midnight.

3318. Μεσοποταμία, Mesopotamia, *mes-op-ot-am-ee´-ah*; from 3319 and 4215; *Mesopotamia* (as lying between the Euphrates and the Tigris; compare 763), a region of Asia:—Mesopotamia.

3319. μέσος, mesos, *mes´-os*; from 3326; *middle* (as adjective or [neuter] noun):—among, × before them, between, + forth, mid [-day, -night], midst, way.

Adjective meaning middle, in the midst. Used to indicate the middle part of something: e.g., the middle of the night (Mt 25:6); the middle of the day (Ac 26:13); the middle of the veil (Lk 23:45). Used in the sense of in the midst, among: e.g., "in the midst of wolves" (Mt 10:16; Lk 10:3). Also Mt 14:24; 18:2; Mk 6:47; Jn 1:26; 19:18; Rev 1:13).

Deriv.: *mesēmbría* (3314), midday; *mesítēs* (3316), mediator, one standing in the middle, a go-between; *mesonúktion* (3317), midnight; *mesótoichon* (3320), a partition, middle wall; *mesouránēma* (3321), mid-sky, midst of heaven; *mesóō* (3322), to be in the middle; *metaxú* (3342), in the midst of.

3320. μεσότοιχον, mesotoichon, *mes-ot´-oy-khon*; from 3319 and 5109; a *partition* (figurative):—middle wall.

3321. μεσουράνημα, mesouranēma, *mes-oo-ran´-ay-mah*; from a presumed compound of 3319 and 3772; *mid-sky*:—midst of heaven.

3322. μεσόω, mesoō, *mes-o´-o*; from 3319; to *form* the *middle*, i.e. (in point of time), to *be halfway* over:—be about the midst.

3323. Μεσσίας, Messias, *mes-see´-as*; of Hebrew origin [4899]; the *Messias* (i.e. *Mashiach*), or Christ:—Messias.

3324. μεστός, mestos, *mes-tos´*; of uncertain derivative; *replete* (literal or figurative):—full.

3325. μεστόω, mestoō, *mes-to´-o*; from 3324; to *replenish*, i.e. (by implication) to *intoxicate*:—fill.

3326. μετά, meta, *met-ah´*; a primary preposition (often used adverb); properly denoting *accompaniment*; "*amid*" (local or causal); modified variously according to the case (general *association*, or accusative *succession*) with which it is joined; occupying an intermediate position between 575 or 1537 and 1519 or 4314; less intimate than 1722, and less close than 4862):—after (-ward), × that be again, against, among, × and, + follow, hence, hereafter, in, of, (up-) on, + our, × and setting, since, (un-) to, + together, when, with (+ -out). Often used in composition, in substantially the same relations of *participation* or *proximity*, and *transfer* or *sequence*.

Preposition governing the gen. and accusative. Its primary meaning is mid, amid, in the midst, with, among, implying accompaniment and thus differing from *sún* (4862), which expresses conjunction, union:

(I) With the genitive, implying companionship, fellowship:

(A) With, in the sense of amid, among, in the midst of, as where one is said to be, sit, or stand (Mt 26:58; Mk 1:13; 14:54, 62; Lk 24:5; Jn 18:5; Ac 20:18; Rev 21:3).

(B) With, in the sense of together with: (1) Particularly, of persons: (a) Where one is said to be, go, remain, sit, or stand with someone, in his company; so also with the notation of place added (Mt 5:25; 9:15; Mk 5:18; Lk 11:7; 15:31; 22:21; Jn 3:26; 7:33; 11:31; 2Ti 4:11; Rev 3:21).

(b) Where one is said to do or suffer something with another, implying joint or mutual action, influence, suffering (Mt 2:3; 12:30, 41; 18:23; Mk 3:6, 7; Lk 5:30; Jn 11:16; 19:18; Ac 24:1; Ro 12:15; 1Th 3:13; Heb 13:23; Rev 3:20). (2) Figuratively, of things: (a) As designating the state or emotion of the mind which accompanies the doing of something or with which one acts, e.g., fear (Mt 28:8). Also Mk 3:5; Lk 14:9; Ac 20:19; 24:3; Eph 4:2; 2Th 3:12; 1Ti 2:9; Heb 10:22. (b) As designating an external action, circumstance, or condition with which another action or event is accompanied, e.g., with an oath (Mt 14:7). Also 24:31; 27:66; Mk 6:25; 10:30; Lk 9:39; 17:20; Ac 5:26; 13:17; 14:23; 24:18; 2Co 8:4; 1Ti 4:14; Heb 5:7; 7:21. Also often where it is equivalent to *kai* (2532), and (Eph 6:23; Col 1:11; 1Ti 1:14; 2:15; 3:4; 2Ti 2:10; Heb 9:19).

(II) With the accusative, *metá* strictly implies motion toward the middle or into the midst of something, and also motion after a person or thing, i.e. either so as to follow and be with a person or to fetch a person or thing. Hence also spoken of succession either in place or time, meaning after:

(A) Of succession in place meaning after, behind (Heb 9:3).

(B) Of succession in time: With a noun of time, e.g., "after six days" (Mt 17:1); also Mt 25:19; Mk 8:31; Lk 15:13; Ac 12:4; 28:11; Gal 1:18. With a noun of person (Ac 5:37; 19:4); with a noun marking an event or point of time (Mt 1:12; Mk 13:24; Lk 9:28; Jn 13:27; 2Pe 1:15).

In composition *metá* denotes: (a) fellowship, partnership, as *metadídōmi* (3330), to impart; *metalambánō* (3335), to participate; *metéchō* (3348), to partake; (b) proximity, contiguity, as *methórios* (3181), border; (c) motion or direction after, as *metapémpō* (3343), to summon or invite; (d) transition, transposition, change, meaning over as in *methístēmi* (3179), to carry away, transfer, remove; *meta-baínō* (3327), to go over, depart; *metatíthēmi* (3346), to remove.

3327. μεταβαίνω, metabainō, *met-ab-ah´ee-no*; from 3326 and the base of 939; to *change place*:—depart, go, pass, remove.

From *metá* (3326), denoting change of place or condition, and *baínō* (n.f.), to go or come. To pass or go from one place to another (Mt 17:20; Lk 10:7); to go away, depart (Mt 8:34; 11:1; 12:9;

15:29; Jn 7:3; 13:1; Ac 18:7). Figuratively, spoken of passing from death to life (Jn 5:24; 1Jn 3:14).

Syn.: *analúō* (360), to depart; *anachōréō* (402), to depart, retire; *apérchomai* (565), to go away; *aphístēmi* (868), to stand off, depart from someone; *metaírō* (3332), to remove; *poreúomai* (4198), to go one's way; *hupágō* (5217), to depart, go; *chōrízō* (5563), to separate, depart.

3328. μεταβάλλω, metaballō, *met-ab-al´-lo*; from 3326 and 906; to *throw over*, i.e. (middle figurative) to *turn about* in opinion:—change mind.

3329. μετάγω, metagō, *met-ag´-o*; from 3326 and 71; to *lead over*, i.e. *transfer* (*direct*):—turn about.

3330. μεταδίδωμι, metadidōmi, *met-ad-id´-o-mee*; from 3326 and 1325; to *give over*, i.e. *share*:—give, impart.

3331. μετάθεσις, metathesis, *met-ath´-es-is*; from 3346; *transposition*, i.e. *transferral* (to heaven), *disestablishment* (of a law):—change, removing, translation.

3332. μεταίρω, metairō, *met-ah´ee-ro*; from 3326 and 142; to *betake* oneself, i.e. *remove* (locally):—depart.

3333. μετακαλέω, metakaleō, *met-ak-al-eh´-o*; from 3326 and 2564; to *call elsewhere*, i.e. *summon*:—call (for, hither).

From *metá* (3326), denoting change of place or condition, and *kaléō* (2564), to call from one place to another, summon. As used in the middle voice, to call to oneself, to call for, to invite (Ac 7:14; 10:32; 20:17; 24:25).

Syn.: *metapémpō* (3343), to send after or for.

3334. μετακινέω, metakineō, *met-ak-ee-nah´-o*; from 3326 and 2795; to *stir* to a place elsewhere, i.e. *remove* (figurative):—move away.

3335. μεταλαμβάνω, metalambanō, *met-al-am-ban´-o*; from 3326 and 2983; to *participate*; genitive to *accept* (and use):—eat, have, be partaker, receive, take.

3336. μετάληψις, metalēpsis, *met-al´-ape-sis*; from 3335; *participation*:—taking.

3337. μεταλλάσσω, metallassō, *met-al-las´-so*; from 3326 and 236; to *exchange*:—change.

From *metá* (3326), denoting change of place or condition, and *allássō* (236), to change. To exchange one thing for another. Used only in a negative sense, exchanging God's revelation for a lie, and exchanging God's plan for man's sexual nature into homosexuality (Ro 1:25, 26).

3338. μεταμέλλομαι, metamellomai, *met-am-el´-lom-ahee*; from 3326 and the middle of 3199; to *care afterwards*, i.e. *regret*:—repent (self).

From *metá* (3326), denoting change of place or condition, and *mélomai*, middle of *mélō* (3199), to concern, to be concerned. To change one's care, etc. Hence to change one's mind or purpose after having done anything (Mt 21:29, 32; Heb 7:21). With the idea of regret, sorrow: to feel sorrow, remorse (Mt 27:3, of Judas; 2Co 7:8).

Deriv.: *ametamélētos* (278), not regretted.

3339. μεταμορφόω, metamorphoō, *met-am-or-fo´-o*; from 3326 and 3445; to *transform* (literal or figurative "metamorphose"):—change, transfigure, transform.

From *metá* (3326), denoting change of place or condition, and *morphóō* (3445), to form. To transform, transfigure, change one's form. In the NT, only in the passive: to be transfigured, transformed. Spoken literally of Christ's transfiguration on the mount (Mt 17:2; Mk 9:2). Spoken figuratively of our being transformed in mind and heart (Ro 12:2; 2Co 3:18).

Syn.: *metastréphō* (3344), to turn from, change; *metaschēmatízō* (3345), to change one's outward form.

3340. μετανοέω, metanoeō, *met-an-o-eh´-o*; from 3326 and 3539; to *think differently* or *afterwards*, i.e. *reconsider* (moral *feel compunction*):—repent.

From *metá* (3326), denoting change of place or condition, and *noéō* (3539), to perceive with the mind, think, comprehend. To repent, change the mind, relent; implying the feeling of regret, sorrow. Distinguished from *metamélomai* (3338), which may mean only to regret, to have remorse:

(I) Generally (Lk 17:3, 4; 2Co 12:21).

(II) In a religious sense, implying pious sorrow for unbelief and sin and a turning from them unto God and the gospel of Christ (Mt 3:2; 4:17; 11:20, 21; 12:41; Mk 1:15; 6:12; Lk

13:3, 5; 15:7, 10; 16:30; Ac 2:38; 3:19; 17:30; 26:20; Rev 2:5, 16, 21; 3:3, 19; 16:9).

Deriv.: *ametanóētos* (279), impenitent *metánoia* (3341), a change of mind, repentance.

3341. μετάνοια, metanoia, *met-an´-oy-ah*; from 3340; (subject) *compunction* (for guilt, including *reformation*); (by implication) *reversal* (of [another's] decision):—repentance.

Noun from *metanoéō* (3340), to repent. A change of mind, repentance: generally (Heb 12:17); in a religious sense, implying pious sorrow for unbelief and sin and a turning from them unto God and the gospel of Christ (Mt 3:8, 11; 9:13; Mk 2:17; Lk 3:8; 5:32; 15:7; Ac 5:31; 20:21; 26:20; Ro 2:4; Heb 6:6; 2Pe 3:9).

3342. μεταξύ, metaxu, *met-ax-oo´*; from 3326 and a form of 4862; *betwixt* (of place or person); (of time) as adjective *intervening*, or (by implication) *adjoining*:—between, meanwhile, next.

3343. μεταπέμπω, metapempō, *met-ap-emp´-o*; from 3326 and 3992; to *send* from *elsewhere*, i.e. (middle) to *summon* or *invite*:—call (send) for.

3344. μεταστρέφω, metastrephō, *met-as-tref´-o*; from 3326 and 4762; to *turn across*, i.e. *transmute* or (figurative) *corrupt*:—pervert, turn.

3345. μετασχηματίζω, metaschēmatizō, *met-askh-ay-mat-id´-zo*; from 3326 and a derivative of 4976; to *transfigure* or *disguise*; (figurative) to *apply* (by accommodation):—transfer, transform (self).

From *metá* (3326), denoting change of place or condition, and *schēmatízō* (n.f.), to form, which is from *schéma* (4976), shape, outward form. To transform, change the outward form or appearance of something (1Co 4:6). Used in a negative sense of false apostles changing their appearance into apostles of Christ and ministers of righteousness (2Co 11:13, 14); and of Satan appearing as an angel of light (2Co 11:15). Used once of the awaited transformation of the bodies of believers into immortal bodies, fitted to the glory of Christ (Php 3:21).

3346. μετατίθημι, metatithēmi, *met-at-ith´-ay-mee*; from 3326 and 5087; to *transfer*, i.e. (literal) *transport*, (by implication) *exchange*,

(reflexive) *change sides*, or (figurative) *pervert*:—carry over, change, remove, translate, turn.

3347. μετέπειτα, metepeita, *met-ep´-i-tah*; from 3326 and 1899; *thereafter*:—afterward.

3348. μετέχω, metechō, *met-ekh´-o*; from 3326 and 2192; to *share* or *participate*; (by implication) *belong* to, *eat* (or *drink*):—be partaker, pertain, take part, use.

From *metá* (3326), with, denoting association, and *échō* (2192), have. To have together with others, to partake of, share in. Generally (1Co 9:10, 12; 10:30; Heb 5:13). Spoken of Christ's partaking of flesh and blood, i.e. becoming flesh and blood like us (Heb 2:14); spoken of partaking of the Lord's Supper (1Co 10:17, 21); spoken of Christ belonging to a tribe other than the one appointed for the priesthood (Heb 7:13).

Deriv.: *metoché* (3352), a partaking, participation, fellowship; *métochos* (3353), a partaker, an associate.

Syn.: *koinōnéō* (2841), to participate, share.

3349. μετεωρίζω, meteōrizō, *met-eh-o-rid´-zo*; from a compound of 3326 and a collative form of 142 or perhaps rather of 109 (compare "meteor"); to *raise in mid-air*, i.e. (figurative) *suspend* (passive *fluctuate* or *be anxious*):—be of doubtful mind.

3350. μετοικεσία, metoikesia, *met-oy-kes-ee´-ah*; from a derivative of a compound of 3326 and 3624; a *change of abode*, i.e. (special) *expatriation*:— × brought, carried (-ying) away (in-) to.

3351. μετοικίζω, metoikizō, *met-oy-kid´-zo*; from the same as 3350; to *transfer* as a *settler* or *captive*, i.e. *colonize* or *exile*:—carry away, remove into.

3352. μετοχή, metoche, *met-okh-ay´*; from 3348; *participation*, i.e. *intercourse*:—fellowship.

3353. μέτοχος, metochos, *met´-okh-os*; from 3348; *participant*, i.e. (as noun) a *sharer*; (by implication) an *associate*:—fellow, partaker, partner.

3354. μετρέω, metreō, *met-reh´-o*; from 3358; to *measure* (i.e. ascertain in size by a fixed standard); (by implication) to *admeasure* (i.e. allot by rule); (figurative) to *estimate*:—measure, mete.

3355. μετρητής, metrētēs, *met-ray-tace´*; from 3354; a *measurer*, i.e. (special) a certain standard *measure* of capacity for liquids:—firkin.

3356. μετριοπαθέω, metriopatheō, *met-ree-op-ath-eh´-o*; from a compound of the base of 3357 and 3806; to *be moderate in passion*, i.e. *gentle* (to *treat indulgently*):—have compassion.

From *metriopathḗs* (n.f.), moderate in passions, which is from *métrios* (n.f.), moderate, and *páthos* (3806), passion. To be moderate in one's passions, to have one's passions moderated; hence to be gentle, indulgent, compassionate. Only in Heb 5:2.

Syn.: *anéchomai* (430), to bear with tolerance; *eleéō* (1653), to have mercy; *makrothuméō* (3114), to be long-suffering; *oikteírō* (3627), to have pity; *splagchnízomai* (4697), to be moved with compassion; *sumpathéō* (4834), to suffer with another, commiserate.

3357. μετρίως, metriōs, *met-ree´-oce*; adverb from a derivative of 3358; *moderately*, i.e. *slightly*:—a little.

3358. μέτρον, metron, *met´-ron*; an apparently primary word; a *measure* ("metre"), literal or figurative; (by implication) a limited *portion* (*degree*):—measure.

3359. μέτωπον, metopon, *met´-o-pon*; from 3326 and ὤψ, *ōps* (the *face*); the *forehead* (as *opposite* the *countenance*):—forehead.

3360. μέχρι, mechri, *mekh´-ree*; or μεχρίς, *mechris, mekh-ris´*; from 3372; *as far as*, i.e. *up to* a certain point (as preposition of extent [denoting the *terminus*, whereas 891 refers especially to the *space* of time or place intervening] or conjecture):—till, (un-) to, until.

3361. μή, mē, *may*; a primary particle of qualified *negation* (whereas 3756 expresses an absolute denial); (adverb) *not*, (conjunction) *lest*; also (as interrogative implying a *negative* answer [whereas 3756 expects an *affirmative* one]) *whether*:—any, but (that), × forbear, + God forbid, + lack, lest, neither, never, no (× wise in), none, nor, [can-] not, nothing, that not, un [-taken], without. Often used in compounds in substantially the same relations. See also 3362, 3363, 3364, 3372, 3373, 3375, 3378.

3362. ἐὰν μή, ean mē, *eh-an´ may*; i.e. 1437 and 3361; *if not*, i.e. *unless*:— × before, but, except, if no, (if, + whosoever) not.

3363. ἵνα μή, hina mē, *hin´-ah may*; i.e. 2443 and 3361; *in order* (or *so*) *that not*:—albeit not, lest, that no (-t, [-thing]).

3364. οὐ μή, ou mē, *oo may*; i.e. 3756 and 3361; a double negative strengthening the denial; *not at all*:—any more, at all, by any (no) means, neither, never, no (at all), in no case (wise), nor ever, not (at all, in any wise). Compare 3378.

3365. μηδαμῶς, mēdamōs, *may-dam-oce´*; adverb from a compound of 3361 and ἁμός, *amos* (*somebody*); *by no means*:—not so.

3366. μηδέ, mēde, *may-deh´*; from 3361 and 1161; *but not, not even*; in a continued negation, *nor*:—neither, nor (yet), (no) not (once, so much as).

3367. μηδείς, mēdeis, *may-dice´*; including the irregular feminine μηδεμία, *mēdemia, may-dem-ee´-ah*, and the neuter μηδέν, *mēden, may-den´*; from 3361 and 1520; *not even one* (man, woman, thing):—any (man, thing), no (man), none, not (at all, any man, a whit), nothing, + without delay.

Adjective from *mēdé* (3366), and not, also not, and *heís* (1520), one. Not even one, no one, i.e. no one whoever he may be. Used with other moods which express potentiality where *oudeís* (3762), no one, would be used with the indicative mood to express actuality.

(I) Generally (Mt 16:20; Mk 6:8; 11:14; Jn 8:10; Ac 4:17, 21; Ro 13:8; 1Co 1:7; 3:18, 21; 2Co 6:3; Php 2:3; Tit 2:15; Heb 10:2; Jas 1:13; 1Pe 3:6).

(II) Neuter *mēdén*, nothing: After verbs of profit or loss, deficiency (Mk 5:26; Lk 4:35; 2Co 11:5; Php 4:6); As an adverb, not at all, in no respect, e.g., without doubting at all (Ac 10:20; 11:12; Jas 1:6).

Syn.: *oudeís* (3762), no one. Also, *mḗtis* (3387), no man, not anyone.

3368. μηδέποτε, mēdepote, *may-dep´-ot-eh*; from 3366 and 4218; *not even ever*:—never.

3369. μηδέπω, mēdepō, *may-dep´-o*; from 3366 and 4452; *not even yet*:—not yet.

3370. Μῆδος, Mēdos, *may´-dos*; of foreign origin [compare 4074]; a *Median*, or inhabitant of Media:—Mede.

3371. μηκέτι, mēketi, *may-ket´-ee*; from 3361 and 2089; *no further*:—any longer, (not) henceforth, hereafter, no henceforward (longer, more, soon), not any more.

3372. μῆκος, mēkos, *may´-kos*; probably akin to 3173; *length* (literal or figurative):—length.

3373. μηκύνω, mēkunō, *may-koo´-no*; from 3372; to *lengthen*, i.e. (middle) to *enlarge*:— grow up.

3374. μηλωτή, mēlōtē, *may-lo-tay´*; from μῆλον, *mēlon* (a *sheep*); a *sheep-skin*:— sheepskin.

3375. μήν, mēn, *mane*; a stronger form of 3303; a particle of affirmation (only with 2229); *assuredly*:— + surely.

3376. μήν, mēn, *mane*; a primary word; a *month*:—month.

3377. μηνύω, mēnuō, *may-noo´-o*; probably from the same base as 3145 and 3415 (i.e. μάω, *maō*, to *strive*); to *disclose* (through the idea of mental *effort* and thus calling to *mind*), i.e. *report, declare, intimate*:—shew, tell.

3378. μὴ οὐκ, mē ouk, *mē ook*; i.e. 3361 and 3756; as interrogative and negative *is it not that?*:—neither (followed by *no*), + never, not. Compare 3364.

3379. μήποτε, mēpote, *may´-pot-eh*; or μή ποτε, *mē pote, may pot´-eh*; from 3361 and 4218; *not ever*; also *if* (or *lest*) *ever* (or *perhaps*):—if peradventure, lest (at any time, haply), not at all, whether or not.

3380. μήπω, mēpō, *may´-po*; from 3361 and 4452; *not yet*:—not yet.

3381. μήπως, mēpōs, *may´-poce*; or μή πως, *mē pōs, may poce*; from 3361 and 4458; *lest somehow*:—lest (by any means, by some means, haply, perhaps).

3382. μηρός, mēros, *may-ros´*; perhaps a primary word; a *thigh*:—thigh.

3383. μήτε, mēte, *may´-teh*; from 3361 and 5037; *not too*, i.e. (in continued negation) *nei-* ther or *nor*; also, *not even*:—neither, (n-) or, so much as.

3384. μήτηρ, mētēr, *may´-tare*; apparently a primary word; a "*mother*" (literal or figurative, immediate or remote):—mother.

3385. μήτι, mēti, *may´-tee*; from 3361 and the neuter of 5100; *whether at all*:—not [*the particle usually not expressed, except by the form of the question*].

3386. μήτιγε, mētige, *may´-tig-eh*; from 3385 and 1065; *not at all then*, i.e. *not to say* (*the rather still*):—how much more.

3387. μήτις, mētis, *may´-tis*; or μή τις, *mē tis, may tis*; from 3361 and 5100; *whether any*:— any [*sometimes unexpressed except by the simple interrogative form of the sentence*].

3388. μήτρα, mētra, *may´-trah*; from 3384; the *matrix*:—womb.

3389. μητραλώας, mētralōias, *may-tral-o´-as*; from 3384 and the base of 257; a *mother-thresher*, i.e. *matricide*:—murderer of mothers.

3390. μητρόπολις, mētropolis, *may-trop´-ol-is*; from 3384 and 4172; a *mother city*, i.e. "*metropolis*":—chiefest city.

3391. μία, mia, *mee´-ah*; irregular feminine of 1520; *one* or *first*:—a (certain), + agree, first, one, × other.

3392. μιαίνω, miainō, *me-ah´ee-no*; perhaps a primary verb; to *sully* or *taint*, i.e. *contaminate* (ceremonial or morally):—defile.

To stain with colour, to tinge. In the NT: pollute, defile:

(I) In the Levitical sense (Jn 18:28).

(II) In a moral sense (Jude 8). Pass.: to be polluted, corrupt (Tit 1:15; Heb 12:15).

Deriv.: *amíantos* (283), undefiled; *míasma* (3393), defilement; *miasmós* (3394), the act of defiling.

Syn.: *molúnō* (3435), to besmear or soil. Also, *diaphtheírō* (1311), to corrupt completely; *kataphtheírō* (2704), to corrupt utterly; *koinóō* (2840), to make common, render unholy or unclean in a ceremonial sense; *sépō* (4595), to make corrupt, to render rotten; *spilóō* (4695), to defile; *phtheírō* (5351), to corrupt.

3393. μίασμα, miasma, *mee´-as-mah*; from 3392 (*"miasma"*); (moral) *foulness* (properly the effect):—pollution.

Noun from *miaínō* (3392), to defile. A colouring, staining; hence pollution, defilement, in a moral sense (2Pe 2:20).

Syn.: *alísgēma* (234), pollution, contamination; *molusmós* (3436), defilement; *spílos* (4696), a spot, moral blemish; *phthorá* (5356), corruption.

3394. μιασμός, miasmos, *mee-as-mos´*; from 3392; (morally) *contamination* (properly the act):—uncleanness.

Noun from *miaínō* (3392), to pollute, defile. Pollution, defilement in a moral sense. Primarily indicates the act of polluting which results in the *míasma* (3393), defilement. Used only in 2Pe 2:10, where it refers to lusts which are polluted.

Syn.: *alísgēma* (234), pollution, contamination; *diaphthorá* (1312), thorough corruption; *molusmós* (3436), defilement; *spílos* (4696), a moral blemish; *phthorá* (5356), corruption.

3395. μίγμα, migma, *mig´-mah*; from 3396; a *compound*:—mixture.

3396. μίγνυμι, mignumi, *mig´-noo-mee*; a primary verb; to *mix*:—mingle.

3397. μικρόν, mikron, *mik-ron´*; masculine or neuter singular of 3398 (as noun); a *small* space of *time* or *degree*:—a (little) (while).

3398. μικρός, mikros, *mik-ros´*; including the comparative **μικρότερος, mikroteros,** *mik-rot´-er-os*; apparently a primary word; *small* (in size, quantity, number or [figurative] dignity):—least, less, little, small.

3399. Μίλητος, Milētos, *mil´-ay-tos*; of uncertain origin; *Miletus*, a city of Asia Minor:—Miletus.

3400. μίλιον, milion, *mil´-ee-on*; of Latin origin; a *thousand* paces, i.e. a *"mile"*:—mile.

3401. μιμέομαι, mimeomai, *mim-eh´-om-ahee*; middle from **μῖμος, mimos** (a *"mimic"*); to *imitate*:—follow.

3402. μιμητής, mimētēs, *mim-ay-tace´*; from 3401; an *imitator*:—follower.

3403. μιμνήσκω, mimnēskō, *mim-nace´-ko*; a prolonged form of 3415 (from which some of the tenses are borrowed); to *remind*, i.e. (middle) to *recall to mind*:—be mindful, remember.

3404. μισέω, miseō, *mis-eh´-o*; from a primary **μῖσος, misos** (*hatred*); to *detest* (especially to *persecute*); by extension to *love less*:—hate (-ful).

3405. μισθαποδοσία, misthapodosia, *mis-thap-od-os-ee´-ah*; from 3406; *requital* (good or bad):—recompence of reward.

Noun from *misthapodótēs* (3406), rewarder. A recompense, whether a reward (Heb 10:35; 11:26) or a punishment (Heb 2:2).

Syn.: With the meaning of reward: *amoibé* (287), recompense; *antapódoma* (468), reward or punishment; *antapódosis* (469), rewards, recompense or punishment; *antimisthía* (489), a reward, requital; *opsōnion* (3800), a soldier's pay. With the meaning of punishment: *díkē* (1349), justice, a sentence; *epitimía* (2009), penalty, punishment; *kólasis* (2851), punishment, the negation of the enjoyment of life; *timōría* (5098), vengeance, punishment, the vindication of honour.

3406. μισθαποδότης, misthapodotēs, *mis-thap-od-ot´-ace*; from 3409 and 591; a *remunerator*:—rewarder.

Noun from *misthós* (3408), a reward, and *apodídōmi* (591), to render. A recompenser, rewarder. Used only in Heb 11:6.

Deriv.: *misthapodosía* (3405), a punishment, recompense.

3407. μίσθιος, misthios, *mis´-thee-os*; from 3408; a *wage-earner*:—hired servant.

Adjective from *misthós* (3408), hire, pay, reward. Hired servant. Used only in Lk 15:17, 19.

Syn.: *ergátēs* (2040), a worker.

3408. μισθός, misthos, *mis-thos´*; apparently a primary word; *pay* for service (literal or figurative), good or bad:—hire, reward, wages.

Noun meaning wages, hire, reward:

(I) Particularly and generally (Mt 20:8; Lk 10:7; Ac 1:18; Ro 4:4; 1Co 3:8; 1Ti 5:18; Jas 5:4; 2Pe 2:15; Jude 11).

(II) In the sense of reward to be received hereafter (Mt 5:12, 46; 6:1, 2, 5, 16; 10:41, 42;

Mk 9:41; Lk 6:23, 35; Jn 4:36; 1Co 3:14; 9:17, 18; 2Jn 8; Rev 11:18; 22:12).

(III) In the sense of retribution, punishment (2Pe 2:13).

Deriv.: *antimisthía* (489), reward, penalty; *misthapodótēs* (3406), rewarder; *místhios* (3407), a day labourer, one paid by the day; *misthóō* (3409), to hire; *misthōtós* (3411), a hired worker.

Syn.: *amoibḗ* (287), recompense; *antapódoma* (468), recompense, what one receives in reward or punishment; *antapódosis* (469), the act of recompensing; *opsṓnion* (3800), rations for soldiers, wages.

3409. μισθόω, misthoō, *mis-tho´-o*; from 3408; to *let* out for wages, i.e. (middle) to *hire*:—hire.

3410. μίσθωμα, misthōma, *mis´-tho-mah*; from 3409; a *rented* building:—hired house.

3411. μισθωτός, misthōtos, *mis-tho-tos´*; from 3409; a *wage-worker* (good or bad):— hired servant, hireling.

Noun from *misthóō* (3409), to hire. One hired, a hired servant (Mk 1:20). Spoken of the hired servant who will leave the sheep in the face of danger (Jn 10:12, 13).

Syn.: *místhios* (3407), hired servant; *ergátēs* (2040), worker.

3412. Μιτυλήνη, Mitulēnē, *mit-oo-lay´-nay*; for **μυτιλήνη, Mutilēnē** (*abounding in shellfish*); *Mitylene* (or *Mytilene*), a town in the island Lesbos:—Mitylene.

3413. Μιχαήλ, Michaēl, *mikh-ah-ale´*; of Hebrew origin [4317]; *Michaël*, an archangel:— Michael.

3414. μνᾶ, mna, *mnah*; of Latin origin; a *mna* (i.e. *mina*), a certain *weight*:—pound.

3415. μνάομαι, mnaomai, *mnah´-om-ahee*; middle of a derivative of 3306 or perhaps of the base of 3145 (through the idea of *fixture* in the mind or of mental *grasp*); to *bear in mind*, i.e. *recollect*; (by implication) to *reward* or *punish*:—be mindful, remember, come (have) in remembrance. Compare 3403.

3416. Μνάσων, Mnasōn, *mnah´-sohn*; of uncertain origin; *Mnason*, a Christian:—Mnason.

3417. μνεία, mneia, *mni´-ah*; from 3415 or 3403; *recollection*; (by implication) *recital*:— mention, remembrance.

3418. μνῆμα, mnēma, *mnay´-mah*; from 3415; a *memorial*, i.e. sepulchral *monument* (*burialplace*):—grave, sepulchre, tomb.

3419. μνημεῖον, mnēmeion, *mnay-mi´-on*; from 3420; a *remembrance*, i.e. *cenotaph* (*place of interment*):—grave, sepulchre, tomb.

3420. μνήμη, mnēmē, *mnay´-may*; from 3403; *memory*:—remembrance.

3421. μνημονεύω, mnēmoneuō, *mnay-mon-yoo´-o*; from a derivative of 3420; to *exercise memory*, i.e. *recollect*; (by implication) to *punish*; also to *rehearse*:—make mention, be mindful, remember.

3422. μνημόσυνον, mnēmosunon, *mnay-mos´-oo-non*; from 3421; a *reminder* (*memorandum*), i.e. *record*:—memorial.

3423. μνηστεύω, mnēsteuō, *mnace-tyoo´-o*; from a derivative of 3415; to *give a souvenir* (engagement present), i.e. *betroth*:—espouse.

3424. μογιλάλος, mogilalos, *mog-il-al´-os*; from 3425 and 2980; *hardly talking*, i.e. *dumb* (*tongue-tied*):—having an impediment in his speech.

3425. μόγις, mogis, *mog´-is*; adverb from a primary **μόγος, mogos** (*toil*); *with difficulty*:— hardly.

3426. μόδιος, modios, *mod´-ee-os*; of Latin origin; a *modius*, i.e. certain measure for things dry (the quantity or the utensil):—bushel.

3427. μοί, moi, *moy*; the simpler form of 1698; *to me*:—I, me, mine, my.

3428. μοιχαλίς, moichalis, *moy-khal-is´*; a prolonged form of the feminine of 3432; an *adulteress* (literal or figurative):—adulteress (-ous, -y).

3429. μοιχάω, moichaō, *moy-khah´-o*; from 3432; (middle) to *commit adultery*:—commit adultery.

3430. μοιχεία, moicheia, *moy-khi´-ah*; from 3431; *adultery*:—adultery.

3431. μοιχεύω, moicheuō, *moy-khyoo´-o*; from 3432; to *commit adultery*:—commit adultery.

3432. μοιχός, moichos, *moy-khos´*; perhaps a primary word; a (male) *paramour*; (figurative) *apostate*:—adulterer.

3433. μόλις, molis, *mol´-is*; probably by variation for 3425; *with difficulty*:—hardly, scarce (-ly), + with much work.

3434. Μολόχ, Moloch, *mol-okh´*; of Hebrew origin [4432]; *Moloch* (i.e. *Molek*), an idol:—Moloch.

3435. μολύνω, molunō, *mol-oo´-no*; probably from 3189; to *soil* (figurative):—defile.

To defile, besmear or soil as with mud or filth (1Co 8:7; Rev 3:4; 14:4).

Deriv.: *molusmós* (3436), defilement, the act of defiling.

Syn.: *miaínō* (3392), to contaminate, defile; *spilóō* (4695), to spot, pollute.

3436. μολυσμός, molusmos, *mol-oos-mos´*; from 3435; a *stain*, i.e. (figurative) *immorality*:—filthiness.

Noun from *molúnō* (3435), to defile. A soiling: defilement, pollution in a moral sense, filthiness. Used only in 2Co 7:1.

Syn.: *diaphthorá* (1312), complete corruption; *míasma* (3393), defilement, the result of defilement; *miasmós* (3394), uncleanness; *phthorá* (5356), corruption.

3437. μομφή, momphē, *mom-fay´*; from 3201; *blame*, i.e. (by implication) a *fault*:—quarrel.

3438. μονή, monē, *mon-ay´*; from 3306; a *staying*, i.e. *residence* (the act or the place):—abode, mansion.

Noun from *ménō* (3306), to remain, dwell. A dwelling place, habitation, abode. Used in Jn 14:2 in the sense of rooms, apartments. Spoken of figuratively in Jn 14:23 in the sense of Jesus and the Father making the believer their resting place.

Syn.: *épaulis* (1886), a country house, cottage, cabin; *katoikētḗrion* (2732), a habitation; *katoikía* (2733), dwelling place; *oikētḗrion* (3613), a habitation; *skēnḗ* (4633), a tent or tabernacle; *skḗnōma* (4638), a pitched tent, metaphorically referring to the body.

3439. μονογενής, monogenēs, *mon-og-en-ace´*; from 3441 and 1096; *only-born*, i.e. *sole*:—only (begotten, child).

Adjective from *mónos* (3441), only, and *génos* (1085), kind, which is from the root of *gínomai* (1096), to become. Only-born, only begotten, i.e. only child (Lk 7:12; 8:42; 9:38; Heb 11:17). In John's writings, spoken only of *ho Lógos* (3056), The Word, the only begotten Son of God in the highest sense, as alone knowing and revealing the essence of the Father (Jn 1:14, 18; 3:16, 18; 1Jn 4:9).

3440. μόνον, monon, *mon´-on*; neuter of 3441 as adverb; *merely*:—alone, but, only.

3441. μόνος, monos, *mon´-os*; probably from 3306; *remaining*, i.e. *sole* or *single*; (by implication) *mere*:—alone, only, by themselves.

3442. μονόφθαλμος, monophthalmos, *mon-of´-thal-mos*; from 3441 and 3788; *one-eyed*:—with one eye.

3443. μονόω, monoō, *mon-o´-o*; from 3441; to *isolate*, i.e. *bereave*:—be desolate.

3444. μορφή, morphē, *mor-fay´*; perhaps from the base of 3313 (through the idea of *adjustment* of parts); *shape*; (figurative) *nature*:—form.

Noun meaning form, shape. Spoken of Jesus appearing in another form, one that was not recognized, to the two disciples on the road to Emmaus (Mk 16:12, see *héteros* [2087], another). Used in the sense of *phúsis* (5449), nature, rather than simply form or shape: spoken of Jesus having been in the "form of God" (Php 2:6, see *Theós* [2316], God), a clear affirmation of His divine nature; contrastly, spoken of Jesus having taken on Himself the "form of a slave" (Php 2:7, see *doulos* [1401], slave) at the incarnation, a clear affirmation of His human nature.

Deriv.: *morphóō* (3445), to form, fashion; *súmmorphos* (4832), conformed to.

3445. μορφόω, morphoō, *mor-fo´-o*; from the same as 3444; to *fashion* (figurative):—form.

From *morphḗ* (3444), form, shape. To form, fashion. Found only in Gal 4:19 where the Christian is described as a little child who needs to mature until his character and conduct project the very image of Christ.

Deriv.: *metamorphóō* (3339), to transform, transfigure; *mórphōsis* (3446), formulation, impression.
Syn.: *plássō* (4111), to shape, form.

3446. μόρφωσις, morphōsis, *mor´-fo-sis*; from 3445; *formation*, i.e. (by implication) *appearance* (*semblance* or [concrete] *formula*):—form.
Noun from *morphóō* (3445), to form. A forming; hence form, appearance, e.g., mere external form (2Ti 3:5); by implication: a prescribed form, a norm (Ro 2:20).
Syn.: *schéma* (4976), fashion; *charaktēr* (5481), exact image.

3447. μοσχοποιέω, moschopoieō, *mos-khop-oy-eh´-o*; from 3448 and 4160; to *fabricate* the image of a *bullock*:—make a calf.

3448. μόσχος, moschos, *mos´-khos*; probably strengthened for ὄσχος, *oschos* (a *shoot*); a young *bullock*:—calf.

3449. μόχθος, mochthos, *mokh´-thos*; from the base of 3425; *toil*, i.e. (by implication) *sadness*:—painfulness, travail.
Noun from *mógos* (n.f.), labour, toil. Wearisome labour, travail; including the idea of painful effect, sorrow. In the NT, always coupled with *kópos* (2873), weariness, labour (2Co 11:27; 1Th 2:9; 2Th 3:8).

3450. μοῦ, mou, *moo*; the simpler form of 1700; *of me*:—I, me, mine (own), my.

3451. μουσικός, mousikos, *moo-sik-os´*; from μουσος, *Mousa* (a *Muse*); "*musical*," i.e. (as noun) a *minstrel*:—musician.

3452. μυελός, muelos, *moo-el-os´*; perhaps a primary word; the *marrow*:—marrow.

3453. μυέω, mueō, *moo-eh´-o*; from the base of 3466; to *initiate*, i.e. (by implication) to *teach*:—instruct.

3454. μῦθος, muthos, *moo´-thos*; perhaps from the same as 3453 (through the idea of *tuition*); a *tale*, i.e. *fiction* ("*myth*"):—fable.
Noun meaning speech, discourse. In the NT: fable, fiction, a mythic tale which will lead men astray from the truth (1Ti 1:4; 4:7; 2Ti 4:4; Tit 1:14; 2Pe 1:16).

3455. μυκάομαι, mukaomai, *moo-kah´-om-ahee*; from a presumed derivative of μύζω, *muzō* (to "*moo*"); to bellow (*roar*):—roar.

3456. μυκτηρίζω, muktērizō, *mook´-tay-rid´-zo*; from a derivative of the base of 3455 (meaning *snout*, as that whence *lowing* proceeds); to *make mouths* at, i.e. *ridicule*:—mock.

3457. μυλικός, mulikos, *moo-lee-kos´*; from 3458; *belonging to a mill*:—mill [-stone].

3458. μύλος, mulos, *moo´-los*; probably ultimately from the base of 3433 (through the idea of *hardship*); a "*mill*," i.e. (by implication) a *grinder* (*millstone*):—millstone.

3459. μύλων, mulōn, *moo´-lone*; from 3458; a *mill-house*:—mill.

3460. Μύρα, Mura, *moo´-rah*; of uncertain derivative; *Myra*, a place in Asia Minor:—Myra.

3461. μυριάς, murias, *moo-ree´-as*; from 3463; a *ten-thousand*; by extension a "*myriad*" or indefinite number:—ten thousand.

3462. μυρίζω, murizō, *moo-rid´-zo*; from 3464; to *apply* (perfumed) *unguent* to:—anoint.

3463. μύριοι, murioi, *moo´-ree-oi*; plural of an apparently primary word (properly meaning *very many*); *ten thousand*; by extension *innumerably* many:—ten thousand.

3464. μύρον, muron, *moo´-ron*; probably of foreign origin [compare 4753, 4666]; "*myrrh*," i.e. (by implication) *perfumed oil*:—ointment.
Any aromatic resin distilling of itself from a tree or plant, especially myrrh. In the NT, generally: ointment, i.e. perfumed oil typically used to anoint oneself for special occasions, or to prepare a body for burial (Mt 26:7, 9, 12; Mk 14:3, 4; Lk 7:37, 38; 23:56; Jn 11:2; 12:3, 5; Rev 18:13).
Deriv.: *murízō* (3462), to anoint for burial, embalm.

3465. Μυσία, Musia, *moo-see´-ah*; of uncertain origin; *Mysia*, a region of Asia Minor:—Mysia.

3466. μυστήριον, mustērion, *moos-tay´-ree-on*; from a derivative of μύω, *muō* (to *shut* the mouth); a *secret* or "*mystery*" (through the idea of *silence* imposed by *initiation* into religious rites):—mystery.

Noun from *mústēs* (n.f.), a person initiated into sacred mysteries, which is from *muéō* (3453), to initiate, learn a secret. A mystery, i.e. something into which one must be initiated or instructed before it can be known; something of itself not obvious and above human insight. In the NT, spoken of facts, doctrines, principles, etc. not previously revealed:

(I) Generally (Mt 13:11; Mk 4:11; Lk 8:10; 1Co 14:2; Eph 5:32; 2Th 2:7; Rev 1:20; 17:5, 7).

(II) Specifically, of the gospel, the Christian dispensation, as having been long hidden and first revealed in later times (Ro 16:25; 1Co 2:7; Eph 3:3, 4, 9; Col 2:2; 4:3; 1Ti 3:9); so of particular doctrines or parts of the gospel (Ro 11:25; 1Co 15:51; Eph 1:9; 1Ti 3:16).

3467. μυωπάζω, muōpazō, *moo-ope-ad´-zo*; from a compound of the base of 3466 and **ὤψ,** *ōps* (the *face*; from 3700); to *shut the eyes,* i.e. *blink* (*see indistinctly*):—cannot see afar off.

3468. μώλωψ, mōlōps, *mo´-lopes*; from **μῶλος,** *mōlos* ("*moil*"; probably akin to the base of 3433) and probably **ὤψ,** *ōps* (the *face*; from 3700); a *mole* ("black eye") or *blow-mark*:—stripe.

3469. μωμάομαι, mōmaomai, *mo-mah´-om-ahee*; from 3470; to *carp* at, i.e. *censure* (*discredit*):—blame.

3470. μῶμος, mōmos, *mo´-mos*; perhaps from 3201; a *flaw* or *blot*, i.e. (figurative) *disgraceful person*:—blemish.

Blame, fault, blemish, disgrace. Used only in 2Pe 2:13. See *ámōmos* (299), without spot.

Deriv.: *ámōmos* (299), blameless, without spot; *momáomai* (3469), to find fault with, blame.

3471. μωραίνω, mōrainō, *mo-rah´ee-no*; from 3474; to *become insipid*; (figurative) to *make* (passive *act*) as a *simpleton*:—become fool, make foolish, lose savour.

3472. μωρία, mōria, *mo-ree´-ah*; from 3474; *silliness,* i.e. *absurdity*:—foolishness.

3473. μωρολογία, mōrologia, *mo-rol-og-ee´-ah*; from a compound of 3474 and 3004; *silly talk,* i.e. *buffoonery*:—foolish talking.

Noun from *mōrológos* (n.f.), speaking foolishly, which is from *mōrós* (3474), foolish, and *légō* (3004), to speak. Foolish talking, empty discourse (Eph 5:4).

3474. μωρός, mōros, *mo-ros´*; probably from the base of 3466; *dull* or *stupid* (as if *shut* up), i.e. *heedless,* (moral) *blockhead,* (apparently) *absurd*:—fool (-ish, × -ishness).

Adjective meaning dull, not acute, e.g., of impressions of the taste: insipid, tasteless. In the NT, of the mind: stupid, foolish; and as a substantive: a fool (Mt 5:22; 7:26; 23:17, 19; 25:2, 3, 8; 1Co 3:18; 4:10). Of things: foolishness (1Co 1:25); foolish things (1Co 1:27; 2Ti 2:23; Tit 3:9).

Deriv.: *mōraínō* (3471), to become dull; *mōría* (3472), foolishness as a personal quality.

Syn.: *anóetos* (453), senseless, one lacking understanding; *ásophos* (781), unwise; *asúnetos* (801), without discernment; *áphrōn* (878), foolish, a fool.

3475. Μωσεύς, Mōseus, *moce-yoos´*; or **Μωσῆς,** *Mōsēs, mo-sace´*; or **Μωϋσῆς, Mōüsēs,** *mo-oo-sace´*; of Hebrew origin; [4872]; *Moseus, Moses* or *Moüses* (i.e. *Mosheh*), the Hebrew lawgiver:—Moses.

N (Nu)

3476. Ναασσών, Naassōn, *nah-as-sone´*; of Hebrew origin [5177]; *Naasson* (i.e. *Nachshon*), an Israelite:—Naasson.

3477. Ναγγαί, Naggai, *nang-gah´ee*; probably of Hebrew origin [compare 5052]; *Nangæ* (i.e. perhaps *Nogach*), an Israelite:—Nagge.

3478. Ναζαρέθ, Nazareth, *nad-zar-eth´*; or **Ναζαρέτ,** *Nazaret,* *nad-zar-et´*; of uncertain derivative; *Nazareth* or *Nazaret,* a place in Palestine:—Nazareth.

3479. Ναζαρηνός, Nazarēnos, *nad-zar-ay-nos´*; from 3478; a *Nazarene,* i.e. inhabitant of Nazareth:—of Nazareth.

3480. Ναζωραῖος, Nazōraios, *nad-zo-rah´-yos*; from 3478; a *Nazoræan,* i.e. inhabitant of Nazareth; by extension a *Christian:*—Nazarene, of Nazareth.

3481. Ναθάν, Nathan, *nath-an´*; of Hebrew origin [5416]; *Nathan,* an Israelite:—Nathan.

3482. Ναθαναήλ, Nathanaēl, *nath-an-ah-ale´*; of Hebrew origin [5417]; *Nathanaël* (i.e. *Nathanel*), an Israelite and Christian:—Nathanael.

3483. ναί, nai, *nahee*; a primary particle of strong affirmation; *yes:*—even so, surely, truth, verily, yea, yes.

3484. Ναΐν, Naïn, *nah-in´*; probably of Hebrew origin [compare 4999]; *Naïn,* a place in Palestine:—Nain.

3485. ναός, naos, *nah-os´*; from a primary **ναίω, naiō** (to *dwell*); a *fane, shrine, temple:*—shrine, temple. Compare 2411.

Noun from *naíō* (n.f.), to dwell. A dwelling, temple, as the dwelling of a god:

(I) Generally, of any temple (Ac 7:48; 17:24; 19:24, referring to the miniature copies of the temple of Diana at Ephesus containing a small image of the goddess. Such shrines of other gods were also common, made of gold, silver or wood, and were purchased by pilgrims and travelers, probably as souvenirs or to be used in their devotions).

(II) Of the temple in Jerusalem or in allusion to it, but only of the actual edifice; in distinction from *hierón* (2411), temple, which included the courts and other appurtenances, *naós* refers to the building itself (Mt 23:16, 17, 21, 35; 26:61; 27:5; 27:40, 51; Mk 14:58; 15:29; Lk 1:9, 21, 22; 23:45; Jn 2:19, 20; 2Th 2:4). See also Rev 11:1, 2.

(III) Of the temple of God in heaven (cf. Rev 3:12; 7:15; 11:19; 14:15, 17; 15:5, 6, 8; 16:1, 17; 21:22).

(IV) Metaphorically, of persons in whom God or His Spirit is said to dwell or act, e.g., the body of Jesus (Jn 2:19, 21); of Christians (1Co 3:16, 17; 6:19; 2Co 6:16; Eph 2:21).

Deriv.: *neōkóros* (3511), a temple servant, worshipper.

Syn.: *tó hágion* (39) the holy place, sanctuary, spoken of the temple.

3486. Ναούμ, Naoum, *nah-oom´*; of Hebrew origin [5151]; *Naüm* (i.e. *Nachum*), an Israelite:—Naum.

3487. νάρδος, nardos, *nar´-dos*; of foreign origin [compare 5373]; "*nard*":—[spike-] nard.

3488. Νάρκισσος, Narkissos, *nar´-kis-sos*; a flower of the same name, from **νάρκη, Narkē** (*stupefaction,* as a "narcotic"); *Narcissus,* a Roman:—Narcissus.

3489. ναυαγέω, nauageō, *now-ag-eh´-o*; from a compound of 3491 and 71; to *be shipwrecked* (*stranded,* "navigate"), literal or figurative:—make (suffer) shipwreck.

3490. ναύκληρος, nauklēros, *now´-klay-ros*; from 3491 and 2819 ("clerk"); a *captain:*—owner of a ship.

3491. ναῦς, **naus,** *nowce*; from νάω, *naō*; or νέω, *neō* (to *float*); a *boat* (of any size):—ship.

3492. ναύτης, **nautēs,** *now´-tace*; from 3491; a *boatman,* i.e. *seaman:*—sailor, shipman.

3493. Ναχώρ, **Nachōr,** *nakh-ore´*; of Hebrew origin [5152]; *Nachor,* the grandfather of Abraham:—Nachor.

3494. νεανίας, **neanias,** *neh-an-ee´-as*; from a derivative of 3501; a *youth* (up to about forty years):—young man.

3495. νεανίσκος, **neaniskos,** *neh-an-is´-kos*; from the same as 3494; a *youth* (under forty):—young man.

3496. Νεάπολις, **Neapolis,** *neh-ap´-ol-is*; from 3501 and 4172; *new town; Neäpolis,* a place in Macedonia:—Neapolis.

3497. Νεεμάν, **Neeman,** *neh-eh-man´*; of Hebrew origin [5283]; *Neëman* (i.e. *Naaman*), a Syrian:—Naaman.

3498. νεκρός, **nekros,** *nek-ros´*; from an apparently primary νέκυς, *nekus* (a *corpse*); *dead* (literal or figurative; also as noun):—dead.

Adjective from *nékus* (n.f.), a corpse. Dead:

(I) As a substantive: a dead person, dead body, corpse (Mt 23:27; Rev 20:13).

(A) As yet unburied (Mt 8:22; Lk 7:15); one slain (Rev 16:3).

(B) As buried, laid in a sepulchre, and therefore the spirit being in Hades (Lk 16:30; Jn 5:25; Ac 10:42; Ro 14:9; 1Th 4:16; Heb 11:35).

(C) Figuratively in the plural, those dead to Christ and His gospel, meaning spiritually dead (Mt 8:22, "Let the spiritually dead bury their dead" [a.t.], meaning let no lesser duty keep you from the one great duty of following Me; Lk 9:60; Ro 6:13; 11:15; Eph 5:14).

(II) As an adjective:

(A) Particularly (Mt 28:4; Ac 20:9; 28:6; Rev 1:17). Figuratively for lost, perished, given up as dead, e.g., the prodigal son (Lk 15:24, 32).

(B) Figuratively, in opposition to the life of the gospel, e.g.: **(1)** Of persons: dead to Christ and His gospel and thus exposed to punishment, spiritually dead (Eph 2:1, 5; Col 2:13; Rev 3:1). Used in the opposite sense, dead to sin, i.e. no longer willingly subject to it (Ro 6:11). **(2)** Of things, dead, i.e. inactive,

inoperative (Ro 7:8; Heb 6:1; 9:14; Jas 2:17, 20, 26).

Deriv.: *nekróō* (3499), to put to death.

3499. νεκρόω, **nekroō,** *nek-ro´-o*; from 3498; to *deaden,* i.e. (figurative) to *subdue:*—be dead, mortify.

3500. νέκρωσις, **nekrōsis,** *nek´-ro-sis*; from 3499; *decease*; (figurative) *impotency:*—deadness, dying.

Noun from *nekróō* (3499), to mortify. The act of killing, putting to death (2Co 4:10, "always carrying about in the body the putting to death of the Lord Jesus" [a.t.], i.e. being exposed to cruelties resembling those which He sustained in His last sufferings). Figuratively: the state of deadness, barrenness as spoken of the womb (Ro 4:19).

3501. νέος, **neos,** *neh´-os*; including the comparative νεώτερος, *neōteros,* *neh-o´-ter-os*; a primary word; "*new,*" i.e. (of persons) *youthful,* or (of things) *fresh*; (figurative) *regenerate:*—new, young.

Adjective meaning young, new:

(I) Particularly of persons: young, youthful (Tit 2:4). In the comparative form: younger (Jn 21:18); in the comparative plural, the younger, the young, as opposed to those older (Ac 5:6; 1Ti 5:1, 2, 11, 14; Tit 2:6; 1Pe 5:5). As implying inferior dignity (Lk 22:26).

(II) Of things: new, recent, e.g., wine (Mt 9:17; Mk 2:22; Lk 5:37, 38, 39). Figuratively of the heart, disposition, nature, as renewed and therefore better: e.g., the new man (Col 3:10); the new covenant (Heb 12:24); Also 1Co 5:7.

Deriv.: *neanías* (3494), a youth; *neanískos* (3495), a youth under forty; *neossós* (3502), a young bird; *neótēs* (3503), youthful age; *neóphutos* (3504), newly planted; *neōterikós* (3512), youthful; *noumēnía* (3561), new moon.

Syn.: *kainós* (2537), new. Also, *prósphatos* (4372), recent, new in the sense of time.

3502. νεοσσός, **neossos,** *neh-os-sos´*; from 3501; a *youngling* (*nestling*):—young.

Masculine noun from *néos* (3501), young. A young animal, or often specifically a young bird. Used only in Lk 2:24.

Deriv.: *nossiá* (3555), a nest of young birds; *nossíon* (3556), a young bird.

3503. νεότης, neotēs, *neh-ot´-ace*; from 3501; *newness,* i.e. *youthfulness*:—youth.

Noun from *néos* (3501), young. Youth, age or time of youth (Mt 19:20; Mk 10:20; Lk 18:21; Ac 26:4); youthfulness, thus Timothy is told to conduct his leadership in such a way that no man despises his *neótēs* (1Ti 4:12). He is at least thirty years old, but leading men much older.

3504. νεόφυτος, neophutos, *neh-of´-oo-tos*; from 3501 and a derivative of 5453; *newly planted,* i.e. (figurative) a *young convert* ("*neophyte*"):—novice.

Adjective from *néos* (3501), new, and *phúō* (5453), to germinate. Newly sprung up or, figuratively, a neophyte, new convert (1Ti 3:6).

Syn.: *ápeiros* (552), inexperienced.

3505. Νέρων, Nerōn, *ner´-ohn*; of Latin origin; *Neron* (i.e. *Nero*), a Roman emperor:—Nero.

3506. νεύω, neuō, *nyoo´-o*; apparently a primary verb; to "*nod*," i.e. (by analogy) to *signal*:—beckon.

3507. νεφέλη, nephelē, *nef-el´-ay*; from 3509; properly *cloudiness,* i.e. (concrete) a *cloud*:—cloud.

3508. Νεφθαλείμ, Nephthaleim, *nef-thal-ime´*; of Hebrew origin [5321]; *Nephthaleim* (i.e. *Naph-thali*), a tribe in Palestine:—Nephthalim.

3509. νέφος, nephos, *nef´-os*; apparently a primary word; a *cloud*:—cloud.

3510. νεφρός, nephros, *nef-ros´*; of uncertain affinity; a *kidney* (plural), i.e. (figurative) the inmost *mind*:—reins.

3511. νεωκόρος, neōkoros, *neh-o-kor´-os*; from a form of 3485 and **κορέω, koreō** (to *sweep*); a *temple-servant,* i.e. (by implication) a *votary*:—worshipper.

3512. νεωτερικός, neōterikos, *neh-o-ter´-ik-os*; from the comparative of 3501; *appertaining to younger* persons, i.e. *juvenile*:—youthful.

3513. νή, nē, *nay*; probably an intensive form of 3483; a particle of attestation (accompanied by the object invoked or appealed to in confirmation); *as sure as*:—I protest by.

3514. νήθω, nēthō, *nay´-tho*; from **νέω, neō** (of like meaning); to *spin*:—spin.

3515. νηπιάζω, nēpiazō, *nay-pee-ad´-zo*; from 3516; to *act* as a *babe,* i.e. (figurative) *innocently*:—be a child.

3516. νήπιος, nēpios, *nay´-pee-os*; from an obsolete particle **νη, ne** (implying *negation*) and 2031; *not speaking,* i.e. an *infant* (*minor*); (figurative) a *simple-minded* person, an *immature* Christian:—babe, child (+ -ish).

Adjective from *nḗ-,* not, and *épos* (2031), word. One who cannot speak, hence, an infant, child, baby without any definite limitation of age.

(I) Particularly (Mt 21:16; 1Co 13:11). By implication: a minor, one not yet of age (Gal 4:1).

(II) Metaphorically: a babe, one unlearned, unenlightened, simple, innocent (Mt 11:25; Lk 10:21; Ro 2:20; Gal 4:3). Implying censure (1Co 3:1; Eph 4:14; Heb 5:13).

Deriv.: *nēpiázō* (3515), to be as a child.

Syn.: *bréphos* (1025), an unborn or a newborn child, infant; *tekníon* (5040), little child; *téknon* (5043), child.

3517. Νηρεύς, Nēreus, *nare-yoos´*; apparently from a derivative of the base of 3491 (meaning *wet*); *Nereus,* a Christian:—Nereus.

3518. Νηρί, Nēri, *nay-ree´*; of Hebrew origin [5374]; *Neri* (i.e. *Nerijah*), an Israelite:—Neri.

3519. νησίον, nēsion, *nay-see´-on*; diminutive of 3520; an *islet*:—island.

3520. νῆσος, nēsos, *nay´-sos*; probably from the base of 3491; an *island*:—island, isle.

3521. νηστεία, nēsteia, *nace-ti´-ah*; from 3522; *abstinence* (from lack of food, or voluntary and religious); specially the *fast* of the Day of Atonement:—fast (-ing).

3522. νηστεύω, nēsteuō, *nace-tyoo´-o*; from 3523; to *abstain* from food (religiously):—fast.

3523. νῆστις, nēstis, *nace´-tis*; from the inseparable negative particle **νη, nē** (*not*) and 2068; *not eating,* i.e. *abstinent* from food (religiously):—fasting.

3524. νηφάλεος, nēphaleos, *nah-fal´-eh-os;* or **νηφάλιος,** *nēphalios, nay-fal´-ee-os;* from 3525; *sober,* i.e. (figurative) *circumspect:*—sober.

3525. νήφω, nēphō, *nay´-fo;* of uncertain affinity; to *abstain* from wine (*keep sober*), i.e. (figurative) *be discreet:*—be sober, watch.

3526. Νίγερ, Niger, *neeg´-er;* of Latin origin; *black; Niger,* a Christian:—Niger.

3527. Νικάνωρ, Nikanōr, *nik-an´-ore;* probably from 3528; *victorious; Nicanor,* a Christian:—Nicanor.

3528. νικάω, nikaō, *nik-ah´-o;* from 3529; to *subdue* (literal or figurative):—conquer, overcome, prevail, get the victory.

3529. νίκη, nikē, *nee´-kay;* apparently a primary word; *conquest* (abstract), i.e. (figurative) the *means of success:*—victory.

3530. Νικόδημος, Nikodēmos, *nik-od´-ay-mos;* from 3534 and 1218; *victorious* among his *people; Nicodemus,* an Israelite:—Nicodemus.

3531. Νικολαΐτης, Nikolaïtēs, *nik-ol-ah-ee´-tace;* from 3532; a *Nicolaïte,* i.e. adherent of *Nicolaüs:*—Nicolaitane.

3532. Νικόλαος, Nikolaos, *nik-ol´-ah-os;* from 3534 and 2994; *victorious* over the *people; Nicolaüs,* a heretic:—Nicolaus.

3533. Νικόπολις, Nikopolis, *nik-op´-ol-is;* from 3534 and 4172; *victorious city; Nicopolis,* a place in Macedonia:—Nicopolis.

3534. νῖκος, nikos, *nee´-kos;* from 3529; a *conquest* (concrete), i.e. (by implication) *triumph:*—victory.

3535. Νινευΐ, Nineuï, *nin-yoo-ee´;* of Hebrew origin [5210]; *Ninevi* (i.e. *Nineveh*), the capital of Assyria:—Nineve.

3536. Νινευΐτης, Nineuïtēs, *nin-yoo-ee´-tace;* from 3535; a *Ninevite,* i.e. inhabitant of Nineveh:—of Nineve, Ninevite.

3537. νιπτήρ, niptēr, *nip-tare´;* from 3538; a *ewer:*—bason.

3538. νίπτω, niptō, *nip´-to;* to *cleanse* (especially the hands or the feet or the face); ceremony to *perform ablution:*—wash. Compare 3068.

To wash some part of the body, as the face, hands or feet. Washing of the hands and feet was very common with the Jews, e.g., of the hands before eating; of the feet, as a mark of hospitality offered to a guest on his arrival, and performed by menial servants or slaves. *Níptō* usually expresses the washing of a part of the body as the hands (Mt 15:2; Mk 7:3), the feet (Jn 13:5, 6, 8, 10, 12, 14; 1Ti 5:10), the face (Mt 6:17), the eyes (Jn 9:7, 11, 15).

Deriv.: *ániptos* (449), unwashed; *aponíptō* (633), to wash off; *niptḗr* (3537), a washbasin.

Syn.: *loúō* (3068), to wash, bathe. Also, *baptízō* (907), baptize, wash ceremonially; *bréchō* (1026), to wet; *plúnō* (4150), to wash things; *rhantízō* (4472), to sprinkle.

3539. νοιέω, noieō, *noy-eh´-o;* from 3563; to *exercise* the *mind* (*observe*), i.e. (figurative) to *comprehend, heed:*—consider, perceive, think, understand.

From *noús* (3563), the mind. To see with the eyes; to perceive, observe. In the NT, used figuratively: to see with the mind, i.e.:

(I) To perceive, understand, comprehend (Mt 15:17; 16:9, 11; Mk 7:18; 8:17; Jn 12:40; Ro 1:20; Eph 3:4, 20; 1Ti 1:7; Heb 11:3).

(II) To have in mind, think about, consider (Mt 24:15; Mk 13:14; 2Ti 2:7).

Deriv.: *agnoéō* (50), not to understand, not know; *anóētos* (453), foolish, unintelligent; *katanoéō* (2657), to ponder, study; *metanoéō* (3340), to repent, change one's mind; *nóēma* (3540), perception, meaning, thought; *pronoéō* (4306), to provide for; *huponoéō* (5282), to conjecture, think, suppose.

Syn.: *ginóskō* (1097) to know experientially; *diaginóskō* (1231), to determine, ascertain exactly, inquire; *dokéō* (1380), to suppose, think; *oída* (1492), to know intuitively or instinctively; *epístamai* (1987), to know; *logízomai* (3049), to reckon, take into account; *punthánomai* (4441), to inquire, understand; *suníēmi* (4920), to understand; *phronéō* (5426), to think.

3540. νόημα, noēma, *no´-ay-mah;* from 3539; a *perception,* i.e. *purpose,* or (by implication) the *intellect, disposition,* itself:—device, mind, thought.

Noun from *noéō* (3539), to perceive. A thought. That which is thought out, planned, devised, in a negative sense (2Co 2:11; 10:5). By metonymy: the mind itself, the understanding (2Co 3:14; 4:4; 11:3; Php 4:7).

Syn.: *dialogismós* (1261), reasoning, thought; *dianóēma* (1270), a thought, machination; *diánoia* (1271), understanding; *enthúmēsis* (1761), an inward reasoning, device, thought; *énnoia* (1771), an inward thought; *epínoia* (1963), a thought; *logismós* (3053), thought, imagination.

3541. νόθος, nothos, *noth´-os*; of uncertain affinity; a *spurious* or *illegitimate* son:—bastard.

3542. νομή, nomē, *nom-ah´*; feminine from the same as 3551; *pasture,* i.e. (the act) *feeding* (figurative, *spreading* of a gangrene), or (the food) *pasturage:*— × eat, pasture.

3543. νομίζω, nomizō, *nom-id´-zo*; from 3551; properly to *do* by *law* (*usage*), i.e. to *accustom* (passive, *be usual*); by extension to *deem* or *regard:*—suppose, think, be wont.

3544. νομικός, nomikos, *nom-ik-os´*; from 3551; *according* (or *pertaining*) *to law,* i.e. *legal* (ceremony); as noun, an *expert in* the (Mosaic) *law:*—about the law, lawyer.

Adjective from *nómos* (3551), law. Pertaining to the law. Generally (Tit 3:9); of persons: one skilled in the law, a lawyer (Tit 3:13). In the Jewish sense: an interpreter and teacher of the Mosaic Law (Mt 22:35; Lk 7:30; 10:25; 11:45, 46, 52; 14:3).

Syn.: *grammateús* (1122), scribe; *nomodidáskalos* (3547), teacher of the law; *nomothétēs* (3550), a lawyer, legislator.

3545. νομίμως, nomimōs, *nom-im´-oce*; adverb from a derivative of 3551; *legitimately* (specially agreeably to the rules of the lists):—lawfully.

3546. νόμισμα, nomisma, *nom´-is-mah*; from 3543; *what is reckoned* as of value (after the Latin *numisma*), i.e. current *coin:*—money.

3547. νομοδιδάσκαλος, nomodidaskalos, *nom-od-id-as´-kal-os*; from 3551 and 1320; an *expounder of* the (Jewish) *law,* i.e. a *Rabbi:*—doctor (teacher) of the law.

3548. νομοθεσία, nomothesia, *nom-oth-es-ee´-ah*; from 3550; *legislation* (specially the *institution of* the Mosaic *code*):—giving of the law.

3549. νομοθετέω, nomotheteō, *nom-oth-et-eh´-o*; from 3550; to *legislate,* i.e. (passive) to *have* (the Mosaic) *enactments* injoined, *be sanctioned* (by them):—establish, receive the law.

3550. νομοθέτης, nomothetēs, *nom-oth-et´-ace*; from 3551 and a derivative of 5087; a *legislator:*—lawgiver.

3551. νόμος, nomos, *nom´-os*; from a primary **νέμω, nemō** (to *parcel* out, especially *food* or *grazing* to animals); *law* (through the idea of prescriptive *usage*), general (*regulation*), special (of Moses [including the volume]; also of the gospel), or figurative (a *principle*):—law.

Noun from *némō* (n.f., see *aponémō* [632]), to divide among, parcel out, allot. Something divided out, allotted; what one has in use and possession; hence, usage, custom. In the NT, law:

(I) Generally, without reference to a particular people or state (Ro 4:15; 5:13; 7:8; 1Ti 1:9).

(II) Specifically, of particular laws, statutes, ordinances, spoken in the NT mostly of the Mosaic statutes:

(A) Spoken of laws relating to civil rights and duties (Jn 7:51; 8:5; Jn 19:7; Ac 23:3; 24:6); spoken of the law of marriage (Ro 7:2, 3; 1Co 7:39); the Levitical priesthood (Heb 7:16); spoken of the ordinance or command respecting the promulgation of the Law (Heb 9:19).

(B) Of laws relating to external religious rites, e.g., purification (Lk 2:22; Heb 9:22); circumcision (Jn 7:23; Ac 15:5; 21:20, 24); sacrifices (Heb 10:8).

(C) Of laws relating to the hearts and conduct of men (Ro 7:7; Heb 8:10; 10:16; Jas 2:8).

(D) By implication for a written law, a law expressly given, i.e. in writing (Ro 2:14).

(III) The Law, i.e. a code or body of laws. In the NT used only of the Mosaic code:

(A) Specifically (Mt 5:18; 22:36; Lk 16:17; Jn 1:17; 7:19; Ac 7:53; Ro 2:13ff.; 5:13; 1Co 15:56; Gal 3:10ff.; 1Ti 1:8; Jas 2:9, 11).

(B) Metaphorically for the Mosaic dispensation (Ro 10:4; Heb 7:12; 10:1).

(C) By metonymy: the Book of the Law, i.e. particularly the books of Moses, the Pentateuch (Mt 12:5; Lk 2:23; 10:26; 1Co 9:8, 9; 14:34). As forming part of the OT, the Law and the prophets (Mt 5:17; Lk 16:16; Jn 1:45; Ac 13:15; 28:23; Ro 3:21); the Law, the prophets, and the Psalms (Lk 24:44); also simply the Law for the OT (Jn 10:34; 12:34; 15:25; 1Co 14:21).

(IV) Metaphorically: the perfect law, meaning the more perfect law for the Christian dispensation, in contrast with that of Moses (Jas 1:25; 2:12; 4:11); of the laws and precepts established by the gospel, e.g., the law of Christ (Ro 13:8, 10; Gal 5:23; 6:2).

(V) Metaphorically, the law, i.e. rule, norm or standard of judging or acting (Ro 3:27; 7:23, 25; 8:2, 7; 9:31). In the sense of a rule of life, discipline (Php 3:5).

Deriv.: *ánomos* (459), without law; *énnomos* (1772), lawful; *nomízō* (3543), to suppose, to think; *nomikós* (3544), lawyer, one learned in the law; *nomodidáskalos* (3547), teacher of the law; *nomothétēs* (3550), a lawgiver.

Syn.: *dógma* (1378), decree, a law; *kanón* (2583), rule.

3552. νοσέω, noseō, *nos-eh´-o*; from 3554; to *be sick,* i.e. (by implication of a diseased appetite) to *hanker* after (figurative, to *harp* upon):— dote.

3553. νόσημα, nosēma, *nos´-ah-ma*; from 3552; an *ailment:*—disease.

3554. νόσος, nosos, *nos´-os*; of uncertain affinity; a *malady* (rarely figurative of moral *disability*):—disease, infirmity, sickness.

Noun meaning disease, sickness (Mt 4:23, 24; 9:35; 10:1; Mk 1:34; 3:15; Lk 4:40; 6:17; 7:21; 9:1; Ac 19:12). Figuratively: pain, sorrow, evil (Mt 8:17).

Deriv.: *noséō* (3552), to be sick.

Syn.: *árrōstos* (732), sick or ill, a disease of a more grievous kind; *asthéneia* (769), sickness, weakness; *malakía* (3119), a slighter infirmity.

3555. νοσσιά, nossia, *nos-see-ah´*; from 3502; a *brood* (of chickens):—brood.

3556. νοσσίον, nossion, *nos-see´-on*; diminutive of 3502; a *birdling:*—chicken.

3557. νοσφίζομαι, nosphizomai, *nos-fid´-som-ahee*; middle from νοσφί, *nosphi* (*apart* or *clandestinely*); to *sequestrate* for oneself, i.e. *embezzle:*—keep back, purloin.

From *nósphi* (n.f.), apart, separated. In the NT, only in the middle, to embezzle, keep back something which belongs to another. Spoken of Ananias and Sapphira keeping back part of the sale price of their property while claiming to give all (Ac 5:2, 3); spoken as a prohibition for Christian slaves (Tit 2:10).

Syn.: *aposteréō* (650), to deprive by fraud; *kléptō* (2813), to steal.

3558. νότος, notos, *not´-os*; of uncertain affinity; the *south* (*-west*) *wind;* by extension the *southern quarter* itself:—south (wind).

3559. νουθεσία, nouthesia, *noo-thes-ee´-ah*; from 3563 and a derivative of 5087; calling *attention* to, i.e. (by implication) mild *rebuke* or *warning:*—admonition.

Feminine noun from *nouthetéō* (3560), to admonish. A putting in mind, i.e. admonition, warning, exhortation (1Co 10:11; Tit 3:10). Linked with *paideía* (3809), discipline, and training (Eph 6:4). *Nouthesía* refers to instruction by word, while *paideía* refers to the wider area of training a child.

Syn.: *epanórthōsis* (1882), correction.

3560. νουθετέω, noutheteō, *noo-thet-eh´-o*; from the same as 3559; to *put in mind,* i.e. (by implication) to *caution* or *reprove* gently:— admonish, warn.

From *noús* (3563), mind, and *títhemi* (5087), to place. To put in mind, to put in one's heart; hence to warn, admonish, exhort (Ac 20:31; Ro 15:14; 1Co 4:14; Col 1:28; 3:16; 1Th 5:12, 14; 2Th 3:15). See *nouthesía* (3559), admonition.

Syn.: *epitimáō* (2008), to rebuke; *paideúō* (3811), to correct by discipline; *parainéō* (3867), to admonish, exhort; *sumbouleúō* (4823), to consult jointly, to counsel; *hupodeíknumi* (5263), forewarn; *chrēmatízō* (5537), to be warned, be admonished.

3561. νουμηνία, noumēnia, *noo-may-nee´-ah*; feminine of a compound of 3501 and 3376 (as noun, by implication of 2250); the festival of *new moon:*—new moon.

3562. νουνεχῶς, nounechōs, *noon-ekh-oce´*; adverb from a compound of the accusative of 3563 and 2192; in a *mind-having* way, i.e. *prudently:*—discreetly.

Adverb from *nounechés* (n.f.), wise, discreet, which is from *noús* (3563), mind, and *échō* (2192), have. Wisely, discreetly, sensibly, as possessing discernment (Mk 12:34).

Syn.: *sōphrónōs* (4996), with sound mind; *phronímōs* (5430), prudently.

3563. νοῦς, nous, *nooce;* probably from the base of 1097; the *intellect,* i.e. *mind* (divine or human; in thought, feeling, or will); (by implication) *meaning:*—mind, understanding. Compare 5590.

Noun meaning the mind:

(I) As the seat of emotions and affections, mode of thinking and feeling, disposition, moral inclination, equivalent to the heart (Ro 1:28; 12:2; 1Co 1:10; Eph 4:17, 23; Col 2:18; 1Ti 6:5; 2Ti 3:8; Tit 1:15); firmness or presence of mind (2Th 2:2); implying heart, reason, conscience, in opposition to fleshly appetites (Ro 7:23, 25).

(II) Understanding, intellect (Lk 24:45; 1Co 14:14, 15, 19; Php 4:7; Rev 13:18).

(III) Metonymically for what is in the mind, thought, counsel, purpose, opinion, of God or Christ (Ro 11:34; 1Co 2:16); of men (Ro 14:5).

(IV) Metaphorically of things: sense, meaning (Rev 17:9).

Deriv.: *ánoia* (454), madness, folly; *énnoia* (1771), notion, intention; *epínoia* (1963), a thought; *noéō* (3539), to perceive, think; *nouthetéō* (3560), to admonish.

Syn.: *diánoia* (1271), the faculty of the mind, intelligence; *nóēma* (3540), thought, intellect; *súnesis* (4907), understanding; *phrónēma* (5427), state of mind, manner of thinking; *phrónēsis* (5428), insight, prudence.

3564. Νυμφᾶς, Numphas, *noom-fas';* probably contracted from a compound of 3565 and 1435; *nymph-given* (i.e. *-born*); *Nymphas,* a Christian:—Nymphas.

3565. νύμφη, numphē, *noom-fay';* from a primary but obsolete verb **νύπτω, nuptō** (to *veil* as a bride; compare Latin *"nupto,"* to *marry*); a young *married* woman (as *veiled*), including a *betrothed* girl; (by implication) a *son's wife:*—bride, daughter-in-law.

3566. νυμφίος, numphios, *noom-fee'-os;* from 3565; a *bridegroom* (literal or figurative):—bridegroom.

3567. νυμφών, numphōn, *noom-fohn';* from 3565; the *bridal* room:—bridechamber.

3568. νῦν, nun, *noon;* a primary particle of present time; *"now"* (as adverb of date, a transition or emphasis); also as noun or adjective *present* or *immediate:*—henceforth, + hereafter, of late, soon, present, this (time). See also 3569, 3570.

3569. τανῦν, tanun, *tan-oon';* or **τὰ νῦν, ta nun,** *tah noon;* from neuter plural of 3588 and 3568; *the* things *now,* i.e. (adverb) *at present:*—(but) now.

3570. νυνί, nuni, *noo-nee';* a prolonged form of 3568 for emphasis; *just now:*—now.

3571. νύξ, nux, *noox;* a primary word; *"night"* (literal or figurative):—(mid-) night.

3572. νύσσω, nussō, *noos'-so;* apparently a primary word; to *prick* ("nudge"):—pierce.

3573. νυστάζω, nustazō, *noos-tad'-zo;* from a presumed derivative of 3506; to *nod,* i.e. (by implication) to *fall asleep;* (figurative) to *delay:*—slumber.

3574. νυχθήμερον, nuchthēmeron, *nookh-thay'-mer-on;* from 3571 and 2250; a *day-and-night,* i.e. full *day* of twenty-four hours:—night and day.

3575. Νῶε, Nōe, *no'-eh;* of Hebrew origin [5146]; *Noë* (i.e. *Noäch*), a patriarch:—Noe.

3576. νωθρός, nōthros, *no-thros';* from a derivative of 3541; *sluggish,* i.e. (literal) *lazy,* or (figurative) *stupid:*—dull, slothful.

Adjective meaning slow, sluggish. Used figuratively in the NT, of the mind: dull, stupid (Heb 5:11; 6:12).

Syn.: *argós* (692), idle, lazy; *bradús* (1021), slow, sluggish; *oknērós* (3636), lazy.

3577. νῶτος, nōtos, *no'-tos;* of uncertain affinity; the *back:*—back.

Ξ (Xi)

3578. ξενία, **xenia,** *xen-ee´-ah*; from 3581; *hospitality*, i.e. (by implication) a *place of entertainment*:—lodging.

3579. ξενίζω, **xenizō,** *xen-id´-xo*; from 3581; to *be a host* (passive a *guest*); (by implication) be (*make, appear*) *strange*:—entertain, lodge, (think it) strange.

3580. ξενοδοχέω, **xenodocheō,** *xen-od-okh-eh´-o*; from a compound of 3581 and 1209; to *be hospitable*:—lodge strangers.

3581. ξένος, **xenos,** *xen´-os*; apparently a primary word; *foreign* (literal, *alien*, or figurative, *novel*); (by implication) a *guest* or (vice-versa) *entertainer*:—host, strange (-r).

3582. ξέστης, **xestēs,** *xes´-tace*; as if from ξέω, *xeō* (properly to *smooth*; by implication [of *friction*] to *boil* or *heat*); a *vessel* (as *fashioned* or for *cooking*) [or perhaps by corruption from the Latin *sextarius*, the *sixth* of a modius, i.e. about a *pint*], i.e. (special) a *measure* for liquids or solids (by analogy, a *pitcher*):—pot.

3583. ξηραίνω, **xērainō,** *xay-rah´ee-no*; from 3584; to *desiccate*; (by implication) to *shrivel*, to *mature*:—dry up, pine away, be ripe, wither (away).

3584. ξηρός, **xēros,** *xay-ros´*; from the base of 3582 (through the idea of *scorching*); *arid*; (by implication) *shrunken, earth* (as opposed to water):—dry, land, withered.

3585. ξύλινος, **xulinos,** *xoo´-lin-os*; from 3586; *wooden*:—of wood.

3586. ξύλον, **xulon,** *xoo´-lon*; from another form of the base of 3582; *timber* (as fuel or material); (by implication) a *stick, club* or *tree* or other wooden article or substance:—staff, stocks, tree, wood.

3587. ξυράω, **xuraō,** *xoo-rah´-o*; from a derivative of the same as 3586 (meaning a *razor*); to *shave* or "*shear*" the hair:—shave.

O (Omicron)

NT Numbers 3588–3801

3588. ὁ, **ho,** *ho*; including the feminine ἡ, **hē,** *hay*; and the neuter τό, **to,** *to*; in all their inflections; the definite article; *the* (sometimes to be supplied, at others omitted, in English idiom):—the, this, that, one, he, she, it, etc.

3589. ὀγδοήκοντα, **ogdoēkonta,** *og-do-ay´-kon-tah*; from 3590; *ten times eight*:—fourscore.

3590. ὄγδοος, **ogdoos,** *og´-do-os*; from 3638; the *eighth*:—eighth.

3591. ὄγκος, **ogkos,** *ong´-kos*; probably from the same as 43; a *mass* (as *bending* or *bulging* by its load), i.e. *burden* (*hindrance*):—weight.

3592. ὅδε, **hode,** *hod´-eh*; including the feminine ἥδε, **hēde,** *hay´-deh*; and the neuter τόδε, **tode,** *tod´-e*; from 3588 and 1161; the *same*, i.e. *this* or *that* one (plural *these* or *those*); often used as personal pronoun:—he, she, such, these, thus.

3593. ὁδεύω, **hodeuō,** *hod-yoo´-o*; from 3598; to *travel*:—journey.

3594. ὁδηγέω, **hodēgeō,** *hod-ayg-eh´-o*; from 3595; to *show* the *way* (literal or figurative [*teach*]):—guide, lead.

3595. ὁδηγός, **hodēgos,** *hod-ayg-os´*; from 3598 and 2233; a *conductor* (literal or figurative [*teacher*]):—guide, leader.

3596. ὁδοιπορέω, **hodoiporeō,** *hod-oy-por-eh´-o*; from a compound of 3598 and 4198; to *be a wayfarer*, i.e. *travel*:—go on a journey.

3597. ὁδοιπορία, **hodoiporia,** *hod-oy-por-ee´-ah*; from the same as 3596; *travel*:—journey (-ing).

3598. ὁδός, **hodos,** *hod-os´*; apparently a primary word; a *road*; (by implication) a *progress* (the route, act or distance); (figurative) a *mode* or *means*:—journey, (high-) way.

(I) In respect to place: a way, highway, road, street:

(A) Used generally (Mt 2:12; 8:28; Mk 2:23; Lk 10:4; Ac 8:26, 36; 25:3; Jas 2:25). Spoken of a pathway between fields (Mt 13:4, 19; Mk 4:4, 15; spoken of a street in a city (Mt 22:9, 10; Lk 14:23). Metonymically for the whole region through which the way leads (Mt 4:15; 10:5).

(B) Figuratively: the way of access; e.g., into the direct presence of God (Heb 9:8).

(C) Figuratively: the way in front of one. Spoken of as the way for a monarch, which is prepared and straightened by envoys beforehand to fill in holes and smooth over rough places, as described in Isa 40:3 (Mt 3:3; 11:10; Mk 1:2, 3; Jn 1:23). Also Rev 16:12.

(D) Spoken by metonymy of Jesus as the way, i.e. the author and medium of access to God and eternal life (Jn 14:6).

(II) In action: a going, journey, progress, course.

(A) Generally: (Mt 15:32; Mk 2:23; 8:3, 27; Lk 9:3; 11:6; Ac 8:39; 9:17, 27; 25:3; 26:13; 1Th 3:11).

(B) Following expressions of time, e.g., a day's journey, the distance covered in one day (Lk 2:44); a Sabbath day's journey, the distance permitted by Rabbinical interpreters, a little less than a mile (Ac 1:12).

(III) Figuratively, a way of life and conduct, a lifestyle:

(A) Spoken of in terms of the people following them; e.g., the way of Baalam (2Pe 2:15). Also Ac 14:16; Ro 3:16, 17; 1Co 4:17; Jas 1:8; 5:20; Jude 1:11).

(B) Spoken of in terms of their characteristics or goals (Mt 21:32; Lk 1:79; Ac 2:28; 16:17; 2Pe 2:2, 21).

(C) The way of God, the way of the Lord, i.e. the way which he approves (Mt 22:16; Lk 20:21; Ac 18:25, 26). Also Mt 21:32; Ac 13:10; Ro 11:33; Heb 3:10; Rev 15:3.

(D) Hence used in an absolute sense for the

Christian way, the Christian religion (Ac 9:2; 19:9, 23; 22:4; 24:14, 22).

Deriv.: *ámphodon* (296), place where two roads meet; *eísodos* (1529), entrance, access; *éxodos* (1841), way out, exodus, an exit; *hodeúō* (3593), to travel, journey; *hodēgós* (3595), guide, leader; *párodos* (3938), a passing or passage; *sunodía* (4923), a caravan.

Syn.: *drómos* (1408), a race, running, career, course; *tríbos* (5147), a worn path; *trochiá* (5163), a track of a wheel, used idiomatically of keeping on the straight path.

3599. ὀδούς, odous, *od-ooce*; perhaps from the base of 2068; a *"tooth"*:—tooth.

3600. ὀδυνάω, odunaō, *od-oo-nah´-o*; from 3601; to *grieve*:—sorrow, torment.

3601. ὀδύνη, odunē, *od-oo´-nay*; from 1416; *grief* (as *dejecting*):—sorrow.

3602. ὀδυρμός, odurmos, *od-oor-mos´*; from a derivative of the base of 1416; *moaning*, i.e. *lamentation*:—mourning.

3603. ὅ ἐστι, ho esti, *ho es-tee´*; from the neuter of 3739 and the third person singular presumed indicative of 1510; *which is*:—called, which is (make), that is (to say).

3604. Ὀζίας, Ozias, *od-zee´-as*; of Hebrew origin [5818]; *Ozias* (i.e. *Uzzijah*), an Israelite:—Ozias.

3605. ὄζω, ozō, *od´-zo*; a primary verb (in a strengthened form); to *scent* (usually an ill "odour"):—stink.

3606. ὅθεν, hothen, *hoth´-en*; from 3739 with the directive enclitic of source; *from which* place or source or cause (adverb or conjecture):—from thence, (from) whence, where (-by, -fore, -upon).

3607. ὀθόνη, othonē, *oth-on´-ay*; of uncertain affinity; a *linen* cloth, i.e. (especially) a *sail*:—sheet.

3608. ὀθόνιον, othonion, *oth-on´-ee-on*; neuter of a presumed derivative of 3607; a linen *bandage*:—linen clothes.

3609. οἰκεῖος, oikeios, *oy-ki´-os*; from 3624; *domestic*, i.e. (as noun), a *relative*, *adherent*:—(those) of the (his own) house (-hold).

Adjective from *oíkos* (3624), a house or household. Belonging to the household. In the

NT, only in the plural: belonging to a certain household (1Ti 5:8). Used figuratively in the NT for associates, kindred of God, children of God (Gal 6:10; Eph 2:19). See *oikétēs* (3610), a household servant.

Syn.: *oikiakós* (3615), belonging to one's household; *suggenḗs* (4773), a relative.

3610. οἰκέτης, oiketēs, *oy-ket´-ace*; from 3611; a fellow *resident*, i.e. menial *domestic*:—(household) servant.

Noun from *oíkos* (3624), house. A domestic servant (Lk 16:13; Ac 10:7; Ro 14:4; 1Pe 2:18).

Syn.: *diákonos* (1249), a servant, minister, deacon; *doúlos* (1401), slave; *therápōn* (2324), attendant; *místhios* (3407), hired servant; *misthōtós* (3411), hired servant; *país* (3816), an attendant, boy, one acting as a servant; *hupērétēs* (5257), an officer, a servant.

3611. οἰκέω, oikeō, *oy-key´-o*; from 3624; to *occupy a house*, i.e. *reside* (figurative, *inhabit*, *remain*, *inhere*); (by implication) to *cohabit*:—dwell. See also 3625.

From *oíkos* (3624), a dwelling. To reside, dwell, abide:

(I) To dwell in: spoken figuratively of the Holy Spirit abiding in Christians (Ro 8:9, 11; 1Co 3:16); spoken figuratively also of sin or a sinful propensity abiding in men (Ro 7:17, 18, 20); spoken of God dwelling in unapproachable light (1Ti 6:16).

(II) To dwell with someone, and as spoken of man and wife, to live together, cohabit (1Co 7:12, 13; Sept.: Pr 21:19 [cf. 1Ki 3:17]).

Deriv.: *enoikéō* (1774), to dwell in; *katoikéō* (2730), to settle down in a dwelling; *oíkēma* (3612), a room, a prison cell; *oikētḗrion* (3613), habitation; *oikouménē* (3625), the inhabited world; *paroikéō* (3939), to sojourn, dwell temporarily; *perioikéō* (4039), to dwell around, as a neighbour; *sunoikéō* (4924), to dwell with.

Syn.: *kataskēnóō* (2681), to lodge; *ménō* (3306), to abide, remain; *skēnóō* (4637), to dwell as if in a tent.

3612. οἴκημα, oikēma, *oy´-kay-mah*; from 3611; a *tenement*, i.e. (special) a *jail*:—prison.

Noun from *oikéō* (3611), to dwell. A house, dwelling. In the NT, and polite Attic Greek usage: a prison (Ac 12:7).

3613. οἰκητήριον, oikētērion, *oy-kay-tay´-ree-on*; neuter of a presumed derivative of 3611 (equivalent to 3612); a *residence* (literal or figurative):—habitation, house.

3614. οἰκία, oikia, *oy-kee´-ah*; from 3624; properly *residence* (abstract), but usually (concrete) an *abode* (literal or figurative); (by implication) a *family* (especially *domestics*):—home, house (-hold).

Noun from *oíkos* (3624), a house. A building, house, dwelling:

(I) In the NT *oikía* is used for an actual house (Mt 2:11; 26:6; Mk 1:29; 14:3; Lk 4:38; 10:5, 7; 22:10, 11; Jn 11:31; 12:3; Ac 4:34; 18:7; 1Co 11:22; 1Ti 5:13; 2Ti 2:20; 3:6; 2Jn 10). Figuratively: spoken of heaven as the dwelling of God (Jn 14:2); spoken of the body as the habitation of the soul (2Co 5:1).

(II) Figuratively: a family, household (Mt 10:13; 12:25; Mk 6:4; 13:35; Jn 4:53; 1Co 16:15). In Mk 10:29 *oikía* may refer to the whole family.

(III) By metonymy: possessions, one's belongings (Mt 23:14; Mk 12:40; Lk 20:47).

Deriv.: *oikiakós* (3615), a relative, pertaining to one's family or household.

3615. οἰκιακός, oikiakos, *oy-kee-ak-os´*; from 3614; *familiar*, i.e. (as noun) *relatives*:—they (them) of (his own) household.

3616. οἰκοδεσποτέω, oikodespoteō, *oy-kod-es-pot-eh´-o*; from 3617; to *be the head of* (i.e. *rule*) *a family*:—guide the house.

3617. οἰκοδεσπότης, oikodespotēs, *oy-kod-es-pot´-ace*; from 3624 and 1203; *the head of a family*:—goodman (of the house), householder, master of the house.

Noun from *oíkos* (3624), a house and *despótēs* (1203), a lord, master. The master of the house, head of a family (Mt 10:25; 24:43; Mk 14:14; Lk 12:39; 13:25; 14:21; 22:11); also a landowner (Mt 13:27; 20:1, 11; 21:33).

Deriv.: *oikodespotéō* (3616), to be head of the house or family.

Syn.: *despótēs* (1203), absolute owner, master; *kúrios* (2962), God, Lord, master.

3618. οἰκοδομέω, oikodomeō, *oy-kod-om-eh´-o*; from the same as 3619; to *be a house-builder*, i.e. *construct* or (figurative) *confirm*:—(be in) build (-er, -ing, up), edify, embolden.

From *oikodómos* (n.f.), builder. To build, construct, erect:

(I) Particularly, to build: e.g., a house (Mt 7:24, 26; Lk 6:48, 49); a tower (Mt 21:33; Mk 12:1; Lk 14:28); a temple (Mk 14:58; Jn 2:20); a barn (Lk 12:18); a synagogue (Lk 7:5). See also Lk 14:30; 17:28; Ac 7:47, 49. The plural participle: builders (Mt 21:42; Mk 12:10; Lk 20:17; Ac 4:11; 1Pe 2:7). Spoken figuratively, to build: of a system of instruction or doctrine (Ro 15:20; Gal 2:18).

(II) By implication: to rebuild or renew a building decayed or destroyed such as the sepulchres of the prophets (Mt 23:29; Lk 11:47, 48). See also Mt 26:61; 27:40; Mk 15:29.

(III) Figuratively: to build up, establish, confirm. Spoken of the Christian Church and its members who are thus compared to a building, a temple of God, erected upon the one and only foundation, Jesus Christ (cf. 1Co 3:9, 10) and ever built up progressively and unceasingly more and more from the foundation:

(A) Externally (Mt 16:18; Ac 9:31; 1Pe 2:5).

(B) Internally, in a good sense: to build up in the faith, to edify, to cause to advance in the divine light (1Co 8:1; 10:23; 14:4, 17; 1Th 5:11). In a bad sense: to embolden (1Co 8:10).

Deriv.: *anoikodoméō* (456), to build again; *epoikodoméō* (2026), to build upon; *sunoikodoméō* (4925), to build together.

Syn.: *kataskeuázō* (2680), to prepare, establish, build; *ktízō* (2936), to create, make.

3619. οἰκοδομή, oikodomē, *oy-kod-om-ay´*; feminine (abstract) of a compound of 3624 and the base of 1430; *architecture*, i.e. (concrete) a *structure*; (figurative) *confirmation*:—building, edify (-ication, -ing).

Noun from *oikódomos*, (n.f.), builder, which is from *oíkos* (3624), house, and *duméō*, to build.

(I) A building up; the act of building. In the NT, only metaphorically: a building up in the faith, edification, advancement in the divine life, spoken of the Christian church and its members (Ro 14:19; 15:2; 1Co 14:5, 12, 26; 2Co 10:8; 12:19; Eph 4:12, 16, 29).

(II) A building, an edifice (Mt 24:1; Mk 13:1, 2). Figuratively, of the Christian church as the temple of God (1Co 3:9; Eph 2:21). Spoken of the future spiritual body as the abode of the soul (2Co 5:1).

Syn.: *endómēsis* (1739), a thing built, structure; *ktísis* (2937), a creation.

3620. οἰκοδομία, oikodomia, *oy-kod-om-ee'-ah*; from the same as 3619; *confirmation*:—edifying.

3621. οἰκονομέω, oikonomeō, *oy-kon-om-eh'-o*; from 3623; to *manage* (a house, i.e. an estate):—be steward.

3622. οἰκονομία, oikonomia, *oy-kon-om-ee'-ah*; from 3623; *administration* (of a household or estate); specially a (religious) *"economy"*:—dispensation, stewardship.

Noun from *oikonoméō* (3621), to be a manager of a household. Management of a household or of household affairs. Particularly: stewardship, administration (Lk 16:2); figuratively: of the apostolic office (1Co 9:17; Eph 1:10; 3:2; Col 1:25). Also, an economy, i.e. a disposition or arrangement of things, a dispensation, scheme (Eph 1: 10).

3623. οἰκονόμος, oikonomos, *oy-kon-om'-os*; from 3624 and the base of 3551; a *house-distributor* (i.e. *manager*), or *overseer*, i.e. an employee in that capacity; by extension a fiscal *agent* (*treasurer*); (figurative) a *preacher* (of the gospel):—chamberlain, governor, steward.

Noun from *oíkos* (3624), house, and *némō* (n.f., see *aponémō* [632]), to deal out, distribute, apportion. An administrator, a house manager, overseer, steward:

(I) Particularly: one who has authority over the servants or slaves of a family to assign their tasks and portions. Along with this was the general management of affairs and accounts (Lk 12:42; 1Co 4:2). Such persons were themselves usually slaves (cf. Eliezer [Ge 15:2] and Joseph [Ge 39:4]). However, free persons appear also to have been thus employed (Lk 16:1, 3, 8; cf. also below in II). The *oikonómoi* also had some charge over the sons of a family, probably in respect to monetary matters, thus differing from the *epítropoi* (2012), guardians or tutors (Gal 4:2 [cf. Ge 24:3]).

(II) In a wider sense: one who administers a public charge or office, a steward, minister, agent; of the fiscal officer of a city or state, treasurer (Ro 16:23). Metaphorically of the apostles and other teachers as stewards or ministers of the gospel (1Co 4:1; Tit 1:7; 1Pe 4:10).

Deriv.: *oikonoméō* (3621), to be a manager of a household.
Syn.: *epítropos* (2012), guardian.

3624. οἰκος, oikos, *oy'-kos*; of uncertain affinity; a *dwelling* (more or less extensive, literal or figurative); (by implication), a *family* (more or less related, literal or figurative):—home, house (-hold), temple.

Noun meaning house, dwelling, home:

(I) Generally (Mt 9:6, 7; Mk 5:19; Lk 1:40; Jn 7:53; Ac 2:46; 5:42; 8:3; 10:22; 20:20; Ro 16:5). With the preposition *en* ([1722] in), *en oíkō*, at home (1Co 11:34; 14:35). Spoken of various kinds of houses or edifices, such as the house of the king, a palace (Mt 11:8). A house of commerce, meaning a bazaar (Jn 2:16). Specifically, house of God, meaning the tabernacle or temple where the presence of God was manifested and where God was said to dwell, e.g., the tabernacle (Mt 12:4; Mk 2:26; Lk 6:4); the temple at Jerusalem (Mt 21:13; Jn 2:16, 17; Ac 7:47, 49); the *ho naós*, sanctuary (Lk 11:51). Figuratively: of Christians as the spiritual house or temple of God (1Pe 2:5); conversely, of one in whom evil spirits dwell (Mt 12:44; Lk 11:24).

(II) By metonymy: a household, family, those who live together in a house (Lk 10:5; Ac 10:2; 11:14; 16:15; 1Co 1:16; 2Ti 1:16; Tit 1:11). Including the idea of household affairs (Ac 7:10; 1Ti 3:4, 5, 12). Metaphorically: *oíkos tou Theoú*, the household of God, i.e. the Christian Church, Christians (1Ti 3:15; Heb 3:6; 10:21; 1Pe 4:17); the Jewish assembly (Heb 3:2, 5).

(III) In a collective sense: the houses and inhabitants of a city or country (Mt 23:38; Lk 13:35).

(IV) By metonymy: family, lineage, posterity, descended from one head or ancestor; e.g., the house of David (Lk 1:27, 69; 2:4). A whole people or nation as descended from one ancestor such as the house or people of Israel (Mt 10:6; 15:24); the house of Jacob (Lk 1:33); the house of Judah (Heb 8:8).

Deriv.: *oikeíos* (3609), of one's own household; *oikétēs* (3610), a fellow resident, a domestic servant; *oikéō* (3611), to reside; *oikía* (3614), a house; *oikodespótēs* (3617), the master of the house; *oikonómos* (3623), steward, manager; *oikourós* (3626), one who stays at home and takes care of it; *panoikí* (3832), with all the house; *pároikos* (3941), a sojourning;

períoikos (4040), someone living near, a neighbour.

Syn.: *skēnḗ* (4633), a tabernacle, tent, temporary dwelling place; *skḗnos* (4636), used of the body as a tabernacle of the soul; *skḗnōma* (4638), a temporary habitation.

3625. οἰκουμένη, oikoumenē, *oy-kou-men´-ay*; feminine participle presumed passive of 3611 (as noun, by implication of 1093); *land*, i.e. the (terrene part of the) *globe*; specially the Roman *empire*:—earth, world.

Noun from *oikéō* (3611), to dwell, abide. The inhabited earth, the world:

(I) Particularly as inhabited by the Greeks, and later by the Greeks and Romans; hence spoken of the Roman empire (Ac 17:6; 24:5), of Palestine and the adjacent countries (Lk 2:1; 21:26; Ac 11:28).

(II) Generally, in later usage: the habitable globe, the earth, the world (Mt 24:14; Ro 10:18; Heb 1:6; Rev 16:14). Metaphorically: the world, for the inhabitants of the earth, mankind (Ac 17:31; 19:27; Rev 3:10; 12:9). Figuratively with *mello* (3195), about to be: the world to come (Heb 2:5).

3626. οἰκουρός, oikouros, *oy-koo-ros´*; from 3624 and οὖρος, *ouros* (a *guard*; be "ware"); a *stayer at home*, i.e. *domestically inclined* (a "good housekeeper"):—keeper at home.

Adjective from *oíkos* (3624), house, and *ourós* (n.f.), a keeper. In the NT, keeping the house, i.e. one who keeps at home, domestic. Used only in Tit 2:5.

3627. οἰκτείρω, oikteirō, *oyk-ti´-ro*; also (in certain tenses) prolonged οἰκτερέω, *oiktereō*, *oyk-ter-eh´-o*; from οἶκτος, *oiktos* (*pity*); to *exercise pity*:—have compassion on.

3628. οἰκτιρμός, oiktirmos, *oyk-tir-mos´*; from 3627; *pity*:—mercy.

3629. οἰκτίρμων, oiktirmōn, *oyk-tir´-mone*; from 3627; *compassionate*:—merciful, of tender mercy.

3630. οἰνοπότης, oinopotēs, *oy-nop-ot´-ace*; from 3631 and a derivative of the alternate of 4095; a *tippler*:—winebibber.

3631. οἶνος, oinos, *oy´-nos*; a primary word (or perhaps of Hebrew origin [3196]); "*wine*" (literal or figurative):—wine.

Noun meaning wine:

(I) Particularly as *oínos néos*, new wine (Mt 9:17; Mk 2:22; Lk 5:37, 38). Also Mk 15:23; Lk 1:15; 10:34; Jn 2:3; 4:46; Ro 14:21; Eph 5:18; 1Ti 3:8; Tit 2:3; Rev 6:6; 18:13.

(II) Figuratively: "the wine of the wrath of God"—the intoxicating cup which God in wrath presents to the nations, and which causes them to reel and stagger to their destruction (Rev 14:10; 16:19; 19:15). Also figuratively: "the wine of wrath of fornication," i.e. a love potion, with which a harlot seduces to fornication (idolatry), and thus brings upon men the wrath of God (Rev 14:8; 18:3; also elliptically in Rev 17:2).

Deriv.: *oinopótēs* (3630), a drinker of wine; *pároinos* (3943), a heavy drinker.

Syn.: *gleúkos* (1098), sweet new wine; *síkera* (4608), strong drink.

3632. οἰνοφλυγία, oinophlugia, *oy-nof-loog-ee´-ah*; from 3631 and a form of the base of 5397; an *overflow* (or surplus) of *wine*, i.e. *vinolency* (*drunkenness*):—excess of wine.

3633. οἴομαι, oiomai, *oy´-om-ahee*; or (shorter) οἶμαι, *oimai*, *oy´-mahee*; middle apparently from 3634; to *make like* (oneself), i.e. *imagine* (*be of the opinion*):—suppose, think.

3634. οἷος, oios, *hoy´-os*; probably akin to 3588, 3739 and 3745; *such* or *what sort of* (as a correlation or exclamation); especially the neuter (adverb) with negative not *so*:—so (as), such as, what (manner of), which.

3635. ὀκνέω, okneō, *ok-neh´-o*; from ὄκνος, *oknos* (*hesitation*); to *be slow* (figurative, *loath*):—delay.

3636. ὀκνηρός, oknēros, *ok-nay-ros´*; from 3635; *tardy*, i.e. *indolent*; (figurative) *irksome*:—grievous, slothful.

3637. ὀκταήμερος, oktaēmeros, *ok-tah-ay´-mer-os*; from 3638 and 2250; an *eight-day* old person or act:—the eighth day.

3638. ὀκτώ, oktō, *ok-to´*; a primary numeral; "*eight*":—eight.

3639. ὄλεθρος, olethros, *ol´-eth-ros*; from a primary ὄλλυμι, *ollumi* (to *destroy*; a prolonged form); *ruin*, i.e. *death, punishment*:—destruction.

Noun from *óllumi* (n.f.), to destroy, kill. Destruction, ruin, death. Spoken of permanent divine punishment (1Th 5:3; 2Th 1:9; 1Ti 6:9); spoken of a temporal destruction of the flesh, leading to restoration and salvation of the soul (1Co 5:5). Some believe *ólethros* here refers to the conquest of fleshly appetites and rebellion against God (cf. 2Co 2:5–11), while others believe that it refers to bodily harm or sickness (cf. Ac 13:9–11).

Deriv.: *olothreúō* (3645), to destroy.

Syn.: *apṓleia* (684), damnation, destruction; *diaphthorá* (1312), corruption, destruction; *phthorá* (5356), corruption.

3640. ὀλιγόπιστος, oligopistos, *ol-ig-op´-is-tos*; from 3641 and 4102; *incredulous*, i.e. *lacking confidence* (in Christ):—of little faith.

Adjective from *olígos* (3641), little, and *pístis* (4102), faith. Of little faith; spoken only by the Lord to believers as a gentle rebuke for anxiety (Mt 6:30; 8:26; 14:31; 16:8; Lk 12:28).

3641. ὀλίγος, oligos, *ol-ee´-gos*; of uncertain affinity; *puny* (in extent, degree, number, duration or value); especially neuter (adverb) *somewhat:*— + almost, brief [-ly], few, (a) little, + long, a season, short, small, a while.

3642. ὀλιγόψυχος, oligopsuchos, *ol-ig-op´-soo-khos*; from 3641 and 5590; *little-spirited*, i.e. *faint-hearted:*—feebleminded.

Adjective from *olígos* (3641), small or little, and *psuchḗ* (5590), soul, mind. Low-spirited, fainthearted, discouraged. Used only in 1Th 5:14.

Syn.: *deilós* (1169), timid, fearful; *ékphobos* (1630), terrified; *éntromos* (1790), terror-stricken.

3643. ὀλιγωρέω, oligōreō, *ol-ig-o-reh´-o*; from a compound of 3641 and ὤρα, *ōra* ("care"); to *have little regard* for, i.e. to *disesteem:*—despise.

3644. ὀλοθρευτής, olothreutēs, *ol-oth-ryoo-tace´*; from 3645; a *ruiner*, i.e. (special) a venomous *serpent:*—destroyer.

3645. ὀλοθρεύω, olothreuō, *ol-oth-ryoo´-o*; from 3639; to *spoil*, i.e. *slay:*—destroy.

3646. ὀλοκαύτωμα, holokautōma, *hol-ok-ow´-to-mah*; from a derivative of a compound of 3650 and a derivative of 2545; a *wholly-consumed* sacrifice ("holocaust"):—(whole) burnt offering.

3647. ὀλοκληρία, holoklēria, *hol-ok-lay-ree´-ah*; from 3648; *integrity*, i.e. physical *wholeness:*—perfect soundness.

3648. ὁλόκληρος, holoklēros, *hol-ok´-lay-ros*; from 3650 and 2819; *complete* in every *part*, i.e. perfectly *sound* (in body):—entire, whole.

Adjective from *hólos* (3650), all, the whole, and *klḗros* (2819), a part, share. Whole in every part, i.e. generally: whole, entire, perfect (1Th 5:23). Figuratively, whole, complete, in a moral sense (Jas 1:4).

Deriv.: *holoklēría* (3647), soundness.

Syn.: *hólos* (3650), whole, complete; *holotelḗs* (3651), complete in every respect; *pantelḗs* (3838), entire, complete.

3649. ὀλολύζω, ololuzō, *ol-ol-ood´-zo*; a reduplicated primary verb; to "*howl*" or "*halloo*," i.e. *shriek:*—howl.

3650. ὅλος, holos, *hol´-os*; a primary word; "*whole*" or "*all*," i.e. *complete* (in extent, amount, time or degree), especially (neuter) as noun or adverb:—all, altogether, every whit, + throughout, whole.

Adjective meaning whole, the whole, all, including every part, e.g., of space, extent, amount (Mt 4:23; 5:29; 16:26; 22:40; Mk 1:33; Lk 1:65; 13:21; Jn 4:53; 19:23; 1Co 5:6). Used of time (Mt 20:6; Lk 5:5; Ac 11:26; 28:30); used of an affection, emotion, condition, e.g., with your whole heart (Mt 22:37; Lk 10:27). Also Jn 9:34; 13:10.

Deriv.: *kathólou* (2527), wholly, entirely; *holóklēros* (3648), entire; *holotelḗs* (3651), wholly, through and through; *hólōs* (3654), at all.

Syn.: *hápas* (537), the whole; *pás* (3956), all; *plḗrōma* (4138), fullness.

3651. ὀλοτελής, holotelēs, *hol-ot-el-ace´*; from 3650 and 5056; *complete* to the *end*, i.e. *absolutely perfect:*—wholly.

Adjective from *hólos* (3650), all, the whole, and *télos* (5056), completion. All or the whole, completely or entirely. Used only in 1Th 5:23.

Syn.: *ártios* (739), complete, perfect; *holóklēros* (3648), whole; *pantelḗs* (3838), entire; *plḗrēs* (4134), full; *téleios* (5046), perfect.

3652. Ὀλυμπᾶς, Olumpas, *ol-oom-pas´*; probably a contracted from Ὀλυμπιόδωρος,

Olumpiodōros (*Olympian-bestowed*, i.e. *heaven-descended*); *Olympas*, a Christian:—Olympas.

3653. ὄλυνθος, **olunthos,** *ol´-oon-thos*; of uncertain derivative; an *unripe* (because out of season) *fig*:—untimely (figurative).

3654. ὅλως, **holōs,** *hol´-oce*; adverb from 3650; *completely*, i.e. *altogether*; (by analogy) *everywhere*; (negative) not *by any means*:—at all, commonly, utterly.

3655. ὄμβρος, **ombros,** *om´-bros*; of uncertain affinity; a thunder *storm*:—shower.

3656. ὁμιλέω, **homileō,** *hom-il-eh´-o*; from 3658; to *be in company* with, i.e. (by implication) to *converse*:—commune, talk.

3657. ὁμιλία, **homilia,** *hom-il-ee´-ah*; from 3658; *companionship* ("homily"), i.e. (by implication) *intercourse*:—communication.

3658. ὅμιλος, **homilos,** *hom´-il-os*; from the base of 3674 and a derivative of the alternate of 138 (meaning a *crowd*); *association together*, i.e. a *multitude*:—company.

3659. ὄμμα, **omma,** *om´-mah*; from 3700; a *sight*, i.e. (by implication) the *eye*:—eye.

3660. ὀμνύω, **omnuō,** *om-noo´-o*; a prolonged form of a primary but obsolete ὄμω, *omō*, for which another prolonged form (ὀμόω, *omoō*, *om-o´-o*) is used in certain tenses; to *swear*, i.e. *take* (or *declare on*) *oath*:—swear.

3661. ὁμοθυμαδόν, **homothumadon,** *hom-oth-oo-mad-on´*; adverb from a compound of the base of 3674 and 2372; *unanimously*:—with one accord (mind).

3662. ὁμοιάζω, **homoiazō,** *hom-oy-ad´-zo*; from 3664; to *resemble*:—agree.

3663. ὁμοιοπαθής, **homoiopathēs,** *hom-oy-op-ath-ace´*; from 3664 and the alternate of 3958; *similarly affected*:—of (subject to) like passions.

3664. ὅμοιος, **homoios,** *hom´-oy-os*; from the base of 3674; *similar* (in appearance or character):—like, + manner.

Adjective from *homós* (n.f., see *homologeō* [3670]), one and the same. Like, similar:

(**I**) Generally, similar in external form and appearance (Jn 9:9; Rev 1:13, 15; 9:7, 10, 19;

13:2, 11; 14:14; 21:11, 18); in kind or nature (Ac 17:29; Gal 5:21); in conduct, character (Mt 11:16; 13:52; Lk 7:31, 32; 12:36; 1Jn 3:2); in conditions, circumstances (Mt 13:31, 33, 44, 45, 47; 20:1; Lk 6:47–49; 13:18, 19, 21; Rev 18:18).

(**II**) Just like, equal, the same with: in kind or nature (Jude 7); in conduct, character (Jn 8:55); in authority, dignity, power (Mt 22:39; Mk 12:31; Rev 13:4).

Deriv.: *homoiázō* (3662), to resemble; *homoiopathḗs* (3663), similarly affected, affected in a like fashion; *homoiótēs* (3665), similarity; *homoióō* (3666), to make like; *homoíōs* (3668), in a similar way, likewise; *parómoios* (3946), similar, much like.

Syn.: *ísos* (2470), equal; *hoíos* (3634), such as; *hopoíos* (3697), what manner; *toiósde* (5107), such, like; *toioútos* (5108), such, of this kind.

3665. ὁμοιότης, **homoiotēs,** *hom-oy-ot´ace*; from 3664; *resemblance*:—like as, similitude.

3666. ὁμοιόω, **homoioō,** *hom-oy-o´-o*; from 3664; to *assimilate*, i.e. *compare*; passive to *become similar*:—be (make) like, (in the) liken (-ess), resemble.

3667. ὁμοίωμα, **homoiōma,** *hom-oy´-o-mah*; from 3666; a *form*; abstract *resemblance*:—made like to, likeness, shape, similitude.

Noun from *homoióō* (3666), to make like. Something made like, a likeness:

(**I**) Generally: likeness, resemblance, similarity, made in the same way (Ro 1:23; 5:14; 6:5; 8:3; Rev 9:7).

(**II**) Particularly: in Php 2:7 *homoíōma* describes more than a mere similarity or resemblance. Jesus became a man. Perhaps *homoíōma* is used here to stress the fact that His humanity did differ from ours in the sense that Jesus' humanity was a sinless one, as was the human nature of Adam and Eve before the Fall (cf. Ro 8:3; Heb 4:15).

Syn.: *morphḗ* (3444), form, nature. Also *schḗma* (4976), form, fashion; *homoiótēs* (3665), similarity but not identical substance, hence, in Jesus, a similar human nature but without participation in man's sinfulness; *homoíōsis* (3669), the action of making alike, similitude, likeness.

3668. ὁμοίως, **homoiōs,** *hom-oy´-oce*; adverb from 3664; *similarly*:—likewise, so.

Adverb from *hómoios* (3664), like, resembling. In like manner, likewise, in the same way (Mt 22:26; 26:35; 27:41; Mk 4:16; 15:31; Lk 3:11; 5:10, 33; 6:31; 10:32, 37; 13:5; 16:25; 17:28, 31; 22:36; Jn 5:19; 6:11; 21:13; Ro 1:27; 1Co 7:3, 4, 22; Heb 9:21; Jas 2:25; 1Pe 3:1, 7; 5:5; Jude 8; Rev 8:12).

Syn.: *paraplēsíōs* (3898), similarly; *hōsaútōs* (5615), thus, in the same way.

3669. ὁμοίωσις, homoiōsis, *hom-oy´-o-sis*; from 3666; *assimilation*, i.e. *resemblance:*—similitude.

Noun from *homoióō* (3666), to make like. A likening, comparison. In the NT: likeness, resemblance. Only in Jas 3:9, in allusion to Ge 1:26.

Syn.: *antítupon* (499), an antitype, something that is stamped out as a true likeness; *eikṓn* (1504), a physical representation, image; *homoiótēs* (3665), likeness, similitude; *homoíōma* (3667), the likeness of something, a resemblance.

3670. ὁμολογέω, homologeō, *hom-ol-og-eh´-o*; from a compound of the base of 3674 and 3056; to *assent*, i.e. *covenant, acknowledge:*—con- (pro-) fess, confession is made, give thanks, promise.

From *homólogos* (n.f.), assenting, which is from *homoú* (3674), together with, and *lógos* (3056), word. To speak or say the same with another, e.g., to say the same things, i.e. to assent, accord, to agree with:

(I) To concede, admit, confess (Ac 24:14); of sins (1Jn 1:9). Hence, to confess publicly, acknowledge openly, profess (Mt 7:23; Jn 9:22; 12:42; Ac 23:8; Ro 10:9, 10; Heb 11:13). Followed by *en* ([1722], in), to confess Christ personally, meaning to profess or acknowledge Him (Mt 10:32; Lk 12:8). Followed by reference to a person: to acknowledge in honour of someone, i.e. to give thanks, to praise (Heb 13:15).

(II) To be in accord with someone, to promise (Mt 14:7).

Deriv.: *anthomologéomai* (437), to confess in return, respond in praise; *exomologéō* (1843), to confess verbally, to profess or acknowledge, promise, praise; *homología* (3671), confession; *homologouménōs* (3672), confessedly, surely, without controversy.

Syn.: *epaggéllō* (1861), to announce, promise,

profess; *eulogéō* (2127), to speak well of; *pháskō* (5335), to assert, affirm, profess.

3671. ὁμολογία, homologia, *hom-ol-og-ee´-ah*; from the same as 3670; *acknowledgment:*—con- (pro-) fession, professed.

Noun from *homologéō* (3670), to agree, confess, say the same. Assent, accord, agreement. In the NT: confession, profession (2Co 9:13; 1Ti 6:12, 13; Heb 10:23). Spoken by metonymy the thing professed, i.e. the Christian religion (Heb 3:1; 4:14).

3672. ὁμολογουμένως, homologoumenōs, *hom-ol-og-ow-men´-oce*; adverb of presumed passive participle of 3670; *confessedly:*—without controversy.

Adverb from *homologéō* (3670), to confess. By consent of all, confessedly, without controversy. Used only in 1Ti 3:16).

Syn.: *alēthṓs* (230), truly; *anantirrḗtōs* (369), without objection; *asphalṓs* (806), assuredly; *óntōs* (3689), verily, certainly; *pántōs* (3843), surely, altogether.

3673. ὁμότεχνος, homotechnos, *hom-ot´-ekh-nos*; from the base of 3674 and 5078; a *fellow artificer:*—of the same craft.

3674. ὁμοῦ, homou, *hom-oo´*; generic of ὁμός, *homos* (the *same*; akin to 260) as adverb; *at the same* place or time:—together.

3675. ὁμόφρων, homophrōn, *hom-of´-rone*; from the base of 3674 and 5424; *like-minded,* i.e. *harmonious:*—of one mind.

3676. ὅμως, homōs, *hom´-oce*; adverb from the base of 3674; *at the same* time, i.e. (conjecture) *notwithstanding, yet still:*—and even, nevertheless, though, but.

3677. ὄναρ, onar, *on´-ar*; of uncertain derivative; a *dream:*—dream.

3678. ὀνάριον, onarion, *on-ar´-ee-on*; neuter of a presumed derivative of 3688; a *little ass:*—young ass.

3679. ὀνειδέζω, oneidezō, *on-i-did´-zo*; from 3681; to *defame,* i.e. *rail at, chide, taunt:*—cast in teeth, (suffer) reproach, revile, upbraid.

3680. ὀνειδισμός, oneidismos, *on-i-dis-mos´*; from 3679; *contumely:*—reproach.

3681. ὄνειδος, **oneidos,** *on´-i-dos*; probably akin to the base of 3686; *notoriety*, i.e. a *taunt* (*disgrace*):—reproach.

3682. Ὀνήσιμος, **Onēsimos,** *on-ay´-sim-os*; from 3685; *profitable; Onesimus,* a Christian:—Onesimus.

3683. Ὀνησίφορος, **Onēsiphoros,** *on-ay-sif´-or-os*; from a derivative of 3685 and 5411; *profit-bearer; Onesiphorus,* a Christian:—Onesiphorus.

3684. ὀνικός, **onikos,** *on-ik-os´*; from 3688; *belonging to* an *ass,* i.e. *large* (so as to be turned by an ass):—millstone.

3685. ὀνίνημι, **oninēmi,** *on-in´-ay-mee*; a prolonged form of an apparent primary verb (ὄνομαι, **onomai,** to slur); for which another prolonged form (ὀνάω, **onaō**); is used as an alternate in some tenses [unless indeed it be identical with the base of 3686 through the idea of *notoriety*]; to *gratify,* i.e. (middle) to *derive pleasure* or *advantage* from:—have joy.

3686. ὄνομα, **onoma,** *on´-om-ah*; from a presumed derivative of the base of 1097 (compare 3685); a "*name*" (literal or figurative) [*authority, character*]:—called, (+ sur-) name (-d).

Noun meaning name; the proper name or appellation of a person:

(**I**) Particularly and generally (Mt 1:21, 23, 25; 10:2; Mk 3:16, 17; 6:14; Lk 1:61, 63; 10:20; Ac 13:8; 1Co 1:13, 15; Php 4:3; Rev 13:1; 17:3; 21:14). By metonymy, "name" is sometimes put for the person or persons bearing that name (Lk 6:22; Ac 1:15; Rev 3:4; 11:13).

(**II**) Used to imply authority, e.g., to come or to do something in or by the name of someone, meaning using his name; as his messenger, envoy, representative; by his authority, with his sanction (Mt 10:41, 42; 18:5; 21:9; 23:39; Mk 9:39; 16:17; Lk 9:49; 10:17; 24:47; Jn 5:43; 10:25; 14:13, 14, 26; Ac 3:6; 4:7, 17, 18; 5:28, 40; 9:27; 1Co 5:4; 2Th 3:6; Jas 5:14). Of impostors (Mt 7:22; Mk 9:38 [presumed]; 13:6; Lk 21:8).

(**III**) Used to imply character, dignity, referring to an honourable appellation, title (Eph 1:21; Php 2:9). See Ac 4:12; Heb 1:4; Rev 19:16. A mere name, as opposed to reality (Rev 3:1).

(**IV**) Used emphatically: the name of God, of the Lord, of Christ, by metonymy as the total expression of God Himself, Christ Himself, in all their being, attributes, relations, manifestations (Mt 6:9; 18:20; 28:19):

(**A**) Spoken of God, where His name is said to be hallowed, revealed, invoked, honored (Mt 6:9; Lk 1:49; 11:2; Jn 12:28; 17:6, 11, 12; Ac 2:21; 9:14, 21; 15:14, 17; Ro 9:17; 10:13; 15:9; 1Co 1:2; Heb 2:12; 6:10; 13:15; Rev 11:18); to baptize in the name of the Lord (Mt 28:19; Ac 2:38; 8:16; 10:48; 19:5); by antithesis, to baptize in the name of Paul (1Co 1:13, 15); the blaspheming of His name (Ro 2:24; 1Ti 6:1).

(**B**) Spoken of Christ as the Messiah where His name is said to be honored, revered, believed on, invoked (Mt 12:21; 18:20; Jn 1:12; 2:23; Ac 8:12; 19:17; Ro 1:5; Php 2:10; 2Th 1:12; Rev 2:13; 3:8); where benefits are said to be received in or through the name of Christ (Jn 20:31; Ac 4:10, 30; 10:43; 1Co 6:11; 1Jn 2:12); where something is done in His name, meaning for His sake, or in and through Him, through faith in Him (Eph 5:20; Col 3:17; 3Jn 7). Where evils and sufferings are endured for the name of Christ (Mt 10:22; 19:29; Mk 13:13; Lk 21:12; Jn 15:21; Ac 5:41; 9:16; 21:13; 1Pe 4:14; Rev 2:3). Where one opposes and blasphemes the name of Christ (Ac 26:9; Jas 2:7).

(**C**) Spoken of the Holy Spirit, to baptize in His name (Mt 28:19).

Deriv.: *euōnumos* (2176), of good name; *onomázō* (3687), to name; *pseudōnumos* (5581), bearing a false name.

3687. ὀνομάζω, **onomazō,** *on-om-ad´-zo*; from 3686; to *name,* i.e. *assign an appellation*; by extension to *utter, mention, profess*:—call, name.

3688. ὄνος, **onos,** *on´-os*; apparently a primary word; a *donkey*:—ass.

3689. ὄντως, **ontōs,** *on´-toce*; adverb of the oblique cases of 5607; *really*:—certainly, clean, indeed, of a truth, verily.

3690. ὄξος, **oxos,** *ox´-os*; from 3691; *vinegar,* i.e. *sour* wine:—vinegar.

3691. ὀξύς, **oxus,** *ox-oos´*; probably akin to the base of 188 ["*acid*"]; *keen*; (by analogy) *rapid*:—sharp, swift.

3692. ὀπή, **opē,** *op-ay´*; probably from 3700; a *hole* (as if for light), i.e. *cavern*; (by analogy) a *spring* (of water):—cave, place.

3693. ὄπισθεν, opisthen, *op´-is-then*; from **ὄπις, opis** (*regard*; from 3700) with enclitic of source; *from the rear* (as a secure *aspect*), i.e. *at* the *back* (adverb and preposition of place or time):—after, backside, behind.

3694. ὀπίσω, opisō, *op-is´-o*; from the same as 3693 with enclitic of direction; *to the back*, i.e. *aback* (as adverb or preposition of time or place; or as noun):—after, back (-ward), (+ get) behind, + follow.

3695. ὁπλίζω, hoplizō, *hop-lid´-zo*; from 3696; to *equip* (with weapons [middle and figurative]):—arm self.

3696. ὅπλον, hoplon, *hop´-lon*; probably from a primary ἔπω, hepō (to be *busy* about); an *implement* or *utensil* or *tool* (literal or figurative, especially offensive for war):—armour, instrument, weapon.

3697. ὁποῖος, hopoios, *hop-oy´-os*; from 3739 and 4169; of *what* kind *that*, i.e. *how* (*as*) *great* (*excellent*) (specially as indefinite correlation to antecedent definite 5108 of quality):—what manner (sort) of, such as, whatsoever.

3698. ὁπότε, hopote, *hop-ot´-eh*; from 3739 and 4218; *what* (-ever) *then*, i.e. (of time) *as soon as*:—when.

3699. ὅπου, hopou, *hop´-oo*; from 3739 and 4225; *what* (-ever) *where*, i.e. *at whichever spot*:—in what place, where (-as, -soever), whither (+ soever).

3700. ὀπτάνομαι, optanomai, *op-tan´-om-ahee*; a (middle) prolonged form of the primary (middle) ὄπτομαι, optomai, *op´-tom-ahee*; which is used for it in certain tenses; and both as alternate of 3708; to *gaze* (i.e. with wide-open eyes, as at something remarkable; and thus differing from 991, which denotes simply *voluntary* observation; and from 1492, which expresses merely mechanical, passive or casual vision; while 2300, and still more emphatically its intensive 2334, signifies an earnest but more continued *inspection*; and 4648 a watching *from a distance*):—appear, look, see, shew self.

3701. ὀπτασία, optasia, *op-tas-ee´-ah*; from a presumed derivative of 3700; *visuality*, i.e. (concretely) an *apparition*:—vision.

3702. ὀπτός, optos, *op-tos´*; from an obsolete verb akin to ἕψω, hepsō (to "*steep*"); *cooked*, i.e. *roasted*:—broiled.

3703. ὀπώρα, opōra, *op-o´-rah*; apparently from the base of 3796 and 5610; properly *eventide* of the (summer) season (*dog-days*), i.e. (by implication) *ripe* fruit:—fruit.

3704. ὅπως, hopōs, *hop´-oce*; from 3739 and 4459; *what* (-ever) *how*, i.e. *in the manner that* (as adverb or conjecture of coincidence, intentional or actual):—because, how, (so) that, to, when.

3705. ὅραμα, horama, *hor´-am-ah*; from 3708; *something gazed at*, i.e. a *spectacle* (especially supernatural):—sight, vision.

3706. ὅρασις, horasis, *hor´-as-is*; from 3708; the act of *gazing*, i.e. (external) an *aspect* or (internal) an inspired *appearance*:—sight, vision.

3707. ὁρατός, horatos, *hor-at-os´*; from 3708; *gazed at*, i.e. (by implication) *capable of being seen*:—visible.

3708. ὁράω, horaō, *hor-ah´-o*; properly to *stare* at [compare 3700], i.e. (by implication) to *discern* clearly (physical or mental); by extension to *attend* to; by Hebrew to *experience*; passive to *appear*:—behold, perceive, see, take heed.

To see, perceive with the eyes, look at, not emphasizing the mere act of seeing, but the actual perception of some object, thus differing from *blépō* (991), to see:

(**I**) To see with the eyes:

(**A**) Particularly, persons or things (Lk 1:22; 9:36; 16:23; 24:23; Jn 4:45; 5:37; 20:18, 25, 29; Ac 7:44; 22:15; Heb 2:8; 1Pe 1:8; 1Jn 1:1).

(**B**) In various modified senses: (**1**) To see face-to-face, to see and converse with, i.e. have personal acquaintance and fellowship with (Jn 6:36; 8:57; 14:9; 15:24; Ac 20:25; Col 2:1). (**2**) To look upon, to behold, to contemplate (Jn 19:37). (**3**) To see take place, to witness (Lk 17:22).

(**C**) Passive: to be seen by someone, to appear to someone: (**1**) Particularly, spoken of things (Rev 11:19; 12:1, 3); spoken of persons, e.g., angels (Lk 1:11; 22:43; Ac 7:30, 35); of God (Ac 7:2); of persons dead (Mt 17:3; Mk 9:4; Lk 9:31); of Jesus after his resurrection (Lk 24:34;

Ac 1:3; 26:16; 1Co 15:5–8; 1Ti 3:16), or of Jesus in the Second Coming (Heb 9:28). **(2)** Middle: to show oneself, present oneself to or before someone (Ac 7:26).

(II) Figuratively, to perceive with the mind or senses.

(A) Particularly, to see God, meaning to know Him, be acquainted with Him, know His character; only in John's writings (Jn 1:18; 6:46; 14:7, 9; 15:24; 1Jn 3:6; 4:20; 3Jn 11). In a wider sense: to see God, i.e. to be admitted to his presence, to enjoy his fellowship and special favour, the figure being drawn from the customs of oriental courts (Mt 5:8; Heb 12:14; Rev 22:4).

(B) Generally: to be aware of, observe (Ac 8:23; Jas 2:24).

(C) Spoken of things: to see and know, to come to know, learn (Jn 3:11, 32; 8:38; Col 2:18).

(D) By Hebraism: to experience, e.g., good, to attain to, to enjoy (Jn 3:36).

(E) In an absolute sense: to see to it, take care, take heed (Heb 8:5); usually followed by *mḗ* ([3361], not), meaning take heed lest, beware (Mt 18:10; 24:6; 1Th 5:15; Rev 19:10; 22:9). Also Mt 8:4; 9:30; Mk 1:44.

Deriv.: *aóratos* (517), invisible; *aphoráō* (872), to look away from one thing so as to see another; *kathoráō* (2529), to see clearly; *hórama* (3705), a spectacle, appearance, vision; *hórasis* (3706), vision, sight; *horatós* (3707), visible; *prooráō* (4308), to foresee.

Syn.: *blépō* (991), to see; *eídō* (1492), to see, perceive; *paratēréō* (3906), to observe; *theáomai* (2300), to look closely; *theōréō* (2334), to see, discern, perceive.

3709. ὀργή, **orgē**, *or-gay´*; from 3713; properly *desire* (as a *reaching* forth or *excitement* of the mind), i.e. (by analogy) violent *passion* (ire, or [justifiable] *abhorrence*); (by implication) *punishment*:—anger, indignation, vengeance, wrath.

Noun from *orégō* (3713), to covet after, desire. The native character, disposition, temper of the mind; impulse, impetus. Hence in the NT: passion, i.e. any violent commotion of mind; indignation, anger, wrath, especially as including desire for vengeance, punishment, and therein differing from *thumós* (2372), wrath:

(I) Generally (Mk 3:5; Ro 12:19; Eph 4:31; Col 3:8; 1Ti 2:8; Jas 1:19, 20). Spoken of God, as implying utter abhorrence of sin and aversion to those who live in it (Ro 9:22; Heb 3:11; 4:3).

(II) By metonymy: wrath, as including the idea of punishment, e.g., as the penalty of law (Ro 4:15; 13:4, 5). Also of the punitive wrath of God, the divine judgements to be inflicted upon the wicked (Mt 3:7; Lk 3:7; 21:23; Jn 3:36; Ro 2:8; 3:5; 5:9; 9:22; Eph 5:6; Col 3:6; 1Th 1:10).

Deriv.: *orgízō* (3710), to make angry, provoke; *orgílos* (3711), angry, quick-tempered.

Syn.: *thumós* (2372), wrath. Also *aganáktēsis* (24), indignation; *eritheía* (2052), partisan strife.

3710. ὀργίζω, **orgizō**, *or-gid´-zo*; from 3709; to *provoke* or *enrage*, i.e. (passive) *become exasperated*:—be angry (wroth).

3711. ὀργίλος, **orgilos**, *org-ee´-los*; from 3709; *irascible*:—soon angry.

3712. ὀργυιά, **orguia**, *org-wee-ah´*; from 3713; a *stretch* of the arms, i.e. a *fathom*:—fathom.

3713. ὀρέγομαι, **oregomai**, *or-eg´-om-ahee*; middle of apparently a prolonged form of an obsolete primary [compare 3735]; to *stretch* oneself, i.e. *reach* out after (*long* for):—covet after, desire.

3714. ὀρεινός, **oreinos**, *or-i-nos´*; from 3735; *mountainous*, i.e. (feminine, by implication of 5561) the *Highlands* (of Judæa):—hill country.

3715. ὄρεξις, **orexis**, *or´-ex-is*; from 3713; *excitement* of the mind, i.e. *longing* after:—lust.

Noun from *orégō* (3713), to desire. A reaching after. Figuratively: longing, lust. Used only in Ro 1:27, spoken of homosexual lust.

Syn.: *epithumía* (1939), desire, longing, lust.

3716. ὀρθοποδέω, **orthopodeō**, *or-thop-od-eh´-o*; from a compound of 3717 and 4228; to *be straight-footed*, i.e. (figurative) to *go directly forward*:—walk uprightly.

3717. ὀρθός, **orthos**, *or-thos´*; probably from the base of 3735; *right* (as *rising*), i.e. (perpendicularly) *erect* (figurative, *honest*), or (horizontally) *level* or *direct*:—straight, upright.

Adjective meaning straight. Spoken of standing straight, erect (Ac 14:10). Straight and level; not crooked or uneven. Used figuratively of paths (Heb 12:13).

Deriv.: *anorthóō* (461), to make straight or

upright again; *orthotoméō* (3718), to rightly divide; *orthós* (3723), rightly.

Syn.: *euthús* (2117), straight.

3718. ὀρθοτομέω, orthotomeō, *or-thot-om-eh´-o*; from a compound of 3717 and the base of 5114; to *make a straight cut*, i.e. (figurative) to *dissect* (*expound*) *correctly* (the divine message):—rightly divide.

From *orthós* (3717), right and *témnō* (n.f., see below), to cut or divide. To cut straight, to divide right. In the NT, used figuratively: to handle correctly, skillfully; to correctly teach the word of truth. Used only in 2Ti 2:15.

Deriv. of *témnō* (n.f.): *peritémnō* (4059), to circumcise; *suntémnō* (4932), to cut short; *tomōteros* (5114), finer edged, sharper.

3719. ὀρθρίζω, orthrizō, *or-thrid´-zo*; from 3722; to *use the dawn*, i.e. (by implication) to *repair betimes*:—come early in the morning.

3720. ὀρθρινός, orthrinos, *or-thrin-os´*; from 3722; *relating to the dawn*, i.e. *matutinal* (as an epithet of Venus, especially brilliant in the early day):—morning.

3721. ὄρθριος, orthrios, *or´-three-os*; from 3722; *in the dawn*, i.e. up *at day-break*:—early.

3722. ὄρθρος, orthros, *or´-thros*; from the same as 3735; *dawn* (as *sunrise*, *rising* of light); by extension *morn*:—early in the morning.

3723. ὀρθῶς, orthōs, *or-thoce´*; adverb from 3717; *in a straight* manner, i.e. (figurative) *correctly* (also morally):—plain, right (-ly).

3724. ὁρίζω, horizō, *hor-id´-zo*; from 3725; to *mark out* or *bound* ("horizon"), i.e. (figurative) to *appoint, decree, specify*:—declare, determine, limit, ordain.

From *hóros* (n.f., see *methórios* [3181]), boundary, limit. To mark out definitely, determine, appoint, set up. Of persons: to set up, appoint (Ro 1:4; Ac 10:42; 17:31); in respect to time, to determine the time (Ac 17:26; Heb 4:7). To determine, resolve, decree (Lk 22:22; Ac 2:23; 11:29).

Deriv.: *aphorízō* (873), to set off by boundary, exclude, separate; *proorízō* (4309), foreordain.

Syn.: *tássō* (5021), ordain, appoint. Also *aphorízō* (873), to set off by boundary, exclude;

diatássō (1299), to arrange thoroughly; *diachōrízō* (1316), to apportion, separate.

3725. ὅριον, horion, *hor´-ee-on*; neuter of a derivative of an apparently primary **ὅρος, horos** (a *bound* or *limit*); a *boundary*-line, i.e. (by implication) a *frontier* (*region*):—border, coast.

3726. ὁρκίζω, horkizō, *hor-kid´-zo*; from 3727; to *put on oath*, i.e. *make swear*; (by analogy) to solemnly *enjoin*:—adjure, charge.

3727. ὅρκος, horkos, *hor´-kos*; from **ἕρκος, herkos** (a *fence*; perhaps akin to 3725); a *limit*, i.e. (sacred) *restraint* (special *oath*):—oath.

3728. ὁρκωμοσία, horkōmosia, *hor-ko-mos-ee´-ah*; from a compound of 3727 and a derivative of 3660; *asseveration on oath*:—oath.

3729. ὁρμάω, hormaō, *hor-mah´-o*; from 3730; to *start, spur* or *urge* on, i.e. (reflexive) to *dash* or *plunge*:—run (violently), rush.

3730. ὁρμή, hormē, *hor-may´*; of uncertain affinity; a violent *impulse*, i.e. *onset*:—assault.

Noun from *órnumi* (n.f.), to excite, arouse. A rushing on, onset, impetus, attempt (Ac 14:5). Figuratively, of the mind: impulse, will, desire (Ac 14:5; Jas 3:4).

Deriv.: *aphormḗ* (874), an occasion; *hormáō* (3729), to rush violently, incite.

Syn.: *bía* (970), force, violence.

3731. ὅρμημα, hormēma, *hor´-may-mah*; from 3730; an *attack*, i.e. (abstract) *precipitancy*:—violence.

3732. ὄρνεον, orneon, *or´-neh-on*; neuter of a presumed derivative of 3733; a *birdling*:—bird, fowl.

3733. ὄρνις, ornis, *or´-nis*; probably from a prolonged form of the base of 3735; a *bird* (as *rising* in the air), i.e. (special) a *hen* (or female domestic fowl):—hen.

3734. ὁροθεσία, horothesia, *hor-oth-es-ee´-ah*; from a compound of the base of 3725 and a derivative of 5087; a *limit-placing*, i.e. (concrete) *boundary-line*:—bound.

3735. ὄρος, oros, *or´-os*; probably from an obsolete **ὄρω, orō** (to *rise* or "*rear*"; perhaps akin to 142; compare 3733); a *mountain* (as *lifting* itself above the plain):—hill, mount (-ain).

3736. ὀρύσσω, orussō, *or-oos´-so*; apparently a primary verb; to *"burrow"* in the ground, i.e. *dig*:—dig.

3737. ὀρφανός, orphanos, *or-fan-os´*; of uncertain affinity; *bereaved* (*"orphan"*), i.e. *parentless*:—comfortless, fatherless.

3738. ὀρχέομαι, orcheomai, *or-kheh´-om-ahee*; middle from **ὄρχος,** *orchos* (a *row* or *ring*); to *dance* (from the *ranklike* or *regular* motion):—dance.

3739. ὅς, hos, *hos*; including feminine ἥ, *hē*, *hay*; and neuter ὅ, *ho*, *ho*; probably a primary word (or perhaps a form of the article 3588); the relative (sometimes demonstrative) pronoun, *who, which, what, that*:—one, (an-, the) other, some, that, what, which, who (-m, -se), etc. See also 3757.

3740. ὁσάκις, hosakis, *hos-ak´-is*; multiple adverb from 3739; *how* (i.e. with 302, *so*) *many times* as:—as oft (-en) as.

3741. ὅσιος, hosios, *hos´-ee-os*; of uncertain affinity; properly *right* (by intrinsic or divine character; thus distinguished from 1342, which refers rather to *human* statutes and relations; from 2413, which denotes formal *consecration*; and from 40, which relates to *purity* from defilement), i.e. *hallowed* (*pious, sacred, sure*):—holy, mercy, shalt be.

Adjective meaning holy, righteous, unpolluted with wickedness, right as conformed to God and His laws, thus distinguished from *díkaios* (1342), which refers more to human laws and duties. Used in the NT:

(I) Of God (Rev 15:4; 16:5; Sept.: Dt 32:4; Ps 145:17); of Christ (Ac 2:27; 13:35; Heb 7:26); of men, meaning pious, godly, careful of all duties toward God (Tit 1:8).

(II) Of things, meaning holy, sacred (1Ti 2:8; Sept.: Pr 22:11). In Ac 13:34, "the sure mercies of David," *hósios* refers to the holy promises (see v. 35; Isa 55:3).

Deriv.: *anósios* (462), unholy, ungodly; *hosiótēs* (3742), sacredness, holiness; *hosíōs* (3743), piously.

Syn.: *hágios* (40), holy with the implication of purity; *áspilos* (784), unblemished; *hieroprepés* (2412), reverent, as is becoming to sacredness.

3742. ὁσιότης, hosiotēs, *hos-ee-ot´-ace*; from 3741; *piety*:—holiness.

Noun from *hósios* (3741), holy, righteous. Holiness manifesting itself in the discharge of pious duties in religious and social life. Twice in the NT joined with *dikaiosúnē* (1343), righteousness (Lk 1:75; Eph 4:24).

Syn.: *hagiótēs* (41), inherent holiness implying pure moral character; *hagiōsúnē* (42), holiness; *theiótēs* (2305), divinity, divine nature.

3743. ὁσίως, hosiōs, *hos-ee´-oce*; adverb from 3741; *piously*:—holily.

3744. ὀσμή, osmē, *os-may´*; from 3605; *fragrance* (literal or figurative):—odour, savour.

3745. ὅσος, hosos, *hos´-os*; by reduplicated from 3739; *as* (*much, great, long,* etc.) *as*:—all (that), as (long, many, much) (as), how great (many, much), [in-] asmuch as, so many as, that (ever), the more, those things, what (great, -soever), wheresoever, wherewithsoever, which, × while, who (-soever).

3746. ὅσπερ, hosper, *hos´-per*; from 3739 and 4007; *who especially*:—whomsoever.

3747. ὀστέον, osteon, *os-teh´-on*; or contrete ὀστοῦν, *ostoun, os-toon´*; of uncertain affinity; a *bone*:—bone.

3748. ὅστις, hostis, *hos´-tis*; including the feminine ἥτις, *hētis, hay´-tis*; and the neuter ὅ τι, *ho ti, hot´-ee*; from 3739 and 5100; *which some,* i.e. *any that;* also (definite) *which same:*—× and (they), (such) as, (they) that, in that they, what (-soever), whereas ye, (they) which, who (-soever). Compare 3754.

Indefinite relative pronoun from *hós* (3739), he who, and *tís* (5100), anyone, someone. Anyone who, someone who, whoever, whatever, differing from *hós* (3739) in referring to a subject only generally as one of a class and not definitely, thus serving to render a proposition as general; usually translated whoever, etc.

(I) When modifying a noun which is already indefinite, *hóstis* will generally be translated in its own clause as if it were a definite relative pronoun, "who, which" (Ac 16:16). Also Mt 7:26; 13:52; 16:28; 25:1; Lk 7:37; Ac 16:16; 24:1; Ro 16:6, 12; 1Co 6:20; 7:13; Php 2:20).

(II) When *hóstis* is used as a substantive in an introductory clause, it will have the idea of everyone who, all who, whosoever, whatsoever: e.g., "whosoever shall exalt himself shall be abased" (Mt 23:12). Also Mt 5:39, 41; 7:24; 10:32, 33; 13:12; 18:4; 23:12; Mk 4:20; 8:34; Lk 14:27; Ac 3:23; Gal 5:10; Rev 1:7.

(III) However, sometimes *hóstis* refers to a definite subject and is then apparently equal to *hós*, who, which: e.g., "the city of David, which is called Bethlehem" (Lk 2:4). Also Jn 8:53; Ac 11:28; 16:12; Ro 16:6, 12; Rev 1:12; 11:8.

3749. ὀστράκινος, **ostrakinos,** *os-tra´-kin-os*; from ὄστρα-κον, *ostrakon*; ["oyster"] (a *tile*, i.e. *terra cotta*); *earthen*-ware, i.e. *clayey*; (by implication) *frail:*—of earth, earthen.

3750. ὄσφρησις, **osphrēsis,** *os´-fray-sis*; from a derivative of 3605; *smell* (the sense):—smelling.

3751. ὀσφύς, **osphus,** *os-foos´*; of uncertain affinity; the *loin* (external), i.e. the *hip*; internal (by extension) *procreative power:*—loin.

3752. ὅταν, **hotan,** *hot´-an*; from 3753 and 302; *whenever* (implying *hypothesis* or more or less *uncertainty*); also causative (conjecture) *inasmuch as:*—as long (soon) as, that, + till, when (-soever), while.

3753. ὅτε, **hote,** *hot´-eh*; from 3739 and 5037; *at which* (thing) *too*, i.e. *when:*—after (that), as soon as, that, when, while. ὅτε, **ho te,** *ho´-teh*; also feminine ἥτε, **hē te,** *hay´-teh*; and neuter τὸ τε, **tō te,** *tot´-eh*; simply the article 3588 followed by 5037; so written (in some editions) to distinguish them from 3752 and 5119.

3754. ὅτι, **hoti,** *hot´-ee*; neuter of 3748 as conjecture; demonstrative *that* (sometimes redundant); causative *because:*—as concerning that, as though, because (that), for (that), how (that), (in) that, though, why.

Conjunction meaning that (demonstrative), because (causal). As a demonstrative it introduces the object, contents, or argument to which the preceding words refer. As a causal, it assigns the cause, motive, ground of something:

(I) As a demonstrative conjunction:

(A) Particularly after demonstrative pronouns (Jn 3:19, "And this is the condemnation, that (*hóti*) light is come into the world . . ."; Ro 2:3; 2Co 5:14; Rev 2:6); after interrogative pronouns (Lk 2:49, "How is it that ye sought me?" Also Mk 2:16; Lk 8:25; Jn 14:22; Ac 5:4, 9; Heb 2:6).

(B) Most frequently *hóti* is put after certain classes of verbs to express the obj. or reference of the verb, e.g., "Moreover I call God for a record upon my soul, that (*hóti*) to spare you I came not as yet unto Corinth" (2Co 1:23); "His disciples remembered that (*hóti*) he had said this unto them" (Jn 2:22). Also Mt 16:21; Mk 2:8, 10; Jn 16:4; Ac 24:26; Ro 8:28, 38; Php 2:24; Heb 11:19; Jas 1:7).

(II) As a causal conjunction: *hóti* is put after certain classes of verbs and also generally to express the cause, reason, motive, occasion of the action or event mentioned, often translated "that," "because," or "for," e.g., "My name is Legion, for [*hóti*] we are many" (Mk 5:9). Also Mt 2:18; Mk 1:27; Lk 4:36; 11:42, 43; 16:3; 23:40; Ro 6:17; 1Co 11:2, 17; 2Co 7:9; Gal 1:6; Rev 5:4; 18:11.

Deriv.: *dióti* (1360), because, for.

3755. ὅτου, **hotou,** *hot´-oo*; for the generic of 3748 (as adverb); during *which same* time, i.e. *whilst:*—whiles.

3756. οὐ, **ou,** *oo*; also (before a vowel) οὐκ, **ouk,** *ook*; and (before an aspirate) οὐχ, **ouch,** *ookh*; a primary word; the absolute negative [compare 3361] adverb; *no* or *not:*— + long, nay, neither, never, no (× man), none, [can-] not, + nothing, + special, un ([-worthy]), when, + without, + yet but. See also 3364, 3372.

3757. οὗ, **hou,** *hoo*; generic of 3739 as adverb; at *which* place, i.e. *where:*—where (-in), whither ([-soever]).

3758. οὐά, **oua,** *oo-ah´*; a primary exclamation of surprise; "*ah*":—ah.

3759. οὐαί, **ouai,** *oo-ah´ee*; a primary exclamation of grief; "*woe*":—alas, woe.

3760. οὐδαμῶς, **oudamōs,** *oo-dam-oce´*; adverb from (the feminine) of 3762; *by no means:*—not.

3761. οὐδέ, **oude,** *oo-deh´*; from 3756 and 1161; *not however*, i.e. *neither, nor, not even:*—neither (indeed), never, no (more, nor, not), nor (yet), (also, even, then) not (even, so much as), + nothing, so much as.

3762. οὐδείς, **oudeis,** *oo-dice´*; including feminine οὐδεμία, **oudemia,** *oo-dem-ee´-ah*; and neuter οὐδέν, **ouden,** *oo-den´*; from 3761 and

1520; *not even one* (man, woman or thing), i.e. *none, nobody, nothing*:—any (man), aught, man, neither any (thing), never (man), no (man), none (+ of these things), not (any, at all, -thing), nought.

Adjective from *ou* (3756), not, and *heís* (1520), one. Not even one, not the least. When it is used in the neuter, *oudén*, it means nothing or not a thing. *Oudeís* is used with the indicative mood to state objectively, where *mēdeís* (3367), not even one, is used with all other moods to state potentially. This distinction parallels the use of the two simple negatives *ou* (3756), not, and *mē* (3361), not. Generally it means no one, nothing, none at all; particularly and emphatically: not even one, not the least.

(I) As a negative adj.: not one, no (Lk 4:24; 23:4; Jn 10:41; 16:29; 18:38; 1Co 8:4).

(II) Used in an absolute sense, as a substantive, *oudeís* means no one, no man, no person (Mt 6:24; 22:16; Mk 5:4; Lk 4:26, 27; 5:36, 37, 39; Jn 5:22; 8:15; 17:12; 18:9; Ac 4:12; 5:13; 9:8; 18:17; 1Co 1:14; 9:15; 2Co 11:9; Eph 5:29; Rev 2:17).

(III) Neuter *oudén*, used in an absolute sense, generally means "nothing" (Mt 10:26; 27:24; Mk 14:60; Lk 4:2; 22:35; Jn 3:27; 8:28; Ac 15:9; 26:26; Gal 2:6; Heb 2:8). The accusative *oudén* as an adverb means in no way, in no respect (2Co 12:11).

Syn.: *mēdeís* (3367), none.

3763. οὐδέποτε, **oudepote**, *oo-dep´-ot-eh*; from 3761 and 4218; *not even at any time*, i.e. *never at all*:—neither at any time, never, nothing at any time.

3764. οὐδέπω, **oudepō**, *oo-dep´-o*; from 3761 and 4452; *not even yet*:—as yet not, never before (yet), (not) yet.

3765. οὐκέτι, **ouketi**, *ook-et´-ee*; also (separately) οὐκ ἔτι, **ouk eti**, *ook et´-ee*; from 3756 and 2089; *not yet, no longer*:—after that (not), (not) any more, henceforth (hereafter) not, no longer (more), not as yet (now), now no more (not), yet (not).

3766. οὐκοῦν, **oukoun**, *ook-oon´*; from 3756 and 3767; is it *not therefore* that, i.e. (affirmative) *hence* or *so*:—then.

3767. οὖν, **oun**, *oon*; apparently a primary word; (adverb) *certainly*, or (conjecture) *accordingly*:—and (so, truly), but, now (then), so (likewise then), then, therefore, verily, wherefore.

3768. οὔπω, **oupō**, *oo´-po*; from 3756 and 4452; *not yet*:—hitherto not, (no …) as yet, not yet.

3769. οὐρά, **oura**, *oo-rah´*; apparently a primary word; a *tail*:—tail.

3770. οὐράνιος, **ouranios**, *oo-ran´-ee-os*; from 3772; *celestial*, i.e. *belonging to* or *coming from the sky*:—heavenly.

Adjective from *ouranós* (3772), heaven. Celestial, heavenly, i.e. dwelling in heaven, as the "Heavenly Father" (Mt 6:14, 26, 32; 15:13), the "heavenly host" (Lk 2:13); a heavenly vision (Ac 26:19).

Syn.: *epouránios* (2032), heavenly.

3771. οὐρανόθεν, **ouranothen**, *oo-ran-oth´-en*; from 3772 and the enclitic of source; *from the sky*:—from heaven.

3772. οὐρανός, **ouranos**, *oo-ran-os´*; perhaps from the same as 3735 (through the idea of *elevation*); the *sky*; by extension *heaven* (as the abode of God); (by implication) *happiness, power, eternity*; specially the *gospel* (*Christianity*):—air, heaven ([-ly]), sky.

Noun meaning heaven, sky, air. Often used in the plural, *hoi ouranoí*, "the heavens," in imitation of the Heb use of the plural *šāmayim* (8064, OT; heavens). The plural is found most often in Matthew, less often in Mark and the epistles of Paul and Peter, only six times in Luke's writings, and not at all in the writings of John and James. However, the singular and plural are used similarly and interchangeably, with no significant difference in meaning between them. In the Hebrew usage, the term was used to speak of the expanse of the sky above, which was regarded as solid and fixed, i.e. the firmament; but was also commonly used to include the regions above the sky where God was said to dwell, and likewise the region underneath and next to the firmament, where the clouds are gathered, the birds fly, etc. Thus, in the NT, *ouranós* is used:

(I) Of the visible heavens and all their phenomena; so where heaven and earth are spoken of together, e.g., as opposites (1Co 8:5; Heb 12:26; 2Pe 3:5); as "heaven and earth," i.e. the universe (Mt 5:18; Mk 13:31; Lk 10:21; Ac 4:24; Col 1:16; Rev 10:6; 14:7). Further, in expressions such as the "present heavens," which are to be destroyed at the final consummation of all things, after which the "new heavens" are to appear (2Pe 3:7, 13; Rev 21:1). Sometimes more than one heaven is spoken of (Eph 4:10; Heb 4:14; 7:26; see more fully in IV, below). Used figuratively in expressions such as "to be exalted to heaven," i.e. to be highly distinguished, renowned (Mt 11:23; Lk 10:15).

(II) Of the firmament itself, the starry heaven, in which the sun, moon, and stars are fixed (Mk 13:25; Heb 11:12). Hence "the powers of heaven," i.e. the host or hosts of heaven; the sun, moon, and stars (Mt 24:29; Mk 13:25; Lk 21:26). Further, the stars are said to "fall from heaven," as emblematic of great commotions and revolutions (Mt 24:29; Rev 6:13; 8:10; 9:1). The firmament itself, which is spread out over the earth as a tent or curtain (Ps 104:2; Isa 40:22), is likewise said to be rolled together as a scroll (Rev 6:14). Used figuratively in Lk 10:18, where the form of expression is in allusion to Isa 14:12, the lightning being emblematic of swiftness.

(III) Of the lower heaven, or region below the firmament, i.e. the air, atmosphere, where clouds and storms are gathered and lightning breaks forth, where the birds fly, etc. Of clouds, i.e. "sky" (Mt 16:2, 3; Mk 14:62; Lk 12:56); of rain and hail (Rev 16:21); of lightning or fire from heaven (Lk 9:54; 17:29; Rev 20:9); of signs, wonders (Mt 16:1; Mk 8:11; Lk 11:16; Ac 2:19; Rev 12:1, 3); of birds (Mt 6:26; 8:20; Lk 8:5; 9:58). Figuratively, in the expression "to shut up the heavens," i.e. to withhold rain (Lk 4:25; Rev 11:6).

(IV) Of the upper or superior heaven, beyond the visible firmament, the abode of God and his glory, of the Messiah, of the angels, the spirits of the righteous after death, and generally everything which is said to be with God:

(A) Generally, e.g., of God (Mt 5:16, 34, 45; 23:22; Mk 11:25, 26; Lk 10:21; Ac 7:49; Eph 6:9; Col 4:1; Heb 8:1; Rev 11:13; 16:11); of the Messiah, the son of God, as coming from heaven (Jn 3:13, 31; 6:33, 38, 41), or as returning there after his resurrection (Mk 16:19; Lk 24:51; Ac 1:10, 11), whence he will again come to judge the world (1Th 1:10; 4:16; 2Th 1:7); of the Holy Spirit (Mt 3:16; Jn 1:32; 1Pe 1:12); of angels (Mt 18:10; 24:36; Mk 12:25; Lk 22:43; Gal 1:8); of the righteous after death, as the seat of their final

glorious reward (Mt 5:12; 6:20; Lk 10:20; 2Co 5:1; Col 1:5; 1Pe 1:4). In heaven also is the spiritual temple with its sacred utensils (Heb 9:23, 24; Rev 11:19; 14:17; 15:5; 16:17); and there also the new Jerusalem is prepared and adorned (Rev 3:12; 21:2, 10). Poetically, the heavens are said to rejoice (Rev 12:12; 18:20).

(B) The expression "caught up to the third heaven" (2Co 12:2), probably in allusion to the three heavens as above specified: the lower, the middle or firmament, and the superior; hence the "third heaven," i.e. the highest heaven, the abode of God and angels and glorified spirits; the spiritual paradise (see 2Co 12:4).

(C) By metonymy, as in Eng., heaven, as the abode of God, is often put for God himself (Mt 21:25; Mk 11:30; Lk 20:4, 5). Also in the formula found so frequently in Matthew, "the kingdom of heaven" (Mt 3:2; 4:17; 5:3, 10; et. al.).

Deriv.: *epouránios* (2032), heavenly, what pertains to or is in heaven; *ouránios* (3770), heavenly; *ouranóthen* (3771), from heaven; *messouránēma* (3321), mid-heaven, the midst of the heavens.

Syn.: *parádeisos* (3857), paradise.

3773. Οὐρβανός, **Ourbanos**, *oor-ban-os´*; of Latin origin; *Urbanus* (*of* the *city*, "*urbane*"), a Christian:—Urbanus.

3774. Οὐρίας, **Ourias**, *oo-ree´-as*; of Hebrew origin [223]; *Urias* (i.e. *Urijah*), a Hittite:—Urias.

3775. οὖς, **ous**, *ooce*; apparently a primary word; the *ear* (physical or mental):—ear.

3776. οὐσία, **ousia**, *oo-see´-ah*; from the feminine of 5607; *substance*, i.e. *property* (*possessions*):—goods, substance.

3777. οὔτε, **oute**, *oo´-teh*; from 3756 and 5037; *not too*, i.e. *neither* or *nor*; (by analogy) *not even*:—neither, none, nor (yet), (no, yet) not, nothing.

3778. οὗτος, **houtos**, *hoo´-tos*; including nominal masculine plural οὗτοι, **houtoi**, *hoo´-toy*; nominal feminine singular αὕτη, **hautē**, *how´-tay*; and nominal feminine plural αὕται, **hautai**, *how´-tahee*; from the article 3588 and 846; *the he* (*she* or *it*), i.e. *this* or *that* (often with article repeated):—he (it was that), hereof, it, she, such as, the same, these, they, this (man, same, woman), which, who.

3779. οὕτω, **houtō**, *hoo´-to*; or (before a vowel) οὕτως, **houtōs**, *hoo´-toce*; adverb from 3778; *in this way* (referring to what precedes or follows):—after that, after (in) this manner, as, even (so), for all that, like (-wise), no more, on this fashion (-wise), so (in like manner), thus, what.

3780. οὐχί, **ouchi**, *oo-khee´*; intensive of 3756; *not indeed*:—nay, not.

3781. ὀφειλέτης, **opheiletēs**, *of-i-let´-ace*; from 3784; an *ower*, i.e. person *indebted*; (figurative) a *delinquent*; morally a *transgressor* (against God):—debtor, which owed, sinner.

Noun from *opheílō* (3784), to owe. A debtor:
(I) One owing money (Mt 18:24). One indebted for favors (Ro 15:27).
(II) One morally bound to the performance of any duty (Ro 1:14; 8:12; Gal 5:3).
(III) Delinquent, one who fails in the performance of duty (Mt 6:12, meaning those who fail in their duty toward us). Generally: a transgressor, sinner (Lk 13:4 [cf. 13:2]).
Deriv.: *chreōpheilétēs* (5533), one who owes a debt.
Syn.: *chreopheilétes* (5533), debtor.

3782. ὀφειλή, **opheilē**, *of-i-lay´*; from 3784; *indebtedness*, i.e. (concrete) a *sum* owed; (figurative) *obligation*, i.e. (conjugal) *duty*:—debt, due.

Noun from *opheílō* (3784), to owe. A debt which must be paid (Mt 18:32), obligation, a service which one owes someone (Ro 13:7; 1Co 7:3).
Syn.: *opheílēma* (3783), an amount due.

3783. ὀφείλημα, **opheilēma**, *of-i´-lay-mah*; from (the alternate of) 3784; *something owed*, i.e. (figurative) a *due*; morally a *fault*:—debt.

Noun from *opheílō* (3784), to owe. A debt, that which is owed, which is strictly due (Ro 4:4). Also an offence; a trespass which requires reparation (Mt 6:12, cf. 6:14).

3784. ὀφείλω, **opheilō**, *of-i´-lo*; or (in certain tenses) its prolonged form ὀφειλέω, **opheileō**, *of-i-leh´-o*; probably from the base of 3786 (through the idea of *accruing*); to owe (pecuniarily); (figurative) to *be under obligation* (*ought, must, should*); (morally) to *fail* in duty:—behove, be bound, (be) debt (-or), (be)

due (-ty), be guilty (indebted), (must) need (-s), ought, owe, should. See also 3785.

To owe, to be indebted:
(I) Primarily of money (Mt 18:28; Lk 7:41; 16:5, 7; Phm 18). Passive participle: what is owed, debt, due (Mt 18:30, 34; 1Co 7:3).
(II) Figuratively, to be bound or obligated to perform a duty, meaning I ought, must. Of what is required by law or duty in general (Mt 23:16, 18; Lk 17:10; Jn 13:14; 19:7; Ro 15:1, 27; 2Co 12:14; Eph 5:28; 2Th 1:3; 2:13; 1Jn 2:6; 3:16; 4:11; 3Jn 8). Also of what the circumstances of time, place, or person render proper: to be fit and proper (Ac 17:29; 1Co 7:36; 11:7, 10; 2Co 12:11; Heb 2:17; 5:3, 12); what is from the nature of the case necessary (1Co 5:10; 9:10).
(III) By implication: to fail in duty, be delinquent, be indebted to someone (Lk 11:4).
Deriv.: *opheilétēs* (3781), debtor; *opheilē* (3782), debt, obligation; *opheílēma* (3783), that which is owed, obligation; *óphelon* (3785), what one wishes to happen; *prosopheílō* (4359), to owe in addition to.
Syn.: *anagkázomai* (315), to be compelled, to have to; *deí* (1163), it is necessary, an obligation out of necessity or inevitability; *prépō* (4241), it is proper or right; *chrē* (5534), it needs be, ought; *chrēzō* (5535), to need.

3785. ὄφελον, **ophelon**, *of´-el-on*; first person singular of a past tense of 3784; *I ought* (*wish*), i.e. (interjection) *oh that!*:—would (to God).

3786. ὄφελος, **ophelos**, *of´-el-os*; from ὀφέλλω, **ophellō** (to *heap* up, i.e. *accumulate* or *benefit*); *gain*:—advantageth, profit.

3787. ὀφθαλμοδουλεία, **ophthalmodouleia**, *of-thal-mod-oo-li´-ah*; from 3788 and 1397; *sight-labour*, i.e. that needs watching (*remissness*):—eye-service.

Noun from *ophthalmós* (3788), eye, and *douleía* (1397), service. Eyeservice, i.e. that is work or service rendered only under the master's eye (Eph 6:6; Col 3:22).

3788. ὀφθαλμός, **ophthalmos**, *of-thal-mos´*; from 3700; the *eye* (literal or figurative); (by implication) *vision*; (figurative) *envy* (from the jealous side-glance):—eye, sight.

3789. ὄφις, **ophis**, *of´-is*; probably from 3700 (through the idea of *sharpness* of vision); a *snake*, figurative (as a type of sly cunning) an artful *malicious* person, especially *Satan*:—serpent.

3790. ὀφρύς, **ophrus**, *of-roos´*; perhaps from 3700 (through the idea of the shading or proximity to the organ of *vision*); the eye-"*brow*" or *forehead*, i.e. (figurative) the *brink* of a precipice:—brow.

3791. ὀχλέω, **ochleō**, *okh-leh´-o*; from 3793; to *mob*, i.e. (by implication) to *harass*:—vex.

3792. ὀχλοποιέω, **ochlopoieō**, *okh-lop-oy-eh´-o*; from 3793 and 4160; to *make a crowd*, i.e. *raise a* public *disturbance*:—gather a company.

3793. ὄχλος, **ochlos**, *okh´-los*; from a derivative of 2192 (meaning a *vehicle*); a *throng* (as *borne* along); (by implication) the *rabble*; by extension a *class* of people; (figurative) a *riot*:—company, multitude, number (of people), people, press.

Noun meaning crowd, a group of people. The size of an *óchlos* is relative. E.g., the *óchlos* of the disciples gathered in the upper room after Christ's ascension is about 120 people, while the crowd described in Lk 12:1 is several thousand.

(I) A crowd, throng, confused multitude. Used in the singular (Mt 9:23, 25; 14:14; 15:33; Mk 2:4; 8:1; Lk 5:1, 29; 6:17; 12:1; Jn 5:13; 12:9; Ac 6:7; 11:24, 26; 14:14; 19:26). Used intensively in the plural with the same sense as the singular: crowds, multitude (Mt 4:25; 5:1; 7:28; Lk 4:42; 5:3, 15; Jn 7:12; Ac 8:6; 17:13).

(II) Sometimes used for the common people, the rabble (Mt 14:5; 21:26; Mk 12:12; Jn 7:12, 49; Ac 16:22; 24:12).

Deriv.: *ochléō* (3791), to excite a crowd, to vex, to harass with crowds; *ochlopoiéō* (3792), to raise a public disturbance.

Syn.: *démos* (1218), a mass of people assembled in a public place; *laós* (2992), people; *pléthos* (4128), a multitude of people, populace.

3794. ὀχύρωμα, **ochurōma**, *okh-oo´-ro-mah*; from a remote derivative of 2192 (meaning to *fortify*, through the idea of *holding* safely); a *castle* (figurative, *argument*):—stronghold.

3795. ὀψάριον, **opsarion**, *op-sar´-ee-on*; neuter of a presumed derivative of the base of 3702; a *relish* to other food (as if cooked *sauce*), i.e. (special) *fish* (presumably salted and dried as a condiment):—fish.

3796. ὀψέ, **opse**, *op-seh´*; from the same as 3694 (through the idea of *backwardness*); (adverb) *late* in the day; by extension *after the close* of the day:—(at) even, in the end.

3797. ὄψιμος, **opsimos**, *op´-sim-os*; from 3796; *later*, i.e. *vernal* (showering):—latter.

3798. ὄψιος, **opsios**, *op´-see-os*; from 3796; *late*; feminine (as noun) *afternoon* (early eve) or *nightfall* (later eve):—even (-ing, [-tide]).

3799. ὄψις, **opsis**, *op´-sis*; from 3700; properly *sight* (the act), i.e. (by implication) the *visage*, an external *show*:—appearance, countenance, face.

3800. ὀψώνιον, **opsōnion**, *op-so´-nee-on*; neuter of a presumed derivative of the same as 3795; *rations* for a soldier, i.e. (by extension) his *stipend* or *pay*:—wages.

Noun from *ópson* (n.f.), meat, and *ōnéomai* (n.f.), to buy. It primarily signifies whatever is bought to be eaten with bread, provisions, supplies for a soldier's pay (Lk 3:14; 1Co 9:7). Metaphorically, it means general wages, recompense (Ro 6:23; 2Co 11:8).

Deriv.: *paropsís* (3953), a dish.

Syn.: *misthós* (3408), pay, wages.

3801. ὁ ὤν ὁ ἦν ὁ ἐρχόμενος, **ho ōn ho ēn ho erchomenos**, *ho own ho ane ho er-khom´-enos*; a phrase combining 3588 with the presumed participle and imperfect of 1510 and the presumed participle of 2064 by means of 2532; *the one being and the one that was and the one coming*, i.e. *the Eternal*, as a divine epithet of Christ:—which art (is, was), and (which) wast (is, was), and art (is) to come (shalt be).

Π (Pi)

NT Numbers 3802–4459

3802. παγιδεύω, pagideuō, *pag-id-yoo´-o*; from 3803; to *ensnare* (figurative):—entangle.

3803. παγίς, pagis, *pag-ece´*; from 4078; a *trap* (as *fastened* by a noose or notch); (figurative) a trick or strategem (*temptation*):—snare.

3804. πάθημα, pathēma, *path´-ay-mah*; from a presumed derivative of 3806; something *undergone*, i.e. *hardship* or *pain*; subject an *emotion* or *influence*:—affection, affliction, motion, suffering.

Noun from *páschō* (3958), to suffer. Suffering, affliction:

(I) Particularly: evil suffered, affliction, distress. Singular (Heb 2:9); plural (Ro 8:18; 2Co 1:5–7; Php 3:10; Col 1:24; 2Ti 3:11; Heb 2:10; 10:32; 1Pe 1:11; 4:13; 5:1, 9).

(II) By metonymy: a passion, i.e. an affection of mind, emotion (Ro 7:5; Gal 5:24).

Syn.: *kakopátheia* (2552), affliction; *páthos* (3806), suffering, passion, lust.

3805. παθητός, pathētos, *path-ay-tos´*; from the same as 3804; *liable* (i.e. *doomed*) *to* experience *pain*:—suffer.

Adjective from *páschō* (3958), to suffer, to undergo pain, inconvenience, or punishment. Liable to suffering. In the NT: destined to suffer (Ac 26:23). See *páthēma* (3804), suffering.

3806. πάθος, pathos, *path´-os*; from the alternate of 3958; properly *suffering* ("*pathos*"), i.e. (subject) a *passion* (especially *concupiscence*):—(inordinate) affection, lust.

Noun from *páschō* (3958), to suffer. Suffering, affliction. In the NT: passion, i.e. affliction of the mind, emotion, especially lustful compassion (Ro 1:26; Col 3:5; 1Th 4:5).

Deriv.: *sumpathḗs* (4835), compassionate, sympathizing; *homoio-pathḗs* (3663), of like passions.

Syn.: *asélgeia* (766), licentiousness; *epithumía* (1939), desire; *órexis* (3715), a longing after; *hormḗ* (3730), violent impulse.

3807. παιδαγωγός, paidagōgos, *pahee-dag-o-gos´*; from 3816 and a reduplicated form of 71; a *boy-leader*, i.e. a servant whose office it was to take the children to school; (by implication [figurative] a *tutor* ["*pædagogue*"]):—instructor, schoolmaster.

Noun from *país* (3816), a child, and *agōgós* (n.f.), a leader, which is from *ágō* (71), to lead. An instructor or teacher of children, a schoolmaster, a pedagogue (1Co 4:15). Usually a slave or freedman to whose care the boys of a family were committed, who trained them up, instructed them at home, and accompanied them to the public schools. In the NT, used figuratively of the Mosaic Law (Gal 3:24, 25).

Syn.: *paideutḗs* (3810), a trainer, instructor. Also *didáskalos* (1320), teacher; *epítropos* (2012), guardian; *kathēgētḗs* (2519), a guide, teacher, master.

3808. παιδάριον, paidarion, *pahee-dar´-ee-on*; neuter of a presumed derivative of 3816; a *little boy*:—child, lad.

3809. παιδεία, paideia, *pahee-di´-ah*; from 3811; *tutorage*, i.e. *education* or *training*; (by implication) disciplinary *correction*:—chastening, chastisement, instruction, nurture.

Noun from *paideúō* (3811), to instruct. Training of a child, and hence generally: education, discipline; instruction as consisting of teaching, admonition, rewards, punishments, etc. Generally (Eph 6:4; 2Ti 3:16); by synecdoche of the part for whole: correction, chastisement (Heb 12:5, 7, 8, 11).

Syn.: *epanórthōsis* (1882), correction; *nouthesía* (3559), instruction, admonition.

3810. παιδευτής, paideutēs, *pahee-dyoo-tace´*; from 3811; a *trainer*, i.e. *teacher* or (by implication) *discipliner*:—which corrected, instructor.

Noun from *paideúō* (3811), to instruct, correct, chastise. An instructor (Ro 2:20); a corrector, a chastiser (Heb 12:9).

Syn.: *paidagōgós* (3807), instructor. Also *didáskalos* (1320), an instructor, teacher; *kathēgētḗs* (2519), a guide, master, teacher.

3811. παιδεύω, paideuō, *pahee-dyoo´-o*; from 3816; to *train* up a child, i.e. *educate,* or (by implication) *discipline* (by punishment):— chasten (-ise), instruct, learn, teach.

From *pais* (3816), child. To train up a child, and hence generally: to educate, to discipline, to instruct:

(I) Generally (Ac 7:22; 22:3). In the sense of to teach; to admonish, by word or deed (1Ti 1:20; 2Ti 2:25; Tit 2:12).

(II) By synecdoche of part for the whole: to correct, to chastise, to chasten, e.g., as children (Heb 12:7, 10). Spoken of chastening from God by afflictions, calamities (1Co 11:32; 2Co 6:9; Heb 12:6; Rev 3:19). Of prisoners: to scourge (Lk 23:16, 22).

Deriv.: *apaídeutos* (521), unlearned; *paideía* (3809), training, chastening; *paideutḗs* (3810), instructor, trainer.

Syn.: *gumnázō* (1128), to train; *didáskō* (1321), to teach; *ektréphō* (1625), to bring up a child; *mastigóō* (3146), to scourge, whip; *hodēgéō* (3594), to show the way, lead, guide; *tréphō* (5142), to bring up a child.

3812. παιδιόθεν, paidiothen, *pahee-dee-oth´-en*; adverb (of *source*) from 3813; *from infancy*:—of a child.

3813. παιδίον, paidion, *pahee-dee´-on*; neuter diminutive of 3816; a *childling* (of either sex), i.e. (properly) an infant, or (by extension) a half-grown *boy* or *girl*; (figurative) an *immature Christian*:—(little, young) child, damsel.

3814. παιδίσκη, paidiskē, *pahee-dis´-kay*; feminine diminutive of 3816; a *girl,* i.e. (special) a *female slave* or *servant*:—bondmaid (-woman), damsel, maid (-en).

3815. παίζω, paizō, *paheed´-zo*; from 3816; to *sport* (as a boy):—play.

3816. παῖς, pais, *paheece*; perhaps from 3817; a *boy* (as often *beaten* with impunity), or (by analogy) a *girl,* and (genitive) a *child*; specially a *slave* or *servant* (especially a *minister* to a king; and by eminence to God):—child, maid (-en), (man) servant, son, young man.

Noun meaning child, male or female; a boy, youth; a girl, maiden. Spoken of all ages from infancy to full grown youth (cf. Mt 2:16, children under two years of age; Ac 20:12, young man):

(I) Particularly and generally (Mt 2:16; 17:18; 21:15; Lk 2:43; 8:51, 54; 9:42; Jn 4:51; Ac 20:12).

(II) Boy, servant:

(A) Particularly and generally, equivalent to *doúlos* (1401), a servant, slave (Mt 8:6, 8, 13 [cf. Lk 7:3]; Lk 7:7 [cf. v. 3]; Lk 12:45; 15:26).

(B) An attendant, minister, as of a king (Mt 14:2; Sept.: Ge 41:38).

(C) The servant of God, spoken of a minister or ambassador of God, called and beloved of God, and sent by Him to perform any service, e.g., of David (Lk 1:69; Ac 4:25); of Israel (Lk 1:54); of Jesus the Messiah (Mt 12:18; Ac 3:13, 26; 4:27, 30).

Deriv.: *paidagōgós* (3807), schoolmaster; *paideúō* (3811), to train, chasten; *paízō* (3815), to play.

Syn.: As a child: *bréphos* (1025), infant; *téknon* (5043), child; *tekníon* (5040), small child. As a servant: *therápōn* (2324), a servant; *oikétēs* (3610), a domestic servant; *paidískē* (3814), a maidservant; *hupērétēs* (5257), a subordinate servant.

3817. παίω, paiō, *pah´-yo*; a primary verb; to *hit* (as if by a single blow and less violently than 5180); specially to *sting* (as a scorpion):—smite, strike.

3818. Πακατιανή, Pakatianē, *pak-at-ee-an-ay´*; feminine of an adjective of uncertain derivative; *Pacatianian,* a section of Phrygia:— Pacatiana.

3819. πάλαι, palai, *pal´-ahee*; probably another form for 3825 (through the idea of *retrocession*); (adverb) *formerly,* or (by relative) *sometime since*; (elliptically as adjective) *ancient*:—any while, a great while ago, (of) old, in time past.

Adverb of time. In the past, long ago, of olden times, formerly, long before now. Particularly (Mt 11:21; Lk 10:13; Heb 1:1; Jude 4). Spoken relative to the present moment: already, at the present time (Mk 15:44).

Deriv.: *ékpalai* (1597), of old; *palaiós* (3820), old.

Syn.: *ékpalai* (1597), of old; *poté* (4218), in time past.

3820. παλαιός, palaios, *pal-ah-yos´*; from 3819; *antique,* i.e. *not recent, worn out:*—old.

Adjective from *pálai* (3819), in the past, long ago. Old, not new, what is of long standing:

(**I**) In age or time, old, former, not recent. Spoken of wine (Lk 5:39); leaven (1Co 5:7, 8); testament (2Co 3:14); a commandment (1Jn 2:7); man (Ro 6:6; Eph 4:22; Col 3:9).

(**II**) From use, meaning old, worn-out, spoken of a garment (Mt 9:16; Mk 2:21; Lk 5:36); wineskins (Mt 9:17; Mk 2:22; Lk 5:37). See also Mt 13:52.

Deriv.: *palaiótēs* (3821), aged, obsolete; *palaióō* (3822), to make old.

Syn.: *archaíos* (744), old, ancient, original, what has exited from the beginning. *Palaiós* is not necessarily from the beginning but just old.

3821. παλαιότης, palaiotēs, *pal-ah-yot´-ace*; from 3820; *antiquatedness:*—oldness.

Noun from *palaiós* (3820), old. Age, antiquity, lengthy existence. Used only in Ro 7:6.

3822. παλαιόω, palaioō, *pal-ah-yo´-o*; from 3820; to *make* (passive *become*) *worn out,* or *declare obsolete:*—decay, make (wax) old.

From *palaiós* (3820), old. In the active, to make old, render obsolete, abrogate (Heb 8:13). In the passive, to grow old, become worn out (Lk 12:33; Heb 1:11).

3823. πάλη, palē, *pal´-ay*; from πάλλω, *pallō* (to *vibrate;* another form for 906); *wrestling:*— + wrestle.

3824. παλιγγενεσία, paliggenesia, *pal-ing-ghen-es-ee´-ah*; from 3825 and 1078; (spiritual) *rebirth* (the state or the act), i.e. (figurative) spiritual *renovation;* specially Messianic *restoration:*—regeneration.

Noun from *pálin* (3825), again, and *génesis* (1078), generation, source. Regeneration, restoration, renewal. In a moral sense: regeneration, new birth, i.e. change by grace from a carnal nature to a Christian life (Tit 3:5). In the sense of renovation, restoration, restitution to a former state; spoken of the complete eternal manifestation of the Messiah's kingdom when all things are to be delivered from their present corruption and restored to spiritual purity and splendour (Mt 19:28).

Syn.: *anakaínōsis* (342), renewing.

3825. πάλιν, palin, *pal´-in*; probably from the same as 3823 (through the idea of *oscillatory* repetition); (adverb) *anew,* i.e. (of place) *back,* (of time) *once more,* or (conjecture) *furthermore* or *on the other hand:*—again.

3826. παμπληθεί, pamplēthei, *pam-play-thi´*; dative (adverb) of a compound of 3956 and 4128; *in full multitude,* i.e. *concertedly* or *simultaneously:*—all at once.

3827. πάμπολυς, pampolus, *pam´-pol-ooce*; from 3956 and 4183; *full many,* i.e. *immense:*— very great.

3828. Παμφυλία, Pamphulia, *pam-fool-ee´-ah*; from a compound of 3956 and 5443; *every-tribal,* i.e. *heterogeneous* (5561 being implication); *Pamphylia,* a region of Asia Minor:— Pamphylia.

3829. πανδοχεῖον, pandocheion, *pan-dokh-i´-on*; neuter of a presumed compound of 3956 and a derivative of 1209; *all-receptive,* i.e. a public *lodging*-place (*caravanserai* or *khan*):—inn.

3830. πανδοχεύς, pandocheus, *pan-dokh-yoos´*; from the same as 3829; an *innkeeper* (*warden of a caravanserai*):—host.

3831. πανήγυρις, panēguris, *pan-ay´-goo-ris*; from 3956 and a derivative of 58; a *mass-meeting,* i.e. (figurative) *universal companionship:*— general assembly.

Noun from *pás* (3956), all, and *águris* (n.f.), an assembly, which is from *agorá* (58), public square, marketplace. An assembly or convocation of the whole people in order to celebrate any public festival or solemnity, as the public games, sacrifices, etc. Hence generally: a festive convocation, joyful assembly. In the NT, used only in Heb 12:23.

Syn.: *ekklēsía* (1577), church, assembly; *sunagōgḗ* (4864), synagogue. These words, however, do not inherently imply gatherings for festivities as *panḗguris* does.

3832. πανοικί, panoiki, *pan-oy-kee´*; adverb from 3956 and 3624; *with* the *whole family:*— with all his house.

3833. πανοπλία, panoplia, *pan-op-lee´-ah*; from a compound of 3956 and 3696; *full armour* ("*panoply*"):—all (whole) armour.

3834. πανουργία, **panourgia,** *pan-oorg-ee´-ah;* from 3835; *adroitness,* i.e. (in a bad sense) *trickery* or *sophistry:*—(cunning) craftiness, subtlety.

3835. πανοῦργος, **panourgos,** *pan-oor´-gos;* from 3956 and 2041; *all-working,* i.e. *adroit* (*shrewd*):—crafty.

3836. πανταχόθεν, **pantachothen,** *pan-takh-oth´-en;* adverb (of *source*) from 3837; *from all* directions:—from every quarter.

3837. πανταχοῦ, **pantachou,** *pan-takh-oo´;* generic (as adverb of *place*) of a presumed derivative of 3956; *universally:*—in all places, everywhere.

3838. παντελής, **panteles,** *pan-tel-ace´;* from 3956 and 5056; *full-ended,* i.e. *entire* (neuter as noun, *completion*):— + in [no] wise, uttermost.

Adjective from *pás* (3956), any, all, and *télos* (5056), end. Complete, whole, entire. In the NT, used adverbially: wholly, entirely, as referring to time: always (Heb 7:25); with a negative, not at all (Lk 13:11).

Syn.: *téleios* (5046), complete. Also *aiōnios* (166), forever, eternal.

3839. πάντη, **pante,** *pan´-tay;* adverb (of *manner*) from 3956; *wholly:*—always.

3840. παντόθεν, **pantothen,** *pan-toth´-en;* adverb (of *source*) from 3956; *from* (i.e. *on*) *all* sides:—on every side, round about.

3841. παντοκράτωρ, **pantokratōr,** *pan-tok-rat´-ore;* from 3956 and 2904; the *all-ruling,* i.e. *God* (as absolute and universal *sovereign*):—Almighty, Omnipotent.

3842. πάντοτε, **pantote,** *pan´-tot-eh;* from 3956 and 3753; *every when,* i.e. *at all* times:—alway (-s), ever (-more).

3843. πάντως, **pantōs,** *pan´-toce;* adverb from 3956; *entirely;* specially *at all events,* (with negative following) *in no event:*—by all means, altogether, at all, needs, no doubt, in [no] wise, surely.

3844. παρά, **para,** *par-ah´;* a primary preposition; properly *near,* i.e. (with general) *from beside* (literal or figurative), (with dative) *at* (or *in*) the *vicinity* of (object or subject), (with accusative) to the *proximity* with (local [especially *beyond* or *opposed* to] or causal [*on account* of]):—above, against, among, at, before, by, contrary to, × friend, from, + give [such things as they], + that [she] had, × his, in, more than, nigh unto, (out) of, past, save, side … by, in the sight of, than, [there-] fore, with. In compounds it retains the same variety of application.

Preposition with the primary meaning of near, nearby, expressing the notion of immediate vicinity or proximity which is differently modified according to the force of each case:

(I) With the gen., expressing the meaning from near, from with. In the NT, only with a gen. of person, implying a going forth or proceeding from the near vicinity of someone, from the presence or side of someone. From:

(A) Particularly after verbs of motion, as of coming, sending (Mk 14:43; Lk 6:19; 8:49; Jn 15:26; 17:8). Also Jn 1:14; 6:46; 7:29.

(B) Figuratively, after verbs of asking, receiving, or those which imply these ideas. After verbs of asking, seeking (Mt 2:4, 7; 20:20; Mk 8:11; Lk 12:48; Jn 1:40; 17:7; Ac 26:22; 28:22; Gal 1:12; Eph 6:8; Php 4:18; 2Pe 1:17).

(C) Figuratively, with the gen. of person as the source, author, director, meaning from whom something proceeds or is derived (Mt 21:42; Lk 1:45; 2:1; Jn 1:6; Ac 22:30).

(II) With the dat. both of person and thing, expressing rest or position, near, hard by, with; and with the dat. plural, meaning among.

(A) Particularly of place, after verbs implying rest or remaining in a place (Mt 6:1; 22:25; 28:15; Lk 9:47; 19:7; Jn 1:39; 8:38; 19:25; Ac 10:6; Col 4:16; 2Ti 4:13; Rev 2:13).

(B) With the dat. of person, the reference being to the person himself without regard to place. **(1)** Particularly and generally meaning with, among (Mt 19:26; 21:25; Lk 1:30; 2:52; Ro 2:11, 13; 1Co 3:19; 2Co 1:17; Gal 3:11; Jas 1:27; 1Pe 2:4, 20; 2Pe 2:11; 3:8).

(III) With the accusative, particularly expressing motion near a place.

(A) Particularly implying motion along the side of something, meaning nearby, by, along (Mt 4:18; 13:4; Mk 2:13; 4:15).

(B) As expressing motion to a place, near to, to, at (Mt 15:29; Lk 8:41; Ac 4:35; 7:58).

(C) Sometimes also expressing the idea of rest or remaining near a place, near, by, at (Mt 13:1; Mk 4:1; 5:21; Lk 5:1; 7:38; Ac 22:3; Heb

11:12). **(2)** Metaphorically, of the ground or reason by or along with which a conclusion follows by reason of, because of, meaning thereby, therefore, on this account (1Co 12:15, 16).

(D) As denoting motion by or past a place. In the NT, only figuratively, as implying a failure to reach the exact point of aim, either falling short or with the general meaning of "other than." **(1)** Aside from, away from, i.e. contrary to, against (Ac 18:13; Ro 1:26; 4:18; 11:24; 16:17; Gal 1:8, 9). **(2)** Beside, with the meaning of falling short (2Co 11:24). **(3)** Past, in the sense of beyond, past (Heb 11:11). More commonly, in the sense of more than, above, beyond (Lk 13:2; Ro 1:25; 12:3; 14:5; Heb 1:4; 2:7; 11:4; 12:24).

(IV) In composition, *pará* implies:

(A) Nearness, proximity, near, by, as in *parakathízō* (3869), to sit down near; *parístēmi* (3936), to stand beside, to aid; *parathalássios* (3864), along the sea.

(B) Motion or direction, near to, by, as in *parabállō* (3846), to throw alongside, compare; *paradídōmi* (3860), to surrender, betray; *paréchō* (3930), to hold near, bring, offer; *parateínō* (3905), to extend along.

(C) Motion, by or past any place, going beyond, as *parágō* (3855), to go beyond; *parérchomai* (3928), to go by, pass by; *parapléō* (3896), to sail by. Used metaphorically, of coming short of or going beyond the true point: *parakoúō* (3878), to mishear, disobey; *paratheōréō* (3865), to overlook, disregard; implying violation, as *parabaínō* (3845), to disobey a command.

Syn.: *eggús* (1451), near; *paraplésion* (3897), close by; *plēsíon* (4139), nearby; *prós* (4314), toward, near; *schedón* (4975), nigh, almost.

3845. παραβαίνω, parabaínō, *par-ab-ah´ee-no*; from 3844 and the base of 939; to *go contrary to*, i.e. *violate* a command:—(by) transgress (-ion).

From *pará* (3844), beyond or contrary to, and *baínō* (n.f., see *metabaínō* [3327]), to go away from, to move. To go aside from, transgress, violate (Mt 15:2, 3; 2Jn 1:9). To lose one's office or position by transgression (Ac 1:25).

Deriv.: *aparábatos* (531), unchangeable; *parábasis* (3847), transgression; *parabátēs* (3848), transgressor.

Syn.: *hamartánō* (264), to sin; *apistéō* (569),

to disbelieve; *paranoméō* (3891), to transgress the law.

3846. παραβάλλω, paraballō, *par-ab-al´-lo*; from 3844 and 906; to *throw alongside*, i.e. (reflexive) to *reach* a place, or (figurative) to *liken*:—arrive, compare.

From *pará* (3844), near, and *bállō* (906), to cast, put. To throw or place side by side; figuratively, to compare (Mk 4:30). Hence, as a nautical term, to come to a place, arrive at (Ac 20:15).

Deriv.: *parabolḗ* (3850), comparison, parable.

Syn.: *homoióō* (3666), to resemble, make similar; *sugkrínō* (4793), to compare.

3847. παράβασις, parabasis, *par-ab´-as-is*; from 3845; *violation*:—breaking, transgression.

Noun from *parabaínō* (3845), to transgress. Transgression, wrongdoing, lawbreaking, a deliberate stepping over a boundary (Ro 2:23; 4:15; 5:14; Gal 3:19; 1Ti 2:14; Heb 2:2; 9:15).

Syn.: *paranomía* (3892), lawbreaking; *paráptōma* (3900), a fault, mistake, error, sin. Also *hamártēma* (265), act of sin; *hamartía* (266), sin.

3848. παραβάτης, parabatēs, *par-ab-at´-ace*; from 3845; a *violator*:—breaker, transgress (-or).

Noun from *parabaínō* (3845), to transgress. Transgressor, violator of the law; used with reference to the imputation of sin to those who having known the law transgress it and deviate from the truth (Ro 2:25, 27; Gal 2:18; Jas 2:9, 11).

Syn.: *hamartōlós* (268), a sinner; *ánomos* (459), lawless person, transgressor.

3849. παραβιάζομαι, parabiazomai, *par-ab-ee-ad´-zom-ahee*; from 3844 and the middle of 971; to *force contrary* to (nature), i.e. *compel* (by entreaty):—constrain.

3850. παραβολή, parabolē, *par-ab-ol-ay´*; from 3846; a *similitude* ("*parable*"), i.e. (symbolic) *fictitious narrative* (of common life conveying a moral), *apothegm* or *adage*:—comparison, figure, parable, proverb.

Noun from *parabállō* (3846), to compare. A parable, a placing side by side. In the NT, a comparison, similitude, parable.

(I) Generally, a comparison (Mk 4:30). In the sense of image, figure, symbol, equivalent to *túpos* (5179), a type (Heb 9:9; 11:19).

(II) Specifically, a parable, i.e. a short story under which something else is figured or in which the fictitious is used to represent and illustrate the real. This common oriental method of teaching was much used by Christ (Mt 13:24, 31, 33; 15:15; 21:33; 22:1; Mk 4:10, 11, 13; 7:17; 12:12; Lk 5:36; 6:39; 8:9–11; 12:16, 41; 13:6; 15:3; 18:1, 9; 19:11; 20:9, 19; 21:29). Parables may be short, one-sentence statements (Mt 13:31, 33), or longer, more involved stories (Mt 13:24–30; 22:1–14; Lk 20:9–19). Although a *parabállō* is usually a positive comparison statement, it may also occur in the form of a question (Lk 6:39), or a proverbial saying (Lk 4:23).

Syn.: *paroimía* (3942), a proverb.

3851. παραβουλεύομαι, parabouleuomai, *par-ab-ool-yoo´-om-ahee*; from 3844 and the middle of 1011; to *misconsult*, i.e. *disregard*:—not (to) regard (-ing).

3852. παραγγελία, paraggelia, *par-ang-gel-ee´-ah*; from 3853; a *mandate*:—charge, command.

Noun from *paraggéllō* (3853), to command. A proclamation, command from a superior. Spoken of those from secular magistrates (Ac 5:28; 16:24), and of those from Paul (1Th 4:2; 1Ti 1:5, 18).

Syn.: *diatagḗ* (1296), arrangement, order; *diátagma* (1297), edict; *éntalma* (1778), an injunction; *entolḗ* (1785), command, precept.

3853. παραγγέλλω, paraggellō, *par-ang-gel´-lo*; from 3844 and the base of 32; to *transmit a message*, i.e. (by implication) to *enjoin*:—(give in) charge, (give) command (-ment), declare.

From *pará* (3844), to the side of, and *aggéllō* (n.f., see *anaggéllō* [312]), to tell, declare. To bring word to anyone. In the NT, to direct, to charge or command (Mk 8:6; Lk 8:29; Ac 10:42; 15:5; 16:18, 23; 17:30; 23:30; 1Co 11:17; 1Th 4:11; 2Th 3:4, 6, 10, 12; 1Ti 5:7; 6:13). Followed by *mḗ* (3361), not, meaning to prohibit (Mt 10:5; Mk 6:8; Lk 8:56; 9:21; Ac 1:4; 4:18; 5:28, 40; 23:22; 1Co 7:10; 1Ti 1:3; 6:17).

Deriv.: *paraggelía* (3852), a commandment.

Syn.: *entéllomai* (1781), to command; *keleúō* (2753), to command, to order.

3854. παραγίνομαι, paraginomai, *par-ag-in´-om-ahee*; from 3844 and 1096; to *become near*, i.e. *approach* (*have arrived*); (by implication) to *appear* publicly:—come, go, be present.

3855. παράγω, paragō, *par-ag´-o*; from 3844 and 71; to *lead near*, i.e. (reflexive or intransitive) to *go along* or *away*:—depart, pass (away, by, forth).

3856. παραδειγματίζω, paradeigmatizō, *par-ad-igue-mat-id´-zo*; from 3844 and 1165; to *show alongside* (the public), i.e. *expose to infamy*:—make a public example, put to an open shame.

3857. παράδεισος, paradeisos, *par-ad´-i-sos*; of Oriental origin [compare 6508]; a *park*, i.e. (special) an *Eden* (place of future happiness, "*paradise*"):—paradise.

3858. παραδέχομαι, paradechomai, *par-ad-ekh´-om-ahee*; from 3844 and 1209; to *accept near*, i.e. *admit* or (by implication) *delight* in:—receive.

From *pará* (3844), from, and *déchomai* (1209), to receive. In the NT, to receive, to accept, to approve something (Mk 4:20; Ac 16:21; 22:18; 1Ti 5:19). Of persons, to receive, to accept as one's child (Heb 12:6).

Syn.: *apodéchomai* (588), to approve, welcome; *anagnōrízō* (319), to recognize.

3859. παραδιατριβή, paradiatribē, *par-ad-ee-at-ree-bay´*; from a compound of 3844 and 1304; *misemployment*, i.e. *meddlesomeness*:—perverse disputing.

3860. παραδίδωμι, paradidōmi, *par-ad-id´-o-mee*; from 3844 and 1325; to *surrender*, i.e. *yield up, intrust, transmit*:—betray, bring forth, cast, commit, deliver (up), give (over, up), hazard, put in prison, recommend.

3861. παράδοξος, paradoxos, *par-ad´-ox-os*; from 3844 and 1391 (in the sense of *seeming*); *contrary to expectation*, i.e. *extraordinary* ("*paradox*"):—strange.

Adjective from *pará* (3844), beyond, and *dóxa* (1391), opinion, expectation, glory. Paradoxical, strange. When used as a noun, something beyond one's expectation, a miracle. Used only in Lk 5:26.

Syn.: *dúnamis* (1411), power, miracle; *éndoxos* (1741), something glorious; *thaumásios* (2297), wonderful thing; *megaleíos* (3167), magnificent thing; *sēmeíon* (4592), sign; *téras* (5059), wonderful thing.

3862. παράδοσις, **paradosis,** *par-ad´-os-is*; from 3860; *transmission*, i.e. (concrete) a *precept*; specially the Jewish *traditionary law*:—ordinance, tradition.

3863. παραζηλόω, **parazēloō,** *par-ad-zay-lo´-o*; from 3844 and 2206; to *stimulate alongside*, i.e. *excite to rivalry*:—provoke to emulation (jealousy).

3864. παραθαλάσσιος, **parathalassios,** *par-ath-al-as´-see-os*; from 3844 and 2281; *along* the *sea*, i.e. *maritime* (*lacustrine*):—upon the sea coast.

3865. παραθεωρέω, **paratheōreō,** *par-ath-eh-o-reh´-o*; from 3844 and 2334; to *overlook* or *disregard*:—neglect.

3866. παραθήκη, **parathēkē,** *par-ath-ah´-kay*; from 3908; a *deposit*, i.e. (figurative) *trust*:—committed unto.

3867. παραινέω, **paraineō,** *par-ahee-neh´-o*; from 3844 and 134; to *mispraise*, i.e. *recommend* or *advise* (a different course):—admonish, exhort.

3868. παραιτέομαι, **paraiteomai,** *par-ahee-teh´-om-ahee*; from 3844 and the middle of 154; to *beg off*, i.e. *deprecate, decline, shun*:—avoid, (make) excuse, entreat, refuse, reject.

From *pará* (3844) aside, implying something more than is proper, hence, wrongly, and *aitéō* (154), to ask, beg. To ask near anyone, i.e. at his hands, to obtain by asking. In the NT, to ask aside or away, to get rid of by asking, similar to the English expression, to beg off of one.

(I) Primarily and generally, to entreat that something may not take place (Ac 25:11; Heb 12:19).

(II) To excuse oneself from an invitation (Lk 14:18, 19).

(III) By implication, not to receive, i.e. to refuse, to reject (1Ti 4:7; 5:11; Heb 12:25). In the sense of to avoid, to shun (2Ti 2:23; Tit 3:10).

Syn.: *egkataleípō* (1459), to forsake, give up.

3869. παρακαθίζω, **parakathizō,** *par-ak-ath-id´-zo*; from 3844 and 2523; to *sit down near*:—sit.

3870. παρακαλέω, **parakaleō,** *par-ak-al-eh´-o*; from 3844 and 2564; to *call near*, i.e. *invite, invoke* (by *imploration, hortation* or *consola-tion*):—beseech, call for, (be of good) comfort, desire, (give) exhort (-ation), entreat, pray.

From *pará* (3844), to the side of, and *kaléō* (2564), to call. To aid, help, comfort, encourage. Translated: to comfort, exhort, desire, call for, beseech with a stronger force than *aitéō* (154).

(I) To invite to come (Ac 28:20).

(II) To call for or upon someone as for aid, to invoke God, to beseech, entreat (Mt 8:5, 31, 34; 18:32; Mk 1:40; 5:17, 18, 23; Lk 8:31; Ac 8:31; 9:38; 16:15, 39; 19:31; 21:12; 24:4; 25:2; 1Co 16:12; 2Co 12:8, 18; Phm 10).

(III) To call upon someone to do something, to exhort, admonish, with the accusative of person (Lk 3:18; Ac 2:40; 11:23; 15:32; 27:33, 34; Ro 2:1, 8; 1Co 1:10; 4:16; 14:31; 2Co 2:8; 5:20; 6:1; 8:6; 10:1; 13:11; Eph 4:1; Php 4:2; 1Th 2:11; 4:1; 1Ti 2:1; 5:1; 6:2; Tit 1:9; 2:15; Heb 3:13; 10:25; 13:19; 1Pe 2:11; 5:1).

(IV) To exhort in the way of consolation, encouragement, to console, comfort (Mt 2:18; 5:4; 2Co 1:4; 2:7; 7:6; Eph 6:22; Col 4:8; 1Th 3:7; 4:18; 2Th 2:17). In the sense of to make glad, in the pass., to be glad, rejoice (Lk 16:25; Ac 20:12).

Deriv.: *paráklēsis* (3874), exhortation, consolation, comfort; *paráklētos* (3875), a counselor, an advocate, a comforter; *sumparakaléō* (4837), to comfort together.

Syn.: *nouthetéō* (3560), to warn, admonish; *paramuthéomai* (3888), to console, comfort.

3871. παρακαλύπτω, **parakaluptō,** *par-ak-al-oop´-to*; from 3844 and 2572; to *cover alongside*, i.e. *veil* (figurative):—hide.

3872. παρακαταθήκη, **parakatathēkē,** *par-ak-at-ath-ay´-kay*; from a compound of 3844 and 2698; something *put down alongside*, i.e. a *deposit* (sacred *trust*):—that (thing) which is committed (un-) to (trust).

3873. παράκειμαι, **parakeimai,** *par-ak´-i-mahee*; from 3844 and 2749; to *lie near*, i.e. *be at hand* (figurative, *be prompt* or *easy*):—be present.

3874. παράκλησις, **paraklēsis,** *par-ak´-lay-sis*; from 3870; *imploration, hortation, solace*:—comfort, consolation, exhortation, entreaty.

Noun from *parakaléō* (3870), to beseech. The act of exhortation, encouragement, comfort.

(I) An entreaty, petition, appeal (2Co 8:4, 17 [cf. v. 6]).

(II) Exhortation, admonition (Ro 12:8; 1Co 14:3; 1Ti 4:13; Heb 12:5; 13:22). In the sense of instruction, teaching, especially teaching that encourages (Ac 13:15; 15:31; 1Th 2:3). This is probably the significance of Ac 4:36 where Barnabas is described as the son of *paraklḗseos*, i.e. son of exhortation, the Aramaic name, Barnabas, probably signifying "son of prophecy."

(III) Consolation, comfort, solace (Ac 9:31; Ro 15:4, 5; 2Co 1:3–7; 7:4, 7, 13; Php 2:1; 2Th 2:16; Phm 7; Heb 6:18). By metonymy, the Messiah as the author of spiritual aid and consolation (Lk 2:25). By implication, joy, gladness (Lk 6:24).

Syn.: *nouthesía* (3559), warning, admonition; *paramuthía* (3889), consolation, comfort.

3875. παράκλητος, paraklētos, *par-ak´-lay-tos*; an *intercessor, consoler*:—advocate, comforter.

Noun from *parakaléō* (3870), to comfort, encourage or exhort. One called upon to help.

(I) An advocate, intercessor; one who pleads the cause of anyone before a judge (1Jn 2:1).

(II) A comforter, bestowing spiritual aid and consolation, spoken of the Holy Spirit (Jn 14:16, 26; 15:26; 16:7).

3876. παρακοή, parakoē, *par-ak-o-ay´*; from 3878; *inattention,* i.e. (by implication) *disobedience*:—disobedience.

Noun from *parakouō* (3878), to disobey. In its strictest sense, it means a failing to hear or mishearing. In the NT, neglect to hear, emphasizing the active disobedience which follows this inattentive or careless hearing (cf. Ro 5:19; 2Co 10:6; Heb 2:2).

Syn.: *apeítheia* (543), disobedience; *parábasis* (3847), transgression.

3877. παρακολουθέω, parakoloutheō, *par-ak-ol-oo-theh´-o*; from 3844 and 190; to *follow near,* i.e. (figurative) *attend* (as a result), *trace out, conform* to:—attain, follow, fully know, have understanding.

3878. παρακούω, parakouō, *par-ak-oo´-o*; from 3844 and 191; to *mishear,* i.e. (by implication) to *disobey*:—neglect to hear.

3879. παρακύπτω, parakuptō, *par-ak-oop´-to*; from 3844 and 2955; to *bend beside,* i.e. *lean over* (so as to *peer within*):—look (into), stoop down.

3880. παραλαμβάνω, paralambanō, *par-al-am-ban´-o*; from 3844 and 2983; to *receive near,* i.e. *associate with* oneself (in any familiar or intimate act or relation); (by analogy) to *assume* an office; (figurative) to *learn*:—receive, take (unto, with).

3881. παραλέγομαι, paralegomai, *par-al-eg´-om-ahee*; from 3844 and the middle of 3004 (in its original sense); (special) to *lay* one's course *near,* i.e. *sail past*:—pass, sail by.

3882. παράλιος, paralios, *par-al´-ee-os*; from 3844 and 251; *beside* the *salt* (*sea*), i.e. *maritime*:—sea coast.

3883. παραλλαγή, parallagē, *par-al-lag-ay´*; from a compound of 3844 and 236; *transmutation* (of phase or orbit), i.e. (figurative) *fickleness*:—variableness.

3884. παραλογίζομαι, paralogizomai, *par-al-og-id´-zom-ahee*; from 3844 and 3049; to *misreckon,* i.e. *delude*:—beguile, deceive.

3885. παραλυτικός, paralutikos, *par-al-oo-tee-kos´*; from a derivative of 3886; as if *dissolved,* i.e. "*paralytic*":—that had (sick of) the palsy.

3886. παραλύω, paraluō, *par-al-oo´-o*; from 3844 and 3089; to *loosen beside,* i.e. *relax* (perfect passive participle *paralyzed* or *enfeebled*):—feeble, sick of the (taken with) palsy.

3887. παραμένω, paramenō, *par-am-en´-o*; from 3844 and 3306; to *stay near,* i.e. *remain* (literal, *tarry*; or figurative, *be permanent, persevere*):—abide, continue.

From *pará* (3844), with, and *ménō* (3306), to remain. To stay, remain nearby with someone, abide (1Co 16:6); to remain, to continue in an office or position; e.g., the priest's office (Heb 7:23). Figuratively, to continue, persevere, e.g., in the law of liberty (Jas 1:25).

Deriv.: *sumparaménō* (4839), to remain together.

Syn.: *diaménō* (1265), to remain throughout or constant; *diateléō* (1300), to continue.

3888. παραμυθέομαι, paramutheomai, *par-am-oo-theh´-om-ahee*; from 3844 and the middle of a derivative of 3454; to *relate near,* i.e. (by implication) *encourage, console*:—comfort.

3889. παραμυθία, paramuthia, *par-am-oo-thee´-ah*; from 3888; *consolation* (properly abstract):—comfort.

3890. παραμύθιον, paramuthion, *par-am-oo´-thee-on*; neuter of 3889; *consolation* (properly concrete):—comfort.

3891. παρανομέω, paranomeō, *par-an-om-eh´-o*; from a compound of 3844 and 3551; to *be opposed to law,* i.e. to *transgress:*—contrary to law.

3892. παρανομία, paranomia, *par-an-om-ee´-ah*; from the same as 3891; *transgression:*—iniquity.

Noun from *paranoméō* (3891), to transgress the law, which is from *pará* (3844), beyond, and *nómos* (3551), law. A transgression or an offence of the law. Used only in 2Pe 2:16. The verb *paranoméō* (3891) occurs in Ac 23:3.

Syn.: *adikía* (93), unrighteousness, injustice, wrong; *hamartía* (266), sin; *anomía* (458), lawlessness; *parábasis* (3847), the act of transgression; *parakoé* (3876), disobedience; *paráptōma* (3900), transgression.

3893. παραπικραίνω, parapikrainō, *par-ap-ik-rah´ee-no*; from 3844 and 4087; to *embitter alongside,* i.e. (figurative) to *exasperate:*—provoke.

3894. παραπικρασμός, parapikrasmos, *par-ap-ik-ras-mos´*; from 3893; *irritation:*—provocation.

3895. παραπίπτω, parapiptō, *par-ap-ip´-to*; from 3844 and 4098; to *fall aside,* i.e. (figurative) to *apostatize:*—fall away.

From *pará* (3844), to the side of or from, implying error, and *píptō* (4098), to fall. In the NT, figuratively, to fall away from the path of duty, to abandon the faith, to apostatize. Used only in Heb 6:6.

Deriv.: *paráptōma* (3900), transgression.

Syn.: *katapíptō* (2667), to fall down.

3896. παραπλέω, parapleō, *par-ap-leh´-o*; from 3844 and 4126; to *sail near:*—sail by.

3897. παραπλήσιον, paraplēsion, *par-ap-lay´-see-on*; neuter of a compound of 3844 and the base of 4139 (as adverb); *close by,* i.e. (figurative) *almost:*—nigh unto.

3898. παραπλησίως, paraplēsiōs, *par-ap-lay-see´-oce*; adverb from the same as 3897; *in a manner near by,* i.e. (figurative) *similarly:*—likewise.

3899. παραπορεύομαι, paraporeuomai, *par-ap-or-yoo´-om-ahee*; from 3844 and 4198; to *travel near:*—go, pass (by).

3900. παράπτωμα, paraptōma, *par-ap´-to-mah*; from 3895; a *side-slip* (*lapse* or *deviation*), i.e. (unintentional) *error* or (willful) *transgression:*—fall, fault, offence, sin, trespass.

Noun from *parapíptō* (3895), to fall by the wayside. A falling aside or away as from right, truth, duty; a lapse, error, fault.

(I) Transgressions committed out of ignorance or carelessness (Mt 6:14, 15; 18:35; Mk 11:25, 26; Gal 6:1; Jas 5:16).

(II) Transgressions which are deliberate, intentional; sins (Ro 4:25; 5:15–18, 20; 11:11, 12; 2Co 5:19; Eph 1:7; 2:1, 5; Col 2:13).

Syn.: *hamartía* (266), offence, sin; *parábasis* (3847), violation, transgression.

3901. παραρρυέω, pararrhueō, *par-ar-hroo-eh´-o*; from 3844 and the alternate of 4482; to *flow by,* i.e. (figurative) carelessly *pass* (*miss*):—let slip.

3902. παράσημος, parasēmos, *par-as´-ay-mos*; from 3844 and the base of 4591; *side-marked,* i.e. *labelled* (with a *badge* [*figure-head*] of a ship):—sign.

3903. παρασκευάζω, paraskeuazō, *par-ask-yoo-ad´-zo*; from 3844 and a derivative of 4632; to *furnish aside,* i.e. *get ready:*—prepare self, be (make) ready.

3904. παρασκευή, paraskeuē, *par-ask-yoo-ay´*; as if from 3903; *readiness:*—preparation.

3905. παρατείνω, parateinō, *par-at-i´-no*; from 3844 and τείνω, *teinō* (to *stretch*); to *extend along,* i.e. *prolong* (in point of time):—continue.

3906. παρατηρέω, paratēreō, *par-at-ay-reh´-o*; from 3844 and 5083; to *inspect alongside,* i.e. *note insidiously* or *scrupulously:*—observe, watch.

From *pará* (3844), near or close to, and *tēréō* (5083), to keep, observe. To watch closely.

(I) To watch closely with a sinister intent. Spoken of the Pharisees watching Jesus to catch him doing anything which they could accuse him of (Mk 3:2; Lk 6:7; 14:1; 20:20). Spoken of the Jews watching the city gates to seize Paul as he left the city (Ac 9:24).

(II) To observe religious days scrupulously, to keep them superstitiously (Gal 4:10).

Deriv.: *paratērēsis* (3907), attentive watching.

Syn.: *blépō* (991), look at; *theáomai* (2300), to look closely at, perceive; *theōréō* (2334), to behold intensely, consider, perceive, see; *horáō* (3708), to see.

3907. παρατήρησις, paratērēsis, *par-at-ay´-ray-sis*; from 3906; *inspection*, i.e. *ocular evidence*:—observation.

Noun from *paratēréō* (3906), to watch closely. Close watching, accurate observation. Used only in Lk 17:20.

3908. παρατίθημι, paratithēmi, *par-at-ith´-ay-mee*; from 3844 and 5087; to *place alongside*, i.e. *present* (food, truth); (by implication) to *deposit* (as a trust or for protection):—allege, commend, commit (the keeping of), put forth, set before.

3909. παρατυγχάνω, paratugchanō, *par-at-oong-khan´-o*; from 3844 and 5177; to *chance near*, i.e. *fall in with*:—meet with.

3910. παραυτίκα, parautika, *par-ow-tee´-kah*; from 3844 and a derivative of 846; *at the very* instant, i.e. *momentary*:—but for a moment.

3911. παραφέρω, parapherō, *par-af-er´-o*; from 3844 and 5342 (including its alternate forms); to *bear along* or *aside*, i.e. *carry off* (literal or figurative); (by implication) to *avert*:—remove, take away.

3912. παραφρονέω, paraphroneō, *par-af-ron-eh´-o*; from 3844 and 5426; to *misthink*, i.e. *be insane* (silly):—as a fool.

3913. παραφρονία, paraphronia, *par-af-ron-ee´-ah*; from 3912; *insanity*, i.e. *foolhardiness*:—madness.

3914. παραχειμάζω, paracheimazō, *par-akh-i-mad´-zo*; from 3844 and 5492; to *winter near*, i.e. *stay* with over the *rainy* season:—winter.

3915. παραχειμασία, paracheimasia, *par-akh-i-mas-ee´-ah*; from 3914; a *wintering over*:—winter in.

3916. παραχρῆμα, parachrēma, *par-akh-ray´-mah*; from 3844 and 5536 (in its original sense); *at the thing* itself, i.e. *instantly*:—forthwith, immediately, presently, straightway, soon.

3917. πάρδαλις, pardalis, *par´-dal-is*; feminine of **πάρδος,** *pardos* (a panther); a *leopard*:—leopard.

3918. πάρειμι, pareimi, *par´-i-mee*; from 3844 and 1510 (including its various forms); to *be near*, i.e. *at hand*; neuter presumed participle (singular) *time being*, or (plural) *property*:—come, × have, be here, + lack, (be here) present.

3919. παρεισάγω, pareisagō, *par-ice-ag´-o*; from 3844 and 1521; to *lead in aside*, i.e. *introduce surreptitiously*:—privily bring in.

3920. παρείσακτος, pareisaktos, *par-ice´-ak-tos*; from 3919; *smuggled in*:—unawares brought in.

3921. παρεισδύνω, pareisdunō, *par-ice-doo´-no*; from 3844 and a compound of 1519 and 1416; to *settle in alongside*, i.e. *lodge stealthily*:—creep in unawares.

3922. παρεισέρχομαι, pareiserchomai, *par-ice-er´-khom-ahee*; from 3844 and 1525; to *come in alongside*, i.e. *supervene additionally* or *stealthily*:—come in privily, enter.

3923. παρεισφέρω, pareispherō, *par-ice-fer´-o*; from 3844 and 1533; to *bear in alongside*, i.e. *introduce simultaneously*:—give.

3924. παρεκτός, parektos, *par-ek-tos´*; from 3844 and 1622; *near outside*, i.e. *besides*:—except, saving, without.

3925. παρεμβολή, parembolē, *par-em-bol-ay´*; from a compound of 3844 and 1685; a *throwing in beside* (juxtaposition); i.e. (special) *battle-array, encampment* or *barracks* (tower Antonia):—army, camp, castle.

3926. παρενοχλέω, parenochleō, *par-en-okh-leh´-o*; from 3844 and 1776; to *harass further*, i.e. *annoy*:—trouble.

3927. παρεπίδημος, parepidēmos, *par-ep-id´-ay-mos*; from 3844 and the base of 1927; an *alien alongside*, i.e. a *resident foreigner*:—pilgrim, stranger.

Adjective from *pará* (3844), near or close to, and *epídēmos* (n.f.), stranger, which is from *epí*

(1909), in or among, and *dḗmos* (1218), a people. A stranger, sojourner; one living among a people not one's own (Heb 11:13; 1Pe 1:1; 2:11). Also from *epídēmos* (n.f.): *epidēméō* (1927), to reside as a stranger, used in Ac 2:10; 17:21.

Syn.: *allogenḗs* (241), one of a different race; *allótrios* (245), stranger; *apódēmos* (590), sojourner, living in another country; *xénos* (3581), a stranger, foreigner; *pároikos* (3941), alien, sojourner.

3928. παρέρχομαι, parerchomai, *par-er'-khom-ahee*; from 3844 and 2064; to *come near* or *aside*, i.e. to *approach* (*arrive*), *go by* (or *away*), (figurative) *perish* or *neglect*, (causative) *avert:*—come (forth), go, pass (away, by, over), past, transgress.

3929. πάρεσις, paresis, *par'-es-is*; from 2935; *prætermission*, i.e. *toleration:*—remission.

Noun from *pariēmi* (3935), to let pass by. A letting pass, remission in the sense of overlooking, not punishing. Used only in Ro 3:25. *Páresis* differs from *áphesis* (859), which implies pardon or forgiveness, i.e. not just an absence of punishment, but the removal of guilt.

3930. παρέχω, parechō, *par-ekh'-o*; from 3844 and 2192; to *hold near*, i.e. *present, afford, exhibit, furnish occasion:*—bring, do, give, keep, minister, offer, shew, + trouble.

From *pará* (3844), unto, at, near, and *échō* (2192), to have, hold. To hold out toward someone, to present, offer.

(**I**) Particularly to offer, e.g., one's cheek (Lk 6:29). Also 1Ti 6:17.

(**II**) Figuratively, meaning to be the cause, source, occasion of something to a person, to make or do, to give or bestow, to occasion something in one's behalf. E.g., with *kópos* (2873), trouble, to give one trouble, to vex (Mt 26:10; Mk 14:6; Lk 11:7; 18:5; Gal 6:17). Also Lk 7:4; Ac 16:16; 17:31; 19:24; 22:2; 28:2; Col 4:1; 1Ti 1:4; Tit 2:7.

Syn.: *prosphérō* (4374), to bring, present, offer.

3931. παρηγορία, parēgoria, *par-ay-gor-ee'-ah*; from a compound of 3844 and a derivative of 58 (meaning to *harangue* an assembly); an *address alongside*, i.e. (special) *consolation:*—comfort.

3932. παρθενία, parthenia, *par-then-ee'-ah*; from 3933; *maidenhood:*—virginity.

3933. παρθένος, parthenos, *par-then'-os*; of unknown origin; a *maiden*; (by implication) an unmarried *daughter:*—virgin.

3934. Πάρθος, Parthos, *par'-thos*; probably of foreign origin; a *Parthian*, i.e. inhabitant of Parthia:—Parthian.

3935. παρίημι, pariēmi, *par-ee'-ay-mi*; from 3844 and ἵημι, *hiēmi* (to *send*); to *let by*, i.e. *relax:*—hang down.

3936. παρίστημι, paristēmi, *par-is'-tay-mee*; or prolonged **παριστάνω, paristanō,** *par-is-tan'-o*; from 3844 and 2476; to *stand beside*, i.e. (transitive) to *exhibit, proffer*, (special) *recommend*, (figurative) *substantiate*; or (intransitive) to *be at hand* (or *ready*), *aid:*—assist, bring before, command, commend, give presently, present, prove, provide, shew, stand (before, by, here, up, with), yield.

3937. Παρμενᾶς, Parmenas, *par-men-as'*; probably by contraction for **Παρμενίδης, Parmenidēs** (a derivative of a compound of 3844 and 3306); *constant; Parmenas*, a Christian:—Parmenas.

3938. πάροδος, parodos, *par'-od-os*; from 3844 and 3598; a *by-road*, i.e. (active) a *route:*—way.

3939. παροικέω, paroikeō, *par-oy-keh'-o*; from 3844 and 3611; to *dwell near*, i.e. *reside* as a *foreigner:*—sojourn in, be a stranger.

From *pará* (3844), near or at, and *oikéō* (3611), to dwell. To dwell near, to be a neighbour. To dwell or sojourn as a stranger (Lk 24:18; Heb 11:9).

Syn.: *epidēméō* (1927), to reside in a foreign country.

3940. παροικία, paroikia, *par-oy-kee'-ah*; from 3941; *foreign residence:*—sojourning, × as strangers.

3941. πάροικος, paroikos, *par'-oy-kos*; from 3844 and 3624; having a *home near*, i.e. (as noun) a *by-dweller* (*alien resident*):—foreigner, sojourn, stranger.

Adjective from *pará* (3844), near or at, and *oíkos* (3624), house. Dwelling near, neighboring; as a substantive: a sojourner, one without the right of citizenship, a foreigner (Ac 7:6, 29). Figuratively, spoken of the saints: as sojourners in this world (1Pe 2:11); as strangers outside the church (Eph 2:19).

Deriv.: *paroikía* (3940), a sojourning.

Syn.: *allótrios* (245), stranger; *parepídēmos* (3927), one sojourning in a strange place. Also *allogenḗs* (241), one of a different race; *xénos* (3581), a stranger, foreigner.

3942. παροιμία, paroimia, *par-oy-mee´-ah*; from a compound of 3844 and perhaps a derivative of 3633; apparently a state *alongside of supposition*, i.e. (concrete) an *adage*; specially an enigmatical or fictitious *illustration*:—parable, proverb.

3943. πάροινος, paroinos, *par´-oy-nos*; from 3844 and 3631; staying *near wine*, i.e. *tippling* (a *toper*):—given to wine.

3944. παροίχομαι, paroichomai, *par-oy´-khom-ahee*; from 3844 and οἴχομαι, *oichomai* (to *depart*); to *escape along*, i.e. *be gone*:—past.

3945. παρομοιάζω, paromoiazō, *par-om-oy-ad´-zo*; from 3946; to *resemble*:—be like unto.

3946. παρόμοιος, paromoios, *par-om´-oy-os*; from 3844 and 3664; *alike nearly*, i.e. *similar*:—like.

3947. παροξύνω, paroxunō, *par-ox-oo´-no*; from 3844 and a derivative of 3691; to *sharpen alongside*, i.e. (figurative) to *exasperate*:—easily provoke, stir.

3948. παροξυσμός, paroxusmos, *par-ox-oos-mos´*; from 3947 ("*paroxysm*"); *incitement* (to good), or *dispute* (in anger):—contention, provoke unto.

3949. παροργίζω, parorgizō, *par-org-id´-zo*; from 3844 and 3710; to *anger alongside*, i.e. *enrage*:—anger, provoke to wrath.

3950. παροργισμός, parorgismos, *par-org-is-mos´*; from 3949; *rage*:—wrath.

Noun from *parorgízō* (3949), to make angry, provoke to violent or bitter anger. Anger provoked, indignation, wrath. Used only in Eph 4:26.

Syn.: *aganáktēsis* (24), indignation.

3951. παροτρύνω, parotrunō, *par-ot-roo´-no*; from 3844 and ὀτρύνω, *otrunō* (to *spur*); to *urge along*, i.e. *stimulate* (to hostility):—stir up.

3952. παρουσία, parousia, *par-oo-see´-ah*; from the presumed participle of 3918; a *being near*, i.e. *advent* (often, *return*; specially of Christ to punish Jerusalem, or finally the wicked); (by implication) physical *aspect*:—coming, presence.

Noun from *parṓn* (participle of *páreimi* [3918], to be present), present, presence, a being present, a coming to a place. Presence, coming or arrival.

(**I**) Presence, the state of being present rather than absent (2Co 10:10; Php 2:12).

(**II**) A coming or visit (1Co 16:17; 2Co 7:6, 7; Php 1:26).

(**III**) Used of the Second Coming of Christ (Mt 24:3; 1Co 15:23; 1Th 2:19; 2Th 2:8; 2Pe 3:4; 1Jn 2:28); the Son of Man (Mt 24:27, 37, 39); the Lord (1Th 3:13; 4:15; 5:23; 2Th 2:1; Jas 5:7, 8; 2Pe 1:16); the day of God (2Pe 3:12). The term *parousía* is used of Christ's Second Coming as a whole, and of individual events (e.g., the Rapture); only context can determine which is being discussed.

(**IV**) Of the coming or manifestation of the man of sin (2Th 2:9 [cf. 2Th 2:3]).

Syn.: *éleusis* (1660), coming.

3953. παροψίς, paropsis, *par-op-sis´*; from 3844 and the base of 3795; a *side-dish* (the receptacle):—platter.

3954. παρρησία, parrhēsia, *par-rhay-see´-ah*; from 3956 and a derivative of 4483; *all out-spokenness*, i.e. *frankness, bluntness, publicity*; (by implication) *assurance*:—bold (× -ly, -ness, -ness of speech), confidence, × freely, × openly, × plainly (-ness).

Noun from *pás* (3956), all, and *rhḗsis* (n.f.), the act of speaking. Literally, "the speaking all one is thinking," i.e. freespokenness as a characteristic of a frank and fearless mind; hence freeness, frankness, boldness in speech and action.

(**I**) Particularly, boldness (Ac 4:13; 2Co 3:12). In adverbial phrases, with openness, openly, plainly (Mk 8:32; Jn 7:4, 13, 26; 10:24; 11:14, 54; 16:25, 29; 18:20; Col 2:15); with boldness, boldly (Ac 2:29; 4:29, 31; 28:31; Eph 6:19; Php 1:20).

(**II**) By implication, the right or authority to speak boldly (1Ti 3:13; Phm 8).

(**III**) By implication, frank reliance, confidence, assurance (2Co 7:4; Eph 3:12; Heb 3:6; 4:16; 10:19, 35; 1Jn 2:28; 3:21; 4:17; 5:14).

Deriv.: *parrēsiázomai* (3955), to speak boldly or freely.

Syn.: *thársos* (2294), courage; *pepoíthēsis* (4006), persuasion, assurance, confidence.

3955. παρρησιάζομαι, parrhēsiazomai, *par-hray-see-ad´-zom-ahee*; middle from 3954; to *be frank* in utterance, or *confident* in spirit and demeanour:—be (wax) bold, (preach, speak) boldly.

From *parrēsía* (3954), freedom or frankness in speaking. To be freespoken, to speak freely, openly, boldly, in speech and action (Ac 9:27, 29; 13:46; 14:3; 18:26; 19:8; 26:26; Eph 6:20; 1Th 2:2).

Syn.: *apotolmáō* (662), to be very bold, to speak boldly; *tharréō* (2292), to be bold, courageous; *tolmáō* (5111), to dare.

3956. πᾶς, pas, *pas*; including all the forms of declension; apparently a primary word; *all, any, every,* the *whole*:—all (manner of, means), alway (-s), any (one), × daily, + ever, every (one, way), as many as, + no (-thing), × thoroughly, whatsoever, whole, whosoever.

Adjective meaning all.

(I) Includes the idea of oneness, a totality or the whole, the same as *hólos* (3650), the whole.

(A) The singular may have the idea of "whole" (Mt 8:32); "every" (Ro 3:19); "all" reference to qualitative nouns, e.g., "all" judgement (Jn 5:22). Also Mt 6:29; Mk 5:33; Lk 1:10; 4:25; Ac 1:8. Used by metonymy with the names of cities or countries to speak of the inhabitants (Mt 3:5; Mk 1:5; Lk 2:1).

(B) In the plural, to signify all of those in a group (Mt 1:17; 4:8; Mk 3:28; Lk 1:6; Ac 5:20; 22:15; Ro 1:5; 5:12, 18).

(II) Also includes the idea of plurality meaning all or every, equivalent to *hékastos* (1538), each one. Everyone who falls into a certain classification.

(A) With the relative pronoun, *hós* (3739), who, everyone who, whoever (Mt 7:24; Jn 6:37, 39; 17:2; Ac 2:21; Ro 10:13; 14:23; Gal 3:10; Col 3:17).

(B) With a participle with the article, it becomes a substantive expressing a class, e.g., everyone who is angry (Mt 5:22). Also Lk 6:47; Jn 6:45; Ac 10:43; Ro 2:10.

(III) All, meaning of all kinds, of every kind and sort including every possible variety.

(A) Generally (Mt 4:23; Ro 1:18, 29; 1Ti 6:10; 1Pe 2:1).

(B) In the sense of all possible, the greatest, utmost, supreme (Mt 28:18; Ac 5:23; 17:11; 23:1; 2Co 12:12; Php 1:20; 2:29; 1Ti 2:2; 2Ti 4:2; Jas 1:2; 1Pe 2:18; Jude 3).

Deriv.: *hápas* (537), whole, all; *diapantós* (1275), continually, always.

Syn.: *hólos* (3650), all, whole. Also *hápas* (537), absolutely all; *hékastos* (1538), each one; *holóklēros* (3648), complete in every part, entire.

3957. πάσχα, pascha, *pas´-khah*; of Chaldee origin [compare 6453]; the *Passover* (the meal, the day, the festival or the special sacrifices connected with it):—Easter, Passover.

3958. πάσχω, paschō, *pas´-kho*; including the forms (πάθω, *pathō, path´-o*) and (πένθω, *penthō, pen´-tho*), used only in certain tenses for it; apparently a primary verb; to *experience* a sensation or impression (usually painful):—feel, passion, suffer, vex.

In the most general sense, to be affected by something from without, to be acted upon, to undergo an experience. In the NT, used of evil, meaning to suffer, be subjected to evil (Mt 17:12; 27:19; Mk 5:26; Lk 13:2; Ac 9:16; 28:5; 1Co 12:26; Gal 3:4; Php 1:29; 1Th 2:14; 2Th 1:5; 2Ti 1:12; Heb 2:18; 5:8; 1Pe 2:19, 20, 23; 3:14, 17; 4:19; 5:10; Rev 2:10). Spoken of the suffering and death of Christ (Mt 16:21; 17:12; Mk 9:12; Lk 17:25; 22:15; 24:26, 46; Ac 1:3; 3:18; 17:3; Heb 9:26; 13:12; 1Pe 2:21; 3:18; 4:1).

Deriv.: a fellow sufferer; *páthēma* (3804), suffering; *pathētós* (3805), subject to suffering; *páthos* (3806), suffering; *propáschō* (4310), to have suffered before; *sumpáschō* (4841), to suffer with.

Syn.: *basanízomai* (the passive of *basanízō* [928]), to be tormented; *kakouchéomai* (the passive of *kakouchéō* [2558]), to be inflicted with harm; *kataponéomai* (the passive of *kataponéō* [2669]), to be oppressed, be vexed; *talaipōréō* (5003), to be afflicted.

3959. Πάταρα, Patara, *pat´-ar-ah*; probably of foreign origin; *Patara*, a place in Asia Minor:—Patara.

3960. πατάσσω, patassō, *pat-as´-so*; probably prolonged from 3817; to *knock* (gently or with a weapon or fatally):—smite, strike. Compare 5180.

3961. πατέω, pateō, *pat-eh´-o;* from a derivative probably of 3817 (meaning a *"path"*); to *trample* (literal or figurative):—tread (down, under foot).

From *pátos* (n.f.), a path, a beaten way. To tread with the feet.

(**I**) To tread down, to trample under foot, i.e. to lay waste (Lk 21:24; Rev 11:2). In the sense of to tread out, as grapes in a wine vat (Rev 14:20; 19:15).

(**II**) To tread on, as to tread upon serpents (Lk 10:19).

Deriv.: *katapatéō* (2662), to trample; *peripatéō* (4043), to walk around.

3962. πατήρ, patēr, *pat-ayr´;* apparently a primary word; a *"father"* (literal or figurative, near or more remote):—father, parent.

A noun, the etymology of which is uncertain. A father, spoken generally of men and in a special sense of God. Progenitor, ancestor, father, mentor, or model.

(**I**) Generally.

(**A**) Particularly one's father, by whom one is begotten (Mt 2:22; 19:5; Mk 5:40; Jn 4:53; Heb 7:10). Plural, parents, both father and mother (Heb 11:23; perhaps Eph 6:4). Of one reputed to be a father or stepfather (Lk 2:48).

(**B**) Of a remote ancestor, forefather, progenitor, or founder of a tribe or people, patriarch. Singular (Mt 3:9; Mk 11:10; Lk 1:32, 73; Jn 4:12; 7:22; Ac 3:13; Ro 9:5; Heb 1:1). Figuratively in a spiritual and moral sense, spoken of Abraham as the father of all who believe (Ro 4:11, 12, 16); spoken of one who leads another to Christ (1Co 4:15). Spoken of Satan as the father of wicked and depraved men (Jn 8:38, 41, 44). He is the model whom sinners resemble, i.e. they have like evil character.

(**C**) As a title of respect and reverence, in direct address (Lk 16:24, 27, 30); of a teacher as exercising paternal care, authority and affection (Mt 23:9; 1Co 4:15 [cf. Php 2:22; 1Th 2:11]. In the plural, fathers, as an honorary title of address used toward older persons (1Jn 2:13, 14); also toward magistrates, members of the Sanhedrin (Ac 7:2; 22:1).

(**D**) Metaphorically with the gen. of a thing; the author, source, beginner of something (Jn 8:44; Ro 4:12).

(**II**) Of God generally as the creator, preserver, governor of all men and things, watching over them with paternal love and care. Thus in the NT God is called Father.

(**A**) Claimed improperly by unsaved Jews (Jn 9:41 [cf. v. 42]).

(**B**) Properly ascribed for all those who are saved (Mt 6:4, 6, 8, 14, 15, 18; Ro 1:7; 8:15; 1Co 1:3; 2Co 6:18).

(**C**) Specifically, God is called the Father of our Lord Jesus Christ in respect to that particular relation in which Christ is the Son of God. See *huiós* (5207), son, where the Father and Son are expressly distinguished (Mt 11:27; 28:19; Mk 13:32; Lk 9:26; 10:22; Jn 1:14, 18; 3:35; 5:26; Ro 15:6; 2Co 1:3; 11:31; Eph 1:3; Col 1:3; Heb 1:5; 1Pe 1:3; 1Jn 2:22; 4:14; 2Jn 3, 9).

(**D**) Metaphorically in Jas 1:17, "the Father of lights" meaning the author or creator of the heavenly luminaries.

Deriv.: *apátōr* (540), literally without father; *patralṓas* (3964), a murderer of fathers; *patriá* (3965), paternal descent; *patriárchēs* (3966), patriarch, progenitor; *patrikós* (3967), paternal, ancestral; *patrís* (3968), a fatherland, native country, town, home; *patroparádotos* (3970), handed down from one's fathers.

Syn.: Related words on family: *mḗtēr* (3384), mother; *huiós* (5207), son; *thugátēr* (2364), daughter; *adelphós* (80), brother; *adelphḗ* (79), sister; *pentherá* (3994), mother-in-law; *pentherós* (3995), father-in-law; *ékgonos* (1549), grandchild, literally a descendant; *mámmē* (3125), a grandmother; *anepsiós* (431), a cousin; *suggenḗs* (4773), a relative; *génos* (1085), family, stock; *oíkos* (3624), family; *goneús* (1118), a parent; *prógonos* (4269), an ancestor, forefather.

3963. Πάτμος, Patmos, *pat´-mos;* of uncertain derivative; *Patmus,* an islet in the Mediterranean:—Patmos.

3964. πατραλῴας, patralōias, *pat-ral-o´-as;* from 3962 and the same as the latter part of 3389; a *parricide:*—murderer of fathers.

3965. πατριά, patria, *pat-ree-ah´;* as if feminine of a derivative of 3962; paternal *descent,* i.e. (concretely) a *group* of families or a whole *race* (*nation*):—family, kindred, lineage.

Noun from *patḗr* (3962), father. Paternal, descent, lineage. In the NT, a family.

(**I**) Particularly, a family which may include several households (Lk 2:4; Eph 3:15).

(II) In a wider sense, a tribe, people, nation (Ac 3:25).

Deriv.: *patriárchēs* (3966), patriarch.

Syn.: *phulḗ* (5443), tribe, race, clan. Also *geneá* (1074), age, generation; *génos* (1085), stock, race, kind; *oíkos* (3624), family.

3966. πατριάρχης, **patriarchēs**, *pat-ree-arkh´-ace*; from 3965 and 757; a *progenitor* ("patriarch"):—patriarch.

3967. πατρικός, **patrikos**, *pat-ree-kos´*; from 3962; *paternal*, i.e. *ancestral*:—of fathers.

3968. πατρίς, **patris**, *pat-rece´*; from 3962; a *father-land*, i.e. *native town*; (figurative) heavenly *home*:—(own) country.

3969. Πατρόβας, **Patrobas**, *pat-rob´-as*; perhaps contraction for Πατρόβιος *Patrobios* (a compound of 3962 and 979); *father's life*; *Patrobas*, a Christian:—Patrobas.

3970. πατροπαράδοτος, **patroparadotos**, *pat-rop-ar-ad´-ot-os*; from 3962 and a derivative of 3860 (in the sense of *handing over* or *down*); *traditionary*:—received by tradition from fathers.

3971. πατρῷος, **patrōios**, *pat-ro´-os*; from 3962; *paternal*, i.e. *hereditary*:—of fathers.

3972. Παῦλος, **Paulos**, *pow´-los*; of Latin origin; (*little*; but remotely from a derivative of 3973, meaning the same); *Paulus*, the name of a Roman and of an apostle:—Paul, Paulus.

3973. παύω, **pauō**, *pow´-o*; a primary verb ("*pause*"); to *stop* (transitive or intransitive), i.e. *restrain, quit, desist, come to an end*:—cease, leave, refrain.

To stop, pause, make an end.

(I) Active, to make one pause, to make one leave off, to restrain. Only in 1Pe 3:10.

(II) More commonly in the middle, to pause, to leave off, to refrain (Lk 5:4; 11:1; Ac 5:42; 6:13; 13:10; 21:32; Eph 1:16; Col 1:9; Heb 10:2; 1Pe 4:1); to cease, to come to an end (Lk 8:24; Ac 20:1; 1Co 13:8).

Deriv.: *anapaúō* (373), to rest; *katapaúō* (2664), to rest.

Syn.: *dialeípō* (1257), to leave off for a time; *hēsucházō* (2270), to become quiet, still, at rest; *katargéō* (2673), to render inactive, abolish;

kopázō (2869), to cease as a result of being tired, relax, subside.

3974. Πάφος, **Paphos**, *paf´-os*; of uncertain derivative; *Paphus*, a place in Cyprus:—Paphos.

3975. παχύνω, **pachunō**, *pakh-oo´-no*; from a derivative of 4078 (meaning *thick*); to *thicken*, i.e. (by implication) to *fatten* (figurative, *stupefy* or *render callous*):—wax gross.

3976. πέδη, **pedē**, *ped´-ay*; ultimately from 4228; a *shackle* for the feet:—fetter.

3977. πεδινός, **pedinos**, *ped-ee-nos´*; from a derivative of 4228 (meaning the *ground*); *level* (as easy for the *feet*):—plain.

3978. πεζεύω, **pezeuō**, *ped-zyoo´-o*; from the same as 3979; to *foot* a journey, i.e. *travel* by land:—go afoot.

3979. πεζῇ, **pezēi**, *ped-zay´*; dative feminine of a derivative of 4228 (as adverb); *foot-wise*, i.e. by *walking*:—a- (on) foot.

3980. πειθαρχέω, **peitharcheō**, *pi-tharkh-eh´-o*; from a compound of 3982 and 757; to *be persuaded* by a *ruler*, i.e. (general) to *submit* to authority; (by analogy) to *conform* to advice:—hearken, obey (magistrates).

3981. πειθός, **peithos**, *pi-thos´*; from 3982; *persuasive*:—enticing.

3982. πείθω, **peithō**, *pi´-tho*; a primary verb; to *convince* (by argument, true or false); (by analogy) to *pacify* or *conciliate* (by other fair means); reflexive or passive to *assent* (to evidence or authority), to *rely* (by inward certainty):—agree, assure, believe, have confidence, be (wax) confident, make a friend, obey, persuade, trust, yield.

To persuade, particularly to move or affect by kind words or motives.

(I) Active voice, to persuade.

(A) Generally, to persuade another to receive a belief, meaning to convince (Mt 27:20; Ac 13:43; 14:19; 18:4; 19:8, 26; 26:28; 28:23; 2Co 5:11).

(B) To bring over to kind feelings, to conciliate. **(1)** Generally, to pacify or quiet an accusing conscience, "our heart" (1Jn 3:19). **(2)** To win over, gain the favour of, make a friend of, with the accusative of person (Gal 1:10); by presents, bribes (Mt 28:14; Ac 12:20).

(II) Middle/passive, meaning to let oneself be persuaded, to be persuaded.

(A) Generally of any truth. Used in an absolute sense, to be convinced, believe (Lk 16:31; 20:6; Ac 17:4; 21:14; Ro 8:38; 14:14; 15:14; 2Ti 1:5, 12; Heb 6:9; 11:13).

(B) To assent to, obey, follow (Ac 5:36, 37; 23:21; 27:11; Ro 2:8; Gal 3:1; 5:7; Heb 13:17; Jas 3:3).

(III) In the perfect tense, to be persuaded, to trust.

(A) To be confident, assured (Ro 2:19; 2Co 2:3; Gal 5:10; Php 1:6, 25; 2Th 3:4; Heb 13:18).

(B) To confide in, rely upon (Mt 27:43; Mk 10:24; Lk 11:22; 18:9; 2Co 1:9; 10:7; Php 1:14; 3:3, 4; Php 1:14; Phm 21; Heb 2:13).

Deriv.: *anapeíthō* (374), to persuade or induce in an evil sense; *apeithḗs* (545), disobedient; *eupeithḗs* (2138), easy to be entreated; *peithós* (3981), persuasive, enticing; *peismonḗ* (3988), persuasion; *pepoíthēsis* (4006), trust, confidence; *pístis* (4102), faith, belief; *pistós* (4103), faithful.

Syn.: *parotrúnō* (3951), to urge along, stimulate; *pisteúō* (4100), to believe, be persuaded of; *pistóō* (4104), to trust or give assurance to; *plērophoréō* (4135), to be fully assured; *sugkatatíthēmi* (4784), to consent; *sumbouleúō* (4823), to give counsel; *sumphōnéō* (4856), to agree; *suntíthēmi* (4934), to assent.

3983. πεινάω, **peinaō**, *pi-nah´-o*; from the same as 3993 (through the idea of pinching *toil*; "*pine*"); to *famish* (absolute or comparatively); (figurative) to *crave*:—be an hungered.

3984. πεῖρα, **peira**, *pi´-rah*; from the base of 4008 (through the idea of *piercing*); a *test*, i.e. *attempt, experience*:—assaying, trial.

Noun from *peírō* (n.f.), to perforate, pierce. An attempt, an experience. In the NT, used only with *lambánō* (2983), to take or make an attempt (Heb 11:29); to take or receive an experience (Heb 11:36).

Deriv.: *ápeiros* (552), inexperienced, unskilled; *peirázō* (3985), to tempt or test; *peiráō* (3987), to try, test, tempt.

Syn.: *dokimḗ* (1382), experience, trial; *dokímion* (1383), trial, proof.

3985. πειράζω, **peirazō**, *pi-rad´-zo*; from 3984; to *test* (object), i.e. *endeavour, scrutinize, entice, discipline*:—assay, examine, go about, prove, tempt (-er), try.

From *peíra* (3984), experience, trial. To make trial of, to try. Similar to *peiráō* (3987), to assay.

(I) Of actions, to attempt, to make an effort (Ac 16:7; 24:6).

(II) Of persons, to tempt, prove, put to the test.

(A) Generally and in a good sense in order to ascertain the character, views, or feelings of someone (Mt 22:35; Jn 6:6; Rev 2:2).

(B) In a bad sense, with ill intent (Mk 8:11; 10:2; 12:15; Lk 11:16; 20:23; Jn 8:6). Hence by implication, to try one's virtue, tempt, solicit to sin (Gal 6:1; Jas 1:13, 14; Rev 2:10); especially by Satan (Mt 4:1, 3; Mk 1:13; Lk 4:2; 1Co 7:5; 1Th 3:5).

(C) In summary, God is said to try men by adversity, to test their faith and confidence in Him (1Co 10:13; Heb 2:18; 11:17, 37; Rev 3:10). Men are said to prove or tempt God by doubting, distrusting His power and aid (1Co 10:9; Heb 3:9); lying to Him (Ac 5:9); and refusing to follow His guidance (Ac 15:10).

Deriv.: *apeírastos* (551), incapable of being tempted; *ekpeirázō* (1598), to try, put to the test; *peirasmós* (3986), testing, temptation.

Syn.: *anakrínō* (350), to examine; *dokimázō* (1381), to prove, test, approve; *exetázō* (1833), to search, question.

3986. πειρασμός, **peirasmos**, *pi-ras-mos´*; from 3985; a putting to *proof* (by experiment [of good], *experience* [of evil], solicitation, discipline or provocation); (by implication) *adversity*:—temptation, × try.

Noun from *peirázō* (3985), to make trial of, try, tempt. Trial, a trial, proof, a putting to the test, spoken of persons only.

(I) Generally, trial of one's character (1Pe 4:12). By implication, trial of one's virtue, temptation, solicitation to sin, especially from Satan (Lk 4:13; 1Ti 6:9).

(II) Trial, temptation.

(A) A state of trial in which God brings His people through adversity and affliction in order to encourage and prove their faith and confidence in Him (1Co 10:13; Jas 1:2, 12; 1Pe 1:6; 2Pe 2:9). Hence used by metonymy for adversity, affliction, sorrow (Lk 22:28; Ac 20:19; Gal 4:14; Rev 3:10). When Christ urges us to pray that God would not lead us or allow us to go into *peirasmós* (Mt 6:13; 26:41; Mk 14:38; Lk 8:13; 11:4; 22:40, 46), he is evidently referring to those enticements to sin that we might not be able to resist in our present stage of spiritual growth.

(B) In the opposite way, man "tempts" God by distrusting Him and complaining to Him (Heb 3:8).

Syn.: *dokimḗ* (1382), trial; *dokímion* (1383), proof.

3987. πειράω, peiraō, *pi-rah´-o*; from 3984; to *test* (subject), i.e. (reflexive) to *attempt*:—assay.

From *peíra* (3984), trial. To try to do something (Ac 9:26; 26:21).

3988. πεισμονή, peismonē, *pice-mon-ay´*; from a presumed derivative of 3982; *persuadableness*, i.e. *credulity*:—persuasion.

3989. πέλαγος, pelagos, *pel´-ag-os*; of uncertain affinity; deep or open *sea*, i.e. the *main*:—depth, sea.

A noun meaning wide expanse of water, the open sea (Ac 27:5). Used with *thálassa* (2281), sea, meaning far out into the sea (Mt 18:6).

3990. πελεκίζω, pelekizō, *pel-ek-id´-zo*; from a derivative of 4141 (meaning an *axe*); to *chop off* (the head), i.e. *truncate*:—behead.

3991. πέμπτος, pemptos, *pemp´-tos*; from 4002; *fifth*:—fifth.

3992. πέμπω, pempō, *pem´-po*; apparently a primary verb; to *dispatch* (from the subject view or point of *departure*, whereas ἵημι, *hiēmi*; [as a stronger form of εἶμι, *eimi*] refers rather to the object point or *terminus ad quem*, and 4724 denotes properly the *orderly* motion involved), especially on a temporary errand; also to *transmit*, *bestow*, or *wield*:—send, thrust in.

3993. πένης, penēs, *pen´-ace*; from a primary πένω, *peno* (to *toil* for daily subsistence); *starving*, i.e. *indigent*:—poor. Compare 4434.

Adjective from *pénomai* (n.f), to work for a living. Poor, needy. Only in 2Co 9:9.

Syn.: *endeḗs* (1729), needy, destitute; *ptōchós* (4434), destitute.

3994. πενθερά, penthera, *pen-ther-ah´*; feminine of 3995; a *wife's mother*:—mother-in-law, wife's mother.

3995. πενθερός, pentheros, *pen-ther-os´*; of uncertain affinity; a *wife's father*:—father-in-law.

3996. πενθέω, pentheo, *pen-theh´-o*; from 3997; to *grieve* (the feeling or the act):—mourn, (be-) wail.

From *pénthos* (3997), mourning. To mourn, lament.

(I) To bewail someone, to grieve for him (2Co 12:21).

(II) To mourn at the death of a friend (Mk 16:10); generally, to be sad, sorrowful (Mt 5:4; 9:15; 1Co 5:2), with *klaíō* (2799), to weep (Lk 6:25; Jas 4:9; Rev 18:11, 15, 19).

Syn.: *thrēnéō* (2354), to bewail; *kóptō* (2875), to beat the breast as an outward sign of inward grief; *lupéō* (3076), to grieve.

3997. πένθος, penthos, *pen´-thos*; strengthened from the alternate of 3958; *grief*:—mourning, sorrow.

3998. πεντιχρός, pentichros, *pen-tikh-ros´*; prolonged from the base of 3993; *necessitous*:—poor.

3999. πεντάκις, pentakis, *pen-tak-ece´*; multiple adverb from 4002; *five times*:—five times.

4000. πεντακισχίλιοι, pentakischilioi, *pen-tak-is-khil´-ee-oy*; from 3999 and 5507; *five times a thousand*:—five thousand.

4001. πεντακόσιοι, pentakosioi, *pen-tak-os´-ee-oy*; from 4002 and 1540; *five hundred*:—five hundred.

4002. πέντε, pente, *pen´-teh*; a primary number; "*five*":—five.

4003. πεντεκαιδέκατος, pentekaidekatos, *pen-tek-ahee-dek´-at-os*; from 4002 and 2532 and 1182; *five and tenth*:—fifteenth.

4004. πεντήκοντα, pentēkonta, *pen-tay´-kon-tah*; multiple of 4002; *fifty*:—fifty.

4005. πεντηκοστή, pentēkostē, *pen-tay-kos-tay´*; feminine of the order of 4004; *fiftieth* (2250 being implied) from Passover, i.e. the festival of "*Pentecost*":—Pentecost.

4006. πεποίθησις, pepoithēsis, *pep-oy´-thay-sis*; from the perfect of the alternate of 3958; *reliance*:—confidence, trust.

Noun meaning trust, confidence (2Co 1:15; 3:4; 8:22; 10:2; Eph 3:12; Php 3:4). See *peithō* (3982, III), to persuade.

Syn.: *elégchos* (1650), conviction; *plērophoría*

(4136), full assurance; *pístis* (4102), faith; *peismoné* (3988), persuasion.

4007. **περ, per,** *per*; from the base of 4008; an enclitic particle significant of *abundance* (*thoroughness*), i.e. *emphasis; much, very* or *ever*:— [whom-] soever.

4008. **πέραν, peran,** *per´-an*; apparently accusative of an obsolete derivative of **πείρω,** *peirō* (to "*pierce*"); *through* (as adverb or prep.), i.e. *across:*—beyond, farther (other) side, over.

4009. **πέρας, peras,** *per´-as*; from the same as 4008; an *extremity:*—end, ut- (ter-) most part.

4010. **Πέργαμος, Pergamos,** *per´-gam-os*; from 4444; *fortified; Pergamus*, a place in Asia Minor:—Pergamos.

4011. **Πέργη, Pergē,** *perg´-ay*; probably from the same as 4010; a *tower; Perga*, a place in Asia Minor:—Perga.

4012. **περί, peri,** *per-ee´*; from the base of 4008; properly *through* (all *over*), i.e. *around*; (figurative) *with respect* to; used in various applications, of place, cause or time (with the generic denoting the *subject* or *occasion* or *superlative* point; with the accusative the *locality, circuit, matter, circumstance* or general *period*):— (there-) about, above, against, at, on behalf of, × and his company, which concern, (as) concerning, for, × how it will go with, ([there-, where-]) of, on, over, pertaining (to), for sake, × (e-) state, (as) touching, [where-] by (in), with. In comparison it retains substantially the same meaning of circuit (*around*), excess (*beyond*), or completeness (*through*).

4013. **περιάγω, periagō,** *per-ee-ag´-o*; from 4012 and 71; to *take around* (as a companion); reflex. to *walk around:*—compass, go (round) about, lead about.

4014. **περιαιρέω, periaireō,** *per-ee-ahee-reh´-o*; from 4012 and 138 (including its alternate); to *remove* all *around*, i.e. *unveil, cast off* (anchor); (figurative) to *expiate:*—take away (up).

From *perí* (4012), around, suggesting completeness, and *hairéomai* (138), to lift up and take away. To take away, abandon.

(**I**) Used transitively (Ac 27:40, "taking up the anchors round about" [a.t. {cf. 27:29}]); of a veil, to remove (2Co 3:16, an allusion to Ex 34:34. Sept.: Ge 41:42; Est 3:10; Jnh 3:6).

(**II**) Metaphorically, to take away completely (Heb 10:11, "completely take away sins" [a.t.], to make complete expiation for sins [cf. Heb 10:4]).

Syn.: *periphérō* (4064), to bear about; *sunépomai* (4902), to accompany; *leípō* (3007), to leave; *kataleípō* (2641), to forsake; *apoleípō* (620), to leave behind; *egkataleípō* (1459), to abandon; *aphíēmi* (863), to leave; *eáō* (1439), to leave alone.

4015. **περιαστράπτω, periastraptō,** *per-ee-astrap´-to*; from 4012 and 797; to *flash* all *around*, i.e. *envelop in light:*—shine round (about).

4016. **περιβάλλω, periballō,** *per-ee-bal´-lo*; from 4012 and 906; to *throw* all *around*, i.e. *invest* (with a palisade or with clothing):— array, cast about, clothe (-d me), put on.

4017. **περιβλέπω, periblepō,** *per-ee-blep´-o*; from 4012 and 991; to *look* all *around:*—look (round) about (on).

4018. **περιβόλαιον, peribolaion,** *per-ib-ol´-ah-yon*; neuter of a presumed derivative of 4016; something *thrown around* one, i.e. a *mantle, veil:*—covering, vesture.

4019. **περιδέω, perideō,** *per-ee-deh´-o*; from 4012 and 1210; to *bind around* one, i.e. *enwrap:*—bind about.

4020. **περιεργάζομαι, periergazomai,** *per-ee-er-gad´-zom-ahee*; from 4012 and 2038; to *work* all *around*, i.e. *bustle about* (*meddle*):—be a busybody.

4021. **περίεργος, periergos,** *per-ee´-er-gos*; from 4012 and 2041; *working* all *around*, i.e. *officious* (*meddlesome*, neuter plural *magic*):— busybody, curious arts.

4022. **περιέρχομαι, perierchomai,** *per-ee-er´-khom-ahee*; from 4012 and 2064 (including its alternate); to *come* all *around*, i.e. *stroll, vacillate, veer:*—fetch a compass, vagabond, wandering about.

4023. **περιέχω, periechō,** *per-ee-ekh´-o*; from 4012 and 2192; to *hold* all *around*, i.e. *include, clasp* (figurative):— + astonished, contain, after [this manner].

4024. περιζώννυμι, perizōnnumi, *per-id-zone´-noo-mee*; from 4012 and 2224; to *gird* all *around*, i.e. (middle or passive) to *fasten on one's belt* (literal or figurative):—gird (about, self).

4025. περίθεσις, perithesis, *per-ith´-es-is*; from 4060; a *putting* all *around*, i.e. *decorating oneself with*:—wearing.

4026. περιΐστημι, periistēmi, *per-ee-is´-tay-mee*; from 4012 and 2476; to *stand* all *around*, i.e. (near) to *be a bystander*, or (aloof) to *keep away from*:—avoid, shun, stand by (round about).

4027. περικάθαρμα, perikatharma, *per-ee-kath´-ar-mah*; from a compound of 4012 and 2508; something *cleaned* off all *around*, i.e. *refuse* (figurative):—filth.

Noun from *perikathaírō* (n.f.), to purge or cleanse all around, which is from *perí* (4012), around, and *kathaírō* (2508), to cleanse. The filth or defilement washed away by cleansing; see *katharismós* (2512), the process of purification. It may be used to denote an expiatory victim or ransom, as cleansing from guilt and punishment (Sept.: Pr 21:18). It is used metonymically in the NT of wretches or outcasts. Paul, in 1Co 4:13, mentions that the disciples of Christ are considered to be the refuse or outcasts of the world.

Syn.: *rhúpos* (4509), dirt, filth; *rhuparía* (4507), filthiness.

4028. περικαλύπτω, perikaluptō, *per-ee-kal-oop´-to*; from 4012 and 2572; to *cover* all *around*, i.e. *entirely* (the face, a surface):—blindfold, cover, overlay.

4029. περίκειμαι, perikeimai, *per-ik´-i-mahee*; from 4012 and 2749; to *lie* all *around*, i.e. *inclose, encircle, hamper* (literal or figurative):—be bound (compassed) with, hang about.

4030. περικεφαλαία, perikephalaia, *per-ee-kef-al-ah´-yah*; feminine of a compound of 4012 and 2776; *encirclement of* the *head*, i.e. a *helmet*:—helmet.

4031. περικρατής, perikratēs, *per-ee-krat-ace´*; from 4012 and 2904; *strong* all *around*, i.e. a *master* (*manager*):— + come by.

4032. περικρύπτω, perikruptō, *per-ee-kroop´-to*; from 4012 and 2928; to *conceal* all *around*, i.e. *entirely*:—hide.

4033. περικυκλόω, perikukloō, *per-ee-koo-klo´-o*; from 4012 and 2944; to *encircle* all *around*, i.e. *blockade completely*:—compass round.

4034. περιλάμπω, perilampō, *per-ee-lam´-po*; from 4012 and 2989; to *illuminate* all *around*, i.e. *invest with a halo*:—shine round about.

4035. περιλείπω, perileipō, *per-ee-li´-po*; from 4012 and 3007; to *leave* all *around*, i.e. (passive) *survive*:—remain.

4036. περίλυπος, perilupos, *per-il´-oo-pos*; from 4012 and 3077; *grieved* all *around*, i.e. *intensely sad*:—exceeding (very) sorry (-owful).

4037. περιμένω, perimenō, *per-ee-men´-o*; from 4012 and 3306; to *stay around*, i.e. *await*:—wait for.

From *perí* (4012), concerning, for, about, and *ménō* (3306), to remain, wait. To wait around. Transitively with an accusative, to wait for (Ac 1:4, waiting for the fulfillment of the promise of the Holy Spirit). See Sept.: Ge 49:18.

Syn.: *ekdéchomai* (1551), expect; *apekdéchomai* (553), to await or expect eagerly; *prosdéchomai* (4327), to look for with patience; *prosdokáō* (4328), to anticipate, await; *anaménō* (362), to wait with expectancy; *epiménō* (1961), to persevere; *prosménō* (4357), to persevere in, stay further in, continue in; *epéchō* (1907), to give heed to; *diatríbō* (1304), to tarry; *proskarteréō* (4342), to continue steadfastly in, wait; *prosedreúō* ([4332] TR) or *paredreúō* (UBS), to sit constantly beside, wait upon, expect.

4038. πέριξ, perix, *per´-ix*; adverb from 4012; all *around*, i.e. (as adjective) *circumjacent*:—round about.

4039. περιοικέω, perioikeō, *per-ee-oy-keh´-o*; from 4012 and 3611; to *reside around*, i.e. *be a neighbour*:—dwell round about.

4040. περίοικος, perioikos, *per-ee´-oy-kos*; from 4012 and 3611; *housed around*, i.e. *neighboring* (elliptically as noun):—neighbour.

4041. περιούσιος, periousios, *per-ee-oo´-see-os*; from the presumed participle feminine of a compound of 4012 and 1510; *being beyond usual*, i.e. *special* (one's *own*):—peculiar.

Adjective from *periousía* (n.f.), what is over and above, abundance, which is from *perí*

(4012), beyond, and *ousía* (3776), substance. Having abundance, superabundant. Used only in Tit 2:14 where by implication, one's own, special, abundant, chosen.

Syn.: *eklektós* (1588), chosen, elect; *polútimos* (4186), extremely valuable.

4042. περιοχή, perioche, *per-ee-okh-ay´*; from 4023; a *being held around*, i.e. (concretely) a *passage* (of Scripture, as *circumscribed*):—place.

4043. περιπατέω, peripateō, *per-ee-pat-eh´-o*; from 4012 and 3961; to *tread* all *around*, i.e. *walk* at large (especially as proof of ability); (figurative) to *live, deport oneself, follow* (as a companion or votary):—go, be occupied with, walk (about).

4044. περιπείρω, peripeirō, *per-ee-pi´-ro*; from 4012 and the base of 4008; to *penetrate entirely*, i.e. *transfix* (figurative):—pierce through.

4045. περιπίπτω, peripiptō, *per-ee-pip´-to*; from 4012 and 4098; to *fall* into something that is all *around*, i.e. *light among* or *upon, be surrounded with*:—fall among (into).

4046. περιποιέομαι, peripoieomai, *per-ee-poy-eh´-om-ahee*; middle from 4012 and 4160; to *make around oneself*, i.e. *acquire* (*buy*):—purchase.

4047. περιποίησις, peripoiēsis, *per-ee-poy´-ay-sis*; from 4046; *acquisition* (the act or the thing); by extension *preservation*:—obtain (-ing), peculiar, purchased, possession, saving.

4048. περιρρήγνυμι, perirrhēgnumi, *per-ir-hrayg´-noo-mee*; from 4012 and 4486; to *tear* all *around*, i.e. *completely away*:—rend off.

4049. περισπάω, perispaō, *per-ee-spah´-o*; from 4012 and 4685; to *drag* all *around*, i.e. (figurative) to *distract* (with care):—cumber.

4050. περισσεία, perisseia, *per-is-si´-ah*; from 4052; *surplusage*, i.e. *superabundance*:—abundance (-ant, [-ly]), superfluity.

Noun from *perissós* (4053), over and above. A superabundance, more than enough (2Co 10:15); spoken of grace (Ro 5:17), joy (2Co 8:2), wickedness (Jas 1:21).

Syn.: *hadrótēs* (100), bounty, abundance; *perísseuma* (4051), abundance, that which

remains over; *huperbolē* (5236), excess, a great measure, more than necessary.

4051. περίσσευμα, perisseuma, *per-is´-syoo-mah*; from 4052; a *surplus*, or *superabundance*:—abundance, that was left, over and above.

Noun from *perisseúō* (4052), to abound. More than enough, abundance.

(I) What is left over, remainder (Mk 8:8).

(II) What is laid up, superabundance. Spoken of material possessions (2Co 8:12). Figuratively, spoken of the thoughts that fill the heart (Mt 12:34; Lk 6:45).

4052. περισσεύω, perisseuō, *per-is-syoo´-o*; from 4053; to *superabound* (in quantity or quality), *be in excess, be superfluous*; also (transposed) to *cause to superabound* or *excel*:—(make, more) abound, (have, have more) abundance, (be more) abundant, be the better, enough and to spare, exceed, excel, increase, be left, redound, remain (over and above).

4053. περισσός, perissos, *per-is-sos´*; from 4012 (in the sense of *beyond*); *superabundant* (in quantity) or *superior* (in quality); (by implication) *excessive*; adverb (with 1537) *violently*; neuter (as noun) *preeminence*:—exceeding abundantly above, more abundantly, advantage, exceedingly, very highly, beyond measure, more, superfluous, vehement [-ly].

Adjective from *perí* (4012), around, above. Over and above, more than enough.

(I) Particularly as exceeding a certain measure, more than (Mt 5:37, 47). In the sense of superfluous (2Co 9:1).

(II) Generally, superabundant, abundant, much, great.

(A) Positively, as an adverb, abundantly, in superabundance (Jn 10:10). With the prep. *ek* (1537), by means of, or expressing measure, beyond measure, exceedingly (Mk 6:51; 14:31; Eph 3:20; 1Th 3:10; 5:13).

(B) By implication, in a comparative sense, advantage (Ro 3:1).

Deriv.: *perisseía* (4050), a superfluity, an overflowing; *perisseúō* (4052), to abound, be exceeding.

Syn.: *mállon* (3123), very much; *meízōn* (3187), greater; *pleíōn* (4119), more than.

4054. περισσότερον, perissoteron, *per-is-sot´-er-on*; neuter of 4055 (as adverb); in a *more* *superabundant* way:—more abundantly, a great deal, far more.

4055. περισσότερος, perissoteros, *per-is-sot´-er-os*; comparative of 4053; *more superabundant* (in number, degree or character):—more abundant, greater (much) more, overmuch.

4056. περισσοτέρως, perissoterōs, *per-is-soter´-oce*; adverb from 4055; *more superabundantly*:—more abundant (-ly), × the more earnest, (more) exceedingly, more frequent, much more, the rather.

4057. περισσῶς, perissōs, *per-is-soce´*; adverb from 4053; *superabundantly*:—exceedingly, out of measure, the more.

4058. περιστερά, peristera, *per-is-ter-ah´*; of uncertain derivative; a *pigeon*:—dove, pigeon.

4059. περιτέμνω, peritemnō, *per-ee-tem´-no*; from 4012 and the base of 5114; to *cut around*, i.e. (special) to *circumcise*:—circumcise.

From *perí* (4012), around, about, and *témnō* (n.f.), to cut off. To cut off or around, to circumcise, to remove the foreskin of the male (Lk 1:59; 2:21; Jn 7:22; Ac 7:8; 15:5; 16:3; 21:21). In the passive (Ac 15:1, 24; 1Co 7:18; Gal 2:3; 5:2, 3; 6:12, 13). Metaphorically in a spiritual sense, meaning to put away impurity (Col 2:11).

Deriv.: *aperítmētos* (564), uncircumcised; *peritomé* (4061), circumcision.

4060. περιτίθημι, peritithēmi, *per-ee-tith´-ay-mee*; from 4012 and 5087; to *place around*; (by implication) to *present*:—bestow upon, hedge round about, put about (on, upon), set about.

4061. περιτομή, peritomē, *per-it-om-ay´*; from 4059; *circumcision* (the rite, the condition or the people, literal or figurative):— × circumcised, circumcision.

Noun from *peritémnō* (4059), to cut around, circumcise. Circumcision. It was practiced by the Jews as a distinguishing sign of the Jewish nation from Abraham on (Ge 17:10f.; Le 12:3; Lk 1:59), and also by several ancient oriental nations and by all of the Muslims.

(I) Spoken of the act of circumcision or cutting off the foreskin (Jn 7:22, 23; Ac 7:8; Ro 4:11; Gal 5:11; Php 3:5).

(II) Spoken of the state of being circumcised (Ro 2:25–27; 3:1; 4:10, 12; 1Co 7:19; Gal 2:12; 5:6; 6:15; Col 4:11; Tit 1:10).

(III) Used figuratively of persons practicing circumcision, the Jews, as opposed to the uncircumcised Gentiles (Ro 3:30; 4:9, 12; 15:8; Gal 2:7–9; Eph 2:11; Col 3:11).

(IV) Spoken figuratively of the spiritual circumcision of the heart and affections, by putting the sins of the flesh off from the body (Ro 2:28, 29; Php 3:3; Col 2:11).

4062. περιτρέπω, peritrepō, *per-ee-trep´-o*; from 4012 and the base of 5157; to *turn around*, i.e. (mental) to *craze*:— + make mad.

4063. περιτρέχω, peritrechō, *per-ee-trekh´-o*; from 4012 and 5143 (including its alternate); to *run around*, i.e. *traverse*:—run through.

4064. περιφέρω, peripherō, *per-ee-fer´-o*; from 4012 and 5342; to *convey around*, i.e. *transport hither and thither*:—bear (carry) about.

4065. περιφρονέω, periphroneō, *per-ee-fron-eh´-o*; from 4012 and 5426; to *think beyond*, i.e. *depreciate* (*condemn*):—despise.

4066. περίχωρος, perichōros, *per-ikh´-o-ros*; from 4012 and 5561; *around the region*, i.e. *circumjacent* (as noun, with 1093 implication *vicinity*):—country (round) about, region (that lieth) round about.

4067. περίψωμα, peripsōma, *per-ip´-so-mah*; from a compound of 4012 and ψάω *psao* (to *rub*); something *brushed* all *around*, i.e. *offscrapings* (figurative, *scum*):—offscouring.

4068. περπερεύομαι, perpereuomai, *per-per-yoo´-om-ahee*; middle from πέρπερος, *perperos* (*braggart*; perhaps by reduplication of the base of 4008); to *boast*:—vaunt itself.

From *pérperos* (n.f.), braggart. To brag or boast (1Co 13:4).

Syn.: *tuphóō* (5187), to be lifted up with pride; *huperaíromai* (5229), to become haughty; *huperphronéō* (5252), to think too highly.

4069. Περσίς, Persis, *per-sece´*; a *Persian* woman; *Persis*, a Christian female:—Persis.

4070. πέρυσι, perusi, *per´-oo-si*; adverb from 4009; the *by-gone*, i.e. (as noun) *last year*:— + a year ago.

4071. πετεινόν, peteinon, *pet-i-non´*; neuter of a derivative of 4072; a *flying* animal, i.e. *bird*:—bird, fowl.

4072. πέτομαι, petomai, *pet´-om-ahee*; or prolonged **πετάομαι,** *petaomai, pet-ah´-om-ahee*; or contracted **πτάομαι,** *ptaomai, ptah´-om-ahee*; middle of a primary verb; to *fly*:—fly (-ing).

4073. πέτρα, petra, *pet´-ra*; feminine of the same as 4074; a (mass of) *rock* (literal or figurative):—rock.

4074. Πέτρος, Petros, *pet´-ros*; apparently a primary word; a (piece of) *rock* (larger than 3037); as a name, *Petrus,* an apostle:—Peter, rock. Compare 2786.

4075. πετρώδης, petrōdēs, *pet-ro´-dace*; from 4073 and 1491; *rock-like,* i.e. *rocky:*—stony.

4076. πήγανον, pēganon, *pay´-gan-on*; from 4078; *rue* (from its *thick* or *fleshy* leaves):—rue.

4077. πηγή, pēgē, *pay-gay´*; probably from 4078 (through the idea of *gushing* plumply); a *fount* (literal or figurative), i.e. *source* or *supply* (of water, blood, enjoyment) (not necessarily the original spring):—fountain, well.

Noun meaning fountain, source of water.

(I) Generally, a fountain of water (Jas 3:11, 12; Rev 8:10; 14:7; 16:4). Figuratively of life-giving water (Jn 4:14); also, an emblem of the highest enjoyment (Rev 7:17; 21:6).

(II) A well (Jn 4:6; 2Pe 2:17).

(III) A discharge or flow of blood from the body (Mk 5:29; Lk 8:44).

4078. πήγνυμι, pēgnumi, *payg´-noo-mee*; a prolonged form of a primary verb (which in its simpler form occurs only as an alternate in certain tenses); to *fix* ("peg"), i.e. (special) to *set up* (a tent):—pitch.

4079. πηδάλιον, pēdalion, *pay-dal´-ee-on*; neuter of a (presumed) derivative of **πηδόν,** *pēdon* (the *blade* of an oar; from the same as 3976); a "*pedal,*" i.e. *helm:*—rudder.

4080. πηλίκος, pēlikos, *pay-lee´-kos*; a quantitative form (the feminine) of the base of 4225; *how much* (as indefinite), i.e. in size or (figurative) dignity:—how great (large).

4081. πηλός, pēlos, *pay-los´*; perhaps a primary word; *clay:*—clay.

4082. πήρα, pēra, *pay´-rah*; of uncertain affinity; a *wallet* or leather *pouch* for food:—scrip.

4083. πῆχυς, pēchus, *pay´-khoos*; of uncertain affinity; the *fore-arm,* i.e. (as a measure) a *cubit:*—cubit.

4084. πιάζω, piazō, *pee-ad´-zo*; probably another form of 971; to *squeeze,* i.e. *seize* (gently by the hand [*press*], or officially [*arrest*], or in hunting [*capture*]):—apprehend, catch, lay hand on, take. Compare 4085.

4085. πιέζω, piezō, *pee-ed´-zo*; another form for 4084; to *pack:*—press down.

4086. πιθανολογία, pithanologia, *pith-an-ol-og-ee´-ah*; from a compound of a derivative of 3982 and 3056; *persuasive language:*—enticing words.

4087. πικραίνω, pikrainō, *pik-rah´ee-no*; from 4089; to *embitter* (literal or figurative):—be (make) bitter.

4088. πικρία, pikria, *pik-ree´-ah*; from 4089; *acridity* (especially *poison*), literal or figurative:—bitterness.

4089. πικρός, pikros, *pik-ros´*; perhaps from 4078 (through the idea of *piercing*); *sharp* (*pungent*), i.e. *acrid* (literal or figurative):—bitter.

4090. πικρῶς, pikrōs, *pik-roce´*; adverb from 4089; *bitterly,* i.e. (figurative) *violently:*—bitterly.

4091. Πιλᾶτος, Pilatos, *pil-at´-os*; of Latin origin; *close-pressed,* i.e. *firm; Pilatus,* a Roman:—Pilate.

4092. πίμπρημι, pimprēmi, *pim´-pray-mee*; a reduplicated and prolonged form of a primary **πρέω,** *preō, preh´-o* (which occurs only as an alternate in certain tenses); to *fire,* i.e. *burn* (figurative and passive *become inflamed* with fever):—be (× should have) swollen.

4093. πινακίδιον, pinakidion, *pin-ak-id´-ee-on*; diminutive of 4094; a *tablet* (for writing on):—writing table.

4094. πίναξ, pinax, *pin´-ax*; apparently a form of 4109; a *plate:*—charger, platter.

4095. πίνω, pinō, *pee´-no*; a prolonged form of **πίω,** *piō, pee´-o*; which (together with another form **πόω,** *poō, po´-o*) occurs only as an alternate in certain tenses; to *imbibe* (literal or figurative):—drink.

4096. πιότης, piotēs, *pee-ot´-ace*; from **πίων,** *piōn* (*fat*; perhaps akin to the alternate of 4095 through the idea of *repletion*); *plumpness,* i.e. (by implication) *richness* (*oiliness*):—fatness.

4097. πιπράσκω, pipraskō, *pip-ras´-ko*; a reduplicated and prolonged form of **πράω,** *praō,* *prah´-o* (which occurs only as an alternate in certain tenses); contracted from **περάω,** *peraō* (to *traverse*; from the base of 4008); to *traffic* (by *travelling*), i.e. *dispose* of as merchandise or into slavery (literal or figurative):—sell.

4098. πίπτω, piptō, *pip´-to*; a reduplicated and contracted form of **πέτω,** *petō,* *pet´-o* (which occurs only as an alternate in certain tenses); probably akin to 4072 through the idea of *alighting*; to *fall* (literal or figurative):—fail, fall (down), light on.

To fall.

(I) Particularly, to fall from a higher to a lower place, spoken of persons and things (Mt 10:29; 13:5, 7, 8; 21:44; 24:29; Mk 4:4, 5; Lk 8:5–8; 20:18; 23:30; Jn 12:24). Figuratively, to fall upon, to seize (Rev 6:13; 11:11).

(II) Of persons, meaning to fall down or prostrate (Mt 2:11; 4:9; 17:6; 18:26, 29; Mk 5:22; 9:20; 14:35; Lk 5:12; 8:41; 17:16; Jn 11:32; 18:6; Ac 5:5; 9:4; 10:25; 22:7; 1Co 14:25; Rev 1:17; 4:10; 5:8; 19:10; 22:8). Spoken of those who fall dead (Lk 21:24; 1Co 10:8; Heb 3:17; Rev 17:10).

(III) Of edifices, meaning to fall, to fall in ruins (Mt 7:25, 27; Lk 6:49; 13:4; Heb 11:30). Figuratively (Lk 11:17; Ac 15:16); in prophetic imagery (Rev 11:13; 14:8; 16:19; 18:2).

(IV) Of a lot, meaning to fall to or upon someone (Ac 1:26).

(V) Metaphorically of persons, meaning to fall from grace or favour (Ro 11:11, 22; 14:4; 1Co 10:12; Heb 4:11; Jas 5:12). Of things, meaning to fall to the ground, to fail, become void (Lk 16:17).

Deriv.: *anapíptō* (377), to fall back, sit down; *antipíptō* (496), to resist; *apopíptō* (634), to fall from; *gonupetéō* (1120), to bow down; *ekpíptō* (1601), to fall out of; *empíptō* (1706), to fall into or among; *epipíptō* (1968), to fall upon; *katapíptō* (2667), to fall down; *parapípto* (3895), to fall beside, to fall down; *peripíptō* (4045), to fall among; *prospíptō* (4363), to fall toward; *ptóma* (4430), a ruin, corpse, dead body; *ptósis* (4431), the act of falling.

Syn.: *katapontízō* (2670), to sink; *rhíptomai* (4496), to fling oneself, to deliberately fall or throw oneself.

4099. Πισιδία, Pisidia, *pis-id-ee´-ah*; probably of foreign origin; *Pisidia,* a region of Asia Minor:—Pisidia.

4100. πιστεύω, pisteuō, *pist-yoo´-o*; from 4102; to *have faith* (in, upon, or with respect to, a person or thing), i.e. *credit*; (by implication) to *entrust* (especially one's spiritual well-being to Christ):—believe (-r), commit (to trust), put in trust with.

From *pístis* (4102), faith. To believe, have faith in, trust. NT meanings:

(I) Particularly, to be firmly persuaded as to something, to believe (Mk 11:23; Ro 6:8; 10:9; 14:2). With the idea of hope and certain expectation (Ac 18:8).

(A) More commonly used of words spoken and things, followed by the dat. of the person whose words one believes and trusts in (Mk 16:13; Jn 4:21; 5:46; Ac 8:12; 1Jn 4:1).

(B) With an adjunct of the words or thing spoken (Mk 1:15; Lk 1:20; 24:25; Jn 4:50; Ac 13:41; 24:14; 2Th 2:11).

(C) With an adjunct of the thing believed (Jn 9:18; 11:26; 14:10; Ro 10:9; 1Co 13:7; 2Th 1:10; 1Jn 4:16).

(D) Used in an absolute sense where the case of person or thing is implied from the context (Mt 24:23; Mk 13:21; Jn 12:47).

(II) Of God, to believe in God, to trust in Him as able and willing to help and answer prayer (Jn 5:24; 14:1; Ac 16:34; 27:25; Ro 4:17, 18, 24; 1 Jn 5:10; 1Pe 1:21).

(III) Of a messenger from God, to believe on and trust in him (when applied to a merely human messenger of God, to credit and trust him, as coming from God and acting under divine authority).

(A) Of John the Baptist, with the dat. (Mt 21:25, 32; Lk 20:5).

(B) Of Jesus as the Messiah, able and ready to help His followers (Mt 8:13; 9:28; Mk 5:36; Jn 4:48; 14:1). (1) Generally, of Jesus as a teacher and the Messiah sent from God (Mt 18:6; Mk 9:42; Jn 1:12; 2:23; 5:38; 8:31; 10:37, 38; 16:27, 30; 17:8, 21; 20:31; Ac 10:43; Ro 10:14; Gal 2:16; 1Pe 1:8). (2) Used in an absolute sense, to believe, meaning to become a Christian (Mk 15:32; Lk 22:67; Jn 1:7; 12:39; Ac 2:44;

4:4, 32; 14:1; 17:12, 34; 19:18; Ro 4:11; 1Co 1:21; Gal 3:22; 1Th 1:7; 1Pe 2:7).

(IV) Transitively, to entrust, commit in trust to someone (Lk 16:11; Jn 2:24). In the passive, to be entrusted with something, to have something committed to one's trust or charge (Ro 3:2; 1Co 9:17; Gal 2:7; 1Th 2:4; 1Ti 1:11; Tit 1:3).

Syn.: *peíthomai* (3982), to be convinced.

4101. πιστικός, pistikos, *pis-tik-os´*; from 4102; *trustworthy,* i.e. *genuine* (*unadulterated*):—spike- [nard].

4102. πίστις, pistis, *pis´-tis*; from 3982; *persuasion,* i.e. *credence*; moral *conviction* (of *religious* truth, or the truthfulness of God or a religious teacher), especially *reliance* upon Christ for salvation; abstract *constancy* in such profession; by extension the system of religious (gospel) *truth* itself:—assurance, belief, believe, faith, fidelity.

Noun from *peíthō* (3982), to win over, persuade. Faith, trust, firm persuasion, confiding belief in the truth, veracity, reality of any person or thing.

(I) In the common Greek usage:

(A) Particularly and generally, a firm persuasion, a belief in the truth of someone or something (Heb 11:1). See also Ro 14:22, 23; 2Co 5:7; 2Th 2:13; 1Pe 1:5. A ground of confidence, reason for belief, proof (Ac 17:31).

(B) Good faith, faithfulness, sincerity (Mt 23:23; Ro 3:3; Gal 5:22; 1Ti 1:19; 2:7; 2Ti 2:22; 3:10; Tit 2:10; Rev 2:19; 13:10).

(II) As a technical term indicative of the means of appropriating what God in Christ has for man, resulting in the transformation of man's character and way of life. Such can be termed gospel faith or Christian faith (Ro 3:22ff.).

(A) Of God, meaning faith in, on, or toward God (Mt 17:20; 21:21; Mk 11:22; Lk 17:5, 6; Ro 1:17; Col 2:12; 1Th 1:8; Heb 4:2; 6:1; 10:22, 38; Jas 1:6; 5:15; 1Pe 1:21). Spoken by analogy of the faith of the patriarchs and pious men from the Old Testament who looked forward in faith and hope to the blessings of the gospel: spoken of Abraham (Ro 4:5, 9, 11–14, 16, 19, 20; Heb 6:12; 11:8, 9), spoken of others (11:4, 5, 7, 11, 13, 17, 20–24, 27–31, 33, 39).

(B) Of Christ, faith in Christ: **(1)** As able to work miracles, to heal the sick (Mt 8:10; 9:2, 22, 29; 15:28; Mk 2:5; 5:34; 10:52; Lk 5:20; 7:9, 50; 8:48; 17:19; 18:42; Ac 3:16). **(2)** Of faith in

Christ's death, as the ground of justification before God, saving faith, found only in Paul's writings (Ro 3:22, 25–28, 30, 31; 1Co 15:14, 17). Generally (Ro 1:17; 5:1, 2; 9:30, 32; 10:6, 17; Gal 2:16, 20; 3:2, 5, 7–9, 11, 12, 14, 22, 24; 5:5, 6; Eph 2:8; 3:12; Php 3:9. (Of the faith of Old Testament saints, see A above.)

(C) By metonymy of the object of Christian faith, meaning the doctrines received and believed, Christian doctrine, the gospel, all that Christianity stands for (Ac 6:7; 14:27; 24:24; Ro 1:5; 10:8; 2Co 1:24; Gal 1:23; 3:23, 25; Eph 4:5; 1Ti 1:2, 4, 19; 3:9; 6:21; Tit 1:4; 2Pe 1:1; 1Jn 5:4; Jude 3, 20).

Deriv.: *oligópistos* (3640), having but little faith; *pisteúō* (4100), to believe, have faith in; *pistikós* (4101), persuasive, faithful.

Syn.: *bebaíōsis* (951), the act of assurance, confirmation; *pepoíthēsis* (4006), reliance, confidence.

4103. πιστός, pistos, *pis-tos´*; from 3982; object *trustworthy*; subject *trustful*:—believe (-ing, -r), faithful (-ly), sure, true.

Adjective from *peíthō* (3982), to win over, persuade. Worthy of belief, trust, or confidence, faithful.

(I) Trustworthy, true, believable, worthy of credit (1Co 7:25; 1Ti 1:12; 2Ti 2:2; 1Pe 4:19; Rev 1:5; 2:13; 3:14; 19:11). Of things, true, sure (Ac 13:34). Used with *lógos* [3056], word or saying (1Ti 1:15; 3:1; 4:3; 2Ti 2:11; Tit 1:9; 3:8; Rev 21:5; 22:6).

(II) Faithful in duty to oneself and to others, of true fidelity (Col 4:9; 1Pe 5:12; Rev 2:10). Of God as faithful to His promises (1Co 1:9; 10:13; 2Co 1:18; 1Th 5:24; 2Th 3:3; Heb 10:23; 11:11; 1Jn 1:9); of Christ (2Ti 2:13). Especially of servants, ministers, who are faithful in the performance of duty (Mt 24:45; 25:21, 23; Lk 12:42; 16:10–12; 19:17; 1Co 4:2; Eph 1:1; 6:21; Col 1:2; 7; 4:7, 9; 1Ti 3:11; Heb 2:17; 3:2, 5).

(III) With an act. sense, firm in faith, confiding, trusting, believing, equivalent to the present participle of *pisteúō* (4100), to believe (Jn 20:27; Gal 3:9). Followed by the dative (1Co 4:17). Used in an absolute sense (Jn 20:20; Ac 10:45; 16:1, 15; 1Co 4:17; 2Co 6:15; Gal 3:9; 1Ti 4:3, 10, 12; 5:16; 6:2; Tit 1:6; Rev 17:14). Used adverbially, faithfully (3Jn 5).

Deriv.: *ápistos* (571), untrustworthy; *pistóō* (4104), to confirm, establish.

Syn.: *áxios* (514), worthy; *aklinḗs* (186), firm, without wavering; *alēthḗs* (227), true; *alēthinós* (228), truthful; *ámemptos* (273), blameless; *anepílēmptos* (423), irreproachable; *apseudḗs* (893), truthful; *bébaios* (949), steadfast, sure; *eilikrinḗs* (1506), sincere.

4104. πιστόω, pistoō, *pis-to´-o*; from 4103; to *assure*:—assure of.

From *pistós* (4103), faithful. To make one faithful, trustworthy. Passive: to be made confident, believing; to be assured. Only in 2Ti 3:14.

Syn.: *bebaióō* (950), to confirm, establish; *diabebaióō* (1236), to strongly affirm; *kuróō* (2964), to ratify.

4105. πλανάω, planaō, *plan-ah´-o*; from 4106; to (properly *cause* to) *roam* (from safety, truth, or virtue):—go astray, deceive, err, seduce, wander, be out of the way.

4106. πλάνη, planē, *plan´-ay*; feminine of 4108 (as abstract); object *fraudulence*; subject a *straying* from orthodoxy or piety:—deceit, to deceive, delusion, error.

4107. πλανήτης, planētēs, *plan-ay´-tace*; from 4108; a *rover* ("planet"), i.e. (figurative) an *erratic* teacher:—wandering.

4108. πλάνος, planos, *plan´-os*; of uncertain affinity; *roving* (as a *tramp*), i.e. (by implication) an *impostor* or *misleader*:—deceiver, seducing.

4109. πλάξ, plax, *plax*; from 4111; a *moulding-board*, i.e. *flat* surface ("plate," or tablet, literal or figurative):—table.

4110. πλάσμα, plasma, *plas´-mah*; from 4111; something *moulded*:—thing formed.

4111. πλάσσω, plassō, *plas´-so*; a primary verb; to *mould*, i.e. *shape* or *fabricate*:—form.

4112. πλαστός, plastos, *plas-tos´*; from 4111; *moulded*, i.e. (by implication) *artificial* or (figurative) *fictitious* (*false*):—feigned.

4113. πλατεῖα, plateia, *plat-i´-ah*; feminine of 4116; a *wide* "*plat*" or "*place*," i.e. open *square*:—street.

4114. πλάτος, platos, *plat´-os*; from 4116; *width*:—breadth.

4115. πλατύνω, platunō, *plat-oo´-no*; from 4116; to *widen* (literal or figurative):—make broad, enlarge.

4116. πλατύς, platus, *plat-oos´*; from 4111; *spread out* "*flat*" ("plot"), i.e. *broad*:—wide.

4117. πλέγμα, plegma, *pleg´-mah*; from 4120; a *plait* (of hair):—broidered hair.

4118. πλεῖστος, pleistos, *plice´-tos*; irregular superlative of 4183; the *largest number* or *very large*:—very great, most.

4119. πλείων, pleiōn, *pli´-own*; neuter **πλεῖον, pleion,** *pli´-on*; or **πλέον, pleon,** *pleh´-on*; comparative of 4183; *more* in quantity, number, or quality; also (in plural) the *major portion*:— × above, + exceed, more excellent, further, (very) great (-er), long (-er), (very) many, greater (more) part, + yet but.

4120. πλέκω, plekō, *plek´-o*; a primary word; to *twine* or *braid*:—plait.

4121. πλεονάζω, pleonazō, *pleh-on-ad´-zo*; from 4119; to *do, make* or *be more*, i.e. *increase* (transitive or intransitive); by extension to *superabound*:—abound, abundant, make to increase, have over.

4122. πλεονεκτέω, pleonekteō, *pleh-on-ek-teh´-o*; from 4123; to *be covetous*, i.e. (by implication) to *overreach*:—get an advantage, defraud, make a gain.

4123. πλεονέκτης, pleonektēs, *pleh-on-ek´-tace*; from 4119 and 2192; *holding* (*desiring*) *more*, i.e. *eager for gain* (*avaricious*, hence a *defrauder*):—covetous.

4124. πλεονεξία, pleonexia, *pleh-on-ex-ee´-ah*; from 4123; *avarice*, i.e. (by implication) *fraudulency, extortion*:—covetous (-ness) practices, greediness.

Noun from *pleonéktēs* (4123), covetous, which is from *pleíōn* (4119), more, and *échō* (2192), to have. The state of having more, a larger portion, advantage. In the NT, the will to have more, i.e. covetousness, greediness for gain, which leads a person to defraud others (Mk 7:22; Lk 12:15; Ro 1:29; 2Co 9:5; Eph 4:19; 5:3; Col 3:5; 1Th 2:5; 2Pe 2:3, 14).

Syn.: *epithumía* (1939), desire, lust; *órexis* (3715), appetite.

4125. πλευρά, pleura, *plyoo-rah´*; of uncertain affinity; a *rib*, i.e. (by extension) *side*:—side.

4126. πλέω, pleo, *pleh´-o*; another form for **πλεύω,** *pleuō, plyoo´-o*, which is used as an alternate in certain tenses; probably a form of 4150 (through the idea of *plunging* through the water); to *pass* in a vessel:—sail. See also 4130.

4127. πληγή, plēgē, *play-gay´*; from 4141; a *stroke*; (by implication) a *wound*; (figurative) a *calamity*:—plague, stripe, wound (-ed).

4128. πλῆθος, plēthos, *play´-thos*; from 4130; a *fulness*, i.e. a *large number, throng, populace*:—bundle, company, multitude.

4129. πληθύνω, plēthunō, *play-thoo´-no*; from another form of 4128; to *increase* (transitive or intransitive):—abound, multiply.

4130. πλήθω, plēthō, *play´-tho*; a prolonged form of a primary **πλέω,** *pleo, pleh´-o* (which appears only as an alternate in certain tenses and in the reduplication form **πίμπλημι,** *pimplēmi*; to *"fill"* (literal or figurative [*imbue, influence, supply*]); specially to *fulfil* (time):—accomplish, full (… come), furnish.

4131. πλήκτης, plēktēs, *plake´-tace*; from 4141; a *smiter*, i.e. *pugnacious* (*quarrelsome*):—striker.

4132. πλημμύρα, plēmmura, *plame-moo´-rah*; prolonged from 4130; *flood-tide*, i.e. (by analogy) a *freshet*:—flood.

4133. πλήν, plēn, *plane*; from 4119; *moreover* (*besides*), i.e. *albeit, save that, rather, yet*:—but (rather), except, nevertheless, notwithstanding, save, than.

4134. πλήρης, plērēs, *play´-race*; from 4130; *replete*, or *covered* over; (by analogy) *complete*:—full.

Adjective from *pléos* (n.f.), full. Full, filled.

(I) Particularly of hollow vessels, e.g., baskets filled with fragments (Mt 14:20; 15:37; Mk 6:43; 8:19). Of a surface, full, fully covered (Lk 5:12).

(II) Figuratively, full, abounding. Spoken of men being filled with something, e.g., of the Holy Spirit (Lk 4:1; Ac 6:3, 5; 7:55; 11:24). See also Jn 1:14; Ac 6:8; 9:36; 13:10; 19:28.

(III) Figuratively, full in the sense of being complete, perfect. Spoken of a full kernel of

grain (Mk 4:28); spoken of a full reward (2Jn 8). **Syn.**: *mestós* (3324), full.

4135. πληροφορέω, plērophoreō, *play-rof-or-eh´-o*; from 4134 and 5409; to *carry* out *fully* (in evidence), i.e. *completely assure* (or *convince*), *entirely accomplish*:—most surely believe, fully know (persuade), make full proof of.

From *plḗrēs* (4134), full, and *phoréō* (5409), to fill. To persuade fully, give full assurance.

(I) Of persons, in the passive, to be fully assured, persuaded (Ro 4:21; 14:5).

(II) Of things, to make fully assured, give full proof of, confirm fully (2Ti 4:5); passive, to be fully established as true (Lk 1:1; 2Ti 4:17).

Deriv.: *plērophoría* (4136), perfect certitude, full conviction.

Syn.: *apodeíknumi* (584), to demonstrate, accredit; *bebaióō* (950), to assure, establish; *kuróō* (2964), to ratify, confirm; *pistóō* (4104), to assure.

4136. πληροφορία, plērophoria, *play-rof-or-ee´-ah*; from 4135; *entire confidence*:—(full) assurance.

Noun from *plērophoréō* (4135), to fulfill. Full assurance, firm persuasion (Col 2:2; 1Th 1:5; Heb 6:11; 10:22).

Syn.: *pepoíthēsis* (4006), reliance, confidence; *pístis* (4102), faith, confidence, dependability.

4137. πληρόω, plēroō, *play-ro´-o*; from 4134; to *make replete*, i.e. (literal) to *cram* (a net), *level* up (a hollow), or (figurative) to *furnish* (or *imbue, diffuse, influence*), *satisfy, execute* (an office), *finish* (a period or task), *verify* (or *coincide* with a prediction), etc.:—accomplish, × after, (be) complete, end, expire, fill (up), fulfil, (be, make) full (come), fully preach, perfect, supply.

From *plḗrēs* (4134), full. To make full, fill, to fill up.

(I) Particularly, to fill a vessel or hollow place; passive (Mt 13:48; Lk 3:5). Figuratively (Mt 23:32, sins). Generally of a place, to fill by diffusing something throughout (Jn 12:3; Ac 2:2; 5:28). Figuratively, to fill one's heart, to take possession of it (Jn 14:6; Ac 5:3).

(II) Figuratively, to fill, supply abundantly with something, impart richly, imbue with; e.g., to fill with joy (Ac 2:28; 13:52; 2Ti 1:4). See also Lk 2:40; Ro 1:29; 15:13, 14; 2Co 7:4; Eph 1:23; 3:19; 4:10; 5:18; Php 1:11; 4:18, 19; Col 1:9; 2:10).

(III) To fulfill, perform fully.

(A) Spoken of duty or obligation (Mt 3:15; Ac 12:25; Col 4:17).

(B) Of a declaration or prophecy, to fulfill or accomplish (Ac 3:18; 13:27). More often in the passive, to be fulfilled, accomplished, to have been accomplished (Mt 2:17; 26:54; 27:9; Mk 15:28; Lk 1:20; 4:21; 21:22; 24:44; Ac 1:16; Jas 2:23).

(IV) To fulfill, bring to a full end, accomplish, complete.

(A) In the passive, of time, to be fulfilled, completed, ended (Mk 1:15; Lk 21:24; Jn 7:8; Ac 7:23, 30; 9:23; 24:27).

(B) Of a business or work, to accomplish, finish, complete (Lk 7:1; 9:31; Ac 13:25; 14:26; 19:21, Ro 15:19; Col 1:25; Rev 6:11).

(C) By implication, to fill out, complete, make perfect, accomplish an end (Mt 5:17; Php 2:2; 2Th 1:11). In the passive, to be made full, complete (Lk 22:16; Jn 3:29; 15:11; 16:24; 17:13; 2Co 10:6; Col 4:12; 1Jn 1:4; 2Jn 12; Rev 3:2).

Deriv.: *anaplēróō* (378), to fill up; *ekplēróō* (1603), to fill, fulfill; *plḗrōma* (4138), fullness; *sumplēróō* (4845), to fill completely.

Syn.: *anaplēróō* (378), to complete, supply, fill up; *gémō* (1073), to be full; *ekplēróō* (1603), to accomplish entirely, fulfill; *epiteléō* (2005), to fulfill, complete, perform; *kuróō* (2964), to make authoritative, ratify; *mestóō* (3325), to fill; *pímplēmi* or *plḗthō* (4130), to fill, accomplish; *teleióō* (5048), to complete, fulfill, finish; *teléō* (5055), to complete, execute, conclude, finish.

4138. πλήρωμα, plḗrōma, *play´-ro-mah*; from 4137; *repletion* or *completion*, i.e. (subject) what *fills* (as contents, supplement, copiousness, multitude), or (object) what is *filled* (as container, performance, period):—which is put in to fill up, piece that filled up, fulfilling, full, fulness.

Noun from *plēróō* (4137), to make full, fill, fill up. Fullness, filling; basically, that with which anything is filled or of which it is full, the contents.

(I) Particularly meaning the contents of the earth (1Co 10:26, 28); of baskets (Mk 8:20); supplement, that which fills up, such as a patch (*epíblēma* [1915]) (Mt 9:16; Mk 2:21).

(II) Figuratively meaning fullness, full measure, abundance.

(A) Generally, of grace and God's provisions (Jn 1:16; Ro 11:12; 15:29; Eph 3:19); of divine perfections (Col 2:9).

(B) Of persons, full number, complement, multitude (Ro 11:25; Eph 1:23).

(III) Fulfillment, full end, completion.

(A) Of time, full period (Gal 4:4; Eph 1:10).

(B) By implication, meaning completeness, reaching the intended goal (Ro 13:10; Eph 1:23; 4:13).

Syn.: *ekplḗrōsis* (1604), completion, accomplishment; *teleiótēs* (5047), completeness; *télos* (5056), end, goal.

4139. πλησίον, plēsíon, *play-see´-on*; neuter of a derivative of **πέλας, pelas** (*near*); (adverb) *close* by; as noun, a *neighbour*, i.e. *fellow* (as man, countryman, Christian or friend):—near, neighbour.

Adverb from *pélas* (n.f.), near, near to. Near, nearby.

(I) Particularly, of places, near, neighboring (Jn 4:5).

(II) Figuratively, used as a substantive, of people: one near, a neighbour, fellow, another person of the same nature, country, class.

(A) Generally, a fellow man, any other member of the human family, as in the precept "Thou shalt love thy neighbour as thyself" (Mt 19:19; 22:39; Mk 12:31; Ro 13:9; Gal 5:14; Jas 2:8). See also Mk 12:33; Lk 10:27, 29, 36; Ro 13:10; Eph 4:25; Heb 8:11.

(B) One of the same people or country, a fellow countryman (Ac 7:27 [cf. 7:24, 26]).

(C) One of the same faith, a fellow Christian (Ro 15:2).

(D) A friend, associate, the opposite of *echthrós* (2190), enemy (Mt 5:43), and the same as *phílos* (5384), friend.

Deriv.: *paraplḗsion* (3897), nearby, close to.

Syn.: *geítōn* (1069), neighbour; *eggús* (1451), near.

4140. πλησμονή, plēsmonḗ, *place-mon-ay´*; from a presumed derivative of 4130; a *filling* up, i.e. (figurative) *gratification*:—satisfying.

4141. πλήσσω, plḗssō, *place´-so*; apparently another form of 4111 (through the idea of *flattening* out); to *pound*, i.e. (figurative) to *inflict* with (calamity):—smite. Compare 5180.

4142. πλοιάριον, ploiárion, *ploy-ar´-ee-on*; neuter of a presumed derivative of 4143; a *boat*:—boat, little (small) ship.

4143. πλοῖον, ploion, *ploy´-on*; from 4126; a *sailer,* i.e. *vessel:*—ship (-ping).

4144. πλόος, ploos, *plo´-os*; from 4126; a *sail,* i.e. *navigation:*—course, sailing, voyage.

4145. πλούσιος, plousios, *ploo´-see-os*; from 4149; *wealthy*; (figurative) *abounding* with:—rich.

4146. πλουσίως, plousiōs, *ploo-see´-oce*; adverb from 4145; *copiously:*—abundantly, richly.

4147. πλουτέω, plouteō, *ploo-teh´-o*; from 4148; to *be* (or *become*) *wealthy* (literal or figurative):—be increased with goods, (be made, wax) rich.

From *ploútos* (4149), wealth. To be rich, restore.

(I) Particularly, to be rich in material possessions (Lk 1:53; 1Co 4:8; 1Ti 6:9; Rev 3:17; 18:5, 15, 19).

(II) Figuratively, to be rich in something spiritual, to be rich in God's blessings (Ro 10:12; 2Co 8:9; Rev 3:18). To be rich in good works (1Ti 6:18); to be rich toward God, in the sense of laying up treasures in heaven by doing good works (Lk 12:21).

4148. πλουτίζω, ploutizō, *ploo-tid´-zo*; from 4149; to *make wealthy* (figurative):—en-(make) rich.

4149. πλοῦτος, ploutos, *ploo´-tos*; from the base of 4130; *wealth* (as *fulness*), i.e. (literal) *money, possessions,* or (figurative) *abundance, richness,* (special) valuable *bestowment:*—riches.

4150. πλύνω, plunō, *ploo´-no*; a prolonged form of an obsolete **πλύω, pluō** (to "*flow*"); to "*plunge,*" i.e. *launder* clothing:—wash. Compare 3068, 3538.

To wash, as garments (Rev 7:14).

Deriv.: *apoplúnō* (637), to wash out.

Syn.: *loúō* (3068), bathe; *níptō* (3538), to wash (part of the body). Also *apoloúō* (628), to bathe off; *aponíptō* (634), to wash off; *bréchō* (1026), to wet, wash; *katharízō* (2511), to cleanse; *kathaírō* (2508), to cleanse, purge.

4151. πνεῦμα, pneuma, *pnyoo´-mah*; from 4154; a *current* of air, i.e. *breath* (*blast*) or a *breeze*; (by analogy or figurative) a *spirit,* i.e. (human) the rational *soul,* (by implication) *vital principle,* mental *disposition,* etc., or (superhuman) an *angel, dæmon,* or (divine) *God,* Christ's *spirit,* the Holy *Spirit:*—ghost, life, spirit (-ual, -ually), mind. Compare 5590.

Noun from *pnéō* (4154), to breathe, to blow.

(I) Breath.

(A) Of the mouth or nostrils, a breathing, blast. Spoken of the destroying power of God (2Th 2:8). Spoken of the vital breath of life (Rev 11:11).

(B) Breath of air, air in motion, a breeze, blast, the wind (Jn 3:8).

(II) Spirit.

(A) The vital spirit or life, the principle of life residing in man. The breath breathed by God into man and again returning to God, the spiritual entity in man (Mt 27:50; Lk 8:55; 23:46; Jn 19:30; Ac 7:59; 1Co 15:45; Rev 13:15).

(B) The rational spirit, mind, element of life. (1) Generally, spirit distinct from the body and soul. In 1Th 5:23, *pneúma, psuché* (soul [5590]), and *sṓma* (body [4983]) are listed together in describing the whole man. Hebrews 4:12 also describes them as being distinct from one another. (2) As referring to the disposition, feeling, temper of mind; e.g., the spirit of gentleness (1Co 4:21; Gal 6:1). Also Lk 9:55; Ro 8:15; 11:8; 1Co 4:21; 2Co 4:13; 12:18; Eph 2:2; 4:23; Php 1:27; 2:1; 2Ti 1:7; Jas 4:5; 1Pe 3:4). (3) As including the understanding, intellect (Mk 2:8; Lk 1:80; 2:40; 1Co 2:11, 12).

(III) A spirit; a simple, incorporeal, immaterial being (thought of as possessing higher capacities than man does in his present state).

(A) Spoken of created spirits: (1) Of the human soul or spirit, after its departure from the body and as existing in a separate state (Heb 12:23; 1Pe 3:19). Of the soul of a person reappearing after death, a spirit, ghost (Lk 24:37, 39; Ac 23:8, 9). (2) Of an evil spirit, demon (Mt 8:16; Mk 9:20; Lk 9:39; 10:20). Used mostly with the adjective *akátharton* (169), unclean, as an unclean spirit (Mt 10:1; 12:43, 45; Mk 1:23, 26, 27; 3:11, 30; 5:2, 8, 13; 6:7; 7:25; Lk 4:36; 6:18; 8:29; 9:42; 11:24, 26; Ac 5:16; 8:7; Rev 16:13; 18:2). Described as evil spirits (Lk 7:21; 8:2; 19:12, 13, 15, 16); as spirits of demons (Lk 4:35; Rev 16:14). Identified on the basis of what they produce: an unspeaking spirit (Mk 9:17); an unspeaking and deaf spirit (Lk 9:25); a spirit causing weakness or sickness (Lk 13:11); a spirit of divination or fortune-telling (Ac 16:16). **(3)** Less often in the plural, of angels as God's ministering spirits (Heb 1:14; Rev 1:4; 3:1; 4:5; 5:6).

(B) Of God in reference to His incorporeality (Jn 4:24).

(C) Of the Spirit of God. In the NT, referred to as "the Spirit of God," "the Holy Spirit," in an absolute sense as "the Spirit"; the Spirit of Christ as being communicated by Him after His resurrection and ascension. The same as the Spirit of Christ (Ro 8:9; 1Pe 1:11); the Spirit of Jesus Christ (Php 1:19); the Spirit of the Lord (2Co 3:17); the Spirit of God's Son (Gal 4:6). The Holy Spirit is everywhere represented as being in intimate union with God the Father and God the Son. The passages with this meaning in the NT may be divided into two classes: those in which being, intelligence, and agency are predicated of the Spirit; and, metonymically, those in which the effects and consequences of this agency are spoken about. **(1)** The Holy Spirit as possessing being, intelligence, agency. **(a)** Joined with the Father and the Son, with the same or with different predicates (Mt 28:19; 1Co 12:4–6; 2Co 13:14; 1Pe 1:2; Jude 20, 21; 1Jn 5:7). **(b)** Spoken of in connection with God the Father, as having intimate union or oneness with Him (Jn 15:26; 1Co 2:10, 11). Described as speaking through the prophets of the OT and the apostles (Ac 1:16; 28:25; Heb 3:7; 9:8; 10:15). Spoken of as imparting new spiritual life to those who believe in the gospel (Jn 3:5, 6, 8), and then dwelling in Christians (Ro 8:9, 11; 1Co 3:16; 6:19; 2Ti 1:14). The Spirit and God the Father are interchanged (Ac 5:3, 9 [cf. 5:4]; Eph 6:17). **(c)** Spoken in connection with or in reference to Christ as an equal, in the form of an oath (Ro 15:30; 1Co 6:11; 2Co 3:17; Heb 10:29). The Holy Spirit is described as descending in a bodily form upon Jesus after His baptism (Mt 3:16; Mk 1:10; Lk 3:22; Jn 1:32, 33). **(d)** As coming to and acting upon Christians, illuminating and empowering them, and remaining with them, imparting to them spiritual knowledge, aid, consolation, sanctification, and making intercession with and for them (Jn 14:17, 26; 15:26; 16:13; Ro 8:14, 16, 26, 27; 14:17; 15:13, 16; 2Co 1:22; 5:5; Eph 3:16; 6:18; 1Th 1:6; 2Th 2:13). Described as the author of revelations to men through the prophets of the OT, being the authority through which prophets and holy men were motivated when they spoke or acted in the Spirit or through the Spirit (Mt 22:43; Mk 12:36; Ac

10:19; 20:23; 21:11; 1Ti 4:1; Rev 19:10). **(2)** The Holy Spirit's influence and effect upon others, such as the power of the Holy Spirit (Ac 1:8). Spoken: **(a)** Of the role of the Holy Spirit in the miraculous conception of the Lord Jesus (Lk 1:35). See also Mt 1:18, 20. **(b)** Of that special authority which rested upon and empowered the Lord Jesus after the descent of the Holy Spirit upon Him at His baptism (Lk 4:1). See also Mt 12:18; Lk 4:18; Jn 3:34; Ac 10:38. As prompting Him to various actions, such as going into the desert and being tempted (Mt 4:1; Mk 1:12; Lk 4:1). See also Mt 12:28; Lk 4:14. **(c)** Of His filling and empowering others (Lk 1:15; 1:41; 1:67; 2:25–27). The technical expression "to be baptized in [or with] the Holy Spirit" refers to the spiritual baptism into the body of Christ for all those who were truly saved (Mt 3:11; Mk 1:8; Lk 3:16; Jn 1:33; Ac 1:5; 11:16; 1Co 12:13). **(d)** Of that authority of the Holy Spirit by which the apostles were qualified to act as directors of the church of Christ (Jn 20:22). Specifically, of the empowerment imparted by the Holy Spirit on and after the Day of Pentecost, by which the apostles and early Christians were endowed with high supernatural qualifications for their work; knowledge equivalent to a full knowledge of gospel truth and the power of prophesying, working miracles, and speaking with languages previously unknown to them; all done in evidence of the baptism of the Holy Spirit (Ac 2:4, 17, 18, 33, 38; 5:32; 8:15, 17–19; 10:44, 45, 47; 11:15, 24; 13:9; 15:8; 19:6; Ro 15:19; 1Co 2:4; 7:40; 12:7–9; 14:2, 32; Gal 3:2, 3, 5, 14; Eph 1:13; 1Th 1:5; 4:8; 5:19; Heb 2:4; 1Pe 1:12). The Holy Spirit prompts one to do or restrain from doing particular actions (Ac 8:29, 39; 13:2, 4; 15:28; 16:6, 7); encourages holy boldness, energy, and zeal in speaking and acting (Ac 4:8, 31); serves the medium of divine communications and revelations (Ac 7:55; 11:28; 21:4; Eph 3:5); and is the source of support, comfort, Christian joy and triumph (Eph 5:18; Php 1:19). **(3)** Metonymically spoken of a person or teacher who acts or professes to act under the inspiration of the Holy Spirit by divine inspiration (1Co 12:10, "discerning of spirits" of teachers, a critical faculty of the mind quickened by the Holy Spirit, consisting not only of the power of discerning who was a prophet and who was not, but also of a distinguishing in the discourses of a teacher what proceeded from the Holy Spirit and what did not. Also 1Jn 4:1–3, 6).

Deriv.: *pneumatikós* (4152), spiritual.
Syn.: *pnoế* (4157), breath, wind.

4152. πνευματικός, pneumatikos, *phyoo-mat-ik-os´*; from 4151; *non-carnal,* i.e. (humanly) *ethereal* (as opposed to gross), or (demonically) a *spirit* (concretely), or (divinely) *supernatural, regenerate, religious*:—spiritual. Compare 5591.

Adjective from *pneúma* (4151), spirit. Spiritual.

(I) Pertaining to the nature of spirits. Spoken of "a spiritual body" (1Co 15:44), i.e. a body dominated by the Spirit or fit for the Spirit, in contrast to a natural or animal body, which obeys one's natural instincts. Spoken of the spiritual forces of wickednesses (Eph 6:12).

(II) Pertaining to or proceeding from the Holy Spirit.

(A) Of persons who are spiritual, i.e. enlightened by the Holy Spirit, enjoying the influences, graces, and gifts of the Holy Spirit (1Co 2:15; 3:1; 14:37; Gal 6:1).

(B) Of things spiritual, i.e. communicated or imparted by the Holy Spirit (Ro 1:11; 7:14; 15:27; 1Co 2:13; 9:11; 12:1; 14:1; Eph 1:3; 5:19; Col 1:9; 3:16). Also spoken of things in a higher and spiritual sense, not literal or corporeal, including also a reference to the Holy Spirit (1Co 10:3, 4; 1Pe 2:5).

Deriv.: *pneumatikôs* (4153), spiritually.

4153. πνευματικῶς, pneumatikōs, *pnyoo-mat-ik-oce´*; adverb from 4152; *non-physically,* i.e. *divinely,* figuratively:—spiritually.

Adverb from *pneumatikós* (4152), spiritual. Spiritually, by the assistance of the Holy Spirit (1Co 2:14), prophetically, allegorically, mystically (Rev 11:8 [cf. Rev 17:5, 7]).

4154. πνέω, pneō, *pneh´-o*; a primary word; to *breathe* hard, i.e. *breeze*:—blow. Compare 5594.

To blow upon, as the wind or air (Mt 7:25, 27; Lk 12:55; Jn 3:8; 6:18; Ac 27:40; Rev 7:1).

Deriv.: *ekpnéō* (1606), to die, expire; *empnéō* (1709), to inhale, breathe, to inspire; *theópneustos* (2315), God-breathed, inspired; *pneúma* (4151), wind, breath, life, spirit; *pnoế* (4157), wind, breath; *hupopnéō* (5285), to blow gently or softly.

Syn.: *rhipízō* (4494), to fan up, to agitate, toss.

4155. πνίγω, pnigō, *pnee´-go*; strengthened from 4154; to *wheeze,* i.e. (causative by implication) to *throttle* or strangle (*drown*):—choke, take by the throat.

4156. πνικτός, pniktos, *pnik-tos´*; from 4155; *throttled,* i.e. (neuter concrete) an animal *choked* to death (*not bled*):—strangled.

4157. πνοή, pnoē, *pno-ay´*; from 4154; *respiration,* a *breeze*:—breath, wind.

Noun from *pnéō* (4154), to breathe, blow. Wind, vital breath, respiration, the ability to breathe (Ac 17:25; a breath of air, a blast of wind (Ac 2:2).

Syn.: *aếr* (109), air; *ánemos* (417), violent wind; *pneúma* (4151), wind.

4158. ποδήρης, podērēs, *pod-ay´-race*; from 4228 and another element of uncertain affinity; a *dress* (2066 implied) *reaching* the *ankles*:—garment down to the foot.

Adjective from *poús* (4228), foot, and *arố* (n.f.), to join, fasten, fit. Reaching down to the feet, spoken of long flowing robes. Used only in Rev 1:13.

Syn.: *stolế* (4749), a long robe worn by people of rank as a mark of distinction. For a list of various types of clothing, see the synonyms under *himátion* (2440), garment.

4159. πόθεν, pothen, *poth´-en*; from the base of 4213 with enclitic adverb of origin; *from which* (as interrogative) or *what* (as relative) place, state, source or cause:—whence.

4160. ποιέω, poieō, *poy-eh´-o*; apparently a prolonged form of an obsolete primary; to *make* or *do* (in a very wide application, more or less direct):—abide, + agree, appoint, × avenge, + band together, be, bear, + bewray, bring (forth), cast out, cause, commit, + content, continue, deal, + without any delay, (would) do (-ing), execute, exercise, fulfil, gain, give, have, hold, × journeying, keep, + lay wait, + lighten the ship, make, × mean, + none of these things move me, observe, ordain, perform, provide, + have purged, purpose, put, + raising up, × secure, shew, × shoot out, spend, take, tarry, + transgress the law, work, yield. Compare 4238.

To make, do, expressing action either as completed or continued.

(I) To make, i.e. to form, produce, bring about, cause; spoken of any external act as manifested in the production of something tangible, corporeal, obvious to the senses, i.e. completed action.

(A) Generally: (1) Particularly and with the accusative (Mt 17:4; Jn 9:11; 18:18; 19:23; Ac 7:40; 9:39; 19:24; Ro 9:20; Heb 12:13; Rev 13:14). (2) Spoken of God, to make, create, with the accusative (Mt 19:4; Lk 11:40; Ac 4:24; 7:50; 14:15; 17:24; Heb 1:2; Rev 14:7).

(B) Figuratively spoken of a state or condition, or of things intangible and incorporeal, and generally of such things as are produced by an inward act of the mind or will; to make, to cause, to bring about, to occasion. (1) Generally to cause, to bring about, e.g., to make peace (Eph 2:15). See also Lk 1:68; Ac 15:3; 24:12; Ro 16:17; 1Co 10:13; Heb 8:9; Ro 15:26; Heb 1:3. Used of mighty deeds, wonders, miracles (Mt 7:22; 13:58; Lk 1:51; Jn 2:11, 23; 4:54; 5:36; 6:30; 11:47; Ac 6:8; 7:36; 15:12). (2) Spoken of a course of action or conduct, to do, execute, exercise, practice; e.g., with *krísin* (2920), judgement, to execute judgement (Jn 5:27; Jude 15). Specifically of right, duty, virtue (Jn 3:21; 5:29; Ro 2:14; 7:19; 10:5; Eph 6:8; Jas 4:17; 1Jn 1:6; 2:29; 3:7; 3Jn 5). (3) Of evil deeds or conduct, to do, commit or practice sin (Mt 13:41; Lk 12:48; Jn 8:34; Ro 1:32; 2:3; 1Co 6:18; 2Co 11:7; 1Jn 3:4; Rev 21:27).

(C) To cause to exist, as spoken of generative power, to beget, to bring forth, to bear. (1) Of trees and plants, to germinate, bring forth fruit, yield (Mt 3:10; 7:17; 13:23, 26; Lk 3:9; Rev 22:2). Metaphorically (Mt 3:8; 21:43; Lk 3:8). Of branches, to shoot forth (Mk 4:32); of a fountain pouring out water (Jas 3:12). (2) Figuratively of persons, to make for oneself, to get, acquire, gain (Lk 12:33; 16:9; Jn 4:1). To profit, advantage, gain (Mt 25:16; Lk 19:18; 1Co 15:29).

(D) Causative, to cause to do or be. E.g., to make someone sit down (Jn 6:10). See also Mt 5:32; 21:13; Mk 1:17; 7:37; 8:25; Lk 5:34; Jn 4:46; 6:15; 11:37; Ac 3:12; 17:26; 1Co 6:15; Col 4:16; Heb 1:7; Rev 13:13).

(II) To do, expressing an action as continued or not yet completed, sometimes, what one does repeatedly, habitually, like *prásso* (4238), to practice.

(A) Followed by the accusative of thing, and without reference to a person as the remote object. (1) Followed by the accusative pron., to do, generally (Mt 5:47; 8:9; 9:28; Mk 11:3; Lk 6:2; 7:8; 20:2; Ac 1:1; 14:11, 15; 1Co 7:36; Gal 2:10; Eph 6:9; Php 2:14; Col 3:17; 1Ti 5:21; Jas 4:15).

(B) Intransitively to do, act, always with an adverbial modifier telling how one acts; e.g., to

act prudently (Lk 16:8). See also Mt 1:24; 12:12; 23:3; 28:15; Lk 2:27; 12:47; Jn 14:31; 1Co 7:37, 38; 16:1).

(C) Followed by the accusative of time, meaning to do or act for a certain time, up to a certain time, to spend, pass (Mt 20:12; Ac 15:33; 18:23; 20:3; 2Co 11:25; Jas 4:13; Rev 13:5).

Deriv.: *eirēnopoiéō* (1517), to make peace; *zōopoiéō* (2227), to make alive; *kakopoiós* (2555), evildoer; *kalopoiéō* (2569), to live virtuously; *moschopoiéō* (3447), to make a calf; *ochlopoiéō* (3792), to make a crowd; *peripoiéō* (4046), to purchase, acquire, preserve, keep; *poíēma* (4161), creation, work, action; *poíēsis* (4162), performance, action; *poiētḗs* (4163), creator, maker, doer; *prospoiéomai* (4364), to pretend; *skēnopoiós* (4635), tentmaker; *cheiropoíētos* (5499), make by hands.

Syn.: *prássō* (4238), to do, to practice, perform. Also *apoteléō* (658), to finish; *douleúō* (1398), to labour as a slave; *ekteléō* (1615), to finish; *energéō* (1754), to be active, efficient; *epiteléō* (2005), to fulfill, perform completely; *ergázomai* (2038), to work; *katergázomai* (2716), to work fully, accomplish; *teléō* (5055), to complete, conclude.

4161. ποίημα, poiēma, *poy´-ay-mah*; from 4160; a *product*, i.e. *fabric* (literal or figurative):—thing that is made, workmanship.

4162. ποίησις, poiēsis, *poy´-ay-sis*; from 4160; *action*, i.e. *performance* (of the law):—deed.

4163. ποιητής, poiētēs, *poy-ay-tace´*; from 4160; a *performer*; specially a "*poet*":—doer, poet.

4164. ποικίλος, poikilos, *poy-kee´-los*; of uncertain derivative; *motley*, i.e. *various* in character:—divers, manifold.

4165. ποιμαίνω, poimainō, *poy-mah´ee-no*; from 4166; to *tend* as a shepherd (or figurative, *supervisor*):—feed (cattle), rule.

From *poimén* (4166), shepherd. To feed a flock or herd, to tend. Used particularly (Lk 17:7, shepherding). Used figuratively, to care for, provide: referring to kings and princes in regard to their people (Mt 2:6; Rev 7:17); in regard to pastors and teachers in the church (Jn 21:16; Ac 20:28; 1Pe 5:2). From the context, to rule, to govern with severity, spoken of Christ ruling with a rod of iron (Rev 2:27; 12:5; 19:15).

In a bad sense, with *heautón* (1438), himself, to feed or cherish oneself, to take care of oneself at the expense of others (Jude 12).

Syn.: *bóskō* (1006), to feed, distinguished from *poimaínō* in that the latter implies the whole office of the shepherd as guiding, guarding, and placing the flock in the fold, as well as leading it to nourishment; *hēgemoneúō* (2230), to act as ruler; *hēgéomai* (2233), to lead; *kateuthúnō* (2720), to guide, direct.

4166. ποιμήν, **poimēn**, *poy-mane´*; of uncertain affinity; a *shepherd* (literal or figurative):— shepherd, pastor.

Noun meaning shepherd, one who generally cares for flocks.

(I) Particularly (Mt 9:36; 25:32; Mk 6:34; Lk 2:8, 15, 18, 20).

(II) Figuratively of Jesus as the Great Shepherd who watches over and provides for the welfare of the Church, His flock (Mt 26:31; Mk 14:27; Jn 10:2, 11, 12, 14, 16; Heb 13:20; 1Pe 2:25); spoken also of the spiritual guide of a particular church (Eph 4:11).

Deriv.: *archipoímēn* (750), chief shepherd; *poimaínō* (4165), to tend, take general care of the flock; *poímnē* (4167) and *poímnion* (4168), flock.

Syn.: *archēgós* (747), leader; *didáskalos* (1320), teacher; *epískopos* (1985), overseer, superintendent; *hēgemṓn* (2232), a leader; *presbúteros* (4245), elder, spiritual leader.

4167. ποίμνη, **poimnē**, *poym´-nay*; contracted from 4165; a *flock* (literal or figurative):—flock, fold.

Noun from *poimén* (4166), shepherd. A flock of sheep (Lk 2:8; 1Co 9:7). Figuratively, the flock of Christ, His disciples, the Church (Mt 26:31; Jn 10:16).

Syn.: *poímnion* (4168), a flock. Also *ekklēsía* (1577), church, assembly.

4168. ποίμνιον, **poimnion**, *poym´-nee-on*; neuter of a presumed derivative of 4167; a *flock*, i.e. (figurative) *group* (of believers):—flock.

Noun from *poimén* (4166), shepherd. A flock. In the NT, it is applied only figuratively for the flock of Christ, his disciples, the Church (Lk 12:32; Ac 20:28, 29; 1Pe 5:2, 3). A diminutive of *poímnē* (4167).

Syn.: *poímnē* (4167), flock. Also *ekklēsía* (1577), church.

4169. ποῖος, **poios**, *poy´-os*; from the base of 4226 and 3634; individualizing interrogative (of character) *what* sort of, or (of number) *which* one:—what (manner of), which.

4170. πολεμέω, **polemeō**, *pol-em-eh´-o*; from 4171; to *be* (engaged) in *warfare*, i.e. to *battle* (literal or figurative):—fight, (make) war.

4171. πόλεμος, **polēmos**, *pol´-em-os*; from πέλομαι, *pelomai* (to bustle); *warfare* (literal or figurative; a single encounter or a series):—battle, fight, war.

(I) Generally, war (Mt 24:6; Mk 13:7; Lk 14:31; 21:9; Rev 11:7; 12:7, 17; 13:7; 19:19).

(II) Particularly, a fight, a battle (1Co 14:8; Heb 11:34; Rev 9:7, 9; 16:14; 20:8). As a hyperbole: referring to strife (Jas 4:1).

Deriv.: *poleméō* (4170), to make war, fight.

Syn.: While *pólemos* embraces the whole course of hostilities, *máchē* (3163), battle, includes the use of arms of hostile armies.

4172. πόλις, **polis**, *pol´-is*; probably from the same as 4171, or perhaps from 4183; a *town* (properly with walls, of greater or less size):—city.

4173. πολιτάρχης, **politarchēs**, *pol-it-ar´-khace*; from 4172 and 757; a *town-officer*, i.e. *magistrate*:—ruler of the city.

4174. πολιτεία, **politeia**, *pol-ee-ti´-ah*; from 4177 ("*polity*"); *citizenship*; concretely a *community*:—commonwealth, freedom.

4175. πολίτευμα, **politeuma**, *pol-it´-yoo-mah*; from 4176; a *community*, i.e. (abstract) *citizenship* (figurative):—conversation.

4176. πολιτεύομαι, **politeuomai**, *pol-it-yoo´-om-ahee*; middle of a derivative of 4177; to *behave* as a citizen (figurative):—let conversation be, live.

4177. πολίτης, **politēs**, *pol-ee´-tace*; from 4172; a *townsman*:—citizen.

4178. πολλάκις, **pollakis**, *pol-lak´-is*; multiple adverb from 4183; *many times*, i.e. *frequently*:—oft(-en, -entimes, -times).

4179. πολλαπλασίων, **pollaplasiōn**, *pol-lap-las-ee´-ohn*; from 4183 and probably a derivative of 4120; *manifold*, i.e. (neuter as noun) *very much more*:—manifold more.

4180. πολυλογία, polulogia, *pol-oo-log-ee´- ah*; from a compound of 4183 and 3056; *loquacity*, i.e. *prolixity:*—much speaking.

4181. πολυμέρως, polumerōs, *pol-oo-mer´- oce*; adverb from a compound of 4183 and 3313; *in many portions*, i.e. *variously* as to time and agency (*piecemeal*):—at sundry times.

4182. πολυποίκιλος, polupoikilos, *pol-oo- poy´-kil-os*; from 4183 and 4164; *much varie-gated*, i.e. *multifarious:*—manifold.

4183. πολύς, polus, *pol-oos´*; including the forms from the alternate **πολλός, polos** (singular) *much* (in any respect) or (plural) *many*; neuter (singular) as adverb *largely*; neuter (plural) as adverb or noun *often, mostly, largely:*—abundant, + alto-gether, common, + far (passed, spent), (+ be of a) great (age, deal, -ly, while), long, many, much, oft (-en [-times]), plenteous, sore, straitly. Com-pare 4118, 4119.

4184. πολύσπλαγχνος, polusplagchnos, *pol-oo´-splankh-nos*; from 4183 and 4698 (figura-tive); *extremely compassionate:*—very pitiful.

4185. πολυτελής, polutelēs, *pol-oo-tel-ace´*; from 4183 and 5056; *extremely expensive:*—costly, very precious, of great price.

4186. πολύτιμος, polutimos, *pol-oot´-ee-mos*; from 4183 and 5092; *extremely valuable:*—very costly, of great price.

4187. πολυτρόπως, polutropōs, *pol-oot-rop´- oce*; adverb from a compound of 4183 and 5158; *in many ways*, i.e. *variously* as to method or form:—in divers manners.

4188. πόμα, poma, *pom´-ah*; from the alter-nate of 4095; a *beverage:*—drink.

4189. πονηρία, ponēria, *pon-ay-ree´-ah*; from 4190; *depravity*, i.e. (special) *malice*; plural (concrete) *plots, sins:*—iniquity, wickedness.

Noun from *ponērós* (4190) evil, malicious. Evil nature, badness. In the NT, only in a moral sense, evil disposition, wickedness, malice (Mt 22:18; Lk 11:39; Ro 1:29; 1Co 5:8; Eph 6:12). In the plural: wicked counsels, wicked deeds (Mk 7:22; Ac 3:26).

Syn.: *kakía* (2549), evil, badness. Also *adíkēma* (92), injustice, misdeed; *adikía* (93), unrighteousness; *hamartía* (266), sin, missing the mark; *anomía* (458), lawlessness; *paranomía*

(3892), law-breaking; *parábasis* (3847), an over-stepping, transgression.

4190. πονηρός, ponēros, *pon-ay-ros´*; from a derivative of 4192; *hurtful*, i.e. *evil* (properly in effect or influence, and thus differing from 2556, which refers rather to *essential* character, as well as from 4550, which indicates *degeneracy* from original virtue); (figurative) *calamitous*; also (passive) *ill*, i.e. *diseased*; but especially (morally) *culpable*, i.e. *derelict, vicious, facinorous*; neuter (singular) *mischief, malice*, or (plural) *guilt*; mas-culine (singular) the *devil*, or (plural) *sinners:*—bad, evil, grievous, harm, lewd, malicious, wicked (-ness). See also 4191.

Adjective from *pónos* (4192), labour, sorrow, pain. Evil in a moral or spiritual sense, wicked, malicious, mischievous.

(I) In an active sense, evil which causes evil to others, evil-disposed, malevolent, malignant, wicked.

(A) Of persons (Mt 5:45; 7:11; 12:34, 35; 13:49; 18:32; Lk 6:35, 45; 11:13; Ac 17:5; 2Th 3:2). With *pneúma* [4151], spirit: evil spirits, malignant demons (Lk 7:21; 8:2; Ac 19:12, 13, 15, 16). With the definite article, the evil one, Satan (Mt 13:19, 38; Eph 6:16; 1Jn 2:13, 14; 3:12; 5:18). Other verses that could be inter-preted this way: Mt 5:37; 6:13; Lk 11:4; Jn 17:15; 1Jn 5:19.

(B) Of things, such as the eye, an evil eye referring to envy (Mt 20:15; Mk 7:22); evil thoughts (1Ti 6:4; Jas 2:4). Particularly as caus-ing pain or hurt, hurtful, with injurious words (Mt 5:11; Ac 28:21; 3Jn 10). Also painful, griev-ous (Rev 16:2). The neuter with the definite arti-cle: evil, evil intent, malice, wickedness (Mt 5:37, 39). Also evil as inflicted, calamity, affliction.

(II) In the passive sense, evil, made evil, evil in nature or quality, bad, ill, vicious.

(A) Morally, wicked, corrupt (Mt 12:39, 45; 16:4; Lk 11:29; 1Co 5:13; Gal 1:4; 2Ti 3:13); of a servant, remiss, slothful (Mt 25:26; Lk 19:22); of things, wicked, corrupt, as of works (Jn 3:19; 7:7; Col 1:21; 2Ti 4:18; 1Jn 3:12; 2Jn 11), also Ac 18:14; 1Th 5:22; Heb 3:12; 10:22; Jas 4:16. Used of times, particularly as full of sorrow and affliction, evil, calamitous (Eph 5:16; 6:13). In the neuter with the definite article: in the sin-gular, evil, wickedness, guilt (Lk 6:45; Ro 12:9; 1Jn 5:19); in the plural, evil things, wicked deeds (Mk 7:23).

(B) In a physical sense, as of external quality and condition, evil, bad, bad fruit (Mt 7:17, 18). Of persons in reference to external state, dress (Mt 22:10).

Deriv.: *ponēría* (4189), evil, wickedness, maliciousness.

Syn.: *kakós* (2556), bad character but not necessarily hurtful or malicious. Also *ádikos* (94), unrighteous; *áthesmos* (113), lawless, contrary to custom; *hamartōlós* (268), a sinner; *anáxios* (370), unworthy; *ánomos* (459), lawless; *kakopoiós* (2555), an evildoer; *kakoúrgos* (2557), an evil worker, malefactor; *parabátēs* (3848), a transgressor; *phaúlos* (5337), slight, trivial, mean, bad, in the sense of being worthless, contemptible.

4191. πονηρότερος, ponēroteros, *pon-ay-rot´-er-os*; comparative of 4190; *more evil*:—more wicked.

4192. πόνος, ponos, *pon´-os*; from the base of 3993; *toil*, i.e. (by implication) *anguish*:—pain.

Noun from *pénomai* (n.f., see *pénēs* [3993]), to labour. Labor, toil, travail. Hence sorrow, pain, anguish (Rev 16:10, 11; 21:4).

Deriv.: *ponērós* (4190), evil, wicked.

Syn.: *kópos* (2873), the weariness resulting from labour; *lúpē* (3077), grief, sorrow; *odúnē* (3601), pain, distress; *pénthos* (3997), mourning, sorrow; *ōdín* (5604), pain, especially of childbirth.

4193. Ποντικός, Pontikos, *pon-tik-os´*; from 4195; a *Pontican*, i.e. native of Pontus:—born in Pontus.

4194. Πόντιος, Pontios, *pon´-tee-os*; of Latin origin; apparently *bridged*; *Pontius*, a Roman:—Pontius.

4195. Πόντος, Pontos, *pon´-tos*; a *sea*; *Pontus*, a region of Asia Minor:—Pontus.

4196. Πόπλιος, Poplios, *pop´-lee-os*; of Latin origin; apparently "*popular*"; *Poplius* (i.e. *Publius*), a Roman:—Publius.

4197. πορεία, poreia, *por-i´-ah*; from 4198; *travel* (by land); figurative (plural) *proceedings*, i.e. *career*:—journey [-ing], ways.

4198. πορεύομαι, poreuomai, *por-yoo´-om-ahee*; middle from a derivative of the same as 3984; to *traverse*, i.e. *travel* (literal or figurative;

especially to *remove* [figurative, *die*], *live*, etc.)—depart, go (away, forth, one's way, up), (make a, take a) journey, walk.

4199. πορθέω, portheō, *por-theh´-o*; prolonged from πέρθω, *porthō* (to *sack*); to *ravage* (figurative):—destroy, waste.

4200. πορισμός, porismos, *por-is-mos´*; from a derivative of πόρος, *poros* (a *way*, i.e. *means*); *furnishing* (*procuring*), i.e. (by implication) *money-getting* (*acquisition*):—gain.

4201. Πόρκιος, Porkios, *por´-kee-os*; of Latin origin; apparently *swinish*; *Porcius*, a Roman:—Porcius.

4202. πορνεία, porneia, *por-ni´-ah*; from 4203; *harlotry* (including *adultery* and *incest*); (figurative) *idolatry*:—fornication.

4203. πορνεύω, porneuō, *porn-yoo´-o*; from 4204; to *act* the *harlot*, i.e. (literal) *indulge unlawful lust* (of either sex), or (figurative) *practise idolatry*:—commit (fornication).

4204. πόρνη, pornē, *por´-nay*; feminine of 4205; a *strumpet*; (figurative) an *idolater*:—harlot, whore.

4205. πόρνος, pornos, *por´-nos*; from πέρνημι, *pernēmi* (to *sell*; akin to the base of 4097); a (male) *prostitute* (as *venal*), i.e. (by analogy) a *debauchee* (*libertine*):—fornicator, whoremonger.

4206. πόρρω, porrhō, *por´-rho*; adverb from 4253; *forwards*, i.e. *at a distance*:—far, a great way off. See also 4207.

4207. πόρρωθεν, porrhōthen, *por´-rho-then*; from 4206 with adverb enclitic of source; *from far*, or (by implication) *at a distance*, i.e. *distantly*:—afar off.

4208. πόρρωτέρω, porrhōterō, *por-rho-ter´-o*; adverb comparative of 4206; *farther*, i.e. *a greater distance*:—further.

4209. πορφύρα, porphura, *por-foo´-rah*; of Latin origin; the "*purple*" mussel, i.e. (by implication) the *red-blue* colour itself, and finally a garment dyed with it:—purple.

4210. πορφυροῦς, porphurous, *por-foo-rooce´*; from 4209; *purpureal*, i.e. *bluish red*:—purple.

4211. πορφυρόπωλις, **porphuropōlis**, *por-foo-rop´-o-lis*; feminine of a compound of 4209 and 4453; a *female trader in purple* cloth:—seller of purple.

4212. ποσάκις, **posakis**, *pos-ak´-is*; multiple from 4214; *how many times*:—how oft (-en).

4213. πόσις, **posis**, *pos´-is*; from the alternate of 4095; a *drinking* (the act), i.e. (concretely) a *draught*:—drink.

4214. πόσος, **posos**, *pos´-os*; from an obsolete πός *pos* (*who, what*) and 3739; interrogative pronoun (of amount) *how much* (*large, long* or [plural] *many*):—how great (long, many), what.

4215. ποταμός, **potamos**, *pot-am-os´*; probably from a derivative of the alternate of 4095 (compare 4224); a *current, brook* or *freshet* (as *drinkable*), i.e. *running water*:—flood, river, stream, water.

4216. ποταμοφόρητος, **potamophorētos**, *pot-am-of-or´-ay-tos*; from 4215 and a derivative of 5409; *riverborne*, i.e. *overwhelmed by a stream*:—carried away of the flood.

4217. ποταπός, **potapos**, *pot-ap-os´*; apparently from 4219 and the base of 4226; interrogative *whatever*, i.e. of *what possible* sort:—what (manner of).

4218. ποτέ, **pote**, *pot-eh´*; from the base of 4225 and 5037; indefinite adverb, at *sometime*, *ever*:—afore- (any, some-) time (-s), at length (the last), (+ n-) ever, in the old time, in time past, once, when.

4219. πότε, **pote**, *pot´-eh*; from the base of 4225 and 5037; interrogative adverb, at *what time*:— + how long, when.

4220. πότερον, **poteron**, *pot´-er-on*; neuter of a comparative of the base of 4226; interrogative as adverb, *which* (of two), i.e. *is it* this or that:—whether.

4221. ποτήριον, **potērion**, *pot-ay´-ree-on*; neuter of a derivative of the alternate of 4095; a *drinking-vessel*; by extension the contents thereof, i.e. a *cupful* (*draught*); (figurative) a *lot* or *fate*:—cup.

4222. ποτίζω, **potizō**, *pot-id´-zo*; from a derivative of the alternate of 4095; to *furnish drink, irrigate*:—give (make) to drink, feed, water.

4223. Ποτίολοι, **Potioloi**, *pot-ee´-ol-oy*; of Latin origin; *little wells*, i.e. *mineral springs; Potioli* (i.e. *Puteoli*), a place in Italy:—Puteoli.

4224. πότος, **potos**, *pot´-os*; from the alternate of 4095; a *drinking-bout* or *carousal*:—banqueting.

Noun from *pínō* (4095), to drink. A drinking match, a drunken bout (1Pe 4:3).

Syn.: *kraipálē* (2897), debauchery, dissipation; *kōmos* (2970), rioting or reveling; *méthē* (3178), drunkeness; *oinophlugía* (3632), excess of wine.

4225. πού, **pou**, *poo*; generic of an indefinite pronoun πός, *pos* (*some*) otherwise obsolete (compare 4214); as adverb of place, *somewhere*, i.e. *nearly*:—about, a certain place.

4226. ποῦ, **pou**, *poo*; generic of an interrogative pronoun πός, *pos* (*what*) otherwise obsolete (perhaps the same as 4225 used with the rising slide of inquiry); as adverb of place; *at* (by implication, *to*) *what* locality:—where, whither.

4227. Πούδης, **Poudēs**, *poo´-dace*; of Latin origin; *modest; Pudes* (i.e. *Pudens*), a Christian:—Pudens.

4228. πούς, **pous**, *pooce*; a primary word; a "*foot*" (figurative or literal):—foot (-stool).

4229. πρᾶγμα, **pragma**, *prag´-mah*; from 4238; a *deed*; (by implication) an *affair*; by extension an *object* (material):—business, matter, thing, work.

4230. πραγματεία, **pragmateia**, *prag-mat-i´-ah*; from 4231; a *transaction*, i.e. *negotiation*:—affair.

4231. πραγματεύομαι, **pragmateuomai**, *prag-mat-yoo´-om-ahee*; from 4229; to *busy oneself* with, i.e. to *trade*:—occupy.

4232. πραιτώριον, **praitōrion**, *prahee-to´-ree-on*; of Latin origin; the *prætorium* or governor's *courtroom* (sometimes including the whole edifice and *camp*):—(common, judgement) hall (of judgement), palace, prætorium.

4233. πράκτωρ, **praktōr**, *prak´-tore*; from a derivative of 4238; a *practiser*, i.e. (special) an official *collector*:—officer.

4234. πρᾶξις, praxis, *prax´-is*; from 4238; *practice,* i.e. (concretely) an *act*; by extension a *function*:—deed, office, work.

4235. πρᾷος, praios, *prah´-os*; a form of 4239, used in certain parts; *gentle,* i.e. *humble*:—meek.

4236. πρᾳότης, praiotēs, *prah-ot´-ace*; from 4235; *gentleness*; (by implication) *humility*:—meekness.

4237. πρασιά, prasia, *pras-ee-ah´*; perhaps from **πράσον, prason** (a *leek,* and so an *onion-patch*); a garden-*plot,* i.e. (by implication, of regular *beds*) a *row* (repeated in plural by Hebrew to indicate an arrangement):—in ranks.

4238. πράσσω, prassō, *pras´-so*; a primary verb; to *"practise,"* i.e. *perform repeatedly* or *habitually* (thus differing from 4160, which properly refers to a *single* act); (by implication) to *execute, accomplish,* etc.; specially to *collect* (dues), *fare* (personally):—commit, deeds, do, exact, keep, require, use arts.

To do, make, perform in general, expressing an action as continued or not yet completed, what one does repeatedly, continually, habitually, like *poiéō* (4160, II). Found in Jn 3:20; 5:29; elsewhere only in the writings of Luke and Paul.

(I) With the accusative of thing, without reference to a person as the remote object:

(A) Spoken of particular deeds, acts, or works done repeatedly or continually, to do, perform, to practice; e.g., to practice magic (Ac 19:19). See also Ac 26:26; 1Th 4:11; 1Co 9:17. Sometimes spoken of doing a single action (Ac 19:36).

(B) Spoken of a course of action or conduct, especially of right, duty, virtue, to do, meaning to exercise, to practice (Ac 26:20; Ro 2:25; 7:15; 9:11; 2Co 5:10; Php 4:9).

(C) More often spoken of evil deeds or conduct, to do, meaning to commit, practice (Lk 22:23; 23:15, 41; Jn 3:20; 5:29; Ac 25:11, 25; 26:31; Ro 1:32; 2:1–3; 7:19; 13:4; 2Co 12:21; Gal 5:21).

(II) Intransitively, to do.

(A) To do or act in a certain way, e.g., ignorantly (Ac 3:17); contrary to the decrees of Caesar (Ac 17:7).

(B) To do, fare, get along in a certain way (Ac 15:29; Eph 6:21).

(III) Spoken in reference to a person, to do something harmful or evil to someone (Ac 5:35; 16:28; 26:9). To change or exact money from someone (Lk 3:13; 19:23).

Deriv.: *prágma* (4229), deed, event, task; *práktōr* (4233), agent; *práxis* (4234), action, deed.

Syn.: *poiéō* (4160), to do. Also *apoteléō* (658), to perform completely; *energéō* (1754), to work energetically; *epiteléō* (2005), to perform fully; *ergázomai* (2038), to work; *katergázomai* (2716), to accomplish.

4239. πραΰς, praüs, *prah-ooce´*; apparently a primary word; *mild,* i.e. (by implication) *humble*:—meek. See also 4235.

Adjective meaning meek, mild, gentle (Mt 5:5; 21:5; 1Pe 3:4). See *praütēs* (4240), meekness for a full discussion of the meaning.

Deriv.: *praütēs* (4240), meekness.

Syn.: *épios* (2261), gentle, of a soothing disposition; *epieikés* (1933), gentle, mild, forbearing; *tapeinós* (5011), humble.

4240. πραΰτης, praütēs, *prah-oo´-tace*; from 4239; *mildness,* i.e. (by implication) *humility*:—meekness.

Noun from *praüs* (4239), meek. Meekness, mildness, forbearance. In the NT it expresses a meekness which differs from the usual connotation of the word in English. *Praütēs,* according to Aristotle, is the middle standing between two extremes, getting angry without reason (*orgilótes* [n.f.]), and not getting angry at all (*aorgēsía* [n.f.]). It is the result of a strong man's choice to control his reactions in submission to God. It is a balance born in strength of character, stemming from confident trust in God, not from weakness or fear (Jas 1:21; 3:13; 1Pe 3:15).

Syn.: *epieíkeia* (1932), fairness, moderation, gentleness; *tapeino-phrosúnē* (5012), humility.

4241. πρέπω, prepō, *prep´-o*; apparently a primary verb; to *tower* up (*be conspicuous*), i.e. (by implication) to *be suitable* or *proper* (third person singular presumed indicative, often used impersonally, it is *fit* or *right*):—become, comely.

4242. πρεσβεία, presbeia, *pres-bi´-ah*; from 4243; *seniority* (*eldership*), i.e. (by implication) an *embassy* (concrete *ambassadors*):—ambassage, message.

4243. πρεσβεύω, presbeuō, *pres-byoo´-o*; from the base of 4245; to be a *senior*, i.e. (by implication) *act as a representative* (figurative, *preacher*):—be an ambassador.

4244. πρεσβυτέριον, presbuterion, *pres-boo-ter´-ee-on*; neuter of a presumed derivative of 4245; the *order of elders*, i.e. (special) Israelite *Sanhedrin* or Christian "*presbytery*":—(estate of) elder (-s), presbytery.

Noun from *presbúteros* (4245), elder. Presbytery, an assembly of aged men, a council of elders, a senate. Spoken of the Jewish Sanhedrin (Lk 22:66; Ac 22:5), which is otherwise called *sunédrion* (4892), a joint session, a council. Spoken of the elders of the Christian church, a governing ecclesiastical body comprised of *presbúteroi* (4245), apparently with reference to the council of elders in a given area (1Ti 4:14). Along with elders there were also *diákonoi* (pl.) (1249), deacons in the local church (Php 1:1). Deacons are never presented as a governing council as are the elders; they exist to assist the elders.

4245. πρεσβύτερος, presbuteros, *pres-boo´-ter-os*; comparative of πρέσβυς, *presbus* (*elderly*); *older*; as noun, a *senior*; specially an Israelite *Sanhedrist* (also figurative, member of the celestial council) or Christian "*presbyter*":—elder (-est), old.

Adjective, the comparative of *présbus* (n.f.), an old man, an ambassador. Older, aged.

(I) Particularly as a comparative adjective (Lk 15:25). As a substantive an older person, senior; in the plural, old men, seniors, the aged (Ac 2:17; 1Ti 5:1, 2; 1Pe 5:5). In the plural, the ancients, the fathers, ancestors (Mt 15:2; Mk 7:3, 5; Heb 11:2).

(II) As a substantive in the Jewish and Christian usage, a title of dignity, an elder, plural elders, meaning persons of ripe age and experience who were called to take part in the management of public affairs. In the NT spoken of:

(A) The members of the Jewish Sanhedrin at Jerusalem (Mt 16:21; 21:23; 26:3, 47, 57, 59; 27:1, 3, 12, 20, 41; 28:11, 12; Mk 8:31; 11:27; 14:43, 53; 15:1; Lk 9:22; 20:1; 22:52; Ac 4:5, 8, 23; 23:14; 24:1; 25:15).

(B) The elders in other cities, such as Capernaum (Lk 7:3).

(C) The elders of Christian churches, presbyters, to whom was committed the direction and government of individual churches (Ac 11:30; 14:23; 15:2, 4, 6, 22, 23; 16:4; 20:17 [cf. 20:28]; 21:18; 1Ti 5:17; Tit 1:5; Jas 5:14; 1Pe 5:1). In the sing., *presbúteros* (1Ti 5:19; 2Jn 1; 3Jn 1).

(D) The twenty-four elders around the throne of God in heaven (Rev 4:4, 10; 5:5, 6, 8, 11, 14; 7:11, 13; 11:16; 14:3; 19:4).

Deriv.: *presbutérion* (4244), a council of elders, an assembly of aged men which acted as the governing body of the church; *sumpresbúteros* (4850), a fellow elder.

Syn.: *epískopos* (1985), overseer, bishop. Also *didáskolos* (1320), teacher; *poimén* (4166), shepherd, pastor.

4246. πρεσβύτης, presbutēs, *pres-boo´-tace*; from the same as 4245; an *old man*:—aged (man), old man.

4247. πρεσβῦτις, presbutis, *pres-boo´-tis*; feminine of 4246; an *old woman*:—aged woman.

4248. πρηνής, prēnēs, *pray-nace´*; from 4253; *leaning* (*falling*) *forward* ("*prone*"), i.e. *head foremost*:—headlong.

4249. πρίζω, prizō, *prid´-zo*; a strengthened form of a primary πρίω, *priō* (to *saw*); to *saw* in two:—saw asunder.

4250. πρίν, prin, *prin*; adverb from 4253; *prior*, *sooner*:—before (that), ere.

4251. Πρίσκα, Priska, *pris´-kah*; of Latin origin; feminine of *Priscus*, *ancient*; *Priska*, a Christian woman:—Prisca. See also 4252.

4252. Πρίσκιλλα, Priscilla, *pris´-cil-lah*; diminutive of 4251; *Priscilla* (i.e. *little Prisca*), a Christian woman:—Priscilla.

4253. πρό, pro, *pro*; a primary preposition; "*fore*," i.e. *in front of*, *prior* (figurative, *superior*) *to*:—above, ago, before, or ever. In comparative it retains the same significations.

4254. προάγω, proagō, *pro-ag´-o*; from 4253 and 71; to *lead forward* (magisterially); intransitive to *precede* (in place or time [participle *previous*]):—bring (forth, out), go before.

From *pró* (4253), before or forth, and *ágō* (71), to go. To go before, bring out.

(I) Transitively, to lead or bring forth, as a prisoner out of prison (Ac 16:30); in a judicial sense, to bring forth to execute (Ac 12:6) or to judge (25:26).

(**II**) Intransitively, to go before, referring either to place or time.

(**A**) Of place, to go before, in front or in advance (Mt 2:9; 21:9; Mk 10:32; 11:9; Lk 18:39).

(**B**) In time, to go first, precede (Mt 14:22; 21:31; 26:32; 28:7; Mk 6:45; 14:28; 16:7; 1Ti 1:18; 5:24; Heb 7:18).

Syn.: *progínomai* (4266), to have transpired already, be past; *proérchomai* (4281), to go before, precede; *proporeúomai* (4313), to go before; *protréchō* (4390), to run forward, precede.

4255. προαιρέομαι, proaireomai, *pro-ahee-reh´-om-ahee*; from 4253 and 138; to *choose* for oneself *before* another thing (*prefer*), i.e. (by implication) to *propose* (*intend*):—purpose.

4256. προαιτιάομαι, proaitiaomai, *pro-ahee-tee-ah´-om-ahee*; from 4253 and a derivative of 156; to *accuse already*, i.e. *previously charge:*—prove before.

4257. προακούω, proakouō, *pro-ak-oo´-o*; from 4253 and 191; to *hear already*, i.e. *anticipate:*—hear before.

4258. προαμαρτάνω, proamartanō, *pro-am-ar-tan´-o*; from 4253 and 264; to *sin previously* (to conversion):—sin already, heretofore sin.

4259. προαύλιον, proaulion, *pro-ow´-lee-on*; neuter of a presumed compound of 4253 and 833; a *forecourt*, i.e. *vestibule* (*alley-way*):—porch.

4260. προβαίνω, probainō, *prob-ah´ee-no*; from 4253 and the base of 939; to *walk forward*, i.e. *advance* (literally or in years):— + be of a great age, go farther (on), be well stricken.

4261. προβάλλω, proballō, *prob-al´-lo*; from 4253 and 906; to *throw forward*, i.e. *push to the front, germinate:*—put forward, shoot forth.

4262. προβατικος, probatikos, *prob-at-ik-os´*; from 4263; *relating to sheep*, i.e. (a *gate*) through which they were led into Jerusalem:—sheep (market).

4263. πρόβατον, probaton, *prob´-at-on*; properly neuter of a presumed derivative of 4260; *something that walks forward* (a *quadruped*), i.e.

(special) a *sheep* (literal or figurative):—sheep ([-fold]).

4264. προβιβάζω, probibazō, *prob-ib-ad´-zo*; from 4253 and a reduplicated form of 971; to *force forward*, i.e. *bring to the front, instigate:*—draw, before instruct.

4265. προβλέπω, problepō, *prob-lep´-o*; from 4253 and 991; to *look* out *beforehand*, i.e. *furnish in advance:*—provide.

4266. προγίνομαι, proginomai, *prog-in´-om-ahee*; from 4253 and 1096; to *be already*, i.e. *have previously transpired:*—be past.

4267. προγινώσκω, proginōskō, *prog-in-oce´-ko*; from 4253 and 1097; to *know beforehand*, i.e. *foresee:*—foreknow (ordain), know (before).

From *pró* (4253), before, and *ginóskō* (1097), to know. To perceive or recognize beforehand, know previously, take into account or specially consider beforehand, to grant prior acknowledgement or recognition to someone, to foreknow.

(**I**) Generally, to know already, to be acquainted with a person or fact beforehand (Ac 26:5; 2Pe 3:17).

(**II**) Used of God's eternal counsel it includes all that He has considered and purposed to do prior to human history. In the language of Scripture, something foreknown is not simply that which God was aware of prior to a certain point. Rather, it is presented as that which God gave prior consent to, that which received His favourable or special recognition. Hence, this term is reserved for those matters which God fabourably, deliberately and freely chose and ordained.

(**A**) Used of persons, to approve of beforehand, to make a previous choice of, as of a special people (Ro 8:29; 11:2). The salvation of every believer is known and determined in the mind of God before its realization in time. *Proginóskō* essentially entails a gracious self-determining on God's part from eternity to extend fellowship with Himself to undeserving sinners. It emphasizes the exercise of God's wisdom and intelligence in regard to His eternal purpose. Compare *proorízō* (4309) which emphasizes the exercise of God's will in regard to these things (Ro 8:29). What He has decreed is what He has decided. He foreordains unto salvation those whom He specially considered and chose in eternity past (see Mt 7:23; Jn 10:14; Ro 11:2; 1Co 8:3; Gal 4:9; 2Ti 2:19).

(B) Used of events, to previously decide or plan, to foreknow for God is to foreordain. First Peter 1:19, 20 presents Christ as the "Lamb of God foreknown from the foundation of the world" (a.t.). He is said to be foreknown because God had planned and determined in His eternal counsel to provide His Son as a sacrifice for His people. It is not merely that God knew ahead of time that Christ would so come and die; God's foreknowledge is given here as the cause for His Son's sacrifice—because He planned and decreed it.

Deriv.: *prógnōsis* (4268), foreknowledge.

Syn.: *problépō* (4265), to look out beforehand, to supply in advance, foresee; *proeídō* (4275) to foresee; *proetoimázō* (4282), to ordain or prepare before; *prolégō* (4302), to tell or say beforehand; *promerimnáō* (4305), to take thought or care beforehand; *pronoéō* (4306), to know or consider in advance; *prooráō* (4308), to foresee; *proorízō* (4309), to set limits in advance, ordain beforehand, predestinate.

4268. **πρόγνωσις, prognōsis,** *prog´-no-sis*; from 4267; *forethought*:—foreknowledge.

Noun from *proginōskō* (4267), to know beforehand. Foreknowledge, recognition or consideration beforehand. In the NT, it is used to denote the foreordained purpose and counsel of God in salvation (Ac 2:23; 1Pe 1:2).

Syn.: *prónoia* (4307), forethought, providence. Also *próthesis* (4286), a setting forth beforehand.

4269. **πρόγονος, progonos,** *prog´-on-os*; from 4266; an *ancestor*, (*grand-*) *parent*:—forefather, parent.

4270. **προγράφω, prographō,** *prog-raf´-o*; from 4253 and 1125; to *write previously*; (figurative) to *announce, prescribe*:—before ordain, evidently set forth, write (afore, aforetime).

4271. **πρόδηλος, prodēlos,** *prod´-ay-los*; from 4253 and 1212; *plain before* all men, i.e. *obvious*:—evident, manifest (open) beforehand.

4272. **προδίδωμι, prodidōmi,** *prod-id´-o-mee*; from 4253 and 1325; to *give before* the other party has given:—first give.

4273. **προδότης, prodotēs,** *prod-ot´-ace*; from 4272 (in the sense of *giving forward* into another's [the enemy's] hands); a *surrender*:—betrayer, traitor.

4274. **πρόδρομος, prodromos,** *prod´-rom-os*; from the alternate of 4390; a *runner ahead*, i.e. *scout* (figurative, *precursor*):—forerunner.

4275. **προείδω, proeidō,** *pro-i´-do*; from 4253 and 1492; *foresee*:—foresee, saw before.

4276. **προελπίζω, proelpizō,** *pro-il-pid´-zo*; from 4253 and 1679; to *hope in advance* of other confirmation:—first trust.

4277. **προέπω, proepō,** *pro-ep´-o*; from 4253 and 2036; to *say already*, to *predict*:—forewarn, say (speak, tell) before. Compare 4280.

4278. **προενάρχομαι, proenarchomai,** *pro´-en-ar´-khom-ahee*; from 4253 and 1728; to *commence already*:—begin (before).

4279. **προεπαγγέλλομαι, proepaggellomai,** *pro-ep-ang-ghel´-lom-ahee*; middle from 4253 and 1861; to *promise of old*:—promise before.

From *pró* (4253), before, and *epaggéllō* (1861), to bring word to, to announce, promise. In the NT, only in the middle *proepaggéllomai*, to proclaim or promise beforehand. Used only in Ro 1:2.

4280. **προερέω, proereō,** *pro-er-eh´-o*; from 4253 and 2046; used as alternate of 4277; to *say already, predict*:—foretell, say (speak, tell) before.

4281. **προέρχομαι, proerchomai,** *pro-er´-khom-ahee*; from 4253 and 2064 (including its alternate); to *go onward, precede* (in place or time):—go before (farther, forward), outgo, pass on.

4282. **προετοιμάζω, proetoimazō,** *pro-et-oy-mad´-zo*; from 4253 and 2090; to *fit up in advance* (literal or figurative):—ordain before, prepare afore.

4283. **προευαγγελίζομαι, proeuaggelizomai,** *pro-yoo-ang-ghel-id´-zom-ahee*; middle from 4253 and 2097; to *announce* glad news *in advance*:—preach before the gospel.

From *pró* (4253), before, and *euaggelízō* (2097), to preach the gospel or the good news. To proclaim the gospel beforehand. Only in Gal 3:8.

Syn.: *prokērússō* (4296), to preach, announce beforehand.

4284. προέχομαι, proechomai, *pro-ekh-om-ahee*; middle from 4253 and 2192; to *hold* oneself *before* others, i.e. (figurative) to *excel*:—be better.

4285. προηγέομαι, proēgeomai, *pro-ay-geh´-om-ahee*; from 4253 and 2233; to *lead the way* for others, i.e. *show deference*:—prefer.

4286. πρόθεσις, prothesis, *proth´-es-is*; from 4388; a *setting forth*, i.e. (figurative) *proposal* (*intention*); specially the *show*-bread (in the temple) as *exposed* before God:—purpose, shew [-bread].

Noun from *protíthēmi* (4388), to purpose or plan. A setting forth, an exposition, a placing in view or openly displaying something.

(I) Particularly, as of food, in an adjectival sense. Spoken of the shewbread, the twelve loaves of bread which were set out fresh every morning on a table in the sanctuary (Mt 12:4; Mk 2:26; Lk 6:4; Heb 9:2). See Le 24:5–9.

(II) Figuratively, what one proposes in one's mind or purposes to himself. Spoken of a purpose, an intent (Ac 27:13); spoken of a firm resolve, a design (Ac 11:23; 2Ti 3:10); spoken of the eternal purpose and counsel of God (Ro 8:28; 9:11; Eph 1:11; 3:11; 2Ti 1:9).

Syn.: *boúlēma* (1013), purpose, will; *thélēma* (2307), desire or will with the power to execute that will; *prógnōsis* (4268), forethought, foreknowledge; *prónoia* (4307), provision, providence, forethought.

4287. προθέσμιος, prothesmios, *proth-es´-mee-os*; from 4253 and a derivative of 5087; *fixed beforehand*, i.e. (feminine with 2250 implication) a *designated* day:—time appointed.

Noun from *pró* (4253), before, and *thesmós* (n.f.), custom, ordinance, which is from *títhēmi* (5087), to set, place, lay. A pre-appointed day or time, the day or time being understood. Used only in Gal 4:2.

4288. προθυμία, prothumia, *proth-oo-mee´-ah*; from 4289; *predisposition*, i.e. *alacrity*:—forwardness of mind, readiness (of mind), ready (willing) mind.

4289. πρόθυμος, prothumos, *proth´-oo-mos*; from 4253 and 2372; *forward* in *spirit*, i.e. pre-disposed*; neuter (as noun) *alacrity*:—ready, willing.

4290. προθύμως, prothumōs, *proth-oo´-moce*; adverb from 4289; *with alacrity*:—willingly.

4291. προΐστημι, proΐstēmi, *pro-is´-tay-mee*; from 4253 and 2476; to *stand before*, i.e. (in rank) to *preside*, or (by implication) to *practise*:—maintain, be over, rule.

4292. προκαλέομαι, prokaleomai, *prok-al-eh´-om-ahee*; middle from 4253 and 2564; to *call forth to oneself* (*challenge*), i.e. (by implication) to *irritate*:—provoke.

4293. προκαταγγέλλω, prokataggellō, *prok-at-ang-ghel´-lo*; from 4253 and 2605; to *announce beforehand*, i.e. *predict*, *promise*:—foretell, have notice, (shew) before.

From *pró* (4253), before, and *kataggéllō* (2605), declare, publish. To announce beforehand, foretell (Ac 3:18, 24; 7:52). To announce beforehand in the sense of promising (2Co 9:5).

Syn.: *proépō* (4277), to tell before; *prolégō* (4302), foretell; *prophēteúō* (4395), to prophesy.

4294. προκαταρτίζω, prokatartizō, *prok-at-ar-tid´-zo*; from 4253 and 2675; to *prepare in advance*:—make up beforehand.

From *pró* (4253), before, and *katartízō* (2675), to establish, set up. To make ready beforehand, make right. Used only in 2Co 9:5 of the offerings for the Jerusalem church which Paul wished to find already prepared.

Syn.: *hetoimázō* (2090), to prepare; *kataskeuázō* (2680), to prepare, make ready or fitting; *paraskeuázō* (3903), to prepare, make ready; *proetoimázō* (4282), to prepare beforehand.

4295. πρόκειμαι, prokeimai, *prok´-i-mahee*; from 4253 and 2749; to *lie before* the view, i.e. (figurative) to *be present* (to the mind), to *stand forth* (as an example or reward):—be first, set before (forth).

4296. προκηρύσσω, prokērussō, *prok-ay-rooce´-so*; from 4253 and 2784; to *herald* (i.e. *proclaim*) *in advance*:—before (first) preach.

4297. προκοπή, prokopē, *prok-op-ay´*; from 4298; *progress*, i.e. *advancement* (subject or object):—furtherance, profit.

4298. προκόπτω, prokoptō, *prok-op´-to*; from 4253 and 2875; to *drive forward* (as if by beating), i.e. (figurative and intransitive) to *advance* (in amount, to *grow*; in time, to *be well along*):—increase, proceed, profit, be far spent, wax.

4299. πρόκριμα, prokrima, *prok´-ree-mah*; from a compound of 4253 and 2919; a *prejudgment* (*prejudice*), i.e. *prepossession*:—prefer one before another.

Noun from *prokrínō* (n.f.), to prefer, which is from *pró* (4253), before, and *krínō* (2919), to judge. A preferring before, a judging beforehand, prejudice. It is an unfavourable prejudgment against one, partiality being the chief attitude of this prejudgment (1Ti 5:21).

4300. προκυρόω, prokuroō, *prok-oo-ro´-o*; from 4253 and 2964; to *ratify previously*:—confirm before.

4301. προλαμβάνω, prolambanō, *prol-am-ban´-o*; from 4253 and 2983; to *take in advance*, i.e. (literal) *eat before* others have an opportunity; (figurative) to *anticipate, surprise*:—come aforehand, overtake, take before.

4302. προλέγω, prolegō, *prol-eg´-o*; from 4253 and 3004; to *say beforehand*, i.e. *predict, forewarn*:—foretell, tell before.

4303. προμαρτύρομαι, promarturomai, *prom-ar-too´-rom-ahee*; from 4253 and 3143; to *be a witness in advance*, i.e. *predict*:—testify beforehand.

4304. προμελετάω, promeletaō, *prom-el-et-ah´-o*; from 4253 and 3191; to *premeditate*:—meditate before.

4305. προμεριμνάω, promerimnaō, *prom-er-im-nah´-o*; from 4253 and 3309; to *care* (anxiously) *in advance*:—take thought beforehand.

4306. προνοέω, pronoeō, *pron-o-eh´-o*; from 4253 and 3539; to *consider in advance*, i.e. *look out for beforehand* (active by way of *maintenance* for others; middle by way of *circumspection* for oneself):—provide (for).

From *pró* (4253), before, and *noéō* (3539), to think, comprehend. To foresee, to perceive beforehand. In the NT, figuratively, to see to beforehand, to care for, to provide for (1Ti 5:8). In the middle voice, to provide for in one's behalf, to apply one's self, to practice diligently (Ro 12:17; 2Co 8:21).

Deriv.: *prónoia* (4307), forethought, providential care.

Syn.: *problépō* (4265) or *prooráō* (4308), to foresee.

4307. πρόνοια, pronoia, *pron´-oy-ah*; from 4306; *forethought*, i.e. *provident care* or *supply*:—providence, provision.

Noun from *pronoéō* (4306), to know ahead. Foresight, providence, care (Ac 24:2); provision, forethought, spoken of in reference to gratifying the lusts of the flesh (Ro 13:14).

Syn.: *epiméleia* (1958), carefulness, attention.

4308. προοράω, prooraō, *pro-or-ah´-o*; from 4253 and 3708; to *behold in advance*, i.e. (active) to *notice* (another) *previously*, or (middle) to *keep in* (one's own) *view*:—foresee, see before.

4309. προορίζω, prooorizō, *pro-or-id´-zo*; from 4253 and 3724; to *limit in advance*, i.e. (figurative) *predetermine*:—determine before, ordain, predestinate.

From *pró* (4253), before, and *horízō* (3724), to determine. To decide or determine beforehand, to foreordain, to predetermine. Used in proclaiming that the actions of Herod and Pontius Pilate in crucifying Jesus Christ were predetermined by the hand and will of God (Ac 4:28). *Proorízō* is used to declare God's eternal decrees of both the objects and goal of His plan of salvation (Ro 8:29, 30), of the glorious benefits that will come from that salvation (1Co 2:7), and of our adoption and inheritance as sons of God (Eph 1:5, 11).

Syn.: *proetoimázō* (4282), to prepare before; *protássō* (4384), to appoint before; *procheirízō* (4400), to appoint beforehand.

4310. προπάσχω, propaschō, *prop-as´-kho*; from 4253 and 3958; to *undergo* hardship *previously*:—suffer before.

4311. προπέμπω, propempō, *prop-em´-po*; from 4253 and 3992; to *send forward*, i.e. *escort* or *aid* in travel:—accompany, bring (forward) on journey (way), conduct forth.

4312. προπετής, propetēs, *prop-et-ace´*; from a compound of 4253 and 4098; *falling forward*, i.e. *headlong* (figurative, *precipitate*):—heady, rash [-ly].

4313. προπορεύομαι, **proporeuomai**, *prop-or-yoo´-om-ahee*; from 4253 and 4198; to *precede* (as guide or herald):—go before.

4314. πρός, **pros**, *pros*; a strengthened form of 4253; a preposition of direction; *forward to*, i.e. *toward* (with the genitive *the side of*, i.e. *pertaining to*; with the dative *by the side of*, i.e. *near to*; usually with the accusative the place, time, occasion, or respect, which is the *destination* of the relation, i.e. *whither* or *for* which it is predicated):—about, according to, against, among, at, because of, before, between, ([where-]) by, for, × at thy house, in, for intent, nigh unto, of, which pertain to, that, to (the end that), + together, to ([you]) -ward, unto, with (-in). In comparative it denotes essentially the same applications, namely, motion *toward*, accession *to*, or nearness *at*.

Preposition meaning toward, to, unto.

(I) Marking the object toward or to which something moves or is directed.

(A) Of place, thing, or person meaning toward, to, unto. **(1)** Particularly of motion or direction after verbs of going, coming, departing (Mt 11:28; 21:34; 26:57; Mk 10:1; Lk 23:7; Jn 3:20; 10:35; 16:7; Ac 9:2; 13:32; 15:25; 22:5; Ro 1:10; 2Co 3:1; Gal 1:17). **(2)** With verbs of falling (Mk 5:22; Lk 16:20; Ac 3:2). **(3)** After verbs implying motion or direction in a close proximity as turning, reaching, looking (Lk 7:44; Ac 9:40; Ro 10:21). **(4)** With verbs of speaking, answering, and praying (Mt 3:15; Lk 1:19; 22:70; Ac 2:38; 3:12; 8:24; Ro 10:1).

(B) Of time: **(1)** Spoken of a time when, meaning toward, near (Lk 24:29). **(2)** Spoken of a time during which, meaning for, at (Lk 8:13; Jn 5:35; 1Co 7:5; Gal 2:5; Heb 12:10, 11; Jas 4:14).

(II) Used figuratively:

(A) After verbs and words implying direction of the mind or will, an affection or disposition toward someone. **(1)** Favorable, meaning toward, to, implying goodwill, confidence (2Co 3:4; 7:4; Col 4:5; 1Th 1:8; 4:12; 5:14; 2Ti 2:24; Tit 3:2; Phm 5). **(2)** Unfavorable, meaning against (Ac 24:19; 25:19; 1Co 6:1; Eph 6:11; Col 3:13, 19; Heb 12:4; Rev 13:6).

(B) Denoting the direction, reference, or relation which one object has toward or to another. **(1)** Toward, in reference or respect to, as to, implying the direction or remote object of an action. **(a)** With reference to persons; e.g., "What is that to us?" (Mt 27:4). See also Jn 21:22, 23. **(b)** With reference to things relating or pertaining to any person or thing or condition, e.g., "things which make for peace" (Lk 19:42). See also Lk 14:32; Ac 28:10; 2Pe 1:3. The things pertaining to God, i.e. divine things (Ro 15:17; Heb 2:17; 5:1). **(2)** Spoken of a rule, norm, or standard, meaning according to, in conformity with (Lk 12:47; 2Co 5:10; Gal 2:14). **(3)** Of the motive, ground, or occasion of an action, meaning on account of, because of, for (Mt 19:8; Mk 10:5). **(4)** As marking the end result, the aim or purpose of an action, meaning for what, why, to what end, for what purpose (Jn 13:28). After verbs expressing the end, aim, tendency of an action or quality (Ac 3:10; Ro 3:26; 15:2; 1Co 6:5; 7:35; 10:11; 2Co 1:20; Eph 4:12; 1Ti 1:16; 4:7; Heb 5:14; 6:11; 1Pe 4:12). Also after nouns and adjectives that express such ends, aims, or tendencies (Jn 4:35; 11:4; Ac 27:12, 34; 2Co 10:4; Eph 4:14, 29; Col 2:23; 2Ti 3:17; Tit 1:16; 1Pe 3:15; 2Pe 3:16; 1Jn 5:16, 17). Followed by the inf. with the neuter definite article *tó*, meaning in order that (Mt 5:28; 6:1; 13:30; 23:5; Mk 13:22; Eph 6:11; Jas 3:3).

(III) Sometimes used after verbs which express simply rest:

(A) Used of places, meaning at, by, in a place (Mk 2:2; 4:1; 5:11; 11:4; 14:54; Lk 19:37; Jn 18:16; 20:12; Rev 1:13).

(B) With persons, meaning with, by, among (Mt 13:56; 26:55; Mk 6:3; 14:49; Jn 1:1; 1Co 16:7; 2Co 1:12; Gal 1:18; 2:5; 4:18; 2Th 2:5; Phm 13).

(IV) In composition *prós* implies:

(A) Motion, direction, reference, meaning toward, to, at, as *prosérchomai* (4334), to come near; *prosdokáō* (4328), to expect, wait for; *proságō* (4317), to lead toward, to approach, bring near; *proseggízō* (4331), to approach near; *prosphilḗs* (4375), friendly toward, acceptable, lovely.

(B) Accession, addition, meaning thereto, over and above, moreover, further, as *prosaitéō* (4319), to ask besides, to beg; *prosapeiléō* (4324), to threaten further. Used intensively as *próspeinos* (4361), intensely hungry.

(C) Nearness, a being or remaining near, at, by, as *prosedreúō* (4332), to attend as a servant, wait on; *prosménō* (4357), remain in a place with someone, abide still.

Syn.: *epí* (1909), upon, at; *eis* (1519), to.

4315. προσάββατον, prosabbaton, *pros-ab´-bat-on*; from 4253 and 4521; a *fore-sabbath,* i.e. the *Sabbath-eve:*—day before the sabbath. Compare 3904.

4316. προσαγορεύω, prosagoreuō, *pros-ag-or-yoo´-o*; from 4314 and a derivative of 58 (meaning to *harangue*); to *address,* i.e. salute by *name:*—call.

From *prós* (4314), to, and *agoreúō* (n.f.), to address, which is from *agorá* (58), the marketplace, also the town square which provided a public platform for speakers. To address, greet. In the NT, to call by name, give a name to. Used only in Heb 5:10.

Syn.: *kaléō* (2564), to call, call a name; *onamázō* (3687), to name.

4317. προσάγω, prosagō, *pros-ag´-o*; from 4314 and 71; to *lead toward,* i.e. (transitive) to *conduct near* (*summon, present*), or (intransitive) to *approach:*—bring, draw near.

From *prós* (4314), to or toward, and *ágō* (71), to bring, come. To lead or conduct to someone, to bring near.

(I) To bring to (Lk 9:41; Ac 16:20); figuratively, to bring near to God, present before God (1Pe 3:18).

(II) To draw near, to approach (Ac 27:27).

Deriv.: *prosagōgé* (4318), access, approach.

Syn.: *anágō* (321), to lead or bring up to; *eiságō* (1521), to lead in, bring in; *epiphérō* (2018), to bring upon, bring forward; *prosérchomai* (4334), to come near, approach; *prosphérō* (4374), to bring to, approach.

4318. προσαγωγή, prosagōgē, *pros-ag-ogue-ay´*; from 4317 (compare 72); *admission:*—access.

Noun from *proságō* (4317), to bring near. A leading or bringing to. In the NT, approach, access, admission, used always of access to God (Ro 5:2; Eph 2:18; 3:12).

Syn.: *eísodos* (1529), entrance.

4319. προσαιτέω, prosaiteō, *pros-ahee-teh´-o*; from 4314 and 154; to *ask repeatedly* (*importune*), i.e. *solicit:*—beg.

From *prós* (4314), for, adding intensity, and *aitéō* (154), to ask, beg. To ask in addition, to demand besides. In the NT, to beg (Mk 10:46; Lk 18:35; Jn 9:8).

4320. προσαναβαίνω, prosanabainō, *pros-an-ab-ah´ee-no*; from 4314 and 305; to *ascend farther,* i.e. *be promoted* (*take an upper* [*more honourable*] *seat*):—go up.

4321. προσαναλίσκω, prosanaliskō, *pros-an-al-is´-ko*; from 4314 and 355; to *expend further:*—spend.

4322. προσαναπληρόω, prosanaplēroō, *pros-an-ap-lay-ro´-o*; from 4314 and 378; to *fill up further,* i.e. *furnish fully:*—supply.

From *prós* (4314), beside, meaning in addition to, and *anaplēróō* (378), to supply. To fill up by adding, to supply fully that which one lacks or needs (2Co 9:12; 11:9).

Syn.: *empíplēmi* (1705), to fill up; *epichorēgéō* (2023), to supply fully, abundantly.

4323. προσανατίθημι, prosanatithēmi, *pros-an-at-ith´-ay-mee*; from 4314 and 394; to *lay up in addition,* i.e. (middle and figurative) to *impart* or (by implication) to *consult:*—in conference add, confer.

4324. προσαπειλέω, prosapeileō, *pros-ap-i-leh´-o*; from 4314 and 546; to *menace additionally:*—threaten further.

4325. προσδαπανάω, prosdapanaō, *pros-dap-an-ah´-o*; from 4314 and 1159; to *expend additionally:*—spend more.

4326. προσδέομαι, prosdeomai, *pros-deh´-om-ahee*; from 4314 and 1189; to *require additionally,* i.e. *want further:*—need.

4327. προσδέχομαι, prosdechomai, *pros-dekh´-om-ahee*; from 4314 and 1209; to *admit* (to intercourse, hospitality, credence or [figurative] endurance); (by implication) to *await* (with confidence or patience):—accept, allow, look (wait) for, take.

From *prós* (4314), unto or for, and *déchomai* (1209), to receive or accept. To receive to oneself, to accept.

(I) Of things, figuratively, to admit, to allow (Ac 24:15; Heb 11:35); of evils, to put up with, endure (Heb 10:34).

(II) Of persons, to receive, to accept into one's presence and kindness (Lk 15:2; Ro 16:2; Php 2:29).

(III) Of things future, to wait for, to expect (Mk 15:43; Lk 2:25, 38; 12:36; 23:51; Ac 23:21; Tit 2:13; Jude 21).

Deriv.: *euprósdektos* (2144), acceptable.

Syn.: *apodéchomai* (588), to accept; *déchomai* (1209), to receive; *lambánō* (2983), to receive; *paralambánō* (3880), to receive from; *proslambánō* (4355), to welcome.

4328. προσδοκάω, prosdokaō, *pros-dok-ah´-o*; from 4314 and **δοκεύω**, *dokeuō* (to *watch*); by implication) *anticipate* (in thought, hope or fear); (by implication) to *await*:—(be in) expect (-ation), look (for), when looked, tarry, wait for.

From *prós* (4314), unto or for, and *dokeúō* (n.f.), to look for. To look for, to wait for.

(I) To expect one's coming (Mt 24:50; Lk 3:15; 12:46; Ac 28:6).

(II) To wait for with hope (Mt 11:3; Lk 1:21; 7:19, 20; 8:40; Ac 3:5; 10:24; 27:33; 28:6; 2Pe 3:12–14).

Deriv.: *prosdokía* (4329) looking for, expectation.

Syn.: *anaménō* (362), to wait for; *elpízō* (1679), to hope; *apekdéchomai* (553), to expect fully, look for.

4329. προσδοκία, prosdokia, *pros-dok-ee´-ah*; from 4328; *apprehension* (of evil); (by implication) *infliction* anticipated:—expectation, looking after.

Noun from *prosdokáō* (4328), to wait, expect. A looking for, an expectation, in the NT only of evils (Lk 21:26; Ac 12:11).

Syn.: *apokaradokía* (603), expectancy, eager longing; *ekdoché* (1561), expectation.

4330. προσεάω, proseaō, *pros-eh-ah´-o*; from 4314 and 1439; to *permit further* progress:—suffer.

4331. προσεγγίζω, proseggizō, *pros-eng-ghid´-zo*; from 4314 and 1448; to *approach near*:—come nigh.

From *prós* (4314), to, and *eggízō* (1448), to approach. To approach or come near to (Mk 2:4).

Syn.: *proságō* (4317), to draw near; *prosérchomai* (4334), to draw near.

4332. προσεδρεύω, prosedreuō, *pros-ed-ryoo´-o*; from a compound of 4314 and the base of 1476; to *sit near*, i.e. *attend* as a servant:—wait at.

4333. προσεργάζομαι, prosergazomai, *pros-er-gad´-zom-ahee*; from 4314 and 2038; to *work additionally*, i.e. (by implication) *acquire besides*:—gain.

4334. προσέρχομαι, proserchomai, *pros-er´-khom-ahee*; from 4314 and 2064 (including its alternate); to *approach*, i.e. (literal) *come near, visit*, or (figurative) *worship, assent to*:—(as soon as he) come (unto), come thereunto, consent, draw near, go (near, to, unto).

From *prós* (4314), to, and *érchomai* (2064), to come. To come to or near any place or person.

(I) Particularly, to come to, approach (Mt 4:3, 11; 8:5; Mk 1:31; 14:45; Lk 8:24; 10:34; 23:52; Jn 12:21; Ac 7:31; 9:1; 28:9; Heb 12:18, 22). With the expanded meaning of to visit, to have conversation with (Ac 10:28; 24:23).

(II) Figuratively:

(A) To come to God, draw near unto Him in prayer, sacrifice, worship, devotion of heart and life (Heb 4:16; 7:25; 11:6); to come to Christ (1Pe 2:4).

(B) To assent to, embrace, accept (1Ti 6:3).

Deriv.: *prosélutos* (4339), a stranger, foreigner.

Syn.: *paragínomai* (3854), to arrive, to be present; *proságō* (4317), to draw or lead near; *proseggízō* (4331), to approach, come near; *prosporeúomai* (4365), to come near to.

4335. προσευχή, proseuchē, *pros-yoo-khay´*; from 4336; *prayer* (*worship*); by implication an *oratory* (*chapel*):— × pray earnestly, prayer.

Noun from *proseúchomai* (4336), to offer prayer. Prayer, prayer to God.

(I) Particularly: in the singular (Mt 17:21; 21:13; 21:22; Mk 9:29; 11:17; Lk 6:12; 19:46; 22:45; Ac 1:14; 3:1; 6:4; 10:31; 12:5; Ro 12:12; 1Co 7:5; Eph 6:18; Php 4:6; Col 4:2; Jas 5:17); in the plural (Ac 2:42; 10:4; Ro 1:10; 15:30; Eph 1:16; Col 4:12; 1Th 1:2; 1Ti 2:1; 5:5; Phm 4, 22; 1Pe 3:7; 4:7; Rev 5:8; 8:3, 4).

(II) Spoken by metonymy for a house or a place of prayer (Ac 16:13, 16). Such places for social prayer and devotion were in the outskirts of those towns where the Jews were unable or not permitted to have a synagogue, and were usually near a river or the seashore for the convenience of ablution (to which the Jews were dedicated).

Syn.: *déesis* (1162), supplication; *paráklēsis* (3874), entreaty.

4336. προσεύχομαι, proseuchomai, *pros-yoo´-khom-ahee*; from 4314 and 2172; *to pray to* God, i.e. *supplicate, worship:*—pray (× earnestly, for), make prayer.

From the preposition *prós* (4314), to, and *eúchomai* (2172), to wish, pray. To pray to God, offer prayer.

(I) In the NT, *proseúchomai* is always directed toward God, whether stated or implied (Mt 6:5–7; 14:23; Mk 1:35; Lk 3:21; Ac 6:6; 1Co 11:4; 1Th 5:17; 1Ti 2:8; Jas 5:13, 18).

(II) The manner in which one prays is expressed either by the dative (1Co 11:5; 14:14, 15; Jas 5:17); or with *en* (1722), in (Eph 6:18; Jude 20).

(III) The object or thing prayed for is put after *hína* (2443), so that (Mt 24:20, neg.; Mk 13:18; 14:35, 38; 1Co 14:13; Php 1:9; Col 1:9), or expressed by the infinitive (Lk 22:40; Jas 5:17).

Deriv.: *proseuché* (4335), prayer.

Syn.: *aitéomai* (154), to ask, as from an inferior to a superior; *déomai* (1189), to make request for particular needs; *erōtáō* (2065), to ask.

4337. προσέχω, prosechō, *pros-ekh´-o*; from 4314 and 2192; (figurative) to *hold* the mind (3563 implication) *toward,* i.e. *pay attention to, be cautious about, apply oneself* to, *adhere to:*—(give) attend (-ance, -ance at, -ance to, unto), beware, be given to, give (take) heed (to, unto) have regard.

4338. προσηλόω, prosēloō, *pros-ay-lo´-o*; from 4314 and a derivative of 2247; to *peg to,* i.e. *spike* fast:—nail to.

4339. προσήλυτος, prosēlutos, *pros-ah´-lootos*; from the alternate of 4334; an *arriver* from a foreign region, i.e. (special) an *acceder* (*convert*) to Judaism ("*proselyte*"):—proselyte.

Noun from *prosérchomai* (4334), to come near, come to. One who comes to another country or people, a stranger, sojourner. In the NT, it is used in the later Jewish sense of the term, for a proselyte, a convert from Paganism to Judaism (Mt 23:15; Ac 2:10; 6:5; 13:43).

4340. πρόσκαιρος, proskairos, *pros´-kaheeros*; from 4314 and 2540; *for the occasion* only, i.e. *temporary:*—dur- [eth] for awhile, endure for a time, for a season, temporal.

4341. προσκαλέομαι, proskaleomai, *pros-kal-eh´-om-ahee*; middle from 4314 and 2564; to *call toward oneself,* i.e. *summon, invite:*—call (for, to, unto).

From *prós* (4314), to, and *kaléō* (2564), to call. To call someone to oneself, bid to come, to summon (Mt 10:1; 15:10, 32; 18:2, 32; 20:25; Mk 3:13, 23; 6:7; 7:14; 8:1, 34; 10:42; 12:43; 15:44; Lk 7:19; 15:26; 16:5; 18:16; Ac 5:40; 6:2; 13:7; 20:1; 23:17, 18, 23; Jas 5:14). Figuratively, to invite men to embrace the gospel (Ac 2:39). Also, to call one to an office or duty, to appoint, to choose (Ac 13:2; 16:10).

Syn.: *metakaléō* (3333), to summon hither, recall; *prosphōnéō* (4377), to call unto.

4342. προσκαρτερέω, proskartereō, *pros-karter-eh´-o*; from 4314 and 2594; to *be earnest toward,* i.e. (to a thing) to *persevere, be constantly* diligent, or (in a place) to *attend* assiduously all the exercises, or (to a person) to *adhere closely* to (as a servitor):—attend (give self) continually (upon), continue (in, instant in, with), wait on (continually).

From *prós* (4314), to, and *karteréō* (2594), to endure. To be strong or firm toward anything, to endure or persevere, to be continually with a person or work.

(I) Spoken of a work or business; to continue or persevere. (Ac 1:14; 2:42, 46; 6:4; Ro 12:12; 13:6; Col 4:2).

(II) Spoken of persons, to remain near, to wait upon, to be in readiness (Mk 3:9; Ac 8:13; 10:7).

Deriv.: *proskartérēsis* (4343), perseverance.

Syn.: *diateléō* (1300), to bring through to an end, to accomplish; *ménō* (3306), to remain; *diaménō* (1265), to continue throughout; *emménō* (1696), to remain in; *epiménō* (1961), to continue in; *para-ménō* (3887), to remain by or near; *prosménō* (4357), to remain with.

4343. προσκαρτέρησις, proskarterēsis, *pros-kar-ter´-ay-sis*; from 4342; *persistency:*—perseverance.

4344. προσκεφάλαιον, proskephalaion, *pros-kef-al´-ahee-on*; neuter of a presumed compound of 4314 and 2776; something *for the head,* i.e. a *cushion:*—pillow.

4345. προσκληρόω, **prosklēroō**, *pros-klay-ro´-o*; from 4314 and 2820; to *give a common lot to*, i.e. (figurative) to *associate with:*—consort with.

4346. πρόσκλισις, **prosklisis**, *pros´-klis-is*; from a compound of 4314 and 2827; a *leaning toward*, i.e. (figurative) *proclivity (favoritism):*—partiality.

4347. προσκολλάω, **proskollaō**, *pros-kol-lay´-o*; from 4314 and 2853; to *glue to*, i.e. (figurative) to *adhere:*—cleave, join (self).

4348. πρόσκομμα, **proskomma**, *pros´-kom-mah*; from 4350; a *stub*, i.e. (figurative) *occasion of apostasy:*—offence, stumbling (block, [-stone]).

4349. προσκοπή, **proskopē**, *pros-kop-ay´*; from 4350; a *stumbling*, i.e. (figurative and concrete) *occasion of sin:*—offence.

4350. προσκόπτω, **proskoptō**, *pros-kop´-to*; from 4314 and 2875; to *strike at*, i.e. *surge against* (as water); specially to *stub on*, i.e. *trip up* (literal or figurative):—beat upon, dash, stumble (at).

From *prós* (4314), to, against, and *kóptō* (2875), to cut, strike. To beat upon anything, to strike against.

(**I**) Generally, to beat against, as floods and winds against a house (Mt 7:27).

(**II**) Particularly, to strike the foot against anything (Mt 4:6; Lk 4:11); to stumble after striking the foot against anything (Jn 11:9, 10). Figuratively, to take offence at something, so as to fall into error and sin (Ro 9:32; 14:21; 1Pe 2:8).

Deriv.: *apróskopos* (677), void of offence, faultless; *próskomma* (4348), a stumbling block, offence, hindrance; *proskopḗ* (4349), stumbling block, offence.

Syn.: *ptaíō* (4417), to stumble; *skandalízō* (4624), to put a snare or stumbling block in the way.

4351. προσκυλίω, **proskuliō**, *pros-koo-lee´-o*; from 4314 and 2947; to *roll toward*, i.e. *block against:*—roll (to).

4352. προσκυνέω, **proskuneō**, *pros-koo-neh´-o*; from 4314 and a probable derivative of 2965 (meaning to *kiss*, like a dog *licking* his master's hand); to *fawn* or *crouch to*, i.e. (literal or figurative) *prostrate* oneself in homage (*do reverence to*, *adore*):—worship.

4353. προσκυνητής, **proskunētēs**, *pros-koo-nay-tace´*; from 4352; an *adorer:*—worshipper.

4354. προσλαλέω, **proslaleō**, *pros-lal-eh´-o*; from 4314 and 2980; to *talk to*, i.e. *converse with:*—speak to (with).

4355. προσλαμβάνω, **proslambanō**, *pros-lam-ban´-o*; from 4314 and 2983; to *take to* oneself, i.e. *use* (food), *lead* (aside), *admit* (to friendship or hospitality):—receive, take (unto).

4356. πρόσληψις, **proslēpsis**, *pros´-lape-sis*; from 4355; *admission:*—receiving.

4357. προσμένω, **prosmenō**, *pros-men´-o*; from 4314 and 3306; to *stay further*, i.e. *remain* in a place, with a person: (figurative) to *adhere to*, *persevere* in:—abide still, be with, cleave unto, continue in (with).

From *prós* (4314), to, with, and *ménō* (3306), to remain. To remain at a place (Ac 18:18; 1Ti 1:3); to remain or continue with a person (Mt 15:32; Mk 8:2). In a figurative sense, to remain faithful to someone (Ac 11:23); to continue in, i.e. to be constant in, to persevere (1Ti 5:5).

Syn.: *proskarteréō* (4342), to continue in, remain constant.

4358. προσορμίζω, **prosormizō**, *pros-or-mid´-zo*; from 4314 and a derivative of the same as 3730 (meaning to *tie* [*anchor*] or *lull*); to *moor to*, i.e. (by implication) *land at:*—draw to the shore.

4359. προσοφείλω, **prosopheilō**, *pros-of-i´-lo*; from 4314 and 3784; to *be indebted additionally:*—over besides.

4360. προσοχθίζω, **prosochthizō**, *pros-okh-thid´-zo*; from 4314 and a form of ὀχθέω, **ochtheō** (to *be vexed* with something irksome); to *feel indignant at:*—be grieved with.

4361. πρόσπεινος, **prospeinos**, *pros´-pi-nos*; from 4314 and the same as 3983; *hungering further*, i.e. *intensely hungry:*—very hungry.

4362. προσπήγνυμι, **prospēgnumi**, *pros-payg´-noo-mee*; from 4314 and 4078; to *fasten to*, i.e. (special) to *impale* (on a cross):—crucify.

4363. προσπίπτω, **prospiptō**, *pros-pip´-to*; from 4314 and 4098; to *fall toward*, i.e. (gently) *prostrate* oneself (in supplication or homage), or (violently) to *rush* upon (in storm):—beat upon, fall (down) at (before).

4364. προσποιέομαι, prospoieomai, *pros-poy-eh´-om-ahee*; middle from 4314 and 4160; to *do forward for oneself*, i.e. *pretend* (as if about to do a thing):—make as though.

4365. προσπορεύομαι, prosporeuomai, *pros-por-yoo´-om-ahee*; from 4314 and 4198; to *journey toward*, i.e. *approach* [not the same as 4313]:—go before.

4366. προσρήγνυμι, prosrēgnumi, *pros-rayg´-noo-mee*; from 4314 and 4486; to *tear toward*, i.e. *burst upon* (as a tempest or flood):—beat vehemently against (upon).

4367. προστάσσω, prostassō, *pros-tas´-so*; from 4314 and 5021; to *arrange toward*, i.e. (figurative) *enjoin*:—bid, command.

4368. προστάτις, prostatis, *pros-tat´-is*; feminine of a derivative of 4291; a *patroness*, i.e. *assistant*:—succourer.

4369. προστίθημι, prostithēmi, *pros-tith´-ay-mee*; from 4314 and 5087; to *place additionally*, i.e. *lay beside, annex, repeat*:—add, again, give more, increase, lay unto, proceed further, speak to any more.

4370. προστρέχω, prostrechō, *pros-trekh´-o*; from 4314 and 5143 (including its alternate); to *run toward*, i.e. *hasten* to meet or join:—run (thither to, to).

4371. προσφάγιον, prosphagion, *pros-fag´-ee-on*; neuter of a presumed derivative of a compound of 4314 and 5315; something *eaten in addition* to bread, i.e. a *relish* (specially *fish*; compare 3795):—meat.

4372. πρόσφατος, prosphatos, *pros´-fat-os*; from 4253 and a derivative of 4969; *previously (recently) slain (fresh)*, i.e. (figurative) *lately made*:—new.

4373. προσφάτως, prosphatōs, *pros-fat´-oce*; adverb from 4372; *recently*:—lately.

4374. προσφέρω, prospherō, *pros-fer´-o*; from 4314 and 5342 (including its alternate); to *bear toward*, i.e. *lead to, tender* (especially to God), *treat*:—bring (to, unto) deal with, do, offer (unto, up), present unto, put to.

4375. προσφιλής, prosphilēs, *pros-fee-lace´*; from a presumed compound of 4314 and 5368; *friendly toward*, i.e. *acceptable*:—lovely.

4376. προσφορά, prosphora, *pros-for-ah´*; from 4374; *presentation*; concretely an *oblation* (bloodless) or *sacrifice*:—offering (up).

4377. προσφωνέω, prosphōneō, *pros-fo-neh´-o*; from 4314 and 5455; to *sound toward*, i.e. *address, exclaim, summon*:—call unto, speak (un-) to.

4378. πρόσχυσις, proschusis, *pros´-khoo-sis*; from a compound of 4314 and χέω, *cheō* (to *pour*); a *shedding forth*, i.e. *affusion*:—sprinkling.

4379. προσψαύω, prospsauo, *pros-psow´-o*; from 4314 and ψαύω, *psauō* (to *touch*); to *impinge*, i.e. *lay a finger on* (in order to relieve):—touch.

4380. προσωποληπτέω, prosōpolēpteō, *proso-o-pol-ape-teh´-o*; from 4381; to *favour an individual*, i.e. *show partiality*:—have respect to persons.

4381. προσωπολήπτης, prosōpolēptēs, *proso-o-pol-ape´-tace*; from 4383 and 2983; an *accepter* of *a face* (*individual*), i.e. (special) one *exhibiting partiality*:—respecter of persons.

4382. προσωποληψία, prosōpolēpsia, *pros-o-pol-ape-see´-ah*; from 4381; *partiality*, i.e. *favoritism*:—respect of persons.

Noun which comes from *prosōpolēptéō* (4380), to show partiality which is from *prósō-pon* (4383), face, and *lambánō* (2983), to receive. A respecting of persons, partiality, favoritism (Ro 2:11; Eph 6:9; Col 3:25; Jas 2:1). This Greek word is found only in the NT.

4383. πρόσωπον, prosōpon, *pros´-o-pon*; from 4314 and ὤψ, *ōps* (the *visage*; from 3700); the *front* (as being *toward view*), i.e. the *countenance, aspect, appearance, surface*; by implication *presence, person*:—(outward) appearance, × before, countenance, face, fashion, (men's) person, presence.

Noun from *prós* (4314), toward, and *ōps* (n.f.), the eye or face, which is from *óptomai* (3700), to see. Literally the part toward, at, or around the eye. Hence, the face, countenance. **(I)** Particularly (Mt 6:16, 17; 17:2; 26:67; Mk 14:65; Lk 9:29; 22:64; 24:5; Ac 6:15; 2Co 3:7, 13,

18; 4:6; 11:20; Gal 1:22; Jas 1:23; Rev 4:7; 9:7; 10:1). Figuratively, to set the face toward, meaning to set forth with fixed purpose toward something (Lk 9:51, 53), to set the face against, meaning to oppose someone or something (1Pe 3:12). *Prósōpon* is used in antithesis to *kardía* (2588), heart, in 1Th 2:17, being separated "in face, not heart," meaning separated physically, but not in spirit or thought. In 2Co 5:12, boasting "in face and not in heart," meaning in external appearances and not in internal realities.

(II) Used by metonymy for presence, person:

(A) Adverbially: (1) from the face, meaning from the presence of someone (Ac 3:19; 5:41; 7:45; 2Th 1:9; Rev 6:16; 12:14; 20:11); (2) in the face, meaning in the presence of someone (Lk 2:31; Ac 2:28; 3:13; 2Co 2:10; 8:24); (3) before the face, meaning before the presence, spoken of messengers who go before someone to announce his coming (Mt 11:10; Mk 1:2; Lk 1:76; 7:27; 9:52; 10:1; Ac 13:24).

(B) As a verbal object: (1) to see the face of someone, meaning to see him, to converse with him (Col 2:1); (2) to behold the face of God, meaning to have access to Him, to be in His presence (Mt 18:10; Rev 22:4); (3) to see the face or receive the face of someone, meaning to regard the external appearance and become partial toward someone, to show favoritism (Mt 22:16; Mk 12:14; Lk 20:21; Gal 2:6).

(C) Once used in an absolute sense as in the later Gr., meaning a person (2Co 1:11, from many faces, meaning from many persons).

(III) Of things meaning face, surface: e.g., the face of the earth, meaning the whole earth (Lk 21:35; Ac 17:26). Hence, equal to the exterior or external appearance: e.g., the face of the sky (Mt 16:3; Lk 12:56); the face of a flower (Jas 1:11).

Deriv.: *prosōpolếptēs* (4381), one who shows partiality.

Syn.: *eídos* (1491), that which strikes the eye, is exposed to view, external appearance, form, shape.

4384. προτάσσω, **protassō**, *prot-as´-so*; from 4253 and 5021; to *pre-arrange*, i.e. *prescribe*:—before appoint.

From *pró* (4253), forth, and *tássō* (5021), to arrange, order. To arrange or set in order before or in front, to appoint before, spoken of times or

seasons being marked out beforehand. Used only in Ac 17:26.

Syn.: *proginốskō* (4267), to foreknow, to consider beforehand; *proetoimázō* (4282), to prepare before; *procheirízō* (4400), to appoint beforehand; *proorízō* (4309), to appoint or decree beforehand.

4385. προτείνω, **proteinō**, *prot-i´-no*; from 4253 and τείνω, *teinō* (to *stretch*); to *protend*, i.e. *tie prostrate* (for scourging):—bind.

4386. πρότερον, **proteron**, *prot´-er-on*; neuter of 4387 as adverb (with or without the article); *previously*:—before, (at the) first, former.

4387. πρότερος, **proteros**, *prot´-er-os*; comparative of 4253; *prior* or *previous*:—former.

4388. προτίθεμαι, **protithemai**, *prot-ith´-em-ahee*; middle from 4253 and 5087; to *place before*, i.e. (for oneself) to *exhibit*; (to oneself) to *propose* (*determine*):—purpose, set forth.

From *pró* (4253), before, forth, and *títhēmi* (5087), to place. To set before someone. In the NT, only in the middle *protíthemai*. To propose, set forth or before the eyes, publicly, for all to see (Ro 3:25); to propose to oneself, to purpose, to plan beforehand (Ro 1:13; Eph 1:9).

Deriv.: *próthesis* (4286), a setting forth, a purpose.

Syn.: *bouleúō* (1011), to resolve, determine, purpose; *boúlomai* (1014), to will, be disposed, intend; *thélō* (2309), to desire, to will.

4389. προτρέπομαι, **protrepomai**, *prot-rep´-om-ahee*; middle from 4253 and the base of 5157; to *turn forward* for oneself, i.e. *encourage*:—exhort.

4390. προτρέχω, **protrechō**, *prot-rekh´-o*; from 4253 and 5143 (including its alternate); to *run forward*, i.e. *outstrip*, *precede*:—outrun, run before.

4391. προϋπάρχω, **proüparchō**, *pro-oop-ar´-kho*; from 4253 and 5225; to *exist before*, i.e. (adverb) to *be* or *do* something *previously*:— + be before (-time).

4392. πρόφασις, **prophasis**, *prof´-as-is*; from a compound of 4253 and 5316; an *outward showing*, i.e. *pretext*:—cloke, colour, pretence, show.

4393. προφέρω, propherō, *prof-er´-o*; from 4253 and 5342; to *bear forward,* i.e. *produce:*—bring forth.

4394. προφητεία, prophēteia, *prof-ay-ti´-ah*; from 4396 ("*prophecy*"); *prediction* (scriptural or other):—prophecy, prophesying.

Noun from *prophēteúō* (4395), to prophesy. A prophesying or prophecy.

(I) Particularly prediction, the foretelling of future events, including the declarations, exhortations, and warnings uttered by the prophets while acting under divine influence; of the prophecies of the OT (Mt 13:14; 2Pe 1:20, 21); the revelations and warnings of the Book of Revelation (Rev 1:3; 22:7, 10, 18, 19). In 1Ti 1:18; 4:14, *prophēteía* seems to refer to the prophetic revelations or directions of the Holy Spirit by which persons were designated as officers and teachers in the primitive church.

(II) Prophecy, meaning the prophetic office, the prophetic gift, spoken in the NT of the special spiritual gift imparted to the teachers of the early church (Ro 12:6; 1Co 12:10; 13:2, 8; 14:22).

(III) By metonymy, the act of prophesying, the exercise of the prophetic office, the acting as an ambassador of God and the interpreter of His mind and will (Rev 11:6). Specifically the exercise of the prophetic gift or charisma in the early church (1Co 14:6; 1Th 5:20).

Syn.: *apokálupsis* (602), revelation.

4395. προφητεύω, prophēteuō, *prof-ate-yoo´-o*; from 4396; to *foretell* events, *divine, speak* under *inspiration, exercise* the prophetic *office:*—prophesy.

From *prophḗtēs* (4396), prophet. To prophesy.

(I) Particularly, to foretell future events, to predict, often representing the idea from the OT of exhorting, reproving, threatening, and everything spoken by the prophets while they were acting under the divine influence as ambassadors of God and as interpreters of His mind and will. Spoken of the OT prophets (Mt 11:13; 15:7; Mk 7:6; 1Pe 1:10; Jude 14), and of the NT prophets (Lk 1:67; Rev 10:11; 11:3). See also Ac 2:17, 18. Spoken once of the high priest, with whose office the gift of prophecy was supposed to be connected (Jn 11:51). Spoken also of false prophets (Mt 7:22). Spoken in mockery by the soldiers commanding Jesus to prophesy

and identify who had hit Him while He was blindfolded (Mt 26:68; Mk 14:65; Lk 22:64).

(II) Specifically of the prophetic gift imparted by the Holy Spirit to the early Christians (Ac 19:6; 21:9; 1Co 11:4, 5; 13:9; 14:1, 3–5, 24, 31, 39).

Deriv.: *prophēteía* (4394), a prophecy.

Syn.: *apokalúptō* (601), to reveal; *prolégō* (4302), to foretell.

4396. προφήτης, prophḗtēs, *prof-ay´-tace*; from a compound of 4253 and 5346; a *foreteller* ("*prophet*"); (by analogy) an *inspired speaker*; by extension a *poet:*—prophet.

Noun from *próphēmi* (n.f.), to tell beforehand, which is from *pró* (4253), before or forth, and *phēmí* (5346), to tell. A prophet, a foreteller of future events, also an interpreter. In the NT *prophḗtēs* corresponds to the person who in the OT spoke under divine influence and inspiration. This included the foretelling of future events and the exhorting, reproving, and threatening of individuals or nations as the ambassador of God and as the interpreter of His will to men (Eze 2). Hence the prophet spoke not his own thoughts but what he received from God, retaining, however, his own consciousness and self-possession (Ex 7:1; 2Pe 1:20, 21; especially 1Co 14:32).

(I) In the NT as spoken of the prophets of the OT:

(A) Used particularly of Isaiah (Mt 1:22; 3:3; Lk 3:4; Jn 1:23); Jeremiah (Mt 2:17); Joel (Ac 2:16); Micah (Mt 2:5); Jonah (Mt 12:39; Lk 11:29); Zechariah (Mt 21:4); Daniel (Mt 24:15; Mk 13:14); Samuel (Ac 13:20); David (Ac 2:30); Elisha (Lk 4:27); Asaph (Mt 13:35); Balaam (2Pe 2:16). In the plural and generally (Mt 2:23; 5:12; 23:29–31, 34, 37; Mk 8:28; Lk 1:70; Ro 1:2; Heb 1:1; Jas 5:10; 1Pe 1:10).

(B) Spoken by metonymy of the prophetic books of the OT (Mt 26:56); generally (Mt 5:17; Mk 1:2; Lk 16:29, 31; 24:27, 44; Ac 8:28; 28:23; Ro 3:21); of the doctrines contained in the prophetic books (Mt 7:12; 22:40; Ac 26:27).

(II) Spoken generally of persons acting by divine influence as prophets and ambassadors of God under the new dispensation, equivalent to a teacher sent from God (Mt 10:41; 13:57; Mk 6:4; Lk 4:24; 13:33; Jn 7:52; Rev 11:10; 16:6; 18:20, 24); specifically of John the Baptist (Mt 11:9; 14:5; Mk 11:32; Lk 1:76; 20:6); of Jesus

(Mt 21:11, 46; Lk 7:16; 24:19; Jn 9:17); the Messiah as a prophet coming into the world (Jn 1:21, 25; 6:14).

(III) Spoken specifically of those who possessed the prophetic gift or charisma imparted by the Holy Spirit to the early churches. Prophets were a class of instructors or preachers who were next in rank to the apostles and before the teachers (1Co 12:28). Like the apostles, however, they did not remain in one place as the teachers did. They seem to have differed from the teachers in that while the latter spoke in a calm, connected, didactic discourse, adapted to instruct and enlighten the hearers, the prophets spoke more from the impulse of sudden inspiration, from the light of a sudden revelation at the moment, as indicated in 1Co 14:30. It seems that this discourse was probably more adapted by means of powerful exhortations to awaken the feeling and consciousness of the hearers. The idea of speaking from an immediate revelation seems here to be fundamental, as relating either to future events or to the mind of the Spirit in general. See also Ac 11:27; see 13:1; 1Co 12:28, 29; 14:29, 32, 37; Eph 2:20; 3:5; 4:11).

(IV) Spoken once in the Greek secular sense of a spokesman of the gods (Tit 1:12).

Deriv.: *prophēteúō* (4395), to prophesy; *prophētikós* (4397), prophetic; *pseudoprophḗtēs* (5578), a false prophet.

4397. προφητικός, prophētikos, *prof-ay-tik-os´*; from 4396; *pertaining to a foreteller* (*"prophetic"*):—of prophecy, of the prophets.

4398. προφῆτις, prophētis, *prof-ay´-tis*; feminine of 4396; a *female foreteller* or an *inspired woman*:—prophetess.

4399. προφθάνω, prophthano, *prof-than´-o*; from 4253 and 5348; to *get an earlier start of*, i.e. *anticipate*:—prevent.

4400. προχειρίζομαι, procheirizomai, *prokh-i-rid´-zom-ahee*; middle from 4253 and a derivative of 5495; to *handle for oneself in advance*, i.e. (figurative) to *purpose*:—choose, make.

4401. προχειροτονέω, procheirotoneō, *prokh-i-rot-on-eh´-o*; from 4253 and 5500; to *elect in advance*:—choose before.

4402. Πρόχορος, Prochoros, *prokh´-or-os*; from 4253 and 5525; *before* the *dance*; *Prochorus*, a Christian:—Prochorus.

4403. πρύμνα, prumna, *proom´-nah*; feminine of πρυμνύς, *prumnus* (*hindmost*); the *stern* of a ship:—hinder part, stern.

4404. πρωΐ, proï, *pro-ee´*; adverb from 4253; at *dawn*; by implication the *day-break* watch:—early (in the morning), (in the) morning.

4405. πρωΐα, prōïa, *pro-ee´-ah*; feminine of a derivative of 4404 as noun; *day-dawn*:—early, morning.

4406. πρώϊμος, prōïmos, *pro´-ee-mos*; from 4404; *dawning*, i.e. (by analogy) *autumnal* (showering, the first of the rainy season):—early.

4407. πρωϊνός, prōïnos, *pro-ee-nos´*; from 4404; pertaining to the *dawn*, i.e. *matutinal*:—morning.

4408. πρώρα, prōra, *pro´-ra*; feminine of a presumed derivative of 4253 as noun; the *prow*, i.e. forward part of a vessel:—forepart (-ship).

4409. πρωτεύω, prōteuō, *prote-yoo´-o*; from 4413; to *be first* (in rank or influence):—have the preeminence.

4410. πρωτοκαθεδρία, prōtokathedria, *pro-tok-ath-ed-ree´-ah*; from 4413 and 2515; a *sitting first* (in the front row), i.e. *preeminence* in council:—chief (highest, uppermost) seat.

4411. πρωτοκλισία, prōtoklisia, *pro-tok-lis-ee´-ah*; from 4413 and 2828; a *reclining first* (in the place of honour) at the dinner-bed, i.e. *preeminence* at meals:—chief (highest, uppermost) room.

4412. πρῶτον, prōton, *pro´-ton*; neuter of 4413 as adverb (with or without 3588); *firstly* (in time, place, order, or importance):—before, at the beginning, chiefly, (at, at the) first (of all).

The neuter of *prṓtos* (4413), first, used as an adverb. First.

(I) Particularly of place, order, time, usually without the article.

(A) Generally (Mt 17:10, 11; Mk 7:27; Lk 9:59, 61; Jn 18:13; Ac 7:12; 15:14; 1Co 11:18; 1Pe 4:17).

(B) Emphatically meaning first of all, before all (Mt 23:26; Ac 13:46; Ro 1:8).

(C) In division or distribution, as referring to a series or succession of circumstances and followed by other adverb of order or time expressed or implied: "First apostles, secondarily ..." (1Co 12:28). See also Mt 5:24; 7:5; Mk 3:27; 4:28; Lk 6:42; 1Th 4:16; Jas 3:17.

(D) Rarely with the article *tó próton*, the first, at first, formerly (Jn 10:40; 12:16; 19:39).

(II) Figuratively of dignity or importance, first, first of all, chiefly, especially (Mt 6:33; Ro 3:2; 1Ti 2:1; 2Pe 1:20; 3:3).

4413. πρῶτος, prōtos, *pro´-tos*; contracted superlative of 4253; *foremost* (in time, place, order or importance):—before, beginning, best, chief (-est), first (of all), former.

Adjective, the superlative of *pró* (4253), forward. Foremost, hence first, the first.

(I) Generally as an adj. spoken of place, order, time. First (Mt 20:8, 10; 21:36; 26:17; Mk 14:12; 16:9; Lk 2:2; Ac 1:1; 12:10; 1Co 15:3, 45; Eph 6:2; Php 1:5; Heb 9:2, 6, 8; Rev 1:17; 4:1, 7; 8:7). *Prôtos* sometimes takes on the idea of former, that which used to be (Mt 12:45; 1Ti 5:12; 2Pe 2:20; Rev 2:4; 21:4). In this respect *prôtos* stands in direct opposition to *kainós* (2537), qualitatively new (Heb 8:13; Rev 21:1).

(II) In an adverbial sense, first, i.e. in the first place (Mt 10:2; Jn 1:41; 8:7; Ac 26:23; Ro 10:19; 1Jn 4:19). Used for the comparative *próteros*, before (Jn 1:15, 30).

(III) Figuratively of rank or dignity, meaning first in importance (Mt 20:27; 22:38; Mk 6:21; 10:44; 12:28–30; Lk 15:22; 19:47; Ac 13:50; 16:12; 17:4; 28:7, 17; Eph 6:2; 1Ti 1:15). Contrasted with *éschatos* [2078], last, in expressions that state that the first shall be last and the last shall be first, meaning those who seem or claim to be first shall be last (Mt 19:30; 20:16; Mk 10:31; Lk 13:30).

Deriv.: *deuteróprotos* (1207), the second after the first; *prōteúō* (4409), to be first; *prōtokathedría* (4410), the first seat or the best seat; *prōtoklisía* (4411), the first place; *próton* (4412), first, at first; *prōtostátēs* (4414), a leader or captain; *prōtótokos* (4416), firstborn, chief in rank, heir.

Syn.: *archē* (746), beginning.

4414. πρωτοστάτης, prōtostatēs, *pro-tos-tat´-ace*; from 4413 and 2476; one *standing first* in the ranks, i.e. a *captain* (*champion*):—ringleader.

4415. πρωτοτόκια, prōtotokia, *pro-tot-ok´-ee-ah*; from 4416; *primogeniture* (as a privilege):—birthright.

4416. πρωτοτόκος, prōtotokos, *pro-tot-ok´-os*; from 4413 and the alternate of 5088; *firstborn* (usually as noun, literal or figurative):—firstbegotten (-born).

Noun from *prôtos* (4413), first, and *tíktō* (5088), to bear, bring forth. Firstborn, preeminent.

(I) Particularly the firstborn of a father or mother (Mt 1:25; Lk 2:7).

(II) Figuratively, the firstborn in the sense of the chief one, the one highly distinguished, so of Christ, as the beloved Son of God before the creation of the world (Col 1:15 [cf. v. 16]; Heb 1:6 [cf. v. 5]), or in relation to His followers (Ro 8:29). Or, as the first to rise from the dead, the leader and prince of those who shall arise (Col 1:18; Rev 1:5).

(III) Firstborn of the saints in heaven, probably those formerly highly distinguished on earth by the favour and love of God, such as patriarchs, prophets, apostles (Heb 12:23).

Deriv.: *prōtotókia* (4415), the rights of the firstborn.

4417. πταίω, ptaiō, *ptah´-yo*; a form of 4098; to *trip*, i.e. (figurative) to *err, sin, fail* (of salvation):—fall, offend, stumble.

4418. πτέρνα, pterna, *pter´-nah*; of uncertain derivative; the *heel* (figurative):—heel.

4419. πτερύγιον, pterugion, *pter-oog´-ee-on*; neuter of a presumed derivative of 4420; a *winglet*, i.e. (figurative) *extremity* (top corner):—pinnacle.

4420. πτέρυξ, pterux, *pter´-oox*; from a derivative of 4072 (meaning a *feather*); a *wing*:—wing.

4421. πτηνόν, ptēnon, *ptay-non´*; contracted from 4071; a *bird*:—bird.

4422. πτοέω, ptoeō, *pto-eh´-o*; probably akin to the alternate of 4098 (through the idea of causing to *fall*) or to 4072 (through that of causing to *fly* away); to *scare*:—frighten.

4423. πτόησις, ptoēsis, *pto´-ay-sis*; from 4422; *alarm*:—amazement.

4424. Πτολεμαΐς, Ptolemaïs, *ptol-em-ah-is´*; from **Πτολεμαῖος** *Ptolemaios* (*Ptolemy*, after whom it was named); *Ptolemaïs*, a place in Palestine:—Ptolemais.

4425. πτύον, ptuon, *ptoo´-on*; from 4429; a *winnowing-fork* (as *scattering* like spittle):—fan.

4426. πτύρω, pturō, *ptoo´-ro*; from a presumed derivative of 4429 (and thus akin to 4422); to *frighten*:—terrify.

4427. πτύσμα, ptusma, *ptoos´-mah*; from 4429; *saliva*:—spittle.

4428. πτύσσω, ptussō, *ptoos´-so*; probably akin to πετάννυμι, *petannumi* (to *spread*; and thus apparently allied to 4072 through the idea of *expansion*, and to 4429 through that of *flattening*; compare 3961); to *fold*, i.e. *furl* a scroll:—close.

4429. πτύω, ptuō, *ptoo´-o*; a primary verb (compare 4428); to *spit*:—spit.

4430. πτῶμα, ptōma, *pto´-mah*; from the alternate of 4098; a *ruin*, i.e. (special) lifeless *body* (*corpse, carrion*):—dead body, carcase, corpse.

4431. πτῶσις, ptōsis, *pto´-sis*; from the alternate of 4098; a *crash*, i.e. *downfall* (literal or figurative):—fall.

4432. πτωχεία, ptōcheia, *pto-khi´-ah*; from 4433; *beggary*, i.e. *indigence* (literal or figurative):—poverty.

4433. πτωχεύω, ptōcheuō, *pto-khyoo´-o*; from 4434; to *be a beggar*, i.e. (by implication) to *become indigent* (figurative):—become poor.

4434. πτωχός, ptōchos, *pto-khos´*; from πτώσσω, *ptōssō* (to *crouch*; akin to 4422 and the alternate of 4098); a *beggar* (as *cringing*), i.e. *pauper* (strictly denoting absolute or public *mendicancy*, although also used in a qualified or relative sense; whereas 3993 properly means only *straitened* circumstances in private), literal (often as noun) or figurative (*distressed*):—beggar (-ly), poor.

Adjective from *ptōssō* (n.f.), to crouch, cower like a beggar. Poor and helpless.

(I) Particularly and often as substantive:

(A) A poor, helpless man and therefore a beggar (Lk 14:13, 21; 16:20, 22; Jn 9:8). Figuratively (Rev 3:17).

(B) In the plural, the poor, meaning the needy, those destitute of the necessities of life and subsisting on the alms from others (Mt 19:21; 26:9, 11; Mk 10:21; 14:5, 7; Lk 6:20;

18:22; 19:8; Jn 12:5, 6, 8; 13:29; Sept.: Est 9:22; Pr 28:27; 31:20).

(C) Generally, poor, needy, contrasted with *pénēs* (3993), one who may be poor but earns his bread by daily labour; also spoken of true poverty, as opposed to the rich, without the idea of begging (Mk 12:42, 43; Lk 21:3; Ro 15:26; 2Co 6:10; Gal 2:10; Jas 2:2, 3, 5, 6; Rev 13:16).

(II) By implication, poor, low, humble, of low estate, including also the idea of being afflicted, distressed (Mt 11:5; Lk 4:18). Figuratively in Mt 5:3, "poor in spirit" means those who recognize their spiritual helplessness.

(III) Figuratively, of things worthless, poor, imperfect (Gal 4:9).

Deriv.: *ptōcheía* (4432), poverty, want, helplessness; *ptocheúō* (4433), to be or become poor.

Syn.: *endeés* (1729), lacking, needy.

4435. πυγμή, pugmē, *poog-may´*; from a primary πύξ, *pux* (the *fist* as a weapon); the clenched *hand*, i.e. (only in dative as adverb) *with the fist* (hard *scrubbing*):—oft.

4436. Πύθων, Puthōn, *poo´-thone*; from Πυθώ, *Puthō* (the name of the region where Delphi, the seat of the famous *oracle*, was located); a *Python*, i.e. (by analogy with the supposed *diviner* there) *inspiration* (*soothsaying*):—divination.

4437. πυκνός, puknos, *pook-nos´*; from the same as 4635; *clasped* (*thick*), i.e. (figurative) *frequent*; neuter plural (as adverb) *frequently*:—often (-er).

4438. πυκτέω, pukteō, *pook-teh´-o*; from a derivative of the same as 4435; to *box* (with the fist), i.e. *contend* (as a boxer) at the games (figurative):—fight.

4439. πύλη, pulē, *poo´-lay*; apparently a primary word; a *gate*, i.e. the leaf or wing of a folding *entrance* (literal or figurative):—gate.

4440. πυλών, pulōn, *poo-lone´*; from 4439; a *gateway, door-way* of a building or city; by implication a *portal* or *vestibule*:—gate, porch.

4441. πυνθάνομαι, punthanomai, *poonthan´-om-ahee*; middle prolonged from a primary πύθω, *puthō* (which occurs only as an alternate in certain tenses); to *question*, i.e. *ascertain* by inquiry (as a matter of *information* merely; and thus differing from 2065, which properly means a *request* as a favour; and from 154, which is strictly a *demand* of something due; as well as from 2212, which implies a *search* for something hidden; and from 1189, which involves the idea of urgent *need*); by implication to *learn* (by casual intelligence):—ask, demand, enquire, understand.

4442. πῦρ, pur, *poor*; a primary word; *"fire"* (literal or figurative, specially *lightning*):—fiery, fire.

4443. πυρά, pura, *poo-rah'*; from 4442; a *fire* (concrete):—fire.

4444. πύργος, purgos, *poor'-gos*; apparently a primary word (*"burgh"*); a *tower* or *castle*:—tower.

4445. πυρέσσω, puressō, *poo-res'-so*; from 4443; to *be on fire*, i.e. (special) to *have a fever*:—be sick of a fever.

4446. πυρετός, puretos, *poo-ret-os'*; from 4445; *inflamed*, i.e. (by implication) *feverish* (as noun, *fever*):—fever.

4447. πύρινος, purinos, *poo'-ree-nos*; from 4443; *fiery*, i.e. (by implication) *flaming*:—of fire.

4448. πυρόω, puroō, *poo-ro'-o*; from 4442; to *kindle*, i.e. (passive) to *be ignited, glow* (literal), *be refined* (by implication), or (figurative) to *be inflamed* (with anger, grief, lust):—burn, fiery, be on fire, try.

4449. πυρράζω, purrhazō, *poor-hrad'-zo*; from 4450; to *redden* (intransitive):—be red.

4450. πυρρός, purrhos, *poor-hros'*; from 4442; *fire-like*, i.e. (special) *flame-coloured*:—red.

4451. πύρωσις, purōsis, *poo'-ro-sis*; from 4448; *ignition*, i.e. (special) *smelting* (figurative, *conflagration, calamity* as a *test*):—burning, trial.

4452. -πω, -pō, *po*; another form of the base of 4458; an enclitic particle of indefiniteness; *yet, even*; used only in comparative. See 3369, 3380, 3764, 3768, 4455.

4453. πωλέω, pōleō, *po-leh'-o*; probably ultimately from πέλομαι, pelomai (to *be busy*, to *trade*); to *barter* (as a *pedlar*), i.e. to *sell*:—sell, whatever is sold.

4454. πῶλος, pōlos, *po'-los*; apparently a primary word; a *"foal"* or *"filly,"* i.e. (special) a *young ass*:—colt.

4455. πώποτε, pōpote, *po'-pot-e*; from 4452 and 4218; *at any time*, i.e. (with negative particle) *at no time*:—at any time, + never (... to any man), + yet never man.

4456. πωρόω, pōroō, *po-ro'-o*; apparently from πῶρος, pōros (a kind of *stone*); to *petrify*, i.e. (figurative) to *indurate* (render stupid or callous):—blind, harden.

From *pôros* (n.f.), a kind of stone. The verb means to harden, make hard like a stone, or callous and insensible to the touch. In the NT only figuratively, to harden, to make dull or stupid. Spoken of the heart being hardened (Mk 6:52; 8:17; Jn 12:40). Spoken of the mind being hardened (2Co 3:14). Its use in Ro 11:7 seems to be an instance where both the heart and the understanding were hardened.

Deriv.: *pôrōsis* (4457), hardening.
Syn.: *sklērúnō* (4645), to harden.

4457. πώρωσις, pōrōsis, *po'-ro-sis*; from 4456; *stupidity* or *callousness*:—blindness, hardness.

Noun from *pōróō* (4456), to harden, petrify, render insensitive. A hardening. In the NT, used only figuratively, hardness of heart or mind, insensitivity (Mk 3:5; Ro 11:25; Eph 4:18).
Syn.: *sklērótēs* (4643), hardness. Also *sklērokardía* (4641), hardness of heart.

4458. πώς, pōs, *poce*; adverb from the base of 4225; an enclitic particle of indefiniteness of manner; *somehow* or *anyhow*; used only in comparative:—haply, by any (some) means, perhaps. See 1513, 3381. Compare 4459.

4459. πῶς, pōs, *poce*; adverb from the base of 4226; an interrogative particle of manner; *in what way?* (sometimes the question is indirect, *how?*); also as exclamation, *how much!*:—how, after (by) what manner (means), that. [*Occasionally unexpressed in English.*]

P (Rho)
NT Numbers 4460–4517

4460. **'Ραάβ, Rhaab,** *hrah-ab´*; of Hebrew origin [7343]; *Raab* (i.e. *Rachab*), a Canaanitess:—Rahab. See also 4477.

4461. **ῥαββί, rhabbi,** *hrab-bee´*; of Hebrew origin [7227 with pronoun suffix]; *my master,* i.e. *Rabbi,* as an official title of honour:—Master, Rabbi.

4462. **ῥαββονί, rhabboni,** *hrab-bon-ee´*; or **ῥαββουνί, rhabbouni,** *hrab-boo-nee´*; of Chaldee origin; corresponding to 4461:—Lord, Rabboni.

4463. **ῥαβδίζω, rhabdizo,** *hrab-did´-zo*; from 4464; to *strike with a stick,* i.e. *bastinado:*—beat (with rods).

4464. **ῥάβδος, rhabdos,** *hrab´-dos*; from the base of 4474; a *stick* or *wand* (as a *cudgel,* a *cane* or a *baton* of royalty):—rod, sceptre, staff.

4465. **ῥαβδοῦχος, rhabdouchos,** *hrab-doo´-khos*; from 4464 and 2192; a *rod-* (the Latin *fasces*) *holder,* i.e. a Roman *lictor* (*constable* or *executioner*):—sergeant.

4466. **'Ραγαῦ, Rhagau,** *hrag-ow´*; of Hebrew origin [7466]; *Ragau* (i.e. *Reü*), a patriarch:—Ragau.

4467. **ῥαδιούργημα, rhaidiourgema,** *hrad-ee-oorg´-ay-mah*; from a compound of **ῥᾳδιος,** *rhaidios* (*easy,* i.e. *reckless*) and 2041; *easy-going behaviour,* i.e. (by extension) a *crime:*—lewdness.

4468. **ῥᾳδιουργία, rhaidiourgia,** *hrad-ee-oorg-ee´-a*; from the same as 4467; *recklessness,* i.e. (by extension) *malignity:*—mischief.

4469. **ῥακά, rhaka,** *hrak-ah´*; of Chaldee or [compare 7386]; O *empty* one, i.e. thou *worthless* (as a term of utter vilification):—Raca.

4470. **ῥάκος, rhakos,** *hrak´-os*; from 4486; a *"rag,"* i.e. *piece* of cloth:—cloth.

4471. **'Ραμᾶ, Rhama,** *hram-ah´*; of Hebrew origin [7414]; *Rama* (i.e. *Ramah*), a place in Palestine:—Rama.

4472. **ῥαντίζω, rhantizo,** *hran-tid´-zo*; from a derivative of **ῥαίνω,** *rhaino* (to *sprinkle*); to *render besprinkled,* i.e. *asperse* (ceremonial or figurative):— sprinkle.

From *rhaíno* (n.f.), to sprinkle. To sprinkle. Spoken of the water of purification made from the ashes of a heifer, and compared to the cleansing power of Christ's blood (Heb 9:13; cf. Nu 19). It is also spoken of the blood of sacrificial animals sprinkled for purification, and compared with the atoning power of Christ's blood, the blood of the new covenant (Heb 9:19, 21; cf. Ex 24:6, 8). Figuratively, spoken of our hearts being sprinkled with the blood of Christ in cleansing from an impure conscience (Heb 10:22). The purpose of describing Christ's redemptive work in terms of Levitical ritualism is to explain how Christ in His atoning death (and triumphant resurrection) accomplished what these things represented, their essential significance, and to say that those rituals are therefore irrelevant and unnecessary. Calvary was both the altar and the mercy seat; Christ was both the priest and the sacrifice.

Deriv.: *rhantismós* (4473), sprinkling.

4473. **ῥαντισμός, rhantismos,** *hran-tis-mos´*; from 4472; *aspersion* (ceremonial or figurative):—sprinkling.

Noun from *rhantízo* (4472), to sprinkle. Sprinkling. In the NT, it is used to identify the blood of Christ as the "blood of sprinkling," corresponding to the OT blood of sprinkling (Heb 12:24; 1Pe 1:2 [cf. Nu 19:9, 13, 20, 21]), even to the blood of Abel's righteous sacrifice, which pointed forward to the sacrifice made by Christ.

4474. **ῥαπίζω, rhapizo,** *hrap-id´-zo*; from a derivative of a primary **ῥέπω,** *rhepo* (to *let fall,* "*rap*"); to *slap*:—smite (with the palm of the hand). Compare 5180.

4475. ῥάπισμα, rhapisma, *hrap´-is-mah*; from 4474; a *slap*:—(+ strike with the) palm of the hand, smite with the hand.

4476. ῥαφίς, rhaphis, *hraf-ece´*; from a primary ῥάπτω, *rhaptō* (to *sew*; perhaps rather akin to the base of 4474 through the idea of *puncturing*); a *needle*:—needle.

4477. Ῥαχάβ, Rhachab, *hrakh-ab´*; from the same as 4460; *Rachab*, a Canaanitess:—Rachab.

4478. Ῥαχήλ, Rhachēl, *hrakh-ale´*; of Hebrew origin [7354]; *Rachel*, the wife of Jacob:—Rachel.

4479. Ῥεβέκκα, Rhebekka, *hreb-bek´-kah*; of Hebrew origin [7259]; *Rebecca* (i.e. *Ribkah*), the wife of Isaac:—Rebecca.

4480. ῥέδα, rheda, *hred´-ah*; of Latin origin; a *rheda*, i.e. four-wheeled *carriage* (*wagon* for riding):—chariot.

4481. Ῥεμφάν, Rhemphan, *hrem-fan´*; by incorrect transliteration for a word of Hebrew origin [3594]; *Remphan* (i.e. *Kijun*), an Egyptian idol:—Remphan.

4482. ῥέω, rheō, *hreh´-o*; a primary verb; for some tenses of which a prolonged form ῥεύω, *rheuō, hryoo´-o*, is used; to *flow* ("*run*," as water):—flow.

4483. ῥέω, rheō, *hreh´-o*; for certain tenses of which a prolonged form ἐρέω, *ereō, er-eh´-o*, is used; and both as alternate for 2036; perhaps akin (or identical) with 4482 (through the idea of *pouring* forth); to *utter*, i.e. *speak* or *say*:—command, make, say, speak (of). Compare 3004.

4484. Ῥήγιον, Rhēgion, *hrayg´-ee-on*; of Latin origin; *Rhegium*, a place in Italy:—Rhegium.

4485. ῥῆγμα, rhēgma, *hrayg´-mah*; from 4486; something *torn*, i.e. a *fragment* (by implication and abstract a *fall*):—ruin.

4486. ῥήγνυμι, rhēgnumi, *hrayg´-noo-mee*; or ῥήσσω, *rhēssō, hrace´-so*; both prolonged forms of ῥήκω, *rhēko* (which appears only in certain forms, and is itself probably a strengthened form of ἄγνυμι, *agnumi*; [see in 2608]); to

"*break*," "*wreck*" or "*crack*," i.e. (especially) to *sunder* (by *separation* of the parts; 2608 being its intensive [with the preposition in comparative], and 2352 a *shattering* to minute fragments; but not a *reduction* to the constituent particles, like 3089) or *disrupt, lacerate*; by implication to *convulse* (with *spasms*); (figurative) to *give vent* to joyful emotions:—break (forth), burst, rend, tear.

4487. ῥῆμα, rhēma, *hray´-mah*; from 4483; an *utterance* (individual, collective or special); by implication a *matter* or *topic* (especially of narration, command or dispute); with a negative *naught* whatever:— + evil, + nothing, saying, word.

Noun from *rhéō* (4483), to speak. That which is spoken, a statement, word.

(I) Particularly a word as uttered by a living voice: a saying, speech, or discourse (Mt 12:36; 26:75; Mk 9:32; 14:72; Lk 1:38; 2:17, 50; 9:45; 18:34; 20:26; Ac 11:16; 28:25). In the plural, words (Lk 2:19, 51; 7:1; 24:8, 11; Ac 2:14; 6:11, 13; 10:44; 16:38; 26:25; Ro 10:18; 2Co 12:4; Heb 12:19).

(II) In the NT, *rhēma* often takes on a particular meaning from its adjuncts or context:

(A) Charge, accusation (Mt 5:11; 18:16; 27:14; 2Co 13:1).

(B) Prediction, prophecy (2Pe 3:2; Jude 17). Also, the sayings of God (Rev 17:17).

(C) Promise from God (Lk 2:29; Heb 6:5).

(D) Command (Lk 5:5; Heb 1:3; 11:3). Alsos Mt 4:4; Lk 4:4, where *rhēma* is used in metonymy for everything which God decrees.

(E) Teaching, precept, doctrine (Lk 3:2; Jn 3:37; 5:47; 6:63, 68; 8:47; 10:21; 12:47, 48; 14:10; 15:7; 17:8; Ac 5:20; 10:22, 37; Ro 10:17; Eph 5:26; 6:17; 1Pe 1:25).

(II) Spoken by metonymy for things spoken of: a matter, a happening (Lk 1:37; 65; 2:15; Ac 5:32).

Syn.: *lógos* (3056), word. Also *épos* (2031), a word.

4488. Ῥησά, Rhēsa, *hray-sah´*; probably of Hebrew origin [apparently for 7509]; *Resa* (i.e. *Rephajah*), an Israelite:—Rhesa.

4489. ῥήτωρ, rhētōr, *hray´-tore*; from 4483; a *speaker*, i.e. (by implication) a forensic *advocate*:—orator.

4490. ῥητῶς, rhētōs, *hray-toce´*; adverb from a derivative of 4483; out-*spokenly*, i.e. *distinctly*:—expressly.

4491. ῥίζα, rhiza, *hrid´-zah*; apparently a primary word; a *"root"* (literal or figurative):—root.

4492. ῥιζόω, rhizoō, *hrid-zo´-o*; from 4491; to *root* (figurative, *become stable*):—root.

4493. ῥιπή, rhipē, *hree-pay´*; from 4496; a *jerk* (of the eye, i.e. [by analogy] an *instant*):—twinkling.

4494. ῥιπίζω, rhipizō, *hrip-id´-zo*; from a derivative of 4496 (meaning a *fan* or *bellows*); to *breeze up*, i.e. (by analogy) to *agitate* (into waves):—toss.

4495. ῥιπτέω, rhipteō, *hrip-teh´-o*; from a derivative of 4496; to *toss* up:—cast off.

4496. ῥίπτω, rhiptō, *hrip´-to*; a primary verb (perhaps rather akin to the base of 4474, through the idea of sudden *motion*); to *fling* (properly with a quick *toss*, thus differing from 906, which denotes a *deliberate* hurl; and from τείνω, *teinō*; [see in 1614], which indicates an *extended* projection); by qualification, to *deposit* (as if a load); by extension to *disperse*:—cast (down, out), scatter abroad, throw.

4497. Ῥοβοάμ, Rhoboam, *hrob-o-am´*; of Hebrew origin [7346]; *Roboäm* (i.e. *Rechabam*), an Israelite:—Roboam.

4498. Ῥόδη, Rhodē, *hrod´-ay*; probably for ῥόδη, *Rhodē* (a *rose*); *Rode*, a servant girl:—Rhoda.

4499. Ῥόδος, Rhodos, *hrod´-os*; probably from ῥόδον, *Rhodon* (a *rose*); *Rhodus*, an island of the Mediterranean:—Rhodes.

4500. ῥοιζηδόν, rhoizēdon, *hroyd-zay-don´*; adverb from a derivative of ῥοῖζος, *rhoizos* (a *whir*); *whizzingly*, i.e. *with a crash*:—with a great noise.

4501. ῥομφαία, rhomphaia, *hrom-fah´-yah*; probably of foreign origin; a *sabre*, i.e. a long and broad *cutlass* (any *weapon* of the kind, literal or figurative):—sword.

4502. Ῥουβήν, Rhoubēn, *hroo-bane´*; of Hebrew origin [7205]; *Ruben* (i.e. *Reuben*), an Israelite:—Reuben.

4503. Ῥούθ, Rhouth, *hrooth*; of Hebrew origin [7827]; *Ruth*, a Moabitess:—Ruth.

4504. Ῥοῦφος, Rhouphos, *hroo´-fos*; of Latin origin; *red*; *Rufus*, a Christian:—Rufus.

4505. ῥύμη, rhumē, *hroo´-may*; prolonged from 4506 in its original sense; an *alley* or *avenue* (as crowded):—lane, street.

4506. ῥύομαι, rhuomai, *rhoo´-om-ahee*; middle of an obsolete verb, akin to 4482 (through the idea of a *current*; compare 4511); to *rush* or *draw* (for oneself), i.e. *rescue*:—deliver (-er).

From *rhúō* (n.f., see *rhúmē* [4505]), to draw, drag along the ground. To draw or snatch from danger, rescue, deliver. In the NT, it is used of God's delivering His saints (Mt 6:13; 27:43; Lk 1:74; 11:4; Ro 7:24; 11:26; 15:31; 2Co 1:10; Col 1:13; 1Th 1:10; 2Th 3:2; 2Ti 3:11; 4:17, 18; 2Pe 2:7, 9).

Syn.: *apallássō* (525), to free from, release, deliver; *apolúō* (630), to dismiss, set free; *eleutheróō* (1659), to deliver, free; *exairéō* (1807), to take out, deliver; *lutróō* (3084), to ransom, redeem; *lúō* (3089), to loose; *sōzō* (4982), to save, deliver, rescue.

4507. ῥυπαρία, rhuparia, *hroo-par-ee´-ah*; from 4508; *dirtiness* (moral):—turpitude.

4508. ῥυπαρός, rhuparos, *rhoo-par-os´*; from 4509; *dirty*, i.e. (relative) *cheap* or *shabby*; moral *wicked*:—vile.

4509. ῥύπος, rhupos, *hroo´-pos*; of uncertain affinity; *dirt*, i.e. (moral) *depravity*:—filth.

4510. ῥυπόω, rhupoō, *rhoo-po´-o*; from 4509; to *soil*, i.e. (intransitive) to *become dirty* (moral):—be filthy.

4511. ῥύσις, rhusis, *hroo´-sis*; from 4506 in the sense of its congener 4482; a *flux* (of blood):—issue.

4512. ῥυτίς, rhutis, *hroo-tece´*; from 4506; a *fold* (as *drawing* together), i.e. a *wrinkle* (especially on the face):—wrinkle.

4513. Ῥωμαϊκός, Rhōmaïkos, *rho-mah-ee-kos´*; from 4514; *Romaïc*, i.e. *Latin*:—Latin.

4514. 'Ρωμαῖος, Rhōmaios, *hro-mah´-yos*; from 4516; *Romæan*, i.e. *Roman* (as noun):— Roman, of Rome.

4515. 'Ρωμαϊστί, Rhōmaïsti, *hro-mah-is-tee´*; adverb from a presumed derivative of 4516; *Romaïstically*, i.e. *in* the *Latin* language:— Latin.

4516. 'Ρώμη, Rhōmē, *hro´-may*; from the base of 4517; *strength; Roma,* the capital of Italy:—Rome.

4517. ῥώννυμι, rhōnnumi, *hrone´-noo-mee*; prolonged from ῥώομαι, *rhōomai* (to *dart*; probably akin to 4506); to *strengthen*, i.e. (impersonal passive) *have health* (as a parting exclamation, *good-bye*):—farewell.

Σ (Sigma)

NT Numbers 4518–4998

4518. σαβαχθανί, **sabachthani,** *sab-akh-than-ee´*; of Chaldee origin [7662 with pronoun suffix]; *thou hast left me; sabachthani* (i.e. *shebakthani*), a cry of distress:—sabachthani.

4519. σαβαώθ, **sabaōth,** *sab-ah-owth´*; of Hebrew origin [6635 in feminine plural]; *armies; sabaoth* (i.e. *tsebaoth*), a military epithet of God:—sabaoth.

4520. σαββατισμός, **sabbatismos,** *sab-bat-is-mos´*; from a derivative of 4521; a "*sabbatism,*" i.e. (figurative) the *repose* of Christianity (as a type of heaven):—rest.

4521. σάββατον, **sabbaton,** *sab´-bat-on*; of Hebrew origin [7676]; the *Sabbath* (i.e. *Shabbath*), or day of weekly *repose* from secular avocations (also the observance or institution itself); by extension a *se'nnight*, i.e. the interval between two Sabbaths; likewise the plural in all the above applications:—sabbath (day), week.

4522. σαγήνη, **sagēnē,** *sag-ay´-nay*; from a derivative of σάττω, *sattō* (to *equip*) meaning *furniture*, especially a *pack-saddle* (which in the East is merely a bag of *netted* rope); a "*seine*" for fishing:—net.

Noun meaning large net, dragnet, seine, used in fishing. It had floats on top and weights on the bottom and was capable of catching many different kinds of fish at once. It could be drawn in either from boats or from the shore. Only used in Mt 13:47.

Syn.: *díktuon* (1350), a net in a general sense; *amphíblēstron* (293), casting net.

4523. Σαδδουκαῖος, **Saddoukaios,** *sad-doo-kah´-yos*; probably a derivative from 4524; a *Sadducæan* (i.e. *Tsadokian*), or follower of a certain heretical Israelite:—Sadducee.

4524. Σαδώκ, **Sadōk,** *sad-oke´*; of Hebrew origin [6659]; *Sadoc* (i.e. *Tsadok*), an Israelite:—Sadoc.

4525. σαίνω, **sainō,** *sah´-ee-no*; akin to 4579; to *wag* (as a dog its tail fawningly), i.e. (genitive) to *shake* (figurative, *disturb*):—move.

4526. σάκκος, **sakkos,** *sak´-kos*; of Hebrew origin [8242]; "*sack*"-*cloth,* i.e. *mohair* (the material or garments made of it, worn as a sign of grief):—sackcloth.

4527. Σαλά, **Sala,** *sal-ah´*; of Hebrew origin [7974]; *Sala* (i.e. *Shelach*), a patriarch:—Sala.

4528. Σαλαθιήλ, **Salathiēl,** *sal-ath-ee-ale´*; of Hebrew origin [7597]; *Salathiël* (i.e. *Sheältiël*), an Israelite:—Salathiel.

4529. Σαλαμίς, **Salamis,** *sal-am-ece´*; probably from 4535 (from the *surge* on the shore); *Salamis,* a place in Cyprus:—Salamis.

4530. Σαλείμ, **Saleim,** *sal-ime´*; probably from the same as 4531; *Salim,* a place in Palestine:—Salim.

4531. σαλεύω, **saleuō,** *sal-yoo´-o*; from 4535; to *waver*, i.e. *agitate, rock, topple* or (by implication) *destroy*; (figurative) to *disturb, incite*:—move, shake (together), which can [-not] be shaken, stir up.

4532. Σαλήμ, **Salēm,** *sal-ame´*; of Hebrew origin [8004]; *Salem* (i.e. *Shalem*), a place in Palestine:—Salem.

4533. Σαλμών, **Salmōn,** *sal-mone´*; of Hebrew origin [8012]; *Salmon,* an Israelite:—Salmon.

4534. Σαλμώνη, **Salmōnē,** *sal-mo´-nay*; perhaps of similar origin to 4529; *Salmone,* a place in Crete:—Salmone.

4535. σάλος, **salos,** *sal´-os*; probably from the base of 4525; a *vibration*, i.e. (special) *billow*:—wave.

4536. σάλπιγξ, **salpigx,** *sal´-pinx*; perhaps from 4535 (through the idea of *quavering* or *reverberation*); a *trumpet*:—trump (-et).

4537. σαλπίζω, **salpizō,** *sal-pid´-zo*; from 4536; to *trumpet,* i.e. *sound a blast* (literal or figurative):—(which are yet to) sound (a trumpet).

4538. σαλπιστής, **salpistēs,** *sal-pis-tace´*; from 4537; a *trumpeter.*—trumpeter.

4539. Σαλώμη, **Salōmē,** *sal-o´-may*; probably of Hebrew origin [feminine from 7965]; *Salomè* (i.e. *Shelomah*), an Israelitess:—Salome.

4540. Σαμάρεια, **Samareia,** *sam-ar´-i-ah*; of Hebrew origin [8111]; *Samaria* (i.e. *Shomeron*), a city and region of Palestine:—Samaria.

4541. Σαμαρείτης, **Samareitēs,** *sam-ar-i´-tace*; from 4540; a *Samarite,* i.e. inhabitant of Samaria:—Samaritan.

4542. Σαμαρεῖτις, **Samareitis,** *sam-ar-i´-tis*; feminine of 4541; a *Samaritess,* i.e. woman of Samaria:—of Samaria.

4543. Σαμοθράκη, **Samothraikē,** *sam-oth-rak´-ay*; from 4544 and Θράκη, *Thraikē* (*Thrace*); *Samo-thracè* (*Samos of Thrace*), an island in the Mediterranean:—Samothracia.

4544. Σάμος, **Samos,** *sam´-os*; of uncertain affinity; *Samus,* an island of the Mediterranean:—Samos.

4545. Σαμουήλ, **Samouēl,** *sam-oo-ale´*; of Hebrew origin [8050]; *Samuel* (i.e. *Shemuel*), an Israelite:—Samuel.

4546. Σαμψών, **Sampsōn,** *samp-sone´*; of Hebrew origin [8123]; *Sampson* (i.e. *Shimshon*), an Israelite:—Samson.

4547. σανδάλιον, **sandalion,** *san-dal´-ee-on*; neuter of a derivative of σάνδαλον, **sandalon** (a "*sandal*"; of uncertain origin); a *slipper* or *sole-pad:*—sandal.

4548. σανίς, **sanis,** *san-ece´*; of uncertain affinity; a *plank:*—board.

4549. Σαούλ, **Saoul,** *sah-ool´*; of Hebrew origin [7586]; *Saül* (i.e. *Shaül*), the Jewish name of *Paul:*—Saul. Compare 4569.

4550. σαπρός, **sapros,** *sap-ros´*; from 4595; *rotten,* i.e. *worthless* (literal or moral):—bad, corrupt. Compare 4190.

4551. Σαπφείρη, **Sappheirē,** *sap-fi´-ray*; feminine of 4552; *Sapphirè,* an Israelitess:—Sapphira.

4552. σάπφειρος, **sappheiros,** *sap´-fi-ros*; of Hebrew origin [5601]; a "*sapphire*" or *lapis-lazuli* gem:—sapphire.

4553. σαργάνη, **sarganē,** *sar-gan´-ay*; apparently of Hebrew origin [8276]; a *basket* (as *interwoven* or *wicker*-work):—basket.

4554. Σάρδεις, **Sardeis,** *sar´-dice*; plural of uncertain derivative; *Sardis,* a place in Asia Minor:—Sardis.

4555. σάρδινος, **sardinos,** *sar´-dee-nos*; from the same as 4556; *sardine* (3037 being implication), i.e. a gem, so called:—sardine.

4556. σάρδιος, **sardios,** *sar´-dee-os*; properly adjective from an uncertain base; *sardian* (3037 being implication), i.e. (as noun) the gem so called:—sardius.

4557. σαρδόνυξ, **sardonux,** *sar-don´-oox*; from the base of 4556 and ὄνυξ, **onux** (the *nail* of a finger; hence the "*onyx*" stone); a "*sardonyx*," i.e. the gem so called:—sardonyx.

4558. Σάρεπτα, **Sarepta,** *sar´-ep-tah*; of Hebrew origin [6886]; *Sarepta* (i.e. *Tsarephath*), a place in Palestine:—Sarepta.

4559. σαρκικός, **sarkikos,** *sar-kee-kos´*; from 4561; *pertaining to flesh,* i.e. (by extension) *bodily, temporal,* or (by implication) *animal, unregenerate:*—carnal, fleshly.

Adjective from *sárx* (4561), flesh. Fleshly, carnal, pertaining to the flesh or body, the opposite of *pneumatikós* (4152), spiritual. Used only in the epistles.

(I) Generally, spoken of things, things of the body, external, temporal (Ro 15:27; 1Co 9:11).

(II) Implying weakness, frailty, imperfection: e.g., of persons as being carnal, worldly (1Co 3:1, 3, 4); of things as carnal, human, frail, transient, temporary (2Co 1:12; 10:4; Heb 7:16).

(III) Spoken of a tendency to satisfy the flesh, implying sinfulness, sinful inclination, carnal (Ro 7:14; 1Pe 2:11).

Syn.: *sōmatikós* (4984), bodily; *phusikós* (5446), physical; *psuchikós* (5591), natural, pertaining to our present body or existence.

4560. σάρκινος, sarkinos, *sar´-kee-nos*; from 4561; *similar to flesh,* i.e. (by analogy) *soft:*— fleshly.

Adjective from *sárx* (4561), flesh, body. Fleshly, material, and therefore soft, yielding to an impression. Only in 2Co 3:3.

4561. σάρξ, sarx, *sarx*; probably from the base of 4563; *flesh* (as *stripped* of the skin), i.e. (strictly) the *meat* of an animal (as food), or (by extension) the *body* (as opposed to the soul [or spirit], or as the symbol of what is external, or as the means of kindred), or (by implication) *human nature* (with its frailties [physical or moral] and passions), or (special) a *human being* (as such):—carnal (-ly, + -ly minded), flesh ([-ly]).

Noun meaning flesh of a living creature in distinction from that of a dead one, which is *kréas* (2907), meat.

(I) Specifically flesh, as one of the constituent parts of the body (Lk 24:39; 1Co 15:39). In the plural, fleshy parts, spoken of as being consumed (Jas 5:3; Rev 17:16; 19:18).

(II) By metonymy, flesh as used for the body, the corpus, the material nature as distinguished from the spiritual and intangible (*pneúma* [4151], the spirit). This usage of *sárx* is far more frequent in the NT than in classical writers.

(A) Generally and without any good or evil quality implied. **(1)** The opposite of *to pneúma*, the spirit expressed (Jn 6:52; Ac 2:26, 31; 1Co 5:5; 2Co 7:1; 12:7; Col 1:24; 2:1, 5, 23; Heb 2:14; 9:10, 13; 1Pe 3:21; Jude 8, 23). Metaphorically in Jn 6:51, "and the bread … is my flesh," meaning that Jesus Himself is the principle of life and nutrition to the regenerated soul (see vv. 53–56). Specifically used of the mortal body in distinction from a future and spiritual existence (2Co 4:11; Gal 2:20; Php 1:22, 24; 1Pe 4:2). **(2)** Used for that which is merely external or only apparent, in opposition to what is spiritual or real (Jn 6:63; 8:15; 1Co 1:26; 2Co 5:16; Eph 6:5; Col 3:22; Phm 16); of outward affliction, trials (1Co 7:28; 2Co 7:5; Gal 4:13, 14; 1Pe 4:1); specifically of the meticulous observance of Judaism as an attempt to earn salvation (Ro 2:28; 4:1; 2Co 11:18; Gal 3:3; Gal 6:12, 13; Eph 2:11; Php 3:3, 4; Col 2:13). **(3)** As the medium of natural generation and descent, and consequently kindred or natural descendants (Jn 1:13; Ac 2:30; Ro 9:3, 8; 1Co

10:18; Gal 4:23, 29; Heb 12:9). Of one's own countrymen (Ro 11:14).

(B) As implying weakness, frailty, imperfection, both physical and moral; the opposite being *pneúma* (4151), the spirit (Mt 16:7; 26:41; Mk 14:38; Jn 3:6; Ro 6:19; 1Co 15:15; 2Co 1:17; 10:2, 3; Gal 1:16; Eph 6:12).

(C) As implying sinfulness, proneness to sin, the carnal nature, the seat of carnal appetites and desires, of sinful passions and affections whether physical or moral (Ro 7:5, 18, 25; 8:3, 7, 8, 12; 13:14; Gal 5:13; Eph 2:3; Col 2:1, 18; 2Pe 2:10, 18; 1Jn 2:16). The Greeks ascribed a similar influence to the body (*sṓma* [4983]), as opposed to *Pneúma* (4151), the Spirit, referring to the Holy Spirit or His influences (Ro 8:1, 4– 6, 9, 13; Gal 5:16, 17, 19, 24; 6:8).

(III) By metonymy, flesh, human nature, man (Mt 24:22; Mk 13:20; Lk 3:6; Jn 17:2; Ac 2:17; Ro 3:20; 1Co 1:29; Gal 2:16; 1Pe 1:24). Figuratively, of the union of husband and wife as one flesh (Mt 19:5, 6; Mk 10:8; 1Co 6:16; Eph 5:31). Compare Jude 7. Used specifically of the incarnation of Christ, His incarnate human nature (Jn 1:14; Ro 1:3; 9:5; Eph 2:15; Col 1:22; 1Ti 3:16; Heb 5:7; 10:20; 1Pe 3:18; 4:1; 1Jn 4:2, 3; 2Jn 7).

Deriv.: *sarkikós* (4559), fleshy, pertaining to the flesh, carnal, sensual; *sárkinos* (4560), of the flesh, made of flesh.

Syn.: *sṓma* (4983), body. Also *kréas* (2907), flesh in the sense of meat; *ptṓma* (4430), a corpse; *chrṓs* (5559), the body, but referring rather to the exterior of it, the surface.

4562. Σαρούχ, Sarouch, *sar-ooch´*; of Hebrew origin [8286]; *Saruch* (i.e. *Serug*), a patriarch:— Saruch.

4563. σαρόω, saroō, *sar-o´-o*; from a derivative of **σαίρω, sairō** (to *brush* off; akin to 4951) meaning a *broom*; to *sweep:*—sweep.

4564. Σάρρα, Sarrha, *sar´-hrah*; of Hebrew origin [8283]; *Sarra* (i.e. *Sarah*), the wife of Abraham:—Sara, Sarah.

4565. Σάρων, Sarōn, *sar´-one*; of Hebrew origin [8289]; *Saron* (i.e. *Sharon*), a district of Palestine:—Saron.

4566. Σατᾶν, Satan, *sat-an´*; of Hebrew origin [7854]; *Satan*, i.e. the *devil:*—Satan. Compare 4567.

4567. Σατανᾶς, Satanas, *sat-an-as´*; of Chaldee origin corresponding to 4566 (with the definite affix); *the accuser,* i.e. the *devil*:—Satan.

Noun transliterated from the Hebrew *Sātān* (7854, OT), adversary. Satan. In the NT, as a transliteration of the Hebrew proper name for the Devil (see *diábolos* [1228], devil). Satan (Mt 4:10; 12:26; Mk 4:15; Lk 10:18; 22:31; 26:18; et al.). As present in men, tempting them to evil (Mt 16:23; Mk 8:33; Lk 22:3; Jn 13:27; Ac 5:3; 2Co 11:14; Rev 12:9).

4568. σάτον, saton, *sat´-on*; of Hebrew origin [5429]; a certain *measure* for things dry:—measure.

4569. Σαῦλος, Saulos, *sow´-los*; of Hebrew origin, the same as 4549; *Saulus* (i.e. *Shaül*), the Jewish name of *Paul*:—Saul.

4570. σβέννυμι, sbennumi, *sben´-noo-mee*; a prolonged form of an apparently primary verb; to *extinguish* (literal or figurative):—go out, quench.

4571. σέ, se, *seh*; accusative singular of 4771; *thee*:—thee, thou, × thy house.

4572. σεαυτοῦ, seautou, *seh-ow-too´*; genitive from 4571 and 846; also dative of the same, **σεαυτῷ, seautōi,** *seh-ow-to´*; and accusative **σεαυτόν, seauton,** *seh-ow-ton´*; likewise contracted **σαυτοῦ, sautou,** *sow-too´*; **σαυτῷ, sautōi,** *sow-to´*; and **σαυτόν, sauton,** *sow-ton´*; respectively; *of* (*with, to*) *thyself*:—thee, thine own self, (thou) thy (-self).

4573. σεβάζομαι, sebazomai, *seb-ad´-zom-ahee*; middle from a derivative of 4576; to *venerate,* i.e. *adore*:—worship.

Middle deponent from *sébas* (n.f.), reverential awe, which is from *sébomai* (4576), to worship, to pay high respect. To be in worship of, to fear. In the NT, to stand in awe of someone, to reverence, venerate, worship. Used only in Ro 1:25.

Deriv.: *sébasma* (4574), object of worship; *sebastós* (4575), venerable, august.

Syn.: *eulabéomai* (2125), to reverence inwardly; *therapeúō* (2323), to serve; *proskunéō* (4352), to make obeisance, worship, reverence; *latreúō* (3000), to perform (religious) service.

4574. σέβασμα, sebasma, *seb´-as-mah*; from 4573; something *adored,* i.e. an *object of worship* (god, altar, etc.):—devotion, that is worshipped.

Noun from *sebázomai* (4573), to worship, venerate. An object of worship, anything venerated and worshiped, e.g., a god (Ac 17:23; 2Th 2:4).

4575. σεβαστός, sebastos, *seb-as-tos´*; from 4573; *venerable* (*august*), i.e. (as noun) a title of the Roman *Emperor,* or (as adjective) *imperial*:—Augustus (-´).

4576. σέβομαι, sebomai, *seb´-om-ahee*; middle of an apparently primary verb; to *revere,* i.e. *adore*:—devout, religious, worship.

To worship, to reverence. In the NT, only in the middle voice (Mt 15:9; Mk 7:7; Ac 16:14; 18:13; 19:27). The participle, used as a substantive, a worshipper of the true God, spoken of Gentile proselytes and the Jews (Ac 13:43, 50; 16:14; 17:4, 17; 18:7).

Deriv.: *asebés* (765), godless; *eusebés* (2152), devout, godly; *theo-sebés* (2318), godly; *semnós* (4586), worthy of respect.

Syn.: *eulabéomai* (2125), to reverence inwardly; *latreúō* (3000), to perform (religious) service; *proskunéō* (4352), to make obeisance, worship, reverence.

4577. σειρά, seira, *si-rah´*; probably from 4951 through its congener **εἴρω, eirō** (to *fasten*; akin to 138); a *chain* (as *binding* or *drawing*):—chain.

4578. σεισμός, seismos, *sice-mos´*; from 4579; a *commotion,* i.e. (of the air) a *gale,* (of the ground) an *earthquake*:—earthquake, tempest.

Noun from *seíō* (4579), to shake. Earthquake, a shaking.

(I) Generally, in the sea meaning a tempest, tornado (Mt 8:24).

(II) Specifically, an earthquake (Mt 24:7; 27:54; 28:2; Mk 13:8; Lk 21:11; Ac 16:26; Rev 6:12; 8:5; 11:13, 19; 16:18).

Syn.: *thúella* (2366), storm, tempest; *laílaps* (2978), a tempest, hurricane; *cheimón* (5494), a winter storm.

4579. σείω, seiō, *si´-o*; apparently a primary verb; to *rock* (*vibrate,* properly sideways or to and fro), i.e. (genitive) to *agitate* (in any direction; cause to *tremble*); (figurative) to throw into a *tremor* (of fear or concern):—move, quake, shake.

4580. Σεκοῦνδος, Sekoundos, *sek-oon´-dos*; of Latin origin; *"second"*; *Secundus*, a Christian:—Secundus.

4581. Σελεύκεια, Seleukeia, *sel-yook´-i-ah*; from **Σέλευκος**, *Seleukos* (*Seleucus*, a Syrian king); *Seleuceia*, a place in Syria:—Seleucia.

4582. σελήνη, selēnē, *sel-ay´-nay*; from **σέλας**, *selas* (*brilliancy*; probably akin to the alternate of 138, through the idea of *attractiveness*); the *moon*:—moon.

4583. σεληνιάζομαι, selēniazomai, *sel-ay-nee-ad´-zom-ahee*; middle or passive from a presumed derivative of 4582; to *be moon-struck*, i.e. *crazy*:—be lunatic.

4584. Σεμΐ, Semi, *sem-eh-ee´*; of Hebrew origin [8096]; *Semeï* (i.e. *Shimi*), an Israelite:—Semei.

4585. σεμίδαλις, semidalis, *sem-id´-al-is*; probably of foreign origin; fine wheaten *flour*:—fine flour.

4586. σεμνός, semnos, *sem-nos´*; from 4576; *venerable*, i.e. *honourable*:—grave, honest.

Adjective from *sébomai* (4576), to worship, venerate. Venerable, respectable, honourable, dignified. In the NT, spoken of things: honourable, reputable (Php 4:8); spoken of persons: grave, dignified (1Ti 3:8, 11; Tit 2:2).

Deriv.: *semnótēs* (4587), gravity.

Syn.: *éntimos* (1784), honourable; *eugenés* (2104), noble; *euschémōn* (2158), honourable, decorous; *hieroprepés* (2412), reverent.

4587. σεμνότης, semnotēs, *sem-not´-ace*; from 4586; *venerableness*, i.e. *probity*:—gravity, honesty.

Noun from *semnós* (4586), venerable. Dignity, honesty, seriousness. Aristotle defined *semnótēs* as standing between not caring if you please anyone and endeavoring at all costs to please everybody (1Ti 2:2; 3:4; Tit 2:7).

Syn.: *aidós* (127), modesty, reverence toward God; *euprépeia* (2143), gracefulness; *eusébeia* (2150), godliness, piety.

4588. Σέργιος, Sergios, *serg´-ee-os*; of Latin origin; *Sergius*, a Roman:—Sergius.

4589. Σήθ, Sēth, *sayth*; of Hebrew origin [8352]; *Seth* (i.e. *Sheth*), a patriarch:—Seth.

4590. Σήμ, Sēm, *same*; of Hebrew origin [8035]; *Sem* (i.e. *Shem*), a patriarch:—Sem.

4591. σημαίνω, sēmainō, *say-mah´ee-no*; from **σῆμα**, *sēma* (a *mark*; of uncertain derivative); to *indicate*:—signify.

4592. σημεῖον, sēmeion, *say-mi´-on*; neuter of a presumed derivative of the base of 4591; an *indication*, especially ceremonial or supernatural:—miracle, sign, token, wonder.

Noun meaning sign of something past, a memorial, a monument. In the NT, a sign, a mark, a token.

(I) Particularly a sign by which something is designated, distinguished, known (Mt 26:48; Ro 4:11). Specifically a sign by which the character and truth of any person or thing is known, a token, proof (Lk 2:12; 2Co 12:12; 2Th 3:17).

(II) A sign by which the divine power in majesty is made known, a supernatural event or act, a token, wonder, or miracle by which the power and presence of God is manifested, either directly or through the agency of those whom He sends (Sept.: Ex 4:8, 17, 28, 30).

(A) As wrought of God (Mt 12:39; 16:4; Lk 11:29; 1Co 14:22). Spoken by metonymy of persons sent from God, whose character and acts are a manifestation of the divine power (Lk 2:34; 11:30). Of signs, wonders, miracles which God did through someone, joined with *térata* (5059), things out of the ordinary, wonders (Ac 2:22, 43; 4:30; 5:12; 14:3; 15:12). Specifically as revealing future events, a sign of future things, a portent, presage (Mt 16:3), the miraculous events and deeds which reveal the coming of the Messiah in His kingdom (Mt 24:3, 30; Mk 13:4; Lk 21:7, 11, 25; Ac 2:19; Rev 12:1, 3; 15:1).

(B) Of signs, wonders, miracles wrought by Jesus and His apostles and the prophets in proof and furtherance of their divine mission (Mt 12:38, 39; 16:1, 4; Mk 8:11, 12; 16:17, 20; Lk 11:16, 29; 23:8; Ac 4:16, 22; 8:6; 1Co 1:22). In John the word is used only in this sense (Jn 2:11, 18, 23; 3:2; 4:54; 6:2, 14, 26, 30; 7:31; 9:16; 10:41; 11:47; 12:18, 37; 20:30).

(C) Spoken by analogy of signs, wonders, wrought by false prophets claiming to act by divine authority (Rev 13:13, 14; 16:14; 19:20); with *térata* (Mt 24:24; Mk 13:22; 2Th 2:9).

Deriv.: *sēmeióō* (4593), to denote, signify.

Syn.: *dúnamis* (1411), mighty work, miracle; *thaúma* (2295), wonder; *thaumásios* (2297), a miracle; *megaleíon* (3167), great work; *téras* (5059), wonder.

4593. σημειόω, sēmeioō, *say-mi-o´-o*; from 4592; to *distinguish*, i.e. *mark* (for avoidance):—note.

4594. σήμερον, sēmeron, *say´-mer-on*; neuter (as adverb) of a presumed compound of the article 3588 (4595, τ changed to σ) and 2250; on *the* (i.e. *this*) *day* (or *night* current or just passed); general *now* (i.e. at *present, hitherto*):—this (to-) day.

4595. σήπω, sēpō, *say´-po*; apparently a primary verb; to *putrefy*, i.e. (figurative) *perish*:—be corrupted.

4596. σηρικός, sērikos, *say-ree-kos´*; from Σήρ, *Sēr* (an Indian tribe from whom *silk* was procured; hence the name of the *silk-worm*); *Seric*, i.e. *silken* (neuter as noun, a *silky* fabric):—silk.

4597. σής, sēs, *sace*; apparently of Hebrew origin [5580]; a *moth*:—moth.

4598. σητόβρωτος, sētobrōtos, *say-tob´-ro-tos*; from 4597 and a derivative of 977; *motheaten*:—motheaten.

4599. σθενόω, sthenoō, *sthen-o´-o*; from σθένος, *sthenos* (bodily *vigour*; probably akin to the base of 2476); to *strengthen*, i.e. (figurative) *confirm* (in spiritual knowledge and power):—strengthen.

From *sthénos* (n.f.), strength. To strengthen, to make one more able to do something. Used only in 1Pe 5:10, where along with *stērízō* (4741), to make firm, it is used to speak of the strength Christ gives those who have endured suffering. The idea of these two Greek words is very similar. However, *stērízō* is used of making one firm, making them more resolved in their belief in the truth, while *sthenóō* is used of making one more capable, more able to endure trials.

Syn.: *endunamóō* (1743), to make strong; *epischúō* (2001), to reinforce, to strengthen more.

4600. σιαγών, siagōn, *see-ag-one´*; of uncertain derivative; the *jaw-bone*, i.e. (by implication) the *cheek* or side of the face:—cheek.

4601. σιγάω, sigaō, *see-gah´-o*; from 4602; to *keep silent* (transitive or intransitive):—keep close (secret, silence), hold peace.

4602. σιγή, sigē, *see-gay´*; apparently from σίζω, *sizō* (to *hiss*, i.e. *hist* or *hush*); *silence*:—silence. Compare 4623.

4603. σιδήρεος, sidēreos, *sid-ay´-reh-os*; from 4604; made *of iron*:—(of) iron.

4604. σίδηρος, sidēros, *sid´-ay-ros*; of uncertain derivative; *iron*:—iron.

4605. Σιδών, Sidōn, *sid-one´*; of Hebrew origin [6721]; *Sidon* (i.e. *Tsidon*), a place in Palestine:—Sidon.

4606. Σιδώνιος, Sidōnios, *sid-o´-nee-os*; from 4605; a *Sidonian*, i.e. inhabitant of Sidon:—of Sidon.

4607. σικάριος, sikarios, *sik-ar´-ee-os*; of Latin origin; a *dagger-man* or *assassin*; a *freebooter* (Jewish *fanatic* outlawed by the Romans):—murderer. Compare 5406.

Noun from the Latin *sicarius*, which is from *sica*, dagger. An assassin, murderer. Only in Ac 21:38. Bands of robbers of this character and referred to by this name were common in Judea under the Roman governors.

4608. σίκερα, sikera, *sik´-er-ah*; of Hebrew origin [7941]; an *intoxicant*, i.e. intensely fermented *liquor*:—strong drink.

Indeclinable noun transliterated from the Hebrew *shēkār* (7941, OT), strong drink. Strong drink, any intoxicating liquor, usually in reference to those prepared from grain, fruit, honey, or dates (Lk 1:15, where it occurs together with *oínos* [3631], wine).

4609. Σίλας, Silas, *see´-las*; contracted from 4610; *Silas*, a Christian:—Silas.

4610. Σιλουανός, Silouanos, *sil-oo-an-os´*; of Latin origin; "*silvan*"; *Silvanus*, a Christian:—Silvanus. Compare 4609.

4611. Σιλωάμ, Silōam, *sil-o-am´*; of Hebrew origin [7975]; *Siloäm* (i.e. *Shiloäch*), a pool of Jerusalem:—Siloam.

4612. σιμικίνθιον, simikinthion, *sim-ee-kin´-thee-on*; of Latin origin; a *semicinctium* or *half-girding,* i.e. narrow covering (*apron*):— apron.

4613. Σίμων, Simōn, *see´-mone*; of Hebrew origin [8095]; *Simon* (i.e. *Shimon*), the name of nine Israelites:—Simon. Compare 4826.

4614. Σινᾶ, Sina, *see-nah´*; of Hebrew origin [5514]; *Sina* (i.e. *Sinai*), a mountain in Arabia:—Sina.

4615. σίναπι, sinapi, *sin´-ap-ee*; perhaps from σίνομαι, *sinomai* (to *hurt,* i.e. *sting*); *mustard* (the plant):—mustard.

4616. σινδών, sindōn, *sin-done´*; of uncertain (perhaps foreign) origin; *byssos,* i.e. bleached *linen* (the cloth or a garment of it):—(fine) linen (cloth).

4617. σινιάζω, siniazō, *sin-ee-ad´-zo*; from σίνιον, *sinion* (a *sieve*); to *riddle* (figurative):—sift.

4618. σιτευτός, siteutos, *sit-yoo-tos´*; from a derivative of 4621; *grain-fed,* i.e. *fattened*:—fatted.

4619. σιτιστός, sitistos, *sit-is-tos´*; from a derivative of 4621; *grained,* i.e. *fatted*:—fatling.

4620. σιτόμετρον, sitometron, *sit-om´-et-ron*; from 4621 and 3358; a *grain-measure,* i.e. (by implication) *ration* (*allowance* of food):—portion of meat.

4621. σῖτος, sitos, *see´-tos*; plural irregular neuter σῖτα, *sita, see´-tah*; of uncertain derivative; *grain,* especially *wheat*:—corn, wheat.

4622. Σιών, Siōn, *see-own´*; of Hebrew origin [6726]; *Sion* (i.e. *Tsijon*), a hill of Jerusalem; (figurative) the *Church* (militant or triumphant):—Sion.

4623. σιωπάω, siōpaō, *see-o-pah´-o*; from σιωπή, *siōpē* (*silence,* i.e. a *hush*; properly *muteness,* i.e. *involuntary* stillness, or *inability* to speak; and thus differing from 4602, which is rather a voluntary *refusal* or *indisposition* to speak, although the terms are often used synonymously); to *be dumb* (but not *deaf* also, like 2974 properly); (figurative) to *be calm* (as *quiet* water):—dumb, (hold) peace.

4624. σκανδαλίζω, skandalizō, *skan-dal-id´-zo*; ("scandalize"); from 4625; to *entrap,* i.e. *trip* up

(figurative, *stumble* [transitive] or *entice* to sin, apostasy or displeasure):—(make to) offend.

From *skándalon* (4625), a trap, stumbling block. To cause to stumble and fall, not found in Greek writers. In the NT, figuratively, in a moral sense, to be a stumbling block to someone, to cause to stumble at or in something, to give a cause of offence to someone.

Transitively:

(I) Generally, to offend, vex, particularly to scandalize (Mt 17:27; Jn 6:61; 1Co 8:13); in the passive voice, to be offended by someone, to take offence at his character, words, conduct, so as to reject him (Mt 11:6; 13:57; 15:12; 26:31, 33; Mk 6:3; 14:27; Lk 7:23).

(II) Causative, to cause to offend, lead astray, lead into sin, be a stumbling block or the occasion of one's sinning (Mt 5:29, 30; 18:6, 8, 9; Mk 9:42, 43, 45, 47; Lk 17:2). Hence in the passive, to be offended, be led astray or into sin, fall away from the truth (Mt 13:21; 24:10; Mk 4:17; Jn 16:1; Ro 14:1; 2Co 11:29).

Syn.: *píptō* (4098), to fail or fall; *proskóptō* (4350), to stumble; *ptaíō* (4417), to offend, stumble, sin.

4625. σκάνδαλον, skandalon, *skan´-dal-on*; ("scandal"); probably from a derivative of 2578; a *trap-stick* (*bent* sapling), i.e. *snare* (figurative, *cause* of displeasure or sin):—occasion to fall (of stumbling), offence, thing that offends, stumbling block.

Noun meaning the trigger of a trap on which the bait is placed, and which, when touched by the animal, springs and causes it to close causing entrapment. In the NT, stumbling block, offence, only figuratively in a moral sense.

(I) Generally as a cause of stumbling, falling, ruin, morally and spiritually. Spoken of Christ as the rock of stumbling (Ro 9:33; 11:9; 1Pe 2:7).

(II) As a cause of offence and indignation (Mt 16:23; 1Co 1:23; Gal 5:11).

(III) As a cause or occasion of sinning or of falling away from the truth (Mt 18:7; Lk 17:1; Ro 14:13; 16:17; 1Jn 2:10; Rev 2:14). By metonymy, spoken of persons (Mt 13:41).

Deriv.: *skandalízō* (4624), to cause to stumble.

Syn.: *próskomma* (4348), an obstacle; *proskopē* (4349), occasion of stumbling.

4626. σκάπτω, skaptō, *skap´-to*; apparently a primary verb; to *dig*:—dig.

4627. σκάφη, skaphē, *skaf´-ay*; a "*skiff*" (as if *dug* out), or *yawl* (carried aboard a large vessel for landing):—boat.

4628. σκέλος, skelos, *skel´-os*; apparently from σκέλλω, skellō (to *parch*; through the idea of *leanness*); the *leg* (as *lank*):—leg.

4629. σκέπασμα, skepasma, *skep´-as-mah*; from a derivative of σκέπας skepas (a *covering*; perhaps akin to the base of 4649 through the idea of *noticeableness*); *clothing*:—raiment.

4630. Σκευᾶς, Skeuas, *skyoo-as´*; apparently of Latin origin; *left-handed*; Scevas (i.e. *Scævus*), an Israelite:—Sceva.

4631. σκευή, skeuē, *skyoo-ay´*; from 4632; *furniture*, i.e. spare *tackle*:—tackling.

4632. σκεῦος, skeuos, *skyoo´-os*; of uncertain affinity; a *vessel*, *implement*, *equipment* or *apparatus* (literal or figurative [specially a *wife* as contributing to the usefulness of the husband]):—goods, sail, stuff, vessel.

4633. σκηνή, skēnē, *skay-nay´*; apparently akin to 4632 and 4639; a *tent* or cloth hut (literal or figurative):—habitation, tabernacle.

4634. σκηνοπηγία, skēnopēgia, *skay-nop-ayg-ee´-ah*; from 4636 and 4078; the *Festival of Tabernacles* (so called from the custom of erecting booths for temporary homes):—tabernacles.

4635. σκηνοποιός, skēnopoios, *skay-nop-oy-os´*; from 4633 and 4160; a *manufacturer of tents*:—tentmaker.

4636. σκῆνος, skēnos, *skay´-nos*; from 4633; a *hut* or temporary residence, i.e. (figurative) the human *body* (as the abode of the spirit):—tabernacle.

4637. σκηνόω, skēnoō, *skay-no´-o*; from 4636; to *tent* or encamp, i.e. (figurative) to *occupy* (as a mansion) or (special) to *reside* (as God did in the tabernacle of old, a symbol of protection and communion):—dwell.

4638. σκήνωμα, skēnōma, *skay´-no-mah*; from 4637; an *encampment*, i.e. (figurative) the *temple* (as God's residence), the *body* (as a tenement for the soul):—tabernacle.

4639. σκιά, skia, *skee´-ah*; apparently a primary word; "*shade*" or a shadow (literal or figurative [darkness of *error* or an *adumbration*]):—shadow.

4640. σκιρτάω, skirtaō, *skeer-tah´-o*; akin to σκαίρω, skairō (to *skip*); to *jump*, i.e. sympathetically *move* (as the *quickening* of a foetus):—leap (for joy).

4641. σκληροκαρδία, sklērokardia, *sklay-rok-ar-dee´-ah*; feminine of a compound of 4642 and 2588; *hardheartedness*, i.e. (special) *destitution of* (spiritual) *perception*:—hardness of heart.

Noun from *sklērós* (4642), hard, and *kardía* (2588), heart. Hardness of heart, stubbornness, obstinacy, perverseness. Spoken of the Jews (Mt 19:8; Mk 10:5). Spoken of the refusal of the disciples to believe those who had seen the resurrected Christ (Mk 16:14).

Syn.: *ástorgos* (794), without natural affection, hard-hearted; *pṓrōsis* (4457), dullness of heart; *sklērótēs* (4643), callousness.

4642. σκληρός, sklēros, *sklay-ros´*; from the base of 4628; *dry*, i.e. *hard* or *tough* (figurative, *harsh*, *severe*):—fierce, hard.

Adjective from *skéllō* (n.f.), to harden, dry up. Dried up, dry, hard, stiff; of the voice or sounds as hoarse or harsh; of things as hard, tough, not soft. Hence, in the NT, hard.

(I) Of winds as fierce, violent (Jas 3:4).

(II) Of things spoken as hard, harsh, offensive, such as words (Jn 6:60; Jude 15). Of things done as being hard, difficult, grievous (Ac 9:5; 26:14).

(III) Of persons as harsh, stern, severe (Mt 25:24).

Deriv.: *sklērokardía* (4641), hardness of heart; *sklērótēs* (4643), hardness; *sklērotráchēlos* (4644), stiff-necked; *sklērúnō* (4645), to make stubborn or hard.

Syn.: *austērós* (840), rough, severe, austere (*Sklērós* always indicates a harsh, brutal character which is not the case with *austērós*); *dúskolos* (1422), difficult, finicky; *chalepós* (5467), perilous.

4643. σκληρότης, sklērotēs, *sklay-rot´-ace*; from 4642; *callousness*, i.e. (figurative) *stubbornness*:—hardness.

Noun from *sklērós* (4642), dry, hard. Hardness, dryness. In the NT, only in Ro 2:5, figuratively of hardness of heart, obstinacy.

Syn.: *pṓrōsis* (4457), a hardening, dullness of the heart.

4644. σκληροτράχηλος, sklērotrachēlos, *sklay-rot-rakh´-ah-los*; from 4642 and 5137; *hardnaped*, i.e. (figurative) *obstinate*:—stiffnecked.

4645. σκληρύνω, sklērunō, *sklay-roo´-no*; from 4642; to *indurate*, i.e. (figurative) *render stubborn*:—harden.

From *sklērós* (4642), hard. To make hard or stiff, make obdurate. In the NT applied only figuratively in a moral sense, to harden, to make obstinate, perverse (Ac 19:9; Ro 9:18; Heb 3:8, 13, 15; 4:7).

Syn.: *pōróō* (4456), to make hard, callous.

4646. σκολιός, skolios, *skol-ee-os´*; from the base of 4628; *warped*, i.e. (figurative) *winding*; (figurative) *perverse*:—crooked, froward, untoward.

4647. σκόλοψ, skolops, *skol´-ops*; perhaps from the base of 4628 and 3700; *withered* at the *front*, i.e. a *point* or *prickle* (figurative, a bodily *annoyance* or *disability*):—thorn.

4648. σκοπέω, skopeō, *skop-eh´-o*; from 4649; to take *aim* at (*spy*), i.e. (figurative) *regard*:— consider, take heed, look at (on), mark. Compare 3700.

From *skopós* (4649), mark, observer. To look, to watch. In the NT, to look at or upon, to behold, to regard (Lk 11:35; 2Co 4:18; Gal 6:1; Php 2:4), to mark to note (Ro 16:17; Php 3:17).

Deriv.: *episkopéō* (1983), to look after; *kataskopéō* (2684), to spy out.

Syn.: *blépō* (991), to watch; *epéchō* (1907), give attention to, mark; *horáō* (3708), to discern clearly; *proséchō* (4337), take heed, beware; *sēmeióō* (4593), to mark, note.

4649. σκοπός, skopos, *skop-os´*; ("scope"); from σκέπτομαι, *skeptomai* (to *peer* about ["skeptic"]; perhaps akin to 4626 through the idea of *concealment*; compare 4629); a *watch* (*sentry* or *scout*), i.e. (by implication) a *goal*:— mark.

Noun from *sképtomai* (n.f.), to look about. Goal, the mark at the end of a race. Particularly, an object set up in the distance, at which one looks and aims, e.g., a mark, a goal. Only in Php 3:14.

Deriv.: *epískopos* (1985), overseer, bishop; *skopéō* (4648), to look toward a goal, give heed.

Syn.: *télos* (5056), the point aimed at, end.

4650. σκορπίζω, skorpizō, *skor-pid´-zo*; apparently from the same as 4651 (through the idea of *penetrating*); to *dissipate*, i.e. (figurative) *put to flight, waste, be liberal*:—disperse abroad, scatter (abroad).

4651. σκορπίος, skorpios, *skor-pee´-os*; probably from an obsolete σκέρπω, *skerpō* (perhaps strengthened from the base of 4649 and meaning to *pierce*); a "*scorpion*" (from its *sting*):— scorpion.

4652. σκοτεινός, skoteinos, *skot-i-nos´*; from 4655; *opaque*, i.e. (figurative) *benighted*:—dark, full of darkness.

4653. σκοτία, skotia, *skot-ee´-ah*; from 4655; *dimness, obscurity* (literal or figurative):—dark (-ness).

Noun from *skótos* (4655), darkness. Darkness, the absence of light (Mt 10:27; Lk 12:3; Jn 6:17; 20:1; 1Jn 2:8, 9, 11). By metonymy, spoken of persons in moral darkness (Jn 1:5).

4654. σκοτίζω, skotizō, *skot-id´-zo*; from 4655; to *obscure* (literal or figurative):—darken.

4655. σκότος, skotos, *skot´-os*; from the base of 4639; *shadiness*, i.e. *obscurity* (literal or figurative):—darkness.

Noun meaning darkness.

(I) Particularly, spoken of physical darkness, such as the darkness that accompanied the crucifixion (Mt 27:45; Mk 15:33; Lk 23:44). Also Ac 2:20; 13:11; 1Co 4:5. Spoken of a dark place where darkness reigns, a place of eternal darkness and punishment called "outer darkness" in the parables of Jesus (Mt 13:12; 22:13; 25:31). See also 2Pe 2:17; Jude 13.

(II) Spoken figuratively of moral darkness, the absence of spiritual light and truth, including the idea of sinfulness and consequent calamity (Mt 4:16; 6:23; Lk 1:79; 11:35; Jn 3:19; Ac 26:18; Ro 2:19; 13:12; 2Co 4:6; 6:14; Eph 5:11). Spoken figuratively of persons in a state of moral darkness, wicked men under the influence of Satan (Lk 22:53; Eph 5:8; 6:12; Col 1:13).

Deriv.: *skoteinós* (4652), dark; *skotía* (4653), darkness; *skotízō* (4654), to darken, deprive of light; *skotóō* (4656), to darken.

Syn.: *achlús* (887), a thick mist, fog; *gnóphos* (1105), a thick dark cloud; *zóphos* (2217), gloom, darkness.

4656. σκοτόω, skotoō, *skot-o´-o*; from 4655; to *obscure* or *blind* (literal or figurative):—be full of darkness.

4657. σκύβαλον, skubalon, *skoo´-bal-on*; neuter of a presumed derivative of 1519 and 2965 and 906; what is *thrown to* the *dogs*, i.e. *refuse* (*ordure*):—dung.

4658. Σκύθης, Skuthēs, *skoo´-thace*; probably of foreign origin; a *Scythene* or *Scythian*, i.e. (by implication) a *savage*:—Scythian.

4659. σκυθρωπός, skuthrōpos, *skoo-thro-pos´*; from **σκυθρός,** *skuthros* (*sullen*) and a derivative of 3700; *angry-visaged*, i.e. *gloomy* or affecting a *mournful* appearance:—of a sad countenance.

4660. σκύλλω, skullō, *skool´-lo*; apparently a primary verb; to *flay*, i.e. (figurative) to *harass*:—trouble (self).

4661. σκῦλον, skulon, *skoo´-lon*; neuter from 4660; something *stripped* (as a *hide*), i.e. *booty*:—spoil.

4662. σκωληκόβρωτος, skōlēkobrōtos, *sko-lay-kob´-ro-tos*; from 4663 and a derivative of 977; *worm-eaten*, i.e. *diseased with maggots*:—eaten of worms.

4663. σκώληξ, skōlēx, *sko´-lakes*; of uncertain derivative; a *grub, maggot* or *earth-worm*:—worm.

4664. σμαράγδινος, smaragdinos, *smar-ag´-dee-nos*; from 4665; consisting *of emerald*:—emerald.

4665. σμάραγδος, smaragdos, *smar´-ag-dos*; of uncertain derivative; the *emerald* or green gem so called:—emerald.

4666. σμύρνα, smurna, *smoor´-nah*; apparently strengthened for 3464; *myrrh*:—myrrh.

4667. Σμύρνα, Smurna, *smoor´-nah*; the same as 4666; *Smyrna*, a place in Asia Minor:—Smyrna.

4668. Σμυρναῖος, Smurnaios, *smmor-nah´-yos*; from 4667; a *Smyrnæan*:—in Smyrna.

4669. σμυρνίζω, smurnizō, *smoor-nid´-zo*; from 4667; to *tincture with myrrh*, i.e. (by analogy) *embitter* (as a narcotic):—mingle with myrrh.

4670. Σόδομα, Sodoma, *sod´-om-ah*; plural of Hebrew origin [5467]; *Sodoma* (i.e. *Sedom*), a place in Palestine:—Sodom.

4671. σοί, soi, *soy*; dative of 4771; *to thee*:—thee, thine own, thou, thy.

4672. Σολομών, Solomōn, *sol-om-one´*; or **Σολομῶν, Solomōn;** of Hebrew origin [8010]; *Solomon* (i.e. *Shelomoh*), the son of David:—Solomon.

4673. σορός, soros, *sor-os´*; probably akin to the base of 4987; a *funereal receptacle* (*urn, coffin*), i.e. (by analogy) a *bier*:—bier.

4674. σός, sos, *sos*; from 4771; *thine*:—thine (own), thy (friend).

4675. σοῦ, sou, *soo*; genitive of 4771; *of thee, thy*:— × home, thee, thine (own), thou, thy.

4676. σουδάριον, soudarion, *soo-dar´-ee-on*; of Latin origin; a *sudarium* (*sweat-cloth*), i.e. *towel* (for wiping the perspiration from the face, or binding the face of a corpse):—handkerchief, napkin.

4677. Σουσάννα, Sousanna, *soo-san´-nah*; of Hebrew origin [7799 feminine]; *lily; Susannah* (i.e. *Shoshannah*), an Israelitess:—Susanna.

4678. σοφία, sophia, *sof-ee´-ah*; from 4680; *wisdom* (higher or lower, worldly or spiritual):—wisdom.

Noun from *sophós* (4680), wise. Wisdom, skill, tact, expertise in any article.

In the NT, it refers to wisdom:

(I) Skill in the affairs of life, practical wisdom, wise management as shown in forming the best plans and selecting the best means, including the idea of sound judgement and good sense (Lk 21:15; Ac 6:3; 7:10: Col 1:28; 3:16; 4:5).

(II) In a higher sense, wisdom, deep knowledge, natural and moral insight, learning, science, implying cultivation of mind and enlightened understanding.

(A) Generally (Mt 12:42; Lk 11:31; Ac 7:22). Implying learned research and a knowledge of hidden things, of enigmatic and symbolic language (Col 2:23; Rev 13:18; 17:9).

(B) Specifically of the learning and philosophy current among the Greeks and Romans in the apostolic age intended to draw away the minds of men from divine truth, and which stood in contrast to the simplicity of the gospel (1Co 1:17, 19–22; 2:1, 4–6, 13; 3:19; 2Co 1:12).

(C) In respect to divine things, wisdom, knowledge, insight, deep understanding, represented everywhere as a divine gift, and including the idea of practical application (Mt 13:54; Mk 6:2; Ac 6:10). *Sophía* stands for divine wisdom, the ability to regulate one's relationship with God (Lk 2:40; 1Co 1:30; 2:6, 7; 12:8; Eph 1:17; Col 1:9; Jas 1:5; 3:13, 15, 17; 2Pe 3:15).

(III) The wisdom of God means the divine wisdom, including the ideas of infinite skill, insight, knowledge, purity (Ro 11:33; 1Co 1:21, 24; Eph 1:8; 3:10; Col 2:3; Rev 5:12; 7:12). Of the divine wisdom as revealed and manifested in Christ and His gospel (Mt 11:19; Lk 7:35; 11:49).

Deriv.: *philósophos* (5386), philosopher.

Syn.: *súnesis* (4907), the capacity for reasoning, intelligence, understanding; *sōphrosúnē* (4997), soundness of mind; *phrónēsis* (5428), prudence, moral insight.

4679. σοφίζω, sophizō, *sof-id´-zo*; from 4680; to *render wise*; in a sinister acceptation, to *form* "*sophisms*," i.e. *continue plausible error*:—cunningly devised, make wise.

4680. σοφός, sophos, *sof-os´*; akin to **σαφής,** *saphḗs* (*clear*); *wise* (in a most general application):—wise. Compare 5429.

Adjective meaning wise, not necessarily implying brilliance or scholastic training, but rather the ability to apply with skill what one knows. In the NT, particularly used of applying spiritual truth in one's life. Hence, the following meanings:

(I) Skillful, expert (1Co 3:10).

(II) Skilled in the affairs of life, discreet, judicious, practically wise (1Co 6:5).

(III) Skilled in learning, learned, intelligent, enlightened, in respect to things human and divine.

(A) Generally, as to things human (Mt 11:25; Lk 10:21; Ro 1:14; 16:19; 1Co 1:25).

(B) Specifically as to the philosophy current among the Greeks and Romans (Ro 1:22; 1Co 1:19, 20, 26, 27; 3:18–20).

(C) In respect to divine things, wise, enlight-

ened, as accompanying purity of heart and life (Eph 5:15; Jas 3:13).

(IV) Spoken of God as surpassing all others in wisdom, being infinite in skill, insight, knowledge, purity (Ro 16:27; 1Ti 1:17; Jude 1:25).

Deriv.: *ásophos* (781), unwise, foolish; *sophízō* (4679), to make wise, instruct.

Syn.: *logikós* (3050), reasonable; *sunetós* (4908), intelligent, prudent; *sōphrōn* (4998), of sound mind; *phrónimos* (5429), prudent, ethical, well-behaved; *epistḗmōn* (1990), scientific, intelligent.

4681. Σπανία, Spania, *span-ee´-ah*; probably of foreign origin; *Spania*, a region of Europe:—Spain.

4682. σπαράσσω, sparassō, *spar-as´-so*; prolonged from **σπαίρω,** *spairō* (to *gasp*; apparently strengthened from 4685 through the idea of *spasmodic* contraction); to *mangle*, i.e. *convulse* with epilepsy:—rend, tear.

4683. σπαργανόω, sparganoō, *spar-gan-o´-o*; from **σπάρ-γανον,** *sparganon* (a *strip*; from a derivative of the base of 4682 meaning to *strap* or *wrap* with strips); to *swathe* (an infant after the Oriental custom):—wrap in swaddling clothes.

4684. σπαταλάω, spatalaō, *spat-al-ah´-o*; from **σπατάλη,** *spatalē* (*luxury*); to *be voluptuous*:—live in pleasure, be wanton.

From *spatálē* (n.f.), luxury in eating and drinking. To live in luxury or pleasure, be self-indulgent. Paul counsels Timothy about the widows who live in pleasure or self-gratification (1Ti 5:6). Also used of wicked rich men (Jas 5:5).

Syn.: *strēniáō* (4763), to live luxuriously, sensuously; *trupháō* (5171), to live in pleasure, self-indulgence.

4685. σπάω, spaō, *spah´-o*; a primary verb; to *draw*:—draw (out).

4686. σπεῖρα, speira, *spi´-rah*; of immediate Latin origin, but ultimately a derivative of 138 in the sense of its cognative 1507; a *coil* (*spira*, "spire"), i.e. (figurative) a *mass* of men (a Roman military *cohort*; also [by analogy] a *squad* of Levitical janitors):—band.

4687. σπείρω, speirō, *spi´-ro*; probably strengthened from 4685 (through the idea of *extending*); to *scatter*, i.e. *sow* (literal or figurative):—sow (-er), receive seed.

4688. σπεκουλάτωρ, spekoulatōr, *spek-oo-lat´-ore*; of Latin origin; a *speculator*, i.e. military scout (*spy* or [by extension] *life-guardsman*):—executioner.

4689. σπένδω, spendō, *spen´-do*; apparently a primary verb; to *pour* out as a libation, i.e. (figurative) to *devote* (one's life or blood, as a sacrifice) ("*spend*"):—(be ready to) be offered.

4690. σπέρμα, sperma, *sper´-mah*; from 4687; something *sown*, i.e. *seed* (including the male "*sperm*"); by implication *offspring*; specially a *remnant* (figurative, as if kept over for planting):—issue, seed.

Noun from *speírō* (4687), to sow. Seed, as sown or scattered, whether of grains, plants or trees.

(I) Particularly, the seed sown (Mt 13:24, 27, 32, 37, 38; Mk 4:31; 1Co 15:38; 2Co 9:10). Used figuratively in 1Jn 3:9 of the work of the indwelling Holy Spirit in Christians that keeps them from practicing sin.

(II) Figuratively of the fertilized egg, the seed of conception (Heb 11:11). Hence, by metonymy, in the sense of children, offspring (Mt 22:24, 25; Mk 12:19–22; Lk 20:28). Generally, seed in the sense of posterity (Lk 1:55; Jn 7:42; 8:33, 37; Ac 3:25; 7:5, 6; 13:23; Ro 1:3; 4:13, 18; 11:1; 2Co 11:22; Gal 3:16, 19; 2Ti 2:8; Heb 2:16; 11:18; Rev 12:17). Hence, Christians are referred to as "the seed of Abraham," in that they are the spiritual children of Abraham, and by faith are heirs of the promises made to him (Ro 4:16; 9:8; Gal 3:29).

(III) By implication, seed in the sense of a remnant, a few survivors, like seed that is kept over from a former year (Ro 9:29).

Deriv.: *spermológos* (4691), seed-gathering, chatterer, babbler.

Syn.: *spóros* (4703), seed; *sporá* (4701), seed, a sowing.

4691. σπερμολόγος, spermologos, *sper-mol-og´-os*; from 4690 and 3004; a *seed-picker* (as the crow), i.e. (figurative) a *sponger*, *loafer* (specially a *gossip* or *trifler* in talk):—babbler.

4692. σπεύδω, speudō, *spyoo´-do*; probably strengthened from 4228; to "*speed*" ("study"), i.e. *urge* on (diligently or earnestly); by implication to *await* eagerly:—(make, with) haste unto.

4693. σπήλαιον, spēlaion, *spay´-lah-yon*; neuter of a presumed derivative of σπέος, *speos* (a grotto); a *cavern*; by implication a *hiding-place* or *resort*:—cave, den.

4694. σπιλάς, spilas, *spee-las´*; of uncertain derivative; a *ledge* or *reef* of rock in the sea:—spot [*by confusion with* 4696].

4695. σπιλόω, spiloō, *spee-lo´-o*; from 4696; to *stain* or *soil* (literal or figurative):—defile, spot.

From *spílos* (4696), a spot, stain. To defile, spot, stain (Jas 3:6; Jude 23).

Syn.: *miaínō* (3392), to defile; *molúnō* (3435), to soil, defile; *rhupóō* (4510), to soil, become dirty.

4696. σπίλος, spilos, *spee´-los*; of uncertain derivative; a *stain* or *blemish*, i.e. (figurative) *defect*, *disgrace*:—spot.

4697. σπλαγχνίζομαι, splagchnizomai, *splangkh-nid´-zom-ahee*; middle from 4698; to have the *bowels* yearn, i.e. (figurative) *feel sympathy*, to *pity*:—have (be moved with) compassion.

4698. σπλάγχνον, splagchnon, *splangkh´-non*; probably strengthened from σπλήν, *splēn* (the "*spleen*"); an *intestine* (plural); (figurative) *pity* or *sympathy*:—bowels, inward affection, + tender mercy.

4699. σπόγγος, spoggos, *spong´-gos*; perhaps of foreign origin; a "*sponge*":—spunge.

4700. σποδός, spodos, *spod-os´*; of uncertain derivative; *ashes*:—ashes.

4701. σπορά, spora, *spor-ah´*; from 4687; a *sowing*, i.e. (by implication) *parentage*:—seed.

4702. σπόριμος, sporimos, *spor´-ee-mos*; from 4703; *sown*, i.e. (neuter plural) a planted *field*:—corn (-field).

4703. σπόρος, sporos, *spor´-os*; from 4687; a *scattering* (of seed), i.e. (concrete) *seed* (as sown):—seed (× sown).

4704. σπουδάζω, spoudazō, *spoo-dad´-zo*; from 4710; to *use speed*, i.e. to *make effort*, be *prompt* or *earnest:*—do (give) diligence, be diligent (forward), endeavour, labour, study.

4705. σπουδαῖος, spoudaios, *spoo-dah´-yos*; from 4710; *prompt, energetic, earnest:*—diligent.

4706. σπουδαιότερον, spoudaioteron, *spoo-dah-yot´-er-on*; neuter of 4707 as adverb; *more earnestly* than others), i.e. very *promptly:*—very diligently.

4707. σπουδαιότερος, spoudaioteros, *spoo-dah-yot´-er-os*; comparative of 4705; *more prompt, more earnest:*—more diligent (forward).

4708. σπουδαιοτέρως, spoudaioterōs, *spoo-dah-yot-er´-oce*; adverb from 4707; *more speedily,* i.e. *sooner* than otherwise:—more carefully.

4709. σπουδαίως, spoudaiōs, *spoo-dah´-yoce*; adverb from 4705; *earnestly, promptly:*—diligently, instantly.

4710. σπουδή, spoudē, *spoo-day´*; from 4692; "*speed,*" i.e. (by implication) *despatch, eagerness, earnestness:*—business, (earnest) care (-fulness), diligence, forwardness, haste.

4711. σπυρίς, spuris, *spoo-rece´*; from 4687 (as *woven*); a *hamper* or *lunch-receptacle:*—basket.

4712. στάδιον, stadion, *stad´-ee-on*; or masculine (in plural) **στάδιος, stadios,** *stad´-ee-os*; from the base of 2476 (as *fixed*); a *stade* or certain measure of distance; by implication a *stadium* or *race-course:*—furlong, race.

4713. στάμνος, stamnos, *stam´-nos*; from the base of 2476 (as *stationary*); a *jar* or earthen *tank:*—pot.

4714. στάσις, stasis, *stas´-is*; from the base of 2476; a *standing* (properly the act), i.e. (by analogy) *position* (*existence*); by implication a popular *uprising*; (figurative) *controversy:*—dissension, insurrection, × standing, uproar.

Noun from *hístēmi* (2476), to stand. A setting up, an erecting, as of a statue. In the NT, a standing.

(I) The act of standing, with *échō* (2192), to have, to stand (Heb 9:8).

(II) In the sense of an uproar:

(A) Particularly, of a public commotion, sedition, insurrection (Mk 15:7; Lk 23:19, 25; Ac 19:40; 24:5).

(B) In a more private sense, dissension, contentions, controversy, with the idea of violence threatened (Ac 15:2; 23:7, 10).

Deriv.: *sustasiastḗs* (4955), a fellow insurgent; *dichostasía* (1370), division, separation.

4715. στατήρ, statēr, *stat-air´*; from the base of 2746; a *stander* (*standard* of value), i.e. (special) a *stater* or certain coin:—piece of money.

4716. σταυρός, stauros, *stow-ros´*; from the base of 2476; a *stake* or *post* (as *set* upright), i.e. (special) a *pole* or *cross* (as an instrument of capital punishment); (figurative) *exposure to death,* i.e. *self-denial*; by implication the *atonement* of Christ:—cross.

Noun from *hístēmi* (2476), to stand. A cross, a stake, often with a crosspiece, on which criminals were nailed for execution. This mode of punishment was known to the Persians (Ezr 6:11; Est 7:10); and the Carthaginians. However, it was most common among the Romans for slaves and criminals, and was introduced among the Jews by the Romans. It was not abolished until the time of Constantine who did so out of regard for Christianity.

Persons sentenced to be crucified were first scourged and then made to bear their own cross to the place of execution. A label or title was usually placed on the chest of or over the criminal.

(I) Particularly, the crosspiece which was fitted upon the upright stake, which Simon was compelled to carry for Jesus (Mt 27:32; Mk 15:21; Lk 23:26; Jn 19:17). Also, the total structure of the cross on which Jesus hung (Mt 27:40, 42; Mk 15:30, 32; Jn 19:19, 25, 31; Php 2:8; Col 1:20; 2:14). Figuratively, in phrases such as "to take up one's cross," or "to bear one's cross," meaning to undergo suffering, trial, punishment; to expose oneself to reproach and death (Mt 10:38; 16:24; Mk 8:34; 10:21; Lk 9:23; 14:27).

(II) By metonymy, spoken of the total experience of dying on the cross. Spoken only of Christ's death as the atonement for our sins (1Co 1:17, 18; Gal 5:11; 6:12, 14; Eph 2:16; Php 3:18; Heb 12:2).

Deriv.: *stauróō* (4717), to crucify.

Syn.: *xúlon* (3586), tree, cross.

4717. σταυρόω, stauroō, *stow-ro´-o*; from 4716; to *impale* on the cross; (figurative) to *extinguish* (*subdue*) passion or selfishness:—crucify.

From *staurós* (4716), cross. To crucify:

(I) Particularly, to crucify, to nail to a cross (Mt 20:19; 23:34; 26:2; 27:22ff.; 28:5; Mk 15:13ff.; 16:6; Lk 23:21ff.; 24:7, 20; Jn 19:6; Ac 2:36).

(II) Figuratively, to crucify the flesh with its affections and lusts, meaning to mortify them, to put them to death, to destroy the power of sinful desires (Gal 5:24; 6:14).

Deriv.: *anastauróō* (388), to recrucify; *sustauróō* (4957), to crucify with.

4718. σταφυλή, staphulē, *staf-oo-lay´*; probably from the base of 4735; a *cluster* of grapes (as if *intertwined*):—grapes.

4719. στάχυς, stachus, *stakh´-oos*; from the base of 2476; a *head* of grain (as *standing* out from the stalk):—ear (of corn).

4720. Στάχυς, Stachus, *stakh´-oos*; the same as 4719; *Stachys*, a Christian:—Stachys.

4721. στέγη, stegē, *steg´-ay*; strengthened from a primary **τέγος**, *tegos* (a "thatch" or "deck" of a building); a *roof*:—roof.

4722. στέγω, stegō, *steg´-o*; from 4721; to *roof* over, i.e. (figurative) to *cover* with silence (*endure* patiently):—(for-) bear, suffer.

4723. στεῖρος, steiros, *sti´-ros*; as contracted from 4731 (as *stiff* and *unnatural*); "*sterile*":—barren.

4724. στέλλω, stellō, *stel´-lo*; probably strengthened from the base of 2476; properly to *set* fast ("*stall*"), i.e. (figurative) to *repress* (reflexive *abstain* from associating with):—avoid, withdraw self.

To set, place, appoint to a position (such as soldiers in battle array). From this original idea of motion into a place comes the usual Greek significance of to send, to dispatch. In the NT, used only in the middle voice, of persons, to shrink from, to withdraw from, to avoid (2Co 8:20; 2Th 3:6).

Deriv.: *apostéllō* (649), to commission, send; *diastéllō* (1291), to differentiate, set oneself apart, order; *epistéllō* (1989), to send one a message; *katastéllō* (2687), repress, curb; *stolé* (4749), a robe, clothing of distinction; *sustéllō* (4958), to draw together, to contract, shorten; *hupostéllō* (5288), to hold back, to lower, draw back.

Syn.: *anachōréō* (402), to withdraw; *apo-*

chōréō (672), to depart, withdraw; *apochōrízō* (673), to separate.

4725. στέμμα, stemma, *stem´-mah*; from the base of 4735; a *wreath* for show:—garland.

4726. στεναγμός, stenagmos, *sten-ag-mos´*; from 4727; a *sigh*:—groaning.

4727. στενάζω, stenazō, *sten-ad´-zo*; from 4728; to *make* (intransitive *be*) *in straits*, i.e. (by implication) to *sigh, murmur, pray* inaudibly:—with grief, groan, grudge, sigh.

4728. στενός, stenos, *sten-os´*; probably from the base of 2476; *narrow* (from obstacles *standing* close about):—strait.

4729. στενοχωρέω, stenochōreō, *sten-okh-o-reh´-o*; from the same as 4730; to *hem* in closely, i.e. (figurative) *cramp*:—distress, straiten.

4730. στενοχωρία, stenochōria, *sten-okh-o-ree´-ah*; from a compound of 4728 and 5561; *narrowness of room*, i.e. (figurative) *calamity*:—anguish, distress.

Noun from *stenós* (4728), narrow, and *chóra* (5561), territory, a space. Distress, trouble, worry, anguish. In most of the verses where *stenochōría* is used in the NT, the word *thlípsis* (2347), tribulation, is also used (Ro 2:9; 8:35; 2Co 6:4). *Thlípsis* refers to troubles from without, such as persecution, affliction, or tribulation. *Stenochōría* has in view distress that arises from within (often caused by *thlípsis*), such as anguish or worry. In 2Co 12:10, Paul lists *stenochōría* as one of the forms of suffering for Christ through which we will be made strong in Him.

Syn.: *kakopátheia* (2552), hardship; *páthēma* (3804), misfortune, affliction; *sunoché* (4928), a restraint, distress, anguish; *talaipōría* (5004), hardship, misery.

4731. στερεός, stereos, *ster-eh-os´*; from 2476; *stiff*, i.e. *solid, stable* (literal or figurative):—steadfast, strong, sure.

4732. στερεόω, stereoō, *ster-eh-o´-o*; from 4731; to *solidify*, i.e. *confirm* (literal or figurative):—establish, receive strength, make strong.

4733. στερέωμα, stereōma, *ster-eh´-o-mah*; from 4732; something *established*, i.e. (abstract) *confirmation* (*stability*):—steadfastness.

4734. Στεφανᾶς, Stephanas, *stef-an-as´*; probably contraction for **στεφανωτός,** *Stephanōtos* (*crowned*; from 4737); *Stephanas*, a Christian:—Stephanas.

4735. στέφανος, stephanos, *stef´-an-os*; from an apparently primary **στέφω** *stephō* (to *twine* or *wreathe*); a *chaplet* (as a badge of royalty, a prize in the public games or a symbol of honour generally; but more conspicuous and elaborate than the simple *fillet*, 1238), literal or figurative:—crown.

A noun meaning crown, wreath.

(I) As the emblem of royal dignity (Rev 6:2; 12:1; 14:14). Ascribed to saints in heaven, elsewhere called kings (see Rev 4:4, 10). Of the crown of thorns set upon Christ in derision as King of the Jews (Mt 27:29; Mk 15:17; Jn 19:2, 5).

(II) As the prize conferred on victors in public games and elsewhere, a wreath (1Co 9:25). Figuratively, a symbol of the reward of eternal life (2Ti 4:8; Jas 1:12; 1Pe 5:4; Rev 2:10; 3:11).

(III) Figuratively, an ornament, honour, glory, that in which one may glory (Php 4:1; 1Th 2:19).

Deriv.: *stephanóō* (4737), to crown.

Syn.: *diádēma* (1238), diadem, a crown marking royal dignity.

4736. Στέφανος, Stephanos, *stef´-an-os*; the same as 4735; *Stephanus*, a Christian:—Stephen.

4737. στεφανόω, stephanoō, *stef-an-o´-o*; from 4735; to *adorn with* an honorary *wreath* (literal or figurative):—crown.

4738. στῆθος, stēthos, *stay´-thos*; from 2476 (as *standing* prominently); the (entire external) *bosom*, i.e. *chest*:—breast.

4739. στήκω, stēkō, *stay´-ko*; from the perfect tense of 2476; to *be stationary*, i.e. (figurative) to *persevere*:—stand (fast).

4740. στηριγμός, stērigmos, *stay-rig-mos´*; from 4741; *stability* (figurative):—steadfastness.

4741. στηρίζω, stērizō, *stay-rid´-zo*; from a presumed derivative of 2476 (like 4731); to *set fast*, i.e. (literal) to *turn resolutely* in a certain direction, or (figurative) to *confirm*:—fix, (e-)stablish, steadfastly set, strengthen.

4742. στίγμα, stigma, *stig´-mah*; from a primary **στίζω,** *stizō* (to "*stick,*" i.e. *prick*); a *mark* incised or punched (for recognition of ownership), i.e. (figurative) *scar* of service:—mark.

4743. στιγμή, stigmē, *stig-may´*; feminine of 4742; a *point* of time, i.e. an *instant*:—moment.

4744. στίλβω, stilbō, *stil´-bo*; apparently a primary verb; to *gleam*, i.e. *flash* intensely:—shining.

4745. στοά, stoa, *sto-ah´*; probably from 2476; a *colonnade* or interior *piazza*:—porch.

4746. στοιβάς, stoibas, *stoy-bas´*; from a primary **στείβω,** *steibō* (to "*step*" or "*stamp*"); a *spread* (as if *tramped* flat) of loose materials for a couch, i.e. (by implication) a *bough* of a tree so employed:—branch.

4747. στοιχεῖον, stoicheion, *stoy-khi´-on*; neuter of a presumed derivative of the base of 4748; something *orderly* in arrangement, i.e. (by implication) a *serial* (*basal, fundamental, initial*) constituent (literal), proposition (figurative):—element, principle, rudiment.

Noun, a diminutive of *stoíchos* (n.f.), a row. Literally, one in a row, one in a series. In the NT, always used in the plural, the basic parts, elements, or components of something.

(I) Generally, the elements of nature, the component parts of the physical world (2Pe 3:10, 12).

(II) Spoken of elementary instruction, in particular of the first principles of Christian doctrine (Heb 5:12). Spoken of the principles of life, philosophy, and religion, particularly in contrasting ceremonial ordinances and the traditions and commandments of men with a true knowledge of Christ (Gal 4:3, 9; Col 2:8, 20).

4748. στοιχέω, stoicheō, *stoy-kheh´-o*; from a derivative of **στείχω,** *steichō* (to *range* in regular line); to *march* in (military) rank (*keep step*), i.e. (figurative) to *conform* to virtue and piety:—walk (orderly).

4749. στολή, stolē, *stol-ay´*; from 4724; *equipment*, i.e. (special) a "*stole*" or long-fitting *gown* (as a mark of dignity):—long clothing (garment), (long) robe.

Noun from *stéllō* (4724), to send. A long flowing robe reaching to the feet, generally worn by persons of high social rank or dignity

(Mk 12:38; 16:5; Lk 15:22; 20:46; Rev 6:11; 7:9, 13, 14).

Deriv.: *katastolē* (2689), long robe of dignity. **Syn.**: *podérēs* (4158), an outer garment reaching to the feet. For a list of various types of clothing, see the synonyms under *himátion* (2440), garment.

4750. στόμα, stoma, *stom´-a*; probably strengthened from a presumed derivative of the base of 5114; the *mouth* (as if a *gash* in the face); by implication *language* (and its relations); (figurative) an *opening* (in the earth); specially the *front* or *edge* (of a weapon):—edge, face, mouth.

4751. στόμαχος, stomachos, *stom´-akh-os*; from 4750; an *orifice* (the *gullet*), i.e. (special) the "*stomach*":—stomach.

4752. στρατεία, strateia, *strat-i´-ah*; from 4754; military *service*, i.e. (figurative) the apostolic *career* (as one of hardship and danger):—warfare.

4753. στράτευμα, strateuma, *strat´-yoo-mah*; from 4754; an *armament*, i.e. (by implication) a body of *troops* (more or less extensive or systematic):—army, soldier, man of war.

4754. στρατεύομαι, strateuomai, *strat-yoo´-om-ahee*; middle from the base of 4756; to *serve* in a military campaign; (figurative) to *execute the apostolate* (with its arduous duties and functions), to *contend* with carnal inclinations:—soldier, (go to) war (-fare).

4755. στρατηγός, stratēgos, *strat-ay-gos´*; from the base of 4756 and 71 or 2233; a *general*, i.e. (by implication or analogy) a (military) *governor* (*prætor*), the *chief* (*præfect*) of the (Levitical) temple-wardens:—captain, magistrate.

4756. στρατία, stratia, *strat-ee´-ah*; feminine of a derivative of **στρατός, stratos** (an *army*; from the base of 4766, as *encamped*); *camp-likeness*, i.e. an *army*, i.e. (figurative) the *angels*, the celestial *luminaries*:—host.

4757. στρατιώτης, stratiōtēs, *strat-ee-o´-tace*; from a presumed derivative of the same as 4756; a *camperout*, i.e. a (common) *warrior* (literal or figurative):—soldier.

4758. στρατολογέω, stratologeō, *strat-ol-og-eh´-o*; from a compound of the base of 4756 and 3004 (in its original sense); to *gather* (or *select*) as a *warrior*, i.e. *enlist* in the army:—choose to be a soldier.

4759. στρατοπεδάρχης, stratopedarchēs, *strat-op-ed-ar´-khace*; from 4760 and 757; a *ruler of an army*, i.e. (special) a Prætorian *præfect*:—captain of the guard.

4760. στρατόπεδον, stratopedon, *strat-op´-ed-on*; from the base of 4756 and the same as 3977; a *camping-ground*, i.e. (by implication) a body of *troops*:—army.

4761. στρεβλόω, strebloō, *streb-lo´-o*; from a derivative of 4762; to *wrench*, i.e. (special) to *torture* (by the rack), but only figurative, to *pervert*:—wrest.

4762. στρέφω, strephō, *stref´-o*; strengthened from the base of 5157; to *twist*, i.e. *turn* quite around or *reverse* (literal or figurative):—convert, turn (again, back again, self, self about).

To turn, turn about.

(**I**) To turn oneself, turn about (Mt 5:39; 7:6; 16:23; Lk 7:9, 44; 9:55; 10:23; 14:25; 22:61; 23:28; Jn 1:38; 20:14, 16; Ac 7:39, 42; 13:46).

(**II**) Figuratively, to turn into something, meaning to convert or change, such as waters into blood (Rev 11:6); of persons, to turn in mind, be converted or changed, become another kind of person, e.g., to become like children (Mt 18:3).

Deriv.: *anastréphō* (390), to overturn, to sojourn; *apostréphō* (654), to turn away or back; *diastréphō* (1294), to turn, twist throughout, pervert; *ekstréphō* (1612), to subvert, pervert; *epistréphō* (1994), to turn back again, turn about; *katastréphō* (2690), to ruin; *metastréphō* (3344), to turn around, change; *sustréphō* (4962), to roll together, to gather; *hupostréphō* (5290), to turn back, return.

Syn.: *metabállō* (3328), to turn about.

4763. στρηνιάω, strēniaō, *stray-nee-ah´-o*; from a presumed derivative of 4764; to *be luxurious*:—live deliciously.

From *strénos* (4764), excessive luxury (Rev 18:3). To revel, to live luxuriously, act with wantonness from abundance (Rev 18:7, 9).

Deriv.: *katastrēniáō* (2691), to become lascivious against.

Syn.: *spataláō* (4684), to live in pleasure, be wanton; *trupháō* (5171), to live in pleasure and luxury.

4764. στρῆνος, **strēnos**, *stray´-nos*; akin to 4731; a *"straining," "strenuousness"* or "strength," i.e. (figurative) *luxury* (*voluptuousness*):—delicacy.

4765. στρουθίον, **strouthion**, *stroo-thee´-on*; diminutive of στρουθός, *strouthos* (a *sparrow*); a *little sparrow*:—sparrow.

4766. στρώννυμι, **strōnnumi**, *strone´-noo-mee*; or simpler στρωννύω, **strōnnuō**, *strone-noo´-o*; prolonged from a still simpler στρόω, *stroō, stro´-o* (used only as an alternate in certain tenses; probably akin to 4731 through the idea of *positing*); to *"strew,"* i.e. *spread* (as a carpet or couch):—make bed, furnish, spread, strew.

4767. στυγνητός, **stugnētos**, *stoog-nay-tos´*; from a derivative of an obsolete apparently primary στύγω, *stugō* (to *hate*); *hated*, i.e. *odious*:—hateful.

4768. στυγνάζω, **stugnazō**, *stoog-nad´-zo*; from the same as 4767; to *render gloomy*, i.e. (by implication) *glower* (*be overcast* with clouds, or *sombreness* of speech):—lower, be sad.

4769. στῦλος, **stulos**, *stoo´-los*; from στύω, *stuō* (to *stiffen*; properly akin to the base of 2476); a *post* (*"style"*), i.e. (figurative) *support*:—pillar.

4770. Στωϊκός, **Stōïkos**, *sto-ik-os´*; from 4745; a *"Stoïc"* (as occupying a particular porch in Athens), i.e. adherent of a certain philosophy:—Stoick.

4771. σύ, **su**, *soo*; the personal pronoun of the second person singular; *thou*:—thou. See also 4571, 4671, 4675; and for the plural 5209, 5210, 5213, 5216.

4772. συγγένεια, **suggeneia**, *soong-ghen´-i-ah*; from 4773; *relationship*, i.e. (concrete) *relatives*:—kindred.

4773. συγγενής, **suggenēs**, *soong-ghen-ace´*; from 4862 and 1085; a *relative* (by blood); by extension a fellow *countryman*:—cousin, kin (-sfolk, -sman).

4774. συγγνώμη, **suggnōmē**, *soong-gno´-may*; from a compound of 4862 and 1097; *fellow knowledge*, i.e. *concession*:—permission. Noun from *sugginóskō* (n.f.), to think alike, agree with, which is from *sún* (4862), with, and

ginóskō (1097), to know. Concession, permission. Used only in 1Co 7:6.

4775. συγκάθημαι, **sugkathēmai**, *soong-kath´-ay-mahee*; from 4862 and 2521; to *seat oneself* in company *with*:—sit with.

4776. συγκαθίζω, **sugkathizō**, *soong-kath-id´-zo*; from 4862 and 2523; to *give* (or *take*) *a seat* in company *with*:—(make) sit (down) together.

4777. συγκακοπαθέω, **sugkakopatheō**, *soong-kak-op-ath-eh´-o*; from 4862 and 2553; to *suffer hardship* in company *with*:—be partaker of afflictions.

From *sún* (4862), together, or with, and *kakopathéō* (2553), to suffer evil or affliction. To suffer hardship, evil or affliction along with someone. Only in 2Ti 1:8.

Syn.: *sugkakouchéō* (4778), to suffer affliction with; *sullupéō* (4818), to sorrow with; *sumpáschō* (4841), to suffer with; *sunōdínō* (4944), to travail in pain together; *sustenázō* (4959), to groan together.

4778. συγκακουχέω, **sugkakoucheō**, *soong-kak-oo-kheh´-o*; from 4862 and 2558; to *maltreat* in company *with*, i.e. (passive) *endure persecution together*:—suffer affliction with.

4779. συγκαλέω, **sugkaleō**, *soong-kal-eh´-o*; from 4862 and 2564; to *convoke*:—call together.

From *sún* (4862), together, and *kaléō* (2564), to call. To call together (Mk 15:16; Lk 9:1; 15:6, 9; 23:13; Ac 5:21; 10:24; 28:17).

4780. συγκαλύπτω, **sugkaluptō**, *soong-kal-oop´-to*; from 4862 and 2572; to *conceal altogether*:—cover.

4781. συγκάμπτω, **sugkamptō**, *soong-kamp´-to*; from 4862 and 2578; to *bend together*, i.e. (figurative) to *afflict*:—bow down.

4782. συγκαταβαίνω, **sugkatabainō**, *soong-kat-ab-ah´ee-no*; from 4862 and 2597; to *descend* in company *with*:—go down with.

4783. συγκατάθεσις, **sugkatathesis**, *soong-kat-ath´-es-is*; from 4784; a *deposition* (of sentiment) in company *with*, i.e. (figurative) *accord* with:—agreement.

4784. συγκατατίθεμαι, **sugkatatithemai**, *soong-kat-at-ith´-em-ahee*; middle from 4862 and 2698; to *deposit* (one's vote or opinion) in company *with*, i.e. (figurative) to *accord* with:—consent.

4785. συγκαταψηφίζω, **sugkatapsēphizō,** *soong-kat-aps-ay-fid´-zo*; from 4862 and a compound of 2596 and 5585; to *count down* in company *with*, i.e. *enroll among*:—number with.

4786. συγκεράννυμι, **sugkerannumi,** *soong-ker-an´-noo-mee*; from 4862 and 2767; to *commingle*, i.e. (figurative) to *combine* or *assimilate*:—mix with, temper together.

4787. συγκινέω, **sugkineō,** *soong-kin-eh´-o*; from 4682 and 2795; to *move together*, i.e. (special) to *excite* as a mass (to sedition):—stir up.

4788. συγκλείω, **sugkleiō,** *soong-kli´-o*; from 4862 and 2808; to *shut together*, i.e. *include* or (figurative) *embrace* in a common subjection to:—conclude, inclose, shut up.

4789. συγκληρονόμος, **sugklēronomos,** *soong-klay-ron-om´-os*; from 4862 and 2818; a *co-heir*, i.e. (by analogy) *participant in common*:—fellow (joint) -heir, heir together, heir with.

Noun from *sún* (4862), together, and *klēronómos* (2818), an heir, a sharer by lot. A co-heir, joint heir, a joint possessor (Ro 8:17; Heb 11:9; 1Pe 3:7). Spoken of the Gentiles as being joint heirs with Israel (Eph 3:6).

Syn.: *summétochos* (4830), a co-participant; *sugkoinōnós* (4791), a partaker with.

4790. συγκοινωνέω, **sugkoinōneō,** *soong-koy-no-neh´-o*; from 4862 and 2841; to *share* in company *with*, i.e. *co-participate* in:—communicate (have fellowship) with, be partaker of.

From *sún* (4862), with, and *koinōnéō* (2841), to partake. To participate in something with others, to share with others in anything. Spoken of in a good sense: sharing material things with someone in need (Php 4:14). Spoken of in a bad sense: sharing guilt with sinners (Eph 5:11; Rev 18:4).

Syn.: *summerízomai* (4829), to share jointly.

4791. συγκοινωνός, **sugkoinōnos,** *soong-koy-no-nos´*; from 4862 and 2844; a *co-participant*:—companion, partake (-r, -r with).

4792. συγκομίζω, **sugkomizō,** *soong-kom-id´-zo*; from 4862 and 2865; to *convey together*, i.e.

collect or *bear* away in company *with* others:—carry.

4793. συγκρίνω, **sugkrinō,** *soong-kree´-no*; from 4862 and 2919; to *judge* of one thing in connection *with* another, i.e. *combine* (spiritual ideas with appropriate expressions) or *collate* (one person with another by way of contrast or resemblance):—compare among (with).

From *sún* (4862), together, and *krínō* (2919), to judge. Literally, to compare one thing with another by noting similarities and differences. In the NT, to place together and estimate the value of each (2Co 10:12). By extension, in the sense of to explain (by comparison), to interpret, to combine into one, e.g., interpreting spiritual things by spiritual things (1Co 2:13).

4794. συγκύπτω, **sugkuptō,** *soong-koop´-to*; from 4862 and 2955; to *stoop altogether*, i.e. *be completely overcome* by:—bow together.

4795. συγκυρία, **sugkuria,** *soong-koo-ree´-ah*; from a compound of 4862 and κυρέω, **ureō** (to *light* or *happen*; from the base of 2962); *concurrence*, i.e. *accident*:—chance.

4796. συγχαίρω, **sugchairō,** *soong-khah´ee-ro*; from 4862 and 5463; to *sympathize in gladness*, *congratulate*:—rejoice in (with).

4797. συγχέω, **sugcheō,** *soong-kheh´-o*; or συγχύνω, **sugchunō,** *soong-khoo´-no*; from 4862 and χέω, **cheō** (to *pour*) or its alternate; to *commingle promiscuously*, i.e. (figurative) to *throw* (an assembly) *into disorder*, to *perplex* (the mind):—confound, confuse, stir up, be in an uproar.

4798. συγχράομαι, **sugchraomai,** *soong-khrah´-om-ahee*; from 4862 and 5530; to *use jointly*, i.e. (by implication) to *hold intercourse in common*:—have dealings with.

4799. σύγχυσις, **sugchusis,** *soong´-khoo-sis*; from 4797; *commixture*, i.e. (figurative) *riotous disturbance*:—confusion.

4800. συζάω, **suzaō,** *sood-zah´-o*; from 4862 and 2198; to *continue* to *live in common with*, i.e. *co-survive* (literal or figurative):—live with.

4801. συζεύγνυμι, **suzeugnumi,** *sood-zyoog´-noo-mee*; from 4862 and the base of 2201; to *yoke together*, i.e. (figurative) *conjoin* (in marriage):—join together.

4802. συζητέω, **suzēteō**, *sood-zay-teh´-o*; from 4862 and 2212; to investigate *jointly*, i.e. *discuss, controvert, cavil:*—dispute (with), enquire, question (with), reason (together).

4803. συζήτησις, **suzētēsis**, *sood-zay´-tay-sis*; from 4802; *mutual questioning*, i.e. *discussion:*—disputation (-ting), reasoning.

4804. συζητητής, **suzētētēs**, *sood-zay-tay-tace´*; from 4802; a *disputant*, i.e. *sophist:*—disputer.

4805. σύζυγος, **suzugos**, *sood´-zoo-gos*; from 4801; *co-yoked*, i.e. (figurative) as noun, a *colleague*; probably rather as proper name; *Syzygus*, a Christian:—yokefellow.

4806. συζωοποιέω, **suzōopoieō**, *sood-zo-op-oy-eh´-o*; from 4862 and 2227; to *reanimate conjointly* with (figurative):—quicken together with.

4807. συκάμινος, **sukaminos**, *soo-kam´-ee-nos*; of Hebrew origin [8256] in imitation of 4809; a *sycamore*-fig tree:—sycamine tree.

4808. συκῆ, **sukē**, *soo-kay´*; from 4810; a *fig tree*:—fig tree.

4809. συκομωραία, **sukomōraia**, *soo-kom-o-rah´-yah*; from 4810 and μόρον, **moron** (the *mulberry*); the *"sycamore"*-fig tree:—sycamore tree. Compare 4807.

4810. σῦκον, **sukon**, *soo´-kon*; apparently a primary word; a *fig*:—fig.

4811. συκοφαντέω, **sukophanteō**, *soo-kof-an-teh´-o*; from a compound of 4810 and a derivative of 5316; to *be a fig-informer* (reporter of the law forbidding the exportation of figs from Greece), *"sycophant,"* i.e. (general and by extension) to *defraud* (*exact* unlawfully, *extort*):—accuse falsely, take by false accusation.

4812. συλαγωγέω, **sulagōgeō**, *soo-lag-ogue-eh´-o*; from the base of 4813 and (the reduplicated form of) 71; to *lead away as booty*, i.e. (figurative) *seduce*:—spoil.

4813. συλάω, **sulaō**, *soo-lah´-o*; from a derivative of σύλλω, **sullō** (to *strip*; probably akin to 138; compare 4661); to *despoil*:—rob.

4814. συλλαλέω, **sullaleō**, *sool-lal-eh´-o*; from 4862 and 2980; to *talk together*, i.e. *converse:*—commune (confer, talk) with, speak among.

4815. συλλαμβάνω, **sullambanō**, *sool-lam-ban´-o*; from 4862 and 2983; to *clasp*, i.e. *seize* (*arrest, capture*); specially to *conceive* (literal or figurative); by implication to *aid:*—catch, conceive, help, take.

4816. συλλέγω, **sullegō**, *sool-leg´-o*; from 4862 and 3004 in its original sense; to *collect:*—gather (together, up).

4817. συλλογίζομαι, **sullogizomai**, *sool-log-id´-zom-ahee*; from 4862 and 3049; to *reckon together* (with oneself), i.e. *deliberate:*—reason with.

4818. συλλυπέω, **sullupeō**, *sool-loop-eh´-o*; from 4862 and 3076; to *afflict jointly*, i.e. (passive) *sorrow at* (on account of) someone:—be grieved.

4819. συμβαίνω, **sumbainō**, *soom-bah´ee-no*; from 4862 and the base of 939; to *walk* (figurative, *transpire*) *together*, i.e. *concur* (*take place*):—be (-fall), happen (unto).

4820. συμβάλλω, **sumballō**, *soom-bal´-lo*; from 4862 and 906; to *combine*, i.e. (in speaking) to *converse, consult, dispute*, (mentally) to *consider*, (by implication) to *aid*, (personally) to *join, attack:*—confer, encounter, help, make, meet with, ponder.

4821. συμβασιλεύω, **sumbasileuō**, *soom-bas-il-yoo´-o*; from 4862 and 936; to *be co-regent* (figurative):—reign with.

4822. συμβιβάζω, **sumbibazō**, *soom-bib-ad´-zo*; from 4862 and βιβάζω, **bibazō** (to *force*; causative [by reduplication] of the base of 939); to *drive together*, i.e. *unite* (in association or affection), (mentally) to *infer, show, teach:*—compact, assuredly gather, intrust, knit together, prove.

4823. συμβουλεύω, **sumbouleuō**, *soom-bool-yoo´-o*; from 4862 and 1011; to *give* (or *take*) *advice jointly*, i.e. *recommend, deliberate* or *determine:*—consult, (give, take) counsel (together).

4824. συμβούλιον, **sumboulion**, *soom-boo´-lee-on*; neuter of a presumed derivative of 4825;

advisement; specially a *deliberative* body, i.e. the provincial *assessors* or lay-court:—consultation, counsel, council.

4825. σύμβουλος, sumboulos, *soom´-boo-los*; from 4862 and 1012; a *consultor*, i.e. *adviser*:— counsellor.

4826. Συμεών, Sumeōn, *soom-eh-one´*; from the same as 4613; *Symeon* (i.e. *Shimon*), the name of five Israelites:—Simeon, Simon.

4827. συμμαθητής, summathētēs, *soom-math-ay-tace´*; from a compound of 4862 and 3129; a *co-learner* (of Christianity):—fellow disciple.

4828. συμμαρτυρέω, summartureō, *soom-mar-too-reh´-o*; from 4862 and 3140; to *testify jointly*, i.e. *corroborate* by (concurrent) evidence:—testify unto, (also) bear witness (with).

4829. συμμερίζομαι, summerizomai, *soom-mer-id´-zom-ahee*; middle from 4862 and 3307; to *share jointly*, i.e. *participate* in:—be partaker with.

4830. συμμέτοχος, summetochos, *soom-met´-okh-os*; from 4862 and 3353; a *co-participant*:—partaker.

4831. συμμιμητής, summimētēs, *soom-mim-ay-tace´*; from a presumed compound of 4862 and 3401; a *co-imitator*, i.e. *fellow votary*:—follower together.

4832. συμμορφός, summorphos, *soom-mor-fos´*; from 4862 and 3444; *jointly formed*, i.e. (figurative) *similar*:—conformed to, fashioned like unto.

Adjective from *sún* (4862), together with, and *morphé* (3444), form. Having like form with or being conformed to something. In the NT, spoken of twice in the sense of our becoming conformed to Christ: our being conformed to his likeness (Ro 8:29), and our bodies being conformed to his glorious body (Php 3:21).

Deriv.: *summorphóō* (4833), becoming conformed.

4833. συμμορφόω, summorphoō, *soom-mor-fo´-o*; from 4832; to *render like*, i.e. (figurative) to *assimilate*:—make conformable unto.

4834. συμπαθέω, sumpatheō, *soom-path-eh´-o*; from 4835; to *feel "sympathy"* with, i.e. (by

implication) to *commiserate*:—have compassion, be touched with a feeling of.

From *sumpathés* (4835), sympathizing. To sympathize with, be compassionate, have compassion upon anyone, to offer sympathizing aid (Heb 4:15; 10:34).

Syn.: *splagchnízomai* (4697), to feel sympathy, to pity, have compassion; *sullupéomai* (the middle of *sullupéō* [4818]), to experience sorrow with, console.

4835. συμπαθής, sumpathēs, *soom-path-ace´*; from 4841; *having a fellow-feeling* ("sympathetic"), i.e. (by implication) *mutually commiserative*:—having compassion one of another.

Adjective from *sún* (4862), together or with, and *páthos* (3806), suffering, misfortune. Compassionate, sympathizing (1Pe 3:8).

Deriv.: *sumpathéō* (4834), to be compassionate.

4836. συμπαραγίνομαι, sumparaginomai, *soom-par-ag-in´-om-ahee*; from 4862 and 3854; to *be present together*, i.e. to *convene*; by implication to *appear in aid*:—come together, stand with.

4837. συμπαρακαλέω, sumparakaleō, *soom-par-ak-al-eh´-o*; from 4862 and 3870; to *console jointly*:—comfort together.

4838. συμπαραλαμβάνω, sumparalambanō, *soom-par-al-am-ban´-o*; from 4862 and 3880; to *take along in company*:—take with.

4839. συμπαραμένω, sumparamenō, *soom-par-am-en´-o*; from 4862 and 3887; to *remain in company*, i.e. *still live*:—continue with.

4840. συμπάρειμι, sumpareimi, *soom-par´-i-mee*; from 4862 and 3918; to *be at hand together*, i.e. *now present*:—be here present with.

4841. συμπάσχω, sumpaschō, *soom-pas´-kho*; from 4862 and 3958 (including its alternate); to *experience pain jointly* or of the *same kind* (specially *persecution*; to "*sympathize*"):—suffer with.

From *sún* (4862), together with, and *páschō* (3958), to suffer. To sympathize with, to suffer together with (1Co 12:26). To endure like sufferings (Ro 8:17).

4842. συμπέμπω, sumpempō, *soom-pem´-po*; from 4862 and 3992; to *despatch in company*:—send with.

4843. συμπεριλαμβάνω, **sumperilambanō,** *soom-per-ee-lam-ban´-o*; from 4862 and a compound of 4012 and 2983; to *take by inclosing altogether*, i.e. *earnestly throw the arms about one:*—embrace.

4844. συμπίνω, **sumpinō,** *soom-pee´-no*; from 4862 and 4095; to *partake a beverage in company:*—drink with.

4845. συμπληρόω, **sumplēroō,** *soom-play-ro´-o*; from 4862 and 4137; to *implenish completely*, i.e. (of space) to *swamp* (a boat), or (of time) to *accomplish* (passive be *complete*):—(fully) come, fill up.

From *sún* (4862), an intensive, and *plēróō* (4137), to fill. To fill to the brim. Used in the passive, to be filled completely, as with water (Lk 8:23). In the passive, used of time, to be fulfilled or fully come (Lk 9:51; Ac 2:1).

Syn.: *apoteléō* (658), to complete fully; *gemízō* (1072), to fill full; *empíplēmi* or *emplḗthō* (1705), to fill full; *pímplēmi* or *plḗthō* (4130), to fill up; *suntelḗō* (4931), to complete fully; *teleióō* (5048), to complete.

4846. συμπνίγω, **sumpnigō,** *soom-pnee´-go*; from 4862 and 4155; to *strangle completely*, i.e. (literal) to *drown*, or (figurative) to *crowd:*—choke, throng.

4847. συμπολίτης, **sumpolitēs,** *soom-pol-ee´-tace*; from 4862 and 4177; a *native of the same town*, i.e. (figurative) *co-religionist* (*fellow Christian*):—fellow citizen.

4848. συμπορεύομαι, **sumporeuomai,** *soom-por-yoo´-om-ahee*; from 4862 and 4198; to *journey together*; by implication to *assemble:*—go with, resort.

4849. συμπόσιον, **sumposion,** *soom-pos´-ee-on*; neuter of a derivative of the alternate of 4844; a *drinking*-party ("*symposium*"), i.e. (by extension) a *room* of guests:—company.

4850. συμπρεσβύτερος, **sumpresbuteros,** *soom-pres-boo´-ter-os*; from 4862 and 4245; a *co-presbyter:*—presbyter, also an elder.

Noun from *sún* (4862), together with, and *presbúteros* (4245), an elder. A fellow elder (1Pe 5:1). Peter reminds the elders of the dignity of their office that they might not forget their duties (5:2, 3).

4851. συμφέρω, **sumpherō,** *soom-fer´-o*; from 4862 and 5342 (including its alternate); to *bear together* (*contribute*), i.e. (literal) to *collect*, or (figurative) to *conduce*; especially (neuter participle as noun) *advantage:*—be better for, bring together, be expedient (for), be good, (be) profit (-able for).

From *sún* (4862), together, and *phérō* (5342), to bring. To bring together.

(I) To bring together in one place (Ac 19:19).

(I) Figuratively, to bring together for anyone, in the sense of contributing, being advantageous, expedient, profitable (Mt 5:29, 30; 18:6; 19:10; Jn 11:50; 16:7; 1Co 6:12; 10:23; 2Co 8:10). The neuter participle may be used as a substantive: in the singular, meaning advantage, profit, benefit (1Co 7:35; 10:33; 12:7; Heb 12:10); or in the plural, meaning things profitable (Ac 20:20).

Syn.: *ōpheléō* (5623), to be useful, to benefit. Also *lusiteléō* (3081), to be advantageous, answer the purpose.

4852. σύμφημι, **sumphēmi,** *soom´-fay-mee*; from 4862 and 5346; to *say jointly*, i.e. *assent to:*—consent unto.

4853. συμφυλέτης, **sumphuletēs,** *soom-foo-let´-ace*; from 4862 and a derivative of 5443; a *co-tribesman*, i.e. *native of the same country:*—countryman.

4854. σύμφυτος, **sumphutos,** *soom´-foo-tos*; from 4862 and a derivative of 5453; *grown along with* (*connate*), i.e. (figurative) closely *united* to:—planted together.

Adjective from *sumphúō* (4855), to grow together, which is from *sún* (4862), together, and *phúō* (5453), to spring up, produce. Brought forth or grown together. In the NT, used only once in a figurative sense, united, at one with, e.g., oneness with Christ in the likeness of His death (Ro 6:5).

4855. συμφύω, **sumphuō,** *soom-foo´-o*; from 4862 and 5453; passive to *grow jointly:*—spring up with.

4856. συμφωνέω, **sumphōneō,** *soom-fo-neh´-o*; from 4859; to be *harmonious*, i.e. (figurative) to *accord* (*be suitable, concur*) or *stipulate* (by compact):—agree (together, with).

4857. συμφόνησις, **sumphonēsis,** *soom-fo´-nay-sis*; from 4856; *accordance:*—concord.

4858. συμφωνία, **sumphōnia,** *soom-fo-nee´-ah*; from 4859; *unison* of sound ("*symphony*"), i.e. a *concert* of instruments (harmonious *note*):—music.

4859. σύμφωνος, **sumphōnos,** *soom´-fo-nos*; from 4862 and 5456; *sounding together* (*alike*), i.e. (figurative) *accordant* (neuter as noun, *agreement*):—consent.

4860. συμψηφίζω, **sumpsēphizō,** *soom-psay-fid´-zo*; from 4862 and 5585; to *compute jointly:*—reckon.

4861. σύμψυχος, **sumpsuchos,** *soom´-psoo-khos*; from 4862 and 5590; *co-spirited*, i.e. *similar in sentiment:*—like-minded.
Adjective from *sún* (4862), together, and *psuchḗ* (5590), soul. Of one mind, joined together, at peace or harmony. Found only in Php 2:2, where it is used to encourage believers to unity and love. In the context of Philippians 2, *súmpsuchos* seems to imply a harmony of feeling as well as thought.
Syn.: *isópsuchos* (2473), like-minded; *súmphōnos* (4859), agreeing, of one accord; *homóphrōn* (3675), like-minded.

4862. σύν, **sun,** *soon*; a primary preposition denoting *union; with* or *together* (but much closer than 3326 or 3844), i.e. by association, companionship, process, resemblance, possession, instrumentality, addition, etc.:—beside, with. In comparative it has similar applications, including *completeness*.
A preposition. Together, with, together with, implying a nearer and closer connection than the preposition *metá* (3326), with.
(I) Particularly of society, companionship, consort, where one is said to be, do, suffer with someone, in connection and company with him. After verbs of sitting, standing, being or remaining with someone (Mk 4:10; Lk 1:56; 2:13; 7:12; 24:29; Ac 4:14; 14:4, 28; 21:16; 1Co 16:4; Col 2:5; 1Th 4:14).
(II) Figuratively of connection, association, as arising from similarity of experiences, from a common lot or event, with, in like manner with, like, e.g., to be dead with Christ (Ro 6:8; Col 2:20). Also 2Co 13:4; Gal 3:9; Col 2:13.
(III) Implying addition, accession, meaning

besides, over and above (Lk 24:21).
(IV) In composition *sún* implies:
(A) Company, companionship, association with, together, same as the English prefix "con-" as in *sunágō* (4863), to bring together, gather. Also *sugkáthēmai* (4775), to sit with; *sunesthíō* (4906), to eat with.
(B) Completeness of an action, meaning altogether, round about, on every side, wholly, and thus intensive as in *sugkalúptō* (4780), to conceal completely; *sumplēróō* (4845), to fill up.
Syn.: *metá* (3326), with; *pará* (3844), near, beside. Also *homoú* (3674), together.

4863. συνάγω, **sunagō,** *soon-ag´-o*; from 4862 and 71; to *lead together*, i.e. *collect* or *convene*; specially to *entertain* (hospitably):— + accompany, assemble (selves, together), bestow, come together, gather (selves together, up, together), lead into, resort, take in.
From *sún* (4862), with, and *ágō* (71), to lead, assemble, gather together.
(I) Generally, to gather things or other people together. Spoken of one gathering things (Mt 3:12; 6:26; 12:30; 13:30, 47; 25:24, 26; Lk 3:17; 11:23; 12:17; 15:13; Jn 4:36; 6:12, 13). Spoken of one gathering people together (Mt 2:4; 22:10; 27:27; Ac 14:27; 15:30; Rev 13:10; 16:14, 16; 20:8). Passive: to be gathered by another (Mt 25:32).
(II) To take into one's house, meaning to give hospitality and protection (Mt 25:35, 38, 43).
Deriv.: *episunágō* (1996), to gather together in one place; *sunagōgḗ* (4864), a gathering, synagogue.
Syn.: *epathroízō* (1865), to accumulate; *sullégō* (4816), to collect or gather up; *sunathroízō* (4867), to gather together; *trugáō* (5166), to gather in as harvest or vintage.

4864. συναγωγή, **sunagōgē,** *soon-ag-o-gay´*; from (the reduplicated form of) 4863; an *assemblage* of persons; specially a Jewish "*synagogue*" (the meeting or the place); (by analogy) a Christian *church*:—assembly, congregation, synagogue.
Noun from *sunágō* (4863), to lead together, assemble. An assembly, a congregation, a synagogue. Spoken of the Jewish Christians. In other places in the NT, it is used as the assembly place of the Jews.
(I) Of a Jewish assembly or congregation, held in the synagogue buildings for prayer,

reading the Scriptures, and exercising certain judicial powers (Mt 10:17; Mk 13:9; Lk 8:41; 12:11; 21:12; Ac 9:2; 13:42, 43; 22:19; 26:11).

(II) By metonymy of a Jewish place of worship, a synagogue, house of assembly. Synagogues appear to have been first introduced during the Babylonian exile when the people were deprived of their usual rites of worship and were accustomed to assemble on the Sabbath to hear portions of the Law read and expounded. After their return from exile, the same custom was continued in Palestine (cf. Ne 8:1ff.).

Assemblies were held in these at first only on the Sabbath and feast days; but subsequently also on the second and fifth days of the week, Mondays and Thursdays. The exercises consisted chiefly in prayers and the public reading of the OT which was expounded from the Hebrew into the vernacular tongue, with suitable exhortation (cf. Lk 4:16ff.; Ac 13:14ff.). The meeting was closed by a short prayer and benediction, to which the assembly responded with "Amen." See Mt 4:23; 6:2, 5; 9:35; 12:9; 13:54; 23:6, 34; Mk 1:21, 23, 29, 39; 3:1; 6:2; 12:39; Lk 4:15, 16, 20, 28, 33, 38, 44; 6:6; 7:5; 11:43; 13:10; 20:46; Jn 6:59; 18:20; Ac 6:9; 9:20; 13:5, 14; 14:1; 15:21; 17:1, 10, 17; 18:4, 7, 19, 26; 19:8; 24:12.

(III) Though synagogue denotes primarily the religious community of Jews (Lk 12:11; Ac 9:2; 26:11), it was also used of Judeo-Christian assemblies or churches (Jas 2:2). Through the Pauline writings, *ekklēsía* became the predominant name for the Christian church.

Deriv.: *aposunágōgos* (656), put out of the synagogue; *archisun-ágōgos* (752), ruler of the synagogue.

Syn.: *ekklēsía* (1577), church, assembly.

4865. συναγωνίζομαι, **sunagōnizomai**, *soon-ag-o-nid´-zom-ahee*; from 4862 and 75; to *struggle* in company *with*, i.e. (figurative) to *be a partner* (*assistant*):—strive together with.

From *sún* (4862), together, and *agōnízomai* (75), to strive, contend for victory, as in the public games. To exert oneself in company with another, to strive alongside, in the sense of aiding or helping. Used only in Ro 15:30, where Paul exhorts others to strive with him through prayer.

Syn.: *sunathléō* (4866), to wrestle in company with, strive together.

4866. συναθλέω, **sunathleō**, *soon-ath-leh´-o*; from 4862 and 118; to *wrestle* in company *with*, i.e. (figurative) to *seek jointly*:—labour with, strive together for.

4867. συναθροίζω, **sunathroizō**, *soon-ath-royd´-zo*; from 4862 and ἀθροίζω, *athroizō* (to *hoard*); to *convene*:—call (gather) together.

4868. συναίρω, **sunairō**, *soon-ah´ee-ro*; from 4862 and 142; to *make up together*, i.e. (figurative) to *compute* (an account):—reckon, take.

4869. συναιχμάλωτος, **sunaichmalōtos**, *soon-aheekh-mal´-o-tos*; from 4862 and 164; a *co-captive*:—fellow prisoner.

4870. συνακολουθέω, **sunakoloutheō**, *soon-ak-ol-oo-theh´-o*; from 4862 and 190; to *accompany*:—follow.

4871. συναλίζω, **sunalizō**, *soon-al-id´-zo*; from 4862 and ἀλίζω, *alizō* (to *throng*); to *accumulate*, i.e. *convene*:—assemble together.

4872. συναναβαίνω, **sunanabainō**, *soon-an-ab-ah´ee-no*; from 4862 and 305; to *ascend* in company *with*:—come up with.

4873. συνανάκειμαι, **sunanakeimai**, *soon-an-ak´-i-mahee*; from 4862 and 345; to *recline* in company *with* (at a meal):—sit (down, at the table, together) with (at meat).

4874. συναναμίγνυμι, **sunanamignumi**, *soon-an-am-ig´-noo-mee*; from 4862 and a compound of 303 and 3396; to *mix up together*, i.e. (figurative) *associate with*:—(have, keep) company (with).

4875. συναναπαύομαι, **sunanapauomai**, *soon-an-ap-ow´-om-ahee*; middle from 4862 and 373; to *recruit oneself* in company *with*:—refresh with.

4876. συναντάω, **sunantaō**, *soon-an-tah´-o*; from 4862 and a derivative of 473; to *meet with*; (figurative) to *occur*:—befall, meet.

4877. συνάντησις, **sunantēsis**, *soon-an´-tay-sis*; from 4876; a *meeting with*:—meet.

4878. συναντιλαμβάνομαι, **sunantilambanomai**, *soon-an-tee-lam-ban´-om-ahee*; from 4862 and 482; to *take hold* of *opposite together*, i.e. *co-operate* (*assist*):—help.

4879. συναπάγω, sunapagō, *soon-ap-ag´-o*; from 4862 and 520; to *take off together*, i.e. *transport with* (*seduce*, passive *yield*):—carry (lead) away with, condescend.

4880. συναποθνῄσκω, sunapothnēskō, *soon-ap-oth-nace´-ko*; from 4862 and 599; to *decease* (literal) in company *with*, or (figurative) similarly *to*:—be dead (die) with.

4881. συναπόλλυμι, sunapollumi, *soon-ap-ol´-loo-mee*; from 4862 and 622; to *destroy* (middle or passive *be slain*) in company *with*:—perish with.

4882. συναποστέλλω, sunapostellō, *soon-ap-os-tel´-lo*; from 4862 and 649; to *despatch* (on an errand) in company *with*:—send with.

4883. συναρμολογέω, sunarmologeō, *soon-ar-mol-og-eh´-o*; from 4862 and a derivative of a compound of 719 and 3004 (in its original sense of *laying*); to *render close-jointed together*, i.e. *organize compactly*:—be fitly framed (joined) together.

4884. συναρπάζω, sunarpazō, *soon-ar-pad´-zo*; from 4862 and 726; to *snatch together*, i.e. *seize*:—catch.

4885. συναυξάνω, sunauxanō, *soon-owx-an´-o*; from 4862 and 837; to *increase* (*grow up*) *together*:—grow together.

4886. σύνδεσμος, sundesmos, *soon´-des-mos*; from 4862 and 1199; a *joint tie*, i.e. *ligament*, (figurative) *uniting principle, control*:—band, bond.

4887. συνδέω, sundeō, *soon-deh´-o*; from 4862 and 1210; to *bind with*, i.e. (passive) *be a fellow prisoner* (figurative):—be bound with.

4888. συνδοξάζω, sundoxazō, *soon-dox-ad´-zo*; from 4862 and 1392; to *exalt* to dignity in company (i.e. *similarly*) *with*:—glorify together.

From *sún* (4862), together, and *doxázō* (1392), to glorify. To glorify together. In the NT used only in Ro 8:17, in the passive, meaning to share in the glory of another. It is used there to express the privilege given to believers in Christ to share in His glory (cf. Jn 17:22).

4889. σύνδουλος, sundoulos, *soon´-doo-los*; from 4862 and 1401; a *co-slave*, i.e. *servitor* or *ministrant of the same master* (human or divine):—fellow servant.

Noun from *sún* (4862), together, and *doúlos* (1401), slave. A fellow slave, fellow servant. Also see the entry for *doúlos*.

(I) Particularly spoken of those in involuntary service (Mt 24:29).

(II) Spoken of those in voluntary service: of Christians serving Christ together (Col 1:7; 4:7; Rev 6:11); of angels serving the Lord God (Rev 19:10; 22:9); and of officials in an oriental court (Mt 18:28, 29, 31, 33).

4890. συνδρομή, sundromē, *soon-drom-ay´*; from (the alternate of) 4936; a *running together*, i.e. (*riotous*) *concourse*:—run together.

4891. συνεγείρω, sunegeirō, *soon-eg-i´-ro*; from 4862 and 1453; to *rouse* (from death) in company *with*, i.e. (figurative) to *revivify* (spiritually) in resemblance *to*:—raise up together, rise with.

From *sún* (4862), together, and *egeírō* (1453), to raise. To raise up together. Used in the NT of being raised up together with Christ. *Sunegeírō* does not refer to merely being raised in the likeness of Christ's resurrection, but rather, it points to a condition or work effected by union with Christ in His resurrection, taking place in and proceeding from it (Eph 2:6; Col 2:12; 3:1). The term, as it is used in the NT, is synonymous with justification (see Ro 4:25; 5:1; Col 2:12, 13).

4892. συνέδριον, sunedrion, *soon-ed´-ree-on*; neuter of a presumed derivative of a compound of 4862 and the base of 1476; a *joint session*, i.e. (special) the Jewish *Sanhedrin*; (by analogy) a subordinate *tribunal*:—council.

4893. συνείδησις, suneidēsis, *soon-i´-day-sis*; from a prolonged form of 4894; *co-perception*, i.e. moral *consciousness*:—conscience.

Noun from *suneídō* (4894), to be conscious of. Conscience.

(I) A knowing of oneself, consciousness; and hence conscience, that faculty of the soul which distinguishes between right and wrong and prompts one to choose the former and avoid the latter (Jn 8:9; Ro 2:15; 9:1; 13:5; 1Co 10:25, 27–29; 2Co 1:12; 8:7; 1Ti 4:2; Tit 1:15; Heb 9:9, 14; 10:2, 22). Spoken of a good conscience (Ac 23:1; 1Ti 1:5, 19; Heb 13:18; 1Pe 3:16, 21); a pure conscience (1Ti 3:9; 2Ti 1:3); a conscience void of offence (Ac 24:16); a weak conscience (1Co 8:7, 10, 12); an evil conscience (Heb 10:22).

(II) Used by metonymy of approval by the consciences of others (2Co 4:2; 5:11).

4894. συνείδω, suneidō, *soon-i´-do*; from 4862 and 1492; to *see completely*; used (like its primary) only in two past tenses, respectively meaning to *understand* or *become aware*, and to *be conscious* or (clandestinely) *informed of:*—consider, know, be privy, be ware of.

From *sún* (4862), together, and *eídō* (1492), to know. To know together, to become aware of.

(I) To know together with someone, to share information (Ac 5:2). To know within oneself, be conscious of (1Co 4:4).

(II) Figuratively, to see in one's own mind, to perceive within oneself, to be aware of (Ac 12:12; 14:6).

Deriv.: *suneídēsis* (4893), conscience.

4895. σύνειμι, suneimi, *soon´-i-mee*; from 4862 and 1510 (including its various inflections); to *be* in company *with*, i.e. *present* at the time:—be with.

4896. σύνειμι, suneimi, *soon´-i-mee*; from 4862 and εἶμι, **eimi** (to go); to *assemble*:—gather together.

4897. συνεισέρχομαι, suneiserchomai, *soon-ice-er´-khom-ahee*; from 4862 and 1525; to *enter* in company *with*:—go in with, go in with into.

4898. συνέκδημος, sunekdēmos, *soon-ek´-day-mos*; from 4862 and the base of 1553; a *co-absentee* from home, i.e. *fellow traveller*:—companion in travel, travel with.

4899. συνεκλεκτός, suneklektos, *soon-ek-lek-tos´*; from a compound of 4862 and 1586; *chosen* in company *with*, i.e. *co-elect* (*fellow Christian*):—elected together with.

4900. συνελαύνω, sunelaunō, *soon-el-ow´-no*; from 4862 and 1643; to *drive together*, i.e. (figurative) *exhort* (to reconciliation):— + set at one again.

4901. συνεπιμαρτυρέω, sunepimartureō, *soon-ep-ee-mar-too-reh´-o*; from 4862 and 1957; to *testify further jointly*, i.e. *unite in adding evidence*:—also bear witness.

4902. συνέπομαι, sunepomai, *soon-ep´-om-ahee*; middle from 4862 and a primary ἔπω, **epō** (to *follow*); to *attend* (*travel*) in company *with*:—accompany.

4903. συνεργέω, sunergeō, *soon-erg-eh´-o*; from 4904; to *be a fellow worker*, i.e. *co-operate*:—help (work) with, work (-er) together.

4904. συνεργός, sunergos, *soon-er-gos´*; from a presumed compound of 4862 and the base of 2041; a *co-labourer*, i.e. *coadjutor*:—companion in labour, (fellow-) helper (-labourer, -worker), labourer together with, workfellow.

4905. συνέρχομαι, sunerchomai, *soon-er´-khom-ahee*; from 4862 and 2064; to *convene*, *depart* in company *with*, *associate* with, or (special) *cohabit* (conjugally):—accompany, assemble (with), come (together), come (company, go) with, resort.

4906. συνεσθίω, sunesthiō, *soon-es-thee´-o*; from 4862 and 2068 (including its alternate); to *take food* in company *with*:—eat with.

4907. σύνεσις, sunesis, *soon´-es-is*; from 4920; a mental *putting together*, i.e. *intelligence* or (concretely) the *intellect*:—knowledge, understanding.

Noun from *suníēmi* (4920), to comprehend, reason out. Literally, a sending or putting together. In the NT, a putting together in the mind, i.e. intelligence, discernment, understanding (Lk 2:47; 1Co 1:19; Eph 3:4; Col 1:9; 2:2; 2Ti 2:7). By metonymy, the mind itself (Mk 12:33).

Syn.: *diánoia* (1271), understanding; *sophía* (4678), wisdom; *phrḗn* (5424), mind, mental perception; *phrónesis* (5428), prudence.

4908. συνετός, sunetos, *soon-et´-os*; from 4920; mentally *put* (or *putting*) *together*, i.e. *sagacious*:—prudent. Compare 5429.

Adjective from *suníēmi* (4920), to reason out, perceive, understand. Literally, capable of putting together in the mind. Hence, intelligent, perceptive, discerning. Having *súnesis* (4907), comprehension (Mt 11:25; Lk 10:21; Ac 13:7; 1Co 1:19).

Deriv.: *asúnetos* (801), unwise, without discernment or understanding.

Syn.: *sophós* (4680), wise; *phrónimos* (5429), discreet, prudent.

4909. συνευδοκέω, **suneudokeō,** *soon-yoo-dok-eh´-o;* from 4862 and 2106; to *think well of in common,* i.e. *assent* to, *feel gratified with:*—allow, assent, be pleased, have pleasure.

4910. συνευωχέω, **suneuōcheō,** *soon-yoo-o-kheh´-o;* from 4862 and a derivative of a presumed compound of 2095 and a derivative of 2192 (meaning to *be in good condition,* i.e. [by implication] to *fare well,* or *feast*); to *entertain* sumptuously in company *with,* i.e. (middle or passive) to *revel together:*—feast with.

4911. συνεφίστημι, **sunephistēmi,** *soon-ef-is´-tay-mee;* from 4862 and 2186; to *stand up together,* i.e. to *resist* (or *assault*) *jointly:*—rise up together.

4912. συνέχω, **sunechō,** *soon-ekh´-o;* from 4862 and 2192; to *hold together,* i.e. to *compress* (the ears, with a crowd or siege) or *arrest* (a prisoner); (figurative) to *compel, perplex, afflict, preoccupy:*—constrain, hold, keep in, press, lie sick of, stop, be in a strait, straiten, be taken with, throng.

From *sún* (4862), an intensive, and *échō* (2192), to have. To hold together, press together; to hold fast, to shut something up:

(I) Particularly, to cover one's ears (Ac 7:57), or of a city besieged, to shut it up (Lk 19:43); of a crowd, to press together (Lk 8:45); of persons having a prisoner in custody, to hold fast (Lk 22:63).

(II) Figuratively, to constrain, compel, press in on (2Co 5:14); in the passive, to be in constraint, distressed, perplexed (Lk 12:50; Ac 28:5; Php 1:23). With the meaning of to be seized, affected, afflicted: with fear (Lk 8:37), with diseases (Mt 4:24; Lk 4:38; Ac 28:8).

Deriv.: *sunoché* (4928), a holding together, a shutting up of the womb.

Syn.: *thlíbō* (2346), to distress, afflict; *piézō* (4885), to press down together; *anagkázō* (315), to compel; *parabiázō* (3849), to constrain.

4913. συνήδομαι, **sunēdomai,** *soon-ay´-dom-ahee;* middle from 4862 and the base of 2237; to *rejoice* in *with* oneself, i.e. *feel satisfaction* concerning:—delight.

4914. συνήθεια, **sunētheia,** *soon-ay´-thi-ah;* from a compound of 4862 and 2239; *mutual habituation,* i.e. *usage:*—custom.

4915. συνηλικιώτης, **sunēlikiōtēs,** *soon-ay-lik-ee-o´-tace;* from 4862 and a derivative of 2244; a *co-aged* person, i.e. *alike* in years:—equal.

4916. συνθάπτω, **sunthaptō,** *soon-thap´-to;* from 4862 and 2290; to *inter* in company *with,* i.e. (figurative) to *assimilate* spiritually (to Christ by a sepulture as to sin):—bury with.

4917. συνθλάω, **sunthlaō,** *soon-thlah´-o;* from 4862 and θλάω, *hlaō* (to *crush*); to *dash together,* i.e. *shatter:*—break.

4918. συνθλίβω, **sunthlibō,** *soon-thlee´-bo;* from 4862 and 2346; to *compress,* i.e. *crowd* on all sides:—throng.

4919. συνθρύπτω, **sunthruptō,** *soon-throop´-to;* from 4862 and θρύπτω, *thruptō* (to *crumble*); to *crush together,* i.e. (figurative) to *dispirit:*—break.

4920. συνίημι, **suniēmi,** *soon-ee´-ay-mee;* from 4862 and ἵημι, *hiēmi* (to *send*); to *put together,* i.e. (mentally) to *comprehend;* by implication to *act piously:*—consider, understand, be wise.

From *sún* (4862), together or together with, and *hiēmi* (n.f.), to send or put. Literally, to send or bring together, as soldiers for a battle. Figuratively, to bring together in the mind, to grasp concepts and see the proper relation between them. Hence, to comprehend, understand, perceive.

In the NT, generally to understand, comprehend (Mt 13:13–15, 19, 23; 15:10; Mk 4:12; 6:52; Lk 8:10; Ac 28:26, 27; Ro 15:21; 2Co 10:12). Followed by those ideas or concepts which are understood (Mt 13:51; 16:12; 17:13; Lk 2:50; 18:34; 24:45; Ac 7:25; Eph 5:17). To understand, be wise, in respect to duty toward God to be upright, righteous, godly (Ro 3:11).

Deriv.: *súnesis* (4907), understanding; *sunetós* (4908), a person who understands.

Syn.: *ginōskō* (1097), to know; *diaginōskō* (1231), to know exactly; *eídō* (1492), to know intuitively; *epiginōskō* (1921), to know fully, discern; *epístamai* (1987), to know well; *suneídō* (4894), to know intuitively, be conscious of; *phronéō* (5426), to think, understand.

4921. συνιστάω, **sunistaō,** *soon-is-tah´-o;* or (strengthened) συνιστάνω, **sunistanō,** *soon-is-*

tan´-o; or **συνίστημι**, *sun-ístēmi, soon-is´-tay-mee*; from 4862 and 2476 (including its collective forms); to *set together*, i.e. (by implication) to *introduce* (fabourably), or (figurative) to *exhibit*; intransitive to *stand near*, or (figurative) to *constitute*:—approve, commend, consist, make, stand (with).

From *sún* (4862), together with, and *hístēmi* (2476), to set, place, stand. Transitively, to cause to stand with; intransitively, to stand with. *Sunistánō* and *sunistáō* are later forms of *sunístēmi*.

(**I**) Transitively, to cause to stand with, to place together. In the NT, to place with or before someone.

(**A**) Of persons, to introduce, present to one's acquaintance for favourable notice; hence, to commend, to present as worthy (Ro 16:1; 2Co 3:1; 4:2; 5:12; 10:12, 18; 12:11).

(**B**) Figuratively, to set forth with or before someone, to declare, show, make known and conspicuous (Ro 3:5; 5:8; 2Co 6:4; 7:11; Gal 2:18).

(**II**) Intransitively, to stand with, together.

(**A**) Particularly of persons (Lk 9:32; Sept.: 1Sa 17:26).

(**B**) Figuratively, from the transitive, to join parts together into a whole, to constitute, restore. In the NT, to be constituted, created, to exist (Col 1:17; 2Pe 3:5).

Deriv.: *sustatikós* (4956), commendatory.

Syn.: *apodeíknumi* (584), to prove by demonstration; *epainéō* (1867), to commend.

4922. συνοδεύω, sunodeuo, *soon-od-yoo´-o*; from 4862 and 3593; to *travel* in company *with*:—journey with.

4923. συνοδία, sunodia, *soon-od-ee´-ah*; from a compound of 4862 and 3598 ("*synod*"); *companionship* on a journey, i.e. (by implication) a *caravan*:—company.

4924. συνοικέω, sunoikeō, *soon-oy-key´-o*; from 4862 and 3611; to *reside together* (as a family):—dwell together.

4925. συνοικοδομέω, sunoikodomeō, *soon-oy-kod-om-eh´-o*; from 4862 and 3618; to *construct*, i.e. (passive) to *compose* (in company with other Christians, figurative):—build together.

4926. συνομιλέω, sunomileō, *soon-om-il-eh´-o*; from 4862 and 3656; to *converse* mutually:—talk with.

4927. συνομορέω, sunomoreō, *soon-om-or-eh´-o*; from 4862 and a derivative of a compound of the base of 3674 and the base of 3725; to *border together*, i.e. *adjoin*:—join hard.

4928. συνοχή, sunochē, *soon-okh´-ay*; from 4912; *restraint*, i.e. (figurative) *anxiety*:—anguish, distress.

4929. συντάσσω, suntassō, *soon-tas´-so*; from 4862 and 5021; to *arrange jointly*, i.e. (figurative) to *direct*:—appoint.

4930. συντέλεια, sunteleia, *soon-tel´-i-ah*; from 4931; *entire completion*, i.e. *consummation* (of a dispensation):—end.

Noun from *suntéléō* (4931), to accomplish. A full end, completion. In the NT, generally, the end, consummation, used only in the expressions *suntéleia toú aiōnos*, "the completion of the age" (Mt 13:39, 40, 49; 24:3; 28:20) and *suntéleia tōn aiōnōn*, "the completion of the ages" (Heb 9:26). The word *aiōn* (165), age, usually translated world, refers to a period of time.

Syn.: *télos* (5056), the end, goal.

4931. συντελέω, sunteleō, *soon-tel-eh´-o*; from 4862 and 5055; to *complete entirely*; genitive to *execute* (literal or figurative):—end, finish, fulfill, make.

From *sún* (4862), together or an intensive, and *teléō* (5055), to finish. In the NT, to end altogether, to finish wholly, to complete.

(**I**) Generally, spoken of finishing an activity (Mt 7:28; Lk 4:13). Spoken of time being ended (Lk 4:2; Ac 21:27). In the sense of to fulfill, to accomplish, e.g., a promise or prophecy (Mk 13:14; Ro 9:28).

(**II**) To finish, to complete in the sense of to make (Heb 8:8).

Deriv.: *suntéleia* (4930), a finishing, consummation, end.

Syn.: *apoteléō* (658), to finish, bring to a goal; *diateléō* (1300), to bring through to an end; *ekplēróō* (1603), to fulfill; *ekteléō* (1615), to finish out, complete; *exartízō* (1822), to fit out, accomplish; *epiteléō* (2005), to complete, accomplish; *pímplēmi* or *pléthō* (4130), to fill; *plēróō* (4137), to fulfill, complete; *poiéō* (4160), to do, fulfill; *sumplēróō* (4845), to fill completely; *teleióō* (5048), to accomplish.

4932. συντέμνω, suntemnō, *soon-tem´-no*; from 4862 and the base of 5114; to *contract* by cutting, i.e. (figurative) *do concisely* (*speedily*):—(cut) short.

4933. συντηρέω, suntēreō, *soon-tay-reh´-o*; from 4862 and 5083; to *keep* closely *together*, i.e. (by implication) to *conserve* (from ruin); mentally to *remember* (and *obey*):—keep, observe, preserve.

　From *sún* (4862), an intensive, and *tēréō* (5083), to guard, keep. To watch or keep together with someone. In the NT:

　(I) To watch or keep in the sense of to keep for oneself. Spoken of Herod keeping John the Baptist in close custody (Mk 6:20). Figuratively, to keep or lay up with oneself in mind (Lk 2:19).

　(II) To keep or preserve together, from loss or destruction. Spoken of wine and the skin bottles in which it is kept (Mt 9:17; Lk 5:38).

　Syn.: *diaphulássō* (1314), to guard carefully; *phulássō* (5442), to preserve.

4934. συντίθεμαι, suntithemai, *soon-tith´-em-ahee*; middle from 4862 and 5087; to *place jointly*, i.e. (figurative) to *consent* (*bargain, stipulate*), *concur*:—agree, assent, covenant.

4935. συντόμως, suntomōs, *soon-tom´-oce*; adverb from a derivative of 4932; *concisely* (*briefly*):—a few words.

4936. συντρέχω, suntrechō, *soon-trekh´-o*; from 4862 and 5143 (including its alternate); to *rush together* (hastily *assemble*) or *headlong* (figurative):—run (together, with).

4937. συντρίβω, suntribō, *soon-tree´-bo*; from 4862 and the base of 5147; to *crush completely*, i.e. to *shatter* (literal or figurative):—break (in pieces), broken to shivers (+ -hearted), bruise.

4938. σύντριμμα, suntrimma, *soon-trim´-mah*; from 4937; *concussion* or utter *fracture* (properly concrete), i.e. complete *ruin*:—destruction.

4939. σύντροφος, suntrophos, *soon´-trof-os*; from 4862 and 5162 (in a passive sense); a *fellow-nursling*, i.e. *comrade*:—brought up with.

4940. συντυγχάνω, suntugchanō, *soon-toong-khan´-o*; from 4862 and 5177; to *chance together*, i.e. *meet* with (*reach*):—come at.

4941. Συντύχη, Suntuchē, *soon-too´-khay*; from 4940; an *accident*; *Syntyche*, a Christian female:—Syntyche.

4942. συνυποκρίνομαι, sunupokrinomai, *soon-oo-pok-rin´-om-ahee*; from 4862 and 5271; to *act hypocritically* in concert *with*:—dissemble with.

4943. συνυπουργέω, sunupourgeō, *soon-oop-oorg-eh´-o*; from 4862 and a derivative of a compound of 5259 and the base of 2041; to *be a co-auxiliary*, i.e. *assist*:—help together.

4944. συνωδίνω, sunōdinō, *soon-o-dee´-no*; from 4862 and 5605; to *have* (parturition) *pangs* in company (concert, simultaneously) *with*, i.e. (figurative) to *sympathize* (in expectation of relief from suffering):—travail in pain together.

4945. συνωμοσία, sunōmosia, *soon-o-mos-ee´-ah*; from a compound of 4862 and 3660; a *swearing together*, i.e. (by implication) a *plot*:—conspiracy.

4946. Συράκουσαι, Surakousai, *soo-rak´-oo-sahee*; plural of uncertain derivative; *Syracusæ*, the capital of Sicily:—Syracuse.

4947. Συρία, Suria, *soo-ree´-ah*; probably of Hebrew origin [6865]; *Syria* (i.e. *Tsyria* or *Tyre*), a region of Asia:—Syria.

4948. Σύρος, Suros, *soo´-ros*; from the same as 4947; a *Syran* (i.e. probably *Tyrian*), a native of Syria:—Syrian.

4949. Συροφοίνισσα, Surophoinissa, *soo-rof-oy´-nis-sah*; feminine of a compound of 4948 and the same as 5403; a *Syro-phoenician* woman, i.e. a female native of Phoenicia in Syria:—Syrophenician.

4950. σύρτις, surtis, *soor´-tis*; from 4951; a *shoal* (from the sand *drawn* thither by the waves), i.e. the *Syrtis* Major or great bay on the north coast of Africa:—quicksands.

4951. σύρω, surō, *soo´-ro*; probably akin to 138; to *trail*:—drag, draw, hale.

　To draw, drag, drag away, to haul. Spoken of things (Jn 21:8; Rev 12:4; Sept.: 2Sa 17:13) or of persons, to drag by force before magistrates or to punishment (Ac 8:3; 14:19; 17:6).

Deriv.: *katasúrō* (2694), to drag down, hale; *súrtis* (4950), a sandbank.

4952. συσπαράσσω, susparassō, *soos-par-as´-so*; from 4862 and 4682; to *rend completely,* i.e. (by analogy) to *convulse* violently:—throw down.

4953. σύσσημον, sussēmon, *soos´-say-mon*; neuter of a compound of 4862 and the base of 4591; a *sign in common,* i.e. preconcerted *signal:*—token.

4954. σύσσωμος, sussōmos, *soos´-so-mos*; from 4862 and 4983; *of a joint body,* i.e. (figurative) a *fellow member* of the Christian community:—of the same body.

Adjective from *sún* (4862), together with, and *sōma* (4983), body. Of the same body with another. Figuratively, spoken in respect to the Christian church as the body of Christ and of the Gentiles as partakers in it. Used only in Eph 3:6.

Syn.: *adelphós* (80), brother.

4955. συστασιαστής, sustasiastēs, *soos-tas-ee-as-tace´*; from a compound of 4862 and a derivative of 4714; a *fellow insurgent:*—make insurrection with.

4956. συστατικός, sustatikos, *soos-tat-ee-kos´*; from a derivative of 4921; *introductory,* i.e. *recommendatory:*—of commendation.

4957. συσταυρόω, sustauroō, *soos-tow-ro´-o*; from 4862 and 4717; to *impale* in company *with* (literal or figurative):—crucify with.

From *sún* (4862), together with, and *stauróō* (4717), to crucify. To crucify with anyone (Mt 27:44; Mk 15:32; Jn 19:32). Figuratively, spoken of the old human nature, which lost its power when Christ was crucifed (Ro 6:6; Gal 2:20).

4958. συστέλλω, sustellō, *soos-tel´-lo*; from 4862 and 4724; to *send (draw) together,* i.e. *enwrap* (enshroud a corpse for burial), *contract* (an interval):—short, wind up.

4959. συστενάζω, sustenazō, *soos-ten-ad´-zo*; from 4862 and 4727; to *moan jointly,* i.e. (figurative) *experience a common calamity:*—groan together.

4960. συστοιχέω, sustoicheō, *soos-toy-kheh´-o*; from 4862 and 4748; to *file together* (as sol-

diers in ranks), i.e. (figurative) to *correspond* to:—answer to.

4961. συστρατιώτης, sustratiōtēs, *soos-trat-ee-o´-tace*; from 4862 and 4757; a *co-campaigner,* i.e. (figurative) an *associate* in Christian toil:—fellowsoldier.

4962. συστρέφω, sustrephō, *soos-tref´-o*; from 4862 and 4762; to *twist together,* i.e. *collect* (a bundle, a crowd):—gather.

4963. συστροφή, sustrophē, *soos-trof-ay´*; from 4962; a *twisting together,* i.e. (figurative) a secret *coalition,* riotous *crowd:*— + band together, concourse.

4964. συσχηματίζω, suschēmatizō, *soos-khay-mat-id´-zo*; from 4862 and a derivative of 4976; to *fashion alike,* i.e. *conform* to the same pattern (figurative):—conform to, fashion self according to.

From *sún* (4862), together with, and *schēmatízō* (n.f.), to fashion. To give the same form with, to conform to anything. In the NT, used only in the middle or passive: to conform oneself (1Pe 1:14) or to be conformed to anything (Ro 12:2).

Syn.: *summorphóō* (4833), to be conformed to.

4965. Συχάρ, Suchar, *soo-khar´*; of Hebrew origin [7941]; *Sychar* (i.e. *Shekar*), a place in Palestine:—Sychar.

4966. Συχέμ, Suchem, *soo-khem´*; of Hebrew origin [7927]; *Sychem* (i.e. *Shekem*), the name of a Canaanite and of a place in Palestine:—Sychem.

4967. σφαγή, sphagē, *sfag-ay´*; from 4969; *butchery* (of animals for food or sacrifice, or [figurative] of men [*destruction*]):—slaughter.

4968. σφάγιον, sphagion, *sfag´-ee-on*; neuter of a derivative of 4967; a *victim* (in sacrifice):—slain beast.

4969. σφάζω, sphazō, *sfad´-zo*; a primary verb; to *butcher* (especially an animal for food or in sacrifice) or (genitive) to *slaughter,* or (special) to *maim* (violently):—kill, slay, wound.

4970. σφόδρα, sphodra, *sfod´-rah*; neuter plural of **σφοδρός, sphodros** (*violent*; of uncertain derivative) as adverb; *vehemently,* i.e. in *a high* *degree, much:*—exceeding (-ly), greatly, sore, very.

4971. σφοδρῶς, sphodrōs, *sfod-roce´*; adverb from the same as 4970; *very much:*—exceedingly.

4972. σφραγίζω, sphragizō, *sfrag-id´-zo*; from 4973; to *stamp* (with a signet or private mark) for security or preservation (literal or figurative); by implication to *keep secret,* to *attest:*—(set a, set to) seal up, stop.

4973. σφραγίς, sphragis, *sfrag-ece´*; probably strengthened from 5420; a *signet* (as *fencing* in or protecting from misappropriation); by implication the *stamp* impressed (as a mark of privacy, or genuineness), literal or figurative:—seal.

4974. σφυρόν, sphuron, *sfoo-ron´*; neuter of a presumed derivative probably of the same as **σφαῖρα, sphaira** (a *ball,* "*sphere*"; compare the feminine **σφῦρα, sphura,** a *hammer*); the *ankle* (as *globular*):—ankle bone.

4975. σχεδόν, schedon, *skhed-on´*; neuter of a presumed derivative of the alternate of 2192 as adverb; *nigh,* i.e. *nearly:*—almost.

4976. σχῆμα, schēma, *skhay´-mah*; from the alternate of 2192; a *figure* (as a *mode* or *circumstance*), i.e. (by implication) external *condition:*—fashion.

Noun from *schein* (n.f.), the 2 aor. inf. of *echō* (2192), have. Fashion, external form, appearance.

In the NT, spoken of specific external circumstances, the state or condition of something (1Co 7:31). In Php 2:8, it refers to the Lord Jesus' whole outward appearance or condition, which bore no difference to that of other men.

Deriv.: *aschēmōn* (809), shapeless, uncomely; *euschēmōn* (2158), comely, well-formed.

4977. σχίζω, schizō, *skhid´-zo*; apparently a primary verb; to *split* or *sever* (literal or figurative):—break, divide, open, rend, make a rent.

4978. σχίσμα, schisma, *skhis´-mah*; from 4977; a *split* or *gap* ("*schism*"), literal or figurative:—division, rent, schism.

Noun from *schízō* (4977), to split, tear. A schism, a rip, a tear, as in a piece of cloth (Mt

9:16; Mk 2:21). Figuratively, a schism, dissension, division as to opinion (Jn 7:43; 9:16; 10:19; 1Co 1:10; 11:18; 12:25).

Syn.: *dichostasía* (1370), division, dissension.

4979. σχοινίον, schoinion, *skhoy-nee´-on*; diminutive of **σχοῖ-νος, schoinos** (a *rush* or *flag*-plant; of uncertain derivative); a *rushlet,* i.e. *grass-withe* or *tie* (general):—small cord, rope.

4980. σχολάζω, scholazō, *skhol-ad´-zo*; from 4981; to *take a holiday,* i.e. *be at leisure* for (by implication *devote oneself* wholly to); figurative, to *be vacant* (of a house):—empty, give self.

4981. σχολή, scholē, *schol-ay´*; probably feminine of a presumed derivative of the alternate of 2192; properly *loitering* (as a *withholding* of oneself from work) or *leisure,* i.e. (by implication) a "*school*" (as *vacation* from physical employment):—school.

4982. σώζω, sōzō, *sode´-zo*; from a primary **σῶς, sōs** (contracted from obsolete **σάος, saos,** "*safe*"); to *save,* i.e. *deliver* or *protect* (literal or figurative):—heal, preserve, save (self), do well, be (make) whole.

From *sós* (n.f.), safe, delivered. To save, deliver, make whole, preserve safe from danger, loss, destruction.

(I) Used particularly of persons, to keep safe, to preserve or deliver out of physical death (Mt 8:25; 14:30; 16:25; 24:22; 27:40, 42; Mk 3:4; 8:35; 13:20; Lk 6:9; 9:24; Jn 12:27; Ac 27:20, 31; Heb 5:7; Jude 5).

(II) Of sick persons, to save from death and (by implication) to heal, restore to health; passively, to be healed, recover (Mt 9:21, 22; Mk 5:23, 28, 34; Lk 7:50; 8:36, 48; Jn 11:12; Ac 4:9; Jas 5:15).

(III) Specifically of salvation from eternal death, sin, and the punishment and misery consequent to sin. To save, and (by implication), to give eternal life (Mt 1:21; 10:22; 18:11; 19:25; 24:13; Mk 10:26; 13:13; 16:16; Lk 8:12; Jn 5:34; 10:9; Ac 2:40; Ro 5:9, 10; 11:14; 1Co 1:21; 5:5; 1Ti 2:15; 4:16; 2Ti 4:18; Heb 7:25; Jas 1:21; 5:20). The participle is used substantively to refer to those being saved, those who have obtained salvation through Christ and are kept by Him (Lk 13:23; Ac 2:47; 1Co 1:18; 2Co 2:15; Rev 21:24).

Deriv.: *diasōzō* (1295), to bring safely through; *sōtēr* (4990), Saviour.

Syn.: *anagennáō* (313), to beget again from above; *diasōzō* (1295), to bring safely through; *therapeúō* (2323), to care for the sick for the purpose of healing; *iáomai* (2390), to heal both physically and spiritually; *phulássō* (5442), to preserve.

4983. σῶμα, sōma, *so´-mah;* from 4982; the *body* (as a *sound* whole), used in a very wide application, literal or figurative:—bodily, body, slave.

A noun meaning body, an organized whole made up of parts and members.

(I) Generally of any material body: spoken of plants (1Co 15:37, 38) and also of celestial bodies: the sun, moon, stars (1Co 15:40 [cf. 41]).

(II) Specifically of creatures, living or dead. **(A)** Spoken of a human body, different from *sárx* (4561), flesh, which word denotes the material of the body. **(1)** A living body (Mt 5:29, 30; 6:25; 26:12; Mk 5:29; 14:8; Lk 12:22, 23; Jn 2:21; Ro 1:24; 4:19; 1Co 6:13; 15:44; 2Co 4:10; 10:10; Col 1:22; 2:23; Heb 10:5; 1Pe 2:24). Spoken in antithesis to *psuchḗ* (5590), soul (Mt 10:28; Lk 12:4), and *pneúma* (4151), spirit (Ro 8:10; 1Co 5:3; 7:34); also used along with *sōma, psuchḗ* and *pneúma* as a periphrasis for the whole man (1Th 5:23). Spoken of the seat of sinful affections and appetites (cf. *sárx* [4561], II, C). See Ro 6:6; 7:24 [cf. v. 23]; 8:13; Col 2:11. **(2)** A dead body, corpse, generally (Mt 14:12; 27:52, 58, 59; Lk 23:52, 55; 24:3, 23; Jn 19:31; Ac 9:40; Jude 9). Specifically spoken of the body of Christ as crucified for the salvation of man (Ro 7:4); spoken figuratively of the communion bread as representing the body of Christ as crucified for the salvation of man (Mt 26:26; Mk 14:22; Lk 22:19; 1Co 10:16; 11:24, 27, 29). **(B)** Spoken of living beasts (Jas 3:3); also of the dead body of a beast, meaning a carcass (Lk 17:37; of victims slain as sacrifices (Heb 13:11).

(III) By metonymy, spoken of the body as the external man, to which is ascribed that which strictly belongs to the person, man, individual; forming a periphrasis for the person himself (Mt 6:22, 23; Lk 11:34, 36; Ro 12:1; Eph 5:28; Php 1:20). Spoken in a figurative sense of anyone having sexual union with a harlot as becoming part of one body with that harlot (1Co 6:16). Spoken of slaves (Rev 18:13).

(IV) Spoken figuratively for a body, meaning a whole, aggregate, collective mass, as spoken of the Christian church, the whole body of Christians collectively, of which Christ is the head (Ro 12:5; 1Co 10:17; 12:13, 27; Eph 1:23; 2:16; 4:4, 12, 16; 5:23, 30; Col 1:18, 24; 2:19; 3:15).

(V) Spoken figuratively in the sense of body, substance, reality as opposed *hē skiá* (4639), the shadow or type of future things (Col 2:17).

Deriv.: *sússōmos* (4954), belonging to the same body, of the same body; *sōmatikós* (4984), corporeal, physical.

4984. σωματικός, sōmatikos, *so-mat-ee-kos´;* from 4983; *corporeal* or *physical:*—bodily.

Adjective from *sōma* (4983), body. Bodily, corporeal, having a shape of (Lk 3:22); pertaining to the body (1Ti 4:8).

Deriv.: *sōmatikṓs* (4985), corporeally, physically, bodily.

Syn.: *sarkikós* (4559), bodily, carnal, fleshly; *sárkinos* (4560), made of flesh; *phusikós* (5446), physical, material, natural.

4985. σωματικῶς, sōmatikōs, *so-mat-ee-koce´;* adverb from 4984; *corporeally* or *physically:*—bodily.

4986. Σώπατρος, Sōpatros, *so´-pat-ros;* from the base of 4982 and 3962; *of a safe father;* Sopatrus, a Christian:—Sopater. Compare 4989.

4987. σωρεύω, sōreuō, *sore-yoo´-o;* from another form of 4673; to *pile* up (literal or figurative):—heap, load.

4988. Σωσθένης, Sōsthenēs, *soce-then´-ace;* from the base of 4982 and that of 4599; *of safe strength;* Sosthenes, a Christian:—Sosthenes.

4989. Σωσίπατρος, Sōsipatros, *so-sip´-at-ros;* prolonged for 4986; Sosipatrus, a Christian:—Sosipater.

4990. σωτήρ, sōtēr, *so-tare´;* from 4982; a *deliverer,* i.e. God or Christ:—saviour.

Noun from *sōzō* (4982), to save. A savior, deliverer, preserver, one who saves from danger or destruction and brings into a state of prosperity and happiness. In Gr. writers, the deliverer and benefactor of an estate. The ancient mythological gods (such as Zeus) were also called *sōtēr.* In the NT, spoken:

(I) Of God as Saviour (Lk 1:47; 1Ti 1:1; 2:3; 4:10; Tit 1:3; 2:10; 3:4; Jude 25).

(II) Of Jesus as the Messiah, the Saviour of men, who saves His people from the guilt and power of sin and from eternal death, from punishment and misery as the consequence of sin, and gives them eternal life and blessedness in His kingdom (Lk 2:11; Jn 4:42; Ac 5:31; 13:23; Eph 5:23; Php 3:20; 2Ti 1:10; Tit 1:4; 2:13; 3:6; 2Pe 1:1, 11; 2:20; 3:2, 18; 1Jn 4:14).

Deriv.: *sōtēría* (4991), salvation; *sōtḗrion* (4992), the means of salvation.

Syn.: *lutrōtḗs* (3086), redeemer; *Messías* (3323), Messiah.

4991. σωτηρία, **sōtēría,** *so-tay-ree´-ah*; feminine of a derivative of 4990 as (properly abstract) noun; *rescue* or *safety* (physical or morally):—deliver, health, salvation, save, saving.

Noun from *sōtḗr* (4990), a savior, deliverer. Safety, deliverance, preservation from danger or destruction.

(I) Particularly and generally: deliverance from danger, slavery, or imprisonment (Lk 1:69, 71; Ac 7:25; Php 1:19; Heb 11:7). By implication victory (Rev 7:10; 12:10; 19:1).

(II) In the Christian sense, *sōtēría* is deliverance from sin and its spiritual consequences and admission to eternal life with blessedness in the kingdom of Christ (Lk 1:77; 19:9; Jn 4:22; Ac 4:12; 13:26; 16:17; Ro 1:16; 10:1, 10; 11:11; 13:11; 2Co 1:6; 7:10; Eph 1:13; Php 1:28; 2:12; 1Th 5:8, 9; 2Th 2:13; 2Ti 2:10; 3:15; Heb 1:14; 2:3, 10; 5:9; 6:9; 9:28; 1Pe 1:5, 9, 10; Jude 3). By metonymy, a source or bringer of salvation, Saviour (Ac 13:47).

Syn.: *lútrōsis* (3085), a ransoming, redemption; *apolútrōsis* (629), salvation, ransom in full; *sōtḗrion* (4992), the means of salvation.

4992. σωτήριον, **sōtḗrion,** *so-tay´-ree-on*; neuter of the same as 4991 as (properly concrete) noun; *defender* or (by implication) *defence*:—salvation.

Adjective from *sōtḗr* (4990), a savior, deliverer. Delivering, saving, bringing salvation. In the NT, only in the Christian sense of saving, bringing salvation (Tit 2:11). Hence, the neuter with the article is used as a substantive for salvation (Eph 6:17), for the doctrine of salvation (Ac 28:28), and, by metonymy, the Saviour (Lk 2:30; 3:6).

Syn.: *antílutron* (487), a redemption price, ransom; *apolútrōsis* (629), redemption, deliverance, salvation; *lútron* (3083), ransom.

4993. σωφρονέω, **sōphroneō,** *so-fron-eh´-o*; from 4998; to *be of sound mind*, i.e. *sane*, (figurative) *moderate*:—be in right mind, be sober (minded), soberly.

4994. σωφρονίζω, **sōphronizō,** *so-fron-id´-zo*; from 4998; to *make of sound mind*, i.e. (figurative) to *discipline* or *correct*:—teach to be sober.

4995. σωφρονισμός, **sōphronismos,** *so-fron-is-mos´*; from 4994; *discipline*, i.e. *self-control*:—sound mind.

4996. σωφρόνως, **sōphronōs,** *so-fron´-oce*; adverb from 4998; *with sound mind*, i.e. *moderately*:—soberly.

4997. σωφροσύνη, **sōphrosunē,** *so-fros-oo´-nay*; from 4998; *soundness of mind*, i.e. (literal) *sanity* or (figurative) *self-control*:—soberness, sobriety.

4998. σώφρων, **sōphrōn,** *so´-frone*; from the base of 4982 and that of 5424; *safe* (*sound*) *in mind*, i.e. *self-controlled* (*moderate* as to opinion or passion):—discreet, sober, temperate.

Adjective from *sṓs* (n.f.), sound, and *phrḗn* (5424), understanding. Discreet, sober, of a sound mind. Hence, spoken of one who follows sound reason and restrains his passions. In the NT, sober minded, having the mind's desires and passions under control (1Ti 3:2; Tit 1:8; 2:2, 5).

Deriv.: *sōphroneō* (4993), to be of sound mind; *sōphronizō* (4994), to teach to be discreet; *sōphrónōs* (4996), temperately; *sōphrosúnē* (4997), sobriety, sanity.

Syn.: *nēphálios* (3524), circumspect, sober; *sophós* (4680), wise; *phrónimos* (5429), prudent.

T (Tau)

NT Numbers 4999–5190

4999. Ταβέρναι, Tabernai, *tab-er´-nahee*; plural of Latin origin; *huts* or *wooden-walled* buildings; *Tabernæ*:—taverns.

5000. Ταβιθά, Tabitha, *tab-ee-thah´*; of Chaldee origin [compare 6646]; *the gazelle; Tabitha* (i.e. *Tabjetha*), a Christian female:—Tabitha.

5001. τάγμα, tagma, *tag´-mah*; from 5021; something orderly in *arrangement* (a *troop*), i.e. (figurative) a *series* or *succession*:—order.

Noun from *tássō* (5021), to arrange in an orderly manner. Anything arranged in order or in array such as a body of troops, a band, cohort. In the NT, order, sequence, or turn (1Co 15:23).

Syn.: *táxis* (5010), regular arrangement, succession.

5002. τακτός, taktos, *tak-tos´*; from 5021; *arranged,* i.e. *appointed* or *stated*:—set.

5003. ταλαιπωρέω, talaipōreō, *tal-ahee-po-reh´-o*; from 5005; to *be wretched,* i.e. *realize* one's own *misery*:—be afflicted.

5004. ταλαιπωρία, talaipōria, *tal-ahee-po-ree´-ah*; from 5005; *wretchedness,* i.e. *calamity*:—misery.

5005. ταλαίπωρος, talaipōros, *tal-ah´ee-po-ros*; from the base of 5007 and a derivative of the base of 3984; *enduring trial,* i.e. *miserable*:—wretched.

5006. ταλαντιαῖος, talantiaios, *tal-an-tee-ah´-yos*; from 5007; *talent-like* in weight:—weight of a talent.

5007. τάλαντον, talanton, *tal´-an-ton*; neuter of a presumed derivative of the original form of τλάω, tlao (to *bear*; equivalent to 5342); a *balance* (as *supporting* weights), i.e. (by implication) a certain *weight* (and thence a *coin* or rather *sum* of money) or "*talent*":—talent.

5008. ταλιθά, talitha, *tal-ee-thah´*; of Chaldee origin [compare 2924]; *the fresh,* i.e. young *girl; talitha* (*O maiden*):—talitha.

5009. ταμεῖον, tameion, *tam-i´-on*; neuter contraction of a presumed derivative of ταμίας, *tamias* (a *dispenser* or *distributor;* akin to τέμνω, *temnō,* to *cut*); a *dispensary* or *magazine,* i.e. a chamber on the ground-floor or interior of an Oriental house (generally used for *storage* or *privacy,* a spot for retirement):—secret chamber, closet, storehouse.

5010. τάξις, taxis, *tax´-is*; from 5021; regular *arrangement,* i.e. (in time) fixed *succession* (of rank or character), official *dignity*:—order.

Noun from *tássō* (5021), to arrange in order. A setting in order; hence, order, arrangement, disposition, especially of troops; an order or rank in a state or in society. In the NT:

(I) Arrangement, disposition, series (Lk 1:8; 1Co 14:40, in proper order, orderly). Figuratively, good order, well-regulated life (Col 2:5).

(II) Rank, quality, character, as in the phrase "a priest according to the order of Melchisedeck" (Heb 5:6, 10; 6:20; 7:11, 17, 21) which means a priest of the same order, rank, or quality as Melchizedek. Also Heb 7:11, not according to the order or rank of Aaron.

Syn.: *tágma* (5001), a group of people that has been arranged in an orderly fashion.

5011. ταπεινός, tapeinos, *tap-i-nos´*; of uncertain derivative; *depressed,* i.e. (figurative) *humiliated* (in circumstances or disposition):—base, cast down, humble, of low degree (estate), lowly.

Adjective. Low, not high, particularly of attitude and social positions.

(I) Of condition or lot, meaning humble, poor, of low degree (Lk 1:52; Jas 1:9).

(II) Of the mind, meaning lowly, humble, modest, including the idea of affliction, depression of mind (Ro 12:16; 2Co 10:1). Elsewhere with an accompanying idea of piety toward God (Mt 11:29; 2Co 7:6; Jas 4:6; 1Pe 5:5).

Deriv.: *tapeinóō* (5013), to humble.

5012. ταπεινοφροσύνη, tapeinophrosunē, *tap-i-nof-ros-oo´-nay*; from a compound of 5011 and the base of 5424; *humiliation of mind*, i.e. *modesty:*—humbleness of mind, humility (of mind), lowliness (of mind).

Noun from *tapeinóphrōn* (n.f.), low-minded, humble, which is from *tapeinós* (5011), lowly, humble. Humility, lowliness of mind, modesty of mind and deportment. Spoken of a genuine humility (Ac 20:19; Eph 4:2; Php 2:3; Col 2:18, 23; 3:12; 1Pe 5:5). Spoken of a mock humility or self-abasement for the wrong reasons (Col 2:18, 23).

Syn.: *praǘtēs* (4240), meekness.

5013. ταπεινόω, tapeinoō, *tap-i-no´-o*; from 5011; to *depress*; (figurative) to *humiliate* (in condition or heart):—abase, bring low, humble (self).

From *tapeinós* (5011), humble. To humble, bring low:

(I) Particularly, spoken of mountains and hills, to be made level (Lk 3:5).

(II) Figuratively as to condition, circumstances, to bring low, to humble, abase. With the reflexive pronoun *heautoú* (1438) oneself, to humble oneself, to make oneself of low condition, to become poor and needy (Mt 18:4; Lk 14:11; 18:14; 2Co 11:7; Php 2:8). In the passive, to be abased, brought low (Php 4:12). Spoken of the mind, to make humble through disappointment (2Co 12:21). In the passive, to be humiliated through disappointment or exposure to shame (Mt 23:12; Lk 14:11; 18:14). Also in the passive, with the idea of contrition and penitence toward God, to humble oneself (Jas 4:10; 1Pe 5:6).

Deriv.: *tapeínōsis* (5014), humility.

Syn.: *kataischúnō* (2617), to shame, disgrace, dishonor.

5014. ταπείνωσις, tapeinōsis, *tap-i´-no-sis*; from 5013; *depression* (in rank or feeling):—humiliation, be made low, low estate, vile.

Noun from *tapeinóō* (5013), to humble, abase. A making low, humiliation. In the NT, the act of being brought low, humiliation (Jas 1:10); spoken of Christ's humiliation (Ac 8:33); a being

low, of humble condition (Php 3:21); spoken by Mary of her unworthiness (Lk 1:48).

Syn.: *aischúnē* (152), shame, disgrace; *atimía* (819), indignity, disgrace.

5015. ταράσσω, tarassō, *tar-as´-so*; of uncertain affinity; to *stir* or *agitate* (*roil* water):—trouble.

5016. ταραχή, tarachē, *tar-akh-ay´*; feminine from 5015; *disturbance*, i.e. (of water) *roiling*, or (of a mob) *sedition:*—trouble (-ing).

5017. τάραχος, tarachos, *tar´-akh-os*; masculine from 5015; a *disturbance*, i.e. (popular) *tumult:*—stir.

5018. Ταρσεύς, Tarseus, *tar-syoos´*; from 5019; a *Tarsean*, i.e. native of Tarsus:—of Tarsus.

5019. Ταρσός, Tarsos, *tar-sos´*; perhaps the same as **ταρσός,** *Tarsos* (a *flat* basket); *Tarsus*, a place in Asia Minor:—Tarsus.

5020. ταρταρόω, tartaroō, *tar-tar-o´-o*; from **Τάρταρος,** *Tartaroō* (the deepest *abyss* of Hades); to *incarcerate* in eternal torment:—cast down to hell.

From *tártaros* (n.f.), the lower part of Hades in Greek mythology where the spirits of the wicked were imprisoned and tormented. In the NT, to thrust down to Tarturus, to cast into Gehenna. Used only in 2Pe 2:4.

5021. τάσσω, tassō, *tas´-so*; a prolonged form of a primary verb (which later appears only in certain tenses); to *arrange* in an orderly manner, i.e. *assign* or *dispose* (to a certain position or lot):—addict, appoint, determine, ordain, set.

To place, arrange, set in order, e.g., to arrange soldiers in order or ranks. In the NT, used figuratively, meaning to set in a certain order, constitute, appoint, used transitively:

(I) Generally, to appoint, ordain to a position or duty (Lk 7:8; Ac 15:2; Ro 13:1; 1Co 16:15); spoken of those appointed to eternal life (Ac 13:48).

(II) To arrange, to appoint details of life; e.g., to arrange a meeting place (Mt 28:16); to arrange a meeting time (Ac 28:23); to ordain things to be done (Ac 22:10).

Deriv.: *anatássomai* (392), to compose in an orderly manner; *antitássō* (498), to resist; *apotássō* (657), to set apart; *átaktos* (813), disorderly, irregular; *diatássō* (1299), set in order, issue orderly and detailed instructions; *epitássō* (2004), to order; *prostássō* (4367), to command; *protássō* (4384), to foreordain; *suntássō* (4929), to arrange or set in order together; *tágma* (5001), an order, arrangement; *taktós* (5002), arranged, appointed; *táxis* (5010), an arrangement; *hupotássō* (5293), to place under, to make subject to.

Syn.: *apókeimai* (606), to be reserved, appointed, laid aside for a certain purpose; *diatíthemai* (1303), to set apart, to appoint; *kathístēmi* (2525), to designate, appoint, place; *títhēmi* (5087), to place, appoint, settle, ordain.

5022. ταῦρος, tauros, *tow´-ros*; apparently a primary word [compare 8450, "*steer*"]; a *bullock*:—bull, ox.

5023. ταῦτα, tauta, *tow´-tah*; nominal or accusative neuter plural of 3778; *these* things:— + afterward, follow, + hereafter, × him, the same, so, such, that, then, these, they, this, those, thus.

5024. ταὐτά, tauta, *tow-tah´*; neuter plural of 3588 and 846 as adverb; in *the same* way:—even thus, (manner) like, so.

5025. ταύταις, tautais, *tow´-taheece*; and **ταύτας, tautas,** *tow´-tas*; dative and accusative feminine plural respectively of 3778; (*to* or *with* or *by*, etc.) *these*:—hence, that, then, these, those.

5026. ταύτῃ, tautēi, *tow-´tay*; and **ταύτην, tautēn,** *tow´-tane*; and **ταύτης, tautēs,** *tow´-tace*; dative, accusative and genitive respectively of the feminine singular of 3778; (*toward* or *of*) *this*:—her, + hereof, it, that, + thereby, the (same), this (same).

5027. ταφή, taphē, *taf-ay´*; feminine from 2290; *burial* (the act):— × bury.

5028. τάφος, taphos, *taf´-os*; masculine from 2290; a *grave* (the place of interment):—sepulchre, tomb.

5029. τάχα, tacha, *takh´-ah*; as if neuter plural of 5036 (adverb); *shortly*, i.e. (figurative) *possibly*:—peradventure (-haps).

5030. ταχέως, tacheōs, *takh-eh´-oce*; adverb from 5036; *briefly*, i.e. (in time) *speedily*, or (in manner) *rapidly*:—hastily, quickly, shortly, soon, suddenly.

5031. ταχινός, tachinos, *takh-ee-nos´*; from 5034; *curt*, i.e. *impending*:—shortly, swift.

5032. τάχιον, tachion, *takh´-ee-on*; neuter singular of the comparative of 5036 (as adverb); *more swiftly*, i.e. (in manner) *more rapidly*, or (in time) *more speedily*:—out [run], quickly, shortly, sooner.

5033. τάχιστα, tachista, *takh´-is-tah*; neuter plural of the superlative of 5036 (as adverb); *most quickly*, i.e. (with 5613 prefixed) *as soon as possible*:— + with all speed.

5034. τάχος, tachos, *takh´-os*; from the same as 5036; a *brief* space (of time), i.e. *with* 1722 (prefixed) in *haste*:— + quickly, + shortly, + speedily.

5035. ταχύ, tachu, *takh-oo´*; neuter singular of 5036 (as adverb); *shortly*, i.e. *without delay*, *soon*, or (by surprise) *suddenly*, or (by implication of ease) *readily*:—lightly, quickly.

5036. ταχύς, tachus, *takh-oos´*; of uncertain affinity; *fleet*, i.e. (figurative) *prompt* or *ready*:—swift.

5037. τε, te, *teh*; a primary particle (enclitic) of connection or addition; *both* or *also* (properly as correlation of 2532):—also, and, both, even, then, whether. Often used in comparative, usually as the latter part.

5038. τεῖχος, teichos, *ti´-khos*; akin to the base of 5088; a *wall* (as *formative* of a house):—wall.

5039. τεκμήριον, tekmērion, *tek-may´-ree-on*; neuter of a presumed derivative of **τεκμάρ, tekmar** (a *goal* or fixed *limit*); a *token* (as *defining* a fact), i.e. *criterion* of certainty:—infallible proof.

5040. τεκνίον, teknion, *tek-nee´-on*; diminutive of 5043; an *infant*, i.e. (plural figurative) *darlings* (Christian *converts*):—little children.

A noun, the diminutive of *téknon* (5043), child. A little child. Used only figuratively and always in the plural. A term of affection by a teacher to his disciples (Jn 13:33; Gal 4:19; 1Jn 2:1, 12, 28; 3:7, 18; 4:4; 5:21).

5041. τεκνογονέω, teknogoneō, *tek-nog-on-eh´-o*; from a compound of 5043 and the base of 1096; to *be a child-bearer*, i.e. *parent* (*mother*):—bear children.

5042. τεκνογονία, teknogonia, *tek-nog-on-ee´-ah*; from the same as 5041; *childbirth* (*parentage*), i.e. (by implication) *maternity* (the performance of *maternal duties*):—childbearing.

5043. τέκνον, teknon, *tek´-non*; from the base of 5098; a *child* (as *produced*):—child, daughter, son.

Noun from *tíktō* (5088), to bring forth, bear children. A child, male or female, son or daughter.

(I) Particularly:

(A) Generally, a child (Mt 10:21; Mk 12:19; Lk 1:7; 7:35; Ac 21:5; Tit 1:6; 2Jn 4, 13; Rev 12:4).

(B) Specifically of a son (Mt 21:28; Ac 21:21; Php 2:22; Rev 12:5).

(II) Spoken in the plural, children, in a wider sense meaning descendants, posterity (Mt 3:9; Lk 1:17; 3:8; Ac 2:39; Ro 9:7, 8; Gal 4:28, 31). Emphatically it means true children, genuine descendants (Jn 8:39; 1Pe 3:6).

(III) Spoken figuratively of one who is the object of parental love and care, or who yields filial love and reverence toward another.

(A) As a tender term of address, equivalent to "my child" or "my son" as from a friend or teacher (Mt 9:2; Mk 2:5; Lk 16:25).

(B) Generally for a pupil, disciple, the spiritual child of someone (1Co 4:14, 17; 1Ti 1:2, 18; 2Ti 1:2; Tit 1:4; 3Jn 4).

(C) Spoken in reference to children of God (see *Theos* [2316], God) in the sense of those whom God loves and cherishes as a Father. Generally of the devout worshippers of God, the righteous, saints, Christians (Jn 1:12; Ro 8:16, 17, 21; 9:8; Eph 5:1; 1Jn 3:1, 2, 10; 5:2). Also spoken of the Jews (Jn 11:52).

(D) Spoken in reference to the children of the devil (see *diábolos* [1228], devil), in the sense of his followers, subjects, in contrast to *tá tékna toú Theoú*, the children of God (1Jn 3:10).

(IV) Spoken in connection with the name of a city or village of a native, an inhabitant, one born or living in that city; e.g., children of Jerusalem (Mt 23:37; Lk 13:34; 19:44). Also see Gal 4:25; Rev 2:23.

(V) Spoken figuratively in connection with a genitive noun in the sense of a child of anything, meaning one connected with, partaking of, or exposed to that thing: e.g., children of light (Eph 5:8); of wisdom (Mt 11:19; Lk 7:35); of obedience (1Pe 1:14); of wrath (Eph 2:3), of a curse (2Pe 2:14).

Deriv.: *áteknos* (815), childless; *teknotrophéō* (5044), to bring up children; *philóteknos* (5388), loving one's children.

5044. τεκνοτροφέω, teknotropheō, *tek-not-rof-eh´-o*; from a compound of 5043 and 5142; to *be a child-rearer*, i.e. *fulfill* the duties of *a female parent*:—bring up children.

5045. τέκτων, tektōn, *tek´-tone*; from the base of 5098; an *artificer* (as *producer* of fabrics), i.e. (special) a *craftsman* in wood:—carpenter.

5046. τέλειος, teleios, *tel´-i-os*; from 5056; *complete* (in various applications of labour, growth, mental and moral character, etc.); neuter (as noun, with 3588) *completeness*:—of full age, man, perfect.

Adjective from *télos* (5056), goal, purpose. Finished, that which has reached its end, term, limit; hence, complete, full, lacking nothing.

(I) Generally (Jas 1:4, 17, 25; 1Jn 4:18). Figuratively, in a moral sense, of persons (Mt 5:48; Mt 19:21; Col 1:28; 4:12; Jas 1:4; 3:2); the will of God (Ro 12:2; Sept.: Ge 6:9; 1Ki 11:4).

(II) Specifically of persons meaning full age, adulthood, full-grown. In the NT, figuratively meaning full-grown in mind and understanding (1Co 14:20); in knowledge of the truth (1Co 2:6; 13:10; Php 3:15; Heb 5:14); in Christian faith and virtue (Eph 4:13).

Deriv.: *teleiótēs* (5047), completeness, perfection; *teleióō* (5048), to complete, perfect; *teleíōs* (5049), completely, without wavering, to the end.

Syn.: *ámemptos* (273), irreproachable, blameless; *ártios* (739), fitted, complete, perfect; *holóklēros* (3648), entire, whole; *plérēs* (4134), complete, full. *Téleios* is not to be confused with *anamártētos* (361), without sin or sinless.

5047. τελειότης, teleiotēs, *tel-i-ot´-ace*; from 5046; (the state) *completeness* (mental or moral):—perfection (-ness).

Noun from *téleios* (5046), perfect, one who reaches a goal. Perfection or perfectness, completeness (Col 3:14; Heb 6:1).

Syn.: *apartismós* (535), completion, finishing; *katartismós* (2677), the act of completing; *plérōma* (4138), a filling up, fulfillment, fullness.

5048. τελειόω, teleioō, *tel-i-o´-o*; from 5046; to *complete*, i.e. (literal) *accomplish*, or (figurative) *consummate* (in character):—consecrate, finish, fulfill, make) perfect.

From *téleios* (5046), complete, mature. To complete, make perfect by reaching the intended goal. Transitively:

(I) Particularly with the meaning to bring to a full end, completion, reaching the intended goal, to finish a work or duty (Lk 13:22; Jn 4:34; 5:36; 17:4); to finish a race or course (Ac 20:24; Php 3:12, probably reflects the same meaning). Of time (Lk 2:43); of prophecy, fulfilled (Jn 19:28).

(II) Figuratively meaning to make perfect in the sense of bringing to a state of completion or fulfillment.

(A) Generally (Jn 17:23; 2Co 12:9; Jas 2:22; 1Jn 2:5; 4:12, 17, 18).

(B) Used in the epistle to the Hebrews in a moral sense meaning to make perfect, to fully cleanse from sin, in contrast to ceremonial cleansing. Moral expiation is the completion or realization of the ceremonial one (Heb 7:19; 9:9; 10:1, 14). Also used of Christ as exalted to be head over all things (Heb 2:10; 5:9; 7:28); of saints advanced to glory (Heb 11:40; 12:23).

Deriv.: *teleíōsis* (5050), the act of completion; *teleiōtés* (5051), a completer, perfecter.

Syn.: *apoteléō* (658), to complete entirely, consummate, finish; *plēróō* (4137), to fill, satisfy, execute, finish, accomplish, complete, fulfill; *sumplēróō* (4845), to fill to the brim, accomplish, fill up, complete; *sunteléō* (4931), to complete entirely, finish, fulfill.

5049. τελείως, teleiōs, *tel-i´-oce*; adverb from 5046; *completely*, i.e. (of hope) *without wavering*:—to the end.

Adverb from *téleios* (5046), perfect, complete. Perfectly, entirely, steadfastly, unwaveringly. Used only in 1Pe 1:13.

Syn.: *hólōs* (3654), completely, altogether, utterly, by any means; *pántē* (3839), wholly, always.

5050. τελείωσις, teleiōsis, *tel-i´-o-sis*; from 5448; (the act) *completion*, i.e. (of prophecy) *verification*, or (of expiation) *absolution*:—perfection, performance.

Noun from *teleióō* (5048), to complete. Completion, perfection. Spoken of a prediction: fulfillment (Lk 1:45). Also spoken of perfect expiation (Heb 7:11).

Syn.: *holoklēría* (3647), integrity, wholeness, soundness; *suntéleia* (4930), completion, consummation.

5051. τελειωτής, teleiōtēs, *tel-i-o-tace´*; from 5048; a *completer*, i.e. *consummater*:—finisher.

Noun from *teleióō* (5048), to complete. A completer, perfecter, particularly one who reaches a goal so as to win the prize. Used only once in Scripture in Heb 12:2 where Jesus is called the "author and finisher of our faith." Compare Heb 2:10 where he is said to bring many sons to glory.

5052. τελεσφορέω, telesphoreō, *tel-es-for-eh´-o*; from a compound of 5056 and 5342; to *be a bearer to completion* (maturity), i.e. to *ripen* fruit (figurative):—bring fruit to perfection.

From *télos* (5056), end, goal, perfection, and *phérō* (5342), to bring, bear. To bring to perfection or maturity, e.g., fruit, grain, etc., to ripen. Used figuratively, only in Lk 8:14.

5053. τελευτάω, teleutaō, *tel-yoo-tah´-o*; from a presumed derivative of 5055; to *finish* life (by implication of 979), i.e. *expire* (*demise*):—be dead, decease, die.

From *teleutē* (5054), death, an end, accomplishment. To end, finish, complete. Intransitively, to end. In the NT, intransitively or with *bíon* (979), earthly life, implied, meaning to end one's life, die (Mt 2:19; 9:18; 22:25; Mk 9:44, 46, 48; Lk 7:2; Ac 2:29; 7:15; Heb 11:22). Of a violent death (Mt 15:4; Mk 7:10).

Syn.: *apothnéskō* (599), to die off; *thnéskō* (2348), to die; *sunapothnéskō* (4880), to die with, together.

5054. τελευτή, teleutē, *tel-yoo-tay´*; from 5053; *decease*:—death.

Noun from *teléō* (5055), to accomplish or complete something. An end, figurative for death. In Mt 2:15, the end of life, death, decease (Sept.: Ge 27:2; Jos 1:1; Jgs 1:1).

Deriv.: *teleutáō* (5053), to end, finish, complete.

Syn.: *thánatos* (2288), death.

5055. τελέω, teleō, *tel-eh´-o*; from 5056; to *end*, i.e. *complete, execute, conclude, discharge* (a debt):—accomplish, make an end, expire, fill up, finish, go over, pay, perform.

From *télos* (5056), end, goal. To make an end or to accomplish, to complete something.

(I) Generally (Mt 10:23; 11:1; 13:53; 19:1; 26:1; Lk 2:39; 2Ti 4:7; Rev 11:7). In the passive (Lk 12:50; Jn 19:28, 30; Rev 10:7; 15:1, 8). Of time in the passive, meaning to be ended, fulfilled (Rev 20:3, 5, 7).

(II) To accomplish, fulfill, execute fully, e.g., a rule or law (Ro 2:27; Gal 5:16; Jas 2:8). Spoken of declarations, prophecy (Lk 18:31; 22:37; Ac 13:29; Rev 17:17).

(III) By implication, to pay off or in full, such as taxes, tribute (Mt 17:24; Ro 13:6).

Deriv.: *apoteléō* (658), to perfect; *diateléō* (1300), to finish completely; *ekteléō* (1615), to complete fully; *epiteléō* (2005), to complete, finish; *sunteléō* (4931), to finish entirely; *teleutḗ* (5054), an end, death.

Syn.: *sumplēróō* (4845), to fill up completely; *teleióō* (5048), to complete, accomplish, consecrate, perfect.

5056. τέλος, telos, *tel´-os*; from a primary **τέλλω, tellō** (to *set out* for a definite point or *goal*); properly the point aimed at as a *limit*, i.e. (by implication) the *conclusion* of an act or state (*termination* [literal, figurative or indefinite], *result* [immediate, ultimate or prophetic], *purpose*); specially an *impost* or *levy* (as *paid*):— + continual, custom, end (-ing), finally, uttermost. Compare 5411.

A noun meaning an end, a term, a termination, completion. Particularly only in respect to time.

(I) Generally (Mt 10:22; 24:6, 13; Mk 3:26; 13:7, 13; Lk 1:33; 21:9; 1Co 1:8; 10:11; 15:24; 2Co 1:13; 3:13; Heb 3:6, 14; 6:11; 7:3; 1Pe 4:7; Rev 2:26). Adverbially in the accusative, finally, at last (1Pe 3:8). With the prep. *eis* (1519), in, unto: to the end, continually, perpetually, forever (Lk 18:5; 1Th 2:16).

(II) Figuratively it means end, outcome, result (Mt 26:58; Lk 22:37; Ro 6:21, 22; 1Co 15:24; 2Co 11:15; Php 3:19; Heb 6:8; 7:3; Jas 5:11; 1Pe 1:9; 4:7, 17).

(III) Figuratively, the meaning can be extended to convey the end or final purpose, that to which all the parts tend and in which they terminate, the sum total (1Ti 1:5).

(IV) Figuratively, it can also be used for a tax, toll, custom, tribute, particularly what is paid for public purposes for the maintenance of the state (Mt 17:25; Ro 13:7).

Deriv.: *entéllomai* (1781), to charge, command; *pantelḗs* (3838), complete, whole, entire; *polutelḗs* (4185), very expensive, costly; *téleios* (5046), finished, complete; *telesphoréō* (5052), to bring to an intended perfection or goal; *teléō* (5055), to finish, complete; *telṓnēs* (5057), a gatherer of taxes or customs.

Syn.: *péras* (4009), a limit, boundary, uttermost part; *suntéleia* (4930), a completion, consummation, fulfillment; *ōméga* (5598), the last letter of the Greek alphabet.

5057. τελώνης, telōnēs, *tel-o´-nace*; from 5056 and 5608; a *tax-farmer*, i.e. *collector of* public *revenue*:—publican.

5058. τελώνιον, telōnion, *tel-o´-nee-on*; neuter of a presumed derivative of 5057; a *tax-gatherer's* place of business:—receipt of custom.

5059. τέρας, teras, *ter´-as*; of uncertain affinity; a *prodigy* or *omen*:—wonder.

A noun meaning wonder or omen. In the NT, it is always associated with *sēmeíon* (4592), sign, and always in the plural translated "wonders" (Ac 2:19, 22). Used of the miracles of Moses (Ac 7:36); of Christ (Jn 4:48); of the apostles and teachers (Ac 2:43; 4:30; 5:12; 6:8; 14:3; 15:12; Ro 15:19; 2Co 12:12; Heb 2:4); and of false prophets or teachers (Mt 24:24; Mk 13:22; 2Th 2:9).

Syn.: *dúnamis* (1411), mighty work, miracle; *thaúma* (2295), wonder; *thaumásios* (2297), a miracle; *megaleíos* (3167), something great; *sēmeíon* (4592), sign.

5060. Τέρτιος, Tertios, *ter´-tee-os*; of Latin origin; *third*; *Tertius*, a Christian:—Tertius.

5061. Τέρτυλλος, Tertullos, *ter´-tool-los*; of uncertain derivative; *Tertullus*, a Roman:—Tertullus.

5062. τεσσαράκοντα, tessarakonta, *tes-sar-ak´-on-tah*; the decade of 5064; *forty*:—forty.

5063. τεσσαρακονταετής, tessarakontaetēs, *tes-sar-ak-on-tah-et-ace´*; from 5062 and 2094; *of forty years* of age:—(+ full, of) forty years (old).

5064. τέσσαρες, tessares, *tes´-sar-es*; neuter **τέσσαρα, tessara,** *tes´-sar-ah*; a plural number; *four*:—four.

5065. τεσσαρεσκαιδέκατος, tessareskaidekatos, *tes-sar-es-kahee-dek´-at-os*; from 5064 and 2532 and 1182; *fourteenth*:—fourteenth.

5066. τεταρταῖος, tetartaios, *tet-ar-tah´-yos*; from 5064; pertaining to the *fourth* day:—four days.

5067. τέταρτος, tetartos, *tet´-ar-tos*; order from 5064; *fourth*:—four (-th).

5068. τετράγωνος, tetragōnos, *tet-rag´-on-nos*; from 5064 and 1137; *four-cornered*, i.e. *square*:—foursquare.

5069. τετράδιον, tetradion, *tet-rad´-ee-on*; neuter of a presumed derivative of τέτρας, *tetras* (a *tetrad*; from 5064); a *quaternion* or squad (picket) of four Roman soldiers:—quaternion.

5070. τετρακισχίλιοι, tetrakischilioi, *tet-rak-is-khil´-ee-oy*; from the multiple adverb of 5064 and 5507; *four times a thousand*:—four thousand.

5071. τετρακόσιοι, tetrakosioi, *tet-rak-os´-ee-oy*; neuter τετρακόσια, *tetrakosia*, *tet-rak-os´-ee-ah*; plural from 5064 and 1540; *four hundred*:—four hundred.

5072. τετράμηνον, tetramēnon, *tet-ram´-ay-non*; neuter of a compound of 5064 and 3376; a *four months´* space:—four months.

5073. τετραπλόος, tetraploos, *tet-rap-lo´-os*; from 5064 and a derivative of the base of 4118; *quadruple*:—fourfold.

5074. τετράπους, tetrapous, *tet-rap´-ooce*; from 5064 and 4228; a *quadruped*:—four-footed beast.

5075. τετραρχέω, tetrarcheō, *tet-rar-kheh´-o*; from 5076; to *be a tetrarch*:—(be) tetrarch.

5076. τετράρχης, tetrarchēs, *tet-rar´-khace*; from 5064 and 757; the *ruler of a fourth* part of a country ("*tetrarch*"):—tetrarch.

5077. τεφρόω, tephroō, *tef-ro´-o*; from τέφρα, *tephra* (*ashes*); to *incinerate*, i.e. *consume*:—turn to ashes.

5078. τέχνη, technē, *tekh´-nay*; from the base of 5088; *art* (as *productive*), i.e. (special) a *trade*, or (genitive) *skill*:—art, craft, occupation.

5079. τεχνίτης, technitēs, *tekh-nee´-tace*; from 5078; an *artisan*; (figurative) a *founder* (*Creator*):—builder, craftsman.

5080. τήκω, tēkō, *tay´-ko*; apparently a primary verb; to *liquefy*:—melt.

5081. τηλαυγῶς, tēlaugōs, *tay-low-goce*; adverb from a compound of a derivative of 5056 and 827; in a *far-shining* manner, i.e. *plainly*:—clearly.

5082. τηλικοῦτος, tēlikoutos, *tay-lik-oo´-tos*; feminine τηλικαύτη, *tēlikautē*, *tay-lik-ow´-tay*; from a compound of 3588 with 2245 and 3778; *such as this*, i.e. (in [figurative] magnitude) so *vast*:—so great, so mighty.

5083. τηρέω, tēreō, *tay-reh´-o*; from τηρός, *teros* (a *watch*; perhaps akin to 2334); to *guard* (from *loss* or *injury*, properly by keeping *the eye* upon; and thus differing from 5442, which is properly to *prevent* escaping; and from 2892, which implies a *fortress* or full military lines of apparatus), i.e. to *note* (a prophecy; figurative, to *fulfill* a command); by implication to *detain* (in custody; figurative, to *maintain*); by extension to *withhold* (for personal ends; figurative, to *keep unmarried*):—hold fast, keep (-er), (pre-, re-) serve, watch.

From *tērós* (n.f.), a warden, guard. To keep an eye on, to watch, and hence to guard, keep, obey, transitively:

(I) Particularly to watch, observe attentively, keep the eyes fixed upon, with the accusative (Rev 1:3, keeping for the fulfillment of the prophecy; 22:7, 9). Figuratively, to obey, observe, keep, fulfill a duty, precept, law, custom, or custom meaning to perform watchfully, vigilantly, spoken of keeping: commandments (Mt 19:17; Jn 14:15, 21; 15:10; 1Ti 6:14; 1Jn 2:3, 4; 3:22, 24; 5:2, 3; Rev 12:17; 14:12); a saying or words (Jn 8:51, 52, 55; 14:23, 24; 15:20; 17:6; 1Jn 2:5; Rev 3:8, 10); the law (Ac 15:5, 24; Jas 2:10); tradition (Mk 7:9); the Sabbath (Jn 9:16). See also Mt 23:3; 28:20; Ac 21:25; Rev 2:26; 3:3).

(II) To keep, guard, e.g., a prisoner (Mt 27:36, 54; 28:4; Ac 12:5, 6; 16:23; 24:23; 25:4, 21). Figuratively, to guard in the sense of keeping someone safe, preserving (Jn 17:11, 12, 15; 1Th 5:23; Jude 1; Rev 3:10). Figuratively, to guard in the sense of preserving something, e.g., the faith (2Ti 4:7); see also Eph 4:3; Jude 6. Figuratively, to guard oneself in the sense of keeping oneself from defilement (1Ti 5:22; Jas 1:27; 1Jn 5:18; Jude 21; Rev 16:15).

(III) To keep back or in store, reserve for later use (Jn 2:10; 12:7; 1Pe 1:4; to keep a daughter at home, unmarried, as opposed to giving her in marriage (1Co 7:37). In a negative sense, to reserve the blackness of eternal condemnation for the wicked (2Pe 2:17; Jude 13); to reserve the wicked for eternal judgement (2Pe 2:4, 9; 3:7).

Deriv.: *diatēréō* (1301) keep, store up; *paratēréō* (3906), to watch closely, guard; *suntēréō* (4933), conserve, keep, protect, preserve; *tḗrēsis* (5084), watch, custody.

Syn.: *phulássō* (5442), to guard, watch, keep by way of protection, observe, protect. Also *diaphulássō* (1314), to guard carefully; *kratéō* (2902), to get possession of, hold fast, keep; *phrouréō* (5432), to keep with a military guard.

5084. τήρησις, tērēsis, *tay´-ray-sis*; from 5083; a *watching*, i.e. (figurative) *observance*, or (concretely) a *prison*:—hold.

Noun from *tēréō* (5083), to keep watch. A custody, keeping, watching.

(I) Figuratively, observance, performance, of precepts (1Co 7:19).

(II) A keeping in the sense of a guarding. In the NT, by metonymy, a place of guarding, a prison (Ac 4:3; 5:18).

Syn.: *desmōtḗrion* (1201), a place of bonds, prison; *phulakḗ* (5438), a guarding or guard, prison, hold.

5085. Τιβεριάς, Tiberias, *tib-er-ee-as´*; from 5086; *Tiberias*, the name of a town and a lake in Palestine:—Tiberias.

5086. Τιβέριος, Tiberios, *tib-er´-ee-os*; of Latin origin; probably *pertaining to the* river *Tiberis* or *Tiber; Tiberius*, a Roman emperor:—Tiberius.

5087. τίθημι, tithēmi, *tith´-ay-mee*; a prolonged form of a primary **θέω, theō,** *theh´-o* (which is used only as alternate in certain tenses); to place (in the widest application, literal and figurative; properly in a passive or horizontal posture, and thus different from 2476, which properly denotes an upright and active position, while 2749 is properly reflexive and utterly prostrate):— + advise, appoint, bow, commit, conceive, give, × kneel down, lay (aside, down, up), make, ordain, purpose, put, set (forth), settle, sink down.

To set, put, place, lay.

(I) Particularly, to set, put, or place a person or thing. To place under a basket (Mt 5:15; Mk 4:21) or under a bed (Lk 8:16). See also Lk 11:33; Jn 2:10; 19:19; Rev 10:2. In the middle, meaning to set or place on one's own behalf, or by one's own order; to put persons in prison (Mt 14:3; Ac 4:3; 5:25; 12:4).

(II) More often of things, to set, put, or lay down. To set in the proper place, assign a place (1Co 12:18).

(A) Particularly spoken of a foundation (Lk 6:48; 14:29; 1Co 3:10, 11); a stone, stumbling stone (Ro 9:33; 1Pe 2:6). Spoken of dead bodies: to lay in a tomb or sepulchre (Mt 27:60; Mk 6:29; 15:47; 16:6; Lk 23:53, 55; Jn 11:34; 19:41, 42; 20:2, 13, 15; Ac 7:16; 13:29; Rev 11:9). Spoken of the knees: to place the knees, to kneel (Mk 15:19; Lk 22:41; Ac 7:60; 9:40; 20:36; 21:5). To place in the sense of to lay off or aside, such as garments (Jn 13:4). See also Mk 10:16; Lk 5:18; Ac 3:2; 4:35, 37; 5:2, 15; 9:37; 1Co 15:25; 16:2; 2Co 3:13.

(B) Figuratively, to lay down one's life (Jn 10:11, 15, 17, 18; 13:37, 38; 15:13; 1Jn 3:16). To place something in the heart or spirit, in the sense of to resolve, to purpose (Lk 21:14; Ac 5:4; 19:21), or in the sense of to ponder (Lk 1:66). See also Mt 12:18; Lk 9:44; 2Co 5:19.

(C) Figuratively, to set, to place in the sense of to appoint, ordain, e.g., to ordain times and seasons (Ac 1:7). To place or ordain someone in a position, to make somebody something; e.g., to make Abraham the father of many nations (Ro 4:17), to make the Son heir of all things (Heb 1:2). To place one into a position of privilege or ministry (Jn 15:16; Ac 13:47; 20:28; 1Co 12:28; 1Ti 1:12; 2:7; 2Ti 1:11). To place or decree a place of subordination for someone (Mt 22:44; Mk 12:36; Lk 20:43; Ac 2:35; Heb 1:13; 10:13) or a punishment for someone (Mt 24:51; Lk 12:46; 1Pe 2:8). To place or give counsel, to advise (Ac 27:12); to place something for others in a certain way, as to give the gospel out freely (1Co 9:18).

Deriv.: *anatíthēmi* (394), to put up or before; *apotíthēmi* (659), to put off from oneself; *diatíthemai* (1303), dispose of, bequeath, to appoint a testator; *ektíthēmi* (1620), to expose, set out; *epitíthēmi* (2007), to lay on; *eúthetos* (2111), well placed, proper; *thḗkē* (2336), receptacle; *thēsaurós* (2344), a receptacle for treasure; *katatíthēmi*

(2698), to lay down; *metatíthēmi* (3346), to transfer, transport, change, remove; *nomothétēs* (3550), a lawgiver; *nouthetéō* (3560), to admonish; *horothesía* (3734), bound; *paratíthēmi* (3908), to place alongside, present, commit, set before; *peritíthēmi* (4060), to place or put around; *prostíthēmi* (4369), to place additionally, lay beside, annex, add to; *protíthemai* (4388), to place before for oneself, propose, purpose; *suntíthemai* (4934), agree, assent, covenant; *huiothesía* (5206) adoption; *hupotíthēmi* (5294), to place under, lay down.

Syn.: *apókeimai* (606), to be laid up, reserved, appointed; *hístēmi* (2476), to make to stand, appoint; *kathízō* (2523), to seat someone, set, appoint; *kathístēmi* (2525), to cause to stand, appoint a person to a position, ordain, set down; *horízō* (3724), to mark by a limit, determine, ordain, define; *procheirízō* (4400), to deliver up, appoint; *tássō* (5021), to place or arrange in order; *cheirotonéō* (5500), to place the hands on, choose by raising of hands, ordain.

5088. τίκτω, tiktō, *tik´-to*; a strengthened form of a primary **τέκω,** *tekō, tek´-o* (which is used only as alternate in certain tenses); to *produce* (from seed, as a mother, a plant, the earth, etc.), literal or figurative:—bear, be born, bring forth, be delivered, be in travail.

To bring forth, bear, bring.

(I) Of women (Mt 1:21, 23, 25; 2:2; Lk 1:31, 57; 2:6, 7, 11; Jn 16:21; Gal 4:27; Heb 11:11; Rev 12:2, 4, 5, 13). Metaphorically of irregular desire as exciting to sin (Jas 1:15).

(II) Of the earth (Heb 6:7).

Deriv.: *prōtótokos* (4416), firstborn; *téknon* (5043), a child; *téchne* (5078), an art, trade, craft, skill; *tókos* (5110), a bringing forth, birth.

Syn.: *apokuéō* (616), to bring forth; *gennáō* (1080), to give birth; *phérō* (5342), to bring or bear.

5089. τίλλω, tillō, *til´-lo*; perhaps akin to the alternate of 138, and thus to 4951; to *pull* off:—pluck.

5090. Τίμαιος, Timaios, *tim´-ah-yos*; probably of Chaldee origin [compare 2931]; *Timæus* (i.e. *Timay*), an Israelite:—Timæus.

5091. τιμάω, timaō, *tim-ah´-o*; from 5093; to *prize*, i.e. *fix a valuation* upon; by implication to *revere*:—honour, value.

5092. τιμή, timē, *tee-may´*; from 5099; a *value*, i.e. *money* paid, or (concretely and collective) *valuables*; (by analogy) *esteem* (especially of the highest degree), or the *dignity* itself:—honour, precious, price, some.

5093. τίμιος, timios, *tim´-ee-os*; including the comparative **τιμιώτερος,** *timiōteros, tim-ee-o´-ter-os*; and the superlative **τιμιώτατος,** *timiōtatos, tim-ee-o´-tat-os*; from 5092; *valuable*, i.e. (object) *costly*, or (subject) *honored, esteemed*, or (figurative) *beloved*:—dear, honourable, (more, most) precious, had in reputation.

5094. τιμιότης, timiotēs, *tim-ee-ot´-ace*; from 5093; *expensiveness*, i.e. (by implication) *magnificence*:—costliness.

5095. Τιμόθεος, Timotheos, *tee-moth´-eh-os*; from 5092 and 2316; *dear to God; Timotheus*, a Christian:—Timotheus, Timothy.

5096. Τίμων, Timōn, *tee´-mone*; from 5092; *valuable; Timon*, a Christian:—Timon.

5097. τιμωρέω, timōreō, *tim-o-reh´-o*; from a compound of 5092 and **οὖρος,** *ouros* (a *guard*); properly to *protect* one's *honour*, i.e. to *avenge* (*inflict a penalty*):—punish.

5098. τιμωρία, timōria, *tee-mo-ree´-ah*; from 5097; *vindication*, i.e. (by implication) a *penalty*:—punishment.

Noun from *timōréō* (5097), to punish. Vindication, retaliation, from the idea of watching out for one's honour, protecting the honour of someone and avenging any violations of one's honour. In the NT, punishment. Used only in Heb 10:29.

Syn.: *díkē* (1349), justice, the execution of a sentence, punishment; *ekdíkēsis* (1557), punishment, retribution; *epitimía* (2009), penalty, punishment; *kólasis* (2851), torment.

5099. τίνω, tinō, *tee´-no*; strengthened for a primary **τίω,** *tiō, tee´-o* (which is only used as an alternate in certain tenses); to *pay* a price, i.e. as a *penalty*:—be punished with.

5100. τίς, tis, *tis*; an encliteral indefinite pronoun; *some* or *any* person or object:—a (kind of), any (man, thing, thing at all), certain (thing), divers, he (every) man, one (× thing), ought, + partly, some (man, -body, -thing,

-what), (+ that no-) thing, what (-soever), × wherewith, whom [-soever], whose ([-soever]).

Indefinite pronoun meaning one, someone, a certain one.

(I) Particularly and generally of some person or thing whom one cannot or does not wish to name or specify particularly. It is used in various constructions:

(A) Simply (Mt 12:29, 47; Lk 9:7–8; Jn 2:25; Ac 5:25; Ro 3:3; 1Co 4:18; 15:12; Php 1:15; Heb 4:6).

(B) Joined with a substantive or adjective taken substantively, a certain person or thing, someone or something (Lk 8:2, 27; 9:19; 17:12; Jn 4:46; Ac 9:19; Gal 6:1; Jude 4).

(C) Followed by the genitive of class or partition of which *tis* expresses a part, e.g., certain of the scribes (Mt 9:3). See also Mt 27:47; Mk 14:47; Lk 14:15; Jn 7:25; 9:16; Ro 11:14; 2Co 10:12.

(II) Emphatically meaning somebody, something, some person or thing of weight and importance, some great one (Ac 5:36; 8:9; 1Co 3:7; 8:2; 10:19; Gal 2:6; 6:15; Heb 10:27).

(III) *Tis* with a substantive or adjective sometimes serves to limit or modify the full meaning, with the idea of somewhat, in some measure, a kind of (Ro 1:11, 13; Jas 1:18).

5101. τίς, tis, *tis*; probably emphatical of 5100; an interrogative pronoun, *who, which* or *what* (in direct or indirect questions):—every man, how (much), + no (-ne, thing), what (manner, thing), where ([-by, -fore, -of, -unto, -with, -withal]), whether, which, who (-m, -se), why.

An interrogative pronoun meaning who?, which?, or what? As an interrogative pronoun it is always written with the acute accent, and is thus distinguished from *tis* or *ti*, as an indefinite pronoun. See *tis* (5100).

(I) Used in direct questions:

(A) Generally: (1) As a substantive: e.g., "who hath warned you" (Mt 3:7). See also Mt 21:23; 27:24; Mk 1:27; 2:7; 9:10; Lk 10:29; 16:2; Jn 1:22, 38; 2:4; 13:25; Ac 7:27; 19:3; Eph 4:9; Heb 3:17, 18; Rev 6:17. (2) With a substantive as an interrogative adjective modifier: e.g., "what man is there ... ?" (Mt 7:9). See also (Mt 5:46; 27:23; Lk 11:11; 14:31; Jn 2:18; Ro 6:21; Heb 7:11). (3) Followed by the gen. of class or of partition, of which *tis* expresses a part: e.g., "which of the prophets?" (Ac 7:52). See also Mt 6:27; 22:28; Lk 10:36; Jn 8:46; Heb 1:5, 13.

(B) The neuter *ti* is sometimes used as an adverb of interrogation. (1) Wherefore? why? for what cause? equivalent to *diá tí*, "because (*dia* [1223]) of what?" (Mt 7:3; 8:26; 17:10; Mk 11:3; Lk 6:2, 41; Jn 1:25; 7:19; Ac 26:14; 1Co 4:7; 10:30; 15:29, 30; Gal 3:19). (2) As to what? how? in what respect? equal to *katá tí*, "according to (*katá* [2596]) what?" (Mt 16:26; 19:20; 22:17; Mk 8:36; Lk 9:25; 1Co 7:16). Also as an intensive meaning how! how greatly! (Lk 12:49).

(C) Equivalent to *póteros* (4220), an interrogative pron. meaning which of two, where two are spoken about meaning who or which of the two? (Mt 9:5; 21:31; 27:21; 23:17, 19; Lk 7:42; 1Co 4:21).

(D) *Tís* with the indicative through the force of the context sometimes approaches to the sense of *poíos* (4169), meaning of what kind or sort? Of persons (Mt 16:13, 15; Mk 8:27, 29; Lk 1:66; 4:36; 24:17; Jn 7:36; Jas 4:12).

(II) Used in indirect questions where it is often equivalent to the indefinite relative pronoun *hóstis* (3748), who or which: e.g., "Let not thy left hand know what thy right hand doeth" where the original question was "What is the right hand doing?" (Mt 6:3). See also Mt 6:25; 9:13; 10:11, 19; Mk 15:24; Lk 6:47; 7:39; 8:9; Jn 19:24; Ac 21:33; Ro 8:26–27; Eph 3:18; Heb 5:12; 1Pe 5:8.

Deriv.: *diatí* (1302), why?, wherefore?

5102. τίτλος, titlos, *tit´-los*; of Latin origin; a *titulus* or "*title*" (*placard*):—title.

5103. Τίτος, Titos, *tee´-tos*; of Latin origin but uncertain significance; *Titus*, a Christian:—Titus.

5104. τοί, toi, *toy*; probably for the dative of 3588; an encliteral particle of *asseveration* by way of contrast; *in sooth*:—[used only with other particles in comparative, as 2544, 3305, 5105, 5106, etc.].

5105. τοιγαροῦν, toigaroun, *toy-gar-oon´*; from 5104 and 1063 and 3767; *truly for then*, i.e. *consequently*:—there- (where-) fore.

5106. τοίνυν, toinun, *toy´-noon*; from 5104 and 3568; *truly now*, i.e. *accordingly*:—then, therefore.

5107. τοιόσδε, toiosde, *toy-os´-deh*; (including the other inflections); from a derivative of

5104 and 1161; *such-like then*, i.e. *so great:*—such.

5108. τοιοῦτος, toioutos, *toy-oo´-tos*; (including the other inflections); from 5104 and 3778; *truly this*, i.e. *of this sort* (to denote character or individuality):—like, such (an one).

5109. τοῖχος, toichos, *toy´-khos*; another form of 5038; a *wall:*—wall.

5110. τόκος, tokos, *tok´-os*; from the base of 5088; *interest* on money loaned (as a *produce*):—usury.

5111. τολμάω, tolmaō, *tol-mah´-o*; from **τόλμα**, *tolma* (*boldness*; probably itself from the base of 5056 through the idea of *extreme* conduct); to *venture* (object or in *act*; while 2292 is rather subject or in *feeling*); by implication to be *courageous:*—be bold, boldly, dare, durst.

5112. τολμηρότερον, tolmēroteron, *tol-may-rot´-er-on*; neuter of the comparative of a derivative of the base of 5111 (as adverb); *more daringly*, i.e. *with greater confidence* than otherwise:—the more boldly.

5113. τολμητής, tolmētēs, *tol-may-tace´*; from 5111; a *daring* (*audacious*) man:—presumptuous.

5114. τομώτερος, tomōteros, *tom-o´-ter-os*; comparative of a derivative of the primary **τέμνω**, *temnō* (to *cut*, more comprehensive or decisive than 2875, as if by a *single* stroke; whereas that implies repeated blows, like *hacking*); *more keen:*—sharper.

5115. τόξον, toxon, *tox´-on*; from the base of 5088; a *bow* (apparently as the simplest fabric):—bow.

5116. τοπάζιον, topazion, *top-ad´-zee-on*; neuter of a presumed derivative (alternate) of **τόπάζος**, *topazos* (a "*topaz*"; of uncertain origin); a gem, probably the *chrysolite:*—topaz.

5117. τόπος, topos, *top´-os*; apparently a primary word; a *spot* (genitive in *space*, but limited by occupancy; whereas 5561 is a larger but particular *locality*), i.e. *location* (as a position, home, tract, etc.); (figurative) *condition, opportunity*; specially a *scabbard:*—coast, licence, place, × plain, quarter, + rock, room, where.

5118. τοσοῦτος, tosoutos, *tos-oo´-tos*; from **τόσος**, *tosos* (*so much*; apparently from 3588 and 3739) and 3778 (including its variations); so *vast as this*, i.e. *such* (in quantity, amount, number or space):—as large, so great (long, many, much), these many.

5119. τότε, tote, *tot´-eh*; from (the neuter of) 3588 and 3753; *the when*, i.e. *at the time* that (of the past or future, also in consecution):—that time, then.

5120. τοῦ, tou, *too*; properly the generic of 3588; sometimes used for 5127; *of this person:*—his.

5121. τοὐναντίον, tounantion, *too-nan-tee´-on*; contracted from the neuter of 3588 and 1726; *on the contrary:*—contrariwise.

5122. τοὔνομα, tounoma, *too´-no-mah*; contracted from the neuter of 3588 and 3686; *the name* (is):—named.

5123. τουτέστι, toutesti, *toot-es´-tee*; contracted from 5124 and 2076; *that is:*—that is (to say).

5124. τοῦτο, touto, *too´-to*; neuter singular nominal or accusative of 3778; *that thing:*—here [-unto], it, partly, self [-same], so, that (intent), the same, there [-fore, -unto], this, thus, where [-fore].

5125. τούτοις, toutois, *too´-toice*; dative plural masculine or neuter of 3778; *to* (*for, in, with* or *by*) *these* (persons or things):—such, them, there [-in, -with], these, this, those.

5126. τοῦτον, touton, *too´-ton*; accusative singular masculine of 3778; *this* (person, as object of verb or preposition):—him, the same, that, this.

5127. τούτου, toutou, *too´-too*; genitive singular masculine or neuter of 3778; *of* (*from* or *concerning*) *this* (person or thing):—here [-by], him, it, + such manner of, that, thence [-forth], thereabout, this, thus.

5128. τούτους, toutous, *too´-tooce*; accusative plural masculine of 3778; *these* (persons, as object of verb or preposition):—such, them, these, this.

5129. τούτῳ, toutōi, *too´-to*; dative singular masculine or neuter of 3778; *to* (*in, with or by*) *this* (person or thing):—here [-by, -in], him, one, the same, there [-in], this.

5130. τούτων, toutōn, *too´-tone*; genitive plural masculine or neuter of 3778; *of* (*from* or *concerning*) *these* (persons or things):—such, their, these (things), they, this sort, those.

5131. τράγος, tragos, *trag´-os*; from the base of 5176; a *he-goat* (as a *gnawer*):—goat.

5132. τράπεζα, trapeza, *trap´-ed-zah*; probably contracted from 5064 and 3979; a *table* or *stool* (as being *four-legged*), usually for food (figurative, a *meal*); also a *counter* for money (figurative, a broker's *office* for loans at interest):—bank, meat, table.

5133. τραπεζίτης, trapezitēs, *trap-ed-zee´-tace*; from 5132; a money-*broker* or *banker*:—exchanger.

5134. τραῦμα, trauma, *trow´-mah*; from the base of τιτρώσκω, *titrōskō* (to *wound*; akin to the base of 2352, 5147, 5149, etc.); a *wound*:—wound.

5135. τραυματίζω, traumatizō, *trow-mat-id´-zo*; from 5134; to *inflict a wound*:—wound.

5136. τραχηλίζω, trachēlizō, *trakh-ay-lid´-zo*; from 5137; to *seize* by *the throat* or *neck*, i.e. to *expose* the *gullet* of a victim for killing (genitive to *lay bare*):—opened.

5137. τράχηλος, trachēlos, *trakh´-ay-los*; probably from 5143 (through the idea of *mobility*); the *throat* (*neck*), i.e. (figurative) *life*:—neck.

5138. τραχύς, trachus, *trakh-oos´*; perhaps strengthened from the base of 4486 (as if *jagged* by rents); *uneven, rocky* (*reefy*):—rock, rough.

5139. Τραχωνῖτις, Trachōnitis, *trakh-o-nee´-tis*; from a derivative of 5138; *rough* district; *Trachonitis*, a region of Syria:—Trachonitis.

5140. τρεῖς, treis, *trice*; neuter τρία, *tria,* *tree´-ah*; a primary (plural) number; "*three*":—three.

5141. τρέμω, tremō, *trem´-o*; strengthened from a primary τρέω, *treō* (to "*dread,*" "*terrify*"); to "*tremble*" or *fear*:—be afraid, trembling.

5142. τρέφω, trephō, *tref´-o*; a primary verb (properly θρέφω, *threphō*; but perhaps strength from the base of 5157 through the idea of *convolution*); properly to *stiffen*, i.e. *fatten* (by implication to *cherish* [with food, etc.], *pamper, rear*):—bring up, feed, nourish.

5143. τρέχω, trechō, *trekh´-o*; apparently a primary verb (properly θρέχω, *threchō*; compare 2359); which uses δρέμω, *dremō, drem´-o* (the base of 1408) as alternate in certain tenses; to *run* or *walk hastily* (literal or figurative):—have course, run.

5144. τριάκοντα, triakonta, *tree-ak´-on-tah*; the decade of 5140; *thirty*:—thirty.

5145. τριακόσιοι, triakosioi, *tree-ak-os´-ee-oy*; plural from 5140 and 1540; *three hundred*:—three hundred.

5146. τρίβολος, tribolos, *trib´-ol-os*; from 5140 and 956; properly a *crow-foot* (*three-pronged* obstruction in war), i.e. (by analogy) a *thorny* plant (*caltrop*):—brier, thistle.

5147. τρίβος, tribos, *tree´-bos*; from τρίβω, *tribō* (to "*rub*"; akin to τείρω, *teirō*; τρύω, *truō*; and the base of 5131, 5134); a *rut* or worn *track*:—path.

5148. τριετία, trietia, *tree-et-ee´-ah*; from a compound of 5140 and 2094; a *three years'* period (*triennium*):—space of three years.

5149. τρίζω, trizō, *trid´-zo*; apparently a primary verb; to *creak* (*squeak*), i.e. (by analogy) to *grate* the teeth (in frenzy):—gnash.

5150. τρίμηνον, trimēnon, *trim´-ay-non*; neuter of a compound of 5140 and 3376 as noun; a *three months'* space:—three months.

5151. τρίς, tris, *trece*; adverb from 5140; *three times*:—three times, thrice.

5152. τρίστεγον, tristegon, *tris´-teg-on*; neuter of a compound of 5140 and 4721 as noun; a *third roof* (*story*):—third loft.

5153. τρισχίλιοι, trischilioi, *tris-khil´-ee-oy*; from 5151 and 5507; *three times a thousand*:—three thousand.

5154. τρίτος, tritos, *tree´-tos*; order from 5140; *third*; neuter (as noun) a *third part*, or (as adverb) a (or the) *third* time, *thirdly:*—third (-ly).

5155. τρίχινος, trichinos, *trikh´-ee-nos*; from 2359; *hairy,* i.e. made *of hair* (*mohair*):—of hair.

5156. τρόμος, tromos, *trom´-os*; from 5141; a "*trembling,*" i.e. quaking with *fear:*— + tremble (-ing).

5157. τροπή, tropē, *trop-ay´*; from an apparently primary **τρέπω, trepō** (to *turn*); a *turn* ("trope"), i.e. *revolution* (figurative, *variation*):—turning.

5158. τρόπος, tropos, *trop´-os*; from the same as 5157; a *turn,* i.e. (by implication) *mode* or *style* (especially with preposition or relative prefix as adverb *like*); (figurative) *deportment* or *character:*—(even) as, conversation, [+ like] manner (+ by any) means, way.

5159. τροποφορέω, tropophoreō, *trop-of-or-eh´-o*; from 5158 and 5409; to *endure* one's *habits:*—suffer the manners.

5160. τροφή, trophē, *trof-ay´*; from 5142; *nourishment* (literal or figurative); by implication *rations* (*wages*):—food, meat.

5161. Τρόφιμος, Trophimos, *trof´-ee-mos*; from 5160; *nutritive; Trophimus,* a Christian:—Trophimus.

5162. τροφός, trophos, *trof-os´*; from 5142; a *nourisher,* i.e. *nurse:*—nurse.

5163. τροχιά, trochia, *trokh-ee-ah´*; from 5164; a *track* (as a wheel-*rut*), i.e. (figurative) a *course* of conduct:—path.

5164. τροχός, trochos, *trokh-os´*; from 5143; a *wheel* (as a *runner*), i.e. (figurative) a *circuit* of physical effects:—course.

5165. τρύβλιον, trublion, *troob´-lee-on*; neuter of a presumed derivative of uncertain affinity; a *bowl:*—dish.

5166. τρυγάω, trugaō, *troo-gah´-o*; from a derivative of **τρύγω, trugō** (to *dry*) meaning ripe *fruit* (as if *dry*); to *collect* the vintage:—gather.

5167. τρυγών, trugōn, *troo-gone´*; from **τρύζω, truzō** (to *murmur*; akin to 5149, but denoting a *duller* sound); a *turtle-dove* (as *cooing*):—turtledove.

5168. τρυμαλιά, trumalia, *troo-mal-ee-ah´*; from a derivative of **τρύω, truō** (to *wear* away; akin to the base of 5134, 5147 and 5176); an *orifice,* i.e. a needle's *eye:*—eye. Compare 5169.

5169. τρύπημα, trupēma, *troo´-pay-mah*; from a derivative of the base of 5168; an *aperture,* i.e. a needle's *eye:*—eye.

5170. Τρύφαινα, Truphaina, *troo´-fahee-nah*; from 5172; *luxurious; Tryphæna,* a Christian woman:—Tryphena.

5171. τρυφάω, truphaō, *troo-fah´-o*; from 5172; to *indulge in luxury:*—live in pleasure.

From *truphḗ* (5172), luxury. To live luxuriously, in pleasure. Used only in Jas 5:5.

Deriv.: *entruphấō* (1792), to revel luxuriously.

Syn.: *spatalấō* (4684), to live in pleasure; *strēniấō* (4763), to live riotously or wantonly.

5172. τρυφή, truphē, *troo-fay´*; from **θρύπτω, thruptō** (to *break* up or [figurative] *enfeeble*, especially the mind and body by indulgence); *effeminacy,* i.e. *luxury* or *debauchery:*—delicately, riot.

5173. Τρυφῶσα, Truphōsa, *troo-fo´-sah*; from 5172; *luxuriating; Tryphosa,* a Christian female:—Tryphosa.

5174. Τρωάς, Trōas, *tro-as´*; from **Τρός, Tros** (a *Trojan*); the *Troad* (or plain of Troy), i.e. *Troas,* a place in Asia Minor:—Troas.

5175. Τρωγύλλιον, Trōgullion, *tro-gool´-lee-on*; of uncertain derivative; *Trogyllium,* a place in Asia Minor:—Trogyllium.

5176. τρώγω, trōgō, *tro´-go*; probably strengthened from a collateral form of the base of 5134 and 5147 through the idea of *corrosion* or *wear*; or perhaps rather of a base of 5167 and 5149 through the idea of a *craunching* sound; to *gnaw* or *chew,* i.e. (genitive) to *eat:*—eat.

5177. τυγχάνω, tugchanō, *toong-khan´-o*; probably for an obsolete **τύχω, tuchō** (for which the middle of another alternate **τεύχω, teuchō**; [to *make ready* or *bring to pass*] is used in certain tenses); akin to the base of 5088 through the idea of *effecting*; properly to *affect*; or (special) to *hit* or *light upon* (as a mark to be reached), i.e. (transitive) to *attain* or *secure* an object or end, or (intransitive) to *happen* (as if *meeting* with);

but in the latter application only impersonal (with 1487), i.e. *perchance*; or (presumed participle) as adjective *usual* (as if commonly *met with*, with 3756, *extraordinary*), neuter (as adverb) *perhaps*; or (with another verb) as adverb by *accident* (*as it were*):—be, chance, enjoy, little, obtain, × refresh … self, + special. Compare 5180.

5178. τυμπανίζω, tumpanizō, *toom-pan-id´-zo*; from a derivative of 5180 (meaning a *drum*, "*tympanum*"); to stretch on an instrument of *torture* resembling a drum, and thus *beat* to death:—torture.

5179. τύπος, tupos, *too´-pos*; from 5180; a *die* (as *struck*), i.e. (by implication) a *stamp* or *scar*; (by analogy) a *shape*, i.e. a *statue*, (figurative) *style* or *resemblance*; specially a *sampler* ("*type*"), i.e. a *model* (for imitation) or *instance* (for warning):—en- (ex-) ample, fashion, figure, form, manner, pattern, print.

Noun from *túptō* (5180), to strike, smite with repeated strokes. A type, i.e. something caused by strokes or blows.

(I) A mark, print, impression (Jn 20:25).

(II) A figure, form.

(A) Of an image, statue (Ac 7:43).

(B) Of the form, manner, or contents of a letter (Ac 23:25); of a doctrine (Ro 6:17).

(C) Spoken figuratively of a person as bearing the form and figure of another, a type, as having a certain resemblance in relations and circumstances (Ro 5:14).

(III) A prototype, pattern.

(A) Spoken particularly of a pattern or model after which something is to be made (Ac 7:44; Heb 8:5).

(B) Spoken figuratively of an example, pattern to be imitated, followed (Php 3:17; 1Th 1:7; 2Th 3:9; 1Ti 4:12; Tit 2:7; 1Pe 5:3). Hence also for admonition, warning (1Co 10:6, 11).

Deriv.: *antítupos* (499), that which corresponds to a type, which represents the real thing; *entupóō* (1795), to impress, stamp.

Syn.: *hupotúpōsis* (5296), a sketch, pattern for imitation.

5180. τύπτω, tuptō, *toop´-to*; a primary verb (in a strengthened form); to "*thump*," i.e. *cudgel* or *pummel* (properly with a stick or *bastinado*), but in any case by *repeated* blows; thus differing from 3817 and 3960, which denote a [usually

single] blow with the hand or any instrument, or 4141 with the *fist* [or a *hammer*], or 4474 with the *palm*; as well as from 5177, an *accidental* collision); by implication to *punish*; (figurative) to *offend* (the conscience):—beat, smite, strike, wound.

To strike, smite with the hand, stick, or other instrument repeatedly.

(I) Particularly and generally.

(A) To smite in enmity with a stick, club, or the fist (Mt 24:49; Lk 12:45; Ac 18:17; 21:32; 23:3); on the cheek (Lk 6:29); on the head (Mt 27:30; Mk 15:19); on the face (Lk 22:64); on the mouth (Ac 23:2).

(B) To beat upon one's chest in strong emotion (Lk 18:13; 23:48).

(C) Figuratively, to smite meaning to punish, inflict evil, afflict with disease, calamity, and spoken only as being done by God (Ac 23:3).

(II) Figuratively, to strike against, meaning to offend, to wound the conscience of someone (1Co 8:12).

Deriv.: *túpos* (5179), stroke, the impression left by striking, a trace or print.

Syn.: *dérō* (1194), to flay, beat, thrash, strike; *paíō* (3817), to strike, sting; *patássō* (3960), to hit, strike, with the hand, fist, or weapon; *pléssō* (4141), to strike as with a plague; *rhabdízō* (4463), to beat with a rod or stick; *rhapízō* (4474), to slap, strike.

5181. Τύραννος, Turannos, *too´-ran-nos*; a provincial form of the derivative of the base of 2962; a "*tyrant*"; *Tyrannus*, an Ephesian:—Tyrannus.

5182. τυρβάζω, turbazō, *toor-bad´-zo*; from τύρβη, *turbē* (Latin *turba*, a *crowd*; akin to 2351); to *make* "*turbid*," i.e. *disturb*:—trouble.

5183. Τύριος, Turios, *too´-ree-os*; from 5184; a *Tyrian*, i.e. inhabitant of Tyrus:—of Tyre.

5184. Τύρος, Turos, *too´-ros*; of Hebrew origin [6865]; *Tyrus* (i.e. *Tsor*), a place in Palestine:—Tyre.

5185. τυφλός, tuphlos, *toof-los´*; from 5187; *opaque* (as if *smoky*), i.e. (by analogy) *blind* (physical or mental):—blind.

5186. τυφλόω, tuphloō, *toof-lo´-o*; from 5185; to *make blind*, i.e. (figurative) to *obscure*:—blind.

5187. τυφόω, tuphoō, *toof-o´-o;* from a derivative of 5188; to envelop with *smoke,* i.e. (figurative) to *inflate* with self-conceit:—high-minded, be lifted up with pride, be proud.

From *túphos* (n.f.), smoke. To smoke, to fume, to surround with smoke. Figuratively, to make conceited, proud, to inflate. In the NT, only in the passive, to be conceited, proud, arrogant (1Ti 3:6; 6:4; 2Ti 3:4).

Deriv.: *tuphlós* (5185), blind.

Syn.: *epaíromai* (1869), to exalt self; *huperaíromai* (5229), to become haughty, proud; *hupsēlophronéō* (5309), to be high-minded; *phusióō* (5448), to inflate, make proud, puff up.

5188. τυφώ, tuphō, *too´-fo;* apparently a primary verb; to make a *smoke,* i.e. slowly *consume* without flame:—smoke.

5189. τυφωνικός, tuphōnikos, *too-fo-nee-kos´;* from a derivative of 5188; *stormy* (as if *smoky*):—tempestuous.

5190. Τυχικός, Tuchikos, *too-khee-kos´;* from a derivative of 5177; *fortuitous,* i.e. *fortunate; Tychicus,* a Christian:—Tychicus.

ϒ (Upsilon)

NT Numbers 5191–5313

5191. ὑακίνθινος, **huakinthinos,** *hoo-ak-in´-thee-nos*; from 5192; "*hyacinthine*" or "*jacinthine*," i.e. deep *blue*:—jacinth.

5192. ὑάκινθος, **huakinthos,** *hoo-ak´-in-thos*; of uncertain derivative; the "*hyacinth*" or "*jacinth*," i.e. some gem of a deep *blue* colour, probably the *zirkon*:—jacinth.

5193. ὑάλινος, **hualinos,** *hoo-al´-ee-nos*; from 5194; *glassy*, i.e. *transparent*:—of glass.

5194. ὕαλος, **hualos,** *hoo´-al-os*; perhaps from the same as 5205 (as being transparent like *rain*); *glass*:—glass.

5195. ὑβρίζω, **hubrizō,** *hoo-brid´-zo;* from 5196; to *exercise violence,* i.e. *abuse*:—use despitefully, reproach, entreat shamefully (spitefully).

5196. ὕβρις, **hubris,** *hoo´-bris*; from 5228; *insolence* (as *over*-bearing), i.e. *insult, injury*:—harm, hurt, reproach.

5197. ὑβριστής, **hubristēs,** *hoo-bris-tace´*; from 5195; an *insulter*, i.e. *maltreater*:—despiteful, injurious.

Noun from *húbris* (5196), arrogance. One who is insolent, contemptuous, injurious. Combines the idea of arrogance and violence against others (Ro 1:30; 1Ti 1:13).

Syn.: *loídoros* (3060), reviler.

5198. ὑγιαίνω, **hugiainō,** *hoog-ee-ah´ee-no*; from 5199; to *have* sound *health,* i.e. *be well* (in body); (figurative) to be *uncorrupt* (*true* in doctrine):—be in health, (be safe and) sound, (be) whole (-some).

From *hugiés* (5199), sound, healthy. To be healthy, sound, in good health.

(I) Particularly, to be healthy (Lk 5:31; 7:10; 3Jn 2). With the meaning to be safe and sound (Lk 15:27).

(II) Metaphorically of persons, to be sound in the faith, meaning sound, pure in respect to

Christian doctrine and life (Tit 1:13; 2:2). Of doctrine, meaning sound doctrine, i.e. true, pure, uncorrupted (1Ti 1:10; 6:3; 2Ti 1:13; 4:3; Tit 1:9; 2:1).

5199. ὑγιής, **hugiēs,** *hoog-ee-ace´*; from the base of 837; *healthy*, i.e. *well* (in body); (figurative) *true* (in doctrine):—sound, whole.

An adjective meaning sound, healthy, in good health.

(I) Particularly of the body or its parts. In the NT always with the idea of becoming whole, being healed of disease and infirmity (Mt 12:13; 15:31; Mk 3:5; 5:34; Lk 6:10; Jn 5:4, 6, 9, 11, 14, 15; 7:23; Ac 4:10).

(II) Figuratively of sound speech or doctrine, in the sense of being true, pure, unadulterated (Tit 2:8).

Deriv.: *hugiaínō* (5198), to be healthy.

Syn.: *hólos* (3650), whole, healthy.

5200. ὑγρός, **hugros,** *hoo-gros´*; from the base of 5205; *wet* (as if with *rain*), i.e. (by implication) *sappy* (*fresh*):—green.

5201. ὑδρία, **hudria,** *hoo-dree-ah´*; from 5204; a *water-jar*, i.e. *receptacle* for family supply:—waterpot.

5202. ὑδροποτέω, **hudropoteō,** *hoo-drop-ot-eh´-o*; from a compound of 5204 and a derivative of 4095; to *be* a *water-drinker,* i.e. to *abstain from vinous beverages*:—drink water.

5203. ὑδρωπικός, **hudrōpikos,** *hoo-dro-pik-os´*; from a compound of 5204 and a derivative of 3700 (as if *looking watery*); to *be* "*dropsical*":—have the dropsy.

5204. ὕδωρ, **hudōr,** *hoo´-dor*; genitive ὕδατος, **hudatos,** *hoo´-dat-os*, etc.; from the base of 5205; *water* (as if *rainy*) literal or figurative:—water.

5205. ὑετός, **huetos,** *hoo-et-os´*; from a primary ὕω, **huō** (to *rain*); *rain*, especially a *shower*:—rain.

941

5206. υἱοθεσία, uihothesia, *hwee-oth-es-ee´-ah*; from a presumed compound of 5207 and a derivative of 5087; the *placing* as a *son,* i.e. *adoption* (figurative, Christian *sonship* in respect to God):— adoption (of children, of sons).

Noun from *huiós* (5207), son, and *títhēmi* (5087), to place. Adoption, the placing as a son or daughter. In the NT, figuratively meaning adoption, sonship, spoken of the state of those whom God through Christ adopts as His sons and thus makes heirs of His covenanted salvation. See *huiós* (5207, II, B). Of the true Israel, the spiritual descendants of Abraham (Ro 9:4 [cf. 6, 7]), especially of Christians, the followers of the Lord Jesus (Ro 8:15, 23; Gal 4:5; Eph 1:5).

5207. υἱός, uihos, *hwee-os´*; apparently a primary word; a *"son"* (sometimes of animals), used very widely of immediate, remote or figurative kinship:—child, foal, son.

A noun meaning son.

(I) Generally.

(A) A male offspring: (1) Strictly spoken only of man (Mt 1:21, 25; 7:9; Mk 6:3; 9:17; Rev 12:5). In Heb 12:8 it is presented emphatically as the opposite of *nóthos* (3541), illegitimate son. Spoken of one who fills the place of a son (Jn 19:26); of an adopted son (Ac 7:21; Heb 11:24). (2) Of the young of animals, "foal of an ass" (Mt 21:5).

(B) Spoken in a wider sense of a descendant, in the plural of descendants, posterity; cf. *téknon* (5043, II), child. (1) Singular. Spoken of Joseph as a son of David (Mt 1:1, 20; Lk 19:9). Spoken of the Messiah as descended from the line of David (Mt 22:42, 45; Mk 12:35, 37; Lk 20:41, 44). Spoken of Jesus as the "son of David" meaning the Messiah (Mt 1:1; 9:27; 12:23; 15:22; 20:30, 31; 21:9, 15; Mk 10:47, 48; Lk 18:38, 39). (2) Plural (Ac 7:16; Heb 7:5); especially the posterity of Abraham, the sons or descendants of Israel, the Israelites (Mt 27:9; Lk 1:16; Ac 5:21; 7:23, 37; Ro 9:27; 2Co 3:7, 13; Gal 3:7; Rev 21:12). (3) Spoken in the title, the Son of Man, in reference to Jesus as the Messiah. See *ánthrōpos* (444, IV), man.

(C) Figuratively, spoken of one who is the object of parental love and care or who yields filial love and reverence toward another, a pupil, disciple, follower, the spiritual child of someone (Heb 2:10; 12:5; 1Pe 5:13; cf. *téknon* [5043, III,

B], child). Spoken of the disciples and followers of the Pharisees (Mt 12:27; Lk 11:19).

(D) Figuratively, spoken with a genitive, the son of something as one connected with, partaking of, or exposed to that thing, often used instead of an adjective. (1) Followed by a genitive of place, condition, or connectivity; e.g., sons of the bridal chamber, bridesmen (Mt 9:15; Mk 2:19; Lk 5:34). Also spoken of the sons of the kingdom (Mt 8:12; 13:38); the sons of the evil one (Mt 13:38); the son of the devil (Ac 13:10); the sons of this world (Lk 16:8; 20:34). (2) Followed by a genitive implying quality, character: e.g., sons of thunder (Mk 3:17). See also Lk 10:6; 16:8; Jn 12:36; Ac 4:36; Eph 2:2; 5:6; Col 3:6; 1Th 5:5. (3) Followed by a genitive of that in which one partakes, to which one is exposed: e.g., "children of the resurrection" meaning partakers in it (Lk 20:36). See also Mt 23:15; Jn 17:12; Ac 3:25.

(II) Specifically *huiós toú Theoú* (gen. of *Theós* [2316], God) son of God, and *huioí toú Theoú,* sons of God. Spoken of:

(A) One who derives his human nature directly from God, and not by ordinary generation: spoken of Jesus (Lk 1:35); implied of Adam (Lk 3:38).

(B) Those whom God loves and cherishes as a father. (1) Generally of pious worshippers of God, the righteous, the saints (Mt 5:9, 45; Lk 6:35; 20:36). (2) Specifically of the Israelites (Ro 9:26; 2Co 6:18). (3) Of Christians (Ro 8:14, 19; Gal 3:26; 4:6, 7; Heb 12:6; Rev 21:7).

(C) Jesus Christ as the Son of God, the Son of the Most High (Mt 27:54; Mk 15:39; Lk 1:32). (1) In the Jewish sense as the Messiah, the Anointed, the Christ, the expected King of the Jewish nation, constituted of God, and ruling in the world (Mt 2:15; 4:3; 8:29; 14:33; 27:40, 43; Mk 3:11; 5:7; Lk 4:3; 8:28; 22:70; Jn 1:34, 49; 9:35). As joined with *ho Christós* (5547), Christ, in explanation (Mt 16:16; 26:63; Mk 14:61; Lk 4:41; Jn 6:69; 11:27; 20:31). (2) In the gospel sense as the Messiah, the Saviour, the Head of the gospel dispensation, as proceeding and sent forth from God, as partaking of the divine nature and being in intimate union with God the Father (Mt 3:17; 11:27; 17:5; 28:19; Mk 13:32; Lk 10:22; Jn 1:18; 3:16–18; 5:26; 10:36; 17:1; Ac 13:33; Ro 1:3, 4, 9; 5:10; 8:3, 29, 32; 1Co 1:9; 15:28; 2Co 1:19; Gal 1:16; 2:20; Eph 4:13; Col 1:13; 1Th 1:10; Heb 1:2, 5;

3:6; 5:5; 6:6; 2Pe 1:17; 1Jn 1:3, 7; 2:22; 4:14; 5:5; 2Jn 3, 9; Rev 2:18).

Deriv.: *huiothesía* (5206), adoption.

Syn.: *népios* (3516), an infant; *paidárion* (3808), a lad; *paidíon* (3813), a young child; *país* (3816), a child or servant; *tekníon* (5040), a little child; *téknon* (5043), a child.

5208. ὕλη, hulē, *hoo´-lay*; perhaps akin to 3586; a *forest*, i.e. (by implication) *fuel*:—matter.

5209. ὑμᾶς, humas, *hoo-mas´*; accusative of 5210; *you* (as the object of a verb or preposition):—ye, you (+ -ward), your (+ own).

5210. ὑμεῖς, humeis, *hoo-mice´*; irregular plural of 4771; *you* (as subject of verb):—ye (yourselves), you.

5211. Ὑμεναῖος, Humenaios, *hoo-men-ah´-yos*; from Ὑμήν, *Humēn* (the god of *weddings*); "*hymnæal*"; *Hymenæus*, an opponent of Christianity:—Hymenæus.

5212. ὑμέτερος, humeteros, *hoo-met´-er-os*; from 5210; *yours*, i.e. *pertaining to you*:—your (own).

5213. ὑμῖν, humin, *hoo-min´*; irregular dative of 5210; *to* (*with* or *by*) *you*:—ye, you, your (-selves).

5214. ὑμνέω, humneō, *hoom-neh´-o*; from 5215; to *hymn*, i.e. sing a religious ode; by implication to *celebrate* (God) in song:—sing an hymn (praise unto).

5215. ὕμνος, humnos, *hoom´-nos*; apparently from a simpler (obsolete) form of ὑδέω, *hudeō* (to *celebrate*; probably akin to 103; compare 5567); a "*hymn*" or religious ode, one of the Psalms):—hymn.

A noun meaning hymn or song of praise. It is used only in Eph 5:19; Col 3:16, where it occurs with *psalmós* (5568), psalm, and *hōdé* (5603), spiritual song.

Deriv.: *humneō* (5214), to sing a hymn.

Syn.: *aínos* (136), praise; *épainos* (1868), commendable thing, praise; *eulogía* (2129), fair speech, blessing, eulogy; *euphēmía* (2162), praise, good report.

5216. ὑμῶν, humōn, *hoo-mone´*; generic of 5210; *of* (*from* or *concerning*) *you*:—ye, you, your (own, -selves).

5217. ὑπάγω, hupagō, *hoop-ag´-o*; from 5259 and 71; to *lead* (oneself) *under*, i.e. *withdraw* or *retire* (as if *sinking* out of sight), literal or figurative:—depart, get hence, go (a-) way.

5218. ὑπακοή, hupakoē, *hoop-ak-o-ay´*; from 5219; *attentive hearkening*, i.e. (by implication) *compliance* or *submission*:—obedience, (make) obedient, obey (-ing).

Noun from *hupakoúō* (5219), to obey. A hearing attentively, a listening, an audience. In the NT, obedience (Ro 1:5; 5:19; 6:16; 15:18; 16:19, 26; 2Co 7:15; 10:5, 6; Phm 21; Heb 5:8; 1Pe 1:2, 14, 22).

Syn.: *hupotagé* (5292), subjection, obedience.

5219. ὑπακούω, hupakouō, *hoop-ak-oo´-o*; from 5259 and 191; to *hear under* (as a *subordinate*), i.e. to *listen attentively*; by implication to *heed* or *conform* to a command or authority:—hearken, be obedient to, obey.

From *hupó* (5259), and *akoúō* (191), to hear. To hearken, obey.

(I) Particularly, to listen to something, hearken with stillness or attention, as a door-keeper would, in order to answer (Ac 12:13).

(II) To yield to a superior command or force.

(A) Spoken of things (Mt 8:27; Mk 4:41; Lk 8:25; 17:6).

(B) Spoken of unclean spirits (Mk 1:27).

(III) To obey one in authority.

(A) Spoken of children obeying parents (Eph 6:1; Col 3:20).

(B) Spoken of slaves obeying their masters (Eph 6:5; Col 3:22).

(C) Spoken of a wife obeying her husband (1Pe 3:6).

(IV) In a spiritual sense, to obey God (Heb 5:9; 11:8); to obey the gospel (Ac 6:7; Ro 10:16; 2Th 1:8); to obey a spiritual leader (Php 2:12; 2Th 3:14).

(V) To obey one's passions, thus becoming enslaved by them (Ro 6:12, 16).

Deriv.: *hupakoē* (5218), obedience; *hupékoos* (5255), obedient.

Syn.: *peitharchéō* (3980), to be submitted to a ruler, to hearken, obey one in authority; *summorphóō* (4833), to conform oneself to.

5220. ὕπανδρος, hupandros, *hoop´-an-dros*; from 5259 and 435; in subjection *under a man*, i.e. a *married* woman:—which hath an husband.

5221. ὑπαντάω, hupantaō, *hoop-an-tah´-o*; from 5259 and a derivative of 473; to *go opposite* (*meet*) *under* (*quietly*), i.e. to *encounter, fall in with*:—(go to) meet.

5222. ὑπάντησις, hupantēsis, *hoop-an´-tay-sis*; from 5221; an *encounter* or *concurrence* (with 1519 for infinite, in order to *fall in with*):—meeting.

5223. ὕπαρξις, huparxis, *hoop´-arx-is*; from 5225; *existency* or *proprietorship*, i.e. (concrete) *property, wealth*:—goods, substance.

5224. ὑπάρχοντα, huparchonta, *hoop-ar´-khon-tah*; neuter plural of presumed participle active of 5225 as noun; things *extant* or *in hand*, i.e. *property* or *possessions*:—goods, that which one has, things which (one) possesseth, substance, that hast.

5225. ὑπάρχω, huparchō, *hoop-ar´-kho*; from 5259 and 756; to *begin under* (*quietly*), i.e. *come into existence* (*be present* or *at hand*); expletively, to *exist* (as copula or subordinate to an adjective, participle, adverb or preposition, or as auxiliary to principal verb):—after, behave, live.

From *hupó* (5259), and *árchōmai* (756), to begin. To begin to be, to come into existence. In the NT, to exist, to be present (Lk 7:25; 16:23; 27:34).

(I) Generally and in an absolute sense, to exist (Ac 19:40; 27:21; 28:18; 1Co 11:18). Used with an adverbial modifier: e.g., the prepositional phrase "in heaven" (Php 3:20). See also Lk 7:25; 16:23; Ac 5:4; 10:12; 17:27; 27:34; Php 2:6). Followed by the dative of person, to be present with someone, implying possession, property (Ac 3:6; 4:37; 28:7; 2Pe 1:8). The participle used as a substantive: things present, in hand, possessions.

(II) To be, the same as *eimí* (1510), to be, logically connecting the subj. and predicate: e.g., his father was a Greek (Ac 16:3). See also (Lk 8:41; 9:48; 11:13; 16:14; 23:50; Ac 2:30; 3:2; 4:34; 7:55; 14:8; 16:20, 37; 17:24, 29; 21:20; 22:3; 27:12; Ro 4:19; 1Co 7:26; 11:7; 12:22; 2Co 8:17; 12:16; Gal 1:14; 2:14; Jas 2:15; 2Pe 2:19; 3:11). As forming a periphrasis for a finite tense of the same verb: they were baptized (Ac 8:16).

Deriv.: *proüpárchō* (4391), to exist before; *húparxis* (5223), possessions, property.

Syn.: *gínomai* (1096), to become; *eimí* (1510), to be. Also *anastréphō* (390), to live, behave, conduct one's life; *záō* (2198), to live.

5226. ὑπείκω, hupeikō, *hoop-i´-ko*; from 5259 and εἴκω, *eikō* (to *yield,* be "*weak*"); to *surrender*:—submit self.

5227. ὑπεναντίος, hupenantios, *hoop-en-an-tee´-os*; from 5259 and 1727; *under* (*covertly*) *contrary* to, i.e. *opposed* or (as noun) an *opponent*:—adversary, against.

5228. ὑπέρ, huper, *hoop-er´*; a primary preposition; "*over,*" i.e. (with the generic) of place, *above, beyond, across,* or causal, *for the sake of, instead, regarding*; with the accusative *superior to, more than*:—(+ exceeding abundantly) above, in (on) behalf of, beyond, by, + very chiefest, concerning, exceeding (above, -ly), for, + very highly, more (than), of, over, on the part of, for sake of, in stead, than, to (-ward), very. In comparative it retains many of the above applications.

A preposition governing the genitive and accusative with the primary meaning of over.

(I) With the gen. particularly of place meaning over, above, across or beyond. In the NT, used only figuratively:

(A) Meaning for, in behalf of, for the sake of, in the sense of protection, care, favour, benefit. (1) Generally (Mk 9:40; Lk 9:50; Jn 17:19; Ac 21:26; Ro 8:31; 1Co 12:25; 2Co 7:7, 12; 8:16; 13:8; Eph 6:20; Php 4:10; Col 1:7; 4:12, 13; Heb 6:20; 13:17). After verbs implying speaking, praying, pleading, or intercession for someone (Mt 5:44; Lk 6:28; Ac 8:24; 12:5; 26:1; Ro 8:26, 27, 34; 10:1; 15:30; 2Co 9:14; Eph 6:19, 20; Php 1:4; Col 1:9; 1Ti 2:1, 2; Heb 7:25; 9:24; Jas 5:16). Often after words implying suffering or even dying on behalf of someone (Lk 22:19, 20; Jn 6:51; 10:11, 15; 11:50–52; 13:37–38; 15:13; 18:14; Ro 5:6–8; 8:32; 9:3; 14:15; 16:4; 1Co 1:13; 5:7; 11:24; 2Co 5:14–15, 21; 12:15; Gal 2:20; Eph 5:2, 25; 1Th 5:10; 1Ti 2:6; Tit 2:14; Heb 2:9; 1Pe 2:21; 3:18; 4:1; 1Jn 3:16). (2) Closely allied to the above is the meaning for, in the stead of someone, in place of (2Co 5:20).

(B) For, because of, on account of, meaning the aim, purpose or objective of an action and implying the ground, motive, occasion of an action: e.g., "for the glory of God," i.e. in order to manifest His glory (Jn 11:4); "for his name" in the sense of for his honour (Ac 5:41; 9:16; 15:26; 21:13; Ro 1:5; 3Jn 7). See also Ro 15:8, 9; 1Co 10:30; 15:3, 29; 2Co 1:6, 11; 12:10, 19; Gal 1:4; Eph 1:16; 3:1, 13; 5:20; Php 1:29; Col 1:24; 2Th 1:5; Heb 5:1, 3; 7:27; 9:7; 10:12).

(C) Over, used with verbs such as speaking or boasting meaning upon, about, concerning (Ro 9:27; 2Co 1:6, 8; 5:12; 7:4, 14; 8:23, 24; 9:2, 3; 12:5, 8; Php 1:7; 2Th 1:4; 2:1).

(II) With the accusative, particularly of place whither, implying motion or direction over or above a place, beyond. In the NT, only figuratively, over, beyond.

(A) Implying superiority in rank, dignity, worth (Mt 10:24; Lk 6:40; Eph 1:22; Phm 16).

(B) Implying excess above a certain measure or standard and spoken comparatively meaning more than (Mt 10:37; Lk 16:8; Ac 26:13; 1Co 4:6; 10:13; 2Co 1:8; 8:3; 12:6, 13; Gal 1:14; Phm 21; Heb 4:12).

(III) In composition, *hupér* implies:

(A) Motion or rest over, above, beyond a place, as *huperaíromai* (5229), to exalt oneself; *huperbaínō* (5233), to transcend, overreach; *huperéchō* (5242), to hold oneself above, to excel.

(B) Protection, aid, for or in behalf of, as *huperentugchánō* (5241), to intercede in behalf of.

(C) Exceeding or surpassing, often with the idea of exaggeration, as *huperbállō* (5235), to throw beyond the usual mark, surpass. Also *huperauxánō* (5232), to grow extraordinarily; *huperekteínō* (5239), to overdo, carry too far; *hupernikáō* (5245), to completely conquer; *huperperisseúō* (5248), to superabound.

Syn.: In the sense of instead of (I, A, 2): *antí* (473), in place of. In the sense of concerning (I, C): *perí* (4012), concerning; *prós* (4314), pertaining to in respect to, in respect to. In the sense of beyond, more than: *epánō* (1883), over; *lían* (3029), exceeding, great, very; *mállon* (3123), more, rather; *meízon* (3185), in a greater degree; *meizóteros* (3186), still larger, greater; *meízōn* (3187), greater; *pámpolus* (3827), very great, immense; *pará* (3844), more than; *pleíon* (4119), more; *péran* (4008), beyond, across; *perissós* (4053), superior, beyond measure, more; *perissóteron* (4054), more abundantly; *perissóteros* (4055), more abundant, greater; *perissotérōs* (4056), more abundantly; *perissós* (4057), exceedingly; *pró* (4253), above,

before; *sphódra* (4970), much, very; *huperánō* (5231), far above, over.

5229. ὑπεραίρομαι, **huperaíromai,** *hoop-er-ah´ee-rom-ahee*; middle from 5228 and 142; to *raise* oneself *over,* i.e. (figurative) to *become haughty:*—exalt self, be exalted above measure.

5230. ὑπέρακμος, **huperakmos,** *hoop-er´-ak-mos*; from 5228 and the base of 188; *beyond* the "*acme,*" i.e. figurative (of a daughter) *past the bloom* (*prime*) of youth:— + pass the flower of (her) age.

5231. ὑπεράνω, **huperanō,** *hoop-er-an´-o*; from 5228 and 507; *above upward,* i.e. *greatly higher* (in place or rank):—far above, over.

5232. ὑπεραυξάνω, **huperauxanō,** *hoop-er-owx-an´-o*; from 5228 and 837; to *increase above* ordinary degree:—grow exceedingly.

5233. ὑπερβαίνω, **huperbaínō,** *hoop-er-bah´ee-no*; from 5228 and the base of 939; to *transcend,* i.e. (figurative) to *overreach:*—go beyond.

From *hupér* (5228), beyond, and *baínō* (n.f., see *anabaínō* [305]), to go. To go or pass over something: e.g., a wall or mountains. Figuratively, to overstep certain limits, to transgress, to go too far, to go beyond what is right. Used only in 1Th 4:6.

Syn.: *parabaínō* (3845), to transgress.

5234. ὑπερβαλλόντως, **huperballontōs,** *hoop-er-bal-lon´-toce*; adverb from presumed participle active of 5235; *excessively:*—beyond measure.

5235. ὑπερβάλλω, **huperballō,** *hoop-er-bal´-lo*; from 5228 and 906; to *throw beyond* the usual mark, i.e. (figurative) to *surpass* (only active participle *supereminent*):—exceeding, excel, pass.

5236. ὑπερβολή, **huperbolē,** *hoop-er-bol-ay´*; from 5235; a *throwing beyond* others, i.e. (figurative) *supereminence*; adverb (with 1519 or 2596) *pre-eminently:*—abundance, (far more) exceeding, excellency, more excellent, beyond (out of) measure.

5237. ὑπερείδω, **hupereidō,** *hoop-er-i´-do*; from 5228 and 1492; to *overlook,* i.e. *not punish:*—wink at.

5238. ὑπερέκεινα, huperekeina, *hoop-er-ek´-i-nah*; from 5228 and the neuter plural of 1565; *above those* parts, i.e. *still farther:*—beyond.

5239. ὑπερεκτείνω, huperekteinō, *hoop-er-ek-ti´-no*; from 5228 and 1614; to *extend inordinately:*—stretch beyond.

5240. ὑπερεκχύνω, huperekchunō, *hoop-er-ek-khoo´-no*; from 5228 and the alternate form of 1632; to *pour out over,* i.e. (passive) to *overflow:*—run over.

5241. ὑπερεντυγχάνω, huperentugchanō, *hoop-er-en-toong-khan´-o*; from 5228 and 1793; to *intercede in behalf of:*—make intercession for.

5242. ὑπερέχω, huperechō, *hoop-er-ekh´-o*; from 5228 and 2192; to *hold* oneself *above,* i.e. (figurative) to *excel;* participle (as adjective, or neuter as noun) *superior, superiority:*—better, excellency, higher, pass, supreme.

5243. ὑπερηφανία, huperēphania, *hoop-er-ay-fan-ee´-ah*; from 5244; *haughtiness:*—pride.

5244. ὑπερήφανος, huperēphanos, *hoop-er-ay´-fan-os*; from 5228 and 5316; *appearing above* others (*conspicuous*), i.e. (figurative) *haughty:*—proud.

Adjective from *hupér* (5228), over, above, and *phaínō* (5316), to shine, show. Appearing over, conspicuous above other persons or things. In the NT, only in the sense of arrogant, haughty, proud. Often associated with those who despise God (Lk 1:51; Ro 1:30; 2Ti 3:2; Jas 4:6; 1Pe 5:5).

Deriv.: *huperēphanía* (5243), arrogance, pride.

5245. ὑπερνικάω, hupernikaō, *hoop-er-nik-ah´-o*; from 5228 and 3528; to *vanquish beyond,* i.e. *gain* a decisive *victory:*—more than conquer.

5246. ὑπέρογκος, huperogkos, *hoop-er´-ong-kos*; from 5228 and 3591; *bulging over,* i.e. (figurative) *insolent:*—great swelling.

5247. ὑπεροχή, huperochē, *hoop-er-okh-ay´*; from 5242; *prominence,* i.e. (figurative) *superiority* (in rank or character):—authority, excellency.

5248. ὑπερπερισσεύω, huperperisseuō, *hoop-er-per-is-syoo´-o*; from 5228 and 4052; to *superabound:*—abound much more, exceeding.

5249. ὑπερπερισσῶς, huperperissōs, *hoop-er-per-is-soce´*; from 5228 and 4057; *superabundantly,* i.e. *exceedingly:*—beyond measure.

5250. ὑπερπλεονάζω, huperpleonazō, *hoop-er-pleh-on-ad´-zo*; from 5228 and 4121; to *superabound:*—be exceeding abundant.

5251. ὑπερυψόω, huperupsoō, *hoop-er-oop-so´-o*; from 5228 and 5312; to *elevate above* others, i.e. *raise* to the *highest* position:—highly exalt.

5252. ὑπερφρονέω, huperphroneō, *hoop-er-fron-eh´-o*; from 5228 and 5426; to *esteem* oneself *overmuch,* i.e. *be vain* or *arrogant:*—think more highly.

5253. ὑπερῷον, huperōion, *hoop-er-o´-on*; neuter of a derivative of 5228; a *higher* part of the house, i.e. apartment in the *third story:*—upper chamber (room).

5254. ὑπέχω, hupechō, *hoop-ekh´-o*; from 5259 and 2192; to *hold* oneself *under,* i.e. *endure* with patience:—suffer.

5255. ὑπήκοος, hupēkoos, *hoop-ay´-ko-os*; from 5219; *attentively listening,* i.e. (by implication) *submissive:*—obedient.

Adjective from *hupakoúō* (5219), to submit to, obey. Listening, obedient (Ac 7:39; 2Co 2:9). Spoken also of Christ being obedient even to death (Php 2:8).

Syn.: *eupeithḗs* (2138), easy to be persuaded, compliant.

5256. ὑπηρετέω, hupēreteō, *hoop-ay-ret-eh´-o*; from 5257; to *be a subordinate,* i.e. (by implication) *subserve:*—minister (unto), serve.

5257. ὑπηρέτης, hupēretēs, *hoop-ay-ret´-ace*; from 5259 and a derivative of ἐρέσσω, *eressō* (to *row*); an *under-oarsman,* i.e. (general) *subordinate* (*assistant, sexton, constable*):—minister, officer, servant.

Noun from *hupó* (5259), under, beneath and *erétēs* (n.f.), a rower. A subordinate, servant, attendant, or assistant in general. In Class. Gr., a common sailor or hired hand as distinguished from *naútēs* (3492), a shipman, seaman. In the NT:

(I) Of those who wait on magistrates or public officials and execute their decrees, a constable or officer, as the attendant on a judge (Mt

5:25). Of the attendants of the Sanhedrin (Mt 26:58; Mk 14:54, 65; Jn 7:32, 45, 46; 18:3, 12, 18, 22; 19:6; Ac 5:22, 26).

(II) Of the attendant in a synagogue who handed the volume to the reader and returned it to its place (Lk 4:20).

(III) Generally, a minister, attendant, associate in any work (Jn 18:36; Ac 13:5). Of a minister of the Word of Christ (Lk 1:2; Ac 26:16; 1Co 4:1).

Deriv.: *hupēretéō* (5256), to serve under the direction of someone else.

Syn.: *diákonos* (1249), a servant, attendant, minister, deacon; *doúlos* (1401), slave, servant; *therápōn* (2324), a servant, attendant; *leitourgós* (3011), a public servant; *místhios* (3407) or *misthōtós* (3411), one who is hired to do a certain task, a hired servant; *oikétēs* (3610), a domestic servant; *país* (3816), servant.

5258. ὕπνος, hupnos, *hoop´-nos*; from an obsolete primary (perhaps akin to 5259 through the idea of *subsilience*); *sleep*, i.e. (figurative) spiritual *torpor*:—sleep.

5259. ὑπό, hupo, *hoop-o´*; a primary prep.; *under*, i.e. (with the generic) of place (*beneath*), or with verbs (the agency or means, *through*); (with the accusative) of place (whither [*underneath*] or where [*below*]) or time (when [*at*]):— among, by, from, in, of, under, with. In comparative it retains the same genitive applications, especially of *inferior* position or condition, and specially *covertly* or *moderately*.

Preposition meaning under, beneath, through.

(I) With the genitive particularly of place meaning whence, from which something comes forth. In the NT, only used in the sense of by, through, from, indicating the agent or the one doing a passive voice action, always indicated in English with the preposition, "by": e.g., that which was spoken by the Lord (Mt 1:22). See also Mt 2:16; 3:6; 4:1; 5:13; 8:24; Lk 7:24; 9:7; 13:17; 14:8; 21:20; Ac 2:24; 4:36; 12:5; 20:3; 23:27; Ro 12:21; 15:15; 1Co 7:25; 10:9; 2Co 1:16; 5:4; 8:19; Gal 1:11; Jas 3:4, 6; 2Pe 2:7, 17; Jude 12; Rev 6:13; et al.). In the same way *hupó* is used after some transitive verbs, where a passive sense is implied: e.g., with *pascho* (3958), to suffer, in the sense of suffering something from someone's hand (Mt 17:12; Mk 5:26; 1Th 2:14). See also Ac 23:30; 2Co 2:6; 11:24; Heb 12:3; Rev 6:8.

(II) With the accusative particularly of place meaning from which; of motion or direction meaning under a place; also of place where something is placed to rest under.

(A) Particularly of place, after verbs of motion or direction meaning under, beneath: e.g., to place something under a bushel (Mt 5:15; Mk 4:21; Lk 11:33). See also Mt 8:8; 23:37; Mk 4:32; Lk 13:34; Jas 2:3).

(B) Of place where, after verbs implying a being or remaining under a place or condition: e.g., to be under heaven (Lk 17:24; Ac 2:5; 4:12; Col 1:23). See also Ro 3:13; 1Co 10:1; Jude 6. Spoken figuratively of what is under the power or authority of any person or thing: e.g., under the Law (Ro 6:14–15; 1Co 9:20; Gal 4:3–5, 21; 5:18). See also Mt 8:9; Lk 7:8; Ro 3:9; 7:14; 16:20; 1Co 15:25, 27; Gal 3:10, 22–23, 25; 4:2– 3; Eph 1:22; 1Ti 6:1; 1Pe 5:6).

(C) Of time, meaning at, during (Ac 5:21).

(III) In composition *hupó* implies:

(A) Place, motion or rest meaning under, beneath, as *hupobállō* (5260), to throw under, bribe secretly; *hupodéō* (5265), to bind under one's feet, put on shoes; *hupopódion* (5286), something under the feet, as a footstool.

(B) Subjection, dependence, the state of being under any person or thing as *húpandros* (5220), under a husband or subject to a husband; *hupotássō* (5293), to subordinate.

(C) Succession, being behind or after, as *hupoleípō* (5275), to leave behind, remain; *hupoménō* (5278), to endure.

(D) *Hupó* in composition also implies something done or happening underhandedly, covertly, by stealth, unperceived, without noise or notice; also by degrees: *huponoéō* (5282), to think privately, surmise, conjecture, oppose; *hupopnéō* (5285), to breathe inaudibly.

5260. ὑποβάλλω, hupoballo, *hoop-ob-al´-lo*; from 5259 and 906; to *throw* in *stealthily*, i.e. *introduce* by collusion:—suborn.

5261. ὑπογραμμός, hupogrammos, *hoop-og-ram-mos´*; from a compound of 5259 and 1125; an *underwriting*, i.e. *copy* for imitation (figurative):—example.

Noun from *hupográphō* (n.f.), to undersign, from *hupó* (5259), before, and *gráphō* (1125), to write. Particularly, a writing example to be copied or imitated by beginning students. In the NT, used figuratively of Christ's suffering as a pattern for us to follow. Used only in 1Pe 2:2.

Syn.: *deígma* (1164), a specimen, example; *homoíōma* (3667), a form, likeness; *túpos* (5179), a type, model, pattern; *hupódeigma* (5262), an example.

5262. ὑπόδειγμα, **hupodeigma**, *hoop-od´-igue-mah*; from 5263; an *exhibit* for imitation or warning (figurative, *specimen, adumbration*):—en- (ex-) ample, pattern.

5263. ὑποδείκνυμι, **hupodeiknumi**, *hoop-od-ike´-noo-mee*; from 5259 and 1166; to *exhibit under* the eyes, i.e. (figurative) to *exemplify* (*instruct, admonish*):—show, (fore-) warn.

5264. ὑποδέχομαι, **hupodechomai**, *hoop-od-ekh´-om-ahee*; from 5259 and 1209; to *admit under* one's roof, i.e. *entertain* hospitably:—receive.

From *hupó* (5259), under, and *déchomai* (1209), to receive. To take to oneself, as if placing the hands or arms under a person or thing, to receive hospitably and kindly. In the NT to receive guests hospitably or to welcome, entertain (Lk 10:38; 19:6; Ac 17:7; Jas 2:25).

Syn.: *apodéchomai* (588), to welcome, receive gladly.

5265. ὑποδέω, **hupodeō**, *hoop-od-eh´-o*; from 5259 and 1210; to *bind under* one's feet, i.e. *put on* shoes or sandals:—bind on, (be) shod.

5266. ὑπόδημα, **hupodēma**, *hoop-od´-ah-mah*; from 5265; something *bound under* the feet, i.e. a *shoe* or *sandal*:—shoe.

5267. ὑπόδικος, **hupodikos**, *hoop-od´-ee-kos*; from 5259 and 1349; *under sentence*, i.e. (by implication) *condemned*:—guilty.

Adjective from *hupó* (5259), under, and *díkē* (1349), judgement, justice. Under sentence, condemned, liable, or subject to prosecution. Used only in Ro 3:19.

Syn.: *énochos* (1777), liable, guilty.

5268. ὑποζύγιον, **hupozugion**, *hoop-od-zoog´-ee-on*; neuter of a compound of 5259 and 2218; an *animal under* the *yoke* (*draught-beast*), i.e. (special) a *donkey*:—ass.

5269. ὑποζώννυμι, **hupozōnnumi**, *hoop-od-zone´-noo-mee*; from 5259 and 2224; to *gird*

under, i.e. *frap* (a vessel with cables across the keel, sides and deck):—undergirt.

5270. ὑποκάτω, **hupokatō**, *hoop-ok-at´-o*; from 5259 and 2736; *down under*, i.e. *beneath*:—under.

5271. ὑποκρίνομαι, **hupokrinomai**, *hoop-ok-rin´-om-ahee*; middle from 5259 and 2919; to *decide* (*speak* or *act*) *under* a false part, i.e. (figurative) *dissemble* (*pretend*):—feign.

From *hupó* (5259), under, indicating secrecy, and *krínō* (2919), to judge. To pretend to be what one is not, to act hypocritically. Originally synonymous with *apokrínomai* (611), to answer, reply. Later, it acquired the meaning to answer upon a stage, to play a part, to act. In the NT, to be a hypocrite, to attempt to fool others. Used only in Lk 20:20.

Deriv.: *anupókritos* (505), one without hypocrisy; *sunupokrínomai* (4942), to play the role of a hypocrite together with; *hupókrisis* (5272), hypocrisy; *hupokritḗs* (5273), hypocrite.

Syn.: *prospoiéomai* (4364), to pretend.

5272. ὑπόκρισις, **hupokrisis**, *hoop-ok´-ree-sis*; from 5271; *acting under* a feigned participle i.e. (figurative) *deceit* ("*hypocrisy*"):—condemnation, dissimulation, hypocrisy.

5273. ὑποκριτής, **hupokritēs**, *hoop-ok-ree-tace´*; from 5271; an *actor under* an assumed character (*stage-player*), i.e. (figurative) a *dissembler* ("*hypocrite*"):—hypocrite.

Noun from *hupokrínomai* (5271), to act as a hypocrite. A stage-player, actor. In the NT, a hypocrite, specifically in respect to religion (Mt 6:2, 5, 16; 7:5; 15:7; 16:3; 22:18; 23:13–15, 23, 25, 27, 29; 24:51; Mk 7:6; Lk 6:42; 11:44; 12:56; 13:15).

5274. ὑπολαμβάνω, **hupolambanō**, *hoop-ol-am-ban´-o*; from 5259 and 2983; to *take from below*, i.e. *carry upward*; (figurative) to *take up*, i.e. *continue* a discourse or topic; mentally to *assume* (*presume*):—answer, receive, suppose.

5275. ὑπολείπω, **hupoleipō**, *hoop-ol-i´-po*; from 5295 and 3007; to *leave under* (*behind*), i.e. (passive) to *remain* (*survive*):—be left.

5276. ὑπολήνιον, **hupolēnion**, *hoop-ol-ah´-nee-on*; neuter of a presumed compound of 5259 and 3025; *vessel* or *receptacle under* the *press*, i.e. *lower winevat*:—winefat.

5277. ὑπολιμπάνω, hupolimpanō, *hoop-ol-im-pan´-o*; a prolonged form for 5275; to *leave behind*, i.e. *bequeath:*—leave.

5278. ὑπομένω, hupomenō, *hoop-om-en´-o*; from 5259 and 3306; to *stay under* (*behind*), i.e. *remain*; (figurative) to *undergo*, i.e. *bear* (trials), *have fortitude, persevere:*—abide, endure, (take) patient (-ly), suffer, tarry behind.

From *hupó* (5259), under, and *ménō* (3306), to remain.

(I) Intransitive, to remain behind after others are gone (Lk 2:43; Ac 17:14).

(I) Transitive, to remain under the approach or presence of any person or thing, in the sense of to await. Hence, in the NT, figuratively, to bear up under, to be patient under, to endure, to suffer (1Co 13:7; 2Ti 2:10; Heb 10:32; 12:2–3, 7; Jas 1:12). Absolute, to endure in the sense of to hold out, to persevere (Mt 10:22; 24:13; Mk 13:13; Ro 12:12; 2Ti 2:12; Jas 5:11; 1Pe 2:20).

Deriv.: *hupomoné* (5281), patience, endurance.

Syn.: *anéchomai* (430), to put up with; *bastázō* (941), to bear; *karteréō* (2594), to be steadfast, patient, to endure; *makrothuméō* (3114), to be long-suffering, patient; *hupéchō* (5254), to endure; *hupophérō* (5297), to bear, endure.

5279. ὑπομιμνήσκω, hupomimnēskō, *hoop-om-im-nace´-ko*; from 5259 and 3403; to *remind quietly*, i.e. *suggest* to the (middle, one's own) memory:—put in mind, remember, bring to (put in) remembrance.

5280. ὑπόμνησις, hupomnēsis, *hoop-om´-nay-sis*; from 5279; a *reminding* or (reflexive) *recollection:*—remembrance.

Noun from *hupomimnéskō* (5279), to recall to one's mind. A putting in mind, a reminding, remembrance, recollection (2Ti 1:5; 2Pe 1:13; 3:1).

Syn.: *anámnēsis* (364), a remembering, recollection; *mneía* (3417), remembrance, mention; *mnémē* (3420), memory, remembrance; *mnēmósunon* (3422), a reminder, memorial.

5281. ὑπομονή, hupomonē, *hoop-om-on-ay´*; from 5278; cheerful (or hopeful) *endurance, constancy:*—enduring, patience, patient continuance (waiting).

Noun from *hupoménō* (5278), to persevere, remain under. A bearing up under, patience, endurance as to things or circumstances. Particularly, with the genitive of thing borne, as evils (2Co 1:6). Generally meaning endurance, patience, perseverance or constancy under suffering in faith and duty (Lk 8:15; 21:19; Ro 2:7; 8:25; 2Co 1:6; 6:4; 12:12; Col 1:11; 1Th 1:3; 2Th 1:4; 3:5; Heb 10:36; 12:1; Jas 1:3, 4; 5:11; 2Pe 1:6; Rev 1:9; 2:2, 3, 19; 3:10; 13:10; 14:12). Specifically patience as a quality of mind, the bearing of evils and suffering with tranquil mind (Ro 5:3, 4; 15:4, 5; 1Ti 6:11; 2Ti 3:10; Tit 2:2).

Syn.: *anochḗ* (463), forbearance, tolerance; *epeíkeia* (1932), clemency, gentleness.

5282. ὑπονοέω, huponoeō, *hoop-on-o-eh´-o*; from 5259 and 3539; to *think under* (*privately*), i.e. to *surmise* or *conjecture:*—think, suppose, deem.

From *hupó* (5259), under, denoting diminution, and *noéō* (3539), to think. To suppose, theorize, suspect. In the NT, in the sense of to conjecture, to suppose, to deem (Ac 13:25; 25:18; 27:27).

Deriv.: *hupónoia* (5283), suspicion, conjecture.

Syn.: *dialogízomai* (1260), to reason, think; *dokéō* (1380), to be of opinion, suppose; *hēgéomai* (2233), to reckon, suppose; *krínō* (2919), to judge, reckon; *logízomai* (3049), to reckon; *nomízō* (3543), to suppose, consider, think; *oíomai* (3633), imagine, suppose; *hupolambánō* (5274), to suppose; *phronéō* (5426), to think.

5283. ὑπόνοια, huponoia, *hoop-on´-oy-ah*; from 5282; *suspicion:*—surmising.

Noun from *huponoéō* (5282), to suspect. Suspicion, surmising, conjecture. Used only in 1Ti 6:4.

5284. ὑποπλέω, hupopleō, *hoop-op-leh´-o*; from 5259 and 4126; to *sail under* the lee of:—sail under.

5285. ὑποπνέω, hupopneō, *hoop-op-neh´-o*; from 5259 and 4154; to *breathe gently*, i.e. *breeze:*—blow softly.

5286. ὑποπόδιον, hupopodion, *hoop-op-od´-ee-on*; neuter of a compound of 5259 and 4228; something *under* the *feet*, i.e. a *foot-rest* (figurative):—footstool.

5287. ὑπόστασις, hupostasis, *hoop-os´-tas-is*; from a compound of 5259 and 2476; a *setting* *under* (*support*), i.e. (figurative) concrete *essence*, or abstract *assurance* (object or subject):—confidence, confident, person, substance.

Noun from *huphístēmi* (n.f.), to place or set under. That which is set under or stands under, the foundation, origin, beginning. In the NT:

(I) The ground of confidence, assurance, guarantee or proof (Heb 3:14; 11:1).

(II) By metonymy, that quality which leads one to stand under, endure, or undertake something, firmness, boldness, confidence (2Co 9:4; 11:17).

(III) Substance, what really exists under any appearance, reality, essential nature. Spoken of God's essence or nature (Heb 1:3).

Syn.: *élegchos* (1650), certainty, proof, demonstration; *phúsis* (5449), nature.

5288. ὑποστέλλω, hupostellō, *hoop-os-tel´-lo*; from 5259 and 4724; to *withhold under* (*out of sight*), i.e. (reflexive) to *cower* or *shrink*, (figurative) to *conceal* (*reserve*):—draw (keep) back, shun, withdraw.

5289. ὑποστολή, hupostolē, *hoop-os-tol-ay´*; from 5288; *shrinkage* (*timidity*), i.e. (by implication) *apostasy*:—draw back.

5290. ὑποστρέφω, hupostrephō, *hoop-os-tref´-o*; from 5259 and 4762; to *turn under* (*behind*), i.e. to *return* (literal or figurative):—come again, return (again, back again), turn back (again).

5291. ὑποστρώννυμι, hupostrōnnumi, *hoop-os-trone´-noo-mee*; from 5259 and 4766; to *strew underneath* (the feet as a carpet):—spread.

5292. ὑποταγή, hupotagē, *hoop-ot-ag-ay´*; from 5293; *subordination*:—subjection.

5293. ὑποτάσσω, hupotassō, *hoop-ot-as´-so*; from 5259 and 5021; to *subordinate*; reflexive to *obey*:—be under obedience (obedient), put under, subdue unto, (be, make) subject (to, unto), be (put) in subjection (to, under), submit self unto.

From *hupó* (5259) and *tássō* (5021), to place in order. To place under, to subordinate, to make subject.

(I) In the active voice, to make others subject, to subordinate, to force others to be subject. Spoken of God bringing all things under

the control of Christ (1Co 15:27–28; Eph 1:22; Heb 2:5, 8). Spoken once of Christ bringing all things under His own control (Php 3:21).

(II) In the passive voice, to be brought under the control of someone else (Lk 10:17, 20; Ro 8:20; 1Co 14:32, 34; 15:27, 28; Eph 5:24; Heb 2:8; 1Pe 3:22).

(III) In the middle voice, to submit oneself, to be subject, to be obedient (Lk 2:51; Ro 8:7; 13:1, 5; 1Co 16:16; Eph 5:21, 22; Col 3:18; Tit 2:5, 9; 3:1; Jas 4:7; 1Pe 2:18; 3:1, 5). Passive voice imperatives have a similar force, to allow oneself to be in subjection, to be obedient (1Pe 2:13). See also 1Pe 5:5, where the passive participle is used with an imperative verb understood. Until God forces the subjection of all, the passive voice in other moods can also signify voluntary submission. For example, the Jews in Paul's day, because of ignorance, were refusing to be submissive (Ro 10:3); and we are encouraged in Heb 12:9 to submit ourselves to God's control.

Deriv.: *anupótaktos* (506), unsubdued; *hupotagē* (5292), submission, dependent position.

5294. ὑποτίθημι, hupotithēmi, *hoop-ot-ith´-ay-mee*; from 5259 and 5087; to *place underneath*, i.e. (figurative) to *hazard*, (reflexive) to *suggest*:—lay down, put in remembrance.

5295. ὑποτρέχω, hupotrechō, *hoop-ot-rekh´-o*; from 5259 and 5143 (including its alternate); to *run under*, i.e. (special) to *sail past*:—run under.

5296. ὑποτύπωσις, hupotupōsis, *hoop-ot-oop´-o-sis*; from a compound of 5259 and a derivative of 5179; *typification under* (*after*), i.e. (concrete) a *sketch* (figurative) for imitation:—form, pattern.

Noun from *hupotupóō* (n.f.), to form or copy slightly, to sketch. Figuratively, a form, sketch, imperfect delineation (2Ti 1:13). By metonymy, a sketch, a pattern for imitation(1Ti 1:16).

Syn.: *eikṓn* (1504), profile, resemblance, image; *hupogrammós* (5261), an underwriting, writing copy, example; *hupódeigma* (5262), copy, example, pattern.

5297. ὑποφέρω, hupopherō, *hoop-of-er´-o*; from 5259 and 5342; to *bear from underneath*, i.e. (figurative) to *undergo* hardship:—bear, endure.

5298. ὑποχωρέω, hupochōreō, *hoop-okh-o-reh´-o;* from 5259 and 5562; to *vacate down,* i.e. *retire* quietly:—go aside, withdraw self.

5299. ὑπωπιάζω, hupōpiazō, *hoop-o-pee-ad´-zo;* from a compound of 5259 and a derivative of 3700; to hit *under* the *eye* (*buffet* or *disable* an antagonist as a pugilist), i.e. (figurative) to *tease* or *annoy* (into compliance), *subdue* (one's passions):—keep under, weary.

5300. ὗς, us, *hoos;* apparently a primary word; a *hog* ("*swine*"):—sow.

5301. ὕσσωπος, hussōpos, *hoos´-so-pos;* of foreign origin [231]; "*hyssop*":—hyssop.

5302. ὑστερέω, hustereō, *hoos-ter-eh´-o;* from 5306; to *be later,* i.e. (by implication) to be *inferior;* genitive to *fall short* (*be deficient*):—come behind (short), be destitute, fail, lack, suffer need, (be in) want, be the worse.

5303. ὑστέρημα, husterēma, *hoos-ter´-ay-mah;* from 5302; a *deficit;* specially *poverty:*—that which is behind, (that which was) lack (-ing), penury, want.

5304. ὑστέρησις, husterēsis, *hoos-ter´-ay-sis;* from 5302; a *falling short,* i.e. (special) *penury:*—want.

5305. ὕστερον, husteron, *hoos´-ter-on;* neuter of 5306 as adverb; *more lately,* i.e. *eventually:*—afterward, (at the) last (of all).

5306. ὕστερος, husteros, *hoos´-ter-os;* comparative from 5259 (in the sense of *behind*); *later:*—latter.

5307. ὑφαντός, huphantos, *hoo-fan-tos´;* from ὑφαίνω, **huphainō** (to *weave*); *woven,* i.e. (perhaps) *knitted:*—woven.

5308. ὑψηλός, hupsēlos, *hoop-say-los´;* from 5311; *lofty* (in place or character):—high (-er, -ly) (esteemed).

5309. ὑψηλοφρονέω, hupsēlophroneō, *hoop-say-lo-fron-eh´-o;* from a compound of 5308 and 5424; to *be lofty in mind,* i.e. *arrogant:*—be high-minded.

5310. ὕψιστος, hupsistos, *hoop´-sis-tos;* superlative from the base of 5311; *highest,* i.e. (masculine singular) the *Supreme* (God), or (neuter plural) the *heavens:*—most high, highest.

5311. ὕψος, hupsos, *hoop´-sos;* from a derivative of 5228; *elevation,* i.e. (abstract) *altitude,* (special) the *sky,* or (figurative) *dignity:*—be exalted, height, (on) high.

5312. ὑψόω, hupsoō, *hoop-so´-o;* from 5311; to *elevate* (literal or figurative):—exalt, lift up.

5313. ὕψωμα, hupsōma, *hoop´-so-mah;* from 5312; an *elevated* place or thing, i.e. (abstract) *altitude,* or (by implication) a *barrier* (figurative):—height, high thing.

Φ (Phi)

NT Numbers 5314–5462

5314. φάγος, phagos, *fag´-os*; from 5315; a *glutton*:—gluttonous.

5315. φάγω, phagō, *fag´-o*; a primary verb (used as an alternate of 2068 in certain tenses); to *eat* (literal or figurative):—eat, meat.

5316. φαίνω, phainō, *fah´ee-no*; prolonged for the base of 5457; to *lighten* (*shine*), i.e. *show* (transitive or intransitive, literal or figurative):—appear, seem, be seen, shine, × think.

From *phốs* (5457), light. To give light, illuminate.

(I) To shine or give light, shine forth as a luminous body (2:16; 8:12; 18:23; 21:23); figuratively, of spiritual light and truth (Jn 1:5; 5:35; Php 2:15; 1Jn 2:8).

(II) To come to light, to appear, be conspicuous, become visible.

(A) Generally to appear, be seen. **(1)** Of persons (Mt 1:20; 2:13, 19; Mk 16:9; Lk 9:8; 1Pe 4:18). With a participle or adjective as predicate in the nominative: e.g., with *díkaios* (1342), righteous, ye appear … righteous (Mt 23:28). See also Mt 6:16, 18; 2Co 13:7. **(2)** Of things (Mt 9:33; 13:26; Heb 11:3); with a predicate adjective as **(1)** above (Mt 23:27; Ro 7:13). Especially of things appearing in the sky or air, meaning phenomena (Mt 2:7; 24:27, 30; Jas 4:14).

(B) Figuratively as referring to the mental eye, to appear, seem (Mk 14:64; Lk 24:11).

Deriv.: *anaphaínō* (398), to be shown or appear openly, to show openly; *aphanḗs* (852), hidden, concealed; *áphantos* (855), invisible; *epiphaínō* (2014), to shine over or upon, to give light, in the pass. to appear; *sukophantéō* (4811), to accuse wrongfully; *huperḗphanos* (5244), one who is conspicuous; *phanerós* (5318), apparent, manifest; *phanós* (5322), lantern; *phantázō* (5324), to cause to appear.

Syn.: *astráptō* (797), to shine forth like lightning; *augázō* (826), to irradiate; *eklámpō* (1584), to shine forth; *lámpō* (2989), to shine; *perias-*

tráptō (4015), to shine round about; *perilámpō* (4034), to shine around; *stílbō* (4744), to glitter.

5317. Φάλεκ, Phalek, *fal´-ek*; of Hebrew origin [6389]; *Phalek* (i.e. *Peleg*), a patriarch:—Phalec.

5318. φανερός, phaneros, *fan-er-os´*; from 5316; *shining*, i.e. *apparent* (literal or figurative); neuter (as adverb) *publicly, externally*:—abroad, + appear, known, manifest, open [+ -ly], outward ([+ -ly]).

Adjective from *phaínō* (5316), to shine, to make to shine or to cause to appear. Apparent, manifest, plain (Ac 4:16; Ro 1:19; Gal 5:19; 1Ti 4:15; 1Jn 3:10); with the verbs *gínomai* (1096), to become, and *érchomai* (2064), to come, to become known, well known, manifest (Mk 4:22; 6:14; Lk 8:17; Ac 7:13; 1Co 3:13; 11:19; 14:25; Php 1:13); with the verb *poiéō* (4160), to make, to make one known or manifest (Mt 12:16; Mk 3:12). With the preposition *en* (1722), in, in the open, openly (Mt 6:4, 6, 18). Also with *en*, in the open in the sense of outwardly, on the outside as opposed to what is on the inside (Ro 2:28).

Deriv.: *phaneróō* (5319), to make manifest or known, show; *phanerốs* (5320), apparently.

Syn.: *gnōstós* (1110), known; *dḗlos* (1212), evident; *dēmósios* (1219), public, open; *ékdēlos* (1552), wholly evident, manifest; *emphanḗs* (1717), manifest; *éxōthen* (1855), outward; *katádēlos* (2612), quite manifest, evident; *pródēlos* (4271), evident, manifest beforehand, clearly evident.

5319. φανερόω, phaneroō, *fan-er-o´-o*; from 5318; to *render apparent* (literal or figurative):—appear, manifestly declare, (make) manifest (forth), shew (self).

From *phanerós* (5318), manifest, visible, conspicuous. To make apparent, manifest, known, to show openly. Transitively:

(I) Of things (Jn 17:6; Ro 1:19). In the passive (Mk 4:22; Jn 2:11; 3:21; 9:3; 17:6; Ro 1:19; 3:21;

16:26; 1Co 4:5; 2Co 2:14; 4:10, 11; 7:12; Eph 5:13; Col 1:26; 4:4; 2Ti 1:10; Heb 9:8; 1Jn 3:2; 4:9; Rev 3:18; 15:4).

(II) Of persons.

(A) Reflexively with *heautón* (1438), oneself, or with the middle or aorist passive used as middle, to manifest oneself, show oneself openly, to appear (Mk 16:12, 14; Jn 7:4; 21:1, 14; 2Co 5:10; Col 3:4; 1Ti 3:16; Heb 9:26; 1Pe 1:20; 5:4; 1Jn 1:2; 2:28; 3:2, 5, 8).

(B) In the passive to be manifested, become or be made manifest, known (Jn 1:31; 2Co 3:3; 5:11; 1Jn 2:19).

Deriv.: *phanérōsis* (5321), manifestation, making known.

Syn.: *anaggéllō* (312) and *apaggéllō* (518), to announce or report; *apokalúptō* (601), to reveal; *gnōrízō* (1107), to make known; *dēlóō* (1213), to make plain; *diaggéllō* (1229), to announce throughout; *diagnōrízō* (1232), to make fully known, reassert; *emphanízō* (1718), to declare plainly, make manifest; *kataggéllō* (2605), to declare; *phrázō* (5419), to declare.

5320. **φανερῶς, phanerōs,** *fan-er-oce´*; adverb from 5318; *plainly*, i.e. *clearly* or *publicly*:—evidently, openly.

5321. **φανέρωσις, phanerōsis,** *fan-er´-o-sis*; from 5319; *exhibition*, i.e. (figurative) *expression*, (by extension) a *bestowment*:—manifestation.

Noun from *phaneróō* (5319), to make manifest. A manifestation, a making visible or observable (1Co 12:7; 2Co 4:2).

Syn.: *apokálupsis* (602), revelation.

5322. **φανός, phanos,** *fan-os´*; from 5316; a *lightener*, i.e. *light; lantern*:—lantern.

5323. **Φανουήλ, Phanouēl,** *fan-oo-ale´*; of Hebrew origin [6439]; *Phanuël* (i.e. *Penuël*), an Israelite:—Phanuel.

5324. **φαντάζω, phantazō,** *fan-tad´-zo*; from a derivative of 5316; to *make apparent*, i.e. (passive) to *appear* (neuter participle as noun, a *spectacle*):—sight.

5325. **φαντασία, phantasia,** *fan-tas-ee´-ah*; from a derivative of 5324; (properly abstract) a (vain) *show* ("fantasy"):—pomp.

5326. **φάντασμα, phantasma,** *fan´-tas-mah*; from 5324; (properly concrete) a (mere) *show* ("phantasm"), i.e. *spectre*:—spirit.

5327. **φάραγξ, pharagx,** *far´-anx*; properly strengthened from the base of 4008 or rather of 4486; a *gap* or *chasm*, i.e. *ravine* (*winter-torrent*):—valley.

5328. **Φαραώ, Pharaō,** *far-ah-o´*; of foreign origin [6547]; *Pharaö* (i.e. *Pharoh*), an Egyptian king:—Pharaoh.

5329. **Φαρές, Phares,** *far-es´*; of Hebrew origin [6557]; *Phares* (i.e. *Perets*), an Israelite:—Phares.

5330. **Φαρισαῖος, Pharisaios,** *far-is-ah´-yos*; of Hebrew origin [compare 6567]; a *separatist*, i.e. exclusively *religious*; a *Pharisæan*, i.e. Jewish sectary:—Pharisee.

5331. **φαρμακεία, pharmakeia,** *far-mak-i´-ah*; from 5332; *medication* ("pharmacy"), i.e. (by extension) *magic* (literal or figurative):—sorcery, witchcraft.

5332. **φαρμακεύς, pharmakeus,** *far-mak-yoos´*; from **φάρμακον, pharmakon** (a *drug*, i.e. *spell-giving potion*); a *druggist* ("pharmacist") or *poisoner*, i.e. (by extension) a *magician*:—sorcerer.

5333. **φαρμακός, pharmakos,** *far-mak-os´*; the same as 5332:—sorcerer.

5334. **φάσις, phasis,** *fas´-is*; from 5346 (not the same as "phase," which is from 5316); a *saying*, i.e. *report*:—tidings.

5335. **φάσκω, phaskō,** *fas´-ko*; prolonged from the same as 5346; to *assert*:—affirm, profess, say.

5336. **φάτνη, phatnē,** *fat´-nay*; from **πατέομαι, pateomai** (to *eat*); a *crib* (for fodder):—manger, stall.

5337. **φαῦλος, phaulos,** *fow´-los*; apparently a primary word; "*foul*" or "*flawy*," i.e. (figurative) *wicked*:—evil.

Adjective meaning bad, worthless, as of food or a garment. In the NT, morally, bad, evil, wicked. Spoken of evil deeds (Jn 3:20; 5:29; Jas 3:16); spoken of wicked statements (Tit 2:8).

Syn.: *kakós* (2556), bad; *ponērós* (4190), malevolent.

5338. φέγγος, pheggos, *feng´-gos*; probably akin to the base of 5457 [compare 5350]; *brilliancy*:—light.

A noun meaning light or brightness, shining. Spoken of the moon (Mt 24:29; Mk 13:24). Spoken of a lamp (Lk 11:33).

Syn.: *phōstér* (5458), luminary, light, light-giving; *phōtismós* (5462), an illumination, light.

5339. φείδομαι, pheidomai, *fi´-dom-ahee*; of uncertain affinity; to *be chary* of, i.e. (subject) to *abstain* or (object) to *treat leniently*:—forbear, spare.

5340. φειδομένως, pheidomenōs, *fi-dom-en´-oce*; adverb from participle of 5339; *abstemiously*, i.e. *stingily*:—sparingly.

5341. φελόνης, phelonēs, *fel-on´-ace*; by transposed for a derivative probably of 5316 (as *showing* outside the other garments); a *mantle* (*surtout*):—cloke.

5342. φέρω, pherō, *fer´-o*; a primary verb (for which other and apparently not cognate ones are used in certain tenses only; namely, οἴω, *oiō*, *oy´-o*; and ἐνέγκω, *enegkō, en-eng´-ko*); to *"bear"* or *carry* (in a very wide application, literal and figurative, as follows):—be, bear, bring (forth), carry, come, + let her drive, be driven, endure, go on, lay, lead, move, reach, rushing, uphold.

To bear, bring.

(**I**) Particularly to bear as a burden, bear up, have or take upon oneself. In the NT, only figuratively.

(**A**) To bear up under or with, to endure, e.g., evils (Ro 9:22; Heb 12:20; 13:13).

(**B**) To bear up something, uphold, have in charge, to direct, govern (Heb 1:3).

(**II**) To bear with the idea of motion, bear along, carry (Lk 23:26). In the passive, to be borne along, as a ship before the wind, to be driven (Ac 27:15, 17). Figuratively to be moved, incited (2Pe 1:21). In the middle, to bear oneself along, move along, rush as a wind (Ac 2:2). Figuratively to go on, advance in teaching (Heb 6:1).

(**III**) To bear, with the idea of motion to a place, bear onward, to bring.

(**A**) Used of things. Generally (Mt 14:11, 18; Mk 6:27, 28; 12:15, 16; Lk 24:1; Jn 2:8; 4:33; 19:39; 20:27; 21:10; 2Ti 4:13; Rev 21:24, 26). Figuratively: of a voice or declaration, in the

passive, to be borne, brought, to come (2Pe 1:17, 18); of good brought to or bestowed on someone (1Pe 1:13); of accusations, charges, to bring forward, present (Jn 18:29; Ac 25:7; 2Pe 2:11); of a doctrine, prophecy, to announce, make known (2Pe 1:21; 2Jn 10). Of a fact or event as reported or testified, to adduce, show, prove (Heb 9:16).

(**B**) Used of persons, to bear, bring, e.g., the sick or afflicted (Mt 17:17; Mk 1:32; 2:3; 7:32; 8:25; 9:17, 19, 20; Lk 5:18; Ac 5:16). See also Mk 15:22; Jn 21:28.

(**IV**) To bear as trees or fields bear their fruits, to yield fruit (Mk 4:8; Jn 12:24; 15:2, 4, 5, 8, 16).

Deriv.: *anaphérō* (399), to carry or bring up, offer up; *apophérō* (667), to carry away; *diaphérō* (1308), to bear through, differ; *eisphérō* (1533), to bring to or into; *ekphérō* (1627), to carry something out, to carry out to burial; *epiphérō* (2018), to bring upon, inflict; *thanatēphóros* (2287), deadly; *karpophóros* (2593), fruitful; *kataphérō* (2702), to bring down; *paraphérō* (3911), to bear along, carry off; *periphérō* (4064), to carry about or around; *prosphérō* (4374), to bring to or before, to offer; *prophérō* (4393), bring forth, produce; *sumphérō* (4851), to bear together, contribute; *telesphoréō* (5052), to bring to an intended perfection or goal; *tropophoréō* (5159), mode or style, deportment, character; *hupophérō* (5297), to bear up under, endure; *phoréō* (5409), to have a burden, bear; *phóros* (5411), a tax; *phórtos* (5414), the freight of a ship.

Syn.: *apokuéō* (616), to bring forth, give birth to, beget; *bastázō* (941), to bear, take up, carry; *gennáō* (1080), to bring forth, give birth to, beget; *tíktō* (5088), to give birth to, beget. Also *paréchō* (3930), to offer, furnish, supply.

5343. φεύγω, pheugō, *fyoo´-go*; apparently a primary verb; to *run away* (literal or figurative); by implication to *shun*; (by analogy) to *vanish*:—escape, flee (away).

5344. Φῆλιξ, Phēlix, *fay´-lix*; of Latin origin; *happy*; *Phelix* (i.e. *Felix*), a Roman:—Felix.

5345. φήμη, phēmē, *fay´-may*; from 5346; a *saying*, i.e. *rumour* ("fame"):—fame.

5346. φημί, phēmi, *fay-mee´*; properly the same as the base of 5457 and 5316; to *show* or *make known* one's thoughts, i.e. *speak* or *say*:—affirm, say. Compare 3004.

From the obsolete *pháō* (n.f.), to shine. Particularly to bring to light by speech; generally to say, speak, utter.

(I) Generally, usually followed by the words that are spoken (Mt 14:8; 26:34, 61; Lk 7:44; Ac 8:36; 10:28, 30, 31; 23:25; 25:5, 22; Ro 3:8; 1Co 6:16; 10:15; 2Co 10:10; Heb 8:5).

(II) As modified by the context, where the sense often lies not so much in *phēmí* as in the adjuncts.

(A) Before interrogations, meaning to ask, inquire (Mt 27:23; Ac 16:30; 21:37).

(B) Before replies, meaning to answer, reply (Mt 4:7; 8:8; 13:29; Lk 23:3; Jn 1:23; Ac 2:38).

(C) Emphatically, meaning to affirm, assert (1Co 7:29; 10:19; 15:50).

Deriv.: *súmphēmi* (4852), to agree with; *phásis* (5334), information; *phḗmē* (5345), fame, rumour.

Syn.: *laléō* (2980), to utter; *légō* (3004), to speak. Also *apophthéggomai* (669), to speak clearly, articulate, give utterance; *diabebaióomai* (1226), to affirm confidently; *diïschurízomai* (1340), to assert vehemently; *eréō* (2046), to say, speak; *homologéō* (3670), to profess, confess; *phthéggomai* (5350), to enunciate clearly.

5347. Φῆστος, Phēstos, *face´-tos*; of Latin derivative; *festal; Phestus* (i.e. *Festus*), a Roman:—Festus.

5348. φθάνω, phthanō, *fthan´-o*; apparently a primary verb; to *be beforehand*, i.e. *anticipate* or *precede*; by extension to *have arrived* at:—(already) attain, come, prevent.

5349. φθαρτός, phthartos, *fthar-tos´*; from 5351; *decayed*, i.e. (by implication) *perishable*:—corruptible.

Adjective from *phtheírō* (5351), to corrupt. Subject to corruption, corruptible, perishable. Spoken of things; corruptible, perishable: e.g., a crown (1Co 9:25); silver or gold (1Pe 1:18); a seed (1Pe 1:23). Spoken of man and the present earthly body (Ro 1:23; 1Co 15:53, 54).

Der.: *áphthartos* (862), incorruptible.

5350. φθέγγομαι, phtheggomai, *ftheng´-gom-ahee*; probably akin to 5338 and thus to 5346; to *utter* a clear sound, i.e. (genitive) to *proclaim*:—speak.

5351. φθείρω, phtheirō, *fthi´-ro*; probably strengthened from φθίω, *phthiō* (to *pine* or

waste); properly to *shrivel* or *wither*, i.e. to *spoil* (by any process) or (genitive) to *ruin* (especially figurative by moral influences, to *deprave*):—corrupt (self), defile, destroy.

From *phthíō* or *phthínō* (n.f.), to waste, pine. To corrupt, destroy. Generally, to bring to a worse state (1Co 3:17). Figuratively, in a moral sense, to corrupt, to make depraved (1Co 15:33; Eph 4:22; Jude 10; Rev 19:2). To corrupt, with the meaning of to subvert or corrupt opinions (2Co 7:2; 11:3).

Deriv.: *diaptheírō* (1311), to corrupt, destroy; *kataphtheírō* (2704), to corrupt, destroy, spoil, deprave; *phthartós* (5349), corruptible; *phthorá* (5356), corruption, both physical and spiritual.

Syn.: *sēpō* (4595), to rot.

5352. φθινοπωρινός, phthinopōrinos, *fthin-op-o-ree-nos´*; from a derivative of φθίνω, *phthinō* (to *wane*; akin to the base of 5351) and 3703 (meaning *late autumn*); *autumnal* (as *stripped* of leaves):—whose fruit withereth.

5353. φθόγγος, phthoggos, *fthong´-gos*; from 5350; *utterance*, i.e. a *musical* note (vocal or instrumental):—sound.

5354. φθονέω, phthoneō, *fthon-eh´-o*; from 5355; to *be jealous* of:—envy.

5355. φθόνος, phthonos, *fthon´-os*; probably akin to the base of 5351; *ill-will* (as *detraction*), i.e. *jealousy* (*spite*):—envy.

A noun meaning envy. Spoken as the motivation for the delivering of Jesus to be crucified (Mt 27:18; Mk 15:10); spoken as characteristic of the old man (Ro 1:29; 1Ti 6:4; Tit 3:3; Jas 4:5). Spoken as the motivation for some to preach the gospel mockingly (Php 1:15). Used in the plural to indicate bursts of envy (Gal 5:21; 1Pe 2:1). While *zēlos* (2205), zeal, and *epithumía* (1939), lust, desire, can have a good connotation, *phthónos* seems to be used only with an evil connotation. However, Jas 4:5 in the NASB Bible seems to denote a good connotation for the word: "God jealously desires the Spirit which He has made to dwell in us." The difference in interpretation is whether one takes the word "spirit" as referring to God or as referring to our spirit, in which case the rest of the verse speaks to our own spirits lusting in envy (see *pneúma* [4151], spirit).

Deriv.: *phthonéō* (5354), to envy.

5356. φθορά, phthora, *fthor-ah´*; from 5351; *decay,* i.e. *ruin* (spontaneous or inflicted, literal or figurative):—corruption, destroy, perish.

5357. φιάλη, phialē, *fee-al´-ay;* of uncertain affinity; a broad shallow *cup* ("phial"):—vial.

5358. φιλάγαθος, philagathos, *fil-ag´-ath-os;* from 5384 and 18; *fond to good,* i.e. a *promoter of virtue:*—love of good men.

Adjective from *phílos* (5384), friend, and *agathós* (18), benevolent. Loving good, a lover of what is good, upright. Used only in Tit 1:8.

Deriv.: *aphilágathos* (865), not loving good.

5359. Φιλαδέλφεια, Philadelpheia, *fil-ad-el´-fee-ah;* from **Φιλάδελφος,** *Philadelphos* (the same as 5361), a king of Pergamos; *Philadelphia,* a place in Asia Minor:—Philadelphia.

5360. φιλαδελφία, philadelphia, *fil-ad-el-fee´-ah;* from 5361; *fraternal affection:*—brotherly love (kindness), love of the brethren.

Noun from *philádelphos* (5361), one who loves his brother. Brotherly love. In the NT, used only of the love of Christians one to another, brotherly love out of a common spiritual life (Ro 12:10; 1Th 4:9; Heb 13:1; 1Pe 1:22; 2Pe 1:7).

Syn.: *eúnoia* (2133), kindness, goodwill, benevolence; *philanthrōpía* (5363), benevolence, philanthropy; *philía* (5373), friendship.

5361. φιλάδελφος, philadelphos, *fil-ad´-el-fos;* from 5384 and 80; *fond of brethren,* i.e. *fraternal:*—love as brethren.

Adjective from *phílos* (5384), friend, and *adelphós* (80), brother. Loving one's brother, brotherly affectionate. In the NT, only in the strictly Christian sense of loving each other as Christian brothers. Used only in 1Pe 3:8.

Deriv.: *Philadélpheia* (5359), Philadelphia; *philadelphía* (5360), brotherly love.

Syn.: *philóstorgos* (5387), having natural love.

5362. φίλανδρος, philandros, *fil´-an-dros;* from 5384 and 435; *fond of man,* i.e. *affectionate* as a wife:—love their husbands.

5363. φιλανθρωπία, philanthrōpia, *fil-an-thro-pee´-ah;* from the same as 5364; *fondness of mankind,* i.e. *benevolence* ("philanthropy"):—kindness, love toward man.

Noun from *philánthropos* (n.f.), a lover of mankind, which is from *phílos* (5384), friend, and *ánthrōpos* (444), human being. Human friendship, philanthropy, benevolence, kindness. Used twice in the NT (Ac 28:2; Tit 3:4).

Syn.: *éleos* (1656), compassion, mercy; *oiktirmós* (3628), compassion; *splágchna* (pl. of *splágchon* [4698]), bowels of compassion.

5364. φιλανθρώπως, philanthrōpōs, *fil-anthro´-poce;* adverb from a compound of 5384 and 444; *fondly to man* ("philanthropically"), i.e. *humanely:*—courteously.

5365. φιλαργυρία, philarguria, *fil-ar-goo-ree´-ah;* from 5366; *avarice:*—love of money.

Noun from *philárguros* (5366), a lover of money, which is from *phílos* (5384), friend, and *árguros* (696), silver. The love of money, covetousness. Used only in 1Ti 6:10.

Syn.: *pleonexía* (4124), covetousness.

5366. φιλάργυρος, philarguros, *fil-ar´-goo-ros;* from 5384 and 696; *fond of silver (money),* i.e. *avaricious:*—covetous.

5367. φίλαυτος, philautos, *fil´-ow-tos;* from 5384 and 846; *fond of self,* i.e. *selfish:*—lover of own self.

Adjective from *phílos* (5384), loving or friend, and *autós* (846), oneself. Self-centered or selfish. Used only in 2Ti 3:2.

5368. φιλέω, phileō, *fil-eh´-o;* from 5384; to be *a friend to (fond of* [an individual or an object]), i.e. *have affection* for (denoting *personal* attachment, as a matter of sentiment or feeling; while 25 is wider, embracing especially the judgement and the *deliberate* assent of the will as a matter of principle, duty and propriety: the two thus stand related very much as 2309 and 1014, or as 2372 and 3563 respectively; the former being chiefly of the *heart* and the latter of the *head*); specially to *kiss* (as a mark of tenderness):—kiss, love.

From *phílos* (5384), loved, dear, friend. To love.

(I) Generally, to have affection for someone (Mt 10:37; Jn 5:20; 11:3, 36; 15:19; 16:27; 20:2; 21:15–17; 1Co 16:22; Tit 3:15; Rev 3:19). Of things, to be fond of, to like (Mt 23:6; Lk 20:46; Jn 12:25; Rev 22:15).

(II) Specifically, to kiss (Mt 26:48; Mk 14:44; Lk 22:47).

(III) Followed by the infinitive with the meaning to love to do something (Mt 6:5).

Deriv.: *kataphiléō* (2705), to kiss affectionately; *phílēma* (5370), a kiss; *philía* (5373), friendship, love.

5369. φιλήδονος, philēdonos, *fil-ay´-don-os*; from 5384 and 2237; *fond of pleasure*, i.e. *voluptuous:*—lover of pleasure.

5370. φίλημα, philēma, *fil´-ay-mah*; from 5368; a *kiss:*—kiss.

5371. Φιλήμων, Philēmōn, *fil-ah´-mone*; from 5368; *friendly; Philemon,* a Christian:—Philemon.

5372. Φιλητός, Philētos, *fil-ay-tos´*; from 5368; *amiable; Philetus,* an opposer of Christianity:—Philetus.

5373. φιλία, philia, *fil-ee´-ah*; from 5384; *fondness:*—friendship.

Noun from *philéō* (5368), to befriend, love, kiss. Love, friendship, fondness. Used only in Jas 4:4.

Syn.: *agápē* (26), love.

5374. Φιλιππήσιος, Philippēsios, *fil-ip-pay´-see-os*; from 5375; a *Philippesian (Philippian),* i.e. native of Philippi:—Philippian.

5375. Φίλιπποι, Philippoi, *fil´-ip-poy*; plural of 5376; *Philippi,* a place in Macedonia:—Philippi.

5376. Φίλιππος, Philippos, *fil´-ip-pos*; from 5384 and 2462; *fond of horses; Philippus,* the name of four Israelites:—Philip.

5377. φιλόθεος, philotheos, *fil-oth´-eh-os*; from 5384 and 2316; *fond of God,* i.e. *pious:*—lover of God.

5378. Φιλόλογος, Philologos, *fil-ol´-og-os*; from 5384 and 3056; *fond of words,* i.e. *talkative* (*argumentative, learned,* "*philological*"); *Philologus,* a Christian:—Philologus.

5379. φιλονεικία, philoneikia, *fil-on-i-kee´-ah*; from 5380; *quarrelsomeness,* i.e. a *dispute:*—strife.

5380. φιλόνεικος, philoneikos, *fil-on´-i-kos*; from 5384 and νεῖκος, *neikos* (a quarrel; probably akin to 3534); *fond of strife,* i.e. *disputatious:*—contentious.

5381. φιλονεξία, philonexia, *fil-on-ex-ee´-ah*; from 5382; *hospitableness:*—entertain strangers, hospitality.

5382. φιλόξενος, philoxenos, *fil-ox´-en-os*; from 5384 and 3581; *fond of guests,* i.e. *hospitable:*—given to (lover of, use) hospitality.

5383. φιλοπρωτεύω, philoprōteuō, *fil-op-rot-yoo´-o*; from a compound of 5384 and 4413; to *be fond of being first,* i.e. *ambitious* of distinction:—love to have the preeminence.

5384. φίλος, philos, *fee´-los*; properly *dear,* i.e. a *friend*; active *fond,* i.e. *friendly* (still as a noun, an *associate, neighbour,* etc.):—friend.

5385. φιλοσοφία, philosophia, *fil-os-of-ee´-ah*; from 5386; "*philosophy*," i.e. (special) Jewish *sophistry:*—philosophy.

5386. φιλόσοφος, philosophos, *fil-os´-of-os*; from 5384 and 4680; *fond of wise things,* i.e. a "*philosopher*":—philosopher.

5387. φιλόστοργος, philostorgos, *fil-os´-tor-gos*; from 5384 and στοργή, *torgē* (*cherishing* one's kindred, especially parents or children); *fond of* natural *relatives,* i.e. *fraternal* toward fellow Christian:—kindly affectioned.

5388. φιλότεκνος, philoteknos, *fil-ot´-ek-nos*; from 5384 and 5043; *fond of* one's *children,* i.e. *maternal:*—love their children.

5389. φιλοτιμέομαι, philotimeomai, *fil-ot-im-eh´-om-ahee*; middle from a compound of 5384 and 5092; to be *fond of honour,* i.e. *emulous* (*eager* or *earnest* to do something):—labour, strive, study.

5390. φιλοφρόνως, philophronōs, *fil-of-ron´-oce*; adverb from 5391; *with friendliness of mind,* i.e. *kindly:*—courteously.

5391. φιλόφρων, philophrōn, *fil-of´-rone*; from 5384 and 5424; *friendly of mind,* i.e. *kind:*—courteous.

5392. φιμόω, phimoō, *fee-mo´-o*; from φιμός, *phimos* (a *muzzle*); to *muzzle:*—muzzle.

5393. Φλέγων, Phlegōn, *fleg´-one*; active participle of the base of 5395; *blazing; Phlegon,* a Christian:—Phlegon.

5394. φλογίζω, phlogizō, *flog-id´-zo*; from 5395; to *cause a blaze*, i.e. *ignite* (figurative, to *inflame* with passion):—set on fire.

5395. φλόξ, phlox, *flox*; from a primary **φλέγω,** *phlego* (to "*flash*" or "*flame*"); a *blaze*:—flame (-ing).

5396. φλυαρέω, phluareō, *floo-ar-eh´-o*; from 5397; to *be a babbler* or *trifler*, i.e. (by implication) to *berate* idly or mischievously:—prate against.

5397. φλύαρος, phluaros, *floo´-ar-os*; from **φλύω,** *phluō* (to *bubble*); a *garrulous* person, i.e. *prater*:—tattler.

5398. φοβερός, phoberos, *fob-er-os´*; from 5401; *frightful*, i.e. (object) *formidable*:—fearful, terrible.

5399. φοβέω, phobeō, *fob-eh´-o*; from 5401; to *frighten*, i.e. (passive) to *be alarmed*; (by analogy) to *be in awe* of, i.e. *revere*:—be (+ sore) afraid, fear (exceedingly), reverence.

From *phóbos* (5401), fear. To put in fear, terrify, frighten. In the Classical Greek, to cause to run away. In the NT, used only in the passive, to become fearful, afraid, terrified.

(I) Particularly:

(A) Intransitively, to be fearful in a certain situation. Used in a command not to fear (Mt 14:27; Mk 5:36; 6:50; Lk 1:13, 30; Ro 13:4). Used generally (Mt 14:30; 17:6; 27:54; Mk 4:41; 10:32; 16:8; Lk 2:9; 1Pe 3:14)　　．

(B) Transitively, to fear someone (Mt 10:26, 28; 14:5; Mk 12:12; Lk 12:4; 20:19; Jn 9:22; Ac 9:26; Ro 13:3; Gal 2:12); to fear something (Heb 11:23, 27; Rev 2:10).

(C) Followed by a negative clause expressing what is feared: e.g., lest "any of you should seem to come short of it [a promise of rest]" (Heb 4:1). See also Ac 27:17, 29; 2Co 11:3; 12:20; Gal 4:11.

(D) Followed by the infinitive, to fear to do something, hesitate (Mt 1:20; 2:22; Mk 9:32; Lk 9:45).

(II) Morally, to fear, reverence, honour.

(A) Generally (Mk 6:20; Eph 5:33).

(B) In regard to the Lord, meaning to reverence God, to stand in awe of God (Lk 18:2, 4; 23:40; Col 3:22; 1Pe 2:17); expressing piety, equivalent to worship, adoration of God (Lk 1:50; Ac 10:22, 35; 13:16, 26; Rev 11:18; 14:7; 15:4; 19:5).

Deriv.: *ékphobos* (1630), very frightened; *phoberós* (5398), fearful; *phóbētron* (5400), that which causes fear, terror.

Syn.: *sébomai* (4576), to revere; *trémō* (5141), to tremble.

5400. φόβητρον, phobētron, *fob´-ay-tron*; neuter of a derivative of 5399; a *frightening* thing, i.e. *terrific* portent:—fearful sight.

5401. φόβος, phobos, *fob´-os*; from a primary **φέβομαι, phebomai** (to *be* put in *fear*); *alarm* or *fright*:—be afraid, + exceedingly, fear, terror.

Noun from *phébomai* (n.f.), to flee in fear. Fear, terror, reverence, respect, honour.

(I) Particularly and generally (Mt 14:26; Lk 1:12; 2:9; 8:37; 21:26; Ro 8:15; 2Co 7:5, 11; 1Ti 5:20; 1Jn 4:18; Rev 11:11). Followed by the genitive of person or thing feared meaning that which inspires fear (Mt 28:4; Jn 7:13; 19:38; 20:19; Heb 2:15; 1Pe 3:14; Rev 18:10, 15). By metonymy, a terror, object of fear (Ro 13:3). Including the idea of astonishment, amazement (Mt 28:8; Mk 4:41; Lk 1:65; 5:26; 7:16; Ac 2:43; 5:5, 11; 19:17).

(II) In a moral sense, fear, reverence, respect, honour (1Pe 1:17; 3:2, 15). Of persons (Ro 13:7); of God or Christ, the fear of God or the Lord meaning a deep and reverential sense of accountability to God or Christ (Ac 9:31; Ro 3:18; 2Co 5:11; 7:1; Eph 5:21; 1Pe 2:18; Jude 23). Used intensively, with *trómos* (5156), trembling, in fear and trembling (1Co 2:3; 2Co 7:15; Eph 6:5; Php 2:12).

Deriv.: *émphobos* (1719), afraid; *phobéō* (5399), to terrify, frighten.

Syn.: *deilía* (1167), timidity, fear; *eulábeia* (2124), fear, reverence, piety; *trómos* (5156), trembling.

5402. Φοίβη, Phoibē, *foy´-bay*; feminine of **Φοῖβος, Phoibos** (*bright*; probably akin to the base of 5457); *Phoebe*, a Christian woman:—Phebe.

5403. Φοινίκη, Phoinikē, *foy-nee´-kay*; from 5404; *palm*-country; *Phoenice* (or *Phoenicia*), a region of Palestine:—Phenice, Phenicia.

5404. φοῖνιξ, phoinix, *foy´-nix*; of uncertain derivative; a *palm*-tree:—palm (tree).

5405. Φοῖνιξ, Phoinix, *foy´-nix*; probably the same as 5404; *Phoenix*, a place in Crete:— Phenice.

5406. φονεύς, phoneus, *fon-yooce´*; from 5408; a *murderer* (always of *criminal* [or at least *intentional*] homicide; which 443 does not necessarily imply; while 4607 is a special term for a *public* bandit):—murderer.

Noun from *phoneúō* (5407), to kill. A manslayer, murderer (Mt 22:7; Ac 3:14; 7:52; 28:4; 1Pe 4:15; Rev 21:8; 22:15).

Syn.: *anthrōpoktónos* (443), manslayer; *sikários* (4607), assassin, murderer.

5407. φονεύω, phoneuō, *fon-yoo´-o*; from 5406; to *be a murderer* (of):—kill, do murder, slay.

5408. φόνος, phonos, *fon´-os*; from an obsolete primary **φένω, phenō** (to *slay*); *murder*:— murder, + be slain with, slaughter.

5409. φορέω, phoreō, *for-eh´-o*; from 5411; to *have a burden*, i.e. (by analogy) to *wear* as clothing or a constant accompaniment:—bear, wear.

5410. Φόρον, Phoron, *for´-on*; of Latin origin; a *forum* or market-place; only in compound with 675; a *station* on the Appian road:— forum.

5411. φόρος, phoros, *for´-os*; from 5342; a *load* (as *borne*), i.e. (figurative) a *tax* (properly an individual *assessment* on persons or property; whereas 5056 is usually a generic *toll* on goods or travel):—tribute.

Noun from *phérō* (5342), to bring. Particularly what is borne, brought; hence a tax or tribute imposed upon persons and their property annually, in distinction from *télos* (5056), toll, which was usually levied on merchandise and travelers (Lk 20:22; 23:2; Ro 13:6, 7).

Syn.: *dídrachmon* (1323), two (or a double) drachmae, the equivalent of a half-shekel, which was the amount of the tribute in the first century A.D., due from every adult Jew for the maintenance of the temple services; *kénsos* (2778), a poll tax.

5412. φορτίζω, phortizō, *for-tid´-zo*; from 5414; to *load* up (properly as a vessel or animal), i.e. (figurative) to *overburden* with ceremony (or spiritual anxiety):—lade, be heavy laden.

5413. φορτίον, phortion, *for-tee´-on*; diminutive of 5414; an *invoice* (as part of *freight*), i.e. (figurative) a *task* or *service*:—burden.

Noun from *phórtos* (5414), a burden, load. A diminutive in form but not in sense. The goods or merchandise carried by a ship, freight, cargo. In the NT, used figuratively: spoken of the burden of ceremonial observances rigorously exacted and increased by human traditions (Mt 23:4; Lk 11:46); spoken of the precepts and requirements of Christ in antithesis to these burdens (Mt 11:30); spoken of the burden of one's own responsibilities and failures (Gal 6:5).

Syn.: *báros* (922), a weight, something pressing on one physically or emotionally; *gómos* (1117), the freight of a ship.

5414. φόρτος, phortos, *for´-tos*; from 5342; something *carried*, i.e. the *cargo* of a ship:— lading.

5415. Φορτουνᾶτος, Phortounatos, *for-too-nat´-os*; of Latin origin; "fortunate"; *Fortunatus*, a Christian:—Fortunatus.

5416. φραγέλλιον, phragellion, *frag-el´-le-on*; neuter of a derivative from the base of 5417; a *whip*, i.e. Roman *lash* as a public punishment:— scourge.

5417. φραγελλόω, phragelloō, *frag-el-lo´-o*; from a presumed equivalent of the Latin *flagellum*; to *whip*, i.e. *lash* as a public punishment:— scourge.

5418. φραγμός, phragmos, *frag-mos´*; from 5420; a *fence*, or inclosing *barrier* (literal or figurative):—hedge (+ round about), partition.

5419. φράζω, phrazō, *frad´-zo*; probably akin to 5420 through the idea of *defining*; to *indicate* (by word or act), i.e. (special) to *expound*:— declare.

5420. φράσσω, phrassō, *fras´-so*; apparently a strengthened form of the base of 5424; to *fence* or enclose, i.e. (special) to *block* up (figurative, to *silence*):—stop.

5421. φρέαρ, phrear, *freh´-ar*; of uncertain derivative; a *hole* in the ground (dug for obtaining or holding water or other purposes), i.e. a *cistern* or *well*; (figurative) an *abyss* (as a *prison*):—well, pit.

A noun meaning well or pit dug in the earth for water, and thus strictly distinguished from *pēgḗ* (4077), fountain, though a well may also be called a fountain. Generally (Lk 14:5; Jn 4:11, 12). Figuratively of any pit, abyss: e.g., in Hades, the bottomless pit (Rev 9:1, 2).

Syn.: *bóthunos* (999), pit, ditch, cistern.

5422. φρεναπατάω, **phrenapataō,** *fren-ap-at-ah´-o;* from 5423; to *be a mind-misleader,* i.e. *delude:*—deceive.

5423. φρεναπάτης, **phrenapatēs,** *fren-ap-at´-ace;* from 5424 and 539; a *mind-misleader,* i.e. *seducer:*—deceiver.

5424. φρήν, **phrēn,** *frane;* probably from an obsolete φράω, **phraō** (to *rein in* or *curb;* compare 5420); the *midrif* (as a *partition* of the body), i.e. (figurative and by implication of sympathy) the *feelings* (or sensitive nature; by extension [also in the plural] the *mind* or cognitive faculties):—understanding.

Literally the diaphragm, the midriff. Figuratively, the supposed seat of all mental and emotional activity. In the NT, by metonymy, meaning the mind, intellect, disposition, feelings. Used only in 1Co 14:20.

Deriv.: *áphrōn* (878), a fool; *homóphrōn* (3675), of the same mind; *sṓphrōn* (4998), of sound mind; *phrenapatáō* (5422), to deceive; *phronéō* (5426), to think.

Syn.: *diánoia* (1271), intellect, mind; *noús* (3563), mind; *súnesis* (4907), discernment, the ability to understand the relationships between ideas.

5425. φρίσσω, **phrissō,** *fris´-so;* apparently a primary verb; to "*bristle*" or *chill,* i.e. *shudder* (*fear*):—tremble.

5426. φρονέω, **phroneō,** *fron-eh´-o;* from 5424; to *exercise* the *mind,* i.e. *entertain* or *have a sentiment* or *opinion;* by implication to *be* (mentally) *disposed* (more or less earnestly in a certain direction); intensive to *interest oneself* in (with concern or obedience):—set the affection on, (be) care (-ful), (be like-, + be of one, + be of the same, + let this) mind (-ed), regard, savour, think.

From *phrḗn* (5424), mind. To think, have a mind-set, be minded. The activity represented by *phronéō* involves the will, affections, and conscience.

(I) Generally, to be of an opinion, to consider (Ac 28:22; Ro 12:3, 16; 1Co 4:6; 13:11; Gal 5:10; Php 1:7). Used of time, to regard, keep (Ro 14:6).

(II) To think, in the sense of having a particular mind-set or attitude. Generally (Php 2:5; 3:15). Used with *autós* (846), same, to be of one mind, one accord, to think the same thing (Ro 15:5; 2Co 13:11; Php 2:2; 3:16; 4:2).

(III) To set one's mind on, to be devoted to (Mt 16:23; Mk 8:33; Ro 8:5; Php 3:19; 4:10; Col 3:2).

Deriv.: *kataphronéō* (2706), to despise; *paraphronéō* (3912), to be foolhardy; *periphronéō* (4065), to despise; *huperphronéō* (5252), to think highly of one's self, to be vain, arrogant; *hupsēlophronéō* (5309), to be proud, arrogant; *philóphrōn* (5391), friendly; *phrónēma* (5427), thought; *phrónēsis* (5428), understanding, prudence; *phrónimos* (5429), thoughtful.

Syn.: *aisthánomai* (143), to perceive, understand; *dokéō* (1380), to think, form an opinion; *epístamai* (1987), to know well; *hēgéomai* (2233), to think; *katanoéō* (2657), to perceive fully, comprehend; *katalambánō* (2638), to apprehend, comprehend; *logízomai* (3049), to reckon, think; *noéō* (3539), to perceive, understand; *nomízō* (3543), to think; *oíomai* (3633) or *oímai,* to suppose, think; *punthánomai* (4441), to ascertain; *suníēmi* (4920), to perceive, understand; *huponoéō* (5282), to suppose; *phrontízō* (5431), to think, consider, be careful.

5427. φρόνημα, **phronēma,** *fron´-ay-mah;* from 5426; (mental) *inclination* or *purpose:*—(be, + be carnally, + be spiritually) mind (-ed).

5428. φρόνησις, **phronēsis,** *fron´-ay-sis;* from 5426; mental *action* or *activity,* i.e. intellectual or moral *insight:*—prudence, wisdom.

Noun from *phronéō* (5426), to think, have a mind-set. Mind, thought, thinking.

(I) A mode of thinking and feeling (Lk 1:17).

(II) Understanding, prudence (Eph 1:8), where it occurs with the noun *sophía* [4678], wisdom).

Syn.: *súnesis* (4907), perception, discernment.

5429. φρόνιμος, **phronimos,** *fron´-ee-mos;* from 5424; *thoughtful,* i.e. *sagacious* or *discreet* (implying a *cautious* character; while 4680 denotes *practical* skill or acumen; and 4908 indicates rather *intelligence* or mental acquirement); in a bad sense *conceited* (also in the comparative):—wise (-r).

Adjective from *phronéō* (5426), to think, have a mind-set. Prudent, sensible, practically wise in relationships with others (Mt 7:24; 10:16; 24:45; 25:2, 4, 8, 9; Lk 12:42; 16:8; 1Co 10:15). In an evil sense, thinking oneself to be prudent or wise because of self-complacency (Ro 11:25; 12:16; used ironically in 1Co 4:10; 2Co 11:19).

Deriv.: *phronímōs* (5430), prudently.

Syn.: *sophós* (4680), wise; *sunetós* (4908), sagacious, understanding, able to reason; *sōphrōn* (4998), of sound mind.

5430. **φρονίμως, phronimōs,** *fron-im´-oce*; adverb from 5429; *prudently*:—wisely.

5431. **φροντίζω, phrontizō,** *fron-tid´-zo*; from a derivative of 5424; to *exercise thought*, i.e. be *anxious*:—be careful.

5432. **φρουρέω, phroureō,** *froo-reh´-o*; from a compound of 4253 and 3708; to *be a watcher in advance*, i.e. to *mount guard* as a sentinel (*post spies* at gates); (figurative) to *hem in, protect*:—keep (with a garrison). Compare 5083.

5433. **φρυάσσω, phruassō,** *froo-as´-so*; akin to 1032, 1031; to *snort* (as a spirited horse), i.e. (figurative) to *make a tumult*:—rage.

5434. **φρύγανον, phruganon,** *froo´-gan-on*; neuter of a presumed derivative of **φρύγω, phrugō** (to *roast* or *parch*; akin to the base of 5395); something *desiccated*, i.e. a dry *twig*:—stick.

5435. **Φρυγία, Phrugia,** *froog-ee´-ah*; probably of foreign origin; *Phrygia*, a region of Asia Minor:—Phrygia.

5436. **Φύγελλος, Phugellos,** *foog´-el-los*; probably from 5343; *fugitive*; *Phygellus*, an apostate Christian:—Phygellus.

5437. **φυγή, phugē,** *foog-ay´*; from 5343; a *fleeing*, i.e. *escape*:—flight.

5438. **φυλακή, phulakē,** *foo-lak-ay´*; from 5442; a *guarding* or (concrete *guard*), the act, the person; figurative the place, the condition, or (special) the time (as a division of day or night), literal or figurative:—cage, hold, (im-) prison (-ment), ward, watch.

Noun from *phulássō* (5442), to keep. A watching, a guarding.

(I) The act of keeping watch, guarding (Lk 2:8).

(II) By metonymy, persons set to watch, a watch, guard or guards (Ac 12:10).

(III) By metonymy, the place where a watch is kept. In the NT figuratively of Babylon as the dwelling place, station, haunt of demons and unclean birds where they resort and hold their vigils or where they are kept in prison (Rev 18:2).

(IV) Spoken by metonymy of the place where someone is watched, guarded, kept in custody, a prison. Generally (Mt 5:25; 14:3, 10; 18:30; 25:36, 39, 43, 44; Mk 6:17, 24; Lk 3:20; 12:58; 21:12; 22:33; 23:19, 25; Jn 3:24; Ac 5:19, 22, 25; 8:3; 12:4–6, 17; 16:23, 24, 27, 37, 40; 22:4; 26:10; Rev 2:10). In the sense of imprisonment (2Co 6:5; 11:23; Heb 11:36). Poetically of the bottomless pit, abyss, Tartarus, as the prison of demons and the souls of wicked men (1Pe 3:19; Rev 20:7). See *tartaróō* (5020), to consign to Tartarus.

(V) By metonymy, the time for a watch of the night, a period of the night during which one watch of soldiers kept guard and were then relieved (Mt 14:25; 24:43; Mk 6:48; Lk 12:38). The ancient Jews, and probably the Greeks, divided the night into three watches of four hours each (Sept.: Jgs 7:19; Ps 90:4). But after the Jews came under the dominion of the Romans, they made four watches of about three hours each as the Romans had. These were either numbered first, second, third, fourth, and were also called *opsé* (3796), late in the day, after the close of the day, evening; *mesonúktion* (3317), midnight; *alektorophōnía* (219), the time of the cock crowing; and *prōí* (4404), morning (cf. Mk 13:35).

Deriv.: *gazophulákion* (1049), a treasury; *phulakízō* (5439), to imprison.

Syn.: *desmōtḗrion* (1201), a prison; *koustōdía* (2892), watch, guard; *tḗrēsis* (5084), a watching, guarding, imprisonment.

5439. **φυλακίζω, phulakizō,** *foo-lak-id´-zo*; from 5441; to *incarcerate*:—imprison.

5440. **φυλακτήριον, phulaktērion,** *foo-lak-tay´-ree-on*; neuter of a derivative of 5442; a *guard-case*, i.e. "*phylactery*" for wearing slips of Scripture texts:—phylactery.

5441. φύλαξ, phulax, *foo´-lax*; from 5442; a *watcher* or *sentry*:—keeper.

5442. φυλάσσω, phulassō, *foo-las´-so*; probably from 5443 through the idea of *isolation*; to *watch*, i.e. *be on guard* (literal or figurative); by implication to *preserve, obey, avoid*:—beware, keep (self), observe, save. Compare 5083.

To watch, keep watch.

(**I**) To watch, guard, keep:

(**A**) Persons or things from escape or violence (Lk 8:29; 11:21; Ac 12:4; 22:20; 23:35; 28:16).

(**B**) Of persons or things kept in safety, to keep, preserve (Lk 2:8; Jn 12:25; 17:12; 2Th 3:3; 1Ti 6:20; 2Ti 1:12, 14; 2Pe 2:5; 1Jn 5:21; Jude 24).

(**C**) In the middle: to protect oneself, to be on one's guard, to beware of, avoid (Lk 12:15; Ac 21:25; 2Ti 4:15; 2Pe 3:17).

(**II**) Figuratively, to keep, observe, not to violate, e.g., precepts, laws. With the accusative (Mt 19:20; Mk 10:20; Lk 11:28; 18:21; Ac 7:53; 16:4; 21:24; Ro 2:26; Gal 6:13; 1Ti 5:21).

Deriv.: *diaphulássō* (1314), to guard carefully, protect; *phulaké* (5438), the act of guarding; *phulaktérion* (5440), phylactery; *phúlax* (5441), a keeper, guard.

Syn.: *blépō* (991), to take heed; *diatēréō* (1301), to keep carefully; *epéchō* (1907), to take heed; *kratéō* (2902), to hold fast; *proséchō* (4337), to be on guard, to beware; *skopéō* (4648), to mark, heed, consider; *suntēréō* (4933), to preserve, keep safe; *tēréō* (5083), to watch over, preserve, keep; *phrouréō* (5432), to guard.

5443. φυλή, phulē, *foo-lay´*; from 5453 (compare 5444); an *offshoot*, i.e. *race* or *clan*:—kindred, tribe.

5444. φύλλον, phullon, *fool´-lon*; from the same as 5443; a *sprout*, i.e. *leaf*:—leaf.

5445. φύραμα, phurama, *foo´-ram-ah*; from a prolonged form of **φύρω, phurō** (to *mix* a liquid with a solid; perhaps akin to 5453 through the idea of *swelling* in bulk), meaning to *knead*; a *mass* of dough:—lump.

5446. φυσικός, phusikos, *foo-see-kos´*; from 5449; "*physical*," i.e. (by implication) *instinctive*:—natural. Compare 5591.

5447. φυσικῶς, phusikōs, *foo-see-koce´*; adverb from 5446; "*physically*," i.e. (by implication) *instinctively*:—naturally.

5448. φυσιόω, phusioō, *foo-see-o´-o*; from 5449 in the primary sense of *blowing*; to *inflate*, i.e. (figurative) *make proud (haughty)*:—puff up.

5449. φύσις, phusis, *foo´-sis*; from 5453; *growth* (by *germination* or *expansion*), i.e. (by implication) natural *production* (lineal *descent*); by extension a *genus* or *sort*; (figurative) native *disposition, constitution* or *usage*:—([man-]) kind, nature ([-al]).

5450. φυσίωσις, phusiōsis, *foo-see´-o-sis*; from 5448; *inflation*, i.e. (figurative) *haughtiness*:—swelling.

5451. φυτεία, phuteia, *foo-ti´-ah*; from 5452; *trans-planting*, i.e. (concrete) a *shrub* or *vegetable*:—plant.

5452. φυτεύω, phuteuō, *foot-yoo´-o*; from a derivative of 5453; to *set out* in the earth, i.e. *implant*; (figurative) to *instill* doctrine:—plant.

5453. φύω, phuō, *foo´-o*; a primary verb; probably original to "*puff*" or *blow*, i.e. to *swell* up; but only used in the implication sense, to *germinate* or *grow* (*sprout, produce*), literal or figurative:—spring (up).

To generate, produce, bring forth, let grow, of plants, fruit, or persons. Usages in the NT:

(**I**) Particularly, to spring up or grow as a plant (Lk 8:6, 8).

(**II**) Figuratively, to spring up, grow up within a person. Spoken of a root of bitterness (Heb 12:15).

Deriv.: *ekphúō* (1631), to produce; *neóphutos* (3504), newly planted, novice; *sumphúō* (4855), to bring forth together; *phulé* (5443), tribe; *phúllon* (5444), a leaf; *phúsis* (5449), nature, natural birth or condition.

Syn.: *auxánō* (837), to grow or increase.

5454. φωλεός, phōleos, *fo-leh-os´*; of uncertain derivative; a *burrow* or *lurking-place*:—hole.

5455. φωνέω, phōneō, *fo-neh´-o*; from 5456 to emit a *sound* (animal, human or instrumental); by implication to *address* in words or by name, also in imitation:—call (for), crow, cry.

5456. φωνή, phōnē, *fo-nay´*; probably akin to 5316 through the idea of *disclosure*; a *tone* (articulate, bestial or artificial); by implication an *address* (for any purpose), *saying* or *language*:—noise, sound, voice.

Noun from *pháō* (n.f.), to shine. A sound or tone made or given forth.

(I) Generally, spoken of things: of a trumpet or other instrument (Mt 24:31; 1Co 14:7, 8; Rev 18:22); the wind (Jn 3:8; Ac 2:6); rushing wings, chariots, waters (Rev 9:9; 14:2; 19:6); of thunder (Rev 4:5; 6:1; 8:5; 11:19; 14:2; 19:6). See also Heb 12:19.

(II) Specifically, the voice or cry of a person.

(A) Particularly and generally as in phrases with verbs of speaking, calling, crying out: e.g., used with *mégas* (3173), great, in the sense of a loud voice (Mt 27:46, 50; Mk 5:7; 15:34, 37; Lk 8:28; 17:15; 23:23; Jn 11:43; Ac 8:7; Rev 1:10; 6:10; 14:15); used with *akoúō* (191), to hear or hear one's voice, in the sense of obeying one's voice or obeying the person himself (Jn 10:16, 27; Heb 3:7, 15; 4:7). Used figuratively, "to change my voice," meaning to change one's tone, to speak in a different manner and spirit (Gal 4:20).

(B) By metonymy, what is uttered by the voice, a word, saying (Ac 13:27; 24:21).

(C) By metonymy, in the sense of the meaning of the voice, language, dialect (1Co 14:10, 11).

Deriv.: *alektorophōnía* (219), crowing of a rooster; *áphōnos* (880), voiceless, mute; *kenophōnía* (2757), empty speaking; *súmphōnos* (4859), agreeable, sounding together, harmonious; *phōnéō* (5455), to address, speak.

Syn.: *boḗ* (995), a cry; *ḗchos* (2279), a loud noise, roar, echo, sound; *kraugḗ* (2906), clamor, crying; *laliá* (2981), talk, speech, saying, prattle; *lógos* (3056), word, speech, discourse; *phthóggos* (5353), utterance, musical note, sound.

5457. φῶς, phōs, *foce*; from an obsolete **φάω, phaō** (to *shine* or make *manifest*, especially by rays; compare 5316, 5346); *luminousness* (in the widest application, natural or artificial, abstract or concrete, literal or figurative):—fire, light.

Noun from *pháō* (n.f.), to shine. Light.

(I) Particularly and generally, spoken:

(A) Of light in itself (Mt 17:2; 2Co 4:6).

(B) Of light as emitted from a luminous body: e.g., of a lamp (Lk 8:16; Rev 18:23); of the sun (Rev 22:5).

(C) Of daylight (Mt 10:27; Lk 12:3; Jn 3:20, 21; 11:9, 10; Eph 5:13).

(D) Of the dazzling light, splendour or glory which surrounds the throne of God in which He dwells (1Ti 6:16; Rev 21:24). Hence, also as surrounding the Lord Jesus Christ in His appearances after His ascension (Ac 9:3; 22:6, 9, 11; 26:13); of angels (Ac 12:7; 2Co 11:14); of glorified saints (Col 1:12).

(II) By metonymy, a light, a luminous body.

(A) A lamp or torch (Ac 16:29).

(B) A fire (Mk 14:54; Lk 22:56).

(C) Spoken of the heavenly luminaries, the sun, moon, and stars of which God is figuratively called the father (Jas 1:17).

(III) Figuratively, moral and spiritual light and knowledge which enlightens the mind, soul or conscience; including also the idea of moral goodness, purity and holiness, and of consequent reward and happiness.

(A) Generally, true knowledge of God and spiritual things, Christian piety (Mt 4:16; Jn 3:19; 8:12; Ac 26:18, 23; Ro 13:12; 2Co 6:14; Eph 5:8; 1Pe 2:9; 1Jn 1:7; 2:8, 10). Hence, true Christians are spoken of as the sons of light or the children of light (Lk 16:8; Jn 12:36; Eph 5:8; 1Th 5:5). Spoken of as exhibited in the life and teaching of someone (Mt 5:16; Jn 5:35).

(B) By metonymy, the author or dispenser of moral and spiritual light, a moral teacher: spoken generally (Ro 2:19) and of the disciples (Mt 5:14; Ac 13:47). Spoken of God (1Jn 1:5). Used especially of Jesus as the great Teacher and Saviour of the world who brought life and immortality to light in His gospel (see Lk 2:32; Jn 1:4, 5, 7–9; 3:19; 8:12; 9:5; 12:35, 36, 46).

(C) By metonymy, the mind or conscience (Mt 6:23; Lk 11:35).

Deriv.: *phaínō* (5316), to give light, illuminate; *phōstḗr* (5458), light, brightness; *phōsphóros* (5459), bearing light, morning star; *phōteinós* (5460), bright, radiant; *phōtízō* (5461), to shine, make known.

Syn.: *apaúgasma* (541), brightness; *lamprótēs* (2987), brilliancy, brightness.

5458. φωστήρ, phōstḗr, *foce-tare´*; from 5457; an *illuminator*, i.e. (concretely) a *luminary*, or (abstract) *brilliancy*:—light.

From *phós* (5457), light. A light, light-giver. In Classical Greek, a window. In the NT, spoken figuratively of a person who gives light to those about him (Php 2:15). By metonymy, also spoken of the radiance of the holy Jerusalem that came from the divine glory (Rev 21:11).

5459. φωσφόρος, phōsphoros, *foce-for´-os*; from 5457 and 5342; *light-bearing* ("phosphorus"), i.e. (special) the *morning-star* (figurative):—day star.

5460. φωτεινός, phōteinos, *fo-ti-nos´*; from 5457; *lustrous*, i.e. *transparent* or *well-illuminated* (figurative):—bright, full of light.

5461. φωτίζω, phōtizō, *fo-tid´-zo*; from 5457; to *shed rays*, i.e. to *shine* or (transitive) to *brighten* up (literal or figurative):—enlighten, illuminate, (bring to, give) light, make to see.

Related to *phós* (5457), light. To give light to.

(I) Particularly (Lk 11:36; Rev 18:1).

(II) Figuratively, to enlighten, shine light upon, to impart moral and spiritual light (Jn 1:9; Eph 1:18; Heb 6:4; 10:32); to illuminate, make one see or understand (Eph 3:9); to bring to light, make known (1Co 4:5; 2Ti 1:10).

Deriv.: *phōtismós* (5462), a shining, illumination.

Syn.: *anáptō* (381), to enkindle, light; *apokalúptō* (601), to take off the cover, disclose, reveal; *dēlóō* (1213), to show, declare; *dialaléō* (1255), to declare publicly; *diasaphéō* (1285), to make clear, declare; *diaugázō* (1306), to shine through, dawn; *diaphēmízō* (1310), to report thoroughly, spread abroad; *diermēneúō* (1329), to explain thoroughly, expound; *exēgéō* (1834), to explain; *hermēneúō* (2059), to interpret; *plērophoréō* (4135), to inform fully, completely assure; *phaneróō* (5319), to make apparent, show, manifest, declare.

5462. φωτισμός, phōtismos, *fo-tis-mos´*; from 5461; *illumination* (figurative):—light.

Noun from *phōtízō* (5461), to lighten. Illumination, light, a bringing to light. In the NT, figuratively of moral and spiritual light (2Co 4:4, 6).

Syn.: *apaúgasma* (541), radiance, brightness; *lamprótēs* (2987), brilliancy, brightness.

X (Chi)

NT Numbers 5463–895

5463. χαίρω, chairō, *khah´ee-ro*; a primary verb; to *be* "*cheer*"*ful*, i.e. calmly *happy* or well-off; impersonal especially as salutation (on meeting or parting), *be well*:—farewell, be glad, God speed, greeting, hail, joy (-fully), rejoice.
To rejoice, be glad.
(I) Particularly, to rejoice, be glad (Mt 2:10; 18:13; Mk 14:11; Lk 6:23; 10:20; Jn 3:29; 11:15; 14:28; Php 1:18; 2:17, 18, 28; 3:1; 4:4, 10; 1Pe 4:13).
(II) The infinitive can be used as a brief formula, similar to the English word "greetings," especially at the beginning of a conversation or of an epistle (Ac 15:23; 23:26; Jas 1:1). The Apostle John commands his readers not to even give a greeting to false teachers (2Jn 10).
Deriv.: *sugchairō* (4796), to rejoice with; *chará* (5479), joy, delight, gladness; *cháris* (5485), grace.
Syn.: *agalliáō* (21), to exult, rejoice greatly; *euthuméō* (2114), to cheer up, make merry; *euphraínō* (2165), to cheer, gladden; *onínēmi* (3685), to gratify; *skirtáō* (4640), to leap for joy.

5464. χάλαζα, chalaza, *khal´-ad-zah*; probably from 5465; *hail*:—hail.

5465. χαλάω, chalaō, *khal-ah´-o*; from the base of 5490; to *lower* (as into a *void*):—let down, strike.

5466. Χαλδαῖος, Chaldaios, *khal-dah´-yos*; probably of Hebrew origin [3778]; a *Chaldæan* (i.e. *Kasdi*), or native of the region of the lower Euphrates:—Chaldæan.

5467. χαλεπός, chalepos, *khal-ep-os´*; perhaps from 5465 through the idea of *reducing* the strength; *difficult*, i.e. *dangerous*, or (by implication) *furious*:—fierce, perilous.

5468. χαλιναγωγέω, chalinagōgeō, *khal-in-ag-ogue-eh´-o*; from a compound of 5469 and the reduplicated form of 71; to *be* a *bit-leader*, i.e. to *curb* (figurative):—bridle.

5469. χαλινός, chalinos, *khal-ee-nos´*; from 5465; a *curb* or *head-stall* (as *curbing* the spirit):—bit, bridle.

5470. χάλκεος, chalkeos, *khal´-key-os*; from 5475; *coppery*:—brass.

5471. χαλκεύς, chalkeus, *khalk-yooce´*; from 5475; a *copper-worker* or *brazier*:—coppersmith.

5472. χαλκηδών, chalkēdōn, *khal-kay-dohn´*; from 5475 and perhaps 1491; *copper-like*, i.e. "*chalcedony*":—chalcedony.

5473. χαλκίον, chalkion, *khal-kee´-on*; diminutive from 5475; a *copper dish*:—brazen vessel.

5474. χαλκολίβανον, chalkalibanon, *khal-kol-ib´-an-on*; neuter of a compound of 5475 and 3030 (in the implication mean of *whiteness* or *brilliancy*); *burnished copper*, an alloy of copper (or gold) and silver having a brilliant lustre:—fine brass.

5475. χαλκός, chalkos, *khal-kos´*; perhaps from 5465 through the idea of *hollowing* out as a vessel (this metal being chiefly used for that purpose); *copper* (the substance, or some implement or coin made of it):—brass, money.

5476. χαμαί, chamai, *kham-ah´ee*; adverb perhaps from the base of 5490 through the idea of a *fissure* in the soil; *earthward*, i.e. *prostrate*:—on (to) the ground.

5477. Χαναάν, Chanaan, *khan-ah-an´*; of Hebrew origin [3667]; *Chanaan* (i.e. *Kenaan*), the early name of Palestine:—Chanaan.

5478. Χαναναῖος, Chanaanaios, *khan-ah-an-ah´-yos*; from 5477; a *Chanaanæan* (i.e. *Kenaanite*), or native of Gentile Palestine:—of Canaan.

5479. χαρά, chara, *khar-ah´*; from 5463; *cheerfulness*, i.e. calm *delight*:—gladness, × greatly, (× be exceeding) joy (-ful, -fully, -fulness, -ous).

965

Noun from *chaírō* (5463), to rejoice. Joy, rejoicing, gladness.

(I) Generally (Mt 2:10; 13:20, 44; 28:8; Mk 4:16; Lk 1:14; 8:13; 15:7, 10; Jn 15:11; 16:20; 17:13; Php 2:2; 1Pe 1:8; 1Jn 1:4; 2Jn 12).

(II) By metonymy, of the cause, ground, occasion of joy (Lk 2:10; Php 4:1; 1Th 2:19, 20; Jas 1:2; 3Jn 4).

(III) By metonymy, of enjoyment, fruition of joy, bliss (Mt 25:21, 23; Heb 12:2).

Syn.: *agallíasis* (20), exultation, exuberant joy; *euphrosúnē* (2167), good cheer, mirth, gladness of heart.

5480. χάραγμα, charagma, *khar´-ag-mah*; from the same as 5482; a *scratch* or *etching,* i.e. *stamp* (as a *badge* of servitude), or *sculptured* figure (*statue*):—graven, mark.

Noun from *charássō* (n.f.), to engrave. An engraving, something engraved or sculptured.

(I) An engraving or sculptured work such as images or idols (Ac 17:29).

(II) A mark cut in or stamped on, a sign: e.g., "the mark of the beast" (Rev 13:16, 17; 14:9, 11; 15:2; 16:2; 19:20; 20:4).

Deriv. of *charássō* (n.f.), to carve: *charaktḗr* (5481), something engraved, an impression; *chárax* (5482), a strong stake used in fortification; *chártēs* (5489), paper.

Syn.: *stígma* (4742), mark, brand; *sphragís* (4973), mark, seal.

5481. χαρακτήρ, charaktēr, *khar-ak-tar´*; from the same as 5482; a *graver* (the tool or the person), i.e. (by implication) *engraving* (["*character*"], the *figure* stamped, i.e. an exact *copy* or [figurative] *representation*):—express image.

Noun from *charássō* (n.f.), to carve. Originally an engraving tool. Later, the impression itself, usually something engraved, cut in, or stamped, a character, letter, mark, or sign. In the NT, an impression, image. Used only in Heb 1:3, where Jesus is described as the *charaktḗr* or the express image of God's nature.

Syn.: *eikṓn* (1504), image; *homoíōsis* (3669), likeness; *homoíōma* (3667), likeness.

5482. χάραξ, charax, *khar´-ax*; from **χαράσσω** *charassō* (to *sharpen* to a point; akin to 1125 through the idea of *scratching*); a *stake,* i.e. (by implication) a *palisade* or *rampart* (military *mound* for circumvallation in a siege):—trench.

5483. χαρίζομαι, charizomai, *khar-id´-zom-ahee*; middle from 5485; to *grant* as a *favour,* i.e. gratuitously, in kindness, pardon or rescue:—deliver, (frankly) forgive, (freely) give, grant.

From *cháris* (5485), grace. To show someone a favour, be kind to.

(I) To give or bestow a thing willingly (Lk 7:21; Ro 8:32; 1Co 2:12; Gal 3:18; Php 1:29; 2:9).

(II) Of persons, to deliver up or over in answer to demands (Ac 3:14; 25:11, 16) or in answer to prayer (Ac 27:24; Phm 22).

(III) Of things, to remit, forgive, not to exact (Lk 7:42, 43). Generally of wrong, sin, to forgive, not to punish (2Co 2:7, 10; 12:13; Eph 4:32; Col 2:13; 5:13).

Deriv.: *chárisma* (5486), a gift of grace.

Syn.: *apolúō* (630), to loose from; *aphíēmi* (863), to send forth, remit; *dídōmi* (1325), to give, bestow; *dōréomai* (1433), to give, make a gift; *paréchō* (3930), to provide, supply; *chorēgéō* (5524), to supply, give.

5484. χάριν, charin, *khar´-in*; accusative of 5485 as prep.; through *favour* of, i.e. *on account of:*—be (for) cause of, for sake of, + ... fore, × reproachfully.

5485. χάρις, charis, *khar´-ece*; from 5463; *graciousness* (as *gratifying*), of manner or act (abstract or concrete; literal, figurative or spiritual; especially the divine influence upon the heart, and its reflection in the life; including *gratitude*):—acceptable, benefit, favour, gift, grace (-ious), joy, liberality, pleasure, thank (-s, -worthy).

Noun from *chaírō* (5463), to rejoice. Grace, particularly that which causes joy, pleasure, gratification.

(I) Grace in reference to the external form or manner, particularly of persons meaning gracefulness, elegance. In the NT only of words or discourses as graciousness, agreeableness, acceptableness (Lk 4:22; Eph 4:29; Col 4:6).

(II) Grace in reference to disposition, attitude toward another, favour, goodwill, benevolence.

(A) Generally favour, goodwill (Lk 1:30; 2:40, 52; Ac 2:47; 4:33; 7:10, 46; 24:27; 25:9; Heb 4:16). Spoken by metonymy of the object of favour, something acceptable (1Pe 2:19, 20).

(B) Spoken of the grace, favour and goodwill of God and Christ as exercised toward men:

where *cháris* is joined with *eirēnē* (1515), peace, *éleos* (1656), mercy, and the like in salutations and in the introduction to most of the epistles, including the idea of every kind of favour, blessing, good, as proceeding from God the Father and the Lord Jesus Christ (Ro 1:7; 1Co 1:3; 2Co 1:2; Gal 1:3; Eph 1:2; Php 1:2; Col 1:2; 1Th 1:1; 2Th 1:2; 1Ti 1:2; 2Ti 1:2; Tit 1:4; Phm 3; 1Pe 1:2; 2Pe 1:2; 2Jn 3; Rev 1:4). Also spoken of the grace of the Lord Jesus Christ in the benedictions at the close of most of the epistles (Ro 16:20, 24; 1Co 16:23; 2Co 13:14; Gal 6:18). Simply with the definite article with equal meaning (Eph 6:24; Col 4:18; 1Ti 6:21; 2Ti 4:22; Tit 3:15; Heb 13:25). Spoken of the grace of Christ in providing salvation for us (Ac 15:11). Also spoken of the grace which God exercises toward us, the unmerited favour which he shows in saving us from sin (Ac 20:24; Ro 3:24; 5:2; 1Co 15:10; 2Co 1:12; 9:14; 12:9; Gal 1:15; Eph 1:6; Heb 2:9; 1Pe 4:10).

(C) Specifically of the divine grace and favour as exercised in conferring gifts, graces and benefits on man. Particularly as manifested in the benefits bestowed in and through Christ and His gospel (Ac 13:43; 2Co 4:15; 6:1; 8:1; Eph 4:7; Php 1:7; Heb 12:15; 13:9; Jas 4:6; 1Pe 1:10, 13; 5:5). Specifically of the grace or gift of the apostleship, the apostolic office (Ro 12:3; 15:15; 1Co 3:10; Gal 2:9; Eph 3:2, 8; 2Ti 2:1). Also of the grace exhibited in the pardon of sins and admission to the divine kingdom, saving grace (Ro 5:15; Gal 2:21; Tit 2:11; 3:7; 1Pe 3:7, "the grace of life"; 5:12).

(III) Gratitude, appreciation, thankfulness in return for favors and benefits. With the verb *échō* (2192), to have, to have thankfulness, to give thanks (Lk 17:9; 1Ti 1:12; 2Ti 1:3; Heb 12:28). Followed by the dative of *Theos* (2316), God, with an understood verb, thanks be given to God (Ro 6:17; 1Co 15:57; 2Co 2:14; 8:16; 9:15). In a question with the verb *estí* (2076), to be, what thanks is it, i.e. what thanks do you deserve (Lk 6:32–34). Used adverbially in the sense of with thankfulness, thankfully (1Co 10:30; Col 3:16).

Deriv.: *charízomai* (5483), to be kind to; *charitóō* (5487), to bestow grace on, highly honour.

Syn.: *dóma* (1390), a gift; *dósis* (1394), a gift or the act of giving; *dōreá* (1431), a free gift; *dórēma* (1434), a favour; *dóron* (1435), a gift; *euergesía* (2108), a benefit; *eulogía* (2129), a

blessing; *eucharistía* (2169), thankfulness, gratitude; *chárisma* (5486), a gift.

5486. χάρισμα, **charisma**, *char´-is-mah*; from 5483; a (divine) *gratuity*, i.e. *deliverance* (from danger or passion); (special) a (spiritual) *endowment*, i.e. (subject) religious *qualification*, or (objective) miraculous *faculty*:—(free) gift.

Noun from *charízomai* (5483), to show favour. A gift of grace, an undeserved benefit. In the NT used only of gifts and graces imparted from God, e.g., deliverance from peril (2Co 1:11); the gift of self-control (1Co 7:7); gifts of Christian knowledge, consolation, confidence (Ro 1:11; 1Co 1:7); redemption, salvation through Christ (Ro 5:15, 16; 6:23; 11:29). Specifically of the gifts and abilities imparted to the early Christians and particularly to Christian teachers by the Holy Spirit (Ro 12:6; 1Co 12:4, 9, 28, 30, 31; 1Pe 4:10). As communicated with the laying on of hands (1Ti 4:14; 2Ti 1:6).

Syn.: *dóma* (1390), a gift; *dósis* (1394), a gift; *dōreá* (1431), a free gift; *dórēma* (1434), a favour, something given; *dóron* (1435), a gift.

5487. χαριτόω, **charitoō**, *khar-ee-to´-o*; from 5485; to *grace*, i.e. indue with special *honour*:—make accepted, be highly favoured.

From *cháris* (5485), grace. To bestow grace, highly honour or greatly favour. In the NT spoken only of the divine favour: to the virgin Mary (Lk 1:28); to all believers (Eph 1:6).

5488. Χαρράν, **Charrhan**, *khar-hran´*; of Hebrew origin [2771]; *Charrhan* (i.e. *Charan*), a place in Mesopotamia:—Charran.

5489. χάρτης, **chartēs**, *khar´-tace*; from the same as 5482; a *sheet* ("chart") of writing-material (as to be *scribbled* over):—paper.

5490. χάσμα, **chasma**, *khas´-mah*; from a form of an obsolete primary χάω **chaō** (to "gape" or "yawn"); a "chasm" or vacancy (impassable *interval*):—gulf.

5491. χεῖλος, **cheilos**, *khi´-los*; from a form of the same as 5490; a *lip* (as a *pouring* place); (figurative) a *margin* (of water):—lip, shore.

5492. χειμάζω, **cheimazō**, *khi-mad´-zo*; from the same as 5494; to *storm*, i.e. (passive) to *labour under a gale*:—be tossed with tempest.

5493. χείμαρρος, cheimarrhos, *khi´-mar-hros*; from the base of 5494 and 4482; a *storm-runlet*, i.e. *winter-torrent*:—brook.

5494. χειμών, cheimōn, *khi-mone´*; from a derivative of **χέω, cheō** (to *pour*; akin to the base of 5490 through the idea of a *channel*), meaning a *storm* (as *pouring* rain); by implication the *rainy* season, i.e. *winter*:—tempest, foul weather, winter.

5495. χείρ, cheir, *khire*; perhaps from the base of 5494 in the sense of its congener the base of 5490 (through the idea of *hollowness* for grasping); the *hand* (literal or figurative [*power*]; especially [by Hebrew] a *means* or *instrument*):—hand.

5496. χειραγωγέω, cheiragōgeō, *khi-rag-ogue-eh´-o*; from 5497; to be a *hand-leader*, i.e. to *guide* (a blind person):—lead by the hand.

5497. χειραγωγός, cheiragōgos, *khi-rag-o-gos´*; from 5495 and a reduplicated form of 71; a *hand-leader*, i.e. personal *conductor* (of a blind person):—some to lead by the hand.

5498. χειρόγραφον, cheirographon, *khi-rog´-raf-on*; neuter of a compound of 5495 and 1125; something *hand-written* ("*chirograph*"), i.e. a *manuscript* (specially a legal *document* or *bond* [figurative]):—handwriting.

5499. χειροποίητος, cheiropoiētos, *khi-rop-oy´-ay-tos*; from 5495 and a derivative of 4160; *manufactured*, i.e. *of human construction*:—made by (make with) hands.

5500. χειροτονέω, cheirotoneō, *khi-rot-on-eh´-o*; from a compound of 5495 and **τείνω, teinō** (to *stretch*); to be a *hand-reacher* or *voter* (by raising the hand), i.e. (genitive) to *select* or *appoint*:—choose, ordain.

From *cheirotónos* (n.f.), stretching out the hands. To stretch out the hand, hold up the hand, as in voting; hence to vote, to give one's vote by holding up the hand. In the NT, to choose by vote, to appoint (Ac 14:23; 2Co 8:19).

Deriv.: *procheirontonéō* (4401), to choose beforehand.

Syn.: *tássō* (5021), to assign; *horízō* (3724), to mark out, specify, ordain; *apostéllō* (649), to set apart; *eklégomai* (1586), to choose.

5501. χείρων, cheirōn, *khi´-rone*; irregular comparative of 2556; from an obsolete equivalent **χέρης, cherēs** (of uncertain derivative); *more evil* or *aggravated* (physical, mental or moral):—sorer, worse.

5502. χερουβίμ, cheroubim, *kher-oo-beem´*; plural of Hebrew origin [3742]; "*cherubim*" (i.e. *cherubs* or *kerubim*):—cherubims.

5503. χήρα, chēra, *khay´-rah*; feminine of a presumed derivative apparently from the base of 5490 through the idea of *deficiency*; a *widow* (as *lacking* a husband), literal or figurative:—widow.

5504. χθές, chthes, *khthes*; of uncertain derivative; "*yesterday*"; by extension *in time past* or *hitherto*:—yesterday.

5505. χιλιάς, chilias, *khil-ee-as´*; from 5507; one *thousand* ("*chiliad*"):—thousand.

5506. χιλίαρχος, chiliarchos, *khil-ee´-ar-khos*; from 5507 and 757; the *commander of a thousand* soldiers ("*chiliarch*"), i.e. *colonel*:—(chief, high) captain.

5507. χίλιοι, chilioi, *khil´-ee-oy*; plural of uncertain affinity; a *thousand*:—thousand.

5508. Χίος, Chios, *khee´-os*; of uncertain derivative; *Chios*, an island in the Mediterranean:—Chios.

5509. χιτών, chitōn, *khee-tone´*; of foreign origin [3801]; a *tunic* or *shirt*:—clothes, coat, garment.

A noun meaning close-fitting inner vest, an inner garment (Mt 5:40; Jn 19:23; Ac 9:39; Jude 23). At times two tunics seem to have been worn, probably of different materials for ornament or luxury (Mt 10:10; Mk 6:9; Lk 3:11; 9:3). Hence it is said of the high priest that he rent his clothes (*chitónas*) or garments (Mk 14:63 where it is used in the plural; Sept.: Ge 37:3; 2Sa 15:32). In Lk 6:29 it is used with *himátion* (2440), an outer cloak as equivalent to *himátia* (Mt 26:65).

Syn.: For a list of various types of clothing, see the synonyms under *himátion* (2440), garment.

5510. χιών, chiōn, *khee-one´*; perhaps akin to the base of 5490 (5465) or 5494 (as *descending* or *empty*); *snow*:—snow.

5511. χλαμύς, chlamus, *khlam-ooce´*; of uncertain derivative; a military *cloak*:—robe.

A feminine noun meaning garment of dignity and office. The purple robe with which our Lord was arrayed in scorn by the mockers in Pilate's judgement hall (Mt 27:28–31). When put over the shoulders of someone, it was an indication that he was assuming a magistracy. It may have been the cast-off cloak of some high Roman officer which they put over the body of Jesus to mock Him as if He were an official person.

Syn.: For a list of various types of clothing, see the synonyms under *himátion* (2440), garment.

5512. χλευάζω, chleuazō, *khlyoo-ad´-zo*; from a derivative probably of 5491; to *throw out* the *lip*, i.e. *jeer* at:—mock.

5513. χλιαρός, chliaros, *khlee-ar-os´*; from χλίω, *chliō* (to *warm*); *tepid*:—lukewarm.

5514. Χλόη, Chloē, *khlo´-ay*; feminine of apparently a primary word; "*green*"; *Chloë*, a Christian female:—Chloe.

5515. χλωρός, chlōros, *khlo-ros´*; from the same as 5514; *greenish*, i.e. *verdant*, *dun-coloured*:—green, pale.

5516. χξς, chi xi stigma, *khee xee stig´-ma*; the twenty-second, fourteenth and an obsolete letter (4742 as a *cross*) of the Greek alphabet (intermediate between the fifth and sixth), used as numbers; denoting respectively six hundred, sixty and six; six hundred sixty-six as a numeral:—six hundred threescore and six.

5517. χοϊκός, choïkos, *kho-ik-os´*; from 5522; *dusty* or *dirty* (*soil*-like), i.e. (by implication) *terrene*:—earthy.

Adjective from *chóos* (5522), earth, dust. Earthy, made of earth or dust (1Co 15:47–49).

Syn.: *ostrákinos* (3749), of earthenware or clay, earthen; *epígeios* (1919), earthly; *katachthónios* (2709), subterranean.

5518. χοῖνιξ, choinix, *khoy´-nix*; of uncertain derivative; a *choenix* or certain dry measure:—measure.

5519. χοῖρος, choiros, *khoy-´ros*; of uncertain derivative; a *hog*:—swine.

5520. χολάω, cholaō, *khol-ah´-o*; from 5521; to be *bilious*, i.e. (by implication) *irritable* (*enraged*, "*choleric*"):—be angry.

5521. χολή, cholē, *khol-ay´*; feminine of an equivalent perhaps akin to the same as 5514 (from the *greenish* hue); "*gall*" or *bile*, i.e. (by analogy) *poison* or an *anodyne* (wormwood, poppy, etc.):—gall.

5522. χόος, choos, *kho´-os*; from the base of 5494; a *heap* (as *poured* out), i.e. *rubbish*; loose *dirt*:—dust.

5523. Χοραζίν, Chorazin, *khor-ad-zin´*; of uncertain derivative; *Chorazin*, a place in Palestine:—Chorazin.

5524. χορηγέω, chorēgeō, *khor-ayg-eh´-o*; from a compound of 5525 and 71; to be a *dance-leader*, i.e. (genitive) to *furnish*:—give, minister.

5525. χορός, choros, *khor-os´*; of uncertain derivative; a *ring*, i.e. round *dance* ("*choir*"):—dancing.

5526. χορτάζω, chortazō, *khor-tad´-zo*; from 5528; to *fodder*, i.e. (genitive) to *gorge* (*supply food* in abundance):—feed, fill, satisfy.

5527. χόρτασμα, chortasma, *khor´-tas-mah*; from 5526; *forage*, i.e. *food*:—sustenance.

5528. χόρτος, chortos, *khor´-tos*; apparently a primary word; a "*court*" or "*garden*," i.e. (by implication of *pasture*) *herbage* or *vegetation*:—blade, grass, hay.

5529. Χουζᾶς, Chouzas, *khood-zas´*; of uncertain origin; *Chuzas*, an officer of Herod:—Chuza.

5530. χράομαι, chraomai, *khrah´-om-ahee*; middle of a primary verb (perhaps rather from 5495, to *handle*); to *furnish* what is needed; (give an *oracle*, "*graze*" [touch slightly], *light* upon, etc.), i.e. (by implication) to *employ* or (by extension) to *act toward* one in a given manner:—entreat, use. Compare 5531, 5534.

Middle deponent of *chráō* (5531), to *lend*. To use, make use of, make the most of, followed by the dat. of things (Ac 27:17; 1Co 7:21, 31; 9:12, 15; 2Co 1:17; 3:12; 1Ti 1:8; 5:23). Of persons meaning to treat well or badly, with the dat. (Ac 27:3; implied 2Co 13:10; Sept.: Ge 16:6; 19:8).

Deriv.: *eúchrēstos* (2173), useful; *katachráomai* (2710), to abuse; *sugchráomai* (4798), to share usage with someone; *chrēma* (5536), something usable as wealth, money; *chrēsimos* (5539), useful, profitable; *chrēsis* (5540), use; *chrēstós* (5543), profitable, good for any use.

Syn.: *apaitéō* (523), to demand back.

5531. χράω, chraō, *khrah´-o*; probably the same as the base of 5530; to *loan*:—lend.

To lend, furnish as a loan (Lk 11:5); the middle voice, *chráomai* (5530), to borrow, receive for use.

5532. χρεία, chreia, *khri´-ah*; from the base of 5530 or 5534; *employment*, i.e. an *affair*; also (by implication) *occasion, demand, requirement* or *destitution*:—business, lack, necessary (-ity), need (-ful), use, want.

Noun from *chréos* (n.f.), debt. Also from *chréos* (n.f.): *chreōpheilétēs* (5533), one who owes a debt.

(I) Use, usage, employment, act of using. In the NT metonymically, that in which one is employed, an employment, affair, business (Ac 6:3).

(II) Need, necessity, want.

(A) Generally (Eph 4:29 meaning merciful, needful edification). With *estí* (2076), is, and the gen. (Lk 10:42, "one thing is needful"). With the inf. (Heb 7:11).

(B) Of personal need, necessity, want (Ac 20:34; 28:10, "such things as were necessary"; Ro 12:13; Php 2:25; 4:16, for one's need or wants; 4:19; Tit 3:14).

(C) Elsewhere only in the phrase *chreían échō* (2192), I have need. **(1)** Generally and followed by the gen. meaning to have need of (Mt 9:12; 21:3; 26:65; Mk 2:17; 11:3; 14:63; Lk 5:31; 9:11; 15:7; 19:31, 34; 22:71; Jn 13:29; 1Co 12:21, 24; Heb 5:12; 10:36; Rev 21:23; 22:5). **(2)** Of personal need, want, with the gen. (Mt 6:8; 1Th 4:12; Rev 3:17). Used in an absolute sense, meaning to have need, to be in need or want (Mk 2:25; Ac 2:45; 4:35; Eph 4:28; 1Jn 3:17). Followed by the inf. act. (Mt 14:16; 1Th 1:8; 4:9); also the inf. pass. (Mt 3:14; 1Th 5:1); by *hína* (2443), so that (Jn 2:25; 16:30; 1Jn 2:27). In the Sept. with the gen. (Pr 18:2; Isa 13:17).

Deriv.: *achreíos* (888), unprofitable; *chrēzō* (5535), to have need of, want, desire.

Syn.: *anágkē* (318), necessity, need; *hustérēsis*

(5304), need; *anagkaíon* (316), necessary, needful; *epánagkes* (1876), necessary; *tó déon*, that which is needful, from *deí* (1163), necessary; *tó prépon* (from *prépō* [4241]), that which is necessary.

5533. χρεωφειλέτης, chreōpheilétēs, *khreh-o-fi-let´-ace*; from a derivative of 5531 and 3781; a *loan-ower*, i.e. *indebted* person:—debtor.

5534. χρή, chrē, *khray*; third person singular of the same as 5530 or 5531 used impersonally; it *needs* (*must* or *should*) be:—ought.

An impersonal verb from *chreía* (5532), need, necessity. It is necessary, it needs to be, ought to be; translated "it is becoming" or "it is appropriate" (Jas 3:10 with the neg. *ou* [3756], not).

5535. χρῄζω, chrēizō, *khrade´-zo*; from 5532; to *make* (i.e. *have*) *necessity*, i.e. *be in want* of:— (have) need.

From *chreía* (5532), need, necessity. Governing a gen., to have need of, want, desire (Mt 6:32; Lk 11:8; 12:30; Ro 16:2).

5536. χρῆμα, chrēma, *khray´-mah*; something *useful* or *needed*, i.e. *wealth, price*:—money, riches.

Noun from *chráomai* (5530), to use, need. Something useful or capable of being used. In both the sing. and plural it means money (Lk 18:24; Ac 4:37; 8:18; 24:26; Sept.: Job 27:17). In Gr. writings it also means thing, matter, business, equal to *prágma* (4229), business, matter, thing, from which is derived *pragmateúomai* (4231), to trade.

Deriv.: *parachrēma* (3916), at the very moment, immediately; *chrēmatízō* (5537), to manage a business.

Syn.: *argúrion* (694), silver, money; *chalkós* (5475), copper, as used for money; *kérma* (2772), a coin, change; *nómisma* (3546), money; *statēr* (4715), a coin, equivalent to four drachmae; *drachmaí* (1406), drachmae, the Greek money; *ploútos* (4149), wealth; *porismós* (4200), gain, a means of gain.

5537. χρηματίζω, chrēmatízō, *khray-mat-id´-zo*; from 5536; to *utter an oracle* (compare the original sense of 5530), i.e. divinely *intimate*; by implication (compare the secular sense of 5532) to constitute a *firm* for business, i.e. (generic) *bear* as a *title*:—be called, be admonished (warned) of God, reveal, speak.

From *chréma* (5536), an affair, business. To have a business affair or dealings, manage a business (Sept.: 1Ki 18:27), especially in trade and money affairs. In the middle *chrématízomai*, to do good business, make a profit, gain. Of kings and magistrates, to do business publicly, to give audience; to answer as to ambassadors, petitioners, to warn, advise, give a response or decision. Hence in the NT:

(I) Spoken in respect to a divine response, oracle, or declaration, to give response, speak as an oracle, warn from God, used in an absolute sense (Heb 12:25 of Moses who consulted God and delivered to the people the divine response, precepts, warnings, and the like). Used of a prophet (Sept.: Jer 26:2); of God (Sept.: Jer 30:2; 36:4). In the pass. of persons, to receive a divine response, warning, to be warned or admonished of God, used in an absolute sense (Heb 8:5 speaking of Moses); followed by *perí* (4012), concerning, with the gen. (Heb 11:7); with *kat' ónar* (*katá* [2596], according, in; *ónar* [3677], dream), in a dream (Mt 2:12, 22). Of things, to be given in response, be revealed (Lk 2:26, by the Holy Spirit).

(II) In later Gr. usage it means to do business under someone's name; hence generally, to take or bear a name, to be named, called, constructed with the name in apposition (Ac 11:26, "named [or called] Christians for the first time" [a.t.]; Ro 7:3, "named an adulteress" [a.t.]).

Deriv.: *chrēmatismós* (5538), an oracle, response or decision.

Syn.: *kaléō* (2564), to call; *onomázō* (3687), to name; *eponomázō* (2028), to surname, call; *apokalúptō* (601), to unveil, reveal; *légō* (3004), to say, speak; *laléō* (2980), to say; *eréō* (2046), to utter, speak, say, tell.

5538. χρηματισμός, **chrēmatismos**, *khray-mat-is-mos´*; from 5537; a divine *response* or *revelation*:—answer of God.

Noun from *chrēmatízō* (5537), to do business, utter an oracle, to be warned of God as by an oracle. An oracle, a reply, response or decision (Ro 11:4).

Syn.: *apókrisis* (612), answer; *apókrima* (610), a judicial sentence, answer of God.

5539. χρήσιμος, **chrēsimos**, *khray´-see-mos*; from 5540; *serviceable*:—profit.

Adjective from *chráomai* (5530), to use, need. Useful, profitable (2Ti 2:14).

Syn.: *eúchrēstos* (2173), useful; *ōphélimos* (5624), useful, profitable; *lusiteleí* (3081), is advantageous, profitable.

5540. χρῆσις, **chrēsis**, *khray´-sis*; from 5530; *employment*, i.e. (special) sexual *intercourse* (as an *occupation* of the body):—use.

Noun from *chráomai* (5530), to use. Use, the act (usage) or manner (use) of using (Ro 1:26, 27 of the use of the body in sexual intercourse).

5541. χρηστεύομαι, **chrēsteuomai**, *khraste-yoo´-om-ahee*; middle from 5543; to *show oneself useful*, i.e. *act benevolently*:—be kind.

5542. χρηστολογία, **chrēstologia**, *khrase-tol-og-ee´-ah*; from a compound of 5543 and 3004; *fair speech*, i.e. *plausibility*:—good words.

5543. χρηστός, **chrēstos**, *khrase-tos´*; from 5530; *employed*, i.e. (by implication) *useful* (in manner or morals):—better, easy, good (-ness), gracious, kind.

Adjective from *chráomai* (5530), to furnish what is needed. Profitable, fit, good for any use.

(I) Of things (Lk 5:39, better for drinking; Sept.: Jer 24:2, 5, good for eating). Figuratively, good, gentle, easy to use or bear; Christ's yoke is *chrestós*, as having nothing harsh or galling about it (Mt 11:30). In a moral sense, moral, useful, good, virtuous (in the proverb in 1Co 15:33 quoted from Menander).

(II) Of persons, useful toward others, hence good-natured, good, gentle, kind (Lk 6:35 of God; Eph 4:32; 1Pe 2:3); *tó chrēstón* (neuter with the article), goodness, kindness, equal to *he chrēstótēs* (5544) (Ro 2:4; Sept.: Ps 86:5).

Deriv.: *áchrēstos* (890), unprofitable, useless; *chrēsteúomai* (5541), to be kind, willing to help; *chrēstótēs* (5544), kindness, usefulness.

Syn.: *epieikés* (1933), seemly, equitable, fair, forbearing, tolerant; *anexíkakos* (420), one who patiently forbears evil; *épios* (2261), mild, gentle; *kalós* (2570), good; *agathós* (18), benevolent; *akéraios* (185), harmless.

5544. χρηστότης, **chrēstotēs**, *khray-stot´-ace*; from 5543; *usefulness*, i.e. moral *excellence* (in character or demeanour):—gentleness, good (-ness), kindness.

Noun from *chrēstós* (5543), useful, profitable. Benignity, kindness, usefulness. It often occurs with *philanthrōpía* (5363), philanthropy; *anochē* (463), forbearance (Ro 2:4), and is the opposite of *apotomía* (663), severity or cutting something short and quickly (Ro 11:22). *Chrēstótēs* is translated "good" (Ro 3:12); "kindness" (2Co 6:6; Eph 2:7; Col 3:12; Tit 3:4); "gentleness" (Gal 5:22). It is the grace which pervades the whole nature, mellowing all which would be harsh and austere. Thus, wine is *chrēstós* (5543), mellowed with age (Lk 5:39). The word is descriptive of one's disposition and does not necessarily entail acts of goodness as does the word *agathōsúnē* (19), active benignity. *Chrēstótēs* has the harmlessness of the dove but not the wisdom of the serpent which *agathōsúnē* shows in sharpness and rebuke.

Syn.: *epieíkeia* (1932), fairness, moderation, clemency, an active dealing with others involving equity and justice; *praütēs* (4240), meekness; *eupoiía* (2140), beneficence, doing that which is good.

5545. χρίσμα, chrisma, *khrís´-mah*; from 5548; an *unguent* or *smearing*, i.e. (figurative) the special *endowment* ("chrism") of the Holy Spirit:—anointing, unction.

Noun from *chríō* (5548), to anoint. The anointing (Ex 29:7; 30:25). The specially prepared anointing oil was called *chrísma hágion* (*hágion* [39], holy). By metonymy used of the Holy Spirit in 1Jn 2:20, 27 where it signifies an anointing which had been experienced, a communication and reception of the Spirit (cf. Jn 16:13). The allusion is to the anointing and consecration of kings and priests (Ex 28:41; 1Sa 10:1). This was emblematic of a divine spirit descending and abiding upon them from God, as was afterwards the laying on of hands (Dt 34:9). In Da 9:26 *chrísma* stands for the Anointed One, Christ (*christós* [5547]), as it stands for the Holy Spirit in 1Jn 2. *Chrísma* is not merely a figurative name for the Spirit as seen from the expressions *chrísma échete* ("you have an anointing" [a.t.], 2:20) and *elábete* ("you received" [a.t.], 2:27). The word seems chosen on the one hand, to give prominence to what the readers had experienced, and on the other hand, by referring to the OT practice, and especially to Christ, to remind them of their calling and mark (1Pe 2:5, 9).

5546. Χριστιανός, Christianos, *khris-tee-an-os´*; from 5547; a *Christian*, i.e. follower of Christ:—Christian.

Noun from *Christós* (5547), Christ. A name given to the disciples or followers of Christ, first adopted at Antioch. It does not occur in the NT as a name commonly used by Christians themselves (Ac 11:26; 26:28; 1Pe 4:16). The believers first became known as Christians as an appellation of ridicule.

Syn.: *mathētēs* (3101), a learner; *pistós* (4103), faithful (one); *adelphós* (80), a brother; *hágios* (40), a saint.

5547. Χριστός, Christos, *khris-tos´*; from 5548; *anointed*, i.e. the Messiah, an epithet of Jesus:—Christ.

Adjective from *chríō* (5548), to anoint. Anointed, a term used in the OT applied to everyone anointed with the holy oil, primarily to the high priesthood (Le 4:5, 16). Also a name applied to others acting as redeemers.

(I) As an appellative and with the article *ho*, the, *Christós*, Christ, it occurs chiefly in the Gospels and means the Messiah (Mk 15:32, "the King of Israel"; Jn 1:41; 4:42 "the Christ, the Saviour of the world"; Ac 2:36; 9:22; 18:28. Also see Mt 1:17; 2:4; 16:16; Mk 12:35; 13:21; Lk 2:11, 26, "the Christ of the Lord" [a.t.]; 4:41; 23:2; Jn 1:20, 25; Ac 2:30; 3:18; Ro 8:11; 1Jn 2:22; 5:1, 6; Rev 11:15; 12:10; Sept.: Ps 2:2 [cf. Da 9:25]). Joined with *Iēsoús* (2424), Jesus, *Iēsoús ho Christós*, Jesus the Christ (Ac 5:42; 9:34; 1Co 3:11), *Iēsoús Christós* (Jn 17:3; Ac 2:38; 3:20; 1Jn 4:2, 3; 2Jn 7), *ho Christós Iēsoús*, the Christ Jesus (Ac 17:3; 18:5, 28; 19:4).

(II) As a proper noun, Christ.

(A) Used in an absolute sense, *Christós* or *ho Christós* chiefly in the epistles referring to the Messiah (Ro 5:6, 8; 8:10; 1Co 1:12; 3:23; Gal 1:6, 7; 2:20; Eph 4:12; Heb 3:6; 5:5; 1Pe 1:11; 4:14).

(B) More often joined with *Iēsoús* (Mt 1:16, "Jesus the One called Christ" [a.t.]); *Iēsoús Christós* in the Gospels (Mt 1:1, 18; Mk 1:1; Jn 1:17; Ac 3:6, "In the name of Jesus Christ"; 4:10; 8:12; 10:36; 28:31; Ro 1:1, 6, 8; 1Co 1:1; 5:4). *Christós Iēsoús*, stressing the deity of Christ first and then His humanity only after His resurrection beginning with Ac 19:4 and often in the epistles (Ro 3:24; 8:2, 39; 15:5; 1Co 1:2, 30; Gal 3:26; 4:14; Php 2:5; 3:3, 8; Col 1:4; Heb 3:1). For the use of *ho Kúrios* (2962), the Lord, in connection with the names *Iēsoús* and *Christós*, see *Kúrios* (2962), Lord (cf. II, B, 2).

(C) Other designations attributed to Christ: (1) The servant of God (*país* [3816], child, servant; Ac 3:13, 26); *tón hágion paída sou* (*hágion* [40], holy; *paída* [3816], child, servant; Ac 4:27, 30). This is a Messianic title of our Lord indicative of humility, submission, vicarious suffering and death (see Ac 8:35; Isa 53:7). (2) Prince and Saviour (*archēgós* [747], chief leader, author or captain; *sōtḗr* [4990], Saviour; Ac 5:31 [cf. Ac 3:15; Heb 2:10; 12:2]). The word *archēgós* reflects the meaning of author or originator as expressed in Ac 3:15, *archēgón tḗs zōḗs* (*zōḗs* [2222], of life), the Originator, Author, and Sustainer of life or the one who inaugurates and controls the Messianic experience of salvation here called *zōḗ*, life (Isa 60:16).

(3) Son of Man, *ho Huiós toú anthrṓpou* (*Huiós* [5207], son; *anthrṓ-pou* [444], of man). This expression occurs eighty-one times in the Gospels, thirty times in Matthew, of which nine passages have direct parallels in both Mark and Luke, four have parallels in Mark only, eight in Luke only, and the remaining nine are peculiar to Matthew.

5548. χρίω, chriō, *khree´-o*; probably akin to 5530 through the idea of *contact*; to *smear* or *rub* with oil, i.e. (by implication) to *consecrate* to an office or religious service:—anoint.

To daub, smear, anoint with oil or ointment, to rub oneself with oil. The practice of anointing is found throughout the biblical record. The following paragraphs discuss its practice and are based upon passages either referring to the concept or employing the key verbs *chríō* or *aleíphō* (218). It was a mark of luxury to use specially scented oils (Am 6:6) such as those Hezekiah kept in his treasure house (2Ki 20:13). The use of ointment was a sign of joy (Pr 27:9), and was discontinued during times of mourning (Da 10:3); thus Joab instructed the woman of Tekoa to appear unanointed before David (2Sa 14:2). On the death of Bathsheba's child, David anointed himself to show that his mourning had ended (2Sa 12:20). The cessation of anointing was to be a mark of God's displeasure if Israel proved rebellious (Dt 28:40; Mic 6:15), and the restoration of the custom was to be a sign of God's returning favor (Isa 61:3). Anointing is used as a symbol of prosperity in Ps 92:10; Ecc 9:8.

Before paying visits of ceremony, the head was anointed. So Naomi told Ruth to anoint herself before visiting Boaz (Ru 3:3). Oil of myrrh was used for this purpose in the harem of Ahasuerus (Est 2:12). This must have been a custom in Palestine as Simon's failure to show hospitality in this respect is commented upon by our Lord in Lk 7:46. Mary's anointing of our Lord was according to this custom.

Rubbing with oil was practiced among the Jews in pre-Christian times as well as by the Apostles (Mk 6:13), recommended by James (Jas 5:14), mentioned in the parable of the Good Samaritan (Lk 10:34), and used as a type of God's forgiving grace when healing the sin-sick soul (Isa 1:6; Eze 16:9). In Egypt and Palestine the application of ointment and spices to the dead body was customary (Mk 16:1; Lk 23:56; Jn 19:40). They were externally applied and did not prevent decomposition (Jn 11:39).

Anointing had the significance of dedication to God. Jacob consecrated the stones at Bethel by pouring oil upon them (Ge 28:18; 35:14), and God recognized the action (Ge 31:13). The tabernacle and its furniture were thus consecrated (Ex 30:26; 40:10; Le 8:11), and the altar of burnt offering was reconsecrated after the sin offering (Ex 29:36). Other offerings, however, were anointed with oil (Le 2:1ff.), but no oil was to be poured on the sin offering (Le 5:11; Nu 5:15).

Priests were set apart by anointing. In the case of Aaron and probably all high priests, this was done twice, first by pouring the holy oil on his head after his robing, but before the sacrifice of consecration (Le 8:12; Ps 133:2), and next by sprinkling after the sacrifice (Le 8:30). The ordinary priests were only sprinkled with oil after the application of the blood of the sacrifice. Hence the high priest is called the anointed priest (Le 4:3, 5).

Kings were designated by anointing, such as Saul (1Sa 10:1) and David (1Sa 16:13). This act was accompanied by the gift of the Spirit. So when David was anointed, the Spirit descended on him and departed from Saul. Also Hazael was anointed over Syria by God's command (1Ki 19:15). Kings thus designated were called the Lord's anointed. David thus speaks of Saul (1Sa 26:11) and of himself (Ps 2:2). This passage is used by the apostles as prophetic of Christ (Ac 4:26). By anointing, kings were installed into office. David was anointed when made king of Judah and a third time when made king of united Israel (2Sa 2:4; 5:3).

Anointing also was used metaphorically to mean setting apart for the prophetic office. Elijah was told to anoint Elisha although the actual event is left unrecorded in Scripture (1Ki 19:16). In Ps 105:15 the words "anointed" and "prophets" are used as synonyms. The servant of the Lord says that he is anointed to preach (Isa 61:1), and Christ tells the people of Nazareth that this prophecy is fulfilled in Him (Lk 4:18).

Similarly in a metaphorical sense someone chosen of God is called an anointed one. Thus Israel as a nation is called God's anointed (Ps 84:9; 89:38, 51; Hab 3:13) being promised deliverance on this account (1Sa 2:10). The name Christ comes from *chríō*, to anoint, equivalent to Messiah. The anointing of Ps 45:7 is taken in Heb 1:9 as prophetic of the Savior's anointing.

Before battle, shields were oiled so that their surfaces might be slippery and shining (Isa 21:5), as was done to the shield of Saul (2Sa 1:21).

NT uses:

(I) Of Jesus as the Messiah, the anointed King (cf. *Christós* [5547], Christ; Ac 4:27, as a prophet; Lk 4:18 from Isa 61:1). With the accusative (Heb 1:9 quoted from Psa 45:7).

(II) Of Christians as anointed or consecrated, set apart to the service and ministry of Christ and His gospel by the gift of the Holy Spirit (cf. *chrísma* [5545], anointing; 2Co 1:21).

Confusion arises in the NT when two distinct words, *chríō* which has a sacred or religious meaning, and *aleíphō* (218), to oil or rub with oil, are translated with the same English word "anoint," without any distinction between the meanings of the words. *Chríō* is consistently translated "anoint" in Lk 4:18; Ac 4:27; 10:38; 2Co 1:21; Heb 1:9. *Aleíphō*, which means to besmear, rub, oil, with a mundane, non-sacred meaning, is also translated "anoint" in every instance of its occurrence (Mt 6:17; Mk 6:13; 16:1; Lk 7:38, 46; Jn 11:2; 12:3; Jas 5:14). Since the English translation "anoint" also bears the connotation of sacredness, dedication, and *aleíphō* does not, and since both words are translated by the same word, much confusion has arisen in the exegesis of the passages (especially where *aleíphō* occurs). Because of the distinction that exists between these two words, it is necessary for us to examine the passages where each occurs.

The verb *aleíphō*, meaning to besmear or oil, is found in Mt 6:17: "But thou when thou fastest, anoint [*áleipsai*, the aor. imper. sing. of *aleíphō*] thine head, and wash thy face." The meaning here is evidently that the person who was fasting should use ointment so that his face would look refreshed and not express a sad countenance. The word here has nothing to do with ceremonial anointing. In Mk 6:13, "and they cast out many devils [demons], and anointed [*éleiphon*, the imperfect of *aleíphō*, they were rubbing with oil as a medicinal means] with oil many that were sick, and healed them." Some have argued that because the works performed here were undoubtedly supernatural then the anointing must have been sacral in nature. Two problems hamper this position. First of all, in sacral anointings, the oil is viewed largely as a visible symbol along with which divine activity occurs. No efficacy is attached to the element itself. God works, we might say, supranaturally (above nature) and coordinately with the human action. However, in the case at hand, the application of oil was an instance of a common medical procedure of that day and was looked upon as the immediate agent of healing. That the healings were instantaneous and thoroughly effectual indeed required a special work by God to accelerate the process and exaggerate the results of the oil's healing power. Yet here God's work was not supranatural (above nature) but supernatural (within nature but extending the normal limits) operating through the oil and not simply alongside it. Lastly, the ritual mode in which sacral anointings were usually administered and the mystery in which they were shrouded are conspicuously absent from this scene. The disciples here are not priestly officials performing cultic ritual; they are the representatives of Jesus sent out to proclaim in word and deed the gospel. In fact, the significance of Jesus' circumventing the Levitical body and its work is critical in understanding the import of the disciples' action. Such a gesture was in effect invalidating or treating as obsolete the OT order and signaling the inception of the NT. In this new economy, all men are priests and all things are sacred. In this light, it would be possible to speak of these healings as quasi-sacramental. Nevertheless, the context of the passage and the teaching of Scripture on the subject would not allow one to classify the disciples' deed as strictly sacral.

Elsewhere, we see that oil was used for medicinal means as in the parable of the Good

Samaritan (Lk 10:34) and also in Jas 5:14 where "anointing him with oil" is *aleípsantes* (aor. act. participle of *aleíphō*) which means "having rubbed the sick person with oil" (a.t.). The injunction by James is that medicinal means should be applied prior to prayer. It is to be remembered that as priests were to show concern for the body, so also the elders of the local church. In Mk 16:1: "And when the Sabbath was passed, Mary Magdalene, and Mary the mother of James, and Salome, had brought sweet spices, that they might come and anoint [*aleípsōsin*, aor. act. subjunctive 3d person plural] him," which clearly meant the application of ointments and spices to the dead body as was customary in Palestine (Lk 23:56; Jn 19:40). Such an application of ointment did not have any resurrection power, nor was it meant to prevent decomposition (Jn 11:39).

However, the distinction between *chríō* and *aleíphō*, while consistently drawn within the NT, is not as clear in the Sept. (Ex 40:15) and especially in patristic writings.

Deriv.: *egchríō* (1472), to anoint, rub in, besmear; *epichríō* (2025), to anoint; *chrísma* (5545), an anointing; *Christós* (5547), Anointed, the Christ.

5549. χρονίζω, chronizō, *khron-id´-zo*; from 5550; to take time, i.e. linger:—delay, tarry.

Of uncertain derivation; a space of *time* (in general, and thus properly distinguished from 2540, which designates a *fixed* or special occasion; and from 165, which denotes a particular *period*) or *interval*; by extensive an individual *opportunity*; by implication *delay*:— + years old, season, space, (× often-) time (-s), (a) while.

5550. χρόνος, chronos, *khron´-os*; of uncertain derivative; a space of time (in general, and thus properly distinguished from 2540, which designates a fixed or special occasion; and from 165, which denotes a particular period) or interval; by extensive an individual opportunity; by implication delay:— + years old, season, space, (5 often-) time (-s), (a) while.

This word perceives time quantitatively as a period measured by the succession of objects and events and denotes the passing of moments. Another word, *kairós* (2540), season, the time of accomplishment, considers time qualitatively as a period characterized by the influence or prevalence of something. *Chrónos* is a period of meas-

ured time, not a period of accomplishment as *kairós*. *Chrónos* embraces all possible *kairoí* (pl.), and is often used as the larger and more inclusive term, but not the converse. In the NT:

(I) Time, particularly and generally.

(A) Mk 9:21; Lk 4:5; Ac 7:23; 14:3, 28; 15:33; 18:23; 27:9; Gal 4:4; Heb 11:32; Rev 2:21; 10:6. With the prep.: *diá* (1223), for (Heb 5:12); *ek* (1537), from (Lk 8:27, "from long times" [a.t.]); *en* (1722), in (Ac 1:21, "at all times" [a.t.]; Sept.: Jos 4:24); *epí* (1909), upon (Lk 18:4, "for a time" [a.t.]; Ac 18:20; Ro 7:1; 1Co 7:39; Gal 4:1); *metá* (3326), after (Mt 25:19, "after a long time"; Heb 4:7).

(B) In the accusative *chrónon*, sing.; *chrónous*, plural, marking duration, time, how long (Mk 2:19; Lk 20:9; Jn 5:6; 7:33; 12:35; 14:9; Ac 13:18; 19:22; 20:18; 1Co 16:7; Rev 6:11; 20:3; Sept.: Dt 12:19; 22:19; Jos 4:14; Isa 54:7).

(C) Dat. *chrónō*, sing.; *chrónois*, plural, marking time meaning when, in, or during which (Lk 8:29, "oftentimes," in, during, since long time; Ac 8:11; Ro 16:25).

(II) Specifically by the force of adjuncts *chrónos* sometimes stands for a time, season, period, like *kairós* (Ac 1:7; 1Th 5:1). Followed by the gen. of event or the like (Mt 2:7; Lk 1:57; Ac 3:21; 7:17; 17:30; 1Pe 1:17; 4:3); with an adj. pron. (Mt 2:16; 2Ti 1:9; Tit 1:2; 1Pe 1:20).

Deriv.: *makrochrónios* (3118), long-lived; *chronízō* (5549), to while away time; *chronotribéō* (5551), to spend time.

Syn.: *hōra* (5610), hour; *hēméra* (2250), day as referring to a period of time; *diástēma* (1292), an interval, space; *étos* (2094) and *eniautós* (1763), a year; *stigmē* (4743), moment.

5551. χρονοτριβέω, chronotribeō, *khron-ot-rib-eh´-o*; from a presumed compound of 5550 and the base of 5147; to be a *time-wearer*, i.e. to *procrastinate* (*linger*):—spend time.

5552. χρύσεος, chruseos, *khroo´-seh-os*; from 5557; made *of gold*:—of gold, golden.

5553. χρυσίον, chrusiŏn, *khroo-see´-on*; diminutive of 5557; a *golden* article, i.e. gold plating, ornament, or coin:—gold.

5554. χρυσοδακτύλιος, chrusodaktulios, *khroo-sod-ak-too´-lee-os*; from 5557 and 1146; *gold-ringed*, i.e. *wearing* a golden finger-ring or similar *jewelry*:—with a gold ring.

5555. χρυσόλιθος, **chrusolithos,** *khroo-sol´-ee-thos*; from 5557 and 3037; *gold-stone,* i.e. a *yellow gem* ("*chrysolite*"):—chrysolite.

5556. χρυσόπρασος, **chrusoprasos,** *khroo-sop´-ras-os*; from 5557 and πράσον, *prason* (a *leek*); a *greenish-yellow* gem ("*chrysoprase*"):—chrysoprase.

5557. χρυσός, **chrusos,** *khroo-sos´*; perhaps from the base of 5530 (through the idea of the *utility* of the metal); *gold*; by extensive a *golden* article, as an ornament or coin:—gold.

5558. χρυσόω, **chrusoō,** *khroo-so´-o*; from 5557; to *gild,* i.e. *bespangle* with golden ornaments:—deck.

5559. χρώς, **chrōs,** *khroce*; probably akin to the base of 5530 through the idea of *handling*; the *body* (properly its *surface* or *skin*):—body.

5560. χωλός, **chōlos,** *kho-los´*; apparently a primary word; "*halt*", i.e. *limping*:—cripple, halt, lame.

5561. χώρα, **chōra,** *kho´-rah*; feminine of a derivative of the base of 5490 through the idea of *empty* expanse; *room,* i.e. a space of *territory* (more or less extensive; often including its inhabitant):—coast, county, fields, ground, land, region. Compare 5117.

5562. χωρέω, **chōreō,** *kho-reh´-o*; from 5561; to *be* in (*give*) *space,* i.e. (intransitive) to *pass, enter,* or (transitive) to *hold, admit* (literal or figurative):—come, contain, go, have place, (can, be room to) receive.

5563. χωρίζω, **chōrizō,** *kho-rid´-zo*; from 5561; to *place room* between, i.e. *part*; reflexive to *go away*:—depart, put asunder, separate.

5564. χωρίον, **chōrion,** *kho-ree´-on*; diminutive of 5561; a *spot* or *plot* of ground:—field, land, parcel of ground, place, possession.

5565. χωρίς, **chōris,** *kho-rece´*; adverb from 5561; *at a space,* i.e. *separately* or *apart* from (often as preposition):—beside, by itself, without.

5566. χῶρος, **chōros,** *kho´-ros*; of Latin origin; the *north-west* wind:—north west.

Ψ (Psi)

NT Numbers 5567–5597

5567. ψάλλω, **psallō,** *psal´-lo*; probably strengthened from ψάω, **psaō** (to *rub* or *touch* the surface; compare 5597); to *twitch* or *twang,* i.e. to *play* on a stringed instrument (*celebrate the divine worship with music* and accompanying odes):—make melody, sing (psalms).

5568. ψαλμός, **psalmos,** *psal-mos´*; from 5567; a set piece of *music,* i.e. a sacred *ode* (accompanied with the voice, harp or other instrument; a "*psalm*"); collective the book of the *Psalms:*—psalm. Compare 5603.

A noun from *psállō* (5567), to sing, chant. Originally a touching, and then a touching of the harp or other stringed instruments with the finger or with the plectrum; later known as the instrument itself, and finally it became known as the song sung with musical accompaniment. This latest stage of its meaning was adopted in the Sept. In all probability the psalms of Eph 5:19; Col 3:16 are the inspired Psalms of the Hebrew Canon (Sept.: Ps 95:1. In superscripts, Ps 3; 4; 5). Specifically of the Psalms as a part of the OT (Lk 20:42; 24:44; Ac 1:20; 13:33). The word certainly designates these on all other occasions when it occurs in the NT, with the one possible exception of 1Co 14:26. These are the old songs to which new hymns and praises are added (Rev 5:9).

Syn.: *húmnos* (5215), a hymn, religious ode; *ōdē* (5603) song of praise.

5569. ψευδάδελφος, **pseudadelphos,** *psyoo-dad´-el-fos*; from 5571 and 80; a *spurious brother,* i.e. *pretended associate:*—false brethren.

A noun from *pseudés* (5571), false, and *adelphós* (80), brother. A false brother. In Gal 2:4 it denotes those who had become outwardly members of the Christian church, sharers in its fellowship of life and love, but in reality were not so inwardly. Therefore, they had no right to be counted as brothers. They had the companionship of the brothers but the real kinship of spiritual life was missing (see 2Co 11:26).

5570. ψευδαπόστολος, **pseudapostolos,** *psyoo-dap-os´-tol-os*; from 5571 and 652; a *spurious apostle,* i.e. *pretended preacher:*—false teacher.

5571. ψευδής, **pseudes,** *psyoo-dace´*; from 5574; *untrue,* i.e. erroneous, deceitful; wicked:—false, liar.

5572. ψευδοδιδάσκαλος, **pseudodidaskalos,** *psyoo-dod-id-as´-kal-os*; from 5571 and 1320; a *spurious teacher,* i.e. *propagator* of *erroneous* Christian *doctrine:*—false teacher.

A noun from *pseudés* (5571), false, and *didáskalos* (1320), a teacher. A false teacher or one who pretends to be a Christian teacher but teaches false doctrine (2Pe 2:1).

5573. ψευδολόγος, **pseudologos,** *psyoo-dol-og´-os*; from 5571 and 3004; *mendacious,* i.e. *promulgating erroneous* Christian *doctrine:*—speaking lies.

5574. ψεύδομαι, **pseudomai,** *psyoo´-dom-ahee*; middle of an apparently primary verb; to *utter an untruth* or attempt to *deceive* by falsehood:—falsely, lie.

5575. ψευδομάρτυρ, **pseudomartur,** *psyoo-dom-ar´-toor*; from 5571 and a kindred form of 3144; a *spurious witness,* i.e. *bearer of untrue testimony:*—false witness.

5576. ψευδομαρτυρέω, **pseudomartureō,** *psyoo-dom-ar-too-reh´-o*; from 5575; to *be an untrue testifier,* i.e. offer *falsehood in evidence:*—be a false witness.

5577. ψευδομαρτυρία, **pseudomarturia,** *psyoo-dom-ar-too-ree´-ah*; from 5575; *untrue testimony:*—false witness.

5578. ψευδοπροφήτης, **pseudoprophētēs,** *psyoo-dop-rof-ay´-tace*; from 5571 and 4396; a *spurious prophet,* i.e. *pretended foreteller* or religious *impostor:*—false prophet.

5579. ψεῦδος, pseudos, *psyoo´-dos*; from 5574; a *falsehood*:—lie, lying.

5580. ψευδόχριστος, pseudochristos, *psyoo-dokh´-ris-tos*; from 5571 and 5547; a *spurious Messiah*:—false Christ.

A noun from *pseudḗs* (5571), false, and *Christós* (5547), Christ. False christ (Mt 24:24; Mk 13:22). The false christ does not necessarily deny the existence of Christ. On the contrary, he builds on the world's expectations of such a person, while he blasphemously appropriates these to himself and affirms that he is the foretold One in whom God's promises and the saint's expectations are fulfilled. He is of the same character as the *antíchristos* (500), antichrist, who opposes the true Christ (1Jn 4:3). The *pseudóchristos* affirms himself to be the Christ. Both are against the Christ of God. The final antichrist will also be a pseudochrist as well. He will usurp to himself Christ's offices, presenting himself to the world as the true center of its hopes, the satisfier of all its needs, and the healer of all its ills. He will be a pseudochrist and antichrist in one.

5581. ψευδώνυμος, pseudōnumos, *psyoo-do´-noo-mos*; from 5571 and 3686; *untruly named*:—falsely so called.

5582. ψεῦσμα, pseusma, *psyoos´-mah*; from 5574; a *fabrication*, i.e. *falsehood*:—lie.

5583. ψεύστης, pseustēs, *psyoos-tace´*; from 5574; a *falsifier*:—liar.

5584. ψηλαφάω, psēlaphaō, *psay-laf-ah´-o*; from the base of 5567 (compare 5586); to *manipulate*, i.e. *verify* by contact; (figurative) to *search* for:—feel after, handle, touch.

To feel an object or to feel for or after an object (Lk 24:39; Ac 17:27; Heb 12:18; 1Jn 1:1; Sept.: Ge 27:12, 21, 22).

Deriv.: of *psáō* (n.f.), to touch lightly: *psállō* (5567), to play a stringed instrument; *psḗphos* (5586), a small stone; *psichíon* (5589), a crumb; *psōmíon* (5596), a sop; *psṓchō* (5597), to rub.

Syn.: *háptomai* (680), to touch, cling to, lay hold of; *thiggánō* (2345), to touch by way of inquiry, to handle.

5585. ψηφίζω, psēphizō, *psay-fid´-zo*; from 5586; to *use pebbles* in enumeration, i.e. (genitive) to *compute*:—count.

5586. ψῆφος, psēphos, *psay´-fos*; from the same as 5584; a *pebble* (as worn smooth by *handling*), i.e. (by implication of use as a *counter* or *ballot*) a *verdict* (of acquittal) or *ticket* (of admission); a *vote*:—stone, voice.

5587. ψιθυρισμός, psithurismos, *psith-oo-ris-mos´*; from a derivative of **ψίθος, psíthŏs** (a *whisper*; by implication a *slander*; probably akin to 5574); *whispering*, i.e. secret *detraction*:—whispering.

5588. ψιθυριστής, psithuristēs, *psith-oo-ris-tace´*; from the same as 5587; a secret *calumniator*:—whisperer.

A noun from *psithurízō* (n.f.), to whisper. A whisperer, a secret slanderer. It is similar to *katálalos* (2637), an accuser, a backbiter who does his slandering openly (Ro 1:29). Also from *psithurízō* (n.f.): *psithurismós* (5587), a whispering.

5589. ψιχίον, psichion, *psikh-ee´-on*; diminutive from a derivative of the base of 5567 (meaning a *crumb*); a *little bit* or *morsel*:—crumb.

5590. ψυχή, psuchē, *psoo-khay´*; from 5594; *breath*, i.e. (by implication) *spirit*, abstract or concrete (the *animal* sentient principle only; thus distinguished on the one hand from 4151, which is the rational and immortal *soul*; and on the other from 2222, which is mere *vitality*, even of plants: these terms thus exactly correspond respectively to the Hebrew 5315, 7307 and 2416):—heart (+ -ily), life, mind, soul, + us, + you.

The soul, that immaterial part of man held in common with animals. One's understanding of this word's relationship to related terms is contingent upon his position regarding biblical anthropology. Dichotomists view man as consisting of two parts (or substances), material and immaterial, with spirit and soul denoting the immaterial and bearing only a functional and not a metaphysical difference. Trichotomists also view man as consisting of two parts (or substances), but with spirit and soul representing in some contexts a real subdivision of the immaterial. This latter view is here adopted. Accordingly, *psuchḗ* is contrasted to *sṓma* (4983), body, and *pneúma* (4151), spirit (1Th 5:23). The *psuchḗ*, no less than the *sárx* (4561), flesh, belongs to the lower region of man's being. Sometimes *psuchē* stands for the immaterial part of man made up of the soul (*psuchē* in the restrictive sense of the life element), and the spirit *pneúma*. However, animals are not said to possess a spirit; this is only in man, giving him the ability to communicate with God. Also breath (Sept.: Ge 1:30; Job 41:12), and in the NT, usually meaning the vital breath, the life element through which the body lives and feels, the principle of life manifested in the breath.

(I) The soul as the vital principle, the animating element in men and animals.

(A) Generally (Lk 12:20; Ac 20:10; Sept.: Ge 35:18; 1Ki 17:21). Of beasts (Rev 8:9).

(B) Metonymically, for life itself (Mt 6:25; 20:28; Mk 3:4; 10:45; Lk 6:9; 12:22, 23; 14:26; 21:19; Ac 15:26; 20:24; 27:10, 22; Ro 16:4; Php 2:30; 1Th 2:8; Rev 12:11). To lay down one's life (Jn 10:11, 15, 17; 13:37, 38; 15:13; 1Jn 3:16). To seek one's life (Mt 2:20; Ro 11:3; Sept.: Ex 4:19). Including the idea of life or the spirit, both natural and eternal (Mt 16:26; Mk 8:36, 37 [cf. Lk 9:25]). In antithetic declarations of the Lord Jesus, *psuchē* refers not only to natural life, but also to life as continued beyond the grave (Mt 10:39; 16:25; Mk 8:35; Lk 9:24; 17:33; Jn 12:25). Generally, the soul of man, his spiritual and immortal nature with its higher and lower powers, its rational and natural faculties (Mt 10:28; 2Co 1:23; Heb 6:19; 10:39; 13:17; Jas 1:21; 5:20; 1Pe 1:9; 2:11, 25; 4:19). Generally the soul (1Co 15:45, a living soul in allusion to Ge 2:7; Rev 16:3; Sept.: Ge 1:24; 2:19; 9:10, 12, 15).

(C) Of a departed soul, separate from the body; spoken in Greek mythology of the ghosts inhabiting Hades (Ac 2:27, 31, quoted from Ps 16:10; Rev 6:9; 20:4).

(II) Specifically the soul as the sentient principle, the seat of the senses, desires, affections, appetites, passions, the lower aspect of one's nature. Distinguished in Pythagorean and Platonic philosophy from the higher rational nature, expressed by *noús* (3563), mind, and *pneúma* (4151), spirit belonging to man only. This distinction is also followed by the Sept. and sometimes in the NT (cf. *pneúma* [4151], spirit, II, B). In 1Th 5:23 the whole man is indicated as consisting of spirit, soul, and body; soul and spirit, the immaterial part of man upon which the word of God is operative (Heb 4:12); "my soul . . . and my spirit," the immaterial part of

personality with which Mary could magnify the Lord (Lk 1:46, 47). Distinguished from *diánoia* (1271), understanding or mind, because soul is related to the affections (Mt 22:37; Mk 12:30; Lk 10:27). From *súnesis* (4907), the ability to put facts together, knowledge, understanding, intellect (Mk 12:33). Sometimes the soul means the mind, feelings (Mt 11:29; Lk 2:35; Jn 10:24; Ac 14:2, 22; 15:24; Heb 12:3; 1Pe 1:22; 2Pe 2:8, 14; Sept.: Ex 23:9; 1Sa 1:15; Isa 44:19). "With all one's soul" (a.t.) means with his entire affection (Mt 22:37; Mk 12:30, 33; Lk 10:27; Sept.: Dt 26:16; 30:2, 6, 10; 2Ch 15:15; 31:21); *Ek psuchḗs* (*ek* [1537], out of), "from the soul" (a.t.), meaning heartily (Eph 6:6; Col 3:23). To be of one soul means to be unanimous, united in affection and will (Ac 4:32; Php 1:27). That which strictly belongs to the person himself, often ascribed to the soul as the seat of the desires, affections, and appetites (Mt 12:18; 26:38; Mk 14:34; Lk 1:46; 12:19; Jn 12:27; Heb 10:38; 3Jn 2; Rev 18:14; Sept.: Ge 27:4, 19; Isa 1:14; 33:18).

(III) Metonymically, a soul, a living thing in which is *hē psuchē*, life.

(A) More often of a man, a soul, a living person, *pása psuchē* (*pás* [3956], every), every soul, every person, everyone (Ac 2:43; 3:23; Ro 13:1). In a periphrasis, *pása psuchē anthrṓpou* ([444], man), "every soul of man" meaning every man (Ro 2:9); *psuchás anthrṓpōn*, "souls of men" (a.t. [Lk 9:56 {TR}; simply *psuchḗ*, Sept.: Ge 17:14; Le 5:1, 2; Dt 24:8]). *Psuchḗ anthrṓpou*, soul of man (Num. 19:11, 13). In enumerations (Ac 2:41, "about three thousand souls"; 7:14; 27:37; 1Pe 3:20; Sept.: Ge 46:15, 18, 26, 27; Ex 1:5; Dt 10:22).

(B) Specifically for a servant, slave (Rev 18:13), probably female slaves in distinction from the preceding *sṓmata* (4983), bodies (cf. *ánthrōpos* [444], man, I, C, 5); Sept.: Ge 12:5.

Deriv.: *ápsuchos* (895), lifeless, inanimate, without life; *dípsuchos* (1374), two-souled, double minded; *isópsuchos* (2473), like-minded; *oligópsuchos* (3642), little-souled, of little spirit, fainthearted, fearful; *súmpsuchos* (4861), joint-souled, agreeing with one accord; *psuchikós* (5591), natural, physical, pertaining to the animal instinct in man.

Syn.: *kardía* (2588), the heart as the seat of life; *diánoia* (1271), understanding; *zōḗ* (2222), life as a principle; *bíos* (979), possessions of life; *bíōsis* (981), the spending of one's life; *agōgḗ* (72), conduct; *noús* (3563), mind, the seat of reflective consciousness; *pneúma* (4151), spirit, only in man as the means of communication with God while soul is held in common with animals as the consciousness of one's environment.

5591. ψυχικός, **psuchikos,** *psoo-khee-kos´*; from 5590; *sensitive*, i.e. *animate* (in distinction on the one hand from 4152, which is the higher or *renovated* nature; and on the other from 5446, which is the lower or *bestial* nature):— natural, sensual.

An adjective meaning soul, the part of the immaterial life held in common with the animals, as contrasted with spirit (*pneúma* [4151]), only in man, enabling him to communicate with God. Natural, pertaining to the natural as distinguished from the spiritual or glorified nature of man. First Corinthians 15:44 refers to a body *psuchikón*, a body governed by the soul or natural and fallen instinct of man, and a body *pneumatikón* (4152), spiritual, governed by the divine quality in man, the spirit. Rendered as "natural" in 1Co 2:14; 15:44, 46 and sensual in Jas 3:15; Jude 19. The term *psuchikós* is not a word of honor even as *sarkikós* (4559), carnal, is not.

5592. ψύχος, **psuchos,** *psoo´-khos*; from 5594; *coolness:*—cold.

5593. ψυχρός, **psuchros,** *psoo-chros´*; from 5592; *chilly* (literal or figurative):—cold.

5594. ψύχω, **psuchō,** *psoo´-kho*; a primary verb; to *breathe* (*voluntarily* but *gently*; thus differing on the one hand from 4154, which denotes properly a *forcible* respiration; and on the other from the base of 109, which refers properly to an inanimate *breeze*), i.e. (by implication of reduction of temperature by evaporation) to *chill* (figurative):—wax cold.

To breathe, blow, refresh with cool air, or breathe naturally. It is from this verb that *psuchē* (5590), soul, is derived. Hence *psuchē* is the breath of a living creature, animal life, and *psuchō* in the pass. *psuchomai*, means to be cool, to grow cool or cold in a spiritual sense, as in Christian love (Mt 24:12).

Deriv.: *anapsuchō* (404), to make cool, refresh; *apopsuchō* (674), to be faint of heart; *ekpsuchō* (1634), to expire, die; *katapsuchō* (2711), to cool off; *psuchē* (5590), soul; *psuchos* (5592), cold; *psuchrós* (5593), cool, fresh, chilly.

5595. ψωμίζω, **psōmizō,** *pso-mid´-zo*; from the base of 5596; to *supply* with *bits*, i.e. (genitive) to *nourish:*—(bestow to) feed.

5596. ψωμίον, **psōmion,** *pso-mee´-on*; diminutive from a derivative of the base of 5597; a *crumb* or *morsel* (as if *rubbed* off), i.e. a *mouthful:*—sop.

5597. ψώχω, **psōchō,** *pso´-kho*; prolonged from the same base as 5567; to *triturate*, i.e. (by analogy) to *rub* out (kernels from husks with the fingers or hand):—rub.

Ω (Omega)

NT Numbers 5598–5624

5598. Ω, Ō, *o´-meg-ah*; the last letter of the Greek alphabet, i.e. (figurative) the *finality*:— Omega.

5599. ὦ, ō, *o*; a primary interjection; as a sign of the vocative *O*; as a note of exclamation, *oh*:— O.

5600. ὦ, ō, *o*; including the oblique forms, as well as ἦς, *ēs, ace*; ἦ, *ē, ay*; etc.; the subjunctive of 1510; (*may, might, can, could, would, should, must*, etc.; also with 1487 and its comparative, as well as with other particles) *be*:— + appear, are, (may, might, should) be, × have, is, + pass the flower of her age, should stand, were.

5601. Ὠβήδ, Ōbēd, *o-bade´*; of Hebrew origin [5744]; *Obed*, an Israelite:—Obed.

5602. ὧδε, hōde, *ho´-deh*; from an adverbial form of 3592; *in this* same spot, i.e. *here* or *hither*:—here, hither, (in) this place, there.

5603. ᾠδή, ōidē, *o-day´*; from 103; a *chant* or "*ode*" (the genitive term for any words sung; while 5215 denotes especially a *religious* metrical composition; and 5568 still more specially a *Hebrew* cantillation):—song.

The original use of singing among both believers and idolaters was in the confessions and praises of the respective gods. Paul qualifies it in Eph 5:19; Col 3:16 as spiritual songs in association with psalms and hymns, because *ōdé* by itself might mean any kind of song, as of battle, harvest, festal, whereas *psalmós* (5568), psalm, from its Hebrew use, and *húmnos* (5215), hymn, from its Greek use, did not require any such qualifying adj. In Rev 5:9; 14:3 *ōdé* is designated as *kainé* (2537), qualitatively new; in Rev 15:3 as the *ōdé* of Moses as celebrating the deliverance of God's people, and the *ōdé* of the Lamb as celebrating redemption by atoning sacrifice (Sept.: Jgs 5:12; 1Ki 4:32; Ps 42:8).

Syn.: *húmnos* (5215), hymn; *psalmós* (5568), psalm.

5604. ὠδίν, ōdin, *o-deen´*; akin to 3601; a *pang* or *throe*, especially of childbirth:—pain, sorrow, travail.

A noun meaning pain, sorrow. Used in the sing. when referring to the pain of childbirth (1Th 5:3). Used in the plural when warning of the sorrows that would follow wars, famines and other catastrophes (Mt 24:8; Mk 13:8; Sept.: Job 21:17; Na 2:10). In Ac 2:24 the *ōdínas thanátou*, the cords or snares of death in allusion to Ps 18:4, 5.

Deriv.: *sunōdínō* (4944), to be in travail together; *ōdínō* (5605), to be in pain, travail.

Syn.: *pónos* (4192), pain of any kind; *lúpē* (3077), sorrow; *móchthos* (3449), labor, travail; *stenochōría* (4730), anguish; *sunoché* (4928), pressure, anguish; *thlípsis* (2347), affliction.

5605. ὠδίνω, ōdinō, *o-dee´-no*; from 5604; to *experience* the *pains* of parturition (literal or figurative):—travail in (birth).

A noun denoting labor pain at the birth of a child. Intransitively, to be in pain as when a woman is in travail (Gal 4:27; Rev 12:2, in both cases applied spiritually to the Church; see Sept.: SS 8:5; Isa 23:4; 26:18; 66:7, 8); transitively with an accusative, to travail in birth of, to be in labor with (Gal 4:19 where Paul applies it in a spiritual sense to himself with respect to the Galatian converts).

Deriv.: *sunōdínō* (4944), to travail together.

Syn.: *tíktō* (5088), to bear, produce, give birth; *basanízō* (928), torture, torment; *skúllō* (4660), to vex, annoy, trouble; *stenochōréō* (4729), to anguish; *kataponéō* (2669), to toil, afflict, oppress.

5606. ὦμος, ōmos, *o´-mos*; perhaps from the alternant of 5342; the *shoulder* (as that on which burdens are *borne*):—shoulder.

5607. ὤν, ōn, *oan*; including the feminine οὖσα, *ŏusa, oo´-sah*; and the neuter ὄν, *ŏn, on*;

presumed participle of 1510; *being:*—be, come, have.

5608. ὠνέομαι, **ōneomai**, *o-neh´-om-ahee*; middle from an apparently primary ὦνος, *ōnos* (a *sum* or *price*); to *purchase* (synonym with the earlier 4092):—buy.

5609. ὠόν, **ōon**, *o-on´*; apparently a primary word; an *"egg":*—egg.

5610. ὥρα, **hōra**, *ho´-rah*; apparently a primary word; an *"hour"* (literal or figurative):—day, hour, instant, season, × short, [even-] tide, (high) time.

A noun meaning hour, a time, season, a definite space or division of time recurring at fixed intervals, as marked by natural or conventional limits. Figuratively, of a season of life, the fresh, full bloom and beauty of youth, the ripeness and vigor of manhood meaning bloom, beauty. In the NT, of shorter intervals, a time, season, hour.

(**I**) Of the day generally, daytime (Mt 14:15; Mk 6:35; 11:11).

(**II**) Of a definite part or division of the day, in earlier writers used only of the greater divisions as morning, noon, evening, night. In the NT, an hour, one of the twelve equal parts into which the natural day and also the night were divided, and which of course, were of different lengths at different seasons of the year.

(**A**) Particularly and generally (Mt 24:36; 25:13; Mk 13:32; Lk 22:59; Jn 4:52; 11:9; Ac 5:7; 10:30; Rev 9:15). Dat. with *én* (1722), in, of time, when (Mt 8:13; 10:19; 24:50; Lk 12:46; Jn 4:53). Accusative of time, meaning how long (Mt 26:40; Mk 14:37; Ac 19:34). With a numeral marking the hour of the day, as counted from sunrise (Mt 20:3, 5, 6, 9; 27:45, 46; Mk 15:25, 33, 34; Lk 23:44; Jn 1:39; 4:6; 19:14; Ac 2:15; 3:1; 10:3, 9, 30). Of the hours of the nights as counted from sunset (Ac 23:23).

(**B**) Figuratively meaning a short time, a brief interval, in the accusative (Rev 17:12); dat. (Rev 18:10, 17, 19). With *prós* (4314), toward (Jn 5:35; 2Co 7:8; Gal 2:5; 1Th 2:17; Phm 15).

(**III**) Metonymically and generally, an hour meaning a time or period as spoken of any definite point or space of time.

(**A**) With adjuncts such as an adj. or pron. as *apó tēs hóras ekeínēs* (*apó* [575], from; *ekeínēs* [gen. fem. of *ekeínos* {1565}, that]), from that hour or that period (Mt 9:22; 15:28; 17:18; Jn

19:27); with *autē* (fem. dat. of *autós* [846], this one, *autē̄ tē̄ hóra*), at this time. Dat. of time, when (Lk 2:38; 24:33; Ac 16:18; 22:13; Sept.: Da 3:6, 15); with the interrogative *poía* the fem dat. of *poíos* (4169), which (*Poía hóra* or *hē̄ hóra* [dat. fem. of *hós* {3739}, which], what hour [Mt 24:42, 44; Lk 12:39, 40]); with *en* ([1722], in; *en autē̄ tē̄ hóra*), in that same hour (Lk 7:21; 10:21; 12:12; 20:19); with *en ekeínē tē̄ hóra*, at that time (Mt 10:19; 18:1; 26:55; Mk 13:11; Rev 11:13). With *áchri* (891), until, *áchri tēs árti* ([*árti* {737}, the present]), until the present time (1Co 4:11). With *pásan* (3956), every, *pásan hóran*, every hour meaning all the time (1Co 15:30; Sept.: Ex 18:22, 26). With an adverb or relative pron.; *érchetai hóra hóte* (*érchetai* [2064] the present indic. 3d person sing. of *érchomai*, I come; *hóte* [3753], when), there comes an hour when (Jn 4:21, 23; 5:25; 16:25); followed by *en* and the relative pron. (Jn 5:28). With *hína* (2443), so that (Jn 12:23; 13:1; 16:2, 32). With the gen. of thing, to be done or to happen (Sept.: Da 9:21, *tē̄ hóra toú deípnou* (*deípnou* [gen. sing. of *deípnon* {1173}, dinner, supper]), at the time of the supper or feast (Lk 1:10; 14:17); temptation (Rev 3:10); judgment (Rev 14:7, 15); one's own (time) (Lk 22:14). With the inf. (Ro 13:11; Sept.: Ge 29:7); the gen. of person, one's time, appointed to him in which he is to do or suffer (Lk 22:53; Jn 16:21), elsewhere of Christ (Jn 2:4; 7:30; 8:20; 13:1).

(**B**) Simply meaning the time spoken of or otherwise understood (Mt 26:45; Mk 14:41; Jn 16:4; 1Jn 2:18). Emphatically (Jn 17:1); by implication meaning time or hour of trial, sorrow, suffering (Mk 14:35; Jn 12:27).

Deriv.: *hēmiórion* (2256), a half hour; *hōraíos* (5611), attractive, comely.

Syn.: *hēméra* (2250), day, the period of natural light; *kairós* (2540), season, time, opportunity; *chrónos* (5550), time duration; *stigmē̄* (4743), instant, moment.

5611. ὡραῖος, **hōraios**, *ho-rah´-yos*; from 5610; *belonging* to the right *hour* or *season* (*timely*), i.e. (by implication) *flourishing* (*beauteous* [figurative]):—beautiful.

An adjective from *hóra* (5610), hour, meaning attractive, comely. Figuratively of a virgin ready for marriage. In the NT only figuratively meaning fair, comely, beautiful, spoken of things (Mt 23:27; Ro 10:15; Sept.: Ge 2:9; 3:6). Of persons (Ge 29:17; 39:6); of a gate of the temple (Ac 3:2, 10), the Beautiful Gate supposed by some to have been the large gate leading from the court of the Gentiles to the court of the Israelites over against the eastern side of the temple, otherwise called the Gate of Nicanor. It was described by Josephus as covered with plates of gold and silver, and was very splendid and massive. However, from Ac 3:3, 8, it would seem rather to have been one of the external gates leading from without into the court of the Gentiles in which also was Solomon's porch (Ac 3:11).

Syn.: *kalós* (2570), beautiful, good; *kósmios* (2887), decorous.

5612. ὠρύομαι, **ōruomai**, *o-roo´-om-ahee*; middle of an apparently primary verb; to "*roar*":—roar.

5613. ὡς, **hōs,** *hoce*; probably adverb of comparative from 3739; *which how*, i.e. *in that manner* (very variously used, as follows):—about, after (that), (according) as (it had been, it were), as soon (as), even as (like), for, how (greatly), like (as, unto), since, so (that), that, to wit, unto, when ([-soever]), while, × with all speed.

A relative adverb from *hós* (3739), who, correlative to *pós* (4459), how, in what manner or way. As, so as, how, sometimes equivalent to a conjunction (cf. IV). For *hōs án*, as if, see *án* ([302], cf. II, A, 1, and B, 3).

(I) In comparisons. In Attic writers *hósper* (5618), just as, is the prevailing word in this usage.

(A) Particularly, fully, with the corresponding demonstrative adverb as *hoútōs* (3779), thus, or the like, either preceding or following, *hoútōs . . . hōs,* so . . . as (Mk 4:26; Jn 7:46, so as if; 1Co 3:15); *hōs amnós . . . hoútōs,* as . . . so (Ac 8:32 quoted from Isa 53:7; Ac 23:11); *hōs gár . . . oútō* (*gár* [1063], and, but, for, therefore; *oútō* [3779], thus), as therefore, "as . . . so also"; Ro 5:15, 18; 2Co 7:14; 11:3; 1Th 2:7; 5:2); *ísos . . . hōs,* (*ísos* [2470], similar, equal), the like, similar, equal gift . . . as (Ac 11:17). *Homoíōs kaí hós* (*homoíōs* [3668], similarly, likewise; *kaí* [2532], and), likewise also as (Lk 17:28); *hōs . . . kaí,* where *hoútōs* ([3779], thus) is strictly implied (cf. *kai* [2532], and, II, B). *Hōs en ouranō̂, kaí epí tēs gēs* (*ouranō̂* [3772], heaven; *gēs* [1063], earth), as in heaven, also on earth (Mt 6:10; Ac 7:51; Gal 1:9). Frequently *hoútōs* is omitted and then *hōs* may often be rendered "so as" or simply "as" (Ac

7:37; Ro 4:17; 5:16). Sometimes the whole clause to which *hōs* refers is omitted as in Mk 4:31, "the kingdom of God" is omitted, which, however, occurs in 4:30.

(B) Generally before a noun or adj. in the nom. or accusative meaning as, like as, like (Mt 6:29; 10:25; Mk 1:22; 6:15; Lk 6:10, 40; 21:35; 10:3, 16; 13:43; 28:3; 22:31; Jn 15:6; Ac 11:5; 1Co 3:10; 14:33; Gal 4:12; 1Th 5:6; Heb 1:11; Heb 6:19; Jas 1:10; 1Pe 2:25; 1Jn 1:7; Jude 10; Rev 1:14; 8:1, 10; 10:1; 20:8; 22:1; Sept.: Jgs 8:18; 1Sa 25:36). Here, too, the construction is often elliptical, e.g., where a part. belonging to the noun before *hōs* is also implied with the noun after *hōs,* as in Lk 10:18 (cf. Mt 3:16; Mk 1:10). Also where the noun before *hōs* is also implied after it, as in Rev 1:10, "as [the voice] of a trumpet"; 16:3; Sept.: Jer 4:31. Sometimes the noun after *hōs* is implied before it (Rev 6:1, "saying with a voice, as it were, the voice of a thunder" [a.t.]). A noun preceded by *hōs* often denotes something like itself, a person or thing like that which the noun refers to, with the meaning "as it were" (Rev 4:6 [UBS], something like a sea of glass, as it were a sea of glass; 8:8, "as it were a great mountain"; 9:7, "as it were crowns like gold" or as if they were golden crowns; 15:2; Sept.: Da 10:18); accusative (Rev 19:1 [UBS], a sound like the voice; 9:6).

(II) Implying quality, character, circumstances as known or supposed to exist in any personal thing; something which is matter of belief or opinion, whether true or false.

(A) Before a part. referring to a preceding noun and expressing a quality or circumstance belonging to that noun, either real or supposed, meaning as, as if, as though. **(1)** Before a nom. as referring to a preceding subject (Lk 16:1, as wasting his goods, being so accounted; Ac 23:20, "as though they would inquire"; 28:19, "not as having" [a.t.], meaning not supposing that I have; 1Co 4:7; 5:3; 7:25; 2Co 6:9, 10; 10:14; 13:2; Col 2:20; 1Th 2:4; Heb 11:27; 13:3, 17; Jas 2:12; Sept.: Ge 27:12). With a part. implied (Eph 6:7; 1Pe 4:11). **(2)** Before a gen. referring to a preceding noun (Heb 12:27). Elliptically (Jn 1:14). Often with a gen. absolute (1Co 4:18, "they, supposing that I shall not come" [a.t.]; 2Co 5:20; 1Pe 4:12; 2Pe 1:3). After *prophásei,* the dat. of *prophasis* (4392), pretense (Ac 27:30, as though they would have cast). **(3)** Before a dat. referring to a preceding noun (Ac 3:12; 1Pe 2:14). **(4)** Before an accusative referring to a preceding object (Ac 23:15; Ro 6:13; 15:15; 2Co 10:2; Rev 5:6). **(5)** Once before an inf. apparently with a part. implied or perhaps instead of the part. construction (2Co 10:9).

(B) Before a substantive or adj. either as predicate or obj. expressing a quality or circumstance known or supposed to belong to a preceding noun, meaning as, as if, as though. Here the part. *ṓn* ([5607] masc., *oúsa* fem., *ón* neuter) or the like, may always be supplied, and the construction is then the same as in section II A above. **(1)** Before the nom. as referring to a preceding subject (Ro 3:7, "as though I were a sinner" [a.t.]; 2Co 6:4, 8, 10; 11:15; 13:7; Eph 5:1, 8, as it becomes children of the light, as they are supposed to walk; 6:6; Col 3:12, 22; Heb 3:5, 6; Jas 2:9; 1Pe 1:14; 2:2, 5, 16; 4:10, 15, 16). Once preceded by *toioútos* (5108), such a one (Phm 9, "being such a one as Paul the aged," such a one as you know Paul to be, your aged teacher and friend). **(2)** Before the gen. as referring to a preceding noun (1Pe 2:12; 3:16 [cf. II, A, 2 in text on word *hōs*]). **(3)** Before the dat. as referring to a preceding noun (1Co 3:1, "as unto spiritual"; 10:15; 2Co 6:13; Heb 12:5, 7; 1Pe 2:13; 3:7; 4:19; 2Pe 1:19), implied (1Pe 1:19). **(4)** Before the accusative as referring to another object (Mt 14:5; Lk 6:22; 15:19; Ro 1:21; 1Co 4:9, 14; 8:7; 2Co 11:16; Heb 11:9). Preceded by *hoútōs* (3779), thus, *hoútōs hōs*, thus as (2Co 9:5).

(C) Before prep. with their cases in the same manner as before part. (cf. II, A). **(1)** With *diá* (1223), through (2Th 2:2); *en* (1722), in (Jn 7:10; Ro 13:13); *ek* (1537), out of, of (Ro 9:32 [cf. 9:31]; 2Co 2:17; 3:5; 1Pe 4:11); *epí* (1909), upon (Mt 26:55, "as though against a robber" [a.t.]; Gal 3:16). **(2)** Before a prep. implying motion to a place, *hōs* qualifies the force of the prep. meaning as if to, toward, in the direction of, leaving it undetermined whether one arrives at the place or not. Used in the NT only once with *epí* (Ac 17:14, "as toward the sea" [a.t.]).

(D) Before numerals meaning as if it were, about, marking a supposed or conjectural number (Mk 5:13, about two thousand; 8:9; Lk 2:37; 8:42; Jn 6:19; 21:8; Ac 1:15; 5:7; 19:34; Sept.: Ru 1:4).

(E) Intensive meaning how! how very! how much! expressing admiration. In the NT only before adj., see below III, C (Ro 10:15, how beautiful the feet; 11:33). Once before the com-

parative (Ac 17:22, how much more religiously inclined do I behold you than other cities or nations; Sept.: Ps 73:1).

(III) Implying manner before a dependent clause qualifying or defining the action of a preceding verb or one that follows.

(A) Generally, meaning as, according as (Mt 1:24; 8:13; 20:14; Lk 14:22; Ro 12:3; 1Co 3:5; Col 2:6; 4:4; Tit 1:5; Rev 9:3; 18:6; 22:12). Once with *hoútō* (3779), thus, corresponding (1Co 7:17). Here in a somewhat more less restrictive *hōs kaí* ([2532], and), like the relative *hós* (3739), he who, serves as a connective particle (Ac 13:33; 17:28; 22:5; 25:10; Ro 9:25).

(B) Before a minor or parenthetic clause which then serves to modify or restrict the general proposition (Mt 27:65; Mk 4:27; 10:1; Lk 3:23; Ac 2:15; 1Co 12:2; 1Pe 5:12; 2Pe 3:9; Rev 2:24).

(C) Before a superlative used as an intensive meaning most speedily, as speedily as possible (Ac 17:15).

(IV) Before dependent clauses expressing the obj. or reference of a preceding verb or word, the nature of the action, the circumstances under which it takes place, and so forth, meaning in what way, how, as, often equivalent to a conjunction.

(A) Generally, meaning how, equivalent to *hópōs* (3704), in the manner that. With the aor. indic. (Mk 12:26; Lk 8:47; 23:55; 24:35; Ac 11:16; Ro 11:2; 2Co 7:15). Pleonastically (Lk 22:61). Once with *toúto* (5124), this, preceding (Lk 6:3, 4). Also followed by *hóti* (3754), that, meaning how that, *hōs hóti*, as that, to wit that. In the NT subjoined to a noun for fuller explanation, usually regarded as pleonastic, but not so in strictness (2Co 5:19; 11:21, "I speak as to the reproach [cast upon us] how that [*hōs hóti*] we are weak, although we were weak" [a.t.]); 2Th 2:2, "nor by letter . . . as that."

(B) Before an obj. clause in a more restrictive sense meaning how, how that, that, with the indic. equivalent to *hóti*, that (cf. *hóti* [3754] I, C) (Ac 10:28, 38; Ro 1:9; 1Th 2:10; 2Ti 1:3; Sept.: 1Sa 13:11).

(C) Before a clause expressing end or purpose meaning as that, so that, equivalent to that, to the end that, like *hína* (2443), so that, or *hópōs* (3704), so that. Followed by the inf. expressing the purpose of a preceding verb meaning so as to, in order to (Ac 20:24, "I count not my life dear so that I may finish" [a.t.]; Heb 7:9, "so to speak" [a.t.], "that I may so speak" [a.t.]).

(D) Before a clause expressing result or consequence, so as that, so that, like *hóste* (5620), so to, so that; with the indic. (Heb 3:11; 4:3 quoted from Ps 95:11).

(E) Before a clause expressing a cause or reason meaning as, that, equivalent to since, because, like *epeí* (1893), thereupon, since, because; *hóti* (3754), that (Gal 6:10, "since we now have opportunity" [a.t.]; perhaps Mt 6:12 [cf. Lk 11:4]).

(F) Before a clause implying time, as when, like *epeí* (1893), thereupon. **(1)** Generally meaning when, in that, while. With the indic. (Mt 28:9; Lk 1:41, 44; 4:25; 19:5; Jn 2:9; Ac 5:24; 28:4). By implication meaning whenever, as often as (Lk 12:58; Sept.: 2Ch 24:11). Also when, with the indic. (Lk 1:23; 2:15, 39; 11:1; Jn 4:1; 6:12, 16; Ac 7:23; 10:7; 13:18, 29). Followed by *tóte* (5119), then, at that time (Jn 7:10). From when, since (Mk 9:21). **(2)** Followed by *án* (302), a particle denoting a supposition, wish, possibility, *hōs án* meaning whensoever, as soon as, with the aor. subjunctive (Ro 15:24 [UBS]; 1Co 11:34, as soon as I come; Php 2:23).

Deriv.: *hōsaútōs* (5615), likewise; *hōseí* (5616), about; *hósper* (5618), just as; *hóste* (5620), therefore.

Syn.: *katá* (2596), according to, as; *katháper* (2509), exactly as; *hoíos* (3739), in the neuter *hoíon*, with a neg., not so, such as; *áchri* (891), until; *méchri* (3360), till (a reference to a space of time).

5614. ὡσαννά, **hōsanna,** *ho-san-nah´*; of Hebrew origin [3467 and 4994]; *oh save!; hosanna* (i.e. *hoshiana*), an exclamation of adoration:—hosanna.

5615. ὡσαύτως, **hōsautōs,** *ho-sow´-toce*; from 5613 and an adverb from 846; *as thus,* i.e. *in the same way:*—even so, likewise, after the same (in like) manner.

5616. ὡσεί, **hōsei,** *ho-si´*; from 5613 and 1487; *as if:*—about, as (it had been, it were), like (as).

A conditional adverb from *hōs* (5613), as, and *ei* (1487), if. As if, as though, followed by the opt. In the NT only before a noun or adj.

(I) In comparisons, as if, as it were, as, like as (cf. *hōs* [5613] I, B) (Mt 9:36; 28:3, 4; Mk 9:26; Lk 22:44; 24:11; Ac 2:3; 6:15; 9:18; Heb 1:12; 11:12; Rev 1:14; Sept.: Job 28:5; 29:25). Elliptically where a part. or inf. belonging to the noun before *hōsei* is also implied with the noun after *hōsei* (Mt 3:16, "as a dove descending" [a.t.]; Mk 1:10; Jn 1:32; inf. Lk 3:22).

(II) Before words of number and measure, as if, as it were, meaning about, approximately (cf. *hōs* [5613] II, D). Before numerals (Mt 14:21, "about five thousand"; Mk 6:44; Lk 1:56; 3:23; 9:14, 28; 22:59; 23:44; Jn 4:6; 6:10; 19:14, 39; Ac 2:41; 4:4; 5:36; 10:3; 19:7; Sept.: Jgs 3:29). Of measure (Lk 22:41).

5617. Ὡσηέ, **Hōsēe,** *ho-say-eh´*; of Hebrew origin [1954]; *Hoseë* (i.e. *Hosheä*), an Israelite:—Osee.

5618. ὥσπερ, **hōsper,** *hoce´-per*; from 5613 and 4007; *just as,* i.e. *exactly like:*—(even, like) as.

5619. ὡσπερεί, **hōsperei,** *hoce-per-i´*; from 5618 and 1487; *just as if,* i.e. *as it were:*—as.

5620. ὥστε, **hōste,** *hoce´-teh*; from 5613 and 5037; *so too,* i.e. *thus therefore* (in various relations of *consecution,* as follow):—(insomuch) as, so that (then), (insomuch) that, therefore, to, wherefore.

5621. ὠτίον, **ōtion,** *o-tee´-on*; diminutive of 3775; an *earlet,* i.e. *one* of the ears, or perhaps the *lobe* of the ear:—ear.

5622. ὠφέλεια, **ōpheleia,** *o-fel´-i-ah*; from a derivative of the base of 5624; *usefulness,* i.e. *benefit:*—advantage, profit.

5623. ὠφελέω, **ōpheleō,** *o-fel-eh´-o*; from the same as 5622; *to be useful,* i.e. *to benefit:*—advantage, better, prevail, profit.

5624. ὠφέλιμος, **ōphelimos,** *o-fel´-ee-mos*; from a form of 3786; *helpful* or *serviceable,* i.e. *advantageous:*—profit (-able).

AMG Publishers is committed to helping you understand the meaning of every word in the original biblical languages. The Strong's numbering system is the easiest and best way to facilitate this endeavor. Enhance your study of the Bible today! AMG's Complete Word Study Series is a comprehensive set of tools for understanding the Hebrew Old Testament and Greek New Testament *without* having to learn the languages.

The Complete Word Study Old Testament (ISBN: 978-089957-665-7) provides a grammatical code and Strong's number right on the words of the English text of the Old Testament. Tools provided at the back of the book allow you to use these codes and numbers to learn more about the words of the Old Testament.

The Complete Word Study Dictionary: Old Testament (ISBN: 978-089957-667-1) is organized by Strong's number and gives extended definitions for each Hebrew/Aramaic word. Also included is a concordance of all the Old Testament verses where the word(s) represented by each Strong's number occurs in the Hebrew Old Testament. Excerpts from this dictionary were used to enhance the *Annotated Strong's Hebrew Dictionary of the Old Testament* contained in this volume.

The Complete Word Study New Testament (ISBN: 978-089957-651-0) gives a grammatical code and Strong's number right on the English text of the New Testament. Also included is a concordance of all the New Testament verses where the word(s) represented by each Strong's number occur in the Greek New Testament. Tools provided at the back of the book allow you to use these codes and numbers to learn more about the words of the New Testament.

The Complete Word Study Dictionary: New Testament (ISBN: 978-089957-663-3) is organized by Strong's number and gives extended definitions for each Greek word. Excerpts from this dictionary were used to enhance the *Annotated Strong's Greek Dictionary of the New Testament* contained in this volume.